The Dictionary of Art · volume fifteen

The Dictionary of Art

CONSULTING EDITOR Hugh Brigstocke

EDITOR Jane Turner

15

Hungary, §VI: Ceramics
TO
Iran, ancient

GROVE

The Dictionary of Art

edited by JANE TURNER, in thirty-four volumes, 1996

This edition is distributed within the United Kingdom and Europe by Macmillan Publishers Limited, London, and within the United States and Canada by Grove's Dictionaries Inc., New York.

Text keyboarded by Wearset Limited, Sunderland, England
Database management by Pindar plc, York, England
Imagesetting by William Clowes Limited, Suffolk, England
Printed in the United States of America by RR Donnelley & Sons Company, Willard, Ohio

British Library Cataloguing in Publication Data

The dictionary of art
1. Art - Dictionaries 2. Art - History - Dictionaries
I. Turner, Jane
703

ISBN 1-884446-00-0

Library of Congress Cataloging in Publication Data

The dictionary of art / editor, Jane Turner.
p. cm.
Includes bibliographical references and index.
Contents: 1. A to Anckerman
ISBN 1-884446-00-0 (alk. paper)
1. Art—Encyclopedias.
I. Turner, Jane, 1956–
N31.D5 1996 96–13628
703—dc20 CIP

Contents

List of Colour Illustrations

General Abbreviations

The abbreviations employed throughout this dictionary, most of which are listed below, do not vary, except for capitalization, regardless of the context in which they are used, including bibliographical citations and for locations of works of art. The principle used to arrive at these abbreviations is that their full form should be easily deducible, and for this reason acronyms have generally been avoided (e.g. Los Angeles Co. Mus. A. instead of LACMA). The same abbreviation is adopted for cognate forms in foreign languages and in most cases for plural and adjectival forms (e.g. A.= Art, Arts, Arte, Arti etc). Not all related forms are listed below. Occasionally, if a name, for instance of an artists' group or exhibiting society, is repeated within the text of one article, it is cited in an abbreviated form after its first mention in full (e.g. The Pre-Raphaelite Brotherhood (PRB) was founded...); the same is true of archaeological periods and eras, which are abbreviated to initial letters in small capitals (e.g. In the Early Minoan (EM) period...). Such abbreviations do not appear in this list. For the reader's convenience, separate full lists of abbreviations for locations, periodical titles and standard reference books and series are included as Appendices A–C in vol. 33.

A. Art, Arts
A.C. Arts Council
Acad. Academy
AD Anno Domini
Add. Additional, Addendum
addn addition
Admin. Administration
Adv. Advances, Advanced
Aesth. Aesthetic(s)
Afr. African
Afrik. Afrikaans, Afrikaner
A.G. Art Gallery
Agrar. Agrarian
Agric. Agriculture
Agron. Agronomy
Agy Agency
AH Anno Hegirae
A. Inst. Art Institute
AK Alaska (USA)
AL Alabama (USA)
Alb. Albanian
Alg. Algerian
Alta Alberta (Canada)
Altern. Alternative
a.m. ante meridiem [before noon]
Amat. Amateur
Amer. American
An. Annals
Anatol. Anatolian
Anc. Ancient
Annu. Annual
Anon. Anonymous(ly)
Ant. Antique
Anthol. Anthology
Anthropol. Anthropology
Antiqua. Antiquarian, Antiquaries
app. appendix
approx. approximately
AR Arkansas (USA)
ARA Associate of the Royal Academy
Arab. Arabic
Archaeol. Archaeology
Archit. Architecture, Architectural
Archv, Archvs Archive(s)
Arg. Argentine
ARHA Associate of the Royal Hibernian Academy
ARIBA Associate of the Royal Institute of British Architects
Armen. Armenian
ARSA Associate of the Royal Scottish Academy
Asiat. Asiatic
Assist. Assistance
Assoc. Association
Astron. Astronomy
AT&T American Telephone & Telegraph Company
attrib. attribution, attributed to
Aug August
Aust. Austrian
Austral. Australian
Auth. Author(s)
Auton. Autonomous
Aux. Auxiliary
Ave. Avenue
AZ Arizona (USA)
Azerbaij. Azerbaijani
B. Bartsch [catalogue of Old Master prints]
b born
BA Bachelor of Arts
Balt. Baltic
bapt baptized
BArch Bachelor of Architecture
Bart Baronet
Bask. Basketry
BBC British Broadcasting Corporation
BC Before Christ
BC British Columbia (Canada)
BE Buddhist era
Beds Bedfordshire (GB)
Behav. Behavioural
Belarus. Belarusian
Belg. Belgian
Berks Berkshire (GB)
Berwicks Berwickshire (GB; old)
BFA Bachelor of Fine Arts
Bibl. Bible, Biblical
Bibliog. Bibliography, Bibliographical
Biblioph. Bibliophile
Biog. Biography, Biographical
Biol. Biology, Biological
bk, bks book(s)
Bkbinder Bookbinder
Bklore Booklore
Bkshop Bookshop
BL British Library
Bld Build
Bldg Building

Bldr	Builder
BLitt	Bachelor of Letters/Literature
BM	British Museum
Boh.	Bohemian
Boliv.	Bolivian
Botan.	Botany, Botanical
BP	Before present (1950)
Braz.	Brazilian
BRD	Bundesrepublik Deutschland [Federal Republic of Germany (West Germany)]
Brecons	Breconshire (GB; old)
Brez.	Brezonek [lang. of Brittany]
Brit.	British
Bros	Brothers
BSc	Bachelor of Science
Bucks	Buckinghamshire (GB)
Bulg.	Bulgarian
Bull.	Bulletin
bur	buried
Burm.	Burmese
Byz.	Byzantine
C	Celsius
C.	Century
c.	*circa* [about]
CA	California
Cab.	Cabinet
Caerns	Caernarvonshire (GB; old)
C.A.G.	City Art Gallery
Cal.	Calendar
Callig.	Calligraphy
Cam.	Camera
Cambs	Cambridgeshire (GB)
can	canonized
Can.	Canadian
Cant.	Canton(s), Cantonal
Capt.	Captain
Cards	Cardiganshire (GB; old)
Carib.	Caribbean
Carms	Carmarthenshire (GB; old)
Cartog.	Cartography
Cat.	Catalan
cat.	catalogue
Cath.	Catholic
CBE	Commander of the Order of the British Empire
Celeb.	Celebration
Celt.	Celtic
Cent.	Centre, Central
Centen.	Centennial
Cer.	Ceramic
cf.	confer [compare]
Chap., Chaps	Chapter(s)
Chem.	Chemistry
Ches	Cheshire (GB)
Chil.	Chilean
Chin.	Chinese
Christ.	Christian, Christianity
Chron.	Chronicle
Cie	Compagnie [French]
Cinema.	Cinematography
Circ.	Circle
Civ.	Civil, Civic
Civiliz.	Civilization(s)
Class.	Classic, Classical
Clin.	Clinical
CO	Colorado (USA)
Co.	Company; County
Cod.	Codex, Codices
Col., Cols	Collection(s); Column(s)
Coll.	College
collab.	in collaboration with, collaborated, collaborative
Collct.	Collecting
Colloq.	Colloquies
Colomb.	Colombian
Colon.	Colonies, Colonial
Colr	Collector
Comm.	Commission; Community
Commerc.	Commercial
Communic.	Communications
Comp.	Comparative; compiled by, compiler
Concent.	Concentration
Concr.	Concrete
Confed.	Confederation
Confer.	Conference
Congol.	Congolese
Congr.	Congress
Conserv.	Conservation; Conservatory
Constr.	Construction(al)
cont.	continued
Contemp.	Contemporary
Contrib.	Contributions, Contributor(s)
Convalesc.	Convalescence
Convent.	Convention
Coop.	Cooperation
Coord.	Coordination
Copt.	Coptic
Corp.	Corporation, Corpus
Corr.	Correspondence
Cors.	Corsican
Cost.	Costume
Cret.	Cretan
Crim.	Criminal
Crit.	Critical, Criticism
Croat.	Croatian
CT	Connecticut (USA)
Cttee	Committee
Cub.	Cuban
Cult.	Cultural, Culture
Cumb.	Cumberland (GB; old)
Cur.	Curator, Curatorial, Curatorship
Curr.	Current(s)
CVO	Commander of the [Royal] Victorian Order
Cyclad.	Cycladic
Cyp.	Cypriot
Czech.	Czechoslovak
$	dollars
d	died
d.	denarius, denarii [penny, pence]
Dalmat.	Dalmatian
Dan.	Danish
DBE	Dame Commander of the Order of the British Empire
DC	District of Columbia (USA)
DDR	Deutsche Demokratische Republik [German Democratic Republic (East Germany)]
DE	Delaware (USA)
Dec	December
Dec.	Decorative
ded.	dedication, dedicated to
Democ.	Democracy, Democratic
Demog.	Demography, Demographic
Denbs	Denbighshire (GB; old)
dep.	deposited at
Dept	Department
Dept.	Departmental, Departments
Derbys	Derbyshire (GB)
Des.	Design
destr.	destroyed
Dev.	Development
Devon	Devonshire (GB)
Dial.	Dialogue
diam.	diameter
Diff.	Diffusion
Dig.	Digest
Dip. Eng.	Diploma in Engineering
Dir.	Direction, Directed
Directrt	Directorate
Disc.	Discussion
diss.	dissertation
Distr.	District
Div.	Division
DLitt	Doctor of Letters/Literature
DM	Deutsche Mark
Doc.	Document(s)
Doss.	Dossier
DPhil	Doctor of Philosophy
Dr	Doctor
Drg, Drgs	Drawing(s)
DSc	Doctor of Science/Historical Sciences
Dut.	Dutch
Dwell.	Dwelling
E.	East(ern)

EC	European (Economic) Community
Eccles.	Ecclesiastical
Econ.	Economic, Economies
Ecuad.	Ecuadorean
ed.	editor, edited (by)
edn	edition
eds	editors
Educ.	Education
e.g.	*exempli gratia* [for example]
Egyp.	Egyptian
Elem.	Element(s), Elementary
Emp.	Empirical
Emul.	Emulation
Enc.	Encyclopedia
Encour.	Encouragement
Eng.	English
Engin.	Engineer, Engineering
Engr., Engrs	Engraving(s)
Envmt	Environment
Epig.	Epigraphy
Episc.	Episcopal
Esp.	Especially
Ess.	Essays
est.	established
etc	*etcetera* [and so on]
Ethnog.	Ethnography
Ethnol.	Ethnology
Etrus.	Etruscan
Eur.	European
Evangel.	Evangelical
Exam.	Examination
Excav.	Excavation, Excavated
Exch.	Exchange
Excurs.	Excursion
exh.	exhibition
Exp.	Exposition
Expermntl	Experimental
Explor.	Exploration
Expn	Expansion
Ext.	External
Extn	Extension
f, ff	following page, following pages
F.A.	Fine Art(s)
Fac.	Faculty
facs.	facsimile
Fam.	Family
fasc.	fascicle
fd	feastday (of a saint)
Feb	February
Fed.	Federation, Federal
Fem.	Feminist
Fest.	Festival
fig.	figure (illustration)
Fig.	Figurative
figs	figures
Filip.	Filipina(s), Filipino(s)
Fin.	Finnish
FL	Florida (USA)
fl	*floruit* [he/she flourished]
Flem.	Flemish
Flints	Flintshire (GB; old)
Flk	Folk
Flklore	Folklore
fol., fols	folio(s)
Found.	Foundation
Fr.	French
frag.	fragment
Fri.	Friday
FRIBA	Fellow of the Royal Institute of British Architects
FRS	Fellow of the Royal Society, London
ft	foot, feet
Furn.	Furniture
Futur.	Futurist, Futurism
g	gram(s)
GA	Georgia (USA)
Gael.	Gaelic
Gal., Gals	Gallery, Galleries
Gaz.	Gazette
GB	Great Britain
Gdn, Gdns	Garden(s)
Gdnr(s)	Gardener(s)
Gen.	General
Geneal.	Genealogy, Genealogist
Gent.	Gentleman, Gentlemen
Geog.	Geography
Geol.	Geology
Geom.	Geometry
Georg.	Georgian
Geosci.	Geoscience
Ger.	German, Germanic
G.I.	Government/General Issue (USA)
Glams	Glamorganshire (GB; old)
Glos	Gloucestershire (GB)
Govt	Government
Gr.	Greek
Grad.	Graduate
Graph.	Graphic
Green.	Greenlandic
Gr.-Roman	Greco-Roman
Gt	Great
Gtr	Greater
Guat.	Guatemalan
Gym.	Gymnasium
h.	height
ha	hectare
Hait.	Haitian
Hants	Hampshire (GB)
Hb.	Handbook
Heb.	Hebrew
Hell.	Hellenic
Her.	Heritage
Herald.	Heraldry, Heraldic
Hereford & Worcs	Hereford & Worcester (GB)
Herts	Hertfordshire (GB)
HI	Hawaii (USA)
Hib.	Hibernia
Hisp.	Hispanic
Hist.	History, Historical
HMS	His/Her Majesty's Ship
Hon.	Honorary, Honourable
Horiz.	Horizon
Hort.	Horticulture
Hosp.	Hospital(s)
HRH	His/Her Royal Highness
Human.	Humanities, Humanism
Hung.	Hungarian
Hunts	Huntingdonshire (GB; old)
IA	Iowa
ibid.	*ibidem* [in the same place]
ICA	Institute of Contemporary Arts
Ice.	Icelandic
Iconog.	Iconography
Iconol.	Iconology
ID	Idaho (USA)
i.e.	*id est* [that is]
IL	Illinois (USA)
Illum.	Illumination
illus.	illustrated, illustration
Imp.	Imperial
IN	Indiana (USA)
in., ins	inch(es)
Inc.	Incorporated
inc.	incomplete
incl.	includes, including, inclusive
Incorp.	Incorporation
Ind.	Indian
Indep.	Independent
Indig.	Indigenous
Indol.	Indology
Indon.	Indonesian
Indust.	Industrial
Inf.	Information
Inq.	Inquiry
Inscr.	Inscribed, Inscription
Inst.	Institute(s)
Inst. A.	Institute of Art
Instr.	Instrument, Instrumental
Int.	International
Intell.	Intelligence
Inter.	Interior(s), Internal
Interdiscip.	Interdisciplinary
intro.	introduced by, introduction
inv.	inventory

Inven.	Invention
Invest.	Investigation(s)
Iran.	Iranian
irreg.	irregular(ly)
Islam.	Islamic
Isr.	Israeli
It.	Italian
J.	Journal
Jam.	Jamaican
Jan	January
Jap.	Japanese
Jav.	Javanese
Jew.	Jewish
Jewel.	Jewellery
Jord.	Jordanian
jr	junior
Juris.	Jurisdiction
KBE	Knight Commander of the Order of the British Empire
KCVO	Knight Commander of the Royal Victorian Order
kg	kilogram(s)
kHz	kilohertz
km	kilometre(s)
Knowl.	Knowledge
Kor.	Korean
KS	Kansas (USA)
KY	Kentucky (USA)
Kyrgyz.	Kyrgyzstani
£	libra, librae [pound, pounds sterling]
l.	length
LA	Louisiana (USA)
Lab.	Laboratory
Lancs	Lancashire (GB)
Lang.	Language(s)
Lat.	Latin
Latv.	Latvian
lb, lbs	pound(s) weight
Leb.	Lebanese
Lect.	Lecture
Legis.	Legislative
Leics	Leicestershire (GB)
Lex.	Lexicon
Lg.	Large
Lib., Libs	Library, Libraries
Liber.	Liberian
Libsp	Librarianship
Lincs	Lincolnshire (GB)
Lit.	Literature
Lith.	Lithuanian
Liturg.	Liturgical
LLB	Bachelor of Laws
LLD	Doctor of Laws
Lt	Lieutenant
Lt-Col.	Lieutenant-Colonel
Ltd	Limited
m	metre(s)
m.	married
M.	Monsieur
MA	Master of Arts; Massachusetts (USA)
Mag.	Magazine
Maint.	Maintenance
Malay.	Malaysian
Man.	Manitoba (Canada); Manual
Manuf.	Manufactures
Mar.	Marine, Maritime
Mason.	Masonic
Mat.	Material(s)
Math.	Mathematic
MBE	Member of the Order of the British Empire
MD	Doctor of Medicine; Maryland (USA)
ME	Maine (USA)
Mech.	Mechanical
Med.	Medieval; Medium, Media
Medic.	Medical, Medicine
Medit.	Mediterranean
Mem.	Memorial(s); Memoir(s)
Merions	Merionethshire (GB; old)
Meso-Amer.	Meso-American
Mesop.	Mesopotamian
Met.	Metropolitan
Metal.	Metallurgy
Mex.	Mexican
MFA	Master of Fine Arts
mg	milligram(s)
Mgmt	Management
Mgr	Monsignor
MI	Michigan
Micrones.	Micronesian
Mid. Amer.	Middle American
Middx	Middlesex (GB; old)
Mid. E.	Middle Eastern
Mid. Eng.	Middle English
Mid Glam.	Mid Glamorgan (GB)
Mil.	Military
Mill.	Millennium
Min.	Ministry; Minutes
Misc.	Miscellaneous
Miss.	Mission(s)
Mlle	Mademoiselle
mm	millimetre(s)
Mme	Madame
MN	Minnesota
Mnmt, Mnmts	Monument(s)
Mnmtl	Monumental
MO	Missouri (USA)
Mod.	Modern, Modernist
Moldav.	Moldavian
Moldov.	Moldovan
MOMA	Museum of Modern Art
Mon.	Monday
Mongol.	Mongolian
Mons	Monmouthshire (GB; old)
Montgoms	Montgomeryshire (GB; old)
Mor.	Moral
Morav.	Moravian
Moroc.	Moroccan
Movt	Movement
MP	Member of Parliament
MPhil	Master of Philosophy
MS	Mississippi (USA)
MS., MSS	manuscript(s)
MSc	Master of Science
MT	Montana (USA)
Mt	Mount
Mthly	Monthly
Mun.	Municipal
Mus.	Museum(s)
Mus. A.	Museum of Art
Mus. F.A.	Museum of Fine Art(s)
Music.	Musicology
N.	North(ern); National
n	refractive index of a medium
n.	note
N.A.G.	National Art Gallery
Nat.	Natural, Nature
Naut.	Nautical
NB	New Brunswick (Canada)
NC	North Carolina (USA)
ND	North Dakota (USA)
n.d.	no date
NE	Nebraska; Northeast(ern)
Neth.	Netherlandish
Newslett.	Newsletter
Nfld	Newfoundland (Canada)
N.G.	National Gallery
N.G.A.	National Gallery of Art
NH	New Hampshire (USA)
Niger.	Nigerian
NJ	New Jersey (USA)
NM	New Mexico (USA)
nm	nanometre (10^{-9} metre)
nn.	notes
no., nos	number(s)
Nord.	Nordic
Norm.	Normal
Northants	Northamptonshire (GB)
Northumb.	Northumberland (GB)
Norw.	Norwegian
Notts	Nottinghamshire (GB)
Nov	November
n.p.	no place (of publication)
N.P.G.	National Portrait Gallery
nr	near

Nr E.	Near Eastern
NS	New Style; Nova Scotia (Canada)
n. s.	new series
NSW	New South Wales (Australia)
NT	National Trust
Ntbk	Notebook
Numi.	Numismatic(s)
NV	Nevada (USA)
NW	Northwest(ern)
NWT	Northwest Territories (Canada)
NY	New York (USA)
NZ	New Zealand
OBE	Officer of the Order of the British Empire
Obj.	Object(s), Objective
Occas.	Occasional
Occident.	Occidental
Ocean.	Oceania
Oct	October
8vo	octavo
OFM	Order of Friars Minor
OH	Ohio (USA)
OK	Oklahoma (USA)
Olymp.	Olympic
OM	Order of Merit
Ont.	Ontario (Canada)
op.	opus
opp.	opposite; opera [pl. of opus]
OR	Oregon (USA)
Org.	Organization
Orient.	Oriental
Orthdx	Orthodox
OSB	Order of St Benedict
Ott.	Ottoman
Oxon	Oxfordshire (GB)
oz.	ounce(s)
p	pence
p., pp.	page(s)
PA	Pennsylvania (USA)
p.a.	per annum
Pak.	Pakistani
Palaeontol.	Palaeontology, Palaeontological
Palest.	Palestinian
Pap.	Paper(s)
para.	paragraph
Parag.	Paraguayan
Parl.	Parliament
Paroch.	Parochial
Patriarch.	Patriarchate
Patriot.	Patriotic
Patrm.	Patrimony
Pav.	Pavilion
PEI	Prince Edward Island (Canada)
Pembs	Pembrokeshire (GB; old)

Per.	Period
Percep.	Perceptions
Perf.	Performance, Performing, Performed
Period.	Periodical(s)
Pers.	Persian
Persp.	Perspectives
Peru.	Peruvian
PhD	Doctor of Philosophy
Philol.	Philology
Philos.	Philosophy
Phoen.	Phoenician
Phot.	Photograph, Photography, Photographic
Phys.	Physician(s), Physics, Physique, Physical
Physiog.	Physiognomy
Physiol.	Physiology
Pict.	Picture(s), Pictorial
pl.	plate; plural
Plan.	Planning
Planet.	Planetarium
Plast.	Plastic
pls	plates
p.m.	post meridiem [after noon]
Polit.	Political
Poly.	Polytechnic
Polynes.	Polynesian
Pop.	Popular
Port.	Portuguese
Port.	Portfolio
Posth.	Posthumous(ly)
Pott.	Pottery
POW	prisoner of war
PRA	President of the Royal Academy
Pract.	Practical
Prefect.	Prefecture, Prefectural
Preserv.	Preservation
prev.	previous(ly)
priv.	private
PRO	Public Record Office
Prob.	Problem(s)
Proc.	Proceedings
Prod.	Production
Prog.	Progress
Proj.	Project(s)
Promot.	Promotion
Prop.	Property, Properties
Prov.	Province(s), Provincial
Proven.	Provenance
Prt, Prts	Print(s)
Prtg	Printing
pseud.	pseudonym
Psych.	Psychiatry, Psychiatric
Psychol.	Psychology, Psychological
pt	part

Ptg(s)	Painting(s)
Pub.	Public
pubd	published
Publ.	Publicity
pubn(s)	publication(s)
PVA	polyvinyl acetate
PVC	polyvinyl chloride
Q.	quarterly
4to	quarto
Qué.	Québec (Canada)
R	reprint
r	*recto*
RA	Royal Academician
Radnors	Radnorshire (GB; old)
RAF	Royal Air Force
Rec.	Record(s)
red.	reduction, reduced for
Ref.	Reference
Refurb.	Refurbishment
reg	*regit* [ruled]
Reg.	Regional
Relig.	Religion, Religious
remod.	remodelled
Ren.	Renaissance
Rep.	Report(s)
repr.	reprint(ed); reproduced, reproduction
Represent.	Representation, Representative
Res.	Research
rest.	restored, restoration
Retro.	Retrospective
rev.	revision, revised (by/for)
Rev.	Reverend; Review
RHA	Royal Hibernian Academician
RI	Rhode Island (USA)
RIBA	Royal Institute of British Architects
RJ	Rio de Janeiro State
Rlwy	Railway
RSA	Royal Scottish Academy
RSFSR	Russian Soviet Federated Socialist Republic
Rt Hon.	Right Honourable
Rur.	Rural
Rus.	Russian
S	San, Santa, Santo, Sant', São [Saint]
S.	South(ern)
s.	solidus, solidi [shilling(s)]
Sask.	Saskatchewan (Canada)
Sat.	Saturday
SC	South Carolina (USA)
Scand.	Scandinavian
Sch.	School
Sci.	Science(s), Scientific
Scot.	Scottish
Sculp.	Sculpture

SD	South Dakota (USA)
SE	Southeast(ern)
Sect.	Section
Sel.	Selected
Semin.	Seminar(s), Seminary
Semiot.	Semiotic
Semit.	Semitic
Sept	September
Ser.	Series
Serb.	Serbian
Serv.	Service(s)
Sess.	Session, Sessional
Settmt(s)	Settlement(s)
S. Glam.	South Glamorgan (GB)
Siber.	Siberian
Sig.	Signature
Sil.	Silesian
Sin.	Singhala
sing.	singular
SJ	Societas Jesu [Society of Jesus]
Skt	Sanskrit
Slav.	Slavic, Slavonic
Slov.	Slovene, Slovenian
Soc.	Society
Social.	Socialism, Socialist
Sociol.	Sociology
Sov.	Soviet
SP	São Paulo State
Sp.	Spanish
sq.	square
sr	senior
Sri L.	Sri Lankan
SS	Saints, Santi, Santissima, Santissimo, Santissimi; Steam ship
SSR	Soviet Socialist Republic
St	Saint, Sankt, Sint, Szent
Staffs	Staffordshire (GB)
Ste	Sainte
Stud.	Study, Studies
Subalp.	Subalpine
Sum.	Sumerian
Sun.	Sunday
Sup.	Superior
suppl., suppls	supplement(s), supplementary
Surv.	Survey
SW	Southwest(ern)
Swed.	Swedish
Swi.	Swiss
Symp.	Symposium
Syr.	Syrian
Tap.	Tapestry
Tas.	Tasmanian
Tech.	Technical, Technique
Technol.	Technology
Territ.	Territory
Theat.	Theatre
Theol.	Theology, Theological
Theor.	Theory, Theoretical
Thurs.	Thursday
Tib.	Tibetan
TN	Tennessee (USA)
Top.	Topography
Trad.	Tradition(s), Traditional
trans.	translation, translated by; transactions
Transafr.	Transafrican
Transatlant.	Transatlantic
Transcarpath.	Transcarpathian
transcr.	transcribed by/for
Triq.	Triquarterly
Tropic.	Tropical
Tues.	Tuesday
Turk.	Turkish
Turkmen.	Turkmenistani
TV	Television
TX	Texas (USA)
U.	University
UK	United Kingdom of Great Britain and Northern Ireland
Ukrain.	Ukrainian
Un.	Union
Underwtr	Underwater
UNESCO	United Nations Educational, Scientific and Cultural Organization
Univl	Universal
unpubd	unpublished
Urb.	Urban
Urug.	Uruguayan
US	United States
USA	United States of America
USSR	Union of Soviet Socialist Republics
UT	Utah
v	*verso*
VA	Virginia (USA)
V&A	Victoria and Albert Museum
Var.	Various
Venez.	Venezuelan
Vern.	Vernacular
Vict.	Victorian
Vid.	Video
Viet.	Vietnamese
viz.	*videlicet* [namely]
vol., vols	volume(s)
vs.	versus
VT	Vermont (USA)
Vulg.	Vulgarisation
W.	West(ern)
w.	width
WA	Washington (USA)
Warwicks	Warwickshire (GB)
Wed.	Wednesday
W. Glam.	West Glamorgan (GB)
WI	Wisconsin (USA)
Wilts	Wiltshire (GB)
Wkly	Weekly
W. Midlands	West Midlands (GB)
Worcs	Worcestershire (GB; old)
Wtrcol.	Watercolour
WV	West Virginia (USA)
WY	Wyoming (USA)
Yb., Y.-b.	Yearbook, Year-book
Yem.	Yemeni
Yorks	Yorkshire (GB; old)
Yug.	Yugoslavian
Zamb.	Zambian
Zimb.	Zimbabwean

A Note on the Use of the Dictionary

This note is intended as a short guide to the basic editorial conventions adopted in this dictionary. For a fuller explanation, please refer to the Introduction, vol. 1, pp. xiii–xx.

Abbreviations in general use in the dictionary are listed on pp. vii–xii; those used in bibliographies and for locations of works of art or exhibition venues are listed in the Appendices in vol. 33.

Alphabetization of headings, which are distinguished in bold typeface, is letter by letter up to the first comma (ignoring spaces, hyphens, accents and any parenthesized or bracketed matter); the same principle applies thereafter. Abbreviations of 'Saint' and its foreign equivalents are alphabetized as if spelt out, and headings with the prefix 'Mc' appear under 'Mac'.

Authors' signatures appear at the end of the article or sequence of articles that the authors have contributed; in multipartite articles, any section that is unsigned is by the author of the next signed section. Where the article was compiled by the editors or in the few cases where an author has wished to remain anonymous, this is indicated by a square box (□) instead of a signature.

Bibliographies are arranged chronologically (within section, where divided) by order of year of first publication and, within years, alphabetically by authors' names. Abbreviations have been used for some standard reference books; these are cited in full in Appendix C in vol. 33, as are abbreviations of periodical titles (Appendix B). Abbreviated references to alphabetically arranged dictionaries and encyclopedias appear at the beginning of the bibliography (or section).

Biographical dates when cited in parentheses in running text at the first mention of a personal name indicate that the individual does not have an entry in the dictionary. The presence of parenthesized regnal dates for rulers and popes, however, does not necessarily indicate the lack of a biography of that person. Where no dates are provided for an artist or patron, the reader may assume that there is a biography of that individual in the dictionary (or, more rarely, that the person is so obscure that dates are not readily available).

Cross-references are distinguished by the use of small capital letters, with a large capital to indicate the initial letter of the entry to which the reader is directed; for example, 'He commissioned LEONARDO DA VINCI . . .' means that the entry is alphabetized under 'L'.

H

[continued]

Hungary, Republic of. [continued]

VI. Ceramics.

Early examples of Hungarian ceramics are mostly remains of building decoration and stove-tiles. During excavations at the royal palace of Buda Castle (1951) it was found that faience had been produced in a workshop in the west wing of the palace from 1470 until 1480 during the reign of Matthias Corvinus (*reg* 1458–90). The works had a triple kiln, where practical and ornamental dishes, and floor- and wall-tiles were produced.

Decoration was in the Renaissance style with laurel wreaths, cornucopia, acanthus leaves and ribbon motifs (examples in Nagytétény, nr Budapest, Castle Mus.). During this period great quantities of faience were imported from Italy, mainly from Milan, which influenced the style in Hungary. It is likely that the designer working at the workshop was also the court illuminator as the motifs and designs are linked to manuscript designs. As well as the Italian style, Hungarian pottery also followed other western European styles.

During the period of Ottoman rule (1541–1699) the occupied territories (central and southern) adopted Turkish pottery techniques, forms and decoration, while in western Hungary, northern Hungary and Transylvania the influence came from the Habáns (a German-speaking sect of the Anabaptists). Two distinctive styles of wares were produced: tin-glazed wares painted with green, blue and lilac floral and geometric motifs, and those with a yellow or blue ground painted with white decoration (e.g. tankard, late 17th century; Zurich, Schweizer. Landesmus.). At first decoration was influenced by Renaissance designs but later by the Baroque.

From 1660 to 1670 the Habáns' connection with the Mennonites of the Netherlands resulted in the adaptation of Delftware mainly decorated with chinoiseries. The Habáns' main areas of production in Hungary were Transylvania (especially Alvinc and the surrounding district), northern Hungary and Transdanubia. Regional styles also emerged in such areas as the lowlands, Transdanubia, northern Hungary and Transylvania. A typical regional style emerged in the lowlands, especially in Hódmezővásárhely, Mezőtur and Szentes. Szentes pottery was black and similar to that produced in Mohács, Transylvania. In Mezőcsát jugs in the form of figures in national costume, known as 'Miska' jugs, and brown, green, brick-red and orange-coloured dishes, plates and human- and animal-shaped pitchers were produced. In the region of Küküllő some plates were decorated with two layers of differently

19. Faience crucifix with wooden cross, h. 718 mm, inscribed HP, made at the Holics Ceramics Factory, 1765–70 (Budapest, Museum of Applied Arts)

coloured slips, which were then decorated with sgraffito and coated with a lead glaze.

In 1743 Francis, Duke of Lorraine (later Holy Roman Emperor, *reg* 1745–65), established the first Hungarian faience factory in Holics (now Holic, Slovakia; *see* HOLICS CERAMICS FACTORY), which mainly supplied wares for aristocratic palaces. Apart from the late application of Baroque and Rococo styles, decoration was influenced by Strasbourg and Vienna. Dinner-services featured yellow or lavender-blue grounds decorated with white chinoiseries in reserves. Following the European style they produced animal-shaped tureens and boxes designed as bunches of grapes, pineapples, bunches of carrots and other fruits and vegetables. Single moulded pieces were mainly produced, including such religious items as crucifixes (see fig. 19), holy-water stoups in the form of St Veronica, as well as Baroque allegories, folk, biblical and mythological figures and characters from the *commedia dell'arte*.

In 1758 another faience factory was established in Tata by Count József Eszterházy, which partly imitated the style of wares from Holics and even employed some Holics workers. Typical products included *trompe l'oeil* wares, which were decorated with red crabs in relief and were called 'Crab' plates (e.g. of 1780; Budapest, Mus. Applied A.). They also made containers for pharmaceutical use and Rococo-style jewellery boxes in the shape of a chest-of-drawers with chinoiserie motifs (e.g. of 1786; Tata, Kuny Mus.). Another important factory was established by Domokos Kuny in Buda. Other smaller faience factories existed in the second half of the 18th century, including those in Cháva, Gács, Kisbér, Stomfa, Pongyelok, Modor, Kosolna, Bolevár and Szobotist.

During the 19th century stoneware began to be made throughout Hungary. Faience and pewter were no longer employed for household goods, and faience factories either changed to the production of stoneware or produced them both in tandem. Most factories also began to experiment with porcelain. Important 19th-century stoneware factories included those in Körmöczbánya (est. 1800), where from 1896 dishes with Hungarian national scenes and traditional decoration were made and attributed to the influence of Clement Massier; Batiz (1805–68), where production was partly influenced by the English factory of Wedgwood; Telkibánya (1827–1907), which originally produced porcelain but from 1870 exclusively made stoneware; Miskolc (est. 1832), where typical works included dishes and ornamental items decorated with embossed and painted grapes and parsley; and Apátfalva (Belapátfalva; early 19th century–early 20th), which produced basketwork wares and items with braided decoration and painted vine leaves.

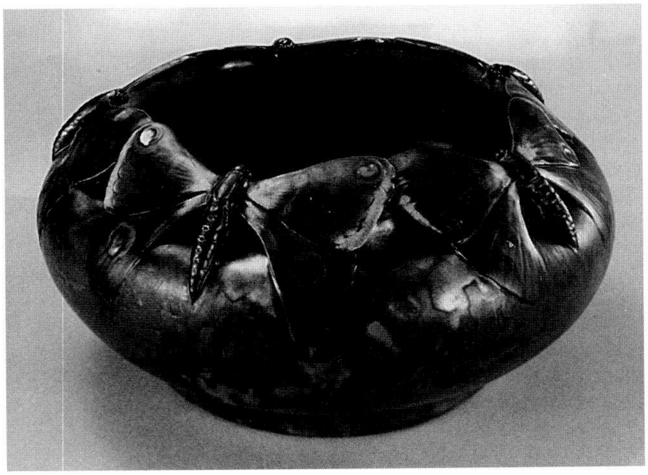

20. Faience vase, h. 166 mm, made by K. Nagy Mihály at the Zsolnay Ceramics Factory, Pécs, 1900–01 (Budapest, Museum of Applied Arts)

The ZSOLNAY CERAMICS FACTORY, established in Pécs in 1851 by Miklós Zsolnay the elder for his son Ignac Zsolnay, was taken in 1865 over by Ignac's brother, Vilmos Zsolnay (1828–1900). Early wares included terracotta building and garden ornaments, clay pipes, bricks and glazed dishes. The factory became internationally famous after the Exposition Universelle of 1878 in Paris, where a collection of faience dishes decorated in high-temperature colours with a porcelain glaze known as 'porcelain faience' was shown. Zsolnay experimented with numerous glazes, the most important of which was the lustred 'Eosin' glaze made with copper-oxide. He also produced ceramic work for Ödön Lechner's buildings, where the decorative effect of colourful tiles was part of an attempt to create a Hungarian style. A range of wares in East Asian and Turkish styles was also produced as a result of the travels in 1887 of Zsolnay's son Miklós Zsolnay the younger. In 1897 Miklós Zsolnay became manager of the factory and employed young artists as designers, including the sculptor Sándor Apáty and the painters Henrik Darilek and Géza Nikelszky. József Rippl-Rónai designed practical and ornamental pieces, dinner-services and tiles. Between 1896 and 1900 products were influenced by the Secession movements, and decoration included flowers, leaves and butterflies (see fig. 20).

The HEREND CERAMICS FACTORY in western Hungary also achieved international recognition. In 1826 Vince Stingl began producing porcelain at the factory, but from 1840 it flourished under the management of Móric Farkasházi-Fischer (1799/1800–80). The factory was famous for reproducing copies of wares from East Asian and 18th-century European porcelain factories including Vienna and Meissen. The factory was very successful at the Great Exhibition of 1851 in London, and Queen Victoria ordered a dinner-service painted with butterflies and flowers, which became known as the 'Victoria' design.

In the 20th century studio potters worked outside the confines of the large factories. Early studio potters included István Gádor (1891–1984), who produced murals, tiles, vases and peasant figures; his later work, however, was abstract in design and painted decoration; Géza Gorka (1894–1971), who produced Habán-style wares and later experimented with simple shapes and crackled glazes; and Margit Kovács, who produced murals, tiles and small figures. The two main centres for studio pottery were the Siklós Centre in Siklós (est. 1969) and the Kecskémet Studio in Kecskémet (est. 1978). In the late 20th century studio potters included Antal Pázmándi (*b* 1943); Gyula Kovács (*b* 1945), who used a variety of textures and glazes; Imre Schrammel (*b* 1933); Katalin Orbán (*b* 1950);

and Levente Thury (*b* 1941), who used Neo-classical and Pop art motifs. Factories still in production in the late 20th century included those in Herend, Zsolnay, Városlöd, Hódmezővásárhely and Hollóháza (*see* HOLLÓHÁZA CERAMICS FACTORY).

BIBLIOGRAPHY

G. Domanovszky: *Népi fazekasság* [Folk pottery] (Budapest, 1942)

K. Csányi: *A magyar kerámia és porcelán története és jegyei* [History of Hungarian ceramics and porcelain] (Budapest, 1954)

G. Sikota: *Herendi porcelán* [Herend porcelain] (Budapest, 1970)

J. Grofcsik: *A magyar finomkerámiaipar története* [The history of Hungarian fine ceramics] (Budapest, 1973)

I. Katona: *A habán kerámia Magyarországon* [Habán ceramics in Hungary] (Budapest, 1974)

——: *A magyar kerámia és porcelán* [Hungarian ceramics and porcelain] (Budapest, 1978)

VII. Glass.

The first reliable reference to the existence of Hungarian glassworks is a document of 1550 in which Georg Krabath of Sparrendorf, secretary to Maria, the widow of Louis II (*reg* 1516–26), offered the purchase of the Sklenoteplice Glassworks along with its house and heated bath to her brother Ferdinand I of Germany (*reg* 1526–64). Krabath claimed that for 200 years the glassworks had supplied mines in Selmec and Körmöc with glass bottles for the storage of aqua-regia (a mixture of nitric and hydrochloric acids), necessary for the disassociation of silver and gold. According to Krabath and other sources the glassworks of Teplicze (now Teplice, Czech Republic) had also been operational from *c.* 1450 chiefly to supply glass to the mining town's aristocracy. Excavations in the 20th century, however, indicate that there was a glassworks operating in Pásztó during the 12th century, which was probably connected to the Benedictine abbey there. The construction of the works was identical to that described in Theophilus's *De diversis artibus* (MS. 12th century). Sources reveal that the Pásztó Glassworks was among the earliest in Europe, and the glass was probably made with the help of German monks. It can be further assumed that before these monastic workshops there were smaller glassworks modelled on the Rhine glasshouses situated in the forests of Germany, which manufactured *Waldglas.*

In the 16th and 17th centuries immigrant Venetian and Murano glassmakers introduced the Italian style of glass to Hungary. These masters worked in the glassworks established on the manorial estates. There is, however, an earlier reference to the probably Venetian glassmaker Antal Olasz, who was a citizen of Buda; he is mentioned in 1419 as 'factor seu laborator vitrorum'. According to the Saxon chronicler Georg Kraus, in 1619–20 Gabriel Bethlen, Prince of Transylvania (*reg* 1613–29), brought glassmakers from Murano to Porumbák where they made crystal. After Bethlen's death, however, they returned to Venice because of their ill-treatment.

The earliest Hungarian glasswares include pitchers (all Budapest, Mus. Applied A.) from Porumbák and from the earlier Transylvanian glassworks at Komána. Their rounded forms are typical of the period; one has a pewter lid while the other two have screw-on tops, which is unusual for the period, and they are known as 'sutus' glass. Two of the jugs are enamelled with the dates 1615 and 1650 and are made from dark-blue, cobalt-oxide glass, which was popular at the beginning of the 17th century. The third jug is transparent and slightly green, covered with a layer of opaque, white glass and dated 1630. Red, white and yellow were the dominant colours used during the period, and the floral motifs decorating these wares suggest the influence of the ceramics of the Habáns (a German-speaking sect of Anabaptists) and to a lesser extent German enamelled glass. Venetian expertise became increasingly important in the production of glass during this period in the manorial glassworks, where window-glass and more decorative utilitarian glass was manufactured.

On 18 July 1635 Pál Pálffy, President of the Hungarian Treasury, wrote a letter about the two types of glassworks: those in the mining towns and those on the manorial estates. He mentioned that the latter were producing wares 'not to satisfy profit motives but for their own pleasure'. Wares from these manorial glassworks include a flask, probably from Porumbák, made by Mikes Mihály and Bethlen Drusián in 1693 (see fig. 21). This flask was made from colourless, transparent glass and decorated with gilded and engraved motifs including trellised, foliate and ribbon decoration, and a crucifix and Lamb of God enclosed in Baroque cartouches. This use of engraved and gilded decoration indicates the influence of enamelled

21. Clear glass flask with silver gilt mount and stopper, h. 230 mm, made by Mikes Mihály and Bethlen Drusián, probably from Porumbák, 1693 (Budapest, Museum of Applied Arts)

18th-century glass from Transylvania and upper northern Hungary with its so-called sealing-wax red decoration. This decoration can be clearly seen on an 18th-century opaque-white jug (Budapest, Mus. Applied A.), which is embedded with sinuous red lines. Until the end of the 18th century blown-glass dominated Hungarian glass production. The primary decorative technique was the 'hot' method, but from the end of the century until the mid-19th century the 'cold' method incorporating cut and engraved decoration became increasingly common.

In 1706 the Parád Glassworks was established by Ferenc II Rákóczy (1676–1735); it moved in 1767 to its present site and changed its name to the Parádvasár Factory. The glassworks manufactured a wide range of everyday and decorative glasswares. The Zlatnó (now Zlatno, Slovakia) Glassworks, established in upper northern Hungary by J. György Zahn in 1807, created high-quality glass in both limited editions and mass-produced wares. During the 1850s it manufactured Czech-influenced cased glass, and in the 1870s and 1880s produced a great deal of luxury and iridescent glass. One of the most significant discoveries during the 19th century, iridescent glass was developed by Valentin Leó Pantocsek at the beginning of the 1860s at Zlatnó. This type was later used for Art Nouveau pieces by such glass artists as Tiffany. The forms of Pantocsek's glass were historical and followed antique prototypes (see fig. 22). His work was shown at the 1873 Weltausstellung in Vienna and promoted by the Austrian glassmaker Ludwig Lobmeyr in his work *Die Glasindustrie: Ihre Geschichte, gegenwärtige Entwicklung und Statistik* (Stuttgart, 1874).

The most significant 19th-century factory for decorating glass was the firm of Henrik Giergl, which was established in 1820; wares were enamelled, gilded and engraved. The two exceptional Hungarian exponents of cut and engraved glass were probably of Czech origin: József Piesche worked in Pest from 1821, and the engraver József Oppitz worked at the Kassa (now Košice, Slovakia) Glassworks between 1840 and 1870. Their most significant works were Piesche's colourless beaker (*c.* 1830; Budapest, Mus. Applied A.), decorated with an engraved mythological scene, and Oppitz's violet-stained goblet (1847; Budapest, Mus. Applied A.), decorated with an engraved scene of Miklós Zríny's battle at Szigetvár in 1556. The most valued glassware during the 1850s was the souvenir spa glass made at such factories as the Parádvasár Factory, of which the most popular type was the 'Forty-Eight' glass depicting the 1848 Revolution and the War of Independence (1848–9), which was generally decorated with the Hungarian coat of arms, flags and commemorative inscriptions.

The politician Lajos Kossuth (1802–94), who played an important role in the development of Hungarian industry, was an inspiring force for glassmakers with his Industrial Society Promotion Exhibitions (1842, 1843 and 1846). Hungarian factories were also particularly successful at the international exhibitions, including the 1862 International Exhibition in London, the 1873 Weltausstellung in Vienna, where the Zayugrócz (now Uhrovec, Slovakia) Glassworks, belonging to J. Schreiber and his nephews, was awarded a medal, and at the 1900 Exposition Universelle in Paris.

22. Iridescent glass bottle in the shape of a stamnium, h. 315 mm, made by Valentin Leó Pantocsek at the Zlatnó Glassworks, *c.* 1860 (Budapest, Museum of Applied Arts)

From 1881 the director of the glass-painting at the Zayugrócz Glassworks studio was ISTVÁN SOVÁNKA. He made historical-style cut, engraved and layered glass (e.g. baptismal font, 1896; Budapest, Mus. Applied A.) and Art Nouveau vases and dishes, which were acid-etched and sometimes iridescent and layered.

Miksa Róth (1865–1944) won a silver medal at the 1900 Exposition Universelle in Paris with his Tiffany-style mosaic *Pax and the Rising Sun* (1900; Budapest, Mus. Applied A.). He was commissioned to make glass for numerous national and international public buildings, including the Gresham Life Insurance Co. Building (1906) and the Ferenc Liszt Academy of Music in Budapest (1907); he executed stained-glass windows including those in the Palace of Culture (1912) in Marosvasárhely (now Tîrgu-Mureş, Romania), which were designed by Ede Thoroczkai Wigand and Sándor Nagy, and the glass cupola for the Teatro Nacional in Mexico City (1910), which was designed by Géza Maróti. He also made the windows for the dining-room in the Andrássy residence in Budapest, which was designed by József Rippl-Ronai.

At the beginning of the 20th century decorative glassware was not always of a high standard. The fundamental problem was that glass painting was taught only in the Industrial Drawing School, and therefore in every glass factory a particular style emerged that was determined by the requirements of the factory. High-quality work, however, was produced: at the beginning of the 1950s the Zoltán Veress Factory made coloured and aventurine glass. Julia Báthory (*b* 1902), who had studied in Munich and at the Bauhaus, started a glass-design course in the Secondary School for the Arts in Budapest, basing her system on German and French traditions. Her work included architectural and Art Deco glass, which often incorporated mirrored, etched and sand-blasted work.

In 1953 a course in glass painting was introduced in the Decorative Arts Department at the School for Applied Arts in Budapest. In 1966 an independent glass design course was started by the painter György Z. Gács (1914–78), who applied architectural and sculptural elements to his glass; similar methods were employed by the sculptors Tibor Vilt and Erzsebet Schaar, who created compositions made of sheets of glass. Zsófia Kanyák (1944–75) designed simple functional objects, decorative wares and lighting fixtures, first in Murano, Venice, and later for the Rosenthal Factory.

Sculptural, studio-glass training was introduced by Zoltán Bohus (*b* 1941), who taught glass design in the School of Applied Arts in Budapest from 1966. Bohus first experimented with the possibilities of combining metal and glass and then examined the relationship between light, glass and space with geometric, cut and cemented layered-glass sculptures. Maria Lugossy (*b* 1950) worked in a similar fashion; her organic forms, however, are softer than those of Bohus. Some of the work of György Buczkó (*b* 1950) also reveals this tendency, but as a multi-media artist he also experimented with etched architectural glass and created various surface effects by using shattered, layered glass. Géza Sigmond (*b* 1950) and Mihály Melcher (*b* 1953) made naturalistic, Post-modernist sculptures using the *pâte de verre* technique. The sculptural work of Endre Gaál (*b* 1957) is of particular interest: it incorporates cut, cemented, carved and shattered glass, stone and other transparent and opaque materials. His work explores the relationship between light, glass and space. Similar work was executed by János Jegenyés (*b* 1946). Márton Horváth (*b* 1941) worked along completely different lines, using the techniques employed in Art Nouveau glass. These artists received both national and international acclaim for their work, winning prizes and taking part in international shows.

BIBLIOGRAPHY

L. Lobmeyr: *Die Glasindustrie: Ihre Geschichte, gegenwärtige Entwicklung und Statistik* (Stuttgart, 1874)
I. Görög: *Az üvegipar: Hivatalos jelentés a Párizsban 1878-ban tartott egyetemes kiállításról* [The glass industry: Official report on the World Fair held in Paris in 1878] (Budapest, 1879)
L. Sághelyi: *A magyar üvegesipar története* [The history of the Hungarian glass industry] (Budapest, 1938)
B. Takács: *Parádi üvegművészet* [Glass art from Parád] (Budapest, 1970)
B. Borsos: *A magyar üvegművesség* [Hungarian glass art] (Budapest, 1974)
V. Varga: *Szecessziós üvegek* [Secession glass] (Budapest, 1980)
M. Bunta and I. Katona: *Az erdélyi üvegművesség a századfordulóig* [Transylvanian glass art at the turn of the century] (Bucharest, 1984)
V. Varga: 'Pantocsek Valentin Leó munkássága: A hialoplasztika, a magyar vas diatretum és as irizáló üveg' [The work of Valentin Leó Pantocsek: glasswork, the Hungarian iron cage-cup (*diatretum*) and iridescent glass], *Építőanyag*, xii (1987), pp. 368–73
——: *Régi magyar üveg* [Old Hungarian glass] (Budapest, 1989)

VERA VARGA

VIII. Metalwork.

1. Gold and silver. 2. Base metals.

1. Gold and silver.

(i) Before 1600. (ii) 1600 and after.

(i) Before 1600. The only mint in Hungary under the Arpád kings was at Esztergom and it has been suggested that a workshop there, perhaps directed by a master trained in Regensburg, might have been responsible for works associated with the court of Stephen I (*reg* 997–1038), including the Gizella Cross (after 1006; Munich, Residenz). Byzantine influence remained strong into the 13th century, for example on a silver-gilt crozier (late 12th century; Kalocsa, Cathedral Treasury; *see* ROMANESQUE, §VI, 5 and fig. 75). It is difficult, however, to identify works from the region that were imported, or to distinguish between those made by foreign and native craftsmen at the court and monastic workshops. Under the Anjou kings the range of influences extended to include Italy, and the only technique employed in the 14th and 15th centuries that may suggest a national style is the use of 'Hungarian enamel' (*see* §IX below; *see also* GOTHIC, §V, 5). As well as the court workshops at Budapest, a metalworkers' guild was established at Kassa (now Košice, Slovakia) in 1376 and there were others in Besztercebánya (now Banská Bystrica), the Szepes region (now Spiš, both Slovakia), Kolozsvár (now Cluj-Napoca) and Nagyvárad (now Oradea, both Romania).

During the period of Turkish rule from 1541 to the end of the 17th century, the goldsmith's art was greatly affected by war, religious intolerance and the frequent melting down of silver objects, yet the high technical and artistic quality of surviving pieces shows that this was the most important period of Hungarian gold- and silversmithing. During this period the Hungarian silver mines, for example in Selmecbánya (now Banská Štiavnica, Slovakia) and Nagybánya (now Baia Mare, Romania), operated partly through state monopolies and were partly leased out. The princes of Transylvania, for example, allowed silversmiths in this region to buy in a certain quantity of precious metals annually, which was often supplemented by the melting down of silver coins. This was also the common practice in the Turkish-occupied region of the Great Plains.

By the second half of the 16th century the official marks of the master silversmith and the assaymasters had been prescribed by the silversmiths' guilds, yet hallmarks were not used on gold objects, and maker's marks on gold items are rare. The price of silverwork was set according to the type and quality of the object, but in the second half of the 16th century the parliament of the Transylvanian principality decided to establish standard prices for silverwork. In the Kingdom of Hungary, however, the administrative institutions of the counties set prices from 1625.

The guilds also regulated the operations of the master silversmiths' workshops, and the increased prestige of the craft meant that silversmiths were appointed to high office in municipal administrations. The guild regulations strictly forbade craftsmen to accept commissions from outside the town or fortifications in which they worked and also forbade the selling of silverware in the countryside, although silversmiths from different guilds often collaborated on particular commissions, resulting in the spread of new techniques and styles. The wide variety of techniques used ranged from embossed and etched decoration, filigree-work and bezelwork to various forms of enamelling.

From 1541 to the 1690s Hungarian silversmiths were well supplied with work. Documentary sources provide an idea of the types of work produced by Hungarian silversmiths (see Szádeczky, 1913). The Saxon silversmiths of Transylvania produced silverwork for the Romanian princes and, along with the Hungarians, made the huge amount of gold- and silverware that was sent to the sultan's court both as gifts and as annual tribute. Works were frequently purchased by envoys in Vienna and Venice, as well as in Istanbul. The aristocrats of northern and western Hungary, for example the ESTERHÁZY family, however, commissioned most of their silver from craftsmen in Augsburg and Nuremberg.

By the early 16th century silversmiths were working in the Renaissance style that had emanated from the royal court in Buda. One of the most distinguished pieces of Hungarian Renaissance silverware is a silver-gilt ewer and basin for wine (1548; Budapest, Mus. Applied A.; see fig. 23) made for Ferdinand I's Chief Cupbearer, Antal Losonczi, by Franciscus Képiró (*fl* 1547–66) of Kolozsvár. This magnificent piece is cast, hammered and enamelled and is decorated with rich Renaissance ornament depicting mythological and biblical scenes. Variations of the late Renaissance style were used in the three different regions. The silversmiths in northern Hungary, living under Habsburg rule, and the Saxon masters of Transylvania were primarily influenced by the German and Dutch Renaissance styles and later by Baroque forms. The native Transylvanian silversmiths developed a more elaborate version of the Italian Renaissance style, while those living under Turkish rule in the south worked in a more austere style. Religious and ideological factors affected the production and style of silverware. The majority of Hungarians in the Protestant parts of the country (mainly the areas occupied by the Turks and Transylvania) worked in the late Renaissance style.

Most of the silverware made in the second half of the 16th century has been destroyed by either religious intolerance or war. The few surviving works are diverse. The Protestant Church became the main patron of silversmiths in this period. There was a great demand for goblets, chalices, cups, plates, bowls, jewellery and metalwork for clothes, as well as weapons. Typically Hungarian objects from the second half of the 16th century include the stemmed cup in Transylvania and the vessels decorated with authentic or imitation ancient Roman coins.

Extant examples of 16th-century silverwork include the badge (Budapest, N. Mus.) of the Brassó guild (now Braşov, Romania), dated 1556. It has a Renaissance shield in relief on the obverse, with an engraved representation

23. Ewer and basin by Franciscus Képiró, silver gilt and enamel, h. (ewer) 750 mm, 1548 (Budapest, Museum of Applied Arts)

of the silversmith's workshop on the reverse. The master who made it is anonymous but denoted by the letters IE. A lidded silver-gilt cup (1578; Budapest, N. Mus.) made by János Lippai (*fl* 1542–78) from Kassa has a cylindrical body decorated with engraved scenes, and on the top there is a statuette of a fighting Roman. These slender, tall, waisted goblets are also often decorated with Gothic foliage. One of the earliest surviving stemmed cups (Budapest, N. Mus.) from Transylvania is the work of György Sturm (*fl* 1589–99), a goldsmith from Nagyszeben (now Sibiu, Romania), made at the end of the 16th century. There are 12 ancient Roman denarii used as decoration on the body. This technique of using antique coins came from southern Germany and became popular in Transylvania through the work of the Saxon goldsmiths there.

(ii) 1600 and after. A greater quantity of gold- and silversmiths' work survives from the beginning of the 17th century, due to the cessation of war in this period. Two important documents concerning silversmithing have also survived: the manuscript of the silversmith W. PÉTER KECSKEMÉTI (published as *Kecskeméti W. Péter ötvöskönyve*, Budapest, 1884), written between 1644 and 1671, which mentions the techniques and working methods of the period, and the collection of silversmiths' designs of András Tar (*fl* 1677–83; Cluj-Napoca, U. Lib.), part of which he produced in a workshop in Debrecen in 1677. At the beginning of the 17th century there was a goldsmiths' guild operating in Debrecen in the territory

under Turkish rule, and the goldsmiths' guild at Kecskemét was founded in the mid-17th century. The objects made by these guilds have distinctive forms and styles.

The work of the guild of Debrecen incorporates more elaborate techniques, richer ornamentation and a wider variety of forms in the late Renaissance style. The most beautiful example is the series of communion flagons made by Márton Szegedi (*fl* 1611–68) that are decorated with columns, the first two of which were made in 1631 (all Debrecen, Calvinist Great Church). Szegedi also used this motif on a cup (1651; Budapest, N. Mus.). Another variation of the work produced in Debrecen is the silver gilt christening flagon (1635–9; Budapest, N. Mus.) made by Bálint Miskolci (*fl* 1627–52).

The work of the gold- and silversmiths of Kecskemét is typified by simple, mostly cylindrical vessels with few decorative elements that are engraved and in the Renaissance style. The best exponent of this style was Illés Tar (*fl* 1640–84), who made a lidded silver-gilt wine flagon in 1642 and a communion plate in 1647 (both Kecskemét, Ráday Mus. Reform Ch.). The work of the guild of Kecskemét also includes finely engraved goblets and plates.

In the principality of Transylvania there were many distinguished goldsmiths' guilds. In Brassó, for example, 169 goldsmiths were recorded in the 17th century. The Transylvanian silversmiths worked in two distinct styles: the Hungarian guilds maintained the colourful, rich traditions of the late Renaissance style, while the closed community of the Saxons was influenced by the work of craftsmen in German-speaking territories, resulting in the use of more elaborate, figural decoration. They were also more receptive to the Baroque style.

The style of the Hungarian silversmiths of Transylvania is represented by the work of István Brózer (*fl* 1628–60), a goldsmith from Kolozsvár, who made a gold chalice (Budapest, N. Mus.) on which the sufferings of Christ are depicted in 18 small, chased gold scenes decorated with coloured, painted and inlaid enamel. The chalice was made for the Protestant church of Kolozsvár on the order of Prince George Rákóczy I (1593–1648). The goldsmiths of Kolozsvár specialized in the production of cups with six-lobed foliage and with faceted bodies and lids, which were made for presentation at Protestant church services. The joint coat of arms of the Rákóczy family and of Transylvania appear on one example (Budapest, N. Mus.), along with Latin inscriptions and chased Renaissance decoration. In Transylvania the hexagonal plate was also popular and was made by both Hungarian and Saxon goldsmiths. A typical example is the silver-gilt plate (1670; Budapest, N. Mus.) made by Daniel Brassai (*fl* 1655–95) of Kolozsvár and inscribed with the name *Teleki Mihály–Vér Judit*.

The style of the silversmiths from the Saxon towns of Transylvania is characterized by the use of repoussé work. Their work is decorated with flower and foliate ornament and engraved with mythological, ancient and biblical subjects. There were a number of masters of this style working in the largest Saxon guilds in Brassó and Nagyszeben. The most important master, SEBASTIAN HANN, worked in Nagyszeben. Eighty-five of his works are extant (Budapest, N. Mus.; Sibiu, Brukenthal Mus.). A cup (1697; Budapest, N. Mus.) decorated with mythological scenes that he made for the imperial judge in Nagyszeben, Bálint Frank (*d* 1697), is typical of the high quality and originality of his work.

The territory in the north that came under Habsburg rule also included important goldsmiths' workshops. The northern part of the country, due to its favourable geographical position, was less afflicted by the almost continuous wars in the south, and many goldsmiths fleeing from the Turks went to the north to find work. Goldsmiths' guilds operated in the capital, Pozsony (now Bratislava, Slovakia), and in the flourishing silvermining towns, for example Besztercebánya, Selmecbánya (now Banská Štiavnica, Slovakia), Körmöcbánya (now Kremnica, Slovakia), where there was also a mint, and in Kassa.

These guilds had mostly German members, and their work is more richly ornamented. A magnificent example is a gold, lidded goblet (*c.* 1645; Budapest, Mus. Applied A.) made by Erasmus Bergman (*fl* 1643; *d* 1647) of Besztercebánya, which is decorated with inlaid enamel, diamonds, rubies and pearls. A more modest example is an ornamental goblet (Budapest, Mus. Applied A.), decorated with mining scenes and with rose quartz and argentite, that was produced in Selmecbánya in 1650, on the occasion of the visit to the town by Ferdinand III to view the new mine shaft named after him. The maker of the goblet was probably the master goldsmith of Selmecbánya. An example of the work of another highly skilled craftsman is the great jewelled plate (Miskolc, Calvinist Church), decorated with stylized female figures, spiral Baroque motifs and garlands of fruit and made by W. Péter Kecskeméti in Kassa. The gilt figures and ornament in bas-relief cover the dish of the plate; the base is chased and nielloed.

With the defeat of the Turks in 1699 and the revolt (1703–11) led by Ferenc II Rákóczy (1674–1735) against the Habsburgs, the political and economic situation changed. This heralded a period when Hungarian traditions were replaced by foreign styles, chiefly the Viennese Baroque. The number of Hungarian craftsmen steadily decreased, and, although traditional techniques and high standards were maintained, they were unable to obtain enough commissions, due to the competition from immigrant craftsmen. The traditional forms made in the 17th century were replaced by western European Baroque forms, and the market was flooded with candlesticks, sugar bowls, coffeespoons and teasets. Due to the success of the Counter-Reformation, the production of ecclesiastical objects again flourished, although forms were influenced by the Austrian and southern German Baroque styles. Objects with highly embossed Baroque cartouches and rocaille forms may be copies of products from either Vienna or Augsburg.

During the 18th century JOHANNES SZILASSY from Löcse (now Levoča, Slovakia) was the most significant and productive goldsmith working in the Hungarian Rococo style. His work is characterized by the use of oval, enamelled, small scenes, sumptuously decorated with jewelled, enamelled flowers and angel heads. His silver-gilt monstrance (1769; Gödöllő, Roman Catholic Church) and chalice (1777; Budapest, Mus. Applied A.) were influential, due to their ingenious and elegant forms. His workshop provided ecclesiastical objects for churches throughout Hungary.

In the 19th century, however, goldsmithing declined, and mass-produced Viennese goods undermined the national market. The most prominent goldsmiths in this period were JÓZEF SZENTPÉTERI, who produced elegant, fine vessels, for example a silver coffee service (1823; Budapest, Mus. Applied A.), and the PRANDTNER family, who worked in Pest. In the mid- and late 19th century, with the rise of Historicism and the Secession movement, specialist goldsmiths were replaced by designers who determined the forms and styles used in goldsmiths' work. One of the most important designers was Pál Horti (1865–1907), who also designed jewellery, for example 'Jewels' (1901–2; Budapest, Mus. Applied A.). In the first half of the 20th century goldsmiths' work was dominated by the historicist and conservative tendencies that enjoyed the support of official cultural policy. During the 1930s more modern designs were introduced by Lajos Bittner (*b* 1899; Budapest, N. Mus.) and by Margit Tevan (1901–78), who used tin in her works in the absence of silver. More recently, the goldsmith's art has moved in new directions, as can be seen in the work of the School of Enamel Art in Kecskemét.

BIBLIOGRAPHY

J. Mihalik: *Kassaváros ötvösségének története* [The history of the goldsmith's art in Kassa] (Budapest, 1900)

L. Szádeczky: *Iparfejlődés és a czéhek története Magyarországon: Okirattárral (1307–1848)* [The history and development of guilds in Hungary: a source study (1307–1848)] (Budapest, 1913)

K. Divald: *A magyar iparmüvészet története* [The history of Hungarian decorative arts] (Budapest, 1929)

E. Koszeghy: *Magyarországi ötvösjegyek a középkortól 1867–ig/Merkzeichen der Goldschmiede Ungarns vom Mittelalter bis 1867* (Budapest, 1936) [bilingual text]

I. B. Bobrovszky: *A XVII. századi mezővárosok iparmüvészete* [17th-century market town decorative arts] (Budapest, 1980)

Az európai iparmüvészet stiluskorszakai: Reneszánsz és manierizmus [European styles of decorative art: Renaissance and Mannerism] (exh. cat., ed. M. Péter; Budapest, Mus. Applied A., 1988)

Az európai iparmüvészet stiluskorszakai: Barokk és rokokó [European styles of decorative art: Baroque and Rococo] (exh. cat., ed. M. Péter; Budapest, Mus. Applied A., 1990)

Az európai iparmüvészet stiluskorszakai: A klasszicizmustói a biedermeierig [European styles of decorative art: from Classicism to Biedermeier] (exh. cat., ed. M. Péter; Budapest, Mus. Applied A., 1990)

Schätze des ungarischen Barock: Eine Ausstellung in Zusammenarbeit mit dem Ungarischen Nationalmuseum (exh. cat., Hanau, Dt. Goldschmiedehaus, 1991)

2. BASE METALS. Knowledge of the Hungarian metalworking industry from the Middle Ages is limited, as most objects have been destroyed, and few contemporary sources mention the production of metalwork. The craftsmen who worked in iron, copper and pewter usually formed common guilds, and consequently there were associations of which bellfounders, gunmakers and pewterers were all members. Pewterers in many towns were probably also members of the coppersmiths' guilds. Metalworkers often practised a wide variety of trades and produced diverse objects. The seals and symbols of their guilds often refer to this practice, in that vessels, jugs, bells and guns are all depicted on them.

During the 16th and 17th centuries northern Hungary and Transylvania became the most important areas of pewter production, and consequently separate pewterers' guilds appeared. Kassa (now Košice, Slovakia) was the centre of the pewter trade in northern Hungary, and in Transylvania the Saxon towns were the main centres. In the 17th century the pewterers' guilds of the largest Hungarian towns were united in one guild. The tin used in the manufacture of pewter was, however, imported. The guilds stipulated that the proportions should be six parts of tin to one of lead. The most commonly used alloy, however, was the 'Nuremberg formula', which was a mixture of ten parts tin to one part lead. Makers' and town marks appeared in the second half of the 16th century, and from the 18th century various marks denoting the quality of tin and lead were used. Documents give a detailed account of the styles of pewter objects made in Hungary from the 16th century. In wealthy households pewter goods were not recorded individually but by the hundredweight. Jugs, flagons, plates, bowls, fruit bowls, trays, baths, salt-cellars, candlesticks and even some coffins and coffin-plates were all made of pewter. Pewter imported from England, Vienna and Nuremberg also influenced the forms and styles used by Hungarian craftsmen, and, after the defeat of the Turks in the late 17th century, many pewterers from Vienna and Brno moved into the former occupied areas in the south.

The most magnificently decorated pewter goods were the guild flagons. One of the most beautiful examples was probably made in Kassa for the bootmakers' guild of Gölnicbánya (1524; Budapest, N. Mus.). This flagon stands on three moulded, dragon-headed legs, and on its body saints are depicted in two rows set in niches defined by columns, with a figure of the Virgin in the centre. The flagon (1693; Budapest, N. Mus.) made for the bootmakers' guild of Sopron is the work of Andreas Schrick (*fl* 1693–1736), who was active in that town. The flagon is wide-bottomed and slender-bodied and decorated with a series of rings. It stands on three legs with angel heads and has a winged eagle as a finial. This type of decorative presentation object was also popular in the 18th century.

Most ecclesiastical and secular pewter objects made in Hungary are, however, generally simple in form and decoration. Most of the pewter produced from the 16th to the 17th centuries consists of flagons, simple rimmed plates and bowls. Plain and ornamented vessels are recorded separately in documents. Pewter vessels are decorated with wrigglework and linear designs and with engraving and embossing. As well as stylized flower patterns, combined with ribbons, foliage, garlands of tulips, carnations, five-petalled roses and pomegranates, there are also often depictions of birds, animals and human figures. A fine example of sumptuous flower decoration is a pewter flagon (Budapest, N.G.) made at the end of the 17th century by Jonas [Johannes] Osterlamb (*fl* 1672–1700) from Eperjes (now Prešov, Slovakia).

Late Renaissance ornament continued to be used in the 18th century. Chased pewter vessels, popular in western Europe, were rare in Hungary, although the guild regulations of the pewterers of Kassa record them in 1762. The conservatism of forms and styles at this time meant that the Baroque and Rococo styles were little used. With the increased production of porcelain and glazed earthenware, however, pewter slowly went out of fashion, and by the early 19th century it was rarely used for domestic objects.

The flowering of the copper industry in Hungary was connected with the rich copper mines in northern Hungary. Most surviving copper objects were produced in this region, as it was less afflicted by war, and, therefore, fewer items were melted down. Coppersmiths' guilds existed by the mid-16th century. The high quality of the work is typified by the seal of the coppersmiths' guild of Kassa (Košice, Mus. E. Slovakia), dated 1595, with a German inscription and a depiction of two eagles holding a flagon with the double-headed Habsburg eagle. A similar seal (Bratislava, Mun. Mus.) was made by one of the guilds in Pozsony (now Bratislava) in 1688. Copper vessels for religious and secular use, including christening sets, bread tins, decorated kettles, wine-coolers, wine-jars, flagons and caskets, were produced in various forms and styles from the 16th to the 19th centuries. In the 19th century JÓZEF SZENTPÉTERI also produced a number of chased and engraved copper panels, for example that depicting *Alexander the Great Crossing the Granicus* (Budapest, Mus. Applied A.).

Guilds for blacksmiths and locksmiths (iron- and steel-workers) existed in the 15th century. These craftsmen often founded joint guilds with carpenters, particularly in Transylvania, but a locksmiths' and gunsmiths' guild in Kassa was also recorded in 1627. Independent locksmiths' guilds existed in Marosvásárhely (now Tîrgu-Mureş, Romania) and in Temesvár (now Timişoara, Romania). At the end of the 18th century a common guild of locksmiths and carpenters was also founded in Kolozsvár (now Cluj-Napoca, Romania). Locksmiths produced iron lamp-stands, railings, irons and bolts, as well as steel locks and keys. Gothic elements continued to be used with the emergent Renaissance style in the 16th century. The earliest extant pieces of cast ironwork were made in the northern highlands of Hungary (now Slovakia) at the end of the 16th century. These include a stove with a depiction of the *Baptism* (1591) and a tombstone for Polyxena Knorr from Selmecbánya (now Banská Štiavnica) in 1598 (both Budapest, Mus. Applied A.).

With the appearance of new techniques and forms in the 17th century, for example the circular cut iron bar, new types of objects were produced, such as the iron bedstead, which was considered a luxury object. Decorative motifs also became richer, and human figures and arabesque forms appeared. Wrought ironwork was decorated with foliage, lambrequins and vase shapes in the 17th-century Baroque style.

The construction of numerous buildings in the 18th century led to an increase in the production of wrought ironwork. In the towns many new forms of ironwork appeared including decorated name plates. The ironwork for the two arcades in the County Hall at Eger is a magnificent example of the Rococo style, as are the gates with the coat of arms of Eger (1758–61; see fig. 24); these were made by Henrik Fazola (*see* FAZOLA), who moved to Eger at the invitation of Ferenc Barkóczy, the Bishop and Lord Lieutenant of Eger, and who worked there until his death. In the late 18th century the style of wrought ironwork became less ornamental.

In the first half of the 19th century wrought ironwork was superseded by cheaper cast iron. The development of the technique of casting iron on a large scale led to industrial manufacture and an increase in production. The most important centre was the foundry at Munkács (now MUKACHEVO, Ukraine). Its first products were copied from patterns brought from Berlin, and the factory produced domestic objects, small statuettes and decorated stoves and tombstones. In the last third of the 19th century, however, there was a revival of wrought ironwork, and such craftsmen as Gyula Jungfer (1841–1908) attempted to develop a historicist style of ironwork. Jungfer also made ironwork and steelwork for a number of important buildings erected in Budapest during this period, for example the Royal Palace, the Vigado Concert Hall, the Customs House, the Parliament Building, the Opera House, the Basilica and the Eastern Railway Station. With the appearance of the Secession style, wrought ironwork continued to be popular, and there are a number of good examples of late 19th-century ironwork both in Hungarian folk styles and with stylized foliate forms in Budapest.

24. Wrought-iron gates by Henrik Fazola, County Hall, Eger, 1758–61

BIBLIOGRAPHY

L. Pusztai: *Magyar öntöttvasművesség* [Hungarian cast-iron work] (Budapest, 1978)

E. Toranová: *Cinárstvo na Slovensky* [Pewterers of Slovakia] (Bratislava, 1980)

G. Németh: 'Felsőmagyarország óuművessége a XVI–XVII. században' [Upper northern Hungarian pewterwork in the XVI–XVII centuries], *Művészettörténeti Értesitő*, xxx/3 (1981), pp. 171–87

K. Pereházy: *Magyarországi kovacsoltvas-művesség* [Hungarian blacksmiths' work] (Budapest, 1982)

G. Németh: *Ónedények* [Pewter vessels], Budapest, N. Mus. cat. (Budapest, 1983)
E. Toranová: *Medi kováčstvo* [Medieval blacksmiths' work] (Bratislava, 1991)

IDA BOD-BOBROVSZKY

IX. Objects of vertu.

The most characteristic feature of Hungarian objects of vertu is the use of a variety of enamel techniques. From the 11th century to the 14th the best goldsmiths were employed by the Hungarian royal court. They produced, among other works, the rich caches of jewellery—mainly rings and buckles decorated with cloisonné enamel—that were discovered in 13th-century royal graves (examples in Budapest, N. Mus.) and the altarpiece (*c.* 1340; New York, Met.) of Queen Elizabeth, wife of Charles Robert of Anjou (*reg* 1308–42).

Most works made from the first half of the 15th century to the 1630s are decorated with filigree enamel, a variation of cloisonné (*see* ENAMEL, §2(i)). The decorated fields, each of a different colour, are lined by twisted silver wires instead of thin silver or gold contours, and the ornamentation is never figural; the decorated surface forms a geometric design sometimes containing stylized leaf and flower motifs. Although this technique probably originated in northern Italy and was disseminated to Hungarian workshops through Venetian and Dalmatian sources, it was so widely practised in Hungary that it is particularly associated with production there. The procedure was followed only sporadically in other European countries, mainly in areas (e.g. southern Poland, the Austrian provinces) that had close economic and artistic connections with Hungary. Most filigree pieces were made for ecclesiastical use, notably the reliquary bust of Ladislas IV (*c.* 1420) in the treasury of Győr Cathedral and Benedek Suky's chalice (mid-15th century; *see* GOTHIC, fig. 89) in the treasury of Esztergom Cathedral; among secular pieces, a fine example is a goblet (*c.* 1480; Wiener Neustadt, Stadtmus.) made for Matthias Corvinus.

While religious symbolism did not appear frequently on 16th- and 17th-century jewels, a significant exception is the depiction on pendants of the Virgin and Child, surrounded by an ornamental baldacchino with the inscription *Patrona Hungariae* (e.g. Budapest, N. Mus.; see fig. 25). This recurrent motif reflects the role of the Virgin as Hungary's celestial patron and the population as believers and defenders of the Catholic faith. Such pendants were worn by people—mostly but not always by women—who were active in the Sodalitates or Confraternitates Marianae, which had been founded and were supported by the Jesuits. A wide variety of jewellery was produced in the 16th and 17th centuries, including necklaces, clasps, rings and the breast pieces favoured by Saxon women in Transylvania. Coloured work was particularly favoured in this region, for example a necklace (early 17th century; Budapest, N. Mus.), made in Kolozsvár, decorated with pearls, rubies and black, white and blue enamel.

In the 17th and 18th centuries medieval enamelling procedures were revived and were practised frequently, especially the *basse taille* (Fr.: 'rounded relief') and *ronde bosse* (Fr.: 'shallow cut') techniques. The former appears on almost all types of objects, whereas the latter appears

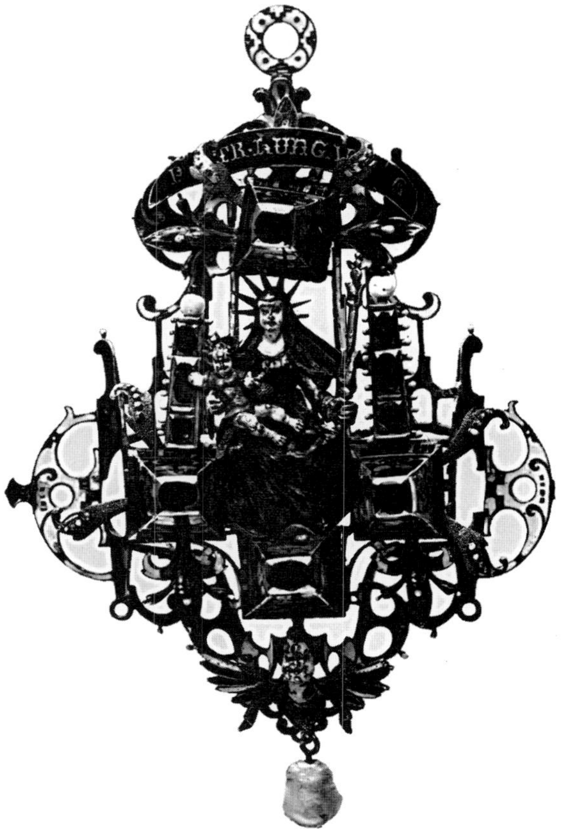

25. Pendant, gold with *basse taille* and *ronde bosse* enamel, inscribed *Patrona Hungariae*, first half of the 17th century (Budapest, Hungarian National Museum)

mainly on jewellery. The most splendid pieces of Hungarian jewellery are pendants and buckles made for women and the aigrettes decorating the high fur caps of men's festive attire. Pendants show the richest and most ingenious variations. Pieces with figural ornamentation were widely produced, especially in the workshops of northern Hungary and Transylvania. These pendants were decorated in *ronde bosse* enamel with such mythological and allegorical figures as Diana or Justice, as well as various figures of animals, mostly birds. These animals often carried symbolic meanings; for example, the motif of the pelican feeding its young with its own blood, which was popular throughout central Europe, had its original religious meaning of self-sacrifice obscured in favour of a more general symbol of marital love.

In the middle and second half of the 18th century the best Hungarian goldsmiths seem to have preferred the enamel painting technique. JOHANNES SZILASSY, for example, was one of the most famous and prolific masters of this technique. Although his oeuvre is represented mostly by such ecclesiastical objects as monstrances and chalices, his workshop also issued other pieces including cases, caskets and boxes ornamented with enamel and precious stones. It was in the wake of his and his contemporaries' contributions that there was a growing taste for several types of objects of vertu. However, these pieces were now mostly imported, mainly from France and Vienna, by members of the landed gentry and the aristocracy. This tendency continued into the 19th century, and in the majority of objects made subsequently it is not so much the influence of local traditions as that of French and Austrian models that is evident.

BIBLIOGRAPHY
S. Mihalik: *Old Hungarian Enamel* (Budapest, 1961)
A. Héjj-Détári: *Old Hungarian Jewellery* (Budapest, 1965)

ANDRÁS SZILÁGYI

X. Textiles.

The most splendid Hungarian textiles are the silk and metal thread embroideries used over a long period to decorate ecclesiastical and secular garments and furnishings. Other trimmings, including metal braids and bobbin laces, were also produced for court use and subsequently became a feature of the clothing and furnishings of well-to-do peasant communities.

1. WOVEN FABRICS. Hungary was never able to develop a competitive weaving industry. Documentary sources show that even in the late medieval period the majority of linen, cotton and woollen fabrics was either purchased abroad or imported by foreign traders: in the years 1457 and 1458, for example, 70–75% of fabrics were imported. An invoice of 1627, among the papers of Gabriel Bethlen, Prince of Transylvania (*reg* 1613–29), mentions only 40 fabrics of Hungarian manufacture but 120 imports (Nagy, 1871). A local textile industry was eventually developed in the 1760s as a protection against such huge imports, but most of the enterprises were short-lived because of lack of capital and the financial policies of the Viennese court.

The industry was based mainly on cotton, the most important factories being those of Ferenc Lotharingiai in Sasvár (1736–1849), Ferenc Kluge in Pápa (1783–1948) and Ferenc Golberger in Óbuda (est. 1784), which still exists. Block and plate printed textiles were produced in polychrome with additional colours added by hand in the pencilling (or painting) technique. By far the greatest quantity, however, was printed in monochrome blue by the indigo resist technique. Rococo motifs were popular, and idyllic landscapes and pastoral scenes adorned the tablecloths and bedcovers.

Between 1783 and 1786 István Valero and Tamás Valero founded in Pest the only silk factory in the country. Its products competed with other European silk goods, and the later designs were in keeping with the Biedermeier fashion of the period. The factory's high technical standards are, however, best illustrated by its woven portraits (examples in Budapest, Mus. Applied A., and Hist. Mus.) of such prominent contemporary figures as Joseph, Palatine of Hungary (*reg* 1796–1847), Ferdinand I, Emperor of Austria (*reg* 1835–48), and the Hungarian revolutionary Lajos Kossuth (1802–94). The factory reached its peak during the period of reform of the first half of the 19th century, but closed after the failure of the 1849 War of Independence.

2. EMBROIDERY. The most outstanding piece of Hungarian Romanesque embroidery is the bell chasuble (Budapest, N. Mus.), which, according to its inscription, was made in 1031 and presented to Székesfehérvár Cathedral by Stephen I (St Stephen, *reg* 997–1038) and his wife Gizella (later it was altered into a cope to become the Hungarian coronation cloak). Although it has been attributed to Regensburg, the chasuble was probably made in Hungary by embroiderers trained in the Byzantine tradition but influenced also by Romanesque art. The purple ground of Byzantine silk is patterned with green rosettes and densely covered with gold and silk embroidery. The figures and the inscriptions linked to them illustrate the *Te Deum* of St Ambrose.

The main evidence for embroidery during the next three centuries is found in archival material: at the end of the 14th century, for example, Etienne le Hongrie (*fl* 1373–1419) is known to have worked for Philip the Bold of Burgundy and other patrons as a painter and embroiderer. A number of embroideries survive from the Late Gothic and early Renaissance periods. Many of them are chasubles made from Italian or Spanish velvets and silks; they are embroidered on the back with cross orphreys and on the front with straight or pillar orphreys. The most common subject was *Christ on the Cross and the Virgin*, though sometimes a *Deposition* or *Resurrection* was depicted. The background was stitched in metal thread couched in geometric patterns, the figures in satin stitch

26. Linen border (detail), embroidered with silk and silver, 0.44×1.80 m, from Transylvania, mid-17th century (Budapest, Museum of Applied Arts)

until the end of the 15th century when they were worked in high relief. These embroideries, along with others from Austria, Bohemia and Poland, represent a specifically central European style.

In the 15th century the professional embroiderers, who worked in metal threads and pearls, were members of the purse- and glove-making guilds, but from the 16th century they tended to work independently in urban workshops and large princely households. They were responsible for velvet and silk embroidery, but much of the linen embroidery was worked by ladies in aristocratic households under the direction of a professional. In the 16th and 17th centuries the style that had evolved in the courts was applied to dress, linen for trousseaus, table and bed linen and the ecclesiastical linen used in the Reformed Church. It is characterized by floral ornamentation worked in silk, silver-gilt thread and metal wire (*see* EMBROIDERY, colour pl. II, fig. 1). Certain motifs, in their form, colour and techniques, were strongly influenced by Turkish embroidery (see fig. 26), but they also reflected the Renaissance ornament of western Europe. After the expulsion of the Turks, Hungarian embroidery increasingly followed western European designs, but the court embroidery motifs are still used in folk textiles.

3. PASSEMENTERIE AND LACE. Passementerie played a significant role in the decoration of clothes and horse trappings in the 15th century, and the guilds, besides making gold and silver braid, cord and buttons, also made lace. In the 16th century metal braids were used to trim garments; in the following century silver gilt and silver bobbin lace often covered the entire surface. The earliest linen bobbin lace comes from Selmecbánya (now Banská Štiavnica, Slovakia) in 1560. In the 17th century Hungarian lace used Milanese and Flemish techniques, and the flower designs that had previously been used only on court embroidery now appeared on lace too. Lace and lacis were often used on shirt sleeves, aprons and antependiums, but the designs were those of western European pattern books.

In the 19th century machine-made lace became widespread, but there was an attempt to revive handmade lace. In 1880 Béla Angyal (1847–1928) established a lace-making school in Körmöcbánya (now Kremnica, Slovakia), and in 1902, in Kiskunhalas, Mária Markovits (1885–1954) created a new type of needle lace following the designs of Árpád Dékáni (1865–1931). This *halas* or 'fishmongers lace' is still made. Dékáni's designs originated in the Secession, but later designers stressed the importance of Hungarian motifs. The third significant development is associated with Aranka and Erzsébet Szontagh, who made 'Csetnek lace' famous. This is actually crochet made in the Irish manner but with Hungarian flower designs.

4. TAPESTRY. There is no tradition of tapestry-weaving in Hungary. The technique was introduced in the last years of the 19th century when designers such as SÁNDOR NAGY, Pál Horti (1865–1907) and János Vaszary (1867–1939) attempted to combine Secession aesthetics with themes from Hungarian peasant life and folk ornamentation. An important work of this period was the *Woman Dressed in Red with a Rose* designed by the painter JÓZSEF RIPPL-RÓNAI and embroidered by his wife Lazarine Boudrion (1898; Budapest, Mus. Applied A.). Sándor Nagy became a member of the GÖDÖLLŐ COLONY, with a tapestry- and carpet-weaving workshop founded in 1904 by ALADÁR KÖRÖSFŐI-KRIESCH, which aimed to create a unity between art, work and life. The artists at Gödöllő worked in many media, but the weaving of tapestries and carpets was one of the most important aspects of their output.

Between the two World Wars the greatest exponent of Hungarian tapestry design was Noémi Ferenczy (*see* FERENCZY, (3)), who trained in Paris and wove her tapestries herself. Her early work was ruled by a pantheistic religious vision, but from the 1920s she concentrated on monumental figures engaged in craft or agricultural work, executed with great splashes of colour. After World War II she had a great influence on the Hungarian tapestry designers of the 1950s.

BIBLIOGRAPHY

I. Nagy: *Áruczikkek szabályzata 1627 és 1706 évekbő* [Merchandise regulations from 1627 to 1706], Magyar Történelmi Tár, xviii (Pest, 1871), pp. 206–12, 214–17

A. Kriesch-Körösfői: 'Hungarian Peasant Art', *Peasant Art in Austria and Hungary*, ed. C. Holme (London, Paris and New York, 1911), pp. 31–46 [*The Studio* special issue]

G. Palotay: *Les Eléments turcs-ottomans des broderies hongroises* (Budapest, 1940) [Fr. and Hung. text]

M. Csernyánszky: *The Art of Lace-making in Hungary* (Budapest, 1962)

M. Varjú-Ember: *Alte ungarische Stickerei* (Budapest, 1963)

——: *Hungarian Domestic Embroidery* (Budapest, 1963) [Eng. and Ger. text]

W. Endrei: *Magyarországi textilmanufakturák a 18. században* [Hungarian textile manufacturers in the 18th century] (Budapest, 1969)

E. Fél: *Peasant Embroidery on Linen and Hemp in Hungary*, Hungarian Folk Art (Budapest, 1976)

M. Kresz: *The Art of the Hungarian Furriers*, Hungarian Folk Art (Budapest, 1979) [largely about appliqué and embroidered decoration]

Historic Hungarian Costume (exh. cat., intro. by E. László; U. Manchester, Whitworth A.G., 1979)

E. Fél: *Hungarian Peasant Embroidery* (London, 1980)

É. Kovács and Z. Lovag: *A magyar koronázási jelvények* [Symbols of the Hungarian coronation]; Eng. ed., rev. as *The Hungarian Crown and Other Regalia* (Budapest, 1980)

M. Varjú-Ember: *Régi textíliák* [Old textiles] (Budapest, 1980); Eng. trans., *The Treasures of the Hungarian National Museum* (Budapest, 1981)

V. Gervers: *The Influence of Ottoman Turkish Textiles and Costume in Eastern Europe, with Particular Reference to Hungary* (Toronto, 1982)

V. Cervers Molnár: *Ipolyi arnold hímzésgyűjteménye az Esztergomi keresztény múzeumban* [The Ipoly embroidery collection in the Museum of Christianity, Esztergom] (Budapest, 1983) [Eng. summary]

W. Endrei: *Patyolat és posztó* [Cambric and broad cloth] (Budapest, 1989)

Képes Kárpitok az Iparművészeti Muzeum gyüjteményében II: Európai és magyar Kárpitok a. XIX. század végétől a II. világháboruig [Tapestries in the collection of the Museum of Applied Arts, II: European and Hungarian tapestries from the end of the 19th century to World War II] (exh. cat. by E. László, Budapest, 1989)

E. LÁSZLÓ

XI. Patronage.

1. Before *c*. 1800. 2. After *c*. 1800.

1. BEFORE *c*. 1800. The Turkish invasion of Buda in 1541 brought an end to several hundred years of patronage by the Hungarian royal court, especially splendid during the reign of MATTHIAS CORVINUS (*reg* 1458–90), when rich collections and royal treasures were assembled and the buildings at Buda Castle were redesigned in Renaissance style (*see* §II, 2 above). In addition to the court's

role in art patronage, a few aristocratic families, notably in Transylvania, established artistic centres and became important patrons. Up to the Turkish invasion, the king and the Catholic Church had been the most active patrons, but with the central region of Hungary now under Turkish rule (*see* §II, 3(i) above), all artistic activity and patronage fell completely outside the domain of European influence.

The complicated political situation, the rapid spread of the Reformation in the 16th century and the fact that Hungary was subjected to an almost constant succession of military campaigns did not help to create an ideal situation for patronage of the arts. Yet necessity, expediency and the need to possess meant that a new form of art patronage was established fairly quickly and was to remain intact until the end of Turkish rule. In the 16th century the most important objective was the building of fortified castles and the manufacture and accumulation of decorative art objects that could be used as gifts. In the early 17th century many castles were built to defend those parts of the country not yet invaded by the Turks. They were commissioned by the Viennese Military Council and constructed by Italian military engineers and architects (*see* §II, 3(i), above). A series of well-equipped fortifications ringed the central region held by the Turks; their designs influenced private building projects and much of the architecture commissioned by the princes of Transylvania. These Italian-style fortification systems suited the demands of the time: instead of asymmetrical and picturesque buildings, properly planned and symmetrical castles were constructed, and this type of military architecture became common practice, being copied in civilian buildings, castles and palaces.

Patronage in the 16th and 17th centuries was circumscribed by the necessity for fortified castles. The aristocracy established regional art centres in these structures, the purpose of which was to protect and further develop the cultural and artistic life of the particular region in which they lived. Archival sources of the period reveal that there was a great interest in the decorative arts. Luxury goods were promoted, the reason being that in uncertain political and military situations it was necessary to have objects that maintained their value and could easily be disposed of. Valuable objects served both as a personal show of wealth and as an investment and were easier to keep safe or were useful to give as ransoms, presents or deposits. Such objects included jewellery, items of gold, weapons, saddlery, expensive clothing and such textiles as embroideries, tapestries, lace and carpets from the Near and Middle East. Most were produced by guild workshops in Hungary, although there was also quite a large number of imports, including a significant proportion of Turkish goods. Aristocrats were the principal owners of such items. For example, in 1629 Gabriel Bethlen (*reg* 1613–29), Prince of Transylvania, was forced by Sultan Murad IV (*reg* 1623–40) to buy items of gold for him in Prague. Orders such as these account for an increased production of a wonderfully inventive range of decorative art objects that drew on Italian Renaissance, Turkish and Baroque art as sources.

In the 17th century portrait painting became popular among the nobility, church dignitaries and the wealthier urban middle classes, and there was an upsurge in the collecting of paintings (*see* §IV, 2 above) and graphic art. As the cult of ancestors developed in the first decades of the century, the nobility began to form collections of portraits in ancestral galleries. Although the most significant portraits were commissioned by the aristocracy, very few of their large galleries have survived; only those of the Batthyány, Nádasdy, Csáky, Esterházy and Zichy families remain in full or partially. There was also a great interest in collecting engraved portraits, the images of which were seen by the public in published form. The commissioning of history paintings for the walls of the banqueting halls of castles was another important area for the history of art patronage: they included paintings of the Turkish–Hungarian conflict. In the mid-17th century, historical paintings appeared that expressed the struggles against the ruling Habsburgs; such works include those depicting the execution of the leaders of the anti-Habsburg Wesselényi conspiracy.

In the 1680s and 1690s the Turks were driven out of Hungarian territory, and the principality of Transylvania came to an end. Hungary was united under the Habsburgs, and this led to changes in the patronage of the arts. New building projects were begun, and it was at this time that the Baroque urban plan became popular, to which aristocratic and bourgeois builders and the Catholic Church equally contributed. The fortified style of castle architecture was replaced by a more graceful style influenced by the new royal palace on Castle Hill in Buda (*see* BUDAPEST, §IV, 1) and incorporating one or two towers and often a *cour d'honneur*, as seen in the Esterházy palace (1714–33) at Cseklész (now Bernolákovo, Slovakia; *see* §II, 3(ii) above). This new type is exemplified by Graf Antal Grassalkovich's palace (1744–7; altered after 1867) at Gödöllő (*see* §II, 3(ii) above). In the 18th century many towns and villages erected plague columns in their central squares; these were free-standing statues dedicated to the Virgin or the Holy Trinity in commemoration of the plague at the beginning of the 18th century. An elaborate example is the Holy Trinity Column (1712–15) on Castle Hill in Budapest, the statue (1715–17) for which was made by Ferenc Antal Hörger (*fl* 1713–37) and Philipp Ungleich (*d c.* 1736).

The unrivalled patron in the 18th century was the Catholic Church, which by this time had completely won back its position of significance in Hungary. The building of new Baroque churches began everywhere, and earlier ones were embellished with Baroque additions. New bishops' palaces, summer palaces and monasteries were also erected. The major ecclesiastical commissions were often given to foreign artists, who usually came to complete specific projects. One of the most exceptional patrons was Count Imre Esterházy, Archbishop of Esztergom (*see* ESTERHÁZY, §II(1)), who at his court in Pozsony (now Bratislava, Slovakia) patronized some of the most important Baroque artists, among them Franz Anton Palko (*see* PALKO, (1)), Antonio Galli-Bibiena (*see* GALLI-BIBIENA, (4)), FRANZ ANTON PILGRAM and Georg Raphael Donner (*see* DONNER, (1)).

2. AFTER *c.* 1800. In the late 18th century portraiture had once more become an important genre, and the rural aristocracy and urban intellectuals showed a great interest

in collecting painted and engraved portraits. In the early 19th century the fashion for portrait busts again became popular. However, society's artistic expectations were beginning to change. Throughout the century new genres of art and new themes appeared, which also signified changes in patronage. Hungary was slowly undergoing a transformation to a bourgeois society, wishing to free itself from Habsburg rule, and the most pressing task was to build and renovate castles and erect public buildings and blocks of flats. The emergence of this secular, chiefly bourgeois, architecture relegated ecclesiastical architecture to second place. In 1808 the Embellishment Committee was established in Pest, the objectives of which were to produce a unified townscape filled with modern buildings of the highest quality. In the first half of the century Neo-classical county halls and town halls were built in many communities—for example Mihály Pollack's County Hall (1828–36) in Szekszárd (*see* POLLACK, (2))—and many museums, theatres, casinos, restaurants, baths and hospitals were constructed or renovated, among them Pollack's Hungarian National Museum (1836–46) and the 16th-century Bath of Bey Veli, later the Császár (Imperial) Baths (extended 1841–5; destr. *c.* 1990) by JÓZSEF HILD, both in Budapest. Public buildings were contracted by the various public bodies. An increasing number of the wealthy bourgeoisie joined the gentry in commissioning private houses. The Hungarian aristocracy were increasingly to be found in Vienna, in order to be close to the Habsburg court, and while there commissioned work from foreign artists. Italian and Austrian architects, sculptors and painters were contracted to design buildings in Hungary and to decorate them, and a significant number of art objects from other countries were imported.

An interest in folk culture also arose in the 19th century. A more secular bourgeois style emerged to replace the old feudal artistic practices. This was served by the founding of the ARTISTS ASSOCIATION OF PEST (active from 1839 to 1869), whose aim was to promote art through exhibitions and art dealing. To satisfy national aspirations, landscape painting became an important genre. In the 1820s the first paintings depicting the landscape of Hungary appeared, pioneered by such artists as Károly Markó the elder. Slightly later, a popular interest arose in the study of folk costumes of different regions. Depictions of colourful and elaborately decorated costumes were published as engravings and sold cheaply to the public. In the 1840s patrons from intellectual circles and the nobility, as well as a small number of the bourgeoisie, became interested in history painting and genre painting and began to make purchases for their collections. Their attempt to raise Hungary's artistic standards to the level of other European countries was temporarily interrupted by the War of Independence in 1848–9. Changes took place only after the Compromise of 1867 with Austria, which resulted in the establishment of the Dual Monarchy.

During the interim absolutist period (1849–67), portrait paintings and still-lifes were most in demand, mainly from civil servants and the wealthy bourgeoisie. In the mid-19th century an interest developed in Romanticism, first evident in genre paintings of country people. Landscape painting and history painting enjoyed renewed popularity, and the appearance of historical themes in art became mainly a device to keep alive ideas of national identity. Competitions for history paintings, and scholarships for artists who practised this genre, were established as part of official cultural policy.

However, at the end of the 19th century the nature of patronage changed radically. The art market began to expand, and patronage came under State control, directed by the Fine Arts Department of the Ministry of Religious and Public Education. The advisory body to this was the Fine Arts Council, which favoured an academic art and a nationally inspired Secessionist art influenced by folk culture. This was reflected in its purchases and competitions, its awarding of commissions and its system of prizes, medals and scholarships. Museums were established (e.g. the Museum of Fine Arts in Budapest in 1896), and various arts societies, artists' associations and artists' colonies were founded. In 1880 Budapest adopted a resolution institutionalizing art patronage, and regular annual loans were made for this purpose.

In the second half of the 19th century rich middle-class patrons had appeared alongside the existing aristocratic ones, but after World War I their numbers were significantly reduced due to a tax on luxury goods introduced in the 1920s and because of the worldwide economic depression that led to their impoverishment. This type of patron was replaced by the art collector or art dealer, and private commissions were contracted only for family tombs. State and public commissions were primarily for monumental sculptural projects or for history paintings and official portraits. During this time numerous heroic monuments were made, among them the statue of *Lajos Kossuth* by Alajos Stróbl (1856–1926) in front of the Parliament Building in Budapest and the Millenary Monument (1894–1900) by György Zala (1858–1937) in Heroes' Square, Budapest. After World War I there was a national campaign to commission war memorials, and, in spite of economic conditions, posters became extremely popular as an art form.

From 1923 on, State purchases were ensured by a certain sum set aside in the budget to be allocated for the development of public collections, the objective of which was to ensure political representation in the arts. The Hungarian National Association for Fine Arts (1859–1945), an organization of artists who favoured the eclectic Historicism popular in Vienna and Munich, also took part in the distribution of prizes and scholarships, but its juries, having conservative tastes, regularly rejected the work of any artist who represented new and creative trends. In order to represent their own interests, the less-traditional artists formed new societies, two of which were the Szinyei Merse Society (1920–51; re-established 1992) and the progressive New Society of Fine Artists (KUT), founded in 1924.

Patronage by the Church was also important, especially that of the Catholic Church. Apart from restoring and redecorating older churches and building new ones, competitions and exhibitions were set up and purchases made for such events as the 900th anniversary of the death of King Stephen I (1938) and the Eucharistic World Congress (1941) (*see* §II, 4(ii) above). From 1930, commissions and purchases were under the jurisdiction of the National

Church Art Council, with the assistance of the Church Art Office.

From 1940, the State decreed that 2% of all construction expenses be allocated for decorative commissions in the fine arts, and after World War II—in accordance with the new Communist social order—State institutions were set up to deal with patronage. The Adult Education Ministry, founded in 1949, established the Hungarian Fine and Decorative Arts Union (1949) and the Fine Arts Foundation, both of which operated in tandem. The Foundation was responsible for State purchases and the distribution of commissions, and from 1954 on only those works approved by the Union could be purchased. In 1956 the Union underwent the first of several transformations that led to a loss of its functions as a patron. Thereafter, the Examiner Department of the Fine Arts Foundation, under ministerial supervision, handled affairs of patronage in its capacity as an administrative organ of the State. The Foundation set up various enterprises and shops under its jurisdiction, producing and circulating designs or actual products bought from artists. In 1963 the State Examiner was founded, its duties being to handle all moneys set aside for purposes of patronage. In 1965 it was the only body that had the authority to judge works of art, and it also initiated a system of scholarships. Due to the economic and political situation in Hungary, individual initiative in the field of patronage ceased completely, and with the collapse of Communism in 1989 patronage of the fine arts was pushed into a sort of 'no-man's land'.

For further discussion *see* BUDAPEST, §II, 2.

BIBLIOGRAPHY

K. Lyka: *Magyar művészet, 1800–1850: A táblabiró világ művészete* [Hungarian art, 1800–1850: The art of provincial Hungary] (Budapest, [*c.* 1900]); 3rd edn as *A táblabiró világ művészete: Magyar művészet, 1800–1850* (Budapest, 1981) [incl. art patronage]

J. Balogh: *A művészet Mátyás király udvarában* [The art of King Matthias's court], 2 vols (Budapest, 1966)

——: *Die Anfänge der Renaissance in Ungarn: Matthias Corvinus und die Kunst* (Graz, 1975)

——: 'Olasz tervrajzok és hazai Későrenaissance épületeink' [Italian designs and the late Renaissance in Hungary], *Magyarországi reneszánsz és barokk: Művészettörténeti tanulmányok* [Hungarian Renaissance and Baroque art historical studies], ed. G. Galavics (Budapest, 1975), pp. 55–135

L. Németh, ed.: *Magyar művészet, 1890–1919* [Hungarian art, 1890–1919] (1981), vi of *A magyarországi művészet története* [The history of art in Hungary], ed. N. Aradi (Budapest, 1981–), pp. 125–41

Matthias Corvinus und die Renaissance in Ungarn, 1458–1541 (exh. cat., ed. J. Balogh and others; Schallaburg, Schloss, 1982)

S. Kontha, ed.: *Magyar művészet, 1919–1945* [Hungarian art, 1919–1945] (1985), vii of *A magyarországi művészet története* [The history of art in Hungary], ed. N. Aradi (Budapest, 1981–), pp. 92–110

G. Galavics: *Kössünk kardot az pogány ellen: Török háborúk és képzőművészete* [Raising our swords against the heathens: Turkish wars and art] (Budapest, 1986)

XII. Collecting and dealing.

Art objects that were not destroyed during Hungary's turbulent history often became part of the Habsburg imperial collections in Vienna. However, the collections of MATTHIAS CORVINUS (*reg* 1458–90) and those of such powerful aristocratic families as the Zrínyis, Nádasdys and Esterházys survived. In the 16th century aristocrats, church dignitaries and humanists followed Matthias Corvinus's example as a collector. They formed impressive *Kunst- und Wunderkammern* (*see* KUNSTKAMMER), to which they often added objects and relics that had supposed connections with historical figures. Humanist scholars were more interested in archaeological objects, numismatology and the collecting of books and manuscripts. Seventeenth-century sources mention such great picture collections as those of the poet and military leader Miklós Zrínyi (1620–64) at his castle at Csáktornya (now Čakovec, Croatia), where he also had a large library and collection of medals. The collection of paintings, coins, medals and decorative arts assembled by Lord Chief Justice Ferenc Nádasdy at his castles at Sárvár and Pottendorf (now in Austria) compared favourably with those in western Europe, although at the time of his execution it became the property of the Habsburgs.

During the relative peace of the 18th century, large collections of paintings by Old Masters were amassed, the best known of which was that owned by the Esterházy family. Their collection, which also included a large number of drawings and engravings, formed the core of the holdings of the Museum of Fine Arts in Budapest (*see* ESTERHÁZY). In the second half of the 18th century, the nature of the ever-increasing collections began to extend to other genres as well. For example, there was a growing interest in collecting Roman remains from the former Roman province of Pannonia (western Hungary). Those objects that were more portable often became part of private collections of antiquities, while larger remains were erected in gardens and parks or restored on site, as was the case with the Roman mosaic pavement found in Bishop János Szily's palace at Szombathely (Lat. Savaria). There was also a demand for historical authenticity at this time, and this was manifested in the formation of collections containing paintings of well-known scholars and others who featured prominently in Hungary's history. A collection of this nature was formed in Marosvásárhely (now Tîrgu Mureş, Romania) by Count Sámuel Teleki (1739–1822), Chancellor of Transylvania, and included a library of more than 36,000 volumes (now Budapest, Lib. Hung. Acad. Sci.). Interest in the country's history was also inspired by such collections of ancient Hungarian artefacts as those of István Marcibányi (1752–1810) and the wood-carver Miklós Jankovich (1773–1846). This romantic and patriotic view of the past was for many years the motivating force behind art collecting in Hungary.

In the 1830s and 1840s a certain art-historical viewpoint with regard to collecting became popular through the activities of Joseph Daniel Böhm (1794–1865), Director of the Graveur-Akademie in Vienna, the consequences of which determined the make-up of Hungarian collections well into the 20th century. Collecting became increasingly specialized, and the principal collectors, most of whom were industrialists, came mainly from the *haute bourgeoisie.* As well as collections of *Hungarica* (solely Hungarian material), these men made significant purchases of western European art by contemporary artists and Old Masters.

The early 20th century is regarded as the 'golden age' of collecting. A number of favourable circumstances helped in the establishment of outstanding collections at this time, and the nature of collecting underwent a gradual change. Though paintings by Old Masters from western Europe continued to be in demand, there was also an increasing interest in collecting 19th-century French and Hungarian paintings. From the 1930s, such individuals as Imre Artinger Oltványi and Lajos Fruchter formed outstanding collections of contemporary art. State collections also benefited from the individual efforts of collectors, an example being the Friends of the Museum of Fine Arts, who contributed greatly to the holdings of the Museum of Fine Arts in Budapest.

After World War II, changes in the field of collecting were effected. Law 12 of 1949 made the State the almost exclusive collector, bringing with it the nationalization of major private collections, and Law 13 of 1949 regulated collectors' duties, including the obligation to declare objects in private collections. Law 9 of 1963 placed local museums under the supervision of county and municipal authorities. This had a great impact on the scope of these museums' holdings, as they began to seek out the work of local and regional artists. By the mid-1970s over 20 memorial museums devoted to contemporary Hungarian artists had been established (e.g. Budapest, Lajos Kassák Mem. Mus.). Private collectors primarily specialized in the more readily accessible work of contemporary artists. Doctors, lawyers, teachers and professionals in the fields of technology and the arts were able to create remarkable collections from humble means.

Art dealers in Hungary existed as early as the reign of Matthias Corvinus; these were Italian dealers who settled in Buda and supplied everything that would have been needed by those at court. Art objects were either bought, commissioned or received as gifts. The Turkish invasion in the early 16th century brought about basic changes to the types of objects being collected and to the nature of collecting itself. Accumulation, luxury and the presentation of gifts became obligatory (*see* §XI, 1 above), resulting in an increase in the production of luxury goods. In the 16th and 17th centuries luxury goods flooded into the western and eastern parts of Hungary. They were brought to Transylvania by Turkish, Greek and Jewish dealers and reached the Habsburg territories in the west through the Turkish-occupied central region. Hungarian delegations returning from Istanbul, the Turkish capital, brought back large numbers of gifts, of which the most desirable were carpets. Such items from the East were often used as a form of tax, as presents given for a favourable outcome at trials or as gifts given to prevent pillaging. At times it was necessary to request them on an exchange basis for a favour. In 1583, for example, Ali, the Pasha of Buda, asked Archduke Ernest, Governor of Hungary, to procure for him a clock and other goods to take to Istanbul as gifts for Sultan Murad III (*reg* 1574–95). More usual methods of obtaining art objects were through the plundering of acquisitions, through ransoms and tribute money and not least through the confiscation of rebels' estates.

In the 18th century traffic in art objects lessened somewhat, yielding to the establishment of a more stable art market that did not merely concern itself with individual deals. At the end of the century there is documentation concerning professional art dealers who helped to build such imposing collections as that of Miklós Jankovich. By 1867, the year of the Compromise between Austria and Hungary that resulted in the establishment of the Dual Monarchy, art-dealing had reached mammoth proportions, and at the end of the century art dealing institutions and auction houses were established. Between 1867 and 1919 a large number of art objects arrived in Hungary, and private collections were established that compared favourably with those elsewhere in Europe. During the short-lived Republic of Councils, set up in 1919 on the Soviet model, many objects were hidden or smuggled out of Hungary to prevent them becoming public property. This activity intensified when the 'X' article of the 1929 bill was issued, which imposed limitations on the export of art objects. During the Depression of 1929–33, many collections owned by the upper middle classes were dispersed, and the events of World War II and its aftermath in Hungary resulted in a further increase in the illegal traffic of goods abroad. Under the new political conditions, the process of collecting was completely transformed; opportunities to collect still existed but were limited in scope.

Although Act XXII of 1888 had provided for the establishment of auction houses (which became part of the art trade), dealing essentially continued to be controlled by art societies through a series of exhibitions held in exhibition halls. More up-to-date ways of dealing evolved after World War I, when a network of trading began to develop, but this system was practically destroyed by the political and social changes after World War II. Dealing came under State control with the foundation of the State Second-hand Store (Bizományi Vállalat), which set up a separate chain of shops to handle art objects. Dealing was carried out not only in these shops but also at auctions and, as earlier, at exhibitions and in the shops of the Fine Art Fund. After 1989, many private art shops and galleries opened; in the 1990s these struggled to carry on dealing in the face of flagging demand.

BIBLIOGRAPHY

L. Siklóssy: *Műkincseink vándorutja Bécsbe* [The route of our art treasures to Vienna] (Budapest, 1919)

G. Entz: *A magyar mügyüjtés történetének vázlata 1850–ig* [A sketch of the history of Hungarian art collecting until 1850] (Budapest, 1937)

J. Balogh: *A művészet Mátyás király udvarában* [The art of King Matthias's court], i (Budapest, 1966)

K. Sinkó: 'Adatok a magyar mügyüjtés történetéhez' [Data about the history of Hungarian art collecting], *Művészet és felvilágosodás: Művészettörténeti tanulmányok* [Art and enlightenment: Art historical studies], ed. A. Zádor and H. Szabolcsi (Budapest, 1978), pp. 545–52

——: 'A magyar mügyüjtés 1850 utan-a magángyüjteményi kiállítás tükrében' [Hungarian art collecting after 1850 reflected by exhibitions in private collections], *Válogatás magyar magángyüjteményekből* [Selections from Hungarian private collections] (exh. cat., ed. G. László and K. Sinkó; Budapest, N.G., 1981), pp. 11–29

L. Mravik: 'Védett-e, ami védett? avagy: Hasznos-e az országnak a mügyüjtés?' [Protect what is protected? or: Is art collecting useful for the country?], *Kritika*, 9 (1989), pp. 10–15

IDA BOD-BOBROVSZKY

XIII. Museums.

The earliest museum in Hungary is the Hungarian National Museum in Budapest, which originated in 1802 when Count Ferenc Széchényi (1754–1820) donated to the nation his collection (items of natural history, archaeological finds and coins) as well as his library, which was the starting point for the National Széchényi Library (now in the Royal Palace complex, Budapest). A Neo-classical building (1836–46) was constructed by MIHÁLY POLLACK to house the collection. The National Museum's Picture Gallery is based on the collection of János László Pyrker, Archbishop of Eger, who bestowed it in 1836, with later additions. The museum now has the leading historical–archaeological collection, and its special Hungarian Historical Picture Collection (founded 1884) includes portraits, landscapes and history paintings. The museum also administers such provincial museums as the Castle Museum, Esztergom, and the Rákóczy Museum, Sárospatak, as well as some important archaeological research centres.

The classification of collections began in 1872 with the founding of the Ethnographic Museum and of the Arts and Crafts Collection (Mus. Applied A. from 1896), both in Budapest. The latter is housed in a Secessionist palace (1893–7) by Ödön Lechner (*see* LECHNER, (1)), and the two museums of Asian art, the Ferenc Hopp Museum of Oriental Art (1919) and the György Ráth Museum (1953), come under its aegis.

Prince Miklós Esterházy II's collection of Hungarian paintings, acquired by Act of Parliament in 1871, formed the basis of the Museum of Fine Arts in Budapest (founded 1896; *see* ESTERHÁZY, §I(4)). The holdings expanded when Bishop Arnold Ipolyi donated his (Ramboux) collection in 1872 and when large purchases were made at the end of the 19th century. The museum building was opened in 1906. It is divided into Egyptian and Classical departments, Old Masters, graphic art, sculpture and modern art. The Hungarian National Gallery was formed in 1957 out of the Museum of Fine Arts' Hungarian collection and was supplemented by items from the former Municipal Picture Gallery. It moved to the Royal Palace complex in 1974.

In addition to the museums that come under the aegis of the Ministry of Culture, there are provincial museums—usually local history museums with an archaeological emphasis—most of which were founded at the end of the 19th century. The Historical Museum of Budapest (founded 1898) moved to the Royal Palace in 1968. Local collections of artistic interest include the Janus Pannonius Museum in Pécs, which displays 20th-century Hungarian art, and a series of museums, also in Pécs, dedicated to individual artists such as Tivadar Csontváry, Ferenc Martyn, Béla Uitz and Victor Vasarely. The Picture Gallery in the István Dobó Castle Museum at Eger contains the former archiepiscopal collection. The Ferenczy Museum, Szentendre, shows the work of 20th-century Hungarian artists, as do several independent museums set up in Szentendre since the 1970s and dedicated to artists who worked there, including Imre Ámos, Jenő Barcsay, Margit Kovács and Lajos Vajda. The Savaria Museum in Szombathely was opened in 1908 and the Szombathely Gallery in 1985.

The earliest and most important national church collection is the Museum of Christianity at ESZTERGOM, founded by Archbishop János Simor in 1875; it includes numerous medieval works of art, many from the Arnold Ipolyi collection. In 1886 the Esztergom Cathedral Treasury was opened to the public. A library and art gallery were set up by the Benedictines at Pannonhalma Abbey. The Roman Catholic bishoprics (Eger, Győr, Veszprém, Kalocsa) established church collections from the 1970s. The Hungarian Reformed Church colleges at Sárospatak, Debrecen and Pápa have collections dating to the 18th century. In 1916 the National Jewish Museum was established in the capital, and the Evangelical Church opened a national museum there in 1973. In Szentendre there is a collection of Serbian Orthodox ecclesiastical art and in Nyíregyháza a collection of Greek Orthodox art.

BIBLIOGRAPHY

H. Horváth: *Budapest művészeti emlékei* [Budapest's monuments of art] (Budapest, 1938)

G. S. Zakariás: *Budapest* (1961), iii of *Magyarország művészeti emlékei* [Hungary's monuments of art] (Budapest, 1959–61)

ERNŐ MAROSÍ

XIV. Art education.

With the exception of the guilds, the origins of art education can be traced back to the early 18th century to the schools run by Piarists (a religious organization established in Rome in 1597 for the education of the poor). As there were no art academies yet established in Hungary, the Piarists offered such courses as architecture and drawing—considered to be part of the bourgeois curriculum—that would usually have been taught in academies. In their secondary schools in Kalocsa, Vác, Tata and Nyitra (now Nitra, Slovakia) the Piarists gave instruction in the basic elements of secular architecture and the design and execution of public buildings, by means of architectural treatises, drawings of building surveys and copies of prints. Writings by the Italians Vincenzo Scamozzi and Andrea Pozzo and the German Leonhard Christoph Sturm in the collections of the school libraries were also carefully consulted. Architectural projects designed by private owners also aroused some public interest, although at this time architecture was viewed primarily as a science and not an art.

In 1782 the Institutum Geometricum (now the Technical University of Budapest) was founded in Buda to teach secular architecture, and it was there that the first engineering degree in Europe was offered. Ferenc Rausch (1743–1816), a teacher at the school, wrote the first textbook on Hungarian architecture, *Elementa architecturae ad structuras oeconomicas applicata* (Buda, 1779), which was published in Latin. The first book in Hungarian on secular architecture, *Várasi építésnek eleji* (The origins of castle building; Buda, 1790), was written by Miklós Révai (1750–1807).

As part of reforms in education initiated by the Habsburg court, drawing schools following German models were set up during the reign of Maria-Theresa (*reg* 1741–80). Under Joseph II (*reg* 1780–90), further developments occurred. In 1783 the principles of, and requirements for, education in drawing schools were established, as were the proposed textbooks and models and the creation of drawing schools on Sundays for students of arts and crafts. A sole director was in charge of all the drawing schools, and for teaching purposes he organized and collected Italian, French and English pattern books from the art archives in Vienna. His staff reported to him annually, and the Akademie der Bildenden Künste and the Council of Governors-General in Vienna supervised the project as a whole. These reforms enabled every town in Hungary to have a drawing school by the last quarter of the 18th century; two of the most distinguished were in Buda and Győr.

Although social conditions for high standards in the fine arts were lacking in Hungary, by 1775 the idea of founding an art academy had taken root. Hungarian aristocrats sought the advice of the Austrian painter Daniel Gran, who outlined a detailed plan of his ideas to the Palatine Lajos Batthyány. During the next ten years, the plan for a national art academy remained on the agenda. In 1791 Leopold II (*reg* 1790–92) set up a committee that would act on behalf of an academy of free artists, and in 1804 Johann Nepomuk Schauff (1757–1827), a drawing teacher from Pozsony (now Bratislava, Slovakia), brought it to public attention. In 1820 the matter was again raised by the Hungarian painter János Mihály Hesz (1768–1833), who lived in Vienna, and six years later the sculptor ISTVÁN FERENCZY put to Parliament his proposal for the creation of a sculpture academy. In 1831 János Joó (1806/7–74), a teacher of drawing, turned to Count István Széchenyi (1791–1860) for assistance in the matter, and in 1841 the critic Imre Henszlmann (1813–88) voiced his concern. In 1846 a change took place when the painter Giacomo Marastoni (1804–60) founded his own private academy in Pest, Első Magyar Festészeti Akadémia (The First Hungarian Painting Academy). Modelled on the Accademia di Belle Arti in Venice and divided into four classes, it inspired and motivated further developments in art education, although most of its pupils were simply preparing for further studies abroad in Vienna, Rome or Munich. It eventually closed in 1860.

In 1871 the State founded the Design and Drawing Teachers' Institute, which in 1908 became the school of the Academy of Fine Arts. Meanwhile, two master schools and one women's school opened in an attempt to counterbalance the conservative and outdated policies of the Institute. Private schools appeared at the end of the 19th century. SIMON HOLLÓSY established principles of teaching at the school he set up in Munich in 1886 that were to be the basis for the colony at Nagybánya (now Baia Mare, Romania), founded in 1896 as the first private art school in Hungary (*see also* NAGYBÁNYA COLONY).

Courses in the decorative arts organized along the lines of the 18th-century drawing schools were taught at the School of Decorative Drawing, founded in 1880 but not opened until 1886; instruction was also given at the School of Decorative Arts, affiliated with the Design and Drawing Teachers' Institute. In 1883 the painter GYULA BENCZÚR was appointed the first Hungarian Director of Art Education.

Major changes in art education took place in the early 20th century. In the 1920s the conservative school of the Academy of Fine Arts was reformed, which involved the merging of training for teachers and artists and the replacement of plaster casts with actual models in the drawing and sculpture classes. A further reform in 1931 paved the way for the pseudo-academic school. The reform of the School of Decorative Arts was repeatedly delayed due to conflicts about its teaching methods in the 1930s. Conservatives wanted its teaching to be based on two-dimensional folk art and representational art, while liberals advocated an approach more responsive to mass production and the needs of industry. The training of architects was also dominated by traditional thinking; as late as the 1930s Eclecticism rather than Modernism was still considered to be the primary model. A truly contemporary approach to art education could only really be found in the various studios and such independent schools as the school of graphic design (1920–50) run by Álmos Jaschik (*b* 1885), the Munka Kör (Working circle) organized by LAJOS KASSÁK and the Atelier Studio School (opened in 1932). After 1945, proposals to reform art education at college level were based on the practice of these private studio schools.

After World War II art education had to meet new challenges set by the large-scale reconstruction of buildings destroyed in the War. Reorganization at this time was supervised by the Hungarian Arts Council, presided over by the musician Zoltán Kodály. Between 1945 and 1949 art students were placed in residential colleges, where new methods of art education along realist lines were introduced. However, after the establishment of the Stalinist regime in 1949, Socialist Realist art on the Soviet model was introduced under the guidance of the Ministry of Welfare. In architectural education, planning courses and site courses were separated, and then a programme based on the 19th-century atelier tradition was adopted. This was followed by a period where the practice was combined with the theory of education. In 1953 a master school was set up to provide further training for talented architects. Educational reform of the school of the Academy of Fine Arts was launched in 1949 with the goal of establishing the hegemony of Socialist Realism. Emulating Soviet practice, the school sought to attain this objective through the revival of 19th-century academic methods. Efforts to reform the School of Decorative Arts began in 1950. Genuine progress became possible only after the establishment in 1964 of design as a main course of study. Changes in the curricula of art schools reached a new phase in the 1990s. Art education at beginner levels came under the jurisdiction of secondary art schools, the numbers of which steadily increased after 1953; many students who went on to art colleges were products of this system.

See also BUDAPEST, §II, 2.

BIBLIOGRAPHY

K. Lyka: *Magyar művészet, 1800–1850: A táblabiró világ művészete* [Hungarian art, 1800–1850: The art of provincial Hungary] (Budapest, [*c.* 1900]); 3rd edn as *A táblabiró világ művészete: Magyar művészet, 1800–1850* (Budapest, 1981)

M. Rabinovszky: 'A művészeti oktatás kezdetei Magyarországon' [The beginnings of art education in Hungary], *Magyar Művészettörténeti Munkaközösség Evkönyve* (1951)

F. Fodor: *Az Institutum Geometricum* (Budapest, 1955)

M. Mojzer: 'Architectura Civilis', *Művészettörténeti Értesítő*, vi/2–3 (1957), pp. 103–18

D. Komárik: 'Építészképzés és mesterfelvétel a XIX. században' [Architectural education and qualifications in the 19th century], *Építés- & Építészettudomány*, iv (1971), pp. 379–418

H. Szabolcsi: *Magyarországi butorművészet a 18–19. század fordulóján* [Hungarian furniture at the end of the 18th century and in the early 19th] (Budapest, 1972) [incl. information of founding and operation of drawing schools]

L. Németh, ed.: *Magyar művészet, 1890–1919* [Hungarian art, 1890–1919] (1981), vi of *A magyarországi művészet története* [The history of art in Hungary], ed. N. Aradi (Budapest, 1981–)

IDA BOD-BOBROVSZKY

XV. Art libraries and photographic collections.

The largest art library in Hungary is housed in the Museum of Fine Arts in Budapest. Specialist art libraries are also held in the Hungarian National Gallery, the Museum of Applied Art and the Hungarian National Museum with its Archaeological Library, all in Budapest. Specialist archives and photo collections are housed in part in the National Museum's archives and in part in their various departments. The department of art history at the Loránd Eötvös University in Budapest has an important art library. Documents pertaining to monuments in Hungary and their preservation are held in Budapest in the National Monument Trust Library, which also contains a photo archive and an archive of plans for, and data pertaining to, buildings. The Hungarian Museum of Architecture in Budapest also operates under the aegis of this institution, which currently organizes occasional exhibitions only. The Hungarian National Academy of Sciences Art Historical Research Group (founded 1969) in Budapest houses a library, archives and collections of photographs and medieval seals, all of which refer to the history of Hungarian art. The most important collections of manuscripts and codices are located in Budapest in the National Széchényi Library, the Loránd Eötvös University Library and the library of the Hungarian National Academy of Sciences and in Esztergom in the Archiepiscopal Library.

BIBLIOGRAPHY

G. S. Zakariás: *Budapest* (1961), iii of *Magyarország művészeti emlékei* [Hungary's monuments of art] (Budapest, 1959–61)

ERNŐ MAROSÍ

Hung-i Kamalvand. *See* ELYMAIS, §5.

Hung-i Nauruzi. *See* ELYMAIS, §3.

Hung-i Yar Alivand. *See* ELYMAIS, §6.

Hung-jen. *See* HONGREN.

Hūns, Kārlis (Teodors) [Gun, Karl (Fyodorovich); Huhn, Carl (Theodor)] (*b* Madliena, nr Riga, 13 Dec 1830; *d* Davos, Switzerland, 28 Jan 1877). Latvian painter and teacher, active in Russia. Having studied (1852–61) at the St Petersburg Academy of Arts under Pyotr Basin (1793–1877), he became attracted to the Romantic Classicism of Karl Bryullov and it was this style that informed much of his early work. However, after graduating in 1861, he travelled across Russia as far as the Ural Mountains with the artist Vasily Petrovich Vereshchagin (1835–1909), and, as a result, his work showed a new versatility and variety of approach, first in his painting of the iconostasis (including a *Virgin* and *Two Evangelists*) in the church of the Protection of the Veil in Yelabuga, Vyatka province, and then in his illustrations of Russian folk life published in T. de Paulys's *Les Peuples de la Russie* (St Petersburg, 1862). From 1863 to 1871 Hūns lived in western Europe—mainly in France—on a scholarship awarded by the St Petersburg Academy of Arts and painted his highly articulate renderings of historical subjects and provincial life, as well as portraits and landscapes. Noteworthy examples are *On the Eve of St Bartholomew's Night* (1868; St Petersburg, Rus. Mus.; version, 1868, Riga, Latv. Mus. F.A.), a depiction of a Roman Catholic noble preparing, with images of Christ, for the Huguenot massacre on 24 August 1572; and the realist *Joiner's Shop, Brittany* (1865; Riga, City A. Mus.). On his return to St Petersburg in 1871 he was made a professor of history painting (1871–4) at the Academy and in 1872, as the Academy sought to respond to the changing times and the waning of its authority, he was appointed to the commission set up to revise its statutes. In November that year he joined the WANDERERS, whereupon he played a major role as an arbitrator between the Wanderers and the Academy in their difficult relations. As the only Latvian to join the Wanderers, he established himself as the foremost initiator of modern Latvian art. He exhibited both at the Academy and with the Wanderers, however, and his work avoided incisive Critical Realism, instead being characterized more by a refined documentary approach, as in *An Outing* (1874) and *After the Storm (10 May 1872, Livonia)* (1872; both Riga, Latv. Mus. F.A.). In 1873–4 he painted the *Awakening of the Day* (destr. 1935), an allegorical ceiling fresco for a staircase in the Anichkov Palace (begun 1741), St Petersburg. In 1874 he contracted tuberculosis, after having effected the showing of the Wanderers' third exhibition in Riga and shortly after his marriage to Vera Monigetti, daughter of the Russian architect IPPOLIT MONIGETTI. His illness forced him to move back to the warmer climates of France and Italy. After his death a posthumous exhibition of his work toured with the Wanderers' sixth show.

BIBLIOGRAPHY

A. Prance: 'Akademikis Profesors Kārlis Hūns', *Illustrēts Žurnals* (1925), no. 7/8, pp. 204–21

A. Eglit: *Karl Fyodorovich Gun* (Riga, 1955)

J. Siliņš: *Latvijas māksla, 1800–1914* [Latvian painting], i (Stockholm, 1979), pp. 207–20

JEREMY HOWARD

Hunt. American family of artists.

(1) William Morris Hunt (*b* Brattleboro, VT, 31 March 1824; *d* Appledore, Isles of Shoals, NH, 8 Sept 1879). Painter, sculptor and teacher. While a student at Harvard College, he exhibited precocious talents in the arts and studied with John Crookshanks King (1806–82), a sculptor working in Boston. In 1843 Hunt went to Europe with his mother and siblings, his father having died of cholera in 1832. They visited Paris and Rome, where he studied briefly under the American Neo-classical sculptor Henry Kirke Brown (1814–86). In 1845 he toured the Near East with his family and Thomas Gold Appleton, a patron and essayist from Boston, visiting Corfu and Athens *en route.* Later that year, he took the advice of Emanuel Leutze and enrolled in the Düsseldorf Academy, but he remained there only nine months. In 1846 Hunt went to Paris with the intention of joining the workshop of the sculptor James Pradier, but he was inspired to become a painter after seeing Thomas Couture's *The Falconer* (1845; Toledo, OH, Mus. A.). Hunt never abandoned his sculptural training, however, and continued to produce work such as the plaster relief of the *Horses of Anahita* (*c.* 1848; New York, Met.). From 1847 to 1852 he worked in Couture's studio, where he rapidly became a favourite pupil. An example of his early figure painting is *La Marguerite* (*c.* 1852; Paris, Louvre), which reflects Couture's influence in its centralized composition, its definition of form through broad masses of light and dark and its rich and elegant textures. Using the same techniques as Couture, Hunt created shaded areas with smooth sepia turpentine washes and contrasted these with dramatic highlights of thick impasto. Couture was a consummate technician, and his pupil assimilated and quickly mastered his doctrine of the primacy of style.

At the Paris Salon Hunt became acquainted with Millet's monumental peasant genre paintings, such as *The Sower* (1850; Boston, MA, Mus. F.A.). He became a close friend of Millet's and in 1853 moved to Barbizon, where he lived and worked until his return to the USA in the summer of 1855. His subject-matter was deeply influenced by Millet, and his *Belated Kid* (see fig.) shows his romantic perception of peasant labour. Under the influence of Millet, Hunt abandoned the painterly flourishes he had learnt from Couture and replaced them with firm brushstrokes and thorough colour blending.

Hunt married the heiress Louisa Dumaresq Perkins on his return to the USA and thus secured his position in Boston society. He lived first at his family home in Brattleboro and then in Newport, RI, where he established an informal studio-school that attracted literati and artists, including Henry James and his brother William, as well as John La Farge. In 1864 Hunt established a studio in Boston, and during the ensuing decades he became a major cultural leader in New England. He was a vigorous spokesman for French modern art, inspiring the American patronage of Millet, Corot and others. Boston's conservative attitude to art prompted Hunt to found the Allston Club in 1866; it existed only two years, but made important purchases, most notably Courbet's *La Curée* (1858; Boston, Mus. F.A.). During the 1860s Hunt was a highly successful portrait painter. In his portraits he used a variety of techniques ranging from a quasi-academic method based on Couture's work to broader, more expressive treatment with looser brushwork. *Mrs Richard Morris Hunt and Child* (1865–6; Boston, MA, Mus. F.A.) exemplifies the artist's desire to capture the sitter's spirit by the most direct means possible.

William Morris Hunt: *Belated Kid*, oil on canvas, 1372×978 mm, 1853–7 (Boston, MA, Museum of Fine Arts)

In 1866 Hunt made a second trip to France and travelled to Dinan with Elihu Vedder and Charles Coleman (1840–1928). After witnessing Millet's triumph at the Exposition Universelle, Paris (1867), and a brief reunion with the artist at Barbizon, he returned to Boston in 1868 and began teaching a class of women art students. During the 1870s he suffered a number of personal tragedies, beginning with a disastrous studio fire in 1872, followed by separation from his wife in 1873 and the suicide of his brother Jonathan in 1874. Partly as emotional solace, he turned his energies increasingly towards landscape painting (e.g. *Sandbank with Willows, Magnolia*, 1877; New York, Met.), and he spent the summer of 1876 touring rural Massachusetts in a horse-drawn cart that functioned as a mobile studio.

Hunt received his most important commission in June 1878, for the decoration of two lunettes in the assembly chamber of the Albany State Capitol. He chose the poetic theme of Anahita, the Persian nature goddess, a subject that had attracted him for many years. One panel, the *Flight of Night*, depicted Anahita in a chariot of clouds and the other, *The Discoverer*, portrayed Christopher Columbus accompanied by Fortune, Faith, Hope and Science. Hunt worked in experimental pigments and painted directly on to the wall; this technique, coupled with the excessive damp in the chamber, led to a rapid deterioration of the decoration. The murals were regarded by his contemporaries as the culmination of Hunt's career, yet the demands of the commission left him physically and emotionally debilitated and led to his nervous collapse and subsequent suicide in 1879.

WRITINGS

H. M. Knowlton, ed.: *Talks on Art* (London, 1878/*R* New York, 1975)

BIBLIOGRAPHY

H. Angell: *Records of William Morris Hunt* (Boston, 1881)
E. D. Cheney: *Gleanings in the Field of Art* (Boston, 1881)
H. M. Knowlton: *Art-life of William Morris Hunt* (Boston, 1889, rev. New York, 2/1971)
M. Shannon: *Boston Days of William Morris Hunt* (Boston, 1923)
The Late Landscapes of William Morris Hunt (exh. cat., College Park, U. MD, 1976)
William Morris Hunt: A Memorial Exhibition (exh. cat. by H. Adams and M. J. Hoppin, Boston, Mus. F.A., 1979)
An International Episode: Millet, Monet and their North American Counterparts (exh. cat. by L. L. Meixner, Memphis, TN, Dixon Gal., 1982)
S. Webster: *William Morris Hunt, 1824–1879* (Cambridge, 1991)

LAURA L. MEIXNER

(2) Richard Morris Hunt (*b* Brattleboro, VT, 31 Oct 1827; *d* Newport, RI, 31 July 1895). Architect, brother of (1) William Morris Hunt. He was the most eminent architect of his time in the US, a prolific designer and the most significant figure of the day in the development of architectural professionalism.

Hunt created several nationally important buildings and was a frequent spokesman for his fellow architects; he was also a champion of high standards in building design. He was much honoured in his lifetime and became widely known, even while fairly young, as 'the dean of American architecture'.

1. TRAINING AND EARLY WORK. In 1843 his widowed mother brought the family to Europe. Except for a brief return to the USA in 1848, Richard remained in Europe for 12 years, eventually attending the Ecole des Beaux-Arts in Paris—the first American to be trained there—and from time to time travelling in Europe, Egypt and the Middle East. In 1846 he was admitted to the Ecole and joined the studio of Hector-Martin Lefuel. He continued his association with the Ecole until 1854, when Lefuel was put in charge of additions to the Louvre, and Hunt was made inspector of works there. In that capacity he assisted Lefuel in the design of the imposing Pavillon de la Bibliothèque.

Hunt returned to the USA in September 1855 as a trained architect and set up an office in New York City. His first commission, a town house on 38th Street (destr.), unexpectedly involved him in a lawsuit when the client refused to pay what Hunt considered his rightful commission. The resulting court case helped affirm a set fee schedule for the work of trained architects and identified Hunt as someone striving to protect professional rights. His earliest major commission was for the Tenth Street Studio Building (51 W Tenth St; destr.) in New York City, the first American structure designed especially for artists. On completion in 1858 it at once became the physical centre of the city's artistic life.

Hunt set up his own training studio there, modelled on those in Paris, and through this studio had considerable impact on subsequent architectural education in the USA. To promote his profession, he also became a founder-member of the American Institute of Architects in 1857, eventually serving as its third national president (1888–91).

In 1861 Hunt married Catharine Clinton Howland; this brought him connections with a wealthy New York merchant family, from whom he later received several commissions. The couple travelled to France, where they remained for over a year. On his return to New York Hunt prepared designs for formal entrances to the south side of Central Park, but his proposals were widely criticized as inappropriate for the new rustic park and were rejected. He was appointed as a judge and commissioner at the Paris Exposition Universelle in 1867, and he and his family once more travelled to Europe, returning to New York in 1868.

1. Richard Morris Hunt: Griswold House, Newport, Rhode Island, 1861–3

2. Richard Morris Hunt: Biltmore House, Asheville, North Carolina, 1888–95

2. MATURE WORK.

(i) Private commissions. Hunt was becoming well known for his domestic architecture, having already constructed the J. N. A. Griswold house (1861–3; see fig. 1) in Newport, RI, an early example of his timber-gabled stick style. It initiated an important series of houses in Newport, including the remodelling of Château-sur-Mer, the Wetmore mansion (1869–79), at that time the largest residence in Newport. Much comment was caused in Boston by Hunt's Brimmer houses (1869–70; destr.), which used French Renaissance details, and in Chicago by the street façade of his mansion for Marshall Field (1871–3), in Second Empire style.

Very large, ornate private houses seemed to give Hunt his greatest satisfaction, and he was given more commissions for these as his career developed. His elegant New York town house for William K. Vanderbilt (1879–82; destr.), 660 Fifth Avenue, designed in a Late Gothic/early French Renaissance style, was widely admired and emulated. The Henry G. Marquand mansion (1881–4; destr.), the Ogden Mills mansion (1885–7; destr.), the William V. Lawrence mansion (1890–91; destr.), the Elbridge T. Gerry mansion (1891–4; destr.) and the very large double residence (1891–5; destr.) on Fifth Avenue for Mrs William B. Astor and her son, Colonel John Jacob Astor, in various styles, all contributed to the decorative elegance of New York's Upper East Side. In Chicago the William Borden mansion (1884–9; destr.) echoed the design of the William Vanderbilt house. Large country houses for clients (who were often personal friends) were also important projects. The Levi P. Morton mansion (1886–7; destr.), near Rhinecliff, NY, was designed as an Elizabethan manor house, and the James W. Pinchot mansion (1884–6) in Milford, PA, the Archibald Rogers mansion (1886–9) in Hyde Park, NY, and the Joseph Busk mansion (1889–91) in Newport were rustic structures in a late medieval French mode.

Hunt is perhaps best remembered today for his huge summer 'cottages' in Newport designed for holiday use and for his great château-style house, Biltmore, in North Carolina; these mansions set the standard for the most opulent way of life in an age of lavish consumption. Ochre Court (1888–92), constructed as a summer home in Newport for Ogden Goelet, who had made a fortune in New York real estate, is in the style of an elegant French château, set on a small town plot. Close by, Marble House (1888–92), erected for William K. and Alva Vanderbilt and modelled in part on the White House in Washington, DC, included the most lavish interiors that Hunt ever designed. Belcourt Castle (1891–4), Newport, commissioned by O. H. P. Belmont and combining French, English and Italian elements, was created as a huge stable and carriage house with living quarters attached. The Breakers (1892–5; for illustration *see* NEWPORT), the grandest of Hunt's Newport houses, commissioned by Cornelius Vanderbilt II, was designed in a 16th-century Genoese style. Biltmore House (1888–95; see fig. 2) was the largest of Hunt's country palaces, erected amid 125,000 acres of farmland and forest preserve close to Asheville, NC, for George Washington Vanderbilt. Boasting more than 250 rooms, it is the largest American house ever constructed. It was enriched by opulent interiors in a picturesque French Late Gothic and early Renaissance mode and surrounded by elaborate formal gardens.

(ii) Monuments and memorials. Hunt's many monuments and memorials, usually in collaboration with the sculptor John Quincy Adams Ward, who favoured a straightforward realism, also brought him public attention. The

Hunt–Ward projects included the *Seventh Regiment* monument (1867–73), Central Park, New York City; the *Matthew C. Perry* statue (1868–72), Newport; the *Yorktown* monument (1880–84), assisted by Henry Van Brunt, in Virginia; the statue of *George Washington* (1883), Wall and Broad Streets, New York City; and the *James Abram Garfield* monument (1884–7), The Mall, Washington, DC. More significant than any of these, however, was Hunt's base and pedestal for Frédéric Auguste Bartholdi's monumental statue of *Liberty Enlightening the World* (1881–6), the most important American statuary project of the 19th century.

(iii) Commercial and public buildings. Hunt was responsible for several significant commercial structures, at first mainly in New York. He built the Presbyterian Hospital (1868–72; destr.), the most modern hospital in the city, for James Lenox, the wealthy merchant and bibliophile, and for the same client designed the elegant Neo-grec Lenox Library (1870–77; destr., now the site of the Frick Museum), facing Central Park. In Newport he built the Travers Block (1870–71) of shops and apartments in Bellevue Avenue, and this still stands prominently, not far from the site of Hunt's own summer home. Also in New York were the Stuyvesant Apartments (1869–70) on East 18th Street, based on the Parisian model; this was the first important American apartment house. The large Stevens House (1870–72; destr.), also built as an apartment house, was later turned into a commercial hotel (The Victoria). Two iron-fronted stores—the Van Rensselaer Building (1871–2; destr.) and the Roosevelt Building (1873–4; *see* NEW YORK, fig. 1), 478–82 Broadway—utilized up-to-date cast-iron technology. The Delaware and Hudson Canal Company Building (1873–6; destr.) was a large and imposing office building. Hunt's Tribune Building (1873–6; destr.), facing City Hall Park, with a clock-tower surmounted by a spire rising from the roof, was for several years the tallest structure in New York.

Following another long visit to Europe in 1874–5, Hunt served as an architectural juror for the Philadelphia Centennial International Exhibition of 1876. His own work became stylistically more varied. Examples are the Scandinavian stave-style St Mark's Chapel and Rectory (1879–80) at Islip, Long Island; the Association Residence for Respectable Aged Indigent Females (1881–3; now the national headquarters for American Youth Hostels), New York City, combining French Gothic Revival elements; the austere Chemical Laboratory (1885–91) at Princeton College (now University), Princeton, NJ; and the Flemish-gabled Free Circulating Library (1887–8), Jackson Square, New York City.

To his contemporaries, Hunt was probably best known for his Beaux-Arts classical Administration Building, with its gold and white dome (1891–3; destr.), at the World's Columbian Exposition held in Chicago (1893). Hunt was chosen by his peers as chairman of the Board of Architects and awarded the commission for the most prominent building of the Exposition. It rose some 80 m over the site of the fair, and placed as it was at the head of the Court of Honor, it set an elegant and dignified tone.

Three further visits to Europe refreshed Hunt's artistic sensibilities; in his final years, while continuing work on great houses and monuments, he also undertook new academic and church commissions. He designed several small buildings (1887–93) for the US Naval Observatory in Washington, DC; for Adelbert College, later Case Western Reserve University, Cleveland, OH, he designed the eclectic Clark Hall (1889–92); and for the United States Military Academy at West Point, a large Academic Building (1889–95), a gymnasium (1889–93; destr.) and a small guard-house (1894–7; destr.), all in a castellated Gothic Revival style. At Trinity Church on lower Broadway in New York City he devised three sets of elaborate bronze entrance doors (1890–94); on the right-hand panel of the principal entrance door the sculptor Karl Bitter (1867–1915) placed a small portrait head of the architect. At Harvard University Hunt designed the Neo-classical Fogg Museum (1893–5; later Hunt Hall; destr.). Hunt's final major commission was for the large Beaux-Arts-style entrance wing (1894–1902) of the Metropolitan Museum of Art, New York. He planned this wing as part of a general expansion of the museum, but his overall plan was not followed. His eldest son, Richard Howland Hunt (*b* 14 March 1862; *d* 12 July 1931), completed the museum entrance wing some years after his father's death.

Hunt designed in many different styles and constructed many building types. Committed to European historicizing styles, he nonetheless attempted to use past ideas for the needs of his time. More than in his buildings, his significance lies in his endeavours to raise the status and standards of his profession. In 1898 several New York art organizations erected a monument to him on Fifth Avenue near 70th Street.

BIBLIOGRAPHY

M. Schuyler: 'The Works of the Late Richard M. Hunt', *Archit. Rec.*, v (Oct–Dec 1895), pp. 97–180

Paul R. Baker: *Richard Morris Hunt* (Cambridge, MA, 1980)

Susan R. Stein, ed.: *The Architecture of Richard Morris Hunt* (Chicago, 1986)

PAUL R. BAKER

Hunt, Alfred William (*b* Liverpool, 15 Nov 1830; *d* London, 3 May 1896). English painter. He was elected a Fellow of Corpus Christi College, Oxford, in 1853 and combined work as an exhibiting artist with an academic career until his early thirties. He resigned his fellowship on his marriage in 1861 and subsequently devoted himself to art. Paintings exhibited at the Royal Academy, London, had already gained the praise of John Ruskin. In 1862 he moved from Oxford to London and became an associate of the Society of Painters in Water-Colours. He was elected a full member the next year and served as vice-president in 1888.

An early model for Hunt's landscapes was provided by the work of David Cox, who was a friend of his father Andrew Hunt (1796–1861), a landscape painter. Cox helped to inspire in Hunt a taste for the dramatic mountain scenery of North Wales that is reflected in *Track of an Ancient Glacier—Cwm Trifaen* (oil, *c.* 1858; London, Tate). Stylistically, however, J. M. W. Turner's watercolours proved more influential, while exposure to the Pre-Raphaelites led to a preoccupation with finish. Hunt's painstaking detail was criticized as excessive, even by such supporters as Ruskin. In some works he scraped and rubbed away his carefully built-up surfaces to achieve a more atmospheric effect, for example in *Tynemouth Pier—Lighting the Lamps at Sundown* (1868; New Haven, CT, Yale Cent. Brit. A.). At his best, Hunt succeeded in fusing the sweep and atmosphere of Turner with Pre-Raphaelite finish and compositional originality.

BIBLIOGRAPHY

DNB

V. Hunt: 'Alfred William Hunt, RWS, 1830–1896', *Old Wtrcol. Soc. Club*, ii (1924–5), pp. 29–47

A. Staley: *The Pre-Raphaelite Landscape* (Oxford, 1973), pp. 144–7

R. Secor: *John Ruskin and Alfred Hunt: New Letters and the Record of a Friendship*, English Literary Studies, 25 (Victoria, BC, 1982)

SCOTT WILCOX

Hunt, John Horbury (*b* Saint John, NB, Oct 1838; *d* Sydney, NSW, 27 Dec 1904). Australian architect of Canadian birth. The son of a carpenter, he trained in Boston, MA, under Edward Clarke Cabot (1818–91). When the American Civil War broke out in 1861 he travelled to India, but on arriving in Sydney in 1863 he decided to stay to work with Edmund Blacket. By 1865 he was Blacket's chief assistant, but he left in May 1869 for a brief partnership with John Hilly (1810–83), establishing his own practice later that year. For the next 30 years his mastery of a complex and asymmetrical free-Gothic style, combined with an outstanding skill in the use of timber and brickwork, was demonstrated in many significant buildings, for example the cathedrals at Armidale (1871) and Grafton (1880) and churches at Denman (1871), Branxton (1873) and Dapto (1882). The stone-vaulted chapel of the Sacred Heart (1896), Rose Bay, is his finest work. His houses, such as Booloominbah (1888) at Armidale, Camelot (1888) at Narellan, Pibrac (1888) at Warrawee and Highlands (1891) at Waitara, are distinctive. As President of the Institute of Architects of New South Wales (1889–95), his campaign for professional status led to schism, with many members resigning under the opposition of its vice-president, John Sulman. However, Hunt succeeded in reconstituting the Institute and oversaw its incorporation (1891) and association (1893) with the RIBA. Eccentric, quick-tempered and argumentative, he was extremely fond of animals and was an active member and vice-president of the Animals Protection Society. His practice collapsed during the economic depression of the 1890s and he spent the last ten years of his life in penury.

BIBLIOGRAPHY

J. M. Freeland: *Architect Extraordinary: The Life and Work of John Horbury Hunt, 1838–1904* (Melbourne, 1970)

PETER REYNOLDS

Hunt, Richard (Howard) (*b* Chicago, IL, 12 Sept 1935). American sculptor. He studied at the School of the Art Institute of Chicago (1948–50), while working part-time in the zoological laboratory of the University of Chicago. In 1953 he encountered the iron sculptures of Julio González at MOMA, New York, which inspired him to establish his own sculpture workshop. Hunt's first works were experiments with assemblages of found objects: broken machine parts and discarded metal from the junk yards of Chicago. Working first in copper and iron, then aluminium and steel, he constructed a series of 'hybrid figures', which made reference to human, animal and plant forms. In the 1960s his work moved from linear and calligraphic structures to more enclosed and monolithic forms, reflecting his growing interest in rock formations and geology. A leading African-American sculptor, Hunt received early recognition, and his work was featured in many museum and gallery exhibitions in the USA. His first retrospective was in 1967 at the Milwaukee Art Center, University of Wisconsin. His commissions include *Expansive Construction* (1960) for Louisiana Southern University, Baton Rouge, and *Centennial Sculpture* (1969) for Loyola University, Chicago. Examples of his work are also in the collections of the Albright-Knox Art Gallery, Buffalo, NY; the Cleveland Museum of Art, OH; the Metropolitan Museum of Art and the Museum of Modern Art, both New York. In November 1969 he was appointed a member of the National Council on the Arts by President Lyndon B. Johnson.

BIBLIOGRAPHY

Richard Hunt: Sculpture and Graphics (exh. cat., Milwaukee, U. WI, 1967)

Richard Hunt: Exhibition of Sculpture (exh. cat., ed. J. Goldman; New York, MOMA, 1971)

The Appropriate Object—9 Artists (exh. cat. by B. Wright, Buffalo, NY, Albright-Knox A.G., 1989)

□

Hunt, William Henry (*b* London, 28 March 1790; *d* London, 10 Feb 1864). English watercolourist. He was apprenticed to John Varley about 1804. Although handicapped by deformed legs, Hunt frequently sketched from nature along the Thames with his fellow apprentice, John Linnell. Together they attended Dr Thomas Monro's Academy, and in 1808 Hunt joined Linnell at the Royal Academy Schools, London. Although he exhibited sporadically with the Society of Painters in Water-Colours from 1814, he did not become an associate until 1824 (having been rejected as a candidate the previous year). He became a full member in 1826.

Hunt's early works are mainly topographical or picturesque views, often executed in a stylish updating of the 18th-century 'tinted drawing' manner. The prominent pen outlines in these works derive from the drawing style of Canaletto, whose work he copied for Dr Monro. Many of his subjects were taken from the countryside around Dr Monro's residence near Bushey in Hertfordshire, where he was a frequent visitor. After his election to the Society, he turned increasingly to figure subjects, often humorous or sentimental in nature, and to still-lifes. In the 1830s he adopted a painstaking method of stippling colour over a ground of heavily gummed Chinese white, a technique which was to be influential on John Frederick Lewis and the Pre-Raphaelites. John Ruskin was an enthusiastic advocate of his work. His meticulous still-lifes of flowers, fruits and birds' nests, which earned him the nickname 'Bird's Nest' Hunt, were widely imitated both in England and America.

BIBLIOGRAPHY

William Henry Hunt, 1790–1864 (exh. cat., Wolverhampton, A.G., 1981)

J. Witt: *William Henry Hunt (1790–1864): Life and Work* (London, 1982)

SCOTT WILCOX

Hunt, William Holman (*b* London, 2 April 1827; *d* London, 7 Sept 1910). English painter.

1. Life and work. 2. Working methods and technique.

1. LIFE AND WORK.

(i) Early career and Pre-Raphaelite Brotherhood. He worked as an office clerk in London from 1839 to 1843, attending drawing classes at a mechanics' institute in the evenings and taking weekly lessons from the portrait painter Henry Rogers. Holman Hunt overcame parental opposition to his choice of career in 1843, and this determined attitude and dedication to art could be seen throughout his working life. In July 1844, at the third attempt, he entered the Royal Academy Schools. His earliest exhibited works, such as *Little Nell and her Grandfather* (exh. British Institution, 1846; Sheffield, Graves A.G.), reveal few traces of originality, but the reading of John Ruskin's *Modern Painters* in 1847 was of crucial importance to Holman Hunt's artistic development. It led him to abandon the ambitious *Christ and the Two Marys* (Adelaide, A.G. S. Australia) in early 1848, when he realized its traditional iconography would leave his contemporaries unmoved. His next major work, the *Flight of Madeline and Porphyro during the Drunkenness Attending the Revelry* (1848; London, Guildhall A.G.), from John Keats's 'Eve of St Agnes', though displaced into a medieval setting, dramatized an issue dear to contemporary poets and central to Holman Hunt's art: love and youthful idealism versus loyalty to one's family. His first mature painting, it focuses on a moment of psychological crisis in a cramped and shallow picture space. The Keatsian source, rich colours and compositional format attracted the attention of Dante Gabriel Rossetti, leading to his friendship with Holman Hunt and thus contributing to the formation of the Pre-Raphaelite Brotherhood (PRB; *see* PRE-RAPHAELITISM) in the autumn of 1848.

Together with Rossetti and John Everett Millais (with whom he had been friendly since *c.* 1844), Holman Hunt developed a powerful graphic style of pen-and-ink outlines in 1848 (e.g. *One Step to the Deathbed*; New Haven, CT, Yale Cent. Brit. A.), but as a young artist with no financial backing he had to base his reputation on exhibition works. Holman Hunt's only oil painting inscribed *PRB* was shown at the Royal Academy in 1849: the landscape of *Rienzi Vowing to Obtain Justice for the Death of his Young Brother, Slain in a Skirmish between the Colonna and Orsini Factions* (priv. col., see 1984 exh. cat., p. 67) had been painted directly from nature the previous summer, an important innovation in terms of a work intended for public consumption. The 14th-century subject-matter was allied to stylistic characteristics (e.g. the pietà-like pose of Rienzi and his murdered brother) that expressed the Pre-Raphaelites' support for the sincerity of the values of the art before Raphael. Rienzi's oath was significant not only in the context of the 1848 European revolutions but also as a metaphor of Holman Hunt's belief in the Pre-Raphaelite Brotherhood as an iconoclastic artistic force.

A *Converted British Family Sheltering a Christian Missionary from the Persecution of the Druids* (exh. RA 1850;

1. William Holman Hunt: *The Hireling Shepherd*, oil on canvas, 764×1095 mm, 1851–2 (Manchester, City Art Gallery)

Oxford, Ashmolean) fuses the medieval element of Pre-Raphaelitism (influenced by Rossetti and Ford Madox Brown) with the 'truth to nature' credo of Ruskin, but the way in which the missionaries function as types of the persecuted Saviour heralded the new form of religious art Holman Hunt was to evolve after the dissolution of the Brotherhood. The Tractarian imagery of the *Druids* was topical but controversial in 1850, a period of religious ferment characterized by fear of conversion to Rome. The picture was purchased by THOMAS COMBE, a Tractarian who became an important patron, friend and business adviser to the artist. Holman Hunt's reputation was far from assured, and his two paintings from Shakespeare, shown at the Royal Academy in 1851 and 1853, can be seen as a deliberate turning away from sensitive religious issues in order to develop the more private theme of sexual morality. *Valentine Rescuing Sylvia from Proteus* (1850–51; Birmingham, Mus. & A.G.) deals with an attempted rape and the betrayal of friendship through lust, while *Claudio and Isabella* (1850–53; London, Tate) reverts to Holman Hunt's preoccupation with the conflict between family loyalty and individual integrity. The emphasis on chastity as a positive virtue is apparent in the artist's treatment of Isabella, an upright figure bathed in sunlight, whose refusal to be manipulated by male desires presages the revelation experienced by the kept woman in Holman Hunt's *Awakening Conscience* of 1853–4 (London, Tate). The model for the latter was Annie Miller (1835–1925), a working-class girl with whom Holman Hunt had fallen in love and whom he had attempted to educate.

Both of these relatively small works are set in enclosed spaces, in contrast to the larger canvases of *Valentine Rescuing Sylvia* and the *Hireling Shepherd* (1851–2; Manchester, C.A.G.; see fig. 1), which include a significant amount of exquisitely detailed *plein-air* painting. The *Hireling Shepherd*, Holman Hunt's first commercial success, is superficially a scene of pastoral dalliance set in a totally naturalistic summer landscape (innovative in terms of its treatment of sunlight); its underlying satire on contemporary sectarianism was to be revealed by the artist in 1897. This is the earliest example of Holman Hunt's ambitious attempt to deal with complex intellectual issues, which inevitably led to his pictures being misinterpreted; for example, reviewers tended to concentrate on the sensational aspect of Holman Hunt's portrayal of the kept woman and her lover in the *Awakening Conscience*, rather than the underlying symbolism of possible redemption.

(ii) Travels to the Near East and later career. Holman Hunt was concerned to expand the frontiers of what could be portrayed in art, whatever challenges this entailed. It was therefore deeply characteristic that, just as his reputation was assured, he left England in January 1854 for the Near East. His desire to paint in the Holy Land stemmed partly from a strong Christian commitment. This was the result of a conversion that, according to Holman Hunt's letter of August 1853 to Thomas Combe, he experienced during the painting of the *Light of the World* (1851–3; Oxford, Keble Coll.), a work destined to become, through replicas and engravings, the most popular Protestant picture of the 19th century.

Holman Hunt arrived in Cairo in February 1854, travelled to Jaffa at the end of May and reached Jerusalem on 3 June 1854. This was his base until 17 October 1855, when he travelled north, via Nazareth, Damascus and the Cedars of Lebanon, to Beirut, where he embarked for the Crimea before returning to England in late January 1856. His love of adventure and strong factual bent led him to adopt the Ruskinian concept of the artist as explorer, morally bound to explain the ways of God to man. The result was several highly accomplished, intensely observed watercolour landscapes, such as *Nazareth* (1855; U. Manchester, Whitworth A.G.), and, in oils, *The Scapegoat* (1854–5; Port Sunlight, Lady Lever A.G.; see fig. 2), the background of which was painted directly on to the canvas at Usdum, on the southern shores of the Dead Sea. Holman Hunt regarded this dangerous and dramatic terrain, thought to be the site of Sodom, as an apt setting for his depiction of the goat described in Leviticus as bearing the sins of the people. However, the correspondence between expiring goat and persecuted Saviour was not immediately apparent and had to be amplified by quotations on the picture frame (itself designed by the artist to elucidate the symbolism) plus a long description in the Royal Academy catalogue of 1856.

Holman Hunt returned to England at the end of January 1856. Although he contributed with Rossetti and Millais to the important illustrated edition of Alfred, Lord Tennyson's *Poems*, published in 1857, the visit to the East had distanced him from his colleagues. The *Finding of the Saviour in the Temple* (Birmingham, Mus. & A.G.), begun from semitic models in Jerusalem in 1854, was not completed until 1860. Its typological symbolism is all-pervasive, but the picture was a great success because it was also comprehensible on the simplest level. The depiction of the Holy Family and rabbis in a carefully researched reconstruction of one of the courts of the second temple fulfilled Thomas Carlyle's plea for 'a veritable contemporary representation of Jesus Christ' (Holman Hunt, 1905, i, p. 356) and initiated a new form of religious art. Ironically, the accumulation of detail allied the work to secular genre painting and detracted from the spiritual significance Holman Hunt wished to convey.

The *Finding* was sold to the dealer Ernest Gambart in 1860 for £5500, including copyright, a record price for a contemporary picture. This not only endorsed Holman Hunt's new policy of exhibiting major works privately, rather than at the Royal Academy (to which he was never elected), but also gave him the freedom to experiment with different types of painting. The *Afterglow in Egypt* (Southampton, C.A.G.), begun at Giza in 1854 and completed in 1863, was the first of his life-size female subject pictures and looked forward to *Isabella and the Pot of Basil* (1866–8; Newcastle upon Tyne, Laing A.G.), painted in Florence and London. This work, with its subject of Isabella mourning her dead lover, bears the weight of the artist's grief following the death of his wife Fanny (née Waugh) in December 1866, after only a year of marriage.

Holman Hunt's *Shadow of Death* (1870–73; Manchester, C.A.G.), his largest canvas to date, was the outcome of his second visit to Jerusalem (Aug 1869 to June 1872), and it was sold in 1873 to Agnew's, together with the oil

2. William Holman Hunt: *The Scapegoat*, oil on canvas, 870 × 1398 mm, 1854–5 (Port Sunlight, Lady Lever Art Gallery)

sketch (1869–73; Leeds, C.A.G.), for £10,500. The unprecedented depiction of Christ as a carpenter ensured its popularity among the working class.

Two years later Holman Hunt married Edith Waugh in Switzerland (as English law proscribed marriage with a deceased wife's sister) and returned once again to Jerusalem. Subsequently he produced only four major oil paintings: the *Triumph of the Innocents* (1876–87; Liverpool, Walker A.G.) and the *Lady of Shalott* (1886–1905; Hartford, CT, Wadsworth Atheneum), both of which incorporate symbolism of a private nature, *May Morning on Magdalen Tower* (1888–91; Port Sunlight, Lady Lever A.G.) and the *Miracle of Sacred Fire in the Church of the Sepulchre, Jerusalem* (1893–9; Cambridge, MA, Fogg), conceived in 1892 on the artist's last visit to the holy city. By about 1899 Holman Hunt's eyesight had so deteriorated that he required some studio assistance.

Holman Hunt's first retrospective exhibition, at the Fine Art Society, London, in 1886, was accompanied by a series of articles on Pre-Raphaelitism, published in the *Contemporary Review*, intended to counteract the prevailing view of the recently deceased Rossetti as the inspiration behind the movement. This formed the basis of Holman Hunt's autobiography, published at the end of 1905, by which date he had been elected to the Order of Merit. The didacticism of his painting was no longer fashionable, and Holman Hunt was alienated from avant-garde trends in English art, which he deplored as excessively influenced by French example. He was, however, greatly loved by the general public, many of whom owned engravings after his pictures. Crowds flocked to see his cremated remains transported from Kensington for interment in St Paul's Cathedral on 12 September 1910.

2. Working methods and technique. Around 1844–5 Holman Hunt discovered that David Wilkie's *Blind Fiddler* (1806; London, Tate) had been executed without any dark priming, 'finishing each bit thoroughly in the day' (Holman Hunt, 1905, i, p. 53). This inspired Holman Hunt to evolve the painstaking technique of painting with small brushes on a wet white ground in order to achieve the brilliant luminosity of colour hitherto confined to watercolours (e.g. the work of John Frederick Lewis). Wet white was employed for portions of *Valentine Rescuing Sylvia*, the *Hireling Shepherd* and *Fairlight Downs—Sunlight on the Sea* (1852–8; London, Andrew Lloyd Webber A. Found.), but the method was too laborious to make it feasible on a large scale.

From 1848 to 1852 Holman Hunt painted landscape backgrounds from nature in the summer and autumn months, adding the figures in the studio in the winter and spring. In only two cases, the *Afterglow in Egypt* and *Shadow of Death*, were the figures painted *en plein air*, and the disjunction between figures and landscape is often apparent, for example in the *Children's Holiday* (1864–5; Torre Abbey, Devon), painted for the industrialist Sir

THOMAS FAIRBAIRN. From the early 1860s, with the *Afterglow in Egypt*, Holman Hunt experimented with a broader technique on a larger canvas. His study of High Renaissance painting during his residence in Florence later in the decade encouraged him to continue with this approach in his major works.

Although Holman Hunt wished to base his reputation on his oils (of which approximately 158 are recorded), his graphic output was considerable. It includes watercolours (e.g. *Asparagus Island*, 1860; priv. col., see 1984 exh. cat., p. 293) produced on his travels, which can be regarded as essentially Pre-Raphaelite in their intensely observed naturalism and exploration of light effects, and several distinguished portrait drawings (e.g. *Dante Gabriel Rossetti*, coloured chalks, 1853; Manchester, C.A.G.).

For a frame design by Holman Hunt, *see* FRAME, fig. 3.

WRITINGS

'The Pre-Raphaelite Brotherhood: A Fight for Art', *Contemp. Rev.*, xlix (1886), pp. 471–88, 737–50, 820–33
'Painting *The Scapegoat*', *Contemp. Rev.*, lii (1887), pp. 21–38, 206–20
Pre-Raphaelitism and the Pre-Raphaelite Brotherhood, 2 vols (London, 1905, rev. 2/1913) [2nd edn contains more pls, a number of important appendices and a slightly abridged text; often inaccurate but remains the standard biog. source]

BIBLIOGRAPHY

F. G. Stephens: *William Holman Hunt, and his Works: A Memoir of the Artist's Life, with Description of his Pictures* (London, 1860) [vetted by Holman Hunt]
P. G. Hamerton: 'Technical Notes: W. Holman Hunt', *Portfolio*, vi (1875), pp. 45–8
J. Ruskin: *Notes on the Pictures of Mr. Holman Hunt: Exhibited at the Rooms of the Fine Art Society* (London, 1886) [collates contemp. reviews]
The Art of W. Holman Hunt (exh. cat., ed. E. Rimbault Dibdin; Liverpool, Walker A.G., 1907)
W. M. Rossetti: 'Reminiscences of Holman Hunt', *Contemp. Rev.*, xcviii (1910), pp. 385–95 [obituary]
R. Davies, ed.: 'William Holman-Hunt, O.M. (1827–1910): Contemporary Notices of his Exhibits in Water Colour', *Old Wtrcol. Soc. Club*, xiii (1935–6), pp. 12–36
M. Lutyens: 'Selling the Missionary', *Apollo*, lxxxvi (1967), pp. 380–87
D. Holman-Hunt: *My Grandfather, his Wives and Loves* (London, 1969)
William Holman Hunt (exh. cat., ed. M. Bennett; Liverpool, Walker A.G., 1969)
M. Bennett: 'Footnotes to the Holman Hunt Exhibition', *Liverpool Bull.*, xiii (1970), pp. 26–64
J. D. Macmillan: 'Holman Hunt's *Hireling Shepherd*: Some Reflections on a Victorian Pastoral', *A. Bull.*, liv (1972), pp. 187–97
M. Lutyens, ed.: 'Letters from ... William Holman Hunt, O.M. (1827–1910) in the Henry E. Huntington Library, San Marino, California', *Walpole Soc.*, xliv (1972–4), pp. 49–73
G. P. Landow: ' "Your Good Influence on Me": The Correspondence of John Ruskin and William Holman Hunt', *Bull. John Rylands Lib.*, lix (1976–7), pp. 95–126, 367–96
R. Parkinson: 'The *Awakening Conscience* and the Still Small Voice', *Tate Gal. Biennial Rep.* (1978), pp. 21–9
G. P. Landow: *William Holman Hunt and Typological Symbolism* (New Haven, 1979)
——: 'William Holman Hunt's "Oriental Mania" and his Uffizi *Self-portrait*', *A. Bull.*, lxiv (1982), pp. 646–55
——: 'Shadows Cast by the *Light of the World*: William Holman Hunt's Religious Paintings, 1893–1905', *A. Bull.*, xlv (1983), pp. 471–8
——: 'William Holman Hunt's Letters to Thomas Seddon', *Bull. John Rylands Lib.*, lxvi (1983–4), pp. 139–72
J. Bronkhurst: ' "An Interesting Series of Adventures to Look Back Upon": William Holman Hunt's Visit to the Dead Sea in November 1854', *Pre-Raphaelite Papers*, ed. L. Parris (London, 1984), pp. 111–25
L. Errington: *Social and Religious Themes in English Art, 1840–1860* (New York, 1984), pp. 210–43, 293–328
D. Holman-Hunt: 'The Holman Hunt Collection: A Personal Recollection', *Pre-Raphaelite Papers*, ed. L. Parris (London, 1984), pp. 206–25
J. S. Maas: *Holman Hunt and the 'Light of the World'* (London, 1984)
The Pre-Raphaelites (exh. cat., ed. L. Parris; London, Tate, 1984)
J. Bronkhurst: 'New Light on Holman Hunt', *Burl. Mag.*, cxxix (1987), pp. 737–9
——: *William Holman Hunt: A Catalogue Raisonné of Paintings and Drawings Executed before his Departure for the Near East on 13 January 1854* (diss., U. London, 1987)
C. Arscott: 'Employer, Husband, Spectator: Thomas Fairbairn's Commission of the *Awakening Conscience*', *The Culture of Capital: Art, Power and the Nineteenth-century Middle Class*, ed. J. Wolff and J. Seed (Manchester, 1988), pp. 159–90
M. Bennett: *The First Generation: The Catalogue of Works in the Walker Art Gallery, Lady Lever Art Gallery and Sudley Art Gallery* (London, 1988), pp. 64–108
K. Flint: 'Reading *The Awakening Conscience* Rightly', *Pre-Raphaelites Re-viewed*, ed. M. Pointon (Manchester, 1989), pp. 45–65
M. Pointon: 'The Artist as Ethnographer: Holman Hunt and the Holy Land', *Pre-Raphaelites Re-viewed*, ed. M. Pointon (Manchester, 1989), pp. 22–44
For further bibliography see W. E. Fredeman: *Pre-Raphaelitism: A Bibliographical Study* (Cambridge, MA, 1965)

JUDITH BRONKHURST

Hunter, Robert (*b* Ulster, 1715–20; *d* Dublin, after 1803). Irish painter. He was possibly the most prolific portrait painter in Dublin during the second half of the 18th century, until the 1790s receiving the leading commissions for state, civic and society paintings. He was acquainted with some of the city's most prominent intellectuals, including founder-members of the Irish Society of Artists. Among them was Samuel Madden, of whom Hunter painted a three-quarter-length portrait (Dublin, Trinity Coll.) and another portrait (1755; untraced) known from a mezzotint by Richard Purcell (*d* 1766).

Hunter's early manner was in the elegant style of such English portrait painters as Francis Cotes and Arthur Devis. His figures are tall and slender but they lack neither modelling nor a sense of presence. Despite his abundant commissions, his official portraiture is accomplished, conveying a good likeness of his sitters. Examples include *William John, Lord Newbattle, later 5th Marquis of Lothian* (1762; Monteviot House, Borders), *Henry, 12th Earl and Marquis of Clanricarde* (1783; Harewood House, W. Yorks) and *George Nugent-Temple-Grenville, 1st Marquis of Buckingham* (*c.* 1783; Dublin, St Patrick's Cathedral). Among his less formal portraits is *A Gentleman with a Gun and Dog* (1775; Dublin, N.G.), depicting a young man reclining in a picturesque landscape after a successful shoot. The composition is assured and the colouring, though rich, is not flashy. Towards the end of his career, by which time he was becoming influenced by the work of Joshua Reynolds, Hunter's position was gradually being eclipsed, initially in the 1780s by Robert Home but more fully after 1790 when Hugh Douglas Hamilton returned to Dublin. In 1792 Hunter organized for himself one of the first one-man shows ever held in the city.

BIBLIOGRAPHY

Strickland; Waterhouse: *18th C.*
A. Pasquin: *Memoirs of the Royal Academicians and an Authentic History of the Artists of Ireland* (London, 1796), p. 13
A. Crookshank and the Knight of Glin: *The Painters of Ireland, c. 1660–1920* (London, 1978), pp. 83–6
——: 'Robert Hunter', *Irish A. Rev. Yb.* (1989–90), pp. 169–85

FINTAN CULLEN

Hunter, William (*b* Kilbride, Western Isles, 23 May 1718; *d* London, 30 March 1783). Scottish physician, patron, collector and museum founder. His father intended him for the Church, but Hunter's desire to practise medicine took him in 1741 to London, where he was assistant to

Dr James Douglas. From 1746 he gave public lectures on anatomy. He obtained his licence from the Royal College of Physicians in 1756 and became an FRS in 1768, when he was also appointed the first Professor of Anatomy at the Royal Academy. Johann Zoffany's painting of *Dr William Hunter Lecturing at the Royal Academy of Arts* (*c.* 1773; London, Royal Coll. Physicians) reveals Hunter's method of lecturing before *écorché* casts modelled from the corpses of criminals executed at Tyburn. Hunter's interest in natural history combined with that in anatomy and dissection induced him to stress the minute study of nature—an emphasis that contrasted with Joshua Reynolds's insistence on the generalized presentation of forms.

Hunter was an avid collector of paintings, books and manuscripts, as well as geological, ethnographic, zoological and anatomical objects. He began collecting at the sale of Richard Mead's art collection (1754), where he purchased portraits of medical men and scientists, including Godfrey Kneller's *Isaac Newton* (*c.* 1702; U. Glasgow, Hunterian A.G.). In 1770 he opened an anatomical theatre in Great Windmill Street, London, with one room serving as a museum, the first science museum in Britain. It also housed Hunter's picture collection, which included Rembrandt's oil sketch of the *Entombment* (*c.* 1639; U. Glasgow, Hunterian A.G.) and, more unusually, three paintings by Chardin: the paired *Cellar Boy* and *Scullery Maid* and a *Lady Taking Tea* (all *c.* 1738; U. Glasgow, Hunterian A.G.). His appreciation of Chardin's work was without equal in England at that time.

Hunter commissioned a portrait of himself from Allan Ramsay (late 1750s; U. Glasgow, Hunterian A.G.), and he employed George Stubbs to paint two exotic animals, *The Nylghau* (*c.* 1771) and *A Moose* (*c.* 1773; both U. Glasgow, Hunterian A.G.); Stubbs's detailed observation of animal anatomy aided Hunter in his study of the comparative anatomy of these creatures. For his medical tract *The Anatomy of the Human Gravid Uterus* (London, 1774) Hunter employed the engraver Charles Grignion from 1751 to depict the various stages of utero-gestation as accurately as possible, based on observation of dissected corpses. Grignion's scrupulously detailed folio plates formed an integral part of the project. In 1781 Hunter became President of the Society of Antiquaries. His desire to keep his collection from dispersal led him to bequeath it in its entirety to the University of Glasgow, where it now forms the principal foundation collection for the Hunterian Art Gallery.

BIBLIOGRAPHY

S. F. Simmons: *An Account of the Life and Writings of the Late William Hunter, MD, FRS, SA* (London, 1783); ed. C. Brock (Glasgow, 1983)

Glasgow University's Pictures (exh. cat. by A. McLaren Young, U. Glasgow, Hunterian A.G., 1973)

M. Kemp, ed.: *Dr William Hunter at the Royal Academy of Arts* (Glasgow, 1975)

——: 'Dr William Hunter on the Windsor Leonardos and his Volume Attributed to Pietro da Cortona', *Burl. Mag.*, cxviii (1976), pp. 144–8

C. H. Brock: 'Dr William Hunter's Museum', *J. Soc. Bibliog. Nat. Hist.*, ix (1980), pp. 403–12

M. Kemp: 'Glasgow University Bicentenary Celebrations of Dr William Hunter (1718–83)', *Burl. Mag.*, cxxv (1983), pp. 380–83

W. D. I. Rolfe: 'A Stubbs Drawing Recognised', *Burl. Mag.*, cxxv (1983), pp. 738–9

——: 'William Hunter (1718–83) on Irish "Elk" and Stubbs's Moose', *Archv. Nat. Hist.*, xi (1983), pp. 263–90

SHEARER WEST

Huntington. American family of railway magnates and collectors. Four members of the family collected art: Collis P(otter) Huntington (1821–1900), Arabella D(uval) Huntington (?1850–1924), Henry E(dwards) Huntington (1850–1927) and Archer M(ilton) Huntington (1870–1955). While Henry assembled the best-known collection, it was Arabella who was the impetus behind the artistic interests of the family; she was married to Collis from 1884 until his death, and to Henry, Collis's nephew, from 1913 until her own death. Archer was her illegitimate son probably by Collis.

Collis's art collection is known through inventories and photographs. An inventory of paintings of 1899 in his San Francisco house (lost in the 1906 earthquake) lists 85; the majority were Barbizon school and related works. Another inventory of his home in 57th Street, New York (undated, but made for Arabella shortly after Collis's death), lists 180 pictures similar to those in San Francisco. During the first decade of the 20th century Arabella, by then a wealthy widow, came under the influence of Joseph Duveen, who raised her collecting ambitions. She bought major paintings, including a Rogier van der Weyden, three Rembrandts, a Hals, a Vermeer and a Velázquez. She bequeathed the 57th Street collection to Archer, who dispersed most of it to museums in gifts designated as the Collis Potter Huntington Memorial Collection (Dutch paintings to New York, Met.; Spanish paintings to New York, Hisp. Soc. America; French decorative art to San Francisco, CA Pal. Legion of Honor; and a miscellaneous group to New Haven, CT, Yale U. A.G.). Archer sold the most famous of Arabella's paintings, Rembrandt's *Aristotle Contemplating the Bust of Homer* (New York, Met.), to Duveen.

By 1910 Arabella's artistic interests had shifted to the house Henry E. Huntington was building on his San Marino ranch near Los Angeles. Henry and Arabella had known each other from at least the 1880s. Although they were not married until 1913, Arabella was active from 1908 in the planning of the San Marino house and collecting art for it. Henry's earlier collecting concentrated on his library of printed books, manuscripts and letters relating primarily to English and American history and literature. His interest in art developed dramatically about 1909. The most distinctive feature of Henry's art collection was its focus on Georgian England, with a fine collection of French sculpture and decorative art of the same time. The decision to specialize in this area appears to have been his, as neither Arabella nor Duveen (Henry's principal dealer) had any special devotion to English art. After some initial wavering, in July 1911 Henry bought, on Arabella's strong recommendation, three of the most important full-length portraits by Gainsborough in the collection: *Lord Ligonier*, *Lady Ligonier* (both 1770) and *Lady Petre* (1788). Within his chosen field Henry specialized in British full-length portraits of the period *c.* 1770–1800, including Gainsborough's '*The Blue Boy*' (*c.* 1770), Lawrence's '*Pinkie*' (1794) and Reynolds's *Mrs Siddons as the Tragic Muse* (1784), miniature portraits by Richard Cosway, Chelsea Gold Anchor ornamental vases, and watercolours by William Blake and Thomas Rowlandson. He deviated from his preferred field only to purchase a group of

Renaissance bronzes from the J. Pierpont Morgan collection in 1917 and to ask Archer for his mother's Renaissance paintings for the separate memorial collection to Arabella in the Henry E. Huntington Library and Art Gallery, which he established in San Marino before his death in 1927.

Archer's interest in collecting was nurtured from an early age by Arabella. He was the most philanthropic of the four Huntingtons, founding and supporting numerous art-related institutions. His principal benefactions were to the Hispanic Society of America, the Museum of the American Indian and the American Academy of Arts and Letters in New York, the Mariners' Museum, Brookgreen Gardens, SC, and the University of Texas (to found a university art gallery). His most abiding interest was Spain. The collections of books, paintings, sculpture and other artefacts he gave to the Hispanic Society were assembled with scholarship in mind. He and his second wife, the sculptress ANNA HYATT HUNTINGTON, brought together a collection of early 20th-century sculpture, much of it commissioned, for the Brookgreen Gardens. Even there he regarded art as subservient to a larger purpose. In this he stood apart from most of the well-known American art collectors of his time, although Henry E. Huntington was guided by similar objectives in forming his library.

UNPUBLISHED SOURCES

San Marino, Huntington Lib. and A. G. [institutional archives]

BIBLIOGRAPHY

B. Gilman Procke: *Archer Milton Huntington* (New York, 1963)

R. R. Wark: 'Arabella Huntington and the Beginnings of the Art Collections', *The Founding of the Henry E. Huntington Library and Art Gallery* (San Marino, 1969)

J. T. Maher: *Twilight of Splendour* (Boston, 1975)

A. Hyatt Mayer and others: *A Century of American Sculpture: Treasures from the Brookgreen Gardens* (New York, [*c.* 1980])

J. Thorpe: *Henry Edwards Huntington: A Biography* (Berkeley, 1994)

ROBERT R. WARK

Huntington, Anna Hyatt. *See* HYATT HUNTINGTON, ANNA.

Huntington, Daniel (*b* New York, 14 Oct 1816; *d* New York, 18 April 1906). American painter. Born into a distinguished New England family, he studied at Yale College and at Hamilton College, New York, where he met and was encouraged by the painter Charles Loring Elliott. In 1835 Huntington went to New York to study with Samuel F. B. Morse and by 1838 had his first pupil, Henry Peters Gray (1819–77). He was elected an Associate of the National Academy of Design in 1839, an Academician in the following year and twice served as its President (1862–9 and 1877–91). Although based in New York, he exhibited at all the major national art institutions as well as at the Royal Academy, London. In 1847 he was a founder-member of the Century Club, over which he presided in 1879–95. He later helped found the Metropolitan Museum of Art and served as its Vice-President from 1871 until 1903.

Huntington early showed an interest in landscape painting, in which he was an associate and stylistic follower of the Hudson River school, but his academic training and religious convictions inspired an ambition to paint historical, particularly religious, subjects. *A Sibyl* (1840; New York, Hist. Soc.) and *Early Christian Martyrs* (1840; Baton Rouge, LA State U.), both painted in Italy, reflect the spiritual earnestness of the German Nazarenes and the technique of Italian Renaissance masters. On his return to New York Huntington established his reputation with *Mercy's Dream* (1841; Philadelphia, PA Acad. F.A.). He rendered this unusual subject, taken from Bunyan's *Pilgrim's Progress*, with a delicacy of form, brushstroke and colour reminiscent of Raphael. Its success suggested another subject from Bunyan, *Christiana and her Children Passing through the Valley of the Shadow of Death* (Philadelphia, PA Acad. F.A.), which he finished on his second trip to Europe in 1843–5. There he also painted an ideal portrait entitled *Italy* (1843; Washington, DC, N. Mus. Amer. A.) and created illustrations for an engraved edition of Longfellow's poems published by Carey & Hart of Philadelphia. In the late 1840s Huntington chose subjects from English history. *Queen Mary Signs the Death Warrant of Lady Jane Grey* (1848; ex-Douglas Putnam priv. col., Marietta, OH) was engraved for distribution by the American Art-Union in 1848.

In 1850 a major one-man exhibition of Huntington's work demonstrated his popularity with fellow artists and public alike. At about this time he turned increasingly to portraiture, for which he tapped a network of family, collegiate, social and artistic connections. He painted about a thousand portraits; the earliest show the influence of Henry Inman in their even surfaces and straightforward compositions. By the 1850s his reputation brought commissions for elaborate, full-scale portraits, which he treated with looser brushwork and dramatic lighting inspired by Titian and Reynolds. On a visit to England in 1851 Huntington painted *Sir Charles Lock Eastlake* (1851; New York, Hist. Soc.) and *John Bird Sumner, Archbishop of Canterbury* (1851; New York, Gen. Theol. Semin.). He made four return visits to Europe between 1852 and 1883. His other distinguished sitters include *William Cullen Bryant* (1866; New York, Brooklyn Mus.) and *Ulysses S. Grant* (1875; New York, Donaldson, Lufkin & Jenrette). The group portrait *American Projectors of the Atlantic Cable* (1894; New York, Chamber of Commerce) includes Cyrus W. Field, Samuel F. B. Morse and a self-portrait.

In 1861 Huntington combined history painting with portraiture in the *Republican Court* (or *Mrs Washington's Reception*, 1861, exh. Paris Exposition 1867; New York, Brooklyn Mus.), which anticipated interest in the Colonial period generated by the Centennial celebrations. It was engraved by Alexander Hay Ritchie (1822–95). With religious allegories such as *Sowing the Word* (1868; New York, Hist. Soc.) he reaffirmed his early ideal of art as a moral force and his admiration for the Old Masters. Fundamentally conservative in both technique and principles, with an engaging personality and a talent for institutional affairs, he exercised considerable influence in the academic establishment of his day. In this role, as well as in his painting, Huntington resisted the changes sweeping American art in the last quarter of the 19th century and clung to the artistic ideals of his youth.

WRITINGS

Catalogue of Paintings, by Daniel Huntington, N.A., Exhibiting at the Art Union Buildings, 497 Broadway (New York, [1850])

BIBLIOGRAPHY

S. G. W. Benjamin: 'Daniel Huntington, President of the National Academy of Design', *Amer. A. Rev.*, ii/1 (1880), pp. 223–8; ii/2 (1881), pp. 1–6

W. H. Gerdts: 'Daniel Huntington's *Mercy's Dream*: A Pilgrimage through Bunyanesque Imagery', *Winterthur Port.*, xiv (1979), pp. 171–94

American Paintings in the Metropolitan Museum of Art, 3 vols (New York, 1980–86), ii, pp. 56–73

WENDY GREENHOUSE

Hunt Painter. *See* VASE PAINTERS, §II.

Hunt & Roskell. *See under* STORR, PAUL.

Hunza. *See* TUNJA.

Huquier, Gabriel (*b* Orléans, 7 May 1695; *d* Paris, 11 June 1772). French collector, engraver, print-publisher and print-seller. He was probably led to study engraving by his taste for collecting prints and drawings. He made no innovations in the engraving process, but used etching lightly reworked with the burin, a method suited to reproducing the sort of drawings that he usually chose as models, most of them coming from his own collection.

Huquier's engravings are mostly of work by contemporaries, sometimes in the form of single engravings, but mostly in books of six, twelve, or sometimes more plates. They are rarely dated. He began by reproducing the works of Claude Gillot, including *La Vie de Notre Seigneur Jésus-Christ* (Bruand, Hébert and Sjöberg, nos 695–754) and *Scènes comiques du Théatre italien* (*c.* 1729–32; BHS 755–66). Among other works by Antoine Watteau, he engraved 12 arabesques (BHS 1711–44) for the Recueil Jullienne. He also engraved Edme Bouchardon's *Livre de vases* (1737; BHS 537–48) and *Apollo and the Muses* (1739; BHS 563–73); and some of François Boucher's drawings, such as *Recueil de fontaines* (1736; BHS 576–82), *Livre de cartouches* (BHS 585–96) and the four series known as *Scènes de la vie chinoise* (BHS 607–66).

Huquier's engravings of ornaments, which helped spread the Rococo style throughout Europe just when it was going out of fashion in France, concentrated on the work of three great designers. He brought out a *Livre d'ornements* (BHS 951–1020) in 115 plates after the compositions of Juste-Aurèle Meissonnier; this was first published in instalments, continuing a series begun in 1730 by the widow of François Chéreau I. Huquier also engraved *c.* 140 plates after Jacques de Lajoüe, including the *Livre de cartouches* (BHS 809-37), the *Livre de buffets* (1735; BHS 838–44), *Divers morceaux d'architecture* (BHS 846–57) and the three series known as *Livre d'architecture* (BHS 858–93). Gilles-Marie Oppenord was the subject of three publications named after their format: *Le Moyen Oppenord* (BHS 1021–80) containing 72 plates (1737–8); *Le Petit Oppenord* (BHS 1081–1248) of 168 plates (before 1748); and *Le Grand Oppenord* (BHS 1249–1368) of 120 plates (1748–51).

As an original engraver, Huquier executed *c.* 500 model or teaching plates, such as *Recueil de vases* (1767; BHS 278–385); *Iconologie* (1768; BHS 62–277); and *Frises d'ornements, arabesques à divers usages* (BHS 392–427). In all, he made more than 2000 pieces. His collections were dispersed at auction in Amsterdam on 14 September 1761 and in Paris in July 1771 and November 1772.

Huquier's son Jacques-Gabriel Huquier (1730–1805) learnt drawing from Boucher and engraving from his father, with whom he collaborated on a few series after Boucher. For a time he carried on the business of his father-in-law, Jacques Chéreau; then, *c.* 1764, he set up on his own account, specializing in the manufacture of fans and also wallpaper. He settled in England *c.* 1770, and there he gave up engraving to paint portraits in pastels.

PRINTS

Recueil de vases (Paris, 1767)
Iconologie (Paris, 1768)
Frises d'ornements, arabesques à divers usages

BIBLIOGRAPHY

Portalis–Beraldi

E. Joullain: *Catalogue du fonds de planches gravées . . . de feu M. Huquier, graveur* (Paris, 1772)

O. Guilmard: *Les Maîtres ornemanistes* (Paris, 1880), pp. 159–60

Y. Bruand: 'Un Grand Collectionneur-marchand de gravures du XVIIIe siècle, Gabriel Huquier', *Gaz. B.-A.*, n. s. 5, xxxvii (1950), pp. 99–114

Y. Bruand, M. Hébert and Y. Sjöberg: *Inventaire du fonds français: Graveurs du dix-huitième siècle*, Paris, Bib. N., Cab. Est. cat., xi (Paris, 1970), pp. 446–545 [BHS]

MADELEINE BARBIN

Huret, Grégoire (*b* Lyon, 24 Oct 1606; *d* Paris, 5 Jan 1670). French engraver, draughtsman and writer. He is thought to have been a pupil of Charles Audran. Early in his career he worked for print-sellers in Lyon. He settled in Paris *c.* 1635 and in 1663 was received (*reçu*) by the Académie Royale with his *Théâtre de la Passion de Nostre Seigneur* (Weigert, nos 407–38), the drawings for which are in the Biblioteca Nacional in Madrid. In 1670 he published a treatise on portraiture, in which he opposed the theories of Gérard Desargues and Abraham Bosse. He left *c.* 490 plates, smooth and silvery in execution, mostly of his own design, but some after works by Sébastien Bourdon, Philippe de Champaigne, Charles Le Brun and Peter Paul Rubens. They comprise *c.* 270 book illustrations, including vignettes and frontispieces, some of them with complex iconography (W 269–90); *c.* 150 scenes from the New Testament and depictions of saints; *c.* 60 portraits; and several images for religious societies, such as that for the Confrérie de St Eustache et de Ste Agnès (W 150). He also made designs for other engravers, notably Claude Charpignon (*fl* mid-17th century), Jean Couvay, Claude Goyrand (*fl* 1627–49), François Ragot (*d* 1670) and Gilles Rousselet.

WRITINGS

L'Optique de portraiture (Paris, 1670)

BIBLIOGRAPHY

R.-A. Weigert: *Inventaire du fonds français: Graveurs du dix-septième siècle*, Paris, Bib. N., Cab. Est. cat., v (Paris, 1968), pp. 294–391 [W]

VÉRONIQUE MEYER

Hurley, (James) Frank [Francis] (*b* Sydney, 15 Oct 1885; *d* Sydney, 16 Jan 1962). Australian photographer, film producer, film maker and writer. He was introduced to photography while working at a steel foundry in Lithgow, NSW, when his foreman would take him on photographic excursions into the nearby Blue Mountains. After an apprenticeship with a photographic postcard firm, where he gained a reputation for achieving spectacular effects with the camera, he was appointed official photographer to the Australian geologist and explorer Douglas Mawson's Antarctic Expedition of 1911–13. The success of his prints and film footage led to his involvement with British explorer Ernest Shackleton's Imperial Trans-Antarctic Expedition (1914–16), where he produced another crop of dramatic images, which told the story of the ill-fated attempt to cross Antarctica. On a visit to England, Hurley was appointed Official War Photographer with the Australian troops, first in Flanders and later in Palestine.

In the early 1920s Hurley undertook two assignments in New Guinea, the resulting films leading to a tour of the USA and the publication in New York of his successful book *Pearls and Savages* (1924). During the 1930s he became involved in the fledgling Australian film industry, working at Cinesound as a cameraman and, less successfully, as a director of his own feature films. During World War II he was again an official photographer and film maker, working in North Africa and the Middle East with both British and Australian troops. After the war he became a prolific producer of photographic books of Australian rural and urban views. Hurley's work showed a pictorialist concern for composition, emotional detachment and fine print quality. Given to rhetorical flourish and disdaining the subtle understatement, his work fitted well into the world of imperialism and 'high endeavour' in exciting places.

PHOTOGRAPHIC PUBLICATIONS

The Blue Mountains and Jenolan Caves (Sydney, 1952)

BIBLIOGRAPHY

D. P. Millar: *From Snowdrift to Shellfire* (Sydney, 1984)

DAVID P. MILLAR

Hurley, William (*fl c.* 1322; *d* 1354). English carpenter. His first recorded work, in royal employment at the Tower of London in 1323–4, shows that he was already a well-known master. In 1326 he was working at the palatine chapel of St Stephen, Westminster, when he possibly designed the timber vault erected by him in 1345–8; in this year he was also employed at Caerphilly Castle, where he probably roofed the remodelled hall. By this date he possessed his own seal. In 1332 he was working at the London Guildhall and was named as 'Keeper of Carpentry for the King's Works'. He was made Chief Carpenter and Surveyor of all the King's Works of Carpentry at the Tower and elsewhere south of the Trent and Humber in 1336. Hurley's only surviving major work is the timber lantern of the octagonal crossing tower at Ely Cathedral. He probably worked there from 1322, when the Romanesque tower collapsed, and was still employed as a consultant up to the time of his death. The lantern's structural system was partly based on recent roofing experiments in chapter houses and towers. The main timber frame supporting the bell chamber is concealed above a wooden vault which is thought not to be load-bearing, although this view has recently been challenged by Wade and Heyman. Stylistic features such as the ogee-lobed quatrefoils and the linking of windows and panelling by mullions show Hurley's awareness of the innovations made by masons working at the chapel of St Stephen. The choir-stalls at Ely were probably also designed by Hurley; they embody ideas that may have been further explored in his later stalls (destr.) for Windsor Castle and for the chapel of St Stephen.

BIBLIOGRAPHY

Harvey
C. A. Hewett: *English Historic Carpentry* (London, 1980)
P. G. Lindley: *The Monastic Cathedral at Ely c. 1320 to c. 1350* (diss., U. Cambridge, 1985)
E. C. Wade and J. Heyman: 'The Timber Octagon of Ely Cathedral', *Proc. Inst. Civ. Engin.*, lxxviii (1985), pp. 1421–36

PHILLIP LINDLEY

Hurlstone, Frederick Yeates (*b* London, 1800; *d* London, 10 June 1869). English painter. After training under William Beechey, Thomas Lawrence and Benjamin Robert Haydon, he entered the Royal Academy Schools in London in 1820. In 1823 his large, ambitious composition, the *Contention between the Archangel Michael and Satan for the Body of Moses*, won a gold medal. Thereafter he exhibited regularly at the Royal Academy and the British Institution, until his election to the Society of British Artists in 1831, after which he rarely showed work elsewhere. In 1835 he was elected President of the Society and continued in office until his death. A successful portrait painter, he preferred to devote his energies to history paintings in the anecdotal or literary vein, and such works as the *Enchantress Armida* (1831) from Torquato Tasso were greatly admired. He visited Italy in 1835, Spain in 1841, 1851 and 1852 and Morocco in 1854. His historical paintings based on these travels earned him the title of the 'British Murillo'; his broad reading in foreign literature, added to first-hand observation, gave vividness and authenticity to such paintings as the *Last Sigh of the Moor*, which won a gold medal at the Exposition Universelle in Paris in 1855. Later he turned to sentimental Spanish and Italian rustic or fancy subjects, as in a *Fisherman's Daughter of Mola di Gaeta* (1858); his technique coarsened, and his reputation declined.

BIBLIOGRAPHY

Obituary, *A. J.* [London], viii (1869), p. 271
E. T. Cook and A. Wedderburn, eds: *The Works of John Ruskin*, xvi (London, 1905)

JUSTINE HOPKINS

Hurrian. Name given to one of the major ethnic groups in the population of northern Mesopotamia and Syria during the 2nd millennium BC. The Hurrians can be identified by their names, which first appear as isolated examples in texts of the second half of the 3rd millennium BC and which show them to have belonged to an Asianic ethno-linguistic group. By about 1700 BC they accounted for a third of the recorded names in the texts of TELL ATCHANA (Alalakh), near Aleppo, and the proportion had risen to half in the 15th century BC. By that time at NUZI, near Kirkuk, they were the dominant element in the population.

There have been several attempts to define Hurrian art. This has been hampered both because nothing is known of the origins of the Hurrians (though they may have been the indigenous population of eastern Anatolia) and because they easily assimilated the culture of Mesopotamia and Syria. The earliest inscriptions in Hurrian probably date to the late 3rd millennium BC; these are on stone tablets held by bronze lions (Paris, Louvre; see fig.; New York, Met.). At the time of their greatest expansion the Hurrians may have been dominated by an Indo-European aristocracy as part of a federation of states known as the

Hurrian bronze lion holding an inscribed limestone tablet, h. 122 mm, from Tell Amuda, north-east Syria, probably late 3rd millennium BC (Paris, Musée du Louvre)

Kingdom of Mitanni, and it is not clear to what extent they or the MITANNIANs should be credited with the fine white on dark painted pottery known as Nuzi ware, intricately coloured glass vessels, distinctive painted friezes and abundant seals, which are found throughout the area. They may have had a predilection for the representation of demons, and they probably played an important role in the transmission of motifs to and from Hittite Anatolia, where the pantheon of Hurrian gods, including the storm god Teshub and goddess Hebat, was carved in the rock shrine of YAZILIKAYA (i).

BIBLIOGRAPHY

M.-T. Barrelet and others: *Méthodologie et critiques I: Problèmes concernant les Hurrites*, Centre National de la Recherche Scientifique (Paris, 1977)

E. Porada: 'Remarks on Mitannian (Hurrian) and Middle Assyrian Glyptic Art', *Akkadica*, xiii (1979), pp. 2–15

M. Salvini and others: *Tell Barri/Kahat* (Rome, 1982), pp. 14–21

M.-T. Barrelet, ed: *Problèmes concernant les Hurrites II*, Editions Recherche sur les Civilisations, Mémoire No. 49 (Paris, 1984)

DOMINIQUE COLLON

Hurtado, Angel (*b* El Tocuyo, 27 Oct 1927). Venezuelan painter and film maker. He studied at the Escuela de Artes Plásticas y Aplicadas in Caracas (1944–8), and then went to Paris, where he studied art history and film at the Sorbonne (1954–9). He returned to Caracas, where he taught film journalism at the Universidad Central de Venezuela, Caracas, and directed the cinema department of Televisora Nacional. Hurtado's painting during this period was articulated around the dynamic interplay of dark bands; his series *Signs of the Zodiac* won him the Venezuelan Premio Nacional de Pintura in 1961. Again in France he worked for television, and in 1970 he moved to Washington, DC, to become head of the film section at the Department of Cultural Affairs of the Organisation for American States, making documentaries on various artists. In later paintings, such as *The Clarity That Never Ceased* (1986; Caracas, Mus. A. Contemp.), he used thinly worked veils of colour.

BIBLIOGRAPHY

R. Delgado: *Angel Hurtado* (Caracas, 1970)

Angel Hurtado: Paisajes interiores y divertimientos (exh. cat., ed. S. Imber; Caracas, Mus. A. Contemp., 1990)

Based on information supplied by DELIA DELGADO

Hurtado de Mendoza. *See* MENDOZA.

Hurtado Izquierdo, Francisco (*b* Lucena, Córdoba, 6 Feb 1669; *d* Priego, Córdoba, 30 June 1725). Spanish architect. He was one of the leading Baroque architects active in southern Spain in the early 18th century. His use of decoration earned him criticism as a 'heretic' by Neo-classical writers (e.g. Llanguno y Amirola). He started as an *ensamblador*, a carver of wooden retables, such as that of the high altar of S Lorenzo, Córdoba (1696). He was practising as an architect almost simultaneously, however: his first attributed work is the *camarín*—a small chapel behind the altar for the display of the sacrament—in the church of La Virgen de la Victoria, Málaga (begun 1693). The octagonal walls and vault are covered with foliated stucco decoration; in a crypt beneath is the rectangular burial chamber of the counts of Buenavista, with groin vaults supported by four central columns. The sacristy (1703) of Córdoba Cathedral, also octagonal but with a dome, has a more modest and architectonic version of the same decoration, which became influential in Andalusia.

The main commissions of Hurtado Izquierdo's middle career were in Granada. When he took over direction of the Sagrario of the Cartuja (1702–20), work had already started on the walls and the base of the tabernacle. He added two lateral chapels at a lower level to strengthen the fabric, and he introduced oculi near the floor to allow a view of the Sacrament from them. The tabernacle and elaborate decorations of the Sagrario were executed in polychrome marble, jasper and porphyry.

Hurtado Izquierdo's Renaissance design for the Sagrario (1704–5) abutting Granada Cathedral, used independently as a parish church, is much more severe and considered and respects Diego de Siloe's designs for the cathedral (begun 1528). It is a Greek cross in plan, with a lining of chapels and tribunes derived from Leonardo de Figueroa's contemporary church of El Salvador, Seville (1696–1711). Work was completed by his follower José de Bada (1691–1755) after 1717. In the Baroque retable (1707) of the Santiago Chapel in Granada Cathedral, Hurtado Izquierdo introduced the use of *estípites*, columns like inverted obelisks, which frequently came to replace solomonic columns as a way of dissolving the architectonic nature of the construction.

As a reward for his work in Granada, Hurtado Izquierdo was appointed a royal tax commissioner in Priego in 1712, where he founded a school of craftsmen that proved influential in Andalusia and the New World. His last work was the Sagrario of the Cartuja of Nuestra Señora del Paular, at Rascafría, near Segovia (begun 1718, completed after his death by his collaborator Teodosio Sánchez de Rueda). This consists of two chambers: the Transparente, a domed octagonal room behind the main altar, and, behind this, a large cruciform anteroom. The anteroom has gilded retables (produced in collaboration with Pedro Duque Cornejo) in the arms, with hexagonal chapels between them, and entrance is by diagonal passages flanking the Sagrario. While the anteroom is lit by oculi in the pendentives, by contrast, the Transparente is brilliantly lit by windows in the dome. The design of the Sacristy of the Cartuja (authorized 1713), Granada, has also been attributed to Hurtado Izquierdo (Taylor, 1962); it was executed posthumously (1730–42) by his assistants the mason Luis de Arévalo and the stuccoist Luis Cabello.

BIBLIOGRAPHY

E. Llaguno y Amirola: *Noticias de los arquitectos e arquitecturas de España* iv, (1829)
R. C. Taylor: 'Francisco Hurtado and his School', *A. Bull.*, xxxii (1950), pp. 25–61
A. Gallego y Burin: *El barroco granadino* (Madrid, 1956)
G. Kubler: *Arquitectura de los siglos XVII y XVIII*, A. Hisp., xiv (Madrid, 1957)
G. Kubler and M. Soria: *Art and Architecture in Spain and Portugal and their American Dominions, 1500–1800*, Pelican Hist. A. (Harmondsworth, 1959)
R. C. Taylor: 'La sacristia de la Cartuja de Granada y sus autores', *Archv Esp. A.*, xxxv (1962), pp. 135–73

ZILAH QUEZADO DECKKER

Hurtrelle [Hurtrel]**, Simon** (*b* Béthune, Pas-de-Calais, 1648; *d* Gennevilliers, Hauts-de-Seine, 11 March 1724). French sculptor. He was the son of a sculptor, Nicolas Hurtrelle (*fl c.* 1650), and studied at the Académie de France in Rome from 1673 to 1682. He returned to France and was employed principally by the crown throughout his career, contributing, often in collaboration with Pierre Mazeline, to the decoration of the château of Versailles, to that of Marly and to the Invalides. He was typical of most of the sculptors assembled by Louis XIV for his great building works: a productive and conscientious interpreter of classicizing designs often provided by others. His work for Versailles included a marble statue of a *Faun Playing the Flute* and a sturdy marble herm of the philosopher *Theophrastus* (1685 and 1686–8; both Versailles, Château).

Hurtrelle also collaborated with Mazeline on a number of important monumental works including a bronze equestrian statue of *Louis XIV* for Montpellier (1686–92, destr. 1792; plaster model, Stockholm, Kun. Slottet) and two important tombs in Paris, that for *Chancellor Michel Le Tellier* in St Gervais-St Protais (marble and bronze, 1686–8; *in situ*) and that of *Charles, Duc de Créqui* in the church of the Capucines (marble and bronze, 1686–9; fragments Paris, St Roch and Dôme des Invalides). Hurtrelle probably took the less important role in the partnership. He was received (*reçu*) into the Académie Royale in 1690 with a moving bronze *Pietà* (Paris, Louvre). He also worked on a small scale, exhibiting a marble group of *Saturn Devouring his Children* at the Salon of 1699 (untraced) and carving a marble group of *Leda and Cupid* (untraced; engr. by Christian Philipp Lindemann (1700–54)) for the royal gallery at Dresden. From 1716 he lived at Niort (Deux-Sèvres).

BIBLIOGRAPHY

Lami; Souchal
J. Guiffrey, ed.: *Comptes* (1891–1901)
F. Souchal: 'Le Monument funéraire du Duc de Créqui à l'Eglise des Capucines', *Archvs A. Fr.*, n. s., xxv (1978), pp. 173–80

FRANÇOISE DE LA MOUREYRE

Hurtu, Jacques (*fl* 1614–19; *d* before 23 June 1623). French designer and engraver. He was of the Protestant faith. Around 1614 he moved from Orléans to Lyon. He engraved *c.* 30 ornamental prints, mostly on black ground, divided into three series (Weigert, nos 1–3). These show watchcases, ornamental foliage, goldsmiths' ornaments, quivers and escutcheons, surrounded by birds, mythological figures and small human figures. Two of the series are dated, one 1614, the other 1619; that of 1614 and the undated one were published in Paris by Pierre Firens (*c.* 1580–1638) and bear only the artist's monogram. He signed himself J. F. on some prints of the series of 1619, *Iacques Hurtu* on others.

BIBLIOGRAPHY

D. Guilmard: *Les Maîtres ornemanistes* (Paris, 1880), p. 41, no. 17
P. Jessen: *Katalog der ornamentischen Sammlung des Kunstgewerbemuseum* (Leipzig, 1894)
M. Audin and R. Vial: *Dictionnaire des artistes et ouvriers d'art de la France: Lyonnais* (Paris, 1918)
R.-A. Weigert: *Inventaire du fonds français: Graveurs du dix-septième siècle*, Paris, Bib. N., Cab. Est. cat., v (Paris, 1968), pp. 391–2

VÉRONIQUE MEYER

Husain, Maqbool Fida (*b* Pandharpur, Maharashtra, ? 17 Sept 1915). Indian painter, printmaker, photographer and film maker. He grew up in Indore, where his family moved in the year of his birth. After studying at the School of Art in Indore for one year he moved to Bombay in 1937 and worked as a painter of cinema hoardings and, from 1941, as a designer of toys and children's nursery furniture. The same year AMRITA SHER-GIL and GEORGE KEYT exhibited their works in Bombay, inspiring Husain to dedicate his life to this creative field. In 1946 FRANCIS NEWTON SOUZA invited him to join his Bombay Progressive Artists' Group. Husain's paintings first attracted notice in Bombay in 1947, when he won an award at the annual exhibition of the Bombay Art Society. He visited Delhi, where he encountered ancient Mathura sculpture and Indian miniature paintings. This was a crucial period in his development as an artist as he assimilated ideas from Western and Indian art. In 1950 he held his first solo exhibition in Bombay and by 1954 had been nominated an eminent artist by the Lalit Kala Akademi, New Delhi. The following year he won the national award at the Lalit Kala Akademi's first national exhibition. By this time he was rapidly becoming the most well-known and influential painter in India. From 1950 he adopted a lifestyle involving extensive travel, including a visit to Europe in 1953 and to New York in 1959. His work was exhibited at the Salon de Mai in Paris in 1951, the Venice biennales of 1953 and 1955, the Tokyo Biennale of 1959 (where he won the International Biennale Award), the São Paulo biennales of 1959 and 1971 (where he was given a major exhibition) and elsewhere. His solo exhibitions began with shows in Zurich (Galerie Palette) and Prague (Mánes) in 1956, Frankfurt (Kunst-Kabinet) and Rome (Paese) in 1960 and Tokyo in 1961. His work was first shown in the USA at India House, New York, in 1964. A major retrospective exhibition of his work was held at the Birla Academy of

Art and Culture, Calcutta, in 1973. He has also had exhibitions of photography and in 1984, at an exhibition in Hannover, he exhibited works on plexiglass.

In his early paintings, prior to 1947, he concentrated on portraits and landscapes. Thereafter his output became more varied. Under the influence of such European painters as Paul Cézanne, Henri Matisse, Pablo Picasso and Paul Klee, he developed a detached expressionist style that retained a keen sense of design. In the painting *Man* (oil, 1.22×2.44 m; 1951; see Alkazi, pl. 2), one of his first powerful statements about modern India, he presented a canvas with broken forms, overturned figures and contrasting flat and textured elements, in which the central figure was an ironical rendering of Auguste Rodin's sculpture *The Thinker.* This painting was followed by *Indian Village* (oil, 1.02×3.35 m, 1955; see Alkazi, pl. 3), in which he combined the techniques of montage, split image, close up and overlapping planes. In 1965–6 he executed a mural (*c.* 30×20 m) on the rear façade of Indraprastha Bharan, New Delhi. In his later work his subject-matter included depictions of women, horses, cities, and mythological and folk themes; a fine mythological painting is *Vishwamitra* (oil on canvas, 1.22×1.52 m, 1973; New Delhi, N.G. Mod. A.). He often explored themes through extended cycles of works, such as a series of paintings based on the *Rāmāyaṇa* and *Mahābhārata* epics, and a series of 45 watercolours completed in 1975 called *Passage through Human Space.* He also acknowledged contemporary events in works such as *Cyclonic Silence* (oil, 1977; see Alkazi, pl. 36), one of a series of paintings in which he responded to a cyclone disaster in Andhra Pradesh. His film *Through the Eyes of a Painter* won the Berlin Film Festival award (Golden Bear) in 1968. His works are to be found in numerous private and public collections throughout the world. He has been honoured with numerous awards, including the Indian Government's Padma Shri, Padma Bhushan and Padma Vibhushan, the highest civilian award.

BIBLIOGRAPHY

A. S. Peerbhoy: *Paintings of Husain* (Bombay, 1955)
S. S. Kapur: *Husain* (New Delhi, 1961)
G. Kapur: *Husain* (Bombay, 1968)
R. L. Bartholomew and S. S. Kapur: *Maqbool Fida Husain* (New York, 1969)
Retrospective Exhibition of M. F. Husain (exh. cat., intro. K. S. Mathur; Calcutta, Birla Acad. A. & Cult., 1973)
E. Alkazi: *M. F. Husain: The Modern Artist and Tradition* (New Delhi, 1978)
G. Kapur: *Contemporary Indian Artists* (New Delhi, 1978), pp. 117–45
Six Indian Painters (exh. cat., London, Tate, 1982)
D. Herwitz: *Husain* (Bombay, 1988)
I. Pal: *Beyond the Canvas: An Unfinished Portrait of M. F. Husain* (New Delhi, 1994)

ANIS FAROOQI

Husayn ʿAli. *See* ʿALI.

Huskisson, Robert (*b* Langar, nr Nottingham, 1820; *d* London, 6 Oct 1861). English painter and illustrator. He lived with his brother Leonard Huskisson (*fl* 1839–59), who was also a painter, and exhibited landscapes, scenes of rural life and works in the fairy genre for which Richard Dadd, his contemporary, is better known. Only four of Huskisson's paintings and two sketches have been traced but the subject-matter of his oeuvre can be reconstructed from its listing as exhibits at the Royal Academy (1839–59) and the British Institution (1851–8) in London, such as the *Dancing Doll* (RA, 1838), *Sunday Morning* (RA, 1842; BI, 1843), *Troublesome Neighbour* (RA, 1843) and *Itinerant Performers* (RA, 1844).

Huskisson's earliest extant work, *Come Unto These Yellow Sands* (oil on panel, 1847; London, Maas priv. col.; engraved in the *Art-Union,* ix, 1 Nov 1847), was not exhibited, perhaps owing to Dadd's success at the Royal Academy in 1842 with a similar picture of the same title (British priv. col.). Taking their text from *The Tempest,* both paintings present richly coloured groups and trains of sparsely dressed female figures and clusters of putti dancing and disporting on a beach, in the night sky and in and around an arching rock. Huskisson's more open, more decoratively coloured version differs compositionally and almost overwhelms with solicitation. With his next work, the *Midsummer Night's Fairies* (1847; London, Tate), shown at the Royal Academy in 1847, Huskisson passed 'within a few months. . .from obscurity to fame', according to the *Art Journal* (London, x, 1848) in which an engraving of the picture appeared. Like Dadd's *Titania Sleeping* (British priv. col.), which had been shown at the Royal Academy in 1841, Huskisson's painting depicted the deluding of Titania's eyes. Where Dadd placed the shadowy figure of Oberon in the cave behind Titania, Huskisson moved him to centre-stage, looking down at Titania already asleep, inclined among nude figures towards the viewer, and where Dadd had his elves ranged airborne in a discrete arch over Titania, Huskisson freed his theatre, peopling it with figures, large and small, sleeping, fighting, freely recapitulating the whole drama. Two surviving sketches provide further evidence of how he sought to compose with variety without losing the central focus: here, towards Titania's highly lit, supine form.

Huskisson's illustrations for Mrs S. C. Hall's *Misdummer Eve: A Fairy Tale of Love* (London, 1848) and an oil painting of the *Mother's Blessing* (*c.* 1870; London, Maas priv. col.), from which the engraved frontispiece derives, show him exercising not only his facility and dexterity but also a compromised capacity to satisfy the elaborate conditions demanded by the identification of the fairy genre with the imagination of the child. Perhaps this difficulty goes some way in accounting for the form of his only other extant picture, *Titania's Elves Robbing the Squirrel's Nest* (British priv. col.), shown at the Royal Academy in 1854, his last recorded exhibited work: a detailed, still highly coloured, circular composition, it lacks the drama of the ambiguities in the earlier works of a sensualized fairy genre.

BIBLIOGRAPHY

A. Graves: *The British Institution, 1806–67; A Complete Dictionary of Contributors and their Work* (London, 1875) [most extensive record of works]
——: *The Royal Academy of Arts: A Complete Dictionary of Contributors and their Works. . .1769 to 1904,* iv (London, 1906)
J. Maas: *Victorian Painters* (London, 1969)
P. Allderidge: *The Late Richard Dadd, 1817–1886* (London, 1974)
B. Phillpotts: *Fairy Paintings* (London, 1978)

LEWIS JOHNSON

Husly [Huslij], **Jacob Otten.** *See* OTTEN-HUSLY, JACOB.

Husn, Tell el-. *See* BETH SHAN.

Hussem, Willem (Frans Karel) (*b* Rotterdam, 29 Jan 1900; *d* The Hague, 21 July 1974). Dutch painter and writer. He was self-taught as an artist, but in 1918–19 he received drawing lessons from Dirk Nijland. He lived in Les Angles, France, from 1919 until 1929, where he painted in a style similar to van Gogh's. Between 1933 and 1936 he lived outside Paris and associated with Georges Vantongerloo and Piet Mondrian. Towards the end of 1939, influenced by Picasso, he started to paint in an abstract manner. In 1944 the influence of Zen philosophy led him to make calligraphic drawings and to write poetry in Haiku-form.

Although Hussem's abstract style caused a public outcry when he was awarded the Jacob Maris prize in 1958, in 1960 he had an exhibition at the Gemeentemuseum in The Hague. From 1959 until 1965 he created virtually monochrome paintings of black, white and brown signs using beige sackcloth-type canvas, influenced by matter painting, for example *Composition with Circle and Verticals 1959 No. 5* (1959; Rotterdam, Boymans–van Beuningen). After 1966 he experimented with a variety of techniques, for example installations made from aluminium (1967); he also produced silk screens. After 1971 he painted solely geometric-abstract canvases, for example *Untitled* (1974; Rotterdam, Boymans–van Beuningen).

BIBLIOGRAPHY

Willem Hussem: De kracht van de penseelstreek [Willem Hussem: the power of the brushstroke] (exh. cat., Utrecht, Cent. Mus., 1984)

JOHN STEEN

Hussey, Philip (*b* Cloyne, Co. Cork, 1713; *d* Dublin, June 1783). Irish painter. He went to sea in his youth, but by the 1740s he was active in Dublin as an artist. Hussey is principally known for his portraits of family groups, some of which are conversation pieces; he may also have specialized in flower-pieces and still-lifes, to judge from the carefully detailed baskets of flowers and other trappings that appear in a number of his portraits. The most important of his group portraits are *The Bateson Family* (1762; Belfast, Ulster Mus.) and *The Corbally Family* (1760s; Dublin, N.G.), both of which depict the families within richly decorated rooms, pride of ownership being the most compelling feature. Hussey visited England on at least two occasions, during which he may have seen and studied conversation pieces by such popular English artists as Arthur Devis.

BIBLIOGRAPHY

Strickland; Waterhouse: *18th C.*
A. Crookshank and the Knight of Glin: *The Painters of Ireland, c. 1660–1920* (London, 1978), pp. 44–6

FINTAN CULLEN

Hussey, Walter (*b* Northampton, 15 May 1909; *d* ?London, 25 July 1985). English clergyman and patron. His first curacy was at St Mary Abbot's Church in Kensington, London; in 1937, he became vicar of St Matthew's Church in Northampton. Convinced of the religious nature of all art as an expression to mankind of God's truths, he commissioned works of art for his church from a number of major British artists. The most celebrated works thus produced were Henry Moore's *Madonna and Child* (1944) and Graham Sutherland's *Crucifixion* (1946). Benjamin Britten wrote a piece of music (the cantata *Rejoice in the Lamb*) for St Matthew's, as did Michael Tippett, Lennox Berkeley, Gerald Finzi and Malcolm Arnold, among others; W. H. Auden produced a litany and anthem. As Dean of Chichester Cathedral between 1955 and 1977, Hussey commissioned a tapestry for the High Altar from John Piper and a stained-glass window from Marc Chagall. A determined proselytizer for modern art, even in the face of opposition and controversy, Hussey befriended most of the artists he patronized. In Kenneth Clark's view he was the Church of England's last great patron of the arts.

PUBLISHED WRITINGS

Patron of Art: The Revival of a Great Tradition among Modern Artists (London, 1985)

MONICA BOHM-DUCHEN

Husson, Jules(-François-Felix). *See* CHAMPFLEURY.

Huszár, Vilmos (*b* Budapest, 5 Jan 1884; *d* Hierden, nr Harderwijk, 8 Sept 1960). Hungarian painter, decorative artist, typographer and writer, active in the Netherlands. He studied at the Academy of Applied Arts in Budapest from 1901 to 1903, and then at the academy in Munich (1904). For a short period he was a member of the artists' colonies of Tecsö and Nagybánya in Hungary, before moving to The Hague in 1906 as a portrait painter to the local aristocracy. Huszár's interest in the work of van Gogh and in modern developments in Paris and London gradually led him from portraits and landscapes in bright colours, such as *Reclining Female* (1913; Otterlo, Kröller-Müller), to an abstract style in painting and stained glass influenced by Cubism and Futurism; an example of this is *Vincent* (1915; Amsterdam, J. P. Smid priv. col.).

In 1916 Huszár met Theo van Doesburg, who admired his work and was influenced by his stained-glass windows. In 1917 he was one of the founders of the periodical DE STIJL. He designed the cover of the magazine, wrote several articles and was probably active as a fund-raiser. His derivation of geometric abstractions from natural shapes, as in *Composition II: Skaters* (1917; The Hague, Gemeentemus.), contributed to the development of NEO-PLASTICISM. One of his totally abstract works was *Composition in Grey* (1918; priv. col.). He also collaborated with architects, such as P. Klaarhamer, on interior design projects, such as *Colour Design for the Bruynzeel Company for a Child's Bedroom* (1919), produced for the De Arendshoeve home in Voorburg. Another interior design was a music-room in The Hague for Til Brugman (1924; *see* NETHERLANDS, THE, §V, 4 and fig. 37). Experiments with a shadow puppet and mechanical theatre show Huszár's interest in creating a form of kinetic light painting. In the mid-1920s he befriended Kurt Schwitters, El Lissitzky and many Hungarian avant-garde artists. He also worked as a typographer and lived in Paris for short periods.

After 1930 Huszár's painting was influenced by Bart van der Leck, as in *Composition 6* (1955–60; Hilversum, priv. col.). During World War II he settled in Harderwijk in the Netherlands, where he owned some land, and where as a Jew he felt relatively safe. He subsequently painted naturalistic landscapes of the countryside around Harderwijk, such as *Hooiberg* (*c.* 1955; The Hague, priv. col.).

BIBLIOGRAPHY

E. Kallai: 'Kubismus und Konstruktivismus', *Neue Malerei in Ungarn* (Leipzig, 1925), pp. 103–11

S. Ex: 'Vilmos Huszár', *De beginjaren van De Stijl, 1917–1922* (Utrecht, 1982), pp. 83–124; Eng. trans. as 'Vilmos Huszár', *De Stijl: The Formative Years* (Cambridge, MA, 1986), pp. 76–121

S. Ex and E. Hoek: *Vilmos Huszár, schilder en ontwerper, 1884–1960* [Vilmos Huszár, painter and designer, 1884–1960] (Utrecht, 1985)

SJAREL EX

Hutcheson, Francis (*b* Drumalig, Co. Down, 8 Aug 1694; *d* Dublin, 8 Aug 1746). Irish philosopher. He attended the University of Glasgow, after which he headed a Presbyterian youth academy in Dublin for about a decade, and then held the chair of moral philosophy at Glasgow from 1730 until his death. He was best known as a moral sense theorist, and was heavily influenced by the theory of perception formulated by John Locke (1632–1704), as well as by the idea of a disinterested, moral sense conceived by ANTHONY ASHLEY COOPER, 3rd Earl of Shaftesbury. His writings give a central role to sensation and feeling in their account of morality and aesthetic value, and as such constitute an important moment in the formation of Enlightenment views about the relation between emotion and rationality. Human nature, in Hutcheson's theory, involves both such external senses as sight and hearing, and internal senses including the moral sense and those connected with beauty, harmony, grandeur (THE SUBLIME) and novelty.

A 'sense' for Hutcheson is any innate capacity of the mind to receive ideas immediately and independently of the will. Since sensations are ideas in the mind that are directly caused by external objects acting on our body, the mind is passive in sensation and has no power to prevent the sensation from occurring. He classified the capacity to perceive beauty as a sense because it is not under the control of our will. Its pleasures do not arise from the 'knowledge of principles, proportions, causes or of the usefulness of the object', and being in this way immediately pleasant, our perceptions of beauty are independent of our own selfish interest. These pleasures are distinct from the joy that arises from the prospect of advantage, and this sense is disinterested in much the same way as Shaftesbury's moral sense.

The main tenets of his aesthetics are contained in the first treatise of *An Inquiry into the Original of our Ideas of Beauty and Virtue* (1725). Of the various aesthetic categories, he devoted most attention to beauty, of which he wrote 'the word *beauty* is taken for the *idea raised in us*, and a *sense* of beauty for *our power of receiving this idea*' (I.ix). Strictly speaking this kind of beauty, which elsewhere he called absolute or original beauty, is not an objective quality of things but rather a simple and pleasurable idea or feeling in the mind caused by our perception in external objects of 'uniformity amidst variety'. He claimed that 'what we call beautiful in objects, to speak in a mathematical style, seems to be in compound ratio of uniformity and variety; so that where the uniformity of bodies is equal, the beauty is as the variety, and where the variety is equal, the beauty is as the uniformity' (II.iii). This type of beauty may be found in our perceptions of both nature and art, in sights and sounds as well as in objects of the intellect, such as geometrical theorems.

The sense of beauty is universal in that in all of mankind the idea of beauty is generally occasioned by uniformity in variety. However, this does not entail that all men have the same taste. Even the beauties recognized by a person with the simplest taste exhibit the quality of uniformity in variety, but without development and refinement of this capacity a person is unable to appreciate the still greater beauty of more complex kinds. Furthermore, two people may observe what is in fact a beautiful object, and nonetheless disagree as to whether it merits approval if one of them associates unpleasant ideas with the beautiful object and hence has an aversion to it.

Hutcheson contrasted absolute beauty with relative or comparative beauty, which he explicated in terms of imitation and resemblance. Relative beauty is founded upon conformity to an original, or the unity of a copy and its archetype (II.iv). Although for the most part the beauty of visual art is of the relative variety, it may also contain either moral beauty or an absolute beauty resulting from a unity of proportion among the parts. In contrast, although music utilizes resemblance to the human voice to induce emotional responses, harmony (or beauty of sound) is typically not the result of imitation, but is absolute. Furthermore, although successful literature achieves its beauty mainly through representation, the chief source of the pleasures of poetry is usually to be found in its moral beauty.

Hutcheson explained the possession of the sense of beauty through an appeal to his rational theology. God is the author and source of human nature, and in order to make the pursuit of scientific inquiry pleasurable he endowed us with an innate capacity to experience pleasure through the perception of uniformity amidst variety. Not only has divine benevolence created natural surroundings pleasant to the senses but it has also guaranteed that the attempt to subsume a plurality of effects under unified causal principles will provide a source of pleasure in the beautiful, since it too involves an awareness of unity in variety.

WRITINGS

An Inquiry into the Original of our Ideas of Beauty and Virtue, in Two Treatises: Treatise I: An Inquiry Concerning Beauty, Order, Harmony, Design; Treatise II: An Inquiry Concerning Moral Good and Evil (London, 1725, 2/1726, 3/1729, 4/1738); Treatise I, ed. P. Kivy (The Hague, 1973)

'Essay on the Nature and Conduct of the Passions', in *Essay on the Nature and Conduct of the Passions and Affections* (London, 1728)

Philosophiae moralis institutio compendiaria (Glasgow, 1742); Eng. trans. as *A Short Introduction to Moral Philosophy* (Glasgow, 1747)

Reflections upon Laughter, and Remarks upon 'The Fable of the Bees' (Glasgow, 1750)

A System of Moral Philosophy, 2 vols (London, 1755)

BIBLIOGRAPHY

T. Fowler: *Shaftesbury and Hutcheson* (London, 1882)

W. R. Scott: *Francis Hutcheson: His Life, Teaching and Position in the History of Philosophy* (Cambridge, 1900)

E. Migliorini: *Studi sul pensiero estetico di Francis Hutcheson* (Padua, 1974)

P. Kivy: *The Seventh Sense: A Study of Francis Hutcheson's Aesthetics and its Influence in Eighteenth-century Britain* (New York, 1976)

ALAN CODE

Hutchinson, John (*b* Owthorpe, Notts, Sept 1615; *d* Deal, Kent, 11 Sept 1664). English parliamentarian and collector. The oldest surviving son of Sir Thomas Hutchinson, a Nottinghamshire gentleman, in July 1638, after studying law, he married Lucy, the daughter of Sir Allen Apsley (?1569–1630), the late Lieutenant of the Tower of London, and retired to his country seat at Owthorpe, Notts. As a Puritan, he sided with Parliament in the Civil War and became Governor of Nottingham, which he held successfully against the Royalist forces. He was returned to parliament in 1646 and was one of the judges who signed the warrant for the execution of Charles I. However, he soon became disillusioned with the rule of Oliver Cromwell and retired from active politics, devoting himself to his estate. He laid out formal gardens and improved the house, adding a 'closet' for his pictures and curiosities. His biography, written by his widow for her children, mentions his delight in 'perspective glasses' and 'artificial' engravings and his 'great judgement in paintings and the liberal arts'. In 1649 he spent *c.* £2000 on buying works of art from the royal collection, which had been given to the royal servants in lieu of wages, or possibly looted; his intention, according to his widow, was to preserve them. On the Restoration of the monarchy in 1660, he was ordered to return the paintings and objects of vertu, without compensation. In 1663 he was imprisoned in the Tower of London, on a groundless suspicion of treason, and later moved to Sandown Castle, where he died a prisoner.

BIBLIOGRAPHY

DNB

L. Hutchinson: *Memoirs of the Life of Colonel Hutchinson* (London, 1806)

DAVID RODGERS

Huth-Schmölz [née Huth], **Walde** (*b* Stuttgart, 29 Jan 1924) German photographer. She was the wife of KARL HUGO SCHMÖLZ. She studied photography at the Schule für Angewandte Kunst und Handwerk, Weimar (1940–43), and she completed her studies by training as a colour photographer with Agfa-Wolfen. In 1945 Huth-Schmölz worked as an industrial photographer at the engineering works in Esslingen. She then worked on commissions for textile companies and leading German fashion magazines, and she was one of the first to use colour photography for these subjects. She was commissioned by the *Frankfurter Illustrierte* to take photographs in Paris (1954–6) and by *Freundin* and *Elegante Welt* to photograph in Florence (1956). Huth-Schmölz set up a studio-house with her husband in Marienburg, Cologne, but suffered a long interruption in her work caused by the demands of her family. She returned to the public eye in the late 1970s with a completely new pictorial style, producing long cycles of high-quality photographs with a strong conceptual basis, such as *One Hundred Unwritten Letters.*

PHOTOGRAPHIC PUBLICATIONS

Ein Wundergewebe durchwandert die Welt (Stuttgart, 1953) [text by W. Semmler]

BIBLIOGRAPHY

L. F. Gruber: 'Walde Huth', *US Cam.*, xx/4 (April 1957)

Aus den Trümmern—Kunst und Kultur im Rheinland und in Westfalen, 1945–1952: Neubeginn und Kontinuität (exh. cat., Bonn, Rhein. Landesmus., 1985)

Sammlung Photographie, Cologne, Mus. Ludwig cat. (Cologne, 1986), pp. 176–80, 247–52

Acht Photographen sehen den Plenarbereich (Heidelberg, 1994)

R. Misselbeck, ed.: *Walde Huth–Augen Weide* (Cologne and Bonn, 1994)

REINHOLD MISSELBECK

Hutin. French family of artists. (1) François Hutin was a painter, engraver and sculptor whose marriage to one of the daughters of the painter Charles-Antoine Hérault (1644–1718) made him part of an artistic clan, typical of *ancien régime* France, that included the Coypel and Roëttiers families as well as Louis Silvestre. Three of François's sons became artists—(2) Charles-François Hutin, who spent much of his career at the Saxon court in Dresden, (3) Pierre-Jules Hutin, who was also active in Dresden, and Jean-Baptiste Hutin (*c.* 1726–after 1786), a painter of mediocre talent, according to his contemporaries.

(1) François Hutin (*b* Paris, 1686; *d* Paris, Aug 1758). Painter, sculptor and engraver. He was a pupil of Bon Boullogne and took part in the student competitions of the Académie Royale in 1709 and 1710. In 1737 he went to Rome with his son (2) Charles-François Hutin, where, although over 50, he was chosen to be a student at the Académie de France, remaining in the city for 7 years, 5 of them as a *pensionnaire.* In 1741, 1742 and 1743 he was entrusted with decorations for the *Chinea* festival (e.g. drawing, Munich, Staatl. Graph. Samml.). He also added sculpture to his list of accomplishments during his stay in Rome, carving among other works a marble bust (Rome, Acad. France). Back in Paris, both he and his wife, the painter Anne-Auguste Hérault (*d* 1771), were members of the Académie de St Luc, and together took the title of Painter to the King of Poland, Duke of Lorraine. François Hutin is known today only for his corpus of engravings, most of which are original prints.

(2) Charles-François Hutin (*b* Paris, 4 July 1715; *d* Dresden, 29 July 1776). Painter, sculptor, draughtsman and engraver, son of (1) François Hutin. He studied painting with François Lemoyne and in 1735 won the Académie Royale's second prize with *Rebecca Receiving from Eleazar the Presents Sent to her by Abraham* (untraced). Two years later he left for Rome with his father. There, on the advice of Jean-François de Troy, the new Director of the Académie de France, he turned in 1739 to sculpture, studying under Sébastien Slodtz. In 1740, a marble head of *Enobarbus* (untraced) by Charles-François was among a group of sculptures sent to France from the Académie in Rome, and in the same year he modelled a small group in antique style of *Faunus and Biblis* (untraced). He returned to Paris in 1742 and in 1744 he was approved (*agréé*) by the Académie Royale as a sculptor. He was received (*reçu*) as a full member in 1747 on presentation of the marble statue *Charon the Ferryman* (Paris, Louvre), a Rococo work whose pathos of expression and whose contorted pose suggest the influence of the work of Gianlorenzo Bernini.

In 1748 Charles-François went to Dresden, accompanied by his brother (3) Pierre-Jules Hutin; here he became First Sculptor to Augustus III. He was, however, chiefly occupied with Pierre-Jules on making drawings of paintings in the Saxon royal collection to be engraved for the *Recueil d'estampes d'après les plus célèbres tableaux de la Galerie Royale de Dresde* (2 vols; Dresden, 1753 and 1757), on which the greatest contemporary French engravers were employed. He also drew most of the plates engraved by Pierre-Jules and by Pierre-Etienne Moitte for the *Recueil d'estampes gravées d'après les tableaux de la galerie et du cabinet de S. E. M. le Comte de Brühl* (Dresden, 1754). In 1762 he was appointed Director of the Dresden Academy, a post at one time held by his uncle, Louis Silvestre. While in Dresden he received decorative commissions for civil and religious buildings including a *Crucifixion* for the Katholische Hofkirche, where he also painted a fresco ceiling in Heilige-Kreuz-Kapelle. He also painted genre pictures with Saxon subjects, such as *Saxon Peasant Woman in her Kitchen* (Madrid, Prado) and *Saxon Girl Reading a Letter* (Dresden, Gemäldegal. Alte Meister). *Hagar and Ishmael* (Budapest, Mus. F.A.) shows the influence of Lemoyne, despite its vigorous execution; Hutin seemed to absorb the styles of more important masters than himself, according to the nature of the work. In 1763 he published his engraved works in a *Recueil de différents sujets composés et gravés par Charles Hutin à Dresden.* His presence in Dresden contributed to the influence and prestige of French art in Germany.

(3) Pierre-Jules Hutin (*b* Paris, 1723–4; *d* Schloss Muskau, Silesia, 1763). Sculptor, draughtsman and engraver, brother of (2) Charles-François Hutin. He was a pupil of Guillaume Coustou (i) and was working at the Sèvres manufactory in 1741. In 1748 he followed his brother Charles-François to Dresden where he assisted him with drawings for the *Recueil d'estampes d'après les plus célèbres tableaux de la Galerie Royale de Dresde* and made engravings for the *Recueil d'estampes gravées d'après les tableaux de la galerie et du cabinet de S. E. M. le Comte de Brühl.* The period of the Seven Years War (1756–63) was not an auspicious moment for the arts and he ended his career at Schloss Muskau, the seat of Graf von Callenberg in Silesia. None of his sculptures is known to survive and he worked mainly as an engraver after the Old Masters and works by his brother Charles-François.

BIBLIOGRAPHY

Lami; Portalis–Béraldi; Thieme–Becker [with extensive early bibliog.]
L. Dussieux: *Les Artistes français à l'étranger* (Paris, 1856)
L. Réau: *Histoire de l'expansion de l'art français: Belgique et Hollande; Suisse; Allemagne et Autriche; Bohême et Hongrie* (Paris, 1928)
Y. Bruand and M. Hebert with Y. Sjöberg: *Inventaire du fonds français: Graveurs du dix-huitième siècle*, Paris, Bib. N., Dépt. Est. cat., ii (Paris, 1970)
H. Marx: 'Zu fünf dekorativen Gemälden von Charles Hutin', *Sächs. Heimatbl.*, xxiii/4 (1977), pp. 147–51

HÉLÈNE GUICHARNAUD

Hutton, Edward (*b* London, 12 April 1875; *d* London, 20 Aug 1969). English writer. He wrote some 36 books, most of them on the history, art and literature of Italy. As a young man he travelled much in Europe, especially Italy, and in 1898, after his marriage, settled in Settignano, Florence, where he was a member of the circle around Bernard Berenson. During World War I he was at the Foreign Office as an expert on Italian affairs and in 1918 was instrumental in founding the British Institute in Florence. That year he returned to England. When World War II broke out he was asked to compile a volume about art treasures in Italy that was used by the Allied Intelligence Corps. Perhaps the most lasting of his works will be his editions of *A New History of Painting in Italy* by J. A. Crowe and G. B. Cavalcaselle and of James Dennistoun's *Memoirs of the Dukes of Urbino* and his own study of the Roman marble workers, *The Cosmati.* It is interesting that his biography of Sigismondo Malatesta, published in 1906, was of great interest to both Ezra Pound and Adrian Stokes. His interest in the history of mosaics led to his designing several mosaic pavements, at Westminster Cathedral (1940) and at Buckfast Abbey (1942–3 and 1944–5), Devon. He owned a painting by Sassetta (*Virgin and Child, c.* 1435; now Washington, DC, N.G.A.). In 1965 he was awarded the Medaglia Culturale d'Oro for his services to Italian art and literature.

WRITINGS

Italy and the Italians (London, 1902)
Studies in the Lives of the Saints (London, 1902)
Sigismondo Pandolfo Malatesta: Lord of Rimini (London, 1906)
ed.: J. A. Crowe and G. B. Cavalcaselle: *A New History of Painting in Italy from the Second to the Sixteenth Century*, 3 vols (London, 3/1908–9)
ed.: J. Dennistoun: *Memoirs of the Dukes of Urbino: Illustrating the Arms, Arts, and Literature of Italy, from 1440 to 1630*, 3 vols (London, 1851, rev. New York, 2/1908, London, 2/1909)
The Franciscans in England, 1224–1538 (London, 1926)
The Cosmati: The Roman Marble Workers of the XII and XIIIth Centuries (London, 1950)

DAVID CAST

Huttunen, Erkki (*b* Alavus, nr Seinäjoki, 18 May 1901; *d* Helsinki, 17 Nov 1956). Finnish architect. He was an important designer of Functionalist office and industrial buildings in Finland. Huttunen trained at the Technical High School in Helsinki between 1921 and 1927, at the same time practising as a painter and caricaturist. He was the architect for the SOK (Suomen Osuuskauppojen Keskuskunta) chain of shops from 1928 to 1942. His first shops were in the classical style, but after 1930 the SOK building division's design principles moved rapidly towards Functionalism through his influence. The rural shop as created by Huttunen (cubic, stuccoed and painted white with a gently sloping roof), as well as streamlined offices and warehouses with horizontal bands of windows, promoted the spread of Modernism in Finland. The mill at Viipuri (1930; now Vyborg, Russian Federation) was constructed entirely of reinforced concrete and steel joists; it was Finland's first Functionalist factory building. Examples of Huttunen's industrial architecture in red brick are the Functionalist complexes for the state alcohol monopoly at Rajamäki near Helsinki (1935) and Enso (1936; now Svetogorsk, Russian Federation). The church at Nakkila, near Pori in the south-west of the country (1937), is one of Finland's few Functionalist ecclesiastical buildings.

Huttunen's private practice was very limited during his directorship of the Ministry of Building (1943–53). His last major project was the SOKOS hotel and restaurant in central Helsinki, completed in 1952. Work on the building had started at the end of the 1930s, and in its design Huttunen used ideas he had encountered during a study trip to the USA in 1937. His Functionalism, which was based on Bauhaus principles, was in form pure International Style, but his design was always governed more by artistic and aesthetic than by strictly theoretical principles.

BIBLIOGRAPHY

Suomen Rakennushallinto, 1911–1961 [The Finnish Ministry of Building, 1911–1961] (Helsinki, 1961)

T. Jokinen: *Erkki Huttunen liikelaitosten ja yhteisöjen arkkitehtina, 1928–1939* [The architect Erkki Huttunen as a designer of business and community buildings, 1928–1939] (diss., U. Jyväskylä, 1992)

TEPPO JOKINEN

Huüs, Pieter. *See* HUYS, (1).

Huy, Godefroid of. *See* GODEFROID OF HUY.

Huy, Jean Pépin de. *See* JEAN PÉPIN DE HUY.

Huy, Rainer of. *See* RAINER OF HUY.

Huydecoper, Joan, I (*b* Amsterdam, 1599; *d* Amsterdam, 26 Oct 1661). Dutch patrician and patron. He consciously pursued the role of the Maecenas of 17th-century Amsterdam. One of the wealthiest men in the city, especially after his second marriage in 1624, he was a patron of architecture, gardening, sculpture, painting, poetry, playwriting and pageantry, as well as mapmaking and publishing. Architecture engaged Huydecoper's particular attention, to the extent that he himself designed villas on paper. His country seat, Goudestein, in Maarssen and his town house (1639–42) by Philips Vingboons on the Singel in Amsterdam became bywords for patrician grandeur. The façade of the town house recalls that of the Palais du Luxembourg in Paris—the palace of Marie de' Medici, whose visit to Amsterdam in 1638 marked the European coming-of-age of the Dutch metropolis. Huydecoper's houses were immortalized by artist–clients of his, especially Jan Vos in poetry and Govaert Flinck in painting.

Through his art patronage, Huydecoper gave expression to his status and international standing. As burgomaster of Amsterdam, a post he occupied six times between 1651 and 1660, he associated himself conspicuously with artistic commissions. Most notably, he assumed much of the credit for the new town hall (now Royal Palace). When the painters, sculptors and art-lovers of Amsterdam joined in a short-lived brotherhood in 1654, Huydecoper was the city father they adopted as their patron. The benefits Huydecoper enjoyed from his protection of poets and artists were sometimes turned to direct advantage. On his return in 1655 from a mission to Berlin as deputy godfather of the child of the Grand Elector, he had Jan Vos organize a triumphal entry into Amsterdam. This display was mocked by other regents, who were offended by Huydecoper's harnessing of the arts to his own glory. His son Joan Huydecoper II followed the family tradition, becoming a burgomaster and an important patron: in 1674 he apparently commissioned Jan van der Heyden to paint a series of paintings of the family estate at Maarssen.

UNPUBLISHED SOURCES

Utrecht, Gemeente Archf [Huydecoper fam. pap., with much inf. on the fam.'s patronage]

BIBLIOGRAPHY

J. E. Elias: *De vroedschap van Amsterdam, 1578–1795* [Amsterdam City Council, 1578–1795], i (Haarlem, 1903), pp. 384–5

G. Schwartz: 'Jan van der Heyden and the Huydecopers of Maarsseveen', *Getty Mus. J.*, xi (1983), pp. 197–220

——: *Rembrandt: His Life, his Paintings* (Harmondsworth, 1985), pp. 134–8

K. Ottenheym: *Philips Vingboons, 1607–1678: Architect* (Zutphen, 1989), pp. 34–45 [Dut. text]

GARY SCHWARTZ

Huygens. Dutch family of courtiers and writers. (1) Constantijn Huygens (i) was secretary to the stadholders Frederick Henry and William II and also served as their art adviser. His diary contains many perceptive remarks about contemporary artists, works by whom he both commissioned and collected. His son (2) Constantijn Huygens (ii) became secretary to William III, with whom he travelled to England. Like his father, he was a keen diarist, as well as being a proficient topographical and landscape draughtsman.

(1) Constantijn [Constantine] **Huygens (i)** (*b* The Hague, 4 Sept 1596; *d* The Hague, 28 March 1687). Courtier, diplomat, writer, patron and collector. He served as a diplomat in Venice and London and in 1625 became secretary to Frederick Henry of Orange Nassau (*reg* 1625–47). On the death of Frederick Henry, Huygens maintained his post under William II (*reg* 1647–50) and later his widow Amalia van Solms. He later became First Councillor under William III (*reg* 1672–1702). Huygens was an educated and cultivated man: he spoke six languages, was a musician and composer as well as a poet (he translated John Donne's poems into Dutch) and received drawing lessons from Hendrik Hondius I. In 1629 he began his autobiography, which contains many references to artists; his greatest praise was for Rubens, but he also wrote discerningly about Rembrandt and Jan Lievens.

As artistic adviser to the stadholder (*see* NETHERLANDS, THE, §XII), Huygens the elder was probably directly responsible for the commission in the 1630s to Rembrandt for a series of paintings on the *Life of Christ*, which included the *Raising of the Cross* (1632) and the *Descent from the Cross* (1633; both Munich, Alte Pin.). Huygens employed Jacob van Campen and Pieter Post to build his own town house (destr.) in The Hague—although, in fact, it was largely of his own design—as well as his country house HOFWIJCK (1639–42), and he influenced Johan Maurits, Count of Nassau-Siegen, in his choice of the same architects to build the Mauritshuis, The Hague (1633–44; now the art museum; for illustration *see* CAMPEN, JACOB VAN).

When Amalia van Solms planned the decorations for Huis ten Bosch (*see* THE HAGUE, §V, 3) Huygens was responsible for the iconographic scheme and the choice of artists for the great Oranjezaal commemorating William II, and he chose those who worked in his preferred High Baroque style inspired by Rubens. His own collection included works by such artists as Thomas de Keyser, Jan Lievens, Adriaen Hanneman, Michiel van Mierevelt, Pieter Saenredam and Gerrit van Honthorst. Portraits of Huygens were painted by both de Keyser (1629–30; Douai, Mus. Mun., on loan to Amsterdam, Rijksmus.) and Lievens (1627; London, N.G.).

WRITINGS

De jeugd van Constantijn Huygens door hem zelf beschreven (MS.; 1629–31); ed. A. H. Kan (Rotterdam and Antwerp, 1946); ed. C. L. Heesakkers (Amsterdam, 1987)

Vitaulium: Hofwijck (The Hague, 1653)

BIBLIOGRAPHY

G. Kamphuis: 'Constantijn Huygens, bouwheer of bouwmeester', *Oud-Holland*, xxvii–xxviii (1962), pp. 151–80

E. K. Sass: *Comments on Rembrandt's 'Passion' Paintings and Constantijn Huygens's Iconography* (Copenhagen, 1971); review by J. Bruyn in *Oud-Holland*, xc (1976), p. 133

N. F. Streekstra and P. E. L. Verkuyl: *Huygens in Noorderlicht: Lezingen van het Groningse Huygens symposium: Groningen, Groninger Mus., 1987*
Huygens herdacht [Huygens commemorated] (exh. cat., ed. A. Eyffinger; The Hague, Kon. Bib., 1987)
V. Freijser, ed.: *Soeticheydt des buyten-levens: Leven en leren op Hofwijck* [The sweetness of country life: life and learning at Hofwijck] (Delft, 1988)

MARIEKE W. BOUMAN

(2) Constantijn [Constantine] **Huygens (ii)** (*b* The Hague, 10 March 1628; *d* The Hague, 2 Nov 1697). Draughtsman, son of (1) Constantijn Huygens (i). He was educated according to the instructions of his father and in 1644 went to Leiden to study in preparation for an official career. He never completed his degree, however, and in 1646 was initiated into the duties of his father, who was the secretary to Frederick Henry. Between 1649 and 1650 Constantijn the younger travelled extensively in Europe and recorded his trip in a diary.

On his return to the Netherlands, Constantijn the younger was unable to obtain a position at court, as the death of Frederick Henry was followed by a 12-year period without a stadholder. During that time he applied himself to drawing, having received drawing lessons in his youth and while a student from Pieter Moninckx (1606–86) and Pieter Kouwenhorn (*c.* 1599–1654) and in the 1660s from Raymond Blavet, a painter from The Hague; he also displayed great interest in the theory of drawing. Initially Huygens drew portraits in chalk and figure studies and, from 1664, landscape drawings with watercolour washes. A number of sheets show many thematic and stylistic similarities with those of his friend, the lawyer and amateur draughtsman Jan de Bisschop. The landscapes and townscapes drawn by Huygens in the 1660s are considerably larger than the travel sketches he was to make in the following decade. These large sheets depict views in the environs of The Hague, the Bommelerwaard and Breda and are considered Huygens's most accomplished work (e.g. the *River Waal at Zaltbommel*, 1669; Paris, Fond. Custodia, Inst. Néer.; see fig.). In 1668 Huygens married Susanna Rijckaert, and the couple lived until 1680 with Constantijn the elder.

In 1672 Huygens the younger became secretary to William III; he kept a diary of William's campaigns in France, Germany and the southern Netherlands. In 1680 he went with the stadholder to Celle and Berlin, during which time he again kept a diary. The most extensive journals, however, cover the period in England and Ireland from 1688 to his resignation from his official post in 1696. Huygens's professional activities kept him extremely busy, and in the war years Huygens's secretariat worked in the field. He sketched whenever he had the opportunity, however: at the IJssel defences (1672) and during the campaign of 1673–8 he regularly made drawings. These often have a high viewpoint and thus give a panoramic picture of the terrain. The works are often sketchy and hastily executed, something he noted in his diary (e.g. *Hunting Scene at Lincent*, 1675; Amsterdam, Rijksmus.). The human figures in Huygens's landscapes take second place, often serving simply as staffage. Virtually all his travel sketches and some of the figure studies are executed in pen and brown ink. The drawings serve as a visual complement to Huygens's diary notes and were primarily

Constantijn Huygens (ii): *River Waal at Zaltbommel*, pen and brown ink, with brown and blue wash, 208×331 mm, 1669 (Paris, Fondation Custodia, Institut Néerlandais)

intended for that purpose. After 1680 he drew rather less; apart from some portraits, which are mentioned in the diaries, virtually no other drawings are known from that period. Huygens's drawings were kept together for a long time but were eventually auctioned in 1823 and have subsequently been dispersed throughout the world, although major groups can be found in the Rijksprentenkabinet, Amsterdam, and at the Musée d'Art Ancien, Brussels.

WRITINGS

Journaal van Constantijn Huygens, den zoon, Werken Hist. Genoot., 4 vols (Utrecht, 1876–88): i [covering the years 1688–91], n. s., 23; ii [1692–6], n. s., 25; iii [1673–8], n. s., 32; iv [1649–50, 1680 and 1682–3], n. s., 46

Register op de journalen van Constantijn Huygens jr, Werken Hist. Genoot., 3rd ser., 22 (Amsterdam, 1906; J. H. Hora Siccama: *Aanteekeningen en verbeteringen op het in 1906 door het Historisch Genootschap uitgegeven register op de journalen van Constantijn Huygens den zoon* [Notes and corrections to the index to the journals of Constantijn Huygens the younger published by the History Society in 1906], Werken Hist. Genoot., 3rd ser., 35 (Amsterdam, 1915))

BIBLIOGRAPHY

Met Huygens op reis: Tekeningen en dagboeknotities van Constantijn Huygens jr (1628–1697), secretaris van stadhouder-koning Willem III [Travels with Huygens: drawings and diary notes of Constantijn Huygens jr (1628–1697), secretary to Stadholder-King William III] (exh. cat. by J. F. Heijbroek and others, Amsterdam, Rijksmus.; Ghent, Mus. S. Kst.; 1982–3)

D. J. Roorda: *Rond prins en patriciaat: Verspreide opstellen* [Concerning prince and nobility: diverse papers] (Weesp, 1984), pp. 94–116

A. Eyffinger, ed.: *Huygens herdacht* [Huygens commemorated] (The Hague, 1987)

A. S. van der Groot: 'Huygens's Final Years as Dutch Secretary', *The Age of William III and Mary II: Power, Politics and Patronage, 1688–1702* (exh. cat., ed. R. P. Maccubin and M. Hamilton-Phillips; Williamsburg, VA, Coll. William & Mary, Swem Lib.; New York, Grolier Club; Washington, DC, Folger Shakespeare Lib.; 1988–9), pp. 60–64

J. F. Heijbroek, ed.: *De verzameling van mr Carel Vosmaer (1826–1886)* [The collection of Mr Carel Vosmaer (1826–1886)] (The Hague and Amsterdam, 1989), pp. 80–92

J. F. HEIJBROEK

Huyot, Jean-Nicolas (*b* Paris, 25 Dec 1780; *d* Paris, 2 Aug 1840). French architect. The son of an architect, he began his training at the Ecole de Dessin, Paris, and in the atelier of the painter Jacques-Louis David, who first directed his studies to Greek architecture. Huyot's mentor in architecture was the leading Neo-classicist Antoine-François Peyre, in whose atelier at the Ecole des Beaux-Arts the historical views of Julien-David Le Roy further stimulated Huyot's interest in architectural evolution. This is reflected in the work he did in Rome, as winner of the *grand prix* (Prix de Rome, 1807), notably a remarkable restoration of the Temple of Fortuna at Praeneste. In 1813 he was selected by Auguste, Comte de Forbin, for an archaeological mission in Greece, Asia Minor and Egypt, travels that extended for nearly a decade, and during which he provided plans for French hospitals at Smyrna (now Izmir) and Constantinople (now Istanbul). These researches formed the basis of his lectures in architectural history in the post created for him at the Ecole in 1819 by his friend Quatremère de Quincy. Huyot took up his duties only on his return to Paris in 1823.

Huyot's revised designs for the Arc de Triomphe (1823) were abandoned as were his two attempts to construct a church: one a project for the new parish church in the Bellechasse quarter, the other a great Early Christian pilgrimage basilica on the heights of Mont Valerin (*c.* 1830). In 1835 a major opportunity was finally provided by a commission to prepare a master plan for the restoration and expansion of the complex of Law Courts on the Ile de la Cité. Huyot died while still attempting to obtain approval for his great scheme (Paris, Mus. Carnavalet), which proposed the French Renaissance as the basis for a new national style of architecture. Work was begun in 1840 on the plans of Louis Duc, who had long been inspired by Huyot's historical views.

UNPUBLISHED SOURCES

U. Paris, Bib. Doucet, MS [*Cours d'histoire d'architecture à l'Ecole Royale des Beaux-Arts,* 4 vols (*c.* 1823–40)]

WRITINGS

Forum romanum: Notes explicatives par Huyot, architecte (Paris [*c.* 1841])

BIBLIOGRAPHY

G. Vauthier: 'J.-N. Huyot, architecte de l'Arc de Triomphe de l'Etoile', *Bull. Soc. Hist. A. Fr.* (1920), pp. 6–19

R. Middleton: 'The Rationalist Interpretations of Léonce Reynaud and Viollet-le-Duc', *AA Files*, xi (1986), pp. 29–48

BARRY BERGDOLL

Huys. Flemish family of artists. The brothers (1) Pieter Huys and (2) Frans Huys both worked as engravers for the print publisher Hieronymus Cock and the firm of Christoph Plantin. Together they were responsible for the engravings in the *Vivae imagines partium corporis humani* (Antwerp, 1566) published by Plantin. Pieter's own style, however, was best expressed in his paintings.

(1) Pieter [Peeter; Peter] **Huys** [Hüis] (*b* Antwerp, *c.* 1520; *d* Antwerp, *c.* 1584). Painter and engraver. He became a master in the Antwerp Guild of St Luke in 1545. Among his other engravings for Plantin are the illustrations of one part of the *Humanae salutis monumenta* (Antwerp, 1571). Huys's style as a painter is apparent in two versions of the *Temptation of St Anthony*, one from early in his career (1547; Paris, Louvre) and the other from later (1577; Antwerp, Mus. Mayer van den Bergh): he shows himself to be a creative follower of Hieronymus Bosch (who was still popular in the second half of the 16th century), but his figures are more lifelike and he used stronger colours and thicker brushwork. The subject-matter of Huys's painting of *Hell* (1570; Madrid, Prado) is entirely in keeping with Bosch, but the colouring is that of Pieter Bruegel the elder. *The Bagpipe-player* (1571; Berlin, Gemäldegal.) shows that Huys not only painted imaginary scenes but was also familiar with recent humanistic and Mannerist developments in painting, especially in Italy. It is a moralizing scene full of symbolism and several layers of meaning. Here he is allied to Jan Sanders van Hemessen, Marinus van Reymerswaele and Pieter Bruegel the elder, all of whom achieved considerable success with such images among Flemish intellectuals. On the basis of these four signed and dated works, other paintings have been attributed to Pieter Huys, though there remains some confusion with the work of Jan Mandijn.

See also FRAME, §V.

BIBLIOGRAPHY

L. Van Puyvelde: *La Peinture flamande au siècle de Bosch et Breughel* (Paris, 1962), pp. 72–5

H. Mund: 'La Peinture de Moeurs chez Pieter Huys', *Rev. Archéol. & Hist. A. Louvain*, xiii (1980), pp. 64–73

G. Unverfehrt: *Hieronymus Bosch: Die Rezeption seiner Kunst im früher 16. Jahrhundert* (Berlin, 1980)

ELS VERMANDERE

(2) Frans Huys (*b* Antwerp, *c.* 1522; *d* Antwerp, before 10 April 1562). Engraver, brother of (1) Pieter Huys. He was evidently a master in the Antwerp Guild of St Luke by 1546, when he had a pupil registered under his name. His earliest dated prints are from 1555, only seven years before his death. He worked for the Antwerp print publishers Hieronymous Cock, Hans Liefrinck I (his brother-in-law) and Bartholomeus de Momper (1535–after 1589) and (in collaboration with his brother Pieter) for the book publisher Christoph Plantin. No paintings or drawings by Frans are known, and his prints all reproduce the work of other artists. Like many Antwerp engravers of the mid-16th century, he was influenced by Italian engraving, probably through the mediation of Giorgio Ghisi, who also worked with Cock. A series of *Grotesque masks* (Hollstein, nos 35–52) is strikingly similar to contemporary Italian work. Frans engraved many portraits of varying quality, chiefly of contemporary rulers, and several humorous genre subjects after Cornelis Massys. His most notable prints, however, were after drawings by Pieter Bruegel I: *Skaters before the Gate of St George* (Hollstein, no. 28), *Naval Battle in the Straits of Messina* (Hollstein, no. 15) and a set of *Warships* (Hollstein, nos 16–26). Frans Huys was perhaps the most successful of all the engravers who worked from Bruegel's designs: his carefully controlled systems of hatching convey subtler effects of light and shade than those of Pieter van der Heyden and are a more faithful reflection of Bruegel's pen lines than the somewhat flashy burin work of Phillip Galle.

BIBLIOGRAPHY

Hollstein: *Dut. & Flem.*; Thieme–Becker
A. J. J. Delen: *Histoire de la gravure dans les anciens Pays-Bas et dans les provinces belges*, II/i (Paris, 1934), pp. 114, 142; II/ii (Paris, 1935), pp. 72–4
Zwischen Renaissance und Barock: Das Zeitalter von Bruegel und Bellange (exh. cat. by K. Oberhuber, Vienna, Albertina, 1967), pp. 38–9, 51–2, 64, 112–13
I. de Ramaix: 'Catalogue de l'oeuvre gravée de Frans Huys', *Livre & Est.*, 55–6 (1968), pp. 258–93; 57–8 (1969), pp. 23–54
T. Riggs: *Hieronymus Cock: Printmaker and Publisher* (New York, 1977), pp. 88–9, 119–20

TIMOTHY RIGGS

Huysing, Hans. *See* HYSING, HANS.

Huysmans [Huysmans van Mechelen]**, Cornelis** (*bapt* Antwerp, 2 April 1648; *d* Mechelen, 1 June 1727). Flemish painter. He was the son of a builder, Hendrik Huysmans, and Catharina van der Meyden. After their deaths he was brought up by his uncle, who apprenticed him to the landscape painter Gaspard de Witte (1624–81) or, according to other sources, to Huysman's half-brother Pieter, though there is nothing to support this in the records of the Antwerp Guild of St Luke. He moved to Brussels to train with Jacques d'Arthois, who, on Huysmans's own testimony, was the most important influence on his development as a painter. On 24 January 1682 he married Maria Anna Schepers in Mechelen and in 1688 signed an agreement with the Mechelen painters' guild, which allowed him, upon payment of 24 guilders and 14 stuivers, to practise his trade there. Perhaps some difficulties he experienced with the guild encouraged his move to Antwerp, where he became a master in 1706–7. In 1716 he returned to Mechelen, where he took on Augustus-Casimir Redel and Jean Edmond Turner as pupils.

Huysmans is generally regarded as a painter of pseudo-Italianate landscapes with mountainous backgrounds, containing figures and motifs borrowed from Nicolas Poussin. However, his art is primarily related to that of Jacques d'Arthois, after whom he painted wide decorative compositions, executed in vigorous brushstrokes and usually depicting the edge of a forest with a sandy bank in the foreground (e.g. *Wooded Landscape*, Vienna, Ksthist. Mus.). His vegetation is less dense than d'Arthois's, with thick individual clumps of foliage allowing less light through and with larger clearings. The diagonal organization of these clearings is a basic structural feature, emphasized by the slant of the tree-trunks. His compositions are defined by sharp light and colour contrasts, for example in the warm and varied autumnal colours of the vegetation and in the contrast between the brightly-lit sand road and the dark tree-trunks and clumps of foliage. His brother Jan Baptist Huysmans (1654–1716), by whom a few signed pictures are known, worked in a similar style, though he made less use of colour, and his pictures were on the whole painted with less vigour. Cornelis's son, Pieter Balthasar Huysmans (1684–1706), also trained as a painter but died young.

BIBLIOGRAPHY

E. Neeffs: 'Corneille Huysmans', *Bull. Comm. Royale A. & Archéol.*, xiii (1874), pp. 1–16
F. J. van den Branden: *Geschiedenis der Antwerpsche schilderschool* (Antwerp, 1883), pp. 1077–8
Y. Thiéry: *Le Paysage flamand au XVIIe siècle* (Paris and Brussels, 1953), pp. 153–5
A. Laes: 'Le Paysage flamand au Musée de Glasgow: Jacques d'Arthois, Corneille Huysmans dit de Malines, Jean Francois van Bloemen dit Orizzonte', *Belg. Tijdschr. Oudhdknd. Kstgesch.*, xxvii (1958), pp. 13–21
Y. Thiéry and M. Kervyn de Meerendré: *Les Peintres flamands de paysage au XVIIe siècle: Le Baroque anversois et l'école bruxelloise* (Brussels, 1987), pp. 182–6, 240

HANS DEVISSCHER

Huysmans [Houseman]**, Jacob** (*b* Antwerp, *c.* 1630; *d* London, 1696). Flemish painter, active in England. He was a pupil of ?Gilles Backereel (?1572–before 1662) and Frans Wouters, presumably in Antwerp, but he came to London before the Restoration. Works painted soon after his arrival in England include small pastiches of mythological and religious subjects by Anthony van Dyck, and much of his mature work is in a flamboyantly Baroque manner that derives ultimately from van Dyck's second Flemish period and suggests, on a larger scale, the influence of Wouters. As a Roman Catholic he was acceptable to Charles II's consort, Catharine of Braganza, and to other Catholics at the English court. Principally as a result of the Queen's patronage, he enjoyed considerable success in the early years of the reign. When Samuel Pepys visited his studio in Westminster on 26 August 1664, he described him as a 'picture-drawer . . . which is said to exceed Lilly [Lely]'. Huysmans's most important portrait of Catharine of Braganza, *Queen Catharine as a Shepherdess* (*c.* 1664; Brit. Royal Col.), was one of the pictures Pepys saw on that occasion. It is an elaborate display in the arcadian manner, the underlying forms rather stiffly articulated and the flesh smoothly worked, but the costume and the riotous display of accessories painted with a bravura, indeed, in places, a vulgarity, that foreshadows passages in the work of Franz Xaver Winterhalter. The colours are highly individual, and the paint is applied with a boldness unparalleled in this period. A pallid orange tone often gives a strange lurid atmosphere to the background of Huysmans's compositions.

The personality of Huysmans's sitters, however, is always conscientiously presented, and this gives charm and intelligence even to his most idiosyncratic compositions: for example the *Portrait of a Woman as a Huntress* (London, Tate), the *Countess of Sunderland* (Blenheim Pal., Oxon), the *Duchess of Powis* (Powis Castle, Powys, NT) and the extravagant *Four Children of John Coke of Melbourne* (Melbourne Hall, Derbys). In the *Coke Children* elements characteristic of van Dyck's work are taken to their extreme limits: the display of costume is very theatrical, and the scene is crowded with lambs, cupids, dogs and flowers. Huysmans's more restrained or conventional portraits (a particularly good series of three-quarter length portraits is in the collection of the Earl of Plymouth) are less technically assured than contemporary works by such artists as Sir Peter Lely. The heads, however, are always interesting, and smaller portraits, such as *Izaak Walton* (*c.* 1675; London, N.P.G.) and *Father John Hudleston* (1685; priv. col.), are restrained in handling and grave in character. He produced impressive images of such Restoration statesmen as *John Maitland, 1st Duke of Lauderdale* (*c.* 1665–70; London, N.P.G.), and *Sir William Morice, Secretary of State* (*c.* 1666; Antony House, Cornwall, NT).

In his later years Huysmans may have found his Catholicism a liability. At the time of the Great Fire of London, for example, he withdrew to Chichester, apprehensive of threats to foreigners in a time of crisis. He continued to enjoy the patronage of Queen Catharine and in 1683 was to be paid £230 for paintings supplied for her chapel in St James's Palace.

BIBLIOGRAPHY

C. H. Collins Baker: *Lely and the Stuart Portrait Painters*, 2 vols (London, 1912), i, pp. 209–19; ii, pp. 154–5

E. Waterhouse: *Painting in Britain, 1530 to 1790* (London, 1953, rev. 4/1978), pp. 104–6

OLIVER MILLAR

Huysmans, Joris-Karl [Charles-Marie-Georges] (*b* Paris, 5 Feb 1848; *d* Paris, 12 May 1907). French writer and critic. His father, Victor-Godfried Huysmans, came from Breda in the Netherlands and worked in Paris as a lithographer and miniaturist. In 1866 Huysmans passed his baccalaureate, then worked temporarily in a humble position in the Ministry of the Interior. After enlisting in 1870 he was wounded during the Franco-Prussian War in 1870–71 and consequently withdrawn from the front line. He then began writing seriously and within the first few years produced *Le Chant du départ* (1871–3), *Le Drageoir aux épices* (1874–5) and *Marthe* (1876), a novel about a prostitute. He made several trips to Belgium during these years.

Huysmans's most significant book was his novel *A rebours* (1884), which is often described as the most important example of French decadent literature (*see* DECADENCE AND DECLINE, §3). Using partly autobiographical material it follows the character Jean Des Esseintes, the last scion of a noble family, who increasingly yields to his leanings towards aestheticism. In the grip of boredom and disgust at the everyday world, Des Esseintes increasingly takes refuge in a world of his own, which depends on the aesthetic harmony of furnishings, food, the daily round, clothes, books, art and music. He can bear to see life and his surroundings only under the conditions that shield him from the other people and phenomena in the world. This alternative world is exaggerated to an almost pathological extent in that it is intended not only to embellish reality but also to replace it. This is promoted by administering precise quantities of drugs and by colour harmonies and orgies of scent in all the objects surrounding him. The character's increasingly neurotic existence, which, much to his sorrow, always only anticipates the sought-after alternative world without ever achieving it, ends after talking to a doctor in his conversion to a new religious awareness that he seeks in strict adherence to Catholicism. *A rebours* was particularly important for popularizing the Symbolist movement (*see* SYMBOLISM). Moreover, his references to Des Esseintes's admiration for the work of the painters Gustave Moreau and Odilon Redon was influential on their success as artists.

Des Esseintes's frame of mind was not dissimilar to Huysmans's own return to Catholicism, a point he emphasized in the foreword he wrote to a new edition of the novel 20 years later. The act of writing the novel was for Huysmans the recognition and expression of his solipsistic tendencies and an escape from them all rolled into one. The new Catholicism described became the exemplar for a number of French intellectuals in the 20th century. The fruits of Huysmans's conversion to Catholicism are shown in the novels that follow a writer-character Durtal, who withdraws from his Bohemian life in Paris having indulged in virtually every conceivable excess to heighten his sensibility (described in *Là-bas*, 1891) and pursues instead the artistic and religious connotations of the famous Chartres Cathedral by means of intensive conversation and meditation (discussed in *En route*, 1895; culminating in *La Cathédrale*, 1898). Durtal's religious awakening is in the manner of a long aesthetic experience: Huysmans included art historical descriptions and analyses of the cathedral ('a book written in stone'), which is solely capable of opening up the mystically conceived path to God. Huysmans's works of art criticism include *L'Art moderne* (1883), *Certaines* (1889) and *Trois primitifs* (1905), the last being a book of essays about the painter Matthias Grünewald. He also contributed to the periodical *La Cravache*, an important forum for the Symbolists, which was edited by Georges Lecomte.

For Huysmans himself his return to Catholicism also brought social recognition; in 1893 he became a member—later an officer—of the Légion d'honneur, and in 1900 he was president of the Académie Goncourt. In 1906 he had to undergo an eye operation but never fully recovered. When he died the following year he was ceremonially buried in the Montparnasse cemetery.

WRITINGS

L'Art moderne (Paris, 1883/*R* Westmead, 1969)
A rebours (Paris, 1884; 2nd edn with preface, 1904; Eng. trans. 1922, 3/1974)
Certaines (Paris, 1889/*R* Westmead, 1970)
Là-bas (Paris, 1891; Eng. trans., 1924)
En route (Paris, 1895/*R* 1989); Eng. trans. by C. K. Paul (London, 1896)
La Cathédrale (Paris, 1898; *R* ed. P. Cogny, Saint-Cyr-sur-Loire, 1986)
Les Grünewald du Musée de Colmar (Paris, 1904; *R* ed. P. Brunet, Paris, 1988)
Trois primitifs: Les Grünewald du Musée de Colmar, le maître de Flémalle et la Florentine du Musée de Francfort-sur-le Main (Paris, 1905)
Oeuvres complètes (Paris, 1926–34)

BIBLIOGRAPHY

E. Hannequin: *Etudes de critique scientifique de quelques écrivains français: Flaubert, Zola, Hugo, Goncourt, Huysmans* (Paris, 1890)
Bull. Soc. Huysmans (1928–39; *R* Geneva, 1975)
G. Ross Ridge: *Joris-Karl Huysmans* (New York, 1968)
H. Trudgian: *L'Esthétique de Joris-Karl Huysmans* (Geneva, 1970)
H. J. Greif: *Huysmans' 'A rebours' und die Dekadenz* (Bonn, 1971)
M. Ach and J. Jörgensen: *Joris-Karl Huysmans und die okkulte Dekadenz* (Cologne, 1980)
F. Garber: *The Autonomy of Self from Richardson to Huysmans* (Princeton, MA, 1981)
G. Stein, ed.: *Dandy–Snob–Flaneur* (Frankfurt am Main, 1985)
R. B. Antoshi: *Reality and Illusion in the Novels of Joris-Karl Huysmans* (Amsterdam, 1986)
M. Y. Viegnes: *La Trilogie de Huysmans* (Paris, 1986)
F. Court-Perez: *Joris-Karl Huysmans: A rebours* (Paris, 1987)
A. Kahn: *Joris-Karl Huysmans: Novelist, Poet, and Art Critic* (Ann Arbor, 1987)
B. Banks: *The Image of Huysmans* (London, 1990)
A. Vircondelet: *Joris-Karl Huysmans* (Paris, 1990)
C. Lloyd: *Joris-Karl Huysmans and the Fin-de-siècle Novel* (Edinburgh, 1991)

ANDREAS KREUL

Huyssens, Peter (*b* Bruges, 6 June 1577; *d* Bruges, 6 June 1637). Flemish architect. The son of a master mason in Bruges, he learnt the same profession there. He joined the Jesuits as a friar in 1597. From 1606 to 1613 he made designs for the church and other buildings of the Jesuit College in Maastricht; he also supervised the construction of the church (converted into a theatre in the 18th century), which was conceived in a wholly traditional Flemish Renaissance style. In 1613 he was sent to Antwerp, where he became assistant to the rector, Franciscus Aguilonius, who had already made the first designs for the city's Jesuit church (now St Carolus Borromeus; *see* ANTWERP, fig. 2). Huyssens took over from Aguilonius after the latter's death in 1617; apart from the two side-chapels, added after 1622, the church was finished in 1621. From the beginning Rubens had taken part in its conception, and his close collaboration with Huyssens produced a church in which Baroque forms were used with an opulence unprecedented in the Netherlands. Even before this church was completed, Huyssens was asked by his superiors to design two others, the first being in Bruges in 1619 (now St Walburga's), the second in Namur in 1621 (now St-Loup's). Both were unfinished when Huyssens died.

Because of his 'inclination to luxury and expenses in designing buildings', Huyssens was ordered to suspend his activities as an architect by the provincial of his order. He also had to leave Antwerp and return to the Jesuit College in Bruges. However, through the intervention of the Infanta Isabella, he was authorized to travel to Italy to study churches there and to choose the marble for a chapel Isabella wished him to design for the palace in Brussels on his return. On 20 November 1626 Huyssens arrived in Rome; about one year later he was back in the southern Netherlands. It is not known whether he designed the chapel for the Infanta, but shortly after his return the abbot of the Benedictine abbey of St Peter in Ghent commissioned him to design a new church for his community (now St-Pieterskerk). Work started in 1629 under Huyssens's direction, but four years later his superiors forbade him to travel constantly between Bruges and Ghent to supervise the construction. The large choir of this church (not finished until 1651), with its impressive row of pillars, shows the strong influence of Roman examples. It was far from completion when Huyssens died and, although his ideas were followed later in the general conception and some essential elements, the style of the dome and of the façade (1719) is different, being more classical in design.

BIBLIOGRAPHY

J. Braun: *Die belgishcen Jesuïtenkirchen* (Freiburg im Breisgau, 1907), pp. 105–12, 129–41, 151–71
M. Konrad: 'Antwerpen Binnenräume im Zeitalter des Rubens', *Belgischen Kunstdenkmäler*, ed. P. Clemen (Munich, 1922), ii, pp. 206–15
J. H. Plantegna: *L'Architecture religieuse dans l'ancien duché de Brabant* (The Hague, 1926), pp. 75–126
J. Vallery-Radot: *Le Recueil des plans d'édifices de la compagnie de Jésus conservé à la Bibliothèque Nationale à Paris* (Rome, 1960), pp. 25, 33, 288, 296, 400–02
H. de Smet: *Sint-Walburga, een Brugse kerk vol geschiedenis* (Bruges, 1982), pp. 77–109
F. Baudouin: 'De toren van de Sint-Carolus-Borromeuskerk te Antwerpen', *Acad. Anlct.: Kl. S. Kst.*, xliv/3 (1983), pp. 15–56
J. L. Meulemeester: 'Huyssens, Rubens, van Mildert en het zeventiende-eeuwse hoofdaltar van de Sint-Donaaskerk in Bruge', *Jb.: Kon. Mus. S. Kst.* (1986), pp. 173–204

FRANS BAUDOUIN

Huysum, van. Dutch family of artists. Caspar van Huysum (*b* 1648) was a painter and etcher in Leeuwarden. His only surviving work is an indifferent etching of a priest, *A. G. van Velsen*. Caspar's younger brother Justus van Huysum I (*b* Amsterdam, 1695; *d* 1716) studied with Nicolaes Berchem and painted many different subjects, such as portraits, marine scenes, landscapes, history and battle paintings, but was best known for his flower paintings, for instance the *Flower Bouquet* (Antwerp, Kon. Mus. S. Kst). This is a flamboyant composition, the flowers contrasting too strongly with their dark background, compared to the subtle and more clearly organized flower paintings of his better-known son (1) Jan van Huysum. At his death, Justus I left a collection of 663 paintings, enough to suggest that he may also have been a dealer. Of his ten children, three others were painters. Justus van Huysum II (*b* 1685; *d* 2 Nov 1707), who before his early death worked in his father's studio, was the only son not to specialize in flower painting but instead painted battle scenes and was also a competent draughtsman. Jacobus van Huysum (*b* Amsterdam, 1687–9; *d* London, 1740) took over the management of his father's studio on the latter's death but in 1721 moved to England to work for Horace Walpole, who was also a patron of Jan. Jacobus was employed to copy paintings in Walpole's collection at Houghton Hall in Norfolk, including works by Caravaggio, Claude and Gaspard Dughet. He also copied paintings by his brother Jan, already a popular painter. After two years, Jacobus was dismissed from Walpole's service for intemperate drinking, a problem that finally caused his death.

His best-known work is a series of paintings representing the *Twelve Months*, symbolized by vases of flowers set against landscape backgrounds (see Grant). The youngest brother, Michiel van Huysum (1704–60), probably studied with Jan. He painted arcadian landscapes and watercolours of fruit and flowers. Only seven oil paintings by him are known, but a large number of watercolours survive (e.g. London, BM), mainly described as copies after his brother Jan. There are also drawings recorded by a Maria van Huysum, a specialist in natural history subjects, who may have been Jan's daughter.

BIBLIOGRAPHY

Thieme–Becker
M. H. Grant: *The Twelve Months of Flowers: Jacobus van Huysum* (Leigh-on-Sea, 1950)
P. Mitchell: *European Flower Painters* (Schiedam, 1981)

□

(1) Jan van Huysum (*b* Amsterdam, 15 April 1682; *d* Amsterdam, 8 Feb 1749). Painter and draughtsman. Although he painted and drew classicizing landscapes, he is best-known as the last important representative of Dutch FLOWER PAINTING, a tradition he carried into the mid-18th century.

1. LIFE AND WORK. In 1704 Jan married Elisabeth Takens and became independent of the family workshop. He lived in Amsterdam throughout his life, apparently never travelling abroad.

(i) Still-lifes. Most of van Huysum's 241 known still-lifes consist of luxuriantly composed flowers in a classicizing vase, standing on a stone plinth or a stone table, often with a bird's nest. Only in the earliest of the dated works, *Flower Still-life* (1706; Hamburg, Kshalle), is there still a traditional, symmetrical pictorial composition. This and other early flower and fruit still-lifes reveal the influence of Cornelis de Heem and Abraham Mignon. The later pictures show flowers with no apparent symmetry in their arrangement; such late Baroque, almost Rococo compositions distinguish van Huysum's pictures clearly from those of other early Dutch flower painters. The flowers luxuriate rampantly, growing forth from the stone vase and nearly flowing over the border, reflecting the interest in nature of the pre-Enlightenment early 18th century (e.g. *Flowers and Fruit*, Amsterdam, Rijksmus., see fig.; and *Flowers in a Vase*, 1726, London, Wallace, *see* FLOWER PAINTING, fig. 3). The flower-pieces from van Huysum's most productive period are presented almost exclusively in an S-shaped arrangement, the only other compositional form being the diagonal—both typical forms of the Rococo. Van Huysum was the first to use a light background and brighter palette; the flowers seem bathed in sunlight under an open sky, a popular feature of his work.

Jan van Huysum: *Flowers and Fruit*, oil on copper, 505×425 mm (Amsterdam, Rijksmuseum)

Van Huysum was most famous, however, for the extreme realism of his fruit and flowers. Despite the extraordinary accuracy of such details as the veins of individual petals, the filaments of the calyxes, dew drops and insects, like other painters he composed his pictures with flowers and fruits from different times of the year. If, as often supposed, he worked only from live models, he must have worked on the same picture at different intervals (some examples bear two dates); he must also have relied heavily on his fine preparatory studies. Besides complete arrangements, he made individual flower studies, capturing bizarre forms of tulips or carnations in full bloom from various points of view (e.g. London, BM). Most of his drawings are in black chalk, ink or graphite, often tinted with grey wash but sometimes also heightened with watercolour.

(ii) Landscapes. In contrast to his flower-pieces, van Huysum's landscape compositions have rarely received much attention. Nevertheless, he produced at least 36 painted classical or arcadian landscapes and numerous related drawings, in a style that represents the final phase of Dutch Italianate landscape painting (*see* DUTCH ITALIANATES). His landscape pictures dating from *c.* 1709 to 1730 reveal a clear dependence on the Amsterdam classicists of *c.* 1700, above all the work of Johannes Glauber (e.g. *Arcadian Landscape*, 1728; Amsterdam, Rijksmus.) as well as the work of Gaspard Dughet. Direct borrowings from Glauber's work can be recognized in the craggy rock formations and 'Mediterranean' form of landscape. Like the flower-pieces, these pictures are distinguished by their extremely fine brushwork and carefully arranged compositions; however, their restrained palette led to a limited acceptance on the part of patrons.

2. CRITICAL RECEPTION AND POSTHUMOUS REPUTATION. Van Huysum's fame as a still-life painter brought him an extended clientele both nationally and internationally. He received commissions from, among others, the

Duc d'Orléans, Prince William of Hesse-Kassel, Frederick-Augustus II, Elector of Saxony and King of Poland, and Frederick William I, King of Prussia, as well as many Amsterdam merchants. In England Horace Walpole commissioned four pictures from him and Sir Gregory Page six. Even during his lifetime, van Huysum's still-lifes commanded high prices.

Van Huysum was a reclusive character; deeply preoccupied with his own art, he interpreted the artistic interest of others in his work as envy. The only pupil he had was Margareta Havermann (*fl c.* 1716–30), whom he allowed, albeit only briefly, to work in his studio. The excellence of his pictures nevertheless inspired imitators throughout the 18th century and into the 19th, among them Wybrand Hendriks, Cornelis van Spaendonck, Paul Theodor van Brussel (1745–95) and Jacobus Linthorst (1745–1815). Paintings by van Huysum are now found in almost all the larger public collections and in some cases were acquired directly from the painter himself. Most were painted on copper or panel and survive in an excellent state thanks to his delicate technique.

BIBLIOGRAPHY

A. M. Hind: *Drawings by Dutch and Flemish Artists*, London, BM cat. (London, 1931), iv, pp. 162–3

M. van Huysum Grant: *Jan van Huysum, 1682–1749: Including a Catalogue Raisonné of the Artist's Fruit and Flower Paintings* (Leigh-on-Sea, 1954)

I. Bergström: *Dutch Still-life Painting in the 17th Century* (London, 1956), pp. 225–7

C. White: *The Flower Drawings of Jan van Huysum* (Leigh-on-Sea, 1964)

C. Kämmerer: *Die klassisch-heroische Landschaftsmalerei, 1675–1750* (Berlin, 1975), pp. 142–50

IRENE HABERLAND

Hwang Chip-jung [*cha* Simang; *ho* Yŏnggok] (*b* 1533; *d* after 1593). Korean painter. The son of a scholar-official, he passed the *chinsa* (literary licentiate) examination in 1576 and took up a civil service career. He was famous for painting grapes and is frequently equated with the bamboo painter Yi Chŏng (i) and the plum-blossom painter Ŏ Mong-nyŏng. In Korea, unlike in China, there is a long-standing tradition of painting grapes that reaches back possibly as far as the Koryŏ period (968–1392). The earliest surviving examples, however, date from the 16th century.

All that remains of Hwang Chip-jung's work are a few small album leaves, which might only be fragments of larger compositions. In *Grapevine* (album leaf, ink and colour on paper; Seoul, Cent. Stud. Kor. A., Kansong A. Mus.), which bears an inscription dated 1593 and the signature *Yŏnggok*, the fruit has nearly all fallen so that the bare stalks show through, partly concealed by a large vine leaf. At the tip of the vine other, smaller leaves seem to sway in a light breeze. Together with the softly blowing tendrils they lend an airy and natural feeling to the painting. The ink tones are finely harmonized, particularly in the representation of the fruit. Two other album leaves attributed to Hwang Chip-jung, *Ink Grapevine* (ink on hemp, 270×221 mm; Seoul, N. Mus.) and *Grapevine* (ink on silk, 320×320 mm; P'yŏngyang, Kor. A.G.), resemble the album leaf described above in their economic composition and light, relaxed strokes, though there is a little more contrast in the ink tones. Hwang Chip-jung can be seen as a follower of Sin Sa-im-dang (*see* YI (i), (1)), who is famous for her depictions of plants and insects. The tradition was carried on by such painters as Yi U, one of Sin Sa-im-dang's sons, Yi Kye-ho and Hong Su-chu (1642–1704). Their compositions are nevertheless much more complex and dynamic with lush and heavy branches.

BIBLIOGRAPHY

An Hwi-jun: *Hanguk hoehwasa* [History of Korean painting] (Seoul, 1980), p. 208

Chōsen bijutsu hakubutsukan [Korean Fine Arts Museum] (Tokyo, 1980), pl. 52

Chŏng Yang-mo, ed.: *Hwajo, sagunja* [Paintings of flowers and birds and the Four Gentlemen] (1985), xviii of *Hanguk-ŭi mi* [Beauties of Korea] (Seoul, 1977–85), pl. 59, pp. 222–3

BURGLIND JUNGMANN

Hwawang-toin. *See* SŎNG SE-CH'ANG.

Hwt-hery-ib. *See* ATHRIBIS.

Hyakurokusanjin. *See* AOKI MOKUBEI.

Hyakusen Sakaki. *See* SAKAKI HYAKUSEN.

Hyatt Huntington, Anna (*b* Cambridge, MA, 10 March 1876; *d* Oct 1973). American sculptor. She was the daughter of the renowned palaeontologist Alpheus Hyatt. She trained at the Art Students League, New York (1895), with H. MacNeil; later she also trained with the American sculptor John Gutzon Borglum (1867–1941). While on a farm at Porto Bello, MD, she began to model domestic animals, and then wildlife in the New York Zoological Park. She worked in Auvers-sur-Oise in France, then in Italy, where she created a public sculpture of lions (installed Oakwood Park, Dayton, OH). Her equestrian statue of *Joan of Arc* was exhibited at the Salon of 1910 in Paris, where it gained an honourable mention. Huntington gained numerous commissions for her accurate interpretations of nature, notably the *Cid Campeador*, an equestrian portrait erected in 1927 in Seville, Spain, and a series of figures and animals sited in the Brookgreen Gardens, New York. Huntington was also involved, after her marriage in 1923 to the collector Archer Milton Huntington, in commissioning and collecting early 20th-century sculpture for the Brookgreen Gardens, South Carolina.

BIBLIOGRAPHY

E. Schaub-Koch: *Anna Hyatt Huntington* (Lisbon, 1957)

P. Hastings Falk: *Who Was Who in American Art* (Madison, CT, 1985)

M. G. Eden: *Energy and Individuality in the Art of Anne Huntington, Sculptor, and Amy Beach, Composer* (Metuchen and London, 1987)

□

Hyde, Edward, 1st Earl of Clarendon (*b* Dinton, Wilts, 18 Feb 1609; *d* Rouen, 9 Dec 1674). English statesman, historian and collector. He fought on the Royalist side in the English Civil War and in 1646 went into exile. After the Restoration of the English monarchy in 1660 he became Secretary of State to Charles II, rising to great power as Lord Chancellor. He was created Baron Hyde in 1660, and Viscount Cornbury, Earl of Clarendon in 1661. In the early 1660s he commissioned Roger Pratt to design a great London residence, Clarendon House, built 1664–7; some interior work was carried out by Robert Streeter, Serjeant-Painter to Charles II. To furnish the building, Hyde, after consulting John Evelyn (1666), embarked on a collection of portraits of 'learned and heroic persons of

England'. As his interest lay in iconography, the quality of the works was not of prime importance. Some, like the group portrait of *James, 7th Earl of Derby, his Lady and Child* by Anthony van Dyck (New York, Frick) were acquired from impoverished Royalist families; other works, such as the portrait of *Edmund Waller* by Peter Lely (Earl of Clarendon, priv. col., on loan to Plymouth, City Mus. & A.G.) are original paintings. However, the majority of the portraits were specially commissioned copies after van Dyck, Lely and Godfrey Kneller.

In 1667 Hyde was dismissed and impeached; he fled to France, where he completed his great *History of the Rebellion* (published 1702–24) and wrote his autobiography. In 1683 his son Henry Hyde, 2nd Earl of Clarendon, moved the paintings to Cornbury, Wilts, where an inventory (Oxford, Bodleian Lib.) of damaged paintings was taken, revealing that the collection included portraits of *Cardinal Wolsey*, *Erasmus*, *Machiavelli* and *Chaucer*.

BIBLIOGRAPHY

DNB
R. Gibson: *Catalogue of Portraits in the Collection of the Earl of Clarendon* (London, 1977)

DAVID RODGERS

Hyde, Eugene (*b* Portland, Jamaica, 25 Jan 1931; *d* St Catherine, 15 June 1980). Jamaican painter. In 1953 he left Jamaica to study advertising design at the Art Center School in Los Angeles. In 1955, however, he moved to the Los Angeles County Art Institute, where he studied painting and graphic art for five years; he returned to Jamaica in the early 1960s and continued to work in advertising while painting and exhibiting regularly. In the 1960s and 1970s, along with Karl Parboosingh, he became a major force in the development of abstract art in Jamaica, and in 1970 he established in Kingston the John Peartree Gallery, which for ten years was to be the principal venue for exhibitions of abstract and modernist art in Jamaica. Hyde's own art ranged from an Expressionism influenced by the American painter Rice Lebrun (*b* 1900) in California in the late 1950s, to a more abstract vision developed in Jamaica in the 1960s and 1970s, where the Abstract Expressionist style of New York provided the technical basis for extended series devoted principally to dance, the female nude and Jamaican flora. After 1975 his figurative Expressionism resurfaced, but with added psychological dimensions inspired by artists such as Francis Bacon. He began to depict the social outcasts, the homeless and deranged who roamed the streets of Kingston, whom he called the 'casualties'. For Hyde, this would be the fate of all Jamaicans if the march towards Communism in Jamaica was not halted. In painting after painting he denounced his country's government.

BIBLIOGRAPHY

Eugene Hyde, 1931–1980, A Retrospective (exh. cat. by R. Smith McRea, Kingston, Inst. Jamaica, N.G., 1984)

DAVID BOXER

Hyderabad, Char Minar, 1591

Hyderabad [Ḥaydarābād]. City in western Andhra Pradesh, India; established in 1591, it flourished especially after 1724. The original seat of the QUTB SHAHI dynasty was GOLCONDA, but in 1591 Muhammad Quli (*reg* 1580–1612) shifted the capital *c.* 8 km east to the south bank of the River Musi. The new city was surrounded by bastioned walls, which have not survived. It was connected with the northern suburbs by four bridges, the first erected in 1593. Muhammad Quli was responsible for the royal and ceremonial structures that formed the original nucleus of Hyderabad. The Char Minar ('four minarets', 1591; see fig.), which stands at the intersection of two streets leading to the four quarters of the original city, has four lofty arched portals supporting an elevated mosque. Additional arched portals, fountains and squares defined the formal north–south axis of the city. Near the centre, the Jami' Masjid (Friday Mosque; 1598) has a prayer chamber opening off a spacious paved court entered to one side. The mosque is notable for the fine stuccowork on the seven cusped arches of the façade and the accompanying inscriptions. Most of the palaces and buildings of this era have disappeared. An exception in the northern part of the old city is the Ashur Khana, still used for ceremonies during Muharram (the Shia commemoration of the martyrdom of Husain). Muhammad Quli's successor, Muhammad (*reg* 1612—26), began work on the Mecca Masjid, which eventually became the largest mosque in the city. 'Abdullah (*reg* 1626–72) built the Toli Mosque. Many other Qutb Shahi mosques stand in the city and suburbs.

Under the MUGHAL occupation from 1687 to 1724 buildings continued to be erected in Hyderabad, and several earlier structures were completed, notably the Mecca Mosque (1693). In 1724 the city once again became the headquarters of a ruling dynasty, the Asaf Shahis. These sultans, otherwise known as the Nizams of Hyderabad, became the most powerful in the Deccan. They were responsible for building the city into a showpiece of wealth and influence. An enclosure containing the graves of a number of these rulers adjoins the Mecca Mosque. The Chaumahalla, situated immediately to the west of this mosque, was the principal headquarters of the Asaf Shahis, but other residences for the Nizams and their ministers were erected throughout the city and its garden suburbs.

European-style architecture was introduced in Hyderabad during the 18th century. Extensions to the Chaumahalla and other palaces made free use of Neo-classical colonnades and pediments. The British Residency, designed by Samuel Russell (son of the artist John Russell) of the Bengal Engineers, was completed in 1806 in a fully fledged Georgian style. The Falaknuma Palace (1872) was an imposing exercise in Neo-classicism inspired by the villas of Andrea Palladio. Under the patronage of the Nizams, the city was provided with a handsome series of civic monuments. The High Court (1916), the Osmania General Hospital (1925) and the State Central Library, all overlooking the River Musi, were built in a revived Qutb Shahi style that adapted traditional modes to 20th-century needs.

See also INDIAN SUBCONTINENT, §§III, 7(ii)(a) and V, 5(vi)(c).

BIBLIOGRAPHY

S. A. A. Bilgrami: *Landmarks of the Deccan: A Comprehensive Guide to the Archaeological Remains of the City and Suburbs of Hyderabad* (Hyderabad, 1927)
J. Burton-Page: 'Ḥaydarābād', *Enc. Islam/2* (Leiden, 1954-)
G. Michell: 'Golconda and Hyderabad', *Islamic Heritage of the Deccan*, ed. G. Michell (Bombay, 1986), pp. 77–85

GEORGE MICHELL

Hydria. Ancient form of vessel, used as a water storage jar (*see* GREECE, ANCIENT, figs 71, 101, 102 and 152).

Hyesan. *See* YU SUK.

Hyewŏn. *See* SIN YUN-BOK.

Hynais, Vojtěch (*b* Vienna, 14 Dec 1854; *d* Prague, 22 Aug 1925). Bohemian painter of Austrian birth. He studied at the Vienna Akademie der Bildenden Künste from 1870, working under Anselm Feuerbach, with whom he kept in contact after leaving for Italy on a scholarship. During two visits to Italy (1874–5 and 1877) he worked on mythological and religious paintings (e.g. *Perseus and Andromeda*, *c.* 1875; priv. col.). He was particularly interested in the Old Masters, especially those of the Baroque period, and most of all in Giovanni Battista Tiepolo. In 1878 he studied under Jean-Léon Gérôme in Paris; during this period he also worked with Paul Baudry. Hynais's later pictures continue to show the influence of their neo-Baroque style of French decorative painting in the academic tradition. Luminism—the dramatization of colours by light—remained much more acceptable to him than the Impressionist treatment of light.

Hynais's first great success was his victory in the contest for the decoration of the Czech National Theatre (1880–83) in Prague. He painted the majority of the works for the staircase and boudoir of the Royal Box. With a new curtain (still in use) which he designed after a fire in the theatre in 1881, he triumphed over his main rival, František Ženíšek. Work for the Court Theatre (the Burgtheater) at Vienna followed, together with some less important work in France. He returned to Prague to carry out a commission at the Pantheon of the National Museum in Prague (1898). His artistic development over this period can be followed in a series of outstanding portraits of his friends and family and official personalities (e.g. *Karl von Hasenauer*, 1890; Brno, Morav. Mus.). By about 1890 he had found his own personal style, based on a combination of semi-photographic naturalism with traditional academic practice. While his studies exemplify the advanced *plein-air* style, his larger canvases, such as the *Judgement of Paris* (1888–93; Prague, Czech. Acad. Sci., Presidium), show him aiming for a refined sensualism.

Hynais also worked in the applied arts, producing porcelain at Sèvres (1889–92) and designing posters (1891–5) that give a foretaste of the future development of Czech poster art; his most important posters were for the Jubilee Exhibition (Prague, 1891) and the Ethnographical Exhibition (Prague, 1895). Even more than his decorative style, the treatment of light and colour in his painting prepared the way for the acceptance of late Impressionism in Czech painting. As a professor at the Prague Academy of the Visual Arts, he was the major influence on young Czech artists.

BIBLIOGRAPHY

Thieme–Becker
J. Neumann: *Modern Czech Painting and the Classical Tradition* (Prague, 1958), pp. 37–9
M. Nováková: 'V. Hynais', *Tschechische Kunst, 1878–1914*, ii (exh. cat., ed. J. Kotalík; Darmstadt, Austellhallen Mathildenhöhe, 1984), pp. 88–91
M. Mžyková: *Vojtěch Hynais* (Prague, 1990)

ROMAN PRAHL

Hynckes, Raoul (*b* Brussels, 11 May 1893; *d* Blaricum, 24 Jan 1973). Dutch painter. He trained at the Koninklijke Academie voor Schone Kunsten in Brussels and the Academie voor Schone Kunsten in Mechelen (1907–12). He came to the Netherlands as a Belgian war victim in 1914. Until 1924 he produced impressionistic work, depicting ports and ships in the vicinity of Volendam, but from then until 1933 he painted cubistic still-lifes. In 1933 he had his first one-man exhibition at the art dealer van Lier in Amsterdam with precisely painted realistic still-lifes of dead game and fowl. From 1933 his work breathed an atmosphere of death and decay. With such artists as Albert Carel Willink and Pyke Koch he was classified as a Magic Realist. Hynckes employed countless mortality symbols in his work; sometimes these were religious, as in *The Sponge of Bitterness* (1934; The Hague, Gemeentemus.). More often, however, he used secular symbols such as skulls, bones or broken chains, as in *Ex est* (1940). His work clearly demonstrates the influence of 16th- and 17th-century *vanitas* painting, as in *The Keys of the Anchoret* (1942–3; Utrecht, Cent. Mus.). After 1945 he produced still-lifes which no longer featured mortality symbols.

WRITINGS

De vrienden van middernacht (Amsterdam, 1973)

BIBLIOGRAPHY

J. van der Hoop: *Raoul Hynckes* (Amsterdam, 1940, 2/1947)

JOHN STEEN

Hyōbu Bokkei. *See under* SOGA.

Hyōgo. *See under* KOBE.

Hyŏndong-ja. *See* AN KYŎN.

Hyŏnjae. *See* SIM SA-JŎNG.

Hyŏnong. *See* YUN, (2).

Hyper Realism. *See* PHOTOREALISM.

Hypnerotomachia Poliphili (Venice, 1499). Illustrated treatise on Italian art. One of the most mysterious books of the Renaissance, it takes the form of a long romance in two parts, written in a curious Italian language that is rich in rare Latinisms and Graecisms. The first part, strongly allegorical in tone, tells the story of a journey made by Poliphilo to meet Polia. He marries her, and together they go off to worship the statue of Venus, the goddess of love. In the second and shorter part, Polia and Poliphilo recall the story of their love, at first beset by problems but afterwards happy. Although precise references to Treviso and to the 1460s create a sense of actuality, the *Hypnerotomachia* adopts the literary convention of pure dream. Hence the strange Graecizing title of the work, which means 'the dream of a battle for love fought by Poliphilo' (i.e. 'lover of Polia').

The initial letters of the 38 chapters of the *Hypnerotomachia* form an acrostic, which reveals this lover of Polia as one 'frater Franciscus Columna'. A 'Francisco alta columna' (literally 'tall column') is in turn indicated as the author of the book in a verse composition that appears printed in a single copy of the *Hypnerotomachia* (Berlin, Staatsbib. Preuss. Kulturbesitz.). If this evidence suffices to rule out recent attributions of the work to Felice Feliciano or Lorenzo de' Medici, the problem of Francesco Colonna's identity remains. A document of 1512, mentioned by the 18th-century scholar Apostolo Zeno, identifies him as a Venetian Dominican friar. This identification has been generally accepted by scholars, and Pozzi and others have contributed supporting evidence. An alternative and less convincing hypothesis (Calvesi) identifies the author as a Roman who was lord of Palestrina and perhaps called 'frater' because he belonged to the Accademia Romana founded by Pomponio Leto.

The *Hypnerotomachia* was printed in Venice for the famous publisher Aldo Manuzio. The edition is a masterpiece of the Renaissance art of the book, exceptionally elegant in the relationship between page and text, the choice of typographical characters and initials, and the design and execution of the woodcut illustrations. This singular emphasis on its visual aspects reflects the author's conviction that the book's appearance forms part of its meaning, a conviction underlined by the pervasive interest in hieroglyphics and symbols that characterizes the *Hypnerotomachia*.

Francesco Colonna must have conceived his work from the start as an illustrated book, and if he himself did not draw the designs for the woodcuts he must have given precise instructions to the artist who did do them. Both in style and in the choice of motifs, these illustrations are deeply rooted in Venetian and Paduan culture, linked with Mantegna, the Lombardo family, Vittore Gambello and Andrea Riccio. Only in rare cases are they derived from ancient monuments preserved outside the Veneto, and these may have come from literary sources or from drawn or painted copies available in the Veneto. Bernardo Parentino's frescoes in the cloister of S Giustina in Padua seem to have played a significant role in the iconography of the book.

A large part of the *Hypnerotomachia* is taken up with tedious descriptions of gardens, architecture, sculptures, goldsmiths' work and other *objets d'art*. The writer's dominant interest was in the visual arts, and this guaranteed the book a secure place in Renaissance artistic literature. The descriptions depend mainly on literary sources, which include numerous ancient writers and the architectural treatise by Leon Battista Alberti and Antonio Filarete, probably known through the Latin version prepared for Matthias Corvinus.

The works of art conjured up by the complicated prose of the *Hypnerotomachia* suggest a dream conceived in the study. Space and form are rarely defined, and the lavish descriptions of ornament are based on improbable ideas derived from literary sources. Thus even the most colossal works described in the *Hypnerotomachia* seem to rise before the protagonist, no less than the reader, merely as objects of aesthetic contemplation, culminating in the imposing but uninhabitable 'relics' of antiquity. Here there is an early indication of the taste for ruins that was to develop and triumph in the early Romanticism of the late 18th century.

The *Hypnerotomachia* had little direct influence on the literature of art, probably because it had scant practical application. However, it was long popular with the creators of devices and emblems as a source of suggestive and curious motifs. In the art of the most diverse High Renaissance painters, from Giorgione to Garofalo and Donato Bramante to Giulio Romano, precise derivations from the text and illustrations of the *Hypnerotomachia* have been discovered. Albrecht Dürer possessed a copy of the book, and the Italian, French and English editions from 1545 on undoubtedly helped to confirm its fascination throughout Europe in the 16th and 17th centuries. While it is true to say that Mannerism is on the whole the artistic style closest to the coded language of the *Hypnerotomachia*, no single work of art renders such brilliant homage to Francesco Colonna's masterpiece as Gianlorenzo Bernini's *Elephant with Obelisk* (Rome, Piazza S Maria Sopra Minerva), a monumental Baroque amplification of one of the wood engravings in the Venetian book.

BIBLIOGRAPHY

F. Colonna: *Poliphili Hypnerotomachia* (Venice, 1499); It. trans. as *La hypnerotomachia di Polifilo* (Venice, 1545); Fr. trans. as *Le Songe de Poliphile* (Paris, 1546); Eng. trans. as *The Strife of Love in a Dream* (London, 1592); ed. G. Pozzi and L. A. Ciapponi, 2 vols ([1964]/*R* Padua, 1980)

C. Huelsen: 'Le illustrazioni dell'*Hypnerotomachia Poliphili* e le antichità di Roma', *La Bibliofilia*, xii (1910–11), pp. 161–76

A. Khomentovskaia: 'Felice Feliciano comme l'auteur de l'*Hypnerotomachia Poliphili*', *La Bibliofilia*, xxxvii (1935), pp. 154–74, 200–212; xxxviii (1936), pp. 20–48, 92–102

A. Blunt: 'The *Hypnerotomachia Poliphili* in 17th-century France', *J. Warb. & Court. Inst.*, i (1937–8), pp. 117–37

E. H. Gombrich: 'Hypnerotomachiana', *J. Warb. & Court. Inst.*, xiv (1951), pp. 119–25

M. T. Casella and G. Pozzi: *Francesco Colonna: Biografia e opere*, 2 vols (Padua, 1959)

G. Pozzi and L. A. Ciapponi: 'La cultura figurativa di Francesco Colonna e l'arte veneta', *Lett. It.*, xiv (1962), pp. 151–69

M. P. Billanovich: 'Una miniera di epigrafi e di antichità: Il chiostro maggiore di S Giustina a Padova', *Italia Med. & Uman.*, xii (1969), pp. 197–292 (265–82)

M. Calvesi: *Il sogno di Polifilo prenestino* (Rome, 1980)

G. Pozzi: 'Il *Polifilo* nella storia del libro illustrato', *Giorgione e l'umanesimo veneziano*, 2 vols (Florence, 1981), i, pp. 71–107
——: 'Colonna, Francesco', *Dizionario critico della letteratura italiana*, 4 vols (Turin, 1986), i, pp. 622–5
M. Calvesi: '*Hypnerotomachia Poliphili*: Nuovi riscontri e nuove evidenze documentarie per Francesco Colonna principe di Preneste', *Stor. A.*, lx (1987), pp. 85–136
S. Danesi Squarzina: 'Francesco Colonna, principe, letterato e la sua cerchia', *Stor. A.*, lx (1987), pp. 138–54

MARCO COLLARETA

Hypocaust [Gr. *hypokauston*, from *hypo*: 'under' and *kaiein*: 'to burn']. Room or place heated from below. Various forms of hypocaust existed in the Classical world, and similar systems of underfloor heating are also known in East Asia.

1. ANCIENT WORLD. The hypocaust was the principal system for heating the floors of Roman baths and the more luxurious villas. Its primitive earlier forms should be differentiated from the true hypocaust, which involved supporting a floor on short, closely spaced pillars (*pilae*) and filling the resultant space with hot gases from a furnace (*praefurnium*) stoked, in simpler systems, from outside (see fig. 1).

Pliny's assertion (*Natural History* IX.lxxix.168) that the hypocaust was invented by the Campanian Sergius Orata (*fl c.* 90–80 BC) is unconvincing. Though Orata did use the system to heat his oyster ponds near Puteoli, after observing the natural hot steam sources of the region, he can only have improved and popularized it. Various simpler forms of subfloor heating existed throughout the eastern Mediterranean from the 5th century BC on, while the earliest archaeological remains of true hypocausts belong to two almost contemporary specimens in Italy and Greece: the Stabian Baths in Pompeii (4th phase; late 2nd century BC) and the Greek Baths at Olympia (4th phase; *c.* 100 BC). Some 60–80 years later, Vitruvius (*On Architecture* V.x.2–3) provided an authoritative description of the system, which was applied with remarkable uniformity in regions as diverse as Syria and Scotland.

Because it was supported by pillars, the floor over a hypocaust was effectively 'suspended', hence its Latin name, *suspensurae*, and references to 'hanging baths' (*balneae pensiles*). It comprised a layer of mortar, 200×400 mm thick, on a smooth bed of 600 mm-square tiles (*bipedales*) or sometimes thin slabs of stone. The pillars were generally constructed of square or round bricks but occasionally of stone, or even sections of terracotta pipe. Their height generally ranged between 0.65 and 1.10 m, but examples 1.5–1.7 m high were not uncommon. Occasionally pillars were replaced by parallel vaults connected to the furnace, which usually burnt wood. The hot furnace gases were only allowed to enter the room itself in small baths that retained primitive heating systems even in later times. Otherwise, a few terracotta pipes embedded in the wall and opening at the springing level of the roof vaults served as chimneys and created the gentle draughts needed to keep the fire burning. The hypocaust system could also be extended to walls, and occasionally to vaults, by means of various types of duct. In the mid-1st century AD Seneca wrote of 'hollow walls' as a recent invention (*Letters* xc.25), and wall heating was only incorporated in the

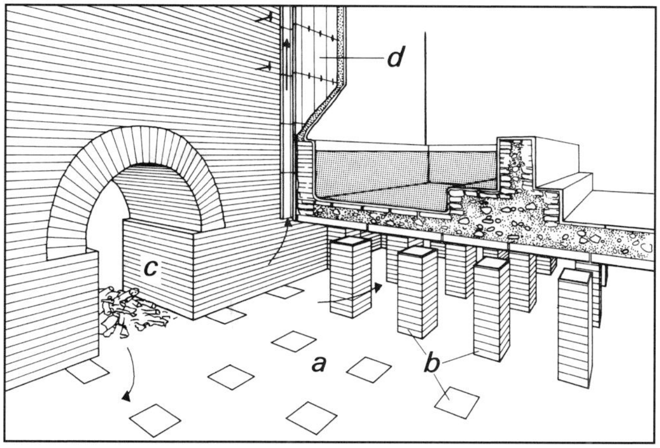

1. Roman hypocaust for heating a bath: (a) hypocaust; (b) pillars; (c) *praefurnium*; (d) *tubuli*

Stabian Baths and Forum Baths at Pompeii during renovation work in the early 1st century AD. The most common and effective system involved installing channels made from hollow terracotta 'box tiles' (*tubuli*) behind the stucco and marble incrustation of the walls. The construction of effective floor and wall heating in Roman baths depended on the ordering and organization of the rooms, so that heating requirements profoundly influenced the planning of Roman baths (*see also* BATH (ii), §1 and fig. 1).

BIBLIOGRAPHY

F. Kretzschmer: 'Hypokausten', *Saalburg Jb.*, xii (1953), pp. 7–41
E. Brodner: 'Untersuchungen an frühen Hypokaustanlagen', *Technol. Gesch.*, xliii (1976), pp. 249–67
A. Sandklef and D. Selling: 'The Heating of Classical Thermae', *Opuscula Romana*, xi (1976), pp. 123–5
T. Rook: 'The Development and Operation of Roman Hypocausted Baths', *J. Archaeol. Sci.*, v (1978), pp. 269–82

FIKRET K. YEGÜL

2. CHINA. Heating a dwelling by baking its floor was a method used in north-western China from ancient times. Several Neolithic sites in the region of Xi'an (e.g. Banpo, Jiangzhai) show layers of hard baked earth that reflect this practice. The baked ground preserved the heat for some time and, when it was exhausted, a new layer was applied and heated. This, however, is heating the floor from above. The first documentary evidence of the use of underfloor heating in élite buildings in northern China dates to the Northern Wei period (AD 386–534). In the *Shui jing zhu* (Commentary on the *Waterways Classic*), Li Daoyuan (*d* 572) described one such system, that was cut in the foundations of the Guanji Monastery (alleged location in present-day Hebei Province, *c.* 150 km east of Beijing). It had four smoke outlets, and a 'web of arteries' that heated the entire main hall 'seating a thousand monks'. During the Qing period (1644–1911) imperial living-quarters were all equipped with hypocaust systems; the rooms were called *nuange* ('heated halls') to distinguish them from other palace buildings heated only by charcoal braziers. The fires for the hypocaust were fed from stokeholes that opened on the marble terrace outside the hall; these gave access to a brick stove chamber, fuelled mostly with charcoal. The hot air circulated through a network of flues

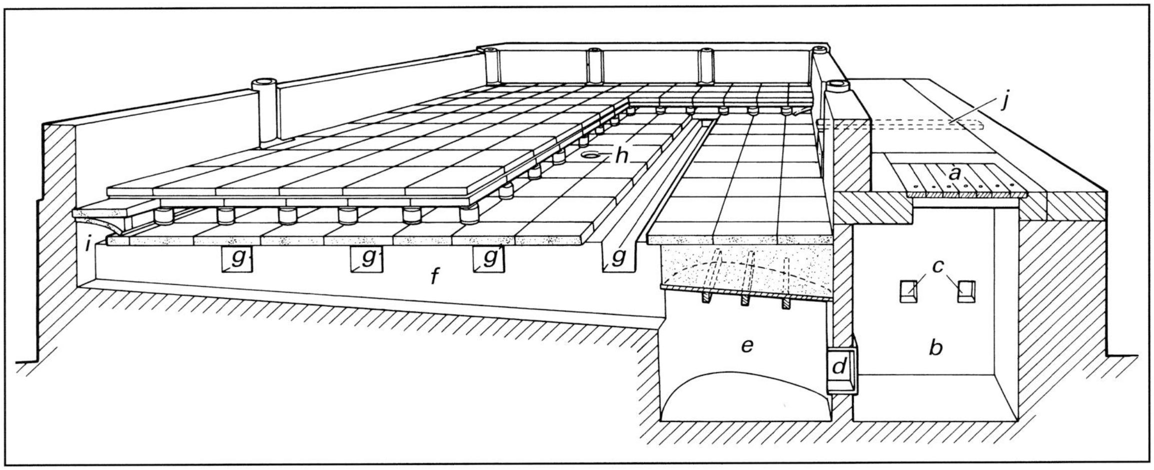

2. Chinese hypocaust heating system, Yihe yuan, Beijing: (a) entrance to stokehole; (b) stokehole; (c) niches for lamps; (d) mouth of stove chamber; (e) stove chamber; (f) main heating flue; (g) winding flue; (h) heat outlet; (i) smoke flue; (j) smoke outlet

under the flagged floor of the hall, smoke and gases being vented through an exterior outlet under the edge of the terrace (see fig. 2). A similar system is still used in stationary yurts in Inner Mongolia.

See also KANG.

BIBLIOGRAPHY

'Heating Devices in Ancient Buildings', *History and Development of Ancient Chinese Architecture*, ed. Zhong Yuanzhou and Chen Yangzheng (Beijing, 1986), pp. 307–11

ELLEN UITZINGER

3. KOREA. Known in Korea as *ondol*, this system of heating was in use there from at least the 4th century BC. It was first developed in north-east China and the north of the Korean peninsula, a region marked by bitter winter cold, and from there spread south throughout the rest of the peninsula. The incorporation of *ondol* into house design has varied with the climatic patterns in Korea (see KOREA, §II, 3(iii)(b)). Its use became widespread by the mid-17th century.

The *ondol* system is thought to have developed within the pit dwellings that were the first known form of housing in Korea. From a source of heat, generally the kitchen fire, a series of flues conveyed hot gases and smoke under the floors of the bedrooms to exit holes in the walls of the house; these might have an exit pipe or chimney attached. The kitchen was built at a lower level than the rest of the house, and brushwood was burnt in the fire, which might be started up several times a day. The *ondol* system was traditionally constructed by laying rough stone slabs in a bed of clay or mortar on supporting rows of stones or bricks, thereby forming smoke ducts. Beaten clay was smoothed over the stone slabs and in turn covered with several layers of coarse paper. Rice paper and, finally, heavy, oiled paper were laid on top to give a smooth finish tight enough to keep fumes from penetrating into the room above.

An *ondol* floor was kept scrupulously clean, since daily activities from sleeping to eating and studying took place upon it. The *ondol* rooms represented the 'closed' element in traditional house-design and were functionally extremely flexible. Korean domestic life is a 'sitting' rather than a 'standing' culture, and the reliance on *ondol* heating has had the effect of reducing the height of much furniture to make it accessible from a seated position. Underfloor heating is still extremely popular in Korea: the traditional *ondol* system based on a kitchen fire may still be found in country areas, but in towns coal briquettes are burnt in a brazier, or a system of underfloor pipes conveying hot water is employed.

BIBLIOGRAPHY

W. Viessman: 'Ondol Radiant Heat in Korea', *Trans. Korea Branch Royal Asiat. Soc.*, xxxi (1948–9), pp. 9–22
Joo Nam Chull [Chu Nam-ch'ŏl]: 'Ondol gwa put'umak-ŭi koch'al' [A study on the *ondol* and *butumak* of traditional Korean architecture], *Munhwajae*, xx (1987), pp. 137–51
Min Kyung-hyun [Min Kyŏng-hyŏn]: *Korean Gardens* (Seoul, 1992), pp. 37, 43, 64

SUSAN PARES

Hypogeum [Gr. 'underground']. The term was used by Herodotus, for example, to refer to the underground tomb chambers of Egypt as well as the sapping tunnels of Persian siege craft. As a specifically architectural term, it can be used for the underground rooms or cellars of buildings. Rules for their construction were given by Vitruvius (*On Architecture* VI.viii), but there is no single type or use for these structures. Vitruvius' instructions can be applied equally to the extensive *cryptoportici* that run underneath some colonnades, particularly those of Roman fora, for example at Arles (*see* ARLES, §1(i)) or Thessaloniki. The function of these is uncertain, although they were ventilated and lit through openings cut into the steps of the colonnade above; they may well have been general storerooms.

Underground chambers were also used for cult purposes, often oracular. Small underground crypt chambers existed in temples, such as that of Apollo at Delphi and the Temple of Zeus at Nemea, although these are really nothing more than rooms within the foundations and are not specifically referred to as hypogea. Otherwise, underground chambers may have been constructed to fulfil or replace natural caves, which were also used for oracular purposes (as at the oracle of Trophonius at Lebadeia). A good example of a more substantially built underground chamber is in the complex of the Nekyomanteion of EPHYRA, where there is a vaulted crypt under a massively vaulted building (late 4th century BC); here a veritable labyrinth of passages leads the worshipper by a succession of ritual stages to the central section above the crypt, which represents the underworld. Another example is the heroön at KALYDON (2nd century BC), the burial place of one Leon 'heroized' as 'the new Herakles', under the main room of a courtyard building. These structures clearly recall vaulted Macedonian tombs (*see* GREECE, ANCIENT, §II, 1(i)(d)), such as that of Philip II (*reg* 359–336 BC), which was associated with an adjacent heroön at ground-level, although the term hypogeum was not used in antiquity to describe them.

Another example at Klaros, in Ionia, lies under the Hellenistic Temple of Apollo, although it would seem to be much older. It was entered by two staircases in the porch of the temple. From these the chamber was again approached by a mazelike passageway and entered only after seven changes of direction. There were two underground rooms: the outer, lined with benches, served as a 'consulting room'; the inner, separated from the outer by a massive wall, was for the diviner alone. The roof of the outer chambers was supported on six arches, the inner on four. The excavations at Klaros were hampered by the waterlogging of the crypt.

Until the development of vaulting techniques, the need to roof any underground structure with flat stone roofs limited their size and reduced their architectural significance to a negligible level. Earlier cist graves in Macedonia (at Vergina) were given roofing supported by timber, or wholly of timber, which rotted. The development of vaulting, probably best regarded here as a Macedonian invention rather than an idea imported to Greece from elsewhere, made possible the construction of the larger Macedonian royal tombs and the later vaulted tombs that imitated their form, although apart from the structure of the roof, the architectural details applied to them were those of normal, above-ground, trabeated Greek architecture.

BIBLIOGRAPHY

E. Dyggve, F. Poulsen and K. Rhomaios: *Das Heroon von Kalydon* (Copenhagen, 1934)

'Summary of Archaeological Research in Turkey in 1957', *Anatol. Stud.*, viii (1958), pp. 17–34 [rep. on Claros, pp. 28–30]

S. I. Dakaris: 'Anaskaphi eis to nekuomanteion tou Acheron' [Excavations at the Nekyomanteion of Acheron], *Praktika Athen. Archaiol. Etaireias* (1961), pp. 108–19

——: 'Das Taubenorakel von Dodona und das Totenorakel bei Ephyra', *Neue Ausgrabungen in Griechenland*, ed. H. A. Cahn and others (Basle, 1963), pp. 35–54

E. Akurgal: *Ancient Civilizations and Ruins of Turkey* (Istanbul, 1967, 4/1978), p. 136

E. Waszink: 'The Location of the Oracle of Trophonius at Lebadeia', *Bull. Ant. Besch.*, xliii (1968), pp. 23–46

R. A. TOMLINSON

Hypostyle [Gr.: 'under columns'] **hall.** Large hall-like structure with a roof supported by numerous columns. Hypostyle halls were built particularly in ancient Egypt, the best-known example being the Temple of Karnak at Luxor (*see* THEBES (i), §II, 1).

□

Hyppolite [Hippolite]**, Hector** (*b* Saint-Marc, 15 Sept 1894; *d* Port-au-Prince, 9 June 1948). Haitian painter. The 250 works produced by him during the last two-and-a-half years of his life dominate the extraordinary achievements of the so-called Haitian primitives. Like his father and grandfather he was a priest of Vodoun. He also worked as a shoemaker and housepainter, and it was interest in some painted doors in a bar in Monrouis, near Saint-Marc, that led him to paint pictures. Hyppolite created his own myth and lived it. His claim to have spent five years in Africa is dubious, but it is certain that he was outside Haiti from 1915 to 1920, perhaps cutting cane in Cuba. Most of his life was lived in penury. The Haitian critic and poet Philippe Thoby-Marcelin brought him to Port-au-Prince in 1945. In the following year André Breton bought his paintings and arranged an exhibition of his work at UNESCO in Paris, writing that Hyppolite's fresh and powerful imagery could reinvigorate European art (Breton). His subjects invite interpretation on many levels. His principal subject, with whom he contracted a spiritual marriage, was woman, in the form of Erzulie the temptress, the queen or the sea goddess. Figures, landscapes and other objects are represented almost summarily in his pictures; he placed little value on perfecting techniques, applying the paint rapidly with chicken feathers and his fingers. In his last year the darker side of magical Vodoun appeared in his pictures.

BIBLIOGRAPHY

S. Rodman: *The Miracle of Haitian Art* (New York, 1974), pp. 24–35

Haitian Art (exh. cat. by U. Stebich, New York, Brooklyn Mus., 1978)

A. Breton: 'Hector Hyppolite', *Kunst aus Haiti* (Berlin, 1979), pp. 218–20

S. Rodman: *Where Art is Joy* (New York, 1988), pp. 47–55

M. P. Lerrebours: *Haïti et ses peintres*, i (Port-au-Prince, 1989), pp. 309–16

DOLORES M. YONKER

Hysing [Huysing]**, Hans** (*b* Stockholm, 1678; *d* London, 1753). Swedish painter, active in England. He was apprenticed to a goldsmith (1691–4), before studying portrait painting under David von Krafft (1655–1724). In 1700 he joined his compatriot Michael Dahl in London and lived with him for some years as pupil and studio assistant. By 1715 he was working independently. Unlike Dahl, whose chief patrons were Tories, Hysing was favoured by both the Hanoverian royal family and the Whig ascendancy. He painted full-length portraits of *Princess Anne*, *Princess Amelia* and *Princess Caroline* in coronation robes (Hertford, Shire Hall) as well as portraits of *Sir Robert Walpole* (Cambridge, King's Coll.) and *Richard Onslow*, Speaker of the House of Commons (Oxford, Wadham Coll.).

Hysing was evidently a painter of stature in his day, since he appears in Gawen Hamilton's group portrait *Conversation of Virtuosis at the Kings Armes* (signed and dated 1735; London, N.P.G.), which is mentioned by George Vertue, whom he painted. He also painted fellow-artists such as Peter Angillis (1685–1734), James Gibbs, Peter Tillemans and Christian Friedrich Zincke.

Many of Hysing's signed and dated works from the period 1715–39 are extant. He was initially influenced by

Dahl, but gradually adopted a personal style, more vigorous in modelling and stronger in colour than that of his mentor, whose later works he surpassed. Hysing's mature style was particularly effective for grand 'parade' portraits; he also produced accomplished portraits of men in uniform, such as that of *Sir Peter Halkett of Pitfirrane* (signed and dated 1735; Edinburgh, N.G.). Hysing provided a link with a younger generation of artists, as Allan Ramsay was his pupil for a time in 1734.

UNPUBLISHED SOURCES

London, N.P.G., Library [MS notes by C. H. Collins Baker]

BIBLIOGRAPHY

Waterhouse: *18th C.*

W. Nisser: *Michael Dahl and the Contemporary Swedish School of Painting* (Uppsala, 1927), pp. 97–105, 131–4

'The Note-books of George Vertue', *Walpole Soc.*, xviii (1930); xxii (1934); xxiv (1936), p. 122; xxx (1948–50), p. 235

Manners and Morals: Hogarth and British Painting, 1700–1760 (exh. cat. by E. Einberg, London, Tate, 1987–8), pp. 94, 244

RICHARD JEFFREE

Hyuhyudang. *See* YI KYE-HO.

Hyzler. Maltese family of painters of German descent. Giuseppe Hyzler (1793–1858) and his brother Vincenzo Hyzler (1813–49) were closely associated with the Nazarene artists, whose noble ideals they propagated with missionary zeal. Their art is explicitly anti-Baroque and stresses the importance of line and good uncluttered design. Giuseppe studied in Rome at the Accademia di S Luca but he was attracted to the circle of Friedrich Overbeck and became a member of the Nazarene community in the monastery of S Isidoro. A *Self-portrait* of this period (Valletta, N. Mus.) shows him wearing the habit of the Nazarenes. He returned to Malta in 1823 and opened an art school that was attended by many of the island's most distinguished citizens. He became an authority on aesthetic matters and was consulted on all important artistic projects. He had an almost dictatorial influence on Maltese artists, and he gathered around him a group of competent but not very remarkable young painters who diffused his ideals and often carried out his many commissions under his supervision. He is best known for the altarpiece of *St Ignatius of Loyola with the Virgin of Manresa* (Gozo, Jesuit Retreat House). Vincenzo was entrusted by Overbeck with the painting of an altarpiece of the *Crucifixion* that had been commissioned for a church in Stresa by Padre Antonio Rosmini, the Catholic theologian and intellectual. His only major painting in Malta is the altarpiece of *St Andrew* (Żejtun, St Catherine), a work that sums up the aesthetic ideals of the Nazarenes.

BIBLIOGRAPHY

M. Buhagiar, ed.: *St Catherine of Alexandria: Her Churches, Paintings and Statues in the Maltese Islands* (Valletta, 1979), p. 211

MARIO BUHAGIAR

I

i. For compound Catalan surnames joined by this conjunction, *see under* the part of the surname that precedes it.

Iacovleff, Alexandre. *See* YAKOVLEV, ALEKSANDR.

Iakovidis, Georgios (*b* Mytilene, Lesbos, 11 Jan 1853; *d* Athens, 13 Dec 1932). Greek painter. He studied painting and sculpture at the School of Fine Arts in Athens (1870–76), and in 1877 he went to the Akademie der Bildenden Künste in Munich to continue his painting studies under Karl Theodor von Piloty. He lived in Munich for 17 years, painting genre pictures, mythological scenes and portraits. Influenced by German academic Realism, his most famous paintings were of children (e.g. *First Steps*, 1890s; Athens, N.G.). In 1900 he was invited by the Greek government to return to Athens to organize the National Gallery, and in 1904 he was appointed Director of the School of Fine Arts. In addition to genre paintings, mythological scenes and some landscapes, at this time he produced formal portraits of eminent Greeks (e.g. *King George I*, 1910; Athens, N. Hist. Mus.). He opposed all new artistic tendencies, including Impressionism and Expressionism, yet his late, rather decorative paintings of nudes, still-lifes and flower compositions oddly betray a form of reserved academic Impressionism (e.g. *Spring*, 1927; Athens, N.G.).

BIBLIOGRAPHY

C. Christou: 'Georgios Iakovidis', *E ellenes zographoi* [The Greek painters], ed. S. Lydakes and A. Karakatsane, i (Athens, 1974), pp. 230–67

L. Iakovidis: *Georgios Iakovidis: Apo tin zoi kai apo tin techni tou* [Georgios Iakovidis: from his life and art] (Athens, 1984)

EVITA ARAPOGLOU

Ialysos. *See under* RHODES.

Iancu, Marcel. *See* JANCO, MARCEL.

Iaşi. Town in eastern Romania. The medieval town dates from the 13th century, according to archaeological remains and written sources. Its urban evolution was connected with the establishment of a princely court in the early 15th century, and with the setting up of the capital of Moldavia there *c.* 1560, a role maintained until the Union of Principalities in 1859. The Princely Court was built around a nucleus created before 1408 by Alexander I (*reg* 1400–32), followed by reconstructions and extensions, the most important ones *c.* 1490 under Stephen III (*reg* 1457–1504), and then under Vasile Lupu (*reg* 1634–53). The palace and its fortified precinct with defence towers and annexes have not been preserved, their remains being revealed only by archaeologists. At the Princely Court, the church of St Nicholas was founded in 1491 by Stephen III and extended at the end of the 17th century but demolished in 1884 by Jean Lecomte du Noüy; a building of little architectural value replaced it. On a hill near Iaşi, Peter IV (*reg* 1574–7, 1578–9 and 1582–91) built the Galata Monastery, whose church combined local traditional forms and such Wallachian elements as the second narthex tower, the new interior spatial conception and the external decoration. The church of the Aroneanu Monastery (1593), with an open porch and polychrome ceramic decoration of eastern origin, was built in a similar spirit of Moldavian–Wallachian synthesis.

The 17th-century architecture of Iaşi is of special interest; it includes several private buildings, for example the Dosoftei House (now a museum), with a loggia on the north. It also included many ecclesiastical buildings: the Barnovschi Church; St John the Baptist; the Bârnova Monastery (outside the town), founded by Prince Miron Barnovschi in 1627–9, with interesting fortifications; and in particular two donations of Vasile Lupu: the churches of the monasteries of the Three Hierarchs (1639) and Golia (1650). The façades of the former were covered entirely with stone sculptures, arranged in registers with Eastern decoration subtly combined with such Western elements as cornices and friezes, representing the type inaugurated at Galata: only fragments of the interior painting are preserved in the church's museum. In the second church, a monument inspired by the 17th-century Polish Baroque, with the exterior worked in smooth stone, the interior followed the Moldavian spatial and decorative tradition, with the painting (extensively restored) very probably executed by Russian artists commissioned by the founder. A simplified version of this was the church at the vast monastic complex at Cetăţuia (1669–72), including a princely house, abbey, cells, bathroom and kitchen, founded by Prince Gheorghe Duca on another hill dominating the city.

In the mid-18th century the Metropolitan Gavril Callimachi erected the new Metropolitan church (St George), whose echoes of the Constantinople Baroque style were a model for some of the churches in the town built by the trade guilds and boyars of modest means. The same type of decoration also appeared on fountains (e.g. at Golia and the Spiridon hospital). The late 18th century and early 19th were characterized by Neo-classicism. A series of landowners built sumptuous dwellings in the town. Ecclesiastical architecture, initially indeterminate (e.g. the Barbol Church), reached the peak of excellence with the Metropolitan church by Alexandru Orascu. The interior painting was executed by Gheorghe Tattarescu. Imposing Neo-classical buildings include the new church at the Frumosa Monastery (1836) and the nearby palace (1899, by the architect Kubelka), and the old University (a private house, rest. 1845).

A major component of urban and architectural taste in Iaşi was the eclecticism of such Gothic-inspired buildings as the Administrative Palace (1922–5; now the House of the Republic), built by the architect D. Berindey on the site of the old Princely Court. This eclecticism marked all building in Iaşi from the end of the 19th century until the mid-20th, when contemporary architecture was limited to a certain banality and uniformity. Significant sculptural monuments include those with historical rather than artistic value: the first Neo-classical composition, the *Obelisk with Lions* in the Copou Garden; the equestrian statue of *Stephen the Great* (1904) by Emmanuel Fremiet in front of the House of the Republic; the standing statue of *Alexandru Ioan Cuza* in Union Place; and busts of writers, cultural personalities and town notables. The House of the Republic houses the Museum of Art, the collection of which is mainly Romanian.

BIBLIOGRAPHY

G. Ionescu: *Istoria arhitecturii in Romania* [The history of architecture in Romania], ii (Bucharest, 1965)

N. Stoicescu: *Repertoriul bibliografic al localităţilor şi monumentelor medievale din Moldova* [Bibliographical repertory of localities and monuments in Moldavia] (Bucharest, 1974)

G. Ionescu: *Arhitectura pe teritoriul Romaniei de- a lungul veacurilor* [The architecture of Romanian territory through the centuries] (Bucharest, 1982)

TEREZA-IRENE SINIGALIA

Ibadan. City in western Nigeria. Founded as a military camp by the allied Yoruba Armies, by the mid-19th century Ibadan was a thriving frontier town, its population swelled by refugees from internecine warfare among the Yorubas. The city evolved a socio-political structure unique to its origins and radically different from other Yoruba political systems. At the base of this republican system is the patriarchal, extended family structure presided over by its 'Mogaji' or 'Oloye', and at the apex is the Olubadan, alternately selected from among the war generals (Balogun) and the civilian leaders (Otun Balogun). Since the Olubadan reigns from his family compound, Ibadan has many large compounds and dwellings intended by their residents to serve as palaces, and the installation of each successive Olubadan shifts the social, economic and political focuses of the city.

Like many African cities that developed rapidly during the 20th century, Ibadan has a mixture of traditional and modern architectural styles. Domestic dwellings may follow traditional courtyard form, being 'activity defined space with an internal and inward-looking orientation'; the modern style house, by contrast, is 'a synthesis of space defined activities with an external street orientation, especially for its private/public spaces' (Aradeon, 1984). Traditional Yoruba buildings display a typical concern for the integration of art with architecture (e.g. the Afin Irefin and the Afin Arẹmọ, royal palaces; *see also* YORUBA, §3).

Religious buildings include Ibadan's most sacred spot, the Okebadan shrine. Here, each February, offerings are made to the spirit of Okebadan for the well-being of Ibadan's citizens. The presence of the priest and custodians and the throng of people create an air of religious festival.

Also within the core of the city, Gbagi (the Central Business District) developed rapidly in the early 20th century, accompanied by the rapid expansion of the peripheral areas. Both were caused by the coming of the Lagos–Kano railway in 1900. The city became a collection and transhipment point for cocoa and palm oil and headquarters for the colonial provincial administration. In the period 1955–8 Ibadan was the regional capital, and since 1967 it has been the state capital. During this period, the population, which was estimated at 175,000 in 1911, grew rapidly so that by 1963 it stood at 627,379. Until the 1960s, the growth of the core city was constrained by colonial zoning regulations and planning laws, and the architecture of the formal and stately bearing of the main house in the Fọkọ (*c.* 1928) and Adebisi Idikan (1929) compounds bears the unmistakable imprint of Mapo Hall (see below).

In contrast, architectural styles in the outskirts are diverse and complex, juxtaposing elements from different sources. Here were built such new institutions as the University College (1948; by Fry Drew and Partners), its affiliate the Teaching Hospital Complex (1958; by Watkins Grey) and the International Institute of Tropical Agriculture (1965; by Becker-Voigt). Housing for the colonial officers in the government reservation (1901) and the Bodija Housing Estate (1959-60; by the Western Nigeria Housing Corporation) grew in direct response to British colonial planning codes and building regulations. The dispersed spatial organization of the University of Ibadan campus was the most pervasive influence on campus planning in Nigeria. Unfortunately, by the 1980s it had become a burden on the resources of the universities, during a period of drastic cuts in university funding.

The challenge faced by non-traditional architecture in Ibadan lies largely in its response to the hilly landscape. The residence of the Colonial District Officer (*c.* 1910), colonial Mapo Hall (1925), Premier Hotel (AMY Architects, Haifa, 1960) and the Cultural Centre (Gideon Associates, 1980) dominate the landscape because of their hilltop locations. In Gbagi two buildings stand out in spite of their flaws: the nine-storey Brokings House has a striking design by the Design Group (1982), although its curtain walls of bronze mirror glass are ill-suited to the tropical climatic environment; and the Cocoa House was a 25-storey office landmark of the 1960s. Unfortunately, the sensitive scale and elegant proportions of the 1962 design by Nickson and Borys were altered by the renovations of Adebayo and Adebayo (1972; damaged by fire 1983).

In the late 1950s Ibadan experienced a flowering of creative and performing arts. This began at the Mbari club and owed its impetus to such literary figures and first-generation University of Ibadan alumni as Chinua Achebe (*b* 1930), Godwin Okigbo (1931-68) and Wole Soyinka (*b* 1934). The Oshogbo (Art) School (*see* NIGERIA, §V) emerged from a series of informal workshops organized at the centre, where Uli and Georgina Beier, Suzanne Wenger (*b* 1915), Bruce Onobrakpeya (*b* 1931; *see* NIGERIA, fig. 4), Uche Okeke (*b* 1933) and Agbo Folarin (*b* 1936) were among those involved. Three of the most famous alumni of the school are Jimoh Buraimoh (*b* 1943), Asiru Olatunde (*b* 1918) and Twin Seven Seven (*b* 1944). In the 1990s other informal centres of artistic activity in Ibadan included the New Culture Studios, founded in Mokola in the 1970s by the painter and sculptor Demas Nwoko (*b* 1935) under the direction of the playwright Gbenga Sonuga.

Crafts produced in the city include the indigo-dyed cloth (*adire*) for which Ibadan is famous, produced using the cassava starch resist technique; *iseyin* cloth, woven on the men's strip weave; as well as leather products, pottery, metal tools and farm implements.

Ethnographic collections are held by the Institute of African Studies at the University of Ibadan, and art exhibitions are held in the United States Information Service Center as well as the British Council.

BIBLIOGRAPHY

K. Morgan: *Akinyele's Outline History of Ibadan* (Lagos, 1946)
D. Aradeon: 'Architecture', *The Living Cultures of Nigeria*, ed. S. O. Biobaku (Lagos, 1976), pp. 38–43
S. B. Aradeon: 'A History of Nigerian Architecture: The Last 100 Years', *Nigeria Mag.*, no. 150 (1984), pp. 1–17
D. Aradeon: 'Architecture and Lifestyle', *A Handbook of Nigerian Culture*, ed. F. Aig-Imoukhuede (Lagos, 1991)

DAVID ARADEON

Ibarra, José de (*b* Guadalajara, Mexico, 1688; *d* Mexico, 1756). Mexican painter. His earliest known work belongs to the 1720s, after which time he produced numerous religious paintings, including a series of panels devoted to female figures in the Gospels such as the *Woman Taken in Adultery*, the *Samaritan Woman* and *Mary Magdalene in Simon's House* (all Mexico City, Pin. Virreinal). Other works include *St Anthony*, the *Dream of St Joseph*, a *Pietà*, the *Coronation of St Rosa* and the *Betrothal of the Virgin* (all Mexico City Cathedral) as well as numerous works in various provincial Mexican churches and museums, such as *Christ Among the Doctors*, the *Death of the Virgin*, the *Assumption of the Virgin*, the *Immaculate Conception*, the *Flagellation* and *St Joseph with Two Benefactors* (all Zacatecas, Mus. Guadalupe). In the cathedral of Puebla are his *Betrothal of the Virgin*, the *Assumption of the Virgin*, *St Michael* and *St Joseph*, and in Querétaro are his *Trinity*, *Circumcision*, *Ecce homo* and *Triumph of the Faith* (Querétaro, Mus. Reg.). Ibarra also painted numerous official portraits, including many of Spanish viceroys, most of which are in the Museo Nacional de Historia del Castillo de Chapultepec, Mexico City. His work is characterized by its rejection of the previous generation's excesses of colour and by its careful draughtsmanship. In 1754 he became president of the newly founded but short-lived Academy of Painting in Mexico.

BIBLIOGRAPHY

M. Toussaint: *Pintura colonial en México* (Mexico City, 1965)
M. C. García Sáiz: 'Aportaciones a la obra de José de Ibarra', *Archv A. Valenc.* (1978)
X. Moyssen: 'El testamento de José de Ibarra', *Bol. Mnmts Hist.*, vi (1981)
S. Sebastian, J. de Mesa and T. Gisbert: *Arte iberoamericano desde la colonización a la independencia* (Madrid, 1985)

MARIA CONCEPCIÓN GARCÍA SÁIZ

Ibarra, Juan de. *See* ALAVA, JUAN DE.

Ibbetson, Julius Caesar, the elder (*b* Leeds, 29 Dec 1759; *d* Masham, N. Yorks, 13 Oct 1817). English painter, printmaker and writer. The son of a clothier, he was apprenticed to John Fletcher, a ship painter in Hull; in 1775 Ibbetson became a scene-painter there. In 1777 he moved to London, where he worked as a scene-painter and picture restorer. He married about three years later. From 1785 he exhibited landscapes, genre scenes and portraits at the Royal Academy. In 1787–8 Ibbetson was personal draughtsman to Col. Charles Cathcart on the first British Mission to Beijing, a voyage that included visits to Madeira, the Cape of Good Hope and Java. His watercolour *False Bay, Cape of Good Hope* (London, V&A), made on this journey, shows a picturesque roughness of foliage and rustic staffage adapted from his English landscape style. Cathcart's death forced Ibbetson to return to England (he exhibited an oil painting, untraced, of the *Burial of Col. Cathcart in Java* at the Royal Academy in 1789); thereafter he lived by painting landscape oils and watercolours, the subjects culled from his frequent tours. He painted occasional portraits throughout his career (e.g. *Young Man*, 1790; Leeds, Temple Newsam House) and contributed to John Boydell's Shakespeare Gallery (e.g. *Scene from 'The Taming of the Shrew'*, untraced, see Waterhouse, p. 192). In 1789 he stayed with John Stuart, 3rd Earl of Bute, at Cardiff Castle and visited the Isle of Wight in 1790. In 1792 he toured Wales and the surrounding area with the painter John 'Warwick' Smith and his companion Robert Fulke Greville, resulting in the publication of his book of engravings, *A Picturesque Guide* (1793). His oil painting of *Aberglasyn: The Flash of Lightning* (Leeds, C.A.G.) evokes the sublimity of the mountainous Welsh terrain; the drama of the storm over Aberglasyn is conveyed by thick impasto and strong chiaroscuro, a way of handling paint that Ibbetson learnt from copying 17th-century Dutch masters while working for a London dealer named Clarke during the late 1770s and early 1780s. He was also an accomplished figure draughtsman and social observer: he showed four humorous paintings of sailors at the Royal Academy in 1800, a topical theme at the height of the Napoleonic Wars. In 1789 he illustrated *Modern Times*, a moralizing tract by John Trusler, and *c.* 1790 painted pastoral scenes on plaster for the library ceiling at Kenwood House, London. From 1793 to 1800 he produced illustrations (engraved by J. Tookey) for John Church's folio *A Cabinet of Quadrupeds* (1805).

In straitened circumstances, Ibbetson moved in 1798 to Liverpool, where he worked for William Roscoe and Thomas Vernon. From that year until his death he lived in the north, at Edinburgh, Rosslyn and the Lake District, finally settling at Masham, N. Yorks, in 1805. He married his second wife in 1799 and was unsuccessful as an ARA candidate the following year. In 1803, while at Ambleside, he published *An Accidence, or Gamut, of Painting in Oils and Water Colours*, part autobiography, part technical handbook. In it he cited Claude Lorrain and Aelbert Cuyp as masters of landscape composition; he also encouraged lady amateurs to paint in oil. Ibbetson's large Lake District oils, for example *At the Ford* (Cardiff, N. Mus.), usually have tree repoussoirs and picturesque rustic figures; they show a sinuous handling of line that has more in common with 17th-century Dutch paintings than the sparer compositions of Romantic art. Ibbetson's finest achievement is in his highly individual watercolours: blue-toned and delicate, they are characterized by astutely balanced elements of landscape, atmosphere and human incident. His eldest son, Julius Caesar Ibbetson the younger (1783–1825), was a drawing-master and innkeeper at Richmond, N. Yorks.

PRINTS

A Picturesque Guide to Bath, Bristol, Hot Wells, the River Avon, and the Adjacent Country (London, 1793)

WRITINGS

An Accidence, or Gamut, of Painting in Oils and Water Colours (London, 1803, 2/1828)

Process of Tinted Drawing (London, 1805)

BIBLIOGRAPHY

Waterhouse: *18th C.*
B. L. K. Henderson: *Morland and Ibbetson* (London, 1923)
——: *Julius Caesar Ibbetson* (London, 1948)
——: 'Ibbetson in the East Indies', *Country Life*, cx (14 Dec 1951), p. 203
Julius Caesar Ibbetson, 1759–1817 (exh. cat., London, Kenwood House, 1957)

SUSAN MORRIS

Ibels, Henri-Gabriel (*b* Paris, 30 Nov 1867; *d* Paris, Feb 1936). French printmaker, illustrator and painter. He became one of the original members of the Nabis as an art student at the Académie Julian, Paris, in 1888–9. He joined in the early group ventures such as printmaking, puppet plays and theatre design, but he was never involved with the more esoteric Symbolist aspirations of some of the group's leading members. He first exhibited at the Salon des Indépendants in 1891 and participated in the Nabis's group shows at Louis Le Barc de Boutteville's gallery. With Edouard Vuillard and Maurice Denis, he was quick to attract public attention, the nature of his work earning him the sobriquet 'le Nabi journaliste'. His art was inspired by contemporary life, with subjects drawn from the spectacle of modern Paris, particularly from the café, circus and boxing ring. Both in subject and technique he can be likened to such artists as Adolphe Willette, Henri de Toulouse-Lautrec and Théophile-Alexandre Steinlen, and his work shares many characteristics with theirs, notably an economy of line and a simplicity of shapes and colours. Such features derived in Ibels's case from the art of Honoré Daumier, Japanese printmakers and Paul Gauguin and the Pont-Aven group.

Ibels held radical political views and shared in the anarchist-socialist determination to make art relevant and useful to society. His witty and unsentimental outlook and ability to simplify and sharpen his observations were ideally adapted to the medium of colour lithography. One of his earliest and most successful posters was created in 1892 for the café-concert singer Jules Mévisto and set the performer's looming profile, in the guise of a proletarian worker, against a backdrop of bleak industrial suburbs (see Saunier, pp. 36–7). He was also employed as a designer of sheet-music covers and theatre programmes. The Théâtre Libre commissioned him to produce a series of eight programmes during their 1892–3 season.

Ibels excelled as a caricaturist and worked for various illustrated journals, including *L'Escarmouche* in 1893–4, for which he designed poster advertisements (e.g. New Brunswick, NJ, Rutgers U., Zimmerli A. Mus.), *L'Estampe originale* from 1893, *Père peinard*, an anarchist journal published by Emile Pouget, *Le Sifflet* and *L'Assiette au beurre*. *Le Sifflet* (Feb 1898–June 1899) was a short-lived publication founded as a riposte to Jean-Louis Forain's anti-Dreyfusard *Psst . . . !*. During the height of the Dreyfus affair, Ibels turned out image-for-image rejoinders to the coarse anti-Semitic caricatures being produced by Forain, and these were collectively published as *Allons-y, histoire contemporaine* (Paris, 1898). Despite this, Ibels and Forain were friends. In collaboration with Toulouse-Lautrec Ibels produced illustrations for G. Montorgeuil's book *Le Café-concert* (1893), a study commissioned by the print dealer André Marty. In 1896 a volume containing Ibels's main posters and prints to date was published by Charpentier and Fasquelle as *Les Demi-cabots*. In 1897 he illustrated Zola's *La Terre*, and after 1900 he wrote several short plays. The success of his career as an illustrator was marked by the State who awarded Ibels the Légion d'honneur in 1913.

BIBLIOGRAPHY

C. Saunier: 'Henri-Gabriel Ibels', *La Plume*, v/9 (1893), pp. 30–37
P. D. Cate: *The Graphic Arts and French Society 1871–1914* (New Brunswick, 1988), pp. 144–58

BELINDA THOMSON

Iberian art. Style of prehistoric art that developed in the Mediterranean areas of the Iberian peninsula (Spain and Portugal) between the 6th–1st centuries BC (*see also* PREHISTORIC EUROPE, §VI).

1. INTRODUCTION. This most westerly civilization of the Mediterranean region provides an important example of a non-Greco-Roman ancient culture, and surviving works reveal both native Iberian elements and the influence of colonizing peoples. The study of Iberian art began in 1860 with the discovery of the sculptures of the Cerro de los Santos in Albacete and the famous 'Dama de Elche' from Alicante (see fig. 1). At first, the style was related to Egyptian, Mesopotamian and Mycenaean art, but further knowledge of its chronology led to the identification of the Archaic Greek influence that developed until the Ibero-Roman period of the 1st century BC. Colonization by the PHOENICIANs and the orientalizing culture of Tartessos are considered to have played a formative role in Iberian culture, which later grew to assimilate Greco-Phocaean and other, still later, elements such as Carthaginian (*see* PUNIC ART) and Hellenistic influences, before disappearing in the rising tide of Romanization. It is also important to evaluate the wide geographical scope of Iberian art, which occurs from Andalusia in southern Spain to Roussillon in southern France, suggesting appreciable cultural and ethnic variations.

The various forms of Iberian art developed in different ways. The sculpture is exceptional and comes mostly from burial sites and such sanctuaries as Cerro de los Santos; it was produced in specialized workshops that made ex-votos in wood or bronze. On the other hand, little

1. Iberian statuette of a princess or queen ('Dama de Elche'), h. 560 mm, *c.* 475 BC (Madrid, Museo Arqueológico Nacional)

architecture or mural painting are known; surviving examples are confined to funerary monuments, although it is likely that palaces existed. The minor arts, however, are well-represented, especially in the fields of gold and silver work and painted pottery, in which distinctive works were produced. As a whole, Iberian art reflects the social structure and beliefs of the society that produced it, rather than the styles of individual artists. During its long development, over more than five centuries, several phases are discernible.

2. CHRONOLOGICAL DEVELOPMENT. The colonizing activity of the Phoenicians and the spread of Tartessian culture from the lower Guadalquivir Valley towards the Mediterranean explain an initial orientalizing phase, datable to the end of the 7th century BC. This phase is characterized by pottery, bronzes and the first carvings in stone. Jewellery ornamented with granulation, filigree and repoussé work, such as that from Crevillente in Alicante, is also typical. In this phase Iberian art acquired its main technical, stylistic and socio-religious characteristics, including techniques for the working of soft sandstones and the adoption of a formal and iconographic vocabulary derived from the eastern Mediterranean. The most representative work of this phase, is the monument from POZO MORO in the highlands between the peninsular Levant and Andalusia (reconstructed in Madrid, Mus. Arqueol. N.; see fig. 2). Dating from *c.* 500 BC, the structure comprises a tower decorated with mythological friezes and set on a stepped base with lions at the corners. Its formal and technical characteristics assist the interpretation of other monuments, known as pillar-stelae, which decorated tombs and of which only the animal carvings, such as lions, bulls or sphinxes, now survive. This form of Iberian sculpture attests to the continuation until Roman times of a strongly hierarchical society whose chiefs were regarded as sacred and made heroes or gods after their death. Such works show the profound assimilation of orientalizing influences before the influence of Greek art supervened.

The numerous pillar-stelae are surmounted by the heads of such animals as lions, bulls, sphinxes and griffins, showing that their models originated in the colonizing world. The activity of the sculptors, who were sometimes itinerant, probably led to the establishment of local workshops, such as those documented in Osuna, Cástulo and Elche. These works were symbols of the economic, social and political power of the chiefs, which explains their frequent intentional destruction.

After the 6th century BC the Phocaean Greeks sought new commercial routes from the Iberian territories of the south-east of the peninsula. This led to a Greco-Iberian phase that produced important works of Iberian art in the region lying between eastern Andalusia and the south-east of the peninsula, including the modern province of Alicante. Further north, however, the absence of a sufficiently developed infrastructure made this Greek stimulus harder to assimilate. The importation of products and craftsmen could explain the increase of Greco-Oriental influence in all fields of Iberian art after the middle of the 6th century BC. This is particularly true of the bronze votive sculptures and the great stone carvings, even though their ideology and significance seem to represent a continuation of the orientalizing phase. From *c.* 550 BC, some carvings of mythical animals began to assume Greek or, more exactly, Archaic Greco-Oriental forms; examples include the *Mermaid* from Corral de Saus, Valencia, and the *Sphinx* from Agost in Alicante. This new style, known as Greco-Iberian, or, more precisely, Ibero-Phocaean, can be seen in the *Bull* from Monforte del Cid, Alicante, or the *Snake* from Balazote in Albacete; parallel carvings of human figures also appeared. These influences extended towards the Guadalquivir Valley, which explains the appearance of the great sculptural groups typical of the region.

The best example of these is the heröon of Porcuna (Córdoba): composed of over 25 almost life-size carvings depicting fights between armed warriors, lions or griffins and divinities such as the 'Lord of the Animals', it confirms the continuity of the heroic ideology of the orientalizing phase. Stylistically, however, it could be included among the great complexes of the Late Archaic period, since the artists seem to have been directed by a sculptor trained in the Greco-Phocaean style current before *c.* 480 BC. The famous female statue known as the 'Dama de Elche' (see fig. 1 above), representing an indigenous goddess of fertility and death, was executed in a severe style suggesting a dating earlier than 450 BC. Similar carvings include the 'Dama de Baza' from Granada dated to *c.*400 BC, which was used as a funerary urn in a princely chamber tomb containing the accoutrements of a warrior. A stele from La Albufereta in Alicante, clearly inspired by a Greek funerary stele of the beginning of the 4th century BC, can probably be attributed to the later part of this phase.

2. Iberian monument to a deified chieftain, sandstone, base 3.65 m square, Pozo Moro, *c.* 500 BC (*in situ*; reconstruction in Madrid, Museo Arqueológico Nacional); reconstruction drawing

This Greco-Iberian tradition, also evident in imitative ceramic vessels and in jewellery such as the Jávea Treasure from Alicante, developed through the 5th and 4th centuries BC towards an increasingly individual style. In this style the full creative scope of Iberian art distinguishes it from Classical art, facilitating the identification of an Iberian phase. Exemplified by the famous Osuna frieze and the silver dishes of Tivissa in Tarragona, the Iberian style is most apparent in the more popular works. However, these can sometimes be hard to date, because the style does not conform to the usual developmental pattern found in élite art, but is characteristic of the socially stratified Iberian culture. Typical works include the stone votive images of the Cerro de los Santos sanctuary, the terracottas of La Serreta de Alcoy (Alicante) and most of the small bronze votive pieces, together with the rich niello work applied to weapons, belts and other objects.

A final Hellenistic or Ibero-Roman phase of the 3rd–1st centuries BC is characterized by the modification of the representation of mythical animals, humans and élite rituals to suit new beliefs and tastes, a trend best seen in the Mallá monument, Barcelona. Carthaginian schemes, such as the hind with a palm tree at Osuna, were one feature of this stylistic development, while Hellenistic models, including new types of funerary lions and sphinxes, were introduced with Romanization. The final influence was the narrative art of Republican Rome, as can be seen in the latest Osuna reliefs. The most important Iberian vase painting styles also date to this period. The symbolic style of Elche, characterized by curved outlines and related to a fertility goddess, differs greatly from the spontaneity and narrative interest of the Lirian style and the sparer, but equally expressive, figures of the Ebro Valley, which are shown participating in fights, dances and rituals. Nonetheless, the grace and individuality of all these creations place them among the best works of the final phase of Iberian art.

BIBLIOGRAPHY

P. Paris: *Essai sur l'art et l'industrie de l'Espagne primitive* (Paris, 1903)
A. Blanco: 'Die klassischen Wurzeln iberischer Kunst', *Madrid. Mitt.*, i (1960), pp. 101–21
M. Tarradell: *Arte ibérico* (Barcelona, 1968)
G. Nicolini: *Bronzes figurés des sanctuaires ibériques* (Paris, 1969)
A. Garcia Bellido: *Iberische Kunst in Spanien* (Mainz, 1971)
F. Presedo: 'La Dama de Baza', *Trab. Prehist.*, xxx (1973), pp. 151–216
M. Almagro: 'Las raices del arte ibérico', *Pap. Lab. Arqueol. Valencia*, xi (1975), pp. 251–80
T. Chapa: *La escultura zoomorfa ibérica en piedra* (Madrid, 1980)
A. Blanco: *Historia del arte hispánico I: La antigüedad*, ii (Madrid, 1981)
M. Almagro-Gorbea: 'Arquitectura y sociedad en la cultura ibérica', *Colloque international 'Architecture et société de l'Archaïsme grec à la fin de la République romaine': Rome, 1983*, pp. 387–414
——: 'Pilares-estela ibéricos', *Homenaje a M. Almagro* (Madrid, 1983), pp. 7–20
J. M. Blazquez and J. González Navarrete: 'The Phokaian Sculpture of Obulco in Southern Spain', *Amer. J. Archaeol.*, lxxxix (1985), pp. 61–9
J. González Navarrete: *Escultura ibérica del Cerrillo Blanco (Porcuna)* (Jaén, 1987)
'Escultura ibérica', *Rev. Arqueol.* [Madrid] (1987) [supernumerary issue]

M. ALMAGRO-GORBEA

Ibi, Sinibaldo (*b c.* 1475; *d c.* 1550). Italian painter. He initially showed great promise, closely following the style of his master Perugino, Raphael and Bernardino Pinturicchio, but the individuality and quality of his work progressively diminished. In 1496, with Berto di Giovanni, Eusebio da San Giorgio, Lattanzio di Giovanni (*d* 1534) and Lodovico di Angelo (1481–1522), he took a year's lease on a workshop near the Porta Eburnea in Perugia. In 1504 he executed a church banner dedicated to St Ubaldo for Gubbio Cathedral (Gubbio, Mus. & Pin. Com.). In 1507 he painted a panel in Gubbio Cathedral for Girolamo and Maddalena Bentivoglio, depicting the *Virgin between SS Sebastian and Ubaldo*. In 1509, commissioned by a lay confraternity, he executed another church banner depicting the *Madonna of Mercy* (Gubbio, Ranghiasci priv. col.). This banner, which strongly reflects the influence of Timoteo Viti, is generally regarded as his best work. Ibi often collaborated with other members of the Perugia school of painting: from 1508 to 1510 he and Berto di Giovanni painted a *Virgin and Child with Saints* for S Agostino, Perugia. In 1512 he is recorded as treasurer of the painters' guild of Perugia, an office he held again in 1523, 1535, 1540 and finally in 1548. He often appears as an assessor of works by his contemporaries, and in 1514 he and Fiorenzo di Lorenzo helped to resolve a dispute involving Eusebio da San Giorgio.

BIBLIOGRAPHY

Thieme–Becker

A. Mariotti: *Lettere pittoriche perugine* (Perugia, 1788/*R* Bologna, 1975)

J. A. Crowe and G. B. Cavalcaselle: *A New History of Painting in Italy* (London, 1866/*R* New York, 1980), pp. 338–9, 344–6

W. Bombe: *Geschichte der Peruginer Malerei*, Italienische Forschungen, v (Berlin, 1912), pp. 334–5

E. Jacobsen: *Umbrische Malerei* (Strasbourg, 1914), p. 139

SUSANNE KIEFHABER

Ibibio. Cluster of peoples speaking Bantu-related languages, inhabiting the south-western or 'mainland' portion of Akwa Ibom State in south-east Nigeria and a small area to the east of the Cross River estuary, including Calabar, the capital of Cross River State. The 4 million Ibibio-speaking peoples are bounded to the north and west by the IGBO, to the south-west by the Ogoni and to the east by the forest groups of south-west Cameroon. There are six distinct sub-groups of the Ibibio: the Annang or Western Ibibio, the Eastern or Ibibio proper, the Northern or Enyong, the Southern or Eket (including Oron), the Delta or Andoni-Ibeno and the Riverain or Efik (Forde and Jones, 1950). The Ibibio seem to have lived in their present location for centuries, although some of their myths suggest migration from an area or place named Ibom, probably in the eastern part of modern Igboland. From the late 1600s the Efik of Calabar carried out highly lucrative trade with the West, acquiring such prestige items as guns and swords for ceremonial use, until south-east Nigeria became a British Protectorate. After initial resistance in a number of areas, all the Ibibio groups were under British rule by 1910, and this, together with intensive missionary activity throughout the 20th century, has had a profound effect upon their traditional socio-political and religious systems and their art.

Ibibio art is well represented in collections of African art all over the world, and there are a number of major holdings (e.g. London, BM), though even these do not do justice to the great variety of Ibibio forms and styles.

1. Artists, materials and tools. 2. Mask and masquerade. 3. Figure sculpture. 4. Funerary arts. 5. Body arts. 6. Puppetry. 7. Drums.

1. ARTISTS, MATERIALS AND TOOLS. The most talented and prolific of Ibibio artists come from the Annang areas of Abak and Ikot Ekpene. In the 1970s there were more than 50 full-time wood-carvers satisfying local demand in the Annang area, while there were only very few working among other Ibibio-speaking groups. In the main, Annang carvers use two types of wood, *ukpo* (*Alstoria congensis*) and *ukot* (*Triplochiton scheroxylon*), both of which are lightweight and soft. Two hardwoods, *nkobia* and *ukwa*, believed to contain powerful spirits, are used only for such special carvings as the most potent Ekpo masks (*see* §2 below). Locally made, iron-bladed tools purchased from Igbo smiths have been replaced by such imported tools as knives, machetes, small axes, adzes, chisels, files and saws. A finished carving is smoothed with the rough side of a *ukuole* leaf or with sandpaper, before being painted, in the past with natural pigments, more recently with imported gloss paint.

In the past, an entire village might commission a carver, sometimes with an apprentice, who would then live in the village for a year or more. He would be provided generously with food and drink and paid handsomely. A good carver was held in high esteem and acclaimed widely. Probably the greatest 20th-century carver was Akpan Chukwu (*d* 1952) of Utu Etim Ekpo. Such communal patronage has declined, sculptors instead working in their own homes where they are visited by their clients. In the 1940s the carvers of Ikot Abia Osom, an Annang village near Ikot Ekpene, formed a cooperative, which flourished to such an extent that Ikot Ekpene became recognized as one of the largest craft centres in West Africa. These carvers have produced works in large quantities and sold them at prices that undercut those of other artists. Although the carving techniques of the cooperative have remained much the same, there have been some important innovations, such as the involvement of women in the decoration of completed carvings, and the incorporation into the repertory of designs from other Ibibio groups.

2. MASK AND MASQUERADE. The most popular artistic genre among the Ibibio is masking. Men, women and children all participate, although the use of carved wooden face masks and cap masks is restricted to youths and men, even when female characters are represented. Boys sometimes wear small, brightly coloured face masks from Ikot Ekpene, but otherwise tend to wear masks of plant fibre or cloth. Women wear headdresses with tableau superstructures; they never use face masks.

The best-known genre is that of the face masks made for the men's ancestor cult, Ekpo, the principal Ibibio regulatory society, exercising administrative, legislative, judicial and ritual functions. Once a year, and at members' funerals, Ekpo maskers impersonate the spirits of the ancestors who have temporarily returned to the land of the living. There are two main types of Ekpo mask, reflecting the dichotomy between restless ghosts (*idiok ekpo*), portrayed by 'ugly' and aggressive characters with fierce expressions or faces distorted or eaten away by disease, and spirits (*mfon ekpo*) who have safely reached the underworld, played by gentle and 'fair' maskers, with sensitively carved features.

Distinctive styles have evolved in different parts of Ibibioland, by far the greatest variety being found among the Annang, where a particular style was often specific to a single village. In the Ikot Abassi (Opobo) area, a common type of Ekpo mask has large hooded eyes, bulging cheeks, a hinged jaw and flapping ears of hide or metal. By contrast, a typical Idiok Ekpo mask from the Annang settlement of Utu Etim Ekpo might consist of one large face, with a smaller face or series of faces on either side, each with double sets of eyes, the whole surmounted by a carved representation of a human skull (see fig. 1). In addition to such black masks with their facial distortions and depending on the area, Idiok Ekpo maskers often blackened their bodies with a charcoal concoction, sometimes with stripes of coloured earth pigment on the legs and body, and with various forms of black raffia bandoleers and skirts. A brass bell was sometimes worn over the

1. Ibibio Idiok Ekpo masker, Utu Etim Ekpo, Abak, Nigeria; from a photograph by Jill Salmons

buttocks, while a weapon, a machete or bow and arrows—with which to attack non-initiates, especially women—was always carried.

In general, Mfon Ekpo masks are in a fairly naturalistic style, representing such aspects of feminine beauty as a small, closed mouth and narrow, petite eyes. The light colours of Mfon Ekpo are said to represent daylight, when *ekpo* spirits return to earth to bring blessings, while *ekpo* ghosts venture out only at night and are therefore represented in black (Messenger, 1973). In some Ibibio communities, however, light-coloured Ekpo maskers are not beneficent. For example, in the Itu area the Ayara Ekpo masker wears a costume of brightly coloured cloth and white goat fur, its limbs dotted with white and yellow clay. Although it moves, like Mfon Ekpo, in a gentle manner, it can execute wrongdoers. In the 1980s, in some Annang groups, Mfon Ekpo face masks were surmounted by a superstructure incorporating mirrors and figures of maidens. As they appear on public occasions, these characters are often referred to as Urua or 'market' Ekpo.

Ekpo society rituals vary considerably from place to place, but, generally, at the commencement of the Ekpo season new members are taken to a lodge in a sacred grove where they are initiated into the society's secrets. They participate in singing, dancing and feasting prior to their first public performance in the local market-place. The maskers are led into the arena by the Akwa Ekpo ('leader of ghosts') who, together with the drummers, invokes each ancestor and dictates individual performances. It is believed that on donning a mask the wearer becomes possessed by the ancestral spirit and thus not wholly responsible for his behaviour, which may include fits of shaking and frenzied dancing, vicious attacks on bystanders and destruction of houses and other property. In order to control the most powerful and feared masks, an escort of up to six non-masked members may be provided. They control their charge with a rope halter and break eggs on the mask to 'cool' it.

In southern Ibibio country small, circular masks are found, as well as representations of round faces on rectangular wood panels arranged in the form of a miniature pitched roof (Neyt, 1979). Little is known about the function of the masks, but their distribution is known to have extended beyond Eket into such other areas as Oron and Okobo. The genre is unusual among Ibibio styles in that the configuration of the mask is often very flat, and the facial features are carved in low relief, with crescentic, moonlike eyes.

The peculiar Cross River forest land trait of covering masks with animal skin (*see* EJAGHAM, §1) was adopted in Ibibioland only temporarily and in a few places. The vehicle for this diffusion was Ikem, a recreational song, dance and masking club for both sexes that originated among the Efut and Efik in the 1890s. Ikem became popular throughout south-east Nigeria in the 1900s and 1910s but had died out by the 1940s. The original masquerade employed skin-covered masks of the type used by the Ejagham, including headdresses in the form of a female human head with an elaborate hornlike coiffure of the type worn by girls in the 'coming-out' ceremony following fattening (*see* §5 below). Another type of skin-covered cap mask was in the form of a male head surmounted by a British-style crown. Such masks, together with accompanying paraphernalia, were bought from the Efik and used in many Ibibio villages. Some Ibibio artists copied the technique of covering wooden sculpture with skin and adopted the mask style to local aesthetic taste. Skin-covered Ikem masks were still in use in the 1970s among the Ika, a small western Ibibio group who do not possess Ekpo and for whom Ikem is the principal funerary and entertainment masquerade. Although Ikem is extinct elsewhere, the horn-coiffure cap mask form has been incorporated into masks used in Ibibio plays. These masks, however, are decorated with modern paints rather than covered with animal skin.

Probably because of the central importance of Ekpo in most Ibibio groups, however, the diffusion of the Ejagham 'Leopard Society', Ngbe, known among the Ibibio as Ekpe, has been rather spasmodic and short-term, except in such villages with strong Efik ties as Oron and Itu, where it is the dominant regulatory society, holding regular meetings and masquerades. Annang craftsmen excel in the production of Ekpe woven string costumes with coloured horizontal stripes. These are either commissioned or bought 'off the peg' at craft stalls in Ikot Ekpene. The same shops supply brass bells of the type worn at the waist by Ekpe masqueraders, as well as raffia and wood models of masquerade figures for the tourist trade.

3. Figure sculpture. A wide range of figure sculpture has been produced in Ibibioland, particularly by Annang carvers. Probably the largest standing figures are those used in the sacred groves of the Ekpo cult and sometimes displayed at masquerades. Two splendid examples are those in the Southern Ibibio style representing Eka Ekpo ('Mother of Ekpo') and Akpan Ekpo ('First Son of Ekpo'), two of the most fearsome and dangerous characters in the Ekpo ensemble (London, BM; for illustration see Talbot, facing p. 188).

Traditionally, when a person was ill or injured he or she consulted the diviner or *abia idiong*, who would identify the moral and mystical cause of the complaint. Such consultations took place in the *idiong* shrine, which was typically furnished with carved wooden animal and human figures and pots containing magical substances. Such shrines are the source of many of the carved dogs and other quadrupeds, owls and other birds, tortoises and human figures found in many African art collections. Dogs play an important role as hunting companions in Ibibio folklore, owls are associated with witchcraft, and tortoises are symbols of the female sex (Talbot). In response to the problem of infertility, for example, the diviner would manipulate wooden figures of a copulating couple as part of magical procedures to induce fertility. Ibibio women's desire to be healthy, plump and sexually attractive was exploited by the institution, known as *mbobo*, involving their pre-nuptial seclusion and fattening (*see* §5 below). In connection with this, seated and standing female figures, often corpulent, in *mbobo* attire and with whitened bodies painted with lines of dark vegetable-dye decoration, were employed by the diviner on behalf of clients who aspired to this condition (see fig. 2). Also connected with *mbobo* is the small wooden carving, called *udeng*, of a woman with a naturalistic head (sometimes two-faced) and a body carved in the form of a paddle. Above the head is a phallic projection forming the handle by which the *udeng* is held while the *mbobo* girls are in procession or dancing.

Among some Ibibio-speaking groups it was customary for a commemorative shrine, known as *ngwomo*, to be erected in honour of a deceased elder and to provide a temporary resting-place for his spirit before its final transmigration to the underworld. Until the early 20th century such shrines were furnished with wooden sculptures representing the deceased's achievements. In one fine example, a column of human figures, each with its feet upon another's head, forms the centre-pole of the *ngwomo*, while other figures are at either side of the pole (for illustration see Talbot, facing p. 142). Another (London, Horniman Mus. Lib.), probably made for a southern Ibibio funerary shrine (*see* §4 below), represents a man seated on a barrel. The figure wears on its head a representation of a fish-eagle feather headdress indicating that the deceased was a holder of one of the most exclusive of Ibibio titles, Inam, initiation into which converted a prominent elder into a semi-deity, in effect preparing the title holder for the transition to life after death.

Ibibio belief in the power of the ancestors is one of the most persistent aspects of the traditional religious system, and figures, as well as masks, representing them provide one of the major channels for Ibibio artistic expression. In Oron, each male ancestor was commemorated in the

2. Ibibio carving of fattening-room girl (*mbobo*), 20th century

form of a hardwood carving, known as *ekpu*, which was kept in the men's meeting-house. Such figures (usually 1.0–1.3 m h.) wore European or African headgear and had bearded faces, bulbous stomachs and emblems of lineage office, often in both hands. More than 600 such carvings were collected by Kenneth Murray in the 1920s, 1930s and 1940s (now Oron, N. Mus.), though not all survived the Nigerian Civil War of 1967–70, when much of the collection was destroyed. In other areas, ancestral shrines sometimes contained figurative sculpture, but few have survived. Rarely, if ever, were women commemorated by carved figures, though they were represented by special pots (Murray).

The prevalent Ibibio belief in water-dwelling spirits, which can bring great fortune or cause fishing grounds to become barren and people to drown, has provided the basis for the powerful sculptural form known in pidgin English as 'Mamy Wata'. This has been shown (Salmons, 1977) to have been influenced by the introduction into

3. Ibibio 'Mamy Wata' sculpture by Joseph Chukwu of Utu Etim Ekpo, Abak, Nigeria

south-east Nigeria *c.* 1900 of a German print of an Indian snake charmer. Following the print's iconography, carved representations of the water spirit represent a large female figure with long, flowing black hair, her chest and arms wreathed with snakes. Such figures are often seated in a canoe accompanied by seven paddlers (see fig. 3). Some *abia idiong* and other priests specializing in Mamy Wata use such carvings, either placed in shrines or as head-dresses, to initiate novices into the Mamy Wata cult, or to relieve them of affliction caused by her. While the calling of a person by spirits such as *inam* and *idiong* is thought to be beneficial, there is an ambivalent attitude to Mamy Wata. Those afflicted are believed to be lured to her watery den, where they become enchanted with wealth and beauty. On their return to the normal world, however, such persons become sterile, mad or both.

4. FUNERARY ARTS. In addition to the wood sculpture placed in the commemorative shrine, or *ngwomo* (*see* §3 above), there are three other spheres of Ibibio funerary arts. Patchwork and appliqué cloths are used to adorn the interior of the *ngwomo*, mural paintings decorate both the inner and outer walls of the female shrine, *nduongo*, and both men and women are commemorated in cement sculpture (Salmons, 1980). In southern, central and western areas of Ibibioland a man's memorial shrine consisted traditionally of a large structure of bamboo poles and palm mats, while that for women consisted of an earth building in the form of a miniature hut thatched with palm mats. In some Annang clans a patchwork cotton cloth, with a central appliquéd panel depicting aspects of the deceased's life, was hung in the *ngwomo* (see fig. 4). To be regarded as a great warrior was one of the primary aspirations of the Ibibio male, and evidence of having taken a man's head in combat was a prerequisite for all those with political ambition. Originally open only to the successful warrior, the Ebie-Owo (Annang) or Ekong (Ibibio) society had become, by the early 20th century, a prestige association open to any wealthy man. Membership of the warriors' society was not only the avenue to political power but also guaranteed provision of an elaborate funeral ceremony and memorial shrine, and it continued well-being in the spirit world. Much of the iconography of the *ngwomo* shrine cloth relates to the part played by the deceased, when he lived, in Ebie-Owo or Ekong.

The traditional female funerary shrine, *nduongo*, contained such items as cooking and water pots, and wooden pestles and mortars. Kenneth Murray's field photographs (now Lagos, N. Mus.) indicate that many *nduongo* were richly decorated with mural paintings stylistically similar to the figures on the appliqué panel of the shrine cloth. Executed in earth pigments, especially white, black, pink and yellow, they symbolized the status of the deceased woman in such institutions as Mbobo and Nyama. This art form appears to have declined severely after the 1930s and 1940s; only one post-1970 example is known to scholars. In 1977 the Annang master carver Udo-Nwa Matthew Ekpe (*d* 1980) of Ikot Obong, near Ikot Ekpene, was commissioned to decorate a woman's shrine at the

4. Ibibio funerary shrine, *ngwomo*, for deceased Annang elder, with patchwork and appliqué cloth by Udoh Umor Aran Ekot of Abiakpong Ikot Essien, Ikot Ekpene, Nigeria; from a photograph by Jill Salmons

National Museum, Oron. No other surviving example of traditional *nduongo* art is known.

The earliest commemorative cement sculptures in Ibibioland date to the 1920s. Starting with the Christian cross, local artists soon developed their own style of tall pedestals on which were modelled seated or standing representations of the deceased. In the 1940s a plaque, in the form of a headstone with a portrait of the deceased modelled upon it, was fashionable. From the early 1970s an open-sided, cement houselike structure, complete with zinc roof, was the setting for naturalistic life-sized figures. From the 1980s Ibibio cement sculpture became increasingly realistic and lifelike, due to the influence of photography and to the extensive work throughout south-east Nigeria of the realist cement sculptor Sunday Jack Akpan (*b c.* 1940) of Ikot Obio Offong, near Uyo (Nicklin and Salmons, 1977).

5. BODY ARTS. The most significant Ibibio body arts relate to the pre-nuptial seclusion and fattening of women (*see also* EJAGHAM, §6). This Ibibio institution was in the hands of the main women's society, Ebre (Nyama among the Annang). At the commencement of her seclusion the young woman, *mbobo*, underwent a form of clitoridectomy believed to ensure easy childbirth in later life and to discourage licentiousness. Senior women subjected the *mbobo* to regular feeding and massage, and to training in such female domestic tasks as cooking, as well as polite decorum. Among the Efik, crafts were practised in the 'fattening-room', including the decoration with intricate pokerwork designs of gourds, fans and musical instruments. Some Efik families taught their *mbobo* to decorate cotton table-linen with delicate appliqué-work, known as *mbufari*, while others taught their girls the craft of relief decoration of figurative, floral and pictographic-script (*nsibidi*) motifs upon brass trays and bowls imported from Birmingham, England.

On a pre-arranged day at the end of the seclusion, all the *mbobo* of the village were decorated by female artists. Their faces and bodies were painted with complex designs and their hair arranged into elaborate coiffures pinned with large brass combs. On their legs they wore brass coils fixed by the blacksmith and around the waist a profusion of bands of coral and imported glass beads. A single large coral bead was often worn at the neck. A bandoleer or chest halter of such rich cloth as velvet or silk and decorated with mirror glass completed the outfit. In some areas each girl would be inspected by Ekpo masqueraders, who would praise plump girls but abuse others, to their and their families' shame. Having passed inspection, the *mbobo* would be carried on a supporter's shoulders to the village square where she would dance before the assembled community. Typically, the *mbobo* would carry an umbrella, a fan or small doll in one hand, while accompanying herself on a whistle or harmonica.

6. PUPPETRY. Traditionally, Ibibio puppet plays were one of the prime activities of the Ekong drama club, not to be confused with the warriors' society, Ekong, found in the Annang, eastern Ibibio and Opobo areas. The main function of the Ekong society was to entertain through plays, songs, stilt-dances, acrobatics and, most of all, puppet plays. Such performances commented upon and satirized local characters and events, serving both to express and channel social tension. In particular, puppet plays were employed to lampoon those people and events that could not normally be commented upon for fear of reprisals.

Ekong was at its height during the 1940s, 1950s and 1960s (Jeffreys, 1951; Messenger, 1971), but performances were still held into the 1980s. Each Ekong group comprised a village-based secret society, the members having to pay an initiation fee and undergo rigorous rehearsals for a period of up to seven years. An Ekong company might have up to a hundred members. At the start of an Ekong performance a 2 m high booth was erected at one side of the village square to serve as changing-room and stage. Carved wooden puppets, with articulated jaws and limbs operated by strings passing through the figure's body, represented a variety of characters. These included the King and Queen of England, the local District Officer, court messengers and policemen, as well as such characters as the Cuckold, the Hausa Trader, the Poor Hunter and the Sexually Lax Woman; dangerous animals and ghouls might also appear. Each puppet was held in one hand while the strings or wires were manipulated with the other to create the movements of limbs and the motion of the lower jaw as if in speech. The puppeteers spoke through reed voice-disguisers, both to ensure anonymity and to emphasize that the characters were spirits rather than living persons. The Ekong puppet institution appears to have been unique to the Ibibio, although their south-western neighbours, the Ogoni, also have puppet plays.

7. DRUMS. In the past, drums were used to summon warriors at times of inter-tribal warfare, to announce the death of a chief or the passing of new laws, and to provide music for masquerade and other performances. Particularly in those parts of Ibibioland bordering Igbo country, gigantic slit-drums (l. *c.* 4 m, diam. 1.3 m), hewn from forest trees, were still to be seen in a few village halls into the 1980s. They are carved in human form, with a head projecting at one end and feet at the other. The sides are decorated with low-relief carvings of such totemic species as pythons and tortoises, and with representations of such human activities as warfare and copulation. Traditionally, a village possessed a complementary pair of male and female drums. Both the drums and the associated cult are known as *ikorok*. Membership of Ikorok demanded the presentation of a human skull taken from an enemy in battle. The carving of a drum could take up to a year, and traditionally the spirit of the new drum required the sacrifice of a human being, preferably that of its carver, before it could be played.

BIBLIOGRAPHY

P. A. Talbot: *Life in Southern Nigeria: The Magic, Beliefs and Customs of the Ibibio Tribe* (London, 1923)

A. J. Udo-Ema: 'Fattening Girls in Oron, Calabar Province', *Nigeria Mag.*, xxi (1940), pp. 386–9

G. I. Jones: 'Masked Plays of South-east Nigeria', *Geog. Mag.*, xviii/5 (1945), pp. 190–99

K. C. Murray: 'Ekpu: The Ancestor Figures of Oron, Southern Nigeria', *Burl. Mag.*, lxxxix (1947), pp. 310–14

D. Forde and G. I. Jones: *The Ibo and Ibibio-speaking Peoples of South-eastern Nigeria* (Oxford, 1950), Ethnographic Survey of Africa, Western Africa, pt 3
M. D. W. Jeffreys: 'The Ekong Players', *E. Anthropologist*, v/1 (1951), pp. 41–7
——: 'The Burial Bird for an Okuku', *Afr. Stud.* [S. Africa], xiv/3 (1955), pp. 134–7
U. Beier: 'Ibibio Monuments', *Nigeria Mag.*, li (1956), pp. 318–36
M. D. W. Jeffreys: 'The Nyama Society of the Ibibio Women', *Afr. Stud.* [S. Africa], lv/1 (1956), pp. 15–28
D. C. Simmons: 'The Depiction of Gangosa on Efik-Ibibio Masks', *Man*, xviii (1957), pp. 1–4, 17–20, pl. B
J. C. Messenger: 'Annang Art, Drama and Social Control', *Afr. Stud. Bull.*, v/2 (1962), pp. 29–35
V. F. Butler: 'Cement Funeral Sculpture in Eastern Nigeria', *Nigeria Mag.*, lxxvii (1963), pp. 117–24
J. C. Messenger: 'Ibibio Drama', *Africa*, lxi/3 (1971), pp. 208–22
——: 'The Carver in Annang Society', *The Traditional Artist in African Societies*, ed. W. L. d'Azevedo (Bloomington and London, 1973), pp. 101–27
K. Nicklin: 'The Ibibio Musical Pot', *Afr. A.*, vii/1 (1973), pp. 50–55, 92
——: 'Ibibio Metalwork', *Afr. A.*, x/1 (1976), pp. 20–23, 98
——: *Guide to the National Museum, Oron* (Lagos, 1977)
K. Nicklin and J. Salmons: 'S. J. Akpan of Nigeria', *Afr. A.*, xi/1 (1977), pp. 30–34
J. Salmons: 'Mamy Wata', *Afr. A.*, x/3 (1977), pp. 8–15, 87–8
F. Neyt: *L'Art Eket collection Azar* (Paris, 1979)
K. W. Nicklin: 'Annang Ibibio Raphia Weaving', *Textiles of Africa*, ed. D. Idiens and K. Ponting (Bath, 1980), pp. 142–62
J. R. Salmons: 'Funerary Shrine Cloths of the Annang-Ibibio, South East Nigeria', *Textiles of Africa*, ed. D. Idiens and K. Ponting (Bath, 1980), pp. 99–141
——: 'Fat Is Beautiful', *A. Links* (September, 1981), pp. 22–5
G. I. Jones: *The Art of Eastern Nigeria* (Cambridge, 1984)
E. Leib and R. Romano: 'Reign of the Leopard: Ngbe Ritual', *Afr. A.*, xviii/1 (1984), pp. 48–57, 94–6
K. Nicklin: 'Cross River Studies', *Afr. A.*, xviii/1 (1984), pp. 24–7, 96
K. Nicklin and J. Salmons: 'Cross River Art Styles', *Afr. A.*, xviii/1 (1984), pp. 28–43, 93–4
J. R. Salmons: 'Martial Arts of the Annang', *Afr. A.*, xix/1 (1985), pp. 57–63, 87–8
K. Nicklin and J. Salmons: '*Ikem*: The History of a Masquerade in Southeast Nigeria', *West African Masks and Cultural Systems*, ed. S. L. Kasfir (Tervuren, 1988), pp. 123–49, pls between pp. 152–3

JILL SALMONS

Ibiza. *See under* BALEARIC ISLANDS.

Ibler, Drago (*b* Zagreb, 14 Aug 1894; *d* Novo Mesto, 12 Sept 1964). Croatian architect and teacher. He gained his Diploma of Architecture at the Technische Hochschule in Dresden. In 1921 he joined the group around Le Corbusier and *L'Esprit Nouveau* in Paris and then studied (1922–4) at the Staatliche Kunstakademie, Berlin, in the studio of Hans Poelzig. Ibler's District Labour Insurance Building (1923), Zagreb, was the first project to reflect the spirit of the Modern Movement in Yugoslavia. Between 1925 and 1935 he established the 'Zagreb School' with fellow architects Drago Galić (*b* 1907), Mladen Kauzlarić, Stjepan Planić and others. In 1929 he founded Zemlja (The Land), a group of progressive artists. He was also a member of CIAM. In the 1920s and 1930s Ibler worked on numerous architectural competitions, but with little success due to ideological resistance to his progressive ideas. He also executed villas on the Island of Korčula, several industrial buildings, and the District Labour Insurance Building (1932), Skopje, which was important in introducing Le Corbusier's principles, including ribbon windows, to Yugoslavia. In 1926 Ibler became a professor at the Zagreb Academy of Fine Arts, where he taught architecture until 1941. He then joined the University of Geneva as a lecturer in architecture. After 1950, again in Zagreb, he led a Master Studio in architecture and returned to teaching at the Academy of Fine Arts. After World War II he encouraged the humanization of architecture by means of more decorative, sculptural and harmonious compositions, for example in his designs for the new opera house (1948; unexecuted) in Belgrade; the Yugoslav Embassy (1959; unexecuted), Moscow; Tito's residence (1961–4), Zagreb; and several residential blocks in Zagreb, in Martićeva, Smičiklasova and Vlaška Streets.

BIBLIOGRAPHY

M. Krleža: 'Slučaj arhitekta Iblera' [The case of the architect Ibler], *Književna Repub.*, iv (1924–5), pp. 170–73
M. Peršen: 'Zagreb u zamislima projektanata' [Zagreb as imagined by the designers], *Vjesnik* (14 March 1954)

PAUL TVRTKOVIĆ

Ibn al-Bawwab [Abū'l-Ḥasan ʿAlī ibn Hilāl al-Bawwāb] (*d* Baghdad, 1022). Arab calligrapher and illuminator. He began as a house decorator but turned to calligraphy and refined the 'proportioned script' developed a century earlier by Ibn Muqla, in which letters were measured in terms of dots, circles and semicircles. An intimate of court circles in Baghdad, Ibn al-Bawwab was appointed librarian to the Buyid ruler Baha' al-Dawla (*reg* 998–1012) at Shiraz. There Ibn al-Bawwab calligraphed the volume missing from a Koran manuscript penned by his predecessor so perfectly that the patron was unable to distinguish the new work from the original. In addition to an epistle and didactic poem on penmanship, Ibn al-Bawwab is said to have copied 64 manuscripts of the Koran, but only one survives: a manuscript copied at Baghdad in 1000–01 (Dublin, Chester Beatty Lib., MS. 1431). The small volume contains 286 folios (trimmed size 175×135 mm). Each page of text has 15 lines in *naskh* script written with a straight-cut reed pen to produce letters of uniform thickness. At the beginning and end of the volume are five double folios of illumination and tables in which brown, white, green and crimson are added to the sepia, blue and gold used on the text pages. The graceful flowing script and the delicately balanced ornament show this manuscript to be a masterpiece of Islamic calligraphy (*see* ISLAMIC ART, §III, 2(iii)(c) and fig. 97).

BIBLIOGRAPHY

Enc. Islam/2
D. S. Rice: *The Unique Ibn al-Bawwab Manuscript in the Chester Beatty Library* (Dublin, 1955/*R* Paris, 1972) [with facs.]
Qur'āns and Bindings from the Chester Beatty Library (exh. cat. by D. James, London, Islam. Cult. Cent., 1980), nos 18–19
Y. Tabbaa: 'The Transformation of Arabic Writing: Part I, Qur'ānic Calligraphy', *A. Orient.*, xxi (1992), pp. 119–48

Ibn Muqla [Abū ʿAlī Muḥammad ibn ʿAlī ibn Muqla] (*b* Baghdad, 885–6; *d* Baghdad, 20 July 940). Arab vizier and calligrapher. He was a tax collector in the province of Fars in south-west Iran and was then made secretary in the central administration in charge of opening and dispatching official letters. He served as vizier to three Abbasid caliphs: al-Muqtadir (*reg* 908–32), al-Qahir (*reg* 932–4) and al-Radi (*reg* 934–40), but due to political intrigue he was imprisoned, had his right hand and his tongue cut off, and died in disgrace. He is renowned as a prophet in the field of handwriting for introducing a new method of writing known as the 'proportioned script' (Arab. *al-khaṭṭ al-mansūb*; *see* ISLAMIC ART, §III, 2(iii)(c)). Applying the nib of the reed pen to the written surface to form a rhombic dot, he reckoned the number of dots used to form a straight-line *alif*, the first letter of the Arabic alphabet, and then calculated all other letters in relation to the *alif*. The script was later perfected by Ibn al-Bawwab, who added artistic elegance to Ibn Muqla's systematized draughtsmanship. No works by Ibn Muqla's hand survive.

BIBLIOGRAPHY

Enc. Islam/2

D. S. Rice: *The Unique Ibn al-Bawwab Manuscript in the Chester Beatty Library* (Dublin, 1955), pp. 5–8

Y. Tabbaa: 'The Transformation of Arabic Writing: Part I, Qur'ānic Calligraphy', *A. Orient.*, xxi (1992), pp. 119–48

NABIL SAIDI

Ibo. *See* IGBO.

Ibrahim Pasha [Nevşehirli Ibrahim Pasha] (*b* Nevşehir, ?1662; *d* Istanbul, 30 Sept 1730). Ottoman patron. He was Grand Vizier to the Ottoman sultan Ahmed III (*see* OTTOMAN, §II(5)) from 1718 to his execution. The son of one Ali Agha, Ibrahim came to Istanbul and rose in the palace service. Under the influence of the Ottoman historian Naima (1655–1716), the ruling élite of the Ottoman empire regarded the glorious apogee of Ottoman power in the 16th century as a model for cultural and political life. Ibrahim was a major contemporary artistic patron, and his active interest in promoting a revival of 16th-century Ottoman culture was in large part responsible for the serious classical revival aspect of the Tulip Period (*Lâle Devri*), the other being a light and playful style best typified by the painting of the court artist LEVNI. Along with the Sultan and Mehmed Yirmisikiz Çelebi, ambassador to France, Ibrahim Pasha also encouraged Ibrahim Müteferrika (*c.* 1670–1745) to open the first printing press in Istanbul (1727; *see* ISLAMIC ART, §III, 8).

Ibrahim Pasha's charitable foundations included various religious and public-service monuments. The most important of his foundations include the mosque complex (1726) bearing his name in the new town of Nevşehir, and the *darülhadis* (a specialized institution of higher learning devoted to studying the traditions of the Prophet Muhammad) and fountain (1720), one of the loveliest in Istanbul, at Şehzadebaşı. Ibrahim Pasha's most significant act of artistic patronage, however—although one that did not long survive him—may have been his attempt to revitalize the moribund Ottoman ceramic industry of Iznik by bringing potters to the Tekfur Saray quarter of Istanbul in 1724 and establishing new ceramic ateliers there to make revetment tiles for important monuments. Iznik ceramics of the 16th century were one of the symbolic touchstones of the Ottoman golden age, and the foundation of the Tekfur Saray ateliers may be seen as self-conscious artistic revival with political and moral overtones. The most splendid example of their use is in the Istanbul mosque (1731) of Hekimoğlu Ali Paşa, Ibrahim Pasha's successor.

BIBLIOGRAPHY

Enc. Islam/2: 'Ibrāhīm Pas̲h̲a, Nevs̲h̲ehirli'; *İslam Ansiklopedesi*: 'Nevşehirli İbrahim Paşa'

T. Öz: *Turkish Ceramics* (Ankara, 1954), pp. 37–42

W. B. Denny: 'Revivalism in Turkish Art: The Hekimoğlu Ali Pasha Mosque in Istanbul', *Seventh International Congress of Turkish Art: Warsaw, 1983*, pp. 81–7

WALTER B. DENNY

Ibrim. *See* QASR IBRIM.

Ica–Chincha. Pre-Columbian culture of South America that extended throughout several valleys on the south coast of Peru and flourished between *c.* AD 1000 and 1476. The Ica–Chincha pottery style was first recognized by the German archaeologist Max Uhle, and regional variations have since been defined by archaeologists from the University of California at Berkeley, especially by Dorothy Menzel. The Ica Valley appears to have been the main cultural centre, while the Chincha Valley seems to have had greater political significance. Commerce was important; pottery was clearly held in high esteem, since it has been found at sites on the central coast and inland in the Río Pampas area near Ayacucho, and it seems, moreover, to have formed the principal indicator of cultural cohesion and diversity between the valleys. The main feature of the decorated wares is a polychrome style, usually with a red base overpainted with white and black designs. Motifs are frequently geometric, with many designs taken from textiles, including diamonds, stepped lines and zigzag lines. There are also many depictions of birds and fish that are difficult to see in the maze of angular designs. A characteristic vessel shape is a jar with a rounded base, globular body, narrow neck and flaring rim. Dishes with a flanged rim are also common. As on NAZCA and HUARI pottery, designs are placed within bands or areas with a black border. The decoration on Ica vessels differs from Chincha vessels: the former have small, closely spaced elements covering much or all of the design surface, while the latter have larger design components; and Ica red is a dark, muted orange-red of a slightly different hue from Chincha red. The arrival of INCA influence after AD 1476 brought little stylistic change, though a few new forms occur, such as a drum bottle with an aryballoid or globular neck.

BIBLIOGRAPHY

M. Uhle: 'Ancient Civilizations of Ica Valley', *U. CA Pubns Amer. Archaeol. & Ethnol.*, xxi (1924), pp. 128–32

——: 'Explorations at Chincha', *U. CA Pubns Amer. Archaeol. & Ethnol.*, xxi (1924), pp. 55–94

P. J. Lyon: 'Innovation through Archaism: The Origins of the Ica Pottery Style', *Ñawpa Pacha*, iv (1966), pp. 31–62

D. Menzel: 'The Pottery of Chincha', *Ñawpa Pacha*, iv (1966), pp. 77–144

——: *Pottery Style and Society in Ancient Peru: Art as a Mirror of History in the Ica Valley, 1350–1570* (Berkeley, 1976)

GEORGE BANKES

Ice-house. Building for storing ice for summer use. Since antiquity ice has been stored in many different structures. In mountain areas it was common to pack ice into deep pits, often lined and roofed with straw or timber. Ice-houses were built of many different materials, such as timber, mud or brick. They were rectangular, square, conical or cylindrical structures, which until the 19th century were usually all or partly underground. The most usual form of British ice-house was an underground, inverted egg-shaped building with a diameter of *c.* 3–6 m and a depth of *c.* 5–10 m, with brick cavity walls, an entrance tunnel and a sump or drain at the base of the well. By contrast, the great ice-houses of Persia reached diameters of 14 m and overall heights of over 16 m. Ice-houses were built as early as the 2nd millennium BC in Mesopotamia and later in China and throughout the Greek and Roman worlds. Ice was always a luxury but a remarkably available one. The Italian courts of the 16th century enjoyed ice in many forms, and Louis XIV of France and his court followed suit, building many ice-houses throughout France in the 17th century. Under Charles II in the 1660s ice-houses were introduced into Britain from France and immediately became fashionable. By the end of the 19th century most English villages and country estates could boast at least one ice-house. In the early 1800s American entrepreneurs built vast timber ice-houses on the banks of the Great Lakes and, with increasingly efficient means of harvesting the ice and insulating timber ice-houses, a vast ice industry evolved, exporting ice all over the world. Ice-houses still exist in many countries, and they are still in use in some areas of the Middle East, Russia, China and Scandinavia. A late 20th-century survey in Britain listed over 3500 extant ice-houses. Australia is the only continent where no known ice-houses were built for the storage of natural ice.

BIBLIOGRAPHY
S. Beamon and S. Roaf: *The Ice-houses of Britain* (London, 1990)

SUSAN ROAF

Iceland, Republic of. Country occupying a large volcanic island (103,000 sq. km) in the North Atlantic Ocean (see fig. 1). It lies just south of the Arctic circle, *c.* 965 km west of Norway, 800 km north-west of Scotland and 260 km south-east of Greenland. Its capital and largest city is REYKJAVÍK. Iceland was uninhabited until Norwegian settlers and some Celtic settlers from Britain arrived in the late 9th century AD. The Alþingi, the representative governing assembly, was formed in 930, and Christianity was adopted in 1000. Iceland was an independent republic with fruitful and uninterrupted contact with other countries throughout Viking times and the early Middle Ages. A rich literary tradition developed from the mid-11th century to the end of the 13th. The Icelandic Commonwealth ended in feudal fightings in the 13th century when Iceland lost its independence and came under the rule of the kings of Norway (*c.* 1263) and later Denmark (1381). Their domination brought artistic stagnation and then decline from the Reformation (1550) until the 19th century. Other factors that contributed to this dark age of Icelandic culture were volcanic eruptions, deterioration in climate, disease, crop failure and famine in the 1740s, a Danish trade monopoly and a decline in the power of the Church. In the 19th century Iceland started to emerge from this period of cultural isolation. Such new technology as steamships and transoceanic cable improved links with other countries, and the influence of the Romantic movement in the early 19th century fuelled a growing spirit of nationalism. In 1863 the National Museum of Iceland (Þjóðminjasafn Íslands) was founded in Reykjavík, followed by the National Gallery of Iceland (Listasafn Íslands) in 1884. By the beginning of the 20th century a broad-based nationalistic and ambitious middle class began to emerge, which grew rapidly and was determined to cut the ties with Denmark. National sovereignty within the Danish Commonwealth in 1918 boosted Icelandic arts and culture, and the establishment of the Icelandic School of Arts and Crafts (Myndlista og Handíðas kóli Íslands) in 1939 provided a focal point for artists who had traditionally trained abroad. In 1944 Iceland declared its independence.

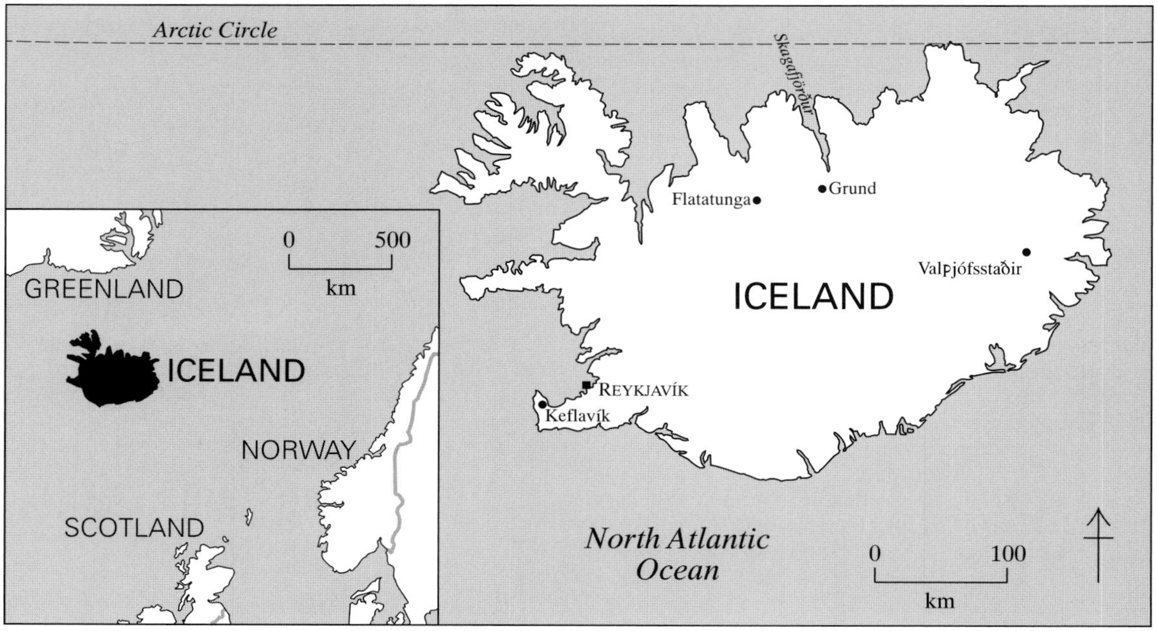

1. Map of Iceland; the capital city of REYKJAVÍK has a separate entry in this dictionary

I. Painting and sculpture. II. Architecture, interior decoration and furniture. III. Ceramics and glass. IV. Metalwork. V. Textiles.

I. Painting and sculpture.

1. BEFORE 1800. Icelandic medieval art has its roots chiefly in VIKING ART, which was part of the cultural heritage brought by the Norwegian settlers. It developed from a mixture of Viking and Romanesque art, with the gradual emergence of specifically Icelandic characteristics, particularly in wood-carving from the beginning of the 11th century. The only patrons in the impoverished, scattered, rural society were the chieftains and the Church. Church inventories from as early as 1185 and 1275 provide evidence of churches and cloisters richly decorated with objects in precious metals, textiles and carvings, most of which were imported. Few of these objects survive: many were destroyed during the Reformation, and many others were taken out of the country, by both Icelanders and foreigners, well into the 19th century. Contact with other countries through trade and travel resulted in a great variety and instability in style and iconography within one period and even within one piece of work. Nor was there a strict chronology of styles: the Romanesque, for example, which was at its most influential in the 12th century, continued to be used into the 19th. A great variety of wood-carvings from the beginning of the Romanesque style in the 11th and 12th centuries has been preserved. The oldest surviving wood panel (11th century; Reykjavík, N. Mus.) is from Flatatunga and is a good example of two different styles in one work. The lower half of the panel depicts holy figures carved in strong, simple outlines, while the upper half shows RINGERIKE ornament. Fragments of a remarkable wood-carving of a Byzantine *Last Judgement* (late 11th century; Reykjavík, N. Mus.), which originally measured 5.2×2.3 m, are believed to have originated from the hall of a chieftain's house in Flatatunga. The earliest preserved Romanesque crucifixion (early 12th century; Reykjavík, N. Mus.) is from Ufsir and shows Christ standing erect, crowned and with open eyes. A carved wooden door from a church at Valþjófsstaðir (*c.* 1200; Reykjavík, N. Mus.) retains only two of its original three circles; one shows scroll-shaped dragons (probably a symbol of evil); the other depicts two scenes from the romance of *Le Chevalier au lion.*

By the beginning of the 13th century a strong artistic tradition had developed in Iceland that incorporated both foreign influences (e.g. Gothic) from imported works and indigenous characteristics. Objects preserved from this time are plentiful and more varied; they include large numbers of mostly religious and legal illuminated manuscripts, which contain the only surviving examples of Icelandic medieval painting. The oldest preserved illuminations are found in a *Physiologus* (*c.* 1200; Reykjavík, Árni Magnusson Inst., AM 673a I–II) in a clear Romanesque style. It is preserved in two fragments of different dates, written in Icelandic and richly decorated. The numerous manuscripts of the 14th century show great variety in style, iconography and execution, reflecting many foreign influences. *Stjórn* (Reykjavík, Árni Magnusson Inst., AM 227) is an example of the height of the Gothic style in Iceland. It preserves chapters from the Old Testament in Icelandic translation and contains seven illuminated leaves of historiated initials with bar borders and numerous chapter initials of foliate design; the illustrations show considerable English influence. The illustrations in the legal manuscripts provide evidence of a strong tradition that made use of several pictorial cycles at the same time, most of which are found in *Jónsbók* (the law book passed by the Alþingi in 1282, which was copied more often than any other Icelandic work) of which the oldest preserved illuminated manuscript dates from *c.* 1300 (Reykjavík, Árni Magnusson Inst., AM 134). One of the major legal manuscripts is *Skarðsbók* (1363; Reykjavík, Árni Magnusson Inst., AM 350 folio), which is beautifully decorated with historiated initials with bar borders (see fig. 2). The style of the miniature is pure Gothic, but the foliate decoration shows strong Romanesque influences. The Icelandic *Sketchbook* (Reykjavík, Árni Magnusson Inst., AM 673a III) shows a range of styles from the 14th to the 16th century. It contains sketches of biblical and secular subjects and decorative motifs that may well have been models for large-scale paintings on church walls and altarpieces. It is possible that such religious paintings may have been common in Iceland but that examples have not survived because of the ephemeral nature of Icelandic building materials.

The production of manuscripts for export, mainly to Norway, came to a halt *c.* 1400. During the period of

2. Historiated initial, 66×65 mm, detail of a leaf from the Icelandic *Skarðsbók*, 1363 (Reykjavík, Árni Magnusson Institute, AM 350 folio, fol 51*r*)

artistic stagnation and economic and physical hardship from the 15th to the 19th century little was produced except for a few oil portraits and a modest amount of work by wood-carvers, silversmiths and weavers. The objects from this period that have been preserved in the National Museum, Reykjavík, show a characteristic Icelandic variety of iconography and styles. The Romanesque acanthus continued to be a dominant motif, with each generation of artists adding its own variations.

BIBLIOGRAPHY

S. Karlsson: *Islandsk bogeksport til Norge i middelalderen* [Icelandic book exports to Norway in the Middle Ages], Maal og minne (Christiania, 1909–)

H. Fett: 'Miniatyrer fra islandske haandskrifter' [Miniatures from Icelandic manuscripts], *Bergens Mus. Åb.*, ii/7 (1910), pp. 3-40

M. Þórðarson: 'Islands middelalderkunst' [The art of medieval Iceland], *Nord. Kult.*, xxvii (1931), pp. 336–43

H. Hermannsson: 'Icelandic Illuminated Manuscripts of the Middle Ages', *Corpus codicum islandicorum medii aevi*, vii (Copenhagen, 1935)

——: 'The Icelandic *Physiologus*', *Islandica*, xxvii (New York, 1938)

——: 'Illuminated Manuscripts of the *Jónsbók*', *Islandica*, xxviii (New York, 1940)

B. Th. Björnsson: *Íslenzka teiknibókin í Árnasafni* [Icelandic sketchbook in the Árnasafn] (Reykjavík, 1954)

K. Eldjárn: *Íslenzk list frá fyrri öldum* [Icelandic art from former times] (Reykjavík, 1957)

S. Jónsdóttir: *Býzönsk dómsdagsmynd i Flatatungu* (Reykjavík, 1959); Eng. trans. as *An 11th-century Byzantine Last Judgement* (London, 1959)

——: 'Gömul krossfestingarmynd' [Old Crucifixion], *Skírnir*, cxxxix (1965), pp. 134–47

M. M. Lárusson: 'Máldagi' [Church inventory], *Kulturhistorisk leksikon for nordisk middelalder* [Dictionary of cultural history for the Nordic Middle Ages], xi (Copenhagen, 1966), pp. 264–6

S. Jónsdóttir: *Lýsingar i Stjórnarhandriti*; Eng. trans. as *Illumination in a Manuscript of Stjórn* (Reykjavík, 1971)

Íslenzk myndlist i 1100 [1100 years of Icelandic art] (exh. cat. by B. Th. Björnsson, Reykjavík, Kjarvalsstaðir, 1974)

S. Jónsdóttir: 'Myndlist á landnáms- og þjóðoveldisöld' [Art in the settlement age and commonwealth], *Saga Íslands*, ii (1975), pp. 261–81

B. Nordal: 'Lögbókarhandritið Gks. 1154 folio: Íslenskt handrit' [The law-book manuscript Gks. 1154 folio: Icelandic manuscripts], *Skírnir*, clix (1985), pp. 160–81

BERA NORDAL

2. 1800 AND AFTER. At the beginning of the 19th century Iceland started to break out of the cultural isolation of the previous two centuries. Þorsteinn Illugason Hjaltalín (1770/1–1817), who styled himself 'the first Icelandic artist', settled in Brunswick, Germany, where he became a respected painter and miniaturist. Helgi Sigurðsson (1815–88) studied drawing at the Kongelige Danske Kunstakademi in Copenhagen, experimented with photography and painted and drew portraits of Icelandic poets and government officials. Sigurður Guðmundsson (1833–74) was the first Icelander to devote himself to art within Iceland and proved the most widely talented of 19th-century Icelandic artists. He studied at the Kongelige Danske Kunstakademi (1849–58) and was a prolific painter of portraits and altarpieces and a theatre designer. He campaigned for the establishment of the National Museum of Iceland (opened 1863), as well as being active in the Romantic movement's struggle for national renaissance. During the 1890s EINAR JÓNSSON, THÓRARINN B. THORLÁKSSON and ÁSGRÍMUR JÓNSSON all studied in Copenhagen, where Einar Jónsson soon came under the influence of the 19th-century Symbolist movement in sculpture, to which in time he added personal religious and occult elements. Thórarinn B. Thorláksson and Ásgrímur Jónsson were landscape painters preoccupied with the qualities of brightness peculiar to the Icelandic wilderness. Ásgrímur Jónsson soon turned away from Romantic realism and adopted a Post-Impressionist and, later, Expressionist style better suited to the interpretation of the massive quality of the Icelandic terrain.

Icelandic painting between 1918 and 1930 was strongly influenced by Post-Impressionism. JÓN STEFÁNSSON, who studied with Matisse (1908–10), introduced to Iceland the ideas of Cézanne and by so doing had a profound influence on the development of Icelandic artistic philosophy. He attracted a large number of followers, including Kristín Jónsdóttir (1888–1959) and JÚLÍANA SVEINSDÓTTIR, the first women artists to study and work in Iceland. However, many painters rejected specific artistic movements and adopted an eclectic position: one of the most notable and complex was JÓHANNES S. KJARVAL, who injected into his depiction of the lava landscapes of Iceland a personal fantasy akin to Symbolism and the Nabis group (see fig. 3). FINNUR JÓNSSON was the sole notable representative of German Expressionism in Icelandic art before 1930. During his studies in Germany (1921–5) he developed a personal quasi-Constructivist abstraction that attracted the attention of Kurt Schwitters, Herwarth Walden and Kandinsky. Icelandic sculptors inclined towards simple, classical forms. Nína Sæmundsson (1892–1965) adopted the southern European softness of Aristide Maillol, while ÁSMUNDUR SVEINSSON chose a much harder style: classicism soon gave ground to Cubism, which later became Expressionism. Around 1950 Sveinsson became one of the most important pioneers of abstract art.

Between 1930 and 1945 there was an ever-increasing internationalism in Icelandic art, with a particular emphasis on the post-Cubism of the Ecole de Paris and Scandinavian Expressionism. Painters turned from landscapes to interpretations of the conditions of the ordinary people at sea or in the countryside. SNORRI ARINBJARNAR, GUNNLAUGUR SCHEVING and THORVALDUR SKÚLASON all introduced Cubist elements into their figurative art. SIGURJÓN ÓLAFSSON was the first Icelandic sculptor to develop his own working methods within an expressionistic primitivism. JÓHANN BRIEM developed paintings in which Expressionism with an element of fantasy, and later existentialism, dealt with the links between the individual and his origins. In contrast JÓN ENGILBERTS emphasized social realism, using stylistic effects reminiscent of Munch and Kirchner.

Between 1945 and 1965 the visual arts were dominated by the abstract movement: geometric abstraction in the early 1950s, with lyrical abstraction beginning to gain adherents after 1956. In the summer of 1945 SVAVAR GUÐNASON, one of the leading colourists in Scandinavian abstract art who had been producing abstract paintings since 1937, held an exhibition of expressionistic abstract works in Reykjavík. The September Exhibitions (*Septembersýningar*) of 1947 and 1948 in Reykjavík paved the way for a Cobra-influenced primitivism; those of 1951 and 1952 were an arena for geometric abstraction. VALTÝR PÉTURSSON and Þorvaldur Skúlason became the main apostles of geometric abstractionism after 1950. A little later this group was joined by HÖRÐUR ÁGÚSTSSON, KARL KVARAN and Svavar Guðnason. The main pioneer of

3. Jóhannes S. Kjarval: *Summer Night at Thingvellir*, oil on canvas, 1×1.5 m, 1931 (Reykjavík, National Gallery of Iceland)

geometric abstraction in sculpture was Gerður Helgadóttir. Meanwhile the cause of lyrical abstraction was promoted by Nína Tryggvadóttir *c.* 1955; ART INFORMEL was pioneered by KRISTJÁN DAVÍÐSSON, who had been educated in the USA and whose painting turned towards Abstract Expressionism *c.* 1960.

There were great changes in Icelandic art after 1965 as the influence of abstract art waned rapidly. New realism, Pop art, and neo-Dada became the dominant movements. In Paris ERRÓ developed his Pop art out of Surrealism in the spirit of Roberto Matta; however, his influence on Icelandic art was indirect, in contrast to that of DIETER ROTH, who lived in Reykjavík from 1957 to 1964 and had an incalculable influence on young artists, becoming the catalyst of the Flúxus movement, which reached its high point in 1969 with the founding of Galleri SÚM. The influence of the sculptor Jóhann Eyfells (*b* 1923), a professor at the University of Orlando, FL, was also felt through his rejection of abstract art and his experiments in three-dimensional art. MAGNÚS PÁLSSON and JÓN GUNNAR ÁRNASON followed in the footsteps of Roth and Eyfells and encouraged the spread of new ideas. After the disbanding of the SÚM movement (1974) its function as an association, collection and gallery was taken over by Nýlistarsafnið (the Living Art Museum), founded in 1979. Other members of SÚM—HREINN FRIÐFINNSSON and the brothers Kristján and Sigurður GUÐMUNDSSON—settled in the Netherlands and did much to strengthen the links between Icelandic and Dutch conceptual art. After 1980 pure conceptual art was on the wane, and young artists turned to painting in the spirit of the New Image, which led to a decline in Dutch influence and closer ties with Germany, Switzerland, Italy and the USA.

BIBLIOGRAPHY

B. Th. Björnsson: *Íslensk myndlist á 19. og 20. öld* [Icelandic art in the 19th and 20th centuries], 2 vols (Reykjavík, 1964–73)

Fjórir frumherjar [Four pioneers] (exh. cat., ed. S. Jónsdóttir; Reykjavík, N.G., 1985) [incl. Eng. trans.]

A. Ingólfsson: 'Iceland', *Northern Poles* (Sneslev, 1986), pp. 48–120

Íslensk abstraktlist [Abstract art in Iceland] (exh. cat., ed. G. B. Kvaran; Reykjavík, Kjarvalsstaðir, 1987)

H. B. Runólfsson: 'Concrete Art in Iceland', *Nordic Concrete Art, 1907–60* (exh. cat., ed. M. Jaukkuri; Helsinki, Nord. A. Cent., 1988) [incl. Eng. trans.]

Aldarspegill [The century in retrospect] (exh. cat., ed. K. Kristjánsdóttir; essay by H. B. Runólfsson; Reykjavík, N.G., 1988) [incl. Eng. trans.]

HALLDÓR BJÖRN RUNÓLFSSON

II. Architecture, interior decoration and furniture.

There is little evidence of interior decoration in Icelandic houses before the 20th century, as until this time the scattered, rural and impoverished population lived in farmhouses built of such short-lived materials as turf and dry-stone walls, turf roofs and pillars and rafters made from driftwood or imported timber. A few also had wood panelling. This type of primitive dwelling served rich and poor alike, although the wealthier houses were more spacious and might have more wood panelling. Around and after the middle of the 18th century some churches and homes for high-ranking public officials were built of cut stone. They were designed by Danish architects and, although almost all are still standing and are preserved as national monuments, their main characteristic is simplicity: decoration is largely confined to simple Baroque patterns on doors, skirting-boards and architraves. Roof decoration is virtually non-existent, as are paintings on walls and ceilings. At the end of the 19th century and the beginning of the 20th, timber and then stone houses were introduced: ornamentation was still used very sparingly. There are one or two examples of decorative paintings on walls, often imitations of wood panelling, which were influenced by a Swiss building style that came to Iceland via Norway, but this style was soon simplified and with the emergence of Functionalism decoration disappeared altogether.

The cramped conditions in small farmhouses did not allow space for much furniture. The main domestic building on a farm (the *baðstofa*) had low ceilings and little floor space, with fixed beds along the walls. Carved wooden bed panels, usually of pine and decorated with acanthus or geometric motifs, the owner's initials and religious verses or blessings, were placed at the front of the fixed beds to prevent bed-linen falling on the ground. Household furniture comprised little cupboards, often carved on the front, and the occasional carved chair. Unpainted carving is the only important form of decoration in Icelandic folk art. Small wooden chests or caskets, often carved, were common, and women had carved workboxes in which they kept their handiwork. The cupboards and chests were used to store personal belongings—clothing and possibly a few books or pieces of jewellery. In the 16th, 17th and 18th centuries carved wooden bed panels, cupboards, chests, boxes, mangles and small chairs were all produced in such imported woods as pine or spruce but also in beech and ash. A wide variety of 17th- and 18th-century cupboards and chests have been preserved (Reykjavík, N. Mus.). The oldest known chair (*c*. 1500; Reykjavík, N. Mus.; see fig. 4) belonged to Þórunn, the daughter of Bishop Jón Arason (1484–1550), and came originally from the church of Grund. A 17th-century church seat and several 19th-century chairs, all decorated with intricate carving, have also been preserved (Reykjavík, N. Mus.).

4. Carved wooden chair, h. 870 mm, from the church of Grund, northern Iceland, *c*. 1500 (Reykjavík, National Museum of Iceland)

In the 20th century increased urbanization, greater prosperity and improved living conditions created a demand for an indigenous furniture industry. Most Icelandic furniture designers trained in Denmark and Sweden, so development in furniture styles followed that of the Scandinavian countries. However, Sveinn Kjarval (1919–81), although working within the Danish tradition, incorporated the older elements of Icelandic design and used native materials in his work. Such contemporary designers as Petur Luttersson (*b* 1936) and Gunnar Magnusson (*b* 1923) have applied modern design to industrial production and specialize in highly functional office furniture.

For further information on architecture *see* REYKJAVÍK.

For bibliography *see* §V below.

III. Ceramics and glass.

Ceramics and glass have been made in Iceland only in the 20th century. Even imported examples are rare, as wooden eating and drinking vessels were usually used. In 1927 the sculptor and painter Guðmundur Einarsson (1895–1963) set up the first ceramic workshop in Reykjavík, where he experimented with Icelandic clay, often using stylized 'Viking' decoration of pierced strapwork and animal forms (e.g. vase, 1939; Reykjavík, priv. col., see 1982 exh. cat., fig. 106).

Einarsson's example was followed by Gestur Thorgrimsson (*b* 1920) and Sigrun Guðjonsdóttir (*b* 1926), who worked together, with Thorgrimsson providing the thrown forms that Guðjonsdóttir decorated. The only ceramic factory in Iceland is Glit Ltd in Reykjavík, founded by Ragnar Kjartansson. In the 1990s some workshops started producing both decorative and practical objects and experimented with mixing ground Icelandic lava ash into the clay. Two potters whose work reflects the forms and textures of the Icelandic landscape are Steinunn Marteinsdóttir (*b* 1936) and Jonina Guðnadóttir (*b* 1943).

The only glass workshop in Iceland was established by Sigrun Olöf Einarsdóttir (*b* 1952), who trained in Denmark. Her blown-glass studio pieces often incorporate human figures; others rely on bold colour composition (e.g. bowls, 1979; artist's col., see 1982 exh. cat., figs 303–4). Such artists as Leifur Breiðfjord (*b* 1945) work in stained glass and have produced windows for churches and for such buildings as the Leifur Eiríksson Terminal at Keflavík airport. The medium is still very young in Iceland, but decorative windows are becoming increasingly popular in new churches.

For bibliography *see* §V below.

IV. Metalwork.

There is a long tradition of skilled metalwork in Iceland due largely to the need for remote farms to be self-sufficient and to the design of the national women's costume, which has much silver and gold filigree ornament. Almost every farm had its own ironsmithy where skilled blacksmiths made iron scythes and horseshoes. Many smiths also used such more refined techniques as copper-casting and brass-making. Fish-oil lamps, which provided the main lighting in homes, were cast in brass, as were women's keyrings, buttons and harness buckles, many of which were skilfully engraved with Romanesque acanthus motifs. During the 17th and 18th centuries decoration included the monogram of Christ, a cross or an inscription. From the 17th to the 19th century richly decorated brass-covered ladies' saddles were made: thin sheets of brass were stamped with pictures of animals and plant decoration (showing Baroque and Rococo influence), and often with the date and the name of the owner, and then fitted into the saddle. The rims of drinking horns might be ornamented with brass or silver (e.g. drinking horn with brass ornament, 18th century; Reykjavík, N. Mus.). Snuff horns, made of sperm-whale tooth and even walrus tusks, were generally decorated with silver rather than carved.

The Icelandic tradition in silverwork goes back to the Middle Ages, when many homes and churches had silver artefacts, a large number of which may have been made in Iceland (e.g. silver and parcel-gilt chalice, 13th century; London, V&A). There were silversmiths in many rural areas who produced the silver ornamentation for women's costumes. Filigree work was especially common on decorative buttons and belts, although many belts were also cast, generally in silver, occasionally in copper or brass. Silversmiths also made silver spoons and small goblets but rarely produced larger objects other than church chalices. Wealthy families acquired larger silver objects from abroad, especially Denmark. In later centuries many Icelandic silversmiths trained in Copenhagen, but could not make a living on their return and produced only occasional pieces (examples in Reykjavík, N. Mus.) One of the most distinguished Icelandic goldsmiths was Sigurður Thorsteinsson (1714–99), who trained in Copenhagen, where he worked as a prolific master craftsman from 1742 to 1799, sending many pieces of his work to Iceland (e.g. silver wafer box, 1774; Reykjavík, N. Mus.). The work of 20th-century metalworkers often reflects the rugged nature of the Icelandic terrain, for example the textured surfaces of the jewellery and vessels of Jens Guðjonsson (*b* 1920), which have influenced a new generation of metalworkers, among them the jeweller Gudbrandur Jezorski (*b* 1943).

For bibliography *see* §V below.

V. Textiles.

Iceland has a long tradition of varied textile work. In the Middle Ages plain homespun woven woollen fabrics in natural or vegetable-dyed colours were produced, as well as tiny quantities of lacis (darned net), knitting and, probably, narrow woven polychrome woollen belts. Linen, silk and patterned textiles were imported. Embroidery was the main means of decorating textiles. The main techniques are *refilsaumur* (laid-and-couched work), *glitsaumur* and *skakkaglit* (straight and slanted-patterned darning), appliqué and stem, long-armed cross and eyelet stitches. These were all worked with wool on woollen or linen grounds, with occasional use of a little silk or metal thread. Only ecclesiastical examples survive from the late medieval period (e.g. antependium with *refilsaumur*, early 14th century; Paris, Mus. Cluny), but records show that embroidery was also used for horse trappings (e.g. saddle-cloths), domestic furnishings and clothing. Medieval embroideries depict a series of circular or polygonal frames enclosing animals, plants, hunting scenes or scenes from the Bible and lives of the saints (e.g. antependium with images of the Virgin and Child with saints, 16th century; Reykjavík, N. Mus.). These designs were based on Byzantine and Islamic silks of the early medieval period, and they survived into the 19th century, used on bedspreads, valances and hangings (see fig. 5). Designs published in foreign pattern books of the 16th and 17th centuries were also used in Iceland (e.g. two panels on altar curtain, 1650 and 1651; Copenhagen, Nmus.). During the 17th century more freely drawn floral patterns were introduced. Worked at first in a variety of stitches, in the late 18th century and the 19th they were embroidered almost exclusively in split stitch with bright polychrome wools on dark, closely woven woollen grounds (e.g. woman's skirt, *c.* 1790; Reykjavík, N. Mus.). There is virtually no information about the production of embroideries. Before the Reformation convents and other major ecclesiastical centres probably provided a focus for the embroiderers; after the Reformation wealthy households were probably the main centres. During the 19th and 20th centuries, Icelandic embroidery was more influenced by international developments, although local tradition remained strong.

European merchants introduced knitting to Iceland in the 16th century. It quickly became popular with men and women, and records of 1582–3 note rent paid by tenant farmers to the Bishop of Holár in knitted stockings. Garments produced were mainly such domestic items as scarves, caps, stockings and mittens, large quantities of which were being exported by 1624. Few knitted garments from this period have survived. Knitting instructions dated 1760 and 1770 have been preserved but are difficult to understand. Two manuscript pattern books (1776 and 1780; Reykjavík, N. Mus.) have squared patterns that inscriptions made clear were intended for knitting. Traditional Icelandic knitting was worked in the round, using five or more needles, in stocking stitch, with rib or garter stitch for the edges. Designs included the eight-pointed star used for coloured insoles, and in north-west Iceland mittens were made with stylized floral, animal and bird motifs. In the early 20th century home knitting-machines became common, and handknitting declined and became women's work. However, during and after World War II, handknitting was revived and was used to produce the Icelandic *lopi* sweater with its round yoke, in white, grey, brown and blackish-brown Icelandic sheep wool. Wool and clothing factories were established at the beginning of the 20th century and used high-quality Icelandic wool. Domestic weaving continued in rural areas until the late 1950s, when it disappeared. However, such artists as Asgerður Búadóttir (*b* 1920) and, more recently, Sigridur

5. Linen bed valance (detail), worked in *glitsaumur* with polychrome wools, 18th century (Reykjavík, National Museum of Iceland)

Johnasdóttir (*b* 1920) and Leifur Breidfjord (*b* 1945) have set up workshops producing woven art textiles. Búadóttir, like Júlíana Sveinsdóttir, approached textile art through painting, producing abstract designs strongly influenced by the colours and textures of the Icelandic landscape (e.g. *Shielded Moon*, 1976; Reykjavík, N.G.). The strong compositions and colours in Breidfjord's designs reflect his background as a stained-glass artist.

BIBLIOGRAPHY

K. Eldjárn: 'Carved Panels from Flatatunga', *Acta Archaeol.* [Copenhagen], xxiv (1954), pp. 81–101

B. Th. Björnsson: *Íslenzk gullsmíði* [Icelandic goldwork] (Reykjavík, 1957)

K. Eldjárn: *Hundrað ár í Thjóðminjasafni* [A hundred years in the Thjóðminjasafn] (Reykjavík, 2/1963) [Eng. summary]

E. M. Mageröy: 'Planteornamentikken i Islands treskurd' [Plant designs in Icelandic wood-carving], *Bibliotheca Arnamagneana Supplementum*, v–vi (Copenhagen, 1967)

T. Magnusson: 'Islandsk folkkunst' [Icelandic folk art], *Nordisk Folkkonst* [Nordic folk art] (Lund, 1972), pp. 77–89

E. E. Godjónsson: 'Icelandic Medieval Embroidery Terms and Techniques', *Studies in Textile History*, ed. V. Gervers (Toronto, 1977)

——: 'Iceland', *Needlework: An Illustrated History*, ed. H. Bridgeman and E. Drury (New York and London, 1978), pp. 259–66

Scandinavian Modern Design, 1880–1980 (exh. cat., ed. D. McFadden; New York, Cooper-Hewitt Mus., 1982)

THOR MAGNUSSON

Ichikawa Beian (*b* Edo [now Tokyo], 1779; *d* Edo, 1858). Japanese calligrapher. Together with MAKI RYŌKO and NUKINA KAIOKU, he was one of the Bakumatsu no Sanpitsu ('Three Brushes of the late Edo period'). His powerful brushwork, known as the Beian *ryū* (Beian school or style), continued to be much admired into the Meiji period (1868–1912). He was the son of Ichikawa Kansai (1749–1820), a poet skilled in calligraphy and the head of the Shōheikō, the official Confucian academy in Edo. From his youth Beian concentrated on calligraphy, studying the works of such famous calligraphers as Yan Zhenqing (AD 709–85), DONG QICHANG of the Ming period (1368–1644) and Mi Fu (*see* MI, (1)) of the Song period (960–1279), and collecting such of their autographs as he could. He modelled himself in particular after Mi Fu, from whom it is said that he took his artist's name, Beian. In 1799 he opened a private calligraphy school, the Shōsanrindō (Hall of the Forested Hill), at Izumibashi in Shitaya, where he began to teach calligraphy. In 1804 he took a pleasure trip to Nagasaki, where he received instruction in calligraphy techniques from a Qing-period Chinese merchant named Hu Tiaoxin and was greatly impressed by the examples he saw of Ming- and Qing-period calligraphy. He especially admired the works of the late Ming-period calligraphers Cai Daoxian, Huang Daozhou and Ni Yuanlu and the *Karayō* (Chinese-style) calligraphy widely disseminated in Japan by Ōbaku (Chin. Huangbo) Zen monks. He had well over 200 students and probably at least 5000 followers, including high-class women, monks, shogunal vassals and daimyo. On certain days of the week he set up a stall in front of his gate and gave public lessons, which were reputedly very popular.

Beian is remembered particularly as a collector and for his writings, principally the *Beika shoketsu* ('Secrets of Bei family calligraphy'), a compilation of Mi Fu's dissertations on calligraphy. Among his other books were *Bokujō hikkei* ('Manual of ink traces'), *Hippu* ('Brush album'), *Shoga daibatsu* ('Calligraphy of the epilogue'), *Beian bokudan* ('Ink talk'; 1812), and *Kaigyōwaihen*, which modern calligraphers continue to find instructive as training manuals. He also made a number of folding calligraphic copybooks and published the *Shōsanrindō shoga bunbōgu zuroku* ('Pictorial catalogue of the writing implements of the Shōsanrindō'), a record of his own collection, which is full of the charm and finesse that were typical of Edo-period literati. In 1822 Beian donated Chinese calligraphy and paintings, 50 examples of stone rubbings, the entire *Nihon kinseki takuhon* ('Folio of rubbings of Japanese monuments'), which his father had assembled, and such manuscripts as the *Jōmō shiryō* to the archives of the Shōheikō (the official Confucian academy in Edo). After the Meiji Restoration of 1868 the collection was given to the nation by the Ichikawa family; the Chinese calligraphy and paintings and the *Nihon kinseki takuhon* are housed in the Tokyo National Museum and the books in the Uchikaku Bunko. Beian died from cholera during an epidemic. His style is reflected in the work of such later artists as Watanabe Kazan and RAI SAN'YŌ; a portrait of Beian by Kazan has survived (1837; Tokyo, Agy Cult. Affairs; for illustration *see* WATANABE KAZAN).

BIBLIOGRAPHY

N. Tsuchida and others: *Gakusha* [Scholars], Sho to jinbutsu [Calligraphy and people], v (Tokyo, 1978)

S. Komatsu: *Karayō* [The Chinese style], Nihon no sho [Japanese calligraphy], xii (Tokyo, 1983)

Masters of Japanese Calligraphy, 8th–19th Century (exh. cat. by Y. Shimizu and J. M. Rosenfield; New York, Japan House Gal. and Asia Soc. Gals, 1984–5)

TADASHI KOBAYASHI

Ichinojō Koretomi. *See* OGATA, (1).

Ichiroku. *See* IWAYA ICHIROKU.

Ichiryūsai. *See* ANDŌ HIROSHIGE.

Icon [Gr. *eikon*: 'image']. Wooden panel with a painting, usually in tempera, of a holy person or one of the traditional images of Orthodox Christianity, the religion of the Byzantine empire practised today mainly in Greece and Russia (*see* EARLY CHRISTIAN AND BYZANTINE ART, §VI, and POST-BYZANTINE ART, §§II, 1 and III, 1). The word also has a range of related but disparate meanings, from the abstract and philosophical to the purely literal. For example, it is still used in modern Greek to mean an image or picture in the ordinary sense. In antiquity, Platonists and Neo-Platonists held that the material, earthly world reflects, or is the image of, the higher and divine cosmos; the Old Testament provides the theme of man as the icon of God in the temple of the world; and St Paul declared that 'Christ is the icon of God' (2 Corinthians 4:4). Thus the idea of the icon is associated with cosmology and the theology of the Incarnation. In the Early Christian period, disputes over such questions as whether or not God can be known or depicted or the invisible can be seen were part of an intense debate surrounding the acceptability, meaning and function of images of Christ. All this was bound up with the complex questions of Christology that exercised the best minds of the period. Whole communities and nations were divided into Orthodox and heretics over the problem of defining the two natures of Christ, the relationship between his humanity and his divinity. The theory and belief system of icons was developed by theologians between the 4th and the 9th centuries, though only a few icons survive from then and up to the 12th century. Once established, however, the doctrinal principles never changed, and the study of icons is as much a matter of theology as of art. Subject-matter, form and composition did not deviate from the established dogma on which they depended; indeed, icons have been called theology in colour (Trubetskoy).

1. HISTORY. Except among Jews, the cult of images in Late Antiquity was widely established. Christianity, spreading in a Hellenistic milieu, had inherited traditions from Greece, Rome, Egypt and the Near East, where gods, demi-gods and even emperors were commemorated or worshipped in the form of statues and paintings. It is not extraordinary, therefore, to find painted images of Christ with the attributes of the sun god Helios and other pagan figures from as early as the 3rd century AD (*see* EARLY CHRISTIAN AND BYZANTINE ART, §§I, 2(i)(a) and III, 2). Christian scenes on the walls of the catacombs (*see* CATACOMB, §3) and in relief carvings on sarcophagi also date to this period (*see* EARLY CHRISTIAN AND BYZANTINE ART, §IV, 2(ii)).

From early on there was opposition to icons. The idea of the representation of a holy person has always had associations with mysterious, not to say magical properties, and the cult of icons depended to a degree on popular belief in their miraculous powers. The principal argument against icons derives from the Old Testament prohibition 'Thou shalt not make unto thyself any graven image, or any likeness of any thing that is in heaven above, or that is in the earth beneath' (Exodus 20:4). Many Church Fathers, including EUSEBIOS OF CAESAREA, argued that the invisible God could not be worshipped in an image and that icons could not be venerated as holy objects. An early defender of icons was St Basil the Great (329–79), who declared that in venerating an icon, one worships the prototype represented there rather than the icon itself.

Antipathy to icons reached a climax in 726, when Emperor Leo III Isaurikos (*reg* 717–41) gave his support to a group of bishops condemning them. Orders were given for the destruction of icons, and the patriarch of Constantinople resigned. These events inaugurated the period known as the iconoclastic controversy (*see* ICONOCLASM). In 754 Constantine V Kopronymos (*reg* 741–75) summoned the Council of Hieria, at which icons were condemned on the grounds that they either separated Christ's human nature from his divine nature or that they confused them. Iconophiles (lovers of icons) held that the Council of Hieria was illegally constituted, but iconoclasts (destroyers of icons), relying on imperial support, began a series of violent actions against icons and against the iconophiles themselves, some of whom were executed.

There was a lull in iconoclasm after Empress EIRENE convened the Second Council of Nicaea (787), which condemned the policy and put forward the theological arguments in favour of icons. Chief among these were the formulation of St Basil the Great, referred to above, and the idea that God's appearance on earth in human form was a precedent that justified the physical depiction of the Second Person of the Holy Trinity in a tangible form, as in a painted image. (It is for this reason that God the Father is not represented in icons but only the Son.) Secondary arguments held that icons could have miraculous powers and that they aided the illiterate in knowing the Gospel. The reinstatement of iconoclasm in 813 lasted until 843, when it was finally defeated with the triumph of Orthodoxy; this victory is marked by an annual feast in the Orthodox Church on the first Sunday in Lent.

The theological background to the problems of iconoclasm forced the Church into defining the use and meaning

1. Icon of the *Entry into Jerusalem*, tempera and gold on panel, 449×335 mm, late 14th century (London, private collection)

of icons in the light of the highest philosophical and intellectual ideals. Through icons the faithful were in touch with the holy persons and events they depicted. For the Orthodox believer the saints are actually present in the church during the liturgy.

2. CATEGORIES AND FUNCTION. Icons can be divided into two main categories: portrait images and scenes illustrating church feasts. The transition from Roman portraits as bust-length frontal images into icons of Christ or of saints is almost imperceptible. This tradition remained more or less unchanged from the 6th to the 16th century. Likewise, icons depicting the feasts of the Church are founded on compositions that were adapted in many cases from antiquity: for example the Entry into Jerusalem is based on the iconography of the arrival of a visiting emperor at the city gates (see fig. 1). In neither portraits nor festival scenes was the artist free to introduce any subjective element into the composition. A painter would no more think of altering the established iconography than the officiating priest would alter the liturgy, in which icons form an essential component (*see* CHRISTIANITY, §III, 2(i)(b), and CHURCH, §IV, 2).

Implicit in all icons and central to their meaning is Christianity's doctrine of salvation: 'God became man in order that man might become God.' The spiritual implications of this idea are evident in icons where techniques of naturalism are not employed; the appearance of visible objects and the three-dimensional world is altered and adapted so that, as in a dream, another reality is discerned in which the logic of sense perception is suspended. The sacred events are not located in earthly space and time. Icons do not convey the rhythms and energy of ordinary life; instead there is an absence of agitation: angels, saints and apostles enact scenes against a background of silence and eternity. Light and shade are not rendered in the western way because, in icons, Christ and the saints are themselves the sources of illumination.

The pictorial language of icons is primarily symbolic. Literal and narrative values are secondary. An icon is a mystical commentary that goes beyond the face value of the historical event. If this is lost, if the image becomes merely narrative or sentimental and decorative, it is no longer an icon, since it is no longer an image of the divine expressed in the physical world.

The icon becomes a living reality when the painter, through prayer and spiritual endeavour, realizes the divine within himself. With this achievement the Incarnation is spiritually re-enacted, transforming the idea into an actual event. This is why the art of icon painting is at its highest when it is associated with schools of mystical prayer such as the *hesychasts* (from Gr. *hesychia*: 'stillness'), who aimed

2. Icon by Andrey Rublyov: *Christ Pantokrator* (detail), tempera on panel, 1.58×1.06 m, 1420 (Moscow, Tret'yakov Gallery)

at transcendental states or *gnosis* ('knowledge of God'). The confluence of mysticism and art reached a climax in Byzantium in the Palaiologan period (1261–1453). In Russia ANDREY RUBLYOV and his school were the greatest exponents of this type of art, as can be seen in his icon of *Christ Pantokrator* (1420; see fig. 2). Although the function of icons was theological, the highest technical and artistic standards were demanded as part of the artist's work of moral perfection and self-transformation. While many icons can be considered works of art, aesthetic delight was not the artist's intention; in the case of Rublyov, his artistic genius, equal to that of his greatest western European contemporaries, is entirely subordinated to his religious mysticism.

From the 12th to the 16th century icons, adhering more or less to the Church's hard-won principles, were expressions of a great medieval culture: powerful, dignified, spiritual, human and often intensely beautiful. After the 16th century, with the decline of Byzantine cultural influence, icon painting in Greece, Russia and eastern Europe gradually weakened and, compromising with Western influence, became increasingly insignificant.

For illustration see colour pls I–III.

BIBLIOGRAPHY

St Basil the Great: *De spiritu sancto* (*c*. 358–79), *PG*, xxxii (Paris, n.d.), p. 149C

E. Trubetskoy: *Umozrenie v kraskakh* [Speculation in colours] (Moscow, 1915–16); Eng. trans. as *Icons: Theology in Color* (New York, 1973)

L. Ouspensky and V. Lossky: *The Meaning of Icons* (New York, 1982)

K. Weitzmann and others: *The Icon* (New York, 1982)

A. P. Kazhdan, ed.: 'Icons', *The Oxford Dictionary of Byzantium*, ii (Oxford and New York, 1991), pp. 977–81

L. Ouspensky: *Theology of the Icon*, 2 vols (New York, 1992)

M. Vassilakis: 'An Icon of the Entry into Jerusalem and a Question of Archetypes, Prototypes and Copies in Late Byzantine Icon-Painting', *Deltion Christ. Archaiol. Etaireias*, xvii (1993)

RICHARD TEMPLE

Silver icon cover with icon of the *Virgin and Child*, late 13th century (Moscow, Tret'yakov Gallery)

Icon cover. Decorative metalwork cover for a Christian icon. The icon cover developed from the ornamental metal plates and silver embossed icons known to have decorated Early Christian altar screens (*see* SCREEN (i), §2). Its appearance and form resulted from a new understanding of the icon and its place in the Orthodox liturgy (*see* EARLY CHRISTIAN AND BYZANTINE ART, §VI, 1), and the silver cover is of particular importance in the Eastern Church. There are three major types of icon cover: those that entirely conceal the painted icon, those that leave the faces, hands and feet of the figures exposed and those that cover only the background and margins of the icon. The first two types of silver cover have a symbolic and eucharistic significance similar to that of the ciborium (*see* CIBORIUM (i)) in which the consecrated elements are kept: they not only have a decorative function, but also serve a ritual purpose as sacred covers. Some icon covers also contained relics, such as that of the 11th–12th-century *Christ Pantokrator* from Esphigmenou Monastery on Mt Athos.

Icon covers that partially conceal the icon are the most common type and are known in Byzantium, the Balkans and Georgia as early as the 10th century. A single icon cover may also combine more than one technique of metalwork, such as silver-gilt, cloisonné enamel and precious stones (*see* EARLY CHRISTIAN AND BYZANTINE ART, §VII, 7(ii), and GEORGIA, §V, 1(ii)). The predominance of one or other type of cover reflects the various religious preoccupations and economic capacities of different times and places. The ornamentation also corresponds to the state of development of the decorative arts and can sometimes be used to identify the attribution of the icon painting itself.

Since icon covers were often provided by particular donors, they are also connected with patronal traditions and with commemorative practices, as is particularly evident in the repoussé images of the saints, which may form part of the cover. A good example is the silver cover of the late 13th-century painted icon of the *Virgin and Child* (Moscow, Tret'yakov Gal.; see fig.). The outer frame of the cover contains busts of St Peter, St Paul, the Four Evangelists and the three medical saints (SS Cosmas, Damian and Panteleimon) as well as the full-length figures of the cover's donors, Constantinos Akropolites and his wife Tornikia Akropolitissa, in the bottom right and left corners respectively.

In eastern Slav territories, the use of icon covers was confined to the most venerated icons, those connected with important personages or events of Church or State and those with dynastic significance. Small icons used for private devotional purposes were sometimes provided with covers adorned with precious stones and were important family heirlooms. Few examples earlier than the 16th century survive, after which there was a considerable increase in the number produced. In Russia, for example, covers were produced for the entire iconostasis, thus effecting considerable change in the aesthetics of the church interior. From the 16th century onwards there was much greater technical uniformity, resulting both from the frequent migrations of the craftsmen who produced the covers and from the durability of the wooden matrices on which the metal covers were beaten out. Gifts of icon covers were made more frequently by rulers and ecclesiastical dignitaries to churches and monasteries at a distance from their place of production.

BIBLIOGRAPHY

S. Radojčić: *Zur Geschichte der silbergetriebenen Reliefs in der byzantinischen Kunst-Tortulae* (1966)

A. Grabar: *Les Revêtements en or et en argent des icônes byzantines* (Venice, 1979)

E. A. Gordienko and A. N. Trifonova: *Katalog serebryanykh okladov Novgorodskogo muzeya-zapovednika* [Catalogue of silver frames in the Novgorod museum-reserve], Muzey-Khudozhestvennye sobraniye, vi (Moscow, 1986)

N. Ševčenko: *Decorated Icons of the Comnenan Period* (1992)

OXANA CLEMINSON

Iconium. *See* KONYA.

Iconoclasm. The destruction of images, particularly for religious reasons. The word is also used more broadly, however, to refer to the suppression of, or simple opposition to, images, whatever the motivation. The study of iconoclasm brings to light general issues concerning the nature and value of imagery, especially in relation to religious doctrines, while historically the nature of those doctrines themselves has determined the role played by iconoclasm within them.

See also CENSORSHIP.

1. Introduction. 2. Regional survey.

1. INTRODUCTION. Iconoclasm may take a number of forms and may be directed against a range of imagery. In its most fundamental form it may involve the total destruction of all images, but other forms might involve the destruction only of anthropomorphic images, or of all images of God, or again of all anthropomorphic images of God. Another form is the destruction of a devotional image that has 'failed', such as the Chinese practice of flogging local earth deities during periods of drought or famine, while other somewhat marginal forms might include the ritual destruction of images, for example during certain Navajo healing ceremonies, in which a sand painting may be prepared by a singer, who then makes the patient sit on the painting. Artists themselves may also be responsible for the iconoclastic destruction of works of art, for example following a spiritual conversion or from a belief that the finished work has failed to meet spiritual or religious criteria. Lastly, and more broadly, the production of a new artistic iconography may be seen as iconoclastic and as a positive interpretation of the iconoclastic impulse insofar as it seeks to displace an existing iconography. Thus Mircea Eliade (1907–86), for example, has analysed much modern art as having a ritual character and as being a manifestation of the modern search for the sacred, involving the destruction of recognizable traditional forms in order to create a new imagery appropriate to contemporary culture.

Historically, the idea of iconoclasm is rooted in the establishment and development of religious monotheism, which in turn fostered the idea of idolatry. In polytheistic religious traditions there has been no history of either condemnation or fear of idolatry. In a monotheistic tradition, however, the singularity and integrity of the one 'true' God is endangered by the visible presence of other deities or objects of worship. In Judaism, for example, idolatry was interpreted as a worship of the creature rather than the creator, impinging on and diminishing the divine integrity of God. The Second Commandment (Exodus 20:2–4) gave formal definition to the censure of the religious imagery of pagan cults and shaped the iconoclasm of 'the chosen people'. This text became the scriptural and the ritual foundation for the iconoclastic attitudes of Christianity and Islam. Idolatry became identified as the worship of an idol, or physical substitute for a 'false' god, and was characterized as a pagan practice by the three Western monotheistic traditions of Judaism, Christianity and Islam.

The very fact of idolatry gave rise to a fundamental debate as to whether the divine can be depicted at all. Once the validity of the image of God was questioned, the basis of all religious, cultic, ritual and even secular imagery was in doubt. The intellectual issues of what constitutes a sacred image, of the relation of the sacred image to the divine, and of the function of sacred images became the theological foundations of the iconoclastic controversies of the monotheistic traditions. In most religious traditions religious images are interpreted as visual mediators of divine energy and protective powers, with the representation of the human and the sacred in religious images being based on the theological question of the relationship between the two worlds. In religious traditions in which the divine is seen as the model for humanity, the human body and sexuality have been seen as positive and natural entities, and religious images have been predominantly figural or symbolic. In religious traditions that see the human as a distortion of the divine, the human body and sexuality have been perceived as negative entities in need of spiritual guidance, and religious images have tended to be primarily geometric or abstract.

Fundamental to both these attitudes has been the fear not only of the power of human sexuality but also of the ability of the image to claim, divert and even control that human energy and power. A central concern of the ecclesiastical hierarchy has therefore been that believers will be dissuaded from 'true' religious practice to 'false' religious practice. For example, one claim is that religious images (of any type) will distract the believers' devotion and attention during worship; descriptions of these 'distractions' range from that of a heightened aesthetic experience to erotic arousal. The condemnation of secular and pagan works of art by the ecclesiastical hierarchy is partly based on the fear that the image's ability to arouse the viewer sexually is a public threat to religion. Religious imagery may also be experienced as a denigration of the integrity of the sacred because anthropomorphic representations humanize, and thereby lessen, divine power and holy effectiveness. The sacred must be represented, therefore, as remote from human sensuality, and erotic arousal as repugnant to divinity, even in religious traditions where such images are acceptable in a secular or other context. In certain religious traditions, moreover, religious images of any kind are a violation of sacred dogma or canon.

Such concerns emphasize the recurrent rivalry in religious traditions between the power of the image and the power of religious authority. In all world religions there has been regular conflict between tradition (i.e. dogma, creeds, the written canon and ecclesiastical hierarchy) and its acceptance and implementation by the laity. In some instances iconoclasm has therefore been seen as a necessary means to reassert traditional authority. On the other hand there have been outbreaks of 'popular' iconoclasm that have been espoused and practised by believers but not advocated by the hierarchy, and conversely there have been injunctions to iconoclasm by the ecclesiastical leadership that have not always been implemented in popular praxis.

2. REGIONAL SURVEY.

(i) Eastern. Although violent iconoclasm has never been sanctioned as such in traditional India, and especially by orthodox Hindus, iconoclastic activities have played various roles. The divine in Hinduism is often understood as an abstraction without parts (Skt *niṣkala*), and images are often abstract symbols or in some cases, for example at Chidambaram, entirely absent (*see* INDIAN SUBCONTINENT, §IV, 1). This lack of figurative imagery has been interpreted as the result of the historical displacement of indigenous icons by the aniconism of the Aryan invaders of north India (*c.* 1500 BC). Religious images and monuments in India were often made of such perishable materials as wood, paper or clay, for single or minimal use, and then intentionally destroyed and replaced; this practice is still prevalent (see fig. 1). The uncompromising monotheism and hostility to idolatry of the 11th-century Muslim invaders resulted in violent outbursts of iconoclasm in north India, notably the destruction of the temple at Somanatha by Mahmud of Ghazna (*reg* 998–1030). The British occupation of India with its religious allegiance to Protestant Christianity inspired the modern iconoclasms of the Brahma Samaj and Arya Samaj (*see* HINDUISM, §1), which eventually led to the development of an esoteric form of Hinduism that advocated philosophical monism and denounced all religious imagery as idolatrous.

Within the Indian traditions, several forms of ritual iconoclasm, including the contextual creation and destruction of ritual *maṇḍala*s, have always been practised. The Tantric tradition espoused the belief that mental worship of the otherwise invisible deities is the highest form of worship, and external worship with imagery the lowest. In actual practice, however, Tantrism is a highly visual and iconic tradition, an example of the disparity between tradition and praxis. SIKHISM began as a devotional and reformist movement within Hinduism and initially rejected the religious use of any and all images. However, images of Guru Nanak began to appear as visual pedagogy and as illustrations to inspire religious piety and good works, precipitating a transition from an iconoclastic to an iconic religious attitude (*see also* INDIAN SUBCONTINENT, §§I, 7, 8, 10 and II, 1–3).

1. *Kali Striding over Shiva*, painted clay images to be honoured and then destroyed at the annual festival of Kali, Krishnanagar, West Bengal, 1980s

In Buddhism iconicism has sometimes tended towards iconolatry, with the image of Buddha becoming an object of worship rather than merely of veneration. Such deification of the Buddha can provoke an iconoclastic reaction against state-imposed Buddhism. This may have been the case at Angkor, the royal capital of the Khmer empire in Cambodia, where, after the death of the Mahayana Buddhist king Jayavarman VII (*reg* 1181–*c.* 1220), it seems that Hindu iconoclasts destroyed or transformed some of the Buddha images in Jayavarman's state temple, the Bayon. On the other hand, the religious conviction that Buddha's nature pervades all things ensures that the forms and motifs of ritual iconoclasm are also present throughout the Buddhist tradition. In line with its emphasis on the unconventional and spontaneous nature of Enlightenment, Buddhism advocates such iconoclastic practices as the temporary cessation of visualization during meditation, the destruction of the formal canon and so on. Moreover, in Zen Buddhism written authority is superseded by the immediate and intuitive relation between master and disciple. The Buddhist ambivalence towards religious imagery is directly related to the individual's stage of spiritual consciousness. Images may be interpreted as necessary vehicles for the development of meditation techniques but are to be transcended; they are also seen as objects of dependence and attachment, material objects from which the Buddhist must extricate him- or herself on the path towards Enlightenment.

(ii) Western. The concentration and commitment to one God as the singular and unique deity transformed the context, canons and rituals of Western religious traditions. This one supreme God was the creator of humanity and the world, unique in substance, and beyond the known characteristics of sexuality, gender, bodily forms or even the visible world. This God created by speaking, thus reinforcing the primacy of the word over the image, and the written canon over religious imagery. Such a deity could be neither limited nor defined by known categories including visual depictions. Although an early style of monotheism, with an integral aniconic attitude towards religious imagery, was advocated by the Egyptian king AKHENATEN, it was the Old Testament religion of Israel that firmly established the Western monotheistic religious tradition and its accompanying prophetic iconoclasm. In an effort to define and identify the unique character of Judaism, the prophets and religious hierarchy distinguished religious and ethical practices from those of the neighbouring cults. In affirming the singularity of God and the primacy of the Word, Judaism nurtured the concept of idolatry. Many scriptural citations attest to the worship of idols by neighbouring cults. Religious pedagogy was focused on the teachings available through the written canon, which were read and interpreted in public worship. As a religious tradition rich in verbal imagery and symbolism, Judaism had little need for the visual image in pedagogy, devotional or ritual practices, cultic observations or spiritual contemplation.

The ambivalent attitude of Early Christianity towards religious imagery was a result of the faith's dual foundation in Hebraic monotheism and Hellenistic philosophy (*see* EARLY CHRISTIAN AND BYZANTINE ART, §I, 2(i)). Some of the Church Fathers were suspicious of and openly hostile to all forms of imagery. Advocating the prophetic iconoclasm of the Hebraic tradition, these patristic texts describe the vanity, sensuality and superstition of idolatry. Christianity eventually recognized the necessity of the visual image as a fundamental component for both religious worship and pedagogy, but the iconoclastic impulse surfaced nevertheless in the iconoclastic controversy (726–843). Emperor Leo III Isaurikos (*reg* 717–41) and Constantine V Kopronymos (*reg* 741–75) were responsible in 726 and 754 for inaugurating the destruction of icons as well as violent actions against iconophiles. This antipathy was influenced by the advent of Islam. Icons were seen as a reversion to pagan idolatry, and the production of such images of God as an act of heresy. The Eucharist was the only true image of God. The triumph of Orthodoxy at the Synod of Constantinople (843) was based on the formulations of St John of Damascus, who defended the icon and defined it as a portrait that must present the recognizable characteristics of a holy person, while at the same time being distinguished from its subject. Carefully defined and prescribed rubrics (including flatness, non-realistic proportions and perspectives, and colour symbolism) distinguished the icon from the idol.

The attitude of the Western Church towards religious imagery during the late 8th century was not without ambivalence or controversy. The *Libri Carolini* (Caroline books; *see* THEODULF) and the Council of Frankfurt (794) delineated a middle-of-the-road position. The image was appropriate for didactic purposes, as aesthetic adornment and as moral inspiration but not as an object of adoration. In the 12th century Cistercian monasticism reaffirmed the simplicity of Benedictine rules, and the abbey churches were cleansed of religious imagery in all media, including stained-glass windows, wall paintings and sculpture. However, religious imagery returned in the 13th century with the relaxing of Cistercian rules (*see* CISTERCIAN ORDER, §III, 2). The occasional outbreaks of the iconoclastic impulse in medieval Christianity focused on the abuses of devotional imagery. The 15th-century Dominican monk GIROLAMO SAVONAROLA preached against the materialism of his contemporaries and inspired others to destroy works of secular and religious art along with profane books. Botticelli and Michelangelo were among those influenced by his preachings. Michelangelo appears to have been highly critical of his own works and mutilated many, including the Florentine *Pietà* (*c.* 1547–55; Florence, Mus. Opera Duomo), although his precise reasons for doing so are unclear.

In the 14th century the English religious reformer John Wycliffe (*c.* 1328–84) and his followers, derisively labelled the Lollards ('mumblers'), can be regarded as Reformation precursors; they argued, among other things, for the destruction of anthropomorphic imagery. The Protestant reformers of the 16th century (*see* CHRISTIANITY, §I, 3(ii)) sought to return to the original foundation of the Christian tradition, and the Hebraic injunction triumphed over the Hellenistic advocacy of divine beauty. Protestantism supported religious worship in prayer, song, music and congregational fellowship. Such austere concentration on the written word reaffirmed the prophetic iconoclasm of the Old Testament. Like the iconoclastic controversies of the 8th and 9th centuries, the iconoclastic impulse that surfaced in the Reformation was thus caused by fundamental changes in the definition of mankind's relationship with God. Some reformers, for example MARTIN LUTHER and Jean Calvin (*see* CALVINISM), were opposed, in varying degrees, to the veneration of images but did not themselves support violent iconoclasm, whereas the destruction of images that swept across northern Europe, particularly in Germany, Switzerland, France, the Netherlands and England, was sanctioned by such figures as Huldrych Zwingli (*see* ZWINGLIANISM) and Andreas Rudolf Bodenstein van Karlstadt (*d* 1541). This iconoclasm ranged through smashing stained glass, breaking heads off statues and the ceremonial burning of paintings and sometimes entire churches (see fig. 2). In turn, several churches founded by Protestants were destroyed during the Counter-Reformation.

Primarily a religion of the Word, Islam quickly formed into an uncompromising monotheism morally committed to the one, eternal and incomparable God (Arab. *allāh*; *see* ISLAM, §I). Basic to the Muslim rejection of images is the theocentric view of God's total power and uniqueness,

2. *Edward VI and the Pope*, oil on canvas, 622×908 mm, *c.* 1548–9 (London, National Portrait Gallery)

often pronounced in the Koran (e.g. ii.255). The distance and distinction between the supreme creator and his created beings are immense. Any association of God with mere creatures is an attempt to humanize God and is perceived as an act of idolatry (Arab. *shirk*). The blasphemy of limiting or categorizing the singularity and supremacy of God in verbal or visual imagery is an unforgivable sin. The Prophet Muhammad (*d* AD 632) protested against the indigenous Arabic practice of idol worship, and the attitude towards religious imagery in the Koran (e.g. v.92) is one of disapproval. Within the first century of Islam violent iconoclasm would occasionally be advocated and practised, especially in public situations such as mosques and churches. Iconoclasm flourished sporadically in some Islamic lands, depending on local interpretations of the Koran. According to some traditions attributed to the Prophet, artists will be among the most severely punished on Judgement Day as they have usurped the function of the creator, and angels will not enter or protect any house with pictures and images. According to another tradition, if imagery is created, it must be flat and shadowless, headless or perforated and without a human face. One tradition advocates making an example of artists or artisans as the 'creators' of images who are unable to breathe life into their images on the Judgement Day and are thereby condemned eternally for their blasphemy. In its most rigorous formulation, Islam stands as the prophetic witness to the one God, the transcendent and invisible creator, who cannot be contained by, or limited to, visible images. Nevertheless, there has been a vibrant and rich tradition of both figural and non-figural art in the Islamic lands (*see also* ISLAMIC ART, esp. §I, 8).

BIBLIOGRAPHY

G. G. Coulton: *Art and the Reformation* (Oxford, 1928)

G. van der Leeuw: *Vom Heiligen in der Kunst* (1932); Eng. trans. as *Sacred and Profane Beauty* (New York, 1963)

E. Bevan: *Holy Images: An Inquiry into Idolatry and Image-worship in Ancient Paganism and Christianity* (London, 1940)

E. R. Goodenough: *Jewish Symbols in the Greco-Roman World*, 8 vols (New York, 1953–8)

M. V. Anastos: 'The Ethical Theory of Images Formulated by the Iconoclasts in 754 and 815', *Dumbarton Oaks Pap.*, 8 (1954), pp. 152–60

E. Kitzinger: 'The Cult of Images in the Age before Iconoclasm', *Dumbarton Oaks Pap.*, 8 (1954), pp. 85–150

C. Garside: *Zwingli and the Arts* (New Haven, 1966)

T. Burckhardt: *Sacred Art in East and West* (London, 1967)

J. Gutmann, ed.: *No Graven Images: Studies in Art and the Hebrew Bible* (New York, 1971)

J. Phillips: *The Reformation of Images: Destruction of Art in England, 1535–1600* (Berkeley, 1973)

A. Bryer and J. Herrin, eds: *Iconoclasm: Papers Given at the Ninth Spring Symposium of Byzantine Studies: Birmingham, AL, 1975*

J. Gutmann, ed.: *The Image and the Word: Confrontations in Judaism, Christianity and Islam* (Missoula, 1977)

C. C. Christensen: *Art and Reformation in Germany* (Athens, 1979)

S. Laeuchli: *Religion and Art in Conflict* (Philadelphia, 1980)

D. L. Eck: *Darsan: Seeing the Divine Image in India* (Chambersburg, PA, 1981)

D. Apostolos-Cappadona: 'To Create a New Universe: Mircea Eliade on Modern Art', *Cross Curr.*, 32 (1982/3), pp. 408–19

D. Apostolos-Cappadona, ed.: *Art, Creativity, and the Sacred* (New York, 1984)

M. Eliade: *Symbolism, the Sacred, and the Arts*, ed. D. Apostolos-Cappadona (New York, 1985)

D. Freedberg: *Iconoclasts and their Motives* (Maarssen, 1985)

J. Elsner: 'Image and Iconoclasm in Byzantium', *A. Hist.*, xi/4 (1988), pp. 471–91
D. Apostolos-Cappadona: 'Picasso's *Guernica* as Mythic Iconoclasm: An Eliadean Reading of Modern Art', *The Problem of Myth in a Post-Eliadean Age*, ed. W. Doniger and L. Patton (Charlottesville, in preparation)

DIANE APOSTOLOS-CAPPADONA

Iconographic handbook. Book regularly consulted by artists and others when required to devise representations of personifications or religious, historical or mythological themes. Such volumes, supplementing the existing literary texts, were particularly widely used in the 16th century, but their origins can arguably be found in Classical representations of mythological subjects.

1. Antiquity. 2. 12th–17th centuries. 3. 18th and 19th centuries.

1. ANTIQUITY. A relationship between art and literature was commonly assumed by ancient writers even before it was summed up in Horace's phrase *ut pictura poesis* ('as with painting, so with poetry'; 19 BC). There are numerous references in Classical texts, notably in Pausanias' *Description of Greece*, to artists using (or departing from) poetic models, especially the great epics. Homer was often seen as the inspiration of painters and sculptors alike; to have surpassed him was the highest compliment that could be paid to an artist, and one that was once accorded Apelles by Pliny the elder. Vase painters may have used pattern books, but there is no evidence for the existence of any kind of compendium or handbook specifically designed to help in devising iconographic inventions. Indeed Classical writers (rightly or wrongly) usually presented artists—the greatest of them at least—as literate and capable of iconographic innovation, a quality sometimes characterized by the terms *ingenium* or *phantasia*. In his dialogue *Zeuxis*, Lucian of Samosata introduces that artist's *Centaur Family*, for example, as a case of a painter being praised only for his novel subject-matter, while even the strangest allegorical figures, such as the *Kairos* (Opportunity) of Lysippos, are treated as inventions of their artists. Doubtless the mythological compilations attributed to Hyginus (*Fabulae* and *Astronomica*) or Apollodoros (*Bibliotheca*; *c*. 61 BC) were useful to painters as well as poets in Late Antiquity.

2. 12TH–17TH CENTURIES.

(i) Christian subject-matter. (ii) Secular history and mythology. (iii) Personification. (iv) Other developments.

(i) Christian subject-matter. Until the 16th century, iconographic handbooks were generally considered unneccessary for depicting religious themes. The Bible and collections of lives of saints, such as the *Golden Legend* (*c*. 1264) of Jacopo da Voragine, were the principal textual sources. The biblical commentary of Peter Comestor (*fl* 1168; *d* 1178–85), the *Historia scholastica*, a book that must have been owned by many parish priests, was a useful supplement. For Hell, poorly described in the canonical texts, there were accounts such as the *Visio Tundalis* and, especially for Tuscan artists, Dante's *Inferno*; Andrea di Cione, for example, followed this, as Ghiberti remarked in his *Commentarii*. One might expect to find compilations listing the attributes of the principal saints, but no such texts seem to have existed. Even in Byzantine art the *Hermeneia tes zoographikes technes* of the monk Dionysios of Furna, which contains detailed specifications of the way in which saints and scriptural subjects should be shown, dates only from the 18th century, so that it cannot be taken, as it once was, as a document of earlier practice. Federico Borromeo's treatise *De pictura sacra* (Milan, 1625), written after the Council of Trent, was concerned with the errors of artists in representing Christian—specifically, Roman Catholic—subjects, at a time when certain prominent clerics, worried about apocryphal stories and doctrinal impropriety, suggested that artists might require instruction in the religious subjects that formed the greater part of their output. Some notable artists even attempted to compose their own handbooks on iconography. Veronese evidently tried but does not seem to have made much progress, while the *Trattato della pittura e scultura, uso ed abuso loro, composto da un theologo e da un pittore* (Florence, 1652) by Pietro da Cortona and the Jesuit Giovanni Domenico Ottonelli was probably largely the work of the theologian. This book was essentially another Counter-Reformation treatise on the avoidance of doctrinal error. The same applies to a great extent to the large section of Francisco Pacheco's *Arte de la pintura* (Seville, 1649), which deals with iconography; and even if it was written by the artist himself he depended much on the advice of learned clerics, whose observations he quotes at length. Pacheco's recommendations had some influence on Sevillian painters, but largely through personal contact.

(ii) Secular history and mythology. In the case of themes from secular history, mythology and allegory, a distinction must be made between reference books of a general kind consulted by both artists and iconographic advisers, and manuals written principally for the use of painters and sculptors. In the first category are texts familiar from medieval times such as the *Gesta Romanorum* (*c*. 1300–1350) and collections of historical *exempla*, of which the *Facta et dicta memorabilia* (AD 31) of Valerius Maximus was the most important. It is worth remembering too that in Italy—and often elsewhere—the references to the ancient stories and characters in Dante's *Divine Comedy* or Petrarch's *Trionfi* regularly provided the initial ideas for historical subjects. For stories from mythology the *locus classicus* was the *Metamorphoses* of Ovid, which was published as 'the Bible of poets' as early as 1493 and by the late 16th century had become the 'painters' Bible'. Ovid's text was most often consulted in translations, usually of a very free kind, for example the Italian paraphrase of Giovanni di Bonsignori (Venice, 1497) and the later versions in verse by Giovanni Andrea dell'Anguillara (Venice, 1561) and Ludovico Dolce (Venice, 1553); there were several French translations available from 1484. Karel van Mander's Dutch epitome and moralization of the *Metamorphoses* was even included as part of his *Schilder-boeck* (Alkmaar, 1604). Joachim von Sandrart in turn inserted a German version of van Mander's commentary into his monumental treatise on art and artists, the *Teutsche Academie* (Frankfurt am Main, 1675–9); a separate volume of the *Metamorphoses* with his own illustrations was published at Nuremberg in 1698. In general, artists tended to favour illustrated versions of Ovid, and in the choice and

method of representation they were as much influenced by the plates as by the text itself. Indeed there were picture books published with the text reduced to minimal 'captions', which are often explicitly addressed to painters and were certainly very useful to them.

In addition to the *Metamorphoses* there was a long tradition of compilations of ancient mythology, ranging from encyclopedic works to much briefer summaries regarding the character, behaviour and appearance of the principal ancient gods. In the first category the most important early text was Boccaccio's *De genealogia deorum* (*c*. 1375), which was still being printed in the 16th century, when it was to some extent superseded by the *Mythologia* of Natale Conti (Comes; Venice, 1567), and by the *De deis gentium varia et multiplex historia* of Lilio Giraldi (Gyraldus; Basle, 1548). The existence of an Italian translation (Venice, 1547) of Boccaccio's book certainly contributed to its lasting popularity; it was still consulted even in the later 17th century. In the same way Conti enjoyed a certain vogue among artists in 17th-century France because his text was available in French from 1599. A much shorter German counterpart was the *Theologia mythologica* (Fribourg and Antwerp, 1532) of Georg Pictor, and a more elaborate one was the *Heydenwelt* (Basle, 1554) of J. Herold, which included illustrations also used in an enlarged edition of Pictor published in 1558. Two important mythological compendia in Spanish—Juan Pérez de Moya's *Philosophia secreta* (Madrid, 1585) and Fray Baltasar de Victoria's *Teatro de los dioses de la gentilidad* (Salamanca, 1620)—relied greatly on the earlier compilations, as did Sandrart's later *Iconologia deorum* (Nuremberg, 1680).

Although these works, and particularly those of Giraldi and Conti, are often cited by historians today in connection with works of art and were certainly used by scholars of the later Renaissance throughout Europe, they enjoyed less success among artists than Vincenzo Cartari's *Imagini de i dei degli antichi* (Venice, 1556), which, as its title suggests, was specifically concerned with Classical iconography. In the preface and elsewhere Cartari alluded to its potential usefulness to artists in devising subjects. Probably for this reason, subsequent editions, of which the earliest was published in Padua in 1571, included illustrations. The *Imagini* was still being printed in the late 17th century and also appeared in translation—in French, English (as J. Lynche: *The Fountain of Ancient Fiction*, London, 1599) and even Latin. In addition to drawing on the compilations of Boccaccio, Giraldi and Conti, Cartari also looked back to the medieval tradition of shorter mythological compendia, such as the 15th-century *Fulgentius metaphoralis* of John Ridewell, and the earliest of all, the so-called *Libellus* of Albricus (Alexander of Neckham), dating from the late 12th century, which was still being printed in the 16th century—as well as to the ancient compendia attributed to Hyginus and Apollodoros mentioned above.

(iii) Personifications. The mythological handbooks were also an important source for personifications. Indeed, the distinction between gods and personifications was often blurred, given that there was a persistent tendency to regard Classical myths as moral allegories—a tradition that goes back to such Late Antique works as Servius' commentary on Virgil (*c*. AD 400), and culminates in the *Ovide moralisé* (Paris, 1509) of Pierre Bersuire and Boccaccio's *Genealogia*. As well as including the principal Classical gods, such as Venus and Mars, which served as personifications of love and war respectively, they also listed a number of other deities such as Fortune, Opportunity and Concord, which were frequently represented by artists. Particularly in the 16th century the range of such personifications employed in pictorial and sculptural decorative schemes greatly increased, but their appearance and attributes were only standardized with the publication of Cesare Ripa's *Iconologia* (Rome, 1593; for illustration *see* RIPA, CESARE; *see also* DISEGNO E COLORE, fig. 1). This work, several times expanded and revised, and provided with illustrations from 1603, was repeatedly published in the principal European languages until well into the 18th century. It is by far the most important of all iconographic handbooks, specifically composed to meet the needs of artists. For allegories of the 17th and 18th centuries it is an indispensable source.

Ripa's text has often been used to identify personifications represented in works of art before 1593, but the validity of this procedure is highly questionable. Although he relied occasionally on earlier products devised by artists and their advisers, notably the 1565 *Mascherata* ordered by Francesco de' Medici in Florence and some frescoes in the Vatican, Ripa usually selected the attributes of his figures from the *Hieroglyphica* (Basle, 1556) of Piero Valeriano, a massive encyclopedia of visual symbols, which again appeared in many editions throughout Europe. Most of Ripa's personifications were therefore effectively his inventions. Valeriano's starting-point had been a short Late Antique compilation, the so-called *Hieroglyphica* (5th century AD) of Horapollo, discovered in the 15th century and first published in Venice in 1505. Iconographic advisers and artists also frequently used manuals of ancient coins, such as Guillaume Du Choul's *Discours de la religion des anciens Romains* (Lyon, 1556), the *Imagines Caesarum* (1548, 1554) of Enea Vico and the *Discorso sopra le medaglie antiche* (Venice, 1559) of Sebastiano Erizzo. The tradition was continued in the work of the Spanish antiquarian Antonio Agostín (1517–86). These texts, several of which were provided with excellent indexes to facilitate consultation, are the principal sources of personifications before Ripa, but the illustrations to the *Ingeniose sorti* (Venice, 1540) of Francesco Marcolini also enjoyed a certain popularity, aided by their being published separately as engravings by Enea Vico.

(iv) Other developments. The absence of ancient handbooks for artists may have prompted Federico Borromeo to suggest that Philostratos had written his *Imagines* (3rd century AD), a fictional account of a picture gallery composed as a theoretical exercise, to correct the mistakes of painters. Horapollo's *Hieroglyphica*, however, was an important source for the *Emblematum liber* (Augsburg, 1531; *see* EMBLEM BOOK, fig. 1) of Andrea Alciati, which initiated the hugely popular and long-lasting European tradition of the emblem book. Such publications, if not iconographic handbooks in the strict sense, were often used by artists, if only for symbolic details. One illustrated book, which is often misleadingly classed as an emblem book, had a direct influence on the subject-matter of

painting. This was the *Microcosmos sive parvus mundus* (Antwerp, 1579) of Willem van Haecht, republished in Dutch by Jan Moerman (Amsterdam, 1608) and subsequently further expanded by Joost van den Vondel as *Den gulden winckel der konstlievende Nederlanders* (Amsterdam, 1613). It consists of a series of pictures, generally of scenes from ancient history, with accompanying commentaries and moralizations. Van Haecht particularly recommended his book to artists to provide new ideas, and it appears to have promoted, for example, themes involving ancient philosophers such as Diogenes.

Other sorts of books frequently consulted by artists and their advisers include the *De inventoribus rerum* (Venice, 1499) of Polydore Vergil, which was used by Annibal Caro in devising frescoes painted by Taddeo and Federico Zuccaro at Caprarola, and the *De gli habiti antichi e moderni* (Venice, 1590) of Cesare Vecellio, a costume book.

It should also be mentioned that one of the most common types of iconographical programme, those devised for triumphal entries and other forms of public ceremonial, gave birth to a specific class of publication. These were detailed descriptions, often lavishly illustrated and widely distributed, which in turn served as indispensable sources for the organizers of later events of the same kind. When Vincenzo Borghini devised the state entry into Florence in 1565 he consulted no less than 30 works of this type, while the illustrated account of Rubens's pageants for the entry of Cardinal-Infante Ferdinand into Antwerp in 1635 was used for some permanent decorative schemes, for example that of the town hall in Amsterdam.

With the growing tendency from the mid-16th century to consult handbooks, writers of treatises on art increasingly included recommendations about subject-matter, as well as lists of useful texts—from the Bible to contemporary works on mythography and ancient history. Giovanni Battista Armenini did this, for example, in his *Dei veri precetti della pittura* (Ravenna, 1586), as did Roger de Piles in his *Remarques sur le poème de . . . Dufresnoy* (Paris, 1667) and Gérard de Lairesse in his *Groote schilderboek* (Amsterdam, 1707).

3. 18TH AND 19TH CENTURIES. There was an increasing interest in antiquarianism in the 18th century, and newer studies on ancient coins, gems and antiquities to some extent replaced the pioneering 16th-century works on the recommended reading lists for artists. Bernard de Montfaucon's monumental *Antiquité expliquée* (Paris, 1719; supplement, 1724; Eng. trans. 1721–5) provided a valuable encyclopedia, while Charles Rollin's *Histoire ancienne* and *Histoire romaine* (Paris, 1731–8; 1738–48) became standard texts for history, frequently republished and epitomized. Johann Joachim Winckelmann's *Versuche eine Allegorie besonders für die Kunst* (Dresden, 1766) was designed to supplant Ripa by providing allegories more closely based on ancient models. Nevertheless the *Iconologia* continued to be consulted, even on occasion by Goya. For Neo-classical painters, too, Ovid remained the principal source for myths, with Plutarch, Livy and Valerius Maximus serving for history. Both David and Ingres, indeed, were well read in ancient literature, which by this time was widely available in translation. Encyclopedic compendia of mythology continued to appear, but now the authors began to emphasize their value for understanding pictorial subject-matter, rather than for devising it. One such publication was the *Dictionnaire abrégé de la fable* (Paris, 1727) of Pierre Chompré, which went through more than 20 editions in France alone before 1850, with translations into Spanish and Polish. Chompré also wrote a *Dictionnaire abrégé de la Bible pour la connoissance des tableaux historiques* (Paris, 1755), but this enjoyed less success. With the exhibitions of the later 19th century, when the notion of a hierarchy of genres and a standard repertory of subjects broke down, iconographic handbooks ceased to be addressed to painters and sculptors. Rather they became art-historical tools, useful for understanding the subject-matter of the art of the past.

BIBLIOGRAPHY

J. Schlosser: *Die Kunstliteratur* (Vienna, 1924); Fr. trans. as *La Littérature artistique* (Paris, 1984)

M. D. Henkel: 'Illustrierte Ausgaben von Ovids Metamorphosen im XV., XVI. und XVII. Jahrhundert', *Vortr. Bib. Warburg*, vi (1926–7), pp. 58–144

J. Seznec: *La Survivance des dieux antiques* (London, 1940/*R* Paris, 1980); Eng. trans. as *The Survival of the Pagan Gods* (New York, 1953)

P. Hetherington: *The 'Painter's Manual' of Dionysius of Fourna* (London, 1974)

J. Brown: *Images and Ideas in Seventeenth-century Spanish Painting* (Princeton, 1978)

J. Białostocki: 'Doctus Artifex and the Library of the Artist in the XVIth and XVIIth Century', *De arte et libris: Festschrift Erasmus, 1934–1984* (Amsterdam, 1984), pp. 11–22

Iconographic programmes. Art historical term probably originating in Germany towards the end of the 19th century. Its use by art historians today is not very consistent: it may be no more than a synonym for the subject-matter of a work of art, which might have been devised entirely by the artist; equally, it may imply a detailed specification of the entire content of a picture or sculpture. Most commonly, however, it describes a scheme of thematically related images, for example a series of arches or pageants for a triumphal entry or a cycle of frescoes, typically devised by someone with scholarly interests. Given its inherent ambiguity, the term is a dangerous one, carrying as it does the implication that any work or group of works of art to which it is applied is both coherent in meaning and learned in content. In this article the term will be used principally in connection with works for which written prescriptions survive.

1. Before *c.* 1420. 2. *c.* 1420–*c.* 1550. 3. From *c.* 1550.

1. BEFORE *c.* 1420. Rightly or wrongly, ancient writers on art are virtually unanimous in crediting artists themselves with the invention of their subject-matter, even in the case of such complex allegories as the *Calumny* of Apelles. The *Tabula Cebetis*, an elaborately symbolic representation of human life in the dialogue attributed to the 1st-century AD philosopher Cebes, might seem the obvious product of a learned programme, having purportedly been dedicated in a temple of Kronos by a 'wise and erudite' man for the instruction of the young, but, as Erasmus already recognized, the picture itself existed only as a rhetorical device. Other literary descriptions of paintings bear more relation to surviving works of ancient art. Two such examples are the pictures of the rescue of

Prometheus and of Andromeda described in Achilles Tatius' *Kleitophon and Leukippe* (III.vi–viii), probably written in the 3rd century AD. These are carefully presented as pendants, thus providing a notional example of an iconographic scheme (*see* EKPHRASIS). Modern scholars have, with more or less ingenuity, discerned similar schemes in Pompeian murals. But the importance of programmes for ancient art has perhaps been overestimated, and attempts to find a single rationale for the choice of all the subjects on, say, the Chest of Cypselus, an object recorded only in the words of Pausanias in the *Guide to Greece* (V.xviii.5), seem misguided, especially if these assume that Pausanias failed to appreciate the true content. Even in the case of the surviving Pergamon altar (*c.* 180–160 BC; Berlin, Pergamonmus.), it is hard to demonstrate that the whole scheme was rigorously coherent. On the other hand, the extensive evidence about inscriptions on ancient works of art implies some collaboration between artists and literary men. Pausanias at times credits scholars with inscriptions, suggesting, for example, that Eumelos of Corinth composed those on the Chest of Cypselus (V.xix.10).

This tradition evidently survived into Christianity in the form of the *tituli* (explanatory inscriptions) composed for the murals and mosaics in churches. The ancient pedagogic device of the description of a work of art flourished during the Middle Ages, but these 'pictures' were generally neither accounts of, nor specifications for, works by real artists, even if artists occasionally may have borrowed personifications from them. Medieval philosophy lent itself to diagrammatic exegesis, and scholastic *schemata* expounding the order of the universe or the hierarchy of the Church are occasionally reflected in monumental works of art, such as the paintings in the crypt at ANAGNI or the frescoes in the Spanish Chapel at S Maria Novella in Florence (*see* FLORENCE, §IV, 6). The habit of drawing parallels, symbolic and typological, influenced the design as well as the content of certain types of religious imagery, such as stained-glass windows (*see* STAINED GLASS, §III, 1). However, the frequent supposition that the figurative decoration of medieval buildings, especially the great cathedrals, was devised according to some elaborate programme, rather than on a piecemeal basis, is not supported by documentary evidence. Even in the field of manuscript illumination the account (Geneva, Bib. Pub. & U., MS. lat. 54) of the humanist Jean Lebègue (1368–1457), written just before 1420, of a series of pictures to illustrate Sallust's *Catiline* is virtually the only surviving example of an entire programme of instructions for an artist.

2. *c.* 1420–*c.* 1550. Evidence of iconographic programmes as such can first be identified in the Renaissance, principally in Italy. Contracts for altarpieces (*see* ALTARPIECE, §2) often specify the subject to be represented, but this usually consists of no more than a list of figures to be included, with an indication of their placing, according to their importance. Significantly, the choice of narrative scenes in the predella is usually left to the painter. Contracts for cycles of narratives, too, very seldom specify the exact subjects and their arrangement, a case in point being the frescoes by Ghirlandaio in S Maria Novella in Florence, where the final disposition does not correspond to the contract. The best-known iconographic programme of the 15th century, a simple list of subjects devised by Leonardo Bruni for Ghiberti's second set of bronze doors for the Florentine Baptistery, was not actually followed by the sculptor, who, as he stated in his *Commentarii*, had chosen to execute the doors according to his own ideas. Even the very elaborate instructions given by Jean de Montagnac, canon of St Agricol, Montagnac, in the contract for Enguerrand Quarton's *Coronation of the Virgin by the Holy Trinity* (1453; Villeneuve-lès-Avignon, Mus. Mun.) gave the artist a certain scope. From at least the mid-15th century to the early 17th the Puy d'Amiens, a society devoted to the praise of the Virgin, invited each year a contribution of a painting on a theme involving a different aspect or attribute of Mary, producing a whole series of unusual and highly determined religious paintings. The programme for the altarpiece of the Brotherhood of the Holy Sacrament at St Pieterskerk, Leuven, in 1464 was less eccentric. Here Dieric Bouts the elder was required to surround the scene of the *Institution of the Eucharist* with straightforwardly typological Old Testament subjects and to follow the advice of two local theologians in the matter.

Documented instances of the involvement of learned laymen in artistic schemes are rare before 1500, and most of them place emphasis on the provision of appropriate inscriptions, rather than on detailed instructions regarding composition. One case of a learned man providing a series of subjects for an artist is the scheme devised by the writer Franco Sacchetti for the painted decoration of the interior of the church of Orsanmichele in Florence, but here the simplicity of the imagery and the lack of coherence between the different elements are notable. Guarino da Verona is known to have provided attributes for a series of *Nine Muses* painted at Belfiore in the *studiolo* of Lionello d'Este, Marquese of Ferrara. In this case the need for learned advice regarding the appearance of figures for which there was no established visual tradition is obvious enough.

That so few Renaissance humanist programmes have survived may be due to the fact that there was no clear precedent for this kind of activity in accounts of ancient art. Thus, even though Marsilio Ficino certainly knew the *Tabula Cebetis*, there is no evidence that he thought of employing an artist to illustrate anything more philosophically complex than the contrast of the laughing Democritus and the weeping Heraclitus. That painting was for his study, and library decoration was generally something of interest to scholars. The most erudite themes can usually be associated with some such context, an outstanding example being Fray José de Sigüenza's elaborate and witty scheme for the library of the Escorial, Spain. Humanists might also concern themselves with the illustrations to books. Konrad Celtis even produced a layout for the title-page to the fourth book of his *Amores* (Nuremberg, 1502), and he similarly provided the specifications for Dürer's woodcut of *Philosophy* (1502). Authors continued to detail the content of title-pages but then sometimes complained about engravers who had not understood their ideas. It is, however, highly unusual to find a scholar giving detailed specifications for the subject of a painting, as Justus Lipsius did when he asked his friend Otto van Veen

1. Perugino: *Battle between Love and Chastity*, oil on canvas, 1.60×1.91 m, 1505 (Paris, Musée du Louvre)

for a picture, now lost, of the exemplary deaths of Arria and Paetus.

The term used in the Renaissance for the choice of a subject was invention, a concept borrowed from rhetoric and accorded relatively little attention in the standard textbooks. In his *De pictura* (1435) Alberti recommended that artists frequent the company of literary men, who could help them with their inventions, and he singled out two notable examples of the genre, the *Calumny* of Apelles and the Three Graces, which, he said, signified Liberality. For Alberti, therefore, a good invention was one that allowed the artist to represent some allegorical theme or abstract concept in attractive visual terms. In the later Renaissance, the role of learned advisers was most commonly related to subjects of this sort. Typically, they suggested appropriate personifications for all kinds of decorative contexts and often proposed suitable identifying attributes. Such advisers, however, seldom gave artists precise instructions regarding compositions. The most celebrated example involved an allegorical subject not dissimilar to the *Calumny*, in which the arrangement and actions of the figures were central to the intended meaning. This is the famous series of instructions provided to Perugino in 1503 for a painting of the *Battle between Love and Chastity* (1505; Paris, Louvre; see fig. 1) for Isabella d'Este, Marchese of Mantua. The scheme, a *psychomachia* (battle for the soul) of a rather conventional kind, was almost certainly devised by the Mantuan courtier Paride Ceresara, who may well have also been responsible for the inventions of the other paintings for the same room, by Mantegna and others, some of which remain unexplained.

Learned advisers also helped in selecting subjects from history or mythology for the decoration of private and public buildings. With their knowledge of ancient literature and access to the relevant texts, they were in a better position than most artists to find, for instance, particularly apposite historical *exempla* for specific contexts or occasions, or groups of individual subjects related to a common theme. Thus, although the documentation has not survived, it is highly likely that an educated layman selected the themes from the works of the Roman historian Valerius Maximus for the stories exemplifying political virtues painted by Domenico Beccafumi on the ceiling of the Sala del Concistoro in the Palazzo Pubblico, Siena, supplementing the text with passages available in the printed commentary. Likewise, Paolo Giovio found or devised historical parallels to events in the lives of Cosimo de' Medici and Lorenzo de' Medici that were then painted in the Medici villa of Poggio a Caiano, near Florence (*see* POGGIO A CAIANO, VILLA MEDICI).

3. FROM *c.* 1550. Written iconographic programmes survive in large numbers from the middle of the 16th century, first in Italy but later elsewhere in Europe. This phenomenon may reflect the richness of the archival evidence surviving from this period and the growing taste for secular decoration in palaces and public buildings, but also the increasing popularity of the ICONOGRAPHIC HANDBOOK. These books, often furnished with excellent indexes, made the task of the devisers of such programmes far easier. Thus it was now possible to exploit readily the corpus of Classical personifications on ancient coins and to use the pseudo-science of hieroglyphics to devise new attributes for personifications. Likewise, mythological compendia provided an invaluable source of images and narrative subjects, just as printed histories and collections of *exempla* offered a wide range of themes.

An analysis of the surviving programmes reveals that such publications were used extensively. Thus Cosimo Bartoli, who supplied several programmes for Vasari's decorations in the Palazzo Vecchio in Florence, evidently consulted Boccaccio's *Genealogia deorum* (*c.* 1350–60; It. trans., Venice, 1547) for mythological subjects, while usually inventing personifications on the basis of a simple association of ideas. Vincenzo Borghini, another of Vasari's collaborators, preferred to base his personifications on Enea Vico's engravings of ancient coins, and in planning the temporary structures for a state entry into Florence in 1565 he studied every available account of earlier pageantry. A series of personifications devised by the Accademia Veneziana in 1560 was based exclusively on Piero Valeriano's *Hieroglyphica* (Basle, 1556), while at about the same time Annibal Caro, in the Stanza dell'Aurora at the Villa Farnese, Caprarola (*see* CAPRAROLA, VILLA FARNESE, §1), relied extensively on Vincenzo Cartari's *Imagini delli dei de gl'antichi* (Venice, 1556, 2/1571, facs ed. M. Bussagli, Genoa, 1987). Both these texts were consulted by Giuseppe Betussi in devising the decoration of the Obizzi castle of Cataio, near Padua, around 1570; but he also used Guillaume Du Choul's study of Roman religion, the *Discours de la religion des anciens Romains* (Lyon, 1556).

Compendia such as those mentioned above remained popular throughout the 17th century, but from its publication in Rome in 1593 the most important manual was Cesare Ripa's dictionary of personifications, the *Iconologia*, which was frequently reissued and revised. It was used, for example, in a scheme for the Palazzo Comunale of Modena devised by Giovanni Castelvetro (1532–1605) in 1604, in a series of programmes of the 1720s by Adolph von Albrecht (1681–1751) for the glorification of the Holy Roman Emperor, Charles VI, and in the library at St Florian Abbey, Austria, in 1746. In none of these programmes, however, was Ripa's name mentioned, and the attributes he recommended were often modified or combined in novel ways.

The devisers of iconographic programmes differed in their taste for obscure historical themes or Classical correctness in their personifications, but the genre itself, once established, did not greatly change until the end of the Baroque era. For the most part devisers depended on a relatively narrow range of reference books and sought to appeal, directly or otherwise, to Classical precedent in the choice of imagery. Almost invariably they were preoccupied with inscriptions, usually in Latin, that offered them an irresistible opportunity to display their wit and learning. Even where the written programmes are missing, the presence of elegant inscriptions is almost always a clear sign of some involvement on the part of an educated adviser. This applies as much to religious as to secular schemes, as is illustrated by the 15th-century typological decoration on the walls of the Sistine Chapel in the Vatican Palace. But where inscriptions are lacking, the possibility that the iconographic invention was devised by the artist alone cannot be excluded. Such, for example, may well have been true of Veronese's frescoes (*c.* 1561) in the Villa Barbaro at Maser (*see* MASER, VILLA BARBARO). Painters might have owned copies of Cartari, Ripa, Vico, Du Choul and Valeriano, and these manuals would certainly have permitted them to produce decorative schemes no less coherent or correct than those of their literary friends and acquaintances. Rubens, admittedly an artist of unusual learning, was even asked to provide programmes for fellow painters.

Although modern scholars often suppose that iconographic programmes were normally imposed on the artists by their patrons, this was certainly not always the case. Thus it was Vasari, not his employer Cosimo I de' Medici, who sought the advice of Bartoli and Borghini, although he did not always follow it. Again, it is clear that programmes varied in their sophistication. In some cases (e.g. the Florentine entry of 1565) every iconographic element was carefully integrated, while in others (e.g. the entry of James I into London in 1603) individual structures were devised by different scholars. The absence of any standard synonym for the modern 'programme' merely underlines the fact that many schemes of decoration were not to any great degree programmatic. Even someone as sophisticated as Caro, in his scheme for the study of Cardinal Alessandro Farnese at Caprarola, described his series of closely related stories and images on the theme of solitude as inventions, in the plural, not as a single invention. That particular programme was a triumphant display of the principle of DECORUM, and organized with unusual care; but it does not follow that every decorative cycle was planned with a comparable degree of rigour or called for the intervention of a learned adviser. It still remains to be established, for example, whether Annibale Carracci's Galleria Farnese in Rome is anything more than a loosely arranged group of familiar mythological subjects on amorous themes that could well have been chosen by the artist himself, and whose disposition in the larger scheme was in most cases without precise significance.

In the 19th century it becomes appropriate to talk of 'programmatic' decorations, as in the many public buildings erected as monuments to culture, commerce and civility, with their encyclopedic schemes intended as expositions of the workings of nature or the progress of history, the arts or the Industrial Revolution. Despite the novelty of many themes and personifications, these often

2. Eugène Delacroix: *Orpheus Bringing the Art of Peace to Primitive Greece* (1845–7), oil and wax medium, half-dome of the library of the Chambre des Députés, Palais-Bourbon, Paris

reflect notions about medieval programmes and on occasion recall Raphael's Stanza della Segnatura in the Vatican Palace. Some notable schemes were still devised along quite traditional lines, for example Delacroix's decorations (1838–47) in the library of the Chambre des Députés in the Palais-Bourbon in Paris, with their Classical *exempla* (see fig. 2) . Interestingly, here the artist himself seems to have been largely responsible for the iconography. In one other respect, too, the 19th-century programmes belong within the tradition: they are meant to be clear. A striking feature of all the documents is the desire to avoid ambiguity and multiple levels of meaning, although these might be invoked *ex post facto* by courtiers in order to demonstrate their wit, a case in point being Vasari's account of the frescoes in the Palazzo Vecchio, Florence, in his *Ragionamenti* (pubd posth., Florence, 1588). The visual language employed in decorative schemes might be obscure, and often unfamiliar even to educated members of the public, but in almost every case it was meant to be amenable to exact, if learned, exegesis, and ephemeral schemes of decoration, perhaps the most characteristic product of the learned adviser, were normally accompanied by explanatory publications. In general, compilers of iconographic programmes rarely took account of the specific skills of the artist, although Borghini explicitly said that painters should not be given precise instructions, because they did their best work when allowed to illustrate their own ideas. The principal interest of such documents lies less in their content, which for the most part is stereotyped and conventional, than in the visual expression subsequently given to it by the painters themselves.

BIBLIOGRAPHY

H. Tietze: 'Programme und Entwürfe zu den grossen österreichischen Barockfresken', *Jb. Ksthist. Samml. Allhöch. Ksrhaus.*, xxx (1911), pp. 1–28

A. Masson: *Le Décor des bibliothèques du moyen âge à la Révolution* (Geneva, 1972)

A.-M. Lecoq: 'Le Puy d'Amiens de 1518: La Loi du genre et l'art du peintre', *Rev. A.* [Paris], xxviii (1977), pp. 63–74

M. Evans: 'The Geometry of the Mind', *Archit. Assoc. Q.*, xii/4 (1980), pp. 32–55

E. P. Garretson: 'Conrad Adolph von Albrecht, Programmer at the Court of Charles VI', *Mitt. Österreich. Gal.*, xxiv–xxv (1980–81), pp. 19–92

R. Guerrini: *Studi su Valerio Massimo* (Pisa, 1981)

C. Hope: 'Artists, Patrons and Advisers in the Italian Renaissance', *Patronage in the Renaissance*, ed. G. F. Lytle and S. Orgel (Princeton, 1981), pp. 293–343

R. A. Scorza: 'Vincenzo Borghini and *Invenzione*: The Florentine *Apparato* of 1565', *J. Warb. & Court. Inst.*, xliv (1981), pp. 57–75

C. Robertson: 'Annibale Caro as Iconographer: Sources and Method', *J. Warb. & Court. Inst.*, xlv (1982), pp. 160–81

R. Brilliant: *Visual Narratives: Storytelling in Etruscan and Roman Art* (Ithaca and London, 1984), pp. 65–89

C. Hope: 'Veronese and the Venetian Tradition of Allegory', *Proc. Brit. Acad.*, lxxxi (1985), pp. 389–428

D. Byrne: 'An Early French Humanist and Sallust: Jean Lebègue and the Iconographical Programme for the *Catiline* and *Jugurtha*', *J. Warb. & Court. Inst.*, xlix (1986), pp. 41–65

A. Hopmans: 'Delacroix's Decorations in the Palais Bourbon Library: A Classic Example of an Unacademic Approach', *Simiolus*, xvii (1987), pp. 240–69

M. Wagner: *Allegorie und Geschichte: Ausstattungsprogramme öffentlicher Gebäude des 19. Jahrhunderts in Deutschland* (Tübingen, 1989)

CHARLES HOPE, ELIZABETH MCGRATH

Iconography and iconology. Terms that refer broadly to the study of subjects and themes in works of art. Iconology, which is based on the results of iconography, is the more wide-ranging and comprehensive. One of the principal concerns of iconography is the discovery of symbolic and allegorical meanings in a work of art (*see* SYMBOL and ALLEGORY). This article is concerned with Western culture and takes its examples primarily from northern European art. However, the principles involved can also be applied *mutatis mutandis* to the art of other cultures (see under separate country surveys).

I. Introduction. II. History of practice. III. Specific studies. IV. Indices and classifications.

I. Introduction.

Historically, the terms 'iconography' and 'iconology' have often been used loosely and interchangeably. However, a distinction between the two can be made: in the modern sense iconography involves the collection, classification and analysis of data, from which the theme or subject of a work of art is deduced. Iconology, on the other hand, starting from the results of iconography, attempts to explain the very basis for the existence of a work of art and its entire meaning. With reference to the broader cultural background, the iconologist pinpoints those features of a work of art that can be seen as symptomatic of a specific culture. Any form of meaningful artistic expression is in principle susceptible to iconographic and iconological study. In practice, however, the focus is chiefly on figurative images and architecture, studying, in particular, the historical perpetuation and transformation of motifs, themes and types. The researcher must be aware of the historical context of the work in question, and an 'iconographic fallacy' can occur when, for example, plainly medieval concepts are incorporated into 17th-century paintings, or when religious and secular genres become intertwined. Together with the histories of style, reception, materials and others, iconography and iconology contribute to the better understanding of a work of art.

II. History of practice.

1. Early history, 16th century to early 19th. 2. Early 19th century to early 20th. 3. The schools of Aby Warburg, G. J. Hoogewerff and Erwin Panofsky.

1. EARLY HISTORY, 16TH CENTURY TO EARLY 19TH. Iconography began in the 16th century and developed along various lines. In the first place there were compendia for artists and art-lovers with indications and explanations of themes and allegorical personifications (*see* ICONOGRAPHIC HANDBOOK). From the humanist and antiquarian traditions came such compendia as the *Iconologia* (1593; first illustrated edition, 1603) of Cesare Ripa, while on the religious side, rooted in the framework of the Counter-Reformation, were such works as Joannes Molanus's *De picturis et imaginibus sacris* (Leuven, 1570). In addition there were artists' (auto)biographies such as Vasari's *Ragionamenti* (1588) and Bellori's *Le vite de' pittori, scultori ed architetti moderni* (1672). Bellori was one of the first to study the literary sources of themes in paintings with a view to thereby establishing the deeper significance and the general symbolic 'idea' of the work of art. In this he was a forerunner not only of modern iconography but of modern iconology as well. There was also a more systematic study of the monuments of antiquity and early Christendom: in *Inlustrium virorum ut extant in urbe expressi vultus* (1569) by Achilles Statius (Aquiles Estaço; 1524–81), concerning ancient portraiture; *Roma sotterranea* (Rome, 1632) by Antonio Bosio, concerning the recently discovered catacombs; and the wide-ranging *Recueil d'antiquités égyptiennes, étrusques, greques, romaines et gauloises* (1752–67) by Anne-Claude-Philippe de Tubières, Comte de Caylus.

The foundations for the scientific approach of iconography were, however, laid by Johann Joachim Winckelmann, who considered the meticulous and objective study of the monuments of antiquity to be a requisite for discovering the significance of their contents, as he contended in *Versuch einer Allegorie besonders für die Kunst* (1766). Meanwhile, following Ripa, the term 'iconology' was employed for what later came to be understood as iconography, while this latter term remained in use for the systematic description of portraits. The famous portrait series (Antwerp, 1645) by Anthony van Dyck appeared in 1759 as *Iconographie ou vie des hommes illustres* (Amsterdam and Leipzig). In archaeology the term 'iconography' retained this meaning for a long time, although by the beginning of the 19th century it was employed in France in the sense that has since become usual.

2. EARLY 19TH CENTURY TO EARLY 20TH. The revival of religiosity during the Romantic period prompted the establishment of the so-called French iconographic school. Its main aim was to recover the substantially lost knowledge of medieval symbolism. The central figure of the first phase of the school was Adolphe-Napoléon Didron, author of *Iconographie chrétienne: Histoire de Dieu* (1843). The school reached its zenith with the monumental *Dictionnaire d'archéologie chrétienne et de liturgie* (1907–53) by Fernand Cabrol (1855–1937) and Henri Leclercq (1869–1945) and in the influential studies of Emile Mâle on the art of the Middle Ages and the Counter-Reformation (e.g. *L'Art religieux du XIIIe siècle en France*; 1898). Mâle realized that in medieval art each form is the container for one concept, and, although this idea later came to be less strictly applied, it continued to dominate Christian iconography. Mâle was also the first to realize the importance of Ripa's *Iconologia* for the iconography of the Counter-Reformation. The French iconographic school systematized Christian iconography. After symbolic character, it emphasized mainly the didactic character of Christian art. It underscored the great importance of studying the liturgy as well as patristics and such large encyclopedias as the *Speculum majus* (Strasbourg, 1473–6) of Vincent of Beauvais (*c.* 1190–1264).

In Germany the beginning of Christian iconography, established rather later than in France, had as its principal representative Anton Springer, who strove for an objective and historical approach to medieval art and its sources instead of a Romantic one. The rules he formulated for this approach were later adopted by, among others, Karl Künstle (1859–1932), as is shown in his *Ikonographie der christlichen Kunst* (1926–8).

The first comprehensive work in the area of secular iconography was Raymond van Marle's *Iconographie de l'art profane* (1931–2), but a more important stimulus for its development was the work of Aby Warburg and Erwin Panofsky.

3. THE SCHOOLS OF ABY WARBURG, G. J. HOOGEWERFF AND ERWIN PANOFSKY. The further development of iconography is for the most part connected with that of iconology. Decisive steps in the development of these disciplines were taken by ABY WARBURG, G. J. HOOGEWERFF and ERWIN PANOFSKY.

In his congress lecture on the painted wall decorations in the Palazzo Schifanoia, Ferrara, in 1912, Warburg showed that the art of a specific period could be connected in numerous ways and in different degrees with the religion, philosophy, literature, science, political and social life of that same period. Moreover, he demonstrated that in some respects an underlying link exists between Classical antiquity, the medieval period and modern times, and, finally, that works of both 'free' and applied art could be seen as valuable historical documents. With his method ('iconological analysis') he argued for the destruction of art history's traditional boundaries. In the circle round him at the Bibliothek Warburg in Hamburg and (from 1933) at the Warburg Institute in London, this method was put into practice. In order to avoid a terminological babel, Hoogewerff, in a conference lecture at Oslo in 1928, attempted to define iconography and iconology and their underlying relationship. He contended that this relationship is equivalent to that between geography and geology: the first is descriptive, fact-collecting and analytical; the second, employing the observations of the first, is explanatory, synoptic and exegetic.

Of greater influence than Hoogewerff's theoretical explanation was Panofsky's, not least on account of his sublimely practical exposition of his theory. Having already presented his theory in a preliminary version in 1932, in 1939 he devised a truly consistent methodology of iconography and iconology, which he propounded in the introduction to his *Studies in Iconology* (1939) and, with minor amendments, in *Meaning in the Visual Arts* (1955). Panofsky distinguished three levels of interpretation: pre-iconographic description (a pseudo-formal analysis), iconographic analysis in the narrow sense, and iconographic interpretation (from 1955 called iconological interpretation) in the deeper sense.

Pre-iconographic description concerns the primary or natural subject, distinguishing between factual subjects (people, animals, objects etc.) and their underlying relationships (identified as situations or events), and expressive subjects ('strong' gestures and attitudes; expression of atmosphere). These 'pure forms', recognized as carriers of primary or natural meaning, constitute the world of artistic motifs. Practical experience is required for the recognition of these subjects (familiarity with objects and events). Iconographic analysis concerns the secondary or

1. Philips Galle: *Triumph of Time*, engraving after Maarten van Heemskerck, 192×264 mm; from the series *Triumphs of Petrarch*, 1565 (Amsterdam, Rijksprentenkabinet)

conventional subject. Artistic motifs or their combinations (compositions) can be brought together using themes and concepts, thus making the world of figures, history and allegories. Knowledge of literary sources is required for their recognition (familiarity with specific themes and concepts). Iconological interpretation concerns the intrinsic meaning or content. Artistic motifs, figures, history and allegories, regarded as manifestations and symptoms of fundamental principles in a culture or period, can be interpreted as what Ernst Cassirer (1874–1945) called 'symbolic' values. Works of art thereby become documents of an artistic personality, a civilization, or a defined religious or philosophical conviction. The researcher requires 'synthetic intuition' (familiarity with the essential goals of the human spirit) for the interpretation, which will inevitably be determined by his personal psychology and conception of the world.

The three levels of interpretation must be approached consecutively: a correct identification of artistic motifs is a requirement for a correct iconographic analysis, which in turn is necessary for a correct iconological interpretation. In all its manifestations, art is influenced by its historical context. This needs to be taken into account when interpreting a work of art, and Panofsky therefore formulated corrective principles for each of the three levels of interpretation. For pre-iconographic description the researcher must be aware of the history of style (the manner whereby, under varying historical conditions, objects and events were expressed in forms); for iconographic analysis, the history of types (the manner whereby, under varying historical conditions, specific themes or concepts were expressed in objects and events); and for iconological interpretation, the history of the culture in general (the manner whereby, under varying historical conditions, essential goals of the human spirit were expressed in specific themes and concepts).

Panofsky's method met with an exceptional response. Although it was developed for the art of the Renaissance, it seemed to be applicable to figurative art of any period. His own studies, and those of, for example, Fritz Saxl, Rudolf Wittkower, Ernst Gombrich, Kurt Weitzmann, Richard Krautheimer, Guy de Tervarent, Henri van de Waal (1910–72) and Jan Białostocki, and, among a younger generation of researchers, Hans Belting (*b* 1935), Eddy de Jongh, Larry Silver, James Henry Marrow (*b* 1941) and Craig Harbison, have made iconography and iconology an extremely important and fruitful branch of art history, comparable with other disciplines in the humanities.

Panofsky's concept of iconology was, however, not without opposition. After a period of some 30 years of consensus (with the exception of Otto Pächt's severe criticism), the epistemological basis of iconology became the subject of dispute, especially with respect to Panofsky's adherence to Ernst Cassirer's theory of symbolic forms. At the same time a more sociologically orientated art history arose, stressing the importance of the function of a work of art with respect to its meaning, thus paying attention to the role of the public. A fundamental criticism of iconology has been developed by the school of art-historical hermeneutics (with Oskar Bätschmann (*b* 1943) as its most prominent spokesman). This school aims at shifting the focus of iconology from that on meaning as such to that on the work of art itself by taking the aesthetic experience as a starting-point for the interpretation of a work of art, and by establishing a relationship between aesthetic experience, art theory, art history and the practical work of an artist following the lines and prescripts of philosophical hermeneutics, or hermeneutics as developed for specific fields of art practice (e.g. literature). Nevertheless, for art history today iconology and iconography continue to be most fruitful as methods for understanding the meaning of art.

III. Specific studies.

1. Analysis of motifs, themes and types. 2. Analysis of symbolic meaning.

1. Analysis of motifs, themes and types.

(i) Introduction. (ii) Transformations. (iii) Imitation theory. (iv) Vehicles of transmission. (v) *Motivkunde.*

(i) Introduction. Form and content are inextricably linked. Iconographic analysis of the content of a work of art is therefore incomplete without a study of its formal aspects, which elucidates the origin and development of a motif, theme or type, with all its sources and variations. In the history of motifs, themes and types, an ongoing tension can be perceived between old and new, continuity and variation. Visual traditions can lead to the canonization of image formulae, which inhibits the development of a theme. Even the influence of a literary source on an existing theme can be diminished if it is not simultaneously

2. *Saturn*, from the *Chronograph of 354*, Renaissance copy (Rome, Vatican, Biblioteca Apostolica, Cod. Barb. Lat. 2154, fol. 8)

3. *Kairos*, marble relief, 600×650 mm, Roman, copy after the late 4th-century BC original by Lysippos (Turin, Museo Civico d'Arte Antica); allegory of Time and Opportunity

strengthened through visual stimuli. In this context, Panofsky (1953) identified resistance to the depiction of the Nativity according to the *Revelationes* (Lübeck, 1492; written *c*. 1360–70) of St Bridget of Sweden (*c*. 1302–73), because it deviated from the traditional scheme.

In a defined period variations in an established scheme appear whenever the contribution of the artist's individuality is greater than that of tradition. The recognition by a new generation of artists of unexploited possibilities in old image formulae (unused because of impediments caused by style) can be seen as one of the driving forces of art. In general, it can be said that art does not stem initially from the direct representation of reality or of a literary datum but rather from other art, i.e. from a visual tradition.

4. Giulio Fontana: *Battle of Cadore*, engraving after a lost wall painting by Titian, 390×530 mm, *c*. 1569 (Paris, Bibliothèque Nationale)

(ii) Transformations. A distinction must be made between the forms that an existing theme or type goes through and that which is chosen for a new theme. The depiction of existing themes and types can be liable to transformation of a general or a specific nature. An example of general transformation is the development at the end of the Middle Ages from iconic to narrative representation, not just of the Man of Sorrows but also of the Passion in general. A specific transformation is that for which Panofsky introduced the term 'pseudomorphosis': Classical personifications that, having acquired a non-Classical expression during the Middle Ages, preserved aspects of the intervening medieval phase when restored to their Classical form. In some cases (for example, Father Time, see figs 1–3; Cupid blindfolded), though not consciously, these aspects were those that expressed the development of these personifications in the Middle Ages.

An important part in the design of new themes was played by the so-called analogy principle: artists sought analogies in older themes, sometimes consciously but more often unconsciously, in relation to content and/or form. For example, for the theme of Batavian history, which had never before been represented, such 17th-century Dutch artists as Otto van Veen looked for connections in biblical, mythological and (ancient) history: for instance, in the theme *Battle on the Bridge* the examples of Giulio Romano's fresco of the *Battle of the Milvian Bridge* (finished 1524; Rome, Vatican, Sala di Constantino) and Titian's *Battle at Cadore* (1537; destr. 1577; ex-Doge's Pal., Venice) were taken as authoritative depictions of the historical events (see figs 4 and 5). Conversely, other themes remained unrepresented for a long time if no suitable analogue was available.

In 1966 JAN BIAŁOSTOCKI introduced the term 'iconographic gravity' for this transposition of an image formula from one theme to another, in which new representations adopt traditional iconographic formulae and are similar not only in the ordering of the visual elements but also in function and spiritual feeling. These image formulae are comparable with topoi in literature. 'Iconographic gravity' is particularly prevalent in what Białostocki called '*Rahmenthemen*' ('encompassing themes', in many respects equivalent to Henri van de Waal's 'iconological groups'). These are themes that possess the potential, in psychological or ideological terms, to be of a more general nature than suggested by their specific subject. As well as the *Battle on the Bridge*, examples include the cavalry battle, the triumph of Virtue over Vice, the hero (and its Christian variant, the martyr), the ruler, the sacrifice, mother with child (Virgin and [Christ] Child, Venus with Amor, motherhood in general), melancholy, inspiration through divine force, and the lamentation of the beloved dead (see figs 6 and 7).

Białostocki observed a break in the occurrence of *Rahmenthemen* in art *c*. 1800, since which time Christian *Rahmenthemen* have become susceptible to secularization, and the expressive elements have been changed into means of expressing emotions. Others, such as Heinz Ladendorf (*b* 1909) and Donat de Chapeaurouge (*b* 1925), saw this break as being earlier, *c.* 1500, when, particularly through the agency of graphics, artists were provided with a greater arsenal of themes and motifs, which they adapted for their own purposes. In an analogous manner, but with connections to the continuance of Classical image formulae in post-Classical art, Warburg had already coined the term '*Pathosformeln*'. These are motifs depicting and giving expression to their significance to such a degree that they constitute part of the 'visual memory' of a culture, a memory that can be suppressed temporarily but not permanently; motifs that in other times become attached to different meanings without difficulty.

In 1947 Saxl described the change in meaning that the winged figure had undergone over time. Existing as the representation of a Sumerian deity, the formula was taken over in Classical Greek art for the representation of Nike, which, with modifications, gave form to the Roman image of Victory. While in Classical art the messenger was represented without wings, and angels also did not possess wings according to the Bible, from the 5th century AD representations of angels align with the prevailing Victory formula (Rome, S Maria Maggiore, first half of the 5th century; Ravenna, S Apollinare Nuovo, 6th century). The conversion of the Roman Victory into a Christian angel was typical of the ways in which 'iconographic gravity' was active in narrative Christian art (5th–6th century AD). Artists given the task of representing biblical themes could seek connections only in the form or content of related mythological themes. 'The primary influence of mythological representations upon Christian scenes was not only widespread, but also formed the basis without which the creation of biblical picture cycles on a vast scale would have been impossible' (Weitzmann, 1960, p. 57). Known examples are the transformation of Hercules into Samson, the lyre-playing Orpheus into psalm-chanting David. Thus also the Early Christian and Byzantine chapel decorations with symbolic representations of Heaven and the Pantocrator in the 'eye' of the chapel are the direct continuation of such cosmological and astrological vault decorations as those in Nero's Domus Aurea (AD 64–8) in Rome and Hadrian's villa (AD 125–35) at Tivoli.

(iii) Imitation theory. The search for formulae and analogies for content in older art was completely consistent with Renaissance imitation or mimesis theory, although the 'study of the Classics' and of the 'great masters' was recommended mainly for overcoming general problems of form and expression. Imitation theory was developed in antiquity by Aristotle and Horace for poetry but from the Renaissance was applied more to visual art. It held on the one hand that the most perfect parts of nature should be imitated and combined in the work of art, thus surpassing nature in perfection (by rejecting accidental imperfections); and on the other hand that, through following and copying the example of great predecessors, the quality of the work would be further heightened. The term 'eclecticism', coined by Winckelmann, had no negative overtone and acquired this only at the end of the 18th century, when opinions about originality and artistic genius altered.

5. Antonio Tempesta: *Battle on the Bridge*, etching after Otto van Veen, 146×209 mm; from the series *War of the Batavians against the Romans*, 1612 (New York, Metropolitan Museum of Art)

One of the consequences of imitation theory was the study and use of Classical sculptures, such as the *Apollo Belvedere* (4th century BC), the Belvedere *Torso* (1st century BC) and the *Laokoon* (*c.* 50 BC; all Rome, Vatican, Mus. Pio-Clementino). The derivations from these works of art could be of a purely formal nature, such as Titian's borrowing of the *Laokoon* (found in 1506) for his *Resurrection* (1522; Brescia, SS Nazaro and Celso): equally for the figure of Christ as, with variations, for the St Sebastian on the right wing of the altarpiece. Titian also made a parody (woodcut, 1543) on the *Laokoon* group, with apes in place of the priest and his children. The appropriation could also be associated with content; that is, a crucial element of the chosen example could be adopted as a model while changing its meaning. For instance, as stated in his *Schriftlicher Nachlass*, Dürer thought that Christ should be represented in a similar manner to depictions of Apollo, because the ancients had represented their 'idol' Apollo in the most beautiful human form, and various borrowings by Dürer from the *Apollo Belvedere* are known. Similarly the *Laokoon* group (or just the head of Laokoon himself) lives on as the *Pathosformel* of suffering: *exemplum doloris*. The most outspoken and liberal of the proponents

6. *Lamentation of Troilus*, miniature from a Neapolitan *Histoire ancienne*, *c.* 1350–60 (London, British Museum, Royal MS. 20 D.I., fol. 145*v*)

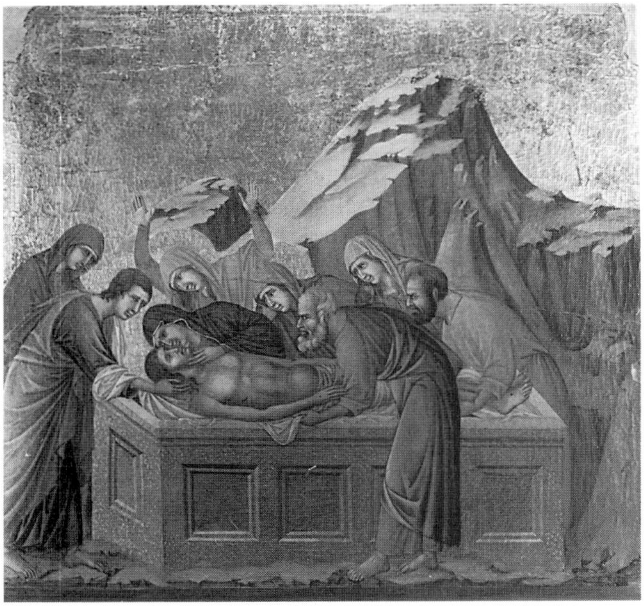

7. Duccio: *Lamentation/Entombment*, tempera on panel, detail from the *Maestà* altarpiece, *c.* 1308–11 (Siena, Museo dell'Opera del Duomo)

of plundering the past in this way was Joshua Reynolds. He specifically defended his practice of 'selective borrowing' set out in the 12th Discourse (1784) of his *Discourses on Art* (1769–90). Throughout his borrowings, a mixture of parody and loftiness is not unusual, as in his allegorical portraits. A peculiarity of his practice is the use of inversion: representing the opposite frame of mind through a minimal change to an existing motif, as in his change of a Classical Maenad (extreme joy) into St Mary Magdalene (extreme suffering; e.g. drawing, 1750–52; London, BM, 201a9, fol. 27 *v*), following Baccio Bandinelli. (Warburg pointed out the same possibilities with the *Pathosformeln*.)

(iv) Vehicles of transmission. Image formulae circulated by a variety of means. In antiquity, the Middle Ages and the Renaissance, antique coins and medals formed an extremely important vehicle for the DISSEMINATION of allegorical personifications. In the Middle Ages the use of seals was modelled on Roman coins. During the Renaissance antique coins and medals were the object of numismatic studies, which in their turn became a source for the further dissemination of antique motifs. After the Crusades, there was a renewed influence of Classical imagery and iconography on that of the (late) medieval regions through the agency of Byzantine art. After the invention of printmaking in the 15th century, and specifically the growth of reproductive graphics in the 16th century, the dissemination of themes and motifs encountered no more obstacles.

(v) Motivkunde. In the 19th century, art motifs came to be regarded as equivalent to those of literature. Pregnant with imagery, they express a spiritual tension and, by combination, they may become elevated into symbols. For the researcher, this necessitated an entirely different approach from that adopted for the transformation of themes and appropriation of motifs discussed above and resulted in the establishment by Heinz Ladendorf and J. Adolf Schmoll (*b* 1915; called Eisenwerth) of what is called *Motivkunde* ('motif knowledge'). Seen as a continuation of iconography and iconology beyond 1800, *Motivkunde* involves the search for both the image-comprising and semantic properties of motifs and constitutes an 'iconology of modern art'.

2. ANALYSIS OF SYMBOLIC MEANING.

(i) Introduction. The retrieval of symbolic and allegorical meanings that may be contained in works of art is an important task of iconography. A symbol is understood to be an object that, according to prevailing convention, indicates a general idea. In contrast, an allegory is a combination of personifications and/or symbols that, in more or less conventional arrangements and on the basis of a consistency between image and concept, represents complex abstract notions. A distinction needs to be made between 'disguised' and 'overt' symbolism. 'Disguised' symbolism operates through a naturalistic form, such that the objects that serve as vehicles for the symbolic meaning can equally be interpreted as merely realistic. With 'overt' symbolism, the symbolic interpretation alone is possible (*see also* SYMBOL, §§2 and 3). For both sorts of symbolism, the meaning can be derived from a wide variety of areas, such as religion (in the broadest sense), philosophy, social and political history, literature and so on. The indicator and equally the condition of the retrievability of a symbol is that it should conform to a specific, definable convention.

(ii) Panofsky's study of Early Netherlandish painting. The term 'disguised symbolism' was introduced by Panofsky in 1934 and further expanded in 1953 in his monumental *Early Netherlandish Painting*. It accompanied the development of naturalism and the perspectival representation of space in painting of the late 14th century and the early 15th. 'A way had to be found to reconcile the new naturalism with a thousand years of Christian tradition' (Panofsky, 1953, p. 141).

The relationship between realism and symbolism is complex. Following the publication of Panofsky's theses, much discussion was given to the question of whether, and to what extent, the process of 'disguising' and rationally structuring could be understood, or whether the naturalist style was merely applied to the pre-existing, symbolic understanding of reality. 'Paradoxically enough, we can only speak safely of "disguised symbolism" if the disguise is inadequate and the symbols betray themselves as such' (Bedaux, 1986, p. 7).

The difficulty that disguised symbolism presents to the modern observer (realistic or symbolic interpretation) did not exist for the medieval observer: for him the visible world was a symbol in its totality. It is a primary iconological problem to decide how long, in what degree and through whom this medieval notion operated. Its decline marked the transition from the Middle Ages into a more modern time, after which it never recovered a position of similar importance. Panofsky was himself well aware of this difficulty (1953, pp. 142–3):

8. Follower of Jan van Eyck: *Annunciation*, tempera and oil on panel, 775×645 mm, *c.* 1425 (New York, Metropolitan Museum of Art)

There is, I am afraid, no other answer to this problem than the use of historical methods tempered, if possible, by common sense. We have to ask ourselves whether or not the symbolical significance of a given motif is a matter of established representational tradition (as is the case with the lilies [in the Mérode altarpiece (*c.* 1425–7; New York, Met.) by the Master of Mérode]); whether or not a symbolical interpretation can be justified by definite texts or agrees with ideas demonstrably alive in the period and presumably familiar to its artists (as is the case with all those symbols revolving around the relationship between the Old and the New Testament [e.g. in the Friedsam *Annunciation* (*c.* 1425; New York, Met.; see fig. 8), attributed to a follower of Jan van Eyck, in which the contrast between the two parts of the Bible is symbolized by architectural and sculptural details]); and to what extent such a symbolic interpretation is in keeping with the historical position and personal tendencies of the individual master.

(iii) Late 20th-century studies of 17th-century Dutch genre painting. Dutch genre painting of the 17th century also incorporated the depiction of abstract ideas in naturalistic form. In 1971 Eddy de Jongh introduced the term '*schijnrealisme*' (apparent realism) for those representations that imitate reality as far as form is concerned but at the same time are an 'abstraction made real' (see figs 9 and 10). For many of these depictions the Horatian '*Ut pictura poesis*' ('As is painting, so is poetry') doctrine provides the art-theoretical foundation, that art serves 'for instruction and entertainment'.

Beginning in the 1980s there was a battle concerning 17th-century Dutch painting between the 'iconological school', of which de Jongh was the leading representative, and Svetlana Alpers (*b* 1936). In Alpers's view (1983) Dutch art is, in contrast to Italian, not 'narrative' but 'descriptive' and directed towards visual knowledge of reality. On these grounds she disputed the implications of disguised moralistic messages and the connections with Italian theories of art.

However, Alpers misunderstood both the existence of a narrative tradition in Dutch art (specifically history painting) and the fact that this art had less to do with developments in the scientific sphere than with the rhetoricians' culture rooted in late medieval traditions. On the other hand, in contemporary writings on art relatively little was said about moralistic teaching, and rather more was mentioned about the imitation of the visible world as a goal of art. Moreover, direct borrowings in painting from the literature of emblems are relatively scarce.

10. Hendrick Goltzius: *Quis evadet?: Homo bulla*, engraving, 191×153 mm, 1594 (Amsterdam, Rijksprentenkabinet); allegory of the transience of human life

9. Frans van Mieris (i): *Boy Blowing Bubbles*, oil on panel, 255×190 mm, 1663 (The Hague, Mauritshuis); allegory of transience and the dangers of unchaste love

Nevertheless, the discovery of an indirect relationship between emblems and the allegorical tradition led to the uncovering of meanings in depictions that were interpreted in the 19th century as pure representations of reality. It seems that precisely such an ambivalent interpretation was intended, in which the choice (to take the moralistic lesson to heart or to enjoy the sublime imitation of nature) was determined ultimately for the spectator by his own cultural background.

IV. Indices and classifications.

Progress in iconographic research has necessitated the development of iconographic classification systems. The *Index of Christian Art*, begun in 1917 by Charles Rufus Morey at Princeton University, Princeton, NJ, grew with each decade into an immense collection of iconographically indexed photographic material on medieval works of art. A strictly maintained method of describing these works formed the basis of a keyword index that referred to the depictions (down to the smallest details) on the photographs.

For medieval art before 1400 the Princeton Index (copies: Washington, DC, Dumbarton Oaks; Rome, Vatican, Pont. Ist. Archeol. Crist.; Utrecht, Iconol. Inst.) forms an indispensable source of iconographically relevant material. The meticulous description of works of art also forms the basis of the thesaurus of themes, depictions, represented objects and their meanings developed in the 1970s and 1980s in France by François Garnier and others.

The above indices are surpassed both qualitatively and quantitatively by *Iconclass*, the iconographic classification system designed by Henri van de Waal and published in 17 parts between 1973 and 1985. *Iconclass* uses a systematic ordering of material in which themes and depictions are hierarchically arranged in clusters, employing the possibilities of a decimal notation system. There are nine head-groups: 1. Religion and magic; 2. Nature; 3. Human being, man in general; 4. Society, civilization, culture; 5. Abstract ideas and concepts; 6. History; 7. Bible; 8. Literature; 9. Classical mythology and ancient history.

Each of these head-groups in the *Iconclass* system is divided into subgroups (primary, secondary, tertiary etc.) by following the notation number with a decimal (the third decimal is exchanged for a capital letter). In this manner for each theme or subject a notation number exists that functions as an easily readable coded title, which also gives it its place in the whole. For example, the notation for 'Madonna', 11 F 4, is constructed as follows: 1=Religion and magic; 11=Christian religion; 11 F=the Virgin Mary; 11 F 4=Madonna. The specific Madonna types form further subdivisions of 11 F 4 (11 F 41, 11 F 42 etc).

The alphabetical index not only indicates the place in the system allocated for a specified theme or depiction but also forms a thesaurus of all the details that play a significant role in the themes and representations covered. So the headword 'kneeling' indicates not only the general motif 'kneeling figure' (31 A 23 3) but also more than 90 themes and representations in which 'kneeling' is mentioned.

Through its breadth, consistency and systematic form, *Iconclass* is truly a *summa* of iconography, which provides museums, print rooms, art-historical libraries and documentation centres with a useful tool for the iconographic opening-up of their collections. *Iconclass* is used by (among others) D.I.A.L. (Decimal Index of the Art of the Low Countries, published by the Rijksbureau voor Kunsthistorische Documentatie at The Hague), a collection of *c.* 10,000 photographs of Dutch art from the 15th century to the 18th, iconographically arranged according to the *Iconclass* system. A second important use of *Iconclass* is the iconographic index of the Bildarchiv Foto Marburg at Marburg an der Lahn (microfiche publication). It also proves its great value through the publication of the most extensive iconographical bibliography.

BIBLIOGRAPHY

EARLY SOURCES

A. Statius: *Inlustrium virorum ut extant in urbe expressi vultus* (Rome, 1569)
J. Molanus: *De picturis et imaginibus sacris* (Leuven, 1570)
G. Vasari: *Ragionamenti* (Florence, 1588)
C. Ripa: *Iconologia* (Rome, 1593, rev. 1603)
G. P. Bellori: *Vite* (1672); ed. E. Borea (1976)
A.-C.-P. de Tubières, Comte de Caylus: *Recueil d'antiquités égyptiennes, étrusques, grecques, romaines et gauloises* (Paris, 1752–67)
J. J. Winckelmann: *Versuch einer Allegorie besonders für die Kunst* (Dresden, 1766)
J. Reynolds: *Discourses on Art* (London, 1769–90)
H. Rupprich, ed.: *Dürer: Schriftlicher Nachlass*, 3 vols (Berlin, 1956–69), esp. vol. ii, p. 104

METHODOLOGY

G. J. Hoogewerff: 'L'Iconologie et son importance pour l'étude systématique de l'art chrétien', *Actes du Congrès international historique: Oslo, 1928*, pp. 53–82
A. M. Warburg: *Gesammelte Schriften*, 2 vols (Leipzig, 1932/*R* 1969)
E. Panofsky: *Studies in Iconology: Humanistic Themes in the Art of the Renaissance* (New York, 1939/*R* 1962)
H. van de Waal: *Drie eeuwen vaderlandsche geschied-uitbeelding, 1500–1800: Een iconologische studie* [Three centuries of Dutch visual representation of history, 1500–1800: an iconological study], 2 vols (The Hague, 1952); review by J. Białostocki, *A. Bull.* (1971), pp. 262–5
E. Panofsky: *Meaning in the Visual Arts* (Garden City, NY, 1955/*R* London, 1970)
E. Cassirer: *Wesen und Wirkung des Symbolbegriffs* (Darmstadt, 1956)
F. Saxl: 'Continuity and Variation in the Meaning of Images', *Lectures*, i (London, 1957), pp. 1–12
H. Ladendorf: 'Die Motivkunde und die Malerei des 19. Jahrhunderts', *Festschrift Dr. h.c. Eduard Trautscholdt* (Hamburg, 1965), pp. 173–88
J. Białostocki: *Stil und Ikonographie: Studien zur Kunstwissenschaft* (Dresden, 1966; rev. Cologne, 2/1981)
G. Hermerén: *Representation and Meaning in the Visual Arts: A Study in the Methodology of Iconography and Iconology* (Lund, 1969)
J. A. Schmoll [Eisenwerth]: 'Zur methodischen Abgrenzung der Motivkunde', *Beiträge zur Motivkunde des 19. Jahrhunderts*, Studien zur Kunst des 19. Jahrhunderts, vi (Munich, 1970), pp. 9–12
E. H. Gombrich: 'Aims and Limits of Iconology', *Symbolic Images: Studies in the Art of the Renaissance* (London, 1972), pp. 1–25
D. de Chapeaurouge: *Wandel und Konstanz in der Bedeutung entlehnter Motive* (Wiesbaden, 1974)
H. Damisch: *Semiotics and Iconography* (Lisse, 1975)
O. Pächt: *Methodisches zur kunsthistorischen Praxis: Ausgewählte Schriften* (Munich, 1977)
E. Kaemmerling, ed.: *Ikonographie und Ikonologie: Theorien, Entwicklung, Probleme* (Cologne, 1979, rev. 3/1984), i of *Bildende Kunst als Zeichensystem*
O. Bätschmann: *Einführung in die kunstgeschichtliche Hermeneutik: Die Auslegung von Bildern* (Darmstadt, 1984, rev. 3/1988)
S. Ferretti: *Cassirer, Panofsky and Warburg: Symbol, Art and History* (New Haven, 1989)
J. P. J. Brandhorst: 'Quantifiability in Iconography', *Knowl. Org.*, xx (1993), pp. 12–19, 29

GENERAL ICONOGRAPHY

M. Lurker: *Bibliographie zur Symbolkunde* (1968), xii of *Bibliotheca bibliographica Aureliana* (Baden-Baden, 1964–8)
——: *Bibliographie zur Symbolik, Ikonographie und Mythologie: Internationales Referateorgan* (Baden-Baden, 1968–)
H. van de Waal: *Iconclass: An Iconographic Classification System*, 17 vols (Amsterdam, 1973–85) [with extensive bibliog.]
J. Hall: *Dictionary of Subjects and Symbols in Art* (London, 1974, rev. 2/1979)
R. Wittkower: *Allegory and the Migration of Symbols* (London, 1977)
J. Hall: *A History of Ideas and Images in Italian Art* (London, 1983)
F. Garnier: *Thesaurus iconographique: Système descriptif des représentations* (Paris, 1984)

CHRISTIAN ICONOGRAPHY

LCI
A.-N. Didron: *Iconographie chrétienne: Histoire de Dieu* (Paris, 1843)
E. Mâle: *L'Art religieux du XIIIe siècle en France: Etude sur l'iconographie du moyen âge et sur ses sources d'inspiration* (Paris, 1898, rev. 9/1958; Eng trans., Princeton, 1984)
F. Cabrol and H. Leclercq, eds: *Dictionnaire d'archéologie chrétienne et de liturgie*, 15 vols (Paris, 1907–53)
K. Künstle: *Ikonographie der christlichen Kunst*, 2 vols (Freiburg im Breisgau, 1926–8)
R. Krautheimer: 'Introduction to an "Iconography of Mediaeval Architecture"', *J. Warb. & Court. Inst.*, v (1942), pp. 1–33; repr. in: *Studies in Early Christian, Mediaeval and Renaissance Art* (New York, 1969/*R* London, 1971), pp. 115–50
L. Réau: *Iconographie de l'art chrétien*, 3 vols (Paris, 1955–9)
K. Weitzmann: 'The Survival of Mythological Representations in Early Christian and Byzantine Art and their Impact on Christian Iconography', *Dumbarton Oaks Pap.*, xiv (1960), pp. 43–68
G. Schiller: *Ikonographie der christlichen Kunst*, 4 vols (Gütersloh, 1966–80)
J. H. Marrow: *Passion Iconography in Northern European Art of the Late Middle Ages and Early Renaissance: A Study of the Transformation of a Sacred Metaphor into Descriptive Narrative* (Kortrijk, 1979)

H. Belting: *Das Bild und sein Publikum im Mittelalter: Form und Funktion früher Bildtafeln der Passion* (Berlin, 1981)
M. Büchsel: 'Ecclesiae symbolorum cursus completus', *Städel-Jb.*, n. s., ix (1983), pp. 69–88
P. Crossley: 'Medieval Architecture and Meaning: The Limits of Iconography', *Burl. Mag.*, cxxx (1988), pp. 116–21
H. Belting: *Likeness and Presence: A History of the Image before the Era of Art* (Eng. trans., Chicago, 1995)

SECULAR AND CLASSICAL ICONOGRAPHY

R. van Marle: *Iconographie de l'art profane au moyen âge et à la Renaissance et la décoration des demeures*, 2 vols (The Hague, 1931–2)
J. Seznec: *La Survivance des dieux antiques: Essai sur le rôle de la tradition mythologique dans l'humanisme et dans l'art de la Renaissance*, Stud. Warb. Inst., xi (London, 1940; Eng. trans., New York, 1953/*R* Princeton, 1972)
G. de Tervarent: *Attributs et symboles dans l'art profane, 1450–1600: Dictionnaire d'un langage perdu*, 3 vols (Geneva, 1958–64)
Lexicon iconographicum mythologiae classicae (Zurich and Munich, 1981–)
P. Preston: *A Dictionary of Pictorial Subjects from Classical Literature: A Guide to their Identification in Works of Art* (New York, 1983)
S. Settis, ed.: *Memoria dell'antico nell'arte italiana*, 3 vols (Turin, 1984–6)

EARLY NETHERLANDISH AND DUTCH ART

E. Panofsky: 'Jan van Eyck's Arnolfini Portrait', *Burl. Mag.*, lxiv (1934), pp. 117–27
——: *Early Netherlandish Painting: Its Origins and Character* (Cambridge, 1953, rev. New York, 1971)
E. de Jongh: 'Realisme en schijnrealisme in de Hollandse schilderkunst van de zeventiende eeuw', *Rembrandt en zijn tijd* [Rembrandt and his time] (exh. cat., Brussels, Pal. B.-A., 1971), pp. 143–94
S. Alpers: 'Realism as a Comic Mode: Low-life Painting Seen through Bredero's Eyes', *Simiolus*, viii (1975–6), pp. 115–44; reply by H. Miedema in *Simiolus*, ix (1977), pp. 205–19; answer by S. Alpers in *Simiolus*, x (1978), pp. 46–50
L. Benjamin: 'Disguised Symbolism Expressed and the History of Early Netherlandish Painting', *Stud. Iconog.*, ii (1976), pp. 11–24
S. Alpers: *The Art of Describing: Dutch Art in the Seventeenth Century* (Chicago and London, 1983); reviews by E. de Jongh, *Simiolus*, xiv (1984), pp. 51–9; J. Białostocki, *A. Bull.*, lxvii (1985), pp. 520–26; A. Grafton and T. DaCosta Kaufmann, *J. Interdiscip. Hist.*, xvi (1985–6), pp. 255–65
C. Harbison: 'Realism and Symbolism in Early Netherlandish Painting', *A. Bull.*, lxvi (1984), pp. 588–602
J. B. Bedaux: 'The Reality of Symbols: The Question of Disguised Symbolism in Jan van Eyck's Arnolfini Portrait', *Simiolus*, xvi (1986), pp. 5–28
P. Hecht: 'The Debate on Symbol and Meaning in Dutch Seventeenth-century Art: An Appeal to Common Sense', *Simiolus*, xvi (1986), pp. 173–87
J. H. Marrow: 'Symbol and Meaning in Northern European Art of the Late Middle Ages and the Early Renaissance', *Simiolus*, xvi (1986), pp. 150–69

WILLEM F. LASH

Iconostasis. Icon-covered screen wall of a Byzantine or Eastern Orthodox church, separating the nave from the chancel (*see* CHURCH, fig. 16; MACEDONIA (ii), fig. 3; and MASEGNE, DALLE, fig. 1); for the equivalent in the Western Church *see* ROOD and SCREEN (i).

□

Idang. *See* KIM ŬN-HO.

Idea art. *See* CONCEPTUAL ART.

Idaean cave. Site on Mt Ida (now Psiloritis) in central Crete. It lies at an altitude of 1498 m and measures some 59×46 m. It was the most important cave in Greek antiquity, identified by many ancient writers as the place where Zeus was born and raised. It was discovered accidentally in 1884 and was excavated first in 1885 by Federico Halbherr, then from 1982 by John Sakellarakis, with funds from the Archaeological Society of Athens. Human presence within the cave is evident from the end of the Late Neolithic period (*c.* 3800 BC) and continued without interruption until the 5th century AD. It was a place of worship from the end of the Middle Minoan period (*c.* 1600 BC). The first object of worship may have been a Minoan male deity who dies and is reborn each year. For this reason, when the Mycenaean Greeks occupied Crete *c.* 1425 BC, Zeus, his successor, was worshipped in the unusual form of a god who dies and is reborn each year. The greatest number of offerings were made during the Late Geometric and the Early Archaic periods (*c.* 700 BC). Best known are the bronze shields with relief decoration, including bosses of eagles and lions, that the mythical Kouretes, guardians of the infant Zeus, were said to clash together to prevent his jealous father Kronos from hearing his cries (Herakleion, Archaeol. Mus.). A large quantity of jewellery, idols, vases, utensils, tools, coins and seals have also been found, dating from all periods.

BIBLIOGRAPHY

F. Halbherr and P. Orsi: *Antichità dell'antro di Zeus ideo* (Florence, 1888)
E. Kunze: *Kretische Bronzereliefs* (Stuttgart, 1931)
J. Boardman: *The Cretan Collection in Oxford* (Oxford, 1961), pp. 79–88
J. A. Sakellarakis: 'Anaskaphe Idaiou Antrou' [Excavation in the Idaean Cave], *Praktika Athen. Archaiol. Etaireias* (1983), pp. 415–500
R. Stock: 'The Secrets of Crete', *New York Times Mag.*, 19 Aug 1984, pp. 94–8, 107–13
J. A. Sakellarakis: 'I nea ereuna sto Idaio Antro (1982–1984)' [New research in the Idaean Cave], *Archaiologia*, xv (1985), pp. 14–22
——: 'L'Antro ideo, cento anni di attività archeologica', *Atti Convegni Lincei*, lxxiv (1985), pp. 19–48

J. A. SAKELLARAKIS

Ideology. Term applied primarily to sets of beliefs that are explicitly held by social groups, are general in scope and have practical implications for participation in social life. The topic of these beliefs need not itself be social; religious beliefs as much as economic theories may be ideological. The term has, however, fallen into loose usage in sociology and other quarters, and there is much debate as to the correct understanding of the concept. This article gives a general definition of ideology and an outline of the ideological analysis of art with particular reference to Marxist theory.

1. Introduction. 2. The ideological analysis of art. 3. Difficulties in the ideological analysis of art.

1. INTRODUCTION. By no means every socially accepted set of beliefs with practical implications counts as an ideology. The following are plausible, although not universally agreed, conditions for a set of beliefs to qualify as an ideology: (1) the set of beliefs demands explanation in terms of its social causes and effects on social relations rather than what (if anything) makes it true; (2) the social effects of the beliefs are more important in perpetuating them than the reasons advanced in their support; (3) the set of beliefs has come into existence because it promotes the interests of a particular social group or at least (in the case of an ascendent class) has the potential for doing so. It follows that ideological analysis is distinct from, and more complex than, the sociology of knowledge. Ideological analysis locates beliefs in their social or historical context and indicates homologies between patterns of beliefs and social structures, but at the same time it

contests their justification. Ideological critique seeks to expose illusions and install true beliefs, thereby undoing social alienation and contributing to human emancipation. In MARXISM, the source and natural home of the theory of ideology, the focus of ideological critique is on identifying the role of beliefs in determining the relations of production, and the interests of different social classes with respect to those relations.

Carrying over ideological analysis to the arts requires some modifications, since works of art cannot be equated directly with sets of beliefs—in common with the other activities and products (e.g. rituals and advertisements) that form a society's cultural superstructure. Cultural phenomena, including art, may nevertheless be regarded as ideological in a derivative sense, insofar as they communicate or serve to reinforce, by whatever oblique means, sets of beliefs that are ideological. Of course, few works of art are explicitly designed with the intention of promoting specific beliefs, and even when this is so, it is rarely the case that such an intention lies at the core of their artistic significance. This is, however, no objection to subjecting them to ideological analysis, which almost invariably assumes that ideological roles are played outside awareness; artist and audience need not be capable of avowing or articulating the ideological role of art.

2. THE IDEOLOGICAL ANALYSIS OF ART. There is more than one way in which the ideological analysis of art may proceed, but its general form will be as follows. A certain theory of society—usually Marxist theory or some variant of it—is taken for granted at the outset. Ideological analysis begins by suspending the natural, internal perspective on a work of art in order to clear the way for awareness of its socio-historical context. Identifying its ideological significance involves viewing the work of art, first, as a 'reflection' of society, that is, as reproducing in some sense the character or form of social life, and, second, as encoding a definite message, or imperative, with repercussions for social life. Ideological analysis may concentrate on different aspects of works of art, including both their manifest representational content and their purely formal properties, there being a vigorous debate as to which of these carries the greater burden of ideological significance. It should also be noted that discursive theories of art of varying scope—ranging from the manifestos of specific artistic movements to methods of art criticism and philosophical theories of the nature of aesthetic experience and judgement—may be classed as ideological on the same sorts of grounds.

The writings on art of Karl Marx (1818–83) consist only of brief and scattered remarks. His earliest writings on the subject—in which he undertook a criticism of Christian and 'feudal Romantic' art in their relation to the Prussian monarchy and its laws of censorship—show him inheriting elements and issues from Hegel's theories of art and religion, and Heinrich Heine's criticism of the German Nazarene school of painting. At this point, Marx appears to have favoured Hellenistic art, with its sensuous depiction of nature, and correspondingly deprecated contemporary Christian art as 'fetishistic'. His later and more theoretical statements on art lay the grounds for the programme of ideological analysis. Marx objected to the theoretical separation of artistic activity from productive labour, claiming that the artist too should be seen as a producer of goods, on account of art's availability for entering into relations of exchange involving surplus value. This carries the important implication that art, like other forms of labour, undergoes alienation in capitalist society, and that the isolated situation of the modern artist is a function of atomistic social conditions and by no means dictated eternally by the nature of artistic activity. In these terms the idealist conception of art as an alternative to material production, opposed to it and associated with a contrary, spiritual realm, is clearly ideological, a means of perpetuating the alienation of existing social forms. Another important concomitant of Marx's perspective is an emphasis on viewing works of art as containing the history of their own production, including the social relations this involves, in opposition to the idealist tendency to divorce the work from that process and view it as an object that is simply 'given'. This also tends to imply an opposition to any deep philosophical contrast between art and technological production or craft.

At the same time, Marx implied that art has at least the potential for playing a role in fulfilling the proper, sensuous needs of man, conceived as a material being, and, indeed, that art provides some sort of prototype or ideal for a future form of non-alienated labour, insofar as it anticipates a condition in which the senses would no longer be alienated—a line of thought intimated in Marx's recognition that the Greek arts 'still afford us artistic pleasure' and 'count as a norm and an unattainable model'. Hence also Marx's statements in *Die deutsche Ideologie* (1845) that the *de facto* uniqueness of artists, which is ideologically misperceived as reflecting a natural inequality of talent, is but a consequence of the division of labour in pre-communist society, and that in communist society, where art would be released from its parochialism, 'there are no painters but at most people who engage in painting among other activities'.

In sum, Marx's writings on art attempt to conceive it in two different ways: first, negatively, as a further expression of the alienation suffered in capitalist society; and second, positively, as a means to social transformation. In the first respect, art is viewed as passive, a reflection of society, its forms limited by social conditions. This is illustrated by Marx's assertion of the dependence of the epic on the technological and productive forms of archaic society. In the second respect, art is conceived as a form of action on society, potentially helping to transform it. In this respect, some avant-garde art—for instance Soviet Constructivism (*see* CONSTRUCTIVISM, §2) and SUPREMATISM, and SURREALISM (as in, for example, André Breton, Diego Rivera and Leon Trotsky: 'Manifesto: Towards a Free Revolutionary Art')—has claimed for itself the title of a revolutionary force by virtue of its aim to destroy established, reactionary forms of artistic perception. Here art itself is conceived as occupying the emancipatory role of ideological critique.

This shows, incidentally, that it is by no means a corollary of Marx's own ideological theory that SOCIALIST REALISM should qualify as an emancipatory artistic form or that ideological analysis need reduce to such bald and repellent claims as that the modernist art of 'late bourgeois society' must necessarily be 'decadent' (the verdict of GEORGY PLEKHANOV on Cubism). The issue of REALISM forms one main line of division between schools of ideological critique, separating on the one hand those who favour realism (figurative representation and idealized forms) as an instrument for representing actual or ideal social conditions (*see* SOCIAL REALISM), and on the other those who locate the distinctive role of art in its power to transcend representation, which is regarded as inescapably prone to ideological contamination (*see also* ABSTRACT ART).

The tension and, arguably, potential for head-on conflict between these two views of the ideological significance of art reappears in many subsequent ideological analyses and leads to such complex notions as that the two ideological roles of art, negative and positive, may be 'doubled up' in a single work. A work of art may simultaneously 'represent' and 'critique' the social form or ideological conception of society out of which it springs. At this point, ideological analysis may come to accord art a privileged cognitive role that is reflexive and partially trans-historical, that of bringing about an awareness of historical development and thus of the relativity of works of art to their own social conditions (*see also* SOCIOLOGY OF ART). This is often referred to as art's function of 'displaying the contradictions' inherent in existing society.

The two ideological dimensions of art in Marx's writings and the possibility of synthesizing them have been extensively developed in the tradition of Marxist aesthetics in the 20th century, where the concept of ideology in all contexts has been revised in multifarious and often highly sophisticated directions. Ideological analysis has also become associated with methods of analysis in SEMIOTICS, STRUCTURALISM and DECONSTRUCTION. Equally, the strategy of ideological critique has been appropriated by non-Marxist—sexually or culturally defined—political forces such as feminism (*see* FEMINISM AND ART) and causes associated with specific ethnic groups. Literary theory has been the principal arena for these developments, but, with appropriate modification, neo- and post-Marxist analyses and theories of literature can be carried over to the visual arts.

3. DIFFICULTIES IN THE IDEOLOGICAL ANALYSIS OF ART. There are, however, logical problems surrounding the notion of ideological analysis of art. These are many and deep, and it is fair to say that they have never been satisfactorily dealt with by ideological theorists, although it would be wrong to think, as some have claimed, that they show the very notion of ideological analysis to be incoherent. The main difficulties are as follows. First, the essential properties of works of art are logically bound up with the ways in which they offer themselves to conscious appreciation; it is a conceptual truth that works of art are constituted by the ways in which they appear and cannot have a real nature independently of these. The fact that ideological analysis appears not to focus, at least primarily, on what is ordinarily thought of as the aesthetic character of works of art casts doubt on its power to catch in its net that which is essential to their identity. If an ideological role is not shown to be central to the identity of works of art, ideological analysis will reduce to an account of the merely contingent properties of works of art, which would leave ideological analysts of art with much weaker claims than they typically wish to uphold.

Second, if the analogy with the ideological analysis of belief is strictly followed through (as, on the face of it, it ought to be), a difficulty arises for the ideological analysis of art—it will have the implication that, just as the 'reasons' supporting ideological beliefs are really 'bad' reasons or not reasons at all, so the distinctively aesthetic properties of works of art that engage viewers and seem to contribute indispensably to their value are really only 'lures', or in some sense deceptive devices for securing the transmission of an ideological message. The ideological analysis of art thus seems to imply that when the appearances of works of art are seen through and their real, ultimately non-aesthetic meaning is correctly discerned, the work will, or should, cease to be available for aesthetic appreciation. It is unlikely that this problem can be resolved, rather than concealed, by granting art, as part of the social superstructure, a degree of 'relative autonomy' with respect to the economic base. In this fashion, the aesthetic significances of works of art either reduce to something else (the operation of broad socio-economic forces) or become merely epiphenomenal, with the result that we are fundamentally mistaken in what we identify as the appeal of art and our grounds for enjoying or valuing it. Such implications are not usually endorsed by ideological analysts, but it is not clear how ideological analysis can avoid them. This difficulty may be viewed as an aggravated instance of the general problem of how didactic theories of art's value may be squared with the apparently non-instrumental nature of our interest in art; in other terms, of how art is ultimately distinguished from PROPAGANDA, and of the acceptability of defining the artist's role as that of 'an engineer of human souls' (Zhdanov's formulation).

A third problem is that the categories of ideological analysis appear coarse—in Marxism there are only three, at most four, stages of historical development—whereas works of art are indefinitely finely individualized objects. This seems to set an a priori limit to the interest and informativeness of ideological analysis and to give reason for taking a greater interest in psychological accounts of the meaning of works of art, since the fineness of meaning in a work of art is something that can be matched by the complexity of the artist's creative mental state (*see* PSYCHOANALYSIS AND ART).

Fourth, there is an epistemological problem for the ideological analysis of art, common to many of the contexts in which the concept of ideology is applied, concerning the criteria on the basis of which the ideological role played by a work of art is to be indentified. The problem is simply that it is all too easy to impute ideological roles, and—since the manifest appeal of art is to a large extent discounted or put in brackets by ideological analysis—there are no firm controls on their ascription.

Finally, there is the problem of how exactly the ideological role of a work of art is related to the psychology of the artist who produced it. In almost all cases, it is not easy to see how the artist could be, or could have been, brought to see the work as having the character that the ideological analyst ascribes to it; nor would it make sense to locate the ideological significance in the unconscious mind of the artist. The question of how ideological significance can nevertheless inhere in works of art cannot fairly be side-stepped, since it must be supposed that at some level ideological roles are mediated by, and realized in, the minds of individuals (*see also* COMMUNICATION THEORY and RECEPTION THEORY).

None of these points, it should be emphasized, provides grounds for an outright rejection of an ideological analysis of art; but the limitations they indicate seem to warrant the conclusion that ideological perspectives on art are not autonomous, and that ideological theory is most plausible when integrated into other, more traditional, forms of aesthetic theory.

BIBLIOGRAPHY

G. Plekhanov: *Iskusstvo i obshchestvennaya zhizn'* (1912); Eng. trans. as *Art and Social Life* (London, 1936)
A. Breton, D. Rivera and L. Trotsky: 'Manifesto: Towards a Free Revolutionary Art', *Partisan Rev.* (Autumn 1938)
Marxism and Aesthetics: A Selected Annotated Bibliography: Books and Articles in the English Language, comp. L. Baxandall (Sussex, 1968)
T. Adorno: *Ästhetische Theorie* (Frankfurt am Main, 1972)
J. Berger: *Ways of Seeing* (Harmondsworth, 1972)
T. J. Clark: *The Absolute Bourgeois: Artist and Politics in France, 1848–1851* (London, 1973)
N. Hadjinicolaou: *Histoire de l'art et lutte des classes* (Paris, 1973)
A. Hauser: *Soziologie der Kunst*, 4 vols (Munich, 1974)
F. Klingender: *Marxism and Modern Art* (London, 1975)
A. Reszler: *Le Marxisme devant la culture* (Paris, 1975)
I. Kulikova and A. Zis, eds: *Marxist–Leninist Aesthetics and Life: A Collection of Articles* (Moscow, 1976)
H. Marcuse: *Die Permanenz der Kunst: Wider eine bestimmte marxistische Ästhetik—ein Essay* (Munich, 1977)
A. Zis: *Foundations of Marxist Aesthetics*, trans. K. Judelson (Moscow, 1977)
P. Bourdieu: *La Distinction: Critique sociale du jugement* (Paris, 1979)
E. M. Swiderski: *The Philosophical Foundations of Soviet Aesthetics: Theories and Controversies in the Post-war Years* (Dordrecht, 1979)
J. Wolff: *The Social Production of Art* (London, 1981)
——: *Aesthetics and the Sociology of Art* (London, 1983)
P. Johnson: *Marxist Aesthetics: The Foundations within Everyday Life for an Emancipated Consciousness* (London, 1984)
M. Rose: *Marx's Lost Aesthetic: Karl Marx and the Visual Arts* (Cambridge, 1984)
T. Crow: *Painters and Public Life in Eighteenth-century Paris* (New Haven, 1985)
T. Eagleton: *The Ideology of the Aesthetic* (Oxford, 1990)

SEBASTIAN GARDNER

Idfū. *See* EDFU.

'Idgāh. *See* MUSALLA.

Idolino [the *Idol*]. Bronze statue (h. 1.50 m) of a youthful nude in sinuous pose, his lower right arm outstretched (*see* STATUE, fig. 3). It is probably a copy by a Roman artist of a Greek original by Polykleitos, although some scholars believe it is Greek and attribute it to Polykleitos himself. It was found in 1530 in the course of building excavations at Pesaro and donated in the same year to Francesco Maria I della Rovere for his Villa Imperiale, which was then under construction near that city. In 1533 the statue was given a pedestal in antique style, with an inscription created for it by Cardinal Pietro Bembo: *ut potui huc veni delphis et fratre relicto.* In 1630 Francesco Maria II della Rovere sent the statue to Ferdinando II de' Medici, who would have inherited it in any case. In 1646–7 it was listed at the Uffizi. Between 1800 and 1803 it was in Palermo to escape the French. In 1889 it was again in the Uffizi, but since 1897 it has been on display at the Museo Archeologico in Florence. The figure was initially identified as Bacchus, and hence the modern pedestal bears decorations that refer to that god. In the early years of its exhibition the statue was decorated with a crown of vine leaves and a bronze branch, with which it was thought to have been discovered. These, however, were almost certainly modern additions influenced by the identification with Bacchus, and they disappeared in the 18th century, when other interpretations prevailed. The statue was then variously identified as a guardian divinity, such as the personification of the god of Luck, a Genius, Mercury, Ganymede and more generically as the idol of an unknown divinity, whence its modern name. Some believe that the figure originally held a lamp.

BIBLIOGRAPHY

A. Furtwängler: *Masterpieces of Greek Sculpture* (London, 1895), p. 286
W. Amelung: *Führer durch die Antiken in Florenz* (Munich, 1897), p. 274
M. Robertson: *A History of Greek Art* (Cambridge, 1975), p. 332
F. Haskell and N. Penny: *Taste and the Antique: The Lure of Classical Sculpture 1500–1900* (New Haven and London, 1981), pp. 240–41

LUCA LEONCINI

Idoma. Kwa-speaking people of central Nigeria, bounded on the north by the Lafia and Nasarawa Emirates, on the south by the Igbo, on the east by the Tiv and on the west by the Igala. They practise yam and millet farming in the wooded savannah that connects the inland steppe with the coastal forest of West Africa. The core group numbers about half a million, with an additional half million of mixed ethnicity in enclaves and border areas. The Idoma encompass a wide variety of religious expression, including Islam and Christianity along with indigenous beliefs. The veneration of ancestors and Aje (the earth) and the propitiation of spirits of the bush are important parts of religious life, manifested in the use of masks and figures. The Idoma consider themselves 'people of Apá', the confederacy of states which controlled the Middle Benue region long before the early 19th-century Islamic jihād of Uthman Dan Fodio. Idoma Division boundaries were set during the colonial period: two Idoma groups now lie outside them. These are the old kingdoms of Keana and Doma (Doma Nokwu), lying north of the Benue and better known by the ethnic label Alago, and a small enclave of Etulo (Utur), totally surrounded by the Tiv. Doma masquerades, cults and kingship rituals are distinct from those south of the Benue, although the underlying precepts of the ancestral cult are shared.

Idoma material culture includes the products of iron-working, brass-casting by the lost-latex technique, weaving on both upright and double-heddle looms, indigo resist-dyeing, body-painting and pottery. Its most distinctive forms, however, are its masking traditions and its figure sculptures. Illustrations can be found in the works listed in the bibliography. Museum collections of Idoma art are detailed below.

1. MASK AND MASQUERADE. There are three basic types of masks among the Idoma, each having a separate origin, patronage group and ritual status. The most powerful are the cloth ancestral masks (*alekwuafia*), which impersonate resurrected fathers. Although the most elaborate and ritually the most significant of Idoma masks, they are buried with the last surviving son and so are not

collectable. Regulatory society masks are second in importance, and the only type of Idoma mask found in collections (e.g. Lagos, N. Mus.; London, BM). These are usually carved from wood to represent human or bush spirits and are controlled by age sets of particular villages. Finally 'slave' masks (e.g. *akatakpa*) are made from raffia fibres or millet stalks and are worn by youths and by the guardian heralds who accompany society masks.

(i) Ancestral masks. Before the onset of British colonial administration *c.* 1910, the ancestral masks were 'owners of the land', holding the power of life and death. The ultimate source of moral authority, ancestors serve as intermediaries between living persons and the powerful forces of Earth (Aje) and the Creator (Owoico). Their periodic manifestation in masquerades assures that this authority is continually reaffirmed. Ancestral masks, dressed in burial shrouds and elongated with a projection beneath the cloth, are found in a wide area on both sides of the Niger and Benue rivers, from Yoruba and Nupe country to Igala, Igbo, Idoma, Ebira and Abakwariga (Hausa) lands. The Idoma mask has a variety of names (e.g. Tall Ghost, Hooded Cobra and The Mask That Leans) and takes the form of an elongated cloth tent terminating at the top in a basketry cone with long cloth filaments and at the bottom in a long train (see fig.). Nowhere is this more elaborate than in central and southern Idoma where the usual indigo-and-white appearance of the burial cloth is supplemented by complex geometric patterns of red and yellow cloth appliqué. Linguistic evidence suggests that the elongated burialcloth mask may have originated in the Idoma homeland before

Idoma ancestral mask (*alekwuafia*), in performance, Igwumale, central Nigeria; from a photograph by Sidney Littlefield Kasfir, 1989

1500 and diffused westward with subsequent population movements (Kasfir, 1985).

(ii) Regulatory society masks. These derive from a different stratum of Idoma life and possess no ancestral authority. The most powerful were such warrior masquerades as Oglinye and Icahoho, which developed out of victory celebrations in pre-colonial times. Eventually these young men's associations became too powerful for the elders to control, and the elders' solution was to turn them into law-enforcement societies (*aiuta*). The painted white-face masks had, from the beginning, a strongly mimetic intention deriving from the former practice of displaying the crania of slain enemies. They are, therefore, far more naturalistic in style than the regulatory masks that depict bush animals. These latter are usually a fused representation of two or more animals and symbolize mythological power. Among the Akweya-speaking subgroup these masks take the place of *alekwuafia* as representations of clan-based ancestral power. (There are examples of the white-face masks in the University of Iowa Museum of Art, Iowa City, and examples of the animal masks in the Musée Barbier–Mueller, Geneva, and the Fowler Museum of Cultural History, UCLA, Los Angeles.) Although the colonial government was compelled to rely on the enforcement powers of the *aiuta* as late as the 1940s, by the 1980s these regulatory societies had nearly given up their law-enforcement function. As an art form, however, their masquerades were proliferating. In 1986 the author attended a funeral in Akpa district featuring a new masquerade complex called Analo. This included sixteen white-face masks, two grotesques and two stilt masks. As in the past, these performances were characterized by youthful exuberance, male bonding and aesthetic spectacle.

(iii) Slave masks. So called because they have no home other than the bush, these raffia and millet stalk masks may be the most ancient form of masking among the Idoma. Before the introduction of weaving to the Benue region, and before the diffusion of Igbo, Akweya and Igede white-face mask genres into central Idoma, these fibre masks were probably the prevalent type. In Doma, isolated from southern influences by the Benue River, raffia masks appear at several levels of the ritual hierarchy. At the end of the 20th century, however, the masks in use south of the Benue in Idomaland proper possessed neither power nor prestige since they were nearly always worn and controlled by youths and younger men. The mask *akatakpa* functions as a trickster, inverting the rules of the social order. These masks might, however, once have been ritually significant.

2. Figure sculpture. Idoma carve several types of figure sculpture for use in the propitiation of water and bush spirits and as agents of socialization. The three main types of female figure—*anjenu*, *anyanmole* and *ekotame*—share a common style. Like the white-face masks, they are intentionally naturalistic, but, unlike the masks, they seek to capture the bloom of young womanhood with their characteristic angular shoulders, jutting breasts and muscular legs. Because it is only size which differentiates *ekotame* and *anyanmole* figures from *anjenu*, some writers have mistakenly assumed that all large female figures are

ekotame (e.g. Neyt, 1985). But only two are clearly identifiable: one in a private London collection and the other, nearly identical, which was until recently in use in an Idoma village (untraced). The latter was made in the late 19th century somewhere in the Tiv-Idoma borderland and was carried at members' funerals by the lineage who owned it. Water spirits, *anjenu*, are represented by a wide range of human and animal types of which the best known are seated mother and child figures. These are metaphoric representations of well-being and fertility that the cult in which they are used seeks to protect. Nearly identical seated figures called *anyanmole* ('women spoil the compound') were used in the late colonial period for the public disciplining of women. There are a few Idoma figure sculptures in public collections (Geneva, Mus. Barbier-Mueller; Oxford U., Pitt Rivers Mus.; New York, Met.).

BIBLIOGRAPHY

R. G. Armstrong: 'The Idoma-speaking Peoples', *Peoples of the Niger–Benue Confluence*, Ethnographic Survey of Africa (London, 1955), pp. 91–152

Sculpture of Northern Nigeria (exh. cat. by R. Sieber, New York, Mus. Primitive A., 1961)

S. L. Kasfir: *The Visual Arts of the Idoma of Central Nigeria* (diss., U. London, SOAS, 1979)

E. O. Erim: *The Idoma Nationality, 1600–1900: Problems of Studying the Origins and Development of Ethnicity* (Enugu, 1981)

S. L. Kasfir: 'Anjenu: Sculpture for Idoma Water Spirits', *Afr. A.*, xv/4 (1982), pp. 47–51, 91–2

——: 'Masks from the Towns of the Dead: The Igbo–Idoma Borderland', *Igbo Arts: Community and Cosmos* (exh. cat. by H. M. Cole and C. C. Aniakor, Los Angeles, UCLA, Mus. Cult. Hist., 1984–6), pp. 163–5

——: *Art in History, History in Art: The Idoma Alekwuafia Masquerade as Historical Evidence*, Boston University Working Papers, 103 (Boston, MA, 1985)

F. Neyt: *The Arts of the Benue: To the Roots of Tradition* (Tielt, 1985)

S. L. Kasfir: 'The Mask of Aja', *Afr. A.*, xix/2 (1986), pp. 83–4

——: 'Celebrating Male Aggression: The Idoma *Oglinye* Masquerade', *West African Masks and Cultural Systems*, ed. S. L. Kasfir (Tervuren, 1988)

——: 'Remembering Ojiji: Portrait of an Idoma Artist', *Afr. A.*, xxii/4 (1989), pp. 44–51, 86–7

SIDNEY LITTLEFIELD KASFIR

Idrisid [Arab. Idrīsī]. Islamic dynasty that ruled in Morocco between AD 789 and 985. It was the first Islamic dynasty to establish an independent state in Morocco and played an important role in the Islamicization of the country. The founder, Idris I (*reg* 789–91), was a descendant of the Prophet Muhammad and was thus regarded by Shi'ites as a rightful successor. Having taken part in a Shi'ite revolt against the Abbasid caliph in 786, Idris fled from Arabia to north-east Morocco, settling in the region of Volubilis, near Meknes, where the local Berber population accepted him as the imam, the temporal and spiritual leader of the Islamic community. His son, Idris II (*reg* 791–828), moved the capital to FEZ, a city founded by his father but subsequently neglected. During Idris II's reign Fez became a flourishing trading, religious and intellectual centre, attracting settlers from the two great metropolises of the western Islamic world, Kairouan and Córdoba. Physical remains from the period are scarce. The Idrisids were responsible for the layout of the old centre of Fez and the division of the city into two distinct quarters (those of the Kairouanis and the Andalusians) separated by the River Fas. In the former was built what is now the Qarawiyyin Mosque, but only its core preserves Idrisid elements. The tomb of Idris I at Moulay Idris near Volubilis and that of Idris II in Fez are the holiest shrines in Morocco. They were completely rebuilt in the 18th century.

BIBLIOGRAPHY

Enc. Islam/2: 'Idrīs I'; 'Idrīs II'; 'Idrīsids'

E. Lévi-Provençal: 'La Fondation de Fès', *An. Inst. Etud. Orient. U. Alger*, iv (1938), pp. 23–53

MARIANNE BARRUCAND

Idromeno, Kol [Nikollë] (*b* Shkodër, 15 Aug 1860; *d* Shkodër, 12 Dec 1939). Albanian painter, architect, sculptor and photographer. His grandfather Andrea Idromeno was a painter and a doctor of theology; his father, Arsen Idromeno, was a furniture designer and painter. Kol Idromeno took private lessons in painting (1871–5) at the studio of the photographer and painter Pietro Marubi (1834–1903). In 1875 he won a competition and began studies at the Accademia di Belle Arti, Venice. However, due to arguments with his teacher, he abandoned the school and continued his studies in one of the large studios in Venice (1876–8).

At first Idromeno produced works with both religious and secular themes that were noted for their highly realistic rendering of the human form (e.g. *St Mary Magdalene*, oil on canvas, 1877; Shkodër Mus.). Many of his biblical works were executed in churches within the Shkodër district, with perhaps his best work being the frescoes of the Orthodox Church in Shkodër, especially the fragment depicting *Hell* (1881), which is painted in a manner quite unlike the traditional post-Byzantine style still prevalent in Albania in the late 19th century. The religious narrative chosen by Idromeno was used by the artist to criticize

Kol Idromeno: *Shköder Wedding*, oil on canvas, 1.35×0.95 m, 1924 (Tiranë, Art Gallery)

contemporary vices. In such portraits as *Sister Tone* (oil on canvas, 1.96×1.69 m, 1883; Tiranë, A.G.) he won acclaim for his attention to detail and his ability to capture the sitter's likeness. In one of his major compositions, *Two Roads* (oil on canvas, 1.96×1.69 m, 1892; Shkodër, A.G.), Idromeno mixed the secular and the religious by placing images of heaven and hell in the corners of an otherwise realist painting. Within the painting are images of every stratum of Albanian society. After World War I he produced such pioneering canvases as *Shkodër Wedding* (1924; Tiranë, A.G.; see fig.), which was praised for its intense realism.

In addition to photography and painting, Idromeno produced decorative sculpture and architecture. He designed approximately 50 public and social buildings, including the bell-tower of Shkodër Cathedral (1910) and Kafja e Madhe (The Big Coffee House) in Shkodër (1935), in which it is possible to see the influence of Western Baroque and Rococo architecture. His decorative works included plaster reliefs and carvings in stone, wood and marble. Among his students were Ndoc Martini and Zef Kolombi.

UNPUBLISHED SOURCES

Shkodër, A.G. [MSS]
Tiranë, A.G. [MSS]

BIBLIOGRAPHY

D. Dhamo: 'Mbi karakterin kombëtar e realist të arteve tona figurative' [On national and realist characteristics of our figurative arts], *Stud. Hist.*, 2 (1971), p. 23
F. Hudhri: 'Vizatimetë K. Idromenos' [Idromeno's drawings], *Nëntori*, 6 (1978), p. 204
M. Prenushi: *Kol Idromeno* (Tiranë, 1984)

GJERGJ FRASHËRI

Idźkowski, Adam (*b* Olszanka, nr Pułtusk, 24 Dec 1798; *d* Lityn, Podole, 3 May 1879). Polish architect and writer. He studied under Antoni Corazzi at the Faculty of Fine Arts of the University of Warsaw (1820–24). In 1824–7 he travelled to Italy, France, England and Germany. In Italy he was awarded membership of the Accademia del Disegno, Florence, for his restoration project for the Temple of Concord (ded. AD 10), Rome. From 1828 he worked as a building adviser in Warsaw to the governmental Commission for Enlightenment. He was also a member of the General Council of Construction to the governmental Commission of Internal Affairs. Idźkowski's major architectural works were the Neo-classical reconstruction (1838–42; destr. 1944) of the Saxon Palace, Warsaw, which was based partly on a plan by Wacław Ritschel (1794–1872); the Gothic Revival reconstruction (1839–42; destr. 1944) of St John's Cathedral, Warsaw, inspired by English Gothic cathedrals; the Gothic Revival railway station (1846) in Skierniewice; and the Neo-classical development (1852) of the Paskiewicz Palace, Homl. He was responsible for several projects in construction and technology, such as a tunnel (1828) under the Vistula River in Warsaw inspired by a tunnel under the Thames in London. Following the theories of Jean-Nicolas-Louis Durand, which were popular until the mid-19th century, Idźkowski declared the equality of all architectural styles and forms of construction. Most of his works, however, bear links to the medieval architecture of England, Germany, France and Italy: in his treatise of 1832 he devoted a whole chapter to the analysis of Gothic architecture and its decoration. Other projects, such as the reconstruction of the Royal Castle, Warsaw (1843; unexecuted), were strongly influenced by Karl Friedrich Schinkel's architectural style. Many of his projects appeared in the collection of works published in 1843, including the unexecuted plans for the Royal Castle and the emperor's castle at Aleje Ujazdowskie, Warsaw.

WRITINGS

Projekt drogi pod rzeką Wisłą dla połączenia Warszawy z Pragą [Project for a passage under the Vistula linking Warsaw and Prague] (Warsaw, 1828)
Kroje architektury obejmujące rozmaite jej kształty uważane jako przedmiot piękności. . . [Types of architecture including its different forms perceived as beautiful. . .] (Warsaw, 1832)
Plany budowli . . . w rozmaitych stylach architektury przez (. . .), Budowniczego Rządowego, członka Akademii Florenckiej Sztuk Pięknych [Architectural plans . . . in various architectural styles by (. . .), State Builder, member of the Florence Academy of Fine Arts] (Warsaw, 1843; Fr. trans., Paris, 1843–52)
Chemin hydroterre ou nouveau système de communications (St Petersburg, 1845)
Chemin de fer statique et ses immenses avantages sur la construction des chemins de fer actuels (Paris, 1857)

BIBLIOGRAPHY

PSB
T. S. Jaroszewski: *O siedzibach neogotyckich w Polsce* [On Gothic Revival residences in Poland] (Warsaw, 1981)

ANDRZEJ ROTTERMUND

Ife. Town in the hilly forest zone of south-western Nigeria. Ife has a Yoruba-speaking population of approximately

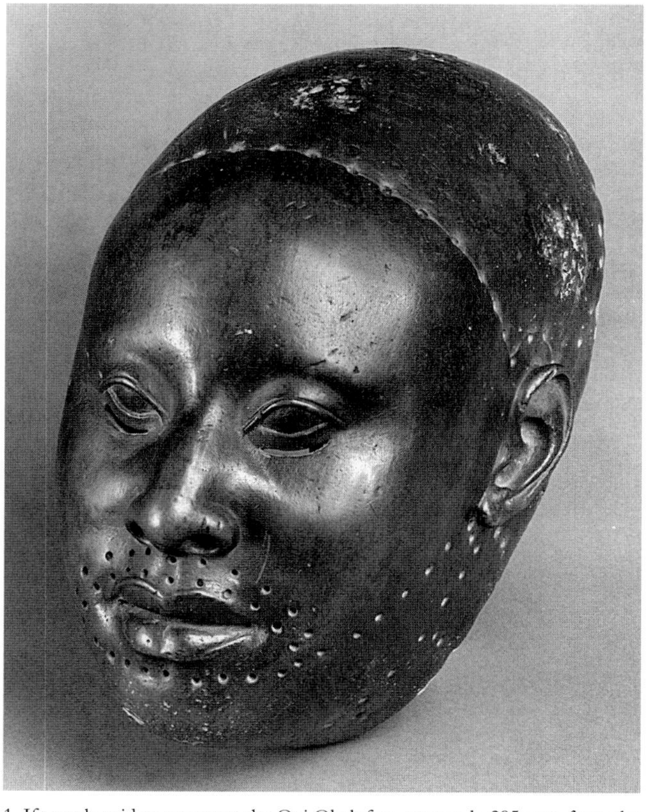

1. Ife mask, said to represent the Oni Obalufon, copper, h. 295 mm, from the Oni's Palace, 11th–15th centuries (Ife, Museum of the Ife Antiquities)

250,000 and has always been held in special regard by the Yoruba peoples as their holy city and the place where the world was created by Oduduwa, the first Oni (king). Its art-historical importance derives primarily from a corpus of 'bronze' and terracotta sculptures, many of them life-size representations of human heads in a remarkably naturalistic style, dating from the 11th to the 15th century (see fig. 1). Excavations at Ife have revealed such other aspects of its ancient material culture as stone sculptures and pavements made from potsherds. Most of the material that has been uncovered is held in Nigerian museums (Lagos, N. Mus.; Ife, Mus. Ant.; U. Ife, Mus. Inst. Afr. Stud.).

1. Discovery and excavation. 2. History. 3. Sculpture.

1. DISCOVERY AND EXCAVATION. In 1911 the German ethnographer Leo Frobenius, having heard that ancient heads accidentally found at Ife were reburied and dug up for ritual purposes, arranged for a well-known bronze head, first discovered in the 19th century, to be excavated from the Olokun Grove outside the town. Given the ritual treatment of the Olokun head and its association with the Yoruba sea goddess of that name, Frobenius concluded that Ife was the lost civilization of Atlantis, but this view was not widely accepted. Frobenius was not allowed to purchase the original Olokun head (Ife, Mus. Ant.), which was identified in the 1950s as a forgery made by using a sand-mould rather than the lost-wax technique, but he did return to Germany with numerous terracotta heads (now Berlin, Mus. Vlkerknd.).

2. Ife head of an Oni, copper with traces of paint, h. 290 mm, from Wunmonije compound, 11th–15th centuries (Ife, Museum of the Ife Antiquities)

In 1938 and 1939 a Yoruba man digging the foundations for a house in the Wunmonije compound, behind the palace at Ife, unearthed 17 copper alloy heads (see fig. 2) and the upper half of a full-length figure (h. 370 mm; Ife, Mus. Ant.), thought to represent an Oni in his regalia. Various estimates were made concerning the date of these brass sculptures, the earliest being the 5th century. The first systematic excavation at Ife was carried out by Bernard Fagg, William Fagg and John Goodwin in 1953. They worked primarily in the sacred groves of Osangangan Obamakin and Olokun Walode, discovering further fragments of sculptures. In 1957 workmen undertaking construction work in a part of Ife known as Ita Yemoo accidentally found more brass items, including a complete full-length figure of an Oni (see fig. 3); a smaller, linked pair of standing figures, interpreted as an Oni and his wife; a small female figure coiled around a bowl on top of a stool; and two staffs and two mace heads portraying human heads. In 1957–8 and 1962–3 Frank Willett excavated the site, revealing two shrines containing terracotta figures as well as potsherd pavements. The pavements may have been the courtyards of houses or the verandahs surrounding them, and they vary in style from simple rows of potsherds or specially made pottery discs, sometimes alternating with white pebbles, to arrangements in herringbone fashion. In 1963–4 Oliver Myers excavated a mound at Igbo Obameri and found several terracotta heads. In 1969 Ekpo Eyo excavated the sites of Odo Ogbe Street and Lafogido, and in 1971–2 Peter Garlake excavated the sites of Obalara's Land and Woye Asiri, revealing a further series of potsherd pavements. That many of these sites lie outside the city walls indicates that Ife had already declined in size by the time these were erected in the 19th century.

2. HISTORY. Ife's position at the centre of a northward bulge of forest made it the focus of a network that drew upon the resources of the River Niger and lesser rivers, the coast and the savannah country to the north. As a result of both local and more widespread trade, Ife developed an internal system of exchange with regular markets. Religious cults emerged to secure the benevolence of the unseen powers of water, earth and sky, and commercial slavery and domestic bondage became an integral part of the social and commercial system, enhancing the wealth and power of the Oni and his entourage and providing the labour that serviced the court, the officials and wealthy traders. At first, the slaves sold to northern traders were probably paid for in salt. As the trading relationship became established and the wealth and power of the Oni increased, such luxury goods as copper, brass, textiles, beads, bracelets, swords and horses were imported from the north in exchange for other indigenous products.

Ife's decline after three centuries of prosperity may have been a result of the rise (*c.* 1400) of Old Oyo (Oyo Ile,

3. Ife figure of an Oni, zinc brass, h. 471 mm, from Ita Yemoo, early 14th century–early 15th (Ife, Museum of the Ife Antiquities)

'Katunga'), situated around 170 km to the north. It has been claimed that Old Oyo was the terminus of an important trans-Saharan caravan route, which provided it with a commercially strategic advantage in controlling the trade to the north. In addition, its situation in the savannah meant that Old Oyo could build up a cavalry-based military power, using horses from the north, in a way that Ife could not. During the early 16th century Ife was again unable to exploit a new source of trade and wealth. This time the arrival of European voyagers and the development of the transatlantic slave trade failed to benefit the city's economy, since it was cut off from the coast to the south by the powers of the Kingdom of Dahomey and of Ijebu. Although Ife sank into economic and artistic decline, it remained the supreme centre of religious observances and was venerated as such.

3. Sculpture. Most Ife sculpture in terracotta, bronze and stone is highly naturalistic, although starkly stylized forms were produced at the same time. Most of the human heads are life-size: some have crowns, while others have holes at the top of the forehead, probably for the attachment of a real crown. Some also have holes in the neck, indicating that they were used in second burial ceremonies for the king, after which they were kept on a shrine in the palace. Examples with holes around the mouth, chin and lower cheeks may indicate that moustaches and beards of real hair were sometimes added. On some of the bronze and terracotta heads the entire face is covered with delicate, linear striations representing scarification, while the neck is often ringed. Several sculptures have 'cat's whiskers' scarification marks radiating from the corners of the lips, resembling those still worn by the Nupe to the north. Numerous pieces retain traces of red and white paint.

Among the full-length figures, those in bronze, representing kings and queens, are heavily laden with beads and necklaces and have a double bow, signifying royal office. In contrast to the naturalism of the facial rendering, the proportions of both bronze and terracotta pieces are shortened, as in much African sculpture. The only known exception is a highly naturalistic, Ife-style seated figure (h. 565 mm; Lagos, N. Mus.) from the Nupe village of Tada, which has been dated by thermoluminescence to the late 13th century or early 14th. Although human forms predominate, such animals as the ram, elephant and hippopotamus are also found. Such representations of animals as an elephant's head from Lafogido (see fig. 4) show greater concentration on surface design than on the subtle modelling of form that characterizes the human heads.

(i) Bronze. Spectographic analysis of the Ife 'bronzes' has revealed that most are alloys of copper with lead or zinc as the main addition. Five of the heads from the Wunmonije compound (e.g. see fig. 2 above), the Obalufon mask (Ife, Mus. Ant.) and the seated figure from Tada are exceptional in that they are cast in copper (in one case with the addition of gold). This was probably achieved by sealing the mould on to the crucible containing the metal, heating the crucible until the metal melted and then inverting the assemblage. By this means it was possible for the copper to run into the mould without contact with the outside air, which would otherwise oxidize the metal and restrict the flow (see 1980–83 exh. cat.). It is possible that the figure from Tada was too large to be cast using this technique; instead the copper may have been poured from open crucibles, requiring at least 20 repairs by casting on.

It has not been established whether the raw materials for the castings were imported or produced locally. Zinc occurs in Nigeria in sufficient quantities to be exploited, but with copper the situation is less clear. Both copper and brass are known to have been transported along the trans-Saharan routes of the Arabs to West Africa. The composition of the Ife castings is totally different from those of the earlier castings of IGBO-UKWU in south-eastern Nigeria, which are made of leaded bronze, and they resemble Benin castings much more closely in composition (*see* BENIN).

(ii) Terracotta. As the terracottas from Ife are much more numerous and varied than the brass castings, they may have been produced over a much longer period and by a greater number of artists. Most of the terracotta sculptures closely resemble the naturalistic brass heads, suggesting the existence of a strong, and perhaps long, tradition of naturalistic representation before the same style was translated into metal. Despite this, no developmental sequence of terracottas has been convincingly established. A ritual vessel (Ife, Mus. Ant.) excavated by Garlake at Obalara's Land bears a depiction of a shrine containing one naturalistic head flanked by two tapering cylindrical heads of a highly conventionalized character (actual examples of which have been found; e.g. Ife, Mus. Ant.). This would indicate that the naturalistic and stylized types of heads were contemporaneous.

Unlike the 'bronzes', the terracottas have often been excavated rather than found accidentally. Some of the heads, including the Lajuwa head (Ife, Mus. Ant.), were evidently intended to be free-standing and never attached to bodies. Other terracotta sculptures are of full-length figures, ranging in height from around 150 mm to near life-size. Some of the figurines may represent sacrificial animals, and some may refer to the animals' behavioural characteristics or to related proverbs.

(iii) Stone. Stone carvings include stools, monoliths, human figures and animal representations. The stools are made of polished quartz, comprising two discs joined by a central column with a large handle-shaped loop on one side. They demonstrate the expertise of carvers in handling such a brittle material. It has been suggested that the shape of these stools derives from that of wooden boxes that have continued to be used into modern times for the storage of ritual objects and as stools (Fagg and Fagg, 1960). Simple four-legged stools were also produced in quartz, granite and soapstone.

Among the varied sizes and forms of monoliths, the Ada Eledisi ('sword of Eledisi'; h. *c.* 1.5 m) is unique in that its upper part curves at right angles to the shaft. However, the most outstanding is the Opa Oranmiyan ('staff of Oranmiyan', one of the offspring of Oduduwa and the founder of Oyo). This is a monolith of granite gneiss (h. more than 5 m), round in section, tapering gently at the top and studded with 140 spiral-headed iron nails. In the sacred Ore Grove of the city there are small standing stones, fragments of stools, stone boxes, a carving of a mudfish (l. *c.* 1 m) and various other artefacts. The grove also contains two human figures, both with hands folded in front of the stomach. The larger, known as Idena ('the gatekeeper'; h. *c.* 1 m), is characterized by naturalistic proportions and is similar to the stone figures situated at Eshure, 150 km east of Ife, and to others scattered around the city. Among the numerous other locations where stone sculpture has been found, the largest and most distinctive

4. Ife elephant head, terracotta, h. 152 mm, from Lafogido, 12th–15th centuries (Ife, Museum of the Ife Antiquities)

corpus (*c.* 1000 carvings) occurs at Esie, some 100 km north of Ife. Most are made of a soft soapstone, and a few have been tentatively dated to the 12th century based on thermoluminescence techniques applied to associated terracotta examples. Although the origin of these works and their links with Ife are not known, it has been suggested that the Esie carvings were dumped there by the Ife faction who migrated northwards, probably following the dynastic strife that led to the founding of Oyo Ile (Old Oyo), or that they emanated from a one-time extensive Oba state.

BIBLIOGRAPHY

K. C. Murray: 'Nigerian Bronzes: Works from Ife', *Antiquity*, xv (1941), pp. 71–80

B. Fagg and W. Fagg: 'The Ritual Stools of Ancient Ife', *Man*, lx (1960), pp. 113–15

F. Willett: 'Ife and its Archaeology', *J. Afr. Hist.*, i/2 (1960), pp. 231–48

W. B. Fagg and F. Willett: 'Ancient Ife: An Ethnographical Summary', *Actes du IVe Congrès Panafricain de Préhistoire: Tervuren, 1962*, iii, pp. 357–73

F. Willett: *Ife in the History of West African Sculpture* (London and New York, 1967); review by A. I. Rubin in *A. Bull.*, lii/31 (1970), pp. 348–54

P. Wheatley: 'The Significance of Traditional Yoruba Urbanism', *Comp. Stud. Soc. & Hist.*, xii/4 (1970), pp. 393–423

F. Willett: *African Art*, World A. (London, 1971/*R* 1977)

E. Eyo: *Two Thousand Years' Nigerian Art* (Lagos, 1977)

P. Garlake: 'Sculpture of Ife and Benin', *The Kingdoms of Africa*, ed. P. Garlake (Oxford, 1978), pp. 111–36

P. Stevens jr.: *The Stone Images of Esie, Nigeria* (Ibadan and Lagos, 1978)

V. E. Chikwendu and A. C. Umeji: 'Local Sources of Raw Materials for the Nigerian Bronze/Brass Industry: With Emphasis on Igbo-Ukwu', *W. Afr. J. Archaeol.*, ix (1979), pp. 151–65

Treasures of Ancient Nigeria (exh. cat. by E. Eyo and F. Willett, Detroit, Inst. A.; Oslo, N.G.; London, RA; and elsewhere; 1980–83)

C. O. Adepegba: 'Ife Art: An Enquiry into the Surface Patterns and the Continuity of the Art Tradition among the Northern Yoruba', *W. Afr. J. Archaeol.*, xii (1982), pp. 95–109

B. W. Andah: 'Urban "Origins" in the Guinea Forest with Special Reference to Benin', *W. Afr. J. Archaeol.*, xii (1982), pp. 63–71

P. T. Craddock: 'Mediaeval Copper Alloy Production and West African Bronze Analyses', *Archaeometry*, xxvii/1 (1985), pp. 17–21; xxviii/1 (1986), pp. 3–32
V. E. Chikwendu and others: 'Nigerian Sources for Copper, Lead and Tin for the Igbo-Ukwu Bronzes', *Archaeometry*, xxxi/1 (1989)

THURSTAN SHAW

Iga. Centre of ceramics production in Japan. It flourished from the late 16th century in the vicinity of Ueno City (now Mie Prefect.; *see* JAPAN, §VIII, 3(ii)). Although Iga is most famous for its aggressively distorted, natural ash-glazed wares for the tea ceremony (*see* JAPAN, §XIV), kilns in the surrounding hills also produced utilitarian wares from at least the second half of the 17th century. It remains unclear if there is any local predecessor to the Iga teawares that emerged in the late 16th century. Sue wares (*see* JAPAN, §VIII, 2(ii)(a)) were fired in the region from the 6th century AD, and unglazed stonewares were manufactured in nearby SHIGARAKI from the 13th century, but since the entire region drew from the same clay source, it is impossible clearly to isolate a proto-Iga ware from the vast amounts of wares made at Shigaraki.

The beginning of Iga teawares is traced through tea ceremony records. The ware is mentioned first in 1581 in the tea diary of Tsuda Sōgyū (*d* 1591) and in 1587 in a record of the tea ceremonies of master SEN NO RIKYŪ. Rikyū's successor FURUTA ORIBE, who favoured boldly distorted forms for his tea ceremony, is recorded as having used Iga ware a number of times in his heyday in the first decade of the 17th century. The Iga wares used by Oribe and his peers were largely confined to flower vases and water jars. Stylistically, they are generous in size and replete with such exaggerated features as protruding knobs, bulging walls and playful, irregular incisions. This sense of bravado was further exaggerated by the firing method. Iga teawares were apparently subject to multiple firings, during which natural ash-glaze deposits and scorch marks appeared on the body. The long exposure to heat made certain wares sag and even crack, effects that came to be highly prized.

It is generally thought that Iga teaware production was inaugurated under the patronage of Tsutsui Sadatsugu (*c.* 1561–1615), lord of Iga Province and a follower of Rikyū and Oribe, but Sadatsugu fell into disfavour with the ruling Tokugawa family in 1608 and was exiled. The Tsutsui were succeeded by the Tōdō clan, and under the headship of Tōdō Takatora (1556–1630) and Takatsugu (1601–76), Iga ware production continued. Takatsugu is known to have invited Kyoto potters to Iga in 1635. Although no systematic investigations have been carried out, an Iga-ware kiln site was discovered in 1935 in the Iga–Ueno Castle site in Ueno City. Shards from the site are now kept at the Sekisui Museum in Tsu City, and other Iga-ware shards have also been collected at sites in the nearby mountain villages of Marubashira and Makiyama. Tōdō clan documents attest to the fact that a domestic glazed-ware industry burgeoned in Marubashira from the 17th century. Teaware manufacture was augmented by production of utilitarian wares, including lidded cooking pots (*donabe*) and large teapots (*dobin*). From the 19th century, when exchange with other kilns was quite common, the potters also made copies of Kyoto ware (*see* KYOTO, §III), ARITA ware, SETO ware and KUTANI ware.

BIBLIOGRAPHY

S. Hayashiya: *Iga* (1975), xiii of *Nippon tōji zenshū* [Complete collection of Japanese ceramics], ed. M. Satō and others (Tokyo, 1975–7)
M. Kawahara: 'Iga no chatō' [Tea ceramics from Iga], vi of *Nihon yakimono shūsei* [Collection of Japanese ceramics], ed. C. Mitsuoka, S. Hayashiya and S. Narasaki (Tokyo, 1981), pp. 119–22
K. Tanimoto: 'Iga no minyō' [Folk ware from Iga], vi of *Nihon yakimono shūsei* (Tokyo, 1981), pp. 123–4
Nihon no tōji [Japanese ceramics] (exh. cat., ed. Y. Yabe; Tokyo, N. Mus., 1985)

RICHARD L. WILSON

Igala. A people living south-east of the confluence of the Niger and Benue rivers in Nigeria. Numbering almost 500,000, they share a common boundary with the Igbo to the south and the Idoma to the east. The narrow strip between the Igala and the Benue River is occupied by the Bassa Nge and Bassa Nkomo; to the west, across the Niger River, live the EDO-speaking peoples, the Ebira and the YORUBA. Igala culture, society and language have much in common with the Yoruba.

The principal Igala art form is wood-carving, particularly of head-pieces used in masquerades. At Idah, the Igala capital on the Niger, there is a set of heavy carved helmets used for the king's masquerades, which appear at royal festivals to control the spectators. These helmets are coloured black, with some details picked out usually in white, and have human features with hairstyles represented by black and red abrus seeds set in gum. Strips of yellow and red cloth hang down from the neckpiece to form a costume. One of these masks, with facial features painted in blue and white, was said to belong to the Achadu, head of the 'Kingmakers', the chiefs responsible for the royal succession (see fig.). Another type of helmet, named *inyelikpi* after a stinging plant, has a distorted mouth and represents a clown.

Igala headpiece for Ugbodu, a masquerade owned by the Achadu in Idah, wood decorated with red and black abrus seeds, facial details picked out in blue and white pigments; from a photograph of 1957

In Ibaji district, south of the capital, a variety of mask forms are used, including black helmet masks, similar to the royal types at Idah, with grooved striations representing facial scars and hairstyles. There are also therianthropic helmets, worn by maskers called *ofogoli* ('the foolish ones'), and horned cap masks with human features in relief. Face-masks are worn here for various plays: the *bogodo* type is characterized by a pierced vertical crest and represents dead members of a title society at an annual funeral ceremony. Headdresses with superimposed figures arranged in tableaux are worn by maskers called *ojamalede* in this district and throughout Igalaland. Some of the headdresses and costumes used by Ibaji Igala are obtained from IGBO artists.

Masking costumes of fibre or fabric are an important art form throughout Igalaland. Cylindrical cloth costumes (h. *c.* 2.44–2.75 m), which taper to a pointed apex, are worn by *egwu afia* maskers who impersonate dead ancestors in the annual Okula festival, a celebration of their return to the community. The headdress of the *olagenyi* masker incorporates a crown of stiff felt, cut to represent feathers; cloth and fibre are both used to produce a bulky and imposing appearance. This figure comes out to honour the dead at funerals and on the occasional ancestral festival. A juvenile dancing masker called *owuna* wears a costume of cloth and fibre with a headdress of white heron feathers. Among the north-eastern Igala, groups of maskers called *ukpoku*, wearing costumes of painted bark cloth and chasing bystanders, are believed to banish witches.

Local Igala carvers also produce fine work, especially the wooden figures (*ojibo*) that are displayed at festivals. Horned wooden figures (*okegga*) occur both in the Ibaji area and in the vicinity of Idah. Smaller examples of these figures symbolize the individual achievements of their owners, while larger figures are owned by clans as symbols of their group achievement. Umale, a wood-carver who lived near Iyale in the northern region of the Igala, produced a distinctive genre of free-standing figures and mirror-frames and boxes decorated with geometric designs. Carved wooden stoppers, in animal or bird forms, are found in the Ankpa area. Igala carvers also produce stools for women, and lidded, zoomorphic boxes are sometimes made for kola nuts or other small possessions.

Smiths in the capital claim to know the technique for casting small brass figures and bells. Weaving is done by both men and women; men weave the narrow strips of cloth, so typical of West Africa, that are sewn together to make white funeral shrouds (*see* AFRICA, §V, 7(i)).

BIBLIOGRAPHY

K. C. Murray: 'Idah Masks', *Niger. Field*, xiv/30 (1949), pp. 85–92
Sculpture of Northern Nigeria (exh. cat. by R. Sieber, New York, Mus. Primitive A., 1961)
J. S. Boston: 'Ceremonial Iron Gongs among the Igala and the Igbo', *Man*, lii (1964), pp. 44–7
——: *The Igala Kingdom* (Ibadan, 1968)
M. Van de Velde-Caremans: 'Some Aspects of the Wood Sculpture of the Central Northern Igala', *Afr. Gandensia*, i (1976), pp. 118–59
J. S. Boston: *Ikenga Figures among the North-west Igbo and the Igala* (Lagos, 1977)
N. C. Neaher: 'Nigerian Bronze Bells', *Afr. A.*, xii/3 (1979), pp. 42–7
P. Chike-Dike: 'Some Items of Igala Regalia', *Afr. A.*, xvii/2 (1984), pp. 70–71
F. Neyt and A. Desirant: *The Arts of the Benue: To the Roots of Tradition* (Ottignies, 1985)
P. Chike-Dike: 'Regalia, Divinity and State in Igala', *Afr. A.*, xx/3 (1987), pp. 75–8
R. A. Sargent: 'Igala Masks: Dynastic History and the Face of the Nation', *West African Masks and Cultural Systems*, ed. S. L. Kasfir (Tervuren, 1988), pp. 17–44

J. S. BOSTON

Igbo [Ibo]. A people living mainly in Anambra and Imo states to the east of the Niger River, Nigeria, although some live to the west, in Bendel state. Numbering about 10 million, the Igbo are bounded to the north by the Igala, Idoma and Tiv; to the east by the Cross River and its numerous small ethnic groups, including the Mbembe, Ejagham and Yako; to the south-east by the Ibibio and Efik; to the south by the Ogoni, Abua and Ijo; and to the west by the Isoko, Urhobo and other Edo-speaking peoples.

Igbo is a modern designation. Outside the core area, such groups as the Ohafia, Ndoki and Ahoada have accepted it only in the 20th century. In precolonial times village groups were the largest political units, although contiguous peoples banded together temporarily in times of war for defence against common enemies. Formerly, therefore, groups were fragmented and semi-autonomous, both politically and culturally. Traditionally, village groups were governed by councils of elders. The Igbo never formed kingdoms, although such towns as Oguta and Onitsha have had rulers called kings.

Artistically the Igbo are most famous for their rich masking traditions and for their figure sculpture, often associated with shrine architecture. However, Igbo artists have produced a wide range of other objects, including tools, textiles, ceramics and furniture, as well as practising a wide range of body arts. Examples of Igbo art objects are held by most museums with African collections (for a select list see Jones, 1989, pp. 68–9). Igbo arts have also been widely illustrated (see works listed in the bibliography below, especially 1984–6 exh. cat.). While few Igbo art forms date from before the late 19th century, the spectacular 10th-century copper alloy and ceramic archaeological finds from IGBO-UKWU have many formal similarities with Igbo arts of the late 19th and 20th centuries.

1. Introduction. 2. Mask and masquerade. 3. Shrines, *mbari* houses and associated arts. 4. Display figures. 5. Titular arts.

1. INTRODUCTION. Not all the forms discussed here are considered 'artistic things' (*ihe nkarinkari*) by Igbo people. Some are of primarily instrumental or ritual importance in Igbo eyes. Sets of small wooden figures in diviners' kits (symbolizing the divination deity, Agwushi, his family and messengers), for example, are normally encrusted with blood and other sacrifices. The same is true of *ofo*, the most powerful instrument of spiritual and ancestral truth. One of these primarily medicinal objects is held by the head of each family and religious cult. It is usually an uncarved stick of sacred wood, although in parts of western Igboland it is cast in brass as a non-specific quadruped, while in the north-west, its anthropomorphic wooden form is embellished with wrought iron. While some *ofo* are well made, few Igbo would describe them as 'artistic things'; they are rarely displayed or even seen.

In the Igbo world every artefact has value. Each object or process may be seen as being located on a continuum between the poles of absolute artistry and absolute power. The Igbo conception of such a continuum may be inferred from the consciously stated oppositions in Igbo thought between male and female, dark things and light ones, elderhood and youth, bad/ugly and good/beautiful, etc. The Igbo world is unified by the tensions and reciprocal interactions between these various poles. While few phenomena can be placed at either of the very ends of the continuum, it is noteworthy that many objects may be seen to have shifted towards the pole of absolute artistry during the 20th century. This may be seen as being a result of European influence and increasing secularization. For example, a masquerade that in 1900 had strong spiritual sanctions and regulatory powers may not have been much more than public entertainment and display in 1980.

In art as elsewhere Igbo men and women have separate roles and use different styles and materials. In addition to being the primary ritual specialists (family heads, diviners and priests), men are the artisans in such durable materials as iron, copper alloys, ivory and wood. Men carve, or model in mud, figures for shrines; they erect buildings; they make masks and control masquerades; and they forge and cast tools, ritual implements and title paraphernalia. Apart from figurative work, male arts tend to be hard-edged, measured, angular, symmetrical and geometrical. Women work softer, more tractable materials, such as fibres and clay, as well as earth and vegetal pigments. They are weavers, painters, ceramicists, decorators, body artists and hair stylists, embellishing surfaces freehand in styles that tend towards the curvilinear, playful and asymmetrical. Except in their ceramic work women's arts are more transient; they are also more decorative and ritually peripheral, while men's are more enduring and centrally connected to rituals.

Artefacts are created in part to cope with and mirror the vagaries of nature, which is venerated as earth, river, forest, sky, leopard, eagle and yam. The vitality of Igbo arts reflects a dynamic world-view that embraces competition, motion and change. For example, the Ijele mask performance (*see* §2(v) below) and the *mbari* monuments (*see* §3 below), perhaps the two most complex and dramatic Igbo art forms, are both dependent on European products (bright cloth and white plates, respectively) for part of their impact and meaning.

2. Mask and masquerade. Masking is one of the few art-related institutions that spans the breadth of Igboland, although few masquerades performed since the late 1960s have had nearly the ritual, political or judicial power of those of the past. The Igbo proverb, 'you do not stand in one place to watch a masquerade', captures the essence of masking as a changing art moving through time and space. The maskers themselves are active, and the arena in which they perform has fluid, changing boundaries. The number of spectators swells and diminishes, and they clap, shout encouragement and move about, stimulated by the music, dance and performance. While women both observe and sometimes participate, about half the characters are female but performed by males, perhaps representing masculine power clothed in feminine beauty. Most of the male population participate in masking, and nearly all take part at some point in their lives. In some areas male children begin playing at masking when they are two or three years old. Forbidden to wear real masks, they fashion imaginative headdresses and costumes out of cloth, cardboard, gourds and leaves. They chase young girls, and sing and dance in emulation of adult maskers. In several areas initiation into Igbo masking societies marks the transition from boyhood to manhood. In the presence of masked spirits, the boy undergoes a symbolic death. The society's secrets and the prescriptions against revealing them are then revealed to him, after which he may be able to dance his first real mask. Thus prepared, he may perform any one of hundreds of less powerful spirit characters that are mildly harassing to women and children, but playful and entertaining rather than ritually powerful.

In all areas of Igboland, despite marked regional variation, the two most important generic mask types may be categorized as 'beauty' (female) and 'the beast' (male). Dozens, and in some areas, hundreds, of other mask types supplement the two constants, so that most regional masking traditions include a range of spirit characters ranging from theatrical, entertaining and often light-coloured beautiful female masks, without much spiritual power, to ritually powerful male or animal masks that are heavy, instrumental agents of socio-spiritual control. Before colonial times these latter masks had very effective powers of social control, occasionally even including the carrying-out of death sentences. Throughout Igboland powerful masked spirits are organized by secret councils of respected elders and priests. Such 'bad spirits' (*ajommuo*) rarely appear. Some are clothed only in darkness, but, when they are embodied in masks and costumes, these are huge, with misshapen features. They also carry weapons and charms.

In all regions, Igbo mask types and styles are shared with their neighbours. When masks lack provenance, as is the case with the thousands that left the country during the Biafran War (1967–70), determining origins is problematic.

(i) North-central. (ii) North-eastern. (iii) Eastern. (iv) South-western. (v) Northern.

(i) North-central. Strong masks of the 'time of the brave' (*mgbedike*) type are widely distributed in the north-central region. Their 'heads' range from 600 to 1200 mm in height, and they have bold features in dark colours, large mouths with menacing teeth, and real or carved horns. They have names like Devours Like Leopard, Can Draw the Knife, Tough, Hero with Bloodshot Eyes, Break my Head and Leopard Killer. All project an aura of mystery, danger, aggression and fearlessness, and they are accompanied by middle-aged men known for their 'deeds of power' as diviners, wrestlers, warriors and farmers. These maskers often carry strong medicines and can be wild and destructive, yet they also perform in public at festivals and at the funerals of important people.

The generic opposites of these heavy masculine spirits are pretty feminine characters who celebrate maidenhood, motherhood and the family. Any large masquerade performance will include a mother spirit with four or five maiden daughters who perform competitive, complex, crowd-pleasing virtuoso dancing with exaggerated gesture and masculine strength both as a group and solo (see fig. 1). The maskers' costumes are bright, appliquéd body suits whose patterns are exaggerated versions of body-painting designs. Similarly, the openwork mask crests are larger and more flamboyant versions of actual hairstyles. The mask features are often small, and delicate, and they are painted white. Thus the masks reaffirm the ideals of maidenhood through exaggeration, making the characters larger than life, which is appropriate as they are danced by tall, strong men. The characters of maidens and mothers are sometimes supplemented by that of a titled male, often played as an awkward buffoon, and by a mischievous, bawdy son. Their actions and slapstick dancing provide a foil for the graceful women.

A variety of lesser spirits may warm up the crowd before the main event, and may also close the activities at dusk. These characters are danced by younger men, who may commission their own masks. Some of these lesser spirits wear carved, detachable masks, while many of them

1. Igbo maiden maskers, near Awka, north-central Igbo region, Nigeria; from a photograph by G. I. Jones, *c.* 1935

wear costumes of raffia, leaves, feathers and appliquéd cloth. The masks themselves represent birds, antelopes and other animals or hybrids, as well as comic and satirical human types, including caricatures of district officers and other whites. These maskers are playful, exuberant and acrobatic.

(ii) North-eastern. Relatively little fieldwork has been done in this area, and in consequence attributions between Igbo and neighbouring peoples are especially difficult. Ogbodo Enyi, a stylized 'elephant spirit', danced by some Igbo in this area, for example, is also known among several non-Igbo groups. The same is true of the face and helmet masks worn in Okperegede dances in this area. Ogbodo Enyi dances alone at funerals and dry-season festivals, representing the collective power of the age-groups that mount and accompany it. Leading its supporters and musicians, Ogbodo Enyi tours the community, alternately running and dancing aggressively. The outings of Ogbodo Enyi, who was once a violent agent of social control, are now festive and non-threatening.

Okperegede is an ensemble of maskers that appears at festivals of ancestral remembrance known as Otutura. Up to nine characters, usually including a mother and her beautiful daughter, herald the performance of their husband and father, Asifu, a legendary leader and fierce warrior. The dance-drama may include horned maskers, who dance erratically with youthful male exuberance; a flirtatious, inept clown; a ragged child; and a colonial district officer. The pantomime centres on the desirable beauty of the daughter, but the awe-inspiring and threatening arrival of Asifu quells this flirtation and all other antics. This three- or four-faced spirit radiates status and authority. He dances violently alone, then with his wife, more calmly, and once again threateningly, to close the festival.

(iii) Eastern. The masquerades of the Afikpo Igbo are well known (Ottenberg), but the arts of other eastern areas have not been studied in depth. Scholarly knowledge of the masks of Ohafiã, Abiriba, Bende, Ngwa and Arochukwu is confused by their similarity to masks of non-Igbo peoples living along the Cross River, and by Igbo interaction with Ibibio, in particular, some of whose artists have carved for Igbo patrons. Afikpo masks are stylistically distinct and include feminine beauties and dark, masculine grotesques among the 12 or so basic types. As elsewhere among the Igbo, secret societies control masking. They mount several festivals featuring more than a hundred masks that together represent the range of human personalities, native and stranger alike, known to Afikpo. The Okumkpa festival features masked leaders, choruses, and a variety of characters that act out didactic, amusing skits lampooning prominent people and non-traditional or devisive behaviour. Another festival features a parade by the members of the age-group who have just completed their initiation, and comprises a variety of masked characters, including children, elders, teachers, clerks, Muslims, young girls, married couples and Europeans, to mention just a few.

Another masquerade, now moribund, was known as Ogbom. This was held to honour the earth and female fertility. It featured finely carved headdresses, some of which were made by Ibibio artists, and several locally distinct masks and headdresses owned by the men's secret societies of Ekpe, Ekong and Okonko. Some of these were skin-covered masks easily confused with those of their non-Igbo neighbours. The masquerade also featured various masked 'runners' in knitted or netted body suits.

(iv) South-western. The two best-documented masquerades among the many in this region are Ekeleke and Okoroshi. They both embody and honour water spirits, *owu*, and may have originated in the Niger Delta to the south. Ekeleke is primarily an entertainment, with elaborate stilt-dancing accompanied by an amusing drama. Ekeleke features between four and eight dancers on low stilts, wearing imported madras cloth, European-made white eyelet lace and long-necked, white-faced carved headdresses lashed on the tops of their heads. Six pieces of music, performed in succession by an orchestra on the edge of the arena, accompany complex group dances and virtuoso solos. The Ekeleke festival lasts for two four-day weeks, dances being held morning and evening, with a progressive build-up to the final two days. This build-up features a small comic play involving an amusing bawdy diviner and a not-very-fierce leopard. Diviner conjures Leopard from the nearby bush so that he may be killed with a toy gun by the lead stilt-dancer, 'good' thus overcoming 'evil'. This drama interrupts the stilt dancing during the final four performances, and the festival is over when Leopard is shot on the final afternoon.

Okoroshi involves weightier spiritual sanctions and occupies eight four-day weeks at the end of the rainy season. The masks in this case are of the two contrasting types: feminine characters, wearing light costumes and white masks, and threatening, dark, masculine ones. Between four and six good/beautiful maskers (*okoroshioma*) are outnumbered by vast numbers of bad/ugly spirit characters (*okoroshiojo*), a hundred or more from each of nine villages. These latter range in character from neutral, through mildly annoying or aggressive but non-destructive, to heavy spirits that once had great destructive power. Most dark maskers wear dark blankets, all wear circlets of sacred young palm leaves, and the most powerful are clothed in masses of dirty, sometimes smelly, raffia. The feminine masks dance prettily before large crowds in spacious arenas on clear sunny days. The masculine masks appear, rain or shine, during the day or at night, and in all parts of the village. Younger, less powerful masks ply the roads and compounds, chasing and harassing women, children and one another. The strongest, darkest spirits emerge towards the end of the season supported by hordes of chanting men carrying clubs. The songs and dances are threatening and militaristic in contrast to the sentimental, melodic songs of the followers of the white-face masks. Dark masks, like the characters they embody, constitute a vast range of shapes, sizes and forms (human, animal and composite), with a similar range of names: Sugarcane, Butterfly, Basket, Sweat, Kingfisher, Jealousy, Lightning, Rat, Snake, Multitude-Is-Power (a proverb), Death-Has-No-Friend (a proverb), Artist, Breaker, Slow Poison,

2. Igbo shrine compound with 'family members' lined up against wall, Oba Uke, Nigeria; from a photograph by Herbert M. Cole, 1983

Elephant, Leopard, Killer. Many of these dark masks are distorted or twisted heads two or three times life-size. Nearly all of them include deliberate violations of the symmetrical, delicate aesthetic embodied in the few pretty white-face masks.

Until the 1950s or so, the masks of Okoroshi had policing and judicial functions and the power to fine and physically punish villagers who had contravened traditional law. In the 1980s the masks still had powerful spiritual sanctions, and their behaviour could be threatening and sometimes destructive.

(v) Northern. During the latter part of the 19th century a number of northern Igbo masks apparently had more or less elaborate superstructures, small tableaux of human figures and animals, either carved as part of the mask or attached to a light cane framework mounted above it and covered with cloth. In the following decades these large masks, or at least their superstructures, became bigger and bigger, probably as a result of inter-community competition, until, *c.* 1910, colossal headdresses were being produced.

Two of these, Ekwe from the Nsukka area and Ijele from the Anambra Valley, are among the largest types of mask known from West Africa. Each has amazing bulk and weight (*c.* 90 kg), yet each is carried by a single man, who unsurprisingly claims supernatural assistance. Ekwe are found in several graded sizes, the largest of which is worn with a 14-kg costume. It features a tableau of multiple wooden figures, animals and vehicles, with as many as 25 separate carvings attached to a central wooden headdress balanced on the wearer's head. The subjects depicted include children, mothers with babies, hunters, leopards, birds, bicyclists, the water-spirit Mamy Wata (*see* IBIBIO, §3), musicians and women with umbrellas, purses or radios.

Ijele feature similar cloth sculptures, though more of them, and they are lighter, being stuffed with grass or foam rubber. Ijele are architectonic structures of cloth-covered wood and, being lighter than Ekwe, can be substantially larger (*c.* 5 m high and 2.5 m in diameter). Colourful figures, animals and groups—including representations of the masquerades of the area—are sewn on to this framework, along with stylized flowers and trees, mirrors and tassels. Most Ijele are surmounted by an equestrian figure and the wooden platform disc on which the complex is constructed is encircled by a large python. The disc is carried on the head, with 12 appliquéd panels hanging down from it to obscure the wearer's body. Two oversized arms project from the superstructure, and a face is appliquéd on to one of the cloth panels, thus giving the giant spirit some anthropomorphic features. It dances with surprising speed and agility. Ijele, usually only called out for the second burial festival celebrating the life of a respected elder, is the dramatic apotheosis of Igbo masquerading. Appropriately, it is called by Igbo the 'king' and 'elephant' of masks.

3. Igbo personal shrine figure (*ikenga*), wood and pigments, h. 743 mm, from Awka region, collected before 1924 (Los Angeles, University of California, Fowler Museum of Cultural History)

3. SHRINES, 'MBARI' HOUSES AND ASSOCIATED ARTS. The family is the linchpin of Igbo culture and the major paradigm for shrine architecture and the associated figural ensembles made for tutelary gods. While implicit in all Igbo mother-and-child imagery, the family is most explicit in community shrines in north-central Igboland. The associated cults seem to have originated at the family level, and are still lineage-based in some areas, but the stronger of them address broad constituencies that cut

across lines of kinship. The deities are sometimes considered as founding ancestors and are commonly linked with and named after markets (and the days on which they are held), rivers, other prominent natural features and sometimes oaths or war. Some of the compounds built for these gods are quite large, and are modelled on those of wealthy families, with several buildings surrounded by a wall covered with elaborate paintings or carved panels. Men and women collaborate in building, decorating and annually refurbishing such compounds and in establishing and adorning its statuary. The latter comprise 'family' groups of eight, nine or more hardwood sculptures, including adult males and females, their children, personal shrine figures (*ikenga*), messengers and, occasionally, animals (see fig. 2). The human figures in this area are very conventionalized in form. They are frontal and symmetrical, with stiff legs slightly apart, arms cut free at the sides, and forearms extended forward with palms up to accept sacrifices and to represent the gods' 'open-handed' honesty. Normally the figures are housed in one room within the shrine compound, lined up against a wall. On their annual festival day, however, they are paraded outside and joined by dozens of lesser deities, their relatives, marshalled from other parts of the community. For this occasion the figures and compounds are redecorated by the women and the figures further adorned with wrappers, caps and other title paraphernalia (*see* §5 below).

While these north-central examples are perhaps the best known, analogous forms are found in the north-east, in eastern or Cross River communities and in the south-west near Owerri. Figural styles and architectural settings vary regionally, but the same spiritual context is common to all areas. The most monumental wooden statuary is found in the community shrines and men's meeting houses in Ohafia and Abiriba near the Cross River. Since the 1950s, for example, that of Asaga Ohafia has housed 22 life-size carvings, comprising a family and diverse entourage for the deified founding ancestor whose figure was placed at the centre of the large room. Other figures included his wives, warriors, a hunter, a court messenger and a white man. The large groups of blocky, rectangular, figures from shrines north of Owerri are less well integrated architecturally, simply being placed along three walls of rather small open buildings. The figures represented here are also diverse.

Shrines may themselves contain other shrines in the form of a personal male shrine or *ikenga* (see fig. 3). Typical *ikenga* take the form of a seated male with horns, symbolizing animal power and persistence, holding in one hand a knife, symbolizing decisive action, and in the other a human trophy head, symbolizing accomplishment. The word *ikenga* itself refers to the strong right arm and thus to physical prowess. *Ikenga* shrines are offered prayers and sacrifices in exchange for personal success. They are

4. Igbo *mbari* house to Obiala, clay and pigments, h. *c.* 8 m, Ndiama Obube, near Owerri, Nigeria; from a photograph by Herbert M. Cole, 1966

carved from hardwoods considered male, and they epitomize the male ethos: individualism and competitiveness, and success and accomplishment resulting from courage, physical strength and aggression.

The largest and most complex stationary works of art recorded among the Igbo are the *mbari* houses made near Owerri in the south-west (see fig. 4). *Mbari* are not shrines but monuments erected in thanksgiving to powerful local tutelary deities, or to placate and honour a god whom divination reveals to have been offended. They will contain more than 100 sculptures and reliefs that are placed in niches on four sides of a rectangular building and in galleries built facing inward around the central house. *Mbari* have been constructed since at least 1902, the largest being built in the 1930s, and fine examples being built up to the 1960s. They are planned by professional master-builders-cum-sculptors who execute much of the sculpture and the complex, illusionistic painting. Much of the manual labour and painting of the varied abstract wall patterns and figures is done by men and women who have been initiated into the secrets and rituals of the building process. The protracted building period is called a 'dance' and is marked by numerous rituals, special dress for the workers, formalized behaviour and several feasts. Before an *mbari* is opened to the public, local elders are invited inside the enclosing fence to assess the workmanship and ensure that it will be acceptable to the god. The subsequent opening ceremonies are lavish, with much music, dancing, fine dress and feasting for hundreds of people.

The sculptures in large *mbari* draw upon nearly all aspects of village life and include figures of gods, spirits and animals, as well as dancers, hunters, wrestlers, women giving birth, diviners and white men. The range of scenes and objects portrayed is vast: women at sewing machines or on the telephone, office buildings, motorcycles, catechists and crucifixes have all appeared. As it has been described: 'They put four things in *mbari*: fearful things, forbidden things, very good (or beautiful) things, and things that cause laughter'.

4. Display figures. In the eyes of most Igbo the single most artistic thing is the youthful female: a virtuous maiden with fine coiffure and elegant body painting. This is the idealized model for countless masks and a small but important group of secular display sculptures carved in the north-central region. Such carvings are called 'the eagle seeks out beauty' (*ugonachonma*) and were commissioned by different age-groups to serve as centrepieces for dances. They are usually life-size images that embody Igbo ideals of maidenhood: a supple, fleshed-out body with high full breasts; a long, graceful neck; a light coloured and delicately featured face; an elaborate hairstyle; a light-skinned body painted with elegant designs; and such accoutrements as coiled-brass leg bangles, ivory armlets and a mirror and umbrella, symbols of vanity and wealth (see fig. 5). Such personal decoration was once affected by marriageable girls. Maiden figures may be compared to the far stiffer, female shrine carvings from the same region. Display figures, though not without conventions, are far more lifelike and naturalistic, as if to reflect their makers' concern with beauty *per se* rather than ritual efficacy.

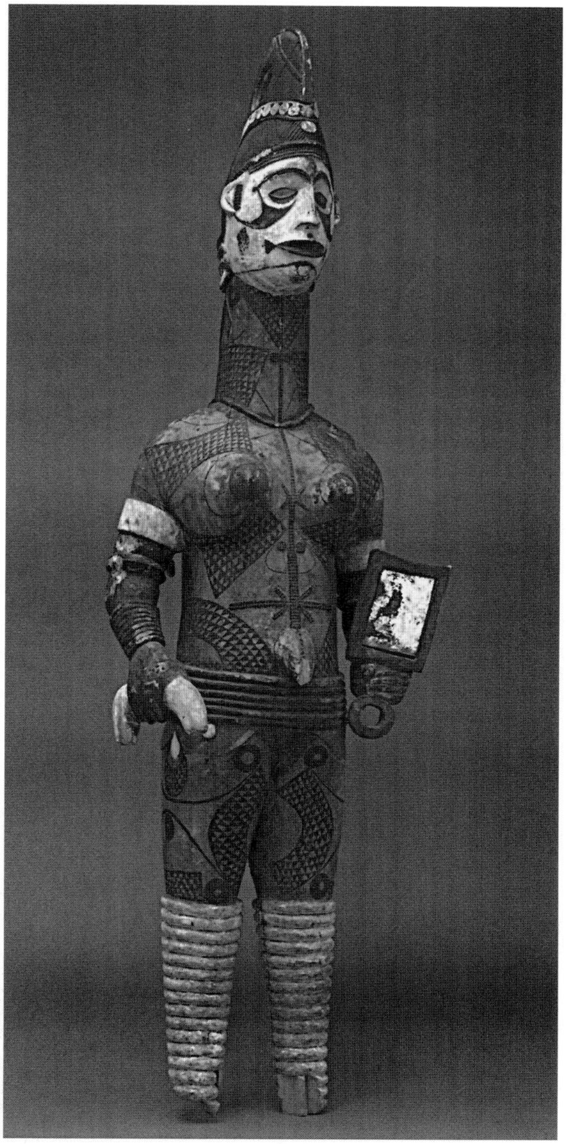

5. Igbo display figure (*ugonachonma*), wood, mirrored glass and pigments, h. 1.27 m, from north-central Igbo region, Nigeria (Seattle, WA, Seattle Art Museum)

5. Titular arts. Like maidens, titled men are represented in art, in large *ikenga* shrine figures and occasionally in masks. On accession to high title a man shows off his beauty through personal decoration, even wearing the same kind of abstract indigo body designs normally worn by young girls. The wealthy man of title is also an idealized eagle: pure and beautiful, strong and aggressive. Titled men also command prerogatives in dress and portable implements symbolic of their wealth and aggressive aura. These include the right to wear eagle feathers in red caps, leopard-tooth necklaces and expensive and exclusive

gowns, once locally woven. They extend their audible power with brass bells and elephant tusk trumpets, some with incised designs. Gestures and manual power are amplified by cow or horse-tail fly-whisks, fans, and spear-like wrought-iron staffs. Physical elevation is achieved by carved stools, which vary regionally and according to specific ranks.

Title prerogatives also include such architectural forms as meeting houses (*obi*), with lofty, thatched or tin roofs that can be seen from a distance. Traditionally, *obi* were faced with panels chip-carved in low relief in several, usually geometric, styles. The higher his title, the more panels a man could display. Carving styles and techniques are often associated with Awka, but artists in the Anambra Valley, around Nsukka in the north, and as far south as Okigwi and Owerri also carved similar forms. Mud sculpture, carved panels and huge doors were used to embellish the portals of wealthy titled men, making their status immediately apparent to passers-by.

Within a man's *obi* and behind an openwork screen called 'eyes of the spirit' (*anyammuo*) were found his personal and lineage shrines, as well as spool-like carvings (*okposi*) symbolizing family ancestors. The *obi* also housed a man's stools, staffs, bells and other title paraphernalia. With other ritual objects, some finely crafted, these constituted an impressive assemblage of prestige and power objects.

BIBLIOGRAPHY

G. T. Basden: *Niger Ibos* (London, 1938)
J. S. Boston: 'Some Northern Ibo Masquerades', *J. Royal Anthropol. Inst. GB & Ireland*, xc (1960), pp. 54–65
R. Henderson: *The King in Every Man* (New Haven, 1972)
S. Ottenberg: *Masked Rituals of Afikpo* (Seattle and London, 1975)
C. C. Aniakor: 'The Igbo Ijele Mask', *Afr. A.*, xi/4 (1978), pp. 42–7, 95
H. M. Cole: *Mbari: Art and Life among the Owerri Igbo* (Bloomington, IN, 1982)
G. I. Jones: *The Art of Eastern Nigeria* (Cambridge, 1984)
Igbo Arts: Community and Cosmos (exh. cat. by H. M. Cole and C. C. Aniakor, Los Angeles, UCLA, Mus. Cult. Hist., 1984–6)
G. I. Jones: *Ibo Art*, Shire Ethnography 13 (Princes Risborough, 1989)

HERBERT M. COLE

Igbo-Ukwu. Town in Nigeria (pop. *c.* 15,000 in the 1990s), situated 40 km south-east of Onitsha, which is on the River Niger. The name means 'Great Igbo' in the Igbo language. It is also the name given to the ancient culture that produced the elaborate metalwork and ceramics, dated to the 10th century AD, that were found at three sites on the outskirts of the town.

1. Introduction. 2. Discovery and excavation. 3. Dating. 4. Interpretation. 5. Materials and manufacture. 6. Art and artefacts.

1. INTRODUCTION. The first site came to light some time before the outbreak of World War II in 1939 while a man, Isaiah Anozie, was digging a cistern. Not far below ground-level he unearthed a highly decorated bronze bowl, and further digging led to the discovery of other bronzes, some of which were given to his neighbours who thought they would make good 'medicine'. The remaining objects were bought by John Field, the area's Assistant District Officer, who published an account of the discovery and presented the collection to the Nigerian Federal Department of Antiquities. At the invitation of the Department, the archaeologist Thurstan Shaw began excavations in 1959. In addition to the original site, two further sites were discovered in the adjacent compounds of Richard and Jonah Anozie, and the sites were accordingly named 'Igbo Isaiah', 'Igbo Richard' and 'Igbo Jonah' respectively. All the finds from the excavations, which were carried out during 1959, 1960 and 1964, were deposited in Nigerian museums, although a few pieces from the original accidental discovery found their way to the British Museum, London. Finds from the sites of Igbo Isaiah and Igbo Richard are in the National Museum, Lagos; those from Igbo Jonah are in the Museum of the Department of Archaeology and Anthropology, University of Ibadan.

2. DISCOVERY AND EXCAVATION. The site of Igbo Isaiah revealed an area *c.* 3×2 m that contained nearly 200 strings of beads and more than 63,000 loose beads of stone and glass, all at the comparatively shallow depth of about half a metre. There were *c.* 25 receptacles in cast bronze, 44 bronze or copper pieces for personal or other adornment, 9 weapon scabbards or hilts, and many other smaller pieces in copper or bronze, as well as knives and blades of iron. Shaw concluded that here were the remains of a shrine or storehouse of regalia housed in a lightly roofed shelter that had been abandoned.

The neighbouring site of Igbo Richard revealed the remains of a shrine containing objects of pottery and copper. At a much greater depth were the remains of a stool, copper artefacts, regalia, beads and other items of jewellery and personal adornment. The site was the burial place of an important person, interred with rich grave goods. From iron clamps and wooden planks found at the lowest level, Shaw concluded that the corpse had been placed in a wood-lined chamber, strapped in a sitting posture on a stool and propped up against a wall or a corner of the chamber, with the arms supported by two copper brackets. Grass matting covered the floor, upon which were placed elephant tusks and a large calabash with a decorated copper handle. The corpse wore ceremonial regalia including strings of beads, a pectoral plate, a bead-studded headdress surmounted by a copper crown, copper anklets and a pair of bead wristlets. A ceremonial fly-whisk was held in one hand, and the fan that was also found may either have been held in the other hand, or stuck into the ground in the same way as a copper rod that supported a bronze leopard skull. An upper group of bones was separated from those of the person of rank by a layer of more than 600 mm in which no human remains were found. This layer was possibly the roof of the tomb, on the top of which five other people were buried.

During the 1920s beads and bronze objects had been found at the site of Igbo Jonah while digging for clay. Excavation revealed a specially dug pit containing much burnt material, a copper wire chain, two blades and other iron objects, and copper and bronze wristlets. A large bronze crotal, or jingle ornament, resembles, but is not identical to, the numerous examples from Igbo Isaiah. The finest bronze objects from this pit were two cylindrical staff ornaments (h. *c.* 105 mm each), which are similar to, but smaller than, those found at Igbo Isaiah. Also in this pit was much pottery resembling that from the other sites, including a particularly magnificent globular vessel, complete except for one of five handles (see fig. 4 below).

Igbo Jonah is the most difficult of the sites to interpret. It is neither a burial site nor a pit dug to conceal 'hidden treasure', nor yet a cistern nor a storage pit; it seems best to describe it as a 'disposal pit'.

3. DATING. When the original accidental find was made at Igbo-Ukwu, it was suggested that the objects could not be very old because textiles were preserved among them. This argument was invalidated by the proximity of cuprous objects, from which copper salts acted as preservatives, inhibiting the action of cloth-destroying bacteria. During the excavations a close look-out was kept for anything that might help to provide dating evidence, such as European glass or ceramics. No such recognizable imports were encountered, although some of the iron objects might have been imported. The lack of smoking pipes suggests a date before *c.* 1600–50. Many of the glass and cornelian beads looked like imports, but it is more likely that they arrived through the Islamic world, perhaps deriving ultimately from India or Arabia. From excavation alone, therefore, it was difficult to assign any date to the Igbo-Ukwu sites, so much depended on radiocarbon dating. Seven such datings pointed to the 10th century, although some scholars found it hard to believe that the superb bronze castings could be several centuries older than those of either IFE (13th–14th centuries) or Benin (*c.* late 15th–19th centuries; *see* BENIN).

4. INTERPRETATION. The objects found at Igbo-Ukwu represent a society with considerable wealth. Given that the economic base of the community responsible was probably subsistence farming, this must have developed into an efficient way of producing plentiful food, assisted by experience in iron smelting and working. In this way considerable surpluses could have been produced, and these translated into the man-hours of artists and craftsmen producing works of art and engaging in such activities as the exploitation of copper. In addition, the economy was doubtless assisted by an internal system of marketing and exchange fostered by local specializations and the region's ecological diversity: savannah products to the north; riverain products from the Niger to the west; deltaic and marine products to the south; and forest products all around.

It is reasonable to assume that there have been no major displacements of population in the last thousand years and that the people who generated and centralized this wealth were the ancestors of the present Igbo. The Igbo are a society without kings or chiefs, having a segmentary form of social organization and being notoriously egalitarian. Status and prestige are not ascribed by birth but achieved by merit, in direct contrast to such societies as Benin, in which kings and courts fostered and concentrated artistic production.

In place of royal or chiefly patronage, the institution of the Lord of Nri (Eze Nri) and the Igbo title-taking system would have fostered Igbo-Ukwu artistic achievements. In all Igbo settlements, the various graded titles culminate in the taking of the Eze (or Ozo, Obi or Nze) title. Once appointed to this, the highest of Igbo politico-ritual titles, the Eze Nri was responsible for securing the fertility of the land, especially the vital yam crop; for removing 'abominations', when taboos had been broken; for settling disputes and ensuring peace among Igbo communities; and for presiding over the title-taking system. He operated through the travelling Nri men who were his officers, and his sanctions were spiritual, not military.

Information given to Jeffreys in 1920 concerning the burial of an Eze Nri accords closely with what was found in the burial chamber at Igbo Richard, including the five bodies above the burial chamber, which may have been of slaves buried at the same time. It is also possible that the Igbo Richard burial may have been that of a rich, senior title-holder. The pit in Igbo Jonah may represent another method of disposing of the regalia of a senior title-holder, perhaps of different rank or at a slightly different date, and it is possible that the vessels and regalia in the repository at Igbo Isaiah were connected with the exercise of the office of either an Eze Nri or a very rich, senior man. Such a person would have an open-sided building or shelter (*obu*), traditionally placed in the centre of the compound of an Igbo lineage head. This *obu* is a kind of temple, in which are kept the ritual and ceremonial materials used in connection with the title system and in conducting relationships with the spirits of deceased members of the lineage in order to secure their favour.

Many of the artistic manifestations of Igbo-Ukwu can be interpreted as belonging to this highly symbolic and ritualized culture and have continuing parallels in the area. For example, the depiction of coiled snakes recalls a taboo against killing and eating the python. The facial scarifications on some bronzes resemble those still made among certain classes of titled men with a small surgical knife and charcoal. The small knives excavated in Igbo Isaiah were perhaps used for this purpose. The occurrence of grasshoppers and beetles as decorative motifs on the Igbo-Ukwu bronzes is suggestive of the ritual power believed to be possessed by the Eze Nri in controlling locusts and yam beetles. The numerous objects described as staff-heads and staff ornaments, together with the fan-holder, are similar to staffs indicative of the politico-ritual/social status of individuals still to be found in the area. Three sizes of bell are attached to the bag carried by an Ozo man to announce his passage. After consecration, such bells are regarded as sacred and kept in the *obu*; this practice may explain bronze bells found at Igbo-Ukwu. Perhaps the significance of three elephant tusks discovered in the burial chamber may be related to the fact that Ozo titled men buy an elephant tusk and have it made into a horn, which they play with pomp and pride at ceremonies, emphasizing their status. Local idioms, folk-tales, songs and sayings refer metaphorically to the chief characteristics of the snail, the tortoise and such insects as flies. The idea of 'headship' and 'leadership' is symbolically represented by animal skulls and by the living leopard and elephant. Although the parallels are not exact, such symbolic meanings relating to the institution of the Eze Nri and the title-taking system could provide explanations of the art of Igbo-Ukwu.

5. MATERIALS AND MANUFACTURE. The highly skilled metal-workers produced works by the lost-wax method, mostly from alloys of copper, tin and lead that provided a composition suitably ductile for casting all the

surface ornamentation. Objects made of copper, which is less suitable for casting, were created by bending and hammering, with surface decoration added subsequently.

More than 100 analyses of Igbo-Ukwu cuprous objects have established that the castings are true bronzes, with scarcely a trace of zinc in their composition. This distinguishes them sharply from the Ife and Benin castings, most of which are brasses (although a few are of copper), and from contemporary developments around the Mediterranean, where brass had increasingly displaced bronze from early in the first millennium AD. Indeed, the use of brass as the principal copper alloy at the time of their manufacture renders the Igbo-Ukwu series of bronze-castings unique, not only in Nigeria and West Africa but also in the wider metal-working world.

Another feature of the Igbo-Ukwu castings is the high silver content, which must have been derived from the copper source and not from an intentional addition. This points to a localized indigenous metal industry, since elsewhere at that time silver was so much more valuable than copper that even a small proportion of it would have been removed by a liquefaction process. The high level of impurities in Igbo-Ukwu copper indicates that it must have been smelted rather than derived from native copper, a hypothesis strengthened by the high levels of arsenic, antimony, lead, nickel and iron in addition to the silver. Investigations in south-east Nigeria have revealed sources of copper that are said to be sufficient to have furnished the Igbo-Ukwu smiths with their needs, although no definite ancient copper workings have been clearly demonstrated as yet. In the majority of castings the proportion of lead exceeds 5% and therefore probably represents a purposeful addition rather than an impurity deriving from the copper ore. There are many potential sources of lead in West Africa: the lead/zinc deposits of the Abakaliki area of south-east Nigeria show signs of pre-colonial exploitation, but it has been supposed that this was for obtaining galena for cosmetic purposes. The major Nigerian sources of tin, in and around the Jos Plateau, were certainly indigenously extracted; there is record of tin being sold to Arab merchants in Kano in the 1830s, but how old this exploitation of Nigerian tin may be is not known.

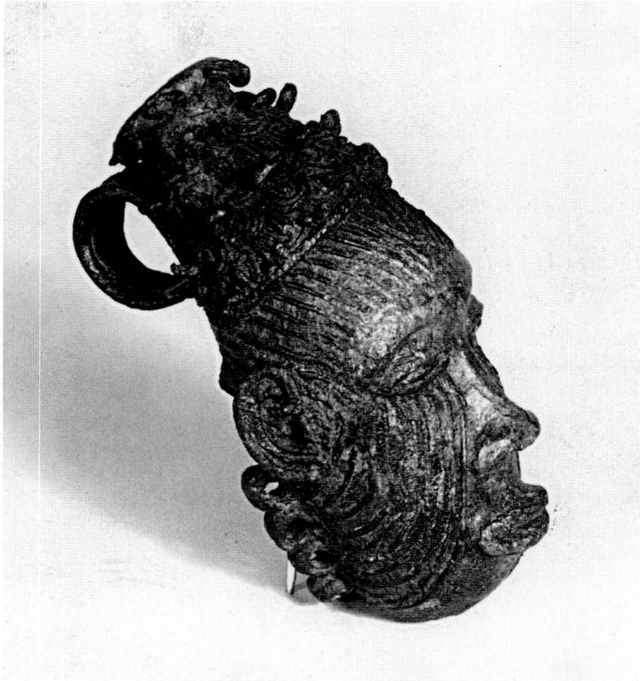

1. Igbo-Ukwu pendant ornament in the form of a human head with typical scarifications, cast bronze, h. 76 mm, probably from Igbo Isaiah, 10th century (Lagos, National Museum)

The bronzes display great technical mastery in the use of the lost-wax technique. Formerly, when the copper was believed to have been imported, it was assumed that knowledge of this technique was imported along with the raw material for casting. However, since the evidence now points to a more localized source of the copper, one has to envisage the possibility of an independent, indigenous invention of both the smelting and the casting techniques.

The large decorated bowls from Igbo-Ukwu are idiosyncratic; in most other metallurgical traditions they would have been made out of sheet metal and the ornamentation attached by riveting or soldering, instead of being part of the whole casting (*see* BRONZE, fig. 3). There are also two castings from Igbo-Ukwu that are made up from more than one piece and that use an adaptation of the casting technique to join the pieces together. Fresh molten metal was poured, or 'burnt in', between two pieces already cast, a technique not in use north of the Sahara. The copper objects from Igbo-Ukwu were not cast but were made by bending, twisting, hammering and annealing when necessary, and then punching in the surface decoration. The copper wire was not drawn but was made by hammering and annealing.

6. ART AND ARTEFACTS. The art of Igbo-Ukwu is unique, not only in its materials and manufacture but also in style, for which no antecedents have been identified. At one time attempts were made to derive the Igbo-Ukwu finds from Benin, only 150 km to the west. Quite apart from the chronological and metallurgical features that disprove such a theory, the art of the sites has a quite distinct style, characterized by technical elaboration and wealth of surface decoration.

(i) Bronze. The greatest number of bronze-castings, including the largest and most outstanding pieces, came from the storehouse at Igbo Isaiah. One remarkable vessel (h. 323 mm) consists of a decorated pyriform water-pot standing on an openwork decorated pot-stand or pedestal; the whole is enclosed with knotted ropework. It is one of two objects from Igbo-Ukwu made by joining together several cast pieces by the 'casting on' process. An elaborate 'altar stand' (h. 274 mm) consists of a cylinder with wide, decorated flanges at top and bottom; opposed solid decorated panels alternating with openwork panels, which carry a pattern of snakes, frogs and spiders; and a male figure on one side and a female on the other. Other items include a decorated annular pot-stand and six large, highly decorated bowls, up to 419 mm in diameter, with a single handle on one side and decorative bosses on the other.

2. Igbo-Ukwu staff ornament, cast bronze, h. 163 mm, probably from Igbo Isaiah, 10th century (Lagos, National Museum)

These bowls are skeuomorphic: numerous handles and bosses of thick, twisted copper wire were excavated, which had been attached to real gourds that had decayed. Skeuomorphs are characteristic of much Igbo-Ukwu work, with translations of weaving, string, knots etc into bronze and of basketry into ceramics. Eleven smaller bronze bowls, crescentic in shape, are skeuomorphic of gourds cut vertically, with the outer surface entirely covered with decorative patterns. Two large bronze vessels (l. *c.* 300 mm), shaped like the shells of the large African land snail (*Achatina achatina*), were perhaps intended for purification ceremonies. They have 'sprinkler' finials at the pointed end and are covered in decorative patterns, including representations of flies. The depiction of insects is characteristic of Igbo-Ukwu work and unknown elsewhere.

Of the dozen pendent ornaments, each equipped with a suspension loop at the back, four represent the heads of elephants, three rams' heads, two human heads and one a leopard's head. Two pendants are in the form of paired eggs surmounted by a bird. Most are highly decorated, and the human heads show scarifications radiating from the bridge of the nose, as on other representations of humans at Igbo-Ukwu (see fig. 1). Each pendant has rows of small loops at the back, from which originally hung copper wire chains carrying beads and small jingle ornaments, or crotals. There were *c.* 13 smaller pendent ornaments, including 4 perforated canine teeth (probably leopard), with half of each tooth skeuomorphically wrapped with string binding. Other highly elaborate objects include a belt composed of small decorated plaques, a conical bell, heads and ornaments for staffs (see fig. 2) and two ornate scabbards, which are skeuomorphic of wood and leather scabbards.

(ii) Copper. Most of the copper objects are smaller and lighter than the castings; many are wristlets, anklets, calabash handles, bosses and chains made from copper wire of various thicknesses. Finds from Igbo Isaiah include six snake finials, made by twisting heavy copper wire into coils, with a spike to fit into a wooden shaft. Two rods, bent over and then back on themselves to form ornamental chapes, were intended to give rigidity to wood and leather scabbards. The copper pectoral, crown and headdress plaques from the Igbo Richard burial chamber were formed from copper that had been beaten into thin flat plates. A fan-holder weighing 737 g must have required substantial working; some of the decoration is heavily

3. Igbo-Ukwu head of a fan-holder with punched decoration, copper, h. 564 mm, from Igbo Richard, 10th century (Lagos, National Museum)

punched in (see fig. 3). The largest number of twisted copper wristlets came from the Igbo Jonah disposal pit.

(iii) Iron. The storehouse deposit in Igbo Isaiah included a pile of small iron knives with copper-decorated handles. Numerous nails and staples around the burial chamber in Igbo Richard were probably used for fastening the planks; two pieces of iron slag in the burial chamber, and more at higher levels, suggest that iron was smelted in the vicinity. Iron objects from Igbo Jonah include two broad blades, a funnel-shaped object, a bar with a hook or eyelet at one end and what may be calabash handles and bosses made from twisted wire.

(iv) Ceramics. The pottery found at Igbo-Ukwu is very elaborate and shows great skill in the treatment of the medium. Almost 1000 pieces excavated at Igbo Isaiah include some very fine, complete or nearly complete vessels. The other two sites produced more than 20,000 pieces of pottery, notably in the supposed shrine in Igbo Richard and the disposal pit in Igbo Jonah. Plain domestic wares include bag-shaped or pyriform water-pots, sometimes decorated around the neck with impressed jabs or a thumb-impressed cordon. Much of the pottery, however, has rich surface decoration and ornament that is comparable to, although not imitative of, that on the cast bronzes. Decoration includes ringed and fluted bosses, and patterns produced by deeply incised parallel lines or deep grooves, often in circular, semicircular or curvilinear configurations. Some bowls stand on conjoined pottery pedestals, with openwork designs or applied snake motifs. Many pots have bifid rims and show decoration derived from basketry. A representation of a human face, probably originally attached to a pottery vessel, is deeply grooved and crudely executed but shows indications of a circular forehead ornament resembling that on the male figure on the bronze altar stand. The most magnificent vessel (h. 406 mm; see fig. 4) came from the disposal pit in Igbo Jonah. It is globular in shape with a wide mouth and a broad out-turned rim, which is joined to the shoulder by five straplike handles, of which four are intact and decorated with ridges and grooving that resemble basketwork. The lower half of the pot is plain, but the upper half is decorated with a series of boldly executed protuberant bosses surrounded by concentric rings of grooving. Superimposed upon this decoration and between the handles are a coiled snake, a chameleon, a ram's head, another snake and an unidentified design consisting of a roughly rectangular piece of material arched up in the middle and covered with crosshatching. It may represent a mat, but, since the other designs are of animate objects, perhaps a tortoise- or turtle-shell was intended.

4. Igbo-Ukwu ceramic vessel, h. 406 mm, from Igbo Jonah, 10th century (Ibadan, University of Ibadan, Museum of the Department of Archaeology and Anthropology)

(v) Other materials. The only wood preserved was that in close contact with bronze or copper, and although it has not been possible to determine its configuration, it is difficult to believe that the high artistic production of Igbo-Ukwu did not include wood-carving. Calabashes would probably have been decorated, since an actual piece of calabash with an incised pattern was excavated. Skeuomorphic representation in bronze and ceramics provides evidence of basketry and grass weaving. Analysis of the fibres of actual textiles preserved where they had been in close contact with copper has demonstrated that they are not cotton but made of an unidentified native product. There are many hints of the skilful combination of different materials, such as copper and iron handles and bosses on calabashes and the use of copper, wood, leather and string in making scabbards.

BIBLIOGRAPHY

M. D. W. Jeffreys: *The Divine (Umundri) Kings of Iboland* (diss., U. London, 1934)
J. O. Field: 'Bronze Castings Found at Igbo, Southern Nigeria', *Man*, xl/1 (1940), pp. 1–6
T. Shaw: *Igbo-Ukwu: An Account of Archaeological Discoveries in Eastern Nigeria*, 2 vols (London and Evanston, 1970)
B. Lawal: 'Dating Problems at Igbo-Ukwu', *J. Afr. Hist.*, xiv/1 (1973), pp. 1–8
T. Shaw: 'Those Igbo-Ukwu Radiocarbon Dates', *J. Afr. Hist.*, xvi/4 (1975), pp. 503–17
M. A. Onwuejeogwu and B. O. Onwuejeogwu: 'The Search for the Missing Links in Dating and Interpreting the Igbo-Ukwu Finds', *Paideuma*, xxlii (1977), pp. 169–88
T. Shaw: *Unearthing Igbo-Ukwu* (London and Ibadan, 1977)
V. E. Chikwendu and A. C. Umeji: 'Local Sources of Raw Materials for the Nigerian Bronze/Brass Industry: With Emphasis on Igbo-Ukwu', *W. Afr. J. Archaeol.*, ix (1979), pp. 151–65
P. T. Craddock: 'Mediaeval Copper Alloy Production and West African Bronze Analyses: Part I', *Archaeometry*, xxvii/1 (1985), pp. 17–41
P. T. Craddock and J. Picton: 'Mediaeval Copper Alloy Production and West African Bronze Analyses: Part II', *Archaeometry*, xxviii/1 (1986), pp. 3–32
V. E. Chikwendu and others: Nigerian Sources for Copper, Lead and Tin for the Igbo-Ukwu Bronzes, *Archaeometry*, xxxi/1 (1989)

THURSTAN SHAW

Iglau. *See* JIHLAVA.

Iglesia, Francisco Ignacio Ruiz de la. *See* RUIZ DE LA IGLESIA, FRANCISCO IGNACIO.

Ignatius Loyola [Iñigo López de Loyola] (*b* Castle of Loyola, Guipúzcoa, Spain, 1491; *d* Rome, 31 July 1556; *can* 1622; *fd* 31 July). Spanish saint. The founder of the Jesuit Order, he came from a noble Basque family and began his career as a soldier. He was wounded at the siege of Pamplona in 1521 and thereafter resolved to become a soldier of Christ. After a year in retreat near Manresa (1522) he embarked on a pilgrimage to Jerusalem, where the local Franciscans prevented him from preaching; he returned to Spain in 1524. Still concerned with the conversion of others, he studied at the universities of Barcelona, Alcalá, Salamanca, and for seven years, from 1528, in Paris. There, among his fellow Spanish students, he found the true disciples he sought. With a committed band of six men he vowed to complete his mission to Jerusalem (1534). They travelled to Venice, but war made the Holy Land inaccessible and Ignatius directed his energies to the founding of a new order, the Society of Jesus, which was recognized by Pope Paul III in 1540.

The Jesuits became well known in Italy for their preaching, teaching and spiritual guidance, and missions were sent abroad for the conversion of heretics and heathens. Increasingly, and lastingly, the emphasis fell on the Jesuits' external roles as missionaries, educators and confessors of the great. Ignatius became the first General of the order, an office granted for life, yet he had no interest in personal aggrandizement and lived in comparative retirement and obscurity in Rome. He refused his followers' requests to have his portrait painted, and their surreptitious introduction of Giovanni Battista Moroni into his presence produced, it seems, a very moderate result (untraced). Similarly Jacopino del Conte, summoned within hours of Ignatius's death to record his likeness (1556; Rome, Casa Gen. Gesuiti), failed (more understandably) to capture his personality. More evocative are the surviving copies of his death mask (e.g. Rome, Casa Gen. Gesuiti), from one of which Alonso Sánchez Coello painted a portrait (1585; destr.). In 1609 Ignatius was beatified by Paul V and in 1622 he was canonized by the first Jesuit-educated Pope, Gregory XV.

Once Ignatius had become a saint, his image became more triumphant, as in Rubens's painting of the *Miracles of St Ignatius* (Vienna, Ksthist. Mus.). Scenes from the new saint's life became popular subjects. Ignatius himself had been very aware of the power of sacred images, both as aids to meditation and as propaganda. In the *Ejercicios espirituales* (written 1521–35; pubd in Latin, 1548), a guide to meditation, each theme is related to a visual image, in order to fix it in the mind. This specificity of image was exemplified by the graphic pictures of tortured saints by Cristoforo Roncalli in the Jesuit novitiate of S Stefano Rotondo, Rome, though with educational rather than artistic results. It has been suggested, too, that the tangibility of the figures in works by Caravaggio is indebted to these meditative techniques, which encourage the participant to re-create scenes in his imagination. Such artists as Rubens and, especially, Gianlorenzo Bernini were devoted to the *Ejercicios*. Bernini's notion of the unified *concetto* animating a work in a variety of media may have been partly inspired by them; certainly his design for the Jesuit church of S Andrea al Quirinale, Rome (1658–70), was a classic exemplar (*see* BERNINI, (2), §3(ii)). His plans for the vault decoration of the Jesuits' mother-church, the Gesù in Rome (*see* ROME, §V, 16), were the basis of Giovanni Battista Gaulli's frescoes (1672–83; *see* GAULLI, GIOVANNI BATTISTA, §1(ii)(a)) and created an explosion of visual propaganda for the Society and the Church, in which the submersion of individual figures into the dramatic sweep of the whole may serve as an effective metaphor for Ignatius's order. The altar dedicated to Ignatius in the same church, designed by the Jesuit Andrea Pozzo and executed (1695–9) by Pierre Legros, Jean Théodon and others, embodies in its spectacular array of sculptural modes and lavish materials a rather less appropriate celebration of the personal, even if chiefly as symbol. Ignatius's modesty in life had already been quickly overturned after his canonization by the foundation of the first church dedicated to him, S Ignazio in Rome (begun 1626), financed by Gregory XV's nephew and designed by the Jesuit ORAZIO GRASSI as an elaboration of the Gesù. In their fantastic theatricality, the ceiling decorations (1684–94) by ANDREA POZZO created a dazzling glorification of Ignatius's work that would have been incomprehensible to him. The magnificent basilica at Loyola (1681–9), designed by Carlo Fontana, makes an instructive contrast with the comparative simplicity of the adjacent castle.

See also JESUIT ORDER, §§I, II and III.

WRITINGS

Exercitia spiritualia (Rome, 1548; Eng. trans., Chicago, 1951)
Sancti Ignatii de Loyola epistolae et instructiones, 12 vols (Madrid, 1903–11)
J. N. Tylends, trans.: *A Pilgrim's Journey* (Wilmington, 1985) [Ignatius's autobiography]

BIBLIOGRAPHY

P. de Ribadaneira: *Vida de Ignacio de Loyola* (Madrid, 1583)
D. Angeli: *Sant'Ignazio da Loyola nella vita e nell'arte* (Lanciano, 1911)
R. Fueloep-Miller: *Macht und Geheimnis der Jesuiten: Eine Kultur- und Geistegeschichte* (Berlin, 1929; Eng. trans., London, 1957)
H. Rahner: *Ignatius von Loyola als Mensch und Theologe* (Freiburg im Breisgau, 1964; Eng. trans., Rome, 1982)
Fontes Documentales de S Ignatio (Rome, 1977)
U. Koenig-Nordhoff: *Ignatius von Loyola: Studien zur Entwicklung einer neuen Heiligen-Ikonographie im Rahmen einer Kanonisationskampagne um 1600* (Berlin, 1982)
P. Caraman: *Ignatius Loyola* (London, 1990)

□

Ignatovich, Boris (Vsevolodovich) (*b* Slutsk, Ukraine [now Belorussia], 3 April 1899; *d* Moscow, 1976). Russian photographer of Ukrainian birth. He worked as a journalist in Moscow, and from 1922 to 1925 he edited several satirical magazines in Leningrad (now St Petersburg) that attracted authors who directed their satire and irony at aspects of the developing Soviet system. Ignatovich took up photography in 1923. In 1927 he was employed as a photojournalist and picture editor by the Moscow newspaper *Bednota*. In 1930–32 he worked as a film cameraman. In the 1930s he was the picture editor on the newspaper *Verchernaya Moskva*, and between 1937 and 1941 he worked as a photographer for the magazine *Stroitelstvo Moskvy*. During the war years he was war photographer on the paper *Boyevoye Znamya*.

Ignatovich found himself at one with other artists seeking new forms of expression, above all with Aleksandr Rodchenko. His themes, often expressed using high or low viewpoints, great detail and diagonal composition, are concerned with the distinctive characteristics of Soviet life, as in *Elections to the Soviets* (1928; see Morozov and Lloyd, p. 108). Ignatovich and Rodchenko laid the foundations of Soviet avant-garde photography in the 1920s and 1930s in their documentation of the changing way of life in the post-revolutionary era. They founded the Oktyabr ('October') group, of which Ignatovich was left as sole leader after Rodchenko resigned over accusations of formalism. Ignatovich himself was also later criticized for formalism, and in 1932 the Oktyabr group was disbanded, but he continued his use of formal innovation and expressive dynamism. In the second half of the 1930s, together with his wife Yelizaveta and sister Ol'ga (*b* 1901), he organized a group of photographers to work for the Soyuzfoto agency; the group pioneered collective photojournalism, signing themselves 'The Ignatovich Brigade'. After World War II he experimented with landscape and portraiture.

BIBLIOGRAPHY

L. Volkov-Lannit: *Boris Ignatovich* (Moscow, 1973)
D. Mrázková and V. Remeš: *Die Sowjetunion zwischen den Kriegen* (Oldenburg, 1981)
S. Morozov and V. Lloyd, eds: *Soviet Photography, 1917–1940: The New Photojournalism* (London, 1984)

DANIELA MRÁZKOVÁ

Ihei Kimura. *See* KIMURA, IHEI.

Ihnasya el-Medina. *See* HERAKLEOPOLIS MAGNA.

Ihnatowicz, Zbigniew (*b* Postawy, Lithuania, 20 July 1906). Polish architect and teacher. After graduating in architecture from Warsaw Technical University (1933), he worked as an architect for the City of Warsaw, first at the District Regional Office and then at the Main Spatial Planning Office (1944–9). His best-known work is the Central Department Store (1948–51; with Jerzy Romański), Jerozolimskie Avenue, Warsaw. It was an essay in canonical early modernism, incorporating all Le Corbusier's 'five points of a new architecture': structural walls were replaced by columns to allow an open plan and fully glazed façades; windows were expressed as continuous horizontal bands of glazing between the exposed edges of the floor slabs; there is a pedestrian way through at ground level beneath the building and a roof terrace, used as an open-air coffee house. From 1949 to 1956 Ihnatowicz was a planning consultant for workers' housing estates and from 1951 to 1964 Chief Architect for Prochem Industrial Buildings design office. Avoiding the pompous and eclectic style prevailing at the time, he employed industrial building techniques in his work, as in the light shell roofs he designed for his rolling stock repair yard (1951), Mińsk Mazowiecki, near Warsaw. Other works included the Start sports stadium (1955; with Jerzy Soltan, Wojciech Fangor and Lech Tomaszewski); another stadium (1955) for Warsaw City Sports Club; the Śródmieście underground railway station (1963; with others), Warsaw; and the Wenecja restaurant (1958–61; with Soltan), Warsaw, the elevations of which were designed as an abstract geometric composition of different textures and colours, based on the rhythm of the structural system. Working with others, he was also involved in the design of many pavilions for international exhibitions, including those in Damascus (1955), New York (1958), Tunis (1962), Budapest (1964, 1965 and 1969), Zagreb (1968) and Lima (1971). In 1956 Ihnatowicz became a teacher at the Academy of Fine Arts, Warsaw, and was appointed Professor in 1973.

BIBLIOGRAPHY

T. P. Szafer: *Polska architektura współczesna* [Polish contemporary architecture] (Warsaw, 1977)
——: *Współczesna architektura polska* [Contemporary Polish architecture] (Warsaw, 1988) [with English and Russian text]

WANDA KEMP-WELCH

Ihne, Ernst Eberhard (*b* Elberfeld, 23 May 1848; *d* Berlin, 21 April 1917). German architect. He trained as an architect in Karlsruhe and Berlin before spending two years (1870–72) at the Ecole des Beaux-Arts, Paris. He returned to Germany and set up practice in Berlin in 1878, concentrating mainly on the design of country houses in the fashionable German Renaissance styles. Ihne's contribution to late 19th-century German architecture was twofold. First, with Robert Dohme (1845–93), he drew attention to and propagated the new type of domestic design and planning that had developed in England and that was later taken up by Hermann Muthesius. Secondly, Ihne became from the 1890s one of the most important architects of the 19th-century imperial German Baroque school. The commission for Schloss Friedrichshof (1889–94; now a hotel), near Kronberg im Taunus, for Empress Victoria, widow of Emperor Frederick, marked the foundation of both developments in Ihne's work. Although he had been to England as early as 1880 and had been the first to report in the German architectural press (1881) on the English Queen Anne Revival, none of his designs of the 1880s, including Villa Meinert (1885), Dessau, was much influenced by these new ideas. Schloss Friedrichshof, however, showed strong English influences in its plan as well as in the use of Tudor-style windows and the emphasis on materials. Ihne developed this approach in his private houses, for example in his villa (*c.* 1891; destr.) for Robert Dohme in Händelstrasse, Berlin.

After the commission for Schloss Friedrichshof, Ihne became architect to Emperor William II and rose to be the foremost official architect of the reign, being ennobled in 1906. In his capacity as the Emperor's architect, Ihne first developed grand, monumental Baroque forms in his refurbishment of the Weisse Saal (1891–5) of the Stadt Schloss, Berlin (destr. 1950). His subsequent public works, for example the Kaiser-Friedrich Museum (1898–1903; now the Bodemuseum), the Königliche Bibliothek (1908–13; now the Staatsbibliothek zu Berlin Preussischer Kulturbesitz) and the Kaiser-Wilhelm Institut (1914–15; now the Max-Planck-Institut für Bildungsforschung), all in Berlin, exemplify this last phase of 19th-century historicism. His architecture, like that of the Reichstag building (1884–95), Berlin, by Paul Wallot, and of Berlin Cathedral (1888–1905) by Julius Raschdorff, epitomized the exaggerated striving for power and dominance by the imperial court and the German ruling classes. Despite all the official honours he received, however, in architectural circles Ihne was often attacked for his Beaux-Arts style. His critics regarded his work as merely copying historic motifs and as mere lifeless eclecticism.

BIBLIOGRAPHY
NDB; Thieme–Becker; Wasmuth
M. Scharabi: *Der Einfluss der Pariser Ecole des Beaux-Arts auf die Berliner Architektur in der 2. Hälfte des 19. Jahrhunderts* (diss., Berlin U., 1968)
S. Muthesius: *Das englische Vorbild*, Stud. Kst 19. Jahrhunderts, xxvi (Munich, 1974)

Ihrwach, Sebastian. *See* IRRWOCH, SEBASTIAN.

Ijjasz de Murcia, Emese. *See under* ALVAREZ IJJASZ MURCIA.

Ijkens, Frans. *See* YKENS, FRANS.

Ijo. Kwa-speaking peoples, numbering between two and three million by the 1990s, occupying most of Delta and Rivers State in the Niger Delta region of Nigeria. This entry focuses on Ijo sculpture in wood, in its various forms of masquerade headdresses, figure sculpture and, most famously, ancestor screens. Examples of Ijo wood sculpture are held by many museums with ethnographic collections, especially in Britain (e.g. London, BM; Oxford, Pitt Rivers Mus.; Liverpool Mus. and Merseyside Co. Mus.), and Geneva (Mus. Barbier-Mueller), for masks, in particular. Ijo textiles and their display, especially at funerals, have also received attention from scholars (see Eicher and Erekosima). The Kalabari Ijo sculptor Sokari Douglas Camp (*b* 1958) has received wide critical acclaim for her innovative work that draws on Ijo forms (for illustration *see* AFRICA, fig. 21).

1. Introduction. 2. Western and Central Ijo. 3. Eastern Ijo.

1. INTRODUCTION. The Ijo peoples share the delta with a number of smaller ethnic groups and are surrounded by the Itsekiri, Isoko, Urhobo and Yoruba to the west and the Igbo, Ogoni and Ibibio to the north and east. Scholars divide the Ijo into three main groups based on linguistic and cultural differences: the Eastern Ijo living to the east of the Nun River; the Central Ijo occupying the area between the Nun and Pennington rivers; and the Western Ijo who live between the Pennington and Forcados rivers. However, a more significant socio-political division occurs at the Nun River: the Eastern Ijo are organized into a series of city states, while the Western and Central Ijo have decentralized clans. The Nun also divides Ijo art into two principal zones, with substantial differences in form and style.

Historical and environmental factors account for differences between the two sectors. The Eastern Ijo migrated from the central delta into a saltwater zone unsuited to farming. This led to intensified trade, first inland and then overseas. Competition between trading concerns resulted in the formation of city states and the introduction or emphasis of certain art forms. In contrast, the Central and Western Ijo lived primarily by fishing and farming. They participated in inland trade but were largely cut off from European trade by Eastern Ijo middlemen. Ijo sub-groups have also been influenced by their different neighbours. The Eastern Ijo 'fattening houses', for example, reflect contact with Ibibio and other Cross Rivers peoples (*see* IBIBIO, §5; EJAGHAM, §6), while the Western Ijo have borrowed their Ifiri cult from the Isoko and Urhobo.

Nevertheless, all Ijo groups share numerous features including a mixed, but mainly matrilineal, descent system; a religion based on beliefs in a female creator, ancestors and nature spirits; and a culture that emphasizes masculine achievement. Cults devoted to clan war gods once operated throughout the delta, often in conjunction with the Peri warrior society, which granted distinction to those who had killed men or leopards.

In art, too, certain themes and motifs are common to all Ijo. In particular, references to trade and warfare abound. Sculptures are equipped with such symbols of military prowess, wealth and prestige as weapons, medicines, trade goods and European finery, while dependants or followers often surround the central figure to indicate the extent of his influence. Like other southern Nigerian groups, the Ijo associate water spirits with trade, but they also seem to have introduced the horizontal headpieces used in masquerade performances to imitate water spirits at play.

Art styles do, however, vary widely across the delta and even within each region. The geometric figure style regarded as most typically Ijo, with its sharp edges and emphatically projecting cylinders and rectangles, seems to be found in its purest form in the centre of the delta, although not all examples from the region conform to this style. To the west, torsos thicken and forms become rounder as Ijo style blends with those of neighbouring groups. Sometimes only the single vertical keloid dividing the forehead suggests an Ijo rather than an Urhobo origin. The masquerade headpieces found west of the Nun adhere more consistently to the geometric style than do the figures. The forms of Eastern Ijo sculpture tend to be softer and less assertive, with their features layered or in low relief.

2. WESTERN AND CENTRAL IJO. Traditionally, the Ijo living west of the Nun were united only by allegiance to clan war-gods for whom they staged annual festivals. There were no village chiefs, and almost constant hostilities between fiercely independent groups made travel treacherous, a situation that may account for the diverse practices and traditions found in the region. Because Europeans and other Nigerians have regarded the region as inhospitable or inaccessible, little Western and Central Ijo sculpture has been collected and even less has been well documented. The art of only one clan, Olodiama of the south-central delta, has been studied in any depth (Anderson). Given significant variations in style, form and practice, even within clans, generalizations are tentative.

The Ijo of this region produce sculptures for nature spirits (*oru*) who communicate through diviners their desire to manifest themselves. Carvings may be commissioned to represent either personal spirit companions or spirits worshipped in shrines. The Ijo of this region differentiate between two types of nature spirits: water spirits (*bini oru*), who reside in underwater towns; and forest or bush spirits (*bou oru*). They characterize the two types as opposite but complementary. The fair-skinned water spirits have long flowing hair and prefer offerings of white cloth and imported foods and beverages. They are generally regarded as beautiful, playful and beneficent beings who may bestow children, money or success in trade. The dark-skinned bush spirits eat local produce and wear black or navy clothing. People describe them as hideous and volatile, but their shrines offer aid in war and wrestling.

Both types of spirit mirror human behaviour and values. A spirit's wealth, the size of his following and the condition of the shrine all attest to his strength and authority. The spirits embody the Ijo ideal of the bold and aggressive individual, and their power to kill makes them effective as agents of social control.

Each shrine is individualized through a complex of images, drum rhythms, praise-names, offerings and rituals. Although carvings may be made for water spirits, many choose to be represented by such imported or mass-produced items as dolls and tableware or by objects found in the river. The majority of figure carvings from this region thus represent forest or bush spirits. Adumu, head of the water spirits, who is associated with the python, is the only major water spirit known to be represented by a carving. Images of Adumu are similar to those made for bush spirits, although they usually wear cowrie-decorated belts instead of war medicines. Like most nature spirits, Adumu appears with a wife and frequently with one or more children, reflecting his status as an adult male. He is also shown with the miniature canoe and other equipment he uses when fishing. These items, like those in Eastern Ijo shrines, are sometimes described as his children or followers.

In contrast to Adumu and a few other major water spirits, bush spirits seem to be worshipped at only one shrine. Although bush spirits themselves are frequently described as handicapped, deformed or otherwise grotesque, Ijo carvings portray them as invincible warriors, decorated with war paint, holding weapons and wearing wooden replicas of medicine gourds as 'bulletproofing'. To add to this military theme, pots of war medicines are placed in their shrines and war songs are sung for them. A number of figures have multiple faces, a feature that seems to indicate the bush spirits' awesome powers.

Some Ijo in this region have adopted the Ivri cult of the Urhobo and Isoko. The Ifiri sculptures, as the Ijo call them, comprise one or more human figures atop an open-mouthed beast. The cult, which attempts to harness or control aggressive tendencies, appears compatible with local beliefs in bush spirits. In areas to which Ifiri has not spread, wrestlers considered to be overly violent may be advised that acquiring a carving to represent a bush spirit companion will alleviate the problem.

The Ijo of this region have a variety of mask and masquerade headpiece forms. Some employ raffia masks to rid their villages of pollution at the end of the rainy season. Their cloth and wooden masquerades (*owu*) are claimed to imitate dances performed by water spirits. Most of the wooden mask headpieces of the region are worn horizontally, imitating water spirits floating on the water (see fig. 1). Their quasi-human features include a visor-like forehead and nose, tubular eyes and a rectangular mouth set on a platform from which heads, fins and other aquatic forms may project. Some masks depict more naturalistic-looking fish, and a few depict upright heads or figures.

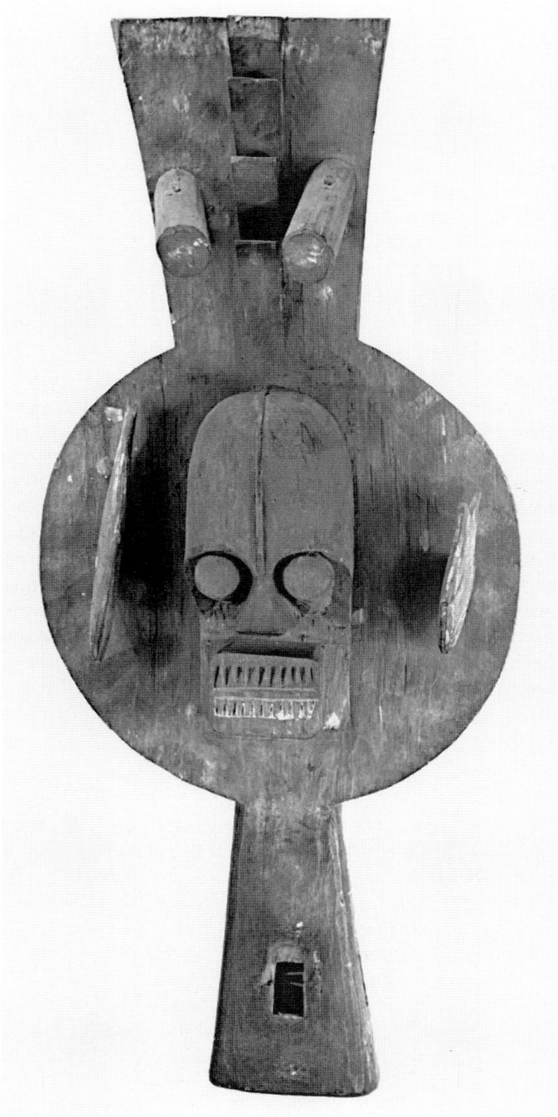

1. Central or Western Ijo masquerade headpiece, worn horizontally with the face turned skyward, wood, h. 660 mm, collected 1937 (Oxford, Oxford University, Pitt Rivers Museum)

The masquerades are largely secular. The spirit Eleke of the Olodiama clan is widely renowned as a ruthless spirit who will kill his invoker's enemies, but most masks are not empowered by spirits and are therefore quite harmless, even though the masqueraders chase the spectators with their machetes. They perform at festivals of various kinds and also at funerals in the south-central area. The Ijo west of the Nun do not appear to have such formally structured masquerade societies as those found east of the Nun (*see* §3 below).

3. Eastern Ijo. Of the art of the four Eastern Ijo city states, only that of Elem Kalabari has been extensively

documented (Horton, 1965). The Kalabari Ijo produce sculptures for three types of beings: the ancestors or dead (*nduen*) who promote the lineage; village heroes (*am'oru*) who promote the village; and the water spirits (*owuamapu*), creative but anti-social beings who provide people with fish but hamper them with storms. The heroes occupy an intermediate position, sharing some traits with both ancestors and water spirits.

The Kalabari commemorate the dead with small stools (*osisi nduen*, 'seat of the dead'), carved on two sides with faces or figures, or with intricate ancestral screens (*c.* 0.5 to 1.5 m high). The screens are called *nduen fobara* ('foreheads of the dead'), and the Kalabari Ijo first began to commission them in the late 18th century. After the death of the head of a canoe house or trading concern, his descendants would order a *nduen fobara* from a family of specialists. On completion the screen would be brought to the compound of another family and a mock battle staged, before it was triumphantly installed in its own compound (Talbot).

The *nduen fobara* is prominently exhibited and designed for visual impact (see fig. 2). The rectangular backdrop, constructed with European joinery techniques, is covered with bamboo slats incorporating geometric designs. Heads and torsos are attached to the screen with arms and legs lashed on separately. Heads representing dependants or followers may be pegged into the top of the screen and the figures equipped with such emblems of rank or power as paddles, weapons, trophy heads, tusks and fans. The central figure, representing the dead leader, commonly displays the markings and attributes of a member of the Peri warrior society and wears either a hat of European or local design or a favourite masquerade headdress. He and the smaller figures flanking him—identified as sons, successors or dependants—may have backbone motifs painted on their torsos. The attendants may also be masked or wear other headgear. The rectangular, relief-like format of the screen and the flanking of the central figure are reminiscent of Benin plaques and suggest some form of contact with the Benin court.

2. Eastern Ijo *nduen fobara*, ancestral screen, wood, split vegetable fibre and pigment, 1.17×0.79×0.33 m, from Kalabari Ijo, collected 1916 (Oxford, Oxford University, Pitt Rivers Museum)

Sculptures for village heroes and water spirits tend to be much simpler in form and less prominently displayed than the ancestral screens. They function primarily to localize spirits rather than to impress their viewers. The pole-like carvings and plaques of village heroes show them wearing distinctive conical caps, but they share other motifs with sculptures of ancestors and water spirits. Carvings for both heroes and water spirits incorporate non-ancestral motifs including figures of pythons, tortoises and bullfrogs, the 'animals of the *oru*'. The immense, truncated images of the major water spirit, Adumu, depict him holding fishing implements, decorated with aquatic animals and painted with designs representing the python. He often wears a European top hat or ruff and may display imported tableware, recalling his ties to European trade. Polychromed spears, paddles and cult objects, decorated with figures of pythons or other animals, represent the central water spirit and his 'followers' in the shrines of other water spirits.

A Kalabari myth explains how a woman named Ekineba, who had been abducted by water spirits, returned to teach her townspeople the plays she had seen under water. She became the patron goddess of the Ekine society (also known as Sekiapu, 'the dancing people') that sponsors a performance of 30 to 50 maskers in each of the Kalabari villages. All of the masks appear in the grand finale called Owo Aro Sun (or 'filling the canoe of the water people'). They then go down to the beach where, screened from the eyes of women and children, they seem to disappear into the water.

Each masker has a distinctive costume, headdress and dance steps. Most have a carved headpiece worn horizontally on top of the head, but this is often hidden by the elaborate costume, with only the surrounding feathers and trinkets being visible. The headpiece itself is not intended to be seen by spectators but to attract the spirit.

Although the maskers manifest supernatural beings, the Kalabari regard the water spirits they represent as fairly innocuous. They stage the masquerades to welcome the spirits into their villages and to entertain them. The masquerades have also served to socialize outsiders, incorporated into the canoe houses to increase their strength, and to display wealth.

Most masks take the form of stylized human faces, which range from a shield shape, like the faces on ancestral screens, to more elongated versions with pointed chins, described by the Kalabari themselves as canoe-shaped. Typically, the nose takes the form of an inverted T, the mouth is a projecting oval or ellipse with exposed teeth, and the eyes are two layered ovals or circles. The maskers wear various types of headgear or crowns, often adorned with pythons, tortoises, birds or lizards. Some headpieces represent animals or combine human features with those of such animals as the crocodile. Otobo, for example, portrays the hippopotamus, its features abstracted and condensed into a rectangular format with projecting, cylindrical tusks and a somewhat human face. A few maskers wear heads mounted vertically. The Kalabari attach the greatest importance to masquerades, while the other Eastern Ijo groups perform *owu* or 'spirit' plays that have similarities to the Kalabari masquerades. The masks used in these plays show only minor differences in style, but they include some types that the Kalabari do not share.

From the 19th century the Nembe Ijo commemorated their kings or leaders with carvings done in an unusually naturalistic style, believed to have been inspired by the figureheads of European ships. The Ijo of Okrika, a pottery-making centre, made vessels decorated with modelled heads to commemorate their ancestors and reportedly carved figures for more prominent and distant ancestors.

BIBLIOGRAPHY

P. A. Talbot: *Tribes of the Niger Delta* (London, 1932)
R. Horton: *The Gods as Guests: An Aspect of Kalabari Religious Life*, Nigeria Magazine Special Publication, 3 (Lagos, 1960)
——: 'The Kalabari Ekine Society: A Borderland of Religion and Art', *Africa*, xxxiii (1963), pp. 94–114
——: *Kalabari Sculpture* (Lagos, 1965)
E. J. Alagoa: *A History of the Niger Delta: An Historical Interpretation of Ijo Oral Tradition* (Ibadan, 1972)
Figurative Sculpture of the Niger Delta (exh. cat., essay by A. Rubin; Los Angeles, Gal. K, 1976)
J. P. Clark: *The Ozidi Saga* (Ibadan, 1977)
M. G. Anderson: *Central Ijo Art: Shrines and Spirit Images* (diss., Bloomington, IN U., 1983)
G. I. Jones: *The Art of Southern Nigeria* (Cambridge, 1984)
N. Barley: 'Pop Art in Africa? The Kalabari Ijo Ancestral Screens', *A. Hist.*, x/3 (1987), pp. 369–80
J. B. Eicher and T. V. Erekosima: 'Kalabari Funerals: Celebration and Display', *Afr. A.*, xxi/1 (1987), pp. 38–45, 87–8
N. Barley: *Foreheads of the Dead: An Anthropological View of Kalabari Ancestral Screens* (Washington, DC, 1988) [pubd on occasion of exh., Washington, DC, N. Mus. Afr. A.; incl. cat. rai. of screens in mus. cols]

MARTHA G. ANDERSON

Ijssewijn, Michiel. *See* YWYNS, MICHIEL.

Ikaniga no Tera. *See* HŌRYŪJI.

Ikdang. *See* KONGMIN.

Ike. Japanese calligraphers and painters. They belonged to the second generation of *Nanga* or *Bunjinga* (literati) painters in the 18th century, who shared an admiration for Chinese culture and the tradition of the scholar–amateur artist, while displaying remarkable individuality. Though deeply moved by Buddhist teachings, (1) Ike Taiga produced mostly secular works and was noted for his style and originality, which became a standard of *Bunjinga* quality. Taiga's wife, (2) Ike Gyokuran, was an accomplished painter in her own right.

See also JAPAN, §VI, 4(vi)(e).

(1) Ike Taiga [Ikeno Mumei; Ikeno Taiga; Ikeno Tsutomu; Kashō, Sangakudōja] (*b* Kyoto, 1723; *d* Kyoto, 1776). His father died when he was very young and from an early age he had to support himself and his mother. He was trained in both Japanese and Chinese calligraphic styles. When, at the age of six, he displayed his calligraphic skill in front of Ōbaku (Chin. Huangbo) Zen priests at the sect's headquarters, the temple of Manpukuji, he was rewarded with laudatory poems. His astonishing dexterity in *kana* (Japanese phonetic) writing at the age of ten is seen in *Two Waka Excerpts from the Kokinshū* (New York, Burke priv. col., see Kosugi, pl. 1). By the age of 12 he was already well versed in four different *kanji* (Chinese character) scripts—*kaisho* (Chin. *kaishu*; regular), *gyōsho* (Chin. *xingshu*; running), *tensho* (Chin. *zhuanshu*; seal) and either *reisho* (Chin. *lishu*; clerical) or *sōsho* (Chin. *caoshu*; grass)—as shown by his *One Hundred Surnames in Four Styles* (ex-Matsuyama priv. col., Osaka; untraced since 1933; only three scripts published; see *Ike Taiga meiga fu*, p. 80, and Matsushita, p. 12). Having mastered basic calligraphic training, he progressed to ink painting and seal engraving. Taiga began selling fans painted in a Chinese style at 14 and chops (seals) engraved in ornate seal script at 15.

Taiga was fortunate to have many good teachers, friends and patrons, including the pioneering literati (*Bunjinga*) painter YANAGISAWA KIEN, who taught him in his mid-teens the unusual skill of ink finger painting (*shitōga*), of which a later example (*c.* 1765) is the hanging scroll *Five Hundred Arhats* (Jap. *rakan*), painted for Manpukuji (Kyoto, N. Mus.; Important Cultural Property). Most of his finger paintings, however, were executed when he was in his 20s and 30s. KŌ FUYŌ, an expert in Chinese Confucian classics and seal engraving, was probably Taiga's closest friend. They shared and nurtured their mutual interest in the classical beauty of Chinese seal engraving from the Han period (206 BC–AD 220). They made at least two extensive trips together, which included climbing famous mountains. Japanese literati artists, following the ideals of Chinese literati, believed that learning from nature was as important as learning from books. KIMURA KENKADŌ, a wealthy sake brewer, was a patron of Taiga as well as a disciple. He was noted for his rich collection of unusual objects, including woodblock-printed Chinese calligraphy books. Taiga, who was by nature taciturn, benefited from his association with Kenkadō and his large coterie of literati painters.

Taiga's major source of pictorial training was Chinese literati-style painting in ink and brush transmitted mainly through woodblock-printed painting manuals, in particular the *Mustard Seed Garden Painting Manual* (Chin. *Jieziyuan huazhuan*, *c.* 1679–1701; Jap. *Kaishien gaden*, 1748 and 1753) and the *Painting Manual of Eight Styles* (Chin. *Bazhong huapu*; Jap. *Hasshū gafu*). Japanese literati artists who studied these manuals tended to produce flatter surface planes and a more prominent use of lines, as opposed to shading, than Chinese literati artists. Taiga successfully employed these features, along with the Japanese trait of decorative abstraction, thereby contributing to the maturity of Japanese literati painting.

As a professional artist, Taiga received commissions from all social strata, from high-ranking samurai to courtesans. His greatest support, however, came from the literate merchant class, who often chose Chinese-style calligraphy and painting as an outlet for their self-expression. Taiga was a prolific artist: about 2000 works are attributed to him, mostly landscapes representing both Chinese themes and scenic Japanese locations. He also painted many figures and the traditional theme of the 'four gentlemen' (orchid, bamboo, plum and chrysanthemum). Most of his works bear his signature (of which he is said to have had more than a hundred forms), sometimes accompanied by Chinese poems or Japanese *waka* (31-syllable classical poems) or *haiku*. Taiga wrote calligraphy in every style available, including the archaic *zattaisho* (miscellaneous script), virtually unknown during his time.

In both calligraphy and painting Taiga was eclectic and versatile. He made great efforts to enrich his literati style by adopting some aspects of other schools. Broad ink wash, seen in the almost abstract handscroll *Scenic Spots of Mutsu Province* (1749; Important Cultural Property; see Suzuki and Sasaki, pl. 4), recalls some ink paintings from the Muromachi period (1333–1568), such as TŌYŌ SESSHŪ's *Habuko Landscape* (1495; Tokyo, N. Mus.). The pooling of ink into puddles, as in the hanging scroll *Catching a Catfish with a Gourd* (Tokyo, Idemitsu Mus. A.) is similar to the *tarashikomi* painting technique (adding pigment to an undried wash to create blurred and pooled effects) used by TAWARAYA SŌTATSU and OGATA KŌRIN of the Rinpa school. His 'true-view' landscapes (*shinkeizu*), in which he was influenced by CHŎNG SŎN, show his fascination with Western linear perspective (e.g. *Mt Asama*, *c.* 1761; see Suzuki and Sasaki, pl. 28). Taiga's imaginative and personalized use of 'realism' encouraged the empiricism in 18th-century literati painting and contributed to laying the foundation for more 'objective' landscape paintings in the 19th and 20th centuries. His painting technique varied from a few abbreviated ink lines to elaborate, large-scale folding screens painted in detail in vivid blues, greens, reds, yellows and even gold. Taiga's early brush works display a serious and sincere style, and his finger paintings an attractive animation. His earliest extant painting is *Willows at Weicheng* (1744; see Suzuki and Sasaki, pl. 21), with title characters in seal script. Although simple and small, the farewell scene in this painting is evocatively expressed by the sensitive and controlled narrow brush lines. In his late 20s Taiga made an attempt to relax his serious brush handling, and for the rest of his life the controlled and the untrammelled styles co-existed in his work.

Modern scholars consider that Taiga did his best work in his 40s. These works show ambitious treatment of composition and sureness of execution; his best quality is a buoyant, poetically enchanted atmosphere embodying the interaction between artist and nature. One of Taiga's most famous works from this period is the *The Ten Conveniences and Ten Pleasures Album* (*Jūben jūgijō*), a collaborative work with the literati painter YOSA BUSON (*c.* 1771; Kamakura, Kawabata Yasunari Mem. Mus.; National Treasure). One leaf from the album, *The Convenience of Fishing* (see fig.), reveals the artist's longing for close contact with nature and is characterized by witty handling of figures and abbreviated strokes to suggest the water and huts. It is embellished with his distinctively distorted and open calligraphy.

Taiga began suffering from an illness, probably kidney failure, some time before the age of 47 and never completely recovered. The works from his 50s consequently lack patience and vitality.

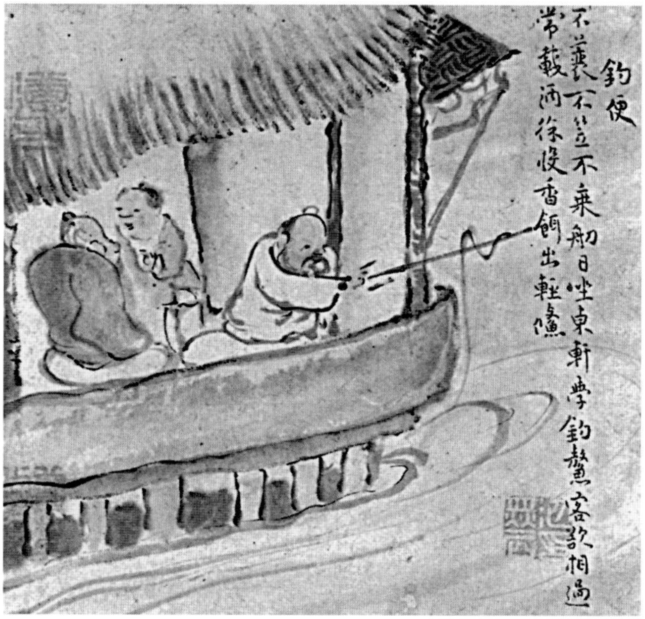

Ike Taiga: *The Convenience of Fishing*, light colours on paper, 180×178 mm, *c.* 1771; leaf from the *Ten Conveniences and Ten Pleasures Album* (Kamakura, Kawabata Yasunari Memorial Museum); National Treasure

BIBLIOGRAPHY

Ike Taiga meiga fu [Collection of famous paintings of Ike Taiga], Kyoto National Museum (Kyoto, 1933)

H. Kosugi, ed.: *Ikeno Taiga sakuhinshū* [Collection of works by Ikeno Taiga], 2 vols (Tokyo, 1960)

Y. Yonezawa and C. Yoshizawa: *Bunjinga*, Nihon no bijutsu [Arts of Japan], xxiii (Tokyo, 1966); Eng. trans. by B. I. Monroe as *Japanese Painting in the Literati Style*, Heibonsha Surv. Jap. A., xxiii (New York and Tokyo, 1974)

H. Matsushita: *Taiga no sho* [Calligraphy of Taiga] (Tokyo, 1970)

Scholar-painters of Japan: The Nanga School (exh. cat. by J. Cahill, New York, Asia House Gals, 1972)

C. Yoshizawa: *Ike Taiga*, Nihon no bijutsu: Bukku obu bukkusu [Arts of Japan: book of books], xxvi (Tokyo, 1973)

Y. Nakata: *Ike Taiga*, Shodō geijutsu [Art of calligraphy], xix (Tokyo, 1975)

S. Suzuki and J. Sasaki: *Ike Taiga* (1980), xviii of *Nihon bijutsu kaiga zenshū* [Complete collection of Japanese painting] (Tokyo, 1980–81)

M. Kōno: *Taiga/Ōkyo*, Meihō Nihon no bijutsu [Rare treasures of Japanese art], xxiv (Tokyo, 1981)

S. Ohki: *Ike Taiga's Karayō calligraphy* (diss., Ann Arbor, U. MI, 1984)

M. Takeuchi: 'True Views: Taiga's *shinkeizu* and the Evolution of Painting Theory in Japan', *J. Asian Stud.*, xlviii (1989), pp. 3–26

——: *Taiga's True Views* (Stanford, 1992)

SADAKO OHKI

(2) Ike [Ikeno Machi] **Gyokuran** (*b* Kyoto, 1727 or 1728; *d* Kyoto, 1784). Wife of (1) Ike Taiga. She was descended from a line of independent, talented women poets and calligraphers. Her grandmother Kaji (*fl* early 18th century), her mother Yuri (1694–1764) and she supported themselves by running the Matsuya tea house in Kyoto's Gion district while composing *waka* (31-syllable classical poetry) as an artistic outlet. At an early age she was encouraged by her mother to study painting. Her first teacher, the literati (*Bunjinga*) painter YANAGISAWA KIEN of Kyoto, gave her the art name (*gō*) Gyokuran ('jade orchid'). She later met and married the famous literati painter Ike Taiga. The two lived an unorthodox life together, showing little concern for money or material possessions. Gyokuran frequently combined her artistic talents by creating simple, small-format paintings on which she inscribed verses, for example *Landscape Fan with Waka* (priv. col.; see 1988 exh. cat., no. 29). She was particularly fond of the intimate fan format, whose limited surface encouraged her impressionistic tendencies in painting and whose curving form complemented the curvilinear script of her poems. She also produced more complex landscape compositions in the Chinese literati style, such as *Spring Landscape* (San Francisco, CA, Asian A. Mus.). Although Taiga's influence is readily visible in her manipulation of space and distinctive outlines, Gyokuran composed her landscapes with an even greater zest for spatial ambiguity. The effect is sometimes startling. Gyokuran outlived Taiga by eight years. Since they had no children and she had no outstanding students, the artistic legacy begun by her grandmother ended with Gyokuran's death.

BIBLIOGRAPHY

S. Suzuki: 'Taiga to Gyokuran', *Kobijutsu*, xliv (1974), pp. 37–48

Japanese Women Artists, 1600–1900 (exh. cat. by P. Fister, Lawrence, U. KS, Spencer Mus. A., 1988)

S. Addiss: 'The Three Women of Gion', *Flowering in the Shadows: Women in the History of Chinese and Japanese Painting*, ed. M. Weidner (Honolulu, 1991)

KAREN M. GERHART

Ikebe, Kiyoshi (*b* Pusan, South Korea, 8 April 1920; *d* Tokyo, 9 Feb 1979). Japanese architect, teacher and writer. He graduated in architecture from the University of Tokyo (1944) and from 1944 to 1946 he worked in the office of Junzō Sakakura. He was then appointed as a lecturer in architecture at the University of Tokyo, became a professor and continued to teach there until his death. One of Ikebe's principal interests was industrialization and modular coordination in building, particularly in housing. Influenced by Le Corbusier's 'Le Modulor', he developed a new modular system, 'GM module', based on the number two. Another prime interest was housing design; he designed about 100 private houses but no large-scale housing complexes because he believed the Japanese building industry was not yet sufficiently well organized to produce good-quality work at that scale. Examples of his residential designs include a series of experimental minimalist houses (1950) in which he explored the standardization of form and space. He also designed the Kagoshima Space Centre (1962–79) for the University of Tokyo, Kagoshima Prefecture. This was Japan's first institute for space science, and Ikebe collaborated with many scientists and engineers, applying systems theory to the industrialized design of the building.

WRITINGS

Sumai [The house] (Tokyo, 1954, rev. 8/1962)
Systematic Design Method (Tokyo, 1968)
Dezain no kagi [The key to design] (Tokyo, 1979)

BIBLIOGRAPHY

'Kagoshima Space Centre, University of Tokyo', *Kenchiku Bunka/Archit. Cult.*, xxi (1966), pp. 55–88

'Industrialisierter Wohnungsbau in Japan', *Dt. Bauztg*, cvi/12 (1972), p. 1311

KAZUHIKO NAMBA

Ikeda, Masuo (*b* Manshū, Manchuria, 23 Feb 1934). Japanese printmaker and painter. From 1952 to 1953 he studied at the National Painting Association Fine Arts Research Institute. In 1955 he met the painter Kyū Ei, and in 1956 he became a member of Ei's Demokurāto Bijutsuka Kyōkai (Democratic Art Society), a group of avant-garde artists. Although at that time he was creating paintings such as *Ruined Town* (1955; Tokyo, Met. A. Mus.), in 1956 he began on Ei's recommendation to produce copperplate etchings. He won prizes at the second, third and fourth Tokyo International Print Biennales, including ones for the drypoints *Wedding Ceremony of Animals* (1962; Tokyo, Met. A. Mus.) and *Woman Applying Make-up* (1964; Tokyo, N. Mus. Mod. A.). In 1961 he received the Award of Excellence at the *Deuxième biennale de Paris*, an exhibition of young artists. In 1965 a one-man exhibition of Ikeda's prints was held at MOMA in New York, and a year later he received the Grand Prize in the print section of the Venice Biennale. In 1972 he settled in New York. In 1983 the exhibition Erosu ni Sasagu—Ikeda Masuo no Shirarezaru Sekai ('Consecration to Eros—the unknown world of Ikeda Masuo') was held at the Ikeda Museum of 20th Century Art in Itō. His style was initially abstract but it later became figurative.

WRITINGS

Watakushi no chōsho—watakushi no gihō [My memorandum—my techniques] (Tokyo, 1976)

PRINTS

Ikeda Masuo—20 nen no zenbō/Zenhanga sakuhin, 1956–1977 [Ikeda Masuo—A full portrait of 20 years complete print works, 1956–77] (Tokyo, 1977)

BIBLIOGRAPHY

Deuxième biennale de Paris (exh. cat., Paris, Mus. A. Mod. Ville Paris, 1961)

'Ikeda Masuo no Subete' [The complete Ikeda Masuo], *Geijutsu shinchō* (March 1977)

Erosu ni sasagu—Ikeda Masuo no shirarezaru sekai [Consecration to Eros—The unknown world of Ikeda Masuo] (exh. cat., Itō, Ikeda Mus. 20th C. A., 1983)

S. Segi, N. Awazu and M. Yonekura: *Ikeda Masuo zenhanga* [Print works of Ikeda Masuo] (Tokyo, 1991) [cat. rais.]

YASUYOSHI SAITO

Ikeda Eisen [Keisai] (*b* Edo [now Tokyo], 1790; *d* 1848). Japanese painter and woodblock-print designer. Having first studied under Kanō Hakkeisei (Jikeisai), he became acquainted *c.* 1810 with the Kanō-style painter Kikukawa Eiji and his son Kikukawa Eizan (1787–1867), a *ukiyoe* ('pictures of the floating world') artist, at that time producing pictures of beautiful women (*bijinga*) in the style of KITAGAWA UTAMARO. Eisen's early works in this genre show Eizan's influence. Eisen subsequently specialized in *bijinga* and *shunga* ('spring paintings', erotic pictures). Eisen's style depicting women, which began to appear around 1821, is characterized by straight lines varying in thickness, sharp angular lines and fine details. Distinctive facial features such as long, slanting eyes, contracted eyebrows and half-open lips touched with green contribute to a strong-minded and vivacious female image. Examples include a series of half-length portraits (*ōkubi-e*) from the early 1820s entitled *Contest of Contemporary Beauties* (*Ukiyo fūzoku mime kurabe*). Eisen later returned to full-length figures. Works of the later 1820s also employed Western-style techniques, such as the use of fine parallel lines for shading. In this period, Eisen began to design landscapes and courtesan prints using shades of blue, known as the *aizurie* ('blue-printed pictures'). In 1835, Eisen began the series *Sixty-nine Stations of the Kisokaidō* (*Kisokaidō rokujūkyū tsugi*; late 1830s; London, BM), which was completed by ANDŌ HIROSHIGE. A major late work was the series commonly known as *Beautiful Women of the Tōkaidō* (*Bijin Tōkaidō*), which features full-length female figures in the foreground and landscape backgrounds. Eisen was also a writer, producing both illustrations and text. In early books, the figure, animal and plant depictions reveal an indebtedness to KATSUSHIKA HOKUSAI, which Eisen himself acknowledged. Later in life, he turned increasingly to writing popular novelettes and other works. Eisen was also author of the *Zoku ukiyoe ruikō* (Compendium of *ukiyoe*, 2nd series), a re-editing of the major sources for the history of *ukiyoe*.

WRITINGS

Zoku ukiyoe ruikō (Tokyo, *c.* 1840s)

BIBLIOGRAPHY

J. Suzuki and I. Oka: *The Decadents: Masterworks of Ukiyo-e* (Tokyo, 1969/*R* 1982)

S. Kikuchi: *Ukiyoe*, Genshoku Nihon no bijutsu [Arts of Japan, illustrated], xvii (Tokyo, 1977)

S. Yoshida: *Ukiyoe no mikata jiten* [Encyclopedia of a view of *ukiyoe*] (Tokyo, 1987)

BRENDA G. JORDAN

Ikenaga Dōun [Ippō; Shiin; San'unsuigetsu Shujin; Ryūkōkaku; Gyokujundō; Seishūken] (*b* Edo [now Tokyo], 1665; *d* Edo, 1737). Japanese seal-carver and calligrapher. The Ikenaga were a powerful provincial family in Odawara, Sagami Province (now Kanagawa Prefect.). In 1593 they moved to Edo, where they ran a pharmacy as well as being the head family of their residential district. Dōun was adopted into the Ikenaga family and became its fifth-generation head. He enjoyed learning from an early age and studied with Sakakibara Kōshū (1655–1706); his close friends included such seal-carvers as HOSOI KŌTAKU (also a distinguished calligrapher) and Imai Junsai (1658–1718). His seal album *Ittō banshō* ('One blade, a myriad images'; 1713; Japan, N. Mizuta priv. col.; *see* JAPAN, §XVI, 20 and fig. 246) was the forerunner of artistic seal albums in Japan. It is in four volumes, the first two showing 328 seals carved in different styles, based on the *Senjimon* (the 'Thousand-character' Chinese classic); the third is a collection of the impressions of 170 private seals in Dōun's own collection. Prefaces from major scholars and Koreans and Chinese resident in Japan, as well as Dōun's own prefatory remarks, are bound together in another volume. Only 100 copies of the *Ittō banshō* were printed, to be distributed exclusively among Dōun's friends or offered to Shinto shrines. He also presented a specially prepared edition, with specially impressed seals, to retired Emperor Reigen (*reg* 1663–87) and another to Hosshin, abbot of the temple Myōhōin. The work is evidence that the practice of seal carving as an art form and the publication of seal albums for aesthetic appreciation began with Dōun. His school became known as the Early Edo school (Shoki Edo ha; *see also* JAPAN, §XVI, 19).

At the age of 50 Dōun passed the Ikenaga lineage to his eldest son Eiriku and retired to the south of the Sumida River in Tokyo, where he lived a leisurely life, reading Buddhist texts and enjoying calligraphy and seal-carving. When he tired of these he would refresh his spirits by playing the *biwa* (Japanese lute). Thirty-three days before he died he took his leave of his relatives and friends, played two tunes on the *biwa* and, when he had completed his will, composed his own epitaph. He was buried at the Juyōin subtemple of Seiganji, Asakusa, Edo. He produced more than 50 volumes of 18 titles, including *Ikenaga Dōun inpu* ('Ikenaga Dōun seal album'; Suita, N. Mizuta Shūhōshitsu priv. col.) and *Renju tenmon* (1722; Sendai, Tohoku U.).

BIBLIOGRAPHY

K. Nakai: *Nihon Injinden* [Accounts of Japanese seal-carvers] (Tokyo, 1915)

Y. Nakata, ed.: *Nihon no tenkoku* [Japanese seal-carving] (Tokyo, 1966)

C. Mimura: *Kinsei nōshoden* [Accounts of pre-modern calligraphy] (Tokyo, 1983), iv of *Mimura Chikusei* [Collected works of Mimura Chikusei] (Tokyo, 1982–7)

NORIHISA MIZUTA

Ikjae. *See* YI CHE-HYŎN.

Ikkei. *See* UKITA IKKEI.

Ikko. *See* NARAHARA, IKKO.

Ikkyū. *See* IKKYŪ SŌJUN.

Ikkyū Sōjun [Kyōunshi] (*b* Kyoto, 1394; *d* Kyoto, 1481). Japanese Zen Buddhist priest, poet, calligrapher and painter. He was one of the most unconventional figures in 15th-century Japan, an uncompromising critic of the Zen establishment, both in his poems, religious statements, paintings and calligraphic works and in his eccentric conduct that sometimes verged on the manic. *Kyōun* ('Crazy Cloud'), his self-mocking sobriquet, is rich in literary connotations and emphasizes his non-attachment to the world, the essential requirement of a committed Zen monk. His famous manuscript of the Chinese verses named *Kyōunshū* ('Crazy Cloud anthology') reveals Ikkyū's unique literary genius and also his mercurial temperament. According to the *Ikkyū Oshō nenpu* ('Chronicle of Reverend Ikkyū'), which is thought to have been compiled shortly after the master's death by his disciple SHŌTŌ BOKUSAI, he was the illegitimate son of Emperor Go-Komatsu (*reg* 1382–1412) and a woman of a branch of the Fujiwara clan, connected with the rival southern court, who was dismissed from the imperial household before her child was born. Although Ikkyū was never recognized as the offspring of an emperor, GoKomatsu received him twice in audience. At the age of five Ikkyū was sent to Ankokuji, a temple in the province of Yamashiro (now part of Kyoto), where he began his training as a Zen monk. In 1406 he went to Kenninji in Kyoto to study Chinese Buddhist and secular classics, but by the age of 17 he had decided to devote himself to the study of Zen and sought instruction from the hermit Ken'ō Sōi. After the death of his master in 1414, he was accepted as a pupil by Kasō Sōdon (Kesō Shūdon; 1352–1428), a Rinzai Zen priest with a reputation for severity, who lived in a hermitage on the shores of Lake Biwa that was affiliated to Daitokuji in Kyoto. Kasō gave him the name Ikkyū ('One Pause' or 'One Rest'), a reference to the dynamic Zen concept of non-duality, in which the narrow path of enlightenment between the two worlds—the material and immaterial, good and evil—is a realm of perfect freedom,

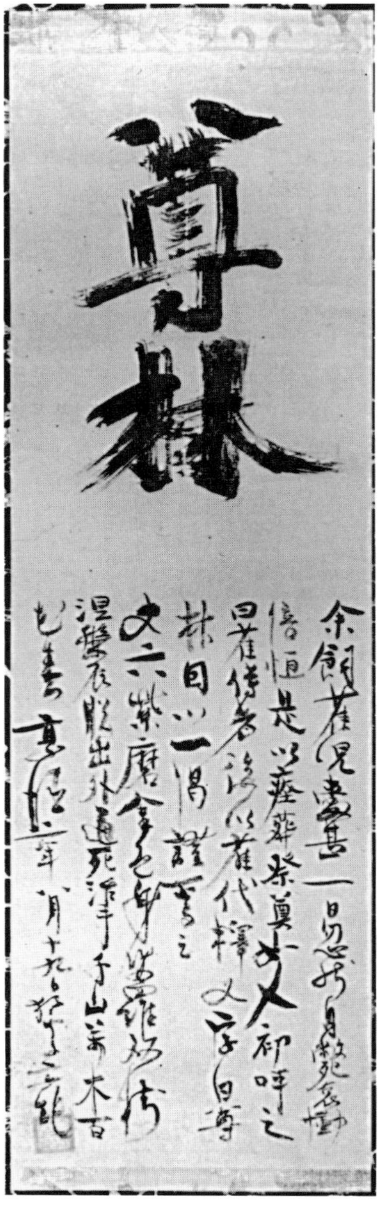

1. Ikkyū Sōjun: *Sonrin* (calligraphy dedicated to a dead sparrow), hanging scroll, ink on paper, 788×245 mm, 1453 (Tokyo, Hatakeyama Collection)

one pause of emptiness. Ikkyū attained enlightenment at the age of 26: while meditating in a boat on Lake Biwa late on a rainy summer night, he was startled by the raucous caw of a crow and cried out in wonder, convinced that he had achieved his ultimate goal. At some point before his master's death he embarked on the itinerant existence that he continued into old age. The unconventional behaviour he cultivated included openly frequenting taverns and brothels. He claimed that he could maintain the pure, original spirit of Zen much more effectively by his profligacy than by observing empty religious conventions. He also wrote statements of faith that explained Zen teachings in colloquial Japanese (*kana-hōgo*).

In 1440 he was invited by the head of Daitokuji, Yōsō Sōi (1376–1458), who had also been a disciple of Kasō, to be abbot of the Nyoian, a subtemple of Daitokuji. Ikkyū refused the honour and accused Yōsō of diluting Kasō's Zen. Ikkyū continued to drift from one small hermitage to another until 1452, when a wealthy patron built him a permanent lodging, which he called Katsuroan ('Blind Donkey's Hermitage'). Four years later he moved to a disused hermitage he found between Kyoto and Nara, which later came to be known as Shūon'an. During the Ōnin Rebellion, which erupted in 1467, Daitokuji and Katsuroan were burnt down, and in 1469 Ikkyū was forced to leave Shūon'an and flee to the Nara area, then to Sakai and finally to Sumiyoshi. In 1474 Ikkyū accepted the emperor's invitation to become abbot of Daitokuji and supervise the temple's reconstruction, although he continued to live at Shūon'an, where he associated with cultural figures such as the *nō* dramatist Konparu Zenchiku (1405–?1468), the linked-verse poet Sōchō (1448–1532), the tea master MURATA JUKŌ and the leading painters of the SOGA school.

The notoriety Ikkyū acquired throughout his life contrasts markedly with his devotion to the essential institutional principles of Zen. In spirit, he identified himself with the old Chinese and Japanese Zen masters, particularly with those of the Daitokuji lineage such as Xutang Zhiyu (1185–1269), one of the most influential Chinese masters, who instructed many Japanese pilgrim monks. The exceptional affinity Ikkyū felt for the fountain-head of Daitokuji Zen is reflected in a number of his poems as well as in inscriptions he provided for paintings. So strongly did he identify with Xutang Zhiyu that four of his numerous portraits (self-inscribed and three dating from 1462, 1464 and 1468 (Kyoto, Daitokuji), the fourth undated (Tokyo, Idemitsu Mus. A.)), represent Ikkyū in the guise of his admired spiritual ancestor. When a rare Xutang portrait was installed at Shūon'an the dreams of Ikkyū's disciples gave them to understand that he was in fact a reincarnation of the Chinese prelate. On his deathbed he still felt great intimacy with the venerated master, to whom he referred in his death poem (*yuige*). This moving document has been treasured, along with other works and his last admonitions to his disciples at Shinjuan, Ikkyū's memorial temple at Daitokuji. Although the four lines of his death poem are written in a straightforward, bold manner, signs of exhaustion and memory lapses may be discerned. The contrasts between deep dark and light grey ink and between wet and dry scratchy brushstrokes add another dimension to this last religious statement.

In his wide range of subject-matter Ikkyū broke the traditional framework of Zen calligraphy. Besides doctrinal statements, aphorisms and treatises on Zen and on venerable masters of the past, sobriquets or 'confirmation names' for disciples, eulogies on religious and secular paintings, including dedicatory inscriptions on his own portraits, he wrote love poems to and about his blind paramour Mori and dedicated a kind of requiem to his dead pet sparrow (see fig. 1). Imitating the Zen practice of bestowing an appropriate sobriquet upon an advanced pupil, Ikkyū named the little bird Sonrin ('Forest of Venerability') and euphemistically compared its death with the passing of the Buddha. This remarkable text (1453, Tokyo, Hatakeyama Col.) reflects Ikkyū's deep concern and respect for all sentient beings, but also expresses his challenge to monastic customs and traditional pieties.

Perhaps his most famous extant work is a pair of hanging scrolls (Daitokuji, Shinjuan; see fig. 2) bearing four large characters: *Shoaku makusa, shūzen bugyō* ('Do no evil, do much good'). For this maxim, derived from the ancient *Shichibutsu tsūkai no ge* ('Verses of the Precepts of the Seven Buddhas') and epitomized in a dialogue between the celebrated Tang period poet Bo Juyi (772–846) and the Chan (Zen) priest Niaoke (741–824), Ikkyū employed a mode of writing known as *ichigyō-sho* ('single line of script') that was not popular among Chinese masters but appears to have been favoured by Zen calligraphers in Japan since about the late 13th century. The narrow, vertical format for a few large-scale characters may have been inspired by similar works of such prominent Zen calligraphers as Wuan Puning (Gottan Funei; 1197–1276), Yishan Yining (Issan Ichinei; 1247–1317), MUSŌ SOSEKI and Tettō Gikō (1295–1369). The first character of each of the two lines is written legibly in a rough but controlled manner, while the following characters dissolve into a swirling dance of the forceful brush. Irregular ink saturation and streaks of bare white within brushstrokes of varying width create an extremely cursive movement. This effect, known in Chinese calligraphy as *feibai* (Jap. *hihaku*; 'flying white'), could be best achieved with a stiff, worn-out brush.

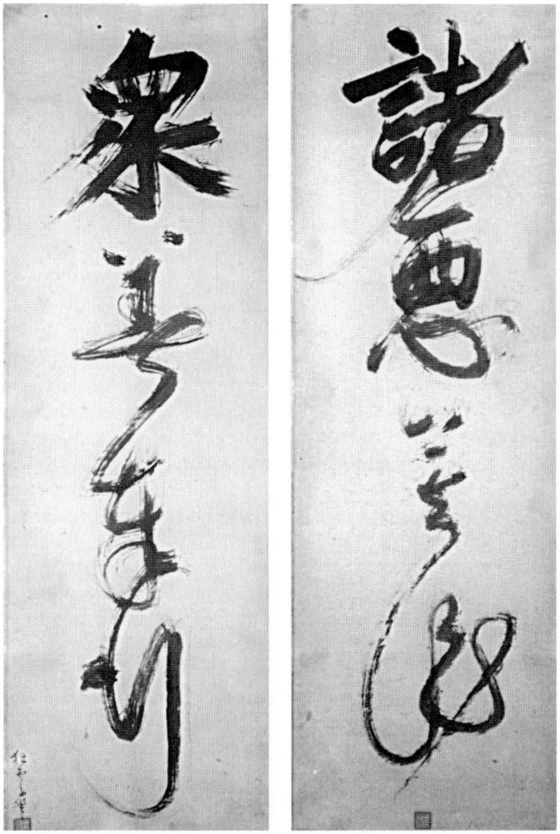

2. Ikkyū Sōjun: *Shoaku makusa, shūzen bugyō* ('Do no evil, do much good'), signed *Kyōunshi hitsu* ('from the brush of Master Crazy Cloud'), pair of hanging scrolls, ink on paper, each 1333×415 mm, second half of the 15th century (Kyoto, Daitokuji, Shinjuan)

Ikkyū was no doubt aware of traditional standards of Chinese calligraphy, but he paid no more attention to them than he paid to the basic codes of monastic conduct or to the rules of Chinese prosody in his poetry. He eschewed such virtues as beauty and harmony, grace and elegance and made no concessions to formal discipline. Freely mixing modes of writing, he brushed his bold characters to the paper with great vigour and impetuosity. Most of his extant works are complex and intense 'ink traces' (*bokuseki*), uncompromising in their individuality, artistically untrammelled and imbued with intense spiritual energy and fiery passion.

WRITINGS

Kyōunshū [Crazy Cloud anthology] (15th century)

BIBLIOGRAPHY

K. Mori, ed.: *Ikkyū Oshō zenshū* [Collected works of Reverend Ikkyū] (Tokyo, 1894)

Ikkyū Oshō nenpu [Chronicle of Reverend Ikkyū], ix/II of *Zoku gunsho ruijū* [Sequel to the collection of historical books and documents] (Tokyo, 1927)

S. Furuta: *Ikkyū* (Tokyo, 1944)

T. Matsushita: 'Ikkyū Oshō no gazō' [The painted portraits by Reverend Ikkyū], *Museum*, 53 (1955), pp. 9–13

H. Tayama: 'Ikkyū Oshō no bokuseki' [The calligraphy of Reverend Ikkyū], *Museum*, 53 (1955), pp. 14–18

Yamato Bunka, 41 (1964) [special number devoted to Ikkyū]

Zen Painting and Calligraphy (exh. cat. by J. Fontein and M. L. Hickman, Boston, MA, Mus. F.A., 1970), nos 51–3

S. Arntzen: *Ikkyū Sōjun: A Zen Monk and his Poetry* (Bellingham, WA, 1973)

H. Brinker: *Die zen-buddhistische Bildnismalerei in China und Japan*, Münchener Ostasiatische Studien, x (Wiesbaden, 1973), pp. 88–91, 158–9, 169–177, figs 26–7, 40, 95–8, 113, 115–23

S. Hirano: *Kyōunshū zenshaku* [Complete commentary on the 'Crazy Cloud anthology'] (Tokyo, 1976)

S. Katō and S. Yanagida: *Nihon no Zen goroku: Ikkyū* [Recorded sayings of Japanese Zen masters] (Tokyo, 1977)

D. Keene: *Some Japanese Portraits* (Tokyo, New York and San Francisco, 1978), pp. 15–25

T. Minakami: *Ikkyū* (Tokyo, 1978)

J. C. Covell with Abbot Sobin Yamada: *Unraveling Zen's Red Thread: Ikkyū's Controversial Way* (Elizabeth, NJ, and Seoul, 1980)

S. Yanagida: *Ikkyū: Kyōunshū no sekai* [Ikkyū: the world of the Crazy Cloud anthology] (Kyoto, 1980)

J. H. Sanford: *Zen-man Ikkyū*, Harvard Studies in World Religions, ii (Chico, CA, 1981)

T. Tamamura: *Gozan zensō denki shūsei* [Collection of biographies of Zen monks of the Five Mountains] (Tokyo, 1983), pp. 31–3

Masters of Japanese Calligraphy, 8th–19th Century (exh. cat. by Y. Shimizu and J. M. Rosenfield, New York, Asia Soc. Gals and Japan House Gal., 1984–5), pp. 116–17, nos 49–51

S. Arntzen: *Ikkyū and the Crazy Cloud Anthology: A Zen Poet of Medieval Japan* (Tokyo, 1986)

Zen. Meister der Meditation in Bildern und Schriften (exh. cat. by H. Brinker and H. Kanazawa, Zurich, Museum Rietberg, 1993), pp. 95–8, plates 30–31, 42, 46

H. Brinker: 'Spuren des Selbst. Schriftzeugnisse zen-buddhistischer Meister aus dem mittelalterlichen Japan', *Das andere China: Festschrift für Wolfgang Bauer*, ed. H. Schmidt-Glintzer (Zurich, 1995)

HELMUT BRINKER

Iktinos (*fl* mid-5th century BC). Greek architect. Ancient sources attribute three buildings to Iktinos: the Parthenon (*c.* 447–432 BC) on the Athenian Acropolis (*see* ATHENS, §II, 1(i)); the Telesterion or Hall of Mysteries (*c.* 430 BC) at ELEUSIS; and the Temple of Apollo at Bassai (*c.* 430–400 BC; *see* BASSAI, §1). On the Parthenon, about which he and the unknown Karpion wrote a treatise (now lost; see Vitruvius), Iktinos collaborated with KALLIKRATES. The exact nature of their collaboration is, however, uncertain, though the theory that Iktinos took the work over from Kallikrates (see R. Carpenter: *The Architects of the Parthenon*, Harmondsworth, 1970, pp. 46, 54, 111) is not widely accepted.

It is possible that Iktinos' treatise on the Parthenon laid down the mathematical concepts underlying its design, since exceptional features of the building are its system of proportion and its refinements. The prevalent proportions are 4:9, 7:12 and 9:14, giving a constant difference of 5. Of these, the most common is 4:9. This governs the relationships between the building's width and length, its height and width, column diameter and interaxial spacing, and height of cornice and height of frieze. The chief refinement, which must have required minute calculations, is the curvature of the temple platform. In addition, the columns incline inwards, as do the cella's side walls, while the antae incline outwards. The columns have entasis, a slight bulge at about one-third of their height, and the corner columns are slightly thickened.

The Parthenon was innovative in other ways. Though Doric, it had many Ionic features. These included an Ionic frieze on the outside of the cella; an external colonnade of 8×17 columns rather than the normal Doric 6×13; and amphiprostyle porches, instead of the traditional distyle *in antis*. The inclusion of four Ionic columns in its end chamber may have been suggested by the combination of a Doric external colonnade with Ionic internal columns in the Stoa Poikile (*c.* 460 BC) in the Athenian Agora. Another innovation was the use of a pi-shaped two-storey Doric internal colonnade in the cella to provide a backdrop for the chryselephantine statue of Athena by PHEIDIAS. The spaciousness of the cella, due to the eight-column façade, also displayed the statue to advantage, suggesting that some innovations may have been prompted by Pheidias himself.

Iktinos' role at Eleusis is less clear, since other architects are also associated with the Telesterion. He is the only recorded architect of the Temple of Apollo at Bassai (*see* GREECE, ANCIENT, fig. 24). This building, however, is paradoxical. Its austere, parochial Doric exterior and unusual plan, perhaps influenced by a predecessor, contrast with an internal colonnade mainly of Ionic columns (but including the earliest example of the Corinthian order) that support a late 5th-century BC Ionic frieze. The pi-shaped internal colonnade recalls the Parthenon, but at Bassai the columns are attached to spur walls and belong to a different order. Their bases and Ionic capitals are quite unlike any in Attica. Though the incorporation of an Ionic frieze in a Doric building also echoes the Parthenon, here the frieze is more naturally placed over Ionic columns and cannot be seen at the same time as the Doric exterior.

BIBLIOGRAPHY

Pausanias: *Guide to Greece*, VIII.xli.9
Plutarch: *Pericles*, XIII.iv
Vitruvius: *On Architecture*, VII. Preface.7
W. B. Dinsmoor: 'The Temple of Apollo at Bassae', *Met. Mus. Stud.*, iv (1933), pp. 204–7
A. Orlandos: *E architektonike tou Parthenonos* [The architecture of the Parthenon] (Athens, 1977)

ANASTASIA N. DINSMOOR

Ikuo Hirayama. *See* HIRAYAMA, IKUO.

Ilchester, 4th Earl of. *See* FOX-STRANGWAYS, W. T. H.

Ilho. *See* NAM KYE-U.

Iliescu-Călineşti, Gheorghe (*b* Călineşti, 1932). Romanian sculptor. He studied with Cornel Medrea at the Nicolae Grigorescu Academy of Art in Bucharest and graduated in 1959. He made his début in 1961 at the annual Salon of Painting and Sculpture in Bucharest. From that date he attended many important national and international exhibitions, and also a series of symposia as a representative of Romania, including the Venice Biennale of 1972. His work belongs to a significant trend in Romanian post-Stalinist sculpture: he attempted to synthesize the essential qualities of Brancusi with a fictitious organic primitivism that was intended to resemble the characteristic features of the wooden tools and domestic objects used in a traditional peasant household. Iliescu-Călineşti's symbolic repertory focused on myths of germination, fertility and the solar cult, deriving from archaic popular beliefs. The energy with which he continually increased his production made him the most active exponent of sculpture in wood in Romania.

BIBLIOGRAPHY

R. Maillard, ed.: *Nouveau dictionnaire de la sculpture moderne* (Paris, 1970)
C. R. Constantinescu: *Iliescu-Călineşti* (Bucharest, 1984)

CĂLIN DAN

Il'in, Lev (Aleksandrovich) (*b* Tambov, 25 June 1880; *d* Leningrad [now St Petersburg], 11 Dec 1942). Russian architect. He studied at the Institute of Civil Engineers, St Petersburg, from 1897 to 1903, and at the architectural faculty of the Academy of Arts, St Petersburg, under Leonty Benois, and in Italy. His early buildings, a house (1903–6; with A. F. Bubyr') on Furshtadtskaya Street 9 and the house (1907) at Petrogradskaya Embankment 8, both in St Petersburg, are in the neo-Baroque style. In 1904 Il'in began working on the reconstruction of some of the bridges of St Petersburg. After his first proposals were rejected as being inconsistent with the city's architectural character, he produced neo-classical designs with extensive use of cast iron for both structural elements and decoration, such as railings and lampposts. Notable examples include the Zelyony Bridge (1904–7) and Sadovy Bridge (1907–8), both on the Moyka Canal, and the Pantaleymonovsky Bridge on the Fontanka Canal. His short-lived enthusiasm for a romantic 'northern' interpretation of Art Nouveau, derived from Scandinavian prototypes, is conveyed by the flats (1907–12) at Zagorodny Prospect 66, St Petersburg.

In 1906 Il'in won the competition to design the 2000-bed Peter the Great Hospital (1908–16; with Alexander Klein and A. V. Rozenberg; now the I. I. Mechnikov Hospital), St Petersburg. Planned on the pavilion system, for a simplified and efficient spatial organization, the hospital's stylistic character follows the model of early 18th-century

St Petersburg Baroque, which was at the time promoted by the World of Art group. Under their influence Il'in experimented with neo-Palladianism too, and he built the subtly arranged complex (1911–13; the lateral wings survive) at Pesochnaya Embankment 24, St Petersburg. However, his experience working on the hospital led to a conviction on his part that the solution of the major problems in architecture lay in the organization of districts, and he thereafter worked mainly as an urban planner.

From 1911 to 1916 Il'in worked on designs (unexecuted) for the village attached to the Lys'vensky Factory, Lysiva, in the Urals and for Liran, a resort on the coast of the Black Sea. After the October Revolution, in Leningrad, he designed the layout for the western end of Yelagin Island, with a granite terrace (1924–5), and completed the city's most important historic ensemble, the public garden (1925–6) on the Strelka, Vasil'yevsky Island, and other projects. Also in Leningrad he produced an urban plan (1924–5) for the district around Stachek Prospect in the south-west area of the city and planned (1925–9) the *c.* 3-km long Bol'shoy Prospect on Vasil'yevsky Island. From 1931 to 1935 he directed the general plan for Leningrad, striving for an organic link between the older parts of the city and the new, fast-growing peripheral areas. In response to a decision by the city administration he drew up a new version of the plan (1935–8), which envisaged a new city centre and development in the southern area, particularly the layout of Moskovsky Prospect. His own vast, monumental residential block (1936–46), at no. 79, set the general tone. From 1930 to 1939 he developed the overall plan for Baku, where he designed the Nagorny Park (1939), with a monument to *Sergey Kirov* (destr. 1991) by the sculptor Pinkhos Sabsay (1893–1980). Il'in was Chief Architect of Leningrad from 1925 to 1928 and of Baku from 1930 to 1936. From 1918 he was director of the City Museum (now the Museum of the History of St Petersburg), Petrograd.

WRITINGS

'Ansambl' v arkhitekture goroda' [The ensemble in city architecture], *Arkhit. SSSR*, 5 (1935), pp. 41–50

'Arkhitekturnyye problemy planirovki Leningrada' [Architectural problems in the layout of Leningrad], *Problemy Arkhitektury*, i/1 (Moscow, 1937), pp. 153–82

'Arkhitekturnyye problemy planirovki Baku' [Architectural problems in the layout of Baku], *Problemy Arkhitektury*, ed. G. Milonov, i/1 (Moscow, 1937), pp. 123–51

'Moy tvorcheskiy put" [My creative path], *Arkhit. Leningrada*, 2 (1938)

BIBLIOGRAPHY

Ye. P. Busyreva: 'Revolyutsiyey prizvannyy' [Called by the Revolution], *Stroitel'stvo & Arkhit. Leningrada*, 11 (1980), pp. 36–40

A. V. IKONNIKOV

Ilion. *See* TROY (i).

Ilkhanid. Dynasty that ruled Iran, Iraq and Anatolia from 1256 to 1353. From 1219, Mongol hordes, commanded originally by Genghis Khan (*reg* 1206–27) and later by members of his family, repeatedly devastated the Iranian world. These campaigns culminated in the sack of Baghdad and the extinction of the ABBASID caliphate in 1258. In the new political order that arose, Iran became a province in a pan-Asiatic empire that at its height comprised much of the Eurasian land mass from Korea to Germany. The Great Khans, descended from Genghis's youngest son Toluy, resided first at Karakorum in Mongolia, and later Beijing. They were supported by three collateral branches: the Golden Horde (*reg* 1226–1502), descended from Genghis's first son Jochi, in southern Russia; the Chaghatayids (*reg* 1227–1370), descended from Genghis's second son, in Central Asia; and the Ilkhanids (*Īl-khān*: 'subordinate khan'), descended from Hulagu (Hülegü; *reg* 1256–65), brother of the Great Khans Qubilay and Mönke, in Iran, Iraq and Anatolia.

The Pax Mongolica imposed on this vast tract of land dramatically facilitated communication between east and west, and Christian missionaries who trekked to the Great Khan's court bearing messages from the pope left vivid accounts of their journeys. For their part, the Mongol khans, especially in Iran, maintained an active correspondence with European rulers, principally in hope of an alliance against the AYYUBID and MAMLUK rulers of Syria and Egypt. Western hopes of converting the Mongols were ill-founded. In religious matters they showed a tolerance remarkable in the medieval period; they themselves practised by turns their ancestral shamanism, Buddhism, Christianity and Islam, following both Sunni and Shiʿite sects. This tolerance created a golden age for Christians and Jews, who repeatedly rose to high administrative office. But the Mongols also imposed their own civil code, the *yasa* (first promulgated by Genghis), which had little in common with the *sharīʿa* code that had traditionally governed Muslim life.

The centre of Ilkhanid power was in north-west Iran, where the fertile uplands were a potent attraction to the still-nomadic Mongol élite. Abaqa (*reg* 1265–82) built a palace on the ruins of a spot already sacred to the Sasanians, TAKHT-I SULAYMAN ('the Throne of Solomon'). Ancient resonances were deliberately exploited by some of the leading Persian intellectuals of the time when the site was decorated with lengthy and carefully chosen quotations from the Persian national epic, the *Shāhnāma* ('Book of kings'). The greatest ruler of the line, Ghazan (*reg* 1295–1304), established his capital at TABRIZ, which became the major international metropolis of the time and a magnet for ambassadors, merchants and artists from most of the known world. An energetic and far-sighted ruler, Ghazan took the momentous decision to embrace Islam and thereby to anchor his own people in Iranian life and culture. He founded a suburb in Tabriz where, in the shadow of his own gigantic tomb, institutions of learning proliferated. He commissioned his vizier RASHID AL-DIN, a physician of Jewish birth, to write a history of the Mongols in the context of a much larger history of the world, the *Jāmiʿ al-tawārīkh* ('Compendium of histories'). Simultaneously, Ghazan reformed the *yasa* to bring it closer to the *sharīʿa* and embarked on an ambitious building programme designed to provide every village in the country with its own mosque, financed by the revenues from the bath (*see* ISLAMIC ART, §II, 6(i)(a)).

Ghazan's brother and successor Uljaytu (Öljeitü; *reg* 1304–16) was an equally lavish patron of architecture who developed SULTANIYYA, a site south-east of Tabriz, as the capital. Its cynosure was the mausoleum of Uljaytu himself (*see* ISLAMIC ART, fig. 48), still one of the finest buildings in Asia. Craftsmen from many areas of the Ilkhanid domains were recruited for this vast project, and on returning home they disseminated the latest fashions and techniques. These vast imperial projects triggered a veritable building boom from 1300 to 1340 that continued for decades thereafter in such cities as Qum, Isfahan, Yazd and Abarquh. The concomitant popularity of Sufi shrines as the focus of local as well as imperial patronage can be seen in such sites as Natanz, Bistam, Ardabil and the shrine of Pir-i Bakran at Linjan near Isfahan (*see* ISLAMIC ART, figs 49 and 77). Ilkhanid architecture largely followed modes established in the Saljuq period (*see* ISLAMIC ART, §II, 5(i)(b)), for example in mausolea and mosque design, but there was a progressive refinement and attenuation of forms, broadly comparable to the transition from Romanesque to Gothic in western Europe. Portals surmounted by paired minarets best express this new trend. Transition zones became less elaborately articulated, while the decorative emphasis shifted from brick patterning to glazed tilework, bringing a dramatic infusion of colour to Iranian architecture (*see* ISLAMIC ART, §II, 9(ii)(b)).

In the arts, pride of place in the Ilkhanid period goes to the book. Ilkhanid scribes and illuminators, especially those of Mosul and Baghdad, rivalled the best artists of the Mamluks and indeed may have laid the foundations for Mamluk work (*see* ISLAMIC ART, §III, 2(iii)(c)). Characteristic of the Ilkhanid school is the use of very large sheets (up to 700×500 mm) of 'Baghdad' paper and corresponding large-scale scripts, especially *muhaqqaq*. The patterns on the gallery vaults of Uljaytu's tomb resemble the frontispieces and carpet pages in manuscripts of the Koran, of which some two dozen have survived. In manuscript painting (*see* ISLAMIC ART, §III, 4(v)(b)), the Mongol interest in science can be seen in the richly illustrated bestiary *Manāfi' al-ḥayawān* ('Usefulness of animals'; Maragha, 1297 or 1299; New York, Pierpont Morgan Lib., MS. M. 500) and al-Biruni's book on calendrical systems *Āthār al-bāqiya* ('Chronology of ancient nations'; 1307–8; Edinburgh U. Lib., Arab. MS. 161), a work that catered to the same interests as the great observatory Hulagu founded at MARAGHA (*c*. 1258). The ferocious battle-scenes from Rashid al-Din's world history (e.g. *see* ISLAMIC ART, fig. 114) are full of Mongol military detail, while the scenes from the Old and New Testaments, the Buddha cycle and Muhammad's life testify to the Mongol curiosity about religion. There was also a sudden upsurge in the production of illustrated copies of the *Shāhnāma*, perhaps in line with the growing commitment by the Mongols to the land they were governing. Several copies, some relatively modest in the scale of their paintings but nevertheless richly illustrated, survive. The masterpiece of Ilkhanid painting is the Great Mongol *Shāhnāma* (dispersed; ex-Demotte), a large manuscript presumably made for the last Ilkhanid, Abu Sa'id (*reg* 1317–35). Of its original 200 or so illustrations, 58 are known (*see* ISLAMIC ART, fig. 115). Full of elements from China and western Europe alike, alive with contemporary allusions and carrying an emotional power never recaptured in later versions of this text, the manuscript expresses at every turn millennial Iranian ideas of royal legitimacy and is therefore an apt metaphor for the resurgence of Iranian national sentiment in later Ilkhanid times.

There was also a steady output of fine pottery (*see* ISLAMIC ART, §V, 4(i)(a)), notably lustre-tiles, overglaze-painted and gilded *lājvardīna* wares (*see* CERAMICS, colour pl. IV, fig. 3) and 'Sultanabad' ceramics with such Chinese motifs as peonies, phoenixes and dragons, but the range and quality of ceramic production was markedly lower than in the previous century. Much the same can be said of metalwork (*see* ISLAMIC ART, §IV, 3(i)(a)), despite the existence of a high-quality centre of production in Fars, in which figural scenes like those in contemporary book-painting were blended with inscription bands that reworked Mamluk modes. The titulature is markedly Iranian, evoking resonances of Solomon and Alexander. Quantities of silks, cottons, linens, woollens, carpets, felts, furs, embroideries and quilting were produced, and one group of textiles with similar selvage construction, paired main warps and gold filé pattern wefts with a silk core, can be assigned to Ilkhanid patronage on the basis of a lampas and compound-weave fabric (Vienna, Dom- & Diözmus.) inscribed with the name of Abu Sa'id (*see* ISLAMIC ART, §VI, 2(ii)(c)).

BIBLIOGRAPHY

D. Wilber: *The Architecture of Islamic Iran: The Il-Khanid Period* (Princeton, 1955/*R* New York, 1969)
L. Golombek: 'The Cult of Saints and Shrine Architecture in the Fourteenth Century', *Near Eastern Numismatics: Iconography, Epigraphy and History: Studies in Honor of George C. Miles* (Beirut, 1974), pp. 419–30
U. Harb: 'Ilkhanidische Stalaktitengewölbe', *Archäol. Mitt. Iran*, suppl. iv (Berlin, 1978)
O. Grabar and S. Blair: *Epic Images and Contemporary History: The Illustrations of the Great Mongol Shah-nama* (Chicago and London, 1980)
A. S. Melikian-Chirvani: 'Le *Shahname*: La Gnose soufie et le pouvoir mongol', *J. Asiat.*, ccxxii (1984), pp. 249–338
D. James: *Qur'āns of the Mamluks* (London, 1988), chaps 4–5
A. E. Wardwell: 'Panni Tartarici: Eastern Islamic Silks Woven with Gold and Silver (13th and 14th Centuries)', *Islam. A.*, iii (1988–9), pp. 95–173
J. L. Abu-Lughod: *Before European Hegemony: The World System, A.D. 1250–1350* (Oxford, 1989)
S. S. Blair: 'The Development of the Illustrated Book in Iran', *Muqarnas*, x (1993), pp. 266–74
——: *Compendium of Chronicles: Rashid al-Din's Illustrated History of the World* (London, 1995)

ROBERT HILLENBRAND

Illouschegg, Franc. *See* JELOVŠEK, FRANC.

Illusionism. In painting, the attempt to make images that seemingly share or extend the three-dimensional space in which the spectator stands. The term is also applied in sculpture, for a presentation of figures that attempts in some way to make them seem alive, and occasionally in architecture, for a presentation of structures that attempts in some way to enhance their dimensions. It was coined by Franz Wickhoff in 1895 and has been used by modernist writers to characterize all methodical attempts to represent, or 'give the illusion of', the visible world. But in current usage it generally denotes work where the intention is that something should seem not so much represented as substantially present.

Such intentions are widespread in sculpture, in work ranging from the statues of ancient Greece—often originally polychromed (*see* STONE, colour pl. VIII, fig. 1)—to Mme Tussaud's wax museum, set up in 1835. The use of the term for a distinct developing tradition is, however, mainly confined to European painting. In painting, three-dimensional illusions tend to lose their hold when the surface, seen closely, yields an identical image to each eye, thus showing its lack of depth: still more so when the spectator moves and the relation of the represented planes fails to change. As a result, illusionist painting falls largely within certain limits of presentation or of imagery. It may be shown to one eye only, in a 'peepshow', or be kept at a distance from the spectator, for instance on a high ceiling, where the two eyes can no longer confidently judge depth. For imagery, the painter may represent a flat surface from which planes jut and recede to a slight depth—the range of effects properly known as *trompe l'oeil*—or alternatively sky and great distance: in both cases the effects of parallax are minimized. The illusion will be stronger if the image is lit in the same way as its location, and in murals it may also share the same architecture, extended into painted vistas. This practice, common in antiquity and in Italian painting from the 15th century, was known in the latter period as *quadratura.*

1. Before *c.* 1450. 2. *c.* 1450–*c.* 1800. 3. After *c.* 1800.

1. BEFORE *c.* 1450. Tales about the lost paintings of ancient Greece show illusionism as a mark of the painter's new power in an age of naturalism. For example, Zeuxis, in the late 5th century BC, is supposed to have painted grapes that birds tried to peck; but when he wished to inspect the work of his rival Parrhasios, the curtain he tried to pluck was itself the painting. Comments by Plato, who deplored these attempts to trick with appearances (*Republic* X.602d), are among the references indicating that illusionistic painting of architecture was used in Greek stage sets, first apparently by Agatharkos for a play by Aeschylus around 430 BC. The mosaicist Sosos, working in the late 3rd century BC, paved the 'unswept room' in Pergamon with *trompe l'oeil* scraps left from a feast (imitation, 2nd century AD; Rome, Vatican, Mus., *see* MOSAIC, fig. 5).

The surviving Roman murals—mostly those buried at Pompeii in AD 79—are thick with illusionistic effects, probably adapted from Greek stage design in order to expand confined interiors. Paintings of the so-called 'First Style' simulate marble, blocks of masonry and columns. The 'Second Style' breaks up these surfaces with seeming windows giving on to vistas of landscape or architecture (e.g. the cubiculum from the villa at Boscoreale, 1st century BC; New York, Met.). Sometimes figures or statuary are introduced, occupying painted ledges or niches. Narrative scenes are enclosed in painted frames. All these features can be seen combined in the House of the Vettii (1st century AD). In other Pompeian mansions, such as the House of the Vestals (1st century BC), shuttered still-life paintings seem to hang from garlanded walls. Architectural features dominate many Roman murals, but the 'garden room' of Livia's villa at Prima Porta (1st century BC; Rome, Mus. N. Romano; *see* WALL PAINTING, colour pl. I, fig. 2) surrounds the spectator with luxuriant foliage, birds and fruit.

Details of Roman murals were preserved in Vitruvius' *On Architecture* (1st century BC). It would seem that illusion was important in the antique enjoyment of painting: Philostratos Lemnios (2nd century AD) wrote lyrically about such 'deceptions', and his grandson Philostratos the younger added: 'To confront objects which do not exist as though they exist, to believe that they do exist, is not this, since no harm can come of it, a suitable and irreproachable means of providing entertainment?' But though Wickhoff first spoke of illusionism in discussing the *Vienna Genesis*, an early 6th-century manuscript, little work from the millennium following Philostratos caters to the taste he describes.

In the late 13th century a renewed interest in solidity led to the painting of *trompe l'oeil* frames around the Assisi frescoes of *Angels* (*c.* 1280), by Cimabue, and the *Legend of St Francis* (*c.* 1300; both Assisi, upper church of S Francesco). Giotto, working in the Arena Chapel in Padua (*c.* 1305–8), initiated grisailles—grey monochromes imitating low relief—and painted, on either side of the central arch, arches that recede concertedly towards a view of the room beyond. Boccaccio wrote of Giotto that whatever he painted 'seemed to be the thing itself, rather than merely resembling it': his innovations made illusion once again a possible and desirable aim for painters.

Over the next century in Italy, pictures were increasingly made in the likeness of recesses or windows opening up imaginary spaces, a development later imitated in the Netherlands. A rule for producing the effect was demonstrated through a carefully presented illusion in 1413, when Brunelleschi first announced his system of artificial perspective by means of a peepshow (untraced). His picture of a church in Florence was viewed from behind, through a small central hole giving on to a mirror that reflected the view back: its sky of burnished silver captured the glare of daylight, so that 'it seemed as if the real thing were seen' according to his biographer Manetti. Masaccio adopted the new system to produce a startlingly powerful architectural recession enclosing the figures in his fresco of the *Trinity* (1427; Florence, S Maria Novella; *see* MASACCIO, fig. 5). The central figures themselves are not, however, foreshortened; to insist on the angle of vision might have lessened their expressive force.

Architectural framing, often continuous with architecture inside the picture, becomes a common feature of the more sophisticated work of the following decades: details jutting from or standing on the ledge of the picture 'window' often link it to its setting. Thus the wing of Jan van Eyck's grisaille Gabriel in his *Annunciation* of 1436 (Madrid, Mus. Thyssen-Bornemisza) casts a shadow beyond the frame of a painted recess, which reflects the supposed statue in its polished back. Filippo Lippi, drawing on van Eyck's unprecedented rendering of textures in oil paint, with its potential for *trompe l'oeil*, introduced the motif of the *cartellino*, an inscribed sheet painted as if pinned to the picture, in the Tarquinia *Madonna* of 1437 (Rome, G.N.A. Ant.) and set a near-tangible fine glass vase before the deeper spaces of his own *Annunciation* (*c.* 1439; Florence, S Lorenzo). In fresco painting, the life-size figures of Andrea del Castagno's *Famous Men and Women* (1449–51; Florence, S Apollonia) seem to step out from niches in a decorative scheme influenced by the current rereading of Vitruvius.

2. *c.* 1450–*c.* 1800.

(i) Large-scale projects. (ii) Small-scale works.

(i) Large-scale projects.

(a) *c.* 1450–*c.* 1600. (b) *c.* 1600–*c.* 1700. (c) *c.* 1700–*c.* 1800.

(a) c. *1450–*c.*1600.* The contrasting depths of a wholly painted environment first stretch to the ceiling overhead in Mantegna's Camera degli Sposi in the Palazzo Ducale, Mantua (1465–74; see fig. 1). Mantegna, elsewhere obsessed with the close-range illusionism of grisailles, showed in this light-hearted virtuoso display the possibilities inherent in opening the ceiling to painted skies. The stationary craning spectator, held at a steady distance, is drawn all the more forcefully upwards by the foreshortenings of figures and of architecture. Such drawing *di sotto in sù* (from below upwards) predominantly lends itself to levity—as here—and awe, or alternatively to gravity and menace, rather than to eliciting sympathy or confronting the viewer directly. Mantegna's innovations, developing on the work of Niccolò Pizzolo (1448–50; destr. 1944) in the Eremitani Church, Padua, were first applied to sacred subjects by Melozzo da Forlì in his decorations (1477–8) for the Santa Casa at Loreto, perching saints and putti within the structure of the dome. Artificial perspective also helped to create imaginary environments in the ingenious *intarsia* (marquetry) covering panels with *trompe l'oeil* contents of cupboards in the *studiolo* of the Palazzo Ducale, Urbino (designed by Francesco di Giorgio, 1476), and the painted apse that seems to extend the architectural

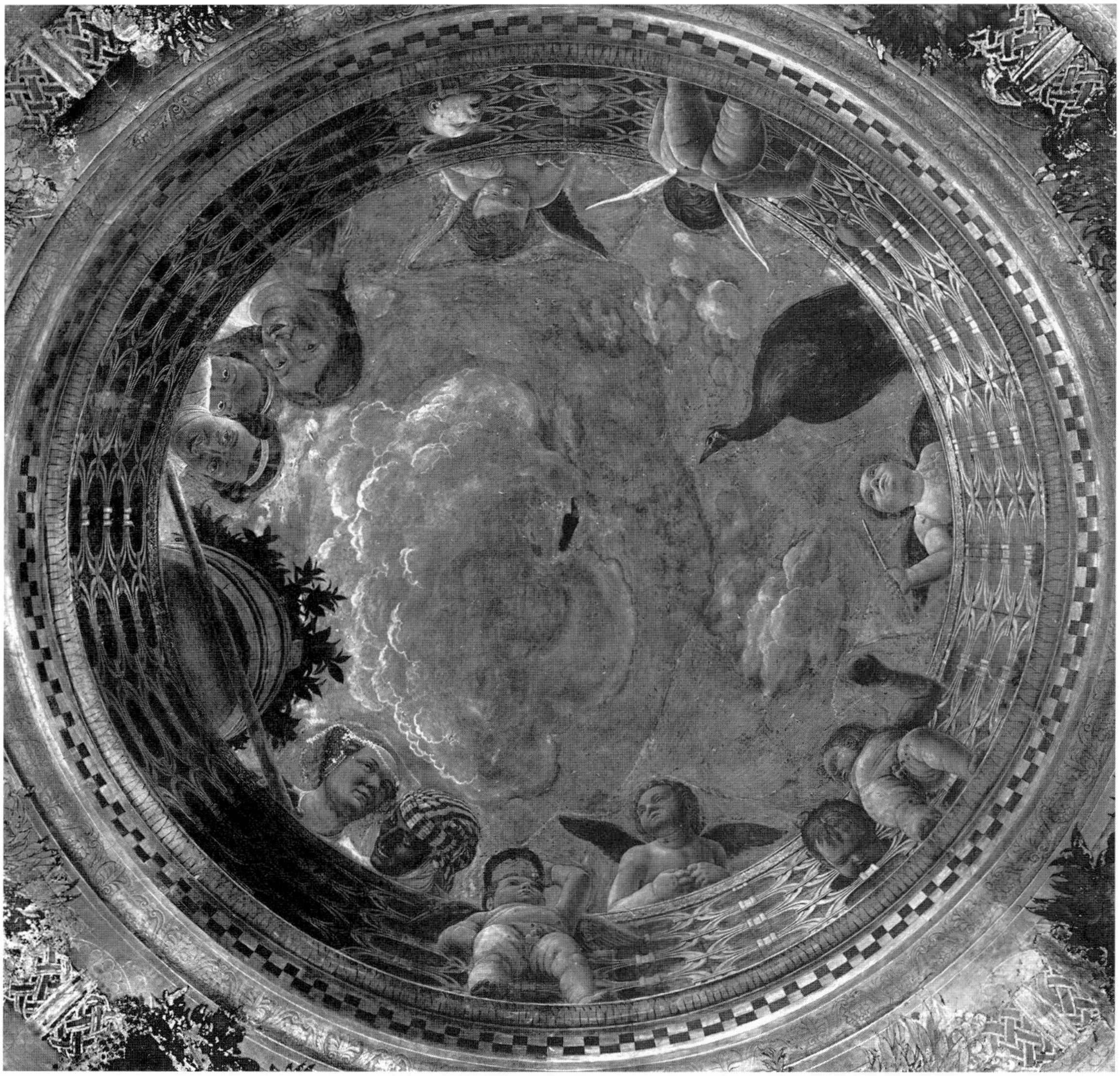

1. Illusionistic ceiling painting (1474) by Andrea Mantegna, Camera degli Sposi, Palazzo Ducale, Mantua

depth of Bramante's S Satiro in Milan (1480). On a miniature scale, a similar spirit informs the fly that seems to have settled on Carlo Crivelli's *SS Catherine and Mary Magdalene* (*c.* 1480–85; London, N.G.).

The full integration of figures—traditionally conveying pathos through postures and gazes—with the involving possibilities of an illusionistic space is seen in Leonardo's *Last Supper* (1490; Milan, S Maria delle Grazie). Often, though, there remains a distinction between the two ways of relating to the spectator; thus the central figures of Michelangelo's Sistine Chapel ceiling (1508–12) are mostly unforeshortened, unlike the supporting *ignudi* and painted architecture, and Raphael in his frescoes for the Galleria Farnese in Rome (1517–19) encloses each narrative incident in a self-contained picture that seems to be framed and hung within the painted architecture. Elsewhere in the Villa Farnesina, its architect Baldassare Peruzzi skilfully opened up the walls of the Sala delle Prospettive (1516–17) with painted vistas showing sites of ancient Rome. The age's most extended illusionism, however, is seen in the very different context of Varallo in Lombardy, where the Milan-based artist Gaudenzio Ferrari between 1505 and 1528 supervised the creation of a progression of permanent tableaux, the sacromonte, showing the life of Christ (*see* SACROMONTE, fig. 1). Constructed sets where painted backdrops seamlessly recede behind polychrome life-size statues, often seen from restricted points of access, engage the spectator's piety with extraordinary directness. This bringing together of contemporary painted techniques with features of medieval effigy-making was amplified here, and repeated elsewhere, until the 18th century.

During the 16th century the main developments of illusionism took place in northern Italy. At Treviso, PORDENONE introduced the distinctly miraculous into ceiling painting, showing *God the Father and Angels* descending into the cathedral dome (1519); in Parma, CORREGGIO made a decisive move further. He dropped architectural painting altogether, creating space instead purely from the lightstruck, animated figures of angels and the risen Christ, seen *di sotto in sù*, in the *Vision of St John on Patmos* (1520–22) at S Giovanni Evangelista. He expanded on this new approach in the tangled angelic ranks spiralling around the *Assumption of the Virgin* (1526–30) in the city's cathedral. Correggio's innovations, imitated by Ferrari at S Maria dei Miracoli, Saronno, in 1534, extended the illusionistic repertory up from the plausible into the imaginative and the transcendent. The imaginative is set in a grotesque tension with the plausible in another notable work of the period, the room of the *Fall of the Giants* (1532–4) in the Palazzo del Tè in Mantua by Giulio Romano. Here the ceiling seems to crash down, under Jove's thunderbolts, not only on the giants but on the spectator's imagination. Giulio's other decorations for the Palazzo make bold use of *di sotto in sù*.

Most work during the later 16th century, the time of the Counter-Reformation, was for private patrons rather than the Church. Francesco Salviati's decorations for the Palazzo Farnese in Rome (begun 1549) teasingly confuse figures painted as if solid with others painted as if woven in tapestry. In Bologna, Pellegrino Tibaldi used a wide range of illusionistic devices to decorate the Palazzo Poggi (1553; now the University), also painting the Poggi at prayer on the walls of their chapel in S Giacomo Maggiore. The most elegant and admired works of the period are Veronese's frescoes (1561) for Palladio's Villa Barbaro at Maser (see colour pl. I, fig. 2), which also exploit a broad repertory of motifs, adding persuasive touches of humour—a little girl peering through a doorway, a broom left leaning against the wall. The practice of ceiling painting was introduced to France by Primaticcio and Niccolò dell'Abbate *c.* 1570, in the Galerie d'Ulysse at Fontainebleau. North of the Alps (where Hans Holbein the younger had made an early importation of architectural illusionism in his designs for the Haus zum Tanz, Basle, *c.* 1520) Friedrich Sustris and Alessandro Scalzi spread the vogue with *commedia dell'arte* characters frescoed on a staircase in Schloss Trausnitz, Landshut (begun 1576; destr. 1961).

Theatre designers had employed architectural illusionism in lost works including sets by Baldassare Peruzzi (sketch, 1515; Turin, Bib. Reale), but the earliest remaining such sets are those designed by Vincenzo Scamozzi in 1585 for Palladio's Teatro Olimpico at Vicenza. The increasing systematization of architectural perspective at this time led to Tommaso Laureti initiating *quadratura* as a distinct practice in Bologna during the 1560s and 1570s. He later worked in the Vatican (e.g. *Triumph of Christian Faith*, 1580s; Rome, Vatican, Sala di Costantino).

(b) c. *1600*–c. *1700.* The much more significant journey from Bologna to Rome of Annibale Carracci in 1595 resulted in a major work, the Galleria Farnese (1597–1604), that does not differ greatly in format from Raphael's work almost a century before: pictures enclosed within a cohesive illusionistic architecture, including grisaille figures and vistas up to the sky. However, Carracci's pupils working after him in or around Rome differed widely in their approaches to ceiling painting. The classicizing Guido Reni distinctly refrained from illusionism, making his *Aurora* (1611; Rome, Pal. Rospigliosi–Pallavicini) a *quadro-riportato*, i.e. a self-contained picture 'repositioned' on the ceiling, while Francesco Albani attempted a unified field of action in the *Fall of Phaethon* (1609; Bassano Romano, Pal. Odescalchi) and Guercino, a later pupil, went for an involving, almost alarming approach in his own *Aurora* (1621; Rome, Villa Ludovisi)—a riposte perhaps to Reni—sending a giant chariot hurtling across a ceiling whose columns seem to fall away in the *quadratura* devised by his Roman collaborator Agostino Tassi. Tassi also worked with Guercino's Bolognese contemporary Domenichino, who sided with the classicizing views advocated by Andrea Sacchi and whose boldest work, the monumental *Four Evangelists* (1624–8) in the pendentives of the dome of S Andrea della Valle, takes the form of *quadri-riportati* set in an orchestrated tension across three-dimensional space. Domenichino in his turn, however, was upstaged by another Carracci pupil, Giovanni Lanfranco, who established himself as the dominant illusionist painter in Rome with his *Assumption of the Virgin* (1625–7; see LANFRANCO, GIOVANNI, fig. 3) in the dome of the same church. The imagery of this is lifted from Correggio's work in Parma, Lanfranco's own native city, but is vastly amplified in scale, in keeping with the larger cosmic conceptions of the age following Galileo and Kepler. Like Domenichino, Lanfranco made the location of his work

subscribe to its meaning, adopting the natural light descending from the dome lantern, where the figure of Christ hovers, to represent supernatural light. Lanfranco went on to work in Naples Cathedral in the 1640s.

Such requisitioning of three-dimensional space to involve the spectator in the intentions of the image, which characterizes much 17th-century art and makes illusionism an important factor in definitions of the Baroque, probably developed in connection with theatrical *mise-en-scène*; it may also be traced in easel paintings of the time, such as Caravaggio's *Supper at Emmaus* (1607; London, N.G.), where an apostle's sharply foreshortened hand seems to reach out to the spectator from the picture. The artist who is often taken to have established the Baroque in Rome, Pietro da Cortona, weaves his free-flying, convulsively busy allegories before and behind the painted architecture of the ceiling of the Palazzo Barberini (1633–9), superseding the distinction between *quadratura* and figure-work in a turbid swirl of energies. His later work for the Pitti Palace, Florence (1640–47) begins to override the distinction between painting and sculpture, with the painted imagery overspilling into moulded stucco clouds and solid figures. Da Cortona's work, brought to France by his pupil Giovanni Francesco Romanelli, helped mould the style of Charles Le Brun in such works as the decorations for the Hôtel Lambert, Paris (*c.* 1650). Dominating all the artistic syntheses of the era was the example and authority of Gianlorenzo Bernini. The great sculptor's use of lighting, location and simulated textures in such works as the *Ecstasy of St Teresa* (1642–52; Rome, S Maria della Vittoria) brings together many developments pioneered by illusionist painters, and it is to his work that the next generation of illusionist painting relates.

Meanwhile in the north the developments of the 16th century were taken up in the 17th by artists such as il Morazzone, who worked in the 1610s and 1620s on ceiling painting and the sacromonte, and by the Bolognese school of *quadraturisti*. The moving force in this was Girolamo Curti, who specialized in enhancing ceilings with imaginary classical architecture (e.g. Sala Urbana, 1630; Bologna, Pal. Com.) and also worked on stage design. His followers Angelo Michele Colonna and Agostino Stanzani Mitelli became celebrated as a team, *figurista* and *quadraturista* respectively, working all over Italy (e.g. Palazzo d'Este, Sassuolo, nr Modena, 1646–7) and also in Spain. Other prominent *quadraturisti* from the Bologna school were Enrico Haffner, Giuseppe Maria Canuti and Andrea Sighizzi (*d* 1684). The latter worked closely with Genoese painters, and during the middle of the 17th century Genoa became an independent centre of the art: its practitioners included Valerio Castello, the artists of the Casa Piola and, most notably, Gregorio de' Ferrari (e.g. the *Four Seasons*, 1688–92; Genoa, Pal. Rosso). It was in Genoa that the painters of the dominant works of late 17th-century Rome were trained.

Giovanni Battista Gaulli and Andrea Pozzo—whose fame has outshone ceiling painters of the 1660s and 1670s such as Giacinto Brandi and the Lucchese team Giovanni Coli and Filippo Gherardi—both worked for the Jesuits: their technical problem of achieving a seemingly seamless ascent into the heavens coincided with the rhetorical programme of Jesuit religion, co-opting a wide diversity of earthly means to promote belief. Gaulli's *Triumph of the Name of Jesus* (1676–9; Rome, Gesù; *see* GAULLI, GIOVANNI BATTISTA, fig. 1) reinvigorates the tradition of Correggio and Lanfranco: it ascends towards the infinite through recessions of radiant figures and clouds, which burst beyond the frame in stucco fixtures and, in a touch of presentation comparable to Bernini, are seen to cast shadows on the giltwork of the vault below—in such areas as have been darkened with a layer of varnish. Pozzo's *Glory of St Ignatius Loyola and the Missionary Work of the Jesuit Order* (1688–94; Rome, S Ignazio), on the other hand, approaches infinity by subordinating its hosts of figures to the most systematic and elaborate *quadratura* ever devised. When seen from the single intended point of view, which is marked by a marble disc on the floor of the nave, the resulting illusion is singularly compelling: as the spectator walks away from the disc the towering architecture seems about to collapse. Pozzo wrote an influential book, *Perspectiva pictorum et architectorum* (Rome, 1693), which explains his working methods and defends his unifocal approach, advising the painter to 'begin your work, with a resolution to draw all the lines thereof to that true point, the glory of God'.

Pozzo's centralizing objectives were not universally shared. In Naples, Lanfranco was succeeded in ceiling painting by Mattia Preti, whose compositions (1661) for the Palazzo Pamphili, Valmontone, scatter, rather than bind, the centres of interest—a development imitated by Francesco Cozza (1605–82) in the Biblioteca Pamphili, Rome (1667–73). Preti's successor in Naples, the vigorous and eclectic Luca Giordano, exported his talents firstly to Venice and later to the Palazzo Medici—Riccardi in Florence. The length of its gallery obliged Giordano in the *Allegory of Human Progress* (1682–3) to bunch the figure-groups that build upwards from the ground of the ceiling's perimeter around a succession of focal points, giving a loping, almost disorientating rhythm to the continuous scene. Giordano subsequently went on to work for the king of Spain in the Escorial (1692–3).

(c) c. *1700*–c. *1800*. At the turn of the 18th century the artistic prestige of Venice was revived by Sebastiano Ricci, whose work was inspired by that of Giordano. Ricci's work in Venice, and that of Jacopo Amigoni, contrasts with the style adopted by Giovanni Battista Piazzetta, whose ceiling paintings (e.g. *Glory of St Dominic*, 1727; Venice, SS Giovanni e Paolo) rely much more heavily on structural understanding and tonal organization, though they too share an approach to composition characterized as Rococo. In this the imagination is directed towards the heavens, not in a single rocketing uplift but in a scattering display of multiple axes and vanishing points. A similar shift in taste informs the innovation by the Galli-Bibbiena family from Bologna of the *scena per angolo*, a stage set that lures the spectator down a multiplicity of tantalizing sideways recessions. These developments, together with an appreciation of the whole tradition from Veronese to Giordano, were combined in the work of the last great figure of Italian illusionism, GIAMBATTISTA TIEPOLO.

Tiepolo's exuberant, light-filled decorative schemes, such as those covering the walls and ceilings of the Palazzo Clerici (1731), Milan, and the Palazzo Labia (1745),

Venice, frequently create vivid, teasing illusions—Antony and Cleopatra, descending a staircase, seem about to enter the Gran Salone of the latter, while in the former the detail of a dwarf leading a monkey by a chain, seemingly part of the painting, is in fact three-dimensional—illusions for the delight of illusions, affirming nothing so much as the power of the artist. He was often assisted in *quadratura* by Girolamo Mengozzi Colonna (*c.* 1688–1766). In 1750 he was called to Würzburg, where he painted a cast of figures representing the *Four Corners of the World* (1750–53; *see* TIEPOLO, (1), fig. 3) around the rim of the vast Kaisersaal in the Residenz, as an earthly interface to the grand cosmic illusion of the opened heavens swaying with receding allegories. Tiepolo went on to work in Spain but had the bitterness shortly before his death in 1770 of seeing his paintings for the church of S Pascal in Aranjuez replaced by those of the Neo-classicist Anton Raphael Mengs.

Italian illusionism had in fact been increasingly in demand abroad since the late 17th century. The version of it recreated by Le Brun in Paris had been taken to England in 1671 by Antonio Verrio, who decorated Chatsworth House, Derbys, and was continued by his assistant Louis Laguerre (e.g. Petworth House, W. Sussex, *c.* 1715). Sebastiano Ricci's nephew Marco Ricci and his pupil Giovanni Battista Pellegrini went to England in 1708 to work for the Earl of Manchester, and in 1712 Sebastiano followed them, producing the ceiling painting of the *Resurrection* (1721; London, Chelsea Hospital). The example of Verrio and Laguerre was, however, inspiring native painters to illusionist work (e.g. William Kent's decorations of 1722–7 for Kensington Palace, London) and when James Thornhill was chosen for the decoration of the cupola of St Paul's Cathedral (1714–17; see colour pl. V) Sebastiano returned to Venice in dudgeon. Elsewhere the Galli-Bibienas had started to export their applications of *quadratura* to stage design in the 1670s and remained a dominant influence on scenography in central and southern Europe for over a century. Francesco Solimena, after Giordano the leading painter in Naples, was in demand internationally for work that, while decorative in effect, maintained a firm sense of structure. His pupil Corrado Giaquinto later took a sweetened variety of the same product to Madrid (e.g. in the Palacio Real, 1759–62).

The main areas where the illusionist tradition took root, however, were Austria and Bavaria. *Quadratura* was brought to Austria in the later 17th century by the Schor family, some of whom had worked with Cortona and Bernini. Johann Michael Rottmayr also brought an Italian training to the Habsburg dominions in masterly fresco cycles ranging from Schloss Frain (1695), Vranov, Moravia, to the Karlskirche (1725–30), Vienna. The arrival of Pozzo in Vienna in 1703 to decorate the Jesuit college church (1703–9) was naturally a stimulus to developments. Ceiling painting took its place within the German-speaking world as a contribution to the *Gesamtkunstwerk*, the encompassing work of art that was the ambition of many aristocratic and ecclesiastical patrons of the time, in which painting, sculpture and architecture were fused, often by means of intricately curvaceous stuccowork. The frescoes of the Bavarian Cosmas Damian Asam, who with his brother Egid Quirin Asam was the most celebrated exponent of the form, often replicate this intricate framing in the complexity of their unfolding narratives (e.g. at Weltenburg, SS Georg und Martin, 1717–21).

Apart from Pozzo's example, many Austrians learnt from another visitor to Vienna, Francesco Solimena; these included Daniel Gran and Paul Troger. Gran was a consummate master of presentation, using classicizing imagery to glorify the Habsburgs (e.g. at Vienna, Österreich. Nbib., 1726–30). Troger, in frescoes including the dome at Stift Altenburg (1733–4), added a Venetian richness of colour and light. The slightly younger Bartolomeo Altomonte worked along similar lines to them.

All these artists, the leading figures among a wealth of practitioners in Austria and Bavaria, maintained characteristics associated with the Baroque, co-opting the spectator into an involvement with religious or dynastic exaltation. A feature that is distinctive to central Europe, however, is the aiming of the image at an oblique, not a central viewpoint. Thus the *quadratura* dome painted (1733) on the ceiling of St Joseph, Obořiště, Czech Republic, staggers almost crazily away from the centre of gravity, and Asam's ceiling (1734) of the Marian prayer-hall at Ingolstadt is an anamorphosis painted to continue the uprights of the altar wall when seen from the door. In the work of Johann Georg Bergmüller, the director of the Augsburg academy from 1730, firm, stocky figures paradoxically inhabit a space splayed to the limits of coherence by these oblique viewpoints (e.g. Steingaden, St Johann Baptist, begun 1742). The direction is pursued by Franz Josef Spiegler, who sends the different axes of approach to the vault at Zwiefalten (1751) spinning up into a dizzy spiral heaven, and by Matthäus Günther, Bergmüller's successor at Augsburg, in the almost equally extreme and disorientating *SS Peter and Paul Driving out Evil Spirits* (1774) at Gotzens, Tyrol. Likewise, Johann Jakob Zeiller's frescoes at Ottobeuren (1763) are designed to move with the moving spectator.

Alongside this interest in eccentricity, other German ceiling-painters of the mid-18th century, such as Johann Baptist Zimmermann, produced work that is airy, diversified and innocuously fantastical (e.g. at Die Wies, 1750). The rich profusion of Rococo decoration in central Germany at this time also includes the work of Johann Zick and the Genoese Carlo Carlone. Further north, Antoine Pesne supplied the Prussian king with illusionistic murals at Schloss Charlottenburg (1740s), and Jakob de Wit introduced ceiling painting to the Netherlands. Meanwhile in the Habsburg dominions the Baroque tradition was continued by Johann Lukas Kracker in Bohemia, and above all by the numerous vast frescoes of Franz Anton Maulbertsch, which reinterpret the illusionistic repertory with a singular mystical emotionality. Nevertheless Maulbertsch, in common with most of the leading painters of central Europe in the late 18th century, eventually adapted his vision to the oncoming Neo-classicism. This new style, with its ideals of simplicity and sobriety, was antithetical to the *quadratura* tradition. Large-scale decorative work, of the sort produced by the Genoese Domenico and Giuseppe Valeriani (e.g. Stupinigi, Pal. Mauriziana, 1733) and Carlo Carlone (Villa Lechi, nr Brescia, 1745), continued on certain levels, accommodating the new desire for restraint in the pastoral decorations (1784) of the pavilion of the Comtesse de Provence at Montreuil; but large-scale illusion was henceforth no longer the object of artistic ambition in Europe.

(ii) Small-scale works. Objects collected and observed, a common concern in northern European art, have been an occasion for *trompe l'oeil* at least since the Master of Mary of Burgundy, or an assistant, painted flowers as if with stems woven into the vellum of a Book of Hours (*c.* 1480; Kraków, Czartoryski Lib.). Independent oil paintings of such objects are often taken to date from the *Still-life with Dead Partridge* of 1504 by Jacopo de' Barbari, a Venetian working in the ambit of Dürer. Below Barbari's partridge, jutting from the same wall, is a *cartellino* in the manner popularized by Antonello da Messina: the flatness of walls and paper have ever since repeatedly invited *trompe l'oeil* treatment. Another feature of Italian painting, the niche, gives an illusionistic setting to early still-lifes such as those of Juan Sánchez Cotán, working in Toledo *c.* 1600, or the Dutch flower-pieces of Ambrosius Bosschaert the elder.

The distinction between levels—walls and paper, two dimensions and three, appearance and reality, transience and the enduring, man's making and God's—the question, in effect, 'What is true?', is the theme contemplatively explored in a countless number of 17th-century still-lifes or *vanitates*, often revolving around a repertory of drawn curtains; tempting, savourable dishes; dark recesses; failing candles; skulls. Conversely, it may be the mere pretext for a bravura display of skill, as in Wallerant Vaillant's *Letter Rack* (?1658; Berlin, Staatl. Museen), the first of an enduringly popular theme. At the same time, however, *trompe l'oeil* was being approached in a scientific spirit of analysis and demonstration. Investigators of perspective following Brunelleschi and Alberti, such as Jacopo Vignola (1583), had codified anamorphosis, the stretching of an image across a plane to produce a familiar likeness when seen from a tangential viewpoint, and Samuel van Hoogstraten applied this to the problem of presenting three-dimensionality. Van Hoogstraten, a Dutchman who wrote a theoretical work about painting—evincing, incidentally, a common northern distrust of Italian ceiling painting—also executed straightforward *trompe l'oeils*, such as the *Head of a Man at a Window Trellis* (1653; Vienna, Ksthist. Mus.; *see* HOOGSTRATEN, SAMUEL VAN, fig. 1), but is mainly celebrated for constructions such as the *Peepshow* (*c.* 1657–61) in the National Gallery in London, which splays a Dutch interior across the insides of a box so as to recombine into a compelling sensation of depth when viewed from either of two holes.

The limits of *trompe l'oeil* as a distinctive form were most thoroughly explored by another Dutchman, Cornelis Gysbrechts (*fl* later 17th century), who worked for the Danish court. Gysbrechts's oeuvre, covering the range of customary motifs—loose papers, curtains, cupboards of curios, woodgrain—sometimes turns painting into a sardonic commentary on itself, as in the picture of skull and gutted candle symbolizing *Vanitas* (Boston, MA, Mus. F.A.) that seems to be ripping away from its own stretchers, or the unadorned, delightfully unsatisfactory *Turned-over Canvas* (Copenhagen, Stat. Mus. Kst). He also seems to have introduced the *chantourné*, a painted board cut to the edges of the objects represented, to stand freely in the room as they would: e.g. *Easel* (Copenhagen, Stat. Mus. Kst). This form was popular in France at the turn of the 18th century, as was the *devant de cheminée*, an illusionistic screen to hide the hearth in summer; notable examples of this were painted by Chardin and the animalist Jean-Baptiste Oudry.

Having grown to fill its tight natural confines, the genre of *trompe l'oeil*, essentially an immediate transaction between skill and visual sensation, is neither truly characterized by development nor reliant on tradition after this time in Europe. It was a widely popular part of visual culture in the 18th century, particularly in France, in work including the grisailles of Louis-Léopold Boilly, the *camaïeux* (also monochromes simulating low relief but in colours other than grey) of Piat-Joseph Sauvage and the remarkable stags' heads of Jean-Jacques Bachelier. But it began to be slighted in estimation at about the time the epithet, with its imputation of deceit, was coined *c.* 1807. Thereafter the innocent pleasures of *trompe l'oeil* were not considered worthy of the attention of serious artists in Europe.

3. AFTER *c.* 1800. It was in the USA that illusionism was taken up with fresh enthusiasm in the late 18th century. Charles Willson Peale's *Staircase Group* (*c.* 1795; Philadelphia, PA, Mus. A.) of two of his sons framed in a doorway—a picture to which George Washington politely bowed in passing by—showed in a sensational way what could be done with painting. The lead was taken up by his son Raphaelle Peale in the obsessively rendered *trompe l'oeil* towel, teasingly hiding a bather, in *After the Bath—a Deception* (1823; Kansas City, MO, Nelson–Atkins Mus. A.), and during the 19th century many little-known painters explored the possibilities of *trompe l'oeil*, creating a sizeable niche for it in the national visual culture. The achievements that dominate the field, however, are those of the 'Philadelphia school'—William Harnett, John F. Peto and John Haberle. The first of these, scrupulously restraining himself to harmonious arrangements of objects that could be flawlessly rendered, such as *Music and Good Luck* (1888; New York, Met., see fig. 2), has become known as the definitive exponent of the whole *trompe l'oeil* genre. Peto's letter racks and Haberle in paintings such as a *Bachelor's Drawer* (New York, Middendorf priv. col.) exploit rather the form's potential for a kind of teasing drollery.

In 20th-century painting uses of illusionistic motifs have been legion. They range from the seeming relief passages of caning etc, introduced by Picasso and Braque into paintings *c.* 1911 to establish the status of the artwork as an object in its own right, to the *trompe l'oeil* ants with which Dalí hoped to subvert psychic composure. But the general purposes informing the often very knowing quotations from the illusionistic repertory have usually had little to do with illusion as an artistic aim. The most ambitious recent development—in scale at least—has been the simulation of architecture on the unbroken walls of city blocks, pioneered by Richard Haas on sites such as the corner of Greene and Prince Streets, New York (1975). Meanwhile the continuing appeal of illusionism for inspiring piety can be seen in the common use for popular devotional images of diffractional foil, a perspex surface the corrugations of which offer variations of the image

2. Illusionistic *trompe l'oeil* painting by William Harnett: *Music and Good Luck*, oil on canvas, 1016×762 mm, 1888 (New York, Metropolitan Museum of Art)

adjusted to bifocal vision, virtually solving the long-standing problem of representing three dimensions in two.

BIBLIOGRAPHY

EWA: 'Prospettici e quadraturisti'
Philostratos: *Imagines*
A. Pozzo: *Perspectiva pictorum et architectorum* (Rome, 1693); Eng. trans. by J. James as *Rules and Examples of Perspective Proper for Painters and Architects* (London, 1707)
W. von Hartel and F. Wickhoff, eds: 'Der Wiener Genesis', *Jb. Ksthist. Samml. Allhöch. Ksrhaus.*, xv/xvi (1895/*R* Graz, 1970)
E. Waterhouse: *Baroque Painting in Rome: The Seventeenth Century* (London, 1937)
E. Feinblatt: 'Jesuit Ceiling Decoration', *A.Q.* [Detroit], x (1947), pp. 239–50
P. Gammelbo: *Study on the Gysbrechts* (Copenhagen, 1955)
A. Blunt: 'Illusionistic Decoration in Central Italian Painting', *J. Royal Soc. A.*, cvii (1959), pp. 309ff
M.-C. Gloton: *Trompe l'oeil et décor plafonnant dans les églises romaines de l'âge baroque* (Rome, 1965)
M. Kitson: *The Age of Baroque* (London, 1966)
J. White: *The Birth and Rebirth of Pictorial Space* (London, 2/1967)
I. Mussa: 'L'architettura illusionistica nelle decorazioni romane', *Capitolium* (Aug/Sept 1969), pp. 41–88
A. Frankenstein: *The Reality of Appearance* (New York, 1970)
M. H. Pirenne: *Optics, Painting and Photography* (Cambridge, 1970), pp. 79–94 [Pozzo]
Gray is the Color: An Exhibition of Grisaille Paintings, XIIth to XXth Centuries (exh. cat. by J. P. Marandel, Houston, TX, Inst. A., 1973)
M. Battersby: *Trompe l'Oeil: The Eye Deceived* (New York, 1974)
M. L. d'Otrange Mastal: *Illusion in Art* (New York, 1975) [thorough survey of *trompe l'oeil*]
J. Shearman: 'Correggio's Illusionism', *La prospettiva rinascimentale. Codificazioni e trasgressioni: Atti de convegno di studi: Milan, 1977*, pp. 281–94
M. Fagiolo and S. Caradini: *L'effimero barocco: Strutture della festa nella Roma del seicento* (Rome, 1977–8)
L. Bellosi: 'La rappresentazione dello spazio', *Ricerche spaziali e tecnologiche*, ed. G. Previtali (Turin, 1980), 1/iv of *Storia dell'arte italiana*, pp. 5–39
N. Spinosa: 'Spazio infinito e decorazione barocca', *Dal cinquecento all' ottocento*, ed. F. Zeri (Turin, 1981), 2/ii of *Storia dell'arte italiana*, pp. 280–343 [with bibliog.]
M. Kubovy: *Psychology, Perspective and Reality in Art* (Cambridge, 1986)

□

Illustratore. *See* MASTERS, ANONYMOUS, AND MONOGRAMMISTS, §I; ILLUSTRATORE.

Ilovšek, Franc. *See* JELOVŠEK, FRANC.

Ilp'yŏnun. *See* SIN YUN-BOK.

'Imad al-Hasani. *See* MIR 'IMAD.

Image, Selwyn (*b* Bodiam, E. Sussex, 17 Feb 1849; *d* London, 21 Aug 1930). English designer. He was educated at Marlborough College and New College, Oxford, where he studied drawing under John Ruskin. Although he took Holy Orders in 1873, he continued to practise as a designer and eventually gave up his clerical duties in 1882, the year in which Arthur Mackmurdo founded the Century Guild of Artists, London. In 1883 Mackmurdo and Image opened the Century Guild Workshops. Image painted panels and inscriptions and designed inlaid decoration for furniture made by the Guild and also produced the title-page woodcut for its magazine *The Hobby Horse*, first published in 1884, which he co-edited from 1886 to 1892. The Guild itself was dissolved in 1888. He undertook design commissions in several fields—stained glass, typography, mosaic and embroidery (for the Royal School of Needlework). He also became active within the Art Workers' Guild, London, of which he became master in 1900. In the same year he began working for the Glasgow furniture manufacturers Wylie & Lochhead, and helped to establish a fashion for plain, leaded glass. He was appointed the first Slade Professor of Fine Art at Oxford in 1910, his tenure to run from 1913 to 1916, and in 1915 he was one of the founder-members of the Design and Industries Association.

BIBLIOGRAPHY

A. Mackmurdo, ed.: *Selwyn Image Letters* (London, 1932)
F. MacCarthy: *All Things Bright and Beautiful* (London, 1972)
J. Cooper: *Victorian and Edwardian Furniture and Interiors* (London, 1987)

JOHN MAWER

Image d'Epinal. Cheap woodcut print, coloured by hand or stencil. Such prints were made in a number of French provincial towns and take their name from the major 19th-century centre of production, where prints are still made. The family dynasties of publishers who made and marketed them are part of the long tradition of French *imagerie populaire*. The 19th-century prints from Epinal treat secular as well as religious subjects; the latter predominated in the 18th century. Secular subjects were produced in large numbers during the French Revolution, by publishers such as Jean-Baptiste Letourmy (in Orleans) and André Basset (in the Rue St Jacques, Paris). Napoleonic themes and portraits became increasingly important particularly during the Second Empire (1852–70). At this time an imagery specifically designed for children emerged, and the Pellerin family built thir business in Epinal into an international success.

See also POPULAR PRINTS and WOODCUT, §II, 5.

BIBLIOGRAPHY

P. L. Duchartre and R. Saulnier: *L'Imagerie parisienne: L'Imagerie de la rue Saint Jacques* (Paris, 1944)
J. Mistler: *Epinal et l'Imagerie Populaire* (Paris, 1961)
J. Adhémar: *L'Imagerie Populaire française* (Paris and Milan, 1968)
French Popular Imagery: Five Centuries of Prints (exh. cat., London, Hayward Gal., 1974)
M. Shapiro: 'Courbet and Popular Imagery: An Essay on Realism and Naïveté', *Modern Art* (1979)
F. Demange, ed.: *Images de la Révolution: L'Imagerie Populaire orléanaise à l'époque révolutionnaire* (Paris, 1989)
N. Garnier: *L'Imagerie Populaire française. Gravures en taille-douce et en taille d'épargne* (1990), i of Réunion des musée nationaux (Paris, 1990–)

□

Imaginistgruppen [Swed.: 'Imaginist group']. Swedish Surrealist group, founded *c.* 1945, which grew out of the short-lived MINOTAURGRUPPEN. Its founders were C. O. Hultén, Max Walter Svanberg and Anders Österlin (*b* 1926), and later its members included the artists Gösta Kriland (1917–89), Bertil Lundberg (*b* 1922), Bengt Orup (*b* 1916), Bertil Gadō (*b* 1916), Lennart Lindfors and Gudrun Åhlberg-Kriland. The Imaginistgruppen followed the example of the Minotaurgruppen by using the styles and techniques characteristic of Surrealism, as in Hultén's *Beach Statue* (*frottage*, 1948; Malmö, Kstmus.). In 1947 the group founded its own publishing house in Malmö, and that year it produced a collection of *frottages*, *Drömmar ur bladens händer* ('Dreams from the hands of leaves'), by Hultén. *Första fasen* ('First phase'), a text on Imaginism written by Svanberg in 1948, was included in the catalogue of an exhibition of his work in Göteborg in 1949. In this 'manifesto', the first part of his *Deklarationer om imaginism i tre utvecklingsfaser* ('Declarations on Imaginism in three phases'), Svanberg discussed the crucial role played by imagination, stressing the free and revolutionary nature of Imaginist art. He claimed that the image, which contained disparate elements, was central and that its realization required the overthrow of traditional art forms, as these were based on reality. These were all familiar Surrealist ideas, and Svanberg developed them further in *Andra fasen* ('Second phase') (1950) and *Tredje fasen* ('Third phase') (1952), so becoming the group's chief theorist. The Imaginistgruppen participated in the Surrealist exhibition held at the Galerie Aleby in Stockholm in 1949, and Imaginistgruppen exhibitions were held in Stockholm in 1951, in Malmö and Göteborg in 1952, at the Galerie de Babylone in Paris in 1953 and at Lund University in 1954. In 1950 the publishing house issued an album of eight lithographs by Svanberg. Svanberg left the group in 1953, claiming to be the only true Imaginist, but the group continued in existence until 1956.

PRINTS

C. O. Hultén: *Drömmar ur bladens händer*, preface M. W. Svanberg (Malmö, 1947)

BIBLIOGRAPHY

C. O. Hultén: Arbeten, 1938–1968 (exh. cat. by C. Dotremont and others, Lund, Ksthall, 1968)

J. Pierre: *Max Walter Svanberg et le règne féminin* (Paris, 1975)

Max Walter Svanberg (exh. cat., Malmö, Ksthall, 1979), pp. 7–12, 21–8 [incl. repr. of *Första fasen*]

□

Imai, Kenji (*b* Tokyo, 11 Jan 1895; *d* Tokyo, 20 May 1987). Japanese architect and teacher. He graduated from Waseda University, Tokyo, in 1919 and immediately began to teach architecture there, continuing to do so until 1965. From 1926 to 1927 he travelled in Europe and studied modern architectural trends in the USSR, Scandinavia, Italy and Spain; he also met Le Corbusier, Ernst May and others. Imai was profoundly impressed by the works of Antoni Gaudí and subsequently played an important role in introducing them to Japan. While his early work as an architect, for example the Library at Waseda University (1925), Tokyo, was Scandinavian in style, Imai was increasingly influenced by Gaudí's work, especially after 1948 when he converted to Catholicism following the death of his Christian wife. This influence is revealed in such works as the Memorial for 26 Martyred Japanese Saints (1962), Nagasaki, and Tōkadō Imperial Palace (1966), Tokyo, which are highly sculptural with Gaudíesque tiling, leaving visible traces of the artist's hands on the surface. Like Tōgo Murano and Takamasa Yoshizaka, who had also trained at Waseda University, Imai consistently promoted an Expressionist approach to architecture. He also introduced the work of Rudolf Steiner to Japan. He was not a prolific architect; his importance lay more in his role as an architectural teacher and for the contribution he made in developing Japanese understanding of modern European architecture.

BIBLIOGRAPHY

I. Kurita, ed.: *Take Motō, Imai Kenji*, Gendai Nihon kenchikuka zenshū [Complete collection of modern Japanese architects], v (Tokyo, 1971)

KATSUYOSHI ARAI

Imai, Toshimitsu (*b* Kyoto, 6 May 1928). Japanese painter. After graduating from Musashi High School he painted impastoed figurative works in a Fauvist style. He went to France in 1952 and in 1955 met the French critic Michel Tapié (1909–87). His style underwent a dramatic change to *Art informel*. His paintings in the late 1950s were aggressively and intensely textured, with vivid colours of red, yellow and black, and a fierce sense of vibration over the entire pictorial surface. However, the grounds of the paintings had the serenely beautiful texture of Chinese porcelain. This East Asian sensibility confirmed Imai's importance for the *Art informel* artists, who were searching for an alternative aesthetic to that of Western modernity. Imai was also an influential activist and after visiting Japan in 1957 with Tapié, Sam Francis and Georges Mathieu, helped to arouse interest in *Art informel* in Japan. His flamboyant gestural paintings of the 1960s were mainly red, with thickly applied paint and dripping lines running in spiral and radial directions. From the 1970s he moved between Japan and Paris. He began to include words in his *peintures-poèmes* and emphasized spontaneous creativity. In 1982 his work changed radically again, using elements of classic Japanese patterns from the early part of the Edo period (1615–1867). Imai developed these into the *Flower, Bird, Wind and Moon* series, characterized by the decorative qualities of the screens of the Rinpa school. Such works as the *Fires of Hell* (acrylic on canvas, 2.2×10 m, 1982; priv. col., see 1982 exh. cat.) combined energetically splattered paint with the elongated proportions of the traditional screens.

WRITINGS

Imai (exh. cat., Paris, Rodolphe Stadler, 1982)

BIBLIOGRAPHY

I. Hariu: *Toshimitsu Imai* (Tokyo, 1975)

Imai, 1950–1989 (exh. cat., Osaka, N. Mus. A., 1989)

AKIRA TATEHATA

Imami [Īmāmī]. Persian family of painters. Working in Isfahan in the later 19th century, they specialized in varnished and painted ('lacquered') objects (*see* ISLAMIC ART, §VIII, 10). Signed works provide the names of some 15 members of the family. Their work is generally confined to the traditional themes of birds and flowers. Their style is less original than that of their contemporaries, the ISFAHANI family, but equally fine in technique. A casket made by Nasrallah Imami in 1865–6 (Tehran, Nigaristan Mus., 75.6.17) includes his typical motif of the hazelnut. A similar floral subject is depicted on the magnificent mirror-case (London, V&A, 922-1869) painted by Riza Imami in 1866 for the Paris Exposition of 1867. Muhammad al-Husayni al-Imami worked in the traditional style in the 1870s and attained the rank of Painter Laureate (Pers. *naqqāsh-bāshī*). Javad al-Imami, who is also known by the name ʿAbd al-Raji, painted a fine spectacle case (1867; Tehran, Mus. Dec. A., 7624) and a penbox (1893; Berne, Hist. Mus., 24-1912), both decorated with flowers and birds.

Many of the later members of the family, such as Mustafa al-Imami, worked in an archaizing style associated with the Safavid dynasty (*reg* 1501–1732). These pieces, such as a mirror-case (New York, Met.), were not only decorated with the languid figures typical of the Safavid style but sometimes provided with spurious inscriptions and dates to the reign of ʿAbbas I (*reg* 1588–1629). Members of the family also painted fine but anachronistic and irrelevant paintings to fill blank spaces or even cover the text in earlier manuscripts, thereby increasing their sale value.

BIBLIOGRAPHY

B. W. Robinson: 'Persian Painting in the Qajar Period', *Highlights of Persian Art*, ed. R. Ettinghausen and E. Yarshater (Boulder, 1979), pp. 331–62

M. A. Karimzada Tabrizi: *Ahvāl u āthār-i naqqāshān-i qadīm-i īrān* [The lives and art of old painters of Iran] (London, 1985), nos 239, 716, 932, 947, 966, 997, 1030, 1062, 1097, 1154, 1228, 1316, 1395 and 1427

L. S. Diba: 'Lacquerwork', *The Arts of Persia*, ed. R. W. Ferrier (New Haven and London, 1989), pp. 243–54

B. W. Robinson: 'Qajar Lacquer', *Muqarnas*, vi (1989), pp. 131–46

□

Imana, Gil (*b* Sucre, 1933). Bolivian painter, sculptor and teacher. From the age of 13 he studied at the Academia de Bellas Artes and in the workshop of Juan Rimsa in Sucre. An extremely active painter, Imana had 58 one-man shows and numerous collective exhibitions after 1950 in cities in Bolivia, Latin America, Europe and the Middle East. He was a member of the artists' group Generación del 52, and in Sucre he was also the founder of the Anteo group of poets, writers and artists. His left-wing ideology linked him to the National Revolution of 1952, within the group of so-called 'social' painters. His subject-matter of social protest centred around the human figure, in particular woman, singly or in groups, with a slight landscape element, and frequently taking the theme of motherhood. He not only painted in oil and acrylic on canvas but also executed frescoes or acrylic murals, such as *The Telephone Company* (1956; Sucre) and *Medicine* (1983; La Paz, Medic. Coll.), and others in Lima and Callao, Peru. In addition, he was a draughtsman and produced graphic work and occasionally sculpture, such as *Crucifix* (1977; La Paz, priv. col.). Imana was the director of the schools of fine art in Sucre and La Paz, as well as a professor in Mérida, Venezuela. He was married to Inés Córdoba, a Bolivian ceramicist and textile artist.

BIBLIOGRAPHY

Art of Latin America since Independence (exh. cat., New Haven, Yale U. A.G.; Austin, U. TX, A. Mus.; 1966)

L. Castedo: *Historia del arte Ibero-americano*, ii (Madrid, 1988)

P. Querejazu: *La pintura boliviana del siglo XX* (Milan, 1989)

PEDRO QUEREJAZU

Imbonate, Anovelo da. *See* ANOVELO DA IMBONATE.

Imera. *See* HIMERA.

Imhof, Heinrich Max (*b* Bürglen, Uri, 13 May 1795; *d* Rome, 4 May 1869). Swiss sculptor. He trained under Franz Abart (1769–1863) and then, with the support of the German geologist and scholar Gottfried Ebel, spent some time in Zurich. There, the Crown Prince of Prussia, later Frederick William IV, King of Prussia, took notice of Imhof and commissioned the sculptor to execute a portrait of him in alabaster (untraced; plaster version, 1819, Altdorf, Hist. Mus.). Through the patronage of Ebel and the Prince, Imhof was able to complete his training in Stuttgart under Johann Heinrich Dannecker. He was soon commissioned to execute a copy of Bertel Thorvaldsen's *Night*, justifying a trip to Rome that he made in 1824 with the Swiss sculptor Johann Jakob Oechslin (1802–73). Unlike the latter, Imhof settled in Rome to pursue the difficult career of the émigré sculptor. Supervised by Thorvaldsen, he executed his first group piece, *Eros and Psyche* (1825), a work steeped in Neo-classicism. The exhibitions organized by the Römischer Kunstverein allowed him to expand his circle of patrons: Frederick William IV, to whom Imhof's *David and Goliath* (1827; plaster version, Berne, Kstmus.; marble version, untraced) much appealed, commissioned him to execute another version of *Eros and Psyche* in marble (Zurich, priv. col.); Ludwig I, King of Bavaria, commissioned from him a colossal bust of *Maximilian I, Elector of Bavaria*, for the German pantheon Walhalla, near Regensburg (*in situ*); and Ludwig I's son, Otto, King of Greece (*reg* 1832–62), summoned Imhof to teach in Athens from 1835 to 1836. Later, Imhof began work on a series of groups with Old Testament subjects, including *Hagar and Ishmael* (1845), which was purchased by a member of the nobility and donated to the Bernische Kunstgesellschaft in Berne. *Eve Before the Fall* (1862–4; Berne, Kstmus.), a life-size work in marble, was acquired to decorate the new Bundeshaus in Berne. Imhof finally achieved official recognition in Switzerland when, in 1865, he was commissioned to create a monument to *William Tell*, to be erected in Altdorf; the work, however, remained unfinished (some drawings, Altdorf, Staatsarchv Uri).

BIBLIOGRAPHY

D. Ulrich: *Die 'Eva vor dem Sündenfall' im Kunstmuseum Bern: Ein spätes Werk von Heinrich Imhof (1795–1869), schweizer Bildhauer in Rom* (diss., U. Zurich, 1988)

P.-A. Jaccard: 'La Lignée germano-romaine: Imhof et Oechslin', *La Sculpture* (1992), vii of A. Helv., ed. F. Deuchler (Disentis, 1987–93), pp. 171–6 [each vol. in Ger., Fr., It. and Romansch]

□

Imhoff. German family of merchants, patrons and collectors. First documented in Nuremberg in the late 14th century, the Imhoffs quickly married into the city's older families and initiated lucrative trading enterprises. From their mercantile offices in southern Germany and Venice, the various family firms rapidly branched out to the rest of Europe. Konrad (*d* 1486) developed silver mines in Saxony. The Imhoffs were one of the great patrician families of Nuremberg during the 15th and 16th centuries. Among their artistic donations to Nuremberg churches, those to St Lorenz (*see* NUREMBERG, §IV, 2) were the most notable. For example Konrad Imhoff (*d* 1449) donated the *Coronation of the Virgin* (1418–22), the artist of which was christened the Master of the Imhoff Altar (also known as the Master of the Deichsler Altar). Hans Imhoff IV (*d* 1499) presented the *St Roch* altar (*c.* 1490) and Adam Kraft's monumental stone tabernacle (1493–6; for illustration, *see* LATE GOTHIC), one of the most famous works of German Late Gothic art.

In the Rochusfriedhof (1518), the cemetery of the parish of St Lorenz, Konrad Imhoff (1463–1519) founded the Rochuskapelle (Imhoff family chapel). A three-bay, single-nave chapel designed by Hans Beheim the elder, it was erected by Paulus Beheim (*fl* 1520–59) and dedicated in July 1521. Wolf Traut painted the wings of the high altar (1521), and Hans Burgkmair I and Sebastian Loscher (*fl* 1510; *d* 1548) created the *Rosary* altar (1522) donated by Konrad Imhoff's children. Veit Hirschvogel produced the stained-glass windows after Dürer's designs. Several paintings by Dürer were replaced in the 17th century with copies by Georg Gärtner I, among others.

Willibald Imhoff (1519–80) built up one of the great Renaissance art collections, based on his inheritance and repurchase of a significant portion of his grandfather Willibald Pirckheimer's holdings of works by Dürer. By 1580 his Dürer collection consisted of at least 10 paintings, numerous watercolours, 29 books filled with woodcuts, engravings and (probably) drawings, and a great book in green parchment that reportedly contained the best of Dürer's work, apparently drawings and illuminations. Willibald also possessed paintings by Lucas Cranach (i), Albrecht Altdorfer, Hans Holbein (ii) and Lucas van Leyden as well as a sizeable collection of Classical coins and sculptures. He also patronized contemporary masters, such as Johann Gregor van der Schardt, who created a life-size terracotta portrait of *Willibald Imhoff* (1570; Berlin, Bodemus.). Although his will (1580) stipulated that his collection was to remain intact, his heirs gradually sold off significant portions to the Holy Roman Emperor Rudolf II, Albert V, Duke of Bavaria, and Thomas Howard, 2nd Earl of Arundel.

BIBLIOGRAPHY

NDB

A. Springer: 'Inventare der Imhoff'schen Kunstkammer zu Nürnberg', *Mitt. Ksr.-Kön. Cent.-Comm. Erforsch. & Erhaltung Baudkml.*, v (1860), pp. 352–7

T. Hampe: 'Kunstfreunde im alten Nürnberg und ihre Sammlungen', *Mitt. Ver. Gesch. Stadt Nürnberg*, xvi (1904), pp. 57–124

W. Schwemmer: 'Aus der Geschichte der Kunstsammlungen der Stadt Nürnberg', *Mitt. Ver. Gesch. Stadt Nürnberg*, xl (1949), pp. 97–206

G. P. Fehring and A. Ress (with W. Schwemmer): *Die Stadt Nürnberg* (Munich, 1961/*R* 1977)

R. von Busch: *Studien zu deutschen Antikensammlungen des 16. Jahrhunderts* (diss., U. Tübingen, 1973), pp. 98–103

C. von Imhoff: 'Die Imhoff-Handelsherren und Kunstliebhaber', *Mitt. Ver. Gesch. Stadt Nürnberg*, lxii (1975), pp. 1–42

Der Mensch um 1500: Werke aus Kirchen und Kunstkammern (exh. cat., ed. H. Gagel; Berlin, Skulpgal., 1977), pp. 47–57

L. Veit: 'Die Imhoff: Handelsherren und Mäzene des ausgehenden Mittelalters und der beginnenden Neuzeit', *Das Schatzhaus der deutschen Geschichte: Das germanische Nationalmuseum*, ed. R. Pörtner (Düsseldorf, 1982), pp. 503–31

P.-R. Jante: *Willibald Imhoff: Kunstfreund und Sammler* (Lüneburg, 1985)

J. C. Smith: 'The Transformations in Patrician Tastes in Renaissance Nuremberg', *New Perspectives on the Art of Renaissance Nuremberg: Five Essays*, ed. J. Chipps Smith (Austin, 1985), pp. 82–100 (91–4)

H. Budde: 'Das "Kunstbuch" des Nürnberger Patriziers Willibald Imhoff und die Tier- und Pflanzenstudien Albrecht Dürers und Hans Hoffmans', *Jb. Ksthist. Samml. Wien*, lxxxii–lxxxiii (1986–7), pp. 213–41

C. Schlief: *Donatio et Memoria: Stifter, Stiftungen und Motivationen an Beispielen aus der Lorenzkirche in Nürnberg* (Munich, 1990), pp. 16–75

H. Pohl: *Willibald Imhoff: Enkel und Erbe Willibald Pirckheimer* (Nuremberg, 1992)

J. C. Smith: *German Sculpture of the Later Renaissance,* c. *1520–1580: Art in an Age of Uncertainty* (Princeton, 1994), pp. 306, 308–9, 352–3, 355, 356, 391–3, 475

JEFFREY CHIPPS SMITH

Imhoff, Peter Joseph (*b* Cologne, 13 July 1768; *d* Cologne, 20 Dec 1844). German sculptor. He came from a family of sculptors resident in Cologne since the early 18th century. He learnt his craft from his father, Johann Joseph Imhoff (1739–1802), and he probably also studied at the Kunstakademie in Düsseldorf. From the 1790s onwards he produced portrait sculptures (most now untraced), sacred and secular figures, as well as decorative sculpture and reproductions after ancient sculpture, working in both stone and terracotta. Surviving early works include terracotta busts of the collector *Johann Wilhelm Baron von Hüpsch* (1786–90; Cologne, Stadtmus.) and his housekeeper *Eva Mechthild Happerts* (1786–90; Darmstadt, Hess. Landesmus.), which show a brilliantly lucid realism emerging from the traditions of Rococo. Around 1800 and for some time afterwards, in striking red sandstone tomb statues and stelae decorated with reliefs, Imhoff evolved a classicizing austerity in the style of Bertel Thorvaldsen (e.g. tombs for *Louise Knobel* (1823) and *Caroline Dornheim* (1826); both Cologne, Reformierte Gemeinde Cemetery). These works were in keeping with the provincial taste of the Rhineland.

Imhoff began to move away from this style, however, when he met Karl Reichsfreiherr vom und zum Stein (1757–1831), an important Prussian reformer, Minister and the founder of a series of antiquarian publications, the *Monumenta Germaniae Historica.* In 1817–19 Imhoff produced sandstone low reliefs, after designs by the painter Heinrich Maximilian Fuchs (1767–1846), for a neo-Gothic octagonal tower, designed in 1814 by Johann Claudius von Lassaulx for Stein's birthplace, the Schloss Nassau. Imhoff's reliefs of the patron saints of the nations allied against Napoleon, together with personifications of the virtues of *Unity*, *Faith in God*, *Bravery* and *Perseverance* (*c.* 2.80 m), are grouped beneath canopies and placed on the pilasters flanking the portals of the tower's base and main section. These figures are the oldest examples of neo-Gothic sculpture in Germany: in an individual and graceful manner, their energetic linearity combines restraint with influences as diverse as Baroque traditions and the art of the Lukasbrüder. The reception of forms from the medieval period, which were seen as 'Old German', expressed a hope for the continuity of national history after the wars of liberation (1813–15), which the tower, with its sculptures and its memorial hall, was intended to commemorate. It is significant, however, that Imhoff did not refer to Gothic prototypes of the same genre: for his reliefs of *St George* and *St Leopold*, for example, he looked to the designs on stained-glass windows (*c.* 1508) in Cologne Cathedral.

Imhoff also based his portrait sculpture on ancient originals: in his herm of the *Freiherr vom Stein* (terracotta and plaster of Paris, 1818) and in the portrait bust of the *Freifrau vom Stein*, produced after her death mask (plaster of Paris, 1819; Nassau, Schloss Stein and Cappenberg-Salm, Schloss Cappenberg), Imhoff combined convincing physiognomic detail with an idealizing overall form. For both Stein and Imhoff the process of immortalizing the dead remained highly classical in approach. Imhoff next received commissions to decorate the Stein family vault in Frucht bei Bad Ems with figurative tomb reliefs for Stein's spouse *Wilhelmine Magdalena Friederike vom Stein* (1821) and mother *Henriette Caroline vom Stein* (1823). Ferdinand Franz Wallraf and Heinrich Maximilian Fuchs designed allegorical representations of motherly love, diligence and religiosity, incorporating features of the two women and their family, according to Stein's precise instructions. The main significance of Imhoff's work was as an early example of the creative power of historicism, which he owed to his patron's purposeful and decisive influence. Without this intellectual element, apart from the liveliness of the early portrait busts, Imhoff's artistic potential would probably have remained limited to a frequently flaccid late classicism, without any particular artistic individuality, as in the late reliefs depicting the *Stations of the Cross*, which Imhoff modelled in about 1844, after drawings by the Lukasbrüder painter, Joseph von Führich, and which have survived in terracotta casts (Brühl and Krefeld) by Imhoff's son, Johann Joseph Imhoff the younger (1796–1860).

BIBLIOGRAPHY
Thieme–Becker
P. Bloch: 'Der Freiherr vom Stein und der Kölner Bildhauer Peter Joseph Imhoff', *Anz. Ger. Nmus.* (1967), pp. 89–116
H. Appuhn: *Das Bildnis des Freiherrn vom Stein* (Cologne, 1975), pp. 51–3, 130, 137
P. Bloch: *Skulpturen des 19. Jahrhunderts im Rheinland* (Düsseldorf, 1975), pp. 8, 16–17, 73
——: 'Gotisierende Skulpturen in Deutschland', *Atti del XXIV congresso internazionale di storia dell'arte: Bologna, 1979*, vi; *La scultura nel XIX secolo*, pp. 143–51
J. Abt and W. Vomm: *Der Kölner Friedhof Melaten* (Cologne, 1980), pp. 149–50, 169, 174–5, 222–3
E. Trier and W. Weyres, eds: *Kunst des 19. Jahrhunderts im Rheinland*, iv (Düsseldorf, 1980)

M. PULS

Imhotep (*fl c.* 2600 BC). Egyptian official and architect. Imhotep, who bore the title 'Greatest of Seers in Heliopolis' and served under the kings Djoser (*reg c.* 2630–*c.* 2611 BC) to Huni (*c.* 2600–*c.* 2575 BC), was traditionally the architect of the step-pyramid complex at SAQQARA. His name was inscribed on the base of a statue of the owner of that monument near the beginning of its entrance colonnade. Imhotep was probably the builder of another step-pyramid complex for Horus Sekhemkhet at Saqqara, where his name appears once more. By the Late Period (*c.* 750–332 BC) Imhotep had been deified, and there are numerous bronze statuettes dating from the Late and Greco-Roman periods (332 BC–AD 395) showing him seated and reading from a papyrus roll (*see* EGYPT, ANCIENT, fig. 41). He was worshipped at the temple of Karnak, Thebes, and an unfinished chapel at Philae was dedicated to his cult. He was traditionally also the builder of the temple at Edfu, and harpists sang about his wisdom, while scribes made a libation to him before they wrote.

The historian Manetho identified him, in the *Aegyptiaca* (*c.* 300 BC), as the physician Asklepios and, more importantly, described him as the inventor of building with ashlar. However, the fact that two large open funerary courts at Saqqara, pre-dating the step-pyramid complexes by some years, are enclosed by great stone walls may cast doubt on this claim. Gunn suggested that there were two Imhoteps, father and son, the former the inventor of building in stone and the latter the architect of the step pyramids. This finds little support in the tradition recorded some two thousand years later that Imhotep's father was a certain 'Kanefer of Krokodilopolis' (Arab. Gebelein).

See also EGYPT, ANCIENT, §II and MAUSOLEUM, §I, 1(i).

BIBLIOGRAPHY
B. Gunn: 'Inscriptions from the Step Pyramid Site', *An. Service Ant. Egypte*, xxviii (1928), pp. 153–74
M. Z. Goneim: *Horus Sekhem-khet* (Cairo, 1957), pp. ix, 4, pl. xiii
D. Wildung: *Imhotep und Amenhotep Gottwerdung im alten Ägypten* (Munich, 1977); Eng. trans. as *Egyptian Saints: Deification in Ancient Egypt* (New York, 1977)
N. Swelim: *Some Problems on the History of the Third Dynasty* (Alexandria, 1983)
——: 'Rollsiegel, Piere de Taille and an Update on a King and Monument Listof the Third Dynasty', *Festschrift Kàkosy* (in preparation)

NABIL SWELIM

Imitation Realism. *See* ANNANDALE IMITATION REALISTS.

Im Lavanttal, St Paul Abbey. Benedictine abbey in Carinthia, Austria, founded in 1091 by Count Engelbert von Spanheim. The present abbey church, dating from *c.* 1175–1210, has a triple-apse east end with shallow absidal chapels flanking a one-bay sanctuary. The sanctuary, transept and first bay of the four-bay nave are covered by quadripartite vaults erected after a fire in 1367. The façade has two towers, the upper parts of which were rebuilt in 1367–75 after the fire. The sculpted capitals in the nave and transept show a transition from Romanesque to Early Gothic forms; the round arches and heavy shafted piers in the nave, however, are entirely Romanesque in appearance. Three bays of the nave and both aisles were given elaborate net and star-ribbed vaults *c.* 1468. The south and west portals have late Romanesque sculpted tympana of the *Adoration of the Magi* and an *Abbot and St Paul before Christ Enthroned.* In the Baroque period a sacristy, a chapel of the Virgin and many conventual buildings were added; there are four Rococo altarpieces (*c.* 1750) in the transept. Wall paintings of 1260–64 show the *Martyrdoms of SS Peter and Paul* in the sanctuary, medallions of saints (*c.* 1468) by Friedrich Pacher in the nave and aisle vaults, and a votive wall painting (1493) in the north transept by Thomas Artula von Villach representing Abbot Sigismund Jöbstl, the founder and his wife, presented by SS Catherine and Benedict. The abbey's collection and library holds many works, some from the abbey of St Blasien in the Black Forest: a Metz ivory of the *Ascension* (*c.* 900); the late 11th-century reliquary cross of Queen Adelheid; a Parisian gold pax (*c.* 1250); two south German embroidered copes of *c.* 1125–50 and 1225–30; and the English early 14th-century Psalter from Ramsey Abbey (MS. 58/1).

BIBLIOGRAPHY
R. Eisler: *Die illuminierten Handschriften in Kärnten: Beschreibendes Verzeichnis der illuminierten Handschriften in Österreich*, iii (Leipzig, 1907), pp. 67–134
K. Ginhart: *Die Kunstdenkmäler der Benediktinerstifts St. Paul im Lavanttal* (Vienna, 1969)

NIGEL J. MORGAN

Immaculates, the. *See* PRECISIONISM.

Immendorff, Jörg (*b* Bleckede, nr Lüneburg, 14 June 1945). German painter, draughtsman and sculptor. He entered the Kunstakademie in Düsseldorf in 1963, spending three semesters studying stage set design before becoming a student of Joseph Beuys. After producing a series of pictures in 1966 using babies as his prime motif, he adopted a word suggestive of baby talk, 'Lidl', for performances and political demonstrations in Düsseldorf and other cities from 1968 to 1970. These activities, for which he enlisted the support of other artists, continued

Icon of the *Archangel Michael*, silver gilt, gold, enamels and hardstones, 10th century (Venice, Tesoro di San Marco)

1. Icon of *St James*, tempera on panel, 13th century (Patmos, Monastery of St John)

2. Icon of the *Virgin Orans*, tempera on panel, 1.93×1.20 m, from Yaroslavl', first third of the 13th century (Moscow, Tret'yakov Gallery)

3. Icon of *Christ Eleimon* ('merciful'), glass mosaic, 745×525 mm, 1100–1150 (Berlin, Dahlem, Museum für Spätantike und Byzantinische Kunst)

Icon of the *Anastasis*, tempera with gilding on panel, 360×265 mm, Byzantine, second half of the 14th century (Baltimore, MD, Walters Art Gallery)

Paolo Veronese: illusionistic frescoes (*c.* 1561), Villa Barbaro, Maser

James Thornhill: grisaille scenes from the *Life of St Paul* (1714–17), cupola and drum of the dome, St Paul's Cathedral, London

1. Edgar Degas: *Dancer on Stage with Bouquet, Acknowledging Applause*, pastel on paper, mounted on canvas, 720×775 mm, 1878 (Paris, Musée d'Orsay)

2. Claude Monet: *Terrace at Sainte-Adresse*, oil on canvas, 981×1299 mm, 1867 (New York, Metropolitan Museum of Art)

Alfred Sisley: *Flood at Port-Marly (Yvelines)*, oil on canvas, 600×810 mm, 1876 (Paris, Musée d'Orsay)

Mary Cassatt: *Woman Sewing*, oil on canvas, 920×630 mm, *c.* 1880–82 (Paris, Musée d'Orsay)

after he began teaching art in 1968 at a secondary school in Düsseldorf; he remained a teacher there until 1980.

Immendorff's renewed application to painting coincided with his first meeting with A. R. Penck in East Berlin in 1976. They wrote a brief manifesto on working collaboratively and met again in 1977, when they decided to organize joint artistic activities and exhibitions. It was at this time that Immendorff began his *Café Deutschland* series, e.g. *Café Deutschland* (1977–8; Aachen, Neue Gal.; *see* GERMANY, fig. 27), using the image of a bar interior as a metaphor for the clash of ideologies between East and West. Having previously explored his political involvement and social commitment through a didactic iconography in a form suggestive of political posters, he began in his new paintings to represent figures in powerfully staged symbolic compositions. The symbolic iconography and condensed corporeality of his pictorial language also found form in painted sculptures carved in wood (e.g. *Saviour*, h. 700 mm, 1983; see 1985 exh. cat., p. 165) or cast in bronze, as in *Worker* (h. 385 mm, 1976; see 1985 exh. cat., p. 160). After working as a visiting lecturer at the Kunsthochschule in Hamburg (1982–3) and the Werkkunstschule in Cologne (1984–5), in 1989 Immendorff was appointed professor at the Städelschule in Frankfurt.

WRITINGS

Hier und jetzt: Das tun, was zu tun ist (Cologne and New York, 1973) [text in Ger. and Eng.]

with A. R. Penck: *Deutschland mal Deutschland: Ein Deutsch-Deutscher Vertrag* (Munich, 1979)

BIBLIOGRAPHY

Jörg Immendorff: Café Deutschland (exh. cat., text D. Koepplin; Basle, Kstmus., 1979)

Jörg Immendorff (exh. cat., ed. W. Bojescul; Brunswick, Kstver., 1985)

ANDREAS FRANZKE

Imola, Innocenzo da. *See* INNOCENZO DA IMOLA.

Imparato, Gerolamo (*fl* Naples, 1571–1607). Italian painter. Documents attest to his career in Naples, but where he came from is a subject of controversy. It is probable that he studied with Silvestro Buono (*fl* 1551–98), with whom he apparently collaborated on a painting of the *Assumption of the Virgin* (Naples, S Pietro in Vinculis) in 1571. His work of the 1590s suggests familiarity with the art of Rome, Venice and Parma, which he might have visited between 1573 and 1587. He may, however, have absorbed this knowledge through his collaboration with Dirck Hendricksz., a Flemish artist thoroughly acquainted with the art of Rome, Venice and Parma, with whom he decorated the ceiling of the church of Donnaromita in Naples. The *Baptism* (1590; Massa Lubrense, nr Naples, parish church), the *Annunciation* (1591; Castiglione Cosentino, nr Cosenza, parish church) and *Christ among the Doctors* (1591–2; S Maria de la Vid, nr Burgos, parish church) all demonstrate a knowledge of such Roman painters of the 1580s as Giovanni Muziano, Cesare Nebbia, Niccolò Circignani and Andrea Lilio. Later works, despite the brief influence of the Neapolitan Mannerist painter Francesco Curia (1538–1610) revealed in the *Madonna del Carmine* (1598; Naples, Spirito Santo), became increasingly Baroque, and Imparato developed his interest in Flemish painters such as Hendricksz. and Paul Bril. However, the *Nativity* (1602–3; Naples, Gesù Nuovo), the ceiling and the small altars (1603–7) of S Maria la Nova, Naples, and the *Immaculate Conception* (1606; Vibo Valentia, church of the Clarisse) move away from the ornate and decorative manner of Curia and Hendricksz., towards a more intimate, emotional style with iridescent colour and broken contours. In his last work, the *Martyrdom of St Peter of Verona* (1607; Naples, S Pietro Martire), Imparato sought softer effects of light and air, probably influenced by Luigi Rodriguez (*fl* 1594–1606), but also in line with Spanish devotional painting, which was well known in Naples. He sent works to Puglia and Calabria; his regular collaborator, at least from 1577, was Giovann'Angelo d'Amato (*fl* 1570s–1610s).

BIBLIOGRAPHY

B. de Dominici: *Vite* (1742–5), ii, pp. 212–18

G. Previtali: *La pittura del cinquecento a Napoli e nel Vicereame* (Turin, 1978), pp. 112–15, 141–6 [full bibliog. and details of early docs]

C. Vargas: 'Inediti di Cardisco, Negroni e Imparato a Massa Lubrense', *Prospettiva*, xlv (1987), pp. 17–28

CARMELA VARGAS

Impasto. Term for paint that is thickly applied to a canvas or panel so that it stands in relief and retains the marks of the brush or palette knife. Early panel paintings show little impasto, but with the adoption of oil painting on canvas, painters such as Titian and Rembrandt explored the possibilities of the technique (*see* REMBRANDT VAN RIJN, fig. 11). Impressionist works may be heavily impasted in many areas.

RUPERT FEATHERSTONE

Imperial Baroque. *See* BAROQUE REVIVAL.

Imperiale. Italian family of bankers, merchants, collectors and patrons. Based in Genoa and engaged in commerce and maritime trade, the family included figures of great significance in the political history of the Genoese Republic, most of whom came from the Sant'Angelo dei Lombardi branch of the family (the name derives from the estate near Avellino acquired in 1631), whose founder was Vincenzo Imperiale (?1518–67). In 1560 he built the family palace in Piazza Campetto, Genoa, and commissioned Luca Cambiaso and Giovanni Battista Castello (i) to decorate it with frescoes. At the same time he also began the construction of a splendid villa at S Pier d'Arena, in the suburbs of Genoa, designed by Giovanni and Domenico PONZELLO. His inheritance passed to his son Gian Giacomo Imperiale (1550–1622), who was Doge of Genoa from 1617 to 1619. He enlarged the palace at Campetto and gave it greater prominence by rearranging the neighbouring buildings and opening up the Via Imperiale (subsequently called the Via Scurreria). He was a devoted patron of Bernardo Castello (ii), whom he commissioned to execute the decoration of the palace and of the villa and to paint some pictures for the family chapel in S Siro, begun in 1600 (severely damaged during World War II).

The extraordinary collection of books and pictures formed by Gian Giacomo's son Gian Vincenzo Imperiale (1582–1648) was housed in the various family residences. A man of profound humanistic culture and lively artistic interests and a prominent figure in Genoa's political circles, Gian Vincenzo's contacts with contemporary artists and an extensive network of correspondents enabled him to form an exceptional library and picture collection (the inventory lists over 300 paintings), both of which testify to his wide-ranging and modern tastes. Among the Genoese artists he patronized were Bernardo Castello (ii), Giovanni Battista Paggi and Domenico Fiasella. He also owned many paintings by Bernardo Strozzi and Sinibaldo Scorza. Rubens and van Dyck were among the foreign artists he met in Genoa, and by 1602 the Imperiale family already owned two paintings by the former: the *Hercules and Omphale* (Paris, Louvre) and the *Death of Adonis* (priv. col.). Van Dyck painted two portraits of *Gian Vincenzo Imperiale* (Washington, DC, N.G.A.; Brussels, Mus. A. Anc.). Gian Vincenzo also collected works by Guido Reni, Pordenone, Palma Giovane and Giulio Cesare Procaccini. He enthusiastically sought out 16th-century Venetian works and acquired paintings by Titian, Giorgione, Tintoretto and Veronese. After Gian Vincenzo's death part of the collection was acquired in 1665 by Francesco Maria Balbi, from whom it passed to Queen Christina of Sweden in Rome and finally to England, where it was dispersed. Some of the works that remained in Genoa were destroyed during the French bombardment of the city in 1684 and others sold. A small number of pictures, mostly family portraits, were transferred to the Villa Imperiale at Terralba, which was acquired in the mid-17th century by Gian Giacomo Imperiale (1627–63), nephew of Gian Vincenzo.

BIBLIOGRAPHY

G. D. Oltrona Visconti: 'Per la genealogia della famiglia Tartaro poi Imperiale (secc. XIII–XV)', *Boll. Ligustico Stor. & Cult. Reg.*, xviii, i/4 (1976), pp. 3–17

R. Martinoni: *Gian Vincenzo Imperiale politico, letterato e collezionista genovese del seicento* (Padua, 1983)

MARIA FONTANA AMORETTI

Imperiali [Fernandi, Francesco] (*b* Milan, 1679; *d* Rome, 1740). Italian painter. After studying with Carlo Vimercati (1600–*c.* 1715) in Milan, he travelled throughout Italy, painting for a period in Palermo (Pio). He arrived in Rome *c.* 1705 and was patronized by Cardinal Giuseppe Renato Imperiali, whose name he took. His earliest Roman works were small cabinet pictures of farmyard birds, animals and fish, such as roosters, rabbits and donkeys (e.g. Holkham Hall, Norfolk, a pair bought in 1714; Penicuik House, Lothian, another pair). Their naturalism and dark colour washes derive from a north Italian tradition and recall the art of Antonio Amorosi or of Sinibaldo Scorza. In his small studies for conversation pieces (examples, Penicuik House) he turned however to the art of Bologna and of Venice; their succinct handling and flickering light and shade are similar in style to Giuseppe Maria Crespi.

Under the influence of Carlo Maratti, Imperiali developed a more elevated style. In 1720–22 (Waterhouse, p. 106) Owen McSwiny commissioned him to paint the *Allegorical Tomb of George I* (Viscount Kemsley priv. col.), one of a series of such paintings commissioned from Italian artists. A group of overdoors, *Tobias before his Father*, *Abraham and the Angels*, *Tuccia* and the *Continence of Scipio*, painted for the Palazzo Reale in Turin (*in situ*) is documented to 1721–2. In these paintings Imperiali established his mature style, characterized by dignified classical setting and drapery, in which the influence of Maratti, Giuseppe Ghezzi and Luigi Garzi was united with a more forceful realism and darker colour. Imperiali's study of Poussin dominates his *Sacrifice of Noah* and *Rebecca Hides her Household Gods from Laban* (both 1720s; Stourhead, Wilts, NT; see fig.). His large altarpiece, the *Martyrdom of St Eustace* (1720s; Rome, S Eustachio), is a dramatic composition that quotes directly from Poussin's *Martyrdom of St Erasmus* (Rome, Pin. Vaticana) in the figures of the priest and naked saint. Poussin also inspired the broadly painted and classically balanced *Martyrdom of SS Valentine and Hilary* and *Beheading of SS Valentine and Hilary*

Imperiali: *Rebecca Hides her Household Gods from Laban*, oil on canvas, 1.37×2.54 m, *c.* 1720 (Stourhead, Wilts, NT)

(before 1724; Viterbo Cathedral, chapel of SS Valentine and Hilary).

Concurrently Imperiali painted many canvases for private commissions and galleries. In his many mythological and biblical paintings of the period he favoured a pastoral, Arcadian setting of wooded landscapes, often with animals. His favourite themes were *Rest on the Flight into Egypt* (untraced example, see Clark, fig. 48), the *Virgin and Child* (e.g. the *Madonna of the Rosary*, *c.* 1732; Vetralla, S Andrea) and the *Meeting of Jacob and Rachel* (versions at Penicuik House, Lothian; San Francisco, CA, Achenbach Found. Graph. A.). Imperiali's independent position put him at odds with the Accademia di S Luca; he was involved in an attempt, led by Michelangelo Cerruti in 1723, to challenge its control over artistic output.

In 1726 a letter from the Abate Gentile to Lothar Franz von Schönborn described Imperiali as one of the leading history painters in Rome. His robust and lively classicism attracted British patrons, and he also acted as an agent on behalf of British collectors. From *c.* 1730 he won distinction as a teacher: Pompeo Girolamo Batoni was his most famous pupil, probably collaborating with Imperiali on the *Madonna of the Rosary*, and his school was favoured by British artists such as William Hoare, Allan Ramsay and James Russel. His last altarpiece, the *Death of St Romuald* (1733 or 1734; Rome, S Gregorio al Celio), is characterized by a vigorous impasto and inspired the direct naturalism of Marco Benefial's *Death of Beata Giacinta Marescotti* (Rome, S Lorenzo in Lucina) (Clark). His last official commission was for a painting called *Liberality, or Alexander Rewards his Generals* (Madrid, Escorial, Real Collegio di Alfonso XIII), which formed part of the decoration devised by Filippo Juvarra for the throne-room of Philip V at La Granja. Here Poussin's classicism is softened by the development of Rococo taste in Rome, a shift also noted in late works in which Imperiali chose literary subjects, set in pastoral, Arcadian landscapes, such as *Erminia Carving her True Love's Name* (London, Y. Ffrench priv. col.; see Clark, fig. 58).

BIBLIOGRAPHY

N. Pio: *Vite* (1724); ed. C. Engass and R. Engass (1977), pp. 40–41, 305

P. De Madrazo: *Viaje artistico de tres siglos par los colleciones de los reyes de Espagna* (Madrid, 1884), p. 199

T. Ashby: 'Thomas Jenkins in Rome', *Pap. Brit. Sch. Rome*, v (1913), p. 489

M. Freeden: *Quellen zur Geschichte des Baroks in Franken unter dem Einfluss des Hauses Schönborn* (Berlin, 1950), i, p. 1041

E. Battisti: 'Juvarra a S Idelfonso', *Commentari*, ix (1958), p. 297

E. Waterhouse: 'Francesco Fernandi detto Imperiali', *A. Lombarda*, iii (1958), pp. 101–6

Il settecento a Roma (exh. cat., ed. S. de Luca; Rome, Pal. Espos., 1959), pp. 38–9

A. M. Clark: 'Imperiali', *Burl. Mag.*, cvi (1964), pp. 226–33

L. Salerno: *Roma communis patria* (Rome, 1968), pp. 85, 191, 223

A Scholar Collects: Selection from the A. M. Clark Bequest (exh. cat., ed. U. W. Hiesinger and A. Percy; Philadelphia, PA, Mus. A., 1980–81), pp. 26–7, n. 15

R. Roli and G. Sestieri: *I disegni italiani del settecento* (Treviso, 1981), p. 83, n. 131

S. Prosperi Valenti Rodinò: 'Il cardinal Giuseppe Renato Imperiali committente e collezionista', *Bol. A.*, n. s. 3, lxxii (1987), pp. 17–60

SIMONETTA PROSPERI VALENTI RODINÒ

Impicchati, Andreino degli. *See* CASTAGNO, ANDREA DEL.

Impresa [pl. imprese; It.: 'badge', 'emblem'; 'undertaking', 'enterprise', 'miltary campaign']. Personal or familial badge or device comprising a design accompanied by an apt word or brief motto suggesting in veiled terms its significance. Imprese were especially fashionable in European court circles from the 16th century to the 18th and were closely related to emblems (*see* EMBLEM BOOK); but the latter, enigmatic inscriptions that only later acquired a pictorial element, were used mostly in devotional literature, and the impresa is distinguishable by its personal character and absence of explanatory inscription.

The use of imprese goes back to at least the end of the 14th century. Discussions of their origin have concentrated on their literary rather than their heraldic antecedents, but while this is important to the way in which they developed in the 16th century, their roots in heraldic devices of the later Middle Ages should not be overlooked. The Greek text of Horapollo's *Hieroglyphika*, discovered by Buondelmonte in 1419, purported to explain the meaning of the Egyptian hieroglyphs and played a role in the 16th-century development of imprese and emblems. Andrea Alciati, in *De verborum significatione* (1522; pubd 1530), linked imprese with hieroglyphics: 'Words indicate, and things are indicated by them. However, things too can indicate, as exemplified by the hieroglyphics of Horus and Chaeremon'. The shields described by the herald in Aeschylus' play *Seven against Thebes* (467 BC; e.g. lines 387–90) were wholly in the spirit of Renaissance imprese and doubtless provided another source of inspiration. Of equal importance, however, were the medieval seal and other personal devices, which were often combined with mottoes similar to those found with imprese. Obviously the refinements laid down in the 16th-century books, for example that they should not be in the language of the country, did not obtain then. The later writers stressed the twofold nature of the impresa: its design, the body; and the accompanying short text, its soul. As most of the apparent imprese used as medal obverse designs by Pisanello lacked such inscriptions, it seems that they were not considered essential at that time.

Few collections of medieval non-armorial seals have been published, but many designs are similar to imprese, including some with interpretative inscriptions (e.g. London, PRO). An eagle with the words *est avis ascendens* on a 14th-century seal-die (London, BM) alludes to the Bestiary story of the eagle flying up to the sun and then diving into water to renew itself. A very popular seal device was a hawk seizing its prey: a seal (1273–4; London, PRO) used by William Burne had this with the text *faus amie seit honie* ('false friend but honest'); another (*c.* 1385–6), used by Robert Bonde, bore a satyr with a hawk on his wrist and the words *tel esquier tel esperver* ('such a squire such a hawk'). A 15th-century seal for Dewrich bore a tree-stump and one shoot, with the motto *thenke and thanke.* Tournament devices, such as the shield for peace on the tomb of *Edward, the Black Prince* (*d* 1376) in Canterbury Cathedral, provide another parallel; and the insignia of the secular orders of knighthood often used impresa-like devices, the Garter (founded *c.* 1346) being the most familiar.

Apart from the medals by Pisanello, early imprese include the Medici diamond ring, in use from *c.* 1448, and tiles from a pavement at Mantua (1494; London, V&A) included imprese for three generations of the Gonzaga family.

Between 1531 and the end of the 17th century numerous emblem books were published, many going through several editions and with translations of the more popular ones into several languages. Other works recorded the imprese used in the public ceremonies of the Renaissance and Baroque courts, especially for coronations, marriages and funerals. One of the largest collections, built up over some 30 years, was kept at Whitehall Palace, London, where a gallery was hung with the painted shields of imprese presented to Elizabeth I by the participants in her Accession Day tilts. Some were described by William Camden and Sir William Segar in the early 17th century, but the inability of these learned heralds to name more than a very few doubtless reflects their ephemeral nature. All were swept away during the Civil War of the 1640s.

Certain prominent Italian families used imprese in works of art made for them. Sometimes the imprese were borne on shields, but most were worked into the general design. Gonzaga imprese, for example, occur in the decoration of the Sala del Fregio (*c.* 1530) in the Palazzo del Te, Mantua, while imprese associated with Isabella d'Este appear on a maiolica service (*c.* 1519; London, V&A). By the mid-16th century the use of imprese had spread north to courts in France and, above all, England under Elizabeth I. Perhaps more than any other late 16th-century monarch she used imprese on medals (e.g. *c.* 1569–70; London, BM), in jewels (as in the armillary sphere worn below an earring in the 'Ditchley' portrait, attributed to Marcus Gheeraerts (ii), *c.* 1592; London, N.P.G.) and generally in her portraits (e.g. the anonymous 'Sieve' portrait, *c.* 1580; Siena, Pin. N.) to enhance their message. Mary, Queen of Scots (*reg* 1542–67) made extensive use of imprese from published collections in her embroideries (Chatsworth, Derbys); others were of her own devising. Imprese could also be set on buildings, along with other devices, on equal terms with the family arms. Scutcheons decorating the palace of Obizzo Alidosio d'Imola, Governor of Cesena in 1508–9, bore his arms and his impresa of the Three Graces, while a slightly earlier doorcase from Gubbio was carved with the arms and imprese of Federico da Montefeltro, Duke of Urbino (all London, V&A). A similar use of imprese combined with arms is shown on an anonymous portrait of *William Burton* (see fig.).

The fashion for using imprese in these quasi-heraldic ways no doubt helped with their introduction into the designs created for the great court festivals of the age. Ceremonial entries to cities drew upon a medieval tradition, but in the 16th century a more classical influence brought about changes that emphasized the importance of imprese. Marriages and funerals also provided scope for the use of imprese, as did coronations and academic festivities. Forty-one emblem books recording the devices used at particular festivals have been recorded, all but two being published between 1551 and 1701: twenty-two described royal funerals and obsequies, one was for the funeral of Michelangelo, ten described ceremonial entries, seven described marriages and one celebrates a royal birth. For some rulers, accounts may be found of their funeral and also of the commemorative obsequies held elsewhere

Impresa incorporated into a portrait of *William Burton*, oil on panel, 902×724 mm, *c.* 1604 (London, Society of Antiquaries of London)

in their domains or by their subjects in foreign countries. Such obsequies, attended by the officers of state and heralds, were held regularly under Elizabeth I. By the end of the 17th century the vogue for imprese was declining, and it is perhaps significant that the two 18th-century funerals (1728 and 1767) recorded by Praz both took place in the New World.

While imprese flourished only for a relatively short time they formed a significant part of Renaissance and Baroque heraldic display. Although some of the classic texts continued to be printed in the 18th century, whether as personal devices or as a recondite way of conveying instruction with pleasure, the creative era of the impresa had come to an end. The scholarly interest in imprese that began to develop in the 19th century has continued, with a greater awareness of both their importance and complexity in assisting comprehension of Renaissance and Baroque thought.

For further illustration *see* ALBERTI, LEON BATTISTA, fig. 1.

BIBLIOGRAPHY

EWA: 'Emblems and Insignia'
A. Alciatus: *De verborum significatione* (Lyon, 1530); ed. P. M. Daly and V. W. Callahan (Toronto and London, 1975)
W. Camden: *Remaines of a Greater Worke Concerning Britaine* (London, 1605)
M. Praz: *A Bibliography of Emblem Books* (1947), ii of *Studies in Seventeenth-century Imagery* (London, 1939–47)
F. Hartt: 'Gonzaga Symbols in the Palazzo del Te', *J. Warb. & Court. Inst.*, xiii (1950), pp. 151–88
J. A. Goodall: 'The Arms of Alidosio', *Coat of Arms*, 6 (1960–61), pp. 2–3
——: 'The Arms and Impreses of Gianfrancesco Gonzaga and Isabella d'Este', *Coat of Arms*, 6 (1960–61), pp. 178–9
R. Strong: *Portraits of Queen Elizabeth I* (Oxford, 1963); rev. as *Gloriana: The Portraits of Queen Elizabeth I* (New York, 1987)

——: *Splendour at Court: Renaissance Spectacle and Illusion* (London, 1973); rev. as *Art and Power: Renaissance Festivals, 1450–1650* (Woodbridge, 1984)
——: *The Cult of Elizabeth: Elizabethan Portraiture and Pageantry* (London, 1977)
J. A. R. Young: *The English Tournament Imprese* (New York, 1988) [AMS Studies in the Emblem, no. 3]
J. A. Goodall: 'All Earliest Imprese: A Study of Some Medieval Seals and Devices', *Antigua J.*, lxxii (1993), pp. 152–7
The Hieroglyphics of Horapollo, trans. by G. Boas, foreword A. Grafton (Princeton, 1993)

JOHN A. GOODALL

Impressionism. Term generally applied to a movement in art in France in the late 19th century. The movement gave rise to such ancillaries as American Impressionism. The primary use of the term Impressionist is for a group of French painters who worked between around 1860 and 1900, especially to describe their works of the later 1860s to mid-1880s. These artists include Frédéric Bazille, Paul Cézanne, Edgar Degas, Edouard Manet, Claude Monet, Berthe Morisot, Camille Pissarro, Auguste Renoir and Alfred Sisley, as well as Mary Cassatt, Gustave Caillebotte (who was also an important early collector), Eva Gonzalès, Armand Guillaumin and Stanislas Lépine. The movement was anti-academic in its formal aspects and involved the establishment of venues other than the official Salon for showing and selling paintings.

The term was first used to characterize the group in response to the first exhibition of independent artists in 1874. Louis Leroy and other hostile critics seized on the title of a painting by Monet, *Impression, Sunrise* (1873; Paris, Mus. Marmottan; see fig. 1), as exemplifying the radically unfinished character of the works. The word 'impression' to describe the immediate effect of a perception was in use at the time by writers on both psychology and art. Jules-Antoine Castagnary's review (1874) demonstrates that it was not always used in a negative way: 'They are *Impressionists* in the sense that they render not the landscape but the sensation produced by the landscape.' The name stuck, despite its lack of precision, and came to be used by the artists themselves.

Typical Impressionist paintings are landscapes or scenes of modern life, especially of bourgeois recreation. These non-narrative paintings demonstrate an attention to momentary effects of light, atmosphere or movement. The paintings are often small in scale and executed in a palette of pure, intense colours, with juxtaposed brushstrokes making up a field without conventional perspectival space or hierarchies of forms. Despite stylistic differences, the artists shared a concern for finding a technical means to express individual sensation.

The term is sometimes used to describe freely executed effects in works of other periods in which the artist has

1. Claude Monet: *Impression, Sunrise*, oil on canvas, 480×630 mm, 1873 (Paris, Musée Marmottan)

presented an impression of the visual appearance of a subject rather than a precise notation. It is also used by analogy in music and literature to describe works that evoke impressions in a subjective way.

1. Sources and emergence of the style. 2. Chronology. 3. Impressionist exhibitions, dealers and patrons. 4. The 'crisis' of Impressionism and later Impressionism. 5. The influence of Impressionism. 6. Criticism and historiography.

1. SOURCES AND EMERGENCE OF THE STYLE. Impressionism grew out of traditions of landscape painting and Realism in France. The immediate predecessors of the Impressionists were Gustave Courbet and the Barbizon painters. The young artists accepted Courbet's notion that the artist's own time and experience were the appropriate subject-matter for art. Courbet's undramatic renderings of scenes from ordinary life were an important example, as was his emphatic handling of paint and opposition to convention. Manet's provocative subject-matter and broad brushstrokes with mere hints of modelling in such paintings as *Déjeuner sur l'herbe* (1863; Paris, Mus. d'Orsay; *see* MANET, EDOUARD, fig. 1) owe much to Courbet. Directly, and through Manet's example, other artists were inspired by Courbet in the 1860s.

The Barbizon artists provided the Impressionists with a model of observed, specific, non-historical landscape with attention to times of day and seasons, often painted out of doors. Many of the Impressionists had direct contact with members of the older generation, whom they sometimes encountered in the 1860s painting in the forest of Fontainebleau. Théodore Rousseau's and Camille Corot's subjects of forest scenes, lanes, villages and fields, Eugène Boudin's and Johan Barthold Jongkind's seascapes and Charles-François Daubigny's river scenes provided the initial inspiration for such paintings as Bazille's *Forest of Fontainebleau* (1865; Paris, Mus. d'Orsay), Sisley's *Village Street at Marlotte* (1866; Buffalo, NY, Albright-Knox A.G.) and Monet's views of the Normandy coast such as *Terrace at Sainte-Adresse* (1867; New York, Met.; see colour pl. VI, fig. 2 and OIL PAINTING, colour pl. III). However, the selfconsciously modern Impressionists did not choose to show the traces of historic France that sometimes appear in Barbizon works, and they avoided sublime natural effects such as sunsets and storms.

2. CHRONOLOGY. The artists who would later be called the Impressionists began to emerge in the 1860s, when most of them were in their twenties. Despite later denials of its importance, most of the Impressionists had formal art training. Manet and Degas were students at the Ecole des Beaux-Arts, Paris, under Thomas Couture and Louis Lamothe (1822–69) respectively. Renoir also entered the Ecole des Beaux-Arts; he met Bazille, Monet and Sisley in the atelier of the academic artist Charles Gleyre and studied there until its closure in 1864. Some of the artists, including Cézanne, Guillaumin, Monet and Pissarro, also worked in 1860–61 at the Académie Suisse, Paris, where there was a model but no instruction. Despite the academic system's emphasis on the figure, the young artists discovered a common enthusiasm for landscape. Bazille, Monet, Sisley and Renoir went to Chailly-en-Bière to paint in the forest of Fontainebleau in 1864 and during the rest of the 1860s concentrated on painting *plein-air* landscapes and figures in landscape. Monet, dissatisfied with his attempt to work from sketches, submitted *Women in the Garden* (Paris, Mus. d'Orsay), a large canvas executed on the spot, to the Salon of 1867, where it was rejected. Renoir achieved some success with paintings of his mistress in outdoor settings such as *Lise with a Parasol* (1867; Essen, Mus. Flkwang). Bazille, who shared studios with Monet and Renoir, also did groups of figures out of doors. Moving away from their Barbizon antecedents, the artists also painted city views and landscapes that show the life of suburbs and seaside resorts. Rather than drawing on past art for their sources of inspiration, they looked to contemporary popular illustration and photographs but above all emphasized direct contact with nature.

Their palettes lightened, and they eliminated earth tones as they moved away from their Barbizon-inspired works of the early 1860s. Monet, Pissarro, Renoir and Sisley worked around Louveciennes in 1868 and 1869. Renoir and Monet painted together at the popular riverside resort called La Grenouillère in 1869 (respectively, Stockholm, Nmus.; London, N.G.; *see* MONET, CLAUDE, fig. 1). In these canvases they began to use smaller, more fragmented brushstrokes and more intense colour in an attempt to suggest the visual appearance of light on rippled water, foliage and figures, without focusing on any detail of the scene.

Manet and Degas, whose families were members of the upper bourgeoisie, moved in different circles from those of Pissarro and the younger generation of Impressionists. Morisot, who met Manet in 1868, was also part of this social group and married Eugène Manet, the artist's brother, in 1874. The figure paintings she exhibited in the late 1860s and early 1870s, such as *Mother and Sister of the Artist* (1869–70; Washington, DC, N.G.A.), show Manet's influence.

During the 1860s both Manet and Degas produced some history paintings, but in a non-academic style; for the most part, however, these artists devoted themselves to subjects they could readily observe. Degas concentrated on portraits of family and friends; because he did not work on commission, he was free to transform this standard genre through his interest in the characteristic gesture, the unexpected angle and the hidden light source. Like most of the artists, he became aware of the compositional possibilities suggested by Japanese prints with their daring cropping, non-Western perspective, simple outlines, lack of modelling and flat areas of colour (*see* JAPONISME). *Musicians of the Orchestra* (1868–9; Paris, Mus. d'Orsay) integrates the portraits into a scene of modern urban life that includes a ballet on stage. Manet also painted contemporary entertainments such as Spanish dancers and people at the races; however, his most notorious works were those such as *Déjeuner sur l'herbe* and *Olympia* (1863; Paris, Mus. d'Orsay), which flouted conventions of spatial construction and finish and, through their presentation of nudes in situations suggesting prostitution, pointed to ambiguities in Second Empire morality. In contrast to the emphasis on painting out of doors by the other Impressionists, these two urban artists worked extensively in the studio.

2. Auguste Renoir: *Monet Working in his Garden at Argenteuil*, oil on canvas, 467×600 mm, 1873 (Hartford, CT, Wadsworth Atheneum)

The Café Guerbois in Montmartre, Paris, provided a place for the artists to meet and to discuss their work. Manet, who was the centre of the group there, began to frequent the café around 1866. He was joined by such critics as Louis-Edmond Duranty, Théodore Duret, Armand Silvestre and Emile Zola, who wrote sympathetically about the new art; Bazille, Degas and Renoir went there regularly and, less frequently, Cézanne, Sisley, Monet and Pissarro, who were living outside Paris. Lively discussions on art provided a forum for the artists to clarify their ideas. They also met some collectors there, including Dr Paul Gachet. The Café de la Nouvelle-Athènes replaced the Café Guerbois in the mid-1870s as the preferred gathering place.

During the 1860s most of the artists received some recognition at the Salon, where about half their submissions were admitted, and sold some works. However, many of them were struggling during this decade. The Franco-Prussian War (1870–71) was a major disruption and a turning-point, after which the artists (with the exception of Bazille, who was killed in 1870) settled into more stable circumstances. The Impressionists' subjects of the 1870s gave no hint of the destruction of the war. In celebrating the French countryside and the new face of Paris, they, like other citizens, seemed to be interested in putting the national humiliation behind them.

A number of the artists settled in places that provided them with consistent motifs, mostly within 50 km of Paris. Pissarro returned to Pontoise, where he had already painted in the late 1860s, and where he remained for the rest of his life. He was joined there in 1872 by Cézanne, who abandoned the dark, turbulent form and content of much of his early work in favour of directly observed landscapes, such as *House of the Hanged Man* (1873; Paris, Mus. d'Orsay; *see* CÉZANNE, PAUL, fig. 2), painted with a varied touch according to Pissarro's teachings on colour. In his subsequent paintings done in the south of France, such as his views of L'Estaque from the later 1870s and early 1880s (e.g. Paris, Mus. d'Orsay; Chicago, IL, A. Inst.), Cézanne continued to work from nature but chose motifs that did not change quickly and began to use a constructive brushstroke. Between 1872 and 1877 Monet lived in Argenteuil, where Renoir, Sisley, Manet and Caillebotte also painted. About 20 minutes from Paris by train, the town was a centre for pleasure-boating on the Seine; more than any other place, it has become identified with Impressionism (e.g. Sisley's *Bridge at Argenteuil*,

1872; Memphis, TN, Brooks Mus. A.; *see* SISLEY, ALFRED, fig. 1).

The paintings of the Impressionists, above all, show scenes of bourgeois recreation: people boating (Manet's *Boating*, 1874; New York, Met.), strolling along rivers, across bridges (Caillebotte's *Pont de l'Europe*, 1876; Geneva, Petit Pal.; for illustration *see* CAILLEBOTTE, GUSTAVE), through fields (Monet's *The Poppies*, 1873; Paris, Mus. d'Orsay) or on the new boulevards of Paris (Caillebotte's *Paris Street: Rainy Weather*, 1877; Chicago, IL, A. Inst.); attending the opera (Cassatt's *Lydia in a Loge*, 1879; Philadelphia, PA, Mus. A.), the café concert (Degas's *At the Café Concert 'Les Ambassadeurs'*, 1876–7; Lyon, Mus. B.-A.), the race-track and other forms of urban entertainment. They also depicted domestic interiors (Morisot's *The Cradle*, 1872; Paris, Mus. d'Orsay); the public park and the private middle-class garden (Renoir's *Monet Working in his Garden at Argenteuil*, 1873; Hartford, CT, Wadsworth Atheneum; see fig. 2); and the rivers, roads and railway lines that made France accessible to travellers (Monet's *Arrival of the Normandy Train at Gare St-Lazare*, 1877; Chicago, IL, A. Inst.; *see also* OIL PAINTING, colour pl. IV). Pissarro showed agricultural activities (e.g. *Harvest at Montfoucault*, 1876; Paris, Mus. d'Orsay), as did Sisley, though to a lesser extent. These subjects, which they shared with more fashionable genre painters and popular illustrators, seemed neutral at the time, although Pissarro's cabbage patches were criticized as vulgar; it was the ways in which they were framed and executed that seemed provocative.

The style of these artists in the 1870s is considered 'classic Impressionism'. They became sophisticated in the manipulation of high-valued colours, in juxtaposed touches and flecks or soft, blended brushstrokes to convey the appearance of reflected light on water, as in Monet's many views of the Seine at Argenteuil (e.g. *Bridge at Argenteuil*, 1874; Washington, DC, N.G.A.; see also colour pl. VII), grass stroked by the wind (Renoir's *High Wind*, *c.* 1872; Cambridge, Fitzwilliam), complementary coloured shadows on frosty ground (Pissarro's *Hoar Frost*, 1873; Paris, Mus. d'Orsay), variations in atmosphere and the effect on the human form of reflections and incidental light (Renoir's *Ball at the Moulin de la Galette*, 1876; Paris, Mus. d'Orsay; *see* RENOIR, AUGUSTE, fig. 1). The lack of concern for academic rules of composition that specified a hierarchy of forms and a clear placement of elements in space, as well as the sketchy quality of the works, suggested rapidity of execution and a direct response to an observed effect. Their technique signified spontaneity and originality, and, to some extent, this manner of execution became in itself a convention of the Impressionists, many of whom in fact worked deliberately.

Manet and Degas remained in Paris, continuing to lead the lives of sophisticated men about town. Degas concentrated increasingly on dancers at the Opéra, in rehearsal and performance, seen in a wide variety of postures from many angles and under different lighting (see colour pl. VI, fig. 1 and PASTEL, colour pl. III). Like Manet, through his contact with the other artists he became more interested in painting outdoor scenes such as *Carriage at the Races* (*c.* 1872; Boston, MA, Mus. F.A.). His increasing use of pastels allowed him to work more freely with both line and colour. Manet also painted more outdoor scenes, such as *At Père Lathuille* (1879; Tournai, Mus. B.-A.), which still show a keen eye for the nuances of social phenomena. Like Degas, he also painted scenes in cafés and places of entertainment, culminating just before his death in *Bar at the Folies-Bergère* (1882; U. London, Courtauld Inst. Gals; *see* MANET, EDOUARD, fig. 3).

3. IMPRESSIONIST EXHIBITIONS, DEALERS AND PATRONS. The Impressionists had some important early patrons: Victor Chocquet, Caillebotte, Ernest Hoschedé, Jean-Baptiste Faure and Dr Gachet and in the later 1870s Eugène Murer (1845–1906) and Paul Gauguin. Some of the early critics, such as Duret, also bought paintings. A few dealers, such as Père Martin and later, and most significantly, Paul Durand-Ruel, sold some of their works. The artists' reputation and hopes for more widespread acceptance and sales, however, depended on their becoming known to the larger public through exhibitions.

At the first exhibition of the Salon des Refusés, established in 1863 by Napoleon III in response to the complaints about the number of rejections from the Salon, works by some of the artists later called Impressionists attracted attention. Although reviews of such works as Manet's *Déjeuner sur l'herbe* were mixed, some critics and members of the public realized that new directions were developing outside the academic mainstream.

The artists' first recognition as a group stemmed from their decision to exhibit outside the Salon. As early as 1867, when Courbet and Manet both held private exhibitions separate from the Exposition Universelle, they had considered showing together, and they continued to investigate various means of showing and selling art, for instance at auction. In 1874 thirty artists showed in an exhibition of the Société Anonyme des Artistes Peintres, Sculpteurs, Graveurs, etc., which took place in the former studio of the photographer Nadar in Paris. These artists banded together to show their work without the sanction of the government and without a jury. The group included Cézanne, Degas, Monet, Morisot, Pissarro, Renoir and Sisley. While it also included Boudin, Guillaumin, Lépine and other artists whose styles had affinities with those of the Impressionists, the exhibition did not promote any stylistic unity and contained works by a number of artists who simply wished to exhibit as independents. Manet, determined to succeed by showing in the official Salon, never participated in the group exhibitions. Nevertheless, critics identified him as the father of the group, the more so when he sent *plein-air* paintings of Argenteuil and other works in a high-key palette to the Salon.

The exhibition attracted the attention of the press, both favourably and unfavourably, and gave the group a name. The term 'Impressionist', which some critics used derisively, was being used in a neutral way in 1876, and in 1877 the artists themselves used it for their exhibition. For later exhibitions, the artists adopted the term 'Indépendants', although the group exhibitions of 1874, 1876, 1877, 1879, 1880, 1881, 1882 and 1886 are commonly referred to as the eight Impressionist exhibitions.

The character of the these exhibitions varied. Disagreements about the nature of the group and the best strategy for presenting and selling work, as well as personal circumstances, led different artists to withdraw at different times. Pissarro was the only one of the core group who showed in all eight exhibitions. Degas's invitations to more conservative Realist artists such as Jean-François Raffaëlli angered his colleagues. At times Cézanne, Monet, Renoir and Sisley chose to send works to the Salon or to the Galerie Georges Petit, thereby forfeiting the right to show with the group. In the early 1880s some of these artists felt it was more advantageous to have solo shows at La Vie Moderne or at Durand-Ruel's gallery. New artists joined in: Caillebotte in 1876; Cassatt in 1879, introduced by Degas; Gauguin and Raffaëlli in 1880; and in 1886 Odilon Redon, as well as Georges Seurat and Paul Signac, brought in by Pissarro, who had joined them in their Neo-Impressionist research. In the last exhibition, of 1886, only Degas, Guillaumin, Morisot and Pissarro remained of the original core group.

Dealers increasingly held individual or group exhibitions of artists whose works they represented. Paul Durand-Ruel, whom Monet and Pissarro had met in London in 1870, was the most important dealer for the Impressionists. He was their best single source of income, at times providing stipends in exchange for their works. Other dealers, such as Georges Petit and the Paris branch of Goupil, where Theo van Gogh worked, also exhibited works of many of the Impressionists during the 1880s. Ambroise Vollard gave Cézanne, whose work had hardly been seen since the group exhibition of 1877, his first solo exhibition in 1895.

4. THE 'CRISIS' OF IMPRESSIONISM AND LATER IMPRESSIONISM. Around 1880 the artists, who were now entering middle age, went through a period of change, which has been referred to as the 'crisis' of Impressionism. It marked the end of the artists' close collaboration and the beginning of a time of individual re-evaluation. The artists had established their subjects and had achieved many of the formal goals implicit in their work of the 1860s and 1870s; they had evolved a complex set of techniques, allowing them to suggest the momentary quality of their perceptions. However, their expectations for the group in terms of support and success had not been fulfilled. They questioned whether the very form of their art might be the reason for the failure of their aspirations. Many of the artists felt dissatisfied with their spontaneous brushwork and casual compositions. Without approaching conventional standards of smooth finish and detailed rendering, the artists chose their motifs more carefully, worked longer on their paintings and considered different ways of arriving at a degree of finish that seemed aimed at making serious works.

Despite Renoir's success with portraits such as *Mme Charpentier and her Children* (1878; New York, Met.), he felt that he had to go back to the beginning again. Inspired by earlier art, especially Raphael's frescoes, he embarked on a study of drawing that led to many paintings in the 1880s of the nude, culminating in his *Bathers* of 1883–7 (Philadelphia, PA, Mus. A.). These were not distinctively modern, unlike Degas's contemporary women bathing in interiors. Later in his life, Renoir reintegrated these figure studies with a more Impressionist handling.

Degas continued to paint urban subjects, though in a more detached way. His dancers were less frequently shown in the context of performance, and, as in his studies of women bathing, he moved closer to his subjects and reduced their context to essentials. His work with monotypes and other prints, as well as with sculpture, revealed an interest in technical and formal experimentation.

Morisot, Cassatt and Pissarro painted figures extensively in the early 1880s (see colour pl. VIII; in contrast to the subjects derived from a bourgeois woman's world, Pissarro concentrated on peasants. Such close-up scenes of peasant women as *Young Peasant Woman Drinking her Coffee* (1881; Chicago, IL, A. Inst.) show both a clarity of composition and an attempt to discipline what he considered the 'romantic' brushwork of Impressionism. The hatched brushstroke deriving from his work with Cézanne was later replaced by the more impersonal dot; seeking a scientific basis for his art in the mid-1880s, Pissarro turned away from the intuitive Impressionist approach to the colour theories and Pointillist technique of Seurat and the Neo-Impressionists. He always supported young artists, whom he encouraged to exhibit with the Impressionist group, and because of his radical politics he was sympathetic to the anarchist causes that some of them espoused.

Monet settled at Giverny in 1883, but he frequently left the familiar sites of the Ile de France and returned to the seacoast, no longer painting the populated resorts but choosing remote places seen from a viewpoint that gave them the strong, flattened shapes he admired in Japanese prints and a more evocative content. His many views of Etretat and Belle Ile in the mid-1880s show his interest in working in extended groups.

Cézanne, who spent most of his time in the south of France, became increasingly sensitive to the interlocking of shapes and the constructive function of brushstroke and colour in his many views of Mont Sainte-Victoire and paintings of bathers, culminating in his large *Bathers* (1900–06; Philadelphia, PA, Mus. A.). Although his formal inventions provided a point of departure for 20th-century artists, his goal of finding a means to realize his sensations remained an Impressionist one.

Sisley's style changed the least of any of the artists. Living in Moret, he continued to paint the same kinds of scene as in the 1870s, although with a shift in palette that was in line with a general change away from primary colours towards pinks, oranges, yellow-greens and other new colours in the 1880s. In the work of a number of the artists, these changes emphasized the subjective and expressive side that had always been a part of Impressionism and that was being explored in a different way in the works of the emerging Symbolist movement.

In the 1890s the Impressionists achieved recognition and, in a number of cases, financial success. Impressionism did not end or stand still while younger artists emerged, as the term POST-IMPRESSIONISM might imply. During their later years many of the Impressionists achieved notable innovations. Critics at the time noticed a trend towards a synthesis of form and expression and towards more decorative effects. Monet exhibited series—large groups of paintings of the same motif—that are in some ways the culmination of the idea of recording subtle shifts in perception (e.g. the series devoted to Rouen Cathedral, including *Rouen Cathedral: The Façade in Sunlight*, 1894; Williamstown, MA, Clark A. Inst.; *see* MONET, CLAUDE, fig. 3), but that are also a way of creating a more monumental form of Impressionism, especially in his *Waterlilies* (e.g. Paris, Mus. Orangerie), painted between 1897 and his death in 1926.

5. THE INFLUENCE OF IMPRESSIONISM. Because Impressionism combined new approaches to formal issues while remaining a naturalist art, it affected a variety of movements in the later 19th century. Although their works were controversial, the Impressionists were acknowledged as a force in the art of their time, and they contributed to an opening up of the art world. The term 'Impressionist' was used widely and imprecisely as a generic word for vanguard artists or to describe some artists who exhibited in the Salon. A lightened palette, looser brushwork and contemporary subject-matter became features of academic Realism. Impressionist colour, compositional innovations and subject-matter provided points of departure for experimental naturalist and Symbolist movements in the late 19th century and the early 20th in other European countries and North America as well as France. Impressionist techniques and approaches were disseminated through direct contact among artists, exhibitions and the adaptations of style and subject by more conservative painters.

Although they seldom took pupils, the original Impressionists influenced those artists with whom they painted as well as younger colleagues to whom they gave advice (and in Pissarro's case his sons, including Lucien). Degas influenced more conservative Realist artists, such as Raffaëlli and Jean-Louis Forain (e.g. *The Fisherman*, 1884; Southampton, C.A.G.; for illustration *see* FORAIN, JEAN-LOUIS), as well as Henri de Toulouse-Lautrec. Monet, who had painted with John Singer Sargent in the 1880s, offered advice in the 1890s to some of the young American artists who had formed a kind of colony at Giverny. Some of them, such as Theodore Robinson, became important American Impressionists. Pissarro advised Gauguin in the early 1880s and encouraged Vincent van Gogh later in the decade, while collaborating with the Neo-Impressionists. Renoir's later style appealed to such artists as Pierre Bonnard, Maurice Denis, Aristide Maillol and Picasso, who were reapproaching the nude or were interested in a new, classic expression.

Gauguin's initial adoption of Impressionist technique, colour and subject-matter and later incorporation of aspects of these into a personal style was characteristic of artists of the next generation who were inspired by Impressionist innovations in colour, composition or facture, while departing from the goal of recording sensations of nature. His paintings of the early 1880s were inspired by Pissarro's work; however, by the end of the decade, Gauguin had renounced a vision that 'neglected the mysterious centres of thought'. Seurat, Signac and their fellow Neo-Impressionists transformed the instinctive Impressionist division of colours and composition through their 'scientific' theories of colour and expression, while retaining the subject-matter of landscapes and urban entertainment.

For artists who felt that the Académie des Beaux-Arts and the Salon were no longer the sole arbiters of taste, the Impressionist paintings they saw exhibited provided a different course from academic teaching. Inspired by the Impressionist exhibitions, the Groupe des Artistes Indépendants, which had its first non-juried exhibition in 1884, provided a venue other than the Salon for younger artists. Many artists of the next generation went through an early Impressionist phase, and features of the style formed the basis for their further explorations. Arriving in Paris in 1886, van Gogh changed from his dark, early palette to one of pure, intense colours, adapting Impressionist subjects and brushwork to his expressive purposes. Toulouse-Lautrec, Bonnard and Edouard Vuillard all went through Impressionist periods. Their work in the 1890s, though flattened, stylized in form and no longer naturalistic in colour, still drew on the imagery of modern life and urban entertainment and extended the Japanese-inspired compositional innovations of the older painters. Henri Matisse's early work was in an Impressionist vein, and he retained an interest in brilliant and contrasting colours.

A third means for the diffusion of Impressionism—and the most important for the pan-European movement—was the absorption of aspects of Impressionist *plein-air* subject-matter, colour and handling into mainstream academic painting. Discussions of 'Impressionism in the Salon' began as early as 1877, referring to modern subjects shown in outdoor light with relatively loosely rendered backgrounds. Jules Bastien-Lepage was an important influence on artists interested in achieving 'Impressionist' light and colour in figure paintings with an appropriate degree of finish. Such works as his *Joan of Arc* (1880; New York, Met.) influenced artists in England, North America and Scandinavia, as well as in France. As a cultural centre for Europe, Paris attracted young artists who then carried Impressionist ideas back to their own countries. Some, such as the Norwegian Frits Thaulow, exhibited in France and were recognized as Impressionists.

American Impressionism was the most unified movement and the one closest in spirit to that of France. In the 1890s and early decades of the 20th century such American artists as Theodore Robinson, Julian Alden Weir, Childe Hassam and John H. Twachtman presented subjects in bright sunlight and used flecked brushwork and intense colour, but frequently retained a more conservative approach to composition and the representation of figures than their French counterparts.

British artists were influenced by the tonal paintings of James McNeill Whistler and the modified academic Impressionism of such artists as Bastien-Lepage. Colour division derived from the Impressionists replaced Barbizon influence. Walter Sickert and Philip Wilson Steer were among those who admired Pissarro, Monet and Degas and evolved a treatment of landscape and figure subjects that drew on aspects of their work.

Later artists found Impressionism liberating in its insistence on the artist's sensibility rather than on academic rules as the determining factor in creating a picture. It provided an example for artists who wished to use colour and brushwork, expressively and who wished to find new ways of composing. Its limitation for later artists seemed to be its reliance on nature for inspiration. Gauguin had predicted that the Impressionists would be the 'officials' of tomorrow, and because of its naturalism, its immediacy and its spontaneous and easily imitated brushwork academic Impressionism became an accepted conservative style in the 20th century. Impressionism has steadily increased in popularity with the public and with buyers. Exhibitions of Impressionists' works draw huge crowds, and paintings sold at auction have continued to break records. Impressionism has often appealed to wealthy buyers who do not identify themselves as part of the Western European tradition: Americans around the turn of the century and, more recently, the Japanese.

6. Criticism and historiography. Writing on individual Impressionists began in the 1860s when their paintings were noticed at the Salon or the Salon des Refusés. Zola was an early defender of Manet and, partly through his boyhood friendship with Cézanne, an early supporter of the other Impressionists. Later, however, his enthusiasm diminished because he felt that the artists had not lived up to their promise.

Early reviews of the Impressionist exhibitions were not overwhelmingly negative, although the negative ones have been frequently quoted. Negative reviewers commented on formal aspects such as the use of crude or violently palpitating colour (especially blues and violets), the exaggerated brushstroke and lack of finish in works that seemed little more than sketches, the negation of elementary rules of drawing and painting and the lack of accuracy. Some reviewers were uneasy about the notion that everything was equally worth painting, but there was little discussion of subjects. Positive critics, such as Duranty in *La Nouvelle Peinture* (1876), commented on the new manner of drawing and use of colour, unusual points of view and the way the artists addressed the psychology of the modern world. Others, such as Castagnary and Silvestre, emphasized the individual sensibility and sensation of the artists. They also remarked on the vividness and naturalism of effect, the direct, unfettered representation of reality and the study of colours in the subject rather than the subject itself, but did not discuss the techniques used to gain these effects.

Duret's pamphlet *Les Peintres impressionnistes* (1878) concentrated on the colourists and landscape painters, excluding Degas and Manet. The difference he pointed to between the artists who emphasized drawing and urban subjects and those who painted primarily in the country with a freer touch was acknowledged by the artists themselves and was a source of division in their exhibitions. Degas was praised for his draughtsmanship by such critics as Zola and Joris-Karl Huysmans, who had reservations about the other artists' lack of finish.

Some writers in the 1880s and 1890s put greater emphasis on the subjective aspects of Impressionism. Jules Laforgue commented on the Impressionist eye and its connection with consciousness. Camille Mauclair and Georges Lecomte compared the artists' effects to poetry and music and pointed to the decorative aspects of their later work.

Many of the early critics and biographers, such as Zola, Duret, Gustave Geffroy and Camille Mauclair, were literary friends of the artists and did not deal with specific aspects of their work. Julius Meier-Graefe, in the early 20th century, began to apply a more analytical approach. Later writers dealt with documentation; Lionello Venturi published documents and produced catalogues raisonnés of Cézanne and Pissarro. Rewald's fundamental history, based on a systematic study of the available information, remains the point of departure for subsequent scholarship. Rewald's approach is empirical and assumes that the artists' subjects were essentially neutral and that their technique was necessitated by the goal of faithful recording. Later writers have stressed the conventionality of the artists' work and the long studio sessions that sometimes underlay their apparently spontaneous effects. Exhibitions in the late 20th century have attempted to set Impressionism in its social and artistic context, a trend also reflected by such writers as T. J. Clark (1984), whose work discusses iconography with subjects interpreted in terms of class ideology.

BIBLIOGRAPHY

EARLY SOURCES

J.-A. Castagnary: 'Exposition du boulevard des Capucines: Les Impressionnistes', *Le Siècle* (29 April 1874); repr. in 1974 Paris exh. cat., pp. 264–5

L. Leroy: 'L'Exposition des impressionnistes', *Le Charivari* (25 April 1874), pp. 2–3; abridged Eng. trans. in Rewald, 1946, pp. 256, 258–61; repr. in 1974 Paris exh. cat.

A. Silvestre: 'Chronique des beaux-arts: L'Exposition des révoltés', *Opinion Nationale* (22 April 1874)

E. Duranty: *La Nouvelle Peinture: A propos du groupe d'artistes qui expose dans les galeries Durand-Ruel* (Paris, 1876); Eng. trans. in 1986 exh. cat., pp. 37–48

S. Mallarmé: 'The Impressionists and Edouard Manet', *A. Mthly Rev. & Phot. Port.*, i/9 (1876), pp. 117–22; repr. in 1986 exh. cat., pp. 28–34

T. Duret: *Les Peintres impressionnistes* (Paris, 1878; 2/1923); repr. in *Critique d'avant garde* (Paris, 1885)

J.-K. Huysmans: *L'Art moderne* (Paris, 1883)

G. Lecomte: *L'Art impressionniste d'après la collection privée de M. Durand-Ruel* (Paris, 1892)

G. Geffroy: *La Vie artistique*, iii: *L'Histoire de l'impressionnisme* (Paris, 1894)

P. Signac: *D'Eugène Delacroix au néo-impressionnisme* (Paris, 1899)

J. Laforgue: *Mélanges posthumes* (Paris, 1903)

C. Mauclair: *The French Impressionists* (London, 1903)

'E. Zola: critical writings', in *Salons*, ed. F. F. Hemmings and R. Niess (Geneva, 1979)

GENERAL

J. Meier-Graefe: *Entwicklungsgeschichte der modernen Kunst*, 3 vols (Stuttgart, 1904)

T. Duret: *Histoire des peintres impressionnistes* (Paris, 1906)

L. Venturi: *Les Archives de l'impressionnisme*, 2 vols (Paris, 1939) [contains lett. written by many of the artists to the dealer Durand-Ruel]

J. Rewald: *History of Impressionism* (New York, 1946, rev. 4/1973) [the standard hist. and basis for further stud.; extensive bibliog.]

——: *Post-Impressionism from van Gogh to Gauguin* (New York, 1956, rev. 3/1978)

J. Lethève: *Impressionnistes et symbolistes devant la presse* (Paris, 1959)

H. White and C. White: *Canvases and Careers: Institutional Change in the French Painting World* (New York, 1965)

L. Nochlin: *Impressionism and Post-Impressionism: Sources and Documents* (Englewood Cliffs, 1966)

M. Roskill: *Van Gogh, Gauguin and the Impressionist Circle* (New York, 1970)

J. Leymarie and M. Melot: *Les Gravures des impressionnistes: Oeuvre complet* (Paris, 1971)

K. Champa: *Studies in Early Impressionism* (New Haven, 1973)

B. White, ed.: *Impressionism in Perspective* (Englewood Cliffs, 1978)

S. Monneret: *L'Impressionnisme et son époque: Dictionnaire international*, 4 vols (Paris, 1978–81)

K. Varnadoe: 'The Artifice of Candor: Impressionism and Photography Reconsidered', *A. America*, lxviii (1980), pp. 66–78

J.-P. Bouillon: 'L'Impressionnisme', *Rev. A.* [Paris], 51 (1981), pp. 75–85

A. Callen: *Techniques of the Impressionists* (London, 1982)

T. J. Clark: *The Painting of Modern Life: Paris in the Art of Manet and his Followers* (Princeton, 1984)
R. Schiff: *Cézanne and the End of Impressionism* (Chicago, 1984)
J. Rewald: *Studies in Impressionism*, ed. I. Gordon and F. Weitzenhofer (New York, 1986)
B. Denvir, ed.: *The Impressionists at First Hand* (London, 1987)
R. Herbert: *Impressionism: Art, Leisure and Parisian Society* (London, 1988)
G. Pollock: 'Modernity and the Spaces of Femininity', *Visions and Difference* (London, 1988), pp. 50–78
A. Distel: *Les Collectionneurs des impressionnistes: Amateurs et marchands* (Dudingen, 1989)

EXHIBITION CATALOGUES

Centenaire de l'impressionnisme (exh. cat. by A. Dayez and others, Paris, Grand Pal., 1974)
Impressionism: Its Masters, its Precursors and its Influence in Britain (exh. cat., ed. J. House; London, RA, 1974)
Japonisme: Japanese Influence on French Art, 1854–1910 (exh. cat. by G. Weisberg and others, Cleveland, OH, Mus. A., 1975)
The Crisis of Impressionism, 1878–1882 (exh. cat., ed. J. Isaacson; Ann Arbor, U. MI, Mus. A., 1980)
A Day in the Country: Impressionism and the French Landscape (exh. cat. by R. Brettell and others, Los Angeles, CA, Co. Mus. A., 1984)
The New Painting: Impressionism, 1874–1886 (exh. cat., ed. C. Moffett; San Francisco, CA, F.A. Museums, 1986)
Art in the Making: Impressionism (exh. cat., ed. D. Bomford and others; London, N.G., 1990)
Impressionism in Britain (exh. cat. by K. McConkey, London, Barbican A.G., 1995)

GRACE SEIBERLING

Imprimatura. Thin transparent coloured paint layer applied over the ground and underdrawing to tone down the brilliant white layer below and to provide a preliminary colour on which to work. Imprimatura may also be loosely applied to any coloured ground layer.

RUPERT FEATHERSTONE

Imstenraedt [Imstenraed], **von.** German family of collectors. Franz Gerhard von Imstenraedt (*b* Cologne, 1632) and Bernhard Albert von Imstenraedt (*b* Cologne, 1634) were the sons of a public notary who presented an altarpiece (Cologne, Walraf-Richartz-Mus.) to the Carmelite church in Cologne, and nephews of the collector Everard Jabach, and thus they received an early introduction to art. In 1650 Franz accompanied Jabach to the auction of the collection of Charles I, King of England and Scotland, from which he bought a portrait by van Dyck of the deposed King and Queen (1632; Kroměříž, Bishop's Pal.). He later acquired important works from the collections of Philip Herbert, 4th Earl of Pembroke, and Thomas Howard, 2nd Earl of Arundel, including three portraits attributed to Dürer and six works by Holbein; among the works acquired from the Arundel collection were Pieter Bruegel I's *Wedding of the Ugly Bride* (*c.* 1566; New York, Met.) and Antonello da Messina's *St Sebastian* (1475–6; Dresden, Gemäldegal. Alte Meister).

In 1667 Franz von Imstenraedt described the collection, for which he claimed responsibility, in a wordy poem in Latin verse, the *Iconophylacium.* He sent a copy to the Holy Roman Emperor Leopold I, who he hoped would acquire the collection, but after initial interest the Emperor rejected the purchase because of the high price. Although there was no interest in the picture lottery that the brothers planned in Vienna, and Charles Eusebius, Prince of Liechtenstein, also rejected it, the collection was acquired by Karl, Graf von Liechtenstein-Castelcorno, Bishop of Olmütz (Olomouc) and Kremsier (Kroměříž) (1624–95), in 1673. An inventory of the collection taken in this year listed 228 pictures, of which the greatest number were Italian, particularly Venetian paintings. History and religious paintings and portraits dominated; there were no genre subjects and only a few landscapes and animal pictures. The most important paintings were housed at Olomouc and were thus spared from the 1752 fire at the summer palace of Kroměříž.

Following the 1673 sale the von Imstenraedt brothers formed a second collection. Although of less impressive quality and lesser value, it was again composed primarily of Italian paintings, though the preference was no longer for Venetian but for Roman and Florentine Mannerist and Baroque works, as well as those by contemporary artists. In 1683 this second collection was sold to Prince Charles Eusebius. The majority of the paintings in the first collection of the von Imstenraedt brothers remain in Olomouc and Kroměříž, at the Archbishop and Bishop's Palaces respectively, although a number of works were sold in 1830. A few paintings, including Sebastiano del Piombo's *Madonna del Velo* (Prague, N.G., Šternberk Pal.) and a fragment from Veronese's *Assumption of the Virgin* (Prague, N.G., Convent of St George), have entered public collections in Europe and the USA.

WRITINGS

F. von Imstenraedt: *Iconophylacium sive artis Appelleae thesaurium* [Picture collection or dictionary of the art of Appelles] (1667; Vienna, Österreich. Nbib., MS. Cod. lat. 10073); repr. in A. Breitenbacher: 'K dějinám arcibiskupské obrazárny v Kroměříži' [Towards the history of the archbishop's gallery in Kroměříž], *Časop. Vlasteneckéno, Mus. Spolku Olomouci, Příloha*, xlv (1932)

BIBLIOGRAPHY

T. von Frimmel: 'Verzeichnis einer Wiener Bilder-Lotterie vom Jahre 1670', *Bl. Gemäldeknd. Beil.*, v (1909), pp. 141–8
A. Breitenbacher: 'Die Sammlung Imstenraedt in der Gemäldesammlung des Erzbistums Olmütz in Kremsier und Olmütz', *Jb. Köln. Geschver.*, xii (1930), pp. 206–20
O. Kurz: 'Holbein and Others in a Seventeenth Century Collection', *Burl. Mag.*, lxxxii (1930), pp. 279–82
F. Grossmann: 'Notes on the Arundel and Imstenraedt Collections', *Burl. Mag.*, lxxxiv (1944), pp. 151–4; lxxxv (1944), pp. 172–6
E. A. Safarik: 'The Origin and Fate of the Imstenraed Collection', *Sborn. Prac. Filoz. Fak. Brn. U.*, viii (1964), pp. 171–82
H. Ley: 'The Imstenraedt Collection', *Apollo*, xciv (1971), pp. 50–59

☐

In. Major school of Japanese Buddhist sculpture of the late Heian (AD 794–1185) and early Kamakura (1185–1333) periods (*see* JAPAN, §V, 3(iii)). The school took its name from Injō (*d* 1108), who was the chief disciple of Kakujō (*d* 1077), son of JŌCHŌ, who had developed a gentle, elegant style of wood sculpture suited to the refined tastes of the mid-Heian aristocracy of the capital (modern Kyoto). Art historians generally consider Kakujō to have been the first-generation master of the school, which specialized in producing for their patrons close formal replicas of Jōchō's imagery. There were two workshops (*bussho*) of the In school in Kyoto: the Shichijō–Ōmiya workshop, established by Injō, and the Rokujō–Madenokōji workshop, set up in the mid-12th century. Initially in competition with the other main exponent of Jōchō's style, the EN school, the In was pre-eminent in the second half of the 12th century. After this, the work of the school became increasingly mannered and began to decline in popularity. In the early Kamakura period it was eclipsed by the dynamic realism of the KEI school. No works by Injō survive. The seated *Amitabha* (h. 2.2 m) at the Hōkongōin in Kyoto is usually attributed to the third-generation master of the school, Inkaku (*fl* 1110–40). The statue is very close in style to Jōchō's *Amitabha* in the Hōōdō (Phoenix Hall) of the Byōdōin (*see* JAPAN, fig. 61). Inkaku was succeeded by Inson (1120–98), the school's leading representative and one of the most powerful sculptors of the time, who received commissions from the retired emperor GoShirakawa (*reg* 1155–8) and participated in refurbishing the temples of Tōdaiji and Kōfukuji at Nara following the fires of 1180 (*see* NARA, §III, 4 and 7). Artists of the school include Inkaku's younger brother Inchō (*fl* 1125–60), Inkei (*d* 1179) and Inshō (*fl* 1175–90).

BIBLIOGRAPHY

Kodansha Enc. Japan

SAMUEL C. MORSE

Inamgaon. Bronze Age site at a small village of the same name, south-east of Pune, Maharashtra, India. Excavations yielded evidence of human habitation from *c.* 1700 to *c.* 900 BC. Initially, the people lived in rectangular houses with low mud walls and thatched roofs, and later (*c.*1200–*c.* 900 BC) in round huts. Among the numerous artefacts from the site are some interesting human figurines of baked or unbaked clay, which are all hand-modelled with curved projections for the hands and stumpy legs. There is no attempt at delineating facial features except for a pinched nose in some examples. Two unbaked female figures, one with head and the other without, seem to be associated with the religious beliefs of the people, for they were found carefully deposited below a house floor dated *c.* 1400 BC. The figurine with a head was placed in a clay box, while the headless figurine was positioned together with an unbaked clay bull on the lid of the container. The unique headless figure has a hole in her abdomen that corresponds with a similar one in the bull for the insertion of a dowel to attach the figurine to the back of the bull. Sculptures of a headless goddess occur in Maharashtra, Andhra Pradesh and Karnataka over a long period (6th century BC–9th century AD). Some of these sculptures are still worshipped by childless women. The Warlis, a tribe living near Bombay, worship a headless goddess named Palghat, which in their language means the position of a woman during childbirth, and paint her picture on the walls of their houses at the time of marriage. A 6th-century AD Sanskrit text also describes a headless rain goddess named Shakambhari. The headless goddess thus seems to be connected with fertility cults. A few unbaked clay male figurines recovered from Inamgaon are characterized by coarse modelling. Similar figures of wheat flour are still made by villagers in Maharashtra at the time of community feasts and are deposited in the river after worshipping.

See also INDIAN SUBCONTINENT, §VII, 18.

BIBLIOGRAPHY

M. K. Dhavalikar: *Masterpieces of Indian Terracottas* (Bombay, 1977)
——: 'Śākambhāri: The Headless Goddess', *An. Bhandarkar Orient. Res. Inst.*, lxviii (1987), pp. 281–93

M. K. DHAVALIKAR

I-nan. *See* YI'NAN.

Inandıktepe. Site of a Hittite temple of the 17th–16th centuries BC, 109 km north of Ankara, beside the ancient route via Çankırı and Kastamonu to the Black Sea. The temple was built on a hill above the fertile valley of the Terme Çayı, and the ruin mound of a village, known as Termehüyük, stands beside the river. Both sites were excavated by Racı Temizer in 1966 and 1967, on behalf of the Directorate General of Ancient Monuments and Museums, after the chance find of fragments of a remarkable cult vessel decorated with reliefs. Finds are in the Museum of Anatolian Civilizations in Ankara.

The mound was occupied sporadically from the Early Bronze Age (3rd millennium BC) to Hellenistic times. In the Old Hittite period its inhabitants built, on a nearby hill, a temple dedicated to the storm god, one of the foremost deities in the Hittite pantheon. The plan, covering an area 70×50 m, is admirably adapted to the shape of the hill, with rectangular two- or even three-storey blocks of rooms set side by side and back to back on terraces rising one above the other to encircle a courtyard on the summit. It was a well-organized, stone-built structure with interior plastering, consisting of storerooms, living-quarters for the priests and priestesses and areas set aside for religious ceremonies. A land grant tablet, written in Akkadian in the cuneiform script and found in one of the jars in a storeroom, dates the building to the reign of Hattusili I (third quarter of the 17th century BC). It is thus the earliest known Hittite temple.

The red-burnished pottery found in the temple is of a high technical standard and belongs to the mature Old Hittite style. The vessels are, however, few in number, and they appear to have had specialized uses. Some have tall beaked spouts and others have bull-headed spouts. Terracotta statues of bulls, used as cult objects, and a crudely modelled god seated inside his shrine were also found. Inandıktepe provides the link between the traditions of the Old Assyrian colony period and later developments in the Hittite empire period (*see* ANATOLIA, ANCIENT, §I, 2(ii)(a) and (b)).

A relief vase known as the Inandık Vase, which came from one of the storerooms, is among the finest examples of Old Hittite pottery. (Fragments of similar relief vases have been found at Bitik and Boğazköy.) It has an ovoid body with four handles, a high wide neck and a flaring rim; the rim was hollow, and libations, poured in through a special opening, flowed into the body of the vessel through the mouths of four bulls' heads. The jar is red-burnished, and the neck and upper part of the body are decorated with figured reliefs in four registers separated from one another by bands of geometric motifs. The faces, hands and legs of the figures are painted red, their long hair is black and they are dressed in creamy yellow or black garments; these colours are also used to pick out details of the scenes. The figures have large pointed noses, almond-shaped eyes, small mouths, thick lips and well-defined, beardless chins. Most of the figures are shown in profile, but a few have their torsos shown frontally, though their heads and legs are in profile. Though small, the figures are lively and well-proportioned so that they give a surprising impression of monumentality.

In the lowest frieze several scenes are shown: the manufacture of vessels for use in a ceremony, gods seated on either side of an altar, musicians playing large and small lyres, cymbals and a lute, and people preparing food for a ceremony. In the second frieze a bull is sacrificed before a statue of a bull (the animal sacred to the storm god), votive offerings are brought, under the guidance of secondary gods accompanied by a lyre-player, and libations are poured before a god who is seated in front of an altar. The third frieze shows male and female deities seated on a bed in front of an altar, and a procession of men and women moving towards a temple in the company of cymbal-players. Finally in the topmost frieze, below the rim, there are musicians with cymbals, lyres and lutes, acrobats and an erotic scene; here the common people are celebrating the sacred marriage depicted in the third frieze. There is no textual evidence for a Hittite sacred marriage ceremony, and the Inandık Vase is the first evidence of its existence. As such it belongs to an Ancient Near Eastern tradition that goes back to the Uruk Vase (Berlin, Pergamonmus.), which depicts roughly the same subject.

The temple was destroyed by a fierce fire in the first decades of the 16th century BC, probably in the reign of Mursili I or, at the latest, in that of Hantili I. Inandıktepe was not reoccupied, and the mound was also abandoned for several centuries.

BIBLIOGRAPHY

T. Özguç: 'The Bitik Vase', *Anatolia*, ii (1957), pp. 57–78

K. Balkan: *Inandık'ta 1966 yılında bulunan Eski Hitit Çağına ait bir bağış belgesi/Eine Schenkungsurkunde aus der althetitischen Zeit, gefunden in Inandık 1966* (Ankara, 1973) [bilingual text]

R. M. Boehmer: *Die Reliefkeramik von Boğazköy* (Berlin, 1983), p. 19

T. Özguç: *Inandıktepe: Eski Hitit Çağına önemli bir kült merkezi/An Important Cult Center in the Old Hittite Period* (Ankara, 1988) [bilingual text]

TAHSIN ÖZGÜÇ

Inariyama tomb. Japanese burial mound at Gyōda, Saitama Prefecture. Dating back to the 6th century AD, it is one of four large mounds, all over 100 m long, in a group of ten known as the Sakitama tomb group. These served as burial places for the powerful Musashi rulers (*kuni no miyatsuko*) in the 6th and 7th centuries. Now partly destroyed, Inariyama was once a moated, keyhole-shaped tomb (*zenpōkōenfun*; *see* Japan, §III, 2(ii)) and is regarded as the oldest of the group.

It was excavated in 1968–9, and one of the two burial trenches contained about 250 items, mostly dating from the early 6th century, including a long sword (Gyōda, Saitama Prefect., Saitama Hist. Park Resource Cent.) bearing a gold inlay inscription of 115 Chinese characters running the length (735 mm) of both sides, discovered in 1978 when it was X-rayed. On the evidence of an analysis of the surface rust the sword appears to have been manufactured by the Chinese *zhaogang* (Jap. *shōkō*) furnace process with imported raw materials (the main component of its steel was magnetite, an iron ore then available only in central China). The sword is an important discovery of a dated object of the Kofun or Tomb period (*c.* AD 300–710) with an inscription relating to political figures known from literary sources. It is dated the 48th year (*xingai*, Jap. *kanotoyi*) of a 60-year cycle, generally interpreted as corresponding to AD 471 (or, less likely, 531). It was made for Wowake no Omi, hereditary Chief Sword Bearer under Ōkimi (Great King) Wakatakeru. Ōkimi Wakatakeru is usually identified with Emperor Yūryaku, who reigned from AD 456 to 479 according to the *Nihon shoki* (or *Nihongi*; 'Chronicle of Japan'; AD 720). The inscription also lists seven generations of the owner's ancestors who had been imperial sword bearers. First on the list is Ō-hiko-no-mikoto, who is mentioned in the *Nihon shoki* as having been sent to the north by the early Emperor Sujin in the late 3rd century. This evidence suggests that by the 3rd century there was already a system of regional rulers with strong allegiance to the Yamato court and a system of ranks bestowed by the emperor.

BIBLIOGRAPHY

S. Murayama and R. A. Miller: 'The Inariyama Tumulus Sword Inscription', *J. Japan. Stud.*, ii (1979), pp. 405–38

T. Saito and H. Otsuka: *Inariyama kofun to Sakitama kofungun* [The Inariyama tumulus and the Sakitama tumuli group] (Tokyo, 1980)

T. Kishi: 'Meibun no shakudoku to kaisetsu' [The decipherment and interpretation of the inscription], *Saitama-Inariyama kofun shingaimei tekken shuri hōkokusho* [Saitama-Inariyama tumulus report on repairs on the iron sword with *xingai* inscription] (Urawa, 1982), pp. 30–37

W. Anazawa and J. Manome: 'Two Inscribed Swords from Japanese Tumuli: Discoveries and Research on Finds from the Saitama-Inariyama and Eta-Funayama Tumuli', *Windows on the Japanese Past: Studies in Archaeology and Pre-history*, ed. R. J. Pearson, G. L. Barnes and K. L. Hutterer (Ann Arbor, 1986), pp. 375–95

J. EDWARD KIDDER JR

Inca. A Pre-Columbian culture of the Central Andean area of South America; the early Inca people are recognizable in the archaeological record of the Late Intermediate Period (*c.* AD 1000–1476), from the 12th century onwards. The Inca empire flourished in the 15th century and early 16th. In a more restricted sense the term refers to the ruling élite and its supreme head, the Sapa Inca. The Inca are alone in having successfully politically unified the vast area of the Central Andes, coastlands and adjacent regions. Their empire endured for only 90 years; it extended 3500 km from north-west to south-east and approximately 320 km inland from the South American coast (see fig. 1). There are widely differing estimates of the total population of Inca and subject peoples at the time of the Spanish arrival in 1532, but a conservative one would be about seven million.

1. Introduction. 2. Architecture and urban planning. 3. Arts and crafts.

1. Introduction.

(i) History. The Inca had no written records, but later accounts of their origins outline their arrival in the Valley of Cuzco (estimated by Rowe as *c.* AD 1200) under the leader Manco Capac, the establishment of their capital at CUZCO and the subjugation of other tribes in the valley and its environs during the reigns of the first eight Inca rulers. The successful defence of Cuzco by Inca Cusi Yupanqui (*reg* 1438–71; the 9th Inca, thereafter called Pachacutec or Pachacuti, meaning 'cataclysm') against the threat of the rival Chanca federation to the north-west left the way clear to consolidate Inca control in the Cuzco region and to expand rapidly beyond it, exploiting a combination of alliances and military conquests. From 1438 onwards Pachacutec extended Inca rule into adjacent mountain regions, north to Cajamarca and south to Lake Titicaca. Further extensions were made by his successor Tupac Inca Yupanqui (*reg c.* 1471–93) into jungle regions

east of Cuzco, north to Ecuador and south into parts of Bolivia, Chile and north-west Argentina. Inca Huayna Capac (*reg* 1493–1525) annexed some north-eastern jungle regions, including Chachapoyas, and subjugated Ecuador as far as the River Ancasmayo. At the death of Huayna Capac, his two sons, Atahuallpa and Huascar, fought for the leadership. In 1532 the Spaniards, led by Francisco Pizarro, landed in Peru during the civil war and turned it to their advantage by kidnapping the recently triumphant Atahuallpa at Cajamarca. Pizarro held Atahuallpa while the Spaniards consolidated their position by acquiring numerous allies from among those subjugated by the Inca. Eventually they had Atahuallpa executed.

(ii) Political and social organization. The Inca called their empire Tahuantinsuyu ('Land of the Four Quarters') and divided it into four provinces: Chinchasuyu (north-west), Antisuyu (north-east), Cuntisuyu (south-west) and Collasuyu (south-east). Cuzco, the capital, was in the centre. Some provinces were divided into smaller units approximating to pre-Inca territories; others were re-divided or adjusted in size. At the local level the *ayllu*, the basic Andean social or kin group, was the organizational or community group. Larger communities were made up of two or more such groups, and new localized groups, unrelated to the kinship system, were occasionally formed for administrative reasons. Cuzco contained ten *ayllu*s, five belonging to Hanan ('Upper') Cuzco and five to Hurin ('Lower') Cuzco. The Inca set themselves up as an élite over their neighbours and subjects. The power of the ruler was absolute; claiming descent from the Sun, the Sapa Inca ('Unique Inca') ruled by divine right. Government was effected through nobles of royal blood and a newly created class of 'Incas by privilege'. The Sapa Inca married his full sister, who was seen as his only legitimate wife (called Coya). When an Inca ruler died his eldest legitimate son, or the most suitable of his legitimate sons, inherited his titles. The rest of his lineage formed a *panaca* (descendant group), inheriting his estates.

Inca organizational genius is illustrated by their modification and transformation of earlier socio-economic organizations based on purely reciprocal arrangements into a complex state system. Extravagant gifts were given by the Sapa Inca in exchange for work or produce, and security and guarantees were offered in exchange for acceptance of Inca sovereignty. Colonists, who formerly had simply extended the range of community access to goods by living in different ecological zones, became a new class of Inca culture-bearers who kept non-Inca populations under subjugation. On coming to power, Pachacutec Inca changed the religious hierarchy so that the Sun god, the ancestor of the Inca themselves, became the chief deity, while the previously dominant older gods, Viracocha and Illapa (creator and thunder gods respectively), were relegated to secondary positions (*see also* SOUTH AMERICA, PRE-COLUMBIAN, §I, 3(i)). This change reinforced the power of the Inca élite through divine right and through the associated calendrical organization of the agricultural cycle, the success of which was vital to the maintenance of power.

Inca society was strongly hierarchical: the Sapa Inca was at the head of a pyramidal organization; his primary

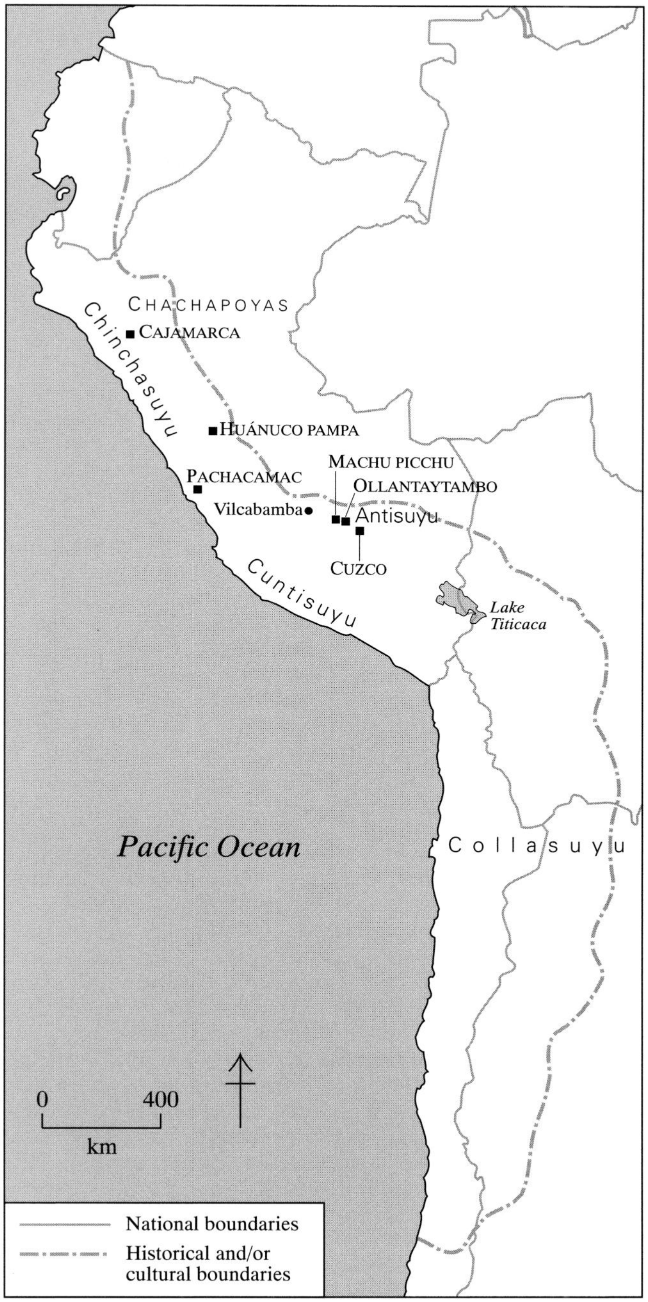

1. Map of the expansion of the Inca empire, *c.* AD 1500; those sites with separate entries in this dictionary are distinguished by CROSS-REFERENCE TYPE

kin formed the class of aristocratic rulers (the council and provincial governors), and his subsidiary kin were their assistants and servants. Native rulers were often allowed to continue to rule their provinces, villages or *ayllu.* Everyone not related to the Inca or native rulers remained householders, who served in the military, on public works and in other government organizations. They also farmed their allotted lands and those belonging to the state and to religious groups. Such households were organized into groups approximated on a decimal system and were supervised by appointed leaders. The accumulation of luxury goods and considerable estates was encouraged among the aristocracy and native rulers but virtually prohibited for commoners. Dress was carefully prescribed according to social rank, and there were many other laws to govern virtually every aspect of everyday life: municipal and agrarian laws, common law, laws of brotherhood (cooperative work), a law governing the distribution of work, domestic law, poor law, and laws regulating travellers, environment and morality. The laws were strictly enforced, and punishments were listed and meted out by government administrators and officials.

The Inca spoke Quechua and spread its use throughout their empire, imposing it on others for purposes of government and for communication between provinces. Quechua-speaking colonists spread the language and educated subjugated peoples in Inca practices and culture. This education was further ensured by requiring defeated leaders to send their eldest sons to the school for the sons of Inca noblemen in Cuzco; daughters could be educated to serve as Sun Virgins in Inca temples. Inca history was kept through oral memory by trained *quipucamayoc*s (court historians) and on illustrated painted boards; the latter, initiated by Pachacutec, were kept in the Coricancha (Sun Temple) in Cuzco. The *quipu* was used to record numerical and statistical information for administrative purposes throughout the empire. It comprised a cord hung with numerous coloured and knotted woollen threads. In the expert hands of the *quipucamayoc*s, *quipu*s were also useful memory aids for histories and literature. Nevertheless, Inca literature was primarily oral, and only fragments of it were recorded at the time of the Spanish Conquest. *Amauta*s ('teachers') composed comedies and dramas for performance at court, acted by members of the élite. Poetry was normally unrhymed verse. Songs and chanted verses were accompanied by various types of flutes. Astronomy had a prominent place in intellectual life and in the organization of religious and agricultural cycles and associated ceremonial occasions. The Inca made precise calendrical observations with the use of horizons in conjunction with architectural features such as pillars, windows, pegs and carved stones called *intihuatana*, and with the help of such shadow-casting objects as plumb bobs.

Ritual games and sport were interwoven with religious ceremony and public occasions. Royal hunts, including many thousands of participants, were organized partly for entertainment and partly for collecting game. Other pastimes included throwing counters and dice, sometimes in forms of gambling.

2. ARCHITECTURE AND URBAN PLANNING. A classic style of Inca architecture is associated with the empire period in Cuzco and with all other government-planned sites built along 40,000 km of all-weather roads, including provincial capitals, residential towns, *tambos* (road-side inns), *chasqui* posts (stops for runners), fortresses, commercial centres, toll gates, look-outs and some special ceremonial centres and shrines. There were two main parallel roads, with important secondary networks, connecting the major provincial capitals, towns and services. Cuzco and the regional capitals had palaces, Sun temples, convents, barracks for housing special groups and government artisans, varied residential sectors for colonists and surrounding populations, storehouses and gathering places (usually at the centre) with a ceremonial dais or platform called *ushnu* (or *usnu*).

The canons of Inca architecture are simple and repetitive. The main building plan was the one-roomed rectangle, of varied size and length but restricted in width. Curved forms were sometimes used in shrines, and the circular plan, in particular, was used for the 'Sunturhuasi', a ceremonial structure connected with ancestor worship. The most important structures were of finely fitted masonry, lesser ones of stone set in mud mortar or adobe bricks or both. All buildings were roofed with thatch set on a wooden frame. Some structures were back-to-back and had gables providing a loft or second storey. Hundreds of storehouses (rectangular, square or circular, according to locality) were built in rows on hillsides near major centres.

Sites were levelled and terraced, and groups of two to eight buildings were arranged around plazas or patios within an enclosure wall, as at the citadel of MACHU PICCHU (see fig. 2). Palaces comprised several such units, linked by a series of doorways. Walls normally measure 700–900 mm in width, incline inwards at an average angle of 5° and are pierced by regularly spaced trapezoidal

2. Inca citadel of Machu Picchu, late 15th century AD–early 16th

doorways, windows and niches, some with double or treble jambs, placed in various patterns.

Since ethnohistorical sources identify the main towns, palaces and estates of the ruling Incas, architectural studies of these provide a basis for an Inca imperial architectural chronology of four phases, plus two post-Conquest phases at the sites of OLLANTAYTAMBO and Vilcabamba. Furniture for use inside buildings was minimal, consisting of low, built-in platforms or protruding rocks, stone pegs set in walls, benches, portable stools, stones set for food preparation and storage pots sometimes sunk into the ground.

There were several contemporaneous styles of imperial masonry, each with variations (*see* SOUTH AMERICA, PRE-COLUMBIAN, §III, 2(iii)). The finely fitted masonry of prestigious buildings is usually of rectangular, regularly coursed blocks with variable depths of sunken joints and smoothness of texture. Right angles are only approximate. Where seams might have been opened, masons ingeniously keyed the ashlars together by alternating the pattern. Polygonal and Cyclopean styles were usually used for monumental terracing and enclosure walls. Stoneworking techniques included the use of massive stone hammers and occasional cutting and polishing with sand and water.

3. ARTS AND CRAFTS. Specially qualified, usually hereditary artisans, such as metalworkers, carpenters, lapidaries and weavers, lived in towns and produced luxury goods. Individual artists or fine craftsmen are not referred to by name in the accounts recorded in ethnohistorical sources, but by tribe: for example the Chimú as excellent goldsmiths or the Colla as fine masons.

(i) Sculpture and carving. In Inca sculpture, as in architecture, the feeling for horizontal planes and mass predominates, and most works are non-representational. Inca stone-carving also includes the sophisticated ornamental shapes given to individual stones in walls, carved planes and steps and abstract shapes on the surfaces of caves and rock masses; such carvings may include figures of a puma (e.g. at Puma Orqo) or a snake (e.g. on some palace doorways). High-relief stone-carvings consist mainly of miniature ceremonial *konapa*s (figures of llamas and alpacas), executed in stones of different colours and textures. Finely carved stone dishes with abstract designs are heavy, finely balanced and sometimes decorated in relief with pumas, snakes or, more rarely, an incised scene (examples in Cuzco, Mus. U.; London, BM). Hammering, and cutting and polishing with sand and water, were employed for monumental stone-carving and to make such figurines and bowls, as well as stone mortars, pestles, axes, clod crushers and weapons such as slingstones and club-heads. Wood-carvings have rarely survived but include carved figures and, from coastal graves, tomb posts carved in the form of architectural implements and ornate carved staffs of office, decorated with paint and sheet metal. Drinking cups (*keros*) were usually of simple shape, with incised geometric patterns or a pattern of small holes inlaid with lead. Cut designs, including stylized floral motifs, were filled with lacquers and fixed with vegetable gum. In the Spanish colonial period such cups were developed into an illustrative art form with lively figurative lacquer-painted scenes showing a mixture of Inca and Spanish culture. Bone, particularly llama bone, was used for ornamental figurines and a wide range of implements. Shell was used for inlay work, for human and animal figurines and in jewellery and lapidary work.

(ii) Pottery. The classic Inca pottery style appears *c.* 1200, well before the classic style of architecture. Pottery was standardized in form and decoration, well-designed and well-proportioned but repetitive. It was produced in many sizes of vessel and varied in provincial areas, where it was copied or integrated with local styles. In Cuzco pottery was made by hand, without the potter's wheel, from carefully prepared clays with added temper. Vessels were made in sections; they are fine-grained, hard, highly polished, with smooth surfaces, finished with a fine liquid clay slip and decorated in white, cream, purple, red and black. Some plain wares were embellished with appliqué strips, and vessels were occasionally modelled. Strap, vertical and horizontal handles, lugs, knobs and other applications were added, and firing was done in an open pit. All ceramic shapes, whether utilitarian or ceremonial, are predominantly functional and include aryballos jars, plates and flat dishes, jugs and bowls, and large jars for storage. Plain wares include cooking pots, pedestal bowls, braziers and colanders. Aryballos jars, for carrying and storing liquids (especially maize beer), have long necks with flaring lips, small lugs and pointed bases below their wide bodies. This form occurs in many variations and with realistic modelling, particularly on the coast. Decoration was organized in zones of parallel bands: continuous triangles or diamonds were used for necks and rims; crosshatching was executed in vertical bands on bodies and horizontal bands on bowls and the insides of plates. Highly stylized motifs, representing plant life, animals and sometimes ceremonial scenes, were painted on.

(iii) Textiles and dress. Textiles preserved in coastal burials include fine tapestry cloth, called *cumbi*, woven in ornate and highly coloured patterns. Inca textiles were not usually embroidered, but feathers were imported from the jungle and sometimes sewn into large shirts and capes. Yarn was spun from llama, alpaca and vicuña wool and used in a range of natural colours or dyed in primary colours. Several dyes were employed: indigo for blue, cochineal for red, the bark of *Chinus mollis* for yellow, and combinations of these. Vicuña wool was used for the finest textiles, but coastal cotton was also used in some Inca textiles. Wide cloth was woven on a vertical loom, while backstrap looms were used for narrow items. Small repetitive geometric designs, such as plain or filled squares, were used on their own, in an infinite variety of patterns or combined with large broad colour areas (*see* TAPESTRY, colour pl. III, fig. 1, and TEXTILE, colour pl. IX). Many designs may have had heraldic significance. Complex combinations of natural dyes for strong and delicate colours were preferred. Precisely planned designs were often calculated to fit the shape of the tunic. Clothing was not tailored but woven into rectangular shapes and used to make tunics, borders, belts, mantles, long sleeveless dresses worn by women and bags used by men for carrying *coca* leaves. Wool and aloe-fibre clothing was worn by both sexes. Distinctive tunics were worn by different army squadrons. Sandals were of

leather or sometimes llama wool. Jewellery was worn by both sexes according to rank and status: the most important pieces for men were large cylindrical ear-plugs, metal disc breast ornaments, wide bracelets of gold and silver and small gold masks on the sandals, shoulders or at the knees. Feathers were widely used in headdresses and collars or were woven into special clothing. Women wore pins for their shoulder mantles, shell necklaces or bone beads. A Coya (queen) might wear two big pins or discs hanging to cover her breasts.

(iv) Metalwork. Metal technology shows evidence of a wide knowledge of different processes and techniques, including hammering, annealing, casting in open and closed moulds (including the lost-wax process), primitive soldering, repoussé, gilding, a type of plating, riveting and drilling. Earlier forms of stone tools and weapons were adapted and copied in copper and bronze, while many elaborate decorative pieces were made in precious metals. Cast tools and weapons included flat trapezoidal axe blades, the *tumi* (a knife or axe with a crescent-shaped blade), chisels, crowbars, slingstones, club-heads, mirrors, tweezers, needles and bells. Gold was the symbolic colour of the Sun and therefore of the Sapa Inca, and silver that of the Moon and of the Coya. These precious metals were used almost entirely for luxury goods, gifts and ceremonial objects, usually with hammer and repoussé ornamentation, riveting and soldering with pulverized copper oxides or copper carbonates mixed with an organic binder. Some figurines and animals were cast in silver or in gold and silver, usually in simple, conventionalized forms. Large-headed human figurines were sometimes inlaid, for example cast silver with gold inlay. Gold and silver drinking cups were decorated and sometimes made in the form of effigy beakers; others were inlaid with turquoise or shell; bowls copied pottery shapes and could also include some figurative modelling.

(v) Musical instruments. Wind instruments included the *queña* flute, made of a joint of cane with as many as eight stops, and panpipes of several joints of cane, or other materials, tied together. Larger bone flutes were used for playing war tunes, and trumpets were made from large conch shells. Other trumpets were made of wood, gourds and metals. Whistles producing only one note were common. Percussion instruments included large drums made from the skins of enemies; drums for important religious ceremonies, decorated with precious metals and stones, and tambourines; metal bells, which were used in festivals; and jingles and rattles, which were tied to the bodies of the dancers who were an integral part of ceremonial occasions and worship.

BIBLIOGRAPHY

F. G. Poma de Ayala: 'Nueva corónica y buen gobierno: Codex péruvien illustré', *Trav. & Mem. Inst. Ethnol.*, xxiii (1936) [whole issue]
J. H. Rowe: 'Inca Culture at the Time of the Spanish Conquest', *Hb. S. Amer. Ind.*, ii, *Bureau Amer. Ethnol. Bull.*, cxliii (1946), pp. 183–330
J. V. Murra: 'Cloth and its Functions in the Inca State', *Amer. Anthropologist*, lxiv (1962), pp. 710–27
J. Jones: *Art of Empire: The Inca of Peru* (New York, 1964)
A. Kendall: *Everyday Life of the Incas* (London, 1973)
G. Graziano and L. Margolies: *Arquitectura inka* (Caracas, 1977; Eng. trans. by P. J. Lyon, Bloomington and London, 1980)
J. Hemming and E. Ranney: *Monuments of the Inca* (Boston, 1982)
A. Kendall: *Aspects of Inca Architecture: Description, Function and Chronology*, 2 vols, Brit. Archaeol. Rep., Int. Ser., ccxlii (Oxford, 1985)
J. H. Hyslop: *Inka Settlement Planning* (Austin, 1990)
A. Kendall: 'An Archaeological Perspective for Late Intermediate Period Inca Development in the Cuzco Region', *Structure, Knowledge and Representation in the Andes*, ed. G. Urton and D. Poole, i (Hamilton, NY, in preparation)

ANN KENDALL

Inca, Juan Tomás Tuyru Tupac. *See* TUYRU TUPAC INCA, JUAN TOMÁS.

Ince, Joseph Murray (*b* Presteign, Powys, 1806; *d* London, 24 Sept 1859). Welsh painter. From December 1823 until early 1826 he was a pupil of David Cox in Hereford. Ince moved to London in 1826, exhibiting at the Royal Academy for the first time in that year; he was an occasional exhibitor at the Royal Academy and the British Institution and a frequent exhibitor at the Society of British Artists until 1858. In 1832 he was in Cambridge, where he was for some time a drawing-master. He returned to Presteign *c.* 1835 and spent much of the rest of his life there.

Ince worked in both watercolours and oils. His subjects were drawn predominantly from rustic England. Following his stay in Cambridge, architectural drawings of the colleges, such as *St Botolph's, Cambridge, and Corpus Christi* (New Haven, CT, Yale Cent. Brit. A.), formed a prominent feature of his work. He also produced some continental townscapes, and several views of Stockholm suggest that he may have visited Scandinavia. His watercolours of the 1830s and 1840s continued to show affinities with Cox's style of the previous decade but with a less assured touch. He frequently resorted to an obtrusive and nervous outlining of form.

BIBLIOGRAPHY

DNB; Redgrave
M. Hardie: *Watercolour Painting in Britain*, iii (London, 1969), p. 19

SCOTT WILCOX

Ince & Mayhew. English partnership of cabinetmakers formed in 1758 by William Ince (*b* ?London, *c.* 1738; *d* London, 6 Jan 1804) and John Mayhew (*b* 1736; *d* London, May 1811). Ince was apprenticed to John West (*fl* 1743–58) of Covent Garden, London, from 1752 until West's death. As the usual age to begin an apprenticeship was 14, he was probably born towards the end of the 1730s. In 1758 Ince formed a partnership with Mayhew. They operated from Broad Street, Carnaby Market, an address formerly occupied by Charles Smith (*fl* 1746–59), whose premises they had purchased. In Mortimer's *Universal Director* (1763) they were described as 'cabinet-makers, carvers and upholders', and by 1778 they were styling themselves 'manufacturers of plate glass' (Ince's father and brother were glass-grinders).

In 1759 the partners began to issue in serial form *The Universal System of Household Furniture*, with Ince executing the bulk of designs. The work, which was dedicated to the 4th Duke of Marlborough and published as a single volume in 1762, consisted of 89 plates, engraved by Matthias Darly, with a further six (of fire-grates) added at the end. Their designs tend to be more cautious versions of those by Thomas Chippendale (i), but they include tripod or 'claw' tables, which are not to be found in

Chippendale's *Gentleman and Cabinet-maker's Director.* Thomas Sheraton judged their work to be 'much inferior to Chippendale's'.

The firm prospered in the 1760s and 1770s, attracting fashionable clients and establishing good relations with such architects as Sir William Chambers, Robert Adam (i) and James Wyatt. They received exclusive commissions from the 4th Duke of Bedford and the 5th to furnish Bedford House, London, and from the 5th Duke at Woburn Abbey, Beds, but in the case of the 6th Earl of Coventry at Croome Court, Worcs, they worked alongside other leading cabinetmakers. When Rococo became less fashionable, Ince & Mayhew readily adapted to the more severe Neo-classical style (e.g. the commodes of 1764 ordered by Lord Coventry, or those of 1767 at Burghley House, Cambs). They developed two characteristic forms for their commodes: the rectilinear, boxlike style of Lord Coventry's commission and the semicircular form of those made for Derby House after a design by Adam (1775; Earl of Derby priv. col.). These commodes, and those of 1773 at Osterley Park House, near London, show Ince & Mayhew's highly accomplished use of marquetry, with large-scale antique motifs and subtle coloration to give an illusion of depth. Their furniture is frequently enriched with ormolu mounts. Another element in their work was antiquarianism: at Burghley they incorporated 17th-century marquetry panels into commodes and corner-cupboards.

In addition to those already mentioned, Ince & Mayhew's patrons included the 4th Duke of Marlborough, the 1st Duke of Northumberland, the 1st Marquess of Lansdowne and the 1st Earl of Caledon. In spite of their prestigious clientele, they were often 'inconvenienced for ready cash', a widespread problem among 18th-century cabinetmakers. A new partnership agreement was signed in 1799, but the last five years of Ince's life were dogged with financial crises. His death in 1804 was followed by acrimonious disputes about money between his widow, Ann, and John Mayhew.

WRITINGS

The Universal System of Household Furniture (London, 1762/*R* 1960)

BIBLIOGRAPHY

M. Hecksher: 'Ince and Mayhew: Bibliographical Notes from New York', *Furn. Hist.*, x (1974), pp. 61–7

P. Kirkham: 'The Partnership of William Ince and John Mayhew', *Furn. Hist.*, x (1974), pp. 56–9

H. Roberts: 'The Derby House Commode', *Burl. Mag.*, cxxvii (1985), pp. 275–82

G. Beard and C. Gilbert, eds: *Dictionary of English Furniture Makers, 1660–1840* (Leeds, 1986)

JAMES YORKE

Inchbold, J(ohn) W(illiam) (*b* Leeds, 29 Aug 1830; *d* Leeds, 23 Jan 1888). English painter. He spent his early years in Leeds, where his father was a newspaper proprietor, but came to London around 1846 to study lithography in the firm of Day & Haghe. His obituary in *The Athenaeum* records that he went on to study at the Royal Academy Schools, but his name does not appear in the registers. He exhibited watercolours at the Society of British Artists in 1849 and 1850 and at the Royal Academy in 1851. At this period his work has a fluidity and a freedom of handling that is closer to Richard Parkes Bonington than to the prevailing style of Victorian watercolours. Around 1852 he came under the influence of the Pre-Raphaelite movement and radically altered his style. His oil painting of the *Chapel, Bolton* (exh. RA 1853; Northampton, Cent. Mus. & A.G.) is a meticulously rendered view of the abbey ruins in the Pre-Raphaelite manner. This was followed the next year by *At Bolton* (Leeds, C.A.G.), another view of Bolton Abbey, this time with a deer prominent in the foreground. Both paintings illustrate lines from William Wordsworth's poem 'The White Doe of Ryleston'. Wordsworth was also the inspiration for the small painting *Study in March* (Oxford, Ashmolean), which is now perhaps Inchbold's best-known work and was highly praised when exhibited at the Royal Academy in 1855. *The Spectator* described it as 'a most delicious little piece—pure and perfect in its soft colour and unsurpassedly tender as a description of the season of early promise'.

It is not known how Inchbold met the Pre-Raphaelites, but the Rossettis knew him well, and he became a close friend of Algernon Charles Swinburne. John Everett Millais admired his work and in a letter to Holman Hunt described *Anstey's Cove, Devon* (Cambridge, Fitzwilliam) as 'a lovely landscape with the sea and cliffs ... quite original and exquisitely truthful and refined'. Inchbold's pictures soon attracted the attention of John Ruskin, and in 1858 he visited Switzerland to paint alpine subjects under Ruskin's supervision. The only picture known from this period is the *Lake of Lucerne* (London, V&A), a tranquil vision of cool reflections and distant mountains. From this point onwards Inchbold's painting changed direction, possibly as a reaction against the bullying he had received from Ruskin. Visits to Venice in 1862 and the following years resulted in a series of ethereal pictures painted with the freedom of his early works and entirely lacking the highly finished technique of his Pre-Raphaelite pictures. The *Certosa, Venice, from the Public Gardens* (Leeds, C.A.G.) is a good example. Inchbold visited Spain in 1865 and 1866 and the Isle of Wight in 1869. Then around 1877 he took up residence at Montreux on the banks of Lake Geneva. Apart from occasional visits to England he remained there for the rest of his life.

Inchbold never married and seems to have had a rather melancholy life. Dante Gabriel Rossetti complained that he was a bore, and Swinburne wrote, 'He had not many friends, being very shy and rather brusque in manner, so that people were apt to think him odd.' Overshadowed by the leading figures of the Pre-Raphaelite Brotherhood his work sank into obscurity after his death.

BIBLIOGRAPHY

Obituary, *The Athenaeum* (4 Feb 1888)

A. Staley: *The Pre-Raphaelite Landscape* (Oxford, 1973)

The Pre-Raphaelites (exh. cat., ed. L. Parris; London, Tate, 1984)

DAVID CORDINGLY

Incunabulum [Lat.: 'swaddling band']. Early stage in the development of something. The term is generally used in its plural form, incunabula, for printed books produced before 1500, and in this sense it is sometimes translated as 'cradle books', since it refers to works made during the infancy of printing.

□

Indau, Johann (*b* 1651; *d* Vienna, 7 Feb 1690). German cabinetmaker and architectural theorist, active in Austria. Probably a native of south Germany, he travelled in Germany and Italy and is recorded in Vienna from 1682. After 1684 he became cabinetmaker to Eleanor Gonzaga (1628–86), widow of the Holy Roman Emperor Ferdinand III (*reg* 1637–57). After her death he was emancipated from guild restrictions.

Indau is known only through his publications. His main work, *Wiennerisches Architectur-Kunst und Säulen-Buch* (Vienna, 1686), is the first treatise on architectural theory published in Austria. Addressed not only to architects, masons and builders but also to carpenters and painters, it follows the tradition of the German *Säulenbücher* of the late 16th century and the 17th as a textbook on the five Classical orders of architecture, with 14 illustrations engraved by Elias Nessenthaler (1664–1714) accompanied by a brief text.

Instead of applying the proportions laid down by Sebastiano Serlio's *Regole generali di architettura* (1537), hitherto the norm in Germany and the Netherlands, Indau proposed his own, simpler method of constructing the orders, in all of which column height, entablature and pedestal were to be in the same proportions. The basis for calculating the other parts of the orders is not, as was usual, the module of half the bottom diameter of the column, but the height of the shaft, constant in all the orders, only the thickness of the columns being variable. Allowing for deviations resulting from different constructional methods, Indau based his proportions on Jacopo Vignola's *Regola delli cinque ordini d'architettura* (Rome, 1562), from which he took over the equality of proportions between the Corinthian and Composite orders; his illustrations too were undoubtedly based on Vignola's. The question of Indau's relation to the *Kurzer doch grundrichtig und deutlicher Bericht von denen in der löblichen Bau-Kunst wohlbekandten und so genandten Fünff Säulen* (?1680s) by Johann Georg Erasmus, which, unlike his own, also followed Vignola in its constructional method, must remain open.

In an appendix of six plates Indau demonstrated the application of the Classical orders: richly decorated variations of the capitals; a palace façade of several storeys as an example of the superpositioning of four orders; two of his own designs for a tabernacle and an altar; and the façade of the Jesuitenkirche Am Hof in Vienna, built 1657–62 and attributed to Philiberto Luchese. Unlike the illustrations in architectural manuals of other 17th-century cabinetmakers, Indau's stress clarity of architectural structure, to which ornamental decoration is always subordinated.

Indau also devoted two series of engravings to the cabinetmaker's art: *Nova invenzione di rabeschi, e fogliami romani* (Vienna, 1686) comprises 12 engravings on 11 sheets with designs for ornamental details, furniture and altars; his designs for the six sheets of *Neue romanische Ziehraten* (Augsburg, before 1686) were engraved by Nessenthaler. In both series he presented acanthus arabesques influenced by Italian ('romanisch') models, thus seeking to replace the traditional cartilaginous conch ornamentation (*Ohrmuschelwerk*), still used by Johann Georg Erasmus, with the floral crocket (*Laubwerk*) of late 17th-century ornamental graphics. Apart from these publications, Indau's only secure attribution is the design (pl. XVIII of his treatise) for the former high altar (1686; destr.) of the Mariahilfkirche in Vienna (not that of the church at Mariazell, Styria, as has been wrongly assumed).

WRITINGS

Neue romanische Ziehraten, inventiert und gemacht durch den kunstberühmbten Johann Indau (Augsburg, before 1686)
Nova invenzione di rabeschi, e fogliami romani (Vienna, 1686)
Wiennerisches Architectur-Kunst und Säulen-Buch (Vienna, 1686; Augsburg, 1713, 1722)

BIBLIOGRAPHY

A. Ilg: 'Das wienerische Architecturbuch Johann Indau's von 1686', *Ber. & Mitt. Altert.-Ver. Wien*, xxiv (1887), pp. 1–10
E. Hajdecki: 'Johann Indau und sein "Wienerisches Architekturbuch" mit einem Exkurs über die Kupferstecher J. Chr. Lauch und Jakob Männl: Eine archivalische Studie', *Ber. & Mitt. Altert.-Ver. Wien*, xl (1907), pp. 89–116
Quellen Gesch. Stadt Wien. I. Abt.: Regesten aus in- und ausländischen Archiven mit Ausnahme des Archives der Stadt Wien, vi (1908), p. 288, no. 11,221
F. Rothe: *Das deutsche Akanthusornament des 17. Jahrhunderts: Zur Frage seiner Selbständigkeit* (Berlin, 1938), pp. 61–6
E. Forssman: *Säule und Ornament: Studien zum Problem des Manierismus in den nordischen Säulenbüchern und Vorlageblättern des 16. und 17. Jahrhunderts* (Stockholm and Cologne, 1956), pp. 219–27, esp. p. 226
U. Schütte: *'Ordnung' und 'Verzierung': Untersuchungen zur deutschsprachigen Architekturtheorie des 18. Jahrhunderts* (diss., U. Heidelberg, 1979), pp. 100–01

HANS H. AURENHAMMER

Independent Group. British group of artists, architects and critics. It met as an informal discussion group at the Institute of Contemporary Arts, London, from 1952 to 1955. Its members, drawn from those of the ICA who were dissatisfied with the Institute's policy towards modernism, included the art critic Lawrence Alloway (1926–90), the design historian Peter Reyner Banham (1922–88), the art historian Toni del Renzio (*b* 1915), the artists Nigel Henderson, Richard Hamilton, Eduardo Paolozzi, William Turnbull and John McHale (1922–78), and the architects Alison and Peter Smithson, James Stirling and Colin St John Wilson.

Reyner Banham convened the first full session (1952–3), during which the Group analysed the philosophy of the Modern Movement. In particular, the theories of Amédée Ozenfant and Le Corbusier were called into question for their failure to deal with consumerism and new technology. Alloway and McHale convened the second term (1955), whose theme was American mass culture and its relationship to fine art. Advertising, car styling, Hollywood films and women's fashion were analysed with a degree of seriousness usually reserved by British art critics for paintings.

The Group's ideas reached a wider audience by means of magazine articles, ICA events and works of art. Hamilton's collage *Just What Is It That Makes Today's Homes So Different, So Appealing?* (1956; Tübingen, Ksthalle; for illustration *see* HAMILTON, RICHARD) captured the essence of the Group's thinking on mass culture. Several Royal College of Art students attending the ICA, particularly Roger Coleman, were influenced by the Group.

See also POP ART.

BIBLIOGRAPHY

L. Alloway: 'The Development of British Pop', *Pop Art*, ed. L. R. Lippard (London, 1978), pp. 27–69

A. Massey and P. Sparke: 'The Myth of the Independent Group', *Block*, 10 (1985), pp. 48–56
A. Massey: 'The Independent Group: Towards a Redefinition', *Burl. Mag.*, cxxix (1987), pp. 232–42
——: *The Independent Group: Modernism and Mass Culture in Britain, 1945–1959* (Manchester, 1995)

ANNE MASSEY

India, Bernardino (*b* Verona, 1528; *d* Verona, 1590). Italian painter. After the death of his father in 1545 he was brought up by his maternal grandparents, from whom he derived the surname India. He is sometimes referred to as India *il vecchio* ('the elder') to distinguish him from his nephew Tullio India. He was trained in the workshop of Gian Francesco Caroto but proved particularly receptive to the Mannerism emanating from Mantua and Parma. He first worked as a fresco painter in buildings designed by Palladio: the Palazzo Thiene, Vicenza, and the Villa Poiana, Poiana Maggiore, near Vicenza. In the Palazzo Thiene, India decorated three rooms with mythological and fantastic scenes (1555–6), the forms of which reveal the influence of Parmigianino. His works (*c*. 1560) in the Villa Poiana are inspired by the Mannerist style of Mantua. The frescoes in the Palazzo Canossa, Vicenza, and the lateral façade of the Palazzo Fiorio della Seta (three panels Verona, Castelvecchio) are of slightly later date. In his later works, beginning in the 1570s, he approached Veronese's use of colour, as can be seen in the numerous altarpieces created for churches in Verona, for example the *Nativity* (1572) and the *Virgin and Child with St Anne* (1579; both Verona, S Bernardino). In the *Conversion of St Paul* (1584; Verona, SS Nazaro e Celso) India created a fusion of Giulio Romano's monumentality and Veronese's use of colour. His final work, the altarpiece depicting the *Martyrdom of St Degnamerita* (1590; Verona, Castelvecchio), demonstrates his skilful use of light.

BIBLIOGRAPHY

Thieme–Becker
L. Magagnato: 'Bernardino India', *Cinquant'anni di pittura veronese, 1580–1630* (exh. cat., Vicenza, 1974), pp. 79–80
B. Mazza: 'Bernardino India', *Maestri della pittura veronese*, ed. P. Brugnoli (Vincenza, 1974), pp. 253–60
Palladio e la Maniera: I pittori vicentini del '500 e i collaboratori del Palladio, 1530–1630 (exh. cat. by V. Sgarbi, Vicenza, S Corona, 1980), pp. 66–73

FILIPPO PEDROCCO

India, Republic of. Country in South Asia founded following the withdrawal of the British from the Indian subcontinent in 1947. Inaugurated in 1950, it was formed from the accession of British and princely India but excluded the territory of what became the Muslim nations of Pakistan and Bangladesh (originally West and East Pakistan), its two neighbours to west and east. In the late 20th century India consists of 26 states and 7 union territories. This survey focuses on the arts produced since 1947. For discussion of earlier periods, *see under* INDIAN SUBCONTINENT.

I. Introduction. II. Architecture. III. Painting. IV. Sculpture. V. Other arts. VI. Village art. VII. Folk textiles. VIII. Urban popular arts. IX. Patronage. X. Art education. XI. Museums and collections. XII. Art legislation. XIII. Art libraries and photographic collections.

I. Introduction.

India is a country of great size and geographical variety. To the north are the Himalaya, the highest mountains in the world. Further south is the massive plain, created over many centuries by rivers running out of the Himalaya and depositing rich alluvium as they drain to the sea. The greatest of these rivers are the Yamuna, the Brahmaputra and, pre-eminently, the Ganga. To the south of the river plains is the broken country of the Vindhya Hills, while the great mass of upland still further south is known as the Deccan. The coastal regions ringing the Deccan plateau are low and flat and are the location of large towns and cities. These fertile tracts become more pronounced in south India, with a commensurate diminution of the upland; much of the state of Tamil Nadu consists of lush lowland.

By the year 2000 India will probably have the largest population of any country in the world. Although India is a secular state, the majority of the population is Hindu; there is, however, a large Muslim minority of about 100 million. Other religious groups include Jainas, Sikhs, Buddhists, Parsis and Christians. Linguistically the variety is also great. Most of the northern Indian languages are Indo-Aryan in origin; in the south the majority are Dravidian. Hindi is widely spoken, especially in the north, though English is the lingua franca of commerce and international activity. Ethnic variety ranges from ancient Austronesian populations to groups originating from Central Asia over many different periods (Indo-Aryans, Kushanas, Turks and Persians) and others descending from European colonists of more recent centuries (Portuguese, Dutch, French and British).

The four great cities of modern India—New Delhi, Calcutta, Bombay and Madras—are all European foundations, although at the first-named city (the capital of the Republic) the new city was planned alongside earlier cities (*see* DELHI). Pre-colonial cities such as Hyderabad and Agra continue to be important urban centres. Although the conurbations boast populations in the millions, at least 70% of India's population still lives in the country, providing a potent and vibrant reservoir of humanity and a continuing link with traditional arts and crafts (*see* §§V, VI and VII below).

BIBLIOGRAPHY

D. C. Ghosh: *Bibliography of Modern Indian Art* (Delhi, 1980)
K. G. Subramanyan: *The Living Tradition: Perspectives on Modern Indian Art* (Calcutta, 1987)

T. RICHARD BLURTON

II. Architecture.

In India after 1947 four distinct kinds of building activity flourished. In order of the volume of building involved these are: the indigenous vernacular modes followed in the vast majority of all rural building and a significant proportion of urban building by people for themselves untouched by official controls and guidance; contemporary popular architecture, mostly domestic and mainly in towns, subject to bye-laws and approval of plans, the latter generally being drawn up by engineers or builders; mainstream work of the architectural profession as taught at schools of architecture and discussed in professional journals; and traditional 'classical' architecture based on the ancient treatises, now mainly restricted to temple building (*see also* INDIAN SUBCONTINENT, §III, 8(ii)). The documentation of Indian architecture of the modern era has concentrated on the output of the architectural profession, which necessarily limits this account. The other three streams provide an important context within which the profession operates, and some of the most fruitful modern works have been generated at the margins between these streams and the official mainstream.

During the British administration the great majority of public-building work was carried out under the direction of engineers, not architects. India's architectural profession is therefore the product of the years since Independence. At Independence (1947), the fledgling architectural culture represented by the country's three schools of architecture and 300 trained architects was involved in a vigorous debate about the style of architecture that would be most appropriate for the new India. The revivalists believed that the way had been shown by the Anglo-Indian syntheses developed during the last phase of British rule, when traditional Indian decorative schemes, motifs and craftsmanship had been incorporated into designs that represented the British architectural mainstream in their arrangement and ordering (*see* INDIAN SUBCONTINENT, §III, 8(i)). Opposing them were a small number of modernists, mostly educated abroad, who were convinced of the need for an entirely new approach, as exemplified by the works of European and American pioneers of modern architecture. In the decade after independence important buildings were built by advocates of both approaches. The Vidhan Soudha Secretariat Building at Bangalore by the State Public Works Department, the Ashoka Hotel, Delhi, by Doctor and the Supreme Court, Delhi, by the Central Public Works Department, all built in the 1950s, represent the revivalists. In contrast, the work of ACHYUT KANVINDE, Durga Bajpai and Habib Rehman throughout the 1950s resulted in influential early modern buildings.

In between these stylistic poles there were continuations of the mixed 'Moderne' and Deco architectural styles of the 1930s. The commissioning of LE CORBUSIER for the planning of CHANDIGARH, the new capital of the Punjab, had a decisive influence on the debate about an appropriate Indian architecture. Le Corbusier, Maxwell E. Fry, Jane Drew and Pierre Jeanneret adapted European modernism to a country without the industrial infrastructure, let alone the modern building industry, that had made possible the new architecture in the West. The innovative use of materials—from bare concrete, for its monumental qualities, to humble brick screens in houses reminiscent of traditional *jālis*—and the ostensibly scientific, a priori method behind the architecture, especially with regard to the climate, made the buildings of Chandigarh a powerful influence on the second generation of Indian architects. A decade later, the work of Louis I. Kahn in Ahmadabad

1. Balkrishna V. Doshi: Gandhi Institute of Labour Studies, Ahmadabad, 1980–84

with a more sophisticated and classical use of brick with arches and an approach to the plan that was more symmetrical and geometrically pure provided a second strong Western influence on Indian architecture.

These powerful influences did not entirely obliterate the conscious search for an Indian form of expression: rather, in the best of the new Indian architecture, they enabled this search to be disciplined by the functionalism and animated by the inventive spirit of modernism. In the Gandhi Memorial Centre at Ahmadabad (1958–63; for illustration *see* CORREA, CHARLES) Charles Correa combined traditional materials and spaces such as courtyards and open pavilions with a modernist open plan and asymmetric planning. A number of architects experimented with the expressive possibilities of plain brick and concrete surfaces in such buildings as the YMCA staff quarters (1961–3), Delhi, by the Design Group, the Ahmadabad School of Architecture (1968) by BALKRISHNA V. DOSHI, the French Embassy Staff quarters (1968–9), Delhi, by RAJ REWAL, and the Indian Statistical Institute (1970–76), Delhi, by Anant Raje (who had worked closely with Louis Kahn in Ahmadabad). Meanwhile, Joseph Allen Stein, an American architect settled in Delhi, was producing highly individual and functionally successful works—for example the India International Centre (1960–62), Delhi, and the Kothari Building (1961–3), Madras—in which the frame of the building was expressed and heavy and light materials contrasted, rather in the tradition represented by Richard Neutra. In spite of examples like these, the work of the majority of architects tended to a simplistic utilitarian modernism with little expressive intent or, in a few cases, to imitation of Le Corbusier or Kahn.

By the late 1960s a substantial industrial infrastructure existed in India capable of producing steel and cement in the quantities to enable large modern blocks of housing and offices to be built, and these increasingly characterized much urban development, especially in such large cities as Bombay. Architecturally important examples of high-rise building are Correa's climatically innovative Kanchenjunga Apartments (1970–83) in Bombay and the New Delhi Civic Centre (1965–83) by Kuldip Singh.

The vast scale and speed of expansion in building for urbanization, industry, commerce, institutions and housing, and the architectural profession's efforts to maintain and increase its role, have conditioned the nature of practice, which generally is to apply models derived from Western precedent. In the late 1960s and early 1970s the search for a different kind of relevance that was engaging more thoughtful architects was intensified by a younger generation, many of them trained abroad, some of whom began to question the relevance of Western models to Indian conditions. Their search for relevance had two aspects: to find opportunities to apply their professional skills to the areas of greatest need, for example housing for rural and poor communities; and to construct an architectural theory (or theories) for the Indian context. In the 1980s and 1990s such explorations and debate took place in an increasingly vital architectural culture with numerous exhibitions, competitions, conferences and the beginnings of architectural journalism and criticism.

The work of many leading architects, as well as many of the next generation, increasingly referred to indigenous sources throughout the 1970s and 1980s: for example Doshi's Indian Institute of Management (1977–85), Bangalore, and Gandhi Institute of Labour Studies (1980–84), Ahmadabad (see fig. 1), Correa's Vidhan Bhavan (begun 1980), Bhopal, and Rewal's Asian Games Village (1981–2) and National Institute of Immunology buildings (1986), Delhi. At the same time, technological development in the construction industry increasingly facilitated the adoption of Western trends.

Are the search for regional identity and 'appropriateness' on the one hand and the continuing fascination with the material and technological primacy of the West on the other opposing and irreconcilable forces? Some reject the latter as irrelevant to Indian conditions and are dedicated—like LAURIE BAKER, the Trivandrum architect, and the many who are experimenting with mud-brick construction—to the development of an inventive, low-cost, 'intermediate technology' architecture based in local practice. At the opposite pole, the overwhelming mass of commercial architecture is indistinguishable, save for a motif here or a feature there, from commercial architecture round the world. Some believe that a dialectic between these forces holds the best possibilities for Indian architecture into the 21st century.

For further illustration *see* DOSHI, BALKRISHNA V.

BIBLIOGRAPHY

S. Cantacuzino: *Charles Correa* (London and Singapore, 1984)
M. Chatterjee: 'The Evolution of Contemporary Indian Architecture', *Architecture in India* (Paris, 1985)
R. Sharma: 'The Search for Roots and Relevance', *Architecture in India* (Paris, 1985)
Charles Correa (exh. cat., Bombay, 1986)
'Indian Identity', *Archit. Rev.* [London], clxxxii/1086 (Aug 1987)
W. J. R. Curtis: *Balkrishna V. Doshi: An Architecture for India* (Ahmadabad, 1988)
V. Bhatt and P. Scriver: *After the Masters* (Ahmadabad, 1990)

SUNAND PRASAD

III. Painting.

The emergence of modern art in India can be traced back to the 1930s (*see* INDIAN SUBCONTINENT, §V, 4(x)), when motifs from Indian classical and folk art were translated into an Expressionist idiom to become statements of contemporary national identity. Indian modernism declared itself in the manifestos for the Progressive Artists' Group in Bombay, which FRANCIS NEWTON SOUZA initiated in 1947 (*see also* BOMBAY, §2). The group included the artists MAQBOOL FIDA HUSAIN and SAYED HAIDER RAZA and staged exhibitions in 1948–9. During Souza's subsequent stay in London, he confirmed his expressionist approach to the human body, while Raza, who settled in Paris in 1950, pursued a sensuous form of abstraction in open allegiance with the painters of the Ecole de Paris. Husain, who did not emigrate to Europe, produced images of peasants, popular gods and secular leaders, all of which seemed to be participating, like the artist himself, in a rejuvenated culture of post-Independence India. It was complemented by the work of SATISH GUJRAL, who was influenced by such Mexican muralists as David Alfaro Siqueiros during his stay in Mexico between 1952 and 1955. Later, a member of the same generation, Tyeb

2. Bhupen Khakhar: *Death in the Family*, oil on canvas, 1.06×1.06 m, 1978 (London, Victoria and Albert Museum)

Mehta, made the logical move from post-war expressionist figuration to a late modernist formalism, but with an iconic intent specific to the Indian context.

The Surrealist concern with primitivism and the unconscious as a subversive element, on the other hand, was the basis of a manifesto formulated by the artist–critic JAGDISH SWAMINATHAN for Group 1890's exhibition in Delhi in October 1963. The Group 1890's exhibition catalogue had a foreword by the Mexican poet and essayist Octavio Paz that invoked a modernist, anarchic spirit specifically rooted in Third World struggles for political and cultural liberation. Beginning in the 1960s another movement, which came to be known as Neo-Tantric art, adopted elements from the esoteric and often erotically symbolized philosophy called Tantra, as a means of stressing Indian identity, while linking up with modernist abstraction. Artists sceptical of cultist mystifications sought an indigenous art that was more informal and witty, as was the case with the mock-pictographic language of K. C. S. PANIKER from 1963. His influence as an art educationist helped turn the art movement in Madras into a swift, diagrammatic mode that claimed to set itself against Western principles of representation. Another artist, K. G. SUBRAMANYAN, also began drawing on indigenous, especially popular, art languages. From 1963, when he made a terracotta mural of architectural proportions in Lucknow, he began to supplement his oil paintings with terracotta reliefs, toys, book designs and weavings, and in 1979 he started to work on glass paintings. As an artist–teacher at the Faculty of Fine Arts in Baroda (now Vadodara) and later at Shantiniketan, Subramanyan influenced a succession of young artists away from an existential concern with identity in favour of a confrontation with the language of art, with invented signs that could mimic and transform contemporary experience into narratives.

The element of kitsch in urban India became a source of imagery and subject-matter for such other Baroda painters as BHUPEN KHAKHAR from the mid-1960s. Khakhar became the first artist to question the élitism of modern Indian art. What began as a local variant of worldwide iconoclasm developed during the 1970s into a specific Indian iconography denoting urban character, class and environment (see fig. 2). The peculiarities of a colonized culture, including the hybrid features of its everyday life and art, gave an edge to the parodic impulse. This new narrative form found its culmination in 1981 in an important exhibition, entitled *Place for People* (see 1981 exh. cat.), which showed the work of six artists, including Khakhar.

The new narratives were given new bases of subjectivity by women artists such as Arpita Singh and Nalini Malani. Indeed, the 1980s consolidated the presence of three generations of women artists comprising a broad feminist front; and their practice, whether painting, sculpture or installation, was by the 1990s at the cutting edge of Indian art. There was an influx of new ideas by the younger generation (often coming from hitherto less important regions in the production of contemporary art, such as Kerala and Karnataka) who reworked the limits of the frame and the pedestal into more open-ended concepts of objects in space. The supreme position that painterly aesthetic had held was challenged. An art practice variously designated as radical or avant-garde came into view in Indian art in the 1990s.

BIBLIOGRAPHY

Progressive Artists' Group (exh. cat. by F. N. Souza, Bombay, Bombay A. Soc. Gal., 1949)
Group 1890 (exh. cat., group manifesto by J. Swaminathan and essay by O. Paz; New Delhi, Rabindra Bhavan A.G., 1963)
S. A. Krishnan, ed.: *Lalit Kala Contemp.*, xii–xiii (1971) [articles on contemporary Neo-Tantric art]
G. Kapur: *Contemporary Indian Artists* (Delhi, 1978)
K. G. Subramanyan: *Moving Focus: Essays on Indian Art* (Delhi, 1978)
D. C. Ghosh: *Bibliography of Modern Indian Art* (Delhi, 1980)
G. Kapur: 'Modern Painting since 1935', *The Arts of India*, ed. B. Gray (Oxford, 1981), pp. 202–16
Place for People (exh. cat. by G. Kapur, New Delhi, Rabindra Bhavan A.G.; Bombay, Jehangir A.G.; 1981)
Contemporary Indian Art: From the Chester and Davida Herwitz Family Collection (exh. cat. by G. Kapur, London, RA, 1982)
India: Myth and Reality, Aspects of Modern Indian Art (exh. cat., ed. D. Elliott and E. Alkazi; Oxford, MOMA, 1982)
Tantra: Philosophie und Bildidee: Aspekte zeitgenössischer indischer Kunst (exh. cat. by L. P. Sihare, Stuttgart, Inst. Auslandsbeziehungen, 1983)
Contemporary Indian Art (exh. cat. by G. Patel, T. W. Sokolowski and D. A. Herwitz, New York, Grey Gal. & Stud. Cent., 1985)
'K. G. Subramanyan: *The Living Tradition: Perspectives on Modern Indian Art* (Calcutta, 1987)
G. Kapur: 'A Stake in Modernity: Brief History of Contemporary Indian Art', *Tradition and Change: Contemporary Art of Asia and the Pacific*, ed. C. Turner (St Lucia, Queensland, 1993), pp. 27–44
Indian Songs: Multiple Streams in Contemporary Indian Art (exh. cat., text by V. Lynn, M. Singh, M. Bawa and H. Shah; Sydney, A.G. NSW, 1993)
Contemporary Indian Art: Glenbarra Art Museum Collection (exh. cat., text by J. James and others; Tokyo, Glenbarra Art Museum, 1993)
A Critical Difference: Contemporary Art from India (exh. cat., text by T. Hyman and others; Aberystwyth Arts Centre; London, Showroom; 1993)
J. Clark: *Modern Indian Art: Some Literature and Problematics*, Research Institute for Asia and the Pacific Occasional Paper No. 26 (Sydney, 1994)
J. A. & Ideas, 27–8 (March 1995) [special issue on studies in modern Indian art]
G. M. Sheikh, ed.: *Contemporary Art in Baroda* (Delhi, 1996)

GEETA KAPUR

IV. Sculpture.

The generalization that Indian sculpture has degenerated into virtual nonexistence since the advent of Islam does not stand up to even cursory analysis. Traditional temple sculpture continued to be produced into the 20th century (although, it is true, on a progressively smaller scale of production), most actively in Tamil Nadu, by such sculptors as V. GANAPATI STHAPATI. Traditions of rural art (e.g. the wood, clay and metal sculptures of Tamil Nadu, Gujarat and Orissa) continue to the present day (*see* BRONZE, fig. 2).

Modernist, urban-centred sculpture originated out of the British art schools established in India in the 19th century (*see also* INDIAN SUBCONTINENT, §V, 5(x)). These schools inculcated an academic, classicizing style that continued into the 20th century. Several artists trained in this style continued to work in the post-Independence period. V. P. Karmakar (1891–1962) was the son of a potter and iconmaker; on the encouragement of a British official in his home district, he became a student at the Sir Jamshetjee Jeejebhoy School of Art, Bombay, in 1910 and from 1920 to 1923 studied in England. Thus grounded in the standard British academic style, he returned to India and received several public commissions, such as the marble statue of *Justice D. N. Mula* (1937) at the Bombay High Court. Such works continue a long-standing tradition of memorial sculpture in modern India. More intimate and romantic in feeling, although equally conservative in style, is the bronze *Fisher Girl* of 1930.

Of more élite family background was D. P. Roy Chowdhuri (1899–1975), who took up the banner of the artist as rebellious individualist. Born into an aristocratic Bengali family, Roy Chowdhuri began his artistic training in his teens, under some family objections, with Abanindranath Tagore (*see* TAGORE, (3)). He also studied with Westerners then living in Calcutta. He received his training in sculpture from Hiranmoy Roy Chowdhury (*d* 1962). His works from the 1930s can be either dryly academic (as in a marble bust of *Dr Annie Besant*, 1936) or daringly expressive (e.g. a bronze bust of *A. Tampoe*, 1930). In the light-catching modulations of the surface, the influence of Auguste Rodin is highly evident in this work, and it was Rodin who provided Roy Chowdhuri with his major inspiration throughout his career, combined with a somewhat prosaic realism that encourages comparisons with Soviet or even Chinese Social Realism. Characteristic works in this vein are *When Winter Comes* (plaster, 1957), the *Triumph of Labour* (bronze, 1954) and the *Martyrs' Memorial* in Patna (bronze, 1956).

RAMKINKER BAIJ was one of the first Indian sculptors to experiment significantly with abstraction, taking as his point of departure the human figure. His famous outdoor *Santal Family* (concrete, 1938; Shantiniketan, Vishva-Bharati U.) exhibits a lyrical, linear distortion of the figures. He moves further in this direction with *Composition* (cement, 1948; Chandigarh, Punjab U. Mus.), which has elements of Cubism and Surrealism. Baij also worked in a more traditional figurative manner. Such works as his bronze bust of *Madura Singh* (1949; New Delhi, N. G. Mod. A.), with roughly modelled surfaces and bold distortions, are best described as expressionistic.

N. G. Pansare (1912–68) trained in India and England, and adapted Western sources very different from those used by artists previously discussed. His architectural reliefs (malad stone, 1948) on the New India Insurance

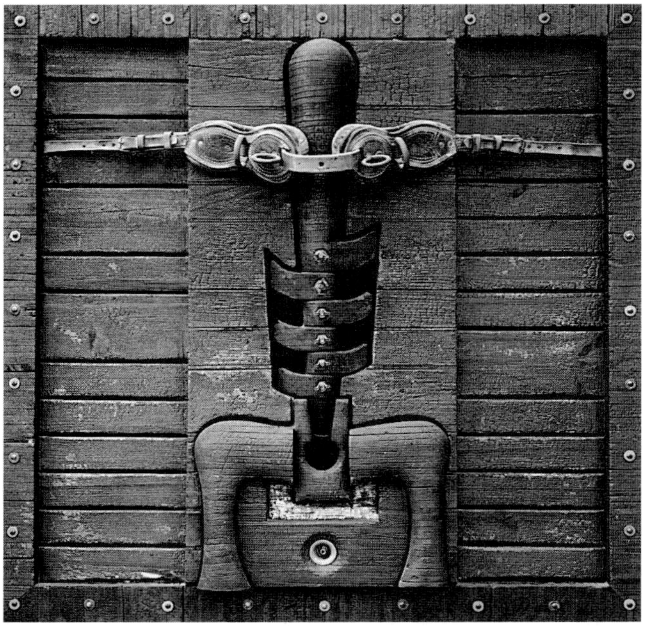

3. Satish Gujral: *Crucifixion*, burnt wood, leather and found objects, 1.23×1.23 m, 1979 (New Delhi, Dhomi Mull Art Centre)

Building, Bombay, translate Indian imagery into the flattened linearized reliefs of the Art Deco style of the 1920s and 1930s. He also carved free-standing human figures, their modelling reduced to broad cubistic planes.

During the 1940s several artists appear whose work initially bears overall resemblance to the realism of D. P. Roy Chowdhuri, but who go on to embrace several varieties of abstraction. By 1975 Pradosh Das Gupta (*b* 1912) was producing such Constantin Brancusi-inspired works as the marble *Egg Bride*. Works by Chintamoni Kar (*b* 1915) from the 1960s and 1970s are strongly indebted to Henry Moore (e.g. *Daedalus and Icarus*, terracotta, 1963; artist's col.). Sankho Chaudhuri (*b* 1916) is also influenced by Moore, but extends his vision towards the Constructivism of Naum Gabo and the Surrealism of Pablo Picasso and Joan Miró (*Music*, aluminium and brass, 1966; *Composition*, metal, 1967). Dhanraj Bhagat (*b* 1917) is another artist using a multitude of sources. It is perhaps via Picasso that he acquired an interest in African art, which informs both his figurative and abstract work (*Three Women*, wood, 1953; New Delhi, Nehru Mem. Mus. & Lib.; *Portrait*, wood, 1963).

The first major sculptor whose mature work dates entirely to the post-Independence period is A. M. Davierwalla (1922–75). Trained as a pharmaceutical chemist, he received only informal instruction in art through his friendship with N. G. Pansare. Works from the late 1940s and early 1950s are in stone or various types of wood. Here various degrees of abstraction are applied to the human figure. The influence of Henry Moore is most obvious, but that of Picasso and possibly Brancusi is equally evident (*Reclining Figure*, stone, 1950; *Water Carrier*, teak-wood, 1955; B. Reporter priv. col.). This mode continued through the 1950s with increasing degrees of inventiveness and sophistication. In the early 1960s works in metal appear, in welded steel (*Crucifixion*, 1962; J. Mango priv. col.) and bronze (*Many-headed Hydra*, 1962; Dara Mistry priv. col.). At this time the influence of Surrealism is increasingly evident. It appears in the use of motifs similar to those used by Paul Klee and Joan Miró, as in *Galaxy* (welded steel, brass and glass, 1966; Bal Chhabda priv. col.), but also in his use of such non-traditional materials as scrap metal and scrap wood. Thus, he makes use of *objets trouvés* in assemblages (*Mother and Child*, scrap wood, 1966; artist's estate). Davierwalla spent 1968 in the United States on a Rockefeller fellowship. This may have provided some of the impetus towards greater abstraction and use of new materials, such as Perspex (*Study in Light and Colour*, 1968). The mode of abstraction in these works is geometric, and in a rather constructivist vein.

Pilloo Pochkhanwalla (*b* 1923) holds much in common with Davierwalla in that she began working as a sculptor relatively late in life (in 1951) and is self-taught. Like him, she is one of India's most inventive assemblage artists. Various monumental welded pieces were commissioned as public sculptures. Roughly textured and emotionally highly charged, her later works express an affinity with the environment and a deep concern with its despoliation (e.g. *Sunblast II*, aluminium alloy, 2.32×1.45 m, 1981; see 1983 exh. cat.; part of the *Homage to the Sun* series).

The artists discussed so far consciously avoided reference to the classical or folk arts of India, feeling in general that their artistic aims were those of individualist moderns, rather than of anonymous artisans producing traditional art forms. One of the first sculptors to counter this trend is MEERA MUKHERJEE, who uses the techniques and forms of metal craftsmen working in villages in Bengal and Orissa as a point of departure for her semi-abstract, powerfully rendered human figurines (e.g. *Woman*, bronze, 1969). Folk techniques that she utilizes include various additive methods, such as winding wax-coated wire around a clay core to produce textural patterns in the final cast-bronze work.

SATISH GUJRAL also takes folk art as a point of departure, combining it with the influence of Surrealism and the expressive power of the Mexican muralists José Clemente Orozco and David Alfaro Sequeiros (the latter of whom he worked with in 1953–4). One of the most cosmopolitan of Indian artists, he studied in India, Mexico and the United States and travelled extensively through Europe. Better known as a painter, his sculptural works are mainly reliefs in wood or ceramic. As reliefs, his works have a frontal, hieratic and iconic quality. Indeed, his *Crucifixion* (wood, 1979; see fig. 3) is essentially a contemporary, abstract icon. His deafness from the age of 13 may account, in part, for both the introspectiveness and the often startling intensity of his work. While highly eclectic, the artist transmutes rather than transcribes his sources, producing highly original works completely at home on the international scene.

P. V. Janakiram (*b* 1930) has also been described as a modern iconmaker. His works in shaped, beaten and repoussé metal are much more readably figurative than Gujral's and more traditional in tone. Stylized facial features and patterns used to render clothing and jewellery recall both Rajput miniature painting and folk art.

A major centre of progressive art training in India is the Vishva-Bharati University at Shantiniketan, West Bengal. Ramkinker Baij studied and later taught there. Sankho Chaudhuri studied there as well, but moved on to the Maharaja Sayajirao University of Baroda (now Vadodara), teaching there through the 1950s and 1960s. This has since become the leading centre in India for the training of sculptors and possesses the most extensive technical facilities in the country. Many notable artists who began as students of Chaudhuri subsequently joined the faculty at Baroda. These include Raghav Kaneria (*b* 1930), who uses scrap metal and other *objets trouvés* in his highly abstracted, surrealistic welded pieces (*Untitled*, *c.* 1980), and Rajnikant Panchal (*b* 1937), whose more recent works have a planar compositional sensibility close to that of Robert Motherwell (*Peep Through*, copper and steel, 1982). After teaching at Baroda during the 1960s, Ajit Chakravarti (*b* 1930) moved to the Vishva-Bharati (All India) University, Shantiniketan, where he was head of the Department of Sculpture in the early 1990s. Biomorphic and figurative surrealist motifs pervade his work (*Bitter Bell*, wood, 1968; artist's col.; *Hero with Spear*, wood, *c.* 1980).

Many sculptors continue in the various modernist styles outlined above. Others are pursuing more inventive modes. The work of Shiv Singh (*b* 1938) bears certain references to minimalism; the clarity of his aesthetic is tempered, however, with lyricism and an affinity with nature (*Formation*, brass, 1980). S. Nandagopal (*b* 1946) is another maker of modern icons. While strongly aware of modernist theories and techniques, he strives to produce a truly Indian contemporary art. In *Deity* (silver-plated brass and copper, 1980; see fig. 4), primitivistic motifs (spirals, lozenges, geometric and linear patterns) are superimposed on an irregularly planar figure to create a contemporary Jagannatha. G. Ravinder Reddy (*b* 1956) has created modern *yakṣīs* (female nature spirits; *c.* 1980) as Pop-art icons. These painted, cast-fibreglass figures dressed in Western garb can be read as unfriendly satires on the modern Indian woman. S. Radhakrishnan (*b c.* 1960) works in clay as a kind of homage to one of India's great traditional art forms. His small-scale 'figures in landscapes', with their strong narrative references, can be sentimental or humorous (e.g. *Wings*, terracotta, 1985). He is of a generation that no longer sees the terms 'modern' and 'Indian' as mutually exclusive.

BIBLIOGRAPHY

J. Appasamy, ed.: *Bhagat* (New Delhi, 1965)
——: *Chintamoni Kar* (New Delhi, 1965)
——: *Sankho Chaudhury* (New Delhi, 1970)
J. Appasamy: *An Introduction to Modern Indian Sculpture* (New Delhi, 1970)
S. A. Krishnan, ed.: *Satish Gujral* (New Delhi, 1970)
J. Appasamy, ed.: *A. M. Davierwalla* (New Delhi, 1971)
——: *P. V. Janakiram* (New Delhi, 1974)
R. Parimoo: *Studies in Modern Indian Art* (New Delhi, 1975)
K. G. Subramanyan: *Moving Focus* (New Delhi, 1978)
P. Daw: *Eminent Indian Sculptors* (Calcutta, 1980)
Indian Sculpture Today 1983 (exh. cat., Bombay, Jehangir A.G., 1983)
Mihika: 'Narrator's Art: Terracotta Sculpture of Radhakrishnan', *Lalit Kala Contemp.*, xxxv (1987), pp. 35–8

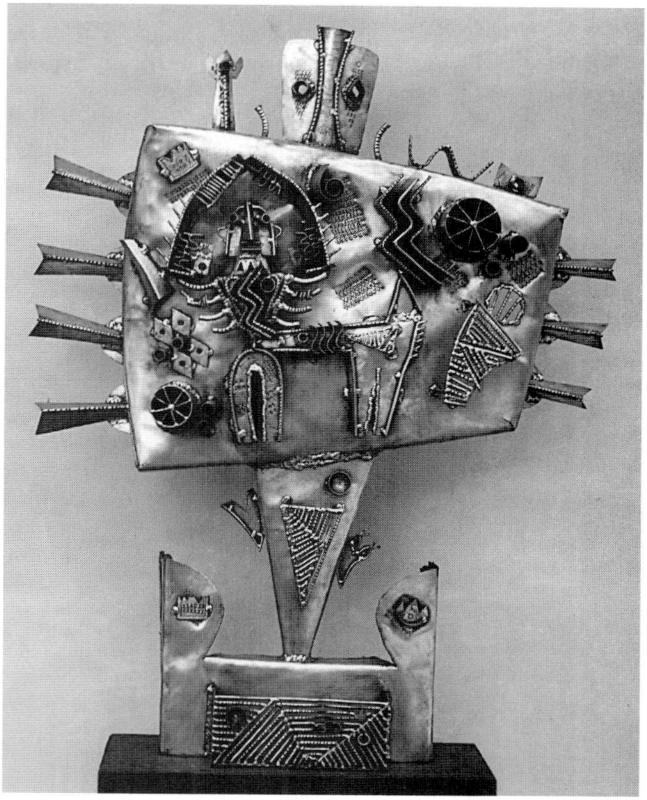

4. S. Nandagopal: *Deity*, silver-plated brass and copper, 1.07×1.09 m, 1980 (New Delhi, Housing and Urban Development Corporation)

V. Other arts.

Within this category are a variety of crafts, most with a long history. Many of these art and craft forms, associated with the traditional life of the village, were in danger of dying out in the wake of greater industrialization and urbanization. In 1952, however, the All-India Handicrafts Board and various regional design centres for training in traditional crafts were established, and thus many practices have been kept alive. A certain transformation has occurred in that various objects traditionally produced for weddings, religious festivals and other occasions are now made for foreign tourists and for the urban Indian market, tending to de-contextualize the works and obscure their original functions. Many of these crafts, however, continue to be produced in the traditional village context (*see* §VI below). Most of the crafts surveyed here are produced in some form all over India. A major repository of Indian crafts is the Crafts Museum, New Delhi.

Utilitarian and decorative objects are woven out of grasses, reeds and bamboo from Assam to Tamil Nadu. In Bihar, golden *sikki* grass is dyed and used in making baskets, toys, figurines in animal and human form, and votive objects. Coils of grass are stitched together with grass or coloured plastic thread. A woman's art, *sikki*-work often makes up part of a dowry. In Kerala, colourful mats of clothlike softness are woven from *kora* grass.

Willow is used to weave baskets and mats in Kashmir. The distinctive *kangri* is a brazier or basket used for heat in the winter and serves as an auspicious object carried by brides to their new homes. In western Orissa, tribal peoples make boxes, traditionally used to hold gifts, out of bamboo, which are decorated with linear designs of lacquer wire.

Extremely popular with tourists are papier-mâché objects painted with coloured lacquer. Best known are the works produced in Kashmir, but lacquered papier-mâché work is also produced in the Punjab, Bihar, Gujarat and Karnataka. In Agra, inlaid marble artefacts are produced primarily for tourist consumption. Replicas of the Taj Mahal, as well as table tops, boxes and the like, are inlaid with precious gems and hardstones, using motifs of Mughal inspiration. The production of enamelwork with Islam-inspired motifs is widespread throughout northern India. The perpetuation of Mughal, as well as Rajput, decorative forms is found in the production of furniture. From Rajasthan and Gujarat particularly, chairs, tables etc are made incorporating the intricate geometric network found in the traditions of Mughal and Rajput architecture, as seen in balconies and window screens carved in wood or stone. Locally derived furniture designs are also found in southern India, particularly in Kerala and Mysore.

Leatherwork, found throughout India, has a distinctive form in the shadow-puppets made of transparent painted leather in Andhra Pradesh; similar traditions are found in Tamil Nadu and Kerala (*see also* INDIAN SUBCONTINENT, §VII, 16). Of all Indian crafts, pottery is probably the least marketable for tourists. Highly utilitarian pottery objects, often unfired, are discarded after use. In Puri, Orissa, potters associated with the Jagannatha Temple continuously produce vessels to feed vast numbers of pilgrims. Throughout India, clay is also used to make images, toys and simple votive lamps.

The most ubiquitous pan-Indian crafts include painted wooden figurines (dolls, toys and votive objects) and cast brass objects (figurines, ritual objects and images of gods). Bidri, a technique of damascening in silver, is particularly associated with Mysore. Fine traditions of jewellery-making also continue, each region of India having its own distinctive styles, such as the silver filigreework of Cuttack, Orissa.

See also §§VI, VII and VIII below and INDIAN SUBCONTINENT, §VII.

BIBLIOGRAPHY

R. F. Bussabarger and B. D. Robins: *The Everyday Art of India* (New York, 1968)
S. Swarup: *5000 Years of Arts and Crafts in India and Pakistan* (Bombay, 1968)
R. Dhamija: *Image India: Heritage of Indian Arts and Crafts* (Delhi, 1971)
L. A. Cort: 'Temple Potters of Puri', *Res*, vii–viii (1984), pp. 33–43
Aditi: The Living Arts of India (Washington, DC, 1985)
J. Jaitly, ed.: *Crafts of Kashmir, Jammu and Ladakh* (New York, 1989)
J. Jaitly: *The Craft Traditions of India* (New Delhi, 1990)

WALTER SMITH

VI. Village art.

Approximately 70% of the population of India is still concentrated in villages. Village life continues to act as a reservoir from which religious and artistic ideas spread to cities. Ideas continue to move from village to city owing to the lure of the latter as a source of lucrative employment. Many town dwellers, though, maintain contact with land or relatives in the country. The village also acts as a conduit through which artistic and other activities of nomadic and tribal groups eventually seep into urban life. Rural life is agricultural and pastoral, and religion and society reflect the importance of gaining a livelihood from the earth.

Indian village art is rarely merely decorative; it invariably has a specific, usually religious, function. It is still largely predicated by the materials available. The most common of these is clay, and both fired and unfired clay sculpture is a feature of almost every region of India. Most of it is conceived within the framework of offerings to the local deities at forest and wayside shrines. These offerings are often in the shape of animals (horses are common). Over the years these may amount to many hundreds of examples lined up in forest or field shrines. Great regional variety is recorded in the production of these offerings, from the 4 m tall horses found in Ayyanar shrines in Tamil Nadu (*see* INDIAN SUBCONTINENT, fig. 359) to the 150 mm high elephant figurines given to celebrate the birth of a boy in Saurashtra, Gujarat. Some are hand-built, while others are part wheel-thrown; some are incised or painted or have an appliqué decoration, or may have all of these together. Votive items, such as parts of the body modelled in clay, may be left at a shrine in the hope of healing. Other clay items include domelike structures in which forest deities are understood to live: examples from Surat District in Gujarat, and also from Orissa, are of great artistic elaboration and ingenuity and resemble miniature stupas. Clay plaques of the gods are well known from Rajasthan, especially Molela, with the figure built up in hollow half relief on a solid background. In Bengal the tradition of making clay figures as offerings to the goddesses Durga and Kali is now most established in the cities but surely had a village origin. The tall-necked horse figurines of Bankura, also from Bengal, are now produced specifically for the middle-class urban market; many city houses are decorated with such items.

Clay, often mixed with cow-dung, is also used as plaster on the walls of village houses. The walls are then often painted. Subjects are now more varied than in the past and include items such as steam trains, as well as the traditional religious scenes that protect the entrance from the attentions of fierce or destructive deities. The change in subject-matter has partly come about because of greater contact with urban life. Some of these traditions—among them the Worli of Maharashtra, the Saora (*see* INDIAN SUBCONTINENT, §X) of Orissa and Bihar, and pre-eminently the villagers of the Mitthila region of Bihar—have been discovered by urban champions of village and tribal art. The wall designs are now also painted on paper (see fig. 5) and sold to grace the walls of upper-class Indian families settled in the cities. The function of these designs is now therefore quite different. One of the most renowned of the remarkable Mitthila (or Madhubani) painters was Ganga Devi. Other traditions of wall painting, such as those in the Bhil regions of Gujarat and Madhya Pradesh, continue unconnected with urban life. A village art allied to wall painting that still flourishes is *rangoli* (many regional names exist). Auspicious diagrams are laid out on the ground before the entrance to the house using white and sometimes coloured powders. The design is first indicated

5. *Durga Riding her Lion-mount*, watercolour on paper, 765×565 mm, from Mitthila, Bihar, 1970s (London, British Museum)

with dots of powder, which are then joined up with continuous lines. The designs—many of great complexity—are handed down from mother to daughter.

Another village art, the function of which has changed over the second half of the 20th century, is metal-casting. Itinerant smiths used to travel through the countryside mending vessels and casting images of the gods (*see* INDIAN SUBCONTINENT, fig. 358). A huge regional variety of folk bronze figures developed over the centuries. This continues to some extent, but, with the advent of plastic and other machine-produced vessels and images, the necessity for the itinerant smith has declined. Some groups, however, such as the Dokra of West Bengal and smiths from the tribal belts of Bastar in eastern Madhya Pradesh, have maintained a livelihood by changing their market. Figures in traditional style are today produced for the urban market, as well as for the tourist and export trade.

Story-telling is another aspect of rural and tribal life that has produced its own art forms, though these are all seriously threatened by cinema and television. Traditionally, in many parts of India itinerant bards sang tales from the epics aided by scroll paintings, paintings on large cotton sheets, sheafs of individual paintings or painted boxes containing scenes of the legends to be narrated (*see also* SCROLL, §2(ii)). This tradition lingers on in parts of Bengal and northern Gujarat (scrolls), Rajasthan (painted sheets) and central Karnataka (painted boxes). Some examples are made specifically for sale as curios rather than to be used.

Textiles (*see* §VII below) are a final area where there is still strength in the village traditions. The dowry was traditionally the means of handing down textile techniques such as weaving, embroidery, appliqué, tie-dyeing and painting. Mahatma Gandhi's emphasis on the merit of hand-spinning and hand-weaving has given traditional Indian textiles some degree of authority among intellectuals, even though Western-style costume and manmade fibres are increasingly popular among the proletariat in both the country and the town.

See also INDIAN SUBCONTINENT, §IX.

BIBLIOGRAPHY

E. Fischer and H. Shah: *Mogra Dev: Tribal Crocodile Gods* (Ahmadabad, 1971)
——: *'Vetra ne Khambha': Memorials for the Dead* (Ahmadabad, 1973)
M. Archer: *Indian Popular Painting in the India Office Library* (London, 1977)
M. Mukherji: *Folk Metal Craft of Eastern India* (New Delhi, 1977)
Y. Vequaud: *The Art of Mithila* (London, 1977)
Gods of the Byways (exh. cat., ed. J. Elliot and D. Elliot; Oxford, MOMA, 1982)
E. M. Gupta: *Brata und Ālpāna in Bengalen*, Beiträge zur Südasien-Forschung, lxxx (Wiesbaden, 1983)
A.-L. Dallapiccola, ed.: *Kult und Alltag: Gelbguss in der Volkskunst Indiens*, Heidelberger Akten der von-Portheim-Stiftung (Heidelberg, 1984)
J. Jain: *Painted Myths of Creation* (New Delhi, 1984)
H. Shah: *Form and Many Forms of Mother Clay* (New Delhi, 1985)
Y. Dalmia: *The Painted World of the Warlis: Art and Ritual of the Tribes of Maharashtra* (New Delhi, 1988)
P. Jayakar: *The Earthen Drum: An Introduction to the Ritual Arts of Rural India* (New Delhi, n.d.)

T. RICHARD BLURTON

VII. Folk textiles.

Indian folk textiles can best be classified as textiles that are made by non-professionals for their personal or domestic use or as gifts. Most folk textiles are costume pieces, decorations for the home and for the household's prized livestock, or objects associated with domestic religious ritual. They are made almost exclusively by women, and the most frequently used decoration is embroidery. Other textile techniques, notably weaving, dyeing and printing, are the preserve of professional craftsmen who are satisfying the demands of the market-place and whose work therefore is rarely expressive of their own personality or imagination. Such textiles lack the personal involvement and individuality that are the essence of a folk textile. A factory-made or professionally woven and dyed cloth can acquire 'folk' status by being embellished to an individual's own taste or with motifs that have a significance for the individual or the community. Similarly, worn-out factory-made cloth may be recycled as appliqué or as padding in a quilt.

In many villages, especially in northern and western India, most of a woman's free time is spent on needlework, and her greatest creative energies are focused on the embellishment of costume. Usually not for her own use, these garments may be for her children; in some communities she also makes special pieces for her daughter's future husband, or for her son's future wife (e.g. Punjabi wedding *bagh*s; large, extensively embroidered cotton shawls). A woman's needlework may also include household textiles to be given to a bride for her new home. These include embroidered bags for possessions, square hangings (Gujarati *chakla*) in which the bride wraps her dowry textiles and which she then hangs on the wall of her house, and bedding covers, often quilted and appliquéd.

The most dazzling variety of embroidered costume is found in Gujarat, especially among the farmers and herdsmen of Kachchh. Each community has its own distinctive style and repertory of embroidery, and dowry customs dictated until recently that a large number of garments be given to a girl on her marriage. The nature of a woman's costume and its decoration is a way of signalling her status in life. In her girlhood her heavily embroidered skirt proclaims her mother's pride in her. In some areas the new bride wears her elaborately decorated wedding garment subsequently every day until it disintegrates; after the first few years of marriage in many areas the amount of decoration on a woman's costume is expected to decline. Embroidered costume in Gujarat is not worn exclusively by women. Men of the Ahir and Rabari communities in particular, especially at fairs and weddings, wear spectacularly embroidered jackets and trousers and carry embroidered purses, shawls and even umbrellas. While Hindu communities such as these cover their textiles with flowers, peacocks and other naturalistic motifs, the Muslims of western India favour small, symmetrical, geometric patterns, often in combination with professionally tie-dyed materials. In Kachchh and western Rajasthan, small pieces of specially produced mirror-glass are embroidered on to wall hangings, bed hangings (see fig. 6) and costume.

Strikingly different from the exuberant, multicoloured embroideries of Gujarat are the angular satin-stitch *bagh*s (shawls) and *phulkari*s (shawls similar to *bagh*s, but less heavily embroidered) of the Punjab. While their production is now a dying tradition, they once formed a significant part of the dowry of a bride, with as many as 20 pieces, given by her father, uncles and mother-in-law, which were the product of several years' work on the part of the women of both the bride's and the groom's family. Traditionally the embroidery of the wedding *bagh* was started at the birth of a male child by his grandmother for use at his wedding. Special *phulkari*s were also given to the bride at significant occasions before the wedding ceremony and when she entered her new home for the first time, and others were distributed among the servants of a well-off household upon a marriage in the family.

In Bengal, embroidered quilts called *kantha*s are often made by women for use in their homes rather than as dowry goods, but the sense of making the object as a gift—an important aspect of the folk tradition—is maintained through the practice of 'dedicating' it to one's father or husband. The finest *kantha*s are made around Jessore (now in Bangladesh), but a coarser variety known as *sujani* comes from Bihar, and especially the Mithila region, where they bear a strong resemblance to the bold wall paintings with which the women decorate their houses on festive occasions. The decorative patterns embroidered on *kantha*s and used in other folk-textile traditions are often similar to the abstract rice-paste decorations made on the mud floors of village homes and are endowed with the same auspicious and protective symbolism. Thus the *aripan* of Bihar, the Bengali *ālpanā*, and the *rangoli* and *mandana* patterns of western India all find parallels in local embroidery styles. While certain classes of decorative motif such as birds and flowers are used indiscriminately, the uses considered suitable for mythological subjects vary. For instance, in Gujarat they are confined to embroidered hangings, while in Punjab scenes from local folk-tales are sometimes embroidered on *phulkari*s.

Appliqué work, most popular in western India, especially Gujarat, is sturdier than embroidery and is thus favoured for canopies for shrines and weddings, wall hangings, bedcovers, and animal and cart decorations. The appliqué hangings made by Kathi families of Saurashtra

6. Textile bed hanging, quilted cotton embroidered with inset mirrors, 0.65×1.40 m, from Saurashtra, Gujarat, 20th century (London, Victoria and Albert Museum)

often combine mythological elements, processions, domestic scenes and geometric designs, while the merchant Mahajans produce non-figurative geometrically patterned pieces. Some large appliqué hangings are produced by professionals. Near Puri in Orissa and in Thanjavur, where the technique is practised to a lesser extent than in western India, appliqué canopies and banners are made professionally for religious festival processions.

As the dowry system, now technically illegal but thriving nonetheless, shifts its emphasis from traditional handmade objects to cash and consumer goods, the art of the folk textile is in varying stages of decline. Textiles may still be given as offerings to shrines and temples, and many Gujarati villagers still wear elaborately embroidered garments, but in some parts of India embroidery has totally fallen from favour. Local handicraft boards are revitalizing some crafts, and tourist demand and foreign trade may keep some skills alive, but in most parts of India the true folk textile is retreating before the advance of factory-made substitutes.

BIBLIOGRAPHY

K. Chattopadhyaya and J. Dhamija, eds: *Marg*, xvii/2 (1964) [embroidery issue]
J. M. Nanavati and others: *The Embroidery and Beadwork of Kutch and Saurashtra* (Baroda, 1966)
J. Irwin and M. Hall: *Indian Embroideries* (Ahmadabad, 1973)
V. Elson: *Dowries from Kutch* (Los Angeles, 1979)
M.-L. Nabholz-Kartaschoff: *Golden Sprays and Scarlet Flowers: Traditional Indian Textiles from the Museum of Ethnography, Basel* (Kyoto, 1986)
J. Gillow and N. Barnard: *Traditional Indian Textiles* (London, 1991)

ROSEMARY CRILL

VIII. Urban popular arts.

Although most of the population of India still live in rural areas, the cities contain more than 200 million people. In the cities, the traditional arts of rural India come into contact with those of the rest of the world. The cities thus represent an arena of artistic ferment and interchange in the fields of both popular, utilitarian art and that consciously produced by artists working from studios (*see also* §§III and IV above). The importance of the image—human or divine—is paramount in India. In the cities the effect of this is immediate and startling; the cityscape is filled with signs and images, many of which are secular. In this respect cities differ from villages, where the emphasis is more usually religious. There is, however, frequent and unwitting cross-over between the categories, and the division is anyway not a distinction that many Indians would find meaningful. However, city imagery can be divided into three main categories: political, cinematic and religious.

Throughout the 20th century, Indian nationalism was a potent force in the production of political images, especially in towns and cities. In a country of low overall literacy, the advantage of using visual imagery to present a political message was quickly seized during the struggle for independence. Popular prints putting over the ideals of the freedom movement were widely disseminated. Some concentrated on the peaceful activities of such leaders as Mahatma Gandhi, while others (still popular today) emphasized the more violent side of the struggle. Indeed, the popularity of these led one commentator to write: 'The warrior–hero theme was, and remains, one of the most celebrated and evocative topics of historical "bazaar" art' (Bayly, p. 395). In more recent decades the heroes of other political systems (Marx, Lenin and Stalin, for instance) have been lauded in colourful popular prints. At election time, posters and prints are produced showing the important achievements of the different candidates, and each party is identified by a different symbol (hand, spinning-wheel, plough etc). Billboard writers and decorators are commissioned to build and paint huge cut-outs, sometimes more than 10 m high, which are then paraded through the streets. Such items were also seen at the time of the assassination of Indira Gandhi, when towering cut-out figures, often skilfully incorporating a map of India and thus recalling the notion of *Bharat Mata* ('Mother India'), appeared on the streets. This idea of large mobile images continues the pan-Indian tradition of mobile religious architecture, most substantially seen in the chariot festival shrines of such temple cities as Puri and Chidambaram.

The Indian cinema industry is the largest in the world, providing entertainment in Hindi, English and all major regional languages. Although many commentators see the popular cinema as a vehicle for nothing more than escapist romances, the cinema also continues the ancient tradition of story-telling. The cinema shares with this tradition its subject-matter (romances, melodramas and mythologies), as well as a necessity to present its message at great length. Another particular feature of the popular cinema is its use of song and dance, often in an apparently incongruous manner, a feature that recalls in the visual arts the interest in pattern and design rather than absolute visual veracity. The Indian cinema makes itself seen throughout the cities of India in huge, hand-painted advertising billboards made up of depictions of the most colourful and lurid scenes from the film. Such images are also seen, on a smaller scale, decorating vehicles of all descriptions. A particular sub-group of this type of popular art is the genre of bright and tinselly items painted for rickshaws—especially the metal plates placed at the back of the seat—found all over India. They frequently show scenes from films, though fantasy and 'Western' lifestyle are also popular. Cinema advertising, while perhaps the most vital secular art form in the cities, is but part of the mass of handmade and machine-produced advertising material seen throughout the cities of India.

Religious imagery is still a major category of popular art in the cities, continuing an ancient tradition that is specific to both place and event. In the former category are paintings such as those produced at the Kalighat shrine in Calcutta, while the latter type are seen in the woodblock prints produced in northern India for the annual *nāgapañcami* festival, a Hindu festival in honour of *nāga*s (snake, generally cobra, divinities) during which it is forbidden to till the earth for fear of killing any snakes. These prints still appear, usually mechanically produced. While popular images from all religious groups are found throughout India, Hindu material is by far the most prominent. Sculptures of the gods in clay, and now in plastic, are frequently seen, but even more common are photomechanically produced prints of the Hindu gods. These fall into two major categories. The first consists of prints produced in such major centres as Delhi, Bombay and Madras that illustrate the gods and goddesses of the Hindu

7. Popular print of Pavagadh Hill, Gujarat, paper, 360×495 mm, 1980s (London, British Museum)

pantheon; these are recognized and popular throughout the Hindu world (including Singapore and parts of urban Britain). Such prints are frequently made into calendars to be placed in an office or shop and have a modern secular function as well as a religious one. The second consists of prints that are place-specific and that record the presence of a particular form of a god or a god who is not known elsewhere. These prints are often disseminated through pilgrimage and show the temple that is the focus of the pilgrim's attention and the way to it. For example, a print (see fig. 7) depicting the *devi* shrine at Pavagadh in eastern Gujarat and its sacred geography includes all the shrines visited on the way to the mountain-top temple of the goddess as well as the means of getting there—train, horse, car, on foot, by bullock-cart, even by palanquin. Such prints continue a long tradition found in Indian painting. Huge paintings on cloth showing these scenes are recorded prior to the development of lithographic presses in the early decades of the 20th century.

The production of prophylactic designs at domestic entrances is a popular art form in both town and country. Known by various regional names—*rangoli*, *kolam*, *āl-panā*—geometric designs, sometimes of great complexity, are prepared in rice paste or other white powders by the women of the household. Each design is built up from an outline of individual dots laid out on the threshold and then joined up. This tradition is allied to the preparation of the complex diagrams (Skt *maṇḍala*s) that are laid out on temple floors at times of special worship (*puja*). This connection is made clear both visually and by the presence of offerings placed within the design.

In towns and cities traditional forms of painting (usually on cloth) continue. These include the *kalamkāri* of Andhra Pradesh, *candarvo* of Gujarat, *pichvāī* and Pabuji *pat* of Rajasthan and Manasa *pat* of Bengal (*see* INDIAN SUBCONTINENT, §VI, 3(iv)).

BIBLIOGRAPHY

V. G. Vitsaxis: *Hindu Epics, Myths and Legends in Popular Illustrations* (Delhi, 1977)

E. M. Gupta: 'Brata und Ālpanā in Bengalen', *Beitr. Südasien-Forsch.*, lxxx (Wiesbaden, 1983)

T. R. Blurton: 'Tradition and Modernism: Contemporary Indian Religious Prints', *S. Asia Res.*, viii/1 (1988), pp. 47–69

T. Guha Thakurta: 'Artists, Artisans and Mass Picture Production in Late Nineteenth- and Early Twentieth-century Calcutta: The Changing Iconography of Popular Prints', *S. Asia Res.*, viii/1 (1988), pp. 3–45

S. Haggard: 'Mass Media and the Visual Arts in Twentieth-century South Asia: Indian Film Posters 1947–Present', *S. Asia Res.*, viii/1 (1988), pp. 71–86

C. A. Bayly, ed.: *The Raj: India and the British, 1600–1947* (London, 1990)

W. H. McLeod: *Popular Sikh Art* (Delhi, 1991)

T. RICHARD BLURTON

IX. Patronage.

After Independence an institutional framework for contemporary Indian art was provided by the State, and the arts received conspicuous state support within the post-Independence policy of planned development. As part of this initiative, two key institutions were set up by the Indian government in Delhi in 1954: the National Gallery of Modern Art and the Lalit Kala Akademi. The brief of the National Gallery of Modern Art is to purchase, preserve and display Indian art works dated after 1860; the number of works is now nearly 13,000. Since the 1970s the National Gallery has also compiled exhibitions for museums abroad and received major exhibitions from foreign collections. The Lalit Kala Akademi, also funded by the government, has been constituted so that its decision-making bodies include a majority of members elected by an all-India electoral roll of artists. The academy supports contemporary artistic practice by exhibiting and purchasing current work; by building studio and workshop facilities in regional art centres; by funding independent art associations all over India; and by maintaining an archive and publishing monographs, journals and reproductions of contemporary art. It has also sent exhibitions to various biennales, and since 1968 it has held the large international Triennale-India in Delhi, with an international jury and a month-long programme of lectures and seminars. The academy also sponsors exhibitions and publications of pre-modern painting and sculpture. An extended cultural exchange programme has helped to bring many exhibitions to India—especially since 1982 when the 'Festival of India' in several countries encouraged reciprocal exhibitions of ancient and modern art and promoted indigenous village crafts.

A growing cultural bureaucracy sponsors and protects the functioning of Indian artists in the competitive museum and gallery circuit abroad. Yet, despite a growing market, it is still very difficult for a professional artist to live in India by his work alone. While the prices of works by better-known artists increase by about three or four times every decade, there has been no substantial enlargement of a commercial gallery system to launch artists. However, Indian buyers, especially at the corporate level, are beginning to invest in art, and there is at least one very large collection of contemporary Indian art in the USA (*see also* INDIAN SUBCONTINENT, §XII, 1).

One distinctive feature of the art scene is the extent to which Indian artists function as a community. A sustained example from 1966 was the artists' village at Cholamandal near Madras, where, under the leadership of K. C. S. PANIKER, 40 artists bought land, built cottages, workshops and galleries, and devised a plan to produce not only their own work but handicrafts for the market to ensure collective survival. The Garhi Studios in Delhi, inaugurated by the Lalit Kala Akademi in 1976, became the model for similar projects in the regional centres of the academy and for the smaller workshops in different parts of the country where artists work together, pooling equipment and skills on a short-term basis.

See also §X below.

GEETA KAPUR

X. Art education.

During the 20th century art education in India became more or less Westernized. The survival of descendants of traditional painters and sculptors in such regions as Rajasthan for courtly and folk styles of painting, folk painting in Bengal and south India, the Sompura family of temple-builders in western India, and in south India classical stone-carving (at Mamallapuram) and bronze-casting (at Swami Malai) owes more to private and government encouragement than to the existence of a well-tried system of art education.

In 1947, on the eve of Independence, the government established a committee to reorganize art education in Bombay. Its report was followed by another one, based on the national seminar on art education organized by the Lalit Kala Akademi in Delhi in 1956, stating what it was hoped would serve as national policy and pattern. Many developments and significant changes in the approach of art schools were more or less due to follow-up action on these reports. The Faculty of Fine Arts established at the Maharaja Sayajirao University of Baroda (now Vadodara) in 1950 took note of modern art movements and instituted a new approach to art education, emphasizing individual inclinations. For the first time the art school could claim to 'train' creative artists, allowing full freedom to students to concentrate entirely on painting, sculpture or printmaking in wide-ranging media and stylistic idioms. With the teaching of the history of art of various civilizations, including Indian art history, it was possible to avoid the feeling of conflict between naturalistic norms, traditional conventions and the style languages of modern movements. University degrees in fine arts subjects were awarded, and art teachers' positions were upgraded on a par with other university staff. Sculpture was given full status as a specialization subject. Furthermore, two-year postgraduate courses were introduced in all fields; young artists and designers were relatively free to develop according to their own temperament and were provided with individual studio spaces and informal working hours as well as upgraded aesthetics and art-history course input. Two-year postgraduate courses were introduced with choices in art history and art criticism involving both Western and Indian art, strengthened with art-historical methodology, as distinct from the limited concern with Indian archaeology and art in the courses offered at Varanasi and Calcutta.

By 1960 the art colleges at Shantiniketan (Kala-Bhavan), West Bengal, and Varanasi had been converted to university-level faculties, and most other government art schools, such as those at Calcutta, Bombay and Madras and newly established ones, had accepted the new pattern of art education. This involved completion of the high school examination as the minimum qualification for pursuing professional-level courses, a common preparatory year (which could be extended to two years), a three-year specialization, and of course languages, aesthetics and history of art; this was termed the National Diploma. The old schools of arts and crafts became colleges of fine arts. Soon there was a clamour to convert national diploma courses to degree courses, and most art schools outside the university system (other than Baroda, Shantiniketan and Varanasi) became affiliated with local universities. Another noteworthy development was the setting up of community workshops for talented young artists after their basic art education. The Lalit Kala Akademi, Delhi, took the lead in 1976 by setting up the Garhi Studios in Delhi and similar workshops under the administration of regional centres at Madras, Calcutta, Lucknow and Bhubaneshwar. A private organization set up similar facilities at Ahmadabad.

Training in architecture has become very specialized. There are several government-funded institutions, while private organizations have also set up schools of architecture—the most noteworthy being that at Ahmadabad—which have widened their scope to include conservation, environmental design and urban planning. Bombay took the lead by separating commercial art from fine arts during the 1950s, while several art schools introduced advertising as an alternative specialization. The setting up of the National Institute of Design at Ahmadabad in 1962 gave a new boost to advertising under the concept of visual communication, thus bringing social education and a social message into its scope, as well as exhibition design. Although a large training school exists at Varanasi for traditional textile technology, the National Institute of Design answers the new technological requirements of India in the context of the industrialization activity over the last 50 years. Some advanced-level Institutes of Technology in the 1980s also established sections for industrial design and visual communication.

BIBLIOGRAPHY

Report of the Committee for Art Education, 1947 (Bombay, 1948)

R. Parimoo, ed.: *UGC Workshop in History of Art, 1977* (Baroda, 1979)

H. Kumar Vyas: *The Designer and the Socio-technology of Small Production* (Ahmadabad, 1990)

R. Parimoo: 'Profile of a Pioneer: N. S. Bendre', *Lalit Kala Contemp.*, xxxvii (1991), pp. 72–86

RATAN PARIMOO

XI. Museums and collections.

This article covers the major public and private collections of Indian art within the Republic of India. For holdings of Indian art elsewhere *see* INDIAN SUBCONTINENT, §XII.

1. Museums. 2. Private collections.

1. MUSEUMS. The museum movement in India, encouraged during the 19th century and the early 20th by the British administration, has been revitalized since Independence in 1947. Today there are over 300 museums of various types: national museums, state museums, archaeological site museums, university museums and such others as the ancestral collections of maharajas and princes. In many cases the individual character of a museum reflects the historical factors that determined its founding, as well as the nature of art in its vicinity. However, since 1947 many museums have also shown a greater awareness of the need for a representative collection to stress the national cultural legacy.

BIBLIOGRAPHY

S. F. Markham and H. Hargreaves: *The Museums of India* (London, 1936)

K. N. Puri: 'Archaeological Museums', *Archaeology in India* (Delhi, 1950), pp. 171–81

C. Sivaramamurti: *Directory of Museums in India* (Delhi, 1959)

R. Morris: 'India', *Art Museums of the World*, ed. V. Jackson (Westport, CT, 1987), i, pp. 484–519

S. Punja: *An Illustrated Guide to Museums of India* (Hong Kong, 1990)

(i) New Delhi. (ii) North-west. (iii) North. (iv) Central. (v) East. (vi) West. (vii) South.

(i) New Delhi. Immediately after Independence the idea of establishing a new museum in New Delhi as a national institution was put into effect. The museums of the Archaeological Survey of India were centralized under one administrative control in 1946, and by 1949 the National Museum in New Delhi had been established. In the 1990s this museum contained over 150,000 items representing Indian art and archaeology from earliest times to the present day. From the Indus Valley civilization (*c.* 2550–*c.* 2000 BC) there are sculptures, inscribed seals, pottery, bronzes and jewellery. Mauryan, Kushana, Gandhara, Sunga and Gupta sculptures are also well represented. The rich collection of medieval sculptures includes the only known bronzes that can be attributed to the Vakataka dynasty, which ruled in the Deccan in the 5th–6th century AD. There is also a vast collection of manuscripts and miniature paintings, including a late 16th-century Mughal *Bāburnāma*, a fine *Rāgamālā* series from the school of Mewar that can be dated *c.* 1660, and richly illuminated copies of the Koran, as well as Indian textiles, jades, metalwork, ivories, woodwork, arms and armour and coins. Central Asian items from the 4th–8th century AD that were acquired during the expeditions of Aurel Stein (and were originally housed in the Central Asian Antiquities Museum in Delhi) are also in the National Museum.

Several other museums founded in New Delhi in the 1950s expressed the post-Independence concern for presenting a national heritage. The Crafts Museum, founded in 1952, has a collection of 20,000 examples of Indian traditional crafts and folk arts, textiles being a speciality. The National Gallery of Modern Art, founded in 1954, contains work by 19th-century European artists who worked in India, early 20th-century Indian painters such as RAVI VARMA, Abanindranath Tagore (*see* TAGORE, (3)), JAMINI ROY, AMRITA SHER-GIL and NANDALAL BOSE, and post-Independence artists. At the Rabindra Bhavan Art Gallery, founded in 1955, is housed the permanent gallery of the Lalit Kala Akademi.

BIBLIOGRAPHY

C. Sivaramamurti: *Bronzes: Guide to the Gallery of the National Museum of India* (Delhi, 1956)

G. Morley: *A Brief Guide to the National Museum* (Delhi, 1962)

C. Sivaramamurti: *Masterpieces of Indian Sculpture in the National Museum* (Delhi, 1971)

(ii) North-west. Important museums are to be found at Srinagar, Chamba, Simla and Chandigarh. At Srinagar, the Sri Pratap Singh Museum contains sculptures from monuments in the central valley of Kashmir; it also houses coins from the Gandhara and Kushana periods. At Chamba, the Bhuri Singh Museum includes 14th–15th-century stone sculptures from local sites and an important collection of Pahari paintings. At Simla, the Himachal State Museum has sculptures from sites throughout Himachal Pradesh, as well as Pahari miniatures. At Chandigarh, the Government Museum and Art Gallery has the finest collection of Gandhara sculptures in India, including standing and seated Buddhist figures, terracotta heads from the 4th–6th-century AD sites of Akhnur and Ushkur, a selection of Hindu and Jaina sculptures from local sites, and a major painting collection.

BIBLIOGRAPHY

J. P. Vogel: *Catalogue of the Bhuri Singh Museum at Chamba (Chamba State, Punjab)* (Calcutta, 1909)

S. D. Sharma: 'Museum and Art Gallery, Chandigarh', *Roopa-Lekha*, xxxviii/1–2 (1968), pp. 247–66

(iii) North. In Uttar Pradesh, the State Museum at Lucknow, founded in 1863, has important collections of sculptures, terracottas, paintings, minor arts, copperplates and coins. The archaeological collection housed in the Kaiserbagh Palace is particularly strong, including over 1000 objects excavated at Mathura during the 1880s. Among the Gupta sculptures (late 4th–late 5th century AD) is a group of dated images that provide a basis for the chronology of sculpture during this period. There are also medieval sculptures from numerous sites. In addition there are some 1500 miniature paintings from the Mughal, Rajasthani and Pahari schools and a collection of minor arts, including Kashmiri shawls from the 18th and 19th centuries, Indian arms and weapons, ivory artefacts and wood-carvings.

The Government Museum, Mathura, which opened in 1880, contains over 4000 pieces of stone sculpture ranging from the 2nd century BC to the 12th century AD. The museum is foremost in India for its collection of Kushana-period art. The earliest stone sculpture in the collection, and a major monument of Indian art, is the colossal statue known as the Parkham *yakṣa* (2nd century BC; *see* INDIAN SUBCONTINENT, fig. 141). At Varanasi, the Bharat Kala Bhavan—founded in 1920 by Rai Krishnadasa and taken over by Banaras Hindu University in 1950—has a rich collection of local stone sculptures, Indian miniature paintings, and textiles, including Kashmiri shawls. Near by, the Archaeological Museum, Sarnath, founded in 1904, has sculptures from the site, including the lion capital of Emperor Ashoka (*reg c.* 269– 232 BC) that now serves as the emblem of the Republic of India. A far more important collection, however, is at the Allahabad Museum, established in 1931; it contains some 500 stone sculptures, which provide a comprehensive collection of sculpture in northern India from the 3rd century BC to the 12th century AD. There is also a large collection of terracotta figurines, including many from Kausambi (3rd century BC–6th century AD). The painting collection includes items from the Mughal, Rajasthani and Pahari schools as well as works by artists from the modern Bengali school.

BIBLIOGRAPHY

J. P. Vogel: *Archaeological Museum at Mathura* (Allahabad, 1910/*R* Delhi, 1971)

V. S. Agrawala: *Mathura Museum Catalogue* (Lucknow, 1952)

S. C. Kala: *Indian Miniatures in the Allahabad Museum* (Allahabad, 1961)

N. P. Joshi: *Mathura Sculptures: A Handbook* (Mathura, 1966)

N. P. Joshi and R. C. Sharma: *Catalogue of Gandhara Sculptures in the State Museum, Lucknow* (Lucknow, 1969)

P. Chandra: *Stone Sculpture in the Allahabad Museum* (Pune, 1971)

R. C. Sharma: *Mathura Museum: Introduction* (Mathura, 1971)

——: *Mathura Museum and Art* (Mathura, 1976)

(iv) Central. In Madhya Pradesh, the State Museum at Bhopal has sculptures from central Indian sites dating from the 10th to the 12th century AD. Also at Bhopal is the Birla Museum, which contains sculptures from 9th–11th-century AD temple sites. The Archaeological Museum at nearby Sanchi contains site material, principally of the Mauryan and Gupta periods. At Gwalior, the Central Archaeological Museum, founded in 1922, has sculptures from local sites and copies of the wall paintings in the Buddhist cave temples at Bagh. At Indore, the Central Museum has a large number of sculptures, many taken from the ruined 11th- and 12th-century temples at Hinglajgarh. At Jabalpur, the Rani Durgavati Museum has 10th- and 11th-century sculptures from sites in the vicinity, among the finest being those from Tewar. At Raipur, the Mahant Ghasi Dass Memorial Museum has sculptures of the 8th and 9th centuries AD from local sites and is known in particular for a series of small Buddhist bronzes from Sirpur. At Sirpur itself, the Archaeological Museum has Buddhist and Hindu sculptures.

BIBLIOGRAPHY

J. H. Marshall, ed.: *Catalogue of the Museum of Archaeology at Sanchi, Bhopal State* (Calcutta, 1922)

(v) East. In Calcutta, the Indian Museum, founded in 1814, received the status of a national museum for eastern India in 1960. It has a vast archaeological collection including terracotta figurines and pictorial seals from Harappa and Mohenjo-daro, and about 400 sculptures from Gandhara, making the Gandhara collection second in India to that at the Government Museum and Art Gallery at Chandigarh. The Indian Museum also contains extensive remains from the stupa at Bharhut in Madhya Pradesh, fine Gupta sculptures of the 5th and 6th centuries AD from various sites in India, and numerous pieces of medieval stone sculpture of the 7th–12th century AD, those from Bihar and Bengal forming a particularly rich collection. There are also sculptures from central and southern India, Nepal and Tibet, as well as ivories, metalwork and textiles from a variety of regions. The collection of Indian paintings includes miniatures from the Mughal and Rajasthani schools and some Deccani and Pahari works. The Indian Museum's coin collection is one of the richest in India, numbering about 46,000.

The Victoria Memorial Hall, Calcutta, founded in 1906, a repository of arts relating to the history of British rule, displays oil and watercolour paintings, miniatures, engravings, sculptures, furniture, textiles, and arms and armour. The Asutosh Museum of Indian Art at Calcutta University, founded in 1937 in memory of the Indian educationist Sir Asutosh Mookerjee, was the first university museum in India. The collection, with a regional character, ranges from the 1st millennium BC to modern times and includes items from the Buddhist sites of Bangarh, Chandraketugarh, Paharpur and Mahasthangarh, terracottas, bronzes, paintings, textiles, and a large collection of folk arts from Bengal and Orissa. Among the other collections of importance in Calcutta is that of the Birla Academy of Art and Culture, which opened in 1967.

The Assam State Museum, Gauhati, founded in 1940, contains stone and copperplate inscriptions dating from the 5th–7th century AD and sculptures from local sites. The Patna Museum, founded in 1917, contains a range of archaeological material, bronzes from south India, arms and armour, and Tibetan paintings. At Bodhgaya, the Archaeological Museum contains the original posts and railings that surrounded the principal temple in the 2nd century BC. At Nalanda the Archaeological Museum, founded in 1958, specializes in Buddhist sculptures. The

Orissa State Museum, Bhubaneshwar, founded in 1932, contains stone sculptures from local sites dating from the 7th century AD, bronzes, palm-leaf manuscripts, temple hangings, arts and crafts, and coins. At Konarak, the Archaeological Museum has pieces from the 13th-century Surya Temple.

BIBLIOGRAPHY

J. Anderson: *Catalogue and Hand-book of the Archaeological Collections of the Indian Museum*, 2 vols (Calcutta, 1883/*R* 1977)
N. G. Majumdar: *Guide to the Sculptures in the Indian Museum* (Delhi, 1937)
C. Sivaramamurti: *A Guide to the Archaeological Galleries of the Indian Museum* (Calcutta, 1954)
C. Kar and T. Mukerjee: *Art Section, Indian Museum Calcutta: A Short Guide* (Calcutta, 1958)
P. D. Chaudhury and M. C. Das: *Ancient Treasures of Assam through Assam State Museum Gauhati* (Gauhati, 1959)
P. L. Gupta, ed.: *Patna Museum Catalogue of Antiquities* (Patna, 1965)
C. Sivaramamurti: *A Guide to the Archaeological Galleries: Indian Museum, Calcutta* (Calcutta, 1976)
K. Khandalavala and S. Doshi: *A Collector's Dream: Indian Art in the Collections of Basant Kumar and Saraladevi Birla and the Birla Academy of Art and Culture* (Bombay, 1987)

(vi) West. In Bombay is the important Prince of Wales Museum of Western India (*see* MUSEUM, fig. 6), which opened to the public in 1922. Its collection of sculptures covers some of the major periods of sculpture in India, including many works from the 8th–12th century. Among the ivories is an 8th-century seated Buddha with attendant figures from Kashmir and several pieces of Christian origin of the 17th and 18th centuries from Goa. There is also carved woodwork from Gujurat of the 10th–17th century and a large Buddhist collection from Nepal and Tibet. The collection of Indian miniature paintings represents all phases of painting from illustrated palm-leaf manuscripts of the 11th–12th century to early 19th-century Pahari paintings. In Pune the Raja Dinkar Kelkar Museum also has some miniature paintings, while the Central Museum, Nagpur, founded in 1863, has various items relating to archaeology, art and ethnology.

In Gujarat, the Museum and Picture Gallery (founded in 1894 and 1920 respectively) at Vadodara form the largest and most important museum in the state. It was created by Maharaja Sayaji Rao III (*reg* 1875–1936), who put together a varied collection while travelling in India and abroad. It contains sculptures from sites in Gujarat, a unique collection of west Indian bronzes discovered at nearby Akota, Jaina carved wooden temple architecture, miniature paintings, modern Indian paintings, and collections of non-Indian art. In 1961 Maharaja Fateh Singh Rao III established the small Maharaja Fateh Singh Museum in Vadodara, the galleries of which were designed by the scholar and museologist Hermann Goetz; this museum contains family portraits, furniture, paintings by the late 19th-century Indian artist Ravi Varma, copies of European paintings and sculptures, and Chinese and Japanese items. At the Maharaja Sayajirao University in Vadodara two collections are noteworthy: the Department of Museology houses 9th-century marble sculptures from Vadaval, while the Department of Archaeology has 4th-century AD finds from the Buddhist monuments at Devinmori. At Ahmadabad, the Calico Museum of Textiles, founded in 1948, has an important collection of Indian textiles and costumes and a Jaina gallery that incorporates several 18th- and 19th-century wooden shrines taken from private residences in Ahmadabad and Patan. Also in Ahmadabad, the Sanskar Kendra Municipal Museum contains the N. C. Mehta Collection of Indian miniature paintings, while the Shreyas Folk Art Museum has traditional mirrorwork and tribal clothes.

In Rajasthan, the Maharaja Sawai Man Singh II Museum in the City Palace at Jaipur, founded in 1959, houses the most important princely collection in India; it includes Persian and Mughal carpets, Mughal and Rajasthani miniature paintings, and arms. The Government Central Museum of Jaipur, on the other hand, has 9th- and 10th-century sculptures from sites in Rajasthan as well as woodwork, jewellery, brasswork and carpets. At Alwar, the City Palace contains more than 7000 manuscripts, Mughal and Rajasthani miniatures, armour and textiles. The Rajputana Museum of Archaeology, Ajmer, founded in 1908, has sculptures, Rajput paintings, arms and armour and coins. The Sardar Museum, Jodhpur, includes 8th–10th-century sculptures and architectural fragments from Osian and Kiradu. At Udaipur, the City Palace Museum has sculptures from Jagat and Nagda.

BIBLIOGRAPHY

O. C. Gangoly: *Critical Catalogue of Miniature Paintings in the Baroda Museum* (Baroda, 1961)
M. K. Dhavalikar: *Mathura Art in the Baroda Museum* (Baroda, 1970)
J. Irwin, ed.: *Historic Textiles of India at the Calico Museum*, 2 vols (Ahmadabad, 1971–3)
M. Chandra: *Indian Art: Prince of Wales Museum of Western India* (Bombay, 1974)
——: *Stone Sculpture in the Prince of Wales Museum* (Bombay, 1974)

(vii) South. In Andhra Pradesh, the State Museum at Hyderabad, founded in 1930, contains sculpture, epigraphy, arms, bidri ware, bronzework, manuscripts, miniatures and paintings (including copies of the Ajanta paintings), textiles, European and modern art, and coins. The Salar Jung Museum, founded in 1951 and since designated a national museum, is based on the acquisitions of the Nawab Salar Jung III (*reg* 1889–1949) and his ancestors, and contains a wide-ranging collection of Eastern and Western paintings, sculptures, textiles, carpets, porcelains, ivories, glass, silver and bronze wares, arms and armour, furniture and toys. There is a rich collection of illuminated Korans and other works by master calligraphers and a significant collection of Indian jades and jewellery. The Karnataka Government Museum and Venkatappa Art Gallery, Bangalore, founded in 1866, contains a range of items, including sculptures of the Hoysala period.

At Madras the important Government Museum and National Art Gallery, founded in 1851, is the second oldest museum in India. Now designated the state museum of Tamil Nadu, it contains antiquities from sites in southern India and the Deccan, including a collection of Amaravati sculptures second only to that at the British Museum, London, and the largest collection of south Indian bronzes in India, the majority of the Chola period. There are also wood-carvings, ivories, ceramics, metalwork and an extensive collection of about 25,000 coins. Elsewhere in Tamil Nadu there is the Archaeological Museum at Mamallapuram and, at Thanjavur, the Art Gallery with fine Chola bronzes. In Kerala at Trivandrum, there is, in addition to the Government Museum of Art and Natural History, the

Sri Chitra Art Gallery, which contains Indian miniature paintings, objects from Tibet, China, Japan and Bali, and contemporary Indian art.

BIBLIOGRAPHY

F. H. Gravely and T. N. Ramachandran: *Catalogue of the South Indian Hindu Metal Images in the Madras Government Museum* (Madras, 1932)
F. H. Gravely and C. Sivaramamurti: *Guide to the Archaeological Galleries: An Introduction to South Indian Temple Architecture and Sculpture* (Madras, 1939)
C. Sivaramamurti: *Amaravati Sculptures in the Madras Government Museum* (Madras, 1942)
V. N. S. Desikan: *Guide to the National Art Gallery* (Madras, 1967)
Journeys in Art through the Salar Jung Museum (Hyderabad, 1971)

S. J. VERNOIT

2. PRIVATE COLLECTIONS. The independence of India in 1947 encouraged the private collection of art there. The well-established recovery and revision of Indian history and the growth of a sense of national identity spurred a taste for art collecting that had already been established in the pre-independence period by such pioneers as ANANDA KENTISH COOMARASWAMY, the TAGORE family, RAI KRISHNADASA, GOPI KRISHNA KANORIA, N. C. Mehta, the lawyer P. C. Manuk, A. C. Ardeshir, Sir Cowasji Jahangir and Dr Alma Latifi. Several of these collectors continued to be active after 1947. Collecting opportunities were enhanced by social changes, including the absorption of the princely states into the Indian union, resulting in certain types of art (especially miniature paintings) being more available to collectors. The 1947–8 Burlington House exhibition in London (see Ashton) drew heavily on private collections. Many of the Indian loans on their return entered the newly formed collection of the National Museum, New Delhi. Indeed, several of the early private collections not dispersed at their owners' deaths are now in institutions both public and private in India or elsewhere. For example, Rai Krishnadasa established the Bharat Kala Bhavan in Varanasi, and P. C. Manuk's collection is in the Victoria and Albert Museum, London, and other British institutions.

The collecting of Indian art increased steadily from the 1950s, paralleling and reinforcing Indian interest in the nation's artistic heritage. Private and public collections in India and abroad prospered. Motichand Khajanchi of Bikaner assembled a collection of Indian miniatures that was shown at the Lalit Kala Akademi in New Delhi in 1960 (now in the National Museum, New Delhi; see Khandalavala, M. Chandra and P. Chandra). Other private collectors continued to be active in the country and to establish institutions. An example of this is the Birla Academy of Art and Culture, Calcutta, founded by BASANT KUMAR BIRLA and Saraladevi Birla in 1962 and opened in 1967. The collection, an extension of their private collection, includes sculpture, miniature painting, decorative arts and contemporary art from India and abroad (Khandalavala and Doshi). The increasingly protective climate of the 1960s and 1970s strengthened existing prohibitions on the legal export of Indian antiquities and led to the 1973 law calling for registration of all art objects in India. Registration has somewhat restrained certain aspects of collection, but several major collectors continue the tradition, mostly in large urban areas.

BIBLIOGRAPHY

L. Ashton, ed.: *The Art of India and Pakistan* (London, 1950)
G. K. Kanoria: *Indian Paintings from Rajasthan from the Collection of Gopi Krishna Kanoria of Calcutta* (London, 1957)
K. Khandalavala, M. Chandra and P. Chandra: *Miniature Painting: A Catalogue of the Exhibition of the Sri Motichand Khajanchi Collection held by the Lalit Kalā Akademi* (New Delhi, 1960)
K. Khandalavala and M. Chandra: *Miniatures and Sculptures from the Collections of the Late Sir Cowasji Jahangir, Bart.* (Bombay, 1965)
R. Skelton: 'Collecting Indian Miniatures', *Indian Miniatures: The Ehrenfeld Collection*, ed. D. Ehnbom (New York, 1985), pp. 9–14
K. Khandalavala and S. Doshi: *A Collector's Dream: Indian Art in the Collections of Basant Kumar Saraladevi Birla and the Birla Academy of Art and Culture* (Bombay, 1987)

DANIEL EHNBOM

XII. Art legislation.

Art legislation in India is based mainly on three acts: the Indian Treasures Act (ITA) of 1878, the Ancient Monuments and Archaeological Sites and Remains Act (AMASRA) of 1958, and the Antiquities and Art Treasures Act (AATA) of 1972.

Operated by the state governments, the ITA has proved to be most effective in regard to the collection of antiquities by the various museums managed by the government. This act defines 'treasure' as 'anything of any value hidden in the soil, or in anything affixed thereto'. 'Treasure' becomes of consequence if it fulfils two criteria: if its value exceeds ten rupees; and if there is proof that it was hidden 100 years before the date of finding. This legislation further stipulates that the finder of any treasure-trove valued at more than ten rupees has to inform the District Collector in writing, with full particulars of the find, its location and date of finding. The finder has either to deposit it in the government treasury or to produce the treasure before the Collector as and when the latter directs. The Collector thereafter has to decide the ownership of the treasure, compensation etc. The act also empowers the Collector to acquire the treasure on behalf of the government whenever necessary or to auction it and dispose of the proceeds according to prescribed rules. It also contains provisions of penalties in the event of default.

The AMASRA of 1958 is operated by the central government, i.e. the Archaeological Survey of India. The principal provisions of the act include: protection of a monument considered to be of national importance, and upkeep and preservation of already notified ancient monuments, remains and sites; regulation of archaeological excavations in protected and unprotected sites; protection of ancient sculptures, carvings and objects; and compulsory acquisition of antiquities. Other provisions include punishment for defacement or destruction of protected monuments and sites, prevention of new constructions and mining close to sites, observation of certain formalities for photography and filming etc, and penalties for violation of the provisions of this act. For the purposes of protection and preservation the act defines monuments, remains, sites and antiquities thus: 'ancient monument' means any structure, erection or monument or any tumulus or place of interment or any cave rock-sculpture, inscription or monolith that is of historical, archaeological or artistic importance and that has been in existence for not less than 100 years and includes both remains of ancient monuments and site of an ancient monument. 'Antiquity' includes any coin, sculpture, manuscript, epigraphy or work of art and craft, any object detached from a structure or any object of historical interest that has been in existence for not less than 100 years.

The AATA of 1972 is implemented through the central and state governments. It aims to regulate trade in antiquities and art treasures, to prevent smuggling and fraudulent dealings in antiquities, and to provide compulsory acquisition of an antiquity in the public interest. It follows nearly the same definition of antiquity as AMASRA and includes such objects of 100 years' standing as are illustrative of science, art or craft, literature, religion, customs, morals or polities of bygone ages. In addition, it calls a manuscript, record or other document of scientific, historical, literary or aesthetic value that has been in existence for not less than 75 years an antiquity. In the terms of this act an art treasure is any human work of art of high aesthetic or artistic value that is not an antiquity, provided its creator is not alive. In order to regulate the export of an antiquity or art treasure the act empowers the Director-General of the Archaeological Survey of India to allow or disallow the export. In case of any dispute as to whether an object is an antiquity or art treasure or not the Director-General is the final authority. The act also has provisions to obtain a licence from the central government for carrying out business in antiquities and compulsory registration, with some exceptions, of certain notified categories of antiquities, e.g. sculpture in various media, paintings and painted manuscripts, through the registering officers and acquisition of antiquities in the public interest, besides penalties for violations.

BIBLIOGRAPHY

H. Sarkar: *Museums and Protection of Monuments and Antiquities in India* (Delhi, 1981)

A. N. Khanna: *Archaeology of India* (New Delhi, 1992)

M. C. JOSHI

XIII. *Art libraries and photographic collections.*

Book collections of artistic significance exist throughout India. The Indira Gandhi National Centre for the Arts in New Delhi has an important art library, begun in 1985; vigorous acquisition of rare books, personal collections, photographic slides and microfilming of manuscripts have made this an international resource. The American Institute of Indian Studies at Varanasi has a well-stocked research library, including a collection of more than 79,000 architectural photographs, largely of Hindu temples. India's largest library, the National Library of India in Calcutta, holds manuscripts, books and journals for research in art and archaeology, including several sizeable donated collections. The National Museum, New Delhi, is one of the very few Indian art museums with a good library. Other museum library collections include those of the Salar Jung Museum in Hyderabad, the Prince of Wales Museum of Western India in Bombay, the Victoria Memorial Hall in Calcutta, the Asutosh Museum of Indian Art at the University of Calcutta, the National Gallery of Modern Art and the Lalit Kala Akademi in New Delhi, and the Indian Museum in Calcutta. The Connemara Public Library, Madras, which serves as library for the Government Museum and National Art Gallery, contains a rich but poorly preserved collection of early books with artistic images of India. India's major resource for study of the Jaina religious tradition along with its visual artistic manifestations is the L. D. Institute of Indology, Ahmadabad. Manuscript archives and many libraries with smaller art book collections—including those in the Asiatic Society of Bombay and of Calcutta, state academies of art, folk art museums and the National Film Archives of India in Pune—are listed in Gupta and in the *World Guide to Libraries*.

Institutional photography collections, with the major exception of the Archaeological Survey of India (for which some guides are published), have developed mostly since 1975. Photography collecting in India has not reached the levels of Europe and America. The Indira Gandhi National Centre for the Arts has begun to build a photographic archive, which contains over 2700 glass-plate negatives by Raja Lala Deen Dayal (*fl* 1860s–70s).

Outside India, the Oriental and India Office collections (incorporating the former India Office Library, 1801–1982) at the British Library, London, constitute the single most important collection of books and manuscripts for the study of Indian art. They hold more than 250,000 photographs of India, half of which are from the 19th century.

BIBLIOGRAPHY

J. Gutman: *Through Indian Eyes* (New York, 1982)

B. M. Gupta and others, eds: *Handbook of Libraries, Archives and Information Centres in India* (New Delhi, 1984–)

The World of Learning (London, rev. 41/1991)

World Guide to Libraries (Munich, rev. 10/1991)

JAMES H. NYE

Indiana [Clark], **Robert** (*b* New Castle, IN, 13 Sept 1928). American painter, sculptor and printmaker. He studied at the Art Institute of Chicago (1949–53), the Skowhegan School of Painting and Sculpture in Maine (summer 1953) and Edinburgh University and Edinburgh College of Art (1953–4), before settling in New York in 1954. There in the late 1950s he began assembling wood sculptures from found materials, often stencilling painted words on to them, as in *Moon* (h. 1.98 m, 1960; New York, MOMA). He called these works *Herms* after the quadrangular, stone stelae guardian figures that served as signposts in crossroads in ancient Greece and Rome. Indiana called himself a 'sign painter' to suggest the humble origins of his artistic activity in the American work ethic and to indicate his fascination with the use of words in signs. Joining his interest in Americana with the formal and signifying elements of signs, he visualized the superficial and illusory American Dream in paintings characterized by flat bright colours and clearly defined contours influenced by the hard-edge paintings by friends such as Ellsworth Kelly and Jack Youngerman (*b* 1926).

Indiana's attention to American themes, use of vibrating bright colour and simple formal configurations and shaped canvases marked him as one of the central figures of American Pop art. He combined the simple Roman numerals and letters found in beckoning American roadside bars and cafés to address serious social issues, as in *The Calumet* (1961; Waltham, MA, Brandeis U., Rose A. Mus.), a celebration of the bonds of peace that united the Native American Indian tribes before the arrival of European settlers. Following the example of Jasper Johns,

Indiana used words in emblems, as in the painting *Figure 5* (1963; Washington, DC, N. Mus. Amer. A.), which includes stencilled words within each side of a pentagon: EAT, USA, ERR, DIE and HUG. Indiana was equally drawn to philosophical themes from the writings of American authors such as Herman Melville, Walt Whitman, William Carlos Williams and Hart Crane, and to the existential aspects of numbers, which he regarded as the basic elements structuring our daily lives, with 1 to 9 representing the spectrum of existence and 0 standing between life and death. His concern for the 'spiritual concept' represented by the word LOVE was expressed in paintings such as *Love* (1966; Indianapolis, IN, Mus. A.) and in related sculptures (e.g. *Love*, carved aluminium, h. 305 mm, edition of six, 1966; see 1977 exh. cat., p. 24); these became his best-known works, and they came also to be regarded as emblems for the hippie generation of the late 1960s. In 1978 he left New York to settle on the remote island of Vinalhaven off the coast of Maine.

BIBLIOGRAPHY

Robert Indiana (exh. cat., intro. J. W. McCoubrey; Philadelphia, U. PA, Inst. Contemp. A.; San Antonio, TX, McNay A. Inst.; Indianapolis, IN, Herron Mus. A.; 1968)

P. Tuchman: 'Pop! Interviews with George Segal, Andy Warhol, Roy Lichtenstein, James Rosenquist and Robert Indiana', *ARTnews*, lxxii/5 (1974), pp. 24–9

Robert Indiana (exh. cat., intro. D. B. Goodall, essays by R. L. B. Tobin and W. Katz; Austin, U. TX, A. Mus., 1977)

Indiana's Indianas (exh. cat., essays by M. B. Peladeau and M. Dibner; Rockland, ME, Farnsworth Lib. & A. Mus., 1982)

Wood Works: Constructions by Robert Indiana (exh. cat. by V. M. Mecklenburg, Washington, DC, N. Mus. Amer. A., 1984)

For further bibliography, *see* POP ART.

KRISTINE STILES

Indian Church. *See* LAMANAI.

Indian subcontinent. Asian region comprising the vast peninsula bounded on the north by the Himalayan range and on the west, south and east by the Arabian Sea, Indian Ocean and Bay of Bengal. This article covers the major arts of modern Pakistan, India and Bangladesh from earliest times until 1947; some of the subsections on minor arts and on tribal and village art also discuss material dating later than 1947. SRI LANKA, NEPAL and BHUTAN are covered separately. For developments after 1947 *see* INDIA, PAKISTAN and, after 1971, BANGLADESH.

Subsections of this survey have been arranged chronologically and geographically. Dynastic appellations have generally been avoided, as regional styles were not necessarily linked to ruling houses, and patronage was often broadly based. The early periods are analysed on a north–south basis, while regional developments in the later periods are covered by geographical area. For purposes of discussion, the term north-west is understood roughly as Haryana, Himachal Pradesh, Jammu and Kashmir and Pakistan; north as Uttar Pradesh (including the Delhi region); central as Madhya Pradesh; west as Rajasthan, Gujarat and Maharashtra; east as Orissa, Bihar, West Bengal and Bangladesh; and south as Tamil Nadu, Kerala, Karnataka and Andhra Pradesh. Historical chronology and geography are discussed briefly at the beginning of many subsections to illuminate contemporary regional divisions.

Translations or explanations have been provided for technical terms in such languages as Sanskrit, Tamil, Persian and Hindi. Transliteration largely conforms to generally accepted scholarly practice. A simplified transliteration system following pronunciation more closely (e.g. 'Chola' rather than 'Cōḷa', 'Shiva' rather than 'Śiva') has been used for all names and terms not in italics.

I. Introduction. II. Iconography and subject-matter. III. Architecture. IV. Urban Planning. V. Sculpture. VI. Painting. VII. Textiles. VIII. Other arts. IX. Colonial-period decorative arts. X. Village art. XI. Tribal art. XII. Patronage. XIII. Collectors and collecting. XIV. Exhibitions. XV. Copies and forgeries.

DETAILED TABLE OF CONTENTS

I. Introduction.

Historically, the Indian subcontinent has been a geographical and cultural unity rather than a political one. Cultural uniqueness has been reinforced by natural barriers, which, until comparatively modern times, separated the inhabitants from neighbouring peoples. The art of the subcontinent was made mostly to serve India's indigenous religions, notably Hinduism, Buddhism (*see* HINDUISM, §I, and BUDDHISM, §III, 1), JAINISM and SIKHISM. Secular arts were also produced for members of the merchant and ruling classes. Treatises composed in Sanskrit and other languages have provided guidelines for the performing arts, architecture and the making of images. This technical literature, together with India's religious and visual arts, has been studied since the 19th century. An increasing variety of approaches characterizes scholarly exploration of the subcontinent's rich artistic traditions.

1. Geography and climate. 2. History. 3. Language groups. 4. Epigraphy. 5. Calendars. 6. Trade and travel. 7. Religions and social order. 8. Concept of art. 9. Status of the artist. 10. Treatises. 11. Historiography.

1. GEOGRAPHY AND CLIMATE. The Indian subcontinent (see fig. 1) forms a vast, irregular diamond with its maximum points between 6° and 36°N and 61° and 97°E. Its northernmost point is the junction of the mountain chains of the Pamirs, Karakoram and Hindu Kush, from which the unbroken barrier of the Himalaya runs south-eastward until it meets the mountains of upper Burma. Lesser but still formidable mountain barriers, combined with deserts, run south-westward from the Hindu Kush, dividing India from Iran, until they reach the sea at the mouth of the Gulf of Oman. From these easternmost and westernmost points, the peninsula of India projects into the Indian Ocean, dividing the Bay of Bengal from the Arabian Sea until its coasts meet at Cape Comorin (Kanya Kumari). The island of Sri Lanka (formerly Ceylon) hangs like a pearl from a point slightly north-east of Cape Comorin.

The upper half of the subcontinent below the Himalaya forms the north Indian alluvial plain, watered by two great river systems. The Indus rises in Tibet but breaks through the mountains to flow south-westward through the alluvial plains of the Punjab and Sind to the Arabian Sea at Karachi. Its principal tributaries flow across the plains of the Punjab from the Himalaya to join the Indus from the east. The Ganga (Ganges) and the Yamuna (Jumna) rise in the middle of the Himalaya, rushing southward to the plains before curving eastward. Their streams, united from Allahabad, are joined in north Bengal by the Brahmaputra, another Tibetan river, which breaks through the mountains into the valley of Assam. This huge volume of water empties into the Bay of Bengal via the vast delta that constitutes the state of Bengal. Between the river systems of the Indus and the Ganga lie the desert and semi-arid region of Rajasthan.

Running across the middle of the subcontinent are the Vindhya and associated mountain ranges and plateaux, with smaller alluvial areas at east and west in coastal Gujarat and Orissa. Historically, the jungle-covered Vindhya have divided north from south India. The south consists mostly of the plateau of the Deccan, some 600 m high and sloping gradually to the east. The Deccan is bordered by the ranges of the Western and Eastern Ghats, which run parallel to the coasts and join in the far south to form the Nilgiri Hills, the highest part of India south of the Himalaya. Below the steep wall of the Western Ghats runs a narrow coastal plain from Bombay to Cape Comorin. The great rivers of the Deccan—the Krishna, Godavari and Kaveri—all flow eastward, and their progress through the Eastern Ghats has created broad valleys and a wider coastal plain.

The Indian year may be divided into the cold, the hot and the rainy seasons. During the so-called cold weather, from October to February, the prevailing north-easterly winds are very dry, being from the interior of Asia. On

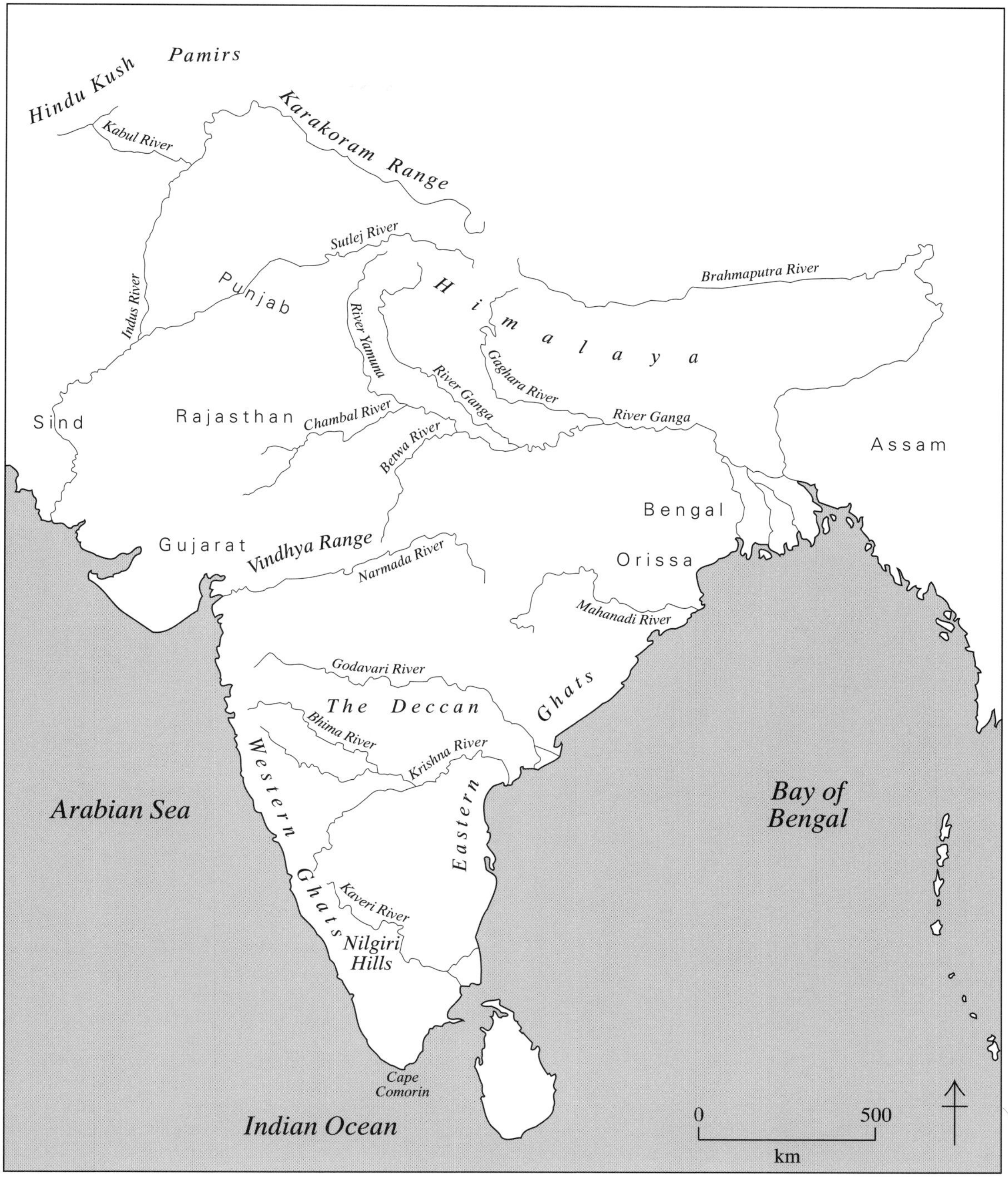

1. Map of the Indian subcontinent

the north Indian plains, daytime temperatures stay warm, but nighttime temperatures in December and January often drop to 0°C. The coastal areas are milder, while the south remains warm. From February to May temperatures increase, attaining 50°C or above on the north Indian plains as the north-east winds fall off. Local storms occur often. From June onwards the south-westerly monsoon winds blow off the Indian Ocean on to the heated land mass, producing heavy and continuous rainfall, especially on the Western Ghats and eastern Himalaya. (The largest annual rainfall ever recorded in India—over 21 m—occurred in Assam in 1861.) The huge volume of water running off the mountains often produces disastrous floods in the lower reaches of the rivers. In late September and October the monsoon winds retreat, and it is from this time to December that the east coast of peninsular India receives its rainfall. The monsoon rains are unevenly distributed, and western and central India, the eastern Deccan and Pakistan have historically been areas liable to severe famine owing to failure of the rains.

In such a climate, human habitation has depended on an adequate supply of water throughout the non-monsoon portion of the year, whether from rivers, irrigation systems or wells. The chief cities and major cultures of the north are to be found on the banks of the perennial rivers, which are fed by both monsoon rains and melting Himalayan snows. The greatest concentrations of population occupy the basins of the major rivers, whose flooding distributes immense quantities of fertile silt over the land. The extreme south, which has a more extensive monsoon period than the rest of India, was one of the earliest centres of Indian culture. In other parts of India, the rivers are fed largely by monsoon rains, so that by summer they fill only a fraction of their beds. Although these areas are of great cultural interest, the cities have remained small until modern times.

Irrigation systems based on dams and tanks, many of them begun in ancient times, have traditionally increased the cropping of the more fertile areas, such as the eastern Punjab and the Kaveri Delta. No south Indian village is without its tank, while the beautiful stepwells of the dry west demonstrate the extreme importance attached to their function (*see* STEPWELL). Devastating though the climate can be, two harvests per year are possible. The summer monsoonal crop, consisting of rice or other crops needing large amounts of water, is sown at the onset of the rains and harvested when they end. The winter crop, often cereals, is sown after the summer harvest and brought in during March, before the summer heat. In the mid-19th century an extensive network of canal systems was begun to harness the major rivers and increase the cropping of drier areas, thus making the feeding of a greatly increased population possible.

BIBLIOGRAPHY

The Imperial Gazetteer of India (Oxford, 1907–9) [still useful for its detailed physical descriptions]

O. H. K. Spate and A. T. A. Learmonth: *India and Pakistan: A General and Regional Geography* (London, 1954, rev. 3/1967)

National Atlas of India (Calcutta, 1977–)

B. L. C. Johnson: *India: Resources and Development* (London, 1979, 2/1983)

2. HISTORY.

(i) Pre- and protohistory (to *c.* 7th century BC). (ii) *c.* 7th century BC–mid-4th century AD. (iii) Mid-4th century AD–*c.* 1000. (iv) Period of Muslim rule (*c.* 1000–1757). (v) British India (1757–1947).

(i) Pre- and protohistory (to c. *7th century* BC). Evidence of human activity in south Asia exists from the remote past in the form of flint tools and associated animal bones. For the Mesolithic (from *c.* 9000 BC) and Neolithic periods, the evidence suggests, unsurprisingly for such a vast area, cultural advances at different rates in toolmaking, village settlement, agriculture and the domestication of animals, pottery, burial and the introduction of copper. The most advanced locale was the north-west. While the earliest settlements there may date from *c.* 8000 BC, none from the south or east is earlier than *c.* 3000 BC. Evidence of artistic activity other than in the north-west is limited to the Mesolithic and Neolithic figural drawings on the rock escarpments of central India and Karnataka. In the Chalcolithic period (from *c.* 5000 BC), pure copper was extensively mined and worked but only rarely alloyed into bronze. Large numbers of copper hoards from the 2nd millennium BC, containing individual objects whose great weight suggests that they were non-utilitarian, have been found in the western Gangetic valley, on the Chota Nagpur plateau and in the northern Deccan. The extreme south remained in the Neolithic until 1000 BC, by which time the Iron Age had already begun in the north. Elaborate funerary rituals, involving both coffin- and urn-burials, often associated with megaliths (*see* MEGALITHIC ARCHITECTURE, §2), distinguish the burial practices of the south. Some of these burials can be dated as early as the Neolithic period, but most belong to the Iron Age.

The earliest urban civilization, found in the Indus Valley, was made possible (as in Egypt and Mesopotamia) by advances in growing wheat and barley in fertile riverine flood-plains. Settled villages first started to use pottery and copper *c.* 5000 BC and established extensive trade networks with both western Central Asia and the Arabian Sea coast. A gradual growth in urbanization can be traced from this date, culminating in a mature civilization *c.* 2550 BC. Identified originally at the site of HARAPPA on the Ravi River in the Punjab and confirmed by the better-preserved remains at MOHENJO-DARO on the Indus in Sind, the Indus civilization is now known from many other sites spread over Pakistan and western India. Of particular importance are KALIBANGAN in Rajasthan and the port city of LOTHAL on the Gulf of Khambhat (Cambay). This civilization is remarkable for its urban planning and extensive bathing and drainage arrangements on a scale unknown elsewhere. Each of the larger cities is marked by a fortified lower town and what appears to have been a citadel; all sites have streets laid out on a grid pattern and brick houses (stone also was used outside the lower Indus plain). Normally built on riverbanks, the towns were protected from floods and possibly human predators by massive ramparts.

Evidence of this people's everyday culture survives in pottery painted in geometric designs enlivened with animal or vegetable motifs, terracotta animals (probably toys), and copper and bronze implements and vessels. Technically, they are of high quality. The few stone or metal sculptures are small in scale. There are no written records, and the civilization's history is unknown. It is usually surmised that these people were the ancestors of the Dravidian peoples, now living mostly in the south. The uniformity of artefacts found at mature Indus sites suggests intensive trading and hence the conditions for a single empire. Some of the most abundant remains are steatite seals and clay sealings, with animal designs and brief inscriptions in an undeciphered ideographic script. These sealings apparently were used for closing bales or bags of merchandise. Some of the larger buildings—often where statues and large numbers of small terracotta figures have been found—have been postulated as temples. There are grounds for believing in a continuity of religious culture with theistic Hinduism (*see* HINDUISM, §I). A divinity on one seal, horned and ithyphallic, much resembles the historic Shiva. The great baths suggest ritual bathing (see fig. 22 below), while the extensive provision for domestic bathing and toilet facilities suggests a spiritual kinship with the ritual ablutions of later Hinduism. However, the considerable evidence of fire-altars at Kalibangan is more suggestive of the next Indo-Aryan phase than of the succeeding theistic Hinduism.

The mature Indus civilization declined rapidly after *c.* 2000 BC. Although significant cultural remains occur from Mohenjo daro after this date, pottery from Harappa suggests a period combining Harappan forms with considerable new influence from Iran. Archaeological evidence from the same period suggesting a distinct cultural change occurs in Harappan-type settlements in Pakistan and in the fire-altars of Kalibangan in particular. Although the cities were abandoned, remains indicate that further east into the subcontinent practices of the Indus civilization type continued with few changes. For historical evidence of this period, it is necessary to examine the Vedas, India's earliest literature. The Vedas were composed (in a still pre-literate society) between *c.* 1500 and the 4th century BC by the Indo-Aryans, the branch of the Indo-European peoples that reached India in the 2nd millennium BC. This literature, the earliest parts of which were composed in the Punjab, speaks of the destruction by fire and sword of the forts of *dāsa*s, described as dark-skinned phallus worshippers. Scholars have tended to identify the forts with the cities of the Indus civilization; indeed, some of the Vedic hymns speak of ruined cities. There is no other evidence that speakers of Vedic—the most archaic form of Sanskrit—took over the Indus cities, and doubt has been cast both on the chronological continuity (the decline of the Indus urban centres seeming to have occurred prior to the arrival of the Indo-Aryans) and on the problem of using linguistic evidence as a guide to historical movements of peoples.

The Aryans were organized in tribes headed by *rāja*s (kings) and worshipped solar and nature gods, headed by Indra, god of thunder, and Agni, god of fire. Their taming and riding of the horse, native to Central Asia, and invention of the horse-chariot and spoked wheel suggest why they were able to extend their rule rapidly over north India. Although little hard history may be learnt from the Vedas, it is evident that by 1000 BC Vedic speakers were moving east and south, assuming a ruling position in indigenous societies as they went. The division of society in the later Vedic period into four classes—priests, warriors, farmers and traders, and an underclass of *śūdra*s (non-Aryans and outcastes)—suggests that the latter represented the indigenous population. The original Indus Valley people would then have been related to the Dravidians. Indeed, attempts have been made to decipher the Indus Valley script in terms of ancient Tamil. The Aryan expansion slowed as it progressed southward, but the declining number of Vedic speakers finally became insufficient to oust the rulers (or languages) of the south (*see also* §§3 and 7 below).

During the Vedic period, the Indo-Aryan heartland shifted to the still thickly forested Gangetic plain; only the spread of iron tools would have made this area habitable. In this region are set the narrative cores of the two great epics of India, the *Mahābhārata* and *Rāmāyaṇa* (early 1st millennium BC), which involve struggles for supremacy between related tribes in the Delhi area and the middle Gangetic region respectively. Archaeological remains of the late Vedic period are comparatively meagre. People evidently lived not in large settlements but in scattered, semi-tribal communities until a second phase of urbanization—at KAUSAMBI and other centres in the Gangetic region—began in the early 1st millennium BC. Wood and brick were used for the buildings of these cities; very few are known to have had stone walls. The absence of long-lasting domestic objects is a characteristic of mature Indian civilization. Two phases of fine pottery are known from this period: Painted Grey Ware (*c.* 1000–450 BC) and Northern Black Polished Ware (*c.* 600–200 BC). The latter was used in the distinctive urban civilization known through the earliest Buddhist and Jaina writings (*see also* §VIII, 5(i) below).

(ii) c. *7th century* BC*–mid-4th century* AD. From Buddhist, Jaina and Hindu sources it is clear that the mid-1st millennium BC was intellectually the most stimulating period in India's history, possibly representing the synthesis of Aryan and Dravidian cultures. The foundations of the various schools of Indian philosophy were laid, and the otherworldly view of life characteristic of the intellectual basis of Indian religions was developed. The framework of Hindu law and morals was established, and the Vedic cult was gradually submerged by theistic Hinduism. Astronomy, mathematics and especially language were fields of concentrated study. It has been claimed that the codification of the Sanskrit language at this time, stifling the development of vernaculars, enabled India to develop a unified culture, extending even to the Dravidian south.

Little of this literature, however, is recognizable as connected history for this period. Following its introduction into India, possibly in the 7th century BC, writing was used for ephemeral purposes rather than for literature. Earlier literature—the Vedas, the epics, Buddhist and Jaina canonical literature—had been entirely oral. Besides these sources there are the king-lists and other historical matter buried in the Puranas (ancient tales and chronicles), although interpreting this evidence is often a matter of conjecture. The major source for internal chronology (apart from some chronicles for peripheral areas such as Kashmir) is inscriptions, on both stone and metal; the first documented use of writing for inscriptions occurred in the 3rd century BC. Inscriptions give connected king-lists, details of political events and royal family relationships and often absolute or at least relative dates, which are supplemented by the legends on coins (*see also* §§4 and VIII, 6(i) below). In addition, accounts written by foreigners, whether Greek, Chinese or Arab, are usually of great value.

Buddhist and Jaina sources indicate that in the 6th and 5th centuries BC, 16 powers divided north India among them, from Gandhara (western Punjab) to Anga (northern Bengal). Other petty kingdoms and tribal republics existed at this time. Kosala (modern Uttar Pradesh) appears to have been the most important of these early powers. Following the Buddha's death in the 5th century BC, Magadha, the chief state in central Bihar, began its slow rise to pre-eminence by absorbing its neighbours. By the

4th century BC, under the Nanda dynasty, it had become the major state. Apart from the ubiquitous Northern Black Polished Ware, there are few physical remains of these cultures other than the walls of Rajgir, Magadha's capital.

Little is known about the political situation in other parts of India at this time, except for the north-west, which formed two satrapies of the Achaemenid Persian empire, namely Gandhara and India (lower Indus region), *c.* 500 BC. The amount of tribute demanded of them suggests that these provinces were extremely wealthy. At the time of the invasion of Alexander the Great in 326–325 BC, they had largely recovered their independence and were being governed either under monarchical systems or in tribal confederacies. Alexander advanced as far as the Beas River, conquering all in his path, but his troops refused to follow him further eastward to the Ganga. Instead, he and his army moved down the rivers of the Punjab to the Arabian Sea, again sweeping all before them. However, even before his death in 323 BC, the Indians had largely recovered their independence (*see also* IRAN, ANCIENT, §I, 2(ii)(b)).

India's first important known empire of subcontinental proportions was founded by Chandragupta MAURYA (*reg c.* 321–297 BC). Around 321 BC Chandragupta seized the throne of Magadha from the Nandas. Within a few years he had extended his empire to cover the whole of north India. He thwarted attempts (*c.* 305 BC) to recover India by Alexander's former general and ruler of Persia Seleukos Nikator, extracting sufficient territory to make the Hindu Kush (India's 'natural frontier') the boundary between the empires. Either Chandragupta or his son Bindusara (*reg c.* 297–*c.* 269 BC) also conquered the Deccan. This vast area was ruled from Pataliputra, a great city on the Ganga and the site of modern Patna. A great deal is known about the administration of the city and the empire from the writings of Megasthenes, the ambassador sent by Seleukos Nikator to Chandragupta in 302 BC, and from the *Artha śāstra*, the writings on political expediency of Kautilya, Chandragupta's minister. Chandragupta's grandson Ashoka (*reg c.* 269–*c.* 232 BC) extended the empire into Orissa at the cost of such great slaughter that he resolved to give up warfare and hunting and rule according to the precepts of Buddhist *dharma* (*see* §7 below). The many inscriptions put up by Ashoka all over his empire presuppose a state of general literacy, and the free-standing pillars on which some of them appear are India's earliest major stone sculptures (*see* §IV, 3(ii) below). Ashoka sent missionaries to Sri Lanka and to the Hellenistic kingdoms of the eastern Mediterranean to convert their rulers to Buddhism, in the former instance meeting with success.

The Maurya empire did not long survive Ashoka's death. It is rarely possible to discuss Indian history thereafter in terms of a unified country, as there were always clear divisions between north and south—and often, in the north, between east and west. The story oscillates between periods when major empires, whether northern or southern, enjoyed relative hegemony and others when various states of equal power jostled for position. There were no fixed boundaries to any of these states. On the ruins of the Maurya empire, two separate kingdoms were established in the north and the south, ruled by the SHUNGA (2nd–1st century BC) and SATAVAHANA (late 1st century BC–early 3rd century AD) dynasties respectively. Together they produced the first great florescence of Buddhist art, seen particularly in the enlargement and decoration of stupa mounds (*see* STUPA, §1) at BHARHUT, SANCHI, AMARAVATI and elsewhere, and in the great series of excavated cave-monasteries of the western Deccan at BHAJA, KARLE and related sites.

Periods of slackening central control in the north often coincided with or were instrumental in causing invasions from the north-west. The Shungas were unable to hold the far north-west, and so-called Indo-Greek and Indo-Parthian kings established themselves there in the 2nd and 1st centuries BC. All in their turn were swept away by the westward advance of the Yueh-chi tribes across Central Asia, one of which established the great Kushana empire linking Transoxiana with the Ganga (*c.* 1st–3rd century AD). Under the Kushana kings, some of whom converted to Buddhism, schools of Indian sculpture flourished at their southern capital Mathura and in Gandhara (*see* §V, 5(i)(a) and (ii)(a) below).

(iii) Mid-4th century AD–*c. 1000.* From the decay of the Kushana empire arose the first major Indian dynasty since the Mauryas, that of the GUPTAs, proclaimed *c.* AD 319 by Chandragupta from the ancient capital Pataliputra. His son Samudragupta (*reg c.* 335–76) conquered much of north India and attempted for the first time since the Mauryas to unite north and south by crossing the Vindhya. The southern kingdoms were only subdued temporarily, and the Vindhya remained the southern boundary of the Gupta realm. The western provinces of Malwa and Gujarat were annexed under Chandragupta II (*reg c.* 380–415). Despite constant warfare, the Gupta period (4th–5th century) has been regarded as India's golden age, with the arts flourishing under a series of remarkable, largely beneficent rulers. If reliance may be placed on their coinage, that most intimate of art forms, its grandeur denotes a truly golden age (see fig. 331 below). From this period date the beginnings of temple architecture in stone and the Gupta transformation of the existing Mathura style, which produced what are now regarded as some of the finest masterpieces of Indian sculpture. Invasions by the Hunas in the late 5th century ended this period, ushering in a century of short-lived and minor kingdoms.

The 7th century witnessed another remarkable empire-building exercise, with the conquests of Harshavardhana (or Harsha; *reg* 606–47 AD). A prince from Thanesar in the Punjab, he took over Kanyakubja (modern Kannauj), the new imperial centre of the Gangetic plain, and was able to enforce his will over most of north India. His empire broke apart after his death, however. Thereafter, no one dynasty was powerful enough to establish hegemony. In the east the Palas had established their power in Bihar and Bengal by the 8th century. Pala power, diminished by the Senas of Bengal, disappeared by the 12th century (*see* PALA AND SENA). During this period the various Rajput clans made their first appearance in western India, establishing kingdoms in Gujarat and Rajasthan. One of these, the GURJARA-PRATIHARA, gained control of Kanyakubja and most of north India in the 9th century.

The history of south India may conveniently be divided between the plateau of the Deccan in the north and the flat country of Tamil Nadu in the extreme south. The Satavahanas (also known as the Andhras) established a formidable, immensely sophisticated kingdom that stretched across the peninsula. In the 3rd century AD they gave way to the Kadambas and then the Chalukyas of Badami (*see* CHALUKYA, §1) in the Deccan, while in the extreme south first the PANDYA and then the PALLAVA dynasties rose to prominence. The Chalukyas and Pallavas disputed the mastership of the south, until both declined in turn. The RASHTRAKUTA dynasty (mid-8th century–late 10th century) ruled the western Deccan, and a Chalukyan branch ruled the eastern (mid-7th century–12th century). A scion of the Chalukyas re-established their power in the western Deccan in AD 973; the Chalukyas of Kalyana (*see* CHALUKYA, §2) flourished for some two centuries before being ousted by the Yadavas of Devagiri (now Daulatabad) and the Hoysalas of Dvarasamudra (now Halebid; *see* HOYSALA and YADAVA). In the far south power was, in Indian tradition, divided among the Chera (of Kerala), Pandya (of Madurai) and the CHOLA rulers (of Tanjore, modern Thanjavur) with the Pallavas (of Kanchipuram) as apparent interlopers. The Pallavas were the first to establish hegemony over the area, between the 6th and 10th centuries, before being supplanted by the Cholas. Under Rajaraja I (*reg* 985–1014) the Cholas established an empire over the whole of south India and the southern Deccan, conquering much of eastern India and invading Sri Lanka and the islands in the Bay of Bengal. It was left to his successors to unite the crowns of the Cholas and eastern Chalukyas and to invade South-east Asia.

During the Gupta period theistic Hinduism (*see* HINDUISM, §I), which had been the dominant religion of Indians for centuries, was firmly established in royal favour. Buddhism had been fading rapidly, except where it was kept alive by royal patronage, as under the Palas. The construction of increasingly larger religious buildings must have consumed ever growing portions of the state revenues, perhaps at the cost of an adequate defence. Only two major temple cities survive from this period, at KHAJURAHO and BHUBANESHWAR, to give some idea of the impressiveness of contemporary cities and monasteries. In the south, despite incessant warfare, this period saw the final phase of the AJANTA caves, the great Hindu cave-temples of ELLORA and ELEPHANTA and the development of Dravidian architecture (*see* §§III, 4(ii) and VI, 1(v) below). The key event of this period, however, was the gradual encroachment of Muslim power in the extreme west.

*(iv) Period of Muslim rule (*c. *1000–1757).* Sind fell to the Arabs in AD 712, and with it the Indus as far up as Multan was in Muslim hands. No significant Muslim expansion occurred after this until Sultan Mahmud of GHAZNA (*reg* 998–1030) launched a series of 15 raids on the wealthiest cities and temples of western India between 999 and 1027. In 1021 he annexed the western Punjab. The Ghaznavids did not remain in power for long after Mahmud's death. From 1176 on, their GHURID successors launched a series of raids into India under Mu'izz al-Din Muhammad ibn Sam (*reg* 1203–6), brother of the reigning Ghurid sultan. In 1191 Mu'izz al-Din gathered an army for the conquest of India. Defeated at Tarain, a hundred miles north of Delhi, by Prithviraja Chauhamana (or Chauhan; *reg* 1178–92), the Rajput king of Ajmer and Delhi, he returned a year later and was victorious. Prithviraja was captured and slain, and his territory as far as Ajmer was annexed. The general Qutb al-Din Aybak was left in charge of the conquered territories, which he extended by the capture of Meerut and Delhi (1193) and Aligarh (1194), making Delhi his capital. Mu'izz al-Din returned to India in 1194 and led his armies down the Ganga, conquering Kannauj and Varanasi. Within a few years the whole of north India had been conquered. When Mu'izz al-Din, who had succeeded his brother on the Ghurid throne, was murdered, his generals in India established their independence.

Delhi's strategic as well as historical advantages made it the natural capital of north India, provided that its possessor was strong enough to maintain power over the fissiparous provinces. By the mid-13th century most of India north of the Vindhya had been conquered, although some areas, such as Rajasthan and Orissa, remained relatively untouched until the 16th century. For the first two centuries of Muslim power, the ruler of Delhi was generally acknowledged as the sovereign of India, especially strong rulers such as 'Ala al-Din KHALJI (*reg* 1296–1316), who organized the first large-scale invasion of the south, and the first three kings of the succeeding TUGHLUQ dynasty (1320–1413). 'Ala al-Din Khalji and Firuz Shah Tughluq (*reg* 1351–88) were both efficient administrators of their vast empires. It was Firuz Shah who introduced the system of remunerating officials by granting them land revenues, which formed the basis of fiscal administration until the 19th century.

After the invasion of Timur in 1398, the Delhi sultanate fell apart; Delhi itself was sacked and fell into a decline from which it did not recover for another century. Throughout the 15th century independent dynasties flourished at Jaunpur (middle Gangetic region), Mandu (Malwa and western central India), Gaur (Bengal) and Ahmadabad (Gujarat). These cities were beautified by mosques and tombs built in styles influenced by indigenous architecture. After the initial impact of the Muslim conquest had subsided, Hindu life continued in the north, although few grandiose temples were erected. One exception was Mewar in Rajasthan, which resisted Muslim power until the 17th century. In Gujarat the wealthy Jaina banking community was still able to build elaborate temple-cities.

India south of the Vindhya range remained untouched by Islam until 'Ala al-Din Khalji led his armies over the Vindhya in 1294, attacking the Yadava kingdom of Devagiri. This was basically a raid for booty, and immense quantities of treasure were taken back from Devagiri and Ellichpur to Delhi, where 'Ala al-Din had his uncle murdered and set himself up as sultan. Devagiri was taken again and annexed in 1307. In 1309–10 'Ala al-Din's general Malik Kafur conquered the Hindu kingdom of Warangal (*see* HANAMKONDA AND WARANGAL) and in 1311 that of the Hoysala dynasty of Dvarasamudra (now Halebid). He then marched to Rameswaram in the extreme south of India before returning to Delhi. Two descendants of the last king of Dvarasamudra were nonetheless able to found the new empire of VIJAYANAGARA (*see also* HAMPI) on the Tungabhadra River in 1336. This empire controlled the southern peninsula for the next two centuries.

Delhi's rulers also proved unable to hold on to the northern Deccan, where 'Ala al-Din Hasan Bahman (*reg* 1347–58) established an independent state based at Gulbarga in 1347. The BAHMANID state endured until 1482. The seizure of power by various provincial governors culminated in the empire's extinction and the establishment of successor kingdoms based at Bidar, Ahmadnagar, Bijapur and Golconda. The Bahmanis' almost constant warfare with their southern neighbour Vijayanagara continued under their successors, except that Vijayanagara sometimes allied itself with one or another of the Muslim states. In 1565 a Muslim alliance defeated Vijayanagara at the Battle of Talikota, and the empire was divided among the victors.

Delhi itself had been taken over from the Tughluqs by the SAYYID dynasty in 1414. The Sayyids in turn were ousted in 1451 by Buhlol LODI (*reg* 1451–89), who sought to re-establish Delhi's control over the provinces. The independent kingdom of JAUNPUR was annexed in 1488, and Buhlol's son Sikandar (*reg* 1489–1517) took over further territory. In 1526 Babur (*reg* 1526–30), a scion of the Timurid line of Ferghana in Central Asia and ruler of Kabul, invaded India and destroyed the power of the Lodi dynasty at the Battle of Panipat (*see also* TIMURID, §I). Babur was the first of the Great Mughals, six consecutive rulers whose conspicuous talents made their offensive nickname (Mughal, meaning Mongol, since Babur was descended from Genghis Khan) synonymous with overwhelming power and riches. At Babur's death in 1530, however, his empire was not even as large as that of the Lodis, and his son Humayun (*reg* 1530–40, 1555–6) was driven from India in 1540 by Sher Shah Sur (*reg* 1538–45; *see* SUR (ii)), an Afghan from the Jaunpur area who had established a power base in eastern India while Humayun was trying to conquer Gujarat. After Sher Shah died in 1545, his successors were unable to secure their power. Humayun, who had been in exile in Iran, recovered Kabul with Iranian help and returned to India in 1555, defeating the Sur forces at Sirhind and reoccupying Delhi. His son Akbar (*reg* 1556–1605), who ascended the throne at the age of 14, may fairly be claimed to have been the true founder of the Mughal empire. Under the able tutelage of his regent, Bayram Khan, until 1560, Akbar recovered Jaunpur and Ajmer. He then embarked on his career of conquest, during which the whole of India north of the Vindhya—from Gujarat to Bengal and including Kashmir, Kabul and Kandahar—was added to his dominions. In 1600 he extended his power southwards into Ahmadnagar. Akbar established an efficient administrative system and found time to pursue inquiries in the areas of religion, philosophy and art. He built a new fort and palace at AGRA and another at LAHORE. The best-preserved site of his time is the palace-city at FATEHPUR SIKRI.

Akbar's son Jahangir (*reg* 1605–27) and grandson Shah Jahan (*reg* 1628–58) raised the Mughal imperium to new heights of grandeur. Early in Shah Jahan's reign, Ahmadnagar was finally incorporated into the empire, and Bijapur and Golconda were reduced to all but vassalage. Shah Jahan's grand projects included renovating the palace at Agra and constructing the Taj Mahal (his wife's mausoleum) and a new palace and city in Delhi (Shahjahanabad), which then became the capital (*see also* §III, 7(i)(a) below). The reign of Shah Jahan's son Aurangzeb (1658–1707) began in murderous fratricidal strife and was marked by incessant wars against both the Deccan kingdoms, which were annexed in 1686–7, and various Rajasthani princes, with whom his ancestors had maintained good relations and intermarried. He upset the delicate equilibrium between Hindus and Muslims and made bitter enemies in Rajasthan and the Deccan, where the Maratha clans were growing increasingly powerful. During the 17th century the succession had been plagued by bitter power struggles, and the succession to Aurangzeb was not settled for a dozen years, during which, under a string of weak monarchs, the most powerful nobles learnt the value of independence from Delhi. Provincial viceroys, whose appointments had hitherto been under Delhi's control, became able to create dynasties of their own. These nobles included Murshid Quli Khan in Bengal, Sa'adat Khan in Avadh and Nizam al-Mulk in Hyderabad. Delhi, desperately weakened, became the prey of successive waves of marauders. Nadir Shah of Iran sacked the city in 1739 and carried off the accumulated treasures of two centuries. Various Afghan and Maratha freebooters followed his example for the rest of the century.

(v) British India (1757–1947). The European powers intruded into the increasingly complex political situation of 18th-century India. The Portuguese, who had arrived as early as 1498, limited themselves largely to securing naval bases from which to control trade in the Indian Ocean. They were followed by the Dutch, the French and the British, all of whom wished to oust them and outmanoeuvre each other in securing privileges from the Mughals for their individual East India companies. At first limiting their presence to the establishment of 'factories' where traders could commission and assemble goods for the next trading season, the French and British companies were tempted into political involvement by India's increasing political instability. They became involved first in the south, in the affairs of the nawabs of the Carnatic area and the nizams of Hyderabad, and then in Bengal. Nawab Suraj al-Daula (*reg* 1756–7) of Bengal attacked and sacked the British town of Calcutta in 1756. The small, highly efficient, modern British navy and army recaptured that city in 1757 and routed the nawab's essentially medieval army at Plassey. By intriguing with dissidents at Murshidabad, the British under Robert Clive were able to make their own nominee, Mir Ja'far (*reg* 1757–60, 1764–5), ruler of Bengal. The East India Company controlled the whole of the province in his name and, within a few years, its own: in 1765 the Mughal emperor Shah 'Alam (*reg* 1760–87) granted the British East India Company official revenue-raising powers in Bengal (*see also* §6 below). From this point on, the Company ruled eastern India in its own name.

The principal struggle between the British and the French for control of the India trade occurred in the south and ended with a British victory in 1761. The rise of Mysore, however, under its dynamic sultans Haydar 'Ali (*reg c.* 1761–82) and Tipu (*reg* 1782–99), involved the British in four wars before their power in the south was secure and they were able to expand their territorial base sufficiently to guarantee the security of Madras. The principal power in the late 18th century was the Maratha confederacy, an alliance of chiefs based throughout western and central India. It was they who controlled the Mughal emperor in Delhi; the British saw them as their principal opponents for the control of India. Lord Wellesley, having destroyed the power of Mysore, turned his attention to the Marathas and pushed British power up the Ganga and Yamuna rivers to win control (in 1803) of Agra and Delhi, where the Mughals exchanged their old master for a new one. During the next 50 years, the British extended their power over the rest of India, through policies of perpetual alliance, war or annexation. By 1857 only a third of the country was ruled by Indians, and the remainder was administered by British officials. This creeping annexation undoubtedly contributed to the mood of disaffection among the Indian population (particularly the sepoys of the East India Company's Bengal army), which resulted in the so-called 'Indian Mutiny' in 1857. Once order had been restored, the company's authority was swept away, and India was ruled in the name of the British Crown and Parliament. A halt was called to the policy of annexation, and the balance of power between British India and the so-called princely states was maintained.

Increasing industrialization and the slow process of democratization brought with them ever-increasing demands for the end of British rule. Exhaustion induced by two world wars, the campaign of non-violence waged by Mahatma Gandhi and the bitter struggle between the Congress Party and the Muslim League (who wanted a separate state on the subcontinent for Muslims) finally convinced the British to leave India, which was partitioned into the states of India and Pakistan in August 1947.

BIBLIOGRAPHY

H. M. Elliot: *The History of India, As Told by its Own Historians*, 8 vols (London, 1867–77/*R* 1966)

E. J. Rapson, W. Haig and H. H. Dodwell, eds: *The Cambridge History of India*, 5 vols (Cambridge, 1922–37)

H. C. Ray: *The Dynastic History of Northern India (Early Mediaeval Period)*, 2 vols (Calcutta, 1931–6, rev. Delhi, 2/1973)

R. C. Majumdar, H. C. Raychaudhuri and K. Datta: *An Advanced History of India* (London, 1946, rev. 3/1967)

R. C. Majumdar and A. D. Pusalkar, eds: *The History and Culture of the Indian People*, 11 vols (Bombay, 1951–77)

A. L. Basham: *The Wonder That Was India* (London, 1954, rev. 1967)

K. A. Nilakantha Sastri: *A History of South India: From Prehistoric Times to the Fall of Vijayanagara* (?Madras, 1955, rev. 2/1958)

H. D. Sankalia: *The Prehistory and Protohistory of India and Pakistan* (Pune, 1962–3, rev. 2/1974)

A. L. Basham: *A Cultural History of India* (Oxford, 1975)

J. E. Schwartzberg, ed.: *An Historical Atlas of South Asia* (Chicago and London, 1978)

B. Allchin and R. Allchin: *The Rise of Civilization in India and Pakistan* (Cambridge, 1982)

I. Habib: *An Atlas of the Mughal Empire* (Delhi, 1982)

C. Renfrew: *Archaeology and Language: The Puzzle of Indo-European Origins* (London, 1987)

C. Bagley, ed.: *The New Cambridge History of India* (in preparation)

J. P. LOSTY

3. LANGUAGE GROUPS. The oldest indigenous languages on the subcontinent probably belong to the Dravidian group, now spoken mainly in south India. Evidence that Dravidian languages were once dominant on most of the subcontinent includes the survival of Brahui in an isolated part of Baluchistan in the extreme north-west and Dravidian influences on later languages. The leading tongue in the group is Tamil (spoken in the state of Tamil Nadu and beyond), which has a vigorous literary tradition going back to about the 3rd century AD and which is used in numerous inscriptions after the 7th century. The three other main Dravidian languages are Malayalam (spoken along the Malabar coast), which developed from Tamil about the 11th century; Kannada (spoken in Karnataka), which is used in inscriptions from the 7th century onwards; and Telugu (spoken on the east coast from Madras to Orissa), which became a literary vehicle after the 12th century and flourished under the empire of Vijayanagara. That Dravidian languages themselves may have been an import is perhaps shown by languages of the Munda group. Spoken in isolated regions in Orissa and neighbouring areas, these languages may be the vestiges of the first aboriginal tongues of India. Some of the Munda languages have been traced back to Austroasiatic roots. Similarly, the Tibeto-Burman group of languages that skirt the northern and eastern perimeter of the subcontinent may once have enjoyed a wider distribution.

About 1500 BC Indo-European speakers migrated into Central Asia, Iran and India, becoming dominant in north India. Their language absorbed indigenous Dravidian features and eventually restricted the scope of Dravidian to ever smaller portions of the south. The earliest evidence for the language of these Indo-Europeans is found in the Vedic texts that were compiled *c.* 1200– *c.* 700 BC. Based on older material, they were written in an archaic form of Sanskrit. In the 5th century BC the natural pace of linguistic change was halted by the development of a systematic Sanskrit grammar and by canonical requirements. Sanskrit (*saṁskṛta*, literally 'well formed') was used side by side with speech that did not conform to the prescriptions of the grammarians and was thus summarily dubbed Prakrit (*prākṛta*, literally 'ill-formed').

Sanskrit has remained virtually unchanged since its formulation, and its influence has been felt all over India and South-east Asia. As the major language of literature and learning, it served to unify Indian civilization through the centuries, for it was understood by educated individuals in every region irrespective of local tongues. By around the 1st century AD, Sanskrit had established itself as the preferred language of inscriptions, dedications and benefactions. It is also the language (albeit corrupt at times) most commonly used in texts dealing with sculpture and architecture (*see* §4 below).

Common speech (Prakrit), which consisted of a number of dialects in different parts of India, continued to develop and change. Its history, only partially documented, is not entirely clear. Pali, for example, is preserved because of its association with Buddhism. The inscriptions of Ashoka, the oldest epigraphs in India, are in Magadhi, a form of Prakrit that prevailed in Magadha (modern Bihar). A hybrid form of Magadhi known as 'half-Magadhi' (*ardhamāgadhī*) became the sacred language of Jainism. Other regional Prakrits are also attested (Maharashtri, Shauraseni etc). Mixed Prakrit-Sanskrit appeared, in which Prakrit words were often 'restored' to a 'true' Sanskrit form. A further development was *apabraṃśa* (literally 'falling away'), a vernacular used by Jaina writers in western India.

These Indo-Aryan languages, some of which began to develop literatures after the 14th century, went through various stages of development before assuming their current forms. The most important is Hindi, which has an old and vigorous literature and is spoken across a large area of north India from Rajasthan to Bihar. Rajasthani dialects (Mewari, Malavi, Jaipuri) are closely related to Hindi, as are those of Bihar (Magadhi, Bhojpuri, Maithili). The Hindi-speaking area can be divided into eastern and western sections; important dialects include Braj (Mathura region), Avadhi (Lucknow region) and Bundelkhandi (Jhansi region). In recent times the Hindi spoken at Delhi has become an important standard. Literary and official forms of Hindi are often highly sanskritized.

Punjabi is widely spoken in north-west India and in Pakistan. Its two main dialects are Dogri, in the Jammu and Kangra valleys, and Lahnda, in the western Punjab. In the group of languages that includes the Kafir dialects of Afghanistan, only Kashmiri possesses a written literature (*see* AFGHANISTAN, §I, 3). The Pahari languages of the Himalaya are offshoots of Rajasthani, apparently the result of colonization. Kachchhi is spoken along the coast of India, and Gujarati, which has a flourishing literature, is spoken in Gujarat, adjacent to Sind in Pakistan. Marathi, with its main centre at Pune, is spoken in Maharashtra and over a wide area of the Deccan. The most easterly of the Indo-Aryan languages are Assamese (spoken in Assam), Oriya (in Orissa) and Bengali (in Bengal and Bangladesh). Bengali has an important literary tradition; like Hindi, its literary forms are often sanskritized.

The appearance of Islam during the 8th century AD brought the Arabic and then the Persian languages to India. Arabic endured as an independent language, particularly in Sind and Gujarat, where trading contacts were established with Arabia and Egypt. As the Turks, who came as conquerors in the 10th century, had been heavily Persianized before their arrival, Turkish remained a minor language in India while Persian flourished. The proximity of Persian, Arabic, Turkish and Indo-Aryan vernaculars resulted in hybrid forms of speech known as Urdu (from Turk. *ordu*: 'army'). As a spoken language, Urdu is now basically the same as Hindi; one simply favours Sanskrit forms, while the other favours Persian ones.

From the 16th century on, the emerging colonial powers brought virtually every European language to the subcontinent. English, a legacy of the long period of British rule, continues to have a role in India, Pakistan and Bangladesh, although more in areas of administration and industry than in culture.

BIBLIOGRAPHY

G. A. Grierson: *The Linguistic Survey of India and the Census of 1911* (Calcutta, 1919)
A. L. Basham: *The Wonder That Was India* (London, 1954, rev. 1967)
C. C. Davis: *An Historical Atlas of the Indian Peninsula* (Oxford, 1959)
T. Burrow: *The Sanskrit Language* (London, 1973)
J. E. Schwartzberg, ed.: *An Historical Atlas of South Asia* (Chicago and London, 1978)
K. B. Vyas, ed.: *Apabhraṃśa of Hemacandra*, Prakrit Text Series, xxiii (Ahmadabad, 1982)

HAROLD COWARD

4. EPIGRAPHY. The total number of pre-Islamic inscriptions from the Indian subcontinent has been estimated at 90,000. Due to the paucity of historically reliable literary sources before Islamic chroniclers appeared in the 12th century, the chronology of Indian art has been built up mainly from the co-occurrence of such inscriptions with sculptures, monuments and other artefacts. In many cases inscriptions are incised directly on buildings and works of art. Materials on which they occur include stone, metal (especially copper, but also bronze, silver and gold), terracotta, brick, pottery, wood, shell, crystal, ivory and cloth.

(i) Subject-matter. Although the contents of inscriptions are varied, two types predominate: land grants engraved on copper plates that record royal donations of villages or other tax-free land holdings, usually to Brahmans (members of the priestly caste), and eulogistic or commemorative inscriptions (Skt *praśasti*) on stone pillars or tablets. The latter are often associated with the foundation or endowment of temples or other religious institutions. Other common categories include pilgrim records recounting visits to holy places, cultic inscriptions recording pious texts or ritual formulae, literary inscriptions containing poetic and dramatic texts, and memorial inscriptions for departed relatives and heroes (*see* SATĪ AND HERO STONES).

Particularly important for the history of art are inscriptions recording the dedication of religious sculptures. Typically incised on the base or pedestal, they usually specify the date, donor and purpose of the gift. Inscriptions labelling narrative scenes or individual images are especially important in the study of iconography. In addition, some inscriptions provide the names of artists and workshops. Architectural studies have benefited from the labels and descriptive inscriptions that are often found on monuments. With the advent of Islam in India, some new uses for inscriptions developed. For example, Muslim tombs include cenotaphs that are often inscribed with verses and historical information. Civil architecture, such as bridges and stepwells, became common, and in some instances these monuments carry bilingual inscriptions in Persian and an Indic vernacular (*see* STEPWELL).

(ii) Scripts and palaeography. The still-undeciphered Indus civilization inscriptions (3rd–2nd millennium BC) are generally treated within the field of archaeology (*see* §2(i) above). The earliest readable inscriptions are in Prakrit. In south India after the 7th century, Dravidian languages, mainly Tamil and Kannada, were commonly used along with and instead of Sanskrit. The appearance of Islam in India brought Arabic and Persian into inscriptional use. Inscriptions in Indian languages are found throughout the subcontinent and in all the neighbouring countries of Asia and South-east Asia.

The study of Indian palaeography effectively begins with the known scripts and languages of the Maurya era (4th–3rd century BC). The epigraphical records of the emperor Ashoka (*reg c.* 269–*c.* 232 BC) were written in two scripts. In the north-west, Kharoshthi, a derivative of the Semitic Aramaic script, was used and continued to prevail there until the 3rd century AD. Elsewhere in India, the Brahmi script was used. Brahmi (probably also derived from Aramaic) first appeared in the Maurya records in a more or less unified form throughout India. This Mauryan or Ashokan Brahmi gradually differentiated itself into regional styles, which began to be discernible in the 2nd and 1st centuries BC. By the first few centuries AD, 'northern' and 'southern' Brahmi had become clearly distinguishable, and by the Gupta period (4th–5th century AD) several local varieties of 'late Brahmi' were in use. These included the northern or Gupta script, broadly subdivided into 'eastern' and 'western' varieties (including the so-called 'nail-headed' script), the 'box-headed' script of central and south India and the 'proto-Kannada-Telugu' of the south. Also notable in this period was the development of highly calligraphic scripts, particularly 'shell script' (*śaṅkha lipi*).

After the Gupta period, between the 7th and 11th centuries AD, the process of regional differentiation of scripts continued and intensified. In the north the late forms of Gupta Brahmi developed into the ornate *siddhamātṛkā* (also referred to as *kuṭila*, or 'acute-angled') scripts, the parent of modern Devanagari. The eastern variety of this script, sometimes referred to as Pala-Sena script, developed into the modern east Indian scripts (in Bengali etc). In the south the Kannada-Telugu script fully established its separate identity. The Tamil script and 'grantha' script, its variant used for Sanskrit, also evolved into distinct forms.

Indic scripts had more or less reached their modern shapes by the 12th century, though some modern scripts, such as Malayalam and Gujarati, developed later. All of the modern Indic scripts—Devanagari, Bengali, Gurmukhi, Oriya, Telugu, Tamil and others—as well as Tibetan and most of the scripts of South-east Asia are ultimately derived from Brahmi. Their common parentage is, however, no longer apparent to the untrained eye. With the establishment of the Delhi Sultanate in the 12th century, the full range of Arabic and Persian scripts entered the inscriptional repertory (for their calligraphy *see* §VIII, 3 below).

(iii) Dating. Indian inscriptions may be dated in continuous or cyclical eras, in a king's regnal years or not at all. Later inscriptions are generally dated in one or more of the continuous eras and can be equated, more or less accurately, to dates in the Gregorian calendar (*see* §5 below). Inscriptions with regnal dates, common in the earlier period and in southern and eastern India, can present difficulties, as the dates of the rulers in question may be known only approximately or not at all. In such cases and in the case of undated inscriptions (which are especially common in the pre-Gupta period), these are assigned estimated dates by comparing their palaeographic characteristics with those of similar inscriptions of known date. Palaeographic dating is, however, an approximate method at best, due to the varying rates of development of different scripts, to regional, stylistic and personal variability and to inadequate documentation and standardization of terminology. Most epigraphists agree that palaeographic dating before the 12th century cannot claim a greater degree of precision than approximately a hundred years in either direction. As many inscriptions of the Islamic period bear dates or the names of known historical figures, palaeographic analysis is a minor concern in this area.

BIBLIOGRAPHY

In addition to works listed below, see individual volumes in the series Corp. Inscr. Indic. (1887– ; i–viii (1887–1978)) and South Ind. Inscr. (1890– ; i–xxvi (1890–1982)) and issues of *Epig. Ind.* (1892– ; i–xli (1892–1976)).

A. H. Dani: *Indian Paleography* (Oxford, 1963)

D. C. Sircar: *Indian Epigraphy* (Delhi, 1965)

——: *Select Inscriptions Bearing on Indian History and Civilization*, i (Calcutta, rev. 1965), ii (Delhi, 1983)

——: *Indian Epigraphical Glossary* (Delhi, 1966)

C. Sivaramamurti: *Indian Epigraphy and South Indian Scripts* (Madras, 1966)

F. M. Asher and G. S. Gai, eds: *Indian Epigraphy: Its Bearing on the History of Art* (New Delhi, 1985)

5. CALENDARS. A variety of calendars and calendrical systems have been used for the dating of inscriptions and other Indian documents. The typical Indian calendar is lunisolar, based on a solar year with 12 (or sometimes 13) lunar months, each composed of two fortnights, the waning, or 'dark', fortnight (Skt *Sktkṛṣṇa* or *bahula pakṣa*) and the waxing, or 'bright', fortnight (*śukla pakṣa*). The days of the month are dated with reference to the true lunar 'day' (*tithi*; defined as the period in which the moon attains 12° of longitudinal elongation from the sun), while the ordinary solar or 'civil' days are assigned the number of the true lunar day current at sunrise. Thus a typical date would be given as 'the ninth *tithi* of the dark half of the month Pausha, Shaka era year 789' (23 December AD 867).

Years in Indian documents are numbered according to some three dozen different eras. The majority of these are continuous or historical eras, of which the most important are the Vikrama, beginning in 57 BC, and the Shaka, beginning in AD 78, still widely current in north and south India respectively. Important defunct historical eras include the Gupta (or Valabhi) era of AD 319 and the Kalachuri-Chedi era of *c.* AD 248. There were also numerous other local eras, for example the Ganga era of *c.* AD 498 in Kalinga and the Kollam era of AD 824 in Kerala.

Cyclical eras were also sometimes used, most importantly the Saptarshi or Laukika era, with a hundred-year cycle, and the sixty-year cycle of Brhaspati (Jupiter), current in north and south India respectively. Following the advent of Islam, the Muslim lunar calendar (starting in AD 622, the year the prophet Muhammad moved from Mecca to Medina) and then the European solar calendar came into wide use.

To ascertain the BC or AD equivalent of an Indian year, the era in question must be determined and the year number converted according to standard formulae: for example, a year of the Shaka era can be roughly correlated to an AD year by adding 78, and a Vikrama year by subtracting 57. However, there are several complicating factors involved in calculating a precise equivalent. First, an Indian year usually begins in Chaitra (March/April), so that it actually overlaps with two years of the Western calendar. Second, Indian years may be counted as either current or expired, and it must be determined which type is intended. The determination of precise equivalents for specific days in Indian documents is more difficult, due to the complexity of the lunisolar dating system as well as to further complications, such as intercalary and expunged days or months introduced to maintain synchronism between the solar and lunar reckonings. Equivalents for specific dates are usually given from the general calculations in Swamikannu Pillai's *An Indian Ephemeris . . .*, but these are not infallible and should be checked and adjusted for local variations.

BIBLIOGRAPHY

R. Sewell and S. B. Dikshit: *The Indian Calendar with Tables for the Conversion of Hindu and Muhammadan into AD Dates...* (London, 1896)

L. D. Swamikannu Pillai: *An Indian Ephemeris, AD 700 to AD 1799*, 7 vols (Madras, 1922–3)

V. B. Ketkar: *Indian and Foreign Chronology with Theory, Practice, and Tables, BC 3102 to 2100 AD . . . Bombay Branch of the Royal Asiatic Journal* (1923), no. 75–A [whole issue]

A. L. Basham: *The Wonder That Was India* (London, 1954, rev. 1967), pp. 494–7 [for a convenient table for the approx. calculation of equivalents of Ind. years, see p. 497]

D. C. Sircar: *Indian Epigraphy* (Delhi, 1965)

RICHARD SALOMON

6. Trade and travel.

(i) External trade. (ii) Internal trade. (iii) Pilgrims and travellers.

(i) External trade. Historically, India has traded with both the West and the East, linking in complex patterns the opposite ends of the Eurasian land-mass. To the north were the immensely difficult passes leading over the Hindu Kush and Karakoram mountains to the trans-Asian highway known as the Silk Route. It was by this route that Buddhism was taken to China in the early centuries AD by Indian traders. From Samarkand or Kashgar caravans went on south-westward to Iran and Syria or eastward to China (*see also* CENTRAL ASIA, §II, 1(iii) and SILK ROUTE). By sea the coastal routes were the first to be utilized. Small trading vessels hugged the shore of the Arabian Sea and moved up the Persian Gulf on the westward route, from which caravans could transport goods onwards to Syria, Egypt and the rest of the Mediterranean. On the east-bound route, boats followed the shores of the Bay of Bengal to the Straits of Malacca and the rich South-east Asian kingdoms, then sailing northward to China. Seals of the Indus civilization (*c.* 2000 BC) found in Sumeria suggest that the coastal route to the Persian Gulf was an ancient one (*see* §2 above). Rice, sandalwood and peacocks are known to have been transported in the 7th century BC.

In the 1st century AD the pattern of the monsoon winds over the Indian Ocean was discovered. Ships sailed directly to India between June and September from the Horn of Africa, using the south-west monsoon, across the open sea and back again, using the north-east winds that prevail during the rest of the year. Ships must also have used the seasonal changes in the prevailing wind to sail directly from south India to South-east Asia. When the movements of nomadic tribes in Central Asia and the Arab conquest of Sogdiana in the 8th century largely closed the ancient road joining India to the Silk Route, maritime routes to both east and west became more important (*see* ISLAMIC ART, §I, 5).

In antiquity India is reported to have exported mostly luxury goods: gold and gems, spices, silks and fine textiles, perfumes, ivory and sandalwood. The anonymous 1st-century AD author of *Periplus maris erythraei* (The periplus of the Erythraean Sea) notes that India exported spices, precious stones and large quantities of muslin and other cotton goods to the West. Pepper and ginger would have been India's own exports, but other spices must have come from further east and been transhipped. India imported gold and silver (i.e. coinage and bullion), brass, copper, tin, lead, coral and cloth. Since India had copper and zinc in abundance, the brass and copper must have been imported through coastal sites purely for reasons of logistical convenience. The total value of the luxury goods imported from India into the Roman world was immense; Pliny the Younger wrote that the annual drain of silver to India was never less than 55 million sesterces. Similar cargoes, of Indian spices, textiles and precious stones in particular, were shipped to South-east Asia and onwards to China, which with its huge population represented an insatiable market. India's capacity to absorb and horde both gold and silver was commented upon by many, for her own import needs were few. In the early period these consisted principally of spices from the East Indies and luxuries such as Chinese silk (before silk was manufactured in India); in the Muslim period imports included war-horses, Chinese porcelain, paper (before it was made locally) and exotic novelties. Textiles were the principal staple of India's export trade, both luxury painted and dyed fabrics and the finest muslins, as well as everyday cottons, 13th-century fragments of which have been found in excavations in Egypt. Indian metallurgy enjoyed a high reputation in this period, and high-quality swords were exported to the Middle East. As ships grew larger, it proved possible to export bulk goods such as teak for shipbuilding in the Arab world, and surplus rice and grains from India's coasts to the other shores of the Indian Ocean.

In ancient times the main west coast ports were Bharuch (Broach), Sopara (near Bombay) and Pattala (on the Indus, in present-day Pakistan), while Tamralipti (modern Tamluk) in Bengal served the east. The ancient port cities in the far south, especially Korkai near Tuticorin (north-east of Cape Comorin), were especially important in the transhipment of goods from China and South-east Asia to the Roman world. Such numbers of Roman coins have been found in the southern ports that they seem to have been used as local currency. All of these ports must also have serviced trade moving eastward. The collapse of the Roman Empire and the expansion of Muslim hegemony led to a decline in the volume of westward trade. This in turn led to an eastward shift of Indian entrepreneurial activity under the PALLAVA and CHOLA dynasties. Although little is known of how goods were shipped by sea in the early period, in the first millennium AD Arab, Indian and Chinese ships competed with one another. The large ships of the Cholas were active throughout South-east Asia and as far as China. However, the increase in Hindu caste-consciousness in the Muslim period (travelling overseas being regarded as impure) led to Arab control of the western trade in the Indian Ocean and Chinese control of the eastern. Even so, Indian Muslims, particularly Gujaratis, successfully carried on much of India's shipping in the Arabian Sea, while Hindu merchants and brokers generally dominated trade and commerce internally and along the eastern shores of the Indian Ocean.

In the 15th century the dominance of the Ottoman Turks over the lands between Europe and India induced the Portuguese and other Europeans to search for a sea-route to India. Vasco da Gama rounded Africa and landed in 1498 at the south Indian port of CALICUT. In the early 16th century the Portuguese made limited conquests to establish a series of strategically placed bases, including Goa (1510), commanding the Arabian Sea; Malacca

(1511), commanding the Spice Islands and the route to China; and Ormuz (Hormuz; 1515), commanding the Persian Gulf. For a century they attempted to control the trade of the entire Indian Ocean either in their own ships or by forcing the cooperation of Asian traders. The system was of limited efficiency, however, and by mid-century the spice trade through the Red Sea and Persian Gulf had resumed, while Indian shippers and merchants carried on their overseas trade as they always had. It has been argued that the extent of European involvement at this time in trade in the Indian Ocean has been much exaggerated.

The decline of Portuguese maritime power in the late 16th century allowed other European powers to elbow their way into what had been a lucrative monopoly. The English and the Dutch, who both established East India trading companies, fought bitterly during the 17th century. The Dutch gradually took control of the trade of the eastern islands and Sri Lanka, while the English established themselves in India. In this period the Dutch supplanted the Portuguese as the main carriers of the inter-Asian trade, which was at least a three-way affair. With India having little need of European goods, and the main source of fine spices being the partially monetarized East Indies, silver with which to buy textiles was exported from Europe to India. With these textiles, mainly the cheaper patterned cottons of the Coromandel coast, the spices of the Moluccas were purchased for shipment to Europe. In addition both the English and the Dutch realized the importance of the European market for Indian textiles, a market that became increasingly important during the 17th century. The English company was in a better position to exploit this opportunity. Indigo, saltpetre and raw silk also became important Indian exports to Europe at this time.

At this period the MUGHAL courts had a near insatiable demand for European luxury goods—paintings, prints, jewels, bijouterie and so on—which European traders imported both for sale and as gifts to gain favours. The principal favours were *farmān*s (Pers. imperial charters) allowing trade unhampered by the numerous customs dues that provided revenue for the Mughal financial system. The Europeans argued that increased trade would greatly increase taxes within the empire, thereby offsetting the lost customs dues. The European companies traded by establishing 'factories' or stations at strategically important places, mostly ports, where resident merchants could commission goods. These were made to order for the following season's ships. By this period, Surat had become the chief port on the west coast where most European companies had factories. In the late 17th century, along the Hugli River in the Gangetic delta of Bengal, a string of European factories was established where muslins, silks and other Bengali textiles were commissioned and gathered together for shipment.

The market for Indian cloth in Europe waned during the 18th century owing to protectionist duties and the growth of local textile manufacturing. With the decline of the Indian aristocracy, the internal market in luxury goods also declined. The pattern of India's exports therefore changed to commodities in bulk. During this period, as the Mughal empire largely disintegrated, the British East India Company was transformed from a trading company into a government that ruled over large parts of India. Simultaneously, the Company's profits from its Indian trade fell inexorably. Meanwhile the more lucrative trade with China in tea, silk and porcelain required bullion. In part to offset this need, the Company encouraged the growing of opium, which became one of India's principal exports, to feed the Chinese market. In 1813 the Company's monopoly of trade between England and India was abolished, and in 1833 its ability to trade with China; neither made sense any longer. The Company's role became entirely governmental. While its monopoly was strictly concerned with direct trade with Europe, the so-called 'country trade'—commerce round the Indian Ocean as far as the Cape of Good Hope and the Straits of Malacca and on to China—was open to all comers, and Asian, European and American vessels competed fiercely for this lucrative business.

(ii) Internal trade. Evidence for the volume and type of internal trade before 1200 is extremely scanty. It has been argued from the literary sources and from coinage that the periods of large empires such as the MAURYA, GUPTA and that of Harsha generally coincided with prosperous economic conditions. Conversely, fragmentation of imperial authority is thought to have coincided with economic depression. Trade and commerce were sufficiently important in Maurya times to have been the province of three of the six boards that regulated the affairs of the capital, Pataliputra (modern PATNA). One board regulated sales and enforced the use of duly stamped weights and measures, while merchants had to pay a licence tax for each commodity. Another board supervised manufacturing, and a third the collection of sales tax (infringements of which were punishable by death). Similar arrangements must have been in force in other large cities of the Maurya empire. The efficient organization of trade, commerce and agriculture, on which any empire's wealth depends, would certainly have been the business of Indian rulers. Only by drawing taxes from sales and revenue from agriculture could enough surplus cash have been raised to keep armies fit for the constant warfare of ancient India.

North India seems to have been economically depressed during the politically fragmented period between the 8th and the 12th centuries, marked by the growth of a feudal society. Sufficient reserves must nonetheless have accumulated in royal treasuries—both from revenues taken increasingly from the peasants and from the surplus from external trade—for noble patrons to indulge in the building of temples and monasteries on a grandiose scale.

Despite the difficulties of road travel within India, there is considerable evidence that vast quantities of food (rice and other grains, sugar, salt and spices in particular) and raw commodities were transported from surplus to deficit areas. Indeed the fact that vast Indian armies and royal households and retainers on the march could be fed suggests that the shipment of immense quantities of food by land never did pose insurmountable problems. Likewise, commodities and materials grown or obtainable only in certain parts of India, including sugar, salt, rice, wheat, iron (from Bihar) and copper (from the Deccan and Rajasthan), could be transported in bulk. There is considerable evidence that textiles were similarly transported, and even the raw materials for them. Raw Bengali silk fed the Gujarati silk industry, while Gujarati cotton fed the Bengali finished cotton business. Luxury goods, finished silks and muslins from Bengal and Gujarat, painted and embroidered textiles from the south and Kashmir, Gujarati leather, mother-of-pearl and lacquerwork, Kashmiri furniture, palanquins and so on were freely traded all over India. The finest-quality goods were ordered specially for imperial or royal consumption; otherwise merchants exposed their wares in the great bazaars in all important towns. There are numerous references in European accounts to both the size of these markets and the comprehensiveness of the goods offered for sale, and to the insignificance of the trade with Europe compared with the vastness of the internal market.

Where rivers were available, they were used for purposes of trade, but their full lengths were only navigable in the monsoon season and for a time thereafter. Otherwise traders had to go overland or, where possible, by coastal routes. Monarchs saw it as one of their duties to build and maintain the roads, which from Maurya times at least linked provincial cities with the capital. The great road linking Pataliputra to TAXILA was already in existence under the Mauryas, and the emperor Ashoka planted groves of trees and built rest-houses to shelter travellers.

In historic times the major north–south routes ran through western India, as the wild country of eastern central India inhibited north–south travel and the development of cities there. Even from so eastern a city as Pataliputra, for example, the major southern route was due west via Prayag (Allahabad), then south-westward to Ujjain in Malwa, on into the Deccan to Pratisthana (Paithan), and to the southern coastal plain via the passes of the Eastern Ghats. As the imperial centres shifted north-westward to KANNAUJ, Agra and Delhi, the cities of Burhanpur and DAULATABAD (formerly Devagiri) replaced Ujjain and Pratisthana. Other major roads ran south-westward from the upper Yamuna, linking the Muslim capitals to Ahmadabad and the Gujarati ports via Ajmer, and to Sind and the Indus ports via Multan in present-day Pakistan (*see also* AGRA, §I and DELHI, §I).

(iii) Pilgrims and travellers. Since Indian literature is not generally a rich source of mundane information, travellers' accounts serve as prime source material, beginning with the writings of Alexander the Great's generals and followers in 326 BC. In the early centuries AD the sacred sites of Buddhism drew pilgrims from outside India, particularly China, and the accounts written by a few of them are a prime source for locating the sites and their buildings and images. These accounts also provide a great deal of information about other religious as well as secular and political matters. Later visitors such as the 11th-century Muslim polymath al-Biruni give invaluable accounts of India. From the late 16th century come the earliest reliable accounts by European visitors, who came as traders, ambassadors or craftsmen, while the 17th-century accounts of Mughal India are numerous and comprehensive. From the late 18th century come the accounts of cultured European travellers, some stationed in India, some on an eastern extension of the Grand Tour.

Despite the historic difficulties of travel within India, its population has always been prepared to travel immense distances on business, family matters and pilgrimage. Throughout Indian history monarchs and their relatives—and the wealthy in general—have seen it as a pious duty, whether Buddhist, Hindu or Muslim, to provide roads with shade, rest-houses and caravanserais and to establish affordable accommodations (Skt *dharmaśālās*) at pilgrimage sites.

As early as 249 BC the emperor Ashoka made the first recorded pilgrimage to the holy places of Buddhism; he was followed by countless others. Some religious centres were famous enough to draw pilgrims from all over India; the most important of these was Banaras (VARANASI), which remains the goal of all pious Hindus. Pilgrimages to other shrines were made at the times of great festivals—the Kumbha Mela every ten years at Allahabad; the festivals at Hardwar, Ajmer, Puri and so on. The great shrine of Jagannatha at Puri in Orissa had thousands of servants who guided pilgrims there from all over India. Indian Muslims also have traditionally gone on pilgrimage, to MECCA (in present-day Saudi Arabia) via the west-coast ports (the Portuguese entry into the Indian Ocean created havoc with their conveyance) and also within India, principally to famous Sufi shrines such as those of Multan, Ajmer and Delhi. Great fairs were held in conjunction with religious festivals, where often the spiritual importance of the place was outstripped by the economic one; merchants used such great concourses of people to sell their wares. Examples include the great elephant and horse fair at the Hariharachattar Mela at Hajipur, on the Ganga opposite Patna, or the Pushkar fair outside Ajmer.

See also §VI, 1 below.

BIBLIOGRAPHY

Periplus maris erythraei (1st century); Eng. trans. by W. H. Schoff as *The Periplus of the Erythraean Sea: Travel and Trade in the Indian Ocean . . .* (New York, 1912)

Hiuen Tsiang: *Si-yu-ki* (7th century); Eng. trans. by S. Beal as *Buddhist Records of the Western World* (London, 1869)

Al-Biruni: *Kitāb fī taḥqīq mā li'l-Hind* [History of India] (*c.* 1030); Eng. trans. by E. C. Sachau as *Alberuni's India*, 2 vols (London, 1914)

F. Bernier: *Histoire de la dernière révolution des états du grand Mogol* (1670); Eng. trans. by I. Brock as *Travels in the Mughal Empire, 1656–58*, ed. A. Constable (London, 1891; rev. V. A. Smith, 1914)

T. Roe: *The Embassy of Sir Thomas Roe to the Court of the Great Mogul, 1615–1619: As Narrated in his Journal and Correspondence*, ed. W. Foster (London, 1899; rev. 1926)

G. Watt: *Dictionary of the Economic Products of India* (London, 1908)

E. H. Warmington: *The Commerce between the Roman Empire and India* (Cambridge, 1928)

R. E. M. Wheeler, A. Ghosh and K. Deva: 'Arikamedu: An Indo-Roman Trading Station on the East Coast of India', *Anc. India*, 2 (1946), pp. 17–124

L. Gopal: *Economic Life of Northern India, 700–1200* (Delhi, 1965)

S. N. Bharadvaj: *Hindu Places of Pilgrimage in India: A Study in Cultural Geography* (London, 1973)

K. N. Chaudhuri: *The Trading World of Asia and the English East India Company, 1660–1760* (Cambridge, 1978)

D. Kumar and T. Raychaudhuri, eds: *The Cambridge Economic History of India*, 2 vols (Cambridge, 1982–3) [comprehensive bibliog.]

N. Lahiri: *The Archaeology of Indian Trade Routes up to c. 200 BC* (Delhi, 1992)

J. P. LOSTY

7. RELIGIONS AND SOCIAL ORDER.

(i) World religions. (ii) Other beliefs and practices.

(i) World religions. The dominant religions of the Indian subcontinent are HINDUISM and ISLAM. SIKHISM, JAINISM, BUDDHISM, CHRISTIANITY and ZOROASTRIANISM are also

present. While Islam, Christianity and Zoroastrianism originated in western Asia, Hinduism, Jainism, Buddhism and Sikhism are indigenous. Since the rise of Jainism and Buddhism (6th century BC) the subcontinent has been a laboratory of co-existing religions, sometimes in harmony, sometimes in strife. Four ideas have evolved that are basic to the indigenous religions, expressed in the Sanskrit terms *anādi*, *karma*, *saṁsāra* and *mokṣa*, or *nirvāṇa*.

Anādi is the notion that the universe is beginningless. There are cycles of creation, each of which encompasses stages of sprouting, growing, maturing and dying, and each of which leaves behind a seed-form out of which the next cycle may arise. The difficult aspect to grasp is that there is no first cycle. The cycles of creation (the image is an agricultural one) are a favourite subject of traditional art.

The concept of *karma* is often misunderstood. There are many definitions of *karma* in the Indian tradition, some of which make it appear rather deterministic. One of the clearest and most influential descriptions is found in the 2nd-century BC *yoga sūtra*s of Patanjali. According to this description, every time one performs an action or thinks a thought, a memory trace or karmic seed is laid down in one's unconscious. There it waits for circumstances conducive to its sprouting forth as an impulse, instinct or predisposition to perform the action or think the thought again. The karmic impulse does not cause anything; it is not mechanistic in nature. It simply predisposes one to perform an action or think a thought. Thus room is left for free will. If one decides to go along with a karmic impulse, it is strengthened. *Karma*s can be good or bad: while good actions and thoughts lay down good karmic traces in the unconscious, evil actions and thoughts do the reverse. Taken together, scripture and tradition distinguish between good and evil.

According to *karma* theory, all of the impulses one experiences result from actions and thoughts in this life. However, if one experiences an impulse, either good or evil, that seems completely out of character with the way one has lived since birth, that impulse is thought to arise from an action or thought in a previous life. This idea introduces the concept of rebirth (*saṁsāra*). One's unconscious contains all of the karmic traces of actions and thoughts from the life before this one, and so on backwards into infinity. One's unconscious is like a huge granary full of karmic seeds or memory traces that sprout as conducive situations arise, impelling one towards good or evil actions or thoughts. The possibility of free choice always allows one to control these impulses, however. Art has been seen as providing a powerful psychological and spiritual tool to use in directing this process.

The concept of rebirth provides the idea of a ladder. At the bottom are animals, in the middle are humans and at the top are the gods. If in a human life one uses one's free choice to act on good karmic impulses and negate evil ones, one will have increased the number of good *karma*s and decreased the number of evil *karma*s in one's unconscious. At death the increase in good *karma*s will automatically cause one to be reborn further up the ladder. Repeating the same procedure over many lifetimes will allow one gradually to ascend to the top of the ladder and be reborn as a god. Unlike humans, gods have no free choice, no power to act. They enjoy the honour of being gods until the merit built up from good choices over countless lives has been used up. Then they are reborn as humans at the top of the human scale, with the prospect of continued birth, death and rebirth to look forward to.

If in this life one uses one's free choice to act on evil karmic impulses, at death one will be reborn a step lower down on the ladder. If this negative pattern is repeated through many lifetimes, one eventually will be reborn as an animal. Animals are human beings in a different karmic form, with no free choice. Their fate is to endure the sufferings caused by their instincts. When they have suffered sufficiently to expiate their bad *karma*, they are reborn as human beings with free choice and a chance to move up the ladder again.

Hinduism provides one response to the prospect of being born, growing old, dying and being reborn endlessly, while Buddhism and Jainism provide others. The Vedas (Hindu scriptures) reveal that there are three different *yoga*s (paths) to release (*mokṣa*). First there is the *yoga* of knowledge. By studying the knowledge revealed in the Vedas under the guidance of a guru, release may be attained. However, in the past this method was open only to the top three classes: priests (*brāhmaṇa*s), warriors or kings (*kṣatriya*s) and farmers, merchants or artisans (*vaiśya*s). The fourth class, the unpropertied labourers or servants (*śūdra*s), was not considered sufficiently pure to study the Vedas. According to a hymn in the *Ṛg veda*, the *Puruṣa sūkta*, caste structure is an integral part of each cycle of creation. Originally, caste seems to have been a functional description of one's karmic nature and the role one played in society. Later, however, as can be seen in the *Mānavadharma śāstra* ('Laws of Manu'; *c*. 200 BC–AD 100), caste came to be understood as a hereditary social structure. Further subdivisions into *varṇa*s ('colour', suggesting a differentiation between fairer- and darker-skinned people) and *jati* (family, caste or sub-caste) also exist. While the constitution of the Republic of India abolished the notion of outcastes, caste remains an important fact of Indian life.

Whereas the *yoga* of study was open only to the top three classes, the other two ways to release—action and devotion—are open to all. The *yoga* of action involves the doing of one's duty (*dharma*) with no thought for the fame, fortune or reward one might receive, but simply as a dedication to God. The *yoga* of devotion (*bhakti*) requires that one similarly engage in prayer, ritual sacrifice, the singing of hymns or the chanting of *mantra*s (special scriptural words or syllables) with no thought for the spiritual merit one might accumulate. Many traditional sculpted or painted images are used as a focus for devotional practice.

Buddhism and Jainism began as reform movements in the 6th century BC. Both rejected the absolute authority of the Vedas and any notion of a god or gods. They also rejected caste distinctions, offering salvation or release to all, regardless of birth. In place of Sanskrit (the language of the Vedic tradition and the upper castes), Buddhism and Jainism employed the dialects of Prakrit (*see* §3 above). The Buddhist response to the prospect of endless rebirth (in the Mahayana school) was world-affirming in that it taught that once the impure *karma* of selfish desire had been purged through the monastic practice of meditation, one would be released from the suffering caused by a life of selfish desire (*dukkha*). Then the world, even during continued rebirths, would be experienced as it really was: beautiful, harmonious and compassionate. The Jaina response to this problem was ascetic and world-denying in the extreme. The only way to obtain release from the *karma* that causes people to harm other beings (e.g. killing animals and plants for food) was to engage in the rigorous practice of *ahiṃsā* (non-violence). Taken to its logical extreme, this meant that the Jaina monk eventually would not move (for fear of stepping on something) or eat (for every form of eating, including vegetarianism, is an act of violence) and would engage in intense meditation to purge the heavy *karma* accumulated in this and previous lives. Once the last *karma* had been removed, the soul (*jīva*) of the Jaina monk would float free to exist externally in the heavens. The magnificent Jaina stone colossus at SHRAVANA BELGOLA shows a saint who had been standing still for so long in *ahiṃsā* meditation that vines had encircled his body.

Christians may have been present in India as early as the arrival of the Apostle Thomas in the 1st century AD. A small community of Jews may also have settled in Malabar at Cochin about the same time. The earliest evidence for Islam in India exists in the western coastal towns and dates from the 8th century AD, trading links with Arabia and Egypt having been established in Roman times. From about AD 1000 Islam became increasingly important in north-west India as the result of invasion and occupation by the Muslim rulers of Afghanistan. In order to escape Muslim persecution in Iran during the 9th century, a group of Zoroastrians settled on the north-west coast of India. Their descendants, especially prominent in Bombay, are known as Parsis. By the 13th and 14th centuries the basic pattern of religious distribution had been established; it prevailed until the 19th century. Throughout the Indo-Gangetic plain, a small, mainly Muslim ruling class governed a mixed population of Muslims and Hindus. In the south, however, a mainly Hindu population was governed by Hindu kings from the mid-14th century to the mid-16th century.

Muslims and Hindus have often had an uneasy, sometimes hostile relationship. In the 15th century the Sikh religion was born with the aim of bringing a peaceful resolution to this conflict. In the *Ādi Grantha* (Sikh scripture), a clear distinction is made between Sikh teachings and practices and those of other religions. Without taking God as revealed to Nanak, the first teacher of Sikhism, as guru (in this context, divine guiding presence), all belief, text and ritual are in vain. Liberation can be achieved only through Sikh contemplation of the name of God. God has personal attributes and is the source of all creation and consciousness, and his will (*hukm*) is the creative principle of all life. Yet he lacks attributes and is formless. Sikhs believe that God can never be incarnated, nor can any image contain him. Nanak also rejected distinctions among people in terms of birth, caste, sex or nationality and saw each human soul as eternal. Human bondage was caused by egoism (*haumai*) separating humanity from God and dimming the divine spark within. This separation could only be overcome by intense love of God and complete surrender to him and his will. Through God's grace one realized reality and was freed from the bondage of ego and the cycle of birth, death and rebirth. Guru Nanak also emphasized moral conduct, self-control, earning a living by one's own labour and sharing its fruits with others.

Islam similarly maintains that there is only one god, who spoke his revelation to the Prophet Muhammad as the Koran. Since God is One, there can be no plurality or division in reality. In the Indian subcontinent prior to 1947, Muslims lived for centuries as minority religious communities within a dominant Hindu culture. Some Hindu practices formally rejected by Islam (e.g. caste distinctions) were adopted by Muslim communities in the subcontinent. This situation led to interesting developments in Islamic theology. The positive Koranic attitude towards Jews and Christians was amplified to include Hindus by recognizing them as 'people of the book'. This recognition allowed for the building of a multi-racial and multi-religious society. Muslims in the subcontinent also extended the interpretation of the sins of idolatry (Arab. *shirk*) and of unbelief stemming from ungratefulness to God (*kufr*), traditionally used to refer to the failings of non-Muslims, to the Muslim community itself. Similarly, the Muslim principle of *jihād* (holy war) against non-believers has been reinterpreted as the spiritual effort or inner war to be waged by each Muslim in order to be truly obedient to God.

In somewhat parallel developments, Hindu reformers such as Swami Vivekananda and Sarvepalli Radhakrishnan extended traditional Hindu concepts to make room for other religions. Buddha, Moses, Jesus Christ and Muhammad are seen as *avatāras* (incarnations) of God. Thus their revelations have been validated and must be practised by their followers in order to progress spiritually. Eventually, when sufficient progress has been made, the Buddhist, Jew, Christian or Muslim can be reborn as a Hindu within the Vedic tradition, which is essential for final release.

While the extension of theological concepts made possible the co-existence of religious communities in the subcontinent, the doctrine of social identification and articulation through separate castes and sub-castes enabled invading and conquered groups, successful and deprived groups to be accommodated into the larger society. Invading conquerors might be deemed members of a warrior sub-caste and therefore of high status. Similarly, a forest tribe might be considered a menial sub-caste. Since each caste had its own duties, the whole society could be accommodated in vertical and horizontal hierarchies. Along with the idea of rebirth, the notion of stages of life, the last two of which freed one from family and caste restrictions, provided ways to escape from permanent entrapment.

BIBLIOGRAPHY

A. L. Basham: *The Wonder That Was India* (London, 1954, rev. 1967)
E. Conze: *Buddhism: Its Essence and Development* (New York, 1959)
J. H. Woods, ed.: *The Yoga System of Patanjali* (Delhi, 1966)
R. H. Robinson: *The Buddhist Religion* (Belmont, 1970)
H. Zimmer: *Philosophies of India* (Princeton, 1971)
T. J. Hopkins: *The Hindu Religious Tradition* (Belmont, 1974)
P. S. Jaini: *The Jaina Path of Purification* (Berkeley, 1979)
H. Singh: *The Heritage of the Sikhs* (Columbia, MO, 1983)
F. Max Muller, ed.: *The Laws of Manu* (Delhi, 1984)
D. L. Eck: *Darśan: Seeing the Divine in India* (Chambersburg, 1985)

H. G. Coward, ed.: *Modern Indian Responses to Religious Pluralism* (Albany, 1987)
K. K. Klostermaier: *A Survey of Hinduism* (Albany, 1989)

HAROLD COWARD

(ii) Other beliefs and practices. There are two ways to gain access to the subcontinent's 'primal' traditions: through the study of pre-literate peoples, such as the Bhil in the west and Toda in the south, as they exist in the more remote regions today, and through a study of folk elements that represent survivals of such earlier traditions.

Several grades of supernatural beings have been identified by scholars of primal religion on the basis of field research. The lowest level consists of malevolent spirits (Skt *preta*), usually male, and malevolent female spirits (*chudail*). The former are said to be spirits who could not make a smooth passage to the next world, usually as a result of untimely or violent death. The latter are usually regarded as the spirits of women who died in childbirth and have become disposed to evil. To be distinguished from both of these groups are malevolent spirits in general, who often are said to reside in certain trees, who are ready to pounce on the unwary and who go by the generic name of ghosts (*bhūta*). The usual way in which spirits of either the general or the specific type disrupt normal life is by causing physical or mental illness, especially fever or possession. Such intrusion can be spontaneous or induced; when induced, it represents a form of black magic (*jādū-ṭonā*). Relief in either case is obtained by recourse to a traditional healer (*ojhā*) who 'shakes off the spirit'.

The next grade of supernatural beings is occupied by local deities. Unlike the lowest-level beings, which are evil *per se*, local deities have both good and evil aspects. If angered, they spell ruin; if appeased, they can be controlled; if pleased, they may even confer benefits, especially when possessed of naturally more benign natures. Thus local deities can be of virulent or benevolent type, in spite of each possessing a dual nature. An example of the former would be the deity of smallpox, Sitala Devi; an example of the latter would be a presiding village deity (*grāmadevatā*). Sitala Devi is virulent, but can be appeased, while a presiding village deity is generally benevolent, but can bring harm if offended. While spirits of the lowest levels make their attacks (usually nocturnal) on individuals, the disposition of local deities may have implications for the community as a whole, though individuals may also be affected.

The next grade of supernatural beings is occupied by indigenous gods appropriated from the pan-Indian pantheon. A local deity might take on a regional aspect en route to assuming a national role. The Vittobha cult of Pandharpur and the Khandoba cult at Gudguddapur could well represent such developments. There is also evidence of the prevalence of monotheism among the Lakher and Thadou Kuki in the north-east. Sometimes, as among the Purum in the same area, a supreme god has been supplanted by a Hindu deity.

In local religious traditions, the soul is often identified with the shadow, as among the Sema Naga of eastern India, or regarded as analogous to it, as among the Oraon in central India. Belief in multiple souls is also common, the favoured number being three. Among the Birhor, in southern Bihar, the shadow is counted as one, the soul that travels in a dream as the second (male) and the soul that continues to animate the body at home as the third (female).

Such religion is not limited to manifestations of spirits in human beings, however. The veneration of the basil plant and pipal tree with offerings of water is an example of sacredness attached to plants and trees in folk religion. Certain animals are also held sacred. Stones with images of cobras are often worshipped, and in some regions a snake-goddess, Manasa, is venerated. Such worship may follow a seasonal cycle, but monthly and weekly cycles are also known. Particular days of the week, associated with the planets, can be important. Thus people afflicted by Mars may fast on Tuesdays and those by Saturn on Saturdays. Each month the days of the new and full moon are important, especially the latter for purposes of fasting. Their Sanskrit names, *Kuhū* and *Rākā*, are of Austric origin. These observances are carried out by women rather than men.

SHAMANISM, or techniques of ecstasy through which the soul is made to ascend to the higher regions or descend to the lower ones, is a well-documented phenomenon of primal religion. In India it is regionally differentiated. Among the Orissan tribe of Saora, the standard pattern involves marriage between the male or female shaman and the spirit. First comes the proposal of marriage. Then problems associated with the proposal lead to a crisis and its final resolution, which ends in the marriage of the shaman with a spirit-spouse. In north and central India the typical features of shamanism include 'supernatural' election, ceremonial initiation, acquisition of a tutelary deity, the use of a winnowing fan rather than a drum as a shamanistic device, the use of ladders, the symbolism of the Cosmic Tree and the summoning of spirits rather than the accompanying of them on their post-mortem journey. Mircea Eliade saw the presence of 'ascension' elements in Indian shamanism as bringing it within the ambit of shamanism as a universal primal phenomenon.

See also §§X and XI below.

BIBLIOGRAPHY

M. Eliade: *Le Chamanisme et les techniques archaïques de l'extase* (Paris, 1951); Eng. trans. as *Shamanism: Archaic Techniques of Ecstasy* (London, 1964)
T. C. Das: 'Religious Beliefs of the Indian Tribes', *The Cultural Heritage of India*, ed. H. Bhattacharyya, iv (Calcutta, 1956), pp. 421–32
G. D. Berreman: *Hindus of the Himalayas* (Berkeley and Los Angeles, 1963)
C. Maury: *Folk Origins of Indian Art* (New York, 1969)
H. H. Presler: *Primitive Religions in India* (Madras, 1971)
B. K. Sarkar: *Folk Elements in Hindu Culture* (Livingstone, 1972)
H. Hermanns: *Die religiös-magische Weltanschauung der Primitivstamme Indiens*, 3 vols (Wiesbaden, 1973)
L. A. Babb: *The Divine Hierarchy: Popular Hinduism in Central India* (New York and London, 1975)
L. P. Vidyarthi and B. K. Rai: *The Tribal Culture of India* (Delhi, 1977)
M.-L. Reiniche: *Les Dieux et les hommes: Etudes des cultes d'un village du Tirunelveli Inde du sud* (The Hague, 1979)
S. N. Parratt: *The Religion of Manipur* (Calcutta, 1980)

ARVIND SHARMA

8. CONCEPT OF ART. Although India has a large body of literature discussing the arts in theoretical terms (*see* §10 below), discussions of the visual arts are almost always confined to technical matters and not to aesthetic considerations. The theoreticians wrote particularly about music,

dancing and Sanskrit court poetry and drama. They did not apply their theories to all Indian literature—the epics and religious literature are conspicuously absent—or to visual works of art. These theoretical works, however, are our main keys to an understanding of how the ancient Indians approached the concept of art. They are concerned with the concept of aesthetic experience and how it was produced. They called such an experience *rasa*, usually translated as 'mood' but originally meaning 'flavour' or 'taste'. The major moods were thought to be eight in number: erotic, humorous, heroic, furious, piteous, wondrous, terrifying and disgusting. A work of art had to have, besides a major mood, various other features, such as accompanying minor moods, determinants and consequents, all of which in varying combinations produced the overall aesthetic experience. Early theoreticians posited that an erotic painting or comic play simply aroused erotic or comic emotions in the spectator, but later, more subtle arguments describe the emotions aroused in the spectator as being sublimated into a generalized aesthetic response. Literary sources suggest that secular and portrait painting could also be appreciated in such terms.

Another body of texts consists of technical literature for the construction of buildings and the making of images. Although secular architecture and painting are dealt with in these texts, their primary purpose is religious. Their writers are concerned not with beauty or aesthetics but with the correct building and adornment of a temple so that it is suitable for the god's house. The rules for making images are sometimes couched in visionary terms: the artist had to imagine the divinity before him in appearance and with attributes as described and even had to become as one with what he was imagining. The artist's prime purpose was to invoke the appropriate religious response, not through the power of his art but through the clarity of the iconography and the correctness of the temple in which the images were housed.

The nearest approach in Sanskrit to the word 'art' in its generalized sense is the word *kala*; in such works as the *Kamasūtra* there are 64 *kala* listed, in which a courtesan was expected to be proficient. These include music, singing and dancing and composing poetry, as well as numerous minor social graces. Another passage in the same text states that the young man-about-town should have a painting board ready in his room and a place for carving and clay-modelling. Plainly the leisured and sophisticated classes in ancient India were expected to appreciate the arts. It is clear that art in Indian terms was a product of high civilization and of court culture in particular. Secular arts such as portrait painting and portrait sculpture are often referred to in literature in terms that indicate that they were meant to be naturalistic, and portraits in particular were expected to seem to breathe. Such three-dimensional aims in painting were to be realized through the use of modelling, shading and foreshortening. What appear in the West as the major achievements of Indian art—religious sculpture and architecture—were evidently not considered as art at all. Religious art, therefore, was outside the terms of reference for early aesthetic enquiry, although the arguments that raged in the theoretical works in the 9th–13th centuries over whether 'peaceful' (*santa*) was the ninth mood (*rasa*) suggest growing unease at the exclusion of works of art, whether literary or visual, intended to suggest the numinous.

From all the different classes of theoretical literature and from remarks elsewhere, it clear that, in order to produce a successful work of art, the artist, having first concentrated on the reality (or summoned it into his mind if it was an image of a divinity), had to reproduce it from the power of his imagination; his images had to be both realistic and ideal, speaking likenesses as well as idealistic summations. Theoretical literature is as uncertain a guide to actual art in India as it is elsewhere, imposing as it does a conceptual framework on what artists do intuitively. Once Indian sculptors had acquired the technical ability in carving to match their imaginations, what obsessed them was the physical power inherent in the human form. As Hinduism and Buddhism developed, and the awesome power of divinities was tempered by their mercy for suffering humankind, then the power of early sculpture gave way to a numinous sensuality. The earliest treatises dealing with the visual arts coincided with the troubled period of the Huna invasions that brought about the end of the Gupta period, when Indian art had reached what appears to have been its classic phase, and doubtless reflect an attempt to preserve what was in danger of being lost.

ANANDA KENTISH COOMARASWAMY remarked on the fact that a general 'flattening' of both sculpture and painting in the late first millennium corresponded to a change in aesthetic values. Although it would perhaps be going too far to say that the technical literature had the effect of altering the course of Indian art, nonetheless the increasing emphasis on iconography in the literature coincided with developments in temple building and decoration that emphasized the structure of the temple at the expense of the quality and variety of its sculpture. The need to display a growing number of recognizable images led to a diminution in the compositional and narrative complexity of Indian sculpture. The even greater shock of the Muslim conquest (*c.* 1200) gave to the iconographical literature an unimpeachable authority. The correct iconographical attributes were all that was required, and indeed they have remained so.

In painting also at this time, plastic techniques gave way to linear ones and subtle gradations of tone to contrasting blocks of pure colour. What is not clear is whether what appear to be such drastic aesthetic changes are due to the wholesale elimination of traditional royal patronage after 1200 or whether such simplified forms had always been favoured by the bourgeois and other patrons who remained. In any event, these new aesthetic values were the ones adopted by Hindu monarchs when they were in a position to resume royal patronage. In the far south there was no such violent disruption to artistic development, and the aesthetic concepts that underlaid south Indian architecture and painting remained unaltered until the 17th century.

The imposition of Muslim rule on much of India from 1200 brought with it an almost diametrically opposed concept of art. In contrast to the crowded and colourful proliferation of images and busy surface detail on Indian buildings, monotheistic Islam offered the austerity of the relatively undecorated mosque. In Islam the divine image is not expressed in artistic terms. In Muslim aesthetics, art is viewed in Platonic terms: artists are not creators, but their work reflects the ideal beauty of creation. Major artistic impulses were expressed in architecture and in the book arts of calligraphy and illumination, particularly in manuscripts of the Koran. In Muslim India it was these arts that naturally received the patronage of the ruling élite.

Since it was to Iran that the Muslim rulers of India looked for cultural inspiration, the tradition of Persian book painting was introduced into India probably in the 14th century. However, this was a private art for the delectation of the discerning patron, and it did not flourish before the later 16th century and the beginnings of the imperial MUGHAL studio. In the more public art of architecture, the earliest Muslim rulers were sufficiently impressed by Hindu buildings to build their first mosques, at AJMER and Delhi (*see* DELHI, §III), out of carved pillars and lintels from the temples they pulled down and to cover the reordered arcades with new corbelled domes. This whole procedure would have been far more time-consuming and labour-intensive than building afresh. These early mosques clearly inspired reverence, for they were extended rather than replaced in later centuries. Later Muslim rulers, however, built mosques, madrasas, tombs and palaces following the classical Islamic principles of arch and dome but using methods and styles different from their models in Iran and Central Asia, consciously adapted to suit the indigenous climate, building materials and work habits (*see* §III, 1 below).

From the 15th century on, cross-fertilization between Hindu and Muslim forms took place in all the arts in the different sultanate kingdoms. The fusion of styles in painting and architecture in the Mughal period is even more striking. Except of course for the Hindu temple, the basic conception of which remained unchanged from the pre-Muslim period, it is clear that in the Mughal imperium two differing concepts of art were fused. The resulting eclectic style was first consciously used by the Mughal emperors in grandiose building projects to overawe their subjects, but it became in the 17th century a pan-Indian manner used by Hindu and Muslim patrons alike. Intruding European influence from the 18th century onwards at first increased this tendency to eclecticism. In the 19th century European concepts of art became widespread through the various art schools set up in the major cities (*see* §9 below). The ideas of art as an end in itself and of the creative artist as an interpreter of life came more and more to dominate the concept of art among the sophisticated urban élites. Art was used by artists as a means of expressing Indianness in order to reawaken Indians to their past, either through heroic subject-matter taken from Indian legends and history or through a reinterpretation of traditional themes in a more modern manner. Art then became linked to the nationalist struggle, and only with its successful ending did Indian artists become free to pursue their own goals irrespective of political content and context.

BIBLIOGRAPHY

E. B. Havell: *Ideals of Indian Art* (London, 1911)
M. R. Anand: *The Hindu View of Art* (London, 1933)
A. K. Coomaraswamy: *The Transformation of Nature in Art* (Cambridge, MA, 1934)
H. Mitra: *Contribution to a Bibliography of Indian Art and Aesthetics* (Santiniketan, 1951)
K. Krishnamoorthy: *Studies in Indian Aesthetics and Criticism* (Mysore, 1979)
T. P. Ramachandran: *The Indian Philosophy of Beauty*, 2 vols, Madras University Philosophical Series, 24 (Madras, 1979–80)
P. Sudhi: *Aesthetic Theories of India* (Pune, 1983–9)
B. Srivastava: *Nature of Indian Aesthetics with Special Reference to Śilpa* (Varanasi, 1985)
A. L. Dallapiccola: *Shastric Traditions in Indian Arts. Vol. I: Texts; Vol. II: References and Documentation* (Wiesbaden, 1989)
R. Thanji: *The Sensuous in Art: Reflections on Indian Aesthetics* (Shimla and Delhi, 1989)
B. S. Miller: *The Powers of Art: Patronage in Indian Culture* (Delhi, 1992)

9. STATUS OF THE ARTIST. Although India has produced objects worthy of being called art for nearly 2500 years, for the majority of this period only a few isolated names of artists survive. Like other craftsmen, artists were organized into guilds (Skt *śreṇi*s) from an early date. Over time these guilds turned into hereditary castes, all of whose members would normally have been expected to follow the same profession. In later periods such castes were invariably of low status, akin to potters or metalworkers, but this was not always the case. In the sophisticated urban civilization of Maurya (4th–3rd century BC) and Gupta (4th–5th century AD) India, where painting and carving were the type of activities that a sophisticated élite was expected to practise, the status of a professional artist was correspondingly higher.

Artists' anonymity was the inevitable concomitant of a society in which illiteracy was the norm and in which those able to write were invariably not concerned with the mundane. The attribution of many texts on architecture and temple construction to divine (e.g. by Vishvakarman or Maya) or royal (e.g. Mandana of Mewar (14th century), Bhoja of Malwa (*c.* 1010–53)) authorship indicates that at least the profession of architect (*sūtradhāra*) was a high calling (*see* §10 below). The architect was usually a Brahman—i.e. a member of the priestly caste—acting on behalf of the patron (*yajamāna*) of the temple, who acquired the merit of the building by paying the architect and his team a fee. The architect would organize the layout of a temple or palace in accordance with the principles handed down to him from his master and would assign work to his team of carvers. The members of this team could have any social status and were not restricted by caste. Such teams moved about as necessary, though the great variation in regional styles, even in early times, suggests that they normally would have worked within given areas. Since images—and probably entire temples—were painted on completion, painters must have been members of such teams. This is indicated by Cave 1 at AJANTA, in which the sculpted Buddha at the back is supported by two painted *bodhisattva*s. Only rarely in ancient India were the names of artists inscribed on their works, and never in contemporary literature.

Following the Muslim conquest of India, calligraphers came to be regarded as the highest of all artists, just as they were in the rest of the Muslim world. With Akbar (*reg* 1556–1605) a change occurred, in that painters were afforded at least equal recognition. Abu'l-Fazl, Akbar's chronicler, was much more enthusiastic in his description of the painters in Akbar's employ than in his dutiful list of calligraphers. Artists in Akbar's studio came from many backgrounds, Hindu as well as Muslim, and were to a considerable extent treated as individuals. The notes of their names on the edges of their paintings were needed for individual payment according to productivity and talent, and librarians' similar notes on the borders of finished manuscript pages let the royal patron know who was responsible in each case. The emperor Jahangir (*reg* 1605–27) claimed to have been able to tell without such notes which of his artists had painted a picture and even who had contributed the parts of a cooperative work. Artists were considered acceptable social companions even for the emperor. Jahangir's close friend MUHAMMAD SHARIF, son of the artist 'ABD AL-SAMAD, was made a grandee of the empire. It is clear from the work of some of Jahangir's artists, such as ABU'L-HASAN and BICHITR, that the emperor had revealed his innermost thoughts and fears for them to render in paint.

Such intimate relations between patron and artist are extremely rare in the history of Indian art, even in the relatively recent past, for which written evidence survives. The names of hundreds of painters are known from the reigns of Akbar, Jahangir and Shah Jahan (*reg* 1628–58), yet for this same period scarcely a dozen names of architects are documented, even though all three rulers were as preoccupied with building as with painting. Official chronicles cast rulers as the builders of palaces and cities, and of course in a sense they were: in any autocracy it is the autocrat who decides where and what to build and in what style. The actual details of building were delegated to a supervisor of construction. In India, with its differing traditions, patronage was the choice made by the ruler as to which tradition to pick. These connections between artists and patrons in India before modern times allowed the basic styles of artists to be modified considerably by patrons. While the fusion of Indian, Iranian and European elements in Mughal painting is perhaps the primary example of stylistic development driven by imperial rather than artistic criteria, this was the usual pattern in Indian patronage. What is unusual is that so much is known about the process. In other situations it is possible to see change and development taking place over several centuries, but what drove these changes is largely opaque, although it was probably patron preference. Yet painters were clearly personalities in their own right and could sometimes impose their wishes on their patrons. Once the latter had decided on the type of painting required, the artist would largely determine its style, whether traditional to the studio or developing from that tradition.

Important artists were allowed to sign their work, and many paintings have reliable attributions. Such artists had high status, and their presence in a patron's studio was a matter of some pride. Even the finest artists, however, were totally dependent on their patrons, who had both the means and the inclination to support them. The studios in which they worked were run by chiefs, not necessarily artists themselves, who apportioned out work in accordance with their perceptions of artists' individual talents. Outside the royal courts, where lesser artists practised their crafts for bourgeois patrons, they were of low account indeed, particularly painters. The traveller François Bernier described the lowly status and (apparently) talent of artists in Delhi at the mercy of the 17th-century nobility, suggesting the dichotomy between court artists and those thrown on to the mercy of the bazaar.

In the 18th century the system of royal patronage began to break down, and an important artist such as Mihr Chand (*fl c.* 1765–75) was able to leave the employ of the powerless emperor to work for the nawab of Avadh and for European patrons. Pahari artists moved from court to court in the Punjab hills. In the early 19th century Delhi artists such as Ghulam Murtaza Khan (*fl c.* 1800–20) and his son Ghulam 'Ali Khan (*fl c.* 1815–40) worked in various styles for the Mughal emperors, the local Muslim and Hindu nobility and British patrons such as William Fraser and James Skinner. Other artists of lesser talent but greater specialization set up their own studios in the 19th century to cater for British taste. Artists in traditional styles, however, continued working at various princely courts until as late as 1947.

This subservience of artist to patron largely ended during the 19th century with the rise of nationalist schools of artists. The establishment of Western-style art colleges in the major cities, ostensibly to train Indian artists in techniques of design, in fact introduced them to the tradition of independence of Western artists. However, it was not the traditional artistic castes who went to such colleges but the urban élite; there was a corresponding radical change in the status of the artist. The Bengal school of artists attempted to interpret traditional Indian painting in a modern manner, while elsewhere such independent artists as RAVI VARMA of Travancore painted traditional Indian stories in the grand Victorian historical manner. Regardless of the individual styles favoured, Indian artists thereafter asserted their artistic independence in the European tradition and followed (albeit at a distance) the developments of the international modern movement.

For relevant bibliography *see* §8 above; *see also* §XII below.

J. P. LOSTY

10. TREATISES. In traditional India, human achievements are assessed according to their compliance with a complex set of interlocking regulations, the observance of which is believed to result in the fulfilment of the treble 'goal of Man' (Skt *puruṣārtha*). This treble goal encompasses activity in the social/legal (*dharma*) and economic/political (*artha*) spheres, as well as the sphere of pleasure, both sexual and aesthetic (*kāma*). Over time a huge body of shastric (from Skt *śāstra*: 'treatise') literature has evolved to codify these regulations. Besides *dharma śāstra*, *artha śāstra* and *kāma śāstra*, this literature includes treatises devoted to nearly all technical fields, including the performing arts (for which the most famous text is the *Nāṭya śāstra* ('Treatise on dance') by Bharata), architecture and the making of images. All these works refer, at least in theory, to a single ideology: the translation of the social hierarchy (*see* §7 above) into practical terms. Shastric literature is not limited to Brahmanical orthodoxy, however. Numerous treatises deal with Buddhist or Jaina topics and even with mosque-building.

(i) Overview. Shastric literature relating to architecture, sculpture and painting is abundant, heterogeneous and not yet fully studied. The main texts are written in Sanskrit,

while numerous others, relying on the same patterns and principles, are written in vernacular languages (*see* §3 above). Besides treatises whose specific subject is art, others with different main subjects deal peripherally with it. Texts concerned specifically with the subject appeared around the 4th and 5th centuries, when the fundamental principles of Indian art were already well established, and they multiplied from the 8th century on.

Treatises on architecture and/or the making of images are generally called *śilpa śāstra* (treatises dealing with craft), a strong indication that artists were considered craftsmen (*śilpin*) in traditional India. A frequent alternate designation is the treatise on dwelling or dwellings (*vastu śāstra*). This does not mean that such texts are confined to architecture but, rather, emphasizes the fact that painting and sculpture were considered subsidiary to building, their usual 'support'. Some works deal comprehensively with architecture (both religious and secular), urban planning and image-making; examples include the 11th-century *Mayamata* (*see* §(ii) below) and the 14th- or 15th-century *Mānasāra* ('Essence of measurement'), a similar text known in Europe as early as 1834 through Ram Raz's *Essay on the Architecture of the Hindus.* However, most of these texts confine themselves to limited subjects. The *Citralakṣaṇa* ('Characteristics of *citra*') of Nagnajit, one of the earliest works on image-making (possibly 5th century), is typical of this category. Following an introduction about the divine origin of image-making, it gives limb by limb instructions for making the image of a universal king, combining measurements and prescriptions regarding form and colour. It ends with short notes on how to modify proportions for making images of lower-status people and of women. As is frequently the case, it is not clear whether the text deals with painting or sculpture; the title is of no help, since *citra* means 'sculpture' as well as 'painting'.

Treatises of every sectarian persuasion dealing with ritual and related subjects comprise more or less comprehensive expositions relating to temple architecture and ornamentation, the making of images and secular, formal and domestic architecture. The Puranas, the main subject of which is the mythological history of the universe, also treat artistic subjects. Thus the *Viṣṇudharmottara purāṇa* ('Virtuous laws of Vishnu') deals with painting, image-making, temple-building, dance, music and literature. The 5th- or 6th-century *Bṛhat saṃhitā* ('Great collection') of Varāhamihira, of which the main topic is astrology, and the *Mānasollāsa*, a 12th-century encyclopedia of royal pleasures, are examples of works with important sections concerning *śilpa śāstra* subjects and methods.

(ii) The Mayamata, *a* vastu śāstra. A summary of the *Mayamata*, a voluminous Sanskrit 'treatise on dwelling' attributed to the mythical architect Maya, indicates how shastric literature deals with artistic subjects. Composed in south India about the 11th century, the *Mayamata* transfers to the theoretical an architecture that came into its own in the 10th and 11th centuries under the Chola dynasty.

First, general topics are dealt with: building sites (with the requisites for each social group); a system of measurements; architects and other technicians; orientation; geometric diagrams (*maṇḍalas*, *padas*) used for layout and ritual; and the planning of cities, forts, villages etc. Then the six fundamental levels of an architectural elevation are presented (base, pillars, entablature, attic, roof and finial), with variations for each marked by different mouldings, proportions and so on. Categories of buildings, defined by the number of levels in their elevation, are then treated: temples (*prāsādas*), which have all six levels; pavilions (*maṇḍapas*), each with base, pillars and entablature; and halls (*sabhās*), each with base, pillars, roof and finial. For each category a description is given of the smallest and simplest type (for example a single-storey temple or four-pillared pavilion) with a square plan; from these are developed types with other plans, sizes and decoration. In a similar way the description of houses is based on that of an elementary one, comprising a single main building (*śālā*) and a verandah (*vāra*, *alindra*), to which other main buildings and verandahs or galleries are added to obtain other types. Descriptions are often enumerative. Thus for palaces, the text provides little more than a bare list of buildings to be installed in concentric courtyards.

The last part of the *Mayamata* deals mainly with divine representations to be installed inside and outside temples. These may be images or symbols such as the *liṅga* (representing the god Shiva), several types of which are described (*see* §II, 1 below), or images. In the latter case iconographic descriptions are given of numerous gods: the number of their arms, their attributes, gestures, postures and colours as well as other details (expression, costume, ornaments). The practical and technical aspects of image-making are confined to scattered details of iconometry. The *Mayamata* also contains long passages devoted to construction rituals as well as to technical points (joinery, roofing, materials), to features such as doors, windows and pedestals, and to other types of buildings (gateways, enclosures etc).

(iii) The śilpa śāstras. Most *śilpa śāstra* texts are in verse. Generally, this is the only indication of the literary skill of their authors, whose Sanskrit is often broken and formulaic. The systematic use of the optative mode ('ought to be', 'must be') enhances the prescriptive nature of the texts. Technical vocabulary is mainly metaphoric and polysemic, abundant but somehow ambiguous. Inverted cyma recta-like mouldings, for example, are often called 'lotuses', but all the many synonyms for 'lotus' in Sanskrit may be applied to one and the same moulding. Terms meaning 'neck' or 'throat' designate all recessed elements, whether narrow recessed mouldings or the full level of elevation just below the roof. In a similar way, terms for 'pillar' (their first meaning often being 'leg' or 'foot') are also applied to pilasters and, by extension, to pilastered and even non-pilastered walls. This linguistic process allows theoretical systematization: the same general rule is valid whether a façade is hypostyle, pseudo-hypostyle or plain. Regional variations occur in the meaning of some terms, as well as in the borrowing of technical words from vernaculars.

Despite its limitations, this technical vocabulary is fairly precise when used to discuss theory. But it is frequently unsuitable for describing actual works of art and often has led to total misunderstandings. Thus, studies in European languages consistently employ the Sanskrit expression *tribhaṅga* to describe images in a hipshot stance, assuming that the Sanskrit designates a pose with three (*tri-*) 'bends' (*bhaṅga*). However, the expression is not descriptive but expletive. It means that a single image may be made in three *different* poses, which are described by indicating degrees of diminution (another meaning of *bhaṅga*) in total body height as well as the measurements of intervals between big toes and between heels.

Like most Indian treatises, the *śilpa śāstra*s codify traditional theories by relating them to divine authority. The human element, if acknowledged at all, is considered the last stage in a process of faithful transmission. Thus they do not refer to monuments or images from which the theories they present have been extrapolated, differing in this sense from such writers as Vitruvius, who based his theories on actual examples. More interest is given to outward appearance than to structural problems: storeys and false storeys are no more differentiated (in description or in vocabulary) than buildings with pillars and those with pilastered walls. In the case of image-making, when details are given about the wooden armatures of clay sculptures, it is because they correspond to the bones of the living deities embodied in the images, just as ropes binding the armatures together are the sinews of the god's body.

Dimensions and proportions play a major role in these treatises. Most include discussions of measurement systems, and all employ conventional units. In architecture these include the module (*daṇḍa*), defined as the width of a pillar top, and intercolumniation (*bhakti*), the horizontal proportions of hypostyle or pseudo-hypostyle buildings. The 'digit' (*aṅgula*) is the conventional unit for image-making. Iconometric canons, evolved from an initial anthropometric one (see the *Bṛhat saṃhitā*), are organized in hierarchic fashion, starting with the most important gods and moving downward to other anthropomorphic gods of lesser status and then, in succession, to men, dwarfs, dwarflike gods and animal forms—e.g. Vishnu-Matsya embodied in a fish (*see* §II, 1 below). A general modular relationship may unite images and buildings.

Intending to be universal, *śilpa śāstra*s and similar texts supplement their descriptions of basic types with long lists of actual or potential, but authorized, variations. Updating is sometimes done by adding new variations in order to acknowledge more recent developments. Such treatises therefore leave a great deal of leeway to artists; this is often emphasized by the prescription to choose a particular option 'in order to fit circumstances' or, more significantly, 'in order to create beauty'. Thus the aesthetics that the texts embody allow faithfulness to virtually any of the numerous variations they propose.

See also §III, 1 below.

BIBLIOGRAPHY

EARLY SOURCES

S. Kramrish: *The Vishnudharmottara (Part III): A Treatise on Indian Painting and Image-Making* (Calcutta, 1928) [partial trans.]

P. K. Acharya: *Architecture of Mānasāra*, Mānasāra Series, iv (London, 1934/*R* Delhi, 1980) [trans.]

U. P. Shah: *Viṣṇudharmottarā Purāna (3rd Khaṇḍa)*, 2 vols, Gaekwads Oriental Series, 130, 137 (Baroda, 1958–61) [crit. edn of Skt text and detailed study]

A. Boner and S. R. Sarma: *Śilpa Prakāśa: Medieval Orissan Sanskrit Text on Temple Architecture* (Leiden, 1966) [Skt text and trans., illus. with rare drgs found in a palm-leaf MS]

B. Dagens: *Mayamata: Traité sanskrit d'architecture*, 2 vols, Institut Français d'Indologie, xl, 1 and 2 (Pondicherry, 1970–76) [Skt text and French trans.]; rev. as *Mayamata: An Indian Treatise on Housing, Architecture and Iconography* (New Delhi, 1985)

V. Gopala Iyengar: *Sakalādhikāra of Sage Agastya*, Tanjore Sarasvati Mahal Ser., cxli (Tanjore, 1973) [Skt text and Eng. trans. of fairly comprehensive treatise on image-making]

A. K. Bhattacharya: *Citralakṣaṇa: A Treatise on Indian Painting* (Calcutta, 1974) [chap. of the 16th-century *śilpa ratna* of Shri Kumara prepared under the patronage of King Devananayana of Travancore]

B. N. Goswamy and A. L. Dahmen-Dallapiccola: *An Early Document on Indian Art: The 'Citralakṣaṇa of Nagnajit'* (Delhi, 1976) [trans.; updated version of B. Laufer: *Dokumente der indischen Kunst: Erstes Heft: Malerei; Das Citralakshaṇa* (Leipzig, 1913)]

M. R. Bhatt: *Varāhamihira's Bṛhat Saṃhitā*, 2 vols (Delhi, 1981–2) [Skt text and trans.]

GENERAL

R. Raz: *Essay on the Architecture of the Hindus* (London, 1834/*R* Varanasi, 1972) [trans. of extracts from the *Mānasāra*]

P. K. Acharya: *An Encyclopaedia of Hindu Architecture*, Mānasāra Series, vii (London, 1946/*R* Delhi, 1979) [dictionary of shastric archit. terms]

H. Mitra: *Contribution to a Bibliography on Indian Art and Aesthetics* (Santiniketan, 1951/*R* 1980) [incomplete, but only available bibliog. of pubd or unpubd shastric texts on art]

K. M. Varma: *The Indian Technique of Clay Modelling* (Santiniketan, 1970)

M. A. Dhaky: 'The Genesis and Development of Māru-Gurjara Temple Architecture', *Studies in Indian Temple Architecture*, ed. P. Chandra (New Delhi, 1975), pp. 166–78

B. Dagens: *Les Enseignements architecturaux de l'Ajitāgama et du Rauravāgama*, Institut Français d'Indologie, lvii (Pondicherry, 1977; rev. as *Architecture in the Ajitāgama and the Rauravāgama* (New Delhi, 1984))

K. M. Varma: *Myth of the So-called 'Tribhaṅga' as a 'Pose', or The Nature and Numbers of Bhaṅgas* (Santiniketan, 1983)

A. L. Dallapiccola, ed.: *Shastric Traditions in Indian Arts*, 2 vols (Wiesbaden, 1991) [see esp. S. Pollock: 'The Idea of Śāstra in Traditional India', pp. 17–26, 301–12; T. S. Maxwell: 'Śilpa versus Śāstra', pp. 5–16; and R. Nath: 'On the Theory of Indo-Muslim Architecture', pp. 187–202]

BRUNO DAGENS

11. HISTORIOGRAPHY. The study of Indian art history was initiated between the mid-19th century and early 20th by Western scholars who applied European norms and methodology to Indian art. More recently, this Eurocentric bias has diminished. Increased familiarity with objects of Indian art and their aesthetic language has led to attempts to understand and explain such objects from the point of view of those for whom they were made.

Most of the 19th-century scholars of European art, who had little access to Indian art objects, derived their dismal view of the art of the subcontinent mainly from sensational travelogues. They saw Indian architecture as subject to no rules, Indian sculpture as dominated by obscene or monstrous forms and Indian painting as a mere exercise in crude, bright colours, lacking such Western techniques as perspective and CHIAROSCURO. GEORG WILHELM FRIEDRICH HEGEL (1835) and JOHN RUSKIN (1859) saw Indian art as irrational or unnatural, flying in the face of 'Classical' (Hegel's term) and Christian values, having reached this state by degeneration from rational origins in ancient Greece.

Such distorted views had begun to fade by the late 18th century and early 19th due to the widespread circulation of aquatints and drawings of Indian monuments by such artists as WILLIAM HODGES and Thomas and William DANIELL, the pioneering work of the Asiatic Society (founded in 1784), the publication of studies on Sanskrit literature and Indian mythology and religion by such scholars as Sir William Jones and Edward Moor, and the interest in Indian history stirred by the decipherments and discoveries of JAMES PRINSEP. By the second half of the 19th century, European museums had begun to collect Indian art. The climate of opinion had changed so much that such influential designers and architects as OWEN JONES, Gottfried Semper and William Morris preferred flat non-illusionistic Indian patterns to illusionistic, mass-produced European industrial designs. In the early 20th century a polygenetic view of world art replaced the primacy of Classical norms. In this atmosphere European artists such as AUGUSTE RODIN and EDGAR DEGAS were moved to high praise for Indian (and other Asian) art.

Classicist prejudices lingered well into the 20th century, however, among archaeologists and art historians working in India itself. These included JAMES FERGUSSON, an architectural historian; Sir ALEXANDER CUNNINGHAM, who helped found the Archaeological Survey of India in 1865 and who became its first director-general; and JAMES BURGESS, who followed Cunningham in that office. Fergusson (1845, 1867, 1876) was exceptional among these scholars in trying to establish a history of architectural styles by using plans, sections and photographs of buildings. Cunningham and Burgess preferred to rely on survey reports, books and the uncertain evidence provided by coins, inscriptions and literary sources. None of these men, including Fergusson, used sculpture to date buildings, seeing no stylistic evolution except a progressive decline. Their interest in sculpture was mainly in identifying the themes of Indian mythology it illustrated.

Even ALFRED CHARLES AUGUSTE FOUCHER and Sir JOHN MARSHALL, who used stylistic analysis to master an enormous body of chaotic material, retained certain Classicist predilections. Foucher studied Gandhara sculpture (1905–23) and traced the origin of the Buddha image to the lingering Hellenism of Bactria. Marshall (1922, 1924), director-general of the Archaeological Survey for much of the first half of the 20th century, explained early Buddhist sculpture as having developed under Greco-Iranian tutelage from an 'Indian' conception of flat relief to a 'Hellenistic' conception of plastic volume. As to the study of painting, which began only in the 20th century, Vincent Smith (1908, 1911) discussed Mughal painting mainly in terms of European and Iranian influences, while Ernst Kühnel (1926) saw it as mere plagiarism of European engraving.

Attempts to look at objects themselves rather than at their foreign roots began with GABRIEL JOUVEAU-DUBREUIL (1914, 1917), who established a chronology of south Indian art on the basis of architectural ornament and iconic attributes. His method was followed by HERMANN GOETZ (1924) in the study of Mughal miniatures, F. H. Gravely and T. N. Ramachandran (1932) in the study of south Indian bronzes, CALAMBUR SIVARAMAMURTI (1942), Philippe Stern and Mirelle Benisti (1961) in their analyses of sculptures in Amaravati, Stern (1954, 1972) in his analyses of Begram and early Indian art and the caves at Ajanta and Ellora, and Odette Viennot (1964) in her work on Indian river goddesses. The study of motifs received a great boost from the iconographic work of Albert Grünwedel (1893), Foucher (1905–18, 1940), T. A. Gopinatha Rao (1914), Benoytosh Bhattacharya (1924), Nalini Bhattasali (1929), Jitendra Nath Banerji (1941) and Marie-Thérèse de Mallmann (1948, 1963, 1964). While useful in classifying a homogeneous group of objects securely tied to one place or time, a methodology relying on the study of motifs has proved misleading for the establishment of a chronology for similar patterns appearing in different places or at different times.

The tyranny of both foreign influences and a methodology relying on motifs was rejected by PAUL MUS, ERNEST BINFIELD HAVELL, ANANDA KENTISH COOMARASWAMY, STELLA KRAMRISCH and Heinrich Zimmer. Mus (1935) laid the foundation for what he called 'comparative religious archaeology', which had important implications for the study of Indian art. Havell (1911) explained Indian art as a reflection of transcendent spiritual ideals rather than of Classical Greek ideals of anatomical realism. Kramrisch (1933, 1946) saw an increasing linearization as the distinguishing factor in Indian sculpture from the late 5th century onwards and explained the symbolism of the Hindu temple as an image of God. Zimmer (1946, 1951, 1955) elucidated the role of Indian images in helping the devotee towards unification with God and explored the function of myths and symbols in Indian art.

However, it was Coomaraswamy who, in a series of remarkable books and essays written in the first half of the 20th century, greatly advanced the study of Indian iconology. Coomaraswamy explained Indian art as a fusion of technical function and symbolic meaning, effected by the interaction not of Indian and foreign techniques but of the linear northern spirit with the plastic southern one. He unearthed the structural and etymological origins of the different parts of the temple from ancient bas-reliefs and texts, demonstrated the use of the temple as the body and house of God, traced Buddhist iconography to pre-Buddhist images and ideas of water cosmology and explained such decorative artistic motifs as the pot overflowing with foliage as incitements to creative abundance. He discovered the Rajput style of painting and analysed it in relation to developments in Indian literature.

Despite the service rendered by these scholars in breaking the grip of Classicism on Indian art history, their reluctance to analyse style made it difficult to chart the evolution they postulated. Moreover, their conclusions did not grow wholly out of an understanding of the intrinsic genius of Indian art but also reflected the ideas of Neo-Platonism (in the case of Havell and Coomaraswamy) and of the cultural historian JOSEF STRZYGOWSKI (in the case of Coomaraswamy and Kramrisch), the philosopher FRIEDRICH NIETZSCHE and the poet Rainer Maria Rilke (in the case of Zimmer) (*see also* NEO-PLATONISM, §1).

A rigorous stylistic analysis, stripped of extraneous speculation, was made for the first time by Ludwig Bachhofer (1929). Though he did not see the history of Indian art as a steady process of decay and rejected psychological speculation, Bachhofer used stylistic polarities and the concept of racial consciousness, developed in European art criticism by HEINRICH WÖLFFLIN, to explain all developments as movements towards or away from the golden age of the art of Stupa 1 at SANCHI. Stylistic analysis was also used by Ivan Stchoukine (1929; *see* SHCHUKIN, (2)) to explain Indian painting from the 16th to the 18th century as part of a process of evolution—going back at least to the 5th century—which had absorbed European and Persian influences. Working from the paintings themselves, Stchoukine made no distinction between a secular Mughal or a religious Rajput style, for example. Using a similar approach, Pramod Chandra (1976) demonstrated the pre-Akbar-period sources of Mughal painting in his analysis of an early manuscript of the *Ṭūṭīnāma* ('Tales of a parrot', *c.* 1560–65; Cleveland, OH, Mus. A., MS.62.279).

Stylistic studies of painting have been furthered since the 1950s by the perceptive connoisseurship of Stuart Carey Welch, Robert Skelton, WILLIAM GEORGE ARCHER and Brijen Goswamy. It is, however, in architecture that the most serious efforts have been made to understand styles by using traditional texts and by consulting scholars and architects. The lead provided by RAM RAZ as early as 1834, was ignored by Fergusson and Burgess, who limited themselves to a Western architectural vocabulary. However, significant progress was made in the first half of the 20th century by Henry Cousens, Manmohan Ganguly, Nirmal Kumar Basu and N. V. Mallaya, and in the second half by Prabha Sankar Sompura, K. R. Srinivasan, Krishna Deva and, above all, M. A. Dhaky. These scholars clarified the technical vocabulary of Indian architecture and gave focus to the analysis of regional styles.

Indian art history has now reached a point where it has begun to reflect on itself. The new awareness is evident, for instance, in Chandra's *On the Study of Indian Art* (1983). Chandra emphasizes the need to study form (in terms of both its origins and its meaning) as well as motifs, to use Western tools for visual analysis as well as Indian manuals of art, to combine traditional and modern scholarship and to define style in terms of time and space rather than power and patronage. With a growing perception of the harmony between function and embellishment and of the interconnectedness of art and life, historians of Indian art are trying with increasing success to integrate an analysis of what art is with an analysis of what it does.

BIBLIOGRAPHY

GENERAL

R. Raz: *Essay on the Architecture of the Hindus* (London, 1834)
G. Hegel: *Vorlesungen über Ästhetik* (Berlin, 1835, rev. 1842); Eng. trans. by T. M. Knox as *Hegel's Aesthetics: Lectures on Fine Art*, 2 vols (Oxford, 1975)
J. Fergusson: *Illustration of the Rock-cut Temples of India* (London, 1845)
J. Ruskin: *The Elements of Perspective* (London, 1859)
J. Fergusson: *History of Indian and Eastern Architecture*, 2 vols; i (London, 1876); ii (New York, 1891), rev. J. Burgess (London, 1910)
A. Grünwedel: *Buddhistische Kunst in Indien* (Berlin, 1893)
V. A. Smith: *The Early History of India from 600 BC to the Muhammadan Conquest, Including the Invasion of Alexander the Great* (Oxford, 1904, rev. 4/1924)
——: *A History of Fine Art in India and Ceylon from the Earliest Time to the Present Day* (Oxford, 1904, rev. London, 3/1962/*R* Bombay, 1969)
A. Foucher: *Etude sur l'iconographie bouddhique de l'Inde d'après des documents nouveaux*, 2 vols (Paris, 1905–18, rev. 1951)
——: *L'Art gréco-bouddhique du Gandhâra*, 3 vols (Paris, 1905–23)
E. Havell: *The Ideals of Indian Art* (London, 1911)
T. A. Gopinatha Rao: *Elements of Hindu Iconography*, 4 vols (Madras, 1914)
G. Jouveau-Dubreuil: *Archéologie du sud de l'Inde*, 2 vols (Paris, 1914)
A. K. Coomaraswamy: *Rajput Painting*, 2 vols (London, 1916)
G. Jouveau-Dubreuil: *Dravidian Architecture* (Madras, 1917)
J. Marshall: 'The Monuments of Ancient India', *Cambridge Hist. India*, i, ed. E. J. Rapson (Cambridge, 1922), pp. 612–49
B. Bhattacharya: *The Indian Buddhist Iconography* (Calcutta, 1924, 2/1968)
H. Goetz: 'Kostüm und Mode an den indischen Fürstenhofen des 16.–19. Jahrhunderts', *Jb. Asiat. Kst*, i (1924), pp. 67–101
E. Kühnel and H. Goetz: *Indische Buchmalerei* [Indian book painting] (Berlin, 1924; Eng. trans., 1926)
A. K. Coomaraswamy: *Catalogue of the Indian Collections in the Museum of Fine Arts, Boston* (Boston, 1926)
——: *History of Indian and Indonesian Art* (Leipzig, London and New York, 1927)
——: 'The Origin of the Buddha Image', *A. Bull.*, ix (1927), pp. 287–317
——: 'Indian Architectural Terms', *J. Amer. Orient. Soc.*, xlviii (1928), pp. 250–75
——: *Yakṣas*, 2 vols (Washington, DC, 1928–31)
L. Bachhofer: *Early Indian Sculpture*, 2 vols (Paris, 1929, rev. New York, 1972); review by A. K. Coomaraswamy in *Int. Studio*, xcv (1930), pp. 2–11
N. K. Bhattasali: *Iconography of Buddhist and Brahmanical Sculptures in the Dacca Museum* (Dhaka, 1929)
I. Stchoukine: *La Peinture indienne à l'époque des Grands Moghols* (Paris, 1929)
A. K. Coomaraswamy: 'Early Indian Architecture: Cities and City-gates, etc.', *E. A.*, ii (1930), pp. 209–35
——: 'Indian Sculpture: A Review', *Rupam*, 42–4 (1930), pp. 2–11
F. H. Gravely and T. N. Ramachandran: *Catalogue of the South Indian Hindu Metal Images in the Madras Government Museum* (Madras, 1932)
S. Kramrisch: *Indian Sculpture* (London, 1933)
P. Mus: *Barabudur: Esquisse d'un histoire du bouddhisme fondée sur la critique archéologique des textes*, 2 vols (Hanoi, 1935)
J. Marshall and A. Foucher: *The Monuments of Sanchi*, 3 vols (London, 1940)
J. N. Banerji: *Development of Hindu Iconography* (Calcutta, 1941)
C. Sivaramamurti: *Amaravati Sculpture in the Madras Government Museum* (Madras, 1942)
S. Kramrisch: *The Hindu Temple* (Calcutta, 1946)
H. Zimmer: *Myths and Symbols in Indian Art and Civilization* (Princeton, 1946/*R* New York, 1962)
M.-T. de Mallmann: *Introduction à l'étude d'Avalokiteśvara* (Paris, 1948)
H. Zimmer: *Philosophies of India* (New York, 1951)
P. Stern: 'Les Ivoires et os découverts à Begram, leur place dans l'évolution de l'art de l'Inde', *Nouvelles recherches archéologiques à Begram*, ed. J. Hackin, 2 vols (Paris, 1954), pp. 19–57
H. Zimmer: *The Art of Indian Asia*, 2 vols (New York, 1955)
P. Stern and M. Benisti: *Evolution du style indien d'Amarāvati* (Paris, 1961)
M.-T. de Mallmann: *Les Enseignements iconographiques de l'Agni Purana* (Paris, 1963)
——: *Etude iconographique sur Mañjuśrī* (Paris, 1964)
O. Viennot: *Les Divinités fluviales Gangā et Yamunā aux portes des sanctuaires de l'Inde* (Paris, 1964)
P. Stern: *Colonnes idiennes d'Ajanta et d'Ellora: Evolution et répercussions* (Paris, 1972)
P. Chandra: *Tti-nma of the Cleveland Museum of Art and the Origins of Mughal Painting* (Graz, 1976)

HISTORIOGRAPHY

J. Fergusson: *On the Study of Indian Architecture* (London, 1867)
S. Kramrisch: 'Influence of Race on Early Indian Art: Notes on the Lecture of Sir John Marshall . . .', *Rupam*, xviii (April 1924), pp. 73–6
J. Marshall: 'Influence of Race on Early Indian Art', *Rupam*, xviii (April 1924), pp. 69–73
J. Strzygowski: 'The Orient or the North', *E. A.*, i (1928), pp. 69–85
A. K. Coomaraswamy: 'Reactions to Art in India', *J. Amer. Orient. Soc.*, cii (1932), pp. 213–20
J. Strzygowski: 'India's Position in the Art of Asia', *J. Ind. Soc. Orient. A.*, i (1933), pp. 7–17
A. K. Coomaraswamy: *Figures of Speech or Figures of Thought* (London, 1945)
R. Schwab: *Le Renaissance orientale* (Paris, 1950)
G. D. Bearce: *British Attitudes towards India* (London, 1961)
A. Imam: *Sir Alexander Cunningham and the Beginnings of Indian Archaeology* (Dhaka, 1966)
S. N. Mukherjee: *Sir William Jones* (Cambridge, 1968)
P. J. Marshall: *The British Discovery of Hinduism* (Cambridge, 1970)
N. Pevsner: 'James Fergusson', *Some Architectural Writings of the Nineteenth Century* (Oxford, 1972), pp. 238–51
P. Mitter: 'Western Bias in the Study of South Indian Aesthetics', *S. Asian Rev.*, vi/2 (1973), pp. 111–14
P. Chandra: 'The Study of Indian Temple Architecture', *Studies in Indian Temple Architecture*, ed. P. Chandra (New Delhi, 1975), pp. 1–39
R. Lipsey: *Coomaraswamy*, 3 vols (Princeton, 1977)
P. Mitter: *Much Maligned Monsters* (Oxford, 1977)

S. D. R. Singam: *Ananda Coomaraswamy—The Bridge Builder* (Petaling Jaya, 1977)
P. Chandra: *On the Study of Indian Art* (Cambridge, MA, 1983)
B. Stoler Miller, ed.: *Exploring India's Sacred Art: Selected Writings of Stella Kramrisch* (Philadelphia, 1983) [with bibliog. by J. Dye]
W. Halbfass: *India and Europe: An Essay in Understanding* (New York, 1988)
S. Arasuratnam: 'Recent Trends in the Historiography of the Indian Ocean, 1500 to 1800', *J. World Hist.*, i/2 (1990), pp. 225–48
K. K. Chakravarty: [review of J. Pereira: *Elements of Indian Architecture* (New Delhi, 1987)], *J. Ind. Soc. Orient. A.*, n.s., xvi (Calcutta, 1991–2)
——: *The Temples at Tala and the Art of Daksina Kosala* (diss., Cambridge, MA, Harvard U., 1992; microfilm, Ann Arbor)
J. Majeed: *Ungoverned Imaginings: James Mills' "The History of India" and Orientalism* (Oxford, 1992)
K. K. Chakravarty: *The Early Buddhist Art at Bodh-Gaya* (New Delhi, in preparation)

KALYAN KUMAR CHAKRAVARTY

II. Iconography and subject-matter.

1. Hindu. 2. Buddhist. 3. Jaina. 4. Epic themes. 5. Other stories and cycles. 6. Erotic and genre themes. 7. Historical themes. 8. Portraits.

1. HINDU. The visual presentation of divine concepts is of key importance in Hinduism. The iconography of the deities of this complex tradition has evolved over centuries as inherited norms and forms have been supplemented with newer themes, motifs and interpretative visualizations.

(i) Early forms. (ii) Shiva. (iii) Vishnu. (iv) Ganesha. (v) The Goddess. (vi) Other deities.

(i) Early forms. The ancient scriptures known collectively as the Vedas and the archaeological finds from such protohistoric sites as those of Baluchistan and of the Indus civilization (*c.* 2550–*c.* 2000 BC) may provide the earliest glimpses of the iconography of the later Hindu tradition. The picture that emerges can be interpreted in various ways. In the three-dimensional objects, many of which are ringlike or cylindrical in shape, discovered at these sites, some scholars have discerned the archetypes of the *yoni* and *liṅga*, symbols of the male and female organs of procreation. If these are in fact emblems of fertility, they may represent the concept of the primordial parents, transformed in later times into the cults of Shiva and Shakti. The small seal showing a seated male figure surrounded by animals, and the torso of a bearded male figure with his gaze directed to the tip of the nose in yogic fashion (discovered at MOHENJO-DARO and HARAPPA respectively), have been interpreted as anticipating Shiva in his roles of Pashupati (Lord of Animals) and Mahayogi (Great Meditator). In the terracotta figurines representing fecund females discovered at sites in Baluchistan as well as those of the Indus civilization, scholars have seen the archetype of the mother goddess that developed into Shakti or Devi. Even the designs and motifs on seals and sealings from the various Indus civilization sites have been interpreted as abstract or aniconic forms of Hindu divinities.

All of this evidence may be representative of non-Aryan, perhaps pre-Vedic, iconography. The corresponding tradition of the Vedic Aryans in the initial stage, as gleaned from the *Ṛg veda*, seems to have been more notional than representational. Several passages of the *Ṛg veda* refer to such divinities as Indra, Varuna and Mithra, often giving them human attributes and patterns of behaviour. But it is doubtful whether the Aryans of the Vedic period (*c.* 2nd–1st millennium BC) represented such divinities in visual form. That the *Ṛg veda* refers derisively to non-Aryans as worshippers of the phallic emblem and of the fetish (*śiśnadeva*, *muradeva*) indicates that devotion to emblems or images was not favoured by Aryans of that time. The performance of sacrificial rites (*yajña*), the keynote of the religious practices of even early Vedic peoples, may have been directed towards deities conceived as apotheosized natural phenomena.

While the texts project the attitudes of a limited stratum of Vedic society, the pre-existing modes of image-worship probably appealed to the majority of people. This may have facilitated the introduction of images into Vedic worship. Although references to images of deities appear in texts postdating the *Ṛg veda*, there are no contemporaneous archaeological finds. The grammarian Panini's aphorisms (*c.* 5th century BC) and the commentaries of the grammarian and author Patanjali (*c.* 2nd century BC) provide the earliest cogent evidence for the making of images. Two examples suggest that the custom of making images of the principal divinities of Hinduism was established before the 1st century AD: the *c.* 2nd-century BC pillar inscription from BESNAGAR recording the erection of a pillar in honour of Vasudeva (a form of the god Vishnu) by the Greek ambassador Heliodorus (*see* §V, 4(ii)(c) below) and the 1st-century BC inscription from Ghosundi referring to the construction of an edifice dedicated to Vasudeva and Samkarshana (another form of Vishnu), presumably enshrining their icons.

Early Indian iconographic themes are heterogeneous in nature. Greek historians report that the army of Poros (*c.* 4th century BC) carried an image of Herakles that has been identified variously as a god—Shiva, Krishna or Indra—or a nature spirit (*yakṣa*), or as one of the guardians of the directions (*dikpālas*) or planetary deities (*grahas*). The four animals—elephant, lion, bull, horse—on the columns of the emperor Ashoka (*reg c.* 269–*c.* 232 BC) have been interpreted as theriomorphic representations of divinities (*see* §IV, 3(ii) below). The deity depicted on early coins from Ujjain has been identified as a form of Shiva by some or as Skanda by others. Shiva appears on coins of the Indo-Scythian ruler Maues (*reg c.* 90–80 BC) and of early rulers of the Kushana dynasty (1st–3rd century AD). The deity Karttikeya is depicted on coins of the minor Yaudheya dynasty (*c.* 1st century BC–6th century AD). A boar, possibly the archetype of the boar incarnation of Vishnu, is found on seals discovered at Basarh (2nd century AD), as is the representation of the goddess Lakshmi lustrated by elephants (Gajalakshmi), while seals from Bhita (near Allahabad) bear Vaishnavite symbols such as the conch and the wheel. Images on Buddhist monuments, such as those at SANCHI and BHARHUT, presumably had antecedents in folk cults and doubtless contributed to the development of Hindu iconography.

Popular traditions appear to have coalesced into bona fide Hindu cults after the 1st century AD. Eventually three gods—Brahma, Vishnu and Shiva—were given the most prominent roles, forming the Trinity (*Trimūrti*). Their respective roles were explained in terms of the universal flux of creation (*sṛiṣṭi*), preservation (*sthiti*) and annihilation (*saṁhāra*). These elemental activities were thought to be dependent on a male–female, passive–active or negative–positive type of partnership, so the concept of female energy (*śakti*) was envisaged to complement the Trinity. However, since no major cult developed around Brahma, Shiva, Vishnu and Shakti or Devi (the Goddess) came to occupy supreme positions in three major cults known as the Shaiva, Vaishnava and Shakta cults. Two other cults, the Ganapatya (with Ganesha or Ganapati at the apex) and the Saura (with Surya, the sun god, at the apex), also developed major followings, though as offshoots of the Shaiva and Vaishnava respectively. These five major cults and a few subsidiary ones developed their own myths, legends, rituals and iconographies. The interactions among them were characterized by both reciprocity and competition. Liberals developed the *pañcopāsanā* system, in which the divinities of all five cults were treated as equals and complements.

(ii) Shiva. Images of Shiva possess such distinctive features as a third eye in his forehead, a crescent moon in his matted hair, a bull as his mount, a tiger skin as his garment, snakes as ornaments and the trident (*triśūla*) and a small drum (*ḍamarū*) as the attributes he holds. His images are often ithyphallic (*ūrdhvaliṅga*), distinguishing him as the symbol of virility. His skin is usually white, and his images have two or more arms.

Shiva's well-known epithet is Pancanana (the Five-headed One). Of the pentad of heads, the front central one, known as Sadyojata, bears a serene expression. Flanking it are the fierce-looking Bhairava on the right and, representing the notion of selfhood, Vamadeva on the left. The rear face, known as Kapila, is wrathful, while the top face, known as Ishana, represents esoteric mysticism. These five faces, often known by alternative names, represent the five elements (*pañcabhūtas*): earth, water, fire, air and ether. When all five faces are shown or implied, the god assumes the form of the Great Lord (Maheshamurti; see fig. 301 below).

Shiva's perennial consort is Parvati (see figs 296 and 358 below). Together they are considered the primordial parents of the cosmos. The universal flux of creation is the result of their perpetual union, an ideology expressed in the abstract Shiva *liṅga* (phallic emblem of Shiva). The oblong vertical *liṅga* is the visual analogue of the male organ of procreation, while the ovoid lower portion represents the *yoni* (vulva). The *liṅga* is often shown as a vertical form and the *yoni* as a triangle, representing Shiva and Shakti, respectively. *Liṅgas* are often represented with faces (*mukhaliṅgas*). The images with one face (*ekamukhaliṅgas*) from Khoh (Allahabad Mus.) and with four faces (*caturmukhaliṅgas*) from NACHNA (Nachna, Mahadeva Temple), both from the 5th century AD, are examples of this form, of which there are 108 varieties. Twelve of these are celebrated as the luminous *liṅgas* (*jyotirliṅgas*), each one being associated with a Shaivite place of pilgrimage (*tīrtha*). A variety made of white stone (*bāṇaliṅga*) represents Shiva's granting of boons to Bana, son of the demon Bali.

Shiva is known as the Mahayogi (Great Meditator) in view of his intimate association with *yoga* (the power of assimilation). This characteristic made him both the leveller of high and low and the harmonizer of discord. His association with ghosts (*bhūtas*), spirits (*pretas*), goblins (*vetālas*) and his dwarflike hordes (*gaṇas*) is doubtless indicative of his pervasive nature. His forms as the Lord of Dance (Nataraja, or Natesha; see fig. 2; see also fig. 211 below) and as the embodiment of wisdom (Dakshinamurti) represent his sophisticated bearing and intellectual qualities. Representations of Shiva's wedding with Parvati (the Kalyanasundaramurti, or Vaivahikamurti) allegorize the importance of marriage as the core of the social system. An 8th-century AD relief at Ellora is among the most celebrated representations of this theme. Images showing Shiva and Parvati seated together in conjugal intimacy (the Umamaheshvaramurti) are also extended expressions of this ideology (see fig. 216 below). Sometimes their divine son Kumara or Skanda is shown between them (the Somaskandamurti).

Shiva assumes his dreadful form (the Ugramurti, or Rudramurti) in order to chastise adversaries and offenders, while in his benevolent form (the Anugrahamurti, or Saumyamurti) he grants favours to the faithful. According to Hindu myth, when Kala or Yama, the god of death,

2. *Natesha*, or *Shiva as the Lord of Dance*, buff sandstone, h. 1.08 m, 8th century AD (Gwalior, Central Archaeological Museum)

dared to touch devotees of Shiva, the latter killed Kala by assuming a particular dreadful form (Kalarimurti). Another form (Kamantakamurti) relates to the episode of Shiva burning Kama, the god of love, to ashes after the latter had disturbed him in meditation. Shiva is also shown as having killed the haughty demon Tripura by destroying the latter's impregnable triple city (the Tripurantakamurti) and as having liquidated the delinquent demon Andhaka (Andhakarimurti).

One of the god's benevolent forms (Gangadharamurti) alludes to the grace he bestowed on his devotees by agreeing to hold the River Ganga on his matted hair. In a variant of this theme, Shiva is shown caressing the breasts of the river goddess, who appears to cling to his body. Shiva giving protection to Markandeya and Chandesha, his ardent devotees, constitutes the theme of other types of the favour-granting form (Anugrahamurti). The demon-king Ravana's shaking of the mountain Kailasa and Shiva's consequent bestowing of grace on him constitute another theme (Ravananugrahamurti), which can be seen in a panel at Ellora (*see* ELLORA, §2). The dancing form (Nrityamurti) of Shiva also belongs to the category of images expressing divine grace. Another important narrative theme related to Shiva alludes to his supremacy in the Trinity. It shows him bursting out of a *liṅga*-like column (Lingodbhavamurti) to the bewilderment of Brahma and Vishnu, who, having failed to ascertain the column's length, were forced to recognize Shiva as the supreme one of the three. Other forms of Shiva appear in narratives of his legends or as iconographic expressions of his many epithets.

(iii) Vishnu. The representations of Vishnu are as varied as those of Shiva. Vishnu's aniconic emblems, including the disc or wheel (*cakra*), the lotus (*padma*) and the mythical half-bird, half-man (Garuda), appear on ancient coins and seals and in other contexts, such as the Besnagar Garuda pillar. The god appears as a human figure as early as the 1st century AD. Three basic divine concepts—the cosmic god Narayana, the Vedic solar god Aditya-Vishnu and the mythico-historical hero–lover Krishna—seem to have coalesced by about that time. This led to the formulation of the Vaishnava cult, at the centre of which was a system (*pāñcarātra*) according to which the subject of devotion had five aspects: the incomprehensible supreme being (*para*), emanations (*vyūha*s), incarnations (*avatāra*s or *vibhava*s), intellectual or spiritual visualizations (*antaryāmin*s) and iconic representations (*arcā*s). The first and fourth of these categories are beyond the comprehension of most worshippers.

While incarnations of Vishnu are numerous, ten of them are fairly standardized: Matsya (fish), Kurma (tortoise), Varaha (boar), Narasimha (man–lion), Vamana (dwarf), Parashurama (Rama with the axe), Krishna, Ramachandra, Buddha and Kalki (the incarnation still to come). In each of these incarnations Vishnu performed a divine feat to save the world from destruction. In representations of them, attributes relevant to the narratives are shown. The variety of such representations is due mainly to the selection of such attributes. The *avatāra*s are sometimes shown in groups on panels and sometimes as independent images. One of the finest examples of the latter is the 5th-century relief at UDAYAGIRI (ii) representing the boar incarnation.

The four prime emanations of Vishnu are Vasudeva, Samkarshana, Pradyumna and Aniruddha. These manifestations are differentiated visually by the order in which the god's four attributes—conch (*śankha*), disc, mace (*mahat*) and lotus (the symbol of Lakshmi, Vishnu's consort and the goddess of fortune)—are held in his four hands, and each manifestation has a distinct cognitive implement. Thus Vasudeva has the disc in the form called Sudarshana, Samkarshana the mace (Kaumaduki), Aniruddha the sword (Nandaka) and Pradyumna the bow (Sharnga). Varying combinations of attributes allowed the four prime emanations to be transformed into 24 forms (*caturviṃśatimūrti*). Independent images of almost all of them exist, as do groups, usually of 4, 12 or 24. Representations of all 24 in art (Narayanashilas) take a variety of forms.

Apart from the four attributes mentioned above, images of Vishnu usually bear some or all of the following features: a blue complexion, yellow garment, long garland of wild flowers (*vanamālā*), jewelled crown (*kirīṭamukuṭa*), gem on his chest (*kaustubha*) and an auspicious mark on his chest (*śrīvatsa*). Garuda serves as his vehicle or attendant and Lakshmi as his consort. In medieval images, particularly those from eastern India, Vishnu is flanked by Bhudevi (the earth goddess) and Shridevi (a goddess of fortune) or by Lakshmi and Sarasvati (the goddess of learning; see fig. 201 below). Six- and eight-armed forms are also known.

The narrative forms of Vishnu relate to the various acts of valour or compassion he performed in his emanations and incarnations. As Vasudeva-Krishna he is extolled as a hero, lover or philosopher, not only in the *Mahābhārata* and its appendix, the *Harivaṁśa*, but in almost all of the Puranas (ancient tales) particularly in the *Bhāgavata purāṇa*. Throughout Indian art these legends, known as the *Kṛiṣṇalīlā*s ('Divine acts of Krishna'), are depicted with variations. Similarly, the legends of Vishnu's Rama incarnation, as told in the epic *Rāmāyaṇa*, are depicted as *Rāmalīlā* episodes in sculpture, painting and other art forms (*see* §§4 and 5 below).

The association of Vishnu with the serpent Shesha or Ananta (the Primordial One) is often depicted (for illustration *see* BUDHANILKANTHA). His forms as Balarama (Krishna's brother) or Samkarshana show the hood of a cobra, signifying this association. During the periodic dissolution of the world (*pralaya*), Vishnu sits or sleeps on the body of this serpent, thus assuming his Anantashayi or Sheshashayi form. The Dashavatara temple at DEOGARH houses a representative 5th-century example of this theme. Another panel in the same temple shows Vishnu rescuing the devout elephant king from the clutches of the crocodile demon (the Gajendramoksha). Krishna's delivery of the message of the *Bhagavadgītā* (a part of the *Mahābhārata*), perhaps evoked by the Nara and Naryana panel at Deogarh, also appears in Indian art, especially in late miniature painting.

The Vaikuntha form of Vishnu, a favourite theme in the arts of Kashmir, Himachal Pradesh and Nepal, has four faces. A serene human one in the front is flanked by the heads of a boar and a lion, and at the rear is a demonic face. These faces symbolize the four qualities that Vishnu upholds and disseminates through his primal forms. In this sense the Vaikuntha form is identified with Vishvarupa, the supreme, all-encompassing form of the god. The *Bhagavadgītā* has a detailed description of this form, which constitutes a favourite theme of Indian art. In another form, that of an enchanting female known as Mohini, Vishnu cheated demons out of their share of the drink of immortality (*amṛita*). In the Vaishnava parallels of images of Shiva and Parvati together, Vishnu is shown with his consort Lakshmi (the Lakshminarayana).

The solar form of Vishnu, presumably derived from the Vedic god Aditya-Vishnu, is represented as Surya, the sun god and supreme divinity of the Saura cult (see fig. 3; see also fig. 205 below). This cult developed from the beginning of the 2nd century BC. On coins of this time, the sun god is represented by a disc or wheel. Possible early representations of the god in human form exist in sculptures from Bhaja and Bodhgaya. In these cases, as on the Lala Bhagat pillar near Kanpur, the god is shown riding in a chariot drawn by four horses. Canonical representations, probably not formulated until the 5th century AD, show seven horses symbolizing the seven colours of the rainbow, seven musical notes and seven poetic metres. The god's charioteer is Aruna. Surya is usually shown holding two lotuses in full bloom. He wears a jewelled crown and elaborate ornaments, particularly earrings with gems (*ratnakuṇḍala*s) and a coat of mail (*avyaṅga*). Often, particularly in north Indian images, he wears boots. His two lieutenants, Dandi (holding a staff) and Pingala (holding paper and pen), and his two female harbingers, Usha and Pratyusha (personifications of the dawn, shown shooting arrows), frequently accompany him. He has four wives—Chhaya, Samjna, Nikshubha and Suvarchasa—at least two of whom often accompany him. Some of his sons, such as Manu, the twin Ashvinikumaras, Yama, Shanaishchara and Revanta, are sometimes represented as attending deities. Independent images of Revanta riding a horse also exist. Several important temples were dedicated to Surya, the most famous at KONARAK, MARTANDA, MODHERA and OSIAN. All of them contain sculptures pertaining to the Saura cult.

3. *Surya*, the solar form of Vishnu, polished black slate, h. 1.65 m, from Ganga Sagar, late 12th century (Philadelphia, PA, Museum of Art)

(iv) Ganesha. Ganesha, or Ganapati—both meaning 'lord of the *gaṇa*s' (hordes)—is the central deity of the Ganapatya cult. The most conspicuous feature of Ganesha's iconography is his elephant head. This has led to the suggestion that this deity developed out of the cult of *yakṣa*s (nature spirits), many of whom had animal heads. In the Puranas, Ganesha is usually referred to as the son of Shiva and Parvati (see fig. 4). However, some Puranic accounts hold that he was Parvati's offspring alone, created without the involvement of a man.

Since Shiva is also known as the lord of the *gaṇa*s, it has been claimed that Ganesha/Ganapati is none other than Shiva himself, and that the Ganapatya sect represents a faction of the Shaiva cult. It seems more likely that the one branched off from the other. Excepting the conspicuous elephant head, Ganesha shares with Shiva a number of iconographic features, such as the sacred thread of serpents (*sarpayajñopavīta*), a third eye in his forehead, a crescent moon on his head and a trident as attribute. In both literature and art, the dancing forms of Shiva and of Ganapati (the Nrityaganapatimurti) are popular. As Heramba-Ganapati the god possesses five heads like Shiva, although all are elephant heads. In this form Ganapati is often shown riding on a lion, although a rat is his conventional mount in his other manifestations.

The four-armed form of Ganesha is the most common in art. His attributes are usually a battle-axe (*paraśu*), rosary (*akṣamālā*), a bowl of sweetmeats (*modakabhāṇḍa*) and a radish (*mūlaka*) or broken tusk (*śūlaka*). He is shown with only one tusk; according to one Puranic account the other one was broken in a fight. Ganesha is invariably shown with a pot-belly. Normally vermilion, his complexion may vary in colour, as do the number of his

4. *Shiva and Parvati with Ganesha* (unfinished), gouache on paper, 178×141 mm, Guler–Kangra style, early 19th century (Oxford, Ashmolean Museum)

arms and certain other features. His consorts are Riddhi and Siddhi; sometimes Lakshmi is also referred to as such. In some images the god is shown with or in the embrace of his consort (the Shaktiganapati form). These images are doubtless the Ganapatya parallels of the similar images of Shiva and Parvati.

There are five or six sub-sects of the Ganapatya cult, each of which has its own interpretation of the god's iconography. The sectarian meaning of his image also changes depending on the position of his trunk. Numerous varieties of his image can be seen in Maharashtra, particularly in Bombay, during the annual week-long celebration in his honour.

Ganesha/Ganapati is a god of wisdom. It is said that only he could act as the divine amanuensis in the difficult task of composing the *Mahābhārata*, the great epic poem about the struggle for supremacy in north India. He is also known as the One Who Bestows Success (Siddhidata) and the One Who Masters Obstacles (Vighnesha). That Ganesha is also an agricultural deity is indicated by the fact that his mount is a rat, whose notoriety as the destroyer of crops is proverbial. The worship of Ganesha is supposed to bring an end to harvest damage.

(v) The Goddess. The Goddess, the pivot of the Shakta cult, is conceived variously as a divine virgin (*kumārī*), wife or female consort (*bhāryā*) or as the principle of female energy (*śakti*). She is also known as the mother (*mātṛikā*) of all children, and of Skanda-Kumara—the divine son of the universal parents, Shiva and Parvati—in particular. As the female energy of a god and as the mother of divine offspring, the Goddess assumes the iconographic form of her male counterpart. Seven goddesses—Brahmani, Maheshvari, Vaishnavi, Kaumari, Indrani, Varahi and Chamunda—were conceived as the spouses of Brahma, Shivamaheshvara, Vishnu, Kumara, Indra, Varaha (Vishnu as a boar) and Shivamahakala (Shiva as Absolute Time). These goddesses are often represented in art as a group of seven mothers (*saptamātṛkās*; see fig. 5) and are frequently shown dancing. Seated images emphasize the goddesses' maternal aspect by including a child on the lap. Smaller groups and independent images also exist. Over time, other gods were accorded spouses, so the number of mother goddesses depicted in art varies.

Shiva's wife is variously known as Parvati (Daughter of the Himalaya), Gauri (a fair-complexioned virgin), Durga (the Invincible One, the Remover of Difficulties), Kali (the Dark-complexioned One), Sabari or Kirati (a member of the Sabara or Kirata tribe) and the like. Many of these names are indicative of the Goddess's iconographic features and functions and the concepts she embodies; her epithets are either descriptive or allude to the narratives in which she plays significant roles. As Sati (a pious woman) or Dakshayani (daughter of Daksha, the Progenitor), she is the first wife of Shiva; she immolated herself, unable to bear the insult her father, Daksha Prajapati, accorded Shiva by excluding him from a ceremonial sacrifice. As Shiva tried to restrain Sati from lodging a protest against this injustice, she created ten illusory manifestations, known as the *mahāvidyās* (embodiments of great wisdom), and coaxed him to relent. These ten forms are Kali, Tara, Shodashi, Bhubaneshvari, Bhairavi, Chhinnamasta, Dhumavati, Vagala, Matangi and Kamala. Some are dreadful and scourging, while others are serene and benevolent. All of the Goddess's forms can be resolved into these two basic aspects.

The Goddess as She Who Rides on a Lion (Simhavahini) is represented on early Indian coins. This aspect is ascribed by some scholars to her possible origin in western Asia. For some of her forms, particularly those having folk or tribal antecedents, a tiger replaces the lion. The Goddess is represented in numerous forms, with varying numbers of arms and different attributes, depending on the specific role she is playing and her association with a particular god. When she is in her benign form, her usual attributes are the lotus and mirror (*darpaṇa*). In her dreadful or militant forms, she carries a variety of weapons, in particular a trident and sword. Usually she bears the iconographic features of Shiva, but as Durga—a composite of all divinities—she exhibits those of other gods as well. One of her dreadful forms is known as Chandi. Interestingly, the *Devīmāhātmya* ('Glorifications of the Goddess') section of the *Mārkaṇḍnya purāṇa*, which deals with her exploits against demons, is known as the *Caṇḍī*. This text describes the Goddess's manifestation in three of her primary forms—Mahasarasvati, Mahalakshmi and Mahakali—in order to liquidate the demons Madhu and Kaitabha, the buffalo demon Mahishasura, and Shumbha and Nishumbha. These divine exploits are depicted in sculpture and painting, particularly in miniature paintings illustrating the *Devīmāhātmya*.

5. *Mother Goddesses*, buff sandstone, 0.83×1.09 m, from Kannauj, Farrukhabad District, 10th century (Kannauj, Archaeological Museum)

The form of the Goddess as Mahishasuramardini (She Who Slays the Buffalo Demon; see fig. 188 below) has been popular in Indian art since perhaps the early Kushana period (1st century AD). In this form the Goddess is usually shown in the act of killing the demon, as can be seen in sculptures from MATHURA. Sometimes an earlier moment in the battle is shown, as in the relief at Mamallapuram. In early examples the Goddess is usually shown as either two- or four-armed, the notable exception being the twelve-armed image at Udaygiri in Madhya Pradesh. Later images show her with more arms according to regional preferences. In Bengal the ten-armed (*daśabhujā*) form became popular, perhaps in the 19th century.

The Mahishasuramardini form of the Goddess is also known as Katyayani, as it was revealed by the Goddess at the hermitage of the sage Katyayana. Of the deity's other dreadful revelations, the Chamunda and Kali forms are better known. In the former, she has an emaciated body (often with a scorpion on it), exposed fangs, sunken eyes and pendulous breasts. Her mount is sometimes an owl, but she is usually shown with a corpse as a mount (the Pretasana form). Chamunda's normal attributes are the skull-cup (*kapāla*) and bed leg (*khaṭvāṅga*). Kali is dark-complexioned and is often shown with a protruding tongue, standing on a corpse that sometimes represents the prostrate figure of Shiva himself. Both Chamunda and Kali are surrounded by a host of *yoginīs* (female adepts), 64 of which are recognized as the Shakta counterparts of Shiva's *gaṇas* (hordes). Images of these *yoginīs*, often with inscribed labels, can be found in temples dedicated to them.

Although all female divinities are manifestations of the Goddess, the spouses of the Trinity are the most popular. Savitri and Gayatri, Brahma's consorts, are invoked in the *Gāyatrī mantra*, of Vedic origin, uttered daily by Hindus, particularly Brahmans. These divinities bear such attributes as a rosary (*akṣamālā*), a water vessel (*kuṇḍikā*) and a book (*pustaka*), which are also relevant to the iconography of Brahma. Shiva's consorts are Sati and Parvati. The former has 51 forms, each sanctifying a pilgrimage centre of the Shakta cult (*śāktapīṭha*). These forms have distinctive iconographic features. Parvati has several other variants, including Uma, Gauri and Haimavati. Their iconographies show subtle differences. Lakshmi and Sarasvati, the consorts of Vishnu, are the goddesses of wealth and wisdom, respectively. The association of the former with a lotus and of the latter with a book is well known. In the iconography of the medieval period, Lakshmi is accorded a pot of treasure (*ratnaghata*) and a sheaf of corn (*dhānyamañjarī*) as her attributes and often an owl (in images from eastern India) as her mount. Her aniconic form is the tuft of hair often shown on Vishnu's chest. An early and enduring representation of the Goddess shows her as Gajalakshmi being bathed by two elephants with water from pots they hold in their upraised trunks. Sarasvati personifies the Vedic river of the same name and is the goddess of all forms of learning, including the performing arts. Like Brahma (with whom she is also sometimes associated), she has a swan as a mount, and she often holds a lute (*vīṇā*). In south India, however, a peacock serves as her mount.

Two other river goddesses, Ganga and Yamuna, are often represented at each side of temple entrances, particularly after the Gupta period (*c.* 4th–5th century). Ganga rides on a mythical crocodile (*makara*) and Yamuna on a tortoise. Ekanamsha is a Vaishnava form of the Goddess, who is usually flanked by the Vasudeva and Samkarshana forms of Vishnu. This trio is apparently the source of the triple divinities—Jagannatha, Balabhadra and Subhadra—who are venerated at the Jagannatha Temple at PURI, where the Rathayatra festival is held every year. Another important goddess is Manasa, who was a daughter of Shiva but who eventually developed into the serpent goddess. That her cult became important, particularly in Bengal, is indicated by the recording of her glorifications in the 17th-century poems known as the *Maṅgalakāvya*s. Shitala, the goddess who relieves smallpox, is still worshipped in villages and towns.

(vi) Other deities. Karttikeya, also known as Skanda or Kumara, is Shiva and Parvati's son (see fig. 203 below), but unlike Ganesha, he did not have an organized cult following. He represents Kandarpa or Kamadeva, the god of love. In legends, Agni, Ganga and the six Pleiads (Krittikas) are also named as his parents. He sometimes has six heads in view of the latter association; this explains his sobriquet Shadanana (One Who Has Six Faces). Various forms of this god exist in art, including representations on Yaudheya and Gupta coins. His distinctive attributes are his mount, a peacock, and a spear (*śakti*) and cock (*kukkuṭa*) held in his hands. He is thought of as the commander-in-chief of the army of the gods (the Devasenapati form) as well as the one who was born to kill the demon Taraka. In view of this, in some of his images, particularly those of the medieval period, he is shown with a bow and arrow. His consort is Devasena. In south India he is popular as Svami (Lord) Subrahmanya.

Of the numerous other divinities, some occur mainly in groups. These include the eight (or ten) guardians of directions (*dikpāla*s), nine planetary deities (*navagraha*s), eight deities of the natural elements (*aṣṭavasu*s), eleven wailing forms of Shiva (*ekādaśarudra*s) and seven sages (*saptaṛṣi*s). Independent images of some of the members of each group also exist. The bearers of wisdom (*vidyādhara*s), divine musicians (*gandharva*s) and heavenly creatures, often part human and part horse or bird (*kinnara*s), are also seen frequently, mostly on reliefs in conjunction with major deities. These semi-divine personages are usually referred to as deities that reside in the space between heaven and earth (*vyayantaradevatā*s).

A number of composite iconographic forms, expressing both syncretic and sectarian developments, also came into being. Well-known examples include the Harihara, Ardhanarishvara, Martandabhairava, Vasudeva-Kamalaja and Shaktiganapati forms, each of which combines important cult deities within a single form. Harihara images have bodies divided vertically, the right sides usually showing Shaivite features and the left those of Vishnu. The Ardhanarishvara form is shared in the same way by Shiva and Parvati (see fig. 6; see also fig. 202 below), and

6. *Ardhanarishvara*, painting, 210×150 mm, ?from Rajasthan, late 18th century–early 19th (London, British Museum)

the Vasudeva-Kamalaja image is the Vaishnava counterpart. Images of Martandabhairava show the combination of Shiva (as Bhairava) and Surya (as Martanda). The Shaktiganapati form combines Ganapati and the Goddess as Shakti.

See also HINDUISM, §1, and §I, 2 and 7 above.

BIBLIOGRAPHY

GENERAL

E. Moor: *The Hindu Pantheon* (London, 1810, rev. by W. O. Simpson, Madras, 1864/*R* 1897)
W. Crooke: *The Popular Religion and Folk Lore of Northern India*, 2 vols (Westminster, 1896)
R. G. Bhandarkar: *Vaisnavism, Saivism and Minor Religious Systems* (Strasbourg, 1913)
T. A. Gopinatha Rao: *Elements of Hindu Iconography*, 4 vols (Madras, 1914–16/*R* New York, 1968)
B. C. Bhattacharya: *Indian Images, Pt 1: The Brahmanical Iconography* (Calcutta and Simla, 1921)
N. K. Bhattasali: *Iconography of Buddhist and Brahmanical Sculptures in the Dacca Museum* (Dhaka, 1929)
S. Kramrisch: *The Hindu Temple*, 2 vols (Calcutta, 1946)
H. Zimmer: *Myths and Symbols in Indian Art and Civilization*, ed. J. Campbell (New York, 1946/*R* 1962)
——: *The Art of Indian Asia: Its Mythology and Transformations*, 2 vols, ed. J. Campbell (New York, 1955)
J. N. Banerji: *The Development of Hindu Iconography* (Calcutta, 1956)
M. T. D. Mallmann: *Les Enseignements iconographiques de l'Agnipurana* (Paris, 1963)
A. Danielous: *Hindu Polytheism* (London, 1964)
B. Srivastav, ed.: *Rupamandana* (Varanasi, 1964)
J. Gonda: *Visnuism and Sivaism: A Comparison* (London, 1970)
B. Dagens: *Mayamata: Traité sanskrit d'architecture*, 2 vols, Institut Français d'Indologie, xl/1–2 (Pondicherry, 1970–76), rev. as *Mayamata: An Indian Treatise on Housing, Architecture and Iconography* (Delhi, 1985)

D. C. Sircar: *Studies in the Religious Life of Ancient and Medieval India* (Delhi, 1971)
S. M. Bhardwaj: *Hindu Places of Pilgrimage in India* (Berkeley, 1973)
B. Sahai: *Iconography of Minor Hindu and Buddhist Deities* (New Delhi, 1975)
G. Liebert: *Iconographic Dictionary of the Indian Religions* (Leiden, 1976)
D. C. Bhattacharyya: *Iconology of Composite Images* (New Delhi, 1980)
P. Pal: *Hindu Religion and Iconography* (Los Angeles, 1981)
K. Vatsyayan: *The Square and the Circle of the Indian Arts* (New Delhi, 1983)

SHIVA

D. N. Lorenzen: *The Kapalikas and the Kalamukhas: Two Lost Saiva Sects* (New Delhi, 1972)
C. Sivaramamurti: *Nataraja in Art, Thought and Literature* (New Delhi, 1974)
B. N. Sharma: *Iconography of Sadasiva* (New Delhi, 1976)
C. Sivaramamurti: *Satarudriya: Vibhuti of Siva Iconography* (New Delhi, 1976)
S. Kramrisch: *The Presence of Siva* (Princeton, 1981)
Manifestations of Shiva (exh. cat. by S. Kramrisch, Philadelphia, PA, Mus. A., 1981)
Proceedings of a Symposium on the Nature of Religious Imagery. Discourses on Siva: Philadelphia and Bombay, 1984

VISHNU

F. O. Sehrader: *Introduction to the Pancaratra and the Ahirbudhnya Samhita* (Madras, 1916)
B. B. Bidyabinod: *Varieties of the Vishnu Image*, Mem. Archaeol. Surv. Ind., ii (Calcutta, 1920)
J. Gonda: *Aspects of Early Visnuism* (Utrecht, 1954)
P. Shah: *Visnudharmottara-Purana (3rd Khanda)* [Virtuous laws of Vishnu], 2 vols, Gackwads Oriental Series 130, 137 (Baroda, 1958–61)
H. D. Smith: *A Source Book of Vaisnava Iconology, According to the Pancaratragama Texts* (Madras, 1969)
L. P. Pandey: *Sun-worship in Ancient India* (Delhi, 1971)
W. Begley: *Visnu's Flaming Wheel: The Iconography of the Sudarsanacakra* (New York, 1973)
K. S. Desai: *Iconography of Visnu* (New Delhi, 1973)
B. N. Sharma: *Iconography of Revanta* (New Delhi, 1975)
C. Sivaramamurti: *Chitrsutra of the Vishnudharmottara* (New Delhi, 1978)
N. P. Joshi: *Iconography of Balarame* (New Delhi, 1979)
N. Krishna: *The Art and Iconography of Vishnu Narayana* (New Delhi, 1980)
R. Champakalaksmi: *Vaisnava Iconography in the Tamil Country* (New Delhi, 1981)
R. Parimoo: *Sculptures of Sesasayi Visnu* (Baroda, 1983)
——: *Vaisnavism in Indian Arts and Culture* (New Delhi, 1987)
T. S. Maxwell: *Visvarupa* (Delhi, 1988)
D. C. Bhattacharyya: *Pratimālakṣaṇa of the Visnudharmottara* (New Delhi, 1991)

GANESHA

A. Getty: *Ganesa* (Oxford, 1936)
B. N. Sharma: *Iconography of Vainayaki* (New Delhi, 1979)
R. L. Brown: *Ganesh: Studies of an Asian God* (Albany, 1991)

THE GODDESS

D. C. Sircar: 'The Sakta-pithas', *J. Royal Asiat. Soc. Bengal*, xiv (1948); also in D. C. Sircar: *The Sakta-pithas* (Delhi, 1973)
P. K. Maity: *Historical Studies in the Cult of the Goddess Manasa (A Socio-cultural Study)* (Calcutta, 1962)
D. C. Sircar, ed.: *Sakti Cult and Tara* (Calcutta, 1967)
B. N. Mukherjee: *Nana on Lion: A Study in Kushana Numismatic Art* (Calcutta, 1969)
R. D. Trivedi: *Iconography of Parvati* (Delhi, 1981)

OTHER DEITIES

J. P. Vogel: *Indian Serpent Lore or the Nagas and Hindu Legend and Art* (London, 1926)
A. K. Chatterjee: *The Cult of Skandakartikeya in Ancient India* (Calcutta, 1970)
K. Sinha: *Karttikeya in Indian Art and Literature* (Delhi, 1979)
R. N. Misra: *Yaksa Cult and Iconography* (New Delhi, 1981)

2. Buddhist.

(i) The Buddha. (ii) *Bodhisattvas*. (iii) *Jinas*. (iv) The Goddess. (v) Other deities.

(i) The Buddha. The pivotal premise of Buddhism being the transience (Pali *aniccam*; Skt *anityam*) of worldly things, the religion was not particularly disposed towards the idea of image-making. Gautama Buddha denounced the concept of a personalized god, and this was a further deterrent. Although during his lifetime he apparently did not allow his own image to be made and worshipped, his was already an apotheosized presence. At the very end of his life he apparently conceded that stupas (reliquary mounds, also known as *caityas*) could be constructed over his earthly remains at crossroads, as was usually done in the case of a 'universal ruler' (*cakravartin*). The eight stupas that were then constructed, as well as many others, became symbols of the Buddha's presence. Eventually, even their ritualistic worship was accepted. Thus the stupa virtually became the Buddha's aniconic image (*see* STUPA, §1).

A few other symbols—a pair of footprints, a vacant seat, a tree (possibly the *bodhi* tree, or pipal), an umbrella, a crown or turban, the mark of the three jewels (*triratna*) comprising the Master (Buddha), the Law (*dharma*) and the Community of monks (*Saṅgha*)—were apparently taken to indicate the Buddha's presence. The Wheel of Law, often atop a pillar or flanked by a pair of deer, was also a dominant symbol. The four animals—elephant, lion, horse and bull—on the columns set up in the Maurya period (*c.* 3rd century BC) can also be understood as emblematic of Gautama Buddha, since the legends of his life are associated with these animals (*see* §V, 3(ii) below). However, until the 1st century AD, anthropomorphic representations of him are not seen, as is evidenced by sculptural remains from Bharhut, Sanchi, Amaravati, Nagarjunakonda, Mathura and Gandhara. Art was predominantly narrative in content until the 3rd century AD, consisting primarily of the *jātakas* (stories of the Buddha's previous incarnations) and *nidānakathās* (episodes of his historical life). The *jātakas* depicted most frequently are the *Mahākapi jātaka* (birth as the Great Monkey), *Vessantara jātaka* (birth as Prince Vessantara), *Ṣaḍdanta jātaka* (birth as a six-tusked elephant) and the *Mṛiga* or *Ruru jātaka* (birth as a deer). Another important episode describes the dream of Maya (the Buddha's mother), who saw a white elephant as the prefigurement of his divine conception.

Of the numerous legends of the Buddha's life, the Eight Great Events (*aṣṭamahāpratihāryas*) are depicted frequently in early Buddhist narrative art, often in a selective group. The eight events are the birth at Lumbini; attainment of wisdom at Bodhgaya; the turning of the Wheel of Law (*dharmacakrapravartana*) near Sarnath; the descent from heaven at Sankasya after the Buddha's meeting with his parents; the taming of the mad elephant Nalagiri at Rajgir; the offering of honey by monkeys at Vaishali; the performance of the miracle of Sravasti and the Great Demise (*mahāparinirvāṇa*) at Kushinagara. The other recurrent themes of early Buddhist narrative art are the Great Departure (*mahābhiniṣkramaṇa*), the receipt of the gift of a garden retreat from the wealthy merchant Anathapindika and the Victory over Evil (*Māravijaya*). Independent images of, or themes related to, deities of pre-Buddhist cults such as *yakṣas* (fem. *yakṣīs*; divinities who control the wealth of nature; see figs 144 and 145 below), *nāgas* (serpent deities) and Hariti and Panchika (protective deities) are also found. Some of these *yakṣas* and *nāgas* are respectfully mentioned in the *Mahāmāyūrī*, a Buddhist work of about the 2nd century AD.

The first human figures of the Buddha were modelled on the iconography of the *yakṣas*. Once created, this type dominated Buddhist art. The Buddha was invariably shown wearing a monk's robe (*saṅghāṭī*) and with the characteristic marks of a great man (*mahāpuruṣa lakṣaṇas*): a protuberance on the head (*uṣṇīṣa*), a tuft of hair between the eyebrows (*ūrṇā*), clockwise-curling hair and webbed fingers and toes. Although they are not all shown in art, 32 major and 64 minor signs of the Buddha are prescribed. The Buddha is represented standing, seated or reclining, the latter only in scenes of the Great Demise. Standing and seated Buddhas exist either as independent images or as principal figures on panels. Five gestures (*mudrās*), some emblematic and some episodic, are common: fearlessness (*abhaya mudrā*), bestowing boons (*varada mudrā*), meditation (*dhyāna mudrā*), touching the earth (*bhūmisparśa mudrā*; see fig. 7) and turning the Wheel of Law. The Buddha is usually shown seated either on a lotus or on a pedestal, the dado of which is often marked with a wheel flanked by a pair of deer. Mostly he sits with crossed legs, a posture that came to be known as adamantine (*vajraparyaṅka*). Occasionally, he is shown sitting with one leg placed across the other thigh (*sattvaparyaṅk āsana*) or with both legs hanging down (*bhadrāsana*). He occasionally holds a begging bowl and, sometimes, the end of his garment in his left hand. Normally, images of the Buddha are unornamented, though in eastern Indian art of the medieval period, crowned, bejewelled images evolved.

Each of the six Buddhas who preceded Gautama—Buddha Vipashvi, Shikhi, Vishvabhu, Krakuchchhanda, Kanakamuni and Kashyapa—is associated with a specific tree. Five of these can be seen at Bharhut, where they are identified by inscriptions. The eighth, or future, Buddha, Maitreya, presently resides in the heaven of contentment (*tuṣita*) as a *bodhisattva*. Several or all of the eight Buddhas may be depicted as a group.

(ii) Bodhisattvas. As Mahayana Buddhism evolved, the concept of the *bodhisattva* became more common, and as a result, all male divinities other than Buddhas came to be known as *bodhisattvas* (see fig. 8; see also fig. 197 below). Four of them—Vajrapani, Avalokiteshvara, Manjushri and Maitreya—were accorded independent status, while others were explained as manifestations or associates of these four. Of the others, several are mentioned, with their iconographic characteristics, in the *Sădhanamălă* ('Series of devotional concepts'; *c.* 1165) and the *Nispannayogăvalī* ('Principles of meditative visualization') of the Buddhist monk Abhayakaragupta (*c.* 12th century). Not all of the *bodhisattvas* are represented in art, however. Vajrapani, holding a thunderbolt (*vajra*), appears even in early Buddhist art as an attendant of the Buddha. He also appears independently but has no emanatory forms. Maitreya also has no emanatory forms. In early iconography he is shown with a water vessel and rosary or in the gesture of fearlessness (*abhaya mudră*) with a small stupa incorporated in his headdress or hair (see fig. 158 below). In later images he holds a flower and turns the Wheel of Law. Manjushri, who personifies wisdom, is usually associated

7. *Seated Buddha*, terracotta plaque, h. 150 mm, from Bodhgaya, eastern India, *c.* 9th century AD (London, British Museum)

with a book, and a miniature figure of the *jina* Akshobhya is shown in his headdress (*see* §(iii) below). Manjushri has several emanatory forms, each of which follows his basic iconic features, except that some show the *jina* Amitabha in his headdress. Manjushri's prominent emanatory forms are: Manjughosha (seated on lion, with the teaching gesture (*dharmacakra mudră*), with Sudhanakumara and Yamantaka, the conqueror of death, as attendants); Manjuvara (similar to Manjughosha but without attendant figures); Siddhaikavira with the boon-giving gesture (*varada mudră*), with Akshobhya in headdress, holding a blue lotus); Vajrananga (usually standing, with six arms, with Akshobhya in headdress); Vagishvara (seated on a lion with one leg hanging down, holding a lotus in the left hand); Manjukumara (three heads, six arms); Manjuvajra (similar to Manjukumara but usually embracing a female consort); Arapachana (accompanied by four *yakṣa/yakṣīs*, Jvalinikumara, Chandraprabha, Keshini and Upakeshini, holding a sword and book); Vadirat (seated on tiger, with the teaching gesture); Namasangiti (three heads, four arms); and Dharmadhatuvagishvara (four heads, eight arms, with Amitabha in headdress).

The *bodhisattva* Avalokiteshvara, also known as Padmapani because he holds a lotus, is also represented in early Buddhist art (see fig. 240 below). He became the most popular of the *bodhisattvas* because he deferred his

8. *Standing Bodhisattva*, schist, h. 1.09 m, from Gandhara, late 2nd century AD (Boston, MA, Museum of Fine Arts)

acceptance of *nirvāṇa* (enlightenment) until all sentient beings had qualified for it. He thus became the apotheosis of mercy (*karuṇā*). The lotus he holds symbolizes the tenderness of his heart. The *jina* Amitabha in his headdress appears to be the other distinguishing feature of his iconography. The most important of his manifestations is a form (the Shadakshari) consisting of Lokeshvara flanked by Manidhara and Mahavidya, each with his/her principal pair of hands palm-to-palm and close to the chest (*añjali mudrā*) and with the other right and left hands holding a rosary and a book respectively. This trio articulates the six-syllabled *mantra* '*Oṁ maṇipadme huṁ*' ('The jewel is in the lotus') and represents the Buddhist Trinity of Master, Law and Community of monks.

The other important manifestations of Avalokiteshvara are Simhanada (seated on lion, with a trident entwined with a snake, and a sword on a lotus, shown to right and left); Khasarpana (right hand in the *varada mudrā* (boon-giving gesture), showering ambrosia that is being drunk by the insatiable spirit Suchimukha, attended by his usual companions Tara, Sudhanakumara, Bhrikuti and Hayagriva, left hand holding a lotus); Lokanatha (*varada mudrā* form, Amitabha on crown, often accompanied by eight other *bodhisattvas*, four minor goddesses and four gate-keeping goddesses); Nilakantha (seated in meditation, two snakes to right and left, holding a skull-cup on his lap); Halahala (three heads, six arms, has female consort); and Vajradharma (seated on peacock, holding a lotus in the left hand and unfolding its petals with the right hand).

(iii) Jinas. With the introduction in the 6th century AD or earlier of Vajrayana or Tantric Buddhism, the pantheon expanded. At the apex of this system were the Adi Buddha (also known as Vajradhara) and Adi Prajna, the primordial parents of all divinities. A female complement (*prajñā*) was attached to each god. The Adi Buddha and Adi Prajna generated the five spiritual offspring (*pañcajina*, or *pañca-Buddhas*): Vairochana, Akshobhya, Amitabha, Ratnasambhava and Amoghasiddhi. They represented the material elements—air, water, ether, fire and earth—and the cosmic ones (*skandhas*)—form (*rūpa*), sensation (*vedanā*), cognition (*saṁjñā*), conformation (*saṁskāra*) and consciousness (*vijñāna*). While not actively participating in the process of creation, they were believed to control the system through spiritual *bodhisattvas* and past Buddhas and acted as the sires or presiding lords (*kuleśas*) of all other deities. A combination of the five was conceived as the sixth *jina*, Vajrasattva, who presided over them. The iconographic characteristics of the *jinas* are as follows: Vairochana (with a peacock as mount, with the *dhyāna mudrā* (meditation gesture), holding a lotus); Akshobhya (with an elephant as mount, with the *bhūmisparśa mudrā* (touching the earth gesture), holding a thunderbolt); Amitabha (with a dragon as mount, with the *dharmacakra mudrā* (turning the Wheel of Law)); Ratnasambhava (with a lion as mount, with the *varada mudrā* (boon-bestowing gesture), holding a jewel); and Amoghasiddhi (with a *garuḍa* as mount, with the *abhaya mudrā* (fearlessness gesture), holding a ritual instrument shaped like a double thunderbolt (*viśvavajra*)). Each *jina* is a different colour and corresponds to a direction (white/centre, blue/east, red/west, yellow-/south and green/north respectively).

Although Buddhist deities, by and large, can be grouped into five families (*kulas*), each presided over by a *jina*, many of them seem to be affiliated with more than one *jina*. Thus any classification based strictly on family relationships is not reliable.

(iv) The Goddess. The supreme goddess of Buddhism is the saviour Tara, the consort of Avalokiteshvara (see fig. 9). In one of her well-known manifestations she is known as the Quintessential Wisdom (Prajnaparamita), while in another form she is the goddess of wealth (Vasudhara). These three forms resemble in concept, and

9. *?Tara Enthroned*, copper alloy, h. 381 mm, from Madhya Pradesh, *c.* 800 AD (Los Angeles, CA, County Museum of Art)

to an extent in iconography, the three prime manifestations of the supreme Goddess of Hinduism, Durga (saviour from perils), Sarasvati (goddess of learning) and Lakshmi (goddess of fortune; *see* §1(v) above). The other important goddesses of Buddhism are Marichi (female version of the Hindu sun god, often shown with a sow's face and riding a chariot drawn by seven pigs); Parnasabari (deified, leaf-clad woman of the Sabara tribe); Kurukulla (goddess of enchantment, often shown shooting a bow and arrow); Chunda (often with four arms, principal hands in *dhyăna mudră*, others holding a rosary or a book, or often with one hand in *varada mudră*); Ushnishavijaya (usually four heads, eight arms, with a stupa in her headdress); Vajragandhari (six heads, twelve arms); Vajravarahi (dancing consort of Heruka, with a sow's face on one side, holding a skull-cup); and Aparajita (dancing on the figure of Ganesha, with the *capetadāna mudră*, gesture of slapping the face of an adversary). All these goddesses have formal variants.

(v) Other deities. Numerous male deities are also known, each having a number of iconographic variants. The most important of the deities are Heruka (known as Hevajra or Samvara when shown in association with his female counterpart, with two, four, six or sixteen arms); Hayagriva (has a horse's head projecting from his own, pot-belly, fierce expression); Yamari (rides or tramples on a buffalo, the mount of Yama, the god of death); Jambhala (god of wealth, usually holds mongoose vomiting treasures); and Kalachakra (four heads, twenty-four arms, fierce expression, represents passing time).

A number of group deities are also known, the most important of whom are the five protectresses (*pañcarakṣās*): Mahapratisara, Mahasahasrapramardini, Mahamayuri, Mahasitavati and Mahamantranusarini. They are usually shown as a group, particularly in manuscript illuminations. However, their independent forms are known from both texts and actual images. Other groups include the 10 directional deities, 4 door-keeping goddesses, 12 goddesses of excellence, 10 goddesses of the spheres and 12 goddesses of mystic spells. Many other deities, often borrowed from the Hindu repertory or transformed with sectarian overtones, were introduced. The concept of the *maṇḍala* (mystic diagram providing spatial definitions of the deities) also added new dimensions to Buddhist iconography.

The themes, motifs and imagery of Buddhist iconography can be more clearly understood if they are studied in the light of such texts as the *Guhyasamăja tantra* ('The discovery of hidden things'; *c.* 4th century AD); the *Sādhanamălă*, *Niṣpannayogăvalī* and *Vajrăvalī* ('Series of inviolable spells') of the 11th- or 12th-century author Abhayakaragupta, and the *Dharmakoṣa-Saṁgraha* ('Collection of the core of the norms') of Amritananda (*c.* 19th century).

See also §I, 7(ii) above.

BIBLIOGRAPHY

GENERAL

A. Foucher: *Etude sur l'iconographie bouddhique de l'Inde*, 2 vols (Paris, 1900–05)
A. Getty: *The Gods of Northern Buddhism* (Oxford, 1914, 2/1928)
B. Bhattacharya: *The Indian Buddhist Iconography* (Calcutta, 1924, 2/1968)
N. K. Bhattasali: *Iconography of Buddhist and Brahmanical Sculptures in the Dacca Museum* (Dhaka, 1929)
B. Bhattacharya, ed.: *Guhyasamăja-Tantra* (Baroda, 1931)
A. K. Coomaraswamy: *Elements of Buddhist Iconography* (Cambridge, MA, 1935)
W. E. Clark: *Two Lamaistic Pantheons*, 2 vols (Cambridge, MA, 1937)
P. C. Bagchi: *Studies in the Tantras*, i (Calcutta, 1939)
A. K. Gordon: *The Iconography of Tibetan Lamaism* (New York, 1939, rev. Tokyo, 1959)
B. Bhattacharya, ed.: *Niṣpannayogăvalī of Mahapandita Abhayakaragupta* (Baroda, 1949)
S. B. Dasgupta: *An Introduction to Tāntric Buddhism* (Calcutta, 1950)
D. L. Snellgrove: *Buddhist Himalayas* (Oxford, 1957)
——: *The Hevajra Tantra: A Critical Study*, 2 vols (Oxford, 1959)
M.-T. de Mallmann: 'Divinités hindoues dans le tantrisme bouddhique', *A. Asiatiques*, x (1964), pp. 67–86
B. Bhattacharya, ed.: *Sădhanamălă*, 2 vols (Baroda, 1968)
D. C. Bhattacharyya with P. Pal: *The Astral Divinities of Nepal* (Varanasi, 1969)
D. Mitra: *Buddhist Monuments* (Calcutta, 1971)
T. Tulku: *The Sacred Art of Tibet* (Berkeley, 1972)
D. C. Bhattacharyya: *Tāntric Buddhist Iconographic Sources* (New Delhi, 1974)
M.-T. de Mallmann: *Introduction à l'iconographie du tantrisme bouddhique* (Paris, 1975)
B. Sahai: *Iconography of Minor Hindu and Buddhist Deities* (New Delhi, 1975)
A. Bharati: *The Tāntric Tradition* (Bombay, 1976)
G. Liebert: *Iconographic Dictionary of the Indian Religions* (Leiden, 1976)
S. K. Saraswati: *Tantrayāna Art: An Album* (Calcutta, 1977)
D. C. Bhattacharyya: *Studies in Buddhist Iconography* (New Delhi, 1978)
M. Khanna: *Yantra: The Tāntric Symbol of Cosmic Unity* (London, 1979)
M. Ghosh: *Development of Buddhist Iconography in Eastern India* (New Delhi, 1980)
D. C. Bhattacharyya: 'The Vajrăvalīnăma-Mandalopăyikă of Abhayăkaragupta', *Tantric and Taoist Studies in Honour of R. A. Stein*, ed. M. Strickmann, Mélanges chinois et bouddhiques, 1/xx (Brussels, 1981), pp. 70–95
Buddhism: Art and Faith (exh. cat. by W. Zwalf, London, BM, 1985)
L. Chandra: *Buddhist Iconography of Tibet*, 2 vols (Kyoto, 1986)
S. Huntington: 'Early Buddhist Art and the Theory of Aniconism', *A. J.* [New York], xlix/4 (1990), pp. 401–8

THE BUDDHA AND BODHISATTVAS

E. B. Cowell: *The Jātaka, or the Stories of the Buddha's Birth*, 6 vols (Cambridge, 1895–1913)
M.-T. de Mallmann: *Introduction à l'étude d'Avalokitecvara* (Paris, 1948)
E. J. Thomas: *The Life of the Buddha as Legend and History* (London, 1949)
M.-T. de Mallmann: *Etude iconographique sur Mañjuśrī* (Paris, 1964)
B. Rowland: *The Evolution of the Buddha Image* (New York, 1968)
S. Beyer: *The Cult of Tără* (Berkeley and Los Angeles, 1978)
D. L. Snellgrove, ed.: *The Image of the Buddha* (Tokyo, 1978)
R. Parimoo: *Life of Buddha in Indian Sculpture: Ashṭa-mahă-pratihărya* (New Delhi, 1982)
Light of Asia: Buddha Sakyamuni in Asian Art (exh. cat. by P. Pal, Los Angeles, CA, Co. Mus. A., 1984)

DIPAK CHANDRA BHATTACHARYYA

3. JAINA. Said to have been propounded by Rishabhanatha, the first *tīrthaṅkara* (literally 'the ford maker'), JAINISM does not admit of a godhead and thus theoretically has no need for images, though Jaina religious images do exist. Differences in interpretation, especially regarding the wearing of clothing by monks, resulted in a schism into two main branches, the Shvetambaras ('white-robed ones') and the Digambaras ('sky-clad (or naked) ones'), at some point between the 5th and 8th centuries AD. Since *tīrthaṅkaras* obtain the highest knowledge after discarding all worldly attachments, including clothes, images created before the schism are nude. Afterwards, images worshipped by the Shvetambara show the figure semi-clad, while icons of the Digambara sect show no drapery.

Rishabhanatha (see fig. 10) was succeeded by 23 other *tīrthaṅkaras*, the last two of whom, Parshvanatha and Mahavira Varddhamana, lived in the 7th or 6th century BC. All of these masters were liberated souls who had attained perfection (*siddhas*) and conquered vice (*jinas*). Images of them exist in two principal postures: seated with crossed legs in the so-called 'lotus position' (*padmāsana*) and standing at ease with straight arms and legs (*kāyotsarga*). An image of a master can be recognized by the attributes with which he is shown (see fig. 11).

Early Jaina literary traditions claim that a wooden portrait sculpture of Mahavira Varddhamana meditating, wearing a crown, ornaments and a loincloth, was fashioned

10. *Jaina tīrthaṅkara Rishabhanatha*, from Chandravati near Mt Abu, *c*. 10th century AD (Zurich, Museum Rietberg)

Tīrthaṅkara	**Attribute**
Rishabhanatha	bull
Ajitanatha	elephant
Sambhavanatha	horse
Abhinandana	monkey
Sumatinatha	*S*/curlew; *D*/red goose
Padmaprabha	red lotus
Suparshva	swastika
Chandraprabha	crescent moon
Pushpadanta/Suvidhinatha	crocodile
Shitalanatha	*S*/*śrīvatsa* (auspicious mark on chest); *D*/*śrīvṛkṣa* (sacred tree) or swastika
Shreyamsanatha	rhinoceros
Vaspujya	buffalo
Vimalanatha	boar
Anantanatha	*S*/falcon; *D*/bear
Dharmanatha	thunderbolt
Shantinatha	deer
Kunthunatha	goat
Aranatha	*S*/*nandyāvarta* diagram; *D*/fish
Mallinatha	water jar
Munisuvrata	tortoise
Naminatha	blue lotus
Neminatha	conch
Parshvanatha	snake
Mahavira	lion

11. The 14 *tīrthaṅkaras* and their attributes; *S* and *D* refer to the two Jaina sects, the Shvetambaras and the Digambaras

during his lifetime. All later images carved or cast in imitation of this portrait were worshipped as images of 'the master when he was alive' (*jīvantaswāmī*). Regular worship in shrines of images of the master as conqueror of vice started about a century or two after Mahavira, however. That image worship may have existed in the 3rd century BC is attested by the highly polished torso and legs of a standing nude figure, perhaps a *tīrthaṅkara*, found during the excavations of a temple site at Lohanipur near Patnfa. Worship of such images reminded the believer of the highest qualities of the soul (*atman*) freed from defilement by action (*karma*); at least this was the explanation advanced in support of image-worship.

Since *tīrthaṅkaras*, freed from all worldly attachments, could not respond to worshippers' pleas for favours, lesser divinities were introduced to perform this function. These were of course subordinated to, and made attendants of, the highest divinity (*devādhideva*). Known as protectors of the church and faith (*śāsanadevatās*) or as nature deities (*yakṣas*/*yakṣīs*), many were borrowed from the Brahmanical pantheon and ancient tree-spirit cults, though with changed names or attributes (*see* §I, 7(ii) above). For example, worship of Vasudeva-Krishna is mentioned in the Jaina canons as having existed during Mahavira's lifetime. Both worship and the imagery of *tīrthaṅkaras* seem to have been influenced by Vasudeva worship and the tree-spirit cults.

To each *tīrthaṅkara* was assigned a *yakṣa* and a *yakṣī* who protected his community of monks and his system of spiritual training. Thus 24 spirits of each sex evolved. Of the 24 *tīrthaṅkaras*, Rishabhanatha, Neminatha, Parshvanatha and Mahavira, along with their female spirit-attendants Chakreshvari, Ambika, Padmavati and Siddhayika, are noteworthy as having been especially popular in Jaina worship.

The Jainas believe in ever-recurring cycles of ages (*ārās*) of human progress and decline (*utsarpiṇī*, *avasarpiṇī*). In each such cycle 24 *tīrthaṅkaras* are born. Sometimes Jainas worship groups of 24 or 72 masters (of past, present and future cycles) or, in single images, groups of two, three, five, seven, eight, eleven or more.

Over time the Jainas came to believe in 16 principal mystical charms (*vidyās*), each of which had its own presiding deity (*vidyādevī*). The 16 principal ones (*mahāvidyās*) existed even before the 8th century, when the *yakṣas* and *yakṣīs* entered the repertory.

Jaina worship has several elements in common with Brahmanical Hinduism. Some were borrowed from the common ancient heritage and some from Brahmanical ritual and mythology. The worship of auspicious symbols—such as the swastika, auspicious mark on the chest, full vase (*pūrṇa kumbha*), mirror and pair of fish (*matsya yuama*)—tree worship and so on are common to both Hinduism and Jainism. The worship of stone plaques (*śilāpaṭas*), an ancient Indian practice, was incorporated into Jaina worship, as can be seen in the *āyāgapaṭas* (votive tablets) of the Kushana period from MATHURA. The Jainas also worship Sarasvati, the goddess of learning well known from Vedic times, who is also called Shrutadevata by the Jainas. Images are also found of Sri-Lakshmi, the goddess of beauty and abundance; of Kubera, the lord of riches (worshipped by the Jainas as the *yakṣa* Sarvanubhuti), and of the mother goddess, worshipped as the *yakṣī* Ambika. The guardians of the directions (*dikpālas*) find a place on the walls of Jaina shrines and in their rituals. The nine planetary deities (*navagrahas*) are shown either at the sides of the *tīrthaṅkara* (in eastern India) or on the pedestals beneath him (in western India). In the medieval period the Hindu gods Kshetrapala and Ganesha also came to be worshipped. Mahishasuramardini, the terrifying Hindu form of Durga, was venerated as Sachchikadevi by the Jainas of Osian and, later, in western India.

Images of Bahubali, the brother of Rishabhanatha, include a colossal image at SRAVANA BELGOLA (see fig. 220 below). Bahubali renounced the world and stood motionless in deep meditation for many years. Ant hills grew around his legs, snakes dwelling in them crawled over his body, and creepers entwined his hands and feet before he ultimately obtained salvation. Images of Bahubali are particularly popular in worship among Digambara Jainas.

The Jainas also revere several symbols, though this practice is generally secondary to those described above. Representations of the eight auspicious marks (*aṣṭamaṅgalas*) and of dreams seen by a *tīrthaṅkara*'s mother can be found in Jaina shrines, as well as plaques mapping different pilgrimage places. Stupa worship, which occurred during the early centuries AD at Mathura, lost favour, although stones and structures erected in memory of saints and laypeople who died by fasting are still popular, especially in south India (see Shah, 1955, pp. 39–130).

Numerous illustrated manuscripts of Jaina texts were produced (*see* §V, 3(ii)(a) below). These were often given to Jaina temples, where they were stored in libraries (*bhaṇḍāras*). Among the most frequently illustrated are the *Kaepa sūtra*, a text on the lives of Mahavira and other *tīrthaṅkaras*, and the *Kālakācaryakathā*, the story of the Jaina monk Kalaka.

See also §1 above and HINDUISM, §I.

BIBLIOGRAPHY

B. C. Bhattacharyya: *Jaina Iconography* (Lahore, 1939; rev. Delhi, 2/1974)
U. P. Shah: *Studies in Jaina Art* (Varanasi, 1955)
A. Ghosh: *Jaina Art and Architecture*, 3 vols (New Delhi, 1974–5)
M. Chandra and U. P. Shah: *New Documents of Jaina Painting* (Bombay, 1975)
J. Jain and E. Fischer: *Jaina Iconography*, 2 vols (Leiden, 1978)
U. P. Shah: *Treasures of Jaina Bhandaras* (Ahmadabad, 1978)
S. Doshi: *Masterpieces of Jain Painting* (Bombay, 1985)
U. P. Shah: *Jaina rūpamandana* [Jaina iconography] (New Delhi, 1987)

U. P. SHAH

4. EPIC THEMES. The two Indian epics, the *Rāmāyaṇa* and the *Mahābhārata*, have had tremendous influence on Indian culture. Both texts have distinct didactic messages based in the Vaishnava cult of Hinduism (*see* HINDUISM, §I). The *Rāmāyaṇa*, attributed to the poet Valmiki, is the story of Rama—the eighth incarnation of the Hindu god Vishnu (*see* §1(iii) above)—who, as the eldest son of Dasharatha, the king of Ayodhya (Uttar Pradesh), destroyed Ravana, the demonic king of Lanka (possibly present-day Sri Lanka; see fig. 277 below), and established the norms of righteousness. The first and last of the seven books (*kaṇḍas*) of the *Rāmāyaṇa* have been identified as later interpolations. The *Mahābhārata*, by contrast, is a historical narrative based on a series of controversial hereditary claims sustained by court intrigues. These intrigues culminated in an 18-day-long civil war fought by the Kauravas and the Pandavas, the two factions of the Bharata family, at the battlefield of Kurukshetra. Krishna, another of Vishnu's incarnations, plays a dominant role in the story. Although the composer of the *Mahābhārata* is traditionally thought to have been Vedavyasa, it was enlarged in transmission; its present version, consisting of 100,000 verses, is sometimes attributed to the sage Vaishampayana. Consisting of 18 progressive segments (*parvas*) plus an appendix, the *Harivaṁśa*, the *Mahābhārata* appears to have been written between the 4th century BC and the 4th century AD.

The places at which these epics were composed cannot be ascertained, as both have regional and sectarian versions. The 1st-century AD Buddhist *Daśaratha jātaka* ('Story of Dasharatha') and the Jaina *Vasudevahindī* ('Wanderings of Vishnu') by the 6th-century author Sanghadasa are excerpted versions of the Rama story. The *Yogavāsiṣṭha Rāmāyaṇa*, a long poetic dialogue between Rama and a Vedic sage, is the Vedantic (metaphysical) supplement to Valmiki's narrative. The 11th-century Jaina *Pampā Rāmāyaṇa*, based on another Jaina text, Vimala Suri's *Paumacariya* ('History of Padma' (i.e. Rama)), became popular in Karnataka. The 10th–12th-century Tamil epic by Kamban, the *Rāmāvatāra* ('Incarnation of Rama'), became popular there and in Tamil Nadu, while the 17th-century *Rāmacaritamānasa* ('Lake of the deeds of Rama') by Tulasidasa reached the hearts of countless thousands, particularly in north India. The Bengali versions of the *Rāmāyaṇa* by Krittivasa Ojha (17th century) and of the *Mahābhārata* by Kashirama Dasa (18th century) are examples of similar adaptations in regional languages. Further, a number of playwrights and poets of ancient India—Bhasa (possibly as early as the 2nd century BC), Kalidasa (*c.* 4th century AD), Bhartrihari (*c.* 7th century), Magha, Bhavabhuti and Bhattanarayana (all *c.* 8th century)—employed in their works themes derived from the epics.

The *Rāmāyaṇa* figures more frequently than the *Mahābhārata* in the visual arts, perhaps due to its linear narrative (see fig. 12). There are no instances in pre-medieval Indian art of representations of themes from the core of the *Mahābhārata*; these appear only in later miniature painting. Early visual evidence of the *Mahābhārata* pertains mostly to subsidiary episodes, such as the confrontation between the hero Arjuna and the god Shiva in the guise of a Kirata—a mountain aboriginal—prior to bestowing his 'irresistible weapon' (*pāśupatāstra*) on Arjuna. This episode is interpreted in poetic form in the 6th-century *Kirātārjunīya* ('Combat between Arjuna and a Kirata') of Bharavi.

Sculptural depictions of well-known episodes of the *Rāmāyaṇa* exist from about the 4th century. A large number of terracotta plaques from Sravasti and from Chandraketugarh (Bengal) show scenes from the *Rāmāyaṇa*, and as many as ten panels from the earliest temple at DEOGARH pertain to this epic. Panels depicting various episodes also exist from temples at NACHNA, Badami, Aihole, PATTADAKAL, Ellora (*see* ELLORA, §2), Paharpur, Bhubaneshwar, Khajuraho, Halebid, Belur and many other sites throughout India. The episodes usually selected for depiction include Rama, his brother Lakshmana and his wife Sita sitting in the forest hermitage or moving through the forest; the attempt by Ravana's sister, Shurpanakha, to entice Lakshmana; Ravana's kidnapping of Sita, his fight with the bird Jatayu, the fight between the brothers Bali and Sugriva and the killing of the former by Rama; Rama and Lakshmana's battle with Ravana's militant entourage; various feats and pranks of Hanuman, Sugriva's minister and general; and Rama's coronation following his exile.

Depictions of themes from the *Rāmāyaṇa* in painting are more elaborate. Important examples include the 18th-century murals with Tamil inscriptions in the temple at Alakarkoyil, near Madurai (*see* §V, 4(vii) below). In iconography and style they can be compared with 16th-century miniatures preserved in the Sarasvati Bahal Library, Thanjavur. A particularly profusely illustrated manuscript of the 17th-century *Rāmacaritamānasa* was executed at Mahishadal in Midnapore during the 18th century (U. Calcutta, Asutosh Mus. Ind. A.). There are several well-known Pahari and Rajasthani sets of *Rāmāyaṇa* paintings. The Shangri *Rāmāyaṇa*, apparently of the 18th century, is famous for its narrative details and visual charm (dispersed 1961; *see* §V, 4(iv)(b) below). The Guler set of the same period by PANDIT SEU (Chandigarh, Govt Mus. & A.G.) is of equal importance. A unique set of *Rāmāyaṇa* drawings by the Kashmiri painter Sudarshana is dated 1816 (Varanasi, Banaras Hindu U., Bharat Kala Bhavan). Of the *Rāmāyaṇa* paintings of the Rajasthani school, the Mewar versions of the various books of the celebrated *Arśa Rāmāyaṇa*, executed in and around Udaipur during the reign of Rana Jagat Singh I (*reg* 1628–52) and his successor Rana Raj Singh I (*reg* 1652–80), are

12. School of Sahibdin: page from the second book of the *Rāmāyaṇa* (detail), 210×385 mm (page size), from Mewar (?Chittaurgarh), 1650 (London, British Library)

notable. Most of these were painted by Sahibdin (*fl* 1628–55) and the contemporary Mewar painter Manohar. Five such sets are now preserved (London, BL, e.g. Add. MS. 15296–97; Bombay, Prince of Wales Mus.), as is an incomplete set of one of the books, the *Sundarakāṇḍa* ('Beautiful book'; London, BL, Orient. & India Office Lib., Skt MS. 3621). Malwa sets also exist. The antecedents for all of these examples come from the period of the Mughal emperor Akbar (*reg* 1556–1605), who had the epic translated into Persian. Of the two best-known Akbar-period illustrated manuscripts, one is an imperial copy (Jaipur, Maharaja Sawai Man Singh II Mus., MS. 07.271; *see* §VI, 4(i)(b) below) and the other a sub-imperial work (Washington, DC, Freer, MS. 07.271; *see* §V, 4(ii) below).

Visual representations of themes from the *Mahābhārata* are comparatively few, and the early examples do not pertain to the principal story. Rather, supplementary episodes such as the *Kṛṣṇalīlā* ('Divine act of Krishna') or *Kirātārjunīya* are depicted in early Indian sculpture and painting. An important illustrated version of the *Āraṇyaka parva* ('Book of the forest') dated 1516 survives (Bombay, Asiat. Soc.). A few Pahari sets of *Mahābhārata* paintings are also known, but even in these, the artists only chose certain episodes for representation. Some sets are restricted to the *Bhagavadgītā*, a section of the *Mahābhārata* concerned with the relationship between philosophy and action, set out in a dialogue between its two protagonists, Krishna and Arjuna. Painters also appear to have been fascinated by the story of the king Nala and his lover Damayanti. The war sequences of the *Mahābhārata* seem to have been of great interest to Mughal painters, as evidenced by the number and treatment of battle scenes in the celebrated Jaipur *Razmnāma* ('Book of wars'; Maharaja Sawai Man Singh II Mus., MS. AG. 1683–1850), the Persian version of the *Mahābhārata* illustrated copiously by painters in the court of Akbar.

Some of the major characters of both epics—Rama, Lakshmana, Sita, Hanuman, Arjuna, Krishna and Balarama—were frequently represented alone or in pairs or trios. Each of them can be distinguished by characteristics described in such iconographic texts as the *Pratimālakṣaṇa* of the *Viṣṇudharmottara* ('Virtuous laws of Vishnu'), though regional and cultic conventions often influenced such representations.

BIBLIOGRAPHY

W. G. Archer: *Indian Paintings from the Punjab Hills: A Survey and History of Pahari Miniature Painting*, 2 vols (London and New York, 1973)
B. N. Goswamy: *Pahari Paintings of the Nala-Damayantī Theme* (New Delhi, 1975)
K. Vatsyayan: *Rāmāyaṇa in the Arts of Asia* (New Delhi, 1975)
S. K. Chatterjee: *The Rāmāyaṇa, Its Character, Genesis, History and Exodus: A Résumé* (Calcutta, 1978)
P. Banerjee: *Rāma in Indian Literature, Art and Thought* (Delhi, 1986)
Manuscript Paintings from the Ramayana (exh. cat. by N. Poovaya-Smith, J. P. Losty and J. Bevan, Bradford, A. Gals & Museums, 1989)
R. Craven, ed.: *Ramayana Pahari Paintings* (Bombay, 1990)

5. OTHER STORIES AND CYCLES. Some texts, while associated with particular religions, have attained general (non-sectarian) acceptance. Among these are the *Pañca tantra* (a compendium of didactic folk stories compiled before the 6th century AD, apparently by Vishnusharma), the *Hitopadeśa* (the version of the *Pañca tantra* composed by Narayana, probably in the 11th century) and the celebrated *Hamzānāma* (the adventures of Amir Hamza, uncle of the Prophet Muhammad), which was illustrated by the court artists of the Mughal emperor Akbar (*see* §VI, 5(i)(b) below).

Several mythological and poetic texts were extensively illustrated with miniature paintings in later periods. The *Naiṣadhacarita* of Shriharsha (*c.* 12th century) is the love story of Prince Nala and Damayanti. The *Meghadūta* ('Cloud messenger') of Kalidasa (*c.* 5th century AD) describes the commissioning of the clouds to convey messages for a forlorn lover. The *Caurapañcāśikā* by Bilhana (*c.* 11th century), which deals with the poet's love for a princess, was illustrated in several sets of illuminations (*see* §VI, 4(ii)(c) below). The *Candāyana*, a popular north Indian Sufi romance composed by Da'ud *c.* 1370, is another important illustrated text (*see* §VI, 4(ii)(f) below). The *Gīta Govinda* (the love story of Krishna and Radha) by Jayadeva (*c.* 12th century) and the *Bālagopālastūti* ('Glorification of the child Krishna') also provided themes of romance and adventure for Indian artists. No illustrated version of any of these texts survives from before the 15th century. Two 16th-century poetic texts, *Rasamanjari* and *Rasikapriya* by Bhanudatta, discuss the various types of heroes (*nāyaka*s) and heroines (*nāyikā*s), and the relevance of sentiments (*rasa*s) and moods (*bhava*s) in the expression of their love.

Sets and cycles of paintings were frequently produced—including, for example, sets of the categories of heroes and heroines. There were thought to be four types of heroes: gentle and inspiring (*dhīrodātta*), quiet and sublime (*dhīrapraśānta*), sensitive and introspective (*dhīralalita*) and haughty (*dhīroddhṛita*). Heroines were also classified under types and sub-types, of which eight were especially popular: a woman whose husband was away on a temporary sojourn (*proṣitabhartṛikā*), an ambivalent woman (*khaṇḍitā*), a nervous woman (*utkaṇṭhitā*), a woman who had quarrelled with her husband (*kalahāntaritā*), a woman whose husband had committed adultery (*vipralabdhā*), a woman awaiting her husband, having been dressed according to his wishes (*vāsakasajjā*), a woman with an independent personality (*svādhinapatikā*) and a woman going to meet her lover (*abhisārikā*; *see* §VI, 5(iii)(b) below).

Rāgamālā cycles combine the arts of painting and music, *rāgamālā* meaning a garland of either colours or musical notes. In the visual arts each note has a specific colour and other iconographic features. Originally, there were 6 masculine notes (*rāga*s) and 36 feminine variations on the *rāga*s (*rāgiṇī*s). Paintings of these are contained in numerous well-known sets.

Another important cycle in miniature painting relates to the 12 months of the year (*bārahmāsa*). Such cycles depict seasonal changes in nature as well as corresponding human emotional and spiritual transformations. The 12 months, beginning with March–April, are Chaitra, Vaishakha, Jyaishtha, Ashadha, Shravana, Bhadrapada or Praushthapada, Ashvina or Ashvayuja, Kartika, Margashirsha or Agrahayana, Pausha or Taisha, Magha and Phalguna. (In earlier times the following names were used: Madhu, Madhava, Shukra, Shuci, Nabhas, Nabhasya, Isha, Urja, Sahas, Sahasya, Tapas and Tapasya.) A variant of this theme represents the so-called six seasons (*ṣaḍṛtu*), each comprised of two months. The six are Vasanta (spring, March–May), Grishma (summer, May–July), Varsha (rainy season, July–September), Sharad (autumn, September–November), Hemanta (winter, November–January) and Shishira (cool season, January–March). Spring is known as the king of the seasons (*ṛturāa*). Such celebrations of nature also occur in literature, as in Kalidasa's *Ṛtusaṁhāra* ('Essence of the seasons').

BIBLIOGRAPHY

K. N. Dikshit: *Excavations at Paharpur, Bengal*, Mem. Archaeol. Surv. India, lv (Delhi, 1938)

W. Waldschmidt and R. Waldschmidt: *Miniatures of Musical Inspiration in the Collection of the Berlin Museum of Indian Art*, 2 vols (Wiesbaden, 1967; Berlin, 1975)

E. Ebeling: *Ragamala Painting* (Basle, 1973)

A. Dahmen-Dallapiccola: *Ragamala-Miniaturen von 1475 bis 1700* (Wiesbaden, 1975)

V. P. Dwivedi: *Barahmasa* (Delhi, 1980)

D. C. Bhattacharyya: *Medieval Indian Sculpture in the Government Museum and Art Gallery, Chandigarli* (Chandigarli, 1981)

6. Erotic and genre themes. Sensuality marks a large number of important themes in Indian art, including bacchanalian motifs, garland-bearing cupids and *mithuna* images. The *mithuna* motif represents an amorous couple (see fig. 13), shown standing or seated, often in an embrace. Such images can be seen throughout Indian art. The couple is often represented holding wine cups and sometimes in the act of drinking (*madhupāna*). Sometimes the female figure is shown with a parrot, which is meant to suggest her sensuous nature; her voluptuous physique expresses the sensuality of the *mithuna* motif. In some examples the couple is shown in sexual union. The *Kāma sūtra*, a treatise on love and sexuality by Vatsyayana (*c.* 2nd century AD), deals extensively with sexual philosophy and practice. Many temple sculptures from KOṆARAK, KHAJURAHO, Bhubaneshvar and other sites appear to illustrate the precepts of the *Kāma sūtra* and later texts on erotics. Themes of sex and fertility occur even in objects of the 2nd millennium BC from the Indus civilization, including female figures with trees issuing from their bodies. Such forms seem to have been the prototypes for erotic themes in Indian art of later periods.

Genre themes, also important in both sculpture and painting, include representations of cities, towns and villages and people of varying status engaged in domestic and collective activities. In the sculpted panels and medallions from monuments at Bharhut and Sanchi (*see* §V, 4(ii)(a) below), for example, men, women and children are shown in routine domestic activities. Scenes of agricultural and cattle farming also occur, and people are shown engaged in various amusements and games of skill. Chess and a board game called *aṣṭapāda* with eight spaces on each side of the board seem to have been popular, even in ancient times, as were wrestling, archery, animal-fighting, swinging in swings and ball games (*kanduka-krīḍā*), the latter probably restricted to women. Festivals are represented, particularly in miniature paintings of the Mughal, Rajasthani and Pahari schools. These include the Kaumudimahotsava (festival of moonlight), Vasanta and Holi (spring festivals), Dipavali (autumnal festival of light) and others. Fairs, carnivals and ceremonial feasts are also represented (*see* §VI, 5, esp. (i), (iii) and (iv)).

13. *Mithuna*, red sandstone, from the west wall, Svarga Brahma Temple, Alampur, AD 688–9

A few genre motifs are depicted repeatedly. The most important one is the mother-and-child motif, found even in sculptures from the Indus civilization. Apart from representations of the Goddess as a mother (*mātṛikā*; *see* §1(v) above), there are several other types that have no religious association and that often highlight the sublimity of motherhood and the innocence of children. The other important related motif is known variously as the tree-damsel (*vṛkṣakā*) or the woman who makes the *śāla* tree bloom (*śālabhañjikā*) and consists of a graceful standing woman holding the branch of a tree that arches over her head (see fig. 145 below). Examples of this motif can be found in sculptures from Bharhut, Sanchi, Mathura and Sanghol. It may have been meant to suggest the fertility of virgin girls. In this connection it is interesting to note that Mayadevi, the mother of the Buddha, is shown in this posture in depictions of the birth. Women are frequently shown looking out of windows, sometimes in groups, in pensive or cheerful moods. Known as the lady in the window (*vātāyanavartinī*), this motif can be seen in the terracotta sculptures decorating 19th-century temples at Birbhum and Bankura (Bengal). Scenes of women at their toilet are also common.

Representations of dancing and music-making have been noteworthy in Indian art since earliest times. In

14. Frieze of musicians and dancers, sandstone, 333×946 mm, from Sikar, Rajasthan, *c.* 973 (Cleveland, OH, Cleveland Museum of Art)

sculpture and painting men and women are shown accompanying dancers on musical instruments (see fig. 14; see also fig. 172 below). In religious art the gods Shiva and Krishna are often associated with dance performances. In some temples all the positions (*karaṇa*s) and movements (*cārī*s) mentioned in the *Nāṭya śāstra* ('Treatise on dance') of Bharata (*c.* 4th century AD) are depicted in great detail.

Other significant scenes of daily life include representations of battles and military movements, travel, scenes depicting construction and other technical activities, hunting scenes and weddings and other social functions. Mughal-period and later manuscripts illustrate the art of falconry (see fig. 264 below) and catalogue various species of flora and fauna (see fig. 313 below).

BIBLIOGRAPHY

O. C. Gangoly: 'The Mithuna in Indian Art', *Rupam*, 22–3 (1925), pp. 54–61

M. P. Foucher: *The Erotic Sculpture of India*, trans. B. Rhys (London, 1959)

C. Sivaramamurti: *Sanskrit Literature and Art—Mirrors of Indian Culture* (Delhi, 1970)

H. Mode: *The Women in Indian Art* (Bombay, 1972)

W. G. Archer: *Indian Painting from the Punjab Hills: A Survey and History of Pahari Miniature Painting*, 2 vols (London and New York, 1973)

M. Chandra: *The World of Courtesans* (Bombay, 1973)

D. Desai: *Erotic Sculpture of India: A Socio-cultural Study* (Delhi, 1975)

7. HISTORICAL THEMES. It is difficult to single out historical themes in the early period, perhaps due to the Indian belief in life as continuous and cyclical. Visual documentation of significant events gradually did become important, however. With representations of Gautama Buddha and the Jaina *tīrthaṅkara* Mahavira Varddhamana, it is difficult to separate historical from legendary elements (*see* §§2 and 3 above). In the secular realm it is easier to make clear differentiations. The numismatic arts provide obvious examples (*see* §VIII, 6(i) below), but themes from history occur in other media as well, with the exploits of rulers taking priority.

In Cave 1 at Ajanta, for example, there is a wall painting of a seated ruler receiving gifts from foreign personages. This panel has been interpreted as the Chalukya king Pulakeshin II (*reg* 609/10–42) receiving an embassy from the Sasanian king Khusraw II (*reg* 596–628), but the painting is probably earlier. Since there is no written record of such an embassy from Persia, this painting may record the diplomatic or cultural relations with foreign embassies of the Mauryan ruler Ashoka (*reg c.* 269–*c.* 232 BC). The 1st-century BC inscription in Cave 14 at Udayagiri in Orissa records the military achievements of King Kharavela (*reg c.* 1st century BC) of the Chedi dynasty. On the ground floor there is a sculptural depiction of the reception of a king, apparently on his return from a victorious campaign, seemingly the visual rendering of the facts mentioned in the inscription. Numerous sculpted and painted panels depict warfare and related activities on the walls of temples at Khajuraho, Bhubaneshwar, Konarak and Thanjavur.

With the advent of the Mughals a plethora of visual documents of historical events was produced. These included a number of biographies of the emperors in manuscript form. Many of the miniatures in the *Bāburnāma* ('History of Babur'), *Akbarnāma* ('History of Akbar'), *Pādshānāma* ('Book of the emperor') and the like record important battles (see figs 263 and 268 below); the capturing of forts or cities; royal births (see fig. 15), coronations and reception ceremonies; manoeuvres of diplomacy and protocol; and the construction and foundation of cities and forts. Rajasthani, Pahari and Sikh miniatures also occasionally portray similar themes. Paintings executed during the period of British rule occasionally record significant moments in Indian history such as the Battle of Plassey (1757) and the Mutiny of 1857. The sensational 19th-century court case between a housewife and the head priest (*mohant*) of the Tarakeshwar Temple near Calcutta is the theme of contemporary paintings from the area near the Kali Temple, Calcutta, that was one of the centres of the picture trade.

See also §§V and VI below.

BIBLIOGRAPHY

G. Yazdani: *Ajanta*, 3 vols (Oxford, 1930–46)

R. N. Saletore: *Life in the Gupta Age* (Bombay, 1943)

J. M. Rosenfield: *The Dynastic Arts of the Kushans* (Berkeley, 1967)

The Imperial Image: Paintings for the Mughal Court (exh. cat. by M. C. Beach, Washington, DC, Freer, 1973)

Room for Wonder: Indian Painting during the British Period, 1760–1880 (exh. cat. by S. C. Welch, New York, Amer. Fed. A., 1978)

Akbar's India: Art from the Mughal City of Victory (exh. cat. by M. Brand and G. Lowry, New York, Asia Soc. Gals; Cambridge, MA, Sackler Mus.; Houston, TX, Mus. F.A.; 1985)

V. Desai: *Life at Court: Art for India's Rulers, 16th–19th Centuries* (Boston, 1985)

DIPAK CHANDRA BHATTACHARYYA

8. PORTRAITS. Although portraiture in the sense of representation of the physical or psychological particularities of an individual is seen in India mainly after the late 16th century, references to the genre and to its varied functions abound in Indian literature beginning in the early centuries AD. The depiction of an individual likeness was understood as an amalgamation of the sitter's visible form and his or her essential qualities, with an emphasis on the latter. In texts such as the *Viṣṇudharmottara purāṇa* ('Virtuous laws of Vishnu'), the Sanskrit word *citra* is generally used to describe the idea of portraiture. Literally translated as 'that which is "conspicuous" or "distinguished"', this noun derives from the Sanskrit root *cit*, which connotes comprehension or perception of essential elements. The fact that in later literature the term *citra* is used to designate both portraiture and all paintings, and that no specific term for portraiture is deemed necessary to distinguish it from other kinds of pictures, suggests that the genre was not seen as a unique form of representation.

(i) North. (ii) South.

(i) North. The earliest identifiable portraits of royalty date from the 1st and 2nd centuries AD in north India. The earliest Kushana royal portraits, on copper and gold coins, show the rulers' physical characteristics: beards, high cheekbones, thinning hairlines and rounded eyes. These numismatic portraits were based on Roman prototypes (*see* §VIII, 6(i) and fig. 331 below). Another group of expressive Kushana portraits consists of small heads of foreigners, monks and other non-royal figures. In contrast, the large stone sculptures of Kushana rulers found near MATHURA apparently make no attempt to render individual particularities. Such generic images represent a fusion of the Buddhist concept of a *cakravartin* (Skt: model ruler) who achieved bloodless victories through the power of *dharma* (righteousness) and the imported cultural ideal of a martial king. These large-scale stone sculptures are identified as portraits of particular kings only by inscriptions, royal insignia such as swords, militaristic clothing and ornamental details.

That the conventions developed during the Kushana period were continued by the Gupta rulers of India is evidenced by the gold coins they issued. Those of Chandragupta II (*reg c.* AD 380–415), for example, often show the king with his queen. Portraits in coeval sculpture are seen at UDAYAGIRI (ii), where figures, apparently of donors, are found at the base of some of the reliefs. The earliest hero stones date to soon after the Gupta period and include busts of deceased warriors at the top with relief panels below showing military exploits, a heroic death and the heavenly felicity awaiting the deceased (*see* SATĪ AND HERO STONES). In these instances the portraits are entirely generalized. The same holds true for the votive stelae with images of donors that were set up by temples. After the Islamic conquest of north India in the 12th century, the most dramatic shift in the development of portraiture occurred in the late 16th century, when the Mughal emperor Akbar (*reg* 1556–1605) commissioned portraits of himself and his grandees (see figs 259 and 260 below). Intended for albums, most early Mughal portraits (dating from *c.* 1580) are single images of the emperor, his courtiers and visiting dignitaries.

15. Mughal school: *The Birth of Prince Murad*, miniature from the *Akbarnāma* (detail), *c.* 1590 (London, Victoria and Albert Museum, I.S. 2–1896 80/117)

The rendition of physiognomic details with a psychological orientation in Mughal portraits is often attributed to the introduction of European art at the Mughal court. However, late 16th-century Mughal portraits bear little resemblance to contemporary European portraits. Typically, they show a single, full-length figure standing in profile against a blank light green or brown background, with a suggestion of grass or rocks. Although the faces are particularized, the bodies generally remain unspecific. Contemporary European portraits of royalty and nobility, on the other hand, usually consist of frontal or three-quarter views with a preference for half- rather than full-length representations. In keeping with his interest in empirical observation, Akbar may have asked his painters to create this new genre. A more logical antecedent may be found, however, in the portraits made in Iran and Central Asia in the late 15th century and early 16th for the Timurids, from whose founder the Mughals were descended (*see* TIMURID and ISLAMIC ART, §III, 4(v)(d)). Similarities include not only the format of the pictures and the postures of the figures but also the execution of the facial features.

The prominence of portraiture in the reign of Jahangir (1605–27) was undoubtedly a result of the Emperor's own preference for more intimate and personalized renditions, the gradual decrease in the production of large, illustrated narratives and the increased presence of Europeans and their art at the Mughal court. The range of portraits produced during his reign includes examples showing physical and psychological observation of specific individuals. Portraits are also included in large, crowded compositions. While some may have been based on direct observation, others were undoubtedly based on tracings and sketches. In the latter part of his reign, Jahangir turned increasingly to allegorical and symbolic portraits in which he is depicted with a halo, flanked by flying putti and equipped with other symbols of eternity and royal grandeur borrowed from the West (see fig. 267 below). This shift may be attributed in part to his need for clear statements of his absolute power. Such symbolic representations of royalty, however, were completely in keeping with Indian traditions.

While the development of formalized public representations of Mughal royalty continued in the reigns of Shah Jahan (1628–58; for illustration *see* HASHIM) and Aurangzeb (1658–1707), the portrayal of lesser courtiers reflected a degree of direct observation and psychological intensity, a sense of informality and a greater understanding of the Western techniques of chiaroscuro and diminishing perspective. A similar freedom of expression is evident in the images of ascetics, teachers and other non-royal subjects.

Inspired by the developments at the Mughal court, Hindu rulers in Rajasthan and the Punjab hills also began to commission portraits. Stylistically, early Rajput portraits are clear imitations of their 17th-century Mughal counterparts. Beginning in the early 18th century, however, portraits of Hindu rulers and courtiers once again emphasized sitters' unique features. Such elements were now used almost as attributes. Together with other royal symbols such as a halo, sword or water pipe, facial features functioned as pictorial conventions, not unlike the attributes of deities (*lakṣaṇas*). The resulting combinations of individualized features and generalized attributes can be found in single images as well as group compositions (see figs 276, 277 and 278 below).

One of the features of 18th-century Rajput portraiture, especially that of Rajasthan, was a decrease in the production of small single images and an increase in the number of large-scale representations of rulers in a variety of celebratory contexts. In these 'contextual' portraits, rulers are shown hunting, watching performances, sitting in a formal *darbār* (Pers.: public audience) or celebrating festivals (see fig. 275 below). Even though such panoramic depictions often represent particular events, and their lengthy inscriptions refer to specific occasions and places, their compositions impart a sense of timelessness. Undoubtedly, there is some accuracy in the depiction of individuals, but this appears not to have been the main intention of such pictures.

Unlike 17th-century Mughal portraits, where there is a great deal of variation in subject-matter and in the treatment of figures, in portraits from Rajasthan and the Punjab hills the focus is primarily on royal figures in formal settings. The most dramatic exception to this phenomenon occurs in the portraits of a ruler of a small principality in the Punjab hills. Resulting from an extraordinary relationship between an artist and his patron, the drawings and paintings by NAINSUKH of Balwant Singh writing a letter in a simple tent (see fig. 299 below), having his beard trimmed or standing alone on a palace roof suggest a more personalized, less formal view of royalty. Although the naturalism of these pictures can be attributed in part to Mughal influence, the selection of informal occasions and portrayal of the ruler without insignia are unprecedented.

Although formal portraits continued to be painted at the Mughal court and most of the Rajput courts in the 19th century, they generally lack the authority of images from the preceding century. The most significant developments of the period were in the use of photography and Western painting techniques, both of which were brought to India by the British. Like their Mughal predecessors, the artist-photographers adapted a new technique to traditional Indian ways of seeing by applying vibrant, opaque colours to their prints to hide the evidence of particular moments and highlight ideal conditions. The rise of the middle class and the decline of royal patronage also contributed to the development of new subject-matter in portraiture at this time.

British influence on the subcontinent in the early 20th century accelerated the process of Westernization, especially in urban centres, and resulted in hybrid notions of self that incorporated some Western attitudes towards individuality. The confluence of conceptual changes, new techniques and broad-based patronage brought Indian portrait traditions into the fold of Western convention.

See also §VI, 5(i) and (iii) below.

BIBLIOGRAPHY

V. Saunders: 'Painted Portrait as a Dramatic Device in Sanskrit Plays', *J. Amer. Soc. Orient. A.*, xxxix (1919), pp. 299–302

R. Cimino, ed.: *Life at Court in Rajasthan* (Turin, 1985)

Life at Court: Art for India's Rulers, 16th–19th Centuries (exh. cat. by V. Desai, Boston, MA, Mus. F.A., 1985)

B. N. Goswamy: 'Essence and Appearance: Some Notes on Indian Portraiture', *Facets of Indian Art*, ed. R. Skelton and others (London, 1986)

R. Brilliant: 'Portraits: The Limitation of Likeness', *A. J.* [New York], xxxxvi (1987)

P. Kaimal: *Stone Portraits at Pallava and Early Chola Temples: Kings, Patrons and Individual Identity* (diss., Berkeley, U. CA, 1988)

A. Roland: *Toward a Psychology of Self in Asia* (Princeton, 1988)

V. N. Desai and D. P. Leidy: *Faces of Asia: Portraits from the Permanent Collection*, Boston, MA, Mus. F.A. cat. (Boston, 1989)

VISHAKHA N. DESAI

(ii) South. Though few portraits survive from south India before Mughal influence penetrated south of the Deccan plateau in the 16th century, those from the first millennium AD are especially intriguing and complex. The majority of surviving portraits are sculpted and invest the entire body with individual character instead of concentrating that character in the face. They ornament sacred places, first the precinct of a Buddhist stupa, later the walls of Hindu

temples. Before the 11th century very few portraits represent women.

It is their intent to represent actual individuals that defines these images as portraits. That intent is expressed in inscriptions adjacent to and contemporary with the portraits. As in the north, some south Indian portraits convey their subjects' individuality through the subtle but clear individuation of one or two distinctive bodily and facial features. A pointed chin, a blunt brow, a rotund belly or skinny legs can distinguish an image from the standardized canon of proportions that governs divine figures. While such subtle distinctions might escape the attention of someone accustomed to portraits that aim at precise physical likeness, even a single unusual feature would command the attention of someone accustomed to highly standardized figural representations.

Beyond this, few generalizations about south Indian portraits are yet possible. The images come from a number of sites and cover a span of several centuries. A relief from Nagarjunakonda (along the Krishna River) includes several portraits of the Ikshvaku king Vashishthiputra Camtamula I (*reg* mid-3rd century AD). An inscription on the panel dates the carving to AD 273. From many years later and far to the south is a portrait of Tirumalai NAYAKA (*reg* 1623–59) in the Minakshi Temple of MADURAI. Although this image was carved after the MUGHAL dynasty had established a strong presence in south India, its form reflects southern rather than Mughal notions of representation in its minimal individuation, its sculptural format and its highly stylized presentation of the human form.

These two portraits show how much south Indian portraits can vary in size and format. The figures of Vashishthiputra Camtamula are well under half a metre in height, whereas the portrait of Tirumalai is over life-size. Vashishthiputra Camtamula is represented four times, once in each of four shallowly carved registers incised on one side of a free-standing stone post. He interacts with other carved figures as he performs royal activities, riding an elephant and sitting in court surrounded by women. Tirumalai Nayaka's image is addorsed to a pillar in one of the many-pillared halls (Skt *maṇḍapa*s) that surround the two main shrines of the Madurai temple. The painted stone portrait stands almost free from the pillar behind it. Tirumalai presses his palms together before his chest in a gesture of prayer or greeting (*añjali mudrā*), and his entire body leans forward eagerly. Interacting with objects beyond the work of art itself, he is meant either to be worshipping the deity some rooms away, or to be welcoming visitors to the temple.

Some of the most interesting south Indian portraits are stone reliefs on the walls of Hindu temples. More than a dozen of these exist outside modern Madras and along the Kaveri River. Within this limited group some patterns emerge among the features that vary so greatly between the Ikshvaku and Nayaka portraits. The portraits outside Madras represent kings of the PALLAVA dynasty (6th century–early 10th), while those along the Kaveri represent royalty of the CHOLA dynasty (9th–13th century) or, more frequently, non-royal individuals. Some of these portraits depict temple donors, while others depict persons dear to patrons of the temple.

One of the non-royal portraits from the 10th century in the Kaveri region depicts a donor identified by an inscription as Daman Amalan (see fig. 16). This image appears on the east wall of the Gomukteshvara Temple in Tiruvaduturai [Tiruvavaduturai], a village roughly 40 km north-east of Thanjavur. Daman Amalan's portrait stresses his deep devotion to the enshrined god. He presses his hands together as he stands before a relief of a *liṅga*, the phallic emblem of the god Shiva. Leaning forward earnestly, his body expresses his reverence; his hips jut strangely and his feet twist sharply towards the *liṅga*. Daman Amalan presents himself to the deity with a demure awkwardness, his being suffused with profound yet almost bashful devotion. His face and body demonstrate the features that distinguished him as an individual. His eyes protrude somewhat, as do the full lips of his narrow mouth. His forehead is short, his cheekbones wide, his jaw sharply slanted, and his chin projects sharply, perhaps indicating a goatee. His body is long in the torso, short in the arms and legs, narrow in the shoulders and fleshy in the belly and hips.

The features that make Daman Amalan's portrait distinctive are not flattering. He was unique because of his imperfections. This modest attitude towards individualism is consistent with the endearing awkwardness of his pose. These features characterize the citizen donor as awkward because the presence of a layperson's image in a temple was unusual, and as clearly recognizable in order to permit a contemporary viewer to link the act of patronage with a known individual.

In contrast south Indian portraits of royalty depict their subjects as relaxed in the august company of the divine, confident in the intimacy that rulers were believed to share

16. Portrait of *Daman Amalan*, granite, h. 320 mm (figure), from the east wall, Gomukteshvara Temple, Tiruvaduturai, 10th century

with the gods. The Adi Varaha Temple at MAMALLAPURAM contains two such images, portraits of Simhavishnu Pallava (*reg c.* 550–70) and Mahendravarman I Pallava (*reg c.* 570–630). These kings pose assertively, their powerful, youthful bodies conveying the steadfast courage and readiness to act that characterized south India's heroic ideal of kings. The portraits, both at least 2 m tall, tower impressively over the viewer. Royal insignia—crown, umbrella, leonine throne—further distinguish the figures from commoners. Portraits of other kings display the club (*daṇḍa*) that connotes the royal power to compel. Since the Adi-Varaha cave and its sculpture were probably commissioned by a descendant of Mahendravarman I, the portraits represent the patron's honoured ancestors.

Another example of a royal portrait commissioned by a devoted relative exists at the Uma-Maheshvara Temple at Konerirajapuram (roughly 40 km east-north-east of Thanjavur). The construction of this temple was sponsored by the Chola queen Shembiyan Mahadevi and dedicated to her husband Gandaraditya (*reg* 954–98), whose portrait appears on the building.

When portraits represent someone dear to the donor, they appear to receive devotion rather than to offer it. These three Pallava and Chola portraits are nonchalant instead of worshipful. The two Pallava kings make no gestures of prayer even though they are in the immediate presence of the temple's central object of worship. Gandaraditya sits while he worships a *liṅga*.

When portraits represent a ruler who was not the monument's patron, individualization is minimal. The type is emphasized rather than the individual, and the attributes of a good king are invoked: power, energy and majesty. Portraits of kings who were themselves temple patrons can give more idiosyncratic information, though not as much as is found on portraits of non-royal donors. This is evident in a series of portraits of the Pallava king Nandivarman II (*reg* 731–96) in KANCHIPURAM, Vaikunthaperumal Temple, a structure funded by Nandivarman himself. The many images consistently depict the king with full cheeks, elongated eyes, a thick waist, large thighs and short legs. These features do not present Nandivarman as a glamorous hero, but they would have made the subject of the portrait easy to identify. This served the needs of the donor portrait: to demonstrate the link between a particular individual's act of generosity and the presence of a temple. The king need not express his love of god with the humility one finds in Daman Amalan's portrait. One relief depicts him enthroned beside a representation of the temple, attended by a queen, a general and other subordinates.

Portraiture in south India seems not to have followed a consistent set of rules. Rather, it seems to have been reinvented to suit the specific needs of each group of sites, period and cultural situation. Individuality, employed variously to make images recognizable and to confess humbly to the flaw of difference, is a frequent element in these portraits.

For portraits in south Indian wall painting *see* §V, 3(i)(b) and 4(vii) below.

BIBLIOGRAPHY

W. Elliott: 'On the Inscription near the Varaha Swami Temple, at Mamallaipuram of the Seven Pagodas, with a Transcript and Translation', *Madras J. Lit. & Sci.*, xiii/2 (1844), pp. 36–47
Annual Report on South Indian Epigraphy (Madras, 1887–)
South Indian Inscriptions (Madras and Delhi, 1890–)
V. Rangacharya: *A Topographical List of the Inscriptions of the Madras Presidency*, 3 vols (Madras, 1919/*R* Delhi, 1985)
R. B. H. Krishna Sastri: *Two Statues of Pallava Kings and Five Pallava Inscriptions in a Rock-Temple at Mahabalipuram*, Mem. Archaeol. Surv. India, xxvi (Calcutta, 1926)
T. G. Aravamuthan: *Portrait Sculpture in South India* (London, 1931)
K. A. Nilkanthasastri: *The Colas*, 2 vols (Madras, 1935–7, rev. 2/1955)
C. Minakshi: *The Historical Sculptures of the Vaikuntaperumal Temple, Kanci*, Mem. Archaeol. Surv. India, lxiii (Delhi, 1941)
Annual Report on Indian Epigraphy (Delhi, 1947/8–)
R. Nagaswamy: 'New Light on Mamallapuram', *Transactions of the Archaeological Society of South India*, Silver Jubilee Vol. (1960–62), pp. 1–50
S. R. Balasubrahmanyam: *Early Chola Art: Part I* (New York, 1966)
T. V. Mahalingam: *Kāñcīpuram in Early South Indian History* (Bombay, 1969)
S. R. Balasubrahmanyam: *Early Chola Temples* (Delhi, 1971)
M. A. Dhaky: 'Cola Sculpture', *Chhavi: Golden Jubilee Volume, 1920–1970*, ed. A. Krishna (Varanasi, 1971)
D. Barrett: *Early Cola Architecture and Sculpture* (London, 1974)
W. Steiner: 'The Semiotics of a Genre: Portraiture in Literature and Painting', *Semiotica*, xxi/1–2 (1977), pp. 111–19
B. Stein: *Peasant State and Society in Medieval South India* (New York, 1980)
B. Frischer: *The Sculpted Word* (Berkeley, 1982)
M. Lockwood: *Mamallapuram and the Pallavas* (Madras, 1982)
B. Stein: *All the Kings' Mana: Papers on Medieval South Indian History* (Madras, 1984)
B. N. Goswamy: 'Essence and Appearance: Some Notes on Indian Portraiture', *Facets of Indian Art*, ed. R. Skelton and others (London, 1986)
R. Brilliant: 'Portraits: The Limitations of Likeness', *A. J.* [New York], xlvi/3 (Fall 1987), pp. 171–2

PADMA KAIMAL

III. Architecture.

The Indian subcontinent has been an unparalleled theatre of building activity for over 4000 years. Architectural enterprise has been fostered by the region's wealth, substantial manpower, relative political stability and abundance of suitable building material. Though much has been destroyed, an extensive architectural heritage has survived; as a consequence, architectural ideas are often more fully explored and well-represented in India than in other parts of the world. For example, in one prolific period of temple building from the 10th to the 12th century, hundreds of structures were erected, many of which are preserved. These provide a more complete record of temple architecture than is available for coeval church building in medieval Europe or the Byzantine world. Much building activity is also evident in the Islamic and colonial periods: in the 11th–18th century hundreds of monuments were constructed in the environs of Delhi alone.

Sustained programmes of temple construction from the 7th century AD led to the development of strong regional traditions of architecture in all parts of India. This development was based on the ascendancy of stone-carving and masonry techniques, but the ancient preference for brick was never set aside, and brick is still a popular building material for all types of building in the subcontinent.

With the appearance of Islam in the 8th century, new requirements were introduced. The earliest Indo-Islamic building borrowed directly from established regional practices of temple construction, but a vibrant new Indo-Islamic style was developed in the Delhi sultanate as it became the pre-eminent political and cultural force in north India during the second half of the 12th century. In different settings, the Indo-Islamic style soon developed regional variations of its own. These variations owed their origin to the pre-existing regional traditions, which were not superseded but survived beside the new Indo-Islamic styles.

In the 16th century the Mughal rulers forged a new architectural dispensation to reflect their imperial ambitions. In many areas, however, ancient traditions of temple architecture lingered, as did regional vestiges of the old Indo-Islamic styles. Curious hybrids, drawing on provincial Mughal, Indo-Islamic and traditional forms, flourished in areas away from the Mughal court, especially as the empire declined in the 18th century. The appearance of Europeans as traders and colonizers brought a new element to Indian architecture, but as in earlier epochs, older practices and traditions were not overtaken entirely. Even in the 20th century ancient temple styles are perpetuated side by side with the most advanced examples of European modernism.

The Indian subcontinent is also important as the source of building forms transmitted to other parts of the world. The rich architectural repertory developed in the service of Buddhism and Hinduism spread to all parts of Asia and beyond, and Indo-Islamic forms have influenced building in South-east Asia, Africa, Europe and America.

The following architectural survey is organized chronologically in the first instance and then along broad sectarian and regional lines. The co-existence of overlapping styles and the lack of distinct transitions from one period or style to the next mean, however, that these subdivisions, particularly chronological ones, are not inviolable.

1. Introduction. 2. Pre- and protohistoric periods. 3. 6th century BC–3rd century AD. 4. 4th–5th centuries AD. 5. 6th–11th centuries. 6. 11th–16th centuries. 7. 16th–19th centuries. 8. 19th century–1947.

1. Introduction.

(i) Forms. (ii) Terminology. (iii) Guilds and craftsmen.

(i) Forms. Through its long history, the Indian subcontinent has shown a remarkable capacity to reformulate its identity to suit new circumstances and needs, an identity characterized, in part, by the agile assimilation of external influences combined with the constant recasting of inherited tradition. India's architects have been adept at absorbing the new and manipulating the old. The result has been a range of building forms of diverse origin and complex meaning within traditions that retain considerable continuity. □

(a) Ancient village and urban forms. (b) Pillar, stupa and altar. (c) Temples. (d) Indo-Islamic and colonial forms.

(a) Ancient village and urban forms. Ancient India's village and urban architecture is known mainly from representations in narrative relief panels ornamenting Buddhist monuments of the last centuries BC and early centuries AD. Village buildings include circular thatched huts with domes, rectangular houses with earthen walls and thatched or shingled peaked roofs, and an occasional oval or apsidal structure with a wattle-and-daub wall and clay finials along the ridge line. The simplest form of circular hut often is associated with the provision of shelter for ascetics, who in some reliefs are shown performing rituals in front of the hut. This role as a shelter for ascetics is reinforced by Buddhist texts and reliefs that present the simple 'fragrant hut' (*gandhakuṭī*) as one of the three structures occupied by the Buddha during his ascetic's retreat in the Jetavana garden (see fig. 17).

17. Gateway relief panel of the Jetavana garden showing a simple round hut and two rectangular buildings, Stupa 1, Sanchi, *c.* 1st century BC

Urban architecture shown in such reliefs includes high earthen city walls with battlements; elaborate buttressed city gates with wooden balconies; gatehouses that follow a variety of village forms; and urban palaces, with several open, pillared storeys above a solid ground storey, corner pavilions, keel-vaulted upper chambers and distinctive barrel-vaulted dormers. Wooden braces support balconies, terraces are enclosed by fencelike balustrades, and perforated screens are used as windows to enclose private spaces.

This wooden architecture in ancient India seems complete and consistent within itself, with a formal vocabulary both original and vibrant that underpins subsequent architectural development across the subcontinent. Though regional and idiomatic variations are evident in relief

18. Rock-cut cave façade mimicking wooden forms, Kondane, 1st century BC

representations, the architectural vocabulary itself justifies the 'pan-Indian' designation given to it by recent scholarship. Remarkably, parts of this vocabulary are preserved in the 20th century in such wooden domestic architecture as that of the Vora community of Gujarat.

The forms of this ancient wooden architecture were mimicked in a number of cave complexes excavated into the rock faces of mountains and hills. The earliest of these rock-cut excavations are in the Barabar hills (*see* BARABAR AND NAGARJUNI) in the eastern state of Bihar. They date to the 3rd century BC, the period of the first great empire in north India, that of the Maurya dynasty. They were intended to give shelter to a sect of wandering ascetics during the rainy season. In two instances, these caves exhibit a simple, stone-carved hut at one end of a rectangular vaulted anteroom. The one façade that survives replicates the vaulted form of a thatched village structure in considerable detail. Though some of these early caves have been finished with a high polish in recognition of their royal patronage, they formally respect their village origins and the symbolism of the hut as an architectural shelter for the ascetic. The best known of these caves, the Lomas Rishi (see fig. 25 below), preserves the name of a great sage.

More elaborate urban architectural forms of wood are reflected in a number of Buddhist assembly hall and monastery complexes excavated out of the mountains along India's western coast near Bombay in the last few centuries BC and early centuries AD. (The only surviving examples of ancient Indian carpentry are the giant wooden joists hung from the rock-cut ceilings of some of these excavations.) Architects within this rock-cut tradition, however, soon began to rearrange wooden forms, creating stone façades for excavations in ways that transformed carpentry sources into a viable decorative surface. This process is already apparent in the 1st century BC at Kondane (see fig. 18). Through clever manipulation of scale, they could make such a façade suggest an almost unlimited range of constructed storeys. If such complex carved façades at first seem intended simply as substitutes for the laborious construction of a wooden original, they also come to represent a process of formal abbreviation and compaction that quickly became a source for architectural creativity in its own right. By the time stone temples began to be built in the 5th century AD, such compaction of architectural form took on an elaborate and self-conscious symbolic vitality.

(b) Pillar, stupa and altar. To the degree that architecture can be defined as an act intended to control space and put it to use, whether functional or symbolic, a series of large sandstone pillars with monolithic shafts and animal capitals

erected in the Maurya period (*c.* 3rd century BC) form India's first surviving monumental architecture. (The Mauryas also built palaces of stone and wood, of which only foundations remain.) The pillars, set up at crossroads along major trade routes and within Buddhist monastic establishments, acted as markers of empire for the Mauryas and in some cases were inscribed with imperial edicts (for illustration *see* SARNATH). Their capitals, composed of ripe lotus-heads supporting imperial emblems, connect royal rule to a well-known water cosmogony (the lotus being a long-standing symbol of the waters). In like manner, lotus-pedestals in later ages supported sacred images. Having no base, the monolithic shafts of Mauryan pillars were rooted in the earth and seemed to span the three-tiered world of earth, air and heaven. The pillars seize space both by marking a centre and by being the centre iconically. Pillars continued to be erected at Buddhist establishments in subsequent centuries (including, for example, KARLE and KANHERI) and were used also to bear Brahmanical emblems, both for ritual purposes and in front of temples. Royal standards shared this iconic value, being carried in battle as focuses for victory. As the *axis mundi*, such pillars centre India's sacred structures, whether Buddhist or Hindu. Later rulers, both Hindu and Muslim, recognized the potency of such pillars by moving and re-establishing them and by constructing victory pillars of their own.

A second form of monumental architecture appearing in early India is the stupa (*see* STUPA, §1), which, though known primarily in a Buddhist context, also served Jaina and Brahmanical purposes. The stupa is a hemispherical solid dome, set sometimes on terraces or a drum, often with a square upper platform crowned by sheltering parasols. Earthen mounds had been used as burial markers for princes in north India from before the 3rd century BC (*see* LAURIYA NANDANGARH), and Buddhist texts record that stupa mounds memorialized the Buddha's relics after his death in the 5th century BC. The stupa, however, is more than a mortuary monument and may contain ritual objects or even a bit of scripture, rather than a relic, placed at its core as the 'seed' to 'enliven' it. The upper square platform functions as a symbolic altar, and the shaft with parasols marks the *axis mundi*, making the monument a giant cosmogram. This programme was elaborated in later stupas, especially those in South-east Asia (*see* BOROBUDUR). With railings or terraces surrounding its base, the stupa provided a focus for ambulatory ritual and became the focus of institutional Buddhism. The stupa further acted as a *caitya* or object towards which worship or reverence was focused. The large rock-cut assembly halls in the Western Ghats are called *caitya* halls because rock-cut stupas stood as the focus of worship in these apsidal excavations. Miniature votive stupas also became common at places sacred to Buddhism.

If an architectural monument can be defined by the ritual potency of its making, then construction of altars was perhaps the ultimate architectural act in ancient India. Texts from the 4th century BC known as the *śulba sūtras* record the constructional techniques necessary to produce a sacred geometry that would make altars efficacious. The square altar replicated creation, expanding from a central point in the cardinal directions to mark the corners of a square universe. Altars, as receptacles of ritual, also became the ground for divine manifestation and a site for the worshipper's personal transformation.

(c) Temples. With the appearance of anthropomorphized images of Hindu deities to represent the force-field of abstractions with which Vedic religion had dealt, the necessity to provide appropriate sheltering structures for the divine became part of India's religious and architectural agenda. The geometry for constructing altars used in early India, as well as the underlying myths and cosmology, exercised control over such structures built to give shelter to divinity after the 4th century AD. The *Bṛhat Saṁhitā* (early 6th century AD) is the first known text to record the application of the altar-grid (Skt *vāstumaṇḍala*) to temple construction. It stated that a grid of 81 squares should be used for cities and houses, but a grid of 64 squares was preferred for temple plans. A slightly later text refers to grids of 64, 81 and 100 squares, and an even later one suggests that each grid 'is fit for all'.

Built into the temple's symbolism were three altars along the vertical axis—those of the sanctum, the base of the superstructure and the open platform at the top—met on the horizontal axis in later temples by a further *maṇḍala* composing the separate structure that shelters the worshipper. One contemporary living tradition records the temple's three vertical levels, using the Sanskrit terms *bhūmi* (earth), *madhya ākāśa* (middle) and *purva ākāśa* (upper) *yantras* (visual tools with magical efficacy).

Northern. Anthropomorphized images of Hindu deities were produced in north India by the Kushana period (*c.* 1st–3rd century AD). It was only from the Gupta period (*c.* 4th–5th century AD), however, that stone temples began to be built. Brick temples were also built in the Gangetic Valley in the Gupta period with terraces supporting cellas, but hardly more than foundations of these remain. Such terraced brick structures were also built at times in later centuries, but the type was replaced for the most part by stone temples with curvilinear towers.

Some scholars have speculated that stone was not originally the preferred material for temples because of its association with funeral monuments in India from megalithic times. In central India at the end of the 4th century AD, however, at a natural sacred site (*tīrtha*) known as UDAYAGIRI (ii) outside the ancient town of Vidisha, Gupta ministers began the excavation of a series of small cave cells, to which constructed porticos were added, that presented a series of newly formulated image-types within their cellas or as friezes on their façades.

The cellas housing images at this site root them in native rock, making the material itself part of the message of manifesting divinity being presented for worship. At some other sites from this period, as at SANCHI, stone temples were constructed that mimicked such cave cells, with cubical walls enclosing the cella, in the form of an altar-like stone structure.

A stone temple at NACHNA (second half of the 5th century) encased just such a cella within a path for circumambulation that was enclosed by walls rusticated to suggest the piled rocks of a mountain slope, either Meru, the mountain at the centre of the Puranic universe, or

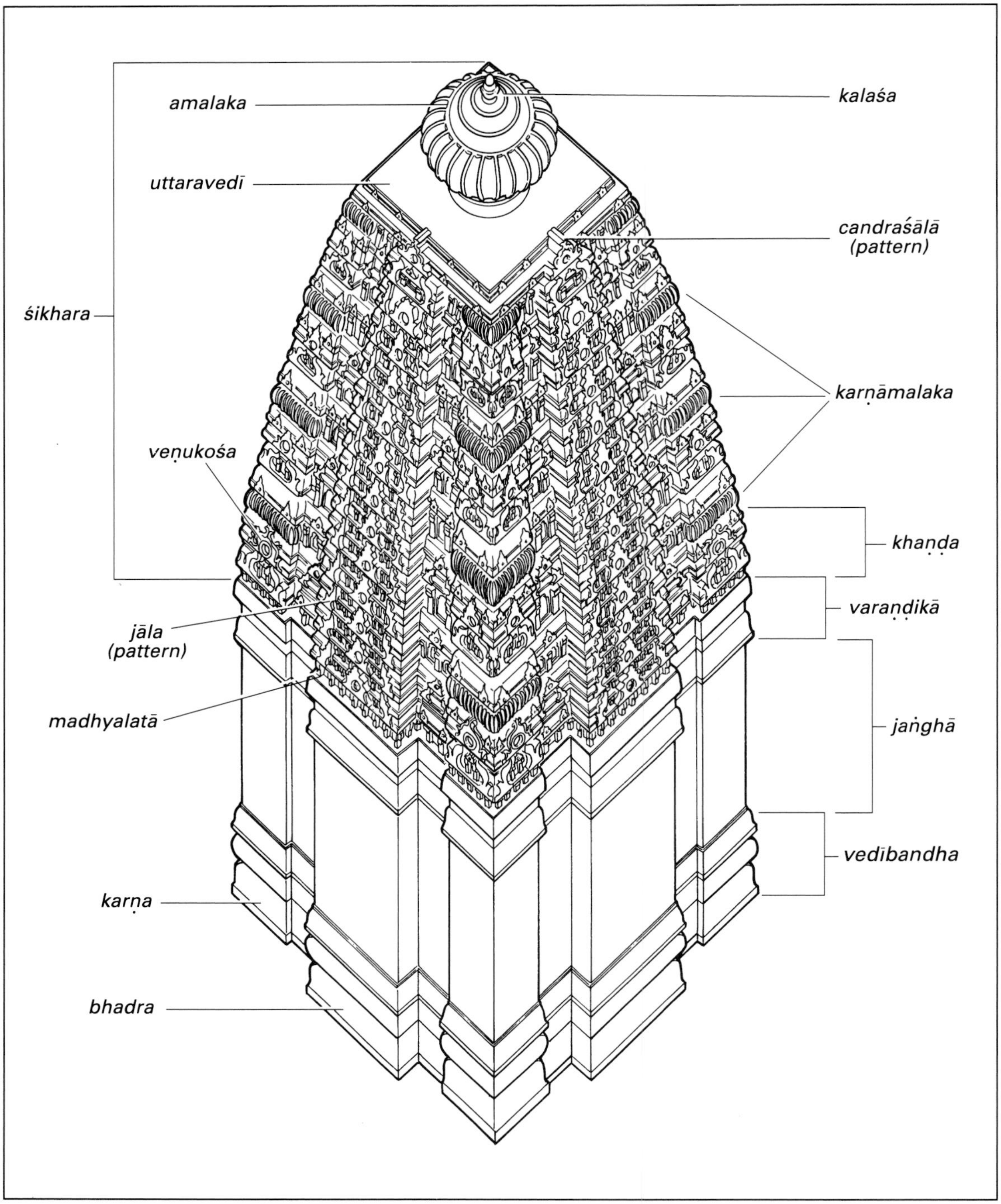

19. North Indian (*nāgara*) temple with *latina* superstructure

more likely Kailasa, on which Shiva's palace was built. Stone as a building material had thus become part of the symbolic message.

At other sites experimentation with architectural forms and symbolism of a greater complexity is evident. Layers of stone were piled to suggest multiple storeys, and the resulting tower was crowned by a ribbed disc (*āmalaka*) modelled on the seed of the small lobed amala fruit. This form had been used in earlier centuries as a pillar capital, in what seems an extension of the cosmogonic symbolism represented by the fruiting lotus at the top of the free-standing monumental stone pillars of the Maurya period.

By using simple cornice layers to suggest storeys and small aediculae with crowning *āmalaka*s to suggest pavilions, these stone temples took on some semblance of a palace's morphology. By abstracting and abbreviating these forms, architects were able to create monuments providing a variety of signals to the initiate. The crowning *āmalaka* marked the ascending axis of a cosmogonic pillar, symbolically passing through the centre of the altar-like body of the structure surrounding the sanctum. Corner aediculae were given the form of small altar platforms, suggesting the plurality of sacred spaces that could share a single identity as a temple. 'All the earth is altar', one of the *śulba sūtra*s had recorded, 'yet for the sake of sacrifice, one must pick a spot and build an altar there'.

The symbolic programme for the temple expressed in the architecture of this period was a constant one. The cavelike cella of the temple became its 'womb' (*garbha*). The temple's vertical axis, marked by the crowning *āmalaka*, was the *axis mundi*, within the symbolic shaft of which divine form could be made visible. The basal cube of the temple and its sanctum was an 'altar' (*vedi*), through the use of which human rituals could become efficacious and within which the anthropomorphized image of divinity could be given shelter. The storeys of the temple with its tower formed a 'palace' (*prāsāda*) appropriate to shelter these manifesting images. The hall or portico in front of the sanctum formed a pavilion giving shelter to the worshipper, from which the religious experience of 'seeing' the divine image (*darśan*) could occur.

Experiments with architectural elements from the 6th century AD led to particular forms in north India that are designated *nāgara*. In its earlier and simpler version (see fig. 19), the *nāgara* temple was characterized by offsets (*bhadra*) projecting as cardinal niches from the cubic cella. The niches were often treated as blind doorways and contained images reflecting various aspects of the sanctum's divinity. Subsidiary projections could provide flanking offsets (*pratiratha*) for these main niches. A curvilinear tower carried these offsets upward to a terminating altar (*uttaravedī*) with the *āmalaka* as crown. A finial, carved as a lustration pot and shown at times with sprouting foliage, was then placed on top of this grooved disc during consecration. Niches with guardian deities (*dikpāla*s) were placed on the corners, and additional offsets were added, occasionally in the form of attached pilasters. This basic type, designated *latina* because of its vertical 'creepers' (*lata*s), was built in a variety of regional styles throughout north India. Some examples had porticos (*mukhacatuṣkī*) placed before the entrance door, some were built on platforms with subsidiary corner shrines (a type known as *pañcāyatana*, or 'five-shrined'), and some were surrounded by sheds to provide a covered path for ambulation. In western India, miniature versions of the central spire began to be placed over the corner piers of the ambulatory walls. This marked the beginning of a multi-spired *nāgara* type often called *śekharī*. Multi-spired forms took on increasing importance from the 11th century, used also on temples without ambulatories, with tiers of subsidiary spires placed over each projecting pier of the sanctum wall. The term *anekāṇḍaka* (many-spired) can also be used for these complex towers (*see* KHAJURAHO, fig. 1). Experimentation included turning the grid that determined the plan of the temple to produce a stellate plan. A group of temples of the 11th century and later, often stellate, carried bands of miniature shrines (*śṛṅga*s) set on pillarets in the superstructure; this temple type is called *bhūmija* after the levels (*bhūmi*) of its superstructure (see fig. 57 below).

Despite the dominance of the curvilinear spire in north India, other forms were also employed. In central India, for example, small votive temples (called *maṇḍapīka*) simulated post-and-plank pavilions of wood. Towers of the *latina* type were superimposed over these shrines by the end of the 9th century. Certain types of images (such as sets of goddesses or a reclining image of Vishnu) required rectangular sanctums. These were often placed in shrines having barrel-vaulted superstructures (*valabhī*). Such barrel vaults were also used to cover the entry spaces or vestibules in front of *latina* temples. This barrel-vaulted element, often containing an image of the god, acted as a fronton (*śukanāsā*) to the main curvilinear tower. Other temples used a pyramidal pentroof superstructure, termed *phāṁsanā* (wedge-shaped), which could employ straight-edged roof forms, curved cornices or ribbed awnings to build up the structure. These towers are often crowned by a fluted bell (*ghaṇṭā*) rather than an *āmalaka*. Except for the temple tradition found in Kashmir, which continued to place pentroofs over the sanctum, this form came to be used primarily over the hall or halls attached along a horizontal axis in front of temples (see, for example, the roof of the hall in fig. 51 below). Like other superstructural types, the *phāṁsanā* was elaborated by the 11th century into a complex form with numerous miniature roofs and finials (*saṁvaraṇā*) clustered around the main elevation.

Southern. Cave temples were excavated in south India in the 5th and 6th centuries AD; temples were constructed in stone from the 7th century, and archaeological excavations suggest an earlier tradition of small shrine complexes in brick and less durable materials. At MAMALLAPURAM, south of Madras, a series of shrines was carved out of the rock in the 7th century. These replicate a range of available types of shelter from thatch huts to elaborate multi-storey palaces. This architecture is generically called *drāviḍa* (of the Dravida country or simply 'southern'). It is typified by a series of terraced storeys, each enclosed by a balustrade and ringed by small architectural aediculae, with a domed structure at the summit (see fig. 20). The aediculae take the form of square-domed structures on the corners (*kūṭa*s) and intermediate barrel-vaulted halls (*śālā*s) connected by segments of a miniature vaulted cloister (*hārā*). As temples in the north can be seen as typically of the *latina* type, those in the south can be collectively designated *kūṭina*. These terms clarify some of the basic differences between north and south, the *latina* having vertical spines or 'creepers' (*latā*) that rise from the offsets and follow the curve of the spire, while the *kūṭina* temple uses terraced storeys and diminishing horizontal tiers of aediculae (*kūṭa*). This formula continued throughout the history of south India's temples, both for the sanctum and for the large gateways (*see* GOPURA) built as entrances to the vast temple enclosures. However, some temples may be classified as *valabhī drāvida* or *valabhī nāgara*, depending on their morphology.

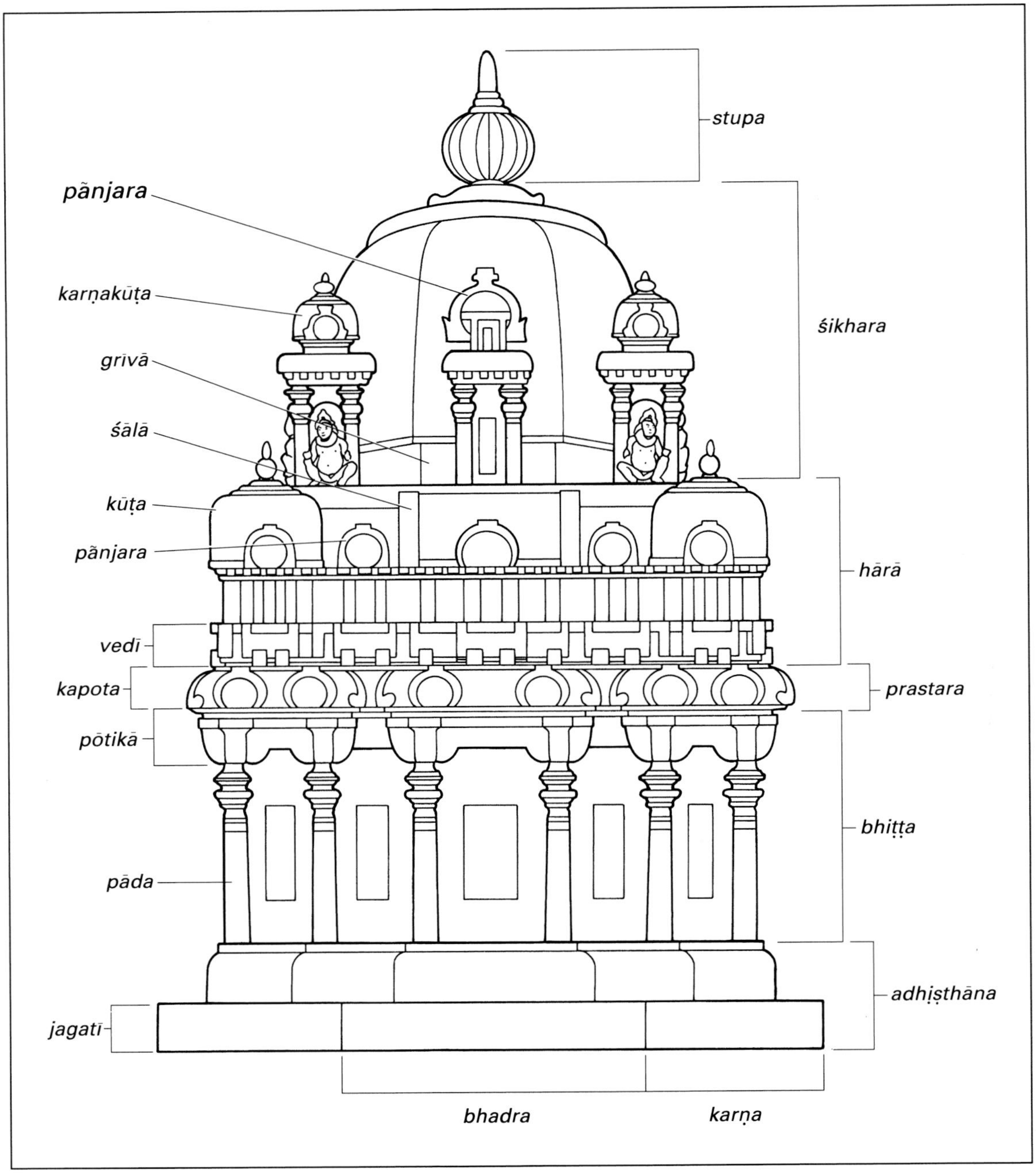

20. South Indian (drāviḍa) temple with *kūṭina* superstructure

Two major regional schools of southern architecture co-existed from the 7th century in the Tamil territory and the Deccan. Tamil temples after the 10th century evolved into huge urban complexes typified by concentric rectangular walled enclosures with gateways of increasing height. The architectural vocabulary used for these enormous structures remained typical of the *kūṭina* order. Temples in the Deccan, on the other hand, interacted with northern forms from the period of the early Chalukya dynasty (7th–8th centuries). Symptoms of this interaction include central projections in the plan, a fronton (*śukanāsā*) over the entrance and a variety of northern mouldings. These *drāviḍa* temples often stand at the same site with *latina* temples clearly of northern inspiration.

Early in the 11th century, architects in the Deccan had begun to create a new hybrid order, described as *vesara* in a few contemporary inscriptions (architectural texts of this school do not appear to have survived). This type exploited the vertical divisions and projecting offsets of *nāgara* architecture, while retaining a *drāviḍa* morphology. The walls of these buildings were often ornamented with an array of architectural models. An inscription from Kuppatur suggests a remarkable self-awareness and confidence in the architects, who describe their work as an 'elegant, equipoised and shapely temple. . .as if built by Vishvakarma [the divine architect] himself. . .freely ornamented with *drāviḍa*, *bhūmija* and *nāgara* [forms, and with] offsets manipulated in many ways'.

(d) Indo-Islamic and colonial forms. Cultural continuities in traditional India are often assumed, while Islam and European imperialism are seen as foreign impositions. The Indian subcontinent, however, has experienced many intrusions, successfully assimilating imported cultures. The coming of Islam to Sind in the early 8th century AD in part only renewed an age-old process of dealing with migrants and warriors from West Asia. Economic contacts led to western Indian communities accommodating Muslim merchants just as communities in south India had accommodated Roman merchants in earlier centuries. A mid-13th-century inscription from Somnath refers to Muhammad as 'the teacher of sailors' who lived near the temple, while other records indicate that Muslims served as ministers under the Rashtrakutas and other Hindu kings. Even before an Islamic political power-base was established in Delhi late in the 12th century, the architectural needs of these Islamic communities were being met by local craftsmen along India's west coast and at places in the hinterland. The mid-12th-century monuments surviving at Bhadreshvar in Kachchh (*see* §5(ii)(a) below), for example, provided a model for the peaceable integration of local craft conventions and new Islamic typologies and for the patronage and guild relationships that could make an Indo-Islamic architecture possible.

The occupation of Delhi and surrounding areas by Turkish rulers at the end of the 12th century initiated a delicate political game of cultural marking. The Quwwat al-Islam mosque in Delhi carries an inscription claiming that the structure was built from the remains of 27 destroyed temples; at Ajmer, a new mosque placed inscriptions from a Sanskrit college face-down in its floor; at Kaman, whole balconies and ceilings from 8th-century structures were reused in a compound built to meet Islamic needs. Such reuse did not necessarily represent plunder, for there is evidence of the participation of indigenous craftsmen and even master architects in the construction of these monuments. The ceilings and pillars at Ajmer were made fresh by Indian craftsmen; at Kaman, the mihrab itself employs Indian ornament. What is new

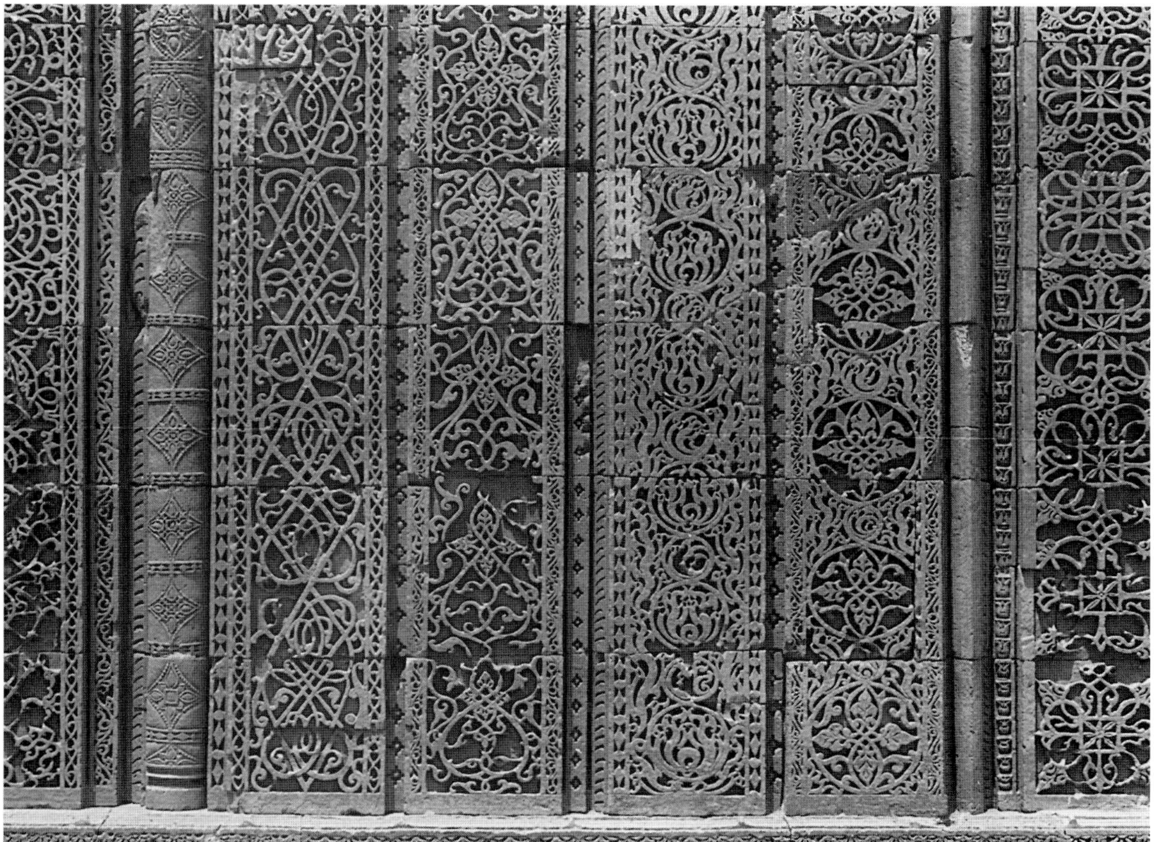

21. Arha'i Din ka Jhonpra Mosque, Ajmer, *c.* 1210–36; detail of screen combining Indian temple mouldings with Islamic decorative motifs

in these buildings is an explicitly Islamic programme, architectural typologies previously unknown in India and vocabularies of forms and ornament that drew on the vast territories of Islam from Arabia to Central Asia. Thus the stone façades of the mosques and tombs at Delhi use Indian vegetal patterns and temple mouldings but combine them with calligraphy and decorative forms taken from Central Asian brickwork (see fig. 21).

Throughout the Islamic period, new infusions of architectural patterns and forms were absorbed in India, understood in Indian terms and then transformed by Indian craftsmen. Traditional Indian forms were put to Islamic use. Craftsmen gave their work a local character that varied according to region and period. The 17th-century palaces of the Mughal and Rajput princes provide a conspicuous instance of how non-Indian forms and elements were assimilated (*see* §7(i)(a) and (ii)(a)-(b) below). Analogous patterns continued in the colonial period when European styles, from the Baroque to Neo-classical, were subject to a process of 'orientalization' (*see* §§7(iii) and 8(i) below). The eclectic styles of the 19th century can be understood, at least in part, as an attempt to co-opt India through the manipulation of her architectural heritage.

In the 20th century architects in the Indian subcontinent have interacted creatively with currents from the rest of the world. Many have trained abroad or have worked with such masters as Louis I. Kahn and Le Corbusier, who were given important commissions following independence. The vast economic development of the subcontinent has led to many opportunities for institutional projects, often on a large scale. The challenge has been to combine the lessons of European modernism with the underlying vernacular understanding (not formal vocabularies) of South Asia. Architects such as BALKRISHNA V. DOSHI, RAJ REWAL, CHARLES M. CORREA and, in the next generation, YASMEEN LARI—all with established international reputations—have struggled to form an architecture that is not just late-modern or post-modern but truly South Asian.

(ii) Terminology.

(a) Introduction. (b) Glossary.

(a) Introduction. Early sources for architectural terminology are various. Some terms first appear in inscriptions, religious texts or even plays and poems that describe cities, palaces or other architectural settings in passing. The earliest systematic (although brief) discussion of building practices for planning cities, houses and temples survives in the *Bṛhat Saṁhitā*, a 6th-century compendium. A chapter on architecture lays out rules for the grid-diagram used to plan all structures. Two subsequent chapters describe water divination and the culture of trees (skills perhaps needed for the placement of temples); a separate chapter then presents special rules for the proportioning of temples. Manuals on architecture, collectively called *śilpa śāstras* and written in Sanskrit, survive from the 11th century AD onward (*see* §I, 10 above). Those from western and central India coordinate closely with building types that survive from the same period. South Indian texts, also in Sanskrit, come from a later period, and more recent texts also have survived in several regional vernaculars.

The Sanskrit terminology employed by the technical manuals can be quite precise; however, there are numerous synonyms, and each text often follows its own conventions. Regional texts were among the first to come to the attention of scholars early in the 20th century, and in some cases vernacular terms derived from these were then employed generally in publications. Oriya terms, for example, spread rapidly into secondary literature concerning many other schools. Such regional terms continue to be useful for the study of contemporary practice. Recent scholarship, however, has attempted to establish a standard Sanskrit terminology based on a comparative study of available texts so that the same architectural element can be called by the same name wherever it occurs. More important than naming or standardization, however, is the ability of this terminology to reveal the symbolic meaning of architectural components and the architect's logic. Sanskrit terms help clarify, for example, which mouldings belong to the platform and which to the base of the temple proper, whether cornices at the top of a wall are one element or two (capping the frieze or acting as the base for the superstructure) and whether offsets are to be taken as planes or piers.

As an example of this technical vocabulary, a north Indian temple (*prāsāda*) often stands on a broad platform (*jagatī*) and may have an ornamented socle (*pīṭha*). Its wall (*maṇḍovara*) consists of base-mouldings (*vedībāndha*), frieze (*jaṅghā*) and cornice (*varaṇḍikā*), broken into vertical corner planes (*karṇa*) and a central projection (*bhadra*), often with flanking offsets (*pratiratha*). The temple's curvilinear superstructure (*śikhara*) may have a single spire or be clustered by miniature spires (*śṛṅga*), each crowned by a large ribbed disc (*āmalaka*) and a water-pot finial (*kalaśa*). Along the axis leading to the inner sanctum there are often a series of closed (*gūḍha-*) or open (*raṅga-*) pillared halls (*maṇḍapa*). A gate (*toraṇa*) may mark the entrance. South Indian temples (*vimāna*) have a different morphology from those in the north as well as a distinct terminology based on the same Sanskrit roots. The '*jagatī*' in south India refers to the platform that forms the sanctum's floor, appearing as a series of mouldings at the base of the wall-frieze. The '*śikhara*' is not the whole spire but refers only to the crowning dome. The halls within a temple compound are given special names, according to their use. The large gateway structures typical of late south Indian compounds are called GOPURAS. The use of appropriate Sanskrit terminology gives descriptions a scientific exactness; it is possible, however, to discuss and understand temple architecture without undue dependence on these terms.

MICHAEL W. MEISTER

(b) Glossary.

Adhiṣṭhāna (i). Moulded basement.

Adhiṣṭhāna (ii). Moulded socle at the base of the wall (*pāda*) in a temple of the southern type.

Alpanāsī (*candraśālā, nāsikā*). Decorative dormer window.

Āmalaka (*āmalasāraka*). Serrated crown or cogged disc that typically surmounts temples of the northern type.

Aṇḍa (*aṇḍaka*). Grooved disc crowning temples of the north Indian variety; see also *āmalaka* above.

Aṅga (i). Projection or receding face of a north Indian temple. Such faces are numbered so that, for example, a building with one main offset and two adjacent portions of wall is regarded as having three faces or limbs (*aṅga*s).

Aṅga (ii). Component or constituent member in a building of the southern variety. For example, a temple composed of a base, wall, cupola and finial is described as *caturaṅga* ('four limbs').

Antarāla. Vestibule or space between the sanctum (*garbhagṛha*) and the hall (*maṇḍapa*).

Antarapaṭṭa (*antarapatra, kandhara, kaṇṭha*). Recess between mouldings.

Ardhamaṇḍapa. See *maṇḍapa* below.

Ardhapadma. Half-lotus decorative motif.

Āsanapaṭṭa (*āsanapaṭṭakā, āsanapaṭṭikā*). Seat slab in a projecting parapet seat.

Bālapañjara. Aedicule, often placed in the vertical crevice (*salilāntara*) of a temple spire.

Bhadra (*bhadraratha, ratha*). Main cardinal offset or projection in a temple's walls.

Bhiṭṭa. Slablike moulding, typically in the plinth (*pīṭha*).

Bhūmija. Superstructural form with four vertical spines (*latā*) having three to five rows (*malā*) of miniature spires (*kūṭastambha*) stacked vertically in the intervening spaces.

Caityagṛha. Hall containing a *caitya* ('sacred object'), typically a Buddhist stupa.

Candraśālā (*alpanāsī, gavākṣa, induśālikā*). Ogee-shaped dormer window.

Chādya. Projecting eave or awning.

Devakulikā (*karṇaprāsāda*). Subsidiary corner temples in a five-shrined or quincunx plan (*pañcāyatana*).

Dhvaja (i). Flagstaff set in a hole pierced through a temple's serrated crown (*āmalasāraka*) and often supported below by a small figure carved in the round (*dhvajadhara*).

Dhvaja (ii). Standard in the form of a free-standing pillar, often for Garuda, the mythic bird associated with Vishnu.

Garbhagṛha. Inner chamber or sanctum of a temple.

Ghaṇṭā (i). Fluted bell surmounting a wedge-shaped (*phāṁsanā*) roof.

Ghaṇṭā (ii). Stellate crown surmounting a temple of the *bhūmija* class.

Ghaṭapallava. Vase overflowing with vegetal scrolls.

Grāsapaṭṭī (*grāsapaṭṭa, grāsapaṭṭikā, grāsamālā*). Band of gorgon or ferocious heads, typically in a temple plinth (*pīṭha*).

Gūḍhamaṇḍapa. See *maṇḍapa* below.

Jāḍyakumbha. Inverted cyma recta in the plinth (*pīṭha*).

Jagatī (i). Terrace or platform upon which a temple and its attendant shrines are placed.

Jagatī (ii). Blocklike base moulding in the socle (*adhiṣṭhāna*) of temples of the south Indian type.

Jāla. Mesh design. Types include *gavākṣajāla*, consisting of interwoven ogee-dormer motifs (*gavākṣa* or *candraśālikā*) and *nāgajāla*, a screen pattern in which the lattice is made up of interlocking serpent (*nāga*) designs.

Jaṅghā. Wall-section exclusive of the podium mouldings (*vedībandha*) and entablature (*varaṇḍikā*). At times termed *kaṭi*.

Kakṣāsana. Top section of a parapet seat that slopes outward and is often decorated with spindles and floral panels.

Kalaśa (i). Torus moulding forming part of a podium (*vedībandha*).

Kalaśa (ii). Finial placed on a temple's serrated crown.

Kalaśa (iii) (*kumbha*). Pot-shaped component of a temple's finial.

Kandhara (*antarapaṭṭa, gala, kaṇṭha*). Broad recess between moulding.

Kailī. Vestibule wall or buffer wall between the sanctum (*garbhagṛha*) and the porch (*mukhacatuṣkī*) or hall (*maṇḍapa*).

Kapota (i). Roll-cornice in an entablature (*varaṇḍikā, prastara*).

Kapota (ii). Roll-cornice serving as a component in a wedge-shaped spire (*phāṁsanā*).

Kapotālī (i) (*kapotapālī, kapotapalika*). Inverted cyma cornice forming the top element of the podium (*vedībandha*).

Kapotālī (ii). Horizontal slab in a wedged-shaped spire (*phāṁsanā*) with an inverted cyma recta profile; also termed *sūrpa*.

Kapotālī (iii). Curved cornice crowning a temple's wall (*jaṅghā*); more commonly termed *varaṇḍikā*.

Karṇa. Corner section of a temple's walls.

Karṇāṇḍaka (*aṇḍa, bhūmyāmalaka, karṇāmalaka*). Subsidiary grooved discs in the corners (*veṇukośa*) of a northern spire.

Karṇaratha (*veṇukośa, karṇalatā, padmakośa*). Corner section of a northern temple spire, typically marked by serrated discs (*karṇāṇḍaka*).

Khura. Square base moulding or foot moulding at the bottom of the podium (*vedībandha*).

Kīrtimukha (*grāsamukha*). Jawless grotesque, usually with pearl festoons or floral motifs spewing from its mouth.

Kumbha (i). Broad moulding with a curved top forming part of a temple's podium moulding (*vedībandha*).

Kumbha (ii). Pot-shaped member of a finial; also termed *kalaśa*.

Kūṭa (i). Subsidiary spire in a multi-spired temple (*śekharī*); also termed *tilaka, śṛṅga*.

Kūṭa (ii). Miniature square shrine set on the entablature (*prastara*) of a south Indian temple. When on a temple's corner it is termed *karṇakūṭa*.

Kūṭa (iii). Square chamber on an upper storey in early Indian architecture; also termed *kūṭāgāra*.

Kūṭina. Generic term for temples of the southern type characterized by the use of aedicules (*kūṭa*s; see fig. 20 above).

Lalāṭabimba. Keystone of a temple doorway that is often carved with an image of a tutelary deity.

Latā (i). Central curving band or cardinal projection of a northern temple spire placed above the sanctum's principal offset (*bhadra*) in buildings with three receding faces (*aṅga*s) in plan; also termed *ratha*.

Latā (ii). Subsidiary projection in the spire between the central spire offset (*madhyalatā*) and corner (*veṇukośa*) in temples with five receding faces (*aṅga*s) in plan.

Latā (iii). Vertical band or spine placed above the cardinal offsets in temples of the *bhūmija* type.

Latina. Curvilinear type of temple superstructure common in north India and characterized by curving spines or creepers (*latā*s; see fig. 19 above).

Madhyalatā. Central projection of northern temple spire.

Mañcikā. String course resting on the podium (*vedībandha*) that often serves as a pedestal for the image niches (*rathikā*s) in the wall (*jaṅghā*).

Maṇḍapa. Hall, typically with pillars supporting the ceiling and roof. Types include *agramaṇḍapa* (forehall), *ardhamaṇḍapa* (half-hall) *āsthānamaṇḍapa* (audience hall), *gūḍhamaṇḍapa* (closed hall), *mukhamaṇḍapa* (entrance hall), *nandimaṇḍapa* (hall or pavilion for Shiva's bull Nandi) and *nṛtyamaṇḍapa* or *raṅgamaṇḍapa* (dance hall).

Maṇḍovara. Portion of the temple elevation from the bottom of the podium (*vedībandha*) to the top of the entablature (*varaṇḍikā*).

Miśraka (i). Pillar with a square or octagonal base, 16-sided middle section and a circular top.

Miśraka (ii). Temple superstructure of a mixed type, most commonly a curvilinear body (*latina*) with a barrel-vaulted crown (*valabhī*).

Nāgapāśa. Decorative motif consisting of interwoven serpents (*nāga*s), often used in doorways.

Nāgaśākhā. See *śākhā* below.

Nāsikā (*alpanāsī*, *alpanāsikā*, *kudu*). Ogee window motif in a temple of the south Indian type.

Nīvrapaṭṭikā. Dentil.

Pakṣabhadra. Short side-wall of a rectangular temple.

Pañcāyatana. Building complex with four subsidiary shrines around the main temple.

Paṭṭī. Band or register. Types include *gagārapaṭṭī* (band of spirals and arrows), *grāsapaṭṭī* (ferocious heads), *kaṅkaṇapatrapaṭṭī* (serrated leaves), *kaṇṭhapaṭṭī* (a decorative frieze set in a recess or *kaṇṭha*), *ratnapaṭṭī* (diamonds) and *śiraḥpaṭṭī* (running festoon placed at the top of the temple wall or *jaṅghā*).

Pedyā. Jamb of a door and relief panel at its base.

Phāṁsanā (i). Wedge-shaped roof composed of horizontal slabs.

Phāṁsanā (ii). Individual slab in a *phāṁsanā*-style roof.

Pīṭha (*jagatīpīṭhā*). Moulded plinth at the base of a temple. Types include *gajapīṭha* (elephant figures), *narapīṭha* (human figures) and *tulāpīṭha* (consisting of joist or dentil ends).

Pradakṣiṇapatha. Ambulatory.

Prāggrīva. Porch.

Praṇāla. Spout for draining water away from an image. It is usually ornamented on the outer end with an open-mouthed lion-head with the water trough behind that pierces the basement mouldings and enters the sanctum beside the image.

Pratiratha (*anuratha*). Subsidiary projection or flanking offset of a temple's walls.

Pṛṣṭhabhadra. Long wall of a rectangular temple.

Raṅgamaṇḍapa. See *maṇḍapa* above.

Rathikā. Framed niche.

Śākhā. Individual side-post or jamb of a doorway. Types include *antaraśākhā* (intermediate jamb); *bahirśākhā* or *bāhyaśākhā* (outer doorjamb); *gaṇaśākhā* (jamb carved with goblin-like figures, or *gaṇa*s), also termed *bhūtaśākhā*; *gandharvaśākhā* (jamb carved with celestial minstrels, or *gandharva*s); *khalvaśākhā* (plain recessed jamb); *mālāśākhā* (outer door-surround carved like a garland); *mithunaśākhā* (jamb adorned with images of couples (*mithuna*s); *nāgaśākhā* (jamb consisting of entwined serpents (*nāga*s), often with Garuda placed in the centre of the lintel and clutching the serpents' tails); *patraśākhā* (jamb adorned with scrollwork); *pratiśākhā* (innermost jamb, typically adorned with scrollwork); *ratnaśākhā* (jamb adorned with diamond-shaped lozenges); *rūpaśākhā* (jamb adorned with figures); *siṁhaśākhā* (jamb adorned with lions or griffins), also termed *vyālaśākhā*; *stambhaśākhā* (jamb shaped like a pillar); and *triśākhā* (door with three jambs).

Salilāntara. Vertical crevice between a temple's receding faces (*aṅga*s).

Śekharī. Multi-spired superstructure.

Śikhara (i). Curvilinear spire or superstructure in a north Indian temple of the *latina* type.

Śikhara (ii). Cupola surmounting a temple of the south Indian *kūṭina* type.

Siṁhakarṇa. Pediment with a triangular shape.

Siṁhamukha. Row of lion-heads.

Śiraḥpaṭṭī. Running festoon at the top of a temple wall; see also *paṭṭī* above.

Skandhavedī. Depressed barrel vault, typically employed on rectangular temples.

Śukanāsā. Arched antefix abutting the superstructure (*śikhara*) above the vestibule (*antarāla*).

Śūrasenaka. Large ogee-shaped dormer, often found at the base of the vertical spines (*latās*) in temples of the *bhūmija* type.

Talacchanda. Ground plan.

Talavitāna. Flat ceiling.

Toraṇa (i). Free-standing arch on two pillars placed before a temple or stupa (for illustration *see* TORAṆA).

Toraṇa (ii). Cusped arch, often over a niche or inside a temple hall; also termed *vandanamālikā*. Other usages include: *citratoraṇa* (ornamental arch) and *makaratoraṇa* (arch spewing from the mouths of mythical crocodiles, or *makaras*).

Ucchālaka. Extension of a pillar above a capital or corbel.

Udambara (*udumbara*). Door-sill or threshold.

Udgama. Pediment typically composed of interlocking window motifs (*candraśālās*); see also *siṁhakarṇa* above.

Ūrdhvacchanda. Ground plan.

Uttarāṅga. Lintel over a door.

Valabhī. Barrel-vaulted roof, typically used to crown a rectangular temple.

Varaṇḍikā. Entablature at the top of a temple's wall-section (*jaṅghā*).

Vedībandha. Podium mouldings used to surround a temple sanctum.

Vedikā (i). Fence or railing surrounding a stupa.

Vedikā (ii). Blind balustrade in a temple balcony or hall composed of pilasters (*stambhikās*) and vertical slabs (*phalakas*).

Veṇukośa (*padmakośa*, *karṇalatā*, *karṇaratha*). Corner section of a northern temple spire, typically marked by serrated discs (*karṇāṇḍakas*).

Vitāna. Ceiling.

MICHAEL D. WILLIS

(iii) Guilds and craftsmen. Guild structures for craftsmen began with the growth of urban centres in the pre-Maurya period and only later took on clear caste overtones. Within the later caste structure of Hinduism, the role of the maker was not a high one, although economic success could raise a guild's status, even to that of a patron within the Buddhist world. Ivory-carvers from the town of Besnagar (ancient Vidisha), for example, contributed to the making of one of the great stone gateways at Sanchi. The distinction between a supervising architect and the workmen who made and assembled the pieces became increasingly significant, however. Master architects had a much higher status and were given the title of *sūtradhāra* (master of the cord used for planning the structure). They controlled the diagrams that governed the temple and made it efficacious, as well as the mnemonic and textual traditions. The *sūtradhāra*'s growing authority may well have been an important source for the rapid innovation that transformed the temple after AD 500. Inscriptional references suggest that the hierarchy of craftsmen within a guild allowed advancement based on ability and that artists of high repute were not anonymous. In the Muslim period such guilds helped make the proliferation of Islamic buildings possible, and they were still in existence to help the British build the new capital in Delhi.

BIBLIOGRAPHY

Enc. Ind. Temple Archit.

P. Brown: *Indian Architecture (Buddhist and Hindu Periods)* (?Bombay, [1941], rev. Bombay, 1956)

——: *Indian Architecture (Islamic Period)* (?Bombay, [1942], rev. Bombay, 1956)

S. Kramrisch: *The Hindu Temple*, 2 vols (Calcutta, 1946)

M. Meister: 'The Two-and-a-Half-Day Mosque', *Orient. A.*, n. s., xviii/1 (1968), pp. 107–13

K. Deva: 'Bhūmija Temples', *Studies in Indian Temple Architecture*, ed. P. Chandra (New Delhi, 1975)

R. N. Misra: *Ancient Artists and Art-activity* (Simla, 1975)

M. Meister: 'Construction and Conception: Maṇḍapikā Shrines of Central India', *E. & W.*, n. s., xxvi (1976), pp. 409–18

M. A. Dhaky: *The Indian Temple Forms in Karnāta Inscriptions and Architecture* (New Delhi, 1977)

B. Dagens, ed.: *Mayamata, an Indian Treatise on Housing Architecture and Iconography* (New Delhi, 1985)

Archit. Rev. [London], clxxxii/1086 (1987) [full issue on 'Indian Identity']

M. Meister, ed.: *Making Things in South Asia: The Role of Artist and Craftsman* (Philadelphia, 1988)

M. Shokoohy: *Bhadreśvar, the Oldest Islamic Monuments in India* (Leiden, 1988)

C. Borden, ed.: *Contemporary Indian Tradition* (Washington, DC, 1989)

M. Meister: 'Prasada as Palace: Kūtina Origins of the Nāgara Temple', *Artibus Asiae*, xlix (1989), pp. 254–80

——: 'Reading Monuments and Seeing Texts', *Shastric Traditions in Indian Arts*, ed. A. L. Dallapiccola (Stuttgart, 1989)

T. Metcalf: *An Imperial Vision: Indian Architecture and Britain's Raj* (Berkeley, 1989)

M. Meister: 'De- and Re-constructing the Indian Temple', *A. J.* [New York], xlix (1990), pp. 395–400

A. Coomaraswamy: *Essays in Early Indian Architecture*, ed. M. Meister (New Delhi, 1992)

MICHAEL W. MEISTER

2. PRE- AND PROTOHISTORIC PERIODS. The impressive diversity of architecture during the protohistoric period in the Indian subcontinent ranges from the simple huts of the Deccan plateau and south India to great cities built of baked brick, such as Harappa and Mohenjo-daro (*c.* 2550–*c.* 2000 BC).

(i) Baluchistan. Sites of the earliest settled communities in the subcontinent have been excavated in Baluchistan, Pakistan. The great settlement of Mehrgarh (*c.* 7000–*c.* 2550 BC), on the lowlands at the foot of the Bolan Pass, has early mud and mud-brick architecture; the buildings seem to conform to a pattern of small, multi-roomed structures with a dividing wall down the centre (Jarrige, 1985; Jarrige and Meadow, 1980).

At a time contemporary to the mature Indus civilization (*c.* 2550–*c.* 2000 BC; *see* §(ii) below) the Kulli culture (Possehl, 1986) arose in southern Baluchistan, also known as Gedrosia. The great site of Nindowari (see Casal), covering some 60 hectares, is almost as large as the lower town of the Indus city of Mohenjo-daro. Nindowari has a high platform built of boulders, which seems to be a monumental expression of architectural patterns seen in the

Quetta Valley to the north at about the same time (see Fairservis; *see also* AFGHANISTAN, §II, 1(i) and QUETTA). Other Kulli sites, especially Kulli itself and Mehi (Stein, pp. 118–27, 154–63), have no signs of monumental architecture but do have structures built of semi-dressed quadrilinear blocks of stone that were carefully laid.

(ii) Indus civilization. The architecture of the Indus or Harappa civilization, which flourished from *c.* 2550 to *c.* 2000 BC, is known from over 1000 sites in Pakistan and India. The largest urban centres are HARAPPA, on the Ravi River, the type site by which the civilization is sometimes known, and MOHENJO-DARO, on the lower Indus in Pakistan. Each of these cities was around 100 ha in size and had a population of 40,000 to 50,000. Other important sites include KALIBANGAN in northern Rajasthan and LOTHAL in Gujarat. A promising site called Ganweriwala in Bahawalpur, Pakistan, as large as Mohenjo-daro, remained unexcavated in the early 1990s. Sites under excavation in the early 1990s included Dholavira, in Kachchh, which produced a unique inscription in the form of a mosaic, and Nausharo, just south of Mehrgarh, where evidence was found for the period of transition between the pre-urban and urban phases of the Indus civilization.

Building in baked brick is extensive in the Indus civilization sites, and beam sockets and other features indicate the use of timber architectural components during at least some periods. Such large civic structures as baths, granaries and warehouses have been identified, as well as such workshops as those of beadworkers at CHANHU-DARO. Residential buildings, often two-storey, generally had a central courtyard on to which opened ranges of relatively small rooms. Little architectural decoration survives at any Indus site, but some buildings have traces of mud plaster covering the brickwork, and tiled floors decorated with intersecting circles remain in some rooms. It has been suggested that these were bathing areas.

Some of the most impressive architectural remains of the Indus civilization (and of the ancient world) are found at Mohenjo-daro. Substantial remains surround the area visible above the valley's surface (see Lohuizen de Leeuw). The city is best known for its orderly layout, based on a grid plan (see Stanislawski), and its sophisticated drainage system (see Marshall). The site is divided into two distinct parts: a high mound (*c.* 400×200 m) to the west, with interesting public buildings, and a lower town (*c.* 80 ha) of domestic architecture, with some evidence for craft activity. The former has sometimes been called the Citadel, but there is no significant evidence to show that it ever functioned in this way. More recent studies refer to it as either the Mound of the Great Bath or the High Mound. The two principal buildings on the mound are the Great Bath itself and a warehouse or granary. (Buildings referred to as the 'College' and 'Assembly Hall' are not well enough known to be included in this discussion.)

The Great Bath is a rectangular 'pool' (11.3×6.7 m with a depth of some 2 m) near the centre of the mound (see fig. 22). It is surrounded by a series of column bases, a circumambulatory with typically Harappan bathing rooms on the western side (see Ardeleanu-Jansen, Franke and Jansen), and is approached on each end by steps, at the bottom of which is a small platform on which the bathers could have stood. The bath was made of baked brick and was waterproofed with a full lining of bitumen. Within the colonnade a well and a drain are present to simplify the changing of water. Most reconstructions of the Great Bath (e.g. Wheeler, p. 16) suggest that it was surrounded by a flat-roofed building, the bath itself being open to the air.

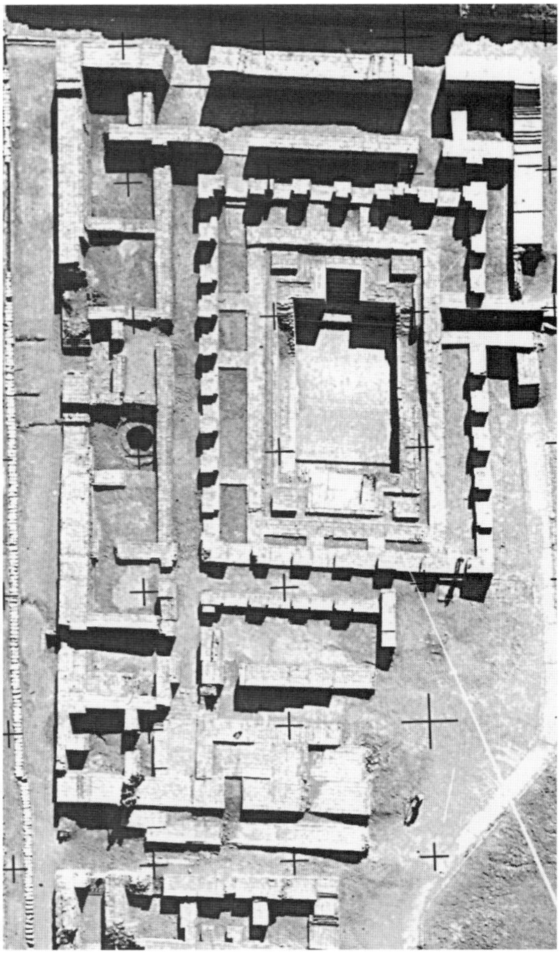

22. The Great Bath, baked brick waterproofed with a bitumen lining, 11.3×6.7×2 m, Mohenjo-daro, Pakistan, *c.* 2400–*c.* 2200 BC

The granary or warehouse is directly adjacent to the Great Bath. The archaeological remains are a series of some 30 solid baked-brick 'cubes' built to a modular unit measuring some 4 m on each side and standing about 1.5 m high. These were apparently the foundations for the building itself, which, according to most reconstructions (e.g. Wheeler, p. 18), would have been made of wood and/or other materials. There is no direct archaeological evidence in the form of package sealings, storage containers or stored products themselves to support the proposed function for this structure. The building at Harappa called the Granary (Wheeler, p. 30) looks nothing like the structure at Mohenjo-daro.

The vast living area of the lower town of Mohenjo-daro, the place of residence for the bulk of the population, contained homes and work places. Craft activities have been documented in the form of kilns for baking pottery, waste products from the smelting of metals and evidence for manufacturing a wide array of products from hardstones (e.g. lapis lazuli, turquoise, carnelian) and shell, some of it from maritime species such as the conch. Most of the lapidary efforts were directed to the manufacture of beads and pendants, and shell was used for bangles and inlays, presumably for furniture, boxes, trays and the like. Faience was also produced in the city. The bead manufacturing and shell bangle production are understood in great detail through the study of wasters, products broken in the course of manufacture, and the finished products themselves (see Vidale in Jansen and Urban, eds, 1987, pp. 113–49; Dales and Kenoyer, 1977).

The lower town was constructed on a grid plan orientated to the cardinal directions, although within the blocks formed from the major arteries the pattern is less regular. The extensive use of baked brick led to splendid preservation; one can enter houses, walk up flights of stairs and peer into wells. The feeling of the place is that of a living community, with the population temporarily out of town. The most useful document on the architecture of Mohenjo-daro is Sir John Marshall's report published in 1931; see also Mackay for this site. For the architecture of other sites see Vats; Thapar; Rao, 1979 and 1985; and Joshi.

(iii) Deccan and south India. On the Deccan plateau of Maharashtra remains of buildings survive from the time of an efflorescence of village life in the 2nd millennium BC. The most extensive mounds are those of Inamgaon (see Sankalia, Ansari and Dhavalikar; Dhavalikar, Sankalia and Ansari). The remains of large rectilinear houses (6.5×4.5 m) with plastered floors lined with post holes, into which the ancient inhabitants had excavated hearths, date to Period I (*c.* 1600–*c.* 1400 BC), termed the Malwa occupation. These structures were equipped with domestic facilities for storage, and evidence suggests they had wattle and daub exterior walls and thatched roofs. Smaller rectilinear houses (5×3 m) are in evidence from Period II (*c.* 1400–*c.* 1000 BC), the Early Jorwe period; there is also a unique structure measuring 10.5×9.15 m. The houses are built in the same architectural tradition as Period I. Some have mud platforms for storage bins, and there are six pit silos and seven mud platforms. A large bund was constructed during this period for the diversion of irrigation water around the settlement. In Period III (*c.* 1000–*c.* 700 BC), the Late Jorwe, the settlement was smaller, with round houses (diam. 2.5–4.25 m). This habitation included a cluster of buildings for craftsmen, one of whom was a goldsmith and another a limemaker. Architecture of the Malwa and Jorwe periods is discussed in detail in Sankalia, Subbarao and Deo; Sankalia, Deo and Ansari, 1969 and 1971; Ansari and Dhavalikar; and Chakravarti, Kumar, Wakankar and Khare.

Throughout most of the 2nd millennium BC the southern Deccan and adjacent regions saw the emergence of the so-called 'Southern Neolithic'. The antecedents of this culture are obscure but cannot be divorced from the origins of the Malwa culture to the north (see Dhavalikar). Architecture consisted of simple wattle and daub structures with thatched roofs (Allchin, 1960 and 1961; Nagaraja Rao and Malhotra; Nagaraja Rao). Settlements are associated with mounds composed of burnt dung, which seem to have been the places of ancient rituals relating to nomadic cattle-keeping (see Allchin, 1963; Allchin and Allchin, 1974).

BIBLIOGRAPHY

ARCHAEOLOGICAL REPORTS

J. Marshall, ed.: *Mohenjo-daro and the Indus Civilization*, 3 vols (London, 1931)

A. Stein: *An Archaeological Tour in Gedrosia*, Mem. Archaeol. Surv. India, xliii (Delhi, 1931)

E. Mackay: *Further Excavations at Mohenjo-daro*, 2 vols (Delhi, 1937–8) [146 figs and pls]

M. S. Vats: *Excavations at Harappa*, 2 vols (Delhi, 1940)

W. Fairservis jr: *Excavations in the Quetta Valley, West Pakistan*, Amer. Mus. Nat. Hist.: Anthropol. Pap., xlv/2 (1956), pp. 169–402

H. Sankalia, B. Subbarao and S. Deo: *The Excavations at Maheshwar and Navdatoli, 1952–53* (Pune and Vadodara, 1958)

F. R. Allchin: *Piklihal Excavations*, Govt Andhra Pradesh, Archaeol. Ser., i (Hyderabad, 1960)

——: *Utnur Excavations*, Govt Andhra Pradesh, Archaeol. Ser., v (Hyderabad, 1961)

——: *Neolithic Cattle Keepers of South India: A Study of Deccan Ashmounds* (Cambridge, 1963)

G. Dales: 'New Investigations at Mohenjo-daro', *Archaeology*, xviii (1965), pp. 145–50

M. Nagaraja Rao and K. Malhotra: *The Stone Age Hill Dwellers of Takkalakota* (Pune, 1965)

J.-M. Casal: 'Nindowari: A Chalcolithic Site in South Baluchistan', *Pakistan Archaeol.*, iii (1966), pp. 10–21

H. Sankalia, S. B. Deo and Z. D. Ansari: *Excavations at Ahar (Tambavati)* (Pune, 1969)

M. Nagaraja Rao: *Protohistoric Cultures of the Tungabhadra Valley: A Report on Hallur Excavations* (Dharwar, 1971)

H. Sankalia, S. Deo and Z. Ansari: *Chalcolithic Navdatoli: The Excavations at Navdatoli 1957–59* (Pune and Vadodara, 1971)

Z. Ansari and M. K. Dhavalikar: *Excavations at Kayatha* (Pune, 1975)

H. Sankalia, Z. Ansari and M. Dhavalikar: 'An Early Farmer's Village in Central India', *Expedition*, xvii/2 (1975), pp. 12–18

G. Dales and J. M. Kenoyer: 'Shell Working at Ancient Balakot, Pakistan', *Expedition*, xix/2 (1977), pp. 13–19

M. Jansen: 'Architectural Problems of the Harappa Culture', *S. Asian Archaeol. 1977*, pp. 405–31

S. Rao: *Lothal: A Harappan Port Town, 1955–62*, Mem. Archaeol. Surv. India, lxxviii/i (Delhi, 1979)

A. Ardeleanu-Jansen, U. Franke and M. Jansen: 'An Approach toward the Replacement of Artifacts into the Architectural Context of the Great Bath at Mohenjo-daro', *Forschungsprojekt Dfg Mohenjodaro*, ed. G. Urban and M. Jansen (Aachen, 1983), pp. 43–6

M. Jansen and G. Urban, eds: *Reports on Field Work Carried Out at Mohenjo-Daro, Pakistan 1982–83 by the IsMeo-Aachen University Mission: Interim Reports Volume 1* (Aachen and Rome, 1983)

J.-F. Jarrige: 'Continuity and Change in the North Kachi Plain (Baluchistan, Pakistan) at the Beginning of the Second Millennium BC', *S. Asian Archaeol.* (1983), pp. 35–68

M. Vidale: 'Surface Evaluation of Craft Activity Areas at Moenjodara, 1982–84', *E. & W.*, xxxiv/4 (1984), pp. 516–28

M. Jansen and G. Urban, eds: *Mohenjo Daro: Report of the Aachen University Mission 1979–1985* (Leiden, 1985)

S. R. Rao: *Lothal: A Harappan Port Town, 1955–62*, Mem. Archaeol. Surv. India, lxxviii/ii (Delhi, 1985)

G. Possehl: *Kulli: An Exploration of Ancient Civilization in South Asia* (Durham, NC, 1986)

M. Jansen and G. Urban, eds: *Reports on Field Work Carried Out at Mohenjo-Daro, Pakistan 1983–84 by the IsMeo-Aachen University Mission: Interim Reports Vol. 2* (Aachen and Rome, 1987)

M. Dhavalikar, H. Sankalia and Z. Ansari: *Excavations at Inamgaon*, i/1–2 (Pune, 1988)

M. Jansen and M. Tosi, eds: *Reports on Field Work Carried Out at Mohenjo-Daro, Pakistan 1983–86 by the IsMeo-Aachen University Mission: Interim Reports Vol. 3* (Aachen and Rome, 1988)

K. Chakravarty, V. Wakankar and M. Khare: *Dangawada Excavations* (Bhopal, 1989)

J. Joshi: *Excavation at Surkotada 1971–72 and Exploration in Kutch*, Mem. Archaeol. Surv. India, lxxxvii (Delhi, 1990)

OTHER SPECIALIST STUDIES

D. Stanislawski: 'The Origin and Spread of the Grid-pattern Town', *Geog. Rev.*, xxxvi (1946), pp. 105–20

M. Wheeler: *Civilizations of the Indus Valley and Beyond* (New York, 1966)

M. Dhavalikar: 'The Genesis of the Jorwe Culture', *Ind. Antiqua.*, n. s. 2, iv/1–4 (1970), pp. 32–41

F. R. Allchin and B. Allchin: 'Some New Thoughts on Indian Cattle', *South Asian Archaeology, 1973*, ed. N. Hammond (Leiden, 1974), pp. 71–7

B. Thapar: 'New Traits of the Indus Civilization at Kalibangan: An Appraisal', *South Asian Archaeology, 1973*, ed. N. Hammond (Leiden, 1974), pp. 85–104

J. van Lohuizen de Leeuw: 'Mohenjo Daro—a Cause of Common Concern', *South Asian Archaeology, 1973*, ed. N. Hammond (Leiden, 1974), pp. 1–11

G. Possehl, ed.: *Ancient Cities of the Indus* (Durham, NC, 1979)

J.-F. Jarrige and R. Meadow: 'The Antecedents of Civilization in the Indus Valley', *Sci. Amer.*, ccxliii/2 (1980), pp. 122–33

Les Cités oubliées de l'Indus: Archéologie du Pakistan (exh. cat., Paris, Mus. Guimet, 1988–9), Eng. trans. as *Forgotten Cities on the Indus: Early Civilization in Pakistan from the 8th to the 2nd Millennium B.C.*, ed. M. Jansen, M. Mulloy and G. Urban (Mainz, 1991)

G. Possehl, ed.: *Harappan Civilization: A Contemporary Perspective* (Delhi, 2/1992)

G. Possehl and P. Rissman: 'The Chronology of Prehistoric India: From Earliest Times to the Iron Age', *Chronologies in Old World Archaeology* (Chicago, 3/1992)

J. Shaffer: 'The Indus Valley, Baluchistan and Helmand Traditions: Neolithic through Bronze Age', *Chronologies in Old World Archaeology* (Chicago, 3/1992)

GREGORY L. POSSEHL

3. 6TH CENTURY BC–3RD CENTURY AD. Although a second wave of urbanization occurred in the Gangetic Valley and other parts of the Indian subcontinent *c.* 6th century BC, few structures from before the 4th century AD survive. Despite the lack of actual buildings, a reasonably complete picture of early Indian architecture can be reconstructed; bas-reliefs from the period are an important source of information. Though most come from Buddhist monuments, the architectural forms they represent are not sectarian. Stone reliefs from BHARHUT (see fig. 24 below), SANCHI (see figs 17 above and 23 below), Bodhgaya (*see* BODHGAYA AND GAYA), MATHURA, AMARAVATI and NAGARJUNAKONDA (2nd century BC to 3rd century AD) show with reasonable accuracy cottages, mansions, palaces, shrines, temples, gateways and fortifications set in leafy forest environs and vivid cityscapes.

23. City-gate, rampart and mansions depicted on relief panel of the *Great Departure from Kapilavastu*, Stupa 1, Sanchi, *c.* 1st century BC

Further information is provided by the rock-cut architecture in Maharashtra and to a lesser extent in eastern India, which imitates in stone the forms of buildings in timber and other impermanent materials. Archaeological excavation of ancient sites, albeit limited, has supplemented and corroborated the information furnished by bas-reliefs and rock-cut examples. Finally, numerous references to architectural structures and their embellishments are found in Sanskrit literature, as well as early Jaina and Buddhist canonical texts. When studied with reference to actual remains, these literary references provide descriptive terminology and a better understanding of early Indian building types.

(i) Cities and palaces. (ii) Religious structures.

(i) Cities and palaces. Most cities appear to have been surrounded by a moat and stone and brick rampart with crenellated parapet, as depicted in bas-reliefs at Sanchi (see fig. 23). The lower portions of such fortifications have been found in excavations at KAUSAMBI and RAJGIR. Entrance to cities was controlled by monumental gatehouses. When strategic and practical concerns allowed, these were placed at the cardinal points, as in the later plan of SISUPALGARH in Orissa (4th century BC onward), where the fortification walls are orientated in the cardinal directions, with two large gateways on each side. Such gatehouses consisted of a pair of projecting towers (Skt *aṭṭāla*) with roofed chambers and overhanging balconies. These were made of wood and could be used to defend the entrance in times of war or as a viewing place for processions. The entrance (*mukha*), between the projecting towers, was high enough to admit an elephant and rider. On the interior, raised platforms (*mañca*) on either side of the road permitted townsfolk to monitor comings and goings. Outside the gate, on the far bank of the moat, there was often a free-standing ornamental gate (*toraṇa*), a simpler version of the gates still standing at Sanchi.

The cities' large avenues and busy streets were lined with shops, emporia, places of worship, public buildings and residences. Palaces and large mansions were built in a consistent style, with high walls surrounding extensive gardens. A glowing account of the parks, gardens and tanks of the palace at Pataliputra is preserved in the accounts of Megasthenes, who in 302 BC was the ambassador of Seleukos I to the court of Chandragupta Maurya (*reg c.* 321–297 BC). The ground floor and lower rooms of palaces and important homes were probably used as kitchens and storage areas and to house domestic animals. The front was often lined with tall octagonal columns. The upper storeys consisted of rectangular, square and, in some cases, apsidal chambers. The form of earthly palaces is reflected in a relief at Bharhut (see fig. 24 below) representing a 'palace of the gods' on the right and a shrine on the left. The main roofing material appears to have been thatch; the walls were predominantly of wattle and daub. A notable feature, found throughout early Indian architecture, is the ogee-shaped dormer window (*gavākṣa*; e.g. in fig. 24 below). Delicate lath or reed screens were set in the *gavākṣa*-type windows to provide privacy and shield the occupants from the elements. Spacious balconies looking down on the avenues below were edged with wooden railings (*vedikā*).

Palaces often had assembly halls. That of the Maurya palace at Pataliputra may be the basis for the architectural description in the 'Book of the Assembly Hall', in the *Mahābhārata* (2[20]:1–4). Possibly inspired by the pillared halls of the Achaemenid kings of Iran, the Pataliputra assembly hall survived into the 5th century AD, when it was visited by Chinese pilgrims who described it in their travel accounts. Excavations in the early 20th century uncovered an extensive hypostyle with stone pillars (*see* PATNA).

(ii) Religious structures.

(a) Stupas. (b) Tree-shrines. (c) Rectilinear, circular and elliptical shrines. (d) Apsidal structures.

(a) Stupas. The stupa, which began as a simple tumulus over the cremated remains of a worthy individual, was adopted by Jainism and Buddhism at an early period. The earliest extant (though altered) examples were built in the 3rd century BC, by which time the stupa was venerated as an aniconic emblem of the Buddha's final release (*nirvāṇa*). With time, the stupa was elaborated by the addition of basal terraces (*medhi*), balustrades (*vedikā*), gates (*toraṇa*) and ornamental designs in plaster on the dome (*aṇḍa*). Free-standing pillars were placed in the vicinity, and a crowning, houselike superstructure (*harmikā*) with a parasol was added on top. The best-preserved example is the main stupa at Sanchi, which achieved its present state *c.* 50 BC (*see* STUPA, fig. 1).

In south India, the basic form continued but was subject to extraordinary decorative embellishment. The chief architectural innovations were the introduction of niches containing Buddha images and clusters of five pillars inside each gateway. The ruined stupa at Amaravati (*c.* 2nd century AD) was of this type (see Brown, pl. xxxv). In the north-western region of Gandhara, the stupa adopted an Indo-Hellenistic style during the first three centuries AD. Stupas at Sirkap (*see* TAXILA), TAKHT-I-BAHI and GULDARA (*see also* AFGHANISTAN, fig. 4) had a square plinth and were articulated with pilasters and pediments in a provincial Mediterranean style. The crowning parasol was multiplied and heightened. Niches with Buddha images were introduced in Gandhara as elsewhere.

(b) Tree-shrines. The simplest form of shrine was a modest dais, usually with a top slab. This sacred platform was called *caitya* ('sacred object'). The word *caitya* was applied to virtually every kind of holy structure, from a ritual altar to a stupa. When a sacred dais or stupa was set inside a building, the result was a *caityagṛha* ('house for the sacred object').

A simple dais was often placed under a tree, a combination depicted in early bas-reliefs. Trees were worshipped from antiquity as symbols of fecundity and the abode of nature-spirits or demigods (*yakṣa*, fem. *yakṣī*). An early representation occurs in a relief at Amaravati (2nd century BC), where a tree enclosed by a railing is labelled in Prakrit *cetiya* (Skt *caitya*; Amaravati, Archaeol. Mus.; see Ghosh and Sarkar, pl. xliiia). Because the Buddha attained liberation under a *bodhi* tree (Skt *pippala*, *aśvattha*; Lat. *Ficus religiosa*), tree-shrines of this species were appropriated by Buddhism as emblems of his enlightenment. Other trees became emblems of past and future Buddhas or were associated with Jaina saints or Hindu deities. The oldest Tamil texts, such as the *Ahananuru*, indicate that the kadamba and banyan trees were the abodes of Murugan and Shiva. Revered trees were enclosed by a wall with a gate; garlands, parasols and auspicious symbols were often added.

Such basic tree-shrines (known as *vṛkṣacaitya* in Sanskrit and *rukkhacetiya* in Prakrit) received elaborate development in the hypaethral *bodhighara* (Pali: 'house for the *bodhi* tree'); the Tamil epic *Silappadikāram* uses the term *podimanram*. These were usually Buddhist shrines of two or more storeys and had timber galleries from which worshippers could lustrate and adore the *bodhi* tree within. A damaged relief from Amaravati (Madras, Govt Mus. & N.A.G.) shows a square *bodhighara* of four or five storeys; other examples were octagonal, round or apsidal. With the decline of earlier Buddhism in India, the *bodhighara* disappeared, but the form continued in Sri Lanka and Java, where ruined examples have been found (see Bandananayake).

(c) Rectilinear, circular and elliptical shrines. Other shrines in ancient India, modelled after modest huts and the prevailing types of domestic architecture, were square, rectangular, circular or elliptical in plan. The simplest examples were single-chambered shrines squarish in plan with a peaked roof. Examples of this basic type are shown in a relief at Sanchi of the shrines at Jetavana (see fig. 17 above). A square pillared pavilion containing a serpent divinity (*nāga*), which also occurs at Sanchi, carries an octagonal ridged roof pierced by *gavākṣa*-type windows. Another pillared pavilion, shown in a Bharhut relief (Washington, DC, Freer), enshrines a wheel, the Buddhist emblem of the law. It has a complete upper storey with an oblong vault and windows.

A number of reliefs from Mathura (Mathura, Govt Mus.) show the development of the square shrine after the 1st century AD. Upper storeys were multiplied and considerably abbreviated. In one relief a multi-storey shrine is shown with the quadripartite moulding known in Sanskrit as *vedībandha* (see Shah, fig. 14). This is the earliest example of a form that becomes virtually universal in the mature temple architecture of northern India. Other stone architectural fragments (e.g. Mathura, Govt Mus., and Lucknow, State Mus.) show that such architectural forms of the Gupta period as the T-shaped doorframe were already present in the first two centuries AD. (The architectural evidence provided by such early fragments has yet to be thoroughly studied.)

Simple huts, the prototype for shrines with circular plans, are represented in numerous reliefs at Mathura, Sanchi and Amaravati. More elaborate is the domed shrine shown in the Bharhut relief (see fig. 24), which consists of an open pillared pavilion with a broad cornice (*kapota*) running around the base of the dome. The entrance portal has the characteristic ogee-arch form. Inside, relics of the Buddha rest on a dais below a parasol. A similar domed shrine containing a miniature stupa is illustrated on a pillar from Amaravati (Madras, Govt Mus. & N.A.G.).

A ruined brick-and-timber shrine (*c.* 3rd century BC) at Bairat (Jaipur District, Rajasthan), the oldest structural temple in India, provides archaeological corroboration for the circular temples illustrated in reliefs. The shrine proper (diam. 8.24 m) was made of lime-plastered panels of brickwork alternating with 26 octagonal wooden columns (see Brown, pl. vi). A circular wall enclosed the building, providing an ambulatory (*pradakṣiṇā*). A small porch preceded the entrance, and the whole was set in a rectangular compound. The elevational aspects of the temple at Bairat can be conjectured from the 3rd-century BC caves at Barabar (Gaya District, Bihar) with inscriptions of the Maurya dynasty. The Sudama Cave, has a circular cell (diam. 5.80 m) with a domical roof and overhanging eaves (in imitation of a timber structure) preceded by a rectangular antechamber with a vaulted roof. The Lomas Rishi Cave is a replica of the Sudama Cave except that the inner cell is oval in plan. The ornate entrance of the Lomas Rishi (see fig. 25) replicates contemporary wooden forms

25. Entrance to the Lomas Rishi Cave, Barabar, 3rd century BC

24. Inscribed relief panel depicting a circular shrine adjacent to a three-storey palace, from Bharhut, mid-2nd century BC (Calcutta, Indian Museum)

in stone. The door has sloping jambs supporting an ogee-shaped frame of laminated planks; the planks rest on rafter-ends and support a finial. The concentric architrave has two registers, one showing latticework and the other a frieze of elephants worshipping cylindrical stupas. The similarities are evident in the configuration of the Lomas Rishi Cave and the buildings represented in the Sanchi and Bharhut reliefs (see figs 24 and 25; see also fig. 17 above).

Circular shrines became more elaborate in the first three centuries AD. A fragmentary relief from Ghantasala in the Andhra region of south India (Paris, Mus. Guimet; see Shah, fig. 12) shows a building of three diminishing 'storeys' crowned by a ridged cupola. Each level, clearly demarcated by a broad cornice, carries projecting niches with balconies and arched windows (*gavākṣa*). The broken lower portion of the relief probably depicted circular walls and mouldings.

A comparison of this relief with contemporary examples from Mathura shows that fundamental differences between northern and southern architecture were beginning to appear by the 2nd century AD. Each of the levels of the Ghantasala superstructure is complete in itself, with all the architectural features carefully replicated. The Mathura examples, in contrast, exhibit considerable abbreviation; the wall-sections of the upper 'storeys' are compressed, and architectural features substantially distorted or eliminated. In some instances, the upper levels are reduced to decorative bands and lattice patterns. The fluid shorthand characteristic of northern architecture is already evident in the Mathura examples; the south elaborates its forms in a more conservative and crystalline manner.

The elliptical plan, a more unusual form, occurs in the inner chamber of the Lomas Rishi Cave at Barabar and in the Gopika Cave at the same site, also a product of the Maurya age. Excavations have revealed that the Vasudeva Temple (*c.* 200 BC) at Beshnagar (near Vidisha, Madhya Pradesh) was a large elliptical structure (8.23×2.97 m), probably of timber, enclosed by an ambulatory and preceded by a rectangular porch (see Khare). A free-standing pillar was added to the precinct *c.* 150 BC. Its inscription describes it as a *garuḍa dhvaja* ('standard of Garuda') of the supreme god Vasudeva (a form of Vishnu). Another elliptical temple (*c.* 1st century BC) was excavated at Nagari (near Chittaurgarh, Rajasthan). Built of timber and enclosed by a monumental wall of dressed stone (90.2×46.05 m), it also seems to have been dedicated to the worship of Vishnu.

An idea of the elevation of these ruined elliptical temples can be gleaned from relief representations. For example, an open pillared pavilion of three storeys is shown in a relief from Jaggayyapeta dating to *c.* 150 BC (Madras, Govt Mus. & N.A.G.; see Burgess). The oval plan was also applied to the *bodhighara* (*see* §(b) above). Related to the elliptical configuration, but not a true oval, were rectangular buildings with semicircular ends (*see* §(d) below). A brick-built example, probably dating to the Maurya period, was unearthed at Kausambi. The building formed part of the monastic complex of Ghositarama, a favourite resort of the Buddha.

(*d*) *Apsidal structures.* The most popular and enduring early building type was the apsidal structure (*cāpa*, later *gajapṛṣṭha*). It was used by all religious sects and was found in all regions of India, from Gandhara and Kashmir in the north to Karnataka in the south. The oldest known apsidal temple appears to be the brick example uncovered at the Buddhist site of SARNATH, near Varanasi. Surviving as a mere foundation, it lies near the Maurya pillar, with which it was probably contemporary. The apsidal Temple 40 (20.4×6.7 m; also *c.* 3rd century BC) at Sanchi was made of stone, stood on a raised plinth and probably had a timber roof. An ambulatory ran around the whole structure. Destroyed by fire *c.* 150 BC, it was rebuilt on several occasions following different plans.

Somewhat better preserved is a large apsidal structure sacred to Jainism excavated out of Udayagiri Hill in Orissa. The temple probably dates to the 1st century BC but appears to have replaced an earlier building on the same site. Constructed of laterite slabs, it was built around a circular dais or sanctum chamber. The roof was probably supported by timber columns set into the brick floor and bedrock. A vestibule and ambulatory were subsequently created inside the temple by adding walls that extended from the sanctum towards the entrance.

26. Interior of rock-cut apsidal temple at Bhaja, 2nd century BC

In excavations at Sonkh, a village near Mathura (see Härtel), two apsidal temples and some of the surrounding habitations were unearthed. Both temples date to the early Kushana period and were built of brick with timber and tile roofs. The more elaborate example (Temple 2) introduces a colonnade around the apse-end that extends down the sides towards the entrance. This structure was set in a square compound with a forecourt. The shrine was dedicated to the worship of a *nāga* (serpent-god); a stone bracket with a *śālabhañjikā* (woman-and-tree motif) and a lintel fragment with a narrative *nāga* panel were the finest artefacts recovered (Mathura, Govt Mus.).

The appearance of the temples at Sonkh may be reflected by a unique stone relief from Mathura (Mathura, Govt Mus.), representing a small apsidal temple outside the walls of a city. The shrine, shown from the side, rests on a square plinth and has three finials on the roof. The exterior is plain. In general appearance, this shrine is similar to the Kapoteshvara Temple at Chezerla, once thought to date to *c.* the 3rd century AD but more probably a product of the 7th or 8th century (*see* §4(ii)(c) below). Extensive excavations south of Nagarjunakonda have unearthed numerous brick-built structures dating to the 2nd and 3rd centuries AD. The apsidal temples there follow the architectural arrangements found elsewhere.

The largest apsidal temple in the subcontinent (39.3×15.5 m) is located at Sirkap, Taxila, in the Gandhara region (see Marshall). Resting on foundations of perhaps the 1st century BC, the building is astylar and set in a rectangular compound, an arrangement seen at Sonkh and Sanchi. (Temple 18 at Sanchi dates to the 7th century but stands on older foundations.) The other apsidal shrines at Taxila are modest structures, varying from the general standard in that they enshrine octagonal stupas and have a corresponding shape on the interior of the apse.

Much about the appearance of no-longer extant apsidal shrines is revealed by the rock-cut apsidal cave temples in Maharashtra. Among the most impressive are those at BHAJA (see fig. 26), PITALKHORA, NASIK, KARLE and Ajanta (caves 9 and 10), dating mainly to the 2nd and 1st centuries BC. The cave temples are earlier than those at Sonkh, but are comparable in that pillars encircle the apse-end (where a monolithic stone stupa stands) and extend towards the entrance. This creates a pair of aisles divided from the central nave by a colonnade. The ceilings carry rafters (in some instances actually wood, in others stone carved to imitate wood); entrances have wide arches of the *gavākṣa* type. The porch interiors and façades are richly decorated with arched niches, balconies and railings. In some cases a wooden façade was placed in front of the temples, as, for example, at Karle, Bedsa and Junnar. Stone versions of residential monastic buildings, known only from foundations elsewhere, are preserved at these sites.

BIBLIOGRAPHY

A. Cunningham: *The Stupa at Bharhut* (London, 1879)
J. Burgess: *The Buddhist Stupa of Amaravati and Jaggayyapeta* (London, 1887)
A. Foucher: *L'Art gréco-bouddhique du Gandhâra*, 2 vols (Paris, 1900–51)
V. A. Smith: *The Jaina Stupa and Other Antiquities of Mathura* (Allahabad, 1901)
A. K. Coomaraswamy: 'Early Indian Architecture I: Cities and City-gates, etc., II: Bodhi-gharas', *E. A.*, ii (1930), pp. 209–35
J. P. Vogel: *La Sculpture de Mathura* (Paris, 1930)
A. K. Coomaraswamy: 'Early Indian Architecture III: Palaces', *E. A.*, iii (1931), pp. 181–217
——: *La Sculpture de Bodhgaya* (Paris, 1935)
V. S. Agrawala: *Handbook of Sculptures in the Curzon Museum of Archaeology, Mathura* (Allahabad, 1939)
J. Marshall and A. Foucher: *The Monuments of Sanchi*, 3 vols (Calcutta and London, 1940)
P. Brown: *Indian Architecture (Buddhist and Hindu Periods)* (Bombay, [1942], rev. Bombay, 1956 with additional photographs)
M. Chandra: 'Architectural Data in Jaina Canonical Literature', *J. Bombay Branch Royal Asiat. Soc.*, xxvi (1951), pp. 168–82
J. Marshall: *Taxila*, 3 vols (Cambridge, 1951)
D. Mitra: *Udayagiri & Khandagiri* (New Delhi, 1960)
Amita Ray: *Villages, Towns and Secular Buildings in Ancient India* (Calcutta, 1964)
A. Ghosh and H. Sarkar: 'Beginnings of Sculptural Art in South-East India: A Stele from Amaravati', *Anc. India*, xx–xxi (1964–5), pp. 168–77
V. S. Agrawala: *Studies in Indian Art* (Varanasi, 1965)
N. P. Joshi: *Mathura Sculpture* (Mathura, 1966)
H. Sarkar: *Studies in Early Buddhist Architecture of India* (Delhi, 1966)
M. D. Khare: 'Discovery of a Vishnu Temple near the Heliodoros Pillar, Besnagar, Dist. Vidisha (M.P.)', *Lalit Kala*, xiii (1967), pp. 21–7
V. Agrawala: 'Ancient Indian Palace Architecture', *Śrī Mahāvīra Jaina Vidyālaya Golden Jubilee*, i (Bombay, 1968), pp. 242–59
V. Dehejia: *Early Buddhist Rock Temples* (London, 1972)
H. Sarkar and B. N. Misra: *Nagarjunakonda* (New Delhi, 1972)
H. Sarkar and S. P. Nainar: *Amaravati* (New Delhi, 1972)
S. Bandaranayake: 'Buddhist Tree-Temples in Sri Lanka', *South Asian Archaeology 1973*, ed. J. E. van Lohuizen-de Leeuw and J. M. M. Ubaghs (Leiden, 1974), pp. 136–59 [fig. 5b, from Amaravati, is incorrectly labelled Mathura]
——: *Sinhalese Monastic Architecture* (Leiden, 1974)
U. P. Shah: 'Beginnings of the Superstructure of Indian Temples', *Studies in Indian Temple Architecture*, ed. P. Chandra (Delhi, 1975), pp. 80–89
H. Härtel: 'Some Results of the Excavations at Sonkh: A Preliminary Report', *German Scholars in India*, ii (New Delhi, 1976), pp. 69–99
S. P. Gupta: *The Roots of Indian Art* (Delhi, 1980)
A. K. Coomaraswamy: 'Early Indian Architecture IV: Huts and Related Temple Types', *Res* (1988), pp. 5–26 [written in the 1930s; ed. with afterword by M. Meister]

KRISHNA DEVA, MICHAEL D. WILLIS

4. 4TH–5TH CENTURIES AD. The kings of the Gupta dynasty and their tributaries controlled the greater part of north India in the 4th and 5th centuries. Their dominion flourished until the Hunas invaded from the north-west in the closing years of the 5th century. To the south of the Narmada River in the Deccan plateau, two branches of the Vakataka house ruled concurrently with the Guptas and are known to have intermarried with them in the early 5th century. The rulers of these dynasties probably built palaces, but no examples survive. The appearance of this architecture is, however, indicated to some extent by the residential structures and gardens depicted in the wall paintings at Ajanta.

While timber and brick continued to be used for residential architecture, the potential of dressed stone began to be appreciated for temple building in north India towards the end of the 4th century. The introduction of stone helped fix the basic components of the temple, the key features being a cella (Skt *garbhagṛha*) for the deity and a portico or hall (*maṇḍapa*) for sheltering devotees. The sanctum entrance was fitted with jambs (*śākhās*), often richly carved and carrying figures of the river goddesses Ganga and Yamuna. Superstructures of storeyed pyramidal form were introduced over the sanctum. South of the Narmada River, structural temples of stone were also built, but the most impressive monuments are the elaborate caves excavated into hillsides and rocky bluffs. This rock-cut architecture, prevalent in the region since the 2nd century BC, was more conservative in character than the structural temples of the north. The principal building types continued to be the apsidal hall (*caityagṛha*) and the monastic enclosure edged by monks' cells (*vihāra*); a lingering debt to timber origins is evident in many architectural features. Innovations include the introduction of images and image-shrines and increasing variety in the design of pillars. The residential aspect of the *vihāra* was also altered so that the monastic court before the image-shrine came to resemble a spacious temple hall.

The development of these various forms was aided by a growing accent on personalized devotion (*bhakti*). This encouraged the installation and worship of popular divinities such as Vasudeva, Varaha, Narasimha and various forms of the goddess. Buddhism in its Mahayana manifestations likewise supported devotional images, the most graphic illustration being Cave 3 at Aurangabad, where the main Buddha image is flanked by carved figures of kneeling worshippers. Inscriptional evidence for patronage is fragmentary, but existing records indicate that royal patronage was the exception rather than the rule; most shrines and temples owed their origin to the king's officers, feudatories and common subjects. □

(i) North of the Narmada River. (ii) South of the Narmada River.

(i) North of the Narmada River. Hundreds of temples were built in the towns and religious centres of north India in the 4th and 5th centuries. Remains have been found as far east as Mahasthan (Bangladesh) and as far west as Murti (Pakistan). Though many temples have been destroyed, surviving buildings are adequate for a basic history of architecture. Chronology is necessarily approximate, as few buildings have dated inscriptions. Analysis is best approached typologically, beginning with simple examples and ending with the most complex. However, the architectural repertory included a range of forms, and simplicity alone does not indicate priority.

(a) Stone temples. (b) Brick temples.

(a) Stone temples. Fragments such as the arcading from Swamighat at Mathura (Mathura, Govt Mus.) indicate that temple building in stone took place in the 4th century. The oldest complete structures, however, date to the 5th century.

Early 5th century. The simplest types are modest in scale, their basic features illustrated by the shrines at SANCHI (Temple 17) and TIGOWA (Kankali Devi Temple; see fig. 27), which are built of sandstone ashlars. Both have a rectangular sanctum (Skt *garbhagṛha*) preceded by a shallow porch (*mukhamaṇḍapa*), with four pillars supporting the porch roof. The buildings are plain internally and externally and rise from rudimentary mouldings. The walls are surmounted by one or two roll-cornices (*kapota*). The roof is made of large slabs; crowning finials and other superstructural features, if any, are not preserved. The pillars of the porch consist of square, octagonal and circular sections. Capitals take the form of an inverted

27. Kankali Devi Temple, Tigowa, sandstone, first half of 5th century AD

lotus (or 'bell') at Sanchi and a pot overflowing with foliage (*ghaṭapallava*) at Tigowa. The pot-and-foliage capital, which became dominant during the 5th century, was widely used in later north Indian architecture. The abaci are carved with *gavākṣa*s (miniature arched window motifs) and support lion brackets, a feature unique to the architecture of the Gupta period. The doors (the only carved portion other than the pillars) display two or three vertical jambs (*śākhā*s) decorated with rosettes and creepers (*patravallī*s). The lintel has lateral extensions, a relic of the timber tradition, which give the doors their characteristic T-shape. Below the extensions of the lintel are panels with sensitively modelled figures of Ganga and Yamuna. These anthropomorphic forms of the river goddesses sanctify the inner chamber by their purifying presence. They are derived from the sensuous *śālabhanjikā* (woman-and-tree motif) used on the brackets of early free-standing gateways.

The caves at UDAYAGIRI (ii), a short distance from Sanchi, throw further light on architecture during the early Gupta period. Of the twenty caves there, three are of architectural interest. Cave 1, which has a rock-cut sanctum and a structural porch, is similar to Temple 17 at Sanchi except that the pillars carry pot-and-foliage capitals. Cave 6 is especially important because an inscription provides the date: Gupta year 82 (AD 401). The cave has a rectangular sanctum and an ornate door with a triple jamb (*triśākha*). The outer pilasters, with bell-shaped capitals, support *śālabhanjikā*s standing on *makara*s (mythical crocodile-like creatures). Resembling the goddess Ganga, they seem to illustrate the transformation of the ancient woman-and-tree motif into the river goddess. Beside the entrance to Cave 6 are guardian figures (*dvārapāla*) in separate panels. The façade also has carvings of Ganesha and Vishnu and of Durga killing the buffalo demon (Mahisasuramardini).

Cave 19 was added to the Udayagiri complex at a later date, probably in the mid-5th century. The interior chamber has a carved lotus-pattern ceiling; four central pillars surround a raised plinth for the image (original missing). The pillars have fluted vase capitals addorsed by rearing leogryphs (*vyāla*s). The cave is entered through an elaborate door adorned with luxuriant creepers, *mithuna* (couples) and panels with birds. The goddess Lakshmi is depicted in the centre of the lintel. As in Cave 6, pilasters support *śālabhanjikā*s standing on crocodiles. However, figures of the river goddesses and door-guardians have been incorporated into the bottom of the jambs. Immediately above the door is a wide relief depicting the *Churning of the Milky Sea.* A hall (*maṇḍapa*), possibly free-standing, preceded the cave, but only a few fragments have survived.

Stylistically similar to the Udayagiri caves and probably contemporary is a dilapidated stone temple, locally known as Bhima ki Chauri, which stands at Darra (or Mukundara) in a wooded valley on the road between Jhalawar and Kota in Rajasthan. Built on an extensive moulded platform with a coping, the structure is approached from the east by lateral flights of steps. The temple consists of a sanctum preceded by a ruined hall (*maṇḍapa*) for Shiva's bull Nandi. The sanctum has an altar enclosed by four stout pillars, providing an inner ambulatory. The pillars are square, and each has an octagonal necking incised with circular grooves fringed by bud projections; the heavy cruciform brackets are carved with floral scrolls. The lintels are relieved by designs of garlands and scrolls, and the flat ceiling (*samatala*) has five lotus flowers. Among loose pieces from the site (Kota Mus. and Kota, Sarasvati Bhandar) are a large ornate *candrásālā* dormer bearing a dwarf (*gaṇa*), beating a tambourine. This may have formed part of the antefix (*śukanāsā*); other pieces include small *candraśālā*s, *āmalaka*s and figures of Ganga as well as *kapota* cornices that seemingly pertained to the temple's ruined superstructure.

ERAN, 75 km to the north of Udayagiri, has an array of monuments of the Gupta period, all in a ruined state. The Narasimha Temple, the earliest shrine, appears to have resembled the temple at Tigowa, though its door was more elaborate. The five jambs are carved with the full range of 5th-century decorative motifs, including rosettes, *mithuna*, creepers and bands of fanciful birds and animals. Images of the river goddesses at the base of the door are flanked by *yakṣa*s (male nature spirits) from whose navels and mouths vegetal scrollwork emanates. A similar theme appears at Deogarh and Nachna (see below). At the centre of the lintel, forming a sort of keystone (*lalāṭabimba*), is Gajalakshmi, or Lakshmi lustrated by elephants. The architrave is lavishly decorated with figures of Ganesha, *vidyādhara*s (flying spirits), *mithuna*s, fanciful birds and animals, and bands of female heads, some in *gavākṣa* arches. The other ruined temples at Eran, enshrining images of Vishnu and Varaha, have rectangular sanctums preceded by a pillared porch.

Later 5th century. The basic architectural repertory was elaborated and a number of new features introduced in

28. Doorframe in Parvati Temple, Nachna, mid-5th century AD

the second half of the 5th century. Features appearing for the first time include a roofed ambulatory around the sanctum, sculpted panels on the façades and rudimentary superstructural forms. Doorframes were further ornamented. These developments are illustrated by the Parvati Temple at NACHNA. Though the building has been heavily altered by restoration, many of its original features can be determined from photographs taken in 1918. The building stands on a raised platform, and the sanctum was surrounded by a roofed ambulatory. The plinth and outer walls were carved with a continuous relief of rock formations and grottoes harbouring wild birds and beasts, an apparent symbolic identification of the temple with Mt Meru, the cosmic mountain at the centre of the universe, or Mount Kailasa, the home of Shiva and Parvati. The upper portions of the outer walls have fallen away; originally the walls were pierced on each side by elaborate grille windows that provided light for the ambulatory passage. These consisted of a post-and-lintel frame carved below with a frieze of *gaṇa*s (dwarf attendants) and surrounded by floral mouldings. A loose grille window shows posts with attached figures and keyhole-shaped openings. On top of the sanctum is a square cell or chamber, forming a second storey. This has no roof at present, but early photographs show vestiges of a further superstructure. The doorframe at Nachna is one of the finest surviving from the Gupta period (see fig. 28). Its decoration includes *mithuna*s, *gaṇa*s and *vidyādhara*s. In the centre of the lintel is a relief of Shiva and Parvati. Prominent door-guardians and figures of the river goddesses flank the entrance.

Other buildings show further elaboration and variation. The ruined Shiva Temple at BHUMARA does not have an ambulatory but introduces two small shrines flanking the entrance steps, as well as the typical suite of mouldings around the base of the temple proper. Collectively termed *vedībandha* ('moulding band about the altar'), these include the following elements: foot-moulding (*khura*), pot-moulding (*kumbha*), torus (*kalaśa*) and cyma-eave (*kapotapālī*). This configuration became virtually universal on north Indian temples after the 5th century.

The doorframe has a triple jamb with figures of the river goddesses at the bottom. The goddesses are canopied by hovering *vidyādhara*s in a cloudscape, an iconography often repeated in later times. The lintel carries an impressive bust of Shiva as a centrepiece. The outer jamb is carved with the *śrīvṛkṣa* motif (decorative band of floriate palmettes). The central jamb carries a standing nature-goddess (*yakṣī*) alternating with a male figure (*yakṣa*). The inner jamb has a bold meander forming half-circles, chevrons and squares set against a lotus ground. A similar meander was employed on the contemporary Shiva Temple at Sakor. (This is in ruins, but portions of its astylar hall survive.)

The walls of the Bhumara Temple originally carried a two-tiered entablature (*varaṇḍikā* or 'waist-section'), which was decorated with *gaṇa*s alternating with ornamental panels and blind keyhole niches. Its appearance can be reconstructed from the Vamana Temple at DEORI KALAN (or Marhia). The temple at Deori Kalan is simpler than the Bhumara Temple, lacking even an entrance porch, but its contemporaneity with Bhumara is evident from such

29. Detail of doorjamb showing aedicula, Dashavatara Temple, Deogarh, second half of the 5th century AD

features as the entablature, the coping stone on the edge of the platform and the wide panels of undulating lotus scrolls on the door. Unlike the temple at Deori Kalan, the temple at Bhumara originally carried some kind of superstructure. As shown by fragments, this was ornamented with ogee-dormers (*gavākṣa*) containing sensitively carved representations of a wide range of deities, including Surya, Brahma, Yama and Indra.

Other buildings indicate that stepped pyramidal *śikharas* were being developed in the second half of the 5th century. The Dashavatara Temple at Deogarh (late 5th century) is the most important example. Unfortunately, the facing stone of the spire has fallen away, leaving a ragged masonry core. The portions still preserved when the first photographs were taken in the 19th century show that the spire was made of superimposed rows of cornices adorned with large *gavākṣa* arch motifs. Fallen fragments show that grooved discs (*āmalakas*) were placed on the corners and at the summit. The original shape of the spire is probably that of the aediculae on the doorjambs (see fig. 29). The entablature at the base of the spire is different from that of the Vamana Temple.

The elaboration characteristic of the second half of the 5th century is evident in other features of the temple. It stands on a large moulded platform edged by reliefs showing scenes from the Rama and Krishna legends. There are steps on all four sides. The remains of small subsidiary shrines on the four corners of the platform indicate that the temple was of the *pañcāyatana* or 'five-shrined' type. The entrance to the main shrine is on the west, and the walls of the other three sides have projections or offsets (*bhadra*) with niches framed by elaborately carved pilasters and jambs. The carved figures within these framed recesses, among the finest and most famous works of the period, represent Vishnu reclining on the serpent Ananta (Vishnu Anantyashayana), the liberation of the elephant Gajendra (Gajendramoksha) and the sages Nara and Narayana.

The door has five lavishly decorated jambs. The inner jamb is carved with rippling lotus scrolls issuing from the navels of *yakṣas* and entwining lively *gaṇas*; the second jamb carries rosettes; the third has amorous couples alternating with atlantids; the fourth consists of an ornate pilaster; and the outer jamb has a garland-like floral pattern (*mālāśākhā*). Vishnu seated under the hooded canopy of the serpent Ananta is the central motif on the lintel. The lower portions of the jambs show the door-guardians and graceful female attendants, the river goddesses occupying the flanks of the lintel, as at Tigowa.

(b) Brick temples. The tradition of building in brick, the material of ancient preference in India, continued in the 5th century, particularly in the Gangetic plain (Madhyadesha), though few brick structures survive. The best preserved is the temple at BHITARGAON (*c.* mid-5th century; see fig. 30), which has a square sanctum and an entrance passage with a wagon-vaulted roof. The wall-section (*jaṅghā*) carries niches with large terracotta images of divinities. The entablature is composed of two roll-cornices; a wide recess between the cornices displays narrative panels and legendary birds and animals with luxuriant scroll-tails. The superstructure is decorated with tiers of arched niches containing a variety of terracotta busts and full figures. They are treated in a muscular style reminiscent of Kushana and Gandhara sculpture. Bhitargaon is the largest and tallest temple to survive from the Gupta period (14.6×10.9 m, h. of the extant spire 21 m). It is the earliest temple to show an emphatic *triratha* plan (cruciform with three offsets). The clear division of the zones of the elevation is also exceptional for the period. They comprise base mouldings (*vedībandha*), wall-section (*jaṅghā*), entablature (*varaṇḍikā*) and shikhara. This arrangement of forms is a universal feature of later temple architecture in northern India.

Ruins of brick structures also survive at SARNATH. The main temple has collapsed, but portions of the base mouldings and wall survive. The mouldings are massive and carry bold dentil ends (*tulāpīṭha*). The wall is articulated with flat pilasters that become five-sided towards the top. The superstructure was probably similar to the aediculae on the carved stone lintels at the site. The temple has a complex cruciform plan with four major projections, each with smaller offsets. (This type of plan was further elaborated in the later shrine at PAHARPUR in eastern India.) Other 5th-century brick structures at Sarnath include a small brick platform (h. *c.* 1 m), possibly a stupa base, east of the main temple. The sides of the platform, divided into two levels, have terracotta decoration. Miniature pilasters alternate with a variety of panels bearing geometric and floral designs. Projecting bosses have lion heads and lotus patterns. The decorative style suggests a date of *c.* the early 6th century.

Stepped terrace temples constructed of brick also survive from the Gupta period. These consist of superimposed platforms of diminishing size, with a sanctum placed at the summit. Derived from the multi-tiered stupa, this type was adapted to Brahmanical worship and canonically designated *eḍuka* in the *Viṣṇudarmottara purāṇa* (III, chap. 84), a *c.* 7th-century text which was translated by C. Venkataramana Sastri (Mysore, 1945). An early 5th-century platform of this type was excavated at Pawaya in

30. Brick temple, Bhitargaon, *c.* mid-5th century AD

1940–42. Some uncovered portions have since disintegrated. The platform had three terraces with the elevation articulated with flat pilasters, cornices and mouldings. It was dedicated to the worship of Vishnu; the fragments of a stone gate (*toraṇa*), carved with narrative reliefs of Vishnu's dwarf *avatāra*, Vamana, were found in front of the structure (Gwalior, Archaeol. Mus.). The loftiest terrace temple (h. 22.8 m) is at AHICHCHHATRA. A massive Shiva *liṅga* is installed on the top, but little remains of the shrine that housed it.

BIBLIOGRAPHY

Enc. Ind. Temple Archit., ii/1
A. Cunningham: 'Eran or Erakaina', *Archaeol. Surv. Ind. Rep.*, x (1874–7/*R* 1966), pp. 76–90
J. Vogel: 'The Temple of Bhitargaon', *Archaeol. Surv. India, Annu. Rep. 1908–9* (1912), pp. 5–16
R. D. Banerji: *The Śiva Temple at Bhūmarā*, Mem. Archaeol. Surv. India, xvi (Calcutta, 1924)
A. K. Coomaraswamy: *History of Indian and Indonesian Art* (New York, 1927/*R* 1965)
R. D. Banerji: *The Age of the Imperial Guptas* (Varanasi, 1933)
Administrative Report of the Archaeological Department, Gwalior State (1939–40, 1940–41 and 1942–6)
S. Saraswati: 'Temple Architecture in the Gupta Age', *J. Ind. Soc. Orient. A.*, viii (1940), pp. 146–58
P. Brown: *Indian Architecture (Buddhist and Hindu Periods)* (Bombay, [1942], rev. 1956), pp. 47–51
M. S. Vats: *The Gupta Temple at Deogarh*, Mem. Archaeol. Surv. India, lxx (Delhi, 1952)
S. Saraswati: 'Architecture', *The Classical Age*, ed. R. C. Majumdar and A. Pusalkar, Hist. & Cult. Ind. People, iii (Bombay, 1954), pp. 471–519
V. S. Agrawala: 'Art in Gupta Period', *The Vakataka Gupta Age*, ed. R. C. Majumdar and A. S. Altekar (Delhi, 1960), pp. 446–71
——: 'A Survey of Gupta Art and Some Sculptures from Nachna and Khoh', *Lalit Kala*, ix (1961), pp. 16–26
N. Ahmed: *Mahasthan* (Karachi, 1964)
D. Mitra: 'Sankar Madha at Kunda, District Jabalpur', *J. Asiat. Soc. Bengal*, viii (1965), pp. 79–81
P. K. Agrawala: *Gupta Temple Architecture* (Varanasi, 1968)
K. Deva: *Temples of North India* (Delhi, 1969), pp. 1–18
P. Chandra: 'A Vāmana Temple at Maṛhiā and Some Reflections on Gupta Architecture', *Artibus Asiae*, xxxii (1970), pp. 125–45
W. Spink: 'A Temple with Four Uchchakalpa(?) Doorways at Nachna Kuthara', *Chhavi, Golden Jubilee Volume, Bharat Kala Bhavan, 1920–1970* (Varanasi, 1971), pp. 161–72
J. Harle: *Gupta Sculpture* (Oxford, 1974)
M. Meister: 'A Note on the Superstructure of the Maṛhiā Temple', *Artibus Asiae*, xxxvi (1974), pp. 81–8
F. Asher: *The Art of Eastern India, 300–800* (Minneapolis, 1980)
M. Zaheer: *The Temple of Bhitargaon* (Delhi, 1981)
J. Williams: *The Art of Gupta India* (Princeton, 1982)

KRISHNA DEVA

(ii) South of the Narmada River. The most impressive architectural achievement of the 4th and 5th centuries in what might roughly be described as south India is the incomparable Buddhist rock-cut monastic complex at AJANTA in the northern Deccan, with a series of more than 20 excavations dating to the second half of the 5th century. (An earlier group of five caves dates to between *c.* 100 BC and *c.* AD 100.) Although Ajanta is south of the Narmada River, it has stylistic links with Gupta-period art in north India, while in some ways also pointing towards the formation of later southern (*drāviḍa*) temple architecture. Related Buddhist caves at nearby Ghatotkaca and at BAGH (Madhya Pradesh) and AURANGABAD (Maharashtra) are of a similar date; all these complexes were probably excavated under the royal and courtly patronage of the Vatsagulma branch of the VAKATAKA dynasty and its feudatories. A few minor foundations in the northern Konkan, around Bombay, may be of the late 5th century (*Enc. Ind. Temple Archit.*, ii/1, pp. 79–92). Several early structural Hindu temples surviving in eastern Maharashtra (anc. Vidarbha) have been ascribed to the 5th-century patronage of the main line of the Vakatakas. These temples, poorly preserved and none with superstructure intact, are mainly of brick, though a number of stone examples are found at RAMTEK (*Enc. Ind. Temple Archit.*, ii/1, pp. 59–71; Bakker). Brick structures also survive at TER (Maharashtra) and CHEZARLA (Andhra Pradesh), but their dates and patronage are disputed. For most of the southern Deccan and peninsular India, virtually no architectural remains are known between the last 4th-century building at NAGARJUNAKONDA in Andhra and the rock-cut temples of the second half of the 6th century at AIHOLE and BADAMI in Karnataka (for the latter, *see* §5(i)(h) below; for the 6th-century rock-cut architecture of Maharashtra, *see* §5(i)(d) below).

(a) Ajanta. (b) Bagh and Aurangabad. (c) Ter and Chezarla.

(a) Ajanta. The 5th-century rock-cut architecture of Ajanta accommodated the proliferating images of Buddhas and *bodhisattvas* characteristic of Mahayana Buddhism. Buddha images were enshrined in the *vihāras* (monasteries) for worship by monks and the lay community (Caves 2, 6, 17), while in *caityagṛhas* (apsidal worship halls) large Buddhas were framed on the front of elaborate stupas (Caves 19, 26). The halls also show smaller seated Buddhas on tiers of niches all over the rock façade and inside along the 'gallery' between the nave colonnade and barrel-vaulted ceiling. In contrast to the relative severity of the earlier aniconic monuments at the site, the Mahayana works were lavishly ornamented. The coarse volcanic traprock was carved into a rich encrustation; painting, not limited to the celebrated narrative murals, was used to colour the carving and to decorate uncarved surfaces. Architecture, sculpture (*see* §V, 6(iii)(c) below) and painting (*see* §VI, 3(i)(a) below) belong to an integral creation.

Though *vihāras* had not been cut in rock for some 300 years, those at Ajanta follow the time-honoured arrangement of a square hall with monks' cells opening along the sides and rear. Into this scheme a Buddha shrine, eventually with a rectangular antechamber (*antarāla*), was excavated in the middle of the rear wall—an innovation anticipated in the Gautamiputra *vihāra* at NASIK, where a stupa was carved in relief on the back wall. Also like the Gautamiputra, the *vihāras* at Ajanta have a pillared veranda across the front, divided from the hall by a wall with a central doorway flanked by windows. Shrines, occasionally with antechambers, appear at the ends of the verandah. Apparently new, at least for rock-cut *vihāras*, is the introduction of a square in the centre of the hall, bounded by a colonnade (from four to eight pillars along each side), leaving narrow aisles around the perimeter.

Special treatment was generally given to the pillars lining the longitudinal axis between the entrance and the image-shrine. This axis progresses towards inner depth, from light to dark, through layers defined by steps, thresholds, symbol-laden doorways and rows of pillars. The flat ceilings were carved with representations of beams and joists, but later these elements were simply painted, becoming a grid for colourful patterns. In positions along the longitudinal axis, notably in the centre of halls, shrine chambers and antechambers, the ceilings were painted with *maṇḍala*-like patterns of concentric rings with a lotus flower in the middle. These prefigure the carved lotus ceilings of later structural temples.

Ajanta has an unprecedented variety of pillar designs. The simplest has a plain, tapered octagonal shaft (originally painted) surmounted by brackets. Also with brackets is a second type, used for pilasters but not for full pillars, with a half roundel hanging down at the head of the square shaft, separated by a narrow polygonal section from a full roundel as, for example, on the lower part of the façade of Cave 19 (see fig. 31). This type is related to Gupta-period pillars and is ultimately derived from early stupa railings with lotus medallions. More complex types have shafts of varied cross-section, usually on square bases and divided horizontally into circular or polygonal zones, the narrower ones treated as richly decorated bands. The polygonal sections, generally octagonal or based on multiples of eight, were often given concave facets to create fluting. Diagonal fluting was also used. A complex variety of elements were placed at the head of this kind of shaft. The brimming vase or vase-of-plenty (*ghaṭapallava*) capital, usually supporting a plain abacus and brackets, was derived from Gupta contacts. Alternatively, a fluted cushion capital (*ghaṭa*) was used, divided by a necking from a

31. Façade of Cave 19, Ajanta, *c.* late 5th century AD

decorated belt (*mālāsthāna*) with pearl-swags (*mālā*). Another type, without brackets, has additional fluted components: a cyma or lotus moulding (*maṇḍi*, *padma*) supporting the abacus and a bulbous element (*laśuna*) between the fluted cushion capital and decorated belt. These are also seen in the Cave 19 façade (see fig. 31), most prominently in the porch.

No masonry precedents are known for these last two types, but more slender wooden versions are depicted in the Ajanta murals. Stockier versions of the type with *padma*, *ghaṭa* and *laśuna* later became characteristic of the 6th-century Brahmanical caves of the region; such pillars were already anticipated in Cave 7, Ajanta. This kind of pillar becomes a standard type in later *drāviḍa* (southern) architecture. Where this type is used as a slender pilaster (as a minor element in the façade of Cave 19 and in several doorways), it can readily be recognized as the future *drāviḍa* pilaster, minus only its crowning brackets.

Ajanta's murals are rich in images of timber-built palaces with thatched roofs. Such architecture, providing a setting for the narrative, is depicted in a stylized manner more informative about how palaces must have been ornamented than about their overall form. Even less literally representational is the carved architectural imagery most conspicuous in the façades of the *caitya* halls, Cave 19 and Cave 26. In these façades the horseshoe-arch gable of the giant sun window cuts through a regularized and repetitive relief representation of a multi-storey building, which provides a framework for enshrining numerous Buddha images. Two conventions used at Ajanta later become indispensable features of *drāviḍa* temple architecture. The first is the treatment of the roll-cornice (*kapota*), representing an overhanging thatched canopy. As in later south Indian temples, this is adorned with regularly spaced horseshoe dormer windows, containing faces of heavenly minstrels (*gandharvamukha*s). It is clear that the beings to which the faces belong are not strictly in scale with the buildings which house them, underlining the symbolic rather than literal evocation of 'heavenly palace' architecture. A second convention of great importance in *drāviḍa* temples is the use of interlinked pavilions in horizontal chains (*hāra*s). A row of barrel-roofed pavilions (*śālā*s) housing Buddha images runs along the top of the façade of Cave 19, and another, sitting over a *kapota*, is placed above the verandah colonnade of Cave 1. Despite these proto-*drāviḍa* characteristics, other elements (of Gupta extraction) point towards later architecture in the northern (*nāgara*) style. For example, the horseshoe gables are all of the northern type (*gavākṣa*s), and ribbed discs (*āmalaka*s), the crowning members of *nāgara* temples, are placed on top of the porch of Cave 19 and the fronton of the stupa in Cave 26. As yet there is no distinction between *nāgara* and *drāviḍa*.

Doorways, with their surrounding sequence of decorative bands (*śākhā*s), were carved with motifs similar to those on 5th-century temples in north India. Uncarved jambs were evidently painted, as shown by traces surviving, for example, on Cave 17. Doors were another location for architecture in miniature, the entablature sometimes being composed of a pair of superimposed *kapota*s adorned with a pattern of *gavākṣa* dormers; the front doorway of Cave 24 has arched pavilions connected by a miniature colonnade. There are, however, no such elaborate chains (*hāras*) of pavilions as seen over doorways at Aurangabad and throughout the Deccan in later times.

(b) Bagh and Aurangabad. Located 215 km from Ajanta just north of the Narmada River (near a trade route also passing by Ajanta), Bagh has sandstone Buddhist caves apparently excavated in AD 470–80 (Spink, 1976–7). Wall paintings, now mostly disintegrated, were closely related to those at Ajanta. (Modern copies are preserved in the Archaeology Museum, Gwalior.) Caves 2 and 4 are the principal excavations, both large monasteries (*vihāras*), similar in general layout to those at Ajanta. At Bagh, however, the shrine at the rear contains a stupa rather than a Buddha image. Another difference is that within the main colonnaded square of the hall a smaller square has been created by the addition of four pillars. In Cave 4, to the sides and rear of the inner square, paired pillars support inward-facing entablatures consisting of two roll-cornices (*kapotas*), with *gavākṣa* dormers. The idea of receding layers of space is given emphasis in Cave 2 by additional transverse beams and by a subtle play of variation among pillar designs.

Pillars at Bagh, being of weaker stone, are more massive than at Ajanta. Correspondences between the details of pillars at the two sites have been found (Spink, 1976–7), but the predominant pillar type at Bagh, with varied cross-sections and brackets at the head of the shaft, is found at Ajanta only in relatively simple versions. Also used at Bagh and much stockier than at Ajanta (except Ajanta Cave 7) is the 'proto-*drāviḍa*' type, with its sequence of elements or mouldings at the head.

32. Carved pillar with 'vase-of-plenty' capital, Cave 3, Aurangabad, *c.* late 5th century AD

Of the nine caves cut into the hillside above Aurangabad, 100 km south-west of Ajanta, two *vihāras*, Caves 1 and 3, are close in style to the latest work at Ajanta. Cave 1 has a verandah with pillars and a richly carved doorway, but beyond this less than a metre of rock has been hollowed out. Cave 3, in contrast, shows a fully developed plan. In addition to the central shrine with a seated Buddha flanked by images of devotees, there is a rectangular antechamber and three cells on either side of the pillared hall. The cells are more carefully integrated into the layout than at Ajanta, with the wider central cells, fronted by a tripartite screen, aligned with the central square. The pillar designs are more lavish and complex permutations of the moulded types at Ajanta. The rich variety in Cave 3, for example, includes the type with 'vase-of-plenty' capital (see fig. 32). The central square has a raised ceiling, and a blind clerestory has been introduced above the pillars—a miniature 'cloister-in-the-air' consisting of interlinked images of shrines. The shrines represented have tiered eaves displaying horseshoe gables and crowned alternately by barrel roofs and ribbed domical roofs. *Hāras* of similar shrine-images sit over the doorways of both Cave 1 and Cave 3.

(c) Ter and Chezarla. The small apsidal, barrel-vaulted shrines at Ter and Chezarla are of plastered brick. Known respectively as the Trivikrameshvara and Kapoteshvara, both are Hindu temples, though Buddhist origins are suggested by a general similarity to apsidal buildings depicted in early Buddhist reliefs and (though lacking aisles) to the rock-cut *caitya* halls. Foundations of apsidal structures are found at Ter itself and at Buddhist sites throughout India. However, an apsidal plan and a barrel roof are not proof of a Buddhist dedication; the configuration appears in Brahmanical *drāviḍa* shrines, most notably the 7th-century Nakula-Sahadeva Ratha at MAMALLAPURAM.

The two buildings are close in overall design and in their details. Both have an apsidal plan and a barrel-vaulted roof, the corbelled underside visible in the interior. Both also have walls capped by a roll-cornice, surmounted by a series of mouldings leading up to the barrel roof. Together these mouldings and the roof make up a superstructure representing an apsidal pavilion. In the terminology of *drāviḍa* temple architecture, this is an apsidal type of one-storey shrine (*ekatala alpa vimāna*), with an apsidal *śālā* superstructure. The *drāviḍa* character extends to the mouldings, which are derived from timber construction. These follow the standard *drāviḍa* sequence and in their simple shapes are close to versions employed in the 7th century (*see* §5(i)(g) below). Furthermore, the walls at Ter have regularly spaced pilasters of the *drāviḍa* type, complete with brackets. None of this precludes Buddhist provenance or a relatively early date; the form of *alpa vimāna* crowned by a square pavilion (*kūṭā*) appears in basic form, though without mouldings, in Gandharan reliefs of as early as the 2nd century AD, and the pilaster type, albeit without brackets, has already been noted at Ajanta. But if these monuments predate the 7th century, then it must be recognized that simple *drāviḍa* temple forms had appeared earlier than is suggested by surviving monuments in Karnataka and Tamil Nadu.

BIBLIOGRAPHY

Enc. Ind. Temple Archit., ii/1, chaps 3-6
J. Marshall and others: *The Bagh Caves* (London, 1927)
D. Levine: 'Aurangabad: A Stylistic Analysis', *Artibus Asiae*, xxviii/2–3 (1966), pp. 175–204
W. Spink: *Ajanta to Ellora* (Bombay, [1967])
——: 'Ajanta's Chronology: The Crucial Cave', *A. Orient.*, x (1975), pp. 143–70
——: 'Bāgh: A Study', *Archvs Asian A.*, xxx (1976–7), pp. 53–84
S. Weiner: *Ajaṇṭā: Its Place in Buddhist Art* (Berkeley and Los Angeles, 1977)
W. Spink: 'Ajanta's Chronology: Politics and Patronage', *Kalādarśana*, ed. J. Williams (New Delhi, 1981), pp. 109–26
C. Berkson: *The Caves at Aurangabad* (New York and Ahmadabad, 1986)
H. Bakker: 'The Antiquities of Ramtek Hill, Maharashtra', *S. Asian Stud.*, v (1989), pp. 79–102

ADAM HARDY

5. 6TH–11TH CENTURIES. After the upheavals of the late 5th century AD, a number of new dynastic powers appeared in various parts of the Indian subcontinent. In the north and north-east, the GURJARA-PRATIHARA and Pala (*see* PALA AND SENA) houses emerged as the most important, while on the Deccan plateau the Chalukyas of Badami (*see* CHALUKYA, §1) were the controlling authority until the advent of the RASHTRAKUTA dynasty in the mid-8th century. In the south the PANDYA and PALLAVA houses were the leading powers.

Architecture flourished in all these kingdoms under the patronage of nobles and their subjects. Little has survived of palace architecture because it was built primarily of timber and brick, but a vast corpus of stone temples has been preserved. Dressed masonry was the preferred material for temples, the potential of stone having been established in north India during the 5th century (*see* §4(i) above). Temple architecture served all indigenous sects, with buildings dedicated to various forms of Shiva, Vishnu and the Goddess, as well as to the saviours of Jainism. As Buddhism declined as a popular faith, its dedications tended to be modest and restricted to monastic schools. The religion of Islam, which became a permanent feature of the Indian social landscape in the 8th century, fostered the development of a new Indo-Islamic architecture (*see* §(ii) below).

During the 10th century the established Indian dynasties declined, and the country was fragmented into a number of competing principalities. Among the regional powers to emerge were the Chalukyas of Kalyana (*see* CHALUKYA, §2) and the CHANDELLA, PARAMARA, CHAMANA, WESTERN GANGA and CHOLA houses. The rulers of these dynasties were vigorous patrons of architecture, and their temple-building projects were often emblematic of clan affiliations and efforts to establish political legitimacy. Scale became a major concern, particularly after the late 10th century. Large temples were first built in north and central India, and by the opening years of the 11th century, buildings of unprecedented size were being constructed in all major centres of the subcontinent.

(i) Indigenous and traditional. (ii) Indo-Islamic.

(i) Indigenous and traditional. In the early decades of the 7th century, temple architecture began to exhibit the regional variations broadly classed as 'northern' (Skt *nāgara*) and 'southern' (*drāviḍa*). Temples in the northern tradition are dominated by tall superstructures with curvilinear profiles (see fig. 19 above). The spires carry vertical spines (*latā*, literally 'creepers') and are thus designated *latina*. In contrast, the superstructures of southern temples are usually rectilinear in profile and composed of miniature shrines or aediculae (*kūṭas*) set in horizontal tiers (see fig. 20 above). This type is designated *kūṭina* (for further discussion of northern and southern temple forms *see* §1(i)(c) above). Northern and southern temples were elaborated with the passage of time. Illustrative of this was the clustering of small spires around the main spire in temples of the northern type, creating a complex, multi-spired form known as *śekharī*. Although southern architecture was more conservative, the number of superstructural levels and aediculae increased steadily. In the Deccan, northern and southern temples were built side by side from the 7th century, leading to the development of a hybrid architecture of considerable vitality.

BIBLIOGRAPHY

K. Deva: *Temples of North India* (Delhi, 1969)
K. R. Srinivasan: *Temples of South India* (Delhi, 1971)
M. A. Dhaky: *The Indian Temple Forms* (Delhi, 1977)
G. Michell: *The Hindu Temple* (London, 1977)
C. Tadgell: *The History of Architecture in India* (London, 1990)

□

(a) North-east. (b) North-west. (c) Rajasthan and Gujarat. (d) Maharashtra. (e) East. (f) Ancient South Kosala. (g) Central. (h) Karnataka and Andhra. (i) Tamil Nadu. (j) Kerala.

(a) North-east. The Gangetic plain, ancient Madhyadesha (Skt: 'middle region'), conforming approximately to the present state of Uttar Pradesh (see fig. 33), was the seat of powerful dynasties between the 6th and 11th centuries. It was also the centre of an important building tradition, now largely lost (like those of previous centuries) as a result of subsequent upheavals and the use of brick as the primary building material. The following outline must therefore rely on ruined buildings and the numerous fragments housed in museums.

6th–7th centuries AD. After the decline of the Gupta dynasty in the late 5th century, the Hunas exercised control over much of north India. No architecture survives in the Gangetic plain from the period of Huna rule, though some sculpture is known (e.g. from Hasilpur, SONDANI and ERAN). Huna power crumbled during the second quarter of the 6th century, and the Maukhari dynasty rose to prominence. An inscription discovered at Haraha (near Lucknow) records the reconstruction of a Shiva Temple in AD 554 by Suryavarman, son of King Ishanavarman (*reg c.* AD 550–76), but any further remains of the temple are yet to be identified. No complete buildings have survived from Harsha's celebrated rule in the first half of the 7th century, but the *Harṣacarita* ('Deeds of Harsha') by the 7th-century writer Bana describes palaces and other structures. Excavation of the extraordinary mounds of KANNAUJ, Harsha's capital, will no doubt yield much information.

This paucity of material makes particularly important the ruined temple of Mundeshvari (anc. Mandalaeshvara), situated atop a hill about 70 km east of Varanasi, in the border districts between Magadha and Madhyadesha. The

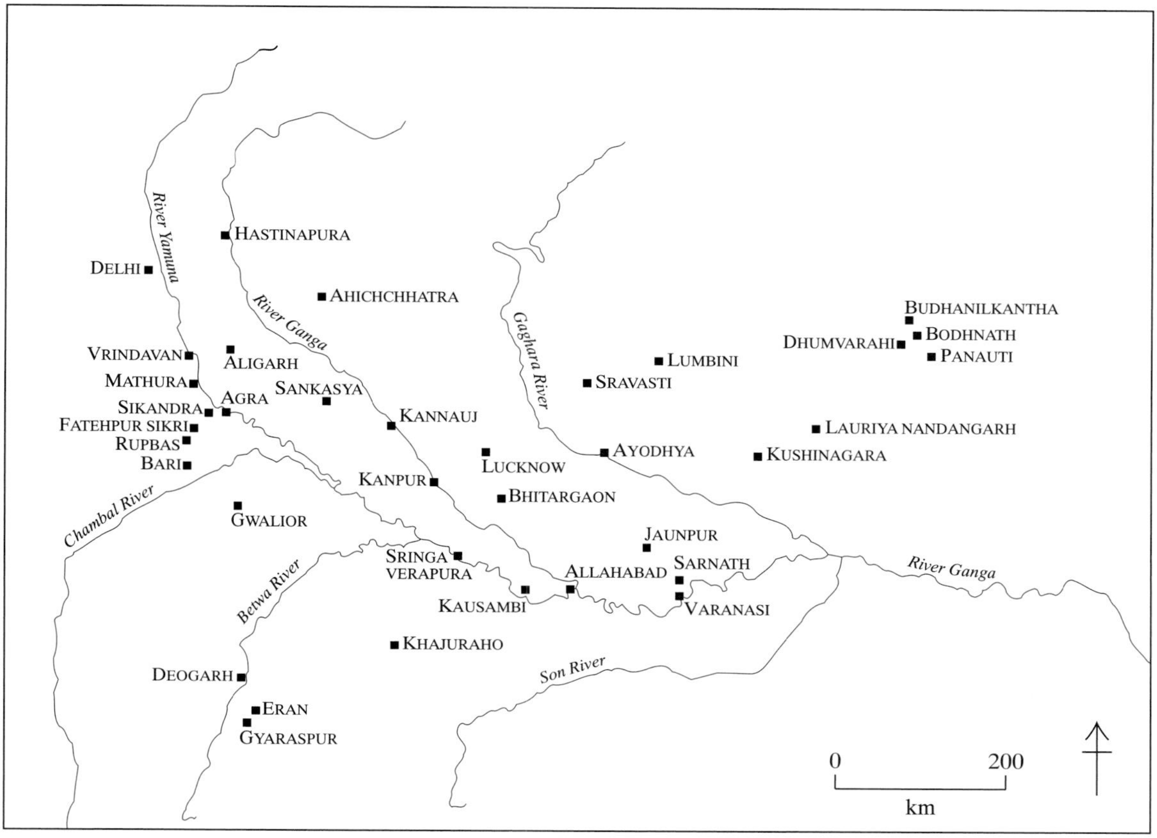

33. Map of north-east Indian subcontinent; those sites with separate entries in this dictionary are distinguished by CROSS-REFERENCE TYPE

temple has an octagonal plan (12 m across) with entrances at the cardinal points. This arrangement indirectly anticipates the stellate (as opposed to orthogonal) configuration found in the later temples of the Gangetic plain (e.g. those at Nimnia Khera and Tahdauli; see below). Internally, the temple at Mundeshvari has a small platform in the centre for a *liṅga*; four pillars support the roof. The external elevation displays eight offsets (*bhadra*s), each girded by *vēdībandha* mouldings of especially massive proportions. The mouldings of the cardinal offsets are interrupted by the entrances. Each of the doorframes has three carved jambs with figures in keyhole-shaped niches at the bottom, a feature characteristic of 6th- and 7th-century architecture. The intermediate projections have matching mouldings, but in lieu of a torus with upturned profile there are large square bosses. Above the intermediate projections are blind windows fitted with jambs and framed by pilasters with overflowing pots. Flanking these are subsidiary niches (now empty) resting on dentil-ends and capped by *gavākṣa* ('cow's-eye') dormers of simple design. The upper portions of the walls and the entire superstructure have collapsed. Numerous fragments around the temple suggest that the building had a superstructure with grooved discs (*bhūmy-āmalaka*s) and *gavākṣa*-style dormers. The Lakshmana Temple at SIRPUR (see fig. 52 below) follows different regional conventions but may provide an indication of the superstructure's original appearance.

The temple at Mundeshvari can be placed in the first half of the 7th century, but its exact date is controversial. Short inscriptions of about the 7th century (some deliberately effaced) on the mouldings do not provide exact chronological information. A long inscription found among the ruins records constructions during the reign of a King Udayasena in year 30 of an unspecified era. If this was the Harsha era, it would be AD 636, a date for the temple that is not unreasonable. The era could, however, equally be a regnal one of Udayasena himself. It is also uncertain which buildings the inscription describes (see Asher); foundations and various fragments indicate that there were once numerous shrines at the site.

A number of fragments from other sites can be tentatively assigned to the period of the temple at Mundeshvari. Many columns from earlier buildings were reused in the late 12th century to construct the pillared arcades of the Quwwat al-Islam Mosque in Delhi (*see* DELHI, §III, 1). One column appears to date to the first half of the 7th century, though most are later. It has a simple square shaft with a large female figure carved into one side. A rudimentary ogee dormer is placed above the figure and an overflowing pot below. Of the same date is a pillar (Lucknow, State Mus. B254) from Rajghat near Varanasi. Carved with figures in keyhole-shaped niches, it was probably part of a temple porch.

34. Relief ornamentation on Dhamekh Stupa, Sarnath, late 7th century AD

Innovations of the second half of the 7th century are best illustrated by temples in central India, for example at Mahua and GYARASPUR (*see* §(g) below). These monuments allow the final enlargement of the Dhamekh Stupa at SARNATH to be placed in the late 7th century. The renovations gave the stupa a stone-faced drum with a bold podium and projections fitted with niches for images (now missing). The attenuated upper cylinder (rising to 30 m), built in brick, was faced with stone carved with frothy floral scrolls, spectacular lotus rhizomes and complex geometric ornament (see fig. 34). In both variety and virtuosity this décor surpasses contemporary work in central and western India. That the Dhamekh style was once more widespread in the Gangetic plain is indicated by a large pillar (Varanasi, Banaras Hindu U., Bharat Kala Bhavan) with circular medallions containing grotesques and exuberant lotus scrolls.

8th–9th centuries AD. During the 8th century, Yashovarman (*reg c.* 720–50) asserted authority over the Gangetic plain, retaining Kannauj as the imperial capital. Though no buildings can be assigned to his patronage, literary accounts mention that he built a temple at AYODHYA. Nothing of Yashovarman's time has been found there, but a variety of sites have yielded 8th-century sculpture, notably Kannauj (see fig. 181 below), Varanasi and Mathura. A rare 8th-century temple survives in a ruined state at Kurtha (or Kuhra, Kanpur District). This building had single projections (*bhadra*s) on each side with the wall section articulated by pilasters. Broad roll-cornices with large dentils mark both the podium (*vēdībandha*) and entablature (*varaṇḍikā*). The superstructure, mostly ruined, is composed of roll-mouldings ornamented on the corners (*veṇukośa*s) with blind arched windows (*candraśālā*s). There are no grooved discs (*karṇāmalaka*s), a common omission in Madhyadesha.

Also dating to the 8th century is the complex at Nimnia Khera (Kanpur District). The main shrine has a stellate plan that is carried through the podium (*vēdībandha*), wall-section (*jaṅghā*) and superstructure (see fig. 35). The projections (*bhadra*s) in the wall are framed by pilasters decorated with narrow string courses. Tiny niches are placed at the cardinal points. The projections in the spire carry a bold mesh (*jāla*) of interlocking arched window motifs, while the angled corners have stellate discs marking the symbolic storeys. The stone door to the sanctum carries river goddesses and floral ornaments on four receding jambs. The nine planets (*navagraha*) are placed in niches on the lintel. Adjacent to the temple are subsidiary brick shrines, one a rectangular structure with a tiered roof (*phāṁsanā*). The temple at Tahdauli (or Tinduli, Fatehpur District), also stellate, dates to the late 9th or early 10th century. It has the same basic features as Nimnia Khera, but the walls and spire are covered with stunning decorative scrollwork carved into the brick (*see* BRICK, fig. 17). The planning and technical skill needed to fit these patterns together successfully represent an unparalleled feat of ceramic engineering. A humbler version of the Nimnia Khera and Tahdauli temples is found at Kherahat, an isolated location near the Chambal River (see Willis). These temples show the fully formed stellate arrangement after several centuries of development in the region. It seems likely that ruins akin to those in South Kosala documenting the emergence of angled and stellate plans (*see* §(f) below) will eventually be discovered in Uttar Pradesh.

A related class of temples is introduced by the remains of small shrines at Parauri (or Parauli, Kanpur District) and Korari (or Kurari, Fatehpur District). These have circular bases and occasionally circular sanctums. The spires are 16-sided, with the decorative mesh (*jāla*) on the spire being carried down into the wall section (*jaṅghā*). Diminutive niches are placed on the cardinal points. The pedigree of these temples seems to stretch back to the 6th-century Maniyar Math in eastern India. The type once had wide currency, for it was exported to Chandrehe and Masaon in central India (*see* §(g) below). Later buildings apparently descended from this type are found at VRINDAVAN and elsewhere.

In the late 8th century the GURJARA-PRATIHARA dynasty consolidated its hold over north India. Nagabhatta II (*reg c.* 810–33) captured Kannauj, and subsequent Pratiharas continued the imperial tradition of retaining that city as capital. Nothing architectural has survived at Kannauj or elsewhere that can be attributed directly to Pratihara patronage, but numerous stone fragments bear elegant if forlorn witness to the metropolitan achievements of the Pratihara age. Examples include a portion of a ceiling (Lucknow, State Mus., 66.277) carved with scrollwork and flying figures in a style related to that of the Sun Temple, Umri, and a late 9th-century doorway (Allahabad Mus.). A screen with richly worked pilasters (Lucknow, State Mus., G134) from Ahar was once fitted into a hall or circumambulatory; the only surviving parallel is the somewhat earlier and more rugged Jaina Temple 12 at DEOGARH. Ahar's extensive ruins have also yielded Pratihara inscriptions. A lintel (Varanasi, Banaras Hindu U., Bharat Kala Bhavan) shows the nine planets (*navagraha*) and a garlanded Shiva *liṅga*; the lintel is delicately executed in a pale sandstone often seen in the Kashi area. A battered river goddess with attendants (Varanasi, Banaras Hindu U., Bharat Kala Bhavan) is particularly poignant. Once part of a temple door, it is twice the size of anything found in central or western India, indicating that north India's most spectacular buildings of the 9th century have been destroyed.

35. Shiva Temple, Nimnia Khera, 8th century AD; main sanctum from the west

10th–11th centuries. The preoccupation with gigantic temple projects under regional dynasties in the 10th and 11th centuries (e.g. KHAJURAHO) suggests that regional rulers were attempting to emulate and surpass earlier achievements in the imperial heartland that no longer survive. Some rulers even undertook building there, a notable instance being the Karna Meru Temple (destr.) at Varanasi, erected by Karna Kalachuri (*reg c.* 1041–72). Ruins indicate that brick continued to be the preferred building material. This is documented at Sarnath, where all subsidiary structures (now reduced to foundations) were made of brick. The precise cutting of decorative patterns and the proliferation of mouldings with sharp profiles indicate that architectural developments paralleled those in central India (*see* §(g) below). This is further shown by the ruined brick temple at Bahua (Fatehpur District), which has a stone doorframe typical of 10th-century Khajuraho. Most of the pillars, brackets and lintels reused in the arcades of the Quwwat al-Islam mosque at Delhi date to the 9th, 10th and 11th centuries. Many examples have festoons, bells on chains and pots overflowing with foliage. There are numerous instances of the flat, stencil-like foliage found throughout north India from the late 10th century. Some pillars have projecting corbels carved in the form of *makara* (aquatic monsters) designed to support struts with dancing musicians and other figures (examples of struts are preserved in the Allahabad Mus.). In some cases figures gird an octagonal shaft that becomes 16-sided and then circular towards the top. Such arrangements are typical of the 11th-century temples of GWALIOR, suggesting that many features were drawn from a repertory developed in Uttar Pradesh. The domical ceilings used in the Quwwat al-Islam Mosque provide further documentation for the vanished temples of the region. Some insight into the general appearance of these later temples is provided by monolithic miniature shrines; well-preserved 10th-century examples are at the Bharat Kala Bhavan, Banaras Hindu University, Varanasi.

A survival of the later architecture of the Gangetic plain is the Shiva Temple at Kandwa, near Varanasi (see Agrawala, 1965). The only specimen from the period of Gahadavala rule (11th–13th century), it is a stone building with a pillared porch; the wall (*jaṅghā*) is divided into two registers suggesting two storeys. The cardinal niches contain images of Shiva Nataraja (Lord of Dance; to the west), Shiva seated in lotus position (south) and Virabhadra (another form of the god; to the north). The spire rises in three storeys to a grooved disc and finial. The sculpture, combining frenzied movement with frozen modelling, is indicative of the final stages of indigenous art before the Islamic conquest.

North India was politically fragmented in the 11th century. The great centres of the Gangetic plain bore the brunt of incursions by Turks and Afghans from West Asia and were repeatedly sacked. Inscriptions and chronicles alike indicate that by the late 12th century hundreds of temples had been destroyed.

For the sculpture of this period in north India *see* §IV, 7(i) below.

BIBLIOGRAPHY

J. P. Vogel: 'The Temple of Bhitargoan', *Archaeol. Surv. India Rep.* (1908–9), pp. 16–21 [deals with later temples in addition to Bhitargoan]

V. S. Agrawala: 'Mathura Terracottas', *J. United Prov. Hist. Soc.*, ix (1936), pp. 6–38

R. S. Tripathi: *The History of Kanauj* (Varanasi, 1937)

B. C. Law: *Panchalas and their Capital Ahichchhatra* (Delhi, 1942)

R. K. Dikshit: 'Kannauj in Literature', *J. Uttar Pradesh Hist. Soc.*, ii (1954), pp. 54–71

M. C. Joshi: 'The Śiva Temple at Nibiyakhera (Distt. Kanpur) and the Chronology of the Brick Temples in the Neighbourhood', *Bhārātī*, viii (1964–5), pp. 65–75

V. S. Agrawala: 'The Kardameśvara Temple at Kandwa, Banaras', *Studies in Indian Art* (Varanasi, 1965), pp. 269–70

——: *The Deeds of Harsha; Being a Cultural Study of Bana's Harshacarita* (Varanasi, 1969)

P. Chandra: *Stone Sculpture in the Allahabad Museum* (Pune, 1970)

S. M. Misra: *Yaśovarman of Kanauj* (Delhi, 1977)

F. M. Asher: *The Art of Eastern India, 300–800* (Minneapolis, 1980)

D. P. Sharma and M. Sharma: 'Decorated Brick Temples of Post-Gupta Period from Fatehpur District of Uttar Pradesh', *History and Culture: B. P. Sinha Felicitation Volume*, ed. B. Sahai (Delhi, 1987), pp. 112–18

M. Willis: 'A Ninth Century Brick Temple', *Artibus Asiae*, lii (1992), pp. 25–46

MICHAEL D. WILLIS

(b) North-west. The Punjab and northern Pakistan have been an important gateway to the Indian subcontinent for centuries (see fig. 36), and many monuments have been lost in the region's numerous upheavals. Some of the earliest temples survive in the Himalayan hill districts, north of the Gangetic plain. The earliest is the Sun Temple at Palethi (near Deoprayag), with a spire of horizontal tiers, built by Kalyanavarman, a local king, during the 7th century. The well-preserved group at Jageshvar, in the hills between Kashmir and Kumaon, was probably established under the patronage of the Katyuri dynasty in the 8th century. The temples have the basic constituents found elsewhere in India but differ in the extreme simplicity of their architectural forms. The same rudimentary style is exhibited at Bheta, Pandukeshwar, Gopeshwar, Lakhmandal and Joshimath, the last of these the site of a temple dedicated to Vasudeva (a form of Vishnu), with an entrance gate and six subsidiary shrines. The Shiva Temple at Jagatsukh (Kulu District) displays a similar style; each side of its simple sanctum is divided into three faces (*triratha*), but its spire is devoid of the usual grooved discs (*bhūmyāmalakas*). The earliest wooden temples in north India are the temples of Shaktidevi at CHHATRADI and Lakshanadevi at BRAHMAUR, both in the Chamba region. These temples, built by King Meruvarman *c.* AD 700, exhibit a rich decorative repertory related to styles on the plains and to those of Kashmir and Nepal.

With the coming of the GURJARA-PRATIHARA dynasty, which ruled most of north India from the early 9th century,

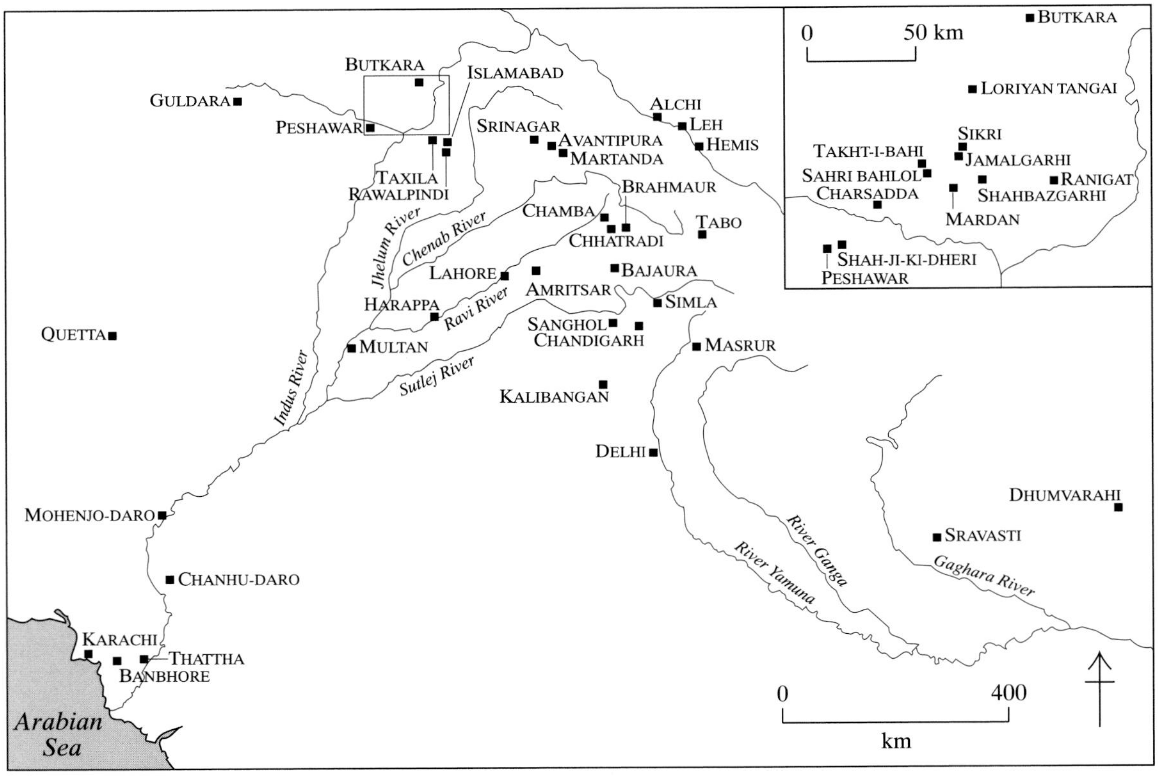

36. Map of north-west Indian subcontinent; those sites with separate entries in this dictionary are distinguished by CROSS-REFERENCE TYPE

a metropolitan style was introduced into the hills. The leading examples of this new 'Pratihara' idiom are the Shiva Temple at BAJAURA and the rock-cut complex at MASRUR. Though damaged, the latter is a monument of considerable architectural significance, recalling the rock-cut temples at Dhamnar. Despite the intrusion of this new idiom, the integrity of the local hill style was maintained in temples such as those at Dwarahat and Adbadari. These buildings have curvilinear (*latina*) spires handled in the 9th-century manner, yet they retain the characteristic simplicity. Most have plain *triratha* sanctums and a paucity of architectural ornament. These traits were continued in the 10th century with the monolithic shrine at Thal and later with the Lakshmi Narayana Temple at Baijnath, near Almora.

The fertile Kashmir Valley, enclosed by mountains, developed a rich and distinctive architectural tradition. Buddhism, introduced in the 3rd century BC in Kashmir, was after the 8th century AD overshadowed by the burgeoning cults of Vaishnavism and Shaivism, and Kashmir became a great seat of Shaiva religion and philosophy. It was also a famous centre of Sanskrit literature between the 6th and 12th centuries. The main source of Kashmir history is the *Rājataraṅgiṇī*, a Sanskrit poetical work written by the 12th-century Kashmiri court-poet Kalhana, who furnished a detailed history of the region from the 6th century until his time. Although the temples in the valley were sacked in the early 15th century, remains survive at such sites as MARTANDA, Parihasapura, Narannag, Narastan, Tapar, AVANTIPURA, Patan and Pandrethan.

The greatest among the Kashmir kings of the Karkota dynasty was Lalitaditya Muktapida (*reg c.* AD 724–*c.* 760), known equally for his military victories and patronage of arts. He founded several towns, including his new capital Parihasapura (modern Paraspur), and built many temples, of which the most celebrated is the Martanda temple dedicated to the Sun god, located in the extreme south-east of the valley. The impressive ruin stands in an open rectangular court (80.5×52 m) edged by a cellular peristyle with fluted columns. The main shrine is set in the centre on a two-tiered platform and faces a gateway that matches the shrine in scale and design. This configuration, derived from Buddhist monastic shrines, was used throughout Kashmir. The temple, with an astylar hall, has prominent projections on each side. These are flanked by pilasters supporting pediments; within each pediment is a trefoil arch. These features are derived from the art of Gandhara, which had assimilated Hellenistic motifs during the 1st and 2nd centuries AD (*see* §IV, 5(ii) below). The upper portions of the pediments and the superstructure have been destroyed, but their former appearance can be deduced from the shrine at Pandrethan (see fig. 37). The pentroof, a characteristic feature of Kashmir architecture, is an archaic version of the tiered pyramidal superstructure (*phāṃsanā*) used throughout north India (*see* §1(i)(c) above).

At the once important centre of Parihasapura little remains except the plinths of a Buddhist monastery, a *caitya* that once enshrined a colossal Buddha image and a grand stupa. The *Rājataraṅgiṇī* attributes the two former buildings and other structures that once stood at the site to Lalitaditya and the stupa to his minister, Chankuna.

37. Shiva Temple, Pandrethan, Srinagar, mid-10th century; view from the south

Lalitaditya also enlarged and embellished the Jyeshthesha and Bhutesha temples at Narannag and built a new Shiva Temple at Narastan. The last is a single-chambered structure in the centre of a courtyard surrounded by an enclosure wall. The shrine stands on a moulded platform. Each side of the sanctum is divided into three faces, the central offset (*bhadra*) having a trefoil recess capped by a high-pitched double pediment. The shrine had a pentroof and is preceded by a porch adorned by two niches bearing figures of six-armed goddesses. A two-chambered gateway pierces the south wall of the enclosure. At Tapar (anc. Pratapapura) only the foundations survive of a large Vishnu Temple, traditionally attributed to Lalitaditya's father, Pratapaditya (*reg c.* 625–61). It was five-shrined (*pañcāyatana*), consisting of a main sanctum and four subsidiary shrines. The sanctum stood on a two-tiered moulded platform and was preceded by a large pillared hall (*maṇḍapa*), in front of which stood a Garuda standard. The gateway is situated centrally in the eastern peristyle.

The remains of two temples survive at Avantipura, established by King Avantivarman (*reg* 855–83), founder of the Utpala dynasty. The Vishnu Temple of Avantisvamin and the Shiva Temple of Avantishvara were built before and after the king's coronation, respectively. The Avantisvamin repeats the plan of Martanda on a smaller scale, eschewing non-essential appendages. Two of its elegant reliefs represent Avantivarman surrounded by queens and attendants. The gateway is lavishly decorated with geometric, floral and figural sculpture, the last representing amorous couples, animals, door-guardians and river goddesses, all placed in pedimented niches. The gateway and other remains of the Shiva Temple of Avantishvara are more austere. Only the platform survives of the main shrine. The square projections on each corner were possibly meant for subsidiary temples, continuing the *pañcāyatana* scheme first seen at the Vishnu Temple, Tapar.

The ruins of several temples survive at Patan (anc. Shankarapattana), a town founded by Shankaravarman (*reg* 883–902). The Vishnu Temple at Buniyar on the Jhelum River (*c*. early 10th century) is one of the best-preserved large temples of Kashmir. Its cellular peristyle has a pedimented superstructure. The columns of the peristyle have voluted capitals adorned with *āmalaka*s, the ribbed crowning element of northern temples. The sanctum stands on a two-tiered plinth with space for perambulation on each tier. The sanctum door is on the west, and prominent *bhadra* recesses on the remaining sides are crowned by pedimented trefoils.

The small mid-10th-century Shiva Temple at Pandrethan (see fig. 37), on the outskirts of Srinagar, is remarkable for its excellent condition, the well-preserved superstructure revealing the appearance of the Martanda and Avantipura temples before their destruction. The shrine was set in a spring-fed tank, and the moulded platform is now submerged. The interior contains one of the finest ceilings in Kashmir. It consists of three intersecting squares formed by diagonally placed lintels. The soffit is decorated with a lotus blossom, while the triangular spaces are filled with *vidyādhara*s (heavenly beings) carrying floral offerings.

In the north-west plains beyond Kashmir there were once many temples, but only a few ruins are preserved, between the Indus and Jhelum rivers in modern Pakistan. At Malot there is a temple of about the 9th century with fluted pilasters and trefoil niches. While these forms recall Kashmir, their elegant handling suggests that this is an independent metropolitan idiom. The use of curvilinear *latina* spires in the pediments shows connections with the main currents of Indian temple architecture. Related ruins are found at Ketas, Amb and Nandan (all in Pakistan). The temples at Bilot and Kafir Kot, further removed from the Kashmir style, retain late Gandharan pilasters but were surmounted by *latina*-type spires.

For sculpture of this period *see* §V, 7(ii) below.

BIBLIOGRAPHY

M. A. Stein: *Kalhaṇa's Rājataraṅgiṇī: A Chronicle of the Kings of Kaśmīr*, 2 vols (London, 1900)

R. C. Kak: *Ancient Monuments of Kashmir* (London, 1933)

P. Brown: *Indian Architecture (Buddhist and Hindu Periods)* (Bombay, [1942], rev. Bombay, 1956)

H. Goetz: *The Early Wooden Temples of Chamba* (Leiden, 1955)

K. P. Nautiyal: *The Archaeology of Kumaon* (Varanasi, 1969)

S. C. Ray: *Early History and Culture of Kashmir* (Delhi, 1970)

D. Mitra: *Pandrethan, Avantipur & Martand* (Delhi, 1977)

S. Huntington and J. Huntington: *The Art of Ancient India, Buddhist, Hindu and Jain* (New York and Tokyo, 1985), pp. 352–74

M. Postel, A. Neven and K. Mankodi: *Antiquities of Himachal* (Bombay, 1985)

J. Harle: *The Art and Architecture of the Indian Subcontinent*, Pelican Hist. A. (Harmondsworth, 1986), pp. 189–98

KRISHNA DEVA

(c) Rajasthan and Gujarat. Three regional styles of temple architecture developed in Rajasthan and Gujarat between the 6th and 11th centuries. The most conservative and oldest in terms of surviving buildings was centred on the Saurashtra peninsula of Gujarat (ancient Surashtra). A different style, based ultimately on conventions established in the Gupta age, emerged in the desert regions of Rajasthan (ancient Marudesha) and neighbouring areas of north India. A third regional style, another variant of the larger northern tradition but with its own distinctive traits, appeared in northern Gujarat and southern Rajasthan (ancient Gurjaradesha).

Saurashtra. The Surashtra style may have arisen under the Garulaka kings as early as the 5th century, flowered under the Maitraka dynasty of Valabhi beginning in the late 6th century and lingered into the 10th century under the Saindhava rulers of Ghumli. Although ground-plans and elevations vary greatly, the more than 100 known structures in this style are characterized by simplicity in terms of both structure and ornament, bold forms, small scale and spare use of figural sculpture. The art historian M. A. Dhaky segregated this group of monuments in the 1950s and coined the term 'Surashtra style' for them (utilizing the ancient spelling as well as geographic boundary). In the varied superstructures of these buildings, Dhaky attempted to trace evidence for a coherent development towards the typical north Indian (*nāgara*) type of superstructure. However, a close examination of the monuments leads to the conclusion that builders in Saurashtra were aware of true *nāgara* in other regions from an early stage but chose to utilize only selected *nāgara* elements. These were integrated with their own local practices in no chronologically coherent fashion.

The Old Temple at Gop is the earliest structural stone monument in Saurashtra. Its tall, square cella now rises from the centre of a high, sculpted, oblong terrace, although it would once have been masked behind ambulatory walls. Its pyramidal superstructure consists of two superimposed pentroofs topped by a bell-shaped finial. Dormers in the form of horseshoe-shaped windows adorn the roofs and originally sheltered sculpted divinities, several of which remain. The terrace, now much abraded, at one time presented the appearance of a large multi-tiered building with projecting entries, colonnades and inhabitants carved in relief. The latter consist primarily of obese dwarfs cavorting in niches around the basement. Although its date is disputed by scholars, stylistic and epigraphic factors point towards a 6th-century date for the temple.

Following Gop, a number of temples were constructed at sites across the Saurashtra peninsula. Preserved structures cluster primarily along the western seacoast. Many are made up of simple cornices, laminated into towers and crowned by ribbed finials. Some have a low profile crowned by a bell-shaped finial, as at Gop. Others have a tall, sometimes curvilinear profile, crowned by a circular ribbed disc (*āmalaka*) as on *nāgara* structures. The cornices on early structures have evenly spaced curved dormer motifs (projecting *candraśālās*). One structure clusters these dormers towards the centre. Some later examples show both the curvature of *nāgara* towers and an interlaced middle band of window motifs in imitation of *nāgara* practices.

Perhaps the earliest extant experimental group of such structures, possibly dating to the late 6th century AD, stands at Bhanasara, south of the mouth of the Bhadar

38. Temple 1, *c.* 7th century AD (left) and Temple 6, *c.* 8th century AD (right), Bhanasara; view from the west

River. The wide variety of architectural elements comprising the superstructures of the six small temples shows a clarity of articulation that suggests an open-walled prototype composed of many levels of balustraded walkways with miniature pavilions marking the corners. This form is most clearly replicated in the early shrines of south India (*see* §§(h) and (i) below). Temple 1 at Bhanasara (see fig. 38) shows this open form as well as a central emphasis of consolidated horseshoe-shaped window motifs that may represent an echo of the larger *nāgara* building tradition. The corners of Temple 1 also bear platforms crowned by small ribbed stones, a configuration that resembles to a certain extent the layered corner segments of the *nāgara* superstructure but that lacks the latter's integration of forms. Other shrines at Bhanasara show only cornice lamination, sometimes with such corner platforms, sometimes without them.

The grandest of Surashtra shrines articulated with corner platforms on each cornice of the superstructure is the temple (probably 8th-century) at Bileshvara. This fairly large structure resembles the temple at Gop in having a simple square sanctum set within a rectangular hall. Its boldly articulated superstructure uses corner aediculae of several forms—some laminated in standard fashion, others consisting of platforms supporting simple ribbed stones, still others crowned by simple domes, suggesting the same variety of sources found in the Bhanasara examples.

A number of structures, beginning with the Surya Temple at Akhodar (see fig. 39), south-west of Junagadh, take the introduction of *nāgara* formulae a step further. These temples show local experimentation with *nāgara* morphology, albeit simplified and applied to the pyramidal tower typical of the Surashtra style. Judging from a number of details reminiscent of Gop and certain early 7th-century monuments, such as the softly carved and fancifully varied faces on the surrounding walls, the temple at Akhodar should date early in the Surashtra tradition.

Simple cornice-layered structures continued to be built alongside *nāgara*-influenced shrines such as at Akhodar and Dhank. The somewhat later example at Sutrapada, built under Saindhava rulers, shows an ossification of the Akhodar formula and sharp, linear stonework.

The remarkable group of structures at Sonkamsari includes the typical corniced type with corner aediculae (Temple 1) as well as a multi-spired variety imitating a Maha-Gurjara type (see below). The more typical 10th-century *nāgara* temples found at Ghumli, Miyani and Prachi suggest that a Surashtra version of Maha-Gurjara was finally imposed on Surashtra itself.

Northern Rajasthan. The term 'Maha-Maru' designates the highly plastic and ornamental variety of *nāgara* architecture that flourished from the 7th to the 10th century in north-west Rajasthan (ancient Marudesha), eastward to

39. Surya Temple, Akhodar, *c.* 7th century AD; view from the south

the Sikar and even Alwar districts of Rajasthan and southward to the area between Chittaurgarh in Rajasthan and westernmost Madhya Pradesh. The terms 'Maha-Maru' and 'Maha-Gurjara' (regional designations implying greater Marudesha and greater Gurjaradesha; see below) and the stylistic groupings they indicate arose from Dhaky's study of western Indian architectural morphology. He noted a fundamental distinction between the architecture of the 8th–10th centuries in northern Rajasthan and contemporaneous building in southern Rajasthan and Gujarat. As this distinction did not mirror political boundaries, he utilized geographically based designations (rather than the dynastic labels of earlier historians) to signify that style formation in this period rested more with local craft-guild development, under local patronage (an idea developed by Meister, 1982 and 1993), than with the generative influence of centralized powers (see Dhaky, 1975).

By looking eastward into Madhya Pradesh, however, it becomes clear that, while the distinction between Maha-Maru and Maha-Gurjara holds true in western India, particularly for carving, the regional schools of Maha-Maru architecture do not stand entirely apart from other direct descendants of the Gupta tradition found in areas of central India such as Gopadri or Dasharnadesha. The Maha-Maru style can best be seen, rather, as forming the western Indian variation of a larger style group, and it is with this inflection that the term 'Maha-Maru' is here employed.

In the 7th and 8th centuries a number of local powers ruled more or less independently in western India. The Pratiharas of Mandor, the MAURYA dynasty of Chittaurgarh, the Chahamanas of Shakambhari and the GURJARA-PRATIHARA dynasty, possibly from the Jalor region of Rajasthan, are particularly important for the development of Maha-Maru building. The Gurjara-Pratihara kings played a leading role in the confederacy that repulsed Arab invaders who entered through the western Indian desert in the second quarter of the 8th century. From that time the Gurjara-Pratiharas began to bring many neighbouring local dynasties into their sphere of control. Early in the 9th century they captured the much-contested city of KANNAUJ in the Gangetic basin, moved their capital there and established an empire.

Although they were feudatories of the Gurjara-Pratiharas throughout the 9th century and early 10th, the local dynasties of northern Rajasthan seem to have retained a large measure of autonomy, resulting in distinct sub-regional building varieties. As Gurjara-Pratihara dominance crumbled towards the mid-10th century, some of these local rulers, such as the Chahamanas, blossomed into strong regional powers capable of lavish patronage.

The Maha-Maru temple usually consists of a sanctum topped with a curved tower, fronted by a porch (*mukha-catuskī*) or an open hall (*raṅgamaṇḍapa*) and porch (see fig. 40). The whole often stands on a platform (*jagatī*). A relatively fixed series of mouldings wraps around the lower portion of the shrine. The platform façade utilizes the same repertory of mouldings as the shrine wall above, but in altered configuration. On the platform the mouldings include several recessed bands, which generally bear patterns such as a merlon-and-half-lotus, wavelike palmiform, checked or swirling foliage, whose prototypes may be found in the Gupta-period temples of central India. Frequently, niches housing deities interrupt these mouldings at regular intervals around the platform.

The sanctum plan shows one or, more usually, two offset planes (*aṅga*s). The shrine floor rises slightly above the platform surface by the addition of several narrow slabs that follow the planes of the wall. The wall of the sanctum (*maṇḍovara*) is divided into three segments: binding mouldings (*vedībhanda*), frieze (*jaṅghā*) and cornice (*varaṇḍikā*). The binding mouldings display a sequence standard for *nāgara* buildings: flat 'hoof' (*khura*), tall shoulder (*kumbha*), half-round (*kalaśa*) and capping inverted cyma recta (*kapotālī*). In some early shrines, 'rafter ends' (square blocks usually bearing decorative carvings) replace the half-round moulding on the central or intermediate offsets, a characteristic seen also in early central Indian buildings and suggestive of the *nāgara* temple's wooden origins.

The frieze of the central (*bhadra*) and corner (*karṇa*) offsets, and frequently of the intermediate offset (*pratiratha*), carries a figure within a large niche surmounted by a tall, lattice-like pediment (*udgama*). The niche on the central offset, containing manifestations of the enshrined deity, is sunk deep into the wall, and its surround, particularly on early temples, resembles that of the sanctum doorway. Although these central niches came to utilize a pillared frame like the corner and intermediary offsets, they continued, as did their central Indian counterparts, to connote a subsidiary sanctum by their depth.

By the late 8th century, a standardized set of the eight divine guardians of the directions (*dikpāla*s) had come to occupy the niches of the corner offsets. The intermediary offsets at first housed subordinate deities. From the 9th

40. Hari-Hara Temple 1, Osian, *c.* second quarter of the 8th century AD; view from the north

century on, however, celestial females, acting as attendants to the deity of the central offset, regularly inhabited this location. At the same time the projecting portion of the intermediary offset shrank to pilaster width, as vertical indentations between the offsets allowed a flexibility of widths to reflect the now hierarchical arrangement of images.

Above the niches on Maha-Maru temples runs a carved garland of flowers or bells. The choice of motif is common to both western and central India, but, as with other elements, the handling is specific to sub-regional schools. Above this garland sits the cornice (*varaṇḍikā*) of the temple. On most Maha-Maru monuments this consists of two inverted cyma-recta mouldings bracketing a decorative recessed band. The band can bear figures—e.g. a narrative sequence from the youth of Krishna—or carry floral and geometric decoration derived from Gupta models, similar to those utilized on the platform.

Springing from the upper cyma moulding, the temple tower of nearly all Maha-Maru shrines rises as a single curvilinear spire. The meshlike surface carving of the superstructure, like the same form on the pediments above the niches, shows a deep undercutting quite distinct from the incised treatment found on contemporaneous Maha-Gurjara-style temples of neighbouring southern Rajasthan and Gujarat (see below).

Several other characteristics of the Maha-Maru superstructure distinguish it from the Maha-Gurjara. The whole is more elongated, the central offset projects to a point above the crowning slab, and the ribbed stone finial is often bulbous. In the earlier shrines, the intermediate offset (*pratilatā*) does not replicate the tightly woven mesh of the central offset (*madhyalatā*), but copies instead that of the corner offsets (*veṇukośas*) punctuated by small ribbed stones replicating the crowning *āmalaka*. A vertical recess intervenes between corner and intermediate offsets, displaying tiny pillars and other architectural elements that are vestiges of pre-stone multi-storey structures (see Meister, 1989). These last two features, as in related temples of central India, seem to have disappeared towards the end of the 8th century and thus act as an indication of a given temple's age.

Sanctum doorways, the final link with the abode of divinity, are sumptuously decorated in Maha-Maru temples. Numerous surrounds are crowded with auspicious, protective and purifying images. One motif that clearly demonstrates the close relationship between buildings of northern Rajasthan and those of Gopadri and Dasharna-desha is the jamb of braided snake coils (*nāgaśākhās*). Other typical features include a foliate capital on the pilaster jamb and a threshold richly decorated with overflowing pots of foliage, lions, fantastic faces and attendants,

41. Kshemankari Temple, Chittaurgarh, *c.* first quarter of the 9th century AD; view from the south

with a central projecting spiral lotus. At the base of the jambs stand river goddesses, guardians and attendants. These form a friezelike composition, so that the positions of individual figures conform only generally to the striations of the surrounds above them, unlike those of the rigidly compartimentalized figures found in this location on Maha-Gurjara doors. The overdoor often displays *nāgara* shrine models and/or pillared niches with pediments, both housing deities.

Maha-Maru temples are also defined by the types of halls that front the shrine. When more than the simple distylar porch is present, the hall tends to be semi-open and pillared. In the case of such halls, the base mouldings match those of the shrine but are surmounted by a blind railing topped with a stone slab that projects into the hall to form permanent seating for an audience. Dwarf vase-and-foliage pillars rest on slabs and slanted seat-backs to brace stone beams that support the ceiling. Elephant brackets, projecting from the seat-slabs to the exterior, mark these junctions. Standing pillars within the hall can form a simple square or aisles, depending on the size and configuration of the hall. A passage is usually left open from the hall to allow external circumambulation of the sanctum. The closed hall so common in Maha-Gurjara temples appears only infrequently in Maha-Maru buildings and then as part of temples with an enclosed ambulatory path.

Dates have been applied to the developmental sequence of Maha-Maru temples not only through comparison with related central Indian monuments dated by inscriptions but also through comparison with a few such monuments within the region. Specifically, an inscription seems to show that the Kalika Temple at Chittaurgarh was built between the mid-7th century and the mid-8th, while the Jaina Mahavira Temple at OSIAN, north of Jodhpur, bears a 10th-century inscription implying that the temple stood as early as *c.* 775. The Vishnu Temple at Buchkala to the east of Osian carries a foundation inscription of AD 815, and the Harasnath Temple in Sikar District, north of Jaipur, can be dated to the third quarter of the 10th century.

Osian has been taken by Dhaky as the type site of Maha-Maru style in its formation and early maturity. The dozen 8th- and 9th-century shrines there illustrate the continuous development of one sub-regional variety of Maha-Maru building. This development began with the early 8th-century Surya Temple 1, which mirrors central Indian *nāgara* temples of the previous century. By the second quarter of the 8th century, the Hari-Hara Temple 1 (see fig. 40) already displayed the distinctive characteristics of later monuments from Osian and neighbouring sites: particularly elaborate sculpted ornamentation, high platforms, deep niches usually filling every offset and frequent subsidiary shrines.

The most significant variations from the Osian type occur to the south and north-east. In the first case, a number of small temples around Chittaurgarh and Kota (*see* KOTA (i)), one possibly as early as the last quarter of the 8th century, show a variety of distinguishing features, including a sub-plinth and the absence of a second cyma moulding topping the recessed band of the cornice. More importantly, they show a distinctive wall treatment with intermediate offsets and often the corners appearing as multiple offset or laminated pilasters bearing foliated capitals. The number of laminations increased throughout the 9th century, and partial niches perpendicular to the wall plane filled the void created at the stepped-in sides of the central and corner offsets (see fig. 41). The wall thus dissolved visually into a series of separated verticals, a characteristic that greatly influenced subsequent developments in the north and west. North-eastern variations of the Maha-Maru style occurred under several local powers, in particular the Chahamana dynasty, whose distinctive practice, including rich, smooth carving, is exemplified by the early 9th-century temple at ABANERI, north-east of Jaipur.

Along with the strengthening of guilds under local political patronage, a second factor that increased the separation of Maha-Maru building from that of central India was the permeability of the borders segregating it from Maha-Gurjara practices to the south. Limited interchange with Maha-Gurjara occurred throughout the 8th and 9th centuries. This can be seen in the mid-9th-century Kameshvara Temple at Auwa, between Jodhpur and Udaipur. With its rectangular plan and roof of layered cornices, Auwa shows a number of unusual variations that are not specific to either style. However, it can be classified as a Maha-Maru structure by the decorative motifs utilized (checker and merlon-and-lotus on the recessed bands;

undercut lattice motif; large, open lotuses within the garland topping the wall; vase-and-foliage pilasters on the niches) as well as by the presence of tall, deep niches surmounted by high pediments. Yet Auwa also displays a number of features typical of Maha-Gurjara style, such as a wide recessed band between the *kalaśa* and *kapotālī* of the *vedībandha*. Although the figural sculpture (*see* §V, 7(iii)(a) below) more closely resembles examples from Marudesha, the clarity of the chiselling and overall aesthetic are reminiscent of contemporary Maha-Gurjara structures such as the slightly later Surya Temple at Varman just to the west (see below).

The process of desolidification—always latent in the Maha-Maru temple with its deep niches and modelled surface and emphasized in the Chittaurgarh-Kota type—reached its apogee in the colonnade-like mid-10th-century Nilakantheshvara Temple at Kekind (modern Jasnagar), north-east of Jodhpur (see fig. 42). This temple clearly belongs to the Maha-Maru tradition. However, it exhibits a number of features—large fluted pilasters behind the side-offset niches, a central niche that projects in the manner of an addorsed sub-shrine, a broken cyma moulding at the frieze base resembling niche pedestals—that became standard in the new Maru-Gurjara style (*see* §6(i)(b) below) that appeared in western India early in the 11th century. This style, as identified by Dhaky, appears to have developed out of a blending of late Maha-Maru practices (exemplified by such buildings as the temple at Kekind) and practices and aesthetic preferences of Maha-Gurjara (see below). Maru-Gurjara had grown into a distinctive and homogeneous style by the second quarter of the 11th century, unifying the architectural production of western India yet preserving its roots in the earlier architecture of northern Rajasthan in numerous details and compositions.

42. Nilakantheshvara Temple, Kekind, *c.* mid-10th century AD; detail of north wall

Southern Rajasthan and Gujarat. The Maha-Gurjara style (again the term was first applied by Dhaky, 1975) flourished from approximately the 7th to the 10th century throughout what is today northern Gujarat and southern Rajasthan, its core being ancient Gurjaradesha. Maha-Gurjara temples are characterized by cleanly chiselled masonry, solid walls and a restrained use of sculptural embellishment. Although related to and often mingling with post-Gupta *nāgara* styles native to northern Rajasthan (see above) and Madhya Pradesh, Maha-Gurjara varies significantly enough from other *nāgara* architecture in detail and conception to warrant a separate designation. During the period in question, numerous dynasties of primarily regional significance, such as the Guhilas of Mewar, Samas of Kachchh (Kutch), Chapas of Wadhwan (modern Surendranagar) and Dvijas of Vasantagadh, rose and fell in the Maha-Gurjara area. Meanwhile the great empires of the Gurjara-Pratiharas of Kannauj in central India and of the Rashtrakuta dynasty of the Deccan contested the territory until the rise and expansion of the powerful Solanki dynasty of Anahilapataka (mod. Patan) late in the 10th century. Throughout the history of Maha-Gurjara building, temples dedicated to the various deities were differentiated by iconographic, not architectural, means. Even Jaina temples can often be distinguished only by the presence of carvings of the Jaina saviour-saints, as the distinctive enclosing compound of later Jaina shrines only began to evolve by the 11th century.

The earliest known temple that can be classified as Maha-Gurjara in style is the ruined Shiva Temple at Kusuma near Abu Road in south-central Rajasthan. Datable by inscription to *c.* AD 636, it displays elements (e.g. a ceiling form clearly derived from bentwood prototypes and an enclosed ambulatory path bearing corner turrets) that give crucial clues to the origins of many features characteristic of, and distinctive to, later Maha-Gurjara building.

RODA, in north-eastern Gujarat, is often taken as the early Maha-Gurjara type site. The small monuments there can be dated on stylistic evidence to the second half of the 8th century (see fig. 43). Each temple consists of a sanctum with a square inner chamber topped by a tower and fronted by a porch. Each structure stands above a moulded plinth (*pītha*) that follows the double or single offset planes of the sanctum wall, a basement configuration distinctive to the Maha-Gurjara style. In addition, some of the Roda temples rest on rectangular platforms, a characteristic more commonly found in the Maha-Maru monuments of northern Rajasthan (see above).

As in all *nāgara* architecture, the wall elevations at Roda consist of three segments: binding mouldings, frieze and cornice. The sequence of binding mouldings is similar to that found in other *nāgara* styles, with the addition of a recessed ornamental band between the half-round moulding and the capping inverted cyma recta. From the earliest examples, these stand above a moulded—and eventually ornamented—plinth. The cornice consists of a single

43. Temple 5, Roda, *c.* second half of the 8th century AD; view from the south-east

similar cyma topped by a recessed band, from which the superstructure springs with no intervening second cyma moulding.

At Roda and on most other 8th- and 9th-century Maha-Gurjara shrines, wall sculpture is limited to a major deity within a single squat, shallow niche placed just above the binding mouldings on each central offset (*see* §V, 7(iii)(a) below). The other offsets bear only a continuous garland of lotus flowers, buds, leaf-and-chain motifs or lion-like faces carved below the cornice.

The pilasters of the niche, projecting beyond the wall surface, support a characteristically short pediment of intertwined horseshoe-shaped decorative motifs that form a lattice-like pattern seen also on the superstructure. In contemporaneous Maha-Maru temples, not only is this central niche larger and more deeply sunk into the wall, with its pediment extending to the cornice, but the subsidiary offsets also bear similar niches housing protective deities and auspicious figures (see above).

At Roda, as in the majority of early *nāgara* temples, the tower-like superstructure above the sanctum is of the single-spired curvilinear type. However, early Maha-Gurjara towers differ from those of neighbouring post-Gupta temples in their squatter proportions; the flat, incised quality of their surface carving; corner offsets flush with central ones (rather than being segregated by indented bands); mimicry of the central rather than of the corner offsets by the intermediate ones; and a particularly wide and flat ribbed crowning stone.

Maha-Gurjara porches and halls are covered by roofs of laminated cornices that step upwards to join with the tower. At Roda the shrine is invariably fronted by at least a distylar porch, and there is one example at the site of a large enclosed hall. An early example of a semi-open pillared hall appears at the site of Methan in eastern Saurashtra, dating to the end of the 8th century or the early 9th. Although it stands separated from the shrine, this hall suggests the variety of options available.

Apart from the wall niches, the focus of the carver's care in early Maha-Gurjara structures was the sanctum doorway. Maha-Gurjara doorways are distinguishable by the clarity of their carving and careful articulation of parts. In general, *nāgara* doorways consist of numerous concentric jambs bearing vegetal or figural motifs and elaborate overdoors and thresholds thronged with tutelary, propitious and protective deities and emblems. The jambs typically show foliate scrolls, lotus petals, strings of jewels or bands of composite animals. Frequently, the central jamb projects as a pilaster with fluted capital, its shaft displaying framed figures or couples. The centre of the sill shows a flat semicircle of carving, while the overdoor usually bears one or two rows of miniature shrines or niches housing deities. At the bases of the inner jambs stand the river goddesses Ganga and Yamuna. Door-guardians (*dvārapālas*) and attendants flank the goddesses, each strictly confined to a single jamb-width.

One of the most significant contributions of Maha-Gurjara architecture to its neighbours and descendants was its development of an elaborate and varied vocabulary of forms for hall ceilings. In the earliest Maha-Gurjara temples, as at Kusuma and Roda, the wooden origins of these ceilings can clearly be discerned. Some are flat, representing crossed beams; some are square slabs decorated with huge lotuses; some show concentric rows of curved ribs receding into cusped semi-domes.

The small, comparatively simple structures at Roda demonstrate the identifying traits of early Maha-Gurjara style. However, within the stylistic boundaries drawn by these common traits there exist numerous differences attributable to disparity of patronage, craftsmanship, chronology and region. It may be possible, as Dhaky has attempted to do, to distinguish regional divisions on the basis of morphology, although the random preservation of monuments has left no region with an uninterrupted record of development. What can be stated is that certain areas seem to have preferred certain forms and that most showed interaction with neighbouring styles to varying degrees.

An example is the border area around Mt Abu in south-western Rajasthan, which once focused on the now levelled city of Chandravati, capital of a branch of the Rajput Paramara dynasty. Preserved temples in this region tend to be encased in an ambulatory pathway from which porches open to the cardinal directions and an enclosed hall fronts the entry, a type rare in other Maha-Gurjara regions. Temples here adopted many details from the Maha-Maru style of neighbouring northern Rajasthan (see above). The late 9th-century Surya Temple at Varman, for example, borrowed such common Maha-Maru forms as the vase-and-foliage pillar and elephant-head bracket but rendered them in the more linear and precise Maha-Gurjara technique. Most aspects of the Surya Temple, however, place it squarely within the Maha-Gurjara tradition. The ceiling of the closed hall forms an elaborate, concentrically cusped semi-dome from whose centre hangs a stalactite of ribbed tiers tapering to an unfolding lotus blossom. Such details prefigure the lavish but delicate carving typical of the style in the 10th century.

Dating of Maha-Gurjara buildings has been accomplished primarily through stylistic comparison, both internally and to firmly dated structures outside the tradition. A few Maha-Gurjara monuments are or may be datable by inscriptions. These are the Mahavira Temple, Ghanerao (dated to AD 954 by a now missing sanctum image); the Durga Temple, Unwas (959–60; dated by an extant foundation inscription); the Ambika (Durga) Temple, JAGAT (960–61, dated by an inscription that notes either repairs or rebuilding; see fig. 44), and the Lakulisha Temple, Eklingji (971–2, dated by an extant foundation inscription; *see* EKLINGJI AND NAGDA). However, as these buildings are concentrated in the Mewar area (home of the Rajput Guhila dynasty) around modern Udaipur, regional variation must be assessed if they are to be used as accurate indicators of date in other regions.

Although Maha-Gurjara architects continued to utilize the single-spired curvilinear tower, they experimented with methods of integrating multiple abutting subsidiary towers, first over temples with enclosed ambulatories. These experiments led to the fully and gracefully consolidated *śekhari* form utilized over much of north India in succeeding centuries. Concomitantly, late 9th- and early 10th-century temples display a consciousness of the correlation between tower form and wall plane not noticeable in contemporaneous buildings in other parts of north India. The most successful solution for non-ambulatory temples was the development of intermediate and corner offsets of equal size, each projecting equilaterally and having recessed inner portions. This format provided square, uniformly sized bases for the minor towers of the superstructure. The Shiva Temple at Kotai in Kachchh, a temple most likely built in the second quarter of the 10th century, is the oldest extant example of this solution (see fig. 45).

Some time early in the 10th century, the sculptural decoration of the wall frieze was expanded and diversified. This may be attributable to the greater planar variation needed for the new superstructures as well as to the general trend towards elaboration. The Kotai temple shows the iconographic composition that had become more or less standard for Maha-Gurjara temples by the mid-10th century, although the option of utilizing a single niche or none at all remained. At Kotai, as at Roda, a major manifestation of the enshrined deity stands within a niche

44. Ambika (Durga) Temple, Jagat, *c.* AD 960–61 or earlier in the 10th century; south wall

45. Shiva Temple, Kotai, ?*c.* second quarter of the 10th century; view from the south

on each of the central offsets. At Kotai, however, composite lion-based animals (*vyālas*) rear in the indentations separating the projections, the intermediary offsets bear graceful attendant women in a variety of poetic postures and the divine regents of the quarters guard the temple's corners.

More specific to 10th-century Maha-Gurjara style than such an iconographic programme, however, is the manner in which figures adhere to the wall. Rather than placing the sculptures within sunken or framed niches, all but the central deity (and at times the corner guardians) back directly on the wall without a frame of any kind. The wall thus remains a solid surface in concept as well as actuality, unlike the conceptually pierced or pillared structures of northern Rajasthan.

Although the intermediary and corner offsets of 10th-century Maha-Gurjara temples came regularly to be treated as pilasters with fluted capitals, the pilasters were clearly intended to look as if they were applied over solid walls and do not seem intended as representations of the pillars of a colonnade, as do those of the contemporaneous Maha-Maru temple at Kekind.

The guardians, female figures and rearing animals on 10th-century Maha-Gurjara temple walls often stand on lotus flowers whose stems sprout from the masonry. This form would seem to render literal the idea that all life proliferates outwards from the sanctum (*garbhagṛha*, 'womb-house'), the dwelling of divine creative force. This feature is found as well from about the mid-10th century on a number of temples in Madhya Pradesh and may have been a Maha-Gurjara borrowing, although the origins of the type are not clear.

Albeit embellished and expanded, base mouldings in the 10th century continued to maintain the above-noted Maha-Gurjara characteristics with the addition of various plinth mouldings such as a band of lion-like faces (*grāsa-paṭṭī*). Niches housing minor deities frequently break the plinth below the central offsets. The cornice doubles into two cyma mouldings, each crowned by a recessed band. With the greater elaboration of the superstructure, small niches containing figures appeared in a number of locations above the wall where once they had been limited to the fronton, as in the exquisitely carved and well-preserved Ambika Temple at Jagat (see fig. 44 above).

The halls, too, were expanded and elaborated. Large enclosed halls (*gūḍhamaṇḍapas*) are common in 10th-century temples. Their interiors are often separated into three aisles by profusely ornamented pillars sometimes linked by florid arches issuing from the mouths of mythical crocodiles (*makara*), as in the Sas Temple at Nagda, Rajasthan (*see* EKLINGJI AND NAGDA). Semi-open halls (raṅgamaṇḍapas) also occur frequently, with side porches giving them a cruciform plan. A stone railing resting on the binding mouldings surrounds this type of hall and is topped by seat slabs projecting into the interior with outward-slanting backrests. Eight dwarf pillars sit at the intersections of the slabs and support often life-size figural brackets and an intricately carved semi-dome.

The interchange with other styles of *nāgara* architecture that the Maha-Gurjara style demonstrates throughout its history is particularly evident with its nearest neighbour, the Maha-Maru style of northern Rajasthan. Towards the end of the 10th century and the beginning of the 11th, all semblance of a regional boundary began to evaporate as, for example, fully fledged Maha-Gurjara temples appeared at Osian, the bastion of early Maha-Maru typology. By the second quarter of the 11th century, the once distinct Maha-Gurjara and Maha-Maru styles had melded into a new and surprisingly homogeneous entity termed 'Maru-Gurjara' (*see* §6(i)(b) below). In the end, perhaps, it was the Maha-Maru with its permeated wall and richness that subsumed the restrained elegance of Maha-Gurjara.

For sculpture of this period *see* §V, 6(iii)(a) and (b), and 7(iii)(a) below.

BIBLIOGRAPHY

Enc. Ind. Temple Archit., ii/1–2

J. Burgess: *Antiquities of Kathiawad and Kacch*, Archaeol. Surv. W. India, Rep. ii (London, 1876)

H. Cousins: *Somanātha and Other Mediaeval Temples of Kāthiāwād*, Archaeol. Surv. India, New Imp. Ser., xlv (Calcutta, 1931)

M. A. Dhaky: 'The Chronology of the Solanki Temples of Gujarat', *J. Madhya Pradesh Itihasa Parishad*, iii (1961), pp. 1–83

J. M. Nanavaty and M. A. Dhaky: 'The Ceilings in the Temples of Gujarat', *Bull. Baroda Mus. & Pict. Gal.*, xvi–xvii (1963–4) [whole issue]

R. C. Agrawala: 'Khajuraho of Rajasthan: The Temple of Ambika at Jagat', *A. Asiatiques*, x (1964), pp. 43–65

M. A. Dhaky: 'Brahmāṇasvāmī Temple at Varman', *J. Orient. Inst., Baroda*, xiv (March–June 1965), pp. 381–7

——: 'The Old Temple at Lamba and Kāmeśvara Temple at Auwa', *J. Asiat. Soc. Calcutta*, viii (1966), pp. 141–8

R. C. Agrawala: 'An Early Pratihāra Temple at Buchkalā', *Bharatiya Vidya*, xxvii (1967), pp. 55–8

K. Deva: 'Extensions of Gupta Art: Art and Architecture of the Pratihara Age', *Seminar on Indian Art History*, ed. M. Chandra (Delhi, 1967), pp. 85–106

M. A. Dhaky: 'Some Early Jaina Temples in Western India', *Sri Mahavira Jaina Vidyalaya Golden Jubilee Volume* (Bombay, 1968), pp. 290–347

J. M. Nanavati and M. A. Dhaky: *The Maitraka and the Saindhava Temples of Gujarat*, Artibus Asiae suppl. xxvi (Ascona, 1969)

M. A. Dhaky: 'The Nīlakaṇṭheśvara Temple at Kekind', *J. Orient. Inst., Baroda*, xxiii/3 (1973), pp. 397–408

M. W. Meister: 'Detective Archaeology: A Preliminary Report on the Śiva Temple at Kusumā', *Archvs Asian A.*, xxvii (1973–4), pp. 77–91

M. A. Dhaky: 'The Genesis and Development of Māru-Gurjara Temple Architecture', *Studies in Indian Temple Architecture*, ed. P. Chandra (Delhi, 1975), pp. 114–65

M. W. Meister: 'A Field Report on the Temples at Kusuma', *Archvs Asian A.*, xxix (1975–6), pp. 23–46

——: 'Phāṁsanā in Western India', *Artibus Asiae*, xxxviii (1976), pp. 167–88

O. Viennot: *Temples de l'Inde centrale et occidentale: Etude stylistique et essai de chronologie relative du VIe au milieu du Xe siècle*, 2 vols (Paris, 1976)

M. W. Meister: 'The Śivaite Sūrya Shrine near Tūsa', *J. Ind. Soc. Orient. A.* (1978), pp. 60–65 [Moti Chandra commemoration vol.]

——: 'Bīṭhū: Individuality and Idiom', *Ars Orientalis*, xiii (1982), pp. 169–86

——: 'On the Development of a Morphology for a Symbolic Architecture', *Res*, xii (Autumn 1986), pp. 33–50

——: 'Prāsāda as Palace: Kūṭia Origins of the Nagara Temple', *Artibus Asiae*, xlix (1989), pp. 254–80

——: 'Style and Idiom in the Art of Uparamāla', *Muqarnas*, x (1993), pp. 344–54

DARIELLE MASON, MICHAEL W. MEISTER

(d) Maharashtra. Surviving architecture of this period in Maharashtra is all of the rock-cut kind. At the opening of the 6th century, numerous small Buddhist caves were excavated in the Konkan (anc. Aparanta), often at such older sites as KANHERI, KONDANE and KARLE (see fig. 46). Inland, new Buddhist work was begun at NASIK (Cave 19), and by the end of the century the sumptuous series at AURANGABAD had been completed. The earliest Hindu cave temples, apart from the architecturally modest Gupta works of UDAYAGIRI (ii) (Madhya Pradesh), are also of the 6th century. Probably belonging to the first half of that century are three important rock-cut monuments in the Konkan, works of the Pashupata Shaiva sect, at Jogeshvari, Mandapeshvara and ELEPHANTA. These have been attributed to the patronage of the Kalachuris (Spink, [1967], p. 9; *see* KALACHURIS OF MAHARASHTRA) or to the local Maurya dynasty (see *Enc. Ind. Temple Archit.*, ii/1, p. 85). The first of the Hindu caves along the scarp at Ellora were probably excavated under the Kalachuris in the second half of the 6th century, and the Buddhist series there may also have been started around this time. Hindu foundations at ELLORA are predominantly Shaiva, their iconography reflecting a strong tradition of goddess worship. Tantric developments in both Hinduism and Buddhism are reflected at Ellora, as they are in Buddhist Caves 6 and 7 at Aurangabad.

Work at Ellora, both Buddhist and Hindu, seems to have continued through the 7th century, when the region was ruled by the early Rashtrakuta dynasty, feudatories of the Chalukyas of Badami (*see* CHALUKYA, §1). Renewed momentum at the site in the 8th century culminated in a burst of activity after about AD 754, when the Rashtrakutas vanquished their former overlords and assumed imperial status. The great Kailasa Temple (*see* ELLORA, §2) was begun shortly afterwards, followed by other Shaiva works on a smaller scale. Patronage of Jaina shrines continued well into the 9th century. After this time virtually no architectural remains are known in Maharashtra (apart from some minor provincial cave sanctuaries) until the 11th century.

Stylistically, the monuments from this period may be divided into two broad phases. In the first phase the legacy of the Vakataka tradition of Ajanta and Aurangabad (sometimes referred to as the 'Vidarbha style', although strictly speaking, ancient Vidarbha was further east; *see* §4(ii)(a) and (b) above) was kept alive at Aurangabad and Ellora and, in provincial versions, at such sites as Nasik. Simultaneously, a related but distinct, less ornate style, typified by Elephanta, characterized the Konkan. Its influence can be seen at Ellora, mixing with the Vakataka heritage (*Enc. Ind. Archit.*, ii/1, 1988, pp. 94–5). The second phase, from the mid-8th century on, corresponded to the first century or so of imperial Rashtrakuta power. Southern influence, notably Chalukya influence from Karnataka, which may have been in evidence for some time before this, became extremely important in Ellora, where it mixed with local traditions.

First phase. By the 6th century the overwhelming presence of sculpture had become intrinsic to the experience of subterranean sacred architecture. Sculpture was present not only in the sanctum itself and in the form of door-guardians (*dvārapālas*) but also in complex panels filling whole bays along the walls of the pillared halls and side chambers. The *vihāra* (monastery) plan, showing a central hall surrounded by monastic cells, is seen at Ajanta and was followed relatively closely at caves 1, 2 and 3 at Ellora. It provided a starting-point for a variety of plans among the Buddhist caves, which in general show an

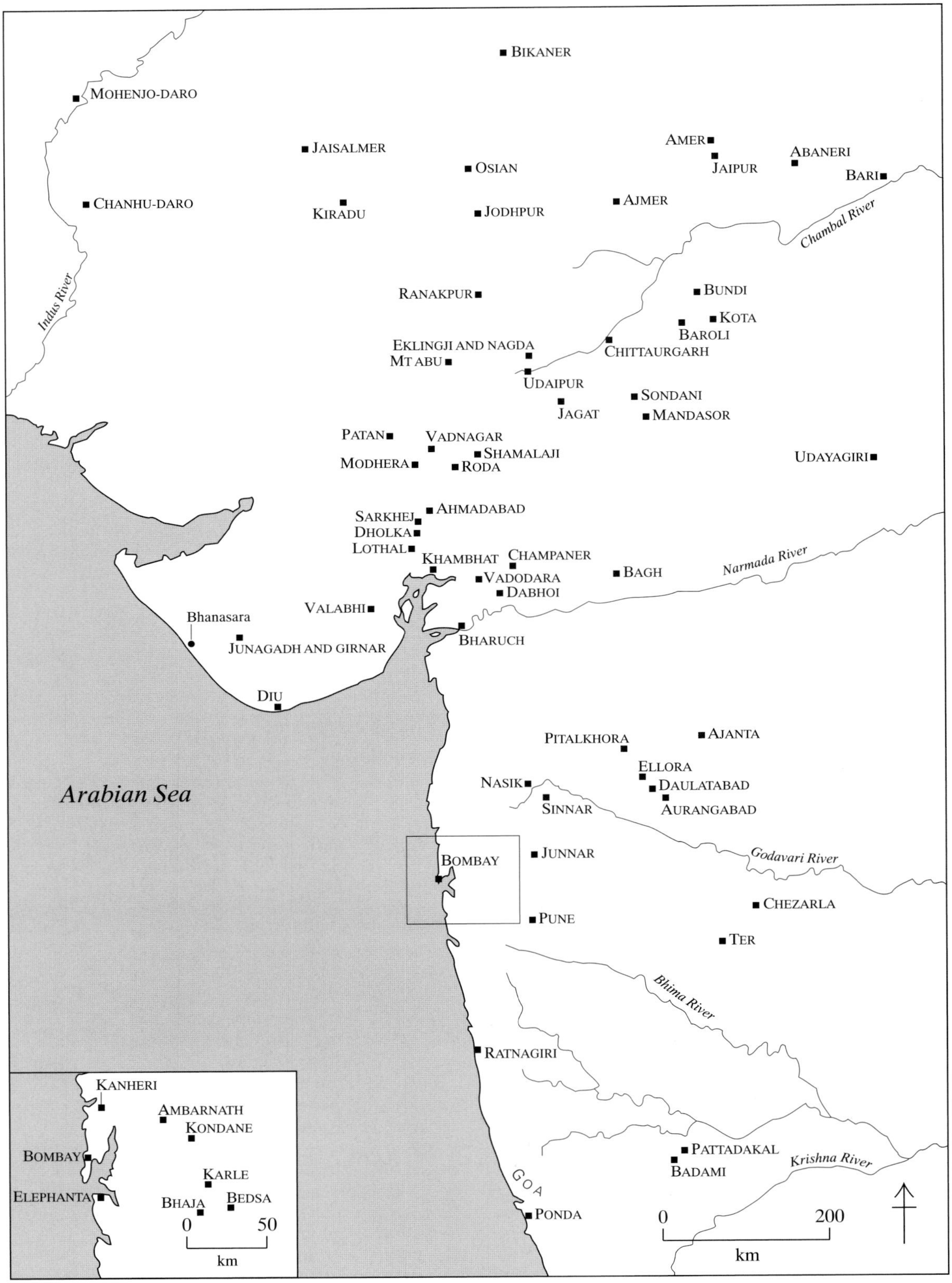

46. Map of western Indian subcontinent; those areas with separate entries in this dictionary are distinguished by CROSS-REFERENCE TYPE

increase in subsidiary shrines opening off the hall, with correspondingly fewer, if any, cells for monks. In caves 6 and 7 at Aurangabad the main Buddha shrine was placed in the middle of the hall to allow circumambulation, thus replacing the former square of pillars. In some instances the basic *vihāra* plan was deepened, as in Cave 5 at Ellora, or widened, as in caves 6, 11 and 12 there. Caves 11 ('Don Thal') and 12 ('Tin Thal'), probably of the late 7th century or early 8th, also show a new, multi-storey conception, with multi-pillared halls of varied design carved one above the other. Cave 10 at Ellora ('Vishvakarma'; see fig. 47), of about the mid-7th century, is the latest of India's rock-cut *caitya* halls; its colonnaded forecourt has an upper storey connected to a musicians' gallery at the front of the hall.

The even greater variety of plan forms among the Hindu cave temples is illustrated by the three Konkani shrines of Jogeshvari, Mandapeshvara and Elephanta. At Jogeshvari an axial sequence of spaces culminates in a *vihāra*-like hall with a central pillared square, in the middle of which (recalling Aurangabad caves 6 and 7) is a sanctum with doorways on all four sides. Mandapeshvara has a wide, shallow hall, alternatively described as a large verandah, with a main, central shrine (with antechamber) at the rear, flanked by subsidiary shrines. Large shrine chambers run across the ends of the verandah, from which they are separated by tripartite screens. This general type is conspicuous among the diverse plans at Ellora, though with only a single sanctum at the rear, sometimes (as in caves 21 and 26) containing a circumambulatory passage. The great cave temple at Elephanta consists of a vast, multi-pillared hall of five square bays by five, with three bays projecting from each side. At the west end of the hall is the free-standing sanctum with entrances on all four sides. Beams emphasize the east–west orientation of the cave and the longitudinal axis running towards the sanctum; a transverse axis leads to the incomparable image of the god Shiva as Maheshvara in the centre of the south wall, the only wall of solid rock, without an entrance. Cave 29 at Ellora ('Dhumar Lena') follows Elephanta closely.

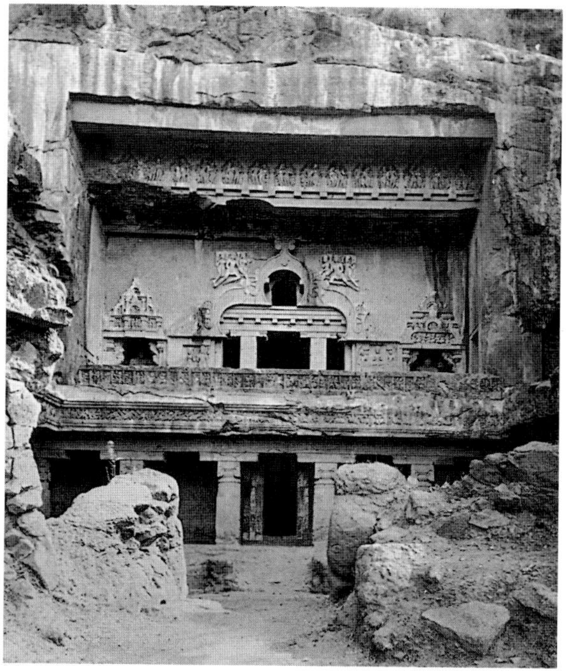

47. Façade of Cave 10, Ellora, mid-7th century AD

Pillar designs most clearly show the differences between the ornate Vakataka tradition and the powerfully chaste 'Elephanta' style. Inherited from the former is the pillar type with mirrored roundels (e.g. caves 6 and 7 at Aurangabad and Cave 5 at Ellora) that had been used earlier at Ajanta only for pilasters. Also of Vakataka provenance and widespread at Ellora is the 'northern' type of pillar with a brimming vase capital (*ghaṭapallava*), usually over a decorated shaft of varied cross-section and with a plain square base. A third major class comprises various 'proto-*drāviḍa*' ('proto-southern') pillars, of which the essential parts are a cushion capital (*ghaṭa*) over a necking and chest (*laśuna*), both usually circular and fluted, often on a square shaft. This form, also with roots at Ajanta and at BAGH, became typical in the Konkan, though the *ghaṭapallava* type is also found there, notably at Mandapeshvara. Early Konkani examples of 'proto-*drāviḍa*' pillars are found at Kanheri (caves 11 and 41) and Lonad, and the type was used at Elephanta in a bold, restrained form with little variation. It is common at Ellora, reflecting its local roots, but sometimes showing clear influence from the Konkan (as at Cave 29). Figural struts angled out from pillars are another legacy from Ajanta to Ellora. At Cave 21 at Ellora these are carved with loving couples (*mithuna*s) as at Cave 3 at BADAMI, dated AD 578.

Clues to the nature of contemporary structural temples of the region may be gained from pillars, from moulded bases (*vēdibandha*s) and, above all, from the architectural imagery carved over doorways and, occasionally (as in caves 14 and 17 at Ellora), on pillar shafts. The images of interlinked shrines found in these positions, prefigured in caves 1 and 3 at Aurangabad (*see* §4(ii)(b) and fig. 32 above), are closer to the northern (*nāgara*) than to the southern (*drāviḍa*) milieu. Their superstructures consisting of superimposed tiers or roll-cornice belong to a general class known as *phaṃsanā* ('wedge-shaped'). They are crowned either by domelike members or by barrel roofs. The overhanging layers of cornice are decorated with horseshoe-arch gables (*gavākṣa*s) arranged in patterns.

A full-size *phaṃsanā* superstructure, in some way reminiscent of Surasthra examples such as the Old Temple at Gop (in Gujarat; *see* §(c) above), is carved in relief over the façade of Cave 9 at Ellora. Here, as in the niche pediments of the adjacent *caitya*-hall façade of Cave 10 (see fig. 47), the *gavākṣa* pattern includes half or split motifs, a device already found in Gupta ornament. A pair of much larger half-*gavākṣa*s belongs to the central portion of Cave 10's façade, surmounted and slightly overlapped by a whole *gavākṣa* opening into the interior. This configuration takes the place of the single large horseshoe arch previously indispensable in *caitya*-hall façades, signalling an ultimate abstraction from timber origins.

At the base of a doorjamb in Cave 12 at Ellora is a small carving of a mature *nāgara* shrine of the *latina* type (see *Enc. Ind. Temple Archit.*, ii/1, pl. 679), which is close to Chalukya examples. Datable perhaps to *c.* AD 700, this carving is symptomatic of the seeping in of influence from Karnataka before the Rashtrakuta period.

Second phase. Mature *drāviḍa* architecture imported to Ellora in the Rashtrakuta period includes India's biggest rock-cut temple, the Kailasa (see fig. 48), two other free-standing monoliths and various elements among the later caves. This architecture derives much from the *drāviḍa* temples of the Chalukyas at PATTADAKAL (*see* §(h) below) from which town craftsmen almost certainly migrated to Ellora. While the *drāviḍa* mode of Ellora is essentially the *drāviḍa* of Karnataka, it is not entirely 'Chalukya'. The coarse Deccani trap lends itself to a chunkier style than the sandstone of the Chalukya heartland, and the imported style was modified (though less than might be imagined) by contact with the indigenous schools of rock-cut (possibly also structural) architecture. Moreover, there are signs of a more direct knowledge of the *drāviḍa* work of the Pallavas in Tamil Nadu than would have been possible purely through Chalukya channels.

The overall plan of the Kailasa Temple is an immediately clear derivation from the Virupaksha Temple at Pattadakal. Within the great excavated pit, which corresponds to the enclosure (*prākāra*) at Pattadakal, the Kailasanath follows the Virupaksha in its sequence of gateway, Nandi pavilion and temple itself, the main shrine (*vimāna*) fronted by a 16-pillar hall (*maṇḍapa*) with porches on the sides and front. At Ellora this sequence of elements is raised on an 8 m-high platform on which, for the temple itself, life-size caryatid elephants and other creatures carry a moulded base of the type arrived at earlier in the 8th century at Pattadakal. The platform is broad enough around the main shrine to provide an exterior circumambulatory path in place of the interior passageway at Pattadakal. Around this pathway are five subsidiary shrines: two square ones at the rear corners and, on the cardinal axes, three rectangular ones with barrel roofs reminiscent of the Mahendravarman shrine of the Kailasa Temple at KANCHIPURAM.

48. Main shrine of Kailasa Temple, Ellora, *c.* mid-8th century AD; view from the south-west

The main shrine of the Kailasa Temple at Ellora has four storeys (*tala*s). In the lower three the aediculae at the centre of each side are crowned by barrel-roofed pavilions (*śālā*s), those at the corners by square pavilions (*kūṭa*s). The top storey, of unitary (*alpavimāna*) form, carries an octagonal dome (*śikhara*) over a platform with reclining bulls at the four corners. While these last two features are of Tamil provenance, the overall composition follows the Karnataka trend towards increasing central emphasis and radial continuity, ensured here by central projections in the walls of the unitary top storey and projecting central elements in each of the lower three, identical in type but expanding in their descent. Yet the effect of dynamic fusion is less powerful than at Pattadakal, partly because the projections, unlike those of the latest Chalukya temples, do not have offsets at the corners and so appear relatively stable and independent. Their concerted effect is also weakened by wide spacing. But although elements are not staggered individually, the whole plan steps forward progressively at the base of the main shrine, where intermediate planes between corners and centre are formed by Chalukya-derived secondary 'wall-shrines' crowned by horseshoe-arched pavilions (*pañjara*s). The barrel-roofed antefix (*śukanāsa*) to the shrine is a further Chalukya feature, derived from *nāgara* temples.

The two other monolithic *vimāna*s at Ellora, dating from about the late 8th century or early 9th, are both Jaina foundations: the 'Little Kailasa' (Chhota Kailasa) and the four-faced (*sarvatōbhadra*) shrine in the Cave 32 ('Indra Sabha') complex, standing in a rock-cut courtyard surrounded by two storeys of cave sanctuaries. These two shrines are variants of one idea, a boldly experimental attempt to create a new shrine form, radically manipulating *drāviḍa* components without departing from the *drāviḍa* language. The usual central barrel-roofed pavilions, much enlarged, have been turned through 90 degrees, so that the horseshoe-arched form usually at either end is now on the front. A cascade of such elements forms a spine to the superstructure, anticipating 11th-century developments in Karnataka.

The Rashtrakuta cave temples occasionally recall the verandah-fronted *vihāra* form. Generally, their plans seem to follow, more closely than before, those of structural temples, being reminiscent of earlier and later examples in Karnataka. The Lankeshvara Cave in the Kailasanath complex, like the main temple, has a sixteen-pillar hall, but the four-pillar type is typical. Flat ceilings, as opposed to the Chalukya 'nave-and-aisles' arrangement, are divided by beams into panels, often with carved lotuses. Once established at Ellora, *drāviḍa* elements began to be used in the façades of cave temples, over openings and decorating railings. In the designs of pillars, more massive than ever, an inventive intermixing of characteristics from Karnataka with local traditions can be seen.

One structure at Ellora is Karnataka *nāgara* in style: the free-standing rock-cut reception hall in front of Cave 15 ('Dashavatara'). An inscription records that this two-storey cave, originally Buddhist, was converted for Brahmanical use by a Rashtrakuta king, Dantidurga (*reg c.* AD 752–8). Dantidurga was probably responsible for the reception hall, which must date from about the time of his victory over the Chalukyas (*c.* AD 754). Niche pediments have complex *gavākṣa* patterns closely related to those of the Papanatha and Kashivishvanatha temples at Pattadakal.

For sculpture of this period *see* §V, 6(iii)(c) and 7(iii)(b) below.

BIBLIOGRAPHY

Enc. Ind. Temple Archit., i/2 and ii/1
J. Fergusson and J. Burgess: *The Cave Temples of India* (London, 1880)
O. C. Gangoli: *The Art of the Rashtrakutas* (Bombay, 1958)
D. B. Levine: 'Aurangabad: A Stylistic Analysis', *Artibus Asiae*, xviii/2–3 (1966), pp. 175–204
W. Spink: *Ajanta to Ellora* (Bombay, [1967])
S. J. Czuma: *The Brahmanical Rāshtrakūta Monuments of Ellora* (diss., U. MI, 1968)
W. Spink: 'Monuments of the Early Kalachuri Period', *J. Ind. Hist.*, xvi, pt 2, no. 137 (Aug 1968), pp. 263–70
K. V. Soundara Rajan: *Cave Temples of the Deccan* (Delhi, 1981)
C. Berkson, G. Michell and W. Doniger O'Flaherty: *Elephanta: The Cave of Shiva* (Princeton, 1983)
G. H. Malandra: *The Buddhist Caves at Ellora* (diss., U. MN, 1983)
C. Berkson: *The Caves at Aurangabad* (New York and Ahmadabad, 1986)
A. Hardy: *Form and Transformation in Indian Temple Architecture: The Karnāta Drāvida Tradition, 7th to 13th Centuries* (Dehli, 1994)

ADAM HARDY

(e) East. Bihar, Bengal and Bangladesh were simply designated 'the east' (*prācya*) in early Indian literature. This large area was divided into a number of ancient provinces, the most important being Magadha, on the south bank of the River Ganga in Bihar. Further east lay Varendra, while Gauda and Vanga occupied the Gangetic delta (see fig. 49). In these regions brick and stucco were the prevalent building materials, a fact that contributed to the destruction of most buildings predating the 11th century. What has survived, however, illustrates the varied and experimental nature of temple architecture in the post-Gupta age. Also discussed below is the architecture of Orissa, which stands somewhat apart from other areas of eastern India in that it developed a regional style of temple-building in stone from the 7th century.

Bihar, Bengal and Bangladesh. The earliest surviving temple in Bihar appears to be that at RAJGIR known as the Maniyar Math, a ruined brick and stucco structure of unusual plan and design. Built on still older ruins, the Maniyar Math consists of a cylindrical sanctum with

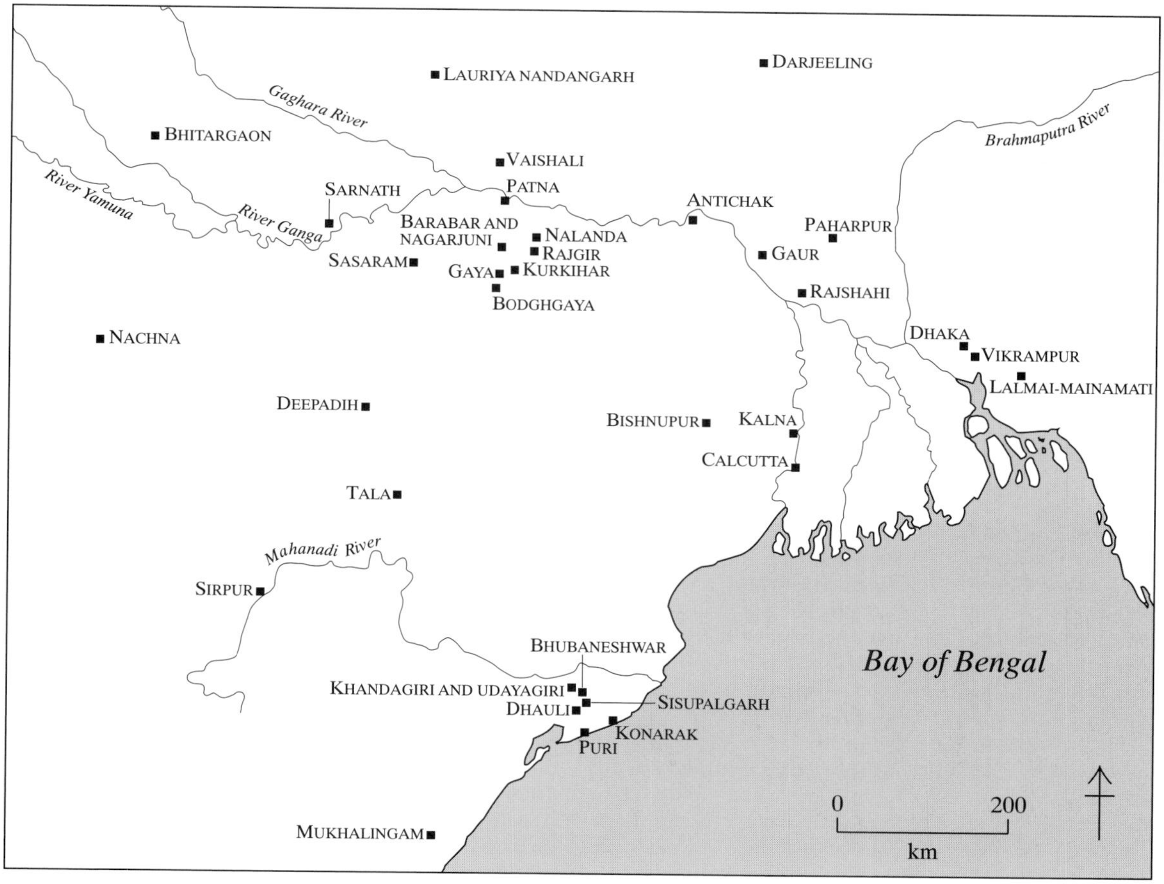

49. Map of eastern Indian subcontinent; those sites with separate entries in this dictionary are distinguished by CROSS-REFERENCE TYPE

50. Mahabodhi Temple, Bodhgaya, *c.* late 6th century AD

circular interior (diam. 3.3 m). Standing on a simple podium of three mouldings, the walls were decorated with at least 13 niches framed by pilasters. The niches contained stucco images that have disintegrated and that are known mainly from old photographs. The projecting cardinal niches held images of the gods Ganesha (north), Dancing Shiva (west) and Vishnu (east). A Shiva *liṅga*, a *nāginī* and five *nāga*s (serpent deities) were also represented. The style of these figures suggests a date in the mid-6th century. The upper portions of the pilasters and niches were subsequently covered by a plain circular wall of larger brick, which constituted the first of several restorations and additions. Inscriptions and the numerous serpent images suggest that the temple served the ancient cult of Maninaga, the tutelary deity of Rajgir.

Near Rajgir is the famous Buddhist monastery of NALANDA, which apparently enjoyed the patronage of the last Gupta kings. Brick-built shrines and monasteries, steadily added to the site from the 6th century, have been reduced in most cases to foundations. The main evidence for architecture comes from Site 3, a complex accumulation of seven successive brick structures. The original stupa was encased and gradually enlarged, with the fifth integument totally altering the character of the building and creating a structure set on a 6 m-high square terrace with multi-storey towers at the corners. The terrace sits on three mouldings and is divided into registers; the corner towers are divided into five registers, the lower three of which are shared with the terrace. The lowest register shows stucco Buddhas and *bodhisattva*s in large niches framed by pilasters with pot-bases and stylized lotus-pedestals, a typical feature of early architecture in this region. The middle register has smaller niches, with those on the corner towers displaying figures within dormers (*gavākṣa*s). The third register, a sham clerestory, has oblong windows similar to those at NACHNA. Each register is finished by a prominent cornice (*kapota*) underpinned by dentils. The fourth register of the corner towers consists of compressed pilasters and a cornice. Above this were cylindrical drums adorned with niches holding Buddhas; the towers were crowned by stupa-like domes, now damaged. The terrace provided an upper ambulatory and supported a sanctum and superstructure (destr.). It was approached from the north by steps on the parapet of which were displayed impressive couchant lions in the round. In architectural conception and decorative treatment, this structure partially follows the Maniyar Math while anticipating such later buildings as the Mahabodhi Temple at Bodhgaya (*see* BODHGAYA AND GAYA). It is thus assignable to the last quarter of the 6th century.

One of the few complete brick structures in eastern India, the Mahabodhi Temple (see fig. 50) is a critical monument for the history of architecture, particularly the development of the northern temple superstructure. The building has been repaired numerous times, the most recent and heavy restoration having taken place in the late 19th century (for pre-restoration photographs, see Burgess). The temple stands on an enormous terrace (12.1×26.8×20.1 m) similar to that of Site 3 at Nalanda, also with a podium of three mouldings. This terrace is embellished with registers of niches and a row of grotesque faces (*kīrttimukha*s) amid floral scrolls. The sanctum (14.9×14.3 m externally) is connected by a passage to a porch. The inner compartments have vaulted roofs like those at BHITARGAON (*see* §4(i) above). The sanctum carries a superstructure (h. 55 m) of seven levels, representing abbreviated storeys stacked one upon the other. Each storey has a row of niches framed by squat pilasters supporting a cornice and pediment. The schematic rendering of these elements, especially the pediments, is typical of the 6th century. The storeys became more compressed towards the top, foreshadowing the radical compression of such levels in temple towers of the 7th and 8th centuries. Each level is marked by large corner discs (*bhūmyāmalaka*s). These discs are incorporated into the fabric of the spire but are still positioned above the storeys they mark, an arrangement that preserves something of their 5th-century function as free-standing finials.

The Mahabodhi spire, often described as rectilinear, has a very gentle convex profile. This curved outline, unknown in the 5th century, was accentuated during the 7th century. Similarly, the offsets are not as pronounced as in later architecture. In the centre of the tower, *gavākṣa* dormers of diminishing size make up a rudimentary central spine (*madhylatā*). The dormers are more interwoven than in 5th-century buildings but have not yet formed the mesh pattern (*jāla*) typical of mature temple architecture. These various features indicate that while older forms are perpetuated at the Mahabodhi, their configuration was in the process of being freed from the predictable logic of Gupta-period architecture. The Mahabodhi is thus a forerunner of temple forms that emerged in the 7th century, making it likely that it is the temple edifice (*prāsāda*) described in the Bodhgaya inscription of AD 598–9 (Gupta year 279, probably not 269 as published; see Fleet). This date is confirmed by the similarity of figural and decorative ornaments to Site 3 at Nalanda (last quarter of the 6th century) and by comparison with the more developed superstructure of the Lakshmana Temple at SIRPUR (*c.* AD 625–50; see fig. 52 below). The date also accords with the description given by the Chinese pilgrim Xuanzang, who visited Bodhgaya *c.* AD 637.

Although stone architecture is atypical of Magadha, an early instance is Temple 2 at Nalanda. This is the only stone structure at the site and the only one devoid of Buddhist imagery. Like the other temples at Nalanda, the building stood on a rectangular platform (35.9×31 m). Though Temple 2 is completely ruined, there are indications at the site that it had a curvilinear spire of the northern type with subsidiary discs (*bhūmyāmalaka*) and a crowning finial (*āmalaka*). The sanctum was connected through an oblong passage to a hall and entrance porch. The plinth, surviving to a height of between 1.5 and 2 m, has minor projections on all sides and steps on the east. Above the lowest moulding is a wide recess in which some 220 figures are framed by ornamented pilasters with palmette brackets. These sculptures represent an array of Brahmanical gods, episodes from the *Rāmāyaṇa* epic and other scenes; the carving suggests the sculptors were more accustomed to working with brick. The recess is topped by a pair of cornices (*kapotas*) ornamented with geese, harpies and mock-dormers (*candraśālikās*).

The ruin of another terraced temple at Aphsad is probably the Vishnu Temple referred to in an inscription of Adityasena (*reg c.* 650–75) of the later Gupta dynasty. The surviving portions comprise a boldly moulded plinth decorated with stucco pilasters and large niches that once contained *Rāmāyaṇa* scenes (now damaged). The pilasters, elaborating types seen earlier at Bodhgaya, show pot-bases resting on lotus petals with square and three-sided shafts. The shafts are incised with half-lotus medallions. Capitals consist of overflowing pots with complex abaci.

Extensive ruins of stupas and Buddhist monasteries (*vihāras*) survive in the LALMAI-MAINAMATI hills and at PAHARPUR and ANTICHAK. The Salban Vihara at Mainamati was probably founded in the 8th century by the Pala king Dharmapala (*reg. c.* 781–812; see Asher). The Somapura Vihara at Paharpur and the ruins of what was probably the Vikramashila Vihara at Antichak are also foundations of Dharmapala. These sites are dominated by terraced temple-stupas of cruciform layout, with prominent image-shrines in each projection. An early example of this plan is found at SARNATH. The best-preserved portion of the two later monuments is the row of terracotta plaques lining the walls that rise from the circumambulatory terrace.

Orissa. The province of Orissa (anc. Kalinga) developed a distinct regional architecture from the mid-7th century. While the forms are analogous to those elsewhere in India, Orissan temples are often described by terms in the Oriya language. These terms derive from local manuscripts that date from the 13th century onwards. Three main types are recognized in this tradition: *rekhā*, a form closely related to the curvilinear *latina* spire in other parts of India; *pīḍhā*, a pyramidal roof made of horizontal tiers and known elsewhere as *phāṁsanā*; and *khākharā*, a barrel-vaulted roof elsewhere termed *valabhī*.

The earliest phase of temple architecture in Orissa is represented by about a dozen buildings at Bhubaneshwar. The best-preserved is the Parashurameshvara (*see* BHUBANESHWAR, §2(i)). This temple consists of a sanctum with a *rekhā*-style superstructure and rectangular hall. The hall is roofed in two sloping tiers with a clerestory between. This configuration represents the *piḍhā*-type superstructure in its most rudimentary form. The exterior walls are covered with low reliefs. The sanctum has bold podium mouldings interrupted by a door with a T-shaped frame in front and by large niches on each of the other sides. The niches hold figures of the deities Ganesha (south) and Karttikeya (east); an image of Parvati (north) has been removed. Corner niches (now empty) on the wall are capped by pediments. The entablature bears a recessed diaper frieze and a variety of figures. The superstructure, the earliest in the region, is a fully developed example of the curvilinear form. While similar to 7th-century spires elsewhere, it exhibits a heavy-shouldered outline typical of Orissa. The arched antefix (*śukanāsa*) on the front of the spire contains figures of Shiva in his forms as Ravananugrahamurti (bestowing his grace on the demon-king Ravana) and Nataraja. The temple has been dated from the early 7th century to the 8th. The architectural and sculptural forms and the palaeography of the short inscriptions suggest a date of about the mid-7th century.

Other 7th-century temples at Bhubaneshwar follow the plan and design of the Parashurameshvara with slight variations. Also belonging to this early period are the Durga Temple at Rameshvara (Cuttack District), with its *khākharā* roof, and the Shiva Temple at Kualo (Dhenkanal District), which has a five-shrined (*pañcāyatana*) configuration.

During the 8th and 9th centuries, the *rekhā* superstructure was articulated with five offsets on each face (*pañcaratha*). This innovation was not universal; some temples retained a tripartite format in the podium and walls. In the podium mouldings, the torus (*kalaśa*) and cornice (*kapōtapālī*) were ornamented with luxuriant foliage. The mouldings were capped by a further course carved with scrolls (*vasanta paṭṭikā*). Simultaneously, walls were adorned with ornate pilasters and niches, elements that were repeated on hall façades. The pediments on the main niches were elaborated; subsidiary niches often terminated in pyramidal pediments (*pīḍhāmundi*). These new forms are seen on the Sisireshvara and Markandeshvara temples at Bhubaneshwar. The Simhanatha Temple on the island of Baramba, assignable to the early 9th century, shows further developments in plan, design and ornamentation. The main offsets are accentuated, and the walls have more ornate pilasters crowned by gorgeous overflowing pots.

51. Mukteshvara Temple, Bhubaneshwar, *c.* mid-10th century AD; view from the south

The hall, with a three-tiered roof, has been lengthened and given a compartmentalized interior. The main building appears to have had four subsidiary shrines, of which only one survives.

A number of *khākharā* structures were built in the 8th and 9th centuries, the leading example being the Vaital Deul at Bhubaneshwar (*see* BHUBANESHWAR, §2(ii)). Dedicated to Tantric worship, the temple enshrines a fearsome image of the goddess Chamunda. The sanctum is rectangular in plan, with the long exterior back wall (*pṛṣṭabhadra*) ornamented with five niches framed by ornate pilasters. The central niche holds a figure of Ardhanarishvara (Shiva and his consort combined in a single body); celestial nymphs (*apsarasas*) appear in the others. The side walls (*pakṣabhadra*) show Parvati with Lakulisha above in a medallion (south) and Durga Mahishasuramardini (i.e. slaying the buffalo demon) with a Hari-Hara above (north).

The superstructure is a mixed type. The top is barrel-vaulted, but the lower portion has the components of a conventional *rekhā* spire. An elaborate antefix, containing Surya in a lower medallion and Shiva Nataraja above, projects towards the rectangular hall on the eastern side of the temple. The hall has four attached corner shrines with *rekhā*-style superstructures.

A southern extension of the Orissan style flourished at MUKHALINGAM. The Madhukeshvara Temple complex, datable to the reign of Kamarnava II (*reg c.* AD 803–53) of the Ganja dynasty, is the oldest and best preserved. The complex is walled and entered through a double gate, the outer one carrying a barrel-vaulted superstructure. The gate leads to a hall for Shiva's bull, Nandi, and then to the main shrine. The superstructure of the main shrine is curvilinear in outline, but composed of horizontal tiers, a mode of construction commonly used on temple halls. The only ornament is a thin, antefix-like projection on each side showing pairs of *gavākṣa* dormers holding Shaiva images. The temple is flanked by shrines of the usual *rekhā* type, with three smaller barrel-vaulted shrines skirting the perimeter wall. The Someshvara Temple, also at Mukhalingam, belongs to the late 9th century and exhibits the decorative exuberance typical of that period. The building has a seven-storey superstructure and displays a wide array of Shaiva images.

Later temples in Orissa are characterized by increasing elaboration and scale, which was a widespread occurrence in 10th- and 11th-century India. The Mukteshvara Temple at Bhubaneshwar (see fig. 51; *see also* BHUBANESHWAR, §2(iii)), a well-preserved building of about the mid-10th century, displays a mixture of early and advanced features and is therefore an ideal monument for understanding the development of Orissan architecture as a whole. The temple's early features include a single register of sculpture on the sanctum, a spire that curves gradually from base to summit and a marked recess in the entablature providing a clear visual break between wall and superstructure. Rising to only 10 m in height, the temple also conforms to the modest scale prevalent before the 10th century. Advanced elements are equally evident. In the podium mouldings, the torus has been transformed into a realistic vase with overflowing foliage. The walls and recesses are carefully segmented and display features (such as pilasters entwined by serpents) that are typical of the mature Orissan style. Rounded discs mark the storeys of the superstructure. Especially characteristic of later architecture is the *bho* motif, a dormer flanked by grinning dwarfs at the base of the superstructure.

The Mukteshvara is also the first temple in which the shoulder slab atop the spire partakes of the projections below, and the decoration of the hall exterior is coordinated with that of the sanctum. Furthermore, the hall has a square plan and a multi-tiered roof of the mature *pīḍhā* type. Earlier halls were usually rectangular with simple slab roofs. Iconographically, the temple is among the earliest to depict charming females (*nāyikā*s) on the walls and all nine planets on the door architrave. Some features of the Mukteshvara are unique, notably the free-standing gate (*see* TORAṆA). Yet other features find their only parallel in central India, including the tall pediments on the niches and cusped coffers on the hall ceiling.

The 10th century was a period of prolific activity. The leading monuments are the temples of Nilamadhava (Vishnu) and Siddheshvara (Shiva) at Gandharadi (Phulbani District), the Gauri Temple at Bhubaneshwar and the three temples at Baudh. All share the advanced architectural and decorative features of the Mukteshvara Temple. The Varahi Temple at Chaurasi (Puri District), a sumptuously ornamented rectangular structure in an exceptional state of preservation, is dedicated to the goddess Varahi (see Boner and Śarmā).

For sculpture of this period *see* §V, 6(v) and 7(v) below.

BIBLIOGRAPHY

Enc. Ind. Temple Archit., ii/1–2
J. F. Fleet: *Inscriptions of the Early Gupta Kings and their Successors*, Corp. Inscr. Indic., iii (Calcutta, 1888); rev. by D. K. Bhandarkar, ed. B. Chhabra and G. S. Gai (Delhi, 1981)
A. Cunningham: *Mahābodhi; or the Great Buddhist Temple under the Bodhi Tree at Buddha-Gayā* (London, 1892)
J. Burgess: *The Ancient Monuments, Temples and Sculptures of India*, 2 vols (London, 1897–[?1911]) [Bodhgaya, pl. 173]
N. K. Bose: *Canons of Orissan Architecture* (Calcutta, 1932)
K. N. Dikshit: *Excavations at Paharpur, Bengal*, Mem. Archaeol. Surv. India, lv (Delhi, 1938)
A. K. Maitra: *The Ancient Monuments of Varendra (North Bengal)* (Rajshahi, [?1949])
K. Deva and V. S. Agrawala: 'The Stone Temple at Nalanda', *J. U.P. Hist. Soc.*, xxiii (1950), pp. 198–212
D. Mitra: *Bhubaneswar* (New Delhi, 1958, 3/1966)
S. Rajguru: *Inscriptions of Orissa*, 4 vols (Bhubaneshwar, 1958–66)
D. Barrett: *Mukhalingam Temples* (Bombay, 1960)
K. C. Panigrahi: *Archaeological Remains at Bhubaneswar* (Bombay, 1961)
C. C. Das Gupta: *Paharpur and its Monuments* (Calcutta, 1963)
F. A. Khan: *Mainamati: A Preliminary Report on Recent Excavations in East Pakistan* (Karachi, 1963)
M. A. A. Qadir: *A Guide to Paharpur* (Karachi, 1963)
A. Boner and S. R. Śarmā: *Śilpa Prakāśa* (Leiden, 1966)
R. R. Mukherji and S. K. Maity: *Corpus of Bengal Inscriptions Bearing on History and Civilization of Bengal* (Calcutta, 1967)
K. Deva: *Temples of North India* (Delhi, 1969)
B. Morrison: *Lalmai: A Cultural Centre of Early Bengal* (Seattle, 1974)
S. K. Saraswati: *Architecture of Bengal* (Calcutta, 1976)
B. Masthanaiah: *The Temples of Mukhalingam: A Study of South Indian Temple Architecture* (Delhi, 1978)
F. M. Asher: *The Art of Eastern India, 300–800* (Minneapolis, 1980)
T. E. Donaldson: *Hindu Temple Art of Orissa*, 3 vols (Leiden, 1985)

(f) Ancient South Kosala. The ancient province of South Kosala, comprising the south-eastern portion of Madhya Pradesh, developed its own style of architecture between the 6th and 8th centuries during the period of the Panduvamshi and Nala kings. Except for the stone temples at TALA, all the monuments in the region are built of brick with stone doorframes and pillars. The two Shiva temples at Tala, the earliest known buildings in South Kosala, were cleared of debris in the 1980s. Only the structure locally called Deorani preserves a significant portion of its elevation. Built on a high plinth, it consists of a sanctum, vestibule, entrance hall and porch. Corpulent attendants of Shiva (*gaṇa*s) guard the steps. The temple walls have plain oblong niches; the largest ones, on the main offsets (*bhadra*s), are surmounted by decorative arches spewing from the mouths of crocodiles (*makaratoraṇa*s). These portions of the elevation find their closest parallel in architecture of the early Chalukya and Pallava dynasties (*see* §§(h) and (i) below). The superstructure at Tala is lost. The sanctum doorframe has six jambs (*śākhā*) stunningly ornamented with scrolls, foliage and multi-stranded garlands. The lintel, carved in two registers, shows Gajalakshmi (the goddess Lakshmi being lustrated by elephants) above and a standing Shiva with attendants below. The broad soffit of the lintel and adjacent faces of the jambs are richly carved with medallions, Shaiva themes and grotesque animal heads (*grāsamukha*s) made up of opulent flowers and foliage. Of the sculptures unearthed by excavation, the most remarkable is a colossal image of Shiva, possibly in his aspect as Kala-Rudra (*see* §V, 6(iv) below). Dating such an unusual monument is difficult in the absence of historical inscriptions. The temple's experimental character recalls the early buildings of Magadha, suggesting that it was built in the 6th century, when conventions for temple architecture were still being formulated.

The monuments at Tala had no direct architectural descendants, and it was the Rajivalochana Temple at RAJIM that introduced the brick tradition of South Kosala. The Rajivalochana stands on a high platform and comprises a sanctum, vestibule and long pillared hall. Due to renovations and additions, only the sanctum is original, though some stone pillars were reused when the hall was reconstructed in the early 8th century. The external walls of the sanctum have a single projection on each side and are dominated by plain square pilasters with brackets of Deccani affiliation. The spire is a straight-edged pyramid four storeys high. The central offsets display four bold dormers of diminishing size, while the corner sections carry small octagonal domes on each level. Each dome is surrounded by spirelets and crowned by a grooved disc. The top of the spire has been restored in an arbitrary fashion.

As with the Mahabodhi Temple at Bodhgaya, the origin of the superstructure in a multi-storey building is readily apparent. Like Bodhgaya also, the architectural elements have been manipulated in a more fluid manner than during the Gupta age. Analogies with the Mahabodhi (with due allowance for regional variation) and comparisons to subsequent buildings in South Kosala suggest that the Rajivalochana can be dated to *c.* AD 600.

The Lakshmana Temple at Sirpur (see fig. 52) provides one of the few fixed points in 7th-century architecture. A dedicatory inscription refers to the establishment of the building by one Vasata, the widowed mother of the Panduvamshi king Mahashivagupta Balarjuna (*reg c.* AD 595–655). An exact year cannot be fixed for the foundation, but it probably occurred in the second quarter of the 7th century. The structure is built of brick and raised on an extensive terrace. It has a sanctum divided into five faces on each side (*pañcaratha*), a vestibule and a long pillared hall (ruined). The long hall, first appearing at Rajim, is a typical feature of South Kosala. The sanctum doorway, in pink sandstone, has five broad jambs lavishly embellished with scrolls, diamonds, amorous couples and Vaishnava themes. Externally, the temple has bold podium mouldings (*vedībandha*s), with each offset in the wall above defined by pilasters of northern and Deccani derivation; the central projections carry blind doorways, and the subsidiary offsets (*pratiratha*s) carry pilaster-framed niches capped by large *gavākṣa* dormers. The two-tiered entablature (*varaṇḍikā*), with a pattern of chequers, carries the massive four-storey spire. Imposing *gavākṣa* dormers of diminishing size were placed on the central offset, with *gavākṣa* arches on the flanking offsets and bulbous grooved discs (*bhūmyāmalaka*s) on the corners. The crowning portion is a modern restoration. The convex outline, the clearly articulated projections and the compressed storeys marked by discs make this spire an immediate precursor of the curvilinear form known as *latina*. A staple of subsequent architecture throughout north India, the *latina* was evidently being developed simultaneously in western and central India, but it is only in the Lakshmana that a formative example has been preserved.

52. Lakshmana Temple, Sirpur, *c.* AD 625–50

Also at Sirpur and coeval with the Lakshmana are two Buddhist monasteries and the Rama Temple. The monasteries follow established conventions with cells around an open court. In the Rama Temple, damaged and shorn of its superstructure, the subsidiary offsets are set at an acute angle, introducing a common feature of buildings in the region. The Shabarinarayana Temple at Kharod (Bilaspur District) has similar angled offsets. The upper portions are like the Lakshmana Temple, but the entablature is less heavily treated, and the spire was given a more curvilinear profile. The building can thus be dated to *c.* AD 650. The Indal Temple at Kharod, made of brick and carrying stucco ornament, replicates the angled offsets of the Shabarinarayana, but introduces figural ornament (damaged) within the *gavākṣa* dormers and on the walls. The curvilinear spire preserves three of its four storeys, each storey being marked by grooved discs on both the corners and subsidiary offsets. The stone doorway is dominated by human-size figures of the river goddesses Ganga and Yamuna, among the finest images in the art of South Kosala. More advanced than the Shabarinarayana, the Indal Temple probably dates to *c.* AD 675.

The Siddheshvara Temple at Palari, probably dating to the end of the 7th century, is a brick-and-stucco construction repeating the design of the Indal Temple at Kharod on a large scale and with more elaborate stucco ornament (for details see Stadtner). The Shiva Temple at Dhobini (Bilaspur District), probably built in the first half of the 8th century, has an exceptional stellate design, based on the rotation of two squares at a 45-degree angle. The lower portions of the building are sandstone, while the spire is brick and stucco. A diamond frieze was introduced into the podium mouldings, while the wall (*jaṅghā*) displays false doorways on the main offsets and *gavākṣa* dormers capped by leogryphs on the corners (*karṇa*s). The spire, intact and three storeys high, is embellished with pilasters combined with bold discs (*āmalaka*s) on the projected offsets.

For sculpture in this period *see* §V, 6(iv) and 7(iv) below.

BIBLIOGRAPHY

K. Deva: 'Laksmana Temple at Sirpur', *J. Madhya Pradesh Itihasa Parishad*, ii (1960), pp. 35–44

D. Stadtner: 'The Siddesvara Temple at Palari and the Art of Kosala during the Seventh and Eighth Centuries', *A. Orient.*, xii (1981), pp. 49–56

KRISHNA DEVA

(g) Central. Numerous temples are preserved in the territory between the Gangetic plain and the Narmada River. This vast area of central India (conforming approximately to the modern state of Madhya Pradesh; see fig. 53) was divided into a number of regions with distinct cultural and artistic traditions: the Dahala country in the east, the Malwa plateau (Malava) in the west, Jejakabhukti (comprising the area of Bundelkhand) in the north and Gopakshetra (the districts around Gwalior) in the north-west. The southern frontier was marked by Anupa and Lata, regions that lay beyond the Narmada. The architecture of these areas developed in synchrony and can be surveyed as a unit, although regional variations are often evident.

53. Map of central Indian subcontinent; those sites with separate entries in this dictionary are distinguished by CROSS-REFERENCE TYPE

54. The 'smaller' Shiva Temple, Mahua, *c.* 7th century AD; view from the south

6th–7th centuries AD. One of the few sites with 6th-century material is SONDANI. Two monumental pillars with massive lion abaci are the chief features of the site (the crowning figures are missing). Inscriptions indicate that these pillars were set up by Yashodharman (*reg c.* AD 525–35) to celebrate his victory over the Huna king Mihirakula. Additional fragments include portions of a doorjamb and a broken lintel (New Delhi, N. Mus.), which may have formed part of a temple door or gate (*toraṇa*). Compared to 5th-century examples, the Sondani pillars are larger and more awkwardly proportioned. The architectural sculpture and scrollwork also show a flattened and simplified rendering of form. Fragments from sites further west, such as Nagari, show similar characteristics.

Modest flat-roofed shrines akin to those developed in the Gupta period survive from the 7th and 8th centuries. One design was built in imitation of wood, with the walls consisting of projecting pilasters and receding panels. This mode of construction, best described as post-and-plank, was facilitated by the easy availability of suitable sandstone blocks and slabs from the Vindhya ranges throughout central India. The earliest example is at Chapara, near BADOH. The moulded podium supports walls of post-and-plank configuration and a heavy entablature (*varaṇḍikā*). The door and pillared portico closely follow 5th-century standards. Directly beside the Chapara shrine is a ruined building of similar design but with small carved images in projecting niches capped with pediments. Similar shrines are located near by at Ramgarh. The flat-roofed 'smaller' Shiva Temple at Mahua is described in the inscription on the structure as a *maṇḍapikā*. (The inscription, which outlines the lineage of some local rulers, was composed by Ishana of Kanyakubja, a poet known from the *Harṣacarita* to have lived in the first half of the 7th century.) Consequently, architectural historians use the term *maṇḍapikā* to designate all temples of post-and-plank construction. The example at Mahua (see fig. 54) shows some elaboration in its richly carved panels and image niches (containing the deities Ganesha, Durga and Varaha). The scrollwork is no longer stiffly pendent, like 6th-century work, but boils with erratic agitation and brooding movement. Aediculae (*kūṭa*s) on the door, which take the shape of temple spires, indicate the emergence of the curvilinear type of superstructure (*latina*).

A second Shiva Temple at Mahua (usually termed the 'larger' Shiva Temple) has the earliest mature superstructure in central India (see fig. 55). The sanctum walls are divided into three vertical faces or sections (*triratha*) and carry prominent projections (*bhadra*s). Pilasters carved with overflowing pots and other richly worked devices articulate the wall surface. The entablature is two-tiered with keyhole niches. The impressive superstructure has a robust pattern of interlocking window motifs on the central projection (*madhyalatā*), while the subsidiary offsets and spire corners (*veṇukośa*s) are marked by substantial grooved discs (*bhūmyāmalaka*s). Diminutive aediculae (*bālapañjara*s) are placed in a deep vertical recess (*salilāntara*). The building faces east and has an elegant T-shaped door with figures of the river goddesses Ganga and Yamuna. The long rectangular area in front of the door may have accommodated a hall, but no trace of it remains. There is no inscription, but a late 7th-century date can be inferred from material elsewhere, notably the Lakshmana Temple at SIRPUR (*c.* AD 600–650) and the temples at ALAMPUR (before AD 690).

A ruined shrine at GYARASPUR (probably late 7th century) is similar in its morphology to the earlier *maṇḍapikā* at Mahua, but the juxtaposition of architectural parts is less awkward and the proportions more attenuated. The frothy scrollwork on the panels, a *tour de force* of architectural ornament, is closely allied to the carving on the larger Shiva Temple at Mahua. A doorframe near the Gyaraspur *maṇḍapikā* is all that remains of another 7th-century building. The only other notable building of the period is the Sitaleshvar Mahadev temple at Chandravati (near Jhalawar). Little survives above the mouldings, but the preserved portions are in the same vigorous style as Gyaraspur.

Such material, limited though it is, indicates that temple architecture in central India underwent a rapid and fundamental transformation in the 7th century. The conventions of the Gupta age were absorbed and overtaken by a new inventiveness, epitomized by the appearance of the curvilinear stone superstructure. The rudimentary components of the mature temple tradition were now in place, providing a foundation for five centuries of dynamic architectural activity.

55. The 'larger' Shiva Temple, Mahua, late 7th century AD; view from the north

8th century AD. The more numerous buildings surviving from the 8th century indicate a consolidation of earlier achievements. Chronology remains relative, however, due to the absence of securely dated monuments. The best-preserved buildings that can be assigned to the first half of the 8th century include two Shiva temples at Amrol, south of GWALIOR. The Rameshvara Mahadeva, the more significant building, has a square sanctum with the walls divided into three faces. A vestibule projects to the east. The sanctum carries a short curvilinear spire and the vestibule an arched antefix (*śukanāsa*). The spire (rebuilt at the top) displays intricate *gavākṣa* ('cow's-eye') arches on the central projection, grooved discs (*karṇāmalakas*) on the corners and aediculae in the recess between. The niches on the walls, with a notable assortment of pediments, show damaged images of the god Shiva's attendants and guardians of the quarters (*dikpālas*). The main niches at the cardinal points display the deities Ganesha, Karttikeya and Uma, the standard iconographic programme for Shiva temples in the Gwalior region during the 8th and 9th centuries. The door has a T-shaped format. The six temples in the gorge at Naresar are similar to those at Amrol and better preserved, but they were executed in a more rugged manner. Additional motifs are found, such as a band of knotted serpents (*nāgapāśa*) forming a doorjamb with Vishnu's mount, Garuda, on the lintel, holding the ends of their tails. Indicative of an early to mid-8th-century date for all these buildings is a substantial lightening of the architectural forms as compared to Mahua. The independence of detail seen in the 7th century has yielded to a carefully chiselled surface and an effort to fit each architectural part into the design scheme. This is shown specifically in the spire by the corner discs and slabs (*kalās*), which are more compressed. Pillars, pediments and other elements have been standardized. Many details, such as pilasters, no longer occur. The net pattern (*jāla*) on the spires and decorative scrollwork on the doors are also flattened and less boldly worked.

The Batesar Mahadeva Temple near Padhaoli is indicative of developments in the second half of the 8th century. The complex stands with nearly 40 shrines of varying sizes on a forested hill. Although it is similar to Amrol and Naresar, certain differences suggest a later date. The arched antefix has been scaled down and integrated with the rest of the structure, and the entablature, purged of some mouldings, plays a less dominant role in the elevation. The spire displays greater compression of architectural elements, and a careful balance has been struck between horizontals (such as the discs) and verticals (such as the recesses and aediculae). A rhythmic precision is evident in the decorative motifs and the tall pediments (*udgamas*) that came into vogue at this time.

Also of 8th-century date are two exceptional buildings: the stellate Shiva Temple at Indor and the rectangular Teli ka Mandir at Gwalior. The Indor Temple has a circular plinth on which are placed 12 square projections alternating with angular corners (*pallavas*); this stellate configuration is carried through the whole elevation. The Teli ka Mandir, rising some 24.4 m in height, is the largest temple in central India from before the 10th century. It has a rectangular plan with a large vestibule. The tall doorway (12.8 m high) recalls the entrances at Batesar and Indor. The walls of the sanctum are adorned with large niches surmounted by pediments in the shape of temple spires. The superstructure is a mixed type, showing a barrel vault (*valabhi*) over two stages of a conventional *latina* base. The temple bears short inscriptions datable to the 8th century; these and the surviving images suggest that the temple was dedicated to the Goddess.

A group of temples at Bandogarh provides evidence that a somewhat simpler idiom was practised in the same period. Still humbler products, at times folkish in character, are found throughout central India and include, for example, the early 8th-century Shiva Temple at Dang and minor shrines at Badoh and Batesar. Many perpetuate the old *maṇḍapikā* type, but some have curvilinear spires. The best-preserved example of the latter is the Shiva Temple at Kuchdon, near DEOGARH.

9th century AD. During the 9th century a more ornate and homogeneous style of architecture appeared throughout central India. To some extent this elegant new idiom may be attributed to the Gurjara-Pratihara dynasty, which ruled most of north India from the time of Nagabhatta II (*reg c*. 810–33). Central India, however, was under a subordinate aristocracy, and inscriptions indicate that it was the main patron of new construction. Most typical of the new 'Pratihara' idiom is the Shiva Temple at Terahi. In scale and general configuration, the temple recalls Naresar, Padhaoli and other 8th-century buildings. However, each elevation has five vertical faces or sections (*pañcaratha*), as well as additional decorative offsets. The walls are more densely ornamented, with slender mock niches filling the recesses and half niches appearing on the corners adjacent to the vestibule wall (*kapilī*). Heavy awnings shelter the images, a feature appearing for the first time in this building. In the superstructure each part plays a subdued role in the elevation, creating a uniform texture. The elimination of the aediculae makes the spire less cluttered and accentuates verticality.

After the mid-9th century, the number of surviving temples increases dramatically. Several buildings of this period are found at Badoh, the most significant being the Gadarmal. This large complex, set on an extensive moulded terrace, comprises a main temple and seven subsidiary shrines. The approach was from the east through an ornate gate that collapsed in the late 19th century or the early 20th (see Burgess). The main temple has a rectangular sanctum, preceded by a vestibule, hall and porch. The podium (*vedībandha*) stands on an ornate socle, and the offsets are adorned with niches with tall pediments. The building is ruined, with virtually everything above the mouldings reset in a haphazard manner. It is clear, however, that the principal offsets were treated as miniature doors with awnings and spirelike pediments. The recesses and intervening spaces between the main niches are partly filled with demigods and nymphs, an important step towards the decorated style of the late 9th century. The well-preserved doorway, with its increased number of jambs, sill (*udambara*) and overdoor (*uttarāṅga*), is a superlative example of the increasing decoration lavished on the finest temples. A figure of Durga is placed in the keystone (*lalāṭabimba*), and a reclining image probably of the goddess Parvati with the infant Karttikeya (Gwalior, Archaeol. Mus.) was once placed in the sanctum. The hall before the temple was of the open type (*raṅga-maṇḍapa*), edged by a parapet with projecting elephant heads. The pillars of the hall are sumptuously decorated with vase-and-foliage decoration on the base and capital; a pillar extension above supports ornate brackets. The ceiling and roof of the hall have collapsed.

The well-preserved Maladevi Temple at Gyaraspur shows further development. The sanctum is surrounded by an ambulatory and preceded by a spacious closed hall (*gūḍhamaṇḍapa*). Both the ambulatory and hall have balconied porches with a low parapet and sloping seat back (*kakṣāsana*). Such balconies, integral to the mature temples of the 10th century, appear in the Maladevi for the first time. Another important innovation is in the multi-spired superstructure, in which the main curvilinear spire is surrounded by eight spirelets. Features that appear on later buildings are the complex domed ceiling and extensive pyramidal roof. No doubt they existed earlier, but there is little evidence for them. The mouldings and doors of the Maladevi exhibit an extraordinary array of carved ornament, executed in the most accomplished 9th-century manner. In the podium, parts of the torus (*kalaśa*) were replaced with square bosses (*tulā*s) carved with grotesques (*kīrttimukha*s) amid floral scrolls. These are among the finest architectural embellishments in central India. The iconography shows Jaina *yakṣa*s and *yakṣī*s (nature deities) and standing figures; some bear labels that can be dated palaeographically to the 9th century.

In the late 9th century, securely dated monuments are found for the first time. The Chaturbhuja Temple at Gwalior is the most instructive example. Inscriptions on the temple record that it was excavated from the rock by an officer of the Pratihara king Mihira Bhoja (*reg* AD 836–85) in 876–7 (Vikrama year 933). The temple is dedicated to Vishnu and shows Varaha, Vishnu and Trivikrama in the main niches, with guardians of the directions on the corners. All the sculpture, including the door, has been mutilated, and the upper portion of the spire has been rebuilt. The building's modest size recalls earlier temples, but the design has changed significantly. Symptomatic of a more decorative style are the less prominent offsets, the double pediments on the main niches and the circular pilasters and griffins used to frame the images. Every architectural element is now carefully sublimated to a controlled scheme of polished elegance and elaboration. In the superstructure a net pattern of unprecedented intricacy has spread out from the central spine to cover the subsidiary offset.

Similar traits are exhibited by the temples at Umri and Madkheda, both dedicated to the god Surya. These buildings preserve a wealth of sculptural ornament, the Madkheda temple being especially notable for its elaborate antefix (*śukanāsa*). Other aspects of late 9th-century architecture are revealed by the ruin known as Char Khamba at Gyaraspur, associated with an inscription (Gwalior, Archaeol. Mus.) dated AD 879–80 (Vikrama year 936). Among the ruins are miniature spires, evidently once part of the multi-spired superstructure. Adjacent to the temple is a gate, the only example to survive from the Pratihara age. It consists of two pillars carved with relief panels, a cross-beam supporting two floral arches and a heavy lintel surmounted by a miniature temple.

The dynamic, linear style of the 10th century is anticipated in such temples as the Jarai Math near Barwa Sagar. The prominence given to goddess imagery on the exterior of this rectangular temple suggests a Tantric dedication. The temple continues 9th-century architectural conventions, but there are sharper distinctions between forms and more precise detail. Scrollwork is regularized and undercut, mouldings have been given a sharper profile, and the temple as a whole has been made subject to more disciplined organization. Figures of Ganga and Yamuna and door-guardians at the base of the doorjambs are sheltered by canopies. The main niches on the north and south sides have been elaborated into niche shrines, complete with miniature doors and pillared porches—a feature elaborated further in the 10th century at Surwaya.

Parallels to the Jarai Math can be found in various parts of central India. In the Dahala region, the Mahadeva Temple at NACHNA has a number of 5th- and 6th-century pieces incorporated into its fabric, but the monument is essentially a forerunner of the Kalachuri style of the 10th century. Near Gwalior, the free-standing hall at Padhaoli anticipates that region's later architecture. The hall is of the open type and stands on a lofty moulded platform that

56. Vishvanatha Temple, Khajuraho, completed 1002; view from the south

was converted into a small fort at a later date (the temple proper is no longer extant). The hall is notable for its profusely carved architraves and exquisite ceilings.

10th–11th centuries: Chandella domains. As the Pratihara empire declined, central India was parcelled into four kingdoms. The Chandella dynasty ruled over Jejakabhukti in the north, the Kalachuris over the Dahala country in the south-east, the Paramara dynasty over Malava in the west and the Kachchhapaghata dynasty over Gopakshetra in the north-west. These powerful houses vied for political supremacy and competed with each other in temple construction. Architecture enjoyed a glorious efflorescence, with buildings of unprecedented scale and complexity being constructed in every part of central India. The common legacy of the Gupta and Pratihara ages meant that temples continued to share many features of plan, design and decorative scheme. Despite this, regional idioms were consolidated. These idioms are generally identified with the prevailing dynasties, for inscriptions show that the kings were active patrons. However, it is difficult to determine whether these idioms owed their origin exclusively to the rulers or whether the dynasties, as regional powers, simply amplified entrenched regional traditions of architecture.

The Chandellas, the most powerful regional dynasty of the 10th–11th century, built forts, tanks and temples throughout their dominion. Important remains are found in north and central India at Kalanjara, Deogarh, Banpur, Dudhai, Madanpur and Mohangarh, with the most distinctive cluster of temples at KHAJURAHO.

Among the finest sandstone temples of Khajuraho are the Lakshmana, Vishvanatha (see fig. 56) and Kandariya Mahadeva temples. An inscription of AD 954–5 (Vikrama year 1011) records the construction of the Lakshmana Temple, the earliest at the site, by King Yashovarman (*reg* 925–54). The temple is set on a lofty terrace (*jagatī*) and consists of a main temple and four subsidiary shrines (*pañcāyatana*). The terrace is ornamented with friezes showing hunting and battle scenes. This is the only temple at Khajuraho to preserve its subsidiary shrines and terrace friezes. The central temple rests on a flaring, emphatically high socle (*pīṭha*). The temple wall (*jaṅghā*) is divided into tiers and heavily embellished with statuary. The superstructure is characterized by an arrangement of subsidiary spires of diminishing size attached to the main spire at graded heights. The clustering of subsidiary peaks and the progressive ascent of the roofs lends a powerful verticality and rhythm to the superstructure. The entrance carries an ornate arch (*makaratoraṇa*), and the interiors display an amazing exuberance of decorative detail, most notably the complex ceilings with their cusped coffers and stamen-like drop finials. The brackets in female form are also an interesting feature. Externally, the halls carry simple pyramidal roofs (*phāṃsanās*), straight-edged in profile and crowned by prominent bell-shaped finials (*ghaṇṭās*).

An architectural zenith was achieved with the Vishvanatha Temple, completed by King Dhanga (*reg c.* 954–1002) in 1002, and the Kandariya Mahadeva (*see* KHAJURAHO, figs 1 and 2), attributable to King Vidyadhara (*reg c.* 1025–50). These buildings have the same basic components as the Lakshmana, but exhibit a more sophisticated handling of the multi-spired form, the Kandariya Mahadeva being the grandest specimen of the type. The projecting balconies, halls, roofs and other features are also more harmoniously integrated into the whole design. Although dynamic and complex, these temples retain a powerful unity of conception. While parallels can be found elsewhere in central India, the Khajuraho temples are the most representative examples of the 11th-century architectural achievement.

10th–11th centuries: Kalachuri domains. Under the Kalachuri kings large temples were built at Tewar (anc. Tripuri) and Gurgi, rivalling those at Khajuraho. The most complete surviving portion is a massive 10th-century gate, now incorporated into Rewa Palace. An account of Kalachuri architecture must therefore be based on lesser buildings. The Shiva Temple at Chandrehi (mid-10th century) is in a remarkably chaste style. It consists of a circular sanctum with 16 offsets, 5 of which are concealed by the vestibule at the lower levels. The circular configuration is found only in the Dahala country and neighbouring areas of the Gangetic plain, where it was used in brick-built temples (*see* §(a) above). The superstructure at Chandrehi has a close-knit group of projections (*ratha*s), one above each wall offset. There are no subsidiary grooved discs. The medallion of the antefix bears a triple head of Shiva. The wall is divided into two tiers, a common feature after the 9th century, but has neither niches nor images. The temple stands on a substantial platform, but the moulded socle is modest and austere like the rest of the building. An inscription records that the temple was constructed by the Shaiva teacher Prabodhashiva, whose disciple constructed the adjacent monastery later, in AD 973. At Masaon, not far from Gurgi, there is a dilapidated Shiva Temple with the same circular configuration.

The Chausath Yogini Temple at Bheraghat presents another unusual type. This temple is a hypaethral circular structure (diam. 42.5 m) containing 81 images, including 64 female adepts (*yoginī*s). The images are labelled in 10th-century characters, but the cloistered roof was provided around the 12th century, when the temple of Gaurishankara also seems to have been added in the centre. This type was widespread in central India, and examples survive at Dudhai, near Deogarh, and at Mitaoli, north of Gwalior. Closely related is the Yogini Temple at Khajuraho, with its cells lining a rectangular court.

More conventional in design is the mid-10th-century Shiva Temple at Nohta, near Damoh. The sanctum is divided into five vertical faces on each side, with the walls carrying two registers of figures. The podium has appliqué niches, and the modest socle some decorated mouldings. The spire was restored using original materials, reset arbitrarily. The temple has an ornate door that provides the entrance to an open hall. Enclosed by a balustrade (*kakṣāsana*), the hall rests on a socle with eight large niches bearing goddesses. Its fine ceiling is supported by square pillars with overflowing pots; these divide the area into nine bays. The central bay has ornate concentric bands (*nabhicchanda*s), while the peripheral ones have flat panels relieved with lotus blossoms. The hall is surmounted externally by a simple pyramidal roof. Closely related to Nohta are the well-preserved Shiva Temple at Maihar and the ruined Shiva Temple at Marai, near Satna.

The Shiva temples at Amarkantak, a pilgrimage centre and source of the rivers Narmada and Son, document the Kalachuri style in the 11th century. Built of a coarse-grained sandstone, they are remarkable for their simplicity of design. The spires are of the curvilinear *latina* type; the walls and doors are devoid of sculpture, the only decoration being diamonds and flat, stencil-like scrolls. The Virateshvara Temple at SOHAGPUR is a late 11th-century temple with many features that are exotic by regional standards. The three rows of sculpture on the sanctum, multi-spired superstructure and closed hall find close parallels in the late temples of Khajuraho.

10th–11th centuries: Paramara domains. The Udayeshvara (or Nilakantheshvara) Temple at UDAIPUR (see fig. 57) is the most famous example of Paramara patronage. This architectural masterwork was completed in 1080 by King Udayaditya (*reg c.* 1080–86). The Udayeshvara stands on an extensive terrace approached by stairs flanked by olossal guardians. Surrounded by eight ruined shrines, the main temple has a stellate sanctum with each side divided into seven faces (*saptaratha*). The socle is smaller than those at Khajuraho; the wall has one row of small niched sculptures. The cardinal offsets are broad and bear figures of the deities Shiva Nataraja (Lord of Dance; south), Andhakantaka (west) and Chamunda (north). The superstructure belongs to a distinctive mode known as *bhūmija* ('earth-born').

Originating in the Malwa country, this class of temple is characterized by four vertical spines (*latā*s), with the intervening quadrants filled with tiers of miniature spires (*kūṭastambha*s). The vertical spines, bearing a complex net pattern, rise from prominent arches (*śūrasenaka*s) placed above each cardinal offset. The superstructure is surmounted by a serrated crown (*ghaṇṭā*). On the east face of the superstructure is an elaborate antefix displaying a figure of dancing Shiva with consorts and other deities (see fig. 195 below). An entrance hall with three identical porches is attached to the vestibule. The hall is supported by ornate pillars capped with atlantid brackets; four central pillars support a chaste circular ceiling of concentric bands with cusped coffers. On the exterior the hall carries a low pyramidal roof with a bell-shaped finial (*saṃvaraṇā*). Placed axially before the temple is a free-standing *sabhā-maṇḍapa*, a low-roofed structure walled with stone screens.

57. Udayeshvara Temple, Udaipur, completed by 1080; view from the south

As a whole, the Udayeshvara Temple is characterized by an architectonic rigour and geometric precision that set it apart from contemporary buildings in other regions.

Temples of the *bhūmija* class were built at many sites in the Malwa region during Paramara times, with fine examples surviving at UN, Nemawar and Jamli. Significant remains of the Paramara period are also found at BHOJPUR, BESNAGAR and Gyaraspur.

10th–11th centuries: Kachchhapaghata domains. The Kachchhapaghata dynasty came to prominence after AD 950 and ruled from the twin centres of Gwalior and Sihoniya; other branches of the family had their seats at Narwar and Dubkund (see Dvivedi). The temples at Narwar have been destroyed, though fragments have been incorporated into later buildings. A reasonably clear picture of 10th-century architecture emerges from the temples at Surwaya, Kadwaha and Terahi, all located south of Narwar. As a rule, they are modest in size and have sanctums divided into five vertical faces. The sanctums are preceded by vestibules and porches. Each building is set on a low socle that is sometimes ornamented; each has the usual podium and a wall displaying two registers of statuary. In the oldest Shiva Temple at Surwaya (mid-10th century), the ceiling of the porch is elaborately ornamented with cusped coffers and friezes. Some of the Vaishnava temples at Kadwaha have relief panels fitted in the sanctums showing Yashoda carrying her infant son Krishna on her lap, the birth of Krishna, and Vishnu reclining on the serpent Ananta. The Mohajamata, the only 10th-century temple at Terahi, shows a rich array of goddess imagery on its walls. An elegant gate, similar to that at Gyaraspur, which stood before the entrance, collapsed in the 1970s.

The superstructures of the temples at Surwaya and Terahi have fallen. The few at Kadwaha that survive include that of the Shiva Temple known locally as 'Murayat'. Its superstructure consists of a central spire with attached half-spires (*uraḥ-śṛṅga*) on each side. The ruined temple at Mandibamora displays vestiges of a similar form. Terahi, Surwaya and Kadwaha also have monastic structures (*maṭha*s), erected as residences for Shaiva ascetics. Each one is two-storey, built around a courtyard and roofed with large stone slabs.

At Dubkund, excavated in the early 1980s, there are remains of numerous ruined shrines. A long inscription, dated AD 1088 and mentioning the Kachchhapaghatas, was found on a pillar in a large Jaina temple. This building consists of a square cloister (24.5 m on each side) lined with shrines carrying pyramidal roofs. The doorjambs are richly carved, as are the pedestals and canopies. The Jaina images have been broken. The plan recalls temples at MT ABU and elsewhere in western India. A related structure of the same period is at Mitaoli, north of Gwalior. Situated on a prominent hill, the temple consists of cells arrayed in a circle around a court. The cells, originally enshrining 64 *yoginī*s, once carried spires, of which only the lowest portions remain. The shrine in the centre is surrounded by a circular pillared verandah.

Grander buildings survive at the Kachchhapaghata capitals of Gwalior and Sihoniya. At Sihoniya the most magnificent building is the Shiva Temple locally designated the Kakanmath. The inscription on the Sas-Bahu Temple at Gwalior indicates that the Kakanmath was built by the ruler Kirttiraja (*reg c.* 1015–35); this date is confirmed by the similarity of some features to the early 11th-century temples at Khajuraho. The Kakanmath stands on a broad terrace and was originally surrounded by at least four subsidiary shrines. The temple plan comprises a sanctum surrounded by an ambulatory with three balconied transepts; in front of this is a vestibule and a closed hall with lateral transepts and a porch approached by stairs from the east. This layout is not unlike temples at Khajuraho. Large standing lions (Gwalior, Archaeol. Mus.) flanked the entrance steps. The socle is elegantly moulded and punctuated by niches with figures of deities. The niches are capped with pediments. The sanctum is girded by the standard podium mouldings.

The Kakanmath is badly damaged, but much of the sanctum remains. The exterior has a single row of large images in niches, one on each of the five offsets. The images are framed by pillars and canopied by miniature arches spewing from the mouths of grotesques (*makara toraṇa*). The intervening projections and recesses are filled with leogryphs and nymphs, and figural friezes run across the top of the wall. The cardinal projections display larger niches, now empty, in the form of miniature doors with ribbed awnings and *phāṃsanā*-style pediments. The sanctum doorway has seven ornate jambs (*śākhā*s), including a row of deities between two bands of couples. The spire above survives to its full height (approx. 37 m), but only the rough masonry core remains. The vestibule and hall have similarly been shorn of their outer walls, revealing clusters of pillars ornamented on the upper quarter and crowned by plain roll brackets. The central ceiling is lost, but peripheral ceilings show designs of cusped coffers. The hall rose to a height of three storeys and was crowned by a bell finial (*ghaṇṭā*).

Two Vaishnava temples in the fortress of Gwalior, not far from Sihoniya, mark the culmination of the Kachchhapaghata style. They are popularly known as Sas-Bahu. A long inscription preserved in the porch of the larger temple indicates that they were begun by King Padmapala (*reg c.* 1085–93) and completed in 1093 by his son Mahipala (*reg c.* 1093–1105). The larger temple comprises a sanctum, vestibule and closed hall. Only the much-restored core of the sanctum remains, the outer walls and superstructure having disappeared. The hall, however, has survived and exhibits grand dimensions and a unique design. Rising to a height of 24.4 m in three storeys, it is surmounted by an elaborate pyramidal roof covered with miniature spires. This is different from Khajuraho, where roofs of simple slabs (*phāṃsanā*s) were preferred. The north and south sides have broad, pillared porticos, and the east has a large, two-storey porch. The main entrance (*see* GWALIOR, fig. 1), with its spiral columns, profusion of doorjambs, complex sill and overdoor, is a superlative example of the mature Kachchhapaghata idiom. The interior is a spacious 12-sided hall with an enormous circular ceiling of concentric rings, supported on 4 massive pillars and 12 pilasters. The images on the exterior are defaced, but the interior retains its original appearance, with stencil-like ornamentation covering every available surface. The smaller temple consists of a porch, open hall and sanctum doorframe. The sanctum itself has completely disappeared. This temple is raised on an ornate moulded socle crowned by running friezes of elephants and human figures. Above this is a parapet wall with sloping seat. The interior has four highly ornate pillars supporting a circular ceiling embellished with figures and cusped coffers. The roof is a smaller version of that of the larger temple.

After the great projects of the 11th century, temple architecture is marked by a slow decline in standards. The later temples at Khajuraho, for example, show a tedious repetition of identical forms. With the arrival of Islam and submission of indigenous dynasties to the sultanate in Delhi, royal patronage of new construction was undermined. Endowments were confiscated, and temple activities, from religious rituals to the refurbishing of old shrines, were curtailed. Guild structure was dislocated, and craftsmen entered the service of Islamic patrons. That these developments caused traditional architecture to decline is well illustrated by a Vishnu Temple at Tilori, near Naresar. The sanctum walls of this building are filled with a random assortment of pillars, chequer patterns and niches. On some of the niches, the pilasters framing the image have been omitted on one side. This random handling of basic architectural forms foreshadows the village shrines of later times, which retain only a garbled memory of the great age of temple building.

For sculpture of this period *see* §V, 6(iv) and 7(iv) below.

BIBLIOGRAPHY

J. Burgess: *The Ancient Monuments, Temples and Sculptures of India*, 2 vols (London, 1897–1910)
K. Deva: 'Temples of Khajuraho', *Anc. India*, xv (1959), pp. 43–65
——: 'Kacchapaghata Temples', *The Researcher*, iii–iv (1963–4), pp. 5–9
——: *Temples of North India* (Delhi, 1969)
——: 'Bhūmija Temples', *Studies in Indian Temple Architecture*, ed. P. Chandra (Delhi, 1975), pp. 90–113
M. Meister: 'Construction and Conception: Maṇḍapikā Shrines of Central India', *E. & W.*, xxvi (1976), pp. 409–18
O. Viennot: *Temples de l'Inde centrale et occidentale*, 2 vols (Paris, 1976) [illustrates many pre-10th-century temples]
S. D. Trivedi: 'Baruāsāgar kā prācīn mandir' [Barwa Sagar's Old Temple], *Betvā Vānī* (Jhansi, 1980), pp. 185–91
H. N. Dvivedi: 'Gopakṣetra ke Kacchapaghata' [Gopaksetra's Kachchhapaghatas], *Gvāliyar Darśan* (Gwalior, 1981), pp. 186–212
D. S. Stadtner: 'Nand Chand and a Central Indian Regional Style', *Artibus Asiae*, xliii (1982), pp. 129–36
K. Deva: 'Teli-ka-Mandir, Gwalior', *Indian Epigraphy: Its Bearing on the History of Art*, ed. F. M. Asher and G. S. Gai (Delhi, 1985), pp. 161–3
S. D. Trivedi: *The Jarāi Temple at Barwā Sāgar* (Jhansi, 1985)
R. D. Trivedi: *Temples of the Pratihāra Period in Central India* (Delhi, 1989)
K. Deva: *Temples of Khajuraho*, 2 vols (Delhi, 1990)
M. Willis: *Inscriptions of Gopakṣetra* (London, 1996)

KRISHNA DEVA, MICHAEL D. WILLIS

(h) Karnataka and Andhra. In this region (see fig. 58), both rock-cut and structural temples date to this period, and the two overlap chronologically. In Karnataka the rock-cut Brahmanical and Jaina cave temples at BADAMI and AIHOLE, royal foundations of the Chalukyas of Badami (*see* CHALUKYA, §1) that belong to the second half of the 6th century AD, predate the earliest surviving structural temples. Andhra's more numerous cave temples, thought to have been excavated under the Vishnukundins, may be slightly later. Brick structural temples have a long history in Andhra; the earliest traces are thought to date to about the 1st century AD. Early forms of 'southern' (*drāviḍa*) temple architecture may have appeared first in the now-vanished buildings of Andhra. However, it is in the Chalukya heartland of northern Karnataka that the formation of a mature *drāviḍa* 'language' from the early years of the 7th century can be traced. This 'language' showed a coherent development over the subsequent 700 years.

It was once held that certain structural temples of the Chalukyas of Badami had been built as early as the 5th century. Most scholars now agree in placing all these monuments in the 7th century and the first half of the 8th, up to AD 753, when the last Chalukya king was overthrown by the Rashtrakuta dynasty. Many of these temples were royal foundations and are concentrated at and around the Chalukya capital, Badami, and neighbouring Aihole, PATTADAKAL and Mahakuta and in western Andhra, especially at ALAMPUR. As well as *drāviḍa* temples, the Chalukyas of Badami built 'northern' (*nāgara*) temples; temples with tiered, pyramidal (*phāṁsana*) roofs; and 'hall temples', in which the sanctum was surrounded by a pillared hall. They also experimented with mixtures of *drāviḍa* and *nāgara* forms. The Chalukya rulers proclaimed themselves devotees of Vishnu until the middle of the 7th century and of Shiva thereafter, but temples to both were patronized at all times. Jainism also flourished, and numerous deities of the Puranic pantheon appear in the iconography.

6th–8th centuries AD*: Rock-cut and* drāviḍa *temples.* The rock-cut cave temples at Badami and Aihole, with their powerful sculptural panels and richly decorated ceilings (*see* §V, 7(vi)(c) below), are the earliest surviving works of the Chalukyas of Badami. Recalling the *vihāra* plan found at AJANTA, each of the Badami caves consists of a pillared hall, with a small, raised sanctum hollowed out at the rear and a verandah across the front. Rows of pillars fill the hall, except in Cave 3, a Vaishnava work dated AD 578, where a square space was created in front of the sanctum. At Aihole the Shaiva cave known as the Ravana Phadi and the smaller Jaina cave relate more closely in plan to Hindu cave sanctuaries in the Konkan (*see* §(d) above), with halls free of pillars and relatively large shrine-chambers to the sides and rear, fronted by tripartite screens (*see* AIHOLE, fig. 1). The rich and varied pillar designs of the caves, deriving largely from Maharashtra, were the starting point for a long tradition in the structural temples of Karnataka. Doorways were surrounded by ornamental bands (*sākhā*s) and flanked by pilasters carrying a rounded or double-curved eaves-cornice (*kapotapālī*) that was crowned by an 'overdoor' comprising a horizontal chain (*hāra*) of pavilions, already recognizable as either proto-*nāgara* or proto-*drāviḍa*.

The Andhra cave temples are stylistically close to the PALLAVA caves of Tamil Nadu (*see* §(i) below). The Andhra caves are generally pillared halls with a single sanctuary or, occasionally, three sanctuaries side by side in the rear wall. Several halls with sanctuaries may have been excavated side by side and interlinked, as in the elaborate three-storey complex at Undavalli. Various *drāviḍa* elements are found in these caves, including a horizontal chain of pavilions on the façade of the Undavalli three-storey complex. Over another of the Undavalli caves and over the Akkanna-Madanna group at Vijayawada, parts of rock-cut proto-*drāviḍa* superstructures survive.

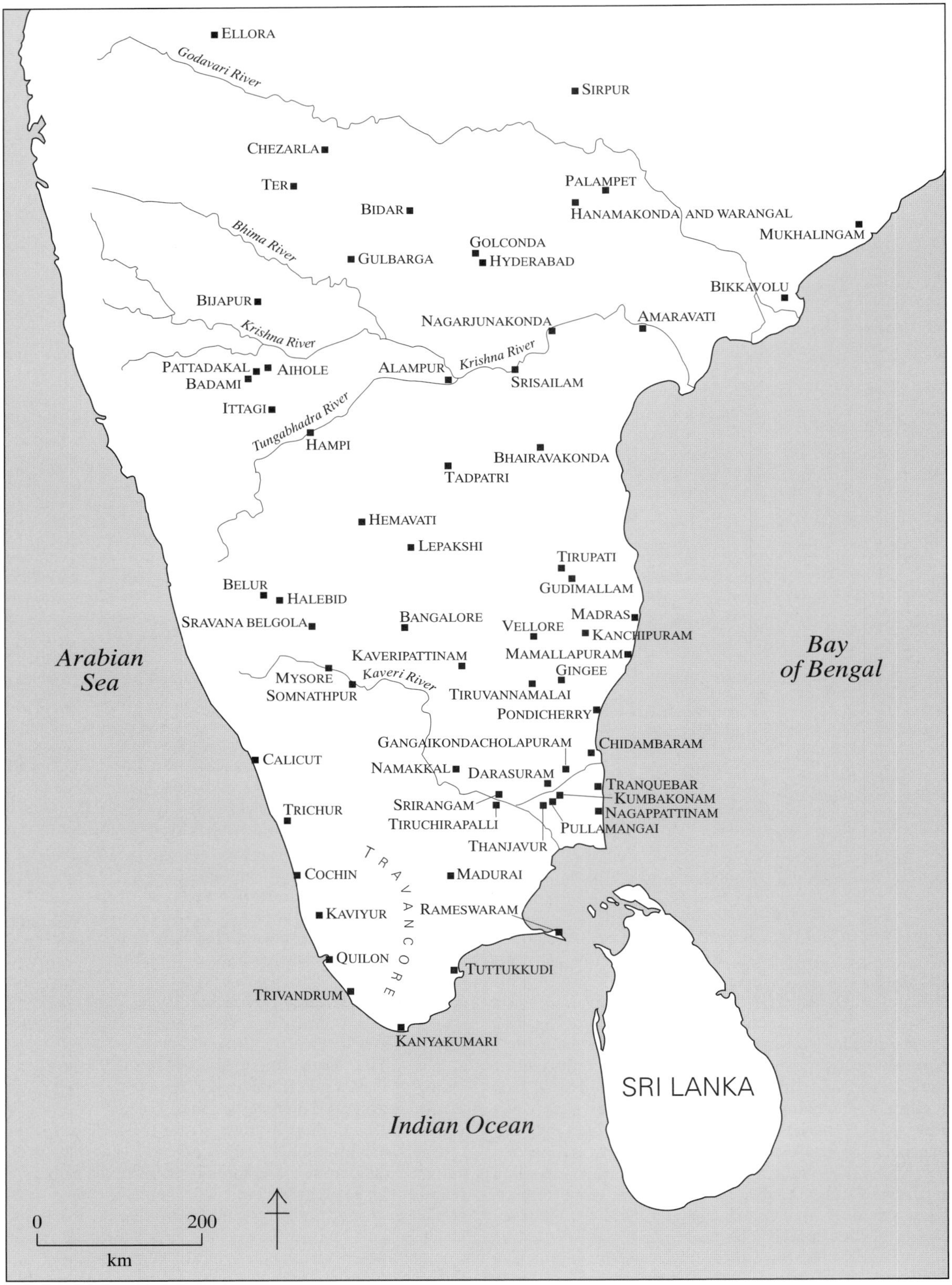

58. Map of southern Indian subcontinent; those areas with separate entries in this dictionary are distinguished by CROSS-REFERENCE TYPE

The simplest form of structural *drāviḍa* temple is the *alpa vimāna* ('minor shrine'), derived from wood-and-thatch prototypes. When rendered in masonry, this type has a moulded base, walls (usually with pilasters), an overhanging canopy or roll-cornice (*kapota*), and a crowning domed pavilion (*kūṭa*), usually square. Alternative *alpa vimāna* forms are rectangular, crowned by a barrel-roofed pavilion (*śālā*), and apsidal (*gajapṛṣṭha*, 'elephant-backed'), crowned by an apsidal *śālā*. *Alpa vimāna*s were almost certainly built in brick before they were built in stone. Probably the earliest surviving structural temple of the Chalukyas, built about the beginning of the 7th century, is a small sandstone *alpa vimāna* fronted by a porch, located south of the Ravana Phadi at Aihole (*see* AIHOLE, fig. 2). The evocation of timber and thatch forms had already been accomplished in the language of masonry by means of an established sequence of superimposed mouldings. At this early stage rather like petrified carpentry, the depiction is symbolic rather than literal. In the crowning pavilion all the superstructure mouldings found in mature *drāviḍa* works are already present, representing the thatched dome (*śikhara*), the necking (*grīvā*) or 'inhabitable' space below the roof, a surrounding railing (*vēdi*) and the edge of a floor, with joist-ends (*pratimālā*s or *vyālamālā*s, where decorated with mythical creatures). This last moulding sits on the roll-cornice, representing thatched eaves. Examples of the apsidal *alpa vimāna* form, possibly considerably older than the Aihole shrine but with the same moulding sequence in the superstructure, are found at TER (Maharashtra) and CHEZARLA (Andhra Pradesh), both brick buildings and originally Buddhist (*see* §4(ii)(c) above). A similar stone shrine at Satyavolu (Andhra Pradesh) has been attributed to the early 8th century (see *Enc. Ind. Temple Archit.*, i/2, p. 53).

A tradition of carving votive shrines in the form of miniature monolithic *alpa vimāna*s, mostly crowned with domed pavilions, was well established in Andhra Pradesh by the 7th century. Images of *alpa vimāna*s, housing fat dwarfs, appear in low relief on either side of the Ravana Phadi façade at Aihole. A row of *alpa vimāna*s topped with domed or barrel-roofed pavilions (*śālā*s) appears over the door to the sanctum of Cave 3 at Badami and in the Undavalli cave superstructure.

Where *alpa vimāna*s are depicted in early Indian relief carvings, they are clearly meant to represent wooden shrines, of narrower proportions than the masonry versions and with a decorated post at each corner to support the canopy and upper pavilion. Such images became basic elements in *drāviḍa* temple design, their timber detailing abstracted into mouldings and their slender pilasters representing the posts. Sometimes they frame images of deities. The earliest shrine images or aediculae to be used in this way, as compositional units, are *kūṭa*- and *śālā*-topped *alpa vimāna*s and will be referred to here as '*kūṭa*-aediculae' and '*śālā*-aediculae', respectively. Appearing later was a third type of aedicula, crowned by a pavilion with horseshoe-arch gables (*pañjara*) representing an end-on view of an apsidal or rectangular *śālā*. These compositional units (see fig. 59), interlinked into 'cloisters' around the storeys (*tala*s) of pyramidal *drāviḍa* shrines, were conceived three-dimensionally, as if embedded in the wall. While the upper pavilions of these aediculae may be read as horizontal chains (*hāra*s) running along the parapets—and indeed are sometimes treated as such without corresponding projections in the wall zone—it is important to be aware of the two-tier *alpa vimāna* concept.

The earliest surviving *drāviḍa* temples based on this idea of multi-aedicular composition are two relatively large Chalukya works belonging to the first half of the 7th century: the Upper Shivalaya, Badami (originally Vaishnava), and the Jaina Meguti, Aihole, dated AD 634. In the first storey of the Upper Shivalaya, *kūṭa*-aediculae project at the corners and *śālā*-aediculae in central positions. Although the Meguti has lost the top of its parapet, it followed a related pattern. In neither temple can such an arrangement be seen in the superstructure. The original tower of the Meguti is missing, while at the Upper Shivalaya a long, piled-up sequence of mouldings was used instead. In both cases a wide ambulatory passage (*pradakṣiṇāpatha*) surrounds the sanctuary, over which the superstructure rises. The *kūṭa*s and *śālā*s over the projections in the outer wall are linked together in a true parapet, as opposed to the 'false' or 'appliqué' parapet on most Chalukya temples.

Whereas in the Meguti and Upper Shivalaya the shrine proper, consisting of sanctuary and superstructure, is contained within the general envelope of the building and not defined externally in the first storey, later *drāviḍa* temples show a gradual differentiation of the shrine proper from the hall (*maṇḍapa*). This trend is evident in a series of medium-sized monuments dating from the later decades of the 7th century and beginning of the 8th. These, in probable chronological order, are the Naganatha at Nagaral, the Mahakuteshvara and slightly later Mallikarjuna at Mahakuta and the Malegitti Shivalaya and later Bhutanatha at Badami. All have three-storey *vimāna*s, with or without ambulatory and with the typically *drāviḍa* stepped-pyramid profile, fronted by a wider hall and then by a porch. The hall has a flat-roofed, three-bay 'nave' with sculpted ceiling panels and a blind 'clerestory' of interlinked aediculae. To either side are 'aisles', over which roof slabs slope gently down to the parapet.

The Malegitti Shivalaya was the first Chalukya temple to show consistent use of full aediculae (i.e. with pilaster-bounded projections corresponding to the *kūṭa*s and *śālā*s of the parapet) throughout the exterior of its shrine proper and hall. In the shrine proper, which is without ambulatory, the first two storeys have *kūṭa*-aediculae at the corners and *śālā*-aediculae on the cardinal axes. The third, top storey, as in the nearby Lower Shivalaya and two *drāviḍa*-style temples at Mahakuta, has a tall, octagonal dome surrounded by a cluster of separate aediculae. The Bhutanatha is similar, though the treatment of its top storey (as an 'upper temple' in the form of a square, *kūṭa*-topped *alpa vimāna*) would, with variations, become the norm in Karnataka for more than three centuries. This is the first of the Chalukya temples in which the shrine proper emerged fully from the adjoining hall, from which it is separated by a narrow recess.

Though a provincial work, the Parvati Temple at Sandur, 100 km south-east of the Chalukya heartland and dating from about the late 7th century, is a very early instance of the fully staggered *vimāna* plan, stepping progressively forward on each face. The *vimāna*, with a curiously *nāgara*

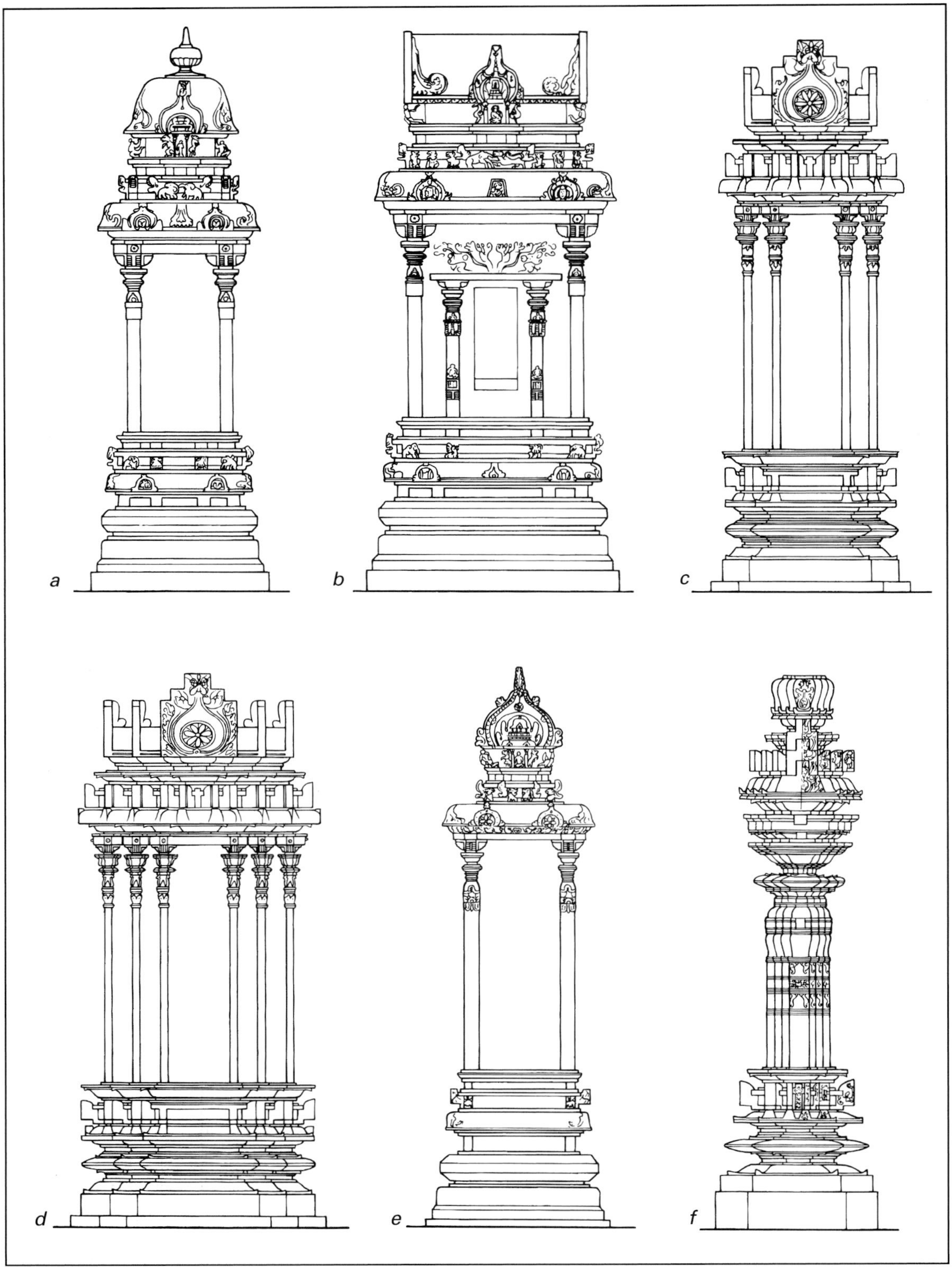

59. *Drāvida* aedicula types, after Dr Adam Hardy: (a) *kūṭa*; (b) *śālā*; (c) staggered *śālā*; (d) double-staggered *śālā*; (e) *pañjara*; (f) *kūṭa-stambha*

curve to its superstructure, is only partly aedicular, the uppermost portions consisting of a sequence of *drāviḍa* mouldings repeated four times.

Towards the end of his reign, the Chalukya king Vijayaditya (*reg c.* AD 696–733) built the Vijayeshvara (now Sangameshvara) at Pattadakal, at the time the largest temple in the Deccan (see fig. 60). It was surpassed in size and splendour by two great *drāviḍa* works of the following reign, the Virupaksha and Mallikarjuna, founded *c.* AD 745 by the two queens of Vikramaditya II (*reg c.* AD 734–47) following his victory over the Pallavas. With their 18 m-high towers, they are comparable in scale to the Kailasa Temple at the Pallava capital, KANCHIPURAM. The basic plan of the later pair was established at the Sangameshvara (now partly ruined), with an ambulatory around the shrine proper, an antechamber with internal subsidiary shrines on the side walls, a 16-pillar hall (nave and double aisles) with a porch on each of the three free sides, and a free-standing pavilion in front (to the east) for the bull Nandi, Shiva's mount. At the Virupaksha these elements are enclosed by a wall (*prākāra*) lined with subsidiary shrines, with gateways to the east and west on the longitudinal axis.

Comparison of the *vimāna* of the Sangameshvara with that of the later Virupaksha (see fig. 61) illustrates certain trends in the *drāviḍa* tradition of Karnataka. In the first storey around the ambulatory, the Sangameshvara, like the earlier Meguti at Aihole, has a pair of *śālā*-aediculae between the corner *kūṭa*-aediculae, so that a recess, containing a traceried window, occupies the central position. Hereafter projecting aediculae would always be placed on the cardinal axes, a prerequisite for the central emphasis that would become increasingly pronounced. Thus, in the Virupaksha, a central *śālā*-aedicula is flanked by intermediate projections taking the form of *pañjara*-aediculae. Over the sanctuary rises a three-tier superstructure in which the first two storeys have central *śālā*-aediculae between corner *kūṭa*-aediculae, and the top storey is a form of *kūṭa*-topped *alpa vimāna*. This is essentially the same as the superstructure of the Sangameshvara, but with an extra storey. However, the overall impression of the Virupaksha is much denser, not only because the projections are much more closely spaced but also because the aedicular language is extended through lower levels of compositional order. A great increase in iconic sculpture on the walls, where almost every projection and recess contains an image, was accompanied by a proliferation of architectural niche-surrounds, mainly monster-flanked archway motifs (*makaratōraṇas*) and secondary *pañjara*-aediculae. At a yet smaller scale are miniature *kūṭa*-aediculae (i.e. *alpa vimānas*) in all the major horseshoe arches.

60. *Vimāna* with unfinished hall, Sangameshvara Temple, Pattadakal, early 8th century AD; view from the north-west

61. *Vimāna*, Virupaksha Temple, Pattadakal, *c*. AD 740 ; view from the south-west

The tendency to emphasize the central portion of the *vimāna* is apparent in the principal difference between the *vimāna*s of the Virupaksa and Mallikarjuna. In the latter the central elements, especially in the first storey, leap dramatically forward, strongly reinforcing the sense of centrifugal swell that would find even greater expression in the later monuments of the region. In this outward surge, parts lose their individuality, the whole impression being one of dynamic fusion. This quality is enhanced by the 'staggering' of corner and central aediculae, where offsets, with additional pilasters in the wall zone, were introduced up to and including the roll-cornice. This treatment is used in the Virupaksha but more insistently in the Mallikarjuna. The effect is to make portions of wall push forward in stages, at the same time as they tend to dissolve the individual elements by breaking down clear boundaries and creating horizontal rhythms and ripples.

Unlike the Sangameshvara, the *vimāna* superstructures of the Virupaksha and Mallikarjuna were given barrel-roofed frontons (*śukanāsa*s)—a *nāgara* feature, though in these examples entirely *drāviḍa* in detail. Earlier examples of the use of this feature in *drāviḍa* temples (it would later become the norm in the Deccan) are the Parvati Temple at Sandur and the Tarka Brahma at ALAMPUR, the only *drāviḍa* monument at that site.

These three great *drāviḍa* works at Pattadakal brought together the range and sequence of mouldings that would be the regional norm in the following centuries. In all three buildings the crowning *kūṭa*s of the superstructure and the various parapets follow the sequence apparent in the early *alpa vimāna* near the Ravana Phadi at Aihole. The moulded base (*adiṣṭhāna*) consists of a foot moulding (*jagatī*) supporting a cushion moulding (*kumuda*), surmounted by a recess (*gala*) sheltered by a roll-cornice (*kapota*). Over these—the moulded base proper—are the moulding representing a floor edge with joist-ends (*vyālamālā*) and the vestigial railing (*vēdī*). Thus the sequence *kapōta–vyālamālā–vēdī* appears on both base and superstructure. Both are now pervaded by a common lush character, the superstructure having lost its earlier blockishness and affinity with carpentry.

It has often been suggested that the *drāviḍa* monuments at Pattadakal show the influence of Pallava architecture from Tamil Nadu, with which they do indeed share many characteristics. But there is virtually no aspect of the Pattadakal temples without precedent in the tradition of the Chalukyas of Badami, of which they can readily be seen as the culmination. Tartakov and Dehejia (1984) have argued that the concept of a broad, shared tradition is more fruitful than a search for influence between one part of south India and another. Nevertheless, essentially different characters were maintained in Karnataka and in Tamil Nadu, both in the composition of individual temples and in the way temple forms developed. While in Karnataka the components became increasingly interconnected through continuities and weakened boundaries, in Tamil Nadu the various parts remained distinct, bound to each other by the general symmetry of the whole rather than through the apparent surge of all-pervasive forces.

6th–8th centuries AD*: Nāgara temples, hybrids and other types.* About the middle of the 7th century, by which time the *drāviḍa* tradition had already been established, *nāgara* temples began to be built in the Chalukya territories. These temples are all in the *latina* mode, the unitary form with a curved spire (*śikhara*). Though among the earliest *latina* shrines in all of India, their *nāgara* vocabulary derived from post-Gupta traditions further north. Elements of this vocabulary were already present in the Badami cave temples, as in the overdoor of Cave 2. Two parallel *nāgara* traditions grew up under the Chalukyas: one in the region of Badami, principally at Aihole and Mahakuta, and the other at Alampur and neighbouring centres in Andhra.

The *nāgara* temples of Aihole and Mahakuta are generally smaller than the Chalukya *drāviḍa* series, though at least as numerous. At these sites there seem to have been no strict divisions between the workshops involved with the different forms of temple: certain moulding and pillar types were shared, and the slender '*drāviḍa*' pilaster type was ubiquitous. Most of the *nāgara* shrines have no ambulatory (an exception is the Huchchimalli Gudi at Aihole), and the sanctuary is fronted by a 'nave-and-aisles' hall with a single porch, or simply by a porch. There is no antechamber to the sanctuary, the antefix (*śukanāsa*) to the superstructure being correspondingly short, and externally there is no recess between the shrine proper (*mūlaprāsāda*) and the hall (*maṇḍapa*). Moulded bases most often consist simply of a foot moulding surmounted by an eaves moulding (*kapotālī*) with a recess in between.

62. Vishva Brahma Temple, Alampur, early 8th century AD

The superstructure generally has three projections, separated by recesses, rising in three stages (*bhūmis*) marked by ribbed discs (*āmalakas*) in the corner projections. From the shoulder platform (*skandha*) rises a thin neck (*grīvā*) supporting a rather bulbous crown (*āmalaka*). Below the superstructure, the walls project only on the cardinal axes, where an image niche may be placed, framed by pilasters. Otherwise the walls are generally plain, without pilasters, and the hall has a roll-cornice but no parapet.

Of the so-called Nava Brahma group of temples at Alampur (all nine are in fact dedicated to Shiva), all but one are *nāgara*. They share some of the characteristics of the Aihole *nāgara* style, but are larger and more lavish. Links with central India are more in evidence, for example in the predominance of vase-and-foliage (*ghaṭapallava*) pillars. The temples originally stood on platforms, and the typical plan, like that of the Upper Shivalaya at Badami, is a single rectangle, sometimes with a porch at one end, containing the 'nave-and-aisles' hall and the sanctuary with its ambulatory. Corresponding to the cardinal axes of the sanctuary are wide, traceried window openings, some combined with sculpted image panels; later examples are sheltered by shallow, two-pillar porches. Moulded bases (*vēdibandhas*) include cushion mouldings (three-faceted *kumudas* or rounded *kalaśas*) and an ornamented dentil course (*tulāpiṭha*) of central Indian origin. The curved spires at Alampur are richer and more complex than those at Aihole and Mahakuta. Though they also have three projections, most rise in four stages, and each recess contains a vertical chain of aediculae. The temple walls are lined with elaborately pedimented projecting niches or wall shrines. Later examples of these wall shrines at Alampur (as in the Vishva Brahma; see fig. 62) are larger and more densely spaced, and their crowns penetrate the roll-cornice.

Provincial sites in Andhra with *nāgara* temples include Satyavolu, Kadamarakalava, Panyam, Mahanadi and Kudaveli. The Sangameshvara at Kudaveli (moved to Alampur to make way for a hydroelectric project) is surrounded by an enclosure wall composed of a chain of *drāviḍa* shrine images. In the Chalukya heartland, influence from Alampur became evident from about AD 700 at Pattadakal, to the extent that the Galaganatha Temple there is clearly the work of craftsmen from Alampur. Four other temples at Pattadakal are *nāgara*, if the Papanatha (a hybrid but predominantly *nāgara* work, in which an 'Alampur plan' is fronted by a slightly later pillared hall) is included. The Kashivishvanatha is the latest *nāgara* temple at Pattadakal, possibly built after the Rashtrakuta conquest of AD 753 but in certain respects still close to the Papanatha. The shrine proper (*mūlaprāsāda*) is divided from the hall by an antechamber, with a corresponding external recess. This is the first shrine in this *nāgara* tradition to have five projections, in the wall zone as well as the superstructure, stepping forward progressively in a staggered plan. There are five stages to the spire, in which the eaves mouldings have proliferated.

In both Karnataka and Andhra, as in other *nāgara* traditions, the superstructure is made up of superimposed eaves mouldings, adorned on the projections with horseshoe-window motifs (*gavākṣa*s). The same principle was employed for the niche pediments, which represent miniature shrine superstructures, and in the aediculae lined up in *nāgara* overdoors, which are essentially the same as the vestigial pavilions marking the stages of the curved *latina* tower. At first the configurations of *gavākṣa*s were relatively simple: a *gavākṣa* between a pair of split or half-*gavākṣa*s or (recalling the cross-section of a *caitya* hall) a *gavākṣa* sitting over a split pair. In the Alampur niche pediments, a smaller version of the second configuration often projects from within a larger one. From the outset a split pair seems to have suggested separation of two formerly united halves, often as a prelude to the emergence from within of another form. In the developed Alampur style, widely spaced split pairs of *gavākṣa*s frame stretches of blind colonnade, with blockish bracketed pillars and a rectilinear second layer leading into the deep background. These miniature colonnades in the air, a multiplication of the pillarets traditionally depicted in half-*gavākṣa*s, give the Alampur works a greater sculptural depth than can be found in other *nāgara* traditions, as well as an incomparable sense of imaginary space within the body of the tower. At the same time, in the mature Alampur style, rather than each tier of *gavākṣa*s being contained within a single eaves moulding, configurations of *gavākṣa*s penetrate two or three mouldings, enhancing the sense of emergence through the wall. Thus the mouldings of the central spine of the superstructure seem torn apart by an expanding cascade of unfurling horseshoe arches.

The superstructure of the Kashivishvanatha at Pattadakal is given a honeycomb appearance by a veil of small, merged and fragmented *gavākṣa*s knitted into a net (*jāla*). The motifs still contain, in their dark eyes, receding planes of colonnades, so that the sense of depth is not entirely lost, as it tends to be in the equivalent *jāla*s of central and western India. While the Kashivishvanatha is the only temple with *jāla*s on the superstructure, the wall shrine pediments of the neighbouring Papanatha, as well as those of the Kashivishvanatha itself, display similar *gavākṣa* nets among other patterns in which proliferated, fragmented, merged and overlapped *gavākṣa* motifs are combined in a variety of exploding constellations. These are the culmination of the Chalukya *nāgara* evolution of *gavākṣa* patterns, an evolution showing a rather rapid version of the kind of development towards 'dynamic fusion' that can be observed in various Indian traditions (not least the *drāviḍa* tradition in Karnataka) in the overall composition of temples.

The monuments of the Chalukyas of Badami, particularly in their Karnataka heartland, contain numerous examples of *nāgara* elements or details in *drāviḍa* temples and vice versa, particularly when they date from the second half of the 7th century and early years of the 8th century. Such intermingling and experimentation are concentrated mainly in the miniature architecture of wall shrines, overdoors and over-windows. However, certain temples may, as a whole, be classified as hybrid or mixed-mode, as they contain a more or less even mixture of *nāgara* and *drāviḍa* characteristics. Two such temples are, in themselves, unique forms: the Jambulinga Temple at Badami, dedicated in AD 699 and perhaps the first three-shrine (*trikūṭa*) Indian temple, and the roughly contemporary Durga Temple at Aihole. The latter is apsidal, consisting of an inner building (similar in its apsidal plan with an ambulatory around the sanctum to a smaller temple at Mahakuta) surrounded by a verandah. In the outer ambulatory so formed, a gallery of fine iconic sculpture is housed in a rich variety of wall shrines of *drāviḍa*, *nāgara* and ingenious hybrid designs. Above the sanctuary rises a *nāgara* spire, probably a slightly later addition.

The Parvati Temple at Sandur (see above), which achieves a *nāgara* character without a single *nāgara* detail, is perhaps the closest approximation in this period to a synthesis of the two modes, though it is not clear whether such a synthesis was consciously sought. The one hybrid temple of the final phase of the Chalukya period is the predominantly *nāgara* Papanatha at Pattadakal, which contains many *drāviḍa* features, most conspicuously a parapet of *kūṭa*s, *śālā*s and *pañjara*s. Another form of parapet pavilion used in the Papanatha Temple shows that hybridization was a conscious game. This motif is a specially invented *kūṭa*, recalling the square, compact form of the *drāviḍa kūṭa*, but with *nāgara* eaves mouldings instead of the usual dome.

Two further identifiable types of temple are found in this period. The first is the *phāṃsanā* form (such as Temple 10 and the Mallikarjuna at Aihole), in which the superstructure, normally without projections, rises in pyramidal fashion through layers of eaves mouldings, alternating with recessed courses treated as blind colonnades. At the summit is a platform supporting an *āmalaka*. Thus the *phāṃsanā* is, at this stage, like a simpler version of the *nāgara*, although the Shiva Temple at Bandatandrapadu in Andhra Pradesh (*c*. mid-7th century) is already crowned with a *drāviḍa kūṭa* dome, like the later *phāṃsanā* shrines of the Deccan. The other temple type is the pillared 'hall temple' peculiar to Aihole. Massive pillars support roof slabs sloping down from a flat portion in one or two spans. The earliest example is probably the Gaudar Gudi (*c*. first half of 7th century), which is rectangular and entirely open apart from the sanctuary. In others the sanctuary is placed against a rear wall, as in the Kunti Gudi group and the well-known Lad Khan, the only hall temple with a partly intact superstructure.

9th–10th centuries AD. Under the Rashtrakutas, artistic activity was concentrated at ELLORA in Maharashtra, and many craftsmen from Karnataka seem to have migrated there (*see* §(d) above). In the former Chalukya heartland and areas to the south, stone temples nonetheless continued to be built. Little is known of the patronage of these monuments. None is securely dated, and most are small, but they form an essential link in the *drāviḍa* tradition of Karnataka. A related but distinct school flourished during the 10th and 11th centuries at Sirval (anc. Shrivolal), some 150 km north of Badami, near the Rashtrakuta capital of

Malkhed. Two fine *drāviḍa* temples that drew on the Chalukya legacy were built early in the 9th century, probably under the Rashtrakutas, at Bhavanasi Sangam in western Andhra.

Three other regions produced important traditions of temple building, mainly *drāviḍa*. In coastal Andhra (anc. Vengidesha) the Chalukyas of Vengi, a collateral branch of the Badami dynasty that was established early in the 7th century, built many temples during the 9th and 10th centuries, notably at BIKKAVOLU. In lower southern Karnataka (anc. Gangavadi) the long-established WESTERN GANGA dynasty of Talkad, who became feudatories of the Rashtrakutas, were active towards the end of the 10th century, especially at SRAVANA BELGOLA and Kambadahalli. At this time upper southern Karnataka and adjacent parts of Andhra Pradesh (anc. Nolambavadi) witnessed a comparable wave of monumental temple building, notably at Nandi, under the NOLAMBA dynasty of HEMAVATI. Close contact with Tamil Nadu is apparent in the final phase of the Vengidesha tradition, while the Gangavadi and Nolambavadi works, though a mixture of the two, could be said to be stylistically more Tamil than Karnata.

Cave temples were excavated under the Chalukyas of Vengi at BHAIRAVAKONDA and Advisomanapalli. No *nāgara* temples survive in upper south India from the 9th and 10th centuries, but *phāṃsanā* shrines are not uncommon. Most temples from this period are Shaiva, but relatively large Jaina shrines were patronized in northern Karnataka, at Hallur and Pattadakal. The most important monuments of Gangavadi are Jaina temples of royal foundation. The typical plan comprised a *vimāna* without ambulatory, linked via an antechamber (*antarāla*) to a closed hall, with a doorway to the east and, sometimes, with a porch. A square defined by four pillars was usual at the centre of the hall, and flat roofs came to supplant the 'nave-and-aisles' section. Multi-*vimāna* temples, dedicated to a number of deities, began to appear during this period. A grouping of three shrines around a square hall was typical. At Kambadahalli there is a complex of five Jaina shrines, which is subdivided into clusters of three and two. Nine *vimāna*s, built in several stages, are interconnected at the Navalinga Temple, Kukkanur. In Vengidesha about the end of the 9th century, there appeared, under influence from Tamil Nadu, temples with wide ambulatories at first-floor level, as in the Bhimeshvara at Cebrolu.

In the former Chalukya heartland, the bold plasticity and soft lushness of the earlier temples were gradually supplanted by a crisp precision and taut sinuousness. Rounded shapes gave way to flexuous double curves, and the imagery of timber and thatch began to be lost in the rhythmic sequences of strata, with their modulated layers of light and shade. The shapes of the blocks from which forms were carved were more in evidence, and the smooth volumes were often left in their blocked-out state. The degree of abstraction was enhanced by an atrophying of the verandah-like recesses of parapet and moulded base (*grīvā* and *gala*), which eventually came to be treated not as separate courses but as mere slots incorporated into the moulding above. The resulting horizontality was complemented by a new vertical continuity created by aligning certain details one above the other. A similar quality is apparent in some 9th-century temples in Vengidesha, such as the Kanchan Gudi at Bikkavolu (see fig. 63). In Gangavadi and Nolambavadi, however, where the shapes and details of mouldings are among the characteristics that show a mixture of Karnataka and Tamil traditions, a sense of massiveness was maintained.

In this period a typical *vimāna* composition can be identified that is also found in Tamil Nadu. It consists of two storeys (*dvitala*), the lower one with central *śālā*-aediculae flanked by corner *kūṭa*-aediculae, the upper one in the form of an *alpa vimāna* with walls of three bays defined by pilasters. The roll-cornice contains, over the outer bays, horseshoe arches (*nāsīs*) that crown *pañjara*-aediculae in the wall below. This typical *vimāna* form is equivalent, in essence, to the top portions of the earlier Sangameshvara or Virupaksha at Pattadakal. The shrines of this form at Kambadahalli in Gangavadi follow the Tamil practice of varying the shape of the dome (*śikhara*), which may be circular, octagonal or the usual square shape. Another influence from Tamil Nadu found here, as elsewhere in southern Karnataka, is the placing of animal figures—lions or Nandi bulls—in the necking (*grīvā*) below the dome.

Three-storey (*tritala*) *vimāna*s of this period combine the repertory of aedicula types in a variety of permutations. The upper storeys are increasingly 'compressed', their lower portions conceptually embedded in the storey below. Usually the top storey consists of an *alpa vimāna* form, the upper two storeys sometimes following the typical composition for two-storey shrines. In Andhra (e.g. the Rupala Sangameshvara at Bhavanasi Sangam and several Eastern Chalukya shrines, e.g. the Kanchan Gudi at

63. Kanchan Gudi, Bikkavolu, first half of the 9th century AD

Bikkavolu; see fig. 63), the top storey may, like the lower storeys, be multi-aedicular, a characteristic not usual in Karnataka before the 11th century. *Pañjara*-aediculae are the usual intermediate elements in five-projection wall schemes, and in Andhra and southern Karnataka (as in Tamil Nadu) the lesser type, with its horseshoe arch incorporated into the roll-cornice, is common. In at least four Chalukya temples at Bikkavolu, a strange, wide form of *śālā*-aedicula is used as a central element; it contains a *pañjara*-aedicula at either end yet has no projection at the centre (see fig. 63).

In general, however, central emphasis continued to increase during this period, accompanied by 'staggering', the proliferation of offsets. Square domes began to receive offsets, and the central bay of *alpa vimāna* forms was treated increasingly as a projection, at first simple, later staggered. A staggered form of *śālā*-aedicula appeared, projecting from the wall in two stages, the offsets (defined in the wall section by pilasters) running up into the crowning *śālā*. In this form, anticipated earlier at Mahakuta, the placing of the central horseshoe arch of the *śālā* over the forward-most projection gives the effect of a *pañjara*-aedicula at the centre of the *śālā*-aedicula. A comparable development took place in the plan of the *vimāna* as a whole. Generally, it was still usual for all of the wall components to project equally, but the central element began to project further than the others, and eventually a progressive stepping forward occurred. These various developments were seen individually throughout upper southern India, but it was in northern Karnataka, notably in the Jaina temple at Pattadakal, that they were brought together to create a powerful sense of expansion.

A striking aspect of temples in northern Karnataka in this period, when compared with monuments built by the Chalukyas of Badami or with contemporary works of other regions, particularly Nolambavadi, is the general absence of sculptural images. If this was due initially to a draining of resources from the region, it corresponded to a new preoccupation with niche surrounds or wall shrines as architectural elements, symbolizing divine presence without necessarily enshrining images of gods. In addition to archway motifs (*makaratōraṇa*s), wall shrines mirror, at a smaller scale, the forms of the primary aediculae on temple walls.

Moulded pillar types, though originating in the earlier rock-cut architecture of the Deccan, were comparatively rare in the structural temples of the Early Chalukyas, where the usual form, supporting brackets, was a rectangular shaft with protruding blocks at the base and near the top, surmounted by part roundels. The typical form in the 9th and 10th centuries combined the two blocks with a series of moulded elements between the upper block and the brackets (*see* §4(ii) above), often with a moulded base under the lower block. As in the early rock-cut precedents, the upper block is often decorated as a belt (*mālāsthāna*) with dangling pearl-swags (*mālā*s). When treated with the full complement of mouldings, this pillar type corresponds to the long-established form for the pilasters of the temple exterior. With the growing preference for double curves, the rectangular portion of the pillars with carved *mālā*s was supplanted, as at the Jaina temple at Pattadakal, by a bell shape. Later examples of the pillar type so formed are often thought, when circular, to have been turned on a lathe, though evidence for this is not conclusive. In the temple walls the bell shape came to replace the *mālā* block in the rectangular pilasters.

Two shrines of the Konti Gudi group at Aihole, perhaps early 9th century, are hall temples, like the earlier shrines in the same group. *Phaṃsanā* shrines were fairly widespread in this period, particularly in western Andhra. A large group, of the 10th and 11th centuries, is found at Papanasi, near Alampur. These are crowned by a variety of *nāgara* and *drāviḍa* elements.

For sculpture of this period, *see* §V, 6(vi) and 7(vi)(c) and (d) below.

BIBLIOGRAPHY

Enc. Ind. Temple Archit., i/2 and ii/1

J. Burgess: 'Rock Cut Temples at Badami in the Dekhan', *Ind. Antiqua.*, vi (1877), pp. 354–66 [*R* Delhi, n.d.]

H. Cousens: *The Chalukyan Architecture of the Kanarese Districts* (Calcutta, 1926)

R. S. Gupte: *The Art and Architecture of Aihole: A Study of Early Chalukyan Art through Temple Architecture and Sculpture* (Bombay, 1967)

K. V. Soundara Rajan: *Early Temple Architecture in Karnataka and its Ramifications* (Dharwar, 1969)

G. Tarr [G. M. Tartakov]: *The Architecture of the Early Western Chalukyas* (diss., U. CA, 1969)

——: 'Chronology and Development of the Chāḷukya Cave Temples', *A. Orient.*, viii (1970), pp. 155–84

O. Divakaran: 'Les Temples d'Alampur et de ses environs au temps des Chalukya de Badami', *A. Asiat.*, xxiv (1971), pp. 51–101

P. Z. Pattibiamin: *Āndhra* (1971), i of *Sanctuaires rupestres de l'Inde du sud* (Pondicherry, 1971–5)

G. Michell: *An Architectural Description and Analysis of Early Western Chalukyan Temples* (London, 1975)

G. M. Tartakov: 'The Beginning of Dravidian Temple Architecture in Stone', *Artibus Asiae*, lxii/1 (1980), pp. 33–99

K. V. Soundara Rajan: *Cave Temples of the Deccan* (Delhi, 1981)

B. R. Prasad: *Chalukyan Temples of Andhradesa* (Delhi, 1983)

G. M. Tartakov and V. Dehejia: 'Sharing, Intrusion and Influence: The Mahiṣāsuramardinī Imagery of the Chalukyas and the Pallavas', *Artibus Asiae*, lxv/4 (1984), pp. 287–345

A. Hardy: *Form and Transformation in Indian Temple Architecture* (Delhi, 1995)

ADAM HARDY

(i) Tamil Nadu.

Early rock-cut architecture. Although there are abundant references to civic, royal and religious buildings in Tamil literature (which survives from the 1st century AD if not earlier), no structural temples or any other buildings can be dated with any certainty prior to the 7th century AD. The earliest surviving monuments in Tamil Nadu are rock-cut. Approximately 100 cave temples are found in the region, each partially emulating structures of wood, brick and plaster that have not survived the vagaries of a tropical climate. Though several may be a century older, the earliest caves of uncontested date are six commissioned by the versatile king Mahendravarman I (*reg c.* 570–630) of the Pallava dynasty. These, together with perhaps a dozen earlier excavations, constitute the first known stage in the development of *drāviḍa* architecture (*see* §1(i)(c) above). Collectively, what the early caves reveal is an emergent regional idiom fully conversant with the basic elements of the pan-Indian repertory of motifs.

Compared to the more lavishly scaled and detailed excavations of the Deccan, early *drāviḍa* caves are modest in plan and austere in the rendering of architectural features. Typically, they consist of a pillared hall (*maṇḍapa*) less than 7 m across and 2.5 m high. Small sanctums (*garbhagṛhas*), 1–2 m square, pierce the rear or side walls of the pillared hall, depending on the orientation sought for the presiding deity. Walls, especially when framing sanctum entrances, are girded at their base (*adhiṣṭhāna*) by a standardized series of mouldings. These invariably incorporate a prominent triple-faceted semicircular moulding (*kumuda*), often separated from the crowning band (*paṭṭikā*) by a neck course from which ends of floor joists appear to project. In subsequent periods these joist blocks were frequently hidden behind elephant or lion antefixes, but they probably existed in perishable materials long before they were included in rock-cut examples of *drāviḍa* architecture. Marking the transition from wall to roof, the entablature (*prastara*), likewise, when included on cave façades or above sanctum entrances, exhibits such ubiquitous pan-Indian motifs as the roll-cornice (*kapota*) adorned with 'cow's eye' dormers (*gavākṣas*), often framing heads to give the impression of residents in a gabled upper storey.

The commonest feature of early *drāviḍa* caves, rarely encountered in other regions, is a simplified pillar type. Massively proportioned and rigidly square in section, except for an octagonal spacer at mid-shaft, the pillar terminates with a flaring bracket capital three times the diameter of the shaft. Often the bracket's lower edge is embellished with a series of 'wave scallops' (*taraṅgas*) bound by a median strip of scrollwork. When not carved in the rock, these motifs and others must have been applied in bright polychromy, as is indicated by traces of green, yellow and red pigment that survive on the façades of two caves at Mamandur, and at Sittanavasal, where ceiling frescoes are also well preserved. Similarly, broad lotus medallions are carved on the top and bottom rectangles of the shaft frequently enough to suggest that they were painted on most others. The lotus-medallion motif provides a vital clue to the origins of this severe but imposing architectural order, as it was also a standard feature of the early railings (*vedikās*) around sacred spaces such as the Buddhist stupas at BHARHUT, SANCHI and AMARAVATI.

*Mahamalla period (*AD *630–68).* In its basic configuration, this archaic formulation of the *drāviḍa* order found widespread acceptance until well into the 8th century, as is evidenced by the Narasimha Cave at Anaimali, near Madurai, which bears an inscription dated in a regnal year equivalent to AD 771. However, the tradition's main stream of development was precipitously transformed in the mid-7th century during the reign of the son of Mahendravarman, Narasimhavarman I Mahamalla (*reg* 630–*c.* 668). To commemorate his great triumph over the Chalukyas of Badami (*see* CHALUKYA, §1) in AD 642, a city was created around a picturesque, boulder-strewn hillside by the sea at MAMALLAPURAM. The distinctive hallmark of the site and period is a radically new pillar type. Shaft bases were fashioned into caryatid-lions, probably in allusion to the king's patron deity, the pillar-born Narasimha, the man–lion incarnation of the god Vishnu. Usually seated on double-lotus pedestals, the lions support bejewelled and faceted shafts that terminate in complex capitals, the bulbous contours of which are abstracted from pot and foliage motifs. Fronted by these taller columns, the caves have more spacious, brighter interiors, and their iconographic programmes are correspondingly amplified with ambitious, wall-filling narrative tableaux in high relief. These include compelling re-enactments of such perennial myths as Durga slaying the buffalo demon, Vishnu asleep on the serpent Ananta, Earth rescued by Varaha (Vishnu as a boar) and Lakshmi (goddess of prosperity) anointed by elephants.

Undoubtedly, the great efflorescence of Pallava art coincided with the creation of Mahamalla's victory-memorial city, as is demonstrated by the ensemble of five monolithic temples known as the Pandava Rathas. These bear the names of the heroes of the epic *Mahābhārata*, assigned at a later date and unassociated with the original dedications (*see* MAMALLAPURAM, fig. 1). The excavation of temple interiors had been commonplace in India for nearly a thousand years, but the reverse, the sculpting of full-scale temple exteriors, was a novel idea. The five contrasting designs were juxtaposed with a remarkable harmoniousness, carved as they were from a single outcrop of gneiss some 60 m in length by 12 m at the highest point.

The historical importance of the Pandava Rathas can scarcely be overstated, as they constitute the earliest prototypes for most developments in *drāviḍa* architecture. Three are square in plan and differ chiefly in the nature of their superstructures. The simplicity of a thatched hut is suggested by the Draupadi Ratha, dedicated to Durga, goddess of victory, whose lion mount stands before it. Multi-pavilioned palaces of extraordinary richness, rising to two and three storeys above the entablature respectively, are evoked by the Arjuna and Dharmaraja Rathas. The former, sharing a plinth with Durga's shrine, was intended for her husband, Shiva, whose bull, Nandi, reclines behind. The Dharmaraja Ratha, engraved with many epithets of the royal patron, was never finished sufficiently to identify the intended occupants of its vertical sequence of three shrines: the crudely carved Somaskanda panel (Shiva with consort and son) in the third-storey sanctum is an intrusive addition made during the reign of Mahamalla's grandson, Parameshvaravarman I (*reg* 669–90). Neither can the Bhima Ratha, with its unfinished interior, be assigned to any particular deity. Its superstructure represents a rare instance of the barrel-vaulted *śāla* type best known in its replicated form as the crowning storey of the towered gateway (*gopura*) of later periods. Finally, the Nakula–Sahadeva Ratha, apsidal in plan, has a corresponding two-storey superstructure known as *gajapṛṣṭha* ('elephant-backed'). Appropriately, an elephant stands to the side, denoting perhaps a shrine intended for Indra, the Vedic god whose mount is the elephant.

Nowhere are the symbolic connotations implicit in the names and forms of the south Indian temple brought closer to the surface than with the Pandava Rathas. The term *ratha* itself, while denoting first a chariot in which festival images are paraded, intersects conceptually with the *vimāna*, a term for the Hindu temple's central structure. The latter also conjures up mythic images of the 'castles in the air' in which gods reside and travel about. Both meanings are congruent with the Pandava Rathas at Mamallapuram: sacred abodes whose locomotive potential is made visible by the alternating lions and elephants that appear to shoulder the plinth shared by the Draupadi and Arjuna Rathas, and the friezes of flying geese and dwarf-attendants (*gaṇa*s) below the cornice on the Arjuna and Dharmaraja Rathas. The superstructures demonstrate fully the palatial aspect of the *vimāna*. Except for the hutlike Draupadi Ratha, each of them rises in a series of diminishing storeys framed by miniature shrines and connecting cloisters. The squared-dome structures (*kūṭa*s) at the corners and intervening *śāla*-aediculae serve as turreted balustrades. The disparity in scale between them, visualized as a protective ring of temples but experienced as guard-rails, is mitigated by the half life-size figural sculptures that inhabit the pilastered inner walls on both levels. In the presence of these smiling deities, the visitor has little difficulty in imagining a supernatural realm where the laws of gravity and perspective are suspended.

A sense of proportion governs each facet of the design of the Pandava Rathas, and structural and figural motifs are handled with a uniform deftness (excluding the lower extremities, which were never completed). It seems that work on the Pandava Rathas terminated with their patron's death *c.* 668, and after a brief reversal in dynastic fortunes brought about by a Chalukya invasion in AD 674, the rock-cut tradition lapsed. Thereafter, with few exceptions, Pallava temples were constructed, block by block, in stone masonry.

*Rajasimha period (*AD *690–728).* Coincident with the change in medium, Pallava temples of the late 7th and 8th centuries embody a significantly altered aesthetic. Though changes were already evident in the monolithic Ganesha Ratha dedicated by Parameshvaravarman, located north of the Pandava Rathas, they are best exemplified by the two greatest monuments of the next generation, the Shore Temple at Mamallapuram (see fig. 64) and the Kailasanatha or Rajasimheshvara at KANCHIPURAM (see fig. 65). Both bear a foundation inscription identifying Parameshvaravarman's son, Narasimhavarman II Rajasimha (*reg* AD 690–728), as patron. Both are also greatly expanded in plan, clustering multiple-shrine structures within the imposing confines of a walled enclosure (*prākāra*). The walled enclosure became a standard feature of *drāviḍa* temples, contributing to the simultaneous growth in importance of towered gateways at cardinal points of entrance, as the temple *vimāna* proper tended to be relatively obscured from view.

64. Shore Temple, Mamallapuram, *c.* AD 700; view from the north

However, the new structural medium and expansion in scale account only partially for the changed aesthetic. Compared to the Pandava Rathas, with their delicate balancing of vertical and horizontal articulations, the Shore Temple's twin *vimāna* towers soar upwards with astonishing boldness and grace. The main expedient for increasing verticality was elimination of the encircling parapet (*hāra*) from the bottom and top storeys of both superstructures. In place of the cloister-connected row of *śāla-* and *kūṭa*-aediculae, seated dwarfs or lions were positioned at their corners. Even the intervening storeys, two on the Kshatriyasimheshvara sanctum and one on the main Rajasimheshvara sanctum (both consecrated with Shiva–Somaskanda panels and *liṅga*s), while preserving the cloistered-parapet motif were radically attenuated by elimination of the passageway between them and the core of the spires. Verticality was further emphasized in the proportions of all the components of the *vimāna*, from pilasters to fluted finials (*stūpikā*s).

Given the corrosive effects of sand and sea air on the Shore Temple's surfaces, exterior decoration is better exemplified by Kanchipuram's Kailasanatha, the largest Indian temple of its day, where embellishment (*alaṁkāra*) became all-important. Its four-storey *vimāna* is buttressed by nine subsidiary sanctuaries and fronted by a pillared hall whose dimensions equal those of the main sanctuary. The temple is also fortified symbolically by a *prākāra* consisting of 58 separate chapels. Narrative and purely decorative compositions spread out across most surfaces. The principle of *horror vacui*, or rather its converse, *amor infiniti*, seems to govern the artistic imagination. For example, the once innovative lion-based column is joined by fantastic variants including, most frequently, rampant horned lions (*vyāla*s) with or without riders, as well as semi-human snakes and gryphon-elephants. In places, a coarseness of surface is apparent, but overall the execution is as crisp as it is exuberant, indicative of changes in taste rather than a qualitative deterioration from the 'classical' mid-7th-century style.

After Rajasimha's reign, the Pallavas continued in power for nearly two centuries, but only one of their 24 later temples is of outstanding historical importance: the Vaikunthaperumal, completed in Kanchipuram as a Vaishnava response to the Shaiva Kailasanatha during the reign of Nandivarman II Pallavamalla (*reg c.* AD 731–96). Like the Dharmaraja Ratha, it affords access to relief-lined galleries and auxiliary sanctums on two upper storeys of the *vimāna*. A unique feature of this temple is a dynastic chronicle in pictures (some with labels in Tamil) that covers in low relief the inner walls of the *prakāra*-cloister. A hymn by Tirumangai Alvar, a major Vaishnava saint and contemporary of Pallavamalla, describes such scenes from the patron's life, providing a rare synchronism between monument and text and a source from which the theologic and ritual underpinnings of the temple's rich iconography can be better understood (see Hudson).

65. Kailasanatha or Rajasimheshvara Temple, Kanchipuram, *c.* AD 700–25; west end of *vimāna*

Non-Pallava monuments. Apart from the widely distributed cave temples mentioned earlier, few non-Pallava monuments in Tamil Nadu can be dated to before the 9th century. One major exception is the monolith at Kalugumalai, Tirunelveli District, in a region once ruled by the Pandya dynasty. Though unfinished below the lower cornice of its two-storey superstructure, it is a fine example of the quintessential *drāviḍa vimāna.* It appears to continue the developments in style of the Pandava Rathas of Mamallapuram and thus probably belongs to the last quarter of the 7th century (though some scholars date it to *c.* 800). The chief difference is the heightened verisimilitude of its figural sculptures. Major deities sit almost completely free of their sumptuously ornamented niches (*devakoṣṭha*s). An encircling frieze of dwarf-attendants beneath the upper cornice is unsurpassed in diversity of pose and characterization.

In architectural terms, the decline of Pallava hegemony in 9th-century Tamil Nadu corresponded with the beginnings of several sub-regional building traditions. Former feudatories who gave substance to their new-found autonomy by constructing stone temples included the Pandyas in the far south, the Bana, Ganga and Nolamba dynasties to the west, and the Muttaraiyars, Irrukuvels and, above all, the Chola dynasty in central Tamil Nadu. The latter rose to prominence at Thanjavur in the delta of the Kaveri River during the last quarter of the 9th century.

To a remarkable degree, stylistic continuities between Pallava precedents and the emerging substyles predominated over changes to the *drāviḍa* order during the 9th and 10th centuries. However, in some buildings, new standards of refinement were established in dressed-stone masonry and figural sculpture alike. The Nageshvarasvami at KUMBAKONAM (*c.* AD 884) consists of a *vimāna* (*c.* 7 m square) and an attached pillared hall of near equal dimensions. Compared to the densely embellished Kailasanatha, the chastely pilastered walls are striking in their structural clarity, providing an understated ground for some of the most convincing studies of the human figure in Indian art. Like most other early-Chola temples, the Nageshvarasvami was constructed of granite only to the level of its entablature. The superstructures of brick and plaster have undergone too many renovations to preserve much sense of their original appearance.

On the basis of its somewhat larger size, greater ornateness and superb finish, a temple situated *c.* 15 km north of Thanjavur at Pullamangai is characterized as a royal endowment, datable to early in the reign of Parantaka I (*reg* AD 907–54). Again, it is the figural sculpture that most impresses. As if dissatisfied by the prominent, but confining, spaces reserved for major deities within split-pilaster niches at cardinal points of the exterior walls, sculpture groupings 'spill over' to include adoring attendants in bold relief against adjacent surfaces. This tendency can be seen to excellent advantage at Shrinivasanallur, 50 km upriver from Tiruchchirapalli, and at Punjai, still further west along the Kaveri, at temples datable by donative inscriptions to *c.* AD 927 and *c.* 940 respectively.

Chola temples were built in increasing numbers during the late 10th century, owing in no small measure to the ardour of the dowager queen Shembiyan Mahadevi. Yet it is safe to say that nothing was added substantially to the tradition until late in the reign of Rajaraja I (*reg c.* AD 985–1014), when Dravidian architecture entered a new phase.

See also §§6(i)(f) and IV, 7(vi)(a) below.

BIBLIOGRAPHY

Enc. Ind. Temple Archit., i/1

A. Rea: *Pallava Architecture*, Archaeol. Surv. India, New Imp. Ser., xxxiv (Madras, 1909/*R* Varanasi, 1970)

G. Jouveau-Dubreuil: 'Les Antiquités de l'époque Pallava', *Rev. Hist. Inde Fr.*, i (1916), pp. 1–78; Eng. trans. by V. S. Swaminadha Dikshitar as *Pallava Antiquities*, 2 vols (London, 1916; Pondicherry, 1918)
——: *Dravidian Architecture* (Madras, 1917)
A. H. Longhurst: *Pallava Architecture*, Mem. Archaeol. Surv. India, xvii, xxxiii, xl (Simla, 1924; Calcutta, 1928, 1930; New Delhi, 1982)
C. Minakshi: *The Historical Sculptures of the Vaikuṇṭhaperumāḷ Temple, Kāñchī*, Mem. Archaeol. Surv. India, lxiii (Delhi, 1941)
P. Brown: *Indian Architecture (Buddhist and Hindu Periods)* (?Bombay [1942], rev. Bombay, 1956)
J. C. Harle: 'The Early Cola Temple at Puḷḷamangai', *Orient. A.*, n. s. iv/3 (1958), pp. 96–108
R. Nagaswamy: 'New Light on Mamallapuram', *Trans. Archaeol. Soc. S. India* (1960–62), pp. 1–50
C. Sivaramamurti: *Kalugumalai and Early Pandyan Rock-cut Shrines* (Bombay, 1961)
K. R. Srinivasan: *Cave Temples of the Pallavas*, Architectural Survey of Temples, 1 (New Delhi, 1964)
S. R. Balasubrahmanyam: *Early Chola Art*, 1 (Bombay, 1966)
K. V. Soundara Rajan: 'Rājasiṁha's Temples in Toṇḍaimaṇḍalam', *Trans. Archaeol. Soc. S. India* 1969), pp. 169–200
S. R. Balasubrahmanyam: *Early Chola Temples, Parantaka I to Rajaraja I: A.D. 907–985* (Bombay, 1971)
D. Barrett: *Early Cola Architecture and Sculpture, 866–1014 A.D.* (London, 1974)
M. Lockwood, G. Siromoney and P. Dayanandan: *Mahabalipuram Studies* (Madras, 1974)
K. V. Soundara Rajan: 'Early Pāṇḍya, Muttarayar and Irrukuveḷ Architecture', *Studies in Indian Temple Architecture*, ed. P. Chandra (New Delhi, 1975), pp. 240–300
K. R. Srinivasan: *The Dharmarāja Ratha and its Sculptures, Mahābalipuram* (New Delhi, 1975)
——: 'Temples of the Later Pallavas', *Studies in Indian Temple Architecture*, ed. P. Chandra (New Delhi, 1975), pp. 197–239
G. Michell: 'The Southern Indian Temple Style, Part One: An Architectural Analysis of the Pallava Temples', *A. & Archaeol. Res. Pap.*, x (1976), pp. 1–10
M. Lockwood: *Mamallapuram and the Pallavas* (Madras, 1982)
O. Divakaran: 'Some Characteristics of the Early Brahmanical Caves in the Pandyan Country', *Kusumanjali*, i (1987), pp. 173–8
M. Hirsh: 'Mahendravarman I Pallava: Artist and Patron of Mamallapuram', *Artibus Asiae*, xlix (1987), pp. 109–30
M. Rabe: *The Monolithic Temples of the Pallava Dynasty: A Chronology* (diss., Minneapolis, U. MN, 1987)
C. Tadgell: *The History of Architecture in India: From the Dawn of Civilization to the End of the Raj* (New Delhi, 1990)
D. Hudson: *The Body of God: Text, Image and Liturgy in the Vaikuntha Perumal Temple at Kanchipuram* (in preparation)

MICHAEL D. RABE

(j) Kerala. In terms of surviving remains, Kerala architecture begins only in the 8th century, with rock-cut temples. The largest number are located in the southern region, some in the Kanyakumari district of modern Tamil Nadu, which was traditionally ruled by Kerala kings. This group shows evidence of contact with the rock-architecture of the Pandya dynasty of southernmost Dravidadesha (*see* §(i) above). The Shaiva excavation at Tirunandikkara consists of an oblong shrine, preceded by a pillared hall and a rudimentary hall before that; the square pillars include an octagonal section and bevelled corbels similar to Pandya examples. The remains of wall painting may be later (*see* §VI, 3(i)(b) below). The Shiva cave temple at KAVIYUR includes relief-carvings depicting a sage (*ṛṣi*), the elephant-headed god Ganapati, a male figure and door-guardians (*dvārapālas*) in the beautifully finished pillared hall (*ardhamaṇḍapa*) in front of the square shrine; in the Kaviyur hall, too, the square pillars have octagonal sections and bevelled corbels. The more northern group of caves, situated in central Kerala, includes fewer examples scattered over a larger area. Parallels seem to exist with Pallava prototypes. There are a number of rock-cut Jaina monuments as well; the most impressive, at Tiruchcharanattumalai (near Chitral), with an inscription of a local king of the late 9th century or early 10th, compares to excavations at Kalugamalai (*see* §(i) above). These early monuments make it clear that Kerala was part of the culture of Dravidadesha in this era.

Structural temples appear to have been introduced into the Kerala region in the early 9th century. Many of these monuments remain in use, but few survive intact. Most have been rebuilt above the granite foundation (*adhiṣṭhana*), in part because the walls of Kerala temples were generally built of laterite, a relatively soft stone, which was then stuccoed. The numerous surviving foundations provide important evidence of temple plans and types. In addition to square and oblong plans, Kerala is distinguished by a significant number of apsidal temples, especially in the north, and numerous circular temples, which are rare in other regions. Shrines of this period include those with and without an enclosed circumambulatory path and those with and without a preceding hall (*mukhamaṇḍapa*). The main shrine, subsidiary structures and stone pedestal or platform for oblations (*balipīṭha*) are contained within a cloistered area (Malayalam *nālambalam*). Temples in Kerala are distinguished by their characteristic sloping roofs supported by wooden superstructures and covered with tile, copper sheeting or thatch, but it is not clear that the present superstructures are representative of those used originally.

Perhaps the only intact temples from the 9th century are associated with the earliest rulers of the Chera or Kulashekhara empire (*c.* 800–1124) and their capital, Tiruvanchikulam or Mahodayapuram (also referred to as Makotai, Muziris, Kodungalur and Cranganur), near the coast of central Kerala. Other early shrines are found in the far south, in the area ruled by the Ay kings.

For sculpture of this period *see* §IV, 6(vi) and 7(vi)(b) below.

BIBLIOGRAPHY

Enc. Ind. Temple Archit., i/1
S. Kramrisch, J. H. Cousins and R. Vasudeva Poduval: *The Arts and Crafts of Travancore* (Oxford, 1952); rev. as *The Arts and Crafts of Kerala* (Cochin, [1970])
M. G. S. Narayanan: *Political and Social Conditions of Kerala under the Kulasekhara Empire (ca. 800 A.D. to 1124 A.D.)* (diss., U. Kerala, 1972)
H. Sarkar: *An Architectural Survey of Temples of Kerala* (Delhi, 1978)
R. M. Bernier: *Temple Arts of Kerala* (Delhi, 1981)

M. E. HESTON

(ii) Indo-Islamic. The first impact of Islam in the north of the Indian subcontinent was felt in AD 711–13 (AH 93–4), when an Arab army under the command of Muhammad b. Qasim invaded Sind. He first conquered the port of Daibul on the coast of the Arabian Sea, before marching north to take over the important city of Brahmanabad, which was renamed al-Mansura al-Mahfuza ('the conquered and protected city') and made the capital of Arab Sind.

The conquest of Multan followed in AD 713. Muslim histories do not record any campaign east of Sind, but there were casual raids towards Rajasthan and Gujarat, some reflected in the inscriptions of Gujara-Pratihara rulers. In the 10th century Sind and Multan were under the control of the Shi'ites, who had links with Fatimid Egypt and Yemen, but in the beginning of the 11th century the orthodox Sunni Sultan Mahmud added the region to the Ghaznavid empire, and early in the 13th century the area was transferred to the recently established Sultanate of Delhi. What little remains of the architecture of Arab Sind shows a strong connection with the Arab lands, but the main monuments are post-Ghaznavid, with stylistic links with Iran and Central Asia.

In southern and western India, the first appearance of Islam came with the Arab and Persian merchants who settled in the ports of the Gujarat, Malabar and Coromandel coasts as well as Ceylon (now Sri Lanka). The Muslim trading communities possessed little political power but developed into a significant economic force. In all regions the local Hindu rulers, whose revenues depended on the commerce of these communities, gave them permission to worship, administer justice and build according to their own religion. The buildings combine the traditions of the settlers' homelands with indigenous technology.

BIBLIOGRAPHY

The Chachnāma [The book of Chach], Eng. trans. by M. K. Fredunbeg (Karachi, 1900)

M. K. Fredunbeg: *History of Sind* (Karachi, 1902), ii

F. C. Murgotten: *The Origins of the Islamic State: Translation from the Arabic with Annotations, Geographic and Historic Notes of the Kitāb futuḥ al-buldān of al-Imām abu'l 'Abbās Aḥmad ibn-Jābir al-Balādhurī*, Studies in History, Economics and Public Law, Faculty of Political Science, Columbia University, lxviii/163A (New York, 1924), pt ii, pp. 209–33

Sayyid Muhammad Ma'sum Bakkari: *Tārīkh-i Sind* [History of Sind] (Pune, 1938)

Abbas H. al-Hamdani: *The Beginnings of the Ismā'īlī Da'wā in Northern India* (Cairo, 1956)

Mumtaz Husain Pathan: *Sind, Arab Period* (Hyderabad and Sind, 1978)

A. Wink: *Early Medieval India and the Expansion of Islam, 7th–11th Centuries*, i of *Al-Hind: The Making of the Indo-Islamic World* (Leiden, 1990)

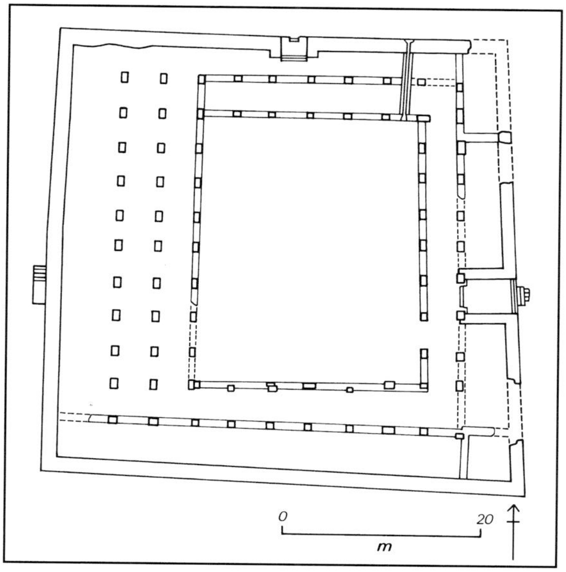

66. Plan of Jami' Mosque, Banbhore, AD 725–6

(a) North-west. The main Muslim towns of Sind were Daybul and al-Mansura. While nothing remains of the superstructure of any buildings, excavations at the coastal village of Banbhore, the site of Daybul, and at the site of al-Mansura have revealed the foundations of two early mosques built during the first two decades of the conquest. At Banbhore the foundations of the Jami' Mosque were discovered, together with an inscription recording the date of its construction as AD 725–6 (AH 107). The foundations show that it was originally built of rubble and mortar and consisted of a colonnade around a courtyard (see fig. 66). This can be termed an 'Arab-type' plan, as such hypostyles were typical of the early mosques in the Arab world. The colonnade was three aisles deep and twelve bays wide on the qibla side (that side facing the Ka'ba in Mecca). On the other three sides of the courtyard, the colonnade was only two aisles deep. Materials from Hindu temples were employed in the construction, including a complete *liṅga*, the symbol of Shiva, reused as a step in front of the entrance.

An important feature of the Banbhore mosque is the absence of a mihrab (niche indicating the direction of prayer) in the foundation of a qibla wall. As the colonnade is divided into 12 bays there would have been no central bay opposite the mihrab. While this does not rule out the possibility of one or more flat mihrabs, or small mihrabs in the form of niches in the original qibla wall, it has been suggested (Creswell) that the mosques of the first century of Islam, such as those in Kufa and Wasit, did not have mihrabs built into their walls, and this may have been the case in the Jami' Mosque of Banbhore.

At al-Mansura, the excavations of the large Jami' Mosque (carried out between 1895 and 1909) revealed only a small section of the western sanctuary, showing the remains of a colonnade which may have been similar to that of Banbhore. As with the Jami' of Banbhore, the foundations were built of masonry, but the excavations give little information on the superstructure of the mosque. The foundations of three smaller mosques were also found, one of which had a mihrab, semicircular in plan, projecting outside the qibla wall. This form is rarely used in buildings in Iran and Afghanistan but is a common feature in Arab buildings. In the 10th and 11th centuries Isma'ilis were prominent in Multan and Sind. The small mosque of al-Mansura may therefore be connected with the Shia government of Sind, which had ties with both Fatimid Egypt and the Shia of the Yemen.

In the 12th century Multan was taken over by the Ghaznavids, who opposed the Isma'ilis. Little is known of its architecture during this period. The only building said to have been founded then is the tomb of Shah Yusuf Gardizi, at MULTAN. Traditionally dated to 1152, the building has been heavily reconstructed. The shrine is a brick structure, rectangular in plan, with a flat roof and a small entrance in the western end of the southern wall. It is covered by glazed tiles of relatively recent date.

BIBLIOGRAPHY

Archaeol. Surv. India, Annu. Rep. (1903–), pp. 132–44; (1908–9), pp. 79–87

H. Cousens: *The Antiquities of Sind*, Archaeol. Surv. India, Imp. Ser., xlvi (Calcutta, 1929), pp. 48–71

F. A. Khan: *Banbore: A Preliminary Report on the Recent Archaeological Excavations at Banbore* (Karachi, 1960, 4/1976)

K. A. C. Creswell: *Early Muslim Architecture* (Oxford, 1969), i/1, p. 4

NATALIE H. SHOKOOHY

67. Shrine of Ibrahim, Bhadreshvar, 1159–60; interior facing west

(b) West. From the early days of Islam Muslim merchants used sea routes across the Arabian Sea to India and Sri Lanka. Al-Istakhri (*d* 957), al-Muqaddasi (writing in 985) and other early Muslim geographers report towns in western India with sizeable Islamic communities where Muslims freely practised their religion and had their own mosques. In Somnath a bilingual inscription of the mid-13th century records that the local ruler permitted the Muslim merchants to build a mosque near the main temple, and in KHAMBHAT (Cambay) there are many Muslim tombstones.

The earliest surviving buildings of one of these trading communities are at Bhadreshvar, an ancient town on the coast of Kachchh (Kutch) in Gujarat known to Ptolemy in the 2nd century AD as Bardaxema (see J. W. McCrindle, ed., *Ancient India as Described by Ptolemy* (London, 1885), p. 33) and to al-Biruni, writing in the 11th century, as Bhadra. The *Jagaducarita* (late 14th century–early 15th) and a local Sanskrit chronicle of the 19th century by the Jaina guru Bantvijaya (published by Burgess) mention the Islamic community and their buildings, describing the Muslims as 'foreigners' and of the Isma'ili sect. The most important Islamic buildings of Bhadreshvar are the Shrine of Ibrahim (see fig. 67) and two mosques, the Solahkhambi Masjid and the Chhoti Masjid. These are all stone structures and date from the mid-12th century AD. The Shrine of Ibrahim (locally known as the Dargah La'l Shahbaz) bears an inscription dated Dhu'l-Hijja AH 554 (Dec 1159–Jan 1160). This is the earliest Islamic date *in situ* on a monument in India. The shrine consists of a square chamber with a corbelled dome; a mihrab is on the western side. There is a portico in front of the entrance on the east. The flat ceiling of the portico is decorated with a grid of squares, each with a lotus motif in the centre. The inscription, carved below the ceiling of the portico, is in a floriated kufic script, with foliations, lobed endings of the letters and floral decoration, a calligraphic style similar to that of Egypt and North Africa.

The Solahkhambi Masjid has an Arab-type plan with an open courtyard surrounded by a colonnade seven bays wide and two aisles deep on the qibla side. On the remaining three sides of the courtyard there is only a single row of columns. An unusual feature of the building is a large hall or portico, seven bays wide and four aisles deep, outside the enclosure wall in front of the eastern entrance. Such halls are not traditional in Islamic buildings and may show the influence of Indian temple architecture. The main mihrab of the mosque is located in the middle of the qibla wall, with a second shallow mihrab on the exterior of the eastern wall. Tombstones outside the mosque date from 1177 (AH 573) to 1227 (AH 624). They indicate the time when the mosque was in use and establish the date of the mosque as earlier than 1177.

The Chhoti Masjid consists of a courtyard to the east and a colonnade leading to a prayer-hall to the west. The colonnade has two rows of four columns, and inside the prayer-hall there is another row of four columns. Two of the entrances to the colonnade have lintels carved in the shape of a semicircular arch, a feature for doorways virtually unknown in India during the 12th century. The form seems to be derived from the archways common in the Islamic buildings of Syria, Egypt and North Africa. The main mihrab is located in the centre of the western wall of the prayer-hall, while a smaller one is situated in the middle of the western wall of the colonnade. The similarity between the architectural elements and decoration of this mosque and those of the Shrine of Ibrahim suggests that the buildings are not only of the same period but were probably designed and constructed by the same craftsmen.

All the Islamic buildings of Bhadreshvar are built of large blocks of stone, without mortar, a method well known in Indian architecture from ancient times, and are constructed using traditional Indian components, including monolithic column shafts surmounted by brackets supporting lintels, roofed with flat slabs and corbelled domes. The column shafts have square, octagonal and circular registers, the form used to represent a Shiva *liṅga*, and also employed in Jaina temples. Early Muslim texts frequently mention the significance of this configuration; its use by the Bhadreshvar merchants indicates the tolerance of the Muslim traders towards the local religion. The Shrine of Ibrahim and the Chhoti Masjid have extensive carved decoration. The columns and pilasters are decorated with a course of pot-and-foliage motifs with vertical strings of carved beads. Further down the shafts, horizontal collars of alternating diamonds and discs pass over the vertical strings. The jambs and lintels of the doors are decorated on the exterior with garlands and with diamond and disc motifs. Similar patterns appear on the brackets and lintels. These decorative motifs were used in local buildings of the mid-12th century and indicate that the Islamic buildings of Bhadreshvar were constructed by local craftsmen, who used the decorative features with which they were familiar. The Muslim patrons did, however, keep to their custom of avoiding images of living creatures. To make the buildings distinctive, Islamic decorative elements were added, for instance the semicircular arches and ornamental kufic script, which at Bhadreshvar is expertly executed. The main innovation at Bhadreshvar was, however, the adaptation of indigenous architectural features to the liturgical requirements of Islam. The practice of burial as opposed to cremation and of collective prayer facing the direction of Mecca introduced new concepts into the architectural tradition of South Asia. Among these the most significant is the precisely calculated orientation of the buildings, marked by the mihrab. All the mihrabs in Bhadreshvar are similar in plan to that in al-Mansura (*see* §(a) above), semicircular and projecting outside the wall. In Bhadreshvar, however, the mihrabs are better preserved. The semicircular form of the mihrab arches, like those of the doorways, closely resembles archways of Syria, Egypt and North Africa. None of the mihrabs is decorated, but around the springing of the arches there are projecting mouldings. These suggest that another decorative mihrab, possibly of carved wood, could have been fitted into the present recess.

Muslim trading communities outside Bhadreshvar must have had their own buildings, but these have not survived. Muslim traders appear to have penetrated inland, however, and with the establishment of Muslim rule throughout most of north India, it is likely that these early buildings served as prototypes for Indo-Muslim architecture during the late 12th century and early 13th.

BIBLIOGRAPHY

al-Biruni: *Kitāb fī Taḥqīq mā li'l-Hind* [A book concerning the study of all aspects of India] (*c.* 1030); Eng. trans. by E. C. Sachau as *Alberuni's India* (London, 1914/*R* Delhi and Bombay, 1964), i, pp. 208–9, 301

J. Burgess: *Memorandum on the Remains at Gumli, Gop, and in Kachh.* Mem. Archaeol. Surv. W. India, iii (Bombay, 1875), pp. 11–19

——: *Report on the Antiquities of Kathiawad and Kachh, 1874–5*, Archaeol. Surv. W. India, ii (London, 1876), pp. 205–10

E. Hultzsch: 'A Grant of Arjunada of Gujarat', *Ind. Antiqua.*, xi (1882), pp. 241–5

G. Bühler: 'The Jagaducharita of Sarvanada: A Historical Romance from Gujarat', *Indian Studies*, i, Sitzungsberichte, cxxvi (1892)

Shams al-din Abu 'Abdullah Muhammad b. Ahmad al-Muqaddasi: *Aḥsan al-taqāsīm* [The finest of land divisions] (Leiden, 1906), pp. 474–86

Abu Ishaq Ibrahim b. Muhammad al-Istakhri: *Al-Masālik wa al-mamālik* [The routes and the countries] (Cairo, 1961), pp. 102, 104–5

Z. A. Desai: 'Arabic Inscriptions of the Rajput Period from Gujarat', *Epig. Ind.: Arab. & Pers. Suppl.* (1961), pp. 1–24

——: 'Kūfī Epitaphs from Bhadreśwar in Gujarat', *Epig. Ind.: Arab. & Pers. Suppl.* (1965), pp. 1–8

M. Shokoohy: *Bhadreśvar: The Oldest Islamic Monuments in India* (Leiden, 1988)

——: 'Muslim Architecture in Gujarat prior to the Islamic Conquest', *Marg*, xxxix/4 (1988)

——: 'Architecture of the Muslim Trading Communities in India', *Islam in Indian Regions*, Beiträge zur Südasienforschung, Südasien-Institut Universität Heidelberg, cxlv (Stuttgart, 1993), pt 1, pp. 291–319; pt 2, pp. 99–101

MEHRDAD SHOKOOHY

6. 11TH–16TH CENTURIES. By the end of the 10th century, north India had become fragmented into a number of competing principalities. Conditions in the south were more stable under the Chalukyas of Kalyana (*see* CHALUKYA, §2) and the CHOLA dynasty of Tamil Nadu. The Chalukyas, who had displaced the Rashtrakutas *c.* AD 973, subsequently controlled the Deccan for two hundred years. Further south, the Cholas were at the height of their power in the 11th century and early 12th; they conquered Sri Lanka, raided northward to the River Ganga and carried out naval expeditions as far as Sumatra. Paralleling the expansionist policies of the Chola kingdom, the Ghaznavid Turks and their successors made raids across the Indus into north India. By the close of the 12th century they had successfully established an Islamic sultanate at Delhi (*see* §(ii)(b) below). The Chalukya and Chola kingdoms meanwhile had begun to disintegrate, their territories being divided among the Yadava, Kakatiya and Hoysala dynasties. This fragmentation favoured the sultanate, and by the time of Muhammad Tughluq (*reg* 1325–51) most of the south had succumbed to Delhi. Delhi's hold over many regions was tenuous, however; a significant revival of temple architecture in the south was inaugurated by the Vijayanagara rulers, and resurgences of traditional architecture occurred sporadically in other areas.

(i) Indigenous and traditional. (ii) Indo-Islamic.

(i) Indigenous and traditional. Temple-building projects of extraordinary elaboration and scale, already under way in north and central India, began to dominate architectural activity in other parts of the subcontinent during the 11th century. Temples of the 11th century and later vary considerably, in keeping with regional styles. (So little survives in the northern heartland that no survey of this region is included below.) In the north-west, stone temples had given way to timber-and-stone shrines with sloping slate roofs by the 13th century. In the east the *nāgara* (Skt: northern) tradition was developed in the great temples of BHUBANESHWAR, PURI and KONARAK. The Maru-Gurjara style dominated in Rajasthan and Gujarat. Buildings in Karnataka attest to a dynamic combination of northern and southern features in a complex mode often termed *vesara*. At the Chola capital of THANJAVUR, the Rajarajeshvara Temple, a building of unprecedented size, represents a grand culmination of the *drāviḍa* (southern) tradition. □

(a) North-west. (b) Rajasthan and Gujarat. (c) Maharashtra. (d) East. (e) Central. (f) Karnataka and Andhra Pradesh. (g) Tamil Nadu. (h) Kerala.

(a) North-west.

Himachal Pradesh. 'Classical' *nāgara* architecture, established in the Himachal region prior to the 11th century, when it was part of the Gurjara-Pratihara empire, is represented by a few surviving later temples. The 11th-century Gauri-Shankara shrine at Dashal near Kulu has a heavy-shouldered *śikhara* and bold *caitya* windows that continue the style of the Vishveshvara Temple at BAJAURA. The Trilokinatha Temple and its subsidiary shrines at Mandi formed an imposing complex; in keeping with its 12th-century date, figural work was employed on a reduced scale. The Shiva Temple at Baijnath (Kangra District) is an earlier monument, but extensive renovation was carried out in 1204. Miniature shrines of the 11th century exist at Nirmand (Kulu District), and architectural fragments and carvings scattered at the sites of scores of later wooden temples suggest that stone temples existed there in earlier times. By the 13th century, the age of the great all-stone temples had passed. Gradually, stone was relegated to the role of mere filling material in temple walls, with all the moulded and carved parts being made of wood.

A large wooden temple of the goddess Kali, known as the Markuladevi, in Udaypur (Lahul-Spiti District) has elements of disparate date, but the shrine door, four out of the six pillars of the hall and all nine of the carved ceiling panels are original. The pediment forms and elongated statuary follow the style of Chamba—indeed, Udaypur is culturally part of Chamba—and the carvings

68. Parashara Temple, Mandi District, 14th century

of Vishnu's incarnations framed under ingenious pediments of interconnected dormers (*udgamas*) bespeak a vigorous tradition. The carving, which shows an evolution over that of the wooden temple of Shaktidevi at CHHATRADI, is datable to the 11th century. A temple of Shiva at Nirmand possesses a wooden doorway of the 11th century. Its five jambs have such 'classical' decorations as niched figures of divinities, creeping vines and pilasters with vase-and-foliage capitals.

Following the advent of Islam in the 11th century, local dynasties in Himachal Pradesh asserted their independence. Indigenous structural forms were introduced gradually in temple buildings, which thus achieved a new vitality. This is why Himachal temples of the 13th to the 18th century blend so well with their surroundings. Such later examples generally consist of a sanctum surrounded by a circumambulatory with a hall, but each temple has its own individuality. The sanctum is often enclosed by a shell of alternate courses of stone and long logs without any cementing material. The superstructure rises up in three or four storeys, each storey marked by a steep, slate-covered roof—a most striking adaptation of the *śikhara* to this area of heavy snowfall.

69. Shiva Temple, Behna, Kulu District, *c.* late 14th century

Not many of these timber-and-stone shrines can be securely dated through inscriptions, two exceptions being the Parashara Temple in Mandi District (14th century; see fig. 68) and the Hirma Temple at Dhungri-Manali (1553). This, combined with the fact that most structures were altered frequently, makes it difficult to establish a chronology. However unsatisfactory, inscribed divine masks (Hindi *mohras*) are the only means of dating most monuments.

The temple of the sage Parashara, on a hill 3000 m above sea-level in Mandi District, is relatively intact. The sanctum is of deodar wood, as are the 12 pillars around it, the whole being enclosed by a stone-and-timber hall. The superstructure has three tiers. Grilled windows and divine figures decorate the walls. Most impressive is the doorway embellished with scrolls and creeping vines, an angular meander, pilasters with vase-and-foliage capitals and intertwined serpents (a Pratihara motif). The square wooden pillars have vase-and-foliage capitals. This temple has traditionally been ascribed to King Ban Sen of Mandi (*d* 1346); the temple conforms to what is known of the style of this period.

Many wooden shrines were built between the 14th and 16th centuries on the trade routes running from Mandi to Kulu-Sultanpur and from the latter to Rampur-Bushahr and Kinnaur, as well as at other sacred places in the interior of Mandi, Kulu and Simla districts. The Shiva Temple at Behna on the old highway linking Sultanpur and the Kullu Valley to Rampur-Bushahr and Kinnaur is another monument that bridges the 'classical' and 'provincial' phases of temple architecture (see fig. 69). A metal bust of a male deity placed in the sanctum provides evidence of artistic activity in the 8th century AD. A few fragmentary sculptures embedded in the temple walls belong to the 10th century. The 11th century is represented by some miniature shrines in the compound of the main temple. The present complex at Behna may date to the late 14th century. It has a rectangular pillared hall with a square sanctum placed at the rear, thus leaving a circumambulatory passage. The low wall of the hall has a long seat that runs along its entire length, and on the outside the wall is relieved with pairs of pilasters. Both these features reproduce in wood forms of the stone temple, namely the seat back (*kakṣāsana*) and railing (*vedikā*). The superstructure has two stages crowned by sloping, shingle-covered roofs. The space separating the roofs is treated as if it were an upper chamber, but there is no approach from below. All four walls have mythological scenes.

The temples of Ambika at Naopano and of Vishnu at Kigas (Mandi District) must have been of imposing dimensions. Their doorframes, latticed windows and statuary closely imitate the more stately carvings of the Parashara Temple, which is a day's walk away. The

Naopano and Kigas temples are datable to the 15th and 16th centuries respectively.

Ladakh. Although Ladakh never came under direct Tibetan political control, Tibet's influence was dominant from the 11th century onwards. After AD 842 the central Tibetan empire of Lhasa collapsed following the death of King Langdarma (*reg* AD 836–42), and his descendants migrated west, forming small kingdoms in Ladakh and elsewhere. The 11th-century Buddhist scholar Rinchen Sangpo went to Kashmir to study and translate religious treatises and initiated the founding of monasteries in Ladakh, Zanskar and Spiti. Most of the earliest monuments in these places are directly credited to him.

As in other parts of India, monasteries and temples were located along the trade routes and close to cities with concentrated wealth. The area from Spituk and Leh up to Hemis, a stretch of some 50 km up the Indus River, has the greatest concentration of monuments. Monasteries, temples and chortens, as well as royal palaces and forts, were constructed of stone and poplar wood. Numerous reconstructions and poor maintenance, especially after the Muslim raids of the 13th century, have obscured the original appearances of these buildings.

The fort and monastery of Nyarma, south of Leh, is among the earliest monuments founded by Rinchen Sangpo. Though only ruins remain, the complex must have been as extensive as ALCHI in the valley of the Indus River. Alchi has the largest, best-preserved concentration in Ladakh of monuments complete with images and painted *maṇḍala*s (cosmic diagrams; for wall painting *see* §VI, 3(i)(c) below). Buildings include the Dukhang (Tibetan: 'assembly hall'), a *sumtsek* (three-tiered temple), a *lhakhang soma* ('new temple'), an old monastery and a chorten. Vairochana is the presiding deity, as in all early temples. The Dukhang includes a square hall with a sanctum attached to its back wall that enshrines a large Vairochana flanked by the four other Buddhas, Akshobhya, Ratnasambhava, Amitabha and Amoghasiddhi. Six *maṇḍala*s of Vairochana's pantheon are painted on the walls, as are some secular scenes. Inscriptions in the Dukhang attribute its construction to a devout personage, Kalden Sherab, who flourished in the 11th–12th century. The style of Kashmir is revealed in the woodwork in the three-storey temple, especially the triangular pediments and the Buddha figures they enshrine, the rafter-ends with prancing lions and the rows of shallow niches on the architraves. Similar forms also exist in the main assembly hall. The temple houses large images of the *bodhisattva*s Maitreya, Manjushri and Avalokiteshvara. The monastic complex at Lamayuru on the Srinagar–Leh road belongs to a branch of the Kadampa Order of Tibetan Buddhism. A small shrine in the monastery, as well as votive chortens with murals and images of Vairochana, point to its founding in the time of Rinchen Sangpo. The main temple at the monastery of Manggyu also enshrines Vairochana, together with other Buddha manifestations and painted *maṇḍala*s.

From the 14th century Ladakh experienced increasing Muslim incursions. Monuments built in open spaces were easy prey. From the 15th century onwards, monasteries were, therefore, placed on high summits and acquired the character of fortresses. The Gelugpa monastery of Spituk was among the first of these constructions. It was built on many levels, and its main assembly hall, with long rows of low seats running from the entrance to the altar at the rear, is in Tibetan style. This and other smaller shrines house images of 11-headed Avalokiteshvara, Tara, Samvara and other Tantric deities.

In the 15th century Ladakh was divided into two parts, under Trakbumde in Leh and Trakpabum in Basgo. Trakbumde's father is said to have built a 'red temple' in Leh, and his grandfather is credited with several chortens. The 'red temple' may be the Maitreya Temple that can still be seen in Leh, though it is much ruined and renovated. Trakbumde also built a three-tiered temple, which has not survived, and a large stupa near Leh with 108 chapels, now ruined. In the 16th century the Basgo house came into prominence and ruled over the whole of Ladakh. King Tashi Namgyel built the 'Peak of Victory' fort in Leh, the first such recorded defensive construction. He also built a temple within the fort, as well as the 'temple of the guardian deities'. Tashi Namgyel's successor, Tshewang Namgyel, built a Maitreya Temple at Basgo, one of the few monuments available for comparative study.

Apart from monasteries, Ladakh also possesses some important royal citadels, those at Tingmogang, Basgo and Shey being particularly significant. Fortifications encircle the citadel and temples of Avalokiteshvara and Maitreya at Tingmogang, datable to the 16th century. Palaces and forts were also built at Leh and Alchi, among other sites, before the 14th century, but they are all in ruins.

See also TIBET, §II, 2 and 3.

BIBLIOGRAPHY

D. L. Snellgrove and T. Skorupski: *The Cultural Heritage of Ladakh*, 2 vols (New Delhi, n.d.)
A. Cunningham: *Ladak: Physical, Statistical and Geographical* (London, 1854/*R* New Delhi, 1941)
J. P. Vogel: *Antiquities of Chamba*, i (Calcutta, 1913)
A. H. Francke: *Antiquities of Indian Tibet*, 2 vols (Calcutta, 1914–26/*R* New Delhi, 1972)
H. Goetz: *The Early Wooden Temples of Chamba* (Leiden, 1955)
M. Postel, A. Neven and K. Mankodi: *Antiquities of Himachal* (Bombay, 1985)
R. Goepper: 'The "Great Stupa" at Alchi', *Artibus Asiae*, liii (1993), pp. 111–43

KIRIT MANKODI

(b) Rajasthan and Gujarat. Early in the 11th century, a new and homogeneous style of temple architecture, the Maru-Gurjara style, spread over western India. The unity of this style was recognized and defined by the art historian M. A. Dhaky through a detailed morphological analysis of western Indian monuments. Dhaky derived the term 'Maru-Gurjara' from the regionally based designations he gave to two earlier styles of western India, 'Maha maru' and 'Maha-Gurjara'. At its peak, Maru-Gurjara style extended from northern Rajasthan down to southern Gujarat and from Sind and Saurashtra across to the eastern border of Madhya Pradesh. In chronological terms it extends from the 11th century to the present.

Although the Maru-Gurjara style did not develop under the patronage of a single dynasty, its spread and homogeneity were due in large part to the patronage of the SOLANKI dynasty (941–mid-13th century) of Gujarat,

70. Someshvara Temple, Kiradu, *c.* 1020; main shrine viewed from the south

which acted as its primary proponent during its development and maturity. Centred around its capital at Anahilapataka (now Patan) in northern Gujarat, by the mid-12th century it had subsumed a number of neighbouring dynasties to assume imperial status. At its peak the Solanki empire stretched over all of modern Gujarat and much of Rajasthan and occupied the region of Malwa in western Madhya Pradesh. Its heir, the Vaghela dynasty, lasted only until the invasion and conquest of Gujarat by the army of the Khalji sultan of Delhi at the end of the 13th century.

Literary records are comparatively copious from this period. Not only is there drama and poetry but also historical accounts of rulers and manuals for artists and architects (*see* §I, 10 above). Thus the vocabulary used for the forms in western Indian architecture tends to be culled from writings of these centuries. Historical accounts and inscriptions allude to a vast number of temple constructions. This is not surprising considering the prosperous economy of the region at this time. Only a minute proportion of structures mentioned are extant, however, although these embrace some of the architectural wonders of the subcontinent.

Whether dedicated to forms of the deities Shiva, Vishnu, Surya (the sun) or the Goddess, Hindu shrines in Maru-Gurjara style share a vocabulary of form and layout. The temple consists of a main shrine connected by buffer walls to either a closed hall or a semi-open pillared hall, the whole fronted by a pillared porch. (Smaller monuments have only the porch.) Only rarely did the main shrine have an enclosed ambulatory path. There may also be detached sub-shrines.

Although utilizing the same vocabulary of forms as Hindu structures, Jaina temples of this period developed an idiosyncratic organization. The main shrine was placed on a high platform, fronting which were a closed hall, vestibule and pillared hall. A row usually composed of 24 or 52 small sub-shrines housing the Jaina saviour-saints (Skt *tīrthaṅkaras*) encircled this central complex. The porches of these sub-shrines formed a continuous cloistered corridor and their rear walls a barrier wall to the outside. Entry was gained through an opening in the platform with a staircase that rose into an entry hall or porch. Unlike Hindu structures, the Jaina temple faces inwards, shielded from the world by a solid exterior wall.

Temples in the Maru-Gurjara style sit elevated on a plinth composed of ornate mouldings that parallel the planes of the orthogonal wall above (see fig. 70). In the mature style, these mouldings number seven or eight. Beginning from the bottom they are an inverted cyma recta, a knife-edged astragal, a recessed band, a cyma recta or hood, a band of lion-like faces, an elephant band, a horse band (rare) and a human band. Below the plinth is a second basement of one or more undecorated courses.

The wall resting on the plinth consists of three segments: base mouldings, frieze and cornice. The base mouldings follow a standard *nāgara* formula, but the faces of the mouldings, especially the large shoulder moulding, tend to be decorated with half-diamonds, lotuses or figural compositions. The frieze usually begins with an interrupted cyma moulding that acts as a pedestal for the niches above. These niches, composed of narrow pillars topped by an awning, shelter standing figures. From the awnings rise short, triangular pediments of lattice pattern matching that on the superstructure. Iconographically, major deities related to the tutelary divinity occupy the central offsets, the corner frames house the regents of the quarters (*dikpālas*), intermediary offsets carry female figures, and the indentations between usually accommodate ascetics.

Above and behind the pediment of the central offset stretches a band of lion-like faces, sometimes continued on the rest of the wall. A round, often fluted pillar shaft, topped by a round capital and foliate impost block, emerges from behind the pediments of all of the side offsets. Conceptually, the wall is a colonnade, a type of organization traceable to late Maha-Maru buildings. The cornice consists of one or more cyma mouldings topped by a recessed band and, just below the superstructure, an overhanging awning or eave.

The curvilinear tower-like superstructure over the main shrine of the typical Maru-Gurjara temple takes one of two forms: single-spired or multi-turreted. The multi-turreted form, developed primarily within the Maha-Gurjara tradition of southern Rajasthan and Gujarat, consists of a central curvilinear tower with abutting half-towers and a number of corner turrets. Over the central offsets and below the abutting half-towers are niches housing deities. At the base of the superstructure, on the entry side, an antefix displays the deity to whom the temple is dedicated. The spire is topped by the usual collection of *nāgara* crowning members.

71. Luna Vasahi Temple, Mt Abu, *c.* 1232–40; ceiling of pillared hall

Roofs over the halls most frequently consist of small slabs of cyma cornices, stepped and placed concentrically, each crowned by a fluted bell finial, a new development from an earlier layered cornice type. The wall of the closed hall imitates the main shrine up to the superstructure. Projecting lateral bays with windows covered by stone screens are additional features.

The semi-open pillared hall duplicates the main shrine only up to the plinth. Above it runs a band of figures or diamond-and-volute patterning. From this band rises a blind railing covered in vegetal and geometric designs alternating with thin pilasters. Resting on the railing is a stone slab whose flat exterior is decorated with miniature stepped roofs. The slab projects into the hall and continues around the sides, forming convenient, permanent seating for an audience. A second slanted slab constitutes the seat back, decorated on the exterior with floral motifs and medallions. Projecting from the seat slab are dwarf vase-and-foliage pillars bearing the ceiling beams and surrounded, on the exterior, by an awning below the roof. On the enclosed Jaina temples, this entire configuration becomes part of the enclosing wall of sub-shrines.

Interiors of both closed and semi-open halls are profusely carved. Columns, usually with bases of four or eight sides, central sections of sixteen sides and circular tops, stand in rows or form an interior octagon. Linking them overhead are wavelike arches elaborately carved with figures or vegetation and often issuing from the mouths of mythical crocodiles (*makaras*).

The bays formed by the pillars are covered by a variety of ceiling types. Flat ceilings carved with floral or figural designs often canopy the smaller bays, while above the central bay rises a dome formed of curved-rib and cuspate mouldings. On the largest ceilings, nearly life-size female figures act as brackets above each pillar of the central octagon, while a lotus pendant hangs in the centre, a type directly descended from 10th-century Maha-Gurjara architecture. In the grand, developed temples, particularly the Jaina structures in which the interior is of paramount importance, these ceilings expand and become breathtaking in their intricacy and delicacy (see fig. 71).

Despite the flamboyance of the typical hall's interior, that of the sanctum remains undecorated apart from an occasional platform or ledge. The exterior of the sanctum doorway, on the other hand, resembles an ordered microcosm: gods, goddesses and personified planets (*navagraha*) inhabit the lintel, while performers, loving couples (*mithunas*), mythical animals, jewels and flowers enrich the jambs. Attendant and guardian divinities (*dvārapālas*) stand prominently on the lower segment of the jambs. The threshold displays a central semicylindrical projection decorated with the spiralling shoots of a lotus stem.

Of standing Maru-Gurjara temples, the largest in size and number are Jaina. Of the Jaina shrines at Dilwara on MT ABU in Rajasthan, those known as the Vimala Vasahi, Luna Vasahi (see fig. 71) and Adinatha Temple are world-famous. Carved primarily of white marble, their interiors dissolve into lacy fantasy. The shrines were built in large part by various Jaina ministers of the Solanki kings. These ministers, like the majority of Jainas, came from the merchant class. (Gujarat, with its long shoreline and numerous ports, has always been a centre for trade and industry.) Consequently, a large proportion of the temples in this area were not royal foundations but donations by private individuals. Some of the other spectacular Jaina temples of the period stand at Kumbharia and Taranga in northern Gujarat and at Mt Girnar and Satrunjaya in Saurashtra.

Much of our knowledge of Maru-Gurjara architecture in its formative stage, however, comes from surviving Hindu monuments. The Someshvara Temple at KIRADU, in the Thar Desert near Barmer, Rajasthan (see fig. 70 above), and the Surya Temple at MODHERA in north Gujarat (exclusive of its detached pillared hall) date from the first half of the 11th century. They retain the clarity of articulation seen in the 10th-century styles as well as the high quality of individual figural sculpture.

In the latter part of the 11th century and even more visibly into the 12th, the integrated patterning of the whole temple engulfed the autonomous parts. Sculptural quality deteriorated, perhaps to be judged more as architectural embellishment. This is evident when comparing the Modhera shrine (*c.* 1026–7) with its own detached hall (*c.* 1070). This new aesthetic seems to be apparent, though combined with a memory of exquisite 10th-century figural carving, in the beautiful but highly stylized sculptures of the Rani Vav at Patan (*c.* 1060–1100; see fig. 189 below). The wealth and skill behind a royal foundation are evident in the seven storeys and three halls of this spectacular monument.

During the 14th century, strong governors of Delhi's Muslim sultans, first Khalji and later Tughluq, ruled Gujarat and parts of Rajasthan. Islamic power eclipsed even the puissant Rajput families of Mewar and Marwar, and temple-building declined, although restorations and additions were made, particularly in the large Jaina complexes. With the deterioration of the Tughluq sultanate and the invasion of Timur (1398), the Islamic governors of Gujarat and Malwa proclaimed their independence. While they consolidated their power, the Rajput dynasties in Saurashtra, Marwar and particularly Mewar revived. Major new temple projects began to occur from early in the 15th century at Jaina sites such as Mt Girnar and Jaisalmer. It was, however, only under the strong rule of Rana Kumbha of Mewar (*reg* 1433–68) that monuments of the first magnitude appeared again. His craftsmen utilized Maru-Gurjara vocabulary not only for the temples they constructed at CHITTAURGARH, the city from which he ruled, but also for two monumental, free-standing towers. They adopted the latter form from mosque elements (minarets and IWAN buttresses) constructed by architects working in the Maru-Gurjara tradition but in the service of sultanate rulers of western India.

Perhaps the single greatest building of this period is the Jaina temple of Adinatha at RANAKPUR. Located between

72. Temple of Adinatha, Ranakpur, *c.* 1440 and later; interior

modern Udaipur and Jodhpur, the Ranakpur structure was built by a wealthy merchant under Rana Kumbha's rule. It shows a new attention to massing and monumental interior space. Although figural sculpture has become awkward and angular, non-figural work has increased, reaching new heights in abstract perfection. As with the Chittaurgarh towers, both changes were due in part to innovations learnt by adapting Maru-Gurjara forms to the predilections of Islamic patrons.

The Ranakpur temple has entries orientated to the four cardinal directions (thus 'four-faced', Skt *caturmukha*). Although most of its individual elements were present in structures of the 12th century, the unified, grandiose three-storey pillared hall demonstrates the adaptability of Maru-Gurjara forms to new requirements. The earlier surround of an open pillared hall with slanting seat backs and seats facing into the hall was reversed and used in the upper storeys, so that the decorated seat back topping a blind railing can be seen by looking up from the hall below, while the seats themselves serve the ambulatory areas on the second and third floors (see fig. 72).

The process of replacing standard forms with forms from other locations is evident in the main superstructure at Ranakpur. The corner offsets of the *nāgara* tower had, up to this time, retained the memory of their origins as corner pavilions by means of the enduring practice of demarcating the storeys with ribbed stones. On the superstructure of the Adinatha Temple, however, the corners of the main tower consist of stacked niches, while the abutting towers display piled pots with overflowing foliage. The latter configuration became a frequent variation and remains popular.

That Maru-Gurjara practices have not died out is due in part to the preservation of architects' manuals. Even today, the Sompura families of Gujarat study and follow treatises handed down over generations.

BIBLIOGRAPHY

M. A. Dhaky: 'The Chronology of the Solanki Temples of Gujarat', *J. Madhya Pradesh Itihasa Parishad*, iii (1961), pp. 1–83

——: 'The Date of the Dancing Hall of the Sun Temple, Modhera', *J. Bombay Branch Royal Asiat. Soc.*, xxxviii (1963), pp. 211–22

J. M. Nanavati and M. A. Dhaky: 'The Ceilings in the Temples of Gujarat', *Bull. Baroda Mus. & Pict. Gal.*, xvi–xvii (1963–4) [whole issue]

M. A. Dhaky: 'Renaissance and the Late Māru-Gurjara Temple Architecture', *J. Ind. Soc. Orient. A.* (1966), pp. 4–22 [special issue]

——: 'Kiradu and the Māru-Gurjara Style of Temple Architecture', *Bull. Amer. Acad. Benares*, i (1967), pp. 35–45

K. F. Sompura: *The Structural Temples of Gujarat (up to 1600 A.D.)*, Thesis Publication Series, iv (Ahmadabad, 1968)

M. A. Dhaky: 'The Genesis and Development of Māru-Gurjara Temple Architecture', *Studies in Indian Temple Architecture*, ed. P. Chandra (New Delhi, 1975), pp. 114–65

——: 'The Western Indian Jaina Temple', *Aspects of Jaina Art and Architecture*, ed. U. P. Shah and M. A. Dhaky (Ahmadabad, 1975), pp. 319–84

H. Singh: *Jaina Temples of Western India* (Varanasi, 1982)

K. Mankodi: *The Queen's Step Well at Patan* (Bombay, 1992)

DARIELLE MASON, MICHAEL W. MEISTER

(c) Maharashtra. During the 11th century a prolific phase of structural temple building was begun under the YADAVA (or Seuna) dynasty and its feudatories. The Yadavas ruled successively from Chandradityapura (now Chanderi), Srinagara (now Sinnar) and Devagiri (now Daulatabad). Seunadesha, the heartland of their power and architectural patronage, corresponded to the north-western portions of modern Maharashtra. After 1311, when the Yadavas were overthrown by Muslim invaders, minor dynasties continued to build Hindu and Jaina temples in the region. Seunadesha, together with Malwa (anc. Malava in western Madhya Pradesh) and the spheres of influence of both regions, formed a single stylistic zone. The Yadava or Seunadesha style was related to the traditions of Karnataka and Andhra Pradesh, not so much in the overall form of temples (which are predominantly *nāgara* rather than *drāviḍa*), but in many details and in pillar design. Antecedents of the style are difficult to trace. It can be assumed to have developed out of a tradition of temple building mainly in brick, but none of these buildings survives. Deccani trap and sandstone are the predominant materials seen in the surviving monuments, most of which are of structural masonry. The rock-cut technique did survive, as in the Jaina cave temple at Tringalvadi (Nasik District).

The grandest temple ensemble is the Gondeshvara at Sinnar (see fig. 73), where the main temple, with its hall (*maṇḍapa*) and free-standing pavilion for Nandi (Shiva's bull), is surrounded by four subsidiary shrines (and is thus *pañcāyatana*; Skt: 'five-shrined'), all raised on a platform and set within an enclosure. Temples with three shrines

73. Gondeshvara Temple, Sinnar, early 13th century

attached to a single hall are not uncommon and include Temple 1 at Balsane, the Mahadeva at Jhodga (see fig. 74), the Bhavani Temple at Takahari and the Lakshmi-Narayana at Pedgaon. As many as 11 sanctuaries surround the hall of Temple 5 at Balsane.

All the major Yadava temples belong to the *bhūmija* mode of *nāgara* temple architecture. In this mode the shrine proper (*mūlaprāsāda*), between the cardinal projections (*bhadras*) of its walls and its superstructure, has a number of vertical chains of *kūṭastambhas*, miniature spires (*śikharas*) sitting on pillar forms (*stambhas*). This way of organizing *nāgara* components is thought to have originated in Malwa (see Deva). The majority of the *bhūmija* monuments in Malwa are stellate, with a plan form based on a square rotated about its centre, while in Seunadesha stellate shrines are outnumbered by orthogonal ones, with parallel projections stepping progressively forward from the corner to the centre of each elevation. Most examples have lost all or part of their superstructures, which may often have been of brick.

One of the largest, most lavish and earliest Yadava temples (1060) is at AMBARNATH. The orthogonal shrine, which is missing its uppermost portions, has seven projections on each elevation. The miniature shrine forms on the *kūṭastambhas* are unusual in being squat with flattened, bell-like crowning members. The later Gondeshvara at Sinnar has seven projections and seven storeys (*bhūmis*) or, in other words, seven *kūṭastambhas* in each vertical chain (see fig. 73 above). Seven-projection shrines (found also at Methi and Changdeva) are outnumbered, however, by five-projection compositions. Later examples follow a 'stepped diamond' plan, in which corner elements are the same size as intermediate ones, a single diagonal line passing through all the salient angles of one quadrant. This plan type, like stellate plans, lends itself to the use of re-entrant projections in the internal angles of the exterior, treated as three-quarters-embedded *kūṭastambhas*. Examples of five-projection, stepped-diamond *bhūmija* shrines are Temple 1 at Balsane (main shrine), the Vishnu Temple at Satgaon (Buldana District), the Siddheshvara at Akola and the Amriteshvara at Ratanvadi (both Ahmadnagar District). The Amriteshvara is complete with five storeys and shares with the temple at Akola the unusual feature of an additional doorway, with porch, at the rear of the sanctum. The main shrine of the Mahadeva at Jhodga (see fig. 74), with seven storeys, follows a stepped-diamond plan with five main projections from corner to corner but with additional, minor projections flanking the central one. These are treated as *kūṭastambha* chains with stylized, hall-like shrine images as crowning elements.

74. Mahadeva Temple, Jhodga, *c.* late 12th century; main shrine viewed from the north

Stellate *bhūmija* shrines in Seunadesha have either three or five vertical chains of *kūṭastambhas* in each quadrant between the cardinal projections, each chain corresponding on plan to a point of the star. These two stellate types are equivalent, in terms of the number of *kūṭastambha* chains, to five- and seven-projection orthogonal shrines respectively. Examples of the first type are Temple 4 at Balsane, the Kalikadevi at Barsi-Talki (Akola District), the Jagadambadevi at Kokamthan (Ahmadnagar District) and the main shrine of the triple temple at Methi. Of the second type are the Mudhaidevi at Vaghali (Jalgaon District), the Mahadeva at Anwa (Aurangabad District), the Maheshvara at Patna (Jalgaon District) and the Daityasudana at Lonar. Normally, the plan type with 3 points in each quadrant was constructed on a star of 16 points, with every fourth point obscured by a cardinal projection, while the type with 5 points in each quadrant was based on a 24-point star, with every sixth point obscured. Sometimes (Meister, pp. 172–3) 20- or 28-point stars were used, with the cardinal axes located between adjacent pairs of obscured points rather than passing through single obscured points. The temple at Kokamthan (Cousens, pl. LXVIII), of perhaps the 14th century, is the only stellate example with a near-complete superstructure; it has five storeys. On the cardinal axes are 'buttresses' in the form of *bhūmija* shrines that rise up beyond the base of the superstructure, recalling the oversized wall shrines of some Hoysala temples in Karnataka.

Temple halls typically contain four pillars defining a central square. Some have ornate corbelled domes, as in the magnificent open hall at Anwa. As in Karnataka, pierced screens sometimes appear around the hall perimeter. Pyramidal (*samvaraṇā*) roofs made up of miniature shrine forms are found at Ambaranath and Sinnar. At Kokamthan and Methi the halls, like the shrines themselves, are stellate.

On the whole the carved surfaces of Seunadesha temples convey a dry, rather mechanical quality. A characteristic shared with certain contemporary schools in

Karnataka and Andhra Pradesh is a profusion of knife-edge mouldings, of thin, deep grooves and of 'flourishes'—excrescences turned up or down—at the corners of mouldings. The base moulding types are shared with other *nāgara* traditions, as is the convention of moulding the wall zone according to the horizontal divisions of pillar design, since the wall contains the pillar portions of the first tier of *kūṭastambhas*. The particular pillar or pilaster design most often employed for the wall zone, as indeed for free-standing pillars, in both Seunadesha and Malwa is almost a hallmark of the temple architecture of those regions. The basic 'proto-*drāviḍa*' pillar type is one in which the upper sequence of components includes a cushion capital (*ghaṭa*), now narrow and pointed. The upper sequence sits over a band decorated with monster faces (*grāsamukhas*) or a hanging leaf motif. Between this band and the tall base block, the shaft is usually decorated with a characteristic ogival 'moonstone' motif. When, in relatively rare instances, a gallery of iconic sculpture runs along the foot of the wall, this may be sheltered by some form of canopy moulding.

Another stylistic hallmark that distinguishes Seunadesha and Malwa from the rest of western and central India is the treatment of horseshoe arches (*gavākṣas*), both as separate motifs and when 'woven' into nets (*jālas*). The type predominant in Seunadesha and Malwa is closer to the *drāviḍa* horsehoe arch (*nāsī*), its lateral 'ears' being foliated (bushy) rather than curvilinear. However, this type also predominates in some *bhūmija* temples of Rajasthan (Menal, Bijolia), suggesting that certain attributes of 'style' could follow the *bhūmija* 'mode', either through the migration of craftsmen or as a conscious idea of appropriate detail for this form of temple.

Not all Seunadesha temples are *bhūmija*. The ruined Temple 8 at Anjaneri (Nasik District) belongs to the *śekharī* mode of *nāgara* (with embedded spire emerging along the cardinal axes). Typically, minor temples are in the *latina* (simple curved spire) mode—several examples exist at Anjaneri—with a miniature spire or other pavilion type at the base of each segment of the superstructure, over a plain wall or combined with a moulded projection to form a *kūṭastambha*. *Phāṁsanā* shrines are found (with pyramidal superstructures of overhanging eaves mouldings), but most notably in eastern Maharashtra, as at RAMTEK.

Dozens of temples in Maharashtra, of various kinds and widely ranging dates, are attributed by legend to one Hemadri, whose historical existence was as minister during the last decades of Yadava rule. Following Cousens (1931), a heavy, plain character is sometimes attributed to Hemadpanti temples, as, for example, in the Siddheshvara at Limpangaon (Ahmadnagar District), just south of Seunadesha proper, which could have been either a *latina* or a *phāṁsanā* shrine (no superstructure remains). No distinct temple type has been convincingly identified with the elusive 'Hemadpanti style', however.

Temple architects in medieval Seunadesha occasionally experimented with the variety of *drāviḍa* architecture found in Karnataka and Andhra Pradesh, just as those southerly regions of the Deccan were, to a much greater extent, conversant with the *nāgara* mode (*see* §(f) below). References to the *drāviḍa* are found in details, as in the barrel-roofed pavilion (*śālā*) over a niche at Anjaneri (Cousens, pl. LX). More significantly, the Ayeshvara at Sinnar, a richly and delicately carved little temple of about the late 11th century, is an entirely Karnata *drāviḍa* work, even down to small details, yet clearly not the creation of any known workshop from Karnataka. The 12th–13th-century triple temple of Bhavani at Takahari has lost its superstructures, but these can be seen more or less intact in an old photograph (Cousens, pl. LXXIV). The two lesser shrines are *bhūmija*, while the main shrine is a hybrid, with a superstructure of Karnata *drāviḍa* components arranged in a *bhūmija* manner.

Outside Seunadesha proper are temples that reflect the style of that region in varying degrees. The Kukdeshvara at Pur (Pune District) has its own lacy quality. Two twenty-four-point stellate *bhūmija* temples geographically and stylistically close to Karnataka are the Mahadeva at Mankeshvara (Osmanabad District), with a stellate hall, and the magnificent Koppeshvara Temple at Khidrapur (or Khedrapur, Kolhapur District), with a stellate open hall in front of a closed hall. Temples extremely close in style to Seunadesha are found as far afield as Jalasangi and Narayanpur in northernmost Karnataka.

BIBLIOGRAPHY

H. Cousens: *Mediaeval Temples of the Dakhan* (Calcutta, 1931)
O. P. Verma: *A Survey of Hemādpanti Temples in Maharashtra* (Nagpur, 1973)
K. Deva: 'Bhūmija Temples', *Studies in Indian Temple Architecture*, ed. P. Chandra (New Delhi, 1975), pp. 90–113
M. W. Meister: 'Reading Monuments and Seeing Texts', *The Shastric Tradition*, ed. A. L. Dallapiccola (Stuttgart, 1989), pp. 167–208

ADAM HARDY

(d) East. Three regional styles of temple architecture can be discerned in eastern India after the 11th century: that of Orissa, of south-west Bengal and of Bihar. In Orissa (anc. Kalinga) monuments are particularly numerous, with major temples surviving at BHUBANESHWAR, PURI and KONARAK. A related idiom was centred in south-west Bengal (anc. Vanga), but the number of surviving buildings is considerably smaller. Most fragmentary of all is the brick tradition of Bihar, which is represented by only a few damaged and relatively late examples.

Kalinga. During the 11th and 12th centuries the temple style of Kalinga remained in a state of transition and experimentation. Though many monuments are preserved, particularly at Bhubaneshwar, inscriptional evidence for royal patronage exists in only two cases: the Brahmeshvara and Megheshvara temples, built by members of the Somavamshi (*c.* 882–1110) and Ganga (*c.* 1077–1435) dynfjasties respectively. Royal patronage is usually assumed for many of the other temples at Bhubaneshwar, but sponsorship by pilgrims, especially from the wealthy merchant classes, should not be discounted.

Major developments in this period included a trend towards increased height and monumentality. The addition of a plinth (*pīṭha*) beneath the temple was a contributing factor. The greatest changes, however, were in the shrine (*prāsāda*) rather than in the hall (*maṇḍapa*). With the Brahmeshvara Temple (*c.* 1060), the forehall became standardized into a square structure with a double-storey pyramidal roof (*pīḍha*). The wall of the shrine and sometimes that of the forehall was divided into two levels or registers separated by a string course (*bandhanā*). The number of levels (*bhūmi*s) in the spire or superstructure was generally increased to ten.

During the highly experimental phase at the beginning of this period, the smooth, continuous contours of temple spires were surrounded by or embedded with clusters of minor spires (*aṅgaśikhara*). The first indications of such multi-spired clusters, known elsewhere in India as *śekharī*, are found in the Gauri Temple at Bhubaneshwar and Varahi Temple at Chaurasi (both *c.* mid-10th century; *see* §5(i)(e) above). In these buildings the wall's vertical salients or projections (*ratha*s) were set off by deep interstices and capped by miniature superstructures. Experimentation continued in the Ekambareshvara and Dakrabhimeshvara temples (*c.* 1000), where, along with miniature superstructures above the narrow salients of the wall, large spire forms were placed against the 'core' turret (*mūlaśikhara*) of the superstructure. These half-spires (*uraḥśṛṅga*s) are apparently of central Indian derivation. With their cumbersome qualities, the Ekambareshvara and Dakrabhimeshvara do not achieve the balance between verticality and outwardly expansive form that marks the Rajarani Temple (*c.* 1030), the most famous example of the spire cluster in Kalinga (see fig. 75). Typical of the Kalinga style, the Rajarani is marked by a sense of massive bulk. Its almost square and somewhat stunted 'core' turret is embedded within a system of smaller versions of itself. Two half-spires emerge from the central projections of the tower's four sides, creating a steplike progression. Between these elements are miniature spires, each capping corresponding projections in the walls and mouldings. The projections, rounded by numerous minor offsets, complement the massiveness of the core and seem almost to bulge outwards, creating a sense of expansion from the centre. Verticality is preserved, however, by the extension of the miniature spires into the lower levels of the main superstructure.

75. Rajarani Temple, Bhubaneshwar, *c.* 1030

Of all the *nāgara* temple styles, that of Kalinga most consistently maintains a close relationship between architectural and sculptural form. On the Rajarani Temple, the column-like salients of the walls bear high-relief figures that seem to stand free from their backdrop of decorative scrollwork and that are instilled with an energy analogous to that in the bounding rhythms of the salients themselves. These sculptures are the final articulation of the burgeoning forth of forms from the temple's core.

Temples of the spire-cluster type are usually considered an anomaly in Kalinga, the dominant concern having been with massive form and uninterrupted verticality from shrine to tower. Spire clusters are nonetheless an important feature in subsequent temples. During the next phase of the Kalinga style there was a shift away from such major features of the Rajarani as prominent spire clusters and the round, column-like wall salients and rounded outline the salients give to the plan. Instead there was a return to a treatment of the shrine as a blocklike cubical mass, although vertical segmentation remained. The Siddheshvara Temple (*c.* 1050) represents the beginning of this phase. Although small spires form a continuous band around the four sides of the trunk of the shrine tower, they are flatly articulated decorative accents, with none of the sculptural quality of the Rajarani. The Brahmeshvara Temple is more monumental and sculpturally richer than the Siddheshvara, although the spire is still squat and square. The vertical salients were cubically conceived, as were the shrine niches on the lower walls and superstructure. High-relief figural sculpture was placed only in the open areas between the salients, where it does not detract from the temple's cubic effect. Miniature spires serve only as minor decorative elements, not as integral parts of the compositional structure.

The Lingaraja Temple (for illustration *see* BHUBANESHWAR), probably built in the late 11th century, synthesizes the sculptural dynamism of the Rajarani with the cubic solidity of the Brahmeshvara. The salients of the superstructure are rounded rather than flattened yet are wholly integrated with the vertical wall. On the vertical salients next to the corners of the superstructure is a series of miniature spires of diminishing sizes imposed one above the other, enhancing the soaring verticality of the tower without interrupting its smooth line. On the lower walls, the sculptural organization echoes that of the Brahmeshvara Temple; the vertical projections bear relief sculptures framed within shrine forms, with the recessed areas between them containing figural sculptures. The sculptures, while carved with a similar level of relief to the Brahmeshvara, are surrounded by more space; the images within the shrine niches also seem less constricted within their frames.

The transition from Somavamshi to Ganga rule did not disrupt the pace of temple building in and around Bhubaneshwar, though some scholars feel that temples of the early Ganga period are unrefined and awkward. This assessment is often applied to the Jagannatha Temple at Puri (*c.* 1140). The temple is inaccessible to non-Hindus and is encased in layers of ritually applied plaster, a common feature of temples in active worship. The temple's general outlines are, however, readily apparent. The spire is massive and the tallest in the Kalinga region (approx. 65 m). Yet its proportions are heavy, and it lacks the soaring verticality of the Lingaraja.

The temples discussed thus far have spires of the *pañcaratha* type, that is, each face of the spire is articulated with five salients or offsets. The spire of the Megheshvara Temple (datable by inscription to *c.* 1190) has three vertical salients flanking the central one, making it seven-faced (*saptaratha*), a form used frequently, but not exclusively, in subsequent periods. The spire of the Megheshvara has an almost circular plan, and a curved horizontal movement is created by the rounded form of the salients and their close placement one beside the other. Small spires, superimposed one above the other, decorate the subsidiary salients as on the Lingaraja. The temple's vertical outline is uninterrupted.

The Lingaraja Temple at Bhubaneshwar served as a model for many of the temples built between *c.* 1250 and *c.* 1350. In this group the number of vertical salients was often multiplied to seven, while the sculptural decoration achieved a new exuberance. Among the finest examples is the Ananta Vasudeva Temple at Bhubaneshwar, datable by inscription to 1278. Though closely related to the Lingaraja, this building is not simply a copy on a smaller scale. The spire has five receding faces like the Lingaraja, but the walls are divided into seven salients. The latter were given a rounded treatment, thus giving the wall surface a curved, almost undulating effect. Echoes of the Lingaraja in the proportions of the shrine and its interrelationship to the forehall are also seen in such temples as the Chitrakarini, Yameshvara and Sari Deul, all in Bhubaneshwar. Their sculptural programmes—both figurative and decorative—are richly conceived and executed, but the work has suffered from erosion due to the softness of the stone.

Also dating to this period are the Surya Temple at Konarak (*c.* 1250) and the Gangeshvari Temple at Beyalispati (between Konarak and Bhubaneshwar). The Surya Temple was conceived as the sun god's chariot, its 24 large wheels (diam. approx. 3 m) representing the signs of the zodiac. The Gangeshvari, dedicated to the Goddess, is the only known 13th-century Kalinga temple with a rectangular rather than square shrine, a format often used for Goddess temples in the 9th and 10th centuries (for example the Varahi Temple at Chaurasi and Vaital Deul at Bhubaneshwar; *see* §5(i)(e) above). In its exuberance, the sculpture at Beyalispati resembles Konarak, with which it is probably contemporary.

Despite a conservative trend dependent primarily on the model of the Lingaraja, new variations were made on the traditional Kalinga temple form. Buildings displaying an experimental use of miniature spires include the Chateshvara Temple at Kisenpur (near Cuttack), datable by inscription to *c.* 1220, and the Gopinatha Temple (*c.* 1250) at Kakudia (near Bhubaneshwar). On the Chateshvara Temple, the central vertical section of the superstructure is covered with rows of projecting miniature spires that become smaller as they ascend. On either side of each central section is a vertical row of four small spires. The latter device was used on the Lingaraja, though the strong three-dimensionality of the Chateshvara's miniature spires suggests links with the Rajarani Temple. Such a relationship is indicated further by various sculptural elements; the figures of the lower walls, for instance, were placed in scrollwork frames rather than in miniature shrine forms. Further adaptations of older temple forms occur in the forehall and include pilasters entwined by serpents and windows with lattice patterns that recall the Mukteshvara Temple at Bhubaneshwar (see fig. 51 above). This borrowing of earlier architectural and sculptural forms is apparent in other 13th-century temples as well. The Gopinatha Temple, for example, offers an unusual variation on the spire-cluster theme. The temple has no forehall, but pillared porticos were placed on each side before the entrance and cardinal niches. Each portico has a pyramidal roof with a cluster of five miniature spires above. This spire design is an adaptation of the Rajarani, but the use of porticos points to inspiration from central India.

A further 'archaistic' or 'eclectic' phase occurred in Kalinga architecture in the late 13th century. Examples include the Lakshmi Temple in the Jagannatha compound at Puri and the Parvati Temple in the Lingaraja compound at Bhubaneshwar. An inscription indicates that the Parvati Temple was in existence in 1275. While both buildings are modelled on the Mukteshvara, the Parvati Temple is more complete, the superstructure of the Lakshmi Temple being uncarved. The vertical wall elements of the Parvati shrine and forehall are essentially taller and thinner versions of those on the Mukteshvara—faceted salients flanked by serpent pilasters. The surface decoration of the spire recalls the Mukteshvara, particularly in its use of an interlocking mesh of decorative window designs (*jāla*). The Parvati Temple, with its attenuated, linear elegance, is a rather mannered variation of the decorative exuberance and weighty form of the Mukteshvara.

A later group of temples (*c.* 1300–50), at first glance similar to the earlier conservative group, displays several variations on the basic Kalinga temple form. These buildings show less concern with sculptural decoration and greater interest in an abstract treatment of various standard architectural forms. The Vakeshvara Temple at Bhubaneshwar is an example (see fig. 76). The plan of the shrine can be described as *navaratha*, the walls and spire being articulated into nine vertical salients on each side, a compression of forms seen in a less attenuated and crowded format on earlier buildings (e.g. the Lingaraja and Ananta Vasudeva). The salients and their shrine niches seem almost squeezed into the wall surface of both the shrine and the forehall. On the spire each salient is flanked by four superimposed miniature spires, as on the Lingaraja. Between the central and corner salients are two narrow vertical divisions consisting of small pyramidal roofs and narrow, rounded mouldings. These divisions contribute to the ascending vertical rhythm of the spire, enlivening a

76. Vakeshvara Temple, Bhubaneshwar, *c.* 1300–50

surface already animated by the play of light and shadow created by the piled horizontal forms.

Other temples in this group are the Varuneshvara, Mitreshvara and Makareshvara, all at Bhubaneshwar. The rounded salients of the Mitreshvara produce a curved horizontal outline (the upper portion of the spire has fallen). The Varuneshvara Temple is better preserved and sculpturally richer than the Mitreshvara, although its proportions are squat and the various architectural elements clumsily articulated. The shrine of the Makareshvara has a squarish format, recalling the Brahmeshvara Temple, although the surface treatment of the spire salients is reminiscent of the Lingaraja.

In the 13th century, two additional structures entered the repertory of architectural forms, the hall of dance (*nāṭāmaṇḍapa*) and hall of offerings (*bhogamaṇḍapa*). The dance hall appears as an integral part of the architectural conception in the Yameshvara Temple at Bhubaneshwar and Surya Temple at Konarak, to name but two examples. In both cases it is a separate structure placed on the same longitudinal axis as the shrine and forehall. Later these halls were added to existing temples, for example the Lingaraja and Ananta Vasudeva. In the latter the halls of dance and offerings are simple, pavilion-like structures with pyramidal roofs and unadorned walls and must date to the 14th century or later.

The mid-14th century marked the end of great temple building activity in Kalinga. The reasons for this decline are difficult to determine. Political events do not seem to have contributed greatly—the Ganga dynasty did not fall until 1435 (nearly a century after the Vakeshvara Temple group was built) and was succeeded by the Suryavamshis, who ruled until 1540.

Only a few significant structures have been assigned to the 15th century, such as the Narasinhanatha Temple at Narasinghnath (Sambalpur District) and the Kapileshvara Temple at Bhubaneshwar. The latter's traditional association with the Suryavamshi king Kapilendradeva (*reg* *c.* 1435–70) has not been corroborated by inscription, and it is possible that the temple even post-dates the 15th century. Its squarish spire, with shallow miniature spire forms around the base, recalls the Brahmeshvara Temple at Bhubaneshwar. The various architectural elements are squat in their proportions; rising to a height of only about 12 m, the temple lacks the monumentality of earlier examples.

Vanga. In the 11th and 12th centuries, a group of temples with common stylistic features was constructed in south-west Bengal and neighbouring portions of northern Orissa. Twenty-six temples at Telkupi (Purulia District, West Bengal) were destroyed in 1957 when a dam was built across the Damodar River. A small number of similar temples survive at other sites, such as Banda (Purulia District), Barakar (Burdwan District) and Khiching (northern Orissa). Ruined examples, with little more than the moulding preserved, have been discovered at Katras and other sites in the neighbourhood of Barakar.

Vanga temples are generally considered to be provincial variants of the Kalinga style. This is particularly true in the case of Temple 4 at Barakar, which derived its general configuration from the 7th-century Parashurameshvara Temple at Bhubaneshwar (*see* §5(i)(e) above). For this reason it has been assigned to the 8th century, but sculptural style suggests a date in the 10th century or later.

The Kinchakeshvari Temple at Khiching is also clearly related to the Kalinga style in the treatment of its base mouldings and the way in which the vertical salients of its lower walls continue along the entire length of the superstructure. Its tall and narrow proportions, never seen at Bhubaneshwar, are comparable to the 'old temple' at Banda and temples 17 and 18 at Telkupi (destr.). The Kinchakeshvari is a reconstructed building on ancient foundations, however, and the accuracy of its rebuilding has been questioned. Judging from the style of the sculpture, the architectural fragments used in the rebuilding date approximately to the 13th century.

The Chandrashekhara Temple at Khiching (see fig. 77) and those at Banda and Telkupi (destr.) bear similarities to the Kalinga style in general outline and in the treatment of some architectural features, but they constitute a distinct idiom. The Chandrashekhara Temple, judging from the sculptural treatment of the doorframe, dates to the late 10th century or the 11th. Though sometimes taken as a later reconstruction (see Donaldson, 1985, i, p. 244), the building's structural integrity seems inarguable, as does its use in illustrating the Vanga style. Each side of the temple is divided into three parts, with the broad central salients housing a projecting, roofed niche. The east side has a projecting entrance; there is no forehall as exists in all Vanga temples. The recessed walls on either side are articulated by a series of pilasters, alternately broad and narrow. These are supported by tall base mouldings, three of which also run across the central projections. These mouldings are a variant of the Kalinga type, consisting of a pot-shaped element (*kalaśa*) placed between square courses (*khura*s). A smaller variant of these is used as a 'capital' for the pilasters. A narrow recess marks the completely undecorated transition between wall and spire. The spires at Telkupi, however, typically had a mesh on the central projection—a decorative form used throughout north India—while the recessed sides had two or more vertical divisions, each composed of horizontal mouldings, as in the early temples of Bhubaneshwar. Even in the Telkupi temples thought to date as late as the 12th century (e.g. Temple 6), the vertical divisions of the spire adhere to the wall mass, which retains a cubic sense in contrast to the rounded forms found in Bhubaneshwar temples of the 11th and 12th centuries.

The later architecture of Vanga is represented by the brick-built Siddheshvara Temple at Bahulara (Bankura District). The sanctum (7.6 m across) shows prominent projections on each side with numerous minor offsets. The two-storey wall carries cardinal niches with pediments in the shapes of spires. The central projections in the spire

77. Chandrashekhara Temple, Khiching, *c.* 13th century

itself carry rows of aediculae, which are surmounted by dormer-like medallions, a feature distantly related to the *gavākṣa* or *candraśālā* motif commonly used in Orissa. The subsidiary salients have been treated as vertical spines worked with a mesh pattern. The corners of the spire (*veṇukośa*s) are divided into storeys by rounded discs. Assignable to the 13th century, this building is a noteworthy culmination to a regional tradition of architecture of which only vestiges remain.

Bihar. The later temple architecture of Bihar is represented by only a few ruined monuments and architectural fragments stored in museums. Though a continuous architectural history is virtually impossible to reconstruct, the buildings at Deo Barnarak give some idea of the buildings that were erected. The largest temple, dedicated to the god Surya, was preceded by a hall (now collapsed) that rested on four stone pillars. One pillar carries an inscription of Jivitagupta (*reg c.* AD 715–25). Neither the pillar nor the temple can be assigned to Jivitagupta's time, however. The pillar follows conventions of the 5th century, while the temple can be placed in the mid- to late 12th century due to the multiplication of cornices in the entablature *(varaṇḍikā)* and the smooth spire with vestigial corner discs (*bhūmyāmalaka*). Also indicative of a late date are the slender offsets terminating in attached half-spires. The ruined brick temples at Konch and Deo Markandeya are assignable to the same period. Another site at which building took place was NALANDA, but little more than foundations are preserved there. Nalanda was sacked by the Khalji rulers of Delhi at the end of the 12th century, after which it fell into ruins. As the sultanate expanded its power in the 13th century, indigenous traditions declined precipitously. It appears that no temples of consequence were constructed in Bihar during the 14th and 15th centuries.

BIBLIOGRAPHY

R. L. Mitra: *Antiquities of Orissa*, 2 vols (Calcutta, 1875–80)
M. M. Ganguly: *Orissa and Her Remains: Ancient and Medieval* (Calcutta, 1912)
R. P. Chanda: *Bhañja Dynasty of Mayurbhanj and their Ancient Capital Khiching* (Baripada, 1929)
N. K. Bose: *Canons of Orissan Architecture* (Calcutta, 1932)
S. K. Sarasvati: 'The Begunia Group of Temples', *J. Ind. Soc. Orient. A.*, i/2 (1933), pp. 124–8
S. Kramrisch: 'Kaliṅga Temples', *J. Ind. Soc. Orient. A.*, ii/1 (1934), pp. 43–60
P. Brown: *Indian Architecture (Buddhist and Hindu Periods)* (Bombay, [1941], rev. Bombay, 1956)
S. Kramrisch: 'The Walls of Orissan Temples', *J. Ind. Soc. Orient. A.*, xv (1947), pp. 178–96
P. P. Acharya: 'Dikpālas and their Śaktis in Temples of Orissa', *Orissa Hist. Res. J.*, xi/2 (1953), pp. 49–52
S. K. Sarasvati: 'Temples of Orissa', *Orissa Hist. Res. J.*, xi/4 (1953), pp. 235–53
D. Mitra: 'Four Little-known Khākahra Temples of Orissa', *J. Asiat. Soc. Bengal*, n. s. 3, ii/1 (1960), pp. 1–23
K. C. Panigrahi: *Archaeological Remains at Bhubaneswar* (Calcutta, 1961)
——: *Chronology of the Bhauma Karas and Somqvaṃśis of Orissa* (Madras, [1961])
A. Banerji: 'An Unfinished Rekha Deul of Purulia', *J. Asiat. Soc.*, vii/3–4 (1965), pp. 163–8
D. Mitra: *Telkupi: A Submerged Temple-site in West Bengal*, Mem. Archaeol. Surv. India, lxxvi (Delhi, 1969)
K. C. Mishra: *The Cult of Jagganātha* (Calcutta, 1971)
T. Donaldson: 'Development of the *Vajra-Mastaka* on Orissan Temples', *E. & W.*, xxvi/3–4 (1976), pp. 419–33
K. Lal: *Temples and Sculptures of Bhubaneswar* (Delhi, 1976)
S. K. Sarasvati: *Architecture of Bengal, i: Ancient Phase* (Calcutta, 1976)
T. Donaldson: 'The Sculptural Program of the Orissan Rekha-Deul', *Sidelights on the History and Culture of Orissa*, ed. M. N. Das (Cuttack, 1977), pp. 563–613
D. Mitra: *Bhubaneswar* (New Delhi, 1977)
T. Donaldson: 'Development of the Nāṭamandira in Orissan Temple Architecture', *Kalādarśana: American Studies in the Art of India*, ed. J. G. Williams (Leiden, 1981), pp. 35–46
K. C. Panigrahi: *History of Orissa (Hindu Period)* (Cuttack, 1981)
A. Joshi: *History and Culture of Khijjingakotta under the Bhanjas* (Delhi, 1983)
T. Donaldson: *Hindu Temple Art of Orissa*, 3 vols (Leiden, 1985)
S. Huntington with J. Huntington: *The Art of Ancient India, Buddhist, Hindu, Jain* (New York and Tokyo, 1985), pp. 415–48
W. Smith: 'The Mukteśvara Temple at Bhubaneswar and Archaism during the Gaṅga Period in Orissa', *Orientations*, xxiv/4 (April 1993), pp. 72–6

WALTER SMITH

(e) Central. After the great building campaigns of the 10th and 11th centuries, architecture in central India entered a period of relative decline. While the basic components of the temple tradition continued, architectural forms became less elaborate and the decoration increasingly stereotyped. This change is attributable mainly to the Islamic conquest of north India and the submission of indigenous princes to the sultanate in Delhi. Temple endowments were eroded and available funds for new construction significantly reduced. Later temples are found at such long-established sites as KHAJURAHO and Naresar as well as such sites as Khojra and Deotaloa, which have groups or individual temples of the later period only.

At Khajuraho, the Duladeo Temple was the last major project before the decline of the Chandella dynasty as a significant power in the 12th century. This building ostensibly maintains earlier building practices, but there are a number of important changes. The temple has a porch, hall and sanctum but lacks an ambulatory, a standard feature of the larger Khajuraho temples. The sanctum has seven projections on each side (*saptaratha*), and the lower walls bear three rows of repetitive sculptures; these are divided by two registers of sharply cut mouldings. The superstructure is multi-spired (*śekharī*), following the nearby precedent of the Kandariya Mahadeva and Vishvanatha temples (*see* §5(i)(g) above). The wall surfaces and projections are dryly executed, but passages of brittle exuberance are seen in the multi-storey pediment facing the superstructure on its east side and the figural groups on the exterior corners of the hall and on its ceiling. Fragmentary inscriptions and mason marks have been used to place the Duladeo in the first half of the 12th century. This date is corroborated by a comparison of the epigraphs with an inscription of 1117–18 (Vikrama year 1174) from the nearly ruined temple of Nilakantha Mahadeva.

The direction of architectural developments towards the end of the 12th century is indicated by work at Naresar (near Gwalior). Art activity appears to have continued there until at least 1192–3 (Vikrama year 1249), the date of a dedicatory inscription on an image pedestal. One large temple (and numerous small shrines) at the site can be assigned to this period. The large temple rests on a moulded plinth and is subject to seven projections on each side. The socle (*vedībandha*) carries a string-course of diamonds and circles; the wall is undecorated save for framed images of divinities on projecting pilasters. The spire (partially reconstructed) lacks any carving except for slim corner discs (*karṇāmalaka*s). The more elaborate doorway has cylindrical pilasters on the jambs that are carved with cork-screw-like bands. Similar designs are found in the later temples of western India.

The temple at Baragaon (Tikamgarh District) is also late 12th century but better preserved and more elaborate in its architectural configuration (see fig. 78). Dedicated to Shiva, this building has a *śekharī* superstructure and hall with a wedge-shaped (*phaṁsanā*) roof. As with many later buildings in the region, the mouldings and walls are constructed of a hard granite that is difficult to carve; consequently the doorway is fitted with a sandstone frame. The spire, lacking carved detail (except for the slim corner discs), anticipates the reduction of the superstructure to a simple turret, an approach that dominates temple architecture from this time forward. Temples similar to that at Baragaon are found at Narainpur and Ahar (both Tikamgarh District). The latter is a Jaina foundation, now heavily reconstructed but associated with an inscription of 1180–81 (Vikrama year 1237).

The development of more modest temples after the 11th century is indicated by shrines at Tilori, Paroli, Chhimka and other sites controlled by the late Kachchhapaghatas, Yajvapalas and other minor rulers of central

78. Shiva Temple, Baragaon, *c.* late 12th century

India. These shrines often continue the long-established *maṇḍapikā*-type temple, with the wall composed of alternating pilasters, slabs and image niches. As a rule, carved ornamentation was reduced with the passage of time. Examples at Naresar have plain exterior walls made of large uncarved slabs of stone; some are capped by wedge-shaped (*phaṁsanā*) superstructures composed of cornices; others carry drastically simplified curvilinear (*latina*) spires. A group of three temples with *phaṁsanā*-type superstructures are found at Deoguna (near Jaso); still others are at Khojra (near Lalitpur) and Sakarra (near Kadwaha).

At Deogarh, which has a long history as a Jaina centre, modest temples were also built during the 11th and 12th centuries. These shrines are generally small cubical cellae, some with attached porches. The walls, like those at Naresar, were often made of simple slabs. Some examples exhibit offsets in plan, but surface articulation is of the utmost simplicity. This severity extends to the superstructures, some of which are smooth, low pyramids. Many temples are reconstructions using older material; inscriptions indicate that Deogarh was an active Jaina centre into the 16th century.

In the Malwa territory of the later Paramara rulers, there are shrines at Chandpur, south of Sanchi, and Rahatgarh, near Gyaraspur. Late temples of the *bhūmija* type (*see* §(c) above) are also found in Malwa. The Shiva Temple at Alirajpur (Jhabua District) has been dated to the late 14th century (Deva, 1975). Its overall design resembles the Udayeshvara Temple at Udaipur (*see* §5(i)(g) above), but the forms are mechanically rendered and conventionalized. Of similar date is the Shiva Temple at Barokhera (Mandsaur District). This is a 'pseudo-*bhūmija*' temple, having vertical rows of aediculae (*kūṭastambha*s) only at the corners of the otherwise standard *latina*-type superstructure. Simple *latina* temples were also built into the 14th century, as evidenced by examples at Udaipur. As is often the case with later temples, the spires are reduced to turrets without decoration.

Ruins in the environs of Chanderi have been associated with the late Pratiharas (see C. B. Trivedi). At the village of Runwaso are a number of Jaina temples, most of them extensively renovated and whitewashed. One small *maṇḍapikā*-shrine, however, is relatively pristine. The decoration on its exterior wall (two superimposed rows of pilasters divided by a narrow band of diamond-shaped lozenges) is simple, repetitive and rather dry, this overall approach to surface articulation becoming standard from the late 11th century. The Vishnu Temple at Marhkhera survives only in fragments. The doorframe of the forehall is the most outstanding feature; it is divided into five bands, all crisply carved. Along with the cluster of figures at the base of the jambs, the overall execution resembles later work at Kadwaha and thus can probably be dated to the late 11th or early 12th century. At Besro, also near Chanderi, the shrine locally known as Devi Marha is the only temple now surviving on a large raised plinth. The broadly articulated *triratha* sanctum is faced by an open-sided hall. No superstructure survives. The stark exterior is devoid of decoration, while the columns of the hall have simply rendered grotesques (*kīrtimukha*) and overflowing-pot (*pūrṇaghaṭa*) motifs. A variety of sculptural fragments are at the site. A short inscription has been assigned on palaeographical grounds to the 13th century, a date supported by the simplification of both sculptural and architectural form. The temples at Ballarpur are similar and probably coeval.

In south-eastern Madhya Pradesh the Haihaya or Kalachuri dynasty remained in power into the 13th century. Later temples are scattered among various sites. The 11th-century Virateshvara Temple at Sohagpur shows a high level of achievement and served as a prototype for later works. Dating to *c.* 1200 is the temple of Gauri-Shankara at Bheraghat, built within the enclosure of the 10th-century hypaethral *yoginī* temple. The Gauri-Shankara is heavily repaired, but the outer walls of the sanctum (*saptaratha* in articulation and divided into two levels by a narrow moulding) retain their original form. Most of the sculptures are broken. A votive inscription near the right doorjamb of the sanctum, dating to the reign of Vijayasimha (*reg c.* 1180–95), indicates the temple's existence at that time.

At Deotalao (about 20 km north of Chandrehe) are three later temples. The Somanatha Temple bears general similarity to the Gauri-Shankhara at Bheraghat and like it is restored. The Bhairava Temple consists of a sanctum only, around which are placed a series of six columns that support a projecting roof. The superstructure resembles the hut-shaped roofs of late Bengali temples. A third, unnamed shrine at the site is similar in form.

Temples of the 12th and 13th centuries in the south-eastern part of Madhya Pradesh are associated with the Ratanpur branch of the Kalachuri dynasty. These are monumental, elaborately ornamented conceptions, showing the continued vitality of temple building in central India. The Mahadeva Temple at Markanda and the Shiva Temple at Pali (*c.* mid-12th century) are *saptaratha* in plan, with continuous bands of sculptures on their lower walls. Both have forehalls, although that of the temple at Pali is rebuilt. The upper portion of the superstructure is modern. The Vishnu Temple at Janjgir (early 13th century) consists of a *saptaratha* sanctum; only the base of the superstructure survives. The walls are densely sculpted. Two bands of images surround the lower walls, and the doorway is flanked by two broad columns, which are completely covered with rectangular relief panels arranged in series of horizontal bands.

BIBLIOGRAPHY

H. V. Trivedi: 'The Yajvapālas of Narwar', *J. Madhya Pradesh Itihasa Parishad*, i (1959), pp. 22–32
K. Bruhn: *The Jina-Images of Deogarh* (Leiden, 1969)
K. Deva: *Temples of North India* (New Delhi, 1969)
Ramasharma: 'Two Inscriptions of Ajayapāladeva', *Epig. Ind.*, xxxviii (1969), pp. 132–4
P. R. Srinivasan: 'Five Gwalior Gangola Tank-bed Inscriptions', *Epig. Ind.*, xxxviii (1970), pp. 305–12
K. Deva: 'Bhumija Temples', *Studies in Indian Temple Architecture*, ed. P. Chandra (New Delhi, 1975), pp. 90–113
B. L. Nagarch: 'Temples at Sakarra', *J. Madhya Pradesh Itihasa Parishad*, x (1976), pp. 55–7
R. Ali: *Art and Architecture of the Kalacuris* (Delhi, 1980)
R. K. Sharma: *The Kalachuris and Their Times* (Delhi, 1980)
C. B. Trivedi: 'Late Pratihara Temples from Bundelkhand', *Madhu: Recent Researches in Indian Archaeology and Art History*, ed. M. S. Nagaraja Rao (Delhi, 1981), pp. 195–8
K. Deva: *Khajuraho* (New Delhi, 1987)

□

(f) Karnataka and Andhra Pradesh.

11th–13th centuries. The predominant temple form in the lower Deccan from about the beginning of the 11th century is what Fergusson (1876) identified as 'Chalukyan', a third category lying between his 'Indo-Aryan' (corresponding to *nāgara*) and 'Dravidian' (*drāviḍa*). It is now widely held that the '*vesara*' mentioned in medieval architectural treatises refers to this 'Chalukyan' form, a view supported by the fact that the term '*vesara*' implies a mule or hybrid, and the temples in question seem to combine *nāgara* and *drāviḍa* characteristics. Their architectural vocabulary, however, is entirely *drāviḍa*. Whatever term may have been used by those who built them, these temples belong to a late stage of development of the Karnata version of *drāviḍa*, which had formed during the 7th and 8th centuries under the Chalukyas of Badami and which had continued to develop in less monumental works under the hegemony of the Rashtrakuta dynasty (*see* §5(i)(h) above). It would be impossible to define at what stage *drāviḍa* became *vesara*, so the term 'Karnata *drāviḍa*' seems most appropriate, as it is for the earlier monuments.

As in the 7th and 8th centuries, a unique variety of temple types was created in the lower Deccan in this period. *Phāṁsanā* temples (with stepped pyramidal superstructures of overhanging eaves) were a widespread, less complex alternative to the Karnata *drāviḍa*. Various modes of *nāgara* developed, and experiments were made in the hybridization of *nāgara* and *drāviḍa*, more self-conscious kinds of mixture than those in the *vesara* temples.

With the advent of the Chalukyas of Kalyana (*see* CHALUKYA, §2), who held sway in Karnataka and beyond, with one brief interregnum, until the end of the 12th century, a new, comparatively dispersed pattern of temple foundation is discernible. It reflects a widespread system of administration under which divisions of territory were ruled by governors. The cultural milieu of the Chalukyas was shared by their feudatories, who built the same kinds of temples. The relatively small scale of the monuments, compared with the 8th-century works of the Chalukyas of Badami, also seems to reflect the decentralized administrative system and a dispersal of available wealth. Soapstone, the fine-grained, grey chloritic schist widely employed from about the mid-11th century, suited this scale of building, as well as the regional predilection for works of great complexity and intricate detail. Patronage of temples, only occasionally by kings, was more often by other members of the court, male or female. Ministers, generals, merchants and their wives are all cited in inscriptions as patrons. Sometimes two or more members of a family founded a temple together, one reason for the growing popularity of multi-shrine temples, in which a number of sanctuaries with superstructures (*vimāna*s)—sometimes as many as five—were attached to a shared hall (*maṇḍapa*). Shaiva temples were the most numerous in this period, but Vaishnava and Jaina foundations were also widespread.

During the first century of rule by the Chalukyas of Kalyana a great increase in temple building took place over a wide area of northern Karnataka. Few Chalukya temples survive in the vicinity of Kalyana, not mentioned as the capital before the mid-11th century. In the earliest phase, when relatively modest shrines were being built in sandstone, activity seems to have been concentrated around the ancient heartland. Busy workshops at AIHOLE and Ron were clearly immediate descendants of local schools active during the Rashtrakuta period. Towards the mid-11th century the Aihole and Ron schools appear to have supplied the craftsmen for more ambitious works, chiefly in areas to the south of the former heartland. Lakkundi, in particular, became the centre for a school responsible for a number of the more important temples sponsored by the Chalukyas of Kalyana, which can thus be seen as the culmination of an unbroken strand of the Karnata *drāviḍa* tradition that may be termed the 'mainstream'.

The last of the mainstream temples, such as the Sarasvati Temple, Gadag, the Dodda Basappa at Dambal and the Mallikarjuna at Kuruvatti, date to about the beginning of the 12th century. Thereafter the mainstream began to be absorbed beyond recognition into other currents that had begun to spring up during the later decades of the 11th century. Karnata *drāviḍa* temples had begun to appear, which, though related to the mainstream, did not belong to it. Non-mainstream works are found over a wide region, in almost every direction from the mainstream core around Lakkundi. Stylistic analysis of mouldings and other details shows that these temples were built by many different workshops or schools, some known only by a single surviving monument (for example the Mukteshvara Temple at Chaudanpur). Others were clearly long-lived and prolific, in particular the school responsible for (among other works) the Siddheshvara Temple at Haveri, the Someshvara and Rameshvara at Gadag and several temples at Lakshmeshvara. Through these various schools the Karnata *drāviḍa* tradition, despite the demise of the Chalukya dynasty, lived on through the 13th century.

Two prolific non-mainstream offshoots were the most distant from the tradition's origins. Early in the 12th century a southern Karnata branch emerged, under the Hoysala rulers of Dorasamudra (now Halebid), who, after 1189, vied with the Yadava dynasty for dominance in the former Chalukya territories of Karnataka. In Telangana (north-western Andhra Pradesh), Karnata *drāviḍa* temples, along with other varieties, were built during the 11th century, while the region was under Chalukya hegemony, and subsequently under the Kakatiya rulers of Hanamkonda and Warangal.

Northern Karnataka. Throughout the period under discussion, the typical temple plan consisted of a single *vimāna* (the shrine proper) attached via an antechamber (*antarāla*) to a hall (*maṇḍapa*). Halls were normally square and flat-roofed, with four pillars at the centre and walls articulated on the exterior by means of the same architectural language as the *vimāna.* An increasingly elaborate, barrel-roofed fronton (*śukanāsa*) rose over the antechamber. Of temples with more than one shrine, the three-*vimāna* type was the most widespread, with the shrines attached to the back and sides of the hall.

From single-cell porches evolved multi-cellular, open pillared halls (*raṅgamaṇḍapa*s) that were used for performances of sacred music and dance, with a seat (*kakṣāsana*) around the perimeter. Often with a serrated outline on plan, an open hall may have been a substitute for the usual closed type (*gūḍhamaṇḍapa*), or it may have been an additional element placed in front. It was in the large, open halls that the characteristic pillars of the period were displayed most effectively; the predominant type was the polished, 'lathe-turned' variety (*see* §5(i)(h) above), with knife-edge mouldings, seeming almost to spin. The open hall of the Tarakeshvara Temple at Hangal contains, at its centre, the most impressive example in Karnataka of a domical, corbelled lotus ceiling.

The composition of the *drāviḍa* (or *vesara*) *vimāna* followed the well-established principle of articulating the tiers of the pyramidal exterior as interlinked aediculae or shrine images: principally, at first, *kūṭa-*, *śālā-* and *pañjara-*aediculae (see fig. 59 above), crowned on the 'parapet' by pavilions that were square-domed, barrel-roofed or horseshoe-gabled, respectively. These forms projected from strata of mouldings that followed the types and sequences established at PATTADAKAL in the early 8th century (*see* §5(i)(h) above). In plan the progressive stepping forward of the *vimāna* walls towards the centre, on each side, became increasingly pronounced and was accompanied by a proliferation of offsets within individual components.

In particular, the staggered *śālā*-aedicula developed in the Rashtrakuta period was further transformed into a double-staggered form. Centrally positioned, this element is essential to the complex, dynamic character of late Karnata *drāviḍa vimāna*s. Conceptually, it is a configuration of five aediculae: a *pañjara*-aedicula (that is, an end-on *śālā*-aedicula) at the centre, with two *śālā*-aediculae emerging one from the other on either side. This double-staggered *śālā*-aedicula, used already by the turn of the 11th century, was the first and most widespread of many ingenious composite, interpenetrating forms.

At first it was usual for the top storey (*tala*) of a *vimāna*, including the crowning 'dome', to be a unitary *alpa vimāna* (squat *kuṭa*-aedicula) form, always staggered. This form was used in the typical, three-storey composition of the beginning of the period, as at Aihole and Ron, and in the Naganatha Temple at Mahakuta. The lower two storeys, with the usual *kuṭa*-aediculae at the corners, had double-staggered *śālā*-aediculae in the centre of the first storey and single-staggered ones in the second storey. A central vertical chain was thereby created, not a chain of identical forms, but a progression downwards from non-aedicular wall to staggered aedicula to double-staggered aedicula with outward-sliding gables. Thus the sense of downward and outward expansion was augmented by a progressive 'unfolding' down the face of the *vimāna.* Elaborations of this principle are the Mallikarjuna Temple at Sudi, with five aedicular projections in the plan and four storeys, and the lavish west *vimāna* of the Kashivishveshvara at Lakkundi, with five projections and three storeys.

By the end of the 11th century it had become the norm that all storeys of a *vimāna*, including the top one supporting the dome, should be of identical, multi-aedicular composition. Thus a continuous radial pattern was created, enhancing the sense of expanding repetition through the descending aedicula-chains. The Kalleshvara Temple at Kukkanur is an early (first half of the 11th century) example of a typical scheme for three-projection *vimāna*s, with three storeys, each with central, double-staggered *śālā*-aediculae flanked by *kūṭa*-aediculae. Kukkanur is also an early example of the use of a motif that augments the central spine of the superstructure and is sometimes mistaken for a 'northern' characteristic of 'Chalukyan' temples. The device in question is an extra horseshoe arch or vegetal archway (*tōrāṇa*) just below the central horseshoe arch of each *śālā*, as if the former is emerging from the latter. A sense that the resulting chain of arch motifs is cascading down the *vimāna* face is enhanced by the depiction of every arch as issuing from the jaws of its monster-face finial.

Horseshoe-arch cascades were incorporated into a characteristic scheme for five-projection *vimāna*s, with four storeys of identical composition, at the Amriteshvara Temple at Annigeri and the Siddheshvara Temple at Havri (see fig. 79) and later at the Mahadeva Temple, ITTAGI (dedicated 1112), and the Tarakeshvara Temple, Hangal (*c.* mid-12th century). In these examples central, double-staggered *śālā*-aediculae and corner *kūṭa*-aediculae are accompanied by a new type of intermediate component. This is a *drāviḍa* form of *kūṭastambha*, comprising an embedded, staggered pillar (*stambha*) crowned by a narrow *kūṭa* pavilion.

This tendency towards a pervasive use of identical aedicula types reached its apogee in stellate shrine forms,

79. Siddheshvara Temple, Havri, late 11th century; main shrine viewed from the north

the most radical transformation of the Karnata *drāviḍa vimāna*. Stellate temples are found at Savadi, Kalagi, Konnur and Dambal. Of these the most ambitious, and the only one to survive virtually intact, is the Dodda Basappa at Dambal, where, unusually, the hall and the *vimāna* are both stellate. The *vimāna* plan is based on a square rotated about its centre to create a star with 24 points, each point locating the salient angle of a *kūṭa*-aedicula. Six further, identical storeys rise to a dome of identical stellate plan. Between the primary elements, re-entrant projections, located on plan by rotated equilateral triangles, are treated as deeply embedded *kūṭastambhas*.

Earlier in Karnataka a preoccupation had developed with secondary aediculae, shrinelike niche-surrounds or wall shrines, more often than not housing no sculpted image (*see* §5(i)(h) above). This tradition continued, wall shrines at first invariably being minor versions of the main aedicular components, especially *kūṭa*-aediculae. During the 11th century there occurred a fertile proliferation of temple architecture in miniature, the 'pediments' of niche frames faithfully representing complex temple superstructures. Stellate as well as orthogonal *drāviḍa* types appeared, as well as *nāgara* and other 'exotic' modes. Contemporary inscriptions boast of the architects' skill in adorning temple walls with these diverse forms (see Dhaky). Experimental compositions are found that were never attempted at full scale.

Often the only wall shrine containing an image is the central one, which, in a series of mainstream temples, appears progressively to burst out of its primary framing aedicula, even penetrating up into the 'parapet', as in the main *vimāna* of the Kashivishveshvara Temple at Lakkundi. This temple's east *vimāna* is unusual for this period in exhibiting a gallery of sculpture—no longer complete—in its walls (*see* §V, 7(vi)(c) below). The images were placed in the recesses, with the projections displaying empty wall shrines. A number of *vimānas* once had a frieze of bracket figures leaning out from the wall pilasters to support the cornice (*kapota*).

The tendencies evident in the development of moulding shapes during the Rashtrakuta period were reinforced under the Chalukyas of Kalyana. Horizontal continuity was emphasized by a flattening and sharpening of certain mouldings, particularly the cushion element (*kumuda*) of the base. The imagery of timber forms became more abstract, with formal aims taking precedence over representational ones. For example, diagonal components appeared at the corners of the joist moulding (*vyālamālā*), and the rim of the eaves moulding (*kapota*) was eventually made wider than the roof portion. Double curves became increasingly taut and sinuous, with flourishes—upturned or downturned excrescences at corners—becoming conspicuous in non-mainstream examples.

The less complex *phāṁsanā* shrines were now crowned by a *drāviḍa* 'dome' and used Karnata *drāviḍa* mouldings and pilasters. Evidence of renewed contact with *nāgara* forms is apparent among 11th-century designs of wall shrines, which include the *śekharī* and *bhūmija* varieties of *nāgara* as well as the basic *latina*. It was probably not before the end of the century that full-size *nāgara* temples began to be built in Karnataka, for the first time in more than 300 years. These seem mainly to have been simple types of *śekharī*, an example of which is the Ganesha Temple at Hangal, though usually the superstructures are lost. Mouldings and details, as well as geographical proximity, point to Malwa and Seunadesha (*see* §(c) above) as the source from which the *nāgara* was reimported. Whereas under the Chalukyas of Badami the *nāgara* had quickly become naturalized and established as one of two familiar alternatives, most of the later *nāgara* temples in northern Karnataka appear to be the products of a Karnata *drāviḍa* vision; on the whole they do not show the same care and mastery as the *drāviḍa*.

As in the earlier period, combinations of *drāviḍa* and *nāgara* are found in the compositions of whole temples, but, as before, many more examples are found in the miniature architecture of wall shrines. *Nāgara* and *drāviḍa* elements often appear side by side, but the most thoroughgoing synthesis of the two 'languages' was achieved when the vocabulary of one was put together according to a mode of organization belonging to the other. At full scale this is best exemplified by the extraordinary Someshvara Temple at Lakshmeshvara, in which *drāviḍa* elements are arranged according to the compositional principles of the *śekharī* mode of *nāgara*.

Southern Karnataka. In southern Karnataka some 300 Hoysala temples survive in various states of preservation, the greatest concentration being in present-day Hassan District, around Halebid. The most spectacular monuments were built during the 12th century, while the dynasty was still nominally a feudatory of the Chalukyas of Kalyana.

Two general characteristics commonly recognized as distinguishing Hoysala temples from those built by the Chalukyas of Kalyana are the abundance of figural sculpture that frequently adorns the walls of the former and the 'ornateness' of Hoysala architecture. This 'ornateness' requires some clarification. It has been suggested that there were two Hoysala styles, one ornate, the other plain. But this apparent difference has largely to do with the degree of elaboration to which surfaces were taken—whether they were fully worked or merely blocked out. In terms of overall, aedicular composition, Hoysala temples are on the whole slightly less complex than their northern Karnata equivalents. By virtue of their richly decorated surfaces, however, they are indeed often more ornate. Mouldings, already at the height of abstraction, were dissolved by carving that fully exploited the possibilities of soapstone. Without destroying the enclosing block outlines, the stone was grooved, bored, drilled and undercut into tangles, where nodular fronds seethe and glitter against dark cavities.

The fact that the predominant mode for Hoysala temples was the Karnata *drāviḍa* ('*vesara*') developed in northern Karnataka is disguised by certain characteristics. One of these, though a detail, has a striking effect on the appearance of the *vimāna*. This is the diagonal type of horseshoe-arch motif occasionally used further north but virtually universal here. The horseshoe arch (*nāsi*), having hitherto represented the gable end of the *śālā* barrel roof, was folded down the middle through a right angle. The monster-face finial was, as it were, folded down the nose, and the dissolutionary expansion implied by the double-staggered *śālā*-aedicula ceased to be orthogonal, seeming now to radiate directly from the heart of the shrine.

Four other special features, by no means ubiquitous, can be seen in various combinations on the more ambitious Hoysala temples. Most widespread is a 'two-tier wall', divided by a continuous eaves moulding (*chādya*) half-way up the wall zone of the first storey. Above this moulding rise the superstructures of the wall shrines, while below runs a dense gallery of sculpture. Secondly, the principal, central wall shrines may be enlarged to become virtually minor *vimāna*s, sometimes containing two shrine chambers (*garbhagṛha*s), one above the other. While attached to the *vimāna* wall, they appear fully emerged, as if having burst out, almost free. Thirdly, for the moulded base of the temple a series of horizontal courses may be substituted, blocked out as rectangular strips with narrow recesses between them and then carved into friezes of animals, narrative scenes and decorative motifs. Lastly (as in northern traditions and as prefigured in northern Karnataka at the Mallikarjuna Temple at Sudi), the whole temple may be raised on a podium, paved on top for circumambulation and reflecting in its plan the general shape of the temple. These four peculiarities, all of which are present in such temples as the Lakshmi-Narayana at Hosaholalu (see fig. 80), contribute to an impression of horizontality, a characteristic further enhanced by the *chādya* canopy invariably placed, as in some other non-mainstream Karnata schools, below the cornice (*kapota*) of the first storey.

Orthogonal *vimāna*s, both three- and five-projection types, were varied simply by permutations of the already

80. Lakshmi-Narayana Temple, Hosaholalu, *c.* 1240; main shrine viewed from the south

existing aedicular repertory of Chalukya tradition, with the special features just outlined providing additional means of variation. These features were also used on stellate *vimāna*s, among which there is more variety than in northern Karnataka (where most types are represented, however, in wall-shrine designs). Two of the earliest Hoysala temples are the two largest and best known: the Chennakeshava at Belur (1117) and the slightly later Hoysaleshvara at Halebid. Belur, as will be discussed presently, is a *nāgara* composition, while Halebid is Karnata *drāviḍa*, neither having a surviving superstructure. Both follow the same plan, based on 16-point rotated-square stars, but with orthogonal central projections (*bhadra*s) putting forth giant wall shrines. (The other three special features were probably first introduced at Halebid, which has two *vimāna*s, with two corresponding halls, side by side and joined at their transepts.) A standard stellate form in the 13th century was a uniform, sixteen-pointed, four-storey *vimāna* composed of *kūṭa*-aediculae. To this type belong the three *vimāna*s of the well-known Keshava Temple at SOMNATHPUR, one of a number of Hoysala temples set in a walled enclosure. More complex stellate geometries, with aedicular forms alternating around the perimeter, are found in temples at Bhadravati, Ramanathapuram and Arsikere.

In contrast to the *śekharī* form predominant among *nāgara* temples in northern Karnataka, the Hoysala versions are *bhūmija*, found in several stellate types with pyramidal superstructures rather than the authentic *nāgara* curvature. The introduction of the *nāgara* into the Hoysala territories must have taken place with the early and prestigious example of the Chennakeshava at Belur. In that temple the northern forms and details seem to have derived from more direct contact with the 'pure' *nāgara* schools of Seunadesha (Maharashtra; *see* §(c) above) than is evident in most of the northern Karnata examples. The salient angles of the stellate shrine do not belong to aediculae, with slender pilasters at the corners, but form thick pillars (*stambhas*), which, in the northern tradition, would have been crowned by 'spires' to form *kūṭastambhas*. The mouldings of the plinth (*vēdībandha*) are *nāgara*. A composition similar to the Chennakeshava is found at the Saumyakeshvara Temple at Nagamangala. In the Mule-Shankareshvara at Turuvekere and the Sadashiva at Nuggihalli, both *bhūmija* in a general sense, *nāgara* components were arranged in ingenious new ways that are thoroughly Karnata in spirit.

A more usual alternative to the Karnata *drāviḍa* is again the *phāṁsanā*. Of the nine *vimānas* within the compound of the Lakshmidevi Temple at Dodda Gaddavalli, eight are *phāṁsanā* and one is Karnata *drāviḍa*.

Telangana. Relatively equal numbers of Karnata *drāviḍa*, *phāṁsanā* and *nāgara* shrines survive from medieval Telangana. Temples in this region were built mainly of grey basalt, often with brick superstructures, many of which have since disappeared. As well as single-shrine temples, a number are found with three shrines or more, and enclosure walls (*prākāras*) survive around several temple groups. The open hall is more widespread than the closed kind, pillars normally being the type with a cuboid block in place of the bell-like element that had become characteristic in Karnataka. In the so-called 'Thousand-pillared' Temple at Hanamkonda (1163; *see* HANAMKONDA AND WARANGAL), a free-standing open hall was placed in front of a three-shrine temple, with which, together with an intervening Nandi pavilion, it shares a raised podium similar to the southern Karnata kind. Such platforms became common in the region during the 12th century.

The Karnata *drāviḍa* temples in Telangana are most closely related to non-mainstream workshops in Karnataka and, in certain ways, to the Hoysala school. Characteristics shared with Hoysala works include the use of the podium (already noted), a predilection for undercut pearl-swag fringes on mouldings and figure sculpture, the rich elaboration of ceiling bays and the use of extra-large central wall shrines, which in the Telangana examples contain three storeys. The Karnata *drāviḍa vimānas* of Telangana are all orthogonal, with little innovation in aedicular composition. The main *vimāna* of the Chennakeshava at Ghanapur (perhaps late 11th century) already has aedicular components of extremely slender proportions. These components became typical in temples of the Kakatiya period, such as the Ramappa Temple at PALAMPET, built shortly before 1213, and well known for the bracket figures and lavish carving of its open hall. The brick superstructure of the five-projection, four-storey *vimāna* has a steeper, loftier profile than its equivalents in Karnataka.

Contact with Kalinga (Orissa) can occasionally be sensed in the details of Telangana temples. On the fringes of Kalinga a stylistic fusion occurred, exemplified in the mid-13th-century Varaha-Narasimha Temple at Simhachalam (Vishakhapatam District), where a *vimāna* entirely Karnata *drāviḍa* in composition clearly was carved by Kalinga craftsmen.

Nāgara temples in Telangana suggest strong contacts with Seunadesha, though the regional idiom is evident, as in the frequent use of Karnata *drāviḍa* base mouldings. The *bhūmija* is the *nāgara* mode that was used, generally with an authentic curvature to the tower. Shrines are mainly orthogonal and typically of the five-projection, five-storey kind, as in the Ramadeva Temple at Pedatumbulam and the Erakeshvara at Pillamari. The shrines of the 'Thousand-pillared Temple' at Hanamkonda, intended to be *bhūmija*, have seven projections but no surviving superstructures. Stellate *bhūmija* shrines, also without superstructures, are found at the Gautameshvara Temple at Manthani and the Shiva Temple at Nagnoor. Like the Chennakeshava at Belur, these are based on stars of 16 points, with the points on the cardinal axes obscured by orthogonal central projections (*bhadras*). The Ramalingeshvara Temple at Nandikundi seems to be the only example in India (other than in miniature depictions in the wall shrines of Karnataka) of a uniform stellate *bhūmija* temple without *bhadras*, the *nāgara* equivalent of the stellate shrines at Dambal, Somnathpur and elsewhere. Based on a sixteen-pointed star, three storeys of *nāgara kūṭastambhas*, creating a *drāviḍa*-like stepped profile rather than a curved *nāgara* one, rise to a stellate cushion member at the summit.

BIBLIOGRAPHY

J. Fergusson: *History of Indian and Eastern Architecture* (London, 1876)
Annu. Rep. Mysore Archaeol. Dept (Mysore, 1886–1956)
A. Rea: *Chalukyan Architecture: Including Examples from the Ballary District, Madras Presidency* (Madras, 1896/*R* Delhi, 1970)
R. Narasimhachar: *The Kesava Temple at Somanathapur* (Mysore, 1917)
——: *The Kesava Temple at Belur* (Mysore, 1919)
——: *The Lakshmidevi Temple at Dodda-Gaddavalli* (Mysore, 1919)
G. Yazdani: *The Temples at Palampet*, Mem. Archaeol. Surv. India, vi (Calcutta, 1922/*R* Delhi, 1977)
H. Cousens: *The Chalukyan Architecture of the Kanarese Districts* (Calcutta, 1926)
S. Settar: *The Hoysala Style of Temple Architecture and Sculpture, Eleventh to Fourteenth Centuries* (diss., U. Cambridge, 1970)
M. Radhakrishna Sarma: *Temples of Telingāṇa: The Architecture, Iconography and Sculpture of the Chalukya and Kakatiya Temples* (Hyderabad, 1972)
M. A. Dhaky: *The Indian Temple Forms in Karṇāṭa Inscriptions and Architecture* (New Delhi, 1977)
R. J. Del Bonta: *The Hoysala Style: Architectural Development and Artists, 12th and 13th Centuries A.D.* (diss., Ann Arbor, U. MI, 1978)
P. B. Wagoner: *Mode and Meaning in the Architecture of Early Medieval Telangana (c. 1000–1300)* (diss., Madison, U. WI, 1986)
A. Hardy: *Form and Transformation in Indian Temple Architecture: The Karṇāṭa Drāviḍa Tradition, 7th to 13th Centuries* (Delhi, 1994)

ADAM HARDY

14th–16th centuries. Following the Islamic invasions at the end of the 13th century and the establishment of the Deccani sultanate (*see* §(ii)(f) below), artistic traditions were severely disrupted; some, such as those sponsored by the Hoysala and Kakatiya dynasties, virtually disappeared. However, as most of south India was brought under the control of the powerful VIJAYANAGARA rulers from the 14th century on, a new, integrated temple style rapidly evolved. By the 16th century, the distinctive style of Vijayanagara temple architecture had been firmly established in almost all of south India. The monumental conception of Vijayanagara-period projects testifies to a substantial economic and artistic investment in temple building, often by royal patrons. Later 16th-century projects sponsored during the reigns of the last Vijayanagara kings (no longer ruling from the capital city of the same name; *see* HAMPI) demonstrate the continuity of architectural traditions (*see also* §§(g) and (h) below).

14th century. The earliest known temples of the Vijayanagara period are modest structures generally built in styles that resemble earlier traditions in the area. Evidently, new artistic traditions in south India were slow to evolve. Temple architecture under the first Vijayanagara kings was executed in granite. Despite its overall plainness, there was often an attempt to create a new, massive style.

At the capital, the first temples to be sponsored by the newly established Sangama dynasty were modest structures, mostly confined to Hemakuta Hill and the periphery. The earliest of them are Shaiva, testifying to the continued importance of this religion in the region. Following previous Deccani practice, Vijayanagara temples often consisted of two or three sanctuaries opening off a common hall approached through an open porch. Walls were generally plain, with moulded bases and cornices. Over the sanctuaries rose pyramidal towers, mostly divided into horizontal strata by deeply recessed mouldings; projections with frontal arched motifs were derived from earlier Deccani styles. So too were the projecting porches with balcony seating and overhanging, deeply curved eaves. The only interior features of interest were columns, mostly with square blocks covered with sculptures, and double capitals with projecting square and circular elements. Ceilings were sometimes provided with raised lotus medallions.

15th century. By the time the Sangama dynasty had come to an end in the mid-15th century, a characteristic Vijayanagara temple style had evolved. While partly dependent on Tamil traditions, especially of the late Chola and Pandya eras (*see* §(g) below), certain Deccani elements also were integrated.

An idea of this style may be had from the Ramachandra complex in the Royal centre at the capital. Probably erected by Deva Raya I (*reg* 1422–46), this shrine served as a state chapel for the king and court. As the first important project at Vijayanagara in the new style, it may have been built by workmen imported from the south. Two shrines stand in the middle of a rectangular enclosure, entered on the east and north through gateways with porches but no towers. The principal shrine consists of an axial alignment of sanctuary, antechamber and columned hall entered through three porches. In elevation the outer walls display typical *drāviḍa* characteristics. The moulded base has petalled motifs and blocks carved with animals. The walls are rhythmically divided into projections by pairs of pilasters; secondary half-pilasters frame deep niches; yet other ornamental pilasters that appear to stand in pots are set into the recesses. Also southern in manner is the method of applying sculpted panels between the pilasters; these illustrate the complete *Rāmāyaṇa* epic. Rising over the sanctuary is a stepped, multi-storey tower built of brick and ornamented with plaster. The capping square-to-domed roof and frontal vaulted projection are typical of Deccani traditions. Of particular interest is the treatment of the columns, with finely sculpted blocks and (on the porches) curved brackets terminating in pendent buds. Also of interest are the friezes of royal processions on the outer face of the enclosure walls.

A survey of other 15th-century examples reveals similar architectural schemes. At Penukonda, a fortified site that served as a later Vijayanagara capital, one of the two temples, believed by some scholars to date from the 15th century although others place it earlier, is dedicated to the god Shiva. It has a rectangular plan consisting of a sanctuary surrounded by a passageway on three sides with a hall in front. The temple is characterized by its long, low elevations, with granite walls covered with sculpted panels between pilasters and a small brick tower capped by a hemispherical roof. Other than columns with sculpted shafts, the interior is unadorned. A similarly modest construction is found at SRISAILAM, an important pilgrimage centre on the Krishna River. Its principal shrine has a pyramidal tower, once sheathed with brass plates; the adjoining hall is entered through three porches. Mythological scenes illustrating Shaiva legends were sculpted on the outer faces of the enclosure walls; these may be compared to similar friezes on the enclosure walls of the Ramachandra Temple.

First half of the 16th century. With the emergence of the Tuluva dynasty at the beginning of the 16th century, the Vijayanagara empire attained its greatest extent and influence. Religious architecture developed a new and monumental expression, especially under the sponsorship of Krishnadeva Raya (*reg* 1509–30) and his successor Achyutadeva Raya (*reg* 1530–42). These and other wealthy patrons were responsible for the increased scale of temple building and the evolution of the planned complex as the ideal temple form. While the typical Vijayanagara complex was modelled on Chola-period examples, it surpassed these models in size and grandeur of conception. A feature of the period was the well-planned and symmetrical religious complex into which different architectural elements were incorporated.

Religious life of this period was characterized by the multiplication of temple divinities, together with their mounts (*vāhanas*), consorts and attendants, all of whom required accommodation in separate shrines and pavilions. The temple complex was also designed to accommodate ever-increasing numbers of priests and worshippers. Another development was the elaboration and codification of devotional rites and the concomitant emphasis on music, dance and theatre as part of the temple's cultural life. Many temple complexes also evolved into educational and economic institutions of regional significance, and their walled enclosures even provided refuge in times of war.

The typical early 16th-century Vijayanagara temple was contained within a vast rectangle of high walls broken by one or more towered gateways (*gopuras*) that were usually aligned with the buildings inside. The gateways revived the form established during the Chola period but exceeded the earlier examples in height and elaboration (*see* §(g) below). Under the Vijayanagara rulers, the *gopura* became an essential feature of south Indian temple architecture. The lower granite portions were usually divided into a high base with walls above; both base and walls were adorned with regular pilasters defining the projections. Bases and cornices were highly elaborated; sculptures were sometimes set into niches. Running through the building was a passageway cut off by one or more sets of doors; pilasters were ornamented with female figures holding branches, multiple images of deities and sometimes even donor portraits. Rising above was a brick construction on a hollow timber framework. This pyramidal mass was arranged in a series of ascending but diminishing storeys, with an angled or slightly concave profile. Each storey was provided with pilastered walls and figural sculptures in plaster, originally brightly coloured. Parapet elements consisting of ornamental roof forms terminated each of the storeys. The tower was capped by an enlarged barrel-vaulted roof with arched ends and potlike finials. This roof was exuberantly ornamented with such motifs as monster masks with protruding eyes, flamelike tufts and crouching figures.

The typical early 16th-century temple was set in an expansive paved courtyard. Lamp columns (*dīpa stambhas*), altars (*bali pīṭhas*), small pavilions and other features were more or less aligned along an axis linking the main shrine with the gateway. Colonnades were built up against the peripheral walls; one or more columned halls (*maṇḍapas*) stood in the middle of the court or were attached to shrines. Great attention was paid to columnar details of these halls and colonnades. Shafts usually displayed carvings on blocks; these constituted a large proportion of all sculpture within the temples. Multi-tiered architectural 'façades' also adorned columnar shafts, a motif derived from Chola-period practice. Characteristic of the early 16th century was the development of the pier into a cluster of colonettes around a central shaft. Peripheral columns or those flanking the central aisles were often sculpturally transformed into rearing lion-like beasts (*yāḷis*) with warrior riders and aquatic monsters (*makaras*). Particular attention was paid to the brackets, which proceeded directly from the shafts, there being no capitals. Brackets

81. View of Kalyana *maṇḍapa*, Vitthala Temple complex, Vijayanagara, mid-16th century

generally had curved, flowing forms and invariably terminated in pendent buds. Ceilings were horizontal, sometimes with raised sections supported on massive crossbeams. An interesting invention of this period was the inverted 'T'-beam that carried massive ceiling slabs.

Halls were raised on moulded bases, sometimes adorned with friezes and miniature niches housing figures. Balustrades flanking access steps were also provided with animal motifs. Overhanging the peripheral columns were double-curved eaves with riblike elements on the undersides. The outer faces of the eaves were delicately ornamented, with upturned, petal-like motifs at the corners. Above rose a brick parapet, which presented a succession of arched niches filled with plaster sculptures and topped by ornamental roof forms.

Other than the sanctuary housing the principal divinity to whom the temple as a whole was dedicated, there were usually other smaller shrines dedicated to subsidiary gods, goddesses and animal mounts standing within the complex or built into the colonnades. The shrines themselves were architecturally less impressive than the towered gateways or columned halls; in fact, many Vijayanagara-period complexes were actually constructed around earlier shrines of modest proportions. Early 16th-century examples were noted for their long, low elevations, dominated by repeated pairs of pilasters, some of which framed deep niches. The typical tower over the sanctuary was multi-storey, with a capping hemispherical or barrel-vaulted roof; invariably, it was considerably lower than that rising over the entrance gateway. Thus the highest, most dramatic elements of the temple were reserved for public display on the outside of the complex.

Within, the sanctuary was approached through a sequence of open columned hall, closed columned hall (*raṅgamaṇḍapa*), antechamber (*ardhamaṇḍapa*) and vestibule (*antarāla*); in larger examples the sanctuary was surrounded by a dark passageway (*pradakṣināpatha*). The interior was massive and plain, except for the treatment of columns and brackets, which resembled those of halls elsewhere. Ornamented doorways were flanked by enlarged guardian figures (*dvārapālas*).

Almost no religious centre of any importance in south India was without its mature Vijayanagara-period renovation or addition. Patrons added columned halls and enclosure walls with towered *gopuras* to earlier shrines, transforming modest sanctuaries into large-scale complexes; they also founded completely new temples, especially at the capital. Several great early 16th-century temples survive at Vijayanagara. The Virupaksha Temple in the sacred centre at Hampi enshrines the guardian divinity of the royal household. Despite the antiquity of its foundation, most of the structure belongs to the era of Krishnadeva Raya. The eastern gateway (1512) is particularly impressive, reaching a height of approximately 52 m. The tower serves as the climax of a colonnaded, paved street still used for chariot (*ratha*) festivals. A large stepped tank is situated outside the walls on the north.

Of more interest artistically is the Vitthala complex at Vijayanagara, parts of which may also date from the era of Krishnadeva Raya (see fig. 81). This temple is celebrated for its finely sculpted bases and columns, both in the free-standing halls of the courtyard and in the hall attached to the shrine itself. Friezes of animals and warriors adorn the base. Peripheral piers are clustered arrangements of colonettes or enlarged rearing animals. Multi-tiered brackets extend outwards to support the massive ceilings. Of unusual interest is the stone chariot that serves as a shrine to Garuda, Vishnu's mount (see fig. 82). Provided with wheels, it was intended to imitate actual chariots that conveyed temple deities. Also of note is the nearby Tiruvengalanatha Temple, assigned to the reign of Achyutadeva Raya. This is a completely planned complex with two sets of enclosure walls, one within the other. Approached from the north, the sanctuary is reached only after passing through two towered gateways, the highest being on the outside.

Some of the finest early 16th-century projects were constructed in the Telugu country. At TADPATRI two complexes survive that testify to the sophistication of artistic traditions at this time. The unfinished gateways of the Ramalingeshvara Temple illustrate an exuberant variant of the Vijayanagara style. All of the elements of these *gopuras* are encrusted with friezes, scrollwork and miniature figures and animals. In contrast the twin shrines are modest structures. The Venkataramana Temple was grandly conceived and finely executed. The outer walls of the sanctuary are completely covered with finely worked pilasters and sculpted panels; the columned hall in front has rearing animals defining an enlarged open space. There is even a small stone chariot treated as a miniature temple. The single-towered gateway is typical in its design.

A related monument is the Virabhadra Temple at LEPAKSHI. Built on an uneven granite outcrop, this complex, with its double set of enclosure walls, has an irregular layout. The principal shrine is approached through a double gateway and an extended open hall. The columnar elements are finely worked, with large-scale sculptures. Mythological friezes adorn the outer walls of the shrine, while narrative murals are preserved on the ceilings (*see* §VI, 4(vii) below).

Another important early 16th-century monument in the Telugu region is found at the celebrated pilgrimage site of Ahobilam. The Narasimha complex of Lower Ahobilam displays most of the typical architectural elements of this period. The temple is contained within a double set of enclosure walls; the gateway has a steeply pyramidal tower. The hall columns have been elaborately treated with sculptures of divinities, musicians and devotees. Also of interest are the pilgrimage temples at the twin sites of Tirupati (*see* TIRUPATI AND CHANDRAGIRI) and Tirumalai, both of which were greatly expanded at this time.

While architecture at the capital was standardized, temples at religious sites were sometimes erected in variant styles. Sringeri was an important centre of Shaiva teachings, with strong connections to the early Vijayanagara rulers. The unusual Vidya Shankara Temple there belongs to the middle of the 16th century. Both its sanctuary with surrounding passageway and its attached hall were provided with numerous wall projections in the typical Hoysala manner; the result is a plan with almost rounded ends. The outer walls have continuous base mouldings and regularly positioned pilasters framing small sculptures. The tower is virtually circular in plan with diminishing storeys capped by a multi-faceted, domelike roof and a pot finial; on the front is a vaulted projection. Elephant balustrades flank the entrance steps, while large guardian figures stand at the doorways. Hall columns are elaborately carved with figures and ornamental motifs.

82. Stone chariot shrine, Vitthala Temple complex, Vijayanagara, 16th century

BIBLIOGRAPHY

P. Brown: *Indian Architecture (Buddhist and Hindu Periods)* (Bombay, [1941], rev. Bombay, 1956), chap. XIX

V. Kameswara Rao: *Select Vijayanagara Temples of Rayalaseema*, Govt Andhra Pradesh, Archaeol. Ser., lxvii (Hyderabad, 1976)

J. M. Fritz, G. Michell and M. S. Nagaraja Rao: *Where Kings and Gods Meet: The Royal Centre at Vijayanagara* (Tucson, 1985)

G. Michell: *Architecture and Art of Southern India: Vijayanagara and the Successor States* (Cambridge, 1994)

GEORGE MICHELL

(g) Tamil Nadu.

11th–13th centuries. During the reign of Rajaraja I (*reg* *c.* 985–1014) the CHOLA kingdom grew from a small principality along the Kaveri River in central Tamil Nadu to become the dominant imperial house of south India. After subjugating perennial rivals further south, most notably the Pandya dynasty of Madurai, and annexing northern Sri Lanka and most of Karnataka, Rajaraja defeated the Chalukyas of Kalyana (*see* §(f) above) and acquired hegemony over what is now Andhra Pradesh (though the rivalry with the Chalukyas continued for another two centuries). In 1004 the Chola ruler's altered status in the region prompted him to assume the title Rajaraja ('King of Kings'). At about the same time he inaugurated work on a temple intended to give appropriate and tangible expression to the newly founded imperium. In the Chola capital of THANJAVUR, at the centre of a double-walled precinct (241×121 m within a 357×235 m outer enclosure wall, or *prākāra*, plus 15 m moat), a structure of unprecedented size was built (see fig. 83). In just three years the central core or shrine (*vimāna*) was completed sufficiently for the king to offer golden flowers to its principal icon, a Shiva *liṅga*. Like the temple rising around it, the *liṅga* installed within the inner sanctum was the largest in India; its black stone shaft, 1.66 m in diameter and twice as tall, was supported by a perforated disc (*yonipīṭha*; diam. 5.4 m). Completion of the *vimāna*'s superstructure took another three years. Then in the year 1010, on the 275th day of Rajaraja's 25th year as king, the temple was officially consecrated to Shiva as Rajarajeshvara ('Lord of the King of Kings'). A commemorative inscription included the information that the crowning pot finial (*stūpikā*) anointed on that occasion weighed 131 kg, including the 16 kg of gold that overlay its copper core. To judge from its monumental proportions, the existing pot finial (h. 3.8 m) may be the original one.

From at least the 17th century, the Rajarajeshvara has also been known as the Brihadeshvara ('Temple of the Large God'). To fully appreciate its magnitude, it may be helpful to compare its dimensions with those of the Rajasimheshvara or Rajasimha-Pallaveshvara (*c.* AD 700) at KANCHIPURAM, the most ambitious structure of the Pallava dynasty and better known as the Kailasanatha. The main temple structures (*vimāna*s) of both are square in plan, but the Chola monument (30.2 m on each side as against the Pallava temple's 15 m) is approximately four times larger in surface area. The differences in elevation are no less striking. From base courses that rise to eye-level at 1.4 m, the Kailasanatha reaches a height of 19.3 m, or just 30% more than its width. The Rajarajeshvara, by contrast, is raised on an imposing reduplicated base (total h. 4.3 m) that soars to 66 m at the tip of its gilded finial: a height over twice its width and nearly three and a half times the height of the Kailasanatha. Both *vimāna*s face east, and each is fronted by an appropriately scaled ceremonial hall that shares its base moulding. However, a major difference lies in the proportionality of these combined structures to their immediate surroundings. Whereas the Kailasanatha is rather confined within a cloistering ring of 55 diminutive chapels, the vast colonnade (264×123 m) of the Rajarajeshvara is set much further back, enclosing a precinct approximately 25 times larger than that at Kanchipuram. It thus provides not only the generous vistas necessary to grasp the entire configuration visually but also ample room for several smaller temples dedicated to the 'family gods'. Not all built concurrently with the main *vimāna*, these include dedications to the mother Amman (the Goddess), the sons Subrahmanya and Ganesha, Nandi (Shiva's bull), the child saint Chandesha and Nataraja, Shiva's manifestation as Lord of Dance. Nataraja's special importance as the Chola dynasty's family deity (*kuladevatā*) is well attested: inscriptions enumerating the festival bronzes presented to the temple

83. Rajarajeshvara or Brihadeshvara Temple, Thanjavur, 1010; view from the south-east

during Rajaraja's lifetime name five Nataraja images, one of which is still in worship; another inscription records the requisitioning of 400 dancing girls (*devadāsis*) from 96 other temples in the realm for exclusive service at the Rajarajeshvara; and a continuous frieze in the upper gallery of the main *vimāna* depicts Shiva performing the dance poses detailed in the Sanskrit treatise on dance, music and drama, the *Nāṭyaśāstra* (though only 81 of 108 were completed).

Though unprecedented in scale, the Rajarajeshvara is best understood as a logical culmination of *drāviḍa*-order architecture rather than as a radical innovation. Base mouldings with the same profiles and embellishing motifs (chiefly lotus petals and leogryphs—composite horned lions—called *vyālas*) were known from the late 7th century AD. Duplication of the vertical wall section with an intervening cornice between two storeys was introduced into the architecture of Tamil Nadu here, but its components are all traditional: projecting offsets (*bhadras*) are framed with pilasters with 'pot capitals' and pierced with doorlike niches (*devakoṣṭhas*). The larger, central offsets on the three visible sides contain screened openings that illuminate the circumambulatory corridors around the inner sanctum. The giant guardians on either side of the first-level openings invite imaginary access to the divine presence within. Shiva's presence is also given anthropomorphic form in the expanded number of niches on each side. The better-known iconic types on each of the lower levels may be identified in circumambulatory order (clockwise from the south) as follows: Bhikshatana (Shiva in his guise as an ascetic); Nataraja; Harihara (the Shiva–Vishnu composite); Lingodbhava (the Infinite Pillar of Light); Ardhanarishvara (the androgyne) and Gangadhara (Shiva as Lord of the River Ganga). Perhaps because more specific signification would be difficult to project from such a height, all the niches on the second storey repeat a bow-wielding form of Shiva as Tripurantaka (Destroyer of Three Demon Cities). On both levels the intervening recesses between the pilaster-framed niches are decorated with depictions of cornucopia-like potted trees.

It is the Rajarajeshvara's superstructure that differs most dramatically from precedents; rarely before had a *drāviḍa vimāna* risen more than three storeys above its initial cornice. The insistent profile of the acute pyramid is subdivided into no less than 13 diminishing terraces. Yet the transformation is more quantitative than substantive, for each terrace supports a sequence of ubiquitous aediculae—square-domed *kūṭas* and barrel-vaulted *śālās*—that had been standardized before the 7th century. With protective deities appearing before some of the larger aediculae, it is clear that the *vimāna* was still perceived as a magical heavenly palace, its airborne potential intimated by the winglike projections on its octagonal cupola (*śikhara*).

In 1012, Rajaraja invested his son Rajendra I (*reg* 1012–44) as co-regent. Five years earlier Rajendra had proved his worth by leading a raid through the heartland of Chalukya territory, sacking the capital and returning with treasure. After his father's death Rajendra continued to expand the Chola empire, first by conquering the rest of Sri Lanka and then by consolidating control of Kerala before turning his attention to the north. With Rajendra's son—the later Rajadhiraja I (*reg* 1044–54)—joining the fray as crown prince, the Chola armies marched victoriously far beyond Andhra, through Orissa, to the banks of the Ganga. In commemoration of this feat, a new capital was constructed some 70 km north-west of Thanjavur and called GANGAIKONDACHOLAPURAM ('City of the Chola who took the Ganga'). South-east of its centre was raised a temple (*c.* 1025) emulating the Rajarajeshvara in every respect and designated the Rajendra Cholishvara.

Though Rajendra's *vimāna* (h. *c.* 50 m) is only three-quarters the height of his father's and is surrounded by a correspondingly reduced walled enclosure, the differences are almost certainly indicative of a desire to create a more harmonious whole rather than of diminished resources or ambition. The slightly increased size of its square plinth (30.7 m on each side) indicates that a building of equal scale was contemplated. Thus the reduction of certain vertical dimensions, together with the increase in others, must have been a deliberate measure to avoid the excessively attenuated, rigid profiles of the Rajarajeshvara. The transition from sub-base (*upapīṭha*) to base (*adhiṣṭhāna*) was emphasized by slightly reducing the height of the sub-base and extending its projection sufficiently to invite circumambulation upon it. The sub-base was also embellished with panels alternately depicting heraldic lions and scrollwork, whereas that at Thanjavur was left plain. The double-storey wall surfaces are remarkably similar in the design of their constituent parts, though a lapse in finishing standards is apparent in places at Gangaikondacholapuram. The major changes are in the superstructure. In an obvious and effective attempt to avoid the monotony inherent in the too uniform stacking of aediculae at Thanjavur, the number of terraces was reduced from 13 to 7, incremental shifts in scale were given prominence by increasing the size of the lowest *kūṭas*, and the overall pyramid profile was given a concave upward sweep.

For nearly two centuries more, Chola power and largesse continued to find expression in the construction of substantial stone temples, often finely detailed with sculptural embellishment but never again on a scale rivalling these two monuments of the early 11th century, which signalled certain changes of direction and priority in the sacred architecture of the region. Beginning with their generous allocation of space for subsidiary chapels, a trend towards the de-emphasis of the central *vimāna*'s visual dominance can be traced. In the important late 12th-century Chola monuments of Darasuram and Tribhuvanam, where the imperial dimension is still evident, the *vimāna* remains the tallest single structure, but the investment of space and creative effort was much more evenly distributed between it and a growing number of other structures. Not the least of the latter were the independent sanctums for the mother goddess and the gods and saints of the Shaiva and Vaishnava pantheons.

During the 13th century, a period coinciding with the ascendancy of the Pandyas, the balance was finally tipped away from the central *vimāna* in favour of peripheral structures. The most important, as a defining characteristic of the south Indian temple's external appearance, was the GOPURA (towered gateway). Whether donated singly, as at Chidambaram, or in complete sets of four with rampart-like *prākāra* walls attached, the operant ideal remained

84. Arunachaleshvara Temple, Tiruvannamalai, 9th–16th century

fixed: any number of *prākāras* might be added to a sanctuary as long as biaxial symmetry was maintained with the cardinal directions and as long as each additional set of *gopuras* completely overshadowed any earlier ones. At the Arunachaleshvara in TIRUVANNAMALAI (see fig. 84), the 11th-century *vimāna* and *gopura* (h. 14 m and 13 m) within the roofed second enclosure are dwarfed by a late 12th-century *gopura* (h. 27 m) and four others dating from the time of Ballala III (*reg* 1291–1342) of the Hoysala dynasty. The west *gopura* (h. 31 m) of the latter set is hidden behind the corresponding *gopura* (h. 44 m) of the fifth *prākāra*, which dates from the late 16th century. Such a series need never end; the south *gopura* of the seventh *prākāra* of the Ranganatha at Srirangam was completed in 1987, becoming one of the tallest in south India (h. 72.6 m).

Various explanations for this curious scale reversal have been offered, none entirely adequate. Certainly, one factor was the great sanctity that temples acquired by association with the canonical pilgrimage hymns of the Tamil saints. From the vantage of royal patrons, the merit to be gained by prominent affiliation with these sites must have seemed greater than that which might accrue from the foundation of new temples. However, the reversal of scale from periphery to centre is perfectly congruent with the spiritual quest that leads from the corporeal to the ethereal, from the mundane exterior to the sacred interior, and the pattern can be found at hundreds of sites in Tamil Nadu and elsewhere in south India.

For the sculpture and painting of this period, *see* §§IV, 7(vi)(a), and III, 3(i)(b) below.

BIBLIOGRAPHY

Enc. Ind. Temple Archit., i/1

E. Hultzsch: 'Inscriptions of Rajaraja I', *S. Ind. Inscr.*, ii (1892)

J. M. Soma Sundaram Pillai: *The Great Temple at Tanjore* (Madras, 1935; Thanjavur, 1958)

K. R. Srinivasan: 'The Last of the Great Cola Temples', *J. Ind. Soc. Orient. A.*, xvi (1948), pp. 11–33

K. A. Nilakanta Sastri: *The Cōḷas*, 2 vols (Madras, 1955)

P. Brown: *Indian Architecture (Buddhist and Hindu Periods)* (Bombay, [1941], rev. Bombay, 1956)

C. Sivaramamurti: *The Choḷa Temples: Tañjāvūr, Gaṅgaikoṇḍachoḷapuram and Dārāsuram* (New Delhi, 1960)

S. R. Balasubrahmanyam: *Four Chola Temples* (Bombay, 1963)

J. C. Harle: *Temple Gateways in South India: The Architecture and Iconography of the Cidambaram Gopuras* (Oxford, 1963)

R. Nagaswamy: *Gangaikondacholapuram* (Madras, 1970)

H. Sarkar: *The Kampahareśvara Temple at Tribhuvanam* (Madras, 1974)

S. R. Balasubrahmanyam: *Middle Chola Temples, Rajaraja I to Kulottunga I (A.D. 985–1070)* (Faridabad, 1975)

——: *Later Chola Temples, Kulottunga I to Rajendra III (A.D. 1070–1280)* (Faridabad, 1979)

B. Venkataraman: *Rājarājeśvaram: The Pinnacle of Chola Art* (Madras, 1985)

F. L'Hernault: *Dārāsuram*, 2 vols (Pondicherry, 1987)

M. L. Reiniche: *La Configuration sociologique du temple Hindou* (1989), iv of *Tiruvannamalai: Un Lieu saint śivaïte du sud de l'Inde* (Pondicherry, 1989–)

C. Guilmoto, M. L. Reiniche and P. Pichard: *La Ville* (1990), v of *Tiruvannamalai: Un Lieu saint śivaïte du sud de l'Inde* (Pondicherry, 1989–)

P. R. Srinivasan: *Inscriptions* (1990), i of *Un Lieu saint śivaïte du sud de l'Inde* (Pondicherry, 1989–)
C. Tadgell: *The History of Architecture in India: From the Dawn of Civilization to the End of the Raj* (New Delhi, 1990)
F. L'Hernault, P. Pichard and J. Deloche: *L'Archéologie du site* (1991), ii of *Tiruvannamalai: Un Lieu saint śivaïte du sud de l'Inde* (Pondicherry, 1989–)

MICHAEL D. RABE

Vijayanagara, 14th–16th centuries. The rulers of south India patronized temple building in the Tamil region as well as in Karnataka and Andhra Pradesh (*see* §(f) above). Under Krishnadeva Raya (*reg* 1509–30) a number of impressive gateways were added to earlier temples. The tower of the Ekambareshvara Temple at KANCHIPURAM, for example, is immense. It has a steeply rising pyramid of ten diminishing storeys that are capped with the usual vaulted roof. The eastern gateway of the Varadaraja Temple, also at Kanchipuram, is similar and may also date from the era of Krishnadeva Raya. Another impressive project can be seen at Kalahasti. The towered gateway erected there was a detached structure remarkable for its impressive proportions. Its finely finished base and walls have delicately modelled mouldings; the tower is a massive pyramid, complete with most of its architectural and sculpted elements. The towered superstructure of the north gateway of the Nataraja Temple at CHIDAMBARAM may also be assigned to this period. Rising over a Chola-period construction, this tower is massive and pyramidal. A portrait sculpture of Krishnadeva Raya within the passageway testifies to the active role of this royal patron in the renovation of the *gopura.*

Despite the loss of the Vijayanagara capital to the Muslims in 1565, the kings and their ministers continued to act as temple patrons, especially in the Tamil country. Temple forms continued to develop, and an idea of the fully evolved Vijayanagara style may be had from the Jalakanteshvara Temple at VELLORE, one of the finest and best-preserved temples of the whole series (see fig. 85). The outer rectangle of walls is only broken by a single towered gateway. Its pyramidal tower has six diminishing storeys with projections and openings in the middle of each long side flanked by guardians. The capping roof form is highly ornamented with monster masks and aquatic beasts. The outer enclosure is reached by passing through the gateway. There stands a columned hall renowned for its magnificent carvings, among the finest of the period and equalled only by those at SRIRANGAM (*see* §V, 7(vi)(a) below). The outer piers were fashioned as richly bridled horses, rearing lion-like monsters and other mythical beasts. The base too is adorned with figurative friezes, and the ceiling of the interior is an elaborate composition combining flowers and birds. A smaller gateway of the standard type leads into the inner enclosure, within which stands the principal temple. A modest building in the typical Vijayanagara manner, it consists of two shrines opening off a common columned hall. Colonnades against the enclosure walls incorporate minor shrines.

Another outstanding example of later Vijayanagara-period architecture is seen within the fourth enclosure of the great Ranganatha Temple at Srirangam. The columned hall there is celebrated for its piers fashioned as mythic beasts or rearing horses with riders and attendant warriors. The animation and virtuosity of these three-dimensional

85. Columned hall in Jalakanteshvara Temple, Vellore, late 16th century or early 17th

carvings rival those at Vellore. At Kanchipuram there is yet another elaborate columned hall dating from this era; it stands within the outer enclosure of the Varadaraja Temple. Almost all of the 96 columns are carved with figures and scenes; peripheral piers were fashioned as enlarged warriors and huntsmen on rearing horses. Sheltering the columns are double-curved eaves ornamented with scrollwork; stone chains for lamps hang from the corners. Episodes from the epic *Rāmāyaṇa* were sculpted on the moulded base.

Towered gateways (*gopuras*) from the end of the 16th century are the most monumental of the Vijayanagara series. These gateways have elaborately finished basements and walls; fully modelled sculptures crowd the upper storeys and capping roof forms. Typical examples can be seen in the Arunachaleshvara Temple at TIRUVANNAMALAI (see above and fig. 84). The ornamentation on the lower architectural elements is highly elaborate, with base, pilasters and eaves all profusely sculpted. Finely carved panels are seen on the outer walls of the eastern tower. Above rise ten diminishing storeys to create the unsculpted, soaring pyramidal mass. This is capped by a vaulted roof with arched ends. Within the gateway, as within that on the north, doorjambs and pilasters are sculpted, and Shaiva subjects appear on the ceilings.

Also found within the Tiruvannamalai complex is an immense thousand-columned hall. Such expansive structures, which appeared in the 16th century, were characteristic of the 17th-century NAYAKA period. In the

Tiruvannamalai example the piers display typical rearing-animal motifs; a dais in the middle has a highly ornamented basement.

BIBLIOGRAPHY

P. Brown: *Indian Architecture (Buddhist and Hindu Periods)* (Bombay, [1941], rev. Bombay, 1956), chap. XIX

G. Michell: *Architecture and Art of Southern India: Vijayanagara and the Successor States* (Cambridge, 1994)

GEORGE MICHELL

(h) Kerala.

11th–14th centuries. During this period Kerala temple architecture developed unified regional patterns; many new structures were created and older ones renovated. Square, circular, apsidal and oblong plans continued to be used; a few elliptical shrines also date from this era. Shrines without enclosed circumabulatory paths (*nirandhāra*) and with them (*sāndhāra*) continued to be built, and notable new types of the latter appeared. Some temples were built with the distinct Kerala pitched roof but actually enclosed miniature *drāviḍa* shrines within them, complete with their own superstructures. Double circumambulatory paths were also common. The exterior walls of Kerala-style temples in stone tended towards simplicity; sometimes the smooth wall areas were decorated with mural paintings, though none survive from this era. Exterior walls of carved wood were common in Kottayam and Alleppey districts.

A dated inscription on the Vadakkunnatha shrine in the Vadakkunnatha Temple complex at TRICHUR indicates an 11th-century date. This single-storey circular temple, with a conical superstructure of wood covered with copper sheeting, encloses a square *drāviḍa* shrine with an octagonal *śikhara* (crowning cupola); two rows of columns line the circumambulatory path, another development of this period. The west-facing shrine has two main entrances; the western one for Vadakkunnatha and the eastern one for his consort; such multiple entrances were also characteristic of this phase. The exterior wall paintings are of much later date; the inner cloistered enclosure (Malay. *nālambalam*) houses multiple shrines.

BIBLIOGRAPHY

Enc. Ind. Temple Archit., i/1

Travancore Archaeological Series (Trivandrum, 1910–36)

Annual Report, Travancore Archaeology Department (Trivandrum, 1922–48)

Annual Report of the Archaeological Department, Cochin State (or *Cochin State Annual Report on Archaeological Researches*) (Ernakulam, 1927–49)

S. Kramrisch, J. H. Cousins and R. Vasudeva Poduval: *The Arts and Crafts of Travancore* (Oxford, 1952); rev. as *The Arts and Crafts of Kerala* (Cochin, [1970])

M. G. S. Narayanan: *Political and Social Conditions of Kerala under the Kulasekhara Empire (ca. 800 A.D. to 1124 A.D.)* (diss., U. Kerala, 1972)

H. Sarkar: *An Architectural Survey of Temples of Kerala* (New Delhi, 1978)

R. M. Bernier: *Temple Arts of Kerala* (Delhi, 1981)

G. Michell: *The Penguin Guide to the Monuments of India*, i (Harmondsworth, 1989)

M. E. HESTON

15th–16th centuries. As protection against the region's frequent rains, sanctuaries, colonnades and gateways were all roofed with sloping tiers of metal sheets or tiles. In plan, sanctuaries were often circular, apse-ended or elliptical, reflecting the survival of ancient building forms. The typical Kerala-style complex had one or more sanctuaries and detached halls of different shapes standing within a rectangular colonnaded compound. The principal gateway was usually demarcated by its multi-tiered roof. Of particular interest is the exuberantly carved woodwork employed on walls, screens, doorways, columns and ceilings. Most of the accompanying paintings are later in date.

The Shiva Temple at Ettumanur, built mostly of timber, is typical. A square sanctuary is contained within a circular columned hall, entered through doorways on three sides. The outer elevation is dominated by the conical metal roof; this rises smoothly to a brass pot finial at the apex. The roof shelters an open wooden screen that admits light to the hall; this is carved with friezes of animals and epic narrative scenes. Angled wooden brackets are carved as deities and other figures; doorways are flanked by guardians and musicians. A detached hall in front of the shrine has a pyramidal roof; the wooden ceiling is divided into 25 panels, each depicting a different deity. Both shrine and hall are set within a rectangular enclosure surrounded by colonnades with double roofs. The entrance is surmounted by a double tier of gabled tiled roofs. Wall paintings found here (*see* §VI, 5(vii) below) are probably later in date. A variant on this scheme is seen at Vaikom, where the square sanctuary is contained within an elliptical columned hall under a smoothly tiled roof. Wood-carvings and paintings are probably later replacements.

The important Jaina centre of Mudabidri, in Karnataka just north of the Kerala border, preserves numerous religious establishments. These were mostly built with the sloping roofs in tiles or copper sheets that are characteristic of the coastal style. Founded in 1429 and added to in later centuries, the Chandranatha Basti consists of a sanctuary preceded by a sequence of three columned halls surrounded by a colonnade; a fourth detached hall has projecting sides. Each hall is roofed with sloping tiers; over the sanctuary is a triple-gabled roof. Stone columns are adorned with carved decoration. In front of the temple is a lofty lamp column.

Other temples illustrating the impact of indigenous practice are seen at Bhatkal. The Ketapai Narayana Temple is entirely roofed with sloping stone tiles. Carved panels and stone railings between peripheral columns of the sanctuary create a screen wall. Of interest is the ceiling design in which a central medallion is surrounded by friezes of miniature figures.

BIBLIOGRAPHY

P. Brown: *Indian Architecture (Buddhist and Hindu Periods)* (Bombay, [1941], rev. Bombay, 1956), chap. XIX

H. Sarkar: *An Architectural Survey of Temples of Kerala* (New Delhi, 1978)

R. M. Bernier: *Temple Arts of Kerala* (Delhi, 1981)

G. Michell: *Architecture and Art of Southern India: Vijayanagara and the Successor States* (Cambridge, 1994)

GEORGE MICHELL

(ii) Indo-Islamic. Ports on the Arabian Sea had been home to Muslim communities since the 8th century AD, but it was not until the invasions of Mahmud of Ghazna (*reg* 998–1030) that Islam became a major political and cultural force in the Indian subcontinent. Displacing the Hindu Shahis of the Punjab and the Carmathians of Multan, the Ghaznavid rulers established a large kingdom that stretched from Thanesar in north India to western Iran. The Ghaznavids were superseded in Iran by the Seljuks and in Afghanistan by the Ghurids, while in north India

the Sultanate of Delhi, established by the commander of the Ghurid army, Qutb al-Din Aybak, gained firm control in the second decade of the 13th century. The Sultanate expanded its power southward until virtually all the subcontinent was under the sway of Delhi in the time of Muhammad ibn Tughluq (*reg* 1325–51).

□

(a) North-west. (b) North. (c) West. (d) East. (e) Central. (f) South.

(a) North-west. The architecture of eastern Punjab and Multan was linked more strongly with Afghanistan and eastern Iran than with the rest of the Indian subcontinent during the Sultanate period. Brick was the main building material, and timber was used for structural and decorative purposes, the relatively dry climate permitting flat roofs of timber and dried mud, and wooden ties in brick walls. Glazed tiles were produced in Multan from the end of the 13th century. The earliest mosque in this area is the ruined Ghaznavid mosque at Rajagira in Swat, Pakistan. It is constructed of stone and schist flakes, which are also used for the floor. The mihrab was originally semicircular in plan but was reconstructed early in its life with a square plan and a horse-shoe arch.

The few surviving early buildings of MULTAN have been restored and in some cases reconstructed. The oldest are the 12th-century mosque of Khalid Walid, with its fine Kufic inscription on the MIHRAB, and the shrine of Shah Yusuf Gardizi, believed to date from 1152 but heavily renovated and covered with later glazed tiles. The shrine is built of brick and is rectangular in plan, with a flat roof and a small entrance in the west end of the south wall. The mihrab appears as an undecorated rectangular projection on the outside of the otherwise plain qibla wall (the wall orientated towards Mecca). A slight batter is seen in the shrine's walls, a feature probably borrowed from vernacular buildings, in which the pisé walls become increasingly narrow towards the top to improve stability. In the village architecture of north Pakistan and Afghanistan this characteristic is still prevalent.

The battering of the walls is more pronounced in the tomb of Shaykh Baha' al-Haqq Zakariya (*d* 1262). One of the largest buildings of Multan, the tomb stands within the perimeter of the old fort and is said to have been constructed by the Shaykh during his lifetime. The general form of the building appears to be original, but the structure has been restored several times, including in the 19th century, and the present tilework and finish of the dome are relatively modern. The tomb consists of a square chamber with plain walls and a hemispherical dome standing on a cylindrical drum. A notable feature of the building is the octagonal transitional zone of the dome. This zone, wider than the dome itself, has an arched opening in each face and appears from the exterior as a separate register. It is almost the same height as the dome and about half the height of the chamber on which it rests. Tall transitional zones are found in Timurid architecture, but the use of square, octagonal and hemispherical registers to enclose a single interior space is peculiar to the Multan region.

The form of Baha' al-Haqq's tomb was repeated in two other structures. One of these is the tomb of Shadna Shahid (*d* 1270), which is almost entirely original but for the modern plaster covering the brickwork. This tomb has a squat dome and is relatively small (5.6 m square on the inside). A second tomb of this type belongs to Shams al-Din Tabrizi (*d* 1276). In this building, believed to have been constructed at the turn of the 13th century by Shams al-Din's grandson, the octagonal register has been increased in height and the square chamber reduced. The octagon has broad arched niches and windows similar in width to the central openings on each side of the chamber. The tomb was heavily restored in 1780, and details such as the turrets and bands of glazed tilework date mainly from that period.

Tombs at Multan may have served as prototypes for the shrines of Shaykh ʿUthman Marvandi Laʿl Shahbaz (*c.* 1340) at Sehwan in Sind and of Shaykh ʿAla' al-Din (1486) at Pakpatan in Punjab, but Multan exerted greater influence on Tughluq architecture in Delhi, which makes extensive use of battered walls (*see* §(b) below). In Multan itself, tomb forms were further developed, notably in the tomb of Rukn-i ʿAlam (see fig. 86), built by Ghiyath al-Din Tughluq in 1320–24. It is octagonal in plan and has heavily battered towers of solid brick at the corners of the first tier. The upper tier, below the hemispherical dome, is comparable to that of the tomb of Shams al-Din Tabrizi, but an arched window was employed in each side instead of a niche. In the tomb of Rukn-i ʿAlam much of the original decoration has survived. The exterior and the interior are extensively decorated with both glazed and unglazed bricks with moulded and cut decoration. While this is derived from the 14th-century architecture of Khurasan and Central Asia, in Multan the colours are limited mainly to blue and white. The finely carved wooden

86. Tomb of Rukn-i ʿAlam, Multan, 1320–24; section from J. Marshall: *The Monuments of Muslim India* (Cambridge, 1928), iii of *Cambridge History of India*, pl. XVI

mihrab of the tomb is the only example of its kind in the Indian subcontinent; the inscription is an excellent example of early Tughluq elongated *naskhī* script. The tomb of Rukn-i ʿAlam was the prototype for a number of later tombs built in the region, including the ruined tombs of Baba Hatam and Bibi Jiwandi, both in Uch. A much later example of the type can be seen in the tomb of Tahar Khan Nahar (1671) in Muzaffargah.

A tradition of building with brick and using glazed tiles also existed in Sind, but the influence of Multan appears to have been minimal; forms derived from the stone architecture of India dominate. The Thambawaro Mosque (13th century or earlier) at Lahori Bandar is now in ruins but was built with temple spolia on a stone platform. It probably had a flat roof resting on monolithic columns. The tomb of Jam Nizam al-Din (1508) in THATTHA represents the later stone architecture of Sind. The tomb is square in plan with a single mihrab projecting well beyond the qibla wall. The building is constructed of rubble and faced with dressed stone decorated with patterns of both Islamic and Indian origin. The tomb has corbelled arches, a system generally abandoned by the early 15th century, and may therefore represent a link between Sind and Nagaur, particularly the Buland Darwaza of the Khanaqah al-Tarikin (1333) at Nagaur (*see* §(c) below). Archaic traditions of stonework continued in Thatta even after the Mughal conquest.

See also §5(ii)(a) above.

BIBLIOGRAPHY

A. Cunningham: *Archaeol. Surv. India Rep.*, v (1875), pp. 114–36
E. D. Maclangan: *Gazetteer of the Multan District, 1901–2* (Lahore, 1902), pp. 326–56
Archaeol. Surv. India, Annu. Rep. (1903–04), pp. 132–44
Archaeol. Surv. India, Annu. Rep. (1908–09), pp. 79–87
Archaeol. Surv. India, Annu. Rep. (1926–27), p. 207
Archaeol. Surv. India, Annu. Rep. (1927–28), pp. 90–91
J. Marshall: *Monuments of Muslim India*, Cambridge Hist. India, iii (Cambridge, 1928), pp. 597–9
H. Cousens: *The Antiquities of Sind*, Archaeol. Surv. India, New Imp. Ser., xlvi (Calcutta, 1929), pp. 48–71
Muzaffargarh District, Punjab District Gazetteers, xxxiv a, 1929 (Lahore, 1931), p. 311
Archaeol. Surv. India, Annu. Rep. (1936–37), pp. 9–10
P. Brown: *Indian Architecture, Islamic Period* (Bombay, [1942], rev. 1956 with additional photographs/*R* 1981), pp. 31–4
M. Wheeler: *Five Thousand Years of Pakistan: An Archaeological Outline* (London, 1950), pp. 61–71
J. Burton-Page: 'Tomb of Rukn-i Alam', *Splendours of the East*, ed. M. Wheeler (London, 1965), pp. 73–81
A. Nabi Khan: 'The Mausoleum of Šaiḥ 'Alā' al-Dīn at Pākpatan (Punjāb): A Significant Example of the Tuġluq Style of Architecture', *E. & W.*, xxiv (1974), pp. 310–26
——: *Multan History and Architecture* (Islamabad, 1983)
U. Scerrato: 'Research on the Archaeology and History of Islamic Art in Pakistan: Excavation of the Ghaznavid Mosque on Mt. Rāja Gīrā, Swat', *E. & W.*, xxxvi/4 (1986), pp. 496–511

NATALIE H. SHOKOOHY

(b) North. Islamic buildings were erected in north India from the end of the 12th century, when the region was conquered by the Ghurid sultan Muhammad ibn Sam (*reg* 1174–1206). Delhi became the centre of rule and the focus of building activity. Architectural developments continued with the expansion and consolidation of territories under subsequent Ghurid slaves (1191–1290), as well as Khalji (1290–1320) and Tughluq (1320–1413) rulers. Political instability and Timur's invasion of north India in 1398–9 weakened the hegemony of the Sultanate, and under the Sayyid (1414–44) and Lodi (1451–1526) dynasties building activity was generally restricted to Delhi and its environs.

Numerous Sultanate buildings have survived in Delhi and in north India, providing a relatively clear picture of architectural developments. Extant buildings include mosques, tombs, madrasas and *ʿidgāh*s (prayer walls used for ʿId and other celebrations; *see* MUSALLA). Secular buildings such as fortifications, stepwells and the remains of bridges and waterworks (dams, reservoirs and canals) are also preserved. Various building materials were employed, including architectural elements from temples demolished by the Muslim conquerors. The early sultans regarded the destruction of temples as a religious duty and the reuse of spolia as an act of symbolic appropriation. Demolition provided a substantial amount of such ready-to-assemble building material as ornamented columns, brackets, lintels, roof slabs and corbelled domes. All these could be reused in the construction of mosques, careful reassembly resulting in buildings with decorative schemes that retained indigenous floral and geometric carved patterns. Human and divine images were defaced, but carvings of animals were sometimes retained. Building materials also included brick, ashlar and dressed stone, typically used in walls with a rubble-and-mortar core. Decorative effects were achieved not only through the reuse of older material but through stone carved specifically for use in Islamic buildings. Carved and painted stucco and ceramic tile were also employed (*see* §VIII, 5(ii) below, and STUCCO AND PLASTERWORK, §III, 6).

A number of architectural and decorative features were imported from Khurasan, the most important of which was a form of the pointed arch. In the decades immediately after the Islamic conquest corbelled rather than true arches were formed by laying blocks of stone horizontally with the upper stone overlapping the one below and the top closed by a long slab. As in Khurasan, calligraphy was a major decorative element (*see also* §VIII, 3 below). The Kufic script became increasingly elaborate and ornamental, while *naskhī* script was the vehicle for informative texts. In Iran, by the time of the Ghurids, the 'Arab-type' plan for mosques, consisting of a colonnade around a courtyard, had given way to a traditionally Persian scheme consisting of two or four iwans (vaulted spaces; *see* IWAN) facing in on a central court. Sometimes the iwans had domed chambers behind. In India, however, the 'Arab-type' plan had been brought to Sind by the Arabs in the 8th century and was employed by early settlers at many sites (*see* §5(ii)(a) and (b) above). This type of plan was not only well established in India but was suitable for the trabeate structures built there; it thus enjoyed continued use under the Ghurids. Façades or screens pierced by arches were added to the Quwwat al-Islam Mosque in Delhi (see below) and the Arha'i Din ka Jhonpra in Ajmer (*see* §(c) below) as a compromise to provide some resemblance to the vaulted iwans and arcades of the Ghurid homelands. The minaret based on a circular plan represents another importation.

Two types of mihrabs can be seen in Ghurid buildings: an 'Arab type' with a semicircular plan and a 'Khurasani type' with a square plan and a pointed two-centred arch, sometimes decorated with lobes. The Khurasani type is found at Delhi, Kaman and Bayana, while the Arab type is found in the early mosques of Sind and Kutch and later at Ajmer and Khatu (*see* §(c) below). Mosques with Khurasani features were generally set on level ground and have entrances that resemble the portals of mosques in Khurasan. Mosques with mihrabs of the Arab type, all in the western regions of Sultanate territory, are usually set on platforms on the side of a hill, with access provided by staircases flanked or surmounted by domed pavilions. This arrangement is often found in the temples of western India. In both architectural form and material there was a tendency to assimilate existing Indian and Arab prototypes with Khurasani elements. This amalgamation eventually led to experimentation and increasingly lighter effects created by the use of arches, vaults and domes carried on squinches and pendentives. This process of assimilating Indian with Arab and Khurasani architectural forms continued into the 16th century.

Delhi and surrounding areas.

Early Sultanate (1191–1290). Two of the earliest Sultanate buildings were the Quwwat al-Islam (Might of Islam) Mosque and the Qutb Minar, a 72.5 m-high minaret, both erected in Delhi to celebrate the Ghurid conquest (see fig. 87; *see also* DELHI, §III, 1). The inscription on the eastern gateway states that the mosque was constructed in 1191 using the material of 27 temples. As a trabeate structure with corbelled domes supported by columns and brackets, the Quwwat al-Islam follows Indian building traditions, but in many respects the design stems from the architecture of Islamic western Asia. It is built on an Arab-type plan, with a large (43×32 m) central courtyard; the mihrab of the original mosque, true to its Ghurid origins, follows the Persian type and consists of a niche, square in plan, with no projection outside the qibla wall. The Arab tradition of projecting the mihrab outside the wall was, however, entrenched in India and is seen in other Ghurid mosques, including a subsequent extension to the Quwwat al-Islam. Another feature of Persian origin is the façade of the prayer-hall, added in 1199. It has five large corbelled arches, the central bay being substantially wider and taller in imitation of an iwan with its flanking chambers. The façade exterior is carved with lotuses and floral motifs of the Indian type as well as Koranic inscriptions in *naskhī* script. The Qutb Minar (*see also* DELHI, fig. 2) is in the style of minarets in Afghanistan and was built at the same time as the mosque, although the two upper tiers were rebuilt several times at later dates. The ground-plan is stellate, with alternating lobes and pointed wedges; the decoration consists of carved bands with arabesques and bold *naskhī* inscriptions. The mosque was increased to three times its original size by Iltutmish (*reg* 1211–36), who extended the qibla wall to the north and south and added new colonnades with entrances aligned with the existing ones on the other three sides, enclosing the original mosque and the Qutb Minar. The screen wall was also extended, incorporating characteristically Khurasani features: pointed four-centred arches rather than the ogee-shaped openings of the earlier screen, and inscriptions in

87. Quwwat al-Islam Mosque, Delhi, *c.* 1191; view of the ruined prayer-hall from the south, with the Qutb Minar beyond

sophisticated *naskhī* and in 'plaited' Kufic script with the terminal strokes formed into interwoven patterns. Coeval mosques outside Delhi include the Chaurasi Khamba in Kaman and a mosque now known as the Ukha Mandir in Bayana (see below). The Chaurasi Khamba is a trabeate building (36×24 m) constructed around a courtyard; the northern and eastern sides are not walled in the usual fashion but have raised platforms with open colonnades above. The main mihrab, rectangular in plan, has an ogee arch decorated with a pierced scroll fringe. The stone minbar, with seven steps and a canopy above the speaker's platform, is the earliest known example in India.

Ghurid *'idgāh*s are located in Bayana and Badaun. Consisting simply of a large open area with a wall that worshippers face during prayer, an *'idgāh* provides a place of assembly for festivals when the Muslims of a whole town gather together. The Bayana *'idgāh* consists of a central mihrab set in a square, domed recess flanked by four smaller niches on either side and a round tower at each end of the wall. The niches are built with corbelled arches of lobed profile. Similar in plan is the brick-built *'idgāh* of Badaun, probably founded by Iltutmish when he was governor of the town but later heavily reconstructed.

The earliest Sultanate tomb is in Delhi. Known as Sultan Ghari, it was built by Iltutmish in 1231–2 (AH 629) and used as the burial place of his son Abu'l-Fath Mahmud. The building consists of a square courtyard (27×27 m) built on a platform and enclosed by a stone wall with a circular tower at each corner; a single-aisled colonnade with a marble mihrab is on the western side. The crypt in the centre of the courtyard is the earliest octagonal structure in India. A second early tomb is said to be that of Iltutmish himself in the Quwwat al-Islam complex, a square chamber (12.5×12.5 m) with entrances on three sides. On the qibla side there are three mihrabs with no projection outside the wall. The corbelled dome, now fallen, was supported by squinches; these are the earliest known examples of such forms in India. While brick-built tomb-chambers in Khurasan served as a prototype, Iltutmish's tomb is executed in stone with a plain exterior that was originally plastered. The interior is lavishly carved with decorative patterns and Koranic inscriptions in *naskhī* and plaited Kufic scripts.

Iltutmish left northern India unified under the Sultanate, but little remains of the architecture of his immediate successors. The tomb of Sultan Balban (*reg* 1266–87) is one of the few surviving monuments. Built with massive rubble-and-mortar walls covered with plaster, it employed true arches and cross vaults and had a true dome (now collapsed) supported by squinches. This new method of construction followed the masonry traditions of Khurasan.

Khaljis (1290–1320). With the Khaljis, true arches became the general rule, and while true domes were often employed, corbelled domes also remained in use. Red sandstone with white-marble inlays was favoured as a building material. 'Ala' al-Din Khalji (*reg* 1296–1316), the dynasty's most prolific builder, extended the Quwwat al-Islam Mosque and began the 'Ala'i Minar. Intended to be double the size of the Qutb Minar, the minaret was left unfinished. The gateway known as the 'Ala'i Darvaza is the most notable part of 'Ala' al-Din's additions to the Quwwat al-Islam. The gate is an elegant structure consisting of a square chamber with true arches and a true dome supported by squinches. Built of red sandstone and white marble, it is carved with geometric patterns and calligraphic borders. Another Khalji-period mosque, the Jama'at Khana in Delhi, has three arched bays, each roofed by a shallow dome, a departure in layout from previous mosques. 'Ala' al-Din also established several fortifications, including the new town of Siri in Delhi, with battered towers and walls built of large blocks of stone, and the fort of Hansi, constructed in brick. The Barsi gate (1303) at Hansi is a massive portal flanked by two towers with semicircular plans and battered walls. Another example of brickwork of this time, the *'idgāh* of Repari, was constructed in 1311–12 (AH 711) and is 47 m long and 10 m high with two battered towers. The structure was plastered and had a band of blue tiles running above its 11 mihrabs.

More modest than the buildings of the Khaljis and their governors are the small vernacular religious buildings at Fatehpur Sikri. The Pathan Masjid and Ambiya Wali Masjid in the village of Nagar at Fatehpur Sikri consist of simple flat-roofed colonnades on the qibla side of the courtyard. They are made of temple spolia, but the mihrabs were carved specifically for the buildings.

Tughluqs (1320–1413). The Tughluq dynasty was established by Ghiyath al-Din Tughluq (*reg* 1320–25), who built the new city of Tughluqabad at Delhi (*see* DELHI, §I). In Tughluq architecture, the emphasis is on space and its manipulation, the exploitation of structural effects and the role of light and shadow. Water was used extensively, often to moderate the temperature. Structural methods based on massive piers and arches became the norm, used side by side with the indigenous system of building with stone beams and brackets. Detailed sculptural designs on the faces of columns and walls were no longer a prime consideration. The traveller Ibn Battuta described the exterior of the palace of Tughluqabad as faced with 'golden bricks', presumably lustre tiles or bricks. Designed on the principle of Iranian fortifications, Tughluqabad is divided into three main areas, the citadel (Pers. *arq*), fort (*qala'* or *bālā shahr*) and fortified town (*shahristān* or *rabd*). The citadel and fort are located not in the centre but in a corner of the fortified town, a configuration that was followed in most Islamic fortifications in India. Tughluqabad had sophisticated waterworks, both for defence and for general use.

To the south-west of the town, Ghiyath al-Din built his tomb, a small fortified structure once surrounded by water and connected to the citadel by a causeway (*see* DELHI, §III, 2). The tomb itself is a square, domed chamber constructed of rubble faced with red sandstone and decorated with white stone. A main feature of the tomb is its battered walls, a form introduced to Delhi from Multan, where Ghiyath al-Din was governor before coming to the throne (*see also* §(a) above). Battered walls became a standard feature of Tughluq buildings.

Muhammad ibn Tughluq's (*reg* 1325–51) main contributions to Delhi were the construction of 'Adilabad, a new fortification to the south of Tughluqabad, and the establishment of the new town of Jahanpanah, including a palace complex, a few miles north of Tughluqabad. The interior decoration of the palace, described by Ibn Battuta, made extensive use of wood-carving, gilt, gold fittings and textiles (especially silk) for carpets, hangings and even trees and artificial flowers. Later Muhammad ibn Tuluq embarked on building a new fortification for Jahanpanah, and adding Siri to the old city of Delhi, but this project was left incomplete. To supply water to Jahanpanah, the Sat Pul was built, a substantial dam with a causeway above and sluices below to control the water. The Bijai Mandal, part of the Jahanpanah palace complex, was constructed of rubble with the usual battered walls. It is a two-tiered structure with a courtyard, all set on a platform. Muhammad ibn Tughluq later moved his capital from Delhi to DAULATABAD in the Deccan, but finding the location unsuitable he re-established the administration in Delhi.

Muhammad ibn Tughluq's successor, Firuz Shah Tughluq (*reg* 1351–88), was a man of the arts, an architect and an engineer who personally designed many of his buildings. His new capital in Delhi was Firuzabad (*see* DELHI, §I). Its citadel was built on the bank of the Jumna Canal, a watercourse constructed with stone banks as a branch of the Yamuna River. The canal was used both for the supply of water and for the transportation of goods and building materials. The Jamiʿ Mosque (Friday Mosque) of Firuzabad, now in ruins, consisted of a courtyard surrounded by a series of vaults or small domes built of rubble and mortar supported on stone columns. The ruins of the mosque stand on a platform with a series of vaulted chambers around it. (Platforms of this kind became common in the Delhi region in the 15th century and the early 16th.) The entrance is a square, domed chamber reached by a pyramidal flight of steps.

To the north of the Jamiʿ Mosque is the Firuz Shah Kotla, a stepped pyramidal structure with three platforms surmounted by a monolithic column of the third Mauryan emperor, Ashoka (*reg c.* 269–*c.* 232 BC), incised with an inscription of the 26th year of the reign. The column—named the Golden Minar (*minara-ye zarrin*)—served as the minaret of the Jamiʿ Mosque. The removal of this column from its original site near Amballa (in Punjab), its transportation and its re-erection were supervised by Firuz Shah, who also designed the building and all the engineering equipment needed for the operation. A circular reservoir near this structure consists of domed chambers above ground and two tiers of corridors below ground with a well in the middle. Its layout departs from the traditional form for Indian stepwells, which are usually oblong with a flight of steps at one end and a circular well at the other. It may be based on a Khurasani type, an example of which survives at Bust in Afghanistan. The form did not become popular in India but was used in a few other places; a Mughal example stands in the fort of Agra.

The mosques constructed in Delhi in the time of Firuz Shah vary considerably. The Begampuri Mosque, for example, is built on a four-iwan plan with domed chambers behind the iwans. The Khirki Mosque is unusual in that it is divided into a grid of 25 squares, with arcades three

88. Madrasa of Firuz Shah, Delhi, *c.* 1320–1415; view from the west

aisles across in a cruciform pattern. The whole area is roofed, leaving four small courtyards to provide light and air. The Sanjar (or Kali) Mosque has a similar plan, but the courtyards are larger. The Kalan Mosque has a modified Arab-type plan. Despite these differences, all the mosques have battered walls, masonry vaults and domes on stone columns as well as columns grouped in pairs round the courtyards. These features, all characteristic of the Firuz Shah period, are also evident in such ruined mosques as the Kalu Sarai Mosque, the mosque in Haud-i Khass and the Chawnsath Khamba Mosque.

Firuz Shah's madrasa in Delhi (see fig. 88) on the bank of the Haud-i Khass reservoir does not follow the traditional plan of a theological college with a courtyard surrounded by cells. Instead, it is arranged on an L-shaped plan and built in two storeys with large halls and arcades open from either side to give pleasant views of the reservoir. The massive retaining wall of the reservoir is faced with ashlar. The ground-level of the building has stone columns supporting heavy masonry arches and vaults; the upper level is a light trabeate structure. At the centre is a domed chamber, with smaller domed rooms at either end. This arrangement gives the building an effect of increasing lightness and plasticity as the eye travels upwards. Firuz Shah's tomb, a square, domed structure with gently battered walls, is located near the madrasa. Its exterior is plain, but the arches and springing of the dome in the interior have borders of carved stucco with calligraphy and floral designs. The dome itself has calligraphic medallions and cartouches, a form of decoration common in Iranian architecture of the period.

One of Firuz Shah's most ambitious projects was the foundation of the town of Hisar-i Firuza (modern Hisar) in a strategically important desert area. He supervised the construction of the town and for the water supply undertook a substantial engineering project to build canals from the Yamuna and Sutlej rivers. The old Jamiʿ Mosque of Hisar, known as the Lat ki Mosque after the column erected in the courtyard, is comparable to the Jamiʿ of Firuzabad but is better preserved, retaining its prayer-hall with masonry vaults and arches supported by columns with monolithic shafts. The surviving parts of the palace of Hisar show that it was originally built in at least three levels. The lower level had arcades with massive piers, the middle level had masonry arcades on monolithic columns, and the upper level (of which little remains) had colonnades. The principle of making the building progressively lighter towards the top is similar to that used in the madrasa at Haud-i Khass. To the north of the palace are the remains of a garden and the Gujari Mahal, a pavilion roofed with nine small domes supported by the walls and four central columns. The Gujari Mahal stands on a high platform with a water channel running underneath. It is comparable to the Bijai Mandal in Siri but is more refined in design. The north wall of the garden, including its gateway and a corner tower, remains intact. The wall has a corridor inside running along its length with arched openings at regular intervals giving views into the garden.

Outside Hisar the Jahaz Kothi ('house in the form of a ship') was probably a madrasa but is named after its shape, which imitates a ship with angular sides and a pointed prow. It has solid battered masonry walls and was surrounded by water. A central arcaded hall with cross vaults leads to a series of chambers and to smaller arcades with secondary courtyards. Hisar and its surroundings have numerous tombs of the time of Firuz Shah. Most consist of a square, domed chamber with battered walls and a single-shelled dome supported by squinches. Any variation is mainly in the decorative treatment; some are stone-clad, others employ carved or painted stucco.

Domed pavilions (*chatrīs*) also served as tombs, as for example in the tomb of Shaykh Salah al-Din Darwish, built in 1339–40 (AH 740) in Delhi, in which the spaces between the columns have been filled with stone screens. A new type of tomb structure was introduced late in the Tughluq period with the tomb of Khan-i Jahan Tilangani (*d* 1368–9). This tomb, also in Delhi, is octagonal in plan with a central domed chamber surrounded by an arcade. The arcade has three openings on each side and is roofed with vaults and small domes. A combination of stone facing and carved stucco was used for the finish of the building. A number of later octagonal tombs were based on this prototype.

Later Delhi Sultanate: Sayyids (1414–44) and Lodis (1451–1526). After the sack of Delhi in 1398–9 by Timur, the Sayyid and Lodi sultans ruled from Delhi over a smaller territory until the establishment of the Mughal empire by Babur (*reg* 1526–30) in 1526. The main architectural remains of this period are mosques and tombs. While the precedents of Tughluq architecture were followed, a number of innovations appeared. By this time the understanding of the load-bearing capabilities of masonry had improved, and buildings were much lighter. The double-shelled dome was introduced from Iran and used in some buildings. The plasticity of cut-stucco decoration added to the effect of lightness, and colour was used more extensively than before. The introduction of tilework in the buildings of Delhi was limited to decorative bands on the exterior walls and occasionally tiled domes. Tiles were also set into red sandstone to provide contrast.

The mosque of the Bara Gunbad complex (1494) at Delhi has tangential arches with sharply curved haunches. This departure from the use of gently curved two- and four-centred arches was not widely used in later times. Built on a platform, the mosque is a five-bayed, single-aisled building with three domes. It has two ornamental corner towers in the qibla wall and a projecting balcony on the north and south sides. The walls are vertical rather than battered. The outside is plastered, and the interior is divided into a lower register in dressed stone and an upper one in cut stucco, far more elaborate than the surface decoration seen previously. The Moth ki Mosque (1505) in Delhi, like the Bara Gunbad, has five bays and three domes, with the interior divided into two registers in stone and cut stucco. Its two corner towers are in the form of octagonal double-storey arcades. The mosque stands on a Tughluq-style platform with arched openings around it. Most other mosques of this period in Delhi are smaller, consisting of three bays with a single aisle and only one dome. Examples are the Nili Mosque, built in 1505–6 (AH 911), the Muhammadiwali Mosque and the mosque of Adham Khan.

The town of Tijara, south-east of Delhi, has many late Sultanate buildings with fine stucco decoration. The La'l Mosque, for example, has cut stucco with floral motifs and Koranic inscriptions. This mosque, with three bays and a single aisle, was roofed by three domes supported by pendentives; the windows have the usual projecting balconies. The mosque in the tomb complex of Hasan Khan in Tijara also has one aisle and three bays roofed by three domes. The tomb is a square, domed chamber.

In Delhi many *'idgāh*s and graveyard enclosures have survived from the 15th century. The enclosures are built on platforms with prayer walls at the western side and have many features in common with mosques, including corner towers, niches or arcades around the platforms, rows of decorative niches in the walls, and decorative turrets on either side of the projection on the exterior of the western wall marking the mihrab. The tombs are of three types: octagonal, domed chambers surrounded by arcades; square, domed chambers; and *chatrī*s (domed pavilions). The octagonal tombs are based on the prototype of the tomb of Khan-i Jahan Tilangani (see above) but are larger and more elaborate. The tomb of the Sayyid ruler Sultan Mubarak Shah (*reg* 1421–34), for example, has six small octagonal *chatrī*s surrounding the high transitional zone of the central dome, which is four-centred in profile. This improves the proportions of the whole and allows the decorative qualities of the upper part of the building to be seen to greater advantage. In the tomb of Muhammad Shah (*reg* 1435–45) the design improvements are taken even further: the octagonal *chatrī*s of the roof are larger and the piers and columns of the arcade slimmer. The dome is hemispherical. The interior is decorated with Koranic inscriptions, cut stucco and red, blue and gold paint. In the tomb of Sikandar Shah Lodi (*reg* 1489–1517) the central dome is double-shelled, a structural advance introduced from Iran and seen earlier at Delhi in the tomb of Shahab al-Din Taj Khan (*d* 1500–01/AH 906). The largest octagonal tomb is that of 'Ala' al-Din 'Alam Shah (*reg* 1446–51) in Tijara. This building is in three tiers rather than two, and the arcades stand on massive piers rather than on dressed stone columns. Octagonal tombs of this type were also built for the Suri sultans in the 16th century.

The square-chamber tombs differ from those of the Tughluq period in that they are generally much larger, the walls are perpendicular, and the exteriors are no longer plain but have a number of niches and windows, sometimes arranged in two or three registers. The best examples are in Delhi and include the Bara Gunbad (1494), the Shish Gunbad, the Dadi ka Gunbad, the tombs of Bare Khan, Chhote Khan and Bhure Khan, and the tomb of Shahab al-Din Taj Khan with its double-shelled dome.

The traditional Indian *chatrī*, octagonal or square, remained popular for tombs. The columns, lintels and brackets are of dressed stone, but in most cases the domes are plastered on both the exterior and interior and many have cut-stucco decoration. In the tomb of Yusuf Qattal in Delhi the spaces between the columns are filled with pierced stone screens carved with geometric patterns.

Other structures of this period in and around Delhi include bridges and STEPWELLS. The stepwells are in the usual Indian style and consist of a flight of steps leading down to the water level, with a series of chambers and corridors in several tiers. They are distinguished from the ancient Indian wells by being arcuate. Two of these are the Rajun ki Ba'in (*c.* 1506–7/AH 912), in Mehrauli, and Ugar Sans Ba'oli, near Connaught Place, off Kasturba Gandhi Road.

Jaunpur. Located mid-way between Delhi and Bengal, JAUNPUR was founded by Firuz Shah Tughluq in 1359. At the time of Timur's invasion the governor, Khwaja Jahan (1394–8), proclaimed his independence and founded the Sharqi Sultanate, which lasted until 1477, when Sikandar Lodi annexed the territory to Delhi. The Tughluq buildings in Jaunpur include the ramparts of the fort, but the walls were largely reconstructed at the time of the Mughal emperor Akbar (*reg* 1556–1605), when a bridge was also built over the Gumti River. The Qal'a Mosque (Fort Mosque) built in 1376 dates from the time of Firuz Shah Tughluq. In its courtyard stands an inscribed commemorative column. The mosque consists of a three-bayed hall with three domes flanked by flat-roofed colonnades. As in other Tughluq buildings the outer rows of columns are set in pairs, a feature adopted in later Sharqi architecture.

The Sharqi sultans erected many buildings, and under their rule the town developed into a centre of learning. However, when Sikandar Lodi took Jaunpur he razed most of the city except for five mosques. These are the only remaining examples of the distinctive architecture that developed in Jaunpur in the 15th century. They indicate that one of its main features was its monumentality, which was initially achieved by building massive structures of exceptional height. Towering screens were used in gateways or in front of prayer-halls, with an effect of lightness obtained by arched openings and niches on the surface. By the end of this period architectural advances included the technique of spanning large halls with arched stone vaults, resulting in buildings that were both lighter in structure and had larger column-free spaces inside.

The Atala Mosque (see fig. 89), built between 1377 and 1404, perhaps as the first Jami' Mosque of Jaunpur, incorporates most of the features associated with Sharqi architecture. It is a square building following an Arab-type plan and is constructed from temple spolia on a grand scale (79 m on each side). Around the exterior of the mosque, except on the qibla side, is a row of chambers with a colonnade in front for accommodating scholars, merchants and travellers. The most arresting feature of the mosque is its central gateway screen in front of the qibla colonnade. The screen has a high central arched recess flanked by square, battered towers with niches in four registers. Three times the height of the prayer-hall, the screen hides the dome over the sanctuary. Two smaller screens on either side balance the otherwise disproportionate effect of the great screen. The interior of the prayer-hall behind the screens is as high as the two-storey colonnade around the courtyard. The north and south ends of the prayer-hall are in two storeys and have royal and women's galleries on the upper floor, with pierced stonework screens and private access from outside.

The Khalis Mukhlis Mosque (*c.* 1430) was built on the same lines as the Atala Mosque but is sparsely decorated. In contrast, the Jhanjhri Mosque of about the same date, of which only the gateway screen remains standing, is an

89. Atala Mosque, Jaunpur, 1377–1404; view of the prayer-hall from the courtyard

example of a carefully proportioned and exquisitely ornamented structure. The screen, like that of the Atala Mosque, consists of an arch flanked by rectangular buttresses. The elevation of the arch is divided into three registers, with pierced stone screens in the top register around which run bands of carved inscriptions in fine overlapping *naskhī* script.

In the La'l Darwaza Mosque (or Shahi Mosque), built *c.* 1450 by the queen of Mahmud Shah, the plan of the Atala Mosque was adapted to suit a medium-sized mosque. As in the Jhanjhri Mosque, columns supporting lintels are used under the arched recess of its gateway screen, but the upper registers of the screen lack elaborate ornament. The prayer-hall has upper galleries for women on either side of the central domed chamber, a departure from the more usual side galleries.

Around 1470, some 60 years after the building of the Atala Mosque, the last Sharqi ruler, Husayn Shah (*reg* 1458–79), built a new Jami' Mosque. This grand structure is set on a high platform, its three gates being reached by broad flights of steps. The exterior chambers are at street level, while above is a two-aisled colonnade around the courtyard of the mosque. A ponderous gateway screen leads to the central domed chamber of the prayer-hall, which benefits from additional light from an open clerestory arcade around the dome. The domed chamber is flanked by colonnades in two storeys with screened areas for women above, as in the La'l Darwaza Mosque. The side halls of the sanctuary (15×12 m) are spanned by arched stone vaults resting on the masonry walls, leaving the whole space free of columns or other supports for the roof. A hundred years earlier, an attempt was made to build a vault of this profile out of brick in the Jami' Mosque of Pandua in Bengal, but the vaults no longer stand. In Jaunpur a more stable structure was achieved by the use of two transverse ribs spanning each hall combined with wall ribs at each end and covered with flat slabs of stone laid horizontally, producing a homogeneous shell.

Bayana. In the early Sultanate period (1191–1290) Bayana emerged as an important provincial centre, and a number of buildings were constructed. The mosque known as the Ukha Mandir (*c.* 1206–7) is a colonnaded building (37×17 m) walled on all sides except the east, where there is an open colonnade with a central entrance gateway surmounted by a corbelled arch. The central mihrab resembles that of the Chaurasi Khamba in Kaman (see above). During the Khalji period the mosque was extended in 1320–21 (AH 720) on its southern side to form the mosque known as the Ukha Mosque, an important monument that influenced later building in Bayana, Agra and the surrounding region. Following the general layout of the earlier building, the eastern elevation of the extension corresponds broadly with the Ukha Mandir and consists of a monumental gateway flanked by open colonnades (see fig. 90). The gateway is built of red sandstone and white marble and originally had two small turrets. Reused materials were employed, but the column shafts

90. Ukha Mosque, Bayana, 1320–21; eastern façade

of the qibla colonnade have been re-dressed. The colonnades on the other sides have an upper level.

Other Khalji architecture includes an elaborate stepwell, the Jhalar Ba'oli, built at Bayana in 1318–19 (AH 718). The tank is square in plan and surrounded by a colonnade, with entrances through round towers on each corner. A village south-west of Bayana near Hindaun has a similar stepwell, and in Hindaun itself the Jachchaw ki Ba'oli is of the same form but without a colonnade.

In the 15th century the region came under the control of the Auhadi Khans, who held it sometimes as tributaries of the Sharqi sultans but mostly as independent rulers. Around 1460 they were replaced by the Jalwanis, who were in turn deposed by Sikandar Lodi. Sikandar Lodi built a new town at Bayana, calling it Sikandra (not to be confused with the Sikandra near Agra); Bayana gradually lost its importance when Sikandar Lodi developed Agra as his new capital.

Auhadi monuments are located in the town of Bayana and in the Vijayamandir fort, 6 km to the west. Within the citadel are a palace, three mosques and many houses, with numerous other houses scattered outside. These houses are among the very few surviving examples of private dwellings from the Sultanate period. Those inside and outside the fort consist of a series of single- or double-storey rooms and colonnades built around a courtyard. The colonnades may have been receiving rooms, with private rooms on the upper floors. The columns and the lintels are of dressed red sandstone, but the stone walls were plastered. A group of houses south of the fort has a different layout. These are all identical in plan, consisting of a central colonnaded hall with a room on either side. Each pair of houses is joined by a party-wall and each has a walled front garden to the north. The structural units, such as column shafts, capitals and lintels, are of the same form and size and are decorated in the same manner. It appears that a modular plan for the area was laid out and executed using mass-produced, prefabricated materials.

Other buildings in the Vijayamandir fort were constructed of modular and prefabricated units, including a colonnaded palace built in two or more storeys around a central courtyard. A red and yellow sandstone gateway in the south-east corner of the courtyard is decorated with blue inlaid tiles. The double columns in front of the building and the brackets decorated with suspended hemispheres are characteristic of Bayana architecture.

The oldest dated Auhadi structure is the Taleti Mosque, built inside the fort in 1417–18 (AH 820) by Karim al-Mulk Auhad Khan (*reg c.* 1400–21; AH 803–24). The prayer colonnade of the mosque projects out from the western wall and occupies only part of the western end of the courtyard, unlike Khalji and Tughluq mosques, in which it stretches the entire length of the western wall. The mosque is decorated with lobed, arched niches and blue tilework. Two similar mosques located in the area are the 'Idgah Mosque in the village of Birambad near Bayana and a ruined mosque in the village of Sikandra. This type of mosque plan became popular in early Mughal building and was used, for example, in the Mosque of Shaykh Salim Chishti at Fatehpur Sikri. The Dawud Khan Mosque, also in the fort, was built in 1447–8 (AH 851) on a more traditional plan, with a colonnaded hall in seven bays and two aisles. The roof is flat and is supported by circular columns of yellow sandstone. Its entrance, flanked by two *chatrīs*, is similar to that of the mosques at Sikandra and at Birambad. The Dawud Khan Mosque has an impressive minaret in yellow and red sandstone that was the prototype for an unfinished minaret, the Ukha Minar, started in 1519–20 (AH 926) for the Ukha Mandir.

Two mosques in the town of Bayana are datable to the Auhadi period: the Muftipara and the Talakini. Both are built on platforms and consist of a courtyard with a flat-roofed gallery on the west side. The monolithic column shafts of the Talakini Mosque are square in plan at each end and octagonal in the middle, a form first seen in the 14th-century columns of the Ukha Mosque and the Jhalar Ba'oli. Such columns can also be found in many 15th-century buildings of Bayana, including a colonnade—probably part of a mosque or a *khānaqāh* (a Sufi hospice or meeting hall)—adjoining a square, domed shrine now in the high school of Bayana. Smaller mosques in the vicinity include the Pahar Mosque and the Delhi Darwaza Mosque, the latter in the village of Sikri.

The Auhadi tombs, numerous in the region, are generally *chatrīs*. The tombs of some members of the Auhadi family are in a graveyard near the Talakini Mosque. The tomb of Auhad Khan (*d* 1421) has a square plan with 12 columns, all finely carved, supporting a corbelled dome decorated on the interior. Near it is another 12-columned, square *chatrī* in which the spaces between the columns are filled with stone panels, some carved with pierced decoration. It has a true dome made of large slabs of stone. Most of the smaller *chatrīs*, mainly with four columns, have either corbelled or true domes. Some, however, have a flat roof with a solid decorative dome resting on the slabs of the roof. Some of the square *chatrīs* have eight columns, one at each corner and one in the middle of each side. A *chatrī* of this type in Hindaun to the south-west bears an inscription with the date 1507–8 (AH 913). Such an arrangement for a *chatrī* is characteristic of Bayana architecture but is uncommon elsewhere in India. In some tombs the form is taken one step further, and an extra column is added in the centre, creating a structure that is not strictly speaking a *chatrī*. In a tomb known as the Bare Kamar, a refined architectural form is achieved by a combination of modular square units. The upper storey of this two-storey structure comprises five *chatrīs*, one in each corner and one in the centre, all with pyramidal roofs.

The architecture of Bayana of the Lodi period (1451–1526) seldom shows influence from Delhi. The secular buildings of the new town, Sikandra, once famous for its gardens, include a gate known as the La'l Darwaza and a reservoir. A similar reservoir, the Ba'oli of Mutam Khan (1512–13; AH 918), is situated north-west of Bayana. It consists of a circular well to the south and a flight of steps with a gateway chamber to the north and has galleries in four levels. The only building constructed entirely in the Delhi style is the main mosque of Sikandra, comparable in design to the Moth ki Mosque in Delhi (see above). The Sikandra mosque, now in ruins, was one of the largest buildings in the area. It was constructed of grey sandstone with decorative string courses of red sandstone. The columns and its 11 mihrabs were also of red sandstone.

In 1496 the Lodi governor Khan-i Khanan Farmuli built a stepwell (*bā'olī*) with three underground levels in the fort at Bayana. The lower storey has a corridor around the reservoir decorated with arched niches, while the upper storeys are built as colonnades. The decorative features of this stepwell, such as the hemispherical forms on the brackets, the high-relief roundels with lotus decoration and the decorative details of the columns, capitals and brackets, are all characteristic of the architecture of north India and the Bayana region in particular. However, in the Ba'oli of Khan-i Khanan the overall effect of the design and decoration strongly resembles that of the palaces of Fatehpur Sikri, suggesting that the Bayana style influenced early Mughal architecture.

See also §5(ii)(b) above.

BIBLIOGRAPHY

A. Cunningham: 'Report of Operations of the Archaeological Surveyor to the Government of India during the Season 1862–63', *Archaeol. Surv. India Rep.*, i (1871), pp. 131–231

——: 'Report of Operations of the Archaeological Surveyor to the Government of India during the Season 1864–65', *Archaeol. Surv. India Rep.*, ii (1871), pp. 252–63

J. D. Beglar: 'Report on Delhi, by Mr J. D. Beglar, Assistant Archaeological Survey of India, for the Half-year Ending September 1871', *Archaeol. Surv. India Rep.*, iv (1874), pp. 1–91

A. C. L. Carlleyle: 'Report on Agra with Notices of Some of the Neighbouring Places by Mr A. C. L. Carlleyle, Assistant Archaeological Survey', *Archaeol. Surv. India Rep.*, iv (1874), pp. 217–21

A. Cunningham: 'Report of Operations of the Archaeological Survey of India for the Season 1872–73', *Archaeol. Surv. India Rep.*, v (1875), pp. 114–44

J. Fergusson: *History of Indian and Eastern Architecture*, ii (1876), rev. J. Burgess (London, 1910), pp. 198–225

A. Cunningham: 'Report of a Tour in Eastern Rajputana in 1871–72 and 1872–73', *Archaeol. Surv. India Rep.*, vi (1878), pp. 40–73

——: 'Report of Tours in the Gangetic Provinces from Badaon to Bihar in 1875–76 and 1877–78', *Archaeol. Surv. India Rep.*, xi (1880), pp. 1–10, 102–26

——: 'Report of a Tour in Eastern Rajputana in 1882–83', *Archaeol. Surv. India Rep.*, xx (1885), pp. 54–92, 114–24, 127–60

H. B. W. Garrick: 'Report of a Tour in the Punjāb and Rājpūtana in 1883–84', *Archaeol. Surv. India Rep.*, xxiii (1887), pp. 11–25, 34–85

A. Führer and W. Smith: *The Sharqī Architecture of Jaunpur*, Archaeol. Surv. India, New Ser., i (Calcutta, 1889)

F. Wetzel: *Islamische Grabbauten in Indien* (1918/*R* Osnabrück, 1970)

Maulvi Zafar Hasan: *A Guide to Nizamu-d Dīn*, Mem. Archaeol. Surv. India, x (Calcutta, 1922)

J. F. Blakinston: *The Jāmi' Masjid at Badaon and Other Buildings in the United Provinces*, Mem. Archaeol. Surv. India, xix (Calcutta, 1926)

J. A. Page: *An Historical Memoir on the Qutb, Delhi*, Mem. Archaeol. Surv. India, xxii (Calcutta, 1926)

J. Marshall: 'The Monuments of Muslim India', *Cambridge History of India*, iii (Cambridge, 1928), pp. 571–97, 622–8

J. A. Page: *A Memoir on Kotla Fīrūz Shāh, Delhi*, Mem. Archaeol. Surv. India, lii (Delhi, 1937)

P. Brown: *Indian Architecture, Islamic Period* (Bombay, [1942], rev. 1956 with additional photographs/*R* 1981), pp. 9–30, 42–7

H. Waddington: ''Adilabad', *Anc. India*, i (1946), pp. 60–76

S. A. A. Naqvi: '*Sulṭān Ghārī*', *Anc. India*, iii (1947), pp. 4–10

T. Yamamoto, M. Ara and T. Tsukinowa: *Delhi: Architectural Remains of the Sultanate Period*, 3 vols (Tokyo, 1967–70)

Z. A. Desai: *Indo-Islamic Architecture* (Faridabad, 1970)

H. Crane and A. Welch: 'The Tughluqs, Master Builders of the Delhi Sultanate', *Muqarnas*, i (1983), pp. 123–66

M. Shokoohy: *Rajasthan I*, Corp. Inscr. Iran., xlix (London, 1986)

M. Shokoohy and N. H. Shokoohy: 'The Architecture of Baha al-din Tughrul in the Region of Bayana, Rajasthan', *Muqarnas*, iv (1987), pp. 114–32

——: *Ḥiṣār-i Fīrūza* (London, 1988)

A. Welch: 'Architectural Patronage and the Past: The Tughluq Sultans of India', *Muqarnas*, x (1993), pp. 311–22

M. Shokoohy and N. H. Shokoohy: 'Tughluqabad: The Earliest Surviving Town of the Delhi Sultanate', *Bull. SOAS* (1994), pp. 516–50, pls 1–16

MEHRDAD SHOKOOHY, NATALIE H. SHOKOOHY

(c) West. Distinctive regional styles of Indo-Islamic architecture developed between the 12th and 16th centuries in western India, an area comprising present-day Gujarat and neighbouring parts of Rajasthan. Influences on Indo-Islamic building styles in this region included the indigenous temple traditions of western India (*see* §5(i)(c) above), the Islamic buildings constructed by Muslim trading communities before the Islamic conquest (*see* §5(ii)(a) above) and, to a lesser extent, the Indo-Islamic architecture of north India and Delhi (*see* §(b) above). The

presence of craftsmen trained in established Indian techniques of building and stone-carving was also an important factor in the richness of the region's Islamic architecture.

Gujarat. Most of Gujarat came under the rule of the Sultanate of Delhi in 1297 during the reign of ʿAla' al-Din Khalji (*reg* 1296–1316). With Timur's sack of Delhi in 1398–9, the governor Zafar Khan assumed the title Muzaffar Shah I and founded the independent Sultanate of Gujarat. This Sultanate lasted until 1572, when the region was annexed to the Mughal empire by Akbar (*reg* 1556–1605).

In the early Sultanate, before the accession of Ahmad Shah (*reg* 1411–42), the buildings, particularly in Saurashtra, were characterized by their layout and decoration following local traditions and by the reuse of materials from temples in the construction of mosques and tombs. Nevertheless, certain components, such as mihrabs, were carved specifically for the mosques and follow the pre-conquest layout with niches semicircular in plan. Monuments surviving from this period are found in Bharuch, Patan, Veraval, Khambhat, Dholka, Mangrol and Petlad. The pre-conquest building tradition of Arab and Iranian trading communities continued into the 13th century. The mosque of Abu'l-Qasim ibn ʿAli al-Idhaji in Junagadh, for example, was built by the chief merchant of the town in 1285–6 (AH 685), 12 years before the area came under the rule of the Khalji sultans of Delhi. The mosque has a colonnaded prayer-hall with a flat roof and a single mihrab, semicircular in plan and with a semicircular arch. In front of the prayer-hall is a portico supported by rows of columns, an arrangement influenced by Hindu and Jaina temples. Pre-conquest mosque and temple architecture continued to exert an influence after the area came under the rule of the Delhi sultans. In Bharuch the Jamiʿ Mosque (*c.* 1297) is in the form of three integrated domed canopies with two extra colonnaded aisles on either side. The building is made from reused material from temples, carefully chosen for its rich ornamentation and skilfully reassembled. The three mihrabs are purposely carved, and while their ground-plan and the way they project outside the wall closely resemble earlier mihrabs, their carved stone interior is enriched with traditional Gujarati motifs.

Sultanate buildings constructed during the reign of Muhammad ibn Tughluq (*reg* 1325–51) include the Jamiʿ Mosque of Veraval, the Jamiʿ Mosque of Khambhat and the Hilal Khan Qadi Mosque at Dholka. The Jamiʿ Mosque of Veraval (1331–2; AH 732) consists of a courtyard and a colonnade to the west, seven bays wide and five aisles deep, with a large dome over the centre. Its single mihrab, similar to those of pre-conquest mosques, is semicircular in plan with a rectangular projection on the exterior wall. It has a semicircular arch. The Jamiʿ Mosque of Khambhat has a façade screen wall in front of the prayer-hall, a feature introduced from Delhi that became an important and highly decorative element in the 15th- and 16th-century architecture of Gujarat. With the Hilal Khan Qadi Mosque (1333) at Dholka a number of distinctive features appear. These include a large domed canopy in front of the eastern entrance and, at the western side of the courtyard, two solid turrets flanking the central arch of the prayer-hall, common features in later Gujarati mosques. The prayer-hall has five interconnected domed canopies, the central one of which is raised above the roof level by means of short columns. The space between the columns is filled up with pierced stonework, creating a clerestory. This arrangement, derived from the temple architecture of Gujarat, is used from this date in most Islamic buildings in the region and occasionally elsewhere in India where the influence of Gujarat was felt.

The Taka (or Tanka) Mosque in Dholka and the Jamiʿ and Chishtiwala mosques in Mangrol were built during the reign of Firuz Shah Tughluq (*reg* 1351–88). The Taka Mosque has a plan similar to that of the Adina Mosque at Pandua (*see* §(d) below), following the arrangement of the Great Mosque of Damascus (*see* DAMASCUS, §3) and the al-Azhar in Cairo (*see* CAIRO, §III, 3).

Under the patronage of Ahmad Shah, the distinctive but provincial Gujarati style reached the height of refinement in his royal buildings and those built by his descendants in the first half of the 15th century. Domes were raised on pillars to create a 'clerestory' and make mosque interiors lighter. This increased emphasis on space and light was accompanied by the use of intricately carved screens, lobed arches and flanking minarets. Although the use of temple spolia on an extensive scale diminished, Indo-Islamic monuments in Gujarat retained a strong indigenous flavour, as both the carving tradition and the architectural vocabulary of the region continued to be employed. The major monuments of this phase of building activity are found at Dholka, Ahmadabad and Sarkhej.

In the buildings of Ahmad Shah's new capital, Ahmadabad, the refinement of Gujarati design was combined with superbly carved stonework. Ahmadabad was laid out on the principles of an Islamic fortified city, with the citadel, the Bhadra, located at one side rather than in the centre. Outside the citadel was a royal square from which a wide thoroughfare led to the Jamiʿ Mosque via the Tin Darvaza, a triumphal arch with three archways. At a later date, the tomb of Ahmad Shah and a second tomb for his wives were built in a square near the Jamiʿ Mosque. The planning of the town reflects this patron's assured use of axial design to create a dramatic architectural ensemble. The Ahmad Shahi Mosque (see fig. 91), built in 1414 inside the Bhadra, was constructed from temple spolia following the plan of older Gujarati mosques. It fits, however, within the distinctive style of the 15th and 16th centuries, as the large central arch in the eastern wall was originally flanked by two minarets, the upper portions of which have fallen. The mihrab is also no longer semicircular in plan. The mosque of Haybat Khan (Ahmad Shah's uncle) is similar but smaller and has a plain façade with a central arch flanked by turrets.

In the mosque of Sayyid ʿAlam (1412), the buttresses of the minarets flanking the central arch are extensively decorated (the upper parts of the minarets have not survived). The screen wall covers only the middle section of the prayer-hall, leaving the columns of the flanking sections visible from the courtyard. The central dome is a true dome, but true domes did not become popular in Gujarat and were used only exceptionally. As the favoured form remained the corbelled dome, and since the diameter of such domes is limited to relatively small spans, the covered space of the mosque was enlarged only by the

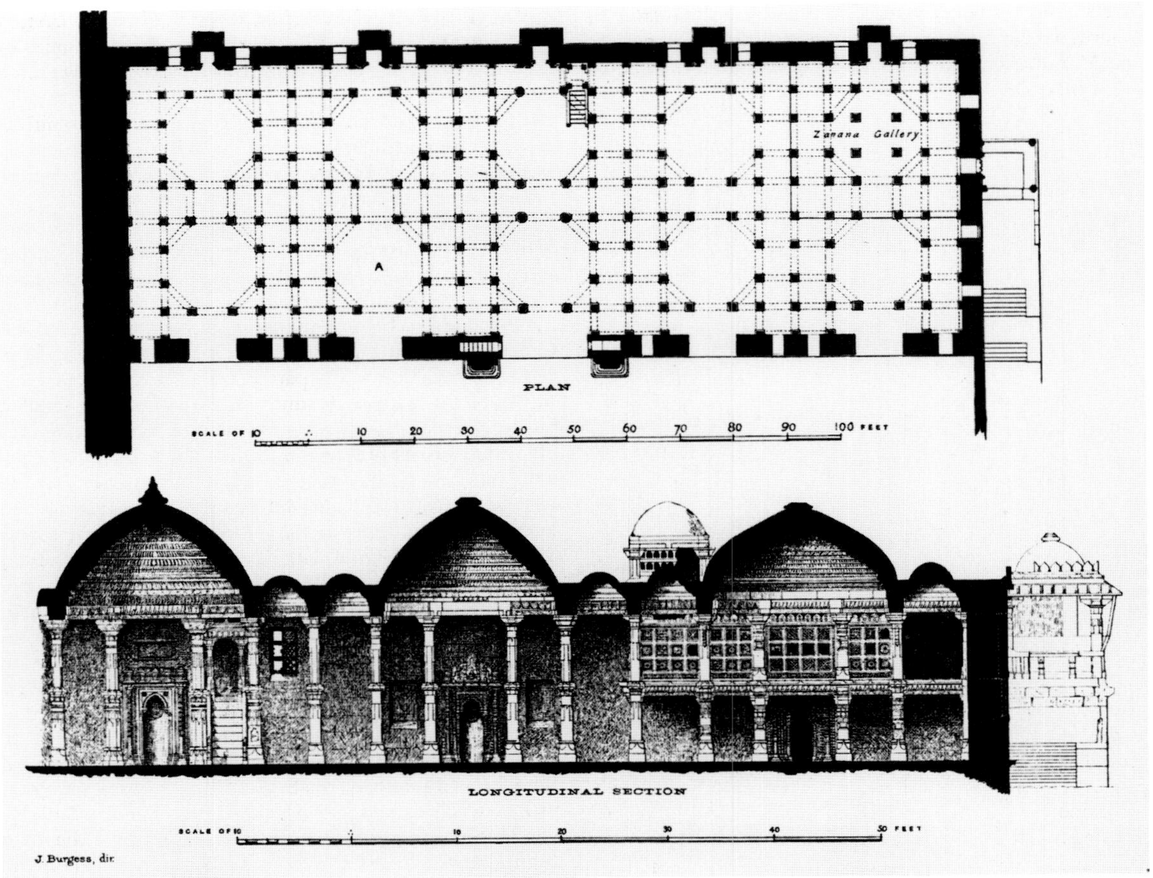

91. Ahmad Shahi Mosque, Ahmadabad, 1414; plan and section from J. Burgess: *The Muhammadan Architecture of Ahmadabad*, i (1900), Archaeological Survey of Western India, Reports, vii (London, 1900–05), pl. XI

multiplication of individual domed units. This was the approach taken in Ahmadabad's largest mosque, the Jamiʿ. Built in 1423–4 (AH 827), the prayer-hall has 15 large corbelled domes and numerous smaller ones as well as flat ceiling slabs. These are supported by some 300 columns of various sizes. The grand effect of the prayer-hall is further emphasized by the restrained scale of the colonnades and entrances to the courtyard. Some of the central domes of the prayer-hall are raised above the level of the roof on pillars in the style of the Hilal Khan Qadi Mosque at Dholka. The spaces around the domes are also raised, providing upper galleries. Most impressive is the treatment of the dome behind the central arch, which, with its gallery, is raised two storeys above roof level, adding further to the height of the building and the light reaching the interior. The screen wall, with three arches, is built only in front of the central part of the prayer-hall, as in the mosque of Sayyid ʿAlam. The central arch is flanked by the buttresses of two minarets, the upper parts of which no longer survive. The mosque is finely decorated with carved geometrical and floral motifs, the carving of the screen wall being particularly notable.

The strong position of the Sultanate of Gujarat from the mid-15th century to the mid-16th permitted the continued evolution of architecture, and Mahmud Bigara (*reg* 1448–1511) was in a position not only to continue to develop the capital, Ahmadabad, but also to found two important cities at Junagadh and Champaner, as well as building palace complexes at Mahmudabad, 27 km from Ahmadabad, and at Sarkhej. Intricately carved screens, windows and ceilings add to the sumptuous effect created by domes, cupolas and colonnades. Some of the finest structures of this period were constructed in CHAMPANER, Mahmud Bigara's new capital, founded in 1485. The city plan was similar to that of Ahmadabad, with the palace in the citadel and outside a royal square leading to a main thoroughfare. The Jamiʿ Mosque of Champaner is a smaller version of the Jamiʿ of Ahmadabad but with more emphasis given to the gateways. The central arch of the prayer-chamber is flanked by two tall minarets with spiral staircases inside; in addition, each corner of the prayer-hall has a shorter, solid minaret. Other monuments in Champaner include the Jaipur Mosque; the Nagina Mosque, a small building with a plan similar to that of the Jamiʿ and constructed of pale yellow stone; the Mandavi, probably a guard-room in the citadel; and the Bohra or Shahr Mosque, a small but elegant building in the citadel.

The impressive number of buildings constructed by Mahmud Bigara at this period include those at Junagadh and Mahmudabad. Further building was also carried out in Ahmadabad and included a number of tombs. The most common tomb type is a square, domed chamber surrounded by a screened colonnade. A notable example is the small tomb of Rani Sipari (*c.* 1515), in which the stone screens have a lacelike delicacy. The mosque of this tomb complex has two slim, tall minarets set in the eastern corners of the prayer-hall, a departure from the usual Gujarati configuration with massive minarets built at either side of the central arch. Other impressive domed tombs with screened colonnades in the Ahmadabad region include that of Shaykh Ahmad Katu in Sarkhej and the Bai Harir tomb (1500–01; AH 906) in Asarwa. Similar structures can be found as far away as Somnath (the Maipuri Dargah) and Una (the Hadrat Shah Pir Dargah).

Among the finest carved screens are those of the small Sidi Sayyid Mosque in Ahmadabad. The screens set into the west wall employ a motif of palms, other trees and creepers endowed with extraordinary movement and life. Extant buildings of the period also include stepwells of the type known in Gujarat as *vāv* and in some other parts of India as *bā'olī* (*see* STEPWELL). These typically consist of a long, narrow reservoir with a circular well in one side and a flight of steps leading down to the water level from the opposite side. The Bai Harir tomb complex in Asarwa near Ahmadabad includes a *vāv* that begins from a platform at the east with a 12-columned *chatrī*. It has five underground landings, each in the form of a colonnaded platform in several tiers. Stepwells were for the daily use of ordinary people and, when constructed for the use of Muslims, were not as a rule highly ornamented. However, the Bai Harir Vav and other examples in Gujarat bear exquisite carvings. One of the finest is in Adalaj, a suburb of Ahmadabad. Although it was built in 1502 during the reign of Mahmud Bigara, it was constructed by Hindus for their own use and has fine carvings of deities associated with water. The Gujarat sultans' tolerance with regard to their Hindu and Jaina subjects is also evident from the number of temples maintained or built during this period.

Rajasthan. The earliest Indo-Islamic structure in Rajasthan, the Arha'i Din ka Jhonpra in AJMER, was built *c.* 1200, following the Ghurid conquest of the area. Constructed of reused temple spolia, it is a trabeate structure comparable with the Quwwat al-Islam Mosque built at about the same time in Delhi (*see* §(b) above). However, in the prayer-hall interior three temple pillars are superimposed to form each column, making the ceiling higher than in any other Ghurid mosque. As in the Quwwat al-Islam, an elegant façade, in this case with seven corbelled arches, was erected in front of the prayer-hall to create the impression of a vaulted iwan. Thus, as in Delhi, the familiar visual forms of Islamic architecture were created through the use of traditional Indian building techniques. While sharing many points with the Quwwat al-Islam Mosque, the Arha'i Din ka Jhonpra differs in important ways, reflecting its western location. The marble mihrab dated 1195 (AH 595) is a stilted semicircle in plan with a five-lobed arch. Semicircular mihrabs of this sort are of the 'Arab type', while mihrabs of Ghurid mosques in Delhi are square in plan, following the Khurasani tradition. Arab-type mihrabs were used in the pre-conquest mosques of the Muslim trading communities (*see* §5(ii)(b) above), and the influence of these buildings may have been felt in Ajmer. The siting of the Arha'i Din ka Jhonpra also differs from Ghurid mosques in north India. While the latter are built on level ground, the Arha'i Din ka Jhonpra is built on a platform (79 m square) on a rocky prominence, a type of location often favoured for temples in western India. The eastern gateway is also reminiscent of a temple entrance, consisting of a flight of steps leading to an arched gateway flanked by square *chatrīs*.

The Shahi Mosque (*c.* 1202–3/AH 599) in Khatu, north of Ajmer, is also built on a platform, in this case partly constructed of stone and partly cut into the rock. A small building, the Shahi Mosque consists of a colonnaded prayer-hall with three domes and one mihrab. A courtyard (19×14 m) is found on the west. The mihrab closely resembles that of the Arha'i din ka Jhonpra, and the calligraphic details of their inscriptions are so similar that they may be the work of the same calligrapher or school. The entrance of the Shahi Mosque also has a flight of steps leading to the courtyard, this time through a narrow passage roofed with a square pavilion that connects to a canopy over the portico. A similar type of entrance can be seen in the temple of Amera Mata on Mt Girnar. At Khatu there are further trabeate mosques, most built in the first two decades of the 14th century. Somewhat exceptional is the shrine of Mahmud Qattal, a modest domical structure with ashlar walls. The mihrab of the Dargah Mosque at Khatu imitates that of the Shahi Mosque but is square in plan, like all mihrabs of the Khalji period (1290–1320). By the beginning of the 14th century the semicircular plan for mihrabs had been abandoned except in coastal Gujarat.

As the area comprising modern Rajasthan was not ruled as a single entity, its architectural development was diverse. In the late 15th century the takeover of Sanchor and Jalor by the sultans of Gujarat brought Gujarati architecture into south Rajasthan. Indicative of the new style are the screen wall added to the older Tupkhana Masjid at Jalor and two new mosques, the Qilaʿ Mosque (1519) and Sand Ba'orivari Mosque, built there entirely in the Gujarati manner under governors appointed by the Gujarat sultans. The Jamiʿ Mosque of Sanchor, south of Jalor, dated 1533–4 (AH 940), was built in the same style.

A distinctive regional idiom influenced by both Delhi and Gujarat developed in Nagaur in western Rajasthan. Said to have been founded by the Ghaznavids, Nagaur was ruled from Delhi until the beginning of the 15th century. The early monuments consist of the mosque of Makhdum Husayn Chishti (1320–21; AH 720) and the Buland Darwaza of the Khanaqah al-Tarikin (1333). The Buland Darwaza, known for its carved decoration and calligraphy, consists of an arched portal leading to a square, domed chamber flanked by two smaller chambers. While the arch is corbelled, the chambers have true domes supported by squinches. The use of *chatrīs* in three tiers on either side of the portal provided a prototype for many later gateways in Rajasthan.

In 1407 the Gujarat Sultan Muzaffar Shah I (*reg* 1391–1411) gave Nagaur to his brother Shams Khan Dandani (*reg* 1405/6–1418/19; AH 808–21), who established an independent dynasty that controlled towns such as Didwana, Khatu, Ladnun and Naraina for over a century. The distinct style that developed in this period is characterized by massive buildings, usually constructed of rubble rather than ashlar. Decoration is simple, and plaster is used extensively on the exterior walls. Between 1412 and 1419 Shams Khan is said to have rebuilt Nagaur to resemble Ahmadabad but on a smaller scale. His plan is, however, unlike that of the capital in that it incorporates the existing town and its massive fort. In the town square in front of the main entrance of the fort he built a three-arched monumental gate similar in design to the Tin Darwaza of Ahmadabad and known by the same name. It is, however, smaller in scale and, following the local tradition, bears simple decoration consisting of mouldings and rosettes.

The impressive Shams Khan Mosque (see fig. 92), on the bank of the large Shams Khan Tala'o (reservoir), incorporates some Gujarati features in its prayer-hall. It is a colonnade with five domes, the central one, now fallen, raised above the level of the roof by means of short columns. The mosque also has a screen wall with five arches, but unlike the Gujarati examples, its surface is plastered. On the roof and at the north-east and south-east corners of the building are two plain round minarets; the form and location of these follow the Delhi model, as do the three mihrabs.

The Ek Minar ki Mosque (Mosque of One Minaret) in Nagaur dates from the time of Mujahid Khan (*reg c.* 1435–67), the son of Shams Khan. It consists of a prayer colonnade (12.2×5.8 m) with the walls battered on the outside, a survival of the Tughluq tradition. The only mihrab of the mosque is decorated with geometrical and floral patterns and resembles the mihrabs of the Shams Khan Mosque. The mosque originally had two solid turrets on the roof, in the same position as the minarets of the Shams Khan Mosque, but the northern turret has fallen, giving rise to the local name for the building. The standing turret is built of rubble and plaster. This form was common in Nagaur during the 15th century and was also used in the old ruined *ʿidgāh* (prayer wall; *see* MUSALLA) of the town. The two standing minarets of the *ʿidgāh* are each about 9.4 m high and 2.8 m in diameter at the base. Solidly built of rubble, they are plastered and have bands of stucco decoration.

Many of Mujahid Khan's buildings are located in the other towns of his territory. In Didwana an inscription from the ruined Delhi Darwaza records his reconstruction of the city wall and this gate in 1436. In Naraina he built a large tank (*c.* 200×200 m) called Mustafa Sar, completing the complex with two gateways and a mosque. The three arches of the eastern gate are flanked on each side by towers in the form of three-tiered *chatrīs* similar to those of the Buland Darwaza of Nagaur. The southern gateway, smaller in size, has a single arch with a chamber topped by a *chatrī* on either side. The Mujahid Khan Mosque (24.5×10.5 m) has a flat-roofed prayer-hall, nine bays wide and four aisles deep. It is built of temple spolia and has a small turret on each corner of the roof, similar to those of Nagaur. The three mihrabs of the mosque are finely decorated, and above each mihrab an inscription in *thulth* script records the construction of the mosque by the order of Mujahid Khan on the birthday of the Prophet, 12th Rabiʿ I, AH 848 (29 June 1444).

Buildings in the district of Nagaur strongly influenced by the Gujarati style include the Qilaʿ Mosque at Didwana and the Shrine of Baba Ishaq Maghribi in Khatu. The eastern entrance of the Qilaʿ Mosque takes the form of a *chatrī*. The courtyard (9.25×10.45 m) is surrounded by a

92. Shams Khan Mosque, Nagaur, *c.* 1407; view from the courtyard

flat-roofed colonnade. On the west in front of the three mihrabs are three small corbelled domes. The building is elegantly constructed and decorated with stonework carved in the Gujarati style. The Qila' Mosque is in many ways similar to the Jami' Mosque at Una on the southernmost point of the Saurashtra peninsula. The Shrine of Baba Ishaq is a square, domed chamber surrounded by a yellow sandstone colonnade with a dome at each corner. The whole building stands above a crypt that appears from the exterior to be a platform (h. 2 m). Tomb buildings of this type, typical of Gujarat, are not seen elsewhere in Rajasthan. The shrine, although constructed in the territory of the Shams Khan dynasty, may have been built under Gujarati patronage.

The surviving buildings of the later Khans of Nagaur are mostly small in scale, with the exception of the fort of Ladnun, restored by Firuz Khan in 1469–70 (AH 874). The only extant parts from this date are the gate and the lower section of the walls. The Firuz Khani Mosque (1495) in Nagaur, in the shrine complex of Bare Pir Sahib, is a small colonnaded mosque. The prayer-hall is five bays wide and two aisles deep with a flat roof and a single mihrab. The Akadwali Mosque (1478) is similar, with the prayer-hall three bays wide and two aisles deep.

The mixed Delhi and Gujarati style of architecture found in Nagaur continued up to the time of the Mughals, with trabeate structures (usually with flat roofs) similar to those of the Firuz Khan period being built into the 16th century. However, distinctive Gujarati features gradually gave way to the established conventions of north India. In 1564–5 (AH 972), at the time of the Mughal emperor Akbar, the imperial style was introduced to Nagaur in the new Jami' Mosque known as the Akbari Mosque, a masonry structure with arches and true domes. These features were not unknown in Nagaur, as true domes had been seen in the Buland Darwaza of the Khanaqah al-Tarikin and remained in use during the Shams Khan dynasty. In the Akbari Mosque the two plain minarets on the roof and on the north-east and south-east corners of the building reflect Nagaur's 15th-century tradition. These minarets are, however, hollow and have a spiral staircase inside leading to a small *chatrī* at the top.

BIBLIOGRAPHY

J. Burgess: *Report on the Antiquities of Kathiawad and Kachh*, Archaeol. Surv. W. India, Rep., ii (London, 1876)

Bombay Gazetteer, viii (1884), pp. 667–8 [Gujarat]

H. B. Garrick: 'Report of a Tour in the Punjab and Rajputana', *Archaeol. Surv. India Rep.*, xxiii (1887), pp. 48–72

J. Burgess: *On the Muhammadan Architecture of Bharoch, Cambay, Dholka, Champanir and Mahmudabad*, Archaeol. Surv. W. India, Rep., vi (London, 1896)

——: *The Muhammadan Architecture of Ahmadabad*, 2 vols, Archaeol. Surv. W. India, Rep., vii (London, 1900–05)

J. Burgess and H. Cousens: *The Architectural Antiquities of Northern Gujarat*, Archaeol. Surv. W. India, Rep., ix (London, 1903)

Archaeol. Surv. India (1907), pp. 6–7; (1908), pp. 3–4; (1909), pp. 9–10; (1949–50), pp. 32–4 [all on sites in Rajasthan]

H. Cousens: *Somnatha and Other Mediaeval Temples in Kathiawad*, Archaeol. Surv. India, Imp. Ser., xlv (Calcutta, 1931)

M. A. Chaghtai: 'Nagaur, a Forgotten Kingdom', *Bull. Deccan Coll. Res. Inst.*, ii (1940–41), pp. 166–83

P. Brown: *Indian Architecture, Islamic Period* (Bombay, [1942], rev. 1956 with additional photographs/*R* 1981), pp. 47–58

Z. A. Desai: 'Inscriptions of the Khanzadas of Nagaur', *Epig. Ind.: Arab. & Pers. Suppl.* (1970), pp. 16–40

M. Shokoohy: *Rajasthan I*, Corp. Inscr. Iran., xlix, pt iv (London, 1986)

M. Shokoohy and N. H. Shokoohy: *Nagaur: Sultanate and Early Mughal History and Architecture of the District of Nagaur, India*, Royal Asiat. Soc. Monographs, xxviii (London, 1993)

(d) East. The Ghurid rulers first conquered Bengal in 1196–7 (AH 593), taking over the ancient city of Lakhnauti (modern Gaur). The area remained under Delhi until 1336, when it came under independent rule, leading to the establishment of the Ilyas Shahi Sultanate six years later. The political independence of Bengal, its tropical climate and distance from Delhi encouraged a local idiom of architecture largely uninfluenced by the rest of India. Pre-Islamic buildings often had a solid core of large-sized bricks laid in horizontal courses without mortar. The stability of these structures was ensured only by their massive weight. Cut and moulded brick embellished the elevations. The Muslims introduced small-sized bricks and the use of mortar, both essential for arches and vaults. At times, the brick was faced with carved stone. That earlier traditions persisted after the 14th century is indicated by the continued massiveness of most structures and the use of carved and moulded brickwork on façades. Bowed roofs and down-turned eaves, apparently derived from common dwellings of bamboo and palm, were also employed in Islamic brick architecture.

Tribeni and Pandua. The early buildings at Gaur are no longer extant, but an indication of their appearance is provided by the mosque and tomb of Zafar Khan Ghazi in Tribeni (Hoogly District). The mihrab, dated 1298–9 (AH 698), and part of the foundation are original and constitute the oldest Islamic remains in the region. The mihrab was built of stone taken from earlier buildings, but the arch was re-dressed in the early Sultanate style. It is two-centred with a pointed lobed fringe. The qibla wall, largely reconstructed, has brickwork niches with a creeper pattern recalling examples in Gujarat. The ruined tomb consists of two square domed chambers; the walls have a masonry core faced with stone taken from temples. The stonework of the entrances and the niches was carefully reset, but on the main surface of the walls the arrangement is haphazard, indicating that they may have been plastered.

The second oldest surviving building is the Adina Mosque at Pandua (near Gaur). Built in 1374–5 (AH 776) by Sikandar Shah I (*reg* 1358–90), the mosque, one of the largest in India, is made of stone up to the imposts of the arches with brick above, a method of construction that was to become popular in Bengal. Extensive use was made of carved and moulded brickwork in a profuse variety of patterns. The prayer-hall is located on the longer side of the courtyard (87×155 m). This arrangement is uncommon but appears in the al-Azhar Mosque in Cairo (*see* CAIRO, §III, 3) and the Great Mosque of Damascus (*see* DAMASCUS, §3), which may have served as a model. As in Damascus, the qibla arcade is broken by a great iwan (vaulted space), with the main mihrab in the centre of the qibla wall and a stone minbar to the north. There are also numerous smaller mihrabs, all built of stone and semicircular in plan, mostly with lobed arches but varying in detail. The form of the arch used for the central mihrab and some of the secondary mihrabs consists of a single semicircular lobe with a smaller lobe on each side. This originated in image niches and is unusual for Indo-Islamic buildings. The tomb of Sikandar Shah adjoins the west wall of the mosque. Originally a square, domed chamber with an adjoining platform to the north, the tomb was probably added to the mosque, possibly after the death of Sikandar Shah in 1393.

The only other building dating from the time of Sikandar Shah is the mosque in Mulla Simla, dated 1375–6 (AH 777). It was originally a single-domed chamber with turrets in each corner. In Chhota Pandua (near Tribeni), the Bari Mosque and Minar may also belong to the time of Sikandar Shah. The brick domes of the qibla arcade of the Bari Mosque are supported by reused monolithic columns. The stone minbar has a domed canopy above and a passage with a three-lobed arch below the speaker's platform. The Minar (h. 38 m) has a circular plan and is built of brick in six registers. The bottom register and the two at the top are plain, while those between are lobed.

Monuments of the 15th and 16th centuries are concentrated in Gaur (see below), but the Eklakhi mausoleum in Pandua is the first building to display some of the characteristic features of later Sultanate architecture in Bengal. The mausoleum dates from the turn of the 14th century and served as a model for a number of later tombs. It consists of a domed brick chamber, square in plan externally but octagonal within. The walls are massive, with octagonal towers in each corner. Entrances pierce each side. The dome has no transitional zone and rises directly from the walls of the octagonal chamber below. The exterior walls are slightly bowed, and the parapet of the roof curves down to each corner in a form derived from local bamboo huts. The façade is divided into two registers by a band of moulded brick, with the brick niches in the upper register imitating carved wooden windows. This decorative façade is perhaps indicative of Bengali houses of the time, of which no examples survive.

Gaur. In Gaur itself, the Hajatgah tomb (early 15th century) and the Putol tomb (late 15th century) are similar to the Eklakhi mausoleum. The Putol tomb (probably once a gatehouse) has foundations and corner towers of dressed stone. The walls, however, are faced with moulded and polychrome glazed bricks. Another example is the mausoleum of Khan-i Jahan Ulugh Khan (*d* 1458–9; AH 863) at Bagerhat in Bangladesh. This tomb has little decoration, and the plain surfaces of the walls may have been plastered. The terracotta mouldings are limited to the wall cornice and four horizontal bands on each tower.

Part of the 15th-century citadel at Gaur built by Nasir al-Din Mahmud (*reg* 1442–60) is preserved, along with the northern gateway, known as the Dakhil Darwaza. Another gate, the Kutwali Darwaza, is now in ruins but appears in a 19th-century drawing by Henry Creighton (see Creighton, pl. IV). The Dakhil Darwaza has a main vaulted corridor with a long narrow hall on either side. The northern and southern elevations of the gateway are similar and consist of an arched portal flanked by towers. The building is of brick but stands on a foundation of dressed stone, with stone also used for the jambs of the arched openings to the corridor and for the decorative band dividing the elevation into two registers. Near the Dakhil Darwaza stands the Chiragh Minar (or Firuza Minar), probably built by Malik Indil Firuz Shah (*reg* 1486–9). The minaret (h. 26 m) is built of brick (some of it with a blue glaze) reinforced with courses of stonework. The first three storeys are polygonal, while the top two are circular. The raised platform is 12-sided. The brickwork is decorated with geometric and floral patterns cut into the clay before firing, a technique commonly used in the decoration of Bengali buildings.

A number of Sultanate-period mosques have survived in Gaur, but the dates of most of them are uncertain, as the only inscriptions found *in situ* are on the Bara Sona (1526), Qadam Rasul (1531) and Jahanian Jahangasht, or Jan Janiyan (1535) mosques. Other monuments at Gaur are associated with dated inscriptions, some of them on the sites of standing buildings. The Chamkatti Mosque, probably built in 1475–6 (AH 880), was originally a single-domed chamber with a three-domed verandah on the eastern side and a tower at each corner. The building had bowed walls and curved cornices; the surface decoration consists of niches and mouldings with floral and geometric patterns executed in glazed brick and moulded terracotta. The arrangement of the plan is characteristic of small mosques in the area and is seen in the Lattan Mosque (see fig. 93), probably built in the reign of Yusuf Shah (*reg* 1474–81). The elevations of the Lattan Mosque are decorated with glazed brickwork. The three mihrabs of the mosque are all semicircular in plan, similar to those of the Adina Mosque. Similar layouts are encountered elsewhere in Bengal, notably in the 16th-century mosque at Sura (Dinajpur District) and the Masjidbari of 1465–6 (AH 870) in Mirzaganj (Bakerganj District). The Masjidbari verandah is barrel-vaulted rather than domed. A late example of the type is the Qadam Rasul in Gaur, erected in 1530–31 (AH 937) under Sultan Nusrat Shah (*reg* 1519–32). This mosque has the usual domed chamber, but the verandah is in the form of a barrel-vaulted corridor running around three sides of the building. The corridor has a three-arched opening to the east and a single-arched opening on the north and south. The main structure is of brick, but the piers supporting the eastern arches of the portico are of dressed stone.

The larger mosques of Gaur also have curved cornices, but the curve is less pronounced and the elevation wider than in the smaller buildings. One of the oldest examples of this type is the Tantipara or 'Umar Ghadi Mosque, datable to 1480–81 (AH 885). Located in the walled city of Gaur, the mosque is two aisles deep and five bays wide, with five mihrabs. It was originally roofed with ten domes supported by monolithic columns taken from earlier buildings. Apart from the columns and a decorative course below the imposts, the rest of the building is brick faced with moulded terracotta.

The technique of using monolithic stone columns below domes, with brick for the rest of the structure, appears in a number of mosques in Gaur, among them the Darasbari Mosque, probably built in 1479–80 (AH 884) during the reign of Yusuf Shah. The prayer-chamber has a vaulted corridor flanked by multi-domed wings; the domed verandah repeats this design. The patterns executed in terracotta in the Darasbari include decorative grilles with roundels of varying design. Creepers fill the decorative arch-shaped areas on the qibla wall. These patterns, although originating from earlier examples in the Adina Mosque and Tantipara

93. Lattan Mosque, Gaur, *c.* 1474–81; view from the north-east

Mosque, resemble the carved stonework of Gujarat. The Sath Gunbad Mosque in Bagerhat is similar to the mosques at Gaur, having a rectangular plan with four corner towers. This mosque, however, was built on a grand scale (49×33 m) with seventy domes and seven curved cross vaults.

In the Gumnant Mosque at Gaur, which has nine bays and three aisles with twenty-four domes supported by monolithic columns, the central bay is vaulted and is supported by arches standing on massive dressed stone piers. The interior of the domes and the central vault is plastered and decorated with cut stucco. While the walls are of brick, the exterior and large areas of the interior were faced with dressed stone. Two other mosques in Gaur, the Chhota Sona Mosque and the Bara Sona Mosque, are built with brick walls faced with stone. The Chhota Sona Mosque, built during the reign of Sayyid ʿAla al-Din Husayn Shah (*reg* 1493–1518), is a relatively small building of five bays and three aisles. The exterior and interior of the walls are faced with slabs of black basalt carved with decoration derived from moulded terracotta. In the Bara Sona Mosque (1525–6; AH 932), the stone surface of the walls is limited to mouldings that follow the lines of the architectural elements. The mosque is much larger than the Chhota Sona and has 4 aisles and 11 bays with 11 mihrabs.

Stone facing was used outside Gaur, as in the mosque at Sura (see above). Another example is the Qutb Shahi Mosque, built in 1582–3 (AH 990) in Pandua, when the area was under the control of the Mughals. The stonework of this mosque is again unornamented, and mouldings are the only decoration on the exterior. This is not the only example of later Bengali architecture constructed in the Sultanate tradition. During the 16th and 17th centuries, while the imperial style of Mughal architecture was being introduced, local practices persisted and were even introduced to other parts of India. In particular, the curved Bengali roof was adopted by Mughal architects during the 17th century and came to be integrated into elaborate late Mughal and post-Mughal buildings, notably in Rajasthan.

BIBLIOGRAPHY

H. Creighton: *The Ruins of Gour* (London, 1817)

H. Blochmann: 'Notes on Places of Historical Interest in the District of Hughly', *J. Asiat. Soc. Bengal*, xxxix (1870), pt 1, pls 8–12; pt 2, pp. 109–25

J. H. Ravenshaw: *Gaur, its Ruins and Inscriptions* (London, 1878)

A. Cunningham: 'Report on a Tour of Bihar and Bengal in 1879–80', *Archaeol. Surv. India Rep.*, xv (1882)

Archaeol. Surv. India, Annu. Rep. (1902–3), pp. 50–59

D. C. Crawford: 'Places of Historical Interest in Hugli District', *Bengal Past & Present*, ii (1908), pp. 288–98

M. Chakravarti: 'Notes on Gaur and Other Old Places in Bengal', *J. Asiat. Soc. Bengal*, n. s., v (1909), pp. 199–235

——: 'Pre-Mughal Mosques of Bengal', *J. Asiat. Soc. Bengal*, n. s., vi (1910), pp. 23–38

J. Marshall: 'The Monuments of Muslim India', *Cambridge History of India*, iii (Cambridge, 1928), ed. W. Haig, pp. 599–608

A. A. Khan: *Memoirs of Gaur and Pandua*, ed. H. E. Stapelton (Calcutta, 1931)

K. S. Sarasvati: 'Indo-Muslim Architecture in Bengal', *J. Ind. Soc. Orient. A.*, ix (1941), pp. 12–36

A. H. Dani: 'Bibliography of the Muslim Inscriptions of Bengal', *J. Asiat. Soc. Pakistan*, ii (1957), appendix

——: *Muslim Architecture of Bengal* (Dhaka, 1961)

S. M. Hasan: *Mosque Architecture of Pre-Mughal Bengal* (Dhaka, 1971)

M. Abdul Qadir: 'The So-called Ladies' Gallery in the Early Mosques of Bangladesh', *J. Varendra Res. Mus.*, vii (1981–2), pp. 161–72

G. Michell, ed.: *The Islamic Heritage of Bengal* (Paris, 1984)

P. Hasan: 'Sultanate Mosques and Continuity in Bengal Architecture', *Muqarnas*, vi (1989), pp. 58–74

(e) Central. The Malwa region of central India began to develop a distinct architectural style after Dilavar Khan

Ghuri broke away from Delhi in 1401 and established an independent kingdom with its capital at Dhar. He was succeeded by his son Hushang Shah (*reg* 1405–35), who transferred the capital to Mandu. In 1436 Mahmud Shah Khalji I (*reg* 1436–69) established a new dynasty in Malwa that lasted until 1531, when the region was annexed to the Sultanate of Gujarat. The particular characteristics that contribute to the distinctiveness of Malwa architecture are the continued development of combinations of trabeate and arcuate features, using the structural principles established in Delhi but no longer followed elsewhere, and the extensive use of colour. Decorative schemes employed polychrome marbles, hardstones such as jasper and agate, ceramic tiles and wall paintings. The Malwa architects were forerunners in the technique of inlaying marble with other stones. They made extensive use of tilework, though little survives, because the glaze has peeled off, probably owing to poor manufacturing methods. Enough has remained to show that in Mandu, perhaps under influence from the Deccan, tilework was not limited to monochrome bands as in Delhi. Rather, polychrome glazed tiles decorated with varying patterns (and at times with calligraphy) were used to cover large architectural surfaces. Wall painting was also popular; surviving examples are few but indicate the variety of colours and subjects chosen. The development of these and other features is documented by the architecture of Dhar, Mandu and Chanderi.

Dhar. Two early mosques survive in Dhar. The Lat ki Mosque (1405–6; AH 808) was named after an ancient iron pillar once erected there but later broken up and left on the site by the Gujarat Sultan Bahadur (*reg* 1526–37). Like other early Indo-Islamic mosques, the Lat ki Mosque was constructed of temple spolia. In the construction of the mosque, the old columns and lintels were carefully chosen and neatly reassembled. The columns were made of two shafts, and in certain places a bracket was set between the shafts to support a decorative arch, a distinctive feature of early Malwa mosques. Each arch consists of two stone segments, and the space above the extrados was left empty. The early 15th-century Kamal Maulana Mosque in Dhar is similar to the Lat ki Mosque but smaller in size. It is part of a larger complex, which includes the tomb of Shaykh Kamal al-Din Malwi (1456–7; AH 861). The walls of the tomb, now whitewashed, were decorated with blue-glazed tiles with medallion patterns, each bearing a religious inscription in *mi'galī* or *bannā'ī* script. Inscribed tilework is rare in Malwa, but these styles of script are frequently seen in the area.

Mandu. MANDU, occupying a commanding position on an outcrop of the Vindhya range, prospered largely for strategic reasons. Although a new phase of architectural development was initiated when Mandu became the capital, a few buildings pre-date the shift, notably the mosque of Dilawar Khan (1405). Similar to the Dhar mosques, it was later connected to the Mandu palaces and used as the royal mosque. That religious architecture at Mandu began to depart from the earlier style of the Malwa region is shown by the mosque of Malik Mughith, dated 1431–2 (AH 835). The prayer colonnade has three large domes, and the arched panels set between the columns are each composed of two pierced stone screens decorated with delicately carved geometric and scroll patterns. The building reflects the innovative arrangements of the 14th-century Tughluq mosques of Delhi, being set on a plinth with corner turrets and a staircase leading to an arcaded portico. The mid-15th-century Jami' Mosque of Mandu also departs from the early Malwa style. This impressive mosque on a central courtyard plan is set on a substantial plinth and has a domed porch on the eastern side. The prayer-hall is an arcaded structure with the arches standing on monolithic columns; the roof is formed of small domes with a single large dome over the central mihrab.

The fort of Mandu and its palaces were begun by Dilawar Khan and completed at the time of Mahmud Shah I (*reg* 1436–69). The impressive gates of the fort, with their two-centred pointed arches with spear-headed fringes, show the direct influence of 13th-century Delhi architecture. The style of the arches makes these 15th-century gates appear older than they actually are. In the mosques at Mandu, archaic methods of construction have the same effect. However, the palaces, dating mainly from the Khalji period, are different in style from the military and religious buildings. The citadel consists of a network of palaces set between parks, gardens and lakes. One of

94. Jahaz Mahal, Mandu, 15th century; view from the west

the most impressive buildings is the Jahaz Mahal (Ship Palace; see fig. 94), built between the banks of two large tanks. The Jahaz Mahal has three storeys with large vaulted halls at ground-level and apartments on the second level. The top level consists of domed pavilions set between open terraces. This arrangement provides covered and open spaces looking over the water, as well as giving a pleasant appearance to the building itself, with its skyline of domes and a silhouette of open colonnades and arches.

The palace complex to the north-east of the Jahaz Mahal includes the ruins of the royal bath, the private royal apartments and a stepwell known as the Champa Ba'oli. The lowest chamber of the stepwell is connected with a basement, the Taikhana, used as a cool retreat during the summer. In the enclosure there are two further stepwells, the Ujala Ba'oli and Andheri Ba'oli. The royal apartments were faced with marble or white plaster decorated with geometric and floral patterns inlaid with coloured stone. The audience hall, known as Hindola Mahal, has a T-shaped plan and exaggeratedly battered walls closely resembling those of Tughluq buildings. At ground-level it has a single vaulted hall with a high ceiling and an antechamber, and above the antechamber there is a gallery with an arched opening overlooking the hall. The gallery is reached by a ramp arranged with half-runs and landings, providing access for palanquins and probably horses. An earlier example of such a ramp is seen in the Tughluq palace at Hisar-i Firuza. The Gada Shah Dukkan in Mandu is another audience hall closely resembling the Hindola Mahal but larger in scale. The entrance façade was clad with marble inlaid with yellow and black stone.

A number of royal buildings are outside the citadel. The Rupmati Pavilion is set on the summit of a hill on the outskirts of the town. Built as a garden pavilion at the turn of the 15th century, it has battered walls and Tughluq-style arches. At each end of the roof of the building is a 12-columned *chatrī*, which, instead of the usual trabeate structure, has a dome supported by arches resting on monolithic columns. *Chatrī*s of this type are common in Mandu and can also be found on other palaces, such as the Baz Bahadur, built by Nasir al-Din Shah Khalji in 1508–9 (AH 914) as a retreat outside the citadel. This palace is a private residence arranged around two courtyards, set on the slope of a hill with a large tank on one side and a view over the valley.

The tombs of Mandu, locally known as *mahal*, are mainly in the form of square, domed chambers. Good examples include the Da'i ka Mahal and Jali Mahal, both of which have massive walls and squinched domes raised on a high transitional zone, octagonal on the exterior. The tombs are set on large square platforms with corner towers and gateways reached by flights of steps. Many tombs of this type can be found in the Malwa territory, the earliest being the tombs of Hushang Shah Ghuri and Mahmud Shah Khalji I. The latter, in the complex known as the Ashrafi Mahal, is in ruins but was once faced with marble inlaid with fine calligraphy and decorative patterns. The tomb of Hushang Shah (for illustration *see* MANDU) stands on a platform and has a massive dome flanked by smaller domes at the corners of the roof. This feature occasionally reappears, a later example being the tomb of Darya Khan dating to the early 16th century. The mausoleum of Hushang Shah is also atypical in having three entrances in the northern and southern walls rather than one on each side.

Chanderi. In the 15th century and the early 16th, the town of Chanderi was an important centre of the Malwa sultans. Many buildings survive from this period, including gates, portions of the city walls and numerous mansions, some still in the hands of the families that built them. The Jamiʿ Mosque follows that at Mandu but is notable for the prominent eaves before the prayer-hall, supported by sinuously curved brackets. The tomb known as Shahzadi-ka Rauza has carved brackets in the same style. Outside the town is the Kushk Mahal, an impressive palace built by the local governor, Sharaf Khan. Square in plan, the building has four vaulted halls opening on to a small central courtyard. The bold ogee arches of these halls are similar to those in the Hindola Mahal at Mandu (see above). Next to the Kushk Mahal are the remains of a free-standing gate; two complete examples, known as the Badal Mahal, and another opening to a graveyard are located below the citadel in the town. These gates each consist of two tapering turrets joined by a pair of ogee arches; pierced screens are placed below the upper arches. A similar free-standing gate is located in the outskirts of Gwalior. Among the notable private mansions of Chanderi are the Raj Mahal, a five-storey stone structure now partly in ruins, and the family house of Kamal Singh, also built of stone but still preserved, with two courtyards, one private and one for general use.

BIBLIOGRAPHY

A. Cunningham: 'Four Reports Made During the Years 1862–63–64–65: Report of 1864–5', *Archaeol. Surv. India Rep.*, ii (1871), pp. 402–12

J. Fergusson: *History of Indian and Eastern Architecture*, ii (1876), rev. J. Burgess (London, 1910), pp. 246–52

J. M. Campbell: 'Mandu', *J. Bombay Branch Royal Asiat. Soc.*, xix (1902), pp. 154–201

E. Barnes: 'Dhar and Mandu', *J. Bombay Branch Royal Asiat. Soc.*, xxi (1904), pp. 339–91

Archaeol. Surv. India, Annu. Rep. (1903–04), pp. 30–48

M. B. Grade: *Guide to Chanderi* (Gwalior, 1928)

J. Marshall: 'The Monuments of Muslim India', *Cambridge History of India* (Cambridge, 1928), pp. 617–25

G. Yazdani: *Mandu, the City of Joy* (Oxford, 1929)

P. Brown: *Indian Architecture, Islamic Period* (Bombay, [1942], rev. 1956 with additional photographs/*R* 1981), pp. 59–65

S. A. Rahim: 'Inscriptions on the Kushk Mahal at Chanderi', *Epig. Ind.: Arab. & Pers. Suppl.* (1965), pp. 19–22

R. Nath: *The Art of Chanderi* (New Delhi, 1979)

(f) South.

Deccan. Islamic rule was first established in the Deccan when ʿAlaʾ al-Din Khalji (*reg* 1296–1316) annexed the area to Delhi two years before becoming sultan. Extant buildings constructed under the Delhi Sultanate include the mosque in the fort at DAULATABAD. It consists of a trabeate prayer-hall built of temple spolia, a type of construction often employed in areas newly conquered by Islam. The mihrabs of the mosque have two-centred lobed arches. When Muhammad ibn Tughluq (*reg* 1325–51) moved his capital from Delhi to Daulatabad in 1340, he built a large mosque on a platform; it follows the 'Arab-type' plan (*see* §(b) above). Other structures dating from this period may include the fortified gateways of Daulatabad and the town's main streets, flanked by a series of vaulted shops.

The history of the Deccan as an independent Islamic state began in 1347 when the Tughluq army revolted and Zafar Khan Hasan Gangu, governor of Gulbarga, declared himself sultan. A Persian adventurer claiming descent from the Sasanian emperors, Zafar Khan assumed the title ʿAla' al-Din Bahman Shah (*reg* 1347–58), thus establishing the BAHMANI dynasty (1347–1527). Architecture during the Bahmani period was derived from Sultanate Delhi, Timurid Central Asia and Iran; the Muslim builders largely ignored Hindu architectural traditions. Two stages of architectural development are associated with the cities that served as the Bahmani capitals, Gulbarga (1347–1424) and Bidar (1424–1518).

Little survives of the fortress of GULBARGA, but the remains of watch-towers, massive ramparts and bastions of Tughluq origin still stand, as well as 16th- and 17th-century reinforcements. Within the irregular space enclosed by the walls were palaces, pavilions and halls, now in ruins. A street of vaulted shops does, however, remain. Mosques and tombs survive in sufficient numbers to chart the development of these forms. The Shah Bazar Mosque, like most early Bahmani structures, follows Tughluq architecture in Delhi. Probably built at the time of Muhammad ibn ʿAla' al-Din (Muhammad I; *reg* 1358–75), the building is set on a platform with a gateway to the east in the form of a square, domed chamber with steps on three sides. The prayer-hall, 15 bays wide and six aisles deep, is roofed by 90 domes resting on masonry arches supported by stone columns. The mosque's walls are battered, as in most early Bahmani buildings. The Jamiʿ Mosque at Firuzabad, probably from the time of Firuz Shah Bahmani (*reg* 1397–1424), is similar in design. More exceptional is the Jamiʿ Mosque in the fortress of Gulbarga. Dating to *c.* 1347, this mosque lacks a courtyard, the whole structure being covered with vaults and small domes. Some interior arches have a wider than normal span with low imposts, a feature that becomes characteristic of later Deccani architecture.

The tombs of the Bahmani rulers and their nobles are located mainly in two groups, one to the west of the Gulbarga fort and the other to the east. All are square domed chambers, the earliest examples being simpler in design with small arched entrances in the centre of each wall. On the qibla side (the wall orientated towards Mecca), a mihrab replaces the arched opening. The walls are plain and battered. Like the early tombs at Delhi, the squinches are built into the walls. The earliest example of this type is the tomb of Ghiyath al-Din Hasan Shah (*reg c.* 1397). Later Bahmani rulers built their mausolea to the east of the fort in a necropolis known as Haft Gunbad (Pers.: 'seven domes'). The tombs of Da'ud Shah (*reg* 1378) and Firuz Shah (*reg* 1397–1422) each consist of a pair of interconnected square, domed chambers. Such double tombs did not become an established form and are found only at this site. The tomb of Da'ud Shah is noteworthy for the extensive use of cut plaster on the interior. Firuz Shah's tomb shows a departure from earlier forms, as the walls are divided into registers decorated with arched niches and windows with pierced stone screens. The exterior walls do not have a heavy batter. All surfaces are plastered, the interior being gilded and painted with polychrome floral and geometric patterns. Later Bahmani tombs retain the double register on the exterior, but their domes are different in that they have a transitional zone above the roof level, usually octagonal in form. Tombs of this late type in Gulbarga include the Chor Gunbaz and the shrine of Gisu Daraz. The latter, built in 1421–2 (AH 825), is the focus of a religious complex with mosques and rest-houses.

Ahmad Shah Wali (*reg* 1422–36) made BIDAR his capital in 1429, radically altering and expanding the citadel. The new fortifications consisted of a triple moat to the south, high ramparts to the north and seven fortified gates. The south-eastern gate of the fort opens to a street leading to a large (124.5×64 m) square known as Laʿl Bagh. The square was surrounded by the main mosque and other royal buildings. The mosque, known as the Solahkhamba Mosque, is the oldest standing building of the Bahmani period in Bidar, having been built in 1423–4 (AH 827). It consists of a single prayer-hall without a courtyard, set directly on the side of the square. The prayer-hall is roofed with small domes, but at the centre before the mihrab is a larger dome similar to that of the Gulbarga Jamiʿ Mosque. The mihrab of the Solahkhamba is semi-octagonal in plan and does not project outside the qibla wall, indicating that the design was influenced by Iranian practice.

The street leading to the Laʿl Bagh is flanked by a palace complex known as the Rangin Mahal. Probably a royal pavilion, the palace adjoins the fortifications and includes an observation tower from which the ruler could review troops. There is also a royal kitchen. The Bahmani structures in the Rangin Mahal include two square, domed chambers to the east of a courtyard; the other buildings were reconstructed in the mid-16th century by the BARID SHAHI rulers. A second palatial structure, to the south of the Laʿl Bagh, is known as the Gagan Mahal. It has two courtyards surrounded by apartments. Originally in three storeys and built in the 15th century, the buildings were heavily renovated under the Barid Shahis. The Tarkash Mahal, adjoining the north side of the Gagan Mahal, also dates from the mid-16th century. Its garden has watercourses and, in the centre, a lobed oval cistern surfaced with carved black stone on a square platform. The uppermost storey of the Tarkash Mahal was a royal apartment overlooking the Laʿl Bagh. The royal bath on the north side of the Laʿl Bagh does not entirely follow the plan of traditional Islamic baths. It has a waiting hall in the form of a portico facing the square and is surrounded by arcades on the other sides. On both the east and west is a series of chambers used for bathing.

From the Laʿl Bagh a street leads to a complex of two audience halls, the Takht Mahal (Throne Palace) and the Diwan-i ʿAm (Hall of Public Audience). Believed to have been built by Ahmad Shah Wali, these buildings are said to have been destroyed in the 17th century to prevent their use by the Mughals. Despite much damage, enough has survived to give us a rare example of audience halls during the 15th century. The larger hall, the Diwan-i ʿAm, stands on the south side of a small garden with a fountain and watercourses. The hall took the form of a pillared portico supported by three rows of wooden columns, six in each row. The ceiling may also have been of wood, as in the later Athar Mahal at Bijapur. At each side of the Diwan-i ʿAm are two long, narrow chambers, originally roofed with shallow vaults, and behind these and the pillared hall itself are seven interconnected chambers. The floor of the central chamber retains its original paving stones in star and hexagon patterns. The lower parts of the walls were covered with glazed tiles with a variety of geometric and floral designs in yellow, red, brown, white, turquoise and cobalt blue; these tiles are close to Timurid examples in Khurasan. The design of the audience hall follows a north Iranian and Central Asian tradition dating back to the 13th century and seen later in the Safavid palaces of ISFAHAN. To the north-west of the Diwan-i ʿAm is the Takht Mahal. Like the Diwan-i ʿAm, the main part of the palace is set on the south side of a courtyard to protect it from direct sun. The portico is small and originally had four wooden columns. It is flanked by two square rooms, and behind it is a larger domed space, probably used as the audience chamber. To the east is a small private courtyard surrounded by rooms and corridors. The spandrel of the main gate was decorated with glazed tiles and includes the emblem of the lion and sun, also used by the Timurids in this period. Outside the complex is a semi-octagonal pavilion built over a crypt with a small portico in front. The pavilion affords views of a lake-size reservoir, the fort and adjacent lowlands.

The town of Bidar was built at the same time as the fort, and the layout of the streets has been little altered since the 15th century. The streets conform to a rough grid with two main avenues on a north–south and an east–west axis. At the centre of the junction is a tower (h. 39.6 m) known as the Chaubara, which rests on a large platform (diam. 17.5 m) pierced with an entrance and a series of niches. The upper part is plain, but there is a single door on the north giving access to a spiral staircase within. The tower seems to have been constructed by Ahmad Shah Wali, and its form may have been taken from Delhi, where a similar building known as the Chor Minar, reminiscent of the towers in the centre of Sasanian towns such as Ardashir-Khurra (Firuzabad), Iran, was built in the Khalji period. The Jamiʿ Mosque, located near the Chaubara, probably dates to the first decades of the 16th century and is similar to the Shah Bazar Masjid in Gulbarga. The mihrab design, however, follows the Solahkhamba Mosque in Bidar fort.

Ahmad Shah Wali was an active patron of Sufism, being first a follower of Gisu Daraz in Gulbarga. After the latter's death and the shift of the capital to Bidar, Ahmad Shah Wali invited Hadrat Khalil'ullah Kirmani from Iran in 1430. Many of Khalil'ullah's descendants set up their own schools (*taʿlīm*s) and monastic establishments (*khānaqāh*s). The largest are those of Shah Wali'ullah Kirmani, Shah Abu'l Faid and ʿAli Husayn Qutb-i Thani, all dating from the 15th century. There are many more *taʿlīm*s and *khānaqāh*s in Bidar. All the *khānaqāh*s have a similar layout and consist of a colonnaded portico at the south of a courtyard flanked by rooms. The *khānaqāh* of Hadrat Khalil'ullah Kirmani has not survived, but the Takht-i Kirmani in the town is believed to be the gate of his residence. It now serves as a shrine. Little of its original decoration can be seen, since the rich stuccowork covering the façade appears to be of the post-Bahmani period. No Bahmani monument shows the influence of Khurasani architecture more clearly than the madrasa of Mahmud Gawan (see fig. 95). Built in 1472–3 (AH 877) by the chief

95. Madrasa of Mahmud Gawan, Bidar, 1472–3; view from the north-east corner of the courtyard

minister of Muhammad Shah III (*reg* 1463–82), the madrasa has a four-iwan plan with a central courtyard. The building is similar to Timurid madrasas of the same period, particularly that in Khargird. The surface of the minaret is covered with glazed tiles set to produce horizontal zigzag patterns.

The Bahmani tombs in Bidar, grouped in a necropolis to the east of the town, depart from earlier examples at Gulbarga. They have relatively thin walls with deep niches, which further reduce the amount of masonry. The domes are squinched and raised on octagonal drums. The oldest of these tombs is that of Ahmad Shah Wali (*d* 1436). The interior is elegantly painted with geometric, floral and decorative calligraphy in red, blue and brown with extensive gilding. The tomb of ʿAlaʾ al-Din Bahmani (*d* 1458) is notable for its exterior tilework, again recalling Timurid designs in Khurasan. Among the tombs of saints, the most notable are those of Hadrat Khalil'ullah Kirmani, situated outside the town, and Multani Padshah, situated inside. Khalil'ullah's tomb is similar to that of ʿAlaʾ al-Din Bahmani but is surrounded by an unroofed octagonal wall with a four-storey elevation built at a later date.

In addition to the buildings at Bidar, examples of later Bahmani architecture are found at Holkonda, Belgaum and Raichur. Mosques also continued to be constructed in the old capital at Gulbarga. Among these are the mosque of Qalandar Khan, the Kali Mosque in Malkhed (near Gulbarga) and the early 15th-century Langar ki Mosque, a small building with masonry vaults that are decorated with unusual plasterwork imitating wooden trusses. A domed minaret known as the Chand Minar at Daulatabad was built in 1435 by a governor of ʿAlaʾ al-Din Bahmani (*reg* 1436–58).

BIBLIOGRAPHY

J. Fergusson: *History of Indian and Eastern Architecture*, ii (1876), rev. by J. Burgess (London, 1910), pp. 262–80
J. Burgess: *Report on the Antiquities in Bidar and Aurangabad*, Archaeol. Surv. W. India, Rep., iii (London, 1878)
H. Cousens: *Lists of the Antiquarian Remains in His Highness the Nizam's Territories*, Archaeol. Surv. India, New Imp. Ser., xxxi (Calcutta, 1900)
Archaeol. Dept Annu. Rep. Nizam's Dominions (1917–41)
G. Yazdani: 'The Antiquities of Bidar', *Archaeol. Surv. India, Annu. Rep.* (1914–15), pp. 132–50
J. Marshall: 'The Monuments of Muslim India', *Cambridge History of India*, iii (Cambridge, 1928), pp. 629–36
P. Brown: *Indian Architecture, Islamic Period* (Bombay, [1942], rev. 1956 with additional photographs/*R* 1981), pp. 66–72
G. Yazdani: *Bidar, its History and Monuments* (Oxford, 1947)
S. Yusuf: *Antiquarian Remains in Hayderabad State* (Hyderabad, 1953)
E. I. Merklinger: 'Seven Tombs at Holkonda: A Preliminary Survey', *Kst Orients*, x/1–2 (1976), pp. 187–97
——: 'The Madrasa of Mahmud Gawan', *Kst Orients*, xi/1–2 (1977), pp. 156–67
E. Schotten-Merklinger: 'The Mosques of Rāičūr: A Preliminary Classification', *Kst Orients*, xii/1–2 (1978–9), pp. 79–94
——: *Indian Islamic Architecture: The Deccan* (Warminster, 1981)
G. Michell, ed.: 'Masterpieces of the Deccan Sultanates', *Marg*, xxxvii/3 (n. d.), pp. 2–87
——: *Islamic Heritage of the Deccan* (Bombay, 1986)
G. Michell and R. Eaton: *Firuzabad, Palace City of the Deccan* (Oxford, 1992)
M. Shokoohy: 'The Sasanian Royal Emblems and their Re-emergence in the 14th Century Deccan', *Muqarnas*, xi (1994), pp. 65–78

Kerala and Tamil Nadu. Muslim settlements were first established along the coast of south India by merchants who arrived from the Persian Gulf and Red Sea. Contacts with the West go back to Greek and Roman times; while an Islamic presence is little documented until the 9th century, the Cheraman Mosque at Cranganur is said to have been founded as early as AD 629–30 (AH 8). The earliest surviving examples of Kerala architecture are the mosques in CALICUT. They differ from other Indo-Islamic buildings in that they closely follow local traditions (*see* §(i)(g) and (h) above) and show links with South-east Asia. The mosques usually have a stone plinth and stone walls with wooden columns supporting hipped or tiered roofs covered with tile. A single mihrab, semicircular in plan, is employed rather than the multiple mihrabs of north India and the Deccan. The Mithqalpalli, or Nakhuda Mithqal Mosque, in Calicut is known to have been founded by Nakhuda Mithqal, a wealthy 14th-century merchant and contemporary of the traveller Ibn Battuta. The mosque (see fig. 96) has a colonnaded prayer-hall and an antechamber at the east, both under a large, three-tiered roof of wood. The roof space was once used as a madrasa. A corridor runs around the ground level of the building, and on the façades are a number of doors and niches with semicircular arch forms carved out of horizontally laid stone blocks. The Jamiʿ Mosque of Calicut may be older than the Mithqalpalli but was restored in 1480–81 (AH 885). It began as a small building but was gradually enlarged, probably since the 16th century, when it was chosen to replace an earlier Jamiʿ destroyed by the Portuguese. In its present form the mosque has an asymmetric prayer-hall with a small antechamber at the east and a porch at the front. The 17th-century coffered ceiling and supporting beams of the porch are finely carved with *naskhī* inscriptions and floral motifs. Inside the prayer-hall are two pools with openings above in the roof to allow the collection of rainwater. Both the Mithqalpalli and the Jamiʿ Mosque have wooden minbars of the 17th century, reconstructed in the 19th. Other old mosques in Calicut are the Allahrapalli, Idrispalli and Muchandipalli. The latter has a 13th- or 14th-century bilingual inscription referring to the construction of the mosque and an Arabic inscription recording restoration work in the 15th century. In front of the Idrispalli is a 15th-century tomb, square in plan, with a masonry dome and finely carved circular windows of wood. Other old Kerala mosques and shrines are found at Kondotti, Tirurangadi, Cochin and Cranganur.

The army of ʿAlaʾ al-Din Khalji (*reg* 1296–1316) took control of Tamil Nadu in 1310, but rule from Delhi ended when the Tughluq governor Jalal al-Din Ahsan claimed independence and established the Sultanate of Maʿbar in 1334. This state lasted until *c.* 1378. Islamic architecture under the Maʿbar sultans has its own characteristics, the buildings being mainly constructed of ashlar with domes or flat roofs made of stone slabs. Wooden structures may once have existed, as some wooden features were imitated in stone. Little influence from north India is found, the builders preferring to follow the architecture of the western seaboard. About 6 km from Madurai, Jalal al-Din founded a new capital, the location of which may be marked by Tiruparangundram, the site of the tomb complex of Sikandar Shah, the last Maʿbar sultan. The prayer-hall there, with its colonnade and antechamber, is similar to mosques in Kerala but is built of stone rather than wood.

96. Nakhuda Mithqal Mosque, or Mithqalpalli, Calicut, 14th century; view from the south

The tomb is located behind the prayer-hall; the tomb door takes the place of the mihrab in the centre of the qibla wall. In Madurai itself is the tomb of Sultan ʿAla' al-Din Udauji. It is known to have been constructed by Sultan Shams al-Din ʿAdil Shah (*d* 1372–3, AH 774), who is also buried there. The tomb is a square-domed chamber on a plinth with a surrounding colonnade; the arrangement is similar to the 15th-century tombs of Gujarat but predates them by a century. The hemispherical dome (diam. 7.5 m) is carved from a single piece of rock, a feature unparalleled in Islamic architecture but not unlike the monolithic cupolas used in Tamil Nadu temples. The Qadi Taj al-Din Mosque in Madurai is comparable in plan to the Calicut mosques but again is constructed of stone.

While many towns in Tamil Nadu have mosques and shrines, apart from those in Madurai the most important examples are found in Nagore and Kayalpatnam. In Nagore, which is probably the old Muslim port of Fatan, the shrine of Hadrat Qadir Wali is one of the holiest places in the south. The domed tomb has many later additions. Kayalpatnam, known to Muslims as Qa'il and to early Europeans as Cael or Coil, is the only town in south India populated almost entirely by Muslims. It possesses two congregational mosques. The greater Jamiʿ Mosque (1336–7; AH 737) is a vast colonnaded hall with a flat roof, fronted by a porch. In the centre of the prayer-hall there was once a pool surrounded by finely carved columns of the 16th or 17th century; the pool has now been filled and the opening covered with a dome. The smaller Jamiʿ Mosque is similar in plan and probably dates to the same period. Both preserve their original minbars. Other mosques in Kayalpatnam follow the same scheme; this is related to the configuration first used at Bhadreshvar in Gujarat in the mid-12th century (*see* §5(ii)(b) above). Few old tombs have survived at Kayalpatnam, but those of Shaykh Sulayman and Shaykh Sam Shahab al-Din, dating to the 17th century, are noteworthy for their stone hipped roofs imitating timber structures.

BIBLIOGRAPHY

S. A. Q. Husaini: 'The History of Madura Sultanate', *J. Asiat. Soc. Pakistan*, ii (1957), pp. 90–130

T. P. Kuttiammu: 'The Mosques of Kerala', *Splendors of Kerala* (Bombay, 1983), pp. 111–15

M. Shokoohy: 'Architecture of the Sultanate of Madura and Other Muslim Monuments in South India', *J. Royal Asiat. Soc., Sri Lankan Branch*, i (1991), pp. 31–92

——: 'Architecture of the Muslim Trading Communities in India', *Islam and Indian Regions*, ed. A. L. Dallapiccola and S. Zingel-Avé Lallemant (Heidelberg, 1993), i, pp. 291–319; ii, pp. 99–113 and pls 23–30

——: 'Architecture of the Muslim Port of Qā'il on the Coromandel Coast, South India: Pt 1, History and the 14th–15th Century Monuments', *S. Asian Stud.*, ix (1993), pp. 139–68

——: 'Architecture of the Muslim Port of Qā'il on the Coromandel Coast, South India: Pt 2, The 16th–19th Century Monuments', *S. Asian Stud.*, x (1994), pp. 161–78

——: 'Epitaphs of Kayalpatnam, South India', *S. Asian Stud.*, xi (1995)

MEHRDAD SHOKOOHY

7. 16TH–19TH CENTURIES.

(i) Mughal. (ii) Regional. (iii) Early colonial.

(i) Mughal. The MUGHAL rulers, descended from Ghengis Khan and Timur, controlled the greater part of India for more than three centuries As the subcontinent's most formidable autocrats, the Mughals developed a powerful architecture that was at once dynastic, Islamic and Indian. Mughal architecture was dynastic because the emperors actively patronized it as an instrument of state and used it throughout their dominions as a visible expression of imperial authority. Mughal architecture was Islamic because the Mughals drew ideas and talent from the Islamic lands to the west, particularly Iran and Transoxiana, the heartland of their forebears. The Mughals also remained orthodox Muslims throughout their history, despite intermarriage and accommodating religious policies. Finally,

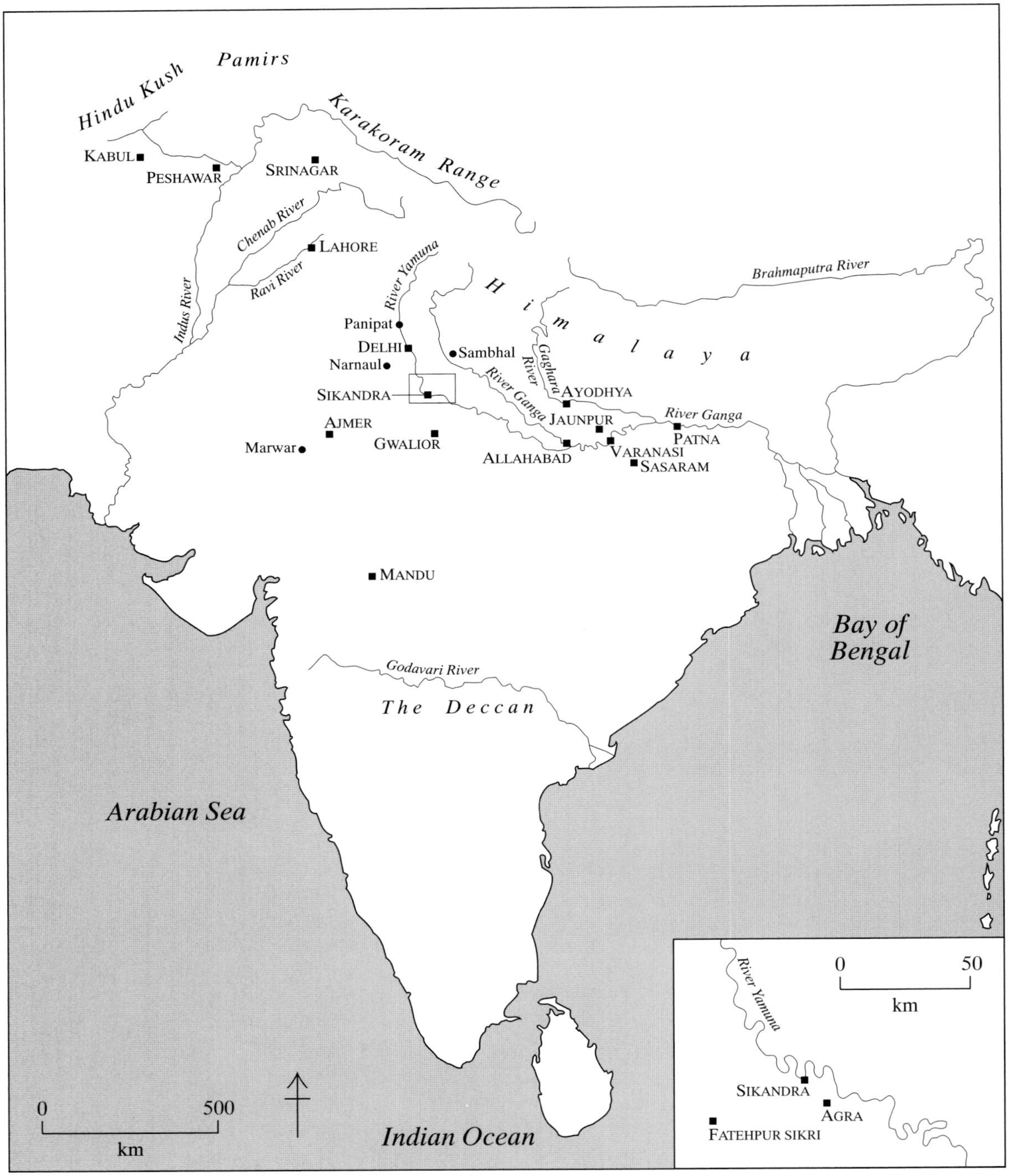

97. Map of Mughal sites; those sites with separate entries in this dictionary are distinguished by CROSS-REFERENCE TYPE

Mughal architecture was Indian because it drew comprehensively on Indo-Islamic and indigenous traditions. Under Mughal patronage, these traditions were welded together with fresh Iranian influences to create a unique new style that absorbed and surpassed its predecessors.

MICHAEL D. WILLIS

(a) Imperial centres. (b) Eastern provinces. (c) Western provinces. (d) Central and southern provinces.

(a) Imperial centres. From the Mughal perspective, the northern part of India stretched from the Indus River in the north-west to the banks of the Ganga near Bihar (see fig. 97). In the centuries before the rise of the Mughal

dynasty, this vast area was loosely linked by trade and pilgrimage. Successive Mughal emperors developed a well-travelled highway, especially between their capitals of Lahore, Delhi and Agra. Each of these northern cities served as a seat of Mughal power and was a centre of important architectural activity. As in ancient India, this was the heartland, and ideas spread out from it to influence all India.

Babur. The first of the Mughal emperors, Babur (*reg* 1526–30), disliked the climate and geography of the Indian plains and had little sympathy for indigenous architecture. He was determined, however, to establish permanent control over the north Indian lands he conquered and immediately began a number of building programmes in his new kingdom. The first projects were a series of symmetrical terraced gardens that contained a variety of small pavilions and the royal tents when the king was present, for Babur disdained city life, preferring garden resorts when not engaged in military campaigns. Several suburban gardens were laid out in the vicinity of Agra, Babur's capital. The pavilions in these gardens were mentioned by Babur in his memoirs, the *Bāburnāma.* No longer extant, the pavilions were probably similar to the gazebos shown in miniature paintings from Khorasan and Bukhara, since two highly placed craftsmen, Mirak Sayyid Ghiyath of Khorasan and Ustad Shah Muhammad, came to India to serve in Babur's employ. Another garden was constructed in 1527 at Sikri (later Fatehpur Sikri). The garden at Dholpur, south of Agra, is the best-preserved example of the period. Known as the Lotus Garden (Pers. Bāgh-i Nīlūfar), it is described in Babur's memoirs, where he notes that he personally chose the site and ordered the construction of a mosque, bath (Arab./Pers. *ḥammām*), well, pillars and rock-cut water courses. The bath and portions of the mosque still remain, along with sections of the water courses. Within the terraced garden is a central octagonal pool and smaller pools resembling lotus petals, recalling the pools in the 15th-century hill-fort at Mandu.

Babur's Indian gardens were modelled on those he had built in Kabul, most notably the Garden of Fidelity (Pers. Bāgh-i Wafā), which was constructed in 1508–9 (AH 914). These gardens conformed to a type known as *chār bāgh* (from Pers. *chahārbāgh*, 'four [plot] garden'), because they were divided into quadrants by water courses. Running water for the courses, where not available, was supplied by water wheels and deep stepwells (Ind.-Pers. *bā'olī*). The arrangement drew on the Timurid tradition, although the use of water courses, instead of planting arrangements, may have been a Mughal innovation. Babur's gardens are symbolic of his efforts to control and order his Indian dominion. Their importance is evident in the numerous *chār bāgh* gardens laid out by his successors and the setting of most Mughal architecture, with the exception of urban mosques, within a *chār bāgh* environment.

Babur also ordered public mosques to be erected. A mosque was constructed by Mir Hindu Beg on Babur's orders at Sambhal in 1526. Another was built at AYODHYA in 1528–9 (AH 935; destr. 1992), on the site of a temple, according to traditions first written down in the 19th century. Temple fragments are incorporated into the fabric of the mosque, a feature unusual for this time. The mosque at Panipat (see fig. 98), dated 1527–8 (AH 934–5), was built directly under Babur's auspices and was located at the site of the Mughal victory over Ibrahim Lodi. These buildings legitimated Babur's rule, serving as visible symbols of the king as a conqueror of 'idolatrous' non-Muslims (Arab. *ghāzī*) and as the supreme protector of holy law (*ẓahīr al-dīn*).

Architecturally these mosques are similar: all have a high central portal and a dome over the prayer chamber, flanked by double-aisled side wings with smaller domes. The façades were plaster-faced. Walls enclosed a large open courtyard. Significantly, neither the mosque at Sambhal nor that at Panipat was constructed in the prevailing single-aisled, multi-bayed mode of Lodi mosques, such as the Moth ki Mosque (*c.* 1505) at Delhi (*see* §6(ii)(b) above). Rather, the buildings are reminiscent of the 15th-century

98. Congregational mosque, Panipat, Babur period, 1527–8; east façade

mosques of JAUNPUR and attempt to emulate the large congregational mosques of Babur's homeland, for example that of Bibi Khanum in Samarkand (*see* SAMARKAND, §3(ii)).

Humayun and the Sur interregnum. Literary sources indicate that Humayun (*reg* 1530–40; 1555–6) was a keen patron of palatial architecture, but the only example from his unsettled reign is the ruined house of his brother Mirza Kamran. It was set in a garden on the north bank of the River Ravi outside Lahore. At Agra, the Kachpura Mosque (named after the locality) is dated the year Humayun acceded to the throne. The building apparently served as the congregational mosque. It resembles Babur's mosque at Panipat, though the central portal is higher and its vaulted chamber more open, allowing for a greater entry of light.

The Purana Qil'a (Old Fort) in Delhi and some of the few remaining structures inside have also been attributed to Humayun. The fort was planned to serve as the focus of Humayun's capital. Khwandamir, a noble at court, remarked that by 1534 the fort's walls and gates were nearly complete, but this was probably an exaggeration. It is difficult to judge how much had been built when Sher Shah Sur (*reg* 1538–45) forced Humayun into exile in 1540. In all probability, Sher Shah completed the fort and constructed the Qil'a-i Kuhna Mosque inside between 1540 and 1545 (*see* DELHI, fig. 5). This building is a single-aisled mosque of five bays. The configuration was a popular one in early 16th-century Delhi, but in this instance the interior and exterior were faced with multicoloured stones, many intricately carved with inscriptions and inlaid to form geometric patterns. The use of multicoloured stone was favoured by the earlier KHALJI dynasty, and the Qil'a-i Kuhna shows a revival of 14th-century practice. As a whole, however, the mosque exhibits a decisive move away from the solid three-dimensional masses of Sultanate building. The architectural forms are pressed into flat panels and the decoration has a precise linear character that directly anticipates later Mughal architecture. Also within the fort is a three-storey octagonal pavilion known as Sher Mandal. Despite the modern name associating it with Sher Shah, the pavilion probably corresponds to the library described in contemporary texts as having been built by Humayun after his return to India in 1555. The library appears to have been modelled on Timurid and Safavid pleasure pavilions.

The funerary architecture of the period is well represented by the tomb of a minor Lodi noble, Ibrahim Sur (*d c.* 1488). Located at Narnaul, 120 km south-west of Delhi, the tomb was built by Ibrahim Sur's grandson Sher Shah in 1542–3, and in its time it was the most elaborate mausoleum in northern India. The domed building has a square plan measuring 20.8 m each side. It is faced with contrasting grey and pink stone, all finely carved, the careful craftsmanship closely related to that of the Qil'a-i Kuhna Mosque in Delhi. Modelled after those built for the most prominent members of the Lodi court, the tomb was evidently intended to project an image of Sher Shah as a just ruler with an elevated genealogy. Similar motives, coupled with the elaboration of older forms, are seen in many concurrent projects, most notably Isa Khan's tomb at Delhi (1547–8) and Sher Shah's own tomb at Sasaram (for illustration *see* SASARAM).

Akbar. The first architectural project of Akbar's reign (*reg* 1556–1605) was a tomb at Delhi for his father, Humayun. Designed by Mirak Mirza Ghiyath (possibly the same Mirak Sayyid Ghiyath of Khorasan who worked for Babur), the tomb was completed in 1571–2 (AH 978) after a decade of work. Situated to the south of the Purana Qil'a not far from the shrine (Pers. *dargāh*) of Nizam al-Din Auliya', the famous saint of the Sufi Chishti order, Humayun's tomb is set in a spacious garden divided by water courses in the *chār bāgh* fashion. The mausoleum, placed on a large platform with arched niches, is built of red sandstone trimmed with white marble. The central space under the dome contains Humayun's cenotaph and is surrounded by two-storey octagonal chambers. These chambers, containing cenotaphs of the king's family, are linked by archways and passages. This arrangement was modelled on the 'eight-paradise' plan (Pers. *hasht bihisht*) of Timurid architecture (*see* ISLAMIC ART, §II, 6(i)(b)). The exterior of the octagonal chambers also shows a debt to Central Asian and Iranian architecture, resembling the palace pavilions seen in early Safavid painting. (Octagonal in plan, these were divided into two storeys and had arched niches.) The tomb's high white marble dome is flanked by cupolas of a more Indian character. The garden setting and the tomb's plan were symbolic of paradise, beginning a long tradition of paradisical imagery in Mughal funerary architecture.

The mausoleum of Ataga Khan, also located near the shrine of Nizam al-Din Auliya' in Delhi, was constructed concurrently with Humayun's tomb but not under imperial auspices. It was built by Ataga Khan's son 'Aziz Kokaltash in 1566. Designed by the architect Ustad Khuda Quli, the small, domed structure has a square plan and is richly embellished with marble and tilework in the manner of the Qil'a-i Kuhna Mosque. The tomb of Adham Khan (who was executed on Akbar's order in 1562 for the murder of Ataga Khan) follows the older octagonal format. It is located in the Mehrauli suburb of Delhi.

Akbar's reign is especially notable for the forts and fortified palaces he built throughout northern India. These extended from Attock on the Indus to that at ALLAHABAD (begun 1573) at the confluence of the Ganga and Yamuna. Akbar also built a fort on Hari Parbat, a hill in SRINAGAR (Kashmir). The gateway at the base of the hill is dated AH 1006 (AD 1597) and constructed of the dark grey stone characteristic of many Mughal monuments in Kashmir. The fort that Akbar built at Lahore served as the seat of government from 1585 to 1598. Few structures from Akbar's time survive except the Masjidi or Masti gate. At Agra, then renamed Akbarabad, a fort was begun flanking the Yamuna River in 1565. Extensive changes were made subsequently, but two gates with their rows of arched niches and colourful decoration have been preserved. Inside, the Jahangiri Mahal dates to before *c.* 1571. The exterior of this palace displays the calm austerity of Humayun's tomb, while the complex interior apartments, with their heavily carved arcades and struts, recall the architecture of Gwalior and western India (*see* GWALIOR, fig. 2). This partially confirms a statement in the *Āyīn-i*

Akbarī that many buildings in the 'fine styles of Bengal and Gujarat' were built by the Emperor within the fort.

The imaginative eclecticism of the Jahangiri Mahal also characterizes Akbar's largest and best-preserved palace city of Fatehpur Sikri. Located 37 km west of Agra, Fatehpur Sikri was begun in 1569–70 (AH 976) on the site of the hospice (Pers. *khānaqāh*) of the Sufi Shaykh Salim Chishti, who had accurately predicted the birth of Akbar's son and heir, the future Jahangir. Most of the construction was finished by 1579. The city was then abandoned in 1585 when the Emperor moved the capital to Lahore and no longer associated himself closely with the Chishti order. The imperial portion of Fatehpur Sikri can be divided into two main sections: the religious area with the mosque and marble tomb of Shaykh Salim Chishti and the residential and administrative areas, mentioned in the *Ṭabaqāt Akbarī* ('Chronicle of Akbar') as the *daulat-khāna* or 'imperial palace'. (For illustrations of buildings, *see* FATEHPUR SIKRI.) The identity of many structures in the palace area has not been established with certainty. The whole complex is an interrelated series of modules, suggesting that it was carefully planned. Constructed almost wholly of red sandstone quarried locally, most of the structures are trabeated and richly carved with a variety of relief ornaments. Many have pillared galleries. The congregational mosque was built on a raised platform and has a large courtyard surrounded by multi-domed arcades. On the north stands the Buland Darvaza, a ceremonial arched entrance of lofty proportions.

One of the most innovative structures of Akbar's time was the temple of Govinda Deva at VRINDAVAN, which employs vaulted and arcuated forms. Built by the high-ranking noble Raja Man Singh in 1590, the Govinda Deva (l. *c.* 154 m) was the largest temple constructed in northern India since the advent of Islam in the 13th century; and its size and style are indicative of Akbar's tolerance towards non-Muslim subjects.

Narnaul, now in Haryana but in the province of Agra under the Mughals, served as a strategic gate to the Rajput stronghold of Marwar, and mosques and stepwells were constructed during the period of Akbar's reign. In 1574–5 (AH 982) Shah Quli Khan built a small octagonal tomb within a garden; it was modelled on the Persian pavilions that inspired the Sher Mandal in Delhi (*see* DELHI, §III, 3). Further projects at Narnaul under Shah Quli Khan include the Jal Mahal (Urdu: Water Palace), built between 1589 and 1592. Set in the middle of an artificial tank, it is a square structure surmounted by five *chatrīs* (small domed pavilions). The façades have deeply recessed arches containing geometric patterns painted in red on burnished plaster.

Jahangir. Like his predecessors, Jahangir (*reg* 1605–27) had substantial interests in architecture, as shown by the surviving monuments and his own memoirs, the *Tūzuk-i Jahāngīrī*. Jahangir's first major project was a tomb for his father at SIKANDRA, near Agra. The tomb may have been started by Akbar, but it is more likely that it was erected mainly under Jahangir's auspices. A poem written by Muhammad Baqir Najm-i Sani in praise of Akbar's tomb specifies Jahangir as its patron and designer. Contemporary histories simply state that Akbar was buried in a garden called the Abode of Paradise (Pers. Bihishtābād). The tomb-garden at Sikandra follows the usual *chār bāgh* arrangement, and inscriptions on the entrance gate (*see* SIKANDRA, fig. 2) refer to the setting as a paradisaical garden. The tomb (*see* SIKANDRA, fig. 1) is set on a broad platform pierced with arched niches, recalling Humayun's tomb. The mausoleum, however, departs from all precedents, both Indo-Islamic and Timurid, consisting of several tiered storeys with pillared galleries and square, domed cupolas. The top storey is marble and contains the cenotaph, which is open to the air. The building was apparently inspired by palatial architecture and referred to the mansions of paradise that are promised in the Koran to the faithful on the Day of Judgement. The complex was completed by 1614 according to inscriptions on the gate by the calligrapher ʿAbd al-Haq Shirazi (later Amanat Khan), who designed the inscriptions on the Taj Mahal. More traditional is the tomb of Anakarli at Lahore, built by Jahangir in 1615–16 (AH 1025). The single-domed building, similar to Khan-i Khanan's tomb in Delhi (*c.* 1600), has been subject to extensive changes throughout its history.

In Lahore, Jahangir expanded and remodelled Akbar's fort; Jahangir's memoirs refer to his additions there in 1612, designed by Khwaja Jahan Muhammad Dust. The Englishman William Finch visited the imperial residence in 1610 and has left a description of some of Jahangir's buildings. The Kala Burj (restored), with paintings of angels and birds in the net-shaped vault, probably belongs to this early phase of construction. More buildings were added in 1617–18 (AH 1027) by the architect ʿAbd al-Karim Maʿmur Khan. Among these are probably the structures of the Jahangiri quadrangle, used as a residential quarter and consisting of a spacious garden and pool surrounded by a series of one-storey pavilions. The pavilions, symmetrically disposed around the edges of the court, have flat roofs and pillared porches with prominent animal brackets. The quadrangle directly abuts a formal audience hall and was built of red sandstone imported from the Agra region, while the fortification walls, also renovated by Jahangir, are of brick and glazed tiles made locally and inlaid to create floral, animal and human forms.

The handsome appearance of Lahore city was praised by European travellers, who admired the splendid mosques, bazaars and mansions constructed by Jahangir's nobles. Few of these structures remain. An exception is the mosque of Shahi Begum, built by Miryam Zamani, the queen mother, and dated AD 1611–12 (AH 1020). Following the precedent of earlier Mughal mosques, the prayer hall has a high central portal and dome with lower flanking wings on each side. The stunning al secco wall paintings on the interior vaults are the best preserved examples of the period. The courtyard had three gates, but only one has survived.

Jahangir and his court had a number of retreats outside of Lahore, including a hunting preserve at Shaikhupura, some 20 km away. There, at the grave of his favourite deer, the Emperor constructed a tank, with a three-storey pavilion in its centre and a tower (Pers. *minār*). These were completed under the direction of Muʿin Khan and Iradat Khan in 1620, although the pavilion was remodelled in Shah Jahan's time. Jahangir was particularly fond of the

99. Tomb of Iʿtimad al-Daula, Agra, Jahangir period, 1626–7; south façade

natural beauty of Kashmir, where he repaired and restored his father's fort, adding palatial structures, throne-kiosks and caravanserais. The mountain slopes of Kashmir were ideal settings for terraced gardens, and Jahangir built one around the falls at Achibal, while his brother-in-law, Asaf Khan, built the Garden of Joy (Pers. Bāgh-i Nishāṭ), a terraced plot of the *chār bāgh* type overlooking Dal Lake. In 1620–21 (AH 1030), Jahangir gave orders for his son, the future Shah Jahan, to dam a stream on Dal Lake at Srinagar; this became Shah Jahan's famous Shalimar Garden (*see* GARDEN, §IV, 2 and fig. 11). Jahangir's favourite retreat in Kashmir was the natural spring at Vernag, south of Srinagar. He mentioned the spring in his memoirs in 1606 and again in 1619–20 (AH 1029), at which time he claimed that an octagonal reservoir, garden and mansion were completed, but inscriptions at the site indicate that the buildings were not finished until 1626–7 (AH 1036). Jahangir built further gardens in the suburbs of Agra. A terraced garden known as Ram Bagh is probably Jahangir's Rose-strewn Garden (Pers. Bāgh-i Gul Afshān). It was completed in 1619 under the supervision of Khwaja Jahan Muhammad Dust. Jahangir subsequently presented this garden to his wife Nur Jahan, changing the name to Light-strewn Garden (Pers. Bāgh-i Nūr Afshān). The Emperor's memoirs indicate that the pillared galleries and closed square chambers that overlook the River Yamuna were complete in 1615. These buildings contain mural paintings.

The nobility became increasingly active patrons during and after Jahangir's reign. One of the most significant architectural activities encouraged by the Emperor was the development of facilities, such as route markers (Pers. *kūs minār*) and caravanserais, to ensure secure communication along the trade routes, especially between the imperial cities of Lahore and Agra. For example, Serai Nur Mahal (Jullundar District), begun in 1618–19 (AH 1028) by Nur Jahan, Jahangir's powerful wife, is a large structure (170 m sq.) faced with imported red sandstone, with elaborately carved gates. Nur Jahan owned another serai (destr.) in Agra, where taxes for goods were collected. Serai Doraha (Ludhiana District) was constructed of brick and faced with glazed tilework; the enclosure (168 m per side) is uninscribed but can be assigned to Jahangir's time on stylistic and historical grounds.

Also symptomatic of the increasing role of the nobility in Mughal architecture is the mausoleum at Agra that Nur Jahan constructed for her parents (see fig. 99). Known as Iʿtimad al-Daula's tomb after her father, the building is set in a *chār bāgh*-type garden. Constructed entirely of white marble, the lower floor is pierced by arched entrances and screened windows. Minarets are set on each corner. The upper storey consists of a small, rectangular, vaulted pavilion, which contains the cenotaphs. The pavilion floor has spectacular inlaid arabesques, and the walls are fitted with stunning marble screens. The interior and exterior walls are heavily inlaid with geometric patterns and arabesques in hardstones. Wine vessels, platters of fruit and cypresses are also shown and invoke the paradisaical images of mystical Persian poetry and the Koran. The tomb of Iʿtimad al-Daula follows the architectural configuration of Akbar's tomb and alludes to the idea of the mausoleum as a 'mansion of paradise'. The architectural components, however, are more carefully integrated into the overall designs and the details are more exquisitely executed.

Construction on the part of imperial princesses, who may have been inspired by Nur Jahan, increased during this period. For example, Sultan al-Nisa Begum, Jahangir's eldest daughter, constructed a square, domed tomb for herself in 1624–5 (AH 1034) and another for her brother, Khusrau, within a garden now called Khusrau Bagh at Allahabad. These tombs are aligned with that of the mother of Jahangir's first wife, Shahi Begum. Another multi-storey structure similar to Akbar's tomb, it was probably built by Jahangir in the early part of his reign.

Shah Jahan. The greatest builder of the Mughal dynasty, Shah Jahan (*reg* 1628–58) immediately issued orders for numerous architectural projects and maintained an active programme of building throughout his reign. His father's tomb was one of the first projects. Jahangir had died in 1627 en route to Kashmir; his body was taken to Lahore and buried in a garden owned by Nur Jahan on the banks of the Ravi. Contemporary texts suggest that the tomb took ten years to complete, but in contrast to Shah Jahan's other projects, the construction is seldom mentioned. This may be due to the fact that Shah Jahan was estranged from his father during the final years of Jahangir's life. The tomb, standing in the centre of the typical *chār bāgh*, is approached through portals on the north and south. It is a large, square platform (85 m each side) with tall, slender towers at each corner. The red sandstone surface is sumptuously inlaid with marble in the shape of wine vessels, flower vases, chevrons and arabesques. The tomb no longer has an upper storey; however, the cenotaph on top was originally surrounded by carved stone screens. Opinion is divided as to whether the cenotaph was covered with a pavilion, as at Iʿtimad al-Daula's tomb, or simply left open to the air. Nur Jahan, who died in 1645, was buried in a similar but smaller tomb a short distance away. In contrast to these imperial tombs is the more traditional mausoleum at Lahore of Asaf Khan (*d* 1641), the brother of Nur Jahan, and an important noble. The tomb, built on Shah Jahan's command, is an octagonal brick and stone structure with a high bulbous dome. Much of the original tile remains, although the marble facing was removed in the 19th century.

Extensive renovations of the forts at Agra and Lahore occupied Shah Jahan immediately on his accession. The work on the fort at Agra (completed in 1640) consisted of three major courtyards: the Divan-i ʿAm (Hall of Public Audience); an area for private audience and treasures now known as the Machchi Bhavan; and a residential area now called Anguri Bagh. The public audience hall is near the fort's entrance, while the private and residential areas overlook the river, a standard arrangement in Mughal palatial architecture by Shah Jahan's time. The area for public audience consisted of an open court with a pillared hall on one side. The hall (62×21 m) has 27 bays of cusped arches supporting a flat roof. The red sandstone fabric was covered with highly burnished plaster imitating marble. The west wall contains the imperial throne-kiosk. Shah Jahan's private and residential chambers were constructed of white marble, while the residential areas have marble galleries with pillars and brackets profusely inlaid with hardstones. A pavilion overlooking the river was used as a *jharokhā* (Ind.-Pers.: 'display window for the royal person'). It has a rounded roof covered with gilt metal; the gleaming roof may have been intended to underscore the Mughal belief that the emperor was an emanation of divine light. While most of the fort at Agra was completed by 1637, the congregational mosque (now known as the Moti Mosque) was not completed until 1653, several years after the capital had been officially shifted to Delhi. This white marble mosque, divided by twelve-sided piers into three aisles, is related to the earlier Jamiʿ Mosque at AJMER but surpasses it in size. In contrast to earlier buildings, the pure white marble of the Agra mosque bears a minimum of ornamentation, which is characteristic of the increasing austerity of Shah Jahan's later religious architecture.

Shah Jahan's additions to the fort at Lahore are similar to those at Agra. The architect ʿAbd al-Karim Maʿmur Khan completed the complex of buildings known as the King's Tower (Pers. Shāhī Burj) in 1631–2 (AH 1041). Especially notable is the so-called Naulakha Pavilion, built of marble and minutely inlaid with hardstones. The heavy roof, with its prominent down-turned eave, has the profile of an inverted parabola. The shape is derived from vernacular Indian forms in perishable materials and shows the degree to which indigenous elements were integrated into a harmonious unified style. In the far north-west, Shah Jahan constructed or modified other forts in Kabul, Kandahar and Balkh in an effort to gain permanent control over Afghanistan.

Among all of Shah Jahan's projects in northern India, none is so well-known as the Taj Mahal at Agra (*see* AGRA, fig. 1). It was built as a tomb for Shah Jahan's favourite wife, Mumtaz Mahal, who died suddenly in 1631. Begun in 1632, the mausoleum was completed in 1647; it was, however, sufficiently finished in 1643 for the memorial services (Ind.-Pers. *ʿurs*) to be performed there. Two supervisors, ʿAbd al-Karim Maʿmur Khan and Makramat Khan, and the architect Ustad Ahmad Lahauri were in charge of the project; the latter is believed to have played a dominant role. Amanat Khan, who had previously worked on Akbar's tomb, designed the calligraphy and, in all probability, the building's symbolic programme. This shows a preoccupation with the Day of Judgement and a vision of the building as the throne of God (see Begley, 1979). The Taj Mahal is a two-storey octagonal structure with prominent arched portals on each side. The tall bulbous dome is flanked by cupolas. Constructed entirely of white marble, the building is ornamented with the inlay and relief characteristic of the period and placed, like all imperial tombs, on a square platform with minarets at each corner. The tomb is flanked by a domed mosque on the west and an identical building on the east and set directly beside the River Yamuna at the end of an enclosed garden of the *chār bāgh* type (308×554 m). A prominent

100. Private audience hall inside the Lal Qilʿa, Delhi, Shah Jahan period, 1639–48; view from the north

gatehouse marks the main entrance. In general appearance, the building was inspired by Humayun's tomb; as in much of Shah Jahan's architecture, the Taj Mahal is notable as a polished synthesis of elements and concepts introduced by earlier emperors.

Just before the Taj Mahal was complete, Ustad Ahmad Lahauri and another architect, Hamid, were charged by the Emperor with the design of a new capital city in Delhi. This city, named Shahjahanabad, included the fortified palace complex now known as Lal Qil'a (Red Fort). The massive project was executed under the supervision of Ghayrat Khan and later Makramat Khan. The foundations were laid in 1639, and the city was first dedicated in 1648. During construction, Shah Jahan visited the site several times and ordered various changes. The audience hall is similar to that in Agra but contains an elevated marble throne with baluster columns supporting a stone canopy of the inverted parabolic type. Behind this were the administrative and residential chambers which, in standard Mughal fashion, overlooked the river. The inner areas, including the private audience hall (see fig. 100), have flat roofs supported by piers with cusped arches. In the Imtiaz Mahal, in garden style, water channels cut through the north–south axis of the complex fed a lotus-shaped pool in the floor. Persian verses on the walls proclaim the rooms to be a paradise on earth. Outside the palace, Shah Jahan began construction of an enormous congregational mosque in 1650. Completed after six years, the mosque is situated on a high plinth and has a massive gate recalling the Buland Darvaza at Fatehpur Sikri. The marble-trimmed façade of the prayer chamber has a prominent central portal and towering minarets at the corners. Three bulbous domes faced with marble are placed over the prayer chamber. Shahjahanabad was not simply a palace but a complete planned city, with broad avenues, markets, mosques, noble houses, gardens and caravanserais. The city's layout underscored the autocratic nature of Mughal administration and the emperor's role as a father to all his subjects.

No account of Shah Jahan's reign would be complete without some reference to landscape architecture. In 1634 his Shalimar Garden in Kashmir was further enlarged with water channels, new terraces and pavilions in the burnished black stone favoured locally. Though rebuilt and replanted, Shalimar retains the beauty that prompted contemporary French travellers to draw comparisons with Versailles. At Lahore, a hydraulic project by 'Ali Mardan Khan and Mulla 'Ala al-Mulk Tuni permitted the construction of an enormous terraced garden in the city. It was modelled on Shah Jahan's garden in Kashmir and is now also called Shalimar; in Mughal times both were known as the Garden Imparting Joy and Bounty (Pers. Bāgh-i Faiz-Bakhsh va Faraḥ-Bakhsh). The garden at Lahore was completed in 1642 under the supervision of Khalil Allah Khan. The terracing and waterworks are well preserved, but many of the pavilions have been destroyed.

Shah Jahan's enthusiasm for building was shared by his family and court. In Delhi, Agra and Lahore, the élite built caravanserais, gardens, mosques and a variety of other structures at their own expense. For example, Jahan Ara, Shah Jahan's favourite daughter, is credited with the construction of several gardens at Lahore; the tile-covered gate known as Chauburji (1646) in that city is probably a product of her patronage. In 1648 she completed the construction of a new congregational mosque in Agra. Faced with red sandstone and white marble trim, the structure adheres generally in plan and elevation to the earliest Mughal mosques. It is, however, greatly refined in ornamentation and design, and in this respect served as a model for later Mughal mosques. Hakim 'Ilm al-Din, known by his title Wazir Khan, was among the more active patrons at Lahore. He embellished the city with baths, markets, caravanserais, palaces and a congregational mosque, known commonly as the mosque of Wazir Khan (1634–5). A more elaborate variation of the Shahi Begum Mosque, it is one of the finest tile-faced structures in the region. Outside the main cities, nobles built a variety of structures. For example, the calligrapher Amanat Khan

101. Badshahi Mosque, Lahore, Pakistan, Aurangzeb period, 1673–4; east front

built a caravanserai on the main route from Lahore to Delhi; it is richly decorated with the master's own calligraphy. In Kashmir, Dara Shikoh, Shah Jahan's favourite son, constructed a school known as Pari Mahal for his religious teacher. Jahan Ara constructed a small cloistered mosque for another religious teacher at Srinagar. Known as the mosque of Mulla Shah Badkhshani, it is located at the foot of the hill called Hari Parbat.

Aurangzeb and the later Mughals. The status of the imperial cities of northern India declined during the reign of Aurangzeb (*reg* 1658–1707), for the Emperor spent much of his time warring in the Deccan in the south. Aurangzeb's reign was also marked by growing conservatism; he abolished many palace rituals and focused on orthodox Islam. His greatest project was the Badshahi Mosque in Lahore (see fig. 101), built in 1673–4 under the supervision of his foster brother, Fidai Khan Koka. This high structure, built adjacent to Lahore Fort, was based on Shah Jahan's congregational mosque in Delhi. Made of red sandstone and decorated with marble, plaster and fresco, the mosque is notable for the use of cusped arches and an array of floral patterns, elements probably derived from palace architecture and ornament.

After the death of Aurangzeb, the authority of the Mughals began to decline, and semi-independent states emerged under powerful nobles. The increased power of the Marathas, Sikhs and British also contributed to the decline of the Mughal dominion. Many of these new powers fostered the arts; their architecture was influenced to varying degrees by Mughal precedent (*see* §(ii)(a) below). In Delhi, the capital of the late Mughals, several monuments in the old tradition were erected. For example, the Qudsiya Bagh Mosque (mid-18th century) displays the ornate surfaces favoured in the imperial mosques of Aurangzeb's time. The tomb of Safdar Jang (1753), modelled on Humayun's tomb, represents a valiant effort to revive early Mughal architecture. However, the decorative flatness of surface and the verticality of the bulbous pointed dome are characteristic of 18th-century style.

UNPUBLISHED SOURCES

London, BL, Orient. & India Office Lib., Pers. MS. 1330 [Muhammad Baqir Najm-i Sani: *Kulliyāt*]

BIBLIOGRAPHY

EARLY SOURCES

Zayn Khan: *Ṭabaqāt-i Bāburī* [Chronicle of Babur] (*c.* 1528–9); Eng. trans. by S. H. Askari (Delhi, 1982)
Zahir al-Din Muhammad Babur: *Bāburnāma* (*c.* 1530); Eng. trans. and ed. A. S. Beveridge, 2 vols (London, 1922/*R* New Delhi, 1970)
Ghiyath al-Din Muhammad Khwand Amir: *Qānūn-i Humāyūnī* [Traditions of Humayun] (*c.* 1533–4); Eng. trans. B. Prasad, ed. M. H. Hosain, 2 vols (Calcutta, 1940)
Baha al-Din Hasan Nithari Bukhari: *Muzakkir-i Aḥbāb* [Remembrance of friends] (*c.* 1566); ed. S. M. Fazlullah (New Delhi, 1969)
ʿAbbas Khan Sarwani: *Tārīkh-i Sher Shāhī* [History of Sher Shah] (*c.* 1579); Eng. trans. and ed. S. M. Imam al-Din (Dacca, 1964)
Muhammad ʿArif Qandahari: *Tārīkh-i Akbarī* [History of Akbar] (*c.* 1580–84]; ed. Muʿin al-Din Nadwi, Azhar ʿAli Dihlavi and Imtiyaz ʿAli ʿArsi (Rampur, 1962) [also known as *Tārīkh-i Qandaharī*]
Gulbadan Begum: *Humāyūnnāma* (*c.* 1587); Eng. trans. by A. S. Beveridge (London, 1902)
Jauhar Aftabchi: *Tezkereh al-Vāqiʿāt* (*c.* 1587); Eng. trans. by C. Stewart as *Tezkereh al-Vakiāt or Private Memoirs of the Moghal Emperor Humayun* (London, 1832/*R* New Delhi, 1970)
Bayazid Biyat: *Tārīkh-i Humāyūn va Akbar* [History of Humayun and Akbar] (*c.* 1591–2); ed. M. Hidayat Hosein (Calcutta, 1941)
Nizam al-Din Ahmad Haravi: *Ṭabaqāt-i Akbarī* [Chronicle of Akbar] (1593); Eng. trans. by B. De, 3 vols (Calcutta, 1911–39)
ʿAbd al-Qadir Badaʿuni: *Muntakhab al-Tawārīkh* [Selections from history] (*c.* 1596); Eng. trans. in 3 vols: vol. i by G. S. A. Ranking; vol. ii by W. H. Lowe; vol. iii by W. Haig (Calcutta, 1884–1925/*R* Patna, 1973)
Abu'l-Fazl: *Āyīn-i Akbarī* [Annals of Akbar] (*c.* 1596–1602); Eng. trans. in 3 vols: i, trans. H. Blochmann, ed. S. L. Gloomer ([Calcutta], 1871/*R* Delhi, 1965); ii and iii, trans. H. S. Jarrett, ed. J. Sarkar (Calcutta, 1948–9/*R* New Delhi, 1972–3)
——: *Akbarnāma* (*c.* 1596–1602); Eng. trans. H. Beveridge, 3 vols (Calcutta, 1907–39/*R* New Delhi, 1972–3)
ʿAbd Allah: *Tārīkh-i Dāʾūdī* [History of Daud] (1605–27); excerpts in H. M. Elliot and J. Dowson, eds: *The History of India as Told by its Own Historians* (London, 1867–77/*R* New York, 1966), iv, pp. 434–513
Muhammad Abu al-Qasim Firishta: *Gulshan-i Ibrāhīmī* [Rose garden of Ibrahim], also known as *Tārīkh-i Firishta* [History of Firishta] (1607); Eng. trans. by J. Briggs as *History of the Rise of Mahomedan Power in India, till the Year 1612* (London, 1909)
Nur al-Din Muhammad Jahangir: *Tūzuk-i Jahāngīrī* [Memoirs of Jahangir] (*c.* 1624); Eng. trans. by A. Rogers, ed. H. Beveridge (London, 1909–14/*R* Delhi, 1968)
ʿAbd al-Hamid Lahauri: *Pādshāhnāma* [Emperor's book] (*c.* 1636–58); ed. 2 vols (Calcutta, 1865–8)
François Bernier: *Travels in the Mogul Empire,* AD *1656–1668*; Eng. trans. by I. Brock, annotated A. Constable, ed. V. A. Smith (Oxford, 1916)
Muhammad Salih Kanbu: *ʿAmal-i Ṣāliḥ* [Work of Salih] (1659–60); ed. 3 vols (Calcutta, 1912/*R* Lahore, 1967)
Muhammad Khafi Khan: *Muntakhab al-Lubāb* [Untarnished selections] (*c.* 1731); Eng. trans. by S. M. Haq as *History of ʿAlamgir* (Karachi, 1975)
Shah Navaz Khan and ʿAbd al-Hayy: *Maʾāthir al-umarā* [Biographies of the nobility] (*c.* 1741–7); ed. Molvi Abdur Rahim and M. A. Ali, 3 vols (Calcutta, 1887–96), Eng. trans. by H. Beveridge and B. Prashad (Calcutta, 1911–53)
Kacchāwan ri Vanśāvalī [Lineage of the Kachchhawas] (*c.* 1834), ed. S. S. Ratnawat (Jaipur, 1981)

GENERAL

Sayyid Ahmad Khan: *Āsār al-Ṣanādīd* [Great heritage] (Delhi, 1847/*R* 1975); Eng. trans. by R. Nath as *Monuments of Delhi: A Historical Study* (New Delhi, 1979)
A. Fuhrer: *The Monumental Antiquities and Inscriptions in the North-Western Provinces and Oudh* (1881/*R* Varanasi, 1969)
S. M. Latif: *Lahore: Its History, Architectural Remains and Antiquities* (Lahore, 1892)
O. von Reuther: *Indische Paläste und Wohnhäuser* (Berlin, 1925)
P. Brown: *Indian Architecture, Islamic Period* (?Bombay, [1942], rev. Bombay, 1956) [rev. edn with additional photographs]
G. M. D. Sufi: *Kashīr*, 2 vols (?1948/*R* New Delhi, 1974)
M. A. Husain: *A Record of All the Quranic and Non-Historical Epigraphs on the Protected Monuments in Delhi Province* (Calcutta, 1963)
J. Hoag: *Islamic Architecture* (New York, 1977)
S. Blake: 'The Patrimonial-Bureaucratic Empire of the Mughals', *J. Asian Stud.*, xxix (1979), pp. 77–94
E. B. Moynihan: *Paradise as a Garden in Persia and Mughal India* (London, 1980)
W. E. Begley: 'Four Mughal Caravanserais Built During the Reigns of Jahangir and Shah Jahan', *Muqarnas*, i (1983), pp. 167–79
E. Koch: *Mughal Architecture: An Outline of its History and Development, 1526–1858* (Munich, 1991)
C. B. Asher: *The Architecture of Mughal India* (Cambridge, 1992)

BABUR, HUMAYUN AND SUR PERIODS

G. Yazdani: 'Narnaul and its Buildings', *J. Asiat. Soc. Bengal*, iii/8 (1907), pp. 581–6, 639–44
K. Qanungo: *Sher Shah and his Times* (Bombay, 1965)
M. A. Husain: 'Inscriptions of Emperor Babur', *Epig. Ind.: Arab. & Pers. Suppl.* (1965), pp. 49–66
C. B. Asher: 'The Qalʿ-i Kuhna Mosque: A Visual Symbol of Royal Aspirations', *Chhavi-2: Rai Krishnadasa Felicitation Volume*, ed. A. Krishna (Varanasi, 1981), pp. 212–17
G. Lowry: *The Tomb of Nasir-ud-Din Muhammad Humayun* (diss., Cambridge, MA, Harvard U., 1981)
C. B. Asher: *The Patronage of Sher Shah Sur: A Study of Form and Meaning in 16th-century Indo-Islamic Architecture* (diss., Minneapolis, U. MN, 1984)
——: 'The Tomb of Ibrahim Sur: Epigraphs and Implications', *Indian Epigraphy: Its Bearing on the History of Art*, ed. F. M. Asher and G. S. Gai (New Delhi, 1985), pp. 275–81

——: 'Legacy and Legitimacy: Sher Shah's Patronage of Imperial Mausolea', *Sharī'at and Ambiguity in Southern Asian Islam*, ed. K. P. Ewing (Berkeley, 1988), pp. 79–97

AKBAR PERIOD

F. Growse: *Mathura: A District Memoir* ([Allahabad], 3/1883)
E. W. Smith: *The Moghul Architecture of Fathpur-Sikri*, 4 pts (Allahabad, 1894–8)
——: *Akbar's Tomb, Sikandarah* (Allahabad, 1909)
S. A. A. Rizvi and J. Flynn: *Fatḥpūr Sīkrī* (Bombay, 1975)
M. Brand and G. Lowry, eds.: *Fatehpur Sikri: A Sourcebook* (Cambridge, MA, 1985)
C. B. Asher: 'Mughal Sub-imperial Patronage: The Architecture of Rāja Mān Singh', *The Powers of Art: Patronage in Indian Culture*, ed. B. S. Miller (New Delhi, 1992), pp. 183–201

JAHANGIR PERIOD

J. Vogel: *Tile Mosaics of the Lahore Fort* (Calcutta, 1920)
S. M. Abdullah: 'Hiran Munara of Shekhupura', *Professor Muhammad Shafi Presentation Volume* (Lahore, 1955), pp. 181–99
Z. A. Desai: 'Inscriptions from the Khusrau Bagh, Allahabad', *Epig. Ind.: Arab. Pers. Suppl.* (1961), pp. 64–8

SHAH JAHAN PERIOD AND LATER

J. P. Thompson: 'The Tomb of the Emperor Jahangir', *J. Punjab Hist. Soc.*, i (1911), pp. 12–30
J. D. Hoag: 'The Tomb of Ulugh Beg and Abdu Razzaq at Ghazni: A Model for the Taj Mahal', *J. Soc. Archit. Historians*, xxvii/4 (1968), pp. 234–48
M. A. Chaghtai: *The Badshahi Masjid* (Lahore, 1972)
——: *The Wazir Khan Mosque* (Lahore, 1975)
W. E. Begley: 'Amanat Khan and the Calligraphy on the Taj Mahal', *Kst Orients*, xii (1978–9), pp. 5–60
——: 'The Myth of the Taj Mahal and a New Theory of its Symbolic Meaning', *A. Bull.*, lvi/1 (1979), pp. 7–37
——: 'The Symbolic Role of Calligraphy on Three Imperial Mosques of Shah Jahan', *Kaladarsana*, ed. J. Williams (New Delhi, 1981), pp. 7–18
E. Koch: 'The Baluster Column: A European Motif in Mughal Architecture and its Meaning', *J. Warb. & Court. Inst.*, xlv (1982), pp. 251–62
——: 'The Lost Colonnade of Shah Jahan's Bath in the Red Fort of Agra', *Burl. Mag.*, cxxiv/951 (1982), pp. 331–9
——: *Shah Jahan and Orpheus* (Graz, 1988)
W. Begley and Z. A. Desai: *Taj Mahal: The Illuminated Tomb* (Cambridge and Seattle, 1989)

(b) Eastern provinces. Eastern India was an important part of the Mughal empire but did not come completely under imperial rule until the late 16th century. Before that date Bihar was a stronghold of nobles of Afghan descent who were loyal to their own kin rather than to any central authority. Outstanding among these was Farid Khan Sur (later Sher Shah), who eventually drove Humayun from India. During the Sur interregnum (1540–55) major monuments were built in Bihar, particularly at Sasaram, the estate (Pers. *jagir*) of Sher Shah and his father Hasan Sur. Such examples of Sur architecture provide key monuments for subsequent Mughal building.

16th century. At Sasaram, Sher Shah began the construction of two monumental tombs *c.* 1538. The larger, his own mausoleum, was set in the middle of an artificial lake (for illustration *see* SASARAM). The building is a three-tiered structure with an octagonal plan and large, low dome. The corners carry *chatrīs* (small domed pavilions). The tomb is based on those built under the LODI dynasty but has an additional storey and more numerous *chatrīs*. Its great scale (diam. 41.5 m) made it in its time the largest tomb in India. Another important feature is the tomb's square platform, an element that was subsequently adopted by the Mughals in all their imperial tombs. The second mausoleum was for his father. Similar to Sher Shah's tomb, it draws on a type that was reserved for royalty in the early 16th century and was apparently meant to elevate Hasan Sur and publicly enhance Sher Shah's ancestry.

Around 1536 Sher Shah captured the fort at Rohtas, south of Sasaram, from a Hindu raja and further fortified it. Dating the various parts of the much renovated fortifications is difficult; there are no inscriptions on any of its walls. The massive structure, measuring approximately 1×1.5 km, has 68 bastions and walls 9 m thick. Some of the 12 monumental entrances are preserved; they have a central archway in an arched recess with oriel windows on each side. This arrangement was of long-standing popularity in India and often featured in later Mughal gates. On the hilltop inside the fort, Haybat Khan, Sher Shah's highest-ranking noble, built a congregational mosque (1543–4). A single-aisled building with three bays, it is the first example in eastern India of the type of small mosque that became popular during Mughal times. Little else inside the fort can be dated to the 16th century or earlier. A multi-bayed mosque of the Sur period at Phulwari Sharif (Patna District), dated 1549–50 (AH 956), is a trabeated structure that conforms to an older regional style. However, some features are consistent with what were to become common characteristics of Mughal architecture: the building material includes red sandstone from Sikri, near Agra, and carved motifs are similar to those that formed a pan-Indian Mughal decorative style.

In the early Akbar period, JAUNPUR was the most important eastern city in the Mughal empire. Khan-i Khanan Muhammad Mu'in Khan, who served as the governor of Jaunpur from 1564 to 1575, constructed a palace within the pre-Mughal fortifications, but only the bathhouse (*ḥammām*) remains. A bridge (1564–7) across the River Gumti was also built under Mu'in Khan; it consists of massive pylons supporting pointed arches, and the top is lined with vaulted pavilions that still provide shade for passing travellers. Mu'in Khan encouraged the building of mosques, some of which are still standing. Although Jaunpur was the governor's residence, the key fortress on the eastern frontier was Chunar. In 1561 Akbar gained control of the fort, and in 1573 fortified gates overlooking the River Ganga were added by Muhammad Sharif Khan. Many of the fort's interior archways and buildings, intricately carved in the early Mughal style, date to this time.

The earliest Mughal building in Rohtas Fort, a mosque constructed by Habash Khan in 1578–9 (AH 986), is similar to the Sur mosque at the same site. A building style more related to that of the imperial court was introduced by Raja Man Singh of Amer, Akbar's leading general, who made Rohtas his official seat while serving as governor of Bihar from 1588 to 1594 and retained Rohtas until 1608. During this 20-year period Man Singh built an enormous palace complex (see fig. 102), generally modelled on the imperial palace at Fatehpur Sikri. He also constructed temples and a number of fortified gates within the fort. A few buildings were provided elsewhere in Bihar by Mughal administrators. For example, Makhsus Khan (brother of an early governor) constructed gardens, wells and a congregational mosque, dated 1587–8 (AH 995), at Hajipur (Vaishali District). Although rebuilt, the original curved

102. Palace of Raja Man Singh, Rohtas, 1596; view from the west

cornice of the entrance gate and façade indicate a continuation of earlier regional traditions. However, the single-aisled, three-bayed plan recalls the congregational mosque at Rohtas and is typical of provincial Mughal mosques.

Further east in Bengal, a number of buildings were erected by rebel nobles prior to the consolidation of Mughal authority. For example, Murad Khan, son of the Jauhar ʿAli Khan Qaqshal, built a single-aisled mosque at Sherpur (Bogra District) in 1582. As in the Hajipur mosque, the curved cornice shows a debt to older regional forms, but the plan reveals an awareness of contemporary practice, the most obvious parallel being the mosques at Rohtas. Appointed governor of Bengal in 1594, Raja Man Singh built a new capital at Rajmahal, then known as Akbarnagar. Among his constructions were a palace, small temple, bridge and large congregational mosque (77×65 m including courtyard). The mosque is ruined, but 19th-century drawings show that it was similar to the imperial congregational mosque at Fatehpur Sikri.

17th century and early 18th. During the reigns of Jahangir and Shah Jahan, the architecture of the imperial centres continued to influence that of eastern India, and the east in its turn contributed to the mature Mughal style. During Jahangir's reign, two fine edifices were constructed at Chunar. One is a multi-chambered portal leading to the shrine of the saint Shah Qasim Sulayman Qadri. Constructed of stone, it is exquisitely carved with floral arabesques and geometric patterns. The style of the ornament and architectural brackets suggests a date early in Jahangir's reign, soon after the saint's death. The second important monument is the tomb of Iftikhar Khan, built in 1616–17 (AH 1022), set within a walled garden laid out on the *chār bāgh* pattern. Square in plan, with the central chamber surrounded by an open verandah, Iftikhar Khan's tomb is similar to the tomb of Muhammad Ghaus at GWALIOR and seems to have served as a model for subsequent tombs in Bihar. The tomb of Shah Daulat (*d* 1608) at Maner, considered to be the finest Mughal edifice in eastern India, is, in fact, a refined version of Iftikhar Khan's tomb. Placed beside a large tank, Shah Daulat's tomb is set on a plinth adjacent to a single-aisled mosque. An elaborate multi-chambered portal marks the entrance. It was built by Ibrahim Khan Kakar, known by the title Dilavar Khan, who was a follower of Shah Daulat and undertook the revitalization of Maner between 1605 and 1608. Maner was the birthplace of Sharaf al-Din Maneri, one of India's noted mystics. Dilavar Khan's constructions include a mosque added to the shrine containing the remains of the saint's father.

In the first half of the 17th century, PATNA was the leading city of Bihar, and the main avenue, paralleling the River Ganga, was lined with mosques, many of them constructed during the reign of Shah Jahan. Complementing these are two structures constructed by Sayf Khan: a religious school and an *ʿīdgāh* (assembly place for prayer on ʿId and other religious occasions; *see* MUSALLA). A further noteworthy building is the Patthar ki Mosque (Urdu: Stone Mosque), dated 1626. The west façade is carved with thin-necked flasks reminiscent of those on the tomb of Iʿtimad al-Daula in Agra (*see* AGRA, §I) and the Khusrau Bagh tombs in ALLAHABAD.

Elsewhere in Bihar, mosques, mansions and entire townships were constructed during the reigns of Jahangir and Shah Jahan. For example, at Khurramabad (Rohtas District) a fort, bridge, caravanserai, baths and a congregational mosque were all built between 1612 and 1618. Bihar Sharif (Nalanda District) drew special attention as the burial place of Sharaf al-Din Maneri. In 1608–9 (AH 1017) a single-aisled, three-domed mosque was built by Shaykh Farid Bukhari, a noted patron throughout the Mughal empire (*see also* §(c) below). Although similar to mosques elsewhere, the polygonal minarets attached to the corners are characteristic of eastern India. Between 1638 and 1646 Habib Khan Sur erected a mosque (similar to that of Farid Bukhari), a tank and an *ʿīdgāh*, all in close proximity to the saint's grave. The largest mosque of the period was built at Kharagpur (Munger District) in 1656–7 (AH 1067) by Indian princes who converted to Islam. It is based on the mosques at Bihar Sharif.

In Bengal, rebels and pirates were a constant threat during the time of Jahangir. Around DHAKA, which was then the capital, small riverine forts were constructed to fend off attacks. In 1624, Shah Jahan himself rebelled against Jahangir, establishing an independent court in Bengal and Bihar. While much of his time was spent in camp, he ordered the construction of a small stone fort at Garhi, now known as Teliagarhi (Santal Parganas District). After Shah Jahan became emperor, he appointed his son Shah Shujaʿ to govern Bengal. During Shah Shujaʿ's long tenure (1639–59) the capital was shifted back to Rajmahal, but building continued in Dhaka. A large caravanserai known as Bara Katra was built in 1644, and a single-aisled, three-domed mosque within the Lalbagh Fort was erected in 1649–50 (AH 1059). The inscription mentioning the mosque indicates that it pre-dates the fort. Rajmahal also flourished under Shah Shujaʿ. Numerous mosques, all probably dating to this time, line the main road to the palace. The so-called Sangi Dalan, the only surviving portion of the royal residence from the time of Shah Shujaʿ, is a rectangular structure with a pronounced down-turned cornice. It is reminiscent of Shah Jahan's balcony for public viewing (Ind.-Pers. *jharokhā*) at Agra Fort (*see* §(a) above). The down-turned outline of the roof that was a common feature of palace architecture during the reign of Shah Jahan seems to have originated in the vernacular architecture of Bengal. At GAUR, the pre-Mughal capital of the independent sultans of Bengal, Shah Shujaʿ constructed a large arched gate before the famous shrine of Qadam Rasul. He also built a tomb for Shah Niʿmat Allah (probably his spiritual adviser), which was based on Iʿtimad al-Daula's tomb at Agra.

Under Aurangzeb, eastern India continued to participate in the mainstream of Mughal architecture, and initially there was little evidence of resurgent regionalism or colonialism. Thus Da'ud Khan Qurayshi, governor of Bihar from 1659–64, founded a caravanserai of the established type at Daudnagar (Aurangabad District). The tomb of Da'ud Khan's nephew, Shamsher Khan, is located a short distance away at Shamshernagar. Probably constructed before 1712, it adheres to the precedent set by Iftikhar Khan's tomb at Chunar. In conformity with 18th-century taste, however, the dome is considerably attenuated.

Patna expanded eastward with the addition of the new section called ʿAzimabad during the governorship of Prince ʿAzim al-Shan (*reg* 1704–12). Two notable monuments within this area are the mosque of Mir Ashraf (a wealthy resident), dated 1773–4 (AH 1187), and the tomb of Nawab Munir al-Daula, dated 1759–60 (AH 1124). The mosque exhibits the elegant decorated surface that characterized imperial architecture in the 18th century. The tomb consists of an open-air cenotaph surrounded by a carved screen and is an elegant example of a grave type that became increasingly popular in the late Mughal period.

In Dhaka, Lalbagh Fort, constructed largely in the late 17th century, probably as a walled garden rather than a fort, contains an audience hall similar to the Sangi Dalan in Rajmahal. The tomb of Bibi Pari, also in the fort, is based on that of Niʿmat Allah at Gaur. The presence of a tomb in a palatial setting marks a departure from established Mughal practice. Many mosques were built in Dhaka as Mughal power declined in the late 17th century and the early 18th. The façades of these buildings are articulated with slender columns and numerous small niches; the interiors of the mosques often have cusped arches. A notable example is the mosque of Haji Khwaja Shahbaz, dated 1679–80 (AH 1089). In the following decades, the architectural treatment drew more on vernacular forms and began to resemble the late Mughal style as it developed throughout India. The curved cornice and down-turned eave, employed earlier in the palaces of Shah Jahan, became a widely used motif. Cusped arches, once restricted to palaces, appear in many different buildings. These trends are seen in the tomb complex of Khwaja Anwar-i Shahid in Burdwan, the last major monumental tomb in Bengal, probably dating to the early 18th century.

In 1703 Murshid Quli Khan, the Mughal governor, moved the capital of Bengal to Murshidabad. By 1717 he had established himself as an independent ruler, but like the nawabs of Avadh he remained ostensibly loyal to the Mughal court. Under the nawabs of Murshidabad, the Mughal legacy in eastern India was carried forward until it merged with the eclectic styles of colonial times (*see* §(ii)(e) below).

For 17th-century Indo-Islamic architecture in the east, *see also* §6(ii)(d) above.

BIBLIOGRAPHY

F. Buchanan-Hamilton: *The History, Antiquities, Topography and Statistics of Eastern India; Comprising the Districts of Behar, Shahabad, Bhagalpoor, Goruckpoor, Dinajepoor, Purianlya, Ronggopoor, and Assam*, 3 vols, ed. M. Martin (London, 1838)
W. Ghose: *Rohtasgarh* (Cuttack, 1908)
S. Z. Ahmad: 'Daud Khan Quraishi, Governor of Bihar and Founder of Daudnagar', *J. Bihar & Orissa Res. Soc.*, iv (1918), pp. 281–97
M. A. A. Khan: *Memoirs of Gaur and Pandua*, ed. H. E. Stapleton (Calcutta, 1931)
M. H. Quraishi: *List of Ancient Monuments Protected under Act VII of 1904 in the Province of Bihar and Orissa* (Calcutta, 1931)
P. Brown: *Indian Architecture, Islamic Period* (?Bombay, [1942], rev. Bombay, 1956) [rev. edn with additional photographs]
A. H. Dani: *Muslim Architecture in Bengal* (Dhaka, 1961)
D. R. Patil: *The Antiquarian Remains of Bihar* (Patna, 1963)
K. Qanungo: *Sher Shah and his Times* (Bombay, 1965)
Z. A. Desai: 'Indo-Islamic Architecture of Bihar', *Islam. Cult.*, xlvi (1972), pp. 17–38
Ahmad Qeyamuddin: *Corpus of Arabic and Persian Inscriptions of Bihar* (Patna, 1973)
C. B. Asher: 'The Mausoleum of Sher Shah Suri', *Artibus Asiae*, xxxix (1977), pp. 273–98
G. Michell, ed.: *Brick Temples of Bengal from the Archives of David McCutchion* (Princeton, 1983)
——: *The Islamic Heritage of Bengal* (Paris, 1984)
C. B. Asher: 'Legacy and Legitimacy: Sher Shah's Patronage of Imperial Mausolea', *Sharīʿat and Ambiguity in Southern Asian Islam*, ed. K. P. Ewing (Berkeley, 1988), pp. 79–97
——: 'Islamic Architecture', *Eastern Indian Art: A Microfiche Archive*, ed. C. B. Asher (Leiden, 1991)
——: 'Mughal Sub-imperial Patronage: The Architecture of Rāja Mān Singh', *The Powers of Art: Patronage in Indian Culture*, ed. B. S. Miller (New Delhi, 1992), pp. 183-201

(c) Western provinces. There are few early Mughal buildings in Sind, Gujarat and Rajasthan, as neither Babur, Humayun nor the Sur dynasty exercised consistent authority over western India. Instead, most early 16th-century building in the area exhibits a continuation of local

regional developments. For example, the Chowk ki Mosque at Nagaur, dated 1553 (AH 960) in the reign of Islam Sur, is a simple trabeated structure with ogee-arched mihrabs that recalls the region's pre-Mughal buildings. During Akbar's reign western India was gradually incorporated into the Mughal empire, but most surviving Mughal buildings are in eastern Rajasthan. The lack of such architecture in the rest of the western region can be explained largely by the hostility of the Raja of Mewar and by Akbar's inability to conquer Gujarat until 1591.

16th century. Architectural activity in the early years of Akbar's rule focused on AJMER and the shrine (Pers. *dargāh*) of Shaykh Mu'in al-Din Chishti. Akbar undertook annual pilgrimages to the shrine from 1569 to 1579. The mosque in the shrine's precinct is not inscribed, but it is known as the Akbari Mosque and is probably a product of the Emperor's patronage. In early Mughal fashion, the building has double-aisled side wings and a high central portal. The serpentine brackets at the entrance and the mosaic stone inlay on the high portal of the prayer-hall are closely related to the congregational mosque and other buildings at Fatehpur Sikri. Following Akbar's example, nobles also made donations to the shrine. For example, Khwaja Hasan rebuilt the dome over Mu'in al-Din's grave in 1579. On the nearby fortified hill known as Taragarh, the shrine of Sayyid Husayn Khing Sawar (a 13th-century saint) was refurbished, and Isma'il Quli Khan, a Mughal noble, added an enormous red sandstone gate in 1570–71 (AH 976). The fort of Ajmer was enlarged by Akbar beginning in 1570. Within three years, the palatial buildings, gardens and fortifications were completed. Portions of the royal residence survive, notably a palace in the centre of a large (71×55 m) courtyard (see fig. 103) entered through an arched gate. The palace is a trabeated structure; its ground-floor is divided into nine bays. Some of the city-gates of this period, brick-built and faced with tile, are also preserved.

Centres of building outside Ajmer include Nagaur, where the local landholder Husayn Quli Khan constructed a congregational mosque in 1564–5 (AH 972). It has three bays and one aisle, the central bay surmounted by a dome. The plan and deeply recessed mihrab show familiarity with architectural practice in Delhi and Agra, but the eastern façade of the mosque and its towering minarets draw on earlier traditions in the region. The most obvious precedent is the 15th-century Shamsi Mosque at Nagaur.

By 1570, the major Rajput princes (with the exception of Mewar) had acknowledged Mughal authority and in return were given important positions in the Mughal military service. The architectural patronage of Raja Man Singh, who came from Amer in Rajasthan and became the highest ranking noble outside the royal family, was widespread (*see* §§(a) and (b) above). Projects in his ancestral domain included his palace at Amer, which seems, in its original state, to have been similar to the one he built at Rohtas. Also much like Rohtas is his palace at Rajgarh, about 50 km from Jaipur, dated 1612. Man Singh constructed the Jagat Shiromani temple at Amer to commemorate the death of his son in 1599.

Early 17th century. In 1613 Jahangir began a campaign against Rana Amar Singh of Mewar and consequently

103. Building in Akbar's palace complex, Ajmer, begun 1570; west façade

resided in Ajmer for three years. His donations to the shrine of Mu'in al-Din Chishti included a gold lattice railing to the saint's tomb. Donations were also made to the tomb of Sayyid Husayn Khing Sawar on Taragarh Hill. Jahangir was fond of Ajmer and built marble palaces (no longer extant) on Ana Sagar Lake. The Emperor's favourite spot was a picturesque valley to the west of Taragarh Hill. There, in 1615, he built the palace known as the Fountain of Light (Chesma-i Nur). It consists of several pillared pavilions and a vaulted one overlooking a waterfall. In the same year Jahangir constructed a palace at Pushkar, about 15 km from Ajmer. The building, originally three pillared chambers on a raised platform, was set beside a lake and used as a hunting-lodge. According to the inscription, it was erected to commemorate victory over the Rana of Mewar.

Jahangir built nothing in AHMADABAD, as he disliked the city. The future Shah Jahan, however, built the mansion known as Shah-i Bagh there during his tenure as governor of Gujarat from 1609 to 1623. The palace, with its interior arched and vaulted chambers, adheres to patterns established in imperial architecture, not to any regional Gujarati developments. Shaykh Farid Bukhari (*see also* §(b) above) served as governor of Gujarat from 1606 to 1609, during which time he added a new quarter to Ahmadabad. As well as administrative buildings, he constructed a tomb for the religious teacher Wajih al-Din, which is based on the nearby shrine at SARKHEJ.

In January 1628, shortly before his coronation, Shah Jahan paid homage to the shrine of Mu'in al-Din Chishti at Ajmer and vowed to build a mosque in thanksgiving for his victory over the Rana of Mewar in 1615. The building was completed, as the inscription indicates, in 1637. Aligned with the saint's tomb, the double-aisled mosque was constructed solely of white marble. It is a key monument for the early history of mosque architecture in Shah Jahan's reign and served as a model for the congregational mosque in the Agra Fort (now the Moti Mosque) built in 1653. Shah Jahan's daughter, Jahan Ara, is said to have built some of the white marble pavilions in the shrine, and other members of the nobility constructed tombs and mosques in the immediate vicinity. Elsewhere at Ajmer, Shah Jahan built open marble pavilions, a private audience hall and a ceremonial viewing balcony on the banks of the Ana Sagar Lake.

Outside Ajmer, architecture in the western provinces often exhibited regional characteristics rather than the pan-Indian Mughal style. For example, an *ʿīdgāh* dated 1656–7 (AH 1066) in Merta (Nagaur District) has prominent corner *chatrīs* recalling the large pavilions set up by Hindus to commemorate the dead. At Narnaul, the façade of the mansion of Rai Mukhund Das appears to draw on the nearby tomb of Ibrahim Sur (1542); the interior of the mansion, however, conforms to other dwellings of the Shah Jahan period. At Amer, the monuments built by Mirza Raja Jai Singh (grandson of the famous Man Singh), who acquired the family seat in 1623, show a lively adaptation of the Mughal style to Rajput needs. The important monuments built during this time include the Shila Mata Temple, the quadrangle containing the Jai Mahal (probably the prince's quarters and audience hall) and the Ganesha Pol (a vaulted gatehouse). Lighter in appearance than its Mughal counterparts, the Ganesha Pol is noted for its fine screens and delicately painted floral decoration (*see also* §(ii)(b) below).

Fine buildings from the Shah Jahan period are also found in Gujarat and Sind. In 1637–8 (AH 1047) at Ahmadabad, Aʿzam Khan (who had been appointed governor in 1635) constructed a large (64×73 m) rectangular caravanserai, which is entered through a multi-storey gateway modelled on contemporary structures in Agra. In THATTHA, the Mughal capital of Sind, Shah Jahan ordered the construction of a congregational mosque (1644–7). The structure bears little resemblance to imperial mosques: it is magnificently faced with tiles and has four large arched portals, similar to those of mosques of Iran. The Mughal-period tombs of Sind, for example the mausoleum of Mirza ʿIsa Khan (*c*. 1640), exhibit a blend of Iranian, Mughal and indigenous styles. The long-standing contacts between Sind and Iran account for this eclectic idiom.

Late 17th century and 18th. During later Mughal rule, architectural activity continued in western India but seldom under imperial auspices. In Ajmer, the white marble tombs of ʿAbd Allah Khan and his wife, dated 1702–3 (AH 1114), maintain the Shah Jahan-period tradition of restrained refinement. The congregational mosque at Merta (1665) is a local interpretation of contemporary imperial buildings. Constructed of red sandstone, it has towering minarets on the corners and is entered through cusped arches. The prayer-hall is five bays wide and three aisles deep; the bulbous central dome is faced with bands of red and white stone.

In those areas ruled by Rajput princes, the Mughal style was assimilated into the local traditions of architecture. This process, begun in the reign of Akbar, continued apace in the 18th century as the authority of the Mughals declined (*see* §(ii)(b) below).

BIBLIOGRAPHY

J. Tod: *Annals and Antiquities of Rajasthan*, 2 vols (1829–32/*R* New Delhi, 1971)
J. Burgess: *The Muhammadan Architecture of Ahmadabad*, 2 vols (Bombay, 1900–05)
G. Yazdani: 'Narnaul and its Buildings', *J. Asiat. Soc. Bengal*, iii (1907), pp. 581–6, 639–44
S. B. Sarda: *Ajmer: Historical and Descriptive* (Ajmer, 1911)
O. von Reuther: *Indische Paläste und Wohnhäuser* (Berlin, 1925)
S. A. I. Tirmizi: *Ajmer through Inscriptions, 1582–1852* (New Delhi, 1968)
Z. A. Desai: *Published Muslim Inscriptions of Rajasthan* (Jaipur, 1971)
E. Koch: *Mughal Architecture: An Outline of its History and Development, 1526–1858* (Munich, 1991)

(d) Central and southern provinces. The southern frontier of the Mughal empire varied considerably in the 16th century. During the time of Babur, Mughal authority reached to the Malwa region, but the most important southern city was Gwalior. Akbar carried Mughal arms across the Narmada River and had incorporated Ahmadnagar into his territory by 1600. The geographical horizon of Mughal architecture in central and south India thus widened significantly during his reign. During Jahangir's reign, campaigns in the Deccan were waged continuously, but territorial expansion was seldom achieved.

16th century. Babur's superintendent of GWALIOR, Rahim Dad, constructed a garden on the *chār bāgh* plan within the fort at the Emperor's behest, but its remains have not been traced. In 1528 Rahim Dad added an arched portal to the Assi Khambha, a pre-Mughal-period building serving as a madrasa (Pers.: Islamic school). The style of the portal is heavily dependent on the 15th-century architecture of CHANDERI and other centres of the Malwa sultans (*see also* §6(ii)(e) above). Humayun built a palace within the fort, but it is no longer extant. In 1531 Yar Muhammad Khan added a domed shop to the side of the Assi Khambha and built a mosque at Antri, a small town to the south of Gwalior.

In the Akbar period a handsome gatehouse was erected in the suburb of Gwalior known as Laderi. A fine shrine was built in the old city for the saint Muhammad Ghaus (*d* 1562). Square in plan and carrying a large dome, the tomb is surrounded by a verandah with spectacularly carved stone screens. The screened verandah recalls a pre-Mughal shrine at SARKHEJ where the saint lived for some time. The design of the mausoleum of Muhammad Ghaus appears to have influenced Iftikhar Khan's tomb at Chunar and Salim Chishti's tomb at Fatehpur Sikri.

The hill fort at MANDU, once a favourite retreat of the sultans of Malwa, was under the command of Budagh Khan in the time of Akbar. He built a palace there on the Emperor's order in 1574–5 (AH 982). Known as Nil Kanth, the mansion consists of a courtyard with arched chambers on three sides. The fourth side is open and overlooks the valley below. Slightly later, Mandu was used as a camp by Akbar during his forays into the Deccan. Inscriptions on the palace walls record Akbar's victories in 1600–01 (AH 1009). In addition to some new construction, Akbar also undertook repairs to a 15th-century gate and the tomb of Mahmud Khalji.

17th century. Jahangir directed his campaigns in the Deccan from Mandu, issuing an order in 1615 for his architect ʿAbd al-Karim Maʿmur Khan to erect new buildings there and repair those of previous kings. The buildings known as the Tauli Mahal and Shah Gada's house are probably the result of this order, for they follow Jahangir's architecture in Agra and Lahore, eschewing regional characteristics.

Mughal headquarters were established in the Deccan at Burhanpur, an important centre on the highway to the

104. Tomb of Dilrus Banu Begum, Aurangabad, completed 1660–61

ports of Gujarat. The leading general ʿAbd al-Rahim Khan-i Khanan built several structures at Burhanpur, including a palatial residence, a garden known as Lal Bagh and a congregational mosque. All conform to imperial prototypes. Khan-i Khanan also built Jahangirpura, an area for the resident nobility.

The Bundella Rajputs, who became vassals of the Mughals during Akbar's reign, built a series of palaces and other monuments at Orchha. Many of the buildings date to the time of Jahangir and were built by Raja Bir Singh. Additions continued until the 18th century. A palace was also built at Datia. As in Rajasthan, this architecture developed a number of unique characteristics (*see* §(ii)(b) below) that distinguish it from imperial architecture.

Gwalior's position on the main route to the Deccan ensured its continued importance. Shah Jahan built a palace there in 1632. A relatively plain structure compared to other imperial examples, it probably replaced the palace of Humayun. Shah Jahan also built a hunting lodge at Bari (Dholpur District), near Gwalior (*see* BARI (i)). While still crown prince and during the first two years of his reign he resided at Burhanpur, where he built a garden and, after damming up a stream, constructed a number of pleasure pavilions. In 1631 his wife Mumtaz Mahal died unexpectedly and was temporarily interred at a second garden at Burhanpur before her remains were transferred to Agra.

A number of buildings were constructed outside Burhanpur by Shah Jahan's officers serving in the Deccan. Most bear a greater resemblance to earlier regional building than to contemporary imperial architecture. These include, for example, the congregational mosque at Biloli (Nander District), built by the regional governor in 1645. However, some notable exceptions are in the pan-Indian Mughal style; among these is the Feria Bagh palace in Ahmadnagar.

In 1687, during Aurangzeb's reign, the ʿAdil Shahi and Qutb Shahi kingdoms were conquered, but a successor state was founded in 1724 by Nizam al-Mulk of Hyderabad. This effectively terminated Mughal rule in the south. The most famous centres in the Deccan under Aurangzeb were Daulatabad and Aurangabad. The citadels at both places contained Mughal buildings, but they are largely ruined. AURANGABAD is best known for the tomb of Aurangzeb's wife, Dilrus Banu Begum (*d* 1657), known locally as Bibi Ka Maqbara (Urdu: Tomb of the Queen), which was built by her son Aʿzam Shah (see fig. 104). ʿAta Allah, the architect, modelled the tomb on the Taj Mahal, which had been designed by his father, Ustad Ahmad. Completed in 1660–61 (AH 1071) under the supervision of Aqa Abu al-Qasim Beg, the tomb is notable for its ornate surfaces and emphasis on verticality, thus anticipating 18th-century developments. Other Aurangzeb-period monuments remain largely unstudied. For example, a congregational mosque and a number of other buildings were constructed in Gwalior by Muʿtamad Khan, the governor. The massive fort at Ater (Bhind District) on the Chambal River was begun by Badan Singh Badoria and completed by Maha Singh in 1668; it contains palatial buildings and an audience hall inspired by imperial examples at Agra.

For 17th-century Indo-Islamic architecture in the south *see also* §6(ii)(f) above.

BIBLIOGRAPHY

Macmillan Enc. Architects: "Ata Allah'

G. Yazdani: *Mandu: City of Joy* (Oxford, 1929)

P. Brown: *Indian Architecture, Islamic Period* (?Bombay, [1942], rev. Bombay, 1956) [rev. edn with additional photographs]

H. N. Dvivedi: *Gvāliyar Rājya ke abhilekha* [Inscriptions of Gwalior kingdom] (Varanasi, 1947)

D. R. Patil: *The Descriptive and Classified List of Archaeological Monuments in Madhya Bharat* (Gwalior, 1952)

N. Ahmad: 'Imam-ud-Din Husain Riadi, the Grandson of Nadir-ul'Asr Ustad Ahmad, the Architect of the Taj Mahal, and his Tadhkira-i-Baghistan', *Islam. Cult.*, xxx (1956), pp. 330–50; xxxi (1957), pp. 60–87

M. Isrisullah: 'Two Persian Inscriptions Carved on the Gate of Bibi ka Maqbara, Aurangabad', *Epig. Ind.: Arab. & Pers. Suppl.* (1956), pp. 34–5

Z. A. Desai: 'Mughal Architecture in the Deccan', *History of the Medieval Deccan, 1295–1724*, ii (Hyderabad, 1974), pp. 305–14

——: 'A Note on the Nagari Inscription of Mughal Emperor Babar from Gwalior Fort', *Sri Dinescandrika: Studies in Indology*, ed. B. N. Mukherjee and others (Delhi, 1983), pp. 67–71

CATHERINE B. ASHER

(ii) Regional. While the Mughals had all but defined Indian architecture from the late 16th century as a result of their great power and numerous building projects, the size and diversity of the subcontinent assured a considerable amount of regional variation even in those areas controlled directly by the court. These regional differences were amplified in the 18th century as the Mughal empire became increasingly decentralized. The latter Mughal period was marked by such new cultural and political forces as the nawabs of Lucknow and Murshidabad and the nizams of Hyderabad. A revived Rajput oligarchy and the Maratha confederacy introduced further complexity and conflicting cultural ambitions. The architecture that appeared under these various entities is notable for its creative eclecticism, dynamic assimilation of Western influence and free use of both Mughal and traditional forms.

(a) Punjab, Avadh, Murshidabad and the Deccan. (b) Rajasthan and central India. (c) Gujarat. (d) East. (e) Himachal Pradesh and Ladakh. (f) South.

(a) Punjab, Avadh, Murshidabad and the Deccan. Regional trends in the Mughal period developed partly from the influence of local building traditions and the use of local materials, as in the Punjab. Regionalism was further encouraged as Mughal authority declined in the 18th century and new cities emerged in Avadh, Murshidabad and the Deccan.

Punjab. Apart from the capital city of LAHORE (*see* §(i)(a) above), the main concentration of buildings was along the royal highway from Agra to Kabul, the major portion of which passed through the Punjab. These buildings included forts, palaces, gardens, caravanserais, bridges, stepwells, route markers (Pers. *kūs-minārs*), madrasas, mansions, mosques and tombs. Since the region is near the capital cities of Delhi and Agra, its buildings closely followed the imperial Mughal style in all respects but one: the lavish use of glazed tile for decoration. Although some buildings adorned with glazed tile exist in other parts of the Mughal empire—e.g. the mausoleum of Mulla Shukrulla Shirazi (*d* 1639), popularly known as Chini ka Rauza, in Agra—this feature was developed to its fullest extent in the Punjab. The reasons for this are the geographical proximity of the region to Iran, the greatest centre of glazed-tile art (*see* ISLAMIC ART, §II, 9(ii)(a) and (b)), and the suitability of this mode of decoration for buildings of brick, the chief building material in the area.

Square tiles utilizing only blue and white were employed on 16th-century buildings of the Punjab. Representative is the tomb of Shaykh Musa Ahangar in Lahore. A clear departure from this tradition is perceptible in the buildings of the early 17th century, for example the portals of the caravanserais at Fatehabad (*c.* 1606) and Doraha (*c.* 1611–27) and the tomb of Muhammad Mumin at Nakodar (1612). In the new style a geometric design was first formed using projecting bricks, then the spaces in between were inlaid with tiles of cobalt blue, turquoise, green and lemon yellow.

After the first quarter of the 17th century, there was another change of style. Entire façades began to be divided into square or rectangular sunken panels that were filled with faience mosaics. The spaces between the panels were covered with plaster painted with simulated brick patterns. The designs consist mainly of flowering trees and vases filled with sprays of flowers. Graceful inscriptions framed arches whose spandrels were usually filled with floral arabesques. The mosaics exhibit a scheme of seven colours: cobalt blue, turquoise, green, orange, cadmium yellow, purple and white. In this kind of work each petal or leaf was formed by a separate tile, and each fragment was of a single colour. The mosque of Wazir Khan in Lahore (1634) is the finest and richest example of this style. Some other specimens of such work may be seen on

105. Tilework on the tomb of Haji Jamal, Nakodar, 1656

the portals of the caravanserai of Amanat Khan (Amritsar District; 1640–41), the Gulabi Bagh gateway in Lahore (1655) and the tomb of Haji Jamal at Nakodar (1656; see fig. 105).

The tile mosaics of Lahore Fort, executed mainly in 1620–30 during renovations begun by Jahangir (*reg* 1605–27), cover an area of about 6688 sq. m and are unique in the Muslim world in the wide range of figurative motifs executed in this medium.

Although tile decoration was mainly limited to the exteriors of buildings, there are stray examples—such as the mosque of Day Anga in Lahore (1635)—where tiles were also used on interior walls. The fashion of faience mosaics began to fade after the third quarter of the 17th century, being too complicated and hence costly and time-consuming. Gradually during the next century there was a reversion to the easier technique of painted tiles of standard size. Begumpuri Mosque in Lahore, built by Zakariya Khan, governor of the Punjab between 1726 and 1745, exemplifies this style.

Towards the end of the 18th century the Sikhs succeeded in wresting political power from the Mughals, and a number of independent Sikh rulers occupied different territories. The glory of the Sikh rule, however, belongs to Maharaja Ranjit Singh (*reg* 1799–1839), who ruled the country across the River Sutlej from his capital at Lahore. A practical man, the Maharaja did not indulge in the luxury of erecting magnificent palaces as did his Mughal predecessors. Except for the Hazuri Bagh pavilion, near the Lahore fort, and a garden at Amritsar built for his personal use; he utilized the existing Mughal palaces of the Lahore fort; he even appropriated some Mughal tombs in the city for officers' residences. Some of his nobles had palatial mansions erected in Lahore and Amritsar; no dominant style emerges from these buildings, however. It was in their religious buildings that the Sikhs succeeded in developing an architectural idiom sufficiently expressive to be referred to as the Sijh style. The Sikh place of worship (*gurdwara*) was the chief form of religious architecture.

The spiritual content of SIKHISM derived from Hinduism as well as from Islam, although it owed more to the former, from which the line of its teachers and most of its followers originally came. The buildings of the faith, however, leaned more towards the Islamic style. The reason for this was that during the early centuries of Muslim rule in India, the Punjab had been cleared of its Hindu monuments and so Sikhs had no prototypes except the existing Islamic buildings. The Rajput element already present in Mughal architecture was, however, exaggerated, probably by the employment of Rajput artisans. The chief architectural elements of the Sikh style were multifoil arches, embowed and domed windows, pilasters following the shape of baluster columns, elliptical eaves with multifoil soffits, domed pavilions (*chatrīs*) on parapets and fluted domes usually covered with gilded copper sheets.

The supreme expression of this Sikh style is the Harmandir, popularly known as the Golden Temple, in AMRITSAR. Originally founded in 1588 and rebuilt about 1764, the shrine owes much of its present appearance (see fig. 106) to Ranjit Singh, who spared no effort in redesigning and adorning the holiest place of his faith. The ground plan of the shrine resolves itself into two parts: the square

106. Harmandir (Golden Temple), Amritsar, founded 1588, rebuilt *c*. 1764

front portion enshrining the Sikh holy book, the Adi Granth, and the semi-octagonal rear portion giving access to the holy water of the tank in the midst of which the shrine stands. The configuration followed in the front portion is what is called a ninefold plan (Pers. *hasht bihisht*), a favourite design for Mughal pleasure-pavilions as well as tombs. The mezzanine floor of the shrine repeats the plan of the ground storey. At the top, each corner of the roof is marked with a *chatrī*, a usual feature of Mughal buildings. The central dome in Mughal buildings was raised higher than the surrounding *chatrīs* by placing its outer shell over a high drum; the space between the ceiling of the building and the outer shell of the dome remained unused. The builders of the Harmandir developed this space into a full-fledged room. In this respect too, however, the tomb of Itimad ud-Daula dated AH 1036–7 (AD 1626–8) at Agra takes precedence.

In the predominance of vegetal motifs, the decorative scheme of the shrine also echoes Islamic taste, as does the use of the pietra dura technique.

See also §VIII, 5(ii) below.

BIBLIOGRAPHY

C. Rodgers: *List of the Objects of Archaeological Interest in the Punjab* (Lahore, 1891)
S. M. Latif: *Lahore: Its History, Architectural Remains and Antiquities* (Lahore, 1892)
F. H. Andrews: 'Wazir Khan's Mosque, Lahore', *J. Ind. A. & Indust.*, x (July 1903), pp. 27–30, pls 22–9
J. P. Vogel: *Tile-mosaics of Lahore Fort* (Calcutta, 1920)
R. E. M. Wheeler: *5000 Years of Pakistan* (London, 1950)
K. M. Walliullah Khan: *Sikh Shrines in Pakistan* (Karachi, 1962)
R. Nath: *Colour Decoration in Mughal Architecture* (Bombay, 1970)
K. S. Kang: 'Art and Architecture of the Golden Temple, Akal Takht, Gurudwara Baba Atal Sahib', *Marg*, xxx/3 (1977), pp. 23–41
M. R. Anand: 'Appreciation of Creative Arts under Maharaja Ranjit Singh: Architecture', *Marg*, xxxiv/1 (1980), pp. 27–33
S. Haider: *Tilework in Pakistan* (Islamabad, n.d. [*c*. 1981–6])
M. Kaur: *The Golden Temple Past and Present* (Amritsar, 1983)
M. Idrees: *Aksa Bahisht* (Lahore, 1985)
S. Parihar: *Mughal Monuments in the Punjab and Haryana* (New Delhi, 1985)
P. S. Arshi: *Sikh Architecture in the Punjab* (Delhi, 1986)

S. Parihar: 'Architectural Design of the Golden Temple: Fact and Fiction', *Punjab U. Res. Bull. (A.)*, xxiii/2 (1992), pp. 89–92, figs 1–7

SUBHASH PARIHAR

Avadh. As the central authority of the MUGHAL dynasty declined after the time of Aurangzeb (*reg* 1658–1707), the emperors became increasingly dependent on their emirs and officers. In Avadh (Oudh), a prosperous province in the Gangetic plain, Muslim state governors known as nawabs (Urdu *nawwāb*, pl. of Arab. *nā'ib*: 'deputy') were appointed during the 18th century. The nawabs became hereditary holders of Avadh and soon found themselves strategic players in the struggle between the British and the Marathas. Mirza Muqim 'Abd al-Mansur Khan, entitled Safdar Jang (*reg* 1739–54), was governor of Avadh and later prime minister under Muhammad Shah (*reg* 1719–48). Safdar Jang's power is well illustrated by his impressive tomb in Delhi, completed in 1753–4 (AH 1167) by his son Nawab Shuja' al-Daula (*reg* 1754–75; *see* DELHI, §I). The tomb, placed on a tall platform, is a two-storey structure (18.3 m sq.) with attached towers on the corners and an elegant bulbous dome faced with white marble. The exterior is red sandstone decorated with marble insets. The spacious garden, which follows the established *chār bāgh* (from Pers. *chahārbāgh*: 'four [plot] garden') pattern, is surrounded by a wall with a gatehouse and three palace pavilions in its perimeter. Safdar Jang's mausoleum is based on the mid-16th-century tomb of Emperor Humayun (*reg* 1530–40, 1555–6; *see* DELHI, fig. 6; *see also* §7(i)(a) above) to such an extent that it can be considered a revival of the early Mughal style. Just as 18th-century classicism in Britain and its colonies marked a reformed dispensation and a return to antique principles, so Safdar Jang's tomb represented a revived Mughal empire under the nawabs.

Safdar Jang's tomb, however, was the last major monument of the Mughal regime. The British victory at Buxar (1764) and the Treaty of Faizabad (1775) reduced Avadh to a dependent buffer state. After this time, the architecture of Avadh seldom looked back to the Mughal past but pursued a decorated blending of Indian and European forms. A key event in these developments was the decision of the fourth nawab of Avadh, Asaf al-Daula (*reg* 1775–97), to make LUCKNOW his capital. This led to the rapid expansion of the city and inaugurated an architectural heyday that lasted until the British annexed the province in 1856.

The religious and palatial complexes added to Lucknow from the time of Asaf al-Daula spread along the south bank of the Gumti River, leaving the older city relatively untouched. The two most important buildings are the Bara (Great) Imambara (1784), built by Asaf al-Daula, and the Farhad Baksh (1781), a mansion built by the European adventurer General Claude Martin. Though much altered over the years, these buildings illustrate the two strands that were to combine in the 19th century to form Lucknow's unique style of architecture.

The Bara Imambara was built to accommodate the Muharram rite of the Shi'ite sect to which the nawabs belonged. Designed by Kifayut 'Ali and constructed of brick and stucco, like most architecture in Lucknow, the complex was undertaken as a famine-relief measure, employing thousands after the rains had failed. The main building consists of an immense (50×16 m) vaulted hall with two subsidiary wings. Above the vaults is a complicated network of galleries. The front elevation is pierced by nine arched doorways and numerous windows, the first and second storeys presenting a battlemented appearance. The building occupies a raised platform with a mosque to the right and a STEPWELL to the left. The stepwell had numerous elaborate rooms and was known as the Baoli Palace. At the basement level of the Imambara are the tombs of the nawab and his wife, noted on the ground floor by simple rectangular outlines.

The Bara Imambara was used to store portable model tombs (*ta'ziya*) of the martyrs Husayn and Hasan, which were taken out in procession during Muharram. A large walled square was created in front of the complex as a processional route for these models. Low battlemented walls echo the theme of the main building, and a large gate (h. 18 m) was constructed on the western side. Known as the Rumi Darvaza (Turkish Gate), it epitomizes the picturesque architecture of the nawabs with its combination of utility and frivolity (see fig. 107). The pottery flower-buds (*guldastā*) at the top of the cusped arch were intended as fountains, but defects in the hydraulic system prevented this fancy from being realized. An eastern gate to the square already existed before 1784, being an entrance to the old Machchi Bhavan fort; this gate was demolished after 1858. It was deemed meritorious for each nawab to add a new *imāmbara* as he came to power, hence the proliferation of these structures in Lucknow.

The Farhad Baksh, the second noteworthy 18th-century building at Lucknow, is a European-style country house that served as the residence of Claude Martin (1735–1800) for almost 20 years. It lies 3.2 km east of the Bara Imambara. A one-storey building capped by little pavilions, its main salon was built on pillars sunk in the river. It was surrounded by a moat on three sides and could only be entered via a drawbridge. Entrances, both outside and within the house, could be closed with thick iron doors. The most curious features, however, were the basement storeys within the banks of the river, which are invisible to the casual viewer. During the hot season Martin would live in these basements, ascending as the annual monsoon caused the river to rise, until by September the basement had flooded and he had reached the ground floor. As the waters receded, the underground rooms would be repainted in preparation for the next year. The engineering skills needed to design such a building are extraordinary, especially considering that Martin was a self-taught architect, much like his contemporary Thomas Jefferson.

The new area of Lucknow that sprang up on the south bank of the Gumti contained many European-style houses similar to the Farhad Baksh but without its whimsical features. Set within their own grounds, these houses were conventional enough of their kind, consisting of a series of rusticated archways at ground level supporting a pillared verandah, usually of the Tuscan order, and topped with a parapeted flat roof. Nawab Asaf al-Daula, in developing his second palace complex, the Daulat Khana, incorporated a Palladian house known as the Asafi Kothi in the scheme. At the same time, domestic architecture of the well-to-do began to undergo a transformation, but social and climatic needs necessitated a modification of European ideals. For example, European-style houses could

107. Rumi Darvaza (Turkish Gate), Lucknow, 1784

not provide the privacy that Indians demanded. Thus the women's quarters (*zanānā*) were usually built as a separate structure and attached to the house by covered passages. This detracted from the ideal symmetry of the building. Such adaptations foreshadowed the mixture of Indian and European forms that characterizes nawabi architecture in the 19th century.

In 1795, while the Daulat Khana of Nawab Asaf al-Daula was still under construction, Claude Martin began Constantia, his most celebrated building (for illustration *see* LUCKNOW). Known also as La Martinière, this remarkable residence exhibits a preoccupation with defence, as in the Farhad Baksh. Constantia has been described as a 'Gothic castle. . .surrounded by a deep ditch, fortified on the outer side by stockades. . .so that the place is sufficiently protected to resist the attacks of any Asiatic power'. Rising over the Gumti, it is a two-storey structure set on a platform; the central square section of the mansion rises another three storeys. Four octagonal shafts running the height of the whole building were sunk into the river bank, and an ingenious system of ducts drew cool air into rooms leading off the shafts. To soften its fortified appearance, Constantia was decorated with a profusion of kiosks and plaster statuary, including lions, Classical figures and Chinese mandarins (the latter lost during the earthquake of 1803). The interior owes much to the contemporary Adam style in Britain (*see* ENGLAND, §II, 4). Plasterwork swags and imitation Wedgwood panels, copied by local craftsmen from imported books, decorate the major rooms. Martin did not live to inhabit this mansion, but his tomb was built into the centre of the basement, barred with thick iron doors like those in the Farhad Baksh.

Constantia had a great influence on the city of Lucknow and initiated a period of high eclecticism there. The statuary and other features were widely copied, being an easy way to 'Europeanize' a house by adding non-structural features in stucco. Spindly Corinthian columns were built up around brick cores, quite out of proportion to the façades they adorned; grandiose architraves were placed over small doorways; façades that should have been fenestrated carried imitation windows in stucco to preserve privacy. These European elements were freely juxtaposed with ribbed and gilded domes, cusped arches and arabesques. Few interiors in this style have been preserved. It is clear, however, that even when faithful copies were made from important pattern books, certain elements were misunderstood or neglected. Grand staircases dwindled into small spirals tucked into corners; fireplaces, often the focal point of a room, were merely decorative. Leading examples of this hybrid style include the Chattar Manzils (see fig. 108), two palaces built for Nawab Nasir al-Din Haydar (*reg* 1827–37), the Chaulakhi Palace of Kaizar Bagh and the gate to Sikandar Bagh, both of the latter built for Nawab Wajid ʿAli Shah (*reg* 1847–56). While these buildings have often been disparaged by architectural critics as corrupt and vulgar, the 19th-century architecture of the nawabs is a genuine product of its age and no more decadent than its Victorian counterparts in England.

Eclecticism dominated Lucknow, but it was not a universal style. The Jamiʿ Mosque of Nawab Muhammad ʿAli Shah (*reg* 1837–42), not completed until 1850, is in a conservative manner that recalls Mughal architecture. Mughal prototypes were apparently viewed as appropriate for religious buildings and symbolic of an older way of life threatened by innovation and progress. In 1856 the British

108. Chhota Chattar Manzil (left) and Darsan Bilas (Chaurukhi Kothi; right), Lucknow, *c.* 1820

finally annexed Avadh and sent Wajid ʿAli Shah into exile, thus ending Lucknow's extraordinary age of architecture. High-handedness in colonial policy, of which this deposition was but a single instance, led to the rebellion of the following year. Considerable military action took place in Lucknow, and many buildings were damaged. As soon as the British were able to reoccupy the city, a programme of systematic destruction was pursued in an attempt to erase the lingering vestiges of nawabi power.

BIBLIOGRAPHY

W. Hodges: *Travels in India during the Years 1780, 81, 82, 83* (London, 1793)

H. A. A. Darogah: *The Lucknow Album* (Calcutta, 1874)

Gazetteer of the Province of Oude, 2 vols (Allahabad, 1877)

P. C. Mookerji: *Pictoral Lucknow* (Lucknow, 1883)

J. Fergusson: *History of Indian and Eastern Architecture*, ii (New York, 1891)

S. C. Hill: *Claude Martin* (Calcutta, 1901)

M. A. Beg: *The Guide to Lucknow* (Lucknow, 1915)

S. Hay: *Historic Lucknow* (Lucknow, 1939)

P. Brown: *Indian Architecture, Islamic Period* (?Bombay, [1942], rev. Bombay, 1956, with additional photographs)

J. Terry: *The Charm of Indo-Islamic Architecture* (London, 1955)

S. Nilsson: *European Architecture in India, 1750–1850* (London, 1968)

Comte de Modave: *Voyage en Inde du comte de Modave, 1773–1776*, annotated by J. Deloche (Paris, 1971)

V. Talwar Oldenburg: *The Making of Colonial Lucknow, 1856–1877* (Princeton, 1984)

R. Llewellyn-Jones: *A Fatal Friendship: The Nawabs, the British and the City of Lucknow* (Delhi, 1985)

——: *A Very Ingenious Man: The Life of Claude Martin* (Delhi, 1992)

ROSIE LLEWELLYN-JONES

Murshidabad. A florescence of building in Murshidabad in the first half of the 18th century accompanied the rise of the high-ranking Mughal emir Murshid Quli Khan. In 1703 he gave the city his name and made it, rather than Dhaka, the capital of Bengal. By 1717 Murshid Quli Khan had combined the offices of revenue collector and governor, giving himself unprecedented power as an officer of the Mughal state. While he regarded himself as an independent ruler, Murshid Quli Khan continued to behave as a Mughal agent, remitting revenue annually to the imperial court at Delhi.

Murshidabad had been founded during Akbar's reign (1556–1605) by Makhsus Khan, brother of the Mughal governor of Bihar, who called the new town Makhsusabad. On making it his capital, Murshid Quli Khan embellished the city with a palace, a new mint, wells, tanks and a Jamiʿ (congregational) Mosque, dated 1724–5 (AH 1137). Only the Jamiʿ Mosque, now known as the Katra Mosque, survives. The building, constructed entirely of brick, has a single-aisled prayer-hall and sits on a raised plinth. The prayer-hall is entered through five arches and originally had five domes (only two survive). Surrounding the plinth on all four sides are domed cloisters for reciters of the Koran. Tall minarets were placed at each corner. With its relatively small entrances, weighty appearance and numerous niches on the façade, the Katra Mosque breaks with the smaller and more refined mosques of DHAKA and Rajmahal, recalling the pre-Mughal architecture of Bengal. Also reminiscent of Bengal's past is the simple tomb of Murshid Quli Khan beneath the east entrance. While contemporary sources relate that this location was chosen as a symbol of his piety, Murshid Quli Khan also probably intended to equate himself with Sikandar Shah (*reg* 1358–90), the first independent ruler of Bengal's Ilyas Shahi dynasty, who was buried beneath the entrance of the Adina Mosque at Pandua. Murshid Quli Khan's daughter ʿAzim al-Nisa Begum maintained this distinctive architecture in her own mosque, as did Nawab Sarfaraz Khan (*reg* 1739–40), who constructed a mosque known today as the Phuti Mosque (Bengali: Broken Mosque).

After this initial period, the architecture of Murshidabad returned to the style of late 17th-century Dhaka, paralleling the need of the nawabs to reaffirm their (albeit token) loyalty to the Mughals as a means of maintaining authority. The mosque built by Nawab ʿAlivardi Khan Mahabat Jang Ghazi (*reg* 1740–56) in 1743–4 (AH 1156) at Roshnibagh is among the first buildings to return to a Mughal aesthetic. The mosque is a small, three-bayed structure entered through three cusped arches. A central dome, flanked by two keel (*chau-chala*) vaults, surmounts the single-aisled prayer hall. Over the central arch is a curved projection with a down-turned eave that emulates a *baṅglā*-style roof; the side arches have projections resembling keel vaults. With similar forms appearing on the side and back, the mosque is typical of 18th-century Mughal architecture elsewhere in India. The Roshnibagh garden in which the mosque is located contains the tomb of Nawab Shujaʿ al-Din, the son-in-law of Murshid Quli Khan. It has been suggested that the construction of the mosque was an attempt by ʿAlivardi Khan to absolve his guilt in the murder of Shujaʿ al-Din's son.

The large mosque at Moti Jheel, built in 1749–50 (AH 1163) by Shahamat Jang (ʿAlivardi Khan's nephew and son-in-law), has an elaborate west façade and stucco interior. Together with the Roshnibagh Mosque, it set a standard of refined elegance for the regional style of Murshidabad as it developed in the 18th century. Perhaps the finest example of this style is the Chowk Mosque, built in 1767–8 (AH 1181) by Munni Begum, widow of Nawab Mir Jaʿfar (*reg* 1757–60; 1764–5). The façade, facing a large court, has seven cusped arches and delicate panels of incised stucco (see fig. 109). The graduated size of the five domes and end keel vaults, flanked by slender minarets, yields an overall appearance of restrained majesty. Undertaken at the height of Munni Begum's influence over her son, the young nawab, the mosque was built on the former grounds of Murshid Quli Khan's public audience hall. Five radial roads led up to the mosque in the city's main chowk (market). While this building may have been intended as the focal point for a rejuvenated Murshidabad under Munni Begum, the real power was now increasingly in the hands of the British.

During much of the 18th century, the nawabs concentrated on building palaces, but none have survived. Religious structures were built within the palace grounds, for example the 18th-century Safed and Zarad mosques (so named because they were painted white and gold). These buildings are similar to the Moti Jheel Mosque, but they have ribbed domes, a feature that appeared at Murshidabad about 1780. Other religious structures are indicative of the Shiʿite beliefs to which the nawabs adhered. For example, a large complex for Muharram rites (*imāmbara*) was provided by Nawab Suraj al-Daula (*reg* 1756–7). The only extant portion is the Medina, a small square building with a bulbous dome flanked by four finials, within the present palace compound. The foundation was packed with earth brought from Kerbala in Iraq. This gesture linked the nawabs and Murshidabad to one of the sacred sites of Shiʿite belief and thus to the sect's source of spiritual authority.

In the 18th and 19th centuries, as in other parts of north India, private patrons played an increasingly important role in architecture. At least 20 inscribed or once-inscribed mosques and religious structures built after the mid-18th century have survived. All the mosques follow the single-aisled, multi-domed format popular in Bengal since the 16th century. The Moti Jheel and Chowk

109. Chowk Mosque, Murshidabad, 1767–8

mosques served as the leading models. An example is the mosque of Miyan Halal (1801–2, AH 1216), which has fluted domes and a fine stucco interior.

A more subdued style came into vogue as the 19th century progressed. Farhat Allah Khan's mosque (1821–2, AH 1237) has no domes, cusping or ornate stucco ornament. The Chhote Chowk ki Mosque, begun by Sadiq ʿAli Khan before 1850 but not completed until 1881, is a single-aisled mosque with three domes. It too is austere and has little stuccowork. Few features of these late mosques show European influence. Private patronage was also responsible for a Husayniya and the Qadam Sharif complex. The Husayniya was used to store portable models (*taʿziya*) of Husayn's tomb, which are part of the Muharram commemorations. It was begun in 1804 by ʿAmbar ʿAli Khan and enlarged in 1854 by Darab ʿAli Khan, both court eunuchs. The Husayniya consists of a rectangular compound with high, white-washed walls and pillared galleries around the interior. The Qadam Sharif complex, the most important structure of which is a shrine housing the Prophet Muhammad's footprints, was built by Itwar ʿAli Khan, the chief eunuch of Nawab Mir Jaʿfar. The mosque in the complex, erected in 1780–81 (AH 1194), follows the established three-dome pattern. The Prophet's footprints had previously been kept at GAUR, and the new shrine (1788), with a single dome and five arched entrances on the south, was based on the earlier building. The transfer of the footprints was aimed at bolstering the religious status of Murshidabad, whose administrative and economic functions had been undermined by the shift of government offices to Calcutta.

By the opening years of the 19th century, Murshidabad's political status rested solely on the fact that it was the seat of the nawab. Increasing British influence is reflected in the new residence of the nawab constructed between 1829 and 1837 (see fig. 125 below). Designed by Duncan McLeod, this palace is entered through a huge portico with a triangular pediment resting on classical columns. Built shortly after Government House in Calcutta (*see* §(iii) below), it is also in a Palladian style. Ten years after the palace had been completed, Nawab Feridun Jah built to its north an enormous *imāmbara* (at 210×95 m the largest in Asia). Like the palace, it shows European influence. Its south façade, facing the palace, is divided into two storeys articulated with pilasters and shuttered windows. The central entrance has a round arch with cusps, flanked by paired Doric columns supporting a cornice. The interior Medina is surrounded by Doric porticos and colonnades. Sadiq ʿAli Khan, the same man who built the Chhote Chowk ki Mosque, was appointed to design the *imāmbara*. Thus while this complex and other official architecture have European forms and motifs, privately patronized religious buildings at Murshidabad, including Sadiq ʿAli's own mosque, lack European influence. This suggests that the architectural style of the Mughals was now seen as an architecture of piety, of Islam and of the passing social order. In contrast, the nawab's buildings, whether religious or secular, represented the progress and increasing dominance of British power in India.

BIBLIOGRAPHY

Munshi Salim Allah: *Tārīkh-i Bangālah* [History of Bengal] (1763), ed. S. M. Imamuddin (Dhaka, 1979)

W. Hodges: *Select Views in India, Drawn on the Spot in the Years 1780, 1781, 1782 and 1783*, ii (London, 1786)

Ghulam Husain Salim: *Riyāẓ al-salāṭīn* [Gardens of the sultans] (1787–8, trans. Abdus Salam, *R* Delhi, 1986)

F. P. Layard: 'The Mausoleum of Ali Verdi Khan and Sooraj ood-Dawlah, at Khooshbagh, near Murshidabad', *J. Asiat. Soc. Bengal*, xxi (1852), pp. 504–11

H. Beveridge: 'Notes on Sirajuddaulah and the Town of Murshidabad, Taken from a Persian Manuscript of the *Tarikh-i Mansuri*', *J. Asiat. Soc.*, xxxvi (1867), pp. 96–9

——: 'Old Places in Murshidabad', *Calcutta Rev.*, xciv (1892), pp. 322–45; xcv (1892), pp. 195–216; xcvi (1893), pp. 234–49

T. J. Till Walsh: *A History of Murshidabad District* (London, 1902)

P. C. Majumdar: *Musnud of Murshidabad (1704–1904)* (Murshidabad, 1905)

Muhammad ʿAbid ʿAli Khan: *Memoirs of Gaur and Pandua* (?Maldah, 1912); ed. and rev. by H. E. Stapleton (Calcutta, 1930)

L. S. S. O'Mally: *Murshidabad*, xxxii of *Bengal District Gazetteers* (Calcutta, 1914)

Annu. Rep. Ind. Epig. (1955–6)

M. Khatun: 'A Persian Inscription in the Indian Museum, Calcutta, from Murshidabad', *Epig. Ind.: Arab. & Pers. Suppl.* (1959–60), pp. 23–6

Shamsud-Din Ahmed: *Inscriptions of Bengal*, iv (Rajshahi, 1960)

A. H. Dani: *Muslim Architecture of Bengal* (Dhaka, 1961)

S. Nilsson: *European Architecture in India, 1750–1850* (London, 1968)

A. Banerji: 'Late Mughal Style Architecture', *J. Asiat. Soc.*, xiv (1972), pp. 1–8

Khan Muhammad Mohsin: *A Bengal District in Transition: Murshidabad, 1765–1793* (Dhaka, 1973)

Annu. Rep. Ind. Epig. (1974–5; 1975–6)

N. R. Ray: *Bengal Nawabs* (Calcutta, 1977)

C. B. Asher: 'Inventory of Key Monuments', *The Islamic Heritage of Bengal*, ed. G. Michell (Paris, 1984), pp. 37–140

——: 'The Mughal and Post-Mughal Periods', *The Islamic Heritage of Bengal*, ed. G. Michell (Paris, 1984), pp. 193–212

——: 'The Architecture of Murshidabad: Regional Revival and Islamic Continuity', *Islam and Indian Regions*, ed. A. L. Dallapiccola and S. Zingel-Ave Lallemant, 2 vols (Stuttgart, 1993), i, pp. 61–74; ii, pls 1–6, figs 1–12

CATHERINE B. ASHER

Deccan. By the beginning of the 16th century the Muslim Bahmani kingdom of the Deccan had broken up into five independent states, each governed by its own line of rulers: the Barid Shahi dynasty of Bidar, the Nizam Shahi dynasty of Ahmadnagar, the ʿImad Shahis of Berar, the ʿAdil Shahi dynasty of Bijapur and the Qutb Shahi dynasty of Golconda and Hyderabad. Though the architecture of each of these dynasties grew out of the common heritage of the Bahmanis at Gulbarga and Bidar, each kingdom developed its own characteristic style. After 1633 the region was invaded by the Mughal dynasty. Bijapur and Golconda-Hyderabad resisted until 1686 and 1687, respectively. For some years thereafter, the Deccan was a province of the Mughal empire, Aurangabad being one of the most important centres. Incursions of the Marathas led eventually to the disintegration of the Mughal empire in 1724, giving local governors such as the Asaf Jahis of Hyderabad opportunities to assert their independence.

The constant threat of invasion and siege led the Deccani sultans to protect their cities with substantial fortifications; these were invariably laid out in circular formation. Ahmadnagar's walls constituted an irregular circuit, reinforced with massive, semicircular bastions; the Shah Husayni Rahmani bastion on the east was trilobed. The principal entrance to the city, on the west, was shielded by a large, semicircular barbican that projects outwards from the walls. BIJAPUR had two concentric circuits of fortifications: the inner walls of the royal citadel in the middle and the outer walls of the city itself. Work on the fortifications and the external moat was completed in 1565. The walls were about 10 m high and no less wide; the inner and outer stone faces concealed a rammed-earth core. They were surmounted by a walkway, with crenellations to provide protection from enemy fire. Numerous semicircular bastions were later used as emplacements for cannons; one circular bastion stood freely inside the walls. Bijapur's five main gates each had an entrance with pointed arches flanked by bastions, some additionally defended by barbicans; inner courts were surrounded by guardrooms. The gates were approached by drawbridges across the moat. The new suburb of Nauraspur, west of Bijapur, was established with its own circuit of fortifications in the early 17th century.

At the death of Quli Qutb al-Mulk (*reg* 1512–43) in 1543, the GOLCONDA citadel was already well established. The Bala Hisar was defended by walls that ran up and over the boulders. The Qutb Shahi headquarters was laid out at the base of the hill, on its northern and eastern flanks, contained within its own set of walls. Beyond the citadel, the city was surrounded by a complete circuit of fortifications, about 2.5 km in diameter. These were extended in 1624 with the addition of the approximately rectangular Naya Qil'a (New Fort) on the north-east. The fortifications, which were massive throughout, rose to an average of 18 m. There were eight strong gates with massive teak doors studded with spikes to resist elephants. Most of the bastions were semicircular; one example in the Naya Qil'a was nine-lobed. The principal entrance to the royal citadel, the Bala Hisar Darvaza, was protected by its own detached, curving barbican. The gate had a pointed-arched entrance, with mythical beasts and lions worked into the plasterwork in the spandrels; beyond the entrance was a lofty domed chamber. Two free-standing portals, with vaults carried on quadruple arches, faced the gateway from outside the walls. These ceremonial structures defined the beginning of the main street of the town.

Ceremonial portals also formed a focal point of HYDERABAD, the newly planned capital of the Qutb Shahis after 1591. The Char Minar stood in the middle of the city, at the intersection of two broad streets. This four-arched gateway, some 30 m square, has four lofty pointed arches, each facing a cardinal point. Above these is an arcaded balcony, running continuously around the building, with a smaller arcade and perforated marble screens above. Minarets (h. over 55 m) at each corner are decorated with double arcaded balconies and had bulbous, petalled domes at the top. At the western end of the open roof was a small mosque, the rest of the roof serving as a court. Near the Char Minar stands another lofty arched portal, the Char Kaman.

Numerous royal structures still stand in the Deccani capitals, testifying to the wealth and culture of the sultanate courts. One of the most important palace complexes of the Nizam Shahis is Hasht Bahish, 3 km north of Ahmadnagar. This has an octagonal pavilion with a double-storey interior chamber used for royal reception; double arcades mark the exterior. Other vaulted halls with small chambers stand near by. The largest royal residence at Ahmadnagar is the Farah Bakhsh, 2 km south of the city, erected in 1577 by the chief minister of Murtaza Nizam Shah (*reg* 1565–88). The complex is dominated by an imposing square pavilion laid out in the Persian manner on a strictly symmetrical plan. Its central, double-height, domed hall is surrounded by smaller vaulted chambers. Monumental arched portals face outwards from the middle of each side towards the surrounding pond. Plasterwork on the multi-faceted interior domes and half-domes was once sumptuously ornamented.

Palace buildings of the 'Adil Shahis at Bijapur include the Gagan Mahal, erected in 1561 by 'Ali I (*reg* 1557–79). Facing north towards a large open space for military displays, the building has a lofty arched portal with narrower arches at either side. The plasterwork in the spandrels forms medallion-and-bracket motifs, the latter being fish-shaped. The nearby Anand Mahal (1589) also has a triple-arched façade leading to a great hall. A large quadrangle marks the core of Bijapur's citadel. Above the north-west corner rises the Sat Manzil, of which only five storeys are intact. The palace dates from 1583 and must have functioned partly as a pleasure palace, since it contained several bathing cisterns. The façade is now merely a set of unadorned arched openings, but the interior was once richly ornamented (the paintings have faded). Immediately to the north is a water pavilion known as the Jal Mandir. This comprises a miniature domed pavilion, ornately decorated with projecting brackets and eaves and crowned with a small petalled dome, standing in the middle of a small pond. On the south side of the quadrangle is the Chini Mahal (so called because of the ceramics excavated near by), which has a long vaulted hall.

The Dad Mahal (Hall of Justice) at Bijapur was erected in 1646; it was later converted into a shrine for a relic of the Prophet Muhammad and renamed the Athar Mahal. This building gives the most complete idea of a Bijapur palace. On the east it has a portico with four double-height teak columns with elaborately carved brackets carrying a painted, panelled ceiling. The large hall on the upper level opens on to the verandah; small chambers at either end are covered with murals. Beside the Athar Mahal is the Jahaz Mahal, now partly demolished, with suites of rooms overlooking a reservoir.

The palace of the Qutb Shahis at Golconda, laid out at the foot of the Bala Hisar, preserves its original sequence of enclosures and vaulted chambers; royal structures are mostly ruined. The first court is marked by the Shila Khana ('Armoury') with its triple arcades. The Dad Mahal with vaulted chambers is located in the second court. On the south side of the third court is the Rani Mahal. It has a raised terrace, probably once a colonnaded verandah with high wooden columns (now lost), adjoining a triple-vaulted hall. The plasterwork is the finest inside the palace, especially in the roundels and panels above the arches. To the south, steps descend to a large hall, now ruined, and beyond to the Shashi Mahal, a private garden with a small central pavilion. The Darbar Hall on the summit of the Bala Hisar is a Mughal-style pavilion with an upper terrace reached by interior steps.

The Asaf Jahi rulers of Hyderabad erected many fine palaces, some of which still occupy large compounds within the city. The popularity of European styles is illustrated in the Chaumahalla, for example, the largest of all the royal complexes. Dating from the time of Asaf Jah I (*reg* 1724–48) and much added to in later times, the complex comprises a linear arrangement of reception halls for state occasions. The entrance on the west side is an arched gateway topped by a slender clock tower. A long garden is flanked on the east and west by Neo-classical wings enlivened with domed finials. The first and earliest of the north-facing residences is a two-storey arcaded building, the upper level set back to create a spacious roof terrace. The projecting corner wings have elaborate plaster ornamentation that imitates earlier work at Golconda. At the upper level the building has projecting corner chambers, each roofed with an open octagonal pavilion. Despite the proliferation of turrets and finials, there is a complete absence of domes. The other residences of the complex are more Neo-classical in design, generally with colonnaded porticos with double-height columns on the north-facing fronts.

Considerable efforts were made to ensure the Deccani cities had regular supplies of water. Bijapur was provided with a sophisticated network of aqueducts, earthen pipes and subterranean water channels with arched masonry tops, the last with storage towers at intervals to regulate pressure. This network transported water from large tanks outside the city to the royal citadel in the middle. Stepped reservoirs within the city walls were monumental structures. The Taj Bauri, in the western end of the city, was a large, square water basin enclosed within high walls. It was entered by a long flight of steps that descended through a broad pointed arch flanked by towers. The steps leading up to Golconda's fortified summit were lined with cisterns and platforms once provided with pulleys by which water was lifted from one level to another; waste water flowed downwards through earthenware pipes embedded in the walls.

Bathhouses (Arab./Pers. *ḥammāms*) were an essential feature of Deccani cities. The Hasht Bahish palace complex south of Ahmadnagar, for instance, had an unusual bathhouse provided with a ventilator tower (*badgir*), a rare instance of this Persian-derived feature in India. The bath itself was set in an underground vaulted chamber, where a pond was fed by water channels. Immediately inside the Bala Hisar Darvaza at Golconda was a royal bathhouse with stone-lined pools contained within vaulted chambers. Holes in the vaults were for escaping steam.

No major examples of mosque architecture survive at Bidar from the Baridi period, or at Ahmadnagar. Under the ʿImad Shahis, however, important mosques were constructed at Gawilgarh and Elichpur. These were built exclusively of ashlar masonry of fine workmanship in a simple style, partly influenced by traditions in neighbouring Malwa (*see* MANDU). The Great Mosque at Gawilgarh may be taken as typical of the ʿImad Shahi style. It stands on a high terrace enclosed on three sides by an arcaded screen wall with battlements. A large gateway with a prominent pointed arch occupies the middle of the east side. The prayer chamber on the west is divided by square pillars into seven aisles, each three bays deep; the rear bays have now collapsed. Domes roof the bays, the central dome in the front row being raised on a high, circular drum decorated with a parapet of trefoil merlons. The arcaded façade is sheltered by an angled eave on slanting rafters. Slender square pylons at the ends of the façade are capped with miniature domed pavilions (*chatrīs*); these have short colonettes with serpentine brackets. Almost the same scheme is repeated in the Chhoti Mosque at Gawilgarh. This was erected in 1577–8, though on a smaller scale and with similar square pylons at the ends of the triple-arched façade. Another variant on this scheme is the prayer-hall of the Jamiʿ Mosque at Elichpur. This building has a spacious hall four bays deep with a façade of eleven arches; the bays are roofed by small domes, some now collapsed.

A quite different style is evident in the mosques of the ʿAdil Shahis. One of the earliest mosques at Bijapur is the small building known as Yusuf's Old Jamiʿ Mosque (1513). This makes use of a single hemispherical dome on a tall, circular drum, the base surrounded by a ring of vertical foliation so that it resembles a bud surrounded by petals. Another early example is Ikhlas Khan's Mosque, possibly the first to show the typical Bijapur device of medallions in the spandrels supported by curved brackets in shallow relief. The monumental Jamiʿ Mosque, erected by ʿAli I in 1576 but never completed, is raised on a high terrace, the open courtyard being reached by a flight of steps. The prayer chamber is sparingly decorated; the central bay of the façade has a cusped arch and medallion-and-bracket decoration in the spandrels; the eave is supported on richly carved brackets. The dome in front of the mihrab is raised on an arcaded square, provided with its own cresting and intermediate finials. The hemisphere has a potlike finial surmounted by a crescent, a typical Bijapur device. The dome is supported by an original vaulting system: intersecting arches on squares meet to form a supporting octagon that projects over the piers beneath, thereby counteracting any side-thrust of the dome. The polygonal mihrab has arched recesses sumptuously decorated with painted foliation.

Malika Jahan's Mosque (1587) at Bijapur is typical of the evolved ʿAdil Shahi style. The masonry has been replaced with finely sculpted stonework, while the dome is a three-quarter sphere above a band of foliation. The Mihtar Mahal is a small mosque gateway belonging to the early 17th century. It has two superimposed chambers with projecting balconies. Angled struts, with delicately carved geese, animals and foliation, support the overhanging eaves; the two slender minarets are crowned by miniature, three-quarter domes. The attached mosque has a triple-arched façade, with finely carved decoration in the spandrels and above the apexes. The angled eave is carried on fully sculpted brackets. The parapet has trefoil battlements, interrupted by a pair of finials in the middle; slender minarets are positioned at the corners.

The ornate ʿAdil Shahi style was the basis for the early mosques of the Qutb Shahis, but surviving examples at Golconda and Hyderabad are generally simpler and more robust in character. The mosque perched at the summit of the Bala Hisar at Golconda, dated to the reign of Quli Qutb Shah (*reg* 1580–1612), is a modest structure with a pair of minarets with arcaded balconies and bulbous domes. More impressive in scale is the Mecca Mosque of Hyderabad, begun in 1617 and completed under the Mughals in 1693. Its prayer-hall has 15 enlarged bays, domed except for the central one, which is roofed with a pointed vault. The arcaded façade is flanked by two somewhat squat minarets with arcaded balconies and bulbous domes.

Eighteenth-century mosques built by the Mughal governors in the Deccan were modelled on examples at Delhi, such as the Moti Mosque of the Lal Qil'a (*see* DELHI, §III, 5). The mosque at Elichpur (1708–9), for example, has a triple-arcaded prayer-hall, the arches with unusual trefoil profiles. Above them rise three bulbous domes with flutings, the central dome being slightly enlarged and raised up on a lofty circular drum.

Funerary monuments constitute a significant proportion of architecture in the Deccan from the 16th to the 18th century. The tombs west of Bidar are the most important record of the Barid Shahis. The mausoleum (1579) of 'Ali Barid Shah (*reg* 1543–79) is the largest of the series. This lofty domed chamber, open on four sides, stands in the middle of a four-square garden (*chār bāgh*). The outer walls have central arched openings flanked by tiers of small arched recesses; above are five horizontal bands for decoration. The parapet and base of the dome, both with trefoil merlons or leaves, are elaborately treated. Fine calligraphic panels of coloured tilework are preserved inside the chamber. Pendentives support the dome, with arabesque plasterwork in the facets. The sarcophagus is of polished black basalt. The tomb of Qasim Barid II (*reg* 1587–91) reverted to earlier schemes. Its squat façade has two tiers of arched recesses on either side and an enlarged single arch in the middle. The diagonal squares in the panels over the doorways recall earlier Bahmani designs, as do the trefoil merlons of the parapet and bands.

Innumerable tombs of the 'Adil Shahis and their nobles still stand in and around Bijapur. The finest of all is the funerary complex (1626) of Ibrahim 'Adil Shah II (*reg* 1579–1627; for illustration *see* BIJAPUR). A tomb and mosque stand on a common plinth in the middle of a garden enclosure. The mausoleum has a square chamber with a verandah running around it with unadorned pointed arches of different widths. The upper portions of the façade are richly sculpted, especially the brackets supporting the overhanging eave and the crested parapet with intermediate finials and corner minarets, both with miniature bulbous domes. The crowning three-quarter dome sitting in a row of outward-curved petals is raised on a square, also provided with corner finials. The cenotaph chamber itself, roofed with a wagon-shaped vault, is covered with superb geometric and calligraphic designs. The mosque opposite, facing towards the tomb, has a similar but smaller dome raised high on petals.

The major 'Adil Shahi monument, and indeed the largest of all Deccani tombs in this period, is the Gol Gumbaz

110. Gol Gumbaz, mausoleum of Muhammad 'Adil Shah, Bijapur, 1656

(see fig. 110), the mausoleum (1656) of Muhammad ʿAdil Shah (*reg* 1627–56). The tomb's design is fundamentally simple: a hemispherical dome, nearly 44 m in external diameter, sits on an almost cubical mass 47.5 m square. Engaged octagonal turrets, with open arcades and capping domes, are positioned at the four corners. The cornice that runs around the building is supported on quadruple tiers of brackets. The exterior blind arches are plain except for plaster medallion-and-bracket motifs in the spandrels. The great dome is supported internally by arches in intersecting squares, exactly as in the Jamiʿ Mosque, Bijapur.

The royal tombs a short distance north-west of Golconda are the most representative examples of the distinctive Qutb Shahi style (see fig. 111). Almost all are square buildings with arcaded lower storeys supported on massive plinths, sometimes also arcaded. The lower storeys are surmounted by crenellated parapets with small bulbous minarets protruding at the corners. Rising above the interior tomb chamber are tall drums, which may be arcaded and balustraded. These support single domes, slightly bulbous in profile, rising from friezes of petals or trefoil merlon motifs. The granite building material is usually covered with plaster designs; this, and the addition of miniature arcaded galleries around the corner minarets, are typical features of the Qutb Shahi style. Among the earlier tombs is that of Jamshid Quli Qutb al-Mulk (*reg* 1543–50), which has an unusual octagonal plan. Elaborate brackets support projecting balconies on two levels. The tomb of Muhammad Quli (*reg* 1580–1612) displays sharply cut plaster decoration that combines exuberant foliate and geometric motifs. Unusual timber columns frame the entrance portals in the middle of each side. One of the last tombs, that erected for ʿAbdullah Qutb Shah (*reg* 1626–72), is a monumental pyramidal composition with almost no ornamentation.

The greatest Mughal monument in the Deccan, the Bibi ka Maqbara ('Tomb of the Queen') at AURANGABAD, was built in 1660–61 for Aurangzeb's queen. The mausoleum was obviously an imitation of the Taj Mahal at Agra, built more than a decade previously (*see* AGRA, §II, 1), but it suffers in any comparison. The Aurangabad tomb, which stands in the middle of a formal garden, is surrounded by four free-standing octagonal minarets, each topped with a

111. Qutb Shahi tombs, Golconda, 16th–17th century

small domed pavilion. The tomb itself is a decidedly vertical composition, with arched portals flanked by double arched recesses on four sides. The central dome is surrounded by smaller domed pavilions.

For painting of this period in the Deccan *see* §VI, 4(vi) below.

BIBLIOGRAPHY

H. Cousens: *Bijapur and its Architectural Remains*, Archaeol. Surv. India, Imp. Ser., xxxvii (Bombay, 1916/*R* New Delhi, 1976)

S. A. A. Bilgrami: *Landmarks of the Deccan: A Comprehensive Guide to the Archaeological Remains of the City and Suburbs of Hyderabad* (Hyderabad, 1927)

G. Yazdani: *Bidar: Its History and Monuments* (Oxford, 1947)

Z. A. Desai: 'Architecture—Bahmani Succession States'; 'Mughal Architecture in the Deccan', *History of Medieval Deccan, 1295–1724*, ed. H. K. Sherwani and P. M. Joshi (Hyderabad, 1974), ii, pp. 253–314

E. S. Merklinger: *Indian Islamic Architecture: The Deccan, 1347–1686* (Warminster, 1981)

K. Rotzer: 'Bijapur: Alimentation en eau d'une ville musulmane du Dekkan aux XIVe–XVIIe siècles', *Bull. Ecole Fr. Extrême-Orient*, lxxiii (1984), pp. 125–95

P. B. Gadre: *Cultural Archaeology of Ahmadnagar during Nizam Shahi Period (1494–1632)* (Delhi, 1986)

G. Michell, ed.: *Islamic Heritage of the Deccan* (Bombay, 1986)

GEORGE MICHELL

(b) Rajasthan and central India. Rajput rulers and their nobles sustained a highly developed court civilization and were among the most prolific architectural patrons in both these regions in the 16th to 18th centuries. These warrior clans had been powerful in north India from the mid-7th century, though with the rise of Islamic hegemony they were increasingly circumscribed, both geographically and politically.

Rajasthan. By the early 17th century all of the Rajput states in the western region now called Rajasthan had been subdued by Mughal forces. Though incorporated into the Mughal empire, the Rajput states continued to enjoy domestic autonomy. Their maharajas became, in many cases, trusted lieutenants of the Mughals while remaining paramount in their own capitals. Building projects sponsored by these rulers and their wealthy subjects ranged from temples, palaces and *hāvelīs* (mansions) to stepwells and hunting-lodges.

In earlier times temple architecture, both Hindu and Jaina, had flourished in the region at sites such as OSIAN, Dilwara (*see* MT ABU) and RANAKPUR (*see* §§5(i)(c) and 6(i)(b) above). This tradition continued in the 17th–18th century under the patronage of the maharajas and their Jaina subjects, who formed a crucial element in the administration and mercantile activities of the Rajput states. The Jagat Shiromani Temple (*c.* 1600) at AMER, built by Raja Man Singh Kachchhwaha (*reg* 1590–1614), was one of a number of temples devoted to the flourishing cult of the god Krishna. In both its dedication and its architectural style, which incorporates pointed arches and other Islamic motifs, it is related to contemporary temples at VRINDAVAN and MATHURA. The Jagannatha (or Jagdish) Temple at UDAIPUR, completed in 1652 under the patronage of Rana Jagat Singh I (*reg* 1628–52), is by comparison an exercise in revivalism, as it follows closely the form of temples built under Rajput patronage of an earlier era, such as the 11th-century Kandariya Mahadeva Temple at KHAJURAHO. This archaism accords with Udaipur's more general conservatism. The economic importance of Jainas in the desert states in particular is reflected in the central location of Jaina temples of this period in the city of BIKANER and fort of JAISALMER.

The construction of other new temples and the further embellishment of existing sites—especially those with royal associations, such as Eklingji (*see* EKLINGJI AND NAGDA)—were naturally both continuing features of the period. In scale and architectural invention, however, these projects rarely competed with those sponsored by contemporary Hindu rulers in other parts of India, such as the Vijayanagara and Nayaka rulers of the south. The special glory of Rajput patronage is, rather, palace architecture.

The fortified palaces of Rajasthan are among the finest secular buildings in north India from the later period, and they embody a distinctive architectural style. The sources for their design are varied. The few fragments of Hindu palaces built before the mid-15th century scarcely admit of stylistic analysis. Taking the archaeological evidence together with literary and visual records, however, enough can be reconstructed to show that the Rajput palaces represent the final phase of a long-sustained north Indian palace tradition. The palace builders also drew heavily for inspiration on local temple architecture and on the Islamic architecture of the neighbouring Delhi and Malwa sultanates (*see* §6(ii)(b) and (e) above).

The Rajput style interacted constantly with the Indo-Islamic mode, including the latter's Mughal phase. The Rajput builders borrowed many structural and decorative motifs from Islamic architecture, including the true arch and the balustered column, while providing in return motifs such as the dripstone (*chajjā*) and corbel capital. Further motifs—notably the cusped arch and Bengali (*baṅglā*) roof with its prominent down-turned eave—were developed jointly in both traditions. The sharing of these and other motifs created a superficial similarity between Rajput and Mughal palace architecture and led to the unsustainable description of the former as a provincial imitation of the latter. The Rajput style—distinguished by its treatment of space and conventional methods of planning and massing—had originated from a quite distinct aesthetic, and in spite of the interaction it retained its individual identity. However similar the parts become, they are typically assembled according to quite different principles.

The most important examples of Rajput palace architecture are to be found in CHITTAURGARH, UDAIPUR, BUNDI and KOTA (i) (in the southern parts of modern Rajasthan); AMER and JAIPUR (in the eastern central parts); JODHPUR, BIKANER and JAISALMER (on the fringes of the Thar Desert); and GWALIOR, Orchha and Datia (in Malwa, outside modern Rajasthan, to the east; for this last group see below). Each of these former state capitals is equipped with one major palace complex that served as the residence (and often the military retreat) of the ruler. In most cases there are in addition several minor palaces for temporary residence and pleasure. The main material in every case is stone, either dressed or plastered. As elsewhere in India at this time, the craftsmen who were responsible for these buildings were for the most part anonymous. They worked in the traditional Indian manner, in which design and execution were parts of a single

112. Palace of Rana Kumbha, Chittaurgarh, north façade, *c.* 1450

process carried out on site by a group of people organized in guilds.

Early: c. *16th century.* The earliest surviving Rajput palaces date from a period not much before the 16th century. They are a palace in the fort of Chittaurgarh built by Rana Kumbha (*reg* 1433–68; see fig. 112), and one in the fort of Gwalior built by his contemporary, Raja Kirtti Singh (*reg* 1454–79). These are among the oldest palaces in India to have survived substantially, although there is evidence of palace building going back at least to the 3rd century BC. From this evidence, enough of the character of India's ancient palaces can be deduced to show that the earliest Rajput examples owe their major functional parts and general arrangement to them. This distinctive character was sustained in 16th-century Rajput palaces, which include two built in Gwalior by Raja Man Singh Tomar (*reg* 1486–1516); the palace of Rana Ratan Singh (*reg* 1528–31) and the houses of Jaimal and Patta in Chittaurgarh (*c.* 1530–60); three palaces in Orchha (1530–1605); and the southernmost court of the palace of Amer, built by Raja Man Singh Kachchhwaha.

Rana Kumbha's palace is an aggregate of many small apartments that are informally grouped on a high substructure to afford protection. The spacious enclosure on the south side is entered through the defensive Tripolia Gate, flanked by domed and tapering octagonal towers. Similar towers articulate the walls enclosing Rana Ratan Singh's palace (at the north end of Chittaurgarh Fort), and a rounded version of them is found on Raja Man Singh's court at Amer. The recurrence of these towers in geographically and historically dispersed palaces is one example of the Rajput builders' consistency and conservatism. Another is provided by Patta's house: though built a century later than Rana Kumbha's palace, it replicates one portion of the palace as a free-standing mansion. The same portion had previously been reproduced to form the Kanwar Pade ka Mahal (Heir-apparent's Palace) that stands adjacent to the main palace, to the west.

Many of the details and motifs employed in these early buildings were taken from the temple architecture of the region. They can be compared with parts of the temples standing adjacent to the palaces or with earlier Rajput temple complexes, such as that at Khajuraho. The commonest kind of column, for example, is a simplified version of the temple column. It has a square base; a shaft that is successively octagonal, 16-sided and cylindrical; and a capital composed of corbels. Sometimes it even has the temple column's decorative carving depicting a vase (Skt *kalaśa*), bells and chains. Window openings are often of a type derived from the temple's external sculpture niche, and the cradle balcony (*jharokhā*) is similarly derived from openings in the temple's ambulatory (Skt *pradakṣiṇapatha*). The dripstone, used in place of a cornice and sometimes as a string course in the palaces, is a feature commonly found around the columned halls (*maṇḍapa*s) of medieval temples. The decorative carving in the palaces, though not bound by any strict iconographical scheme, incorporates motifs such as lotus-petal friezes, which were also common on temple plinths.

The palaces of this early period, however, differ from the temples in their treatment and assembly of these details. In a temple such details are grouped closely and in a definite programme, and the massing is heavy. The palaces are less dense in the grouping of parts, more varied in plan and more economical in construction. In the palaces there is an alternation of open and enclosed spaces, with ranges of small chambers around courtyards at various levels. In some instances the plan is controlled by a general symmetry, as in Man Singh's court in Amer, but other palaces (including Rana Kumbha's) are entirely irregular, with apartments arranged in a picturesque assembly.

The palaces are further distinguished from their temple progenitors by the pronounced influence of the Islamic architecture in the neighbouring sultanates. The single most transforming element of Islamic influence on the secular tradition of indigenous architecture was the introduction of the true, or radiating, arch. Though perhaps known previously, the true arch was rare; even at this date it was not employed conspicuously, though use was made of its technological advantages (for example in the huge vaulted substructures of some of the palaces). The structural dome was a more visible feature, copied from the same source. Further Islamic influence is apparent in architectural decoration, especially coloured tilework, though often the technique employed Indian motifs (*see* §VIII, 5(ii) below). More generally, the effect of sultanate architecture was seemingly to make Rajput design more experimental, by presenting Hindu craftsmen with alternatives to their own traditions. But the disparate sources of early Rajput palace design were not always resolved into a homogeneous style; sometimes richly carved brackets and corbels were juxtaposed oddly with severe pointed arches and domes.

Middle: c. *17th century.* A more successful fusion of the various sources into a resolved style was achieved in a middle phase corresponding roughly to the 17th century. The major fortified palace complexes in the Rajput state capitals were mostly built over very long periods of time, as successive maharajas of each dynasty added their own suites of rooms, often altering or destroying those of their predecessors. Most have some parts dating from the 17th century (though these may be disguised under the accretions of later periods).

In the palace of Amer, Mirza Raja Jai Singh (*reg* 1623–67) added the Divan-i ʻAm (Pers.: 'common hall', audience hall), an impressive columned hall constructed of red and buff sandstones and cream marble. The same patron was responsible for the palace's central court, where the Jess Mandir and Jai Mandir together form a two-storey marble pavilion that faces a terrace with a fountain and formal garden. In the Udaipur Palace (see fig. 113), the Chandra Mahal, Dilkushal Mahal and Mor Chowk with its flanking chambers were all added early in the 17th century (though much of their decoration is later), and the Badi Mahal was added at the end of the century. In the last, the most

113. Udaipur Palace, east façade, begun *c.* 1570

elegant courtyard of the palace, a marble cloister surrounds a hanging garden with a central tank. In Jodhpur, extensive women's apartments (Pers. *zanānā*) were added to the palace during the reign of Maharaja Jaswant Singh (*reg* 1638–78); these are distinguished by the particularly intricate stone-carving that covers whole façades, turning them into lacelike screens (see fig. 114). In Jaisalmer, apartments were added to the palace in the fort around the Hawa Pol, including the somewhat archaic Juna Mahal. In the Bikaner Palace, the Lal Niwas is one of the few apartments surviving from the early 17th century; the Karan Mahal was added about 1650 and the Anup Mahal at the end of the century. All three are small audience halls with increasingly sumptuous decoration. In the Bundi Palace (see fig. 115), the robustly styled Ratan Daulat Hall was added at the beginning of the century and the more delicate Chatar Mahal and the Chitra Shali in the middle. The earliest parts of the Kota Palace, dating from the reign of Rao Madho Singh (*reg* 1625–48), include the Hathian Pol (the palace's main entrance, embellished with sculptures of elephants), the Arjun Mahal and the majestically scaled Raj Mahal.

Each of these palaces is strictly divided on lines of gender. The *zanānā* was intended for the accommodation of women—for the maharaja's usually numerous wives, other female relations and their female servants. It is often subdivided into independent apartments for individual maharanis and is provided with its own entrance and a temple. The male domain (*mardānā*) is divided into a public area, with a Divan-i ʿAm, and the private residence of the maharaja. The latter might include a Chitra Shala (Skt: 'painted gallery') and Sheesh Mahal (Pers.: 'mirror palace'), decorated with glass and used as a bedroom. Though usually the most frequently remodelled and most lavishly embellished part of the palace, the male domain is in many cases smaller than the women's quarters, reflecting its smaller number of permanent residents.

114. Fort Palace, Jodhpur, women's apartments, 1630s

An impression of how the palaces were originally furnished and used can be obtained from contemporary miniature paintings depicting palace interiors. These indicate that furnishings were almost entirely soft: carpets and bolsters were strewn on the floor, blinds were hung over arcades, canopies were stretched over courtyards; there was little solid furniture. The ease with which such trappings could be rearranged enhanced the versatility of the rooms. Many rooms were designed to serve a range of domestic activities; this is reflected in their names, which refer not to their functions but to their patrons.

In the course of the 17th century, certain changes occurred in the repertory of architectural details and motifs. The temple column (a patently archaic form) was used less, often supplanted by a simple pier or by a balustered and fluted column borrowed from Mughal architecture. The Bengali roof was introduced, especially in Amer and the desert states (Jodhpur, Bikaner and Jaisalmer). The cusped arch was used increasingly in place of the lintel or corbelled arch (though the construction remained technically trabeate, for the arches were commonly too small to require voussoir construction). These changes meant that the Rajput style kept pace with Mughal architecture. These two traditions, which drew from common sources, namely the Hindu temple tradition and early sultanate architecture, remained related as they developed—a relationship characterized not by the dominant influence of one over the other but by mutual awareness and creative interaction.

Though the Rajput and Mughal palace styles each achieved a synthesis of antecedent indigenous and Islamic sources, the results are quite different, exhibiting a number of distinguishing features. At the level of superficial details, the decoration differs. Though Mughal-style schemes were sometimes attempted in Rajput palaces, the more typical Rajput decoration is based on local folk art. The painting of walls, doors and shutters and the mirrorwork of the Sheesh Mahals often employ the motifs and patterns of local handicrafts and embroidery. While mature Mughal decoration is generally impeccably refined, Rajput decoration, even at its most sophisticated as in Chitra Shala murals—tends to be bold in scale, vivid in colouring and seemingly casual in design. Its subject-matter is often religious: the amours of Krishna are a favourite theme, and images of the god Ganesha are also common. Even some of the features that are common to the two styles are employed differently. In Mughal palaces, pierced stone screens (*jālīs*) are used as a decorative and shading device, most commonly in the male domain (they are also used in the verandahs of Mughal tombs). In Rajput palaces they are used in the women's apartments, where they facilitated the inhabitants' seclusion.

The more fundamental differences between the Rajput and Mughal styles, however, concern planning and the

115. Bundi Palace, south façade, mostly 17th century

relation of parts. While a Mughal palace consists of detached pavilions, in a Rajput palace the apartments are linked in a single congeries. The parts of a Mughal palace are usually formally grouped. A few of the Rajput palaces are symmetrical in plan, but in most the parts adhere in complex and irregular patterns, the result not only of the palaces' piecemeal growth over time but also of a deliberate evasion of predictable symmetry and a preference for picturesque and varied grouping. Mughal palaces were built on level ground, while most Rajput palaces were built on hillsides and exploit changes in height for both defensive and aesthetic ends. Each Mughal palace is surrounded by an outer fortification wall, but while many Rajput palaces are similarly situated within or adjacent to forts, there are always additional fortifications contiguous with the palace buildings themselves, as integral parts of their structure.

On a few occasions, it is true, a Rajput maharaja commissioned a palace apartment in the Mughal style: the court of the Jai Mandir in the Amer Palace, for example, is a fairly close imitation of Shah Jahan's Anguri Bagh in Agra Fort (*see* AGRA, §II, 3). Like Akbar's commissioning of the Rajput-style women's apartments at FATEHPUR SIKRI, this indicates that the attachment of patrons to particular styles could be loose. But such trading of styles between their customary patrons did not diminish the differences between the styles themselves.

In addition to the major palaces described above, most of the Rajput capitals contain a number of lesser palaces. These include further women's apartments, such as the Taleti Mahal in Jodhpur (early 17th century); hunting-lodges, such as the Sikar Burj in Bundi (18th century); gardens with pavilions, such as the Ek Thamba Mahal at Mandor (early 18th century); and summer retreats by water, such as the Jag Mandir in Udaipur (begun in the 1620s) and the Amar Sagar Palace outside Jaisalmer (late 17th century). In the details of their architectural style, these small pleasure palaces closely follow the larger ones, but they generally have few storeys and are more open and unprotected, lacking fortifications.

Examples of other types of buildings also survive from the middle phase. The sites of royal (and to some degree other) funeral pyres are marked by cenotaphs (*devals*). These are popularly known as *chatrīs* ('umbrellas', domed pavilions) because they commonly take the form of this standard architectural feature, placed over a platform. Among the countless examples throughout the region, especially impressive groups are to be found at Bada Bagh outside Jaisalmer, Devi Kund outside Bikaner and Ahar outside Udaipur. The cenotaphs of the rulers of Jodhpur, at Mandor, depart from the usual pattern and are formed like temples.

Buildings also include the architectural adjuncts of wells and of artificial lakes constructed for both royal pleasure and public benefit. Stepwells, such as the Raniji ki Talab in Bundi, are often highly complex architectural conceptions, sometimes enriched with elaborate decorative carving. The dams of lakes are usually provided with broad steps into the water (*ghāts*) and may be embellished with pavilions, as at Rajsamand, north of Udaipur (1660s). A few examples of courtyard houses (Hindi *hāvelīs*) built in the cities by nobles and rich merchants also survive from this period.

Late: c. *18th century.* Although the Rajput style reached a level of maturity in the 17th century, building activity continued copiously in the region in a late phase corresponding roughly to the 18th century. Some entirely new palaces were built. The city and palace of Jaipur were begun in 1727, when the Kachchhwaha Rajputs moved their capital there from Amer, and the palace of Bharatpur (1733) and garden palace at Dig (1760s) were built in the Rajput style, though under the patronage of Jats.

The laying out of the city of Jaipur on a fresh site provided the opportunity for a remarkable fulfilment of planning principles dictated by ancient *śilpa śāstras* (Skt: architectural treatises; *see* §I, 10 above), an exercise that in part reflected the scholarly interests of the patron, Maharaja Sawai Jai Singh II (*reg* 1700–43). The palace centres on a seven-storey block, the Chandra Mahal, again fulfilling shastric convention; subsequent additions to it, however, reveal a turning to Mughal planning principles, with independent pavilions in courtyards. The Bharatpur Palace follows the standard type of high-walled, fortified block. Rather more innovative is the palace at Dig, built by Raja Suraj Mal (*reg* 1755–63). The most sophisticated of Rajasthan's garden palaces, it ingeniously combines Mughal and local garden conventions and even makes architectural allusions to a Hindu literary tradition concerned with the monsoon season.

This period also saw considerable extension and redecoration in older palaces. In the palace at Jodhpur, Maharaja Ajit Singh (*reg* 1707–24) added many apartments, including the Daulat Khana, Moti Mahal and Sheesh Mahal. The Phul Mahal was added later in the century. In the Kota Palace, the Bhim Mahal and Bada Mahal were added by Rao Bhim Singh (*reg* 1707–20). In Bikaner, the additions to the palace made by Maharaja Gaj Singh (*reg* 1745–87) include the Gaj Mandir. In the Udaipur Palace at this period there was extensive remodelling and redecoration of existing apartments, especially those around Mor Chowk and in the Dilkushal Mahal. Such remodelling was a common habit in many of the Rajput capitals and continued into the 19th century; the designs usually sustained something of the traditional Rajput exuberance.

The palaces mentioned are only the most impressive among a much larger number: other examples are to be found in the capitals of smaller states, such as Dungarpur and Deolia, and in the provincial towns that were controlled by the maharajas' chief nobles, such as Samod (north of Jaipur). These too generally cover long historical spans; in the 18th century many of them were decorated with fine murals. Many courtyard houses also survive from this period. Especially notable are those in Jaipur and the towns of Shekhawati District. The plan of these houses was adapted to create a new form of temple architecture, of which there are examples in the important pilgrimage towns of Nathdwara and Pushkar.

In some respects this period of frantic productivity was also one of stylistic decline. Features such as balconies, domed pavilions and arcades formerly had given façades great depth and openness. But on later buildings, surfaces

116. Patua ki Haveli, Jaisalmer, façade, *c.* 1805

tend to be flat, and details too are flattened and sometimes rendered only as carved relief decoration. The features are smaller and multiplied in number, so that they do not fulfil their original functions but form a decorative crust. This last development is most marked in some buildings of about 1800, including the Hawa Mahal in Jaipur (1799) and the houses of merchants and ministers in Jaisalmer, such as the Patua ki Haveli (*c.* 1805; see fig. 116) and Salim Singh ki Haveli (*c.* 1815). What had been lost in architectonics was made up for in decorative wealth. This situation was to persist until the transformations wrought by European influence in the late 19th century.

For painting of this period in Rajasthan *see* §VI, 5(iii) below.

BIBLIOGRAPHY

J. Tod: *Annals and Antiquities of Rajast'han*, 2 vols (London, 1829–32, 4/1972)
L. Rousselet: *India and its Native Princes*, ed. Lt. Col. Buckle (London, 1876)
J. P. Stratton: *Chitor and the Mewar Family* (Allahabad, 1881)
F. L. Mehta: *Handbook of Meywar and Guide to its Principal Objects of Interest* (Bombay, 1888)
S. S. Jacob: *Jeypore Portfolio of Architectural Details*, 12 vols (London, 1890–1913)
B. J. Sahai: *History of Bhurtpore* (Calcutta, 1898)
A. Adams: *The Western Rajputana States* (London, 1899)
O. Reuther: *Indische Paläste und Wohnhäuser* (Berlin, 1925)
B. N. Reu: *Glories of Marwar and the Glorious Rathors* (Jodhpur, 1943)
H. Goetz: *The Art and Architecture of Bikaner State* (Oxford, 1950)
R. C. Agrawala: 'Some Famous Sculptors and Architects of Mewar', *Ind. Hist. Q.*, xxxiii (1957), pp. 321–34

S. Toy: *The Strongholds of India* (London, 1957)
G. S. Ghurye: *Rajput Architecture* (Bombay, 1968)
M. C. Joshi: *Dig* (New Delhi, 1968, 2/1971/*R* 1982)
G. N. Sharma: *Social Life in Medieval Rajasthan* (Agra, 1968)
K. C. Jain: *Ancient Cities and Towns of Rajasthan* (Delhi, 1972)
B. M. Singh Parmar: 'Murals of Hadaoti', *Cultural Contours of Hadaoti*, ed. Gahlot (Jodhpur, 1976), pp. 35–8
R. A. Agarawala: *Marwar Murals* (Delhi, 1977)
A. K. Roy: 'The Dream and the Plan', *Marg*, xxx/4 (1977), pp. 25–6
H. Goetz: *Rajput Art and Architecture*, ed. J. Jain and J. Jain-Neubauer (Wiesbaden, 1978)
A. K. Roy: *History of the Jaipur City* (New Delhi, 1978)
R. A. Agarawala: *History, Art and Architecture of Jaisalmer* (Delhi, 1979)
A. Topsfield: *Painting from Rajasthan in the National Gallery of Victoria* (Melbourne, 1980)
V. S. Srivastava: 'Junagadha Fort, Bikaner', *Son of the Soil, Maharaja Ganga Singh*, ed. Y. P. Singh (Bikaner, 1981), pp. 225–8
M. Carapetian: 'Jaipur: The Pink City', *Archit. Rev.*, clxxii/1027 (1982), pp. 35–43
A. Nath and F. Wacziarg: *Rajasthan: The Painted Walls of Shekhavati* (New Delhi, 1982)
R. M. Cimino, ed.: *Life at Court in Rajasthan* (Florence, 1985)
G. H. R. Tillotson: *The Rajput Palaces: The Development of an Architectural Style, 1450–1750* (London, 1987)
S. Gole: *Indian Maps and Plans: From Earliest Times to the Advent of European Surveys* (New Delhi, 1989)
G. H. R. Tillotson: 'The Rajput Aesthetic', *South Asian Archaeology 1987*, ed. M. Taddei (Rome, 1990), pp. 1165–80

Gwalior, Orchha and Datia. In central India in the 16th–17th century, the patronage of Rajput maharajas was responsible for a number of palaces and other structures. Sharing important design features, these constitute a coherent series and present a variation on the Rajput style established by the more numerous contemporary buildings of Rajasthan (see above).

The earliest in the series is the Man Mandir in the fort of Gwalior (*see* GWALIOR, fig. 2), residence of the Tomar Rajput ruler Raja Man Singh (*reg* 1486–1516). Its eastern face, some 90 m long, forms a part of the fort's curtain wall and overlooks the ascent ramp. In the northern part of the palace, a spacious courtyard is surrounded by plain chambers for the accommodation of servants. The royal area, at the southern end, has many small apartments grouped around two small internal courts, roughly 10 and 11 m sq. respectively. These rooms and their elevations on to the courts are all profusely decorated with carving and tilework. Many of the motifs, especially of the carving, are unique in palace architecture; they are derived, with modifications, from temple decoration. In a similar manner, the pronounced corrugated dripstones (*chajjās*) are an exaggerated version of the 11th-century ribbed dripstones on the smaller of the Sas Bahu temples within the fort. The tile decoration is most extensive on the exterior walls. The dominant blue colour and the technique are both derived from the architecture of the Malwa sultanate (especially that of its northern capital, CHANDERI), but the motifs include such traditional Indian emblems as ducks, crocodiles and elephants. The influence of Chanderi is also responsible for the engaged and domed round towers and for some internal structural techniques. The main courts of the palace are at a raised level, with dimly lit apartments below. In the outwork of the fort, Man Singh also built a separate *zanānā* (women's quarters), the Gujari Mahal. This shares many of the stylistic features of the Man Mandir, but is even more regular in plan, with apartments grouped symmetrically about a square courtyard.

117. Jahangir Mandir, Orchha, interior, *c.* 1605

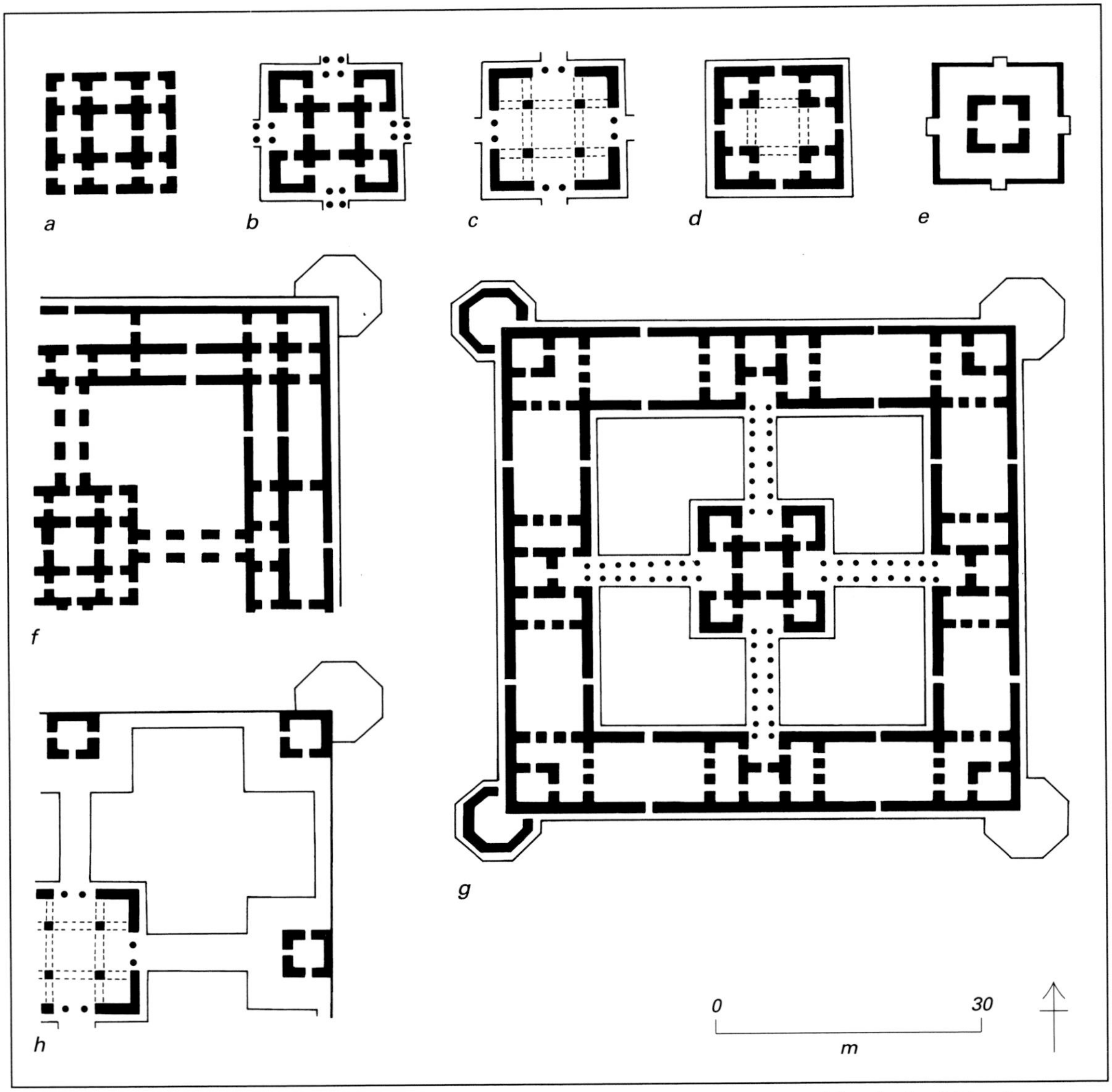

118. Plans of Govind Mandir, Datia, *c.* 1620: (a)–(e) floor plans of the central tower with (a) at ground-floor level and (e) at the uppermost level; (f) north-east quadrant at ground-floor level; (g) building plan at first-floor level; (h) north-east quadrant at second-floor level

In 1518 Sultan Ibrahim Lodi (*reg* 1517–26) successfully concluded a two-year siege of Gwalior, and from this point (until 1754) the city remained in the possession of the Delhi sultanate. While this put an end to Rajput patronage at the site, the existing buildings continued to exert an influence. Man Singh's palaces are distinguished from most of the palaces in Rajasthan by their regular plans and by their high outer walls, relieved by ornament but without openings—so that the palace's external appearance is that of a decorated, boxlike fortress. These features were sustained and developed in the palaces of the adjacent Rajput state to the south, Bundelkhand.

The earliest of three palaces at Orchha, the former capital of Bundelkhand, is the Ramji Mandir (1531–54). Though partly collapsed and much altered through conversion into a temple, its original design is still apparent. Regular ranges in two storeys surround an open, square courtyard, while on the roof of the upper storey stand detached, square chambers, capped by domes. This basic pattern was repeated and complicated in the second palace in the group, the Raj Mandir (1554–91), built on an island in the Betwa River. The centre of each range was brought forward to create a more varied plan and complex internal massing, but without abandoning the overall square form and strict symmetry. The outer retaining wall still has few openings and pronounced string courses.

The pattern developed in these buildings was followed elsewhere. Variations on it include the court of the women's quarters in the UDAIPUR Palace (*c.* 1570) and the southern court of the AMER Palace. Also belonging to this sequence is the *zanānā* court at FATEHPUR SIKRI known as Jodh Bai's Palace (*c.* 1571). (An earlier instance of this region providing ideas for early Mughal architecture is the echo of the inner courts of Gwalior's Man Mandir in the interior of the 'Jahangiri Mahal' in the Agra Fort (*c.* 1565).) The pattern was continued further in Orchha with the construction of the Jahangir Mandir (*c.* 1605; see fig. 117), built by Raja Bir Singh Deo (*reg* 1605–27) and named in honour of his imperial Mughal patron, Jahangir. In the Jahangir Mandir the plan was slightly modified and enlarged, but it retains the ranges (with alternating apartments and terraces) and the domed square chambers at the top.

After long experimentation, the pattern achieved an apotheosis in the Govind Mandir, built by the same patron towards the end of his reign (*c.* 1620) at Datia (24 km north-west of Orchha). The Govind Mandir closely reproduces the arrangement of the Jahangir Mandir with one transforming difference: in the centre of the courtyard rises a five-storey tower (for plan see fig. 118). This contains the main royal apartments and is linked to the surrounding ranges by bridges. While maintaining symmetry, this addition enormously complicates the internal massing and enhances the dynamics of the design; it also ingeniously adapts both the form and meaning of the *maṇḍala* (Skt: cosmological diagram) on which the plans of the whole sequence of Bundelkhand palaces are based. The plastered and tiled surfaces within the Govind Mandir have deteriorated, but in terms of planning it is one of the most arresting buildings in India.

Scarcely less remarkable than its palaces is the state's major contribution to temple architecture, the Chaturbuj Temple in Orchha (1558–73). Its gigantic massing and plain surfaces relieved by arched openings make it a singular object in temple design, though it has some affinities with contemporary temples at VRINDAVAN, MATHURA and Amer. The use of Islamic forms is especially bold: a large, sultanate-style dome nestles among the temple towers (*śikhara*s). South of the temple, strung out along the riverbank, are the cenotaphs (*deval*s) of the state's rulers. Departing from the usual domed pavilion (*chatrī*) pattern, each of these is a square-planned, two-storey structure, surmounted by four large domed chambers around a central conical tower like a *śikhara*. The largest of the group (partly ruined) is that of Bir Singh Deo.

BIBLIOGRAPHY

A. Cunningham: *Four Reports Made during the Years 1862, 63, 64, 65*, ii (Simla, 1871), pp. 330–53
L. Griffin: *Famous Monuments of Central India* (London, 1891)
M. B. Garde: *A Handbook of Gwalior* (Gwalior, 1936)
H. Goetz: 'Bundela Art' (1938), repr. in *Rajput Art and Architecture*, ed. J. Jain and J. Jain-Neubauer (Wiesbaden, 1978)
P. Brown: *Indian Architecture: Islamic Period* (?Bombay, [1942], rev. Bombay, 1956 with additional photographs)
P. Chetwode: 'Orchha: A City Left to the Jungle'; 'Assassin's Palace at Datia', *Country Life*, clxii/4191–2 (1977), pp. 1194–5, 1284–5
K. Chakravarty: *Art of India: Orchha* (Delhi, 1984)
——: *Gwalior Fort: Art, Culture and History* (Delhi, 1984)
D. P. Kambo and R. Rewal: 'Datia and Orchha', *Architecture in India*, ed. R. Rewal and others (Paris, 1985), pp. 46–51
G. H. R. Tillotson: *The Rajput Palaces: The Development of an Architectural Style, 1450–1750* (London, 1987)
D. H. A. Kloff: *Naukar, Rajput and Sepoy* (New York, 1990)

G. H. R. TILLOTSON

(*c*) *Gujarat.* In the 18th century, as the Mughal empire disintegrated, the Maratha armies of the Gaekwad, Holkar and Scindia moved into the northern and western parts of the subcontinent. In Gujarat they were led by Damaji Gaekwad I. The administrative headquarters of the Marathas was initially Songadh, then Patan. The seat of power was transferred to Baroda (now Vadodara) after the death of Damaji Gaekwad II (*reg* 1734–68) in 1768. In subsequent years there were constant struggles for the throne, but this changed with the accession of Sayajirao III in 1875. Thereafter British architects and designers (particularly Charles Mant (1839–81) and ROBERT FELLOWES CHISHOLM) were responsible for most of the important state buildings constructed.

The Marathas contributed little to the architecture of Gujarat. Their most significant introduction was the *wada*, a form of residential dwelling that developed in almost all areas ruled by the Marathas. In Gujarat it is found predominantly in Baroda and other major centres of Maratha power. Though the origin of the *wada* can be traced to the ordinary rural house, it came to be associated with royalty, the nobility and their confidants, and owing to its political and economic importance, Baroda became a city where many *wada*s were built. The earliest surviving example dates from around 1750. All are known by family names and almost all have become multi-family dwellings.

A *wada* is basically a house built around a courtyard. Entry is through a large, deep gate, which has a cattle shed and hay store on one side and a caretaker's room on the other. The courtyard, both a circulation and a social space, is usually lined with columns. Behind the colonnade is the living area. The upper floor has a narrow circulation space connecting the rooms on that storey. The balcony forming this space often projects into the courtyard. The upper façades have a number of door-type windows. The first floor is usually provided with a long, decorated room serving as a 'darbar hall', or office, the prime domain of male family members. A family temple, a small room for arms and sleeping quarters on the upper storeys are other common features. Segregation of male and female domains was achieved by carefully positioned staircases. The number of staircases, their location and accessibility forced a fixed pattern of movement and increased privacy. These architectural elements constituted the basic parts of the *wada*; any expansion was achieved by varying the number of courtyards and other key features. The height of the plinths and decorative articulation of woodwork reflected the owner's status.

Horse carriages and animals were often kept in the adjoining property, where there were quarters for both servants and attendants. Stone was used for plinths and column bases, with brick and mud or lime mortar for walls and wood for the structure. Wooden columns and half columns were embedded in the wall so as to show on the wall surface. The columns and beams were finished, while unfinished timbers were often used as joists for the floors. These joists were covered with wooden planks or stone slabs, which were in turn covered with a thick layer of mud with brick rubble. The final layer was of cowdung mixed with clay; this served as a good insulation for heat and sound.

The Bhadra, the original palace at Baroda, was converted into a *wada* by the Gaekwad; its spaces are organized around two courtyards and seven staircases. The first Maratha palace was the Sarkar Wada (*c.* 1780–1800). With the longest wooden façades in the city, it is organized around three courtyards and has a number of staircases. Bhaskar Vithalrao Wada is a two-courtyard structure with nine staircases embedded in walls a metre thick. Bhau Shinde Wada has a rural character with two courtyards set lengthwise; the first is residential, while the second contains a free-standing temple. Tambekar Wada (mid-19th century; see fig. 119) is a single-courtyard structure with four staircases, the front wing being three-storey, and has a remarkable series of wall paintings in the first floor 'darbar hall' (audience hall).

Perhaps the most notable example of these residential buildings is the Oze Wada (*c.* first quarter of the 19th century). This is a 33.5×45.7-m structure with three courtyards and an ancillary building with an additional courtyard. It has a long, colonnaded corridor with three entry steps on the side nearest the road. The original ground floor was a predominantly transparent space with free-standing columns. The right wing has a family temple six bays wide and ten bays long, beside which is a small courtyard with priestly family houses; the middle bays are opened to double height, the upper portion being used by the women of the family. A family temple of this type is typical of *wada*s in Gujarat. Four flights of main staircases serve the house, rendering the side nearest the road into the male domain, while the female quarters are at the rear. On the road side a staircase leads up to the 'darbar hall', which consists of a wide bay flanked by two narrow aisles; the hall has decorated columns and ceiling. On the road side as well as in the courtyard, the door-type windows open on to a narrow circulation balcony cantilevered from the ground-floor columns.

119. Tambekar Wada, Vadodara, front façade, 19th century

In spite of prolonged Muslim rule in Gujarat, the majority Hindu and Jaina population was able to pursue its religion. Their temples continued to be built, one of the significant forms being the *hāvelī* temple. In Hindu mythology, a temple is treated as a divine residence as well as a cosmological statement. This residential aspect was elaborated by a Vaishnava sect in the *hāvelī* temple, a form seen as a replica of Lord Krishna's home. The temple is seen as a symbolic manifestation of places and spaces associated with the daily and seasonal life of Krishna, especially the Vraj Bhumi in Mathura, the place where Krishna is believed to have been born. In plan and spatial articulation it has the quality of a *hāvelī*—a residence with added elements of the royal palace as well as the privacy required for a temple. The Lord is treated as a living being, gently awakened with music, dressed, sent to graze the cows, given lunch, rested in the afternoon, offered recreation and put to bed, each activity constituting a separate ritual. The sect's devotional focus is the Lord as a child of up to eleven and a half years of age.

In studying the temple form, the physical manifestation of these rituals becomes clear. A complete *hāvelī* temple consists of the following elements. Above the first gateway is the music room, behind which are the Govardhan court, where some festivals are celebrated, and entrance steps guarded by lions and the welcoming gate flanked by peacocks and elephants. This is in the form of a long colonnade where devotees could meet. Through the Vaikunth (Heaven) Door is the Vraj court, where devotees gather for prayers. The water place (Jamuna Tat), the swing room and the rooms for milk, flowers, ornaments, storage etc are located on three sides of the Brij court. In the front flank is located the sanctum. A private temple, evening prayer temple and sleeping quarters are located around the core. The ground floor is strictly for use as a temple, but the first floor and higher floors are used by the Maharaj Shri (the person looking after the Lord); the *hāvelī* is often owned by his family. The development of devotional theism in the 16th century was the prime reason for the development of this temple form that departed from the traditional monumental typology, i.e. caused the removal of spires, turrets and domes.

The *hāvelī* temple is found in most parts of Gujarat, Saurashtra and Rajasthan. One example is the Gokulnathji Temple, constructed in the mid-19th century in one of the richest parts of Nadiad. It has a high plinth, and the ground floor opens to the street via large windows in a colonnaded verandah. The balconies, the distinguishing element in the façade, are typical of *hāvelī*s. Devotional spaces are located on the northern side, organized in the same order as described above. The first floor is used for residential purposes, while the floor above is for storage. In this trabeate structural system, wood is used for all structural members. Some external walls are thick brick walls; in other parts brick infilling can be seen. The flooring was originally of stone.

BIBLIOGRAPHY

J. Burgess and H. Cousens: *The Architectural Antiquities of Northern Gujarat, More Especially of the Districts Included in the Baroda State* (Delhi, 1903)
C. Batley: *Indian Architecture* (London, 1934)
M. S. Mate: *Maratha Architecture, 1650 A.D. to 1850 A.D.* (diss., Poona, U. Poona, 1959)
V. S. Pramar: *Wooden Houses and Mansions of Gujarat* (Ahmadabad, 1989)
S. Khandwala: *A Study of Haveli Mandirs of Gujarat* (diss., Ahmadabad, School of Architecture, C.E.P.T., 1993)

MIKI DESAI

(d) East.

Orissa. At the beginning of the 17th century, much of Orissa was brought under the control of the Garhjat dynasty, which established a series of feudatory states. These remained more or less independent during the Mughal, Maratha and even British periods. While the Garhjat chiefs never attained the glory of their predecessors, they acted as temple sponsors over a period of more than two centuries. This was not, however, an era of innovation in sacred architecture; temples were small in scale and usually influenced by earlier Orissan architectural traditions (*see* §§5(i)(e) and 6(i)(d) above).

The dominant form was the towered sanctuary, with a curvilinear spire (*śikhara*) topped by a large, ribbed, circular crowning element (*āmalaka*) and pot finial (*kalaśa*). Generally the outer surface of the spire was provided with shallow projections in the middle of each side, sometimes also a reduced model of the overall tower in relief. While smaller towers were usually unadorned, the surfaces of larger examples were entirely covered with narrow horizontal mouldings. The sanctum was approached through one or more square halls; each had a pyramidal roof, characteristically divided by deep recesses into horizontal eave-like mouldings. Lion-like beasts sometimes projected outwards from the middle of each side; at the summit was a pot finial. Interiors were massive and plain, dominated by corbelled ceilings.

Typical examples of the late Orissan temple style are seen in the towns that served as headquarters for the chieftains of the different feudatory states. Temples were often dedicated to Jagannatha, originally a god worshipped only at PURI. By the beginning of the 18th century, however, Jagannatha was established as a deity of regional importance. At Ranpur, Baramba and Keonijhar, for instance, Jagannatha temples erected in the 18th century demonstrate the survival of the earlier Orissan style. But there was no accompanying sculptural tradition. The outer surfaces of the buildings are invariably plain.

BIBLIOGRAPHY

A. Eschmann, H. Kulke and G. C. Tripathi: *The Cult of Ragannatha and the Regional Tradition of Orissa* (New Delhi, 1978)

Bengal. The Hindu revival inspired by the teachings of Chaitanya, the 16th-century Bengali saint, led to a renewal of temple building in that region. Such construction continued to flourish during the British period, diminishing only at the end of the 19th century. In the 17th century the main patrons were the local Malla rulers of BISHNUPUR. Economic and social changes in the 18th and 19th centuries, resulting mainly from the wealth generated from trade with Europe, led to the emergence of a new élite of local landowners (*zamīndār*s), who became the main sponsors of temple building.

The temples of this period form a distinctive group that inherited both Islamic and Hindu techniques and forms. As in earlier Islamic architecture in the region (*see* §6(ii)(d) above), brick was the chief building material. Arches, domes and vaulted forms, derived from mosque and temple architecture, were of particular importance in roofing interior space. From Hindu traditions, especially those of neighbouring Orissa, came the curvilinear spire, its outer surfaces divided into horizontal mouldings. Influences from European architecture, especially Neo-classical elements, were also absorbed by the beginning of the 18th century. These included pilasters and mouldings applied in lime plaster to building exteriors. But by far the most important stylistic influence was indigenous. The typical Bengali hut (*baṅglā*), with its curved ridge and cornice, was usually constructed of bamboo and thatch. Widely imitated in masonry (in both mosques and temples), the sloping roof with curved ridge and cornice became the most obvious feature of the Bengal style. The interaction of these different traditions resulted in an astonishing variety of temple forms.

In the 17th and 18th centuries, in particular, a vivid terracotta art (*see* §VII, 18 below) was used in temple decoration. Façades were covered with small bricks and plaques illustrating mythological episodes, narrative epics and scenes from daily life. Pastimes of the élite—processions, boating, receptions and hunting parties—were a common subject, perhaps reflecting the habits or aspirations of donors. Designs also included deities, attendant and guardian figures and a host of ornamental motifs. The animation and diversity of such terracotta decoration testify to the continued vitality of artistic tradition in the region.

The Raghunatha Temple (1633) at Ghurisa, an early example of the style, consists of a single domed chamber roofed with a pyramidal vault; above each wall are curved cornices. A variant of this scheme, the contemporary Radha Vallabha Temple at Krishnanagar, has a central domed chamber approached through a triple-arched entrance. Above the walls are curved cornices; rising on the roof is an upper chamber capped with a pyramidal roof. No figurative themes are depicted in the terracotta decoration, which is restricted to stylized foliate and geometric motifs, thus betraying the influence of earlier Muslim practice in the region. A slightly later development of this scheme, the Vasudeva Temple (1679) at Bansberia, has a central domed chamber surrounded by verandahs on three sides. Elevated on the roof is an octagonal pavilion with a pyramidal vault. Terracotta ornamentation on the principal façade includes images of the god Krishna as well as friezes depicting scenes from the epics and secular subjects.

The numerous monuments at Bishnupur, capital of the local Malla rulers, illustrate the range of temple forms that had developed by the mid-17th century. One of the finest examples is the Shyama Raya Temple (1643), which was built on two levels. On the lower level a central domed chamber is approached through vaulted verandahs on each side, which form small chambers at the corners; the upper level has an octagonal chamber roofed with a

120. Keshta Raya Temple, Bishnupur, 1655

pyramidal vault and four detached smaller towered chambers at the corners. Each façade has a triple-arched entrance capped by a curved cornice. Terracotta ornamentation is elaborate and decorates the verandahs and sanctum as well as the exterior walls. Frequently repeated depictions include Krishna with the cowherds and scenes from the *Rāmāyaṇa*. The Keshta Raya Temple (1655) at Bishnupur illustrates particularly clearly the impact of local traditions (see fig. 120). Laid out as a double hut (*jor baṅglā*), the building appears from the outside as two large vaulted chambers, each with curved ridges and cornices; above rises a smaller square chamber with a pyramidal roof. In contrast the interior has a single central domed chamber surrounded by vaulted corridors.

Indigenous influence is also evident in an 18th-century monument at Baranagar. Four hut-like brick temples are arranged around a square court facing each other. Each is roofed with a curved vault and entered through a triple-arched verandah. The principal façades are covered with terracotta plaques, many depicting epic battles from the *Rāmāyaṇa*.

During the 18th century temple architecture in Bengal developed variant schemes. At KALNA, for instance, the Lalji (1739) and Krishna Chandra (1751–2) temples are multi-storey constructions, each with 25 miniature towers distributed on three ascending roof levels. Each miniature tower has a curved profile (derived from the curvilinear spire) and is adorned with horizontal mouldings. Beneath, domed sanctuaries are flanked by vaulted chambers; projecting entrance porches are roofed with curved, hut-like vaults.

By the 19th century, temple forms generally had been reduced in scale and somewhat simplified. A fine example is the Pratapeshvara Temple (1849), also at Kalna. It consists of a single chamber above which rises a curved spire, enlivened with typical narrow mouldings. Horizontal cornices replace the more usual curved variety. Each façade is richly embellished with delicately modelled terracotta plaques.

The impact of Neo-classical elements on 19th-century temple architecture is evident in the Gopala Lakshmi Temple at Ghurisa. The building has a Neo-classical socle and pilasters, and the cornices are all of Neo-classical design. Nine curved turrets on two levels create a pyramidal roof composition. Sculptures are of plaster; socle friezes include figures in European dress.

BIBLIOGRAPHY

G. Michell, ed.: *Brick Temples of Bengal: From the Archives of David McCutchion* (Princeton, 1983)

Assam and Tripura. Temple forms developed independently in Assam and Tripura, drawing inspiration from both Bengal and the Buddhist traditions of neighbouring Burma. An interesting example is the temple at the pilgrimage centre on Kamakhya Hill near Gauhati, capital of the Koch rulers of western Assam. Though established in the 16th century, most of the present building dates from a later period. The temple presents a long, low elevation divided into a sanctum and three halls, each with a differently shaped roof. Octagonal and 16-sided dome-like towers rise over the sanctum and adjoining hall. Constructed of brick, these towers are divided into horizontal layers by mouldings and capped with tiers of pot finials. The second hall has a hut-like roof with curved cornices; the outermost apsidal hall has a long, low roof. Sculpted stone panels are set into the unadorned brick walls.

During this period eastern Assam was under the rule of the Ahom kings. Whitewashed temples at their capital at Sibsagar are typical of the region's unique style of religious architecture. The characteristic feature of these temples is their curved towers, which have central curvilinear projections crowned with tiers of pot finials; similar but larger finials crown the summits. Most sanctums adjoin halls with vaulted roofs and curved eaves. Usually there is no ornamentation, but the Vishadol Temple is an exception. Its walls have shallow niches housing figurative panels; above are miniature turrets.

Brick temples at Udaipur in Tripura display influences from neighbouring Burma. The typical example consists of a square sanctum and adjoining hall; both are roofed with vaults with curved eaves. Rising over the sanctum is a large hemispherical superstructure, rather like a Buddhist stupa in shape but with a circular ribbed finial. Walls are unadorned except for corner buttresses and horizontal mouldings.

BIBLIOGRAPHY

A. Banerji: *Temples of Tripura* (Varanasi, 1968)

GEORGE MICHELL

(e) Himachal Pradesh and Ladakh. Such kingdoms as Mandi, Kulu and Chamba remained vigorous until the 18th century. Though hundreds of temples were built, surviving examples are in many instances late and unprepossessing. Evidence for earlier temples is only indirect and takes the form of numerous silver and brass masks (*mohrās*) of divinities worshipped in villages (*see* §VIII, 14(i) below).

The Hirmadevi Temple at Dhungri on the outskirts of Manali preserves an inscription of 1553 of Raja Bahadur Singh of Kulu on its wooden doorframe. Deeply undercut diamonds, floral scrolls and stiff figural carving continue the tradition of the temple of the sage Parashara in Mandi (*see* §6(i)(a) above), but the work has lost the verve of that shrine. All other parts of the Hirmadevi Temple, including the three-part superstructure, are much later. The wooden temple of Adi Brahma at Khokhan, near BAJAURA in Kulu, is square in plan, with a pillared verandah running around it. The superstructure (see fig. 121), with four sloping roofs, is unusually high. Twisted wooden brackets impart a distinctive look to the structure. A few fragments of an earlier stone temple of the 11th century remain at the site. Inscribed silver masks of Raja Tedhi Singh of Kulu (*reg* 1742–67) with dates equivalent to 1746 are the cult objects, and the temple may well be mid-18th century.

During this period, Ladakh's control over its own destiny grew quite weak, the result of repeated invasions. The architecture of the region gradually came to depend more and more on stylistic inspiration from Tibet. The oldest monuments of LEH are the temple of the guardian deities and the castle built by Tashi Namgyel in the 16th century. Senge Namgyel (*reg c.* 1570–1642), nephew of Tshewang Namgyel, built the great fortlike palace at Leh, the Serzang Temple at Basgo and a temple of Shakyamuni Buddha, as well as chortens (*see* STUPA, §5) and prayer-halls. He also promoted the Kadampa school of Tibetan Buddhism (*see* BUDDHISM, §III, 6) and founded the monasteries of HEMIS, Stakna and Chendey. His queen probably built a smaller temple at Shey, as is recorded in an inscription of 1642. Some distance away, there is an 'old temple' (*lhakhang Nyingpa*) that has fine murals of the mid-18th century and, at a higher level, several smaller shrines. The small monastery at Stakna possesses an

121. Adi Brahma Temple, Khokhan, superstructure, ?mid-18th century

assembly hall (*dukhang*) and residential quarters for monks. The Chendey Monastery has an image of its founder, Taktshang Repa, and murals of Shakyamuni, as well as cosmic diagrams (Skt *maṇḍalas*) of Kalachakra and Akshobhya. Senge Namgyel's successor, Dedan (*reg c.* 1642–75), built a long *maṇi* wall decorated with inscriptions below Leh as well as 'two-storey' images of Buddha Shakyamuni and the *bodhisattva* Avalokiteshvara.

See also TIBET, §II.

BIBLIOGRAPHY

J. P. Vogel: *Antiquities of Chamba*, i (Calcutta, 1913)
A. Cunningham: *Ladak: Physical, Statistical and Geographical* (London, 1854/*R* New Delhi, 1941)
H. Goetz: *The Early Wooden Temples of Chamba* (Leiden, 1955)
A. H. Francke: *Antiquities of Indian Tibet*, 2 vols (Calcutta, 1914–26/*R* New Delhi, 1972)
M. Postel, A. Neven and K. Mankodi: *Antiquities of Himachal* (Bombay, 1985)
D. L. Snellgrove and T. Skorupski: *The Cultural Heritage of Ladakh*, 2 vols (New Delhi, n.d.)

KIRIT MANKODI

(f) South. By the beginning of the 17th century, the Vijayanagara empire had disintegrated and much of south India was divided between powerful local governors, known as Nayakas. These rulers continued to patronize temple architecture on an impressive scale; earlier Hindu temples were renovated and transformed into vast, well-planned complexes, and new projects were initiated. As Nayaka influence lessened towards the end of the 17th century, other dynasties asserted their independence. These included the Sethupatis of Ramnad and the rulers of TRAVANCORE, who, in the 18th century, acted as temple patrons and were responsible for substantial architectural projects.

Nayaka-period temples. Architecture of this period was a direct continuation of Vijayanagara-period traditions (*see* §6(i)(f) above); indeed it is not always possible to distinguish between the two styles. Features that generally characterize Nayaka-period complexes include a rigorous symmetry carried out in overall planning on a vast scale. A typical development was the multiplication of high walls (Skt *prākāras*) surrounding the main sanctuary to create a concentric series of square or rectangular enclosures or courtyards. Towered gateways (*gopuras*) increasing in height from the inner to the outer enclosures were usually positioned in the middle of each of the four sides and aligned with structures of the innermost sanctuary. There were invariably separate sanctums for the male and female aspects of the principal cult divinity, as well as shrines for a host of lesser deities, animal 'vehicles' (*vāhanas*) and guardians. Many of these small shrines were contained within the columned corridor that encircled the four sides of the principal sanctum. The outer enclosures were crowded with subsidiary structures, especially columned halls, including those designated as 'thousand-columned', as well as colonnades, storerooms, stepwells, lamp columns, altars and other structures. These testify to both the elaboration of temple rituals during this period and the diverse economic, educational and cultural functions of religious complexes.

As in the Vijayanagara period, architecture and sculpture were closely linked. Figures on column shafts, so deeply

122. Minakshi Sundareshvara Temple gateway, Madurai, 17th century

carved as to be nearly in the round, included not only the principal cult divinities but also temple donors and their families, for whom the columns along the central aisles were typically reserved. Rearing beasts adorned peripheral piers. Enlarged brackets extended outwards from crouching animals in a series of curved elements, each provided with a pendent bud. Receding perspectives of such brackets projecting from decorated piers were a typical feature of Nayaka-period architecture. Interiors were enlivened by brightly coloured paintings that adorned walls and ceilings (*see* §VI, (4)(vii) below).

The superstructures of towered gateways were crowded with sculpture, mainly brightly coloured plaster figures depicting deities, semi-divine beings and guardians. The arched ends of the crowning barrel-vaulted roofs (*śālā*s) were embellished with exuberantly finished monster masks (*kīrttimukha*s) and aquatic beasts (*makara*s); pot finials (*stūpī*s) were displayed along the ridge. While in most temples these sculptures have been renovated many times, there has been little alteration in the overall schemes.

As the nucleus of the town, the typical Nayaka-period temple dominated the layout of the surrounding streets, which usually included wide thoroughfares used in the annual chariot (*ratha*) festivals. Free-standing colonnades, axially aligned with the principal gateways of the temple, provided a link between town life and religious activities. Outside the temple walls were large rectangular tanks (*teppamkulam*s), with stepped sides and pavilions in the middle, which served as venues for float festivals.

Four branches of Nayakas ruled respectively from Ikkeri, MADURAI, GINGEE and THANJAVUR. The architecture sponsored in the 16th and 17th centuries by the Nayaka rulers of Ikkeri in the south-western part of the Deccan was influenced by earlier traditions in the region. The largest of the monuments, the Aghoreshvara Temple, is typical. It consists of a sanctum (*garbhagṛha*) surrounded by an ambulatory adjoining a spacious hall. The plain outer walls of the sanctum are framed by a deeply moulded socle and cornice; niches surmounted by tower-like elements are positioned in the middle of each side. Above rises the multi-storey pyramidal superstructure crowned by a cupola and pot finial. Friezes of shallow pilasters with towered motifs ornament the hall walls, which are overhung by steeply angled eaves. The interior hall columns are ornately treated, some with rearing animals in the typical Vijayanagara-period manner. A detached pavilion for Shiva's vehicle, the bull Nandi, has similar elaborately carved columns.

The Madurai rulers, who had effectively become independent by the end of the 16th century, were probably the most powerful Nayakas of south India. Under their patronage, especially that of Tirumalai (*reg* 1623–59), large-scale temple projects were initiated, the most impressive being the great Minakshi Sundareshvara Temple at Madurai. The temple complex is contained within an immense rectangular area surrounded by high enclosure walls and entered through four towering gateways, one in the middle of each side (see fig. 122). Within the enclosure is a dense cluster of colonnades, columned halls, tanks, storerooms, shrines and, at the core, the temple of Shiva as Sundareshvara and that of his consort Minakshi.

Though not the highest gateways of the Nayaka period, the examples at Madurai are among the most elaborately ornamented. The upper portions are completely covered with plaster sculptures of divinities, celestial beings, mythical monsters, guardians and animal mounts, all periodically renovated and repainted in brilliant colours. The gateways are exceptional for their elongated proportions and elegantly curved profiles achieving a dramatic upward sweep. Other outstanding features of the complex include its large stepwell, which is surrounded by a colonnade with wall paintings (*see* §VI, 4(vii) below). The columns on the west side of the tank are elaborately carved. Such columns have almost free-standing sculptures of divinities, musicians and animals. Outside the complex, opposite the east gateway, is a magnificently adorned hall. This contains perhaps the finest carvings, especially rearing beasts and portrait sculptures of the Nayaka rulers and their ministers; projecting brackets are carried on seated animals. A small pavilion within the hall is fashioned of polished black granite. East of the hall stands the lowest storey of a colossal but unfinished gateway begun by Tirumalai.

Other projects patronized by Tirumalai include the great Shiva Temple at Suchindram, a sacred site near the southernmost tip of the Indian peninsula. The temple is contained within a rectangular enclosure, with the principal seven-storey gateway on the east. This gateway is preceded by a long colonnade with elaborate columns sculpted with donor figures and attendant maidens. Within the courtyard are several halls with highly ornamented columns, some with clusters of colonettes and multiple brackets, which are among the finest of the Nayaka period.

While there are only a few modest temples at the fortified capital of Gingee, its Nayaka rulers sponsored several larger projects at nearby sacred sites. Perhaps the most impressive is the Ekambareshvara Temple at KANCHIPURAM. Earlier shrines, altars, pavilions and even lamp columns were incorporated into an extensive columned hall in front of the entrance to the main temple. With the exception of an impressive Vijayanagara-period gateway, the remainder of the temple is largely a Nayaka-period structure. A striking feature of the complex is the corridor surrounding the principal shrine, presenting a continuous sequence of piers with animal and lotus brackets projecting outwards in the Nayaka-period manner. The principal Shiva sanctum and several other smaller shrines open off the corridor.

The great complex at Kalahasti was substantially rebuilt in the 17th century. As at Kanchipuram, the principal sanctuary is contained within a colonnaded space, with a corridor on four sides. The piers are sculpted with mythical beasts and animals with riders and have projecting brackets with pendent buds. Accessory shrines and cult images are situated along the corridor.

The outer gateway of the Govindaraja Temple at Tirupati is a fine example in the Nayaka-period style (*see* TIRUPATI AND CHANDRAGIRI). Completed in 1624, it has a high double socle with pilastered walls. The (restored) concrete superstructure has seven storeys surmounted by the usual barrel-vaulted roof (*śālā*) with gilded finials. Pavilions used for swing festivals (ritual placing of gods' images in swings), also Nayaka-period structures, have columns ornamented with delicately carved scrollwork.

The Nayakas of Thanjavur were mainly responsible for developing the Ranganatha temple complex on the sacred island of SRIRANGAM. While structures of the inner enclosures of this temple were erected under the patronage of a succession of Chola, Hoysala and Vijayanagara rulers (*see* §6(i)(f) above), under the Nayakas the temple was transformed into a vast complex laid out in a series of seven concentric rectangular enclosures defined by high walls. Towered gateways in the middle of each side are aligned along roads that proceed axially inwards towards the main sanctum. The east gateway of the fourth enclosure is an elegantly proportioned structure; the tower has double projections in the middle of each side and a slightly concave profile. Nayaka-period additions include the hall on the south side of the third enclosure, which has columns adorned with donor portraits and the usual array of sculpted figures.

Though not as large a complex, the Jambukeshvara Temple at Tiruvannaikovil on Srirangam island is another fine example of Nayaka-period architecture. The seven towered gateways that still stand in the four concentric enclosure walls are monumental constructions, impressively proportioned and highly ornamented. The west gateway of the outermost enclosure leads directly into a columned hall; another similar structure is situated on the left. Decorated piers with extended brackets are supported on large seated animals; end columns are adorned with maidens sculpted in high relief.

Though less well known, the Bhu Varaha Temple at Srimushnam is another notable example of the Nayaka style. The complex is entered through two gateways with clearly articulated socles and walls; their six-storey superstructures have painted plaster sculptures. Two columned halls that precede the principal shrine are distinguished by the highly ornate treatment of the column shafts, which are covered with figurative panels. Corner piers have clusters of colonettes, while those in between are embellished with vigorous depictions of riders on prancing beasts. The columns of the central aisles have fully modelled portraits of Nayaka nobles. Lotus medallions are delicately incised on the ceilings.

The Subrahmanya shrine within the courtyard of the Brihadeshvara Temple at Thanjavur is an exquisitely finished Nayaka-period monument illustrating the survival of earlier Chola-period features. The shrine consists of a sanctum, enclosed hall and porch. The walls, raised on delicately modelled socles, are regularly divided by closely positioned slender pilasters with double capitals. Other pilasters frame niches; pilasters standing in pots fill shallow recesses. Over the sanctum rises the brick superstructure in a pyramidal series of diminishing storeys, with a cupola at the summit. Brick parapet elements (*hāra*s) appear above the hall walls.

Other important Nayaka-period temples are located at KUMBAKONAM. The Sarangapani temple complex is typical of the later series at this town. Entered through a soaring ten-storey gateway of standard design, the complex contains columned halls and sanctuaries ornamented in the Nayaka-period manner. Carved elephants, horses and wheels ornament the socle of the hall attached to the principal shrine. The stepped Mahamakham tank, a popular place of pilgrimage within the town, has four shrines on each side, all small pavilions with domelike brick roofs. One shrine, dedicated to Tulabhava, has a sculpted ceiling.

At the holy site of RAMESWARAM, a temple with a foundation dating back to the Chola period was transformed, with endowments of the Sethupati rulers, into the vast Ramalingeshvara complex. A concentric series of enclosures is formed by high walls with towered gateways in the middles of three sides. The east gateway is positioned in the second set of enclosure walls; two entrances in the peripheral walls on this side are approached through columned halls. The superstructures of the gateways, which follow the standard scheme, are unusually constructed of stone rather than brick, but only those on the east and west are completed, and this comparatively recently. A spacious corridor surrounds the second enclosure wall on four sides, incorporating subsidiary shrines and a stepwell. The colonnade is exceptional both for its great length (205 m north to south) and for the fine workmanship of its piers (see fig. 123). Enlarged pendent lotus brackets rest on crouching lion-like beasts (*yāli*s). Only traces remain of painted medallions with figures that decorated the ceilings. The west colonnade is interrupted by another corridor with piers sculpted as rearing animals, warriors and maidens. Within the innermost enclosure are the two principal shrines of the temple, both dedicated to Shiva, as well as a Nandi pavilion, a smaller goddess sanctuary, a tank and a columned hall. Portraits of royal donors and their ministers are sculpted on the columns of the innermost enclosure.

Much of the Padmanabhasvami Temple at TRIVANDRUM was built in the 18th century under the patronage of the Travancore rulers. The temple is of interest architecturally because it combines Kerala and Nayaka features. The rectangular sanctuary at the heart of the complex

123. Ramalingeshvara Temple, Rameswaram, outer colonnade, 18th century

enshrining a large image of the god Vishnu reclining on the serpent Ananta is built in the typical Kerala style (*see* §6(i)(h) above). The outer walls, covered with murals, are sheltered by a double tier of angled roofs. Together with subsidiary shrines, the sanctuary stands within a court. On the north is an entrance with a multi-tiered gabled roof. More closely linked with contemporary Nayaka-period practice is the exceptionally broad east gateway with a soaring superstructure of seven ascending storeys. Both the colonnade surrounding the shrine and the expansive hall have elaborately treated columns.

For sculpture and painting of this period in Tamil Nadu *see* §§V, 7(vi)(a) and VI, 4(vii) below.

BIBLIOGRAPHY

P. Brown: *Indian Architecture (Buddhist and Hindu Periods)* (?Bombay, [1941], rev. Bombay, 1956), pp. 95–100

K. Thiagarajan: *Meenakshi Temple, Madurai* (Madras, 1965)

H. Sarkar: *An Architectural Survey of the Temples of Kerala* (Delhi, 1978)

W. Noble: 'The Architecture and Organization of Kerala Style Hindu Temples', *Anthropos*, lxxvi (1981), pp. 1–24

R. Bernier: *Temple Arts of Kerala: A South Indian Tradition* (Delhi, 1982)

G. Michell: *Architecture and Art of Southern India: Vijayanagara and the Successor States* (Cambridge, 1994)

GEORGE MICHELL

Kerala palaces. In Kerala numerous palaces built from the 16th to the 19th century preserve ancient indigenous forms. Palaces were built of wood and laterite, with steeply pitched gabled roofs covered with thatch or tiles. Though varied in size, scale, complexity and decoration, most palaces involve a traditional square or rectangular structure with a sunken central courtyard open to the sky, called a *nālukeṭṭu* (Malayalam: four buildings; literally 'four parts tied together'). The orientation and organization of space around this courtyard follow conventional patterns based on principles laid out in ancient architectural treatises (*see* §I, 10 above). The *nālukeṭṭu* was a type of domestic architecture shared by upper-caste Hindus of Kerala. While the kings of the largest kingdoms sometimes built on a grander scale, in general Kerala palaces are characterized by their understatement and simplicity compared to palaces in most other parts of India.

Among the earliest palaces to survive is the Mattancheri Palace in COCHIN (i), capital of the rajas of Cochin, traditionally believed to have been built for them by the Portuguese in the mid-16th century. The Portuguese attribution cannot be confirmed, but there is evidence for the early date. The scale is distinct from other local examples; the central courtyard is much larger than elsewhere and contains a shrine dedicated to the family goddess, Pazhayannur Bhagavati. Also unique is the use of the ground storey as the temple enclosure; the palace proper occupies the second storey. A number of these rooms contain handsomely carved wooden coffered ceilings in the traditional local mode, and the mural paintings that decorate the walls of some rooms, particularly those depicting the *Rāmāyaṇa* epic, are among the finest in India (*see* §V, 5(vii) below).

The palace at Padmanabhapuram in the far south was begun about 1600 and attained its final form in the mid-18th century; in Kanniyakumari District of modern Tamil Nadu, Padmanabhapuram was the capital of the TRAVANCORE kings during the 17th and 18th centuries. No other true palace complex survives in Kerala; the palace of the Zamorin, or Samudri, kings of Calicut (now Kozhikode) was destroyed in the 18th century.

The Padmanabhapuram complex, approached from its main gate on the west, includes various residential, official, administrative and religious structures within its fortified walls. The oldest residential structure within the complex is the Thaikottaram (Mother Palace), a *nālukeṭṭu* of laterite and wood. Its entrance porch on the south-west resembles the type often used locally for musical and dramatic performances, with a handsomely carved wooden ceiling supported by an exquisitely carved wooden pillar. The structure is surrounded by an exterior verandah on both the first and second storeys (see fig. 124, right). The tiled roof is supported by wooden pillars, while the verandah 'wall' is actually a screen of wooden slats carried on carved wooden struts that curve out to meet the overhang of the roof. This widely used local convention also appears on the upper two storeys of the four-storey *uparika mālika* ('superior building'), forming a cantilevered exterior balcony (see fig. 124, left). The room in the uppermost chamber contains 18th-century mural paintings depicting various Hindu deities, including Sri Padmanabhasvami, tutelary deity of the royal family, after whom the site is named. The mid-18th-century palace at Krishnapuram (near Kayankulam), built by the same kings, follows the

124. Padmanabhapuram Palace, interior of compound from north, *c.* 1600–mid-18th century; right: Thaikottaram; left: *uparika māḷika*

example of Padmanabhapuram, though it is a single large structure enclosing multiple courtyards.

By the early 19th century, Tiruvanandapuram (now TRIVANDRUM) had begun to serve as the main capital of Kerala. The fort area surrounding the Padmanabhasvami Temple contains numerous palaces built by successive Travancore kings throughout the 19th century. The palace of Svati Thirunal (*reg* 1829–47) continues ancient indigenous traditions but on a grander scale and with increasingly lavish decoration. Palaces built in the second half of the 19th century are essentially Neo-classical buildings based on British colonial styles (*see* §(iii) below) with tiled and gabled roofs retained from the local school.

Colonial styles were adopted for palace architecture by the rajas of Cochin much earlier than in Travancore. The 18th-century Vadakkekkara Palace at TRICHUR attaches a conventional *nālukeṭṭu* to a colonial Neo-classical structure; other palaces at Tripunittura, the family seat, likewise join European-style buildings to adjacent *nālukeṭṭu*s. The latest example of this, the Hill Palace at Tripunittura, places a grand Neo-classical structure (built in three phases beginning in the late 19th century) in a vast formal garden; attached to it by a covered walkway is a traditional *nālukeṭṭu* palace.

For sculpture and painting of this period in Kerala *see* §§V, 7(vi)(b) and VI, 4(vii) below.

BIBLIOGRAPHY

Travancore Archaeological Series (Trivandrum, 1910–36)
Annual Report, Travancore Archaeology Department (Trivandrum, 1922–48)
Annual Report of the Archaeological Department, Cochin State (or *Cochin State Annual Report on Archaeological Researches*) (Ernakulam, 1927–49)
S. Desivinayagam Pillai: 'Ancient Forts at Kalkulam and Udayagiri', *Kerala Soc. Pap.*, 6th ser. (1930), pp. 313–16
V. R. Chitra and T. N. Srinivasan: *Cochin Murals*, 2 vols (Cochin, 1940)
R. V. Poduval: 'Travancore's Ancient Capital: Padmanabhapuram', *D. R. Bhandarkar Volume*, ed. B. C. Law (Calcutta, 1940), pp. 319–23
Annual Report of the Archaeology Department, Travancore—Cochin State (Trivandrum, 1950–56)
S. Kramrisch, J. H. Cousins and R. V. Poduval: *The Arts and Crafts of Travancore* (Oxford, 1952); rev. as *The Arts and Crafts of Kerala* (Cochin, [1970])
H. Sarkar: *An Architectural Survey of the Temples of Kerala* (Delhi, 1978)
Splendours of Kerala (Bombay, 1979/*R* 1983)
R. M. Bernier: *Temple Arts of Kerala: A South Indian Tradition* (Delhi, 1981)
M. C. Heston: *The Mattancheri Palace Murals of Kerala, India: A Stylistic Study* (diss., Columbus, OH State U., 1985)
K. T. Ravindran: 'Le Palais de Padmanabhapuram', *Architectures en Inde* (Milan and Paris, 1985), pp. 36–40
R. Rewal and K. T. Ravindran: 'An Indian Portfolio: Padmanabhapuram Palace', *Mimar*, xxi (July–Sept 1986), pp. 61–7
M. B. Heston: 'The Palace Murals at Padmanabhapuram: The Politics of an Image', *Potpourri of Indian Art*, ed. P. Pal (Bombay, 1989), pp. 115–31
M. Moore: 'The Kerala House as Hindu Cosmos', *Contrib. Ind. Sociol.*, xxiii/1 (1989), pp. 169–202
M. B. Heston: 'Images from the Past, Vision of the Future: The Art of Marttanda Varma', *Perceptions of India's Visual Past*, ed. C. B. Asher and T. R. Metcalf (New Delhi, 1994), pp. 199–210
——: 'Nalukettu Palaces: Developments in Cochin and Travancore, Sixteenth to Twentieth Centuries', *Pazhaya Kerala*, i (in preparation)

M. E. HESTON

(iii) Early colonial. The Portuguese were the first Europeans to build extensively in India. In 1510 Don Afonso de Albuquerque founded a settlement comprising domestic, administrative and religious buildings in GOA, and a Portuguese fort, factory and settlement had previously been established at COCHIN in Kerala. Early buildings were wooden, fortified with palisades, but by the mid-16th century fortified stone structures were being constructed at such sites as DIU, Daman and Bassein. Danish, Dutch, French and English settlements followed. The Dutch (1616), British (1612) and French (1668) factories at Surat in Gujarat were long, low, defensive buildings, facing inwards on to courtyards, which acted both as communal dwellings and as warehouses. Initially built of mud and brick, they were later constructed in more permanent materials.

Later colonists settled around Madras (*see* MADRAS, §1) and THANJAVUR in the south and in Bengal. In the mid-18th century, Dutch, Portuguese and Danish influence declined, but the French provided impressive residences for their governors at Pondicherry in Tamil Nadu and in Bengal. The magnificent Baroque Government House in Pondicherry was commissioned by Marquis Joseph de Dupleix (1697–1764; governor of Pondicherry 1741–54) and built in 1752, only to be destroyed by the British in 1761; it was rebuilt in the Rococo style from 1766. After the conquest of Pondicherry, the British led in both commercial and architectural matters. In 1690, Calcutta became the headquarters of the East India Company, and after the Battle of Plassey the new Fort William was begun in 1758 (*see* MILITARY ARCHITECTURE & FORTIFICATION, §III, 2(v)(e) and fig. 19). Bricklayers and carpenters recruited from England acted as instructors for local Indian labour. The more settled colonial life and thriving trade

125. Palace of the nawab, Murshidabad, designed by Duncan McLeod, 1829–37

necessitated a variety of building types: churches, residences, tombs, monuments and official, legal and administrative buildings, as well as a town hall and a mint. The Writers' Buildings existed by the 1780s, and by 1794 the Government House, Council House, Accountant General's Office and Supreme Court had all been built, only to be replaced within ten years by grander edifices.

Alongside official architecture, domestic building developed. Mercantile expansion allowed wealthy merchants to live lavishly in large town houses requiring 50–100 servants. Sophisticated country or garden houses on the outskirts of cities may have been influenced by the designs of Andrea Palladio and John Nash, with the addition of wide verandahs on the south side for shade and cloth ceiling fans (*punkhas*) to aid air circulation. The commoner rustic bungalows originated in Bengal but were also built in northern India, where they were adapted to local conditions. The clay and thatch originally used in their construction were eventually superseded by stone walls and roof tiles.

Up to the 1820s (when a course in civilian architecture was introduced), architectural commissions remained in the hands of military engineers. Previously, study of *La Science des ingénieurs* (1739) by Bernard Forest de Bélidor (?1697–1761) and consultation with patrons had produced, for example, the new Government House at Calcutta (1799–1803; *see* CALCUTTA, §2). It was designed by Charles Wyatt (*b* 1758) and inspired by James Paine's design for Kedleston Hall, Derbys. John Garstin (*b* 1756), also a military engineer, designed among other buildings a remarkable circular granary known as the Golghar (1786) at Bankipore, a district of modern Patna, and the Calcutta Town Hall (1805–13). Monuments commemorating military successes include the circular, domed Rohilla Monument in Calcutta (1817). In 1803 the Freedom of Amiens was celebrated with a Tuscan–Doric Banqueting Hall built at Madras by John Goldingham (1765/6–1849), a Danish-born astronomer and mathematician. The British Residency at HYDERABAD, intended for extravagant state occasions, was begun by Lieutenant Samuel Russell (*fl* 1790–1810) in the same year. At Lucknow, General Martin's palace-cum-tomb Constantia had no parallel in Europe (for illustration *see* LUCKNOW).

By the end of the 18th century, smaller towns were developing away from Calcutta. Barrackpore (modern Barakpur), the country seat of the governor of Bengal, was a military cantonment where officers lived in bungalows and soldiers in tents. In this new urban pattern, developed to meet the army's need for mobility and speed, troops were located away from the old forts in permanent camps built around a large open space (Pers. *maydan*) used for gatherings and parades. Berhampore, which grew up in much the same way, was a large brigade station with a large cemetery containing numerous Neo-classical tombs and monuments. At Murshidabad, a Palladian palace was built on the river front by military engineers to the design of Duncan McLeod between 1829 and 1837 (see fig. 125; *see also* §(ii)(a) above).

Although the majority of architects working in India during this period were British and Irish, Edward Tiretta (*fl* 1760s–90s), an East India Company architect, was Italian. European architectural books in circulation included the works of James Gibbs, James Paine, the Adam brothers and William Chambers, as well as James Leoni's editions of the works of Leon Battista Alberti and Palladio, Sebastien de Vauban's work on fortifications and the works of Jacopo Vignola. Among the many churches derived from James Gibbs's St Martin-in-the-Fields, London, which had been included in his *Book of Architecture* (1728), were the church of St Mary (1825) in Pune; those of St John (1787) and St Andrew (1818) in Calcutta; and St George's Cathedral (1816) and St Andrew's Church

(1818–21) in Madras, the last based on drawings by Colonel Thomas Fiott de Havilland (1775–1866). Catholic churches often adopted a southern European Baroque style derived from Il Gesù, Rome. The Gothic style was rarely used at this time; exceptions are St Peter's Church in Fort William (1826) and St Paul's Cathedral (1829–47), both in Calcutta. From *c.* 1820 until the mid-19th century Neo-classicism dominated colonial architecture in India; Madras was known as the 'Grecian city'. This Greek revival was introduced by such architects as William Nairn Forbes (*b* 1796), who designed the Calcutta Mint (1824–31), and Thomas Cowper (*b* 1780), architect of the Town Hall, Bombay (1820–23). Both were inspired by James Stuart and Nicholas Revett's drawings of Greek architecture: Forbes's Doric order on the Calcutta Silver Mint was derived from the Parthenon. These large Doric structures of the early 19th century were constructed on the same Grecian model as contemporary buildings in Europe, America and the Caribbean, in keeping with the spirit of an era dominated by large-scale, formal architecture.

BIBLIOGRAPHY

M. Archer: 'Company Architects and their Influences in India', *RIBA J.* vii (Aug 8 1963), pp. 317–21
P. Spear: *The Nabobs* (London, 1963)
S. Nilsson: *European Architecture in India, 1750–1850* (London, 1968)
——: *The New Capitals of India, Pakistan and Bangladesh* (Lund, 1973)
J. Pieper: *Die anglo-indische Station* (Bonn, 1975)
A. King: *Colonial Urban Development* (London, 1976)
R. G. Irving: *Indian Summer—Lutyens, Baker and Imperial Delhi* (New Haven and London, 1981)
G. Stamp: 'British Architecture in India, 1857–1947', *J. Royal Soc. A.*, cxxix (May 1981), pp. 357–79
Lotus Int., 26 (1981) [issue on hybrid archit.]
J. Morris: *Stones of Empire* (London, 1982)
G. Tindall: *City of Gold: The Biography of Bombay* (London, 1982)
Lotus Int., 34 (1982) [issue on India]
P. Davies: *Splendours of the Raj* (London, 1985)
J. Morris and others: *Architecture of the British Empire* (London, 1986)

STEN ÅKE NILSSON,
GERALDINE SMITH-PARR

8. 19TH CENTURY–1947. Late colonial British building was mainly civic (government edifices, railway stations, memorial gateways), and its syncretic styles incorporating Indian elements with Western forms carried a political message. Building in indigenous styles continued—with a certain eclecticism also evident in the development of the Hindu temple. Meanwhile, in Europe and America, a growing knowledge of the 'East' inspired interest in enlivening Western architecture and design with Indian elements. □

(i) Late colonial architecture. (ii) Continuing traditions. (iii) Indian architecture and the West.

(i) Late colonial architecture. During the first half of the 19th century the British employed a classical architecture to announce that their empire, like that of Rome, embodied enduring ideals of law and order. After the upheaval of the 1857 rebellion, the British were determined to reconstitute their empire and to establish themselves as legitimate rulers with direct links to the Mughal dynasty and hence to India's own past. Although European forms were not abandoned, the British began to incorporate indigenous styles into their buildings as they conceived the Mughals had done in the 16th and 17th centuries.

British understanding of India's architecture was shaped by the architectural historian JAMES FERGUSSON, who insisted, particularly in his influential *History of Indian and Eastern Architecture* (1876), that all building in India was expressive of religious affiliation and could be classed as either Hindu, Buddhist or Muslim. As they set out to represent their own empire as authentically Indian, the British were drawn not to 'Hindu' architecture but to the soaring domes and arches of the so-called 'Saracenic' style. For the British this style was more aesthetically satisfying and, as the style favoured by the Mughals, appropriately imperial. At no time did the British conceive of their building in the Saracenic mode as an antiquarian exercise. Its 'traditional' forms were always put to modern uses in the construction of railway stations, banks, post offices and other utilitarian structures. With rare exceptions the British made no attempt to be faithful to the style of any given period of India's past. In their vision, shaped by Orientalist discourse in Europe, India was fundamentally different and timeless (*see* ORIENTALISM). Thus India's architecture was not an on-going tradition in which the British worked, but a static set of architectural forms from which elements could be chosen to serve the needs of empire.

The first British builders to incorporate Indic elements into their work were ROBERT FELLOWES CHISHOLM and Charles Mant (1839–81) (*see also* VADODARA). From his initial designs in the early 1870s for the Madras Board of Revenue and University Senate House (the latter incorporating Byzantine elements), Chisholm went on to design structures in the Saracenic style for the Maharaja of Baroda and in various south Indian cities. At the end of his career he designed an East India Museum (never built) on the south bank of the Thames in London. Mant's most famous design was for Mayo College, Ajmer; it joined Rajput and Mughal forms with a soaring clock tower (see fig. 126). The most prolific of the late 19th-century British Indian builders was SAMUEL SWINTON JACOB. Employed as state engineer by the maharajas of Jaipur, Jacob designed not only the widely admired Albert Hall in Jaipur (now Government Central Museum of Jaipur) but also post offices, colleges and other civic buildings throughout north India. In addition he put together an influential builders' handbook, *Jeypore Portfolio of Indian Architectural Details* (1890).

India's two largest cities, Calcutta and Bombay, remained mostly unaffected by Saracenic eclecticism. With its coastal site and maritime orientation, a prospering Bombay looked to Europe, above all to the contemporaneous GOTHIC REVIVAL, for its architectural styles. The University Hall (1869–78) was designed by George Gilbert Scott (*see* SCOTT (ii), (1)), while FREDRICK WILLIAM STEVENS's Victoria Terminus (1878–87), inspired by St Pancras Station, London, was the largest and most spectacular structure erected by the British in 19th-century India (*see* BOMBAY, fig. 1). Nevertheless, two of the city's most prominent structures, the Prince of Wales Museum and the Gateway of India (*see* BOMBAY, fig. 2), both built in the first decade of the 20th century, incorporate Indic design elements.

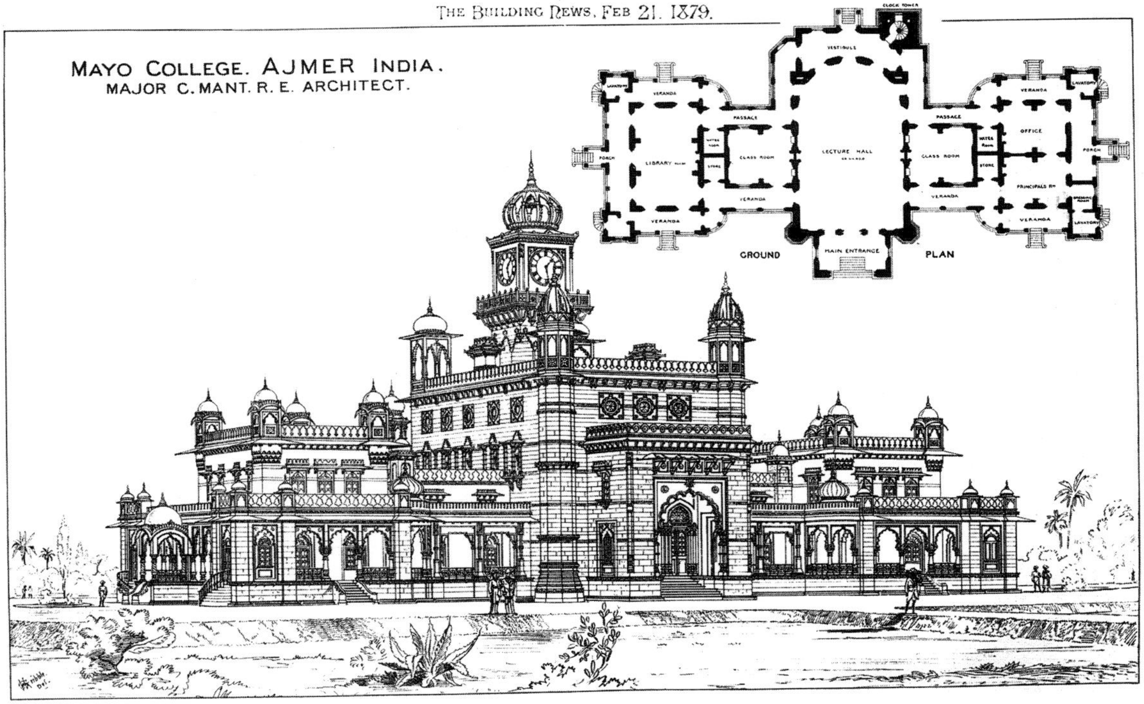

126. Design for Mayo College, Ajmer, by Charles Mant; from *Building News* (21 Feb 1879)

In India, as elsewhere, the Edwardian era saw a revival of classical architecture associated with resurgent imperialism. Lord Curzon, as viceroy, preferred the Neo-classical forms of Palladian design (*see* PALLADIANISM) for the building meant above all others to represent the Raj in stone: the Victoria Memorial (1905), Calcutta. By its classicism the memorial sought to impress not only the Indians and the British at home but England's continental rivals as well. The decision, in 1911, to shift the capital from Calcutta to Delhi and to create a new city there offered the British a further—and, in the end, a final—opportunity for a monumental imperial architecture (*see* DELHI, §I). Not surprisingly, this decision precipitated an intense struggle between those who saw in the relocation of the capital to the Mughal heartland an unparalleled opportunity for the British to define their rule as 'Indian' in the style of Akbar (*reg* 1556–1605) and those who insisted that the new city must embody the classical forms of a worldwide empire. Foremost among the latter was HERBERT BAKER, designer of the Renaissance-style Union Buildings (1909) in Pretoria, South Africa. For Baker, classical forms alone possessed the 'constructive and geometrical' qualities necessary to embody the idea of law and order the British had brought to India. For New Delhi, Baker designed secretariat buildings that sought an orientalized classicism, with a combination of columns, porticos, pierced stone screens and domed kiosks that proclaimed the Raj to be Indian as well as British.

The principal designer of New Delhi was Edwin Lutyens. At once authoritarian and rigorously logical, his overall layout for the city (*see* LUTYENS, EDWIN, fig. 3), shaped by a hexagonal radial form, focused on the Viceroy's House (now Rashtrapati Bhavan) set on Raisina Hill. Lutyens created in New Delhi, especially in the Viceroy's House, an architecture stamped with a unique personal genius. Though ideals of classicism underlay his work (he disdained all of India's historic architecture as 'childish'), the classical forms he employed were stripped to their essentials and then reconstituted so that they contained indigenous ornamentation and detail. The younger Delhi architects who had worked with Lutyens and Baker kept alive into the 1930s one of the last flowerings of the classical tradition. But the nationalist challenge as it took shape under Mahatma Gandhi, together with a lack of funds, left the British in India increasingly demoralized. In the end India's nationalists repudiated both the classical and the colonial 'Indo-Saracenic' modes in favour of international MODERNISM.

See also §§V, 8(ii); VI, 4(ix) and (x); and IX below.

BIBLIOGRAPHY

J. Fergusson: *History of Indian and Eastern Architecture* (London, 1876)
S. Jacob: *Jeypore Portfolio of Indian Architectural Details* (London, 1890)
A. D. King: *Colonial Urban Development* (London, 1976)
R. Irving: *Indian Summer: Lutyens, Baker and Imperial Delhi* (New Haven, 1981)
G. Stamp: 'British Architecture in India, 1857–1947', *J. Royal Soc. A.*, cxxix (1981), pp. 357–79
P. Davies: *Splendours of the Raj* (London, 1985)
N. Evenson: *The Indian Metropolis: A View towards the West* (New Haven, 1989)
T. R. Metcalf: *An Imperial Vision: Indian Architecture and Britain's Raj* (Berkeley, 1989)
G. H. R. Tillotson: *The Tradition of Indian Architecture: Continuity, Controversy and Change since 1850* (New Haven, 1989)

THOMAS R. METCALF

(ii) Continuing traditions. The Orientalists condemned nearly all traditional Indian art later than the 13th century (*see* ORIENTALISM), and this prejudice has lingered. Thus, among scholars, temple building in the 19th and early 20th centuries has largely been ignored. Trends in this continuing tradition are discernible. The established movement towards regional differentiation continued, while forms (e.g. arches and domes) associated with architectural splendour continued to be developed for temple use. In some cases distinctive features associated with various regions and times were intentionally mixed to make an ecumenical statement. Particularly from the early 20th century, temples were consciously built in a distinctive regional style (e.g. southern) for migrants from that region relocated in distant parts (e.g. Delhi).

The continuing development of regional forms can be seen in the Sumari Temple at Ramnagar, across the Ganga from VARANASI, where the northern (Skt *nāgara*) tradition achieved a new sweeping verticality and textural richness. This stone temple to the Goddess (*c.* 1800) was raised over an arcade of the sort common to many post-Mughal buildings. Its body is quilted with narrative and iconic panels comparable to, yet distinct from, those on contemporary temples with terracotta decoration in Bengal. Traditional forms have thus become more geometric while taking on a new decorative finish. Distinct elements such as the grooved finial (*āmalasāraka*) and vase-and-foliage pilasters reveal a delicate cusping and floral detailing that mark post-Mughal architecture throughout north India.

The Bhonda Mahadev Mandir at Nagpur (*c.* 1818) also shows regional continuity, despite being built by artists from Rajasthan for a Mysore pundit at the expense of the East India Company. In western India the styles of Girnar and Shatrunjaya continued to develop with only occasional breaks. At Shatrunjaya the Motishah Tuk (1836) elaborates the underlying formal logic of the SOLANKI period and furthers its geometric reticulation of towers and walls. Refurbishment and additions of figurative sculpture were still being carried out in the 1990s; artisans headed by the Sompura family continued to build Gujarati-style temples following practices established for over a millennium.

In eastern India the building of brick temples in Bengal continued into the 19th century (*see* §7(ii)(e) above). This style, however, came to a halt as both artists and patrons shifted to such new commercial centres as Calcutta. Simpler structures, lacking terracotta figurative panels, continued to be built. Calcutta's Kalighat (1809) and Dakshineshwar (1855) temples maintained the tradition while adapting decorative elements from European colonial architecture (much as the temple building tradition in Gujarat assimilated the prestige and luxury effect of western Asian domes, a feature of that region's architecture of power in the 14th century and after).

In north India traditional imagery is typified by the style created for the Birla family, first in the Lakshmi Narayana Temple in New Delhi (see fig. 127) and later in cities including Varanasi, Bhopal, Hyderabad and Calcutta. These structures offer a blandly abstract version of the *nāgara*-type temple, eclectically synthesizing 12th-century Orissan tower profiles with elements imitating 2nd-century BC railings (*vedikās*) and gateways (*toraṇas*). The interiors are colourful amalgams of updated medieval decorative details and wall paintings in the style of the Bengali renaissance (*see* §VI, 4(x) below). The reliefs, by contrast, are marked by pictorial distortions based on the foreshortening that occurs in photographs. The range of deities and concepts honoured in the Birla temples extends ecumenically to embrace the widest range of Indian beliefs, including Buddhism, Jainism and Sikhism.

127. Lakshmi Narayana Temple, New Delhi, 1938; interior facing main sanctum

South India maintained greater continuity with the past than the north did during this period. The outermost gateways of SRIRANGAM, begun in about the 13th century, continued towards completion during the 20th century in forms that are difficult to distinguish from those of their forerunners. The temples within the MYSORE Palace date back to the 15th century and forward to as late as 1953, when the last maharaja dedicated a triple-shrined temple to the goddesses Savitri, Gayatri and Lakshmi. The general forms are derived from established tradition, with parapet shrines of the Vijayanagara period set over severe walls. Less standard, but no less traditional, are the temples of Karnataka's coast, which blend age-old Deccani features with Malabar wooden forms (usually associated with Kerala in the south) and imported Portuguese details (originating from Goa to the north).

Sikh religious complexes (*gurdwārās*) built in the 18th and 19th centuries draw on a variety of elements in the existing élite tradition. The Harmandir (Golden Temple) at AMRITSAR (see fig. 106 above) solidified this distinctive combination. Like a temple, it is a palatial structure enshrining an object, but like a mosque it has no idol; within is the Granth Sahib, the community's holy book.

The Harmandir, reconstructed in 1765, was given its present form under Ranjit Singh (*reg* 1799–1839) in the first decade of the 19th century. Its rectangular block is crowned by a central dome fringed with pinnacled pavilions (*chatrīs*) sheathed in marble and gilded copper. Most subsequent examples are white marble halls articulated with the domed pavilions of traditional temple architecture and detailed with the vocabulary of post-Mughal decorative forms.

The 20th-century rebirth of Buddhism, after a break of seven centuries, has produced two quite different styles. First there have been the historicizing temples of the Mahabodhi Society, as seen at Sarnath, and the similar revivalist stupas sponsored by the Japanese in the 1960s in Orissa and Bihar. In contrast, a genuinely original transformation of ancient Buddhist forms has been developed by followers of B. R. Ambedkar (1891–1956). The major monuments of this new tradition are at Nagpur's Dikshabhumi ('conversion ground') and at the site of Ambedkar's cremation in Bombay. The reinforced concrete stupas exhibit a shift of the cosmic dome symbolism from a solid mass indicating the Buddha's final extinction to an open hall where the faithful meet to organize the new Buddhist future.

A significant 20th-century development has been the spread of regional forms in response to the national integration of the subcontinent. An increasing number of Indians working in commerce, government service and other fields have moved from one region to another and have erected structures at their new locations in the idioms of their home regions. For example, in Madras a reinforced-concrete temple in the timber style of Kerala was built for the Ayappan community of Sabrimalai and a white marble Jaina temple for the west Indian Jaina community. Similarly, a red sandstone Rajasthani temple was constructed in Pune. South Indian gateway and temple forms can be seen in VRINDAVAN, UJJAIN and New Delhi. The patently Gujarati form of the Svami Narayana Mandir in the centre of Varanasi reveals this practice emerging in the 19th century.

See also §V, 8(i) below.

BIBLIOGRAPHY

J. Burgess: *The Temples of Śatruñjaya in Kathiawad* (Bombay, 1869/*R* Gandhinagar, 1976)

H. Cousens: *The Architectural Antiquities of Northern Gujarat, More Especially of the Districts Included in the Baroda State*, Archaeol. Surv. India, New Imp. Ser., xxxii (London, 1903) [incl. mat. on artisans]

G. Sanderson: *Types of Modern Indian Buildings* (Allahabad, 1913)

M. S. Mate: *Maratha Architecture, 1650 A.D. to 1850 A.D.* (Pune, 1959)

Temples of North India (Delhi, 1959), pp. 32–44

M. Edwards: *Indian Temples and Palaces* (London, 1969), pp. 137–49 [Hari Mandir]

M. A. Dhaky and H. P. Shastri: *The Riddle of the Temple of Somanatha* (Varanasi, 1974)

Mehar Singh: *Sikh Shrines in India* (Delhi, 1975)

P. O. Sompura: 'The Vāstuvidyā of Viśvakarmā', *Studies in Indian Temple Architecture*, ed. P. Chandra (Delhi, 1975), pp. 47–56

'Homage to Amritsar', *Marg*, xxx/3 (June 1977)

H. Sanyal: 'Temple Building in Bengal from the Fifteenth to the Nineteenth Century', *Historical Dimensions*, i of *Perspectives in Social Science* (Calcutta, 1977), pp. 120–77 [mat. on artisans]

S. Lewandowski: 'The Hindu Temple in South India', *Buildings in Society: Essays in Social Development of the Built Environment*, ed. A. D. King (London, 1980), pp. 123–48

J. R. Macy and E. Zelliot: 'Tradition and Innovation in Contemporary Indian Buddhism', *Studies in History of Buddhism*, ed. A. K. Narain (Delhi, 1980), pp. 133–53

M. S. Nagaraja Rao: 'The Mysore Palace: Its History and Architecture', *Dasarah Cultural Festivities, 1980 Souvenir* (Mysore, 1980), pp. 23–34

S. Chaturvedi: *Nagar Shaili ke naye Hindu mandir* [The new Hindu temples of Nagar Shaili] (Delhi, 1982)

A. A. Kanchansagarsuri: *Shri Shatrunjay Giriraj Darshan in Sculptures and Architecture* (Palitana, 1982)

G. Michell, ed.: *Brick Temples of Bengal: From the Archives of David McCutchion* (Princeton, 1983)

Shri Lakshminarayan Temple (Delhi, 1983)

A. B. Khare: *Vārānasī kā uttar madhya kālin devālaya sthapatya* [Later medieval temple construction of Varanasi] (diss., Varanasi, Banaras Hindu U., 1988)

C. Tadgell: *The History of Architecture in India: From the Dawn of Civilization to the End of the Raj* (London, 1990)

G. M. Tartakov: 'Art and Identity: The Rise of a New Buddhist Imagery', *A. J.* [New York], xlix/4 (1990), pp. 409–16

GARY MICHAEL TARTAKOV

(iii) Indian architecture and the West. Western interest in Indian architecture in the 19th and early 20th centuries had its roots in the 1700s. European interest in the subject was stimulated in the second half of the 18th century by the drawings and paintings of Western artists who visited India. Among the first was WILLIAM HODGES, who toured India from 1780 to 1783, subsequently exhibiting his paintings at the Royal Academy, London. The appeal of Indian architecture was in its irregular outlines and intricate detail at a time when picturesque forms in imaginative settings were in vogue. Plain classicism of the Palladian kind had fallen into disrepute; Joshua Reynolds, President of the Royal Academy, suggested in his *Discourse* of 1786 that architects should study Hodges's views for hints for creating new forms with greater appeal to the imagination.

One of the first architects to respond to Reynolds's ideas was George Dance, who in his restoration of the south front of the Guildhall in the City of London (1788) gave it a tripartite form with cusped windows and pseudo-minaret finials (*see* DANCE, (3)). The architect Samuel Pepys Cockerell (*see* COCKERELL, (1)) added a 'Mughal' dome to an otherwise classical house at Daylesford, Gloucestershire, in 1788. At Coleorton, Shropshire (1803), and Ashburnham Place, Sussex (1812–13), Dance combined Indian details with Tudor forms. Cockerell's finest achievement was Sezincote, Gloucestershire (1805), a brilliant synthesis of Grecian and Mughal styles designed for his nabob brother Sir Charles Cockerell (see fig. 128).

The artists Thomas and William DANIELL toured India from 1784 to 1794 and brought back more detailed information than Hodges, whose paintings were rather impressionistic. From 1795 on they published *Oriental Scenery*, a remarkable series of aquatint views of India that were greatly admired in Britain and Europe. In 1799 Thomas Daniell painted views of Indian architecture to decorate an 'Indian Room' in the Duchess Street mansion of Thomas Hope (*see* HOPE, (1)) in London. In 1800 Daniell designed a garden monument in the shape of a Hindu temple in Bihar for Major John Osborne at Melchet Park, Wiltshire. He also collaborated with S. P. Cockerell on the Indian details of Sezincote and designed the garden monuments there.

The success of the Daniells' aquatints seems to have encouraged the Prince Regent, who liked Indian styles of architecture, to ask WILLIAM PORDEN to design a stable

128. Sezincote, Gloucestershire, designed by Samuel Pepys Cockerell, 1805; engraving by F. C. Lewis after the drawing (1817) by John Martin (London, British Library)

block at Brighton in the Indian style (1804–8). When the Prince contemplated remodelling his pavilion at Brighton, HUMPHRY REPTON, an otherwise conservative designer opposed to the importation of foreign ideas, selected an Indian style for his designs (1806) for the pavilion. Like Dance and Cockerell, he was indebted to the Daniells' studies. Repton argued that the growing links between India and Britain made it more appropriate to build the pavilion in an Indian rather than a Grecian style. In the event his designs were not used. It was JOHN NASH who produced a pavilion (1815–21) in a fantasy style, including his own version of Indian columns, domes and minarets (for illustration *see* BRIGHTON).

Nash's pavilion was influential in Britain and abroad. Amon Henry Wilds (*c.* 1790–*c.* 1850) 'Indianized' his home on Western Terrace, Brighton, in the 1820s and used the style again for a spa (1835) at Gravesend, Kent. In Germany the pavilion influenced Albert Schadow's palm house at Peacock Island, Berlin (1829–31), and Jeffry Wyatville's unexecuted designs (1837) for an Indian-style house for the Duke of Sax-Meiningen (*see* WYATT, (3)). In the United States the designs of William Ranlett (*fl* 1840–62) for a villa in the Indian style to be built on Staten Island, New York, were reproduced in his *The Architect: A Series of Original Designs* (1847). From the mid-1840s to the 1860s the Connecticut architect HENRY AUSTIN produced many designs for villas, country houses and railway stations, which had Indian details applied to Tuscan forms. In a less serious mood, Iranistan (1847) was a copy by Leopold Eidlitz (see EIDLITZ, (1)) of the Brighton Pavilion executed at the request of the circus owner P. T. Barnum.

From the mid-19th century on, Indian craftsmanship became more widely known and respected in the West. Indian handicrafts were displayed at the Great Exhibition of 1851 in London. Indian craftsmen's mastery in wood, stone, metalwork and textiles and their understanding of surface decoration were praised by such connoisseurs as OWEN JONES, HENRY COLE and the Berlin art historian GUSTAV FRIEDRICH WAAGEN, who suggested that all students of art should study them.

In India the British were apathetic regarding Indian traditions until the rebellion of 1857 forced a reappraisal of their attitudes (*see* §(i) above). John Lockwood Kipling (1837–1911), Principal of the School of Art at Lahore in the 1870s and 1880s, appreciated Indian design and encouraged his students to use traditional techniques. He was particularly interested in wood-carving and in finding Western outlets for the talents and skills of Indian carvers. In 1883 a chance meeting with the Duke of Connaught at the Calcutta Exhibition led to a commission for a suite of rooms at the Duke's home, Bagshot Park, Surrey. Between 1884 and 1890, under the direction of Kipling and Sardar Ram Singh, the teacher of wood-carving, the students produced over 200 intricately carved panels to line a billiard room, as well as furniture and furnishings. The Duke's mother, Queen Victoria (*reg* 1837–1901), liked the Bagshot scheme and in 1890 commissioned Kipling to create an 'Indian dining room' (later called the Durbar Room) for Osborne, Isle of Wight. Bhai Ram Singh lived on the estate while construction took place. Both Kipling and the Duke hoped these schemes would be influential, but few further commissions followed.

In the late 1880s the Hungarian architect Ödön Lechner (*see* LECHNER, (1)) saw photographs of Anglo-Indian buildings while on a visit to London, greatly admired them and introduced Indian elements into his own designs. At a time of Austrian domination, Hungarians began to look for their national roots, which many believed were in India. Hence the use of Indian elements in Lechner's Museum of Applied Arts, Budapest (1893–7).

In the United States, Associated Artists, a group formed in 1879 that included the designers CANDACE WHEELER, Louis Comfort Tiffany (*see* TIFFANY, §2), SAMUEL COLMAN (ii) and Lockwood de Forest (1850–1932), was developing a new style of interior design less reliant on European influence. In this endeavour Indian woodcarvers played a major role. De Forest, who was responsible for wood-carving, went to India in 1881 and met the Hutheesingh family, who had workshops in Ahmadabad; he commissioned them to produce items for schemes in the United States. At the request of de Forest the carvers copied details and panels from many buildings in Ahmadabad, especially the Sidi Sayyid and Rani Sipri mosques. The first examples were used as overmantels in the Hamilton Fish House, New York (1883). Others were used in the decoration of the William S. Kimball House, Rochester, New York (1883), and in the houses of other wealthy clients on the East Coast and in Chicago. De Forest's own house (1886) on East 26th Street, New York, incorporates a copy of a carved bay window from Ahmadabad. His finest interior was probably that at the Deanery (1904) at Bryn Mawr College, Pennsylvania. In these schemes Tiffany and de Forest used Indian woodwork with Western fabrics and materials to create original effects rather than pastiche Indian interiors.

From the late 18th century on, 'Indian' and 'Moorish' elements were added to the vocabulary of fantasy styles. In 1797 William Porden exhibited a 'Design for a Place of Public Amusement in the Style of the Mohametan Architecture of Hindostan'. Such fantasy buildings were featured at spas, seaside resorts and other places of entertainment. Theatres and cinemas with Indian interiors included Mondielli's St Charles Theatre, New Orleans (1843), which was one of the first, and a striking 'Mughal' interior by Frank E. Edbrooke (*see* EDBROOKE, (1)) for the Broadway Theatre (1890) in Denver, Colorado. Thomas Lamb (1871–1942) designed several Indian interiors, notably the Loew's, 175th Street, New York (1930), remarkable for its fidelity to its sources, the cave temples of Ellora and Elephanta. In Britain, FRANK MATCHAM, a leading theatre architect, used Indian forms in his Empire Palace, Edinburgh (1892), Grand Opera House, Belfast (1895), and Hippodrome, Brighton (1900).

In the early 20th century tastes began to change in favour of simplicity and the austerity of Modern Movement ideas. Generally speaking, variety and intricacy, the keynotes of Indian architecture, could play no part. Buildings showing Indian influence that continued to be built in the West included the various Western headquarters of Indian religions. The Old Vedanta Temple, Webster Street, San Francisco (1905–8), is the earliest of such buildings. Other isolated examples include the Rajasthani pavilion (1978) in the Vienna travel bureau scheme by HANS HOLLEIN and, in Japan, the Mirror House (1979) by Monta Mozuna (*b* 1941), inspired by the observatory in New Delhi built by Jai Singh (*reg* 1700–43).

BIBLIOGRAPHY

H. Repton with J. A. Repton and G. S. Repton: *Designs for a Pavillon at Brighton* (London, 1808)
L. de Forest: *Indian Domestic Architecture* (Boston, 1885)
——: *Indian Architecture and Ornament* (Boston, 1887)
——: *Illustrations of Design* (Boston, 1912)
C. Lancaster: 'Oriental Forms in American Architecture, 1800–1870', *A. Bull.*, xxix (1947), pp. 183–93
M. Archer: *Indian Architecture and the British* (London, 1969)
A. S. Lewis: *Lockwood de Forest: Painter, Importer, Decorator* (Huntingdon, NY, 1975)
P. Mitter: *Much Maligned Monsters* (Oxford, 1977)
M. Archer: *Early Views in India* (London, 1979)
P. Conner: *Oriental Architecture in the West* (London, 1979)
R. Head: 'Bagshot Park and Indian Crafts', *Sources of Inspiration for Victorian Art and Architecture*, ed. S. Macready and F. Thompson (London, 1985)
——: *The Indian Style* (London, 1986)
S. Koppelkamm: *Exotische Architekturen im 18. und 19. Jahrhundert* (Berlin, 1987)
R. Head: 'Indian Crafts and Western Design', *J. R. Soc. A.*, cxxxvi (1988), pp. 116–31
——: *Catalogue of Paintings, Drawings, Engravings and Busts in the Royal Asiatic Society, London* (London, 1991)

RAYMOND HEAD

IV. Urban planning.

Although the Indian subcontinent is agrarian, it is also a land of major cities. Some, such as Varanasi and Patna, have had long, continuous histories; others are more recent; some have come and gone. From the Aryan settlements until the coming of Europeans, the morphology of these cities reflected the mingling of indigenous and invaders' cultures.

1. *c.* 3000–*c.* 500 BC. 2. *c.* 500 BC–*c.* AD 600. 3. *c.* AD 600–1947.

1. *c.* 3000–*c.* 500 BC. The earliest known villages, dating from about 7000 BC, have been excavated in Baluchistan, Pakistan. From 3000 BC on, a network of villages and townships formed part of a unified civilization in the Indus Valley and Saurashtra (part of modern Gujarat). Agricultural development there was sufficient to support a number of trading towns and at least three major cities. Two, it appears, were capitals—MOHENJO-DARO and HARAPPA—each with about 25,000 inhabitants and located some 550 km apart on the Indus. The third, LOTHAL, was smaller and a seaport on the Gulf of Khambhat (Cambay).

Mohenjo-daro and Harappa were both divided by the Indus, each with a raised citadel containing granaries and public buildings on their western banks. Their main streets formed rectangular grids orientated to the cardinal points. Alleys meandered within each block. Each city had a highly organized water supply and drainage system. The reasons for the decline of the Indus civilization are unknown, but in the 2nd millennium BC Aryan invaders from Central Asia moved into the valley. Their villages had a single large tree symbolizing the centre of the universe at their centre and a ceremonial path around the settlement.

The impact of Harappan and Aryan ideas on future Indian urban plans is conjectural. It seems the fusion of Aryan Vedas (India's earliest scriptures) with the beliefs of the indigenous people about 1000 BC provided the basis for later Hindu philosophical treatises and, possibly, for the *vāstu vidyā*, the science of architecture and urban planning (*see* §I, 10 above). The central component of the *vāstu vidyā* is the diagram known in Sanskrit as a *vāstu puruṣa maṇḍala*. The square, related to cosmic space by its orientation to the cardinal points, is the geometric form that indicates the absolute. The *maṇḍala* is subdivided into further squares, each representing a god, with the central square assigned to Brahma. Architectural manuals (*vāstu śāstras*) give 32 ways of subdividing the *maṇḍala*. For urban planning, the priest would choose the astrologically auspicious pattern possessing the number of subdivisions (*pādas*) sufficient for the intended population. Each subdivision, housing a specific caste, would form a square, but within this it could be developed along alleys. As settlements were built of sun-baked brick until Mughal times and have therefore not survived, it is difficult to assess the impact of such dicta on town design.

2. *c.* 500 BC–*c.* AD 600. In north India by the beginning of the 6th century BC or earlier, a second wave of urbanization occurred as many villages grew into towns, centres of industry and trade. Some, such as SRAVASTI, Rajagriha (RAJGIR), AYODHYA, KAUSAMBI and Kashi (VARANASI), were of importance on the Ganga plains; others, such as VAISHALI, UJJAIN, TAXILA and the port of Bharukachchha (BHARUCH), had wider significance. Rajagriha was possibly the first stone-walled fortified city in India (*c.* 6th century BC). By the 3rd century BC the Maurya capital, Pataliputra (modern PATNA), stretched for 14 km along the Ganga and was surrounded by a wall and moat with 64 gates.

From 180 BC the Maurya empire disintegrated slowly. Under a variety of rulers, the mercantile community—including traders from West and Central Asia in the north and Romans and Chinese in the south—developed, and guilds sponsored urban development, temples and charitable organizations (*see* §I, 6 above). In the north, towns grew on the caravan routes (e.g. Taxila and Bharuch). Through trade, West Asian and European ideas influenced India, and Indian ideas were taken to West Asia and east into Cambodia and Indonesia. In the south, continued trade made ports (e.g. KAVERIPATTINAM) important. Arikamedu (near Pondicherry) had a Roman trading station from the 1st century BC to the 2nd century AD.

Few buildings survive from the Gupta period (*c.* 4th–5th centuries AD), possibly because of later Muslim iconoclasm, but, more likely, because of the buildings' small scale and later development of the same sites. Most cities from this era that have been excavated have simple grid plans orientated to the cardinal points. Markets were located in the main thoroughfares, which had houses with balconies overlooking the streets. Wells and drains were frequent features. Large houses were located behind the main streets, while slums were located on the periphery. Affluent houses were built of brick or stone, and comfortable living extended into the middle classes. Formal education was available in Brahmanical institutions and Buddhist monasteries. In such cities, building codes were developed to control the spread of fires. As trade developed further, well-located towns gained in importance. Kannauj (in western Uttar Pradesh), MATHURA and Varanasi became centres both of textile production and of religion. Thaneswar was important because it controlled the upper Ganga. The country being predominantly rural, most public works consisted of irrigation improvements, road building, the planting of trees for shade and the construction of rest-houses.

3. *c.* AD 600–1947. From the 7th to the 12th century, when Hinduism was at its zenith, India was dotted with temple cities that acted as nodes in an arterial network (e.g. *see* BHUBANESHWAR, §1). The Chola monarchs, a major south Indian power from *c.* AD 980, sponsored the development of urban temple cities (e.g. THANJAVUR). Following the weakening of their power in the 12th century, Vijayanagara, 'City of Victory' (*see* HAMPI), became a major capital of the south. Founded in 1336 on the Tungabhadra River, Vijayanagara controlled the spice trade and had cotton industries. It was enclosed by seven rows of fortifications and consisted of a number of zones: a sacred centre at Tungabahadra, an intermediate irrigated valley, a fortified urban core and a royal centre. Although no full explanation exists for its plan, Vijayanagara was an urban realization of cosmic principles. Circumambulation of the sacred core was important, from the royal centre to the Ramachandra Temple (Rama being the prime god of the kings).

Arab traders had provided a Muslim presence in India from the founding of Islam, but Muslim rule only started in the late 12th century with the conquests of the Turko-Pathan sultans. The Muslims gave life to existing cities and founded new ones as centres of administration, trade and manufacturing. Lahore (in modern Pakistan), Delhi and Patna were raised to new levels. AHMADABAD was founded by Sultan Ahmad Shah (*reg* 1411–42) in 1411; Agra became the seat of government for Sultan Sikandar Lodi (*reg* 1489–1517). ALLAHABAD, Fatehpur Sikri and Attock (in modern Pakistan) owed their foundation to the Mughal emperor Akbar (*reg* 1556–1605). Contemporaneously, Faridabad was founded by Shaykh Farid Bukhari. Later new towns included Farrukhabad, Moradabad, Shikohabad, Najibabad and Faizabad (all in modern Uttar Pradesh).

The new cities were protected by walls, within which was a further protected citadel with paved roads, the royal palace, quarters for staff and its own water supply. The chief mosque was close by, and shops were on the main streets. Housing took the form of protected, often gated, neighbourhoods (*mohallas*, *pols*), in which clan groups resided. The neighbourhoods appear to have had haphazard layouts—good for defence—and to have consisted of terraced courtyard houses on narrow alleys; a central open space (chowk) might have a platform under a tree where the elders gathered.

DELHI, founded in the 1st century BC or before, was established as the capital of the Delhi sultanate and continued as such under the Mughals until it was replaced by AGRA. It was re-established as capital by Shah Jahan (*reg* 1628–58) in 1639. The city went through several changes in location due to adjustments in the course of the river Yamuna and was sacked a number of times. Sultan Islam Shah Sur (*reg* 1545–54) constructed Salimgarh

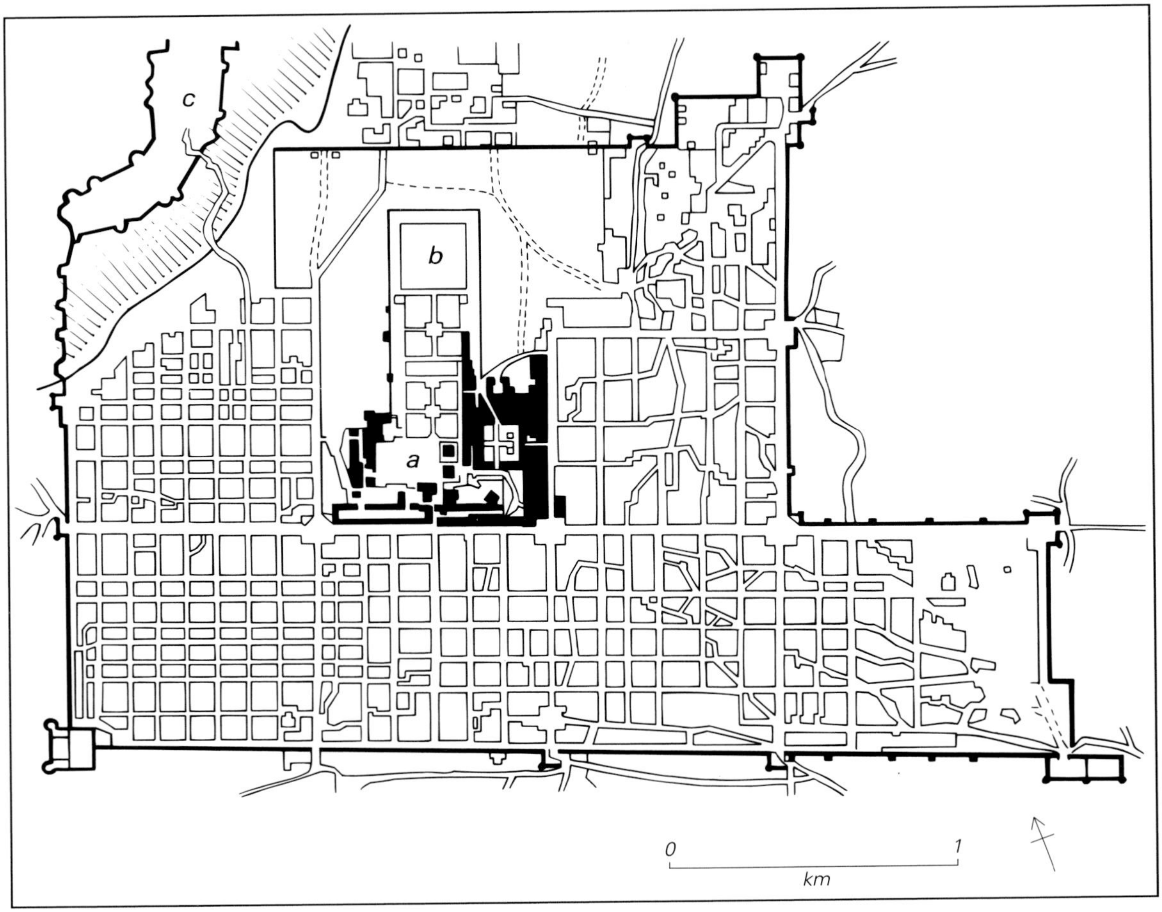

129. City plan of Jaipur, founded 1727: (a) City Palace; (b) Brahmapuri; (c) Nahargarh (Tiger) Fort

Fort, and Emperor Humayun (*reg* 1530–40, 1555–6) and Sher Shah Sur (*reg* 1538–45) both built new cities. Delhi owes its imperial splendour to Shah Jahan, who built a new fort (now Lal Qil'a or Red Fort), which was also the imperial palace, and to its west the city of Shahjahanabad. The city was walled, with gates opening to the arterial roads. Its central road, Chandi Chowk, lined with merchants' shops and houses, ran east–west to the fort and had a small canal running down its centre. The Jami' Mosque (Friday Mosque) still stands near its eastern end, towards the south, but other mosques, tombs and charitable institutions existed throughout the community.

Lahore was transformed from a village into a camp town by the sultans of Delhi to control their western holdings. Sultan Balban (*reg* 1266–87) strengthened its fort and encouraged merchants to settle, Emperor Akbar shifted his court to Lahore in 1584, and Jahangir (*reg* 1605–27) and Shah Jahan added to its commercial activities and beauty.

Under Mughal rule, Hindu traditions persisted in the adaptation of Islamic design principles, as at Fatehpur Sikri, and in urban layout, as at Jaipur. FATEHPUR SIKRI, founded by Akbar, was inhabited for only 18 years before the lack of water, summer heat, inaccessibility and other factors led to its abandonment in 1584. The city is surrounded by a wall, with the palace on the ridge. There appear to be no contemporary accounts of housing in the town, and no housing survives. The palace plan and architecture show a fusion of indigenous and Islamic concepts. The overall plan and use of water channels is Mughal, but the organization into broken grid symmetries is Hindu.

JAIPUR (see fig. 129), founded in 1727 by Maharaja Sawai Jai Singh (*reg* 1699–1743) of Amer, both follows and deviates from the *śāstras*. Broad main streets form a nine-square but unevenly divided *maṇḍala*, with one square displaced to a corner due to the site's topography. The town's orientation is not due north, possibly due to astrological considerations and the necessity of including an earlier palace in the plan. The palace is in the central square, and each subdivision, internally served by small streets and alleys, was reserved for a particular occupational group in accordance with the *vāstu vidyā*.

European settlements in India began with Portuguese factories (at CALICUT *c.* 1500 and COCHIN in the same year). The Portuguese were followed by the Dutch (at Masulipatam in 1605 and then on both Indian coasts) and the English (in Surat in 1611 and then throughout India).

The East India Company founded the three settlements that have grown into India's major metropolises: Bombay, received from the Portuguese (1661–5), Madras (1639) and Calcutta (1690). Danish and French factories developed from 1668 onwards. While the original factories were simply walled trading posts consisting of houses, warehouses and offices, they soon gave way to forts and permanent settlements.

In building their settlements, the Europeans re-created their home environments in India. Panaji in GOA is a city of narrow streets, white-washed churches and red-tiled roofs. PONDICHERRY, a grid-planned city founded by the French in 1674, has a central square, an *hôtel de ville* and wide roads and is punctuated by public gardens. Nagapatam was neatly laid out by the Dutch in squares with canals. British urban planning can be divided into two periods: before 1857, when control was under the East India Company, and thereafter. Madras and Calcutta were established as trading posts within forts. Fort St George (Madras) was built adjacent to the decaying Portuguese settlement of São Thomé, and Fort William (Calcutta) at the highest reach on the Hoogly for ships. Both were developed as English cities with Neo-classical architecture and gardens of the type in vogue 'at home'. Population growth accompanied commercial success. While Bombay continued to be highly diverse, with considerable economic power in the hands of the Parsis, in both Calcutta and Madras distinct 'white' and 'black' towns developed, the former with suburbs of BUNGALOWS set in gardens (the opposite of the traditional Hindu or Muslim house built around a courtyard) and the latter largely unplanned, except for a grid street layout. European architecture was adopted by many wealthy Indians.

After 1857, the consolidation of British power and the building of railways hardly changed the pace of urbanization, as the majority of Indians continued to live in villages. British India was, however, divided into districts (comparable to the *sarkar*s of Mughal India), in which administrative headquarters developed into the most important towns of their respective districts. A number of these towns had two additional features: Civil Lines and cantonments. Both were suburbs, the former for civil servants and business people and the latter for the army. Both were laid out as grid-planned communities. Their central roads were wide malls, streets were tree-lined, building plots were divided regularly, and the houses were bungalows. Churches, cemeteries, clubs and race and golf courses followed. Major road-widening schemes were run through congested areas, and sanitation improvements were made. New towns were also built: settlements in the arid parts of the Punjab and hill stations to house British administrators during the summer months. The former had either grid plans or roads radiating from a central chowk (e.g. Lyallpur, Faisalabad in modern Pakistan). The hill stations followed British plans and architectural styles. SIMLA, for example, consisted of the clutter of a small English country town with a parish church and an Elizabethan great house.

The era of British planning in India culminated in the city of New Delhi, inaugurated in 1931. (The imperial capital had been moved from Calcutta to Delhi in 1911.) Designed by EDWIN LUTYENS and HERBERT BAKER, New Delhi was planned along 'City Beautiful' lines, with radiating axial roads and important buildings or monuments terminating the vistas (*see* CITY BEAUTIFUL MOVEMENT). The viceroy's palace was located at the end of the major axis—now the Raj Path—with secretariat buildings on either side. The architecture is Neo-classical with Indian decorative elements.

New industrial cities (e.g. for steel manufacturing) were built in the 20th century. Jamshedpur, conceived by Jamshedi Tata, a Parsi industrialist, in 1908, had a series of master plans by European architects. The plans generally followed GARDEN CITY principles, with segregated land use, zoning, neighbourhood units and slum clearance projects.

BIBLIOGRAPHY

G. Hambly and W. Swaan: *Cities of Mughul India* (New York, 1968)
S. A. Nilsson: *European Architecture in India, 1750–1850* (London, 1968)
A. Volwashen: *Living Architecture: Indian* (New York, 1969)
R. L. Singh, ed.: *Morphology of Indian Cities* (Varanasi, 1971)
B. V. Begde: *Ancient and Medieval Town Planning in India* (New Delhi, 1978)
B. Bhattacharya: *Urban Development in India (Since Pre-historic Times)* (Delhi, 1979)
G. L. Possehl, ed.: *Harappan Civilization: A Contemporary Perspective* (Warminster, 1982)
C. Tadgell: *The History of Architecture in India from the Dawn of Civilization to the End of the Raj* (London, 1990)
I. Banga, ed.: *The City in Indian History* (Columbia, MO, 1991)
J. Gollings: *City of Victory, Vijayanagara: The Medieval Hindu Capital of Southern India* (New York, 1991)
V. Nand: 'Urbanism, Tradition and Continuity in Ahmedabad', *Mimar*, xxxviii (1991), pp. 26–36

JON LANG

V. Sculpture.

Although figurines in terracotta, bronze and other materials were produced in the Indian subcontinent from the second millennium BC, the history of monumental sculpture begins only with the Maurya dynasty in the 3rd century BC. Soon after this short-lived house collapsed, Indian sculpture began to develop regional characteristics. The formation of these idioms is little understood, since ties among artists, patrons and styles are difficult to assess. Multiple idioms often co-existed within the same political realm, and boundaries between kingdoms were constantly in flux. Recent scholarship has therefore emphasized regional traditions that transcended the rise and eclipse of individual dynasties. Consequently, this survey of Indian sculpture is organized along geographical and chronological lines, with some exceptions made where related works spill over regional or chronological divisions. Dynastic appellations are used in cases in which a distinctive style was restricted to a political realm during a specific period. However, there is no evidence to suggest that rulers directly shaped sculptural styles, apart from fostering environments in which the creation of art could flourish. Rulers competed for territory but also exchanged sons and daughters in marriage alliances that are recorded in inscriptions. It is documented also that playwrights, poets, merchants, ascetics and pilgrims travelled widely throughout the subcontinent. Such evidence expresses the common cultural bonds that unite the subcontinent's diverse regions and also provides a partial explanation for the artistic homogeneity embodied in sculpture and its iconography.

1. Introduction. 2. Pre- and protohistoric periods. 3. Early historic period–3rd century BC. 4. 2nd–1st century BC. 5. 1st–3rd century AD. 6. 4th–6th century AD. 7. 7th–18th century. 8. 19th century–1947.

1. INTRODUCTION. The subcontinent's religions have determined most of the themes depicted by sculptors over the centuries. In ancient Vedic rituals the gods received offerings through elaborate sacrifices, but they were not seen as concrete personalities. Rather, the gods were invisible yet powerful impulses of intelligence who could be approached only through metaphor. This concept of divinity may account for the fact that there is little sculpture, religious or otherwise, until several centuries after the second stage of urbanization in the Gangetic valley (*c.* 6th century BC). The early Indus civilization (*c.* 2550–*c.* 2000 BC) did, however, produce small works in stone and metal (see fig. 130 and §2 below) but no monumental images. Terracotta figurines, some apparently of the mother goddess, were also made in the early Indian and Gangetic cultures (*see* §VIII, 18 below). These two strands, one literary and abstract, the other popular and focused on images, foreshadowed the dual character of all subsequent sculpture in India. Thus while the gods came to be represented in concrete form, the mythopoetic legacy of the Vedic tradition assured that such representations were seen as metaphorical. This emphasis on the subtle nature of the divine is indicated by the widespread use of aniconic symbols. The most well-known and prevalent instance is the *liṅga*, a phallus-like stone emblematic of the god Shiva; it is considered the most appropriate and profound representation of that god. An extreme case is found at CHIDAMBARAM, where part of the temple sanctum is empty—to illustrate the non-particularized nature of the divine. Similarly, the sun is sometimes shown as a simple disc, and in the earliest stone sculpture, the Buddha and the saviours of Jainism are represented by symbolic attributes.

Such abstractions, however profound, did not fulfil popular devotional needs. Alongside the high tradition there was an enduring veneration of the divine both through images and as manifested in such things as trees, rivers and rock formations. This need for the tangible eventually led to anthropomorphic representations of the Buddha and the gods of the Brahmanical pantheon. Such sculptures were produced without denying the abstract potency of symbols. In India old traditions are seldom repudiated; rather they are absorbed into an eclectic hierarchy that views established practices and beliefs as part of a greater truth. Thus images are regarded both as symbols of higher reality and as actual manifestations to whom prayers, flowers, incense and food can be offered directly. This combination of the subtle and the substantial is neatly summarized by the geometric designs often incised on pedestals beneath images; in the ordinary course of events, these were never seen once the sculptures had been installed. The collective result of these ideas is that images are regarded as having a hidden power that captures a range of reality from the immediate to the transcendent. This deep conviction accounts for the extraordinary vitality of Indian sculpture over many centuries.

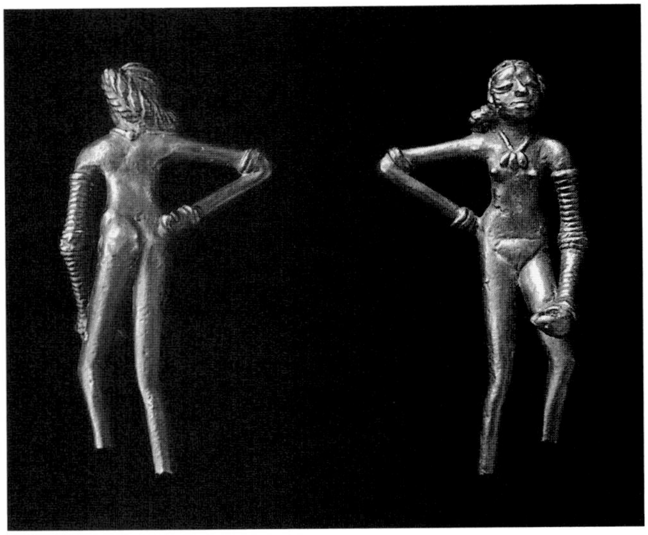

130. Female figure, bronze, from Mohenjo-daro, *c.* 2000 BC; front and back views (New Delhi, National Museum)

The earliest monuments with significant sculpture are dedicated to Buddhism. Gradually, however, production was given over to Vishnu and Shiva, the two major gods of Hinduism. Numerous deities are associated with these gods as consorts, offspring and attendants. Adherents of Jainism, the third religion with a substantial following in the subcontinent, have been responsible for roughly one-quarter of all the sculpture produced there, a quantity that far outweighs the Jaina community's relative size. (For discussions of these three religions and the related iconographic traditions, *see* §II, 1–3 above; BUDDHISM, §III, 1; HINDUISM, §1; and JAINISM.)

(i) Architectural context. (ii) Materials and techniques. (iii) Sculptors. (iv) Stylistic overview.

(i) Architectural context. For the most part sculpture did not exist apart from architecture in pre-modern India. Changing architectural styles and religious practices have meant, however, that the relationship between sculpture and architecture has varied considerably over the ages. The buildings of the Indus civilization, constructed of fired brick, appear to have been devoid of sculptural decoration (*see* §III, 2 above). After the second stage of urbanization, literary references suggest that ornament in stucco and paint developed, but as the architecture itself was primarily of wood, no examples have survived. Some idea of its appearance is provided by depictions in relief on early Buddhist monuments (2nd–1st century BC). These reliefs indicate that figural sculpture, almost certainly in wood, played only a minor role and consisted of such things as female figures on architectural struts. This restricted use of wood sculpture continued until the 19th century in regions where brick and timber architecture prevailed, most notably in the Kathmandu Valley and neighbouring regions of the Himalayas (*see* NEPAL, §III). However, the early Buddhist monuments themselves, particularly those at BHARHUT, SANCHI and AMARAVATI, herald not only the beginning of major monuments in stone but also the intimate relationship between sculpture and architecture, an important feature of Indian art. The gates of the Great Stupa at Sanchi (*c.* 50 BC) are completely

covered with reliefs from top to bottom; the spaces between architectural members are fitted with sculpture in the round. Within the gates, the dome of the stupa was decorated with festoons and other sculptural ornament, probably in stucco (*see* STUPA, §1). At Amaravati (*c.* 1st century AD), narrative and floral reliefs decorated the stupa railing. A thousand years later, the mature stone temples of KHAJURAHO displayed a similar decorative conception, illustrating the ancient Indian ideal that sees ornamentation (*alaṅkara*) as an essential ingredient of artistic effort.

While the ideal of ornament was finding expression in stone, brick temples continued to be built for popular deities. Examples from the KUSHANA period (1st–3rd century AD) employed stone for such pieces as the doorframes, window-surrounds and brackets. These portions were carved in relief, but the temple walls (none of which has survived above the foundations) seem to have been simply whitewashed. By the 5th century AD, the amount of ornamentation had increased to include decorative mouldings, pilasters and terracotta panels with figures or floral designs. These were fitted into niches on exterior walls or in the plinth; examples are seen at BHITARGAON, SARNATH and PAHARPUR. Occasionally, near life-size terracotta figures appear, as at AHICHCHHATRA. Details were also modelled out of stucco applied over brick (*see* §III, 5(i)(e) above). In later brick architecture, as exemplified by Tahdauli (9th century), the complex floral patterns covering the entire structure were cut into the bricks before the temple was erected (*see* BRICK, §II, 6).

Early stone temples, like their brick counterparts, were not heavily encrusted with relief. Only the doorframes (see fig. 134 below), pillars and image niches were singled out for exceptional embellishment. With time, however, the number of decorative mouldings increased, and these carried ornamental devices. Temple walls were subject to offsets that contained niches with sculpture. The main sculptures were seen as manifestations or projections of the divinity within the sanctum. Subsidiary images often depicted the guardians of the quarters (*dikpālas*), who simultaneously protected the building and incorporated the universe within it. The superstructure, originally conceived as a multi-storey mansion, was decorated with arched window-motifs and often with sculpture (see fig. 135 below). Notable exceptions are utilitarian structures such as the 11th-century monastic residences and remains of fortifications at Surwaya and Kadwaha. Apparently continuing ancient practices, these buildings are virtually devoid of decoration.

Because most work was destined for specific architectural settings, Indian sculpture has been dominated by the relief tradition. Individual stelae were typically set in niches or enshrined in a sanctum; thus in many cases even those pieces rendered on both sides, and therefore ostensibly in the round, give the impression of two reliefs brought together. Despite the prevalence of relief, examples of sculpture in the round were produced in every period. The pillars of the Maurya age (*c.* 3rd century BC) carried animals in the round (see fig. 131), and the popular nature spirits known as *yakṣīs* (female) and *yakṣas* (male) that were sculpted in subsequent centuries were treated similarly (see for example figs 141 and 144 below). After the 6th century Nandi (the bull that served as the mount of the god Shiva), often sited to face a temple in admiration of the main image within the sanctum, was always carved in the round. The fact that a significant number of these figures were required led to an accomplished handling of the Nandi theme. Another popular image for representation in the round was Varaha, Vishnu's boar incarnation. Often colossal in scale and free-standing, the Varaha was evidently meant to be circumambulated and viewed from all sides.

131. Bull capital, polished sandstone, from Rampurva, *c.* 3rd century BC (Delhi, Rashtrapati Bhavan)

From the 11th century the Islamic conquest disrupted sculptural practices in the subcontinent. However, many traditions continued, albeit circumscribed, under the patronage of the Jaina and Hindu communities. Sculptural embellishment became a characteristic of some Islamic buildings, including panels with elephants and other animals, brackets rendered as birds, floral arabesques and pilasters of carved stucco. Most spectacular are the large stone screens of the Mughal period (16th–18th century), which are pierced with complex geometric and floral patterns (*see also* §III, 1 above).

(ii) Materials and techniques. Indian sculpture was produced in every available material, from terracotta and wood to basalt and jade. Terracotta figurines have been produced steadily over the ages, whether as folk art or in styles established by stone sculpture. In areas where brick was the major building material, particularly the Gangetic plain, terracotta-carving was on a par with stonework. Wood was another material used in India from earliest times. Its perishable character has meant that little of significant age has survived, although examples of ornament from the 19th century provide instructive suggestions about it (*see* §VIII, 19 below).

Stone in its many varieties has been the major medium for figural sculpture. Generally, sculptors have employed what was available locally. There have been exceptions, however. The monumental pillars and sculptures of the Maurya period are mainly of a speckled buff sandstone quarried at Chunar in eastern India. Between the 1st and 6th centuries AD, MATHURA emerged as a leading centre of sculpture (*see* §5(i) below); many images in a red sandstone with buff flecks were produced, and examples were transported to important locales throughout India. In later periods, Jaina images in marble and burnished black basalt were also transported over considerable distances. These practices continued under the Mughals, who used white marble from Rajasthan and a speckled red sandstone (quarried at FATEHPUR SIKRI) for some imperial buildings.

Bronze-casting achieved a high degree of perfection, as is indicated by the extensive and well-known corpus of images from south India after the 9th century (*see* §7(vi)(a) below). Eastern and western India also had long-standing metal traditions, but many important images have been destroyed (for example *see* PAHARPUR). Few precious-metal images have survived. Stucco images were gilded in imitation of cast gold, a practice perpetuated in South-east Asia. Kashmiri bronzes were inlaid with silver, a technique elaborated in Nepal and Tibet by the insetting of gems.

The examination of standing temples built between the 8th and 13th centuries suggests that stone sculptors worked on site. This is indicated by the numerous unfinished blocks set into otherwise complete buildings. In some instances the decoration on such blocks is complete at one point but trails off into incised lines and then the smooth slab. In such cases it appears that work ceased because funding was withdrawn. Sculptors working on large projects appear to have been divided into two teams working on opposite sides of buildings or rock excavations. At times there was little coordination between teams. Numerous unfinished sculptural pieces, usually abandoned because of flaws in the stone, suggest that compositions were initially roughed out and then detailed from the top down. The detailing may have been left to a master.

Former dynastic capitals must have been centres of production, but in the north little has survived in such capital cities as Dhara, Tripuri and Kanyakubja. Other centres of sculpture such as Khajuraho were established for reasons that are less clear. Some centres, such as Chidambaram or Mt Abu, were selected because local myths stressed the sacredness of their locations (*see* MT ABU, §1). Monuments were built on naturally fortified hilltops (such as Kalanjar), near trade routes (such as the cave temples of western India) or at important pilgrimage centres (as at VARANASI).

(iii) Sculptors. India developed a carefully stratified society at an early period, and sculptors, along with others who engaged in manual crafts, were organized into well-defined class groups. Though akin to guilds, they occupied a different and fundamentally less powerful social position than their counterparts in late medieval Europe. The internal organization of artist families is not well documented, detailed information appearing in inscriptions only after the 10th century. Judging from the way engravers of stone and copperplate inscriptions referred to members of their families following the same profession, membership was apparently hereditary. Workshops were organized into a number of specializations, the least skilled workers being delegated to quarries. (Ancient chisel marks can still be detected in some locations.) Master artists were responsible for important figural sculpture on shrine walls and within sanctums. Most craftsmen, however, dressed ashlar blocks and produced the carved registers that formed temple plinths and superstructures (see fig. 132). Other specialists modelled and burnished plaster, while still others did woodwork or cast bronze. The fact that individual artists, though bound by traditional practices and shared conventions, appear to have enjoyed tremendous creative latitude is indicated by the diversity of detail on many major monuments.

132. *Masons at Work*, stone, from Khajuraho, 11th century (Khajuraho, Archaeological Museum)

Sculpture workshops do not appear to have moved over wide areas, and it is only rarely and in later periods that a 'guild' link can be established between monuments. Leading architects, in contrast, seem to have travelled extensively. The names of individual artists, often prefixed by the word 'craftsman' (*śilpi*), are found in short inscriptions from the Kushana period. Standing temples carry names and masons' marks from at least the 8th century (*see* for example PATTADAKAL). In some cases the names appear to be actual signatures—that is, proclamations of authorship; in others it seems that names simply document work on a complex temple project. Sculptors in traditional India were not artistic personalities in the modern sense, but the idea that they were anonymous craftsmen working in a timeless spiritual world is likewise an exaggeration.

However much sculpture was admired and revered in its religious setting, manual crafts were always seen as degrading activities by the learned élite. Thus texts discussing religious images are often theoretical and detached from actual practice; alternatively, a text could be a cryptic manual from the hands of craftsmen with little formal training in the Sanskrit language. Clear correlations between the surviving texts (*see* §I, 10 above) and the rich heritage of sculpture in all its regional variety and chronological complexity are seldom traceable.

DONALD M. STADTNER, MICHAEL D. WILLIS

(iv) Stylistic overview. Sculptures of the human figure, whether objects of cult worship or components of narrative relief, have typically communicated their meaning through a profound and complex iconography. Coupled with these devices are two perennial stylistic components of Indian sculpture, volumetric modelling and a certain fluidity of form.

A subtle tension suggesting close observation is apparent in the body of a metal female figurine from the Indus Valley site of Mohenjo-daro, though the figure's overelongated, sticklike limbs show a stylization perhaps related to the technique of working in metal (see fig. 130 above; *see also* §2(ii)(a) below). The figurine's pose anticipates that of south Indian metal images of the much later Chola period (9th–13th century). The marked volumetric form of a male figure from Mohenjo-daro, carved in stone though of diminutive size, heralds the less powerfully modelled bulk of 3rd-century BC colossal stone statues from Patna (ancient Pataliputra) in eastern India. More angular are the copper sculptures in the round of a chariot with charioteer and animal figures (New Delhi, N. Mus.) found at Daimabad in Maharashtra and variously dated between *c.* 2000 and *c.* 1000 BC.

Sculpture is almost completely lacking between the time of the Indus or Harappa civilization (*c.* 2550–*c.* 2000 BC) and *c.* 300 BC. Exceptions are copper harpoons and hominid plaques of unknown function or significance found in the Gangetic plain, which have a powerful and elegant form. From *c.* 300 BC onward sculpture in stone emerges in different categories: as volumetric statuary, as part of an architectural context and as rock-cut monuments. The capitals of the free-standing pillars utilized by the emperor Ashoka (*reg c.* 269–*c.* 232 BC) to promulgate his edicts juxtapose stylized lotus shapes and single or addorsed animals sculpted in the round. The style of these animal sculptures in the round is either 'naturalistic' in its fulsome modelling of convex planes (reminiscent of the miniature carvings on the seals of the Indus civilization), as in the bull capital from Rampurva (see fig. 131 above), or more stylized in the manner of contemporary Persian sculpture (*see* IRAN, ANCIENT, §III, 3), as in the lion capital from Sarnath (for illustration *see* SARNATH). Among large statues carved in the round is the statue of a whisk bearer from Didarganj, an apogee of the Indian ideal of femininity (see fig. 139 below).

'Naturalistic accents' were integrated with the accoutrements of colossal male figures from 2nd-century BC sites in Bihar and Madhya Pradesh (see fig. 141 below). Contrasting with their unified bulk are the crisp and delicate terracotta figurines from Patna and Tamluk. The small facial features of the latter are set off by the extravaganzas of clay pellets affixed to their headdresses and garments.

Indian sculpture from the centuries following the Maurya period is predominantly Buddhist. The posts and beams of the stone railings surrounding Buddhist stupas are carved with relief panels full of lotus motifs and narrative scenes from the life of the Buddha teeming with human figures and symbols, though the Buddha does not figure among them (see fig. 133). From the 1st century BC and with increasing frequency, the Buddha himself was represented as a male figure endowed with special characteristics, including the *uṣṇīṣa* (cranial protuberance). The gestures of his hands (*mudrā*s) also became part of the

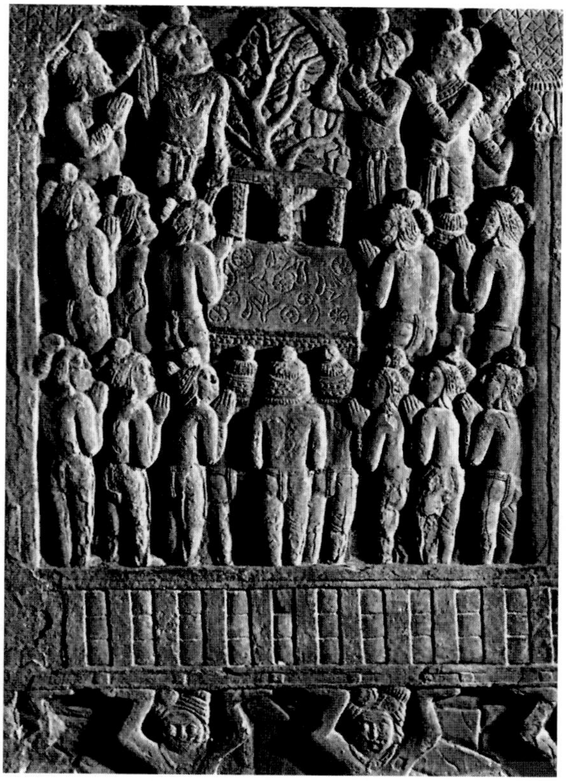

133. *Great Miracle at Sravasti*, carved on a pillar from Bharhut, mid-2nd century BC (Calcutta, Indian Museum)

iconography of the Buddha image (*see* §II, 2 above). Icons, whether Buddhist, Jaina or Brahmanical, from this time were set up in ever growing numbers. The subjects and motifs of early Buddhist art fall into two broad categories: a relief mode, the main subject of which was the lotus, and a narrative mode filled with human activity. Lotus plants and stalks are conduits of a linear movement that also flows in the branches of trees and the limbs of human figures, filling the reliefs.

Fluid convex shapes distinguish the sculpture of north India from the 2nd century BC to the 1st century AD and extend into Andhra Pradesh, where a more compacted modelling accentuates the structure of the human body, as in the liṅga at Gudimallam (see fig. 150 below). This fluidity can be seen in both structural and rock-cut sculptures. It is carried not only by the linear rhythms of the undulating lotus stalk—of which the railing panels at Stupa 2 at Sanchi are a clear example—but also in the reliefs of BHAJA, which spread like a seemingly viscous mass over the walls of the rock-cut monastery (*see* §4(ii)–(iii) below).

Under Shaka rule sculpture in Mathura continued these longstanding traditions. However, a new, hybrid form of sculpture came into being in the late 1st century BC in the north-west (now Afghanistan and Pakistan), an area traversed and inhabited by nomadic groups from western Asia. This part of the subcontinent was thus exposed to Hellenistic and Roman idioms. Known as Gandhara, the region followed a stylistic course of its own characterized by 'Classical' physiognomy and cumbersome drapery imposed on typically ample Indian figures (*see* §5(ii) below). The Mathura school of sculpture's plasticity of form remained unaffected by the conventions that evolved in the north-west.

The Mathura railing posts of the early 1st century BC, in addition to being decorated with panels and roundels full of symbolic or narrative reliefs, were adorned with large figures of *yakṣa*s and *yakṣī*s and serpent divinities, kings in their own realm rendering homage, worship and protection to the stupa. In the Kushana-period sculptures of Mathura (*see* §5(i) below), three centuries later, the opulent figures of the *yakṣī*s sculpted in much higher relief (almost in the round) have assumed a provocative stance and facial expression. The plastic means by which they fulfil their role descend directly from the fluidity of form of which the lotus stem was the prime symbol. Its convex planes, however, are now distended and particularized in their fullness.

For half a millennium, sculpture in Andhra Pradesh kept pace with the transformations of style in Mathura. At AMARAVATI, sculpture achieved an unprecedented delicacy and intensity of style and emotion. The motif of the simple lotus creeper, moreover, having displayed its convex shapes on the flat ground of the relief, was augmented by the 4th century by a more richly foliate creeper; the leaves, obliquely carved against their ground, brought a new sculptural texture, and the concave planes, cut at various angles, introduced variations of light and shade into panels filled with foliage. Such relief panels on temple walls were entirely filled with vegetation, which for several centuries would set off the smooth shapes of the human figures on the same buildings. Regional styles are distinct from one another as much in the early centuries AD as half a millennium later. The ponderousness of western Indian sculpture persisted from KARLE to AJANTA, while the impassioned elegance of Amaravati was inherited to an extent by Pallava sculpture of the late 6th century to the 9th in the south (*see* §7(vi)(a) below).

By the 5th century an economy and subtlety of modelling seem to carry the indwelling breath of the image through its surging and intersecting planes. This quality graces Indian sculpture particularly in the school of Sarnath (*see* §6(i) below). The faces of its images portray states of meditation and harmony. In the 5th and 6th centuries, Indian sculptors transformed stone into an apparently palpitating medium. In this period the most subtle and powerful sculptures were carved from living rock in central India, the Deccan and the south. These include examples from Udayagiri, Ajanta, Elephanta, Ellora, Badami, Mamallapuram and Kalugumalai. As the forms of structural architecture developed into the 13th century, the sculptures with which they were decorated continued to embody the ancient traditions, but with regional variations. Metal sculpture attained its peak in south India between the 9th and 12th centuries (*see* §7(vi)(a) below). The plastic single figure thus had its place both as a free-standing form and as an element of temple décor, for example on the doorframes of 'early' temples (see fig. 134). With increasing programmatic complexity, images were assigned positions in relation both to the sanctum and to the four

134. Parvati Temple, Nachna, lower part of the left doorway, *c.* late 5th century AD

directions (see fig. 135). The sanctum as a rule holds only one image or a symbol, such as the *liṅga*. The figures on the outside of the walls, however, are also integral to the temple (*prasāda*), as are the sculptural multiples of miniature aediculae or miniature towers on the superstructure. In the unfolding of its meaning, the entire surface of the building, of which the architectural and the anthropomorphic carvings are part, achieves an effect that is uniquely that of Indian sculpture.

STELLA KRAMRISCH

BIBLIOGRAPHY

A. K. Coomaraswamy: *Introduction to Indian and Indonesian Art* (London, 1927)
——: *Yakṣas*, 2 vols (Washington, DC, 1928–31/*R* New Delhi, 1971)
S. Kramrisch: *Indian Sculpture* (Oxford, 1933)
A. K. Coomaraswamy: *Transformation of Nature in Art* (Cambridge, 1934)
S. Kramrisch: 'Ornament', *A. Bull.*, xxi (1939), pp. 375–82
A. L. Basham: *The Wonder That Was India* (London, 1954, rev. 1967)
H. Zimmer: *The Art of Indian Asia: Its Mythology and Transformations*, 2 vols, ed. J. Campbell (New York, 1955)
Marg, xii/3 (March 1959) [issue on Rajasthani sculpture]
F. D. K. Bosch: *The Golden Germ: An Introduction to Indian Symbolism* (The Hague, 1960)
C. Sivaramamurti: *Indian Sculpture* (Bombay, 1961)
H. Zimmer: *Myths and Symbols in Indian Art and Civilization* (Princeton, 1963)
Master Bronzes of India (exh. cat. by P. Chandra, Chicago, IL, A. Inst.; Kansas City, MO, Nelson–Atkins Mus. A.; 1965)
Marg, xxvi/3 (June 1973) [issue on Madhya Pradesh sculptures]
J. Irwin: '"Asokan" Pillars: A Reassessment of the Evidence. Part III: Capitals', *Burl. Mag.*, cxvii (Oct 1975), pp. 631–43
R. N. Misra: *Ancient Artists and Art Activity* (Simla, 1975)
P. Pal: *Bronzes of Kashmir* (New York, 1975)
C. Sivaramamurti: *The Art of India* (New York, 1977)
A. de Lippe: *Indian Medieval Sculpture* (Amsterdam, 1978)
H. D. Sankalia: *Pre-historic Art in India* (Durham, 1978)
C. Sivaramamurti: *Chitrasutra of the Vishnudharmottara* (New Delhi, 1978)
A. N. Heeramaneck: *Masterpieces of Indian Sculpture from the Former Collections of Nasli M. Heeramaneck* (New York, 1979)
Manifestations of Shiva (exh. cat. by S. Kramrisch, Philadelphia, PA, Mus. A., 1981)
P. Mazumdar: 'Guilds in Early Medieval North India (*c*. AD 606–1206)', *Aspects of Indian Art*, ed. J. Chakrabarty and D. C. Bhattacharyya (Calcutta, 1983), pp. 48–55
B. S. Miller, ed.: *Exploring India's Sacred Art: Selected Writings of Stella Kramrisch* (Philadelphia, 1983)
R. Nagaswamy: *Masterpieces of Early South Indian Bronzes* (New Delhi, 1983)
S. Z. Czuma: *Kushan Sculpture: Images from Early India* (Cleveland, 1985)
S. L. Huntington: *The Art of Ancient India: Buddhist, Hindu, Jain* (Tokyo, 1985)
The Sculpture of India, 3000 BC*–1300* AD (exh. cat., ed. P. Chandra; Washington, DC, N.G.A., 1985)
J. C. Harle: *The Art and Architecture of the Indian Subcontinent* (New York, 1986)
From Indian Earth: 4,000 Years of Terracotta Art (exh. cat., ed. A. Poster; New York, Brooklyn Mus., 1986)
P. Pal: *Indian Sculpture* (New York, 1987)
G. Schopen: 'On Monks, Nuns, and "Vulgar" Practices: The Introduction of the Image Cult into Indian Buddhism', *Artibus Asiae*, xlix/1–2 (1988–9), pp. 153–68
J. Williams: 'From the Fifth to the Twentieth Century and Back', *A. J.* [New York], xlix (1990), pp. 363–9

STELLA KRAMRISCH, DONALD M. STADTNER, MICHAEL D. WILLIS

2. Pre- and protohistoric periods. Eleven significant pieces of sculpture of human and divine subjects survive from sites of the Indus (or Harappan) civilization (*c*. 2550–*c*. 2000 BC; *see* §I, 2 above). Two pieces are from Harappa, the remainder from Mohenjo-daro (both sites in modern Pakistan). All these pieces are now in museums in Pakistan, unless stated otherwise, circulating

135. *Vishnu*, carved on lower part of west side of superstructure, Vettuvankovil cave temple, Kalugumalai, *c*. 8th century AD

between Karachi, Lahore and Mohenjo-daro. Fine small-scale carvings occur on stamp seals from Harappa, Mohenjo-daro and other sites. Numerous terracotta figurines survive from the Indus civilization and from cultures that preceded it by several millennia.

(i) Stone and bronze figures. (ii) Seals. (iii) Terracotta figurines.

(i) Stone and bronze figures. The most controversial piece, found at Harappa, is a red jasper male torso (New Delhi, N. Mus.; see fig. 136) discovered in 1928–9 by M. S. Vats, who came upon it in the vicinity of the circular brick threshing floors to the south of the Great Granary. It has been ascribed to an intermediate level of the site (Vats, 1940, pp. 74–5). Made of dense, unflawed stone and a deep, even red, it is 95 mm high and broken at the legs, with the head and arms missing. There are holes for the attachment of the head and arms, but none is apparent for the legs. Prominent circular indentations, probably made by a tube drill, are located on the front of each shoulder. Although their function is unknown, they indicate the attachment position for a garment or places to inlay ornaments (Marshall, 1931, p. 46). Holes at the nipples may have taken inlay. The piece is a frontal nude, with the genitalia carefully modelled, although now defaced.

Vats insisted from the beginning that the piece should be attributed to the Harappan civilization, citing the use of the tube drill and the facts that the sculpture was made in pieces (not a practice in historic India for small sculpture) and that there is no piece of sculpture from the historic period made of the same material. Sir John Marshall countered this claim by stating that the torso had not been created from parts but had been broken and repaired in antiquity. He preferred to attribute it to a historic age, possibly the Gupta period (4th–5th century AD), and referred to it in relation to other Harappan sculpture as follows: 'They are, without exception, crude, archaic and lacking in anatomical correctness, whereas the

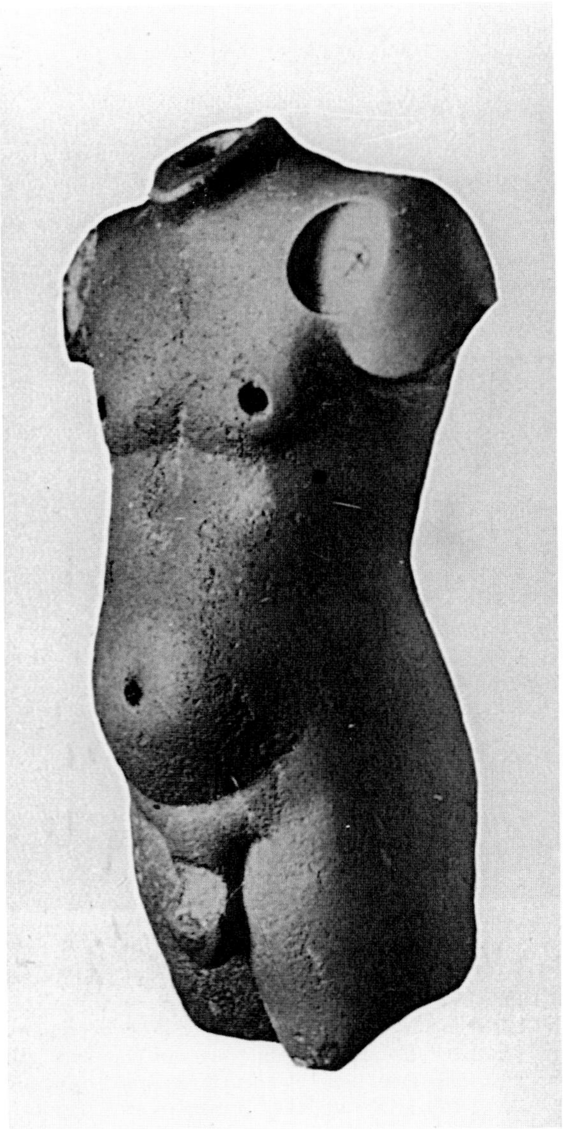

136. Male torso, red jasper, h. 95 mm, from Harappa, ?3rd millennium BC (New Delhi, National Museum)

figure in question is anatomically correct and the work of a sculptor in possession of an advanced technique' (Marshall, in Vats, 1928–9, p. 79). This position softened somewhat as Marshall considered other Harappan art. Noting the exquisite portrayal of a zebu on a seal from Mohenjo-daro (Marshall, 1931, no. 337), he stated: 'Experienced sculptors whom I have consulted take the view that an artist who could engrave the seal in question would have had little difficulty in carving the statuette' (Marshall, 1931, p. 47). Sir Mortimer Wheeler considered the torso to be 'disputed' (Wheeler, pp. 86, 89).

The broken torso of a dancing figure, made of dark grey stone, was found by Rai Bahadur Daya Ram Sahni during his excavations at Harappa. Vats believed that the torso was uncovered on Mound F near the Great Granary (Vats, 1940, p. 22). This would have been about 150 m north of the spot where the red jasper torso was found. Everything in this part of the site can be safely assigned to the Mature or Urban Phase Harappan (*c.* 2550–*c.* 2000 BC), so gross chronology is not a problem. The torso is 99 mm high, with the head, arms and legs missing. While the legs were broken off, there are holes for attaching the arms and head. The pose is that of a dancer with his right leg fixed and left one lifted. The twist of the torso gives the figure a wonderful sense of movement. Nothing remains to suggest the arms' position. Marshall felt it likely that the figure was 'ithyphallic, since the *membrum virile* was made in a separate piece'. From the thickness of the neck, he inferred 'that the dancer was three-headed, or at any rate three-faced' and conjectured that it may have represented Shiva as Lord of Dance (Nataraja) or an animal-headed deity (Marshall, 1931, p. 46). Wheeler (1953, p. 90) agreed that the identification with Shiva Nataraja was plausible.

There are two small metal figurines of what are generally called 'dancing girls' from Mohenjo-daro. The best of these (New Delhi, N. Mus.; see fig. 130 above) was found in a small house by Rai Bahadur Daya Ram Sahni during the 1926–7 field season, deep within the urban maze of the south-western quarter of the city. Now 108 mm high, it was solid cast in bronze, using the lost-wax process. It represents a thin young woman, standing with her head tilted slightly back. The figurine is highly stylized; the legs and arms are sticklike, and there is no sense of flesh on the body or of anatomy to the joints. The left leg is bent at the knee. The right arm is also bent, with the hand placed provocatively on the back of the hip, the thumb outside a clenched fist. The left arm rests slightly bent on the left thigh. The left thumb and forefinger form a circle, and it is apparent that the figurine once held a small object, now missing.

The *Dancing Girl* is naked except for some adornments. Around her neck is a small necklace with three large pendent beads. On her left arm she wears 24 or 25 bangles that would severely restrict the mobility of an actual elbow joint. The right arm has four bangles, two at the wrist and two above the elbow. The hair is worn in a kind of loose bun, rendered in some detail and much the same as some Indian coiffures today.

The second metal *Dancing Girl* was found by Ernest J. H. Mackay in an otherwise undistinguished building during his final full season at Mohenjo-daro (1930–31; Mackay, 1930–34, p. 60). The mirror image of the first example, this figurine is 132 mm high. The legs are straighter than those of the other example, and the hair is tied back with a bow. This sculpture's state of preservation is not as fine as that of the first example, but as Mackay observed, 'despite the damage by corrosion it is clear that the workmanship and finish of this later figure is inferior to that found earlier' (Mackay, 1930–34, p. 60).

Much of the stone sculpture from Mohenjo-daro is described just as it came from the earth in the preliminary reports that were published annually until the field season of 1936–7. Mackay (1937–8) assembled the first comprehensive review of this material. Alexandra Ardeleanu-Jansen's survey (1983) is by far the most comprehensive treatment of the topic. Her later paper (1991), using a more stylistic approach, is more widely available.

The so-called *Priest-King* from Mohenjo-daro (see fig. 137) has probably come to symbolize the Harappan civilization more than any other single object. This steatite bust was found by Rao Bahadur K. N. Dikshit during the 1925–6 season (Marshall, 1925–6, pp. 90–91, pl. XLIIIa). It was recovered from a small enclosure with some curious parallel walls that Mackay (1931, p. 356, pl. XCVIII, 1–4) suggested might have enclosed the hypocaust for an ancient bath. The find-spot of the *Priest-King* can be attributed to the Late Period at Mohenjo-daro.

Though Mackay described this sculpture in great detail, some observations will help to place the piece in context. The statue is broken at the bottom and survives to only 180 mm. It represents a male figure dressed in a toga-like garment draped over the left shoulder and under the right arm. This garment is covered in the trefoil pattern found on other objects from Indus civilization sites. One hole is present below each ear, apparently to hold a necklace in place. The back of the head is smooth, and it may be that the sculpture was intended to be placed in a niche with a sloping back. The broken nose is straight but does not seem to have dominated the face. The eyes appear to be partially closed or hooded but not of Asian type, at least according to Mackay (1931, p. 357). One shell eye-inlay still survived when the piece was found. The ears are

137. *Priest-King*, steatite, h. 180 mm, from Mohenjo-daro, Late Period (Karachi, National Museum of Pakistan)

fashioned rather crudely as the simple 'C'-shapes characteristic of Harappan sculpture. In fact they are quite out of place, the figure's other physical features being far more sophisticated in their representation. The hair is cropped short, eliminating the bun common to many Harappan figures, both male and female. It is parted in the middle and kept in place by a simple band that hangs down the back of the head to below the shoulders. The beard is close cropped, and there may or may not be a moustache (Mackay, 1931, p. 357; Wheeler, p. 86). The suggestion that this work portrays a priest was first made by Mackay (in Marshall, 1925–6, p. 91; see also Mackay, 1931, p. 357). Wheeler seems to have coined the term 'Priest-King' (p. 65), a phrase perfectly in line with his vision of the Harappan civilization. That the individual portrayed was either a 'priest' or a 'king', let alone both, is without foundation. Nor can it be demonstrated that the work is a portrait or even a representation of a human being, since it is quite conceivable that it represents a deity and was intended for veneration (Mackay, 1931, p. 357; Wheeler, p. 87).

Harold Hargreaves found a well-preserved limestone head in a large building in a Late Period context. This piece was fully described by Mackay (1931, p. 359). It survives to a height of 175 mm and has no trace of colour or other finish. Some features offer contrasts to the *Priest-King*. Since the sculpture is broken at the neck, there is no trace of dress. An attempt was made to represent long, wavy hair arranged in a bun at the back of the head and held in place with a string fillet and small hairpin with a round top, clearly visible on the sculpture's left side. The limestone head has a short beard, and the subject's upper lip seems definitely to have been shaved. The mouth is held in a slight smile, and the lips, which are not full, are slightly pursed. The nose is of medium size, but broken. Each ear is a simple, almost closed oval rather than the more usual 'C'. The almond-shaped eyes, possibly inlaid at one time, contrast with the heavily lidded eyes of the *Priest-King*. More lifelike than the latter, this head may have been an attempt at portraiture.

Ernest Mackay found a headless, seated male statue of grey alabaster in a chamber in the southern half of the Mound of the Great Bath (Mackay, 1926–7, p. 966; 1931, pp. 358–9, pl. C, 1–3; Ardeleanu-Jansen, 1991, p. 166). It can be attributed to the Late Period at the site. The statue survives to 292 mm in height. Based on the thickness of the clothing around the waist, Mackay hypothesized that the figure was meant to be wearing a thick, kiltlike garment. This was covered by a thinner garment or shawl that went over the left shoulder and under the right arm, just as in the case of the *Priest-King*. The left arm lies along the outer side of the left leg, which is raised and bent at the knee, while the right hand rests on the right knee. The hands are crudely rendered. A 'rope' of hair hangs down the back, asymmetrically to the right. According to Mackay, 'a squarish projection at the back of the head is evidently intended to represent a knot of hair. It is, however, unfinished and shows the chisel marks of the preliminary stone dressing' (1931, p. 359). This statue is seated and costumed in the same manner as some males in Bactrian art. Whether the other pieces of sculpture from Mohenjo-daro originally were posed this way is conjectural, although

Ardeleanu-Jansen's reconstruction of the *Priest-King* in this posture is quite convincing (1991, pp. 167–9).

The so-called *Official of L Area* is a yellow limestone piece found in a chamber on the southern half of the Mound of the Great Bath; it can be ascribed to the Late Period at Mohenjo-daro. Surviving to a height of 197 mm it represents a beardless personage, thought to be a male. This notion is based on the arrangement of the hair in a bun at the back and held in place by a fillet extending around from the front. The mouth is full and straight, without expression. The nose is broken but appears to have been carved in a fashion not unlike the other sculptures from Mohenjo-daro. The eyes are hollow, drilled to take inlay of some kind. Once again the ear is a simple crescent. This piece and the well-preserved limestone head may have been created by the same hand.

A badly weathered head of a female in grey limestone also comes from L Area. Found in 1926–7, it can be assigned to the Late Period of the site (Mackay, 1926–7, pl. XIX, 1–3; 1931, pp. 357–8, pl. XCIX, 1–3). This work is in a bad state of preservation, the nose, mouth and ears being completely weathered away. It survives to a height of 150 mm. According to Mackay, 'it apparently represents a female, for there is no beard, and the hair, which is slightly curly, hangs down the back of the head. The eyes beneath the receding brows are long and narrow and the original inlay of the right eye, which is made of a whiter stone than the head, is still in place' (1931, p. 358).

The headless body of the poorly preserved alabaster statue of a half-kneeling male was found by Hargreaves lying on the top of a wall during the 1925–6 field season (Marshall, 1925–6, p. 85; Mackay, 1931, pp. 359–60). Three days later, part of the head was found elsewhere at the site and, the next day, the final fragment. Known as the *Sad Man*, this sculpture can be attributed to the Late Period at Mohenjo-daro. Its broken, scattered state indicates that it was damaged during, or just after, the abandonment of the area in which it was found, which may have been a temple (Wheeler, pp. 52–3). The *Sad Man* survives to 420 mm in height. It is badly weathered, and many of the features are damaged or obliterated. The original posture is difficult to determine. The left leg is folded under the figure, with the left hand resting on the knee. The right leg is bent, with the knee slightly raised and the right hand resting on it. If this position were assumed in life, it would be extremely uncomfortable, perhaps explaining the man's dour countenance. The head is disproportionately large. The face is long, the nose straight, the mouth probably open and the eyes narrow and sad, although some of these details of appearance may be due to weathering. Traces of a beard are present. The hair seems to be short, possibly parted in the middle, with a fillet around the front that hangs in two strands down the back, not unlike that of the *Priest-King*. The *Sad Man* was dressed in a skirt hung on a cord, which can be seen from the rear, and is naked from the waist up. Mackay (1931, p. 360) suggested that this figure may represent a deity in some grotesque form. The fact that the statue is certainly not a realistic portrayal of a human being could be due to a lack of skill on the part of the carver.

One of the finds from the 1931 season is the brown limestone bust of a male from a Late level of the site (Ardeleanu-Jansen, 1983, p. 140). The bust was cleanly broken at the neck and is not severely weathered, although the nose is broken. It is 145 mm high. The expression is not very animated but if viewed from the left appears to be a scowl. The mouth is almost straight, with only a slight downturn. The chin is short. The face is unbearded, but the hair is depicted in a herringbone pattern that suggests waves like that of the Late Period limestone head. The hair is worn in a bun at the back of the head and held in place by a fillet; the latter was either tied in a bow or used in conjunction with a hair clip or two pins. There are two bands hanging from the fillet on the back of the head. The ears are prominent, simple 'C' shapes, much like those of other sculptures from Mohenjo-daro. The eyes are ovate. Elisabeth C. L. During Caspers has suggested that this indicates a 'Sino-Tibetan of Mongoloid descent' (p. 228). Such a determination depends on the degree to which this sculpture might be thought of as a portrait. Some linguistic data do suggest that one of the languages of the greater Indus region in antiquity was of Sino-Tibetan affinity.

(ii) Seals. The stamp seals of the Indus civilization are the finest expression of the art of these ancient peoples. For the most part they are small (*c*. 40×40 mm) steatite objects with a flat engraved face and a perforated boss on the back. The face carries a short message in the yet to be deciphered Indus script, generally four to seven characters in length. Below the line of writing is a device, usually a bull, either humped or unhumped. The carving was done intaglio, at times with great skill.

Approximately 1814 of these seals have been found. They occur in almost all of the sites of the Mature or Urban phase of the Harappan civilization, not just the cities, although the largest collection does come from Mohenjo-daro itself. Inscribed objects other than the 1814 stamp seals include 135 copper tablets, 511 sealings, 11 copper/bronze tools and 435 miscellaneous objects, including 350 miniature objects found at Harappa and not paralleled at other sites. The copper tablets seem to occur only at Mohenjo-daro (Mahadevan, p. 9). The sealings are composed of impressions taken from the standard stamp seal, as well as special moulded and baked objects that were apparently manufactured in their own right. The longest Indus inscription, 26 characters in length, occurs on two identical mouldings from Mohenjo-daro. (For republished illustrations of seals and other glyptic materials, see Joshi and Parpola; Shah and Parpola.)

The composition of the standard stamp seal suggests that it was used to identify its owner—by name, place of origin or some other such designation. The most frequent device below the writing is the so-called 'unicorn'—a bull shown in profile, which may have a single horn or may have two, one hidden behind the other. There are 1159 examples of the 'unicorn' seal (Mahadevan, table 8). Other devices include the zebu (54 examples), the rhinoceros (55) and the short-horned bull, which may be the Indian gaur (95). Steatite or some other related soft stone was used for carving most of the seals, but examples also exist in copper and terracotta. It has been demonstrated that there is a northern group of seals, associated with the Harappa domain, and a southern group, associated with

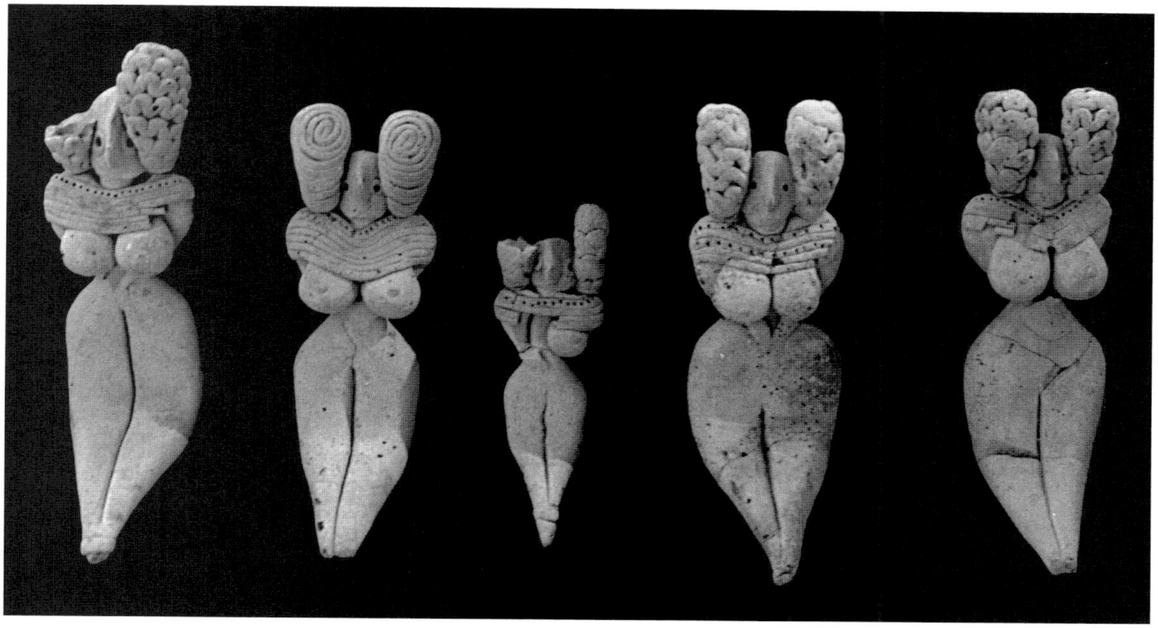

138. Female figurines, terracotta, from Mehrgarh, Period VI (Paris, Musée Guimet)

Mohenjo-daro (Rissman). A provincial carving style is also evident.

In addition to the standard, square stamp seal there are examples of a bar seal, without a device below the writing, and narrative seals that picture much more than the usual simple device. Good examples of the latter are seal number 420 (the 'Proto-Shiva' seal of Mohenjo-daro) and number 430 (the 'Seal of Divine Adoration'). There are nine cylinder seals in protohistorical contexts in South Asia. A clay 'bead' decorated in a way that yields a design when rolled out comes from Mehrgarh, Period IIB (J.-F. Jarrige, p. 25). Three cylinder seals were found at Mohenjo-daro (Mackay, 1937–8, pp. 325, 344–5, pls LXXXIV, 78; LXXXIX, 376; XCVI, 488); one at Kalibangan from the Urban Phase Harappan levels (Thapar, 1975); two at Sibri similar to those from Margiana, southern central Asia, *c.* 2400–*c.* 1900 BC (Santoni, p. 57); one at Daimabad, from the Jorwe levels (*c.* 1400–*c.* 1000 BC; Sali, pp. 508–11, fig. 108, pl. CXLI); and one at Maski. The last, a terracotta seal showing a man driving an elephant, is a surface find, but B. K. Thapar assigns it to a Chalcolithic period at the site (*c.* 1700–*c.* 400 BC; Thapar, 1957, pp. 21–4, fig. 3, pl. XVII, B). Finally, a Mesopotamian-style cylinder seal (Nagpur, Cent. Mus.; Lal, p. 101, pl. XXIV, 4, and Suboor) may have come to India as a gift during colonial times, the benefactor having acquired it in the course of travel in the Middle East. B. B. Lal, however, feels that there is a chance that the seal was as important to India in ancient times.

(iii) Terracotta figurines. Both human and animal figurines occur as early as the Neolithic era, as documented at Mehrgarh Periods I and II. The earliest representations are small seated humans, without arms and with legs joined together. Some are decorated with jewellery and may be coloured with red ochre (C. Jarrige, 1991, p. 87, pl. 73). Human figurines are not present in Period III at Mehrgarh, but those of Period IV show some continuity with the Neolithic examples in that they are seated, armless and with legs joined. Elaborate hairstyles and prominent breasts appear on female figurines in Period V, and these features are even more exaggerated in Period VI (see fig. 138). In Period VII there is some diversity of style, and distinctly male figurines appear.

These figurines give some sense of dress, hairstyles and conventions for wearing jewellery in ancient times. Ethnic diversity may be documented in differences presented. Figurine styles from Mehrgarh are also found in upland Baluchistan, the Zhob Valley and as far away as Central Asia, regions that were one vast interaction sphere in antiquity.

The figurines of the Mature Indus civilization are far more diverse than those of Mehrgarh. These are amply illustrated in excavation reports for Mohenjo-daro (Marshall, 1931; Mackay, 1937–8), Harappa (Vats, 1940); Chanhu-daro (Mackay, 1943); and Lothal (Rao). Humans, both male and female, are dressed and decorated in a number of ways, again suggesting the ethnic diversity of the Harappan peoples. The range of hats and other head coverings is especially interesting. Large female figurines, such as the one often illustrated from Mohenjo-daro (Mackay, 1937–8, pl. LXXV, no. 21–3), are confined to that site. They may, or may not, be 'mother goddesses'. Males can often be distinguished from females by breasts and genitalia. If these are taken as sound guides, some Mature Harappan figurines may be hermaphroditic (Mackay, 1937–8, pl. LXXIL, no. 8). One style of Mature Harappan male figurine has been found at Mohenjo-daro, Chanhu-daro and Nippur (Dales). Scientific testing has demonstrated that the Chanhu-daro figurine was made in the Indus Valley and that the Nippur example is of Mesopotamian origin.

A wide-ranging assortment of animals are shown in the terracotta art of the Indus civilization. These include superbly modelled bulls, squirrels and monkeys from Mohenjo-daro. Rhinoceroses, dogs (several breeds, some with collars), hogs, rabbits, elephants, turtles and birds also occur, sometimes as puppets, with separate, movable body parts. Somewhat curiously, there are no representations of lions, although they were a part of the Harappan environment. On the whole the animal figurines seem to be toys or items of delight and not a part of the Harappan religious system.

The Kulli culture in southern Baluchistan, contemporary with the Mature Harappan civilization, has a distinctive tradition of terracotta figurines. The bulls, which are generally found in large numbers at Kulli sites, are painted, possibly indicating that bullocks were decorated in antiquity. The male and female figurines are generally torsos and heads set on small stands. They are rather flat in section, often with hands on hips, and are sometimes elaborately decked in jewels. Painting is held to a minimum, but the diversity of hairstyles is impressive (C. Jarrige, 1984; Possehl).

BIBLIOGRAPHY

M. A. Suboor: 'A Note on a Babylonian Seal in the Central Museum, Nagpur', *J. Asiat. Soc. Bengal*, x (1914), pp. 461–3

J. Marshall: 'Exploration, Western Circle, Mohenjo-daro', *Archaeol. Surv. India, Annu. Rep.* (1925–6), pp. 72–98

E. J. H. Mackay: '"L" Area', *Archaeol. Surv. India, Annu. Rep.* (1926–7), pp. 89–97

Sir J. Marshall: 'The Indus Culture', *Archaeol. Surv. India, Annu. Rep.* (1926–7), pp. 51–60

M. S. Vats: 'Excavations at Harappa', *Archaeol. Surv. India, Annu. Rep.* (1928–9), pp. 76–85

E. J. H. Mackay: 'Excavations at Mohenjo-daro', *Archaeol. Surv. India, Annu. Rep.* (1930–34), pp. 51–71

——: 'Statuary', *Mohenjo-Daro and the Indus Civilization*, ed. J. Marshall, i (London, 1931), pp. 356–64

J. Marshall, ed.: *Mohenjo-Daro and the Indus Civilization*, 3 vols (London, 1931)

E. J. H. Mackay: *Further Excavations at Mohenjo-daro*, 2 vols (Delhi, 1937–8)

M. S. Vats: *Excavations at Harappa*, 2 vols (Delhi, 1940)

E. J. H. Mackay: *Chanhu-Daro Excavations, 1935–36*, American Oriental Series, xx (New Haven, 1943)

B. B. Lal: 'Protohistoric Investigation', *Anc. India*, ix (1953), pp. 80–102

M. Wheeler: *The Indus Civilization* (Cambridge, 1953/*R* 1968)

B. K. Thapar: 'Maski 1954: A Chalcolithic Site of the Southern Deccan', *Anc. India*, xiii (1957), pp. 4–142

G. F. Dales: 'Of Dice and Men', *Essays in Memory of E. A. Speiser*, ed. W. W. Hallow, *J. Amer. Orient. Soc.*, lxxxviii/1 (1968), pp. 14–23

B. K. Thapar: 'Kalibangan: A Harappan Metropolis beyond the Indus Valley', *Expedition*, xvii, no. 2 (1975), pp. 19–32

I. Mahadevan: *The Indus Script: Texts, Concordance and Tables*, Mem. Archaeol. Surv. India, lxx (New Delhi, 1977)

A. Ardeleanu-Jansen: 'Stone Sculptures from Mohenjo-daro', *Reports on Field Work Carried Out at Mohenjo-Daro, Pakistan 1982–83 by the Ismeo-Aachen University Mission: Interim Reports Vol. 1* (Aachen and Rome, 1983), pp. 139–57

C. Jarrige: 'Terracotta Human Figurines from Nindowari', *South Asian Archaeology, 1981*, ed. B. Allchin (Cambridge, 1984), pp. 129–34

J.-F. Jarrige: 'Chronology of the Earlier Periods of the Greater Indus as Seen from Mehrgarh, Pakistan', *South Asian Archaeology, 1981*, ed. B. Allchin (Cambridge, 1984), pp. 21–9

M. Santoni: 'Sibri and the South Cemetery of Mehrgarh: 3rd Millennium Connections between the Northern Kachi Plain (Pakistan) and Central Asia', *South Asian Archaeology, 1981*, ed. B. Allchin (Cambridge, 1984), pp. 52–60

E. C. L. During Caspers: 'A Possible Harappan Contact with the Aegean World', *South Asian Archaeology, 1983*, ed. J. Schotsmans and M. Taddei, Istituto Universitario Orientale, Dipartimento di Studi Asiatici, Serie Minore, xxiii (Naples, 1985), pp. 435–52

G. L. Possehl: *Kulli* (Durham, NC, 1986)

S. R. Rao: *Lothal: A Harappan Port Town, 1955–62*, Mem. Archaeol. Surv. India, lxxviii (Durham, NC, 1986)

S. A. Sali: *Daimabad, 1976–79*, Mem. Archaeol. Surv. India, lxxxiii (New Delhi, 1986)

J. P. Joshi and A. Parpola, eds: *Collections in India*, Corpus of Indus Seals and Inscriptions, i (Helsinki, 1987)

P. C. Rissman: 'The Organization of Seal Production in the Harappan Civilization', *Old Problems and New Perspectives in the Archaeology of South Asia*, ed. J. M. Kenoyer, Wisconsin Archaeological Reports, ii (1989), pp. 159–70

A. Ardeleanu-Jansen: 'The Sculptural Art of the Harappa Culture', *Forgotten Cities on the Indus: Early Civilization in Pakistan from the 8th to the 2nd Millennium B.C.*, ed. M. Jansen, M. Mulloy and G. Urban (Mainz, 1991), pp. 167–78

C. Jarrige: 'The Terracotta Figurines from Mehrgarh', *Forgotten Cities on the Indus: Early Civilization in Pakistan from the 8th to the 2nd Millennium B.C.*, ed. M. Jansen, M. Mulloy and G. Urban (Mainz, 1991), pp. 87–94

S. G. M. Shah and A. Parpola, eds: *Collections in Pakistan*, Corpus of Indus Seals and Inscriptions, ii (Helsinki, 1991)

GREGORY L. POSSEHL

3. EARLY HISTORIC PERIOD–3RD CENTURY BC. Few sculptures are known from the period between the decline of the Indus civilization (*c.* 2000 BC) and the establishment of the Maurya empire in the 3rd century BC. The maturity of Indian sculpture of the 3rd century BC in the absence of similar accomplishment in the immediately preceding and succeeding periods has led some scholars to see Maurya sculpture as an isolated phenomenon, executed through intervention of Greek or Persian sculptors. However, perhaps a continuity of decorative motifs and, to some extent, plastic feeling can be traced from the sculpture of the Indus civilization (*see* §2 above) through the bronze animals and charioteer from Daimabad (*c.* 1500–1000 BC), the superb weapons of the so-called copperhoard culture of Uttar Pradesh (*c.* 1000 BC or later) and the lustrous, volumetrically conceived pottery from the Gangetic plain (*c.* 500 BC). Characterized by a combination of naturalism and abstraction, of rounded, modelled volumes and of textured surface, such works seem to anticipate the co-existence of diverse styles in the 3rd century BC.

(i) Style and dating. The absence of firm archaeological or documentary evidence makes it difficult to establish a coherent chronological sequence for 3rd-century BC sculpture. Further, the variety of techniques and motifs seems to represent a diversity of artistic choice and skills rather than a pattern of development. A remarkable unity of plastic conception characterizes all the objects and distinguishes them from the cubical modelling of the 2nd-century BC sculpture of Bharhut. The homogeneity of style, together with the evidence of some Ashokan edicts, suggests that much of this sculpture was created during the reign of Ashoka (*reg c.* 269–*c.* 232 BC), though some examples are probably pre-Ashokan, as Ashoka apparently directed the engraving of inscriptions on pre-existing pillars.

The variety of techniques and styles is demonstrated most effectively by the free-standing pillars found especially at sites sacred to Buddhism. Of the roughly 20 pillars of which remains are known, the shaft, the capital, the abacus and the crowning animals show a variety of treatments. The shaft and capital may be squat or slender, with varying ratios of breadth to height. The abacus may be square and plain or round and carved. Crowning animals are single (see fig. 131 above) or addorsed (for illustration *see* SARNATH), and animal capitals occur on both inscribed and uninscribed pillars. Some pillars employ conventions more appropriate to wood, while others show a mastery of the medium of stone. Some are characterized by an integration of parts, others by a lack of integration.

The decorative scheme of the abacus frequently consists of combinations of geese and honeysuckle or the bull, horse, lion and elephant along with the wheel. The animal surmounting the pillars is most frequently the lion, as in examples from Sarnath, Rampurva, Lauriya-Nandangarh, Vaishali and Sanchi, though the bull and elephant are also depicted, as at Rampurva and Sankasya respectively. The lions are characterized by geometric tensions and accentuated planes; the qualities of clear definition and fluid rhythm are best combined in the bull of the Rampurva pillar (see fig. 131 above). The animals and birds in relief on the abacus tend to be softer and fuller in modelling than the heraldic animals in the round at the top. The vegetal motifs on the abacus, though articulated with stylized regularity by faceting, ribbing and scooping, are characterized by a lifelike quality.

Also firmly related to the reign of Ashoka by an inscription is the elephant shown as if emerging from the rock at DHAULI. Different in style from the pillar sculptures, it is the most softly rendered of all the works. The elephants and *makaras* (crocodilian beasts) on the entrance of Lomas Rishi Cave (*see* BARABAR AND NAGARJUNI; see also fig. 25 above) can be dated to the Maurya period by both their context and style.

Though often dated later, a number of sculptures are clearly related in form to the pillar sculptures and can thus be assigned to the Maurya period. This group includes the Didarganj *Whisk-bearer* (see fig. 139), two *yakṣas* from Patna and the Lohanipur torso (all Patna Mus.) as well as a variety of lesser-known examples: the pair of griffins from Kumrahar, the head of a lion from Masarh, the seven-hooded *nāga* canopy from Rajgir (all four Calcutta, Ind. Mus.), the bull capitals of Salempur and Lohanipur, the bird fragments from Sarnath and two heads from Kumrahar and Lohanipur (all Patna Mus.). These works are related to the sculpture of the pillars by a combination of naturalism and stylization, monumentality and frontality, fluently merging plans and harsh, precise incisions, as well as by a lustrous polish, which appears to be more usual in this period than later. On the other hand, a *nilgāi* (blue bull) head and seven fragments of human heads recovered from Sarnath (all Sarnath, Archaeol. Mus.) show a combination of physical vehemence, anatomical naturalism and cubical volumes that suggest a transition to the 2nd-century BC sculpture of Bharhut.

139. *Whisk-bearer*, polished sandstone, h. (without base) 1.63 m, from Didarganj, near Patna, 3rd century BC (Patna, Patna Museum)

A similar co-existence of styles and motifs also characterizes sculpted ring stones (possibly designed as jewellery moulds). The ring stones range in diameter from about 50 to 80 mm. Most of them are of soapstone, and many have a hole in the centre, giving rise to their name. One group is distinguished by refined workmanship and a clear rendering of such motifs as mother-goddess figures, honeysuckle, palm trees, pyramids, unicorns and sphinxes, some of which may be of western Asiatic derivation. Examples have been found at Taxila, Rupar, Mathura, Sankasya, Kausambi, Rajghat, Jhusi and Vaishali (e.g. Calcutta, Ind. Mus.; Varanasi, Banaras Hindu U., Bharat Kala Bhavan). A second group of ring stones, mostly found at Murtaziganj in Patna (e.g. Patna Mus.), is of somewhat rougher workmanship. Their decoration includes, along with mother-goddess figures, such 'Indianizing' motifs as naturalistic birds and animals, lotuses, and stellate, taurine and crescent designs. A third group, all of which are from Kausambi (e.g. Allahabad Mus.), combines the exquisite workmanship of the first group with motifs such as the honeysuckle stem and rosettes of the second. It is perhaps transitional between the first and second groups.

(ii) Symbolism and interpretation. In translating Vedic, Upanishadic or epic ideas and Greek or Persian or other Western Asiatic motifs into stone, the 3rd-century BC sculptor appears to have reinterpreted them syncretically. The pillar had been conceived in earlier Brahmanical literature primarily as an *axis mundi*, variously expressed as burial post, sacrificial stake, portable victory standard, Tree of Life or cosmic mountain. It had been represented also in ancient Near Eastern reliefs. In all these various forms, it was seen in ancient India as a symbol of the myth of creation, suggesting the eternal, life-giving, cyclical passage of water between earth and heaven. In Persian palaces or Greek temples, the pillar was used as a load-bearing element, seemingly divested of such explicit symbolic functions. The monumental Maurya pillars, however, appear to have taken over the pre-Buddhist symbolism of the pillar. They seem to identify the law of the Buddha with the law of the state and to represent the Buddha as the universal emperor, turning the Wheel of the Law and re-enacting the primordial drama of creation by separation and reintegration of life-giving elements. The birds, animals and plants of the pillars appeared to harmonize with the theme of the cyclic flow of waters.

In keeping with their intended symbolism, Maurya pillars are not load-bearing; they stand free with no bases rising straight from the earth. Rather than the additive jointing and setting procedures used for Greek or Persian pillars, Maurya pillars were created by subtractive cutting into a monolithic block of stone. Their shafts are smooth rather than fluted. The so-called 'Persian bell capitals' resemble the bases rather than the capitals of Persepolitan pillars. The drooping sepals of the Persian examples have become the petals of lotus-form Maurya capitals, which have been given a greater bulge at the top. An abacus with reliefs was introduced. Western Asiatic motifs were used in both the pillars and the ring stones but given a greater fullness and smoothness and a more curvilinear rhythm than in Persia or Greece. The harsh expression of Persian animals was softened, and the frenzied disquiet or passivity of Greek animals was replaced by lucid repose or gliding motion in Indian examples.

Though 3rd-century BC sculpture still poses unresolved questions, its legacy clearly survived in later art. The pillars were imitated in free-standing and structural forms. The combined use of organic and geometric motifs seen in the ring stones is echoed in the medallions of Bharhut and in Mathura reliefs, as well as in the mystical and cosmic diagrams of the Jaina religion—*yantras*, *ayāgapaṭas* and *saptacakras*. The *yakṣī* served as model for the *śālabhañjika*, and the *yakṣa* became the precursor of the Buddha image and images of Jaina *tīrthaṅkaras* (teachers). The tension between plastic and linear styles continued. Indian sculpture of the 3rd century BC was, therefore, not an exotic or ephemeral phenomenon, but a part of continuing development.

BIBLIOGRAPHY

L. Waddell: *Report on the Excavations at Pataliputra* (Calcutta, 1903)
V. Smith: 'The Monolithic Pillars or Columns of Asoka', *Z. Dt. Mrgländ. Ges.*, lxv (1911)
R. P. Chanda: *The Beginnings of Art in Eastern India* (Calcutta, 1927)
N. R. Ray: *Maurya and Sunga Art* (Calcutta, 1945)
R. E. M. Wheeler: 'Iran and India in Pre-Islamic Times', *Anc. Ind. (1947–8)*, pp. 85–103
K. A. N. Sastri, ed.: *Age of the Nandas and Mauryas* (Varanasi, 1952)
R. E. M. Wheeler: *Civilizations of the Indus Valley and Beyond* (London, 1966)
B. P. Sinha and L. A. Narain: *Pataliputra Excavation, 1955–56* (Patna, 1970)
S. Paranavitana: *The Greeks and the Mauryas* (Columbo, 1971)
J. Irwin: '"Asokan" Pillars: A Reassessment of the Evidence', *Burl. Mag.*, cxv (1973), pp. 706–20; cxvi (1974), pp. 712–27; cxvii (1975), pp. 631–43; cxviii (1976), pp. 734–53
J. C. Huntington: 'The Lomas Rsi: Another Look', *Archvs Asian A.*, xxviii (1974–5), pp. 34–56
S. P. Gupta: *The Roots of Indian Art* (Delhi, 1980)
J. Irwin: 'The Prayaga Bull-Pillar: Another Pre-Asokan Monument?', *South Asian Archaeology*, ed. H. Hartel (Berlin, 1981), pp. 313–40
——: 'The Lat Bhairo at Benaras (Varanasi): Another Pre-Asokan Monument?', *Z. Dt. Mrgländ. Ges.*, cxxxiii/2 (1983), pp. 321–52

4. 2ND–1ST CENTURIES BC. The more three-dimensional treatment of the sculpture of the previous century gave way to a basically two-dimensional treatment in the 2nd century BC. At the same time, the earlier repertory of motifs was vastly enlarged, and human figures were introduced on a large scale in narrative reliefs. Popular divinities were given iconic form in stone, and the foundations for the iconographic vocabulary of later Indian art were laid. It has been suggested that the rolled-up volutes of gates, the shape of the relief medallions and the use of continuous narration might derive from portable pictorial scrolls carried in the festive processions. The sharp, perpendicular cut at such sites as Bharhut has, on the other hand, been seen as a translation of techniques practised in wood. While the sculptor of this period, faced with the prospect of relating elaborate stories, might have had recourse to earlier pictorial or woodworking traditions, no examples of these survive. One of the most interesting aspects of the 2nd to 1st century BC is the transition that can be traced from the flat cubic forms and austere beauty of the sculpture of Bharhut to the soft, rounded forms and exuberance of the gateways of Stupa 1 at Sanchi.

(i) North. (ii) Central. (iii) West. (iv) East. (v) South.

(i) North. In ancient times the Gangetic plain was regarded as the core area of Indian civilization. Due to continuous rebuilding, invasions and wars, the early sculpture of this region is known mainly from fragments, however. Perhaps most representative of the sculpture of north India in the 2nd century BC is surviving work from the stupa site at Bharhut in present-day Madhya Pradesh. Fragments have been recovered at Mathura and at scattered sites including Sarnath, Kausambi, Rajghat, Musanagar (near Kanpur) and Deoria (near Allahabad). These consist of reliefs, mainly from railings and gateways, and images in the round depicting popular divinities, principally *yakṣas* and *yakṣīs* (male and female nature spirits).

(a) Bharhut. (b) Related work of the 2nd century BC. (c) 1st century BC at Sarnath, Mathura and other sites.

(a) Bharhut. Before its discovery by Alexander Cunningham in 1873, the stupa at Bharhut had been so

thoroughly despoiled that only portions of the eastern gateway and of the railing could be recovered (the major portion is in Calcutta, Ind. Mus., with fragments in other collections, e.g. Washington, DC, Freer; Seattle, WA, A. Mus.; New Delhi, N. Mus.; Allahabad Mus.). An inscription on the eastern gateway recording its erection by Dhanabhati in the reign of the SHUNGA dynasty (*c.* 184–75 BC) and other votive records on the railing suggest an early to mid-2nd-century BC date for the sculpture.

The railing of the stupa, consisting of uprights pierced by three rows of crossbars crowned by a coping, was provided with four gateways. Each gateway comprised two pillars with bell-shaped lotus capitals and abaci crowned by addorsed animals, supporting three voluted architraves. The railing pillars and crossbars were carved in relief with medallions representing stories of the Buddha's life or the *jātaka* tales of the Buddha's previous births. The Buddha's life and work were represented aniconically through such symbols as the horse with or without an umbrella held above it (great departure), the *bodhi* tree (enlightenment), the wheel (first sermon), the ladder (descent from the heaven of the 33 gods) and the stupa (decease). His presence was suggested by his seat beneath a tree (see fig. 133 above), his sandals, headgear or footprints. The Buddha, his law and the monastic community were shown by the triple jewel motif. Such animals as the elephant, the lion, the bull and the deer were associated with Buddha and his worship. In the tales of his past lives, which were identified by labels, he was shown as bird, beast or man, performing acts of charity and self-sacrifice. The central theme of Buddha's life was accompanied by lotuses and plants issuing from pots and from the mouths and navels of animals and dwarfs representing the abundance of nature. The concept of abundance was also represented by large tutelary figures of male and female divinities, serpent gods and dryads. A railing post is carved with the *yakṣī* Chandra (see fig. 140) who grasps a flowering tree with one hand while the gesture of the other suggests the birth of a flowering stem from her womb. The same theme of abundance was suggested by the sculpture on the coping. It was carved on the inner face with a wish-fulfilling creeper issuing from the mouth of an elephant and yielding the good things of life such as clothes, jewellery and food or displaying edificatory scenes. On the outer face, it was carved with a lotus rhizome. On both sides it was bordered with decorative or auspicious motifs of stepped merlons and lotuses as well as bells and chains. The gateway was decorated with sacred animals worshipping the *bodhi* tree, crocodilian *makara*s with coiled tails, standard-bearing riders, honeysuckle and the triple-jewel ornament. The apparent purpose of all this sculpture was to announce and beautify the stupa as the central object of worship and to educate people in the sacred lore of Buddhism (for discussion of Buddhist iconography *see* §II, 2 above).

Ostensibly in response to this religious purpose, the Bharhut sculptors adopted an extremely self-conscious, solemn and hieratic style, at once elegant and affected as well as appealing and fresh, conscientiously observant in specific details but abstract and distant in general effect. They conceived their figures as two-dimensional reliefs, sandwiched between the ground and an imaginary frontal

140. *Yakṣī Chandra*, railing post from Bharhut, *c.* 100–*c.* 80 BC (Calcutta, Indian Museum)

plane. They carved the details of the figures by flat, stratified planes, sharply detached from one another by an incisive, sure, vertical cut. The feet of figures were splayed to the sides, their arms were often folded close to their chests. Their outer silhouette and surface contours were made relentlessly rectilinear and rendered by a shallow undercutting, creating thin, sharp, broken shadows, harshly outlining the different parts. All units of the composition, both figural and non-figural, were described by similar geometric means. Muscular transitions of the body, tattoo or other marks on the face, drapery, jewellery, leaves of trees, petals of flowers, feathers of birds and ripples of water were described meticulously by various combinations of parallel ridges or incisions, wavy lines, hooks or whorls. Figures flex their limbs in sharp angular bends, and both animate and inanimate elements tilt over at impossible angles to adapt to the size of the frame. Figures and units were arrayed vertically, positioned above rather than behind one another. Their size was determined by their relative importance and not by a realistic scale or by distance from the viewer. Figures are viewed uncompromisingly from the front or back or in profile, but within a scene a multiplicity of viewpoints was presented. Continuous narration is sometimes adopted with the same figures appearing at different places and times within a composition. Figures lack animation and weight; their eyes are open, vacant, protruding diamonds, their mouths thin, unsmiling lines, their faces and expressions remote and aloof. The respect for detail was thus united with a pervasive mood of rigorous austerity. Organic and inorganic motifs were stylized, serving as decorative symbols compelling devotion to a religion accepting but transcending this world.

(b) Related work of the 2nd century BC. The hieratic solemnity and narrative wealth of Bharhut sculpture stands alone in the 2nd century BC. However, sequels to its style can be found in sculptures all over India in the later half of the century. While sharing the cubic forms of Bharhut, these sculptures also showed a certain relaxation, anticipating the more fluid plastic styles best known from the gateways of Stupa 1 at Sanchi (*c.* mid-1st century BC; *see* §(ii)(d) below) and the railing at Bodhgaya (*c.* early 1st century BC; *see* §(iv)(a) below). Relief sculptures are found mainly on fragments of railings and gateways, while sculpture in the round is represented by a group of *yakṣas* and *yakṣīs*.

Mathura and its suburbs and adjacent areas (e.g. Gayatri Tila, Kankali Tila, Bhuteshvar, Junsuiti, Katra) appear to have been the most important centres for such transitional sculptures. Examples of fragmentary reliefs include a carved railing post, a *yakṣa* holding a sword and a child, another bearing a *caurī* and a *yakṣī* tying a sash around her waist. Closely related are relief fragments showing couples, processions of winged animals, cooking and city scenes (all Mathura, Govt Mus.). A second group of carvings (Lucknow, State Mus.) depicts the god Balarama, a dancer performing in a thatched hut, a horse and rider, two women revering a pillar with a lion capital and a stupa revered by horse-headed mythical animals (*kinnaras*) and winged mythical creatures (*suparṇas*). In all these examples the human figures are clearly related to those of Bharhut stylistically in their flat, cubical modelling, perpendicular cutting and precisely delineated features with ridged eyelids and eyebrows, as well as in their stiff and jutting elbows and knees, limited gestures and masklike expressions. Parallels with Bharhut in clothing and jewellery include massive turbans secured by a fillet, throat clasps with rosettes, multi-strand necklaces with buckle clasps, 'fleur-de-lis' armlets, beaded bracelets and triangular aprons. On the other hand, these works show a stylistic proximity to Bodhgaya and Sanchi in their fullness, relaxation and animation and greater weight and volume. Arms and feet are positioned so that they are viewed from the front rather than the side. Clothing motifs common to later sculpture include cylindrical, inclined headdresses for women and bulging turbans extending over the ear for men. The architectural and group compositions reveal a more logical perspective and more leisurely spacing of units. Animals are less schematized and more pliant. A further relief on a railing crossbar showing an elephant and two riders (from Gayatri Tila; New Delhi, N. Mus.) shares these transitional features that presage a more plastic style. A fragmentary dryad from Mehrauli (New Delhi, N. Mus.), one of the finest carvings of the period, is allied to finds from Mathura and retains a Bharhut-like propensity for decorative detailing.

A number of sculptures in the round from Mathura and nearby areas—mainly of *yakṣas*—show similar transitional traits. They include *yakṣas* from Parkham (see fig. 141) and Baroda (both Mathura, Govt Mus.), Palwal (Lucknow, State Mus.) and Noh (Bharatpur, State Mus.) and a *yakṣī* from Jhing ka Nagra (Mathura, Govt Mus.). The flat, slablike backs of the Parkham and Baroda *yakṣas*, the cursory indication of their buttocks by a shallow, curving line and the harsh transition from stomach to legs gives way in the Noh and Palwal *yakṣas* to a greater modulation and relaxation of the back and a softer transition to the legs. In the latter two examples earrings are less massive and the topknot tiered. Epigraphic evidence suggests a link between the Jhing ka Nagra *yakṣī* and the Parkham *yakṣa*. While an evolution is apparent within this group, their cubic modelling is closer to the Bharhut style of the 2nd century BC than to the softer forms of the next century.

Similar transitional works have been found at SARNATH. These include a headless *yakṣī* (Calcutta, Ind. Mus.), a few railing posts, a coping and a doorway lintel (all New Delhi, N. Mus.). Carved on the architectural fragments are stupas, leogryphs, a trident, winged figures and club-bearing women riding lions as well as motifs such as the pot with foliage, honeysuckle and lotus. While the rendering is in the orderly, flat, additive style of Bharhut, the Sarnath reliefs show greater movement and ornamental restraint. Several reliefs in a similar style were found at KAUSAMBI (Allahabad Mus.). Two railings are carved with *yakṣas*, one with a *yakṣī* and a fourth apparently with a figure of the Buddha's mother, Maya, grasping a branch of a tree. (The latter carries a short donative inscription.) Fragments of a coping are decorated with lotuses and lotus rhizomes. Figures are cubic and inorganic, with limbs and drapery carved with sharp, projecting angles, but the vertical cut of Bharhut has given way to a more rounded modelling. Bodies are enlivened by bends that set hips, shoulders and

141. *Yakṣa*, pinkish-beige sandstone, h. 2.64 m, from Parkham, *c.* 2nd–1st century BC (Mathura, Government Museum)

head at different angles, and drapery edges are given more substance and movement. The nodes and leaves of lotus rhizomes are broader, heavier and less symmetrical. The same transitional tension between textured surface and modelled forms is exhibited by a small *yakṣa* from Musanagar, near Kanpur (Lucknow, State Mus.). Images in the round from these regions that provide a bridge from Bharhut to the next century include an image of a *yakṣa* from Rajghat (Varanasi, Banaras Hindu U., Bharat Kala Bhavan) and a *yakṣa* from Deoria (at local school premises).

(c) 1st century BC *at Sarnath, Mathura and other sites.* A few further transitional works are known from the early 1st century BC; sculpture of the mid- to late 1st century BC approximates the sculptural gateways of Stupa 1 at Sanchi in central India (*see* §(ii)(d) below) and the somewhat simpler work from Bodhgaya in eastern India (*see* §(iv)(a) below). Fragmentary works found at Sarnath, Mathura and other isolated north Indian sites (like their counterparts at Sanchi and Bodhgaya) demonstrate the victory of modelled over linear forms.

At the head of the transitional phase of the early 1st century BC are two pillars (New Delhi, N. Mus.) from Amin (Karnal District, Punjab) with donative inscriptions (see Agrawala). They are carved with a lotus-bearing *yakṣa* and a standing couple. The figures are carved with a greater sense of movement as well as a new sense of volume, weight and mutual perception. A number of broken railing posts, copings and reliefs from Musanagar and various locations in Mathura and its environs show similar transitional traits (Mathura, Govt Mus., and Lucknow, State Mus.). A *śālabhañjikā* (woman and tree) on a railing post and a representation of Gajalakshmi (the goddess lustrated by elephants) on a gateway (*toraṇa*) architrave from Kausambi, as well as a standing female figure in the round from the same site, headless and broken off below the knees (all Allahabad Mus.), also tend to anticipate the modelling of later work. On the other hand a lingering hardness, flatness and squarishness indicate an idiom slightly earlier than the mid-1st century BC.

A figure of a headless *yakṣī* holding a multi-strand garland found at Sarnath (Calcutta, Ind. Mus.) approximates the style of the better-known Bodhgaya figure of a standing *yakṣī* identified as the goddess Sri (*see* §(iv)(a) below). Both have high, constricted waists, full, flaring hips and a lower garment with drapery shown falling in parallel, diagonal folds. In both, the transparent lower garment clings to the body revealing its curves, and the modelling of the flesh is soft yet resilient. A female head in a medallion (Sarnath, Archaeol. Mus.), with her braided and clustered rolls of hair, inclined cap with rows of fluted patterns, full cheeks, broad nose and bemused expression, is a clear prototype for the heads in the Bodhgaya medallions. A capital with volutes (Sarnath, Archaeol. Mus.), showing an elephant with a mahout and a standard bearer in relief on one side and a prancing horse with a rider waving flowers on the other, is reminiscent of the prancing horses, the centaur with upraised arms and the elephant carved on Bodhgaya railing panels. As at Sanchi, the curved shape of the rolled volutes is carefully blended with the curving bodies of the moving horse and elephant. The flowers, seemingly weighed down with sap, and the deeply carved background are closer to the rich, full and sensuous style of the gateways of Stupa 1 at Sanchi than to the simple Bodhgaya style. Several carved railing posts

(Sarnath, Archaeol. Mus., and Lucknow, State Mus.), a few fragments showing the worship of a stupa by an elephant and a mythical creature, possibly a *kinnara*, and a few volutes with rosettes (all Sarnath, Archaeol. Mus.), a medallion head and a crossbar carved with a bull-rider from Mathura (Mathura, Govt Mus.) are rendered with similar soft, relaxed, deeply carved surfaces and are assignable to the same period. Sculptures in the round that recall Sanchi include a figure of a *yakṣa* holding a stick and a massive torso from Mora, a village near Mathura (both Mathura, Govt Mus.). The chronological position of the Mora torso is indicated by its gliding outlines and ample forms, which are strongly analogous to the figures on the Sanchi gates. Further, the Mora torso was found in conjunction with a Vaishnava inscription of a local ruler (*mahākshatrapa*), one Rajuvala, who may have reigned in the 1st century BC. Also dating to this period is a palm-leaf capital (Lucknow, State Mus.; see fig. 142). Capitals have been recovered also at Beshnagar and Pawaya (*see* §(ii)(c) and (d) below). The voluminous modelling of the Mathura capital, like that of the example from Pawaya, makes it a clear parallel to the mature Sanchi style.

BIBLIOGRAPHY

A. Cunningham: *The Stupa of Bharhut* (London, 1879)
J. Marshall and S. Konow: 'Sarnath', *Archaeol. Surv. India, Annu. Rep.* (1906–7), pp. 68–101
J. P. Vogel: 'Mathura School of Sculpture', *Archaeol. Surv. India, Annu. Rep.* (1906–7), pp. 137–60; (1909–10), pp. 63–70
H. Hargreaves: 'Excavations at Sarnath', *Archaeol. Surv. India, Annu. Rep.* (1914–15), pp. 97–131
L. Bachhofer: *Early Indian Sculpture* (New York, 1929)
J. P. Vogel: *La Sculpture de Mathura*, A. Asiat.: Etud. & Doc., xv (Paris, 1930)
C. L. Fabri: 'Mathura of the Gods', *Marg*, vii (1954), pp. 8–22
Marg, xv (1962) [issue on Mathura]
N. P. Joshi: *Mathura Sculptures* (Mathura, 1966)
R. C. Agrawala: 'Sunga Pillars from Amin, near Kurukshetra', *Lalit Kala*, xiv (1969), pp. 50–52
——: 'Unpublished Bharhut Reliefs in the National Museum, New Delhi', *Lalit Kala*, xiv (1969), pp. 53–5
P. Chandra: *Stone Sculpture in the Allahabad Museum* (Pune, 1970)
R. C. Sharma: *Mathura Museum and Art* (Mathura, 1976)
C. L. Bodien: 'An Early Yaksha from near Aktha near Sarnath (Varanasi District, U.P.)', *Chhavi*, ii (1981), pp. 294–7
R. Morris: 'The Early Sculptures of Sarnath', *Estratta da indologica taurinensia*, x (1982), pp. 155–68

142. Palm-leaf capital from Mathura, 1st century BC (Lucknow, State Museum)

(ii) Central. Despite the fact that the main centres of Indian civilization during the last two centuries BC were located in the north, a larger number of monuments and individual works have been preserved in central India. BESNAGAR (anc. Vidisha) and UJJAIN were important cities, but remains have been found at sites throughout the region, indicating that styles and conventions were widespread. Dating is still debated; the chronology outlined below is based both on the evidence of inscriptions and on stylistic development. (The site of Bharhut, though located in central India, is discussed with stylistically related material from the north; *see* §(i) above).

(a) Sanchi, Stupa 2. (b) *Yakṣa* and *yakṣī* images from Besnagar. (c) Monumental pillars. (d) Sanchi, Stupa 1 and related work.

(a) Sanchi, Stupa 2. Relief sculpture from the Besnagar region datable to *c.* late 2nd century BC shows a growing sense of volume and movement as well as a growing sensitivity to the sensuous and tactile possibilities of the human form. This development is well illustrated by the railing carvings of Stupa 2 at SANCHI. The palaeography of inscriptions on the railing suggests the stupa was built in the last quarter of the 2nd century BC. Though the structure has been shorn of its crowning members, berm and stairway balustrades (surviving portions in Sanchi, Archaeol. Mus.), 85 of the original 88 posts of the ground railing survive *in situ*. This makes Stupa 2 the best preserved monument of the period and critical for understanding early relief sculpture in its original context.

The railing posts are carved on two sides, occasionally on three, with relief medallions in the centre and half medallions above and below. A few posts are decorated with rectangular panels, and a few have additional ornamentation between the medallions. Motifs and themes are similar to those at Bharhut, but the iconography is substantially simplified. The programme includes major events in the Buddha's life, such as his birth, enlightenment, first sermon and death. The lotus, a symbol of rich and varied meaning that was associated with the Buddha's miraculous conception, occurs in 70 variations; out of 455 medallions, nearly 300 are monopolized by this theme. The lotus also partly intrudes on 126 other medallions. The celebratory character of its symbolism is indicated by the necklaces, cables and wreaths that gird it and by the curling, curving, interwinding and multiplying of its petals. The lotus is also shown surging from auspicious vases with leaves, buds and flowers. Associations of the Buddha's birth with animal cults (*mahājāneya paśu*) are suggested by elephants (shown crouching and floating on clouds or holding lotuses in their trunks), the lion (presumably the lion of the Shakya race, i.e. the Buddha), the bull (*nandīpada*, a symbol of the taurine constellation) and the horse and rider. The goddess of abundance, Sri, is linked to the Buddha's birth by the association of the Buddha's mother, Maya, with Gajalakshmi, the goddess Sri lustrated by elephants. Maya is also associated with the *śālabhañjikā* (woman-and-tree figure) as she holds a branch of the Shala or Ashoka tree while giving birth to the Buddha in the Lumbini garden. In this early phase the child emerging from her side is not represented.

The Great Departure (*mahābhiniṣkramaṇa*) of the Buddha, when he left behind his princely life and renounced the world, is commemorated by a horse with or without a rider or parasol-bearing grooms. The Buddha's Enlightenment (*sambodhi*) is shown by the *bodhi* tree, hung with garlands and crowned by parasols. The tree is enclosed by a railing and is often shown worshipped by mythical creatures. The First Sermon (*dharmacakrapravartana*) is symbolized by a wheel, which is often mounted on a throne or framed by lotuses. The wheel is also depicted as the crowning element on posts with lion or elephant capitals. The wheel is often shown in association with deer, bulls, lions or human worshippers. The Final Release (*mahāparinirvāṇa*) is shown by representations of the stupa.

Jātaka stories and other Buddhist tales are also represented at Stupa 2. For example, a horse-headed figure depicted in one of the medallions has been identified as the *yakṣī* Assamukhi converted by the Buddha from eating humans. Allusions to the Buddha's earlier appearances may be intended by peacocks, geese, sporting elephants in bowers (see fig. 143), deer and even generic hunting or fighting scenes. A further range of mythical, vegetal and animal elements, drawn from diverse sources and mingled with vividness and imagination, indicates a continuation of the wide-ranging eclecticism that first appeared at Bharhut.

Attempts have been made (see Marshall and Foucher) to characterize Stupa 2 as the beginning of a popular, indigenous art of relief as opposed to an imperial Greco-Persian-inspired sculpture in the round sponsored by the Maurya dynasty; to detect evidence of this in the greater familiarity of Sanchi artists with animals and plants than with human figures; to identify the better-modelled and hybrid forms of Stupa 2 as having been inspired by Asiatic Greek art; and to see the elegant, crowded compositions of Bharhut as later than the simpler compositions of Stupa 2. Such attempts fail because an earthy, popular idiom co-existed with the heraldic, courtly style even in Maurya days; because sculptures continued to be made in the round in the period of Stupa 2; and because the hybrid motifs were cognates drawn from an Asiatic heritage shared by Indians and Greeks alike. Moreover, seemingly contradictory elements co-exist in the sculpture of Stupa 2: disjointed and organic modelling, angular and curvilinear contours, free and compass-drawn curves, hieratic and natural forms, feet splayed to the sides or pointing to the front, knowledge of perspective, overlapping and foreshortening and the deliberate rejection of such knowledge for combining frontal and profile views. This co-existence of seemingly contradictory elements takes the reliefs of

143. Elephant relief medallion carved on a railing post, Stupa 2, Sanchi, late 2nd century BC

Stupa 2 beyond the uncompromisingly hieratic, additive and rectilinear style of Bharhut.

(b) Yakṣa *and* yakṣī *images from Besnagar.* That the Maurya tradition of making sculpture in the round was continued in this period is evident from several free-standing images recovered from Besnagar in the neighbourhood of Vidisha. These consist of a colossal standing image of the *yakṣa* Kubera, two standing images of *yakṣīs* (Vidisha, Distr. Archaeol. Mus.; Calcutta, Ind. Mus.) and a fragmentary *yakṣī* with a mutilated face (Gwalior, Archaeol. Mus.). These sculptures, probably only a sample of those originally made, indicate that Besnagar (anc. Vidisha) was an important centre of the *yakṣa* cult. *Yakṣa* images, symbolizing the mysterious spirit of life and creation, would have been placed in shrines (Pkt *yakkha cetiya*) and served as objects of popular devotion in *yakṣa* festivals (*yakkha mahā*). Devotional needs probably determined that the images should be frontally posed for face-to-face contact and carved in the round for circumambulation. Such sculptures came to serve as ready models for all sects when they wanted to translate abstract conceptions of the godhead into concrete objects for popular devotion.

Over 3 m tall, immense in girth and in contained vehemence, the *yakṣa Kubera* (see fig. 144) is identifiable by the money bag clenched in his left hand. The armlets with 'fleur-de-lis' motif, the five bracelets comprising cylindrical beads and rosettes, the heavy, spiral earrings, the thick knotted girdle with knobbed tassels and the *paryastaka* (ornamental piece of cloth between the legs) that adorn this image hark back to Bharhut. On the other hand, the lower garment falling in pleated folds over the left leg, the scarf stretched over the torso, and the necklace fitted with beads, rosettes, studs and prancing animals all

144. *Yakṣa Kubera*, sandstone, h. 3.43 m (with base), from Besnagar, *c.* late 2nd century BC (Vidisha, Archaeological Museum)

have acquired a greater volume and weight than at Bharhut. The body is more organically and less additively modelled than in sculpture at Stupa 2 at Sanchi. The figure's large, inclined hair-knot, *saṅku karṇa* (animal ears), open, bulging eyes and massive shoulders and arms presage the *yakṣa*s produced at Mathura in the first three centuries AD.

Though the other *yakṣa* and *yakṣī* images vary in detail, like the *yakṣa Kubera* they probably date to the end of the 2nd century BC. They share certain features related to the sculpture of Bharhut such as the rendering of the *paryastaka*, but most other draperies have greater volume and weight. These figures have also eschewed the archaic flexions and inorganic construction of Bharhut; they seem to have moved even beyond the sculpture of Stupa 2 in this regard. However, various motifs, such as multi-strand necklaces, cylindrical spacers and rectangular clasps, and the general presentation of the figures in stiff frontal poses with abrupt contours tie this group of *yakṣa*s and *yakṣī*s to the period of Stupa 2. This is confirmed by the fact that the forms lack the sensuous, relaxed style that appeared at Sanchi in the 1st century BC.

(c) Monumental pillars. As with the *yakṣa*s, popular devotion also played a role in the erection of votive standards or columns (*dhvaja*s). The most complete example from the 2nd century BC is located just north of Besnagar. According to the inscription on the pillar, it is a *garuda dhvaja* (standard of Garuda) set up in honour of Vasudeva (a form of the god Vishnu) by Heliodorus, an ambassador sent by King Antialkidas of Taxila to King Bhagabhadra of Vidisha. Historical events place these rulers between *c.* 150 and 100 BC (*see* BACTRIAN AND INDO-GREEK MONARCHIES). The BESNAGAR pillar is about half the size of an Ashokan pillar, and the shaft is divided into three sections with 8, 16 and 32 sides. The top portion is round and culminates in a bell capital with a cable necking and an abacus with geese and honeysuckle. The shaft is also carved with garlands and lotus medallions similar to those on the railing of Stupa 2 at Sanchi. The crowning *garuḍa* figure is missing, but some fragments and the foundations of an adjacent temple were found during excavations (*see* §III, 3 above). The broken shaft of another *garuḍa* pillar was found in the modern town of Vidisha (Gwalior, Gujarimahal Mus.). The inscription mentions the erection of a temple of Bhagavat by one Gautamiputra during the reign of King Bhagavata. Capitals from other columns, without the shafts, have also been found. One is in the form of a *makara* (mythic crocodile) and the other a *tāla* (fan palm; both Gwalior, Archaeol. Mus.). These can be attributed to the 2nd century BC. The *makara* in particular retains a debt to the cubic conception of form seen at Bharhut. A theory has been put forward (see Banarjea) that these pillar and capital fragments represent a cult of Vasudeva-Krishna and his brothers as emanations of the god Vishnu (*see* §II, 1(iii) above).

Several other capitals dating to the 2nd century BC have been found in the Vidisha region. The broken stump of a pillar (with the bell capital now set beside it) is located adjacent to Stupa 1 at Sanchi; in Vidisha itself a capital was found on the hill known as Lohangi Pir (see Stadtner); a bell capital with a crouching lion (Gwalior, Archaeol. Mus.) has animals carved on a wide abacus. These resemble the reliefs of Stupa 2 at Sanchi. Still more interesting is a capital carved in the shape of a banyan tree (Calcutta, Ind.

Mus.). The tree is hung with a conch shell, a lotus, two vases exuding coins and four bags tied by strings; the foot of the tree is enclosed by a lattice fence and set on a square railed base that serves as the abacus. This sculpture has been variously identified as the wish-giving tree (*kalpa vṛkṣa*), the banyan tree of the *Mahāvāṇija jātaka* and the sacred tree (*sthala vṛkṣa*) hung with treasures (*aṣṭanidhi*) that is associated with shrines of such deities as Kubera, Vaishravana, Sri or Padmini.

(d) Sanchi, Stupa 1 and related work. Stupa 1 at SANCHI, a remarkable structure carefully restored in the 20th century, is the most complete stupa in India (*see* STUPA, fig. 1). A number of phases in its history can be discerned. The brick core of the present structure, apparently the first stupa on the site, was built in the 3rd century BC during the Maurya period, possibly as part of efforts by the emperor Ashoka (*reg c.* 269–*c.* 232 BC) to spread the unifying message of Buddhism. A pillar with a lion capital (Sanchi, Archaeol. Mus.), set up beside the brick stupa, is a typical example of Maurya workmanship. The stupa was enlarged, faced with stone and encircled by two railings in about the 2nd century BC. One railing is at ground level, and the second is on the berm. The berm railing has some minor reliefs, but the complete absence of sculpture on the outer railing is in marked contrast to both Bharhut and Stupa 2 at Sanchi, with which it is contemporary. Around the mid-1st century BC, four carved gateways (*toraṇa*s) were added at the cardinal points; in a remarkable state of preservation, these are critical for the history of early sculpture on the subcontinent. The posts of the gates have narrative panels from top to bottom (see fig. 17 above). Capitals of various types support architraves, also carved with narrative scenes. Bracket figures and some figures between the architraves are carved in the round (some portions in Sanchi, Archaeol. Mus.). The date of the gateways is debated. (They are sometimes placed in the early 1st century AD.) A date in the mid-1st century BC is borne out by the palaeography of the votive inscriptions on them, by the mention of one Ananda, foreman of the artisans of the early SATAVAHANA king Satakarni, in an inscription on the south gate and, finally, by the reliefs themselves, which are a clear culmination of earlier traditions in central India.

The gateway sculptures follow and elaborate the iconographic conventions developed at Bharhut and Stupa 2 at Sanchi. The person of the Buddha is represented aniconically, but the attempt to describe the redeeming mission of his present and past lives anticipated many ideas of Mahayana ('Greater Vehicle') Buddhism. Austere Buddhist ideals of ethical conduct and renunciation are presented in popular garb through didactic stories set at court and in the city and jungle. Vegetation and symbols of water cosmology not only continue to evoke ideas of fertility and abundance but also take on more Buddhist associations. The use of ivory-carvers from Vidisha (indicated by a south gateway inscription) also suggests the adaptation to the service of Buddhism of age-old motifs familiar to local craftsmen.

Jātaka stories on the Sanchi gates illustrate such ethical teachings as self-sacrifice for the good of others and the pursuit of excellence (*pāramitā*) through the *bodhisattva*s' living example. Thus on a north gateway architrave, Prince Vessantara demonstrates excellence in giving (*dānapāramitā*) by giving away everything he has for the sake of others. On another architrave of the same gateway the *bodhisattva* instructs his child, Isisinga, in the excellence of wisdom (*prajñapāramitā*) by warning him against the wiles of women. On a west gateway pillar, the *bodhisattva* as the Great Monkey (*mahākapi*) illustrates excellence in heroism and compassion (*vīrya* and *karuṇā*) by spanning a river with his body to help the monkeys under his leadership to escape. Lessons in equanimity (*upekṣā*) and endurance (*kṣānti*) are given by the *bodhisattva* as the six-tusked elephant who allowed a hunter to saw off his tusks to satisfy his jealous ex-wife, reborn as queen of Varanasi. Another scene on a west gateway pillar illustrates the *sāma jātaka*, which celebrates the filial love of the *bodhisattva* who is mortally wounded by a hunter-king when serving his blind anchorite parents.

Though the Buddha is not represented in human form, his life and mission are recapitulated on the gateways. A symbolic reference to the miraculous conception of the Buddha-to-be may be intended by lotuses emerging from vases and by Gajalakshmi (associated with the Buddha's mother, Maya) lustrated by elephants, as well as by the heavenly elephant entering the side of the sleeping queen. Sensuous *śālabhañjikā*s (woman-and-tree figures), which serve as brackets (see fig. 145) and appear in other contexts, not only symbolize abundance but also probably refer to Maya giving birth in the Lumbini garden. The repeated figures of riderless horses, above which parasols are held, and auspicious footprints on the north gate and

145. *Śālabhañjikā*, bracket on east gateway, Stupa 1, Sanchi, 1st century BC

east gate architraves suggest the Great Departure (*mahābhiniṣkramaṇa*), when Gautama set aside princely pleasures for the life of a recluse. The pillars of the south gate show the worship of Gautama's hair by the gods after he had cut it off in renunciation. The offering of milk-rice to Gautama by Sujata is represented on the north architrave, while the south pillar (Sanchi, Archaeol. Mus.) shows the gift of grass by Svastika, a grass-cutter. The defeat of Mara (*māradharṣaṇa*), who attempted to disturb the Buddha's meditation and rob him of his enlightenment, is depicted on a north architrave by the pell-mell flight of Mara's demonic hordes. Mara is seen presiding over a world of unsubdued and monotonous passion on a pillar of the east gate. The amorous couples (playful and evidently intoxicated), together with the treasure-yielding creepers (*kalpalatā*s) on the north, west and east gates, represent the pleasures that must be abjured as a step towards Buddhahood. On the north gateway pillar, the wish-giving creeper, rising from footprints and crowned by lotuses and *triratna* ('triple jewel', i.e. the Buddha, the teaching and the community of monks), is described in an inscription as the 'height-measuring rod' of Lord Buddha himself. Thus creepers of desire are transformed into ladders of Buddhahood, and Mara becomes the prototype of all who must purge their passions to become the Buddha. The conflict of Buddha with Mara is made into a conflict internal to human nature.

The Buddha's enlightenment (*sambodhi*) is shown by the adamantine throne (*vajrāsana*) and *bodhi* tree, enclosed by later railings and shrines. Seven weeks after his enlightenment, the Buddha decided to preach the law (*dharma*). The events of the seven weeks are shown on a south gateway pillar (Sarnath, Archaeol. Mus.). They include the sheltering from the rain under the hood of the *nāga* (serpent) king Muchalinda, the offering of barley cakes and honey by the merchants Tapussa and Bhallika and the gift from the *lokapāla*s ('guardians of the world') of four begging bowls, welded into one by the Buddha to accept the merchants' offering. On the east and west gateway pillars the gods, led by Indra and Brahma, approach the Buddha to persuade him to help men wavering between truth and untruth. The Buddha's 45-year-long ministry was heralded by the First Sermon, or Turning of the Wheel of Law (*dharmacakrapravartana*). This is symbolized at Sanchi by a wheel mounted on a low, thronelike slab or crowning a pillar. Numerous miracles performed by the Buddha are represented. On an east gateway pillar, he is shown converting the Kashyapas by walking on a river in flood (the Buddha probably indicated by a calm slablike space among the waves) and by overcoming a fire-spitting serpent. In the panels of a north gateway pillar, the Buddha walks in the air to convert the Shakyas (the Buddha is not represented, but a similar scene from Bharhut has an identifying inscription) and causes a mango tree to sprout so as to overwhelm heretics. Another panel shows the Buddha's descent from heaven after preaching to his mother. At the top an empty throne beneath a tree represents the sermon in heaven, a stairway marks the Buddha's path to earth, and at the bottom an empty throne beneath a tree surrounded by human followers represents his return. The background of palaces, towns, processions and ongoing domestic activity indicates the busy drama of the Buddha's proselytizing life (see fig. 23 above). An impression is thus created of the Buddha as a man of contemplation and action.

The ministry of the Buddha culminated in the Great Demise (*mahāparinirvāṇa*) at Kushinagara. This is represented on the architraves by stupas. Crowned with umbrellas, encircled by perambulatory terraces and watched by guardians of the quarters, the stupa is the body of the Buddha himself, both teacher and saviour, lying in state and traversing the tetradic cosmos. On the north gateway pillar, a stupa is shown flanked by joyous Mallas of Kushinagara. Incessant festivals seem to be occurring around the tumuli and temples shown in the reliefs. Thus the Buddha's decease is shown not as an occasion for grief but as a celebration of the idea that any person can break the spell of rebirth and attain the extinction of desire. This is emphasized by the stupas and trees of the seven Buddhas who preceded Gautama and by the stupa and tree of the future Maitreya. The ever-living possibility of Buddhahood in the past, present and future is thereby established.

After the Buddha's demise, his early monastic ideals were slowly humanized and universalized. That this process was accompanied by a gradual assertion of his superhuman character is indicated by the depiction of miracles and by the adoption of the places of his activities as centres of pilgrimage. Symbols of his activities became mementos for veneration. The beginning of these developments is shown on the south and west gateway architraves by the representation of the siege of Kushinagara, in the threatened war over the division of the Buddha's relics. On an architrave of the south gateway the armies of seven claimants for the Buddha's relics are shown advancing on the town, engaging in action and returning with their share. The emperor Ashoka, who is reported to have distributed the relics of the seven original stupas all over India, is shown on a south gateway architrave in his abortive mission to open the stupa at Ramagrama, which was jealously guarded by *nāga*s (serpent deities). Ashoka is also seen on an east architrave wilting in distress on seeing that the *bodhi* tree has been poisoned. The tree is then shown revived by lustration and music-making worshippers.

The gateways at Sanchi represent a powerful culmination of two centuries of sculpture in central India. While different hands were clearly at work, the appearance of the same names in donative inscriptions indicates that all the sculptures were executed in a relatively short period of time. The style is characterized by graceful movement, complex compositions and an increased feeling for the sensuous qualities of flesh. Despite occasional archaisms, the reliefs demonstrate a greater sense of modelling, contour and volume than work from either Bharhut or Stupa 2 at Sanchi. The sketching or incising of forms on stone has been replaced by three-dimensional modelling. The cut is oblique rather than perpendicular; thus sharp, inert shadows have yielded to a bichromatic play of light over projecting and receding planes. Contours, once abrupt and broken, have become smooth and uninterrupted. Forms have gained volume and weight and are filled with the surging essence of life. Human couples have given up their remote expressions and become psychologically differentiated and mutually aware. Details are no longer scattered over the composition, colliding with the frame (as often happens at Bharhut); instead the forms swell from within and spill over the edges of reliefs, emphasizing thematic unity and, in the theme itself, the central event.

The style of the Sanchi gates had an impact on that of other monuments. For example, a corner pillar of Stupa 2 was recarved in a closely related style. Scenes depicted include the worship of the *bodhi* tree and the wheel. While the compositions on this pillar are characterized by the finest qualities of the Stupa 1 gateways, the elongation of the lotus-bearing women and the symmetrical lotus rhizomes framing them anticipate features that appear at the end of the 1st century BC.

The style of the Sanchi gates also has parallels in other parts of central India. This is shown by a palm-leaf capital (Gwalior, Archaeol. Mus.) found at Pawaya, site of the ancient city of Padmavati. With its voluminous and sensitively rendered forms, the capital is a clear cognate of the sculpture at Sanchi. A standing figure of a *yakṣa* (Gwalior, Archaeol. Mus.), found at Pawaya and identified as Bhagavat Manibhadra in the inscription on the pedestal, documents the continuation of *yakṣa* cults in the 1st century BC. The ponderous form of this image parallels the *yakṣa*s on the stupa gates at Sanchi.

The final stages of early Indian sculpture in central India are documented by Stupa 3 at Sanchi. This stupa was constructed around the 2nd century BC to rehouse relics of the Buddha's disciples. The stupa acquired a single gateway around the late 1st century BC or early 1st century AD. The gateway repeats, in a stereotypical manner, the themes of Stupa 1. Some iconographic variations were introduced, however, and the volutes of one architrave were changed into coils of serpents. In the individual reliefs the profuse opulence of Stupa 1 was transformed into an untidy clutter. The earlier feeling for pulsating forms was lost, and figures are no longer posed diagonally in depth but frontally on the surface plane. At times the proportions are unduly distorted. Plants have lost their swaying motion, and lotus medallions have become flat and prolix. These changes augured an end to the early traditions of sculpture in central India.

BIBLIOGRAPHY

J. P. Vogel: 'The Garuda Pillar of Besnagar', *Archaeol. Surv. India, Annu. Rep.* (1908–9), pp. 126–9

H. H. Lake: 'Besnagar', *J. Bombay Branch Royal Asiat. Soc.*, xxiii (1910), pp. 135–46

D. R. Bhandarkar: 'Excavations at Besnagar', *Archaeol. Surv. India, Annu. Rep.* (1913–14), pp. 186–226

J. Marshall: *A Guide to Sanchi* (Calcutta, 1918, 3/Delhi, 1955)

L. Bachhofer: *Early Indian Sculpture*, 2 vols (Paris, 1929)

J. Marshall and A. Foucher: *The Monuments of Sanchi*, 3 vols (London, 1940)

J. N. Banarjea: 'The Holy Pañchavīras of the Vṛishṇis', *J. Ind. Soc. Orient. A.*, x (1942), pp. 65–8

——: *The Development of Hindu Iconography* (Calcutta, 1956)

P. Chandra: 'Yaksha and Yakshi Images from Vidisha', *A. Orient.*, vi (1966), pp. 157–63

M. D. Khare: 'Discovery of a Vishnu Temple near the Heliodoros Pillar, Besnagar, Dist. Vidisha (M.P.)', *Lalit Kala*, xiii (1967), pp. 21–7

R. C. Agrawala: 'Unpublished Yaksha-Yakshi Statues from Besnagar', *Lalit Kala*, xiv (1969), pp. 47–9

P. Chandra: *Stone Sculpture in the Allahabad Museum* (Pune, 1970)

D. Mitra: *Sanchi* (New Delhi, 1973)

J. Irwin: 'The Heliodorus Pillar: A Fresh Appraisal', *A. & Archaeol. Res. Pap.*, vi (1974), pp. 1–13

D. M. Stadtner: 'A Śuṅga Capital from Vidisha', *Artibus Asiae*, xxxvii (1976), pp. 101–4

R. N. Misra: *Yakṣa Cult and Iconography* (Delhi, 1981)

M. D. Khare: *Vidisha* (Bhopal, 1985)

K. K. Chakravarty, ed.: *Vidisha through the Ages* (Vidisha, 1989)

(iii) West. Sculpture of the 2nd century BC from western India is preserved mainly in rock-cut excavations at BHAJA and PITALKHORA in Maharashtra. Works at these two sites mark a break with the full modelling and plastic conception of the Maurya period and approach the flatter, more two-dimensional, 2nd-century BC style of BHARHUT in central India (*see* §(i)(a) above). Incisions and ridges were substituted for Maurya-period modelling, and bodies are less organic and facial expressions more abstract. The distinctive western Indian traits exhibited by works at both sites include the high, soft relief in which bodies and ornaments have been rendered, the pliant, agitated line of the drapery and the additive, amorphous spread of the modelling. Such qualities may be rooted in the appliqué technique of terracotta. The way in which the figures seem to burst from the stone, negating the nature of the material, also contrasts with the selfconscious grace and orderly elegance of the art of Bharhut.

(a) Bhaja. (b) Pitalkhora. (c) Nasik and related sites. (d) Karle.

(a) Bhaja. Many of the sculptures that survive at Bhaja are on the façade of a large *caitya* hall (one in which an object or area of reverence is located), Cave 12, where human figures are carved as though looking out from balconies (for illustration *see* BHAJA), and on the verandah of a *vihāra* (monastery), Cave 19. The most famous sculptures are two narrative reliefs flanking the entrance to Cave 19. One shows a king accompanied by whisk-bearers driving a four-horse chariot across the backs of two obese nude demons. The other shows an elephant with a rider holding a goad and an attendant carrying a standard and spear (see fig. 146). A tree is shown several times: uprooted by the elephant, surrounded by a railing and bedecked with garlands, and bearing dangling or falling human beings. Near the tree are a king enjoying music and dance and a horse-headed female figure holding a man. These complex sculptures have provoked a variety of interpretations. The charioteer has been identified as the sun god Surya making his daily way across the sky and the elephant-rider as the god Indra on his mount, Airavata. The presence of these Hindu deities on a Buddhist monastic dwelling has been explained by their identification with the Buddha, with Surya representing the latter's spiritual power and ability to illuminate and Indra representing his temporal power and stabilization of the universe. However, the charioteer has also been identified as the universal king (*cakravartin*) Mandhata conquering the mythic land of Uttarakura, whose citizens lived in eternal youth and happiness under wish-fulfilling trees. Both the elephant-rider and the king seated near the trees have been identified as Mara, the demon of passion, who attempted to disturb the Buddha's meditation. The horse-headed figure alone appears indisputably to be the *yakṣī* (female nature spirit) Ashvamukhi, who was converted from her cannibalistic habits by the Buddha. These figures may express multiple layers of meaning with both Hindu and Buddhist connotations. They seem to personify the forces

146. *Elephant rider*, verandah of Cave 19, Bhaja, 2nd century BC

of nature, directly confronting our senses and invoking elemental powers.

The sculpture on the verandah of Cave 19 also includes load-bearing *yakṣa*s (male nature spirits), guardian figures, figures with human heads and the bodies of bulls, and a depiction of bulls fighting over the body of a man.

Bhaja's sculpture can be dated to the 2nd century BC both on stylistic grounds and on the basis of two inscriptions carved on roof beams of the *caitya* hall. Specific parallels with the contemporary sculpture of Bharhut and Stupa 2 at Sanchi include such stylistic conventions for human figures as ridged eyelids and eyebrows, pointed elbows and knees and feet with arched insteps, as well as jewellery motifs such as 'fleur-de-lis' armlets and beaded bracelets. Parallels in composition include the repetition of elements in continuous narration, the combination of frontal and profile views and meticulously detailed and crowded scenes. Stylistic features unique to western India include a sense of bodies appearing to grow out of the stone rather than to be carved into it, an elongation of limbs and a sense of energy and movement.

(b) Pitalkhora. Of the 13 caves excavated at Pitalkhora, numbers 3 and 4 are significant for their sculptural remains. While the sculptures of Bhaja are fairly homogeneous in style, those at Pitalkhora show four phases of evolution, moving from the flat, additive style of the 2nd century BC at Bharhut to the full, organically integrated forms seen in the 1st-century BC sculpture of the gateway of Stupa 1 at Sanchi in central India and at Bodhgaya in eastern India (*see* §§(ii)(d) above and (iv)(a) below). This stylistic evolution is supported by the palaeography of inscriptions at the site.

The first phase (mid-2nd century BC) is represented by such works as the winged horses, *yakṣa*s and guardian figures (*dvārapāla*s) of Cave 3 and the composite animals on the pillar capitals of Cave 4. The cubic modelling of these figures is similar to that of Bhaja and Bharhut. The human figures have the same glittering open eyes with prominent irises, eerie smiles, finlike ears and deep navels. A free-standing sculpture of a plump, tightly modelled standing dwarf with upraised arms (New Delhi, N. Mus.) is attributed by an inscription to Kanha Dasa, a goldsmith. Its open, staring, protruding eyes, sharply incised pupils, hair in ringlets arranged in two geometrical rows, the chiselled, linear clarity of its armlets, wristlets and the necklace framing its chest, with its flowers, human heads and *triratna* (triple gem) motifs, and the knife edges of the pleated skirt covering its hips, are typical of this phase. Parallels in jewellery types include broad necklaces impressed with rosettes, bracelets composed of four circles, armlets with three plaits and serpentine earrings.

The second phase (*c.* 150–*c.* 125 BC) is seen in figures such as the elephants and elephant-riders and guardians at the entrance and on the plinth of Cave 4. While these works are still reminiscent of Bharhut, they are enlivened by subtle modelling. The figures have acquired a slight inclination and sway, and their expressions are less abstract.

The third phase (*c.* 125–*c.* 100 BC) moved further away from the flatness of the Bharhut style. The rounded, plastic style of the 1st century BC was anticipated but not fully realized. Works from this period include, in Cave 4, a representation of Gajalakshmi (badly damaged) as well as horses with attendants and loving couples (*mithuna*s). The lustration of Lakshmi was represented in the 2nd century BC at Bharhut and in the 1st century BC at Bodhgaya. The example at Pitalkhora is similar to the former in that the soles of Lakshmi's feet touch, a posture not seen later. Her hour-glass torso and more relaxed stance, however, presage the Bodhgaya style, though the lotus stalks held in her hand do not yet have the sweeping movement seen there. Nevertheless, the lotus petals have shed their harsh edges and become more rounded. The loving couples of Cave 4 are similar to those of Bharhut in the jutting angles of their bodies but are heavier and planted more firmly on the ground. The rigidity of Bharhut has yielded to greater relaxation.

The fourth phase (after *c.* 100 BC) marked a new era of sensitivity and grace closely approximating the modelled 1st-century BC style of Bodhgaya and the sculpture on the gateways of Stupa 1 at Sanchi. Two pieces recovered from the debris of Cave 4 exemplify the work of this period (both New Delhi, N. Mus.). A royal couple with attendants captures the emotional relationship between the figures, while a carving of a stag, with quivering flesh and nostrils, is delicately modelled.

(c) Nasik and related sites. Early work from the *caitya* hall at NASIK can also be dated to the second half of the 1st century BC. The doorway arch displays carved representations of wooden ribs interspersed with horses, elephants and bulls in the manner of Pithalkhora, with the differences that the ribs at Nasik are knotted with the *triratna* motif in the centre and that alternate beams have been carved into human heads. A guardian at the entrance retains the archaistic pose of one arm hanging down and one arm raised and appears uncomfortably compressed on to its narrow shelf of space. (For Caves 3 and 10 at Nasik, *see* §6(iii)(c) below.)

A damaged animal-eared *yakṣa* head from the façade of the *caitya* at KONDANE also seems to belong to the same phase, though it features decorative details in the headdress. The four dancing couples above the entrance hall of the same *caitya* or the gracefully posed warriors holding bow and arrow, club or shield also show a growing sophistication in modelling. The hands and legs of the dancers swing in harmony, and their bent heads and slanted eyes exhibit a sense of intimacy and mutual awareness. The *caitya* façade has an inscription datable to the first half of the 1st century BC.

The *caitya* at BEDSA has inscriptions above the verandah doorway from the latter half of the 1st century BC. The petals of the bell capitals in the verandah are more clearly articulated than earlier examples. Each one is surmounted by an *āmalaka* (ribbed disc) in a square frame and a stepped abacus, crowned by addorsed horses, elephants and single bulls with male or female riders. The figures are somewhat stiffer than those on the gates at Sanchi and are sturdily modelled. The horses are shown with their heads bent to the side, with flared nostrils and accentuated bones and muscles. The riders look out at the viewer.

(d) Karle. The culmination of the tradition of western Indian cave sculpture occurred at KARLE in the magnificent *caitya* hall and three *vihāras*. While the inscriptions recording donations of different parts of the *caitya* range from *c.* 70 BC to AD 120, the sculptures of Karle can be dated stylistically to the late 1st century BC and early 1st century AD. (Some scholars place the sculpture as much as a century later; for dating questions *see* §6(iii)(c) below and SATAVAHANA.)

Of the two enormous stone columns (*kirttīstambhas*) that originally stood in front of the *caitya* hall, only one survives. It rises to a height of 11.4 m above a circular drum carved with rail patterns (now defaced) and consists of a shaft with 16 facets, an inverted lotus capital, an *āmalaka* in a square frame and a stepped abacus crowned by four addorsed sejant lions. The cap of the pillar is connected with the screen wall of the vestibule behind it by a rock attachment with a square mortice. A similar attachment on the other side has vanished. The pillar appears originally to have supported a wheel (*cakra*), thus increasing its height to around 15 m.

Half life-size elephants, originally fitted with ivory tusks and metal ornaments, rest their forequarters on a base carved with rail patterns. Originally they supported a framed frieze with rail designs, which was replaced in the Gupta period by figures of the Buddha and his attendants.

On either side of the central entrance of the vestibule are *yakṣa/yakṣī* couples. They wear massive *kuṇḍalas* (earrings) and clustered beaded bracelets. The women wear multi-strand girdles and thick, heavy ankle-rings. The male usually holds one end of his *uttarīya* in one hand with his other arm draped fondly around his partner's shoulder. The female figures lean or move towards their companions and hold them by either the shoulder or the waist. Their dress, indicated by the pendent drapery between their legs (*paryastaka*), is diaphanous; in one case even this drapery is missing. Two *mithunas* are carved on a smaller scale above the elephants in the verandah (see fig. 147), and two dancing couples are skilfully accommodated within the curve formed by the springing of the *caitya* arch. The dancers glide diagonally up the curve, each with one arm wrapped around the other person and the

147. *Mithuna* couple, Karle, late 1st century BC–early 1st century AD

other raised. Their heads are bent and look out at the viewer, and their garments and garlands echo their motion.

Inside the cave there are 37 pillars, 15 of which are arranged on each side of the nave, and 7 of which are installed around the apse. The pillars have vase-of-foliage bases and crowns and octagonal shafts. Each capital supports two kneeling elephants (with either male and female or two female riders) facing the nave or addorsed horses or sphinxes facing the aisles. The eighth pillar on the right shows, in low relief, a stupa, a mounted wheel, two deer and a lion pillar carved on its 16-sided shaft. The seven pillars around the apse are octagonal without base or capital.

The sculptures of Karle show clear and emphatic advances over earlier cave sculpture. The figures are in much higher relief. Instead of being splayed, their feet are placed diagonally. Their legs are flexed, bent or crossed. The pendent drapery between the legs, immovably centred in earlier examples, swings with the movement of the body. The dancing couples vibrate with movement, their sashes floating away from their bodies, the dancers' legs occasionally breaking out beyond the frame. The combination of front and profile views, while still used, is less awkward than before, and the bodies are fuller and fleshier. The women are narrow-waisted and wide-hipped, with full breasts and thighs. The men have powerful shoulders, long arms and strong, thick legs. The flesh of the stomach is modelled and the navel deeply sunk. The nudity of the female figures is frankly and sensuously emphasized. The women's pert mannerisms and bold stares and the intimacy of the embraces are new qualities in the history of Indian sculpture. The couples and animals lean towards the nave, suggesting an audience listening to a discourse. The repetition and alternation of the richly sculpted and closely spaced pillar shafts in the hall create an orchestrated rhythm of decorative and symbolic elements. Illumination that filters through screen and grills is modulated by the continuous high relief of the pillars and emphasized by the darkness in the aisles. The sculptures of Karle and allied sites anticipate the massive, swelling weight, sensuous modelling, radiant energy, languorous movement and joy that are the salient characteristics of Mathura sculptures in the first three centuries AD (*see* §5 below).

BIBLIOGRAPHY

J. Fergusson and J. Burgess: *The Cave Temples of India* (London, 1880)
J. Burgess and B. L. Indraji: *Inscriptions from Cave Temples of Western India*, Archaeol. Surv. W. India, x (Bombay, 1881)
J. Burgess: *Report on the Buddhist Cave Temples*, Archaeol. Surv. India, New Imp. Ser., iv (London, 1883)
J. Marshall: 'The Monuments of Ancient India', *Cambridge History of India*, i (Cambridge, 1922), pp. 618-49; also in *Cambridge History of India*, i, ed. E. J. Rapson, W. Haig and H. H. Dodwell (Delhi, 1968), pp. 555–88
L. Bachhofer: *Early Indian Sculpture*, ii (Paris, 1929)
R. S. Wauchope: *Buddhist Cave Temples of India* (Calcutta, 1933)
E. H. Johnston: 'Two Buddhist Scenes at Bhaja', *J. Ind. Soc. Orient. A.*, vii (1939), pp. 1–7
R. G. Gyani: 'Identification of the So-called Surya and Indra Figures in Cave No. 20 of the Bhaja Group', *Prince of Wales Mus. Bull.* (1950–51), pp. 15–21
S. K. Saraswati: 'Art and Architecture', *The Age of Imperial Unity*, History and Culture of the Indian People, ii (Bombay, 1951), pp. 483–505
W. Spink: 'On the Development of Early Buddhist Art in India', *A. Bull.*, xl (1958), pp. 95–104
M. N. Deshpande: 'Important Epigraphical Records from the *Caitya* Cave, Bhaja', *Lalit Kala*, vi (1959), pp. 30–32
——: 'The Rock-cut Caves of Pitalkhora in the Deccan', *Anc. India*, xv (1959), pp. 66–93
G. Yazdani: *The Early History of Deccan* (London, 1960)
Cambridge Hist. India, i, ed. E. J. Rapson, W. Haig and H. H. Dodwell (Delhi, 1968), pp. 555–88
D. Mitra: *Buddhist Monuments* (Calcutta, 1971)
V. Dehejia: *Early Buddhist Rock Temples: A Chronological Study* (London, 1972)
O. C. Kail: *Buddhist Cave Temples of India* (Bombay, 1975)
S. Nagaraju: *Buddhist Architecture of Western India* (Delhi, 1981)
K. K. Chakravarty: *Early Buddhist Art of Bodh-Gaya* (Delhi, in preparation)

KALYAN KUMAR CHAKRAVARTY

(iv) East. While little evidence has emerged of royal patronage for monuments in eastern India from the 2nd century BC to the 3rd century AD, remains are ample. Examples of sculpture from the 2nd–1st century BC are widely scattered, and it seems likely that artists worked in key locations such as Pataliputra (modern Patna) and Bodhgaya and from there distributed works on commission. As in other parts of India in the first two centuries BC, chronology is far from exact. Iconographic, palaeographic and formal comparisons with Bharhut and Sanchi (*see* §§(i) and (ii) above) are the basic tools for building a history of the early eastern style.

(a) Bodhgaya and related sites. The only site in ancient Magadha (part of modern northern Bihar) with a significant concentration of sculpture is Bodhgaya, the place of the Buddha's enlightenment and an important pilgrimage centre (*see* BODHGAYA AND GAYA). A relief from BHARHUT (2nd century BC) suggests that a hypaethral wooden structure once enshrined the *bodhi* tree (*see* BUDDHISM, §I). Although this temple has disappeared, parts of a stone railing adorned with relief sculptures have survived (Bodhgaya, Archaeol. Mus.; Calcutta, Ind. Mus.; London, V&A). Votive inscriptions on the railing mention gifts by queens and intimates of some Mitra kings, who apparently ruled in the first century BC. Like the somewhat earlier railings at Stupa 2, Sanchi, and at Bharhut, the Bodhgaya railing has reliefs in medallions on the crossbars and at the centre of the uprights; at the top and bottom of the uprights are three-quarter medallions. The uprights at the entrances carry full-length figures and, in a few instances, reliefs in rectangular panels. The reliefs are sparsely carved compared to Bharhut and Stupa 2 at Sanchi, and both reliefs and figures are more fully modelled. These features are regional characteristics more than chronological indicators. While the Bharhut reliefs, generally labelled, illustrate scenes of the historical Buddha's life and of his previous incarnations, the Bodhgaya examples are mostly busts in lotus medallions and animals, both real and mythical. Of the scenes that can be confidently identified, one illustrates the purchase of the Jetavana garden so that it could be given to the Buddha. In contrast with the more detailed illustration of this episode at Bharhut, only three figures cover the garden with gold coins. Similarly, the full-length figures, though more sensitively modelled than their counterparts at Bharhut and Stupa 2, Sanchi, show considerably less linear detail in the rendering of accoutrements. This may be seen on the male figure, probably a *yakṣa*, boosting his female counterpart into a tree and on the figure generally identified as the god Indra (see fig. 148). A *yakṣī* standing on a bulbous pot (identified with the

148. *Indra*, railing post, stone, h. 1.71 m, Bodhgaya, *c.* 100 BC

goddess Sri) also indicates a decisive move away from the sharp, linear style of the 2nd century BC. As with sculpture elsewhere, the Bodhgaya railing documents the assimilation of pre-Buddhist divine and popular cults into Buddhist iconography. One panel may represent Surya, the sun god, who is shown on a chariot drawn by four horses. The palaeography of the Bodhgaya inscriptions and the style of the sculptures, which precede and occasionally overlap with the relaxed forms of the gateways of Stupa 1 at Sanchi, support a date of *c.* 100 BC. When the Mahabodhi temple was reconstructed in the 6th century AD, the railing apparently was reset. At this time some replacement uprights were made, which are rare examples of copies in an archaizing style.

At least one other product of the artists who made the Bodhgaya railing has survived. This is a post carved with a standing female figure at Rajasan on the outskirts of Hajipur (Vaisali District). The loose modelling of the figure is virtually identical to the figural style at Bodhgaya. The post may have been part of a railing, but since it lacks mortices it could also have been free-standing. The distance that separates the post from Bodhgaya (about 110 km) indicates that products of this workshop were widespread and probably more numerous than remains suggest.

(b) Khandagiri and Udayagiri. Close to the famous temple site of Bhubaneshwar are two short ranges of hills known as KHANDAGIRI AND UDAYAGIRI. In these hills are 35 rock-cut cave shrines containing the most important early sculpture in the Kalinga region. Unlike the Barabar caves in ancient Magadha (*see* BARABAR AND NAGARJUNI) or those in the Deccan, which are carved consecutively along a path, these shrines appear to have been randomly placed. The caves were probably excavated for the use of Jainas, since the monarch Kharavela (*c.* 1st century BC), whose lengthy inscription is carved on the cave known as Hathigumpha, was a follower of Jainism. Later images and temples in the hills also belong to the Jaina faith. Several of the shrines are adorned with relief sculpture, most notably the Hathigumpha, the Manchipuri cave, the Ananatagumpha and the two-storey Ranigumpha. The sculpture is generally restricted to friezes tucked under the eaves or lining the porch ceilings of the caves. The friezes are

149. *Sacred Tree Surrounded by a Railing*, Cave 5, Udayagiri, 1st century BC

placed on railing-type bands supported by corbels and interrupted at intervals by arched entrances. The extrados of each arch is carved with lotus rhizomes or prancing animals. Occasionally there are guardian figures and full-relief panels extending to the ground. The reliefs show a variety of narrative scenes, flying *vidyādharas* (minor deities), trees and elephants (see fig. 149). With the exception of auspicious symbols and themes such as the Gajalakshmi, the subjects of most of the reliefs have not been identified. The style, however, recalls the sculpture on the gateways of Stupa 1 at Sanchi and so suggests a date in the 1st century BC. As at Sanchi, the reliefs are densely detailed and remarkable for their opulent vitality.

BIBLIOGRAPHY

L. Bachhofer: *Early Indian Sculpture* (New York, 1929)
A. K. Coomaraswamy: *La Sculpture de Bodhgayā*, Ars Asiatica: Etudes et Documents, xviii (Paris, 1935)
N. R. Ray: *Maurya and Sunga Art* (Calcutta, 1945, rev. 1965); rev. as *Maurya and Post-Maurya Art* (Delhi, 1975)
D. Mitra: *Udayagiri and Khandagiri* (New Delhi, 1960)
S. K. Saraswati: *Early Sculpture of Bengal* (Calcutta, 1962)
P. L. Gupta: *Patna Museum Catalogue of Antiquities (Stone Sculptures, Metal Images, Terracottas and Minor Antiquities)* (Patna, 1965)
N. R. Ray, K. Kandalavala and S. Gorakshkar: *Eastern Indian Bronzes* (New Delhi, 1986)
S. L. Huntington and J. C. Huntington: *Leaves from the Bodhi Tree* (Dayton, OH, 1989)

FREDERICK M. ASHER

(v) South. In the Andhra region, situated on the lower reaches of the Krishna River, monumental stupas decorated subsequently with reliefs executed in the marble-like limestone of Palnad were constructed from the 3rd century BC. Perhaps the most celebrated is the former stupa at AMARAVATI, which was established in Maurya times. Lesser stupas with sculptural reliefs were erected at Goli, Bhattiprolu, Ghantashala and Jaggayyapeta. Reliefs on an Amaravati limestone stele (Amaravati, Archaeol. Mus.), in the style of Bharut (*see* §(i)(a) above) and, as there, provided with descriptive inscriptions (not employed later on in Andhra), prove beyond doubt the penetration of the Bharhut style around 250–100 BC.

In the later phase of the early period (*c.* 1st century BC) at Amaravati, even the simplest decoration was imaginatively and sensitively rendered. To this phase belong those fragments of the rail coping that depict flat-faced dwarfs carrying a heavy undulating garland and others that bear images of running youths with broad faces and staring eyes directing a series of fabulous animals (Madras, Govt Mus.; London, BM), and also a drum slab carving of the *Enlightenment of the Buddha* in low relief (London, BM). An inscribed headless life-size statue probably of a king with his folded hands raised in a gesture of adoration (Madras, Govt Mus.) is an elegant and monumental example of the art of Amaravati apparently of the late 1st century BC

Stylistically, the decoration of the Jaggayyapeta stupa drum is roughly contemporary with the Amaravati sculptures from the end of the early period. One of the best examples at Jaggayyapeta is the relief depicting the *cakravartin* (world-emperor) Mandhata (Madras, Govt Mus.); a similar sculpture in higher relief is in Paris (Mus. Guimet). The large figure of the emperor is shown surrounded by the symbols of his exalted state (his queen, his minister, his general and his horse). Stylistic characteristics such as the rather flat, masklike face of the monarch are conventions that can also be seen in the art of Mathura prior to the Kushana period (*see* §(i)(a) above). The manner in which the men's lower garments curl around their legs (in the figures of the minister and general) resembles the dress of the life-size headless image of a king from Amaravati. However, the Jaggayyapeta figures have attenuated limbs, and their feet do not appear to stand firmly on the ground.

Further south, the only sculpture of any importance (one for which various dates have been proposed) is the famous stone *liṅga* (sacred phallus) faced with a standing figure of the god Shiva (see fig. 150). It is still worshipped in a temple at Gudimallam near Madras. Carved from

150. Shiva *liṅga*, stone, h. of Shiva figure 800 mm, Gudimallam, *c.* 1st century BC

brown igneous rock and highly polished, it is unique owing to the presence of a square fence (as depicted on reliefs), with the original shrine open to the sky. Shiva's figure is modelled on that of a *yakṣa*. His curls are arranged on top of his head in the manner of an ascetic and take the form of a turban. Two-armed, he holds in his right hand a ram ready for sacrifice and in his left hand a lance and a vessel for water or ghee. He wears heavy earrings, a wide necklace and bracelets. His diaphanous undergarment, which emphasizes his sexual organ, is tied tightly above his thighs and held in position by a waistband. He stands on a grinning dwarf *yakṣa*. There is no similar sculpture of this period anywhere in south India. The Gudimallam Shiva with his slanted eyes, corpulent body and resolute stance contrasts with the more remote *yakṣa*s depicted at Bharhut. There are a number of relief panels from Amaravati in a more relaxed and fluid style reminiscent of the gateways of Stupa 1 at Sanchi (e.g. London, BM; Boston, MA, Mus. F.A.). The chronological position of these panels is controversial, as the dating of Sanchi and sites with analogous sculpture in western India has ranged from the 1st century BC to the 1st century AD. In the opinion of this author, however, it seems unlikely that the period of early maturity at Amaravati precedes the 1st century AD.

BIBLIOGRAPHY

D. Barrett: *Sculptures from Amaravati in the British Museum* (London, 1954)

Bull. Madras Govt Mus., iv (1956) [issue on Amaravati sculptures in the Madras Government Museum]

P. R. Srinivasam: 'Recently Discovered Early Inscriptions from Amaravati and their Significance', *Lalit Kala*, x (1961), pl. XIV, fig. 3

A. Ghosh and H. Sarkar: 'Beginnings of Sculptural Art in South-east India: A Stele from Amarāvatī', *Anc. India*, xx–xxi (1964–5), pp. 168–77

D. Barrett: 'The Early Phase at Amarāvatī', *BM Q.*, xxxii (1967–8), pp. 35–48

V. Dehejia: 'Early Activity at Amaravati', *Archvs Asian A.*, xxiii (1969–70), pp. 41–54

I. K. Sarma: 'New Light on Art through Archaeological Conservation', *J. Ind. Soc. Orient. A.*, x (1978–9), pp. 48–54

D. Barrett: 'Style and Palaeography at Amarāvatī', *Orient. A.*, xxxvi/2 (1990), pp. 77–82

R. Knox: *Amaravati: Buddhist Sculpture from the Great Stūpa* (London, 1992)

A. Roy: *Amarāvatī Stūpa: A Critical Comparison of Epigraphic, Architectural and Sculptural Evidence* (Delhi, 1994)

O. M. STARZA-MAJEWSKI

5. 1st–3rd centuries AD.

(i) North. (ii) North-west. (iii) West. (iv) Central. (v) East. (vi) South.

(i) North. The name given to the Kshatrapa (satrap) families who probably ruled north India during the 1st century AD suggests that they were provincial governors, although no overlord to whom they were responsible has been identified. Mathura may have served as the capital of the Kshatrapa ruler Rajula, but it was more widely recognized as a religious centre than as a political headquarters. Inscriptions on a lion capital (London, BM) found at the Saptarshi Tila, Mathura, imply that after some time, Rajula assumed the more elevated title Mahakshatrapa and was joined in rule by his son Sodasa, who took the title Kshatrapa. The Kshatrapas were eventually superseded by the KUSHANA dynasty of the 1st–2nd century, whose origins may be traced to eastern Central Asia. The extent to which the first recorded Kushana monarchs, Kujula Kadphises and Vima Kadphises, actually ruled north India is uncertain, but their successor Kanishka certainly extended Kushana authority over much of north India.

Under Kushana rule, Mathura flourished, becoming the premier centre for artistic production in north India; indeed, while the production of sculpture flourished at Mathura, very little was produced elsewhere in the Gangetic plain. While large-scale religious sculptures were made at Mathura and many Buddhist works were widely exported across north India, artistic production elsewhere in the region largely ceased (for example at Sanchi in Madhya Pradesh) and was only resumed after the period of Kushana dominance. A similar hiatus also occurred at this time in the excavation of western Indian rock-cut sanctuaries and in the workshops of eastern India.

(a) Religious. (b) Secular.

(a) Religious.

Buddhist. A major innovation of Kushana times was the development of an anthropomorphic image of the Buddha. That the introduction of the image in north India coincided with the arrival of the Kushanas, as inscriptional evidence suggests, is not certain; on the basis of stylistic evidence, some images have been assigned a date prior to the reign of Kanishka, the first major Kushana emperor in India. However, there seems to be no evident link between Kushana authority and the creation of anthropomorphic Buddha images, since all the inscriptions on statues indicate that they were donated by monks, nuns or, occasionally, by lay worshippers but never by the royal family. The introduction of these images is an issue that has consumed a great deal of scholarly attention, in large measure because scholars have been involved in a debate centring on whether they were first made in the north-western region of Gandhara (*see* §(ii) below) or at Mathura. The debate has often assumed political overtones, with proponents of a Gandhara origin (most often European scholars) arguing for Greek or Roman influence as the stimulus, and proponents of a Mathura origin (most often Indian scholars) arguing for Mathura and pre-Kushana art as the source. For the most part, the debate has focused on images of the Buddha, although images of major Hindu deities and large numbers of Jaina saints, or *tīrthaṅkara*s, were also produced from the early Kushana period.

The earliest documented image of the Buddha from north India, a headless standing figure from Kausambi (Allahabad Mus.; see fig. 151) is dated to Kanishka's second year. Both the style and the use of the characteristic local red mottled sandstone suggest that the piece was produced at Mathura. The figure was provided by the nun Buddhamitra, who in no way implies in her dedicatory inscription that the image is exceptional in the sense of being a radical departure from previous practice. Buddhamitra was an active patron of Buddha images; her name is associated with at least two other works, one an export from Mathura (see below). Such circumstances suggest that she may have been involved in facilitating the cult of image worship. Although the Kausambi statue has the appearance of a Buddha image in that it is shown wearing only a simple monastic robe and no jewellery, the inscription refers to it as representing a *bodhisattva*. This apparent discrepancy is characteristic of inscriptions on

151. *Buddha*, red sandstone, h. 1.20 m, probably made at Mathura, from Kausambi, year 2, reign of Kanishka, AD 80 (Allahabad, Allahabad Museum)

Kushana images that iconographically appear to represent the Buddha. Various explanations include the notion that the term *bodhisattva* was to be taken literally as any being bearing the essence of Buddhahood, including the Buddha himself. Such a complex explanation may not, however, be necessary if it is assumed that the patrons meant precisely what their scribes wrote: that the images represent *bodhisattvas*, in this case probably Shakyamuni in the phase between his renunciation and his enlightenment.

The nun Buddhamitra was also involved in the provision of the most celebrated early Kushana image, a Buddha figure found at Sarnath, Uttar Pradesh, but carved of the characteristic mottled Mathura stone and dated in Kanishka's third year (Sarnath, Archaeol. Mus.). Since the primary patron of this figure was the monk Bala, it is commonly called the *Friar Bala Buddha*, although it too is identified as a *bodhisattva* in the inscription. This over life-size sculpture, with softly modelled abdomen and swelling chest, is better preserved than the Kausambi example. The head is intact, and part of the halo is evident. A huge umbrella, carved separately, was intended for placement on an inscribed shaft running behind the image. Bala's role in the provision of anthropomorphic Buddha (or *bodhisattva*) images was considerable, for others bear his name, including one found at Sravasti, Uttar Pradesh, but again apparently made at Mathura (Calcutta, Ind. Mus.); a patron a generation later (the daughter of Buddhamitra's niece) records that she was Bala's disciple.

A well-known image from the Katra Mound, Mathura (see fig. 152), is iconographically more complete. Although it too is identified as a *bodhisattva* in the dedicatory inscription, it has no adornments but displays several identifying marks of a Buddha (*lakṣaṇas*): the cranial protrusion (*uṣṇīṣa*), the raised dot between the eyebrows (*ūrṇā*), the Wheel of the Law (*dharmacakra*) marked on the hands and feet, and a nimbus. Characteristic of Buddha images from Mathura, the figure raises the right hand in the reassuring gesture (*abhaya mudrā*), probably perpetuating a convention derived from earlier north Indian art, in which figures were frequently portrayed with the right hand raised, for example holding a whisk or grasping the branch of a tree. Although inscribed, the image bears no date; because the system of noting the monarch's name and regnal year was apparently first used during Kanishka's reign and is generally applied in Kushana inscriptions,

152. *Seated Buddha*, mottled red sandstone, h. 690 mm, from the Katra Mound, Mathura, early 2nd century AD (Mathura, Government Museum)

many scholars therefore believe that this places the image just prior to Kanishka's accession. In any event, the soft modelling of the abdomen and chest and the naturalistic proportions suggest a date close to the time of Kanishka. However, there is much debate about the actual dates of his reign (see Basham). Some believe that it began in AD 78, while others argue for dates of *c.* AD 110, 128 or 144. Because so many images are dated in the era that began with Kanishka, it would be useful to resolve his regnal dates in terms of the common era, but this has not yet been achieved. Nevertheless, Kushana-era dates in inscriptions at least provide an indication of sculptures' dates relative to each other and thus furnish a means of determining the development of sculpture during the period. It is thus known, for example, from a *Buddha* (Calcutta, Ind. Mus.) dated the year 39 (i.e. during the reign of Huvishka) that artists began to work in a more formalized fashion after the time of Kanishka, as suggested by the relatively flattened abdomen, tubular limbs and more sharply protruding nipples. Later images assumed an even more formalized appearance, with virtually no modelling of the torso and the head very large in proportion to the body. Some of these highly formalized figures, such as one from Sravasti (Lucknow, State Mus.; see fig. 153), are draped with a garment the folds of which are clearly indicated, still further obscuring the natural form of the body. This fashion is quite unlike that of the earlier Kushana Buddhist images, which are invariably draped in diaphanous garments. The Sravasti Buddha, which is carved from lighter-coloured sandstone than most Mathura images and is thus possibly a local product, bears no date but closely relates to Jaina images inscribed in the reign of Vasudeva, Huvishka's successor. It is curious that there are no extant Kushana-period images inscribed later than the year AD 98, presumably the last year of Vasudeva's reign: Vasudeva was apparently the last in the Kushana imperial line, and perhaps because of this the dating system commencing with the beginning of Kanishka's reign seems to have lost favour at this time. In consequence, plotting the evolution of late Kushana sculpture and the transition to the Gupta style cannot be reliably based on inscriptional evidence. However, it has been proposed that the digit indicating the century was occasionally omitted; thus a *Seated Buddha* from Mathura (Lucknow, State Mus.) dated in the year 36 of the Kushana era might in fact belong to the year [1]36. This would help to explain the formalized style of the figure and the fold-marked treatment of the garment. An alternative proposal is that a new era began with the reign of Kanishka II, who succeeded Vasudeva (*see also* §(ii)(a) below).

153. *Seated Buddha*, white sandstone, h. 300 mm, from Sravasti, *c.* 2nd–3rd century AD (Lucknow, State Museum)

At least some north Indian Buddha images of this period were made outside Mathura and may bear regnal dates of monarchs other than the Kushanas. The ruined Ghositarama monastery at Kausambi yielded a number of sculptures, including two bearing inscriptions dated year 83 (probably of Kanishka's era) during the reign of Bhadramagha. The dynasty to which this king belonged is often called the Maghas; they appear to have ruled during the later part of the 2nd century in what is today eastern Uttar Pradesh. One of these sculptures (Allahabad U., Archaeol. Mus.) is a *Seated Buddha* draped in a heavy-looking garment with folds clearly indicated. This heavy, pleated style of garment appeared as early as the year 51 on a Buddha image from Anyor, just north of Mathura (Mathura, Govt Mus.); like the Kausambi figure, the Anyor *Buddha* was made for the Mahasanghika sect.

Besides those images that appear to represent the Buddha despite inscriptions identifying them as *bodhisattvas*, there are some Kushana works that clearly portray *bodhisattvas*. These include an image from Ahichchhatra, Uttar Pradesh, with inscriptions identifying it as a representation of *Maitreya*, the Buddha of the Future (New Delhi, N. Mus.). This figure probably dates to the reign of Kanishka or early in that of Huvishka and holds a flask of ambrosia in the manner of contemporary Maitreya images. There is no question that, by the year 29, early in Huvishka's reign, images of Maitreya were produced; one example from Girdhapur (Mathura, Govt Mus.) also holds the flask, though the figure is not identified by inscription. The identities of other Kushana-period *bodhisattva* images from north India are less certain: for example, some figures from Serai Azampur, on the outskirts of Mathura (Mathura, Govt Mus.), hold a lotus (*padma*) in the upraised right hand and so may represent Padmapani, a form of Avalokiteshvara. A figure in the Kronos Collection, New York, is shown seated with one leg pendent and the other crossed on top of it and two fingers of the right hand raised as if to support the head. A similarly posed figure from Gandhara (Calcutta, Ind. Mus.) holds the lotus in the left hand and so may also be identified as Padmapani/Avalokiteshvara. These *bodhisattva* figures generally wear a large plaquette placed centrally in the turban, together with such other adornments as necklaces and bracelets, which readily distinguish them from the austerely dressed figures of the Buddha. In reliefs such figures are sometimes shown as the objects of devotion, for example in a relief from Maholi (Mathura, Govt Mus.).

The development of Buddhism during this period is documented by sculpture and related works, a notable example being a fragmentary *Buddha Amitabha* (Mathura, Govt Mus.) dedicated in the year 26 during the reign of Huvishka. Only the pedestal survives, but its inscription is an important record of the evolution of Mahayana Buddhism, as it may indicate the existence at this time of such paradise cults as that described in the *Sukhavatī Vyūha* ('Arrangement of Amitabha's heaven'), which had been translated into Chinese by the mid-2nd century. Buddhist narrative relief was another feature of Kushana art at Mathura. Episodes in the life of the Buddha continued to be depicted, but with anthropomorphic images replacing the symbols used earlier at such sites as Bharhut and Sanchi. A relief from Rajghat, Mathura (Mathura, Govt Mus.), characteristically represents these episodes in narrative order from right to left: in this case, the birth of the Buddha is followed by the Buddha overcoming Mara, the Buddha's Descent at Sankasya, the Miracle at Sravasti and finally the *parinirvāṇa*. Each scene spans two registers. The order enables each episode to be 'read' by a devotee circumambulating the stupa or temple in the traditional clockwise direction; this was in itself an innovation, as the reliefs of earlier monuments were not generally organized according to narrative sequence but rather seem to have been arranged according to the place where the episodes occurred. This arrangement can be seen on a broken relief from Mathura often described as a lintel (Lucknow, State Mus.). From the right, the episodes represent the Buddha overcoming Mara, the First Sermon (showing the Buddha turning the rim of a wheel to indicate his setting in motion the Wheel of the Law), and the Buddha in the Indrashala Cave being implored by Indra and other deities to return to the leadership of his order. On the far right, in place of the expected scene showing the birth of the Buddha, is an image of the solar deity, Surya, apparently an example of the solar metaphors widely used to describe the Buddha's birth, for example in the *Buddhacarita* of Ashvaghosha, probably written about the time of Kanishka.

A different sort of order is apparent in a series of pillars from a stupa railing found at Bhuteshar on the northern outskirts of Mathura. On one side of each pillar is a voluptuous female figure standing on a dwarflike vehicle; above, as if on the verandah of a building, is a couple, playfully engaged. On the reverse is a relief of an episode from the life of the Buddha or from his previous lives; there is one story—almost invariably recounted in three panels—on each pillar. Themes include the story of the Buddha quelling the elephant Nalagiri at Rajgir and the *Vessantara jātaka*. Earlier railing pillars do not display this regular order. It is likely that the female figures faced outward, confronting the mundane world beyond the stupa precinct, while the sacred stories could be 'read' by the devotee in the course of circumambulation. Railing pillars adorned on one side with female figures were widely employed in north India during this period. Their sectarian affiliation, however, can be difficult to ascertain because they have no narrative reliefs that might indicate whether they defined the circumambulatory pathway of a Buddhist stupa or enclosed the precinct of a monument of another faith. Many such pillars were found at Mathura, but others, carved in the characteristic Mathura sandstone and in a style indistinguishable from that of Mathura, were found some distance away, for example a railing from Sanghol in Haryana (New Delhi, N. Mus.).

Jaina. Although some of the dates inscribed on anthropomorphic images of Jaina *tīrthaṅkaras* are problematic, it appears that this form appeared at about the same time as anthropomorphic Buddha images were introduced in north India; an image of the year 48 (Lucknow, State Mus.; see fig. 154) identifies Huvishka as the reigning monarch. Other inscribed *tīrthaṅkara* images bear even earlier dates: two examples (both Lucknow, State Mus.) date to the year 4, and three more (two Lucknow, State Mus., one Mathura, Govt Mus.) date to the year 5. Of the latter group, one piece has an inscription mentioning the name of Kanishka (though not necessarily Kanishka I) and indicating that the figure represented is Vardhamana, i.e. Mahavira, the founder of JAINISM. Other *tīrthaṅkaras* named in inscriptions include Arishtanemi on a piece dated year 18 and Shantinatha in an inscription of the following year (both Lucknow, State Mus.). Some images, while not identified by inscription, clearly depict other *tīrthaṅkaras* such as Parshvanatha. All of these figures, together with others dated to the reign of Vasudeva and many probably even later, were found at the Mathura site

154. *Tīrthaṅkara*, red sandstone, h. 600 mm, from Kankali Tila, Mathura, year 48, reign of Huvishka (Lucknow, State Museum)

known as the Kankali Tila, described by late 19th-century excavators as the site of a Jaina stupa.

The stylistic evolution of these figures—if they are arranged according to the dates in their inscriptions—is somewhat perplexing. For example, while a figure dated year 7 with an inscription identifying Kanishka as the reigning monarch (Lucknow, State Mus.) appears squatter and more heavily set than Buddhist figures of the same period, and the detailed carving on the pedestal is more typical of later in the Kushana period, the image of the year 48 naming Huvishka as the reigning monarch is quite similar to contemporary Buddha images. If it is assumed that Indian sculptures made at about the same time and in the same area for adherents of different faiths rarely, if ever, differ, then some explanation for these apparent discrepancies must be sought. It is not adequate to conclude that Jaina works often differ from contemporary Buddhist pieces. One explanation, probably correct, is that the Jaina image of the year 7 was in fact made in the year 107 (see discussion above) and that the monarch identified in the inscription is not Kanishka I but a subsequent king of the same name. Thus the earliest dated *tīrthaṅkara* figures would be those of Huvishka's reign (e.g. the piece dated to the year 48), while that of the year 31 should be interpreted as dating to the year 131 and thus made during the reign of Kanishka III.

Besides the *tīrthaṅkara* images, a great many square plaques known as *āyāgapaṭa*s dating to this period were found, primarily at the Kankali Tila in Mathura. These generally feature a central image of a seated *tīrthaṅkara* set within a circular frame and surrounded by auspicious symbols—most commonly the eight called *aṣṭamaṅgala*—usually arranged concentrically. On a few examples a wheel was substituted for the figure. Two pieces (Mathura, Govt Mus., and Lucknow, State Mus.) represent a stupa, perhaps the one that once stood at the Kankali Tila; their style recalls comparable representations of stupas at Amaravati and Nagarjunakonda. The plaques are almost invariably inscribed, generally beginning with a salutation to the *arhat*s (i.e. the *tīrthaṅkara*s) and continuing with the name and identity of the donor. Almost all were provided by women; this suggests that they may have been given for a particular purpose (e.g. in the hope of achieving fertility), although women also played a significant role in the provision of other types of Jaina and Buddhist images. They did so apparently on their own authority and with independent funds, for there is nothing in the inscription to suggest any sort of dependent status. The only dated plaque was set up by a woman named Amohini, a lay disciple of Jaina ascetics, and is dated in the year 42 of the reign of the Kshatrapa Sodasa. Its design shows a large central female figure shielded by a parasol or umbrella, the characteristic royal perquisite, and flanked by attendants. It may be earlier than the other pieces, which can probably be assigned to the time of Kanishka. However, it has been argued on the basis of palaeography that the *āyāgapaṭa*s are prior to Kanishka's reign and may have provided a model for anthropomorphic images of the Buddha. The practice of inscribing sculptures, common in north India during this period, is indicative of the attention to record-keeping that might be expected among the business communities that flourished in such urban areas as Mathura.

Hindu. At about the same time that stone anthropomorphic Buddha and *tīrthaṅkara* images were first made, images of the major Hindu deities also began to be produced in stone, primarily at Mathura. Most of the surviving figures are very small, as in the case of a number of standing Vishnu images all under 250 mm high (Mathura, Govt Mus.). A significant majority of these were discovered in wells, as if they had been placed there intentionally, perhaps for protection or ritual purposes. Iconographically, they are well developed; Vishnu is shown with a tall crown and four arms holding his four characteristic attributes: the mace, the conch shell, the wheel and the lotus. However, the style of the figures is difficult to analyse, because they are rendered more summarily than the larger contemporary Buddhist and Jaina figures. No large images of Vishnu survive from this period, but other small images of Hindu deities (again, mostly found in wells) include several of Gaja-Lakshmi (e.g. Allahabad U., Archaeol. Mus.) and others of Durga slaying the buffalo demon (e.g. Berlin, Mus. Ind. Kst). Indeed, virtually the full Hindu pantheon appears among the small sculptures of this time. An unusual exception to the small scale of the period is a complex figure, commonly identified as Indra but possibly representing Vishnu, from the Saptasamundri Well on the site of the Government Museum, Mathura. From the crown of the central male figure the bust of a second figure rises; a serpent deity (*nāga*) emerges from the main figure's right shoulder, and a comparable figure apparently originally emerged from the left shoulder. A mace is attached below the serpent deity emerging from the right shoulder, though its present placement may represent a faulty reconstruction. The figure's iconography remains to be resolved, but it is most probably a Hindu image; the modelling and the treatment of the facial features suggest a date in the reign of Huvishka or Vasudeva.

The only surviving large-scale Hindu figures of the Kushana period are Shiva *liṅga*s (phallic emblems of Shiva) or reliefs showing *liṅga* worship. One large and complex example with figures ascending all four sides still stands at Nand in Ajmer District, Rajasthan; carved from Sikri sandstone, it was probably exported from Mathura. Another, showing a single head emerging from each of four clustered *liṅga*s, was found in the Saptasamundri Well at Mathura (Mathura, Govt Mus.). This unusual form anticipates the more conventional four-faced (*caturmukha*) *liṅga* (e.g. New Delhi, N. Mus.) that must have been developed during the Kushana period. An example of this more conventional type is in the National Museum of India, New Delhi. The provenance of this figure is unrecorded, but it is carved from the mottled red sandstone generally used at Mathura. Shiva in his *liṅga* form is also shown in a narrative context, the only Hindu deity shown in this fashion in relief sculpture of this time. One such work (Mathura, Govt Mus.) illustrates a Shiva *liṅga* being worshipped by two garland-bearing figures in the costume commonly called 'northern dress': high boots and trousers and a flaring, long-sleeved coat (a type of dress also used to depict Kushana rulers). This scene may be taken as a parallel to the reliefs illustrating stupa worship. Another such relief from Mathura (Lucknow, State Mus.) is rendered with remarkable perspective suggesting depth; it shows a one-faced *liṅga* on a pedestal with two figures, apparently *gaṇa*s (members of Shiva's retinue).

A number of Kushana-period sculptures depict the solar deity Surya, although their sectarian affiliation is uncertain. They may be Buddhist images, for Surya appears in several Buddhist contexts prior to the Kushana period and on a Kushana-period plaque from Mathura illustrating episodes in the Buddha's life (see above). Surya is also a Brahmanical deity of considerable antiquity and was later worshipped independently. It is therefore unclear whether the considerable numbers of Kushana images of Surya are Buddhist or Hindu, or perhaps icons of an independent cult. The god wears northern dress and is invariably shown squatting, as if in a chariot; there are often two leaping horses on the pedestal. His right hand holds the handle of a dagger, while in the left is an object generally identified as a lotus, although its appearance is quite unlike the full-blown form seen in later images. So close are these Surya images to depictions of the Kushana monarchs that the identity of some figures has been confused. This is particularly true of one example from the Kankali Tila at Mathura (Mathura, Govt Mus.), which is perhaps intentionally ambiguous; a dot between the eyebrows is reminiscent of the Buddha's *ūrṇā*, and standing animals at the side of the pedestal (maybe horses) resemble those on the Buddha's lion throne.

Another category of north Indian images, found particularly at Mathura, is a group of serpent divinities (*nāga*s). These are generally represented as male figures beneath serpent canopies; sometimes they hold a flask. An inscribed example found at Ral Bhadar, *c.* 12 km north-west of Mathura, and dated in the year 8 of Kanishka's reign, was made for the dedication of a tank, as was a better-known piece from Chargaon (*c.* 16 km south of Mathura), inscribed in the year 40, during Huvishka's reign (both Mathura, Govt Mus.). The latter figure is full-sized, with a vitality shown by few of the more rigidly erect figures; the deity leans to the right while raising his right hand back over his head for balance. If these two inscribed figures were intended to commemorate the dedication of tanks, it seems likely that other *nāga* images of this period served the same purpose, although the tradition does not appear to have persisted in north India beyond the 3rd century.

(b) Secular. Images of the Kushana rulers appear both on coins and as a group of portrait statues found at Mat, a site just north of Mathura. The largest of these is a figure of *Vima Kadphises* seated on a lion throne, possibly executed during the period of his reign (Mathura, Govt Mus.). It may be intentional that the figure is seated on a throne similar to those used for Buddha images and wearing the northern dress, otherwise used for images of Surya, as if to imply godlike qualities; even the figure's hand positions are similar to those seen in Surya images, although the objects they held have not been preserved. This interpretation is reinforced by the king's title, *devaputra* ('son of god'), and by the fact that the statue was installed in a temple. Such interpretations should not be forced or overextended, since the lion throne was already common to royal imagery and thus was among the emblems adopted by early Buddhists; similarly, the costume was among the repertory of Iranian and Central Asian imagery adopted both by the Kushanas and by the worshippers of Surya, whose cult was stimulated by the arrival in India of the sun-worshipping Iranian Maghas.

The other statues in the temple at Mat were probably added after the figure of Vima Kadphises. Best known of these is a (headless) standing figure of Kanishka (see fig. 155). He is dressed in a long coat worn over a tunic, pants and boots; the inscription identifying him runs along the lower hem of the coat. His right hand rests on the handle of a sword, the left on the handle of a long mace. The two-dimensionality of the figure is a departure from works actually dated to Kanishka's time and may suggest a date later in the Kushana period, as if his image were added as a memorial.

However, there may be other explanations for the unusual style of this sculpture; for example, a foreign artist may have been brought to Mathura specifically to produce royal images. A similarly dressed figure found in the Mat temple has an incomplete inscription that has been read as the name of the western Kshatrapa ruler Chastana. However, since that reading is incorrect, it is inappropriate to draw historical conclusions from it. Other figures wearing this type of costume, often called 'donor figures', are common at Mathura, though their relationship to the Kushana royal family is uncertain.

155. Headless figure of Kanishka, mottled red sandstone, h. 1.5 m, from Mat, *c.* AD 100 (Mathura, Government Museum)

An especially interesting group of sculptures represents inebriated figures in what are generally described as 'Bacchanalian' scenes. This is not to suggest that a cult of Bacchus actually flourished at Mathura, although the reliefs may be taken as evidence of religious practices not widely prevalent elsewhere in India; during Kushana times Mathura was very much an international city, even though it was not the political capital. The scenes are usually carved on both sides of a relatively thick stone slab with a depression at the top, probably intended to hold a bowl. Stone bowls carved with vine-leaf motifs and what might be bunches of grapes were found in the Sardar Bazaar and Palikhera districts of Mathura (both Mathura, Govt Mus.). The subject of the reliefs is generally quite explicit. The example from Palikhera shows on one side a pot-bellied figure, possibly the *yakṣa* Kubera (a bucolic deity), seated at ease while drawing a cup towards his head. Two standing companions join him or replenish his cup (it is not clear which) while a diminutive figure, apparently a servant, stands by his pendent leg; behind are two figures, one of them goat-headed, an image that appears in other 'Bacchanalian' works. On the reverse of the slab, the pot-bellied figure is depicted in clear need of support from his companions and attendants. A similar theme is suggested by a double-sided relief from Maholi, Mathura. On one side a dishevelled courtesan, attended by a tiny servant holding a parasol, appears intoxicated and stands with such difficulty that she clutches her own scarf as if to gain balance; a male figure is firmly supported by an attendant. On the opposite side the courtesan has fallen, while her male companion and the now-scowling attendant try to help her stand; an old woman looks on scornfully. Although it has been suggested that one side of this relief depicts the virtuous courtesan Vasantasena (a character from the drama *Mṛcchakatikā*) as a contrast with the scene of intoxication on the opposite side, it seems more likely and in keeping with other double-sided 'Bacchanalian' reliefs of Mathura that both sides depict drunkenness.

BIBLIOGRAPHY

V. A. Smith: *The Jain Stupa and Other Antiquities of Mathura*, Archaeol. Surv. India, New Imp. Ser., xx (Allahabad, 1901/*R* Varanasi, 1969)

J. P. Vogel: *La Sculpture de Mathura*, Ars Asiatica, xv (Paris, 1930)

V. S. Agrawala: 'Catalogue of the Mathurā Museum: Buddha and Bodhisattva Images', *J. United Prov. Hist. Soc.*, xxi (1948), pp. 43–98

——: 'A Catalogue of the Images of Brahmā, Vishṇu, and Śiva in Mathurā Art', *J. United Prov. Hist. Soc.*, xxii (1949), pp. 102–210

J. E. van Lohuizen-de Leeuw: *The 'Scythian' Period: An Approach to the History, Art, Epigraphy and Paleography of North India from the 1st Century B.C. to the 3rd Century A.D.* (Leiden, 1949)

V. S. Agrawala: 'Catalogue of the Mathura Museum: Jaina Tīrthaṅkaras and Other Miscellaneous Figures', *J. United Prov. Hist. Soc.*, xxiii (1950), pp. 35–107

——: 'Catalogue of the Mathura Museum: Architectural Pieces', *J. United Prov. Hist. Soc.*, xxiv–xxv (1951–2), pp. 1–160

H. Lüders: 'Mathurā Inscriptions: Unpublished Papers Edited by Klaus Janert', *Abh. Akad. Wiss. Göttingen, Philol.-Hist. Kl.*, 3rd ser., xlvii (1961)

J. M. Rosenfield: *The Dynastic Arts of the Kushans* (Berkeley, 1967)

A. L. Basham, ed.: *Papers on the Date of Kaniṣka* (Leiden, 1968)

M. M. Carter: 'Dionysiac Aspects of Kushān Art', *A. Orient.*, vii (1968), pp. 121–46

N. P. Joshi: *Catalogue of the Brahmanical Sculptures in the State Museum, Lucknow*, pt 1 (Lucknow, 1972)

S. Czuma: *Kushan Sculpture: Images from Early India* (Cleveland, 1985)

G. von Mitterwallner: *Kuṣāṇa Coins and Kuṣāṇa Sculptures from Mathurā*, Government Museum, Mathura Growse Memorial Lectures no. 4 (Mathura, 1986)

D. M. Srinivasan, ed.: *Mathura: The Cultural Heritage* (New Delhi, 1989)

J. S. Yadav: *Cultural Heritage of Mathura: A Bibliography* (New Delhi, 1991)

FREDERICK M. ASHER

(ii) North-west. The north-west portion of the Indian subcontinent was known from the late 6th century BC as GANDHARA (Behistun Inscription 6, Herodotus, *Histories* III.xci, Strabo, *Geography* XV.i.26). The nucleus of this region, bounded by the Indus and Kabul rivers, north-east of Peshawar, lay on the principal trade and migration routes between Central Asia and India. The term Gandhara is also applied to a 'school' of Buddhist art and architecture, dated *c.* 1st–5th century AD, the remains of which stretch beyond the Peshawar Valley to Taxila and Manikyala in the south, along the valleys of the Kabul River and its tributaries northwards and westwards into Swat, Bajaur and Afghanistan. Close links in style and subject-matter are also visible in Central Asia (*see* AFGHANISTAN, §II, 1(i)(c), (ii)(c) and (iii)(b); CENTRAL ASIA, §I, 2(i)(b), 3(ii) and 4(iii)).

(a) Historical background. (b) Early period. (c) 2nd–3rd centuries AD.

(a) Historical background. The heterogeneous nature of Gandharan art is best understood in its historical context. The history of the region has been primarily reconstructed from limited references in inscriptions and in Western and Chinese texts, combined with numismatic evidence. From *c.* 508 BC Gandhara was a province of the ACHAEMENID empire until conquered by Alexander the Great in 327–326 BC. The Greeks ceded the territory *c.* 305 BC to the MAURYA ruler Chandragupta (*reg c.* 321–297 BC). The earliest Buddhist stupas in Gandhara (e.g. Butkara I (*see* BUTKARA) and Dharmarajika at Taxila) appear to have been founded in the Mauryan period, probably during the reign of Ashoka (*c.* 269–232 BC). In the early 2nd century BC Greek kings from Bactria established a principality in Gandhara (*see* BACTRIAN AND INDO-GREEK MONARCHIES) with cities at Sirkap (*see* TAXILA) and Shaikhan Dheri (*see* CHARSADDA). During the 1st century BC, with the establishment of Maues at Taxila (*c.* 90–80 BC), control gradually passed to the Scythians or Shakas from Central Asia. In the 1st century AD, forces under Gondophares (*c.* AD 20–50) founded an INDO-PARTHIAN kingdom at Taxila. From about the mid-1st century AD, the KUSHANA empire expanded from Bactria to the Gangetic basin in the south and Kashmir in the east under the rulers Kujula Kadphises, Vima Kadphises and Kanishka. The consolidation of such a vast area under Kushana rule gave them control over the growing trade between India, China and the Roman Empire. This coincided with, and no doubt accelerated, an expansion of Buddhism, which spread along the trade routes into Central Asia and China (*see* SILK ROUTE).

Kushana chronology is uncertain and controversial (*see also* §(i)(a) above). Inscriptions dated in the so-called Kanishka era give succeeding kings as Kanishka I (years 1–23), Huvishka (26–60) and Vasudeva I (64–99). The most widely accepted dates for the first year of Kanishka range between AD 78 and 144. Arguments for a second century, with the sequence Kanishka II ([10]5–[1]17), Vasishka ([1]22–[1]30), Kanishka III ([1]41), are based on numismatic and sculptural evidence. A controversial

156. *Visit to the Indrashala Cave*, schist relief, h. 762 mm, from Mamane Dheri, dated in the year 89 of an unknown era, *c.* 2nd–3rd century AD (Peshawar, Peshawar Museum)

Buddhist triad relief of the year 5, for example (Lohuizen-de Leeuw, 1986, fig. 7), is generally considered to be dated [10]5 because the sculpture is in a fully developed style related to that of the *Indrashala Cave* relief from Mamane Dheri, dated year 89 (see fig. 156). Also disputed is the identification of the unspecified era used in the majority of dated inscriptions and on three images (Vogel, pl. LXIXa–c; Konow, nos XL, LIII, LX): a *Buddha* from LORIYAN TANGAI (year 318; Calcutta, Ind. Mus.), a pedestal from Hashtnagar (year 384; London, BM) and a *Hariti* from Skarah Dheri (year 399; Chandigarh Mus.). A key, but enigmatic, piece is a bronze reliquary from the stupa of SHAH-JI-KI-DHERI, a site identifiable as the legendary foundation of Kanishka I (*see* RELIQUARY, fig. 6). The syncretic images on the casket show a Kushana king flanked by putti with an undulating garland that supports in its upper loops seated Buddhas and other figures, including the Iranian sun and moon gods, Miiro and Mao, holding rings of investiture. On the lid, a Buddha seated on a lotus is worshipped by Indra and Brahma. Whether the royal figure represents Kanishka I, II or III is disputed, while three different readings of the inscription variously link the casket with the Kanishka era and/or Kanishka's monastery (see 1992 exh. cat., no. 193).

(b) Early period. Pre-Kushana sculpture is little known because the investigation of earlier sites has been extremely limited. Small moulded terracotta figurines from Akra Mound (Bannu District, south-east of Peshawar; Harle, figs 7–8), Shaikhan Dheri (Dani, pp. 46–54, pls XXIII–XXXIII) and Taxila (Marshall, 1951, pls 132–3) show the co-existence in the 1st century BC to 1st century AD of separate Hellenistic and Indian stylistic traditions. Included in the Indian group are a terracotta female nature spirit, or *yakṣī*, from Mohra Moradu, Taxila (London, V&A; Hallade, fig. 8), and two almost identical bronze statuettes from Bannu (Oxford, Ashmolean: see 1992 exh. cat., no. 113; and Peshawar Mus.: Harle, fig. 9). All these images have 'bicornate' headdresses, Indian attire and jewellery that correspond closely with representations found on 1st-century BC terracottas from AHICHCCHATRA.

The distinctive sculpted stone toilet trays or palettes of Gandhara also appear to be primarily pre-Kushana in date, since numerous examples were found in the Indo-Greek and Indo-Parthian levels at Sirkap (Marshall, 1951, pls 144–6). Mythological and profane themes on the palettes include Artemis and Actaeon (from Akra Mound; London, BM), Aphrodite chastising Eros (from Narai, Peshawar Valley; London, BM), Dionysiac banqueting scenes and nymphs and satyrs (Francfort, nos 1–2 and 8; 1992 exh. cat., nos 153–6). In more Indianized examples Hellenistic sea monsters are replaced by a crocodilian beast (*makara*), the lotus is included, and busts of couples predominate (Francfort, nos 9, 42–4 and 56–63).

A small group of schist sculptures in the round from Sirkap and Dharmarajika may also be considered pre-Kushana in that they exhibit an archaic rigid frontality, round staring eyes and schematized incised drapery (Marshall, 1951, pls 211–13). The images include *yakṣīs* and female donors, seated or standing draped male statuettes and winged bracket figures in devotional poses or holding gifts (Fabrègues, figs 7–10; Nehru, figs 115–24). Friezes of this period from Butkara and Dharmarajika have alternating ovolo patterns, palmettes, lotus rosettes, winged cupids, eagles, lion masks or a row of male busts in low relief (Fabrègues, figs 1–6). The same archaic characteristics are apparent in stucco heads of *c.* mid-1st century AD from the apsidal temple at Sirkap, except for two examples—a fragmentary bearded head and a satyr—that are more Hellenistic in style (Marshall, 1951, pl. 148; Nehru, figs 130–37). That the modelling of large sculptures in clay was also practised is indicated by fragments of colossal images that had been accidentally fired when the apsidal temple was burnt down (Cunningham, p. 127).

The earliest seated Buddha images in Gandhara belong stylistically to the beginning of the 1st century AD (Lohuizen-de Leeuw, 1981, figs 6–7, 9–19 and 32–4). Standing figures on the gold casket from Bimaran, Afghanistan (London, BM), datable by coins from the same stupa deposit, show that the iconography of the Buddha image was already fully developed by the mid-1st century AD (*see* AFGHANISTAN, §§I, 4 and II, 1(iv)(c) and fig. 14; see also 1992 exh. cat., pp. 186–92).

(c) 2nd–3rd centuries AD. Although chronology is uncertain, by the early 2nd century the diverse artistic traditions of the pre-Kushana period had merged to form a distinct Gandharan style. Coin designs of Kanishka I labelled 'Boddo' (Buddha), 'Sakamano Boudo' (Shakyamuni Buddha) and 'Metrago Boudo' (Maitreya Buddha) show that both standing and seated types had been standardized by this time. Independent statues were designed to be placed on pedestals against walls, so the backs are rarely worked and the images are usually depicted in strict frontal posture. The Buddha is portrayed as a barefooted adept but with the auspicious marks (*lakṣaṇas*) of a great being (*mahāpuruṣa*) and world ruler (*cakravartin*).

These marks include the nimbus, the sacred mark between the eyebrows (*ūrṇā*) and the cranial protuberance indicating wisdom (*uṣṇīṣa*). The latter appears as a topknot of wavy hair tied with a band, or, more rarely, follows textual references to the Buddha's attributes and is concealed by rows of tight curls coiled to the right (Zwalf, fig. 14). Ear lobes devoid of the jewellery that made them elongated symbolize the renunciation of worldly goods and aspirations. Some images are shown with moustaches.

Monastic robes cover both shoulders on standing images, but on seated figures, following the Indian example, the robes may be draped over the left shoulder only. Some standing figures (Foucher, fig. 594; Ingholt, fig. 211) have the robe bound like a sling round the right arm, a device that may derive from a Western prototype since it is also found in Roman reliefs (e.g. the Augustan Altar of Peace dated 13–9 BC; *see* ROME, ANCIENT, §IV, 1(iv)(b)). The standing Buddha generally has the right hand raised in *abhaya mudrā*, the gesture signifying reassurance or protection, while the seated Buddha can also be depicted in *dhyāna mudrā* (meditation), *dharmacakra mudrā* (preaching) or *bhūmisparśa mudrā* (calling the earth goddess to affirm his Enlightenment). Although most seated examples are depicted cross-legged in the lotus position, a few assume the 'European' pose, which is more commonly reserved for kings or subsidiary deities within the Buddhist pantheon (Rosenfield, fig. 166). A greater variety of poses occurs in the narrative reliefs, where the Buddha may appear in three-quarters view, walking or, in *parinirvāṇa* scenes, lying on his right side.

Bodhisattvas serve as cult images or illustrate the life and previous births of the historical Buddha. In an early relief of *Siddhartha Going to School*, the young prince is depicted as a small bejewelled Buddha (see fig. 157). The meditating, emaciated, ascetic image of the *Fasting Siddhartha* is also more akin to that of a seated Buddha (Foucher, fig. 193; Ingholt, figs 52–3). More usually, *bodhisattvas* appear as royal figures with richly ornamented hair or headdresses, earrings, bangles, necklaces, a sacred thread across one shoulder and a cord of amulets strung across the chest (see fig. 8 above; Tissot, pls XXII–XXIV, figs 105–18). Headdresses may be decorated with mythical animals, putti, a lion mask, bird protome or *garuḍa* and *nāgī* emblem (Tissot, pls XXVII–XXXI). Attributes identifying specific *bodhisattvas* are held in the hands and worn as turban jewels. Siddhartha has a turban, or a topknot and long curly hair. Maitreya usually has a topknot comprising a double loop of bound hair. He holds a flask containing *amṛta*, the Elixir of Life symbolizing the promise of future salvation, and may be in *abhaya*, *dhyāna* or *dharmacakra mudrā* (see fig. 158). The turban crest in rare depictions of Avalokiteshvara carries an image of his spiritual father, Amitabha, the celestial Buddha of the western paradise (Tissot, fig. 184). *Bodhisattvas* holding a lotus have been tentatively identified as Padmapani, a form of Avalokiteshvara associated with creation in Mahayana Buddhism; those holding a palm leaf perhaps represent Manjushri.

Although Vajrapani is a prominent *bodhisattva* in later Buddhism, in Gandhara his status, together with Indra (Vedic god of war and weather) and Brahma (god of creation), is that of an acolyte of the Buddha. Syncretism

157. *Siddhartha Going to School*, schist relief, 325×350 mm, from Charsadda District, *c.* 2nd century AD (London, Victoria and Albert Museum)

158. The Buddha seated between an unidentified *bodhisattva* and Maitreya, with Brahma and Indra in the background, schist relief, h. 543 mm, from Sahri Bahlol Mound C, *c.* 3rd century AD (Peshawar, Peshawar Museum)

is evident in depictions of Vajrapani, who is equated with such Bacchic figures as Pan, Dionysos and Eros, but most frequently with Herakles, complete with lionskin (*see* AFGHANISTAN, fig. 7; Ingholt, fig. 99; Foucher, figs 327 and 330; Flood, fig. 1). He also appears as a nude, bearded, Zeus-type figure (Foucher, fig. 257; Flood, fig. 2). He always holds a thunderbolt, thus being linked with Zeus and Indra. He may also carry the fly-whisk attribute of

Brahma. Both Indra and Brahma also appear as separate entities in the reliefs, often with Vajrapani. Indra wears a distinctive flat-topped hat; Brahma appears as an ascetic, with a flask and fly-whisk.

Other subsidiary deities in the Buddhist pantheon are similarly correlated with their Hellenistic, Iranian and Indian equivalents, a wide range of labels and attributes being used to cover a relatively uniform set of such sub-religious roles as fertility, prosperity and defence of the faith. The so-called *Athena* of Lahore Museum (Ingholt, fig. 443) shows a goddess in an Attic helmet holding a spear and perhaps originally a shield. She is identified as Roma on coins of Huvishka and is affiliated with the figures of female palace guards in reliefs depicting Siddhartha's Renunciation (Foucher, fig. 391). Most favoured are representations of the so-called tutelary couple, usually identified as Panchika, general of the *yakṣa* army, and his consort Hariti, the legendary devourer of children converted by the Buddha into a protectress: the inscription on her image of the year 399 from Skarah Dheri requests that she heal and protect children (Konow, no. LX, pp. 124–7, pl. XXIII.8).

The beneficent and fertility aspects of Hariti are emphasized in depictions of the tutelary couple. The pair are attended by children and genii with money bags, symbolizing prosperity. She often carries a cornucopia, the attribute of Tyche or Fortuna and the Iranian goddess Ardochsho, or a lotus flower of the equivalent Indian goddess, Lakshmi. Representations of Panchika as a corpulent, jewelled figure with a moustache, ornate cap and long spear link him with corresponding images of Kubera, god of wealth and Lord of the Northern Quadrant (Tissot, pls XVII.7 and XIX.12–14, figs 158–61). In an example from Sahri Bahlol (Peshawar Mus.; Ingholt, fig. 345), the male figure has the knobbed staff and winged cap of Pharro, the Iranian god of good fortune, who also appears on Kushana coins. Dionysiac overtones are evident on several reliefs where Panchika drinks from a kantharos, and the cornucopia held by Hariti devolves into an antelope-head rhyton or drinking horn (Tissot, figs 139–40).

An affiliated image appears to be a goddess seated between two lions (Chandigarh Mus.; Taddei, fig. 12) who holds a cup and a horned animal head (identified as a severed ram's head on a *c.* 4th-century image of a female deity in the Fujii-Yurinkan Museum, Kyoto: see Taddei, pp. 357–60, figs 9–10). These attributes may refer to the goddess Durga, consort of Shiva, as does the trident held by a later statue of *Hariti* from Sahri Bahlol (Peshawar Mus.; Ingholt, fig. 341). An ithyphallic Shiva with a trident and flask also appears as one of six figures emanating from a seated *bodhisattva* on a fragmentary relief (Peshawar Mus.; Taddei, pp. 349–55, fig. 1). Kushana coins of the 1st–3rd century depict figures holding these and other Shaivite attributes, such as the elephant goad, thunderbolt, bull or a small animal resembling an antelope. The coin legends, however, identify the images as Wesho, a Zoroastrian wind god, which implies that the correlation of attributes with specific deities had not yet been strictly formalized.

Narrative reliefs, primarily of schist, illustrate the eight Great Events (e.g. Birth, Enlightenment, First Sermon), lesser episodes and miracles in the life of the Buddha (see fig. 157) or scenes from his previous incarnations (*jātakas*). These were carved on large stelae, pedestals of statues, within arched frames or on elongated panels arranged horizontally or in vertical tiers. The continuous horizontal friezes may depict either a single scene or a series of episodes from each story, not necessarily in chronological order, and separated from each other by trees or pilasters. An exception to the norm is the *Dīpaṅkara jātaka* (concerning the first of 24 preceding Buddhas), which usually follows the early Indian convention of representing all the episodes of the story within a single frame.

A subsidiary group of decorative reliefs illustrates primarily Classical motifs of centaurs, marine deities and monsters, drinking scenes or vine scrolls interspersed with Dionysiac figures and animals. A direct reference to Classical mythology with no apparent Buddhist connection is seen in reliefs illustrating the story of the Trojan Horse (see 1992 exh. cat., no. 133). The popular motif of putti carrying garlands is stylistically closer to Western examples than to its Indian counterpart (Ingholt, figs 374–80; Ackermann, pls LXXXVI–LXXXIX). Crouching winged Atlas figures alternating with lions and elephants bearing mahouts are placed below mouldings and entablatures (Marshall, 1951, pls 58 and 157–8).

Pilasters and free-standing columns are derived from Persepolitan or Corinthian models. Reliefs show Indo-Persepolitan columns mounted by lions at the corners of the stupa platform. Indo-Corinthian capitals were used as mounts for stupas and *triratna* symbols, the 'three jewels' representing Buddha, *dharma* (Buddhist law) and *saṅgha* (Buddhist community). They also formed part of the umbrella superstructure of stupas. Small Buddha, *bodhisattva* or other figures are often inserted into the hollows of the foliage (Marshall, 1951, pls 73a and 79a; Faccenna, figs 11–12; Tissot, pl. IX.4, figs 33, 46–7 and 79–84; 1992 exh. cat., no. 203).

Most schist sculptures were buried beneath the debris of collapsed buildings, and few pieces have been found *in situ* on their original monuments. Stucco relief decoration survived on the lower levels of stupas and shrines where it was protected by fallen rubble. Both schist and stucco were used from the beginning, but as stucco had to be constantly maintained, only later work in the medium is generally preserved.

Stucco also gradually replaced schist as the preferred medium for the mass production of images (*see also* STUCCO, §III, 6). The numerous stucco heads that survive were originally attached to less durable clay bodies covered with only a thin coating of painted stucco. Buddha faces *c.* 1 m high and the remains of colossal feet at TAKHT-I-BAHI indicate that some enormous acrolithic cult images were produced in this way (Hargreaves, pl. XX; *see also* AFGHANISTAN, §II, 1(ii)).

A large proportion of sculpture, particularly from 19th-century collections, has no site provenance. Analysis of any chronological development is further hampered by site and regional variations in style (particularly noticeable between Peshawar Valley and Swat sculptures), the diversity of influences and the absence of securely dated images. In broad terms, narrative reliefs appear to have been superseded by large panels of Paradise or similar scenes, usually containing a dominant Buddha figure seated on a lotus surrounded by smaller Buddha and *bodhisattva* images (see fig. 158 above). Later, multiple images of the Buddha predominated (*see* §IV, 6(ii) below).

BIBLIOGRAPHY

A. Cunningham: 'Taxila, or Takshasila', *Archaeol. Surv. India Rep. 1863–4*, ii (Simla, 1871), pp. 111–35

J. P. Vogel: 'Inscribed Gandhāra Sculptures', *Archaeol. Surv. India, Annu. Rep.* (1903–4), pp. 244–60

A. Foucher: *L'Art gréco-bouddique du Gandhâra*, 2 vols (Paris, 1905–18)

H. Hargreaves: 'Excavations at Takht-i-Bāhī', *Archaeol. Surv. India, Annu. Rep.* (1910–11), pp. 33–9

S. Konow: *Kharoshṭhī Inscriptions with the Exception of those of Aśoka*, Corp. Inscr. Indic., ii/1 (Calcutta, 1929/*R* Delhi, 1991)

J. Marshall: *Taxila*, 3 vols (Cambridge, 1951/*R* Delhi, 1975)

H. Ingholt and I. Lyons: *Gandharan Art in Pakistan* (New York, 1957)

D. Faccenna and M. Taddei: *Sculptures from the Sacred Area of Butkara I (Swāt, W. Pakistan)*, 2 vols, Ist. It. Medio & Estrem. Orient. Rep. & Mem., ii/2–3 (Rome, 1962–4)

A. H. Dani: 'Shaikhan Dheri Excavation (1963 and 1964 Seasons)', *Ancient Pakistan*, ii (1965–6), pp. 17–134, pls XVI–XXIII, XXVIII–XXXIII

J. Rosenfield: *The Dynastic Arts of the Kushans* (Berkeley, 1967)

K. W. Dobbins: 'Gandharan Buddha Images with Inscribed Dates', *E. & W.*, xviii (1968), pp. 281–8

M. Hallade: *The Gandhara Style* (London, 1968)

H. C. Ackermann: *Narrative Stone Reliefs from Gandhara in the Victoria and Albert Museum in London*, Ist. It. Medio & Estrem. Orient. Rep. & Mem., xvii (Rome, 1975)

H.-P. Francfort: *Les Palettes du Gandhāra*, Mém.: Dél. Archéol. Fr. Afghanistan, xxiii (Paris, 1979)

W. Zwalf: *The Shrines of Gandhara* (London, 1979)

J. Huntington: 'A Gandhāran Image of Amitāyus' Sukhāvatī', *AION*, n. s., xl (1980), pp. 651–72

J. E. van Lohuizen-de Leeuw: 'New Evidence with Regard to the Origin of the Buddha Image', *South Asian Archaeology 1979*, ed. H. Härtel (Berlin, 1981), pp. 377–400

D. Faccenna: 'Note Gandhariche 1: Ricostruzione di un pilastro con *cakra* nell'area sacra di Butkara I (Swāt, Pakistan)', *AION*, xliv (1984), pp. 319–38

J. Cribb: 'A Re-examination of the Buddha Images on the Coins of King Kaniṣka: New Light on the Origins of the Buddha Image in Gandharan Art', *Studies in Buddhist Art of South Asia*, ed. A. K. Narain (Delhi, 1985), pp. 59–87

F. Tissot: *Gandhâra* (Paris, 1985); Eng. trans., abridged, as *The Art of Gandhâra* (Paris, 1986)

J. E. van Lohuizen-de Leeuw: 'The Second Century of the Kanishka Era', *S. Asian Stud.*, ii (1986), pp. 1–9

C. Fabrègues: 'The Indo-Parthian Beginnings of Gandhara Sculpture', *Bull. Asia Inst.*, i (1987), pp. 33–43

G. Fussman: 'Numismatic and Epigraphic Evidence for the Chronology of Early Gandharan Art', *Investigating Indian Art*, ed. M. Yaldiz (Berlin, 1987), pp. 67–88

M. Taddei: 'Non-Buddhist Deities in Gandharan Art: Some New Evidence', *Investigating Indian Art*, ed. M. Yaldiz (Berlin, 1987), pp. 349–62

G. Verardi: 'The Buddha's Dhūnī', *Investigating Indian Art*, ed. M. Yaldiz (Berlin, 1987), pp. 369–82

F. B. Flood: 'Herakles and the "Perpetual Acolyte" of the Buddha: Some Observations on the Iconography of Vajrapani in Gandharan Art', *S. Asian Stud.*, v (1989), pp. 17–27

L. Nehru: *Origins of the Gandhāran Style: A Study of Contributory Influences* (Delhi, 1989)

J. C. Harle: 'Artefacts of the Historical Period from Bannu', *South Asian Archaeology 1987*, ed. M. Taddei (Rome, 1990), pp. 643–55

A.-M. Quagliotti: 'The Buddha, the Solar Disk and the Cosmic Tree: A Relief in the Victoria and Albert Museum', *Silk Road Art and Archaeology*, ii (1991–2), pp. 73–105

K. Tanabe: 'OHPÞO: Another Kushan Wind God', *Silk Road Art and Archaeology*, ii (1991–2), pp. 51–71

The Crossroads of Asia: Transformation in Image and Symbol in the Art of Ancient Afghanistan and Pakistan (exh. cat., ed. E. Errington and J. Cribb; Cambridge, Fitzwilliam, 1992)

E. ERRINGTON

(iii) West.

(a) Rajasthan and Gujarat. (b) Maharashtra.

(a) Rajasthan and Gujarat. Like most of north India in the first three centuries AD, western India was ruled by a mosaic of individual lineages that held local control over a network of circumscribed territories. Some of these rose to positions of prominence. The Malavas, for example, exercised control over large tracts of Rajasthan in the 1st century AD, only to have their sovereignty temporarily usurped by the Shaka Kshatrapas, whose power extended from Gujarat across portions of Rajasthan. By the 3rd century the Malavas once ruled at least some parts of their former realm. Two other prominent powers were the Arjunayanas and the Yaudheyas, whose territories abutted the KUSHANA dominions.

Sculptural remains from western India are scanty. Not unexpectedly, the most numerous examples have been found in Bharatpur District, a short distance south of MATHURA in the heart of Arjunayana territory. Both the medium—a spotted red sandstone—and the style of these figures correspond directly to the mainstream style that was disseminated from Mathura during the Kushana period (1st–3rd century AD; *see* §(i) above). A now headless *nāga* (serpent deity) figure from Bareh (Bharatpur, State Mus.) is closely allied to Mathura in its wide-legged stance, sturdy physique and ornamentation. While a water-pot in one hand and the remains of serpent coils identify this image as a *nāga*, it is of the same genre as the numerous *yakṣa* and *bodhisattva* figures found at Mathura. This is especially evident in the bare torso, the thick, ropelike belt at the waist, wide swag of a scarf draped across the hips and flat beaded necklace. Similarly, a stout, dwarflike *yakṣa* from Aghapur, bearing the remains of a bowl on its head (Bharatpur, State Mus.), is related to the majestic *yakṣa* from Ahichchhatra (New Delhi, N. Mus.), although it is considerably less refined. The broad, round faces with heavy, blunt facial features and thick moustaches are comparable in these examples, as are the sagging chests that top immensely rotund stomachs. Other examples, such as a seated male figure flanked by worshippers from Bharatpur (Mathura, Govt Mus.) and a row of four standing male figures (perhaps representations of the *bodhisattva* Maitreya) with turbans, water-pots and hands raised in *abhaya mudrā* (the gesture of fearlessness) from Noh (Bharatpur, State Mus.), also echo the dominant style at Mathura. Scattered examples of a variety of different types of images—both human and divine—from Sambhar, west of Jaipur, have also been found (Sharma, p. 58).

Terracottas from Rang Mahal (Bikaner, Govt Mus.), in the north-west desert reaches of Rajasthan, exhibit a local style departing somewhat from the Kushana Mathura norm in its liveliness and naturalism, qualities that are partially explained by the freer handling of form that terracotta allows. While the dating of these pieces remains controversial (*see* §6(iii)(a) below), it appears that some of them can be attributed to the late Kushana period. A number of the Rang Mahal female figures are particularly reminiscent of Kushana female figures from Bhuteshvara, near Mathura (Calcutta, Ind. Mus.), but they are distinguished by an arresting sense of spontaneity and animation.

Scattered figures of both terracotta and stone that come from sites in the south-west, including SHAMALAJI, Devni Mori, Junagadh and Amreli (all in Gujarat), also demonstrate regional conventions that differ from those of the Kushana-dominated north. The general emphasis on a squatter, denser and more naturalistic formulation of the figure suggests ties to contemporary Shaka Kshatrapa and Satavahana sites further south and west in Maharashtra and Madhya Pradesh (*see* §(b) below). However, a more coherent understanding of style must await further research.

BIBLIOGRAPHY

U. P. Shah: 'Terracottas from Former Bikaner State', *Lalit Kala*, viii (1960), pp. 55–62

D. S. Sharma: *Rajasthan through the Ages*, i (Bikaner, 1966)

Kushan Sculpture: Images from Early India (exh. cat. by S. Czuma, Cleveland, OH, Mus. A., 1985)

CYNTHIA PACKERT ATHERTON

(b) Maharashtra. Free-standing images have been recovered at a range of sites in Maharashtra. At the major cave temple complexes of the Western Ghats there was a lull in sculptural activity during the 1st century AD with significant work coming only from KARLE. Sculpture at such other major cave temple sites as NASIK and KANHERI advanced beyond maturity the style so elegantly realized at Karle. The dating of Karle varies according to scholarly approach. In general, scholars tracing sequential stylistic development in northern, eastern and central India tend to date the gateways of Stupa 1 at Sanchi to *c.* 1st century BC and, on the basis of stylistic similarities, place much of the sculpture at Karle to the same period or slightly later, as in §4(iii)(b) above. Scholars such as the present author using arguments relevant to SATAVAHANA inscriptions, such classical texts as the *Periplus of the Erythraean Sea*, and the stylistic sequence in western Indian sculpture tend to place Karle in the second half of the 1st century AD and, in turn, to date the gateways of Stupa 1 at Sanchi to the early decades of the 1st century AD. Other works are dated in relation to these two key sites.

Pauni, Ter and Bhokardan. At Pauni, a major stupa site on the scale of Bharhut, sculptures on the railing pillars display the frontal stance, generalized body contours and emphasis on surface details characteristic of sculpture from BHARHUT, SANCHI, BHAJA and PITALKHORA in the previous two centuries (*in situ*; see Deo and Joshi, pls XIX–XXVI; *see* §4 above). Dated palaeographically to the early years of the first century AD, the pillar images of Muchalinda, king of the *nāga*s (serpent deities), go farther with this style than their predecessors. The guardian figures tuck their chins in gracefully as they worship the snake king; the deeper relief around their chins and within the folds of their turbans enlivens faces made even more distinctive by heavily lidded, almond-shaped eyes and thin, protruding lips. These features are in marked contrast to the flaccid arms and flatter relief of the lower bodies. The *yakṣi* on a related pillar shares this style, while exhibiting a more subtle overall treatment of her body: a gracefully angled hip and right shoulder just hidden behind her large earring suggest a three-dimensionality not seen earlier. Similar in conception to images from Pitalkhora, but less polished in overall details than those from Bharhut, the Pauni sculptures are works of a regional school interpreting widespread stylistic conventions, not copying them point for point.

Ivory statuettes from TER and Bhokardan, and a terracotta figure from Brahmapuri, reflect the application of this style to objects on a smaller scale. The Brahmapuri female (see Sankalia and Dikshit, pl. XXI), from the 1st–2nd century, wears a typically elaborate coiffure, the details of which contrast with her smooth, generalized body forms. Surface detail is emphasized, particularly on her flattish, rounded face, with its heavily rimmed eyes, bulging cheeks and receding mouth. The ivory figure from Bhokardan, broken above the waist (1st century AD; see Deo and Gupte, pl. LVI, figs 37–9), stands frontally, one leg crossed behind the other. She wears ornaments at her waist and on her ankles but appears to be nude otherwise. Her attendants twist slightly so that only one shoulder appears in front of the main image, a sophisticated use of the three-dimensional ivory medium. This image is strikingly similar in composition and style to a well-known ivory *yakṣi* found in the ruins of Pompeii in Italy; the similarity suggests that the Pompeii ivory was produced by a Satavahana workshop and underscores the role Bhokardan played as an international emporium. An ivory *yakṣi* from Ter (priv. col.; see Dehejia, pl. 85), by contrast, represents the same conception of female beauty but in a strikingly different style. This figure has a longer, thinner face, more deeply inset eyes, a simpler headdress, more pendulous breasts, thinner legs portrayed with raised knobs to indicate kneecaps and deeper overall relief. Coming from a site located on a trade route that extended from the coast to the region south and east of Maharashtra, this figure illustrates the effect influence from the south (possibly AMARAVATI) may have had in the development of an early Maharashtra sculptural style (*see* §6(vi) below).

Karle, Nasik, Kanheri and related sites. The façade of the rock-cut *caitya* hall (a hall with a sacred object or area of reverence) at Karle represents the exciting integration of sculpture and architecture at the peak of the Maharashtra style seen earlier at Bhaja and Pitalkhora (*see* §4(iii)(b) above). The magnificent life-size elephants that 'support' the side wings of the verandah are carved in deep relief so as to appear to emerge directly from the rock wall behind them. Their delicately wrinkled ears, taut hides, sensitively carved trunks and tapered legs show an increased sculptural sophistication compared with their predecessors at Pitalkhora. The male and female loving couples (*mithuna*s) are accomplished works that reveal an exceptionally refined approach to standard compositions (see fig. 147 above). Related to the Karle *mithuna* are four figures, two male and two female, portrayed in the same sinuous pose on the *caitya* window of the contemporary Bhuta Lena group of caves at Junnar. There, however, relief-carving is shallower than at Karle. The *mithuna* sculptures of Cave 6 at Kuda (see Dhavalikar, fig. XXVa, b), variously dated but probably of the late 3rd century, show a growing attention to three-dimensional, almost spherical body forms within relief-carving, intensified in 5th- and 6th-century sculpture from sites such as Ajanta (*see* AJANTA, §2; *see also* §6(iii)(c) below) and AURANGABAD.

Nasik, whose relief sculptures followed shortly upon Karle's, displays another characteristic of Maharashtra style, where traditional forms are presented but combined in entirely novel ways. Thus the smaller-scale dwarf from Pitalkhora (which apparently supported an object or architectural member on its head) was transformed into larger-scale figures supporting the porch of Cave 3, a residence hall called the Guatamiputra Cave after the *in situ* inscription naming this Satavahana ruler. Round-faced, short-necked and bulging-eyed, these figures are flatter, generalized versions of the more individualized Pitalkhora dwarf. A similar shift can be seen in the male door-guardians of this hall. They stand in the square, frontal posture seen earlier at Pitalkhora and Karle, but details appear to have been glossed over. The elaborate turbans, belts and jewels are disproportionately enlarged, and while an attempt was made to separate the figures from the wall behind them with deep relief cuts under the arms, the overall effect of the heavy clothing is to push them back into the wall. At the same time they are part of an extraordinary composition that includes the doorframe and lintel of the main hall entrance. Carved in an elaborate series of niches housing loving couples, surmounted by a lintel that projects to either side in an elaborate pattern of scrolls supported by rearing lions, the doorway translates into relief sculpture the free-standing *toraṇa*s created on an even larger scale at Sanchi. Inside, two females stand (or dance) in worship of a stupa carved in shallow relief against the rear wall. Here, too, their postures mimic the lyrical gestures of the Karle *mithuna* couples (and are also reminiscent of the elaborately twisted figures in Amaravati relief carvings of the same period), but in a flatter, stiffer, more generalized way. The shallow, almost schematic sculptural style contrasts with the originality of the subject-matter, a trait that is seen in later periods as well.

Kanheri's *caitya* façade sculpture well represents a transition in the evolution of Maharashtra's classical sculptural style. *Mithuna* couples (see fig. 159) are cut in deeper relief than at Nasik and display rounded, taut forms related to those at Karle. However, the style has become stiff and stylized; figures have a thick-limbed, heavy appearance. Their bent posture is awkward, their legs too far apart. Their coiffures are flatter, a symptom of a more generalized change in surface treatment, which had become less detailed. These images lack the liveliness and individuality of their predecessors at Karle. At the same time, certain details of ornament and iconography are more specific; for instance, the male figures hold clusters of blossoms, which were to become a standard device on *bodhisattva* images of the 5th and 6th centuries. Small Buddha images carved on the large courtyard pillar of this cave represent the beginning of an even more important sculptural tradition. These images—the first to portray the Buddha in anthropomorphic form in Maharashtra— were carved in shallow relief. Standing frontally, with very round heads and short necks, they are similar to Buddha images of the 2nd and 3rd centuries AD from Amaravati, as well as to 2nd-century images from SARNATH in the north. Appearing nearly simultaneously with their counterparts to the north and south, they reveal the singular receptivity to new ideas that would transform the style and content of Maharashtrian sculpture in coming centuries into a distinctive regional version of great 'classical' Indian art.

159. *Mithuna* couples, *caitya* hall façade, Kanheri, *c.* late 2nd century AD

BIBLIOGRAPHY

H. D. Sankalia and M. G. Dikshit: *Excavations at Brahmapuri (Kolhapur) 1945–46* (Pune, 1952)
K. Khandalavala and M. Chandra: 'The Date of the Karle Chaitya', *Lalit Kala*, iii–iv (1956–7), pp. 11–26
D. Barrett: *A Guide to the Karla Caves*, Ancient Monuments of India, i (Bombay, 1957)
M. Chandra: 'Ancient Indian Ivories', *Prince of Wales Mus. Bull.*, vi (1957–9), pp. 4–63, pls 3a, 3b
——: 'An Ivory Figure from Ter', *Lalit Kala*, viii (1960), pp. 7–14
M. N. Deshpande: 'Some Observations on the Ivory Figure from Ter', *Lalit Kala*, x (1961), pp. 55–6
J. L. Trabold: 'A Chronology of Indian Sculpture: The Satavahana Chronology at Nasik', *Artibus Asiae*, xxxii/1 (1970), pp. 49–88
V. Dehejia: *Early Buddhist Rock Temples: A Chronological Study* (London, 1972)
S. B. Deo and J. P. Joshi: *Pauni Excavation, 1969–70* (Nagpur, 1972)
S. P. Deo and R. S. Gupte, eds: *Excavations at Bhokardan (Bhogavardhana), 1973* (Nagpur, 1974)
M. K. Dhavalikar: *Late Hinayana Caves of Western India* (Pune, 1974)
M. Leese: 'The Early Buddhist Icons in Kanheri's Cave 3', *Artibus Asiae*, xli (1979), pp. 83–93

GERI H. MALANDRA

(iv) Central. During the first three centuries AD, the regions south of the Yamuna River played a relatively minor role in the history of sculpture. Such early examples of the period as the gate of Stupa 3 at Sanchi (*see* §4(ii) above) and an image of the *yakṣa Manibhadra* from Pawaya (Gwalior, Archaeol. Mus.) indicate how the majestic style of the 1st century BC underwent a process of disintegration. Human figures were no longer modelled as gently voluminous forms but as clusters of independent parts and harshly modulated planes. This treatment anticipated early Kushana images such as the *bodhisattva* from Ganeshra (Lucknow, State Mus.) and suggests that a local variation of the Kushana style developed in central India in the opening years of the 1st century.

This local idiom appears to have been completely overtaken by the style of MATHURA as that city emerged as the leading centre of Indian sculpture in the second half of the 1st century. Its overwhelming importance is indicated by a number of imported images at Sanchi (Archaeol. Mus.), including a headless *bodhisattva* seated in *padmāsana* (lotus position), dated year 28 of the Kushana era (*c.* AD 106), and the pedestal of a Buddha image, dated year 22 (*c.* AD 199). Better preserved is a 2nd-century AD seated Buddha in the pose of meditation (*dhyāna mudrā*). This image has both shoulders covered with symmetrically arranged pleats in the robe, a common feature in the later art of Mathura. That this type of work was copied locally is indicated by a small, virtually identical Buddha (Sanchi, Archaeol. Mus.). Similar imports and local derivatives are found at other places in central India. For example, a small standing Buddha in the mottled red sandstone of Mathura was found at Lashkar (Gwalior, Archaeol. Mus.). Local work inspired by such examples is represented by a small seated Buddha made of buff-coloured stone (Gwalior, Maharaja Jiwaji Rao Scindia Mus.).

While Mathura was the main source of images, sculpture from Gandhara was also brought into central India. This is indicated by a standing Buddha from Gharighat (Jabalpur) (Bhopal, State Mus.). Other fragments of the Kushana period have been found at several sites in western Madhya Pradesh. Most of this material awaits systematic study. A notable piece still *in situ* is a large Shiva *liṅga* at Pingaleshvar, 16 km from Ujjain. The date is controversial, but the faces carved into the base of the *liṅga*, particularly that of Shiva in his benign aspect, recall the *bodhisattva* heads from Mathura dating to the second half of the 1st century AD.

BIBLIOGRAPHY

J. Marshall and others: *Catalogue of the Museum of Archaeology at Sanchi, Bhopal State* (Calcutta, 1922)
J. Marshall and A. Foucher: *The Monuments of Sanchi* (London, 1940)
J. M. Rosenfield: *The Dynastic Arts of the Kushans* (Berkeley, 1967)
Kushan Sculpture: Images from Early India (exh. cat. by S. Czuma, Cleveland, OH, Mus. A., 1985)

MICHAEL D. WILLIS

(v) East.

(a) Stone. Finds of Kushana coins in Bihar, Bengal and Orissa suggest that eastern India, like the north, fell in the Kushana domain. Kushana sculptures exported from Mathura also have been found in eastern India. At RAJGIR, for example, a relief carved in characteristic Mathura stone was found at the site of the Maniyar Math (New Delhi, N. Mus.). The relief illustrates two standing *nāgas* (serpent deities). Much further east, at Chandraketugarh, a small red sandstone Buddha image, probably of Mathura origin, was found (U. Calcutta, Asutosh Mus. Ind. A.). The style of the figure follows closely that of Kushana Buddha images from Mathura (*see* §(i) above) and was likely an import to Chandraketugarh. During the Kushana period, then, Mathura served as a major source of imagery for other parts of India, echoing the practice many centuries earlier, during the Maurya period, when a single centre produced pillars and possibly other works for distant distribution.

Mathura was, however, not the only source of sculptural imagery during the Kushana period. A *bodhisattva* torso from the village of Kumrahar, just south of Patna (ancient Pataliputra), is fashioned from buff sandstone but closely follows Kushana models at Mathura, while a standing figure of the Hindu god *Karttikeya* from Mahasthan reflects Kushana fashion and is even carved from red sandstone in imitation of Mathura stone, though not from Mathura stone itself. Double-sided reliefs, often with a female figure on each side and probably serving as brackets, were commonly made during the Kushana period at Mathura. Similar reliefs were made in eastern India. An example at Nayatola, adjacent to the site of Kumrahar, shows a female figure clasping the branches of a tree on

160. Female figure clasping a tree, polished sandstone, double-sided relief, from Rajendranagar, 1st–3rd century AD (Patna, Patna Museum)

each side of the relief. A second such relief, quite similar in form, carved from buff sandstone and brilliantly polished, was found at Rajendranagar, also near Kumrahar (see fig. 160). This relief is particularly important in confirming the persistence of a polished finish, often considered a Maurya characteristic but in fact a feature of much Kushana and earlier sculpture from Pataliputra. Not all Kushana-period works from eastern India imitate the Mathura models, however. The famous *Whisk-bearer* from Didarganj (see fig. 139 above) may be a product of Kushana times, for the fashion of many of the accoutrements recalls Kushana works at Mathura, such as the pillar figures of Bhuteshar. The figure itself adheres more closely to the style long in vogue in Pataliputra, however. (This piece is attributed by some scholars to the Maurya period; *see* §3 above.)

(b) Bronze and terracotta. The hoard of Jaina metal objects recovered at Chausa in Bihar (Patna Mus.) includes a superbly rendered *Wheel of Law* (*dharmacakra*) (*see* §II, 2 above) that apparently served as the finial of a staff. It is fully rendered on both sides, anticipating later wheels with figures carved against both faces. Around the rim is a band of trilobed motifs that may represent flames but are more probably the *śrīvatsa* symbol of good fortune. The wheel is supported by a pair of crocodile-like animals (*makara*s) with a delicately rendered female figure perched on the snout of each. The figures' stance recalls the dryads characteristic of the period between the 2nd century BC and the 2nd century AD. A similar wheel, but without figural decoration, was found at TAXILA. It was dated by the excavators to the 1st century AD, making it likely that the Chausa example is of the same period (see Marshall and Foucher, vol. iii, pl. 177, no. 393). Most of the other works from the Chausa hoard are later.

Terracotta sculptures are found widely in eastern India from the Maurya period to the 5th–6th century AD (*see also* §VIII, 16 below), after which time they become less common due to the accessibility of stone from the Dalma hills. Buxar in ancient Magadha has yielded a great many terracotta sculptures. Other such sites in Bihar include Patna, LAURIYA NANDANGARH, VAISHALI and Belwa. In Bengal significant finds have been made at Chandraketugarh and Tamralipta. Some of the terracottas parallel stone sculpture in style. For example a terracotta bust (Patna, Kanoria priv. col.) shares many stylistic features with the Bharhut reliefs (*see* §4(i)(a) above).

BIBLIOGRAPHY

J. Marshall and A. Foucher: *The Monuments of Sanchi*, 3 vols (London, 1940)
N. R. Ray: *Maurya and Sunga Art* (Calcutta, 1945, rev. 1965); rev. as *Maurya and Post-Maurya Art* (Delhi, 1975)
J. Marshall: *Taxila*, iii (Cambridge, 1951/*R* Delhi, 1975), pl. 177, no. 393
S. K. Saraswati: *Early Sculpture of Bengal* (Calcutta, 1962)
P. L. Gupta: *Patna Museum Catalogue of Antiquities, Stone Sculptures, Metal Images, Terracottas and Minor Antiquities* (Patna, 1965)
F. M. Asher: *The Art of Eastern India, 300–800* (Minneapolis, 1980)
N. R. Ray, K. Khandalavala and S. Gorakshkar: *Eastern Indian Bronzes* (New Delhi, 1986)
S. L. Huntington and J. C. Huntington: *Leaves from the Bodhi Tree* (Dayton, OH, 1989)

FREDERICK M. ASHER

(vi) South. In the Tamil country and the region of modern Kerala early sacred shrines were built in the perishable media of wood, brick and stucco, and little sculpture survives. However, stone and, to a lesser extent, metal were used for sculpture in the 1st–3rd centuries AD in the region comprising the states of Karnataka and Andhra Pradesh. Satavahana power was extended to Andhra during the reign of Vasishthiputra Pulumavi (*c.* AD 110–38 or 130–58). Although the early decoration of the drum of the celebrated stupa at AMARAVATI pre-dates Andhra becoming a Satavahana province (*see* §4(v) above), the early carved section of the Amaravati railing probably dates to the refurbishment of the monument begun at the time of Pulumavi. Prior to the consolidation of Satavahana power in the Krishna Delta, the Buddha was represented by symbols; compositions were simple, and ornamentation was modest. The occasional and tentative introduction of the Buddha figure at Amaravati probably coincided with the issue of the Satavahana coins of Pulumavi with their remarkable royal portrait heads.

During the mature period of sculptural art at Amaravati (second half of 2nd century–first quarter of 3rd century), the inner and outer faces of the railing pillars were most delicately carved with full and half-lotus medallions (sometimes with crowded scenes from Buddhist legend) accompanied by figures, decorative motifs and various minor scenes. The medallions on the crossbars, projecting as they do from the curved cross-section forming tondi, are one of the glories of Indian art. Compositions from the first phase of the mature period are still uncomplicated, but the extraordinarily supple and willowy figures are deeply cut, allowing for the overlapping of forms on several planes. One of the finest examples from the 2nd century AD is a fragment that represents the *Adoration of the Buddha*. The women are turned at various angles towards each other and the ground, and have fully rounded faces and limbs.

Reliefs from the second phase of the mature period are remarkable for their swirling rhythms and frenzied dramatic action (see fig. 161). The sculptural decoration of the Amaravati railing probably reached its zenith during the reign of Yajna Srisatakarni (*c.* AD 175–203), who is known from his elegant portrait head on his coins. In Amaravati sculptures from the last phase *c.* AD 250, the movement to a proto-Nagarjunakonda mannerist style, with elongated limbs and flatter, drier faces, is clearly visible.

In the early 3rd century the Ikshvaku dynasty replaced the Satavahanas as the principal rulers of the eastern Deccan. Their capital was at NAGARJUNAKONDA in a secluded valley of Andhra beside the Krishna River. Although the Ikshvakus were Hindus, Nagarjunakonda is better known for its 30 Buddhist monasteries and for the main stupa (Pkt *mahācetiya*), built by Queen Chandasiri, which contained a relic of the Buddha. The site is datable to the late 3rd century AD and the 4th century by means of inscriptions recording donations by female members of the Ikshvaku family. The projecting platforms at the base of the large stupa provided the main focus for decoration, bearing sculptures representing scenes from the life of Buddha. Interesting as the reliefs are (the remains are now housed in Nagarjunakonda, Govt Mus.), they indicate that a great decline had occurred since the mature period at Amaravati. Though cut equally deep, the figures are less

161. Drum slab showing four events surrounding the birth of the Buddha, stone relief, 1.58x0.96m, from the stupa at Amaravati, 2nd century AD (London, British Museum)

delicately rendered. Mannerisms appear, such as elongated, even spidery human legs and protuberant eyes. The flatness common to all the figures makes them easily distinguishable from the mature Amaravati style with its rounded faces, bodies and limbs.

Early Andhra sculpture also includes statues in the round, made on a larger scale than that customarily found on the stupas. Two male torsos (untraced; see Barrett, 1960, pls 2–3) from Nagaram, about 96 km north-west of Jaggayyapeta on the lower reaches of the Krishna River, are in a mature Amaravati style. The aesthetic conception of the human body is as fully and even more sensitively expressed in these two examples as in the finest Kushana-period images from Mathura (*see* §5(i) above). Of the rare early south Indian bronze figures, the finest is perhaps a little family group of royal riders on an elephant in a pure Satavahana style of the 2nd century AD (Kolhapur Mus.).

BIBLIOGRAPHY

D. Barrett: *Sculptures from Amaravati in the British Museum* (London, 1954)
——: *Ter* (Bombay, 1960)
J. C. Harle: *The Art and Architecture of the Indian Subcontinent* (Harmondsworth, 1986)
D. Barrett: 'Style and Palaeography at Amarāvatī', *Orient. A.*, xxxvi/2 (1990), pp. 77–82
R. Knox: *Amaravati: Buddhist Sculpture from the Great Stūpa* (London, 1992)

O. M. STARZA-MAJEWSKI

6. 4TH–6TH CENTURIES AD. From the 4th century AD the codification of such texts as the *Mahābhārata* and early *Purāṇa*s gave canonical shape to the central myths and cults of religious life. Standardized forms of Vishnu, Shiva, the goddess and other divinities appeared for the first time, indicating a significant growth in popular theism. Skill and technical expertise are indicated not only by the many stone sculptures that were produced but also by the iron pillar at Delhi, a remarkable feat of metallurgy that has resisted corrosion over 15 centuries. The Gupta kings ruled north India during the 4th and 5th centuries; these monarchs sponsored elaborate Vedic sacrifices and with the Vakatakas of the Deccan wielded a degree of political power over India that had not been seen since the disintegration of the Mauryan empire. This notable period is appropriately if somewhat tritely described as a golden age. Embracing practically all fields of endeavour, a movement of revitalization fostered the vigorous yet beatific vision that informed the period's great works of literature and sculptural art.

(i) North. (ii) North-west. (iii) West. (iv) Central. (v) East. (vi) South.

□

(i) North. Between the 4th and 6th centuries AD, the leading centres of Indian sculpture in the Gangetic plain were MATHURA and SARNATH—both producing images of the highest calibre. These images had a wide influence: Mathura sculptures, following patterns established in the KUSHANA period, were exported to various parts of the subcontinent, and Sarnath conventions of iconography were imitated in Maharashtra, eastern India and South-east Asia. The workshops of Mathura catered equally to all religions, whether Buddhist, Jaina, Vaishnava or Shaiva. Sarnath was a Buddhist retreat and its sculpture entirely Buddhist in content. Nearby VARANASI, however, was a centre for followers of other sects, as Brahmanical images attest. The importance of Mathura and Sarnath between the 4th and 6th centuries appears to have been primarily religious and cultural; neither seems to have been a 'capital' of the ruling Gupta dynasty. There is little evidence that the Gupta monarchs were directly involved in the patronage of temples or religious images (*see* §XI, 1 below). The sculpture of this period is thus 'Gupta' only to the extent that it was produced when the Gupta dynasty was in power.

(a) Late 4th century. (b) *c.* 400–430. (c) *c.* 430–60. (d) *c.* 460–500. (e) *c.* 500–550. (f) *c.* 550–600.

(a) Late 4th century. Towards the end of the 4th century, north Indian sculpture underwent a profound change, well documented by a *Seated Bodhisattva* (Calcutta, Ind. Mus.) dated to year 64 probably of the Gupta era (AD 383–4). The *Bodhisattva* shows a debt to iconographic conventions established in the Kushana period, but the form is removed from anything produced in the 3rd century. The face has a subtle and inward beneficence anticipating later images; the limbs and torso, while retaining a certain Kushana ruggedness, are noticeably softened and seem to expand gently from within. The image was recovered at Bodhgaya but was probably brought there from Mathura soon after it was carved. A wide distribution of Mathura images is indicated by such other examples as a 4th-century *Standing Buddha* at Sanchi (Archaeol. Mus.), identifiable as an export from Mathura by its mottled red sandstone and vigorous style.

(b) c. *400–430.* The formative qualities of the *bodhisattva* figure in the Indian Museum, Calcutta, and other works of the late 4th century were quickly transformed in the opening years of the 5th century. The style matured with astonishing forcefulness, the most complete evidence for this development being the caves and reliefs at UDAYAGIRI (ii). Most of the sculpture at Udayagiri can be dated to Gupta year 82 (AD 401–2). Parallels to the Udayagiri reliefs are found at a number of sites in the Gangetic plain. The brick temple at BHITARGAON, for example, carries terracotta panels, some of which are close to Udayagiri in iconography and the treatment of bodily form. The large terracotta images of the river goddesses Ganga and Yamuna from AHICHCHHATRA (New Delhi, N. Mus.) also belong to this period.

Stone sculpture of the early 5th century is well represented by a seated Jaina *Tīrthaṅkara* (saint, teacher) from Mathura (Lucknow, State Mus.). This image is heavily cast and powerful but displays greater formal elegance and control when compared to the late 4th-century *Bodhisattva* in the Indian Museum. Another piece belonging to the early 5th century is a mock dormer, probably once part of a temple spire (Mathura, Govt Mus.). The richly worked floral scrolls and modelling of the face within the dormer arch are close to the Mathura *Tīrthaṅkara.* Also of the early 5th century are the carved pillars at Bilsadh, 150 km east of Mathura. The figures in the reliefs sit in bold frontal poses and are robustly modelled; a similar robustness is displayed in the seething floral scrolls that completely cover one side of the pillars. An inscription dated Gupta year 96 (AD 415–16) is incised in duplicate on two nearby columns and records the construction of a temple, gatehouse (*pratoli*) and other buildings. The assertive style of the carvings points to a date in the opening years of the 5th century, indicating that the relief pillars were complete when the dedicatory inscriptions were prepared.

A number of sculptures belonging to the early 5th century have been found further east in the Gangetic plain, at the ancient centres of KAUSAMBI and Varanasi or in their immediate environs. A *Standing Buddha* from Sarnath (New Delhi, N. Mus.), like early 5th-century sculpture at Mathura, has a bold, assertive quality, even though a reductive modelling of the flesh and a simplified iconography are immediately evident. The same qualities are found in contemporary images of the god Vishnu from Unchdih and Jhusi (Allahabad Mus.). This idiom, with its focus on thematic and plastic essence, characterizes much of the art of the eastern Gangetic plain and has its roots in the earliest known carvings in the region (*see* §4(i) above). Though restrained, it could occasion stunning results. A *Krishna Govardhana* (Varanasi, Banaras Hindu U., Bharat Kala Bhavan) captures the god's omnipotence and beneficence and ranks in monumental grandeur with the celebrated *Varaha* (Vishnu in his boar incarnation) at Udayagiri (*see* §(iv)(b) below).

(c) c. *430–60.* The development of sculpture in the mid-5th century can be charted on the basis of a considerable number of dated images. From Mathura comes a damaged *Tīrthaṅkara* (Lucknow, State Mus.) dated Gupta year 113 (AD 432–3). More complete and more useful for understanding the mid-5th century is a *Standing Buddha* from Govindnagar (Mathura, Govt Mus.) dated Gupta year 115 (AD 434–5). Around these two images can be clustered a number of sculptures, such as the famous *Standing Buddha* dedicated by the monk Yashadinna and the spectacular torso from Jaisinhapur (both Mathura, Govt Mus.). A standing image of *Vishnu* (New Delhi, N. Mus.) can also be dated to *c.* 435. These examples show that sculpture had acquired a calm, flawless magnificence by the third decade of the 5th century. Torsos and limbs have a gentle fullness and substance and are no longer modelled with the seething forcefulness that is so evident in works created during the opening years of the century. Likewise the faces have become more slender and introspective, creating a mood of sober maturity. These are

162. *Standing Buddha*, buff sandstone, h. 1.45 m, from Sarnath, *c.* AD 435 (London, British Museum)

images of great strength, but it is the subtle strength of divinity in repose.

Parallels to the Mathura sculptures of *c.* 435 have been found at other sites. A *Seated Buddha* (Lucknow, State Mus.) dated Gupta year 109 (AD 429) documents the beginnings of the mature 5th-century style in the eastern Doab. This image was found at Mankuwar, a village near Allahabad. A mid-5th-century *Standing Buddha* from Sarnath (London, BM; see fig. 162) is close to the Mankuwar *Buddha*. The style of these sculptures has departed decisively from the aggressive modelling of earlier images in the region and has assumed the restrained qualities of the Govindnagar *Buddha* of AD 434–5. This shows both that the idioms of Mathura and Sarnath developed in synchrony and that the east maintained its unique emphasis on cursory modelling and iconographic simplicity.

These and many other images were once installed in temples. Among the more important architectural fragments to have survived is a bracket from Mathura carved with the personification of a river goddess (Mathura, Govt Mus.). Conceived with the same mellifluous outline and calm volume as other sculptures of the mid-5th century, this rectangular panel (1.33 m long) was originally fitted on a doorframe outside the jambs. A complete door of the type is found at Udayagiri (Cave 19). If the Mathura panel came from a doorway of similar proportions, then the original was 4.5 m high, more than twice the size of any surviving door in central India. Of equal scale is a richly carved lintel with scenes of the *Kṣāntivādin jātaka* 'Proclaiming patience' from Sarnath (Sarnath Mus.).

While Mathura and Sarnath dominated 5th-century sculpture, a number of minor centres appear to have developed. This is suggested by a *Standing Buddha* from Bazidpur (Lucknow, State Mus.). The body of this figure is modelled after the simple fashion of Sarnath, with no pleats in the robe. Pleats do appear, however, where the robe is draped around the neck. This is characteristic of Mathura. The head and nimbus are also akin to Mathura examples. The mixed idiom of this *Buddha* is perhaps due to its production at Bazidpur, a town equidistant between Mathura and Sarnath. Another indication of sub-centres is a Buddha head in the Los Angeles County Museum. While related to Sarnath, it has a precision and sultry verve not usually found in work from that centre and it may have been produced at Kanshambi.

(d) c. *460–500.* Towards the end of the 5th century, the art of north India became progressively more serene and refined, continuing trends already set in motion by *c.* 435. No dated examples from Mathura have been found, but three images of the Buddha unearthed at Sarnath (Sarnath Mus.) bear inscriptions recording their dedication in Gupta years 154 (AD 474) and 157 (AD 477). Closely related to these dated images are standing figures of the *bodhisattva Avalokiteshvara* and the goddess *Tara* (Calcutta, Ind. Mus.); the most celebrated image in this style is the *Seated Buddha* in the pose of teaching (see fig. 163). In this group of sculptures all sense of movement, even of breath, has been stilled by a yogic calm. A transcendent simplicity, stripped of all non-essentials, permeates the forms. In an effort to capture an underlying Buddha essence, their makers have created images removed from the mundane world. This is the most mature and eloquent statement of the eastern idiom.

Mathura shared in this increasing refinement while retaining its proclivity for more robust modelling. An image of *Vishnu* and a headless figure of the Buddha standing in a mandorla (both Mathura, Govt Mus.) are Mathura parallels to the Sarnath work of *c.* 475. The style of these two sculptures clearly indicates the changes that occurred in the four decades following the Govindnagar *Buddha*. In the earlier image the body pulsates with inner life, and the pleats of the robe curl over the chest like waves.

In contrast, the forms of the later images are subtly flattened and simplified. The folds of the Buddha's robe have a methodical rhythm, and the loose drapery ends fall stiffly at his side. A more precise outline accentuates the triangular shape of his torso. These traits make the images abstract and distant. Contributing to this is a slight contrapposto that lightens the image's visual impact. Contrapposto was rarely used in the early sculpture of Mathura, and its appearance in the late 5th century may be attributed to influence from Sarnath. Such influence

163. *Seated Buddha*, buff sandstone, h. 1.61 m, from Sarnath, *c.* AD 475 (Sarnath, Archaeological Museum)

seems to show that Sarnath, and perhaps other centres as well, were beginning to challenge the primacy of Mathura.

The refined style prevalent *c.* 475 is best known from the much-lauded Buddhas produced at Sarnath, but it appears that the style soon faltered. This is indicated by a pillar from Varanasi (Banaras Hindu U., Bharat Kala Bhavan) dated Gupta year 159 (AD 478–9). The reliefs on the pillar, showing incarnations of Vishnu, have a ponderous quality, somewhat like 5th-century sculpture in Bihar (*see* §(v) below). While the pillar is a relatively humble work, the reliefs nonetheless display a disturbing crudity. The evidence seems to indicate that the dated sculptures of Sarnath were the last vigorous expression of 5th-century art in the eastern Doab. A rapid decline is also indicated by sculptures at ERAN in central India, notably the *garuḍa* pillar dated Gupta year 165 (AD 484–5) and the colossal *Varaha* dated in the first regnal year of Toramana (*c.* 490; *see* §(iv)(b) below). These sculptures, like the Varanasi pillar, exhibit faltering outlines and limp modelling.

(e) c. *500–550.* No securely dated sculptures from the first half of the 6th century have been found in north India, but the remains at SONDANI in central India are datable to *c.* 525–35 (*see* §(iv)(c) below). The best-preserved images include a flying *vidyādhara* couple (minor divinities; New Delhi, N. Mus.) and two life-size guardians in high relief (*in situ*). Although superficially similar to earlier work, the Sondani carvings display a radically different concept of form. The supple elegance of *c.* 475 has yielded to a dramatic overstatement that cannot compensate for a coarsening of detail and tightening of plastic feeling. The limbs and torsos are no longer imbued with quiet voluminousness but are starkly modelled and somewhat distorted. The hair, drapery and ornaments have lost their playful fullness in favour of sharp outlines and linear accents.

Cognates of the Sondani style can be found in the Gangetic plain. A *Standing Buddha* from Mathura (Calcutta, Ind. Mus.) is the best surviving example (see fig. 164). This sculpture is a forced attempt to achieve the grandeur of the *Buddha* dedicated by Yashadinna and other masterpieces of a century before. Though iconographically similar, the sculpture is radically altered in substance. The torso is flattened and less sensitively modelled; the neck and head are not gracefully integrated with the shoulders and chest. The legs are disproportionately long, and the stance is awkward. Especially telling are the drapery folds over the body, which have been reduced to a mechanically organized pattern that no longer reflects the body's inner life. These qualities extend to the face, which has a frozen precision and little of the soft, swelling grace seen in earlier Buddhas. The craftsman seems to have carved the block down from the outside, rather than simply releasing a living conception from within the stone. This 'negative plastic modelling', despite regional differences, is closely related to the sculpture at Sondani.

Another example from Mathura belonging to the first half of the 6th century is a colossal head of the Buddha from Chamunda Tila (Mathura, Govt Mus.). The head no longer embodies the calm beneficence of the 5th-century Buddhas but has a cool and forbidding grandeur. The face is modelled with tight severity; the lower lip does not swell sympathetically but protrudes harshly and is strongly outlined. As in other images of this period, great size attempts to compensate for the debasement of significant form. Works like these from Mathura speak of an art tenaciously clinging to tradition but with no spiritual vitality animating the studied repetition of earlier achievements; all that remains is an intimidating abstraction devoid of compassion and grace.

164. *Standing Buddha*, reddish sandstone, h. 1.46 m, from Mathura, *c.* AD 525 (Calcutta, Indian Museum)

Analogous developments at Sarnath are illustrated by a *Standing Buddha* with the right hand lowered in the gesture of bestowing boons (*varada mudrā*; Sarnath Mus.). It shows a debt to the Sarnath Buddhas of *c.* 475 in that the emphasis on iconographic simplicity and delicate form has been maintained, but the conception of form has been significantly altered. The body has lost its plastic wholeness, and the right hand and fingers are especially harsh and additive. Again the stele seems to have been cut down from the outside in 'negative plastic modelling'. A number of relief panels with Buddhist narrative scenes (often placed in the 5th century) are more likely products of the first half of the 6th century. A metal *Standing Buddha* (New York, Asia Soc. Gals) is also representative of trends in the first half of the 6th century, but the heavier treatment of form suggests that it may have been produced in Bihar. The influence of Sarnath was particularly strong in both Bihar and Maharashtra at this time.

(f) c. *550–600.* The only dated stone sculpture from the second half of the 6th century is the *Standing Buddha* from Mathura (Lucknow, State Mus.) belonging to Gupta year 280 (AD 599–600). This *Buddha* has cumbersome, swelling forms quite different from those of images produced *c.* 535 (for example, fig. 164). In the *Buddha* of AD 599–600, the cautious delicacy and crisp linearity have been superseded by ponderous shapes that billow outward with uncouth vigour. The pleats of the robe have been rendered as bold, sweeping lines, as against the fastidious folds used in the first half of the 6th century. A *Standing Buddha* from Govindnagar (Mathura, Govt Mus.) is closely related to the example dated AD 599–600, but the face has been treated in an even more harshly additive manner. The smooth robe of this particular *Buddha* recalls Sarnath, indicating again Sarnath's increasing influence from the late 5th century onwards. Another important document of this period is a terracotta seal of the Maukhari king Sarvavarman (*reg c.* 576–80). The procession depicted at the top of the seal shows two *gaṇa*s (dwarflike demigods) escorting Shiva's bull, Nandi. These figures exhibit the same flaccid outline and exaggerated modelling as the *Buddha* of AD 599–600, though some allowance must be made for the fact that *gaṇa*s are by nature somewhat squat and deformed. The figures on the seal have a rustic vitality that marks them off from the studied qualities seen in the reliefs from Sarnath with repetitive scenes of the life of the Buddha. As a whole, the late 6th-century sculpture of the Gangetic plain seems to represent a regression, and in terms of 5th-century standards this is certainly so. Looking to the future, however, it is precisely the crumbling of established canons that allowed a radically new and dynamic art to emerge in the 7th century.

BIBLIOGRAPHY

J. C. Harle: *Gupta Sculpture* (Oxford, 1974)

J. Williams: *The Art of Gupta India: Empire and Province* (Princeton, 1982)

The Sculpture of India (exh. cat. by P. Chandra, Washington, DC, N.G.A., 1985)

MICHAEL D. WILLIS

(ii) North-west. Unlike the Gupta empire, the north-west (including Gandhara, the western Punjab and Kashmir) was fractured into small kingdoms between the 4th and 6th centuries and presented an easy target for invaders from Central Asia. By the mid-3rd century, the northern part of the Kushana empire, including Gandhara, from the south of the Hindu Kush to Peshawar and possibly Taxila, was taken over by the semi-independent Kushano-Sasanians, under the suzerainty of the Sasanians in Iran. By the end of the 4th century, Sasanian rule had been replaced by the Kidarites, who controlled the Bactro-Gandharan region and appeared as inheritors of the old Kushana empire, though they never coalesced into a powerful centralized state. By the mid-5th century the Hephthalite, or White, Hunas had swept down from Bactria into Gandhara and the Punjab (*see* IRAN, ANCIENT, §I, 2(ii)(b)). The 6th-century Huna chief Mihirakula is infamous in Buddhist history as a destroyer. Yet it is unclear if the decline of Buddhist centres was due solely to Huna destruction or if the economic chaos that followed the invasions dried up the revenues necessary to sustain the large monastic establishments. Many of the Huna chiefs, following the example of Mihirakula, were militant Shaivites, but some were patrons of Buddhism, which continued to thrive in Kashmir through the Karkota era (*c.* AD 600–855).

Art historians generally have tended to use this 'dark age' of the 4th–6th centuries in the north-west as a dumping ground for problematic works (i.e. those that appear to be too late for the Kushana era but too early for the Karkota dynasty of Kashmir or the Shahi states of Gandhara and Upper Indus highlands, *c.* 7th–10th centuries). On the Afghan threshold between Kabul and Jalalabad, Buddhist sculpture appears to have continued to flourish at such sites as HADDA after the Kushana decline (*see* AFGHANISTAN, §II, 1(ii)(d)). Further east in the heart of Gandhara, the situation looks more bleak. The monastery of Jaulian flourished peacefully under Kidarite rule, as did others around Taxila that were thoroughly studied by Sir John Marshall. This era ended abruptly *c.* AD 460, when a Hephthalite invasion of Gandhara and the Punjab left Taxila and its monuments in ruins. Buddhist Taxila between *c.* 300 and 450 reveals a style of sculpture in stucco very similar to that found at Hadda. Subjects include multiple meditating Buddhas in elaborate arcuated settings on votive stupas and large single Buddha icons or set pieces of the Buddha with *bodhisattva*s and adorers. These works place little emphasis on narrative. After the destruction of Huna power, Buddhism returned to the region, but Taxila never recovered.

Further east in Kashmir, a number of terracotta heads have been found at Akhnur and Ushkur that combine Kushana Gandhara style with a rich Gupta sensuousness to a greater extent than at Taxila or Hadda. Akhnur, probably the earlier site of the two, falls more completely within the 4th to 6th century. By far the most famous and enigmatic Kashmiri monument of this era was a Buddhist (perhaps originally an Ajivika) shrine at Harwan. In the courtyard of an apsidal building, a pavement of figured terracotta tiles and a low surround of similar plaques displayed a most unusual array of stamped low-relief designs. Some of the motifs are clearly indigenous in inspiration, but others show scenes such as hunting on horseback that appear to belong to an alien tradition. The strangest plaques are those with a repeating design of emaciated ascetics in a foetal position below a band of paired profile heads above a balustrade (see fig. 165). These motifs suggest links with Central Asia and Iran at a

165. Stamped plaque with figures, terracotta, 527×289×70 mm, from Harwan, *c.* 4th century AD (Los Angeles, CA, County Museum of Art)

time when the empire of the Hunas had opened the north-west region to outside influences.

Little is known of monumental stone sculpture in Kashmir before the Karkota period. There are a few works, however, which suggest that the Gandharan tradition continued, albeit modified by strong Gupta influence. Centres of artisanship were mainly devoted to the production of images of Brahmanical deities. Some notable works of this era from Bejbehara (ancient Vijayeshvara), a Shaiva centre, include a richly detailed, six-armed *Karttikeya*, reminiscent of Gandhara *bodhisattva* images, and a stolid four-armed figure of the goddess *Durga* draped in a surprisingly Hellenistic manner (both Srinagar, Sri Pratap Singh Mus.). Another important pre-Karkota Kashmiri site for the production of Brahmanical stone images is Baramula, work from which is probably slightly later as it is closer in style to the Gupta tradition.

A few small bronze statuettes, such as a *Standing Buddha* with a large radiate nimbus dated *c.* AD 400 (Kansas City, MO, Nelson–Atkins Mus. A.), show strong Gupta influence superimposed on the older Gandharan tradition. A fine standing *Vishnu* with a human head flanked by a lion head and a boar's head (Berlin, Mus. Ind. Kst) and a standing *bodhisattva Maitreya* in a beckoning pose (Los Angeles, CA, Co. Mus. A.) are dated to the 6th century. A large bronze mask of a *nāga-rāja*, found in Peshawar, is identified by its inscription as Haradeva, an epithet of Shiva. Stylistically, these works presage the far more numerous small bronzes from the Karkota era in the same region.

BIBLIOGRAPHY

S. Beal: *Si-yu-ki: Buddhist Records of the Western World*, 2 vols (London, 1884)

J. Barthoux: *Figures et figurines*, i of *Les Fouilles de Hadda*, Mém.: Dél. Archéol. Afghanistan, iii (Paris and Brussels, 1930)

J. Marshall: *Taxila*, 3 vols (Cambridge, 1951)

P. Pal: *Bronzes of Kashmir* (New Delhi, 1975)

H. Alam: 'Akhnur Terracottas in Lahore Museum', *Lahore Museum Bulletin*, i/2 (1988), pp. 69–92

P. Pal, ed.: *The Art and Architecture of Ancient Kashmir* (Bombay, 1989) [see articles by R. Fisher on Harwan and by J. Siudmak on early stone and terracotta sculp.]

G. Fussman: 'Le "Masque Court": Une Effigie en laiton de Šiva au Gandhara', *J. Asiat.*, cclxxix/1–2 (1991), pp. 137–74

The Crossroads of Asia: Transformation in Image and Symbol in the Art of Ancient Afghanistan and Pakistan, exh. cat. Cambridge, Fitzwilliam Museum 6 Oct–13 Dec 1992, ed. E. Errington and J. Cribb (Cambridge, 1992), nos 210–12, 220–21, pp. 218–23, 234–40

MARTHA L. CARTER

(iii) West.

(a) Rajasthan. (b) Gujarat. (c) Maharashtra.

(a) Rajasthan. With the gradual consolidation of Gupta rule across most of north India, the political history of western India becomes clearer. While the Shaka Kshatrapas continued to be powerful, they lost their sovereign status after their defeat late in the 4th century AD by Chandragupta II (*reg c.* 380–415). Such other rulers as Yaudheyas and Arjunayana maintained their local rule while acknowledging Gupta suzerainty. The Malavas persisted under a similar arrangement, as did a related branch, the Aulikaras. As Gupta power declined through the 5th century, the empire fragmented; furthermore, a violent threat to stability was posed in the 6th century by the Huna invasions from the north-west. These events paved the way for the gradual rise to power of numerous local and regional dynasties that characterized the early medieval period.

Sculptural remains from Rajasthan during this period suggest that, unlike much of north India under the Guptas, there was no clear, unifying style in Rajasthan. Instead there was a conglomeration of loosely related regional and local idioms, some of which were to have more enduring importance than others. Two tall doorposts from Mandor (Jodhpur, Sardar Mus.) that depict episodes from the life of Krishna and that are datable to the late 4th or early 5th century preserve a style that is individual and unique for the region of ancient Marwar. The energetic exposition of the Krishna legend is enlivened by a rich naturalism, seen especially in the scene representing Krishna's lifting up of Mt Govardhana. The craggy mountainside is populated by a lion and his mate, while *nāga*s (serpent deities) twist in tight coils behind the robust figure of Krishna himself. The formulation of the figures, not far from the *yakṣa* types of preceding centuries, is more powerful, with more fluid contours and surface detail. The narrative is also less hieratic and more spontaneous than was seen in the Kushana period. This animated quality is also characteristic of terracottas from Rang Mahal (Bikaner, Govt Mus.), some of which may date to the 4th century and later (*see* §5(iii)(a) above).

In some cases it is possible to trace the beginnings of what would become identifiable regional idioms in subsequent centuries. Several important examples from the Malwa region, which once united a large area including parts of the modern states of south-eastern Rajasthan, northern Gujarat and western Madhya Pradesh, exhibit stylistic trends that persisted for centuries. The architectural ornamentation of the late 5th-century temple at Mukundarra and such related fragments as a door-jamb figure and a musician from this temple framed within the curvilinear confines of a *candraśāla* (arch-shaped blind dormer; both Kota, Govt Mus.) show a soft, fluid figural style coupled with a virtuosic display of luxuriant foliage and elegantly carved *makara*s (mythological aquatic creatures). The Malwa area at this time was ruled by the Aulikara dynasty, which appears to have acknowledged Gupta suzerainty. The regional style modified the era's overall tendency towards detailed refinement in favour of a more lissome expression. Some scholars have attributed the forging of this elegant local variation to infusions from the VAKATAKA realm further south and west (*see* §(c) below).

The segments of a gateway (TORAṆA) of the early 6th century from Nagari (*in situ*) also share decorative features that are characteristic of Mukundarra. In addition there are other connections in the Malwa region to contemporary sites in neighbouring Mandasor District (Madhya Pradesh), at Khilichipur and SONDANI. (These sites are discussed in the context of central Indian sculpture in §(iv)(c) below.) A *dvārapāla* (door-guardian) at the base of one of the Nagari *toraṇa* posts, while relatively simply adorned, displays a suave litheness and neatly controlled ornamentation that make it a quieter version of its extraordinarily refined early 6th-century counterpart at Khilichipur. The latter site exhibits a style that complements smoothly contoured figures with precisely detailed ornament. Sixth-century *dvārapāla* figures from nearby Sondani (see fig. 166) also display a tendency towards tall figures adorned with the most elegantly and lightly worked surfaces, with a particular interest in depicting the transparency of cloth and stylish intricacies of headdresses and hairstyles.

The strongest case for regional identity and stylistic continuity is seen in examples from southern Rajasthan and northern Gujarat (the ancient Mewar and Abu regions in Rajasthan; Idar in Gujarat). In ancient times this area formed more of a coherent unit than it does today; most scholars believe that it constituted the western reaches of ancient Malwa. The basic hallmarks of regional style are seen most clearly in late Gupta examples of the 6th century from SHAMALAJI in northern Gujarat (*see* §(b) below) and are echoed in related works from a number of sites in the region. The material—a greyish, friable schist—is also distinctive for works from this area. The most numerous examples have been found at Tanesara-Mahadeva, including a poignant *mātṛkā* (divine mother) image (see fig. 167). Particularly unusual are the convincing naturalism of the pose, the sense of maternal benevolence and the lushly volumetric rendering of form. Another characteristic example is a fragmented image of *Shiva* from Dungarpur (Los Angeles, CA, Co. Mus. A.). This image is endowed with a quiet sense of divine power, and its graceful surfaces are enlivened by prominent yet elegant ornament. Its relative attenuation and linear stylization suggest an attribution to the late 6th century.

166. *Dvārapāla* (door-guardian), beige sandstone, h. 2.6 m, from Sondani, *c.* 6th century AD

167. *Mātṛkā* (divine mother), schist, h. 762 mm, from Tanesara-Mahadeva, *c*. 6th century AD (Los Angeles, CA, County Museum of Art)

BIBLIOGRAPHY

Enc. Ind. Temple Archit., ii/1, pp. 30–32, 139–49

U. P. Shah: 'Terracottas from Former Bikaner State', *Lalit Kala*, viii (1960), pp. 55–62

D. S. Sharma: *Rajasthan through the Ages*, i (Bikaner, 1966)

P. Pal: 'Some Rajasthani Sculptures of the Gupta Period', *Bull. Allen Mem. A. Mus.*, xxviii (1971), pp. 104–18

J. Williams: 'The Sculpture of Mandasor', *Archvs Asian A.*, xxvi (1972–3), pp. 50–66

J. C. Harle: *Gupta Sculpture: Indian Sculpture of the Fourth to the Sixth Centuries A.D.* (Oxford, 1974)

P. Pal: *The Ideal Image* (New York, 1978)

J. Williams: *The Art of Gupta India, Empire and Province* (Princeton, 1982)

(b) Gujarat. Under the aegis of the Gupta rulers and their tributaries, a complex, though relatively limited, sculptural idiom developed in Gujarat. This idiom incorporated aspects of the prevalent Indian style while introducing features unique to the region. This synthesis of region and centre is also apparent in the polity of the area. The Kshatrapas (also known as Shakas) maintained control until the last quarter of the 4th century AD, and a reference to them in the ALLAHABAD pillar inscription of Samudragupta (*reg c.* 335–76) suggests that they held an elevated status during the early years of Gupta hegemony. It was not until the reign of Chandragupta II (*reg c.* 380–415) that they were brought fully under Gupta control.

The development of sculpture in this area emerges from hazy beginnings with limited and scattered examples, indicating that a definable 'school' did not exist prior to the 4th century. The major sculptural remains from Gujarat for the 4th–6th centuries are located within a very small geographical area centred primarily on the adjacent sites of Devni Mori and SHAMALAJI. Devni Mori is the earliest site, a Buddhist centre once marked by two monasteries (Skt *vihāras*), a temple, a large stupa and numerous votive stupas (the area was flooded for a reservoir in the 1960s). All the buildings were constructed of brick, the large stupa being embellished with decorative architectural motifs of carved brick and a number of terracotta Buddha figures. From the stupa core excavators recovered an inscribed relic casket; its inscription, dated in the year 127, refers to a stupa built during the reign of Rudrasena. Some scholars have referred this date of year 127 to the Kalachuri era, an interpretation that yields an equivalent of *c.* AD 375 and is concomitant with the reign of the Kshatrapa ruler Rudrasena III. Coins were also recovered from the stupa mound that date from other Kshatrapa reigns in the 3rd and 4th centuries. A Maitraka-dynasty coin from the late 5th century was also found. In view of a possible date of *c.* 375, some have considered Devni Mori a primary source for the development and dissemination of the Gupta style. This interpretation, however, has been embroiled in controversy, and other scholars question both the reading of the inscription and the relative dating of the stupa and its sculptures. Alternative proposals suggest the relic casket was an earlier artefact inserted in the stupa when it was reconstructed in the early 5th century.

Reconstruction of the Devni Mori stupa in the 5th century would best account for the style of the sculptures. These represent a local amalgamation of influences derived from both Mathura and late Gandhara traditions. The earliest possible date for these influences is the late 4th century. A terracotta *Seated Buddha* in the lotus position (Skt *padmāsana*) admirably demonstrates this area's eclectic style (see fig. 168). The sharply delineated facial features and robe covering both shoulders are Gandharan conventions, but these elements are fused with Mathura practices of string-fold draperies and neat rows of snail-shell curls. Other examples show a mixture of characteristics, such as Gandharan-style wavy hair, robust Mathura body types or Mathura-style bared shoulders. The downcast eyes of the

168. *Seated Buddha*, terracotta, h. 660 mm, from Devni Mori stupa, *c.* AD 375 (Vadodara, Maharaja Sayajirao University, Department of Archaeology and Ancient History)

figures also align them with later trends derived from such images as the *Bodhisattva* found at Bodhgaya that is dated in the year 64 of the Gupta era (*see* §(i)(a) above).

A hiatus in production at Devni Mori appears to have occurred in the late 5th or early 6th century. In part this may be attributed to the tumultuous political events in the region. This period was marked by a struggle for control of the western Malwa area by the Guptas, Vakathakas, Hunas and Aulikaras. Devni Mori and Shamalaji fell within the boundaries of the Malwa territory, which encompassed portions of northern Gujarat as well as southern Rajasthan. After an initial victory by the Hunas between *c.* 500 and 510, the Aulikaras prevailed under Prakashadharman and Yashodharman between 515 and 530. In the midst of these events Devni Mori declined in importance, and Shamalaji experienced a brief but important surge of artistic activity in the first half of the 6th century. This shift was accompanied by two major changes: the brick and terracotta media at Devni Mori gave way to stone (specifically schist) at Shamalaji, and the religious orientation of the imagery shifted from Buddhist to Brahmanical.

From the transitional period of *c.* 500 are some dwarf (*gaṇa*) or nature spirit (*yakṣa*) figures from Shamalaji (Vadodara, Mus. & Pict. Gal.), whose blunt, stocky physiques and cheerful demeanour recall Kushana-period *yakṣa* figures of the 2nd and 3rd centuries AD. Their slightly more articulated and naturalistic formulation, combined with the fact that they are made of stone at a time when stoneworking was just being introduced, suggests that they form the genesis of the Shamalaji sculptural tradition.

By the end of the first quarter of the 6th century stone sculpture had achieved an extraordinary sophistication, indicated by the remains of a mother goddess group accompanied by Skanda (Vadodara, Mus. & Pict. Gal.). Two of the mothers (*mātṛkā*s), representations of Brahmi and Chamunda, are depicted standing, with their respective vehicles (*vāhana*s) and the remains of a small child or weapon at their feet. Broad hips are canted to one side, with a slight bend of the opposite knee, and they face forward with radiant, open visages. Much attention is paid to such details as bouffant, elaborate coiffures and finely chiselled folds of the lower garments. The Skanda figure is more stiffly frontal, with thicker swags of drapery wrapped across the hips and twisted below the waist into a regionally distinctive loop. Directly succeeding this group are the remains of another set of mother goddesses accompanied by a standing Ganesha and a four-armed Shiva (for illustration *see* SHAMALAJI). These figures exhibit a different organization of vehicles and attributes while showing greater *déhanchement*, more attention to detail and more elegantly disposed drapery folds. Aside from these attributes, a sense of immediacy, directness and spontaneity imbues all Shamalaji figures, resulting in a singular idiom. Also noteworthy is the liveliness of such details as Ganesha's sinuously upward-curving trunk and spirited attendant. Shiva's expression is animated and the quartet of arms freely disposed. Other fragments of mother images suggest the possibility of a third set roughly contemporary with the second and dating to *c.* 525–30. These images lack distinguishing vehicles, simply depicting standing mothers with playful children on their hips. These are characterized by a particularly arresting sense of maternal tenderness and engaging naturalness.

Several other images remain from what must have been a 6th-century Shaiva temple at Shamalaji, probably contemporary with the later *mātṛkā* figures. One of a pair of tall, suave guardians (*dvārapāla*s; Bombay, Prince of Wales Mus.) is distinguished from the *mātṛkā* group by its polished surface, elongated limbs, thicker physique and slightly stiffer posture. The image also shows a more meticulous approach to detail. The complex enumeration of attributes and surface textures is skilfully and inventively rendered, ranging from the craggy backdrop against which the figure is positioned to the serpent's scales and the stylish ornamentation. These figures are similar to examples from Sondani and Khilchipura not far to the east (*see* §(iv)(c) and fig. 166 above); these and other correspondences suggest considerable interchange between allied sites in western India.

Although the figures at Shamalaji are predominantly Shaiva, there remain a few Vaishnava images that bring an iconographic and stylistic close to the span of artistic activity at the site. These depict Vishnu in his cosmic Vishvarupa form, and one example (New Delhi, N. Mus.) represents the god's emanatory power in full and resplendent glory. The figure type, with its robust physique, elongated torso and iconographic complexity, is directly aligned with the later Shaiva figures and *dvārapāla*, all of which may be dated to *c.* 530.

The Shamalaji style was relatively contained and quite short-lived. Related examples have been found at the nearby sites of Devni Mori, Vartol, Tintoi, Koteshvara and Mahudi. Some of these specimens are dated late in the 6th century or perhaps in the early 7th. Actual production at Shamalaji, however, seems to have come to a halt in the second quarter of the 6th century, and artistic production shifted eastwards. This shift is attested by the spate of related *mātṛkā* imagery that occurred at Jagat, Tanesara (see fig. 167 above) and Amjhara in south-east Rajasthan. These images display a cognate style that is contemporary with the last Shamalaji works, with some examples post-dating Shamalaji by as much as 20 years.

In other areas of Gujarat, sculptural production for this period is negligible and less regional in its stylistic definition. The 5th-century caves at Uparkot, the 'Upper Fort' of Junagadh, show carved columns whose figural décor aligns them with mid-5th-century trends imported from the central regions at Udayagiri, Sarnath and MATHURA (see figs 162 and 163 above and fig. 173 below). Like other examples from Gujarat, the images are infused with a local spirit of inventiveness and energy. Under the Maitraka rulers, numerous structural temples were also built in this region, the oldest being the so-called 'Old Temple' at Gop, originally a Shaiva temple. The date is controversial and has ranged from *c.* 525 to 600. Some minor figures of *gaṇa*s remain, as do individual images of doorkeepers, Vishnu, Surya and a goddess. Though abraded, these display a squat, dense formulation that lacks the innovative elegance of the examples at Shamalaji.

BIBLIOGRAPHY

Enc. Ind. Temple Archit., ii/1

R. C. Agrawala: 'Some Unpublished Sculptures from Southwestern Rajasthan', *Lalit Kala*, vi (1959), pp. 63–71

U. P. Shah: *Sculptures from Śāmalājī and Roḍā (North Gujarat) in the Baroda Museum* (Baroda, 1960)

R. C. Agrawala: 'Some More Unpublished Sculptures from Rajasthan', *Lalit Kala*, x (1961), pp. 31–3

R. N. Mehta and S. N. Chowdhary: *Excavation at Devnimori* (Baroda, 1962)

U. P. Shah: 'Western Indian Sculpture and the So-called Gupta Influence', *Aspects of Indian Art*, ed. P. Pal (Leiden, 1972), pp. 44–8

J. C. Harle: *Gupta Sculpture* (Oxford, 1974)

J. G. Williams: *The Art of Gupta India: Empire and Province* (Princeton, 1982)

S. Schastok: *The Śāmalājī Sculptures and 6th Century Art in Western India* (Leiden, 1985)

R. Salomon: 'New Inscriptional Evidence for the History of the Aulikaras of Mandasor', *Indo-Iran. J.*, xxxii (1989), pp. 1–39

CYNTHIA PACKERT ATHERTON

(c) Maharashtra. Although cave temples continued to be excavated at the end of the 3rd century, there was a drastic reduction in sculptural productions; few if any images can be ascribed with confidence to the 4th century. When artistic production resumed in the 5th century, it was in Vidarbha, in eastern Maharashtra, and in the western cave temples.

Vidarbha. In Vidarbha a number of sites cluster around Nagardhan (ancient Nandivardhana), one of the centres of the Vakataka empire in the 4th and 5th centuries. Three images in particular illustrate the distinctive character of this region. An image of *Shiva* in the form of a corpulent dwarf, from Manasar (see fig. 169), embodies the spirit of the mid-5th century. The curls bubbling from its topknot,

169. *Shiva* in the form of a dwarf, stone, Manasar, *c.* AD 420–50 (New Delhi, National Museum)

the delicately incised and arched eyebrows and gently smiling lips, the chubby yet graceful arms and hands, the soft, realistic drape of the jewelled necklace, the amusingly cocked right toe—such details reflect a creative combination of individualization and iconographic specificity. This unique image is most comparable to the massive *yakṣa*s (nature deities) carved on either side of the *caitya* window of Cave 19 at Ajanta (*in situ*; see Spink, *Ajanta to Ellora*, p. 49, figs 1, 2; *see also* AJANTA, §2). These *yakṣa*s share with the Manasar *Shiva* gently tilted heads, taut body forms, delicate fingers, finely etched facial features and a powerful, confident corpulence, yet they are somewhat harder-edged (for instance in the more schematic folds under the breasts). Since the Ajanta images should be dated *c.* 465–85, the Manasar *Shiva* is likely to belong to *c.* 420–50, when the Vakatakas were prominent in eastern Maharashtra.

A second image, portraying the god *Vishnu Trivikrama* (Conqueror of the Three Worlds) from the temple of the same name at RAMTEK, represents well the fresh ideas penetrating Maharashtra in the 5th century (*in situ*; see *Enc. Ind. Temple Archit.*, figs 108, 109). Part of a group of temples attesting to the growth of Vaishnava worship in Vidarbha, this *Trivikrama* exudes a bold energy, expressed in the sharply uplifted kicking leg, the tautly arched torso and the head and neck drawn back as if to balance the kick. Although this is a free-standing image, it preserves a frontality familiar from art of preceding centuries. The symmetrical rolls of flesh at the waist seem to conflict with the otherwise muscular body, suggesting iconographic convention more than the individualization of the Manasar *Shiva*. The elongated, subtly twisted, slender torso carries a suggestion of the slightly earlier sculptural style of AMARAVATI and NAGARJUNAKONDA to the south (*see* §5(vi) above). Yet there are also links to developments further west. The head is backed by a small fluted or spoked halo, a feature also represented on the *yakṣa*s at Ajanta. (It appears on many images of the 6th century in Maharashtra, starting with Jogeshvari and Elephanta and, later in the century, further south at Badami Chalukya sites as well.) Unique to this region and general period, the *Vishnu Trivikrama* may be assigned a date *c.* 500.

Third, and equally distinctive, is the life-size image of the river goddess *Ganga* from Pavnar (*in situ*; see Williams, 1983, pl. 23) of the early 6th century. Like the Ramtek *Vishnu Trivikrama* image, this *Ganga* image is characterized by slim, fluid lines, though perhaps more softly modelled than in the more vigorous *Vishnu*. The caplike curly hairstyle, narrow oval face with slightly tucked-in chin, elongated upper chest and narrow ankles contribute to a streamlined effect. Like the proportions of the small *Ganga* image on the upper right lintel of the south porch doorway at Jogeshvari (Spink, 1978, fig. 25), from *c.* AD 530–60, the Pavnar image anticipates the proportions of the female in the *mithuna* couple of the Lakshmana Temple at SIRPUR, also of the 6th century (Williams, 1983, figs 247, 248). In this the image exemplifies the multiple cross-regional links of Maharashtrian style, connecting it to east and west even in the formative years of its 'classical' period. Yet small, conventional details reveal its 5th-century Vidarbha character: for instance, its diaphanous lower garment drapes over the right shin, revealed only by a very narrow ridge at the hemline, similar in delicacy to the hem of a fragmentary *dvārapāla* (door-guardian) image from Ramtek (*Enc. Ind. Temple Archit.*, fig. 123).

Ajanta and Jogeshvari. Sculptures of such high quality amplify the pool of features that characterize 4th- to 6th-century sculptural style. Yet they are outnumbered by the vast body of 5th- and 6th-century sculpture from the Buddhist and Hindu cave temples of western and coastal Maharashtra. Among these, AJANTA remains the premier site where, in the period from *c.* 460 to 485, sculptural practices with roots in the 2nd and 3rd centuries were combined with new themes in Buddhist art. This explosive doctrinal and artistic leap was fuelled by the patronage of Vakataka ministers and other local rulers.

By this time anthropomorphic Buddha images—only tentatively represented on a small scale earlier at Kanheri (*see* §5(iii)(b) above)—were being carved with abandon, from primary, superhuman-sized shrine images to hundreds of smaller-scale images carved in relief panels on the façades and walls of many of Ajanta's caves. Although technically still relief-carvings attached to the parent rock, the compositions were carved deeply enough to create a convincing three-dimensional effect. The images' massive, square, frontal poses, more than stylistic conventions, were necessary to convey the majestic force of the teaching Buddha (see Spink, *Ajanta to Ellora*, p. 24, fig. 3). Even as the ponderous proportions of the earlier (*c.* 470) Buddhas were tempered into the slimmer type of the latest ones (*c.* 480; see Spink, *Ajanta to Ellora*, p. 28, fig. 8), as in Cave 26, the square, hieratic style continued to exist.

This style is in marked contrast to the rhythmic individualism of a wide variety of attendant figures. The monumental *yakṣa*s on the façade of Cave 19 exemplify this difference, as does the deservedly famous *Snake King and Queen* (*nāga/nāginī*) panel to the left of the cave's courtyard (see fig. 170). Cut in deep relief, the figures lean gently against one another, conveying an emotional connection anticipated in the earlier Karle and Kuda *mithuna* couples (*see* §§4(iii)(d) and 5(iii)(b) above). The king's slightly inclined head and gently curved waist, along with the queen's drooping breasts and hips tilted back as she raises her left leg, all convey a sense of languor and beneficence. While the composition as a whole is balanced, no details are symmetrical; like the Manasar *Shiva*, these figures are enlivened by a multitude of subtle variations. The connection between Cave 19 at Ajanta and Amaravati and Nagarjunakonda is suggested by small details and the overall scheme of this cave's façade. Although gentle, the opposed twists of the snake queen's head and hips are reminiscent of the more forceful angular movements of relief carving from these places. Her very rounded face, like the round faces of the Buddha figures flanking the cave's entrance door (Zimmer, fig. 178), reflects an element of the earlier southern style (Zimmer, fig. 98) more than the slimmer, crisper aesthetic of Buddha images from,

170. *Snake King and Queen*, relief, Cave 19, Ajanta, *c.* AD 475

for example, SARNATH of approximately the same time (Zimmer, fig. 102).

In the first half of the 6th century, Brahmanical shrines appeared in the western caves, incorporating elements from Ajanta's style together with dramatic new iconographical themes. These developments were coterminous with political activities that brought Maharashtra's rulers into contact and conflict with dynasties further north. Under the emergent Kalachuri dynasty (*see* KALACHURIS OF MAHARASHTRA), Jogeshvari, the earliest Brahmanical cave temple (*c.* 525–30), well illustrates a rapid conjunction of cultural themes. As noted above, the slim, graceful river goddess on the south porch doorway is similar to the Pavnar *Ganga*, while the composition of the lintel itself clearly follows the Ajanta style, with multiple figures portrayed in small shrines across the top of the door, embedded in a series of borders embellished with a luxurious variety of vegetal and anthropomorphic relief sculpture. The east entrance to the main hall presents a startling contrast: the demon Ravana shaking Mt Kailasa, Shiva's abode, is carved above the lintel in shallow but detailed relief (Spink, 1978, pl. 1, no. 3). A well-known theme that would reappear on a larger scale at Elephanta and Ellora, this first version at Jogeshvari betrays no single precedent, although the closely overlapping arms of the demon are reminiscent of another multi-armed image, the *Vishnu Vishvarupa* of *c.* 535–40 from SHAMALAJI (Schastok, fig. 34). This comparison is more suggestive of contemporaneity than of influence in either direction. The tightly constructed scene of figures surrounding Shiva may be compared to the Parel (Bombay) stele (*in situ*; Schastok, fig. 112) of *c.* 525–30, a Shiva image with clearer ties both to contemporary sculpture from Shamalaji and to predecessors at Ajanta. Shiva's face—with its crisp but serene features—and full but gently modelled upper torso are more like sculpture from Ajanta than like the harder contours of the Shamalaji figure.

Elephanta. By the middle of the 6th century, Maharashtra's sculpture had reached a new height of sophisticated style and iconographic innovation in the great Shaiva cave temple at ELEPHANTA, dated to *c.* 535–50. Like Ajanta in the previous century, Elephanta appears to have been the result of an artistic and doctrinal burst that was surely the product of political patronage and intensified sectarian teachings, linked with the commissioning of the most skilled artists. Somewhat round-faced figures line the cave walls in a series of relief panels, whether Shiva in his many forms, his consorts or his numerous attendants. The relief depicting *Shiva Gangadhara* (receiving the Ganga in his hair) exemplifies the Elephanta style, sharing with both the Parel stele and Ajanta's earlier figures a serenity and the full but not taut bodily forms that are the hallmarks of classic Maharashtrian sculpture. The slender, fluid flying figures above, attendant deities, and dwarfs below all turn to face or gaze up or down at Shiva and his consort, Parvati. Like the *Snake Queen* of Cave 19 at Ajanta, the *Parvati* is portrayed with subtly drooping breasts, head tilted gently towards her left shoulder and full lips barely parted. She and Shiva do not look at one another, but they are powerfully connected by their movement, standing close together but swaying in opposition, so that their shoulders almost touch while their hips angle apart in perfect balance.

171. *Shivamahadeva* (detail), Elephanta, *c.* AD 550

Most extraordinary is the colossal, three-faced image of *Shivamahadeva*, carved on the central panel of the south wall (see fig. 171). Planned to be viewed from the distance of the hall entrance, all details have been more crisply released from the stone than in the surrounding, smaller-scale images. This can be seen, for instance, in the sharp line at the edge of the central face's protruding lower lip. Each visible face represents a different aspect of Shiva (two more are implied, one behind the image and one to be seen only from above). From the viewer's left these are: the fierce Aghora, snarling, hook-nosed and moustached; the central Sadyojata, with hair piled up in an ascetic's topknot inside elaborate garlands of pearls and elaborate crests of jewels; and the blissful Vamadeva on the right, with a peaceful expression and hair dressed with tight curls and jewelled swags. In profile Vamadeva's face appears almost angular, with flat forehead, sharply triangular nose and square chin. This sharpness is moderated by the mouth, which is relieved by the asymmetrically larger lower lip. With complete mastery the artist has portrayed multiple contrasts: massive scale versus fine detail; material sensuousness of ornament versus unmarked flesh suffused with divine power; traditional motifs versus original composition.

Ellora and Aurangabad. During the last half of the 6th century, Buddhist and Brahmanical sculptural activity intensified at ELLORA and AURANGABAD, cave temple sites further inland. At Ellora, themes introduced at Elephanta were repeated in several Shaiva excavations, the

172. *Dancer and Musicians*, relief, Cave 7, Aurangabad, *c.* AD 575–600

more stolid and schematic style of which reflects experience more than inspiration. Thus the Ravananugraha scenes (showing Ravana shaking Mt Kailasa) in caves 29 and 21 at Ellora are rather literally composed, with a linear register of deities at the top, a middle ground filled with the protagonists, and Ravana confined beneath another linear register, placidly lifting Mt Kailasa, without the fury conveyed despite the smaller scale at Jogeshvari (Spink, *Ajanta to Ellora*, p. 66, figs 10, 12, 13). Although a certain subtlety was lost during this period, high craftsmanship is still evident, particularly in Cave 21 at Ellora, a jewel-like Shaiva excavation of *c.* 575, notable for its sensuous variety of female figures. The range includes a majestically calm *Ganga* on the north entrance wall (Spink, *Ajanta to Ellora*, p. 35, fig. 4), bemusingly varied tree nymphs carved in the porch pillars and images of Parvati—for instance the one in the Umamaheshvara scene on an interior relief panel (Spink, *Ajanta to Ellora*, p. 65, fig. 9) in which the goddess is shown flinging dice in the midst of a board game. Compared with the *Snake Queen* in Cave 19 at Ajanta or with the *Parvati* at Elephanta, this image is somewhat harder in its contours. The breasts are now perfectly spherical instead of more naturally drooping; the head is perfectly straight instead of gently tilted; the headdress involves a gorgeous, if rigid, array of ringlets and jewels.

Female imagery plays an equally important role in Buddhist excavations of this period, as it would in the 7th and 8th centuries. In Cave 7 at Aurangabad, *c.* 575–600, unique compositions depict female deities in hieratic poses surrounded by attendants (Berkson and others, pp. 136–7; *see* AURANGABAD). In an extraordinary scene inside the shrine a central dancing figure, caught in mid-step, is surrounded by musicians (see fig. 172). With heavy, intricately decorated headdresses, bulging, spherical breasts, narrow waists and wide hips, these figures are a more florid version of the hardened style of Cave 21 at Ellora. As would be the case in the 7th century, sculptors experimented with many themes never before rendered in rock-cut relief. However, the thematic innovations were not to be matched by brilliance of style, which, after Elephanta, remained competent but not compelling.

See also §III, 4(ii) above.

BIBLIOGRAPHY

Enc. Ind. Temple Archit., ii/1, pp. 59–71
H. Zimmer: *The Art of Indian Asia*, ii (Princeton, 1955)
W. Spink: *Ajanta to Ellora* (Bombay, 1967)
——: 'Ellora's Earliest Phase', *Bull. Amer. Acad. Benares*, i (1967), pp. 11–22
S. L. Weiner: *Ajanta: Its Place in Buddhist Art* (Berkeley, 1977)
W. Spink: 'Jogeswari: A Brief Analysis', *J. Ind. Soc. Orient. A.* (1978), pp. 1–35 [Moti Chandra commemorative issue]
K. V. Soundara Rajan: *Art of South India—Deccan* (Delhi, 1980)
S. Kramrisch: 'The Great Cave Temple of Siva on the Island of Elephanta', *The Presence of Siva* (Princeton, 1981), pp. 443–68
J. G. Williams: *The Art of Gupta India, Empire and Province* (Princeton, 1982)
C. Berkson and others: *Elephanta: The Cave of Shiva* (Princeton, 1983)
W. Spink: 'The Great Cave at Elephanta: A Study of Sources', *Essays on Gupta Culture*, ed. B. L. Smith (Delhi, 1983), pp. 235–82
J. G. Williams: 'Vakataka Art and the Gupta Mainstream', *Essays on Gupta Culture*, ed. B. L. Smith (Delhi, 1983), pp. 215–33
S. L. Schastok: *The Samalaji Sculptures and 6th Century Art in Western India* (Leiden, 1985)
The Sculpture of India, 3000 B.C.–1300 A.D. (exh. cat. by P. Chandra, Washington, DC, N.G.A., 1985)
C. Berkson: *The Caves at Aurangabad: Early Buddhist Tantric Art in India* (New York and Ahmadabad, 1986)
C. D. Collins: *The Iconography and Ritual of Siva at Elephanta* (Albany, 1988)

GERI H. MALANDRA

(iv) Central. Between the 4th and 6th centuries AD, trends established in early Indian art found fruition, and the vocabulary of medieval Indian art took shape. It has been argued that as Gupta power waned under foreign onslaught, martial postures in 'Gupta' sculpture gave way to ascetic attitudes. However, except perhaps for three images of Jaina *tīrthaṅkaras* (teachers, saints) from Durjanpura near Vidisha (*see* BESNAGAR), dedicated by the shadowy Ramagupta (*reg c.* AD 376–80), who does not even find a place in dynastic chronology, no sculpture from this period in central India can be associated directly with a Gupta ruler. Moreover, even after the five great Gupta kings (*c.* AD 320–467) were followed by weak Gupta rulers, sculpture of great power continued to be produced, even from areas outside the Gupta realm, well into the 6th century. The style of this sculpture varied geographically rather than dynastically. At the same time, dynastic boundaries did not restrict the movement of artists and patrons, so despite local variations, a broadly unified style emerged.

The evolution of central Indian sculpture between the 4th and 6th centuries can best be charted by looking at the sculpture itself and by relating undated examples to the few dated images of the period. Seen thus, the three centuries tentatively arrange themselves into three broad stylistic phases: formative (*c.* 320–400), high (*c.* 400–500) and late (*c.* 500–600). These broad phases can be divided into chronological sub-phases, which can be divided in turn by artistic province.

(a) Formative phase (*c.* 320–400). (b) High phase (*c.* 400–500). (c) Late phase (*c.* 500–600).

*(a) Formative phase (*c. *320–400).* The formative phase is characterized by strong memories of the sensuousness, fleshiness, extroversion, tactile volume, additive contours and lateral emphasis of Kushana Mathura.

c. *320–70.* The earliest images of this phase are a standing *Vishnu* and a standing guardian figure carved in high relief on slabs found at GARH DHANAURA in the tribal district of Bastar in south-eastern Madhya Pradesh, followed closely by a *Seated Buddha* in the lotus position (*padmāsana*) discovered at Bhongapal in the same district. The wide shoulders of the *Vishnu*—stressed by a broad necklace, sacred thread, garland and halo—and the stiff, inert curves of the swinging garment, the fleshy lips, ridged eyebrows and powerful frontal stance recall Buddha images of Mathura. However, the open stares, vapid smiles and accentuated nipples and male organs of the Mathura figures, as well as their athletic tension and earthiness, have given way to an indrawn look, a relaxation in posture and—in the *Vishnu*—elegant, meticulously designed ornament. Even the somewhat cruder guardian image has luxuriant, intermeshed locks framing his head like a halo. The short, stunted legs, the squarish form of the Garh Dhanaura images, the massive head of the Bhongapal image and the latter's dryness and relative lack of animation indicate that these objects pre-date early 5th-century images at Udayagiri.

c. *370–400.* The Bastar images appear to be followed by the three Jaina *tīrthaṅkaras*, dedicated by inscriptions of Ramagupta and found at Durjanpura, near Vidisha in north-western Madhya Pradesh (Vidisha, Distr. Archaeol. Mus.). All three have *śrīvatsas* (auspicious symbols) on their chests, are seated on lion thrones in the lotus posture and are attended by male whisk-bearers. Memories of Kushana Buddhas survive in the sharply etched eyes of the attendants and in the broad-shouldered bodies, deeply grooved navels, spread legs and open gazes of the *tīrthaṅkaras* themselves. However, the sharp, additive contours of Kushana images have begun to give way to mutually responsive curves. The stone between the body and the bent part of the arms has been cut away, creating a new interaction of solids and voids. The flat, harshly incised triangles and half-circles in the halo have been replaced by elegantly double-cut, scalloped and beaded borders, enclosing overlapping lotus petals of some volume. The uncompromising frontality of Kushana attendants has been replaced by a sideways inclination. Instead of sitting up stiffly, bodies tautened like bows, the main images have acquired a slight forward sway, and the lions supporting the throne rest easily on all fours. In spite of strong Kushana links, the idiom is freer, lighter, bouncier.

*(b) High phase (*c. *400–500).* The tentative experimentation of the 4th century was replaced by a fully fledged style of great assurance and charm in the early 5th century. The vestiges of Kushana tension and vehemence were firmly harnessed to a mood of exultant introspection.

c. *400–425.* This change in mood is evident in the cave sculptures of UDAYAGIRI (ii). These are firmly dated by an inscription of AD 401 from a Sanakanika feudatory of the emperor Chandragupta (*reg* 319/20–35) in Cave 6 and by a further inscription of Shaba Virasena, a minister of the same emperor, in Cave 7, recording a gift to Shambhu (a form of the god Shiva). The only image of Shambhu at the site is the *ekamukhaliṅga* (single-faced *liṅga*) in Cave 4. Shiva's consort, Parvati, is shown as the goddess Durga beside caves 4, 6 and 17, pressing down the haunch of the buffalo demon with her arm or upending it and placing her foot on its head, symbolizing victory over evil (Mahishasuramardini). Among the children of Shiva and Parvati, Ganesha, who overcomes obstacles, and Karttikeya, who overcame the demon Taraka, figure in caves 6 and 9, respectively. There are also, outside caves 4 and 6, two damaged groups of the 'seven mothers' (*saptamātṛkās*), who helped Shiva destroy ignorance, represented by the demon Andhaka (*see* §II, 1 above).

Vishnu, however, is the dominant figure, shown twice outside Cave 6, standing frontally posed with arms lowered, adorned with a garland that reaches to his knees and a high crown comprising a quatrefoil pattern, a lion head spouting pearl strands, and wide side bands. In one example Vishnu places his hands on the figures of Gadadevi and Cakrapurusha, who personify the power of his weapons (mace and discus respectively) to destroy ignorance. On either side of the entrance to Cave 6 are two *dvārapālas*, identified as Vishnu's attendants Jaya and Vijaya (see fig. 173). Vishnu is also represented reclining on the coiled serpent Shesha. Arranged on the wall behind him are the goddess Lakshmi, holding a lotus; the god Brahma, the creator, seated on a lotus sprung from Vishnu's navel; the personified attributes mace (*mahat*), discus (*cakra*) and conch (*śankha*); the kneeling narrator,

173. *Dvārapāla* (door-guardian) with trident, Cave 6, Udayagiri, *c.* AD 400–425

the sage Markandeya; and the two demons Madhu and Kaitabha, poised to slay Brahma.

The most remarkable representation of Vishnu is his boar incarnation (Varaha) in Cave 5. As Varaha he heaves exultantly upwards, lifting the earth goddess Bhudevi from the primal waters with his tusk. The waters themselves are indicated by the wavy lines on the back and side walls; by the serpent Shesha, over which Varaha presses forward and upward; by the lotus on which Bhudevi's feet are perched; by the similar lotus on which Lakshmi stands, holding a long-stalked lotus as a sun-shade over Varaha; by the kneeling, worshipful figures of Varuna and Samudra ('Ocean'); and, finally, by the two great rivers, Ganga and Yamuna. Shown on the door pilasters of Cave 6 as *vṛkṣakā*s (tree nymphs) standing on crocodiles under mango and *aśoka* trees, Ganga and Yamuna are differentiated in Cave 6 by their respective vehicles, a crocodile and a tortoise. Rows of figures rise on the wall behind Varaha, standing with one hand clenched on their hips, the other extended in praise of their lord. These figures include gods—among them Brahma and Shiva—12 *āditya*s (celestial deities associated with the sun) with solar halos, 8 *vasu*s (atmospheric powers), 11 ithyphallic *Rudra*s (manifestations of the god Shiva) and bearded sages. This graphic celebration of the rescue of the earth has been interpreted as the description of the *varāha* rite, performed to save the world from a deluge of iniquity. It has also been interpreted as a depiction of the victorious exertions of Chandragupta II (*reg c.* 380–415) in recovering the heartland of the Gupta empire from the Shaka invaders and wresting Queen Dhruvadevi, identified here with the pliant figure of Bhudevi, from the Shaka king (*see* §II, 1(iii) above).

Apart from these Shaiva and Vaishnava sculptures, the doorjamb, pilasters and columns of Cave 19 are carved with load-bearing dwarfs, vegetal scrolls and *kīrttimukha*s (beastlike 'faces of glory') emitting strings of pearls, while the lintel, in two registers, shows flying figures and the churning of the ocean. A fragment of a lotus ceiling (Gwalior, Archaeol. Mus.) with seated images that represent zodiacal signs and a doorjamb carved with addorsed lions were also found on the hilltop at Udayagiri (on site).

Strong Kushana-period memories are evident in the Udayagiri figures' ridged eyebrows, staring eyes, short chins, full lips, thick necks, barrel chests, hands clenched at hips, exuberant vitality and voluminous drapery. However, the flabby forms of the Vidisha *tīrthaṅkara*s and the stunted proportions of Garh Dhanaura have been replaced by tighter, firmer, better-proportioned bodies that are electric with muscular tension. The dryness and frozen stillness of Kushana Buddhas have been relieved by a self-conscious use of ornament, posture and gesture, by swinging garlands, fluttering drapery, tumbling curls and dainty pleats and ruffles in belts and sashes. Even when standing still, bodies now appear galvanized by arrested breath. The figures seem to tremble with a carefully orchestrated tension between the bent and straight, the free and engaged leg, the raised and lowered shoulder, while the numerous curves of body, drapery and ornament answer one another, building a harmonious rhythm.

Other sculptures from central India that can be assigned to the early period are the standing *Narasimha* (Vishnu's incarnation as man-lion from ERAN; U. Sagar, Archaeol. Mus.), the *bodhisattva Vajrapani* from Sanchi (Sanchi, Archaeol. Mus.) and the ithyphallic *Harihara* (symbolizing the syncretic union of Shiva and Vishnu; New Delhi, N. Mus.). These figures' massive round heads and shoulders, accentuated by powerful, flaring arms, broad torques or streaming hair, their swelling chests and male organs, pushing against their constricting robes and the surging buoyancy of their poses, negating their physical volume, all link them with the Udayagiri style. In the case of the Sanchi Vajrapani, dating based on stylistic analysis is supported by an inscription of AD 412–13 recording the gift of a Vajrapani pillar.

Closely related to both the *mātṛkā* groups outside caves 5 and 6 at Udayagiri and the Mahishasuramardini images outside caves 6 and 17, and therefore assignable to the same early phase, are rock-cut reliefs showing the *saptamatṛkā*s and Virabhadra (a form of Shiva) at BADOH, in Vidisha District, and a few other *mātṛkā*s, also from Vidisha (Gwalior, Archaeol. Mus.; and New Delhi, N. Mus.). These objects are linked by such characteristics as broad shoulders, outspread arms, powerful chests, squat legs, bolt upright poses, rigid frontality, sharp bifurcation of the waist and legs, flat-topped female or periwig-style male headdresses, heavy necklaces, divided circular rings and multiple bangles. This stylistic grouping is supported, in the case of the Badoh relief, by the palaeography of its inscription mentioning King Jayanta Sena and, generally, by a broad resemblance to the seated images on Chandragupta II's 'archer-type' coins.

c. *425–50.* Sculpture from this period is marked by an emphatic change in mood and idiom. The volume and physical tension of earlier works have been harmonized with a sense of spiritual repose. The human body has become more youthful and pliant, consciously modelled on vegetal or animal forms, relaxed into a placid, gently breathing expanse of robe and flesh and full of quiet power and grace. It no longer seems to thrust against an imaginary frontal plane. The stance has become easier, with arms and legs held more closely to the body. Sharp, precipitous bodily transitions have been replaced by a reticent, smoothly flowing, curvilinear contour, unbroken by heavy girdles, belts or fleshy cords around the chest. Proportions have become balanced and stabilized. Gestures and postures have been standardized and energized. Motifs have become more elegant and graceful. In most cases scalloped haloes have been replaced by lotus-centred ones, thick robes with engraved folds by diaphanous robes with relief folds, lion thrones by lotus thrones. In major centres outside central India at this time, the attempt was made to embody the Buddha's limitless compassion and meditation rather than his messianic zeal for world reform. The change in central Indian style must be read in the light of a desire to harmonize sensuality and spirituality, extroversion and introversion, strength and grace, swelling volume and chastening line, form and ornament.

To this extraordinary moment can be assigned the fragments of the gateway (*toraṇa*) lintel found at Pawaya near Gwalior (Gwalior, Archaeol. Mus.). On one side of this lintel is shown the churning of the ocean, surrounded by figures seated with splayed legs: Vishnu's mount, Garuda, Karttikeya and his 12-armed consort Sashthi. On the other side appears a magnificent scene of a female dancer with an all-female orchestra. Female figures look out in dismay from palace windows at a scene below, in which the demon-king Bali appears beside a sacrificial platform, pouring water into the hands of the Vamana *avatāra* of Vishnu, as a token of a gift of land measuring three steps. Vishnu claims this gift in three world-spanning strides in an adjacent scene as Trivikrama (Conqueror of the Three Worlds), depriving Bali of his kingdom and power. A figure on two prancing horses, framed by a crescent, represents the sun and moon witnessing the scene. Other figures of this phase from Pawaya include a Vishnu in *abhaya mudrā* (the gesture granting fearlessness) and a Janus pair atop a capital (both Gwalior, Archaeol. Mus.), identified variously as *cakrapuruṣa*s (personifications of Vishnu's wheel), the gods Indra and Upendra, or Nara and Narayana.

Several other sculptures belong to the same phase, including an image of the river goddess *Ganga* (Boston, MA, Mus. F.A.); a head of Vishnu from Vidisha (Cleveland, OH, Mus. A.); a *nāga* (snake king), two seated Buddhas and a head of the *bodhisattva Avalokiteshvara* from Sanchi (Sanchi, Archaeol. Mus.); a lion pillar capital at Sanchi; a standing *Vishnu* from Pipariya (U. Sagar, Archaeol. Mus.); and a standing Vishnu (Allahabad Mus.) and *ekamukhaliṅga* from Khoh (see fig. 174). A doorjamb at Tumain shows Lakshmi's lustration by elephants and the 'eight auspicious objects' (*aṣṭamaṅgala*) on the lintel. The porch of the Narsing Temple at TIGOWA has capitals and pilasters bearing lions separated by trees or clutching small human beings in their paws, doubled *candraśālā*s (motifs suggesting rounded window-like openings) framing lion or human heads, doorjambs carved with river goddesses, and a lotus ceiling. A lintel fragment at Eran shows alternating lion and human heads, *gaṇa*s (dwarfs), *makara*s (mythical aquatic animals) and the god Ganesha, and a capital there has addorsed lions above *candraśālā*s enclosing human heads.

A comparison between the seated Buddhas of Sanchi from this phase and the sculptures from Garh Dhanaura or Udayagiri shows how the plastic volume of the earlier phases was subdued and how the Buddha as a '*yakṣa* in monk's clothing' made way for the transcendent master of law. Similarly, the harsh, congealed volumes, ridged, connected eyebrows, open, protruding eyes and hard

174. *Ekamukhaliṅga* (single-faced *liṅga*), from Khoh, *c.* AD 425–50 (Allahabad, Allahabad Museum)

175. *Seated Buddha* in *dhyāna mudrā*, sandstone, h. 1.52 m, from Sanchi, *c.* AD 450–51 (Sanchi, Archaeological Museum)

cheeks and squarish head jutting out of the *ekamukhaliṅga* at Udayagiri were transformed. In the *ekamukhaliṅga* from Khoh, softly defined locks of hair, eyebrows and eyelids merge imperceptibly in the oval head, which occupies the shaft unobtrusively. Its vision has become more withdrawn and hooded. The emphatic accentuation of the distinctive volumes or contours of the body, robe and ornament of the Udayagiri *Vishnu* and the abrupt bifurcation of the upper and lower body of the Vidisha *saptamatṛkā*s have been discarded. Instead, the Shankargadh *Vishnu*, Pawaya lintel dancer and Tigowa river goddesses are characterized by soft, unaccented modelling, fluid, curvilinear contours, graceful, effortless flexion, spare ornament and reticent mood. Their limbs appear to be filled with surging sap, imitating the luscious, twining plants that often frame them.

c. *450–75.* This unique balance was, however, fragile and transient and gave way to a transitional period (*c.* 450–75) characterized by an ambivalence regarding the rendering of physical proportions and a negation or accentuation of volumes in different parts of the same image, heralding the rarification, elongation and abstraction of the late phase. Most important in this transitional period are the four Buddhas, originally seated under canopies, in the ambulatory adjoining the lower railing of Stupa 1 at Sanchi, one opposite each entrance. An inscription of 450–51 on the crossbar of the railing records an endowment by a female devotee, Harisvamini, for maintaining lamps in the place of the four Buddhas and probably refers to these. The Buddhas are seated in the lotus position, on lotus seats, in the *dhyāna mudrā* (pose of meditation; see fig. 175). They are flanked by whisk-bearing *bodhisattva*s and, at the south gate, by the gods Indra and Brahma. Their haloes are formed by triangular rays and floriate scrolls and framed by flying *gandharva*s bearing offerings. A few *tirthaṅkara* images from NACHNA (on site; Rajendra Udyan Garden, Panna, Madhya Pradesh; cave, Siddh-ka Pahar Hill), especially an image of Parshvanatha (on site), appear to be analogous. All of these sculptures are characterized by the juxtapositions of an elongated torso with spread legs and of a full face with a flat chest in which the earlier fleshiness has nearly dissolved. Substantial floriate designs are combined with gossamer-thin, lacelike patterns in the haloes.

The sculptures of the BAGH caves in western Madhya Pradesh also belong to this transitional phase. It has been suggested, on the strength of transitional architectural features and sculptural motifs, that the art of Bagh shows the influence of earlier work at Ajanta and influenced, in turn, a later phase there, thus falling in the period between *c.* 462 and 480. Bagh represents, it is felt, an intermediate phase in the development of Buddhist sectarian iconography in which the non-iconic stupa and rock-cut icons of Buddhas and *bodhisattva*s coexisted. A late 5th-century copperplate inscription of King Subandhu, found in Cave 2, mentions repairs to this 'abode of art', thus supporting the chronological presumption. The elongation of limbs, dematerialization of surfaces, uncertainty about proportions and growing abstraction detected in the Sanchi Buddhas are held in check at Bagh by an enlargement of scale and volume, a formal sluggishness, accentuation of the sacred thread or necklace and the leavening of meditative composure by mannerism.

Such are the stylistic features of the *dvārapāla*s, Buddhas, *bodhisattva* attendants and *bodhisattva*s Maitreya and Padmapani Avalokiteshvara in Cave 2. The Buddhas grasp the hems of their garments with their left hands and hold their right palms open in the *varada mudrā* (the pose of bestowing boons). The attendants hold the edges of their knotted garments, fly whisks or lotus stalks. The lotus-bearing *bodhisattva*s wear matted hair with inset Buddhas in *abhaya mudrā* (the pose granting fearlessness). In Cave 9 the pillars are carved with real or fabulous animals emerging from acanthus leaves. The door lintel in Cave 9 displays seated Buddhas and *candraśālā*s framing busts with knotted coiffures or cascading locks, fluttering ribbons or scarfs, plump cheeks and full breasts. The doorjambs carry river goddesses with dwarf attendants emerging from *makara* (crocodile) mouths. The verandahs of caves 2 and 4 include a corpulent *yakṣa* king accompanied by *makara* heads, stupas and flying figures and a snake king and queen, crowned by an abraded panel of the Buddha preaching his first sermon.

The sculptures of the Shiva Temple at BHUMARA also appear to belong to this transitional phase. Most of these have been found in oblong slabs with sunken friezes framed by *candraśālā*s that formed part of the superstructure. Shiva appears as the central bust on a lintel in the form of an *ekamukhaliṅga*, resembling a similar *liṅga* in the neighbouring village of Khamharia. Durga Mahishasuramardini, Karttikeya, Ganesha, the sun god Surya, Brahma, the wealth god Kubera and Shiva dancing and riding his bull appear in the *candraśālā*s. The *gaṇa*s appear in the friezes as megalophallic, with heads of boars, monkeys, parrots or bulls and with lion or demon heads on their stomachs. They are represented running, dancing, playing musical instruments, standing with one hand clenched at their hips, sitting pensively or expressing contained joy with slightly parted lips. Their hair, parted in the middle, streams down on their shoulders in ringlets or is occasionally made into topknots like that worn by the god Krishna or into smooth skullcaps. The *gaṇa*s often give way to female figures that stand with their heads inclined in reflection or alternate with *gaṇa*s climbing meandering lotus creepers (see fig. 176) or waves with curling crests. The doorjamb shows river goddesses with attendants, figures standing alone or in couples. The lintel is carved with flying, garland-bearing *vidyādhara*s, *candraśālā*s, corrugated fan-palm leaves and *kīrttimukha*s.

Transitional features are evident in the juxtaposition of the elongated bodies, short, stunted legs, round faces and square crowns of the gods; in the band of flesh bifurcating the chests and bellies of the *gaṇa*s; in the hair of the *kīrttimukha*s, crumbling into vegetal forms; in the complex variety of the poses of the *gaṇa*s; and in the exhaustive, syncretic iconography. The lotus rhizomes have lost the quiet, soft, feathery quality of Mukandara and resemble the heaving surf of a raging sea, with deep, churning pools of shadow. The calm simplicity of the hairstyle, the single, beaded necklace and the full meditative head, held straight in the *ekamukhaliṅga* at Khoh, have given way to a complexity of intermeshed locks of hair, ornate necklaces and crown, and to a linearized, bemused, introspective head, held at a slight downward inclination, in the *ekamukhaliṅga*s of Bhumara and Khamharia.

Closely allied to the style of Bhumara was the sculpture of the so-called Dashavatara Vishnu temple (*c*. 475) at DEOGARH. Originally a five-shrine (*pañcāyatana*) complex on a square plinth, the temple still stands with vestiges of the base of four shrines at the corners. It displays growing iconographic complexity and ornamental prolixity. The lintels and the jambs of its west-facing doorway have multiplied since those of the simple doorways of Udayagiri and are filled with floral motifs, standing couples, dwarfs, whisk-bearers, guardian figures and the river goddesses, Ganga and Yamuna, at the top left and right corner. The central panel above the entrance shows Vishnu seated on the coiled body of the serpent Sesha. The open hood of the serpent forms a halo behind Vishnu's head. Lakshmi massages his foot. His man-lion (Narasimha) and dwarf (Vamana) incarnations flank him, and flying, garland-bearing celestial figures converge towards him.

For the devotee circumambulating the temples, Vishnu appears in niches framed by ornate jambs, lintels and vase-foliage pilasters on the three walls of the temple. On the south, Vishnu lies on the serpent Sesha, the *anantashayana* form (see fig.177). Lakshmi, flanked by Garuda, massages his right foot. Brahma, flanked by Indra, Karttikeya, Shiva and Parvati, appears above him. The demons Madhu and Kaitabha and male and female personifications of Vishnu's weapons, namely bow, sword and mace, strike martial

176. Floral scroll with *gaṇa*s (detail), from Bhumara, *c*. AD 450–75 (Allahabad, Allahabad Museum)

poses below. This panel evokes the myth of the creation of Brahma, the creator, by Vishnu from his navel. Lying prone in the primeval waters, Vishnu rescues the beginning of the world from dark, invading forces, an act that is

177. *Vishnu Anantashayana* (Vishnu sleeping on the cosmic serpent Ananta), Vishnu Temple, Deogarh, *c.* AD 475

celebrated by the gods and goddesses who overcome obstacles, fight evil and embody good fortune.

In the eastern niche, in a rocky wilderness occupied by deer and lions, Vishnu appears as two-armed Nara and four-armed Narayana, ascetics with matted hair incarnating devotion, righteousness and non-violence. His presence is celebrated by flying, garland-bearing angels, the celestial maiden Urvashi and Brahma on a lotus seat. Vishnu appears in the northern niche in his Gajanugrahamurti form: he is shown, mounted on the flying Garuda, descending to rescue a royal devotee changed into an elephant (Gajendramoksha), who has been seized by an aquatic monster, represented here by a serpent couple. The rescue from ignorance is epitomized in this panel. The rescuer, the rescued and the assailant forces from which rescue is effected are bound in a single composition in a relationship of benediction and devotion, the victorious attainment of release (*mokṣa*) being celebrated by flying angels, bearing a crown, assembling from all sides at the top.

Compared with the sculpture of Bhumara, the human figures of Deogarh have become harder and more angular in outline. Their eyes and throat line are more harshly delineated. They are more heavily cluttered with ornamentation. Their legs are cleft by a robe that also sharply bifurcates the waist from the legs. The necklace lacks the volume of Bhumara and seems to be plastered on the body. The lotus scrolls are less deeply cut than at Bhumara and vibrate less with the play of light and shadow. Deogarh figures also show greater mannerism, an exaggeration of gestures and postures. This change is seen in such features as the fingers curving in feminine contours around a staff, the over-accentuated sideways sway of figures in the *Nara and Narayana* and *Gajendramoksha* reliefs, the pretentious poses of the combatants below *Vishnu Anantashayana* and their slender legs, disproportionate to their broad-shouldered trunk. Otherwise, the broad shoulders, cascading curls, elongation and the luxuriant depiction of foliage in the overhead bower link Deogarh sculptures with the slightly earlier ones at Bhumara and the slightly later ones at Nachna.

c. *475–500.* The movement toward idealism in this period, best known from the Buddhas of AD 474 and 477 from Sarnath in north India, remained hesitant in central India, tied as it was to the heavier, earthier idiom of western India (*see* §§(i) and (iii) above). The experiments of the immediately preceding decades do not appear to have been followed to their logical conclusions at later sites such as Nachna, DEORI KALAN, Pipariya, Shankargadh or Eran.

At Nachna the walls of the Shiva-Parvati Temple are rusticated to imitate rocky slopes inhabited by wild animals.

A bear and boar with heads turned to look behind them, a bull resting with its head tucked between its legs, a boar scratching its belly with its tusk, stags licking their feet or scratching their heads (Nachna; Satna, Tulsi Sangrahalaya, Ramvan) help to conjure up the forest habitat. The temple doorjamb is carved with river goddesses standing below trees, on lotuses or *makaras*, beside door-guardians; with flying and amorous couples; with *gaṇas* holding lotus rhizomes; and with diagonal bands of overlapping leaves, while the lintel carries worshippers converging towards the figures of Shiva and Parvati. A rear window carries such motifs as pots and palmettes, *kīrtimukhas* and delicately flexed human figures. The doorways or window lintels, inset in the adjacent Kumramath and Mahadeva temples, show Vishnu in his Varaha and Narasimha incarnations; Surya with his archer-wives, attendants, charioteer, horses and worshippers; interlocked palmettes; lotus rhizomes and leogryphs with riders. Nachna also has a four-faced *liṅga* from Lakhorabagh, showing Shiva as the embodiment of the elements of earth, water, fire and air, as Sadyojata, Vamadevi, Aghora and Tatpurusha respectively. Finally, there are six panels of the *Rāmāyaṇa* epic set in charming sylvan retreats, complete with zigzag walls formed of cubic boulders and bent trees with enormous flowers and thick leaves. Among other scenes, Sita is shown conversing with her husband Rama and offering alms to the demon king Ravana, disguised as a mendicant. Hanuman is represented appearing before Rama and Lakshmana, his brother, at the behest of Sugriva and again allowing himself to be brought before Ravana after wrecking Lanka, Ravana's capital.

The sculptures in the two storeys of the superstructure in the Vamana Temple at Deori Kalan are found in recessed dies, alternating with countersunk panels and, in turn, larger central panels. The niches are filled with amorous couples, voluptuous female figures, flower-bearing worshippers and dwarfs engaged in dance and music. The countersunk panels contain *kīrttimukhas*, *makaras*, birds with floriate tails and floriate arches. The central panels show Vishnu in his incarnations as Narasimha and Hayagriva. The doorjamb is decorated with lotus rhizomes and *śrīvṛkṣa* (auspicious tree), emerging from *śaṅkhanidhis* (conch-treasures) and overflowing pots, respectively, and with guardians wearing haloes of spiked rays. In the lintel Vishnu is carried by his mount, Garuda, who frames the god with his outspread wings, and jawless lion masks flank a central human head. A four-legged image, broken at the waist and equipped with a *makara* gargoyle (*in situ*), may have represented the Vamana incarnation of Vishnu and stood as the presiding deity of the temple.

Sculpture from nearby Pipariya includes a doorway carved with the seven planets (*in situ*); Krishna killing the bull and horse demons; Varaha and Narasimha on the lintel; and a capital carrying a *gaṇa* head with protruding fangs and foliate hair, Vishnu and personified attributes of Vishnu's wheel and mace. A rock-cut Shiva and Parvati from Shankargadh (*in situ*) can also be grouped with the Deori Kalan and Pipariya sculptures.

The complete dematerialization, abstraction, linearity and attenuation that are the hallmarks of the Sarnath style in this period were never fully accepted at any of these central Indian sites. In spite of the emphatic attenuation to the waist and lower legs, the chest and thighs are still broad, and the sexual organs, instead of being suppressed, as at Sarnath, are revealed below the robes. Though the robes themselves are more clinging and transparent than before, their volume is still stressed in raised edges and in the bunched-up portion across the thighs. The powerful frontality in vogue earlier has given way to a 'shot hip' posture, but the lithe, soaring, weightless quality of work from Sarnath is missing. The dainty, prettified pose and manner of the Nachna or Deori Kalan guardians, the delicate, wan grace of the Nachna animals, the quiet, subdued mood of introspection and the layering of light, space and shadow in the *Rāmāyaṇa* panels are no doubt late features. They belong, however, to an earthier, somewhat folkish idiom and do not conjure up the mood of implacable austerity evoked by the Sarnath images of this period. The crisp, ornamental carving of the foliage and intertwined lotus rhizomes on doors and windows and the meticulous attention to ornamental details speak of a preference for the earlier style of Mathura and Sanchi rather than for the severe, unadorned simplicity of Sarnath.

More squat proportions characterize the inscribed pillar of AD 485 and the inscribed theriomorphic Varaha image of about the same period erected by the royal brothers Matrvishnu and Dhanyavishnu at Eran. Unlike the lion capital from the early phase at Sanchi, the Eran pillar capital has straight, closely spaced, sharp-edged petals with harsh arrises. The heads of the lions, compared with those of a pillar capital from the middle phase at Sanchi, have become disproportionately larger and cruder and are much more abruptly sunk on cursorily jointed legs. At the summit the Janus image of Garuda, framed by a wheel and holding a snake, is also thick and stunted in appearance.

The theriomorphic boar is also a vast, amorphous, inert bulk, adorned with rows of bearded sages and beardless figures of the seven planets. The boar wears a garland carved with alternating male and female figures, as well as a scorpion, probably representing the signs of the zodiac. The cube atop the boar's head, with corpulent figures on three sides, has been interpreted as a sacrificial post or as the god Brahma. A flying angel inside the boar's ear, a female figure, probably personifying speech, above the tongue and two intertwined *nāgas* take shelter on the body of the lord against the deluge. The earth goddess hangs slack and flabby from his tusk, which protrudes from its squared-off, ridged snout. The crowding of lumpy figures, devoid of the force or momentum of earlier examples, stamps this image unmistakably as late.

(c) Late phase (c. *500–600)*. In the 6th century, sculpture in central India became very large in size, but there was no undue accentuation or minimization of any one part of the body. The variety in ornament, costume, dress or hairstyle increased, but these never became too coarse or too abundant and never hid or distorted the body. Mannerisms became more conspicuous, but without sacrificing dignity. Gesture and scale were never substituted completely for modelling or expression. The flexion or torsion of the body was never exaggerated to the point that it lost balance. As the century wore on there was a gradual coarsening of the idiom.

c. *500–525.* This period in central India is dominated by two Shiva temples, the Deorani and Jethani at TALA in eastern Madhya Pradesh. Enormous guardian figures, now lying broken on the ground, appear to have stood on both sides of the steps, facing inward. Massive four-faced pillars carved with standing images were raised on the south steps of Jethani over lions, load-bearing dwarfs and *makara*s. Architraves carved with lion heads, dwarfs, couples, the Narasimha incarnation or Karttikeya spanned these pillars. The Deorani doorjamb is a marvel of skilfully chiselled diagonal bands of floral motifs intertwined with animals, birds and human riders. The side panels inside the doorjamb show Kubera with his entourage, *kīrttimukha*s, and Shiva and Parvati dallying and gambling. The lintel shows the lustration of Lakshmi, elephants, trees and a standing Shiva. The lotus medallion on a ceiling fragment from Jethani was replaced in the ceiling of the Deorani by a medallion in which ascetics take the place of petals. An image of the god Varuna, as well as fragments carved with nymphs, river goddesses and grinning *gaṇa* heads were also found at the site.

In 1987 a unique image of *Shiva* was found at the Deorani Temple. Its headgear, waist and chest bands, halo and fingernails are made of snakes; its ear and earring of peacocks; its eyebrows and nose of a descending lizard with outspread legs; its chin of a crab; its shoulder-straps of crocodiles; its knees of lion heads; its phallus of a tortoise; its testicles of bells and its eyeballs, chest, stomach and thighs of demon or dwarf heads. It stands frontally posed, in the round, against a slab. While there is no iconographic or textual precedent for this image, it may have multiple meanings, among which may be the merging of *paśu* (beings) with *pati* (supra-being) by the annihilation of *pāśa* (bonds) in the body of Pashupati (Lord of Animals). The *lakuta* ('staff') held by the image and its erect phallus suggest an association with Lakulisa, the Shaiva teacher of the Pashupata school. The Pashupata associations of Tala are also indicated by several images of *Shaiva* ascetics, with staffs in hand, as well as by broken images of Shiva as an ascetic in tigerskin. The combination of a terrible countenance with unassailable dignity and calm and the apparent reconciliation of mutually hostile animals in the unique *Shiva* image also appear to embody the union of the malignance of Rudra with the benignancy of Shiva. This beneficent aspect is emphasized in another massive head of Shiva found at the site. Adorned with matted locks, a crescent moon and a third eye, it is an image of beatific calm, its expression closely rivalling that of the mid-5th-century *ekamukhaliṅga* from Khoh (see fig. 174 above).

The massive height and weight and lack of buoyancy of the Tala images, the hardening and elongation of their legs, the use of Sarnath-style plain, clinging drapery, cleft by the legs, the variety in their ornament and hairstyle, the invasion of the *kīrttimukha*s by foliate patterns, the fastidious, finespun foliate relief on pillars and the complex undercutting of the foliate bands of the doorjamb all indicate an enhancement of late 5th-century stylistic features. The Tala style is characterized by careful observation and a sense of secular humanism, undimmed by the lofty spiritualism of late 5th-century Sarnath or by the increasing symmetrization characteristic of 6th-century sites outside central India. The relatively pallid or lumpy forms of sculpture from Nachna or of the Eran capital, respectively, have been renounced for figures full of pent-up power and vehemence. The disenchantment, boredom, nonchalance or pain of the load-bearing dwarfs have been caught unerringly. The impact of relentless penance is mirrored faithfully in the wasted skulls of Shaiva ascetics. The movement of the wind is reflected in the trembling lotus leaves and fluttering clothes. The swell of toes, raised edges of nails, lines on palms and pulsations of flesh are infallibly reproduced. Flowers also show great fidelity to forms in nature. This sculpture has affinities with the Vakataka sculptures of Vidarbha (*see* §(iii)(c) above), though some pillars and jambs from Turturiya, Malhar and Senakapat in the areas of Raipur and Bilaspur have been tentatively assigned to this style. A 6th-century coin of the Sharabhpuriya king Prasannamatra, found in the sanctum of the Jethani Temple, is about the only external chronological evidence, indirectly supporting this evidence of style.

c. *525–50.* This period is represented mainly by the school of Mandasor in western Madhya Pradesh (discussed also in the context of Rajasthan in §(iii)(a) above). The sculptures of this school found at SONDANI comprise fragments of two pillars crowned by addorsed lions framing a central lion head; two colossal *dvārapāla*s holding *triśūla*s (tridents) emerging from *triśulapuruṣa*s (personified tridents); and two doorjambs carved with rosettes, *mithuna*s, checkered bands, double *candraśālā*s and Shiva and Parvati. A few fragments carry a flying *vidyādhara* with consort (New Delhi, N. Mus.), and lotus-bearing males and couples with dwarf companions (Gwalior, Archaeol. Mus.). One pillar from Khilichipur (Mandasor Fort) is carved with *dvārapāla*s accompanied by *triśūlapuruṣa*s, the river goddess Yamuna on a turtle, lotus medallions and intermeshed foliage. Another pillar, from Afzalpur (Mandasor Fort), carries an ithyphallic, trident-bearing Shiva. The head (recut) bears a headdress composed of a skull, *makara*s and a jewel. The figure is accompanied by *gaṇa*s. Six musicians and a male dancer appear on the base.

Although all of the Mandasor sculptures may not belong to the same year, their style—read together with an inscription dated AD 533–4 of King Yashodharman of Mandasor and an allied inscription on a Sondani pillar, praising the same king as the conqueror of the Huna Mihirakula—puts them *c.* 525–50. The massive scale, cascading hair and hand hooked in the robe, bunched across the thighs, are features that survive from the preceding phase. However, the quivering lines of drapery visible earlier at Tala, appearing to respond to the pulsating flesh beneath, have been lost. Instead, the drapery folds have been rendered symmetrically in radiating lines, while the frozen layers of the flying *uttarīya*s (upper garments) are piled rigidly upon one another. The idiom has become florid, with agitated 'vermicular' headdresses and fussy, explosive lines of drapery. Bodies are modelled less evenly than at Tala, accentuating the breast and depressing the groin. Arms and legs seem merely additive. The easy flexion of Tala has been replaced by a sharp, angular, sideways thrust of the legs, almost tipping the body off balance. The winding rhizomes and the flying *vidyādhara* couple are harder and flatter than motifs from Tala and appear lifeless and still in comparison. The Mandasor style is closely anticipated or paralleled by sculptures from SHAMALAJI, Jhalawa, JAGAT, Kotyark, Tanesara and Nagari in adjacent areas of Gujarat and Rajasthan in western India (*see* §(iii) above).

c. *550–600.* The last phase of the 6th century is represented by a Shaiva *dvārapāla* from Nachna, two guardians with attendants, a standing *Maheshvari* and *Vaishnavi* (two of the *saptamātṛkās*) at Nandchand and a seated *Maheshvari* (U. Sagar, Archaeol. Mus.), all from eastern Madhya Pradesh. The preference for superhuman scale continued, but the sense of proportion surviving at Mandasor was almost lost. The arms are bloated, stiff and spread out unnaturally like bows, terminating in enormous fingers. The animation implicit in the sideways bodily flexion at Mandasor has been destroyed in the stiff, columnar legs and rigid, frontal pose. The more rounded proportions of Mandasor have given way to squared-off bodies and heads. The transitions within the body have become precipitous and abrupt. The heavy incised swags of cloth and sacred thread falling to the knees are drained of life and movement. The *mātṛkā* images show the same dry style, with heads sunken on their shoulders, puffed-up faces, squat, congealed, ponderous bodies and spread legs. Similarities with the *dvārapālas* in Cave 27 at Ellora and the sculptures at the Varaha Temple at DEOGARH, with their swelling bodies and curved arms, come to mind.

BIBLIOGRAPHY

M. Garde: 'The Site of Padmāvatī', *Archaeol. Surv. India, Annu. Rep.* (1915–16), pp. 100–110
R. D. Banerji: *The Temple of Śiva at Bhūmarā*, Mem. Archaeol. Surv. India, xvi (Calcutta, 1924)
J. Marshall and others: *The Bāgh Caves* (London, 1927)
J. Marshall, A. Foucher and N. G. Majumdar: *The Monuments of Sanchi*, 3 vols (Calcutta, 1940)
D. R. Patil: *Monuments of the Udayagiri Hill* (Gwalior, 1948)
M. S. Vats: *The Gupta Temple at Deogarh*, Mem. Archaeol. Surv. India (Delhi, 1952)
U. P. Shah: *The Sculptures from Śāmlāji and Rodā* (Baroda, 1960)
V. S. Agrawala: 'A Survey of Gupta Art and Some Sculptures from Nāchnā Kuthārā and Khoh', *Lalit Kala*, ix (1961), pp. 16–26
K. S. Dikshit: *A Guide to the Central Archaeological Museum, Gwalior* (Gwalior, 1962)
D. Mitra: 'Varāha-Cave of Udayagiri: An Iconographical Study', *J. Asiat. Soc.*, v/3–4 (1963), pp. 99–103
J. Rosenfield: 'On Dated Carvings of Sarnath', *Artibus Asiae*, xxvi/1 (1963), pp. 10–26
U. V. Singh: 'Execution at Eran', *J. Madhya Pradesh Itihasa Parishad*, iv (1963), pp. 41–4
D. Mitra: 'Śaṅkar-Maḍha at Kundā, District Jabalpur', *J. Asiat. Soc.*, vii (1965), pp. 70–81
P. K. Agrawala: 'A Note on the So-called Sūrya Statue from Pawāyā', *Bull. Anc. Ind. Hist. & Archaeol.*, xi (1968), pp. 67–9
R. C. Agrawala: 'Newly Discovered Sculptures from Vidiśā', *J. Orient. Inst., Baroda*, xviii/3 (1969), pp. 250–53
G. S. Gai: 'Three Inscriptions of Rāmagupta', *J. Bhandarkar Res. Inst.*, xviii/3 (1969), pp. 245–51
P. Chandra: *Stone Sculpture in the Allahabad Museum* (Pune, 1970)
——: 'A Vāmana Temple at Marhiā and Some Reflections on Gupta Architecture', *Artibus Asiae*, xxxii (1970), pp. 125–45
W. Spink: 'A Temple with Four Ucchakalpa Doorways at Nāchnā-Kuthārā', *Chhavi* (1971), pp. 161–72
J. C. Harle: 'On the Mahiṣasuramardinī Images of the Udayagiri Hill Caves', *J. Ind. Soc. Orient. A.*, iv (1971–2), pp. 44–8
U. P. Shah: 'Western Indian Sculpture and the So-called Gupta Influence', *Aspects of Indian Art*, ed. P. Pal (Leiden, 1972), pp. 44–8
J. Williams: 'The Sculptures of Māndāsor', *Archvs Asian A.*, xxvi (1972–3), pp. 50–66
——: 'A Recut Asokan Capital and the Gupta Attitude toward the Past', *Artibus Asiae*, xxxv (1973), pp. 225–40
M. Meister: 'A Note on the Superstructure of the Marhiā Temple', *Artibus Asiae*, xxxvi (1974), pp. 81–8
O. Viennot: 'Le Temple ruiné de Mukundara entre Mālwa et Rajasthan', *South Asian Archaeology, 1973* (Leiden, 1974), pp. 116–27
J. Williams: 'New Nāga Images from the Sanchi Area', *Oriental A.*, xxii/2 (1976), pp. 174–9
W. Spink: 'Bāgh: A Study', *Archvs Asian A.*, xxx (1976–7), pp. 53–84
C. Berkson: 'Some New Finds at Ramgar Hill, Vidisha District', *Artibus Asiae*, xl (1978), pp. 215–32
D. M. Stadtner: 'A Sixth-century Temple from Kośala', *Archvs Asian A.*, xxxiii (1980), pp. 38–48
——: 'Nāndchānd and a Central Indian Regional Style', *Artibus Asiae*, xliii (1981–2), pp. 129–36

KALYAN KUMAR CHAKRAVARTY

(v) East. The capital of the GUPTA dynasty (possibly of eastern Indian origin) may have been Prayag (modern ALLAHABAD), where an inscription of the monarch Samudragupta (*reg c.* 335–76) proclaims the territory that was included within his realm (*see* §(i) above). Although the claims are likely exaggerated, all of eastern India probably fell within Gupta territory. In central India, stone temples and many stone sculptures form a Gupta legacy (*see* §(iv) above). In eastern India, Gupta remains are more scant, though inscriptions indicate that Gupta art was once more extensive there. The architecture was brick and was often covered with stucco sculpture, even more fragile. Monuments such as the apsidal temple known as the Maniyar Math at RAJGIR, a brick structure whose central cylinder was adorned with magnificent stucco sculptures, give a sense of Gupta art in eastern India. A sensitively rendered image of the god *Vishnu*, a dancing *Shiva* and a superb *nāginī* (female serpent divinity) were among the fine stucco sculptures dating from *c.* 500 that were revealed when the Maniyar Math was excavated; only a short time later they were lost to the environment.

Little can be surmised about the architecture of temples in eastern India in this period, though there is inscriptional evidence for a number that are no longer extant at such sites as Jagdishpur, Baigram and Damodarpur in Bangladesh. Beautifully carved columns with small narrative panels once probably formed part of the largely brick temple at Rajaona (Munger District, Bihar), perhaps supporting the ceiling slab of a porch (*maṇḍapa*). Two large rectangular panels illustrating episodes of the *Rāmāyaṇa* epic, perhaps also forming part of this temple, were found at the site (see fig. 178). The sensitive modelling of the figures and rich carving of floral motifs corresponds well with fine Gupta art elsewhere in India. Only at the Sonbhandar caves of Rajgir, close to the Maniyar Math, do temple walls remain partially intact, in this case because these Jaina sanctuaries are rock-cut.

A number of other Gupta-period monuments are known from the area corresponding to modern Munger and Bhagalpur districts, Bihar. At Shahkund, for example, a superb 5th-century image of Vishnu's incarnation as the Man-Lion (*Narasimha*) remains in a modern temple. North of that site, at Sultanganj, is an island in the Ganga River, essentially a tall, rocky outcropping whose surface is carved with reliefs. The earliest of these sculptures, dating to *c.* 500, include a sensitive image of *Vishnu* reclining on the coils of the serpent Ananta or Sesha; the

178. *Rāmāyaṇa* panel, from Rajaona, *c.* late 5th century AD–early 6th

Ganga at the rock's base may have been equated, at least metaphorically, with the primordial waters on which the serpent floated. Just 55 km to the east, at Patharghata, are reliefs also illustrating Vishnu, particularly in his incarnation as Krishna, that date to about the same time. These are on a cliff overlooking the Ganga.

In Bengal, where stone is especially scarce, few Gupta sculptures are known. One, a Buddha figure from Biharail in Bangladesh, was probably imported from Sarnath, so closely does it resemble 5th-century work there (*see* §(i) above). A Vishnu figure from Narhatta, also in Bangladesh, is a local product. It is carved from dark grey stone and shares sufficient similarities with the Narasimha of Shahkund to be assigned a similar date.

Private patronage provided for these monuments and for Gupta sculpture and architecture elsewhere. That is, individuals (not the Gupta monarchs) seeking the merit believed to accrue from religious endowments paid for the works. The only known works provided by the Guptas themselves were at Nalanda, the great Buddhist monastery in Bihar that may in fact have been founded by them—literary evidence such as that of the 7th-century Chinese pilgrim Xuanzang is corroborated by the discovery at Nalanda of many Gupta royal seals, likely once attached to documents that recorded gifts of land to support the monastery. No monument prior to 550 survives at Nalanda, but a number of works there may be assigned to the 7th century (*see* §7(iv) below).

BIBLIOGRAPHY

R. D. Banerji: *Eastern Indian School of Medieval Sculpture*, Archaeol. Surv. India, New Imp. Ser., xlvii (Delhi, 1933)

S. K. Saraswati: *Early Sculpture of Bengal* (Calcutta, 1962)

P. L. Gupta: *Patna Museum Catalogue of Antiquities, Stone Sculptures, Metal Images, Terracottas and Minor Antiquities* (Patna, 1965)

F. M. Asher: *The Art of Eastern India, 300–800* (Minneapolis, 1980)

N. R. Ray, K. Khandalavala and S. Gorakshkar: *Eastern Indian Bronzes* (New Delhi, 1986)

S. L. Huntington and J. C. Huntington: *Leaves from the Bodhi Tree* (Dayton, OH, 1989)

FREDERICK M. ASHER

(vi) South. The stupa at Goli of *c.* early 4th century AD is probably the last major work of the early school of Amaravati (*see also* §5(vi) above). The transition from the mature Amaravati style to the later one can be traced particularly well in the free-standing Buddhas. The most distinctive feature of examples of this type datable to the 3rd–4th century from the Amaravati stupa area and from Uppukonduru (Madras, Govt Mus. & N.A.G.; Hyderabad, State Mus.) is the treatment of the thick upper robe, which, leaving the right shoulder bare, is drawn to the left side of the body, making a heavy swag at the bottom hem. This type, with the hair and cranial bump (*uṣṇīṣa*) covered with curls and the left hand held at shoulder height with its back turned towards the spectator, holding part of the robe, had been the model for the standing Buddhas produced in Tamil Nadu, Sri Lanka (*see* SRI LANKA, §IV, 1) and South-east Asia. A notable over life-size stone example in the round, datable to the 6th century, was recovered at Kanchipuram (Madras, Govt Mus. & N.A.G.; see Dehejia, p. 54, pl. 1). It exhibits the same features as the early Amaravati style. The face of this *Buddha* is full, though unsmiling; his body is robust but has protuberant flesh along the waistline; the right shoulder is bare, and the robe has a heavy swag at the bottom edge. The rather broad shoulders and the thickening of the hips suggest a date in the 6th century.

Early metal images are rare, but attention may be drawn to the surviving upper part of an exceptionally fine small *bodhisattva Avalokiteshvara* (London, V&A), which is probably from the Krishna Delta, where a number of Buddhist bronzes have been found. Its style combines the aesthetic tradition of the north-west Deccan with developments in the Andhra country. The treatment of the hair and even the flower ornament in the headdress recall an *Avalokiteshvara* at Kanheri, while the gesture of the surviving left hand is similar to a *bodhisattva* holding a lotus flower in Cave 1 at Ajanta. However, the full face is reminiscent of the mature phase at Amaravati. This bronze perhaps dates from *c.* 600.

Apart from the single sculptures just mentioned, the first substantial monuments after those at Amaravati and Nagarjunakonda are the cave shrines of modest size associated with the Chalukyas of Badami (*see* CHALUKYA, §1). At the height of their power the Chalukyas controlled most of the Deccan, their only significant rival being the Pallava dynasty to the south. The Chalukyas first excavated cave temples at AIHOLE and BADAMI and then, from the 7th century, built structural monuments at various sites in their realm. The Hindu cave shrines carved out of the red sandstone cliffs at Badami are all Vaishnava with two exceptions (one Shaiva, one Jaina). Only the most elaborate, Cave 3, is dated by inscription to AD 578. This epigraph is inscribed next to a large sculptural panel on the verandah showing Vishnu as Varaha, his boar incarnation, rescuing the Earth Goddess (see fig. 179). The allegorical identification of Varaha with the king as saviour and protector of the earth seems likely given that Varaha was used by the Chalukyas as a dynastic emblem. Another verandah panel shows the majestic *Vishnu Seated upon Shesha* (the coiled serpent of infinite time). A third panel represents *Vishnu Trivikrama*, striding across the universe. Some of these figures tend to be brutish and are usually shown standing rigidly with thick-set legs and oversized hands. However, the gods' jewellery is rendered with sensitivity, and some of the attendant figures are stylishly mannered in the true Gupta style. The quality is uneven, but the seated Vishnu is exceptional. Cave 3 shares with the Rameshvara at Ellora the charming feature of human couples as brackets. The Badami caves are notable less for the sculpted representations of deities than for the finely carved attendant figures and the decorative motifs on the ceilings.

179. *Vishnu as Varaha, Rescuing the Earth Goddess*, relief panel, Cave 3, Badami, 6th century AD

The Aihole caves, Brahmanical and Jaina, are equally finely decorated inside. The Shaiva Ravana Phadi has a splendid *Shiva Nataraja*, the Lord of Dance, flanked by dancing and standing mother goddesses (*mātṛkās*), an *Ardhanarishvara* (Shiva as half-man, half-woman) and an exceptional *Gangadhara* (Shiva receiving the River Ganga on his head) with his consort and the three river goddesses. A fine *Durga* slaying the buffalo-demon and a *Varaha* are carved on either side of the passageway into the sanctum. The tall-crowned figures with rather rounded faces are among the finest works of the early Chalukya period. They are highly individual. The legs are slender and delicately done, and the drapery is indicated by means of deeply scored parallel lines. Stylistically they have no counterparts in the caves at Badami, and they have neither predecessors nor successors in Karnataka. The same applies to the pair of doorkeepers in 'Scythian' costume outside the entrance to the Ravana Phadi. A softer and quite charming early post-Gupta style marks the faces of the graceful Aihole images, which were probably carved *c.* 600.

Early caves are also found at Mogulrajapuram, near Vijayawada, in the Andhra country. These shrines were excavated when the eastern branch of the Chalukyas had established itself on the lower reaches of the Krishna River. Cave 4, probably dating from the end of the 6th century, is particularly important for its fine dancing *Shiva*, which combines the northern penchant for a multi-armed figure with the southern theme of the god trampling a dwarf demon. On either side of the entrance to this cave are guardian figures, one of them horned, which are the precursors of the door-keepers in Pallava-period caves (*see* §7(vi)(a) below).

For discussions of contemporary architecture in south India *see* §III, 4(ii) above.

BIBLIOGRAPHY

D. Barrett: 'The Later School of Amarāvatī and its Influences', *A. & Lett.*, xxviii/2 (1954), pp. 41–53
G. Tartakov: 'Chronology and Development of the Chalukya Cave Temples', *A. Orient.*, viii (1970), pp. 156–84
J. C. Harle: 'Two Yavana Dvārapālas at Aihole', *The Professor K. A. Nilakantha Sastri 80th Birthday Commemoration Volume* (Madras, 1971), pp. 210–13
——: 'Some Remarks on Early Western Caluliya Sculpture', *Aspects of Indian Art*, ed. P. Pal (Leiden, 1972)
A. de Lippe: 'The Sculpture and Architecture of Southern India', *The Arts of India*, ed. B. Gray (Oxford, 1981), pp. 53–82
W. Zwalf: *Buddhism: Art and Faith* (London, 1985)
J. C. Harle: *The Art and Architecture of the Indian Subcontinent* (Harmondsworth, 1986)
V. Dehejia: 'The Persistence of Buddhism in Tamilnadu', *Marg*, xxxix/4 (?1988), pp. 53–74 [issue on new studies in Buddhist art]

O. M. STARZA-MAJEWSKI

7. 7TH–18TH CENTURIES. Sculptures were produced in great numbers from the 7th century, chiefly to embellish temples constructed by regional rulers and their subjects. (The period is sometimes designated 'medieval', a term of European origin that many scholars find problematic in an Indian context.) All the major gods and goddesses of the Brahmanical pantheon were represented as well as a host of minor deities. New conventions emerged for ornament and the iconography of images, while the forms of Vishnu and Shiva inherited from the 5th century were elaborated and regularized. Jaina saviours and attendant deities were the chief figures represented on numerous

Jaina temples. Buddhism generated a complex Tantric pantheon that had a profound impact on Buddhist art beyond India. The extraordinary art activity of the period may be linked with significant changes in the nature of Indian kingship, as royal Vedic sacrifices, patronized up to the 5th century, were set aside in favour of temple construction and the allegorical use of religious images to establish legitimacy.

Islam had been a feature of the Indian cultural landscape from the 8th century, but its impact on sculpture was negligible until the establishment of the Delhi Sultanate. In the 13th and 14th centuries, the Sultanate's expansionist policies led to the conquest of virtually all the subcontinent. This conquest was frequently accompanied by iconoclasm and brought about a decline in the indigenous élites that once patronized temple sculpture. The hold of Delhi over the south was weak, however, and a revival soon began under the Vijayanagara rulers; Timur's invasion of 1398–9 destroyed the hegemony of the Sultanate and allowed for further revivals of traditional art, particularly in western India. Away from these revivals, popular religious beliefs, essentially conservative and Hindu, fostered a vigorous folk tradition that still produces images in various media.

(i) North. (ii) North-west. (iii) West. (iv) Central. (v) East. (vi) South.

(i) North. In the 7th century centres of sculpture such as MATHURA and SARNATH (*see also* §5(i) above) declined in importance. KANNAUJ (ancient Kanyakubja) emerged as the imperial capital, and the cults surrounding the Hindu gods Vishnu and Shiva grew in popularity—as is attested by the Vaishnava and Shaiva images found at many sites. Upheavals accompanying Islamic incursions (from *c.* 1000) led to the destruction of virtually all the early temples in the Gangetic plain; few sculptures are preserved in their original context, and few can be associated with dated inscriptions. Architectural settings and the chronology of sculpture must therefore be reconstructed from what survives in neighbouring areas.

(a) 7th century. (b) 8th century. (c) 9th century. (d) 10th century and later.

(a) 7th century. During the first half of the 7th century Harshavardhana (*reg* 606–47) became the leading ruler of north India. Considerable information about him can be gleaned from the *Harṣacarita*, Bana's contemporary Sanskrit text (part history and part panegyric), and the memoirs of Xuanzang, the celebrated Chinese Buddhist pilgrim who spent several years in Harsha's kingdom. These accounts (exceptional when compared to how little has survived for other Indian kings) give detailed information about Harsha's reign and the public rituals he sponsored, which included large donative ceremonies and the veneration of Buddhist images. No temples or images, however, have been discovered that can be attributed to his patronage.

Outside Kannauj, the only building that can be attributed to Harsha's time is the ruined Shiva Temple at Mundeshvari, 70 km east of Varanasi. Located on the western edge of Bihar, the temple is best considered an extension of northern traditions and styles (*see* §III, 5(i)(a) above). Guardian figures are included in the niches at the bases of the doorjambs, and Brahmanical images were found scattered about the site (many now in Patna Mus.). While some pieces (such as a damaged set of *mātṛkās*, mother goddesses) date back to the 5th century, most belong to the first half of the 7th century. As a group these images are heavily cast and imbued with brooding rhythms. The faces have a sensuous fullness, but the limbs are often slightly distorted. An image of the sun God *Surya* found at Khairadih (Lucknow, State Mus.; see fig. 180) also displays these characteristics. A date for this figure in the first half of the 7th century is suggested by the ponderously rendered hands, broad shoulders and slightly awkward construction, a feature especially apparent in the attendant figures. The fussy detailing and symmetrical disposition of the ornaments in the crown are also typical of the period. This image was apparently carved from a capital of the MAURYA period, as is evidenced by the round base and fragmentary beaded border.

An analysis of the Mundeshvari and Khairadih sculptures (as well as of examples of the same date from Mahua, Vidisha (*see* BESNAGAR) and Sagar in central India) makes it possible to assign some sculptures from Kannauj to the first half of the 7th century. The most important is a standing figure of Shiva's consort, *Parvati* (Kannauj, Puratattva Sangrahalaya). This figure has heavy forms and

180. *Surya*, sandstone, 920×510 mm, from Khairadih, Uttar Pradesh, first half of the 7th century AD (Lucknow, State Museum)

a fully modelled face; there is a propensity for distortion and awkward construction, but these qualities are subdued compared to examples away from the capital. The roots of this figural style can be found in the *Buddha* from Mathura (Lucknow, State Mus.) dated Gupta year 280 (AD 599–600; *see* §6(i)(f) above). Its rude, ballooning forms represent the collapse of conventions established in the Gupta period, but also anticipate the full-bodied figures of the 7th century.

After Harshavardhana's death without issue in 647, the history of north India becomes difficult to chart. Inscriptions provide no evidence for important dynastic patrons, and—to judge from the number of surviving pieces—production evidently declined. Important developments were nonetheless taking place. Sculptures from eastern and central India show that the awkward touches seen in the first half of the 7th century were set aside, and a style of sensuous heaviness and extraordinary vigour emerged. Examples of this style in the Gangetic plain include a figure of the goddess *Durga Seated on a Lion* (Calcutta, Ind. Mus.) and a weather-worn figure of *Durga Killing the Buffalo Demon* (Chicago, IL, A. Inst.). Both were executed in the mottled red sandstone of Mathura. A figure of the god *Ganesha* from Ramnathpur (Allahabad Mus.) may also date to the second half of the 7th century.

(b) 8th century. Although no dated pieces of the 8th century have survived in the Gangetic plain, works from adjacent regions show that a more controlled handling of form emerged. The rippling modulations of flesh so typical of the 7th century were subdued; ornaments and draperies were also treated less ponderously. A standing *Vishnu* from Mathura (Lucknow, State Mus.) illustrates these qualities. The arms and legs of this figure have calm, taut surfaces, while the hour-glass torso displays a subtle breadth quite removed from the opulent modelling and vigorous lateral expansion favoured in the 7th century. The garlands and draperies have lost their plastic bulk and have been given flat, linear accents. The handling of the face is identical to that of an early 8th-century figure of *Brahmi* (consort of the god Brahma) from Kota (Gwalior, Archaeol. Mus.). The intricately wrought crown, which retains a degree of earlier heaviness, may be compared to ornaments on such images as the *Ganesha* from Gangola Tal, Gwalior Fort (Gwalior, Archaeol. Mus.).

These steps towards a more controlled style continued throughout the 8th century. An *Ardhanarishvara* image (half Shiva, half Parvati) from Kannauj (Kannauj, Puratattva Sangrahalaya) is indicative of mid-8th-century work (see fig. 181). A sense of rhythm sweeps through the whole form; the ornaments, while still sumptuous, have been firmly subordinated to the overall composition. The handling has not yet become tight or brittle, but the plastic feeling is more subdued than during the 7th century or the early 8th. With subdued modelling, the limbs have begun to take on a tubular quality, but the overt clumsiness and naivety often found in the regional idioms of central India have been avoided. Likewise the sense of rhythm has been held confidently in hand, never threatening the coherence of the image. An essential difference is discernible between the regional idioms and their metropolitan counterparts: while the former exhibit a tenacious effort

181. *Ardhanarishvara* (half Shiva, half Parvati), sandstone, from Kannauj, Uttar Pradesh, mid-8th century AD (Kannauj, Puratattva Sangrahalaya)

at excellence, those produced in Kannauj display an easy mastery and accomplishment. The *Ardhanarishvara* was probably made during the time of Yashovarman (*reg c.* 720–50), and while no sculptures can be attributed to royal patronage, this piece makes it clear that the sculptors of greatest skill worked in the capital.

Dated material at Kanswa (a suburb of Kota in Rajasthan) helps to fix the date of the *Ardhanarishvara*, providing at least one absolute point of reference for 8th-century sculpture. The most useful piece there from a chronological standpoint is a Shiva *liṅga* that is probably coeval with an inscription recording the foundation of a Shiva Temple in Malava year 795 (AD 738–9). One of the faces on the *liṅga* is nearly identical to the *Ardhanarishvara*, having the same arching eyebrows, carefully cut almond-shaped eyes, matted locks and delicate ornaments. The softer volume exhibited in the Kanswa sculpture may be due either to regional variation or to a slight difference in date. In either case the *liṅga* places the *Ardhanarishvara* firmly in the middle decades of the 8th century.

182. *Bhairava*, sandstone, from Kannauj, Uttar Pradesh, mid-9th century AD (Kannauj, Puratattva Sangrahalaya)

Sculptures of the late 8th century have survived in considerable numbers in central India, and developments in the Gangetic plain can be reconstructed from these examples. That a high standard of production was maintained is shown by an image of the river goddess *Ganga* from Etah (Varanasi, Banaras Hindu U., Bharat Kala Bhavan). This figure, which would have come from a temple doorframe, closely parallels the late 8th-century figures on the Gargaj Mahadev Temple at Indor in central India. The faces and limbs show the same precisely cut features and restrained modelling. In comparison to the *Ardhanarishvara* from Kannauj, the limbs are less tubular; a more fundamental difference, however, is the way in which the forms have been drained of their voluminousness. The ornaments have been regularized and rendered with precision. This sleek sculptural style directly anticipates developments in the 9th century.

Other examples from the late 8th century are found in a ruined temple of Shiva at Pathari, about 10 km from Jhansi (portions now in Jhansi Mus.). Of superlative quality, this work may have been executed by craftsmen from the Gangetic plain. Images of *Haragauri* (Shiva and his consort) from Mathura (New Delhi, N. Mus.) and of *Vishnu* from Kannauj (Vadodara, Mus. & Pict. Gal.) show the late 8th-century style at a less august level.

(c) 9th century. During the 9th century the GURJARA-PRATIHARA rulers of Rajasthan gained control of the Gangetic plain as well as portions of eastern and central India. Nagabhatta II (*reg c.* 810–33) was responsible for capturing Kannauj and making it the dynasty's capital. While no inscriptions have survived to indicate that he was a patron of the arts, Nagabhatta's reign can be used to bracket developments during the first part of the 9th century. Sculpture from his time is marked by a lyrical richness of detail and smooth coherence of modelling. The most splendid example is a four-faced Shiva *liṅga* from Kannauj (Kannauj, priv. col.). A measured restraint in the modelling has imbued the faces on the *liṅga* with unprecedented delicacy and beneficence. Gone are the heavy facial features and awkward modulations typical of the 8th century. The ornaments and coiffure are carefully detailed without being coolly precise. The Kannauj *liṅga* represents what is best in early 9th-century sculpture. It is a superlative summation of the period's style and a reminder that Kannauj was the imperial capital of north India and the source of its finest works. That sculpture approaching this calibre was made in other centres is evidenced by the torso of a *bodhisattva* from Sarnath (New Delhi, N. Mus.).

The long reign of Mihira Bhoja (*reg c.* 836–85) marked the pinnacle of Gurjara-Pratihara power and was likewise a highpoint in the sculpture of north India. As before, there are no inscriptions linking royalty to specific pieces, but many outstanding sculptures from Kannauj can be attributed to this period. A small figure of *Bhairava*, the terrifying form of Shiva (Kannauj, Puratattva Sangrahalaya; see fig. 182), demonstrates that the high standard of earlier years was maintained. The sleek and efficient modelling, an important characteristic of the mid-9th century, has been handled with unparalleled urbanity and ease. The same powerful assurance is flaunted in a pair of colossal images of *Vishnu Vishvarupa*, in the Makran Nagar Temple, Kannauj. Although the faces of these figures have been reworked, the rest shows how every detail, indeed every chisel stroke, was directed towards a single concentrated purpose.

Other important examples of mid-9th-century sculpture include a dancing *Ganesha* (Kannauj, priv. col.) and several images of Surya, Skanda and other Brahmanical gods (Kannauj, Puratattva Sangrahalaya). The finest specimens from outside the capital come from KAUSAMBI and include an image of the Jaina *tīrthaṅkara* (teacher) *Chandraprabha* and a richly carved doorframe from a vanished temple (both Allahabad Mus.).

The final stages of 9th-century sculpture coincide with the reign of Mahendrapala I (*reg c.* 885–910). Earlier conventions were maintained, but close inspection shows a tighter conception of form and greater sharpness of details. A well-known piece of the late 9th century is a panel of the *Kalyanasundara* (Marriage of Shiva and Parvati; Kannauj, priv. col.). The treatment of the forms on this stele, especially the handling of the faces, shows the increased emphasis on precision and line. In comparison to the earlier *Bhairava* from Kannauj, forms have been conceived less plastically. Also dating to this period is a seated *Tīrthaṅkara* from Potra Kund, Mathura (Mathura, Govt Mus.).

A broken image of *Uma-Maheshvara* (Shiva with Parvati; Kannauj, Puratattva Sangrahalaya; see fig. 183) probably dates to the opening years of the 10th century. The interest in decorative surface and lavish ornament that developed in the 10th century finds expression in a supple chiselling of coiffures and ornamental details. The waving drapery held delicately between Uma's fingers shows how the sculptor exploited every opportunity for a display of virtuosity. In this convincing and powerful image, Shiva and Parvati do not stare aimlessly but gaze passionately upon one another with an eternal dignity befitting their divine status. This special insight and strength of conception characterizes the sculpture from ancient Kannauj. Outside the capital, the metropolitan idiom of the early 10th century is seen in the temple known as Jarai Math near Barwa Sagar. Most of the images there have been mutilated, however.

(d) 10th century and later. The power of the Gurjara-Pratiharas rapidly declined during the time of Mahipala (*reg c.* 912–45) as strong regional kings emerged. The Lakshmana Temple (AD 954–5) at KHAJURAHO, built under the CHANDELLA dynasty (9th–12th century), heralds the hard, angular style that dominated sculpture in north and central India until the end of the 12th century. This style is characterized by sharp noses, pinched lips and prominent chins that are not convincingly incorporated into the rest of the face. Similarly, torsos are fragmented into a series of harsh planes and limbs arranged to accentuate dynamic line. When clustered together on temple walls, these sculptures create a vibrant and compelling surface, but the images cannot maintain their strength when removed from the architectural setting. An example illustrating this is a *Kalyanasundara* panel from Etah (Varanasi, Banaras Hindu U., Bharat Kala Bhavan). The consistency and widespread nature of this dynamic style may be explained by the increasing demand for sculpture that drew craftsmen from their home regions to places where large temple projects were underway.

In the 11th century, Afghans and Turks began to make incursions into north India. The most dramatic events in the doab were the sacking of Mathura and Kannauj by Mahmud of Ghazna in 1017–18. Chroniclers indicate that hundreds of idols were overthrown and their temples destroyed. In the upheavals that followed these raids, the Pratihara lineage was eventually extinguished, and the city of Kannauj seems to have entered a period of decline. The Kalachuri rulers played an increasingly important role in the region. While Kalachuri hegemony was challenged by the Chandella and PARAMARA dynasties, Karna Kalachuri (*reg c.* 1041–72) was able to control Varanasi and is recorded to have built a temple there (the building has not survived). The dynasties competing with the Kalachuris also built actively in cities under their control. Fragments from Kausambi and elsewhere testify to a vigorous campaign of reconstruction after the Ghaznavid raids. A preoccupation with increasing scale—the most conspicuous feature of temple architecture in the 11th century—

183. *Uma-Maheshvara* (Shiva with Parvati), sandstone, from Kannauj, Uttar Pradesh, early 10th century (Kannauj, Puratattva Sangrahalaya)

led to a general decline in the quality of individual images. Sculpture became increasingly conventional. Traits that first appeared at Khajuraho in the mid-10th century were accentuated; figures were starkly distinguished from their ground, and details became increasingly sharp. Scrollwork was reduced to flat, stencil-like patterns, a feature often seen in surviving temple fragments.

After the mid-11th century, the Ghaznavids were unable to pursue their Indian conquests. The Gahadavala dynasty rose to prominence in the eastern doab and maintained Varanasi as their capital; a temple of the period is preserved at Kandwa, on the outskirts of the city. While this building carries some sculpture, more representative examples have been recovered from the large ruin at Jamsot. These sculptures (Allahabad Mus.) display a hard, metallic quality, their frenzied movements and expressions being stylized to the extreme. The brittle forms are bedecked by crisply rendered ornaments; large necklaces with radiating spikes are especially characteristic. In the western doab the pillars in the Quwwat al-Islam Mosque at Delhi provide a comprehensive picture of 12th-century ornament (*see* DELHI, §III, 1). The most instructive sculpture is an image of *Vishnu* (New Delhi, N. Mus.) recovered from the Quwwat al-Islam precinct, which bears an inscription dated Vikrama era 1204 (AD 1147–8). The style is identical to Jamsot and indicative of the rigidity of Indian sculpture on the eve of the Islamic conquest.

From the late 12th century on, north India was an integral part of the Delhi sultanate. Although traditional practices were severely disrupted by the conquest, sculptors soon found new employment. The façade of the Quwwat al-Islam Mosque, dated Dhu'l-Qa'da, AH 594 (September 1198), was constructed by Indian craftsmen and exhibits the wholesale transfer of indigenous motifs to the repertory of Indo-Islamic architecture. The scrollwork and floral sprays on the façade are entirely Indian, but they were rendered with a freshness and vigour that would have been impossible before the conquest. This creative dynamism is symptomatic of the positive effort of the GHURID dynasty to forge a new Islamic dispensation that assimilated and surpassed its predecessors.

See also §III, 5(i)(a), and 6(i)(a) and (ii)(b) above.

BIBLIOGRAPHY

J. P. Vogel: *Catalogue of the Archaeological Museum at Mathura* (Allahabad, 1910)
V. S. Agrawala: *A Short Guide Book to the Archaeological Section of the Provincial Museum, Lucknow* (Allahabad, 1940)
——: 'Buddha and Bodhisattva Images', *J. United Prov. Hist. Soc.*, xxi (1948), pp. 43–98
——: 'Images of Brahma, Vishnu and Siva, etc.', *J. United Prov. Hist. Soc.*, xxii (1949), pp. 102–210
——: 'Jaina Tirthankaras and Other Miscellaneous Figures', *J. United Prov. Hist. Soc.*, xxiii (1950), pp. 35–147
——: 'Architectural Pieces', *J. United Prov. Hist. Soc.*, xxiv (1951), pp. 1–160 [the foregoing articles constitute a cat. of the Govt Mus., Mathura]
P. Chandra: *Stone Sculpture in the Allahabad Museum* (Pune, 1970)
N. P. Joshi: *Catalogue of the Brahmanical Sculptures in the State Museum, Lucknow* (Lucknow, 1972)
F. M. Asher: *The Art of Eastern India, 300–800* (Minneapolis, 1980)
S. Huntington with J. Huntington: *The Art of Ancient India: Buddhist, Hindu, Jain* (New York and Tokyo, 1985) [Kannauj sculp. are illus. as figs 20.3, 20.4]

MICHAEL D. WILLIS

(ii) North-west. Sculptures in the 6th–7th-century style of north India have been found all over the north-west, while Jammu and Kashmir also have yielded sculptures in the style of Gandhara (*see* §§6 (i) and (ii), and 7(i) above). Surviving bronzes come mostly from the hilly areas. Except for Himachal Pradesh, north-west India suffered heavy destruction of cultural property during and after the Muslim conquest, which began *c.* 1000. The gigantic images of the Buddha and Brahmanic deities that are mentioned in Kalhana's *Rājataraṅgiṇī* ('River of kings'; 12th century) have not survived.

(a) Jammu and Kashmir. (b) Himachal Pradesh. (c) Punjab. (d) Haryana.

(a) Jammu and Kashmir. Kashmir became prosperous and strong in the late 7th century. The Karkota ruler Lalitaditya Muktapida (*reg c.* 724–760), who controlled large parts of India and Central Asia in the 8th century, built several huge temples enshrining numerous images in metal and stone. The commingling of the sculptural idioms of GUPTA-period north India and of Gandhara, and the assimilation of motifs from Iran, Central Asia and China, contributed to the creation in the 8th century of a well-defined but still essentially Indian school of sculpture in Kashmir. In these works mass is delineated gracefully, and modelling is naturalistic. Torsos appear powerful, with prominent pectoral muscles and creased abdomens; faces are generally broad and eyebrows arched and well marked; eyes are usually conspicuous and elongated; noses are broad and mouths, though small, are well modelled. Exquisite finish and precise detailing enhance the beauty of Kashmiri sculpture, whether in metal or stone. Except for architectural reliefs, chlorite was generally popular for free-standing sculpture, since it allowed polishing and the precise rendering of details. The *saptamātṛkā* images from Pandrethan (Srinagar, Sri Pratap Singh Mus.) represent old traditions of Kashmiri sculpture continuing into the 8th century. These images are strongly modelled and have rounded contours. Their garments, whether based on Iranian or local conventions, cling to their bodies, revealing the forms underneath in the Indian manner. A crowned *Buddha* from the Parihasapura stupa (built by Chankuna, a Tocharian minister of Lalitaditya), though Indian in spirit, shows Chinese influence in the modelling of the face, while the crown and its side streamers are Sasanian.

Having crystallized by the mid-8th century, the Kashmiri style continued for over 300 years with only minor changes. An 8th-century brass image of a *Preaching Buddha* (Richmond, VA Mus. F.A.) exhibits ponderous modelling that nonetheless appears naturalistic and vital. The proportions of the 9th-century sculptures of AVANTIPURA are slightly different. In comparison, the bronze *Lokeshvara* (a form of the *bodhisattva* Avalokiteshvara) of the early 11th century (Srinagar, Sri Pratap Singh Mus.) is

184. *Shiva*, stone, h. 470 mm, from Akhnur, Jammu, 9th century AD (Jammu, Dogra Art Gallery)

tightly modelled. While the face of the main figure is broad, those of the attendants are narrow. By the 10th century silver and copper were being used to inlay eyes, lips, nails and sometimes garments. Most Kashmiri bronzes of deities have a nimbus and body aureole; this practice extended even to small bronzes from adjoining areas.

Literary sources indicate that the worship of the god Vishnu provided a strong stimulus for Kashmiri sculpture from the Gupta period on. The *Pāñcarātra* doctrine, centring around the god and his emanations (*vyūha*s; *see* §II, 1 above) was popular. Images of him are usually four-faced, the two faces at the sides being those of a boar and a lion. Archaeological evidence and references in the *Rājataraṅgiṇī* and other texts suggest that Shaivism, too, was popular; indeed, Kashmir has its own Shaiva school. Hari-Hara images, representing the unity of Vishnu and Shiva were made in Kashmir from the 9th century. A 9th-century three-faced *Shiva* from Akhnur in Kashmiri style (see fig. 184) is reminiscent of Vishnu images. Both the plumpness of the faces and the way in which the braided hair frames the two faces on the sides point to influence from Central Asia. The god's inner necklace is of north Indian type, but the unusual outer necklace, which appears to be made of hardstones or possibly bone pieces, suggests outside influence during this period.

Buddhism was equally popular in Kashmir. Sculptures from the regions of Ladakh and Lahul are in Kashmiri style, though sometimes they differ in minor ways. Many bronze images by Kashmiri artists are still worshipped in monasteries in these areas.

(b) Himachal Pradesh. Sculpture of Himachal Pradesh represents several styles. A 7th-century stone sculpture of *Surya*, the sun god, in the north Indian style has a Sasanian costume and hairstyle (from Gum, now Chamba, Bhuri Singh Mus.). The splendid early 8th-century brass images from BRAHMAUR and CHHATRADI, the work of an artisan called Gugga, are in a style that was in vogue over a large area. In one figure, of a goddess named in an inscription as *Lakshana*, the slender waist contrasts with full hips and thighs. Similar sculptures of a slightly later date survive at several sites in this region. The *Shaktidevi* image (a personification of feminine energy) from Chhatradi, a later work by Gugga, shows a slightly different style. It appears angular, and the modelling is somewhat tight. The brass image of *Narasimha* (Vishnu's *avatāra* as a man-lion) at Brahmaur shows close iconographic and stylistic affinity with a late 8th-century stone image of the same deity from Kashmir (Srinagar, Sri Pratap Singh Mus.). The brass images of *Vishnu Caturmurti* (9th century) and *Shiva with Parvati* (10th century) under worship in temples at Chamba exhibit Kashmiri characteristics in their modelling—particularly the torsos—and in the use of silver and copper inlay. Stone sculptures here generally follow Kashmiri style.

While some sculptures in Kashmiri style have been discovered in Kangra (Lahore Mus.; Simla, Himachal State Mus.; Dharamsala, Kangra A. Mus.), works of the 7th–8th century from that site show affinities in modelling and the rendering of drapery with sculpture of the Gangetic plains. The sculptures at the late 8th-century rock-cut temples of MASRUR are in a distinct style generally different from that of Kashmir, but various motifs and architectural features peculiar to the latter area are nonetheless seen here. The Masrur sculptures and others at Kangra Fort emphasize curves in their modelling, and the surfaces appear sensitive and smooth.

Sculptures from Kulu, figures of Garuda and Surya from BAJAURA (Simla, Himachal State Mus.), and the wooden images of a *yakṣī* (nature spirit) and other figures at Gazan (Kulu), in the temple of the *devī*s (goddesses) Docha and Mocha, all follow the idioms of the Gangetic plains from the period leading up to the 7th century. Later works, however, show an assimilation of Kashmiri traits. The sculpture of south-eastern Himachal Pradesh indicates that this area was influenced by Uttar Pradesh; some works, products of workshops in the plains, have also been discovered here. The Spiti Valley has yielded sculpture showing clear Kashmiri affiliations as well as pieces in a local style developed by assimilating influences from Kashmir itself (the strongest influence), north India and western Tibet. Some sculptures in marble seen in temples at Chamba and Lahul suggest contacts with the north-west; marble was commonly used for images in the Shahi kingdom of Kashmir (6th–9th century).

Metal plaques with images of Brahmanic and local deities or of ancestors, showing a fully rounded face and a summary rendering of part of the bust, are peculiar to Sirmur, the Simla Hills, Mandi and Kulu, all situated on an old trade route from Uttar Pradesh to Ladakh and Kashmir. This kind of image, locally called a *mohra*, is cast in the lost-wax process. Such sculptures were in vogue first in Sirmur and the hills of Uttar Pradesh, and the oldest examples have a stylistic affinity with sculpture from the Gangetic plains. The tradition travelled from the south-east to the north-west right up to Kulu. Later works show angular treatment of faces and eyes. Busts made of metal sheets are later in date, and their technique indicates Tibetan influence.

(c) Punjab. Stone sculptures have been discovered at several sites, including Dholbaha, Ghanauli, Majhoor and Mandian. Sculptures at Dholba from different periods and in different styles indicate the general movements that influenced the area. A *Vishnu* image of *c.* 7th century, discovered at Dholbaha, is modelled in a full and simple manner. The deity's crown is of the north Indian Gupta-period type. Sculptures of the 8th century of *Shiva with Parvati* and of *Mahishamardini* (Durga slaying the buffalo demon) are not fully modelled. Later sculptures show traces of Kashmiri influence. A *Vishnu* head of *c.* 10th century, with a round face, narrow, long eyes, clearly marked eyebrows and a well-modelled, small mouth, is in the Kashmiri style, even though the cylindrical crown decorated with a lion and strings of pearls is of north Indian type. The modelling of a dancing figure of the god *Ganesha* and the crown he wears with crescents containing lotuses show Kashmiri affiliation.

Sculptures of the 11th century and later, such as an *Uma-Maheshvara* seated on the bull Nandi, are different in style. The figures are slim and are embellished with ornaments treated in the manner associated with central India from the 10th century on (*see* §7(iv) below). Another sculpture shows excessively elongated figures with small heads and tightly modelled legs, a type seen at Chandravati and other sites in Rajasthan of the 11th–12th century. In a sculpture of *Uma-Maheshvara* of *c.* 11th century from Ghanauli, the faces appear softly modelled, but are expressionless and disproportionate to the bodies. Other figures carved on this stele are in strict horizontal and vertical registers, as was the practice during this period in Uttar Pradesh and Rajasthan. Most of these sculptures are preserved in the Punjab Government Museum, Sadhu Ashram, Hoshiarpur.

(d) Haryana. A large number of sculptures have survived in Haryana (many are preserved in Haryana Archaeol. Mus.). Sculptures of the 8th century show an overall simplicity of expression and sensitive plastic surface, as seen in the figures of the wealth god, *Kubera*, from Sirsa and the god *Brahma*, from Pehowa. In a sculpture of *Vishnu with Gadadevi and Chakrapursha* from Agroha (see fig. 185), the modelling of the three faces shows different approaches. The face of Gadadevi is narrow, while that of Vishnu is broad. The upper part of Vishnu's torso is well modelled, but the lower part, the legs in particular, appear tightly modelled. A tendency towards such a treatment of limbs can be seen in sculpture of this region from the late 7th century on. The heavy breasts and slender waist of a sculpture of *Mahishamardini* from Sirsa (late 9th century) are softly modelled. However, the somewhat tightly modelled limbs and their angular disposition indicate the style of the period.

The figures in later sculptures are loaded with decorative attributes and appear relatively stiff, with blank expressions. At Pinjaur sculptures and the remains of an extensive temple of *c.* 9th–10th century are preserved *in situ.* The former show stylistic affinities with the sculptures of Himachal Pradesh. Somewhat later sculptures from Pinjaur have affinities with the elongated figures from Chandravati and related sites in Rajasthan and similar work in the Punjab.

See also §III, 5(i)(b).

185. *Vishnu with Gadadevi and Chakrapursha*, stone, h. 1.45 m, from Agroha, Haryana, 9th century AD (Chandigarh, Government Museum and Art Gallery)

BIBLIOGRAPHY

J. P. Vogel: *Antiquities of Chamba State* (Calcutta, 1911)
R. C. Kak: *Handbook of the Archaeological and Numismatic Sections of the Sri Pratap Singh Museum, Srinagar* (Calcutta, 1923)
H. Goetz: *The Early Wooden Temples of Chamba* (Leiden, 1955)
D. Barrett: 'Bronzes from Northwest India and Western Pakistan', *Lalit Kala*, xi (1965), pp. 35–44
S. E. Lee: 'Clothed in the Sun: A Buddha and a Surya from Kashmir', *Bull. Cleveland Mus. A.*, lxvii/2 (1967), pp. 42–50
M. Singh: *Himalayan Art* (Greenwich, 1968)
H. Goetz: *Studies in the History and Art of Kashmir and the Indian Himalaya* (Wiesbaden, 1969)
V. C. Ohri: *Arts of Himachal* (Simla, 1975)
P. Pal: *Bronzes of Kashmir* (Graz, 1975)
D. L. Snellgrove and T. Shorupski: *The Cultural Heritage of Ladakh*, 2 vols (Warminster, 1977–80)
H. Diserens: 'Six Unpublished Anthropomorphic Wooden Sculptures at Gazan (Kulu)', *Cent. Asia. J.*, xxv/3–4 (1981), pp. 163–73
D. C. Bhattacharyya: *Medieval Indian Sculpture in the Government Museum and Art Gallery Chandigarh* (Chandigarh, 1981)
U. von Schroeder: *Indo-Tibetan Bronzes* (Hong Kong, 1981)
D. E. Klimburg-Salter: *The Silk Route and the Diamond Path: Esoteric Buddhist Art on the Trans-Himalayan Trade Routes* (Los Angeles, 1982)
S. Huntington with J. Huntington: *The Art of Ancient India: Buddhist, Hindu, Jain* (New York and Tokyo, 1985)
M. Postel, A. Neven and K. Mankodi: *Antiquities of Himachal* (Bombay, 1985)
The Sculpture of India: 300 BC–1300 AD (exh. cat. by P. Chandra, Washington, DC, N.G.A., 1985)
J. C. Harle: *The Art and Architecture of the Indian Subcontinent* (Harmondsworth, 1986, rev. 1987/*R* 1990)
V. C. Ohri: *Sculpture of the Western Himalayas* (New Delhi, 1991)

VISHWA CHANDER OHRI

(iii) West.

(a) Rajasthan and Gujarat. (b) Maharashtra.

(a) Rajasthan and Gujarat. While the idea of a unified empire and a coherent stylistic norm has been argued for much of north India during the period of Gupta supremacy, in western India this cohesiveness is a less viable concept, as sculptors either pursued independent directions or responded in a localized fashion to the overall stylistic trends of the 5th century (*see* §6(iii)(a) and (b) above). In the centuries after the Gupta period a rapid diversification and clarification of regional identities occurred in western India. There, as elsewhere, regional

permutations of artistic norms can often be informative about political and historical events.

7th–9th centuries. Between the 7th and the 9th centuries several Rajput clans, the most renowned of which was the GURJARA-PRATIHARA clan, rose to prominence. This powerful family distinguished itself in the middle of the 8th century in the wake of Arab raids on India's western coast and frontiers. The family's subsequent history dominated the course of events in Rajasthan. Its members advanced (possibly from a home base in ancient Gurjaradesha, at the junction of the south-west portion of modern Rajasthan and northern Gujarat), gaining control of the imperial capital at Kannauj in the early 9th century. While the power bases of other clans were not as extensive or powerful as that of the Gurjara-Pratiharas, they established strong local identities that in many cases persisted for centuries. In Rajasthan the Chahamanas in Sapadalaksha and Guhilas in Mewar were particularly prominent among the several lineages that governed portions of the region. In Gujarat the Maitrakas of Valabhi ruled over the Saurashtra peninsula from about the late 5th century to the 8th century.

The terms of stylistic transition in western India after the 6th century differed little from the response in other areas. There was a general shedding of overt refinement, a renewed vitality accompanied at times by a naive clumsiness, and a tendency towards ponderosity. Often described as the disintegration of a 'classical' apogee of artistic accomplishment, the style of this period is frequently uneven and inconsistent; nonetheless, it can also be fresh, with a less self-conscious aesthetic than that of the Gupta period. It heralds a new way of handling the human figure, one that coalesced later into a style that successfully mediated between embellished naturalism and iconic exactness. This formulation was yet to be worked out successfully in the 7th and 8th centuries, and the transformation of the early style into its most mature exposition was not achieved until the 9th century.

South-western Rajasthan (including the Sirohi, Abu, Udaipur and Dungarpur regions) appears to have formed an important plexus of artistic activity in the 7th century, as is attested by the remains of a Shiva Temple at Kusuma and a number of images of goddesses and of Surya, the sun god. These compare well with sculptures found throughout neighbouring northern Gujarat, and indeed it seems that most of the sculptural remains from this area of Rajasthan are later offshoots of the SHAMALAJI stylistic complex.

The Shiva Temple at Kusuma has been associated with an inscription of AD 636 (Vikrama era 693) recovered from its ruins, and stylistic features accord with a 7th-century date. The figures of a female celestial and of a door-guardian (in situ) that originally occupied the over-door retain the suave, somewhat refined hallmarks of such late Gupta-era examples as a 6th-century Shamalaji guardian figure (Bombay, Prince of Wales Mus.), with which they have a clear affinity (*see* §6(iii) (b) above). A shift towards a simpler, more summary formulation indicates a move away from the overt aestheticism of the 6th century, however. The three-headed *Maheshamurti* bust (Shiva as Great Lord) that occupies the sanctum at Kusuma is quite ornate in the superb detailing of the three faces and the subtle distinctions between the emanations' ornaments and headdresses. Yet despite the attention to detail, 6th-century naturalism and equilibrium have given way to a new formulation, seen in the broad, flattened central face, the disproportionately small arms and hands and the stiffness in the carving, which renders the image more distant and iconic.

Echoes of the Shamalaji style are also apparent in the numerous *mātṛkā* (mother goddess) and other goddess images from Udaipur, Mt Abu and other related sites in both Rajasthan and northern Gujarat, most of which date from the 7th century and early 8th. They typically feature a single seated image of a squat, curvaceous goddess with attributes and, if a *mātṛkā*, with a child. They are distinguished by their extremely taut, dense modelling, lateral description of form and weighty stasis. These tendencies are repeated in a pair of bronze *jina*s (Jaina teachers), dated to AD 697 (Vikrama era 744), recovered from a cache discovered in a Jaina temple at Vasantgarh (now in a Jaina temple, Pindavada, Rajasthan). These figures are modelled with a strained clarity that emphasizes breadth and that is most obvious in the expansive chests and full thighs; this is not simply a 7th-century trait but an enduring characteristic of sculpture from this region.

Further east, the Sitaleshvara Mahadeva Temple at Jhalrapatan (Chandrabhaga), datable to 689–90, stands as one exemplar of style from the Jhalawar region. Sculptural style in this area is related to that of central India and undoubtedly formed part of a larger stylistic continuum that stretched across the Malwa region. Connections to earlier monuments, such as the 5th-century temple at Mukundarra (*see* §6(iii)(a) above), survive in modified form, as can be seen in the shallow, slightly more programmatic floriate carving on the pillars and inner door-jambs and in the river goddess and attendant figures at their bases. Compared to a Mukundarra jamb fragment (Kota, Govt Mus.), the attendants at Jhalrapatan seem more restless and less serenely balanced, introducing a measure of angularity and broadness of contour. More indicative of larger regional characteristics are the figures of *Ardhanarishvara* (half Shiva and half Parvati) and *Durga Mahishasuramardini* (Durga vanquishing the buffalo demon) that were also recovered from Jhalrapatan (Jhalawar, Archaeol. Mus.). Their tall, lithe figures with squared shoulders, long waists, rounded bellies, slim hips and tubular limbs presage the remarkably similar formulation of the renowned stele depicting a royal couple with groom, produced in central India approximately half a century later (U. Sagar, Archaeol. Mus.; *see* §(iv) below).

Finally, a grouping of the *saptamātṛkā*s (seven mother goddesses) accompanied by Shiva and Ganesha that is carved into the face of a large rock near Mandor Fort is one of the few early examples from ancient Marwar, the desert heartland of Rajasthan. The panel has been dated to the 7th century on the basis of stylistic considerations and its purported association with a nearby inscription of AD 685. The bluntly modelled figures are particularly massive, awkward and somewhat rough.

The change in style from the 7th to the 8th century was subtle but definitive; sculpture in western India for the most part followed trends established in north India (*see*

§(i) above). There was a growing interest in rich ornament, and the expansiveness so characteristic of the 7th century was modified in favour of more constricted surfaces, angular posturing and robust, lively expressiveness. While forms were still broadly simplified, they were contained within stronger contours. As a consequence, implied movements seem more controlled and coherent. These trends are particularly evident in the figures that occupy the niches of the Surya Temple 1 at OSIAN, for example in the powerful figure of *Ganesha* in the southern central niche (*bhadra*). Also falling within the first half of the 8th century is the Mahadeva Temple at Bithu, just over the border from Jodhpur into Pali District, where the figures are more restrained and graceful than their hardy counterparts at Osian.

A more sophisticated idiom is exemplified by the Kumbhashyama and Kalika temples at CHITTAURGARH, where a Malwa style of Mukundarra and Chandrabhaga is subject to a particularly ornate and agitated stylization. Regional differences are pronounced: in contrast with the sharper-edged, deeper and more geometrically abrupt detail on the contemporary Surya Temple 1 at Osian, the ornament on the Kalika and Kumbhashyama temples is shallowly carved and animates surfaces with a show of decorative linear virtuosity. The tall, relatively languid figure of the god *Varuna* from the Kalika sanctum's northwest *karṇa* (corner wall division) exemplifies this, standing on his vehicle, the *makara* (crocodile-like mythical water beast), who is provided with a florid, upswept tail. The Malwa predilection for surface ornament and a tubular conception of the body can be seen in simpler form in the two sub-shrines (known as no. 1 and no. 2) at Menal.

The prodigious amount of temple building through the 8th and 9th centuries, particularly across Rajasthan, reflected the gradual consolidation of power and patronage under the Gurjara-Pratiharas and their powerful tributaries. Indeed, the burgeoning power of the former dominated politics not only in Rajasthan but also in large tracts of north India through the 8th and 9th centuries, and a seemingly responsive burst of artistic production accompanied their rise. At Osian the presence of the Gurjara-Pratiharas in the second half of the 8th century is recorded in a 10th-century inscription found in the Mahavira Temple complex, and Osian provides a virtual laboratory for the ongoing experiments of the 8th and 9th centuries.

Paradigmatic of the type of male physique particularly favoured throughout the latter half of the 8th century at Osian is a figure of the *dikpāla* (directional guardian) *Indra*, located on the south-east *karṇa* of the Mahavira Temple. The body has become a geometric assembly of parts that is more abstract than natural in its description of form. Ornament is intensely decorative and often borders on the extravagant, a trait taken to great heights on the roughly contemporary Hari-Hara 2 and 3 temples and one characteristic of the site. In addition, sculpture at this point was executed with a greater sense of spatial independence and more salient treatment of detail and ornament. At Osian a dramatic change in the description of figures occurred at the end of the century. What had been massive robustness as seen on the Surya Temple 1 became geometric clarity. Architectural and sculptural ornament also became more profuse and complex, with figures integrated into more complicated decorative schemes. That the end of the 8th century was a time of transition can be seen in the mixed character of the images of the Surya 3 temple. The singular figure of *Durga Mahishasuramardini* from the north *bhadra* niche is described with a forceful clarity and powerful naturalism, bearing her weapons authoritatively and brandishing her arsenal of attributes in a seemingly effortless display. The surrounding space is animated by her gestures and by her aggressive projection from the confines of the niche. These features would prompt a dating at the very end of the century or even at the beginning of the 9th, but subsidiary figures on the temple retain characteristics consonant with slightly earlier developments at the site.

Some general stylistic features—notably the burgeoning independence and animation of the figures and the increasing vitality of ornamental detail—are shared by examples from other areas of western India. Yet despite many common characteristics, regional differences in the formulation of the figures are pervasive and continuous. This is demonstrated in an unusual grouping of figures of nude *yoginīs* (goddesses who practise yoga) stored in a small temple at Jhalrapatan. These figures are strikingly analogous to the mid-8th-century stele cited above that depicts a royal couple. With it they share such features as lanky bodies, tubular limbs and prominent breasts set high over attenuated waists and narrow hips. The broader development of sculptural style in this period must be understood along with regional nuances; in the case of the Jhalrapatan *yoginīs*, a central Indian idiom (in particular that of Malwa and related regions) is clearly the strongest determinant of style.

Temples were also built in increasing numbers in Gujarat. Despite the lush sculptural heritage of the Shamalaji examples, temples in Gujarat from the 7th through the 9th century were not provided with the extensive sculptural ornamentation that typifies monuments to the north and east. There was instead a stronger commitment to structural and decorative lucidity, with figural sculpture held modestly in check and confined to the doorways and central niches (*bhadras*) of exterior walls. The figures that ornament the doorframe of Temple 3 at RODA are softer, more fluid and less ornamented versions of their contemporaries on Osian's Mahavira and Hari-Hara 2 and 3 temples. A seated *Surya* on the west wall of Temple 6 is simply and solidly stated, with embellishment judiciously applied to the headdress and tunic.

The pursuit of a new artistic norm through the 7th and 8th centuries coalesced in the 9th into a mature expression that marks the apex of this era of experimentation. The definitive stylization of the latter half of the 8th century was maintained but in a more relaxed fashion. Figures were less dense and not as tied to their architectural framework. This increased salience from the architectural matrix resulted in a growing complexity in the postures of, and space around, the figures. Hallmarks of the era are a controlled, coherent description of form, a concentrated dynamism and a greater feeling of naturalism. Regional differentiations continued to be marked.

For the 9th century the only complete, dated temples in Rajasthan are the two modest shrines at Buchkala, dedicated in AD 815 (Vikrama era 872) during the reign of the Gurjara-Pratihara ruler Nagabhatta II (*reg* AD 810–33). Reference to dated images from outside western India—in particular Madhya Pradesh—is thus necessary to provide the foundation on which to build an understanding of the development of style. Regional variations must be borne in mind, however, when extrapolating from such monuments as the AD 860–61 (Vikrama era 917) pillar at BADOH, a column dated AD 862 at DEOGARH and the Chaturbhuja Temple at Gwalior of AD 875–6 (Vikrama era 932; *see* §7(iv) below and GWALIOR, fig. 1).

Despite the worn condition and abbreviated rendering of the Buchkala shrine figures, seen for example in the *Trivikrama* (Vishnu as Conqueror of the Three Worlds) from the south *bhadra*, subtle stylistic changes are discernible. These are amplified and more clearly stated in the energetic and spatially complex figure of *Mahishasuramardini* in the north *bhadra* niche on the Shiva Temple at Bhundana, where the advances presaged in the Surya 3 *Durga* are taken further. A less successful example from this same time frame is the Pipla Devi Temple at Osian, where the figures exhibit 9th-century characteristics in diluted fashion.

The Harshatmata Temple at ABANERI, sometimes dated to the late 8th century (*see* §III, 5(i)(c)) but more likely of the early 9th, stands in ruins, and its sculptural programme is mostly lost. Clearly, it was an exceptional and lavishly adorned monument. What does remain is distinguished by both the consummate quality of its sculptural embellishment and the unusual subject-matter represented on the exterior of the circumambulatory passage. In a series of 12 sculpted panels, scenes of a male royal figure paired with a consort and surrounded by attendants are rendered in a lush, sensuous manner full of surprising and often whimsical details (see fig. 186). The extraordinary delicacy of the carving, executed with a goldsmith's precision, and the range and depth of the figures' expressiveness are highly accomplished and unparalleled elsewhere. In addition, fragments near the temple and stored in a nearby STEPWELL attest to a rich iconographic tradition drawing on both Vaishnava and Shaiva imagery.

A softer variation of this elegant style is seen in a number of images from Kaman, a site in Bharatpur District not far from Mathura. A rendering of *Shiva and Parvati*, his consort, from the late 8th century (Ajmer, Govt Mus.) and another from the mid-9th century (Bharatpur, State Mus.) perpetuate the distinctive characteristics of the Mathura region in their heavy, smoothly volumetric figures and emphasis on shapely, rounded contours. A Shiva *liṅga* (Bharatpur, State Mus.) distinguished by its weighty sobriety and delicate ornamentation also falls in this category.

The stylistic features that differentiate sculpture from south-western Rajasthan and much of northern Gujarat, notably a solid sense of form and a pervasive fluid curvaceousness, are exhibited in the 9th-century Kameshvara Temple at Auwa. That temple's mediating position between north and south is, however, seen in the way in which the figures are enlivened by refined surface ornamentation that is reminiscent of trends seen at Osian. From the Sirohi area, two contemporary female figures, a *Gajalakshmi* (the goddess Lakshmi being lustrated by elephants) from Varman and a *Durga Mahishasuramardini* from the Surya Temple at Karoridhwaja, exhibit enduring stylistic features of the region in their dense physiques, lushness and appealing naturalism. Ultimately, as was the case in the preceding centuries, the style of Sirohi continued to be dependent on trends set in northern Gujarat. Particularly striking is the similarity to a female *whisk-bearer* from Akota (Vadodara, Mus. & Pict. Gal.), a site that has yielded a number of bronzes characterized by extraordinary technical accomplishment. While the Akota bronze is more elaborately bejewelled and costumed than the Sirohi goddesses, their facial features and physiques are virtually identical. The voluptuous physiques and smooth contours so characteristic of this region are also seen in a set of fine *mātṛkā*s (mother goddesses) from Vadaval, where the spontaneous naturalism and expressiveness of much earlier work from Shamalaji and related sites was sustained.

186. *Seated couple*, stone, upper terrace, Harshatmata Temple, Abaneri, Rajasthan, *c.* early 9th century AD

As the 9th century progressed, the experimentation, confidence, energy, immediacy and naturalism of the first half of the century were shed in favour of more complicated systems of embellishment that tended to rely on the multiplication of architectural details, more complicated frame types and disjointed wall surfaces. Figural sculpture became correspondingly less active, more repetitive and conservative and virtually indistinguishable within the decorative whole. Formerly distinctive regional affiliations were less predominant, and there was an increasing predictability to sculptural programmes. Vishnu Temple 2 at Osian, the Kshemankari Temple in Chittaurgarh and the Naktimata Temple at Bhavanipura (near Jaipur) are all examples of this late phase. The Naktimata Temple is the most successful example. While its sculpture is clearly not the equal of that produced in the first half of the century, it nonetheless has its own relaxed appeal. While the figures are refreshing and easy, they are unquestionably a conservative element in the overall schema; they demand little of the viewer, and their place in the fabric of the temple is much less prominent than on earlier monuments. A final example, the Surya Temple at Varman, remains true to the style of the south-west in its relative lack of ornamentation and smooth sense of form, but its surviving sculpture demonstrates clear moves towards the elegant and decorative tendencies of the 10th century.

10th century. Beginning in the 10th century, a consolidation of regional power occurred across western India in the wake of the decline of the Gurjara-Pratiharas. There was a concurrent burgeoning of temple patronage and construction as monumental temple architecture served increasingly as a forum to broadcast clan and regional sovereignty. Through the 10th and 11th centuries temples became progressively more grandiose, with seemingly endless permutations of iconographic and decorative possibilities. This development was accomplished at the expense of overall quality and command of the sculptural programme, a trend that was repeated across most of north India. Nevertheless, western India preserves some superb examples from this elaborate era.

No dated monuments are extant in western India with which to document the transition between the 9th and 10th centuries. Numerous dated examples from the second half of the 10th century do, however, provide a coherent picture of stylistic developments. From the region of ancient Shakhambari, the Chahamana clan claimed dominion over western India against the last vestiges of Gurjara-Pratihara sovereignty. A lengthy inscription records the construction in AD 956 of a lofty temple to Shiva known as the Harasnath Temple, on a hill near Sikar known as Harshagiri. The scanty but tantalizing remains of that temple suggest that it was of exceptional quality. At the beginning of the 20th century, rebuilding of the temple resulted in the displacement of numerous images. The sanctum now preserves a monumental image of *Parvati* performing *pañcāgni tapas* ('five-fire meditation') to gain the favour of Shiva, who is present in the form of a *liṅga* below her in the sanctum; flanking her in a tightly organized pattern is a host of attendant female musicians and *yoginīs*. All these figures were presumably once stationed on the temple's exterior walls. The rigidity of Parvati, the highly mannered torsion of the other figures and the meticulously detailed, almost obsessive profusion of ornament throughout depart from the more vibrant and naturalistic mode favoured in the previous century. This period is characterized by an increasing interest in creating larger, more complex compositions consisting of numbers of aggrandized, ornate figures organized in self-consciously decorative patterns. These features are also present in two single images of Vishnu (both Jaipur, Hawa Mahal Mus.) from Shambar, the original capital of the Chahamanas, and Chatsa, near Jaipur.

Regional distinctions that were discernible in previous centuries were consistent in the 10th, although the increasing predilection for formal and iconographic complexity resulted in a gradual uniformity for much of it. For example, a 10th-century Shiva *liṅga* from Kaman departs from the straightforward rendering of the 9th-century example from the same site (noted above) in its richer symbolic and ornamental vocabulary. The iconography, augmented with emanations of Shiva's four faces and additional attendants and with such decorative accretions as colonnettes and a gateway (*toraṇa*) framework, results in a more complicated visual whole.

A similarly ornate aesthetic dominates the contemporary Nilakantheshvara Temple at Kekind (modern Jasnagar), not far from the pilgrimage place of Pushkar. The general style of the figures aligns them with the Harasnath Temple and related examples, but unlike the monumentality of figures at the former site, those at Kekind are extremely lithe and attenuated, clearly signalling a differing regional sensibility. In overall effect, the figures on the temple exterior appear fused—or knit—into the fabric of the wall itself, functioning as a delicate embroidery. Throughout the 10th century, figural sculpture participated increasingly in its architectural environment in a way that resulted in a visual synthesis.

Different regions had different responses to this tendency, however. In the Ghateshvara Mahadeva Temple at BAROLI, also from the first half of the 10th century, architectural details and figural imagery reflecting its heritage in the Malwa idioms of Chittaurgarh and Jhalrapatan were grafted onto the chaste, elegant architectural features of south-west Rajasthan. The *Shiva Natesha* from the west *bhadra* niche of this temple (see fig. 187) is a particularly elegant example of the lithe fluid style endemic to the region, as is the *Chamunda* from the north *bhadra* niche. The latter horrific figure is analogous to images of this goddess from nearby HINGLAJGARH in Madhya Pradesh

187. *Shiva Natesha*, stone, west wall, Ghateshvara Mahadeva Temple, Baroli, Rajasthan, first half of the 10th century

in her lean attenuation and in the framing elements and ornamental details. Modern boundaries belie the relative stylistic and historical unity of the ancient Malwa region.

The strongest representation of 10th-century developments and a harbinger of the future is seen in a cluster of monuments from southern Rajasthan. In subsequent centuries sculptural activity intensified in northern Gujarat, where the emergence of large numbers of grand temples—particularly Jaina ones—attests to increased patronage by the mercantile classes. There was a concurrent atrophying of monumental temple construction in northern Rajasthan as attention shifted in subsequent centuries towards the building of palaces and forts and the development of the renowned Rajput painting ateliers (*see* §VI, 4(iii) below).

Although it is located in the southernmost part of Rajasthan, the sculpture of the Mahavira Temple at Ghanerao participates fully in the stylistic genre characteristic of the south-western region. The temple is dated to *c.* AD 954 on the basis of a purported inscription (now lost) on the pedestal of the sanctum image and displays many ornamental features characteristic of the 10th century. These are tempered, however, by a sober restraint and weighty simplicity that are maintained in the architecture and figural imagery. Details are precise and heavy, lacking the decorative specificity and elaboration seen in the north. A more overtly decorative and aggressively sculptural variation is seen on the remarkable Ambika (Durga) Temple at JAGAT, of *c.* AD 960–61, which features images of Durga Mahishasuramardini in each of its *bhadra* niches (see fig. 188). Like those at Ghanerao, the figures are sturdy and monumental, and regional continuity is seen in the striking resemblance of the female figures to earlier examples from Sirohi, Mt Abu, Udaipur and northern Gujarat. Finally, the Lakulisha Temple at Eklingji, built in AD 971–2 under Guhila patronage, displays a much more austere approach. Figural imagery is limited to the goddess *Sarasvati* in a *karṇa* niche flanking the doorway (*see* EKLINGJI AND NAGDA). Similarly, the so-called Sas-Bahu temples at Nagda, extremely close to the Eklingji temple, add little to the stylistic profile of late 10th-century sculpture from the region. Both of these monuments relegate most of their figural decoration to the halls that precede the sanctum, and there are images stationed on the *bhadra* projections, but the quality of the carving is at best uninspired.

11th–16th centuries. From the 10th century on, shifting patterns of political alliance and interconnection resulted in a bewilderingly diverse network of clans distributed across most of western India. Yet as the contours of political control over the west became more distinctive and complex, sculptural style became more uniform, and an enduring homogeneity can be traced across most monuments constructed from the 11th century onwards.

Emerging from this web as the pre-eminent power were the Gujarat-based SOLANKI clan, one of the four original Rajput clans purported to have arisen from a sacrificial fire-pit on Mt Abu. Numbers of grandiose temples attest to the Solankis' lavish and extensive patronage of the arts, the impact of which was felt across most of western India. One of the most magnificent examples from this era is the Surya Temple at MODHERA, which has an inscription

188. *Durga Mahishasuramardini* (slaying the buffalo demon), west wall, Ambika Temple, Jagat, Rajasthan, *c.* AD 960–61

of 1026–7 (Vikrama era 1083) added sometime after its construction. This structure stands as an exemplar of 11th-century style, in which temples combine increasingly ambitious plans with opulent sculptural programmes. Sculpture cloaks both exteriors and interiors and is remarkable for its grand scale, copious ornamentation and finely tuned attention to detail. The figures on the Modhera temple retain their regional affiliation in their close resemblance to the examples cited from southern Rajasthan and northern Gujarat and are particularly analogous to the Ambika Temple at Jagat. While the stately, smoothly modulated bodies with broad, somewhat flattened faces correspond to the style of the earlier temple, at Modhera the aggrandized scale and increased embellishment of the images and their framing elements are markers signalling their later date.

From this time on, the surfaces of temples and related monuments were almost unrelieved in their decorative intensity. Yet while virtually no space was left unadorned, and the overall effect is impressive, this surfeit generally resulted in a decline in the quality of the imagery. Faces are masklike and blank, and features are often generic, repetitive and harshly carved. Individual figures are no longer discernible; instead, they participate in profusely populated sculptural programmes that are increasingly conventionalized. Surfaces are broken up with details rendered in terse, linear terms, and decorative elements are often regimentally ordered; moreover, the subtleties of modelling are eschewed in favour of virtuosic posturing. Nevertheless, some impressive monuments were produced in the midst of this overall decline. One of the most ambitious is the Rani Vav at PATAN (i), an enormous STEPWELL produced under the patronage of a Solanki queen in the 11th century. The otherwise mechanical carving is mitigated by the staggering quantity of the sculpture, which blankets every available surface, and its extraordinary decorative intensity (see fig. 189).

Perhaps the most renowned of the many opulent temples constructed during this prolific era are at Dilwara on Mt Abu, which preserves a complex of Jaina temples from the 11th century and later. Their fortress-like white marble exteriors reveal, upon entering, a dazzling spectacle of intricate and inventive carving. There is astounding variety, ranging from ceiling panels with interlaced figures in dexterous poses to forests of extravagantly carved pillars. Despite the skilfulness of the ensembles, however, the individual figures are machine-like in their angular, geometric perfection and devoid of any sense of sensuality or rhythm in their highly mannered contortions, a point that is underscored by the use of chaste white marble. Aside from lavish temple patronage, the wealthy Jaina community also produced bronze sculptures for installation in temples and shrines that differ little in style from those carved in stone. A characteristic example is a bronze *Shantinatha* (one of the 24 Jaina teachers or saints) from *c.* 1188 (London, V&A).

While artistic style from the 11th century could be called predictable, the political situation in this and the ensuing centuries was fragmented and disrupted. Indeed, any sense of stylistic uniformity may owe much to the far-reaching effects of the ongoing Muslim incursions into the subcontinent. As more emphasis was laid on markers of clan and religious solidarity, the more subtle distinctions of regional style or preferences of individual patrons may have been subsumed. From this point on, Rajasthan and Gujarat followed somewhat different artistic paths. In Rajasthan the earlier bombast was perpetuated well into the 15th and 16th centuries, when the preoccupation with the Muslim threat was supplanted by the dynamics of Rajput rivalries and conflicting claims to regional power. However, clan identity was expressed less in the form of monumental temples and more in the form of secular architecture, such as palaces and forts, which were seldom

189. *Vishnu*, *Shiva* and female figures, stairway of the Rani Vav ('Queen's stepwell'), Patan, Gujarat, *c.* 1060

adorned with anything but the most minimal and decorative sculpture. What sculpture remains—as for example on the Adbhutnath Temple or the massive Manastambha and Kirtistambha pillars (all in Chittaurgarh) erected under the patronage of Chittaurgarh's Rana Kumbha (*reg* 1433–68)—do little more than awkwardly repeat established formulas. One notable exception is the Jaina temple of Adinatha at RANAKPUR in southern Rajasthan, dated to 1440 and later, which perpetuates the virtuosic sculptural tenor set by its predecessors at Dilwara on Mt Abu.

In Gujarat, Jaina temples in particular continued to be built and decorated, and vast temple complexes were constructed at such important sites as Satrunjaya and Girnar. But little can be said about sculptural style except that it is orderly and profuse, with an almost obsessive interest in decorative multiplicity.

17th–18th centuries. Much less sculpture was produced in western India in the 17th and 18th centuries than in previous centuries, and it departed little from trends established earlier. The Jagdish Temple in Udaipur, built in 1651 by Jagat Singh I (*reg* 1628–52), differs only in its choice of model. Meant to emulate the magnificent monuments produced at KHAJURAHO in Madhya Pradesh, it succeeds only in providing a much-abridged quotation. While sculpture was produced in Rajasthan between the 16th and 19th centuries, it was increasingly limited to the garnishing of secular architecture. Sculpted tablets honouring revered rulers and ancestors were produced for royal cenotaphs such as those at Ahar, Mandor and JAISALMER; important local heroes were also lauded in this fashion. In general these tablets feature abbreviated, conventionalized images of rulers and their consorts, or they depict heroic figures—often on horseback or in battle. As they were meant to be markers and not portraits, the carving is folkish and summary (*see also* SATI AND HERO STONES).

In addition to stone and bronze sculpture, Gujarat is known for an ancient and opulent wood-carving tradition, of which many late examples are preserved (New Delhi, N. Mus., and National Handicrafts and Handlooms Museum; Vadodara, Mus. & Pict. Gal.; Bombay, Prince of Wales Mus.). The carving that adorns the altars, pillars and halls of small-scale personal shrines and secular architecture, while skilful, is also folkish and fraught with ornamental detail.

See also §III, 5(i)(c), 6(i)(b) and 7(ii)(b) above.

BIBLIOGRAPHY

GENERAL WORKS

N. L. Dey: *The Geographical Dictionary of Ancient and Medieval India* (Calcutta, 1899, rev. 1927/*R* Delhi, 1984)

K. K. Handiqui: *Yaśastilaka and Indian Culture* (Sholapur, 1949)

B. N. Puri: *The History of the Gurjara-Pratihāras* (Bombay, 1957)

D. S. Sharma: *Early Cauhān Dynasties* (Delhi, 1959/*R* 1975)

M. A. Dhaky: 'The Chronology of the Solanki Temples of Gujarat', *J. Madhya Pradesh Itihasa Parishad*, iii (1961), pp. 1–83

D. C. Sircar: *The Guhilas of Kiṣkindhā* (Calcutta, 1965)

D. S. Sharma: *Rajasthan through the Ages* (Bikaner, 1966)

G. S. Ghurye: *Rajput Architecture* (Bombay, 1968)

K. C. Jain: *Malwa through the Ages* (Delhi, 1972)

A. Ghosh, ed.: *Jaina Art and Architecture*, 3 vols (New Delhi, 1974–5)

L. K. Tripathi: *The Temples of Baroli* (Varanasi, 1975)

J. Jain-Neubauer: *The Stepwells of Gujarat in Art-historical Perspective* (Delhi, 1981)

M. Meister: 'Forest and Cave', *Archvs Asian A.*, xxxiv (1981), pp. 56–73

A. Kalia: *Art of Osiāñ Temples* (Delhi, 1982)

M. Meister: 'Bīṭhū: Individuality and Idiom', *A. Orient.*, xiii (1982), pp. 169–86

D. Handa: *Osiāñ: History, Archaeology, Art and Architecture* (Delhi, 1984)

S. Schastok: *The Śāmalajī Sculptures and 6th Century Art in Western India* (Leiden, 1985)

M. Meister: 'Regional Variations in Mātṛkā Conventions', *Artibus Asiae*, xlvii (1986), pp. 233–46

SPECIALIST STUDIES

U. P. Shah: 'Ancient Sculptures from Gujarat and Saurashtra', *J. Ind. Mus.*, viii (1952), pp. 49–57

R. C. Agrawala: 'Sculptures from Ābānerī, Rajasthan', *Lalit Kala*, i–ii (1955–6), pp. 130–35

P. Jayakar: 'Notes on Some Sculptures in Situ at Ābānerī, Rajasthan', *Lalit Kala*, i–ii (1955–6), pp. 139–44

U. P. Shah: 'Bronze Hoard from Vasantgaḍh', *Lalit Kala*, i–ii (1955–6), pp. 55–65

R. C. Agrawala: 'Some Unpublished Sculptures from Southwestern Rajasthan', *Lalit Kala*, vi (1959), pp. 63–71

K. V. Soundara Rajan and R. T. Parikh: 'A Magnificent Saptamatrika Group and Parvati from Vadval, North Gujarat', *Prince of Wales Mus. Bull.*, vii (1959–62), pp. 46–54

R. C. Agrawala: 'Some Interesting Sculptures from Devāngaṇa, Rajasthan', *Lalit Kala*, viii (1960), pp. 69–71

U. P. Shah: 'Sculptures from Śāmalajī and Roḍa', *Bull. Baroda Mus. & Pict. Gal.*, xiii (1960), pp. 1–136

R. C. Agrawala: 'Some More Unpublished Sculptures from Rajasthan', *Lalit Kala*, x (1961), pp. 31–3

——: 'A Newly Discovered Sun Temple at Tusa', *Bhāratīya Vidyā*, xxiii (1963), pp. 56–8

——: 'Khajuraho of Rajasthan, the Temple of Ambikā at Jagat', *A. Asiat.*, x (1964), pp. 43–65

V. S. Srivastava: 'The Ancient Śiva Temple at Mt Harsha, Sikar', *The Researcher*, v–vi (1964–5), pp. 17–32

R. C. Agrawala: 'Inscriptions from Jagat, Rajasthan', *J. Orient. Inst., Baroda*, xiv (1965), pp. 75–8

——: 'Unpublished Temples of Rajasthan', *A. Asiat.*, xi (1965), pp. 53–72

M. A. Dhaky: 'Brahmāṇaswāmī Temple at Varman', *J. Orient. Inst., Baroda*, xiv (1965), pp. 381–7

R. C. Agrawala: 'Sculptures of Mewad in the Sixteenth Century', *J. Ind. Soc. Orient. A.*, i (1965–6), pp. 30–33

M. A. Dhaky: 'Renaissance and the Late Māru-Gurjara Temple Architecture', *J. Ind. Soc. Orient. A.*, i (1965–6), pp. 4–22

——: 'The Old Temple at Lamba and Kāmeśvara Temple at Auwa', *J. Asiat. Soc.*, viii (1966), pp. 141–8

——: 'Some Early Jaina Temples in Western India', *Śrī Mahāvīra Jaina Vidyālaya Golden Jubilee Volume*, 2 vols (Bombay, 1968), i, pp. 290–347

——: 'The Aruneśvara Temple at Kasindra', *J. Orient. Inst., Baroda,* xix (1969), pp. 157–9

M. A. Dhaky and J. M. Nanavati: *The Maitraka and Saindhava Temples of Gujarat* (Ascona, 1969)

R. C. Agrawala: 'Mātṛkā Reliefs in Early Indian Art', *E. & W.*, xxi (1971), pp. 79–89

S. P. Shrivastav: 'A Recently Discovered Gurjara Pratihāra Temple in Rajasthan', *J. Ind. Soc. Orient. A.*, v (1971–3), pp. 12–14

R. C. Agrawala: 'Pratihāra Sculptures from Choti-Khātu, Rajasthan', *J. Orient. Inst., Baroda*, xxiii (1973), pp. 72–4

M. A. Dhaky: 'The Nīlakaṇṭheśvara Temple at Kekind', *J. Orient. Inst., Baroda*, xxii (1973), pp. 397–408

M. Meister: 'Detective Archaeology: Preliminary Report on the Śiva Temple at Kusumā', *Archvs Asian A.*, xxvii (1973–4), pp. 77–91

M. A. Dhaky: 'Genesis and Development of Māru-Gurjara Temple Architecture', *Studies in Indian Temple Architecture*, ed. P. Chandra (New Delhi, 1975), pp. 114–65

M. Meister: 'A Field Report on the Temples at Kusumā', *Archvs Asian A.*, xxxix (1975–6), pp. 23–46

C. Lin-Bodien: 'The Chronology of Candrāvatī, Kusumā, Chitorgarh: A Case Study in the Use of Epigraphic and Stylistic Evidence', *Archvs Asian A.*, xxxiii (1980), pp. 49–64

CYNTHIA PACKERT ATHERTON

(b) Maharashtra. From the 7th to the 18th century, sculpture in Maharashtra continued to reflect the cultural and political mixture that had characterized earlier periods.

The great works of the Vakataka, Kalachuris of Maharashtra and Rashtrakuta periods, most notably the rock-cut temples at ELLORA, preserve an energized local style, displayed on a scale that was not to be equalled in subsequent times. Later in the period, with the advent of built temples across the region controlled by the Yadava dynasty, architectural elements were emphasized at the expense of sculptural elaboration. Nonetheless, the quality of later sculpture reflects both continued skill in artists' workshops and an on-going ability to absorb and integrate styles from other regions. After the 13th century, even this production was greatly reduced, partly in response to Muslim advances across the Deccan. Sculpture of the succeeding Maratha period, most often in stucco rather than stone, was more an accessory to architecture than a primary component of it, prolonging into modern times a trend first seen in the Yadava period.

The corpus of stylistic ideas and skills built up in the 6th century at the Brahmanical cave temples of ELEPHANTA and Ellora and Buddhist caves at AURANGABAD (*see* §6(iii)(c) above) were transferred directly to the Buddhist caves at Ellora in the 7th century. In Cave 6 at Ellora, the sculptural style and architectural details of the refined late 6th-century Cave 21 at the same site (Spink, p. 45, figs 25, 28) were adopted almost verbatim, while certain of the sculptures of female figures and *bodhisattvas* in Cave 8 at Ellora, a mid-7th-century excavation, show clear connections to earlier work in caves 7 and 9 at Aurangabad. By the end of the 7th century, as the Rashtrakuta dynasty began to expand, a new, more 'southern' idiom was introduced in the last of the Buddhist excavations, caves 11 and 12, anticipating the mature Rashtrakuta style of the mid-8th century. The earlier squarish profiles of head-dresses and shoulders gave way to figures with more streamlined forms. The headdresses were almost pointed, the eyes became narrower, shoulders sloped, facial contours were smoothed out, and relief, while still deep, became flatter (Parimoo and others, fig. 31). Applied to small- and large-scale Buddhist sculpture, this style spread over western Maharashtra and can also be seen in 8th-century Buddhist bronzes from Sopara (Bombay, Asiat. Soc.; Gorakshar, figs 13, 14, 17) and in the rock-cut sculptures of Panhale Kaji.

This kind of change was not merely regional. A 7th-century stone sculpture of *Uma-Maheshvara* (Shiva with his consort, Parvati; Los Angeles, CA, Co. Mus. A.; 1981 exh. cat., fig. 49) from the temple complex at Markandi, across Maharashtra in the eastern district of Chandrapur, shares with 7th-century Ellora sculpture a late 'classical' roundness of form and squareness of profile inspired more by central and western Indian styles than by the cave temples. In the case of the *Uma-Maheshvara*, however, the highly arched, sinuous eyebrows, heavily projecting top eyelids and scalloped lips anticipate the style of 11th-century sculptures on the Markandeshvara Temple at Markandi, which themselves project not a southern but a northern ambience. In this regard they are comparable to images on the temples at KHAJURAHO.

It is the great Kailasa Temple (Cave 16) at Ellora, of *c.* 750–800, that epitomizes the early medieval sculpture of Maharashtra (*see* ELLORA, §2). Many features carry on traditions established in the earliest rock-cut cave temples there, but these are presented with a new energy and compositional complexity, adopted in part from earlier Chalukya sculpture, that are hallmarks of Rashtrakuta style. The temple, cut from the basaltic cliff to resemble a built edifice, 'rests' on the backs of over life-size elephants (Dhavalikar, pl. 23) that are similar in function to those at KARLE from the 1st century AD. Cut in such deep relief that their effect is three-dimensional, they face out from the base of the temple, lifting bunches of leaves as they graze. This 'naturalism' is extended to small details: even the vein structure of their ears is depicted with precision.

Extended narrative relief sculpture, not used in Maharashtrian sculpture before this time, was introduced on the porch base of the Kailasa Tample. In these scenes from the epic *Mahābhārata* and *Rāmāyaṇa*, the background is cut away to create a strongly three-dimensional sense even within essentially two-dimensional, linear compositions (Dhavalikar, pls 26, 27). This effect, noteworthy, for example, in the lacy network formed by the bows and lunging figures of soldiers in battle scenes from the *Mahābhārata*, contrasts with 12th-century Yadava relief sculpture such as that on the lintel of the temple at Satgaon (Deshpande, 1985, pl. XIVa). There, a lacy, almost calligraphic intertwining of limbs and ornaments produces an overall filigree effect that overwhelms the *saptamātṛkā* images and the shrines in which they are portrayed.

Perhaps the most famous of the Kailasa sculptures, a major image of the demon *Ravana Shaking Mt Kailasa*, Shiva's abode in the Himalayas (see fig. 190), was carved into the base of the temple plinth, underscoring the meaning of the entire complex as the god's mountain

190. *Ravana Shaking Mt Kailasa*, Kailasa Temple, Cave 16, Ellora, Maharashtra, *c.* AD 750–800

home, to which worshippers' prayers would be transported. Portraying a theme seen earlier at Jogeshvari, Elephanta and Ellora's first Brahmanical caves, this scene has been transformed by elongated, tapered, energized figural types cut in dramatically deep relief. Shiva's composure contrasts with Ravana's frenzy as he tries to displace the great god and his consort, Parvati. Location, meaning and emotional contrasts have been integrated in a quintessential example of Maharashtrian medieval sculptural achievement.

The emotional intensity of 8th- and 9th-century Maharashtrian sculpture is embodied in sculptures of the Kailasa complex's *yajñaśālā* (sacrifice hall; Dhavalikar, pls 55–9). The horrific god Kala, with contorted face and schematically rendered ribs and muscles, presides in angular frenzy over his victims, fallen in a twisted pile beneath his feet, one serving as his mount. Meanwhile the goddess Durga sits serenely on her lion, her calm pose in sharp contrast to its snarling ferocity. Details have become stylized, and have not lost their cumulative, inner energy: thin ridges pick out details of the lion's face and the snail-shell curls of its mane and of the goddess's eyes, mouth, hairline, small, half-spherical breasts and necklaces hanging in symmetrical loops between them, and heavily beaded belts. Across the cell a queen and her attendants form an even more relaxed group, each leaning in a slightly different direction as all observe the goddesses of the *saptamātṛkā* group near by. The contrast between Kala's fury, Durga's serenity and the royal group's more human tranquillity exemplifies Rashtrakuta artists' ability to portray a range of emotional states.

Extended to sculpture in Ellora's 9th-century Jaina caves, this style maintained its inner energy, contained within forms bursting with surface tension, even in a context that required more staid emotional states (Zimmer, pls 242–3, 246). It was sustained in translation into smaller, portable images as well, for instance in the 10th-century Jaina bronze images from Rajnapur Khinkhini (Nagpur, Cent. Mus.; Gorakshar, figs 10, 19). The latter's tapered volumes, smooth surfaces and distinctively curled hairstyles also recall details of the nearby and slightly earlier NOLAMBA sculptures of HEMAVATI in Andhra Pradesh (*see* §(vi)(b) below), thus reiterating the Maharashtrian tendency to absorb stylistic traits from neighbouring traditions.

With the commencement of Yadava rule over Maharashtra in the 11th century, sculptural context and style underwent a considerable change, again influenced by art of other regions. Built temples, adapting styles from Gujarat and Malwa, replaced cave temple architecture, making it possible to distribute shrines across the state without the geographical restrictions imposed by the location of suitable rock cliffs. Resources were thus also distributed more widely, with the result that after the 10th century, no single temple complex could rival the concentrated efforts at Ajanta, Elephanta or Ellora. Although many of the built temples were devoid of external sculpture, where present it continued to reveal the technical skill of Maharashtrian artists. Along the west coast near Bombay, a crisp, slightly angular style was achieved, exemplified by 11th-century images from Jondhali Baug (Bombay, Prince of Wales Mus.; Chandra, figs 119–21) and by contemporary female figures on the Chakreshvara Temple at Sopara (Kramrisch, 1965, fig. 130). Thin eyebrows arched in mild frowns, narrow noses and thin, slightly pursed lips contribute to the crisp effect. Still revealing a Maharashtrian ambience, these images' full volumes, with round cheeks, spherical breasts and wide shoulders, contrast with the otherwise similar style of contemporary sculpture from Madhya Pradesh (*see* §(iv) below). At the Ambarnath Mahadeva Temple, also in Thana District, such sculptures are clearly accessories to the overall architectural scheme, appearing from a distance to form a decorative pattern that draws attention away from the individual characteristics or effects of the sculpture (Deglurkar, pls IV, V).

The 11th-century images of eastern Maharashtra on the Markandeshvara Temple at Markandi (Jamkhedkar, figs 20, 23), are related to the sculptural style of Khajurako in their detail, sophistication and polish. Hard, thin lines etch eyebrows, eyes and mouths, and elaborate ornaments are flattened against flesh, with many details schematically and symmetrically rendered. Even less fluid than contemporary sculpture from further west, the Markandi images underscore the continued pan-Maharashtra predilection for cultural borrowing and adaptation, even as medieval art forms reached their end.

By the 18th century, Maratha temple sculpture was being eclipsed by the structural and ornamental details of the buildings themselves. Images were placed in small niches, as on the mid-18th-century Khandoba Temple at Pali (Mate, 1981, p. 49, fig. d). Earlier rounded body forms were replaced by a sharper, more angular, style; breasts were no longer of the stylized spherical gourd type, but smaller and more pointed. Facial features, too, were more sharply defined, with smaller eyes and narrower noses. These stucco images, often still brightly painted, reflect a contemporary charm more than the monumental grandeur of Maharashtra's classical and medieval sculpture.

See also §III, 5(i)(e) and 6(i)(b) above.

BIBLIOGRAPHY

H. Goetz: 'The Kailasa of Ellora and the Chronology of Rashtrakuta Art', *Artibus Asiae*, xv (1952), pp. 84–107
H. Zimmer: *The Art of Indian Asia*, ii (Princeton, 1955)
S. Kramrisch: *The Art of India* (London, 1965)
W. Spink: *Ajanta to Ellora* (Bombay, 1967)
S. J. Czuma: *The Brahmanical Rashtrakuta Monuments of Ellora* (diss., U. MI., 1968)
M. Chandra: *Stone Sculptures in the Prince of Wales Museum* (Bombay, 1974)
G. B. Deglurkar: *Temple Architecture and Sculpture of Maharashtra* (Nagpur, 1974)
D. C. Chatham: *The Stylistic Sources and Relationships of the Kailasa Temple at Ellora* (diss., Berkeley, U. CA, 1977)
M. S. Mate: 'Temple Architecture', *Marg*, xxxiv/2 (1981), pp. 41–52 [issue on the art of the Chhatrapatis and Peshwas]
Manifestations of Shiva (exh. cat. by S. Kramrisch, Philadelphia, PA, Mus. A., 1981)
M. K. Dhavalikar: *Masterpieces of Rashtrakuta Art: The Kailas* (Bombay, 1983)
S. Gorakshar: 'Ancient Metal Images', *Marg*, xxxvi/4 (1983), pp. 37–48 [issue on Maharashtra: traditions in art]
A. P. Jamkhedkar: 'Ancient Structures', *Marg*, xxxvii/1 (1984), pp. 25–36 [issue on Maharashtra: religious and secular architecture]
S. R. Deshpande: *Yadava Sculpture* (Delhi, 1985)
M. N. Deshpande: *The Caves of Panhale-Kaji (Ancient Pranalaka)*, Mem. Archaeol. Surv. India, lxxxiv (New Delhi, 1986)
B. S. Deshmukh: *Iconography of the Hindu Temples in Marathwada* (Jaipur, 1987)

R. Parimoo and others: *Ellora Caves: Sculptures and Architecture* (New Delhi, 1988)

GERI H. MALANDRA

(iv) Central. The central part of northern India (conforming approximately to the modern state of Madhya Pradesh) was divided into a number of regions in the 7th century and later. These were never defined with exact boundaries but tended to endure as cultural entities. The eastern portion was known as the Dahala country. This extended from the upper reaches of the Narmada River near Jabalpur to the banks of the Ganga near Allahabad. To the south was the province of South Kosala, with its centres at Rajim and Sirpur. In this area links with adjacent Orissa were often apparent. The western part of central India, dominated by a large plateau, was known as Malava or Malwa from the 9th century onwards. The most important centres there were Vidisha and Ujjain. The northern portion of central India was divided into two areas, Gopakhshetra and Jejakabhukti. Gopakhshetra was the area around the city of Gwalior, while Jejakabhukti conformed to the large region called Bundelkhand, bounded on the north by the Yamuna River and on the west and east by the Betwa and Ken rivers.

With the slow improvement of transportation over the centuries and the advent of Mughal power after 1550, these regions began to coalesce, though still to some extent preserving their cultural identity. Regionalism was stronger in some centuries, while in others differences were submerged. These patterns have not been studied systematically, and no standard nomenclature has been devised for sculpture after the 7th century. In addition the inventory of sites and monuments, especially from later periods, is far from complete. What follows is necessarily a provisional history.

(a) 7th century. (b) 8th–9th centuries. (c) 10th–13th centuries. (d) 14th–18th centuries.

(a) 7th century. Dated material from the 7th century is scarce. Central Indian parallels can, however, be found for a dated *Standing Buddha* from Mathura (Lucknow, State Mus.). The date on the pedestal is 284; though unspecified, the Gupta era is the only likely possibility, giving an equivalent of AD 599–600. This date is supported by the object's style. Despite an obvious debt to 5th-century conventions, the image displays loose, swelling forms that retain little of the careful grandeur of earlier sculpture. The ponderous limbs billow outwards with a graceless and uncontrolled vigour, a manifestation of the breakdown of the artistic canons of the Gupta age. Parallels to the Mathura image in central India include a number of Buddhas at SANCHI (Sanchi, Archaeol. Mus.) showing a distorted treatment of earlier types, characteristic of decay. The rock-cut relief panels in the Naharghati at DEOGARH also illustrate these developments. A standing figure of the god *Vishnu* has bulging limbs and crudely cut ornaments that give the figure a massive and savage presence; an emphatically rustic quality is also seen in the panel of mother goddesses a few steps away. These images bear an undated inscription that has been placed at the end of the 6th century on palaeographic grounds. Similar sculptures have been found at Keldhar (Shivpuri, Distr. Mus.).

The crumbling of Gupta standards was a long process, but as these conventions fell apart, vital new types of sculpture began to emerge. This is apparent in the Shiva shrine (*maṇḍapikā*) at Mahua, which can be placed in the first half of the 7th century. Images of the deities *Ganesha*, *Durga* and *Varaha* on the building show occasional distortion but not crude, ballooning forms; instead they are animated with fresh volume and brooding rhythm. The scrollwork is no longer stiff but boils upwards with imaginative, if erratic, agitation. A sculpture of *Vishnu* from Vidisha (Vidisha, Distr. Archaeol. Mus.; *see* BESNAGAR) shows similar qualities appearing in the Malwa region. Kindred developments with distinct regional traits are seen in the Lakshmana Temple at SIRPUR. This building is associated by inscription with King Shivagupta, who ruled in South Kosala during the first half of the 7th century. As elsewhere, the sculptural forms have a new vitality that combines an opulent plastic sense with unresolved movement and complexity. In contrast, a contemporary image of the goddess *Parvati* from Sagar (New Delhi, N. Mus.) has the simple beauty and directness that are often found in work from the Dahala country. A rock-cut set of mother goddesses at Deogarh are a somewhat rustic parallel to the *Parvati* image. These examples (others could be added) show that in the first half of the 7th century old canons were discarded, while pioneering efforts were undertaken in form and iconography. Regional idioms were particularly prominent.

In the second half of the 7th century an artistic explosion of extraordinary force occurred. In central India the most remarkable and complete monument is another building at Mahua, the Shiva Temple. The lavishly carved door has images of river goddesses at its base. These figures are animated by sensuousness and vigour, with none of the distortion and uneasy movement seen in the early part of the century. The change in the treatment of floral scrolls is equally dramatic; they have lost their uneven, agitated qualities and have become a vibrant, frothy spray. Parallels to the Mahua temple are numerous. A small shrine at GYARASPUR has large panels carved with floral scrolls similar to those at Mahua. In terms of figural imagery, the most spectacular example is the main *Varaha* image (the boar incarnation of Vishnu) in the ruined Varaha Temple at Deogarh Fort (see fig. 191; the temple ruins are of a later date). This monumental figure has the same ponderous elegance as the Mahua river goddesses and bristles with sureness, vitality and power. Other works include an *Ambika* from Gyaraspur (Gwalior, Archaeol. Mus.) and a doorjamb from Temple 18 at Sanchi. In all these sculptures the lyrical calm and naturalism of the Gupta age have been superseded by dynamic tension, rhythm and increasing complexity. The 7th century was therefore a crucial turning-point and the beginning of a new era in the history of Indian sculpture.

(b) 8th–9th centuries. The innovations of the 7th century were steadily consolidated and elaborated during the 8th and 9th centuries. Though regional idioms continued to exist, the strength of regionalism gradually waned. In the early 8th century forms were gradually controlled and simplified. Rich modelling was balanced by a rhythmic linearity and growing precision in the description of detail.

191. *Varaha*, red sandstone, from the ruined Varaha Temple, Deogarh Fort, Madhya Pradesh, late 7th century AD

These developments are well illustrated by the door and various sculptures at the Rajivalochana Temple at RAJIM in South Kosala. A similar reduction of plastic vitality is found in the Shiva Temple at Dang, in an image of *Ganesha* from Gwalior (Gwalior, Archaeol. Mus.) and in the well-preserved rock-cut image of Durga slaying the buffalo demon (*Durga Mahishasuramardini*) at Deogarh. The chronology of early 8th-century sculpture is aided by datable works, notably a *Gajalakshmi* (the goddess Lakshmi being lustrated by elephants; Indore, Cent. Mus.) found at Indragarh, near Bhanpura, in conjunction with an inscription providing a date of AD 710–11 (Vikrama era 767).

A large stele depicting a *Royal Couple with Horse and Groom* (see fig. 192) bears an inscription of the Kalachuri king Shankaragana (*reg c.* 750–75). The figures' limbs are tubular in conception, and the general outline is strongly linear. An identical figural style is found in many parts of the Dahala country, notably Nandchand, TIGOWA, Bargoan and Chhoti Deori. Similar work is also seen on the Teli ka Mandir at Gwalior and on the temples at nearby Naresar. More sophisticated, but clearly contemporary, are the splendid mother goddesses from the village of Kota, near Shivpuri (Gwalior, Archaeol. Mus.).

Towards the end of the 8th century, the energy that once had given conviction to volume and form was applied instead to rich and active decorative surfaces. Examples include the sculpture of the Gargaj Mahadev Temple at Indor. The figure of *Ishana* (a *dikpāla* or directional guardian) on the south side of the building, one of the finest works of the late 8th century, shows that sculpture had become an increasingly passive backdrop for the display of gesture and intricate decoration. Decorative scrollwork had acquired a lashing briskness and sharp, frilly quality that differed markedly from the supple opulence of earlier work. Individual sculptures of the late 8th century survive in considerable numbers. One of the best preserved is a bust of *Shiva*, possibly from BADOH (Gwalior, Archaeol. Mus.). In South Kosala a parallel is found in sculpture of the Siddheshvara Temple at Palari.

Ninth-century sculpture is characterized by unsurpassed elegance, by an internal coherence and sleek simplicity of form. Volumes were carefully controlled and detail carefully focused. The finest work of this period displays a degree of mature assurance and accomplishment not seen since the Gupta era. Dated monuments (the earliest in the region) include a free-standing monumental pillar at BADOH (AD 861, Vikrama era 917), a stray column at Deogarh (AD 862, Vikrama era 919), a ruin at Gyaraspur known as Char Khambha (AD 879–80, Vikrama era 936) and the rock-cut Chaturbhuja Temple at Gwalior (AD 876–7, Vikrama era 933; *see* GWALIOR, fig. 1). The figural sculpture on these monuments is badly damaged, but what survives indicates that a growing homogeneity of style was emerging in central India. The dated material can be related to well-preserved buildings such as the Maladevi Temple at Gyaraspur and the Surya Temple at Madkheda. The

192. *Royal Couple with Horse and Groom*, red sandstone, probably from Sagar, Madhya Pradesh, *c.* AD 750–75 (Sagar, University of Sagar, Archaeological Museum)

Madkheda Temple in particular is a stunning visual catalogue of Hindu imagery. Individual stelae and fragments from the 9th century survive in considerable numbers; a bust of the god *Indra* from Badoh (Gwalior, Archaeol. Mus.) is unusually well-preserved.

(c) 10th–13th centuries. An overall trend, sometimes termed 'medieval', that emerged in the first half of the 10th century was characterized by a growing emphasis on dynamic line and the geometric arrangement of form. These qualities are already apparent in a hero stone from Terhai dated AD 904 (Vikrama era 960; Gwalior, Archaeol. Mus.). More important is the pillared hall at Paroli, datable to approximately the same period. This little-known building contains a wealth of sculpture on its massive lintels and intricately carved ceilings, for the most part perfectly preserved. All the major gods of the Hindu pantheon are displayed, along with running friezes depicting Shaiva rites and events from the life of Krishna. Especially notable is a ferocious dancing image of the goddess Chamunda with attendants. That the first half of the 10th century was a period of prolific sculptural activity is also indicated by the Jarai Math at Barwa Sagar and the well-known Lakshmana Temple at KHAJURAHO (see fig. 193; *see also* §III, 5(i)(b) above). The Lakshmana Temple is associated with an inscription of AD 954–5 (Vikrama era 1011). In these buildings the complete temple wall (*jaṅghā*) was carved with images; especially at Barwa Sagar, the sculpture exhibits stunning decorative variety.

193. Shrine doorway and interior, red sandstone, Lakshmana Temple, Khajuraho, Madhya Pradesh, *c.* AD 954–5

194. *Shiva Slaying the Demon Andhaka*, red sandstone, from Sohagpur, Madhya Pradesh, *c.* AD 925 (Shahdol, private collection)

A distinct and accomplished idiom also appeared in the Dahala country in the first half of the 10th century. Characterized by a masterful sense of internal modelling and proportion, the idiom is well illustrated by a sculpture from Sohagpur showing *Shiva Slaying the Demon Andhaka* (see fig. 194). The tight treatment of the flesh is enlivened by overlays of ornament, spirited poses and a vibrant play of light and shadow. In nearby Singhpur, a number of images and a spectacular shrine doorway are products of the same workshop. Other notable products of this period include a group of images of *yoginis* (goddesses who practise yoga) from various places in Shahdol, Jabalpur and Rewa districts (Dubhela Mus.), all produced in the territory ruled by the Kalachuri kings. As in sculpture produced under the Chandella, Paramara and other dynasties of the period, work from the Dahala country exhibits a style that seems particular to the Kalachuri domain. It is difficult to determine, however, whether such idioms owed their origin to particular rulers or whether the dynasties, as regional powers, simply drew on entrenched regional traditions.

By the late 10th century the inventiveness of the preceding decades had begun to wane. The new tendencies that emerged are evident in the river-goddess figures in a monastery building at Chandrehe, dated by inscription to AD 973 (Kalachuri-Chedi era 724). Similar work is found in the *yogini* images of the Chausath Yogini Temple at Bheraghat and those on an enormous gateway from Gurgi, now incorporated into the palace at Rewa. These works exhibit mannered poses and a weakening of plastic feeling. Ornaments have acquired a biting precision, and scroll-work has been tightened and undercut. The same characteristics are seen in sculpture at Khajuraho and Surwaya that dates to the second half of the 10th century.

During the 11th century large temples were built in great numbers in central India. As quantity took precedence over quality, figural sculpture tended to become perfunctory and to show an increased hardening of form. Representative work is seen at the Sas-Bahu Temple in Gwalior. Closely related but with better preserved sculpture is the ruined Shiva Temple (known as Kakanmath) at Sihoniya. Some of the temples at Kadwaha also date to this period. In the Malwa region, the most outstanding monument is the Udayeshvara Temple at UDAIPUR, datable to *c.* 1080. Some sculpture retains a coherent sense of form (see fig. 195), but most of the images have stereotypical poses; the limbs are decked with ornaments that conceal rather than enhance the flesh. The faces, now disturbingly masklike, have sharply delineated features. Many sculptures combine frenzied, angular movement with a mechanical concern with modelling. In the floral scrolls and other carved ornaments, flat, stencil-like patterns have taken over the surfaces and cast a crisp frosting over the entire structure. This is an agitated linear style, purged of almost every vestige of plastic feeling.

These characteristics were accentuated during the 12th century, from which period a number of dated works have survived. In Jejakabhukti, a gigantic *Standing Jina* (a liberated soul who has conquered vice) at Ahar (near Chhatarpur) is associated with an inscription of 1180–81 (Vikrama era 1237). The Duladeo Temple at Khajuraho is probably datable to the first half of the 12th century, and the crudeness of its sculpture provides a compelling contrast to the mid-10th-century work at the same site. Ajayagarh, the last centre associated with the Chandella dynasty, has sculptures executed in the same unyielding and rigid manner. A Jaina image at Bahuriband, dated in the reign of the Kalachuri ruler Gayakarna (*reg c.* 1123–53), shows that similar works were produced in the Dahala country. Comparable work in the Gwalior region includes an image of *Vishnu Seated on his Mount Garuda*, dated 1185–6 (Vikrama era 1242; Gwalior, Archaeol. Mus.). A group of goddesses from Naresar, dated 1188–9 (Vikrama era 1245; Gwalior, Archaeol. Mus.), shows how the emphatic rigidity of the 12th-century style led to a degeneration of workmanship and disintegration of forms.

In the 13th century, as Islamic dynasties asserted their influence, temples were abandoned or destroyed in central India, and craftsmen were drawn from indigenous practice to the service of Muslim patrons. Thus figural sculpture diminished in importance, while Indian decorative motifs were transferred wholesale to Indo-Islamic art (*see* §III, 5(ii) and 6(ii) above). In central India material from this period is scarce, but some evidence is provided by a fragment of Arabic calligraphy from Gwalior (Scindia School) that dates to the early 13th century. The letters are set on a background of lotus flowers and flat, stencil-like scrolls that recall temple decoration. Figural sculpture in the 13th century was restricted to minor dedications, typically for the Jaina community. These were small individual stelae, often inscribed with dates and personal details. For example, a Jaina image of the *tīrthaṅkara* (divine master) *Neminatha* (Calgary, Bumper Dev. Corp.), characterized by a conservative repetition of forms, carries an inscription recording its establishment by one Damdhala in 1263 (Vikrama era 1319). Such works show that by the 13th century sculpture had lost vitality.

195. Medallion with Shiva below and in his dancing form as Natesha above, red sandstone, Udayeshvara Temple, Udaipur, Madhya Pradesh, *c.* 1080 (Gwalior, Archaeological Museum)

(d) 14th–18th centuries. In the 14th century figural sculpture for non-Muslim patrons persisted in central India, but historical circumstances indicate that support

for large-scale Hindu monuments was substantially undermined. An unyielding and uncritical adherence to received art practice seems to have been typical.

The Jaina images carved into the cliff face of Gwalior Fort during the 15th century provide good examples. They are mostly standing figures of considerable size, set in niches with architectural frames and ornaments (the images were mutilated by Babur (*reg* 1526–30) in the Mughal period and restored in the 20th century). These Jaina figures show almost no perceptible change in iconographic conception from those produced in the 13th century. Attempts were made to retain the vigorously linear style of earlier times, but the organization of forms shows clear signs of distortion and disintegration. In work on Hindu temples the decline was equally severe. A folk art emerged at the village level that is characterized by the use of stick figures (*see* §X below and SATI AND HERO STONES). Numerous images of the popular god Hanuman also date to this time. More sophisticated, but also representative, is a little-known image of *Chamunda* with 20 arms at Narayanpur.

A revival took place in the 15th century, coinciding with a widespread 'renaissance' of devotional religion, notably the worship of Krishna. In Gwalior a series of buildings was erected by the Tomar Rajputs in the 15th and early 16th centuries. The courtyard of the Man Mandir (*see* GWALIOR, fig. 2) has sumptuously carved arcades and a number of fascinating brackets in the form of peacocks. Stone screens with spiralling arabesques and dancers in silhouette show varying degrees of Islamic influence. In the Gujari Mahal, also at Gwalior, elephants carved in high relief occupy pavilions over the doors (see fig. 196). To a limited extent similar work was produced in other parts of central India, though it must be viewed in the context of the contemporary, more vigorous revival that took place in Rajasthan (*see* §(iii)(a) above).

Indigenous forms of sculpture continued well into the 18th century. The silver *liṅga* of the Mahakala Temple at Ujjain is a good example of the endurance of old traditions. It is both remarkable and symptomatic, however, that the reconstruction of this temple, one of the most sacred in India, was carried out in 1745 with reused pillars and other items and not a single piece of new stone-carving.

See also §III, 5(i)(b), 6(i)(e) and 7(ii)(b) above.

196. Elephant, buff sandstone, Gujari Mahal, Gwalior, Madhya Pradesh, 15th century

BIBLIOGRAPHY

P. C. Mukerji: *Report on the Antiquities in the District of Lalitpur, N. W. Provinces, India* (Roorkee, 1899)
D. R. Patil: *The Descriptive and Classified List of Archaeological Monuments in Madhya Bharat* (Gwalior, 1952)
H. V. Trivedi: *The Bibliography of Madhya-Bharat Archaeology* (Gwalior, 1953)
P. Chandra: 'The Kaula-Kapālika Cults at Khajurāho', *Lalit Kalā*, i–ii (1955–6), pp. 98–107
O. Viennot: *Les Divinités fluviales Ganga et Yamuna aux portes des sanctuaires de l'Inde* (Paris, 1964)
K. Deva: 'Extensions of Gupta Art: Art and Archaeology in the Pratihāra Age', *Seminar on Indian Art and Archaeology, 1962* (New Delhi, 1965), pp. 85–106
K. Bruhn: *The Jina-Images of Deogarh* (Leiden, 1969)
P. Chandra: *Stone Sculpture in the Allahabad Museum* (Bombay, 1971)
O. Viennot: *Temples de l'Inde centrale et occidentale* (Paris, 1976)
J. Harle: 'The Post-Gupta Style in Indian Temple Architecture and Sculpture', *J. Royal Soc. A.*, cxxv, no. 5253 (1977), pp. 570–89
A. de Lippe: *Indian Medieval Sculpture* (Amsterdam, 1978)
H. V. Trivedi: *Inscriptions of the Paramāras, Chandellas Kachchhapagliālas and Two Minor Dynasties*, Corp. Inscr. Indic., vii (New Delhi, 1978)
R. K. Sharma, ed.: *Art of the Paramaras of Malwa* (Delhi, 1979)
A. Rahman: *Art and Architecture of the Kalacuris* (Delhi, 1980)
E. Lascarides Zannas: 'The Big Sukanasa of Udayesvara Temple at Udaipur, Madhya Pradesh', *Madhu: Recent Researches in Indian Archaeology and Art History*, ed. M. S. Nagaraja Rao (Delhi, 1981), pp. 187–94
D. Stadtner: 'The Śaṅkaragaṇa Panel in the Sāgar University Art Museum', *Indian Epigraphy: Its Bearing on the History of Art*, ed. F. M. Asher and G. S. Gai (Delhi, 1985), pp. 165–8
R. N. Misra: *Sculptures of Dāhala and Dakṣina Kosala and their Background* (Delhi, 1987)
R. Salomon and M. Willis: 'A Ninth-century Umāmaheśvara Image', *Artibus Asiae*, l (1990), pp. 148–55
R. D. Trivedi: *Temples of the Pratīhāra Period in Central India* (Delhi, 1990)
Gods, Guardians and Lovers: Temple Sculptures from North India AD 700–1200 (exh. cat., ed. V. N. Desai and D. Mason; New York, Asia Soc. Gals, 1993)

DONALD M. STADTNER, MICHAEL D. WILLIS

(v) East

(a) Bihar and Bengal. (b) Orissa.

(a) Bihar and Bengal. From the 8th to the 12th centuries the region that now comprises the Indian states of Bihar and West Bengal and the nation of Bangladesh (the latter two referred to as Bengal below) was ruled by a number of dynasties. Many were short-lived and highly localized, but one, the Pala dynasty, was prominent throughout the period, at times controlling virtually the whole of Bihar and Bengal. A number of Pala kings were Buddhists, others were Hindus, but all were apparently tolerant, and under them religious art flourished. Some of the Palas are known to have patronized religious establishments, though

it has not been possible to link any of the kings to the creation of specific surviving works of art. A second dynasty, the Senas, ruled much of the Bengal region for a fairly limited period in the 12th century. Though they were no more important than many lesser-known dynasties of the Bihar–Bengal region, such as the Khadgas, Varmans and Chandras, the Sena name has been appended to that of the Palas. Thus the entire period from the 8th to 12th century is often called the Pala–Sena period, and its art is identified as that of the Pala–Sena school (*see* PALA AND SENA).

Chronological development. The stylistic developments and variations of the sculpture of the so-called Pala–Sena period are comparatively well documented. Some 75 surviving metal and stone images bear inscriptions that date their manufacture. Consequently, a secure chronology for this approximately 400-year period has been established, and even undated works can be assigned their correct chronological place with considerable certainty. Sculptures from this school survive in great quantities (some 6,000 images and votive stupas are known), providing a fairly complete record of the prodigious artistic and religious activity during this period. The survival of many examples of sculpture from a number of sites, clusters of sites and well-defined regions within the broader Bihar and Bengal area makes it possible to identify some of the substyles that flourished within the Pala–Sena school.

From these substyles it may be inferred that some of the major religious sites, as well as major dynastic capitals, had their own workshops or guilds of artists who worked locally. In Bihar important religious centres that have yielded strong evidence of local artistic activity include Bodhgaya (*see* BODHGAYA AND GAYA), NALANDA, KURKIHAR and Uddandapura. In Bengal a similar concentration of religious and artistic energy may have occurred at major sites such as PAHARPUR, Mahasthangarh and Mainamati. However, many images have also been found in villages where only a single Pala-period temple seems to have existed. The distinction between the pattern of distribution of sculptures in what was mainly Buddhist Bihar and mainly Hindu Bengal may be related to differing practices of lay worship, the concentration of holy sites in Bihar and other aspects of religious life.

The early phase of the Pala school (8th–10th century) took place mainly in Bihar, particularly south of the Ganga River in the region known as Magadha. As the ancient homeland of Shakyamuni Buddha, Magadha included many sites that had become sacred to Buddhists because of their association with events in the life of the historical Buddha. Some of these sites, such as Bodhgaya, where the Buddha attained enlightenment, became especially prominent during the Pala period. Numerous large and small monasteries (*vihāra*s) were also located at sites in Bihar unrelated to events in the life of Shakyamuni. (The ubiquity of monasteries in the region is echoed in the modern name, Bihar, which is a corruption of the term *vihāra*.) Some of the monasteries, particularly Nalanda, were eminent institutions of higher learning with rigorous entrance requirements, at which the great Buddhist thinkers and teachers of the period propounded highly progressive forms of Buddhism.

Pala art in the Bihar region was partly an outgrowth of an already well-established local tradition, but it was also indebted to nearby centres such as SARNATH. Artistic remains prior to the Gupta period are scarcer in the Bengal region; it is likely that the first major fluorescence of the art of Bengal occurred in the Pala period, and the tradition flourished particularly in the later phase (11th–12th century). The art of this later Pala phase was primarily Hindu (mainly Vaishnava).

Materials and techniques. Most surviving images from the Pala–Sena period are made of stone, but there is a considerable corpus of metal images as well; fewer surviving examples are of terracotta and stucco, while only a handful are made of wood (*see also* §VIII, 15, 18 and 19 below). This is not surprising due to the relative durability of the respective media. The stone employed was primarily grey, grey-black or black in colour and was apparently quarried from a number of different sites. Stone types include phyllite and biotite or chloritic schists (rather than what have commonly been called, simply, 'chlorite' or 'basalt'). Stone images range in size from only a few centimetres in height to well over life-size.

Surviving metal sculptures that have been analysed are primarily fabricated of bronze (copper alloyed with tin), brass (copper alloyed with zinc), or varying amounts of tin, zinc and lead either singly or together. A few surviving examples are made of silver or gold and may represent an extensive practice of creating images in precious metals. Many metal images were gilded, and some were inlaid with metals of contrasting colours. Metal images were probably placed on altars and may have served in smaller, more personal shrines. They range from miniatures only a few centimetres high to extraordinary technical achievements a metre or more in height. The famous metal *Buddha* from Sultanganj (Birmingham, Mus. & A.G.), a pre-Pala period work of *c.* the 7th century, is well over life-size and suggests the existence of a monumental metalworking tradition that may have continued into the Pala–Sena period. Smaller pieces were generally solid cast, though larger ones are generally hollow. Frequently, the finished piece consisted of the main figure(s) and pedestal and a halo that was cast separately and inserted into the base of the image. Unlike south Indian metal pieces of the Chola period and later (*see* §(vi)(a) below), images from Bihar and Bengal do not have lugs or holes in the bases for being carried in processions.

The vast majority of terracotta and stucco sculptures take the form of panels that were set into the walls of temples or stupas as part of their exterior decoration. Most important among the terracottas are those at ANTICHAK in Bihar and Paharpur in Bangladesh; important stuccos are found at Nalanda and Apsadh, both in Bihar.

Format and style. Both Buddhist and Hindu images were created in similar formats and were stylistically similar (except during one brief phase in the late pre-Pala and early Pala period, when Buddhist and Hindu images apparently were sometimes created by artists trained in different traditions). Stone sculptures were most commonly executed as stelae with a large central figure and surrounding elements, such as a *kīrttimukha* (face of a lion-like mythical creature) at the top. (These motifs are

197. *Standing Bodhisattva*, black stone, h. 2 m, from Nalanda, Bihar, *c.* 7th century AD (Nalanda, Archaeological Museum)

also seen in metal images; see figs 198 and 201 below.) The format usually includes attendant figures flanking the main figure and *vidyādharas* ('bearers of wisdom') flying above, a decorated lotus pedestal and base on which the central figure stands and a halo or throne behind the main figure. From the 8th to the 10th century the back slab was usually rounded at the top, but in the 11th and 12th centuries it was pointed. Such stelae were apparently primarily used as images in shrines or were set into niches in the walls of temples. The majority of buildings were apparently made of brick, but few survive; there are no examples of Pala-period monuments with stone sculptures in the places originally intended by their makers. However, an idea of the original relationship between the carved stone images and the temples may be surmised from many of the intact structures at Pagan in Burma (now Mayanmar; *see* BURMA, §IV, 2), which were clearly modelled on Pala-period prototypes.

The Pala–Sena sculpture style evolved from a somewhat simple, Gupta-derived tradition. This is seen most clearly in the stucco images adorning Stupa/Temple 3 (*c.* late 6th century or 7th century) at Nalanda, in the early metal images (particularly the huge *Buddha* figure from Sultanganj and numerous pieces from Nalanda) and in a handful of stone images (see fig. 197). The style gradually developed towards increasing elaboration over the centuries. Greater detail appeared in specific elements, such as lotus petals, haloes, jewellery and garments, and there was also an increasing tendency to fill in every bit of space on an image with detail. As the style developed, images were often more three-dimensional. In particular, the central figures were often executed completely in the round and, in the case of stone images, detached from the stele background. Many of the later images are also larger in scale than earlier works. Later figures are more attenuated, less rounded and more angular and are often posed in the thrice-bent posture (*tribhaṅga*). Headdresses and crowns are high and elaborate in the later phase, and jewellery is even more detailed and richer. These developments may indicate growing technical proficiency on the part of the artists, but they also parallel the trend towards enrichment of form seen elsewhere in India during these centuries.

198. *Buddha* in *bhūmisparśa mudrā*, metal with silver inlay, h. 330 mm, from Kurkihar, Bihar, late 9th century AD or early 10th (Patna, Patna Museum)

199. *Avalokiteshvara*, gilded metal, h. 255 mm, from Kurkihar, Bihar, *c.* 12th century (Patna, Patna Museum)

Subject-matter. The most common subject among the Buddhist images of this period is the Buddha displaying the *bhūmisparśa mudrā* (earth-touching gesture; see fig. 198). This gesture refers to a specific event in the life of Shakyamuni that occurred while he sat under the famous *bodhi* tree at Bodhgaya. Through this gesture, he called the earth to witness his renunciation and his triumph over Mara, god of death and lust, thus assuring his own enlightenment. The special prominence given to the Buddha in *bhūmisparśa mudrā*, and hence the notion of the defeat of Mara (Maravijaya) at Bodhgaya, may be related to religious factors that brought that site and the concept of Buddhist attainment into prominence during the Pala period. Just as Sarnath, where the Buddha performed his first teaching, was prominent in the Gupta period and the image of the preaching Buddha prevailed in Gupta and Gupta-related art, the site of Bodhgaya, depicted through the earth-touching Buddha, was in all likelihood the paradigm for the Pala period. The emphasis on this image type in Pala lands led to its prominence throughout the Buddhist world, particularly in Burma and Tibet as well as in Java, Nepal and Thailand (*see* BURMA, §I, 3; INDONESIA, §I, 3; and THAILAND, §I, 3). Indeed, the internationalism of images popular during the Pala period is clearly manifested in the Buddhist art of nearby regions. Records of the visits of Buddhist pilgrims from outside India, most notably from China and Burma, document the strength of international activity during the Pala period in Magadha, the Buddhist homeland, and explain something of the means of transmission of art forms and ideas.

Many Buddhist stone stelae show a central Buddha, most commonly the Buddha in *bhūmisparśa mudrā*, surrounded by seven other scenes, the total group representing what had by then become a standard set of eight major events in the life of the Buddha. During the later Pala period representations of Buddhas wearing crowns and ornaments became relatively common. Such figures document the practice of esoteric forms of Buddhism, namely Vajrayana/Tantra (*see* BUDDHISM, §§I and III, 1). A few surviving representations of figures in *yuganaddha* (sexually joined) pose, further demonstrate the existence of esoteric Buddhism.

Bodhisattvas, particularly Avalokiteshvara (see fig. 199), are also shown in art, as are female figures, including, among others, Tara (see fig. 200), Prajnaparamita and Chunda. Votive stupas, most often carved in stone but sometimes cast in metal, commonly bore representations of Buddha figures that referred to events in his life, but other subjects were also sometimes depicted. Many miniature images were produced during this period, as is documented especially at Nalanda; the subject-matter of

200. *Tara*, black stone, h. 1.22 m, from Tetrawan, Bihar, *c.* last quarter of the 11th century (Calcutta, Indian Museum)

201. *Vishnu Trivikrama*, silver, h. 250 mm, from Vikrampura, Bangladesh, *c.* 12th century (Calcutta, Indian Museum)

these tiny stone stelae parallels that seen in the larger images. Tantric Buddhist figures, such as Heruka, Vajrasattva, Vairochana, Samvara and the *jina* Buddhas, were also included in the artistic repertory of Pala–Sena-period art, which is probably the most extensive of all the surviving Buddhist pantheons in India.

Among images of Hindu deities, those of Vishnu predominate, most commonly as Trivikrama (see fig. 201), one of his 24 icon forms determined by the order of the attributes he holds in his hands. (This form should not be confused with Trivikrama as one of the ten major incarnations of Vishnu.) Shaiva images are also well represented in the surviving Pala-period corpus and include a wide range of manifestations of Shiva alone or with his consort, Parvati. One striking example shows the divine pair joined in one body that is half-male and half-female in the form known as Ardhanarishvara (see fig. 202). Hindu images also include individual representations of Surya, Brahma, Agni, Karttikeya, Durga, Ganesha, Balarama and many of

202. *Ardhanarishvara*, black stone, h. 1.06 m, from Purapara, Bangladesh, late 11th century–early 12th (Rajshahi, Varendra Research Museum)

the other by then standard gods of the religion. A number of apparently unique conceptions must also be credited to the Bihar and Bengal artists. Among these is a distinctive form of the dancing Shiva in which the god stands on the back of his vehicle, the bull Nandi (see Huntington, 1985, fig. 18.31).

By the 13th century the Pala–Sena school was declining in Bihar and Bengal, due perhaps to the collapse of strong imperial control of the region by Buddhist and Hindu kings and the advent of the Muslims. However, the school took root elsewhere in Asia, particularly in Burma, Tibet and Nepal, where Pala style and imagery formed the foundation of local art traditions. Even earlier, during the fluorescence of the art of Bihar and Bengal, the styles had been exported (for example to Java). Thus the legacy of the Pala–Sena school of art lies not only in the large surviving body of work produced in India but also in its influence on international schools of Buddhist art.

See also §III, 5(i)(c), 6(i)(d) and 7(ii)(e) above.

(b) Orissa. Extensive textual sources are preserved defining the canons of Orissan architecture. Surviving Orissan sculpture is, for the most part, an integral part of an architectural setting. This contrasts with the situation in Bihar and Bengal, where surviving images were set into what are now lost architectural contexts but were not actually part of the fabric of the buildings. Orissan sculpture can only be fully understood within the context of the limitations imposed by the relevant architectural schemes.

The principal surviving architectural and sculptural monuments of the Orissa region date from the 7th through the 13th century. It is uncertain whether an extensive earlier tradition once existed but can no longer be traced, or whether the few existing early monuments, such as those at KHANDAGIRI AND UDAYAGIRI, represent a sporadic and intermittent art production prior to the 7th century.

Surviving examples indicate that stone was widely used in the 7th century both in constructing buildings and in the sculptural arts. The stone building tradition was probably introduced in Orissa by the Shailodbhava dynasty, which came into prominence in the second quarter of the 6th century and continued to rule until the second half of the 8th century. The stimulus for using stone may have come from outside the region, perhaps from the Deccan, as is suggested by stylistic associations between the 7th-century stone monuments of Orissa and those of the Early Western Chalukya dynasty of the Deccan (*see* CHALUKYA, §1). The Orissan sculptural style of the 7th century appears to have been influenced by the Gupta tradition, which had been widespread throughout north India in the preceding two centuries (*see* §6(i) above), as well as the contemporary art of neighbouring regions such as Madhya Pradesh (the location of ancient SIRPUR), Bihar, Andhra Pradesh and the Deccan. Such influences could easily have spread into Orissa during the early 7th century, when three rival kings—Shashanka of Bengal, Harsha of Kannauj and Pulakeshin II of the Early Western Chalukya dynasty—were apparently contenders for control over portions of the region. Indeed Shashanka, a devotee of Shiva, is traditionally credited with building the first Shaiva temple in Orissa, at the site of Tribhuvaneshvara (Bhubaneshwar).

Surviving sculpture represents both Hindu and Buddhist themes, though Hinduism was the prevailing religion in the region. Sculptures were created to be enshrined in temples, placed in niches or used as part of the richly carved surface decoration of temple walls. For example, in Bhubaneshwar, which has the greatest concentration of Hindu monuments, the Parashurameshvara Temple (*c.* 7th century) has a richly textured exterior carved with architectural motifs such as repeating *candraśālās* (arch shapes) as well as carved figures in niches (*see* BHUBANESHWAR, §2(i)). An image of *Karttikeya* (see fig. 203) in a niche on the east side of the temple's tower (*śikhara*) exemplifies the 7th-century style: the figure is full and fleshy, and the contours are soft, ultimately revealing a Gupta source as well as ties to contemporary Hindu works from neighbouring Bihar (*see* §(a) above). Although the figure is ornamented, the work is much simpler than the evolved Orissan style of later centuries, which is characterized (like other late Indian sculpture) by richness of ornamentation.

This later Orissan style, dominant by the late 10th century, is exemplified by a female figure (see fig. 204) from the Rajarani Temple at Bhubaneshwar (*see* BHUBANESHWAR, §2(iv)). The figure is voluptuous, with full, round breasts and large hips, and shows the thrust hip and thrice-bent posture (*tribhaṅga*) typical of *c.* 11th-century figures. The highly refined decorative details, especially in motifs such as the strands of gems and floral scrolls, are clearly derived from Gupta-related sources. Carved ornamentation on the exteriors of Orissan temples from the 10th century and later is generally deeply undercut, so that

203. *Karttikeya*, stone, Parashurameshvara Temple, Bhubaneshwar, Orissa, *c.* 7th century AD

204. Female figure, stone, Rajarani Temple, Bhubaneshwar, Orissa, *c.* 11th century

sunlight clearly distinguishes the forms. Figures are animated and carved with a crisper outline than is seen in earlier sculptures, lending a hardened quality rather than a soft fleshiness to the bodies. Figures from the mid-11th century adorning the famed Lingaraja Temple at Bhubaneshwar, for example, are in even more exaggerated and angular postures, and the forms of the body have been simplified, so that legs and arms are sometimes tubular, with little sense of fleshiness and definition of structure (*see* BHUBANESHWAR, §2(v)).

Orissa's numerous other sites with artistic remains include KONARAK, PURI, Chaurasi, Jajpur and Khiching. At Konarak, one of the largest Hindu temples ever constructed in India was built in the 13th century by the ruler Narasimha I (*reg* 1238–64) of the Ganga dynasty. The monument, the so-called Surya Temple, is believed to have taken some 20 years to construct. Fine chlorite was used for the carving of major images and doorframes, while laterite and khondalite (an easily weathered stone) were used for the main fabric of the structure. Carved of these more porous rocks, the exterior decoration of the monument lacks the precision and crispness of the chlorite images. Textual sources reveal that the major images were carved by master craftsmen, an importance suggested also by the allotment of the better-quality stone for their work. As the temple was dedicated to the sun god, it is not surprising that several of the finest carvings represent this deity (see fig. 205). A number of other chlorite carvings show Narasimha I himself. Free-standing sculptures atop

205. *Surya*, chlorite, Surya Temple, Konarak, Orissa, *c.* 1238–58

the forehall (*jagamohan*) of the temple depict musicians and fierce deities known as *bhairavas*. These images are massive and solid, and the figures are bulky and thick. The exterior walls of the temple bear female figures in various poses, as well as loving couples (*mithunas*).

The repertory of images in Hindu Orissan art includes many of the by then standard images of Hindu deities, such as Shiva and Vishnu in many of their forms and manifestations, Karttikeya, Ganesha, guardian/directional deities (*dikpālas*), Surya and goddesses such as Parvati, Lakshmi and Sarasvati. Orissa gives strong evidence of *sakta* (great goddess) cults, as well as other female cults, such as that of the 64 *yoginīs* (female ascetics). Two temples dedicated to the *yoginīs* survive in the region at Hirapur and Ranipur Jharial. There is also an emphasis on erotic imagery, namely the presence of *mithunas*, particularly at Konarak.

Architectural sculpture adorning the exterior walls of Orissan temples, highly organized into horizontal and vertical divisions, includes not only figurative sculpture in limited zones but also decorative motifs such as lions, *nāgas* (snake deities) and other symbolic forms, scrollwork and door and window decoration. Fully developed doorways often included a series of specific motifs, such as *dvārapālas* (guardians), a *navagraha* ('nine-planets') lintel and depictions of the river goddesses. A few exceptional temples, such as the Mukteshvara in Bhubaneswar, also have sculpted interior walls.

Orissa's numerous Buddhist monuments, less well known than their Hindu counterparts, were constructed in the 8th to the 12th century. After that time, as was true elsewhere in India, Buddhism ceased to be a major religious tradition, and important art works were rarely produced for Buddhist establishments. The Bhauma (Kara) kings of the 8th century were apparently early patrons of Buddhist art, which was also fostered by other dynasties. The style and materials used for Buddhist monuments do not differ significantly from those used in Hindu contexts, and the same artists may have worked on both Buddhist and Hindu projects. Strong ties to the Buddhist art of the adjacent state of Andhra Pradesh are apparent (*see* §(vi) below); indeed, many of the Orissan Buddhist sites were part of a cluster of centres that spanned both Orissa and northern Andhra Pradesh. In particular, stylistic ties are evident between the art of the Assia Hills in Orissa and the art at Salihundam in Andhra Pradesh. Four famous sites in the Assia Hills have yielded much of Orissa's known Buddhist art: RATNAGIRI, Lalitagiri (which is also called Nilitagiri), Udayagiri (not to be confused with Udayagiri-Khandagiri in Orissa or Udayagiri in Madhya Pradesh) and Vajragiri.

The dating of Orissan Buddhist sculpture relies on comparison with more securely dated Hindu monuments in Orissa and in nearby regions, since dated inscriptions are rare, and archaeological excavation has not yet been extensive. The Buddhist images of this period in Orissa are strictly Mahayana and Vajrayana/Tantric. Typical representations include Buddha figures, *bodhisattvas* (e.g. Avalokiteshvara; see fig. 206) and Tantric deities such as Samvara. Female figures, such as Tara, are also known. Images often have many arms and display other features

206. *Khasarpana Avalokiteshvara*, depicted as if within Mt Potalaka, speckled beige stone, h. *c.* 2 m, Udayagiri, Orissa, late 9th century AD or 10th

of 'later' art from elsewhere in India, such as the *tribhaṅga* posture and the use of rich ornamentation.

The rather grainy, porous stone used for Orissan Buddhist sculpture lends the images a soft appearance, in contrast to many contemporary images from Bihar and Bengal. The Orissan Buddhist style also seems to perpetuate Gupta aesthetics, so that even images from the 11th and 12th centuries are often softly modelled and gracefully posed and use a curved, rather than angular, outline for the body. As in Gupta images, eyes are often depicted in a downcast fashion rather than as if wide open. Coiffures recall the high, piled up and curled locks seen so commonly in Gupta images.

Fewer metal images are known from Orissa than from Bihar and Bengal, but those that survive suggest a once-flourishing metalworking tradition. The most important cache of metal pieces (Bhubaneshwar, Orissa Mus.) was found at Achutrajpur (near Banpur), where some 95 figures along with 20 stupas, a bell, a spouted pot and numerous other fragments and pieces were unearthed in 1963. Only five of the images are Hindu, ten are Jaina and the remainder are Buddhist, reflecting the fact that they were found in a ruined ancient Buddhist monastic site. That the monastery may have been founded as early as the 7th century is suggested by the discovery near by of copper-plate inscriptions of the Shailodbhava dynasty of Kongoda. The metal pieces, however, date primarily from the 9th and 10th centuries and show close stylistic affinities with the metal sculptures of Bihar, particularly those found at Nalanda. The diversity of styles and the resemblance of some of the pieces to works known to have been made outside Orissa suggest that some of the pieces were manufactured elsewhere and imported into the region.

After the 13th century lavish Hindu and Buddhist monuments ceased to be created in Orissa. The end of the era of large-scale temple construction does not seem to have been due to a lack of vigour in the religion and culture, as is indicated by the ambitiousness and technical proficiency of the later monuments. Instead political problems, perhaps caused by the advent of Muslims into the region, may have been a major factor in bringing the Orissan tradition to a close.

See also §III, 6(i)(d), and 7(ii)(d) above.

BIBLIOGRAPHY

BIHAR AND BENGAL

A. Broadley: 'The Buddhistic Remains of Bihar', *J. Asiat. Soc. Bengal*, xli (1872), pp. 209–312 [as booklet (Varanasi, 1979)]

J. Anderson: *Catalogue and Handbook of the Archaeological Collections of the Indian Museum*, ii (Calcutta, 1883), sections 1, 3

A Descriptive List of Sculptures and Coins in the Museum of the Bangiya Sahitya Parishad (Calcutta, 1911)

R. Basak and D. C. Bhattacharya: *A Catalogue of the Relics in the Museum of the Varenda Research Society, Rajshahi* (Rajshahi, 1919)

M. Ganguly: *Handbook to the Sculptures in the Museum of the Bangiya Sahitya Parishad* (Calcutta, 1922)

J. French: *The Art of the Pal Empire* (London, 1928)

N. K. Bhattasali: *Iconography of Buddhist and Brahmanical Sculptures in the Dacca Museum* (Dacca, 1929)

S. Kramrisch: 'Pala and Sena Sculpture', *Rupam*, xl (Oct 1929), pp. 107–26

R. D. Banerji: *Eastern Indian School of Mediaeval Sculpture*, Archaeol. Surv. India, New Imp. Ser., xlvii (New Delhi, 1933)

K. P. Jayaswal: 'Metal Images of Kurkihar Monastery', *J. Ind. Soc. Orient A.*, ii, no. 2 (Dec 1934), pp. 70–82

S. K. Saraswati: *Early Sculpture of Bengal* (Calcutta, 1937, 2/1962)

D. R. Patil: *The Antiquarian Remains in Bihar* (Patna, 1963)

P. L. Gupta, ed.: *Patna Museum Catalogue of Antiquities* (Patna, 1965), pp. 52–82, 118–59

E. Haque: *The Iconography of the Hindu Sculptures of Bengal, up to Circa 1200 AD* (diss., Oxford U., 1973)

J. Naudou, P. Stern and C. Picron: 'La Stele Pala-Sena: Evolution et chronologie', *Au Service d'une biologie de l'art*, i (Lille, 1978), pp. 57–97

S. K. Mitra, ed.: *East Indian Bronzes* (Calcutta, 1979)

Arts of Bengal: The Heritage of Bangladesh and Eastern India: (exh. cat., eds R. Skelton and M. Francis; London, Whitechapel A. G.; Manchester, C.A.G.; 1979–80)

F. Asher: *The Art of Eastern India, 300–800* (Minneapolis, 1980)

B. Bandyopadhyay: *Metal Sculptures of Eastern India* (New Delhi, 1981)

U. von Schroeder: *Indo-Tibetan Bronzes* (Hong Kong, 1981)

D. Mitra: *Bronzes from Bangladesh: A Study of Buddhist Images from District Chittagong* (New Delhi, 1982)

S. Huntington: 'Pre-Pala and Pala Period Sculptures in the Rockefeller Collection', *Apollo* (Nov 1983), pp. 370–78

——: *The Pala-Sena Schools of Sculpture* (Leiden, 1984)

S. Huntington with J. Huntington: *The Art of Ancient India: Buddhist, Hindu, Jain* (New York and Tokyo, 1985)

Leaves from the Bodhi Tree: The Art of Pāla India (8th to 12th Centuries) and its International Legacy (exh. cat. by S. Huntington and J. Huntington; Dayton, OH, A. Inst.; Baltimore, MD, Walters A.G.; Newark, NJ, Mus.; U. Chicago, IL, Smart Mus. A.; 1990)

S. Huntington, ed.: *Archive of Bihar and Bengal Art*, Microfilm Archive of the American Committee for South Asian Art (1994)

ORISSA

R. L. Mitra: *The Antiquities of Orissa*, 2 vols (Calcutta, 1875–80/*R* 1961–3)

K. Fischer: 'Orissan Art in the Evolution of Postmediaeval Indian Culture', *Orissa Hist. Res. J.*, iii/1 (1954), pp. 20–30

O. C. Gangoly: *Orissan Sculpture and Architecture* (Calcutta, 1956)

K. C. Panigrahi: *Archaeological Remains at Bhubaneswar* (Bombay, 1961)

P. Acharya: 'Varieties of Stones Used in Building Temples and Making Images in Orissa', *Orissa Hist. Res. J.*, xiii/2 (1965), pp. 9–20

K. Lal: *Temples and Sculptures of Bhubaneswar* (New Delhi, 1970)

A. Boner, S. R. Sarma and R. P. Das: *New Light on the Sun Temple of Koṇārka* (Varanasi, 1972)

D. Mitra: *Bronzes from Achutrajpur* (New Delhi, 1978)

V. Dehejia: *Early Stone Temples of Orissa* (New Delhi, 1979)

D. Mitra: *Ratnagiri (1958–61)*, 2 vols, Mem. Archaeol. Surv. India, lxxx (New Delhi, 1981–3)

T. Donaldson: *Hindu Temple Art of Orissa*, 3 vols (Leiden,1985–7)

SUSAN L. HUNTINGTON

(vi) South.

(a) Tamil Nadu. (b) Kerala. (c) Karnataka. (d) Andhradesha.

(a) Tamil Nadu. As elsewhere in India, the history of sculpture in the south-eastern state of Tamil Nadu is inextricably linked to the history of sacred architecture. Most sculpture was intended either to be seen in a niche or to function structurally as a figural pillar, antefix block, bordering frieze or other architectural member. Even the free-standing festival bronzes for which the region is famous have spent their ritual lives behind the protective bars of auxiliary shrine rooms, never to be seen, except frontally, by any but administering priests. On annual car-festival days (*rathostava*), when they are paraded beyond the temple precincts, these portable images are so richly bejewelled and garlanded as to be completely hidden from view, save for the faces.

Given this predominantly architectural context, the sculpture of Tamil Nadu can best be understood, in both iconographic and stylistic terms, when presented within a chronological framework defined by leading examples of temple architecture, beginning with the upper cave temple at Tiruchchirapalli, dedicated by the Pallava king Mahendravarman I (*reg c.* AD 570–630), and ending with the Minakshi Sundareshvara Temple in Madurai, largely rebuilt by Tirumalai Nayaka (*reg* 1623–59). The most significant monuments in this remarkably long tradition were commissioned by kings belonging to the Pallava dynasty of Kanchipuram (late 3rd–early 10th century) and the Chola dynasty of Thanjavur (late 9th–late 13th century). After a hiatus ushered in by Islamic invasions and protracted by Hindu resistance under the Vijayanagara empire, the 17th-century Nayaka rulers oversaw a final flurry of indigenous creativity that continued into the 20th century.

This dynastic periodization is time-honoured and convenient, but it should be used with caution for three reasons. First, the artistic remains of the entire region where the Tamil language is spoken (including northern Sri Lanka) present a picture of great homogeneity. Continuities in style and substance always predominated over disjunctive changes from one period to the next. In fact, more dramatic change sometimes occurred during a single generation than is apparent, for example, between monuments patronized by late Pallava and early Chola kings, respectively. Second, the shift of capitals—from Kanchipuram in northern Tamil Nadu to Thanjavur in the Kaveri River midland, then to Madurai, just opposite northern Sri Lanka—should not lead one to expect Pallava, Chola and Nayaka monuments to be confined to their respective portions of the region. Rather, each dynasty used the patronage of temples to project a visible, divinely sanctioned presence beyond the boundaries of its immediate territory. Third, overemphasis on dynastic labels obscures substantial contributions of feudatory powers. Patronage of major stone temples was a royal prerogative, but pledges of fealty and tribute did not prevent provincial rulers from participating in the meritorious activity of temple building. In short, dynastic labels are necessary but almost exclusively temporal in significance, little more than abbreviated references to period characteristics.

Sculptural art in early cave temples. The first substantial corpus of sculpture in Tamil Nadu consists almost exclusively of pairs of door-keepers or guardians (*dvārapālas*) carved in relief at the entrances to cave-temple sanctuaries. Approximately 80 caves with guardians are found in Tamil Nadu, many of them little known beyond their immediate vicinity, either because they lie abandoned on barren hillsides or because they are still in worship as the original cellae (*mūlasthāna garbhagṛhas*) of later structural temples that surround and hide them from view. The cave sanctuaries themselves are mostly devoid of sculpture contemporary with their excavation. Many empty cellae preserve tenon holes cut into altar-like projections, indicative of detached images now lost, perhaps made of wood, plaster or metal. Others, when dedicated to Shiva, house substantial *liṅgapīṭhas*, cylindrical phallic symbols set into square or octagonal pedestals, signifying an androgynous godhead. Only after the late 7th century was a Somaskanda panel (depicting Shiva enthroned with his consort, Uma, and son Skanda and attended by the other two members of a Hindu trinity, Brahma and Vishnu) sometimes set into the rear wall of a Shaiva sanctum behind the *liṅga*. As a rule, rock-cut images of other deities did not appear in cave sanctuaries until the mid-7th century.

Images of door-keepers are not uncommon elsewhere, but those found in the early caves of Tamil Nadu constitute a distinct regional type. With analogues in neighbouring Andhra Pradesh, the *dvārapāla* figures tend by their iconographic features to indicate the deity of the sanctum they guard. Most numerous are Shaiva guardians, who lean forward on heavy clubs that sometimes have snakes coiled about them. Some are crowned with trident tines, their partners with an axe blade, identifying them as personifications of Shiva's two most common attributive weapons. Vaishnava guardians are never armed, but motion towards the sanctuary with a spread-finger gesture of adoration called *vismaya mudrā*. In at least two cases, a sanctuary's dedication to Brahma is marked by the presence of bearded attendants in priestly attire holding lotuses or water-gourds. Female guardians (*dvārapālikās*) armed with bow and arrows or sword and shield signify dedications to the victory goddess Durga.

Only three cave temples in Tamil Nadu bear dated inscriptions. All are deep in the south, in the area controlled by the PANDYA dynasty, and have yielded the relatively late dates of AD 670, 770 and 773. Since only ten other caves are engraved with the dedications of kings whose regnal dates are known, comparative analysis of guardian figures is an essential means of ascertaining the relative chronology of the monuments. The series can be anchored near its beginning by a group of five caves that bear dedications naming a single king as patron, Mahendravarman I of the PALLAVA dynasty: these are the upper cave at Tiruchchirapalli, Mamandur North, Mandagappattu, Mahendravadi and Pallavaram. The largest of three caves at Vallam was dedicated by a vassal of Mahendravarman (but consecrated in the name of the vassal's father). Two others, at Dalavanur and Shiyamangalam, are usually also ascribed to Mahendravarman, although their inscriptions are sufficiently ambiguous to permit attribution to his father Simhavishnu (*reg c.* 550–70). A pre-Mahendravarman dating for Dalavanur and Shiyamangalam is posited by the relatively archaic appearance of their figural sculptures. Still earlier, stylistically, are the guardian figures of Mamandur South and Kuranganilmuttam, and of the Kotikal and Dharmaraja Mandapams at Mamallapuram.

The main stylistic common denominator of pre-Mahendravarman *dvārapālas* is a restrictive adherence to the ground plane. Regardless of pose, all limbs tend to project an equal distance from the matrix, giving the appearance of figures immobilized, half-buried in the wall. The workmanship suggests that the artists were relatively inexperienced in carving the extremely intractable medium, a coarse gneiss. Little trace of awkwardness survives in the guardians of Mahendravarman's time. With limbs disposed in conformity with the basic principles of foreshortening, and body axes shifting freely from strict alignment with the ground plane, they stand convincingly at ease within their niches. Seen to best advantage at Tiruchchirapalli and Mandagappattu, the life-size guardians look well muscled, their faces scowling, fangs bared at would-be intruders. By contrast the earlier *dvārapālas* seem incongruously childlike, much smaller than life-size as a rule, with disproportionately large heads and vacuous smiles or completely expressionless faces.

However, the dating of the rock-cut monuments of Tamil Nadu remains highly controversial, and stylistic approaches have been largely frustrated by the misinterpretation of a single inscription. From Mahendravarman's Mandagappattu cave dedication the inference has been made (gaining the certitude of fact in secondary literature on Indian art) that he initiated the art of rock-carving in Tamil Nadu, nearly a thousand years after the BARABAR AND NAGARJUNI caves were excavated in Bihar under the MAURYA dynasty. Referring to Mahendravarman by a title he is known to have assumed owing to his wide-ranging accomplishments, the Sanskrit verse can be translated as: 'Without brick or timber, metal or mortar, by the king Vichitra-citta ("multifarious mind") was this distinguished sanctuary designed for Brahma, Shiva and Vishnu' (adapted from Gopinath Rao). Given this striking circumlocution for rock-cut architecture, the presumption was made that the Mandagappattu cave constituted a novelty in the region when it was created. However, the phrase can better be construed as exemplifying the patron's brilliance as a poet; each of five quatrain dedications commonly attributed to Mahendravarman is composed in a different poetic metre and refers to the temple and its patron in unique, colourful (*vicitra*) phrases. This reading is more satisfactory because it permits recognition of the Mandagappattu guardian figures' relative maturity of style. It is also reinforced by knowledge of Mahendravarman's

207. *Shiva Gangadhara*, rock-cut granite, 2.2×2.6 m (panel), upper cave temple, Tiruchchirapalli, Tamil Nadu, *c.* AD 625

other, largely literary, accomplishments. A long but abraded inscription at Mamandur cites his authorship of two Sanskrit comedies (both still extant in the repertory of Kathakali troupes), a history of south Indian painting (now lost, together with the pictures) and an improved system of musical notation. He also claimed, among other things, to be a great statesman, soldier, lover, designer of musical instruments, composer, perfume distiller, architect, sculptor and 'tiger-among-painters' (*citrakārapuli*; see Ramachandran, 1933). Such an accomplished individual is surely not demeaned if the inauguration of rock architecture in Tamil Nadu is denied him.

Elimination of Mandagappattu as a false starting-point clears the way for possible recognition of other pre-Mahendravarman-period sculpture in the region. For example, some of the numerous Jaina inscriptions found in natural rock shelters throughout Tamil Nadu unquestionably predate the entire Pallava period, but little progress has been made in establishing the relative chronology of the low-relief icon panels that sometimes accompany them. Similarly, several cave temples excavated beyond the boundaries of active Pallava control, in the south in Pandya territory especially, must almost certainly be coeval with those named above, rather than later as is often assumed. One likely example of a pre-Mahendravarman cave in Pandya country is Pillaiyarpatti, a Shaiva cave with a rock-cut *liṅga* in its sanctuary and several figural sculptures in its antechamber (*mukhamaṇḍapa*), including a large relief image of the elephant-headed Ganesha (Tamil Pillaiyar: 'son [of Shiva]'). A probable dating is provided by the label inscription engraved on one of the pillars that has been placed palaeographically in the 5th century (see Nagaswamy, 1965).

While the relative chronology of the most archaic cave temples in Tamil Nadu is fraught with controversy, there is no disputing the region's oldest sculptural masterpiece. By virtue of its patronage by Mahendravarman and its matchless refinement and subtlety, the Gangadhara panel in the upper cave at TIRUCHCHIRAPALLI deserves recognition as one of those rare works of art which successfully embody a civilization's highest ideals (see fig. 207). Facing the cella (now empty) in a large eight-pillared hall (*maṇḍapa*) excavated high on the rock face of a citadel in territory that the Pallavas had conquered only a short time previously, the narrative relief's ostensible subject is the famous myth of Shiva's support and control of the River Ganga when it descended from the heavens. Standing at the centre with imperious ease, Shiva is shown about to catch the mermaid-like river goddess on two outstretched strands of his locks (*jaṭā*s). Surrounding deities, priests and royal devotees gesticulate their wonder in the gesture of *vismaya mudrā*.

Additional grounds for adulation become apparent from an eight-verse dedication engraved on the relief's framing pilasters. The inscription is organized in such a way that the first and last of four verses on either side refer directly to the 'matchless stone-body' between them. The first verse on the left introduces the parallel between Shiva as Gangadhara ('Ganga-holder') and the Pallava king as lord of the Kaveri River, which flows past the city below (Hultzsch, 1907–8):

> Being afraid that the god who is fond of rivers (*Śiva*), having perceived the Kâvîrî, whose waters please the eye, who wears a garland of gardens, and who possesses lovely qualities, might fall in love (*with her*), the daughter of the mountain (*Pârvatî*) [Shiva's wife], has, I think, left her father's family [the Himalayas] and resides permanently on this mountain, calling this river the beloved of the Pallava (*king*).

Anyone reading the verse *in situ* would realize that the adjacent sculpture visualizes the shared relationship, the ambiguities of which are heightened since the names Kaveri and Pallava are also euphemisms for courtesan and libertine (Srinivasan, 1964). Other verses on both sides of the panel reinforce the duality of reference, with epithets applicable to both deity and king and repeated suggestions to the effect that the sculpture is simultaneously a divine icon and a royal portrait.

Although there seems to be a remarkable bond between the image and its patron's own versified gloss, it must be acknowledged that this interpretation of the Tiruchchirapalli panel is not universally held. Some scholars, following Hultzsch, have presumed that a separate portrait of the king was installed in the cella, while others have denied that one was even contemplated. Only Michael Lockwood and his colleagues have also interpreted the Gangadhara relief as a dual god-king portrayal and thus an important precursor of the *devarāja* cults of the great temple-building monarchies of South-east Asia.

Appropriately enough for a work of such historical importance, the *Shiva Gangadhara* panel exemplifies wonderful mastery of the rock-carving medium as well as stylistic maturity. The most outstanding trait of sculpture of this period is its unprecedented naturalism. Mahendravarman was one of the most artistically inclined sovereigns known to Indian history, and it was perhaps at his behest that the Tiruchchirapalli master informed his work with a new sensitivity to human anatomy and posture and a corresponding attention to the substantiality of drapery and metalwork. A true sense of corporality is seen, for example, in the pliant bulge of Shiva's midriff, the creases between arm and chest, and the finely honed contours of all faces and limbs of the panel. Shiva's lower garment (*veṣṭhi*) and its trappings are rendered with a remarkable fondness for irregular, wavy pattern. In place of the schematic, parallel pleats seen on the earlier door-keepers, the major folds relate to the volume and position of the legs beneath, and the overlaid sashes have a crumpled alternation of girth and direction that suggests actual, starched fabric. Their languorous swags are echoed above by the arc of the padded sacred cord (*yajñopavīta*). Below, heavily welted hemlines have as counterpoint ribbons of the utmost delicacy, which cinch the belt and flutter down the columnar left leg (embodying Shiva's epithet Sthanu, meaning 'stationary' or 'postlike').

Further accentuation is provided by metallic ornaments: a locket slung about the waist on a thin double chain, jewelled studs on the belt and a wealth of filigree work on the pectoral, bracelets, armbands (*keyura*s), zoomorphic earrings and plaquettes of the crown. Yet for all their richness, these accoutrements do not overpower the organic forms they adorn. The sculptor has further harmonized the composition by repetition of sinuous curves. Like a musical leitmotif, undulations are introduced horizontally by the double strand of hair that Shiva extends to snare the goddess Ganga, then vertically in the taut coils of the cobra held in his lower right hand. Throughout the composition, echoing curves recur in such details as locks of hair, piled high and cascading over shoulders, chest and waistbands, even in the gently arched legs of the flying *deva*s; every figure is charged with the same rhythmic pulse.

The increased sophistication with which spatial effects were achieved in the poses of Mahendravarman-period door-keepers is also fully evident in the Gangadhara relief. No longer did the Pallava sculptor betray the least difficulty in separating figures from ground plane. The successful illusion of free-standing figures is even more remarkable considering the hieratic formality of the composition. Basically, all the figures face front and centre, and all are brought forward to the surface plane. Thus, without recourse to the conventions of foreshortening, which came into use in the following generation, the sculptor made the figures seem freely posed, unencumbered by the wall to which they adhere. This was accomplished by carving the figures in much higher relief than previously (undercut limbs seem to be modelled in the round) and by a judicious modulation of relief levels. With respect to the latter point, one can cite the obvious difference between Shiva's upper and lower arms at Tiruchchirapalli and the slightly earlier image at Shiyamangalam. Even more impressive is the continuous reduction of relief in the flying figures: from heads that are nearly disengaged from the wall to feet that just break through the surface. Clearly, this anticipates the dramatic spatial effects attained during the reign of Mahendravarman's son at Mamallapuram.

The Gangadhara relief was composed so as to create a hieratic statement of utmost formality without loss of naturalistic vitality. Matching pairs of subsidiary figures encircle the supreme deity, yet the resultant symmetry has been relieved with great subtlety. Across the top, for example, the two flying figures have their legs tucked up in virtually identical form, while their upper body poses are mirror opposites: outer hands resting at the hip, inner ones expressing adoration in *vismayā mudrā*. Minor variations in attire and coiffure sustain interest in the individuality of the two otherwise identical princely ascetics (*rājarṣi*s) below. These and other details preserve a sense of the natural within the rarefied atmosphere that surrounds Shiva, whose spellbinding presence draws everything else into line. He stands at royal ease, shifting his weight on the head of a dwarf-attendant (*gaṇa*) to catch the falling river goddess with studied nonchalance. Such peerless accomplishment deserves no lesser parting commendation than the patron/subject's own words. In translation from the right pilaster's opening verse (Hultzsch, 1907–8):

> When king Guṇabhara ['virtue-laden', i.e. Mahendravarman] placed a stone-figure in the wonderful stone-temple on the top of the best of mountains, he made in this way Sthâṇu ['stationary'] (*Śiva*) true to his name and became himself stationary [*sthāṇu*] (i.e., *immortal*) in the worlds together with him.

'Classical' Pallava sculpture. Judging from its frequent mention in later records of the dynasty, the greatest military triumph of the Pallavas was the sack of Badami, the capital of the Chalukyas of Badami (*see* CHALUKYA, §1), in AD 642 by Mahendravarman's son, Narasimhavarman I Mahamalla (*reg c.* 630–68). As a direct consequence of this decisive victory over Pulakeshin II (*reg* 609/10–42) the Pallavas enjoyed a respite for a quarter of a century from border wars to the north-west. During this period the majority of their most ambitious and successfully realized rock-cut monuments were created. Pulakeshin's defeat by Mahamalla ('the Great Wrestler') terminated an unprecedented chain of conquests and aggrandizement by the Pallavas' arch-rival for hegemony over south India. During the previous three decades, the Chalukya empire had far outgrown the borders of Karnataka to include much of Maharashtra, Gujarat and Andhra Pradesh, and Pulakeshin had even defeated the great north Indian sovereign Harshavardhana (*reg* 606–47) on the banks of the Narmada River. Consequently, the treasury that Mahamalla's forces plundered must have been vast, and to some degree the ensuing building campaign at MAMALLAPURAM represents the brief golden age that it financed.

If nothing but the five monolithic temples commonly named after the Pandavas, the heroes of the *Mahābhārata* epic, had survived from the reign of Mahamalla (*see* MAMALLAPURAM, fig. 1), the perpetuation of his memory by the site name Mamallapuram ('city of the great wrestler') would be justly deserved. But his fame does not rest just on these, or on the fact that more rock-cut monuments were produced during his reign than in all previous generations of Pallava patronage. Without doubt his glory is best reflected by the immense cliffside relief known as *Arjuna's Penance* or *Descent of the Ganga* (see fig. 208).

208. *Arjuna's Penance* or *Descent of the Ganga* (centre detail), rock-cut gneiss, 12×25 m, Mamallapuram, Tamil Nadu, *c.* AD 650

The relief sculpture, India's largest (12×25 m), has attracted considerable scholarly attention since 1914, when problems with the received tradition that it represents Arjuna's Penance were first enunciated (jointly by Jouveau-Dubreuil and Goloubew; much of the literature is cited by Willetts and Ramaswami). Equally serious objections to their alternative interpretation that the relief depicts the Descent of the Ganga were raised in a lengthy defence of the traditional view (see Ramachandran, 1950–51). The controversy is best resolved if both myths, together with several others, are accepted as constituting a series of allegorical tributes to the patron, Mahamalla himself.

His father's *Shiva Gangadhara* panel at Tiruchchirapalli, with Sanskrit commentary attached, provides the immediate precedent for recognizing Mahamalla as the ultimate subject of this great relief at Mamallapuram. Vital corroboration, together with much of the relief's proclamatory content, comes from contemporary *praśasti* texts, dynastic panegyrics that started to appear in the 7th century as preambles to royal land grants and other documents. Like them the relief eulogizes the reigning king, his attributes, accomplishments and ancestry, traceable back through epic times and, ultimately, to divine origins. The major difference between written *praśasti*s and this visual example is a function of medium; whereas words must be read sequentially in a fixed order, many details of a picture can be apprehended simultaneously or in an indefinite variety of sequences. Thus the visual medium is more conducive to the layering of meanings, and in full consciousness of this potential the relief was designed with multiple identities in mind for several of its major figures. As in the written *praśasti*s, mythic characters appear variously as putative ancestors through whom the king's lineage is traced or as archetypes of his character and achievements.

Since two mythic characters have been recognized most frequently, albeit as mutually exclusive subjects of the relief's iconography, they are best introduced first and together. The ascetic standing just above the temple scene can be interpreted as depicting both the Pandava prince Arjuna, in pursuit of divine weapons, and Bhagiratha, at whose behest the Ganga came to earth. Both Arjuna and Bhagiratha performed austerities (*tapas*) in the Himalayas, staring at the sun through clenched fingers while standing for long periods on one foot. Both were ultimately rewarded by manifestations of Shiva, who is shown in the relief displaying the gesture of fulfilling vows (*varada mudrā*). In further consonance between the myths and the relief's iconography, both moments of revelation are described in the *Mahābhārata* as witnessed by throngs of divine and semi-divine beings, including part-bird musicians (*kinnaras*) and aquatic snake deities (*nāgas*). The latter form a prominent heptad in and beside the central crevice, identification of which as the River Ganga is fixed, in part, by the humorous vignette of the cat deceiving mice by feigned austerities, a fable always situated by the Ganga in its several textual variants (see Heras). The river itself, the prominence of which near the relief's centre was originally augmented by actual running water, illustrates the rich multivalence with which the entire composition must be read. While obviously representing in its descent the dénouement of Bhagiratha's penance, the Ganga defines the setting where Arjuna practised his austerities. It also serves to locate Badaritpovana, represented by the temple scene below, where Arjuna (in an earlier incarnation as Nara, with Narayana (Vishnu, enshrined in the temple)) practised the austerities that empowered him—according to Shiva, shown pointing out the connection—to wrestle with the god and to be worthy to receive the Pashupata weapon, personified as the mask-bellied dwarf.

The question remains how these overlapping myths appear as the visual *praśasti* of the king. For Arjuna the analogies are reasonably apparent. Later inscriptions indicate that Pallava kings assumed titles meaning 'Arjuna's equal in battle' (*Yuddhārjuna*, *Samaradhanaṁjaya Pārthāvikrama*; see Hultzsch, 1909–10, and Krishna Sastri). But it is Narasimhavarman's prime title, Mahamalla, that cognoscenti recognized in the magnificent depiction of Arjuna's penance (and subsequent wrestling with Shiva). In effect the relief is an immense visual gloss upon the name of the place where it is located: Mamallapuram, 'City of the Great Wrestler'.

With the myth of Bhagiratha and the Descent of the Ganga, it is again a later inscription that preserves an analogical reference to the king. Composed one century after Mahamalla's reign, a verse in the Kashakudi plates praises the Pallava dynasty with a *double entendre* on the word *avatāra* ('descent'; Hultzsch, 1891):

> From him [Ashokavarman, son of Pallava, a mythic progenitor] descended the powerful, spotless race of the Pallavas

[*vaṁśāvatāra*], which resembled a partial incarnation [*aṁśāvatāra*] of Vishnu, as it displayed unbroken courage in conquering the circle of the world with all its parts, (*and*) as it enforced the special rules of all castes and orders, and which resembled the descent of the Ganga [*Gaṅgāvatāra*] (*on earth*), as it purified the whole world.

Since Arjuna and Nara, his earlier incarnation, are considered fractional incarnations (*aṁśāvatāras*) of Vishnu, the Kashakudi verse may be said to verbalize the bipolar organization of the relief. On the left, in direct alignment with the enshrined icon of Vishnu, his series of full and partial incarnations is recalled, starting with Kurma, the tortoise perched directly beneath the temple, through Nara (seated in horizontal equity with Vishnu), to Arjuna and, ultimately, the patron whose palace was constructed on the hill above the relief. Meanwhile, like the purifying waters of the Ganga, blessings flow from the unbroken succession of Pallava rulers through the centuries. The 7th-century sculptor integrated both myths in a revolving cycle that rises on the left and descends on the right. In terminology borrowed from ancient Indian aesthetics, the relief amounts to a visual *prahelikā*, a sumptuous 'confection'-like conundrum. As if posing a riddle, its ambiguous iconography prompts one to question whether the chief protagonist is Arjuna or Bhagiratha. But the question is rigged, since the correct answer is 'both to a degree, but ultimately neither'. Both are archetypes for, but are not themselves, the principal subject, who is the Pallava king Mahamalla.

To the extent that the relief's iconography can accommodate at least three separate narratives, it exemplifies that most recondite of Sanskrit literary genres, the simultaneous narrative (*saṁdhānakāvya*). Significantly, the earliest textual example is attributed to the famous Pallava court poet, Dandin (who is known from the autobiographical prologue of his romance *Avantisundarīkathā* ('Story of Avantisundari') to have visited 'Mahamallapuram' just two or three decades after the relief was created). His *Rāghava-Pāṅdavīya* was a sustained conflation of India's two great epics, the *Rāmāyaṇa* and *Mahābhārata.* Though lost but for a single stanza, it survives in later versions, in which each verse can be read as furthering two or more story lines at once. All the major figures in the relief at Mamallapuram function in the same manner. Once this propensity is recognized, both in the literary circles of the Pallava court and, specifically, in the relief's iconography, the multiple identities of many other figures in the composition are revealed. Typically, each serves either to highlight the patron's own character or to represent one or more of his illustrious ancestors. Frequently, adjacent figures provide the necessary iconographic clues to establish an identification, serving, in effect, as pictographic labels.

In lieu of an exhaustive reading of the relief's iconography, it must suffice to show how one character is incorporated into the royal panegyric. The Vedic seer Agastya, chief patriarch of Brahmanical culture in south India, is represented by the third (now headless) figure seated immediately behind the youth shouldering a water-pot. By carrying the water-pot in one hand and pointing at this ascetic with the other, the youth offers a charade-like identification of Agastya, the 'pot-born' (*kumbhayoni*). Agastya's presence is called for and reiterated in several written *praśastis* of the dynasty, because his destruction of the demon Vatapi, when first taming the south, foreshadowed Mahamalla's conquest of the Chalukya capital Vatapi (now Badami). More clearly than any other element of iconography, the presence of Vatapi-slaying Agastya confirms the characterization of the great relief as a royal eulogy, purposefully created at the centre of Mahamalla's victory-memorial city.

As regards a stylistic assessment of Mahamalla-period sculpture, clearly the virtuosity of Pallava sculptors was at its height during the third quarter of the 7th century. Their style can be defined in terms of four partially antithetical characteristics. To a degree rarely matched in other regions or periods of Indian art, they seemed to strive simultaneously for naturalism and for stylized accentuation, for stark simplifications of surface combined with spatial effects of great sophistication.

The skilful harmonizing of the first two seemingly polarized tendencies, that is towards naturalism and stylization, was already in evidence during the previous generation. The Shiva Gangadhara figure at Tiruchchirapalli was laden with jewelled accoutrements of utmost richness without diminishing the sense of corpulent flesh. At Mamallapuram the sculptors managed to incorporate still greater degrees of naturalism and stylization within a single composition without losing cohesiveness of style.

For example, in the principal trio of the relief, Arjuna is depicted much more naturalistically than either Shiva, who is presenting him with a spirit-weapon, or the personified weapon itself. The differences between them are greater than is necessary for advancing the narrative, as if the artist was intentionally contrasting an individualized human being with more conventionalized deity types. This is particularly true of the facial renderings. As befits a hero who coerced the spirit realm by will-power alone, Arjuna's features show great strength of character and resolve. His head is thrown back in defiance, with angular brows that accentuate his stare. Compared to the generalized roundness of facial planes and the bland smiles of Shiva and the Pashupata weapon-personification, Arjuna's prominent cheek-bones, flared nostrils and broadly set mouth look as if they were modelled on a specific individual. Consistent with these more realistically observed features, anatomic detail was executed with remarkable specificity. Arjuna's sunken ribcage may be somewhat overdone, but the way wiry muscles and ligaments are shown adhering to protruding elbows and knees is very convincing, as are deft finishing touches such as the painfully taut arch of the raised foot and the thin moustache that overlays his beard.

Elsewhere on the relief, visibly human youths are shown performing their daily ablutions in the Ganga alongside fanciful riverine serpents. The same dichotomy between convincingly human individuals and conventionalized supernatural creatures can be seen throughout Mamallapuram. Among the monolithic temples at the site, the first gallery of the Dharmaraja Ratha has a quartet of priests who are far more individualized and naturalistically proportioned than the equally well-carved but ineffable deities near by. In the cave temple known as the Adi Varaha Mandapam, the labelled images of the Pallava kings

Simhavishnu and Mahendravarman are convincing portraits, not only compared to adjacent Shiva and Brahma icons but even within their own panels in comparison to their wraith-like consorts. The reason for the deliberate stylization of their queens is that they represent personifications of Prosperity (Lakshmi) and the Earth (Bhudevi) rather than actual human wives. This metaphysical difference between portrait and personification has been evoked by giving the goddesses extremely prominent noses, small but full lips, and sinewy limbs that seem to stretch to impossible lengths. Yet, remarkably, their charms are not diminished by their stylized unearthliness. In taking note of this formal dualism at Mamallapuram between 'intensive naturalism (for men and animals) and appropriately abstract canon of proportions' for deities, one art historian expressed the opinion that it typified Indian art generally (Rowland). However true this may be, it is no accident that the discussion arose in the context of the great relief and contemporary sculptures at Mamallapuram, for nowhere else are these polar tendencies pushed further apart. To the extent that later artists sometimes strove to emulate this delicate balance, Pallava art of the Mahamalla period may justifiably be characterized as 'classical'.

The other two distinguishing aspects of this 'classical' Pallava style, the simplification of surface and effective spatial illusion, are not as antithetical as naturalism and stylization, but they are rarely combined with such assurance elsewhere in Indian art. The simplicity is most evident in the very sparing use of ornament against sleekly streamlined organic forms. The extreme hardness of the region's rock (gneiss) was taken by some scholars to account for this simplified, 'stonier' style, as opposed to the more easily carved sandstone, schist and trap that predominate further north at sites such as Badami, Ellora and Ajanta. It is true that this may have fostered a tendency to concentrate upon essential forms and forgo the luxuriant frameworks and jewelled accoutrements that are ubiquitous in Indian art. But difficulties inherent in the medium cannot fully account for the remarkable restraint and effectiveness with which such limited ornament was applied. This was pre-eminently an art of the human figure. Mahamalla's sculptors recognized the value of large, plain surfaces for positioning their dynamic figures in spacious, stagelike niches and for offsetting without distraction the fluid, linear contours of organic form.

To substantiate this characterization it may be noted that walls surrounding sculpture niches on the Dharmaraja Ratha and within the Mahishasuramardini Mandapam are completely devoid of embellishment (*see* MAMALLAPURAM, figs 1 and 2). Not as much as a single straight line is scored around the bordering framework. Proof that this resulted from conscious restraint rather than the exigencies of working in an obdurate material is plentiful. At a sufficient distance from the all-important human figures so as not to overpower them, the full range of embellishments is replicated. Inhabited dormers (*gavākṣa*s), theriomorphic joist-ends, human and animal gargoyle spouts perforated to function and richly scrolled simulations of metal sheathings are all unstintingly detailed. Even gratuitous touches of humour appear where scarcely noticeable, for example in the endless variety of coiffure, expression and even ethnic type among the miniature heads that peer from the dormers like denizens of heaven.

The fourth distinguishing quality of 'classical' Pallava sculpture, adeptness in the treatment of space, is perhaps the most distinctive trait of the period. This is because the modes of positioning figures in relief involve deliberate conventions that are less subject to personal whim or qualitative differences in skill among contemporary artists than the other three qualities discussed above. Consequently, spatial conventions tend to be quite uniform for any given period. They can also be shown to have developed progressively from one period to the next as techniques were attempted, refined and passed on. Thus by contrast to the archaic female guardians of the pre-Mahendravarman-period Kotikal Mandapam, which appear embedded in the sanctuary walls, identically equipped 'classical' counterparts on the Draupadi Ratha are clearly the work of a sculptor fully conversant with foreshortening techniques. This ability to free figure from ground is in evidence throughout Mamallapuram. Roy Craven has effectively characterized Pallava narrative reliefs as appearing 'as if the action took place behind a gossamer screen which expands with the straining forms but always holds them to a constant plane'.

This assessment of Pallava sculpture dating from the third quarter of the 7th century as embodying a 'classical' style receives rare corroboration from Dandin's autobiographical prologue to his *Avantisundarīkathā*. The Pallava court poet once visited Mamallapuram as the guest of a master sculptor, Lalitalaya. The sculptor was seeking the poet's commendation for his restoration of a beach-front reclining Vishnu image, perhaps the very one that survives near the centre of the Shore Temple complex. Lalitalaya's skilful mend of a severed arm was duly praised, after which the sculptor modestly conceded that his father Mandhatar had been a far superior artist. Since Dandin's visit is best dated to the years immediately preceding the Shore Temple's construction (*c.* 700), Mandhatar may have headed the Pallava atelier at the site during its heyday in the time of Mahamalla. By contrast with his father's era, Lalitalaya went on to characterize his own as one in which artists had become dispirited, their efforts thwarted by a precipitous decline in royal patronage. An explanation for the apparently abrupt end of the 'classical' Pallava period is alluded to by Dandin. During his childhood, in 674 to be precise, the Chalukyas finally managed to exact revenge for Mahamalla's rout of Pulakeshin in 642: in a reversal of dynastic fortunes the Pallava capital was sacked, though the ruler at that time, Parameshvaravarman I (*reg c.* 669–90), managed to survive in a tactical retreat.

Judging from the physical evidence of temple patronage that survives from the ensuing years of Parameshvaravarman's reign, the sculptor Lalitalaya's lament was fully justified. Only one new monument at Mamallapuram can be securely attributed to Parameshvaravarman, while inscriptions indicate that he appropriated at least four of his predecessors' temples, namely the Dharmaraja Ratha and the Dharmaraja, Adi Varaha and Ramanuja Mandapams. The one original excavation, the Ganesha Ratha, certainly confirms stylistically that a disruption in the arts must have coincided with reversals on the battlefield; its diminutive *dvārapāla*s are awkwardly disposed, and the other carving on the monolith is coarse by previous standards. Similar inelegancies of proportion and finish betray two bas-reliefs elsewhere at Mamallapuram as intrusive additions to their respective sanctuaries, datable on stylistic grounds to this period of relative decline. Situated in the third-storey cella of the Dharmaraja Ratha and the central sanctuary of the Mahishasuramardini Mandapam, both are Somaskanda panels, depicting Shiva, his consort Uma and their son Skanda. In iconographic terms their importance cannot be overstated, as they constitute the earliest formulations of the most recurrent icon type of the late Pallava period. Since both include as subordinate attendants the other two major gods of the Hindu trinity, Brahma and Vishnu, the popularity of the type can be explained, in part, as registering partisan Shaiva sentiments. But the existence of an implicit political dimension is not surprising, given the uses to which religious iconography had been put by earlier Pallava kings.

The late Pallava 'embellished' style. Somaskanda iconography became closely associated with the Pallava dynasty during the reign of Narasimhavarman II Rajasimha (*reg* 690–728). Significantly, he was the son of Parameshvaravarman I, during whose reign the icon type was initiated. Inscriptions in two of the numerous structural temples he commissioned during a period of revived prosperity for the kingdom draw explicit parallels between the Shaiva holy family and Rajasimha's relationship to his father. In foundation inscriptions of both the Talagirishvara at Panamalai and the Kailasanatha at KANCHIPURAM, Rajasimha is equated with the war god Skanda by virtue of their fathers' common name, Parameshvara, and their shared propensity to be victorious over enemies (see Hultzsch, 1890, and Rangacharya).

As in the panegyrics of his predecessors and successors, Rajasimha's inscriptions draw numerous other parallels between king and mythic archetypes. Likewise the proliferation of iconographic themes visualized in the sculptural programmes of his temples is quite impressive. Nevertheless, the prominence accorded to this single, highly formalized configuration of the Somaskanda icon was unprecedented. Well over 40 low-relief Somaskanda panels survive from the temples of Rajasimha, plus fragments of numerous others that were merely painted in the peripheral chapels around the Kailasanatha's courtyard. Most were enshrined in positions of supreme sanctity directly behind the *liṅga* in the innermost cella of their respective temple. Clearly the fusion they constituted between the prerogatives of deity and kingship was extraordinarily complete and satisfying to the patron and to several of his successors, who perpetuated use of the type. In a relatively minor example that appears over a subsidiary shrine door at the rear of the Kailasanatha (see fig. 65 above), Shiva in a towering crown is enthroned with his consort seated dutifully to his left holding their son, like an heir apparent, on her lap. Behind them, like ministers of church and state, the priestly creator Brahma and order-preserving Vishnu raise approving hands in benediction. Curiously, the royal parasol is always shown off-centre over consort and son rather than over Lord Shiva himself, indicative perhaps of an emphasis on the dissemination of powers and legitimacy.

The same rear wall of the Kailasanatha provides an excellent sampling of the iconographic riches with which Rajasimha-period temples were constructed and adorned. Dramatically projecting from every corner, rampant lions prompt simultaneous recollection of the patron's official regnal name and favoured epithet: Narasimhavarman, meaning the 'protected by the man-lion' incarnation of Vishnu who burst from a column, and Rajasimha, the mauling 'royal lion (in the face of) dense troops of the elephants of his daring foes' (from the foundation inscription; see Hultzsch, 1890). Given the density with which heraldic lion pilasters are distributed on its walls, it is no surprise that the temple's official designation was not Kailasanatha, as it is commonly known today, but Rajasimha-Pallaveshvara. Strictly speaking, the name refers to Shiva as 'Lord of the Pallava Lion among Kings', but a hint of deified kingship is also implied. In other words, the temple may be said to confer lordship on the Pallava king Rajasimha himself by deliberately coalescing the identities of patron-deity and king. The names of several earlier Pallava temples conform to this same formula, which persisted as long as kings governed south India, but nowhere is there stronger iconographic support than here for the royal apotheosis. Similarly, an encircling band of several hundred royal epithets, repeated in four different scripts on the base mouldings of the enclosure's chapels, serves to permeate the entire complex with glories of the king. Some are expressions of piety and devotion to Shiva, but many others are deliberately multi-referential, as applicable to the supreme deity as to a king of kings. To cite one example, 'He Whose Sign Is the Bull' pertains equally to Shiva, whose totemic vehicle is the bull Nandi, and to any Pallava king, the dynastic crest bearing the same animal.

Nandi appears in rare semi-anthropomorphic form dancing beside Shiva Nataraja, the Lord of Dance, in a niche at the rear of the Kailasanatha Temple. While Brahma and Vishnu look on approvingly from countersunk panels to the sides, eight-armed Shiva kicks one leg aloft in a dance pose known as *ūrdhva tāṇḍava* ('upright dance'). Only a dwarf flautist survives on the lower panel of accompanists, while another dwarf dances on the side opposite Nandi. Overhead a pedestalled image of elephant-headed Ganesha presides, and a jewelled festoon arches from the mouths of floriated water-spirits (*makaras*) being ridden, or tamed into symmetry, by two more playful dwarfs. The narrative occasion that unites so many disparate elements is the myth of Shiva's victory over the goddess Kali in a dancers' duel. As recounted, for example, in the foundation myth of the temple at Tiruvelangadu, where the duel is said to have occurred, the great goddess matched every move of Shiva's cosmic dance until he sent galaxies colliding with one swift vertical kick—not that she was unable to follow suit, but doing splits was unlady-like (Sivaramamurti, 1974).

The Kailasanatha's walls are densely adorned with sculptural elements, with many subsidiary figures stacked between pilasters and the entire assembly bound top and bottom by floral and animate friezes. Clearly the governing aesthetic was one that saw each surface area as a void to be filled and, as such, the contrast with Mahamalla-period 'classicism' could hardly be more dramatic or complete.

Apparently, the lapse in artistic activity and standards during the intervening reign of Parameshvaravarman I was short-lived. Technical proficiency was fully restored, but the premium formerly placed on naturalistic form and understatement was negated in favour of maximizing surface richness.

To call the resultant style 'embellished' is to grant due recognition to the paramount status of ornament (*alaṁkāra*) in the conceptual framework of Indian aesthetics, particularly during the 8th century. This was the period when Dandin and his contemporary *alaṁkārikā*s defined the excellence of poetry in terms of ever-expanding lists of figures of speech (*alaṁkāra*s). Subsequently, a unified theory of suggestion gained ascendancy in literary circles, but in the visual arts it is safe to say that the preoccupation with ornamental embellishment remained constant, with rare exceptions, to the present day. Even liturgically, the adornment of images (*alaṁkāraṇam*) with jewellery, vestments, flowers or coloured pastes remains a primary activity of temple priests, and nowhere more so than in Tamil Nadu.

Little of artistic excellence remains to be seen at the other temples that Rajasimha sponsored at Kanchipuram, Mamallapuram, Panamalai and elsewhere, primarily because the soft sandstone has not weathered well. Many surfaces, even of the Kailasanatha, are further obscured beneath thick layers of well-intentioned but generally disfiguring plaster restoration of uncertain date. The same is true for most later Pallava temples of the 8th and 9th centuries. Modest in scale as a rule and unremarkable for any innovative contribution to the south Indian temple tradition, they seem to be indicative of the ever diminishing resources, if not ambition, of a dynasty losing control of its feudatories.

Chola sculpture in stone and bronze. Not surprisingly, perhaps, the first indications of fresh artistic life coincided with the rise of the Cholas to supremacy in the late 9th century. The transfer of regional dominance from the Pallavas of Kanchipuram to the Cholas of THANJAVUR occurred gradually during this period, and the emergence of a new artistic idiom was equally gradual. Vijayalaya (*reg c.* 846–71), the first ruler at Thanjavur to resurrect the name Chola from purely literary annals of the Sangam age (*c.* 1st–3rd centuries AD), never renounced fealty to the Pallavas, and early Chola temples faithfully exemplify adherence to long-established norms in plan and iconography. Only late in his reign did the second Chola king, Aditya I (*reg c.* 871–907), openly revolt, effectively ending Pallava rule in 903. Thus it may be appropriate to identify the first innovative trends in the greatest temple assigned to his reign, the Nageshvarasvami (*c.* 886) at KUMBAKONAM. Exquisite taste in the execution and distribution of its sculptures sets the Nageshvarasvami apart from other 9th-century temples in the region. Perhaps never before or since was bolder use made of unadorned wall surfaces to offset and accentuate a few figure sculptures. Only a rigorous grid of undecorated plank mouldings and chastely profiled pilasters serves to stabilize and separate figures. Beneath intersection points are set miniature panels of narrative relief, scenes from the *Rāmāyaṇa* mostly, on the scale and with the delicacy of ivory-carving. But it is the almost palpable sense of the living presence of the major niche figures that sets the Nageshvarasvami apart. For the first time in over two centuries an unabashed embrace of naturalism seems to have inspired sculptors

209. *Victorious Durga*, granite, 1.5×0.5 m (centre panel), Brahmapurishvara Temple, Pullamangai, Tamil Nadu, *c.* AD 910

and with such success that most scholars are convinced that the figures are portraits of specific individuals, though these have not yet been identified.

Something of this new-found interest and skill in depicting the human figure animates the deities that inhabit niches (*devakoṣṭha*s) at the cardinal points of the Brahmapurishvara (*c.* 910) at Pullamangai (see fig. 209) and a few other Chola temples of the early 10th century. In an iconographic formula that dates back at least to the 7th century, Durga stands victorious on the severed head of the buffalo demon. Her *tribhaṅga* ('triple-bend') contrapposto also exemplifies a much older tradition. But her faultless proportions and earnest expression, the latter intensified by the slight tilt of her head, mark the sculpture as the work of one who was as intent on living models as he was faithful to inherited canons.

Five donative records engraved on the Brahmapurishvara are ascribed to the time of Parantaka I (*reg c.* 907–54), the earliest dated to his third regnal year. None is a foundation inscription *per se*, but the superlative quality of the temple's sculptures and the lavish application of ornamental embellishment, such as the jewelled bands and scrollwork of each pilaster, leave little doubt that Parantaka I was the principal donor. As befits a royal chapel, numerous episodes of epic valour are depicted in miniature on the 'necking-blocks' beneath each half and full pilaster of the exterior walls. The split-pilaster niche in which Durga is installed (and still worshipped) does not differ in its basic configuration and location from innumerable others dating back to the earliest stone temples of the 7th century. For reasons that no longer are entirely clear, on the region's Shiva temples victorious Durga images invariably occupy a niche on the north side of the antechamber (*ardhamaṇḍapa*). This positioning remains constant whether the temple faces east, as is most common, or west. Similarly, at Pullamangai a stately *Ganesha* occupies its standard position on the opposite (south) wall of the antechamber. In keeping with the literal meaning of his name ('Lord of the *gaṇa*s'), he is surrounded by seven varied dwarfs with belted pot-bellies similar to his own; they minister to him with musical instruments and bowls of his favourite sweets. On the temple proper (*vimāna*) the niches are occupied by the most common sequence of the period: images of *Shiva Dakshinamurti* (the supreme teacher) and *Shiva Lingodbhava* (the infinite pillar of light) on the south and west respectively, the former obscured by a later subshrine, and Brahma the creator, with three visible faces, on the north.

Parantaka enjoyed a long and for the most part successful reign until Krishna III (*reg c.* 939–68), an invader of the RASHTRAKUTA dynasty from Karnataka, won a decisive victory against him in 949. Though Chola power remained at a low ebb through several reigns for the rest of the 10th century, no corresponding decline is evident in the figural art of the region. On the contrary, mastery of the human figure by sculptors working in stone and in bronze was maintained at levels rarely matched after the early 11th century. This can be corroborated by a number of museums in Europe and North America that possess members of a unique and exquisite set of goddess images from Kanchipuram. Arriving in Paris in 1927 (with reliable but as yet unpublished confirmation of the Kanchipuram provenance), they were dispersed as follows: three to the Musée Guimet, Paris, and one each to the British Museum, London; Royal Ontario Museum, Toronto (see fig. 210); Detroit Institute of Arts; Minneapolis Institute of Arts; Nelson–Atkins Museum of Art, Kansas City, MO; and the Arthur M. Sackler Gallery in Washington, D.C.

All nine sculptures depict approximately life-size goddesses seated in the same cross-legged position against rounded back slabs. While each of the goddesses holds a different weapon, six of the nine hold identical skull-bowls (*kapāla*s), and the other three must have done so before they were damaged. This shared attribute and an appetite for blood offerings are the best evidence that they may represent aspects of the goddess Durga. Her association with animal sacrifice and even blood and flesh offerings from self-inflicted wounds is testified to by a sizeable number of sculptural panels of the Pallava and Chola periods, such as the one at Pullamangai. Additional support for this identification (proposed here in the absence of any other plausible explanation) appears on the pedestal of the Detroit figure. In place of the more usual animal vehicle (*vāhana*), a decapitated human corpse is lightly engraved beneath her feet. But to call her Chamunda, as some scholars have done, is incorrect, as the complete set

210. *Goddess*, possibly one of the *navadurgā*s, granite, 1.11×0.71 m, from Kanchipuram, Tamil Nadu, *c.* AD 950 (Toronto, Royal Ontario Museum)

does not constitute a grouping of the well-known *saptamātṛkas*, the personified energies (*śaktis*) of seven gods, Chamunda being associated with Yama (Death).

Identification of the goddesses as a unique grouping commonly known in texts as the *navadurgās* (the nine manifestations of the great goddess) is also not without difficulties. First, a (now headless) figure in the same pose and style (Madras, Govt Mus. & N.A.G.) may have come from the same, as yet unidentified, temple in Kanchipuram. This would mean a total of ten images, making a single grouping of nine impossible. Second, no textual description of *navadurgās* has yet been found that matches these in the configuration of their upraised weapons. This latter difficulty is not unduly troubling, however, since the *āgamas* and *tantras* in which they are mentioned are ritual texts, which never coincide closely with the visualizations of sculptors. The chance of a match between text and image is especially remote in Tantric contexts such as this, such contexts being, almost by definition, highly esoteric.

As for the probable date of these accomplished sculptures, the third quarter of the 10th century is suggested by certain stylistic peculiarities. These range from such generalities as pose and shape of the slab to specific elements of iconography: for example, the miniature animal vehicles placed beneath the feet and birds perched in ear-disks of some figures, including the one illustrated. Together they point to an infusion of Karnatic influence best dated to the years immediately following the Rashtrakuta conquest of northern Tamil Nadu in 949. In fact, Krishna III is known to have commissioned a temple near Kanchipuram at Kaveripakkam, where a large number of stylistically comparable images have been found.

In both Tamil Nadu and Karnataka the art of bronze-casting had attained a high order by the 10th century. Earlier masterpieces are known and assigned to the 9th century (if not the 8th) on stylistic grounds, but the first securely dated examples belong to the 10th century. These examples are, in Tamil Nadu, the image at Karaiviram of Shiva's consort, *Uma*, dated to 917 (Nagaswamy, 1983), and in Karnataka, at the Manjunatha Temple in Kadiri, the *Lokeshvara*, a rare Buddhist image still in worship as Brahma and dated to 968 (Srinivasan, 1963; see fig. 222 below).

The corpus of datable bronze images increases for the early 11th century. Significantly, this period coincided with full restoration of the Chola imperium under the leadership of the dynasty's two greatest rulers and patrons, Rajaraja I (*reg c.* 985–1014) and his son, Rajendra I (*reg* 1012–44). No fewer than 66 metal icons, cast variously in gold, silver or alloys of mostly copper, are enumerated, together with many ornaments in gold, pearls and precious stones, in the copious donor inscriptions of Rajaraja's crowning achievement, the Rajarajeshvara, or Brihadeshvara, Temple at Thanjavur (see Hultzsch, 1891). At least one of those listed is thought to survive: the truly magnificent *Shiva Nataraja* still installed for worship in the temple's subsidiary dance sanctuary (see fig. 211). Though it is impossible to say which this is of the four Nataraja images Rajaraja personally donated, its date should be close to that of the temple's final consecration ceremony on the 275th day of the king's 25th year (AD 1010).

211. *Shiva Nataraja*, bronze, 1.1×1.35 m, Brihadeshvara Temple, Thanjavur, Tamil Nadu, *c.* 1010

Given the pride of place accorded by the Cholas to Shiva's dancing manifestation (claimed as the dynasty's patron deity (*kuladevatā*)), one cannot imagine a more important sculpture surviving from Rajaraja's reign. The lower half of its flaming aureole appears to be later restoration work, as do the crudely misshapen ends of the lotus pedestal and the thicker anklet on the right foot, covering a mend. But the rest of the sculpture radiates a brilliance unsurpassed by any others of the period or by the innumerable later examples of the type that have emanated from the foundries of Thanjavur District to so many museums and private collections of the world.

Like other Chola-period bronzes still in worship, Rajaraja's *Nataraja* in the pose known as *ānanda tāṇḍava* ('dance of bliss') is a surprisingly bright, coppery hue. It was probably cast in some combination of the five-metal alloy (*pañcaloha*; generally gold, silver, copper, lead and tin) prescribed by texts, and ceremonial bathings have prevented accretion of the green patina common to museum pieces. Over the centuries these libations have also effectively softened the definition of its cast ornamentations and facial features, but unlike the near-contemporary and more famous Tiruvelangadu *Nataraja* (Madras, Govt Mus. & N.A.G.), its eyes and brows have never been marred by recutting.

Technical excellence apart, it is the consummate balance between visual power and symbolic profundity that has earned such Chola Nataraja images recognition as the quintessential Hindu icon. Its interpreters are many, dating back to the earliest Tamil literature, though no visual example of the type survives from before the 6th-century cave relief at Shiyamangalam (see Zvelebil). In mythic terms, its rich vein of associated meanings can best be tapped by introducing a second Chola bronze, whose narrative occasion immediately precedes that of Shiva's dance in the *ānanda tāṇḍava* pose. No finer image of Shiva as Bhikshatana, the beggar god, is known than the one discovered in 1951 as part of a treasure-trove of eight major figures at Tiruvengadu (Thanjavur, A.G.; see fig. 212). An inscription on the Svetaranyasvami Temple at Tiruvengadu records its installation in a specially constructed hall in the year 1048. The donor, named though not otherwise identified, also presented land to support its regular worship and ornaments of gold and silver that are enumerated in a separate inscription.

The Tiruvengadu *Bhikshatana* and other bronzes from the same temple have been frequently published and justly rank among the foremost creations of the Chola period. They include a *Vrishabhavahana* (Shiva posed as if leaning on a bull) dated to 1011 and his consort, named *Uma Parameshvari* in a presentation inscription of the following year (both Thanjavur, Rajaraja Mus.); and a *Nataraja* dating from before 1013, in which year gold was offered on its behalf. The *Nataraja* (*in situ*) is less well known because it was restored to worship after recovery in 1925. Most notable aesthetically among the score of other bronzes that have been recovered from the fields surrounding Tiruvengadu is the *Ardhanarishvara*, Shiva as half-female, discovered in 1960 (Madras, Govt Mus. & N.A.G.). Characteristic of the entire group is the gracious poise with which the mendicant *Bhikshatana* appears to advance, his aura of irresistible charm made more graphic by the deer's eagerness to feed from his hand. Also characteristic of these early 11th-century bronzes is the vibrancy with which organic forms are contoured, always with acute attention to natural proportions and sparing use of metallic accents. This degree of naturalism did not persist much after the *Bhikshatana*'s date, as the repetition of increasingly codified formulae progressively ossified the surfaces of stone and metal images alike.

212. *Bhikshatana*, bronze, h. 800 mm, from Tiruvengadu, Tamil Nadu, 800 mm, 1048 (Thanjavur, Art Gallery)

Returning to the narrative thread that links the images of Shiva as beggar and dancer, it is said that Vedic *ṛṣi*s (sages or seers), obsessed by ritual observance, had become virtually atheistic. In order to confute them, Shiva took the form of a preternaturally beautiful wandering youth and, accompanied by Vishnu as the seductress Mohini, approached the sages' settlement in the Pine Forest. While the sages themselves were completely distracted by Mohini's presence, their wives disappeared one by one with the ash-smeared boy with a skull-bowl in his hand. When they eventually became aware of the double seduction, the infuriated sages sought revenge by conjuring up monsters from their sacrificial fires. But their consternation only increased when in quick succession Shiva overcame these monsters: he flayed a leaping tiger with his fingernails, wrapping its hide around his waist, coiled snakes as ornaments about his arms and head and finally jumped on the demonic dwarf Muyalaka and began to dance. The sages were converted. In a localizing twist of the myth, at the request of the universe-supporting snake, Adishesha, Shiva agreed to perform the apocalyptic dance in perpetuity at Chidambaram.

The truly cosmic reverberations of Shiva's 'dance of bliss' have been the subject of philosophical analysis for many centuries. Texts even older than Rajaraja's image of *c.* 1010 try to reconcile its by then standard iconography with such seemingly disparate concepts as the five divine functions (*pañcakṛiya*), the supragender personality of godhead and the paradoxes or antinomies of life and death, time and eternity, matter and spirit, motion and stillness, the One and the Many. To illustrate only the five divine functions: the *Nataraja*'s rattle-like drum in the upper right hand signifies creation, for sound is said to be the subtlest empirical element; fire raised in the opposite hand foretells destruction; in their midst the raised palm offers reassurance, while the arm slung across the body points out the veiling power of ignorance, personified by the dwarf, Muyalaka or Apasmara, below; finally, the icon's most striking feature, the kick with the left leg, is said to promise eventual liberation.

Once the *ānanda tāṇḍava* Nataraja received definitive formulation—its earliest dated appearance is in a niche of the Uma-Maheshvara at Konerirajapuram (969–76)—it continued to be reproduced, with negligible changes in iconography, centuries after the Cholas had disappeared from the political landscape in the late 13th century. For example, a rare dated *Nataraja* (Madras, Govt Mus. & N.A.G.) was cast in Belur, Karnataka, and inscribed with a date equivalent to 1511 (Kali Yuga 4611). This remarkably vigorous though conservative spirit is manifest across a vast spectrum of iconographic types, both Shaiva and Vaishnava, all of which persisted throughout the Chola,

Vijayanagara and Nayaka periods, despite the jolts the region suffered at the hands of Islamic raiders from north India, primarily in the early 14th century.

Stylistic developments are more difficult to plot in the absence of specific examples. It is nevertheless safe to say that the great expansion in scale of temple complexes, beginning with Rajaraja's Brihadeshvara at Thanjavur, came at the expense of qualitative consistency. Individual masterpieces of stone-carving can be found wherever royal benefaction was sufficiently generous, but the predominant trend was towards increasingly mechanical reiteration of forms many generations removed from their original conception. The cohabitation of some good art with a lot of bad is perhaps best exemplified by the niche sculptures of the Rajendra-Cholishvara (*c.* 1035–44) at GANGAIKONDACHOLAPURAM. As befits the central memorial of an empire that extended to north India and included Sri Lanka and possibly much of Indonesia, Rajendra's temple, also called Gangaikondacholishvara (lord of the Chola who seized the Ganga), is adorned with colossal, majestic guardians and several imposing bas-reliefs, including the famous depiction of an enthroned Shiva conferring a crown of flowers on the boy saint Chandesha. Significantly, the *Chandeshanugraha* panel is set prominently into the sanctuary wall directly beside a major staircase, thus maximizing its visual impact. But just around the corner, panels of equal scale but set far above eye-level are exceedingly coarse.

One other trend in Indian art, by no means unique to Tamil Nadu, was the seeming emulation of metalwork in stone. Perhaps it was the greater sanctity and celebrity accorded to the festival bronzes that prompted stone-carvers to try to reproduce their appearance. At Gangaikondacholapuram, for example, a niche contains an *ānanda tāṇḍava Nataraja* so faithful to the bronze ideal that an unsightly vertical strut was required to support its projecting left leg. Niche sculptures from the 11th century were regularly provided with floral pedestals that only free-standing images require for stability. Thus at such late Chola temples as the Airavateshvara at DARASURAM, built by Rajaraja II (*reg c.* 1146–72), the uniformly refined niche figures look more like stone replicas of bronzes than images of living deities; they are twice removed, in effect, from the original sources of inspirations, whether physical or spiritual. This impression is heightened by use of an almost black stone for these niche images, compared to the light buff colour of the surrounding walls. The more finely grained darker stone also fostered crisper, and hence more metallic, rendering of each figure's jewellery and weapons.

Vijayanagara and Nayaka periods. In 1336 a south Indian prince named Harihara renounced vassalage to the Delhi sultanate and founded the kingdom of VIJAYANAGARA. For more than two centuries his successors were successful in enforcing the claim that they ruled the entire peninsula south of the Krishna River on behalf of their tutelary deity, Shiva Virupaksha. Thus, while much of the rest of India was being transformed by the dictates of Islam, the south was unified by a heightened consciousness of being non-Muslim. It is difficult to determine whether the perception of relative homogeneity in the face of external threat served to solidify political unity or was itself a by-product of successful administration by the rulers of Vijayanagara. In either case the visible dividends of such a protracted period of internal peace and increased prosperity in the south were great. Once evolved, the distinctive idiom of Vijayanagara architecture (*see* §III, 6(i)(g) above) was utilized throughout Karnataka and Tamil Nadu, usually for the purpose of expanding pre-existing temples by the addition of richly articulated ceremonial halls and towered gateways (*gopuras*).

In purely formal terms the multi-pillared halls of the Vijayanagara period represent a logical culmination of several trends. In the famous 'Horse Court' (otherwise known as the Sheshagiri Mandapa; see fig. 213) in the Ranganatha Temple at Srirangam, for example, the predominant motif of the colonnade is a rank of leaping animals. The triumphant spirit that obviously charges each equestrian figure and the gladiators duelling with tigers below is not really different from that which had inspired Rajasimha's rampant-lion pilasters 900 years before. The theme remained constant while the forms grew more elaborate. The addition of auxiliary halls and subsidiary family-deity shrines within the precincts of existing temples took precedence over the founding of new temples from at least the middle Chola period. This was a direct consequence of the great sanctity accorded to many places of pilgrimage in the canonical hymns of the early devotional (*bhakti*) saints. The Ranganatha at Srirangam, for instance, on an island in the Kaveri, is perhaps the most sacred place for Sri Vaishnavas, taking its name from an icon of Vishnu reclining on the primordial waters. Finally,

213. Granite pillars, h. 5.5 m, Sheshagiri Mandapa, Ranganatha Temple, Srirangam, Tamil Nadu, *c.* 1590

Vijayanagara-period halls exemplify the final triumph of what may be called the 'more is better' aesthetic. Despite the few exceptions noted at 7th-century Mamallapuram and 9th-century Kumbakonam, south Indian temples tended to become ever more embellished with the passage of time. By the late 16th century at Srirangam, on piers (h. 5.5 m) of overwhelming complexity, not a single architectonic facet or organic limb can be found that is devoid of jewelled or floral ornament. Yet through imposition of rigorous logic in the distribution of recurrent elements and through careful graduation of carving depths—always proportional to iconic significance—a sense of orderliness pervades the whole.

The iconography of Vijayanagara-period halls is no less complex or characteristic of the age. Most of the motifs have a long history, even beyond the boundaries of the south, and constitute a fusion of courtly pursuits with conceptions of the divine. Miniature shrine models represent palaces or chariots of the gods. The replicated icons in vertical tiers show the gods enthroned and giving audience (*darśana*) to their subjects, while the 'entertainments' registered on two levels below correspond exactly to the dance, music, dramatic and martial performances that were conducted with equal frequency in the royal and sacred audience halls of the period. As for the rampant mounted warriors, the predominant motif at Srirangam and numerous other Vijayanagara halls, it has been persuasively argued that they embody the vibrant spirit of that age whose chivalry and romance were not unlike those of medieval Europe. Both the Crusades and the defence of Vijayanagara called for 'the highest valour and personal heroism' (Brown). So strong were the institutions of state and religious life in the Vijayanagara period that they continued unabated in most of the south for well over a century after the capital itself was devastated by the combined forces of the Islamic Deccan in 1556.

The following century is known as the NAYAKA period, after the term for local governors of the Vijayanagara empire who continued to rule, independently of one another, following the collapse of the imperial lines. Greatest of these leaders, as both political force and patron of art, was Tirumalai (*reg* 1623–59) of MADURAI. It was during his reign that the combined Minakshi Sundareshvara Temple at Madurai, one of the largest in India, assumed its present form. High walls of the outer enclosure (*prākāra*) separate a precinct (258×218 m) from the surrounding city streets. From a distance only the *gopuras* (gateways) at the mid-point of each side are visible above the skyline. Completely lined with figures of deities standing before embellished pavilions on each of nine upper storeys, the *gopuras* are supreme examples of this quintessential feature of the south Indian temple (see fig. 122 above). Also characteristic is the enclosure beneath a single roof of the entire inner *prākāra*, except for the rectangular stepped pool known as the 'Golden Lily Tank' at one corner. This inner section (*c.* 95×130 m) contains the two principal sanctuaries, dedicated to Shiva as Sundareshvara and Minakshi, his consort. To enter this cavernous area from any of four smaller *gopuras* is to be presented with long vistas in all directions, stretching farther than the eye can penetrate in dim light and lined with the endless variety of massive pillars in which the sculptors of the Vijayanagara and Nayaka periods invested their most imaginative efforts. Except for the regimented files of rampant lions alternating with elephant-trunked lion-like beasts (*yāḷi*s), the major figural sculptures seem completely free from any architectonic function. These figures of gods, mythic heroes and the royal donors stand, sit or appear to dance almost completely in the round, not quite detached from the more structural portions of the shafts behind them.

The iconographic programme of these corridors, covered courtyards and halls designated for dance, marriage or royal audience, is not at all obvious. At one place or another one might see most members of the Hindu pantheon, but favourites reappear sufficiently often to give an impression of relatively free variation. In Madurai's

214. *Rati on a Goose*, granite, h. 1.7 m (figure), Thousand-pillared Hall, Minakshi Sundareshvara Temple, Madurai, Tamil Nadu, *c.* 1600

'Thousand-pillared Hall' (a Nayaka-period addition to a surprising number of temples), only the central aisle and two bays across the front are lined with major figures. While some may be generic heavenly musicians or guardians, others are obviously intended to provoke recollection of specific myths. For example, as one approaches the Nataraja shrine at the heart of the hall, the culminating pillars depict *Vishnu Mohini* and *Bhikshatana*. In smaller-scale panels beside them, the *ṛṣi*s of the Pine Forest and their wives clamour towards their respective apparitions of desire. These episodes immediately preceded Shiva's initial cosmic dance. Like sentinels, the pillars block further access to the sacred until all human pride has been abased. If this reading is correct, then the strategic placement of Rati, sexual pleasure personified (see fig. 214), consort of Kama (Love), along the central aisle was intended to be cautionary rather than enticing. In either case she serves as a fitting final example of the history of architectural sculpture in Tamil Nadu. The perfunctory treatment of the base and the floral boss above the whisk-bearing attendant only heightens, by contrast, one's awareness of the love and patience with which the figure was rendered. It would be difficult to find a more perfect example of the Indian artist's command of ornamentation than the execution of Rati's vehicle, the goose (*haṁsa*), with its wonderfully detailed breast, wings and tail.

See also §III, 6(i)(f) and 7(ii)(f) above.

BIBLIOGRAPHY

GENERAL

Enc. Ind. Temple Archit., i/1
G. Jouveau-Dubreuil: *Dravidian Architecture* (Madras, 1917/*R* Varanasi, 1972)
S. Kramrisch: *Indian Sculpture* (Calcutta, 1933/*R* Delhi, 1981)
P. Brown: *Indian Architecture (Buddhist and Hindu Periods)* (Bombay, [1941], rev. 1956)
B. Rowland: *The Art and Architecture of India: Hindu, Buddhist, Jain* (Harmondsworth, 1953, rev. Baltimore, 4/1977)
P. R. Srinivasan: 'Bronzes of South India', *Bull. Govt Mus., Madras*, n. s. viii (1963)
E. Gerow: *A Glossary of Indian Figures of Speech* (The Hague, 1971)
C. Sivaramamurti: *Nataraja in Art, Thought and Literature* (New Delhi, 1974)
M. Adiceam: 'Les Images de Śiva dans l'Inde. XV: Gaṅgādharamūrti', *A. Asiat.*, xxxii (1976), pp. 99–139
R. Craven: *A Concise History of Indian Art* (New York and London, 1976)
F. L'Hernault: *L'Iconographie de Subrahmanya au Tamilnad* (Pondicherry, 1978)
A. de Lippe: *Indian Mediaeval Sculpture* (Amsterdam and New York, 1978)
C. Sivaramamurti: *Panorama of Jain Art* (New Delhi, 1983)
M. Rabe: 'Victorious Durgā, the Buffalo Slayer', *Muse: Annu. Mus. A. & Archaeol., U. Mo-Columbia*, xx (1986), pp. 50–65
C. Tadgell: *The History of Architecture in India: From the Dawn of Civilization to the End of the Raj* (New Delhi, 1990)

PALLAVA PERIOD

Dandin: *Avantisundarī* (*c.* 7th century); Trivandrum Skt Ser., clxii (Trivandrum, 1954)
E. Hultzsch: 'The Pallava Inscriptions of the Kailasanatha Temple at Kanchipuram', *S. Ind. Inscr.*, i (1890), pp. 14–21
——: 'Kasakudi Plates of Nandivarman Pallavamalla', *S. Ind. Inscr.*, ii (1891), pp. 342–60
——: 'Two Cave-inscriptions from the Triśirapalli Rock', *Epig. Ind.*, ix (1907–8), pp. 58–60
A. Rea: *Pallava Architecture*, Archaeol. Surv. India, New Imp. Ser., xxxiv (Madras, 1909/*R* Varanasi, 1970)
E. Hultzsch: 'The Pallava Inscriptions of the Seven Pagodas', *Epig. Ind.*, x (1909–10), pp. 1–14
V. Goloubew: 'La Falaise d'Arjuna de Māvalipuram et la descente de la Gaṅgā sur la terre, selon le Rāmāyaṇa et le Mahābhārata', *J. Asiat.*, 4 (1914), pp. 210–12
G. Jouveau-Dubreuil: *Les Antiquités de l'époque Pallava*, 2 vols (Pondicherry; Eng. trans., 1916–18)
T. A. Gopinath Rao: 'Mandagappattu Inscription of Vichitra-chitta', *Epig. Ind.*, xvii (1923–4), pp. 14–17
A. H. Longhurst: *Pallava Architecture*, Mem. Archaeol. Surv. India, xvii, xxxiii, xl (Simla, 1924; Calcutta, 1928, 1930/*R* New Delhi, 1982)
H. Krishna Sastri: 'The Vayalur Pillar Inscription of Rajasimha II', *Epig. Ind.*, xviii (1925–6), pp. 145–52
V. Rangacharya: 'Two Inscriptions of the Pallava King Rajasimha-Narasimhavarman II', *Epig. Ind.*, xix (1927–8), pp. 105–15
G. Jouveau-Dubreuil: 'La Descente de la Ganga à Mahabalipuram', *Etud. Orient.*, ii (1932), pp. 293–7
T. N. Ramachandran: 'The Royal Artist, Mahendravarman I', *J. Orient. Res.*, vii (1933), pp. 219–46, 303–30
C. Minakshi: *The Historical Sculptures of the Vaikuṇṭhaperumāḷ Temple, Kāñchī*, Mem. Archaeol. Surv. India, lxiii (Delhi, 1941)
T. N. Ramachandran: 'The *Kirātārjunīyam* or "Arjuna's Penance" in Indian Art', *J. Ind. Soc. Orient. A.*, xviii (1950–51), pp. 1–111
Father H. Heras: 'The Hypocritical Cat', *Tamil Cult.*, i (1952), pp. 286–319
C. Sivaramamurti: *Kalugumalai and Early Pandyan Rock-cut Shrines* (Bombay, 1961)
P. R. Srinivasan: 'Sculptures in the Two Rock-cut Vaishnava Cave Temples of Nāmakkal', *Artibus Asiae*, xxiv (1961), pp. 107–16
K. R. Srinivasan: *Cave Temples of the Pallavas*, Architectural Survey of Temples, i (New Delhi, 1964)
R. Nagaswamy: 'Some Contributions of the Pāṇḍya to South Indian Art', *Artibus Asiae*, xxvii/3 (1965), pp. 264–74
W. Willetts: *An Illustrated Annotated Annual Bibliography of Mahabalipuram on the Coromandel Coast of India: 1582–1962* (Kuala Lumpur, 1966)
K. V. Soundara Rajan: 'Rājasiṁha's Temples in Toṇḍaimaṇḍalam', *Trans. Archaeol. Soc. S. India* (Madras, 1969), pp. 169–200
M. Lockwood, G. Siromoney and P. Dayanandan: *Mahabalipuram Studies* (Madras, 1974)
J. Dumarçay and F. L'Hernault: *Temples Pallava construits* (Paris, 1975)
P. Z. Pattabiramin: *Tamilnāḍu et Kerala* (1975), ii of *Sanctuaires rupestres de l'Inde du sud* (Pondicherry, 1971–5)
K. R. Srinivasan: *The Dharmarāja Ratha and its Sculptures, Mahābālipuram* (New Delhi, 1975)
V. Dehejia: *Nāmakkal Caves* (Madras, 1977)
N. S. Ramaswami: *Māmallapuram: An Annotated Bibliography* (Madras, 1980)
M. D. Rabe: *The Monolithic Temples of the Pallava Dynasty: A Chronology* (diss., Minneapolis, U. MN, 1987)

CHOLA PERIOD AND LATER

E. Hultzsch: 'Inscriptions of Rajaraja I', *S. Ind. Inscr.*, ii (1892)
A. Rodin: 'La Danse de Çiva', *A. Asiat.*, iii (1921), pp. 9–13
P. R. Srinivasan: 'Important Works of Art of the Early Chola Period from near Tanjore', *Trans. Archaeol. Soc. S. India*, ii (1956–7), pp. 36–61
J. C. Harle: *The Brahmapurisvara Temple at Pullamangai* (Bombay, 1958)
——: 'The Early Cola Temple at Puḷḷamangai', *Orient. A.*, n. s. iv/3 (1958), pp. 96–108
S. R. Balasubrahmanyam: *Four Chola Temples* (Bombay, 1963)
J. C. Harle: *Temple Gateways in South India: The Architecture and Iconography of the Cidambaram Gopuras* (Oxford, 1963)
C. Sivaramamurti: *South Indian Bronzes* (Delhi, 1963)
D. Barrett: *Early Cōla Bronzes* (Bombay, 1965)
S. R. Balasubrahmanyam: *Early Chola Art, Part One* (Bombay, 1966)
R. Nagaswamy: *Gangaikondacholapuram* (Madras, 1970)
S. R. Balasubrahmanyam: *Early Chola Temples, Parantaka I to Rajaraja I: A.D. 907–985* (Bombay, 1971)
M. A. Dhaky: 'Cōla Sculpture', *Chhavi, Golden Jubilee Volume, Bharat Kala Bhavan, 1920–1970* (Varanasi, 1971), pp. 263–89
D. Barrett: *Early Cōla Architecture and Sculpture, A.D. 866–1014* (London, 1974)
S. R. Balasubrahmanyam: *Middle Chola Temples, Rajaraja I to Kulottunga I (A.D. 985–1070)* (Faridabad, 1975)
G. Schwindler: *The Dating of South Indian Metal Sculptures* (diss., Los Angeles, UCLA, 1975)
K. V. Soundara Rajan: 'Early Pāṇḍya, Muttarayar and Irrukuveḷ Architecture', *Studies in Indian Temple Architecture*, ed. P. Chandra (New Delhi, 1975), pp. 240–300

S. R. Balasubrahmanyam: *Later Chola Temples, Kulottunga I to Rajendra III (A.D. 1070–1280)* (Faridabad, 1979)
S. Rathnasabapathy: *The Thanjavur Art Gallery Bronze Sculptures*, i (Thanjavur, 1982)
R. Nagaswamy: *Masterpieces of Early South Indian Bronzes* (New Delhi, 1983)
B. Venkataraman: *Rājarājeśvaram: The Pinnacle of Chola Art* (Madras, 1985)
K. Zvelebil: *Ānanda-Tāṇḍava of Śiva Sadānṛttamūrti* (Madras, 1985)
G. Yocum: 'Brahmin, King, Sannyāsi, and the Goddess in a Cage: Reflections on the Conceptual Order of Hinduism at a Tamil Śaiva Temple', *Contributions Ind. Sociol.*, n. s. xx (1986), pp. 15–39
F. L'Hernault: *Dārāsuram*, 2 vols (Pondicherry, 1987)
V. Dehejia: *Art of the Imperial Cholas* (New York, 1990)
F. L'Hernault, P. Pichard and J. Deloche: *L'Archaeologie du site* (1991), ii of *Tiruvannamalai: un lieu saint śivaïte du sud de l'Inde* (Pondicherry, 1989–)

MICHAEL D. RABE

(b) Kerala. Stretching along the Arabian Sea in extreme south-west India, Kerala is separated from the rest of the subcontinent by the Western Ghat. The region emerged as a distinct linguistic and cultural zone after about the 13th century; earlier it consisted of three major areas: northern Kerala, or Malabar; central Kerala, or the territory corresponding approximately to the later kingdom of Cochin; and southern Kerala, or the territory of the later kingdom of Travancore. These local identities persisted into modern times. The northern area is the least documented.

The lack of works inscribed with dates makes any chronology of Kerala sculpture relative and provisional. Early remains are dated primarily by comparison with other south Indian styles in which Kerala shared; a characteristic Kerala style probably first developed between the 13th and 15th centuries. As in other parts of India, much of the sculpture was made to decorate temples, and many devotional images are still used in worship.

. Human figure in the hall (*ardhamaṇḍapa*) of the cave temple at Kaviyur, ...ala, *c.* 8th century AD

7th–9th centuries. During this period northern Kerala was ruled first by the Nannanas and then by the Musakas, central Kerala by the Cheras and the south by the Ays. The earliest sculpture from Kerala is ascribed to this period and includes Buddhist and Hindu remains. The few scattered Buddha images all hail from the south, though there is no clear evidence of Ay authorship; these works are linked stylistically to contemporary Tamil Nadu and Sri Lanka. For example, a seated stone Buddha (Krishnapuram Pal. Mus.) shows ties to the 4th- to 6th-century south Indian school associated with AMARAVATI and KANCHIPURAM (*see* §6(vi) above), especially in the heavy torso, the drapery created with raised ridges, the full face with large eyes and the hair in loose curls. A seated stone *Buddha in Meditation* at Mavelikara has the pose, slim torso, broad shoulders and smooth, clinging drapery of a seated *Buddha in Meditation* of around the 6th to 8th century at Anuradhapura in Sri Lanka, though parallels also exist to Jaina figures believed to be from 9th-century Tamil Nadu and the lower Deccan (Los Angeles, CA, Co. Mus. A.; New York, Asia Soc.) and to Buddhist images from NAGAPPATTINAM (Madras, Govt Mus. & N.A.G.) of the 9th to 11th century. Other Buddha images likewise represent a range of styles, suggesting that Kerala probably was in contact with a variety of Buddhist centres, both overland and by sea.

The earliest known bronze from Kerala, a figure of the god *Vishnu* (Trivandrum [Thiruvananthapuram], Govt Mus. A. & Nat. Hist.), is usually ascribed to the 8th or 9th century. Three of its four arms are broken, but the tall cylindrical crown indicates the figure's Vaishnava identity. The slim waist, broad shoulders and thick garland or sacred thread (*upāvīta*) over the left arm, the waistband (*kaṭisūtra*) falling in a semicircle over the upper thighs and the loops of the sash extending to either side of the hips compare to Pallava-period bronzes of the 8th to 9th century (*see* §(a) above) and attest to the penetration of this style into Kerala, though the eyes inset with rock crystal and the unusual division of the arms simultaneously set the image apart from the general trends of contemporary south Indian bronze art.

A number of Hindu rock-cut temples may also predate the 9th century; several in the central region suggest Pallava and Chalukya inspiration. For example, a seated Shaiva figure believed to depict *Shiva Dakshinamurti* (the embodiment of wisdom) from the cave temple at Irunilakode has the long, slender proportions, broad, graceful sacred thread touching the waist and relative simplicity of form usually associated with the Pallava style. However, the limbs are more attenuated and the pose more lively and complex than in most Pallava works, features that compare with certain caves at AIHOLE. Epigraphs of the Chalukyas of Badami that mention the conquest and subjugation of Kerala apparently refer only to the Kongunad area (modern Coimbatore and Salem districts, Tamil

Nadu), though the Brahmanical culture of Kerala as a whole bears a strong Chalukya imprint.

The southern cave temples partake of the Pallava and PANDYA-period styles of Tamil Nadu. The hall (*ardha-maṇḍapa*) preceding the shrine of the cave temple at KAVIYUR contains the loveliest of all Kerala cave reliefs, including a human figure, a guardian figure (*dvārapāla*), a sage (*ṛṣi*) and a representation of Ganapati (one of the names of the god Ganesha). The human figure (see fig. 215), perhaps a chieftain or donor, is a compelling presence, with his slightly cocked head, broad shoulders and powerful arms folded across his slim torso. The simplified treatment of the body and ornaments recalls Pallava-period carving, while the hairstyle bears a close resemblance to those of figures in the Pandya caves at Tirumayam and Virasikhamani. The unfinished excavation at Vizhiñjam (near Trivandrum [Thiruvananthapuram]), the seaport and capital of the Ays, has uncovered a depiction of *Shiva Kiratamurti* (Shiva in the guise of a hunter) holding a bow, arrow and battle-axe; stylistic parallels exist both to Pallava work and to the lively *Shiva* at Tirumalapuram, which is associated with the Pandyas. Since the latter captured Vizhiñjam in the 8th century, it is possible that this monument was actually excavated by Pandya patrons.

9th–12th centuries. This was the only period when Kerala was united under a single authority, that of the Kulashekharas (*c.* 800–1124). This did not, however, translate into a unified artistic style or even into a distinct Kerala idiom, and the tendency to regional divisions continued in the creation of districts ruled by Kulashekhara governors.

Various sources describe the Kulashekhara capital, Makotai (Skt Mahodayapuram), near Tiruvanchikulam and adjacent to or part of Kodungalur (now Cranganur), one of the many sites to benefit from the introduction of stone structural temples into Kerala. Tradition associates the origins of the Krishna Temple at Tirukkulashekharapuram, a suburb of Makotai, with Kulashekhara Alvar (*reg c.* 9th century), an early Kulashekhara king and a saint of the Hindu devotional (*bhakti*) movement that swept through south India during this period. The shrine wall niches (*devakōṣṭhas*), containing six figures in relief, are believed to belong to the original construction; the sculptures therefore represent rare examples of early sculpture surviving *in situ*, since most walls in Kerala temples, usually built of laterite, were replaced in subsequent renovations. Features pointing to an early date include the simplified forms of the bodies, jewellery and garments, the thick sacred thread falling to the waist at the left and the semicircular curve of the lower sash falling across the upper thighs. The earliest inscription from the temple, which palaeographic analysis places *c.* the 11th century, is dated in the 195th year of the building's construction, which would place its origin in the 9th century. This date seems to agree with both the sculptural and architectural styles and the association with Kulashekhara Alvar. A group of granite figures carved in the round from the Kizhtali Shiva Temple at Tiruvanchikulam (Trichur, Archaeol. Mus. & Pict. Gal.) includes a Dakshinamurti and four of the *saptamātṛkā*s (seven mother goddesses), also believed to be early 9th century on stylistic grounds.

A standing stone *Vishnu* in a subshrine of the Mahadeva Temple at Kazhakuttam is an example from the south of about the same period. The *samabhaṅga* (a four-armed image standing upright) holds a conch (*śaṅkha*) and discus (*cakra*) in its upright hands. The lower right hand is placed on the waist, and the lower left displays the gesture of bestowing boons (*varada mudrā*), a common iconography among Vishnu images of the Pallava, Pandya and early Chola periods. Among the features suggesting a date as early as the 9th century are the pronounced inward curve of the upper arms, the broad sacred thread falling across the left arm, the semicircular loop of the lower waistband falling across the thighs and the *cakra* held with its edge towards the viewer. A stone *samabhaṅga Vishnu* from the Chalappuratta shrine (*ambalam*) at Eramam in the far north bears a number of similar early elements, some related to traditions of Dravidadesha and others to the lower Deccan; evidence points to a late 9th- or early 10th-century date. Some scholars have also attributed a number of bronzes that appear to represent a unique variation of the Pallava- and early Chola-period bronze tradition of Tamil Nadu to the Kerala region (see Pal, 1969–70). Of uncertain date and provenance, these controversial works anticipate later Kerala bronzes but relate more clearly to 9th- to 11th-century Tamil Nadu.

Jaina monuments also survive from the Kulashekhara era. At Tiruchcharanattumalai, near Chittral in the far south, rock-cut reliefs depict *jina* figures, their attendant female nature spirits (*yakṣī*s) and a number of inscribed votive images. Among the figures are standing images of Parshvanatha and Padmavatidevi sheltered by a multi-headed cobra; a large niche with a Mahavira seated beneath a tree and parasol (*chattra*) and between two standing attendants; an adjacent niche with a female in 'triple-bend' posture (*tribhaṅga*) standing on a lotus pedestal accompanied by attendants; and numerous other figures seated beneath triple-tiered parasols. An inscription of the Ay king Vikramaditya Varaguna (*reg c.* AD 880–920) is assumed to represent the founding of the site and the approximate date of the earliest carving. This and other early Jaina rock shelters were later converted to Bhagavati (Hindu) shrines and are still in use. Free-standing Jaina figures (Trichur, Archaeol. Mus. & Pict. Gal.) from Godapura in central Kerala (near Alathur) include Parshvanatha, in standing meditation (*kāyotsarga*) beneath a triple-headed cobra, rendered with the slim, somewhat elongated proportions associated with the 9th century. The patrons in this case are unknown.

The growth of Chola power in south India also affected Kerala. Though it is uncertain that the Cholas actually occupied the region, inscriptions attest to their invasions in the far south in the late 10th century, while hostilities between them and the Kulashekharas continued into the early 12th century. Growing Chola artistic hegemony in the 11th century is suggested both in architecture and in the introduction of certain iconographic types. The practice of placing dwarf figures beneath the water chute or drain (*praṇāḷa*) of a shrine was adopted from the Cholas, and these drains conform to Chola stylistic conventions. Two shrines of the Vadakkunnatha Temple complex at TRICHUR, one of which has an inscription of the 11th century, include dwarfs with hair and large circular earrings recalling Chola artistic vocabulary. Also borrowed from the Cholas in the 11th century is the stairway (*sōpāna*) with carved side panels depicting deities and dance scenes. In the Vishnu Temple at Trivikramangalam (near Trivandrum), the carved panel figures are framed within a beaded garland that emerges from the open mouth of a rearing griffin (*vyāla*). One dancer is depicted in an animated and complex pose, twisted so that her lower body is viewed from the rear while her upper body is seen frontally. Guardian figures from the same temple also reflect the important role of Chola traditions in this region at the time. The impact of the Chola style was also felt in the region around the Kulashekhara capital. This is apparent in the dance scene on the banister of the Govardhana shrine in the Krishna Temple at Kulashekharapuram, which displays a figure style and composition typical of Chola art.

13th–15th centuries. It was only in the era following the final collapse of the Kulashekhara empire (*c.* 1124) and the complete withdrawal of the Cholas from Kerala politics that a distinct Kerala idiom began to develop in sculpture, paralleling a growth in Malayalam literature, but exactly when, where and how this occurred is not yet understood. It is likely that subregional trends developed in the several major kingdoms and numerous principalities that inherited the legacy of the Kulashekharas, especially the Kolattiris of Kolattunad in the north, the Zamorins of Kozhikode (Calicut) and the Perumpadappu Svarupam of Cochin in north-central and central Kerala, and the Trippappur Svarupam of Venadu (Travancore) in the south.

A fresh wave of Jainism, inspired by a revival in the Deccan, seems to have taken root in the 13th century in northern Kerala. The direct source for this new development was Tulu Nadu, contiguous with northern Kerala, and parallels exist between monuments in these areas. The temple at Manjeshwar in northernmost Kerala houses numerous Jaina bronzes of different sizes and types that have been dated as early as the 12th century and as late as the 16th century.

A number of Hindu bronzes from Kerala that do not fit the known patterns of development for other south Indian bronze traditions have been given dates as early as the 14th to 15th century and as late as the 16th to 17th. An *Uma-Maheshvara* (Shiva with Uma, his consort) is characteristic of this group (see fig. 216). Shiva is seated with one leg folded and one pendant (*lalitāsana*) on a lotus pedestal, with Uma on his lap, holding a battle-axe and a deer; his lower left hand is in the gift-bestowing gesture, and the lower right encircles Uma. The image surround (*prabhāmaṇḍala*) is actually an elaborate motif of swirling scroll patterns that arises behind the bodies and encircles and canopies them in a manner related to the florid stone-carving of Karnataka from the 12th and 13th centuries (*see* §(c) below). The robust figural style is also reminiscent of HOYSALA sculpture and is distinct from the slender bodies that normally characterize Chola-period bronzes, while the full faces with large eyes and thick lips are elements specific to Kerala. Many authors have made comparisons between the evolved Kerala style and the art of the Mysore region during the Hoysala period, especially as regards the often heavy quality of the figures and the love of ornament; these may have been inspired by artists from the Mysore region moving into northern Kerala after the fall of the Hoysala dynasty in the 14th century. While lacking the refined and elegant sophistication of Chola-period and later south Indian bronzes, the Kerala pieces, with vigorous and lively poses, animated faces, a strongly plastic sense of modelling and a love of three-dimensional ornament, suggest a new direction in local bronze-casting following the break with the Chola past. This pronounced change in taste produced such works as another *Uma-Maheshvara* (New Delhi, N. Mus.) and a figure of the god *Ganesha* (Denver, CO, A. Mus.). By the 15th or 16th century, this new trend had broken forth with great energy to create the mature Kerala idiom, a rich, vigorous and distinctive south Indian regional style.

216. *Uma-Maheshvara*, bronze, h. 191 mm, Kerala, *c.* 14th–15th century (Los Angeles, private collection)

16th–18th centuries. Even in this late period, securely datable works are scarce. Stone was probably never the preferred medium for sculpture in Kerala, since in general the local stone is of poor quality for carving. Wood, metal and even ivory sculpture survives in considerable quantity and attests to the strength and vitality of the Kerala school through the 18th century.

Wood-carving played an important role in Kerala temple decoration, especially in the Kottayam and Alleppey districts, which are rich in timber. Sometimes the entire shrine wall was made of wood and carved with images of deities, scenes from the Puranas and vegetal and floral ornament. Even in areas where wood was less abundant, it was often used for the struts that supported deeply overhanging eaves and might depict figures or mythical creatures. Wood was also used in the gables of superstructures and

217. *Dvārapāla* (door-guardian), wood, h. *c.* 1.3 m, on the shrine wall of the Shiva Temple at Kaviyur, Kerala, 17th–18th century

in the richly carved ceilings and entablatures of detached pillared halls (*namaskāra maṇḍapa*s) and temple theatres (Mal. *kūttambalam*s), where Sanskrit drama was performed. A carved wooden guardian figure at the Shiva Temple at KAVIYUR (see fig. 217) represents the fully developed Kerala style. Inscriptions on the plinth (*adhiṣṭhāna*) provide dates of AD 950 and 951 (Kali era 4051 and 4052), but the temple has been rebuilt above the foundation, and it is unlikely that any of the wooden portions are much older than the 17th or 18th century. The broad proportions of the figure are particularly well suited to the heroic (*vīrya*) qualities of the guardian, whose wide eyes are also expressive of his nature. The profusion of ornament in his necklaces, arm- and ankle-bands, earrings, crown and garment is made more elaborate by a recurrent beaded design and contrasts with the swelling flesh of the body. The crown with attached halo rises in tiers, surmounted by a lotus bud, while large circular earrings, locks of hair and tassels frame the face. In the carved ceilings of halls and stage pavilions (raised platforms within temple theatres supporting a carved wooden ceiling), mandalic diagrams of the guardians of the eight directions (*aṣṭadikpāla*s) are also treated in a style fairly close to those on temple walls, while strut figures and other carved architectural elements display a greater stylistic range, suggesting the simultaneous practice of different idioms within Kerala. Other buildings with important wood sculpture include the Shiva Temple, Ettumanur, and the Narasimha Temple, Chengannur.

Many of the stylistic conventions of temple sculpture *in situ* carried over into bronzes of this period. For example, a superb female figure (see fig. 218), while longer-legged than the guardian at Kaviyur, displays numerous related stylistic features, including the tiered crown with a lotus-bud finial and attached halo and the large, circular earrings decorated with beading and framed by vegetal sprays. Beaded ornament adorns her jewellery and lower garment, and her lower body is given greater girth by the tassels flaring to either side. This elaborate ornament contrasts dramatically with the soft, swelling forms of the body, while the face has the large, double-outlined eyes and strong nose characteristic of Kerala. The treatment of the torso, lower body, crown and ornaments compares closely with that of a bronze *Sri Devi* (Trichur, Archaeol. Mus. & Pict. Gal.). The rigidity of the feet and ankles is common to these and many other such bronzes, including representations of *Rama* (Denver, CO, A. Mus.), *Virabhadra* (Trivandrum, Govt Mus. A. & Nat. Hist.) and *Devi* (Madras, Govt Mus. & N.A.G.), which must all belong to the same era. The extreme elaboration that sometimes characterizes this mode is seen in a pair of nearly life-size bronze guardians (Trichur, Archaeol. Mus. & Pict. Gal.). These stunning figures, in which the profuse ornament serves as a foil for the softly modelled flesh, bear the hallmarks of the Hoysala tradition in the three-dimensional treatment of the decorative detail and the flared tassels framing the face and shoulders. Whether these remnants of the Hoysala style in Kerala represented a recent infusion of Hoysala artists into the region (which would argue for an earlier date) or archaic conventions continuing into a later period is uncertain.

While such examples provide evidence of new developments in late Kerala sculpture, other conventions continued as well. Local museums and temples house sculpture that relates to works produced in other areas of south India between the 16th and 18th centuries and demonstates Kerala's continuing interaction with artistic traditions beyond its borders. In the southernmost part of the region—an area that passed back and forth between local kings and Tamil conquerors throughout the centuries—NAYAKA-inspired figures appear in temple halls at a number of sites. The dance hall and Devi shrine of the palace at Padmanabhapuram, chief palace of the kings of Venadu, include pillars with attached female lamp-bearers carved virtually in the round. Nearly identical figures form the entire covered circumambulatory path at the Adikeshava Temple, Tiruvattar, Sthanunathasvami Temple, Suchindram (both near Padmanabhapuram), and Padmanabhasvami Temple, Trivandrum. Highly animated figural pillars, comparable to those at the Minakshi Temple, Madurai (see fig. 214 above), appear in a number of temples in the south.

Kerala was also home to a Christian community that may have settled there in the early centuries AD. With the arrival of European merchants and conquerors between the 16th and 19th centuries, new schools of Christianity and new artistic traditions were introduced. Numerous Christian churches of various denominations—both Syrian and European—have carved beams and wooden ceilings that resemble those in Hindu temples and palaces. Similar features, but without images, are found in the Islamic buildings of the Kerala coast (see Shokoohy). The carved and painted wooden altarpieces used in Christian churches may represent a hybrid style, while images in the round of Christian subjects—which are more rare—are based directly on European prototypes. The latter were probably brought to Kerala by European missionaries.

See also §III, 5(i)(j), 6(i)(h) and 7(ii)(k) above.

BIBLIOGRAPHY

Enc. Inst. Temple Archit., i/1
Travancore Archaeological Series (Trivandrum, 1910–36)
Annu. Rep., Travancore Archaeol. Dept (Trivandrum, 1922–48)
Annu. Rep. Archaeol. Dept, Cochin State [*Cochin State Annu. Rep. Archaeol. Res.*] (Ernakulam, 1927–49)
F. H. Gravely and T. N. Ramachandran: *Catalogue of the South Indian Hindu Metal Images in the Madras Government Museum* (Madras, 1932)
S. Kramrisch, J. H. Cousins and R. Vasudeva Poduval: *The Arts and Crafts of Travancore* (Trivandrum, 1948); rev. as *The Arts and Crafts of Kerala* (Cochin, [1970])
Annu. Rep. Archaeol. Dept, Travancore-Cochin State (Trivandrum, 1950–56)
K. K. Pillay: *The Śucīndran Temple* (Adyar, 1952)
Kerala Dept Archaeol. Admin. Rep. (Trivandrum, 1956–)
R. Nagaswamy: 'Rare Bronzes from Koṅgu Country', *Lalit Kala*, ix (1961), pp. 7–10
C. Sivaramamurti: *South Indian Bronzes* (New Delhi, 1963/*R* 1981)
C. R. Jones: *The Temple Theatre of Kerala: Its History and Description* (diss., Philadelphia, U. PA, 1967)
J. L. Davidson: *Art of the Indian Subcontinent from Los Angeles Collections* (Los Angeles, 1968)
P. Pal: 'South Indian Sculptures: A Reappraisal', *Boston Mus. Bull.*, lxvii (1969), pp. 153–73
——: 'Some Interesting South Indian Bronzes', *Archvs Asian A.*, xxiii (1969–70), pp. 151–73
R. Nagaswamy: 'Koṅgu Bronzes in the Victoria and Albert Museum', *Lalit Kala*, xv (1972), pp. 41–3
M. G. S. Narayanan: *Political and Social Conditions of Kerala under the Kulaśēkhara Empire (Ca. 800 A.D. to 1124 A.D.)* (diss., Trivandrum, U. Kerala, 1972)
B. N. Sharma: 'Unpublished Bronzes in the National Museum, New Delhi', *Lalit Kala*, xv (1972), pp. 52–3
——: 'Further Unpublished Bronzes in the National Museum, New Delhi', *Lalit Kala*, xvii (1974), pp. 40–41
A. Ghosh, ed.: *Jaina Art and Archaeology*, 3 vols (New Delhi, 1974–5)
R. Y. Otsuka and M. C. Lanius: *South Asian Sculpture: The Harold P. and Jane F. Ullman Collection* (Denver, 1975)
U. P. Shah and M. A. Dhaky: *Aspects of Jaina Art and Archaeology* (Ahmadabad, 1975)
P. Pal: *The Divine Presence: Asian Sculptures from the Collection of Mr. and Mrs. Harry Lenart* (Los Angeles, 1978)
H. Sarkar: *An Architectural Survey of Temples of Kerala* (New Delhi, 1978)
Splendours of Kerala (Bombay, 1979/*R* 1983)
R. M. Bernier: *Temple Arts of Kerala* (Delhi, 1981)
J. C. Harle: *The Art and Architecture of the Indian Subcontinent* (Harmondsworth, 1986, rev. 1987/*R* 1990)
R. Nagaswamy: *Masterpieces of Early South Indian Bronzes* (New Delhi, 1983)
C. Sivaramamurti: *Panorama of Jain Art* (New Delhi, 1983)
M. C. Heston: *The Maṭṭāncheri Palace Murals of Kērala, India: A Stylistic Study* (diss., Columbus, OH State U., 1985), pp. 251–61.
S. L. Huntington with J. C. Huntington: *The Art of Ancient India: Buddhist, Hindu, Jain* (New York and Tokyo, 1985), pp. 601–15
G. Michell: *The Penguin Guide to the Monuments of India*, i (Harmondsworth, 1989)
M. Shokoohy: 'Architecture of the Sultanate of Ma'bar in Madura, and Other Muslim Monuments in South India', *J. Royal Asiat. Soc. GB & Ireland*, n. s. 2, i (1991), pp. 31–92
G. Michell, ed.: *Living Wood: Sculptural Traditions of Southern India* (Bombay, 1992)

M. E. HESTON

(c) Karnataka. The state of Karnataka, in south-central peninsular India, constitutes an ancient cultural region known as Karnata or Kuntaladesha, from which diverse sculptural traditions emerged and proliferated, often in conjunction with the many dynastic families of the area. Because temples and the accompanying rituals to enshrined deities had an intricate role within regional polity—royalty required overlord deities for legitimacy and sustenance—regional temple styles are often labelled as dynastic art. Ostentatious temples speak of dynastic puissance. While it might be true that royalty, or royal surrogates, had some impact on the appearance of monuments within their realm, there are no consistent dynastic artistic styles, and stylistic discrepancies within a given political realm are frequent. Contributing to regional diversity are temples built by smaller dynastic families, which, even if politically subordinate to a regional sovereign, constructed monuments according to their own requirements.

218. Female figure, bronze, h. 356 mm, Kerala, *c.* 16th–18th century (Los Angeles, private collection)

Two generalizations can be made regarding monuments in Karnataka. First, in this region architectural and sculptural elements labelled 'northern' (*nāgara*) and 'southern' (*drāviḍa*) were utilized freely (*see* §III, 1(i)(c) above). This was true under the early Chalukyas of Badami (*see* CHALUKYAS, §1), whose temples with northern superstructures sit beside temples with southern characteristics, and it remained true throughout the region's history. This mixing and sharing of elements and motifs demonstrate how easily artisans appropriated ideas to suit their immediate needs in order to formulate new regional mannerisms.

Second, Karnataka sculptors favoured ornamental surfaces. Architectural elements such as doorways, pillars and ceiling panels are usually embellished, as are images' clothing and jewels. This trend started with the earliest Chalukya sculptures, which are distinguished from other southern work because they are more decorative—relative to the contemporaneous austere PALLAVA tradition, for instance—and climaxed with HOYSALA sculptures, which are famed for their surface exuberance.

7th century–mid-8th. The Chalukyas of Badami were avid supporters of structural temples, and the largest number of early Indian temples date from this period. Major sites in Karnataka include BADAMI and nearby Mahakuta, PATTADAKAL and AIHOLE. Additionally, temples or ruins are located at Sandur, Nagaral and Banavasi. At first most sculptural reliefs were subsidiary and decorative, but soon large sculptures, such as deity images in niches or loving couples (*mithunas*) on pillars, became well integrated with the architecture. Door-guardians (*dvārapālas*), for instance, started as small, symbolic images but by the end of the Chalukya period had become intimidating, life-size protectors.

A few shrines might date earlier, but the first to have a datable inscription, to AD 634–5 (Shaka era 556), is the Jaina Meguti Temple at Aihole. Except for reliefs of animals and *ganas* (dwarfs), the walls lack large imagery. Other shrines from the 7th century at Aihole, such as the Gaudar Gudi and Huchchappayya Gudi, have floral and scroll doorway reliefs and other animal and *gana* reliefs that are exquisitely lyrical but lack monumentality. This early pattern of nicely executed subsidiary panels is seen at the upper and lower Shivalaya temples at Badami. In addition to scroll, *gana* and animal motifs, both shrines have small narrative reliefs: the upper Shivalaya has scenes from the *Rāmacarita* (a version of the *Rāmāyaṇa* epic) and the *Kṛṣṇacarita* ('Deeds of Krishna'), and the lower Shivalaya had *Kṛṣṇacarita* scenes (removed to Badami Mus.).

Variously dated from the mid-7th century to the early 8th, the Malegitti Shivalaya at Badami, designed by the architect Aryaminci Upadhyaya, is a finely proportioned temple that has large niche sculptures. From this period on, wall imagery became increasingly popular. Besides the *gana*, animal and floral wall reliefs and ornamental doorways encountered elsewhere, this temple has an increased number of relief panels, many of which show deities. Originally, the temple was probably dedicated to the sun god Surya (also called Aditya), a representation of whom is prominently displayed in the central panel over the shrine doorway and who is seen elsewhere, along with associated guardians, on the temple walls. In the exterior wall niche to the south is a majestic *Vishnu*, and the north wall niche has a figure of *Shiva*. Both are presented frontally. Though well executed, the figures are broad with rather tubular limbs.

Two temples at Aihole, the Lad Khan and the Durga Temple, though considered enigmatic in form and controversial in dating are now usually assigned to the late 7th century to early 8th. Both temples have graceful *mithunas* in high relief on exterior pillars. These figures, though still a bit stocky and tubular, are compositionally sophisticated, as can be seen in the manner in which their bodies twist and embrace. The faces convey contentment, a sign of the sculptors' growing skills. Doorways, pillar reliefs and ceiling panels are more elaborately carved at these temples. At the Durga Temple, originally dedicated to the sun god, there is an increased number of exterior-pillar *mithunas* as well as additional niche figures of deities in the ambulatory. The *Shiva* and *Durga* niche sculptures are among the finest works from the Chalukya period. In graceful triple-bend pose, multi-armed Shiva leans on his bull, Nandi, with self-absorbed dignity. Durga stands in the same pose, but the arrangement of her many arms and her pose in relation to her pathetically defeated foe, the buffalo demon Mahishasura, suggest an active deity, whereas Shiva appears passive.

The refinement of the Durga Temple sculptures is also evident in other Aihole monuments. Figures became more slender and naturalistic, as is seen, for example, in the ceiling of the north-west temple of the Konti Gudi group (Shrine 1), a panel of which depicts *Vishnu Reclining on Shesha*. Some sculptural changes might be attributable to the slow influx of ideas and mannerisms from ALAMPUR, an important Chalukya site in Andhra Pradesh (*see* §(d) below). Another group of ceiling panels (Bombay, Prince of Wales Mus.) from the Huchchappayya Math, Aihole, demonstrate the maturing of the Chalukya-period style. The panels depicting Shiva, Vishnu and Brahma (see fig. 219) with a host of attendants can be credited to a particular sculptor, Narasobba, and his assistant Ganasobba.

The latest Chalukya temples and the grandest in scale and are in Pattadakal. The three largest shrines have dynastic affiliation. Vijayaditya (*reg c.* AD 696–733) had the Vijayeshvara, also known as the Sangameshvara, built, but it was unfinished at his death. During the reign of his son and successor, Vikramaditya II (*reg c.* AD 733–45), the Virupaksha was founded (*c.* 745) by the king's senior queen, Loka Mahadevi; Loka Mahadevi's sister, Queen Trailokya Mahadevi, founded the Trailokeshvara (now called Mallikarjuna) in 755. Sculptural manners of previous monuments are mixed together, blending elements from Telingana (Andhra Pradesh) with local idiosyncracies. The large *dvārapālas*, *mithunas*, niche figures of deities, pillar reliefs and so on epitomize the Chalukya sculptural style at its climax.

The Virupaksha, originally called Lokeshvara, was built to celebrate Vikramaditya II's victory over the Pallavas. Many of the niche figures are of forms of Shiva, to whom the temple is dedicated. Contained within deep niches, these figures are sturdy yet slender and often dramatically posed. For example, on the south wall of the forehall, Natesha dynamically conveys motion. Especially theatrical are the large guardians carved in high relief on the porch pilasters. Whereas most of the guardians appear to be at rest because their backs are engaged with the pilasters, one guardian in particular, on the south porch, has only his right side engaged, thus successfully conveying the illusion that he is stepping away. Other porch reliefs include *mithunas* similar to the ones already mentioned from Aihole, except that here they have taken on an even more urbane demeanour. Numerous figural sculptures are in evidence. As had been the case since the Chalukya cave

219. *Brahma*, ceiling relief by Narasobba and his assistant Ganasobba, from Huchchappayya Math, Aihole, Karnataka, 7th century AD (Bombay, Prince of Wales Museum of Western India)

temples, the interior is embellished with ceiling, doorway and pillar reliefs. Of the two subshrines, one is dedicated to Ganesha and the other to Durga—the latter has a powerful representation of the victorious goddess. These temple sculptures are testaments to the glory of the Chalukya dynasty and early Karnataka sculptors.

Mid-8th century–late 10th. In the mid-8th century the RASHTRAKUTA dynasty seized control of the Deccan, and for the next two centuries its members remained India's paramount rulers. Karnataka and Maharashtra formed the nucleus of the Rashtrakutas' lands; it is in the latter area, at Ellora, that they built their greatest imperial monuments (*see* ELLORA, §1; and *see also* §(iii)(b) above). Temple sites in Karnataka include Aihole, Pattadakal, Kukkanur, Hallur, Sirval and Bagli, most of which are sculpturally unimpressive. Malkhed (anc. Manyakheta; Gulbarga District), once a Rashtrakuta capital, now has little more than ruins with uninspired pillar reliefs.

Generally, temples built in Karnataka during Rashtrakuta times tend towards conservatism: while some elements popularized during the previous century continued, most sculptural embellishments were reduced. Interior pillar-relief narratives became fewer in number, and ceiling panels with deities were often replaced by large, full-blossomed lotus motifs. Exterior niche figures were minimized or eliminated. At Sirval over 20 shrines were constructed during the early 10th century. While these temples might be of architectural interest, sculpturally they lack distinction. Exterior walls were articulated by means of engaged pilaster variations rather than added sculpture.

Local architectural mannerisms developed during the Chalukya period were dominant at Aihole from the late 9th century to the early 10th. This is seen at the Konti Gudi group of shrines (nos 2 and 3), the Hallibasappa Gudi (no. 11) and temples 52 and 53. The exterior walls of these shrines, however, do not have niche figures or any significant sculptural embellishments, and the interior pillar and doorway reliefs lack the crisp elegance seen on earlier temples. Figures are stiff and crudely proportioned, no longer showing the relaxed naturalism attained during the height of the Chalukya idiom. Yet a contemporaneous set of pillars from Kadur (now in front of Mysore, Govt Karnataka, Dept Archaeol.) has vigorous reliefs depicting Shaiva narratives bordered by exuberant animal and floral motifs. There was a trend towards subregional idioms during this period.

Especially within Rashtrakuta Karnataka, many questions have yet to be answered about who actually sponsored temples and how best to discuss the question of 'idiom'. It is only in connection with Ellora that an imperial Rashtrakuta style can be identified. Much of the vast Rashtrakuta empire was overseen by feudatories who had their own subregional identifications and self-interest. As a consequence, there are numerous instances of subregional sculptural styles that display a comingling of Rashtrakuta (i.e. Ellora) elements with local idioms. For example, pillars in the Navalinga group at Kukkanur are carved in a manner that shares characteristics with pillars popularized in Nolambavadi (the territory controlled by the NOLAMBA dynasty; see below). Variant pillar shapes (including the proto-'lathe-turned' type) seen at the Rashtrakuta-period Jaina temple at Pattadakal developed simultaneously in Nolambavadi and Gangavadi (the territory controlled by the Ganga dynasty). The Kalleshvara Temple at Bagli, most often noted for the small erotic sculptures on the exterior wall below the superstructure, also shares architectural and sculptural elements with temples in Nolambavadi. Thus while there was no distinct 'Rashtrakuta' sculptural style in Karnataka, there are some monuments distinctly identifiable as 'Ganga' or 'Nolamba'—two dynastic families that, although less powerful militarily than the Rashtrakuta dynasty, played important roles in the history of the area.

The WESTERN GANGA dynasty was the longest-lived such family in Karnataka, having a presence in the southern part of the region from the mid-4th century to the early 11th. Situated as they were between the dominant dynasties of northern Karnataka (i.e. Chalukyas of Badami, Rashtrakutas and Chalukyas of Kalyana) and the Pallava, Pandya and Chola rulers in Tamil Nadu (*see* §(a) above), the Gangas had a politically precarious position. Important Western Ganga temple sites include SRAVANA BELGOLA, Manne, Kambadahalli, Begur, Varuna, Narasamangalam and Talakad (their capital, which is now mostly buried under silt from the Kaveri River). Many elements displayed in their temples, most of which date to the 10th century, are shared with contemporaneous monuments elsewhere. Since this is a propensity already apparent in Rashtrakuta-period temples, it does not imply that artistic inferiority was a corollary of political subordination. Although the Rashtrakutas were the dominant political power of their time, their artistic presence in Karnataka was muted, while the Gangas sponsored a monument at Sravana Belgola that is unique in art history.

The Gangas developed the sacred Sravana Belgola site as the pre-eminent supporters of JAINISM (Digambara sect) in the south. On the smaller hill, the Chandragiri (anc. Katavapra), where, legend has it, Chandragupta Maurya (*reg c.* 321–297 BC) resided as a Jaina ascetic, there are a number of shrines dating from the 9th to the 13th century. The Chandragupta Basti (which some scholars date to the 9th century but which might date to the 10th century) is sculpturally noteworthy for its 12th-century carvings. Especially significant are the stone screens with some 90 episodes from the life of Chandragupta Maurya and the great teacher Bhadrabahu, executed by the artist Dasoja, who has other signed sculptures at the Hoysala temples at BELUR and HALEBID. Nearby is one of the finest of the Ganga-period temples, the Chamundaraya Basti. Sponsored by Chamundaraya, general and minister to the Western Ganga king Rajamalla IV (*reg c.* AD 974–99), the temple dates to *c.* 982, though the superstructure was completed *c.* 995 through the aid of Chamundaraya's son Jinadevana. The exterior walls, though devoid of sculptures, have above them on all sides handsomely rendered images of seated *jina*s, *yakṣa*s and *yakṣī*s. More of these figures grace the upper storeys of the superstructure. All have an understated, naturalistic and relaxed mien.

At the summit of the larger hill, the Vindhyagiri, stands the world's tallest monolithic free-standing sculpture (h. *c.* 18 m) called, in Kannada, *Gommateshvara* (see fig. 220). Sponsored by Chamundaraya and dedicated in AD 981 or 983, this image is of Bahubali, the son to the first Jaina *tīrthaṅkara* ('enlightened master'), Risabhanatha (also called Adinatha). Nude except for the vines that grew around his legs and arms during his years of meditation, Bahubali stands majestically upright. As is appropriate for a Jaina saint, he is ideally proportioned, with wide shoulders and narrow waist; an alert face with the slightest smile signifies his blissful enlightenment. Still in pristine condition after a thousand years, Bahubali over the centuries has served as the model for other Jaina colossi in Karnataka, none of which equal him in artistic charm.

220. *Gommateshvara* (*Bahubali*), h. *c.* 18 m, Sravana Belgola, Karnataka, dedicated AD 981 or 983

At Kambadahalli the five-shrine Panchakuta Basti, dating from *c.* 975, and the twin-shrine Shantinatha Basti, from the late 10th century, have several Jaina images sculpted in the same handsome style as the Sravana Belgola images. Sculptures here, especially *yakṣī*, *yakṣa* and guardian figures, are more richly bejewelled than in coeval northern Karnataka (Rashtrakuta) temples. Some temples in the Western Ganga territories have large lotus-motif ceilings, a trait shared with Rashtrakuta-period temples, but at Kambadahalli (and at Begur and Narasmangalam) there are ceiling reliefs showing the eight guardians of the directions (*aṣṭadikpāla*s). This is a characteristic shared with temples in the Nolamba territory, where ceiling panels, and sculptures in general, are often elaborately carved.

The Shaiva temples at Begur (twin-temple complex) and Narasmangalam (the Ramalingeshvara Temple) have architectural characteristics that demonstrate a sharing of elements with monuments in Tamil Nadu. At Sravana Belgola and Kambadahalli, exterior wall space is broken only by engaged pilasters (similar to those on temples in northern Karnataka), but at Begur and Narasmangalam walls are broken into deep recessions and projections, edged with pilasters. To illustrate further how regional 'styles' were mixed and shared in the 10th century, a partial set of *mātṛkās* (mother goddesses) from Begur (Bangalore, Karnataka Govt Mus. & Venkatappa A.G.) are low-relief granite figures with little ornamentation (as in Tamil Nadu), whereas other sculptures within the twin shrines (especially two Mahishasuramardinis and a Surya) are carved from dark schist and appear stylistically related to images from Nolambavadi. Also related in style to temples there, especially the ones at Nandi and Avani, are the pillar reliefs and the ceiling panels depicting the guardians of the directions. The stucco images on the superstructure at the Ramalingeshvara Temple, Narasmangalam, which might date from the time of the temple, are a peculiar feature.

Members of the Nolamba (Nolamba-Pallava) dynasty were at times politically and matrimonially related to the Gangas and at other times in direct competition with them. From the 8th century to the early 11th the Nolambas controlled south-east Karnataka and limited contiguous sections of Andhra Pradesh and Tamil Nadu, which made up Nolambavadi. Though HEMAVATI (anc. Henjeru), the Nolamba capital, is located in the portion of Andhra Pradesh that protrudes into the Tumkur District of Karnataka, its monuments rightfully belong within a discussion of Karnataka sculptures. A distinguished (Nolamba) sculptural idiom was centred here, with stylistically related monuments at Pathasivarama, Baraguru and Aralaguppe (the latter two in Tumkur District, as is the less important site of Nonavinakere). Although architectural and sculptural traits were shared elsewhere in Nolambavadi, there were idiomatic shifts. Temples from Nandi and Avani blend elements from Hemavati with characteristics from Gangavadi monuments. In their appearance the Nolamba temples at Dharmapuri (Tamil Nadu) are more *drāviḍa* ('southern') but have Nolambavadi traits; hence the temples are more sculpturally elaborate (for example, the pillar reliefs and the ceiling panels showing the eight guardians of the directions) than was common in the deep south. Ornamentation became increasingly popular in Nolambavadi. Doorways, pillar reliefs, perforated window-carvings and ceiling panels, all of which were sculptural elements developed during the early Chalukya period but then reduced, became areas of attention. The intensification of this trend in the 11th century under the Chalukyas of Kalyana (*see* CHALUKYA, §2) may be explained by the fact that the Nolambas moved to Bellary District, presumably along with their artisans, becoming absorbed into the Chalukya realm.

Possibly the most elegant late 9th- or early 10th-century temple in Karnataka is the Bhoganandishvara at Nandi. The exterior walls lack niche images, but the windows have perforated carvings of lively dancers, musicians, *gaṇas* and deities. On all sides above the walls and throughout the superstructure are deities (mostly forms of Shiva, to whom the temple is dedicated) and subsidiary figures, all exquisitely sculpted. The naturalistic, relaxed figures are surrounded by exuberant ornament in the form of animal and vegetal motifs and celestial beings. The otherwise granite temple has eight black schist sculptures at the top of the tower (*grīvaśikhara* level), which are especially majestic: four couchant Nandis interspersed with two Shivas, a Brahma and a Vishnu.

In the same compound the Arunachaleshvara Temple is a close duplicate of the Bhoganandishvara. Only the walls, including some fine perforated window-carvings, date from the 10th century. The complete Arunachaleshvara tower is by much later sculptors who were trying to archaize their work in order to conform with the earlier Bhoganandishvara model (*see* §XV below). A VIJAYANAGARA-period shrine, in a recognizably 16th-century style, was built in between the two temples.

Avani (anc. Avantikaksetra; a site rich in *Rāmāyaṇa* lore) boasts many epigraphs and shrines. The Lakshmaneshvara Temple dates to the reign of King Vira Nolamba (also called Anniga; *reg c.* 923–40), except for the tower, which is a Vijayanagara-period replacement. The temple is unusual in that its walls have reliefs of deities (mostly goddesses) or attendants, plus a portrait of Vira Nolamba and the religious leader Tribhuvanakarata. During the 10th century, exterior walls generally lacked significant deity reliefs—at Nandi and Sravana Belgola, for instance, sculptures appeared above the walls. These reliefs and the peculiar iconographic scheme make the Lakshmaneshvara Temple a curiosity. The mostly renovated Bharateshvara Temple has an inscription (*c.* 980) claiming that the Nolamba queen Divambika had it built. Both temples have interior ceiling panels with central figures of Shiva and Parvati surrounded by representations of the eight guardians of the directions akin to the panels at the Bhoganandishvara at Nandi.

The prevailing goddess imagery on the Lakshmaneshvara is a visual reminder that goddess worship became increasingly popular from the 10th century. A coeval *Goddess* image from Avani (locally called *Mutyalamma*, 'the pearl-like mother'), once installed in a separate shrine (Bangalore, Karnataka Govt Mus. & Venkatappa A.G.), is a striking image demanding attention, as the defeated foe below the seated goddess has learnt. Another vigorous image that attests further to the importance of goddess worship in this area is the enshrined Kolaramma *Goddess* at the Kolaramma Temple in nearby Kolar. Within an 11th-century shrine in the temple, the *Goddess* might date from the late 10th century.

Enshrined within the Siddeshvara Temple at Hemavati is an imposing image of *Bhairava* (locally called *Henjappa*) (see fig. 221), which illustrates the Nolamba idiom at its finest. Adornments complement the robust figure, harmonizing idealism with naturalism. Because the Virashaivas (a Shaiva sect) usually replaced enshrined anthropomorphized icons in this region from the 12th century, *Bhairava*, dating from the late 9th or early 10th century, is especially distinctive. An equally grand image represents the goddess *Kali* (Madras, Govt Mus. N.A.G.). Sculpted and adorned in the same manner as the *Bhairava*—both images are black schist and approximately 1.5 m high—this majestic *Kali* most certainly was created for special worship. Other splendid sculptures from Hemavati are kept at the same museum: a particularly handsome seated *Umasahita* (Shiva and Parvati) displays exemplary figural form with delicate embellishments. During the Nolamba period ornamentation was neither superfluous nor

221. *Bhairava*, Siddeshvara Temple, Hemavati, Andhra Pradesh, late 9th century–early 10th

detrimental to the form; rather, there was an elemental balance between the two. This is seen in the ubiquitous pillar reliefs, the intricate doorways (e.g. at the Doddeshvara and Virupaksha temples) and, especially, the ceiling panels, such as the loose panels at Hemavati and Pathasivarama and those in the Kalleshvara Temple at Aralaguppe. There, carved in high relief, Shiva dances with extreme vigour surrounded by four celestial garland-bearers (carved in the round and attached at their backs to the ceiling) and guardians of the directions. Also at Aralaguppe a large (h. 1.5 m) *Umasahita* stele exemplifies the late 10th-century trend towards heightened embellishment.

Before proceeding to the 11th century, two more smaller dynastic families, the Santaras and the Alupas, require brief discussion. Active sponsors of Jainism, the Santaras were located in the hills of western Karnataka. Not a notable martial family (probably the reason most modern historians have ignored their presence), the Santaras sponsored monuments but only in their capital city, Humcha. Dating from the late 9th century and the 10th, sculptures surviving in Humcha display a crisp vigour rarely encountered in work associated with the Rashtrakutas in Karnataka. The reliefs on the Bogara Basti, such as the small *jina*s and subsidiary figures sculpted above the exterior walls and especially the interior pillar-carvings, are exceptional. Although the *jina*s and other pillar images were rendered in a slender, graceful manner, the lively decorative motifs (e.g. *kīrttimukha*s (demon masks), lotus scrolls and jewels) best portray the sculptors' skill. Humcha remained an artistic centre into the 12th century; the guardians in the Panchakuta Basti, dedicated in 1077, combine ideal figural form with enthusiastic ornamentation and are similar in style to the best sculptures produced under the coeval Chalukyas of Kalyana.

South-west Karnataka—ancient Tulu Nadu (southern Kanara District and adjacent northern Kerala)—was the traditional land of the Alupa dynasty. Temple sites include Udiyavara, Polali, Ullala and Kadiri (near Mangalore). Although worship of the *saptamātṛkā*s (seven mother goddesses) and Durga was popular in this area, three exceptional Buddhist bronzes at Kadiri are most noteworthy. In AD 968 the Alupa king Kundavarman (*reg c.* 950–80) inscribed and installed a bronze image of *Lokeshvara*. Generally considered to represent the Mahayana Halahala Lọkeshvara, the figure is seated, three-faced and six-armed; some have argued that it represents a form of Shiva. This image, probably the largest bronze in Karnataka (h. 1.37 m), is not an isolated example: at the same site there is a coeval image of *Avalokiteshvara*, with one head and four arms (see fig. 222). Both images were superbly cast and are imbued with grace. A third image, possibly slightly later in date, is a seated *Buddha* that

222. *Avalokiteshvara*, bronze, Manjunatha Temple, Kadiri, Karnataka, dedicated *c.* AD 968

displays stylistic affinities with Buddhas from NAGAPPATTINAM, Tamil Nadu.

Although the *Buddha* does resemble bronzes from Chola territory (*see* §(a) above), other bronzes in Karnataka have been incorrectly labelled 'Chola' in style. For instance the bronze *Kali* from Malangi, near Talakad (Bangalore, Karnataka Govt Mus. & Venkatappa A.G.), though often called 'Chola', is more likely 'Ganga'. A number of Jaina bronzes are in the Ganga idiom, some at the Sravana Belgola Math and others in various collections; a *Bahubali* (Bombay, Prince of Wales Mus.) is a fine example. A *Somaskanda* (Shiva seated with Parvati; Bangalore, Karnataka Govt Mus.) from Nandi and another representation of the same theme (Pasadena, CA, Norton Simon Mus.) might be in the Nolamba idiom. The latter two are close in style to 11th-century bronzes made under the Chalukyas of Kalyana. A large *Shiva and Parvati* (h. of Shiva figure 665 mm; London, BM) appears to be late 10th century or 11th and requires further investigation, as do other bronzes too numerous to list. Once Karnataka bronzes receive systematic study, it will be possible to assign them more accurately to idiom appellations.

11th–13th centuries. From AD 973, when the Rashtrakutas were irremediably defeated, until 1189 (except for a 25-year hiatus of Kalachuri control) the Chalukyas of Kalyana were the primary power in the Deccan. In northern Karnataka—in Belgaum, Bijapur, Bidar, Raichur, Dharwar and Gulbarga districts—temple construction proliferated during this period. Major sites include ITTAGI, Lakkundi, Haveri, Hangal, Gadag and Dambal, and many other lesser known sites also exist. Famed for their architectural innovations, temples during the Chalukya period became divergent in form, with a heightened dependency on sculptural embellishment. Greater attention to minute details was possible by the use of a malleable, fine-grained, greenish or blue–black chloritic schist. Besides figural images, a popular wall motif was a pilaster crowned by a miniature pavilion. Early forms are at the 11th-century Jaina temple at Lakkundi and the Siddheshvara at Haveri. Artisans' knowledge of disparate architectural traditions is indicated by the pavilion form, which duplicates temple superstructure shapes from other regions of India. Pillar reliefs from this period are less common because of the intricate shape of pillars themselves; the 'lathe-turned' type was popular and remained so into the 14th century. Occasionally, pillar bracket figures were used. When carved, ceiling panels have elaborate representations of the directional guardians. Doorways, too, are ornate.

An example of a mature temple built under the Chalukyas of Kalyana is the Mahadeva at Ittagi (the topmost part of the tower is rebuilt). Sponsored by Mahadeva, a general to King Vikramaditya VI (*reg c.* 1076–1126), the monument was dedicated in 1112 (Shaka era 1034). Such architectural elements as the elaborately carved miniature pavilion motif that decorates the walls above the deep niches or engaged pilasters and repeats up the tower and the open eastern pavilion with its numerous, complex 'lathe-turned' pillars distinguish this (and coeval Chalukya) temples. There are lively small-scale figural reliefs on the walls and pillar bases. The interior lantern ceiling has attendants watching the spirited dancing Shiva. The 12th-century Kashivishveshvara Temple at Lakkundi has more numerous figural reliefs on the walls and doorway carvings that are especially elaborate. The latter are composed of female and guardian figures at the bottom and, above them, bands of jewels and vegetal motifs interwoven with dancing and embracing couples, musicians, dwarfs, horned lions (*yāḷis*) and so on, all of which were carefully sculpted in high relief. The walls and superstructure have small-scale figural carvings (complementing the pilaster-pavilion,

223. Female musician, Dharwar District, Karnataka, *c.* 1100 (Los Angeles, CA, County Museum of Art)

or deep niche pavilion wall motif), many of which have Shaiva themes. Delineated throughout the temple are energetic *gaṇa*s and *yāḷi*s.

Though temples were becoming increasingly elaborate in shape and embellishment, their sculptures were not overwhelmed by ponderous extras. Some sculptures from this period are outstanding for their elegant understatement, for example a representation of the *tīrthaṅkara Parshvanatha* (London, V&A) originally from Gulbarga District. (That Jainism at times suffered in this area is indicated by this sculpture's epigraph, which states that the image was enshrined after a period of persecution.) Sculpted by Chakravarti Paloja, this work is handsome and slender, though rigidly frontal and without ornamentation, as a Jaina saint should be. Most figural sculptures from this period have delicate ornaments whose volumes overlay and supplement the slightly elongated bodies beneath them. Two sculptures—an *Uma-Maheshvara* from Balligrama (Shimonoga, Govt Mus.) and a female musician pillar bracket from Dharwar District (see fig. 223; similar figures in Bombay, Prince of Wales Mus.)—are indicative of the late 11th-century–early 12th-century style. Hundreds of other examples (including bronzes) have survived. The *Uma-Maheshvara*, though it shows the idiosyncrasies of its time, is not too distant stylistically from Nolamba-period antecedents (such as Aralaguppe), while the female musician has affinities with the better-known coeval and later Hoysala female bracket images (such as those at Belur).

The proclivity for profuse ornamentation culminated when the HOYSALA dynasty, erstwhile feudatories to the Chalukyas, seized power over southern Karnataka. Originating in the Malanad Hills in the Western Ghats, the Hoysalas moved east into the heartland of former Gangavadi and established their imperial capital at Halebid (anc. Dorasamudra). Inscriptions indicate that some sculptors moved from Chalukya to Hoysala territory, bringing with them mannerisms that contributed strongly to the so-called 'ornate style'. While this term is used to denote the period of extensive temple construction under the Hoysalas, the majority of temples were not so complex and closely resemble buildings of the Chalukyas of Kalyana (for example the Lakshmidevi Temple at Dodda Gaddavalli, dedicated in 1113, or the Malleshvara at Kikkeri). The famous ornate temple sites include BELUR, HALEBID and SOMNATHPUR. Complex in shape, these buildings' exterior surfaces are veiled with sculptural embellishments. Interiors, too, are ornate, with extensively carved doorways, ceilings and pillar-bracket figures. Pillars are 'lathe-turned' or have other elaborate forms. Figures tend to have portly bodies overlaid with profuse ornamentation, often with delicate filigree. Artists signed works during other periods, but at Hoysala monuments this is especially common, though not as a statement of individuality. Although individual masters can be identified, sculptors harmonized within a style norm (competing workshops had to work together on monuments). In addition to the famous sites mentioned above, many other Hoysala-period sites exist, including Nuggehalli, Basral, Koravangalam, Arsikere, Angadi, Mosale and Amritapur. These locations were Sri Vaishnava or Shaiva centres (this was a time of active devotional (*bhakti*) movements), and Jainism enjoyed continued support, especially at Sravana Belgola.

224. Exterior relief, Hoysaleshvara Temple, Halebid, Karnataka, *c.* 1121–60

The Chennakeshava Temple at Belur, dedicated in 1117, was erected to commemorate the victory of Vishnuvardhana (*reg* 1108–42) at Talakad over the Cholas, who had occupied portions of southern Karnataka. The first of the famed ornate Hoysala shrines, this monument has walls covered with richly embellished iconic panels. The original appearance of the temple is altered by the perforated stone screens between the exterior pillars of the *maṇḍapa*, added during the reign of Ballala II (*reg* 1173–1220), the king who secured regional supremacy by defeating the tottering Chalukyas in the north and intruding into Chola territory in the south. This temple and those at Halebid and Somnathpur are visually overwhelming. Placed below the *maṇḍapa* roof are 38 figural bracket images (Kannada *madanakai*) depicting females in alluring poses (there are 4 more in the interior). With delicately carved ornaments, plump, seductive bodies and a lace foliate motif overhead, these figures—22 of which are signed by their artists—deserve the acclaim they have received.

During Vishnuvardhana's reign, two temples were constructed at Halebid, the Jaina Parshvanatha (1133) and the Hoysaleshvara (*c.* 1121–60). Also at Halebid, the Jaina Santinatha (1196) and Kedareshvara (1219) were built during the reign of Ballala II. The famed twin-shrined Hoysaleshvara was first sponsored *c.* 1121 by Vishnuvardhana's officer Ketamalla, but it was not completed until *c.* 1160, during the reign of Narasimha I (1142–73), by the architect Kedaroja. Sculptural scenes and motifs shroud this temple's surface. The temple basement has small relief bands with thousands of figures extending around the monument, and above on the main wall surface there are over 400 high-relief figural sculptures (see fig. 224). The profusely ornate interior has detailed coffered ceilings, carved and 'lathe-turned' pillars, bracket figures and doorways richly decorated with intimidating, almost life-size guardians. Though prodigious with accoutrements, the sculpted figures retain a vitality that was eroded in later Hoysala sculpture. At the ornate and architecturally best-preserved Keshava at Somnathpur, which was founded in 1268 by Somanatha, general to King Narasimha III (*reg c.* 1263–91), some of the figural sculptures appear more frozen and stubby compared to their predecessors. The inventiveness and grandeur of embellishments that characterize the Hoysala ornate style became repetitive and restrictive in its final 13th-century phase.

14th–17th centuries. Muslim incursions from the north devastated the traditional ruling families of the south. Founded in 1366, Vijayanagara ('City of Victory', in modern Bellary District) became the centre for 'Hindu' resistance to Muslim forces until 1565, when the city was plundered. The sculptural style popularized during the Vijayanagara period—the result of mixing mannerisms indigenous to Karnataka, Tamil Nadu and Andhra Pradesh—spread throughout the south, with some vicissitudes, and continued into the NAYAKA period.

Often during the Vijayanagara period, temple complexes of earlier times were refurbished and expanded. When making renovations directly on to older monuments, sculptors often tried to archaize their work. More distinctively in the 'Vijayanagara style' are the enormous gateway towers (*gopuras*) with stucco figures and 'thousand-pillared' halls that were added to established shrines. Columns were extensively carved, often with engaged rearing animals projecting forwards, almost in the round. Partly because the preferred medium was granite, sculptures were no longer ornately embellished. Massive temples had low-relief panels depicting martial acts, fantastic animals and religious myths. At times sculptures appear repetitive, and bodies, facial features and dress seem formulaic and without vigour. Delightful exceptions are known (especially at the Vitthala, Hazararama and Virupaksha temples at the site of VIJAYANAGARA), including some delicate bronzes. The colossal monolithic Narasimha (h. 6.7 m) and Ganesha (h. 4.5 m) at Vijayanagara are perhaps the grandest and most powerful single images.

After the fall of Vijayanagara, prominent Nayakas of Ikkeri, Keladi, Madhugiri and Chitradurga and the Wodeyars of Mysore ruled independently (as did the BAHMANI sultans in north Karnataka). The Aghoreshvara Temple at Ikkeri and the Vidyashankara Temple at Sringeri have sculptures similar to those found at Vijayanagara. At the latter temple, low-relief basement panels, though awkwardly presented, depict scenes from the epic poem *Kirātārjunīyam* ('The combat of Arjuna and a Kirata'), and other deities and narratives are found throughout the monument. Painting and wood-carving, such as the pillar and ceiling panels at the Chauter palace at Mudabidri (17th century), became popular during this period. The Wodeyars of Mysore sponsored impressive monuments, of which the monolithic Nandi (1664) on Chamuneshvari Hill is an imposing example. However, the grandest Nayaka sites are in Andhra Pradesh and Tamil Nadu, most notably at MADURAI.

See also §III, 5(i)(f) and 6(i)(f).

BIBLIOGRAPHY

Enc. Ind. Temple Archit., i/2H. Cousens: *The Chalukyan Architecture of the Kanarese Districts* (Calcutta, 1926)
D. Barrett: *Nolamba Temples at Hemavati* (Bombay, 1958)
C. Sivaramamurti: 'Nolamba Sculptures (brought from Hemāvātī) in the Madras Government Museum', *Bull. Govt Mus., Madras*, n. s., ix, no. 1 (1964) [whole issue]
G. Tarr: 'Chronology and Development of the Early Chalukya Cave Temples', *A. Orient.*, viii (1970), pp. 155–84
M. A. Dhaky: 'Santara Sculpture', *J. Ind. Soc. Orient. A.*, n. s., *Dr. Vasuder Saran Agrawala Commemoration Volume*, pt i, vol. iv (1972), pp. 78–97
——: 'Ganga Jaina Sculpture', *Aspects of Jaina Art and Architecture* (Ahmadabad, 1973)
R. Del Bonta: *The Hoysala Style: Architectural Development and Artists, 12th and 13th Centuries* (diss., Ann Arbor, U. MI, 1978)
G. Michell and V. Filliozat, eds: *Splendours of the Vijayanagara Empire: Hampi* (Bombay, 1981)
C. Radcliffe: *Early Chalukya Sculpture* (diss., New York U., 1981)
A. L. Cohen: *Temple Architecture and Sculpture in Nolambavadi* (diss., U. Chicago, 1989)
K. Collyer: *The Hoysala Artists: Their Identity and Styles* (Mysore, 1990)
A. L. Cohen: 'The King and the Goddess: The Nolamba Period Laksmanesvara Temple at Avani', *Artibus Asiae*, lii (1992), nos 1–2, pp. 7–24
A. Dallapiccola, ed.: *The Ramachandra Temple at Vijayanagara* (Delhi, 1992)
S. Settar: *Hoysala Temples* (Dharwad, 1992)

ANDREW L. COHEN

(d) Andhradesha. Occupying the eastern Deccan in peninsular India, the Andhra region comprises ancient Vengi, parts of Kalinga, Telangana (Trilinga or Tailangana), Renandu and parts of Nolambavadi. Vengi, a centre of art activity from early times, lay in coastal Andhra. This

region's celebrated centres during and after the 7th century AD included Vijayawada, Bikkavolu and Samarlakota. The Kalinga region stretched northwards from Vengi into Orissa and had Mukhalingam as one of its most distinguished sites. The north-west portion of the Andhra country constituted ancient Telangana. Covering a large area, Telangana included such important centres as Palampet and Hanamkonda. Southern Andhra incorporated the Renandu and Nolambavadi regions. Bhairavakonda and Chilamkuru were significant in Renandu. Nolambavadi lay in south-western Andhra with Hemavati as its capital; substantial portions of this region are now in the state of Karnataka (its sculpture is discussed in the context of that area, *see* §(c) above).

These different regions emerged gradually between the 7th and 11th centuries AD, but their boundaries tended to vary. A cohesive integration began under the Kakatiya dynasty (11th–14th century) and was further reinforced during the time of the Vijayanagara rulers (14th–16th century).

7th century. Stylistic considerations, aided by inscriptions and reign periods, allow the earliest built temples in Andhra to be placed between 635 and 696. Rock-cut monuments pre-date these temples and exhibit influences from neighbouring Vidarbha and Tamil Nadu (*see* §(iii)(b) and (a) above). These early monuments show that the beginnings of sculptural art in the 7th century were hesitant as alternatives were explored between the rock-cut and structural modes and their respective schemes of figural composition. The rock-cut mode was ultimately favoured, as is indicated by the excavations at BHAIRAVAKONDA and at Undavalli near Vijayawada. The shrines at Bhairavakonda were probably excavated in the early 7th century, although they also contain reliefs of later periods. The pillars with lion bases (*simhapāda*) and the leogryph (*vyāla*) decorations on the cornices display a local idiom intermixed with impulses from Tamil Nadu. The exteriors of caves VI, VII, IX and X are dominated by massive reliefs of the two door-guardians (*dvārapāla*s), Nandikeshvara and Bhairava, standing cross-legged and leaning on heavy clubs in typical Andhra fashion. The levels of stylistic expression vary in the figure work, the portly, well-modelled guardians exhibiting a graceful flamboyance while reliefs of Brahma and Vishnu are distinctly rugged. The dating of the Andhra caves, including the cave at Adivisomapalli, remains controversial, but the inspiration of the rock-cut tradition of the 6th century and early 7th century in the western Deccan is obvious.

During the second half of the 7th century, sculptural production became more prolific as structural temples were built in increasing numbers. Starting at Bandatandrapadu in western Andhra (*c.* 635–42) with images of the elephant-headed Ganesha, Karttikeya and Durga Mahishasuramardini (the Goddess defeating the buffalo demon) that follow the tradition of neighbouring Karnataka, sculpture grew more spirited in the temples at ALAMPUR, Kudaveli and Kadamarakalava (between AD 655 and 681). Relief work and sculpture in the round at these sites are sparse and consist of floral scrolls and friezes with figural motifs in addition to the prominent images of guardians and the river goddesses Ganga and Yamuna carved on temple doorways. In the Kumara Brahma Temple at Alampur (mid-7th century), these motifs recall the delicate 'classical' treatment found in the early Vidarbha idiom of the VAKATAKA period (mid-3rd century AD to late 5th). There is, however, considerable variation, and the images of Trivikrama (a form of Vishnu) and Natesha (a dancing form of Shiva) on the exterior of the Svarga Brahma Temple (AD 688–9) are heavier in volume and relatively squat in their proportions. Such features in the imagery at Kudaveli (between AD 655 and 681) recall the later art of Vidarbha produced under the KALACHURIS OF MAHARASHTRA. The connection is particularly noticeable in the figures of Natesha and the personified 'treasures' Sankhanidhi and Padmanidhi.

The *Durga Mahishasuramardini* image (Alampur, Site Mus.) adheres to this idiom in portraying a sensitively modelled feminine form, imperious in mien yet endowed with a tranquil expression. The images of Kubera (the god of wealth) and attendants (*pratihārī*s; Alampur, Site Mus.) have the same portly breadth and controlled volume. But two guardian figures from Vijayawada are matchless for their sheer majesty and overwhelming form (see fig. 225). In every detail, from the knitted brows to the defiant

225. *Dvārapāla* (door-guardian), attributed to the artist Gundaya, granite, from Vijayawada, Andhra Pradesh, 7th century AD (Madras, Government Museum and National Art Gallery)

posture with legs crossed and hand resting on a huge club, these works have a surging volume and an audacious grandeur. An inscription on one of these images indicates that it was carved by the artist Gundaya of Vengi.

The 7th century is characterized by a preponderance of Shaiva themes, though Vaishnava figures occur occasionally. Some motifs are widespread. Nandikeshvara, the 'horned guardian' denoting the personified Nandi (Shiva's bull), occurs at Alampur in the Svarga Brahma and Padma Brahma temples as well as at Bhairavakonda; it is also represented in the cave temples of the Pallava dynasty in Tamil Nadu. Decorative motifs, including dance groups and amorous couples (*mithunas*), were depicted effectively throughout the period. The panels on the pillars of the Shivanandishvara Temple at Kadamarakalava (dating between 656 and 681) depict episodes from the epics. Sculpture was not yet encumbered with excessive detail and retained its formal coherence. A *Ganesha* (Madras, Govt Mus. & N.A.G.) from Vijayawada is typical. It has two arms, a naturalistic head and trunk, and on its head a lotus flower but no crown. The matrix of this art lay in the Karnataka region, and an idiom that can be described as specific to Andhra had yet to develop.

8th century. Alampur and Satyavolu in western Andhra still emulated the Karnataka tradition in the 8th century AD. In addition, Dravidian or southern modes were introduced into Vengi at Pondugula. The relevant sculptures at Alampur and Satyavolu were completed in 734, but the earliest may go back to 690. Sculpture, despite its refreshing vitality, continued to be subservient to its architectural setting. Such figural motifs as amorous couples, dwarfs (*gaṇas*), celestial musicians (*gandharvas*), couples in a flying posture, female attendants and river goddesses are common during the 8th century and are rendered with aplomb. These and such other motifs as the leogryph, swan, elephant and vegetal scroll are prominent in the repertory of the period. Variations in the posture and juxtaposition of figures abound. In the anthropomorphic images the round, swelling faces, elegant hairstyles and ornaments are sensitively rendered. Gestures are mildly intimate, as is illustrated by a relief of a *gandharva* couple on the Garuda Brahma Temple (built between 696 and 734) at Alampur, which shows a coquettish *apsarās* (minor female sky divinity) tenderly touching the shoulder of a celestial musician (Prasad, 1980, pl. 27). The amorous couples in the Vishva Brahma Temple at Alampur, of the same date, derive their sensitive modelling from a conceptual form (*rūpa*) idealized in classical poetry. Though small in size, the female figures are slender and well-modelled, with sensuous, rhythmic contours; their male counterparts are elegant, well-built youths of ideal proportions. Some inspired work is also found in the Vengi region. The image of *Simhanada Lokeshvara* (Madras, Govt Mus. & N.A.G.) from Amaravati is an eloquent example of a pervasive simplicity and charm. Sculpture from a number of sites, however, suggests a decline. The bas-reliefs of Vishnu, Brahma and Andhakasura on the ceiling of the main entrance (*mahādvāra*) to the fortified area containing temples at Alampur, dated to 780 by an inscription, are rigid in composition. At Bhairavakonda (Cave V) the three-headed *Maheshamurti* (Great Lord; Shiva) is patently archaic.

Shaiva themes remained predominant in the cult images, which had greater clarity in composition and iconography. The Gangadhara, Natesha and Vyakhyana-Dakshina images of Shiva and the Karivarada and Trivikrama forms of Vishnu on the Vishva Brahma Temple at Alampur are examples of such iconographic precision. The figure of the fire god Agni on the exterior of the Ramalingeshvara Temple at Satyavolu in western Andhra is surrounded by a halo that is marked by tufts of flame at regular intervals, anticipating the pattern in the images of Natesha encountered later in Chola metalwork (*see* §(a) above). The impact of the southern tradition is noticeable in the Dakshinamurti images of Shiva as the supreme teacher at Satyavolu, where the figures have a strong provincial character defined by rigidity of stance and ethnic undertones in the cut of the face and head (Prasad, 1978, p. 25).

The 8th-century sculpture of Andhra is thus marked by a disintegration of older idioms and the advent of new regional currents. A universal Andhra style, homogeneous in form and character, had yet to be established, but developments in the following century facilitated that trend without reducing the decorative and thematic content of sculpture.

9th century. By discarding its strong dependence on Karnataka and by subsuming the traditions of Tamil Nadu and Kalinga within its mould, Andhra was able to redefine its artistic identity during the 9th century. Jammidoddi, Vijawada, Bikkavolu and other sites in Vengi became the loci of significant art activity, which can be assigned to the time of Vijayaditya II (*reg* 806–46) and Vijayaditya III (*reg* 848–91) of the Eastern Chalukya dynasty. A balance between plasticity and precise, angular forms emerged, with figures more elongated and expressive of varied moods and gestures. The roots of this style lay ultimately in the Kalinga region. Parallels are evident in the decorative devices, the choice of images—for example Karttikeya, Ganesha, Durga, Natesha and Lakulisha (the legendary founder of the Pashupata sect considered an incarnation of Shiva)—and the scheme of their placement on temple walls. The most significant parallel with Kalinga is seen in the lyrical charm of the figurative sculpture, apparent, for example, in two panels from Jammidoddi (Vijayawada, Archaeol. Office). One of these depicts six dancers in different poses with the figure of an ascetic at the top. The panel is remarkable for its coherent grouping, perspective and narrative quality. The short, adipose, youthful figures have a tenderness matching those in Kalinga. The richly carved ornaments and the high conical crown worn by each figure add to their grace. A pillar at Vijayawada, dated by an inscription to the 9th century, bears the *Kirātārjunīya* story in relief in three registers. It displays reduced plasticity, but the episodes of this tale of Arjuna's fight with Shiva as a hunter (*kirāta*) are succinctly depicted.

Bikkavolu, in eastern Andhra, exhibits a blending of influences from different sources, those from Kalinga again being particularly evident. The northern version of Surya, the sun god, holding a lotus in both hands and accompanied by his attendants Dandi, Pingala and Aruna (the god of the morning), the latter wearing boots, occurs on the Golingeshvara Temple. Northern sources similarly explain the *Lakulisha* seen on the southern offset of the Golingeshvara in place of Dakshinamurti (Sivaramamurti, 1962). Influences from other regions also persisted. *Ganga* and *Yamuna* on the doorway of the Virabhadra Temple show the impress of Karnataka forms as used in western Andhra. The image of *Karttikeya* on the central offset of the Rajarajeshvara Temple and the *Ganesha* and *Durga Mahishasuramardini* in other niches are remarkable for their simplicity of detail and their combination of Karnataka and Kalinga modes of form and iconography. Ganesha has a crown of matted locks, a Kalinga feature. *Surya* (see fig. 226), on the central offset of the east wall of the Virabhadra Temple, is typical of the style that crystallized at Bikkavolu. The elongation with a touch of solidity, the fleshy pelvic region and tubular legs define the anatomy of the figure. Drapery and ornaments exhibit economy of detail, and the *makara toraṇa* (arch formed by aquatic creatures) above the figure, especially the floriated tails, has none of the agitated sweep and intensity that occur in the Kalinga region. Interestingly, the image is carved on two separate blocks of stone. The compositions at Bikkavolu are marked by a controlled dynamism.

At MUKHALINGAM, in the extreme north-east of Andhra, ties with neighbouring Orissa are particularly evident. The Madhukeshvara Temple, a treasure-house of figural imagery and motifs, partakes directly of trends shaped at Bhubaneshwar (*see* BHUBANESHWAR, §1) and marks the start of a substantial alteration and refinement in the art of the immediate area. The 'secular' vignettes in particular have an abiding charm. This is especially true of the *mithuna* couples, who exhibit an infinite variety of poses expressive of endearment, 'coquettish modesty' and 'clinging embracement' (Donaldson, 1985, i, p. 156). Animal motifs reveal many spirited forms, but the scrollwork on the doorframes shows extraordinary delicacy and skill of craftsmanship. The figure of a bashful, indolent tree goddess (*śālabhañjikā*) is lost in the lyrical exuberance of sweeping foliage and floral scrolls (see fig. 227). The cult images include *Ganesha*, *Karttikeya*, *Durga Mahishasuramardini* and different forms of Shiva and Vishnu, among them *Lakulisha* and *Natesha* and the incarnations of Vishnu.

226. *Surya*, sandstone, Virabhadra Temple, Bikkavolu, Andhra Pradesh, 9th century AD

227. *Śālabhañjikā*, sandstone, Madhukeshvara Temple, Mukhalingam, Andhra Pradesh, 9th century AD

In sum, the 9th century marked the culminating phase of trends that first surfaced in the 7th century. In the process of evolution, figurework became considerably more chaste, and sculptural form achieved greater unity and harmony. Depictions became more precise, with volume and planes better controlled and details handled with greater economy. This flair for economizing on detail is noticeable everywhere: in figural motifs, in jewellery and drapery and in decorative devices.

10th century. During this period art activity became fairly pervasive, and examples of sculpture are found at most sites throughout the Andhra region. The style matured, assuming distinct Andhra characteristics. The early phase of these developments falls within the reign of the Eastern Chalukya king Bhima I (*reg* 892–922) and was centred in the eastern Andhra sites of Chebrolu, Draksarama and Samarlakota. The accent was on a profusion of reliefs and sculptures on temples. Interiors received greater attention, and figurework was liberally employed on doorways. Gajalakshmi (Lakshmi being sprinkled with water by elephants, signifying prosperity and abundance) on lintels, Ganga, Yamuna and personifications of wealth (*nidhi*s) on jambs, and guardians of the four quarters (*dikpāla*s) on ceilings became part of the generally accepted decorative programme for shrine interiors. Pillars were skilfully carved with episodes from the epics and a variety of other themes.

While the statuary came to have a powerful presence, cult icons became more stereotyped and tended to be frontally conceived, rigid forms with precise iconography but masklike expressions. The *Karttikeya* image on the Bhimeshvara Temple at Samarlakota is a typical example, with its repetitive depiction of the peacock, stylized mode of drapery, masklike smiling face, staring eyes and disproportionate fleshiness. An image of *Shiva* (Madras, Govt Mus. & N.A.G.) from Bikkavolu exhibits similar schematization. On the other hand, the panel depicting the *saptamātṛkā*s (seven mother goddesses) built into the south-west corner of the Bhimeshvara Temple at Draksarama, is a spirited example retaining a certain grace despite the repetitive nature of the imagery, and there are similar images of Uma-Maheshvara (Parvati and Shiva), Natesha, Karttikeya with his consort Valli, and Durga Mahishasuramardini (Alampur, Site Mus.). Individual sculptures at the Mandava Narayana Temple, Samarlakota, are remarkable for the richly cut, beaded ornaments recalling wood-carving. Metal images were also cast; a notable example is the standing *Buddha* from Nagarjunakonda (Chandigarh, Govt Mus. & A.G.).

The finest figurework of the mid- to late 10th century is seen at MUKHALINGAM and HEMAVATI (for the latter, *see* §(c) above). An extremely exuberant idiom characterizes Mukhalingam. Following the patterns of the Madhukeshvara Temple of the preceding century, the figurework on the Someshvara Temple shows maturity and lyrical grace, evident in the ornamental motifs that adorn the niches on the temple walls. The swirling scrollwork and meandering stalks containing amorous couples and females and other figures are masterpieces of Kalinga decorative art. The floriated scrolls—oblique or vertical—rise ecstatically, adhering closely to the wall surface, producing a rich effect of light and shade. Among the figural motifs, warriors with females (sometimes erotic in nature) are a notable addition. Some reliefs point to Tantric ritual practices attributed to the Kapalika sect of Shaivism. Cult figures represent a well-developed iconographic programme; *Lakulisha* (see fig. 228) on the south wall of the Someshvara Temple is a typical example. However, the artistic idiom of Kalinga began to decline soon after the mid-10th century, as is evidenced by the later sculpture at Simhachalam, Sarapalli and Jayati.

The figurework on the Agastyeshvara Temple at Chilamkuru in the Renandu region of southern Andhra compares well with that at Hemavati in the second half of the 10th century. Similarities are evident in the themes and the form of reliefs on pillars and in the different iconographic representations of Shiva and Vishnu. Fanciful imagery is created by the meandering creepers enclosing the pillar reliefs with lions shown frontally or in profile. Subsequent manifestations of this style occur in the Agastyeshvara Temple at Attirala.

228. *Lakulisha*, sandstone, Someshvara Temple, Mukhalingam, Andhra Pradesh, 10th century

11th–13th centuries. After the 10th century Andhra art was reshaped considerably, the Telangana region forming the core area of the new style. In this development the content remained generally the same, but the form was redefined. Sculptures display a preference for short and plump forms, with male and female figures shown wearing heavy jewellery of pearled ornaments. Bodies are rendered with a crisp yet dynamic sensuousness. Early 11th-century examples are known from Patancheru (notably a *Whisk-bearer*; New Delhi, N. Mus.) and from the Ramalingeshvara Temple at Nandikandi. The statuary on the mid-11th-century Pachchala Someshvara Temple at Panagal shows the style gathering strength, with the figures articulated in a trim and shapely manner. The floridity and voluptuousness often seen in the sculpture of Karnataka are avoided. Images generally have a simple, rhythmic grace, although harsh lines are occasionally evident, as in the face of the

229. Right doorjamb (detail), granite, Rudreshvara Shrine, Thousand-pillared Temple, Hanamkonda, Andhra Pradesh, 1162

Ardhanarishvara (Shiva as half-female) from Panagal (Shrine 3, west wall). The *sālabhañjikā* image and the *Dancing Shiva* on the Pachchala Someshvara Temple and the creeper around them have the same plasticity and rhythmic grace.

Northern Karnataka had a strong impact on Andhra at this time, but sculpture was generally less florid. The sculptures on the mid-11th-century Chennakeshava Temple at Gangapura clearly convey this difference. For instance the guardian figures on the eastern doorway of the temple have the lateral stance, profusion of jewelled decoration, high, tiered crowns and floral canopies commonly found in the late Chalukya art of Karnataka, but the overall treatment is markedly less lavish.

Sculptures emulating earlier forms co-existed with the new style, the indigenous art of eastern Andhra being illustrated best by the massive, independent image of *Shiva Virabhadra* at Chebrolu. Generally, however, reliefwork is characterized by smooth, firm carving with meticulous attention to detail, whether the motifs be creepers, tendrils, stalks and foliage or jewellery and crowns. Such carving recalls the techniques used in working ivory. Sculptures also acquired a lustrous, almost metallic polish.

In the 12th century, developments reached a peak in the Thousand-pillared Temple (1162; Shaka era 1084) at Hanamkonda (*see* HANAMKONDA AND WARANGAL). While clearly there is a relationship with the art of Karnataka, a definite Andhra identity is evident from the ornate but less florid figures and the pleasing patterns of decoration, which are profuse but not overdone (see fig. 229). Human figures appear more elongated, though in the dancing female figures on walls and brackets the fleshy, plump form was not entirely abandoned. A lintel from Warangal (New Delhi, N. Mus.) depicting the dancing Shiva, Brahma and Vishnu is an exquisite example of the period. The style represented by these remains became ubiquitous with the rise of the KAKATIYA dynasty and was spread through the followers of the Shaiva Siddhanta and Kalamukha sects.

Hanamkonda had an abiding effect on the art of the Andhra country, and its idiom recurs consistently in the figures at Kondaparti (1203), Pillalamarri (Nameshvara Temple, 1202; Erakeshvara Temple, 1208), Kalabagura (?1210), Katachapura (*c.* 1230) and Bhutapura (*c.* 1270), among other places in western and northern Andhra. In southern Andhra, the figurework at Tripurantakam repeats the same style. The statuary on the Ramappa Temple (1213) at PALAMPET and on the 13th-century temples at Nagulapadu emulates this idiom, but the forms are somewhat stereotyped. Rows of dancers, amorous couples and tree goddesses, as well as delicately carved rosettes and animal motifs, occur on the *kakṣāsana*s (seat backs) of the Ramappa Temple. The figures of dancers, *nāginī*s (female serpent deities) and tree spirits on the brackets of the hall are elongated, supple, fleshy and full of a sense of movement. The reliefs of Shiva, a mother goddess and dancing Ganesha on a lintel in the temple are remarkable, while the massive figure of Nandi (1211; Shaka era 1135), profusely decorated with jewellery, displays consummate ease in the handling of volume.

Despite the pervasiveness of the Telangana style, regional idioms continued to survive. The later phase of the Kalinga style is seen on the Narasimha Temple (1268; reconstructed) at Simhachalam. Its sculptures and relief-work are characterized by a severity of expression, yet the decorative jewellery lends grace to the images, as in a female bust from Ghanapura (see fig. 230). In southern Andhra, Nandlur and Pushpagiri (the latter dated to 1254) afford examples of the intermixing of Telangana features with the local idiom. A number of metal sculptures have also survived from this period. A *Natesha* from Draksarama, Dipalakshmi images from Warangal and *jina*s (Jaina saints) from Bapatla deserve mention (Prasad, 1980, p. 199).

The statuary of the 13th century, particularly the iconographic programme of cult images, was severely restricted by the dictates of the canons. But other motifs—for example amorous couples, dancers, tree goddesses, erotic figures, animal friezes and narratives following the epics and other sources—still reveal some vitality. Creepers, tendrils and bunches of flowers are delicately rendered. Thirteenth-century work includes hero stones (*vīragal*s; examples Hyderabad, State Mus.; Golconda, Khajana Bldg Mus.), depicting persons immortalized for their heroic deaths (*see also* SATĪ AND HERO STONES).

14th–15th centuries. Widespread social and political change occurred throughout peninsular India as a result of the expansion of Tughluq power in the 14th century. However, the traditional Telangana idiom survived in the Palnad and Guntur districts of Andhra. Older forms continued while new themes were added to the repertory. Scenes from the lives of Shaiva saints on the enclosing walls of the Shiva temples at SRISAILAM are significant in this respect.

The second quarter of the 14th century was marked by the advent of the VIJAYANAGARA kingdom. With the kingdom seldom exercising control of territories north of the River Krishna, the geographical distribution of the type of monuments associated with Vijayanagara is limited to southern Andhra, Karnataka and Tamil Nadu. The earliest work in what can be considered the Vijayanagara style is seen in the Andhra region at Kadiri (Lakshmi Narasimhasvami Temple, 1352), Gorantla (Madhavarayasvami Temple, 1354) and Penukonda (Shiva and Rama temples, 1354). The cornices carved with lion heads (*simhalalāṭa*) and the niches containing *Dakshinamurti*, *Virabhadra*, *Brahma* and *Ganga* at Penukonda are the most notable sculptures. The bas-reliefs in two registers on the Rama Temple are similarly significant and were repeated later at Tadpatri. The dedication of the temple at Penukonda to Rama is indicative of the rising popularity of devotional Vaishnavism in the 14th century. At Kadiri the pillars are surmounted by pillarets and bear leogryphs, *apsarasās* and floral motifs on the shafts, which recall earlier Telangana configurations. These forms persisted at

230. Female bust, black stone, 580×420 mm, Ghanapura, Andhra Pradesh, 13th century or earlier (Hyderabad, Department of Archaeology and Museums)

Godlavidu (1362) in southern Andhra and Ganapuram (1380) in western Andhra.

The Vijayanagara style reveals a standard pattern of figural composition from the 15th century. Bold, stylized figures of lions ride on the backs of elephants on pillars with leogryphs forming the brackets. Deities are prominently depicted on the shafts of pillars. Spirited examples of such forms occur at LEPAKSHI. Both plain and decorated doorways are encountered, the latter having male and female door-keepers, scrollwork with lion and elephant figures, vase motifs on the jambs and Gajalakshmi on the lintel. Cornices are carved minutely with rings and chains. Exterior decoration takes many forms. Temple bases carry friezes with swans, elephants, lions and horses depicted in rows. Walls were sometimes left plain but, when decorated, contain figures in low relief in two or three registers. Niches are covered with semicircular arches composed of stylized animal figures. A *makara* (crocodile-like aquatic creature) at the base and a lion head at the centre top often adorn these niches. *Makara toraṇa*s sometimes have plumage flowing downwards or resting on top of the pilasters. In these patterns Vijayanagara art followed established conventions. Panels showing a deity or a full-blown lotus flower form the centrepiece of ceilings. Reliefwork is handled skilfully, both in the carving of tiny details and in larger figures. Cult images representing Shaiva and Vaishnava forms, among others, acquired much prominence on the walls of towered gateways (*see* GOPURA), as did acrobats, shepherds, cowherds and life-size monkeys.

The best 15th-century work is seen in the Ramalingeshvara Temple (*c.* 1450) and its complementary edifices (1509) at TADPATRI. Kevalamurti and the different types of Shiva Dakshinamurti occur prominently on the southern *gopura.* The temple also contains scenes from the *Rāmāyaṇa*, including the subjugation of Taraka, Maricha and Ravana by Rama, the abduction of Sita and the Lanka cycle of Hanuman's exploits. The *apsarasas* on the pillars of the hall in the Parvati shrine rank among the finest specimens, retaining some elegance despite a general stiffness in pose and form. Similarly impressive is the figure of *Ganga* on the doorway of the Ramalingeshvara Temple (*c.* 1450); the river goddess is shown clasping the round curve of a floral stalk as it turns upwards. Other notable 15th-century monuments are found at Srisailam and Pushpagiri. Forms and motifs surviving from earlier phases also occur at these sites, with some variation on doorways, pillars, cornices, brackets and temple exteriors. At Srisailam the scenes depicting tribal myths (Mallikarjuna Temple, 1456; reconstructed second quarter of 16th century) compel attention. With a strong Shaiva content, these include episodes relating the fascination of a maiden of the Chenchu Andhra tribe for Shiva, a Chenchu warrior receiving Shiva's grace by accident, and Shiva as the hunter god killing a boar with the assistance of a Chenchu girl. The art at Srisailam also evinces Tantric influences in cult images, notably in an icon of *Ganesha and his Consort* on the western enclosing wall of the Mallikarjuna Temple, with Ganesha touching his consort's *yoni* (vulva) with his trunk.

On the 15th-century Satanamalleshvara Temple at Pushpagiri the pilasters with deities carved below and rich scrollwork above have a delicate quality. The female figures standing under creepers guarding the entrance of the *gopura* and the depiction of the *Kirātājunīya* episodes are also remarkable. The Chennakeshava Temple (1436; reconstructed) at Pushpagiri has more varied imagery. Well-ordered patterns, including friezes of swans, horses, leogryphs, warriors and elephants, are carved at the base of the temple. The wall niches containing figures of deities are imaginatively composed of lotus petals that rise from the base and develop into a *makara* and arabesque. The spaces between such niches are also carved with divinities. Sculpture of the 15th century is also found at Tirupati (*see* TIRUPATI AND CHANDRAGIRI), the most significant work being the massive, monolithic images of Ranganatha (Vishnu reclining on the serpent Ananta), Chakrapurusha (Vishnu's *chakra* or discus personified), Panduranga and guardian figures fashioned after the celebrated Nrisimha or Narasimha (Vishnu as man–lion) and Ganesha at HAMPI (Sivaramamurti, 1961, p. 132). All the figures are encountered on the Govindaraja Temple at Tirupati.

16th–18th centuries. In the early 16th century the Vijayanagara style continued to flourish; Adoni, Chandragiri, Markapuram, Jatprolu and Tadpatri were the leading centres. Lepakshi in southern Andhra rose to prominence with the construction of the Virabhadra Temple complex (16th century). The walls of the main temple are plain, but the *śikhara* (spire over the shrine) has seated Vishnu figures on each side. Large figures of Brahma, the sages Dattatreya and Narada, Natesha and the nymph Rambha are carved on the shafts of the pillars in the hall. The sanctum contains an image of *Virabhadra.* Narrative reliefs extend, in stages, from the east to the north walls of the hall. Despite the immensity of the sculptures on the monuments of the complex, forms appear devoid of vitality; the figures look frozen in stance and expression. Lines are harsh, postures rigid and the faces have a vacant look. The *apsarasas* and the *Durga Mahishasuramardini* (see fig. 231) in the hall illustrate these traits.

During the Vijayanagara era the production of portrait sculptures, typically of royal personages, flourished, and examples are preserved in the Andhra region. Notables are depicted on the 16th-century Chennakeshava Temple at Somapalem, while the Vijayanagara ruler *Vira Narasimha* (*reg c.* 1503–9) of the Tuluva dynasty is shown on the south *gopura* of the Ramalingeshvara Temple at

231. *Durga Mahishasuramardini*, stone, Virabhadra Temple complex, Lepakshi, Andhra Pradesh, 16th century

Tadpatri. The Venkateshvara Temple at Tirumala, Chittoor District, has metal images of the Tuluva ruler *Krishna Deva Raya* (*reg* 1509–30) and his two queens, *Chinnadevi* and *Tirumaladevi*, with their names inscribed on their shoulders.

After the fall of Vijayanagara in 1565, sculpture ceased to be fashioned for want of patronage. Motifs recalling earlier patterns continued to occur sporadically in military architecture and related structures. For instance, a small floral relief flanked by roaring lions occurs on a lintel on a gate of the fort (16th century) at Medak. The base of the gate jambs is decorated with a large figure of an elephant with a diminutive rider. The *kīrtimukha* (face-and-floral scroll motif) on the brackets of one of the main gates, the Fateh Darvaza, at GOLCONDA and the lions and leogryphs on the side walls of the entrance to the Bala Hisar, Golconda's citadel, recall earlier patterns but are bereft of vitality. Similar leogryphs are seen on the west gate of the citadel at Warangal. While sculpture diminished, traditional iconographies were carried down in manuscript painting (*see* §VI, 4(vii)(d) below).

See also §III, 5(i)(g) and (h), and 6(i)(f) above.

BIBLIOGRAPHY

Enc. Ind. Temple Archit., i/1–2, ii/1

C. Sivaramamurti: 'Early Eastern Chāḷukya Sculpture', *Bull. Govt Mus., Madras*, n. s. vii/2 (Madras, 1957/*R* 1962), pp. 1–59

——: *Indian Sculpture* (New Delhi, 1961)

M. S. G. Murti: *Jain Vestiges in Andhra* (Hyderabad, 1963)

K. V. Soundara Rajan: *Architecture of the Early Hindu Temples of Andhra Pradesh*, Govt Andhra Pradesh, Archaeol. Ser., xxi (Hyderabad, 1965)

M. Rama Rao: *The Temples of Sri Sailam* (Hyderabad, 1967)

A. G. Rao: *Lepakshi* (Hyderabad, 1969)

S. G. Murti: *The Art of Lepakshi* (Hyderabad, n.d.)

M. R. Sarma: *Temples of Teliṅgāṇa: The Architecture, Iconography and Sculpture of the Cāḷukya and Kākatīya Temples* (Hyderabad, 1972)

A. W. Khan: *Stone Sculptures in the Alampur Museum* (Hyderabad, 1976)

N. S. Ramaswami: *Temples of Tadpatri* (Hyderabad, 1976)

V. Kameswara Rao: *Select Vijayanagara Temples of Rāyalaseema*, Govt Andhra Pradesh, Archaeol. Ser., xlvii (Hyderabad, 1976)

B. R. Prasad: *Temple Sculptures of Andhra Pradesh* (New Delhi, 1978)

C. Sivaramamurti: *Early Āndhra Art and Iconography* (Hyderabad, 1979)

M. L. Nigam: *Sculptural Art of Andhra* (New Delhi, 1980)

B. R. Prasad: *Art of South India: Andhra Pradesh* (New Delhi, 1980)

P. V. Begde: *Forts and Palaces of India* (New Delhi, 1982)

T. E. Donaldson: *Hindu Temple Art of Orissa*, 3 vols (Leiden, 1985)

G. Michell: 'Golconda and Hyderabad', *Islamic Heritage of the Deccan*, ed. G. Michell (Bombay, 1986), pp. 77–85

P. B. Wagoner: *Mode and Meaning in the Architecture of Early Medieval Telangana* (diss., Madison, U. WI, 1986)

R. N. MISRA

8. 19TH CENTURY–1947. Indian sculpture from the 19th century and early 20th century can be broadly viewed in terms of three categories: a continuing tradition of temple and related sculpture following the conventions of earlier ages, a tradition of folk or rural art centred in villages (*see* §§X and XI below) and works deriving from or influenced by European models. There are also many examples of interaction between indigenous and imported styles.

(i) Traditional styles and forms. The most strongly 'classical' school of sculpture survived (as it does to the present; *see* INDIA, REPUBLIC OF, §IV) in southern India, in Tamil Nadu. Artists working in stone, cast bronze and wood continued to create icons bearing the same formal and iconographic conventions seen in Chola art (*see* §7(vi)(a) above). Centres of activity included Mahabalipuram, Madurai, Kumbakonam, and Nagarkovil. Many artists continued to consult *śāstra*s (Skt: treatises; *see* §I, 10 above) on sculpture for traditionally correct proportions and measurements, and continued to work in a traditional manner drawing diagrams on the stone or wood block as a mnemonic device for the direct transmission of correct forms.

'Classicizing' sculpture in stone, wood and clay was also produced in Orissa, although artists did not seem to be in as close touch with the textual tradition as their Tamil counterparts. Pandits were consulted when strict accord with the *śāstra*s was desired. Temples such as the Viranchi Narayana in Buguda and the Jagannatha in Belaguntha have elaborately carved wooden doors consisting typically of arrangements of square panels bearing iconic or narrative imagery, and lintels and doorframes with figurative, vegetal or abstract forms.

In Kerala, wood-carving and metal-casting continued into the 20th century, but with steadily diminishing output. Keralan sculpture is often described as having an almost ferocious intensity, this quality becoming more pronounced in the late period, along with greater stiffness and angularity. The qualities are evident, for example, in a 19th-century image of *Shasta* (Aiyanar; Trivandrum [Tiruvananthapuram], Govt Mus. A. & Nat. Hist.) and in sculptures from the Shiva Temple at Kurati. Surprising delicacy appears, however, in carvings from the palace of Swati Tirunal (*reg* 1827–47) in Trivandrum Fort. Karnataka also has a tradition of wood-carving surviving into the 20th century. Sandalwood icons, averaging a third of a metre in height, were produced in a cosmeticized Hoysala style (*see* §7(i) above), as were wooden panels bearing crowded narrative compositions.

In Bengal, brick temples profusely decorated with terracotta sculptures were built as early as the 16th century, and the tradition continued into the 20th, with buildings dating into the 1930s. Their sculpture was characterized by a continuity of traditional forms, along with absorption of various contemporary (including European) influences. Major centres were Birbhum, Burdwan, Mindapore and Hooghly districts. Subject-matter includes episodes from the *Rāmāyaṇa* and *Mahābhārata*, genre scenes and depictions of Europeans. Friezes are the most prominent format. Imagery is organized into static figural groupings and crowded compositions, with a tendency towards high relief and profuse surface detail, often delicately applied. Aside from costume and architectural elements, European influence is seen in the tendency towards a more naturalistic representation, particularly in terms of modelling. A decline in patronage after *c.* 1850 is attributed to the increasing Westernization of the wealthy Bengali middle classes. After this time terracotta sculptures are increasingly replaced by cheaper stuccowork (*see also* §III, 7(ii)(e) above).

In Gujarat and Rajasthan, sculpture in the tradition of the great medieval temples continued. Examples include the carvings from the inner courtyard of the Swaminarayana Temple in Ahmadabad. The overall treatment becomes rather broadened and generalized. In Gujarat, in particular, sculptors carved wooden house façades. In

232. *Dvārapālas* (door-guardians), sandstone, probably from Rajasthan, late 19th century (London, Sotherby's, 11 October, 1990)

Rajasthan, royal palaces and elaborate household shrines continued to be embellished. A pair of door-guardians (see fig. 232), probably produced in Rajasthan in the late 19th century, are skilfully carved and show a continuing interest in detail but lack the power of earlier work.

Several sculptural forms continued to be produced throughout India. Miniature icons were created of brass, silver and other metals in virtually every state, as were painted wood carvings. Styles vary from the naturalistic to the elementally abstract. These works functioned as votive images or as household icons. Metal masks depicting various deities were produced in Himachal Pradesh, Maharashtra, Karnataka and Kerala. They are generally placed over aniconic *liṅgas*, abstract goddess icons or over the face of a stone or wood image.

BIBLIOGRAPHY

R. F. Bussabarger and B. D. Robins: *The Everday Art of India* (New York, 1968)

S. Kramrisch, J. H. Cousins, R. V. Poduval: *The Arts and Crafts of Kerala* (Cochin, 1970)

P. K. Bose: *Traditional Craft in a Changing Society: Potters and their Craft in Gujarat* (Surat, 1980)

E. Fischer and others: *Orissa: Kunst und Kultur in Nordost-Indien* (Zurich, 1980)

K. K. Das Gupta: *Catalogue of the Wood Carvings in the Indian Museum* (Calcutta, 1981)

N. K. Behura: *Peasant Potters of Orissa* (New Delhi, 1982)

P. M. Gardner: 'Creative Performance in South Indian Sculpture: An Ethnographic Approach', *A. Hist.*, v/4 (Dec 1982), pp. 472–9

S. R. Sarma: 'A Living Tradition of Śilpa in Orissa', *Rūpa Pratirūpa; Alice Boner Commemoration Volume*, ed. B. Bäumer (New Delhi, 1982), pp. 187–8

G. Michell, ed.: *Brick Temples of Bengal: From the Archives of David McCutchion* (Princeton, 1983)

J. F. Mosteller: 'A New Approach for the Study of Indian Art', *J. Amer. Orient. Soc.*, cvii/1 (1987), pp. 55–69

WALTER SMITH

(ii) European works and influences. In the 19th century, sculptures that were produced in England and then transported to India brought a new visual element to Indian cities, the subjects often being depicted in Classical dress. The prevailing mode in colonial architecture was the Palladian (*see* PALLADIANISM), introduced by the British, who valued not only its suitability to the local climate but also its association with Imperial Rome, and Neo-classical statues of such statesmen as Lords Mayo, Cornwallis, Dalhousie and Wellesley and John Malcolm were erected, Lord Mayo's in AJMER, Lord Dalhousie's in Calcutta. John Bacon jr sculpted the statues of both Cornwallis and Wellesley. Malcolm's statue stood inside the Bombay Town Hall. Many Neo-classical funeral monuments to Europeans are also found from this time; examples include the marble memorial sculpture in St George's Cathedral, Madras, or the fragments of sculpted tombstones showing the *thanatos* (Gr: 'death') motif in Park Street Cemetery, Calcutta.

These European sculptures were permanent, commemorative, didactic and usually classical. The exception was work produced in GOA, where the wood-carving tradition included Christian themes. Settled by the Portuguese in the late 15th century and possessing a large Christian population, Goa produced sculpture that followed the lead of Iberian Baroque (*see* PORTUGAL, §II, 2).

After 1857 and the so-called 'Indian Mutiny', much of India came under direct British control. An emphasis on defence and the military necessitated clean water and food supplies. Public fountains were erected, such as Richard Norman Shaw's Flora (Frere) fountain or the Crawford Markets fountain designed by William Emerson and John Lockwood Kipling (both in Bombay). Most sculpture after 1857 was additional to public buildings and food markets, as for example, Lockwood Kipling's bas-reliefs of rural life over the doorways of Crawford Markets. As Anglicanism was the major religion of the colonizers, little religious sculpture was required.

In India as in Britain, the thrust of 19th-century thought was towards improvement and uplift, so edifying subjects adorned public buildings. Personifications of Science, Commerce, Justice and Agriculture decorated the roofline of the Writers' Building, Calcutta. In the 1860s art schools opened in Bombay, Calcutta, Madras and, later, Jaipur (*see* BOMBAY, §2; CALCUTTA, §3; and MADRAS, §2). Students were to be trained by European methods. What remains from the late 19th century are small silver presentation pieces, such as *Bhistī* ('Water-carrier', *c.* 1893; Oxford, Ashmolean), which is modelled with a naturalism rarely seen previously in India.

20th-century sculpture before 1947 was mainly a decorative accompaniment to major building programmes. Pomeroy sculpted *Lord Curzon* for the Victoria Memorial, Calcutta, where a statue of *Victoria* herself was also sited. Rao Bahadur Khetre's *George V* stood on the Apollo Bunder in Bombay. He and Queen Mary were also commemorated in Sir EDWIN LUTYENS's plan for New

Delhi, the proposed new capital city. This building programme afforded opportunities for animal as well as human subjects. Bulls, elephants, lions and cobras are all lovingly represented in sandstone or bronze, a reference to the decoration of temple and palace complexes in classical India, which Lutyens drew on in his plan (*see* DELHI, §I).

The work of traditional sculptors also came under colonial influence. For example, in Bengal, the Pal caste sculptors from Krishnanagar had a long tradition of modelling human figures as well as *pūjā* (devotional) images in clay. In the early 20th century they began to produce European-style sculpture such as the portrait bust, in Nadia District, of the pioneering surgeon and philanthropist *Dr Umadas Banerji*. Heroes of the Independence movement, such as *Netaji Subhas Bose* and *Mahatma Gandhi*, carved by the sculptors of Krishnanagar, fill the pedestals once occupied by colonial officials.

See also §III, 7(iii) and 8.

BIBLIOGRAPHY

R. F. Bussabarger and B. Dashew Robbins: *The Everyday Art of India* (London, 1968)

S. Nilsson: *European Architecture in India, 1750–1850* (London, 1968)

Maharaja of Baroda and V. Fass: *The Palaces of India* (London, 1980)

R. Grant Irving: *Indian Summer: Lutyens, Baker and Imperial Delhi* (New Haven, 1981)

T. R. Metcalf: *An Imperial Vision: Indian Architecture and Britain's Raj* (Berkeley, 1989)

C. A. Bayley, ed.: *The Raj: India and the British, 1600–1947* (London, 1990)

J. Guy and D. Swallow, eds: *Arts of India, 1550–1900* (London, 1990)

GERALDINE SMITH-PARR BANERJI

VI. Painting.

The art of painting was practised in India from ancient times, though little early work remains. Some paintings in caves, rock shelters and on rock faces is assumed to be prehistoric but may be of relatively recent tribal manufacture. Painted pottery from the prehistoric period is restricted in decoration principally to geometric, vegetal and animal motifs; human representation is extremely rare. Information about painting in much of the historical period comes more from literary sources than from surviving examples. There are frequent references to painting in religious texts, the epics, poetry and plays, and several important texts describe painting practices.

GENERAL BIBLIOGRAPHY

A. K. Coomaraswamy: *The History of Indian and Indonesian Art* (Leipzig, New York and London, 1927)

——: 'The Technique and Theory of Indian Painting', *Techn. Stud. Field F.A.*, iii/2 (1934), pp. 58–89; reprinted *J. United Prov. Hist. Soc.*, xxiii (1950), pp. 1–34

D. Barrett and B. Gray: *Painting of India* (Lausanne, 1963)

R. P. Hinograni: *Painting in South Asia: A Bibliography* (Delhi, 1978)

J. C. Harle: *The Art and Architecture of the Indian Subcontinent* (Harmondsworth, 1986)

1. Introduction. 2. Prehistoric. 3. 1st century BC–16th century AD. 4. 16th century–1947.

1. INTRODUCTION.

(i) Overview. (ii) Materials and techniques. (iii) Subject-matter. (iv) Painters. (v) Literary references.

(i) Overview.

(a) Wall painting. (b) Manuscripts.

(a) Wall painting. Significant painted remains from the historical period do not survive from before *c.* 1st century BC. Caves 10 and 11 at Ajanta contain ravaged remains in a fluid and naturalistic style that is closely comparable to contemporary sculpture (*see* §3(i)(a) below); these are the sole survivors of what literary sources reveal to have been a rich tradition of wall painting in religious and secular buildings. A gap of several centuries follows these examples until the wall paintings of the later caves at Ajanta; most of these, and the best-preserved examples, are in Caves 1, 2, 16 and 17 (see figs 238-41 below). The dating of these paintings is problematic, but it is reasonable to place them in the 5th century AD. Similar, though much less well-preserved examples survive at Bagh. The style of the 5th century emphasizes the suggestion of three-dimensional form through the use of colour modelling and, like its predecessors, is the perfect two-dimensional counterpart of the sculptural style of the period. Except for poorly preserved fragments that reveal that wall painting was widespread in the monasteries of ancient Gandhara, the remains at Ajanta and Bagh are the only physical evidence of Indian painting from the 5th century and earlier. Though these remains are limited, the styles must have been widely distributed, perhaps even pan-Indian. Not only are regional expressions of the parallel sculptural style widely distributed, but the imprint of the 5th-century painting style is seen in the later idioms of both north and south India. The splendid 6th-century wall paintings in Cave 3 at Badami are clearly derived from the style typified by Ajanta, though they are more linear in execution. Other extensions of the idiom are in Sri Lanka at the site of Sigiriya (*see* SRI LANKA, §V, 2).

Examples from the 8th century survive at a Jaina cave temple at Sittannavasal in Tamil Nadu and on the ceiling of the Kailasa Temple at Ellora in Maharashtra. Both show technical continuity with earlier traditions, and both exhibit a tendency towards greater linearity, though this is much more marked at Ellora. Also at Ellora are wall paintings in a Jaina cave, in which linearity begins to dominate the three-dimensional modelling and unity of form of the classical period.

In the south, the traditions of wall painting (and of painting temples and sculpture) enjoyed a vigorous development into the modern period. Among significant examples to survive are those at the great Rajarajeshvara Temple at Thanjavur (early 11th century; see fig. 244 below), the wall paintings at Lepakshi in Andhra Pradesh (*c.* 1540) and numerous examples in temples and palaces in Kerala of the 16th–18th century, including the Mahadeva Temple at Ettamanur and the Mattancheri Palace in Cochin (see fig. 233; *see also* §4(vii) below). The situation in the north is somewhat less clear. Later medieval wall paintings do survive in temples, but they are very few. This is taken by some scholars to indicate a withering of the tradition in favour of manuscript illumination. Nevertheless, there is considerable evidence for the continuation of wall painting in the north. Literary sources frequently describe painted interiors; the palace of Firuz Shah Tughluq (*reg* 1351–88) in Delhi is known to have been decorated inside with wall paintings; Mughal and

233. Wall painting depicting Vishnu (detail), from *Rāmayāṇa* cycle, Mattancheri Palace, Cochin, *c.* late 16th century–early 17th

other paintings abound in representations of painted interiors; and wall paintings survive in palaces, mosques and tombs in increasingly large numbers from the 15th century, with important examples at Gwalior, Fatehpur Sikri, Delhi, Agra, Lahore and Amer. At a folk level, wall painting survives in north India in the late 20th century.

See also §3(i) below.

DANIEL J. EHNBOM

(b) Manuscripts. No manuscripts of an early date have survived from India itself. The physical evidence of the Indian manuscript tradition for the first millennium AD depends almost entirely on material from Central Asia, where Indian traditions spread along with Buddhism (*see* CENTRAL ASIA, §II, 5(ii)). A few manuscripts on palm leaves from India and Nepal dating from the later first millennium were preserved in the Singh Darbar (Secretariat Library) in Kathmandu (now in Kathmandu, N. Archvs), while a cache of manuscripts on birch bark, palm leaves and paper dating between the 6th and 10th centuries were found at Gilgit (now mostly New Delhi, N. Archvs). Although calligraphy evidently flourished among the Buddhists, illumination was scarcely practised at all. Some larger birch-bark folios from Gilgit (7th–8th century; London, BL, Or. MS. 11878A; see 1982 exh. cat., pp. 29–30) have colophon pages decorated with large roundels or stylized lotuses, in ink and without colours. A few 8th–10th-century Central Asian paper manuscripts have similar roundels, some with colours, marking chapter ends. Occasionally a Buddha is also found in these roundels, while a few manuscripts have Buddha images in the margins. But the number of such decorated manuscripts is extremely small (scarcely a dozen), and almost all of them are in Buddhist texts translated into Khotanese (Zwalf, chap. 3), suggesting the influence of the traditional Iranian love of sumptuous manuscripts. In India proper at this time, it seems there was no tradition of decorating manuscripts other than with the simplest ink designs. The inherent antipathy of the Indian tradition to the value of the written word and the comparatively short survival expectation of manuscripts in the climate are perhaps two elements contributing to this austerity. Where the palm-leaf tradition survived into the 19th century, this restraint persisted. Physically too, birch-bark manuscripts are practically impossible to decorate with pigments because of the friable nature of the surface layers of the bark. Palm leaves can be coloured, but there is no physical evidence that they were until the early 11th century (*see* §3(ii)(c) below) and no textual evidence at all. The more stable surfaces provided by the wooden covers were perhaps illustrated earlier than the leaves themselves.

From the available evidence, manuscript illumination would seem to have been first practised in a specifically Tantric Buddhist environment in the monasteries of eastern India and Nepal in the late 10th century and early 11th. The subjects are almost totally confined to the various Buddhas, *bodhisattvas* and other divinities, both beneficent and terrifying, who make up the Vajrayana pantheon (see fig. 234). These manuscripts coincide with the development of texts describing objects of devotion in the minutest iconographic detail. From later Tibetan evidence, monks not only meditated on divinities in this way but actually painted them so, and the practice in Indian monasteries may have been similar, although guilds of professional artists were also involved. Two texts provide the vast majority of such manuscripts, the *Prajñāpāramitā* ('Perfection of wisdom'; see fig. 251 below) and the *Pañcarakṣā* ('Five protections'; spells addressed to the five Raksha goddesses). With two known exceptions (a *Kāraṇḍavyūha*, London, BL, Or. MS 13940, and a *Prajñāpāramitā*, Boston, MA, Mus. F.A., 20.589), none of these miniatures makes any attempt to illustrate the contents of the text; instead they serve protective and merit-acquiring roles. Palm-leaf manuscripts with similar iconic miniatures, but of the founders of the Jaina system, were illuminated in western and southern India slightly later than the Buddhist examples from the east (*see* §3(ii)(a) below). The reasons for the commencement of the art in this case are more obscure. Simple emulation of this new development in Buddhist art for the same meritorious purposes is doubtless a reason. Meditation on divinities and their depiction in paint for the same reasons as in Buddhist manuscripts may also be of relevance. Wooden covers of the 12th century and later show historical events of great importance to the Jaina church. But on the leaves themselves the miniatures do not illustrate the text of the manuscripts, even though the range of Jaina texts with miniatures is wider than those of the Buddhists. There is no evidence that any Hindu manuscripts were illuminated

234. Palm-leaf manuscript, each folio *c.* 72×432 mm, Pala style, from Vikramashila Monastery, Bihar, *c.* 1145 (London, British Library, Or. MS. 6902, fols 163*v*, 164*r*)

in India itself at this time. A few Hindu illuminated leaves and painted covers survive from 12th-century Nepal. A pair of covers of this period (London, BM, 1965–6–142) was evidently painted in a Buddhist studio. Hardly any contemporary Hindu manuscripts survive. Buddhist manuscripts owe their survival to the Buddhist monastic libraries of Nepal and Tibet; Jaina manuscripts owe theirs to the temple libraries of Rajasthan, Gujarat and Karnataka.

Early Islamic period. Few manuscripts have survived from the first two centuries of Muslim rule, but those that have are for the most part indistinguishable from those in the Iranian tradition. Timur's invasion in 1398 precipitated the destruction of the unified Sultanate, with its close ties to the Islamic heartlands, and thereafter Indian Koranic scripts and illumination began to differ significantly from Middle Eastern models. Illustrated manuscripts of the Persian classic poetic texts, apparently done in India and emulating work from the commercial studios of Shiraz, are found from the 1430s. Although there is no evidence whatever as to provenance at this period, artists trained in the Iranian tradition must have sought employment at the Muslim courts of India, taking examples of their work with them (see Ettinghausen and Fraad; Adahl; and Brend). Further influence from the commercial Shiraz studios (and indeed those of Herat and Bukhara) is felt in India in various Sultanate, or Indo-Persian, styles right up to the period of the hegemony of the Mughal style (*see* §3(ii)(d) below). From *c.* 1500 the Indian studios included Indian artists trained in other traditions, as their work is incorporated into these manuscripts (see Khandalavala and Chandra).

Jaina manuscript painting survived the Muslim conquest, and illustrated palm-leaf manuscripts were produced up to the 14th century, when paper ones first became commonplace. The major change was in the type of illustration, when the range of texts illustrated was reduced almost to one, the *Kalpa sūtra*, and the content of the illustration changed from the iconic to the narrative (*see* §3(ii)(b) below). Very possibly the Iranian tradition of narrative illustration served as the catalyst for this change in attitude. From the 14th to the 16th century large numbers of manuscripts of this text were produced, commissioned by pious laymen for donation to the temple library (*bhaṇḍār*) of their spiritual preceptor.

As mentioned, few Hindu illustrated manuscripts survive from before the 15th and 16th centuries, when the tradition had become one largely of manuscripts with full-page paintings with a verse inscribed above or on the verso. Either every verse of a fairly short text is illustrated, or nearly every side of each folio carries illustrations. This type of manuscript illustration, in which the burden of carrying the story is borne by the pictures rather than the text, arose almost certainly through the problems of linguistic incomprehension in an area with so many varied literary traditions. The type of manuscript with a full-size picture on every folio is the typically Indian way of illustrating manuscripts, in contrast to the Iranian one of fully integrating text and miniatures.

Mughal. Books were among the most precious possessions of the Mughals, who established themselves as the rulers of northern India during the 16th century. The founder of the dynasty, Babur (*reg* 1526–30), a descendant of Timur, brought with him into India his ancestral devotion to books and presumably to painting. Safavid artists at his son Humayun's court in Kabul and then in Delhi (when Humayun (*reg* 1530–40; 1555–6) was able to regain his Indian dominions in 1555) brought to India the latest developments in the Iranian book tradition: elaborate and highly finished paintings by master artists; fine calligraphy; illumination in double carpet pages, head-pieces and *shamsa*s (Pers.: 'sun-bursts'), and other pieces scattered throughout the text in profusion; sumptuously illuminated margins painted in gold with individual designs; bindings, sometimes painted and lacquered boards rather than simply in tooled and painted leather; and a burgeoning interest in portraiture and the assembling of albums (*see* §4(i)(a) below; *see also* ALBUM, §2). All these features were incorporated into Mughal manuscripts. The

235. Basavan, assisted by Chatar Muni: *Akbar Taming the Elephant Hava'i*, from the *Akbarnāma*, gouache on paper, Mughal, *c.* 1590 (London, Victoria and Albert Museum, I.S.2–1896, 21 and 22/117)

norms of Safavid illumination and calligraphy were also applied to Koranic manuscripts and rapidly displaced the Sultanate styles and scripts. Mughal illumination thereafter developed independently, with greater use of black and orange in particular. Manuscript illumination from the Deccani court studios is especially sumptuous.

Under Akbar (*reg* 1556–1605) whole libraries were eagerly acquired. But the royal library (*kitābkhāna*) was more than a collection of books; it was also the centre for their production, and the period is most notable for Akbar's lavish commissioning of illustrated manuscripts, which in their scale and quantity mark him out from all other Muslim patrons of the book (*see also* §4(i)(b) below). At least 100 artists were recruited in India to join the few Safavid masters whom Humayun had brought back from exile, while the scale of production required large numbers of calligraphers, papermakers, burnishers, gilders, illuminators and binders. In Mughal India, as in the rest of the Islamic world, calligraphers, especially the Timurid ones, were accorded the first place above mere artists, although both literary and visual sources indicate the high regard in which the latter were held. Relatively few names are known of Mughal calligraphers, some of the more important of whom were given soubriquets such as 'Golden-pen', 'Amber-pen', 'Musky-pen' etc (*see also* §VIII, 3 below). Akbar's artists produced the most heavily illustrated manuscripts ever seen in the Islamic world and in greater numbers than ever before. Conscious efforts were made to expand the repertory of illustrated texts, the size and number of folios in each manuscript and the expanse of paintable surface by ignoring the ruled margins and painting up to the folio's edge. Creative tension is apparent in some manuscripts between those artists favouring the Iranian approach to book illustration and those preferring the Indian method. In the last 20 years of Akbar's reign, the studio produced manuscripts that were the most refined and beautiful of their age (1982 exh. cat., nos 64–6). The miniatures are all by single artists and of the highest finish (see fig. 235), the calligraphy and illuminations are of the same high standard, the margins are decorated with animal and floral designs in gold and colours (Losty, 1985), and for the first time on Mughal manuscripts there are painted and lacquered covers. The boards, instead of being covered with leather, were carefully prepared and then painted, both outside and on the *doublures*, and finally covered with layers of lacquer to protect the paint (e.g. the *Khamsa* of Nizami, 1595; London, BL, Or. MS. 12208; *Khamsa* of Amir Khusrau, 1597; Baltimore, MD, Walters A.G., W. 624; *see also* Bookbinding, colour pl. IV, fig. 1).

Such immense undertakings, often in progress simultaneously, required the most careful organization. The head of the studio received directions from the Emperor as to what texts to prepare and, no doubt in consultation with him, worked out the numbers and subjects of illustrations, perhaps even the apportioning of the work among the available artists. Artists' work was presented regularly to Akbar, with notes on the edges ascribing the work; artists were paid and given handsome presents according to the reception that their work received. These notes were later covered by the ruled gilded margins when the manuscript was being assembled, although occasionally an inefficient gilder neglected to do his work properly. Sometimes vital information has survived from these notes, as in the British Library's *Akbarnāma* ('History of Akbar'; Or. MS. 12988), a date on one painting being the sole evidence for the production of this vast but incomplete manuscript. After the painting had been appropriately placed in the assembled manuscript, the court librarian made a more formal note on the border of the page, although later remargining often removed this. Artists rarely signed their work at this period.

The indigenous Indian tradition favoured book illustration with full-page paintings and accompanying text on the verso. Although the Mughal tradition never quite got this far, nonetheless from the reign of Jahangir (*reg* 1605–27) paintings in manuscripts rarely incorporate text within the area of the painting, though occasionally a line or two at top or bottom is seen. Jahangir and his son Shah Jahan (*reg* 1628–58) preferred artists to work on individual paintings rather than book illustrations, whether portraits or historical or natural history scenes (*see* §4(i)(c) and (d) below). In these the Mughal artist was released from subservience to the written text, and his compositions were free to follow their own logic.

The Mughal emperor Humayun (*reg* 1530–40, 1555–6) brought back with him from Iran the idea of compilation of albums, which formed portable art galleries of individual paintings (*see also* ALBUM, §2). Unlike manuscripts, where miniature and text were painted and written on the same piece of paper (or in the Mughal tradition, pieces of paper, since these manuscripts use layers of paper glued together to produce a fairly thick and highly burnished product), an album leaf is, as it were, a frame to contain the painting, which is painted on another sheet. Album leaves are much thicker than manuscript leaves; indeed, they are cards, made from many layers of paper glued together but with cut-outs in the upper layers to accommodate the painting being incorporated. Extremely skilled craftsmen assembled the Mughal albums, where the leaves give the appearance of being entirely uniform, and the skill lay in meticulous preparation of surfaces and gluing to prevent cockling. Akbar's albums appear to have been quite plain, but Jahangir's albums have margins that are most sumptuously and freely embellished (see fig. 265 below). Jahangir's albums alternate double pages of calligraphy and pictures. In the former the margins contain figurative designs from the whole repertory of Mughal composition in gold and colours, while in the latter the designs are more sober arabesques and floral designs to avoid detracting from the pictures. In the albums of Shah Jahan, both kinds of marginalia become stiffer and more stylized, and the key distinctions are no longer observed. Figures echoing the subject of a portrait are painted in the margins, while floral subjects, reminiscent of the pietra dura work in white marble in Mughal architecture, frequently surround pages of calligraphy. Such themes formed the stock-in-trade of marginalia in albums for as long as they continued to be compiled.

Late tradition. The most important non-Muslim studios in the 17th–18th century were those of the Rajput kingdoms, many of whose rulers maintained studios for the production of manuscripts of the Hindu epics and religious texts and of individual paintings, especially portraits. After some experimentation with format and the balance between text and paintings in the early 17th century, the Rajput manuscript format clarified into the large *pothī* format, with paintings occupying the full size of the folio and text on the reverse and on intervening folios. In Mughal manuscript illustration, the dramatic incidents in a story invariably were chosen for illustration. In Rajput manuscripts, several connected incidents from a story quite often were illustrated in the same picture in continuous narration. Convenient screens of rocks or trees, or sometimes separate registers or panels, separate the different parts (see fig. 236). The best artists, such as Sahibdin (*fl* 1628–55) in Mewar, sometimes did not bother with such framing devices but contrived to convey the onward momentum of a story through their composition skills (*see* §4(iii)(a) below). Manuscripts of the 17th century are heavily illustrated but are still recognizable as manuscripts, with unillustrated folios separating the pictures. From the early 18th century they are more like picture books, and there is a general continuation of the format of pre-Mughal manuscripts, with a full-page picture on one side of every folio and accompanying text on the reverse. The next stage of this development, found particularly in the Rajput court studios of the Punjab Hills from the mid-18th century, is the reduction of the full Sanskrit text to a selection of verses or a summary in Hindi. In these late manuscripts may be seen the final development of the Indian conception of book illustration. For smaller texts the Rajput studios developed an upright *pothī* format (*see* §(ii)(b) below), like the unbound leaves of a normal book, except that they were often made of thick card. Texts such as the *Rāgamālā* (verses expounding musical modes) were illustrated one verse at a time, usually with a text panel at the top of the page and the painting underneath. The painting was usually provided with ruled margins, while the outer border was always coloured and sometimes illuminated. Versos in this format are always blank. Very rarely are such sets bound; they seem to be a Hindu response to the Muslim albums.

In the south of India the palm-leaf tradition was maintained until the 19th century (*see* MANUSCRIPT, fig. 3). The original austerity of the format was scarcely alleviated until the close of the tradition, except by an occasional illustrated folio or decorated covers and by being made into fanciful shapes such as those of cows or *liṅga*s (phallic emblems of Shiva). That it was possible to illustrate palm leaves is shown by examples of the school of Orissa from the 17th century, where text and illustrations are incised and inked, with colour added in later examples (*see* §4(v)(b)

236. *Bharata Brings News of his Father's Death to Rama*, from the *Rāmāyaṇa*, *c.* 205×388 mm, Mewar, 1650 (London, British Library, Add. MS. 15296(1), fol. 114a)

below). In Assam, where the bark of the aloe tree had long been the traditional medium alongside rough country paper cut to the same shape as the strips of bark, a school of illustration developed in the Vaishnava monasteries from at least the 17th century. The art was also patronized by the rulers, and the original vigorous style was subjected to a process of bland conformity to late Mughal ideals. These massive and brightly coloured manuscripts of many hundreds of pink or yellow bark folios were produced until 1838.

In the centuries after Muslim power became predominant in India the two very different book traditions developed side by side, influencing each other in painting styles but scarcely at all in format until the 18th century. Calligraphy had never been an art that Hindu patrons or scribes cared much about, and even the grandest Rajput manuscripts are full of careless mistakes and erasures. However, in the 18th century a few determined patrons, such as Raja Jai Singh II (*reg* 1699–1743) of Amer and his successors, commissioned manuscripts of sacred Hindu texts with standards of calligraphy and illumination rivalling those of contemporary manuscripts of the Koran. Some of his scribes came from Kashmir, where the traditional birch-bark manuscripts had been sewn and bound, sometimes in leather, from about the 15th century. Even in the plains of India some types of Hindu manuscripts were crudely sewn, usually in a single section, and bound from the 17th century. Sewing and binding of Hindu manuscripts became much more common towards the end of the 18th century, along either the short or long edge. The boards were sometimes painted or lacquered but more usually were covered in cloth and embroidered. At the same time there was a revival of the ancient scroll format, which once had been of cloth but now was usually of paper, often handsomely illuminated.

J. P. LOSTY

(ii) Materials and techniques.

(a) Wall painting. Fifth- and sixth-century AD wall paintings at Ajanta, Bagh in Malwa and Badami reveal a high level of technical accomplishment. The works are executed in secco, a technique that does not utilize the wet plaster typical of European wall painting (though true fresco is occasionally found in later times; *see* §3(i)(b) below). Instead, the roughened stone surface was covered with a mixture of mud, cow dung and chopped straw. The resulting smooth, durable surface was covered with a thin layer of plaster, which was allowed to dry. The artists applied red underdrawing to the prepared surface with tampons and frequently utilized underpainting in red or green. Most of the colours were made of local minerals, though lampblack and imported lapis-lazuli blue were also used; colours were applied with animal-hair brushes. Glue was used as a binding medium, and the final surface was burnished to a subtle shine that survives to the present (see Ghosh). Also preserved at Ajanta are remains of the same practices applied to the decoration of sculpture. As in the ancient and medieval West sculptures and architecture were originally richly painted, but little has survived with the original surface intact.

There was also painting on cloth and on wooden boards, no ancient examples of which survive. The tradition of cloth painting persisted, however, and spread with Buddhism far beyond India proper. It was important throughout the history of Indian painting and survives in the late 20th century as a folk art (*see* § VII, 3(iv)(b) below).

DANIEL J. EHNBOM

(b) Manuscripts. The material normally used for manuscripts in ancient India was the leaf of the talipat palm (*Corypha umbraculifera*). When cut and prepared through smoothing, boiling and drying, the finished leaf (Skt *pattra*) formed a long, narrow rectangle with a smooth, flexible,

light brown surface. A pile of such leaves had wooden covers (*paṭas*) of the same size at top and bottom and an off-centre hole bored through the pile through which a cord (*nādī*) was tied round the whole bundle. Wider manuscripts had two holes, a third of the way from each end, but it was not usual to use the second hole for the cord. The text was written parallel to the long side, either with pen and ink in the northern tradition or inscribed with a stylus in the southern, although literary sources suggest a less clear-cut distinction. The term for such a book is *pustaka* in Sanskrit and *pothī* in Hindi. Such books would seem to have first been used towards the end of the first millennium BC.

The *pothī* was the norm for manuscripts until it was supplanted by paper between the 13th and 15th centuries in northern India. In the south the palm-leaf tradition, with a change from the talipat to the palmyra palm (*Borassus flabellifer*), continued until the 19th century. Cloth, metals and ivory were also used in the same *pothī* shape, as were the inner bark of the Himalayan birch (*bhūrja-pattra*; *Betula utilis*) and the aloe (*sāñcī*; *Aquilaria agallocha*) and paper. Although originally used widely over northern India, birch-bark manuscripts are found only from Kashmir and the north-west Himalaya. The attractive surface is naturally brown and streaked in various shades. The sheets were cut to the same shape as talipat manuscripts, although the finest manuscripts had a much larger folio size in the 7th and 8th centuries. Under Muslim influence in Kashmir from the 15th century, birch-bark leaves are found sewn up in codex format. The aloe tree, yielding a much tougher material than birch bark, seems to have been used only in Assam from the 6th century. The natural shade is a beige colour, but folios could be dyed pink or yellow.

Paper was manufactured in the north-west Himalaya region from at least the 6th century and in Nepal from the 11th century. Nonetheless, its use was not widespread, birch bark and palm leaves being much the preferred media even in those areas. However, the Muslim conquest of much of northern India in the early 13th century introduced into the plains of India first imported papers from the Middle East and then paper manufactories, which rapidly undermined the palm leaf in western India. Scarcely any palm-leaf manuscripts from Gujarat or Rajasthan are later than 1400. In the south, however, it was only in the 19th century that the palm-leaf manuscript finally yielded to paper. The new material was adapted to Indian ways. It was cut to the *pothī* shape, with writing continuing parallel to the longer edge. An off-centre margin between the two columns of text, corresponding to that containing the string-hole in a palm-leaf manuscript, was long retained, with a red medallion marking the site of the hole. This and other medallions marking foliation points in ancient manuscripts became in later centuries the foci of minor decoration. Jaina and Hindu manuscripts kept to these traditions until the 18th century. Wooden covers were replaced among the Jainas by folded card manuscript holders, painted or covered with textiles.

The traditions of the book as understood in the Middle East and Iran were introduced under the Muslim Sultanate of Delhi, founded in 1193. The codex of paper, sewn, bound and covered in leather, became the normal medium for writing among Indian Muslims, who used Arabic as a religious language (as befitted the language of the Koran) and Persian or occasionally Turkish as the language of communication and of literature.

J. P. LOSTY

(iii) Subject-matter. The earliest surviving paintings at Ajanta are Buddhist in subject, but this is certainly an accident of preservation. The subjects of ancient painting in India were far more diverse than surviving works indicate. For example, the closely related paintings at Badami in the south Deccan adorn a shrine consecrated to Vishnu and thus indicate the non-sectarian nature of Indian painting styles. Eastern and western Indian painting was overwhelmingly religious, though again it is not clear to what degree this is an accident of survival. Most manuscripts illustrated in the eastern Indian style depict scenes from Buddhist texts, primarily the *Aṣṭasāhasrikā Prajñāpāramitā* (Skt: 'The perfection of wisdom in 8000 sections'; see fig. 251 below); the western Indian style favours the scriptures of the Jainas, especially the *Kalpa sūtra* ('Book of the ritual') and the *Kālakācāryakathā* ('The story of the monk Kalaka'), although many surviving manuscripts illustrate Hindu, Islamic and what might loosely be called 'secular' texts (*see* §3(ii)(a) and (b) below).

Indo-Persian manuscripts (the term refers to works produced in India but following Persian stylistic models) illustrate literary works and histories in Persian, some of which were written in India, for example the *Khamsa* ('Five poems') of Amir Khusrau (see fig. 252 below). The *Caurapañcāśikā* and *Candāyana* group styles attest to the non-sectarian subject-matter of Indian painting. In the first group are such diverse subjects as the *Caurapañcāśikā* (Skt: '50 stanzas of a thief'), a 12th-century love poem by Bilhana (see figs 255-6 below); the *Bhāgavata purāṇa* (the principal scripture of worshippers of Vishnu, especially in his Krishna form); the *Gīta Govinda* of Jayadeva (a 12th-century Sanskrit devotional poem celebrating the mystical aspects of Krishna's eroticism); the *Devīmāhātmya* (a hymn of praise to the Goddess); *Rāgamālā* themes (Skt and Hindi: 'garland of melodies'; personifications of musical modes); and Jaina and Islamic texts. *Candāyana* group manuscripts are very rare. Two illustrate the *Candāyana* itself, a 14th-century Sufi romance that was popular in India (see fig. 257 below). The third, known from a single surviving leaf in the National Museum, New Delhi, illustrates the *Gīta Govinda.*

Mughal painting considerably enlarged the subject-matter of Indian painting. To the subjects that had previously been illustrated in Indo-Persian styles the Mughals added the repertory of Persian poetical and historical illustrated texts (including regnal and other histories of their own) and adopted Persian translations of the Indian epics, the *Mahābhārata* (the national epic of India chronicling a dynastic struggle that took place *c.* 1000 BC), the *Rāmāyaṇa* (the account of Vishnu's incarnation as Rama and the war that resulted from the abduction of his wife Sita by the demon king Ravana) and other Sanskrit texts. Albums of portraits, animal studies and genre paintings were popular.

Subsequent regional styles in Rajasthan, the Punjab Hills and elsewhere in north India are overwhelmingly religious in subject. They combined the themes of the early 16th-century *Caurapañcāśikā* group with portraits, historical subjects and genre scenes inspired by Mughal models. Medieval Hindi and Sanskrit literature was often illustrated. Especially popular were such rhetorical texts as the *Rasikapriyā* of the poet Keshav Das, completed in 1591 in Orchha, the *Rasamañjarī* by Bhanudatta and the *Satasaī* by Bihari. These works classified heroes (*nāyaka*s) and heroines (*nāyikā*s) and were so well known that series illustrating these subjects often had little or no text, as is also true of religious subjects and representations of musical modes. Though the *Mahābhārata* remains a very popular text, curiously enough it was rarely illustrated, unlike the *Rāmāyaṇa*, second only to the tenth book of the *Bhāgavata purāṇa* in popularity for illustration (see for example fig. 274 below).

In south India, the Muslim courts of the Deccan favoured poetical and historical manuscripts, similar typologically though not necessarily textually to Mughal examples. They also produced portraits and genre scenes that became increasingly 'Mughalized' over time. The more conservative styles illustrated primarily religious subjects in wall paintings and some manuscripts, especially Shaivite subjects, the *Rāmāyaṇa* and the *Bhāgavata purāṇa*.

(iv) Painters. There is very little information about professional painters in ancient India. Few names are known, and the small amount of work that has survived is anonymous. It is likely that most artists were craftsmen in family workshops, and some Buddhist monks probably were trained as artists. Artists of the eastern and western Indian schools were primarily monks and in many cases were also scribes. It seems likely that at least some professional artists of the early 16th century were members of a caste of scribes (*kāyastha*s). Artists of the Mughal period came from a wide variety of backgrounds, both Indian and Persian. They worked within a centralized, imperially sponsored workshop, but this seems to have been the exception rather than the norm. Little is known about the lives of these painters, but their names are plentiful, and some emerge as distinct artists whose work can be discerned even when signatures or scribal ascriptions are missing. The best among them were well paid and highly regarded.

It is generally accepted that artists of the regional schools functioned as anonymous craftsmen, and it is true that there are fewer known names and even less biographical information than for the members of the Mughal workshop. Nevertheless, much important information can be gleaned from inscriptions on paintings: for example, that many painters were Muslims who painted Hindu subject-matter for their Hindu patrons. The typical workshop was based on the family (see Goswamy). Examination of genealogical and archival sources continues to reveal detailed information—long thought lost—on the histories of painters' families.

See also §I, 9 above.

(v) Literary references. The earliest surviving discussion of technical aspects of painting is in the *Nāṭya śastra* (*c.* 1st century BC–1st century AD), a broad textbook on all the arts traditionally assigned to the ancient sage Bharata. The *Kāma sūtra* of Vatsyayana (*c.* 4th century AD), a manual of social and sexual behaviour, describes painting boards, paint boxes and brushes as essential possessions of the cultured. A commentary on this text by Yashodhara may be much later, but it probably refers to 4th–6th-century sources when it lists aesthetic principles of painting that are intended more for the cultivated aristocrat than for the humble craftsman. As interpreted by Ananda Kentish Coomaraswamy (p. 88), the six 'limbs' (Skt *ṣaḍaṅga*s) of painting given by Yashodhara are distinction of types (*rūpabheda*), ideal proportions (*pramāna*), expression of mood (*bhāva*), embodiment of charm (*lāvaṇyavojana*), points of view, stances etc. (*sādṛśya*) and preparation of colours (*varṇikabhaṅga*). The implications of these categories have been variously explained by more recent scholars (Sivaramamurti, 1968, p. 17, and Agrawala, pp. 47–84), but their general import is fairly clear, and directly or indirectly they informed traditional texts on painting for over a millennium.

More technical manuals (*śilpa*s), such as the *Citra sūtra* section of the *Viṣṇudharmottara purāṇa* (*c.* 4th–7th century), deal with both practical and aesthetic issues of painting and outline matters such as the preparation of panel, cloth and wall surfaces for painting and the preparation of various pigments, but they may still have been intended primarily for an educated audience rather than a purely professional one. Such early sources are augmented and clarified by sections on painting in later encyclopedic texts such as the *Samarāṅgaṇa sūtradhāra*, traditionally assigned to the Paramara king Bhoja of Dhara (*reg c.* 11th century), the closely related and probably later *Aparājitapṛcchā* by Bhuvanadeva (both from the Malwa region), and the *Abhilaṣitārtha cintāmaṇi* or *Mānasollāsa*, traditionally assigned to the Western Chalukya king Someshvara (*reg c.* 12th century). Painting is only one of many arts that these works discuss, stressing both implicitly and explicitly the close interconnections of all the arts in traditional India. There are, in addition, many references to painting in religious works and epic literature, plays, rhetorical works and other poetry that help to make more comprehensible the practice and place of painting in ancient and early medieval India.

From these sources it is clear that there were distinct groups of painting practitioners in early India. One group of painters was professional (*see* §(iv) above). As is typical in ancient societies, the social status of professional painters in general was rather low, but skill and the importance of their art in both secular and sacred contexts placed the best individuals high in the regard of their patrons. Religious communities included painters among their numbers. Another significant group was aristocratic men and women who, as cultivated members of society, were expected not only to know and judge the quality of painting but also to produce it, though sometimes such painters were satirized as mere dilettantes and mocked for their cultural pretensions. No portraits on panel survive, but there are extant examples of technically related wooden bookcovers from the 11th century and later. Portraits on panel seem to have been especially important, primarily as images of potential marriage partners for young men and women of high birth. This tradition of courtly and aristocratic achievements in the arts was of long duration and was paralleled in later periods by the emphasis on painting as a suitable pursuit for princes of such Indo-Islamic dynasties as the Mughals.

Taken together, the texts present a fairly clear description of painting practices and techniques (*see also* §(ii) above). Wall painting for palaces and temples, where paint was applied to a carefully prepared and polished dry plaster surface, took pride of place. There are extensive instructions for the preparation of grounds for painting that suggest techniques even more developed than analysis of the few surviving vestiges of early painting implies. The techniques of painting on wood and cloth are less thoroughly discussed and are lacking entirely in some sources, but it is known that surfaces were primed and burnished in preparation for painting. Artists used styli, crayons and several types of brushes made of animal hair, bark fibres and grasses, with wooden (generally bamboo) handles. Individual colours had an elaborately detailed symbolic significance (*see also* COLOUR, §III) and were derived from indigenous animal, mineral and vegetable sources, except for ultramarine blue, which was imported from ancient sources in Afghanistan. Binding media were adhesives made from both animal and vegetable sources. The recipes and techniques of colour preparation remained remarkably consistent, and some persisted even into the late medieval and modern periods before being replaced by chemical dyes in the 19th century.

In any composition, great emphasis was placed on the positioning of the various elements and the correct proportions of the figures (*see also* §(iii) above). Preliminary sketches were followed by filling and modelling with colour, careful outlining with ochre and shading with lampblack to suggest three-dimensional form. Detailed instructions ensure the correct depiction of human, animal and decorative forms. Males and females fall into five basic types, each determined by their proportions. Nine possible stances are enumerated by most authorities, of which the five frontal types are the most important. Extensive guidelines for the foreshortening of figures also appear. Animal types and decorative forms are discussed in slightly less detail.

DANIEL J. EHNBOM

BIBLIOGRAPHY

WALL PAINTINGS AND MANUSCRIPTS

A. F. R. Hoernle: 'An Epigraphical Note on Palm-leaf, Paper and Birch-bark', *J. Asiat. Soc.*, lxix (1901), pp. 93–134

H. Glück: *Die indischen Miniaturen des Hamzae Romanes* (Vienna, 1925)

I. Stchoukine: *La Peinture indienne à l'époque des Grands Moghols* (Paris, 1929)

G. Yazdani: *Ajanta*, 4 vols (Oxford, 1930–55)

M. M. Haq: 'The Khan Khanan and his Painters, Illuminators and Calligraphers', *Islam. Cult.*, v (1931), pp. 621–31

A. K. Coomaraswamy: 'The Technique and Theory of Indian Painting', *Techn. Stud. Field F.A.*, iii/2 (Oct 1934), pp. 59–89; repr. in *J. United Prov. Hist. Soc.*, xxiii (1950), pp. 1–34

T. W. Arnold: *The Library of A. Chester Beatty: A Catalogue of the Indian Miniatures*, 3 vols, rev. and ed. J. V. S. Wilkinson (Oxford, 1936)

M. Chandra: *Jain Miniature Painting from Western India* (Ahmadabad, 1949)

——: *The Techniques of Mughal Painting* (Lucknow, 1949)

M. A. Chagatai: *Painting during the Sultanate Period* (Lahore, 1963)

S. Doshi: 'Twelfth Century Illustrated Manuscripts from Mudabidri', *Prince of Wales Mus. Bull.*, viii (1965), pp. 29–36

A. Ghosh, ed.: *Ajanta Murals: An Album of Eighty-five Reproductions in Colour* (New Delhi, 1967)

B. N. Goswamy: 'Pahari Painting: The Family as the Basis of Style', *Marg*, xxi (1968), pp. 21–62

C. Sivaramamurti: *South Indian Paintings* (New Delhi, 1968)

K. Khandalavala and M. Chandra: *New Documents of Indian Painting: A Reappraisal* (Bombay, 1969)

R. Ettinghausen and I. Fraad: 'Sultanate Painting in Persian Style', *Chhavi* (1971), pp. 48–66

R. Das Gupta: *Eastern Indian Manuscript Painting* (Bombay, 1972)

G. L. Trehan: *Learning and Libraries in Ancient India: A Study* (Chandigarh, 1975)

A. K. Bhattacharya: *Technique of Indian Painting* (Calcutta, 1976)

U. P. Shah: *Treasures of Jaina Bhandaras* (Ahmadabad, 1978)

J. P. Losty: *Krishna, a Hindu Vision of God: Scenes from the Life of Krishna Illustrated in Orissan and Other Eastern Indian Manuscripts in the British Library* (London, 1980)

K. Adahl: *A Khamsa of Nizami of 1439: Origin of the Miniatures, a Presentation and Analysis* (Uppsala, 1981)

G. Bosch, J. Carswell and E. Petherbridge: *Islamic Bindings and Bookmaking* (Chicago, 1981)

The Imperial Image: Paintings for the Mughal Court (exh. cat. by M. C. Beach, Washington, DC, Freer, 1981–2)

J. Guy: *Palm Leaf and Paper: Illustrated Manuscripts of India and Southeast Asia* (Melbourne, 1982)

The Art of the Book in India (exh. cat. by J. P. Losty, London, BL, 1982)

U. Ranade: *Manuscript Illustration of the Medieval Deccan* (Delhi, 1983)

J. P. Das: *Illustrated Palm-leaf Manuscripts from Orissa* (New Delhi, 1985)

J. P. Losty: 'The "Bute Hafiz" and the Development of Border Decoration in the Manuscript Studio of the Mughals', *Burl. Mag.*, cxxvii (1985), pp. 855–70

W. Zwalf, ed.: *Buddhism: Art and Faith* (London, 1985)

B. Brend: 'The British Library's Shahnama of 1438 as a Sultanate Manuscript', *Facets of Indian Art* (London, 1986), pp. 87–93

J. P. Losty: *Indian Book Painting* (London, 1986)

——: 'Bengal, Bihar, Nepal: Problems of Provenance in 12th Century Buddhist Manuscripts', *Artibus Asiae* (in preparation)

——: 'An Early Indian Manuscript of the *Karandavyuhasutra*', *N. K. Bhattasali Centenary Volume*, ed. G. Bhattacharya and D. Mitra (in preparation)

ALBUMS

E. Kühnel and H. Goetz: *Indian Bookpainting from Jahangir's Album in the State Library in Berlin* (London, 1926)

M. C. Beach: 'The Gulshan Album and its European Sources', *Bull. Mus. F.A. Boston*, lxiii (1965), pp. 63–91

R. Hickmann and V. Enderlein: *Indische Albumblätter: Miniaturen und Kalligraphien aus der Zeit der Moghul-Kaiser* (Leipzig, 1979)

T. Falk and M. Archer: *Indian Miniatures in the India Office Library* (London, 1981)

LITERARY REFERENCES

S. Kramrisch: *The Vishnudharmottaram: Part III, A Treatise on Indian Painting* (Calcutta, 1924/*R* 1928)

A. K. Coomaraswamy: *The History of Indian and Indonesian Art* (New York, 1927)

S. Digby: 'The Literary Evidence for Painting in the Delhi Sultanate', *Bull. Amer. Acad. Benares*, i (1967), pp. 47–58

C. Sivaramamurti: *South Indian Paintings* (New Delhi, 1968)

M. Chandra: *Early Indian Painting* (London, 1975)

C. Sivaramamurti: *Chitrasūtra of the Vishṇudharmottara* (New Delhi, 1978)

P. K. Agrawala: *On the Ṣadaṅga Canons of Painting* (Varanasi, 1981)

DANIEL J. EHNBOM, J. P. LOSTY

2. PREHISTORIC. The first examples of rock art were identified in the sandstone Vindhya Hills of central India by Archibald Carllyle, a superintendent of the Archaeological Survey of India, in 1867. Carllyle was the first scholar to attribute these works in red ochre to the Stone Age toolmakers who occupied the rock shelters. D. H. Gordon, a career soldier and amateur archaeologist, attempted to classify the paintings, dating the bulk of them to the 5th–10th century AD and assigning the very earliest to *c.* 700 BC. A genuine appreciation of these works started only after the discovery in 1957 of the galleries of rock paintings (see fig. 237) at Bhimbetka in Raisan District, Madhya Pradesh, by Vishnu Shridhar Wakankar. Wakankar secured

237. Rock painting at Zoo Rock, Bhimbetka, Madhya Pradesh, *c.* 12,000–6000 BP

evidence that some of these paintings dated from the Mesolithic period (*c.* 12,000–6000 BP). The excavation by Allahabad University of rock shelters in the Mirzapur region yielded similar evidence. Wakankar and the German scholar Erwin Neumayer, assisted by regional workers in different parts of India, explored new sites and made copies of paintings in more than 3000 rock shelters; these are stored at the Institute of Rock Art, Ujjain, or are in Neumayer's private collection. Wakankar also established a tentative chronology based on superimpositions and stylistic patterns. The majority of the shelter groups he studied are in Madhya Pradesh.

The earliest paintings were done with green mineral pigments and seem to date from the Upper Palaeolithic, as seen at Bhimbetka in shelters BHIM. III A+28, 30, and BHIM. II A.30 A and B, where the paintings can be tentatively assigned a date of earlier than 40,000 BP. These green paintings are largely confined to scenes of dancing and hunting of bovids. The human figures typically show an unusual bend of body between shoulders and hips that must have been inspired by the movements of the body while dancing. The faces in some paintings are extremely naturalistic, in others schematic. Animal figures in green are either cattle or deer. Figures were then introduced in a purple or dark red pigment made from haematite. The drawings in red were often associated with green, and two-colour pictures were made.

In the Mesolithic, with the improvement in climatic conditions, more cultural activity was undertaken and more elaborate rituals were developed. Highly stylized depictions of female figures probably indicate a mother cult. The union of male and female is rarely shown, but pregnant women, childbirth, and mother and child are drawn occasionally. Women are also depicted as load bearers, most often with a cylindrical basket on the back suspended from a flat strap or band tied on or over the head. Among the rituals, dancers are often depicted in a line of 10, 12, 20 or 30, sometimes clapping their hands over the head or under the raised knee. Figures in sophisticated masks and costumes are shown dancing with alternate male and female dancers with horned head-dresses. Magical cures must have played an important role in the society, as sweeping the body with brooms or putting spells on the sick are shown. A burial ceremony with weeping participants is painted with deep pathos. In Mesolithic drawings, a dark, purplish red was the predominant colour, though red and white are also very common. During the Upper Palaeolithic period the upper part of the rocks was most commonly painted, but during the Mesolithic period all surfaces could be used.

Within a short time it should be possible to classify the chronological development of all the Mesolithic styles. The most interesting style, used for depicting deified animals, is a honeycomb pattern and variants. Sometimes geometric patterns were added to fill up the body, and spirals and zigzag patterns were often used to decorate rectangular masses. Deified animals were drawn extremely large, and animals such as bison, wild cattle, rhinoceros, antelope, deer and panther were depicted. Sometimes composite animals were shown. Stories or incidents of tribal strife were rendered symbolically.

By the time Malwa was occupied by agricultural communities from the north, the Mesolithic shelter-dwellers had developed their art to its classical stage. They would have encountered these incoming hordes, who travelled either on horseback or in chariots drawn by horses and humped bulls, two animals new to Malwa. Chariots drawn by antelope, deer, horses and bulls are often depicted in the rock art in the Shahad-Karad, Dharmpuri, Jaora Malkhar, Chiklod and Mirzapur areas. An exchange of commodities with these newcomers brought changes in the structure of the society, including the introduction of pottery and copper. Their artistic tastes changed, and they tried to develop a new style inspired by the geometric patterns on Malwa pottery. Even their animal drawings were modified, and the dynamic drawing and naturalistic outline were lost to conventional, schematic forms.

BIBLIOGRAPHY

J. Cockburn: 'On the Recent Existence of Rhinoceros Indicus in the North-western Provinces, and a Description of a Tracing of an Archaic Rock Painting from Mirzapur Representing the Hunting of this Animal', *J. Asiat. Soc. Bengal*, lii/2 (1883), pp. 56–64

A. Carllyle: 'Cave Paintings of the Kaimur Range', *Journal of the Royal Asiatic Society of Bengal* (1899)

J. Cockburn: 'Cave Paintings in the Kaimur Range, North-west Provinces', *J. Royal Asiat. Soc. GB & Ireland*, xxxi (1899), pp. 89–97

M. N. Ghosh: *Rock Paintings and Other Antiquities of Prehistoric and Later Times*, Mem. Archaeol. Surv. India, xxiv (Delhi, 1932)

D. H. Gordon: *The Prehistoric Background of Indian Culture* (Bombay, 1958)

Y. Mathpal: 'Rock Art of India', *J. Ind. Hist.*, liv/1 (1976), pp. 27–51

V. S. Wakankar: 'Bhimbetka—The Prehistoric Paradise', *Prachya Pratibha*, iii/2 (1976), pp. 7–29

V. S. Wakankar and R. R. R. Brooks: *Stone Age Painting in India* (New Haven, London and Bombay, 1976)

S. A. Brandt and others: 'Rockshelters with Painting. . .and an Account of. . .the Mesolithic Occupation at the Gagharia I Shelter', *Palaeoenvironments and Prehistory in the Middle Son Valley*, ed. G. R. Sharma and J. D. Clark (Allahabad, 1983), pp. 205–39

E. Neumayer: *Prehistoric Indian Rock Paintings* (Delhi, 1983)

Y. Mathpal: *Prehistoric Rock Paintings of Bhimbetka, Central India* (New Delhi, 1984)

——: 'The Hunter-gatherer Way of Life Depicted in the Mesolithic Rock Paintings of Central India', *Recent Advances in Indo-Pacific Prehistory*, ed. V. N. Misra and P. Bellwood (Delhi, 1985), pp. 177–83

V. S. Wakankar: 'Bhimbetka: The Stone Tool Industries and Rock Paintings', *Recent Advances in Indo-Pacific Prehistory*, ed. V. N. Misra and P. Bellwood (Delhi, 1985), pp. 175–6
B. F. Sinha: 'Origins of Art in the Central Gangetic Valley', *Archaeology and History: Essays in Memory of Sh. A. Ghosh*, ed. B. M. Pande and B. D. Chattopdhyaya (Delhi, 1987), pp. 445–50
V. S. Wakankar: 'Rock Art of India', *Archaeology and History: Essays in Memory of Sh. A. Ghosh*, ed. B. M. Pande and B. D. Chattopdhyaya (Delhi, 1987), pp. 583–97
E. Neumayer: 'Wheeled Vehicles and Mounted Animals in Prehistoric Indian Rock Art', *Man and Environment*, xvi/2 (1991), pp. 39–70
V. S. Wakankar: 'Rock Art of South India', *Indian Archaeological Heritage: Shri K. V. Soundara Rajan Festschrift*, ed. C. Margabandhu and others (Delhi, 1991), pp. 91–100
E. Neumayer: 'Rock Pictures in Orissa', *Puratattva*, xxii (1992), pp. 13–24
——: 'Music and Musical Instruments in Indian Rock-art', *Puratattva*, xxiii (1993), pp. 69–73

VISHNU SHRIDHAR WAKANKAR

3. 1ST CENTURY BC–16TH CENTURY AD.

(i) Wall painting. (ii) Miniature and other painting.

(i) Wall painting. Literary sources record that wall painting was a highly developed and respected art in ancient India. Though most of the lavishly painted palaces and temples they describe have long since perished, significant examples of wall painting survive in varied regional contexts.

(a) West. (b) South. (c) Himalaya. (d) Northern plains.

(a) West. Of the remains of wall painting in western India, by far the most extensive are those of the famous cave site of AJANTA, which was begun *c.* 100 BC and remained at least sporadically active until its great period of final flowering under Vakataka patronage in the 460s and 470s AD. In the early phase (*c.* 100 BC–AD 100), representations of the Buddha were never shown, but they are almost omnipresent in the 5th-century AD phase of work. The paintings of this latter period owe their remarkable state of preservation to the fact that the site was essentially abandoned after the late 5th century AD. Other sites with traces of paintings, sometimes dating from the early phase but more often from the 5th century, include BHAJA, JUNNAR and PITALKHORA. The remains of 8th- and 9th-century paintings survive at ELLORA mainly in the context of Hindu and Jaina rock-cut shrines, but many surfaces were repainted at later dates into the 18th century.

Ajanta. The cave site of Ajanta is located in a remote gorge a few kilometres from the town of Ajanta in the Sahyadri range of the Western Ghats in the Deccan. An important ancient trade route passed through the plains near by, which may explain why a monastic complex first developed at the site *c.* 100 BC–AD 100. At this time two impressive *caitya* halls (temples), Caves 9 and 10, and four associated *vihāra*s (monastic residences), Caves 8, 12, 13 and 15A, were excavated in the gorge's steep scarp. As was customary, all were decorated with paintings, after a layer of lime plaster had first been applied to the smoothed rock surfaces.

Most of Ajanta's paintings from the early phase either have been lost through damage and abrasion or have been obscured by subsequent paintings applied in the 5th century. However, in Cave 10, the larger of the two early *caitya* halls, traces of beautifully rendered floral and geometric patterns survive on many of the interior pillars, though largely covered by later Buddha images. These early designs bear a striking resemblance to some of the carved ornament on the gates at Sanchi (variously dated to the 1st century BC or 1st century AD; *see* §V, 4(ii)(b) above) and belong to the same general period. The lotus roundels on the aisle ceilings of Cave 9 are also from the early phase of work, and this cave retains traces of an early frieze of men and animals just above its interior pillars. The well-known but darkened and damaged *jātaka* scenes (illustrating stories of the Buddha's previous lives) on the walls of Cave 10 belong to the early phase but are painted on an area of plaster that once obscured an inscription on the wall beneath. Thus these elaborate paintings, showing scenes of daily life again reminiscent of the carvings at Sanchi, must have been added to the cave some years after it was excavated. There are somewhat similar *jātaka* scenes on the front wall of the interior of Cave 9, but they have been largely obscured by a subsequent series of painted Buddhas dating from the 5th century.

More than 20 caves at Ajanta were excavated in the 5th century in a great burst of pride and piety by a group of kings, courtiers, powerful monks and laymen. Carefully programmed painted decoration characterizes the great period of patronage during the reign of the Vakataka emperor Harishena (*reg c.* 460–78). The first paintings of this phase date no earlier than 466 or 467, by which time a few excavations had reached a point where plastering and then painting could begin. However, all the well-laid plans fell into disarray in the late 470s, when the Vakatakas suddenly lost control of the site due to a developing insurrection by their feudatories, instigated by the powerful Ashmakas.

Workers at Ajanta in the 5th century, with no experience at excavating rock-cut halls, modelled both the form and the decoration of their excavations on contemporary structural buildings. While the patrons' inscriptions suggest that their caves were supposed to emulate 'the palaces of the lord of the gods', a more immediate source was the splendid palaces and temples built by earthly kings, the type of lavishly decorated structures depicted in Ajanta's wall paintings. Such structural references are particularly evident in the decorated ceilings of the caves (see fig. 238). These typically show a painted beam and crossbeam structure, sometimes with large painted medallions at crucial points and always with exuberant ornamentation in the 'coffers' between the crossing 'beams'. It is fascinating to see the evolution of subject and composition over the decade or so in which such ceiling paintings were executed. The coffers in early examples, for instance in Caves 16 and Lower 6, are filled almost exclusively with simple floral and geometric motifs and a few representations of birds; in later ceiling paintings, such as those in Caves 1 and 2, more and more zoomorphic and anthropomorphic forms appear, and the complexity of the compositions and the colour arrangements increases. Given the short period in which it occurred, such an evolution, which can be seen just as clearly in the decoration of doorways, windows and pillars, can have nothing to do with what is normally considered to be 'stylistic development'. It must be explained by 'internal pressures', as eager artists and patrons watched their rivals' productions and aimed to improve upon them.

The artisans who came to Ajanta at the behest of prestigious patrons were already highly skilled. On the

238. Cave 2 at Ajanta, *c.* AD 475–8; interior from right front

basis of later evidence it appears such craftsmen could operate as painters, sculptors or architects, as the situation required. However, being ordered to cut a 'palace' in a cliff was a sobering assignment, especially if one had never faced a cliff before, while there is little difference between painting the walls of a palace (as the artists had certainly done) and painting murals on the walls of a cave or a conventional pattern on a ceiling surface. Thus, although Ajanta's architectural and sculptural forms (*see* §§III, 4(ii)(a) and V, 6(iii)(c) above) developed during the early years of activity at the site with diffidence and difficulty from relatively simple forms to increasingly complex ones, as the sculptors' confidence grew, paintings could be applied in the old familiar ways from the start. This explains why some of the most sophisticated paintings at the site, often assigned to the 7th or even 8th century, appear in the earliest contexts. They really belong, like all of the others, to this single brief period of Vakataka patronage.

The painting of the porch ceiling of Cave 17, which all scholars agree belongs to Harishena's reign, provides a case in point. Painted in a freehand and frankly slapdash style by a group of related artists who must have done this type of work in structural buildings many times before, it includes a central medallion with curiously conjoined figures, rendered with strikingly orange-coloured and highlighted flesh tones. These figures are clearly related to certain paintings in Caves 2 and 26 that, not being in such firmly dated contexts, were once assigned to the 6th, 7th or even 8th century because of their 'advanced style'. On the basis of such a comparison, however, such an ascription cannot be sustained.

Though it was some time after the excavators started cutting the rock-cut *caitya* halls and *vihāras* into Ajanta's awesome scarp that decoration began, the development of the site proceeded with an obvious urgency. Ajanta's many unfinished excavations provide clear evidence that as soon as a porch had been cut out, it was often (although not invariably) plastered (in this later phase mud plaster was usually applied rather than lime plaster) and then painted, even though the process of cutting out the interior was still under way. As soon as the front portions of the interior were defined, the plasterers and the painters would continue their work, while the excavators continued chiselling out the cave's rear portions. Although it may seem that the various workers were treading on each other's heels in their desire (or that of their patrons) to get their work done as soon as possible, this system had the advantage of allowing the more skilled artists at the site to concentrate sooner on the finer and more demanding work. No more than five years after the second phase of patronage began at Ajanta, the porches of some of the earliest excavations, such as that of the impressive Cave 16, were already plastered and painted. When *c.* 468–9 work on the cave was interrupted for a time because of hostilities in the region, the decoration of the more forward portions of the interior was already in progress, even though the rear portions of the cave were still solid rock. It is clear in this cave, as in the equally early Cave 11, how far the painted decoration had progressed in this early phase, for the artists were never able to complete the original painting programme. The various painted Buddha images, some bearing hastily written donative inscriptions, that appear on wall surfaces already plastered but not yet painted when the first phase of work on these two caves was interrupted, are all intrusive votive donations, placed here in a characteristically helter-skelter fashion by anxious donors during the last year or two of disrupted activity at the site.

Although work on many caves at the site suffered a similar interruption in about 468–9, this was not true of the donations of Upendragupta, the Vakataka feudatory king who controlled the Ajanta region until his defeat by the rival Ashmakas *c.* 472. His demise occurred when his sumptuous *caitya* hall, Cave 19, and the handsome associated *vihāra*, Cave 17, were largely completed. Beautifully decorated and well preserved, they reveal the character and quality of Ajanta's painting at its height.

The paintings in Cave 17's porch (see above) and the interior of the cave are done in a variety of styles and vary in quality as well as type. It is hardly surprising that the general level of competence is high; Upendragupta was the king of the region and a great patron. As he says in his inscription, he 'expended abundant wealth' on this 'measureless hall', which 'cannot even be imagined by little-souled men' (Mirashi, pp. 127–9). Undoubtedly, he brought the most skilled artists from his capital to do the work. Indeed, artists probably came from far-flung regions in greater and greater numbers to work at Ajanta, and this alone would account for the fusion, and confusion, of so many different but contemporaneous styles in the paintings throughout the caves.

A striking example of two different artists working in close conjunction can be seen on Cave 17's splendidly decorated porch doorway. The overall design of the surrounding painted mouldings is consistently organized, and the whole enframement must have been laid out according to a single master design. However, it is evident upon close examination that the left side of the door was decorated by a different artist from the right side, as the specific detailing of the floral, geometric and figured forms varies. Furthermore, the two artists had quite different pigments on their palettes, even though most of these must have come from local sources; for instance, the colours used for painting the Buddhas' flesh-tones by the 'left-hand' artist are now almost black from oxidation, whereas those on the right have changed little.

Most of the colours used throughout the site fall into a somewhat limited range, in which greens, reds, ochres and umbers predominate. Most were derived from the many colourful deposits found in the region's basaltic hills or from local organic sources. Hues such as lapis lazuli blue (used sparingly, at least in the earlier paintings) were clearly imports, obtained through trade or purchase.

On the pilasters of Cave 17's porch doorway, as on the carved pillars and various sculptures throughout this and other caves, the painted and the sculpted details are all part of a single conception probably often executed by the same artist; the brush enhanced the work of the chisel, as colourful highlights or extra 'grace notes' were added to the carved designs. In some cases painting was used to effect economies: it is common, for instance, for the less visible faces of pillar capitals or bases to be merely painted (sometimes with evident haste) while the more prominent parts are carefully detailed with the chisel, at a greater cost of both time and money.

Whereas the painted porch and interior ceilings of Cave 17 combine motifs with both structural and ornamental references, the paintings on the walls concentrate on scenes from the Buddha's present or previous existences. Evidence from unfinished caves indicates that painting typically began at ceiling level and proceeded downward. The narrative compositions on the walls spread out expediently in order to include whatever episodes the artist wanted to show; there are no strictly defined 'frames' dividing one scene from the other. However, even though the many stories depicted seem to be arranged almost at random, the areas closest to the cave's axis are generally reserved for motifs of particular significance. Large paired *bodhisattvas* (now largely lost) once flanked the porch doorway, scenes of the Buddha's miracles occupied the side walls of the shrine antechamber, and impressive standing Buddhas framed the doorway to the shrine. There is an even more insistent concentration of Buddha imagery in Upendragupta's adjacent 'perfumed hall', the *caitya* Cave 19. While the façade is covered with carved Buddha images, and many others are carved on the capitals and friezes of the interior, still more were painted in repetitive but impressive groups along the aisle walls and in the cave's vault, making the cave interior into a veritable 'radiation chamber'.

Unfortunately, most of the paintings in Cave 17's interior have suffered greatly from their exposure to soot from oil lamps and incense, since the image here, like one in the similarly blackened Cave Lower 6, was finished relatively early and must have been used for worship for nearly a decade. Cleaning the wall surfaces of these caves has proved difficult, particularly because it is almost impossible to remove all of the carbon-based soot without damaging the black outlines, also composed of carbon, that are an essential part of many of the compositions. The most remarkably preserved paintings, at least in terms of their pristine surface condition, are those in Cave 1, which are ascribed here to the patronage of the great Vakataka emperor Harishena. Ironically, it is the sad history of his reign that is responsible for the generally happy state of his paintings, since it appears that he died suddenly just as his cave was nearing completion *c.* 477. His cave was apparently never dedicated or put into worship, and only a few years after his demise Ajanta was abandoned altogether. Thus the surfaces of the Cave 1 paintings remained amazingly clean, even though the lower portions of most of them, and even the higher levels of those in the porch, were destroyed by the damp debris that built up in the cave over the course of many centuries, dissolving both the tempera-based paintings and their mud-plaster support wherever it came into contact with them.

Although the paintings in most of the more fully decorated caves at Ajanta, such as caves 2, 16 and 17, do not seem to have been arranged according to any obvious iconographic programme, those in Cave 1 appear to have been intentionally focused on the theme of kingship. This is yet a further argument for ascribing the cave to Harishena's patronage. The many *jātaka*s depicted on the walls of the main hall (e.g. see fig. 239) all have this insistent 'royal' emphasis. Two of them involve *nāga*s (snake divinities) who were kings; this is especially appropriate as the Vakataka house traced its origins back to *nāga* forebears. The splendid painted hall ceiling also has a kingly figure in the centre of each of its quadrants. Even the scenes along the cave's main axis, such as those depicting the Buddha's temptation by Mara or his miracle at Sravasti (both in the shrine antechamber), or the sculpted scenes of war and dalliance and of the visit of Prince Siddhartha to the garden on the cave's façade, do not break this pattern, since the Buddha was, after all, a prince who gave up his royal prerogatives in order to follow a different path.

The two most famous paintings in Cave 1 are the colossal figures of the *bodhisattva*s *Padmapani* (holding his lotus; see fig. 240) and *Vajrapani* (leaning on a personification of his thunderbolt; see fig. 241) on the rear wall of the cave, flanking the approach to the shrine. Complementing Harishena's own royal status with their crowns, and painted with a consummate confidence, they are treated with a lavishness that typifies the aesthetic of the day. Proclaiming the delights of paradise even more than the release of *nirvāṇa*, they express the high artistic standards as well as the radiant optimism of these times. Linked to the gods Brahma and Indra, connected with priestly, spiritual virtues on one hand and kingly, temporal virtues on the other, they perfectly characterize the dual forces that sponsored and sustained the site. The fact that the *Padmapani*, like so many of the other paintings in this cave, seems to derive from a southern tradition and the *Vajrapani* from a northern one, despite the fact that they form a pair and are precisely contemporary, also tells us much about the complexity of this site's development and the fusion of forces and traditions that brought it into being.

On the accession of Harishena's weak successor *c.* 477, the Ashmakas, who now controlled the Ajanta region, asserted their independence and turned their attention to

239. *Mahājanaka jātaka*, Prince Mahājanaka before Renouncing his Kingdom, left wall of Cave 1, Ajanta, *c.* AD 477

240. *Padmapani*, on rear wall to left of shrine antechamber, Cave 1, Ajanta, *c.* AD 477

overthrowing their Vakataka overlords. Soon the material support for Ajanta began to wither away, and the great programmes of excavation and decoration throughout the site came to a halt.

By *c.* 479 the old patrons no longer exercised control over the caves that they had so proudly sponsored, while new donors, mostly monks still resident at the site in these declining days, donated a generally scrambled array of Buddha images, locating them wherever unpainted wall areas were still available in caves that had already been dedicated and put into worship (unlike Cave 1, which has no such intrusions). These images, whether painted or sculpted, have nothing to do with the original programmes of decoration and generally have a disruptive effect. Only in rare cases are they effectively composed, as in the shrine antechamber of Cave 2, where only the ceiling had been decorated when the cave's main Buddha image was rushed to completion by the cave's original donor *c.* 478. After this a number of new and different donors sponsored the array of multiple Buddha images that cover the antechamber walls.

The early caves dating to the 1st centuries BC and AD suffered the same treatment. In Cave 10 the semicircular vaults over the aisles were filled with a series of hastily painted seated and standing Buddhas, all of which were probably completed within the course of a few days or weeks at the behest of a single patron or group of patrons. In contrast, the pillars of caves 9 and 10 were covered with an array of single images or small groups of images, donated by different individual devotees and often separately inscribed with conventional votive formulae. While the arrangement appears random, careful study shows that the first of these painted Buddhas were those done on the more convenient lower level of the pillars, generally starting with the most readily visible surfaces. As these areas filled up, the upper and rear surfaces of the pillars were utilized. This expedient fashion of painting the pillars and the fact that the painted images were given by many different donors suggest that this work (in contrast to the carefully programmed repainting of the cave's ceiling) was part of the anxious late phase of donative activity *c.* 479–80. It is possible that these donors, most of whom, as the inscriptions prove, were monks still living at the site, were particularly interested in placing their votive images in the evidently sacred context of these old *caitya* halls at a time when the loosening of administrative controls at the site allowed them to 'invade' these caves with their personal donations.

Ellora. While so many marvellous paintings have survived at Ajanta, only fragmentary and obscured traces of painting remain at subsequent cave sites made over the course of the next two or three centuries in the Traikutaka, Early Kalachuri and Chalukya periods. It is not until the beginning of Rashtrakuta patronage in the mid-8th century that significant examples are preserved, and even these

241. *Vajrapani*, on rear wall to right of shrine antechamber, Cave 1, Ajanta, *c.* AD 477

seem sparse after Ajanta's abundance. The most interesting remains are in the great Kailasa Temple at Ellora (Cave 16). That it is still called the Rang Mahal (Painted Palace) hints at its previous splendours, even though its original decoration, dating from the reign of Krishna I (*reg c.* 758–73), has been largely obscured by later layers. A few figures, including a fine but hardly visible *Dancing Shiva* on the ceiling inside the main hall, appear to date from the time the temple was first decorated.

The clearest early remains occupy a small section of the ceiling of the main porch, where an early composition of a god, apparently Shiva, riding a mythical creature attended by flying celestials is visible because two later painted surfaces have partly fallen away. The second layer reveals a figure of *Vishnu on Garuda* and may date from the following century, judging from its increased sharpness of feature and linear emphasis. The final layer, tentatively assigned to the 12th century on epigraphic grounds, shows vigorous battle scenes done in a manner anticipating the medieval Jaina manuscript style. Much of the surface of the temple was replastered and then painted in the 18th century at the behest of the Holkar princess Ahilyadevi.

A Jaina cave complex at the northern end of the site was at one time lavishly painted. Recent restoration has enhanced the visibility of the colourful ornamental and figurative motifs with which the ceilings and walls were covered when the caves were created, probably in the reign of Amoghavarsha (*reg* 814–73). The most impressive series of paintings, mainly showing flying celestials, are found in the Indra Sabha (Cave 32) and have strong links with the contemporary art of south India.

BIBLIOGRAPHY

J. Fergusson and J. Burgess: *The Cave Temples of India* (London, 1880), pp. 280–349

J. Griffiths: *The Paintings in the Buddhist Cave-Temples of Ajanta, Khandesh (India)*, 2 vols (London, 1896)

G. Yazdani: *Ajanta*, 4 vols (Oxford, 1930–55)

S. Kramrisch: *A Survey of Painting in the Deccan* (Hyderabad, 1937), pp. 3–69

V. Mirashi: *Inscriptions of the Vākāṭakas*, Corp. Inscr. Indicarum, v (Ootacamund, 1963)

M. Singh: *The Cave Paintings of Ajanta* (London, 1965)

A. Ghosh, ed.: *Ajanta Murals: An Album of Eighty-five Reproductions in Colour* (New Delhi, 1967)

O. Takata: *Ajanta* (Tokyo, 1971) [excellent plates]

W. Spink: 'The Splendours of Indra's Crown: A Study of Mahayana Developments at Ajanta', *J. Royal Soc. A.*, cxxii (1974), pp. 743–67

——: 'Ajanta's Chronology: Cave 1's Patronage', *Chhavi-2: Rai Krishnadasa Felicitation Volume*, ed. A. Krishna (Varanasi, 1981), pp. 144–57

D. Schlingloff: *Studies in the Ajanta Paintings: Identifications and Interpretations* (Delhi, 1987)

K. Khandalavala, ed.: *The Golden Age: Gupta Art—Empire, Province and Influence* (Bombay, 1991)

R. Parimoo and others, eds: *The Art of Ajanta*, 2 vols (New Delhi, 1991)

D. Schlingloff: *Ajanta Paintings* (Delhi, 1991)

W. Spink: 'The Archaeology of Ajanta', *A. Orient.*, xxi (1991)

WALTER SPINK

(*b*) *South.*

Earliest examples. Among the earliest vestiges of painting in south India are the few fragments preserved in Cave 3 at BADAMI, first published by Stella Kramrisch (1936). According to the dedicatory inscription, this temple of the god Vishnu was excavated in AD 578. The inscription encourages the visitor to observe the wonderful decoration of the cave, the work of the King's craftsmen (see fig. 242). Especially noteworthy is the eave over the entrance, on the inner face of which is a huge carved image of Vishnu's mount, *Garuda*, flanked by flying figures. On either side of the *Garuda* are faint traces of wall paintings depicting courtly scenes, music and dance and royal personages. One of the latter, possibly a portrait of King Kirtivarman, faces the central shrine as if paying eternal homage to Vishnu.

242. *Maidens*, detail of a wall painting from Cave 3, Badami, *c.* AD 578

8th–12th centuries. The earliest surviving paintings in Tamil Nadu are dated about the 8th century. However, frequent references to painted walls and ceilings are found in literature from the period between *c.* 100 BC and AD 250. For example, the *Paripatāl*, an anthology of religious poetry from about the 1st century AD, refers to a pavilion in the temple of Subrahmanya, near Madurai, which had on its ceiling pictures of the Hindu divinities Kama, Rati, Indra and Ahalya. It is interesting to note that pavilions with representations of Kama and Rati are plentiful from the Vijayanagara and Nayaka periods (*see* §(vii) below). None of this early material survives, however.

As a rule, monuments from this era, whether excavated or structural, were decorated with paintings, and sculptures were generally painted. Patches of colour are still visible at MAMALLAPURAM (e.g. Adi Varaha cave). The earliest extant paintings are to be found in the Kailasanatha Temple complex at KANCHIPURAM, built during the reign of the Pallava ruler Narasimhavarman II Rajasimha (*reg* *c.* 690–728; *see* §III, 5(i)(i) above, esp. fig. 65). The walls of the small shrines surrounding the sanctuary were once painted. Fragmentary Somaskanda scenes, showing the god Shiva with Uma (another name for his consort, Parvati) and their child Skanda between them, and scenes of Shiva accompanied by Vishnu and Brahma occur frequently in the shrines along the south, west and north walls. The Somaskanda group, an iconographic innovation of the Pallava artists, appears frequently. Several other scenes discovered in recent years have yet to be properly identified. Elegant floral and geometric designs seem to have been popular as a means of embellishing architectural elements such as beams and doorframes.

A second example of what must have been a large number of paintings can be found in the Talagirishvara Temple at Panamalai (South Arcot District), built about the same time as the Kailasanatha in Kanchipuram. The outer shrines were once adorned with paintings. A fragment on the back wall of the north shrine shows a much defaced rendering of Shiva performing the 'dance of total devastation'. Parvati watches from the side wall (see fig. 243). She is shown standing under a parasol with one leg folded and one hand supporting her chin in a relaxed attitude, contrasting sharply with the energetic dance of her spouse.

Perhaps the best-known paintings in Tamil Nadu are those of the Sittannavasal Jaina cave temple, probably executed between the 8th and 9th centuries. Although associated with the early Pandya period (*c.* 7th–9th centuries), the cave bears a strong resemblance, in its layout and in the form of its columns, to earlier Pallava monuments. During the reign of the Pandya ruler of Madurai Srimara Srivallabha (also called Avanipashekhara; *reg* *c.* 815–62), additions were made to the cave, and the original Pallava works were painted over. An inscription found near by celebrates the ruler and praises the piety of the Jaina monk Ilam Gautama, 'hailing from Madurai, who enlarged the inner *maṇḍapa* of the cave and renovated the whole complex'.

Every part of this monument was decorated with paintings, some of which have survived. Among these are 'portraits', possibly of the royal couple, a representation of a monk and scenes of dancing. The pillars and the

243. *Parvati*, detail of a wall painting from Talagirishvara Temple, Panamalai, 7th–8th century AD

beams of the verandah are decorated with scroll motifs. On the ceiling of the *maṇḍapa* is the most famous scene: a large lotus pond in which people gather lotus flowers, elephants sport, and fish swim about. A lovely fragment in the hall shows a dancing maiden. The ceiling of the antechamber is embellished with textile patterns, a recurrent motif in Jaina painting. In the far south at Tirumalaipuram, there are other paintings produced within the Pandya domain, depicting textile motifs and birds.

The continuation of earlier styles is evident at Tirunandikkara in southern Kerala. In the Shaiva cave temple a fragment, probably executed in the 9th century, shows the head of a male deity. This figure formed part of a large panel, of which only the upper section remains. Traces of hands and heads can be seen among flowers, clouds and rocks. On another fragmentary panel architectural elements, and elephant and lion faces appear. The elegance and sensitivity of line are reminiscent of the Kanchipuram wall paintings.

After the Cholas came to power in the 9th century, they began to build small temples in the Pudukkottai region. In the mid-9th-century Vijayalaya Cholishvara Temple, dramatically perched on the hill at Narttamalai (Pudukkottai

District), are remains of a painting showing a dancing figure, perhaps Shiva, on the wall of the antechamber. Flying *gandharvas* (celestial divinities) are depicted on the ceiling. The most remarkable painting is that of *Bhairava* (a form of Shiva) accompanied by his dog and surrounded by an aureole of flames. An image of the goddess *Durga* with attendants is barely visible.

Probably the most important monument of the Chola period is the Rajarajeshvara Temple at Thanjavur, built by Rajaraja I (*reg* 985–1014). The paintings on the walls of the circumambulatory passage around the sanctum were first brought to the attention of scholars in 1930 by S. K. Govindaswami. There were actually two layers: a top one dating from the 17th or 18th century and a lower one from the 11th century. The later paintings have been removed, and the ones coeval with the construction of the temple have been exposed. They are found on the south wall, on the two 'wings' of the west wall and on the north wall.

Mostly large in size, these paintings provide an exceptional source for the study of Chola religious and social life. Their main themes are the various aspects of Shiva and the life of famous Shaiva saints (see fig. 244). On the southern wall is the painted image of Shiva as the embodiment of wisdom (*Dakshinamurti*) seated under a banyan tree. His head, faintly visible, shows matted locks tied around it. The tree and its surroundings are enlivened by the presence of various animals. A little to the left of it are *Bhairava* in adoration with his dog. The next painting of importance, on one of the wings of the west wall in the circumambulatory passage, depicts the life of the famous saint Sundara. The lively narrative begins with his marriage

244. Detail of a wall painting in the circumambulatory passage, Rajarajeshvara Temple, Thanjavur, 1014

and culminates in his visit to Mt Kailasa. The other 'wing' of the wall shows the temple of CHIDAMBARAM.

Another important theme in the Rajarajeshvara Temple is the courtly portrait. A bearded royal figure is shown accompanied by three queens paying homage to the goddess Kali. The identification of these figures is still uncertain, although they may represent Rajaraja I and his queens. In the north-western corner of the passage is a panel depicting two male standing figures, said to be portraits of Rajaraja I and his court poet Karur (Karuvur; Karuvarur) Devar visiting the temple.

The panel on the north wall of the passage showing Shiva destroying the three fortresses of the *asuras* (demons) depicts the god's face aglow with rage and the *asuras* flying away in fear, fighting and eventually dying. It is one of the finest creations of the Chola period. Scenes of music and dance complete the cycle.

The final phase of Chola painting is exemplified at Tirumalai (North Arcot District). The temple on the hill above the village is called Kundavi Jinalayam. Its popularity is attested to by inscriptions that range in date from AD 910 to the 14th century. The fact that the temple is named after Kundavi, Rajaraja I's sister, indicates the extent of royal patronage. The temple was repeatedly expanded and redecorated. The main hall is divided by brick walls into three small cells, with fragments of Chola painting on the ceilings. These consist of textile designs at the centre and *kīrtimukhas* (demon masks) at the corners. There are also some incomplete paintings in which only outlines showing geese and flowers are visible. On either side of the entrance are paintings of armed door-guardians.

Study of these paintings reveals a number of features that were important throughout this period. There is a close similarity between the paintings and contemporaneous sculptures. Thus, for instance, the painted renderings of the Somaskanda group in the Kailasanatha Temple at Kanchipuram are exact replicas of the reliefs of the same theme (*see* §V, 7(vi)(a) above). Painted *gandharvas* and composite beings have sculpted counterparts in the cave and structural temples. Such parallels are so strong that it is possible to determine the exact stance of a partially destroyed painted figure. This can be illustrated by comparing the disfigured *Dancing Shiva* at Panamalai with a sculpture of the same theme.

The majority of the aspects of Shiva depicted in the paintings of the Rajarajeshvara in Thanjavur follow the same iconographic traditions as are seen in contemporary sculpture. Despite the relatively limited repertory of subjects—mainly mythological themes and persons—painters were able to convey some idea of everyday life by inserting elements drawn from their immediate surroundings. Contemporary fashions, coiffures, jewellery and textiles are carefully documented in their work. Portraits were also important in this period. Rulers are shown as donors, worshipping their family deity or engaged in conversations with their gurus. There was a marked tendency to show the king as protector of the religious establishment, making gifts to temples and appearing as a devotee.

Paintings from between the 8th and 12th centuries tend towards simple compositions and are carefully laid out and finely executed. Overlapping figures or figures on different planes are depicted with great mastery. Compositions are never crowded, and the transitions from one plane to another are gradual. Such paintings had to be executed while the plaster on the walls was still wet. An analysis of the paintings at the Rajarajeshvara at Thanjavur reveals that the artists worked not only quickly but also so carefully that the joints indicating different days' work could not be detected.

13th century–c. 1525. Although the architecture and sculpture of Karnataka under the Hoysala dynasty (mid-11th–mid-14th century) is well known, no Hoysala wall paintings have been discovered. There are, however, paintings on palm leaves from about the 13th century preserved in the Jaina Basadi at Mudabidri. They deal with Jaina canonical subjects and are, like the script accompanying them, exceptionally elegant. After a gap of almost three centuries, building and painting activity was resumed in the 14th century by the energetic VIJAYANAGARA rulers. However, no remains of Vijayanagara paintings from before the 16th century have survived (*see* §(vii) below).

BIBLIOGRAPHY

S. Kramrisch: 'Paintings at Badami', *J. Ind. Soc. Orient. A.*, iv/1 (June 1936), pp. 57–61

——: *Drāvida and Kerala in the Art of Travancore* (Ascona, 1961) [suppl. xi of *Artibus Asiae*, xxiv (1961)]

T. N. Ramachandran: 'Cave Temple and Paintings of Sittannavasal', *Lalit Kala*, ix (1961), pp. 30–54

C. Sivaramamurti: *South Indian Paintings* (Delhi, 1968)

A. Gopala Rao: *Lepakshi* (Hyderabad, 1969)

I. Thomas: *Painting in Tamilnadu, A.D. 1350–1650* (diss., Ann Arbor, U. MI, 1979; microfilm, Ann Arbor, 1979)

R. Nagaswamy: 'Tamil Paintings', *Marg*, xxxiii/2 (1979–80), pp. 73–95

V. Kameshwara Rao: *The Lepakshi Temple* (Tirupati, 1982)

G. Michell: *The Penguin Guide to the Monuments of India*, 1 (Harmondsworth, 1989)

A. L. DALLAPICCOLA

(c) Himalaya. Among the most notable wall paintings of the region are those of the Buddhist monastery at ALCHI, which stands some 64 km west of Leh on the Indus River in Ladakh, Jammu and Kashmir. The complex consists of five main buildings standing close together within the confines of a ruined enclosure wall. The earliest paintings are contained in the two oldest buildings, the three-storey Sumtsek Lhakhang and the Dukhang, which contain inscriptions that record their construction by Tsultrim Ö and Kalden Sherab and are thought by most scholars to date from the mid-11th century to the early 12th. They are executed in a similar style to those of the nearby Manggyu monastery, which are less well preserved, and the less interesting paintings of Sumda monastery, at the back of the mountain ridge behind. The other buildings are the Lhakhang Soma (New Temple), which contains wall paintings in the style of the 12th or 13th century; the Manjushri Lhakhang (Manjushri Temple) with sculptures of Manjushri but no wall paintings; and the Lotsava Lhakhang (Temple of the Great Translator), which contains paintings in a later style.

The wall paintings of the Sumtsek and the Dukhang are the greatest surviving monument to what Pal has designated the Kashmiri–Tibetan style, the main features of which derive from late Kashmiri art. The style was initiated by Rinchen Sangpo (958–1055), who individually or with his sponsor, the priest-king Yeshe Ö, is said to have founded 108 monasteries in the western Himalaya, including that of Nyarma in Ladakh (ruined). Few have survived, though during his tour of the Sutlej Valley in 1909 Francke found ample evidence of these foundations in both inscriptions and local legends. Rinchen Sangpo brought 32 artists from Kashmir to the kingdom of Guge, western Tibet, where they worked in the monasteries of THOLING, TABO and TSAPARANG. These artists, probably working with others trained in the earlier central Tibetan tradition, created a new conglomerate style. No work can be directly attributed to them, and the wall paintings of the Dukhang of Tabo monastery are probably the closest surviving examples. These date from a major renovation of the building in the mid-11th century, 46 years after its foundation, recorded by an inscription. It is probable that the work of decorating the newly founded temples lasted several generations, and the more advanced style of the Alchi paintings places it at least a generation later than that of Tabo. However, many close parallels can still be found with late Kashmiri sculpture in the facial type, dress and ornament, especially in the tight-fitting short tunic used for female figures. There is also a close resemblance in architectural motifs: the Mahastupa has a lantern ceiling similar to those of the Kashmiri temples of Pandrethan and Payar.

Within the Sumtsek are three alcoves containing large-scale painted stucco sculptures of the future Buddha, *Maitreya*, flanked by the *bodhisattva*s *Avalokiteshvara* and *Manjushri*. The three images and the depictions on interior walls are richly painted in a bright, fresh palette. In the inaccessible uppermost storey is a small lineage group of nine religious teachers painted in the same style as the lower walls; they are each identified by inscriptions below, the most recent being *Drigungpa* (1143–1216/17). This has been taken as evidence that the paintings of the Sumtsek date from the third decade of the 13th century at the earliest (see Goepper, 'Clues for a Dating'). Certain problems are raised by this dating, however. First, as the style was initiated in the early 11th century, it would mean that it had maintained its momentum and freshness for more than 200 years, which seems unlikely. The art of Kashmir itself was in terminal decline at this stage, though Goepper believes these paintings to be the work of Kashmiri artists. Second, a 13th-century date would place the work more or less at the same time as that of the Lhakhang Soma, whose style is heavily influenced by the late Pala art of north India. Many cloth paintings (*tangka*s) in this style from Tibetan monasteries are now dated as early as the 12th century. The inscriptions may have been added later, and it seems more judicious to maintain the traditional dating until other evidence appears.

The temples belonged to the Kadampa order of Tibetan Buddhism, and the central pictorial theme is of the Family Buddha, Vairochana. The walls of the Sumtsek are painted with groups of *maṇḍala*s and single depictions of the enthroned Vairochana and other Buddhas, *bodhisattva*s and their consorts, surrounded by smaller figures (*see* TIBET, fig. 4). The protector deity *Mahakala* is depicted over the doorway (as in the other buildings), and there is a large painting of the *Eleven-headed Avalokiteshvara* (see fig. 245). The figures are very lively. Depth is created

245. *Eleven-headed Avalokiteshvara*, detail of a wall painting in the Sumtsek, Alchi, Ladakh, *c.* 11th–13th century

through heavy outlining and shading and through the extensive use of profile, a noteworthy feature being the projecting eye concealed in profile, a prominent feature of western Indian painting up to the 15th century (*see* §(ii)(a) below). The draped garments of the three stucco sculptures are also painted: that of *Maitreya* in the central alcove facing the entrance has roundels illustrating the past and present lives of the Buddha; that of *Manjushri* in the right-hand alcove has stepped lozenge medallions enclosing scenes of *mahāsiddhas* (Tantric *yogins*); and the garment of *Avalokiteshvara* in the left-hand alcove is freely painted with a landscape of temple buildings, many resembling those of Kashmir, deities, celestial beings and princely figures, many of whom are mounted on horseback and accompanied by attendants. A 16th-century inscription at the base of the sculpture recording restoration work has been interpreted (see Francke) as indicating major repainting by a Mughal artist, a conclusion probably suggested by the figures of horsemen wearing turbans and elaborately decorated cloaks, one of whom carries a hawk. This interpretation may be discounted, however, since any restoration would have respected the original design. Rather, these scenes reflect a rich cosmopolitan milieu encompassing an area connected by the trade routes linking Afghanistan, Central Asia and the Himalaya. Many of the figures represented, including some of the deities, wear garments with designs of mounted horsemen and animals enclosed in pearl-bordered roundels. Such textiles, known elsewhere from paintings, were probably produced in Central Asia, and their designs are also seen in the decoration of the ceiling with rows of mounted archers performing the backwards 'Parthian shot'. These ceiling paintings may imitate a widespread practice of lining the ceiling with cloth still evident in Baltistan, Ladakh and Tibet; the subject-matter must have been copied directly from patterned textiles.

The rear wall of the Dukhang features a painted stucco image of *Vairochana* that has been frequently repainted and repaired. The walls are painted in the same style as the Sumtsek, including rows of *bodhisattvas*, a 'wall of a thousand Buddhas' and a drinking scene. The Lhakhang Soma is painted in a completely different style influenced by the late Pala art of north-east India and is stylistically very close to a group of *tangkas* dated before 1227 found at Karakhoto in eastern Central Asia (St Petersburg, Hermitage). The facial type is notably different from the previous style, and the eyebrows and eyelids are drawn in an undulating line rather than as single curved lines. The ornamentation is more elaborate; a tiered conical crown with small triangular projections replaces the earlier three-leaf triangular crown, and a set of necklaces with long pendants replaces the simple pearl necklace. The composition is highly schematic and resembles a group of *tangkas* joined together. The individual compositions are more hierarchically organized, with the central deity surrounded by his retinue or other deities in horizontal and vertical rows. The majority face forward, creating a more linear effect; in those in profile, the depiction of the projecting concealed eye is less evident. Vairochana continues to be the principal theme, but he is joined by a complex array of deities, including some of terrifying appearance. The style of the wall paintings of the Lotsava Lhakhang, which probably dates from the 14th century, is a stylized version of that of the Lhakhang Soma, though certain features such as the wide festooned border around the top of the wall derive from the style of the Sumtsek. The ornamentation of the figures is simplified, and the rich textile designs of the earlier two styles are less apparent. The iconography too is different. The central theme is the Buddhist trinity of Shakyamuni Buddha accompanied by Rinchen Sangpo, representing the monastic order (*sangha*), and Shadakshari, representing the doctrine (*dharma*), surrounded by various *maṇḍalas* and multiple forms of seated Buddhas.

See also TIBET, §IV.

BIBLIOGRAPHY

A. H. Francke: *Antiquities of Indian Tibet*, Archaeol. Surv. India, New Imp. Ser. (Calcutta, 1914/*R* New Delhi, 1972)

R. Khosla: *Buddhist Monasteries in the Western Himalayas* (Kathmandu, 1979)

D. L. Snellgrove and T. Skorupski: *The Cultural Heritage of Ladakh*, 2 vols (New Delhi, 1979–80)

P. Pal: *A Buddhist Paradise: The Murals of Alchi, Western Himalayas* (Hong Kong, 1982)

R. Goepper: *Alchi: Buddhas, Goddesses, Mandalas* (Cologne, 1984)

——: 'The "Great Stūpa" at Alchi', *Artibus Asiae*, liii/1–2 (1990), pp. 159–69

——: 'Clues for a Dating of the Three-storeyed Temple (Sumstek) in Alchi, Ladakh', *Asiat. Stud.*, xliv/2 (1990), pp. 159–76

M. Piotrovsky: *Lost Empire of the Silk Road: Buddhist Art from Khara Khoto, X–XIIIth Century* (Milan, 1993)

JOHN SIUDMAK

(d) Northern plains. Virtually nothing survives of the wall paintings of north India from this period. However, literary evidence, contemporary material elsewhere, comparison with the manuscript tradition and later material evidence combine with the few remains to give some idea of the paintings that once covered the walls of temples and palaces, many themselves now in ruins or destroyed. Though a version of the eastern Indian style undoubtedly prevailed at first in Bihar and Bengal, elsewhere (and after around the 12th century even in the east) the idioms were probably variants (though on a larger scale) of the prevailing western Indian style, which was not restricted to the geographic confines of western India (Chandra, pp. 12–16). Surviving scroll and banner paintings hint at a lost tradition of wall painting, as does the famous dictum that Rajput painting 'historically, indeed, is a reduced wall painting' (Coomaraswamy, p. 128). South Indian and Himalayan examples, too, suggest what has been lost in the northern plains. It can reasonably be assumed that ancient traditions of palace decoration persisted, but if temple paintings have essentially vanished, palace wall paintings have fared only slightly better. Literary evidence documents the extensive use of painted decoration in the palaces of both Muslims and non-Muslims from the 13th century to the Mughal conquest of 1526, apparently with special emphasis on royal, heroic and erotic themes (see Digby).

BIBLIOGRAPHY

A. K. Coomaraswamy: *The History of Indian and Indonesian Art* (London, Leipzig and New York, 1927)

M. Chandra: *Jain Miniature Paintings from Western India* (Ahmadabad, 1949)

S. Digby: 'The Literary Sources for Painting in the Delhi Sultanate', *Bull. Amer. Acad. Benares*, i (1967), pp. 47–58

DANIEL J. EHNBOM

(ii) Miniature and other painting.

(a) Western Indian style. (b) Regional variants of Western Indian style. (c) Eastern Indian style. (d) Indo-Persian style. (e) *Caurapañcāśikā* group. (f) *Candāyana* group.

(a) Western Indian style.

Before c. *1350.* JAINISM, like other religions of India, began as an oral tradition. After the death of Mahavira in 527 BC, the theological teachings and philosophical dogmas imprinted in the collective memory were perpetuated from preceptor to pupil, a continuity disrupted in the 4th century BC when many Jaina monks died in a severe famine and much sacred lore was lost. A Jaina council of monks was convened to compile the surviving fragments of their canon. This conclave was the first of several attempts to record and preserve Jaina beliefs. Their efforts gathered momentum after the 6th century AD, when the concept of temple libraries began to take concrete shape, and over the centuries thousands of manuscripts, some illustrated, were deposited in such libraries.

The oldest extant group of illustrated Jaina documents consists of palm-leaf manuscripts (Hindi *poṭhī*) and wooden book covers of the 11th and 12th centuries. Most of the manuscripts contain only a few illustrations, which were placed in the centre and/or at the ends of the folios. The pagination number was marked in letters on the left and as a number on the right. A study of these manuscripts shows that the work began with the scribe, who first divided the folio into columns and margins and then demarcated the spaces for receiving paintings. He transcribed the text across the length of the folio, leaving empty the space reserved for illustration. To guide the artist, the scribe frequently provided a brief caption or a rapid thumbnail sketch in the margin. The manuscript was then submitted to the artist, who proceeded in sequential order. The folios of a finished manuscript were strung together by means of a cord. Sometimes the manuscript was enclosed within plain or painted wooden book covers and the whole bundle enveloped securely in a piece of cloth. The subjects illustrated in palm-leaf manuscripts are hieratic in intent and depict *tīrthaṅkaras* (Jaina saints), iconic portrayals of divinities from the Jaina pantheon and conventional representations of monks, worshippers and donors. Many illustrations feature animals, geometrical lotus medallions and rosettes. In most compositions the importance of the chief figure is conveyed by the imposing proportions. These miniatures bear no relationship to the text, neither illustrating nor elucidating it; their presence appears to have a purely magical value that served to sanctify and protect the sacred texts. These holy books were also revered as objects of worship. Buddhist illustrated manuscripts of this period exhibit a similar tradition. In both Jainism and Buddhism this practice can be traced to the influence of Tantrism.

Curiously, the constraints that conditioned the pictorial contents of the Jaina palm-leaf manuscripts did not apply to the wooden book covers. The paintings on wooden book covers show a remarkable freedom in their execution and selection of subjects. The artists drew on the existing repertory of decorative motifs such as the undulating lotus rhizome and other auspicious symbols. Some book covers feature scenes from the lives of the *tīrthaṅkaras* and legendary heroes; others portray events of historical significance to the Jaina church, such as the consecration of a temple in Marwad or a disputation between a Shvetambara and a Digambara monk at the court of Siddharaja Jaisimha of Gujarat. The paintings on the covers reveal a liveliness that is absent in the iconographic representations in palm-leaf manuscripts.

The illustrations in the palm-leaf manuscripts and wooden book covers employ the Western Indian style of painting, the origins of which lie in the 8th-century wall paintings of Ellora (*see* §(i)(a) above). This style is characterized by linear energy and angular rendering. Its distinguishing feature is the far eye, which protrudes beyond the outline of the face. Sometimes the style exhibits a concern for naturalism, conveying roundness of form through flowing lines and gradations of tone. At other times paintings show flat colouring with brittle delineation. As the style developed over time, the linear expression with its angular distortions and exaggerations eclipsed the naturalistic grace of the style: all traces of modelling disappear, and there is a noticeable predilection for abstract form.

Towards the end of the 13th century the pictorial content of the palm-leaf manuscripts was widened in scope to include the narration of Jaina legends. The paintings in such manuscripts not only increased in number but also featured descriptive details of landscape and architecture. They employed the ancient method of continuous narration whereby two or three episodes were compressed in the same miniature, and the protagonist involved was depicted in each episode. Apart from this innovation there was no attempt to enlarge the field of the composition or to change the relationship between the pictorial and the textual matter: in line, form and colour, the style of painting in Jaina manuscripts and wooden book covers remained unaffected until the mid-14th century.

See also §1(ii)(b) above.

c. *1350–1550.* Gujarat came under Muslim domination at the end of the 13th century, but the Jaina tradition of illustrated manuscripts not only did not abate but gathered strength and momentum. Many manuscripts were illustrated in the 14th century; the number grew further in the 15th century but in the 16th century began to decline. From 1350 to 1550 the Western Indian style of painting, with its exaggeratedly angular rendering of the human figure and faces characterized by the distinctive protruding eye, continued to be centred largely in Gujarat and Rajasthan, though it was not confined to those areas. It was practised in other regions such as Delhi, Gwalior, Mandu and Jaunpur (*see* §(b) below) but on an extremely limited scale; these places produced less than ten manuscripts each, while in Gujarat and Rajasthan hundreds were written and illustrated.

The Western Indian style used in Shvetambara Jaina manuscript illustration progressed steadily along established lines into the 14th century, but *c.* 1350 it abruptly swerved from its path, exhibiting noticeable improvements in drawing and colouring. The miniatures painted after this date are greatly superior in quality to earlier examples. As the manuscript of the *Kalpa sūtra* and the *Kālakācāryakathā* (*c.* 1375; Bombay, Prince of Wales Mus.) reveals, the line is flowing and increasingly fluent in its articulation, the palette is broader with accents of gold and silver for heightened effect, and the composition is more complex in the structuring of its constituent elements. The miniatures are divided into panels, each portraying an episode from the story. The narrative moves from one panel to an adjacent one placed either above, below or on the side, and an individual is often depicted more than once in the same miniature. The imposing proportions of the chief figure—monk, king or queen—indicate its relative importance, as is entirely in keeping with the hieratic character of the art. No attempt is made to depict spatial depth, not even by means of overlapping figures. Also, the narrative rather than the iconographic aspect of the scriptures receives the greater emphasis: the miniatures include many descriptive details of the material culture of the times, such as contemporary architecture with wooden trellises, richly furnished interiors with objects of everyday use and textiles of exquisite quality.

A break from the earlier tradition occurs also in the substitution of paper for palm leaf as the carrier for sacred texts *c.* 1350. It has been suggested that the smoothness of paper, as against the textured surface of palm leaf, contributed to the superior workmanship of paper manuscripts. This premise is belied by the many superb palm-leaf miniatures, equally refined in their execution. The shift in the style reflects, perhaps, a change in the sensibility of patrons: the precision and elegance in execution answer a new need. In the initial stages palm-leaf manuscripts served as prototypes for paper manuscripts in their format and in their system of marking pagination numbers on the folios in letters on the left and numbers on the right. The custom of indicating the string-hole was retained even though the folios of a paper manuscript were seldom strung together. Later, when the potential of paper was fully grasped, the folios tended to become broader and shorter without abandoning the horizontal *poṭhī* format.

Interestingly, the refined expression of the style first appeared in themes not previously illustrated: in the miniatures of the *Kalpa sūtra* and the *Kālakācāryakathā.* These two texts, though unrelated to each other thematically, were frequently transcribed together as one manuscript, with the *Kālakācāryakathā* invariably appended to the *Kalpa sūtra.* The *Kalpa sūtra* is a hagiographical work on the first and the last three of the twenty-four Jaina *tīrthaṅkaras* (*see* JAINISM). The *Kālakācāryakathā* recounts the story of the monk Kalaka, who sought the aid of Sahis (foreigners from beyond the River Indus) to defeat Gardhabhilla, the tyrannical king of Ujjaini. To portray Sahis in the Kalaka tale the artist turned to Arab or Persian painting or to Persian pottery and devised a figural type with round face, slanted eyes and long hair tied in a tasselled plait. Attire consisted of long robes and high boots and a heavy metal collar encircling the neck and shoulders (see fig. 246). Unlike other figures in the Western Indian style, Sahis are generally depicted without the protruding eye.

As the refined version of the Western Indian style developed, the manuscript of the *Supasanahachariyam* of 1413, written and illustrated in Delvada, Mewar, enlarged the field of the illustration to cover the entire folio. Despite its appeal, this practice was restricted to merely one or two folios in a few manuscripts. Many episodes hitherto not illustrated were introduced, thereby increasing the number of miniatures in a manuscript. Also, the colour scheme resorted to a lavish use of gold. Borrowings from Persian painting, such as prancing or dappled horses and the colour carmine, were integrated. Even so, the style began to lose its pristine beauty: the line weakened, the palette narrowed to predominantly red and gold, and the compositions continued to be structured on solutions formulated when the style was at its most expressive. Undeniably, the style still retained a certain vitality, but monotony had crept in. A few decades later, *c.* 1470, angularities and distortions in drawing became increasingly pronounced, and ultramarine or lapis lazuli blue superseded red as the preferred colour. In the larger compositions the additional space was not used imaginatively but the area was merely filled with a multiplication of motifs. Thus, instead of one, there would be four attendants serving a queen. The predilection for decorative effects expressed itself in the margins of several manuscripts in ornamental scrollwork or medallions. The style is only superficially striking, its sumptuousness obscuring the indifferent workmanship.

The desire for ostentation in Shvetambara Jaina manuscript illustration culminated in a cluster of manuscripts termed ‘opulent’. They are written in golden ink on a

246. Western Indian style: *Monk and Sahi King* (above) and *King and Queen* (below), from the *Kālakācāryakathā*, gouache on paper, each 90×305 mm, *c.* 1375–*c.* 1400 (Bombay, Prince of Wales Museum of Western India)

coloured ground—blue, black, red or purple—that heightens their grandeur, and all the folios are further embellished with border decorations. This trend begins *c.* 1400. In the early examples, the borders generally portray floral and geometrical motifs, but after 1450 they become more ambitious, incorporating trees, flowering sprays and undulating creepers, floral or geometrical motifs (including those derived from designs on Islamic tiles and carpets as well as indigenous woodwork) and a variety of motifs enclosed in circles, squares or spirals, birds, animals, and human figures engaged in different activities. Except in occasional instances, such as a *Kalpa sūtra* of 1459 from Patan and a Digambara Jaina manuscript of the *Yaśodhara carita* of 1494, where the border panels on certain folios either illustrate the text or supplement the episode featured on the same folio, they usually serve an ornamental and subsidiary function. Hence, they are free of hieratic constraints (for illustration *see* JAINISM).

Of the opulent group of manuscripts, painted *c.* 1475–1500, the manuscript of the *Kalpa sūtra* and *Kālakācāryakathā* in the Devasano Pado private collection, Ahmadabad, remains unparalleled in the unusual treatment accorded to the subject and the borders. Some Sahis are painted in a different manner from that generally encountered in such manuscripts and appear to be based on documents painted in either the Persian style or its close derivative, the Indo-Persian style (*see* §(d) below). Apart from the imaginative rendering of prevailing motifs, the border decorations of the Devasano Pado manuscript contain charming representations of terms for dance and music in the form of Indian or Sahi women dancers and musicians, as well as such diverse subjects as wrestlers, duelling horsemen, cavalrymen accompanied by foot soldiers, women acrobats forming an elephant or a cart, genre scenes of people bathing in a pool or monks on their peregrinations. Some interesting panels are pure landscapes: animals in a forest, a palm entwined with creepers, a sailing ship on the high seas, rain clouds with birds winging homeward or deer running through a field of giant flower stalks. More fascinating are the subjects with Persian affiliations, such as the fable of Bahram Gur, or Persian horsemen or animal trainers. Curiously, none of the documents in the opulent group employs gold in its border decorations; their bright pigments act as a perfect foil to the dazzling gold script on the folios.

After this gloriously extravagant achievement the style of painting in western India, which had already begun to falter, degenerated: the line became brittle, the execution poor and the compositions mechanical. Emptied of content, the Western Indian style was displaced *c.* 1580 by a new expression in Gujarat. However, because so many examples of the *Kalpa sūtra* employed the blue-and-gold version of the Western Indian style, the theme is inextricably identified with the style, and later *Kalpa sūtra* series continued to use that idiom. During the 14th and 15th centuries several cloth paintings (*paṭas*) featuring sacred *yantra* diagrams (see fig. 247) or occasionally a pilgrimage

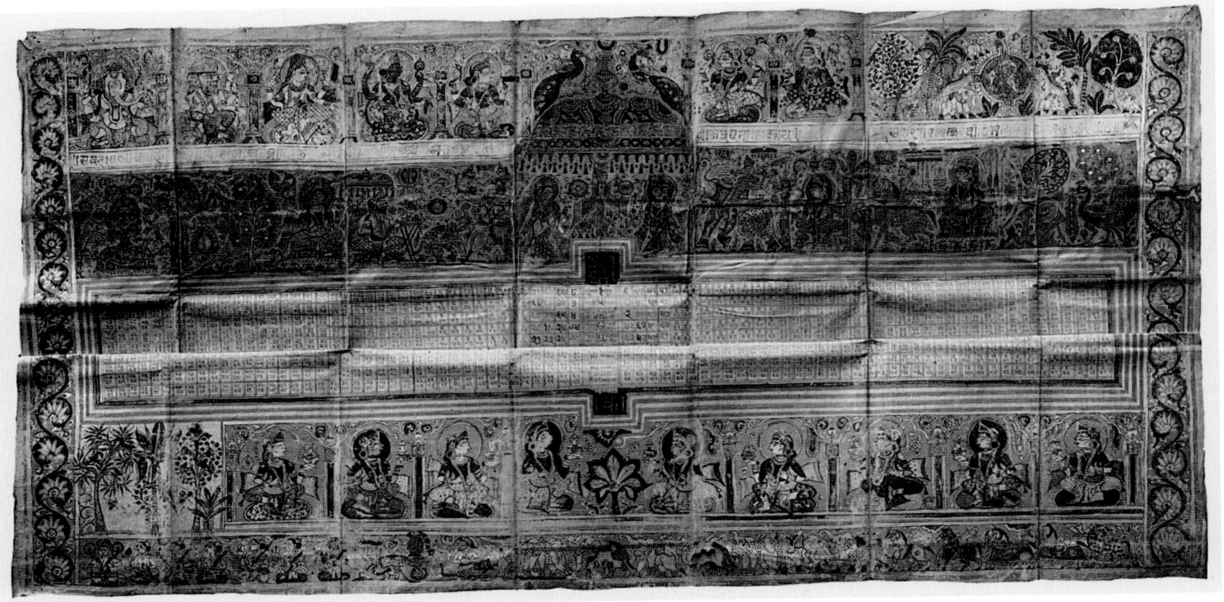

247. Western Indian style: *Paṭa* (cloth painting) with *yantra* diagrams, tempera on cotton cloth, 1447 (London, Victoria and Albert Museum)

place were painted. They reflect the same stylistic nuances as the manuscripts of the period.

There can be little doubt that the Digambara Jainas of this region also commissioned illustrated copies of their texts, but only one example (1494), featuring the *Yaśodhara carita*, the legend of King Yashodhara (a popular theme among the Digambaras), survives. In style, concept and execution this manuscript is indistinguishable from its contemporary counterparts from the opulent group of the Shvetambara sect. Its text is written in gold letters on different colour grounds, the illustrations are painted in blue and gold, and it has decorative borders. However, the illustrations of this manuscript are more lively and interesting because of the theme.

Several Hindu manuscripts reveal Vaishnava and occasionally Shakta affiliations. Those belonging to the latter group are of the *Devī māhātmya* and are datable to *c.* 1400. Most of the Vaishnava documents attributable to *c.* 1425–50 illustrate the text of the *Bālagopālastuti* ('Praise of the youthful Krishna') dealing with Krishna's childhood (see fig. 248). The style employs conventions typical of the Western Indian style of *c.* 1425 prior to the extensive use of gold. And yet these Vaishnava paintings have their own character and are different from Jaina examples. Very similar in style and of the same period is a manuscript of the *Gīta Govinda* depicting love episodes between Radha and Krishna.

Of the extant secular documents the most interesting is the *Vasanta vilāsa*, a poem celebrating the festival of spring, while others feature the *Rati-Rahasya*, a work on erotics. The *Vasanta vilāsa*, a painted scroll on cloth executed in Ahmadabad in 1451, unrolls vertically and is divided horizontally into alternating panels of text and illustration. The paintings, which show men and women seated in pavilions or gardens against a backdrop of trees, flowering bushes and creepers, capture the spirit of the poem. Freed of hieratic constraints, they reveal a liveliness that is absent in the sacred iconographical representations of the Jainas. Also, for the first time in the Western Indian style, landscape becomes important.

(b) Regional variants of Western Indian style. From its stronghold in Gujarat and Rajasthan the Western Indian style of painting spread to Delhi, Mandu, Jaunpur and Gwalior, where lay votaries of the Jaina Shvetambara sect patronized it to illustrate the *Kalpa sūtra* and the *Kālakācāryakathā*.

Delhi. The earliest example painted outside Gujarat and Rajasthan is a paper manuscript of the *Kālakācāryakathā* executed in 1366 in Yoginipur (Delhi). The refined execution of the three illustrations of iconographical significance conforms so completely to the tenets of the Western Indian style in Gujarat and Rajasthan that, were it not for the colophon, this manuscript would surely have been attributed to that region. More interesting in terms of the style as it developed in Delhi is a *Kalpa sūtra* executed in 1466 in Yoginipur. Its two miniatures correspond to contemporaneous manuscripts from western India, yet differences exist in the colour tonalities, the architectural motifs and the rendering of the female attendant figure, which resembles the figures in the Digambara Jaina *Mahāpurāṇa* attributed to Delhi (*c.* 1420; Delhi, Shri Digambara Jaina Naya Mandir; see below). In this context it is important to note that, in most *Kalpa sūtra* manuscripts executed outside Gujarat and Rajasthan, the rendering of motifs that are of no hieratic significance—such as trees, clouds, rocks, architecture and such figures of minor importance as attendants—often betrays a high degree of local influence.

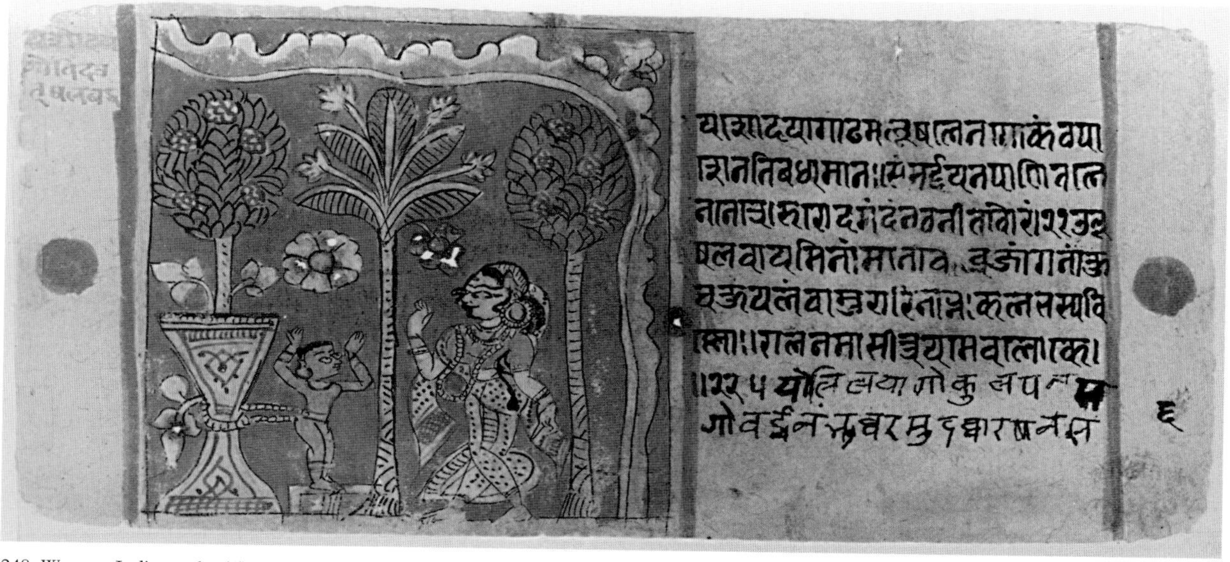

248. Western Indian style: *The Infant Krishna Tied to a Mortar*, from the *Bālagopālastuti*, gouache and ink on paper, 105×230 mm, late 15th century (London, Victoria and Albert Museum)

That there were idioms other than the refined version of the Western Indian style in Delhi is supported by a Digambara Jaina document of the *Adi purāṇa* painted in Yoginipur in 1404. Only the first illustration is complete; the spaces demarcated for illustrations in the remaining 257 folios remain blank. Despite this major deficiency, the manuscript appears different from its concurrent counterparts in western India in its organization of the textual and illustrated areas on the folios and its schema of illustrations (the number of illustrations, their size and their position). The solitary miniature in the manuscript portrays the 16 lucky dreams (according to the Digambara tradition) of Marudevi. Stylistic considerations different from those in western India shape the uncluttered composition, the incisive line (as if made by stylus) and the restricted palette of primary colours without gold and silver. The coarser pictorial expression of this manuscript has little in common with the concurrent refined idiom in western India. Its style in its spirit and workmanship instead shows analogies to the previous phase of Jaina miniature painting in western India. It represents a logical progression and perpetuation of that style even though the intermediate links are missing. The discovery of this and other later manuscripts from the region of Delhi and Gwalior establishes the fact that, during the 15th century, two closely related but distinct variants of the Western Indian style existed: one in western India, the other in northern India.

A clearer picture of the prevailing style in Delhi emerges from a Digambara Jaina text of the *Mahāpurāṇa* (Delhi, Shri Digambara Jaina Naya Mandir). Neither the date nor the place of execution is mentioned, but it can be assigned to Delhi, *c.* 1420. Many folios of this manuscript are lost, but enough survive to indicate that it is a continuation of the 1404 Delhi *Adi purāṇa* and that it defines the divergences existing between the two coeval regional idioms of the Western Indian style. Although both manuscripts employ the same basic colours, there is a difference in the tonalities of their miniatures, because in the 1404 *Adi purāṇa* the red colour has flaked away, while in the Naya Mandir *Mahāpurāṇa* the coat of yellow lacquer on the illustration changes the original colour values. In the schema of illustrations, the Naya Mandir *Mahāpurāṇa* is comparatively conservative. This manuscript observes the stylistic conventions of the Western Indian style, yet its miniatures differ from those painted in western India in several ways. For instance, its workmanship is rougher, lacking both refinement and finish, the compositions are larger and much simpler, lacking the descriptive details of the material culture of the times, and its palette is limited in its range. Nevertheless, it is imbued with a vitality that lessens the rigidity inherent in the Western Indian style. Further stylistic differences can be noted in motifs used for architecture and landscape, costumes and particularly textiles: the coarse cloth with elementary patterns from northern India contrasts poorly with the fine, diaphanous fabrics with exquisitely woven or printed designs from western India. Though insignificant in themselves, these stylistic discrepancies establish that there existed in the northern region another variant of the Western Indian style.

Mandu. In the 15th century, in Mandapadurga (Mandu) in central India, the capital of the sultans of Malwa, Jaina merchants and bankers commissioned illustrated copies of religious texts for the edification of the adherents of the faith and for preserving and perpetuating the religious lore. Two illustrated *Kalpa sūtra*s state specifically that they were executed at Mandu. The earlier, an exceptional document dated 1439 (see fig. 249), is painted in an evolved style with neatly arranged compositions, a subdued colour scheme accented in gold and assured as well as

249. *The Parents of the Jina Mahavira, Siddhartha and Trishala*, colours on paper with gold text on a crimson ground, 100×70 mm, from the *Kalpa sūtra* executed at Mandu, 1439 (New Delhi, National Museum)

accomplished draughtsmanship. Again, this manuscript features unusual episodes in its illustrations. Apart from its distilled style, the manuscript is especially notable for the delineation of its human figures. For the first time, the faces of both the men and women are cast in a distinctive squarish mould, and the far eye, though present, is barely attached; it appears to be on the verge of being eliminated. The rendering of the bodies is free of excessive angularities and distortions. The costumes also strike a new note in their type, design and the manner in which they are worn: some women drape the *sāṛī* over the head and across the chest in a broad band, while the men wear a short *dhotī* and an *uttarīya*, which flows down in front from the neck and shoulders. The ends of all these garments flare out stiffly. The thick textiles with simplistic patterns contrast sharply with the intricately designed and finely textured fabrics in miniatures from western India. In its treatment of landscape as well as architecture, this manuscript differs from those in western India. Thus, though it is within the definitions of the Western Indian style as practised in Gujarat and Rajasthan, it exhibits significant divergences in the treatment of its human figures, in the motifs it employs for architecture and landscape and in the events of the story it illustrates. These departures signify a new inspiration.

Almost identical in style to the 1439 Mandu *Kalpa sūtra* is a manuscript of a *Kālakācāryakathā*, of which the overall character in general, and the treatment of the human figures and costumes in particular, suggest that it must also have been made in Mandu *c.* 1440. Interestingly, in one of its compositions a line of the text runs through the illustration separating the clouds from the scene below. This new device shows a loosening of the rigid relationship between the text and the illustration in manuscripts from western India, and an acceptance of the flexibility exercised in these matters in Islamic book illustration. In the same miniature, the style of dress of the native Indian soldiers underlines the Islamic influence.

While the two manuscripts discussed above represent the progressive stylistic strand of the western variant of the Western Indian style, a *Kalpa sūtra* executed at Mandu and painted in the blue-and-gold palette represents its regular version. On grounds of style this manuscript can be assigned to *c.* 1470. Thus, during the 15th century two versions of the western variant of the Western Indian style existed side by side at Mandu, one in its original form, the other in its slightly altered, progressive form.

Jaunpur. In this capital of the Sharqi sultans was painted a *Kalpa sūtra* with varied and interesting marginal decorations. The forces of change that affected the Mandu *Kalpa sūtra* of 1439 appear to have exercised their influence on this manuscript executed in Jaunpur in 1465 as well, though not in as elegant a fashion (see fig. 250). Their influence is particularly visible in the unusual rendering of its human figures with squarish faces and the far protruding eye, which no longer functions as an organic part of the physiognomy. Again, the costumes of the men and women and the manner in which they are draped—with flaring ends—recall those of the 1439 Mandu *Kalpa sūtra.* Also similar is the treatment of the wavy cloud in the upper corner of the illustration, while the rendering of the tree signals a new approach. In all other aspects, such as its composition, its colour scheme and its border decorations, the 1465 Jaunpur *Kalpa sūtra* follows the tenets of the Western Indian style then current in western India.

Gwalior. In the disintegration that followed Timur's conquest of the Delhi Sultanate, the territory of Gwalior became an independent kingdom under the rule of the Tomara Rajputs. The Jaina poet Raidhu lived in Gwalior during the 15th century, and four illustrated copies of his composition are known, the earliest being a *Pāsanāhacariu* dated 1441 in Gwalior. Clearly, the style of painting from Delhi stretched to Gwalior, for this *Pāsanāhacariu* is modelled on the Naya Mandir *Mahāpurāṇa* in its colour scheme, including the lacquer coating, as well as in its

250. *Mahavira in the Puspottara Heaven*, 114×292 mm, from a *Kalpa sūtra* manuscript executed in Jaunpur, *c.* 1465 (Charlottesville, University of Virginia, Bayly Art Museum)

schema of illustrations, which is even more rigid in its arrangements, being symptomatic of the growing conservativeness of the northern variant. Though poor in its rendering, the *Pāsanāhacariu* is extremely interesting stylistically because it portrays the human figures with squarish heads and the far, protruding eye does not function as an integral feature of the face. The costumes consist of a blouse with a *sāṛī* made of thick material worn over the head and across the chest in a broad, stiff, flaring band. The men, generally, wear a *dhotī* and an *uttarīya* flowing down from the shoulders but occasionally also the *jama* and the *pajama* (items of dress not encountered in the manuscripts painted in Gujarat and Rajasthan except in the case of the Sahi figures, who represented a foreign ethnic group in their native attire). Departures from the Naya Mandir manuscript are apparent in the costumes and the treatment of the landscape and architecture.

The surviving latter part of another manuscript, a *Jasaharacariu* featuring Raidhu's compositions, bears the date 1454. It can be assigned to Gwalior because its schema of illustrations is comparable to the *Pāsanāhacariu*, as is the style, except that it has already begun to stultify. To this region can be attributed two more manuscripts painted in the same style and featuring Raidhu's compositions: a *Jasaharacariu* of *c.* 1450 and a *Sāntināhacariu* of *c.* 1460.

Though painted in a crude version of the northern variant, this group of four Gwalior manuscripts assumes immense importance because they exhibit several stylistic features that are analogous to those found in the 1439 Mandu *Kalpa sūtra* and the 1465 Jaunpur *Kalpa sūtra*. The parallels are apparent particularly in the rendering of the figures, their squarish heads and faces in profile with the farther eye being merely attached to it. Also comparable are their postures and their sartorial styles. The relationship of these four Digambara manuscripts to the Mandu and Jaunpur *Kalpa sūtras* is further underlined in the treatment of landscape and architecture. Undoubtedly, the Digambara and Shvetambara manuscripts outside the region of Gujarat and Rajasthan represent a group not limited by hidebound conventions.

Other. In a style that is an extension of the northern variant of the Western Indian style are a few folios of the *Devī māhātmya* painted in 1485 in Pimpalner, Malwa (Varanasi, Banaras Hindu U., Bharat Kala Bhavan). Though painted in a highly mannered idiom that accentuates the stylistic angularities, this document reveals affinities to the Naya Mandir *Mahāpurāṇa* in the treatment of the figures, the colour scheme, the compositional device of arches above figures, the rudimentary designs on coarse fabrics and above all in its sense of energetic movement. A few folios from a fragmentary manuscript of the *Pañca tantra* ('Five tales'; Varanasi, Banaras Hindu U., Bharat Kala Bhavan), a collection of animal tales with moral teachings, exhibit in their choice of colours and the rendering of their figures close connections to the Naya Mandir *Mahāpurāṇa* of *c.* 1420. They can therefore be attributed to the same date.

The manuscripts of the 1439 Mandu *Kalpa sūtra* and the 1465 Jaunpur *Kalpa sūtra* have been given pivotal importance in the study of the development of style in miniature painting. Their stylistic characteristics—the squarish face, the far protruding eye no longer an integral part of the face, the distinctive dress and the treatment of landscape—have been interpreted as signifying the stirrings of a new spirit in the Western Indian style that effloresced into the vibrant *Caurapañcāśikā* style (*see* §(e) below).

BIBLIOGRAPHY

W. N. Brown: *Miniature Paintings of the Jain Kalpa-Sutra* (Washington, DC, 1934)
——: *The Story of Kalka* (Washington, DC, 1934)
M. Chandra: *Jain Miniature Paintings from Western India* (Ahmadabad, 1949)
——'An Illustrated MS. of Mahāpurāṇa in the Collection of Sri Digambar Naya Mandir, Delhi', *Lalit Kala*, v (1959), pp. 68–81
P. Chandra: 'Notes on Mandu Kalpasutra of A.D. 1439', *Marg*, xii (1959), pp. 51–4
M. Chandra and K. Khandalavala: 'An Illustrated Kalpasūtra Painted at Jaunpur in A.D. 1465', *Lalit Kala*, xii (1962), pp. 8–15
M. Chandra: *Studies in Early Indian Painting* (Bombay, 1967)

M. Chandra and U. P. Shah: 'New Documents in Jain Painting', *Shri Mahavira Jaina Vidyalaya Golden Jubilee Volume* (Bombay, 1968)
K. Khandalavala and M. Chandra: *New Documents of Indian Painting: A Reappraisal* (Bombay, 1969)
S. V. Doshi: 'An Illustrated Ādipurāṇa of 1404 A.D. from Yoginīpur', *Chhavi: Golden Jubilee Volume* (Varanasi, 1971), pp. 382–94
K. Khandalavala and S. Doshi: 'Miniature Paintings', *Jain Art and Architecture*, iii (Delhi, 1975)
K. Krishna: 'Illustrated Leaves from a Pancatantra Manuscript of the 15th Century', *Aspects of Jaina Art and Architecture*, ed. U. P. Shah and M. A. Dhaky (Ahmadabad, 1975), pp. 405–13
S. Doshi: *Masterpieces of Jain Painting* (Bombay, 1985)

SARYU V. DOSHI

(c) Eastern Indian style. Surviving paintings from eastern India of this period seem to suggest that painting was an exclusively Buddhist activity confined to the great monasteries of Bihar and Bengal and perhaps Orissa. Though there is no evidence of non-Buddhist painting, it must have been practised. The surviving material suggests also that painting was used exclusively in manuscripts, but Buddhist monasteries in eastern India, like their later Tibetan counterparts, were richly frescoed and hung with banner paintings, though no examples appear to have survived. On the other hand, a considerable body of paintings in palm-leaf manuscripts has been preserved, mostly formerly in the collections of Nepalese monasteries.

General features. Miniatures normally occupy the central position on the long leaves of palm-leaf manuscripts, and there are sometimes flanking miniatures. The viewpoint is normally frontal, and apart from a few trees the vista behind is of empty space. Because of the tiny compass of these miniatures, never exceeding around 80 mm square, there is not much room for iconographical complexity. The wooden covers enclosing the manuscript offered more scope but were rarely taken advantage of for more extensive painting: a row of images is the norm, but Indian covers are rarer than their more adventurous Nepalese counterparts (*see* NEPAL, §V, 1(i)). The text most often used is the metaphysical *Aṣṭasāhasrikā Prajñāpāramitā* ('Perfection of wisdom in 8000 sections'). Pairs of miniatures occur either at the beginning, middle and end of the manuscript or at the beginning of each of the 32 chapters. The subjects thus painted include the Buddha (transcendent and historical) and *bodhisattvas* and other divinities, both beneficent and terrifying, of the Tantric Buddhist pantheon. The second most popular text for illumination, the *Pañcarakṣā*, contains miniatures of the five goddesses whose protection is invoked, sometimes with each goddess's appropriate transcendent Buddha.

No painting has been generally accepted to be much earlier than AD 1000 (Lerner suggests a 10th-century date for a cover in the Metropolitan Museum, New York). The art declined with the abandonment of the Buddhist monasteries after the Muslim takeover of eastern India in the 13th century, so that the timespan of this monastic style is about 250 years. Most of the surviving manuscripts are stylistically linked to those dated in the regnal years of Pala monarchs (*see* PALA AND SENA), and hence are generally called Pala in style. Broadly speaking, the Pala kings were patrons of Buddhism, but there is no evidence that they themselves commissioned such manuscripts, although one of their queens did. For the last two centuries of the Pala dominion the kings ruled little more than Bihar.

Bihar. As the Pala manuscripts are dated in the regnal years of kings who sometimes have the same name (two Mahipala, three Vigrahapala etc) some flexibility of dating is possible, allowing for two interpretations of the stylistic development of Pala painting. Saraswati (1971, 1977) and others have argued that the style was derived directly from Gupta (*c.* 4th–6th century) painting, that the intervening manuscripts conforming most to Gupta ideals have been lost, and that therefore the earliest surviving manuscripts display the classical ideals of harmonious composition and of modelling with colour. Those manuscripts whose style is more linear and flat are thus later, since they conform more to the medieval style. Two manuscripts in widely differing styles but both dated in the early years of one Mahipala are a case in point: that dated in his 4th year (Calcutta, Asiat. Soc.) is judged more classical and early, while the lack of colour modelling and the brittle line of that dated in his 5th year (Cambridge, U. Lib., Add. 1464) suggests a later date. The former has thus been assigned to the first Mahipala, *c.* 1000, and the latter to the second, *c.* 1070. Alternatively, it has been argued (see 1982 exh. cat.) that such flexibility is possible only in the 11th century and that even assigning the 'medieval-style' Cambridge manuscript to *c.* 1070 still puts it earlier than the culmination of the Pala style in the reign of Ramapala (*reg c.* 1072–*c.* 1126 [other scholars suggest *c.* 1087–*c.* 1141]; e.g. Oxford, Bodleian Lib.; Varanasi, Banaras Hindu U., Bharat Kala Bhavan; London, V&A) and the reign of Gopala III (*reg c.* 1128–*c.* 1143; e.g. London, BL, and Boston, MA, Mus. F.A.). All of these examples conform to classical ideals of modelling and volume. Further, as all the 11th-century manuscripts show considerable divergences in style and iconography both among themselves and from the later examples, it would seem to follow that such manuscript illumination was essentially a new development in Indian art. All 11th-century examples, therefore, would seem experimental, before a general stylistic consensus was reached in Bihar *c.* 1100.

Only a small number of such manuscripts have their provenances noted in the colophon, the monastic complex of Nalanda being responsible for most of them. Although Nalanda's early style seems somewhat experimental (manuscripts in Calcutta and Oxford), it was apparently sufficiently standardized by the late 11th century to serve as the model for such late Ramapala-period manuscripts as the famous Vredenburg manuscript dated in Ramapala's

251. Eastern Indian style: The *Bodhisattva Samantabhadra*, miniature from an *Aṣṭasāhasrikā Prajñāpāramitā*, from Bihar, *c.* 1118 (London, Victoria and Albert Museum, IS.4.1958)

36th year (London, V&A, IS.4.1958; see fig. 251). One manuscript is from the monastery of Vikramashila on the Bengal–Bihar border (London, BL, MS. Or. 6902; see fig. 234 above); its stylistic peculiarities, in particular the penchant for placing its divinities within shrines, suggests it is intermediary between the Bihari version of the style and its contemporary in Bengal.

Bengal. A small number of manuscripts seem to have a provenance in Bengal rather than Bihar. That most securely linked to Bengal (Vadodara, Mus. & Pict. Gal.; see Bhattacharya) is dated *c.* 1100 in the reign of Harivarman of south-east Bengal. Its style is much simpler than that of Bihar, with only perfunctory modelling, a nervous line, grimacing faces and a fondness for placing divinities within shrines and for using trees as background fillers. Stylistically related but apparently from south-west Bengal is a heavily illustrated manuscript of the *Kāraṇḍavyūha sūtra*, a Buddhist text in honour of the *bodhisattva* Avalokiteshvara (London, BL, MS, Or. 13940; see Losty, 1989, 'An Early Indian Manuscript'), which is unusual in its use of narrative illustration. Intermediary between the southern Bengal style and that of Bihar is another *Aṣṭasāhasrikā Prajñāpāramitā* manuscript (London, BL, MS. Or. 14282; see Losty, 1989, 'Bengal, Bihar, Nepal'). Contrary to the text the manuscript has a preponderance of terrifying divinities, suggesting a heavily Tantric monastic environment such as the monastery at Somapura in north Bengal, which had close links with Vikramashila. The last Buddhist illuminated manuscript known from Bengal is dated as late as 1289 (Calcutta, Asiat. Soc.).

BIBLIOGRAPHY

B. Bhattacharya: 'Twenty-two Buddhist Miniatures from Bengal (11th Century AD)', *Bull. Baroda State Mus. & Pict. Gal.*, i (1944), pp. 17–36

S. K. Saraswati: 'East Indian Manuscript Painting', *Chhavi: Golden Jubilee Volume of the Bharat Kala Bhavan* (Varanasi, 1971), pp. 243–62

——: *Tantrayāna Art: An Album* (Calcutta, 1977)

The Art of the Book in India (exh. cat. by J. P. Losty, London, BL, 1982), pp. 18–36

M. Lerner: *The Flame and the Lotus: Indian and Southeast Asian Art from the Kronos Collection* (New York, 1984)

J. P. Losty: 'An Early Indian Manuscript of the *Kāraṇḍavyūhasūtra*', *Nalinikānta Śatavarṣikī: Studies in Art and Archaeology of Bihar and Bengal*, ed. G. Bhattacharya and D. Mitra (New Delhi, 1989), pp. 1–21

——: 'Bengal, Bihar, Nepal: Problems of Provenance in 12th Century Illuminated Buddhist Manuscripts', *Orient. A.*, xxxv/2–3 (1989), pp. 86–96, 140–49

J. P. LOSTY

(d) Indo-Persian style. The term 'Indo-Persian' or 'Sultanate' painting is applied to works made during the 15th and 16th centuries under pre-Mughal Muslim patronage in India. These paintings almost invariably illustrate literary texts, usually in Persian but sometimes in the Avadhi language written in the Perso-Arabic script. Following the publication of Indo-Persian paintings from the *Ni'matnāma* ('Book of delicacies'), a cookery book, and other manuscripts, attempts have been made to relocate in India the production of paintings hitherto regarded as provincial Persian works of uncertain provenance. Dating mainly from the 15th century, these are frequently related in style to works of the Timurid and commercial Turkoman schools of Shiraz (*see* ISLAMIC ART, §III, 4(v)(d) and (e)). Most of these attributions are speculative, although some of the works may eventually be confirmed as Indian. It is clear, however, that prior to the Mughal period Shiraz was the Persian centre of painting that most influenced painting in India, the other principal influence being that of Mamluk Egypt, with which there were vigorous trading links (*see* ISLAMIC ART, §III, 4(v)(a)).

252. Indo-Persian style: *A Couple Converse*, from a manuscript of the *Khamsa* of Amir Khusraw, gouache on paper, 93×201 mm, Delhi, *c.* 1450 (Washington, DC, Arthur M. Sackler Gallery)

15th century. A combination of these two influences has been recognized in a group of manuscripts of which the key example is a dispersed copy of the *Khamsa* ('Five poems') by the Indo-Persian poet Amir Khusraw (1253–1325) of Delhi (e.g. Washington, DC, Freer and Sackler Gal.; see fig. 252). In this case the Shirazi features are those of the short-lived style that flourished under the Mongol Injuid dynasty (*c.* 1303–57) and is characterized by rather loose drawing within a square or horizontal frame (*see* ISLAMIC ART, §III, 4(v)(b)). The subjects are seen from a horizontal viewpoint with no sense of depth and with stylized landscape elements shown against a flat red or yellow background. This style shows affinities with both Arab and East Asian painting, but the elements of Arab origin in the Amir Khusraw miniatures are more pronounced and can clearly be associated with a style that was already established in Iraq by the early 13th century and continued in Egypt and Syria under the Mamluks (1250–1517).

Mamluk paintings, like those of the Injuid dynasty, tend to be square or horizontal in format, but the picture area is not always fully coloured; garments are usually shown with a pattern of stylized folds, and the vegetation often includes unusually large flowering plants. Apart from the uncoloured backgrounds, these features occur in the Amir Khusraw miniatures together with an elaboration of the Mamluk convention in which the sky is represented by banded arcs resembling one or more canopies sagging at the centre; costume details are similar to Mamluk court dress. The somewhat carelessly written text, suggesting patronage by a member of the bourgeois merchant community rather than a royal establishment, is sufficiently related to the *nasta'līq* script (introduced *c.* 1400) to favour a date in the second half of the 15th century. The degree of Mamluk influence argues for a western Indian provenance, since the Egyptian trading contacts were primarily with the ports of Gujarat and other centres on the western seaboard.

The Mamluk style was still current in Egypt when the Amir Khusraw manuscript was illustrated, but its Injuid-derived red backgrounds, datable to at least a century after the last known examples of Injuid painting, suggest that the early development of Indo-Islamic manuscript illustration in the Sultanate period must already have been taking place when Sultan Firuz Shah Tughluq (*reg* 1351–88) promulgated his edict against figural paintings in royal apartments. This view is supported by developments in the illustration of Jaina texts of the *Kālakācāryakathā* in western India during the late 14th century, in which Mamluk and possibly Persian pictorial conventions are used to depict Indo-Scythian invaders (Sahis; *see* §(a) above).

Some *Shāhnāma* ('Book of kings') illustrations in the Bharat Kala Bhavan, Banaras Hindu University, Varanasi, executed in the same style as the Amir Khusraw manuscript, are evidently of similar date and provenance to illustrations to the *Masnavī*, a poem by Jalal al-Din Rumi (Paris, priv. col.). In contrast to these manuscripts, likely to have been copied in commercial scriptoria, a *Khamsa* of Nizami (Rome, Bib. Accad. N. Lincei & Corsiniana, MS. Caetani 36), illustrated with small neat pictures in this style, has a finely calligraphed *nasta'līq* text set within carefully drawn gold rules. This suggests that the style may have been practised in at least one court workshop and was perhaps of wider currency than has hitherto been assumed. To some extent this is also true of several dispersed pages from Nizami's *Iskandarnāma* ('Book of Alexander') (e.g. London, V&A, IS. 31–1980), but some of these also show the influence of provincial Timurid painting, particularly in the treatment of female costumes and the presence of distorted Chinese cloud forms. Such

253. Indo-Persian style: *Wedding of Kaikāūs and Sūdāba*, from a manuscript of the *Shāhnāma* of Firdawsi, gouache on paper, 113×138 mm, *c.* 1450 (Paris, Musée Guimet)

changes may be due to the presence of imported manuscripts in Indian collections rather than the arrival of artists from Iran. A *Shāhnāma* dated AH 843 (AD 1439–40; Bankipur, Patna, Khuda Baksh Lib., MS. 3787) with seals of Gujarat sultans is illustrated in the contemporary Timurid style of Shiraz. It was probably imported from there, but a recently arrived Shirazi artist could equally have been responsible for its miniatures.

A profusely illustrated Persian anthology copied by two scribes from Isfahan between 1435 and 1436 (Dublin, Chester Beatty Lib., MS. Pers. 124) is more likely to have been illustrated in India, almost certainly for the library of the Deccani sultanate of Bidar. It subsequently entered the library of Isma'il 'Adil Shah at Bijapur in 1514. The manuscript is illustrated in a provincial Persian style with rhythmic and decorative elements suggestive of an Indian origin. These include motifs identical to those found on tile panels formerly in the public audience hall of the fort of Ahmad I Wali (*reg* 1422–36); he was the Bahmani sultan in whose reign the writing of the manuscript was started at Bidar. A *Shāhnāma* dated AH 841 (AD 1438; London, BL, Or. 1403) has also been attributed to the Bahmanid court, but it differs significantly in style from the anthology, and its Indian origin has been disputed.

No such problem occurs with another group of manuscripts illustrating Persian or Avadhi texts that are clearly the work of Indian painters trained in the indigenous medieval styles normally associated with Jaina painting. Here they incorporate elements from Persian or Mamluk sources in an attempt to meet the requirements of bourgeois Muslim patronage. Two of these manuscripts are of well-known literary texts, the *Iskandarnāma* and *Shāhnāma*, which were often illustrated by Persian artists, but a third work in Persian is a version of the *Hamzanāma*, rarely illustrated tales of the Amir Hamza that belong to popular oral rather than literary tradition. The remaining two works in the group are the earliest of five known illustrated copies of the *Candāyana*, a poetical romance composed in 1379 in Avadhi Hindi by the Sufi Mulla Da'ud. None of the manuscripts has a colophon, but there is general agreement that they are roughly contemporary with the group centred around the Amir Khusraw manuscript, i.e. of the late 15th century.

The strongest analogies with Jaina painting are seen in the *Shāhnāma*, which appeared on the European art market in 1987 (e.g. Zurich, Mus. Rietberg; Paris, Mus. Guimet; see fig. 253). In it, the royal figures of Iran's national epic closely resemble the Sahi kings seen in late 14th-century and early 15th-century copies of the *Kālakācāryakathā*. In both the Jaina manuscripts and the *Shāhnāma* these royal figures wear richly patterned cloud collars, which derive from neither Mamluk nor Injuid sources but can be seen in paintings made in the 1370s for the Jalayirid rulers of Tabriz and Baghdad and for the Muzaffarids, who replaced the Injuid rulers of Shiraz in the 1350s until their massacre by Timur in 1393 (*see* ISLAMIC ART, §III, 4(v)(c)). However, the *Shāhnāma* miniatures feature the more archaic horizontal format, red backgrounds and two-dimensionality of Injuid painting rather than the vertical format and high viewpoint favoured by the Jalayirids and Muzaffarids. The faces are all shown in three-quarter view with pupils in the corners of the eyes except for demons, who are goggle-eyed. Like the highest-quality Jaina miniatures, the *Shāhnāma* paintings contain much richly detailed patterning of textiles and architectural decoration, whereas other manuscripts of this group show less invention in this respect.

The *Iskandarnāma* (Ahmadabad, Cult. Cent., Mehta Col., and Bombay, Prince of Wales Mus.) also employs the horizontal format, mainly without square or vertical compartments and with no more than four figures within the frame. Landscape and architectural features are minimal, there is no skyline, and the traditional profile face with protruding eye is restricted to such figures as boatmen. A similar but less summary approach is found in the *Hamzanāma* (Berlin, Staatsbib. Preuss. Kultbes., MS. Or. 4181). In particular, there is a greater variety of tree types than in other works of this group, and the sky is occasionally rendered by undulating bands of colour; faces are mostly in three-quarter view.

By contrast with these illustrations to Persian texts, the full-page paintings in the two *Candāyana* manuscripts are necessarily in the vertical format of the Near Eastern codex with text written in spacious *naskh* script on the reverse of each page. Of these, the six detached pages in the Bharat Kala Bhavan, Banaras Hindu University, Varanasi, are almost entirely within the indigenous stylistic tradition with profile faces and protruding eyes, although areas of empty space clarifying the narrative are partly the result of lessons drawn from Persian or Mamluk painting. Compared with the archaic qualities of these miniatures, those of the second *Candāyana* (Berlin, Staatsbib. Preuss. Kultbes., MS. Or. 3014) reveal the inheritance of more varied pictorial sources and possess a dramatic and emotional tension not seen in any other Indo-Persian paintings. In one respect they conform to indigenous traditions in their use of rather square facial types with the projecting eye and the choice of native sword types rather than the sabres seen in the *Hamzanāma* or the Varanasi *Shāhnāma*. However, they also incorporate distorted motifs from Iranian and Mamluk painting. The painters were confused in the rendition of horizon and cloud forms. Bands of colour, ultimately of Mamluk origin, at times imitate the curved horizon of Timurid Shiraz painting or are occasionally contorted into a parody of Chinese cloud pattern. Debased forms of embroidered cloud collars signify further Iranian influence.

No such problems arise in the case of manuscripts executed for known royal patrons. The first to be recognized, the *Ni'matnāma* (London, BL, Orient. & India Office Lib., MS. Pers. 149; see fig. 254), was started for the epicure Ghiyath al-Din Khalji (*reg* 1469–1500) of Malwa and completed for his son, ʿAbd al-Muzaffar Nasir Shah (*reg* 1500–10), following Ghiyath Shah's forced abdication. The two artists who collaborated on the manuscript emphasized different features of the contemporary commercial Turkoman style of Shiraz; the more skilled and inventive of the pair also introduced sophisticated representations of indigenous costumes and facial types. Such innovations are also seen in paintings associated with the *Caurapañcāśikā* series (*see* §(e) below) and suggest that an early Rajput style was already in the course of development at the end of the 15th century, with reciprocal

254. Indo-Persian style: *Sultan Ghiyath al-Din of Malwa Tests the Preparation of Betel*, from a manuscript of the *Ni'matnāma*, gouache and gold on paper, 133×120 mm, Mandu, *c.* 1500 (London, British Library, Oriental and India Office Library)

influences at work between centres of Hindu and Muslim patronage.

16th century. The source of the Persian style adopted by these Indian artists is revealed in the illustrations to a glossary of rare words, the *Miftāḥ al-fuzalā* ('Key of the learned') by Da'ud ibn Muhammad ibn Mahmud, whose *nisbat* (pen-name), *Shadiyabadi*, shows him to have been a native of Mandu. The miniatures of this manuscript are all in a pure Shirazi style of *c.* 1490 and are evidently the work of a Persian immigrant. More than a decade later, Da'ud ibn Muhammad was commissioned to translate al-Jazari's Arabic treatise on automata for Nasir Shah under the title *ʿAjā'īb al-ṣanā'iʿ* ('Wonders of craft'). Like many other later versions of the Arabic work, its illustrations are copied with minor variations from a Mamluk original—further evidence that earlier Egyptian or Syrian manuscripts were available as models in the libraries of Sultanate India.

Yet another style represented in the Mandu workshop is that of contemporary Herat, found in a copy of Sa'di's *Būstān* ('Orchard') made for Nasir Shah between 1500 and 1503 by the scribe Shahsawar, who calligraphed the *Miftāḥ al-fuzalā*, and a certain Haji Mahmud, who claims in the title heading to have executed both illuminations and paintings. This is the first instance of a metropolitan Persian style appearing in India, but although the *Būstān*'s miniatures contain no overtly Indian features, they lack the refinement of Timurid painting under Husayn Bayqara. Like the Bukhara school of the later 16th century, this is clearly Herat painting at one remove from its late 15th-century inspiration but still competent and capable of lively narration. It is unclear whether painting continued to be patronized at Mandu after Nasir Shah's death in 1510, but the cultural synthesis evidenced in certain *Ni'matnāma* miniatures is echoed in three further manuscripts of the *Candāyana*, in which the paintings represent stylistic advances on those in earlier copies of the text (*see* §(f) below).

Ignoring later 16th-century manuscripts produced outside the Mughal boundaries for sultans of the Deccan, the last of these is a copy of the first part of Nizami's *Iskandarnāma*, the *Sharafnāma* ('Book of the noble'; London, BL, Or. 13836), commissioned by Sultan Nusrat Shah (*reg* 1519–31) of Bengal and completed in the last year of his reign. In this manuscript there is very little assimilation of indigenous pictorial elements into what is basically mid-15th-century Persian painting of the Shiraz school. Nevertheless, there are also features of even earlier Shirazi painting, such as rocks painted in the Muzaffarid manner of the late 14th century. These would already have been archaisms in mid-15th-century Shiraz, and their presence supports the view that foreign influences in painting during the Sultanate period were introduced and assimilated over a long timespan, although certain stages in this process have been obscured through the loss of libraries during dynastic conflicts.

See also ISLAMIC ART, §III, 4(v)(g).

BIBLIOGRAPHY

R. Ettinghausen: 'The Bustan Manuscript of Sultan Nasir-Shah Khalji', *Marg*, xii/3 (1959), pp. 40–43

R. Skelton: 'The Ni'mat nama: A Landmark in Malwa Painting', *Marg*, xi/3 (1959), pp. 44–8

K. Khandalavala and others: 'A New Document of Indian Painting', *Lalit Kala*, x (1962), pp. 45–54

K. Khandalavala and M. Chandra: 'Three New Documents of Indian Painting', *Prince of Wales Mus. Bull.*, vii (1964), pp. 23–34

S. Digby: 'The Literary Evidence for Painting in the Delhi Sultanate', *Bull. Amer. Acad. Benares*, i (1967), pp. 47–58

K. Khandalavala and M. Chandra: *New Documents of Indian Painting: A Reappraisal* (Bombay, 1969)

I. L. Fraad and R. Ettinghausen: 'Sultanate Painting in Persian Style, Primarily from the First Half of the Fifteenth Century: A Preliminary Study', *Chhavi* (1971), pp. 48–66

R. Skelton: 'The Iskandar Nama of Nusrat Shah: A Royal Sultanate Manuscript Dated 1531–2', *Indian Painting: Mughal and Rajput and a Sultanate Manuscript* (London, 1978), pp. 135–53

K. Adahl: *A Khamsa of Nizami of 1439: Origin of the Miniatures—A Presentation and Analysis* (Uppsala, 1981), pp. 81 and 84–92

The Art of the Book in India (exh. cat. by J. P. Losty, London, BL, 1982)

N. M. Titley: *Persian Miniature Painting and its Influence on the Art of Turkey and India* (London, 1983), pp. 161–85

B. Brend: 'The British Library's Shahnama of 1438 as a Sultanate Manuscript', *Facets of Indian Art* (London, 1986), pp. 87–93

B. N. Goswamy: *A Jainesque Sultanate Shahnama and the Context of Pre-Mughal Painting in India* (Zurich, 1988)

B. W. Robinson: *Fifteenth Century Persian Painting: Problems and Issues* (New York and London, 1991), pp. 61–75

ROBERT SKELTON

(e) Caurapañcāśikā group. A number of stylistically related works known collectively as the *Caurapañcāśikā* group have helped to clarify the development of Indian miniature painting in the first half of the 16th century. The group is particularly important since it appears to represent the dominant style of painting in north India in that period. Consisting of manuscripts and sets of illustrations with little or no text, the group derives its name from a central work, a series of illustrations of the *Caurapañcāśikā* (hereafter CPS), the poet Bilhana's Sanskrit love lyric (Ahmadabad, Cult. Cent., Mehta Col.; see fig. 255).

The texts of the CPS group are both sacred and secular and served the purposes of Muslims, Jainas and Hindus (both Vaishnavites and Shaivites). Given this range, the style cannot be described as Hindu; sectarian identification does not determine the essential character or development of the style. It is generally characterized by large areas of bright colour strongly juxtaposed, marked flatness and abstraction of form, vigorous rhythms and bold line. These traditional elements derive from the Western Indian style, particularly the 15th-century progressive variants of the Delhi–Gwalior region, Jaunpur (now eastern Uttar Pradesh), and Mandu (Malwa; *see* §§(a) and (b) above). Although most CPS group examples follow the horizontal page format typical of Indian painting, a few use a vertical format in the Persian and Indo-Persian manner.

Two manuscripts in the style bear firm evidence of their date and place of production. The first, painted in 1516 (Vikrama era 1573) at the river fort of Kachchhauva (near Agra), is the *Āraṇyaka parva* ('Book of the forest'; Bombay, Asiat. Soc., MS. B.D. 245), the third book of the great Hindu epic the *Mahābhārata*. The second, a Jaina text, the *Mahāpurāṇa* (Jaipur, Dig. Jaina Atisaya Kshetra), was painted in 1540 (Vikrama era 1597) in the Delhi suburb of Palam. The two manuscripts confirm that the style was practised in the Delhi–Agra region during the first half of the 16th century. Though both are clear and attractive in execution, neither is of the highest quality. Both were painted by *kāyastha*s (members of a class of scribes and painters).

Like the dated works, several of the undated manuscripts in the group are modest productions. These include a manuscript of Qutban's romantic lyric *Mṛgāvata* (Varanasi, Banaras Hindu U., Bharat Kala Bhavan, nos 7742–7991) written in Avadhi (eastern Hindi) in the early 16th century, which is likely on linguistic and stylistic evidence to have been painted in what is now eastern Uttar Pradesh. Of a similar quality are a *Rāgamālā* series (ex-Vijayendrasuri priv. col.; Bombay, Jagdish Goenka priv. col.) illustrating the various modes of Indian music and a section of another manuscript of the Jaina *Mahāpurāṇa* (Sagar, Jain Temple Lib.). These were probably produced between 1516 and 1540, but slightly earlier or later dates are also possible.

Another category consists of works of a high quality, described here in likely chronological order. First are three classic Sanskrit Hindu texts: a splendid manuscript of the 10th book of the *Bhāgavata purāṇa* (dispersed; see fig. 256) recounting the exploits of Krishna; a manuscript of selections from the *Devī māhātmya* (Simla, Himachal State Mus.) praising the goddess and bearing a date that cannot be read with certainty; and a manuscript of the *Gīta Govinda* (Bombay, Prince of Wales Mus., MS. 54.37–46), Jayadeva's 12th-century poem celebrating the love of

Radha and Krishna. These are followed by a *Candāyana* (Lahore Mus. and Chandigarh, Govt Mus. & A.G.), Da'ud's Sufi romance of Lauraka and Chanda written in Avadhi; a single surviving leaf from another *Bhāgavata pūraṇa* (Bombay, the late Madhuri Desai priv. col.); a *Rāgamālā* series, of which only one leaf is known to survive (London, V&A, IS. 110-1955); and the *Caurapañcāśika* itself. It is virtually certain that not all of these were painted in the same place, but they are very closely related. The chronology suggested is based on stylistic evolution from a relatively free and spontaneous execution, typified by the dispersed *Bhāgavata pūraṇa*, to a highly finished and dry elegance, typified by the CPS illustrations (see fig. 255 above). Though it is impossible to assign firm dates to this process, a range from *c.* 1520 to *c.* 1560 is reasonable.

There is a third category of works of the CPS group that exhibit strong Mughal influence and must thus be dated after *c.* 1560–65, after the founding of the Mughal style (*see* §4(i) below). Examples of this type include a series known after the place of its discovery in Rajasthan as the Issarda *Bhāgavata purāṇa* (dispersed); two more *Bhāgavata purāṇa* series (New Delhi, Goenka Acad. A. & Music, and Kankroli, priv. col.); a *Gīta Govinda* series (New Delhi, N. Mus.); and a *Rāgamālā* series (Varanasi, Banaras Hindu U., Bharat Kala Bhavan; Patna, G. K. Kanoria priv. col.; and other collections). These represent the final stage of the style's development, which ended *c.* 1600.

Except for the identification of the patrons of the 1516 and 1540 manuscripts as petty aristocrats, little is known about the patrons of the CPS group beyond the fact that they came from several religions. Explicit and implicit in most literature on the group is the assumption that the patrons were nobles and princes. Some may have been, but there is no reason to assume all were. Indeed, if the CPS group style derived from Western Indian painting, perhaps similar patronage patterns prevailed: Western Indian painting is strongly identified with patronage from wealthy merchant classes.

The CPS group style inherited the traditions of the Western Indian style, the dominant idiom in Indian painting from around the 10th or 11th centuries to the end of the 15th. While certainly the CPS group dominated north Indian painting during the first half of the 16th century, its importance continued well beyond mid-century and its influence even longer. It was a major source for the emergence of Mughal painting under Akbar (*reg* 1556–1605), a process revealed by an illustrated manuscript of the *Ṭūṭīnāma* ('Tales of a parrot'; *c.* 1560–65; Cleveland, OH, Mus. A., MS. 62.279), produced for the young Akbar (*see* §4(i)(b) below). Artists trained in the CPS group style provided the most significant Indian contribution to the fledgling Mughal idiom, a heritage evident in details of costume, figure type and, perhaps most important of all, compositional elements. During the last quarter of the 16th century Mughal-influenced works such as those of the late CPS group may have acted as vehicles for the spread of Mughal style.

In addition to its importance in the development of the Mughal idiom, the CPS group also preserved the essentially abstract traditions of Indian painting and transmitted them

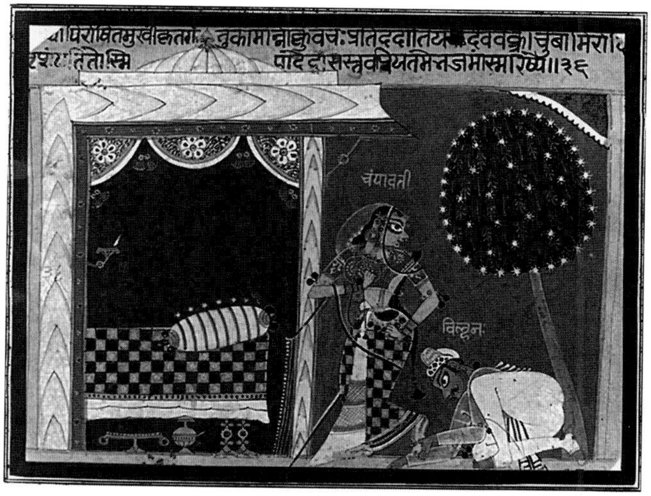

255. *Caurapañcāśikā* group: *The Poet Bilhana and his Mistress, the Lady Campavati*, opaque colour on paper, *c.* 164× *c.*218 mm; from Bilhana: *Caurapañcāśikā*, *c.* 1550–60 (Ahmadabad, Culture Centre, Late N. C. Mehta Collection)

256. *Caurapañcāśikā* group: *The Marriage of Krishna's Parents*, opaque colour on paper, 175×238 mm; from a *Bhāgavata purāṇa* manuscript, *c.* 1520–30 (London, Victoria and Albert Museum)

to late 16th- and 17th-century styles of Rajasthan, Malwa and contiguous regions (*see* §4(iii) below) and elsewhere. How this process took place is not clear, although the broad geographic range of the parent style of the CPS group and the broad range of its heirs strongly suggest that the group was not restricted to the Delhi–Agra region. It probably represented a style that was practised throughout much of north India in the 16th century.

The CPS group has prompted much scholarly disagreement. Because of its central place in the history of Indian painting after 1500, these controversies have had a far-reaching influence on painting scholarship in general. Early assessments of the group tentatively suggested a close connection with Mughal painting under Akbar (see Gray), but the idea lost favour to a view that any Mughal connections were the result of a 17th-century date for the group as a whole (see Khandalavala). This opinion was based on analysis of costume and decorative motifs. However, the discovery of the dated manuscripts proved dates earlier in the 16th century, and the stylistic evidence of the Cleveland *Ṭūṭīnāma* removed all question of the debt of Mughal painting to the CPS group (see Chandra).

Though the firmly dated examples of the CPS group fall into the 16th century, and the group style was presumably still prevalent at the inception of Mughal painting, there are persuasive arguments that the style may have originated during the 15th century (see Doshi and 1982 exh. cat.). This view sees the dated and related modest productions as provincial expressions of an earlier style that may have originated under direct courtly patronage. Thus, related elements found in Western Indian painting would be reflections, rather than precursors, of the CPS group style. This view cannot be confirmed or rejected, but the case for an early chronology is weakened perhaps by its assumption that the CPS group was in decline just as it made its fundamental contribution to the emerging Mughal style.

BIBLIOGRAPHY

B. Gray: *Rajput Painting* (London, 1949)
K. Khandalavala: 'Leaves from Rajasthan', *Marg*, iv/3 (1950), pp. 2–24, 49–56
D. Barrett and B. Gray: *Painting of India* (Geneva, 1963/*R* London, 1978)
M. Chandra and K. Khandalavala: *New Documents of Indian Painting: A Reappraisal* (Bombay, 1969)
——: *An Illustrated Āranyaka Parvan in the Asiatic Society of Bombay* (Bombay, 1974)
P. Chandra: *The Ṭūṭī-nāma of the Cleveland Museum of Art and the Origins of Mughal Painting* (Graz, 1976)
S. Doshi: 'A Fifteenth-century Jain Manuscript from Gwalior and some Thoughts on the *Caurapañcāśikā* Style', *J. Ind. Soc. Orient. A.*, x (1978–9), pp. 30–40
The Art of the Book in India (exh. cat. by J. P. Losty, London, BL, 1982)
D. J. Ehnbom: *An Analysis and Reconstruction of the Dispersed Bhāgavata Purāṇa from the Caurapañcāśikā Group* (diss., U. Chicago, IL, 1984)

(f) Candāyana group. Like the *Caurapañcāśikā* group (*see* §(e) above), this imperfectly understood group of three illustrated manuscripts occupies a place of great importance in the history of Indian painting, providing major examples of a pre-Mughal style. None of the manuscripts has a colophon, but similarities with better-documented material suggest a date in the first half of the 16th century (roughly contemporary with the *Caurapañcāśikā* group) and a place (or places) of execution in north India. The group is named after two of the three texts, both of which are manuscripts of the *Candāyana*, a late 14th-century devotional Sufi romance (Bombay, Prince of Wales Mus., a portion of which is dispersed; and Manchester, John Rylands U. Lib., Hindustani MS. 1). This text, lost to modern readers until its rediscovery in the mid-20th century, was written in Avadhi (eastern Hindi) by the Muslim divine Da'ud. The author narrates the tribulations of the soul in search of union with the divine through the symbolic device of an adulterous love affair. The surviving text is incomplete, lacking both its beginning and end. That the work was popular in its time is confirmed by its mention in 16th-century records and the existence of several illustrated and unillustrated manuscripts. (There are other illustrated *Candāyana* manuscripts in 15th- and 16th-century Indian styles outside this group.) For reasons that are not clearly understood, the story sank into oblivion. The third manuscript, of which only a single leaf is known to survive (New Delhi, N. Mus.), illustrates the *Gīta Govinda* of Jayadeva, a 12th-century devotional poem in Sanskrit celebrating the mystical dimensions of Krishna's amorous exploits. It has been unflaggingly popular since its composition.

The style of the *Candāyana* group is best illustrated by the Bombay manuscript, presumably the earlier of the group's two copies of this text. The colour scheme is cool and restrained, dominated by soft blue, pink, mauve, white and yellow and enlivened with a liberal application of gold. The line is extremely fine, in marked contrast to that of most Indian painting of the period. A typical composition consists of a few figures under a large tree with dense foliage, the whole set below a high, curving horizon line, as, for instance, in the painting *Lauraka Lamenting the Death of Chanda* (see fig. 257). The pale ground is generally dotted with decorative devices representing plants; the sky is almost invariably filled with arabesque cloud forms. These stylistic elements point to Persian prototypes, although Indian elements are also strong, including the square-headed figure type, frequent use of uncompromising horizontal registers in compositions and certain details of costume. The *Candāyana* group as a whole represents a distinct strain of Indo-Persian painting. The two manuscripts illustrating the *Candāyana* share interesting characteristics. They invariably consist of vertical, full-page

257. *Candāyana* group: *Lauraka Lamenting the Death of Chanda*, opaque colour and gold on paper, 190×138 mm; from a *Candāyana* manuscript, *c.* 1500–50 (Bombay, Prince of Wales Museum of Western India)

illustrations with texts in Arabic script on the backs of the leaves. The pictures are compositionally conservative, and though individual leaves may be splendid, the constant repetition of stock devices lessens their overall impact. This is equally true of *Candāyana* manuscripts illustrated in other styles and may indicate the widespread survival of illustrative traditions directly associated with the text.

There is little evidence of the religion or social status of patrons who commissioned works in the *Candāyana* group. Any assumption that a Persian-derived style used to illustrate a Sufi romance would be restricted to Muslim patrons is seriously challenged by the evidence that it was also used to illustrate the *Gīta Govinda*. The generous use of gold and other expensive pigments suggests that the patrons were sufficiently wealthy to afford the best materials, but they need not have been princes and might well have been wealthy merchants.

In addition to the significance of the *Candāyana* group in suggesting the diversity of artistic patronage in 16th-century India, it was also of major importance for the inception of Mughal painting *c.* 1560–65 under Akbar (*see* §4(i)(b) below). Artists trained in the *Candāyana* group idiom were included in the fledgling Mughal workshop and thus contributed Indo-Persian elements to the new style. This is especially obvious in the *Ṭūṭīnāma* ('Tales of a parrot'; *c.* 1560–65; Cleveland, OH, Mus. A., MS. 62.279), a manuscript produced for Akbar that documents the formation of the Mughal style from its many sources. The most important of the early Mughal masters who had received training in the *Candāyana* group style was BASAWAN.

BIBLIOGRAPHY

P. L. Gupta, ed.: *Candāyana* (Bombay, 1964)
A. Krishna: *Malwa Painting* (Banaras, 1964), p. 9
M. Chandra and K. Khandalavala: *New Documents of Indian Painting: A Reappraisal* (Bombay, 1969)
P. Chandra: *The Ṭūṭī-nāma of the Cleveland Museum of Art and the Origins of Mughal Painting* (Graz, 1976)

DANIEL J. EHNBOM

4. 16TH CENTURY–1947.

(i) Mughal styles. (ii) Sub-imperial styles. (iii) Styles of Rajasthan and contiguous regions. (iv) Pahari styles. (v) Eastern Indian styles. (vi) Deccani styles. (vii) South Indian styles. (viii) Kashmiri styles. (ix) Company styles. (x) Early modern styles.

(i) Mughal styles. Under the patronage of the Mughal emperors, diverse pre-Mughal styles such as those represented by the *Caurapañcāśikā* and *Candāyana* groups (*see* §3(ii)(e) and (f) above) were merged with other stylistic elements, some coming directly from Iran and perhaps Europe, to create a distinctive new idiom. The Mughals were descended from a noble line of Timurids who had long cultivated such princely refinements as painting and literature. For such Muslim rulers, libraries were indicative of wealth, power and learning; they were equally repositories of sacred and secular wisdom (*see* ISLAMIC ART, §III). The ability to support artists for the copying and illumination of books and to locate and acquire the fine materials for those artists' use (including, on occasion, pigments of gold and silver), was an activity of the highest social level. Both illustrated manuscripts and individual works, often bound in albums, were produced in the Mughal royal atelier. This body of work continues to be admired not only for its sumptuousness and fine detail but also for its subtlety and vitality.

Although the Mughal dynasty begins with the conquest of Hindustan in 1526, what has come to be known as the Mughal style did not develop fully until the reign of Akbar (*reg* 1556–1605). Nevertheless, the patronage of his two predecessors, Babur (*reg* 1526–30) and Humayun (*reg* 1530–40; 1555–6), is included here, for Mughal art was already in an embryonic state during their reigns, with key ingredients being slowly set in place.

BIBLIOGRAPHY

E. M. Elliot and J. Dowson: *The History of India as Told by its Own Historians (the Muhammedan Period)*, 8 vols (London, 1867–77/*R* Allahabad, 1964)
F. R. Martin: *Miniature Painting and Painters of Persia, India and Turkey* (London, 1912)
L. Binyon and T. W. Arnold: *The Court Painters of the Grand Moguls* (Oxford, 1921)
P. Brown: *Indian Painting under the Mughals* (Oxford, 1924)
I. Stchoukine: *La Peinture indienne à l'époque des Grands Moghols* (Paris, 1929)
T. W. Arnold: *The Library of A. Chester Beatty: A Catalogue of Indian Miniatures*, 3 vols, rev. and ed. by J. V. S. Wilkinson (London, 1936)
M. Chandra: *Techniques of Mughal Painting* (Lucknow, 1949)
R. Ettinghausen: *Paintings of the Sultans and Emperors of India in American Collections* (New Delhi, 1961)
A. A. Ivanov, T. V. Grek and O. F. Akimushkin: *Albom indiyskikh i persidskikh miniatyur xvi–xviii v.v: vostochnaya miniatyura i kalligrafiya v Leningradskikh sobraniyakh* [Albums of Indian and Persian miniatures, 16th–18th centuries: Oriental miniatures and calligraphy in Leningrad collections] (Moscow, 1962)
The Art of Mughal India: Painting and Precious Objects (exh. cat. by S. C. Welch, New York, Asia Soc. Gals, 1963/*R* 1976)
A. K. Das: 'Mughal Royal Hunt in Miniature Paintings', *Ind. Mus. Bull.*, ii (1967), pp. 19–23
E. Binney III: *Indian Miniature Paintings from the Collection of Edwin Binney III: The Mughal and Deccani Schools with Some Related Sultanate Material* (Portland, OR, 1973)
P. Chandra: *The Ṭūṭī-nāma of the Cleveland Museum of Art and the Origins of Mughal Painting* (Graz, 1976)
B. W. Robinson and others: *Islamic Painting and the Arts of the Book* (London, 1976)
Paintings from the Muslim Courts of India (exh. cat. by R. Pinder-Wilson, London, BM, 1976)
Persian and Mughal Art (exh. cat., London, Colnaghi's, 1976)
S. C. Welch: *Imperial Mughal Painting* (New York, 1978)
The Grand Mogul: Imperial Painting in India, 1600–1660 (exh. cat. by M. C. Beach, Williamstown, MA, Clark A. Inst.; Baltimore, MD, Walters A.G.; Boston, MA, Mus. F.A.; New York, Asia Soc. Gals; 1978–9)
A. K. Das: 'Calligraphers and Painters in Early Mughal Painting', *Chhavi 2: Rai Krishnadasa Felicitation Volume*, ed. A. Krishna (Varanasi, 1981), pp. 92–7
The Imperial Image: Paintings for the Mughal Court (exh. cat. by M. C. Beach, Washington, DC, Freer, 1981)
The Art of the Book in India (exh. cat. by J. P. Losty, London, BL, 1982)
The Indian Heritage: Court Life and Arts under Mughal Rule (exh. cat., ed. R. Skelton; London, V&A, 1982)
D. Walker and E. Smart: *Pride of the Princes: Indian Art of the Mughal Era in the Cincinnati Art Museum* (Cincinnati, 1985)
India: Art and Culture, 1300–1900 (exh. cat. by S. C. Welch, New York, Met., 1985)
A. K. Das: *Splendours of Mughal Painting* (Bombay, 1986)
A la Cour du Grand Moghol (exh. cat., Paris, Gal. Mausart, 1986)
Wonders of a Golden Age: Painting at the Court of the Grand Mughals (exh. cat. by B. N. Goswamy and E. Fischer, Zurich, Mus. Rietberg, 1987)

□

(a) Babur and Humayun periods. (b) Akbar period. (c) Jahangir period. (d) Shah Jahan period. (e) Aurangzeb period. (f) Later periods.

(a) Babur and Humayun periods. Scarce though material is from the reigns of the first two Mughal emperors, enough has survived to allow a basic description of early

developments. Babur (*reg* 1526–30), in his memoir, the *Bāburnāma*, reveals the discerning eye of a connoisseur in comments on such painters as Bihzad and Shah Muzaffar. He is known to have collected books: his seal is found in a number of manuscripts, including a Timurid *Shāhnāma* ('Book of kings'; London, Royal Asiat. Soc.) dating from the first half of the 15th century. A *Tīmūrnāma* ('History of Timur') of Mulla Hatifi, apparently illustrated by Bihzad, also seems to have formed part of his library. Many contemporaries of Babur, including his cousin Mirza Muhammad Haydar, practised calligraphy and painting. Thus while no illustrated manuscripts can be assigned to Babur's patronage, a number of early 16th-century works from eastern Iran with no specific provenance may have been prepared for him.

Babur's son Humayun (*reg* 1530–40; 1555–6) inherited his father's library. Literary references indicate that Humayun employed painters, including them among his entourage even as he wandered in exile after 1540. His brother Mirza Kamran, who governed Kabul and neighbouring regions from 1530, had a reputation for literary pursuits and built a pleasure garden (now ruined) outside Lahore. A manuscript of *Yūsuf and Zulaykha* (New York, Pub. Lib.) carries a colophon stating that it was written for Mirza Kamran by the calligrapher ʿAbdallah Shirazi. It is not dated but was probably produced *c.* 1530–53. The manuscript has 143 leaves and 6 miniatures in the provincial Bukhara style, one of many idioms that went into the making of the Mughal style. A finer single page, *Loving Musicians* (USA, priv. col.; see fig. 258), may also have been painted for Kamran.

Humayun spent much of his exile in Iran as a guest of Shah Tahmasp. While there, he took an interest in the leading artists of the Safavid court, enticing some into his service, for it was around 1544 that Shah Tahmasp was losing interest in painting. Humayun began his return to India with the capture of Kabul from his brother in 1545, and Kabul remained the centre of Humayun's court until November 1554. Kamran was captured and blinded in August 1553. While direct links have not been established by signatures or attributions, some of the painters of Kamran's manuscripts may have entered Humayun's workshop in Kabul. Maulana Dust served both Humayun and Kamran, but only one ascribed work by him is known, a portrait of *Shah Abu al-Maʿali* (priv. col., sold London, Sotheby's, 11 April 1972, lot 18). The atelier expanded with artists and craftsmen arriving from Iran. These included Khwaja ʿABD AL-SAMAD and MIR SAYYID ʿALI, put in charge of the imperial painting workshops under Akbar. MIR MUSAVVIR, the Safavid master and father of Mir Sayyid ʿAli, also served Humayun.

The most important manuscript of the Humayun period is a *Khamsa* ('Five poems') of Nizami (Ahmadabad, priv. col., see Chandra, pls 102–5), with thirty-four miniatures and two handsomely illuminated title-pages. There are no historical inscriptions, but two miniatures are attributable to Mir Musavvir. The remaining paintings are by ten anonymous artists working in Bukhara, Safavid, Indo-Persian and *Candāyana*-influenced idioms. Of special interest are works by Indian artists, particularly the painter who did the entire Layla and Majnun section. This unknown master actively blended various styles and gave

258. *Loving Musicians*, opaque colour on paper, 195×118 mm, Humayun period, *c.* 1550 (USA, private collection)

his work an emotional vitality and realism. The *Khamsa* thus foreshadows developments that came to fruition in the time of Akbar (*see* §(b) below).

Humayun's interests appear to have included pictures of historical events as well as portraits and natural history studies, themes further developed by Akbar and his successors. Studies of court life giving accurate portrayals of the imperial circle and anticipating the historical paintings long considered an innovation of Akbar include *Akbar Presenting a Painting to Humayun in a Tree House* (Tehran, Gulistan Pal. Lib.) by ʿAbd al-Samad and *Humayun and his Brothers in a Landscape*, attributed to Dust Muhammad (Berlin, Staatsbib. Preuss. Kultbes.).

BIBLIOGRAPHY

Zahir al-Din Muhammad Babur: *Bāburnāma* (*c.* 1530); Eng. trans. and ed. by A. S. Beveridge, 2 vols (London, 1922/*R* New Delhi, 1970)
Mahfuz al-Haq: 'Persian Painters, Illuminators and Calligraphists etc in the XVIth century', *J. & Proc. Asiat. Soc. Bengal*, xxviii (1932), pp. 239–49
S. K. Banerji: 'Humayun's Early Relations with Kamran (1514–33)', *Ind. Hist. Q.*, xii (1936), pp. 287–93
P. Chandra: *The Ṭūṭī-nāma of the Cleveland Museum of Art and the Origins of Mughal Painting* (Graz, 1976)
A. Welch: *Artists for the Shah* (New Haven, 1976)
Islamic Art from India (exh. cat., London, Spink & Son, 1980) [*Yūsuf and Zulaykha*, MS., colour pl. 60, p. 35]

H. Elgood: 'The Earliest Extant Illustrated Manuscript for a Prince of the Mughal Family', *A. & Islam. World*, iii (1985), pp. 34–9, 95
India: Art & Culture, 1300–1900 (exh. cat. by S. C. Welch, New York, Met., 1985), pp. 144–6

MILO CLEVELAND BEACH, MICHAEL D. WILLIS

(b) Akbar period. On inheriting the kingdom from Humayan, Akbar (*reg* 1556–1605) came into possession of his father's well-stocked library and a small workshop of artists and artisans who made books. As his political power grew, so did the impact and richness of the books he commissioned.

Early works, c. *1560–1580.* One of the first manuscripts produced for Akbar (who came to the throne at the age of 13) was the *Ṭūṭīnāma* ('Tales of a parrot'; *c.* 1560–65; Cleveland, OH, Mus. A., MS. 62.279), a fanciful collection of 52 stories related by a parrot to its mistress in an attempt to keep her at home at night while her husband was away. Each tale is followed by a moral lesson, so the stories both entertain and instruct. The illustrations are fresh, spontaneous and enormously lively. They reveal the stylistic components of the imperial Mughal style at a formative stage: many of the backgrounds are spatially deep rather than flat; the compositions are more varied and less friezelike; and a few of the figures are shown in three-quarter view rather than in strict profile. The book is important in presenting the earliest work of several of the greatest Mughal artists, DASWANTH and BASAWAN in particular. Marginal inscriptions name both artists and a few others, but since the margins were severely retrimmed in a past remounting of the pages, most names are lost. The *Ṭūṭīnāma* also underscores the increasing significance of an artist's individual style within the Mughal tradition. Through changes of attitude in patronage (several emperors took an intense interest in individual artists), Mughal painters were encouraged to develop more personal styles. However, even though some illustrations are closely related to the work of the two great Persian Safavid painters Mir Sayyid ʿAli and ʿAbd al-Samad, the majority are in regional Indian styles. This is particularly evident in the figure types, which show that a number of the artists who worked on the *Ṭūṭīnāma* were probably trained in the pre-Mughal styles represented by the *Caurapañcāśikā* and *Candāyana* groups (*see* §3(ii)(e)–(f) above).

Although the *Ṭūṭīnāma* was earlier, the first major manuscript made for Akbar was the *Dāstān-i Amir Ḥamza* or *Ḥamzanāma* ('Tales of Hamza'; dispersed). The *Ḥamzanāma* describes the adventures of Hamza, an uncle of the Prophet Muhammad, but mixed with this narrative are legends and folk tales, and the result is a work of wild fantasy. The story, which centres on Hamza's attempts to convert the world to Islam, may have been seen in relation to Akbar's own activities conquering and consolidating the varied religious and social factions within India. Contemporary texts relate that there were originally 14 volumes, each with 100 illustrations, which took 14 years to complete. While there is not complete scholarly agreement about its dates, the work was probably executed between 1562 and 1577. Remains of wall painting at the new imperial city of Fatehpur Sikri (begun 1569) appear to be contemporary with this manuscript. The unusually large size of the *Ḥamzanāma* illustrations (about 676×513 mm) inspired solutions unique to that format and effects closer to those of wall painting than was customary in manuscript folios.

Overall supervision of the project was assigned first to Mir Sayyid ʿAli and then to ʿAbd al-Samad. Their influence is perhaps most apparent in the fact that the sophisticated formal solutions first introduced in the *Ṭūṭīnāma* for the depiction of figures, landscape and architecture seem here to be fully 'accepted' and in the process of being simply extended and refined. Yet the majority of the illustrations are in a vitally new style that developed only in part from Persian (Iranian) precedents. Painters trained in various local and pre-Mughal Indian schools were certainly present in the Mughal workshops at this time, for visual references to these early styles are found throughout the work. The clear presentation of narrative action, the choice and strength of the colours used and the large, bold forms found in many illustrations are characteristics more common in Indian than Iranian painting. These features are clear, for instance, in the illustration *Badi ʿal-Zaman Emerging from a Chest* (Cincinnati, OH, A. Mus.; see fig. 259), which represents the moment in which Badi, a friend of Hamza, jumps fully armed from a chest in which he had floated down-river. After skirmishes, he kills the local ruler and converts the populace to Islam. Like most illustrations in the manuscript, the scene stresses dramatic encounter; the action is expressed through large, direct

259. *Badi ʿal-Zaman Emerging from a Chest*, opaque colour, gold, silver and mica on cotton cloth, 795×640 mm; from a *Ḥamzanāma* manuscript, Akbar period, *c.* 1562–77 (Cincinnati, OH, Cincinnati Art Museum)

forms that are spatially close to the viewer and compositionally central. Nothing distracts from the main figures and the action, for the goal of the Indian painter was to relate and intensify the story. Similarly exciting scenes appear on each of the manuscript folios, indicating the directness of the young Akbar's taste at this time.

A collection of animal fables of about the same period, the *Anvār-i Suhaylī* ('Lights of Canopus'; 1570; U. London, SOAS, Lib., MS. 10102), is similar in scale to the *Ṭūṭīnāma*. None of its 27 illustrations bear any ascription of authorship, but there is considerable stylistic unity, with the exception of two scenes in a style almost directly derived from the provincial Persian centre at Bukhara. The works are still simple and direct, and there remains little extraneous to the narrative, but the overtly Indian elements so obvious and so varied in the *Ṭūṭīnāma* have been altered to accord with new and distinctively Mughal interests: the workmanship of the *Anvār-i Suhaylī* is finer, the colours more varied, less strong and less strongly contrasted, and the drama is presented in a quieter, less assertive manner. This indicates that central control was becoming increasingly important in Akbar's Mughal workshops.

By the mid-1570s Akbar also began commissioning portraits of major nobles and personalities at court as well as interesting character types that he or his artists encountered. These early portrait studies are primarily concerned with personality, shown through physiognomy as well as pose and gesture. A portrait of *Mota Raja Udai Singh* (Boston, MA, Mus. F.A.; see fig. 260) combines an acute portrayal of the face of this important Hindu Raja with an emphatic statement about his acknowledged corpulence. There is no background space, and the Raja's bulk serves more to set off his strong face and quizzical expression than to create a sense of weight and volume. The technique is rather rough, but this imparts a visual and descriptive liveliness greater than that found in many later, more elegant works. As the portrait tradition developed, increasing attention was paid to objects and materials (the textures of clothing, for example, or the careful description of weaponry) often to the detriment of psychological penetration. Few individual portraits of Akbar himself exist, compared to the profusion of imperial images produced under his successors, although he is shown on most pages of the various manuscripts of the *Akbarnāma*, which recounts the history of his reign.

Generally speaking, however, during his early years Akbar seems to have preferred narratives recounting fictional and fantastic adventures to portraits and texts based on actual events. A *Dārābnāma* manuscript (*c*. 1580; London, BL, Or. MS. 4615) recounting the life of the grandfather of Alexander the Great directly continues the narrative and artistic developments initiated by the *Ṭūṭīnāma* and *Anvār-i Suhaylī* volumes. Many of its 157 illustrations are inscribed with the artists' names, and the range and character of the artistic personalities expressed in these scenes are further evidence of Akbar's slowly increasing interest in individual personality traits of the artists. The illustrations of this manuscript, however, lack the evenness of quality that had already developed in the *Anvār-i Suhaylī* of 1570. Some are of the highest imperial calibre, others are not. It is usual to claim that the book was assembled over a long period of time, the 'better' illustrations being later additions. Such a conclusion is unwarranted until more is known about how workshops were set up and what procedures were used by patrons to finance and prepare volumes. Many Mughal manuscripts, for instance, show a similarly wide range of quality. It has also been suggested (Seyller, 1985) that style and quality were perhaps determined less by the taste of the patron than by the character of the text and the purpose and economic determinants of the commission.

260. *Mota Raja Udai Singh*, opaque colour on paper, 112×75 mm, Akbar period, *c*. 1575–80 (Boston, MA, Museum of Fine Arts)

Later works, c. *1580–1605.* Evidence suggests that Mughal painters were influenced by European prints by at least the beginning of Akbar's reign. Even the *Ṭūṭīnāma* shows receptiveness to such foreign sources, as is clear from the attempts at chiaroscuro modelling. However, in 1580, at Akbar's invitation, a mission of Jesuit priests came from Goa to the Mughal court, bringing with them gifts for the Emperor, among which was the Royal Polyglot Bible, an eight-volume work printed in Antwerp between 1568 and 1573 by Christoph Plantin. It was illustrated with engravings that were studied, copied and adapted by imperial artists. This gift was followed by a virtual flood of European prints, most of which were northern European and from workshops in Antwerp, the main port from which ships sailed to India. Given as gifts to Akbar and members of the imperial circle, they were distributed in the hope of an eventual conversion of the Emperor (and then of his court) to Christianity. Many prints by Albrecht Dürer and his followers were sent as well; in fact, he was the artist most frequently used as a source for Mughal studies in the European manner. (Whether original Dürer prints were sent, or copies made in the Antwerp workshops and elsewhere from the mid-16th century onwards, has yet to be satisfactorily determined; this could clarify the date the first prints were available for artists to study.) After 1580 few Mughal artists were unaffected by European influence, including its imagery. The artists Basawan and KESU DAS were at the forefront of those painters particularly receptive to European ideas. While Kesu Das's paintings and drawings remained relatively faithful to the European originals, Basawan was far more inventive in absorbing and adapting the imported style, as in the drawing attributed to him of a *Seated Man* (*c.* 1580–85; Washington, DC, Freer; see fig. 261). A sincere interest in learning from European example remained strong into the middle years of the reign of Akbar's son Jahangir (*reg* 1605–27), after which references to Europe generally became superficial exoticisms thrown in to enliven a declining tradition.

In the early 1580s Akbar also apparently consciously shifted the emphasis of his interests from fictional adventure and spiritual enquiry to history and the interpretation of actual events. This followed a religious vision that he experienced in 1579 during a hunt. Abu'l-Fazl, his court biographer, claimed it gave him a sense of the 'glory of unity'. This experience seems to climax years of religious questioning and to mark a new orientation reflected in the kinds of manuscripts he commissioned. The imperial copy of the *Razmnāma* ('Book of wars'; Jaipur, Maharaja Sawai Man Singh II Mus., MS. AG. 1683–1850), a Persian translation of the great Hindu epic the *Mahābhārata*, which Akbar had made between 1582 and 1586, provides a perfect transition from one interest to the other. It is one of the two finest examples of Hindu texts that Akbar had translated into Persian and illustrated, a project reflecting his interest in the character and traditions of the people over whom he ruled. The other was a translation of the *Rāmāyaṇa* (imperial copy, Jaipur, Maharaja Sawai Man Singh II Mus., MS. AG. 1851–2026). Akbar commanded his courtiers to make copies of these imperial translations so that Muslims would gain familiarity with the Hindu tradition. One such copy of the *Rāmāyaṇa* (Washington, DC, Freer, MS. 07.271) throws light on developments in style at the sub-imperial level of patronage (*see* §(ii) below).

The imperial *Razmnāma* is dominated by the work of Daswanth, a painter who established a particularly close rapport with the Emperor. Daswanth's illustrations of fantastic and otherworldly events are especially powerful. The painter's death by suicide in 1584 is often associated with the changing character of the books Akbar commissioned. Whether Akbar's waning interest in the subjects in which Daswanth specialized was a contributing factor in his death, or the impact of Daswanth's suicide was a

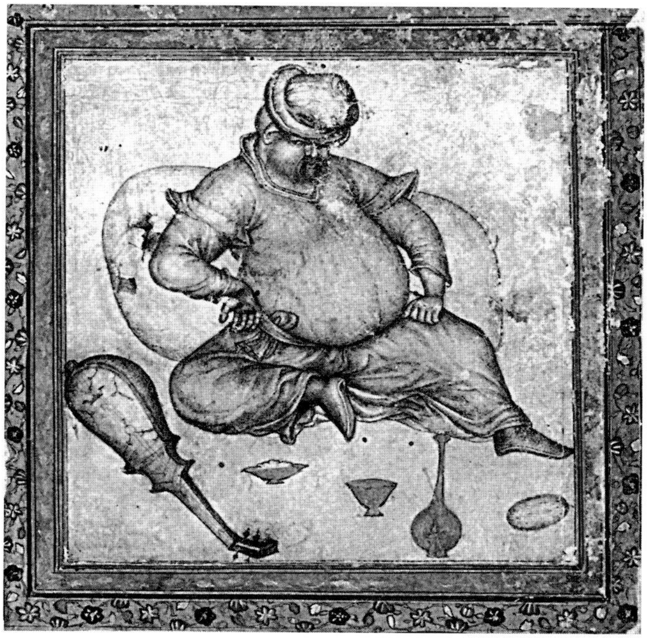

261. Basawan (attrib.): *Seated Man*, black ink and some gold on brownish paper, 85×80 mm, Akbar period, *c.* 1580–85 (Washington, DC, Freer Gallery of Art)

further reason for Akbar's change in taste remains uncertain. The shift in emphasis from fantastic subjects towards historical themes seems to have resulted from a variety of factors, including Akbar's growing sense of his own historical role.

Further evidence of this trend is Akbar's commission in the early 1580s of the *Ta'rīkh-i alfī* ('History of the millennium'), a historical account of Islam to mark the coming of the year 1000 AH. Only a few dispersed pages of this manuscript are known. At about the same time he commissioned an illustrated copy of the *Tīmūrnāma* ('History of Timur'; Bankipur, Patna, Khuda Bakhsh Lib.); Timur was increasingly invoked as the dynastic progenitor of the Mughals. The imperial copies of the *Ta'rīkh-i alfī* and *Tīmūrnāma* manuscripts would have contained text and illustrations relating to Akbar's reign, for each brought its narrative up to the date it was written. Each therefore demanded new skills of its artists, for they had to include scenes familiar to or even witnessed by many of the viewers. A few artists took advantage of opportunities to paint such actual events from memory or observation. Most artists, however, were accustomed to adapting accepted compositional prototypes, adding details or rearranging figures to make the scene more topical and specific. Not all painters could create new compositions that had the visual immediacy demanded by the text. Nonetheless, it was a time when old standards were changing, and many artists were seeking new sources of inspiration.

Between 1569 and 1585 Akbar's court centred on Fatehpur Sikri, a new city he built to celebrate the birth of his first son, Salim, later Jahangir. Between 1585 and 1598, the imperial capital was at Lahore. It is convenient to use these two capital cities to define stages in the development of Mughal art. The years at Fatehpur Sikri were characterized by religious and artistic experimentation. By 1585 Akbar was highly conscious of his place in a revived Timurid dynasty, his succession was secured, and his wealth and political power were unassailable. Judging by the works of art that he commissioned, he was insistent on an image of unquestioned imperial splendour. The years at Lahore represent the culmination of Akbari art, a period of self-assured maturity, artistic consolidation and refinement. In architecture as well as painting an assertive sense of dynastic power is evident (*see also* §III, 7(i)(a) above).

A translation into Persian of the memoirs of Akbar's grandfather, Babur, was presented to the Emperor in 1589, and the original text was almost certainly illustrated. Additional copies of the *Bāburnāma* ('History of Babur') were quickly commissioned and completed, probably for other members of the imperial family as well as for presentation. Illustrations included the major historical events of the reign, as well as studies depicting the flowers and animals that Babur's text described so carefully. Some years earlier Akbar's father, Humayun, commissioned his painters to record the appearance of remarkable creatures that he encountered. The inclusion of natural history studies in the Akbari *Bāburnāmas* is therefore a continuation of established imperial Mughal subject-matter. Specific inspiration for the form and combination of these natural history studies may have been found in European herbals circulating on the subcontinent.

In 1590–91 a history of Akbar's reign, the *Akbarnāma*, was commissioned from Abu'l-Fazl, the Emperor's friend and confidant. The first section of that text, covering the years between Babur's arrival in 1526 and 1572, was presented to Akbar in 1596. Another volume, bringing the narrative up to date, was finished two years later (London, V&A, MS. IS. 2-1896 and dispersed; the V&A holds the main portion, which includes events dating between 1560 and 1578; see fig. 262). The illustrations were probably completed in the mid-1590s. This first known *Akbarnāma* manuscript, when complete, would have had several hundred illustrations. It seems that the paintings included were originally intended for an earlier, no longer extant manuscript of *c.* 1586–7 describing the same historical period (Seyller, 1990). There is now evidence that it was normal procedure for paintings to be added to and removed from manuscripts according to changes in the interpretation of events, the creation of new, more accurate texts or simply whim. The production of the *Akbarnāma* was accomplished by a centrally controlled allocation of tasks. Major artists designed the compositions, which were carried out by younger or less skilled artists who filled in the colours and completed some details. Additional master artists were sometimes assigned specific portraits within each scene. As one might expect, some partnerships worked brilliantly, while others produced only perfunctory results.

This complex workshop method is found most often in those manuscripts that were meant to impress by their size and the quantity of illustrations (e.g. the *Razmnāma*, *Tīmūrnāma* and *Akbarnāma*). The purpose of such volumes may have been to impress state visitors (manuscripts that seem to have been produced for Akbar himself have a different character). The *Akbarnāma* is the last of a series of historical manuscripts seemingly calculated to confirm the political power and dynastic grandeur of the Emperor. The *Ta'rīkh-i alfi* placed Akbar within the overall history of Islam, while the *Tīmūrnāma* proclaimed his role, which was by no means universally accepted, as direct descendant of the founder of the Timurid dynasty. The *Bāburnāma* glorified the first Mughal ruler, while the *Akbarnāma*, beginning with Babur's reign, concentrated on Akbar himself as the greatest of the Mughals. Many of the illustrations for this *Akbarnāma* were based on scenes in the *Tīmūrnāma*, suggesting that this work too was consciously intended to help to establish Akbar's claims to the Timurid throne.

262. Basawan, assisted by Chatar Muni: *Akbar Restraining the Enraged Elephant Hawa'i*, double page miniature, opaque colour on paper, 345×217 mm each, from an *Akbarnāma* manuscript, Akbar period, *c.* 1590 (London, Victoria and Albert Museum)

A group of exquisite and opulent manuscripts was produced at Lahore late in Akbar's reign, most of them illustrated Persian poetical anthologies. These manuscripts are smaller and more personal than the illustrated historical volumes. Most of the paintings are by one artist working alone. Akbar's taste is revealed in these works to be imperial and epicurean. One manuscript from the Lahore period that was certainly made for the Emperor's private use is a *Dīvān* (collected poems) of Anvari (1588; Cambridge, MA, Sackler Mus., MS. 1960.117.15). It is very small (the pages measure 140×73 mm) and uses a thin paper of extraordinarily fine quality. The 15 illustrations in the Anvari volume are individual works by the greatest artists in Akbar's workshops.

In the mid-1590s a series of similar books was produced at Lahore, of which the following are the most important: a *Khamsa* ('Five poems') of Nizami (1595; London, BL, Or. MS. 12208, and Baltimore, MD, Walters A.G., MS. W. 613); a *Bahāristān* ('Spring garden') of Jami (1595; Oxford, Bodleian Lib., MS. Elliot 254); a *Khamsa* of Amir Khusrau Dihlavi (1597–8; Baltimore, MD, Walters A.G., MS. W. 624, and New York, Met., MS. 13.288.33); and an *Anvār-i Suhaylī* (1596–7; Varanasi, Banaras Hindu U., Bharat Kala Bhavan, MS. 9069/1–27). These Lahori works all show superb technical control, with subtle, highly variegated colouring and expertise in the depiction of human interrelationships. There is also increasing concern for volume and spatial recession and for accurate, or at least convincingly portrait-like, characterizations. All of this bespeaks a patron and painters who knew exactly what they wanted and how they could achieve it. This is not an experimental art but a highly polished refinement of accepted taste, and the refinement and sophistication of that taste makes this phase of Mughal painting similar to the earlier imperial styles of Iran.

While in the *Ṭūṭīnāma* there were several different stylistic traditions in simultaneous use by its various artists, by the 1580s each manuscript (e.g. the *Tīmūrnāma*) had interior consistency but might differ markedly in character from other works. In the Lahore period illustrated pages from imperial manuscripts seem interchangeable. At this point, central control in the workshops was all-important.

The painter who seems to have been most important in this evolution was ʿABD AL-SAMAD, by whom there are inscribed paintings dated in the late 1580s. He also contributed to the 1595 manuscript of the *Khamsa* of Nizami. He was director of the Mughal workshop at the time of the *Ḥamzanāma*, and it was under his guidance that Mughal style came to maturity. The direction of Mughal painting increasingly came to follow the aims pursued by ʿAbd al-Samad. It is likely that the increased central control that became evident by the Lahore period can be attributed to this artist. He must have died in the last years of the 16th century.

The last great historical manuscript probably initiated by Akbar is a second *Akbarnāma* manuscript (*c.* 1596–7; London, BL, Or. MS. 12988; Dublin, Chester Beatty Lib., MS. 3; and dispersed). Its style stems directly from the developments at Lahore. Less rugged and experimental than the earlier illustrations to the same text, it is a quiet, epicurean work. Many of Akbar's greatest painters were still involved in its production, but the younger masters also took part. *Mughal Troops Chasing the Armies of Da'ud Khan* (Washington, DC, Freer; see fig. 263) demonstrates the artist's ability to depict forms twisting in space and his interest in the patterns of cloth and the placement of colour, rather than the violence and chaos of a battle, which is felt acutely throughout the first *Akbarnāma*.

A comparison of the *Tīmūrnāma* with the two *Akbarnāmas* is useful for understanding Mughal attitudes to historical texts. The *Tīmūrnāma* (*c.* 1580) provides compositional prototypes for several of the paintings in the first *Akbarnāma*, but the importance of this extends

263. *Mughal Troops Chasing the Armies of Da'ud Khan*, opaque colour on paper, 242×128 mm (full size); from an *Akbarnāma* manuscript, Akbar period, *c.* 1596–7 (Washington, DC, Freer Gallery of Art)

beyond simple compositional affiliation. When a scene showing Timur hunting becomes the prototype for a scene of Akbar hunting, it can perhaps be inferred that the two rulers are being linked and that Akbar is being proclaimed as Timur's successor. The second *Akbarnāma*, on the other hand, is quite independent of the first copy of that text, in compositional designs as well as in the polish of its technique. By the end of the 16th century the link between Akbar and Timur was no longer a point to be made, and artists could concentrate on a more direct presentation of events and settings. Architectural realism in this manuscript is such that several buildings shown are still recognizable. It was on the increased realism of late Akbar-period painting that subsequent Mughal styles were founded.

Akbar left Lahore in 1598. Painting during the remainder of his reign, judging by those works that survive, concentrated on texts and illustrations that had personal and intense meaning for the Emperor rather than dynastic or state documents. Books were almost all small in scale and had few illustrations. Space was shallower, and the painters concentrated even further on human portraiture and the psychology of human contact and interchange. A copy of the 15th-century Persian poet Jami's *Nafaḥāt al-uns* ('Fragrant breezes of friendship'; 1604–5; London, BL, Or. MS. 1362), recounting the lives of saints and Sufis, is a fine example of this new direction. It contains 17 illustrations, each the work of a single painter.

More important in defining the artistic transition that occurred when Akbar died in 1605 is a manuscript of the *Kulliyyāt* ('Complete works') of Sa'di (*c.* 1604; Geneva, Prince Sadruddin Aga Khan priv. col.). Several of its illustrations are by such master painters as LAL, one of the most prolific of all Akbar's artists, and they continue the visual and spatial complexity of which Akbar was fond; others, however, are by younger artists (e.g. Govardhan) who reached maturity only under Jahangir's patronage. The increasing calmness of this manuscript indicates the direction that Mughal style was to take in the coming decades.

BIBLIOGRAPHY

Abu'l-Fazl: *Āyīn-i Akbarī* [Annals of Akbar] (*c.* 1596–1602); Eng. trans. in 3 vols: i, trans. H. Blochmann, ed. S. L. Gloomer ([Calcutta], 1871/*R* Delhi, 1965); ii and iii, trans. H. S. Jarrett, ed. J. Sarkar (Calcutta, 1948–9/*R* Delhi, 1972–3)

——: *Akbarnāma* (*c.* 1596–1602); Eng. trans. H. Beveridge, 3 vols (Calcutta, 1907–39/*R* Delhi, 1972–3)

S. C. Welch: 'The Paintings of Basawan', *Lalit Kala*, x (1961), pp. 7–17

P. Chandra: *The Ṭūṭī-nāma of the Cleveland Museum of Art and the Origins of Mughal Painting* (Graz, 1976)

M. C. Beach: 'The Mughal Painter Daswanth', *A. Orient.*, xiii (1982), pp. 121–33

A. Schimmel and S. C. Welch: *Anvari's Divan: A Pocket Book for Akbar* (New York, 1983)

Akbar's India: Art from the Mughal City of Victory (exh. cat. by M. Brand and G. Lowry, New York, Asia Soc. Gals; Cambridge, MA, Sackler Mus.; Houston, TX, Mus. F.A.; 1985–6)

J. Seyller: 'The School of Oriental and African Studies *Anvār-i Suhaylī*: The Illustration of a *de luxe* Mughal Manuscript', *A. Orient.*, xvi (1986), pp. 119–51

M. C. Beach: *Early Mughal Painting* (Cambridge, MA, 1987)

J. Seyller: 'Scribal Notes on Mughal Manuscript Illustrations', *Artibus Asiae*, xlviii/3–4 (1987), pp. 247–77

Miniatures de l'Inde impériale: Les Peintres de la cour d'Akbar, 1556–1605 (exh. cat., Paris, Mus. Guimet, 1989)

J. Seyller: 'Codicological Aspects of the Victoria and Albert Museum *Akbarnāma* and their Historical Implications', *A. J.* [New York], xlix/4 (1990), pp. 379–87

——: 'Overpainting in the Cleveland Ṭūṭīnāma', *Artibus Asiae*, lii/3–4 (1992), pp. 283–318

MILO CLEVELAND BEACH

(c) Jahangir period. Akbar's son and successor, Jahangir (*reg* 1605–27), inherited an empire that was extensive, secure and well-administered. This allowed him the leisure to develop a deep and lively interest in art. A patron with a critical mind and sophisticated taste, he prided himself on his connoisseur's eye. He wrote in his memoirs, the *Tūzuk-i Jahāngīrī* (ii, pp. 20–21):

> As regards myself, my liking for painting and my practice in judging it have arrived at such a point that when any work is brought before me, either of deceased artists or of those of the present day, without the names being told me, I say on the spur of the moment that it is the work of such and such a man. And if there be a picture containing many portraits, and each face is the work of a different master, I can discover which face is the work of each of them. If any other person has put in the eyes and eyebrows of a face, I can perceive whose work the original face is and who has painted the eye and the eyebrow.

This passion for discernment influenced the development of painting. Though skilled at picking out the work of individual painters, Jahangir did not favour the practice of joint authorship that had prevailed in his father's time. Then it was common for a senior artist to draw the outline of a miniature, while a junior painter filled in the colour. Often a portrait specialist retouched important faces. Jahangir preferred each painting to be the work of an individual artist. Works produced for him thus tend to have a greater creative unity. Furthermore, he encouraged his painters to develop their particular talents and interests. His workshops consisted of small groups of highly talented specialists: for example, Manohar, Daulat and Bishan Das for portrait painting, Abu'l-Hasan for large court scenes, Mansur for natural history drawing.

This arrangement also suited Jahangir's preference for smaller books with fewer illustrations, all of a high quality. Rather than state documents meant to impress, the books produced for Jahangir seem intended for personal enjoyment. Remarkable for their refinement and serenity, they are characterized by delicate painting showing great technical skill, a devotion to detail and an emphasis on psychological penetration rather than narrative action. Faces show individuality and portraiture reaches new levels of realism.

Before 1605. Jahangir's individual tastes were already apparent when in 1587–8 he founded his own workshop, supervised by AQA RIZA, an émigré painter from Herat and the father of Abu'l-Hasan. Still a Mughal prince (known as Prince Salim until he chose the name Nur al-Din Jahangir on his accession in 1605), at the age of 20 he was already a self-confident patron and collector. In 1599 Prince Salim rebelled against his father and set up his own court at Allahabad, assuming the title Shah Salim. (The title 'Shah' had previously been reserved for the emperor.) His close confidants joined him there, and Aqa Riza was put in charge of the painting workshop. Of varied subject-matter, paintings produced for Jahangir at Allahabad include a *Dīvān* (collected poems) of Amir Najm al-Din Hasan Dihlavi (Baltimore, MD, Walters A.G., MS. W.650), completed in 1602, and a manuscript of the *Rāj kunwār* ('King's son'; Dublin, Chester Beatty Lib., MS. 37), a romance in Persian that is perhaps a translation of an Indian story, and a *Hālnāma* ('Book of ecstasy'; Paris, Bib. N., MS. Or. Smith-Lesonef 198), both completed in 1603–4. An *Anvār-i Suhaylī* ('Lights of Canopus'; London, BL, Add. MS. 18579), illustrating the animal tales commissioned some three decades earlier by Akbar, was begun in 1604, possibly at Allahabad, but completed only in 1610–11. An undated copy of the *Dvadasa bhāva* (dispersed), a Hindu text translated into Persian from Sanskrit, may be assigned to this period on stylistic grounds. Miniatures of the period have a mellow colour scheme and uncluttered composition. Stylistically, they fall mainly into two groups: those in which Persian elements are dominant (perhaps due largely to the influence of Aqa Riza, who favoured a Persian style) and those in a simplified Akbari style, resulting in part from the fact that most of the best painters had been employed by Akbar himself.

1605–1618/19. Jahangir was reconciled with his father and returned to the imperial court before Akbar died in 1605. On assuming the throne, he took charge of his father's enormous library and painting workshops. The work produced for Jahangir after he ascended the throne shows less Persian influence. His preference for specialist painters and for a small group of highly skilled artists led to important changes in the imperial workshops. It seems likely that many minor painters were released from imperial service and that some found employment with nobles while others migrated to nearby courts and outlying areas where local patrons had previously managed with talent available in the region. This dispersal of artists apparently contributed to the style now loosely called Sub-imperial or Popular Mughal (*see* §(ii) below). Maktub Khan, a scholarly courtier, was made superintendent of the library, and Jahangir's personal seal and autograph were put on the fly-leaves of many important volumes. A number of old and rare volumes were altered in a variety of ways: new miniatures and marginal decorations, including realistic figural drawings, were added, and some old miniatures were partially repainted. Manuscripts on which such work was carried out include a *Dīvān* (collected poems) of Hafiz (*c.* 1605; London, BL, Or. MS. 7573), a *Khamsa* ('Five poems') of Mir ʿAlishir Nava'i (Windsor Castle, Berks, Royal Col., MS. A.8), a *Būstān* ('Scented garden') of Saʿdi (Cambridge, MA, Philip Hofer priv. col.), a *Gulistān* ('Rose garden') of Saʿdi (1567; London, BL, Or. MS. 5302), the *Khamsa* of Nizami (1595; London, BL, Or. MS. 12208, and Baltimore, MD, Walters A.G., MS. W.613) and a *Shāhnāma* ('Book of kings'; dispersed).

A number of paintings have been identified that were probably intended for a *Jahāngīrnāma* ('History of Jahangir'). Unlike the illustrated narrative of the *Akbarnāma*, parts of the *Jahāngīrnāma* might have resembled an album, since Jahangir preferred commissioning individual paintings. The text of Jahangir's memoirs, known as the *Tūzuk-i Jahāngīrī*, survives, but if one or more illustrated manuscripts were completed, none of these remains intact. However, some dispersed paintings have been matched with the text. For example, *Jahangir Weighing Prince Khurram* (London, BM) represents the ceremonial weighing of the Prince (the future Emperor Shah Jahan) against gold and silver on his 16th birthday, celebrations that are described in Jahangir's memoirs for the year 1607–8, where he notes that they took place at Khurram's residence in the Urta garden at Kabul. The date of the picture is considerably later, as is *Jahangir Watching a Snake and Spider Fight* (Rampur, Raza Lib.), which illustrates a spectacle recorded in the Emperor's memoirs for the same year. *Jahangir Punishing Prince Khusrau* (Rampur, Raza Lib.), recording the trial of the Emperor's rebellious son, relates to an event described in Jahangir's memoirs for the year 1606–7.

In his memoirs Jahangir included detailed and sensitive descriptions of the animals and plants he saw. His interest in natural history led him to instruct his painters to make visual records of rare and unusual birds and animals he encountered. Many of these, according to a note in his memoirs, were to be included in the *Jahāngīrnāma*. For instance, in 1612 Jahangir sent to Goa an envoy, who on his return presented the Emperor with a collection of the rarities found there. One of these was a turkey cock. A fine painting of an elegant turkey survives (London, V&A) and is perhaps the one intended for the *Jahangīrnāma*. The painter Mansur specialized in bird and animal studies, and his mastery of natural history subjects is evident in such works as *Falcon on a Bird-rest* (see fig. 264). He based his studies on the observation of birds and animals and successfully captured their movements, as here in the twist of the falcon's neck.

Many paintings and specimens of calligraphy collected by Jahangir were bound into albums (*muraqqa*). Though albums were assembled somewhat earlier in Iran, and Akbar had portraits of his nobles and courtiers bound into an album (dispersed), Jahangir's are among the finest known Indian examples. So far one complete album, the *Muraqqaʿ-i gulshan* (Tehran, Gulestan Pal. Lib., MS. 1663/64), and 25 pages of a second (Berlin, Staatsbib. Preuss. Kultbes., MS. A.117), as well as a number of stray folios detached from these or other albums, have been identified. The albums contain Persian paintings by such artists as Bihzad, Qasim ʿAli and Mahmud Muzahib, works by Akbar's master painters, European engravings and

264. Mansur: *Falcon on a Bird-rest*, opaque colour on paper, 237×146 mm; from a dispersed Mughal album, Jahangir period, *c.* 1619 (Jaipur, Maharaja Sawai Man Singh II Museum)

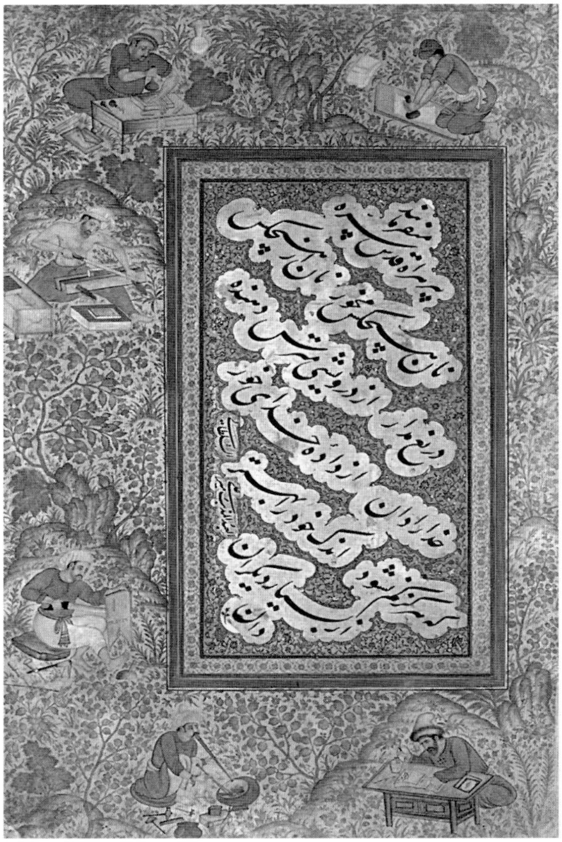

265. Decorated border (detail) showing workers in the Emperor's library, surrounding calligraphy by Mir ʿAli Herati, opaque colour on paper, 425×266 mm; detached folio from an album, Jahangir period, 1599–1600 (Washington, DC, Freer Gallery of Art)

paintings that flowed in with the Jesuit missionaries to Akbar's court, paintings commissioned by Jahangir himself and works by such renowned calligraphers as Mir ʿAli and Sultan ʿAli Mashhadi. When Jahangir failed to acquire a work he admired, he instructed his painters to copy it; these copies are also mounted in his albums. Through copying European art, a number of Jahangir's artists gained an understanding of its principles and absorbed these in their own work. Consequently, shading and modelling were used to give greater substance to figures, anatomical details became more realistic, spatial depth was explored through the use of European perspective, and painting took on a greater naturalism.

Much care was lavished on the preparation of these albums. The folios, which are bound in fine leather or lacquered covers, are highly glazed and fairly thick, made up of layers of light blue, pink or buff coloured paper. They are arranged so that facing pages of paintings alternate with calligraphy. Usually two to four paintings are mounted on a single folio, though in some cases one large painting is mounted alone. The margins are uniformly wide on the top, at the bottom and on the side further from the spine. Borders are decorated with exquisitely drawn creeping and flowering plants, hillocks and streams, birds and animals, curious clouds, arabesques and geometrical patterns in gold. These were inspired perhaps by the border decorations in a fine group of small manuscripts produced for Akbar in the 1590s, including the *Bahāristān* ('Spring garden') of Jami of 1595 (Oxford, Bodleian Lib., MS. Elliot 254), the above-mentioned *Khamsa* of the same year and the *Khamsa* of Amir Khusrau Dihlavi (1597–8; Baltimore, MD, Walters A.G., MS. W.624, and New York, Met., MS. 13.288.33). These, in turn, may have been inspired by Safavid border decorations. Especially where the openings in Jahangir's albums consist of two specimens of calligraphy, the borders often contain painted sketches of human figures: princes, nobles, foreigners, soldiers, hunters, falconers, dervishes, retainers and workers of the treasury, garden, mint or library (see fig. 265; see also fig. 260 above). Subjects taken from European paintings and engravings were also incorporated in these border decorations.

Portraiture was also highly developed in Jahangir-period painting and was practised by a number of skilled artists, including BISHAN DAS, NANHA, DAULAT, MANOHAR, ABU'L-HASAN, FARRUKH BEG and HASHIM. They created authentic likenesses, recording the wide variety of skin tones and facial features encountered at Jahangir's court. Portraits appeared in a variety of formats, from individual

266. Bishan Das: *Shah ʿAbbas Receiving the Mughal Envoy Khan ʿAlam*, opaque colour on paper, 365×250 mm, Jahangir period, *c.* 1619 (Boston, MA, Museum of Fine Arts)

standing figures shown in profile to court scenes with dozens of nobles and courtiers, each given an individual identity. Some portraits achieve a remarkable depth of psychological penetration; emotional currents are recorded in revealing glances and facial expressions. At times portraits could be startlingly realistic, as in the *Dying ʿInayat Khan* (study, Boston, MA, Mus. F.A.; finished painting, Oxford, Bodleian Lib.), which was commissioned by the Emperor, who had been moved by the sight of the dying man's emaciated features.

Jahangir sometimes went to great lengths to obtain authentic portraits. In 1613 Bishan Das was sent with Jahangir's official envoy, Khan ʿAlam, to Iran to the court of Shah ʿAbbas I and instructed to bring back authentic likenesses of the Shah, members of his family and important courtiers. Among the surviving signed depictions by Bishan Das of Shah ʿAbbas and his nobles is a miniature of *Shah ʿAbbas Receiving the Mughal Envoy Khan ʿAlam* (Boston, MA, Mus. F.A.; see fig. 266). Bishan Das's uncle, the painter Nanha, may have accompanied Prince Khurram on a similar mission to Udaipur. There are signed depictions by both artists of the *Maharana of Mewar* and his sons. A remarkable study of *Sultan Ibrahim ʿAdil Shah II* (*reg* 1579–1627) of Bijapur in the Deccan is preserved in a detached folio of a Jahangir album (Prague, Náprstek Mus. Asian, Afr. & Amer. Cult.). An inscription gives a date of 1610–11 and names the artist as Farrukh Beg, a Persian painter who migrated to India and worked for both Akbar and Jahangir. It has been suggested (Skelton, 1957) that Farrukh Beg travelled to the Deccan and worked there for some time for Ibrahim ʿAdil Shah. The portrait (possibly a copy of an original made for the Deccani Sultan) may have been presented to Jahangir on the artist's return.

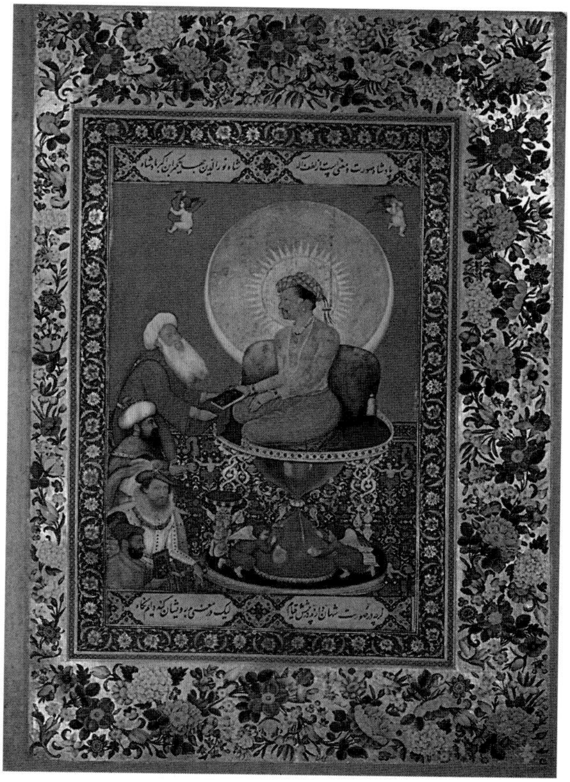

267. Bichitr: *Jahangir Preferring a Sufi Shaykh to Kings*, opaque colour on paper, 295×183 mm, Jahangir period, *c.* 1620 (Washington, DC, Freer Gallery of Art)

1618/19–1627. Paintings completed towards the end of Jahangir's reign and perhaps also intended for a *Jahāngīrnāma* are different in character. The Emperor's health was failing and his authority diminishing; the political situation was further strained by the rebellion of his ambitious son (the future emperor Shah Jahan). The mood of this later period is conveyed in two somewhat different types of paintings. Works showing Jahangir meeting ascetics and holy men and bestowing favours on them increased in number. Although this theme had occurred throughout Jahangir's reign, from his earliest days on the throne (when he was portrayed discussing religion and philosophy with the pious and learned and looking after the needs of sincere devotees), the numerous later examples may have been intended to emphasize the divine right to kingship of an ailing emperor. The second group of paintings is allegorical: Jahangir is shown in imaginary assemblies, performing impossible feats and receiving divine inspirations. In his memoirs Jahangir noted that some of these highly symbolic paintings were meant to represent his dreams.

In these allegorical works painters such as Abu'l-Hasan, BICHITR, GOVARDHAN and Hashim created a new style of miniature, giving form to Jahangir's imaginative world. One of the finest examples is Bichitr's work *Jahangir Preferring a Sufi Shaykh to Kings* (see fig. 267). Ignoring kings—including James I of England, Sultan Mehmed II of Turkey and possibly Sultan Ibrahim ʿAdil Shah II of Bijapur—Jahangir directs his attention to a Sufi shaykh. (The fourth figure, holding a painting, has alternatively been identified as the painter himself.) Jahangir is surrounded by an immense halo composed of the sun and moon, an allusion to his name Nur al-Din ('Light of religion'). Some of the imagery (e.g. the hourglass throne and the putti) is derived from the European prints Jahangir collected. Though the iconography of the painting presents the Emperor as glorified and divinely destined, the face is a telling portrait of an ageing, troubled and distant ruler.

Other allegorical paintings are equally extraordinary. In Abu'l-Hasan's *Jahangir's Dream of Shah ʿAbbas I's Visit* (*c.* 1618–20; Washington, DC, Freer; for illustration *see* ABU'L-HASAN), the two embracing rulers, who in fact never met, stand astride a globe. At the feet of Jahangir is a lion, at the feet of Shah ʿAbbas a lamb. When the wishful amiability of the picture proved false, and Shah ʿAbbas attacked the disputed province of Kandahar, Jahangir banned him from all future depictions. *Jahangir Shooting the Head of Malik ʿAmbar* (*c.* 1615–20; Dublin, Chester Beatty Lib.) shows the Emperor astride a globe shooting an arrow at the severed head of an enemy he never succeeded in conquering. Thus an ageing, contemplative emperor achieved in his paintings what was impossible in life. Drawing on his imaginative world, his painters created allegorical and highly symbolic imperial iconographies unique in the Islamic art of India.

BIBLIOGRAPHY

Nur al-Din Muhammad Jahangir: *Tūzuk-i Jahāngīrī* (*c.* 1624); Eng. trans. by A. Rogers, ed. by H. Beveridge (London, 1909–14/*R* Delhi, 1968)

R. Skelton: 'Mughal Artist Farrokh Beg', *A. Orient.*, ii (1957), pp. 393–411

R. Ettinghausen: 'The Emperor's Choice', *Essays in Honor of Erwin Panofsky*, ed. M. Meiss (New York, 1961), pp. 98–120

M. C. Beach: 'The Gulshan Album and its European Sources', *Bull. Mus. F.A., Boston*, lxiii/332 (1965), pp. 62–91

R. Skelton: 'Two Mughal Lion Hunts', *V&A Mus. Yb.* (1969), pp. 33–48

A. K. Das: 'Bishndas', *Chhavi, Golden Jubilee Volume: Bharat Kala Bhavan, 1920–1970*, ed. A. Krishna (Varanasi, 1971), pp. 183–91

B. W. Robinson: 'Shah Abbas and the Mughal Ambassador Khan Alan: The Pictorial Record', *Burl. Mag.*, cxiv (1972), pp. 58–63

A. K. Das: 'Ustad Mansur', *Lalit Kala*, xvii (1974), pp. 32–9

——: 'Some More Mansur Drawings', *Lalit Kala*, xviii (1977), pp. 26–31

——: *Mughal Painting during Jahangir's Time* (Calcutta, 1978)

M. C. Beach: 'The Mughal Painter Abu'l Hasan and Some English Sources of his Style', *J. Walters A.G.*, xxxviii (1980), pp. 6–33

P. Chandra: 'The Judgment of Khusrad in the Garden of Mīrzā Kāmrān: An Illustration to the *Tūzuk-i Jahāngīrī*', *Chhavi-2: Rai Krishnadasa Felicitation Volume*, ed. A. Krishna (Varanasi, 1981), pp. 43–6

ASOK KUMAR DAS

(d) Shah Jahan period. Formal perfection became the dominant characteristic of painting under Shah Jahan (*reg* 1628–58), whose principal aesthetic concern was architecture (*see* §III, 7(i)(a) above), projects aimed at expressing Mughal imperial grandeur. The technical precision characteristic of painting in his father's reign continued, but formal grandeur was achieved largely at the cost of the naturalism of the earlier period. Full of lovely detail, many of the paintings produced for him are nevertheless rather stiff and cold. As the masters of Jahangir's workshops disappeared one by one from the scene, it appears that little training was undertaken of new artists, and numbers declined.

Like his father, Shah Jahan was not particularly interested in book illustrations, as the imperial style had become an unsuitable medium for illustrating all but the grandest of manuscripts. However, two illustrated Persian literary texts by Sa'di, a *Būstān* ('Scented garden'; London, BL, Add. MS. 27262) and a *Gulistān* ('Rose garden'; Dublin, Chester Beatty Lib., MS. 22), were produced in 1628–9. In format they are similar to a *Gulistān* of Sa'di commissioned by Jahangir (*c.* 1610; Baltimore, MD, Walters A.G., 7 paintings, MS. W.668, and priv. cols.). In these two manuscripts the illustrations are restricted to horizontal sections in the middle of the page with calligraphy above and below surrounded by wide coloured borders with gold outlined drawings. The rich but stiff effect may explain why such experiments were not repeated. An exception is the repainting (*c.* 1635–40; priv. col., see 1985 exh. cat., no. 158) of the six miniatures in a Timurid *Gulistān* of Sa'di dated 1468, which had apparently been damaged.

Many of the greatest paintings of the period are found in a manuscript of the *Pādshāhnāma* ('History of the Emperor'; Windsor Castle, Royal Lib. MS. HB.149; folio numbers cited follow the Royal Library refoliation of *c.* 1980). The writing of the history of the reign proved more complicated than anticipated. In 1636 Muhammad 'Amin Qazvini began the official history of the first ten years (1628–38). On presentation his work was rejected, and 'Abd al-Hamid Lahauri was commissioned to rewrite Qazvini's work and to continue it. The revision of the first decade was apparently completed by 1641; the history of the second decade was finished by 1648. Lahauri died in 1654–5, and his work was taken up to the end of the third decade (1658) by his pupil Muhammad Waris. The single existing volume of the imperial copy of the *Pādshāhnāma*, in Lahauri's version, copied by the scribe Muhammad 'Amin of Mashhad and dated 1657–8, covers only the first decade of Shah Jahan's reign and contains 44 paintings. Another dozen or so paintings in various collections may have been intended for it or for subsequent volumes, which were never completed.

The manuscript presents many problems of interpretation. Whereas the years covered in the text are 1628–38, some seven paintings seem out of sequence: four refer to events before Shah Jahan's accession, and three, including the manuscript's frontispiece, show Shah Jahan in old age. Shortly after the text was copied, Shah Jahan was dethroned by his third son, Aurangzeb, in 1658. It has been suggested that the manuscript was put together rapidly at the close of the reign with whatever materials were available and that paintings of pre-accession events were inserted at random. However, studies have shown (see Begley, 1986) that these paintings relate to sequences in the text where Shah Jahan dreams of earlier events and that they are in the correct places. Two paintings intended for subsequent decades were inserted at appropriate spaces. Many of the paintings belong stylistically to the 1630s, whereas Lahauri's text of the first decade was not ready until 1641. Dated paintings were executed within a few years of the events depicted and must have been intended for Qazvini's original text. Only a few paintings are dated or datable to the 1640s. Delays in writing the text may have caused the Emperor to cease commissioning paintings for it shortly after 1640, when he was fully occupied with his building projects.

The quality of the paintings varies between brilliant and luminous studies by great masters of the studio (principally Balchand, Lalchand, Bichitr, Payag, 'Abid and Murad) and work that, while never less than competent, seems forced and derivative in comparison. For many years it was believed that this latter work was done in the 18th century, possibly in Lucknow (see Barrett and Gray and 1982 exh. cat.) since the manuscript had found its way there by 1776, where it was remargined and rebound. However, it now seems more likely that these pages were painted late in Shah Jahan's reign with what artists were left in the studio when the manuscript was finally being assembled.

Formal scenes at court predominate in the manuscript, and such scenes are rendered static by the lack of contact between the Emperor, depicted as a superior being, always in profile, nimbused and placed high on his throne platform, and the courtiers below. The actors and spectators in the lower part of the picture are mainly shown in full profile, so that they stare at each other across the usually empty centre of the picture. What little vitality there is in these formal and stylized compositions occurs only when one of the princes is received onto the upper platform in face-to-face contact with the Emperor or where some action is introduced among the courtiers below. The layered compositions resulting from this hierarchical necessity reinstate a traditional Indian compositional device of painting in several registers. The intersection of the horizontal lines with the vertical ones of pillars in these *darbar* scenes creates an oddly geometrical effect, as if complex compositions were no longer possible without such obvious schematization. The result is usually a brilliant surface lacking any depth. The necessity for accuracy in the depiction of the courtiers present, whose names would have been recorded in the court annals, meant that most of the faces were drawn from studies or *charba*s (perforated gazelle skins used with pounce) kept on file. In such circumstances, only the greatest artists, such as Balchand and Bichitr, could produce more than the mere brilliance of surface decoration. The basic design of such scenes was inherited from similar court settings in the illustrations to Jahangir's memoirs, but the balance between formalism and naturalism maintained by earlier artists shifted decisively towards the former.

The greatest technical developments occur in the less formal paintings. Battle scenes, which had been alien to Jahangir's aesthetic, were particularly valuable for artists seeking to expand the limitations of Mughal landscape painting. Renditions of both distant views and crowds were refined by artists such as Payag and ʿAbid, who were able to control the recession from foreground to background of the painting through purely painterly means, without needing text panels to conceal the awkward joins. In crowd scenes in the *Pādshāhnāma*, the sense of mass on mass of soldiers is vividly conveyed at last by blurring those at the back so that they merge into the background, a radical development in technique. In such paintings as the *Battle of Hooghly* (see fig. 268) or the *Aged Shah Jahan Hunting Deer* (fol. 165*r*), recession in landscape is effortlessly suggested, while in the latter the Emperor and his party merge into the landscape in the European manner.

Various albums were compiled for Shah Jahan, now for the most part dispersed. The Minto Album (London, V&A, IM. 8-1925 to 28-1925, and Dublin, Chester Beatty Lib., MS. 7) is possibly the only one that represents something like the original. Several other existing albums, for example the Wantage Album (London, V&A) and the Kevorkian Album (New York, Met., 55.121.10, and Washington, DC, Freer; see Welch and others), date only in part from the Shah Jahan period. The 17th-century paintings in these albums date from Shah Jahan's father's reign and his own; those from the latter are almost invariably portraits, datable up to the mid-1640s. They are mounted within illuminated borders decorated with clumps of flowers with heavy gold outlining. Although these floral borders are among the most charming work of the 17th-century Mughal studio, they are increasingly stiff and formal.

This formality of approach, even to the borders around portraits, is more apparent in the so-called Late Shah Jahan Album (dispersed), which contained paintings mainly of the 1650s. Here the personality of the sitter is often echoed in the small portraits in the borders, which are set against a background of flowers in lightly brushed gold. The combination was apparently an attempt to revive Jahangir-period border illuminations, but it suffers in the comparison. In Jahangir's albums, figural composition in colour is reserved only for pages of calligraphy, while inventive gold designs with very subdued colours are mainly used around

268. *Battle of Hooghly*, opaque colour on paper, 355×250 mm; from the *Pādshāhnāma*, Shah Jahan period, *c*. 1636–58 (Windsor, Windsor Castle, Royal Library, MS. HB.149, fol. 117*r*)

paintings. In the Late Shah Jahan Album the border figures echo the central portrait in their stiffness and formality.

In considering the work of the artists of the Shah Jahan period, a natural division is obvious around 1640, by which time most of the great painters inherited from the Jahangir period were no longer active; few works by them are dated or attributable much after that date. Abu'l-Hasan's last definite work is from about 1628, a portrait of *Shah Jahan* on the jewelled throne (Baltimore, MD, Walters A.G., W. 688, fol. 45). Other great artists of the Jahangir period, such as BALCHAND and BICHITR, were working in the 1630s, Bichitr up to about 1645, and both contributed splendid pages to the *Pādshāhnāma*. Neither shows any significant change from his earlier style: Balchand's work (fols 43*v*, 72*v* and 135*v*) is in characteristic soft tones, while Bichitr's single contribution (fol. 50*v*) is brilliantly lit and diamond hard. PAYAG contributed at least four pages to the *Pādshāhnāma* (fols 102*v*, 176*v*, 195*r* and 214*v*), which it seems best to consider as work of the 1630s. He later developed into a specialist in night scenes and holy men, showing in his rendering of light and shade considerable European influence. His subject range continued the work of GOVARDHAN, one of the greatest painters of the period still active up to 1640 but whose style and preoccupations seem to have excluded him from working on the *Pādshāhnāma*. ʿABID painted probably four paintings for the *Pādshāhnāma*, of which two remain in the

Windsor manuscript (fols 94*v*, 192*v*; others Oxford, Bodleian Lib. Ousely Add. 173, and Washington, DC, Sackler Gal.). His surviving work is attributable entirely to the 1630s and shows a brilliant if idiosyncratic command of surface detail. The artist whose greatest and almost only known work is found in the *Pādshāhnāma* is Murad, a pupil of Abu'l-Hasan, whom he sought to emulate in his realistic modelling and in the classical balance of his compositions. Apart from Murad, only Hashim and Chitarman (*fl c.* 1630–70) can be considered primarily as Shah Jahan-period artists working right up to the end of his reign and beyond, and their known work is confined almost entirely to portraits (e.g. Chitarman's portrait of *Dara Shikoh*, *c.* 1645; London, V&A, Minto Album). Hashim's work, in particular, epitomizes the late Shah Jahan style of portraiture, its subject caught in uninvolved, clinically brilliant detail against the lightest of backgrounds (for illustration *see* HASHIM).

Apart from work done for the Emperor, a considerable body of work has survived from his reign done for his eldest son, Dara Shikoh, in an album assembled between 1633, when the prince was 18 and married to his cousin Nadira Begum, and 1642, when it was formally presented to her according to an inscription on the fly-leaf in the prince's hand (London, BL, Orient. & India Office Lib., MS. Add. Or. 3129; see Falk and Archer). It represents the work of a small group of artists, of whom only one is named, Muhammad Khan (*fl* 1630s), who worked in a markedly Persian idiom. The album contains the usual mix of calligraphy and paintings, the latter being confined almost entirely to portraits of youths or maidens (none inscribed) and bird and flower studies.

BIBLIOGRAPHY

'Abd al-Hamid Lahauri: *Pādshāhnāma* (*c.* 1636–58); 2 vols (Calcutta, 1865–8; trans. by W. E. Begley and Z. A. Desai, in preparation)

B. A. Saksena: *History of Shahjahan of Delhi* (Allahabad, 1932)

D. Barrett and B. Gray: *Painting of India* (Geneva, 1963/*R* London, 1978)

T. Falk and M. Archer: *Indian Miniatures in the India Office Library* (London, 1981)

W. Komala: *The Windsor Castle Badshah Nama and its Place in the Development of Historical Painting during the Reign of Shah Jahan* (diss., Iowa City, U. IA, 1982)

The Art of the Book in India (exh. cat. by J. P. Losty, London, BL, 1982)

W. E. Begley: 'Illustrated Histories of Shah Jahan: New Identifications of Some Dispersed Paintings and Problems of the Windsor Castle Padshahnama', *Facets of Indian Art*, ed. R. Skelton and others (London, 1986), pp. 139–52

S. C. Welch and others: *The Emperor's Album: Images of Mughal India* (New York, 1987) [incl. Kevorkian Album]

W. E. Begley and Z. A. Desai, eds: *Shah Jahan Nama of Inayat Khan: An Abridged History of the Mughal Emperor Shah Jahan* (New Delhi, 1990/*R* Oxford, 1991)

(*e*) *Aurangzeb period.* The imprisonment of the emperor Shah Jahan in 1658 by his son Aurangzeb (*reg* 1658–1707) and the latter's victory in the ensuing fratricidal struggle brought to an end the great age of imperial patronage. Aurangzeb was a strict Sunni Muslim, and although his religious orthodoxy has often been cited as the cause of the decline of Mughal painting in the later 17th century, other factors were also important. It was only enlightened patronage that made possible the technical experiments that occurred early in Shah Jahan's reign and resulted in the grand paintings of his *Pādshāhnāma.* In its absence under Aurangzeb, Mughal painting stopped developing, and those artists who were left in the imperial studio remained content with the technical and stylistic plateau they had already reached. Their work is characterized by a retreat from realism and a reversion to more traditional Indian concepts of composition.

Artists must have remained in the imperial studio until at least 1680, when Aurangzeb became more orthodox and banned music and painting at his court. Despite his ostensible disapproval, portraits of Aurangzeb and other paintings of imperial quality were still produced, apparently under imperial patronage. Two fine scenes date from early in his reign, the *Darbar of the Emperor Aurangzeb* (*c.* 1658; Cambridge, MA, Fogg) and *Emperor Aurangzeb Shooting Nilgai* (*c.* 1660; Dublin, Chester Beatty Lib.). Paintings of obvious imperial provenance continued to be produced, whether from Delhi or from his encampments in the Deccan, where he pursued his continuous campaigns against the Deccani kingdoms and the Marathas. However, the absence of a connoisseur as patron meant that the aesthetic content of painting was reduced in favour of the practical art of portraiture. Some compositions have been simplified almost to the point of caricature when compared with those produced under Shah Jahan. The basic composition of standing portraits is unaltered, but apart from a few paintings by Hashim in his old age, the life has largely gone out of them. The sketchiness of background detail favoured by Hashim became general. Equestrian portraits, often with the horse rearing, became fashionable about 1680. Their theatricality was increased by streaks of orange and gold forming curtain-like swags at the top of the picture. Window portraits, with only the subject's head and shoulders showing within a painted window-frame, also became increasingly popular. Some of these paintings, for example *Equestrian Portrait of Aurangzeb* (*c.* 1680; London, BL, Orient. & India Office Lib.), are fine enough to have been made for the Emperor. However, much of this work, which survives in larger quantities than from earlier in the century, was done for private patrons taking advantage of the dispersal of artists from the imperial studio.

(*f*) *Later periods.* After Aurangzeb's death in 1707, the arts flourished in Delhi again. However, the power of the Mughal emperors was permanently weakened, and lavish patronage was no longer possible. An attempt to revive the formal *darbar* (audience) paintings of Shah Jahan's period under the emperor Bahadur Shah I (*reg* 1707–12) is seen in the painting *Bahadur Shah Enthroned* (priv. col.), but the rows of courtiers and horses lack grandeur. Considerably finer is a similar portrait of Bahadur Shah's second son, *'Azim al-Shan on a Jewelled Throne* (Paris, Bib. N.), a posthumous portrait made after his son Farrukhsiyar became emperor (*reg* 1712–19). Vividness of colour almost to the point of garishness is characteristic of paintings at this time.

Under the next emperor, Muhammad Shah (*reg* 1719–48), these vivid colours are contrasted increasingly with large areas of white used, for instance, for buildings, walls and garments. Muhammad Shah was the first emperor since Shah Jahan with a connoisseur's interest in painting. His reign was long enough for a distinctive style to flower. Fine artists such as Chitarman (*fl c.* 1720–30; a namesake of the Shah Jahan-period painter), Muhammad Faqirallah

Khan (*fl c.* 1740), Muhammad Afzal (*fl c.* 1740) and Govardhan (*fl c.* 1720–40; a namesake of the Jahangir-period artist) were active in the imperial studio. Formal scenes were foreign to Muhammad Shah's taste, and his own commissions show him to have been a pleasure-loving man, as in *Muhammad Shah Viewing a Garden* (Boston, MA, Mus. F.A.) in which he is shown being carried in a palanquin; *Muhammad Shah Making Love* by Chitarman (London, BL, Orient. & India Office Lib.); or *Muhammad Shah Smoking a Hooka in his Private Apartments* (Oxford, Bodleian Lib., MS. Douce Or. A3, fol. 14; see fig. 269).

Between 1733 and 1738 Govardhan painted the 37 miniatures of a manuscript of the *Kārnāma-i 'ishq* ('Book of affairs of love'; London, BL, Orient. & India Office Lib.), a romantic tale in Persian composed in 1731 by Rai Anand Ram, known by the pen-name 'Mukhlis', and dedicated to Muhammad Shah. An imperial illustrated manuscript is unusual for this period and allows an analysis of the artist's style. Govardhan has the sureness of technique of the best 17th-century painting, but his works display a hardness of line and icy formality and stiffness. His palette combines splashes of brilliant colour with cool greys, greens and whites. Other artists in their individual studies concentrated on scenes of entertainment, particularly involving groups of women. Few artists attempted to break out of the increasing standardization of subjects: terrace scenes with a Mughal pavilion occupying one side, with water, landscape and low hills beyond, form the standard settings. In all these pictures gentleness and calm seem to be the prevailing moods of the period, while a love of order is expressed in formally balanced compositions. The only experimentation is in the rendition of night scenes, using chiaroscuro techniques. This practice may reflect a direct borrowing from European prints or perhaps a second-hand influence from studying the works of such 17th-century Mughal masters as Payag. As usual, the artist made what he wanted of his models and did not slavishly copy them. The dark sky was embellished with stars and moon, and the figures are brilliantly lit by an often yellowish light but without any obvious light source. Characteristic of all the artists of the period is perfunctoriness of line and modelling; all follow accepted stylizations in drawing, little is freshly observed, while the minimal modelling yields a hard, masklike quality to faces.

The tranquillity of Delhi was shattered in 1739 by the invasion of the Afghan Nadir Shah, who had already made himself master of Iran. Delhi was sacked and the accumulated treasures of two centuries carted off to Tehran. The end of the imperial capital's inviolability was the signal for yet more marauders to descend on it from Afghanistan and from its hinterland. All who could flee from Delhi did so. Many painters made their way to the Punjab Hills, where the Mughal style greatly influenced the styles of the Rajput courts there (*see* §(iii) below); other artists fled eastward to Avadh and to Allahabad.

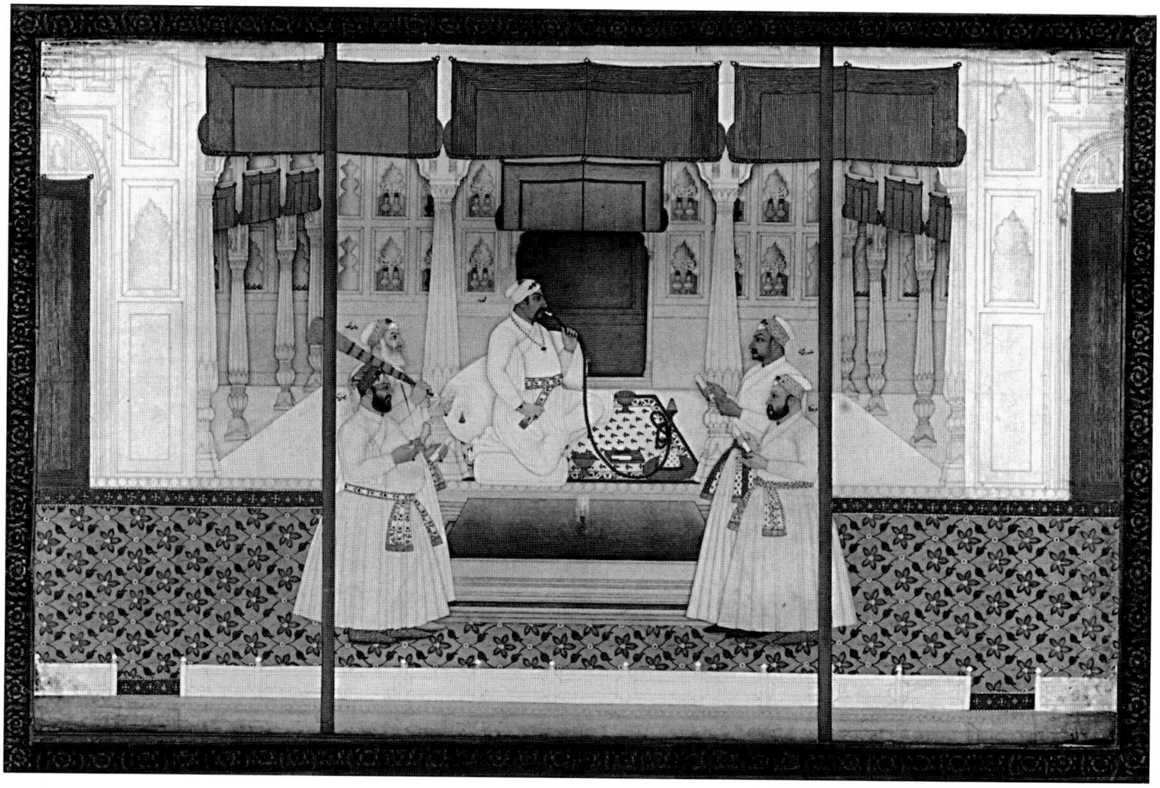

269. *Muhammad Shah Smoking a Hookah in his Private Apartments*, opaque colour on paper, 350×505 mm, *c.* 1719–48 (Oxford, Bodleian Library, MS. Douce Or. A3, fol. 14)

The complex history of this period in India does much to explain the changes in patronage and hence painting styles. Painting continued under Muhammad Shah in Delhi after 1739, albeit in a diminished but still recognizably Mughal way. The courts at Lucknow, Patna and Murshidabad became more or less independent from Delhi with the decline of Mughal power. All could be expected to have employed painters from the 1730s, but the products are so similar to imperial work from Delhi that they cannot readily be distinguished. State portraits of the type of *Muhammad Shah on a Terrace with Sa'adat Khan of Avadh* (London, BL, Orient. & India Office Lib.) are possibly representative of work done in Lucknow *c.* 1730.

The situation changed in 1758 when the heir apparent, Shah ʿAlam II, fled Delhi. He was proclaimed emperor in 1759 following his father's murder and spent the next 14 years in Allahabad under the protection of the nawab of Avadh and the British. The intellectual and artistic centre of northern India shifted eastwards with him, and scholars, poets and artists took refuge in Lucknow and Faizabad. The career of the artist Mihr Chand (*fl c.* 1765–75) exemplifies the pattern of dispersal. Mihr Chand painted Shah ʿAlam's portrait (Berlin, Pergamonmus.) in Patna or Allahabad in the 1760s in a purely Mughal style. He subsequently moved to Faizabad, the capital of Avadh for the last 10 years of the reign of Shujaʿ al-Daula (*reg* 1754–75), and it is at this time that he came under increasing European influence along with other artists working in Avadh. Not only were there European prints in abundance, there were actual professional European artists as well (*see* §(ix) below). There were also Europeans active in Avadh collecting and commissioning paintings, and as patrons they influenced their artists' work. Given this complex artistic situation in Avadh, there were several variant styles in use at the same time. The two greatest artists, Mihr Chand and Mir Kalan Khan (*fl c.* 1725–80) are vividly contrasted, although both are heavily influenced by European art, especially in the way they abandoned the traditional profile in favour of a more natural approach to facial representation. Mir Kalan Khan was trained in the Mughal style of Delhi (two attributed paintings, one dated 1724, are in the St Petersburg Album; St Petersburg, Acad. Sci.) but was in later life influenced by Dutch and Flemish landscape prints, the distant vistas of which he combined with his Mughal vision as in *Village Life in Kashmir* (London, BL, Orient. & India Office Lib.). He was also fascinated by Bijapuri paintings, and in such works as *Princess Watching a Maid Kill a Snake* (London, BL, Orient. & India Office Lib.) the women are dressed in rich Bijapur costumes of about 1600. It is debatable whether these are actually copies of Bijapur originals; rather, they may be idealized visions of alien societies, rather like his versions of European originals. Chiaroscuro plays a considerable part in his work, with brilliantly lit figures, illuminated from the side, positioned against dark backgrounds. He never seems to have assayed portraiture, and his rich style seems to have had no followers

In contrast, Mihr Chand is known mostly for his portraits, in which many European conventions were adopted. He made this change in his style apparently even before the English painter Tilly Kettle arrived in Faizabad in 1771–2, as is shown in his *European Courtesan* (*c.* 1765; London, BL, Orient. & India Office Lib.). All of Mihr Chand's portraits of Shujaʿ al-Daula have the same format as those by Tilly Kettle, but the conventional view that they are copied from Kettle's work is open to question. All Kettle's known portraits of Shujaʿ al-Daula make use of just two set positions of the face, and those of his son, Asaf al-Daula (*reg* 1775–97), only one, combined with extremely stiff and grand positions of the body. Although the nawab appreciated Kettle's work, he is unlikely to have sat for him very long, so that it is equally possible that Kettle based his iconography on existing portraits by Mihr Chand.

In his landscape work, Mihr Chand pioneered a flat plain behind the sitter, peppered with tiny trees and with small distant hills beyond, which was much used in later Lucknow painting and in Murshidabad. He had several followers, the most influential being Bahadur Singh, who was capable of producing work in several styles to suit his patrons. In addition to his master's style, he worked in a revivalist Mughal style of about 1630, with a lovely soft technique reminiscent of Balchand, while for European patrons he produced precise tinted drawings. Other artists active in Lucknow in 1760–90 made similar changes of style to suit their patrons. Thereafter, the increasingly Europeanized taste of the nawabs and the nobility, as well as British patronage, changed the style into a variant of Company school painting (*see* §(ix)(f) below).

In Farrukhabad, between Lucknow and Delhi, a variant of the Avadh style flourished briefly during the reign of Ahmad Khan Bangash (*reg* ?1749–71), a Rohilla Afghan whose ancestors had migrated to India a century earlier. A small group of pictures centred round the activities of the nawab, and, briefly, his successor, show great fondness for autumnal colouring and elongated, sharp-featured women (e.g. London, BL, Orient. & India Office Lib. and V&A; Paris, Bib. N.; and other collections).

The city of Murshidabad in western Bengal was the political centre of eastern India from 1704. There is no conclusive evidence of painting there during the earlier 18th century, but under ʿAlivardi Khan (*reg* 1740–56) a distinct variant of late Mughal painting developed. Works such as *Nawab ʿAlivardi Khan Hunting Roebuck* and *Nawab ʿAlivardi Khan and Companions Seated on a Garden Terrace* (both London, V&A) were probably commissioned by him. Mughal artists probably migrated eastwards from Patna, where there is some evidence of painting activity earlier in the century. Under the successors of ʿAlivardi Khan to 1770, a style emerged, highly formal and much colder than the contemporary Avadh style but with, if anything, an even more brilliant use of colour. The landscape style is quite distinctive, often with huge rounded hills composed of separate ribbons of colour, and with wonderfully vivid trees (e.g. London, BL, Orient. & India Office Lib. and V&A). Unlike the style of Avadh with its plethora of artists' names, scarcely any names of artists from Murshidabad are known. The subject-matter is confined almost entirely to *Rāgamālā* painting (illustrating the modes of Indian music) and to portraiture in the earlier period (1750–70). With the waning power and interest of the nawabs, the British in Calcutta and in other stations on the river between the two cities became much more important as patrons. Illustrations of Hindu themes became more numerous from 1770 onwards. After this date there is a rapid stylistic degeneration. As in Lucknow, British patronage changed the basic elements of technique, substituting washes of watercolour for the meticulous brushwork of the indigenous style.

Patna, another centre where Mughal painting flourished in northern India, was by 1760 part of the dominions of the nawab of Bengal. A group of artists with links to Murshidabad worked there in the 1760s, particularly Dip Chand, who worked especially for a Company official named William Fullarton. A portrait of a British official (London, V&A) signed by Dip Chand probably depicts Fullarton himself. Slightly later another group of artists from Patna was employed in Calcutta by Lady Impey, wife of the Chief Justice Sir Elijah Impey, in the portrayal of natural history subjects among others. Two works painted for her by Shaykh Zain al-Din, *Lady Impey Supervising her Household* and the *Impey Children and their Attendants* (Impey priv. col., see 1985 exh. cat.), are among the finest of late 18th-century Mughal paintings.

The return of Shah ʿAlam to Delhi in 1771 under the patronage of the Marathas did something to stabilize the Mughal imperium for a brief period and to attract some artists back to Delhi. However, the Mughal defences were powerless to stop the Rohilla bandit Ghulam Qadir from seizing the Emperor and putting out his eyes in 1788 on discovering that the fabled treasures of the Mughals were all gone. Few paintings of distinction were produced in Delhi at this period, apart from a particularly moving one of the blind emperor sitting on his pastiche throne (USA, priv. col., see 1978 exh. cat., no. 43) by Khairallah (*fl c.* 1790–1800). In 1803 the Maratha presence in Delhi was replaced by a British one, and Shah ʿAlam and his successors, Akbar II (*reg* 1806–37) and Bahadur Shah II (*reg* 1837–58), lived out the twilight of the Mughal empire under its protection. In the peace that came to Delhi the arts flourished again, and a handful of fine artists recorded the end of the Mughals, in particular Ghulam Murtaza Khan (*fl c.* 1800–35) and his (probable) son Ghulam ʿAli Khan (*fl c.* 1815–55). Both men worked for European patrons and perforce adopted many of the techniques of European portraiture and landscape. Their realism spills over into their work for the Mughals as, for instance, in a fine *darbar* scene of Akbar II by Ghulam Murtaza Khan (London, BL, Orient. & India Office Lib.), whose son seems to have inherited his father's position as court painter. The last great Mughal paintings are Ghulam ʿAli Khan's 'coronation' portraits of *Bahadur Shah II* from 1837; there are several versions of this work (signed version, Switzerland, priv. col.), in which the Emperor is shown seated on his throne in front of Shah Jahan's scales of justice in the Delhi palace. The Mughal school retained its meticulous attention to detail along with its technique to the last, but despite the static formalism inherited from the 17th century, the portraits are expressed in the language of European realism; these faces convey not only self-knowledge, but also knowledge of the imminent end.

BIBLIOGRAPHY

E. Kühnel: 'Mir Tschand, ein unbekannter Mogulmaler', *Berliner Mus.: Ber. Staatl. Mus. Preuss. Kultbes.*, xliii (1922), pp. 115–22
——: *Indische Miniaturen aus dem Besitz der Staatlichen Museen zu Berlin* (Berlin, 1937)
R. Skelton: 'Murshidabad Painting', *Marg*, x (1956), pp. 10–12
Room for Wonder: Indian Painting during the British Period, 1760–1880 (exh. cat by S. C. Welch, New York, Asia House Gals and Amer. Fed. A., 1978)
M. Archer: *India and British Portraiture, 1770–1825* (London, 1979)
R. Hickmann and V. Enderlein: *Indische Albumblätter, Miniaturen und Kalligraphien aus der Zeit der Moghul-Kaiser* (Leipzig, 1979)
Arts of Bengal (exh. cat., London, Whitechapel A.G., 1979)
India: Art and Culture, 1300–1900 (exh. cat. by S. C. Welch, New York, Met., 1985), nos 281c–d

J. P. LOSTY

(ii) Sub-imperial styles. The great quantity of paintings produced in the imperial Mughal workshop at the end of the 16th century sparked an unprecedented interest in painting in the Mughal style among some members of the nobility and merchant class. Sub-imperial Mughal painting, as the work produced for these patrons is known, broadly follows the subject-matter and style of imperial painting (*see* §(i) above) but shows a greater proclivity to illustrate subjects from Hindu literature and to employ the simpler compositional patterns and brighter colours of traditional Indian painting. It flourished as a hybrid style combining Mughal and indigenous Indian elements from *c.* 1600 to 1620, a period that coincides with the reduction of the size of the imperial atelier and the narrowing of its range of subjects under Jahangir (*reg* 1605–27). Although the patrons, artists and provenance of most Sub-imperial paintings are unknown, one major patron has been identified: ʿAbd al-Rahim Khan-i Khanan (1561–1626/27), the commander-in-chief of the Mughal armies under both Akbar and Jahangir (*see* §(a) below). The names of a few other nobles have been associated with specific manuscripts (*see* §(b) below). A variant strain of Sub-imperial painting is identified as Popular Mughal, since it appears to have been less directly dependent on models and developments in the imperial atelier (*see* §(c) below). After *c.* 1620 the hybrid style of Sub-imperial painting was subsumed within the increasingly distinct regional schools, such as those of Rajasthan, the Punjab Hills and central India.

(a) Works created under ʿAbd al-Rahim Khan-i Khanan. (b) Works created under other Sub-imperial patrons. (c) Popular Mughal painting.

(a) Works created under ʿAbd al-Rahim Khan-i Khanan. Mughal nobles commonly owned libraries, but it is only in ʿAbd al-Rahim's case that it can be documented that the library establishment included an independent workshop for the production and illumination of books. Some 20 artists worked for ʿAbd al-Rahim over a period of nearly 30 years, and 7 manuscripts can be associated with him. The 130 illustrations preserved in a copy of the Hindu epic the *Rāmāyaṇa* (Washington, DC, Freer, MS. 07.271) commissioned by ʿAbd al-Rahim are the earliest known Sub-imperial paintings, with the exception of a single painting by the artist Mushfiq (1595–6; London, BM, 1947.10–11.02). In a lengthy note on the *Rāmāyaṇa*'s flyleaf, ʿAbd al-Rahim described the valorous Rama, the circumstances by which the copy was made in emulation of Akbar's profusely illustrated manuscript of the same Hindu text (Jaipur, Maharaja Sawai Man Singh II Mus., MS. AG. 1851-2026; *see* §(i)(b) above), the number of paintings and folios, the dates of the project's inception (1587–8/AH 996) and completion (1598–9/AH 1007) and

the name of the supervisor, Maulana Shakibi Imami. This detailed inscription has long been considered evidence that ʿAbd al-Rahim took a great personal interest in painting, so much so that he began work on his copy of the *Rāmāyaṇa* even before the imperial manuscript was completed, apparently *c.* 1591–2. However, five dates within the manuscript, ranging from 1597–8 (AH 1006) to 1604–5 (AH 1013), contradict ʿAbd al-Rahim's chronology, thereby undermining the precision of his testimony and the assumption of active connoisseurship.

The style of the illustrations changed during the manuscript's seven-year production, apparently as different artists assumed control of the project. Paintings early in the manuscript, particularly those by Govardhan, compare closely to contemporary imperial works. For instance, in the painting *Rishyashringa Travelling to Ayodhya with Shanta* (see fig. 270), Rishyashringa, his wife and their attendants wear strongly modelled Indian garments; their fine features in profile are set off from the brightly coloured ground by considerable shading. The multicoloured outcrop, gold- and blue-streaked sky and subtle articulation of the trees and hills provide further links with imperial painting and distinguish this artist's work from the schematic forms and insistent registration that are more characteristic of the rest of the manuscript.

270. Govardhan: *Rishyashringa Travelling to Ayodhya with Shanta*, Sub-imperial style, opaque colour on paper, 265×139 mm; from a *Rāmāyaṇa* manuscript, *c.* 1597 (Washington, DC, Freer Gallery of Art, MS. 07.721, fol. 22*r*)

The artists Shyama Sundara and Fazl each played dominant roles in large portions of the painting cycle. Their compositions are generally marked by arbitrary, flat zones of colour, their figures by ungainly features and schematic drapery. Nonetheless, the sheer boldness of design and brilliance of colouring of several of their paintings, as well as others by Mushfiq, Nadim, Yusuf ʿAli, Qasim and Kamal, rival the visual impact of many imperial works. Indeed, it is clear from stylistic evidence in the *Rāmāyaṇa* in Jaipur and the *Bāburnāma* of 1597–9 (New Delhi, N. Mus.) that at least two artists active in ʿAbd al-Rahim's workshop, Ghulam ʿAli and Banavari, were once members of the imperial atelier.

An album with 30 paintings (Oxford, Bodleian Lib., MS. Laud. Or. 149), whose provenance was once one of the most controversial issues of early 17th-century Indian painting, can also be linked with the atelier of ʿAbd al-Rahim. Known as the Laud *Rāgamālā* (18 of the paintings are part of a *Rāgamālā* cycle, a 'garland of ragas' illustrating the musical modes), the album was given by Archbishop Laud to the Bodleian Library in 1640, the earliest date a group of Indian paintings entered a European collection. One painting is inscribed with the name of Kala Pahar, a painter whose work is otherwise known only in ʿAbd al-Rahim's *Rāmāyaṇa*. The 18 paintings of the *Rāgamālā* series show strong connections to the vigorous figure types of Fazl and Qasim. The album also contains illuminated borders with pronounced affinities to other manuscripts produced by the atelier.

A dispersed manuscript of the *Razmnāma* ('Book of war'; the Persian translation of the Hindu epic the *Mahābhārata*), dated on the basis of two miniatures to 1616–17, develops many features seen in the Freer *Rāmāyaṇa* and the Laud *Rāgamālā*. ʿAbd al-Rahim's commission of a copy of the *Razmnāma* was certainly inspired by Akbar's imperial manuscript of the Hindu epic (1582–6; Jaipur, Maharaja Sawai Man Singh II Mus., MS. AG. 1683–1850), the painting cycle of which it reflects quite closely. Sizeable panels of text are often incorporated in the compositional field, a layout that had fallen out of favour in imperial painting by the late 1580s. Like illustrations in the *Rāmāyaṇa*, the compositions of the *Razmnāma* regularly employ zones of flat colour in the hilly backgrounds, but the units are smaller, and the effect is thus less mannered. Similarly, the draughtsmanship of figures and settings alike surpasses that of paintings produced by the same artists a decade before.

ʿAbd al-Rahim's artists used a more Persianate style of painting to illustrate manuscripts of classical Persian poetry, probably because this correlation of style and subject was considered appropriate. A *Panj Ganj* ('Five treasures') of Jami (Dublin, Chester Beatty Lib., MS. 20), a poetical manuscript copied in 1520 by Sultan ʿAli, was decorated by Mushfiq in 1603–4 (AH 1012) with corner illuminations of delicate birds, animals and a few figures.

A *Khamsa* ('Five poems') of Amir Khusraw Dihlavi (Berlin, Dt. Staatsbib., MS. Or. 1278) contains a note written on the fly-leaf by 'Abd al-Rahim that describes the piecemeal purchase of the manuscript in Gujarat beginning in 1603–4. It is evident from the note that he based his high estimation of its value on his erroneous belief that the famous Sultan 'Ali wrote the manuscript and that the legendary Bihzad painted it. His atelier refurbished the manuscript, which is recorded as entering the library in 1617 (AH 1026); a detached painting by Mushfiq now in a private collection is dated 1610–11 (AH 1019). The seven miniatures still in the manuscript are the most refined works of the atelier. 'Abd al-Rahim's artists also painted 90 miniatures for a *Shāhnāma* ('Book of kings'; 1616; London, BL, Add. MS. 5600), and a *Zafarnāma* ('Book of victory'; *c.* 1610; priv. col.) can also be attributed to his workshop. Though 'Abd al-Rahim is the best known Sub-imperial patron, painting was apparently not his main interest. His own literary accomplishments, avid sponsorship of poetry and the notes by him on the fly-leaves of several manuscripts (which contain a number of errors) support the view that his interest in books focused neither on the style nor even presence of the illustrations, but on their texts, calligraphy and sheer material value.

(b) Works created under other Sub-imperial patrons. A few other manuscripts can be associated with the names of specific nobles. Two sparsely illuminated manuscripts dated to 1613 (AH 1022), a *Khamsa* of Nizami and a *Silsilat al-Dhahab* ('Chain of gold') of Jami (both Dublin, Chester Beatty Lib., MS. 14 and MS. 8), bear inscriptions with the respective names of Nawab Bahadur Khan and Nawab Murtaza Quli Bukhari . The former was written at Agra, the most likely provenance of many Sub-imperial works. The colophon of an astrological manuscript, the *Kitāb-i Sā'at* ('Book of time'), states that it was written for Mirza 'Aziz Koka Muhammad Khan 'Azam (*c.* 1542–1624) at Hajipur, near Patna, in 1583 (AH 991). Mirza 'Aziz Koka was Akbar's foster brother. The style of the 12 miniatures illustrating the manuscript is so close to that of a *Ṭūṭīnāma* ('Tales of a parrot'; *c.* 1580; Dublin, Chester Beatty Lib., MS. 21), apparently produced for Akbar, that it is probable that imperial artists were assigned temporarily to this project. The possibility that imperial artists produced paintings for a manuscript commissioned by a non-imperial patron raises the question of whether every manuscript produced in the imperial atelier or by its artists was made for the emperor himself and underscores the speculative nature of the identification of other patrons. The rarity of inscriptions on Sub-imperial works other than those produced for 'Abd al-Rahim has made it difficult to trace the links between Sub-imperial painters and the Mughal atelier. However, a painter's level of experience with the imperial idiom can usually be ascertained by the thoroughness of his grasp of its formal features.

Two other manuscripts associated with Mirza 'Aziz Koka (see 1982 exh. cat.) raise further questions about non-imperial patronage. The first is a copy of the *Anvār-i Suhaylī* ('Lights of Canopus'; London, BL, Or. MS. 6317; see fig. 271) with an inscription stating that it was written at Ahmadabad in 1600–01 (AH 1009). Mirza 'Aziz Koka

271. *The Tortoise Borne by the Geese into the Sky*, Sub-imperial style, opaque colour on paper, 239×178 mm; from an *Anvār-i Suhaylī* manuscript, 1600–01 (London, British Library, Or. MS. 6317, fol. 56*v*)

was at that time governor of the wealthy province of Gujarat with its capital at Ahmadabad. However, the L-shaped format, dessicated figures, bright pastel ground overlaid with decorative tufts, and spatial incongruities of the manuscript's 43 illustrations bear little relation to the earlier miniatures of the *Kitāb-i Sā'at.* Mirza 'Aziz Koka may have been the patron, but it seems he employed different artists. A manuscript of the *Zafarnāma* (1600–01; London, BL, Or. MS. 1052) with stylistically similar illustrations was probably produced by the same atelier as the *Anvār-i Suhaylī.* The simple compositions and blank gazes of the figures in both manuscripts demonstrate a greater affinity with conventions current in the 1580s than with those of contemporary imperial painting. That even the most accomplished Sub-imperial painting is marked by this generally old-fashioned quality suggests that an artist's awareness of the rapid stylistic developments of the imperial atelier dropped off immediately after he left the stimulation of its collective activity.

Sub-imperial copies of the *Shāhnāma* are surprisingly abundant. Their illustrations are characterized by Persianate compositional and figural elements repeated schematically. The best of these manuscripts (Berlin, Dt. Staatsbib., MS. Or. fol. 172) exhibits a subtle pastel palette and carefully drawn figures accentuated by eddies in the green ground. More representative is a copy (1601; New York, Met., MS. 13.228.22) whose 72 small illustrations display cruder, oversized figures set against simple backgrounds. The absence of any information about the artists and patrons of the numerous examples of this text implies that Sub-imperial painting had become commercial in nature, produced not only for intimates of the court but increasingly for an anonymous market of merchants and others eager to own decorated books.

(c) Popular Mughal painting. This vein of Sub-imperial painting appears to have been less closely connected with developments in the imperial atelier. Within the stylistic spectrum, some examples employ more Mughal features than others. A set of *Rāmāyaṇa* paintings (dispersed, e.g. New Delhi, N. Mus.) contains miniatures that are quite close to imperial paintings in both colour and fineness of execution. The figures, typically endowed with small heads with expressive, linear features, often assume active poses in complex groups. Subtle formations of rocks and trees create more naturalistic spatial progressions than in the landscapes of most Sub-imperial paintings. Conversely, such architectural settings as court scenes or the besieged fortress of Lanka are flattened by the prominent use of bright geometric patterns and large areas of gold. This unique series was initially dated to *c.* 1610, but most scholars now agree that it may well be as early as *c.* 1595.

A number of *Rāgamālā* series illustrated in the first two decades of the 17th century demonstrate the increasingly superficial understanding of the imperial idiom in Popular Mughal painting. A dispersed series dated 1605 enlists the typical vertical format with short Sanskrit captions in the upper border. The figures retain the basic facial features and costumes of Mughal painting but without any semblance of modelling, and the shallow settings are articulated with crudely drawn details and matte pastel colours. The 34 miniatures of a *Rāgamālā* set known as the Manley *Rāgamālā* (*c.* 1610; London, BM, 1973.9.17) include richer colours, more developed architectural settings and figures whose squat proportions and squarish heads are akin to those of early 17th-century Rajasthani painting. Noting such resemblances to later, better-documented schools, several scholars have advanced various regions in north India as centres of Popular Mughal painting. The range of two Hindi dialects used in these *Rāgamāla* sets suggests Uttar Pradesh (possibly even Agra) as their provenance. Other areas cited as centres of Popular Mughal style include Rajasthan and Bundelkhand.

The only secure provenance for this variety of Popular Mughal painting, however, is Agra, the name inscribed in a long scroll illustrated by Ustad Salivahana in 1610 on behalf of a Jaina community (2857×322 mm; Ahmadabad, L. D. Inst. Indol.; see fig. 272). The scroll represents two scenes: the proclamation of an order by Jahangir prohibiting the slaughter of animals during a Jaina sacred feast and its joyous reception among the Jaina community. The artist claimed proudly that he was a member of the imperial atelier and that he had actually witnessed the Emperor's order. He emphasized the documentary nature of the painting with a quite convincing portrait of Jahangir and numerous labels identifying the members of the Emperor's entourage, who are arrayed in hierarchical registers across the narrow scroll. The lively, albeit flatly rendered courtiers, musicians and gatekeepers are all stock characters of Mughal painting, but their even positioning across the broad zones of the green and dull pink ground exemplifies the uncomplicated figural groupings characteristic of Popular Mughal painting. Below this scene, Salivahana depicted an imaginary one of Vijayasena Suri, a renowned Jaina monk, being presented with the imperial decree. The subsequent celebrations among the Jaina nuns and laity, including brightly coloured musicians and a woman scattering rice, appear at the bottom of the scroll.

272. Ustad Salivahana: *The Jaina Community Celebrating the Proclamation of the Emperor Jahangir* (detail), Popular Mughal-style scroll, opaque colour on paper, 2857×322 mm (full size), 1610 (Ahmadabad, L. D. Institute of Indology)

Ustad Salivahana emerges even more clearly from the anonymity of most Popular Mughal artists as the painter of illustrations in a manuscript of the *Śalibhadra caritra* (Calcutta, priv. col.), the colophon of which indicates that it was made in 1624 for a family of Jaina merchants. The treatment of faces, particularly the enlarged eyes of figures seen in profile, is highly reminiscent of contemporary painting produced in Rajasthan, especially in the school of Mewar (*see* §(iii)(a) below). Although Salivahana must rank among the most accomplished of Popular Mughal artists, the limited aspects of Mughal naturalism in his two known works make his claim to training in the imperial atelier suspect.

The fact that Popular Mughal painting was produced in Agra, the Mughal capital, demonstrates that such works need not be provincial and suggests that artistic distance from the imperial idiom need not correspond with geographic distance. The heightened awareness of the customs of the nearby Mughal court and the ready availability of artists with some knowledge of the prestigious imperial idiom must have made Agra the most important centre of Sub-imperial Mughal painting.

BIBLIOGRAPHY

T. Arnold and A. Grohmann: *The Islamic Book* (Leipzig, 1929)
A. Coomaraswamy: *Catalogue of the Indian Collections of the Museum of Fine Arts, Boston*, vi (Cambridge, MA, 1930), pp. 19–29
M. Haq: 'The Khan-i Khanan and his Painters, Illuminators, and Calligraphists', *Islam. Cult.* (1931), pp. 621–30
P. Nahar: 'An Illustrated Salibhadra MS.', *J. Ind. Soc. Orient. A.*, i (1933), pp. 63–7
T. W. Arnold: *The Library of A. Chester Beatty: A Catalogue of the Indian Miniatures*, 3 vols, rev. and ed. by J. V. S. Wilkinson (London, 1936)
H. Stooke and K. Khandalavala: *The Laud Ragamala Miniatures* (Oxford, 1953)
P. Chandra: 'A Series of Ramayana Paintings of the Popular Mughal School', *Prince of Wales Mus. Bull.*, vi (1959), pp. 64–70
——: 'Ustād Sālivāhana and the Development of a Popular Mughal Art', *Lalit Kala*, viii (1960), pp. 25–46
Miniature Painting: A Catalogue of the Exhibition of the Sri Motichand Khajanchi Collection (exh. cat. by K. Khandalavala, M. Chandra and P. Chandra, New Delhi, Lalit Kala Akad., 1960)
R. Ettinghausen: *Paintings of the Sultans and Emperors of India from American Collections* (New Delhi, 1961)
R. Pinder-Wilson: 'An Illustrated Mughal Manuscript from Ahmadabad', *Paintings from Islamic Lands*, ed. R. Pinder-Wilson (Oxford, 1971), pp. 160–71
S. Andhare: 'An Early Ragamala from the Kankroli Collection', *Prince of Wales Mus. Bull.*, xii (1973), pp. 58–64
E. Binney III: *Indian Miniature Painting from the Collection of Edwin Binney III: The Mughal and Deccani Schools with Some Related Sultanate Material* (Portland, 1973)
S. Digby: 'A Shah-nama Illustrated in a Popular Mughal Style', *The Royal Asiatic Society: Its History and Treasures* (London, 1979), pp. 111–15
R. Cran: 'The Manley Ragamala: An Album of Indian Illustrated Modes', *BM Yb.*, iv (1980), pp. 181–206
The Imperial Image: Paintings for the Mughal Court (exh. cat. by M. C. Beach, Washington, DC, Freer, 1981–2)
The Art of the Book in India (exh. cat. by J. P. Losty, London, BL, 1982)
J. Seyller: 'Model and Copy: The Illustration of Three *Razmnama* Manuscripts', *Archvs Asian A.*, xxxviii (1985), pp. 37–66
——: *The Freer Rāmāyaṇa and the Atelier of 'Abd al-Rahīm* (diss., Cambridge, MA, Harvard U., 1986)
——: 'A Subimperial Manuscript: The *Ramayana* of 'Abd al-Rahim Khankhanan', *The Legend of Rama: Artistic Visions*, ed. V. Dehejia (in preparation)

JOHN SEYLLER

(iii) Styles of Rajasthan and contiguous regions. The painting styles of Rajasthan and contiguous regions (see fig. 273) exhibit wide variety. Some styles (e.g. Mewar and Malwa) are the inheritors of the pre-Mughal *Caurapañcāśikā* group idiom (*see* §3(ii)(e) above) and carry its essentially conservative values of flatness, abstraction, bold line and bright colour into the 17th century and beyond. Other styles (e.g. Bundi, Bikaner and Kishangarh) exhibit a refined line and controlled palette derived directly from Mughal painting (*see* §(i) above). In spite of their apparent differences, the extremes of style in this area should not be considered as polar opposites but as ends of a stylistic continuum. □

(a) Mewar. (b) Malwa. (c) Bundi, Kota and related schools. (d) Bikaner. (e) Amer, Jaipur and Shekhavati. (f) Kishangarh. (g) Marwar. (h) Gujarat. (i) Kachchh.

(a) Mewar. The kingdom of Mewar was one of the most important and prolific centres of Rajasthani court painting. The style that flourished at Udaipur, its last capital, from the 17th century or earlier until the mid-20th century is characterized by bold outline drawing, a vibrant palette and a robust use of such semi-archaic compositional conventions as multiple narration, in which the painting includes several consecutive scenes or episodes. While each century brought marked changes to the prevailing style, a coherent artistic vision endured throughout, whether the artist was depicting the divine sports of Krishna or the reigning monarch in *darbar* (audience). This continuity of vision in the face of strong Mughal, Deccani or European influences is attributable to the conservatism of the hereditary artist families and to their steady response over the ages to the Mewar landscape, flora and fauna and to the architectural forms of the Udaipur palaces. Their artistic conservatism was itself a reflection of the unchanging social and cultural values of this most traditionalist of Rajput courts.

273. Map showing painting schools in Rajasthan and contiguous regions; those sites with separate entries in this dictionary are distinguished by CROSS-REFERENCE TYPE

From the 14th century Mewar was ruled by the chiefs of the Sisodiya clan, a branch of the Guhilot Rajputs who had controlled the region from the 8th century. Over the centuries they distinguished themselves as adversaries of successive Muslim invaders and as rigorous upholders of the Rajput martial code and Hindu cultural traditions. They were the last Rajput power to capitulate to the Mughals, and thereafter they remained aloof from the imperial court. Regarded as the premier Rajput chiefs, the Mewar rulers held the hereditary title of Rana (or Maharana).

Several of the earlier Ranas, notably Rana Kumbha (*reg* 1433–68), were important patrons of the arts, but few documented examples of painting survive from the pre-Mughal period (those that do are Jaina manuscripts in a conventional Western Indian style, *see* §3(ii)(a) above). Many royal manuscripts may have perished in the repeated sacking of the fortress capital of Chitor, which fell for the last time to the emperor Akbar in 1568. The new capital at Udaipur was founded at this time by Udai Singh (*reg* 1536–72), and following the enforced acceptance of Mughal suzerainty by Amar Singh I (*reg* 1597–1620) in 1615, it became a flourishing centre of painting. From the second quarter of the 17th century the indigenous tradition of poetical and mythological manuscript illustration underwent a brilliant renascence. By the early 18th century a new phase had begun, with a greater emphasis on Mughal-inspired court portraiture and reportage. This developed at Udaipur into a uniquely versatile and often grandiose form of documentary art. The virtually continuous artistic tradition of Mewar was finally ended by the dissolution of the princely states after 1947.

Early to mid-17th century. The first dated document of Mewar painting under Rajput patronage, a *Rāgamālā* ('Garland of *rāga*s', with illustrations of musical modes) of 1605 (Patna, Kanoria priv. col., and dispersed; illustrated in Kanoria), shows a strong stylistic relationship with manuscripts in the 16th-century *Caurapañcāśikā* group (*see* §3(ii)(e) above). It is likely that Chitor had been a centre of the *Caurapañcāśikā* group style before 1568 and that that tradition formed the basis for the developments in manuscript illustration at Udaipur in the following century. The *Rāgamālā* is by a Muslim artist, Nasiruddin, working at Chawand, a temporary capital of the Ranas (1585–1609) during the period of Mughal invasions. Nasiruddin painted in a coarse but still lively *Caurapañcāśikā* manner. Other related fragmentary series of the late 16th century or early 17th of possible Mewari origin include a small group of *Gīta Govinda* pages (e.g. New Delhi, N. Mus.) and a set of vividly coloured *Rāgamālā* pages (e.g. Varanasi, Banaras Hindu U., Bharat Kala Bhavan).

After Rana Amar Singh's capitulation to Jahangir in 1615, the heir apparent, Karan Singh (*reg* 1620–28), was obliged to attend the Mughal court, where he was befriended by the future emperor Shah Jahan. No inscribed paintings from Karan Singh's reign have come to light, but it is possible that he favoured the Sub-imperial or Popular Mughal style of manuscript illustration then in vogue among the Rajput princes (*see* §(ii) above). The influence of this style is evident in the compositions and figure drawing of a *Rāgamālā* of 1628 (New Delhi, N. Mus., and dispersed), the earliest work of Sahibdin (*fl* 1628–55), the leading artist working for Rana Jagat Singh I (*reg* 1628–52). Nevertheless, Sahibdin's joyously vibrant use of primary colours, quite unlike the muddy Sub-imperial palette, reveals him as essentially a follower of the tradition of Nasiruddin, to whom he may have been related. A close correspondence can be seen, for example, between their respective versions of *Mārū rāginī*, the forty-second and last page in the *Rāgamālā* series of 1605 and 1628 (Patna, Kanoria priv. col., and New Delhi, N. Mus.). But while Nasiruddin's pair of lovers on a jaunty camel with attendants are set against old-fashioned flat colour areas, Sahibdin's grouping reveals a Popular Mughal refinement of line and an open foreground shown in spatial recession.

After 1628 Sahibdin continued to adapt the older style in versions of poetical subjects that vary from the staidly literal to the brilliantly expressive. His growing mastery is seen in the *Gīta Govinda* of 1629 (Jodhpur, Pal. Lib., and dispersed) and still more in his illustrations of *c.* 1630–35 to the *Rasikapriyā*, a Hindi rhetorical poem on ideal types of lovers by Keshav Das (Udaipur, Govt Mus., and dispersed; *see* COLOUR, colour pl. VII, fig. 2). In the following decade Jagat Singh began to commission ambitious epic or genealogical series that called for a more elaborately narrative style of illustration. A number of manuscripts revert from a vertical to the traditional horizontal format, facilitating more diffuse and active compositions, which sometimes employ multiple narration within a single frame. These include Sahibdin's *Sūryavaṁśaprakāśa* ('Genealogy of the Solar dynasty', i.e. the Sisodia Rajputs) of 1645 (Udaipur, City Pal. Mus., and dispersed) and the great *Bhāgavata purāṇa* (relating the mythology of Vishnu) of 1648 (books 8, 9, 11 and 12 survive in Pune, Bhandarkar Orient. Res. Inst.). Sahibdin's finest later work appears in two books (the second and sixth) of a collaborative *Rāmāyaṇa* series that was Jagat Singh's final and most ambitious commission: the *Ayodhyākāṇḍa* ('Book of Ayodhya') of 1650 and the *Yuddhakāṇḍa* ('Book of the battle') of 1652 (London, BL, Add. MS. 15296–97). The vigorous scene in the *Yuddhakāṇḍa* of Rama and his monkey allies besieging Ravana and his demons in the schematically represented city of Lanka (see fig. 274) shows Sahibdin's mature compositional technique at its best. His last known work, the *Sukarakṣetramāhātmya* of 1655 (Calcutta, priv. col.), another mythological series, was executed once more in a tall vertical format.

Although Sahibdin's style fundamentally influenced later manuscript illustration at Udaipur, its effects are not yet evident in several works of *c.* 1625–30. These include a *Rasamañjarī* (a rhetorical treatise on lovers by Bhanudatta) by several hands, showing Sub-imperial as well as archaic provincial features (New Delhi, N. Mus., and dispersed), and a *Ḍholā–Mārū* (the romance of Dhola and Maru) from Ahar (New Delhi, N. Mus.).

A later contemporary of Sahibdin, working in a harsher and less flexible idiom, was Manohar, whose work is found in a few pages of the *Bhāgavata purāṇa* of 1648 and in the *Bālakāṇḍa* ('Book of childhood'), dated 1649, of the great *Rāmāyaṇa* (Bombay, Prince of Wales Mus., and Jehangir A. G.). He also had followers, as is shown by the *Āranyakāṇḍa* ('Book of the forest') of 1651 (Udaipur, Rajasthan Orient. Res. Inst.), possibly by Manohar himself, and the cruder *Uttarakāṇḍa* ('Last book') of 1653 from the same manuscript (London, BL, Add. MS. 15297), and by other series of *c.* 1650–60, such as a vigorous *Sūr sāgar* (Hindi devotional poems to Krishna by Sur Das; Patna, Kanoria priv. col., and dispersed; see M. Chandra, pl. 3) and the Gem Palace *Rāgamālā* (New Delhi, N. Mus.; named after the shop in Jaipur where it first came to light).

An exotic but short-lived stylistic influx from the Deccan is seen in the fourth and fifth books of Rana Jagat Singh's *Rāmāyaṇa*, the *Kiṣkindhākāṇḍa* ('Book of Kishkindha'; London, BL, Add. MS. 15296) of 1653 and the undated *Sundarakāṇḍa* ('Beautiful book'; 18 surviving pages in London, BL, Orient. & India Office Lib., Skt. MS. 3621), with their enlarged figure drawing, unified compositions and more varied palette using pinks and

274. Sahibdin: *Rama and his Monkey Allies Besieging Lanka*, Mewar school, opaque colour on paper, 180×360 mm; from a manuscript of the *Yuddhakāṇḍa* of the *Rāmāyaṇa*, 1652 (London, British Library, Add. MS. 15297 (1), fol. 27)

other intermediate tones. A similar style has sometimes been associated with Aurangabad in the Deccan (*see* §(vi)(e) below), where Rajput nobles serving with the Mughal armies were stationed in the mid-17th century. However, at least some of these works, including two almost identical *Gīta Govinda* series (Udaipur, Rajasthan Orient. Res. Inst., and dispersed), may well have been painted in Mewar itself.

Late 17th century and after: manuscript and mythological painting. Later manuscript painting at Udaipur seldom ventured beyond imitation or occasionally inspired elaboration of Sahibdin's achievement. A number of lengthy and uninspired mythological series (e.g. Udaipur, Govt Mus.), some by Mun (*fl* 1680s), can be ascribed to the reigns of Rana Raj Singh I (*reg* 1652–80) and Rana Jai Singh (*reg* 1680–98). Other manuscripts from the end of the 17th century include a *Rāgamālā* in an unusually tall format (Boston, MA, Mus. F.A., and dispersed). Some exceptionally large and fine *Sūr sāgar* illustrations with multiple narrative compositions (dispersed; see Topsfield, 1980, no. 62) were probably made for Rana Amar Singh II (*reg* 1698–1710).

Under Sangram Singh II (*reg* 1710–34), another patron who valued quantity over quality, the manuscript painters' prodigious output exhausted their imaginative powers. Dated series of this reign include a repetitive *Gīta Govinda* of 1714 (Udaipur, Govt Mus.), a *Sat saī* (700 poems of Bihārī Lāl) of 1719 and a *Sundarśṛṇgāra*, a treatise on lovers by Sundar Das (both Udaipur, Sarasvati Bhavan Lib., and dispersed), of 1723. There are many pages of charm and humour in the unusual *Mulla dupiāẓa* ('Mulla two-onions'; Udaipur, Govt Mus.) of *c.* 1720, a series of sometimes ribald aphorisms of a legendary buffoon at the Mughal court. But from the early 18th century the best artists had increasingly devoted themselves to the newer genre of court portraiture.

In the later 18th century and the 19th few significant additions of illustrated manuscripts were made to the royal library, though as late as 1876 a lavish book of the *Rasikapriyā* (ex-Sarasvati Bhavan Lib., Udaipur; held by the Udaipur courts as an object of litigation at the time of publication) was completed after 15 years' work by the artists Shivalal (*fl* 1858–93) and Parasuram (*fl c.* 1859–80), who mainly specialized in portraiture (see fig. 276 below) and hunting scenes. Some generations before this, however, the centre of mythological painting in Mewar had shifted to the pilgrimage town of Nathdwara, north of Udaipur, where artists from various parts of Rajasthan gathered near the temple of Shri Nathji (a form of Krishna) to produce large devotional cloth paintings (*pichvāī*) depicting the exploits of the god and the ceremonies of his cult. These static, iconic subjects, often elaborately compartmented, were skilfully painted in rich colours, and *pichvāī* production of increasing garishness has continued to the present day.

Late 17th century and after: portraiture and court scenes. As a result of the Maharanas' isolation from the imperial court, the Mughal-inspired taste for naturalistic portraiture and court reportage reached Udaipur later than elsewhere in Rajasthan, and in an assimilated form owing much to earlier experimentation at Bundi. The first inscribed works appeared in the reign of Raj Singh I, the earliest dated example being a portrait of the Rana on a rearing horse accompanied by retainers (1670; priv. col.). Further conventional studies of royal family groups were painted for Jai Singh. However, a new verve and originality are evident in the period of Amar Singh II, who was depicted by his anonymous leading artist in an unprecedented variety of scenes, not only standing, riding or holding court but also celebrating festivals, hunting, playing polo or consorting with his ladies. The viewpoint is often close and intimate, with a spare and confident linear idiom and an unusually cool palette. Many works are in a sparsely coloured, heavily stippled grisaille, an adaptation of a Mughal–Deccani convention that may also owe something to the example of European prints. A large study of the Rana at worship at the Eklingji temple (Oxford, Ashmolean) is a notable example of this genre. A few other large compositions (the largest being painted on cloth) also depicted life at court against a topographically accurate background of the palaces and gardens of Udaipur. The most brilliant example is the painting of Amar Singh's revels with his nobles at the Holi festival in the Sabrat Vilas gardens (Melbourne, N.G. Victoria; see fig. 275), with its refined execution, symmetrical composition and vivid play of reds and greens.

This innovation of court reportage above all determined the course of the later Udaipur school. Under Sangram Singh II, scenes of *darbars*, festivals, hunts, temple visits, animal fights and other spectacles became ever larger and more populous and detailed, providing a comprehensive record of the ruler's public life and the activities of his court. Earlier Mughal models became submerged in the vigorous, sometimes naively archaic compositions of the Mewar artists, who continued to experiment with consecutive narration and multiple viewpoints dependent on the nimbate figure of the Rana. Their imaginative zest compensated for a certain coarsening of style. One of the most impressive examples is the panoramic scene of Sangram Singh's procession around Pichola Lake on the night of the Gangaur festival (*c.* 1715–20; Udaipur, City Pal. Mus.), in which the royal barge is depicted three times at successive stages of the procession. In the background of this picture there is an unusual flirtation with European chiaroscuro.

275. *Rana Amar Singh II Celebrating the Holi Festival in a Garden*, Mewar school, opaque colour on paper, 470×405 mm, *c.* 1708–10 (Melbourne, National Gallery of Victoria)

Under Jagat Singh II (*reg* 1734–51) the political and economic decline of Mewar began to accelerate as a result of the Maratha incursions from the south. From this period the Maharanas succumbed to an escapist mentality, indulging in extravagant festivals and displays that were recorded in careful detail by the court artists. Jagat Singh was a liberal patron of the arts, and during his reign the style developed under his two predecessors reached full maturity. Artists' names were for the first time recorded in some numbers in the inscriptions on the backs of pictures. One of the most influential was Jai Ram (*fl c.* 1720–51), who had earlier worked for Sangram Singh. His was the guiding hand behind an ambitious series of at least ten large paintings depicting the *Rāsalīlā* (religious dance dramas) performed in the palace for Jagat Singh on an autumn night in 1736 (Melbourne, N.G. Victoria, and dispersed).

The Mewar style continued with the momentum it had gained under Jagat Singh through the two brief and undistinguished reigns that followed and into that of Ari Singh (*reg* 1761–73), an arrogant and divisive ruler but an active patron of painting. His artists included, among others, Jugarsi, Kesu Ram, Bhima, Jiva and the young Bakhta (*fl* 1756–1811). Much of the early work of Ari Singh's reign, including hundreds of portraits of himself and his horses and elephants, is mechanically executed, but a number of fine larger works were still produced. The most spectacular is an unsigned painting of 1767 depicting Ari Singh six times in continuous narration as he promenades with his ladies at the lake palace of Jagmandir (Udaipur, City Pal. Mus.).

After this date painting at Udaipur fell into decline until the early 19th century. Some of the royal artists took up employment at the minor courts of the nobles, among them Bakhta, who spent the remainder of a long career working for the Rawats of Deogarh in northern Mewar. Here a vigorous variant of the Udaipur style flourished for at least three generations, especially under Rawat Gokul Das II (*reg* 1786–1821). Bakhta, his son Chokha (*fl* 1799–1824) and Chokha's son Baijnath (*fl c.* 1825–40), as well as other artists, produced confident, boldly coloured work of a quality superior to the stagnant Udaipur school. Bakhta was the most gifted of them, revealing in the portraiture of his *darbar* groups and procession scenes a sensitivity to personality sometimes verging on humorous caricature; a splendid example is his painting of 1806 of *Gokul Das and Courtiers* seated in *darbar* on a vast floral carpet against a mustard-yellow landscape (New Delhi, N. Mus.). Chokha, who in many respects followed his father's style, was also, within his limits, an expressive and engaging painter. His small, dense compositions are peopled with squat, large-eyed figures possessed by a dreamy sensuality.

At different periods in the first quarter of the 19th century Chokha worked not only at Deogarh for Gokul Das but at Udaipur for Rana Bhim Singh (*reg* 1778–1828), portraying this amiably sybaritic ruler in warmly intimate studies. For much of his reign Bhim Singh was too impoverished to maintain more than a modest standard of painting. However, a number of more ambitious works, including the murals in the Chitram ki Burj apartments of the City Palace, may date from his prosperous later years following the acceptance of British suzerainty in 1818. The later artists working for Bhim Singh and Jawan Singh (*reg* 1828–38), such as Ghasi (*fl c.* 1820–36) and Rama (*fl c.* 1835), were generally competent but uninspired. The work of the latter reign was especially hackneyed.

Sarup Singh (*reg* 1842–61) proved to be a more discerning patron, and in the work of his leading artist, Tara (*fl* 1836–68), the Udaipur style became to some extent rejuvenated. Tara began his career with conventional equestrian portraits of Jawan Singh, but from the late 1840s he produced many spirited larger compositions, such as two paintings of 1850–51 showing the Holi festival played on elephant- and horseback at the City Palace under riotously colourful clouds of powder (Udaipur, City Pal. Mus., and priv. col.). Tara's style was carried on in an elaborated form by his son Shivalal and follower Parasuram, whose stippled grisaille equestrian portrait of Sarup Singh in the classic Tara manner (London, priv. col.; see fig. 276) shows the influence of contemporary European engraving technique.

Although Sajjan Singh (*reg* 1871–84) had begun to show a taste for European-style portraits in oils, the early reign of Fateh Singh (*reg* 1884–1930), an ultra-conservative ruler and a devoted huntsman, is noteworthy for many large and meticulously detailed hunting scenes set in the hills and jungles of southern and eastern Mewar, the best of them painted by Shivalal in 1885–90 (Udaipur, City Pal. Mus.). In the first half of the 20th century Pannalal (son of Parasuram; *fl c.* 1910–45) and his son Chhaganlal (*fl c.* 1915–45) were the main artists who carried on the manner of Shivalal, albeit under increasing European influence. Accomplished *darbar*, festival and hunting scenes (e.g. Udaipur, City Pal. Mus.) were produced as late as the reign of Bhupal Singh (1930–55). But after 1949 the abolition of princely powers brought an end to royal patronage and this last residue of the Mewar tradition.

276. Parasuram: *Maharana Sarup Singh on Horseback*, Mewar school, opaque colour on paper, 323×228 mm, 1859 (London, private collection)

BIBLIOGRAPHY

A. K. Coomaraswamy: 'An Illustrated Śvetāmbara Jain Manuscript of A.D. 1260', *E. A.*, ii (1930), pp. 237–8
M. L. Menaria: *A Catalogue of Manuscripts in the Library of H. H. the Maharana of Udaipur* (Udaipur, 1943)
K. Khandalavala: 'Leaves from Rajasthan', *Marg*, iv (1950), pp. 2–24, 49–56
G. K. Kanoria: 'An Early Dated Rajasthani Rāgamālā', *J. Ind. Soc. Orient. A.*, xix (1952–3), pp. 1–5
P. Chandra: 'A Rāgamālā Set of the Mewar School in the National Museum of India', *Lalit Kala*, iii–iv (1956–7), pp. 46–54
M. Chandra: *Mewar Painting in the Seventeenth Century* (New Delhi, 1957)
H. Goetz: 'The First Golden Age of Udaipur', *A. Orient.*, ii (1957), pp. 427–37
S. M. Nawab: *The Oldest Rajasthani Paintings from Jain Bhandars* (Ahmadabad, 1959)
Miniature Painting: A Catalogue of the Exhibition of the Sri Motichand Khajanchi Collection (exh. cat. by K. Khandalavala, M. Chandra and P. Chandra, New Delhi, Lalit Kala Akad., 1960)
D. Barrett and B. Gray: *Painting of India* (Geneva, 1963/*R* London, 1978), pp. 133–8
S. Andhare: 'Painting from the Ṭhikānā of Deogarh', *Prince of Wales Mus. Bull.*, x (1967), pp. 43–53
M. C. Beach: 'Painting at Devgarh', *Archvs Asian A.*, xxiv (1970–71), pp. 23–35
S. Doshi: 'An Illustrated Manuscript from Aurangabad Dated AD 1650', *Lalit Kala*, xv (1972), pp. 19–28
Rajasthani Temple Hangings of the Krishna Cult (exh. cat. by R. Skelton, New York, Amer. Fed. A., 1973)
S. Andhare and N. Singh: *Deogarh Painting* (New Delhi, 1977/*R* 1983)
K. Talwar and K. Krishna: *Indian Pigment Paintings on Cloth* (Ahmadabad, 1979)
A. Topsfield: *Paintings from Rajasthan in the National Gallery of Victoria* (Melbourne, 1980)
——: 'Sāhibdīn's *Gīta-Govinda* Illustrations', *Chhavi-2: Rai Krishnadasa Felicitation Volume*, ed. A. Krishna (Varanasi, 1981), pp. 231–8
R. Parimoo: 'More Paintings from the Deogarh Ṭhikānā', *Lalit Kala*, ii (1982), pp. 12–15
The Art of the Book in India (exh. cat. by J. P. Losty, London, BL, 1982)
O. P. Sharma: 'An Illustrated Manuscript of the Ḍholā Mārū', *Bull. N. Mus. New Delhi*, iv–vi (1983), pp. 118–21
A. Topsfield: 'Ketelaar's Embassy and the *Farangi* Theme in the Art of Udaipur', *Orient. A.*, xxx (1984), pp. 350–67
R. K. Vashistha: *Mewāḍ kī citrāṅkan paramparā* [The tradition of Mewar painting] (Jaipur, 1984)
Life at Court in Rajasthan (exh. cat. by R. M. Cimino and others, Turin, Pal. Reale, 1985)
S. Andhare: 'Mewar Painters: Their Status and Genealogies', *Facets of Indian Art*, ed. R. Skelton and others (London, 1986), pp. 176–84
A. Topsfield: 'Sahibdin's Illustrations to the *Rasikapriyā*', *Orientations*, xvii (March 1986), pp. 18–31
S. Andhare: *Chronology of Mewar Painting* (Delhi, 1987)
A. Topsfield: 'Udaipur Paintings of the *Raslīlā*', *A. Bull. Victoria*, xxviii (1987), pp. 54–70
——: 'Udaipur Paintings of the 18th and 19th Centuries', *Indian Miniature Painting* (exh. cat., London, Spink & Son, 1987), pp. 73–96
K. Vatsyayan: *Mewari Gita-Govinda* (New Delhi, 1987)
A. Topsfield: *The City Palace Museum, Udaipur: Paintings of Mewar Court Life* (Ahmadabad, 1990)

——: 'A Dispersed *Gīta Govinda* Series in the Mewar–Deccani Style', *Makaranda: Essays in Honour of Dr James C. Harle*, ed. C. Bautze-Picron (Delhi, 1990), pp. 215–26
——: 'The Royal Paintings Inventory at Udaipur', *Indian Art and Connoisseurship: Essays in Honour of Douglas Barrett*, ed. J. Guy (Ahmadabad, in preparation)
J. P. Losty: 'Aurangabad or Mewar? The Influence of the Deccan on Rana Jagat Singh's *Ramayana* of 1649–53', *Karl Khandalavala Felicitation Volume*, ed. B. N. Goswamy (Ahmadabad, in preparation)

ANDREW TOPSFIELD

(b) Malwa. For some decades a school of painting has been assigned to Malwa (though its place of production is still uncertain) and dated to the 17th century; previously, however, this same school had been designated 'Primitive Rajasthani', tentatively assigned to Bundelkhand and dated to the second half of the 16th century (see Coomaraswamy, pp. 3, 69–78, pls i–ix). Its earliest known examples are in a *Rasikapriyā* manuscript dated VS 1690 (AD 1634; dispersed, first published by Khandalavala, and pp. 14, 51, fig. 15). The work illustrates Hindi verses by the poet Keshav Das, depicting traditional heroes (*nāyakas*) and heroines (*nāyikās*) in prescribed amorous moods. Despite their unpretentious 'primitive' appearance, the illustrations are indicative of a well-established tradition, already, to some extent, in an over-mature state. Most scenes are standardized; they include a kiosk-topped pavilion, often to one side, with a bed in the interior. Backgrounds are plain blocks of colour; a patch of sky hangs at the top of the work, with a broad white band indicating the horizon line. Figures and a tree are often set against the monochrome ground; in rare instances a richer background is created with tall and decorative trees. Works of this early phase of the school exhibit characteristic figure types with oval heads and beady eyes. Also distinctive are the women's striped skirts and short bodices. Amorous emotion is conveyed through gesture rather than facial expression; sulking heroines suffering pangs of separation heighten some leaves.

Stylistic evolution is displayed in a *Rāmāyaṇa* manuscript of only a few years later (*c.* 1640; e.g. Varanasi, Banaras Hindu U., Bharat Kala Bhavan, nos 6756–815; Patna, Kanoria priv. col.). The earlier treatment of landscape persists, and new developments include fragile, nervous, topographic-like contours formed by waves of thin lines over red-ochre boulders and a more pronounced horizon line in the sky. The treatment of faces, dress and trees continues as before, but the compositions are more complex than in 1634. For example, in *Rama's Party Returning from the Lankan Conquest* (see fig. 277), the chariot bearing Rama, Sita and Hanuman is depicted literally flying through the centre of the painting, while the horses drawing it proceed along a diagonal path. Six well-wishers on the left are balanced by two trees and a pair of geese on the right.

277. Malwa school: *Rama's Party Returning from the Lankan Conquest*, opaque colour on paper, 165×222 mm, from a *Rāmāyaṇa* series, *c.* 1640 (Patna, Kanoria private collection)

A complete, undated *Rāgamālā* set (Varanasi, Banaras Hindu U., Bharat Kala Bhavan, nos 7450–83) can be assigned to *c.* 1650. The style peaks in this and other related works, including a dispersed *Rāgamālā* set (e.g. Patna, Kanoria priv. col). The line is bold and the abstracted forms pulsate with brilliant colour. The treatment of each theme is distinctive, avoiding the repetition of the *Rasikapriyā* of 1634. *Gaurī rāgiṇī* (see fig. 278) from the *Rāgamālā* set in the Kanoria collection, for example, shows a woman and her confidante traversing a flowering forest inhabited by mischievous monkeys. This fine expression of Malwa painting has been designated Style A. The idiom continues throughout the second half of the century.

Around the middle of the 17th century another strain of Malwa painting, called Style B, appears in an *Amarū śataka* ('One hundred verses of Amaru'; 1652; dispersed, see Mehta). This sub-style, a refined version of Style A, shows Mughal influence. The heroes, heroines and maids, mainly the traditional characterizations of lovers described in the poet Amaru's verses, are rendered with delicate faces and gentle movements. Colours are subdued, with a plain slate, mauve or black usually chosen for the background. Text relating to the illustration appears at the tops of leaves, a floral scroll in the bottom band. All the illustrations have virtually the same setting: a pavilion with open verandah topped with domes and kiosks, with little indication of landscape surroundings.

Style B left a lasting mark on the Malwa school, and the two strains influenced each other in the succeeding decades. Works in Malwa Style A showing the influence of Style B include illustrations of the *Rasabelī*, the poet Puhakara's verses on the traditional classification of lovers (*c.* 1670; New Delhi, N. Mus., MS. 51.63/1–25); painted by the artist Sukhadeva, these show a mellowing of the stark expression of the *Rasikapriyā* of 1634 and the *Rāmāyaṇa* of *c.* 1640. Fine blending of the two strains resulted in elegant, tall figures with expressive faces. The *jāmā* ('coat') worn by the men is usually transparent and sensitively rendered. The trees retain their traditional decorative character yet are more delicate and are entwined with swaying vines. Sukhadeva delighted in blending green and blue tonalities. Related examples by a different hand and with a distinctive brick-red colour illustrate a *Rasikapriyā* (Varanasi, Banaras Hindu U., Bharat Kala Bhavan, nos 448–9, 1426).

A set known as the Narsyang Shahar *Rāgamālā* (New Delhi, N. Mus., see Khandalavala, figs 24–5), named after its place of production (usually identified with the modern

278. Malwa school: *Gaurī rāgiṇī*, opaque colour on paper, 190×183 mm, from a *Rāgamālā* series, *c.* 1650–60 (Patna, Kanoria private collection)

Narsinghgarh in Malwa, though this is not certain), is a key work in that it is also dated VS 1737 (AD 1680) and the painter is identified as Madho Das. In this and related *Rāgamālā*s (Varanasi, Banaras Hindu U., Bharat Kala Bhavan, nos 1387–401) scenes are standardized and presented with only minor variations. Nevertheless, they do not lack in freshness and creativity. This stage of Malwa painting represents a culmination of Style B, in which a borrowed naturalism is exquisitely blended with the style's inherent decorativism. Human forms are even more delicate, and the traditional stark facial type is further mellowed. Traditional elements are used with innovative skill. Architectural forms, which often dominate, as well as thick forestscapes are presented decoratively and with sensitivity. Walls are multicoloured and sometimes have brick facing. A white band demarcates the sky from the richly forested landscape. Another *Amarū śataka* set (*c.* 1680; Bombay, Prince of Wales Mus., see M. Chandra) is a product of an atelier working in Style B as developed by Madho Das. A floral scroll is also represented at the bottom of these works.

In the next decade a watered-down application of this great tradition is found in sundry semi-folk illustrations and even at higher levels of production. The last major illustrations in the Malwa style are several *Bhāgavata purāṇa* sets, one of which is in two parts, with dates equivalent to 1686 (dispersed) and 1688 (Patna, Kanoria priv. col.). These paintings are known for their narrative quality. The field is divided arbitrarily into small or large rectangular compartments, the main event from the Krishna story depicted in the large panel and minor events in the smaller compartments. The main scenes are particularly lively, showing creativity in design and in visualization of the event.

The great Malwa tradition declined in the 1690s but nevertheless left a mark on styles of the neighbouring regions. Its influence, in varying degrees, is evident in Maratha court painting, especially from central Indian centres. Large numbers of related paintings have variously been attributed to central India, Burhanpur, Ahmadnagar or Amer.

BIBLIOGRAPHY

A. K. Coomaraswamy: *Catalogue of the Indian Collection in the Museum of Fine Arts, Boston*, v (Cambridge, MA, 1926)

N. C. Mehta: 'A Note on Ragamala', *J. Ind. Soc. Orient. A.*, iii/2 (1935), pp. 145–7

K. Khandalavala: 'Leaves from Rajasthan', *Marg*, iv/3 (1950), pp. 2–24, 49–56

M. Chandra: 'An Illustrated Set of the Amaru Sataka', *Prince of Wales Mus. Bull.*, ii (1951–2), pp. 1–63

W. G. Archer: *Central Indian Painting* (London, 1958)

P. Chandra: 'Ustad Salivahana and the Development of Popular Mughal Art', *Lalit Kala*, viii (Oct 1960), pp. 25–46

A. Krishna: *Malwa Painting* (Varanasi, 1962)

ANAND KRISHNA

(c) Bundi, Kota and related schools. A prolific and dynamic school of painting developed in BUNDI, the capital of a district of the same name in south-eastern Rajasthan, from the late 16th century to the 19th. As early as the 17th century related painting styles such as those of Kota, Indargarh, Khatoli, Toda Rai Singh, Raghugarh, Uniara and Kapren developed out of the school that was originally sponsored solely by the rulers of Bundi. These are to be evaluated as idioms of the Bundi school and together provide a complex picture of the *Bundikalam* ('Bundi school of painting'). The stylistic nuances of the two major centres of the *Bundikalam*, Bundi and Kota, are closely related.

Bundi. Bundi was a more or less independent kingdom under the Hara Rajputs, but it is difficult to reconstruct the early history of the state before the 16th century. In 1569 the Mughal emperor Akbar (*reg* 1556–1605) conquered the fortress of Ranthambhor, then under the command of the Bundi ruler Rao Surjan (*reg* 1554–85), who became a feudatory of the Mughals with a privileged status. The oldest portrait of a Bundi ruler is a Mughal painting of Rao Surjan in the *Akbarnāma* ('History of Akbar') of *c.* 1590 (London, V&A, MS. IS. 2–1896; some scholars date this MS. *c.* 1586–7), which depicts him bowing before Akbar. In 1575 Akbar sent Rao Surjan to Varanasi as commander of the fortress of Chunar, a site associated with the earliest dated paintings of the Bundi school, the so-called Chunar *Rāgamālā*, a fragmentary set now dispersed (e.g. London, V&A; Varanasi, Banaras Hindu U., Bharat Kala Bhavan; Allahabad Mus.; San Diego, CA, Mus. A.). An inscription on a page from the Chunar *Rāgamālā* (Washington, DC, Freer) states that it was painted in Chunar in 1591 by artists trained in the imperial Mughal workshop. Rao Bhoj (*reg* 1585–1606), who is often cited as the patron, is not mentioned in the inscription. However, he spent a few years in Varanasi before being transferred to Agra, a leading centre for Sub-imperial Mughal painting. Since the Chuna *Rāgamālā* is related stylistically to sub-imperial painting, Rao Bhoj's connections with both Agra and Chunar are of special significance.

It is not until the rule of Rao Ratan Singh (*reg* 1607–31), successor to Rao Bhoj, that the evolution of Bundi painting can be documented on the basis of datable miniatures and wall paintings. Since the evidence of wall paintings is crucial in assigning miniatures of insecure date and provenance to specific periods and centres of production, they are discussed side by side here. Among the finest known paintings produced for Rao Ratan Singh are the wall paintings of that part of the Bundi palace complex known as the Badal Mahal. The ceilings and upper areas of the walls, including the domes and half-domes, are covered with paintings, as are the surfaces of the vaulting system below. The iconographic scheme is almost entirely Hindu with a few imported elements. One of these is the dragon, which was brought to India by the Mughals and occurs frequently in wall paintings produced during the reign of Jahangir (*reg* 1605–27); another is the mythical bird, the Persian simurgh; both appear in conjunction with the genuinely Indian *garuḍa*, the mythical bird-vehicle of the god Vishnu. The wall paintings depict the Hindu gods and goddesses, elephant fights, polo matches, processions and, above all, hunting scenes (see fig. 279). The style is reminiscent of Popular Mughal painting (*see* §(ii)(c) above), except for the female figures, which display the rounder head forms characteristic of the Bundi school. A significant feature in the landscape paintings is the depiction of symmetrical, fan-shaped plantain trees, which remain a trademark of Bundi painting for centuries. Faces in three-quarter profile derived from Akbar-period painting still appear often, though full profile became standard in Bundi painting later in the 17th century. Portrait painting initially adhered closely to contemporary Jahangir-period formulae: the robe is darkened under the armpits, the turban is flat, the hair is painted to show each separate strand, and the general impression is of smoothly flowing lines.

Under Rao Shatru Sal (Chattar Sal; *reg* 1631–58) artists sought greater individuality and independence from Mughal painting, becoming more experimental. Disproportionally large faces are depicted in profile and take on an oval form; noses are pointed. Yet men are still shown with the darkening of the robe under the armpits and with flat turbans, as, for instance, in a portrait of Rao Shatru Sal (priv. col.; see Beach, 1974, fig. 34). More conservative is a *Bhāgavata purāṇa* series (Kota, Govt Mus., and a single folio each in London, V&A, MS. IS. 150–1949, Washington, DC, Freer, and Patna, priv. col.) depicting scenes from the life of Krishna. The perspective follows Akbar-period conventions, the early 17th-century style of turban with loose hair at the back of the head is retained, and in many cases the three-quarter profile is still in evidence. Towards the end of the reign of Shatru Sal, paintings of the ruler riding on an elephant were introduced, for example *Rao Shatru Sal on the State Elephant Sundar Gaj* (*c.* 1650; Patna, V. K. Kanoria priv. col.; see Archer, fig. 3). These are derived from imperial Mughal painting under Shah Jahan (*reg* 1628–58).

279. Bundi school: *Hunting Scene*, detail of a wall painting from the Badal Mahal, Bundi palace complex, 1620–30

In the time of Rao Bhao Singh (*reg* 1658–81) and Rao Anurad Singh (*reg* 1681–95) Bundi painting acquired its definitive and distinctive character. Two paintings, *Couple Watching a Pigeon* (?1662; Varanasi, Banaras Hindu U., Bharat Kala Bhavan) and *Couple in a Pavilion* (1682; Bombay, C. D. Gujarati priv. col.), embody the delicacy and vividness of the mature Bundi style. The faces, which are always painted in profile, are evenly round and have a straight, occasionally pointed nose. In pictures with landscapes the horizon has been shifted towards the upper edge of the picture, and the sky sometimes includes stylized cloud formations. The characteristic plantain trees, used sparingly, are like the painted backdrop of a stage set. While the background elements of these miniatures are colourful with lush depictions of flowers and foliage or elaborate architectural forms, the background of portraits is generally monochrome and devoid of architectural and landscape elements.

The repertory of Bundi painting in the second half of the 17th century is considerably widened. During the reigns of Rao Bhao Singh and Rao Anurad Singh, *Rāgamālā* series were particularly popular, as were genealogical series of posthumous portraits of Bundi rulers going back to the 15th century. It was in this period that a gifted Bundi artist, Mohan, painted *Lovers Pointing to the Crescent Moon* (1689; Bombay, Prince of Wales Mus.). The figures are proportionally and delicately rendered, the patterns on the clothing as carefully and precisely articulated as the profusion of flowers in the landscape.

Rao Raja Budh Singh (*reg* 1695–1739) commissioned the most lyrical paintings of the school, the wall paintings in the Chattar Mahal in the Bundi palace complex. Landscapes are luxuriant, with the indispensable plantain trees and a variety of other vegetation inhabited by numerous birds, while ducks, crocodiles and fish sport among the lotuses in the water. The rich palette is bright but slightly more subdued than in earlier periods. The sky, for example, often glows in the most varied vivid tones of red. The women (and Budh Singh himself) have a horizontal, occasionally crescent-shaped mark on their foreheads. The turban acquires a twist at the back of the head in the form of a hornlike protuberance, a fashion in Bundi turbans up to the 19th century.

Wall paintings and miniatures produced in the second half of the 18th century reflect the entire repertory of Rajput themes. They include *darbar* (audience) scenes, *Rāgamālā* sets, scenes from the life of Krishna and *Bārahmāsā* sets, with an illustration for each of the 12 months of the year. Equestrian portraits became increasingly popular, with an ever-growing number of servants and bearers of insignia and weapons crowded around the horse and rider. Erotic subjects and scenes from the women's quarters of the palace occur, including the popular theme of women bathing as in *After the Bath* (Allahabad Mus.).

Wall paintings in the Bundi palace complex dating from the early 19th century include those of the part of the palace known as the Chitrashala and the lower floor of the Badal Mahal. The latter depict mainly Maharao Raja Ram Singh (*reg* 1821–89), either hunting, celebrating festivals such as Holi or in long processions. Striking features of these paintings are the variety of viewpoints and the variable uses of perspective employed by the painters. In some cases figures are painted one above the other in an archaic fashion, though they are meant to be perceived as standing one behind the other. In other paintings European single-point perspective is erratically included. Miniature painting also continued into the 19th century, mainly in the form of standing portraits that concentrate more on decorative effect than on individual physiognomy. By the end of the 19th century Bundi painting was replaced by photography.

Kota. The earliest known paintings from Kota date to the second half of the 17th century. Located to the south of Bundi just across the Chambal River, Kota officially became an independent state under a decree passed in 1631 by the Mughal emperor Shah Jahan (*reg* 1628–58). Its first ruler, Rao Madho Singh (*reg* 1625–48), was the second son of Rao Ratan of Bundi. Given the geographical proximity and family ties, it is not surprising that paintings produced at Kota and Bundi are stylistically similar.

Surviving portraits of Rao Madho Singh are posthumous works, probably based on a contemporary original. Kota painting is not firmly documented until the reign of Rao Jagat Singh (*reg* 1658–84), when a mature school of painting flourished. Portraits of the ruler, such as *Jagat Singh of Kota with his Zenana* (Patna, V. K. Kanoria priv. col.) and *Jagat Singh of Kota in a Garden* (priv. col., on dep. Cambridge, MA, Fogg), are delicately and subtly executed, and the technique shows close affinities with imperial Mughal portraiture. Strong linear rhythms underscore the movement and grace of the figures. Faces are well modelled, the eyes comparatively narrow, with a more or less heavily emphasized double outline, which is also sometimes found in Bundi paintings.

In the late 17th century and the early 18th, hunting scenes became increasingly popular. Several fine examples survive, including *Rao Ram Singh of Kota Hunting at Mukundgarh* (*c.* 1695; priv. col., see Beach, 1974, fig. 60) and *Rao Ram Singh of Kota Pursuing a Rhinoceros* (*c.* 1690; S. C. Welch priv. col.). In the overall effect of tense excitement, as well as in the detailed execution of such areas as the heads of antelopes or the eyes of the elephant, these miniatures exemplify the vivacity of design and technical skill achieved by the artists of Kota in the late 17th century.

In the early 18th century, fine wall paintings were executed in the part of the Kota palace complex known as the Chattar Mahal, including hunting scenes full of surging action. However, not all of the many hunting scenes produced in the early 18th century depict actual events. Some compositions were pieced together from several different scenes or copied from earlier works, in some cases from works originating in Bundi. Paintings from the reign of Maharao Arjun Singh (*reg* 1720–23) include portraits, hunting scenes and *Rāgamālā* sets. The portraits are characterized by a pointed and sometimes hooked or curved nose, as seen in contemporary portraits of Arjun Singh himself, such as *Arjun Singh of Kota Inspecting a Horse* (Boston, MA, Mus. F.A.).

A *Rāgamālā* set (1768; Udaipur, Sarasvati Bhavar Lib.) with over 240 paintings was painted during the reign of Guman Singh (*reg* 1764–70). An inscription provides the name of the artist, Dalu. Under Maharao Umed Singh (*reg* 1770–1819), large-format miniature paintings of hunting scenes were produced, often inscribed with such details as the names of those participating in the hunt, its precise dates and the name of the artist. Master painters known from these works (early 1780s) include Shaykh Taju, Hans Raj Joshi, Bhimsen and Gumani. The composition usually features the hunter, often Umed Singh himself, sitting in a hiding place in the trees, surrounded by exotic vegetation that recalls the works of Henri Rousseau. These paintings, which owe as much to artistic imagination as to actual observation of the hunt, employ a powerful use of line and colour. Examples include *Hunting Scene* (525×655 mm, 1788; Kota, M. H. Brijraj Singh priv. col.) by Gumani and *Umed Singh Hunting in the Jungle* (546×826 mm, 1781; Switzerland, priv. col.) by Shaykh Taju. One of the largest hunting scenes of Kota was executed around 1780 and runs the entire length of a room in the Jhala ki Haveli, a detached residence within the Kota palace complex. The wall paintings of this building also include scenes honouring the main Vaishnavite deities of Kota. Also from the period of Umed Singh is a manuscript dated 1804 (Kota, Govt Mus., MS. 1950–3454) that illustrates in 38 miniatures the festivities of Brijnathji, Brijrayji and Mathureshji, major deities of the Vallabhacharya Sampradaya, a Hindu sect stressing personal devotion to Krishna that was founded by the 15th-century Vaishnava teacher Vallabhacharya.

Painting in Kota received its last important impetus under Maharao Ram Singh (*reg* 1827–66), who sponsored wall paintings and miniatures focusing on his own activities, such as scenes of hunting and festivals in which he is the protagonist. These subjects contrast with those of the wall paintings of the Bade Devtaji ki Haveli, Kota (near the old palace), commissioned by the Bade Devtaji (royal priest), executed a few years earlier. These show a revival of classical Rajput themes, including *Bārahmāsā* scenes and *Nāyaka–Nāyikā Bheda* (a classification of heroes and heroines). In most portraits painted under Maharao Ram Singh, including those of Europeans, the line of the ruler's profile is applied to the facial contours of the sitter. Large-scale cloth paintings, occasionally as high as 4 m but painted with the delicacy of miniatures, were also produced during the reign of Ram Singh. These include a painting of *Maharao Ram Singh's Visit to the Lal Qil'a ('Red Fort') in Delhi in 1842* (4.52×2.59 m; Kota, City Palace, Rao Madho Singh Mus.), which provides a bird's-eye view of Shahjahanabad with detailed glimpses of people and animals in the streets and gardens.

Maharao Shatru Sal (*reg* 1866–89) was the last important patron of Kota painting. He had the Kanvarpada ka Mahal of the Kota palace complex decorated with paintings between 1866 and 1867, and later the Raj Mahal, the Anand Mahal, the Arjun Mahal and the verandah of the Lakshmi Bhandar (part of the old palace). Among the most interesting are the murals of the Raj Mahal, depicting scenes from the life of Krishna as well as scenes of hunting and a group representing Kota rulers. By the end of the 19th century Kota painting disappeared altogether.

Indargarh. From the 17th to the 19th century paintings in a style related to that of Bundi were produced at Indargarh, founded about 52 km to the north-east by Indar Sal, the eldest brother of Shatru Sal of Bundi. The oldest extant wall paintings in the Indargarh palace complex were painted during the reign of Indar Sal's son and successor, Maharaja Gaj Singh (*reg c.* 1660–80). One particularly important room inside the palace contains a complete set of 36 *Rāgamālā* paintings as well as depictions of animals (including the uncharacteristic turkey), hunting and procession scenes and a number of Hindu deities. Wall paintings and miniatures (many unpublished), including portraits of the rulers (see fig. 280), indicate that the Indargarh school of painting lasted until the 19th century. However, by the beginning of the 19th century the spontaneity was increasingly lost, the depiction of landscape was subordinated to geometric and decorative principles, and human features were rendered devoid of expression.

Khatoli. Another stylistically discrete idiom of the Bundi school developed from the Indargarh school in 1673, when Amar Singh, second son of Gaj Singh, conquered Khatoli in the vicinity of Indargarh. A portrait of him, *Amar Singh Smoking a Water-pipe* (Boston, MA, Mus. F.A., 66.156), is clearly derived from the Indargarh school in both composition and style. Khatoli miniatures from the second half of the 18th century are distinguished by their economic treatment of the background and by the way in which doll-like human figures frozen in their movements are dotted around the painting like statues (e.g. Hyderabad, Mittal Mus. Ind. A.; Secundarabad, R. K. Tandon priv. col.; and Jaipur, priv. cols).

280. Indargarh school: *Maharajah Megh Singh of Indargarh Hunting Wild Boar*, opaque watercolour on paper, 250×198 mm, from Indargarh, *c.* 1800 (Uniara, Rajendra Singh private collection)

Toda Rai Singh. Another separate idiom of the Bundi school is represented by the wall paintings in the palace of Toda Rai Singh, 65 km north of Bundi, the oldest of which was executed around the end of the 17th century. The depiction of the vegetation and of women's clothing is especially reminiscent of paintings generally ascribed to Bundi. The school seems to have survived into the 18th century. Unfortunately, few examples have been published.

Raghugarh. Paintings stylistically related to those of the Bundi school were also produced in the 17th century for Rajput rulers of the Khichi Chauhan clan, whose capital was at Raghugarh in Malwa in central India. Raghugarh miniatures from the end of the 17th century are particularly close to the wall paintings and miniatures of Bundi. Figures often have delicate limbs, small waists and somewhat elongated heads with large eyes (e.g. Patna, V. K. Kanoria priv. col.; Hyderabad, Mittal Mus. Ind. A.). The exact link between Bundi and Raghugarh is as yet unclear. A large number of later Raghugarh paintings, including portraits of the rulers, have been preserved in a single collection (New Delhi, N. Mus.). Raghugarh painting lasted into the 19th century and was indebted to the Bundi school to a greater or lesser extent at various times.

Uniara. In the mid-18th century yet another idiom of the Bundi school developed in Uniara, some 65 km north-east of Bundi. The colophon of an illustrated manuscript of the *Hitopadeśa* (London, BL, Or. MS. 13934), a collection of ancient Indian fables, states that it was produced for the young prince Jasvant Singh of Uniara during the reign of his father Rao Raja Sardar Singh (*reg* 1740–77). The colophon says further that the painter (who produced 132 illustrations for the manuscript) was Dhano from Bundi, which explains the stylistic links with Bundi painting. Other illustrated manuscripts produced at Uniara include a *Bhāgavata purāṇa* (Uniara, Rajendra Singh priv. col.) with several hundred illustrations of scenes from the life of Krishna. According to the colophon, it was completed in 1759 and painted by Mira Bagas. Many single miniatures from Uniara are known, including portraits as well as *darbar* and hunting scenes (e.g. Uniara, Rajendra Singh priv. col.; Jaipur, Sangram Singh priv. col.). In the late 18th century painting in Uniara was heavily influenced by Jaipur, with which Uniara had close ties, its rulers of the Naruka clan being a lesser branch of the Kacchawaha Rajputs of Jaipur.

Wall paintings in the Jagat Shiromani Temple in Uniara date from the late 1770s. They are stylistically close to the wall paintings in the hunting-lodge at Nagar and a temple in Badoli, both in the former Uniara state. The wall paintings in the part of the Uniara palace complex known as the Rangshala were mainly executed in the early 19th century and show some influence of the Jaipur school of painting.

Kapren. Paintings influenced by those of Bundi were also produced in the mid-18th century in Kapren, some 42 km west of Bundi. This particular Bundi idiom owes its existence to a brother of Raoraja Umed Singh of Bundi (*reg* 1739–70), Dip Singh, who in 1760 was given Kapren to rule together with 27 other villages. Paintings produced in Kapren in the 18th century can be distinguished from those of Bundi by their more profuse decoration. The portrait of *Maharaja Sultan Singh of Kapren* (see fig. 281) is a good 19th-century example; 19th-century Kapren miniatures are stylistically almost indistinguishable from those of Bundi.

281. Kapren school: *Maharajah Sultan Singh of Kapren*, opaque watercolour and gold on paper, 235×190 mm, from Kapren, *c.* 1800 (Kapren, Kesri Singh private collection)

BIBLIOGRAPHY

K. Khandalavala: 'A Group of Bundi Miniatures in the Prince of Wales Museum', *Prince of Wales Mus. Bull.*, iii (1953), pp. 25–35

A. Banerji: 'Illustrations to the Rasikapriya from Bundi-Kotah', *Lalit Kala*, iii–iv (1957), pp. 67–73

K. Khandalavala: 'Five Bundi Paintings of the Late 17th Century A.D.', *Prince of Wales Mus. Bull.*, v (1957), pp. 50–56

W. G. Archer: *Indian Painting in Bundi and Kotah* (London, 1959)

P. Chandra: *Bundi Painting* (New Delhi, 1959)

K. Khandalavala, M. Chandra and P. Chandra: *Miniature Painting* (New Delhi, 1960) [from the Sri Motichand Khajanchi Col.]

M. M. Shastri: *Catalogue to Government Museum, Kota* (Jaipur, 1961)

M. C. Beach: 'Painting of the Later Eighteenth Century at Bundi and Kota', *Aspects of Indian Art*, ed. P. Pal (Leiden, 1972), pp. 124–9

——: *Rajput Painting at Bundi and Kota* (Ascona, 1974)

R. Skelton: 'Shaykh Phūl and the Origins of Bundi Painting', *Chhavi 2: Rai Krishnadasa Felicitation Volume* (Banaras, 1981), pp. 123–9

R. K. Tandon: *Indian Miniature Painting: 16th through 19th Centuries* (Bangalore, 1982)

The Art of the Book in India (exh. cat. by J. P. Losty, London, BL, 1982)

G. Sen: *Paintings from the Akbar Nama* (Calcutta, 1984)

J. Bautze: 'Drei Miniaturmalereien aus Kota im Linden-Museum', *Tribus*, xxxiv (1985), pp. 89–120

——: 'Portraits of Bhao Singh Hara', *Berlin. Indol. Stud.*, i (1985), pp. 107–22

——: 'Zuordnungsfragen bei Kota-Malereien', *Z. Dt. Mrgländ. Ges.*, suppl. vi (1985), pp. 438–44

M. K. B. Singh: *The Kingdom that was Kotah: Paintings from Kotah* (New Delhi, 1985)

J. Bautze: 'A Contemporary and Inscribed Equestrian Portrait of Jagat Singh of Kota', *Deyadharma: Studies in Memory of Dr. D. C. Sircar* (New Delhi, 1986), pp. 47–64

——: 'Eine Garudastandarte aus Kota im Linden Museum', *Tribus*, xxxv (1986), pp. 57–82
——: 'Mughal and Deccani Influence on Early 17th-century Murals of Bundi', *Facets of Indian Art*, ed. R. Skelton and others (London, 1986), pp. 168–75
——: 'The Murals in the Jagatśiromaniji Temple in Uniara, Rajasthan', *Proceedings of the XXXII International Conference for Asian and North African Studies: Hamburg, 1986*, pp. 84–8
——: 'Portraits of Rao Ratan and Madho Singh Hara', *Berlin. Indol. Stud.*, ii (1986), pp. 87–106
——: 'Sporting Pastimes of the Hara Kings: Murals of Bundi and Kota', *India Mag.*, vi (1986), pp. 64–71
——: *Drei 'Bundi'-Rāgamālās: Ein Beitrag zur Geschichte der rajputischen Wandmalerei* (Stuttgart, 1987)
——: Une Représentation des bārahmāsā dans la Baḍe Devtājī kī Havelī de Kota', *Berlin. Indol. Stud.*, iii (1987), pp. 195–252
——: 'Portraitmalerei unter Maharao Ram Singh von Kota', *Artibus Asiae*, xlix/3–4 (1988–9), pp. 316–50
——: 'Deckenmalereien Ost-Rajasthans im 17. Jahrhundert am Beispiel des "Badal Mahal" in Bundi', *Z. Dt. Mrgländ. Ges.*, suppl. vii (1989), pp. 666–81
——: 'Ikonographie und Datierung der späteren Jagdszenen und Portraits Bundis', *Tribus*, xxxix (1990), pp. 87–112
——: 'Painting at Khatoli: The Later Phase', *Makaranda: Essays in Honour of Dr. James C. Harle*, ed. C. Bautze-Picron (New Delhi, 1990), pp. 227–33
——: 'Portraitmalerei unter Maharao Raja Ram Singh von Bundi', *Das Bildnis in der Kunst des Orients*, ed. M. Kraatz and others (Stuttgart, 1990), pp. 135–46
——: 'New Documents on Seventeenth Century Portrait-painting at Indargarh', *Lalit Kala*, xxvi (1992), pp. 18–21

JOACHIM BAUTZE

(d) Bikaner. Best known for its lyrical paintings in soft colours, the Bikaner school may have a starting date as early as the late 16th century. Situated in the semi-barren Thar Desert in north-west Rajasthan, the state was founded in 1478 and from the late 16th century was closely allied with the Mughals. As a result, a sophisticated Mughal-influenced taste emerged in its court and élite society.

Though little is known of the lives of individual artists, surviving royal archival accounts and numerous inscriptions on paintings make Bikaner one of the best-documented Rajput schools. Evidence indicates that the Maharajas of Bikaner recruited Mughal school painters but also patronized other artists, mainly local Muslims but also some Hindus and Jains. The royal workshop followed the Mughal pattern, and one or more monitors (senior artists called *gajadhars*) served as links between the patron and the painter. They secured material, supervised the production of paintings and disbursed stipends to other artists. Senior artists appear to have maintained their own workshops, training younger artists, applying finishing touches to their works and contributing an element of individual style to the traditional royal school. Records indicate that some 500 artists worked at one time or another at the Bikaner court, producing over 15,000 individual paintings as well as numerous illustrated manuscripts. They worked mainly on paper but also on wood, hide, cloth and ivory. Wall paintings (fine examples survive at Bikaner Fort) and paintings on doors and furniture are in the same style and appear to be by the same artists.

282. 'Ali Raza 'of Delhi': *Vaikuñtha darśana*, Bikaner school, opaque colour on paper, 80×222 mm, *c.* 1650 (Varanasi, Banaras Hindu University, Bharat Kala Bhavan)

Subject-matter was drawn from both Mughal and traditional Jaina and Hindu sources. Court splendour was projected in depictions of royalty and studies of women inspired by Mughal models. More traditional themes included *Rāgamālā* sets depicting the modes of music, *Bārahmāsā* sets illustrating the 12 months of the year and scenes from the *Vaikuñtha darśana* ('Vision of Vishnu's paradise'). Special to Bikaner are small portraits of dignitaries and depictions of Hindu divinities created as offerings (Ind.-Pers. *nazar*) for presentation on birthdays or during the mourning period after a death. Talented artists received high recognition and rewards, including money, land and secure employment.

The first documented patron of Bikaner painting is Maharaja Karan Singh (*reg* 1631–69). Work from his reign draws heavily on Mughal prototypes of the Shah Jahan period (1628–58) and contemporary Jodhpur paintings. The creations of the great masters of the period are impressive: the *Vaikuñtha darśana* (*c.* 1650; Varanasi, Banaras Hindu U., Bharat Kala Bhavan; see fig. 282) was executed by the painter 'Ali Raza 'of Delhi' (*fl c.* 1645–65). *Ladies' Party* (*c.* 1665; untraced, see Goetz, fig. 83) is the work of Ruknuddin (*fl c.* 1650–1700) and *Lady Looking into a Mirror* (1665; San Diego, CA, Mus. A., Binney Col.) the work of Natthu (*fl c.* 1650–95). These artists also executed fine portraits. While emulating Mughal works in their naturalism, these paintings have a particular charm and freshness. A more stylized and flatter idiom also began to emerge in this phase.

Bikaner painting assumed a distinct character during the reign of Maharaja Anup Singh (*reg* 1669–98), a great connoisseur of painting. It might best be described as a Rajput adaptation of Mughal refinement combined with an intense, Deccani-influenced palette. 'Ali Raza's style was important in the formation of the idiom developed in the second half of the 17th century by such local masters as Ruknuddin, Natthu, Isa (*fl c.* 1650–1715) and Rashid (*fl c.* 1675–95). Patrons of the period seem to have favoured two lineages of painters, the Umarani and Lalani, whose names derive from their founders. Ruknuddin, from the Umarani house, and his son Ibrahim (*fl c.* 1675–1700) supervised Anup Singh's workshop.

The 18th-century workshop is particularly well documented by numerous inscriptions on paintings, mainly in

Marwari dialect but occasionally in Persian script. These reveal dates and artists' names and in some cases other information, such as the place of production and occasion for which a painting was produced. Paintings executed for Maharaja Sujan Singh (*reg* 1700–36) tend to be simple and direct (e.g. see Goetz, fig. 84). A set of the *Rasikapriyā* (produced *c.* 1674–*c.* 1714) and a *Bhāgavata purāṇa* (produced *c.* 1725–40) were major undertakings and influenced Bikaner painters for decades. The royal atelier during Sujan Singh's reign seems to have been under the supervision of the painter Nure (*fl c.* 1646–1715), and from this point onwards Ruknuddin's successors lost their monopoly, and the sons of Nure and Natthu dominated the royal workshop. Murad, son of Lufa, was also important in this period (see Ehnbom exh. cat., 1985, no. 66). Human figures, trees and architecture became slender and elongated. Though some artists continued to favour Ruknuddin's squarish faces, the majority followed Nure's preference for small oval faces. Until the third quarter of the century human expressions remained lively, and landscape was well treated, if conventional. However, paintings lost their subtlety, and compositions were less well integrated.

Matrimonial ties with Jodhpur and Jaipur in the latter years of the reign of Zorawar Singh (*reg* 1736–45) and the first half of that of Gaj Singh (*reg* 1746–87) had an impact on painting. Some works maintain earlier conventions, but others show a dominating Jodhpur influence. Portraits include *Zorawar Singh Hunting* (*c.* 1740; New Delhi, N. Mus., BKN.35) with its sinuous lines and delicate colours. Gaj Singh patronized over 200 artists (supervised by Abu, son of Kasam), who have left a delightful record of the splendours of his court (e.g. see Goetz, fig. 85). While they excelled in precision and refinement, they showed little interest in psychological penetration, and their style became hard and artificial (e.g. see Goetz, fig. 82). Continued political and matrimonial ties with Jaipur led to a further influx of Jaipur artists into the court workshops during the reigns of Surat Singh (*reg* 1787–1827) and Ratan Singh (*reg* 1827–51). Jaipur artists soon usurped the prestige and landholdings of practising painters of local lineages such as Abu, his son Ahmad (*fl c.* 1804) and Ibrahim (*fl c.* 1764). Interaction between an already degenerate Jaipur style and the Bikaner idiom created a new hybrid style at Bikaner. It is characterized by crudely modelled figures, ornamental foliage and trees and a preference for an unusual shade of an almost acidic green. The style seems to have been initiated by Katiram of Jaipur (*fl c.* 1815) and Sukharam and his son Balu (*fl c.* 1754–60) and to have been taken up by local artists.

A treaty signed with the British in 1818 and the advent of the Company school of painting (*see* §(ix) below) dealt a heavy blow to the Bikaner school. However, a small group of artists continued to work in the declining royal ateliers of Maharaja Saradar Singh (*reg* 1851–72) and his successors.

BIBLIOGRAPHY

H. Goetz: *The Art and Architecture of Bikaner State* (Oxford, 1950)
Miniature Paintings: A Catalogue of the Exhibition of the Sri Motichand Khajanchi Collection (exh. cat. by K. Khandalavala, M. Chandra and P. Chandra, New Delhi, Lalit Kala Akad., 1960)
N. Krishna: 'Bikaner Miniature Painting Workshops of Ruknuddin, Ibrahim and Natthu', *Lalit Kala*, xxi (1985), pp. 23–7
India: Art and Culture, 1300–1900 (exh. cat. by S. C. Welch, New York, Met., 1985), nos 247 and 252
Indian Minatures: The Ehrenfeld Collection (exh. cat. by D. J. Ehnbom, New York, Amer. Fed. A., 1985)
N. Krishna: *Bikaner Painting* (in preparation)
——: *Socio-economic Conditions of Bikaner Artists* (in preparation)

NAVAL KRISHNA

(e) Amer, Jaipur and Shekhavati. Three centres of painting are particularly important in the region ruled by Rajputs of the Kachchhwaha clan. Painting developed first at Amer (Amber) in the early 17th century, and work continued from 1728 at Jaipur, the new capital that Sawai Jai Singh II (*reg* 1699–1743) established 8 km south of Amer. Shekhavati, a region in the old Jaipur state, is known for extensive wall paintings on the 19th-century mansions (*havelīs*) of merchant families.

Amer. The earliest references to painting occur in two contemporary biographical accounts of Raja Man Singh of Amer (*reg* 1590–1614): the *Mānacaritakāvya* by Atma Rai (1613; Jaipur, Maharaja Sawai Man Singh II Mus., MS. 1401) and the *Mānacaritra* by Narottama Kavi (Jaipur, Maharaja Sawai Man Singh II Mus., MS. 1977). These reveal that Man Singh, an important member at the court of the Mughal emperors Akbar (*reg* 1556–1605) and Jahangir (*reg* 1605–27), had the walls of his new palace at Amer embellished with panels illustrating scenes from Krishna's life, *Rāgamālā* themes, folk stories and erotic subjects; painted between the panels were peacocks, cranes and parrots, animals, flowers and flowering plants. Traces of such wall paintings have been discovered not only in the Man Singh Palace there but also in the cenotaphs (*chatrīs*), pavilions and temple domes at Amer and the nearby towns of Bairat and Mozumabad. Though damaged and weathered, the paintings reveal a mixture of local idiom with Mughal elements and technique. Raja Man Singh was a patron of literature, drama, art and architecture and actively fostered their development in his court. Outside the court Jaina manuscripts were illustrated in a late Western Indian style (*see* §3(ii)(a) above). Examples are known from Amer and Mozumabad (1591 and 1606 respectively; both Jaipur, Dig. Jaina Atisaya Kshetra), further indicating a thriving art tradition in this region.

Mirza Raja Jai Singh (*reg* 1623–67), an equally powerful personality who also occupied a high position in the Mughal court, constructed new palaces and audience halls in Amer, modelled on Mughal palaces in Agra and Delhi, and acquired fine carpets and decorative art objects. However, the vigorous local style continued to predominate in painting, except in portraiture, which was modelled on Mughal court style. Typical of the Amer portrait style is the double portrait of *Mirza Raja Jai Singh and his Grandson Kishan Singh*, who died as a prince in 1682 (London, BL, Orient. & India Office Lib., Add. Or. MS. 4244). An unusually long (138.99 m) horoscope (*janmapatra*) was prepared for this short-lived prince, containing pictures of planets, stars, deities, portents, directional divinities (*dikpālas*) and portraits painted in a similar but less opulent style (Jaipur, Maharaja Sawai Man Singh II Mus., MS. 1458; all further works cited are in this collection unless otherwise indicated). A manuscript on music (MS. 6790/1), one of the Prince's interests, with four illustrations in a mixed local style, was prepared in 1679 at

Jaisinghpura, near Aurangabad; a manuscript on massage (Jaipur, priv. col.) has numerous illustrations drawn in a simple and unsophisticated style.

Maharaja Sawai Jai Singh (*reg* 1699–1743) was a perceptive man with original ideas, interested in religion, literature, astronomy, architecture, urban planning and painting. He commissioned sets of illustrations on such themes as *Rāgamālā* (the modes of music), *Bārahmāsā* (the 12 months) and *Saḍṛtuvarṇam* (the six seasons). A *Rāgamālā* set painted at Amer in 1709 (Kankroli, Maharaj of Kankroli priv. col.) and related illustrations (dispersed) show the flowering of a mature local idiom with elements of late Mughal and Deccani styles. Large flowering plants on the dados of pavilions and buildings shown in these paintings and some architectural details can also be found in buildings constructed by Sawai Jai Singh in Amer and Jaigarh.

Jaipur. Sawai Jai Singh established in his new city, Jaipur, a sprawling complex devoted to the arts of the book. Painters, calligraphers, papermakers and bookbinders from Delhi, Agra and elsewhere worked side by side with local recruits. Taking advantage of political uncertainty in Delhi, Sawai Jai Singh acquired a large number of Mughal albums, portraits and illustrated manuscripts. The painters of the workshop prepared albums bound with fine textiles, in which Jai Singh's large collection of Mughal, Deccani and Rajasthani paintings was mounted. An inventory compiled in 1745 (Bikaner, Rajasthan State Archv) records numerous albums and illustrated manuscripts and nearly 2500 individual paintings.

One of the most interesting productions from the period of Sawai Jai Singh is an illustrated manuscript on poetics, the *Sarasarasagrantha*, dated 1737, with 39 high-quality miniatures (MS. 7743/JS). The style is lively, the colouring vibrant, the work evocative of the world of romance and poetry effectively created by the painters of Emperor Muhammad Shah (*reg* 1719–48) at Delhi. A young painter, Sahibram (*fl c.* 1740–1805), came to prominence as a portraitist. He prepared over life-size portraits of Sawai Jai Singh (e.g. AG.1402) in a personal style that became standard. He continued to work for five successive rulers, painting on cloth in the same style over life-size portraits of Sawai Ishwari Singh (AG.1403), Sawai Madho Singh I (AG.1404), Sawai Prithvi Singh (Jaipur, priv. col.), Sawai Pratap Singh (AG.1405, 1406 and 1407) and Sawai Jagat Singh (AG.1408).

Maharaja Sawai Madho Singh I (*reg* 1750–68), the offspring of Sawai Jai Singh's marriage with a Mewar princess, was also a connoisseur of art and architecture. He enlarged the workshop by appointing new painters and kept them busy with commissions of portraits, albums and illustrated manuscripts. A large number of portraits of the corpulent ruler, his sports and pastimes and his courtiers have survived. Some of these reveal a welcome departure from the earlier style incorporating Mewar elements. Painters gave more attention to courtly ceremonies and animal fights, and the compositions are often panoramic, with bright, luxuriant colouring.

The Jaipur school reached its zenith under Maharaja Sawai Pratap Singh (*reg* 1778–1803), an ardent devotee of Radha and Krishna and a poet, composer and connoisseur of painting. The workshop flourished under his attention; the names of 25 painters are known, among them Sahibram, Gopal, Jivan, Ramjidas, Hira, Ghasi and Mangal. Among the most notable illustrated manuscripts and sets of paintings are a *Rāgamālā* set of 43 miniatures (AG.546–586), a long *Rāmāyaṇa* series (Jaipur, priv. col.), a *Bhāgavata purāṇa* completed in 1792 with 366 illustrations (AG.102–467) and a *Devī māhātmya* dated 1799 with 102 illustrations (AG.1–101).

The *Rāgamālā* set, painted by Mangal and Jivan, is very well-finished though somewhat formalized (see fig. 283). The *Devī māhātmya* set is more vigorous and exhibits a distinctive palette, with lighter shades of blue, yellow, grey and green not used before. Large individual compositions were made, including a painting of Radha and Krishna dancing with musicians and milkmaids, a remarkable painting of Krishna's circle dance or *Rāsalīlā* (see fig. 284) and one showing Krishna lifting Mt Govardhana to protect the villagers. Large preliminary drawings of the painting of Krishna's dance were collected by A. K. Coomaraswamy from the successors of Sahibram (e.g. New York, MOMA; Boston, MA, Mus. F.A.; Calcutta, Ind. Mus.). Ramjidas and other artists also prepared a large number of lively drawings and thumbnail sketches of nobles and such humble retainers as musicians, writers, painters, tailors, barbers, elephant drivers and timekeepers (see Das, 1981).

283. Jivan: *Rāginī varārī*, Jaipur school, opaque colour on paper, 315×185 mm, from a *Rāgamālā* series made for Maharaja Sawai Pratap Singh, *c.* 1778–85 (Jaipur, Maharaja Sawai Man Singh II Museum)

284. Jaipur school: *Rāsalīlā*, opaque colour on paper, 650×490 mm, *c.* 1790 (Jaipur, Maharaja Sawai Man Singh II Museum)

Patronage of painting continued during the troubled reign of Maharaja Sawai Jagat Singh (*reg* 1803–18), who commissioned extensive wall paintings in several rooms of the Chandra Mahal and in various mansions, temples and pavilions. However, after his death painters left the workshop in search of other employment. Maharaja Sawai Ram Singh II (*reg* 1835–80) founded a school of art to train students in Western art, craft and even photography; the Amer–Jaipur style declined.

Shekhavati. From the beginning of the 19th century many traders from the desert area of Shekhavati, in the northern part of the old Jaipur state, migrated to Calcutta, Bombay, Delhi and other cities and within a short time accumulated substantial wealth. They spent a considerable part of their riches in constructing enormous mansions and brought the finest woodworkers, masons and painters to decorate them. These mansions are found in such small towns and *thikānas* (districts ruled by local *thakurs* who paid revenue and swore allegiance to the Maharaja) as Fatehpur, Ramgarh, Nawalgarh, Dundlod, Mukandgarh, Jhunjhunu, Pilani, Chirawa, Bissau and Malsisar. The wall paintings decorating these structures are distinctive and show a mixture of folk and classical idioms, perhaps reflecting the unsophisticated taste of their merchant patrons. The paintings embellishing the exteriors and interiors of these sprawling mansions depict religious and mythological subjects, birds, animals, floral and geometrical motifs and scenes from contemporary life. Gods and goddesses co-exist with ordinary mortals, trains, cars, brass bands, bicycles, sewing machines and marriage processions. The artists painted in a simple and vigorous narrative style, the tradition continuing until the third decade of the 20th century. In the 1980s efforts were begun to preserve the paintings.

BIBLIOGRAPHY

S. K. Andhare: 'A Dated Amber Ragamala and the Problem of Provenance of the Eighteenth Century Jaipur Painting', *Lalit Kala*, xv (1972), pp. 47–51

——: 'An Early Ragamala from the Kankroli Collection', *Prince of Wales Mus. Bull.*, xii (1973), pp. 58–64

K. Khandalavala: *Wall Paintings of Amber*, New Delhi, Lalit Kala Akad. (New Delhi, 1974)

A. K. Das: 'Miniature', *Marg* (Sept 1977), pp. 77–94, 102

——: 'Ramjidas Chatera: An Eighteenth Century Portrait Painter from Jaipur', *Cultural Contours of India: Dr. Satya Prakash Felicitation Volume*, ed. V. S. Srivastava (New Delhi, 1981), pp. 317–23

F. Wacziarg and A. Nath: *Rajasthan: The Painted Walls of Shekhavati* (New Delhi, 1982)

A. K. Das: 'Glimpses of Social Life as Depicted by a Group of Jaipur Drawings of "Ordinary" People', *Sodhak*, xiv/40 (1985), pp. 35–46

——: 'An Illustrated Manuscript of Durga Path of Jaipur School Dated AD 1799', *Dimensions of Indian Art: Pupul Jayakar Seventy*, ed. L. Chandra, J. Jain and A. Prasad (New Delhi, 1986), pp. 85–92

——: *Amber–Jaipur Painting*, v of *Treasures of Indian Painting*, (Jaipur, 1986)

I. Cooper: *The Guide to Painted Towns of Shekhawati* (Churu, n.d.)

ASOK KUMAR DAS

(f) Kishangarh. In the mid-18th century the artists of Kishangarh, a small state located between Ajmer and Jaipur, produced miniature paintings characterized by a unique lyrical sensibility. Despite its relatively minor political status among the principalities of Rajasthan and the relatively short span of its artistic production from the late 17th century to the late 19th, the brilliance of these works secures Kishangarh's important position among the numerous schools of Indian painting.

Kishangarh was founded in 1609 by Kishan Singh (*reg* 1609–15), the eighth son of Raja Udai Singh of Jodhpur. Its fine school of painting was unknown to Western art historians until 1943, when Eric Dickinson, Professor of English Literature at Government College in Lahore and an Indian miniature enthusiast, was invited to see the Kishangarh Darbar Collection, still in the possession of the ruling family. The collection comprised approximately 800 pictures. Dickinson immediately recognized the significance of a portfolio of unusually large miniatures, which are now regarded as among the finest paintings of the school. Although they depicted a wide range of subjects, Kishangarh artists favoured romantic scenes of courtly love. Many of these miniatures were based on the stories of Radha and Krishna. Other subjects included portraits, historical events, studies derived from European prints, studies of horses, floral subjects, hunting scenes, genre scenes and *darbar* (audience) scenes.

Before 1740. The earliest dated Kishangarh painting (1694; Kishangarh, Darbar Col.) was executed during the reign of Raja Man Singh (*reg* 1658–1706) and is a portrait of his son *Raj Singh*, showing him on a horse spearing a black buck. In this and other known early works, Kishangarh paintings demonstrate a close stylistic affinity to contemporary Mughal painting, a characteristic shared with work from Bikaner and in contrast to contemporary painting from Mewar and Malwa. As ruler of Kishangarh,

Raj Singh (*reg* 1706–48) was an enthusiastic patron of the arts and a painter himself, as is known from a portrait in the Kishangarh Darbar Collection ascribed to him. Darbar records yield the names of several artists at work during Raj Singh's reign, including three who migrated from Delhi: Bhavani Das, Dalchand and Kalyan Das. Bhavani Das joined the Kishangarh workshop in 1719 and is recorded in archival documents as being active in Kishangarh in 1722. Dalchand and Kalyan Das followed in 1726. Archival records listing artists' salaries up to 1742 show that Bhavani Das received the highest wage of any artist of the atelier. Paintings attributed to him include *Raja Sahasmal with Falconers* (Kishangarh, Darbar Col., see Dickinson and Khandalavala, p. 35), probably from Raj Singh's reign. As in the 1694 portrait of *Raj Singh*, contemporary Mughal compositional conventions have been adopted, and the painting shows the fine technical execution associated with Mughal artists. Two other paintings attributed to Bhavani Das are a *Queen Listening to Music* and a *Princess Enjoying Fireworks* (both New Delhi, N. Mus.). Dalchand must also have achieved a level of esteem, for an inscription on a painting of a horse by him states that the work was presented to the Mughal emperor Farrukhsiyar (*reg* 1712–19). In a delicately executed miniature of *c.* 1740 (Patna, G. K. Kanoria priv. col., see 1985 exh. cat., p. 371) Raj Singh is depicted resting after a hunt: he is shown seated regally under a tree surrounded by female attendants in a composition strongly evocative of portrayals of Krishna and his female companions and anticipating work that would be associated with his son and successor Savant Singh.

1740–70. The flowering of the Kishangarh idiom, which has been assigned to the period 1740 to 1770, has traditionally been attributed to the influence of Savant Singh (*reg* 1748–64). Like his father Raj Singh, Savant Singh was a devotee of Krishna and the arts. From the time of Kishan Singh there appears to have been a continuous association between the Kishangarh rulers and Vaishnavite teachers. Both Savant Singh and Raj Singh were followers of the 15th-century teacher Vallabhacharya, who propounded the *Pushṭimārga* ('Way of grace') in which salvation is found through personal devotion to Krishna. Under the pen-name Nagari Das, Savant Singh attained renown as a Hindi poet, writing frequently on the theme of the love of Radha and Krishna. Verses from his works were illustrated by Kishangarh painters. Savant Singh was also accomplished in music and art. Four sketches in the Kishangarh Darbar Collection are ascribed to him, including a sketch of a *yoginī* (female ascetic) with a Hindi couplet written in his hand. Savant Singh had close connections with the Mughal court and was an ally of both Farrukhsiyar and Muhammad Shah (*reg* 1719–48). A portrait of *Savant Singh in a Garden Pavilion* (priv. col., see Randhawa, p. 15), dated on the reverse to the 25th regnal year of Muhammad Shah (i.e. 1744), reflects the highly refined technique and attentiveness to detail that Kishangarh painting shared with contemporary Mughal painting. The background, with its romantic depiction of distant vistas and forested rolling hills on the horizon, is also characteristic of Kishangarh painting.

Works associated with the artist Nihal Chand (*fl* 1735–1757 or 1773) represent the quintessential Kishangarh idiom, and it has been assumed that the classic Kishangarh style resulted from the relationship between Savant Singh and this uniquely gifted artist, who held an eminent position at court and was given a *jāgīr* (land grant). Nihal Chand's father was the painter Bhik Chand, and two descendants, Sitaram and Badan Singh, were also painters. Nihal Chand's paintings characteristically depict the idealized lovers Radha and Krishna in luscious surroundings and feature the idealized female figure type of attenuated elegance that is distinctive to Kishangarh painting. The faces are elongated and distinguished by long, curving, lotus-bud eyes, high arching eyebrows, a long, sharply pointed nose and pointed chin. Dickinson and Khandalavala suggested that this female facial type is a stylistic exaggeration of the distinctive beauty of Bani Thani, a singer, poet and devotee of Krishna.

Nihal Chand's painting *Courtly Paradise* (Kishangarh, Darbar Col., see Dickinson and Khandalavala, p. 21) depicts Radha and Krishna portrayed as a Rajput prince and his mistress in a marble pavilion being entertained by an ensemble of female musicians. The symmetry, gleaming white colour and clarity of the delineation of the pavilion provide a striking contrast to the lush forest painted in deep green tones in the background. The artist's virtuosity is apparent in his treatment of the diverse foliage of the forest and its varied bird life. Also characteristic of his work is the brilliantly painted sunset which serves to enhance the romantic ambience. This painting also features the figure of Krishna wearing a distinctive turban that Savant Singh is said to have seen in a vision and subsequently ordered his painters to depict.

The painting *Fireworks Exhibition at Night* (Kishangarh, Darbar Col., see Dickinson and Khandalavala, p. 41), attributed to Nihal Chand, depicts a theme also popular in late Mughal paintings produced for Muhammad Shah. The Kishangarh work is inscribed on the *verso* with the poetry of Nagari Das/Savant Singh, describing the glowing love of Radha and Krishna (who are present in the work) in imagery as evocative as the fireworks depicted in the painting: 'The scented smoke of incense floats around the fitful beauty of a stream of shining lamps; while showers of dazzling sparks create a scintillating fairy land' (Dickinson and Khandalavala, p. 40). It was this painting that led to Dickinson's realization that some Kishangarh miniatures were illustrations of verses by Nagari Das and that Nagari Das was the pen-name of Maharaja Savant Singh of Kishangarh.

Nihal Chand is also named as the artist in a Persian inscription on the *Boat of Love* (New Delhi, N. Mus.; see fig. 285), illustrating a verse from *Bihārī chandrikā*, a volume of poetry by Savant Singh. The sequential illustration represents (in the distance) Krishna and Radha seated with female attendants on a hillock against a brilliant sunset; (in the middle register) the lovers with female attendants in a boat floating on a lotus-covered lake, along the far bank of which is a view of temples and palaces; and (in the foreground) the pair standing alone under a tree in a verdant forest. This painting is imbued with all the lyrical romanticism and exquisite detail that distinguishes the paintings associated with both Nihal Chand

285. Nihal Chand: *Boat of Love*, Kishangarn school, opaque colour on paper, *c.* 1750 (New Delhi, National Museum)

and the height of the Kishangarh school during the mid-18th century. Other extant works by Nihal Chand include an illustration from the *Bhāgavata purāṇa* (1757; Kishangarh, Darbar Col.), also with an inscription naming him as the painter. Although he was noted for his paintings of Vaishnavite themes, archival records of Kishangarh reveal that he was once commissioned to illustrate a series of scenes from the *Shāhnāma* ('Book of kings'; dispersed), the 10th–11th-century poet Firdausi's Persian epic on the ancient kings of Iran.

Also from the mid-18th century is the painting *Raja Sardar Singh Presiding at a Music Party in the Palace at Rupnagar* (Kishangarh, Darbar Col., see Dickinson and Khandalavala, p. 39). On the *verso* is a Hindi inscription naming the painter as Amar Chand, a contemporary of Nihal Chand, said to have been trained in Delhi. According to the inscription, Amar Chand had an enthusiasm for architectural décor. His elaborate depiction of architecture points to Mughal influence, as do the refined technique and the rather static symmetrical composition. Also indicative of the close cultural ties between the Mughal court and Kishangarh, the principal performer is identified as the singer Pana of Shahjahanabad (Delhi). The figures depicted in the painting are identified in gold in *devanāgrī* script, and one of those watching the entertainment is the painter Nihal Chand. His inclusion here among court officials is yet another indication of his high standing.

Although painting continued at Kishangarh under later rulers, by the late 18th century the early delicacy was often replaced by a hardening of the line and an exaggeration of the distinctive Kishangarh facial features that result in near caricature. The 23 illustrations of a *Gīta Govinda* (1820; priv. col., see Randhawa, p. 45), painted for Raja Kalyan Singh (*reg* 1797–1838), reflect a movement away from the Mughal-influenced idiom of the 18th century and towards the general Rajasthani style of the 19th. Gone is the characteristic Kishangarh female facial type of the mid-18th century, as too are the refined execution and air of romantic nostalgia.

Reflecting the closer stylistic relationships to contemporary Rajasthani schools is a painting of *Mokhan Singh* (*reg* 1838–41) standing with his courtiers by a lake (Cambridge, MA, Fogg), with an inscription naming the artist as Nanak Ram. The open vistas and a register of dense foliage behind the line of figures are reminiscent of 18th-century Kishangarh painting, but the palette and quality of line are typical of the 19th century. A slightly later work from the reign of Prithvi Singh (*reg* 1841–80), *Prithvi Singh Riding with his Sons in a Deserted Landscape* (priv. col., see 1965 exh. cat.; 1965, p. 110), shows the decline from the sensitive refinement of execution and mood that had characterized Kishangarh painting at its height.

BIBLIOGRAPHY

E. Dickinson: 'The Way of Pleasure', *Marg*, iii (1949), pp. 29–35

E. Dickinson and K. Khandalavala: *Kishangarh Painting* (New Delhi, 1959)

Gods, Thrones and Peacocks: Northern Indian Painting from Two Traditions, Fifteenth to Nineteenth Centuries (exh. cat. by S. C. Welch and M. C. Beach, New York, 1965)

E. Binney III and W. G. Archer: *Rajput Miniatures from the Collection of Edwin Binney III* (Portland, 1968)

A Flower from Every Meadow: Indian Paintings from American Collections (exh. cat. by S. C. Welch, New York, Asia Soc. Gals; San Francisco, CA, Cent. Asian A. & Cult.; Buffalo, NY, Albright-Knox A. G.; 1973)

F. A. Khan: 'The Painters of Kishangarh', *Roopa-Lekha*, li (1980), pp. 61–9

M. S. Randhawa and D. S. Randhawa: *Kishangarh Painting* (Bombay, 1980)

India: Art and Culture, 1300–1900 (exh. cat. by S. C. Welch, New York, Met., 1985)

MARSHA TAJIMA

(g) Marwar. Marwar painting is the name given to a range of related styles that were practised in the huge and largely desert territory of Marwar or Marudesh, which covers much of western Rajasthan, with its capital at Jodhpur. The far west of the region, around Jaisalmer, is geographically remote, and painting there remained to some extent untouched by Mughal courtly styles, maintaining simple compositions and a distinctive angularity close to folk art. Painting in more easterly centres, nearer to Delhi and situated on important trade routes, was open to greater Mughal influence, especially after the Rathor rulers of Jodhpur capitulated to the Mughal emperor Akbar (*reg* 1556–1605) in the late 16th century, thereafter serving as courtiers to a succession of Mughal rulers. While later Marwar painting, especially that of early 19th-century Jodhpur with its bold colours, spiralling clouds and swirling skirts, is well known and well represented in many collections, its early development remains unclear.

17th century. The most important early landmark in Marwar painting is a set of *Rāgamālā* paintings dated 1623 (VS 1680; Jaipur, Sangram Singh priv. col., and New Delhi, N. Mus.). Known as the Pali *Rāgamālā*, it was produced not in Jodhpur itself but in the provincial town of Pali, a prosperous trading centre on the route between Marwar and Mewar and between the coast and northern India. The *Rāgamālā* set is complete, with 36 illustrations representing the six *rāgas* (musical modes), each with six *rāgiṇīs* ('wives of the *rāgas*' or subordinate modes), plus one extra *rāgiṇī*. The colophon states that it was written and painted by Pandit Virji under the patronage of Bithal Das, ruler of Pali. The paintings are in a lively folk style strongly influenced by the Western Indian tradition of earlier Jaina manuscripts (*see* §3(ii)(a) and (b) above and §(h) below). They are in an archaic horizontal format, reflecting the shape of earlier palm-leaf manuscripts. The use of architectural elements and decorative textiles and even the poses of many of the figures strongly recall Gujarati manuscript illustration, but certain elements show the early stages of a distinctive Marwari style. Faces are characterized by sloping foreheads, pointed noses, almond eyes and pouting lips, features that recur throughout the later development of Marwari painting, and the colour scheme, a somewhat sombre and earthy palette of yellows, greens and greys, remains characteristic until the exuberant outbursts of the 19th century.

Dispersed single leaves from other 17th-century manuscripts, predominantly *Rāgamālās*, show an eclectic style, which in its early stages is still heavily influenced by Jaina painting. These include, for example, two illustrated folios from an *Upadeśamālā prakāśaṇa* (New Delhi, N. Mus.), a long poem containing moral instructions for Jaina lay followers and nuns, dated 1634 (vs 1691–2). The horizontal format, however, was abandoned before the middle of the 17th century. Paintings then change their emphasis to the darker tones and vertically layered composition seen in contemporary Malwa painting (*see* §(b) above). The influence of the Mughal court was already present in the early manuscripts, for instance in costume elements such as the four-pointed *jāmā* ('robe') and flat turban. By the middle of the 17th century it began to exert itself more strongly in terms of subject-matter and composition. Maharajas Gaj Singh (*reg* 1620–38) and Jaswant Singh (*reg* 1638–78) were both eminent figures at the court of Shah Jahan, and Mughal-trained artists and architects were working at Jodhpur under their patronage. Concurrent with the traditional style of religious manuscript and *Rāgamālā* illustration, a new fashion for Mughal-style portraits and group scenes evolved. For the first time finely detailed, recognizable studies of individuals started to appear in Jodhpur, most notably a group of fine portraits of Jaswant Singh, alone or with nobles or ladies (e.g. London, BM and V&A; Melbourne, N.G. Victoria). Other portraits, presumably inspired by Mughal prototypes, including, for example, a posthumously painted head of *Gaj Singh* (New Delhi, N. Mus.), show less naturalism and favour stylized 'sculptural' curls of hair and stiff-looking turbans. Other *darbar* (audience) scenes showing Gaj Singh or Jaswant Singh with their nobles exhibit the formality of contemporary Mughal court scenes but are set against the sparser surroundings of the Jodhpur court. These prefigure the favoured 18th-century and early 19th-century Marwari composition, reflecting real-life *darbar* protocol, of ranks of nobles seated on either side of the ruler (see fig. 286).

286. Marwar school: *Maharaja Bhim Singh of Jodhpur with his Nobles*, opaque colour on paper, 408×315 mm, from Jodhpur, *c*. 1790 (London, Victoria and Albert Museum)

18th century. With the death of Jaswant Singh in 1678, Jodhpur was taken under Mughal control by Aurangzeb, a situation that lasted until the Emperor's death in 1707, when Maharaja Ajit Singh (*reg* 1707–24) was able to recapture his kingdom. A taste for equestrian portraiture had come to Jodhpur with the Mughals, and during the 18th century stately, sparsely-composed paintings of Rathor noblemen, in tall turbans, on horseback with retainers or standing stiffly facing other local nobles, were produced in large numbers, painted predominantly in earth tones of yellow, brown, orange and green. Although largely stylized, the subjects, and often their horses, have some degree of individuality, and a finely detailed rendering of textile patterns, horse trappings and turban cloths is characteristic of these portraits. Some of the most impressive equestrian portraits were done for Maharaja Ram Singh (*reg* 1750–51) and his nobles, especially Thakur Sher Singh of Riyan.

The virtuosity and formality of 18th-century painting in Marwar are epitomized by its most gifted exponent, Dalchand (*fl c*. 1720–50), a Mughal-trained artist who worked at Jodhpur under Maharaja Abhai Singh (*reg* 1724–49). A portrait of the Maharaja by him (Jodhpur, Umaid Bhavan Pal. Lib., see Ashton, p. 431) displays the Mughal fondness for the equestrian portrait with detailed distant landscape and finely patterned textiles, as well as the use of the nimbus around the ruler's head. That Dalchand came from the Mughal court is confirmed both by his obviously Mughal style of painting and by an inscription on the *verso* of another portrait by him, *Abhai Singh with a Courtier* (Copenhagen, Davids Saml.), which names him as 'the Delhi artist' (*dillī rā chitārā*) Dalchand. Further documentation on the artist includes a portrait of him (London, BL, Orient. & India Office Lib., Johnson album 58, no. 1) and a painting by his student Maharai (London, V&A, IM. 88-1922).

During the 18th century painting studios emerged in several smaller *thikānas* of Marwar (districts ruled by local *thakurs* who paid revenue and swore allegiance to the Maharaja). Notable among these was Ghanerao, between Jodhpur and Udaipur, whose rulers Padam Singh (*reg* 1720–42) and Viram Dev (*reg* 1743–78) were patrons to artists who used a bold, lively style to illustrate court scenes. One of the most accomplished of the Ghanerao artists was Chhajju (*fl c.* 1720–40), who may have come from Jodhpur. His formal portraits transcend the static and convey much of the subject's personality (for illustrations see Sharma, pl. 70; Archer, p. 57). Another Ghanerao artist, Kripa Ram (*fl c.* 1717–*c.*1740), is known through his portrait of *Padam Singh*, dated 1717 (Jaipur, Sangram Singh priv. col.), and it appears from a double portrait of *Viram Dev and Durjan Singh* dated 1774 (priv. col.) that the painter Sahibdin (*fl* 1770s), a Bikaner artist, also worked in Ghanerao as well as Jodhpur, where he painted *Maharaja Ram Singh* (*reg* 1750–51; Jaipur, Sangram Singh priv. col.). Under Ajit Singh (*reg* 1800–56), painting in Ghanerao became heavily influenced by the contemporary Man Singh (*reg* 1803–43) style of Jodhpur painting (see below). For example, a scene of a ruler and nobles watching dancing girls (Jaipur, Sangram Singh priv. col.), signed by the painter Shiv Lal and dated 1812 (VS 1869), shows typical ingredients of snail-like clouds, stylized trees and skirts that curl up along the hemline.

The fortress town of Nagaur, to the north-east of Jodhpur, also had a flourishing studio in the 18th century. Ajit Singh of Jodhpur had placed Nagaur under his son Bakhat Singh, and after Ajit Singh's death in 1724 Nagaur became an important centre from which Bakhat Singh planned the overthrow of his brother Abhai Singh, who had succeeded to the throne of Jodhpur. The art of portraiture, for which there is some evidence at Nagaur during its years as a Mughal satellite almost a hundred years earlier, was revived. Several fine and often large-scale portraits were painted, sometimes with the entire picture space filled with only the head and shoulders of the subject (e.g. Jodhpur, Umaid Bhavan Pal. Lib.). Bakhat Singh commissioned extensive mural decorations for the new palace he had built within the older fort. They are in a Sub-Imperial Mughal style and are of flying peris (heavenly beings) amid clouds on the ceilings, and, on the walls, scenes of music, dancing, wrestling and girls bathing or offering food at shrines. The colour scheme, although now much perished, seems to be a simple one, particularly favouring the use of green. When Bakhat Singh became Maharaja of Jodhpur in 1752, ruling for one year only, Nagaur lapsed into relative insignificance. It seems likely that some of the artists from Nagaur followed Bakhat Singh to Jodhpur: one portrait of his successor *Bijay Singh* (*reg* 1752–93; Jodhpur, Umaid Bhavan Pal. Lib.) is signed by a Muslim artist from Nagaur named Kayim.

Around the third quarter of the 18th century, under Bijay Singh, portraiture in Marwar began to anticipate stylistic developments of the early 19th century. Horses, often painted blue, prance more jauntily, bearing nobles whose turbans, no longer towering above them in the fashion of the 1750s, became lower and eventually small and round and whose beards and pleated *jāmās* are depicted in curling outlines.

19th century. Marwar painting entered its most prolific phase in the early 19th century. Maharaja Man Singh (*reg* 1803–43) was an enthusiastic patron of the arts, as well as a devoutly religious man. Dominated by his gurus, he ultimately became a recluse. Numerous paintings depict him with his spiritual mentor, Devnath, a *kānphaṭa* yogi, or with Jallandarnath, a leader of the Nath sect, in whose honour he built the Mahamandir (Great Temple) in Jodhpur. It was dedicated in 1805 and decorated with wall paintings depicting the saints of the Nath sect in meditation or yoga *āsaṇas* (postures). Several paintings on paper from this period are signed by Misridas of Mahamandir, who may also have executed the temple murals. Man Singh also commissioned *c.* 1820 several large-sized sets, mostly of 70 or more paintings, illustrating both religious and secular texts (Jodhpur, Umaid Bhavan Pal. Lib., with the exception of a few single pages). Religious subjects include the *Bhāgavatgīta* the great Hindu epic the *Rāmāyaṇa*; the *Nāth caritra*, relating the history of the Nath sect; the *Gajendra moksha*, a devotional text recounting the salvation of the elephant king through the benevolence of the god Vishnu; the *Śiva purāṇa*, relating the mythology of the god Shiva; and the *Durga caritra*, telling the story of the goddess Durga's triumph over demons. Secular subjects include the Rajasthani romance *Dholā–Mārū*; the *Pāñca tantra*, a collection of animal tales with moral teachings; and the *Sūraj prakāsh*, a history of the solar races by Karnidan that traces the origins of the Rathor Rajputs and recounts their history down to Abhai Singh's time. The illustrations in these sets are characterized by a large horizontal format, bold colours and fantastic and stylized rocks, clouds and trees.

Man Singh's courtly activities were also well documented. Many exuberant paintings show him in gardens, in palaces, with his nobles, with his womenfolk, in procession and alone (e.g. Jodhpur, Umaid Bhavan Pal. Lib.). In these secular scenes, lush vegetation and palace architecture often dominate, almost overwhelming the figures with huge green leaves or white arcades. The curling outlines that had begun to appear 30 years earlier are now adopted exclusively, with rhythmic rows of swinging bell-like skirts and *jāmās* and curling *dupaṭṭās* (veil-like scarves) predominating.

Several named artists are known from this period, the most prolific and competent being Amar Das and Shiv Das, as well as Dana, Bulaki Das, Moti Ram, Udai Ram and Bhatti Shankar (all *fl c.* 1820–50). Both Shiv Das and Dana also sometimes appended to their signatures the surname 'Bhatti', which as well as being the clan name of the ruling house of Jaisalmer was also adopted by non-Rajput artisans in the Jodhpur region. Although the desert city of Jaisalmer had probably had an active painting studio in its heyday as an important trading centre, it is unlikely that an artist would have been of the ruling Rajput clan.

Several of Man Singh's artists continued to work under his successor Takhat Singh (*reg* 1843–73), producing secular paintings still in the Man Singh style. Lively wall paintings depicting events in the life of Krishna, scenes from the *Dholā–Mārū* romance and a variety of other subjects were painted to decorate rooms in the palace. During the reign of Jaswant Singh II (*reg* 1873–95) wall painting came under the influence of Jaipur, one set of *Rāgamālā* scenes in the Phul Mahal in Jodhpur Fort reportedly being executed over a 15-year period by a Jaipur artist (Hendley, p. 64). Miniature painting declined sharply under Jaswant Singh, a progressive and Western-looking ruler who was more strongly committed to improving social welfare and communications than to patronizing the arts. In emulation of Victorian England, he recorded courtly life and the nobles of neighbour states by photograph, and the flow of paintings so liberally commissioned even by his immediate predecessor ceased abruptly.

BIBLIOGRAPHY

T. H. Hendley: *Memorials of the Jeypore Exhibition*, i (London, 1883)
H. Goetz: 'The Marwar School of Rajput Painting', *Bull. Baroda Mus. & Pict. Gal.*, iv, part 1 (1947), pp. 43–54
——: 'The Nagaur School of Rajput Painting (18th century)', *Artibus Asiae*, xii (1949), pp. 89–98
L. Ashton, ed.: *The Art of India and Pakistan* (London, 1950)
H. Goetz: 'Marwar (with Some Paintings from Jodhpur in the Collection of Kumar Sangram Singh)', *Marg*, xi/2 (1958), pp. 42–9
K. Khandalavala: 'The Origin and Development of Rajput Painting', *Marg*, xi/2 (1958), pp. 4–17
W. G. Archer: *Indian Miniatures* (London, 1960)
Sangram Singh: 'An Early *Ragamala* MS from Pali (Marwar School) Dated 1623 AD', *Lalit Kala*, vii (1960), pp. 76–81
Miniature Painting: A Catalogue of the Sri Motichand Khajanchi Collection (exh. cat. by K. Khandalavala, M. Chandra and P. Chandra, New Delhi, Lalit Kala Akad., 1960)
K. Ebeling: *Ragamala Painting* (Basle, 1973)
O. P. Sharma: *Indian Miniature Painting* (Brussels, 1974)
R. A. Agrawal: *Marwar Murals* (New Delhi, 1979)
A. Topsfield: *Paintings from Rajasthan in the National Gallery of Victoria* (Melbourne, 1980)
R. Cimino, ed.: *Life at Court in Rajasthan* (Turin, 1985)

ROSEMARY CRILL

(h) Gujarat. Painting in Gujarat from *c.* 1500 to *c.* 1900 drew inspiration from numerous religious, cultural, artistic and political sources. The region was always a stronghold of JAINISM, especially the Shvetambara sect, but its proximity to the Islamic hinterland and important seaports of Sind meant that it was also one of the earliest parts of the subcontinent to receive and absorb political and cultural influences from the Islamic world. However, although both these streams found expression in Gujarati painting, paucity of material and difficulty of identification have led art historians to neglect the local Islamic 'Sultanate' style in favour of Jaina painting.

Most painting in Gujarat was done for a mainly Jaina, but occasionally Hindu, merchant clientele, generally labelled as favouring strong conservatism in painting. Canonical scriptures and other important literary works were copied to be donated to monks or temple libraries in order to earn the donor religious merit. This may explain why such earlier conventions as showing both eyes with the face in profile, angularity in the depiction of the human body and the aperspectival treatment of architecture, landscape or narrative sequences continued into the first half of the 16th century, along with abstract pictorial imagery reflecting religious and philosophical phenomena understood only by instructed viewers. These characteristics slowly gave way to more innovative expressions influenced by contemporary trends from other regions. Among the few examples of illustrated Hindu manuscripts, some depict the legends of Krishna, as in the *Gīta Govinda* (Boston, MA, Mus. F.A.) or the *Bālagopālastuti* (Vadodara, Mus. & Pict. Gal.), and others such famous literary works as the *Vasanta vilāsa* (Washington, DC, Freer), the *Meghadūta* (1668; Ahmadabad, L. D. Inst. Indol.), the *Mādhavānala-Kāmakandalākathā* (1494; Ahmadabad, Muni Sri Punyavijayaji priv. col.), the *Pancatantra* (see Krishna) and the *Devī māhātmya* (1719; Bombay, Prince of Wales Mus.).

A large number of *Kalpa sūtra* and *Kālakācāryakathā* manuscripts were painted during the 16th and 17th centuries, often with abundant use of gold script and colouring. The *Kalpa sūtra*, the most revered book of the Shvetambara sect, forms part of Jaina canonical literature, whereas the *Kālakācāryakathā* is a Shvetambara legend often appended to it (*see also* §3(ii)(a) above). A beautiful manuscript of the *Kalpa sūtra Kālakācāryakathā* painted in 1501 in Patan has more than 150 folio sheets (Jamnagar, Ancalagaccha priv. col.). Its elaborate figurative and narrative borders and hieratic half-page illustrations are interpreted as having been directly inspired by the contemporary Islamic ruling class in Gujarat and display a well-knit synthesis of Persian and indigenous elements, the chief innovation being the inclusion of Persian-type figures within the borders. Cosmographic texts such as the *Saṁgrahaṇī sūtra* (see fig. 287) and the *Kṣetramāsa* were frequently illustrated up to the 17th century; 16th-century examples include those in the Muni Sri Punyavijayaji private collection and the Dehla Jaina Upashraya Bhandara, both in Ahmadabad. Educational manuscripts such as the *Uttarādhyayana sūtra*, known from palm-leaf manuscripts of the 13th and 14th centuries, were often copied and illustrated throughout this period; examples are found in the Museum and Picture Gallery and the Hamsavijayaji private collection in Vadodara and the Muni Sri Punyavijayaji collection in Ahmadabad. Other illustrated Jaina texts of the period include the *Sthānāṅga sūtra*, the *Subāhucaritra*, the *Supārśvanātha caritra* and the *Śālibhadra Caupai.*

A group of paintings of the late 16th century or early 17th (e.g. a *Yaśodhara caritra* painted in 1596; Jaipur, Dig. Jaina Atisaya Kshetra) shows some resemblance to the *Caurapañcāśikā* style (*see* §3(ii)(e) above) in some of their pictorial devices, indicating that this style also prevailed in Gujarat. By the 17th century a truly characteristic style had emerged, as can be seen in a *Saṁgrahaṇī sūtra* of 1601 (New Delhi, Mahavira Jaina Lib.); a *Saṁgrahaṇī sūtra* of 1604; a *Yaśodhara caritra* of 1636 from Idar (Jaipur, Dig. Jaina Atisaya Kshetra); a *Yaśodhara caritra* of 1687 from Surat (Karanja, Sena Gana Mandir priv. col.); and a *Lokaprakāśa* painted in 1657 (Ahmadabad, L. D. Inst. Indol.). A manuscript of the *Upadeśamālā*, an ancient Shvetambara didactic text (1708; Ahmadabad, Devasano Pado priv. col.), is a complete departure from earlier conventions, resembling the Sirohi–Marwar style of neighbouring Rajasthan, characterized by figures with wide-open eyes and a certain effort to depict perspective. A

287. *Doctrine of Six Léśyas*, folio from a manuscript of the *Saṁgrahaṇī sūtra*, gouache on paper, 184×95 mm, Gujarat, *c.* 1625 (Madison, WI, University of Wisconsin, Elvehjem Art Center)

Meghadūta of 1699 (Ahmadabad, L. D. Inst. Indol.) appears to have absorbed elements from early Rajasthani painting in terms of the treatment of the human body and architectural details, while illustrated manuscripts of the *Kumārasaṁbhava* dated 1644 and 1675 (Ahmadabad, L. D. Inst. Indol.; New Delhi, N. Mus.) integrated some features of popular Mughal painting in the use of colour and the depiction of facial forms and male costume.

Rāsa texts relating local Jaina legends were popularly illustrated in Gujarat from the 16th century: examples include a *Śreṇika-Saṁyaktva rāsa* of *c.* 1550 (Vadodara, Jnana Mandir priv. col.); two *Candarāja rāsa* manuscripts dated 1655 and 1812 (both Ahmadabad, Muni Sri Punyavijayaji priv. col.); a late 17th-century *Ārdrakumāra rāsa* (Ahmadabad, Muni Sri Punyavijayaji priv. col.); a *Śrīpāla rāsa*, dated 1829 (Ahmadabad, L. D. Inst. Indol.); and a *Haribala Caupāi* dated 1687 (Ahmadabad, Devasano Pado priv. col.). During this period, *vijñaptipatras*—illustrated invitation scrolls sent out by Jaina communities to invite monks to spend the four months of the rainy season with them—formed an important category of painting in Gujarat (*see* §VII, 13 below). These paper or cloth scrolls are usually beautifully illustrated with scenes of the town or village issuing the invitation and representations of the 14 auspicious dreams and events in the lives of the *tīrthaṅkaras*, the Jaina saints. In 1610, the painter Shalivahana, trained in a Mughal studio, created a magnificent scroll on behalf of the Shvetambara Jainas of Agra, inviting the monk Vijayendra Suri of Gujarat (Doshi, p. 77).

The diversity found within Gujarati painting of the 18th and 19th centuries testifies to the versatility achieved by the painters of the various sub-regions—mainland Gujarat, the Saurashtra peninsula, north Gujarat, the Jamnagar area and Kachchh (*see also* §(i) below).

BIBLIOGRAPHY

W. N. Brown: *Miniature Paintings of the Jaina Kalpasutra* (Washington, DC, 1934)

M. Chandra: *Jain Miniature Paintings from Western India* (Ahmadabad, 1949)

S. M. Nawab: *The Oldest Rajasthani Paintings from Jain Bhandaras* (Ahmadabad, 1959)

O. C. Gangoly: *Critical Catalogue of Miniature Paintings in the Baroda Museum* (Vadodara, 1961)

P. Chandra: *Indian Miniature Painting: The Collection of Earnest C. and Jane Werner Watson* (Madison, 1971)

M. Chandra and U. P. Shah: *New Documents of Jaina Painting* (Bombay, 1975)

K. Krishna: 'Illustrated Leaves from a Pancatantra Manuscript of the 15th Century', *Aspects of Jaina Art and Architecture*, ed. U. P. Shah and M. A. Dhaky (Ahmadabad, 1975), pp. 405–13

J. Jain and E. Fischer: *Jaina Iconography*, Iconography of Religions, xiii/12–13 (Leiden, 1978)

U. P. Shah, ed.: *Treasures of Jaina Bhandaras*, L. D. Series, lxix (Ahmadabad, 1978)

S. Doshi: *Masterpieces of Jain Painting* (Bombay, 1985)

J. Jain-Neubauer: 'Of Kings, Krishna, Malwa Girls and Opium: Wall Paintings in the Palace of Jamnagar, Gujarat', *Felicitation Volume for Karl Khandalawala* (Ahmadabad, in preparation)

JUTTA JAIN-NEUBAUER

(i) Kachchh. The earliest known paintings from Kachchh (Kutch) were produced *c.* 1725. Though contact on the part of Rao Bharmal (*reg* 1585–1631) with Mughal painters is attested by a surviving portrait in the Minto Album (an album of paintings collected by the Earl of Minto in 1807–13; London, V&A), a regional tradition in Kachchh emerges only from the time of Rao Desalji (*reg* 1718–41). The suddenness of its beginning and absence of an earlier known tradition of painting in the region raise questions about sources that are not yet fully resolved.

Two distinct phases are evident in Kachchh painting. The first, exemplified by a portrait of *Rao Desalji* (see fig. 288), was probably a wholly indigenous development, though influence from nearby regions is possible. There is a broad family resemblance between works from Kachchh and those in the Rajasthani styles of Mewar and Jodhpur in Marwar (*see* §§(a) and (g) above). Political and cultural contacts existed with Mewar, and works from that region, including portraits of rulers and court scenes, formed part of the Kachchh royal collection. Moreover, there is Kachchh work based directly on Mewar painting: a splendid festival scene set on Lake Pichola in Udaipur (Mannheim, Städt. Reiss-Mus.) conveys an overall feeling

288. Kachchh school: *Rao Desalji*, opaque colour on paper, *c.* 1725–50

of Mewar painting, but differences in details, including figure treatment, suggest a Kachchh version of a Mewar original. Numerous political and family links with Marwar included the marriage of a Kachchh princess with a Jodhpur prince. Contact between the rulers of the two states is documented by a large *darbar* (audience) painting depicting the meeting of Rao Lakhpatji (*reg* 1741–60) and Bakhat Singh of Nagaur/Jodhpur, each with his retinue (Heidelberg, Kirsch priv. col., see Goswamy and Dallapiccola, pl. vi). Among the most sumptuous works of its kind from Kachchh, the painting has an immediacy that suggests it was based on actual observation, while its style reveals a strong Jodhpur influence.

The source of the second phase of Kachchh painting is European. Contact with Western art is documented by a sizeable group of European prints, mostly etchings and engravings, imported into Kachchh. These were carefully mounted and collected in albums, the French and English captions translated into Gujarati and Kachchhi (see Goswamy and Dallapiccola, pls xv, xvi, figs 18, 19, 24). The prints, small in size and mainly from the mid-18th century, range from scenes from William Hogarth's *'Progresses'* series (e.g. *The Rake's Progress*, *c.* 1733) to portraits of Catherine the Great of Russia. They include views of Italian cities, Viennese palaces, and buildings and parks in England, as well as depictions of historical events and scenes from well-known adventure tales. There are also 19th-century illustrations of Queen Victoria and the British royal family and stray leaves from Parisian fashion magazines.

Kachchh painters were particularly fascinated by townscapes, which they copied, trying to understand techniques such as the rendering of perspective and effects of light and shade. In this second phase of Kachchh painting the focus shifts from people to landscapes. By the early 19th century Kachchh painters, having assimilated European conventions, turned to landscapes of their own country, creating views of Anjar, Bhuj and Mundra and of palaces and mansions, characterized by a delicate line and subdued palette (see Goswamy and Dallapiccola, pls xviii, xxvi, figs 26–33). After 1820 painting production slowed; some surviving coarse wall painting was probably done in the 19th century. At this time there is another development: painted doors and windows, which were produced until the end of the 19th century (e.g. Mannheim, Städt. Reiss-Mus.). Their unusually vibrant colouring and the boldness of design and figures on their lacquer-finished surfaces contrast with work of the first quarter of the 19th century.

BIBLIOGRAPHY

B. N. Goswamy and A. L. Dallapiccola: *A Place Apart: Painting in Kutch, 1720–1820* (New Delhi, 1983)

A. L. DALLAPICCOLA

(iv) Pahari styles. The Pahari (Hindi: 'of or pertaining to mountains or hills') styles of Punjab and the Himalayan foothills (see fig. 289), like those of Rajasthan and contiguous regions (*see* §(iii) above), range from essentially conservative idioms that preserve traditional values of bright colour, flatness and abstract form (e.g. Basohli and Kulu) to those showing greater Mughal impact in their refinement and cool colour (e.g. Kangra and related styles). □

(a) Basohli. (b) Kulu. (c) Mankot. (d) Nurpur. (e) Bilaspur. (f) Chamba. (g) Garhwal. (h) Guler. (i) Jammu. (j) Jasrota. (k) Kangra. (l) Mandi.

(a) Basohli. This capital of a relatively modest hill state not far from Jammu has come to be associated with a major regional painting style of the mid-17th century to mid-18th that has been described as having 'barbaric magnificence' and an 'air of wild sophisticated luxury' (see Archer). Its characteristics include rich, monochromatic backgrounds; a strong, bounding line; exaggerated but superbly controlled drawing of faces and forms; arbitrary but brilliant use of architectural and decorative design; and, for a period of time, the use of beetle wing-cases stuck on to paintings suggesting, through their dazzling effect of colour and lustre, emeralds in jewellery and clothing.

Early in the 20th century, when Pahari paintings had just started to be discussed, those of Basohli were not given any prominence. What later came to be termed Basohli work was at that time designated as being from Jammu, especially by Ananda Kentish Coomaraswamy, who used the term to distinguish this early, more passionate, style from the later, more fluent and naturalistic Kangra style. It was not until 1929 that Ajit Ghose succeeded in establishing the term Basohli. Several Basohli substyles were subsequently identified (see Randhawa), and Karl Khandalavala defined various regional idioms that share such common elements as vitality, emphatic stylization and strong colouring.

However, it is extremely doubtful that all work classified as Basohli comes from that state. No major family of artists based in Basohli has so far come to the notice of scholars, and although it was undoubtedly an important centre of Pahari painting, much work grouped under the umbrella of its name seems to have been done elsewhere or by artists originating in other states and working, perhaps temporarily, under the patronage of the ruling house of Basohli.

Several sets of paintings have been linked with the Basohli style, sometimes on very inadequate grounds. These include a magnificent series depicting the Tantric forms of Devi, the Goddess, and dated to the third quarter of the 17th century. Linked with this dispersed set (examples at Lahore Mus.; Chandigarh, Govt Mus. & A.G.; New Delhi, N. Mus.; Zurich, Mus. Rietberg; and elsewhere) is a contemporary *Rasamañjarī* ('Posy of delights') series (pages in Boston, MA, Mus. F.A.; London, V&A; Cleveland, OH, Mus. A.; Cambridge, MA, Fogg; and elsewhere; see fig. 290). Neither series names the patron, place of execution, painter or date; the works are associated with Basohli on account of their obvious stylistic connection with a somewhat later dated set of the *Rasamañjarī*, the colophon of which mentions that it was painted at Basohli by Devidas in 1694–5 for Raja Kripal Pal. Devidas seems to have come from a well-known and extensive family of painters settled in the neighbouring state of Nurpur (*see* §(d) below). The stylistic connection between Devidas's *Rasamañjarī* and the earlier version of this love poem is so strong that it has been suggested that both the early *Rasamañjarī* and the Devi series may have been painted by Devidas's father, Kripal of Nurpur. However, there is no reason to believe that Kripal ever worked at Basohli, while Devidas may only have been temporarily employed there by Raja Kripal Pal, who was obviously a lover of paintings. (For illustration of another *Rasamañjarī* folio from a Nurpur–Basohli workshop *see* COLOUR, colour pl. VI, fig. 1.)

The first major set of 18th-century paintings linked with Basohli is a *Gīta Govinda* series, dated 1730, which carries a colophon naming the painter MANAKU and a patroness, Malini. There is no mention, however, of the place of execution, and there is strong reason to doubt that the work has anything to do with Basohli. Manaku was a member of a famous painting family of Guler. While the possibility that Manaku travelled to Basohli cannot be ruled out, there is no evidence to suggest that he ever worked there: reliance on his use of beetle wing-cases in the *Gīta Govinda* as evidence of the work having been done at Basohli is unjustified, since it has yet to be proved that only Basohli painters used this device. There thus seems also to be no clear case for linking Manaku's *Bhāgavata purāṇa* (*c.* 1740; dispersed; Lahore Mus.; Chandigarh, Govt Mus. & A.G.; and Udaipur) with Basohli. The same is true of the later, enlarged version of the tenth book of the *Bhāgavata purāṇa* (*c.* 1760–65; dispersed; New Delhi; London, V&A; and USA), which may have been executed by one of his two sons. The description of this last series by Archer as being in the 'Guler–Basohli' style acknowledges its synthesis of the early, energetic and highly stylized Basohli mode with the slightly later, naturalistic Guler mode, a combination that eventually led to the remarkably fluent and lyrical Kangra style (*see* §§(h) and (k) below).

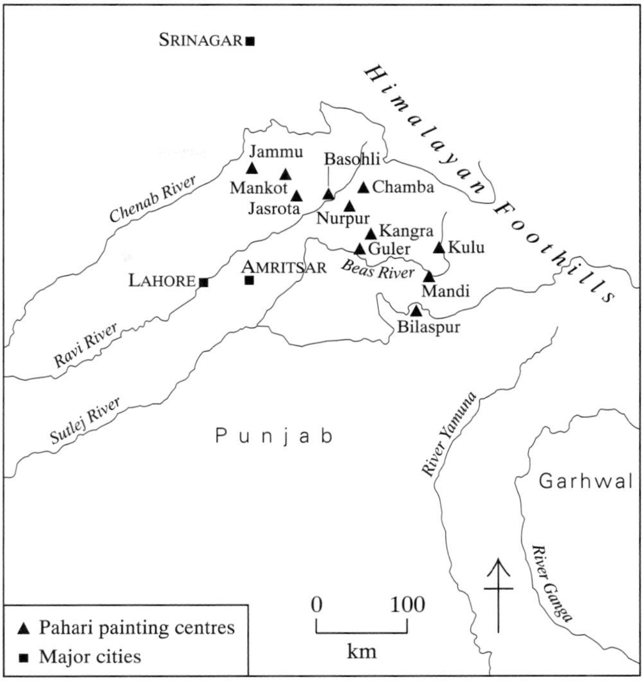

289. Map showing Pahari painting schools; those sites with separate entries in this dictionary are distinguished by CROSS-REFERENCE TYPE

Portraits of members of the royal house of Basohli, from Sangram Pal (*reg* 1635–73) to Medini Pal (*reg* 1722–36), both imagined and drawn from nature, were executed in the early stylized manner. However, from the reign of Amrit Pal (*reg* 1757–78), the style of royal portraiture changed dramatically to the naturalistic style favoured by NAINSUKH, originally of Guler, who seems to have migrated to Basohli *c.* 1765 and settled on lands granted by Amrit Pal.

To Nainsukh's youngest son, Ranjha, may be attributed the celebrated series of *Nala and Damayanti* paintings and drawings (paintings: Jammu, Karan Singh priv. col.; drawings: dispersed). The fact that this delicate series, executed in an extremely fluent, poetic style, belonged to the royal collection of Basohli strongly suggests that the rulers of Basohli took an interest in and patronized painting for nearly a century and a half. As a centre of painting, however, Basohli seems to have declined rapidly from the mid-19th century; no work of any significance is associated with it after that period.

BIBLIOGRAPHY

M. S. Randhawa: *Basohli Painting* (New Delhi, 1959)
M. S. Randhawa and S. D. Bhambri: 'Basohli Paintings of Bhanudatta's Rasamanjari', *Roopa-Lekha*, xxxvi/1–2 (1967), pp. 1–124

290. Basohli school: *A Lady Blames her Cat for Scratches Inflicted by her Lover*, scene from the *Rasamañjarī*, gouache on paper, 235×325 mm, *c.* 1660–70 (London, Victoria and Albert Museum, IS 20–1958)

W. G. Archer: *Indian Painting from the Punjab Hills*, 2 vols (London, 1973)
R. K. Tandan: *The Ragamala Paintings from Basohli* (New Delhi, 1980)
B. Gray, ed.: *The Arts of India* (Oxford, 1981)
R. K. Tandan: *Pahari Ragamalas* (Bangalore, 1983)
Pahari-Meister (exh. cat. by B. N. Goswamy and E. Fischer, Zurich, Mus. Rietberg, 1990)

B. N. GOSWAMY

(b) Kulu. Documentation is scarce on early painting in Kulu (Kullu), one of the most remote states of the Punjab Hills. Portraits of early Kulu rulers, which might serve to establish a chronology, are problematic. For instance, though a portrait is known of *Raja Jagat Singh* (*reg* 1637–72; Varanasi, Banaras Hindu U., Bharat Kala Bhavan), its style reveals that it is not contemporary with his reign. A portrait of *Raja Man Singh* (*reg* 1688–1719; Ahmadabad, Cult. Cent., Mehta Col.), showing Mughal influence in colouring and other features, has an inscription in a dialect connecting it with Mandi rather than Kulu. None of the four portraits of Raja Jai Singh (*reg* 1731–42; London, V&A; San Diego, CA, Mus. A., Binney Col.; Calcutta, G. K. Kanoria priv. col.; anonymous priv. col., see Archer, ii, p. 6, figs 10 and 11) is in a Kulu style. (Archer attributed three to the hill state of Baghal and one to Kahlur.)

Several artists from Basohli apparently migrated to Kulu in the last quarter of the 17th century. Their early work has affinities with Basohli painting (*see* §(a) above) but also shows a separate development of style, perhaps due to their isolation in Kulu. Colours are generally less brilliant than in Basohli painting; the emphasis is on decorative patterns rather than naturalistic landscapes. A possible example of their early work is *Radha and Krishna in the Forest* (Bombay, Khandalavala priv. col., see Archer, ii, p. 244, fig. 6).

A superb *Rāmāyaṇa* series of 270 paintings is a central but imperfectly understood work. Known as the Shangri *Rāmāyaṇa*, it was in the possession of Raja Raghubir Singh of Shangri, a fiefdom of Kulu in the Simla Hills. According to family tradition, the series was painted in Kulu by Kashmiri Brahman artists. Dispersed in 1961 (168 paintings are in New Delhi, N. Mus.; examples also in Varanasi, Banaras Hindu U., Bharat Kala Bhavan; London, V&A; and San Diego, CA, Mus. A., Binney Col.), the series has been classified into four styles and ascribed to the period from *c.* 1690 to *c.* 1710 (Archer). Scholarship is divided, however, on questions of both dating and place of production. (Bahu in Jammu has been suggested; see Goswamy and Fischer.) An inscription on a painting in the latter part of the series (New Delhi, N. Mus.), though not indisputably clear, indicates a date of [17]65 and mentions Mandi. Compositions of works in the early part of the series (mainly the first two books, the *Bālakānda* and *Ayodhyākānda*) are characterized by a lack of regard for orderly arrangement, creating a sense of agitated movement. People and objects break the constraints of the frame, protruding into the border. Trees are stylized with geometric rosettes for leaves and jagged, twisted trunks. An equestrian portrait of a prince accompanied by attendants (Ahmadabad, Cult. Cent., Mehta Col.), possibly an early work of an immigrant artist, appears to be the prototype for these paintings. In the latter part of the *Rāmāyaṇa* series, compositions are more balanced and the faces of people and animals more expressive.

The *Rāmāyaṇa* series shares a number of features with other works that can be assigned to Kulu at about the same period. These include a *Rāgamālā* series (London, V&A), a *Nāyikābheda* series and illustrations of the Krishna legend. Figures are often rendered with exaggerated features, including thick necks and heavy jaws; legs are long and torsos short. Young men are depicted with straggling locks ending in dishevelled strands. A three-dot pattern is commonly used for textiles, which later develops into a pattern of four or five dots. Many works have willow trees and creepers, often with white flowers; a willow-sprig motif occurs in the foreground and as a decorative motif on textiles. Lotuses are used in a variety of decorative patterns and in lotus-flower crowns.

Paintings from *c.* 1710–40 have simplified compositions and colour schemes showing a preference for mauve and blue. Common features include a willow tree with drooping branches framing a central figure, and swirling clouds with curly outlines. Paintings of the mid-18th century and later retain traits of the local style but also exhibit the influence of other centres of Pahari painting. A more naturalistic treatment is evident in a portrait of *Raja Tedhi Singh* (*reg* 1742–67; London, V&A, IS. 112-1954). In *Krishna and Radha Rising from the Pines* (London, V&A, IS. 112-1955) facial features are regular, lacking the exaggeration of earlier examples, and this type, with slight variations, is common in later painting. A distinctive use is made of architecture as a compositional device for juxtaposing contrasting blocks of colour, frequently setting off a solitary female figure, as in *Lady Writing a Letter* (Simla, Himachal State Mus.; see fig. 291).

Late 18th-century work includes a series illustrating the *Bhāgavata purāṇa* (dispersed, e.g. New Delhi, N. Mus.; London, V&A) painted by the artist Bhagwan for Raja Pritam Singh (*reg* 1767–1806) in 1794. At least two sets of the love story *Madhu-Malati* (both dated in the 1790s; e.g. Hyderabad, Mittal Mus. Ind. A., and Boston, MA, Mus. F.A.) were painted by the same artist in his individual style: compositions are animated, figures tall and graceful, colours dominated by reds and blues. Little development of the regional style occurred in the 19th century. Wall paintings (one large panel is in New Delhi, N. Mus.) are in a late Kangra style (*see* §(k) below). The murals of the Devi temple at Bhakli, above Kulu town, are the work of Gulabu Ram of Samloti, near Kangra. They were executed *c.* 1930 and clearly show the influence of Western painting.

BIBLIOGRAPHY

J. C. French: *Himalayan Art* (Oxford, 1931)
K. Khandalavala: *Pahari Miniature Painting* (Bombay, 1958)
J. Mittal: 'An Illustrated Manuscript of *Madhu Malati* and other Paintings from Kulu', *Lalit Kala*, iii–iv (1958), pp. 90–95
——: 'The Devi Mural at Kulu by Sajnu', *Roopa-Lekha*, xxxii/2 (1961), pp. 85–97

291. Kulu school: *Lady Writing a Letter*, opaque colour on paper, 216×145 mm, *c.* 1770–86 (Simla, Himachal State Museum)

W. G. Archer: *Indian Paintings from the Punjab Hills*, 2 vols (London, 1973)
F. S. Aijazuddin: *Pahari Paintings and Sikh Portraits* (London, 1977)
B. N. Goswamy and E. Fischer: *Pahari-Meister* (Zurich, 1990); Eng. trans. as *Pahari Masters: Court Painters of Northern India* (Zurich, 1992)

(c) Mankot. Central to the study of painting in Mankot (Ramkot state), one of the smallest of the Punjab Hill states, are some 250 paintings (Chandigarh, Govt Mus. & A.G.) formerly in the possession of Inder Vijai Singh, a descendant of the Mankot rulers. Portraits from the Mankot court and related paintings in this collection helped to define the Mankot school and to identify with Mankot other paintings that had been considered a local idiom of the Basohli style (*see* §(a) above). Portraiture, derived from Mughal examples under the emperor Shah Jahan (*reg* 1627–58), was introduced at Mankot in the mid-17th century and remained the main concern of Mankot painters until *c.* 1700. From this period are keenly observed portraits of rulers, courtiers, nobles and even ordinary men, including a fine study of the priest *Gokul* (Chandigarh, Govt Mus. & A.G.), who, according to the inscription, served the blind Raja Sital Dev (*reg c.* 1630–50) well. Two portraits of Sital Dev are known (Bombay, Khandalavala priv. col., and ex-Latifi priv. col., Bombay; see Archer, ii, p. 284, nos 1 and 3). The borders of such works are usually red, and the sitters are usually set against stark backgrounds of rich yellow or sage green and seated on colourful floral or

striped carpets, which enhance the painting's decorative effect.

Works from *c.* 1700–20 show greater distortion, a feature shared with Basohli painting, but the idiom is distinctively Mankot. Examples from the period, among the best of Mankot paintings, include illustrations of the *Bhāgavata purāṇa* (Chandigarh, Govt Mus. and A.G.) and *Rāgamālā* series (e.g. London, V&A). The *Bhāgavata purāṇa* illustration *Krishna Uprooting Two Trees* (see fig. 292) is typical of such works in its avoidance of intricate detail in favour of a narrow focus on the drama of the scene. On the left Krishna's mother, Yashoda, is discussing his mischievous behaviour with a friend, who bites her own finger in amazement. Meanwhile, on the right, a delightfully naughty Krishna, tied to a mortar to keep him out of trouble, happily drags it between two trees, uprooting them but also performing a good deed in freeing two trapped spirits. The colours are bright, and the sturdy figures pulsate with energy. The charming Yashoda and her companion have faces characteristic of Mankot: long, thin strands of hair flow along the cheeks, the nose is sharp, the forehead receding, the chin unobtrusive, the eyes large and eloquent. This and other illustrations of the series show the artists understood the texts and the spirit of the episodes they depicted. As in other Mankot works, they capture in these paintings an 'air of swaggering elation' (Archer, i, p. 376). In *Kalayavana Pursuing Krishna* from the same series, both figures wear half-sleeved coats, a style of Central Asian origin. A similar garment is worn by Nurpur rulers in some 17th-century portraits (e.g. Varanasi, Banaras Hindu U., Bharat Kala Bhavan; Lahore Mus.). Artists in Mankot were apparently aware of trends in painting at Basohli and Nurpur (*see* §(d) below) and assimilated elements from both styles.

Paintings of the 2nd quarter of the 17th century indicate influences from still other centres. Impressive portraits of the Mankot ruler Ajmat Dev (*reg c.* 1730–60; e.g. Chandigarh, Govt Mus. & A.G.) show the linearity and angularity of portraits from Bandralta to the north of Mankot. The Jammu (or Jasrota) practice of drawing naturalistic portraits with uncoloured backgrounds (*see* §§(i) and (j) below) was adopted by Mankot painters for a short period. Changes in the physiognomy of the face, adjusting it to a more rectangular form, are evident in paintings of both Mankot and Chamba (*see* §(f) below), suggesting contacts between the artists of these centres. In works after *c.* 1750 faces generally appear slightly heavier, and figures are shorter and squatter. Colours are more muted; compositions frequently employ clumps of foliage. A good example of this phase is *Raja Tedhi Singh Worshipping Krishna* (*c.* 1750–60; Chandigarh, Govt Mus. & A.G.).

With the political intervention of the Sikhs in the Jammu region in the 18th and 19th centuries, court life at Mankot was also affected, and a general decline in painting set in. By 1846 Mankot and other principalities in the region had ceased to exist independently. The few portraits from Mankot dating to this period of political and artistic decline exhibit poor draughtsmanship, particularly in the depiction of faces.

292. Mankot school: *Krishna Uprooting Two Trees*, opaque colour on paper, 201×296 mm, 1700–10 (Chandigarh, Government Museum and Art Gallery)

BIBLIOGRAPHY

M. S. Randhawa: 'Paintings from Mankot' *Lalit Kala*, vi (1960), pp. 72–5

D. Barrett and B. Gray: *Painting of India* (Geneva, 1963/*R* London, 1978)

W. G. Archer: *Indian Paintings from the Punjab Hills*, 2 vols (London, 1973)

B. N. Goswamy: 'The Bhāgavata Paintings from Mankot', *Lalit Kala*, 17 (1978)

Essence of Indian Art (exh. cat. by B. N. Goswamy, San Francisco, CA, Asian A. Mus., 1986)

(d) Nurpur. Lying close to the Punjab plains, Nurpur was less isolated than other states of the Punjab Hills. Its rulers served as generals and governors in the Mughal empire throughout the early 17th century. The earliest known Nurpur painting, depicting Raja Jagat Singh (*reg* 1618–46) and his brother Madhu Singh worshipping Lakshmi-Narayana at a household shrine (*c.* 1620; Varanasi, Banaras Hindu U., Bharat Kala Bhavan; see fig. 293), is stylistically distinct but also indicates a debt to Mughal works. A date of *c.* 1620 is confirmed by the subject: after an estrangement between the two brothers in 1623, Madhu Singh was not heard of again. The date is further supported by the presence of two young sons of Jagat Singh in the painting. The artist has brought out the characters of the sturdy Jagat Singh and of his weak brother, shown smaller and with a timid expression. Lines are fine and the drawing precise. The red border contains naturalistic studies of flowers and animals in a Mughal-derived manner. As the stylistic origins of Pahari painting are obscure, this early portrait from the hills is of special importance. A sketch portrait of *Jagat Singh* in a similar style is also known (see K. Goswamy, p. 63). Another portrait (Chandigarh, Govt Mus. & A.G.) shows a slight shift from naturalism towards stylization and a preference for warm colours. Portraits from the mid-17th century show some stylistic progression but remain closely linked to Mughal models. For example,

293. Nurpur school: *Raja Jagat Singh of Nurpur and his Brother Madhu Singh Worshipping Lakshmi-Narayana*, opaque colour on paper, 246×230 mm, *c.* 1620 (Varanasi, Banaras Hindu University, Bharat Kala Bhavan)

two portraits of Raja Man Dhata (*reg* 1661–1700), one standing and the other a seated window portrait (both New Delhi, N. Mus.), show him wearing a short-sleeved fur-trimmed coat, of the type worn in Mughal portraits of the period. However, in contrast to Mughal works, the standing portrait has a plain yellow background.

In the same period a bolder style was adopted for *Rāgamālā* illustrations and for pictures on themes of *Dasavatāra* (the ten incarnations of Vishnu) and the Krishna legend. Typical of such works is *Vāmana avatāra* ('The dwarf incarnation'; Zurich, Mus. Rietberg; see 1961 exh. cat., p. 67, where the work is illustrated but not assigned to any school). Stylistic affinities in the mid-17th century between Nurpur and Chamba, also in the Punjab Hills, arise from the migration of Nurpur artists to Chamba (*see* §(f) below), which was under Nurpur control from 1623 to 1641.

The two 17th-century Nurpur styles coalesced in the early 18th century. In paintings illustrating court events and literary texts facial features are less exaggerated, and colour is controlled. Landscapes, however, are not naturalistic—trees are rendered in a stylized and decorative manner until the mid-18th century. In a series illustrating the love poem *Rasamañjarī* (e.g. Ahmadabad, Lalbhai priv. col., see Archer, ii, pp. 307–9, figs 14 i–vi), the figure of the hero is clearly modelled on the young Raja Daya Dhat (*reg* 1700–35), thus revealing period and place of production. These paintings are stylistically distinct, employing a naturalistic treatment of figures and a sober palette with considerable use of mauve and blue. However, the compositions and iconography follow the Basohli *Rasamañjarī* series painted by Devidas in the late 17th century (see Archer, ii, pp. 29–30, figs 15, i–v). The series is attributed to Golu, the son of Devidas, who is still remembered in Nurpur. (For illustration of another *Rasamañjarī* folio from a Nurpur–Basohli workshop *see* COLOUR, colour pl. VI, fig. 1.) Slightly later but also important is a *Rāmāyaṇa* series with distinctive figure types and inventive depictions of trees (e.g. Lahore Mus.; Chandigarh, Govt Mus. & A.G.).

Paintings from around the mid-18th century are markedly different, showing the influence of Guler and Jammu (or Jasrota; *see* §§(h)–(j) below). Pictures of Nurpur princes watching dance performances (e.g. London, V&A, IS. 175-1951) are rendered in a delicate and naturalistic manner, similar to Jammu (or Jasrota) painting. The picture format is often vertical, and a number of paintings feature tall, graceful female figures with smallish heads. Several types of female faces are common: some with small pointed noses and others with rounded sensitive features. The only two known signed works in the Nurpur style are from the mid-18th century: *The Two Gosains* by Gur Baksh (Chandigarh, Govt Mus. & A.G.) and *Lady on a Terrace* by Har Jaimal. The names of several other artists are known from records. Wall paintings of the 3rd quarter of the 18th century in the Brijrajswami Temple, Nurpur, appear to be the work of three artists, including Golu, to whom the paintings on the panels are attributed, characterized by well-planned, complex compositions and a vibrant but judicious use of colour.

Changed political conditions in the Punjab from the 3rd quarter of the 18th century diminished court life at

Nurpur. No major work was done and no new style evolved. Portraits of the last ruler, Bir Singh (*reg* 1789 or 1805–1815), are not in the Nurpur style (see Archer, i, p. 404). Wall paintings in the Damthal Temple near Nurpur are in the Kangra style (*see* §(k) below), suggesting that the local idiom did not continue beyond the 18th century.

BIBLIOGRAPHY

J. C. French: *Himalayan Art* (Oxford, 1931)
W. G. Archer and M. S. Randhawa: 'Some Nurpur Paintings', *Marg*, viii/3 (1955), pp. 8–25
K. Khandalavala: *Pahari Miniature Painting* (Bombay, 1958)
B. N. Goswamy: 'The Pahari Artists', *Roopa-Lekha*, xxxii/2 (1961), pp. 31–50
Miniature indiane dal XV al XIX secolo (exh. cat. by R. Skelton, Venice, Fond. Cini, 1961; Eng. trans., 1961) [exh. held 1960; colour pl. 50 ascribed to Nurpur]
K. C. Aryan: 'Nurpur', *Marg*, xvii/3 (1964), p. 61
M. S. Randhawa and S. D. Bhambri: 'Basohli Paintings of Bhanudatta's Rasamanjari', *Roopa-Lekha*, xxxvi/1 and 2 (1967) [figs 1, 15, 19, 21, 29, 31, 38–42, 45, 55, 57, 60, 61, 63, 77 and 78 are Nurpur paintings]
B. N. Goswamy: 'A Document of Nurpur Painting', *Roopa-Lekha*, xxxix/1 (1971), pp. 38–43
W. G. Archer: *Indian Paintings from the Punjab Hills*, 2 vols (London, 1973)
K. Goswamy: 'An Early 17th Century Painting from Nurpur', *Arts of Himachal* (Simla, 1975), pp. 51–6
F. S. Aijazuddin: *Pahari Paintings and Sikh Portraits in the Lahore Museum* (London, 1977)
U. Bhatia: 'Paintings from the Bathu Manuscript', *Lalit Kala*, xx (1982), pp. 28–33
K. Khandalavala: *Pahari Miniature Paintings in the N. C. Mehta Collection* (Ahmadabad, [1983])
A. Okada: 'Une Illustration insolite du Narasimhāvatāra', *Rev. Louvre* (Oct 1985), pp. 285–8
V. C. Ohri: *On the Origins of Pahari Painting* (Simla, 1991)

VISHWA CHANDER OHRI

(e) Bilaspur. Located in the Sutlej River valley of the Punjab Hills, Bilaspur was a centre of painting for over a century from *c.* 1650. The clan name for the ruling house is Kahlur, and the state was known as Kahluria until the mid-17th century, when the ruler Dip Chand (*reg* 1650–67) moved the capital to a new site on the left bank of the Sutlej and named it Byaspur, later modified to Bilaspur. Dip Chand served the Mughal ruler Aurangzeb (*reg* 1658–1707), and it is perhaps this direct association combined with his marriage to a princess from the neighbouring state of Mandi, which also had relations with the Mughals and had established a painting atelier around 1650 (*see* §(l) below), that motivated his interest in establishing a painting workshop.

It was the secular aspect of Mughal painting that influenced the earliest phase (*c.* 1660–80) of painting in Bilaspur. The majority of paintings from this period are portraits, not religious subjects. If the painting tradition had sprung up indigenously, as a corollary to the local sculpture tradition, one would expect to see the predominance of religious themes, the subject-matter of most sculpture. There are some paintings depicting scenes from the *Rāmāyaṇa* and *Rāgamālā*s with Krishna and Vishnu occupying the central positions (see Archer, 1973, ii, p. 169, fig. 2), but these are far less numerous than portraits.

The relatively naturalistic portraits done in the third quarter of the 17th century manifest an interest in the raja, his family and members of his administration and entourage. A portrait of *Prince Dan Chand* (see fig. 294),

294. Bilaspur school: *Prince Dan Chand*, opaque colour on paper, 200×137 mm, *c.* 1670 (San Diego, CA, San Diego Museum of Art)

identified by inscription on the reverse, shows the extent of Mughal influence in Bilaspur around 1670 (see Welch and others, pp. 216, 219, 226–7). After the initial infusion of Mughal influence, subsequent painting in Bilaspur followed a course not unlike other Pahari schools in terms of subject-matter, though keeping throughout its history a refinement of style reflecting its early Mughal beginnings. There is a predilection for flat backgrounds of dark green, brown or mauve. Figures are presented as slightly elongated, dressed in muted colours. Brushwork is usually fine, though excessive detailing or use of stippling does not occur.

From the end of the 17th century to the middle of the 18th, painting continued to be stylistically refined, employing subtle colours and accomplished techniques, though traditional subjects such as episodes from the *Bhāgavata purāṇa*, *Rāmāyaṇa* and *Rāgamālā* as well as devotional works of Shiva, Vishnu and the Goddess became more prevalent (see Archer, 1973, ii, pp. 171–82, figs 6–37). During this period portraiture was not as highly regarded and is restricted mainly to standard representations of the ruler. During the last decades of the 18th century, influences from other painting schools, namely Guler and Kangra (*see* §§(h) and (k) below), began to dominate Bilaspur work. By the first decades of the 19th century, painting in Bilaspur had declined, showing little relationship to its origins and losing its former significance.

BIBLIOGRAPHY

J. C. French: *Himalayan Art* (Oxford, 1931), pp. 23, 24, 98–100

J. Hutchison and J. P. Vogel: *History of the Punjab Hill States* (Lahore, 1933), ii, pp. 494–513

W. G. Archer: *Indian Painting in the Punjab Hills* (London, 1952), figs 8, 9

M. S. Randhawa: *Kangra Valley Painting* (New Delhi, 1954), pls 32, 34, 36–7

K. Khandalavala: *Pahari Miniature Painting* (Bombay, 1958), figs 10, 11, 38, 43–4 and pls F and XI; nos 44, 53, 67, 160

Miniature indiane dal XV al XIX secolo (exh. cat. by R. Skelton, Venice, Fond. Cini, 1961; Eng. trans., 1961) [exh. held 1960], pls 38, 49, 71–3, 87

E. Waldschmidt and R. L. Waldschmidt: *Miniatures of Musical Inspiration* (Wiesbaden, 1967), pls B, C, D; figs 1–69

W. G. Archer and E. Binney III: *Rajput Miniatures from the Collection of Edwin Binney III* (Portland, 1968), figs 70a and b, 72–4

W. G. Archer: *Indian Paintings from the Punjab Hills* (London, 1973), i, pp. 223–43; ii, pp. 169–91

V. C. Ohri: *Art of Himachal* (Simla, 1975), pp. 40, 127, 144, 157

C. Glynn: 'Early Painting in Mandi', *Artibus Asiae*, xliv/1 (1983)

S. C. Welch and others: *The Emperor's Album: Images of Mughal India* (New York, 1987)

CATHERINE GLYNN

(f) Chamba. The sheltered location of this large state in the Punjab Hills helped to preserve its records and cultural heritage. The earliest painting definitively connected with Chamba is of the second quarter of the 17th century, while the earliest documents evidencing the presence of painters of Gujarati origin in Chamba date from 1670 and 1676 (see B. N. Goswamy, 1989). The earliest Chamba painting portrays *Balabhadra Varman and his Son Bishambhar* (Simla, Himachal State Mus.); its style is distinct. A mannerism, especially in the depiction of hands, is seen in this work, suggesting a period of experimentation of some decades. It seems some painters had come to Chamba from north India in the late 16th century or early 17th when, as the result of the expansion of the territory of the Mughal empire, Raja Bas Dev of Nurpur (*reg* 1580–1613) transferred his state capital from Pathankot to Dhameri, and some artisans and artists he brought in from outside went to the neighbouring Chamba. The early drawings and paintings (mostly Hyderabad, Mittal Mus. Ind. A.) and the development of Chamba painting in the first half of the 17th century suggest the arrival of more northern Indian painters in Chamba. A painting of a *Princess with a Hawk Attended by Maids* (Los Angeles, CA, Co. Mus. A.) is a fine example exhibiting the mixed traits of Deccani and early Chamba painting. Another painting, *Lady with the Tambour* (Zurich, Mus. Rietberg), in a different hand also shows the clear influence of Deccani painting. Both these works are of the mid-17th century. A Chamba drawing of *c.* 1660 (Hyderabad, Mittal Mus. Ind. A.), an illustration to the *Rasamañjarī* text discovered at Chamba and exhibiting the influence of Rajasthani–Deccani painting, bears an inscription in Takri, a script peculiar to the Punjab Hills. Paintings related to the periods of all the rulers succeeding Balabhadra Varman (*reg* 1589–1613; 1623–41) are known.

The figures in works painted before the later years of Chattar Singh (*reg* 1664–90) are rendered in a naturalistic manner. Slim wrists and a distinctive treatment of hands are noted in early Chamba paintings. Subdued, pale colours were generally preferred, and painters were usually required to do portraits. The *Dāsavatāra* (ten incarnations of Vishnu) series remained popular over a long period. Early Chamba paintings depicting *Narasimha Slaying Hiranayakashipu* are well known (Paris, Mus. Guimet), the lion head rendered in a naturalistic manner. Chamba rulers generally professed Vaishnavism, and the worship of Rama became more popular from the mid-17th century. In a painting of the third quarter of the 17th century, *Rama with Three Brothers, Sita and Hanuman*, the distinctive traits of early Chamba painting are seen, and the tigers below the throne are rendered realistically (Simla, Himachal State Mus.). A portrait of *Young Raja Udai Singh* (*reg* 1690–1720) uses colours of deeper shades, and a carpet bears a floral design (New Delhi, N. Mus.). Decorative trees also started appearing in Chamba painting of the late 17th century, indicating the adoption of some elements of Basohli-style painting (*see* §(a) above). A series of paintings on the theme of *Pārijatāharaṇa* ('Abduction of Parijata'; Chandigarh, Govt Mus. & A.G.) seems to belong to the late 17th century. Rich, warm colours are used, and the treatment of the trees is decorative and stylized. Some paintings of the *Rāgamālā* ('garland of *rāgas*' illustrating musical modes) theme of this period, with a vertical composition following broadly the same colour schemes but depicting different facial types, are known (Zurich, Mus. Rietberg; Chandigarh. Govt Mus. & A.G.). A peculiar idiom for modelling was used by Chamba painters: a series of fine, long lines drawn clearly and at regular intervals on garments was employed for indicating volume, especially of the arms. Although this modelling is also seen in a few paintings from Mankot and Nurpur, at Chamba it remained in practice for several decades in the 18th century. Jagdish Mittal suggests that a painting of the *Nayaka-nayika-bheda* (classification of heroes and heroines) series in a horizontal format of the beginning of the 18th century that was ascribed to Kahlur–Bilaspur (Archer, 1973, ii, p. 173, no. 10) is a Chamba work. Not only is the use of the above-mentioned modelling seen in the painting, but the figural types depicted appear in several other Chamba paintings and on an illustrated paper book-cover acquired from Chamba (Simla, Himachal State Mus.).

Two broad styles are noticeable in a period of about three decades after *c.* 1690: one with clear indigenous figural types but exhibiting the influence of the Basohli style in other elements, the other much more influenced by the Basohli style. A series of *Dasavatara* paintings in a horizontal composition and characterized by a rare vitality was painted *c.* 1700 at Chamba. The colouring, though somewhat different, is close in intensity to Basohli-style painting as seen in one example from this series, *Balarama Diverting the River Jamuna* (Bombay, Prince of Wales Mus.). Another *Dasavatara* series in a vertical format (two paintings are in Chamba, Bhuri Singh Mus.) was painted about two decades later. A *Rāgamālā* series of roughly square dimensions (two examples in Chamba, Bhuri Singh Mus.) appears stylistically close to the Mankot–Basohli style, but the detailing is not as fine. Despite these various influences, a study of the drawings discovered among painter families at Chamba (mostly Hyderabad, Mittal Mus. Ind. A.) has suggested that Mughal–Deccani styles continued to influence Chamba painting until *c.* 1720 (see Mittal, 1989). Some paintings and a set of tinted drawings illustrating the Puranic story of Dhruva, a prince who became an ascetic (dispersed; formerly Chamba, Dharam

Pal priv. col.) and the wall paintings in the Shakti-Devi Temple at Gand-dehra (see below) indicate the underlying traits of Deccani painting.

A painting of *Ugar Singh with Ladies* (London, V&A) is ascribed by Archer (1973) to Jammu. The facial type of the women is different from that seen in Chamba paintings of the earlier period. Ugar Singh (*reg* 1720–35) had lived in Jammu for some years and gained the throne of Chamba with the help of the ruler of Jammu. The development of Chamba painting from this period on suggests the presence of one or more painters from Jammu at Chamba. Some paintings possessing a stylistic affinity with the painting of Ugar Singh are in the Bhuri Singh Museum, Chamba. Only a few paintings of this period survive. Several paintings attributable to Laharu and Mahesh, painters active during the reign of Umed Singh (*reg* 1748–64), are known. Laharu's name is mentioned on a dated painting of the *Bhāgavata* series (1757; Chamba, Bhuri Singh Mus.). The sharply receding foreheads and the distinctive treatment of the eyes are the salient idioms of the work of this artist. Rectangular and squarish facial types are seen in paintings of this period. Several new elements appeared in two sets of the *Rāmāyaṇa* and in a *Bhāgavata* series. Both the *Rāmāyaṇa* sets are in the horizontal format, and the older series is smaller. Goetz (1954) believes traits of provincial Mughal painting were adopted in Chamba at this period. The treatment of female faces in the *Bhāgavata* series is impressive and shows a deviation from the earlier types. The architectural designs, complex and often dominant in the *Rāmāyaṇa* series, have a clear relationship with Mughal architecture. Green, particularly in a dark tone, is much used in the *Bhāgavata* paintings. The colouring in the paintings of the *Rāmāyaṇa* series is different; a rich yellow predominates in several compositions. The figural types of women in the paintings of the early part of the series show a development influenced by a type seen in works attributable to the period of Ugar Singh. Floating streaks of clouds, or bubble-like clouds, are painted over the blue of the sky, and the treatment of water, showing waves and ripples, is also distinctive, with a dark grey used for the undercoat.

A large number of drawings of the *Bhāgavata* and *Rāmāyaṇa* series and a few of the *Rāgamālā* theme have survived (Hyderabad, Mittal Mus. Ind. A.; Chamba, Bhuri Singh Mus. and elsewhere). In these drawings the quality of line is different from the firm and bold draughtsmanship of the paintings influenced by the Basohli style. The lines are fine, light and graceful, the stylization of figures is distinct, and the simplified forms are pleasing, indicating an indirect influence, probably from Guler, where new developments were taking place (*see* §(h) below). A family of carpenter-painters of Guler was working for the Chamba rulers, as is indicated by a portrait of *Udai Singh* painted *c.* 1715–20 by Kuku (Chandigarh, Govt Mus. & A.G.). Umed Singh's son Raj Singh (*reg* 1764–94) gave land in the Rihlu area to descendants of the painter Pandit Seu of Guler, including Nikka (son of NAINSUKH). The names of two of Nikka's sons, Harkhu and Chhajju, appear

295. Mahesh (attrib.): *Narasimha, the Man–lion Incarnation of Vishnu*, Chamba school, 194×287 mm, 1725–50 (Zurich, Museum Rietberg Zürich)

on two paintings of *c.* 1800 (Hyderabad, Mittal Mus. Ind. A.). Paintings done in the style native to Chamba show distinctive figural types, often naturalistic in treatment, and the compositions are simple and spacious except in the paintings of the *Rāmāyaṇa* series. Subjects are of a sacred nature, and there is a preference for paintings depicting the incarnations of Vishnu (see fig. 295). Painting at Chamba was in a state of experimentation when *c.* 1770 Guler painters working in a poetic and more refined and expressive style arrived at Chamba, and a clear shift in themes took place. In place of Krishna's childhood exploits, such romantic themes as *Rukmiṇī and maṅgala* (on the abduction of Rukmini by Krishna from a temple and their marriage; e.g. Chamba, Bhuri Singh Mus.) were painted. Similarly the celebrated *Anirudda Usha* paintings of this period (e.g. Chamba, Bhuri Singh Mus.) are related to a love story. Paintings related to poetry with clear romantic overtones such as *Bārāmāsā* (themes of the 12 months; e.g. Hyderabad, Mittal Mus. Ind. A.) and *Astha-nayika* (the classification of eight heroines; e.g. Hyderabad, Mittal Mus. Ind. A.; London, V&A) were also done. Rulers were portrayed with their consorts or watching dancing-girls and musicians. Some of the portraits of Raj Singh by Guler painters (e.g. Hyderabad, Mittal Mus. Ind. A.) show his indomitable character.

The invasion of Kangra by the Gurkhas of Nepal, and the occupation of Kangra fort and its surroundings by the Sikh Maharaja Ranjit Singh in 1809 rapidly changed the political situation in the Punjab Hills. Though Chamba state escaped annexation, it lost the fertile tract of Rihlu in 1821, and Guler painters left the service of Chamba. However, paintings done for Chamba by Guler painters living at Rihlu are known after 1821. For about five decades from that date paintings were done in three distinct styles at Chamba: the first with roots in the Guler style, the second possessing affinity with late Kangra painting and the third exhibiting close affinity with the contemporary style of the Punjab. Examples of these three styles are seen in wall paintings in Chamba. Chemical or aniline colours appeared from the mid-19th century. In the latter half of the 19th century excessive modelling on faces is seen in several paintings. The painter Durga did some wall paintings in the Rang Mahal as well as some miniatures in the third quarter of the 19th century. Tara Singh, a Rajput (*d* ?1912), painted some works on Tantric themes in the late 19th century; his style shows affinity with late Kangra painting. Sohnu and Jawahar, two brothers from a Gujarati painter family at Chamba, painted several works in the late 19th century and early 20th (Chamba, Bhuri Singh Mus.). Jawahar also painted figures on *peepal* leaf for an Englishman working as an engineer at Chamba in the early 20th century. Wall paintings have survived at several places: Shakti–Devi Temple (1720–30), Gand-dehra; Chamunda–Devi Temple (1754), Devi-ri-kothi; Shiva Temple (1840–50), Obri-Chambra; and the Rang Mahal (19th century), Chamba. The panels removed from the latter palace are in the National Museum, New Delhi, the Himachal State Museum, Simla, and the Bhuri Singh Museum, Chamba.

BIBLIOGRAPHY

J. Ph. Vogel: *Catalogue of the Bhuri Singh Museum at Chamba* (Calcutta, 1909)
——: 'Portrait Painting in Kangra and Chamba', *Artibus Asiae*, x/3 (1947), pp. 200–15
J. C. French: 'Art in Chamba', *A. & Lett.*, xxv/2 (1951), pp. 45–8
W. G. Archer: *Indian Painting in the Punjab Hills* (London, 1952)
J. Mittal: 'Mural Paintings in Chamba', *J. Ind. Soc. Orient. A.*, xix (1952–3), pp. 11–18
H. Goetz: 'Rajput Sculpture and Painting under Raja Umed Singh of Chamba', *Marg*, vii/4 (1954), pp. 23–34
J. Mittal: 'Some Ramayana and Bhagwata Drawings of Chamba', *Marg*, viii/3 (1955), pp. 26–31
——: 'The Wall Paintings of Chamba', *Marg*, viii/3 (1955), pp. 38–42, 97
K. Khandalavala: 'An *Aniruddha Usha* Series from Chamba and the Painter Ram Lal', *Lalit Kala*, 1–2 (1955–6), pp. 37–44
H. Goetz: 'The Art of Chamba in the Islamic Period: Part II', *J. Orient. Inst., Baroda*, xi/3 (1961–2), pp. 217–36
J. Mittal: 'Chamba Murals', *Marg*, xvii/3 (1964), pp. 23–7
B. N. Goswamy: 'Painting in Chamba: A Study of New Documents', *Asian Rev.*, ii/2 (1965), pp. 53–8
——: 'The Artist-family of Rajol: New Light on an Old Problem', *Roopa-Lekha*, xxxv/1–2 (1966), pp. 15–23
M. S. Randhawa: *Chamba Painting* (New Delhi, 1967)
B. N. Goswamy: 'Pahari Painting: The Family as the Basis of Style', *Marg*, xxi/4 (1968), pp. 17–62
V. C. Ohri: 'Laharu and Mahesh: Miniature Painters at Chamba in the Mid-18th Century', *Lalit Kala*, xiii (n.d.), p. 50
W. G. Archer: *Indian Paintings from the Punjab Hills*, 2 vols (London, 1973)
B. N. Goswamy: 'Genealogies of Some Artist Families of Chamba', *A Western Himalayan Kingdom: History and Culture of the Chamba State*, ed. V. C. Ohri (New Delhi, 1989), pp. 171–89
K. Goswamy: 'Portraits from Chamba: Some Notes on their Meaning and Context', *A Western Himalayan Kingdom: History and Culture of the Chamba State* (New Delhi, 1989), pp. 206–14
J. Mittal: 'Chamba Painting: Circa 1650–Circa 1850 A.D.', *A Western Himalayan Kingdom: History and Culture of the Chamba State* (New Delhi, 1989), pp. 190–205
——: *Indian Drawings 16th–19th Century: Jagdish & Kamla Mittal Museum of Indian Art, Hyderabad* (Hyderabad, 1989)
B. N. Goswamy and E. Fischer: *Pahari-Meister* (Zurich, 1990); Eng. trans. as *Pahari Masters: Court Painters of Northern India* (Zurich, 1992)
V. C. Ohri: *On the Origins of Pahari Painting* (Simla, 1991)

(g) Garhwal. Located to the extreme south-east of the Punjab Hills, Garhwal was a centre of painting from the second half of the 18th century to the late 19th. Though the corpus of Garhwal work is small, the school's contribution is significant. Its distinctive features include precise drawing, strong compositions, vigorous line, expressive figures, luxurious and atmospheric landscapes and a brilliancy of colour.

Two Mughal artists came to the capital city, Srinagar, in 1658 with Prince Sulayman Shikoh, who sought asylum there after the defeat of his father, Dara Shikoh, in a war of succession. No work by these artists has survived, but the painter, poet and collector Mola Ram (*c.* 1750–1833) was descended from them. Works by him in a late Mughal style include a depiction of a *Courtesan Drinking Wine* dated 1771 (see Lal, 1948–9, pl. 1). His subsequent work is in a more Pahari idiom, a rather stiff and clumsy version of the Kangra style (*see* §(k) below). The earliest known example of this type is dated 1775 (London, V&A, IS. 122-1955). Dates and Hindi verses by Mola Ram are often inscribed on his paintings.

Among Garhwal's finest paintings is a group of works from the second half of the 18th century, including *Shiva and Parvati* (Boston, MA, Mus. F.A.; see fig. 296). A number of scholars have attributed these to outside artists

296. Garhwal school: *Shiva and Parvati*, opaque colour on paper, 295×213 mm, late 18th century (Boston, MA, Museum of Fine Arts)

whose presence in Garhwal is indirectly indicated by jeremiads in verses written by Mola Ram in 1769 and 1775. It has been documented that prototypes of some Garhwal paintings of the Krishna legend (Chamba, Bhuri Singh Mus.) are the work of Guler artists (*see* §(h) below). This and stylistic affinities between Garhwal and Guler painting suggest that Guler painters settled in Garhwal. Opinion, however, is divided; scholars have suggested alternatively that artists from Pahari centres other than Guler migrated to Garhwal, that Garhwal painters travelled to other Pahari centres for apprenticeship or that the Garhwal style was developed independently by local artists.

Yet Garhwal masterpieces such as *Shiva and Parvati* have an individuality that distinguishes them from the work of other Pahari centres. Landscapes exhibit some Guler idioms but contain certain elements of the local environment. In a number of works, for instance, a large tree with leafless branches is dramatically set against the sky. Women are rendered with sinuous graceful figures, sharp facial features and slender wrists and fingers. The use of Shaivite crescent-shaped marks on foreheads (not generally seen in paintings from other centres) was a common and consistent feature at Garhwal. Other typical features include a pair of tiger or leopard cubs placed in the background, paired birds, a lotus pond and floral sprays with pointed ends.

Artistic activity in Garhwal waned in the early 19th century. Srinagar was severely damaged by an earthquake in 1802, and the state was occupied by the Gurkhas of Nepal the following year. Raja Praduman Shah (*reg* 1785–1803) died in 1804 fighting against them, and they remained in power until 1815, when they were driven out by the British, who annexed the southern part of the state. When Praduman Shah's son, Sudarshan Shah (*reg* 1815–59), moved in 1816 to the new capital, Tehri, artists again assembled there. The basic traits of Garhwal are present in their works, consisting mainly of series illustrating Hindu mythology or romantic themes of Hindi literature. But the sophistication of the compositions and panoramic landscapes of earlier works is greatly simplified. With a few exceptions, the work shows a gradual decline. Mola Ram's son Jwala Ram, who worked at Srinagar under the British Commissioner, continued to paint, but his line is heavy and his colour somewhat crude (see Archer, ii, p. 89, no. 31). Excellent works were produced, however, by the painter Chetu (Chaitu; *fl c.* 1830–*c.* 1860) and other artists from Guler/Kangra who worked for the Tehri-Garhwal court during this period (see Archer, ii, p. 90, no. 35). Their works are characterized by fluid female figures, but instead of the luxuriant landscapes for which Garhwal painting is famous, sparse compositions with bloblike trees are typical. A colophon dated 1866 on a painting of a *Rukmini and Krishna* series (see Archer, i, p. 122; ii, p. 91, nos 37i and ii) testifies to the continuity of painting activity. By this time crude versions of old paintings were produced, and no new style had developed.

BIBLIOGRAPHY

J. C. French: *Himalayan Art* (Oxford, 1931)
M. Lal: 'Garhwal School of Painting (1658–1858)', *Roopa-Lekha*, xx/2 (1948–9), pp. 114–24; xxi/1 (1949–50), pp. 17–33; xxi/2 (1950), pp. 12–28; xxii/1 (1951), pp. 32–46; xxii/2 (1951), pp. 27–41; xxiii/1–2 (1952), pp. 37–50
W. G. Archer: *Garhwal Painting* (London, 1954)
K. Khandalavala: *Pahari Miniature Painting* (Bombay, 1958)
W. G. Archer and D. Bhattacharya: *Love Songs of Vidyapati* (London, 1963)
D. Barrett and B. Gray: *Painting of India* (Geneva, 1963/*R* London, 1978)
B. N. Goswamy: 'Pahari Painting: The Family as the Basis of Style', *Marg*, xxi/4 (1968), pp. 17–62
M. Lal: *Garhwal Painting* (New Delhi, 1968)
W. G. Archer: *Indian Paintings from the Punjab Hills*, 2 vols (London, 1973)
V. C. Ohri: 'Some Problems of Garhwal Painting: A Brief Discussion', *Arts of Himachal*, ed. V. C. Ohri (Simla, 1975)
S. Singh Panwar: 'Garhwal Painting: Some Erroneous Impressions Corrected', *Lalit Kala*, xix (1979), pp. 51–6
Manifestations of Shiva (exh. cat. by S. Kramrisch, Philadelphia, PA, Mus. A., 1981) [excellent example, p. 213]
K. Khandalavala: *Pahari Miniature Paintings in the N. C. Mehta Collection* (Ahmadabad, [1983])

VISHWA CHANDER OHRI

(h) Guler. The small principality of Guler, in the eastern group of Pahari hill states, was the seat of some of the most gifted artist families who flourished in the region during the 18th and 19th centuries. Both the capital, Haripur, and its twin town, Guler, appear in Pahari paintings of the 18th century. Members of the ruling house of Guler were often sent on expeditions to distant regions by their Mughal overlords: the rajas Rup Chand (*reg c.* 1610–*c.* 1635), Man Singh (*reg c.* 1635–*c.* 1661) and Bikram Singh (*reg c.* 1661–*c.* 1685) all campaigned with success, quelling rebellions or acting as governors of subdued lands. It is not unlikely that this sustained connection with the Mughals bears some relationship to

the rise and development of painting at Guler, at least from the early 18th century, for paintings often formed the subject of gifts and exchanges. However, there is no documentation, apart from later, highly stylized portraits of 17th-century rulers, to suggest that painting was actually practised at Guler any earlier than the 18th century. However, a manuscript account of the reign of Dilip Singh (*reg c.* 1695–1741), the *Dilīparañjanī* by Uttam Kavi (1703), mentions painters prominently among the craftsmen settled in the Guler domains. Although no painter is mentioned by name, it is likely that one of the families alluded to in its pages is the celebrated family of PANDIT SEU. Pandit Seu himself seems to have worked for Dilip Singh, producing for him, apart from an early *Rāmāyaṇa* series (*c.* 1720), a series of 'succession portraits' comprising a number of different leaves, each showing a ruler on elephantback accompanied by his heir-apparent who is seated behind him in a subordinate position, holding a fly-whisk over the ruler's head. The series represents the royal succession up to the time of Dilip Singh, who is shown with his son Gowardhan Chand as heir-apparent.

The Brahmin family to which Pandit Seu belonged fell from caste on account of having taken up painting and became submerged in the painter community. Its ancestry is known from an entry of 1763 in a pilgrims' book at Hardwar written by Seu's painter son, NAINSUKH. By this time the family seems to have been securely established at Guler, where they were regarded as 'natives'. Both Nainsukh and his elder brother MANAKU worked there, suggesting the existence of discriminating patronage on an extensive scale. Various members of the family travelled widely, but although they also migrated elsewhere in the generations that followed, there is little doubt that they continued to regard Guler as their home. It was there that they evolved the remarkably refined Guler style of painting, which retained its Pahari intensity but integrated into it the naturalism and airy atmosphere of late Mughal painting (see fig. 297). Pandit Seu himself may have been responsible for this change, possibly under the influence of the Mughal paintings that seem to have arrived in the hills *c.* 1725. The style adopted by Pandit Seu in his last years and by Nainsukh from 1735 is variously described as 'Guler' (Archer) and 'pre-Kangra' by Karl Khandalavala, and M. S. Randhawa spoke of Guler as the 'birthplace of Kangra art'; however, it is perhaps best spoken of as the Seu–Nainsukh family style.

Among the many other known families of painters that originated in Guler are those of Dhumun and PURKHU, later settled at Samloti, and Basia and Siba, later settled at Ustehar. It would seem that painting continued at Guler into the last quarter of the 18th century under Raja Govardhan Chand (*reg* 1741–73) and his son Prakash Chand (*reg* 1773–90). Migrations from Guler to the Kangra or Chamba territories may have taken place when the painter families expanded and large-scale patronage became available in other states. Other families include that of Punnu and Gwal, active in the second quarter of the 18th century; that of Lahori, Birbal and Sipahi, who flourished in the late 18th century and early 19th; that of Fauju and Lalman, also active in the early 19th century; and that of Ghathu, son of Biba, who flourished in the second half of the 19th century. All had Guler affiliations and may have been distantly linked to the family of Pandit Seu. In any case, their works are strongly influenced by the work of the Pandit Seu family, who had established some kind of artistic norm in the Pahari hills by the mid-18th century.

297. Guler school: *Lady with a Hawk*, gouache on paper, 206×111 mm, *c.* 1760 (London, Victoria and Albert Museum, IS 178–1950)

In the 19th century, painting at Guler declined; the few known artists include Muhammad Baksh, who may have come from outside to work in Guler. In the 20th century no painters turned out any significant work at Guler, but the memory of the great work done in the past was revived when the large collection of the royal family was disposed of by Raja Baldev Singh (*reg* 1922–59).

BIBLIOGRAPHY

M. S. Randhawa: *Basohli Painting* (New Delhi, 1959)
M. C. Beach: 'A Bhagavata Purana from the Punjab Hills and Related Paintings', *Bull. Mus. F.A. Boston*, lxiii (1965), pp. 169–72
W. G. Archer: *Indian Paintings from the Punjab Hills*, i (London, 1973)
F. S. Aijazuddin: *Pahari Paintings and Sikh Portraits in the Lahore Museum* (London, 1977)

B. N. Goswamy: *Essence of Indian Art* (San Francisco, 1986)
Pahari-Meister (exh. cat. by B. N. Goswamy and E. Fischer, Zurich, Mus. Rietberg, 1990)

(i) Jammu. The Rajput hill state of Jammu, with its capital town of the same name, was once the principal power in the group of states that lay west of the Ravi River in the Pahari hills. However, perceptions of its importance as a centre of painting have undergone several changes. Its political eminence led ANANDA KENTISH COOMARASWAMY, writing early in the 20th century, to associate with it a cluster of early Pahari styles marked by a certain 'savage vitality', with paintings 'well and vigorously designed, often with a decorative simplicity very suggestive of large-scale mural art': hot colours, monochromatic backgrounds, emphatic drawing, and a high degree of stylization in the rendering of figures, space and architecture. The elements in these paintings were seen to have been put together with boldness of imagination, the painters taking extraordinary liberties with appearance while bringing out the inherent poetry of the situations, thus emphasizing feeling over description. Coomaraswamy distinguished this style from that of Kangra (*see* §(k) below), which he associated with later, more lyrical and graceful work characterized by easy rhythms and fluent line. However, Coomaraswamy's categories slowly gave way to others as more facts were discovered and more material came to light. In particular, his Jammu category was generally replaced by the term Basohli, largely on account of the assertions of Ajit Ghose in 1929; Basohli subsequently gained currency as a generic term for the early energetic regional style (*see* §(a) above).

The mid-18th century at Jammu was associated with a major Pahari painter, NAINSUKH, who was believed by many writers, including William George Archer, Karl Khandalavala and M. S. Randhawa, to have worked for Prince Balwant Singh (1724–63), thought to be the youngest brother of Jammu's most famous ruler, Ranjit Dev. But even this claim of Jammu to fame seems to have been misplaced, for that distinguished patron Balwant Singh is now believed to have belonged to the small principality of Jasrota (*see* §(j) below).

A major 18th-century style of painting in Jammu is exemplified by the remarkable series of Shangri *Rāmāyaṇa* paintings formerly ascribed to Kulu (*see* §(b) above) but probably produced by a family of painters based at Bahu, the former capital of Jammu. One series, the Bahu Shangri *Rāmāyaṇa* (dispersed: examples in New Delhi, N. Mus., and priv. cols; see fig. 298), is almost certainly a Jammu product. One of the major series of paintings from the Pahari hills, its leaves burst with colour; it is flamboyant in design, inventive in composition and packed with the feeling that runs through this moving epic. The style does not appear to have been long-lived, however, for it flowered at exactly the time that the new, naturalistic styles beginning to appear in the region were slowly supplanting all existing styles. Although the rulers of Jammu must have attracted painters from time to time, it was not until the establishment of the powerful Dogra dynasty under Maharaja Gulab Singh in the mid-19th century that Jammu emerged as a centre, drawing artists from considerable distances. Members of painter families from such other hill states as Guler and Kangra (*see* §(h) above and §(k)

298. Jammu school: *Jatayu, King of the Vultures, Promises to Guard Sita*, from the Bahu Shangri *Rāmāyaṇa*, gouache on paper, 184×288 mm, *c*. 1710 (private collection)

below) and from the Punjab plains are known to have worked at Jammu under the Dogra rulers; among them were Ruldu and Kanchanu of Samloti, Arjun of Guler, Haricharan of Thanpuri and Aziz, possibly from the Punjab plains. However, the work they produced only echoed the past; this style trailed on into the 20th century, when traditional work at Jammu came to an end.

BIBLIOGRAPHY

Pahari-Meister (exh. cat. by B. N. Goswamy and E. Fischer, Zurich, Mus. Rietberg, 1990)

(j) Jasrota. The remarkably small size and negligible resources of the Rajput state of Jasrota, lying west of the Ravi River in the Pahari hills, belie the significance of the paintings produced there in the 18th and 19th centuries. This tiny state, ruled by a Rajput house that prided itself on its long history, was clearly overshadowed by the much larger state of Jammu, under which it came in the 19th century. No work of any significance can be associated with Jasrota before the second quarter of the 18th century, when it suddenly came into prominence, principally because of the presence there of the great painter NAINSUKH. The date of Nainsukh's migration from Guler to Jasrota and his reasons for doing so are unclear, but it is almost certain that when he arrived there *c.* 1740 he started working for Mian Zorawar Singh and other members of the royal clan. Surviving works of this period include fine portraits of Mian Zorawar Singh and Mian Mukund Dev that demonstrate that Nainsukh was already in command of the wonderfully fluent line associated with him.

However, it was under Mian Zorawar Singh's son, Balwant Singh (1724–63), that Nainsukh launched upon an extraordinary series of portraits and intimate scenes inseparably associated with Pahari painting. Although Balwant Singh never occupied the throne of Jasrota, Nainsukh seems to have found in him a patron of uncommon discernment and passion and stayed with him as his retained artist until the prince's death. Over this period of almost a quarter of a century Nainsukh's works conjured into being an extraordinary world in which Balwant Singh is always the principal figure, whether portrayed alone, in state or in intimate company, out on a hunt, watching a dance performance, sitting writing a letter (see fig. 299), regarding with amusement a group of mimics poking fun at him, examining the points of a horse, having his beard trimmed, stalking a duck from behind the cover of a buffalo, supervising construction, or watching his horse kick a wild boar to death. There is not only wit and great observation in these works but, more than that, a warmth that goes straight to the heart. Clearly, while rendering his prince, Nainsukh was indulging his fancy too, for Balwant Singh never commanded the resources with which he is shown surrounded; rather, the paintings seem to represent a mildly inebriated world that painter and patron appear to have conspired to bring into being.

299. Nainsukh: *Balwant Singh Writing in his Tent*, Jasrota school, gouache on paper, 215×290 mm, *c.* 1750 (Bombay, Prince of Wales Museum of Western India)

The identity of Balwant Singh has been a matter of controversy among scholars, most (including William George Archer, Karl Khandalavala and M. S. Randhawa) placing him in Jammu and seeing him as the youngest brother of the famous Ranjit Dev. However, there is now enough evidence to establish that Balwant Singh was a prince of Jasrota for whom Nainsukh worked.

Painting in Jasrota declined rapidly after Balwant Singh's death. Nainsukh seems to have moved to Basohli, where he spent the last years of his life working for Raja Amrit Pal. At Jasrota, very minor work continued to be done. In the second quarter of the 19th century the state ceased to be a political entity when the Maharaja of Lahore, Ranjit Singh (*reg* 1799–1839), granted it as a fief to a favourite noble, Suchet Singh.

BIBLIOGRAPHY

B. N. Goswamy: 'The Problem of the Artist Nainsukh of Jasrota', *Artibus Asiae*, xxviii (1966), pp. 205–10

Pahari-Meister (exh. cat. by B. N. Goswamy and E. Fischer, Zurich, Mus. Rietberg, 1990)

(k) Kangra. An ancient Rajput kingdom ensconced in the Pahari hills, Kangra has long been associated with a major regional painting tradition of the 18th–20th centuries. Although it was a principal centre of painting, with several families of painters active, the work produced there was so varied that it is difficult to speak of a general Kangra style. However, common characteristics include its great delicacy and refinement; a fluent, rhythmic line; vivid but discreet colouring; idealized rendering of forms, especially the female figure; fine characterization, even of minor figures; a relaxed air in composition; and a marked sensitivity for landscape. The principal artists associated with Kangra painting are the grandsons of PANDIT SEU, Fattu and Khushala, both sons of MANAKU, and Kama, Gaudhu, Nikka and Ranjha, the sons of NAINSUKH. Although there are extremely few signed works by these painters, evidence suggests that at least some of them worked for Maharaja Sansar Chand (*reg* 1775–1823), one of the most important patrons of painting in the hills.

Among the large, extensive series of Kangra paintings known to have been executed in the late 18th century and early 19th are a dispersed *Bhāgavata purāṇa*; a *Gīta Govinda* ('Song of the herdsman') generally referred to as the Tehri-Garhwal *Gīta Govinda*; a *Rāmāyaṇa* once in the collection of the art dealer C. L. Bharany; a Bihari *Satsai* (New York, Kronos Col.; see fig. 300); a *Rāgamālā* (New Delhi, N. Mus.); a *Nala and Damayanti* (Jammu, Karan Singh priv. col.); and a *Rasikapriyā–Kavipriyā* (dispersed). Shorter series include a *Rukmini Harana* (dispersed), an *Usha and Aniruddha* (mostly Chamba, Bhuri Singh Mus.) and a *Sudama carita* (dispersed). Countless isolated leaves deal with such themes as archetypal heroes and heroines (*nayaka*s and *nayika*s) or poetic scenes of rural life. Whatever the theme, these painters seem to have had the ability to steep themselves completely in its spirit. It is they, more than anyone, who created that magic world in which, as the art historian Ananda Kentish Coomaraswamy said, 'all men are heroic, and all women beautiful and passionate and shy'. If it is the childhood of Krishna they render, they are able to conjure into being a world where all that matters is the divine child, and everything else happens with reference to him. His parents seem to

300. Kangra school: *The Village Beauty*, from a Bihari *Satsai* series, gouache on paper, 190×130 mm, *c.* 1785 (New York, Kronos Collection)

lead no lives of their own; the milkmaids speak the whole day of nothing but his deeds; his boyish companions and their adoring herd of cows hang upon his every word. When the painters turn to the tender love story of Nala and Damayanti, they interpret with singular refinement the lovers' states of mind: the distraction of Nala as he turns away from affairs of state to contemplate Damayanti's beauty; the 'fires of separation' that scorch and burn Damayanti, who longs ceaselessly for her lover; and the tender exchanges between the lovers when they are finally united in marriage. The painters turn with supreme ease and with equal effect from one sentiment to another. All this is done within the parameters of a style that constantly treads a narrow path between passionate feeling and reticent expression. However, the style could not maintain this delicate balance for long, and from the second quarter of the 19th century it started to slip into excessive sweetness. Although competent work continued to be done by later descendants of Pandit Seu until the end of the century, the freshness went out of the style, which often lapsed into sentimentality and dull repetition.

Many other families of artists in the region originally came from Kangra but moved in the early 19th century to such villages as Samloti and Ustehar. Prominent among the artists settled in these two villages were PURKHU and Bassia, son of Uttam. The work of Purkhu largely comprises a colourful record of the Kangra court. The work captures admirably the atmosphere of the court and recreates, in vivid detail, the personalities, assemblies, festivals and meetings that Purkhu must have witnessed. Although his drawing lacks the verve seen in the works of Pandit Seu's descendants and displays little penetration of character in the portraits, it is unfair to dismiss his work as merely journalistic. His compositions are often innovative and daring, and his sensitivity to colours is quite remarkable: some of his leaves are truly dazzling in their effect.

Apart from a large group of paintings recording the life and times of Maharaja Sansar Chand and his family, Purkhu and his two brothers Buddhu and Rattu seem to have been involved in working on very extensive series of paintings that include a *Śiva purāṇa* (mostly Chandigarh, Govt Mus. & A.G.), a *Parijata Harana* (New Delhi, N. Mus.), a *Rāmāyaṇa* and a *Rasikapriya* (both dispersed). Purkhu's four sons—Ramkrishna, Ramdayal, Chandanu and Ruldu—continued to work in the 19th century at other centres of painting, notably Jammu and Mandi.

BIBLIOGRAPHY

M. S. Randhawa: *Kangra Paintings of the Bhagavata Purana* (New Delhi, 1960)

——: *Kangra Paintings of the Gita Govinda* (New Delhi, 1963)

W. G. Archer: *Indian Paintings from the Punjab Hills*, 2 vols (London, 1973)

F. S. Aijazuddin: *Pahari Paintings and Sikh Portraits in the Lahore Museum* (London, 1977)

B. N. Goswamy: *Essence of Indian Art* (San Francisco, 1986)

Pahari-Meister (exh. cat. by B. N. Goswamy and E. Fischer, Zurich, Mus. Rietberg, 1990)

B. N. GOSWAMY

(l) Mandi. The isolated situation of Mandi in the narrow Beas Valley of the Punjab Hills is reflected both in the region's distinctive dialect and in its unusual paintings. Portrait painting in the Mughal style was introduced in the reign of Raja Hari Sen (*reg* 1623–37), whose early portraits are finely executed and naturalistic in treatment (e.g. Chandigarh, Govt Mus. & A.G.). Also in this Mughal-influenced style is a painting of two Turkmans shown with faces in the typical Mughal three-quarter view (Ahmadabad, Cult. Cent., Mehta Col.). There are slightly later portraits of Hari Sen by hill painters whose work is less refined in style.

For a period of about 30 years in the mid-17th century a regional style of miniature painting was practised that retained certain Mughal-derived characteristics. Examples include such works as the *Killing of the Demon Pralambasura*, a leaf from a *Bhāgavata purāṇa* series (Chandigarh, Govt Mus. & A.G.). The elaborate compositions of these paintings employ receding planes; the line, though somewhat coarsened, is still relatively fine; the architecture is realistic, and the faces are well modelled. Some of the female facial types are derived from Mughal prototypes of the Shah Jahan period (1628–58). Features such as birds shown in flight at the top of a picture and the use of deep blue for the sky may have been borrowed from Deccani painting (*see* §(vi) below). Certain of these conventions persist over a long period.

Mandi painting acquired a highly distinctive character under Raja Sidh Sen (*reg* 1684–1727), whose personality influenced the development of the style. He was a man of enormous stature and a great warrior as well as a deeply religious devotee of the god Shiva. Portraits of him include the *Young Raja Sidh Sen* (*c*. 1675–1700; Hyderabad, Mittal Mus. Ind. A.) and *Raja Sidh Sen in Audience* (*c*. 1700–20; New Delhi, N. Mus.). In several works he was depicted as an incarnation of Shiva.

Mandi painting during Rajah Sidh Sen's reign is characterized by bold, sweeping lines. Important figures are given emphasis by strong modelling on faces and other parts of the body. Compositions are simple and colours progressively more controlled. Space is often divided in three horizontal registers: a narrow foreground, monochrome background (usually in light green but occasionally in cream or light pink) and a white and blue strip at the top for the sky. The palette consists of muted colours, light blue and chocolate brown.

Numerous temples to the god Shiva and Devi, the Goddess, were built in the 17th and 18th centuries in Mandi, and the primitive vitality that characterizes the sculptures produced in the period appears to have influenced the statuesque and bold depiction of figures in some pictures. Paintings of images under worship were also produced. The forms of Shiva are frequent subjects, as in *Shiva Enthroned* (see fig. 301). Portraiture and subjects related to Shiva, Devi and Tantric themes were more popular than purely literary themes. Even Rajas and nobles wear the typical Shaivite mark of horizontal lines on the forehead. The figures are mannered in form: heads, hands

301. Mandi school: *Shiva Enthroned*, opaque colour on paper, 270×187 mm, *c*. 1730–40 (London, Victoria and Albert Museum)

and sometimes feet are greatly enlarged in paintings of the early 18th century. Trees are depicted with bunches of sparse foliage, over each of which are blossoms of white or light green (e.g. *Krishna Collecting a Toll from the Gopis*, New Delhi, N. Mus.). The influence of Tibetan painting is suggested by padded garments (seen occasionally) and to some extent by colours, especially in depictions of flames, as in the paintings of the Tantric goddess *Tripura Sundari* (Varanasi, Banaras Hindu U., Bharat Kala Bhavan) and *Krishna Swallowing the Forest Fire* from a *Bhāgavata purāṇa* series (New Delhi, N. Mus.). It is also possible that the unusual elements seen in these Mandi paintings had been introduced there by Kashmir painters familiar with Persian painting. Depictions of the Krishna legend in folk style were produced for the common people. From after *c.* 1750 to *c.* 1770 there is a coarsening of line and colour. Later paintings show bright colours and a fluent, more refined line. Distinct facial types have prominent eyes and noses.

The third and last phase of Mandi painting started after *c.* 1805, when a painter from Guler named Sajnu migrated to Mandi. Works by him painted for Raja Ishwari Sen (*reg* 1788–1826) include the portrait *Raja Ishwari Sen Worshipping Shiva* (Varanasi, Banaras Hindu U., Bharat Kala Bhavan; see Archer, ii, p. 275) and a series of 21 illustrations of the *Hamir hath*, a ballad relating the downfall of Hamir, the overlord of Ranthambhor Fort in Rajasthan (dispersed; see Archer, ii, p. 273). Colour, facial types and architecture in his works are related to Guler painting, but Sajnu used more crowded compositions full of detail. Buildings in his paintings are placed at angles, a compositional innovation, and groups of figures, hills and rocks are arranged in marked diagonals. For the first time in Mandi, borders of paintings are decorated; devices include the Shiva *liṅga* and figures of gods and devotees. Several artists from Guler, Kangra and Nurpur came to Mandi in the second quarter of the 19th century. Adverse political conditions from 1840 onwards, however, hastened the decline of art.

One of the most extensive collections of Mandi painting was that of the Mandi Palace Library (now dispersed). Works from this collection bear rubber stamp marks with no legend and contain handwritten inventory numbers. Some wall paintings survive (mainly in the house of Kanwar Samsher Singh at Mandi), but these are not earlier than the 19th century.

BIBLIOGRAPHY

K. Khandalavala: *Pahari Miniature Painting* (Bombay, 1958) [pls xii and xiv; figs 9, 23, 25–6, 28 and 35; and suppl. nos 146–9 and 152]

Miniature indiane dal XV al XIX secolo (exh. cat. by R. Skelton, Venice, Fond. Cini, 1961; exh. held 1960; Eng. trans. 1961)

M. R. A. [Mulk Raj Anand]: 'Mandi', *Marg*, xvii/3 (1964), pp. 55–7

W. G. Archer: *Indian Paintings from the Punjab Hills*, 2 vols (London, 1973)

Chandramani [Singh]: 'On Mandi Paintings', *Chhavi-2: Rai Krishnadasa Felicitation Volume*, ed. A. Krishna (Varanasi, 1981), pp. 206–11

Manifestations of Shiva (exh. cat. by S. Kramrisch, Philadelphia, PA, Mus. A., 1981)

C. Glynn: 'Early Painting in Mandi', *Artibus Asiae*, xliv/1 (1983), pp. 21–64

K. Khandalavala: *Pahari Miniature Paintings in the N. C. Mehta Collection* (Ahmadabad, [1983])

Essence of Indian Art (exh. cat. by B. N. Goswamy, San Francisco, 1986)

VISHWA CHANDER OHRI

(v) Eastern Indian styles.

(a) *Bengal.* Bengal is unique in India for the variety of its pictorial art. Initially it might appear that one was dealing with an arbitrary geographical abstraction rather than a single cultural tradition. However, these different, very distinct styles all reflect a common phenomenon of Bengali culture. From the imposition of Muslim rule *c.* 1203, Bengali culture had a dual aspect, either looking to the external traditions of the rulers or to the traditionally orientated folk art of the masses. As Mughal rule was replaced by that of the British, cultural interchange became increasingly complex.

The Pala Buddhist palm-leaf illuminated manuscript tradition (*see* §3(ii)(c) above) set the pattern for later Hindu manuscripts throughout Bengal and eastern India. The format of long rectangular scenes in joined series illustrating various legends survived the transition from palm leaf to paper and continued in villages well into the 20th century. At least six styles were produced by artists (*patua*s) with distinctions of style and palette but more markedly of subject-matter. Such universal Hindu themes as the *Rāmāyaṇa*, as well as regional Bengali themes such as the life of Shri Chaitanya (1485–1533), ending with depictions of hell, or the story of the goddess Manasa, Muslim stories of the tiger controlling the Sufi saints Satya Pir and Badekhan Gazi, and the creation legends of the Santal tribes were depicted. In Birbhum, Muslim artists produced such paintings for Hindus; elsewhere, Hindu artists produced them for Santal tribespeople.

The decline of Mughal central government led to the establishment of a provincial court at Murshidabad after 1740 that patronized the arts. While it has been suggested that the personality of the austere ʿAlivardi Khan (*reg* 1740–56) or the hedonistic Suraj al-Daula (*reg* 1756–7) is reflected in their patronage of painting, these distinctions were expressed in the common language of Mughal art. Murshidabad painting was dominated by the Mughal themes of formal portraits of rulers and their courtiers and court activities from the *darbar* (audience) to hunting, as well as by *Rāgamālā* series illustrating musical theory. Increasing British influence is first seen by the appearance of oddly dressed central figures in the equivalent of the formal *darbar* portrait. Progressively, as the nawabs lost even the appearance of power, court scenes were replaced by Muslim festival scenes, particularly of Muharrum, a festival that grew greatly in importance at this time and gave rise to much artistic activity. Hindu festivals and shrine scenes (see fig. 302) were also shown. Stylistically, European modelling and perspective became increasingly important, but the decline in the status of the artist and the undiscriminating nature of foreign patronage led to an increasing crudity (*see* §(ix)(b) below).

Away from Murshidabad, at Calcutta, Muslim artists painted flower series and scenes of Anglo-Indian life down to horses and dogs. Meanwhile, at the great Kali Temple in Calcutta, artists began to create the first urban popular art in India. The style differed considerably from the style of the rural artists, as it concentrated on a single scene or figure, highly simplified but slightly modelled, painted on an upright rectangular sheet of European paper. Not only were the perennial subjects of the *Rāmāyaṇa*, the Goddess

302. Murshidabad school: *Scene at a Shrine*, *c.* 1760 (London, British Library, Oriental and India Office Library)

and the love of Krishna and Radha depicted, but also semi-naked courtesans, still-life scenes of fish illustrating proverbs and news stories of scandalous murders. Elsewhere in Calcutta engravers of the *svarnakar* caste began to turn out black-and-white or hastily coloured prints. Differing from Kalighat paintings in their interest in detail and the crowded scenes they depict, they are frequently signed. As well as the Goddess these also illustrated the *Rāmāyaṇa* and *Mahābhārata* epics, Radha–Krishna legends and such Bengali favourites as the life of Shri Chaitanya, the goddess Manasa and the river goddess Ganga.

A few years later the modern technique of chromolithography began to be used. This was the work of a group of former students of the Calcutta Art School, who took the name Calcutta Art Studio. The results of their highly classical European art training are immediately apparent, though put at the service of popular Hinduism. As well as universal images of Hinduism, they also concentrated on images of Kali, associated with militant Bengali nationalism, and scenes from Sanskrit literature. These changes point towards a somewhat puritan, reformist, Bengali and Indian nationalism and led the way for the more revolutionary ideas of Ernest Binfield Havell, Principal of the Calcutta Art School from 1896, and members of the TAGORE family (*see* §(x) below).

BIBLIOGRAPHY

T. Falk and M. Archer: *Indian Miniatures in the India Office Library* (London, 1981)
T. R. Blurton: *Hindu Art* (London, 1993)

DAVID JONES

(b) Orissa. Surviving examples of Orissan miniature painting appear to be no earlier than the mid-16th century. One of the best known, discovered in Ranpur (Puri District), shows the reception of the *Embassy of the Mughal Emperor Akbar by the Orissan King Mukunda Harichandana* (*reg* 1559–67; U. Calcutta, Asutosh Mus. Ind. A.). The monarch, with his guard and two attendants, is seated in his palace before the five Muslim ambassadors, who wear magnificent robes and extravagantly tied turbans. The style of this painting derives its force and inspiration from medieval art but also reveals Mughal, Deccani and Vijayanagara influences. However, the vigour of the drawing with its superb characterization, the excellence of the linear design and the sumptuous colour are unique in contemporary Indian painting.

Probably to the same period belong four pages, painted on both sides and found near Ranpur at Nayagarh, depicting gracefully drawn herdswomen on the moonlit banks of the River Jumna together with delicately tinted animal and tree forms (U. Calcutta, Asutosh Mus. Ind. A.). From Nayagarh is also an excellent sketch of cavalry

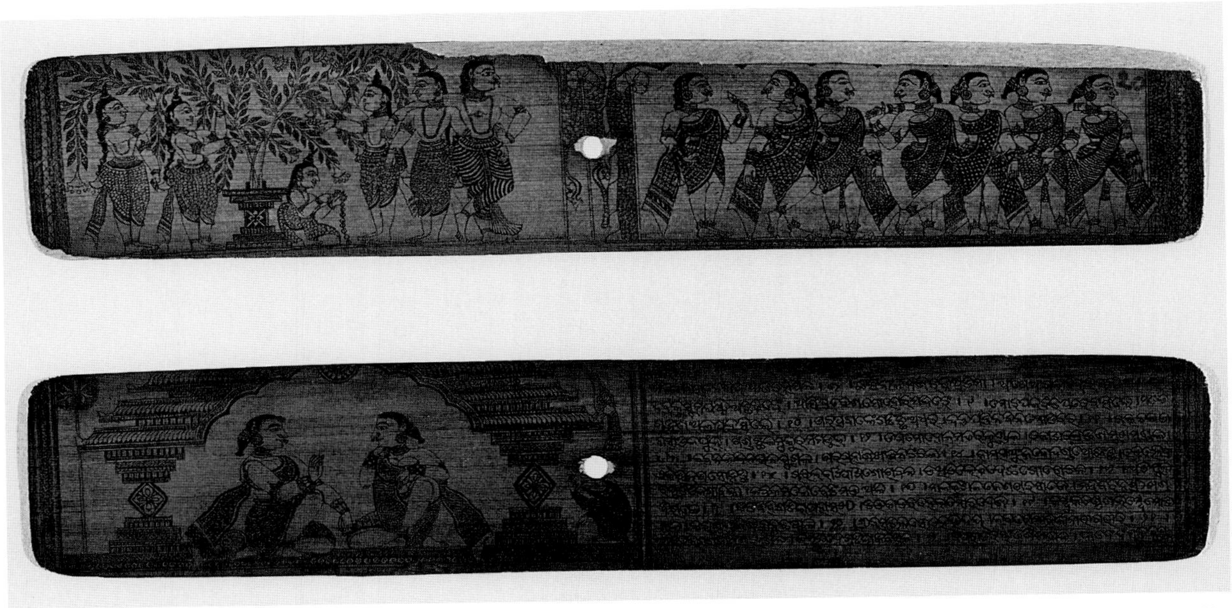

303. Orissan school: *The Sport of Radha and Krishna*, palm-leaf manuscript, mid-17th century (London, British Library, Oriental and India Office Library)

in light brown and blue with yellow tones dating from the 16th century; a slightly later, 17th-century coloured drawing shows a princely archer inside a chariot in the characteristic linear style (both U. Calcutta, Asutosh Mus. Ind. A.).

These works give some idea of the quality of the contemporary wall paintings in the great religious centre at Puri. It is unlikely that the heavily overpainted wall paintings in the Jagannatha Temple are much earlier than the 17th century, but some may be based on earlier compositions. The Puri cult of Krishna as Jagannatha spread to distant parts of Orissa together with the iconography of the god. The connection between the Puri wall paintings and those found in the Jagannatha Temple at Dharakot and the Chaitanya Temple at Chikiti (both in Ganjam District) and at Srikurmam (now in Andhra Pradesh) is a close but complex one. The latter do not appear to be earlier than the 18th century and are in the metropolitan Puri style. However, those in the Virinchi Narayana Temple in Buguda (Ganjam District) are in a style close to the traditional painting of south India (*see* §(vii) below).

The best-known Orissan painted cloth hangings (*paṭa*s) are from the Jagannatha Temple, Puri; commissioned by pilgrims, they show symbolic plans of the sacral complex. One of the earliest of the group is a splendid painting executed in 1670 (London, V&A). It depicts both a frontal view of the wooden divinities (which are painted annually in a folk style before taking part in the famous car festival) installed in the shrine proper and a cross-section of the three halls surrounded by the subsidiary temples. Particularly beautiful are the tones of the picture: delicate earth reds, yellows, shades of orange and green-black. The style is eclectic, combining elements of the linear medieval Orissan style with contemporary developments in painting in south-western Bihar. Certain decorative elements go back to the well-known *Embassy* miniature; others appear in contemporary Orissan illustrated palm-leaf manuscripts (see fig. 303). The architectonic composition is retained and developed in the fine early 19th-century Puri plan once in Berlin but lost during World War II. Unable perhaps to rival the technical mastery of their predecessors in refined drawing, later artists paid less attention to elaborate detail. This technique degenerated in the late 19th century into less elegant cloth hangings with almost garish colours; however, the example acquired by the Bibliothèque Nationale, Paris, in 1894 is still of considerable beauty.

Although early examples of Orissan illustrated palm-leaf manuscripts are not coloured, the *Song of the Cowherd* of Jayadeva, illustrated by Dhananjaya *c.* 1690, includes many passages of red, yellow, blue and green, applied mostly to clothes and sometimes to figures. The 18th-century palm-leaf examples show all the characteristics of Orissan illustration at this time, with immensely ponderous limbs and sharply pointed features. In the 19th century the technique of adding tints to palm-leaf illustrations degenerated into a general wash of reds and yellows. Raghunatha Prusti (*fl* 1886), one of the greatest late 19th-century illustrators, used no colour but had a keen eye for detail.

BIBLIOGRAPHY

O. C. Gangoly: 'Summary Survey of Orissan Painting', *Marg*, viii/4 (1955), pp. 47–56

D. P. Ghosh: 'Eastern School of Mediaeval Indian Painting', *Chhavi: Golden Jubilee Volume* (1971), pp. 91–103

E. Fischer and others: *Orissa: Kunst und Kultur in Nordost-Indien* (Zurich, 1980)

J. P. Losty: *Krishna, a Hindu Vision of God: Scenes from the Life of Krishna Illustrated in Orissan and Other Eastern Indian Manuscripts in the British Library* (London, 1980)

S. Chandra: 'The Art and Craft of Patta Painting', *A. Asia*, xxi/4 (1991), pp. 139–45
O. M. Starza-Majewski: 'A Seventeenth Century Ritual *Pata* from the Jagannatha Temple, Puri', *S. Asian Stud.*, ix (1993), pp. 47–60

O. M. STARZA-MAJEWSKI

(vi) Deccani styles. The Deccan (derived from Skt: 'south') is a broad plateau that covers much of south India (see fig. 304). The distinctive painting styles of its Muslim courts show a wide range of indigenous and foreign influences, though their individual differences were eventually submerged in a heavily Mughalized idiom that dominated painting in the region after the imperial conquests of the late 17th century.

(a) Ahmadnagar. (b) Bijapur. (c) Golconda. (d) Aurangabad.

(a) Ahmadnagar. Founded in the late 15th century, Ahmadnagar was for the most part absorbed into the Mughal empire in 1600, preserving its independence for a shorter time than either Bijapur or Golconda (*see* §§(b) and (c) below). Under Iranian influence, the court converted to the Shia sect of Islam. Ahmadnagar's painting is the rarest of the Deccani schools and has been the most elusive to reconstruct. Despite the small number of surviving works—only about 20 items can be ascribed to this centre—Ahmadnagar painting undoubtedly represents the earliest and most original flowering of the art of painting in the Deccan. Many of the pictures are royal portraits, a theme eminently suited to the unique Ahmadnagar style: majestically austere figures, a sensitivity to human relationships, gentle colours, a fondness for plain gold backgrounds and an overall mood of noble restraint. The works span the last four decades of the 16th century and the reigns of three art-loving sultans: Husayn Nizam Shah I (*reg* 1554–65) and his sons Murtaza I (*reg* 1565–88) and Burhan II (*reg* 1591–5).

The earliest examples of painting are the 12 illustrations to the history of the reign of Sultan Husayn Nizam Shah I, the *Tarif-i Husayn Shahi* (Pune, Bharata Itihasa Samshodhaka Mandala). Husayn led a victorious Muslim coalition against Vijayanagara in 1565, just before his death. The *Tarif-i Husayn Shahi* describes the Sultan's virtues, as well as those of his wife Humayun. The book was probably written in 1565, after his victory, which is mentioned, but before his death, which is not. The six pictures depicting court life are the most lyrical of the book, using strong indigenous patterns, vibrant colours and simply drawn figures. In several of the court scenes a mysteriously damaged female figure shares Husayn's throne, probably Queen Humayun. If this identification is correct, these are the only female royal portraits in Islamic art. Perhaps her images were obliterated at the order of her son when he seized power and ended her regency in 1569.

These charming images hardly anticipate two grand portraits of the Sultan of Ahmadnagar executed a decade or so later, both by the same anonymous artist and both inscribed with the dynastic title *niẓām shāh* (Rampur, Raza Lib., and Paris, Bib. N., Suppl. Pers. 1572, fol. 26; see fig. 305); of extraordinary quality, they exhibit a rare marriage of visionary splendour with humanistic dignity. In the picture in Paris a young king, sitting on a splendidly

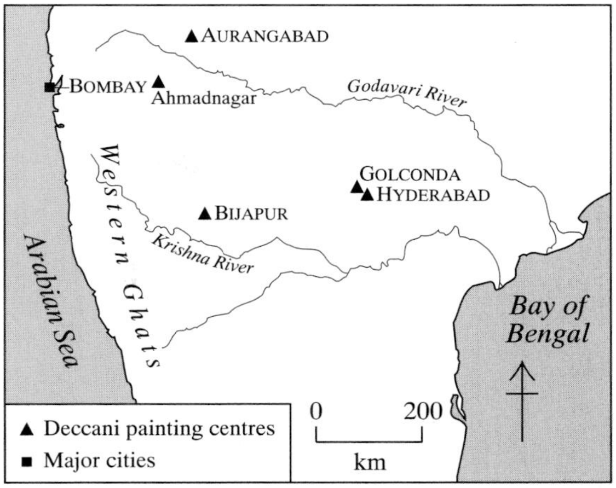

304. Map showing Deccani painting schools; those sites with separate entries in this dictionary are distinguished by CROSS-REFERENCE TYPE

inlaid throne, presents gold to a courtier while a young boy races up offering betel-nut. In the portrait in Rampur the same king, in similar clothes, stretches out on a bed, gripping large bolsters. A third picture by the same artist, completing his known work, depicts a royal adolescent galloping on a piebald horse through a field of swaying golden plants.

The sudden appearance of this superb school of portraiture suggests there may have been earlier painting of a more sophisticated kind than the illustrations of the *Tarif-i Hasayn Shahi*, though it has not survived. Certain

305. Ahmadnagar school: *Sultan of Ahmadnagar Enthroned*, opaque colour on paper, 235×205 mm, *c.* 1575 (Paris, Bibliothèque Nationale, Supplément Pers. 1572, fol. 26)

paintings do seem to anticipate late 16th-century developments, but it is unclear if they were painted in Iran, with which Ahmadnagar had close ties, or in India. Two drawings of Turkman warriors, both by the same hand and meant to face each other in the same album (Washington, DC, Freer, and Boston, MA, Mus. F.A.) may represent the kind of painting that eventually gave rise to the style of the portraits in Paris and Rampur. Originally described as *c.* 1430, Timurid school (see Martin), they are probably 16th century in date and exhibit an emphasis on the weight and volume of the human body that is more Indian than Iranian, as are details of costume. A third portrait, of a dervish (Bombay, Jehangir A.G.), is similar in mood and style.

A group of five superb line drawings belong to a slightly later phase of Ahmadnagar art, dating possibly to the reign of Sultan Burhan II in the late 16th century. It would not be surprising if after years of exile at the court of the Mughal emperor Akbar (*reg* 1556–1605), on his return to the Deccan the Sultan patronized painting that was strongly marked by Mughal taste. The *Running Elephant* (USA, priv. col.) has the turbulent mood of Akbar's manuscript illustrations. The *Royal Picnic* (London, BL, Orient. & India Office Lib.) probably depicts Burhan himself seated on a canopied throne in a garden and about to begin a sumptuous feast. Three other drawings, a *Scholar Meditating before an Open Book* (Paris, Mus. Guimet, E.O. 35776), a *Young Prince Embraced by a Small Girl* (San Diego, CA, Mus. A., Binney Col.) and a *Kneeling Youth* (untraced, see Zebrowski, fig. 20) exemplify the Ahmadnagar taste for elegant drawings in the Persian manner.

BIBLIOGRAPHY

F. R. Martin: *The Miniature Painting and Painters of Persia, India and Turkey* (London, 1912)
E. Blochet: *Les Enluminures des manuscrits orientaux de la Bibliothèque Nationale* (Paris, 1926)
D. Barrett: *Painting of the Deccan* (London, 1958)
D. Barrett and B. Gray: *Painting of India* (Geneva, 1963/*R* London, 1978)
S. C. Welch: 'Mughal and Deccani Paintings from a Private Collection', *A. Orient.*, v (1963), pp. 221–33
K. Khandalavala and M. Chandra: *Miniatures and Sculptures from the Collection of the Late Sir Cowasji Jahangir, Bart.* (Bombay, 1965)
E. Binney III: *Indian Miniature Painting from the Collection of Edwin Binney III: The Mughal and Deccani Schools with Some Related Sultanate Materials* (Portland, 1973)
T. Falk and M. Archer: *Indian Miniatures in the India Office Library* (London, 1981)
M. Zebrowski: *Deccani Painting* (London, 1983)
India: Art and Culture, 1300–1900 (exh. cat. by S. C. Welch, New York, Met., 1985)

(b) Bijapur. From 1489, the year Yusuf ʿAdil Shah established an independent kingdom, until 1686, the year the Mughals took the city, Bijapur's position as an artistic centre was second only to the Mughal capital, Delhi. The rulers of Bijapur, Shia Muslims, looked to Iran as a cultural model. Like Iranian rulers, the ʿAdil Shahi sultans were great patrons of painting, architecture and literature. Stylistic evidence indicates that painters were mostly Indian by birth but infused with Iranian sensibilities, producing a pungent and vigorous school of painting rivalling the best Mughal and Safavid work. Subjects were usually local rulers and princes portrayed in moments of intimacy: strolling in a garden, embracing a lover or simply dozing on heaps of pillows. Following Iranian example, line is eloquently calligraphic, while the south Indian taste for fleshy nudes in painting and sculpture gives sensuality and drama.

The earliest Bijapur pictures are small illustrations to a Persian manuscript on astronomy, the *Nujūm al-ʿulūm* ('Stars of science'; 1570–71 (AH 978); Dublin, Chester Beatty Lib.). Closely related are two other manuscripts, both on music and dance, the *Javāhir al-mūsīkat* (London, BL, Or. MS. 12857) and the *Rasapradipa tika* (Jaipur, Maharaja Sawai Man Singh II Mus.). All three are in a coarse but lively style and were probably executed for Sultan ʿAli ʿAdil Shah I (*reg* 1557–79).

His successor, Sultan Ibrahim ʿAdil Shah II (*reg* 1579–1627), was Bijapur's greatest king and patron of the arts. As at neighbouring Ahmadnagar, painting suddenly erupted with unexpected brilliance from provincial roots, although here with a more understandable cause, for Ibrahim was a poet, calligrapher, musician and mystic, attracting men of culture to his court from all over the Islamic world. From a surviving handful of great royal portraits, the work by four major anonymous painters can be identified. The fragmentary *Procession of Sultan Ibrahim ʿAdil Shah II* (Bikaner, Chandra Pal.) and the bust portrait of the same king as a chubby adolescent (priv. col., see Zebrowski, colour pl. vi) are by an artist working *c.* 1590 whose skill in handling the mass and movement of the human body, whose talent for characterization and whose mastery of both robust form and ornament are unique in Indo-Islamic art, though there is some affinity to the Mughal style of the *Ḥamzanāma* (*see* §(i)(b) above).

Two decades later, a second anonymous master executed a series of courtly portraits with graceful poses, restrained colour, meditative expressions and moods of quiet dignity, attesting to a vastly different sensibility. His masterpiece is the *Dervish Receiving a Visitor* (Oxford, Bodleian Lib., MS. Douce Or. b.2 (I), fol. 1a). The dark-skinned visitor, wearing the white garb of a penitent and strongly resembling the Sultan himself, stands with downcast eyes begging blessings from the saint, a grizzled, white-bearded figure with long, clawlike fingernails. This strange picture may record a real incident in the Sultan's religious life. This painter's other works show the same change from the explosive idiom of the procession scene in Bikaner to an elegantly meditative mood, much akin to the transformations in Mughal art from the reign of Akbar (*reg* 1556–1605) to that of Jahangir (*reg* 1605–27). The artist's *Stout Courtier* (London, BM, 1937 4–10 03) portrays a corpulent nobleman in a moment of uneasy quiet, perhaps after having discovered some unsettling news. *The Mullah* (London, BL, Orient. & India Office Lib.) depicts a severe religious leader carrying a sumptuously decorated Koran, also lost in thought, identical in style and even in size to the *Stout Courtier. Sultan Ibrahim ʿAdil Shah II* (London, BM, 1937 4–10 02; see fig. 306) and the *Kneeling Dervish* in the Gulshan Album (Tehran, Gulistan Pal. Lib.) are more opulently dressed figures, but there is the same mood of distant, gentle reverie. The *Fighting Cranes* (Paris, Mus. Guimet, M.G. 9150) completes the group of known examples of this painter's supremely poetic, graceful and jewel-like work.

A third artist was responsible for the larger-scale *Sultan Ibrahim ʿAdil Shah II Hawking* in the Leningrad Album

306. Bijapur school: *Sultan Ibrahim ʿAdil Shah II*, opaque colour on paper, 170×102 mm, 1610–20 (London, British Museum, 1937 4–10 02)

(*c.* 1590; St Petersburg, Acad. Sci., fol. 2). He worked in a mode characterized by gold arabesque, grand calligraphic contours and paradisical garden settings, rivalling and perhaps surpassing the lyricism of the previous artist. He may be Farrukh Husayn, mentioned by the poet–historian Zuhuri in his account of Sultan Ibrahim's illustrious court. In this picture, Ibrahim rides a henna-dyed horse through a fantastic world of verdant meadows, blossoming trees and shimmering rocks, a setting that is more like the eternal spring of Persian mystical poetry than the dusty Deccan plateau. This brilliant picture captures the artistic temperament of the Sultan and his court. A tiny painting (141×105 mm) of *Ibrahim Riding an Elephant* (priv. col., see Zebrowski, figs 71–2) has a similar, equally magical landscape and can be attributed to the same artist. The mount may be the famous elephant Atash Khan, whom Ibrahim praised lavishly in his book of Urdu songs, the *Kitāb-i nauras.* Another elephant picture by the same artist (Varanasi, Sitaram Sahu priv. col.) may also depict Atash Khan, loaded down with massive gold ornaments. The garden of delights setting has become more Indian, ethereal greens replacing the iridescent Iranian tones of the picture in St Petersburg. A small picture of a *Groom Calming his Horse* (London, V&A, IS. 88–1965) may have been painted *c.* 1610 when the artist was in advanced age, for his style has become loose and abbreviated, with thin washes of colour and rapidly applied dabs of paint.

The fourth major artist in Ibrahim's studio began his career as one of several painters who executed the pleasant but unremarkable illustrations for the Deccani Urdu manuscript the *Pem nem* (London, BL, Add. MS. 16880). One of his best pages (fol. 46a) shows the meeting between a youthful prince and an ashen-faced *yoginī* (female ascetic), perhaps a reference to Ibrahim's interest in the occult. During the next two decades this painter developed into an artist of great technical skill and decorative strength, though, in the end, less original than the previous three. His greatest work, a *Yoginī* (Dublin, Chester Beatty Lib., MS. 11a, fol. 3), a dark brooding image of female mystery, develops the theme touched on in the *Pem nem. The Kiss* (Istanbul, Topkapı Pal. Mus.) is a light-hearted depiction of elegant lovers embracing. Equal to the *Yoginī* in power is the dozing prince, dubbed *The Siesta* (Berlin, Pergamonmus., T. 4595, fol. 36). A youthful prince, perhaps Ibrahim himself, overcome by the heat of day, has collapsed on a heap of cushions while pages fan and massage him, and even the garden trees bend down to shade him. It is one of the most enchanting visions of the heat and leisure of India and—like *Sultan Ibrahim ʿAdil Shah II Hawking*—a reflection of the relaxed, refined tone of the Bijapur court. The same artist's *Ascetic Visited by a Yoginī* (Berlin, Pergamonmus., T. 4596, fol. 49), set in a marvellous crystalline garden, presents the mysterious male counterpart to his *Yoginī* in Dublin (both works have also been assigned to Golconda; *see* §(c) below).

During the reign of Sultan Muhammad ʿAdil Shah (*reg* 1627–56) both Bijapur's political situation and the character of its art changed. The kingdom of Ahmadnagar, directly to the north, had been conquered by the Mughals, who appointed a viceroy of the Deccan, resident at Aurangabad. The Mughal emperor, his court and his army were frequently there, readying for the final push to conquer Bijapur and Golconda. The presence in the Deccan of the Mughal nobility and military commanders—many of whom, including the Rajasthani maharajas, were patrons of the arts in their own kingdoms and carried artists and craftsmen to the Deccan in their vast entourage—exerted a northern influence on the Bijapur school. Portraits became more factual, figures more realistic, colours more restrained, the sense of mystery lessened, and the typical Mughal subject of marching armies and formal court ceremony began to replace depictions of the private lives of the sultans.

A series of portraits of Muhammad ʿAdil Shah, executed between 1630 and 1650, exemplify this trend. A Mughal and a Deccani artist collaborated on the earliest picture in this style (ex-Kevorkian priv. col., New York; see Zebrowski, fig. 92). The figure of the Sultan standing rigidly at attention, his hand placed firmly on his sword, was executed by the northern painter, while the dreamy violet-hued setting of palaces, iridescent trees and a wine flask on a column is undoubtedly the work of a local artist. This picture suggests that Muhammad had a taste for Mughal paintings and was engaging Mughal artists for his most important artistic endeavours. Also because of Mughal example, there was a new interest in recording such details of the painting as the authorship or the subject on the picture itself. The grand *Darbar of Sultan Muhammad 'Adil Shah* (Jaipur, Maharaja Sawai Man Singh II Mus., AG. 771), depicting the Sultan puffing on his waterpipe, relaxing on a bedlike throne and surrounded by the chief members of his court, is inscribed with the artist's name (Muhammad Khan, son of Miyan Chand), the date (1651) and the fact that the picture records the royal gift to the painter (whose self-portrait appears in the lower right-hand corner) of a daily allowance for his 'accomplishments of the pen'.

A large painting of Muhammad on an elephant with his African prime minister, Ikhlas Khan (priv. col., see Zebrowski, fig. 100), is a sumptuously coloured work with an inscription in fine gold *naskh* script recording the names of two artists, Haydar Ali and Ibrahim Khan. This inscription suggests that the early Mughal division of labour on a single picture, with artists specializing in line, colour or faces, had perhaps been adopted at Bijapur, though the precise details of the allocation of tasks usually given in Mughal inscriptions are not given here. Abdul Karim, a fourth artist working at Bijapur at this time whose name is known from inscriptions, is responsible for the most powerful work to have survived from the reign: a large drawing of the Sultan with 42 courtiers and mullahs, performing religious rites in a spacious pillared shrine housing a golden reliquary box inscribed with the names Allah and Muhammad (priv. col.). The hall is almost certainly the Asar Mahal, where a hair from the Prophet's beard is kept and periodically viewed amid great celebration, probably the event depicted in the drawing. The inscription giving the artist's name is on an open book held by a courtier—possibly this figure is a self-portrait of the artist.

During the reigns of the last two sultans of Bijapur, 'Ali 'Adil Shah II (*reg* 1656–72) and Sikandar (*reg* 1672–86), the kingdom was constantly under Mughal threat, finally falling in 1686. Painting, nevertheless, achieved a new brilliance. Line casts off Mughal formality, eyes arch gracefully upwards, rich colours reappear, gestures and glances among figures create a compositional coherence often lacking in contemporary Mughal portraits. A portrait of *'Ali and Four Courtiers* (ex-Moti Chandra priv. col., Bombay, see Zebrowski, fig. 107) may record the temporary reconciliation between the Sultan and the Maratha ruler Shivaji. The rippling, reclining figure of the Sultan dominates the picture in a dazzling way, while the palette of green, blue, yellow and maroon proves that Deccani artists were still brilliant colourists. The *Deer Hunt* (USA, priv. col., see Zebrowski, fig. 115) is at once dashing, lyrical and full of pathos. An ambitious genealogical picture depicting an imaginary assembly of all the sultans of the 'Adil Shah dynasty, posed formally on their thrones before a fantastic green and violet landscape (New York, Met.), compares well with earlier paintings. It is the last surviving picture that can be connected with certainty to Bijapur, executed for the last Sultan, the boy Sikandar, who was soon to fall into Mughal hands and be confined for the rest of his short life.

BIBLIOGRAPHY

Ibrahim 'Adil Shah II: *Kitāb-i nauras* [The book of nine essences] (*c.* 1600); Eng. trans. and ed. N. Ahmad (New Delhi, 1959)

H. Cousens: *Notes on the Buildings and Other Antiquarian Remains at Bijapur* (Bombay, 1890)

H. Goetz: 'La Peinture indienne: Les Ecoles du Dekkan', *Gaz. B.-A.*, n.s. 5, xiii (1935), pp. 275–88

S. Kramrisch: *A Survey of Painting in the Deccan* (London, 1937)

H. Goetz: *The Art and Architecture of Bikaner State* (Oxford, 1950)

R. Skelton: 'The Mughal Artist Farrokh Beg', *A. Orient.*, ii (1957), pp. 393–411

D. Barrett: *Painting of the Deccan* (London, 1958)

R. Skelton: 'Documents for the Study of Painting at Bijapur', *A. Asiat.*, v/2 (1958), pp. 97–125

D. Barrett: 'Some Unpublished Deccan Miniatures', *Lalit Kala*, vii (1960), pp. 9–13

D. Barrett and B. Gray: *Painting of India* (Geneva, 1963/*R* London, 1978)

J. Mittal: 'Paintings of the Hyderabad School', *Marg*, xvi/2 (1963), pp. 43–56 [also 'Portfolio', pp. 17–22]

D. Barrett: 'Painting at Bijapur', *Paintings from Islamic Lands*, ed. R. Pindar-Wilson (Oxford, 1969), pp. 142–59

M. Zebrowski: *Deccani Painting* (London, 1983)

India: Art and Culture, 1300–1900 (exh. cat. by S. C. Welch, New York, Met., 1985)

MARK ZEBROWSKI

(c) Golconda. Paintings from Golconda are characterized by a richness appropriate to one of the wealthiest cities of medieval India. Originally a provincial capital of the Muslim Bahmanid rulers (1347–1512), the fortress city of Golconda became the centre of an independent kingdom under the Qutb Shahi dynasty (*reg* 1512–1687). The Qutb Shahis were Shia Muslims and thought of themselves as receiving their royal authority from the foremost Shia dynasty, the Safavids of Iran. Links with Iran were close throughout the period of Golconda independence, and like their mentors the Golconda sultans maintained studios and libraries and patronized scholars, poets and artists from all over the Muslim world.

Before c. *1636.* The earliest paintings associated with Golconda occur in manuscripts with clear Iranian links. Influence from Bukhara is paramount in a copy of Hatifi's *Khusrau and Shirin* (1569; Bankipur, Patna, Khuda Bakhsh Lib.); Khorasani influence is evident in the frontispiece to a medical encyclopedia (1572; Dublin, Chester Beatty Lib. MS. 30); and influence from Shiraz dominates a *Sindbad-nāma* ('Story of Sindbad'; *c.* 1575; London, BL, Orient. & India Office Lib., MS. 3214) and an *Anvār-i Suhaylī* ('Lights of Canopus'; 1582; London, V&A, MS. IS. 13-1962). Only the medical encyclopedia, with illuminated decoration rather than illustrations, is of royal quality. The others show to a greater or lesser degree an Indo-Persian style derived from Shiraz in the late 15th century overlaid with the more up-to-date Iranian influences (see 1982 exh. cat., pp. 53–4, 70–71). Characteristic of this style and of later Golconda painting are an interest in surface pattern (rather than recession into depth), cluttered compositions and an opulent, thick palette. The earliest Golconda manuscript to combine these characteristics in a single, coherent style is the *Kulliyāt* ('Collected works'; Hyderabad, Salar Jung Mus.) of Sultan Muhammad Quli Qutb Shah (*reg* 1580–1612). Six of the miniatures, with their dense compositions in sumptuous colours and a paint surface so thick that it has developed craquelure, show the Golconda style in formation. The compositions are often still Iranian, yet full of Indian details. Safavid influence remains strong: the Safavid baton turban is depicted long after its use had been discontinued in Iran itself. The remaining two miniatures are in a Bukharan style derived from the *Khusrau and Shirin* manuscript. A date of *c.* 1590 seems probable for the *Kulliyāt*, although it may have been in production for much of the ensuing decade as the royal author continued his poetic outpourings.

Related to this manuscript in style are five paintings showing a ruler with courtiers and dancers in landscape and architectural settings (London, BM, 1974-6-17-06(1–5)). The ruler may be either the young Muhammad Quli, *c.* 1590, or his successor Muhammad (*reg* 1612–26) early in his reign (see Barrett, 1958 and 1960). Since there is no surviving contemporary Golconda portrait of the former monarch and only problematic ones of the latter, it is difficult to be sure; stylistic archaisms such as the use of compositional registers suggest an early date but not earlier than the *Kulliyāt* itself. It has been suggested that these are archaistic productions of *c.* 1630 showing the young ʿAbdallah Qutb Shah (*reg* 1626–72) and that a portrait of a Golconda ruler in *darbar* (London, BM, 1937-4-10-1; see fig. 307) identified by Barrett (1958, pl. 8) as Muhammad Qutb Shah *c.* 1612 is in fact his successor, ʿAbdallah (Skelton, pp. 186–7; Zebrowski, pp. 178–81). These new

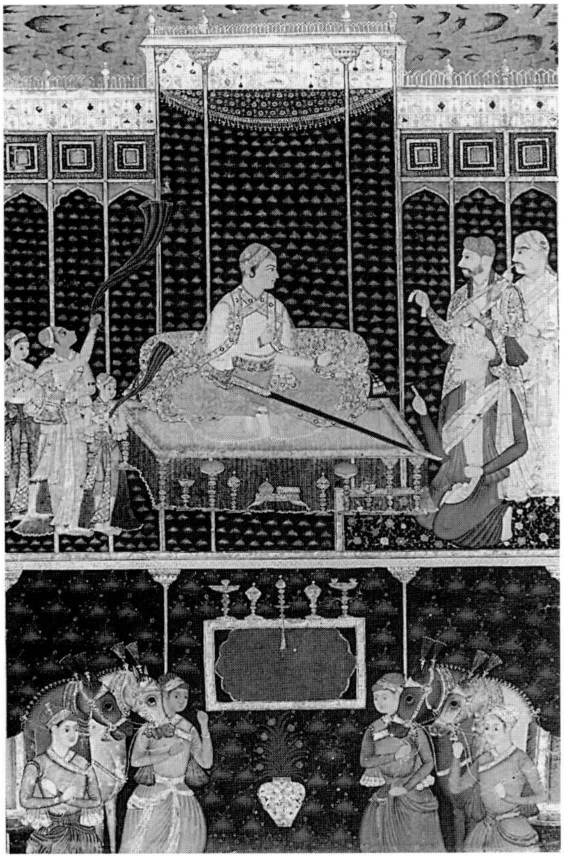

307. Golconda school: *Portrait of a Ruler (probably Muhammad Qutb Shah) in Darbar*, opaque colour on paper, 248×160 mm, *c.* 1612 (London, British Museum, 1937–4–10–1)

datings, however, make any coherent chronological development of the Golconda style impossible (Losty, 1995); it is difficult to conceive of these works being later than the lushly romantic paintings attributable to the 1620s (see below).

The disputed British Museum portrait is best seen as one of *Muhammad Qutb Shah* and datable *c.* 1612; it is the first great work of Golconda painting. The young king, wearing the typical rich Golconda royal costume, sits enthroned on a couch in the centre of the painting, a great sword across his knees, his face in full profile turned towards a group of his ministers on the right. In a lower register four men hold the reins of horses; all these are in three-quarter profile. No attempt has been made at the realism that was preoccupying the contemporary Mughal and Bijapur schools (*see* §§(i) and (vi)(b) above). The figures are puppets, the full profile coming from the earliest known Deccani paintings, while the three-quarter profiles reveal a Persian rather than Mughal source in their blank, doll-like expressions. There is no attempt at perspective or placing figures in space. Yet the painting works as an expression of royal power partly because of these limitations. The composition is restrained and static, the colours are bold and sumptuous, the balance is perfect.

A portrait of the same monarch from *c.* 1620 (priv. col., see 1976 exh. cat., no. 187; Zebrowski, no. 142, a later copy) shows him standing in a meadow against a dark ground. He is dressed similarly and holding the great straight sword but has more angular features and a small moustache. In contrast to the contemporary Mughal portrait of this king by Hashim (London, V&A, IM. 22-1925), with its mood of introspective realism, the Golconda portrait is all swagger and opulence. It probably should not be taken as a realistic portrait. The full profile and unmodelled features are still derived from the earliest schools of the Deccan and not from the vogue for portraiture in full profile in the Mughal studio introduced by the emperor Jahangir (*reg* 1605–27). There are no other undisputed contemporary Golconda portraits with which to compare it. Other paintings of this period still show little Mughal influence.

More characteristic of the romantically opulent Golconda school in the 1620s is the painting *A Prince Hawking* (London, BL, Orient. & India Office Lib., Johnson Album 67, no. 3). The prince, wearing a long green *jāmā* ('robe') and magnificent gold shawl, rides in a flowery meadow through which a stream meanders. Old-fashioned qualities include the way the landscape builds in registers of different shades of green to a solid pink wall of rock, the extreme flatness of the composition and the careful edging of the verges of the stream (an Indo-Persian convention from the 15th century). White palaces on the mountain beyond have been thought to indicate that this painting may be based on an original from Bijapur, where this convention was employed in a group of paintings of the early 17th century. The best-known examples are the famous *Yoginī* (Dublin, Chester Beatty Lib., MS. 11A, fol. 3) and *Ascetic Visited by a Yoginī* (Berlin, Pergamonmus., T.4596, fol. 4a; for both *see also* §(b) above). Like *A Prince Hawking*, these use registers to build up the landscape and show an inability to suggest landscape recession, despite Bijapuri artists having solved this problem in other works (see Zebrowski, pp. 92–8). It may yet turn out that Barrett was right in 1958 when he attributed the *Yoginī* to Golconda.

c. *1636–87.* Mughal influence is seen directly in Golconda painting from *c.* 1636, when a strong Mughal presence was established in the Deccan with the final defeat of Ahmadnagar. The Mughal viceroy in the Deccan, always an important noble and sometimes a son of the emperor himself, had with him a great army staffed by some of the most important nobles in the empire, who brought to the south all the comforts of Mughal civilization as well as its artistic tastes. Deccani artists were exposed to the Mughal tradition of portraiture, and standard Mughal iconography was adopted even though interpreted in the Deccani manner. Golconda royal portraits were henceforth painted as if their suitability as gifts had to be borne in mind. Faces were modelled in full profile in the Mughal manner, the costume changed to the Mughal knee-length *jāmā*, although enlivened by the bold draping of the shawl round the body, and a halo surrounded the head of the sovereign. A portrait of ʿAbdallah Qutb Shah seated on a terrace (*c.* 1635–40; Oxford, Ashmolean, 1960.203) exemplifies this new manner; there are later standing portraits of the Shah in the same basic style. The opulence of the palette and the lavishness of the gold continue the rich Golconda tradition, but a northern sobriety is also evident. The swagger, however, continued in the work of some artists, as in a portrait of the last Golconda sultan *Abu'l-Hasan* (*reg* 1672–87; San Diego, CA, Mus. A., Binney Col., see Zebrowski, fig. 156). Something of the grandeur of contemporary Mughal historical painting has perhaps influenced one of the most important paintings from ʿAbdallah's reign, a procession scene in the new capital Hyderabad (St Petersburg, Saltykov-Shchedrin Pub. Lib., Dorn 489, fol. 18b). ʿAbdallah seems about aged 40, which dates the picture to *c.* 1650. The unknown artist has absorbed techniques such as perspective used in the Mughal manner. Still typical of the Golconda style are the size of the King, taller than anybody else in the procession, and the principal courtiers, who are taller than the musicians or the members of the crowd.

Throughout the 17th century, however, a strand deriving directly from Iran continued in Golconda painting. The calligraphic drawings of Riza Abbasi and his followers were imitated in Golconda (Zebrowski, figs 140, 148 etc) but given solidity in an Indian manner. In the second half of the 17th century particularly important connections between the Iranian painters SHAYKH ʿABBASI and his sons and a strand of Golconda painting suggests influence in both directions (Zebrowski, pp. 195–206). The wonderful *Sleeping Girl* (Berlin, Pergamonmus., F.4589, fol. 1), with its all-important line, heavy shading and subdued colouring, best exemplifies this style. There was likewise mutual influence in the painting of lacquered articles.

After 1687. Golconda fell to the Mughal emperor Aurangzeb (*reg* 1658–1707) in 1687, and the lavish patronage of the sultans, which had kept Golconda painting distinctive, was at an end. Aurangzeb appointed Mughals based at Hyderabad as governors of the Deccan. Mughal hegemony in the Deccan from 1685 to 1724 resulted in, among other things, a style of painting combining Mughal and Deccani elements. Any of the various cities of the northern Deccan occupied by the Mughal forces could have served as locations for this work. Deccani sumptuousness is still present in many paintings. The numbers of potential patrons, in the old Golconda kingdom at any rate, seems to have increased rather than decreased. Although compositions are stiff in the contemporary Mughal manner, the exuberance of colour and extravagance of detail more than compensate. The conventional horse portrait of the late Aurangzeb period has been totally transformed in such paintings as *A Young Prince Hawking* (priv. col., see Zebrowski, no. 183), with its delicate blue stallion, rich colours and fantastic Deccan landscape, or the even richer colours of a similar equestrian portrait (London, BM, 1947-9-20-06), in which the stallion's curled mane cascades almost to its hooves against a wonderful landscape of lake and hills. Such styles were translated to Rajasthan by Rajput nobles serving the Mughals in the Deccan and greatly influenced schools such as those of Bikaner and Kishangarh (*see* §(iii)(d) and (f) above). Besides such fine work, a tradition of bazaar painting for a European clientele continued from the late Golconda period. (Dutch, English and French traders were regularly at Golconda.) These are mainly albums of portraits of the Deccani rulers and Mughal notables (e.g. London, BM; Amsterdam, Rijksmus.).

In 1724 the Mughal viceroy of the Deccan, Nizam al-Mulk, threw off Mughal hegemony and declared his independence of Delhi under the title Asaf Jah, nizam of Hyderabad. This secessionist movement coincided with those in Avadh and Bengal, but while political independence in these two states resulted in a resurgence of the arts, no comparable revival occurred in Hyderabad. The finest work of the 18th century is found in various albums of *Rāgamālā* paintings that follow a standard, if variant, iconography peculiar to the Deccan (see Ebeling, pp. 194–6). Among the finest is the Johnson Album (London, BL, Orient. & India Office Lib.; see Falk and Archer, no. 426), which was acquired in Hyderabad by Richard Johnson, the British Resident there from 1783 to 1785. It is undated but was probably painted *c.* 1750–60. Such sets combine a brilliant sense of colour with an almost cloying sentimentality in their concentration on the female form. Indeed, 18th-century Hyderabad painting gives particular emphasis to the harem and its inhabitants. There is little portraiture, apart from sets of Hyderabad rulers and important officials produced at the end of the century, and many of these are stiff and graceless. More interesting work, if in a minor vein, was done in such provincial centres as Kurnool or Shorapur.

BIBLIOGRAPHY

S. Kramrisch: *A Survey of Painting in the Deccan* (London, 1938)
D. Barrett: *Painting of the Deccan* (London, 1958)
H. Goetz: *Indian and Persian Paintings in the Rijksprentenkabinet* (Amsterdam, 1958)
J. Irwin: 'Golconda Cotton Painting of the Early Seventeenth Century', *Lalit Kala*, v (1959), pp. 11–48
D. Barrett: 'Some Unpublished Deccan Miniatures', *Lalit Kala*, vii (1960), pp. 9–13
S. C. Welch: 'Mughal and Deccani Paintings from a Private Collection', *A. Orient.*, v (1963), pp. 221–33
H. K. Sherwani: *Muhammad Quli Qutb Shah* (London, 1967)

E. Binney III: *Indian Miniature Paintings from the Collection of Edwin Binney III: The Mughal and Deccani Schools with Some Related Sultanate Material* (Portland, 1968)
K. Ebeling: *Ragamala Painting* (Paris, 1973)
R. Skelton: 'Early Golconda Painting', *Indologen-Tagung 1971*, ed. H. Härtel and V. Moeller (Wiesbaden, 1973)
Paintings from the Muslim Courts of India (exh. cat. by R. H. Pinder-Wilson, London, BM, 1976), pp. 93–5
R. Hickmann and V. Enderlein: *Miniaturen und Kalligraphien aus der Zeit der Moghul-Kaiser* (Leipzig, 1979)
T. Falk and M. Archer: *Indian Miniatures in the India Office Library* (London, 1981)
The Art of the Book in India (exh. cat. by J. P. Losty, London, BL, 1982)
M. Zebrowski: *Deccani Painting* (London, 1983), pp. 153–206; review by J. P. Losty in *Bull. SOAS*, xlvii (1984), pp. 577–9
G. Michell, ed.: *Islamic Heritage of the Deccan* (Bombay, 1986)
J. P. Losty: 'The Development of the Golconda Style', *Douglas Barrett Felicitation Volume*, ed. J. Guy (Ahmadabad, 1995)

(d) Aurangabad. The so-called 'Aurangabad style' is one of the more problematic in Indian painting. It is named after the city of Aurangabad (originally Kharki), which was founded by the Ahmadnagar general Malik Ambar in 1610 and later in the century served as the Mughal headquarters in the Deccan. Aurangzeb was Mughal governor there from 1636 and again from 1653, and it was apparently during the latter period that the city was officially renamed after him. Works to which the term 'Aurangabad style' has been applied combine elements of the sumptuous Deccani palette and landscape tradition along with Rajput compositions and figural types, the latter modified by the modelling of features.

Paintings in this style were assigned to Aurangabad by Doshi in her publication of an illustrated manuscript of a *Rasamañjarī* ('Cluster of delights'; 1650; originally Udaipur, Jain Lib., now dispersed) by Darya Khan. The use of the name Aurangabad in the colophon seems slightly premature, but the name may have been used by the inhabitants before being officially sanctioned from Delhi. Other manuscripts are linked to the atelier that produced this work. The finest, a *Rāgamālā* ('Garland of *rāgas*'; dispersed, see Welch and Beach, no. 18) found at Ghanerao (a vassal state of Mewar in the 17th century), was previously thought to represent the style of Nagaur. An illustrated manuscript of Jayadeva's 12th-century devotional poem, the *Gīta Govinda* ('Cowherd's song'; dispersed, see Topsfield) is in a slightly less refined style. Paintings of female figures in a similar style were found at Ghanerao Palace placed under glass in the Shish Mahal (see Zebrowski, pp. 48–50). The basic Rajput style in all these examples is specifically that of Mewar; all sets are contemporary with the *Rasamañjarī* of 1650. The use of the term 'Aurangabad style' to refer to miscellaneous paintings combining Rajput, Mughal and Deccani influence cannot be justified. It was from Aurangabad that Mughal influence spread to the Deccani styles after 1630, and as the city was a centre for the movement of works of art, many of these problematic hybrids may have passed through it, without actually having been painted there.

Large numbers of Rajput nobles served in the Mughal army, frequently in the Deccan, including at various times the rulers of Marwar, Bundi, Kota, Bikaner and other states, but not those of Mewar. Although it is an attractive theory that artists accompanied Rajput rulers to the Deccan and were then influenced by local styles, there is little evidence to support it. On the contrary, it appears that the shift of paintings and artists was from the Deccan to Rajasthan. While the great rajas may have had a few artists with them in the Deccan principally to take portraits, the major painting activity in mid-17th-century Mewar was manuscript illustration, an art that could not be conducted successfully in camp. Bearing in mind that all the 'Aurangabad' material was found in Mewar or the vicinity and that its basic elements are those of Mewar about 1650, it seems best to consider the style as a variant of that of Mewar when exposed to Deccani influence and actually painted in Mewar itself (*see* §(iii)(a) above). The manuscript of the *Rasamañjarī*, which was actually commissioned by a prince of a branch of the Mewar ruling family, was copied in Aurangabad and then brought back to Udaipur for illustration, a not uncommon practice.

That Deccani artists were present in Udaipur is demonstrated by the use of the 'Aurangabad style' for two books of an illustrated manuscript of the Hindu epic the *Rāmāyaṇa* commissioned by Rana Jagat Singh I (*reg* 1628–52) of Mewar between 1649 and 1653. It seems that one or more Deccani artists painted some of the finest paintings in the *Kiṣkindhākāṇḍa* ('Book of Kishkindha'; London, BL, Add. MS. 15296(2)) and organized the work, while other artists were native to Mewar (Losty, in preparation). The incomplete *Sundarakāṇḍa* ('Beautiful book'; London, BL, Orient. & India Office Lib., MS. Skt 3621) has some paintings in a closely linked style as well as others in which the characteristics of the 'Aurangabad style' are well to the fore (Falk and Archer). The 'Aurangabad style' thus appears to be the result of one or more Deccani artists' presence in Udaipur at the end of Jagat Singh's reign. The style disappeared as an individual idiom thereafter in the general collapse of painting in the next two reigns, but it did leave its mark on Mewar painting from early in the next century.

BIBLIOGRAPHY

S. C. Welch and M. C. Beach: *Gods, Thrones and Peacocks* (New York, 1965)
S. Doshi: 'An Illustrated Manuscript from Aurangabad Dated 1650 AD', *Lalit Kala*, xv (1972), pp. 19–28
T. Falk and M. Archer: *Indian Miniatures in the India Office Library* (London, 1981), pp. 257–9
M. Zebrowski: *Deccani Painting* (London, 1983), pp. 46–59
L. Y. Leach: *Indian Miniature Paintings and Drawings*, i of *The Cleveland Museum Catalogue of Oriental Art* (Cleveland, 1986), pp. 150–51
J. P. Losty: *Indian Paintings in the British Library* (New Delhi, 1986), pp. 38–41
A. Topsfield: 'A Dispersed *Gita Govinda* Series in the Mewar–Deccam Style', *Makaranda: Essays in Honour of Dr James C. Harle*, ed. C. Bantze (New Delhi, 1990), pp. 215–26
J. P. Losty: 'Aurangabad or Mewar? The Influence of the Deccan on Rānā, Jagat Singh's *Rāmāyana* of 1649–53, *Karl Khandalavala Felicitation Volume*, ed. B. N. Gosvamy (in preparation)

J. P. LOSTY

(vii) South Indian styles. The majority of surviving wall paintings in south India date from the VIJAYANAGARA and NAYAKA periods, i.e. the 14th to 18th centuries. Wall painting appears to have been the favoured form of pictorial expression in south India; however, miniature paintings do survive, executed on paper and cloth. Painted hangings were produced for religious and secular contexts and painted scrolls for performances by story-tellers.

(a) Vijayanagara painting. (b) Nayaka painting. (c) Thanjavur or Maratha painting. (d) Other post-Vijayanagara painting.

(a) Vijayanagara painting. Adorning the walls and especially the ceilings of halls and colonnades, painting on plaster is a characteristic feature of Vijayanagara-period temple architecture (14th–16th centuries). Paintings depict themes from the epics (*Rāmāyaṇa, Mahābhārata*) and Puranas (*see* §II, 4(i) and 5(i) above), as well as legends connected to specific temples (Skt *sthāla purāṇa*s). Such foundation legends increased in importance during the Vijayanagara era, possibly due to the emergence of provincial capitals as seats of power and the growth of pilgrimage centres within territory controlled by the dynasty. Occasionally, significant cult divinities were also depicted. Generally, paintings were set out in narrow bands or registers. In larger ceiling compositions, the surface was divided into panels that could be viewed from different directions. Architectural elements, often imitating those in contemporary temples and palaces, were commonly employed as framing devices. Such panels were frequently accompanied by explanatory inscriptions, or the characters of given episodes were identified. Surviving colours indicate a palette dominated by yellows, browns and ochres; reds, greens and blues were employed as highlights. As in earlier south Indian painting, fluid line work dominates the renderings of figures, animals and architectural elements (*see* §3(i)(b) above).

By far the most impressive paintings dating from the 16th century are the remarkably well-preserved paintings in the Virabhadra Temple at LEPAKSHI. The elegant line work, vibrant colours and details of costume and facial types are the hallmarks of the Vijayanagara style. The most important of these paintings, depicting episodes drawn from Shaiva mythology, are in the ceiling bays of the *maṇḍapa* in front of the main shrine (see fig. 308). Among the most famous scenes are the marriages of Shiva and Parvati and of Arjuna and Draupadi and the *Kirātārjunīya* ('Arjuna's penance'). In the latter the scene of the boar attacking the sages is especially impressive (see fig. 309). Other themes are the story of Ravana receiving the *ātma liṅga* from Shiva and the story of King Manuchola and the cow, a legend connected to the Tiruvarur Temple (*see* §(c) below). Aspects of Shiva and other mythological figures complete this programme.

The ten *avatāra*s are illustrated on the ceiling of the Raghunathalaya at Lepakshi. A huge representation of *Virabhadra*, a form of Shiva (*c*. 7.5×4.2 m), is surrounded by eight guardians of the directions (*dikpāla*s), and *Shiva and Parvati* occupy the ceiling in front of the Virabhadra shrine. Portraits of the donor, Virupanna, and his wife are seen below. Other paintings occupy the walls of the corridor surrounding the main sanctum, the ceiling behind the Parvati shrine and the ceiling of a verandah on the south side of the temple. These are in a poor state of preservation, however.

308. Vijayanagara style: *Ladies Attending Parvati*, detail of a ceiling painting from Virabhadra Temple, Lepakshi, 16th century

309. Vijayanagara style: *Boar Attacking a Group of Sages*, from the *Kirātārjunīya* ('Arjuna's penance'), detail of a ceiling painting from Virabhadra Temple, Lepakshi, 16th century

Lepakshi painting is two-dimensional, with no suggestion of depth by means of shading or of multiple planes. The most important feature of this style is the emphasis on line; entire paintings have the appearance of coloured drawings. Nonetheless they are full of movement, expression and drama. Most of the human figures are shown in three-quarter profile, while deities are posed frontally. Several standing human figures are slightly twisted, suggesting subdued animation. The figures are clad in a variety of textiles and display an equally varied selection of headdresses, coiffures and jewellery. Architectural elements are simple. The panels invariably have exquisite painted borders, a peculiarity not seen elsewhere. The colours used are few: earth-red, black, green, yellow ochre, white and grey.

Other Vijayanagara paintings survive at TADPATRI, on the ceilings of the pillared hall and north porch of the Chintala Venkataramana Temple. A substantial series of paintings, now poorly preserved, was at one time visible on the ceiling of the Chennakeshava Temple at Somapalayam (Chittoor District). The surviving scenes of court life and battle suggest that these once formed part of an elaborate presentation of the *Rāmāyaṇa*. Medallions on the undersides of the beams incorporate animal and foliate motifs.

Frescoes similar in style and layout to the Lepakshi paintings once existed at the Kapardishvara Temple at Tiruvalanjuli (Thanjavur District) in Tamil Nadu. Also no longer extant is the exquisite series of frescoes illustrating episodes from the *Rāmāyaṇa* at the Pundarikaswami Temple at Tiruvellarai, near Tiruchchirapalli. Fortunately, the paintings in the Sri Tenupurishvara Temple at Pattisvaram (Thanjavur District) have survived. Traces of paintings are to be found in almost every part of the temple, though their fragmentary state does not always allow precise identification of the subject. A magnificent *Shiva Nataraja* (Shiva as Lord of Dance) adorns the ceiling of the *gopura* (gateway). To the left of the dancing god, following contemporary sculptural representations, stands *Shivakami* (another name for Parvati). The two figures, which might be representations of the processional images stored in the temple, are set off against a dramatic dark background. A small figure of *Shiva Dakshinamurti* (the god as the embodiment of wisdom) flanked by animals appears on the adjoining beam. The painting continues downward along the pillar; the damaged figures may have represented rows of devotees.

Towards the courtyard there is yet another important painting on the ceiling of the *gopura*. It shows Shiva and Parvati bestowing a pearl canopy on the saint Tirujnana Sambandar, an event shown as having occurred at Pattisvaram while the saint sang Shiva's praises under a scorching sun while wandering through the Thanjavur District. There are scenes from other myths connected with the temple on the walls of the main shrine and ceiling of the *amman* shrine, dedicated to the god's female counterpart. Fragments of a series of depictions of sacred bathing places (*tirtha*s) along the Kaveri River survive on the ceiling of the cloisters surrounding the main shrine.

Some of the frescoes of the Kundavi Jinalayam at Tirumalai near Polur (North Arcot District) have also been dated to the Vijayanagara period. These include *Neminatha*, the Jaina *tīrthaṅkara* (*see* §II, 3 above), addressing his sermon to a great congregation (*samavasaraṇa*); episodes from the story of Agnila (a pious lady) and Varadatta (a Jaina ascetic); two *dvarapala*s (semi-divine guardian figures) and on the ceiling decorative motifs with rows of geese and textile patterns.

Of a later date are the wall paintings within the five-storey *gopura* of the Narumbunatha Temple at Tiruppudaimarudur (Ambasamudram District), which were discovered by the State Archaeological Survey of Tamil Nadu in the late 1970s. Forceful line work characterizes these paintings, which are noteworthy for the inclusion of local legends and court and battle scenes. The most renowned of the scenes is a lively rendering of an Arab boat transporting horses.

Cloth hangings were commonly used in the columned halls and colonnades of temples and palaces. Such textiles helped define the spaces within these open structures, and their painted images provided appropriate settings for both religious and courtly rituals. The most common technique of painting was that of directly applying line work in black or ochre and then filling in with a limited range of colours, especially reds, greens and browns. Compositions were clearly related to those seen in murals, which were similarly subdivided into friezes and panels. Architectural elements used as framing devices were often developed into elaborate motifs.

Particularly interesting among the painted cloths are some 17th-century (late Vijayanagara-period) examples illustrating courtly subjects. Among these is a series of hangings showing scenes of royal reception (New York, Brooklyn Mus.). Seated royal figures are shown with a variety of visitors, including foreigners readily identifiable by their attire. More animated are the crowded court scenes on a large painted hanging in Paris (Krishna Riboud priv. col.). In this work royal couples seated in niches are entertained by music and dance, and animals and warriors are shown in procession.

The earliest painted cloths intended for the European market were made at about this time. An example datable to the mid-17th century shows Dutchmen feasting with Indian maidens (London, V&A). The surrounding borders display floral patterns that imitate contemporary Golconda textiles (*see* §VII, 3(iv)(a) below).

(b) Nayaka painting. From the late 16th century, wall paintings were added to newly built or renovated temples patronized by the Nayakas of MADURAI, GINGEE and THANJAVUR. Typical of these later paintings are bright colours, often dominated by red backgrounds, and sharply defined line work. Narratives are usually laid out in narrow bands and provided with identifying inscriptions.

Dating from the late Vijayanagara or early Nayaka period, a substantial series of frescoes is found in the Vardhamana Temple at Tirupparuttikunram, on the outskirts of KANCHIPURAM. Brightly coloured friezes adorn the ceiling of the open hall leading to the twin shrines. These paintings illustrate episodes from the lives of Rishabhanatha and Neminatha, two Jaina *tīrthankaras*, as well as from the legend of the Hindu god Krishna (*see* §II, 1 above). Identifying inscriptions accompany each scene.

Apart from the few fragments of wall paintings still extant at Gingee, a good example of the mature Nayaka style that developed there may be seen in the Venugopala Parthasarathi Temple at Chengam (North Arcot District), erected in the 17th century. The central part of the friezes on the ceiling of the outer hall is sufficiently preserved to allow identification of episodes from the *Yuddhakāṇḍa* ('Book of the battle') of the *Rāmāyaṇa*. The paintings are laid out in narrow, concentric registers, and each incident is identified with short bilingual labels in Telugu and Tamil. Some scenes are drawn from the Telugu cultural tradition, for example one in which Hanuman is depicted dragging the demon Ravana's queen, Mandodari, by the hair. The crisp line work, compositions and lively figural poses suggest a connection with contemporary manuscript illumination in Andhra Pradesh (*see* §(d) below).

The Chennaraya Perumal at Adamankottai (Dharmapuri District) has an important series of paintings, probably from the mid-17th century or early 18th. Scenes from the *Mahābhārata* and *Rāmāyaṇa* can be seen in the lateral bays. Especially remarkable is a superb rendering of *Prince Rama's Coronation* at the end of the northern bay. The central bay is occupied by a gigantic depiction of *Vishvarupa* (*see* §II, 1(iii) above). Also significant are the paintings surviving in the Shivakamasundari Temple within the 12th-century Nataraja Temple complex at CHIDAMBARAM. Legends connected with the temple and various shrines near it, the life of the Shaiva saint Manikkavasagar, a plan of the temple and a rendering of the temple chariot festival are illustrated in a lively, colourful style. The most renowned paintings in this group are those narrating the story of Shiva as Bhikshatana (his aspect as a mendicant), seducing the wives of the *ṛṣis* (sages), and of Vishnu in his feminine form as Mohini (north bay). Brief explanatory inscriptions occur here and there. In the southernmost bay, the life of Manikkavasagar is set out in a series of dramatic panels, including such gory details as jackals devouring horses or the impalement of the Jainas. Red, black, ochre and white dominate the palette, and the drawing is strong and expressionistic.

A good example of the MADURAI style are the paintings of the great Minakshi Sundareshvara Temple, where there is a panel depicting the *Marriage of Minakshi and Sundareshvara* (an aspect of Shiva) on the ceiling of the Unjal hall (*maṇḍapa*) at the western end of the 'Golden Lily' tank. In the group are Mangammal, the queen of Madurai, Prince Muthu Vijayaranga Chokkanatha Nayaka and the commander Dalavay Ramappaiah. Their portraits are labelled in both Tamil and Telugu. The 18th-century friezes that once decorated the walls along the northern and eastern sides of the tank, refurbished in 1894, are in a sad state of preservation. Recent copies in the Temple Museum give some idea of the originals. These long narrative friezes represented the 64 *līlās* (appearances, miracles) Shiva is claimed to have performed in and around Madurai. The paintings are notable for their vividly drawn figures and distinctive brown and ochre colouring.

At Alagar Koil, about 20 km to the north of Madurai, is the famous temple of Kallalagar, named for an aspect of Vishnu, 'the beautiful lord of the Kallars'. In a separate building to the south of the main temple complex is the Vasanta *maṇḍapa* with the extensive remains of an 18th-century painted *Rāmāyaṇa* series. The narrative is laid out along the *maṇḍapa* walls and on the ceilings of the eastern corridor and central pavilion. The style is remarkable for its inventiveness and spiritedness. Long captions in Tamil accompany the paintings.

In the 18th century the *Rāmāyaṇa* was very popular with artists and patrons. An impressive series of panels illustrating the entire epic covers the porch ceiling of the Thirugokarneshvara Temple at Thirugokarna (Pudukkottai District). A fragmentary series of panels probably contemporary with these can be seen on the ceiling of the Sri Andal Temple at Srivilliputtur.

Comparable mythological friezes may also be found in a number of *maṇḍapa*s at the Vaishnava Ranganatha Temple at SRIRANGAM. On the ceilings of the inner *prākāra* (covered walk-way serving as an enclosure wall) around the shrine of Ranganatha, local legends related to the island on which the temple is located and a complete *Viṣṇu purāṇa* cycle are to be seen. These paintings are arranged in registers, each of which is divided into compartments by architectural elements. Each register bears a Telugu caption. The paintings were commissioned by Vijayaranga Chokkanatha Nayaka of Madurai *c.* 1720. His portrait and those of his queens worshipping Sri Ranganatha appear at the end of the friezes. According to epigraphical sources, the poetry on which the paintings are based was the work of Kavi Ramabhadriah, an intimate friend of the Nayakas, and the artist was Rajasri Pattabhiramayyagaru. This is one of the rare instances in which patron, poet and artist are known.

Temples were not the only places to be adorned with paintings, nor was subject-matter drawn exclusively from mythology. The Ramalinga Vilas, the palace of the Sethupati rulers in Ramanathapuram, is the only building in south India to have an extensive cycle of wall paintings depicting secular subjects. Side by side with exquisite renderings of scenes from the *Rāmāyaṇa*, the *Bhāgavata purāṇa* and the local *sthāla purāṇa*, there is a series of paintings narrating the life of the Sethupatis, in particular Muthu Vijayaraghunatha Sethupati (*reg* 1710–20). These scenes, together with those from the *sthāla purāṇa*, appear in the entrance hall. They include forceful, detailed renderings of the battles between Muthu Vijayaraghunatha Sethupati and the Thanjavur Marathas as well as his reception of several Europeans, including a Jesuit priest. The paintings devoted to episodes from the *Bhāgavata purāṇa* are in the next hall. In the Darbar Hall are paintings depicting episodes from the *Bālakāṇḍa*, the first book of the *Rāmāyaṇa*, culminating in the marriage of the Ikshvaku princes and Mithila princesses. Portraits of the ruler in various garments and poses and engaged in various activities occupy the arches. The most striking scene shows him receiving the sceptre from the goddess Rajarajeshwari, the tutelary deity of his family. The paintings on the upper storey show Muthu Vijayaraghunatha Sethupati listening to music, watching dancers, drinking in the company of his mistress and making love.

Typical painted textiles from the Nayaka period include temple banners and hangings. The fields are invariably divided into panels filled with figures of divinities, consorts and guardians; more rarely, episodes from the *Rāmāyaṇa* or from the story of Krishna occupy narrow bands. As in wall paintings, backgrounds are often brilliant red or dark blue; the wide variety of colour is introduced in the rendering of the figures.

There were also paintings on scrolls, which were unfolded slowly during performances by story-tellers to illustrate the episodes being narrated. The subject-matter of the scrolls is generally related to mythology. The earliest known south Indian example, probably executed in the first quarter of the 17th century (Hyderabad, Mittal Mus., 76.469), recounts the legend of the origin of the Padmasali community. Made of fine, hand-woven cotton, it is painted in a sophisticated style that reflects the artist's debt to works produced for the contemporary Nayaka rulers. The human figures are agile in appearance; the heavenly beings are richly clad in floating scarves and heavily adorned with jewellery. A firm, vigorous outline encloses areas of bright, flat colour set against a dominant cinnabar ground.

(c) Thanjavur or Maratha painting. With the advent of Maratha rule *c.* 1670, western Indian traditions were introduced into the south on a more vigorous scale. The Darbar Hall erected inside the Thanjavur Palace bears testimony to this. The paintings, which have only recently been exposed, show the continuing tradition of the Nayaka school (the hall was repainted in the 19th century). On the rear wall is a portrait of Shivaji, leader of the Maratha rebellion against the Mughal rulers of India, with his ministers. In addition there are images of deities such as Sri Ranganatha, Krishna, Subrahmanya and Panduranga. Exquisite painted stuccowork decorates the architectural elements.

In the Thyagaraja Temple at Tiruvarur (Thanjavur District), the thousand-pillared Devasiriya *maṇḍapa*, an important structure in its own right, houses on its ceiling an impressive series of paintings of the *sthāla purāṇa*. Another set of paintings precisely documents the annual temple chariot festival.

The fame of the Thanjavur or Maratha school is based, however, on paintings on canvas glued to wooden supports and framed. These were meant to be hung on the walls of domestic *pūjā* (worship) rooms or in *bhājan* halls (spaces set aside for the chanting of hymns). The subjects are usually deities, holy places and portraits. The dazzling palette consists mainly of vivid reds, deep greens, chalk white and turquoise blue. Lavish use was made of gold, glass beads and, sometimes, precious stones. The majority of these paintings are characterized by their large formats and relatively simple compositions. This school, greatly influenced by European techniques, was the most popular one in Tamil Nadu until the beginning of the 20th century, when the RAVI VARMA school began the mass production of images of deities, which led eventually to the popular graphics known as 'calendar prints'. The Sarasvati Mahal Library, Thanjavur, holds a number of painted leaves and manuscripts on paper. One of the most famous is the leaf illustrating the 17th-century Telugu version of *Bālakāṇḍa* of the *Rāmāyaṇa*.

(d) Other post-Vijayanagara painting.

Andhra Pradesh. Apart from the vestiges of wall paintings at Tadpatri and Somapalayam, there is not much in Andhra Pradesh to document the development of pictorial art immediately after the fall of Vijayanagara. However, an important series of paintings on the ceiling of the Siddheshvara Temple at Holalagundi, a village in Kurnool District, was rediscovered at the beginning of the 1980s. The paintings, probably from the late 18th century or early 19th, have a strong thematic and stylistic affinity with those on the ceiling of the open hall (*raṅga-maṇḍapa*) of the Virupaksha Temple at HAMPI (Vijayanagara; see Karnataka below). The subjects were drawn mainly from the Puranas and epics, although the artists were also inspired by contemporary events, as is apparent from the scene of the battle between a local chief and the British. As at Vijayanagara, the *Marriage of Rama and Sita*, the *Marriage of Shiva and Parvati* and *Shiva Destroying the Three Celestial Fortresses of the Asuras* (demons) have been included. The main stylistic features are the square or rectangular shape of the panels and figures shown either in profile or frontally (only rarely in three-quarter profile). It is mostly divine beings that have been depicted frontally. The predominant colours are sky blue, black, grey, red and dark blue. Characters and episodes are identified by an inscription in black.

Karnataka. The history of Karnataka painting recommences, after an apparent gap of some nine centuries, with the 16th-century fragments on the ceiling of the dilapidated Uchhayappa *maṭha* (monastery) at Anegundi. From literary sources it is known that paintings decorated temples, dancing halls and palaces in Karnataka and that the art was highly acclaimed. The vast majority of surviving paintings in Karnataka date from the post-Vijayanagara epoch. In the second half of the 16th century, after the fall of the capital, artists and craftsmen who had worked under the patronage of the Vijayanagara rulers migrated southwards in search of work at the small Hindu courts. A large number of these artists were employed by Raja Wodeyar (*reg* 1578–1617), the first powerful ruler of the emerging Wodeyar dynasty of Mysore. Little is known of this early phase of Mysore painting, as no significant examples survive. It is to be assumed that such painters followed the Vijayanagara idiom.

Highly sophisticated paintings on paper and cotton were prepared, probably in Srirangapattana, in the second half of the 17th century. This town, which became the Wodeyar capital in 1610, continued to be a cultural centre until the end of the century. A few leaves from a dispersed *Mahābhārata* manuscript on paper (e.g. a spirited battle scene, Los Angeles, LA, Co. Mus. A., M.88.29.2; Hyderabad, Salar Jang Mus.) bear testimony to the existence of a mature and refined school of painting. The colophon bears the date *Samvat* 1592 (AD 1670) as well as the name of the scribe, Govind Sharma, son of Ratnakar. The Brahman for whom the manuscript was prepared, one Timmaji *paṇḍita*, possibly an important priest or official of the Wodeyars, is portrayed on the colophon pages by an artist other than the one responsible for the text illustrations. A particularly striking illustration represents a forest landscape with a river (Hyderabad, Mittal Mus. Ind. A., 76.528). Pure landscapes like this are rare in Indian art. The artist clearly delighted in the rendering of a grove of flowering trees on the shores of a river with abundant fish and a crocodile. The battle scenes depicted on other leaves are filled with movement. Adversaries ride furiously against each other in horse-drawn chariots. The stark profiles, beaklike noses, large oval eyes and partially frontal poses betray the painter's debt to the Vijayanagara tradition, for which these illuminations otherwise show little affinity. The figures are short and solid, and the unusual modelling makes them appear to be infused with superhuman strength and vigour.

This manuscript style did not change much during the following half-century. A series representing the ten incarnations (*avatāras*) of Vishnu was probably executed in the early 18th century at Srirangapattana. The paintings (dispersed; e.g. Hyderabad, Mittal Mus. Ind. A., 76.535 and 76.537, both depicting *Kṛṣṇalīlā* themes) are on cotton pasted on cardboard. The figures are larger in scale. In most of the examples a single figure stands beneath an arch decorated with floral garlands as if in a shrine, almost filling the entire picture space. Some of the gods have been portrayed frontally, emphasizing their hypnotic stares. Others are shown in full profile with their feet twisted sideways and their bodies in the combined front/side view typical of Vijayanagara painting. The palette is richer and livelier than in the dispersed *Mahābhārata* series.

A substantial series of impressive paintings of the late 18th century can be found on the east and west outer walls of the Darya Daulat Bagh, the summer palace of Tipu Sultan (*reg* 1782–99). On the west wall to the right of the entrance are portraits of *Tipu* and his predecessor *Haydar ʿAli* (*reg* ?1761–82) riding at the head of their troops with their ministers. On the same wall to the left of the entrance there is a representation of episodes from the second Anglo-Mysore War. On the east wall are, among other things, portraits of Tipu Sultan's contemporaries, the rajas of Thanjavur and Kodagu and the nawabs of Avadh, Savanur, Arcot and Cuddapah.

The most renowned of the Karnataka paintings are the frescoes on the ceiling of the open hall of the Virupaksha Temple at Vijayanagara. Especially forceful are the two central panels depicting the god of love, Manmatha, disturbing Shiva's penance—an incident connected with the local *sthāla purāṇa*—and Shiva as the destroyer of the fortresses of the *asuras*. Since Hampi (Vijayanagara) was allegedly the place where the marriage of Virupaksha (one of the names of Shiva) and the goddess Pampa took place, the conjugal theme is emphasized. An entire register is devoted to the depiction of the divine wedding, while other panels show Arjuna, one of the heroes of the *Mahābhārata*, securing Draupadi's hand by hitting a revolving fish-target and (from the *Rāmāyaṇa*) Rama winning the archery contest that led to his marriage to Sita. Contemporary events also have a place in the iconographic programme. The last register shows the procession accompanying Vidyaranya on his visit to the shrine of Virupaksha. The frescoes are generally considered to be contemporary with the construction of the temple's open hall (1510); however, it is possible that they were executed at a much later date. Stylistic features such as the subdivision of the panels, the emphasis on architectural features as framing devices, the deities shown frontally instead of in three-quarter or full profile and details of costume and headgear suggest a mid- or late 18th-century date. Thematic and stylistic affinities with an important set of frescoes discovered on the ceiling of the Siddheshvara Temple at Holalagundi and with the frescoes in the open hall of the Narasimhasvami Temple at Sibi seem to support this view.

Mysore. The early phase of the Mysore school can be studied in the paintings of the Mallikarjunasvami Temple at Mudukutore (Mysore District); the Narasimhasvami Temple at Sibi (Chitradurga District); the Jaina *maṭha* (monastery) at SRAVANA BELGOLA and the Chitramandapa (Painted Hall) of the Prasanna Venkataramanasvami Temple at Mysore itself. All these works were executed during the early 19th century under Krishnaraja III Wodeyar (*reg* 1799–1831), who ascended the throne after the fall of Tipu Sultan. Painting gained a new impetus at this time due to comparatively peaceful conditions and the munificent patronage of the ruling family.

The Mudukutore and Sibi paintings illustrate stories drawn both from Shaiva (e.g. Mallikarjunasvami Temple: *Shiva's Wedding*) and Vaishnava (e.g. Narasimhasvami Temple: *Vishvarupa*) mythology and portray contemporary historical personalities and events. The figures are sensitively drawn, and the colour scheme is bright and harmonious against a monochromatic background. The walls of the Jaina *maṭha* at Shravana Belgola are decorated with paintings mostly illustrating scenes from the lives of certain Jainas and their kings. The Chitramandapa of the Prasanna Venkataramanasvami Temple is lined with painted wooden panels. Four painted doors said to have been in the Mysore Palace are now in this *maṇḍapa*. Bearing the portraits of the 12 Mysore kings from Raja Wodeyar (*reg* 1578–1617) to Khasa Chamaraja VIII (*reg* 1776–96), they are inscribed with the rulers' names and regnal years. On the walls are found mythological scenes and maps of holy places in south India, e.g. Hampi, Melkote, Srirangapattana, Tirupati, all identified by inscriptions.

The second phase of the Mysore school probably evolved during the second half of the 19th century. The most representative examples of this style are the illustrated manuscripts of the encyclopedic work *Śrītattvanidhi*, compiled and illustrated under the guidance of the now-deposed Krishnaraja III Wodeyar. The three known manuscripts are all on imported paper. Backgrounds are generally left plain, but faces, drapery folds, façades, palace interiors, trees and hills are shaded in darker tones. All the figures are finished with fine, flowing black outlines. The palette is limited, and although the overall effect of these illustrations is diagrammatical, the forms, proportions and methods of representing deities became the prototype for all later Mysore schools. A more colourful and ornate version of this style can be seen in the superb manuscript of the *Sundarakāṇḍa* ('Beautiful book') of the *Rāmāyaṇa* in the Mysore Palace Sarasvati Bhandar Library. It is lavishly illustrated with a profusion of goldwork in the paintings, which seem to show a convergence of various traditions of Indian manuscript painting, most notably those from the Deccan (*see* §(vi) above).

The late Mysore style reveals many innovations, having been influenced by an increasing familiarity with European paintings, prints and photographs and by the availability of paper and new, factory-made pigments. Instead of narrative scenes done in horizontal bands against plain backgrounds, the artists painted deities within niches and under ornate arches in the manner of certain formal portraits. Outdoor scenes were set against a deep blue sky, with naturalistic hills, trees, rocks and flowering plants. Episodes in continuous narratives were divided not by formal borders but by realistic scenic or architectural elements. Many new bright colours were introduced, including synthetic ultramarine, vermilion, emerald green and crimson. The use of gold leaf and gesso also became common. Familiarity with photography induced many traditional artists to shade faces and textile folds to make them appear more lifelike. However, many traditional decorative elements, such as abundant jewellery, intricate textile patterns and symmetrically placed attributes, were retained. Most of the Mysore paintings that decorate old homes and *bhājan* halls in and around the city are examples of this late mixed style. During and after the reign of Chamaraja IX (*reg* 1881–94) an eclectic style evolved, based on a synthesis of Western-style photographic realism and traditional elements. Oil paintings on canvas of mythological subjects and portraits were quite common.

Kerala. The first surviving document of Kerala painting after the *c.* 9th-century fragment at Tirunandikkara is the magnificent depiction of *Shiva Nataraja* (3.6×2.4 m) in the *gopura* of the temple at Ettumanur, which may date from the 16th century.

About 1555 the Mattancheri Palace at COCHIN was built by the Portuguese and presented to the ruler Vira-keralavarma (*reg* 1537–61). There can be found the most extensive and best-preserved group of wall paintings from a tradition that flourished throughout the Kerala region from at least the 15th century to the 19th. Remarkable for their extensiveness and state of preservation, these paintings are representative of the stylistic diversity that informs the Kerala tradition. Their chronology is debated. Scenes from the *Rāmāyaṇa* occupying the walls of the royal bedchamber were probably executed in the late 16th century or early 17th. The frescoes in the staircase room at the south-eastern end of the palace were painted at the beginning of the 18th century. The main themes there are of deities, for example *Mahalakshmi*, *Shiva as Kirata*, the *Coronation of Rama*, *Vishnu Reclining on the Serpent Shesha* and *Shiva and Uma* (*see* §II, 1 above). Towards the end of the 18th century and beginning of the 19th, other chambers in the palace were decorated with paintings. This time the inspiration was predominantly Vaishnava, for example scenes showing *Krishna and the Cowherds* (*gopi*s) or *Krishna Lifting Mt Govardhana* over his head to save the community from a flood.

The paintings from the temple at TRICHUR, which come close to the 'middle phase' at Mattancheri in date, style and spirit of execution, show a popular subject in this region: Rama in the attitude of teaching, surrounded by sages and his brothers, while Hanuman reads from a manuscript he holds. The temple at Trichur also has one of the most forceful interpretations of the final battle between Rama and Ravana.

The leading schools of Kerala painting continued to exist into the 18th century, when impressive, large-scale compositions were painted in the palaces of Padmanabhapuram and Krishnapuram. Typical of 18th-century TRAVANCORE are the frescoes in the royal bedchamber on the top floor of the Padmanabhapuram palace complex. The walls of this relatively large room are covered with mythological paintings, each in its own panel. Especially

310. *Rama and Sita Enthroned, Conversing with Sages, Monkeys and Rama's Brothers*, opaque colour on paper, 310×324 mm, from Rajamundry, Andhra Pradesh, 1757 (Hamburg, Museum für Völkerkunde)

noteworthy are the scenes showing the worship of the elephant-headed god Ganesha and the hunter-god Shasta riding through the forest with his hounds. Most impressive, however, are the renderings of *Bhairava*, a terrifying form of Shiva, with his dog, and the goddess *Durga* standing on the severed head of a buffalo. The Krishnapuram palace frescoes are contemporary with those at Padmanabhapuram but are not as well preserved. The only scene to have survived in pristine splendour is that of *Vishnu on his Mount, Garuda*, coming to the rescue of the king of the elephants, Gajendra.

Surviving miniature paintings compare favourably with those produced elsewhere. One of the most famous series is a *Rāmāyaṇa* with text in Telugu script from the first quarter of the 18th century (Hyderabad, State Mus.). Figures, costumes and ornaments in this manuscript are in accord with the aesthetic conventions adopted by local painters from the post-Vijayanagara traditions current in south India at the time. The sophisticated style recalls the Chengam ceiling paintings. Most of the paintings are in watercolours, the colour scheme is sombre, and the backgrounds are plain. The highly imaginative artist relied on the power and expressiveness of line and composition to convey the various moods of the narrative. All the illustrations of this series are on handmade European paper backed with cotton cloth.

Another important set of paintings, including scenes from the *Rāmāyaṇa* and other mythological subjects, was prepared at Rajahmundry in Andhra Pradesh *c.* 1757 for a French official, Pierre Duplant de Laval (Hamburg, Mus. Vlkerknd.). The general characteristics of this album include simple compositions, the rendering of the few figures in one plane, minimal elements of nature, architecture, furniture and carpets, directness of narration and two-dimensional space. The palette includes lively colours; the support is thick, handmade paper. These pages are significant both because they are datable and because they supply information about a hitherto unknown Rajahmundry school of painting (see fig. 310). Moreover, the set exemplifies the existence of a regional style of painting that was distinct in every way from work done at the courts of the Deccani sultans (*see* §(vi) above).

See also §III, 7(ii)(k) above.

BIBLIOGRAPHY

C. Hayavadana Rao, ed.: *Mysore Gazetteer* (Bangalore, 1930), pp. 334–41
C. Sivaramamurti: *South Indian Paintings* (Delhi, 1968)
J. Mittal: *Andhra Paintings of the Ramayana* (Hyderabad, 1969)
R. Nagaswamy: *Studies in Ancient Tamil Law and Society* (Madras, 1978)
S. Kramrisch: 'The Forms of Kerala Paintings', *Marg*, xxxii/2 (1979), pp. 57–65
I. J. Thomas: *Painting in Tamilnadu, A.D. 1350–1650* (diss., U. Ann Arbor, MI, 1979; microfilm, Ann Arbor, 1979)
R. Nagaswamy: 'Tamil Paintings', *Marg*, xxxiii/2 (1979–80), pp. 73–95
J. Appasamy: *Thanjavur Painting of the Maratha Period* (Delhi, 1980)
S. Rajasekhara: *Holalagundi Paintings* (Dharwad, 1982)
Master Dyers to the World: Technique and Trade in Early Indian Dyed Cotton Textiles (exh. cat. by M. Gittinger, Washington, DC, Textile Mus., 1982)
J. Mittal: 'An Illustrated Deccani Manuscript from Rajahmundry: A Hitherto Unknown Centre of Painting in the Deccan', *Mitt. Mus. Vlkerknd. Hamburg*, n. s., xiv (1985), pp. 41–62
India: Art and Culture, 1300–1900 (exh. cat. by S. C. Welch, New York, Met., 1985)
M. C. Heston: *The Mattancheri Palace Mural Paintings of Kerala, India: A Stylistic Study* (diss., Columbus, OH State U., 1986; microfilm, Ann Arbor, 1987)
G. Michell: *The Penguin Guide to the Monuments of India*, i (Harmondsworth, 1989)
Sivapriyananda: 'Mysore School of Traditional Painting', *Marg*, xli/4 (1990), pp. 68–71

A. L. DALLAPICCOLA

(viii) Kashmiri styles. From the 15th century, the arts and crafts of Kashmir had received an extraordinary fillip under the celebrated Sultan Zayn al-Abidin (*reg* 1420–70). During his reign, which came not long after the introduction of paper in the region, the Sultan seems to have invited to Kashmir large numbers of painters and other craftsmen from centres in Persia and to have encouraged Kashmiri craftsmen to go to Persia for training. The sudden blossoming of the production of illuminated manuscripts undoubtedly belongs to this period. Although dated manuscripts are rare, surviving works include sumptuously illuminated copies of the Koran and a manuscript of Sa'di's *Būstān* ('Orchard'), completed in the 'city of Kashmir' in AH 911 (AD 1505; Cambridge, Fitzwilliam). Later, large numbers of works drawing on the repertory of manuscript painters working at Shiraz and elsewhere were produced in Kashmir itself. From the 18th century, impressive quantities of such popular Persian works as the *Shāhnāma* ('Book of kings') of Firdausi (e.g. London, BL, Add. MS. 18804), the *Gulistān* ('Rose garden') of Sa'di, the *Dīvān* (collected poems) of Hafiz (see fig. 311), the *Panj ganj* ('Five treasures') of Jami and the *Qissā-i cāhār darves* ('Story of the four dervishes'), were produced. Standard iconographies were developed, images were shared between different works and a measure of predictability began to appear in manuscripts that were obviously produced in quantity in response to popular demand.

311. Kashmiri style: illustrated manuscript page from a *Dīvān* of Hafiz, shown without its border, 143×91 mm, *c.* 1796 (London, British Library, Oriental and India Office Library, Add. MS. 7763, fol. 111*r*)

Patronage of such work mostly came from the middle class, from men devoted to Persian learning and with a taste for the arts; illustrated works produced for royal patrons are rare. From the late 18th century and early 19th, Hindu names occur among the patrons mentioned in colophons, indicating that Persian learning was seen by this time as a heritage common to both the Muslims and the Hindus of Kashmir. The interests of Hindu patrons were, however, wider, and it is clear from surviving works that several illustrated Hindu classics began to be written in Persian as well as the *devanāgarī* and *sharada* scripts: numerous copies of such works as Valmiki's *Rāmāyaṇa*, the *Mahābhārata*, the *Bhāgavata purāṇa* and Tulasi's *Rāmacaritamānasa* ('Holy lake of the acts of Rama'), often profusely illustrated, survive. Pocket-sized manuscripts containing sacred and ritual texts for daily use (e.g. the *Bhāgavadgīta*, the *Śivamahimnā sūtra*, the *Pañcastavī*, the *Sargīta*, the *Viṣṇusahasranāmā*), as well as *tantra* and *kavacha* texts, were also produced in large numbers, although these were often sparsely illustrated. Interestingly, in the matter of the iconographies used in these illustrations, the painters—who clearly owed allegiance to a provincial Persian style—drew on images and conventions rooted in the much earlier Hindu–Buddhist tradition of the region, for example when showing deities with multiple arms and heads or multicoloured limbs. Works of this kind continued to be produced up to the beginning of the 20th century, when new techniques such as lithography and block printing took over, virtually ending the tradition of book painting in Kashmir. Illuminated manuscripts of the *Guru Granth Sahib*, the sacred book of the Sikhs, formerly produced in some numbers, also became scarcer.

Kashmiri paintings are often recognizable by the distinctive thin, glazed paper and dramatic range of colours, flaming orange, deep moss green and a peculiar mauve-violet being the painters' particular favourites. Although there is little interest or merit in the drawing, which generally tends to be weak and routine in character, the colours in Kashmiri painting, embellished with gold, glow and shimmer with remarkable brightness. What stands out most in Kashmiri paintings, however, is the occasional boldness of composition. While the standard, repeated renderings of battle scenes and drinking bouts tend not to hold the viewer's interest for long, painters often startle with their innovation and daring when called on to render a fresh scene.

BIBLIOGRAPHY

F. Nowotny: *Eine durch Miniaturen erläuterte Doctrina Mystica aus Srinagar* (The Hague, 1958)

H. Goetz: 'Two Illustrated Persian Manuscripts from Kashmir', *A. Asiatiques*, ix/1–2 (1962–3), pp. 61–72

M.-T. de Mallmann: 'Sur un manuscrit du Kasmir', *A. Asiatiques*, xv (1967), pp. 29–46

A. Adamova and T. Greck: *Miniatures from Kashmirian Manuscripts* (Leningrad, 1976)

L. Y. Leach: 'Painting in Kashmir from 1600 to 1650', *Facets of Indian Art*, ed. R. Skelton and others (London, 1982), pp. 124–31

K. Goswamy: 'Itinerant Kashmiri Artists: Notes on the Spread of Style', *Making Things in South Asia. Proceedings of the South Asia Seminar: Philadelphia, 1986*, pp. 86–95

R. Hickmann: 'Die Kashmir Miniaturen des staatlichen Museums für Völkerkunde, Dresden', *Abh. & Ber. Staatl. Mus. Vlkerknd., Dresden* (1986)

K. Goswamy: *The Glory of the Great Goddess: An Illustrated Manuscript from Kashmir from the Alice Boner Collection* (Zurich, 1989)

KARUNA GOSWAMY

(ix) Company styles. The term 'Company painting' is used by art historians to denote a special type of painting in a semi-European style that was made by Indian artists in the 18th and 19th centuries for Europeans working for the British, French, Dutch and Danish East India Companies trading in India. Miniature painting had flourished in India for centuries before the arrival of the Europeans. But as the Mughal empire collapsed and its tradition of patronage declined (*see* §(i)(f) above) and as wealth and power shifted to European hands, Indian artists accepted commissions from European patrons and strove to produce paintings that appealed to their tastes.

Most Company paintings were made for the British, who by the late 18th century had assumed wide political and administrative functions in India. The pictures they commissioned reflected the range of their interests, from the costumes and occupations of Indians to architectural drawings of mosques, temples and forts, scenes of spectacular religious festivals and drawings of species of flowers, birds and animals that were new to them. One of the earliest examples of such patronage is a set of paintings (*c.* 1686; Paris, Bib. N., MS. Od.45 and Venice, Bib. N. Marciana) made for the Italian adventurer Niccolo Manucci, depicting Mughal emperors and Deccani rulers and nobles as well as various forms of transport such as litters and palanquins.

(a) South India. (b) Murshidabad. (c) Patna. (d) Calcutta. (e) Varanasi. (f) Lucknow. (g) Delhi.

(a) South India. By the 18th century the British were becoming firmly installed in India, especially in the south. During the Mysore Wars of 1767–99 numerous British army officers were stationed there, frequently passing through Madras. In 1785 Peter Boileau, a Company servant, had a set of drawings made in Madras (London, V&A, 1.5.75 (1–42)–1954) depicting people of various castes and occupations, each illustration featuring a man and woman from the respective groups. The earliest sets produced in considerable numbers for sale to the British were apparently made in Tanjavur (e.g. London, V&A, E.I.D.93.B.36, and BM, Or. MS. 54e). They show a man and woman facing each other, holding the implements of their trade: for example a washerman and woman, a tailor and his wife or a dancer and her musician. These popular illustrations were the Indian equivalent of paintings of Picturesque subjects, such as whalebone scrapers or peat-cutters, which were then in vogue in England. In the early Tanjavur paintings, the backgrounds are plain yellow, green or blue with a line of cloud drawn across the top. As time passed the background became more complex, the cloud grew bigger, and a line of small trees and houses rimmed the horizon. Company paintings of the local rulers were also made showing Raja Tulsaji (*reg* 1765–86), Raja Amar Singh (*reg* 1787–98) and Raja Sarabhoji (*reg* 1798–1832) passing through the city in colourful processions (e.g. London, V&A, IM.319–21, and Cambridge, MA, Fogg).

In Tiruchirapalli (Trichinopoly) sets of paintings were made depicting the famous temples of the south. Artists there also produced sets of mica paintings of occupations etc, executed in brilliant green and yellow ochre, opaque colours on thin, transparent sheets of mica (e.g. London, V&A). Most mica paintings were small; sets were sold in boxes, and individual paintings could be mounted in albums in the same way as paintings on paper.

Although closely related to other south Indian paintings, a minor school of Company painting developed in Malabar *c.* 1810–30: its distinctive and elegant style used sombre colourings of brown, cream and fawn to depict mainly occupations, especially those connected with the cultivation and use of the coconut palm (e.g. London, V&A and BL, Orient. & India Office Lib.).

(b) Murshidabad. Company painting soon developed in eastern India at Murshidabad, a city situated on the River Bagirathi (a tributary of the Ganga) and on the great highway from Calcutta to Upper India. Ruled by a nawab, by the early 18th century it had become the political and commercial centre of eastern India. The city was well known for its artists who worked in a late Mughal style (*see* §(i)(f) above), producing for the nawab and the local gentry miniature paintings of scenes of court life, portraits of rulers and *Rāgamālā* series, illustrating the modes of Indian music. In 1775 a British Resident was appointed to the nawab's court. Ten years later the British artist George Farington came to work in Murshidabad for three years

312. Company style: *Mubarak al-Daula Celebrating the Holi Festival*, opaque watercolour on paper, 450×750 mm, from Murshidabad, *c.* 1790–1800 (London, British Library, Oriental and India Office Library); after a painting by George Farington, 1785–8 (untraced)

and made paintings for the nawab. Local artists were able to observe European techniques at first hand and to make copies of his paintings. One such copy depicts the Resident, Sir John D'Oyly, seated in *darbar* (audience) with Nawab Mubarak al-Daula. Another, *Mubarak al-Daula Celebrating the Holi Festival* (*c.* 1790–1800; London, BL, Orient. & India Office Lib.; see fig. 312), shows the Muslim nawab celebrating a Hindu festival and being entertained by dancers and musicians. The local artist attempted to copy not only Farington's composition but also his approach to figure drawing and his use of light, shadow and perspective; the result was a work far removed from the Indian tradition. Murshidabad was especially famous for its lavish celebration of such Muslim festivals as Id and Khwaja Khizr, when lamps were floated on the river. These festivals were also depicted in paintings for the British by Murshidabad artists, as were the various stages of Muharram, the annual commemoration among Shias of the death at Karbala' of Husayn, grandson of the Prophet, along with his family and followers.

As in the south, mica paintings for sale to the British developed in Murshidabad in the late 18th century. Mica was abundant in the nearby hills of Chota Nagpur, and it had long been used for the painted lanterns and the great *ta'zia*s, symbolic models of the tombs of those who died at Karbala', which were carried through the streets in processions and erected in mosques during Muharram. Mica paintings, a speciality of Murshidabad artists throughout the 19th century, included series devoted to costumes, occupations, methods of transport, festivals and ceremonies.

(c) Patna. By 1770 a Council had been appointed by the British in Patna to take control of the revenue administration of eastern India. The city grew rapidly, attracting Murshidabad artists, one of whom was Sewak Ram (*fl c.* 1770–1830), well known for his paintings of festival scenes and occupations (examples in London, V&A, and BL, Orient. & India Office Lib.; and Dublin, Chester Beatty Lib.). British influence also reached Patna painters first-hand: Sir Charles D'Oyly, British Opium Agent and later Commercial Resident (1821–33), was a skilled amateur artist. He initiated a sketching club for the British of the district, imported a lithographic press from England and trained a Patna painter, Jairam Das, to operate it. Jairam Das also made prints of his own drawings (e.g. London, BL, Orient. & India Office Lib.). Other surviving works by him include a book of 36 drawings in watercolour and pencil (London, Royal Asiat. Soc.) with an inscription naming him as the artist and a number of miniature portraits on ivory (Patna Mus.), which are unsigned but attributable to him. Other paintings dating from *c.* 1800 to *c.* 1880 have survived by such Patna artists as Hulas Lal (*fl c.* 1810–75), Fakir Chand Lal (*fl c.* 1810–65), his son Shiva Lal (*fl c.* 1840–87), Tuni Lal (*fl c.* 1820–60) and his son Shiva Dayal Lal (*fl c.* 1840–80), the majority depicting festivals, servants and occupations (e.g. Dublin, Chester Beatty Lib.; and London, V&A). The earlier paintings are executed in soft shades of sepia, dull blue and green, but over the years the palette brightened.

Drawings by Patna painters were also purchased by travellers halting at the river ghats on their way up-country. After about 1880 British patronage gradually declined. The grandson of Shiva Lal, the artist Ishwari Prasad, migrated to Calcutta to look for work. From 1904 he was employed by the British art historian E. B. Havell on the staff of the Calcutta School of Art. He provided Havell and others interested in Indian art, such as Percy Brown and W. G. Archer, with much information concerning the traditional techniques and work of Patna artists, including members of his own family.

(d) Calcutta. Founded in 1690 as a small British trading station, Calcutta grew rapidly and by 1773 had become the virtual capital of British India. As early as 1770 artists began to migrate there. Sir Elijah Impey, the Chief Justice, and his wife employed three painters, who described themselves in their signatures as 'artists of Azimabad' (i.e. Patna): Zayn al-Din, Ram Das and Bhawani Das. Between 1777 and 1782 they painted a series of about 200 bird and animal studies, working first-hand from the extensive menagerie assembled by Lady Impey in Calcutta. Of the 120 surviving paintings, which are among the finest surviving Company works, over 100 are of birds. The fine detail of feathers, leaves and flowers, seen for instance in Zayn al-Din's *Sulphur-crested Cockatoo on a Flowering Asoka-tree Branch* (see fig. 313), suggests that the artists were trained in the discipline of Mughal court painting, a tradition in which natural history studies formed an important part. British interest in ornithology and the recording of new species also led to the official employment of artists by the East India Company to make illustrations of specimens at the Calcutta Botanic Garden and later at the Barrackpore Menagerie (e.g. Cambridge, MA, Fogg).

Artists such as E. C. Das and Shaykh Muhammad Amir specialized in painting dignified views of the houses of local British residents and portraits of their household staff (e.g. London, V&A, and BL, Orient. & India Office Lib., and Marquis of Dufferin and Ava priv. col.), the latter becoming a particularly popular subject. Some artists marketed similar paintings sent to them by their castefellows in Patna and Varanasi. Methods of transport such as palanquins and carriages were also added to the repertory of subjects.

Sometimes Calcutta artists were recruited to travel with a British officer on tour to record scenes or objects of interest. Lord Amherst, Governor General *c.* 1825–8, took a Calcutta artist with him on his embassy to Burma, and Sir Walter Raleigh Gilbert, Political Agent for the South-West Frontier and aide-de-camp (1812–14) to Sir George Nugent, made a tour from Hazaribagh in Bihar to Surguja in the Central Provinces, which was recorded by a Calcutta artist.

(e) Varanasi. Before the development of Company painting, local artists decorated the walls of houses and made designs for textiles. In the early years of the 19th century, however, several artists from Patna, including Dallu Lal (*fl c.* 1810–60), migrated to Varanasi and set up shops at the ghats where many travellers up the Ganga disembarked to view the temples; they sold pictures of

313. Zayn al-Din: *Sulphur-crested Cockatoo on a Flowering Asoka-tree Branch*, Company style, opaque colour on paper, 535×755 mm, 1777 (Oxford, Ashmolean Museum)

ascetics, dancing girls and musicians and other 'occupations'. Raja Iswari Narain Singh (1835–89) employed two artists, Gopal Chand and Lal Chand, trained by Dallu Lal in the Company style, to make portraits of courtiers as well as drawings of birds and flowers (e.g. Varanasi, Banaras Hindu U., Bharat Kala Bhavan).

Painting on mica became popular also in Varanasi, persisting until the end of the 19th century. Sets depicting dancing girls and other occupations were painted in bright pinks, reds and blues (e.g. London, V&A). A novelty made in Varanasi consisted of a card painted with a head and a landscape background over which mica overlays depicting costumes could be superimposed (e.g. London, V&A).

(f) Lucknow. Company painting flourished in Avadh at Faizabad, where the nawab Shujaʿ al-Daula (*reg* 1754–75) had his court, and then Lucknow, where Asaf al-Daula (*reg* 1775–97) shifted the court and where it remained. Painters trained in the Mughal tradition in Delhi migrated to Faizabad and Lucknow, and in the second half of the 18th century paintings were produced there in a variety of styles ranging from works close to the contemporary late Mughal idiom in Delhi to European-influenced Company painting (*see also* §(i)(f) above).

The nawabs' wealth and reputation as generous patrons of the arts attracted a number of European artists. During the reigns of Shujaʿ al-Daula and Asaf al-Daula, TILLY KETTLE, JOHAN ZOFFANY, Francesco Renaldi (1755–*c.* 1790) and OZIAS HUMPHRY painted in Faizabad and Lucknow (see Archer, 1979). Their technique was observed and their paintings copied by local artists (e.g. London, V&A, and BL, Orient. & India Office Lib.).

A number of European adventurers who served the nawabs themselves became patrons of the arts, among them the colonels Jean Baptiste Gentil, Antoine Polier and Claude Martin, who collected earlier paintings and commissioned works from both visiting European artists and local painters. Works commissioned by Gentil include an Indian atlas decorated with drawings of the products of various areas and a volume of drawings depicting mainly the customs of the court of Avadh (both London, V&A). A fine set of bird drawings was produced for Martin (dispersed; e.g. London, V&A). By 1773 a British Resident was appointed in Avadh, and several British officials stationed there collected and commissioned paintings, including Richard Johnson (Assistant Resident 1780–84; the bulk of his collection is in London, BL, Orient. & India Office Lib.).

With the accession of Sa'adat Ali (*reg* 1798–1814), painting in the Late Mughal idiom died out, and paintings produced for the nawabs by Indian artists are in a range of European-influenced styles. British artists continued to visit Lucknow until the middle of the 19th century. Robert Home (1752–1834) was court artist to Ghazi al-Din

Haydar (*reg* 1814–27); George Beechy (1798–1852) settled there until his death, working for several nawabs.

The variety of patrons is reflected in the wide range of subjects represented in 19th-century Lucknow Company painting, from typical sets of 'occupations' and paintings of the houses of British inhabitants to copies of European paintings and court portraits and entertainments produced for the nawabs, in which the British Resident is often featured among the guests (e.g. London, BL, Orient & India Office Lib.). Lucknow artists also produced panoramas reflecting the contemporary English vogue. A large surviving example, a *Procession of Ghazi al-Din Haider through the Streets of Lucknow* (1.23×4.83 m; London, V&A), is hectic and crowded, with shades of blue predominating.

The last nawab of Avadh, Wajid 'Ali Shah (*reg* 1847–56), wrote poetry in Urdu and Persian, and among the works surviving from his reign are 118 paintings illustrating a volume of what appears to be his own verse, the *Nizām 'ishqnāma* ('A king's book of love', dated 1849–50; Windsor Castle, Royal Lib.). The paintings, in a highly Europeanized style, show the nawab in his palaces, which are decorated and furnished in the European fashion.

(g) Delhi. Not surprisingly, the finest Company paintings were made in Delhi. There Indian artists painting in the indigenous miniature style still flourished, but as they gradually lost court patronage many began to produce paintings for the British, who in the late 18th century and the early 19th were visiting Delhi and Agra in increasing numbers. The earliest examples were painted in the Mughal miniature technique and represent the Mughal monuments and ruins in Delhi, Agra and Fatehpur Sikri that the British came to see. By *c.* 1808 local artists were producing large architectural drawings depicting a range of Mughal monuments (e.g. London, V&A, and BL, Orient. & India Office Lib.; see fig. 314). They were executed on large sheets of European paper (often 600 mm wide) in soft watercolour washes of cream, grey and pink with touches of gold, green and blue for the inlay work, using a style similar to that of the British engineer–draughtsman. The Indian artists' skill in painting the minute detail of inlay and mosaic work delighted the British visitors. As with Company painters in other centres, the names of the artists are rarely known, but one Agra artist, Latif, became well known for his skilled work. Two drawings by him were reproduced in Fanny Parks's memoirs, *Wanderings of a Pilgrim in Search of the Picturesque* (1850). By the middle of the 19th century the drawings of monuments were smaller in format and usually sold in sets but depicted a wider range of tombs and mosques.

Delhi artists also painted pictures of the Delhi rulers. Sometimes these were isolated portraits, but frequently the emperor was shown either seated surrounded by his courtiers or being carried in his palanquin accompanied by the heir apparent riding on horseback; both types of scenes often included the British Resident, for instance Sir David Ochterlony or Sir Charles Metcalfe. By the 1840s artists produced long panoramic scrolls showing the emperor in procession, for example to the mosque for the Id celebrations. Among the finest Delhi paintings are portraits commissioned by Colonel James Skinner from

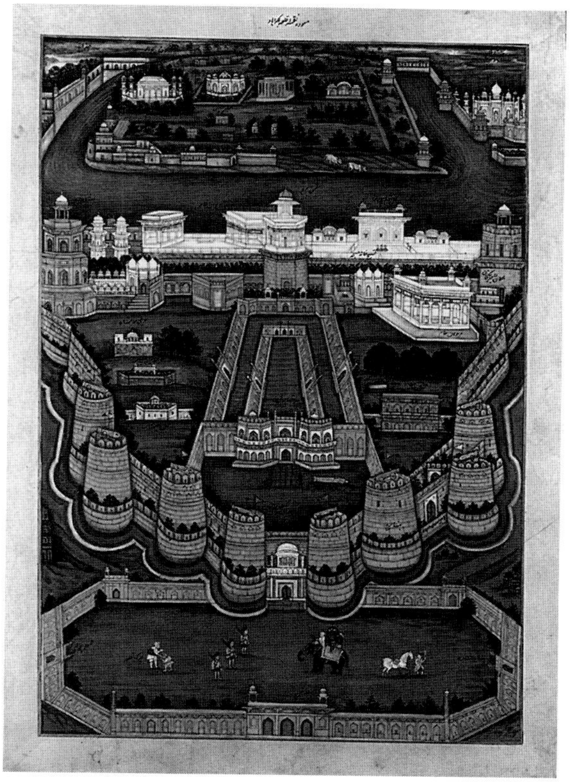

314. Company style: *Agra Fort*, opaque watercolour on paper, 355×520 mm, from Delhi, *c.* 1770–80 (London, Victoria and Albert Museum)

the artist Ghulam 'Ali Khan (three in London, N. Army Mus.; most dispersed, some repr. in Archer and Falk): these depict Skinner in *darbar* at Hansi, reviewing his troops or inspecting his farm. Skinner also had portraits made of his troops and Indian friends. An outstanding series of portraits was made for William Fraser, First Assistant to the Delhi Resident, Sir Charles Metcalfe, and his brother James (dispersed; e.g. London, BL, Orient. & India Office Lib.). The name of the artist (or artists) is not known, but the collection represents the range of people to be seen in Delhi and its environs and includes portraits of the emperor, his courtiers, dancing girls, musicians, Afghan horse-dealers, ascetics and villagers bringing in their rent. Fraser also had paintings made while travelling with his brother James through the Himalaya on their return from the Nepal War of 1814–15.

During the 19th century Company painting gradually declined, largely as a result of the invention of photography. A few Delhi artists continued to make paintings on ivory of various sizes depicting the Mughal emperors, Mughal ladies and the Delhi and Agra monuments. The larger paintings could be bought separately or mounted on sandalwood boxes or fire-screens; the smallest were used on earrings, studs and brooches.

BIBLIOGRAPHY

F. Parks: *Wanderings of a Pilgrim in Search of the Picturesque*, 2 vols (London, 1850/*R* Karachi, 1975)

M. Archer: *Patna Painting* (London, 1947)
——: *Indian Painting for the British* (Oxford, 1955)
——: *Natural History Drawings in the India Office Library* (London, 1962)
——: *British Drawings in the India Office Library* (London, 1969)
——: *Company Drawings in the India Office Library* (London, 1972)
——: *India and British Portraiture, 1770–1825* (London, 1979)
Room for Wonder: Indian Painting during the British Period (exh. cat. by S. C. Welch, New York, Asia Soc. Gals, 1979)
M. Archer: 'Exotic Commissions', *Interiors* (March 1982), pp. 71–9
Birds in an Indian Garden (exh. cat. by T. Falk and G. Hayter, London, M. Guidhuis Gal., 1984)
British Watercolours and Drawings, 16th–20th Century (exh. cat. by M. Archer, London, Eyre and Hobhouse Gal., 1984)
P. Pal and V. Dehejia: *From Merchant to Emperor* (New York, 1986)
M. Archer and T. Falk: *India Revealed* (London, 1989)

MILDRED ARCHER

(x) Early modern styles. Three prominent characteristics mark the emergence of modern painting in the Indian subcontinent: the transformation or quickening of the local art scene under the impact of alien art forms; the rise of independent professional artists drawn from all strata of society and trained in open academies, not traditional workshops; and the appearance of creative non-professionals concerned more with the expression of personal experiences than with responding to patrons' behests.

By the mid-19th century the British (represented by the East India Company) had strengthened their hold over India and ventured to introduce a new educational system (1835) and establish professional institutions, including art schools, that the new Indian élite demanded. Some schools were started by private initiative and then taken over by the government. The Madras Art School was established (1850) on the initiative of Alexander Hunter, a surgeon in the army. That at Bombay was conceived by two Parsi businessmen, one of whom, Jamshetjee Jeejheebhoy, gave the British government a large donation in 1853 to institute a 'school of art and manufacture'; on his insistence, it was established in 1856 as the Jamshetjee Jeejheebhoy (later the Sir Jamshetjee Jeejheebhoy) School of Art. The school at Calcutta (first called the School of Industrial Art) came into being in 1854 on the initiative of a group of private enthusiasts; it was taken over by the government about ten years later.

315. Nandalal Bose: *Tiller of the Soil*, tempera on paper, 580×560 mm, 1938 (New Delhi, National Gallery of Modern Art)

All these schools were established with the intention of revivifying the local art and craft scene and in the early stages were run by people sympathetic to this. Some of them—Henry Hover Locke (who arrived in India in 1864), John Lockwood Kipling (1865), John Griffith (1865) and Ernest Binfield Havell (1884; *see* HAVELL, (3))—were graduates of the School of Art and Design (later the Royal College of Art) attached to the South Kensington Museum (now the Victoria and Albert Museum), London. Although Locke (who encouraged an Indian colleague to write a book on the arts of ancient India in the local language) and John Griffith (who copied and brought to light the much-admired paintings of the caves at Ajanta) had enthusiasm for the local arts, the training in the schools answered the new professional needs: realistic illustration, engraving for reproduction, painting of realistic portraits and landscapes, sculpture of commemorative statues and monuments (*see also* §V, 8(ii) above) in the established Victorian academic style. So when Havell arrived at the Calcutta Art School (1896) and tried to give it an indigenous orientation, in 1904 selling its collection of copies of Italian and British art, there was a public uproar; some students left the school and set up a rival institution. This broke the artistic community into two groups, one made up of professionals attached to Victorian academicism, the other of creative artists (members of neither the old, indigenous, nor the new, post-colonial, professional scene), who rebelled against the rigidities and limitations of this kind of art, which followed outlandish norms and isolated them from their ancient heritage.

Rabindranath Tagore (*see* TAGORE, (1)), the renowned Bengali poet and a key figure in India's cultural renaissance, came to Havell's defence, saying that while he was not against Western art, the works Havell had disposed of were poor examples of it, and besides, no novice could truly appreciate another country's art until he had learnt to appreciate his own. Abanindranath Tagore (*see* TAGORE, (3)), nephew of Rabindranath, followed in his wake. Although Abanindranath learnt his skills from foreign art school instructors, he earnestly wanted to work back to his indigenous roots and produce painting that was both personal and poetic, responding directly to an inner urge, not an outer need. Contact with Tenshin Okakura, a Japanese aristocrat and art scholar who was himself trying to persuade Western-influenced Japanese artists to take interest in their traditional roots, strengthened Abanindranath's resolve; besides, the removed naturalism of Japanese art (as against the surface realism of the West or the symbolic iconography of traditional Indian art) seemed to him more appropriate to the new circumstances. This interest in Japan continued even after Okakura's death in 1916. Just as the artists of the European academicist persuasion sought to enlarge their horizons by looking towards British and European art centres, so Abanindranath Tagore and his followers had a predilection for East Asia, seeing there a community of interest, even of philosophic approach. After a visit to Japan in 1916 Rabindranath Tagore too came back very impressed by that country's art environment.

As the first to view modern artists as creative non-professionals, the Tagores should be considered the real progenitors of the modern Indian art movement. The professional painters who preceded them had no decided views and were mainly concerned with the minutiae of practice. Around the turn of the century, Abanindranath Tagore and his brother Gaganendranath gathered a group of artists and art lovers to launch what was called the Neo-Bengal art movement. They also formed the Indian Society of Oriental Art (1907) to educate the public about the niceties of art, particularly Eastern art, through exhibitions, lectures and publications. In 1905 Havell invited Abanindranath Tagore to teach at the Government Art School in Calcutta. Firm in his belief that art cannot be taught, especially in such schools with a structured routine, Abanindranath only accepted because of his great respect for Havell, whom he called his *guru* or teacher. Havell made him Vice-Principal with full freedom to handle teaching in his own way, and when Havell went on leave in 1906 for health reasons Abanindranath was Acting Principal for three years. During this time he trained a group of students who became the torch-bearers of his art movement. Among them was NANDALAL BOSE (see fig. 315), who had much greater talent, versatility and sense of mission than the rest and whom Rabindranath Tagore involved with his non-conformist educational venture in Shantiniketan, where creative arts played a major role. The Tagores were also the first to think of art education on modern lines, linking the past and the present, East and West, high arts and low arts, and exposing the novice to as wide a spectrum of art as possible, giving him complete freedom of choice. In his institution Rabindranath brought together artists and artisans from East and West, traditionalists and modernists, art historians and theorists, and let them interact. He built a library of world art at Shantiniketan that was remarkable for its time and in 1922 was instrumental in bringing to Calcutta an exhibition of German Expressionist works.

The efforts of Havell, Abanindranath and Rabindranath Tagore and Bose did not find favour with such protagonists of academicist art as Cecil Burns (1863–1925) and Gladstone Solomon (1880–1965), both principals of the Jamshetjee Jeejheebhoy School of Art in Bombay. Nevertheless, Abanindranath's disciples entered the government art schools as teachers of Indian painting and motivated students to look beyond academicist realist art practice, even if their own work was not particularly distinctive or influential.

Realism of the European kind never struck deep roots in the Indian painting scene, although a number of Indian professional artists practised realistic painting from the latter part of the 19th century: among them RAVI VARMA (see fig. 316), Hamendranath Majumdar (1857–1948), Fanindranath Bose (1888–1915), V. P. Karmarkar (1891–1967) and Atul Bose (1898–1977). Some of these painters had learnt their craft under European teachers or had gone to European institutions for advanced training. This was probably due to a general absence among Indians of a firm belief in a materialist philosophy. To them reality was more often than not an inscrutable entity that came in a variety of guises and costumes, the realistic one being only one of them. In the absence of an established realistic stance there was no anti-realist aftermath as in the Western art scene, nor a step-ladder ascent or descent from a tangible object to an intangible abstraction. So most Indian painters of the early 20th century, informed as they were directly or indirectly of movements in the Western art scene, never abandoned figuration. This was the case with BENODE BEHARI MUKHERJEE and RAMKINKER BAIJ, who knew the Western art scene indirectly, and AMRITA SHER-GIL, who studied painting in Paris from 1929 to 1934 and so had a chance to view it at close quarters.

316. Ravi Varma: *Woman Holding a Fan*, oil on canvas, 530×350 mm, *c.* 1895 (London, Victoria and Albert Museum)

Until India became independent in 1947, such painters lived in a fairly closed situation; they did not have a regular audience, let alone patrons or collectors on a noticeable scale. They sought their public through All India Exhibitions, such as the Calcutta art exhibition supported by the government in 1871, or the exhibitions of the Bombay Art Society (1888), the Indian Society of Oriental Art (1907) and of such later societies as the All India Fine Arts and Crafts Society of Delhi (1931) and the Academy of Fine Arts, Calcutta (1936). The prizes awarded and the notice received at these exhibitions worked as a kind of accreditation for artists, and their works were collected in small numbers by certain museums and individuals. By and large, painters subsisted on the admiration and criticism of a sympathetic coterie alongside clubs and associations. The general public knew of artists and their work mainly through colour reproductions in such well-established journals as the *Modern Review* or its Bengali counterpart *Prabasi.* Reproductions from these journals, compiled as *Chatterjee's Picture Albums*, reached a much wider Indian audience. The only serious art journals to carry expositions or criticisms of modern Indian art were *Rupam* (1933) and its sequel, the *Journal of the Indian Society of Oriental Art*, and occasional unscheduled publications such as the *Śilpa pushpanjali.*

BIBLIOGRAPHY

A. K. Coomaraswamy: *Art and Swadeshi* (Madras, 1911)
E. B. Havell: *Essays on Indian Art, Industry and Education* (Madras, 1918)
A. Tagore: *Vageswari silpa prabandhavali* [Vageswari lectures on art] (Calcutta, 1941)
P. R. Ramachandra Rao: *Modern Indian Painting* (Madras, 1953)
W. G. Archer: *India and Modern Art* (London, 1959)
P. Neogi, ed.: *Tagore on Art and Aesthetics* (New Delhi, 1961)
J. Appasamy: *Abanindranath and the Art of his Times* (New Delhi, 1968)
K. G. Subramanyan: *Moving Focus: Essays on Indian Art* (New Delhi, 1978)
Nandalal Bose: Centenary Exhibition (exh. cat., ed. L. P. Sihare; New Delhi, N.G. Mod. A., 1983)
B. B. Mukherjee: *Chitrakatha* [Essays on art] (Calcutta, 1984)
N. L. Bose: *Drishti o shristi* [Creation and vision] (Calcutta, 1985) [Collected writings of Nandalal Bose]
K. G. Subramanyan: *The Living Tradition: Perspectives on Modern Indian Art* (Calcutta, 1987)

K. G. SUBRAMANYAN

VII. Textiles.

From the late 17th century to the early 19th India was the textile workshop of the world. Today, although mill production and shifting economic trade patterns have limited the role of the subcontinent's hand-produced textiles, this highly skilled, immensely rich and varied industry survives and remains a part of the area's living culture. Though the emphasis in the following sections is on the period before 1947, the present tense is often used to reflect the continuity of the traditions. (For textiles in the post-independence period *see* INDIA, REPUBLIC OF, §VII; PAKISTAN, §V; and BANGLADESH, §5.)

1. Introduction. 2. Woven fabrics and raw materials. 3. Decorative techniques.

1. INTRODUCTION. Clothing, like food, is of immense social importance, being one of the main means by which social differentiation is demonstrated publicly in this highly stratified society. As has been true for over three millennia, gifts of cloth are still essential to the performance of life-cycle rites, to the worship of the gods and as payment in kind to specialist service castes. The pre-eminence of the indigenous industry has depended on a number of key factors. First, raw materials are readily available. Cotton, the most important, is widely grown. Wool, flax and silk (both indigenous wild silks and the cultivated silk introduced from China in the early Christian era) are all available. Second, important technical skills, particularly the knowledge of cotton-dyeing and a wide range of decorative techniques, developed early in the region. Third, besides widespread cotton production for local consumption, specialist caste and guild organizations produced luxury and export textiles using well-established regional and inter-regional trading systems.

The earliest remains of Indian textiles are fragments of dyed cotton yarn from the Indus Valley site of Mohenjo-daro (*c.* 2550–2000 BC). Indirect evidence of sophisticated textile technology is found in literature, sculpture, painting and inscriptional sources from the Vedic period (*c.* 1500 BC) onwards. Classical Greek and Roman text record the importance of early trade with the West, and accounts of Chinese Buddhist pilgrims who visited India between 400 and 700 AD document textile trade with East Asia. The earliest physical evidence of textile exports, fragments of block-printed cottons from Gujarat excavated in Fustat on the southern edge of modern Cairo, dates back to the 13th century. However, no complete textiles, either domestic or export, survive from before the 17th century. From the Roman period onwards three main areas excelled in luxury and export textile manufacture: western India, with Gujarat, Sind and Rajasthan as the focus; the Coromandel coast of south India; and north-east India, including Bengal, Orissa and the Ganga Valley.

Textiles in pre-Islamic India were either plain, like the muslins exported to the Roman world; geometrically patterned with chevrons, stripes, diagonal bands or stylized rosettes; or decorated with stylized figurative processions of sacred animals and birds. The colour range included basic reds, ochres, yellows, blacks, blues and greens. From the 13th century onwards the Turkish and Afghan Muslim rulers of the Delhi Sultanate (*c.* 1200–1526) and their successors, the Mughals (1526–1857), increasingly influenced textile production. They imported craftsmen from Iran and Turkey, patronized and enhanced existing élite production and set up imperial workshops. They encouraged woollen carpet and shawl production, but overall their greatest influence was on design and colour range (which expanded) rather than on technology. Flowering plant motifs inspired by the natural world and by European herbals were introduced under the emperors Jahangir (*reg* 1605–27) and Shah Jahan (*reg* 1628–58). These appeared on court dress, turbans, shawls, sashes, floor-spreads, cushions and hangings for walls (*see* EMBROIDERY, colour pl. I, fig. 2), doors and windows as well as panels and screen walls for tented camps.

The height of the Mughal empire (16th century to early 18th) coincided with the expansion of Portuguese, Dutch, French and British trading activities in the region and their growing involvement in regional and international trade in cloth. The Europeans initially sought spices and markets for their own cloth and purchased the printed and painted cottons that Gujarat and the Coromandel coast exported to South-east Asia and the Middle East as barter in the spice trade with the Malay archipelago and as items for re-export to the Levant. Some chintzes (painted and printed textiles; *see* TEXTILE, colour pl. II, fig. 2) reached Europe. Colour schemes and designs were adapted to European taste, and direct trade developed. By the late 17th century painted and printed cottons had become high fashion in the West, as had the silks, silk and cotton mixes and the fine plain and embroidered muslins that Bengal produced.

Their designs, a synthesis of Indian, Chinese and European elements, have influenced Western textile design ever since. The main centres of luxury and export production retained their positions well into the 19th century, despite protective legislation against imports into Europe in the early 18th century and internal political disturbances in the late 18th century as Mughal power weakened and the British East India Company expanded its economic and political control.

By the mid-19th century the tide of trade had turned, and India was flooded with cheap cotton imports from British mills. The indigenous handloom industry survived, however, despite the collapse of the export market in the West, the penetration of the Indian market, particularly in the north, and the pauperization of large groups of weavers. Cotton production increased, and weavers continued to supply local communities. In the early years of the 20th century handloom cloth woven with handspun yarn (*khadi*) became a symbol of national pride and economic self-sufficiency. Since independence, the governments of the region, while supporting the mill sector, have consciously protected the handloom industry. The pattern of traditional regional styles and local cloth specialities is still evident.

An analytical distinction can be made between cloths produced locally or regionally for popular or ritual use, which reflect the continuity of tradition from the pre-Islamic period, and those produced for courtly or élite secular consumption, which show greater evidence of now well-absorbed external influences. The former, including textiles made by specialist weavers and cloths made or decorated by village and tribal women for their own use, depend for their effect on a sense of mass, volume, colour or texture. Strong, simple, often geometric patterns are created by basic yarn-dyeing, and yarn and cloth resist-dyeing techniques. Pattern is subordinate to colour or texture, and in Hindu contexts both colour and material have symbolic and ritual associations. The dominant colour palette and technique vary regionally. Strong, deep colours (particularly reds), block-printing, resist-dyeing and embroidery techniques characterize the north-west. In the Deccan, colours are darker and more subdued. In Malabar white plain weaves are dominant. In the north and north-east, pattern emerges from weaving technique, and colour gives way to texture. Textiles produced for courtly or élite secular consumption show a rich combination of Indian, Sino-Islamic and European influences and are always a product of specialist skill. They depend stylistically on linear surface treatment and neutral backgrounds setting off the pattern, whether woven, embroidered or painted and dyed.

Hand-produced Indian textiles are increasingly sought after for public and private collections. Museums with major holdings include the Calico Museum of Textiles, Ahmadabad; the City Palace Museum, Udaipur; the Bharat Kala Bhavan, Banaras Hindu University, Varanasi; the National Museum, New Delhi; the Victoria and Albert Museum, London; the Museum of Modern Art, New York; the Museum of Fine Arts, Boston; the Los Angeles County Museum; the Association pour l'Etude et la Documentation des Textiles d'Asie, Paris, and the Museum für Völkerkunde, Basle.

The following subsections will examine the main woven textiles (cotton, silk, wool and the mixed-fabric *maśrū*) and the main decorative techniques (printing, resist-dyeing, painting and embroidery). For the history of Indian carpets *see* §VII, 4 below.

UNPUBLISHED SOURCES

Paris, Bib. N., MS. Fr. 14614 [a copy of the diary (1678–80) of Georges Roques, a French trader in western and central India, with examples of Indian textile products and observations on Indian textile-workers]

BIBLIOGRAPHY

GENERAL

D. Macpherson: *History of European Commerce with India* (London, 1812)
J. Yates: *Textrinum Antiquarum* (London, 1843)
J. Forbes Watson: *The Textile Manufactures and Costumes of the People of India* (London, 1866)
B. Baden-Powell: *Handbook of the Manufactures and Arts of the Punjab* (1872), ii of *Handbook of the Economic Products of the Punjab* (Lahore, 1868–72)
J. Forbes Watson: *Collection of Specimens and Illustrations of the Textile Manufactures of India*, 13 vols (London, 1873–80)
W. Heyd: *Geschichte des Levanthandels im Mittelalter*, 2 vols (Stuttgart, 1879); rev. as *Histoire du commerce du Levant au moyen-âge*, 2 vols (Leipzig, 1885–6)
G. Birdwood: *The Industrial Arts of India*, 2 vols (London, 1880)
T. Mukharji: *Art Manufactures of India* (Calcutta, 1888)
E. Kumsch: *Muster orientalischer Gewebe und Druckstoffe* (Dresden, 1893)
Letters Received by the East India Company from its Servants in the East: A Calendar of Papers of the East India Company of London between 1602 and 1617, 6 vols (London, 1896–1902)
Indian Art at Delhi, 1903: Being the Official Catalogue of the Delhi Exhibition, 1902–1903 (exh. cat. by G. Watt and P. Brown, New Delhi, Qudsia Gdns, 1902–3) [sections on the various classes of textiles]
The English Factories in India, 1618–99: A Calendar of Documents in the India Office Library, London; the Library of the British Museum; and the Public Record Office, London, 13 vols (Oxford, 1906–27)
J. Jasper and M. Pirngadie: *De inlandsche kunstnijverheid in Nederlandische Indie*, 4 vols (The Hague, 1912–30)
H. Dodwell: 'The Madras Weavers under the Company', *Ind. Hist. Rec. Comm., Proc.*, iv/41 (1922)
R. Meyer-Riefstahl: *Persian and Indian Textiles from the Late 16th to Early 19th Century* (New York, 1923)
M. Dupont: *Décoration hindoue* (Paris, 1925)
G. Fernandes: *Report on Art-crafts of the Bombay Presidency* (Bombay, 1932)
C. Fawcett, ed.: *The English Factories in India: New Series*, 4 vols (Oxford, 1936–56)
R. Pfister: *Les Toiles imprimées de Fostat et l'Hindoustan* (Paris, 1938)
M. Cagigal e Silva: *Alguns motivos decorativos orientais no arte indo-portuguesa* (diss., 1949) [typescript at Lisbon, Mus. N. A. Ant.]
K. de B. Adrington, J. Irwin and B. Gray, eds: *The Art of India and Pakistan: A Commemorative Catalogue of the Exhibition Held at the Royal Academy of Arts, London, 1947* (London, 1950) [intro. to the textile col. by J. Irwin]
A. Mookerjee, ed.: *Designs in Indian Textiles* (Calcutta, 1950)
A. Geijer: *Oriental Textiles in Sweden* (Copenhagen, 1951)
A. Weibel: *Two Thousand Years of Textiles* (New York, 1952)
M. Cagigal e Silva: *A arte indo-portuguesa*, vi of *As artes decoratives*, ed. J. Barreira (Lisbon, 1953)
J. Irwin and P. Jayakar: *Textiles and Ornaments of India* (New York, 1956)
B. Sandesara, ed.: *Varnakasamuhchaya*, 2 vols (Baroda, 1956–9) [The *Varnakas* are stock-lists compiled by Gujarati writers, 14th–18th centuries]
S. Swarup: *The Arts and Crafts of India and Pakistan* (Bombay, 1957)
A. Mookerjee, ed.: *5000 Indian Designs and Motifs* (Calcutta, 1958)
'Handloom Sari Industry of Maheshwar', *Census of India*, viii–viia-2 (1961)
'Handlooms', *Marg*, xv/4 (1962) [whole issue]
S. Mookerjee: *Indo kodai senshoku* [Old textiles of India] (Kyoto, 1965) [Eng. captions]
K. Tatsumura: *Meibutsu-gire ruishū* [Collections of fragments of masterpieces], 10 vols (Kyoto, 1965–9) [outstanding textile fragments from Persia, India, China etc.]
S. Robinson: *A History of Dyed Textiles* (London, 1969)
R. Mehta: *Masterpieces of Indian Textiles, Hand-spun, Hand-woven, Traditional* (Bombay, 1970)

S. Chaudhuri: *Trade and Commercial Organization in Bengal, 1650–1720; with Special Reference to the English East India Company* (Calcutta, 1975)
C. Singh: *Textiles and Costumes from the Maharaja Sawai Man Singh II Museum* (Jaipur, 1979)
C. Singh and D. Ahivasi: *Woollen Textiles and Costumes from Bharat Kala Bhavan* (Varanasi, 1981)
The Indian Heritage: Court Life and Arts under Mughal Rule (exh. cat. by R. Skelton and others, London, V&A, 1982), pp. 78–102
The Living Arts of India: Craftsmen at Work (exh. cat. by S. Grayson, London, Serpentine Gal.; Glasgow, Third Eye Cent.; Bradford, Cartwright Hall; and elsewhere; 1982)
V. Ramaswamy: *Textiles and Weavers in Mediaeval South India* (Delhi, 1985)
M.-L. Nabholz-Kartaschoff: *Golden Sprays and Scarlet Flowers: Traditional Indian Textiles from the Museum of Ethnography, Basel* (Kyoto, 1986)
Woven Air: The Muslin and Kantha Traditions of Bangladesh (exh. cat., London, Whitechapel A.G., 1988)
B. N. Goswamy: *Indian Costumes in the Collection of the Calico Museum of Textiles* (1993), v of *Historical Textiles of India at the Calico Museum* (Ahmadabad)

SPECIALIST STUDIES

J. Chandra Ray: 'Textile Industry in Ancient India', *J. Bihar & Orissa Res. Soc.*, iii/2 (1917), pp. 180–245
A. Weibel: 'Indian Textiles', *Bull. Detroit Inst. A.*, xxi (1942)
R. Sergeant: 'Material for a History of Islamic Textiles up to the Mongol Conquest', *A. Islam.*, xi–xii (1946), pp. 57, 118–19
K. de B. Codrington: 'The Minor Arts of India', *Indian Art*, ed. R. Winstedt (London, 1947)
M. Chandra: 'Kashmir Shawls', *Prince of Wales Mus. Bull.*, iii (1954), pp. 3–4, 8
A. Geijer: 'Some Evidence of Indo-European Commerce in Pre-Mughal Times', *J. Ind. Textile Hist.*, i (1955), p. 34
H. Goetz: 'Some Early Indo-Muslim Textiles', *Orient. A.*, n. s., i/1 (1955), pp. 22–7
J. Irwin: 'Reflections on Indo-Portuguese Art', *Burl. Mag.*, xcvii (1955), pp. 106–14
——: 'Origins of the "Oriental" Style in English Decorative Art', *Burl. Mag.*, xcvii (1955), pp. 386–8
——: 'Indian Textile Trade in the 17th Century', *J. Ind. Textile Hist.*, i (1955), ii (1956), iii (1957), iv (1959) [four pts: 'Western India', 'Coromandel Coast', 'Bengal' and 'Foreign Influences']
V. Agrawala: 'Reference to Textiles in Bana's Harshacharita', *J. Ind. Textile Hist.*, iv (1959), p. 65
M. Chandra: 'Costumes and Textiles of the Sultanate Period', *J. Ind. Textile Hist.*, vi (1961)
Lallanji Gopal: 'Textiles in Ancient India', *J. Econ. & Soc. Hist. Orient*, iv (1961), pp. 53–69
E. Olson: 'The Textiles and Costumes of India', *The Museum* [Newark, NJ], n. s., xvii/3–4 (1965), pp.1–38
J. Irwin and P. R. Schwartz: *Studies in Indo-European Textile History* (Ahmadabad, 1966) [repr. of articles first published in serial in the *J. Ind. Textile Hist.*]
Vijay Krishna: 'Flowers in Indian Textile Design', *J. Ind. Textile Hist.*, vii (1967), pp. 1–20
J. C. Irwin and M. Hall: *Indian Embroideries* (1973), ii of *Historical Textiles of India at the Calico Museum* (Ahmadabad)
A. Buhler, E. Fischer and M.-L. Nabholz: *Indian Tie-dyed Fabrics* (1980), iv of *Historical Textiles of India at the Calico Museum* (Ahmadabad)
B. C. Mohanty: *Brocaded Fabrics of India*, Study of Contemporary Textile Crafts of India (Ahmadabad, 1984)
S. Cohen: 'Textiles', *Islamic Heritage of the Deccan*, ed. G. Michell (Bombay, 1986), pp. 118–28
B. C. Mohanty, K. V. Chandramouli and H. D. Naik: *Natural Dyeing Processes of India*, Study of Contemporary Textile Crafts of India (Ahmadabad, 1987)
V. Murphy and R. Crill: *Tie-dyed Textiles of India: Tradition and Trade* (London and Ahmadabad, 1991)
T. Roy: *Artisans and Industrialisation: Indian Weaving in the Twentieth Century* (Delhi, 1993)

D. A. SWALLOW

2. WOVEN FABRICS AND RAW MATERIALS. Most of the Indian subcontinent's rich array of traditional woven textiles were produced with simple apparatus; the fine quality resulted from an understanding and sympathetic use of the local environment, an intimate knowledge of the materials and skill of the hands. The many weaver subcastes ranked low in the hierarchy of the caste system, and their earnings were small despite long hours of work. In the main cotton-growing and silk-producing areas, the weavers supplied cloth lengths to the intermediate merchants (Hindi *baniyā*). The merchants supplied cloth to printers and other craftsmen and to other merchants for trade through the towns. Weavers worked within a close-knit family structure; children assisted with simple tasks, assimilating the skills and experience of their elders and eventually passing them on to a new generation.

(i) Cotton. (ii) Silk. (iii) Cotton and silk mixtures. (iv) Wool.

□

(i) Cotton. Plain cotton cloth has for centuries been the basic ground for varied decorative and folk arts. The cotton plant (*Gossypium herbacum* and its varieties) has always been India's staple textile fibre; it was and is grown widely, the quality of the fibre varying according to local conditions. The finest cotton is grown in the west in the fertile lands of Gujarat and the valley of the Tapti River in Maharashtra; in the east in the rich soil of Bengal; and in the south in the lower valley of the Kistna River and in the coastal plains around Madras. The plains and foothills of the Punjab produce a coarser fibre, yielding a substantial fabric well suited to local conditions. The hills of Assam yield an excellent strong, firm cotton.

The spinning of cotton thread has been done on the spinning wheel (*carkhā*) for the past two or three centuries (or earlier), though in isolated areas hand-spinning on the spindle continued until towards the end of the 19th century. Early archaeological sites yield spindle-whorls; other tools, being of wood, have not survived. Until the 19th century, the winding of the warp was done on rows of sticks erected in the ground to the length of the cloth piece required, the warper crossing and re-crossing the threads as he walked, so that the threads were held in order for the simple handloom. The handlooms for cotton were of standard breadths and accommodated standard lengths, as most ordinary people wore a draped garment made from an uncut cloth length. The length for a *dhotī* (man's loin-cloth) or a *sāṛī* varied from region to region. In western India, the *sāṛī* was comparatively short; in Bengal and in parts of south India, it was long. For a shoulder wrap (*cādar*) or a woman's head cloth (*orhanī*), two breadths of cloth were stitched together; the term *dupaṭṭā*, sometimes used for a woman's head covering, literally means 'two cloths'. In areas with a large Muslim population, where cut-and-stitched garments were worn, a *thān* (length of cloth to make a garment) would also be woven.

Indian cotton thread was comparatively loosely spun, giving the finished cloth a soft texture. It was the practice of the Indian cotton weavers to stretch the warp after tying the crossings of the threads and to brush in a starch of rice-paste (*koie*) before setting up the loom. The warp threads were thus strong and supple during weaving. The finished cloth was washed to remove all trace of starch; it was then bleached by drying in the sun.

Among India's most prized cotton textiles were its muslins, especially white cotton muslins from Dhaka (Bangladesh). Their fine quality has been attributed to a number of factors, including the variety of cotton plant grown in the region. Dhaka cotton grew especially well in the lands along the Brahmaputra River and its tributaries, where annual flooding brought alluvial and saline deposits. The cotton fibre produced was fine and soft and was spun on a small iron spindle, known locally as a *takwa*. Women spun the yarn (the supple hands of younger women were said to produce the finest) and men did the weaving. As some moisture in the air was necessary to keep the thread supple, the spinners worked from soon after dawn until the sun dissipated the morning dew, and then for a short time in the late afternoon before sunset. The jawbone of the boalee fish (*Siluris boalis*) was used in carding the fibre before spinning. Its small, curved, closely-set teeth were ideal for combing out coarse fibres and extraneous matter and straightening the fine threads.

The starching of the warp thread with rice-paste, while the weft thread remained as spun, and the use of a small, smooth shuttle were also important factors. The soft, fine cloth produced was known by such names as *bāftāhavā* ('woven air') and *śabnam* ('evening dew'). Patterned muslins (*jamadānī*) were woven with floral sprigs (Hindi *būṭī*) brocaded in thicker, softer white cotton on the delicate white ground.

Fine hand-woven muslins were also produced in other parts of Bengal, in the Tapti Valley, around Madras. In Rajasthan, cotton from Gujarat was used to weave fine muslin *sāṛī*s with richly patterned coloured borders. The muslin *sāṛī*s of Rajastan were often printed.

BIBLIOGRAPHY

J. Taylor: *A Descriptive and Historical Account of the Cotton Manufactures of Dacca, in Bengal* (London, 1851)

E. Thurston: 'The Cotton Fabric Industry of Madras Presidency', *J. Ind. A. & Indust.*, vii/59 (1897), pp. 20–24, pls 81–8

H. F. Samman: 'The Cotton Fabrics of Assam', *J. Ind. A. & Indust.*, x/82 (1904), pp. 21–2, pl. 13

C. A. Silberrad: 'Cotton Fabrics of the North-western Provinces and Oudh', *J. Ind. A. & Indust.*, x/82 (1904), pp. 23–4

See also general bibliography following §1 above.

(ii) Silk. The silk moth genus *Bombyx mori*, from which the cultivated silk of China, Central Asia and Europe was produced, is not native to India. The climate is too hot and dry in summer, and in some areas too cold in winter, for the larvae to survive. The distinctive soft, matt qualities of Indian silk textiles derive from the larvae of the wild silk moths native to central and north-east India, of which the three main types are known as *tasar*, *eri* and *mūṅgā*. The cocoons of some other wild species were formerly collected locally, but they were usually too tangled and broken to unwind satisfactorily, so were suitable only for rough peasant cloth. Indian silk moths are multivoltine, producing two, three or more crops during the year, while the *Bombycidae* are mainly univoltine, yielding only one crop.

Tasar moths (varieties of *Anthereae pernyi* with many local names) are abundant in the wild in central India and eastern India, particularly Bengal. In some localities, *tasar* silk has been improved by selection of the largest cocoons from which to breed, but full domestication is not easy, and in the 19th century many villagers still gathered local wild cocoons from the trees. The *tasar* silkworm produces an attractive, pale brownish silk, which bleaches and dyes well. The *eri* (*Attacus ricini*) is native mainly to Assam and eastern India and feeds on *Ricinus communis*, the castor oil plant. The *eri* cocoon is soft and white or yellowish; it is less easy to unwind, but *eri* silk also dyes satisfactorily. The *mūṅgā* or *mūgā* (*Antheraeopsis* or *Antheraea assama*) is native to Assam and parts of Bangladesh. The cocoon yields a beautiful yellow silk, which is often used in its natural state in woven and embroidered textiles of this area.

The Punjab has no natural supplies of silkmoths, due to the unsuitable climate, and for centuries skeins of raw silk were imported for weaving. The main sources of supply were Bukhara and Khorasan in Central Asia. The bales of raw silk were brought through the mountain passes to Amritsar, Lahore, Multan and other trading centres. In Kashmir, where the climate was more suitable, cultivation of *Bombyx mori* was introduced from Central Asia at an early date for the excellent local silk industry. In Bengal a few mulberry plantations for moths of the *Bombyx* species were successfully established in the 19th century, and cultivated silk was produced for trade.

The methods used by a group of village communities in a remote part of central India to prepare the cocoons and reel and weave silk cloth were recorded by a 19th-century district administrator (see Dewar). These simple methods seem to have been a precedent for all Indian reeling before the development of more sophisticated reeling and spinning tools. Women boiled or steamed the cocoons to soften and clean them, peeled away the outer layer of silk and then unwound the filament. To reel the silk the woman placed about six or eight cleaned cocoons in a bowl by her side, gathered the filaments together in her left hand, while her right hand rhythmically twirled the *natwa*, a smooth, sticklike, wooden tool shaped to receive the silk thread. It was the softness of reeling—even after more sophisticated equipment was developed in the main silk-weaving centres—that gave Indian silk cloth its characteristic mellow texture. To provide a firmer thread for the warp, able to withstand the tension of the loom, two fine threads were 'thrown' or twisted together, generally on a spinning wheel. The weaving of the cloth was usually done by men, using a simple handloom. For illustrations of the warping process and a variety of traditional silk looms see *Journal of Indian Art and Industry* issues in bibliography below. For a general discussion of techniques of reeling, spinning and weaving *see* TEXTILE, §I, 2(v).

(a) Plain, striped and chequered silks. Plain silk (Hindi *daryai* or *doriya*) was either produced in natural shades or dyed. (Silk was usually dyed in the skein before weaving, *see* §3 (i) below.) One of the most beautiful traditional silk fabrics was the *dhūp chānh* ('light-and-shade'), a plain shot-silk with indigo warp and crimson weft, giving a variety of luminous purples, violets or maroon-reds, according to the quality and colour of the yarns. In the Punjab, silk-dyers were particularly skilled in producing reds and bright greens (*see* §3(i) below) and wove a *dhūp chānh* with these colours. In Kashmir a plain silk fabric called *par-ī tāūs* (Pers. 'peacock feathers') was shot in many colours.

Striped silk (*gulbadān*) was the most common of all the traditional fabrics. The stripes were laid in the warp, and even the simplest patterns had vibrancy from the juxtaposition of colours, often enhanced by contrasting 'separating-stripes' of only two threads between the main sequences of the design. In the more elaborate *gulbadān*s, the grouping of the stripes was sometimes delineated between bands of tiny chequers, often in black and white, or of chevrons in contrasting colours, woven over as few as four threads. A main use for *gulbadān*s was trousering for wealthier Hindus and Sikhs. Striped *maśrū* (*see* §(iii)(a) below) was worn by Muslims. Silk muslin (Hindi *malmal*) and netlike fabrics (*dalmiyan*), woven for ladies' garments, were often printed with gold.

During the 19th century the manufacture of silk fabrics for European women settled in India became an important trade. Chequered fabrics (Pers. *carkhānā*) were fashionable from the mid-19th century. The Indian weavers' subtle exploitation of mellow colour, often given brilliancy by the insertion of just two contrasting threads, was enhanced by the delicate 'secondary colours' where the warp and weft threads interwove. The rich depth of the traditional Indian *dhūp chānh* was transformed to a shimmering cluster of blue-greys and greens or a glowing medley of soft yellows, orange and salmon-pinks.

Bengal was originally the main producer of plain and patterned silk fabrics for European taste. South India was by tradition a cotton-producing area, having no natural silk supplies, but during the 19th century the increase in the Indian silk trade led to the establishment of silk factories in the vicinity of Madras, using both Bengali and European silk yarn. Factories were also opened in Bombay where Chinese imported silk yarn was also used, especially for the satins, which were popular for tie-dyed and embroidered garments in Gujarat (*see* §3(iii)(b) and (v) below). As commercial production increased, it became necessary to use machine-spun yarn from Europe in order to withstand the greater tensions and frictions of machine looms. In the 20th century, wild silk of natural colour has been used successfully in new contexts—for example tailored suits for men and luxurious furnishing fabrics.

(b) Silk brocades. The origins of brocade-weaving in India are obscure. Due to the fragility of silk and the ravages of the Indian climate, no silk textiles of an early date survive. Likewise, no pre-Mughal brocades, which might have been woven in central or eastern India (where indigenous silkmoths are found), are known. However, a technique of 'loom-embroidery'—working geometric and other highly stylized motifs over hand-picked threads—occurs in the borders of tribal textiles of north-east India and Assam (see Hall). Thus a highly conventionalized mode of pattern-weaving almost certainly existed in India from an early period.

The Mughal emperor Akbar (*reg* 1556–1605) established workshops for weaving brocade at Lahore, Agra and Fatehpur Sikri, bringing skilled workmen to India from Safavid Iran according to the *Āyīn-i Akbarī* ('Annals of Akbar', *c.* 1596–1602; i, p. 87, *āyīn* 31). However, these records show that the trading of silk fabrics from Iran and Central Asia into north-west India was already long established (*Āyīn–i Akbarī*, i, p. 92, *āyīn* 32). Kashmir, which had ancient cultural links with Iran, had a silk industry of its own that produced flowered silks in an 'Indo-Islamic' style. Under Akbar's successors Jahangir (*reg* 1605–27) and Shah Jahan (*reg* 1628–58), brocade weaving was introduced into royal workshops in provincial capitals. Ahmadabad, in Gujarat, famous for textile production since the Ahmad Shahi dynasty (1398–1572), became a leading centre for fine brocades. Burhanpur, in Khandesh, a provincial capital under Shah Jahan, gained renown and must have had considerable influence in introducing the technique to other centres in central India. As Mughal influence extended across Bengal, the technical advances merged with the ancient traditions of the finest silk-producing districts in India.

The chief designs of Mughal brocades were small conventional plants or flowers (Hindi *būṭī*) repeated as a sprig pattern, a running pattern of flowers and leaves all over the textile (*phulvār*), and a network or trellis (*jāl*) of lines, scrolls or leaves, each mesh enclosing a flower. The brocade loom used to weave them was more complex than the simple silk looms. Numerous heddles to raise and lower the threads were harnessed in groups (*nakṣa*) in accordance with the pattern.

Design styles in silk brocades can be studied in miniature paintings of the 17th to 19th centuries. Practical knowledge of Indian silk brocades, however, is derived mainly from surviving garment pieces dating from the 19th century, which have a soft lustrous texture and rich mellow colour. Women's *sāṛī*s and *oṛhanī*s (head veils) and men's *cādar*s (shoulder wraps) were woven with a plain or patterned field and distinctive patterned borders. Selvedge borders often have a small geometric pattern (*moṭhaṛā*) or a running floral meander or scroll (*bēl*) enclosed between plain or patterned guard borders. The deep decorative panels (*ānchāl* or *palla*) at the ends of the cloth were of more elaborate design, usually a row of large conventionalized flowering plants (*būṭā*) with the characteristic 'drooping bud' at the top, enclosed between cross-borders of *bēl*.

By the 19th century, Bengal, with its natural resources in wild and cultivated silk and supreme skills in dyeing, had developed a sophisticated style, blending Mughal-style finely balanced floral ornament with imaginative indigenous figurative design. The expansion of Calcutta from the 18th century onwards had brought secure patronage. Mushidabad became a renowned centre of trade in woven silk brocades, both for the European settlers and for wealthier Indians. The variety and individuality of Bengali brocades results in part from their production in scattered villages, particularly around the towns of Azamgarh, Baluchar and Marshidabad.

In the mid-19th century distinctive *sāṛī*s were produced by communities of highly skilled weavers near Baluchar. The fields and selvedge borders were of traditional floral designs; the exceptionally long end panels were decorated with one or more large central floral motifs (*butā*), surrounded by rows of small panels containing a variety of pictorial subjects—elephants, horseriders, men smoking hookas and sometimes figures of Europeans. In one such *sāṛī* (see fig. 317) the end panel includes in the design a bridegroom on horseback attended by a canopy-bearer and a woman bearing a lamp. The Baluchar *sāṛī*s became popular with Europeans as collectors' pieces.

317. Silk brocade *sāṛī*, 860×1110 mm, from Baluchar, Bengal, *c.* 1860 (London, Victoria and Albert Museum)

(c) Kamkhābs (silk and gold brocades). The richest patterned fabrics of India are the *kamkhābs*, brocades woven from silk with a weft pattern in gold or silver thread. It was a tradition of the Mughal court to award a fine textile, the *khil'at*, as a mark of special honour; a *kamkhāb* was an appropriate offering. The metal thread (*kalābattū*) was made from fine wire, heated and pulled through holes of diminishing sizes in a steel drawplate, then flattened by hammering lightly and twisted around a core of silk. As pure gold would have been too soft, gilded silver wire was used; the gold surface, which remained intact, was hardened by the wire-drawing and hammering.

The most famous centre of *kamkhāb*-weaving is Varanasi, where a tradition of fine design and superb technique has prevailed since the 17th century. A typical example is a *kamkhāb* (London, V&A; see fig. 318) originally purchased for the former Indian Museum, London, in 1855. The floral motifs are Indian poppy plants, skilfully designed within the discipline of the handloom technique, requiring a master-weaver and at least two assistants. The threads of the pattern were lifted and depressed by the *pāgia*, a complex harnessing of the heddles of the loom. The ground of the cloth was built up on a warp and weft of silk; tiny spools of metal thread were used to weave each floral motif separately across the breadth of the cloth as the work progressed, using silver thread for the leaves and gold for the blossoms. The technique of holding the metal threads firmly in place by picking fine diagonal lines across the pattern can be clearly seen in the textile. In the second half of the 19th century, the elaborate European brocades woven on the Jacquard loom dominated fashion and influenced Indian design. Many Varanasi brocades of the second half of the 19th century are technical masterpieces, with birds and animals enshrined amid a profusion of floral ornament.

Kamkhābs produced in Ahmadabad in the 19th century were woven with a 'floating weft' technique, in which the silver and gold threads were carried on the shuttle across the breadth of the cloth, passing across the back of the cloth between the motifs, instead of true brocading, as at Varanasi and elsewhere, in which each motif was woven separately with its own tiny spools of thread. The Ahmadabad brocades are bolder in style, and motifs tend to be more closely set to avoid unduly long, loose threads at the back.

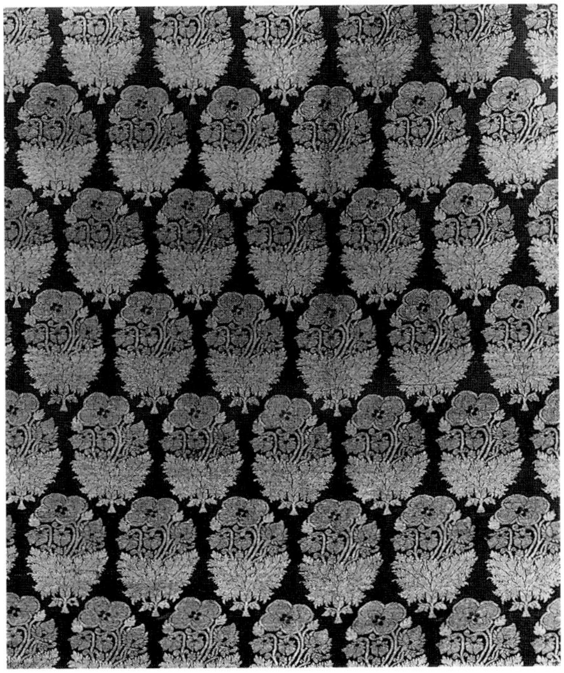

318. *Kamkhāb*, red silk brocaded with gold and silver thread, 1200×755 mm, from Varanasi, *c.* 1855 (London, Victoria and Albert Museum)

In Rajasthan and Bengal the *kamkhāb* was of a lighter, more gauzelike texture, sometimes on a fine cotton muslin base, rather than silk. In Rajasthan deep end borders (*anchāl* or *palla*) of *sāṛīs* or *oṛhanīs* were often worked in the *mīnākārī* (Pers.: 'enamelled') style, in coloured silks on a gold ground, the pattern usually being floral *būṭās* interspersed with birds and flowers.

BIBLIOGRAPHY

Abu al-Fazl: *Āyīn-i Akbarī* [Annals of Akbar] (*c.* 1596–1602); Eng. trans. in 3 vols: vol. i trans. H. Blochmann, ed. S. L. Gloomer ([Calcutta], 1871/*R* Delhi, 1965); vols ii and iii trans. H. S. Jarrett, ed. J. Sarkar (Calcutta, 1948–9/*R* Delhi, 1972–3)

N. G. Mookerji: 'The Silk Industries of Moorshedabad', *J. Ind. A. & Indust.*, v/38 (1894), pp. 1–8, pls 1–7

A. Yusuf Ali: *A Monograph on Silk Fabrics in the North-Western Provinces and Oudh* (Allahabad, 1903/*R* Ahmadabad, 1974)

F. Dewar: 'Silk Fabrics of Central Provinces', *J. Ind. A. & Indust.*, x/81 (1904), pp. 7–12, pls 4–6

S. M. Edwards: 'Silk Fabrics of the Bombay Presidency', *J. Ind. A. & Indust.*, x/81 (1904), pp. 1–6, pls 1–3

W. M. Hailey: 'Silk in the Punjab', *J. Ind. A. & Indust.*, x/81 (1904), pp. 13–16, pls 7–9

R. A. Krishna and V. Krishna: *Banaras Brocades* (New Delhi, 1966)

M. Hall: 'India and Pakistan: Tribal Textiles', *5000 Years of Textiles* (London, 1993), pp. 114–17 and fig. 121

See also general bibliography following §1 above.

(iii) Cotton and silk mixtures. Mixed fabrics of cotton and silk were probably produced in India from an early date. By the 19th century, plain silk-warped textile with a satin-like appearance (*ghaṭṭā*) was widely traded throughout India, to be used as a ground fabric for embroidered garments or (in Gujarat) for tie-dyed cloth; it was also used for lining garments, and sometimes for embroidered bed-covers and furnishings for Europeans in India. Mixed fabrics had the practical advantage of being cool and comfortable to wear in a hot climate, the cotton content giving ventilation and absorbency. However, increased imports of glossy satinettes from China in the late 19th century led to a decline in their production.

(a) Maśrū. According to Muslim traditions, the wearing of pure silk was prohibited for men, except in war. Mixed fabrics of cotton and silk had the softness and sheen of silk but did not infringe religious injunction. Cloth known as *maśrū* (Per.: 'permitted') was woven either with a warp of silk and weft of cotton or less commonly with a warp of cotton and weft of silk. The most striking *maśrūs* have a rich, satin-like appearance from a closely set silk warp, the soft cotton weft tending to lie below. Silk-warp *maśrūs* are particularly effective in vertical striped designs, the sheen adding vibrancy to the soft, rich colours of the natural dyes. Striped *maśrūs* were used for trousering for Muslim men. *Maśrūs* were also used for women's trousers (*śalvar*) and for garment linings. Saddle cloths and elephant trappings of silk or velvet were usually lined with satin *maśrū*, often patterned in fine stripes.

The main centres of *maśrū* weaving were in regions where Islamic influence was—or had been—prevalent. Even after regional changes in dominance, the established centres tended to retain their craft, as trade prospered with other parts of India and with the Islamic countries of the Middle East. In the north-west *maśrū* was produced at Lahore, Amritsar, Multan and other towns in the Punjab and Sind. Important centres in Gujarat were Surat and Ahmadabad; and in north India, Delhi, Varanasi, Azamgarh, Jalaun and other towns. Centres in the Deccan included Ahmadnagar, Bijapur and Hyderabad. From the 19th century *maśrū* was produced in south India in Madras and other towns. In some designs, the warp of some of the main stripes was tie-dyed, so that tiny chevron-shaped flecks of white were reserved on the coloured ground. In the *khanjari* ('wavy') pattern, the entire silk warp is tie-dyed at regular intervals. When stretched on the loom, the threads are adjusted so that the tie-dyed (reserved) bands produce fine wavy or zigzag lines across the breadth of the cloth. (For examples of *khanjari maśrūs* from Varanasi see Forbes Watson, ii, nos 459–62; from Hyderabad, no. 469; from Thanjavur, nos 478–9; and from Tiruchirapalli, nos 494–5.)

A type of *maśrū* with cotton warp and silk weft, sometimes known as *sūfī* ('lawful') or as *garbha-sūtī*, was woven in plain colours or simple stripes chiefly in the Punjab and Sind, in Belgaum, Pune and Nasik and in Bengal at Bankura and Manbhum. These cloths are somewhat stiffer than the silk-warped *maśrūs*. More elaborate *sūfī* fabrics with intricately patterned stripes, known as *sūja khāni* (probably after the person who had originally produced them), were among the products of Bahawalpur in the Punjab; these were sometimes glazed with a mucilaginous emulsion of quince seeds.

(b) Himrū. A distinctive brocaded silk and cotton, *himrū* ('cold season', and thus a textile mainly for that time of year) was woven chiefly in the Deccan. The cloth is woven from thick, soft cotton, both in warp and weft. The surface pattern was brocaded with an additional weft

of silk, the spare threads carried loosely across the back of the cloth, between the motifs, in the 'floating weft' technique. These loose silk threads form an extra lower layer to the cloth, providing additional warmth. When made up into traditional coats and trousers, *himrūs* were often lined.

Aurangabad was the greatest centre of *himrū* production. Its designs included elegant and refined floral and geometric patterns. Striped *himrūs* were made for trousering, the main stripes brocaded along their length with small floral sprigs (*būṭīdār*) with fine coloured borderlines set between the stripes. Among the most striking are those with delicate colours brocaded on a main ground of dark blue, dark maroon or black. (For examples of *himrū* from Aurangabad see Forbes Watson, ii, nos 507–16 and 518; from Hyderabad, no. 519; and from Tiruchirapalli, no. 520.)

(c) Amarū. Similar to Deccani *himrū*, *amarū*, produced in Varanasi, was usually woven of cotton (or sometimes cotton weft on *tasar* silk warp), with floral sprigs (*būṭī*) brocaded with silk. The designs resemble those of the Varanasi silk brocades and *kamkhābs*, for which *amarū* was a less expensive alternative.

(d) Azizulla. Woven in the region of Dhaka, *azizulla* (*ajiji*) consists of fine white cotton and rich yellow *mūṅgā* silk woven in alternate stripes or in chequers. It is a particularly beautiful blend of natural materials in a simple yet effective design. In addition to garment lengths (*thān*), special pieces were woven for *sāṛīs*, shawls, sashes and turbans, with integrated side borders and end borders of silk. These fabrics were often finished with embroidery in *mūṅgā* silk, subtly blended into the design of the woven cloth (for examples see Forbes Watson, v, nos 642, 648–9).

(iv) Wool. Traditional woollen textiles were woven in India in the colder areas of the north-west, especially Himalayan regions such as Kashmir, Kulu, Kangra, Chamba, Ladakh, Lahul and Spiti. Woollen industries were established during the 19th century at Lahore, Amritsar, Ludhiana and other towns in the Punjab; some of these were offshoots of the Kashmir shawl industry. In the late 19th century, a few urban commercial enterprises produced factory-woven fabric of European style, using imported wool, for trade to European settlements in the cold regions; but these woollen fabrics are not true Indian textiles.

Sheep are not indigenous to India; the lovely woollen textiles of the Himalayan valleys are produced mainly from the wool of mountain goats, the different qualities being sorted for different types of cloth. The fleece of wild mountain goats is softer and finer than that of the domesticated animal. Kashmir shawl wool, which is known in the West as pashmina (from Pers. *paśam*: 'wool') or incorrectly as cashmere (from an old spelling of Kashmir), came mainly from a Central Asian species, the long-haired *Capra hircus*. The best was imported from Tibet, from the wild goats of Changthan and Rodokh. Beneath their rough outer hair, the animals grew a soft inner fleece as extra protection during the severe winter, shedding it at the approach of summer. It was laboriously collected from the rocks and bushes on which the animals had rubbed themselves; the softest and finest (*asālī tūs*) grew from the under-belly and was reserved for the finest shawls. A second grade of wool, derived from domesticated goats but still of fine quality, was used for the main production of shawls and for weaving both plain shawl cloth (Arab. *alwān*) and patterned shawl cloth (Pers. *jāmavār*) to be made into garments. Lower grades were used for ordinary cloth. Sheep's wool was sometimes imported from Kirman in Iran and from Bukhara and Yarkand in Central Asia. Attempts were made in the 19th century under European influence to establish herds of sheep in the north-west, but this was successful only in a few suitable fertile valleys such as Kulu.

(a) Kashmir shawls. One of the world's finest woven textiles, the Kashmir shawl, was produced in the Kashmir Valley, where cultural links with Iran and Central Asia were strong. The industry is recorded from the early Mughal period, by which time it was already mature; William Moorcroft, an official of the East India Company, described shawl production in 1820–23. Kashmir shawls were woven on horizontal treadle looms, using the twill-tapestry technique. The design was drawn by a pattern draughtsman (Arab. *naqqāś*) and then worked through by a 'colour caller' (Urdu *tarah gurū*), who decided the number of warp threads over which each colour must pass. A pattern master (*ta'līm gurū*) transcribed this in pattern instructions (*ta'līm*) written in a code understood by weavers (see Irwin, pl. 4).

A master weaver and one or two assistants worked side by side at a shawl loom. The heddles of the loom were threaded for the main weft, forming the web of the cloth. Before each weaver lay his wools for the pattern, each colour was wound on a separate spool (*tolji*). After each row of the pattern had been worked according to the pattern instructions, a weft thread was laid across the entire breadth and made firm with the batten. Traditionally a fine shawl was produced on one loom, taking some 18 months to complete. A shawl with a plain field, however, might have the plain cloth woven on a simple loom and joined to the patterned pieces of the borders by a skilled needleworker (*rafūgar*), with almost imperceptible stitches. Moorcroft described as a recent practice the sharing out of a shawl between several looms so that the complex requirements of European merchants could be met. The elaborate patterns of the mid-19th century (see fig. 319) were invariably woven in pieces and joined in this way (the shawl illustrated was, however, in the possession of an Indian nobleman and had at some time been mounted on a backing and used as a door-curtain or *pardah*).

In the Mughal period the shawl was a male garment worn wrapped around the shoulders or, in a narrower width, as a sash. The Mughal emperor Akbar is said to have possessed a number of them (*Āyīn-i Akbarī*, i, p. 92, *āyīn* 32). A Kashmir shawl was sometimes presented by the emperor as a *khil'at* (garment presented as a mark of favour). Fine shawls were traded throughout India and Central Asia.

The earliest surviving Kashmir shawl fragments (e.g. London, V&A; Ahmadabad, Calico Mus. Textiles) date from the late 17th century or early 18th. Shawls of the 17th and 18th centuries followed the traditional style of

319. Kashmir shawl, loom-woven from fine goats' fleece using the twill-tapestry technique, 2.17×1.37 m, *c.* 1860 (London, Victoria and Albert Museum)

Indian garment cloths: at each end was a patterned border with a row of conventional flowering plant motifs (*būṭā*). The end borders were enclosed by narrow, patterned cross borders (*tanjir*). Most shawls had patterned side borders (Arab. *hāśiyā*), which were sometimes woven separately and sewn to the finished piece. The field (*matan*) might be plain or patterned. In the increasing elaboration of the 18th century the ground of the end borders between the plant motifs was often filled with ornament (*jāl*), usually a running pattern of small, conventional leaves or flowers (see Irwin, pp. 41–2, figs a–g).

The motif known in the West as the Kashmir 'cone' or 'pine' (or later incorrectly as the 'Paisley' pattern) developed from the flowering plant motif or *būṭā*. The Mughal *būṭā* of the 17th century was a graceful plant with roots, flowers and a 'drooping bud' creating a curve at the top. By the end of the 17th century the motif was sometimes transformed to a stylized Indo-Persian 'vase of flowers'. By the mid-18th century the flower pattern was severely confined within a firm contour, the 'drooping bud' becoming the conventional curved summital feature (the transition is illustrated in Irwin, 1973, figs 1–6).

Kashmir shawls began to attract the attention of European traders towards the end of the 18th century. Their warmth, softness and lightness were particularly admired in France, where this elegant draped garment blended well with the current fashions. Shawl traders in Paris influenced design, requiring the end borders to be much longer. The floral motifs consequently became taller. French drawings were sent to Kashmir showing the flower motifs with smoother curves and incorporating the fashionable Neo-classical 'scroll'. In a portrait of *Empress Josephine* (1809; Nice, Mus. Masséna) by Antoine-Jean Gros the Empress wears a dress made from a white Kashmir shawl, the deep end borders in soft colours forming the hem border and the side borders used as trimmings for the bodice; a red Kashmir shawl is draped regally over her shoulders (see Lévy-Strauss, p. 24).

Such shawls also became popular elsewhere in Europe, exports reaching their peak in the early 19th century. The earliest imitations were produced in Europe towards the end of the 18th century, and during the second quarter of the 19th century, as large patterns became increasingly fashionable, the shawl manufacturers of France and Britain used the Jacquard attachment to weave shawl designs of great complexity. By the mid-19th century, pressure from these European machine-made shawls forced the weavers of Kashmir to achieve technical marvels (see fig. 319 above), though under great strain. The elaboration of design and refinement of detail in such shawls are as fine as those of the best European shawls, while the softness of texture and colour harmony of natural dyes are far superior. Needleworkers were increasingly employed to sharpen small details of the pattern. By the 1860s it was quicker and cheaper to work an entire shawl by embroidery rather than the laborious weaving technique. By the end of the 19th century, factory competition, European import restrictions and taxes imposed in Kashmir upon the weavers led to the decline of the Kashmir woven shawl industry. Embroidered shawls (Arab. *ʿamlī*) of a high quality were produced, but by the end of the century such high standards were no longer maintained. During the 1860s and later, many Kashmiri weavers migrated to Amritsar and other cities in Punjab, where they produced plain and patterned shawl cloth of a coarser wool than the Kashmir shawl.

(b) Himalayan homecrafts. In the mountain valleys of the Himalaya, the weaving of woollen cloth from goats' fleece was a traditional homecraft. The fabric was woven on a simple narrow handloom, usually in widths of less than half a metre. Four or more pieces were sewn together to make a large shawl or wrap. The cloth was usually the natural colour of wool (Urdu *khud raṅg*), but sometimes coloured stripes or chequers or coloured borders were woven. The dark, luminous brownish-black that appears as the ground colour or as chequers on pieces from Kulu and Kangra is not dyed but a natural colour of the fleece of some goats. Wool was traded between the valleys.

Even in the remote northerly valleys of Lahul and Spiti, villagers kept a few goats, augmenting their supplies of wool with purchases both from shepherds from other regions, who rented their grazing land in the summer, and from traders from Ladakh. Spiti cloth, which is particularly good, is often woven with patterned stripes. (For examples from Kulu and Kangra, see Forbes Watson, xii, nos 1056–

8 and 1062; from Lahul, xiii, nos 1101–2; and from Ladakh, nos 113–16.)

UNPUBLISHED SOURCES

London, BL, Orient. & India Office Lib., MS. Eur. F.38 [William Moorcroft's letters to C. T. Metcalfe written in Kashmir, 1812–20, reporting on shawl manufacture and trade]; MS. Eur. D.260 [William Moorcroft: *Notice of Particulars Respecting the Manufacture of Shawls in Kashmir*, MS. dated 25 April 1821]; MS. Eur. D.264 [William Moorcroft: *Shawl Manufacture*, 97-page MS. dated 1823]; MS. Eur. E.113 [shorter 49-page version of *Shawl Manufacture*]

BIBLIOGRAPHY

Abu al-Fazl: *Āyīn-i Akbarī* [Annals of Akbar] (*c*. 1596–1602); Eng. trans. in 3 vols: vol. i trans. H. Blochmann, ed. S. L. Gloomer ([Calcutta], 1871/*R* Delhi, 1965); vols ii and iii trans. H. S. Jarrett, ed. J. Sarkar (Calcutta, 1948–9/*R* Delhi, 1972–3)

J. Rey: *Etudes pour servir à l'histoire des châles* (Paris, 1823)

W. Simpson: *India Ancient and Modern* (London, 1867) [pls of shawl-weavers and embroiderers]

J. Forbes Watson: *Collection of Specimens and Illustrations of the Textile Manufacturers of India*, 13 vols (London, 1873–80)

Kashmeer and its Shawls (London, 1875)

M. Chandra: 'Kashmir Shawls', *Prince of Wales Mus. Bull.*, iii (1954), pp. 3–4, 8

J. Irwin: *Shawls: A Study of Indo-European Influences*, V&A Mus. Monograph 9 (London, 1955); rev. as *The Kashmir Shawl* (London, 1973)

M. D. Mamgain: *Himachal Pradesh District Gazetteers: Lahul and Spiti* (Chandigarh, 1975), pp. 34–5, 128–30, 156–7

M. Lévy-Strauss: *The Romance of the Cashmere Shawl* (Milan, 1986; Eng. trans. Ahmadabad, 1987)

See also general bibliography following §1 above.

3. DECORATIVE TECHNIQUES. Patterned textiles were created either by weaving yarns that were already dyed (*see* §2 above and §(i) below) or by block-printing, resist-dyeing, painting or embroidering fabric once it was woven (*see* §§(ii)–(v) below). Frequently a number of different decorative techniques were combined for a single textile (see fig. 320 below). For example, printing was often combined with other techniques, such as resist-dyeing or embroidery; printed patterns were also occasionally finished by painting additional colours—yellows, oranges or greens—which, however, are not entirely fast. □

(i) Dyeing. (ii) Printing. (iii) Resist-dyeing. (iv) Painting. (v) Embroidery.

(i) Dyeing. The natural dyes used for traditional Indian textiles were derived from various parts of plants and trees—roots, fruits, flowers, leaves, seeds, bark, wood and galls—and from other sources, including insects. The techniques and many of the materials used for dyeing silk differ from the methods used for cotton, due to the different constitution of the fibres. Synthetic chemical dyes were introduced in the late 19th century but did not totally replace the traditional dyes discussed below. The preparation and use of dyestuffs was the result of generations of experience, and many families guarded their methods carefully.

The mellow beauty of Indian natural dyes is dependent upon the Indian environment: the quality of the waters in the local rivers and long seasons of sun for continuous work, i.e. the facility to dry intricate work quickly before it became blurred, especially in the processes of printing, resist-dyeing and *kalamkārī* (see §§(ii)–(iv) below), which combines the craft of dyeing with that of skilled painting.

(a) Reds. Plants and trees that yield alizarin from the roots or bark were used to produce glowing red colours on Indian cotton. The loveliest of the crimson-red cotton dyes is from the long tap-root of the chay plant (*Oldenlandia umbellata*; Tamil *cāya ver* or *saya ver*; Telegu *tśeri vello*), which grows on sandy ground along the Coromandel coast in south India. Plants from the Kistna Delta yielded the finest colour, because the ground is impregnated with broken, rotting shells; calcium is an essential ingredient of the dyeing process.

A distinctive warm brick-red, widely used all over northern and western India, is produced from *āl* or *saranguy*, the young cultivated roots of the tree *Morinda citrifolia*. Other trees of the same family, such as *Morinda tinctoria*, yield red of varying quality. In western India, crimson was obtained from manjeet, a plant of the madder family cultivated near Bombay. The madder plant (*Rubia tinctorum*), however, is not native to India, though some cultivation was introduced during the 18th century by the East India Company, mainly for their own trade goods.

Alizarin-dyeing on cotton requires a mordant, a substance that combines with the colouring matter to fix the dye in the fibres of the thread. The yarn or cloth is steeped in the mordant before dyeing. Alizarin yields crimson when mordanted with alum; a lovely brownish-black when mordanted with oxidized iron; and a range of violets and browns when mordanted with a solution of alum and iron. Astringents and other substances to assist the dyeing varied locally.

Cottons of a distinctive dark wine-red were produced in the far south of India, particularly near Madurai, where the fine quality of the dyeing is attributed to the waters of the Vaigai River. The red dye was prepared from roots of *timbúr*, a small shrub growing on the banks of the Vaigai, to which were added dried powdered *kaya* leaf and gingelly (a species of sesame) oil. The mordant was made from the ashes of *umarī* (*Salicornia indica*), a plant growing wild on sandy banks near the coast. Dyers achieved a dark, fast colour by steeping the white cloth in the mordant for three or four days, then in the dye-bath for two days, leaving it in shallow running river water for a day, drying it in the sun, then dipping, washing and drying repeatedly for ten or eleven days.

The main red dyestuffs used in India for silk were not vegetable dyes but were derived from certain insects whose bodies (under certain conditions) yield alizarin. Silk takes an alizarin-red without the use of an alum mordant, though various auxiliaries were used locally to enhance the colour; sometimes such auxiliaries are described as 'mordants' (not always strictly accurately). The earliest accounts of silk dyeing date from the mid- to late 19th century and are incomplete; most are by local officials, who were concerned that indigenous processes were being lost with the increasing use of commercial dyes.

The crimson red characteristic of silks from central India and Bengal was obtained from lac, an incrustation formed by an insect, the *Kerria lacca* Kerr on the branches of various trees. The lac was collected and made into cakes, which were sold all over India. The cakes were powdered by the dyers, and *sajjīmiṭṭī* (Fuller's earth) and other substances were added as mordants and auxiliaries. Shades from pink to deep crimson were obtained by altering the strength of the dye-bath or by repeated dippings. In north-west India, however, the crimson silk dye was obtained from the dried bodies of *Kermes vermillio* Planchon (an insect similar to cochineal), with *bozgand* (the galls of *Pistasia terebinthus*) as a mordant. The dyers of the Punjab produced a brilliant scarlet by dyeing first in kermes and then in the yellow of *harasingār* (the flowers of *Nyctanthes arbor-tristis*, the night-flowering jasmine). Indian silk-dyers were also skilled in obtaining an extraordinary wide range of orange and salmon-pink tints by various combinations of red and yellow dyes.

(b) Blues. The indigo plant (*Indigofera tinctorum*) yields the deep rich blue that is a feature of many Indian textiles. The dyestuff is contained in indican, a glucose substance in the leaves. A fermentation process was used to convert this to indigo-white, which was then transformed by oxidization (achieved through beating) to insoluble indigo-blue. This coagulated into flakes and sank to the bottom of the tank. The sediment was collected and pressed into cakes or cubes, which were traded all over India and abroad.

To form a fast dye on cotton yarn or cloth, indigo-blue pigment had to be temporarily returned to its soluble state (indigo-white) to permeate the fibres. This was carried out in another fermentation vat. The cloth was steeped until the dyer judged from his experience that the required depth of colour had been achieved. When lifted from the vat the fabric was yellowish in colour, but on exposure to the air the indigo-white was reconverted by oxidization to indigo-blue, which was fast to light and to washing. Indigo dyers were of low caste and lived on the edge of a town, downstream, because of the pollution of the water caused by their work.

The technique of dyeing silk differed from the laborious process for cotton. Methods varied locally; sometimes the yarn or cloth was first steeped in *sajjīmiṭṭī* to clean the silk and prepare it for the dye-bath of indigo with an astringent to give greater fastness to the colour. In other places the cakes of indigo-blue were powdered by the dyers, then mixed with some auxiliary alkaline ingredient, such as *sajjīmiṭṭī*, together with molasses (treacle). The silk was dipped in this solution and allowed to dry; the dipping and drying were repeated until the required depth of colour was achieved. Purple could be obtained by dipping in crimson and (after drying) a second dipping in indigo. Black could be obtained from indigo used in combination with an acid substance, or with protosulphate of iron.

(c) Yellows and greens. The rhizome of turmeric (*Curcuma longa*), especially the main rhizome, yields *haldī*, a deep yellow dye that is especially good as a strong, fast dye on cotton and on *tasar* silk. *Haldī* is also the colorant used in Indian cookery. Saffron was widely used for silk; the dried flowers were used with an alkaline substance such as wood ashes or the ashes of plantain leaves. Other yellow dyes, used mainly for silks, include dried *kamala* fruits (*Mallotus philippinensis*), which yields a yellow dye from a reddish powder in the epidermal glands; the *latkan* tree (*Bixa orellana*), which yields a range of deep yellow, orange and reddish dyes from the seeds; and the flowers of *harasiṅgār* (*Nyctanthes arbor-tristis*), which yield a deep yellow or orange dye used mainly as an auxiliary to enhance other dyes.

Few plants produce a good green dye, other than a light green for painting. A good green, stated to be fast on cotton, was achieved in northern and western India by dyeing first in indigo and then in *haldī*.

BIBLIOGRAPHY

N. N. Banerjei: 'Dyes and Dyeing in Bengal', *J. Ind. Art & Indust.*, vii/59 (1897), pp. 11–20

B. C. Mohanty, K. V. Chandramouli and H. D. Naik: *Natural Dyeing Processes of India* (Ahmadabad, 1987)

See also general bibliography following §VI, 1 above.

(ii) Printing. The most famous of India's patterned textiles produced for popular use were block-printed cottons, and the block-printing tradition survives to the present day. Indian print-blocks are carved from smooth hardwood with the design on the lower side and a handgrip on the upper side. The printer works rhythmically, placing the block in position, then impressing the pattern with a double blow of his clenched hand. The dominant colours of most Indian traditional block-printed fabrics were red and black, from an alizarin-based dye. In western and north-west India the dyestuff was usually *āl*, in south India usually chay or other local plants or tree roots. It was, however, the mordant that was printed and not the dyestuff. The alum (for red) or iron oxide (for black) was thickened with gum to make it workable on the print-block; two shades of red were obtained by adding more gum for the lighter colour. The cloth was immersed in the heated dye-bath and, after washing, the design appeared in its full range of colours. The red was less pure and rich in a printed textile than in a painted one because of the presence of gum in the mordant. Other colours, such as light yellows and greens, were often painted by hand but were not entirely fast. In the modern period commercial alizarin has been used instead of natural dye plants. Turmeric (*haldī*) can be used directly for printing yellow, if thickened by gum.

It is not practical to use natural indigo for direct printing, because the soluble form of the dye would oxidize more quickly than the print-block could be manipulated. However, an indigo ground is often found on older printed cottons. After printing, the motifs were covered with resist-paste or wax and the cloth dyed. The result was a dark blue cloth with the motifs printed in colour. In western India, a dark green ground was obtained by resist-dyeing first in indigo, then in *haldī*. Since the introduction of European commercial dyes in the late 19th century, any colour can be directly printed.

Many types of printed cottons were cheap and thus widely used for everyday garment pieces. Fine cotton muslins were printed and sometimes further embellished with gold, usually in the form of an overprinted final outline to the motifs. The parts to be gilded were printed with gum, then gold leaf (Hindi *varaq*) was applied and, when the gum had dried, burnished. Silver was similarly used. In cheaper grades of gold printing, gold powder was used instead of gold leaf. In still cheaper work, powdered mica—or in modern times metallic powder—has been applied in the same way, to provide a glitter to the textile. This type of printing, not fast to washing and liable to damage by abrasion, was often used for garments for festive occasions and textiles for ceremonial use. Larger articles such as ceremonial banners were sometimes printed entirely in gold and silver on a coloured ground.

Various regions developed distinctive styles from their local traditions. One of the most famous south Indian centres was Machhilipatanam (Masulipatam), which had been a centre of the Indo-European chintz trade in the 17th and 18th centuries and a centre for the textile trade with Persia from even earlier. Fine surviving 19th-century examples include a printed cotton quilt cover or *razaī* (see fig. 320) in an Indo-Islamic style, with central medallion, quarter medallions in the corners of the field and deep end borders. Four breadths of narrow handloom cotton were used for the *razaī*. The delicate flowers in the broad border show the intricacy of the finely cut blocks for the mordant-printing. The green leaves were indigo-dyed with a wax resist, then overpainted for green. An interesting feature is the fine wax-drawn pattern of running leaf-stem reserved in white on a mordant-dyed red ground in the main end borders of large conventional flowering plants (*būṭās*). The central field of the *razaī* was mordant-dyed red after the printing was completed, the small plant motifs (*būṭī*), medallions and borders having been protected with wax. The *razaī* has a glazed surface typical of the printed cottons of Machilipatnam, which is created by burnishing the lightly starched cloth after printing. By the mid-19th century, the cotton printers of Machilipatnam were producing dress fabrics for European women settled in India,

320. Printed cotton quilt cover (*razaī*) that was also mordant-dyed and resist-dyed, 2.58×1.85 m, from Machhilipatanam, *c.* 1880 (London, Victoria and Albert Museum)

in a blend of Indian-style plant motifs and European sprig patterns. Cheaper work, bolder in style, was done in the regions around Madras, notably at North Arcot.

According to early records of the East India Company, in western India the finest chintzes were obtained at Burhanpur, in the 17th century a Mughal provincial capital on the Tapti River and a trade centre for southern Rajasthan and the northern Deccan. A few cotton textiles from Burhanpur region survive, made for Indian use and stylistically of the early 18th century, with refined floral ornament in the best late-Mughal tradition (see Irwin and Hall, colour pl. iv and pl. 8). The outlines were mordant-printed in black and red from beautifully cut small print-blocks, and the colouring was finished by painting. Political disturbances in the region in the mid-17th century disrupted the chintz trade, resulting in a decline in the European trade in this area.

Ahmadabad was known for mordant-printing in black and red. (The style can be recognized as that described in the diary of the French trader Georges Roques, who visited the region in the 17th century; see Schwartz.) The designs have deep end borders with a band of simple flowering plants and numerous narrow lines of small geometric and floral patterns. The print-blocks are boldly cut; the colour scheme of black and red is completed by details freely painted in yellow and green. Until the 1970s a community of cotton-printers in Ahmadabad produced these traditional garment cloths and printed quilt covers in a similar style.

A living art in Ahmadabad is the printing of *pacheḍī*, large cotton temple cloths in the traditional black and red, for the worship of the mother goddess as practised in some of the villages (see Irwin and Hall, pls 49–51). The cloths literally are the temple: four are erected as walls, and a canopy cloth is hung overhead. The central part of each cloth is printed with a representation of the goddess; printed above, below and to either side are animals and birds, musicians, dancers and bands of worshippers carrying offerings and flowers. The *pacheḍīs* are printed by families who have practised the art for generations and who regard their task as sacred.

The distinctive bold style of cotton-printing in the Punjab in north India arose from the texture of the cloth: it was necessary to cut blocks with larger and less complicated patterns as the nap of these thicker fabrics would not take a fine impression. Printed cotton was used for floorspreads, canopies and door curtains; quilt covers (*razaī*) were printed in pairs and stitched together with an interlining of cotton wool. (The usual decoration for garment cloths, especially for women, was embroidery; *see* §(v) below and INDIA, REPUBLIC OF, §VII.) Bold floral designs abound, often arranged within an architectural framework of Islamic style or within a trellis or ogee. In colouring, the bold brick-red of the *āl* root predominates, with the associated brownish-black and a dull but pleasant violet. Contrast is provided by the deep yellow of turmeric and green.

The cotton-printers of Rajasthan in western India created especially fine garment fabrics. Paintings from the Rajput courts in the 18th and 19th centuries capture the delicacy and romanticism of court dress, with extensive use of light gauzy fabrics for women's *oṛhanīs* (large veils that cover the head and hang over the shoulders) and soft cottons and muslins for men's *jāma*s (court coats). Designs of *sāṛī*s and *oṛhanī*s feature deep end borders of flowering plants, peacocks and other birds, in soft colours and gold. Surviving 19th-century examples confirm that Rajasthan had a fine standard of fabric printing (see Irwin and Hall, pls 67–74). This tradition has been continuously maintained from at least the early 18th century at Sanganer, near Jaipur. Until the mid-20th century, the Sanganer printers were reserved to the Jaipur court; tax stamps feature on all printed cottons supplied outside the court. The Sanganer style was based on mordant-printing in black and red, but to meet European demands, later textiles employed the fuller range of colours available with commercial dyes. The printers had earlier made extensive use of overprinting with gold on court dress pieces. Some of the modern export fabrics feature gold printing in modern metallic gilt, providing a touch of exoticism.

Printing on silk is a comparatively modern innovation in India. The traditional silk dyes are not suitable for block-printing techniques, although a little printing on silk was done in Bengal and central India in the late 19th century, after the introduction of commercial dyes. Since the mid-20th century, the introduction of screenprinting into India has proved increasingly popular, and both cottons and silks are printed by this technique, in both traditional and modern designs.

BIBLIOGRAPHY

J. L. Kipling: 'Panjab Cotton Prints', *J. Ind. A. & Indust.*, i/14 (1886), p. 104, pl. 6

W. S. Hadaway: *Cotton Painting and Printing in the Madras Presidency* (Madras, 1917)

P. R. Schwarz: 'L'Impression sur coton à Ahmedabad, Inde, en 1678', *Bull. Soc. Indust. Mulhouse* (1966); Eng. trans. by M. Hall (Ahmadabad, 1969) [extracts from the diary of Georges Roques, 1678–80, with notes]

S. Robinson: *A History of Printed Textiles* (London, 1969)

J. Irwin and M. Hall: *Indian Painted and Printed Fabrics* (1971), i of *Historic Textiles of India in the Calico Museum* (Ahmadabad, 1971–)

F. Cousins: *Tissus imprimés du Rajasthan* (Paris, 1986)

See also general bibliography following §1 above.

MARGARET HALL

(iii) Resist-dyeing. Method of creating simple, but effective patterns of spots, flowers and geometric ornament by shielding (or 'reserving') certain areas of cloth or yarn from dye. It encompasses a wide range of reserve techniques, including the use of substances such as paste or wax, which are applied to parts of the fabric to prevent the dye from penetrating (*see* §(b) below; the use of wax in this way is elsewhere known by its Malay term 'BATIK'), and tie-dyeing (*see* §(a) below), in which cotton thread or other material is wrapped around the fabric or yarn. Tie-dyeing techniques fall into two basic types. In the first the design is produced by resist-dyeing individual areas of a woven cloth; when the term 'tie-dyeing' is used in the West, it usually refers to this technique. In the second—usually but not always a more elaborate process—the threads are dyed according to the projected pattern before they are woven; this technique is most often known in the West by the Malay term 'ikat'. Both types of tie-dyeing are referred to in India by derivations of the verb *bāṅdhnā* (Hindi: 'to tie'); hence English 'bandanna', the spotted cloth, usually handkerchiefs, imported from India since the 18th century.

(a) Tie-dyeing. (b) Other methods.

(a) Tie-dyeing. The earliest evidence for tie-dyeing in India is found in the 5th-century wall paintings in Cave 1 at Ajanta, in which women are shown wearing fabrics of several identifiably tie-dyed designs. The first known written record is the *Harṣacarita*, a history of King Harsha (*reg* AD 606–48) by Bana, in which tie-dyed textiles and the women skilled in making them are specifically mentioned. Printed textiles in imitation of tie-dyeing, probably dating from the 15th century, have been excavated at Fustat in Egypt.

Tie-dyed designs produced by resist-dyeing individual areas of a woven cloth are found all over India but are particularly associated with the western states of Rajasthan and Gujarat, where tie-dyed cloth in cotton, wool and silk is widely used for turban cloths, women's head coverings, shawls and skirts. The more complicated designs are made up of a succession of small tie-dyed dots, a type of pattern known as *cunarī* (see fig. 321), or similar regional variants. The dots (*dhanak* or *bindī*) are formed by individually wrapping, usually with cotton thread, tiny sections of cloth that have been raised up with the aid either of a board on which the design is outlined in nails or of a dextrous finger or specially cultivated fingernail. Mud or paste is sometimes added over the cotton binding to ensure the resistance to dye. To attain symmetry and to save time, the cloth is folded into halves or quarters before being tied. When the wrapping, with a long continuous thread, is completed the cloth is dyed, with the lightest colour first if the design is to be multicoloured. Small areas of colour, such as the

321. Tie-dyed silk *sāṛī* (detail), from Gujarat, late 19th century (London, Victoria and Albert Museum)

centres of circles, may be individually dipped in dye or painted after the final dyeing.

In Rajasthan the two most commonly encountered uses for this type of tie-dye are the turban cloth and the *oṛhanī* (head cloth). The most popular turban pattern is red with a design of tiny squares in green and yellow, and the most favoured *oṛhanī* is that given to a mother on the birth of a son, a yellow cloth known as *pīliyā* (from *pīlā*: 'yellow'), with a large red and white tie-dyed circle and a red border. Tie-dyed cloths worn by women tend to be symbolic of love, either for husband or child, and allusions to *bāṅdhnā* cloth occur frequently in song and poetry.

Produced on the same principles as the dotted *cunarī*, but visually different, is the form of tie-dyeing resulting in a striped pattern. Known in Rajasthan, its chief area of manufacture, as *lahariyā* ('wavy'), it is produced by rolling a length of fine cotton into a long rope and binding it tightly at intervals. A zigzag stripe results from pleating the cloth like a fan, and a chequered pattern can be obtained by repeating the process along the opposite diagonal of the cloth so that the stripes cross, an effect known as *moṭharā* (from *moṭh*, a type of lentil, which the tiny checks created in the finer varieties resemble). *Lahariyā* and *moṭharā* fabrics are much favoured as turbans in Rajasthan. The *lahariyā* pattern carries connotations of water and fertility, as indicated by its name and that of the multicoloured version *samdar lahar* (*samdar* from *samudra* meaning 'sea', thus 'waves of the sea'). It is worn during the spring, around the Holi festival, when tie-dyed cloths in red and watery pale blue are also worn. *Lahariyā* cloths symbolizing rain are traditionally given by men to their sisters at the Teej festival during the rainy season. Printed imitations of tie-dyed *oṛhanī*s and turbans are common, and genuine tie-dyed fabrics are thus usually sold still wrapped as proof of their authenticity. Most towns in Rajasthan have a local tie-dye industry, but notable centres are Jaipur, Sikar, Jodhpur, Udaipur and Bikaner.

Gujarati tie-dye, mainly of the dotted *cunarī* type, employs a wider range of motifs and additional materials, notably silk and wool, which are not commonly used in Rajasthan. Pictorial designs for *sāṛī*s with animals (especially elephants), birds, flowers, dancing girls or sometimes the *rāsa maṇḍala* (featuring Krishna dancing with his female devotees) have been popular since the mid-19th century. Particularly sought after are the *gharcholū* wedding *sāṛī*s, which have tie-dyed patterns of female dancers, musicians and animals within gold brocade squares. The large Muslim community requires the production of non-representational pieces; particularly striking are the red-on-black compositions of Khatri Muslim silk wedding garments, which include a head cover, dress and matching trousers, all tie-dyed to a high degree of technical excellence. Traditionally, tie-dyeing is the preserve of the Khatri community, whose members may be either Hindu or Muslim. The tying of the pattern is done by women and girls, the dyeing by men. Work of the finest quality is no longer done and the best examples date, at the latest, from the early 20th century. The woollen shawls of the Rabari shepherd community of Saurashtra are tie-dyed in a basic design with a central circle, usually in black, red and yellow. The main centres for tie-dyeing in Gujarat are Jamnagar, Porbandar, Bhuj and Anjar, although countless villages and small towns are also involved in tie-dye production.

Tie-dye techniques are found throughout most of north India and in some parts of the south, for example in the Gujarati-settled area around Madurai. In Assam a coarse and boldly-patterned brown and yellow tie-dyed cloth was made in the 19th century, and finer but equally large-scale cotton examples exist from the Punjab. Berhampur and Murshidabad in West Bengal produced beautiful, simply patterned silk *sāṛī*s usually of a plain colour with sparse groups of small dots, as well as the spotted tie-dyed handkerchiefs, exported to Britain in the 18th and 19th centuries, that were the original 'bandannas'. The Parsis of Bombay favoured dark silk *sāṛī*s with a field sprinkled with coloured dots and an embroidered border; printed imitations were also popular.

Ikat, the tie-dyeing of yarn before weaving a cloth, is widely practised in India and has been since at least the 5th century AD, when ikat cloths were depicted in the Ajanta wall paintings. 'Proto-ikat', in which threads are dyed as if for ikat cloth but remain unwoven, is made by the Naga tribes in north-eastern India and used as decorative fringes; this primitive method of decoration may be a forerunner of woven ikat. As with the *cunarī* type of tie-dyeing, the area of production of the most splendid Indian ikats is Gujarat, but there are also important centres in Andhra Pradesh and Orissa. The ikat technique involves the binding and dyeing of the warp or weft threads, or both, before weaving. As the basis of the designs is more linear than in *cunarī*, the resistant barrier with which the threads are bound can be of a wider material, such as tree bark or rubber tubing. Ikat is a technically demanding method, as it requires expert setting-up of the threads on the loom and exact weaving to ensure the coordination of the outlines of the design, although much of the appeal of ikat textiles lies in the slight blurring of motifs that it necessarily entails. The most complex in design and execution of all Indian ikats is the *paṭolū* (pl. *paṭolā*) of Gujarat. This is a double ikat silk, woven in a limited range of traditional designs, which is so highly valued that it has acquired a semi-sacred status and is worn only on certain auspicious occasions such as marriages, when the mother of the groom may wear it as a *sāṛī* (but not the bride herself), or the groom may use it as a saddle cloth or shoulder cloth. In upper-class social life in Gujarat, it may be worn occasionally by high-caste Hindus and Jainas and some Isma'ili Muslims. Painted *paṭolu* patterns are used as decoration on the walls of palaces and temples in Kerala. Throughout their history (they are mentioned in Gujarati texts of the 12th century) *paṭolā* have been highly prized and an important export to South-east Asia, where they became the preserve of royalty and were confined to ceremonial and ritual use. Some designs and shapes of *paṭolā* were made for export only, perhaps the most striking being the long narrow cloths with a large-scale elephant design, apparently made for use in Indonesia. *Paṭolā* made for the domestic market have patterns of flowers, roundels, tigers, elephants or dancing girls in jewel-like tones dominated by red and yellow. Formerly produced in several centres in Gujarat, by the late 1980s they were being made by only two families in the town of Patan, near Ahmadabad.

In Andhra Pradesh double ikat is used for cotton *teliyā rumāl*s (Hindi: 'oil cloths'), so called because the cloth is steeped in oil (*tel*) before dyeing. *Teliyā rumāl*s, usually about a metre square, are worn in a basic form as lungis and turbans by local fishermen but are best known for their use in the courtly dress of Hyderabadi women in the 19th and early 20th century. Usually in simple geometric patterns in dark blues, reds and browns, but sometimes incorporating embroidery and gold thread when made for the upper classes, the *rumāl*s were woven in pairs, to be worn by men singly as a type of turban or by women doubly as a *dupaṭṭā* draped over the head. The sombre colours are produced by the use of iron filings and vinegar, alone to produce black and in conjunction with alizarin dyes for reds. The ikat industry of Andhra Pradesh grew up in the late 19th century, and from the 1920s to the 1950s ikats from Chirala in eastern Andhra were exported from Hyderabad to the Middle East. For the most part these were versions of *teliyā rumāl*s with figurative patterns in squares, sometimes incorporating modern motifs such as aeroplanes, clocks or gramophones. Ikat-weaving was introduced into Pochampalli about 1920, and since the 1960s Pochampalli and neighbouring villages have largely taken over from Chirala as the main centre, manufacturing a wide variety of ikat cloths that cater for both the thriving local market of lungis and *sāṛī*s, and the increasing demand from Europe, where ikat has become popular as clothing and furnishing fabric. Even Japanese ikat designs supplied by Western and Indian textile buyers have in modern times been produced in Andhra Pradesh for export.

Ikat production in Orissa, notably in the Cuttack, Bolangir and Sambalpur districts, grew up probably only in the 19th century. The combinations of geometric and figurative designs often recall the Andhra ikats, but the Orissan examples (mostly *sāṛī*s) tend to be characterized by large chequerboard patterns with borders incorporating fish or animal motifs. Orissan ikats frequently, but not exclusively, use dark purples and muted browns and pinks, but in Cuttack District red and yellow ikats woven with written text from the *Gita-govinda*, Jayadeva's 12th-century poem on the love of Radha and Krishna, are made for the Jagannath temple at nearby Puri. In both Andhra and Orissa the most usual technique is weft ikat, but warp and double ikat are also produced.

Maśrū, a warp-faced satin-weave fabric usually with silk warp and cotton weft (*see* §2(iii)(a) above), was often dyed in a simple arrowhead ikat pattern or with zigzag rows of a contrasting colour, a design known as *khañjari* ('like a dagger'). In the 19th century, the ikat patterns and the satin fabric became so interlinked that some commentators inaccurately use '*maśrū*' exclusively to mean those with ikat designs, identifying plain *maśrū* as 'satin' or 'atlas'. *Maśrū* ikats were formerly made in Varanasi, Aurangabad, Hyderabad and, especially, Tiruchirapalli (Trichinopoly) and are frequently seen made up into trousers and jacket linings in early 19th-century Thanjavur paintings.

BIBLIOGRAPHY

C. R. Das: 'Tie and Dye Work', *J. Ind. A. & Indust.*, ii/23 (1888), pp. 63–4, pls 11–13

T. H. Hendley: 'The Arts and Manufactures of Ajmere-Merwara', *J. Ind. A. & Indust.*, iii/25 (1890), pp. 5–9

P. Jayakar: 'A Neglected Group of Indian Ikat Fabrics', *J. Ind. Textile Hist.*, i (1955), pp. 55–65 [*teliyā rumāl*s]

V. S. Agrawala: 'References to Textiles in Bana's Harshacharita', *J. Ind. Textile Hist.*, iv (1959), pp. 65–8

B. C. Mohanty and K. Krishna: *Ikat Fabrics of Orissa and Andhra Pradesh* (Ahmadabad, 1974)

J. L. Larsen and others: *The Dyer's Art: Ikat, Batik, Plangi* (New York, 1976)

A. Buhler and E. Fischer: *The Patola of Gujarat*, 2 vols (Basle, 1979)

A. Buhler and others: *Indian Tie-dyed Fabrics* (1980), iv of *Historic Textiles of India in the Calico Museum* (Ahmadabad, 1971–)

V. Murphy and R. Crill: *Tie-dyed Textiles of India* (London and Ahmadabad, 1991)

See also general bibliography following §1 above.

ROSEMARY CRILL

(*b*) *Other methods*. The process of making a pattern on cloth by resist-dyeing must be one of the oldest in India. Before dyeing, the pattern on the cloth was drawn or printed with a paste or with wax, which formed a resist to prevent the dye from entering the pattern. After dyeing, the resist substance was scraped and washed away, and the finished work appeared as a coloured cloth with the pattern reserved in white. Resist-dyeing with indigo, probably the earliest form of the craft, is seen on fragments of cotton textiles, the remains of medieval (and later) trade goods from India, found in excavations at Fostat, near Cairo (see Irwin and Hall, pp. 1–13 and pl. 3–5; Nabholz-Kartaschoff, pl. 84). In western India, especially Gujarat, a resist-paste composed of clay, cow-dung, resin and rice-paste was used, giving an attractive, bold, free effect. A little dye often seeped through, creating a contrast of rich dark blue and bluish-white. In south India, wax, the most effective resist substance, was usually used. It was especially suited to indigo-dyeing, which does not require heat, so the fine detail of the pattern was not spoilt. A printed or painted cloth could be given a coloured ground by applying a resist over the patterned motifs to protect them. South Indian dyers produced designs of fine white lines on a red (mordant-dyed) ground by drawing the lines in wax before the mordant was applied. When the fabric was immersed in the dye-bath, the colour would adhere only where the mordant was absorbed.

Among the finest surviving examples of resist-dyeing on mordant-dyed cloth are the rare garment cloths made until the end of the 19th century in the village of Karuppur for the Rajas of Tanjavur and their court (see Irwin and Hall, colour pl. 13, pls 80–85). The borders of the fine white cotton *dhotī*s were brocaded with gold thread in a simple design of flowers and leaves. The woven design was then further embellished with a delicate floral leaf-stem pattern drawn in wax to provide a resist. The main bands of the woven design were painted with the alum mordant, while the iron mordant was painted over the narrow bands. The field of the *dhotī* thus remained white; the borders were dyed deep red with narrow black bands, and a floral design in fine white lines remained where the wax had been applied. The gold thread, which had a cotton core, attained a rich warm tint in the dye-bath. *Sāṛī*s for the ladies of the court, produced by the same process, were usually patterned in the field and had a long, richly patterned end panel.

Resist-dyeing, using a wax resist, was an essential stage in the complex processes of *kalamkārī* for the motifs where indigo blue (or indigo overpainted with yellow for dark green) was required (*see* §(iv)(a) below).

(iv) Painting.

(a) Kalamkārī. Among the finest textiles of India are the *kalamkārī* (lit. 'pen work'; from *qalam*: 'pen'), produced in south India by a series of processes combining the craft of dyeing with that of skilled painting. The cloth was given a firm surface before painting by steeping it in astringent, then in buffalo milk, drying it in the sun and then burnishing it with a small tool. The first stage was the painting of the mordants (*see* §(i) above) for the reds, blacks, browns and violets. The painter drew the outline of the design with the iron mordant for black and the alum mordant (lightly tinted with sappan wood so that he could see his work) for outlines of the parts that were to be red. Fine white lines were created within the red areas by painting in wax, which acted as a resist to prevent the mordant from penetrating the cloth. The various parts of the design were then painted with appropriate mordants, diluting the mordant for paler shades. After the alizarin-based dye-bath, the complete range of colours appeared, fast to both light and washing. Because the mordants were liquid, without the gum necessary for printing, the colours were pure and clear. The second stage, to produce the blue and dark green, was performed by a separate group of craftsmen, the indigo dyers. The entire cloth was covered with wax, except for the places where blue or green were required, to protect the delicate painting from damage in the indigo vat. After dyeing, the wax was scraped and washed away, and the cloth returned to the painters. Where dark green was required, the blue was overpainted with a yellow or a pale green dye from local dye-plants, which were, however, not fast to light or washing. The introduction of dark green was required mainly in the *kalamkārīs* made for the Indo-European chintz trade; in older chintzes the overpainting has often washed out in use. Pale green and yellow were obtained by painting with dye from local dye-plants.

Among surviving examples from the 17th century is a large cotton floorspread from the Amber palace near Jaipur (London, V&A; see Irwin and Brett, pl. 1). It was painted in the region of Machhilipatanam, at that time in the kingdom of Golconda, and is mordant-dyed from painted mordants in the beautiful range of reds, pinks, violets, light browns and brownish-black that are yielded by the chay plant of the Kistna Delta. Trade records show that fine *kalamkārīs* from this region were traded to Iran as well as to Indian courts. The design of the field comprises two opposed rows of flowering trees and flowering plants that link to form a pattern over the ground, with points of emphasis made by large, carefully spaced flowers. Within the border are lively figures of huntsmen, animals and birds, and a charming scene of a courtier and girl. The little blue that occurs in such early Golconda *kalamkārīs* is always pale. This is because the cloth could not be exposed long in an indigo dye-bath, to avoid damage to the intricate painting. Sometimes the blue appears to be painted and thus not entirely fast. Other 17th-century examples from the Coromandel Coast include large wall hangings with courtly figures, some in European dress (*see* TEXTILE, colour pl. VI, fig. 2).

Vivid Hindu temple cloths were produced using the *kalamkārī* technique at such centres as Kalahasti, Pallakollu and Madurai. Temple cloths from Kalahasti are distinguished by a deep rich blue achieved by highly skilled dyeing in indigo. After the design was painted and mordant-dyed for the reds, violets, browns and black, the entire cloth—except for the parts intended to be dyed blue—was covered with protective wax. It was then immersed in the indigo dye-vat until the required depth of colour was achieved; judgement had to be exact, for

322. Painted cotton temple cloth (*kalamkārī*) that was also mordant-dyed and resist-dyed, 1.85×3.89 m, from Kalahasti, *c.* 1880–85 (London, Victoria and Albert Museum)

repeated immersion would damage the earlier painting. Fine examples from Kalahasti include a 19th-century temple cloth (see fig. 322) shown at the Indian and Colonial Exhibition in 1886. The production of *kalamkārī* temple cloths still continues in south India. They are used to drape the temple carts (*ratha*) that carry images of the gods in processions held for religious festivals.

(*b*) *Pigment paintings on cloth.* India has a long tradition of religious paintings on a cotton base, lightly primed with a paste of rice or other grain. These cloths are mainly temple hangings, votive cloths and various types of *maṇḍala* (Skt: cosmic diagram for contemplation) painted with powdered pigment colours from earths and metallic minerals used with a binding of gum. They are not truly 'textiles' (though sometimes loosely discussed as such) but votive paintings. Pigment paintings on cloth are liable to damage by abrasion or damp, especially when folded and stored. There is thus a continuous tradition of producing new paintings, for damaged cloths are considered unfit for religious service. A pioneer collection of these paintings was begun in the 1950s by the Calico Museum of Textiles, Ahmadabad, which was greatly expanded during the 1960s and 1970s (see Talwar and Krishna).

The oldest surviving examples, some dating from the 16th century, are the *paṭṭas* of the Jainas, some depicting cosmic diagrams and others symbolic representations of *tīrtha* or places of pilgrimage (see Talwar and Krishna, pp. 92–8, pls 86–102 and colour pls ix–x). *Picchavāī*s, hangings for the shrines of the Vallabhacharya sect who worship Krishna in his aspect of Shri Nathaji, combine the gay stories of Krishna's childhood and youth among the cowherds with his deeper significance as a mature and powerful god. They illustrate the religious festivals of Krishna's life and the seasons. The *picchavāī*s are hung in the shrine appropriately for each festival, for each season and for the time of the day, at each *darśana* ('showing') of the image of Shri Nathaji, which is revealed to devotees eight times in each day. *Picchavāī*s are still painted in the little town of Nathdwara, in Rajasthan, the centre of the Vallabhacharya sect; versions of traditional subjects are also painted on paper and on cloth, for sale to devotees and visitors (see Talwar and Krishna, pp. 1–81, pls 1–85 and several colour pls). Some Vallabhacharya hangings are embroidered with silk or gold, which may be how they came to be thought of as 'textiles'.

*Pañcāṅga*s, 'calendars' for the Hindu religious year, are long, narrow cotton scrolls, written in black, with a traditional series of paintings at the head (Talwar and Krishna, pp. 103–5, pl. 107, a and b). In an entirely different tradition are the *phāḍa*s from Marwar, Rajasthan. These are very large folk paintings on thick, strong cotton or jute cloth used by the travelling *bhopā*s (ballad singers). The *phāḍa* is held aloft on two bamboo poles to augment performances of folk legends and historic and religious stories in the villages (Talwar and Krishna, pp. 99–103, pls 103–5). The hero of the ballad is depicted large in the centre; a myriad of smaller scenes are illustrated all over the main cloth. The *bhopā*s illuminate each scene with their lamp, as the story unfolds in the open air at nightfall.

UNPUBLISHED SOURCES

Paris, Mus. N. Hist. Nat. Lib., MS. 193(i) [The Beaulieu MS., *c.* 1734, an account of a demonstration by a chintz painter at Pondicherry, with sample pieces of cloth showing the stages of his work]

BIBLIOGRAPHY

W. S. Hadaway: *Cotton Painting and Printing in the Madras Presidency* (Madras, 1917)

P. R. Schwartz: 'French Documents in Indian Cotton Painting: The Beaulieu MS., c. 1734', *J. Ind. Textile Hist.*, ii (1956), pp. 5–20, pls 1–3

R. N. Mehta: 'Picchavais: Temple Hangings of the Vallabhacarya Sect', *J. Ind. Textile Hist.*, iii (1957), pp. 4–14

J. Irwin and K. B. Brett: *Origins of Chintz, with a Catalogue of Indo-European Cotton-paintings in the Victoria & Albert Museum, London, and the Royal Ontario Museum, Toronto* (London, 1970)

J. Irwin and M. Hall: *Indian Painted and Printed Fabrics* (1971), i of *Historic Textiles of India in the Calico Museum* (Ahmadabad, 1971–)

'Homage to Kalamkāri', *Marg*, xxxi/4 (1978) [whole issue]

K. Talwar and K. Krishna: *Indian Pigment Paintings on Cloth* (1979), iii of *Historic Textiles of India in the Calico Museum* (Ahmadabad, 1971–)

M.-L. Nabholz-Kartaschoff: *Golden Sprays and Scarlet Flowers: Traditional Indian Textiles from the Museum of Ethnography, Basel* (Kyoto, 1986)

See also general bibliography following §1 above.

MARGARET HALL

(*v*) *Embroidery.* The history of embroidery in India is long, but its beginnings are obscure. Bronze needles were excavated at Mohenjo-daro (*c.* 2550–2000 BC), and these may have been used for embroidery. Early written references to decorated or flowered textiles could refer equally to embroidered, woven or printed designs, and this usually applies also to representations of textiles in sculpture and early paintings, for example at Ajanta. The earliest specific reference to embroidery is by Marco Polo, writing at the end of the 14th century, who comments on leather mats with designs in gold and silver thread that were produced in Gujarat. This area of western India has continued to produce the finest embroidery in India, usually in a fine silk chain stitch that is directly derived from a leather-working embroidery technique using a hooked implement (*ārī*) rather than a needle. Such embroideries were done by professional male craftsmen for courtly, temple and domestic use and are distinct in style from the folk embroideries (*see* INDIA, REPUBLIC OF, §VII) done by Gujarati women for their own families. The earliest known surviving examples of Indian embroidery are two pieces done for the Jaina community in Gujarat (Ahmadabad, Calico Mus. Textiles, 983; Paris, Assoc. Etude & Doc. Textiles Asie, 2381). Probably made for presentation to Jaina nuns, these two panels date from the early 16th century (or possibly late 15th) and are embroidered in silk satin stitch and couching on cotton; they retain traces of inscriptions embroidered in *kuśa* grass.

Bengal in the east was also a centre for embroidery in the 16th century. Vasco da Gama mentions bed-canopies embroidered in white as early as 1502, and other Portuguese references to fine Bengal embroidery occur throughout the 16th century. Surviving examples of Bengal embroidery date mainly from the late 16th century and early 17th. These are quilts done in Satgaon on the Hughli River for the Portuguese market (although they were also highly prized in England). They are embroidered in yellow silk chain stitch on a white cotton ground and often combine Christian and Hindu mythological themes as well as the coats of arms of Portuguese patrons. The production of these splendid quilts declined sharply after 1632, when the Portuguese were expelled by the Mughals from their trading centre at Hughli, although similar quilts for the European trade were produced, often in non-representational designs, throughout the 18th century. Similar quilts (Port. *colchas*) were produced in Portugal itself as the trade with India declined. The Bengal tradition survives in the simpler forms of domestic quilts (*kānthās* and *sujanīs*; *see* INDIA, REPUBLIC OF, §VII), and Bengali embroidery known as *kaśīdā* still employs natural gold-coloured *mūga* silk on white cotton.

High-quality embroidery for the European market was also produced in Gujarat at least from the beginning of the 17th century. The earliest surviving export piece is a bedspread embroidered with flowers and angels (Hardwick Hall, Derbys, NT) that appears in a Hardwick Hall inventory dated 1603. Embroidered quilts and hangings from Gujarat were commanding high prices in London by 1641 according to East India Company records. Designs were modified to suit European taste and were frequently based, like those of contemporary chintz hangings, on English crewelwork embroideries. The Indian trade embroideries, however, were done in fine floss silk chain stitch on a cotton or cotton-and-linen twill ground. During the 18th century, designs for both chintz and embroidered hangings were influenced by the European vogue for Chinese painted wallpapers, and Chinese-style trees on silk grounds became popular.

Embroidery flourished in the 17th century as a courtly art for the Mughal emperors and nobility. Again, Gujarati professional chain-stitch embroiderers were foremost among the craftsmen in the imperial workshops. Embroidery in the ubiquitous floral patterns beloved by the Mughal emperors was used for costume—robes, turbans and sashes—floor-coverings, screens, hangings (see fig. 323 and EMBROIDERY, colour pl. I, fig. 2) and tent-linings and was at least as highly prized as brocaded or painted textiles. A magnificent embroidered coat (London, V&A; see Guy and Swallow, pl. 61) is perhaps the finest example of the court embroiderer's art. Gold and silver thread was often incorporated into floral designs, in which satin stitch was often used as an alternative to chain stitch. Sequins, metal foil and beetles' wing cases were also used, especially during the 18th and 19th centuries, to add sparkle to court dress.

Regional courts emulated Mughal furnishings and dress, but some also developed their own styles. A group of famous chain-stitch embroideries, probably made for the royal family of Jaipur in the 18th century, seems to have been based on paintings from Bundi in Rajasthan (e.g. Ahmadabad, Calico Mus. Textiles; Jaipur, Maharaja Sawai Man Singh II Mus.; Richmond, VA Mus. F.A.). Professional artists also must have provided cartoons for the exquisite satin-stitch embroideries done at the court of Chamba and other Punjab Hill states in the 18th and 19th centuries. These *rūmāls* (coverlets) often depict scenes from the love story of Krishna and Radha in a style that reflects the Mughal-influenced paintings of the Hill states. Some impressive large hangings from this group also show battle scenes (e.g. London, V&A; New York, Met.; Ahmadabad, Calico Mus. Textiles). *Rūmāls* in coarser

323. Embroidered hanging for a wall or the interior of a tent, cotton ground with silk chain stitch, 1700×810 mm, made by professional Gujarati embroiderers for the Mughal court, second half of the 17th century (London, Victoria and Albert Museum)

materials, and sometimes in abstract designs, were done throughout the Hill states up to the early 20th century.

Reputedly introduced to India by the Portuguese, the use of gold thread (*zarī* or *zardozī*) became increasingly popular in courtly embroidery during the 18th century and continued throughout the 19th century for ceremonial dress, throne covers, canopies, saddle cloths and elephant trappings, often worked in heavy padded patterns on velvet. The metal thread was formed by wrapping thin silver, gold or silver gilt strips around a silk core. Flat metal strips could also be laid on to the fabric, usually crimped into a zigzag pattern. *Zarī* embroidery is still done by specialist male professionals, mostly in Delhi, on satin and velvet for caps, bags and belts. Pictorial embroideries in *zarī* work were done on satin for Europeans in Delhi and Agra in the 19th and early 20th centuries.

Fine embroidery done in white cotton on muslin, sometimes in combination with undyed silk, was a speciality of the male Muslim embroiderers of Lucknow. Known as *cikan* or *cikankārī*, it seems to have originated in Bengal, probably as a derivative of the delicate woven *jāmdānī* muslins rather than the heavier Bengali quilting tradition. Floral designs were adapted from European whitework patterns of the 18th century, and openwork panels similar to drawn thread work were incorporated, with the important difference that Indian openwork (*jālī*) is formed by pushing threads aside and securing them with tiny buttonhole stitches, not by pulling them out of the fabric. *Cikan* work has not been produced in Bengal since the late 19th century, but it grew to great prominence in Lucknow around the mid-19th century. It was popular with both local and European patrons, and work of incredible fineness, using a traditional and limited range of stitches, was done in Lucknow up to the 1980s, when the last two master craftsmen died. Whitework embroidery was also done in the Punjab, but it had more in common with the Afghan (Kandahar) and Baluch style of embroidery, which was used mainly on shirts and *burqās* (all-enveloping women's garments). *Cikan* work is still being produced commercially in Lucknow, now mostly by local girls.

The fine embroidered shawls of Kashmir originated as a way of imitating woven shawl designs in a less time-consuming, and therefore less costly, technique. The embroidered or *'amlī* shawl is said to have been introduced into Kashmir by an Armenian merchant named Khwaja Yusuf in 1803, and professional embroiderers from Kirman reputedly taught the Kashmiris the technique of shawl embroidery. Needlework was already involved in shawl manufacture, as professional darners (*rafūgars*) were employed to sew woven sections together. The embroidery was done in *paśam*—the same goat hair as the shawl itself, to maximize its similarity to a woven one—in satin stitch or darn stitch. Usually the designs mirrored exactly the woven patterns, but other possibilities were introduced with embroidery, notably the trend of embroidering maps of Kashmir and plans of Srinagar on to a shawl (e.g. London, V&A, IS13–1970). As the 19th century progressed, the embroidery became coarser and was sometimes done in floss silk. Towards the end of the 19th century in Kashmir, heavy embroidery in wool chain stitch on felt and coarse cotton became popular. Embroidered felt rugs (*namdās*) and heavy crewelwork curtains, which found a large market among Europeans, are still produced in Kashmir.

During the 19th and early 20th century in Gujarat, particularly in Kachchh, local people and temples were important patrons of embroidery. Embroiderers of the Mochi community produced fine chain-stitch embroidery, usually on satin, for clothing, especially women's skirts and bodices, and for temple hangings (*pichvāī*) for shrines to Krishna. Designs are usually floral for costume, frequently with borders of peacocks or parrots, and figurative scenes showing Krishna with female devotees or cows for the *pichvāīs*. Mochi embroidery as carried out in Kathiawar sometimes combined chain stitch with satin or herringbone stitches on wall hangings and doorway decorations (*torans*) for local customers. Most of the home decorations in Kathiawar are embroidered by local women for their own use (*see* INDIA, REPUBLIC OF, §VII), but some are also made by local Muslim craftsmen.

Beadwork is a speciality of Kathiawar but seems to be of fairly recent origin, probably dating from the mid-19th century. Designs are made not by sewing beads on to a cloth base but by threading them together in rows. Beadwork is used to make all sorts of household decorations in rural Gujarat as well as cart and animal trappings. Originally produced only by professional craftsmen, beadwork became a domestic craft during the 20th century.

BIBLIOGRAPHY

G. Watt: *Indian Art at Delhi* (London, 1904)
J. Irwin: 'The Commercial Embroidery of Gujarat in the Seventeenth Century', *J. Ind. Soc. Orient. A.*, xvii (1949), pp. 51–6
——: *Indian Embroidery* (London, 1951)
Marg, xvii/2 (1964) [full issue devoted to embroidery]
J. M. Nanavati and others: *The Embroidery and Beadwork of Kutch and Saurashtra* (Baroda, 1966)
A. K. Bhattacharya: *Chamba Rumal* (Calcutta, 1968)
J. Irwin and B. Hanish: 'The Use of the Hook in Indian Embroidery', *Bull. Needle & Bobbin Club*, liii/1 & 2 (New York, 1970), pp. 3–16
J. Irwin: *The Kashmir Shawl* (London, 1973)
J. Irwin and M. Hall: *Indian Embroideries* (Ahmadabad, 1973)
R. Skelton and M. Francis, eds: *Arts of Bengal* (London, 1979)
M.-L. Nabholz-Kartaschoff: *Golden Sprays and Scarlet Flowers: Traditional Indian Textiles from the Museum of Ethnography, Basel* (Kyoto, 1986)
S. Paine: *Chikan Embroidery* (Aylesbury, 1989)
J. Guy and D. Swallow, eds: *Arts of India, 1550–1900* (London, 1990)
S. Aryan: *Folk Embroidery of Himachal Pradesh* (New Delhi, 1992)

ROSEMARY CRILL

VIII. Other arts.

1. Arms and armour. 2. Books and prints. 3. Calligraphy. 4. Carpets. 5. Ceramics. 6. Coins. 7. Dress. 8. Furniture. 9. Glass. 10. Ivory. 11. Jade, agate and crystal. 12. Jewellery. 13. Maps. 14. Masks. 15. Metalwork. 16. Puppets. 17. Tents. 18. Terracotta. 19. Woodwork.

1. ARMS AND ARMOUR. The development of arms and armour on the Indian subcontinent spans a period of many thousands of years, from the flint spearpoints and arrowheads of the Neolithic period to the introduction of European armaments in the 19th and 20th centuries, and includes the elaborate ritual weapons of the medieval period and the intricately wrought ceremonial arms of the Mughal era.

(i) Before 1200. Early Indian arms and armour are known from excavated material, sculpture and literary sources. The first two provide only limited evidence. The literature is richer in detail, although somewhat idealized; it is nevertheless clear that the bow was regarded as the supreme weapon. Shiva's bow was called Pinaka, Vishnu's Stranga, while the epic hero Arjuna used the bow Gandiva. Arjuna's bow was made of horn, the other two of bamboo, indicating the early existence of reflex and single-curve bows, as can also be verified from visual sources. The *Dhanur veda* ('Science of archery') describes the bow in warfare. Often in Vedic literature the bow serves the dramatic purpose of demonstrating strength, skill and unavoidable fate, its symbolism made all the more potent by its acknowledged supremacy in battle. The spear, sword, dagger, axe, club, quoit and shield also appear in the hands of gods and warriors. However, because of the symbolic nature of the weapons carried by gods, they are often represented in stylized or exaggerated forms and therefore must be used with caution to document contemporary weaponry. One example of a symbolic weapon is Vishnu's club, which represents authority or the power of knowledge. Similarly, Rama's bow came to symbolize his virtues and figures prominently in his life story. The philosophical view that creation is achieved by the interaction of order and chaos demands that the powers of evil be allowed to rise up and challenge the powers of good, to be repeatedly, inevitably and temporarily defeated. The weapons of the gods are central to this process, and the manner in which they are used in the epic literature served as an exemplar to the warrior caste and strongly affected weaponry and

324. *Archers*, detail of a relief on the exterior of Cave 3, Badami, Kerala, AD 578

the conduct of warfare in the subcontinent until modern times.

Excavated material supports the literary evidence that bows reached a high level of effectiveness at an early date in the subcontinent. The Indus Valley culture (*c.* 2550–*c.* 2000 BC) produced bronze and copper arrowheads with long narrow barbs, and elaborate arrowheads of the 1st century AD have been excavated at Taxila. The Classical authors Arrian and Strabo pay tribute to Indian archers' skill and the penetrative power of their arrows against shield or breastplate, and Herodotus, writing in the 5th century BC, describes Indians as having cane bows and iron-tipped arrows. Representations of weapons can be seen on coins—for example the 'archer type', first struck in the reign of Samudragupta (*reg c.* AD 335–76)—and in sculpture. Reliefs at Bharhut, Sanchi and other sites show swords, daggers, spears, axes, shields, tridents and elephant goads, and 6th-century friezes at Badami represent archers (see fig. 324). Although their place of manufacture is debated (see Pant, pp. 19, 20), the earliest metal swords are from the Indus Valley; they are copper double-edged weapons with a strong central rib. Subsequent Indo-Aryan sword forms can be traced from 1st-century BC statuary from Mathura, Bharhut and Sanchi that depicts a hilt with a broad platform pommel, a round guard and two types of short, double-edged blade. In one type the blade is straight-sided and in the other spoon-shaped or waisted; this latter type is a recurring form in Indian blades. In the Kushana period (1st–3rd century AD), 2nd-century iron swords excavated at Taxila are all of Roman type. In contrast, those shown in contemporary sculptures from Mathura are of the Indian waisted type, with the exception of two examples that were clearly imported from Central Asia. In the Gupta period (4th–5th century AD), the waisted blade evolved into a form recognizable as the *khanda* (thrusting dagger). Across India there was considerable uniformity in blade shapes, but with a variety of hilts reflecting regional and external influences. The *khanda* and the forward-angled *kopis* blade appear in the wall paintings at Ajanta. Over time the *kopis* blade developed into the flamboyant south Indian sword, which in later times became a vehicle for ostentatious and non-functional decoration, serving a ritual rather than a fighting purpose.

Throughout the Pala and Sena periods (8th–13th century) the swords of eastern India as shown in sculpture indicate a retrospective and symbolic approach. Further south, the *khanda* gave way to the Tamil sword tradition. The earliest examples of swords in the south date from the 2nd or 1st century BC and were excavated at Adichalanur (see Gordon). These iron swords are of three types. Two are similar to the short, double-edged swords with straight or spoon-shaped blades found in the north at this period. The third has a straight, tapering blade with a pronounced midrib and appears to be unique to south India. In the Deccan there was also a preference for straight blades of this general type, although no Indian evidence survives from the early medieval period to support continuous usage. Because of the importance of Indian Ocean trade in the Deccan, the straight swords of Sasanian Persia or pre-Islamic Arabia may have been an influence. However, Indian weaponry seems otherwise to have resisted outside influence until the arrival of the Mughals in the 16th century.

(ii) 1200 and after. Information on arms and armour in the subcontinent prior to the 16th century is extremely

limited. There is little excavated material from the Sultanate period (*c.* 1200–1526), and information is largely derived from such literary sources as Fakhr-i Muddabir's *Ādāb al-ḥarb wa'l-shajā'a* ('Art of war and courage') and the evidence of such travellers as Ibn Battuta. Sculpture in western India shows a continuation of traditional Indian weaponry forms; these can also be seen in stylized form in western Indian paintings from the 14th century. A number of bronze swords of indeterminate date from south India relate in appearance to pre-16th-century temple swords, but this may merely reflect the intense conservatism of the later period in matters of ritual. It is not until the late 16th century and early 17th that sufficient pieces survive to permit comparison with the weaponry in Mughal-period miniature paintings; these sources, along with the few dated or historically inscribed pieces, enable a reasonably accurate chronology of arms to be established. From the *Ṭūṭīnāma* and the *Ḥamzanāma*, it is possible to distinguish between indigenous Indian types and those imported by the Mughals from their Central Asian nomad tradition (*see* §VI, 4(i)(b) above). Inter-dynastic marriages between the Mughal and Rajput rulers began in 1562 and resulted in a change of the Mughal attitude to arms design and decoration. For example, the Timurid use of jade for sword and dagger handles, which appears to have been unknown in pre-Mughal India, can be found in the 17th century in forms that echo Indian metal prototypes. The evidence from Mughal miniatures is supplemented by Abu'l-Fazl's *Āyīn-i Akbarī* ('Annals of Akbar'), which records in considerable detail Akbar's love of weaponry and his interest in the manufacture of firearms. The gift of bejewelled swords and daggers is frequently mentioned in other sources, notably memoirs of Jahangir (*reg* 1605–27). Famous swords include that of Dara Shikoh (1615–69), stamped with the date AH 1050 (AD 1640–41; see fig. 325). A steel sword with a gold hilt and watered blade with stamped and gold-inlaid inscriptions, it was sheathed in a wooden scabbard covered with green velvet and red brocade with enamelled gold mounts.

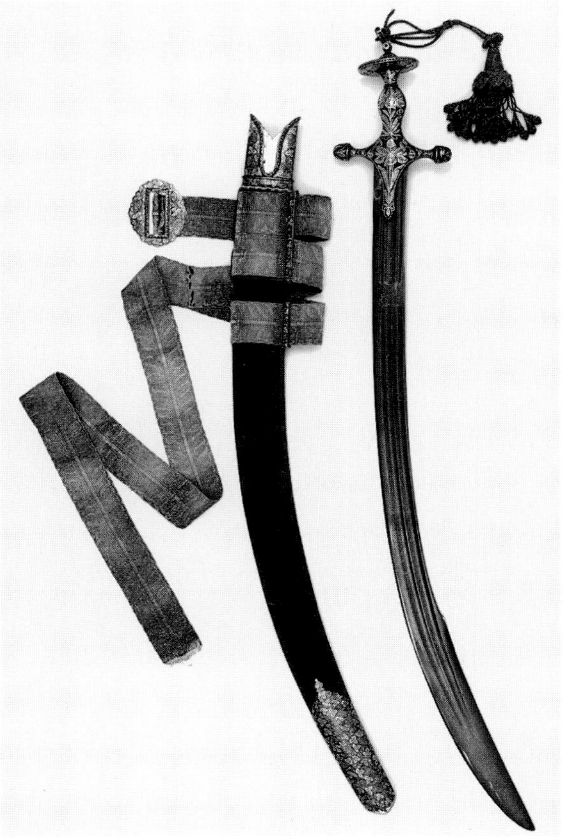

325. Sword (right), steel with gold hilt, inscribed as belonging to Dara Shikoh, l. 851 mm, Mughal period, dated AH 1050 (AD 1640–41); scabband (left), wood with velvet, brocade and gold (London, Victoria and Albert Museum)

Of particular importance at this time was the introduction of firearms to Indian warfare. Little credence is currently given to the view that firearms are documented by Sanskrit texts. Although rockets may have been used in ancient Indian warfare, the evidence as a whole suggests that Muslim armies introduced firearms into the subcontinent. The Arabs brought naphtha to India in the early 8th century AD, and natural saltpetre and sulphur were widely found. The army of Sultan Mahmud resisted Timur's invasion of 1398 with the use of grenades, rockets and thunderflashes to frighten the opposing cavalry. Cannon were introduced into the Deccan in the second half of the 14th century and became common in the 15th century owing to maritime links with Egypt and Turkey. Muhammad I (*reg c.* 1358–75) of the Bahmani dynasty set up an arms factory as early as 1365. In contrast, the Rajputs cherished the skills of the traditional mounted warrior on which their social structure in part rested. Tod, writing as late as the 1820s, refers to 'the Rajpoot, who still curses those vile guns; which render of comparative little value the lance of many a gallant soldier, and he still prefers falling with dignity from his steed, to descending to an equality with his mercenary antagonists'. Tod further describes how no prince or chief in Rajasthan in the early 19th century was without his *silākhāna*, or armoury, where he would pass hours viewing and arranging his weapons: 'Every favourite weapon, whether sword, matchlock, spear, dagger or bow, has a distinctive epithet and the Keeper of the Armoury is one of the most confidential officers about the person of the Prince. These arms are beautiful and costly.'

The Turks, particularly Turkish artillery and arquebus men, played an important role in the establishment of firearms in India, but they were superseded in the 17th century by European merchant companies, which constructed fortified bases and recruited local forces to man them. In the 18th century the merchant companies set up arsenals, initially for themselves (as at Pondicherry) but subsequently for local rulers (as at Lucknow, Agra and Seringapatam). In the 19th century, such local Indian centres of manufacture as Monghyr in Bengal (famous for pistols), Lahore, Sialkot, Gujarat, Shahpur and Kashmir were destroyed by foreign imports. European technology and tactics, particularly with regard to firearms, also destroyed the power of rulers and the traditional arms-production jobs of their subjects. The time-honoured weapons of India—the bow, lance, sword, dagger, mace, *katāra* and quoit—together with mail and plate, remained in general use until the uprising of 1857; their ceremonial role as a link with a great martial tradition continued until 1947 and the dissolution of the princely states.

See also §§10(iii) and 15(v) below and ISLAMIC ART, §VIII, 1(ii).

BIBLIOGRAPHY

Enc. Islam/2: 'Barud'

J. Tod: *Annals and Antiquities of Rajast'han* (London, 1829–32/*R* New Delhi, 1971)

G. Oppert: *Weapons, Army Organisation and Political Maxims of the Ancient Hindus, with Special Reference to Gunpowder and Firearms* (London, 1880)

W. Egerton: *A Description of Indian and Oriental Armour* (London, 1896/*R* London, 1968)

W. Irvine: *The Army of the Indian Moghuls* (London, 1896/*R* New Delhi, 1962)

S. Sen: *Military System of the Marathas* (Calcutta, 1928)

V. R. R. Dikshitar: *War in Ancient India* (Calcutta and London, 1944)

D. H. Gordon: 'The Early Use of Metals in India and Pakistan', *J. Royal Anthropol. Inst. GB & Ireland*, lxxx/1–2 (1950), pp. 55–78

S. D. Singh: *Ancient Indian Warfare with Special Reference to the Vedic Period* (Leiden, 1965)

H. R. Robinson: *Oriental Armour* (London, 1967)

P. S. Rawson: *The Indian Sword* (London, 1968)

G. N. Pant: *Studies in Indian Weapons and Warfare* (New Delhi, 1970)

S. Digby: *War-horse and Elephant in the Delhi Sultanate: A Study of Military Supplies* (Oxford, 1971)

S. P. Verma: *Art and Material Culture in the Paintings of Akbar's Court* (New Delhi, 1978)

The Indian Heritage: Court Life and Arts under Mughal Rule (exh. cat., ed. R. Skelton; London, V&A, 1982)

R. K. Saxena: *The Army of the Rajputs* (Udaipur, 1989)

F. Wilkinson: 'India and Southeast Asia', *Swords and Hilt Weapons* (London, 1993), pp. 186–203

ROBERT ELGOOD

2. BOOKS AND PRINTS. Except for the Chinese method of block-printing used in Tibetan areas (*see* TIBET, §V, 9), the technology for mechanically reproducing texts and images was introduced into South Asia by European colonial powers. The production of printed books as well as single prints and broadsheets was initially controlled by colonial officials and European missionaries, who established printing presses at colonial ports. Printing began in Portuguese Goa in 1556 and is recorded at the British colony of Bombay in 1674, at the Danish colony of Tranquebar by 1792 and in Bengal by 1778. The first Devanagari founts were developed in Calcutta to print Hindi and Sanskrit text. Charles Wilkins, working at the Fort William College in Calcutta, and William Carey, at his Serampore mission, developed founts for printing the scripts of many regional South and South-east Asian languages.

With the proliferation of presses that could print South Asian languages, vernacular newspapers quickly appeared. These early newspapers included some of the first printed graphic art produced by Indian artists. By the 1830s, traditional *patua* painters of Calcutta who had learnt the printer's trade began designing and producing individual woodblock-engravings of Hindu themes for the local market. These engravings often included printed text and were embellished with watercolours after printing. The introduction of lithographic printing to India in the 1820s enhanced possibilities for illustrations with the inclusion of cursive script as well as the possibility of colour reproduction (see fig. 326). Initially, colour lithography was restricted to expensive prints in the orientalist mode established by 18th-century English aquatints such as those by WILLIAM HODGES and Thomas and William DANIELL. These prints of Indian monuments, racial types and scenery were primarily intended for a European clientele in India and abroad. However, by the 1880s, middle-class Indian artists, particularly those at the Calcutta School of Art (*see* CALCUTTA, §3), were working

326. Lithograph frontispiece from Charan Dasji: *Svarodayasara* ('Treatise on divination') (Kasi, 1882)

with a variety of colour-printing technologies, and lithography, oleography and finally chromolithography came to be used to produce popular religious pictures for the growing Indian market. RAVI VARMA was the most prominent painter to reproduce his work mechanically through prints.

BIBLIOGRAPHY

A. Paul, ed.: *Woodcut Prints of Nineteenth-century Calcutta* (Calcutta, 1983)

B. S. Kesavan: *History of Printing and Publishing in India*, 2 vols (Delhi, 1985)

T. G. Thakurta: 'Artists, Artisans and Mass Picture Production in Late Nineteenth- and Early Twentieth-century Calcutta', *S. Asia Res.*, viii/1 (1988), pp. 3–46

P. Godrej and P. Rohatgi, eds: *India: A Pageant of Prints* (Bombay, 1989)

WOODMAN TAYLOR

3. CALLIGRAPHY. Since no Indian alphabet is based on an intellectual concept of artistic writing, calligraphy is synonymous with the Islamic scripts used for writing Arabic, Persian, Urdu and Sindhi. The Arabic script, used for all these languages, is composed according to specific mathematical rules and is thus most suited to a variety of artistic forms and flourishes. Calligraphy came to enjoy a unique status among the arts of the subcontinent, as seen elsewhere in the Islamic world, and was practised from the first appearance of Muslims there. Among the earliest examples are the floriated kufic inscriptions at Banbhore in Sind (one dated AH 294, AD 906–7) and at Bhadreshvar, Gujarat (12th century). Initially restricted to architecture, calligraphy later appeared on metalwork, manuscripts and woodwork. In Kerala and Kashmir, where wood was the easily available building material, inscriptions carved on rectangular wooden panels are found. Two inscriptions in wood from Ahmadabad (see *Annu. Rep. Ind. Epig.* (1959–60), App. D, nos 48–9) and one from the Darya Mahal Palace at Surab, Pakistan (Bombay, Prince of Wales Mus.), are also known.

While Indian calligraphers generally adhered to the conventional six styles of penmanship (*see* ISLAMIC ART, §III, 2(iii)(c)), in the eastern part of the subcontinent a new style was devised in the 13th century. Called *bihār*, perhaps after its area of origin, this script was at first exclusively used on stone, then mostly restricted to copies of the Koran in the 14th–15th century, after which it seems to have gone out of vogue. From the 18th century, new, purely decorative, calligraphic scripts, mostly for paper panels (*waṣlīs*), were devised; these include *gulzār* (in which letters are drawn in outline and the hollows filled with floral motifs), *ṭā'ūs* ('peacock'), *māhī* ('fish'), *zulf-i'arūs* ('bride's tresses'), *larza* (in which the letters are drawn as if with a shaky hand) and *ghubār* ('dust script').

In the 12th and 13th centuries calligraphic inscriptions executed against floral and geometric designs formed the chief theme of architectural decoration. Such Sultanate-period buildings as the Quwwat al-Islam Mosque (1192–8), the Qutb Minar (*c.* 1198–1215) and the Tomb of Sultan Iltutmish (*c.* 1236) at Delhi and the Arha'i Din ka Jhompra Mosque (*c.* 1200) at Ajmer incorporate elaborate specimens of kufic and monumental *thuluth* calligraphy (see fig. 327). A variety of conventional and non-conventional calligraphy occurs up to the end of the Sultanate period in monuments and gravestones throughout India: *naskh* script with *riqā'* and *tauqī'* flourishes appears on 13th–14th-century tombstones in Gujarat, while epigraphs in *ṭughrā thuluth*, found on mosques and tombs in Bengal, Gujarat and Rajasthan, were used to create the impression of such motifs as a bow and arrow, an arched colonnade, an earthen lamp, a flying bird, a swimming duck or a hooded serpent. Exquisite examples of *ṭughrā thuluth* calligraphy are found in Hyderabad and elsewhere in Andhra Pradesh.

327. Monumental calligraphy on the façade and interior (central part, from east) of the Tomb of Sultan Iltutmish (*c.* 1236), Quwwat al-Islam Mosque, Delhi, 1192–8

Manuscript calligraphy was cultivated on a much wider scale under the Mughal dynasty and reached its zenith under Akbar (*reg* 1556–1605) and his successors. At the same time, monumental calligraphy in the *naskh*, *thuluth* and *nasta'līq* scripts continued to be practised, as can be seen in inscriptions on Mughal buildings at Agra, Delhi, Ahmadabad, Allahabad and Ajmer. Outstanding specimens of the *thuluth* script, executed in faience by the calligrapher of the Taj Mahal at Agra, 'Abd al-Haq Shirazi (later Amanat Khan), occur on two gateways of a caravanserai at Sarai Amanat Khan, near Atari, and even after the decline of Mughal power fine examples of stone calligraphy are found in small principalities such as Kalyana (modern

Basava-Kalyan) in Karnataka, Khambhat in Gujarat and Vellore in Tamil Nadu. Mughal emperors and such art-loving nobles as Mirza ʿAbd al-Rahim Khan-i-Khanan attracted master calligraphers from Iran and Central Asia. Outstanding calligraphers of Akbar's period include ʿABD AL-SAMAD and Muhammad Husayn Kashmiri, who was acclaimed by later artists and critics as the most talented *nastaʿlīq* writer of India. The latter calligrapher also worked under Jahangir (*reg* 1605–27); other masters of this time included MUHAMMAD SHARIF, ʿAbd al-Rahim Hirewi, ʿAbd al-Rahim ʿAmbarim-Qalam and ʿAbd al-Latif ʿAbbasi. To the period of Shah Jahan (*reg* 1628–58) belongs ʿAbd al-Rashid Dailami, nephew of the celebrated Mir ʿImad of Iran, whose name became a byword among later generations of Indian *nastaʿlīq* writers. Under Aurangzeb (*reg* 1658–1707) and his successors calligraphy continued to flourish through such master penmen as Hidayat Allah Zarrin-Qalam, Afdal al-Husayni, Hafiz Nur Allah, Sarb Sukh Rai, Sayyid Muhammad, Amir Panja Kash, Agha Mirza and Ghulam Muhammad Warith, author of the *Tadhkira-i khushnavīsān* ('Biography of calligraphers'; composed *c.* 1822–3, pubd Calcutta, 1910). To the first half of the 19th century belong Muhammad ʿAli and Muhammad Baqir. The last Mughal emperor, Bahadur Shah II (*reg* 1837–58), was himself a calligrapher.

During the 14th–17th centuries at provincial capitals such as Bidar, Ahmadnagar, Bijapur, Golconda and Hyderabad, the Bahmani dynasty and its successors commissioned exquisite specimens of calligraphy from Iranian and indigenous artists, most of them known only through their monumental work; they include the Bahmani Sultan Shihab al-Din Mahmud (*reg* 1482–1518) and Jalal al-Din Muhammad al-Fakhkhar Shirazi, some of whose album pages also survive (Istanbul, Topkapı Pal. Lib.; Tehran, Royal Lib., incl. a work entitled *Bahjatul-Mabāhij*). The royal libraries of Bijapur, Golconda and Hyderabad employed first-grade masters of calligraphy, such as ʿAbd al-Latif Mustafa, Khalil Allah and ʿAbd al-Halim (Bijapur) and Habib Allah Gilani, ʿArab Shirazi and Zain al-ʿAbidin (Golconda), whose album pages and manuscripts adorn various collections. Judging from the outstanding examples of monumental calligraphy, Gujarat, like Bengal, has a rich heritage of this art, although most work (including an outstanding example on the Jamiʿ Mosque (Friday Mosque), Ahmadabad) is unsigned. Few specimens survive on paper. Among the few penmen of note is ʿAbd al-Hayy. After the advent of the British, the rulers and the local élite of such princely states as Hyderabad, Lucknow and Rampur kept the art of calligraphy flourishing.

Among the most talented contemporary calligraphers was Maulana Khalil Tonki (*d* 1994) of Delhi. In the late 20th century the chief patrons of calligraphy were the Government of India, through its Bureau of Promotion of Urdu, and the state governments, through their Urdu academies and research institutes (as at Tonk, Rajasthan). Examples of calligraphy are preserved in many major museums, manuscript libraries and private collections, both in the subcontinent and abroad. The largest such collections are at the Salar Jung Museum, Hyderabad, and the National Museum, New Delhi.

See also ISLAMIC ART, §III, 2(v).

BIBLIOGRAPHY

M. A. Chughtai: *Pak wa Hind min islāmī khaṭṭāṭī* [Islamic calligraphy in Pakistan and Hindustan] (Lahore, 1976)
M. A. Ghafur: *The Calligraphers of Thatta* (Karachi, 1978)
A. Rahmani: *Barr-i ṣaghīr Pak wa Hind min khaṭṭāṭī* [Calligraphy in the Indo-Pak subcontinent] (Lahore, 1978)
P. I. S. M. Rahman: *Islamic Calligraphy in Medieval India* (Dhaka, 1979)
A. Schimmel: *Calligraphy and Islamic Culture* (New York, 1984)
India: Art and Culture, 1300–1900 (exh. cat. by S. C. Welch, New York, Met., 1985)
Monumental Islamic Calligraphy from India (exh. cat. by W. E. Begley, Houston, TX, Sewali Art Gallery; Cambridge, MA, Harvard U., Semit. Mus.; Columbus, OH, U. Gal. F.A.; and elsewhere; 1985–6)
Z. A. Desai: 'Islamic Calligraphy in India', *India* (Moscow and New Delhi, 1987), pp. 185–91

ZIYAUD-DIN DESAI

4. CARPETS. Woollen knotted-pile carpets have probably been manufactured in India for at least two millennia, but they have never been the subcontinent's predominant floor covering. Traditionally, the majority of the population has relied more on cotton floorspreads, cotton and woollen flatweaves, thick cushions, grass mats and even felts.

(i) Early sources. (ii) Mughal period. (iii) 18th century–early 20th.

(i) Early sources. The earliest written records of carpets in north India are contained in Buddhist texts such as the Pali *Bramajāl sutta* (probably compiled *c.* 3rd–5th century AD). Such texts mention curious carpet types such as *uddalomī* (Pali: 'rugs with "fur" on both sides'), *ekantalomī* ('rugs with "fur" on one side') and *kuttakaṃ* ('rugs large enough for 16 dancers') as well as *namatakaṃ* ('felt rugs'). The *Ārtha śāstra*, a Sanskrit text on statecraft perhaps written in the 3rd century BC, though it existed in oral form much earlier, and the preserved version is apparently of a later date, mentions *āstaraṇa* as a carpet type to be taxed at internal toll stations. Chinese records are another valuable source of information. The Han general Ban Yong, in a report to the emperor of *c.* AD 125, noted that India produced woollen carpets of good quality. The Chinese Buddhist monk Xuanzang on pilgrimage in India *c.* AD 629–45 referred to woollen garments and carpets as common gifts to novice monks in north India, and the monk Yijing (travelled 671–95) mentioned the widespread use of the *nisīdana* (Pali and Skt: a rectangular, stitched cloth mat with attached fringe) as a religiously sanctioned carpet for monks. Chinese records of the 8th century also state that 'gold-embroidered carpets' were among the products of Kashmir.

The Arab conquest of Sind in 712 and expanding Muslim control of north India encouraged Arab writers to compile accounts of the customs and economic products of India. These records are particularly valuable owing to their accuracy in commercial matters and use of common Arabic and Persian carpet terms. Maqdisi wrote in *c.* 985 of the *busuṭ* (Arab.: 'carpets') manufactured in Sind and favourably compared them to contemporary Iranian products from Kuhistan and Khorasan, and ʿAbd al-Latif mentioned *c.* 1203 the coloured palm-leaf mats exported from Maʿbar on India's south-eastern coast. The Venetian Marco Polo wrote of the embroidered, appliquéd leather mats of Gujarat *c.* 1298. An inscribed copper boundary document from the Hindu Deccani kingdom of Vijayanagara dated 1382 mentions *jambukhāna* (Skt form of Kanada *jāmkhānī*: 'cotton flatwoven carpets').

During the Sultanate period (*c.* 1200–1526), with the establishment of powerful Muslim kingdoms in north India and the Deccan, extensive royal demand for carpets is well documented. *Farrāshkhānas* (Pers.: 'carpet departments') were created within the general state *kārkhānas* (bureaux to control the manufacture and/or procurement of required goods). It is not known to what degree locally manufactured carpets satisfied requirements or to what extent the *farrāshkhānas* depended on imports. Under Tughluq sultans such as Firuz Shah (*reg* 1351–88) the carpet department was particularly massive and well funded. The Arab traveller Ibn Battuta reported *c.* 1320–51 that woollen carpets were imported into Sultanate India from Aksaray in Anatolia, while Gujarati merchants' lists of the 14th–15th centuries state that *kathīvū* (Indianized form of Arab. *al-qaṭīfa*: 'knotted-pile carpet' or 'thick velvet') were manufactured in the Gujarati town of Patan. The possibility of early Gujarati manufacture of knotted-pile carpets is reinforced by the Portuguese seaman Duarte Barbosa's statement of *c.* 1502–14 that thick *al-qaṭīfas* were made in the Gujarati port of Khambhat (Cambay). His preceding statement that velvets were also manufactured in Khambhat removes the possibility that Barbosa might have intended the term *al-qaṭīfa* to refer to velvets instead of carpets.

(ii) Mughal period. The textual evidence suggests that woollen knotted-pile carpets were produced in India before the reign of the third Mughal emperor, Akbar (*reg* 1556–1605), and not introduced by him, as is often assumed. The *Āyīn-i Akbarī*, Abu'l-Fazl's contemporary account of the court, states that during Akbar's reign 'wonderful varieties of *kilims*' (Pers.: 'flat-woven carpets', though in 16th-century India the term may also have been used for knotted-pile carpets) were produced in the royal workshops. This documents Akbar's patronage of carpet production but not his introduction of it. Weavers of knotted-pile carpets settled in Agra, Fatehpur Sikri, Lahore and other towns, but carpets were still imported into India from Iran.

Until the 19th century, Indian carpets were never dated or signed. Evidence from other dated media (such as miniature paintings) can sometimes be used to assign approximate dates. The most common carpet design appearing in Mughal miniature paintings of the Akbar period are blue-ground, red-bordered carpets dominated by symmetric vine scrolls and simple palmettes, in some cases with the ground and border colours reversed and with the addition of 'in-and-out' palmette borders. Such carpets correspond roughly to the most ubiquitous of all surviving classical carpet types, known variously as 'Herat', 'Indo-Isfahan' or 'Indo-Persian' carpets. Controversy often surrounds attempts to establish the provenance and date of such carpets, as they were woven both in Iran (possibly in Herat but also in Isfahan) and in India, and the design has been continuously produced since the end of the 16th century.

A small number of surviving woollen knotted-pile carpets have ground patterns resembling miniature paintings; these are known as 'picture-format' carpets. Unlike 16th-century Persian carpets, scenes of animal combats or groupings of mythical personages are not treated as isolated details of an unrelated ground pattern but are integrated into a visually coherent image encompassing the entire field. This concept was previously unknown in other carpet-weaving centres and must be considered to be an original Mughal contribution. Dating, however, still poses difficulties. The narrative style of domestic and mythological scenes portrayed on the Ames Carpet (Boston, MA, Mus. F.A., 93.1480) approximates miniature paintings of the late Akbar period (*c.* 1590s), but the carpet may be later. It is unknown how long it took for such designs to be transmitted from one medium to another or how long they remained popular. A second example (Vienna, Österreich. Mus. Angewandte Kst, 0292) with birds, trees and flowers is drawn in the style of the late Akbar period or early Jahangir period (*reg* 1605–28). A third example, the Widener Carpet (Washington, DC, N.G.A., C-328), combines elements of the painterly style with a more conventional format of animal combats and individual vignettes within floral scrolls. The borders of all three carpets contain monstrous faces within palmettes (imagery borrowed from carpets of Safavid Iran), while their fields display features that are considered characteristic of Indian carpets, including *ton-sur-ton* (unoutlined floral elements in light shades of one colour superimposed on darker shades of the same colour) and the display of sinuous, wisteria-like racemes. Other probable Akbari-period carpets include at least 16 fragments of a red-ground 'grotesque' animal carpet or carpets, possibly woven in Lahore for the wealthy Rajput rulers of Amer/Jaipur in the late 16th century or early 17th (e.g. Detroit, MI, Inst. A., 31.64, and Glasgow, Burrell Col., 9/1).

The best documented of all Mughal examples, the somewhat later Girdlers Carpet (*c.* 1631; London, Girdlers' Co.) and the Fremlin Carpet (*c.* 1640; London, V&A, IM 1-1936), borrow minor details from 'picture-format' carpets to create what are essentially standard 'Indo-Persian' carpets modified for the European market. Both were woven in Lahore as commissions for resident Europeans. The Girdlers Carpet superimposes five European heraldic motifs on a considerably narrowed red central ground. The borders are conventional in-and-out palmette meanders, and the field is decorated with standard scrolling vines, buds, blossoms, elaborate palmettes and wisteria-like racemes. *Ton-sur-ton* colouring is much in evidence. The Fremlin Carpet has European heraldic devices superimposed on both the in-and-out palmette borders and the field. The basic vine scroll and palmette pattern of the field is largely obscured by disjointed vignettes of animal combats amid blossoming trees. The simple drafting of the floral elements of these two carpets conforms to the earlier Akbar-period style and demonstrates the difficulty of assigning dates to Mughal carpets solely on the basis of comparable styles in other media.

Similar carpets without heraldic devices include the large Morgan Carpet (New York, Met., 17.190.858), in which the field is composed of symmetrically repeated animal combats under trees. It is better drawn and coloured than the Fremlin Carpet, and its finely composed border of interpenetrating stars and cartouches suggests the existence of workshop production capable of modifying both the level of quality and the design elements of a basic repertory. A fourth carpet, known as the Illchester (England, priv. col.; see 1983 exh. cat., no. 76), reflects the drafting and colour saturation of the Girdlers Carpet, while its blue ground exhibits even more skilfully drawn animals than the Fremlin Carpet. All four carpets were probably woven in Lahore between 1630 and 1650.

Carpets with floral elements within niches represent another original Mughal format, one that can be more precisely associated with stylistic developments within painting. Mughal artists began depicting flowers in a new manner in the 1620s as a result of encouragement from the emperor, Jahangir (see Skelton, 1972, and 1982 exh. cat., *The Indian Heritage*). The Mannerist naturalism of newly introduced European herbals was copied and then modified to produce sensitive studies of Kashmiri flora. This unique Mughal floral style was not pure naturalism; relative proportions were ignored, and elements of one genus were often combined with those of another. One result of this decorative innovation was a small number of Mughal carpets featuring a single, large flowering plant arising from a mound, enclosed within a cusped arch. Often known as 'prayer rugs' but more probably wall or tent hangings, these carpets range in quality from the relatively coarse construction of the McMullan Carpet to the superb silk foundation and fine goat-hair pile of the Altman fragment (both New York, Met., 1974.149.2 and 14.40.722). Production was gradually expanded to include carpets with several horizontal registers of large, alternating flowering plants or trees. The finest example is the Frick 'Tree' Carpet (New York, Frick). All of these examples were probably produced between the late 1620s and *c.* 1650.

By the middle of the 17th century the standard 'Indo-Persian' carpet was still popular and was produced in vast numbers, but more elaborate variations were also woven. In its most sophisticated form, the standard in-and-out palmette border was replaced by bands of elaborate strapwork, stars and cartouches or graceful double guilloches supporting twisting leaves, bracts and colourful rosettes. The spiralling vines of the ground were similarly enhanced by a detailed elaboration and increased variety of buds, blossoms, palmettes and racemes. This is best observed in the Gulbenkian fragment (Lisbon, Mus. Gulbenkian, T.72). Other carpets emphasized the centre of the field by producing single or multiple central medallions (e.g. Detroit, MI, Inst. A., 29.242, and Lisbon, Mus. Gulbenkian, T.62). As more complex borders and a greater variety of larger floral elements were added to carpets with animal combat motifs, the animals came to play a less important role (e.g. New York, Met., 17.190.857) and eventually disappeared.

The large, well-drafted flowers and trees of the earlier examples became more regimented during the second half of the 17th century. Unconventionally shaped and rectangular carpets woven in Lahore and purchased for use in the Rajput palace of Amer (Jaipur, Maharaja Sawai Man Singh II Mus.) bear acquisition labels ranging from 1664 to 1673. Graceful but static rows of small flowering plants cover their fields, and their borders usually consist of a single column of similar plants. The field of an exceptional pair of floral carpets purchased for the Jaipur palace in 1656 also displays those same flowers on a rich red ground, while its borders consist of more conventional leaf and blossom meanders (see fig. 328). Another common treatment of flowers in the carpets of this period is their enclosure within lattices. Single blossoms, groupings of two or more floral varieties or bouquets rising from vases were used to fill uniform diamond or ogival lattices formed by serrated lancet leaves or European strapwork (e.g. Paris, Mus. A. Déc., 4407; Los Angeles, CA, Co. Mus. A., M70.37; New York, Met., 14.40.723). Floral lattice carpets of the late Shah Jahan period are the most finely constructed of all classical knotted-pile carpets. They are characterized by striped, coloured silk warps, silk wefts and fine goat-hair pile. The knot density of one example (Washington, DC, Textile Mus., 63.00.22), 2070 knots per

328. Carpet, woollen knotted-pile over cotton foundation, 4.37×2.01 m, probably made in Lahore, Mughal period, *c.* 1650 (New York, Metropolitan Museum of Art)

square inch (3105 knots per square decimetre), is unequalled by any other contemporary carpet.

During the third quarter of the 17th century simple lattices were replaced by more complex arrangements of alternating shapes and sizes. Individual recognizable blossoms evolved into composite floral fantasies combining elements from different plants. The abandonment of robust draughtsmanship in favour of precise, small-scale detailing eventually produced the *millefleurs* carpets of the early 18th century to the early 19th. Every surface (borders and field) of these superbly constructed carpets was filled with tiny, repetitive floral patterns. When this aesthetic was applied to lattice carpets, the floral elements were miniaturized and the framework eventually eliminated (e.g. Oxford, Ashmolean). When the model was the single plant within a cusped arch, the result was the *millefleurs* 'prayer carpet' (e.g. Vienna, Österreich. Mus. Angewandte Kst, T.1539).

(iii) 18th century–early 20th. With the decline of Mughal political power during the 18th century, patronage was withdrawn from many carpet-weavers. Artisans of all crafts migrated to emerging provincial centres in Rajasthan, the Punjab, Avadh (Lucknow), Bengal (Murshidabad) and the Deccan (Hyderabad), where many 18th-century carpets were woven. While *millefleurs* and other small-pattern carpets appear in 18th-century miniature paintings, little else is known about Indian carpet-weaving during that century other than that earlier carpet types were copied and some bizarrely modified. In the first two decades of the 19th century bold 'tile pattern' carpets with fields of interlocked stars and crosses appear in miniature paintings. Similar carpets with unconventional blue cotton wefts are known and must represent an early 19th-century development.

Knotted-pile carpets had been woven at Eluru, Godovari District, in the Deccan since the 17th century, and the establishment in the early 18th century of the nizam's court at Hyderabad encouraged new production in old centres such as Warangal and Machhilipatanam (Masulipatam). Simply drawn silk pile lattice carpets in the north Indian style of the second half of the 17th century were probably woven in the Deccan or at Ayyampet in Thanjavur District during the 18th century and early 19th (e.g. Kuwait City, N. Mus., LNS 20R, and Lyon, Mus. Hist. Tissus, 31.090). A series of woollen knotted-pile *safs* (Arab.: 'multiple-niche prayer rugs') as well as a number of distinctive *dari* (Urdu and Hindi: 'cotton flatweave carpet') *safs* may also be attributed on the basis of colouring and construction to Deccani centres in the late 18th century or early 19th (e.g. Washington, DC, Textile Mus., R. 63.00.15, and Ahmadabad, Calico Mus. Textiles, 1388).

By the second half of the 19th century the knotted-pile carpet industry was virtually extinct in north India. *Daris* were still produced in vast numbers, and fine *millefleurs* carpets (e.g. London, V&A, 0744.15IS) were still being made in the Deccan for the Hyderabad court, but elsewhere the demand for traditional carpets was insufficient to support large-scale, high-quality weaving.

After the 1870s an entirely new knotted-pile carpet industry using modern materials and techniques was established by Europeans to produce inexpensive copies of Persian, Chinese, French and simplified Indian carpets for the European and North American markets. A small number of high-quality, knotted-pile carpets were produced in Indian prisons, where the most technically superior pictorial *daris* ever woven were made from *c.* 1900 to 1920. In the 20th century India became one of the world's largest exporters of woollen knotted-pile carpets and cotton flatweaves.

BIBLIOGRAPHY

EARLY SOURCES

Abu'l-Fazl: *Akbarnāma* (*c.* 1596–1602); Eng. trans. H. Beveridge, 3 vols (Calcutta, 1907–39/*R* Delhi, 1972–3)

——: *Āyīn-i Akbarī* [Annals of Akbar] (*c.* 1596–1602); Eng. trans. in 3 vols: i, Eng. trans. H. Blochmann, ed. S. L. Gloomer ([Calcutta], 1871/*R* Delhi, 1965); ii and iii, Eng. trans. H. S. Jarrett, ed. J. Sarkar (Calcutta, 1948–9/*R* Delhi, 1972–3)

D. Barbosa: *A Description of the Coasts of East Africa and Malabar in the Beginning of the Sixteenth Century*, ed. and trans. by H. Stanley (London, 1866), p. 65

H. Elliot: *The History of India as Told by its Own Historians (The Muhammedan Period)*, iii (London, 1867), p. 356

T. Rhys Davids and J. Carpenter, trans.: *The Digha Nikay*, i (Oxford, 1890), p. 7

I-Tsing: *Nan-hai-zhi-kuei-nai-fa-cha'uan* [Record of the inner law sent home from the southern sea]; Eng. trans. by J. Takakusu as *A Record of the Buddhist Religion as Practiced in India and the Malay Archipelago A.D. 671–695* (London, 1896/*R* Delhi, 1966), pp. 54–5, 110–12, 123

T. Rhys Davids, trans.: *Dialogues of the Buddha*, Sacred Books of the Buddhists, ii/1 (London, 1899), pp. 11–13

M. Stein: *Kalhaṇa's Rājataraṅgiṇī: A Chronicle of the Kings of Kashmir*, i/7 (London, 1900), p. 342, n. 955

T. Watters: *On Yuan Chwang's Travels in India*, i (London, 1904–5/*R* New Delhi, 1973), pp. 80, 295, 398

H. Yule, ed. and trans.: *The Book of Ser Marco Polo*, ii (London, 1926), pp. 393–4

M. Dames, ed.: *The Book of Duarte Barbosa*, i (London, 1928), p. 141

R. Shamasastry, trans.: *Kauṭilya's Arthaśāstra* (Mysore, 1929), pp. 81–2, 124

K. Shastri: *Foreign Notices of South India from Megasthenes to Ma Huan* (Madras, 1939), p. 11, 148

N. Sen: *Accounts of India and Kashmir in the Dynastic Histories of the Tang Period* (Santiniketan, 1968), p. 31

MONOGRAPHS

K. Chattopadhyay[a]: *Indian Carpets and Floor Coverings* (New Delhi, n.d.)

T. Hendley: *Asian Carpets: 16th and 17th Century Designs from the Jaipur Palaces* (London, 1905)

C. Latimer: *A Monograph on Carpet-making in the Punjab, 1905–6* (Lahore, 1907)

N. Mukerji: *A Monograph on Carpet Weaving in Bengal* (Calcutta, 1907)

K. Prasad: *Monograph on Carpet Making in the United Provinces* (Allahabad, 1907)

H. Twigg: *A Monograph on the Art and Practice of Carpet Making in the Bombay Presidency* (Bombay, 1907)

H. Harris: *A Monograph on the Carpet Industry of South India* (Madras, 1908)

F. Martin: *A History of Oriental Carpets before 1800* (Vienna, 1908)

W. Bode and E. Kühnel: *Vorderasiatische Knupfteppiche aus alterer Zeit* (Leipzig, 1913); Eng. trans. by C. Ellis (London, 1922, rev. 1958/*R* 1970)

A. Kendrick and C. Tattersall: *Hand-woven Carpets: Oriental and European* (London, 1922)

F. Sarre and H. Trenkwald: *Altorientalische Teppiche*, ii (Vienna, 1928); Eng. trans. by A. Kendrick (Vienna, 1929)

Kevorkian Foundation Collection of Oriental Carpets; Special Exhibition (exh. cat. by M. Dimand, New York, 1966)

K. Erdmann: *Siebenhundert Jahre Orientteppich: Zu seiner Geschichte und Erforschung* (Herford, 1966); Eng. trans. by M. Beattie and H. Herzog as *Seven Hundred Years of Oriental Carpets* (London, 1970)

M. Beattie: *Thyssen–Bornemisza Collection of Oriental Rugs at Villa Favorita, Castagnola* (Castagnola, 1972)

M. Dimand and J. Mailey: *Oriental Rugs in the Metropolitan Museum of Art* (New York, 1973), pp. 117–72

Carpets of Central Persia: With Special Reference to Rugs of Kirman (exh. cat., ed. M. H. Beatie; Sheffield, Mappin A.G.; Birmingham, Mus. & A.G.; 1976)
I. Bennet, ed.: *Rugs and Carpets of the World* (London, 1977), pp. 122–37
M. Eiland: *Chinese and Exotic Rugs* (Boston, 1979), pp. 128–87
C. Singh: *Textiles and Costumes from the Maharaja Sawai Man Singh II Museum* (Jaipur, 1979), p. 155
C. Singh and D. Ahivasi: *Woollen Textiles and Costumes from Bharat Kala Bhavan* (Varanasi, 1981), p. 2
The Indian Heritage: Court Life and Arts under Mughal Rule (exh. cat. by R. Skelton, R. Crill, V. Murphy and others, London, V&A, 1982), pp. 44, 73–6
The Unappreciated Dhurrie (exh. cat. by S. Cohen, London, David Black Orient. Carpets, 1982)
The Eastern Carpet in the Western World (exh. cat. by D. King and D. Sylvester, London, Hayward Gal., 1983)
E. Gans-Ruedin: *Indian Carpets* (London, 1984)
D. Black, ed.: *World Rugs and Carpets* (London, 1985), pp. 79–85, 194–201
S. Cohen: *The Development of Indian Floorcoverings and their Appearance in Miniature Paintings* (diss., U. London, 1986)
N. Kajitani and K. Yoshida: *Gion matsurī yama hoko kensōhin chōsa hōkokusho* [Survey report on textiles used to decorate floats in the Gion Festival] (Kyoto, 1992) [on 18th-century Ind. carpets; Jap., with Eng. contribution by D. Walker]

ARTICLES

A. F. Kendrick: 'Pile Carpet Belonging to the Worshipful Company of Girdlers', *A. Workers' Q.*, iii (1904), pp. 97–9
F. Andrews: 'Indian Carpets and Rugs', *J. Ind. A. & Indust.*, xi/89–94 (1905–6), pp. 5–10
A. Juvet-Michel: 'The Great Centres of Production of Ancient Oriental Carpets', *Ciba Z.*, xv (1938), pp. 506–10
K. Erdmann: 'The Art of Carpet Making', *A. Islam.*, viii (1941), pp. 121–91
R. Sergeant: 'Material for a History of Islamic Textiles up to the Mongol Conquest', *A. Islam.*, xi–xii (1946), pp. 57, 118–19
K. Erdmann: 'Der indische Knupfteppich', *Indol.-Tagung* (1959), pp. 104–14
M. Chandra: 'Costumes and Textiles of the Sultanate Period', *J. Ind. Textile Hist.*, vi (1961)
'Carpets of India', *Marg*, xviii/4 (1965) [whole issue]
R. Skelton: 'A Decorative Motif in Mughal Art', *Aspects of Indian Art*, ed. P. Pal (Leiden, 1972), pp. 147–52
——: 'Persian Carpet Design in Relation to Miniature Paintings and Manuscript Decoration', *Carpets of Central Persia, with Special Reference to Rugs of Kirman. Proceedings of the Colloquium Held in Conjunction with the Exhibition: Sheffield, 1978*, pp. 33–6
D. Walker: 'Classical Indian Rugs', *Hali*, iv (1982), pp. 255–7
S. Cohen: 'Textiles', *Islamic Heritage of the Deccan*, ed. G. Michell (Bombay, 1986), pp. 118–28
——: 'Indian and Kashmiri Carpets: Their Perceived History', *Orient. Carpet & Textile Stud.*, iii/1 (1987), pp. 119–26

STEVEN COHEN

5. CERAMICS. The emphasis of 20th-century archaeology on prehistoric sites and, in the few historical excavations, on architectural and sculptural remains has meant that relatively little attention has been given to ceramics after the Maurya period (3rd century BC). Although most of the later sherds recovered are generally slipped in buff, red or reduction black, each type has its own identity, much as the potters of each region of the Indian subcontinent continue to produce vessels with distinctive shapes and decorative styles.

(i) Pottery. The shapes, styles and production techniques used to manufacture earthenware vessels in the Indian subcontinent in the 20th century represent an inheritance of 5000 years of craftsmanship. Many of these vessels are virtually interchangeable with those found in excavations of prehistoric and historic sites, as are the potters' wheels, anvils, mallets and decorating tools used in their production. In many cases, the documentation of the work of 20th-century traditional potters and the uses of their products aids in the construction of hypotheses about the manufacture and function of ancient earthenware. Many different forms of potters' wheels—heavy or light, fast or slow, stick-propelled or hand-turned—are used; flat dishes and shallow bowls may be finished while still on the wheel, but most pots are cut from it while incomplete and beaten into their final forms (usually round-bottomed), using mallets and stone anvils. Working on the wheel is exclusively a man's prerogative, while women generally decorate the vessels, painting them either before or after firing using closely guarded techniques. Firing is generally conducted in temporary field kilns, although permanent kilns are also employed in many parts of the subcontinent. As the porous terracotta is easily contaminated, earthenware is regularly broken and replaced by Hindu families at seasonal junctures, festivals and other times of transition, providing a continuous demand for pottery and causing community refuse sites to be filled with broken pottery, even as they were in earlier times.

Excavations of Chalcolithic sites in the Quetta Valley in Baluchistan have yielded some bichrome and polychrome pottery (dated *c.* 3000–*c.* 2300 BC), but the large majority comprises buff-slipped bowls and dishes painted with brown geometric, vegetal and zoomorphic designs that suggest strong links with southern Turkmenistan. Many of the innumerable sherds from wheel-thrown pottery dating from *c.* 2300 to *c.* 1750 BC found at Harappa and contemporaneous sites in north-western India closely correspond in substance and technique to those found in Mesopotamia. Although some polychromatic slips have been discovered, most Harappan earthenware has a red base slip intricately painted in black with crowded motifs including geometric bands, fishscales, intersecting circles and foliate and animal forms; the results are similar to some 20th-century vessels from Gujarat, Sind and Rajasthan. After the end of the Harappan culture, Black-and-Red Ware was widely produced, and sherds have been found throughout northern India. Similar wares are still made and constitute the most common Indian pottery. Much of this ware had red exterior walls (sometimes painted with black or brown designs) with solid black interiors. This effect was achieved by using the same overall base slip, which turned black on the interior when it was sealed during firing, a form of partial reduction firing still practised in western Uttar Pradesh in the late 20th century. More exceptional are the types now commonly called Painted Grey Ware and Northern Black Polished Ware. The former, popular across north India from *c.* 1000 to *c.* 300 BC, had a plain grey, overall slip decorated with simple geometric black and brown designs. Northern Black Polished Ware and other closely related wares were produced between *c.* 600 and *c.* 100 BC over a wide area, the main centres being in the Gangetic Plain. The ware is recognizable by its black or bluish lustre achieved by the use of high-fired, highly burnished ferrous oxide slips (see fig. 329). A 20th-century counterpart is hand-formed by women in Manipur.

South Indian megalithic burial sites from the early first millennium BC have produced large (5×5×2 m) buff or

329. Pottery reliquary, Northern Black Polished Ware, h. 110 mm, w. 195 mm, *c*. 3rd century BC (London, British Museum)

red-slipped terracotta sarcophagi alongside quantities of Black-and-Red Ware and Plain Red Ware. The sarcophagi, some with multi-legged bases, were constructed using a combination of wheel and coil-and-slab techniques (a method similar to that used to build large storage jars); some were minimally decorated with geometric designs along the rim. Some, such as the famous ram sarcophagus excavated at Sankhavaram in Andhra Pradesh, had sculpted lids, while smaller burial jars from the Nilgiri Hills were decorated with modelled images of bulls, deer and humans.

Glazed pottery was not popular in pre-Islamic India. From the 12th century AD, west Asian craftsmen were imported to set up workshops in north India catering to the demands of aristocratic Muslims and associated Hindu courts. These centres produced glazed tiles and vessels, most often in pale blue accented with dark blue designs; similar wares are still made in Jaipur and Delhi.

BIBLIOGRAPHY

R. Nath: *Colour Decoration in Mughal Architecture* (Bombay, 1970)
O. Manchanda: *A Study of Harappan Pottery* (Delhi, 1972)
N. Hammond, ed.: *South Asian Archaeology* (London, 1973)
B. Saraswati: *Pottery-making Cultures and Indian Civilization* (New Delhi, 1979)
K. S. Ramachandra: *Archaeology of South India: Tamil Nadu* (Delhi, 1980)
O. P. Jaggi: *Technology in Ancient India*, i (Delhi, 1981)
V. V. K. Sastry: *The Proto and Early Historical Cultures of Andhra Pradesh* (Hyderabad, 1983)
S. L. Huntington: *The Art of Ancient India* (New York, 1985)
S. P. Huyler: *Gifts of Earth: Traditional Terracottas and Clay Sculptures in Contemporary India* (Ahmadabad, 1992)

STEPHEN P. HUYLER

(ii) Tiles. The extensive use and production of glazed tiles in the Indian subcontinent evolved only with the advent of Muslim rule. Earlier evidence for glazed tiles is sparse. For example, although the Chinese pilgrim Xuanzang (in India AD 629–45) records a tile roof of brilliant colours at the monastery of Nalanda, this may have been of glass and pottery fragments set in mortar, a practice preserved in 20th-century Buddhist monuments of South-east Asia. Distinct centres of tilework appeared only in the 13th century, notably in regions with an established brick building tradition. The most important locations were the Punjab, Sind, Malwa, Bengal and the Deccan. The earliest centre of tilework was in and around Multan, where tile decoration was applied to tombs. One of the earliest and most elaborate examples is the tomb of the saint Rukn al-Din ʿAlam (*c*. 1325). The tilework, in turquoise, blue and white, is arranged in bands around the tapering turrets of the building and alternates with unglazed brickwork. The style is strongly reminiscent of Seljuk-period decoration in Iran. Specific to Multan are monochrome relief tiles and relief tile mosaic. The favoured patterns were interlocking squares, hexagons and a honeycomb design. This early style of tilework persisted at Multan and the nearby town of Uchh into the Mughal period (1526–1858).

During the 15th and 16th centuries, tile decoration became increasingly popular throughout the subcontinent. In the Sultanate capital of Delhi, the earliest examples are isolated specimens in turquoise, blue and yellow on tombs of the Lodi dynasty. Best preserved is the tomb of Maulana Jamali (begun *c*. 1528), where the tiles are combined with cut plaster. In addition to geometric designs set in round medallions, winding tiled scrollwork decorates the window frames. Tiles were also used in Mandu and other cities of the Malwa sultans. In Gwalior, the Man Mandir Palace, built by the local Tomar Rajputs in the late 15th century to early 16th, represents one of the most exceptional displays of tilework in India. Small pieces of tile are set in the carved stone decorations of the interior, while the exterior is covered with large-scale tile scenes of whisk-bearers, plantain trees, birds, elephants, tigers and cheetahs executed in faience mosaic set into slabs of sandstone (see fig. 330). Their figural style and colouring conform to the *Caurapañcāśikā* group of manuscripts (*see* §VI, 3(ii)(e) above). The Gujari Mahal, also in Gwalior, carries a remarkable Persian and Arabic inscription in blue tile mentioning Raja Man Singh (*reg* 1486–1516). In the Deccan, tilework was used on monuments of the Bahmani kingdom. At Bidar, elaborate floral designs embellish the audience hall of the fort, and the Islamic college of Mahmud Gawan (founded 1472) represents a clear transplant of the Timurid-style mosaic faience of Iran. Bengal had a distinct tilework tradition characterized by moulded plaques. Typically incorporated into the façades of buildings, these plaques carry vigorous floral motifs and geometric patterns: a good example is the Darasbari Mosque at Gaur (*c*. 1479). In later periods, especially the 17th and 18th centuries, Bengali temples were often covered with terracotta plaques of religious images and daily life scenes (*see* §18(e) below).

Tilework of the Mughal period survives at Lahore and to a lesser extent at Agra, Delhi and a number of caravanserais linking these cities (see Begley). Its style conforms to that introduced by the Mughals in various other decorative media: flowering plants, formally arranged on a plain ground in a medallion or square arched panel, are the most common devices. These could be fixed to the whole façade of a building, as in the tomb known as Chini ka Rauza in Agra (*c*. 1639), or they could make up the dado, as in the tomb of Jahangir at Lahore (*c*. 1627–37). Spandrels were often filled with tile arabesques and scrollwork in a manner recalling Timurid and Safavid decoration. Elaborate examples are found on the mosque of Wazir Khan (1634–5), Lahore, which also has prominent glazed inscriptions. The panels on the Hathi Pol gateway at Lahore Fort are notable for the great variety of coloured tiles used, while the north wall of the fort, finished in 1631–2, is exceptional for its depictions of court officials, fighting animals, caravans and angels. Most Mughal tilework comprises mosaics of small tesserae cut according to the design. Colours include blue, turquoise, white, purple, green, orange and yellow. In addition, there are polychrome glazed tiles directly inspired by the *haft rang* ('seven-coloured tiles') of Safavid Iran, which were employed on the tomb of Asaf Khan at Lahore (*c.* 1637) and on that of Madin Sahib in Kashmir. Tiles from these tombs are in the Victoria and Albert Museum, London; other examples from Lahore are in the Field Museum of Natural History, Chicago. The quality of Mughal tilework declined in the 18th century.

The imperial fashion was not followed throughout the Mughal empire. In Thatta during the 16th and 17th centuries a distinct tradition of blue, turquoise and white tile mosaic was favoured in addition to underglaze-painted tiles. In the 18th and 19th centuries, tilework appeared on a large scale in Sind, where Hala became a centre for glazed tile production, specifically slip-painted tiles usually covered with brownish or greenish glazes. Blue-and-white underglaze tiles were also produced at Hala and Multan.

See also §III, 6(ii)(a), (e) and (f) above.

BIBLIOGRAPHY

E. W. Smith: *Moghul Colour Decoration of Agra* (Allahabad, 1901)
W. Furnival: *Leadless Decorative Tiles, Faience and Mosaic* (London, 1904)
J. P. Vogel: *Tile Mosaic of the Lahore Fort* (Calcutta, 1920)
R. Nath: *Colour Decoration of the Mughal Architecture* (Bombay, 1970)
H. N. Dvivedi: 'Gujarīmahal ke dvāra par arabī-phārsī lekha' [Arabic-Persian inscription of the door of the Gujari Mahal], *Gvāliyar Darśan*, ed. H. N. Dvivedi (Gwalior, 1980), pp. 363–5
W. Begley: 'Four Mughal Caravanserais Built in the Reigns of Jahangir and Shah Jahan', *Muqarnas*, i (1983), pp. 167–79
A. Khan: *Multan, History and Architecture* (Islamabad, 1983)

JULIA GONNELLA

330. Tilework cheetah, Man Mandir Palace, Gwalior, late 15th century–early 16th

6. COINS. The concept of coinage apparently came to ancient India from the Greek world via the Achaemenid empire of Iran. Indian coinage, however, developed within a local tradition with characteristics of its own that distinguished it from coinage originating in the Greek world. This indigenous tradition has survived into the 20th century despite repeated waves of foreign influence.

(i) 4th century BC*–3rd century* AD. Although the precise date and process of the introduction of coinage in India is debated, it is certain that by the mid-4th century BC silver coins with locally created designs were already in use in the north-west of the subcontinent. Now known as punch-marked coins, they were made from small, rectangular or oval slabs of metal stamped on one face with one or more non-pictorial emblematic designs. From the north-west the production of punch-marked silver coins spread into the heartland of India; by the end of the 4th century BC it flourished in the Gangetic plain. In the same region copper coinages were initially made in the same way, but casting was soon introduced. Also rectangular, the cast coins had designs similar to those on punched coins moulded on both sides during the casting process.

After an initial phase in which punch-marked coins were generally stamped with four circular non-pictorial designs, some stamps featuring symbolic representations of animals (mostly elephants and bulls), plants and other natural objects, such as the sun, rivers and mountains, also began to appear. The introduction of these emblems, which also appear on cast copper coins, was followed by an increase in the number of stamps to five. Five-stamped punch-marked coins, issued widely and found throughout the subcontinent and Afghanistan, are thought to have been issues of the Mauryan empire (*c.* 321–*c.* 185 BC; see fig. 331a). Although the function of the stamps is little understood beyond the recognition that they served to identify the pieces of metal bearing them as coins, the repertory of designs is closely related both to marks found on Maurya-period artefacts (e.g. pottery stamps and metalwork) and to emblems used in petroglyphs in north India. The use of such emblems is a recurring theme in Indian coin design, particularly in south India.

By the 1st century BC Indian coins struck with a single design on each side were being produced. This transformation in the technology of coin-making in India seems

331. Indian coins, actual size: (a) punch-marked silver *karshapana*, Maurya period, 3rd century BC; (b) silver tetradrachm of the Greek king Menander, with Kharosthi inscription, north-west India, *c.* 150 BC; (c) gold double stater of the Kushana king Vima Kadphises, with Greek inscription, north-west India, *c.* AD 90; (d) gold *dinara* of the Gupta king Samudragupta, showing him playing a stringed instrument, north India, *c.* AD 370; (e) silver *tanka* of Ghiyath al-Din Tughluq, Sultan of Delhi, 1320–25; (f) gold *mohur* of the Mughal emperor Jahangir, Lahore, 1607 (London, British Museum)

to reflect the influence of the Greek kingdoms established in the north-west during the 2nd century BC (331b). The influence of these Greek kingdoms also probably accounts for the use of divine images in Indian coin design. Small aniconic representations of deities had already appeared in a few rare instances in the last phase of the punch-marked silver coinage; the earliest examples on two-sided coins were of the same type, but during the 1st century BC representational imagery was also employed, particularly on coins from the city of Ujjain. During the 1st century BC it also became usual for Indian coins to have an inscription, although Brahmi inscriptions had already occasionally appeared on punch-marked and cast copper coins of the 2nd century BC. As inscriptions became more popular, the Greek practice of placing them in a circle around the edge of the main design was adopted.

During the 1st century AD Indian coinage underwent a further transformation under the Kushana dynasty of the 1st–3rd centuries AD (331c). The Kushanas adopted a Hellenized style of coinage from their Scythian and Iranian neighbours, who had inherited the Indo-Greek kingdoms of the north-west, and their coin design may also have been influenced by the Roman coins imported into India during the 1st and 2nd centuries. The predominant designs used by the Kushanas were royal portraits on the front of the coins, either half, or more commonly full length, and divine images on the back. Both obverse and reverse designs were normally accompanied by identifying inscriptions. Representations include the Hindu deity Shiva, called Oesho by the Kushanas, and the Buddha, who is represented in a style similar to that of contemporary north-west Indian sculptures. A contemporary series of silver coins mixed Greek royal portrait designs with local emblematic motifs. During the 1st century AD the Scythian satraps of western India initiated a coinage based on surviving Greek coins from the north-west and on imported Roman coins. After the first few issues the Greek inscriptions around the royal portrait became unintelligible, but the same design was retained over the next three centuries.

From the time of the Kushanas south Indian coinage maintained a relative degree of isolation from other coinage. Under the influence of the Scythian rulers of western India, however, during the 1st and 2nd centuries AD silver portrait coins were issued by the Satavahana kings of the south (late 1st century BC–early 3rd century AD). Most of their coins, however, followed the traditional pattern, with emblematic symbols as the predominant design, often combined with a surrounding Brahmi inscription: stylized representations of lions, elephants, bulls and horses are the commonest emblematic designs. The successors of the Satavahanas in the south maintained the same traditions of coin design until the 10th century AD, when a revival of punch-marked coins took place. These multi-stamped uniface coins were made of gold and have from three to eleven stamps. The designs on the punches were either symbolic emblems, like those used on earlier coins, or inscriptions.

(ii) 4th–12th centuries. As Kushana power waned in north India, local issues of coins following Kushana prototypes were produced. The most notable of these are the issues of the Gupta king Samudragupta (*reg c.* 335–76) and his successors, which represent a high point in Indian coin design (331d). The Kushana formula of royal portrait and divine image was exploited by artists aware of contemporary trends in sculptural and pictorial art to produce splendid representations of the king and images of such Hindu deities as Lakshmi, Ganga and Kartikkeya.

At the same time, a fresh wave of Western influence penetrated the north-west as Iranian and then Hun invaders took over the former Kushana territories. The Iranian invaders introduced Sasanian coin designs into the north-west during the 3rd and 4th centuries, and during the 5th and 6th centuries the same designs were carried further into India by the Huns. These designs, ultimately of Greek origin and inherited by the Sasanians from their Parthian predecessors in Iran, used a royal portrait as the main design on the front and a religious design representing the sacred fire-altar of the Zoroastrian religion on the back. Within India the Huns combined Sasanian designs with local emblems and with Kushana and Gupta designs, but the distinctive portrait design remained important; in western India it survived into the medieval period. From about the 9th century until the Muslim conquest of north India (1192) mixed designs predominated. In the north-west, Turkish rulers issued coins with a horseman and bull design loosely based on Hun versions of Kushana and Gupta designs. In western and central India, stylized versions of Hun copies of Sasanian silver coins, some with an image of boar-headed Vishnu replacing the royal bust, were in use alongside modified versions of Gupta gold coins with a three-line Nagari inscription in place of the royal portrait.

(iii) 13th–18th centuries. Initially the Ghurid conqueror Muhammad ibn Sam (*reg* 1174–1203) issued his own versions of local Indian coins, but soon coins using designs from Afghanistan were issued for use in India. As the new coins were without pictorial designs (in keeping with the aniconic Islamic tradition), inscriptions formed their main design element. With only a few exceptions coins were decorated with boldly written and symmetrically arranged inscriptions in a cursive form of Arabic script. On many coins the central part of the inscription was contained within an ornamental frame, which was often a square reminiscent of earlier Indian coins.

The coin designs of the Delhi Sultanate (*c.* 1200–1526; (331e)) were continued by smaller sultanates. In Bengal and Jaunpur during the 14th–15th century, remarkable calligraphic designs combined the sultan's name and titles into a united frame with tall, vertical fencelike strokes. The 15th-century Malwa sultans adapted the use of the square frame design by producing square coins. In south India, however, earlier traditions were consolidated during the 14th century in the coinage of Vijayanagara, which featured emblematic religious designs and inscriptions.

Afghan designs were reintroduced to India by the Mughal dynasty (1526–1858). Decoratively written and arranged cursive inscriptions within ornamental frames remained the main features, although the language changed from Arabic to Persian (331f). However, the Mughal emperors Akbar (*reg* 1556–1605) and Jahangir (*reg* 1605–27) departed from strict Islamic tradition by issuing special gold coins with pictorial designs, including royal portraits and signs of the zodiac. In the 18th century the power of the Mughal empire disintegrated as local princes and European invaders began to establish control over large parts of India. The Mughal emperors, however, continued to issue their own coins, while both local rulers and the Europeans issued copies of Mughal coinage distinguished by their mint names and by the use of small emblematic designs.

(iv) 19th–20th centuries. During the 19th century the coin designs of the local princes and the European colonists gradually moved away from those of the Mughals. Emblematic designs replaced the main inscriptional design on some local coins, which were often inscribed in an Indian script rather than Arabic or Persian; European symbols were used on the European coins. From 1835 the British monarch's head appeared on the coins of British-ruled territories, and as British control was extended; Western-style coins gradually replaced local issues. The coins of the local princes continued to be used in some regions until 1947. A new national coinage replacing the British issues appeared in 1950. The design of the Republic of India's first coins, Western in style, illustrates well the continuity of the Indian coinage tradition. The emblems used (including the lion, bull and horse inspired by Maurya-period sculptures) and the square shape of the half-anna and two-anna denominations refer back to the early phase of coinage in India.

BIBLIOGRAPHY

J. Allen: *British Museum Catalogue of the Coins of Ancient India* (London, 1936)

J. M. Rosenfield: *The Dynastic Art of the Kushans* (Berkeley, 1967)

P. L. Gupta: *Coins* (New Delhi, 1969, rev. 2/1979)

C. Bruce and others: *The Standard Guide to South Asian Coins and Paper Money since 1556 AD* (Iola, 1981)

JOE CRIBB

7. Dress. As few complete examples of Indian dress survive from before the 18th century, the main sources for the study of costume are the descriptions found in various texts and representations in sculpture and painting. Sculpture is the key source before the 17th century; painting begins to play a particularly important role from the 16th and 17th centuries, when the Mughals (and eventually the British) encouraged a more 'naturalistic' approach to representation. Terracotta figures, known from all periods of Indian art, and the finest coins of the Kushana, Gupta and later monarchs also document prevalent costume types. Any study of Indian dress must take into consideration the warm climatic conditions of the subcontinent and the fact that artists could show the dress lighter than it actually was to reveal the body.

See also §VII above.

(i) To the 17th century. (ii) 18th century and after.

(i) To the 17th century. The main sources for the study of early Indian dress are textual descriptions and visual representations of the anthropomorphic Indian gods, some of whom wear special types of costume. Stone and terracotta figures from the Indus Valley civilization (*c.* 2550–*c.* 2000 BC) show dress types, and in the Vedas (*c.* 1500–*c.* 1200 BC) the term *suvasana* is applied to a well-dressed person. Excavations have revealed that in the Indus Valley civilization both men and women wore a strip of cotton or woollen cloth wound around the waist; shawls, sometimes patterned, and wraps were also popular. Deities were represented wearing fan-shaped headgear (*see* §IV, 2 above). From the Vedic literature, both sewn (Skt *vāsana*) and unsewn (*vāsas*) garments were worn. Male dress comprised an overgarment (*drāpi* or *atka*) worn with a wrap (*paryāṇahana*) and a waistcloth. Women wore a breast-band (*pratidhi*), a skirt (*nīvī*) and a belt (*rasanā*). The late Vedic and Buddhist literature is rich in references to such sewing implements as needles, thimbles and scissors, suggesting the increased adoption of sewn garments; such details as undergarments, wraps and headgear also indicate the wearing of more elaborate dress. *Yakṣa* figures (male nature deities) of this period or a little later wear a shawl thrown over the left shoulder and a waistband ending in a big knot; *yakṣīs* (female nature deities) wear a veil thrown over the head. The sash (*paṭṭikā*) was also popular. Evidence for dress in the Maurya and Shunga periods (*c.* 4th–1st century BC) includes the *Artha śāstra*

of Kautilya (*see* §I, 10 above), which mentions baggy pants known as *samputikā* or *sūthana*; Megasthenes, the Indo-Greek ambassador to the Mauryan court, refers in his *Indica* to flowered muslin and gold-embroidered dress.

Stone sculpture began to be produced in quantity in the 2nd century BC, providing a vivid impression of Indian costume and jewellery. Garments for women were thin, with a narrow cloth wrapped around the waist and a broad sash hanging down in front. Sewn garments are most commonly represented on figures of foreigners, for example an Iranian guard or an Indo-Greek devotee. Both men and women wore elaborate turbans, which in the Andhra region had a ball-like front. Stone images of Kushana emperors from Mat, near Mathura, show the Central Asian dress styles they favoured in the 1st–3rd century AD. A headless figure of Kanishka wears an overgarment, trousers and heavy boots (see fig. 155 above); another wears a long, tightly fitted coat secured by a belt. A separate stone head (possibly representing a Kushana chief) has the characteristic conical cap. These were the established conventions used to represent people from the north-west as well as Surya, the sun god. Surya is invariably represented wearing a tailored coat with pointed tails, a type introduced by the Kushana emperors, who are represented on coins of this period dressed in such coats worn with tight trousers and a peaked cap or turban. This long-tailed coat is common in Gupta-period sculpture, in which women also wear similar tunics with a pointed hem. In the wall paintings at Ajanta these costume types appear with the addition of numerous details. Carved stone panels such as those found at Deogarh, Uttar Pradesh, provide evidence of the broad-hemmed skirt, loose blouse and scarf worn by peasant women. Although most of society went bareheaded, cowherds, elephant drivers and those in allied occupations wore long caps, and traders may have worn turbans. Some Jaina texts provide further insight into the clothing of the Gupta and post-Gupta period. It included stitched (*bahuparikarma*) or unstitched (*yathakṛtam*) garments, everyday costumes (*nityanivāsana*) and formal dress (*kṣaṇotsavikam*). Clothing was washed, starched, pressed and perfumed. Another custom is described by the 11th-century Chalukya emperor Someshvara, who lays down in his work *Mānasollāsa* ('The splendour of thought') that kings should change their way of dress according to the season.

Manuscript illustrations of the 12th–16th century usually depict standardized costume types; in general these represent a continuation of older traditions, although a variety of textile designs appear in women's dress. In 15th-century manuscripts in the western Indian style, the princes (known as 'Sahi figures') of the *Kālakācāryakathā* story are shown in double-breasted coats with heavy floral patterns, evidently the Persian or Indo-Persian dress of the period. They also wear pointed crowns and tight trousers. Some manuscripts also show women wearing long Persian tunics. In the *Ni'matnāma* (London, BL, Orient. & India Office Lib.), some of the women attendants are shown dressed in a long coat of plain white and a turban with a small central protrusion (*kulah*); in contrast, the Indian women in the manuscript are dressed in a short bodice (*cholī*) and skirt (*ghāghrā*) with a starched transparent scarf (*oṛhnī*), a dress type that continued for several centuries (see fig. 332).

Paintings of the 16th century provide fuller documentation of north Indian costume. Abu'l-Fazl, the Mughal court chronicler, remarks in his *Āyīn-i Akbarī* ('Annals of Akbar') that the emperor Akbar (*reg* 1556–1605) adopted Rajput dress. Its appearance is known from pre-Mughal paintings in the *Caurapañcāśikā* style (*see* §VI, 3(ii)(e) above). The costume types in these manuscripts are standardized; women's dress has bold checked patterns, and the ends of the scarf (*dupaṭṭā*) are edged with large pompoms. Men wear a transparent tunic with pointed ends (*chākdār jāmā*), tight *pājāmā* pants and a turban with a central protrusion; Akbar later changed the turban to the flat *aṭapaṭī* Rajput type and the tunic to the round-skirted type worn with minor variations in both the Rajput and Mughal courts over the succeeding centuries. The tunic was tied with a long, knotted sash, which was shortened around the middle of the 17th century; Abu'l-Fazl notes that the distinction between Hindus and Muslims lay in which side the lapel was tied. Women at court wore the traditional scarf and skirt, but later changed to the *sāṛī*, a one-piece, unsewn garment. Both male and female costumes were embellished with geometric or floral designs, which are helpful in dating them. Persian dress

332. Indian dress of the 16th century, detail from a manuscript of the *Ni'matnāma*, *c*. 1500 (London, British Library, Oriental and India Office Library)

was occasionally worn, and some princesses and female courtiers wore the Muslim style of dress, comprising a tunic with a long skirt (*pishvāz*) and tight pantaloons; in rare instances they also wore the Persian cap. Upper-class Deccani men wore a heavy tunic with a more elaborate sash than their Mughal counterparts. It appears that Humayun (*reg* 1530–40, 1555–6) used to dress according to the colour of the planet of the day, and Abdur Qadir Badaoni records in his *Muntakhab al-tawārīkh* ('Selection of histories') that Akbar also followed this tradition at certain times. Both Akbar and Jahangir (*reg* 1605–27) occasionally wore Portuguese dress, and in rare instances Indian court ladies are shown dressed in European fashion. In his memoirs, Jahangir refers to a sleeveless overgarment of Persian derivation, originally called *kurdī*; he redesignated it *nādirī* and made it a favoured present to a noble. From the mid-17th century it became fashionable for men to wear a transparent white tunic over a coloured undergarment (*nīm astīn*) on the chest to create an especially colourful effect. Also from the mid-17th century, Rajasthani and Pahari paintings document the subtle variation of Indian costume from region to region and from people to people.

BIBLIOGRAPHY

Abu'l-Fazl: *Āyīn-i Akbarī* [Annals of Akbar] (*c*. 1596–1602); Eng. trans. in 3 vols: i, trans. H. Blochmann, ed. S. L. Gloomer ([Calcutta], 1871/*R* Delhi, 1965)
W. Foster: *Early Travels in India* (London, 1921)
M. Chandra: *Prāchīn Bhāratīya Veśa Bhūsā* (Prayag, 1950)
A. H. Sharar: *Gujishtā Lucknow* (New Delhi, 1971)
Abdur Qadir Badaoni: *Muntakhab al-tawārīkh* [Selection of histories], Eng. trans. W. H. Lowe (Delhi, 1973)
M. Chandra: *Costumes, Textiles, Cosmetics and Coiffure in Ancient and Mediaeval India* (New Delhi, 1973)
S. Saccidananda: *Indian Costume, Coiffure and Ornament* (New Delhi, 1975)
I. P. Pandey: *Dress and Ornaments in Ancient India* (Delhi, 1988)
M. Verma: *Dress and Ornaments in Ancient India: The Maurya and Sunga Periods* (Delhi, 1989)

KALYAN KRISHNA

333. Man's robe, painted and dyed cotton, h. 1.05 m, from Burhanpur, 18th century (London, Victoria and Albert Museum)

(ii) 18th century and after. Historically, Indian dress was regional in character and only secondarily revealed the wearer's social standing and community. Regional homogeneity of dress applied across the entire social spectrum from nomadic and tribal peoples through rural and urban populations to the royal court; despite its refinement of line and exaggerated features, royal dress never really lost touch with its regional roots. The nature of raw materials constituted the key difference between each segment of the social spectrum, as all garments maintained a shared design vocabulary. Thus the coarsest cottons and wools were used in tribal and mountain areas; finer cottons (see fig. 333), some silk and limited use of gold and silver were worn in rural and urban contexts, and the finest wools and muslins, gossamer silks and ornate brocades were favoured at court (*see* §VII above). Certain types of garment, including the pre-tied turban and numerous overgarments, originated at court, along with the use of footwear, which was previously unknown in large areas of the subcontinent. For the mass of the population, normal dress comprised a one- or two-piece unsewn garment; under Islamic influence, the two-piece sewn garment became accepted, especially in the north and west, by the 18th century.

The modern era in Indian dress has been a period of change that started in the late 18th century, accelerated in the 19th century and continued at a fast pace into the late 20th century. It was initially brought on by exposure to colonial influence and the sudden availability of such European goods as sewing accessories, buttons, hooks and sewing machines. There were significant changes over these 200 years in both men's and women's apparel. Male attire began the process of change with a mild adaptation of traditional dress and then embarked on a phase imitative of European styles, while women updated their traditional forms of dress more gradually, maintaining a greater sense of continuity while moving out of the home and into public life. This process of change was uneven in proportion to the degree of colonial exposure received by an area or social class.

A brief geographical overview of the prevailing norms of dress at the end of the 18th century indicates that Indian dress remained strongly regional. In the mountainous areas of the north the basic dress for both men and women comprised a tunic or jacket reaching to the thigh or knee and worn over loose trousers narrowing at the calf or ankle. In Himachal Pradesh women wore skirts instead of trousers, and in Ladakh female costume comprised an ankle-length tunic over a close-fitting undergarment. Footwear for both sexes generally consisted of rope or leather sandals or slippers of leather or wood; in Ladakh, knee-high boots of embroidered cloth bound with leather were worn. Except for Ladakh, where men wore woollen hats, male headgear throughout the region was either the turban or the cloth cap (*topi*). However, there was considerable variation in women's headgear: in Punjab, Jammu and Himachal Pradesh a headscarf or veil was the norm, but in Kashmir a circular, cushioned headdress with a veil was worn and in Ladakh a fur-based headdress studded with turquoise and gold nuggets. In the west of the subcontinent women wore a veil and a very full gathered skirt under a blouse or tunic, while men wore a large, colourful, draped or pre-tied turban and a hip-length tunic over a long loincloth (*dhotī*); both sexes wore slippers or enclosed leather sandals with curled or pointed toes (*jūtī*). In central, eastern and southern regions dress revealed greater religious influence. Muslim men and women both wore loose trousers (*pājāmā*), which were either flared or gathered at the ankle; the female upper garment was either a hip-length tunic (*qamīz*) or a fitted bodice flared to the knees, while men wore a knee-length tunic. The costume of the non-Muslim population was far simpler, both male and female clothing comprising a single unsewn garment: a loincloth for men and a *sāṛī* for women, the latter sometimes worn with a blouse (*cholī*). Men of all faiths also wore a shawl or shoulder-cloth. Muslim men wore a variety of cloth caps as headgear, while others wore draped or pre-tied turbans. Muslim women wore veils; those of other faiths simply draped the ends of their *sāṛī*s over their heads. Footwear in these areas was virtually unknown, although some members of the Muslim community wore light slippers of cloth or leather. With increasing exposure to the lifestyles and dress of European traders and colonists, the Indian nobility began to adapt their code of dress. The changes they initiated brought a greater uniformity of dress across the subcontinent, minimizing regional differences.

In male dress, the earliest signs of these changes appeared in the high-collared, buttoned jackets and European-style coats that began to be worn over the traditional long loincloth or loose trousers; at the same time shoes replaced bare feet or sandals. The Jodhpur pants evolved into the Indian equivalent of trousers and were worn with a shortened coat, a turban and boots or shoes. From the mid-19th century, when foreigners increasingly became employers for men of various classes and communities, employees began to adopt full European dress for work while retaining their traditional dress for home wear. The Indian university culture of the late 19th century simplified the cut of the loose *pājāmā* trousers, an important variation in the north being the straight, narrow Aligarh pants, worn with the high-collared jacket (*ackan*) or the knee-length jacket (*kurtā*). In the first half of the 20th century, the Gandhian movement allayed the switch to Western clothes among the common people if not the upper classes. The turban was almost completely replaced by the 'Gandhi *topī*', a cloth cap that disguised caste and community origins, enabling men of diverse backgrounds to integrate within the independence movement. Nonetheless, except for certain nomadic, rural and tribal segments all over the country where traditional dress is worn, late 20th-century India has seen a large-scale conversion to Western dress; only since the 1970s has there been a rediscovery of traditional costume among the urban élite.

In women's dress, the first signs of experimentation with *sāṛī* styles appeared in the 1870s, when ladies in such cosmopolitan centres as Bombay and Calcutta began to appear at public gatherings. The Bengalis, inspired by the Parsis, initiated the addition of the blouse and petticoat and the permutations of length, width and drape that characterize the modern *sāṛī*. By the early 20th century, the standard 6-m-long *sāṛī* worn with pleats in front and the end-piece passed over the left shoulder had become the most visible symbol of the growing urban élite in towns across the subcontinent, infiltrating even traditionally non-*sāṛī*-wearing areas. Imported textiles such as chiffon, net fabric and lace began to overshadow traditional Indian silks and cottons, while the natural weight of traditional borders and end-pieces was replaced by artificial attachments applied to the surface or used as a backing. In reaction to this, the *khadi sāṛī* of the Gandhian movement represented a revival of the traditional heavier handspun and handwoven cloth that had been replaced by imported and home-produced mill fabrics. Although the *sāṛī* is still widely worn in the late 20th century, since the 1960s young women have increasingly preferred the greater mobility provided by the two-piece Punjabi dress (*salwar-qamīz*), comprising a long tunic and loose, cuffed trousers worn with a veil or scarf. The educated élite have also taken to Western dress. The modern dress code remains in a process of evolution, caught between the dual attractions of ethnic identity and Western culture.

BIBLIOGRAPHY

J. Forbes Watson: *Textile Manufactures and the Costumes of the People of India* (London, 1866/*R* Varanasi, 1982)

G. Watt: *Indian Art at Delhi, Being the Official Catalogue of the Delhi Exhibition, 1902–1903* (Calcutta, 1903)

C. L. Fabri: *A History of Indian Dress* (Calcutta, 1961)

B. Walker: *The Hindu World: An Encyclopedic Survey of Hinduism*, 2 vols (London and New York, 1968/*R* New Delhi, 1983)

S. N. Dar: *Costumes of India and Pakistan* (Bombay, 1969)

Indian Women from Village and City, 1850–1960 (exh. cat., ed. J. M. Scarce; Edinburgh, Royal Mus. Scotland, 1984)

H. Hossain: *The Company Weavers of Bengal: The East India Company and the Organization of Textile Production in Bengal, 1750–1813* (Delhi, 1988)

M. Banga and A. Shah: *The Rabari of Ahmedabad: A Study of their Costumes* (Ahmadabad, 1992)

ṚTA KAPUR CHISHTI

8. FURNITURE. Apart from the archetypal Indian cot (Hindi *cārpāī*), little furniture was used in the Indian subcontinent before the arrival of European colonists in the 16th century. The Portuguese were the first to employ Indian carvers of wood and ivory who had formerly embellished temples and palaces to provide items such as communion tables and church furnishings for the Portuguese Asian export market. These were decorated with Christian motifs and subsidiary Indian designs and are known to have existed from the 1580s. Portuguese-designed furniture was generally of hardwood with inlaid decoration in the Mughal style. Ebony was particularly prized for its hardness, durability and grain, taking a brilliant polish and providing a dark, lustrous background for applied decoration in ivory and bone (*see* MARQUETRY,

colour pl. VIII, fig. 2). Ivory caskets produced in Sri Lanka were despatched to Portugal as diplomatic gifts (*see* SRI LANKA, §VI, 5). These, with the communion tables, are the earliest datable examples of Indo-Portuguese art. Furniture from different production centres in the Indian subcontinent, including Sind, Gujarat and the Deccan, was assembled in Goa for shipment to Europe; both the Portuguese and later the Dutch were involved in this trade. Rattan cane first appeared in Indo-Dutch export trade furniture of the 17th century and within a generation was known all over Europe.

Indian-made furniture was produced almost exclusively for the European market until the 18th century, when increasing numbers of European settlers created a significant local demand. Indian craftsmen reinterpreted models from imported pattern books ('musters') or copied them from original pieces. Two major centres of furniture-making at this time were Murshidabad in Bengal and Vizagapatam (now Vishakhapatnam) in south India, each close to a colonial administrative centre and each with traditions of ivory-carving, veneering and inlaying. In the 18th century, furniture generally followed the style of Chippendale and later of Hepplewhite and Sheraton pieces, and the ivory-workers of the Murshidabad court produced ivory furniture strongly influenced by the Neo-classical style. Furniture from Vizagapatam was either of wood with an ivory inlay (see fig. 334) or was veneered with sheets of ivory on a wooden core. The ivory was decorated by incising a pattern and filling the depressions with black resin (lac). The monochrome black on work for Europeans probably results from the engravings provided for craftsmen to copy. Later examples of furniture from Berhampore are of ebony with ivory embellishments. The size and importance of the 18th-century market for European-style furniture are demonstrated by the opulent Kat Gola complex near Murshidabad; this large Neo-classical mansion was built on the profits from such furniture.

In the early 19th century the artist Robert Home (1752–1834) was appointed court painter in Lucknow, and 'School of Home' furniture designs flourished across north India and survived, at least in Benares (Varanasi), as late as 1880. Thrones, however, normally retained their traditional Indian shape. Often octagonal, they were portable, the upper section lifting off the base, to enable them to be used in camp as well as at court. The Vizagapatam style fell out of favour in the 19th century as more middle-class Europeans went to India. While the important officials who had arrived earlier had lived in style and commissioned furniture to take back to Europe, these later arrivals were administrators without capital who bought and sold their furniture at auction. Furniture therefore began to be adapted to the needs of these middle classes, becoming more transportable, and was usually finished in a simpler manner with a black shellac finish known as 'French polish'. At this time, Indians also began to use European-style furniture. Travelling furniture, bound with brass corners and edges to prevent damage, was popular. The reclining armchair with a swivelling or sliding footrest section and a caned seat was also developed at this time. Beds had reeded, turned, tapering legs, bulbous reeded supports (for mosquito curtains) and spindled railings. In Calcutta, the new, grand Government House (1803) contained a large suite of furniture in the Regency Revival style that is known to have been made in India. The visit of Edward, Prince of Wales, in 1876 occasioned the purchase of a suite of Louis XVI style chairs from Paris. By the late 19th century, furniture manufacturing and retailing shops existed in such major cities as Calcutta, where the firm of Lazarus and Tomlin produced Rococo Revival furniture, and Whiteway and Laidlaw's department store provided transportable campaign furniture. Late 19th-century households in India had much of the clutter of Victorian homes. For the wealthy, there was lavish display including even glass and crystal furniture, much of which was manufactured in Belgium; a suite is known from the palace in Udaipur.

334. Writing-cabinet and table, wood inlaid with ivory, with hinges and handles of chased silver, table 800×756×501 mm, overall h. 1.56 mm, made under European patronage at Vizagapatam, 18th century (London, Victoria and Albert Museum)

From the 1920s to the late 1940s, Art Deco found favour among avant-garde collectors and Rajput princes. Indian princes had begun travelling more frequently to Europe, and the princely palaces at Jaipur and Jodhpur both have Art Deco furnishings. Alternating with Art Deco was the more official 'Lutyens Baroque' of the 1920s and 1930s, introduced *c.* 1929 when EDWIN LUTYENS furnished the Viceroy's House in New Delhi. The caned *bergère*-style suites of furniture mirrored the taste of the aristocratic and wealthy clients for whom Lutyens had designed country houses in England. These styles lingered on into the late 1940s and early 1950s. After 1947, the modern movement reached India via France and Le Corbusier, who worked in the subcontinent for a time. Modernist furniture, copied by Indian carpenters, was based on Scandinavian, American and British designs.

See also §§10 and 19 below.

BIBLIOGRAPHY

T. Falk: 'Inlaid and Ebony Furniture from British India', *Orientations*, xvii/3 (1986), pp. 47–56

J. Guy and D. Swallow, eds: *Arts of India, 1500–1900* (London, 1990)

GERALDINE SMITH-PARR BANERJI

9. GLASS. Although the manufacture of vitreous material at the time of the Indus or Harappan civilization (*c*. 2550–*c*. 2000 BC) has been suggested, and there is a small, probably indigenous body of material (beads, bangles and seals) from the Painted Grey Ware phase (*see* §5(i) above), Indian glass manufacture only becomes clearly evident under the Maurya dynasty (*c*. 321–*c*. 185 BC). Finds at Taxila included earrings of distinctly Indian form, and the Patna sites of Kumrahar and Bulandibagh produced glass seals that have been dated to *c*. 300–200 BC. A number of sites of the Satavahana dynasty (*c*. 1st century BC–*c*. 3rd century AD) have yielded beads, bangles and ear ornaments. Analysis of excavated material showed that the glass was of soda lime silica composition, which is found until at least the late 19th century. Many foreign imports were also found at these sites, and it seems plausible that glass technology developed as a result of contact with other areas, particularly Achaemenid Iran. There is no satisfactory evidence for glass furnaces from ancient Indian archaeology, but lumps of unworked glass have been found at an unexcavated site at Kopia, Basti, Uttar Pradesh.

From the end of the Maurya period until the late 16th century there are only scattered finds, mostly of bangles and beads (see Dikshit). The Deccan has significant finds at sites associated with both the Muslim Bahmani rulers (mid-14th century to early 16th) and the Hindu kings of Vijayanagara (mid-14th century to mid-16th). The *Āyīn-i Akbarī* ('Annals of Akbar') notes glass-making centres at Alwar and Bihar in the late 16th century under the Mughal ruler Akbar (*reg* 1556–1605), though no objects have survived. Good examples of the 18th and 19th centuries in public collections show that the range of glass included hooka bases, vessels, rosewater sprinklers, small dishes and moulded bottles (*see* GLASS, colour pl. V, fig. 1). Although European glass was highly valued at court, particularly in the 17th century, the techniques used in India depended more on surface decoration (by appliqué or wheel-cutting, gilding or cold-painting) than on manipulation of the molten metal. The metal is usually of rather poor quality, though the painted or gilt decoration is often extremely fine (see fig. 335; see also Markel and 1991 exh. cat., nos 6–8). Other seemingly Indian products are of lead glass and were probably made in England for the Indian market (see 1982 exh. cat., no. 394). In the 19th century,

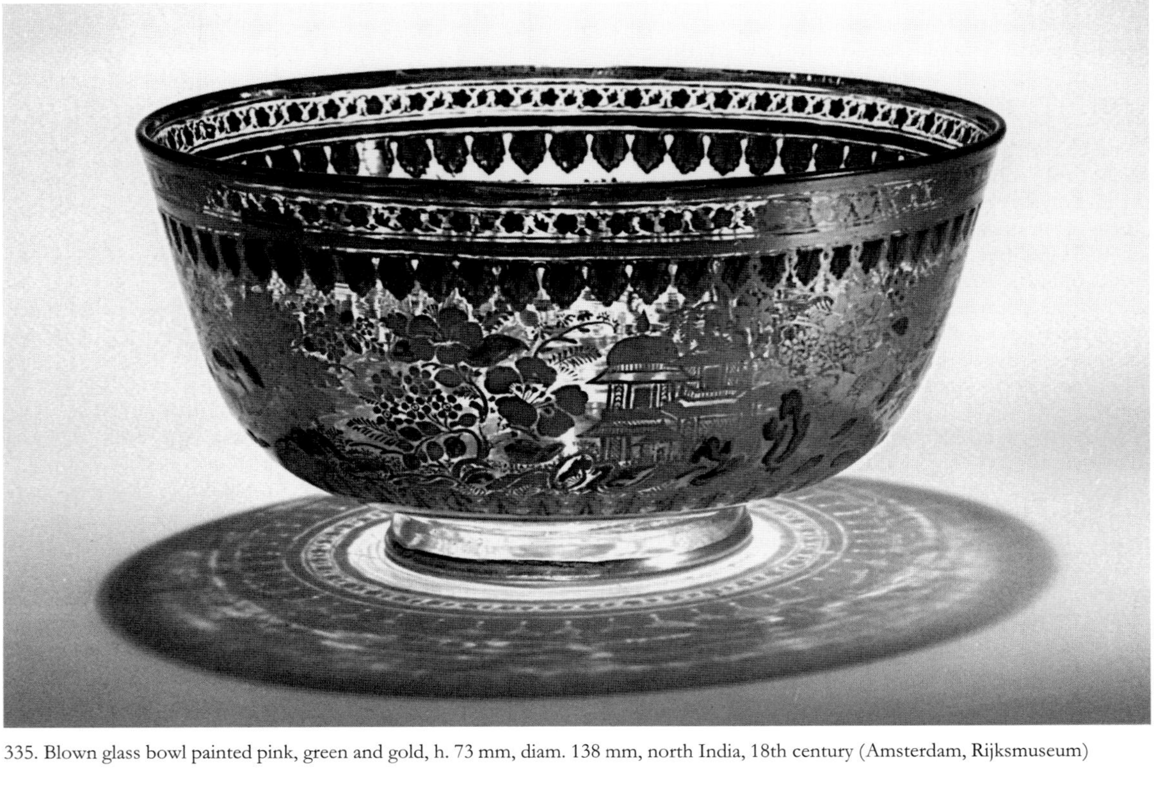

335. Blown glass bowl painted pink, green and gold, h. 73 mm, diam. 138 mm, north India, 18th century (Amsterdam, Rijksmuseum)

studies were made of the various centres of glass production; a journey made by Buchanan in 1800 produced the first description of Indian glass manufacture. Attempts were made by the British to establish a developed industry but failed in the absence of a strongly rooted tradition. Owing to the difficulty of finding suitable raw materials and the loss of courtly patronage, the indigenous industry contracted and reverted to the production of bangles and small vessels of inferior quality.

BIBLIOGRAPHY

F. Buchanan: *A Journey from Madras through the Countries of Mysore, Canaras and Malabar*, i (Madras, 1870)

C. J. Hallifax: 'Pottery and Glass Industries of the Punjab', *J. Ind. A. & Indust.*, v (1894), pp. 36–49

H. R. C. Dobbs: *A Monograph on the Pottery and Glass Industries of the North-western Provinces and Oudh* (Allahabad, 1895)

K. P. Jayaswal: 'Brahmi Seals Newly Discovered at Patna', *J. Bihar & Orissa Res. Soc.*, x/3 (1924), pp. 189–93

M. G. Dikshit: *History of Indian Glass* (Bombay, 1969)

S. Digby: 'A Corpus of "Mughal" Glass', *Bull. SOAS*, xxvi/1 (1973), pp. 80–96

The Indian Heritage: Court Life and Arts under Mughal Rule (exh. cat., ed. R. Skelton; London, V&A, 1982)

M. Postel: *Ear Ornaments of Ancient India* (Bombay, 1989)

S. Markel: 'Indian and "Indianate" Glass Vessels in the Los Angeles County Museum of Art', *J. Glass Stud.*, xxxiii (1991), pp. 82–92

Hoofse snuisterijen uit India [Court gems from India] (exh. cat. by P. L. Scheurleer, Amsterdam, Rijksmus., 1991)

SUSAN STRONGE

10. Ivory.

(i) To the 3rd century AD. The earliest known use of ivory in the Indian subcontinent can be traced to the Indus or Harappan civilization (*c.* 2550–*c.* 2000 BC). This highly developed culture had centres at Harappa, Mohenjo-daro and Kalibangan and traded with the village culture of Baluchistan, the Deccan and western India. Further trade links were established with Afghanistan and Persia, thus accounting for the similarity of many Harappan ivory objects to those found in contemporary Near Eastern cultures. The objects most commonly found at various Indus Valley sites include inlay fragments, miniature fish, small animal figures, pierced rods, batons, pegs, small vessels, cylinder seals, mirror-handles, combs, kohl-sticks, hairpins, dice and beads. The decoration of these objects seems to have been restricted to the occasional application of colour and cross-hatched, linear or circle-dot incisions. The elephant is one of about six animals to appear on the distinctive Harappan steatite seals, which are thought to have denoted ownership, and tusks and skeletal remains have been excavated at Mohenjo-daro. This site has produced some of the most significant finds, not least the earliest known Indian ivory representing the human form. This fragmentary plaque (*c.* 2300–1750 BC) depicts a standing male figure wearing a loincloth, with his hands on his hips and a spear or quiver above his left shoulder. Other finds from Mohenjo-daro include quantities of small and much-handled ivory fish, their bodies hatched to take coloured pigments, which are thought to have been used either as part of a religious ritual or simply as gaming-pieces. The most commonly found ivory object, however, is the comb, examples of which have been found at almost all Indus Valley sites.

Few ivory objects appear to have been made during the Neolithic (*c.* 2375–1000 BC) and Chalcolithic (*c.* 2000–1100 BC) periods, but numerous domestic ivory and bone carvings survive from the 8th–3rd century BC, when the mother-goddess cult of previous millennia continued sporadically. A group of highly stylized ivory female figures decorated with linear incisions and circle-dot motifs was excavated in 1955–6 at Prabhasa, Gujarat. These figures are thought to date from *c.* 600–200 BC and relate to others found at Taxila, Nagda, Ujjain and Avra, the entire group probably deriving from a terracotta prototype originating in the Near East. In contrast, an ivory female figure (*c.* 600–500 BC) from Champanagar, Bihar, carved in sections, is of naturalistic form. From the Mauryan period (4th–2nd century BC) only utilitarian objects—seals, antimony rods—survive. A number of small figures of the Shunga period are known, including a doll-like ivory male figure from Bhir Mound, Taxila, a headless ivory soldier found at Patna, and three bone fragmentary female figures from Mathura, Ahichchhatra and Ter. The three female figures share such distinctive characteristics as broad bodies, angular faces, rows of anklets and necklaces falling between the breasts. A small ivory comb fragment depicting two lovers amid leaves (London, V&A), from Malwa (southern Rajasthan), has been dated to the 1st century BC. Perhaps the finest find of this period, however, is the ivory female figure recovered at Pompeii (Naples, Mus. Archaeol. N.).

In 1937–9 the French archaeologist Joseph Hackin (1886–1941) and his wife, excavating at the summer palace of the Kushana kings at BEGRAM, Afghanistan, discovered a hoard of some 600 ivory plaques (Kabul Mus.; Paris, Mus. Guimet) in a concealed cellar room. Both the date and the original purpose of the plaques remain speculative, but it is thought they may have been applied to furniture. They provide a fascinating insight into Kushana courtly life and in particular the everyday preoccupations of the bejewelled and scantily dressed ladies most of them depict. They are also highly significant in that they bear close comparison with finds at Mathura, Amaravati, Nagarjunakonda, Sanchi and Bharhut in terms of figural style, costume, decorative elements and architectural motifs.

(ii) 4th–15th centuries. There is little evidence of any strong tradition of ivory-carving, other than that employed for minor objects of everyday use, in either the Gupta (4th–5th century AD) or post-Gupta periods. During the 8th–9th century, however, a remarkable group of painted miniature Buddhist ivories was produced in Kashmir. Although these are scattered in at least 14 museums and private collections in Europe, the USA and India, there can be no doubting the synchronism of the minutely detailed style, which treats subjects already familiar in Gandharan art, scenes from the life of the Buddha. A closely related bone reliquary depicting a bejewelled Buddha (New York, Met.) has been dated to the 9th–10th centuries. A group of 15 ivory panels (London, BM) depicting Hindu court ladies and carved in an archaizing style, discovered (1856) at Brahmanabad, Sind, has been dated to the 10th century. These panels can be related to contemporary temple sculpture and may originally have formed a casket. An ivory chesspiece said to have belonged to Charlemagne, with a nobleman riding an elephant surrounded by soldiers (Paris, Bib. N., Cab. Médailles),

first mentioned in a Paris inventory of 1505, has been described as of the Sultanate period (11th–12th century) from north-west India. It bears an Arabic inscription in kufic script: 'from the work of Yusuf al-Bahlili'. Each of a pair of vigorously carved ivory lions (London, V&A) dating from the 12th century, probably throne supports , bears a dedicatory inscription in proto-Bengali translating respectively as 'auspicious co-heiress' and 'great middle-born'.

There are numerous ancient epigraphical and literary references to ivory-carvers from the *Rāmāyaṇa* onwards, and Orissan craftsmen are mentioned repeatedly, particularly in the context of furniture. From palanquins and thrones to throne legs, litters, chariots, royal beds, balconies and couches, a vast amount and variety of furniture seem to have adorned royal palaces. It is therefore surprising to find little pre-dating the construction in the mid-13th century of the Sun Temple at Konarak. The Jagannatha Temple (*c.* 1198) in Puri, however, bears an interesting 15th-century inscription recording a royal gift of eight ivory thrones. At least a dozen throne legs, elaborately carved with an elephant-headed lion (Skt *gajasiṁha*) variously clutching a warrior or surrounded by hunters, are dispersed in museums in India and the USA. The earliest (Philadelphia, PA, Mus. A.) bears close comparison with larger-scale temple carvings at Konarak and may therefore be datable to the 13th century. A fine 14th–15th-century seated figure of the elephant-headed god Ganesha (New York, Met.) has also been attributed to Orissa. A series of small ivory openwork panels depicting lovers reclining on a bed with bolsters surrounded by a foliate arch and columns, which are thought to have been set into wooden beds, display distinctive Orissan features and vary in date from the 13th to the 17th century (London, BM; Los Angeles, CA, Co. Mus. A.).

(iii) 16th century and after. Between the 16th and 18th centuries the Mughals, Deccani rulers and provincial courts of Rajasthan employed ivory primarily in the art of warfare. Exquisite weapons with gold-damascened blades and ivory or hardstone hilts set with gold, silver and gemstones were worn at court by emperors, princes and courtiers. Walrus and hippopotamus ivory had long been used in preference to elephant ivory for sword- and dagger-hilts as they gave a better grip. Ivory was further used to decorate the wooden stocks of matchlock rifles, inlaid in elaborate designs. It also served to mount scabbards with carved chape and locket, as arrowheads and for the manufacture of powder-horns and primers. A series of the latter was produced in the 17th century; a number found their way into European collections and are typified by a composition of animals of the chase consuming each other (London, V&A; Dresden, Hist. Mus.; Copenhagen, Nmus.). Walrus ivory was also used for the carving of archers' thumb-rings (more common in jade), an exceptional example of which is in the Maharaja Sawai Man Singh II Museum in the City Palace, Jaipur.

Ivory and ivory-inlaid caskets were made for courts throughout the subcontinent, as well as for the European market in Gujarat and Sind from the late 16th century. Numerous ivory boxes, carved with such typically Mughal motifs as a single flower below a cusped arch and sometimes embellished with copper-gilt mounts, were produced during the 17th and 18th centuries. Boxes from the Deccan, Orissa, Punjab and Rajasthan were produced according to local traditions of design and decoration and were frequently painted or gilded. In the south, too, patronage revolved around the princely states, and the main centres of ivory-carving were Madras, Madurai, Mysore and Trivandrum. Some of the finest examples include a 17th-century figural box-panel from Madurai (Richmond, VA, Mus. F. A.; see fig. 336), an 18th-century princely couple from Srirangam (Berlin, Mus. Ind. Kst), two 17th-century Madras ivory figures of a tribal woman and Balarama (Edinburgh, Royal Mus. Scotland) and a Tamil Nadu casket panel depicting Shiva and Parvati dated

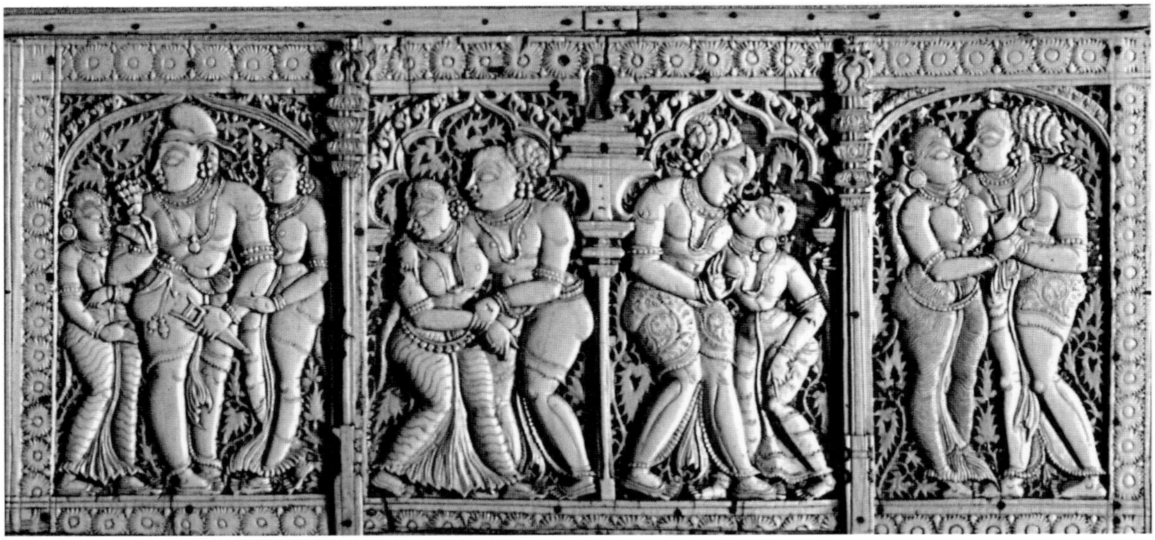

336. Ivory panel from a cosmetics box, 152×314 mm, from Madurai, 17th century (Richmond, VA, Virginia Museum of Fine Arts)

337. Ivory armchair, carved, painted and gilt, 920×780 m, south India, late 18th century (London, Victoria and Albert Museum)

1766 (London, V&A). An exceptional and little-known group of around 20 mainly figural Nayaka-period ivories of the 17th and 18th centuries is in the Minakshi Sundareshvara Temple Museum, Madurai.

With the increasing affluence of the Europeans settled in such cities as Calcutta and Madras during the second half of the 18th century, craftsmen began to produce ivory or ivory-veneered furniture that skilfully copied European designs (see fig. 337; *see also* §8 above). A series of parcel-gilt ivory chairs of hybrid design with foliate backs, lion-head finials and cabriole legs, often attributed to Murshidabad, is thought to have originally furnished Warren Hastings's Calcutta house (Calcutta, Victoria Mem. Hall; London, Soane Mus. and V&A). The typically lac-decorated, ivory-veneered furniture of Vizagapatam (Vishakhapatnam) on the east coast is perhaps more familiar in Europe today; production in quantity seems to have continued well into the 19th century. Examples of Chippendale-style chairs, grandiose cabinets with disproportionate broken pediments, slender-limbed late Georgian tables, mirror-cabinets and numerous boxes can be found in museums, country houses and private collections (e.g. Hyderabad, Salar Jung Mus.; London, St James's Pal., Royal Col.; London, V&A; Powis Castle, Powys, NT; Copenhagen, Kstindustmus.). The decline of the Mughal empire and increasing British power led to the demise of the princely courts, and despite valiant efforts to revive court arts for the Great Exhibition of 1851 in London and numerous successive exhibitions, culminating with that at Delhi in 1902–3, a tradition spanning nearly 2000 years was dwindling to an end. However, the richly carved throne and footstool produced by the Maharaja of Travancore's craftsmen and presented to Queen Victoria at the Great Exhibition of 1851 cannot easily be equalled (London, Kensington Pal., Royal Col.). Ivory continued to be used in a traditional way for throne or chair backs, bed legs, weapons, fly-whisk handles, fans and scent bottles until the late 19th century.

BIBLIOGRAPHY

G. Birdwood: *The Industrial Arts of India* (London, 1880)
J. L. Kipling: 'Indian Ivory Carving', *J. Ind. A. & Indust.*, i/7 (1885), pp. 49–53
Art and the East India Trade (exh. cat. by J. Irwin, London, V&A, 1970)
V. P. Dwivedi: *Indian Ivories: A Survey. . .from the Earliest Times to Modern Times* (New Delhi, 1976)
M. Chandra: *Indian Ivories* (New Delhi, 1977/*R* London, 1978)
The Indian Heritage: Court Life and Arts under Mughal Rule (exh. cat., ed. R. Skelton; London, V&A, 1982)
F. St Aubyn, ed.: *Ivory: A History and Collectors' Guide* (London, 1987)
D. Swallow and J. Guy: *Arts of India, 1550–1900* (London, 1990)

BRENDAN LYNCH

11. JADE, AGATE AND CRYSTAL. The earliest and most persistent form of hardstone-working in India was the manufacture of beads, most commonly of chalcedony, particularly cornelian and banded or variegated agates, which were produced in large numbers from prehistoric times down to the late 20th century. Although varieties of these stones have been quarried or found in river beds in various parts of the subcontinent, the most important centre of production was always the lower valley of the Narmada River, Gujarat, where the ancient port of Broach (Bharuch) and, from medieval times, Cambay (Khambhat) provided access to domestic and foreign markets. Another important centre was Arikamedu near Pondicherry, Tamil Nadu, an entrepôt for trade with Rome, where there was a hardstone bead-making industry. A fragment of a fine, thin-walled onyx cup or bowl (Pondicherry Museum) suggests that vessels were also made there for export to the West.

(i) 3rd century BC*–14th century* AD. The hardstones of Gujarat were particularly celebrated in the Mediterranean region during the Classical period and were mentioned by Greek and Roman writers, including the author of *Periplus Maris Erythraei* ('Periplus of the Erythraean Sea'; *c.* AD 75) and Pliny, who refers to several varieties of chalcedony from India and quotes Zenothemis' description of pieces of sardonyx large enough for the manufacture of sword hilts (*Natural History* XXXVII.xxiii.87–8). He also states that Indian rock crystal is preferred to any other (XXXVII.ix.23) and that some authors mention a crystal vessel from India with a capacity of just over 2 litres (XXXVII.x.27). Another allusion to the size of Indian hardstone-carvings in the 3rd century AD is found in Philostratus the younger's *Life of Apollonius of Tyana*, in which the small size of stones imported into Greece is contrasted with pieces worked in India that were 'turned into decanters and wine coolers, because they are so large, and into goblets of such size that from a single one of them four persons can slake their thirst' (III.27). Although

no confirmed examples of exported Indian vessels had been identified among collections of antique hardstones by the mid-1990s, within India several crystal reliquaries have been excavated at Buddhist sites. These include a finely executed piece in the form of a goose from Taxila (*c.* 1st century AD; see fig. 338) and model stupas, such as that from Bhojpur, Madhya Pradesh (3rd–2nd century BC; London, V&A, I.M. 223–1921). Excavations at such sites as Taxila have also resulted in the discovery of chalcedony and crystal intaglio seals influenced by Greek or Roman models. Pliny, quoting Zenothemis (*Natural History* XXXVII.xiii.87–8), states that sardonyx was not held in high regard by Indians but was popular in the Roman empire as almost the only gemstone that, when engraved as a signet, did not carry the sealing wax with it. Pliny adds that later they persuaded the Indians to share their appreciation of it. It is difficult to find evidence of hardstone-carving during the Gupta (4th–5th century) and subsequent periods, but the picture becomes clearer from the 15th century.

(ii) 15th century and after. In 1468, the Sultan of Malwa included vessels of agate and crystal among gifts sent to the Timurid king Abu Sa'id Mirza (*reg* 1459–69), and in the next century a rock-crystal image of a Jaina *Tīrthaṅkara* was made in Gujarat for a brass shrine dated 1515 (Vikrama year 1572; London, V&A, I.M. 3–1939). Around 1518, the Portuguese official Duarte Barbosa wrote that cornelian was worked both at Cambay (Khambhat) and at Limadura (modern Limodra) near the Ratanpur mines for export via Cambay (see M. L. Dames, *The Book of Duarte Barbosa*, London, 1918–21). Barbosa also echoed Pliny in referring to the manufacture of knife handles; Jean Baptiste Tavernier, who visited Cambay in the mid-17th century, wrote that 'here those beautiful agates which come from India are cut into cups, handles of knives, beads and other objects of workmanship'.

Although such objects exist in European collections formed in the 16th and 17th centuries, their Indian origin has yet to be established. An agate cup and archer's ring (London, V&A; see 1982 exh. cat., nos 381–2) have been plausibly attributed to the 17th century, as have a few rock-crystal vessels and weapon handles. One of two cameos (London, V&A) made for the Mughal emperor Shah Jahan (*reg* 1628–58) by a European immigrant is inscribed with his title, 'Kan Attam' ('supreme engraver'), but the only other documented object—apart from engraved seals—is a green quartz drinking bowl dated AH 1021 (AD 1612–13) and inscribed for the Mughal emperor Jahangir (*reg* 1605–27; Providence, RI Sch. Des., Mus. A.). Otherwise, it is not until the 19th century that agate vessels made in Cambay can be firmly dated by their inclusion in international exhibitions and museum collections.

By contrast with the working of indigenous Indian hardstones, whose recorded use over several millennia has been substantiated by few significant examples, the much shorter duration of jade craftsmanship in India has resulted in many extant works. This can be explained by the fact that the craft was fostered by the Mughal emperors, whose Timurid ancestors had patronized jadeworkers in eastern Central Asia and eastern Iran during the 15th century. Mughal jade-carvers used only the nephrite (calcium magnesium silicate) found in the Yurungkash and Karakash rivers in the neighbourhood of Khotan in China's Xinjiang Uygur Autonomous Region. A dark green dish dated AH 915 (AD 1509–10) and decorated with an engraved arabesque medallion is inscribed as belonging to the Mughal emperor Babur (*reg* 1526–30), but although

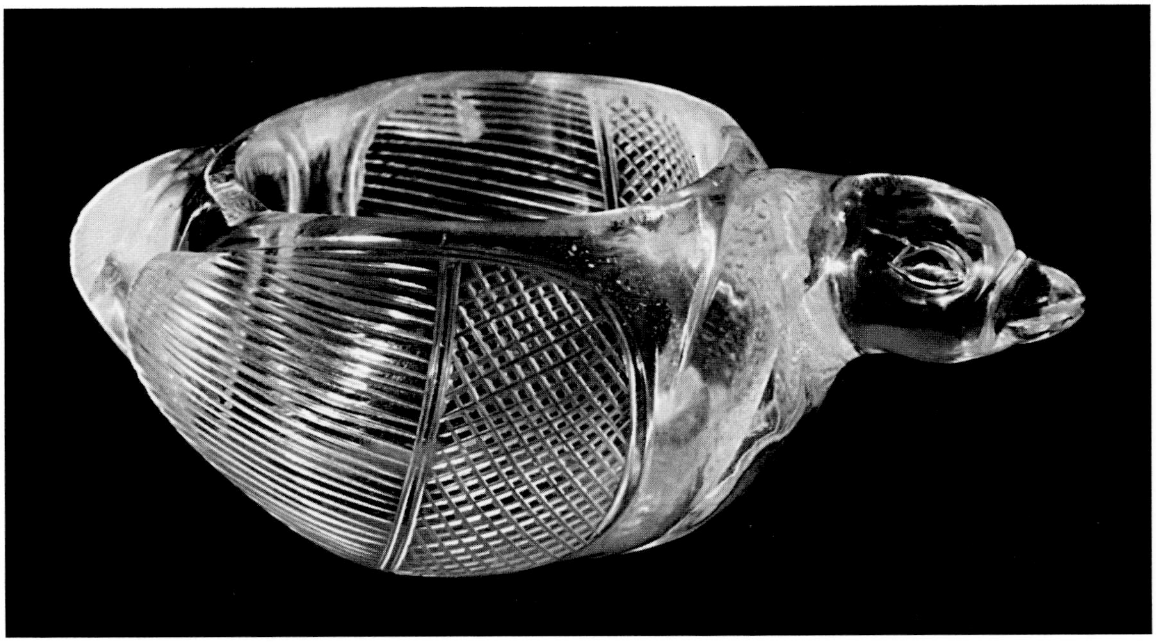

338. Crystal reliquary in the form of a goose, h. 32 mm, l. 100 mm, Taxila, *c.* 1st century AD (London, British Museum)

this shows that the founder of the dynasty was familiar with jade before arriving in India, his conquest of Delhi removed him from proximity to the source of supply. This situation evidently changed in 1562 when Khwaja Mu'in of Kashgar, the proprietor of the jade riverbed, visited the court of Babur's grandson Akbar (*reg* 1556–1605) and presented rare merchandise from his locality. However, Khwaja Mu'in died too soon to exploit any Mughal taste for jade, and the attribution of jades to Akbar's reign is, on the whole, speculative. An exception is a white archer's thumb-ring inscribed 'Shah Salim'—the title adopted by the heir apparent during his rebellion at the end of Akbar's reign (Varanasi, Banaras Hindu U., Bharat Kala Bhavan). It was originally decorated with a gold inlay of floral arabesques of the type seen in later Timurid and Safavid decorative art, suggesting that the craftsman was among those attracted to the court from Iran or neighbouring regions.

Following his accession as Jahangir, the new emperor continued to commission jade objects and collected pieces made for Ulughbeg Mirza and other descendants of his ancestor Timur. Like the Timurid pieces, early Mughal jades imitate porcelain or metal forms. Thus a small cup dated AH 1016 (AD 1607–8; priv. col., on loan to New York, Brooklyn Mus.), bearing Persian quatrains and the titles of Jahangir, copies the form of a type of porcelain of the Chinese Ming period (1368–1644) imported into India, while the quartz vessel mentioned above and a jade inkpot made by Mu'min Jahangiri in AH 1028 (AD 1618–19; New York, Met.) are modelled after chased brass prototypes. A decisive change from these models to organic forms is marked by a small perfume phial in the form of a flower bud made for Jahangir in AH 1036 (AD 1626–7; London, V&A; see 1982 exh. cat., no. 354). This trend continued during the reign of Shah Jahan, culminating in the emperor's white nephrite cup of AH 1067 (AD 1657; see fig. 339). The craftsman responsible for this masterpiece combined Chinese, European and indigenous design features with absolute assurance, and this successful eclecticism defined the future direction of Indian jade production.

By the mid-17th century, the imported raw material was readily available to wider sections of the wealthy classes, and a great variety of objects were made, including animal-headed and pistol-grip dagger handles, powder horns, cups, bowls, ewers, sweetmeat boxes, trays, hooka bowls, Koran stands, amulets and mirrors (*see* MIRROR, §III). Many of these were encrusted with gemstones or enamel set in gold inlay (*see* JADE, colour pl. III, fig. 2). Motifs carved in relief echoed those used in marble decoration and included acanthus or flowering plant designs of the type seen on Mughal buildings from the reign of Shah Jahan onwards. Towards the end of the 18th century these motifs tended to become more flamboyant, finally becoming stilted and overcrowded as tastes and modes of patronage changed under British rule in the 19th century.

BIBLIOGRAPHY

J. B. Tavernier: *Nouvelle relation du serrail du Grand Signior* (Paris, 1675); *Les Six Voyages de Jean Baptiste Tavernier, Ecuyer Baron d'Aubonne, qu'il a fait en Turquie, en Perse, et aux Indes* (Paris, 1676); Eng. trans. of both by V. Ball, ed. W. Crooke, as *Travels in India*, 2 vols (Oxford, 1925)

E. H. Warmington: *The Commerce between the Roman Empire and India* (Cambridge, 1928)

A. J. Arkell: 'Cambay and the Bead Trade', *Antiquity*, x/3 (1936), pp. 292–304

M. Chandra: 'The Art of Cutting Hardstone Ware in Ancient and Modern India', *J. Gujarat Res. Soc.*, i (1939), pp. 71–85

R. K. Trivedi: *Agate Industry of Cambay*, Census of India, 1961, v, pt VII-A(1) (Delhi, 1964)

R. Skelton: 'The Shah Jahan Cup', *V&A Mus. Bull.*, ii/3 (1966), pp. 108–9

——: 'The Relations between the Chinese and Indian Jade Carving Traditions', *The Westward Influence of the Chinese Arts from the 14th to the 18th Century*, Colloq. A. & Archaeol. Asia, iii (London, 1972), pp. 98–110

M. Chandra: *Trade and Trade Routes in Ancient India* (Delhi, 1977)

The Indian Heritage: Court Life and Arts under Mughal Rule (exh. cat., ed. R. Skelton; London, V&A, 1982)

A. Riazuddin: *History of Handicrafts: Pakistan–India* (Islamabad, 1988)

S. Markel: 'Fit for an Emperor: Inscribed Works of Decorative Art Acquired by the Great Mughals', *Orientations*, xxi/8 (1990), pp. 22–36

R. Skelton: 'Islamic and Mughal Jades', *Jade*, ed. R. Keverne (London, 1991), pp. 274–95

S. Markel: 'Inception and Maturation in Mughal Jades', *The World of Jade*, ed. S. Markel (Bombay, 1992), pp. 49–64

ROBERT SKELTON

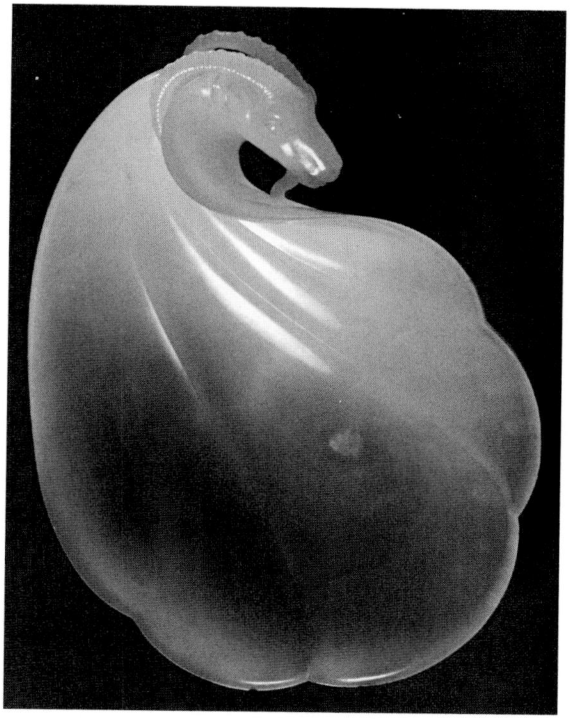

339. Nephrite jade drinking cup of Shah Jahan, l. 187 mm, dated AH 1067 (AD 1657) (London, Victoria and Albert Museum)

12. JEWELLERY. Since the Indus Valley civilizations of the 2nd millennium BC, jewellery in India has played a central role in both personal ornament and religious iconography. Both gold and silver were worked with great skill and set with gems or hardstones or decorated with enamel.

(i) Before the 16th century. (ii) 16th–18th centuries. (iii) 19th–20th centuries.

(i) Before the 16th century. The famous bronze statuette from Mohenjo-daro of a girl naked but for her jewellery

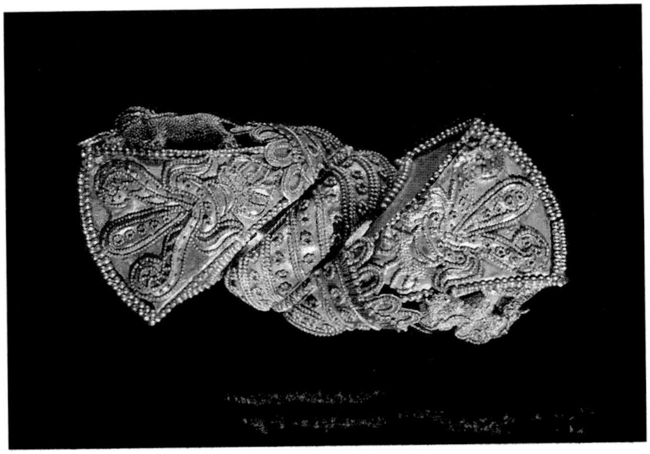

340. Gold earring with granulated and repoussé decoration, *c.* 1st century BC (New York, Metropolitan Museum of Art)

(New Delhi, N. Mus.; see fig. 130 above) illustrates the preoccupation with personal adornment that has persisted in the Indian subcontinent throughout the ages. Besides the evidence of jewellery finds from the Indus Valley sites, goldsmiths' tools and pots resembling crucibles have also been discovered, as have jewellers' weights and balances. On the evidence of archaeology, the range of jewellery worn included armlets, rings, hairpins, necklaces, hair fillets, bangles, girdles and ear ornaments. Mackay (1939) argued that the Indus Valley goldsmiths could make artefacts from moulds, produce thin sheets of gold, draw wire and mix alloys of copper and silver with gold. He also noted (1937–8) that bangles and other items were sometimes made from tubes of sheet gold filled with lac to produce the effect of substantial jewellery more cheaply. Ornaments were also made of silver and copper, and the lost-wax casting method was used to manufacture such small items as animal-shaped amulets. As in later times, a wide range of other materials, including gemstones and hardstones, steatite, faience, shell and terracotta, was also used in jewellery. Some pottery bangles seem to have been glazed (Chandra, 1964); however, early evidence for glass, used particularly for bangles throughout Indian history, is ambiguous, and not until the Maurya period (4th–3rd century BC) did bangles, glass seals and earrings of indigenous manufacture become clearly evident in the archaeological record (*see also* §9 above). Chandra describes the different phases of Indus Valley jewellery, noting the influence of contacts with other cultures, and provides appendices of the many names for types of jewellery found in such ancient texts as the *Ṛg veda.* J. Brijbhusan also surveys references to jewellery in ancient literature, including the *Rāmāyaṇa* and the *Artha śāstra* of Kautilya.

On the evidence of sculpture, jewellery of the 2nd and 1st centuries BC could be wildly extravagant, implying a period of technical experimentation. The sculptures of Bharhut depict figures weighed down with lavish ornamentation of often bizarre form, as do such small-scale Bengali terracotta figurines as the famous *yakṣī* from Tamluk (Oxford, Ashmolean; see fig. 351 below). Although the proportions of the figures seem to be exaggerated, the ornaments appear to be depicted realistically, with technical features visible. For instance, the loop-in-loop type of chain found in Buddhist jewellery (Marshall, 1904) is also seen on a Bharhut *yakṣī* (Calcutta, Ind. Mus.; see fig. 140 above). An important pair of gold royal earrings with granulated and repoussé decoration (see fig. 340) is also related to sculptural depictions, most closely to the figure of the universal monarch (*cakravartin*) on the 1st-century BC stupa at Jaggayyapeta, Andhra Pradesh, with which the earrings are thought to be contemporary. Remarkable for their size, their regal links are indicated by the winged lions and elephants (both symbols of royalty) worked in granulation. A bead and two pendants with dense gold granulated motifs are probably of the same period (Postel, p. 197).

A major outside influence on the development of jewellery came from Greece and the Hellenistic world, from Alexander's invasion of the Punjab (326–325 BC) to the end of the Maurya period. Sculpture again provides the main evidence, but there is a small amount of excavated jewellery, notably from the Taxila area (Marshall, 1951). Unfortunately, few sites provide a clear picture of the development of Indo-Greek art, and little jewellery has been dated with any certainty. Motifs such as cupids, classical urns and creatures or characters from Greek mythology frequently occur, and Rai Govind Chandra (1979) suggests that certain techniques may have been introduced from the Greek or Hellenistic worlds. As examples he cites granulation, die-casting, repoussé work using finely carved dies, and sophisticated engraving on hardstones; however, at least some of these techniques must have been introduced from Iran.

While the jewellery represented on stone *bodhisattva* images shows Hellenistic and Iranian influence, its design suggests that jewellery styles were dependent on a highly developed indigenous tradition whose practitioners were able to absorb and advance new techniques and fashions. A rare gold amulet case (London, BM) found at Ahinposh near Jalalabad, Afghanistan, and dated to the 2nd–3rd century AD can be compared with examples represented being worn on cords by *bodhisattvas* in images from Gandhara (London, BM; see 1988 exh. cat., no. 17). The form, Iranian in origin, survived in south Indian jewellery into the 19th century. Another Buddhist piece, part of a gold bracelet in the form of gold flowers set with sapphires and linked by gold conch shells, was found at Bodhgaya by Sir Alexander Cunningham and is dated, uncertainly, to the early centuries AD (London, BM; see 1988 exh. cat., no. 18). By the 2nd century AD two distinct types of *bodhisattva* image predominated: the first is adorned by a bead diadem, the second has a turban, richly encrusted with jewels or ornamented metal plaques (Schmidt). Both types also wear conventional ensembles of jewellery, some of which, like the collar necklaces and armbands, have long pedigrees in Indic culture (*see* CENTRAL ASIA, fig. 77). On the basis of archaeological finds, these pieces seem to have been set most frequently with garnets, lapis lazuli or pearls, all of which had symbolic value.

In south India, two archaeological finds provide meagre evidence of early jewellery in the region. A group of gold pieces from Souttoukeny, Tamil Nadu, dates from the 2nd century BC; the second group, from the Nilgiri Hills, has a much more uncertain dating, definable only as the second half of the first millennium BC (Knox). Finds include ear ornaments, pendants and beads made from sheet gold fabricated into three-dimensional shapes or from flat gold ornamented with applied gold wires or granulation; some pieces are also set with cabochon stones.

From the Kushana period (1st–3rd century AD) are pieces depicting the goddess Hariti, sometimes with her consort Panchika (also known as Kubera), both folk deities who were absorbed into the Buddhist pantheon. The couple are shown in repoussé on a gold plaque (London, V&A) wearing Hellenistic and Kushana clothes; a similar plaque representing them in Indian costume was among the contents of a gilded schist reliquary (Cleveland, OH, Mus. A.). Two gold medallion discs showing Hariti dressed in a short Hellenistic tunic and wearing a diadem of the kind seen on Western Classical deities are set with garnets and pearls (London, V&A; Cleveland, OH, Mus. A.).

Little research has been done on jewellery produced between the end of this early period of Indian history and the Mughal age (16th–19th century). Sculpture is the main source for style, with some additional information from wall paintings, especially those in the Buddhist cave temples of Ajanta, which depict jewellery characterized by the use of less gold and more gemstones. The few pieces that have so far been identified from this intermediate period include a gold armlet found at Godagiri in Rajshahi District, Bangladesh (*c.* 5th century AD; Dhaka, N. Mus. Bangladesh), a Pala-period (8th–12th century) bronze bangle (New York, Met.) and a Kashmiri diadem of the 9th–10th century. However, during this period the literature concerning precious stones developed (*see* GEM-ENGRAVING, §I, 6). Louis Finot surveyed the *ratna śāstra* treatises on jewels, which typically list nine precious stones and include a detailed classification of each. Each stone represents one of the nine planets of the Indian system and falls into one of two classes, *mahāratnani* (*mahāratna*: 'most precious of all jewels') or *uparatnani* (secondary or inferior gems). Ruby (the sun), pearl (the moon), diamond (Venus), emerald (Mercury) and sapphire (Saturn) are in the first class; jacinth (Rahu), topaz (Jupiter), cat's eye (Ketu) and coral (Mars) are in the second. As the stones have either beneficial or malevolent qualities, all nine are often worn together in the *nauratan* setting to neutralize the bad influences and attract the good (see Untracht).

(ii) 16th–18th centuries.

(a) North. The most important source for north Indian jewellery traditions in the Mughal period is the *Āyīn-i Akbarī* ('Annals of Akbar'; *c.* 1596–1602) of Abu'l-Fazl, which includes a passage listing the ornaments worn in Hindustan. The author lists 37 types, their names carefully transliterated from Hindi to Persian. A manuscript copy of 1621 (London, BL) includes very small illustrations of these types. Milstein gives an analysis of a later illustrated version; the section on jewellery is followed by a description of metalcrafting techniques, including that of *kuṃdan*, by which gemstones are set into gold. Usually combined with enamelling (*see* §15(iv) below and JEWELLERY, colour pl. II, fig. 1), this technique was used in all Mughal jewellery until claw settings were introduced from Europe in the 19th century. Each setting was made from a gold sheet hammered on to a die and then pierced to take a stone. This shell was then soldered together; alternatively, it could be cast in one piece by using the lost-wax process. After engraving and enamelling, the piece was prepared for setting; it was filled with shellac, overlaid at the apertures for the stones by thin sheets of silver alloyed with a small amount of pure gold. To enhance the colour of inferior stones, these sheets could be tinted with a transparent colour. The stone itself was then cold-set using a strip of pure gold wire, pressed and pushed into place. The setting was the most highly paid part of the process; at the time of Akbar (*reg* 1556–1605), according to the *Āyīn-i Akbarī*, the stone-setter was paid more than the enameller.

The jewellery that was worn in abundance at every level of society often drew the comments of foreign travellers. François Bernier, in India from 1658 to 1659, noted that the empire was an 'abyss of gold and silver. . .because so much was melted, remelted and wasted in fabricating women's bracelets both for the hands and feet, charms, earrings, nose and finger rings. . .the quantity of these articles made in India is incredible'. The royal treasuries were filled with enormous quantities of uncut gemstones, turban jewels, rings and necklaces. The jewellery worn by Akbar in miniature paintings shows a mixture of Hindu and Iranian influences; female styles, on the scant evidence of the depiction of women in painting at that time, seem to have been more clearly demarcated. Miniature paintings of the reign of Jahangir (*reg* 1605–27) illustrate a revolution in personal ornamentation, which became very elaborate, reflecting the wealth and stability of the empire; the emperor's interest in foreign rarities must also have contributed to aspects of the change. In particular, Portuguese jewellery brought to court was almost certainly copied by the royal craftsmen, and Jahangir also sent agents to purchase expensive exotica. European models also inspired a new variant of the royal turban aigrette, which had originally followed Iranian fashions (Stronge, 1985). New materials such as jade probably began to be used at this time, although the most famous jade jewels, characteristically set with gemstones in gold, date from the time of Shah Jahan (*reg* 1628–58; London, V&A; see 1988 exh. cat., nos 62, 304 and 309). Also from the time of Shah Jahan are two cameos, one a portrait of the emperor (see fig. 341), the other representing an incident when he was attacked by a lion (Paris, Bib. N.; see 1982 exh. cat., no. 377); both are thought to have been made by Europeans at court. A third cameo portrait of the emperor probably dates to *c.* 1660 (New York, Met.).

As most of the information concerning 17th-century Indian jewellery derives from paintings and contemporary descriptions rather than from actual pieces, generalization is difficult. It may be inferred by comparison with other artistic areas and from the evidence of paintings that innovation continued through the reigns of Akbar, Jahangir and Shah Jahan and that in the time of Aurangzeb (*reg* 1658–1707) styles were generally repeated without much change. Despite being renowned for his personal

341. Cameo portrait of Shah Jahan, sardonyx, 23×20 mm, *c.* 1630–40, (London, Victoria and Albert Museum)

austerity, Aurangzeb was impressively adorned for his appearance on state occasions according to contemporary European accounts. Elsewhere, provincial rulers took over courtly Mughal jewellery styles and followed their emblematic significance.

More jewellery has survived from the 18th century, though almost entirely without precise provenance. The exceptions are a group of aigrettes from Jaipur and the Mughal court and the turban jewels presented to Admiral Charles Watson by Mir Ja'far 'Ali Khan after the Battle of Plassey (*see* §15(iv) below; all London, V&A). A key document of the same period is an illustrated album prepared for the French Colonel Gentil in 1774, which depicts male and female jewellery (London, V&A). Information on jewellery below courtly levels in the Mughal period is almost non-existent, but as 'Company painting' developed in the 18th century, various illustrations of castes and occupations provided glimpses of a more humble but equally decorated society.

(b) South. The jewellery of Hindu south India was designed on completely different aesthetic foundations from that of the Mughal-influenced north and displays incomparably greater diversity in form, style and decoration. At a tribal level, jewellery could be made from seeds, flowers and chopped grasses. At a higher social level, these were imitated in metal and used as pendants or beads. Structurally, southern jewellery is usually more complicated; for example, flat sheets of gold are decorated with minute applied granules, discs and wires. A strong geometricism in many pieces is combined with animal heads or masks from nature or mythology, portrayed realistically or in semi-abstract form. Temple jewellery is massive and is usually decorated with religious motifs worked in repoussé; J. Filliozat and P. Z. Pattabiramin illustrate an array of ornaments from temple collections, none precisely datable but probably not of any great age. The jewellery, generally, is rich in symbolism. For example, the *rudrākṣa* bead, a seed sacred to Shiva, could be strung in a rosary or worn by *yogi*s or widows. The rare double nut, symbolizing the union of Shiva and Parvati, is particularly sacred and may be encased in the sacred metal, gold, to form the focal point of a necklace; the casing may be embellished with representations of the deities, sometimes riding on the bull Nandi and attended by fan-bearers (Bolon and Sarin).

Havell noted the complexity of female ornaments for the hair and ears found in the Madras region; six different types were worn as a set for the ear, and the hair was adorned with gold pieces representing the sun and moon (London, V&A). He also gave an informative description of the *thālī*, the Hindu marriage necklace presented to temples, which attains particularly complicated forms in the south. The diversity of southern jewellery contrasts markedly with areas under Mughal rule, where a more general style permeated jewellery made for both Muslims and Hindus. Only at a lower level, where jewellery is made of silver or base metal, are there obvious regional differences in the north. Courtly jewellery in the south was certainly as splendid as that found at the Mughal court. Domingo de Paes, visiting the king of Vijayanagara in the 16th century, especially noted the lavish apparel and ornaments of the queen's personal maids, who wore silk clothes and startling quantities of necklaces, jewelled girdles, anklets and bracelets.

(iii) 19th–20th centuries. Jewellery of this period is much better documented, chiefly as the result of the systematic documentation of Indian material culture conducted in the 19th century but also because of the collecting activities of European institutions, which were stimulated by the great international exhibitions of the time. Also, as European women increasingly began to live in the Indian subcontinent in the 18th century, they turned to local goldsmiths to make jewellery according to Western fashions, Indian jewellery not having any appeal for them. The copying of European styles and techniques led to the incorporation of claw settings and *cannetille* filigree into jewellery made for Indians. As greater numbers of Europeans settled during the 19th century, firms developed wares appealing specifically to that market. One of the most notable, the British firm of P. Orr & Sons of Madras, became renowned for jewellery decorated with figures from Hindu mythology made by its Indian craftsmen and marketed as 'swami ware' (from the Sanskrit adjectives *svami* and *svamini*, meaning 'male' and 'female' and used to denote a god, goddess, lord, master, etc; see fig. 342). These wares achieved international renown through the medium of the great exhibitions, as did the delicate glass and gold jewellery of Partabgarh (Rajasthan) and Ratlam (Madhya Pradesh). The renowned enamellers of Jaipur also supplied the European market, sending their wares to the exhibitions. However, the generally poor quality of the material collected for these Western exhibitions prevented it having the impact on European design that textiles, in particular, had. It was not until the firm of Cartier became involved with trade in India after the Delhi Durbar held in 1911 to mark the coronation of George V that Indian influence began to make a significant impact on Western jewellery. Cartier also refashioned some of the Indian princely collections in Art Deco style, incidentally causing a revolutionary shift away from gold to platinum. Thus the traditional jewellery styles and techniques of the subcontinent were spurned in fashionable circles and did not regain general appeal for several decades.

342. 'Swami ware' necklace, from a pattern book of P. Orr & Sons, Madras, 19th century (London, Victoria and Albert Museum)

BIBLIOGRAPHY

E. B. Havell: 'The Art Industries of the Madras Presidency: Jewellery', *J. Ind. A. & Indust.*, iv/34 (1891); v/40 (1892), pp. 29–34 and plates; vi/48 (1894), pp. 70–71 and plates

L. Finot: *Les Lapidaires indiens* (Paris, 1896)

J. Marshall: 'Buddhist Gold Jewellery', *Archaeol. Surv. India, Annu. Rep., 1902–03* (1904), pp. 185–94

T. H. Hendley: 'Indian Jewellery', *J. Ind. A. & Indust.*, xii (1909) [series of articles published as set]

E. J. H. Mackay: *Further Excavations at Mohenjodaro* (New Delhi, 1937–8)

——: 'Arts and Crafts in the Time of Mohenjodaro', *Ind. A. & Lett.*, xiii/2 (1939), pp. 73–89

J. Marshall: *Taxila*, 3 vols (Cambridge, 1951)

R. G. Chandra: *Studies in the Development of Ornaments and Jewellery in Proto-historic India*, Chowkhamba Sanskrit Series, xli (Varanasi, 1964)

J. Filliozat and P. Z. Pattabiramin: *Parures divines du sud de l'Inde* (Pondicherry, 1966)

J. Brijbhusan: *Masterpieces of Indian Jewellery* (Bombay, 1979)

R. G. Chandra: *Indo-Greek Jewellery* (New Delhi, 1979)

M. Latif: *Bijoux moghols/Mogol juwelen/Mughal Jewels* (exh. cat. by M. Latif, Brussels, Soc. Gén. de Banque; Musées Royaux A. & Hist.; 1982)

The Indian Heritage: Court Life and Arts under Mughal Rule (exh. cat., ed. R. Skelton; London, V&A, 1982)

Z. Haque: *Gahana: Jewellery of Bangladesh* (Dhaka, 1984)

M. Lerner: *The Flame and the Lotus: Indian and South-east Asian Art from the Kronos Collections* (New York, 1984)

S. J. Czuma: *Kushan Sculpture: Images from Early India* (Cleveland, 1985)

R. Knox: 'Jewellery from the Nilgiri Hills, a Model of Diversity', *South Asian Archaeology; 1983*, ii, ed. J. Schotsmans and M. Taddei (Naples, 1985), pp. 523–33

S. Stronge: 'Jewels for the Mughal Court', *V&A Mus. Album*, v (1986), pp. 308–17

R. Milstein: 'Indian Jewellery in an Illustrated 'A'in-i Akbari', *Jewellery and Goldsmithing in the Islamic World*, ed. N. Brosh (Jerusalem, 1987), pp. 105–12

O. Untracht: 'The Nava-ratna', *Islamic and Hindu Jewellery* (London, 1988), pp. 17–30

A Golden Treasury: Jewellery from the Indian Subcontinent (exh. cat. by S. Stronge, N. Smith and J. Harle, Bradford, Cartwright Hall, 1988)

M. Postel: *Ear Ornaments of Ancient India* (Bombay, 1989)

C. W. Schmidt: 'The Age of the Kusanas', *India Mag.*, xii (1991), pp. 30–41

Hoofse snuisterijen uit India [Court gems from India] (exh. cat. by P. L. Scheurleer, Amsterdam, Rijksmus., 1991)

C. R. Bolon and A. V. Sarin: 'Metaphors in Gold: The Jewelry of India', *Asian A.*, iv/4 (1993), pp. 1143

S. Stronge: 'Indian Jewellery and the Great Exhibitions', *The Jewels of India*, ed. S. Stronge (Bombay, 1995)

O. Untracht: 'Swami Jewellery: Cross-Cultural Ornaments', *The Jewels of India*, ed. S. Stronge (Bombay, 1995)

SUSAN STRONGE

13. MAPS. Although maps were produced in India before the advent of European cartographers in the 18th and 19th centuries, few have been dated. Despite their artistic merit, such maps were not valued by Europeans because they had no projection or scale and appeared to have been drawn without scientific principles.

The best-known early expressions of spatial relationships from the subcontinent are the Hindu, Buddhist and

Jaina cosmographical diagrams and paintings (e.g. Ahmadabad, Calico Mus. Textiles, 961). These were produced from the 16th century in a variety of shapes—round, oval, square or humanoid—on paper, cloth and stone; globes are also known. Representing the entire universe, the maps usually centre on Mt Meru (the mountain believed to exist at the centre of the universe) and include depictions of trees, animals and fish as well as rivers, mountains and buildings. The few surviving world maps show some European influence in the representation of geographical features, although their treatment is Asian. Even Persian-influenced maps include such decorative elements as trees, buildings, towns and ships. A fine, late 18th-century world map (Berlin, Mus. Islam. Kst), probably from the Deccan, includes numerous painted miniature scenes such as peasant life in Africa and red horses swimming in the Caspian Sea.

The most decorative maps, however, are probably those depicting religious sites. Long scrolls (*vijñapatipatra*; e.g. 12×0.23 m, 1859; Vadodara, Maharaja Sayajirao U., 7572) sent to invite Jaina monks to bless a town by their presence during the monsoon season depicted the journey there in great detail: the shops they might pass, dancing girls in welcoming poses, temples and other important buildings and frequently an elevation of the desired destination. Elaborate paintings of popular pilgrimage sites, executed partly in plan and partly in elevation, were prepared for visitors to take home for contemplation or as souvenirs. Here, as in most Indian cartography, the importance of the religious element overruled scale and projection. The elaborate maps of the Jagannatha Temple at Puri, Orissa (see fig. 343), which depict each shrine in great detail, are mental maps rather than strict geographical representations. A large number of plans of the holy circumambulation around Vraj, the birthplace of Krishna, were produced in a variety of styles. Some are in the form of a leaf or a lotus (e.g. Vrindavan, Vrindavan Shudh Sansthan, 4706); others show the various sites in stylized elevation on either side of the banks of the River Yamuna. One map of Varanasi, another popular pilgrimage site, is a large painting on cloth (3.25×2.29 m), crowded with buildings ranged along the River Ganga and stretching inland to the roads thronged with pilgrims making their way along the seven paths around the city (New Delhi, N. Mus., 61.935). Another depicts the major shrines along the pilgrimage route, with each divine image carefully delineated, rivers emphasized by fish in the water and trees along the banks, and a richly caparisoned bull as the focal centre (Paris, priv. col.). Two other examples of 18th-century scroll maps have survived, one depicting the Ali Mardan Khan Canal, which flowed south to Delhi and the Yamuna (Hyderabad, Andhra Pradesh State Archives), and the other representing the road from Delhi to Kandahar (London, BL, Pers. MSS 4380, 4725). Both are richly decorated. The canal map shows each irrigation outlet, and distant towns and villages are named without regard for their geographical location. Along the canal banks tigers and deer are shown, as well as a variety of flora. At one point an elephant is shown partly submerged to indicate the depth of the water. The road map depicts the view from the centre of the road to either side, with plans of the forts and towns encountered along the way, as well as wells, bridges and a wealth of other information on the surrounding countryside. Much simpler and less decorative route maps accompanied a manuscript detailing travels of the saints of Islam. Similar route maps were still produced in the late 20th century (*see* INDIA, REPUBLIC OF, fig. 7).

The region of Kashmir appears to have attracted a large number of cartographers. Kashmiri maps of the 18th and 19th centuries range from large paintings on cloth (e.g.

343. Map of the Jagannatha Temple, Puri, Orissa, painted cloth, 1.5×2.7 m, ? late 19th century (Paris, Bibliothèque Nationale)

London, BL) to a series of carefully depicted sheets for individual administrative districts; every hamlet is named, each stream and bridge is shown, but not a single road (e.g. Amritsar, Maharaja Ranjit Singh Mus., Acc. M/829). There are also hundreds of stylized 19th-century plans of the many sacred springs of the region (e.g. Srinagar, Sri Pratap Singh Mus., 58:2063, 59:2066) and maps of Srinagar embroidered on shawls (e.g. London, V&A, I.S.31.1970). Other town plans include an elaborate 18th-century cloth map of Surat (Jaipur, Maharaja Sawai Man Singh II Mus., 118), the town's commercial importance being marked by the large number of ships depicted on the river. Nasik, too, is shown on a finely detailed map that is undoubtedly based on a survey (Pune, Peshwe Daftar). Two 18th-century maps of the main streets of Shahjahanabad (now Delhi) are similar to the route maps in that they show the buildings on either side in elevation as they might appear to a pedestrian (London, V&A, AL 1762–4).

The largest extant collection of Indian maps is held at the Maharaja Sawai Man Singh II Museum, Jaipur, and includes maps of military campaigns, sketches showing how a valley might change if a dam were constructed, engineers' plans for the repair of a fortress wall, plans for the construction of Jaipur, maps of Bengal and Assam and many hundreds of others.

BIBLIOGRAPHY

S. Gole: *India within the Ganges* (New Dehli, 1983)

——: *Indian Maps and Plans from Earliest Times to the Advent of European Surveys* (New Delhi, 1989)

G. N. Bahura and C. Singh: *Catalogue of Historical Documents in Kapad-Dwara Jaipur: Maps and Plans* (Jaipur, 1990)

J. E. Schwartzberg: *Cartography in the Traditional Islamic and South Asian Societies*, ii/1 of *The History of Cartography*, ed. J. B. Harley and D. Woodward (Chicago, 1992)

SUSAN GOLE

14. MASKS. Ritual masks have been produced on the Indian subcontinent since the third millennium BC, as can be seen from a Harappan mask found at Kalibangan in Rajasthan. In the late 20th century, numerous regional variants of traditional masks continue to be manufactured, despite the erosion of many traditions. The main mask tradition is associated with the re-enactment of the Hindu *Mahābhārata* and *Rāmāyana* epics and other Hindu legends derived from Puranic texts. Popular themes include the destruction of demons by the goddess Kali and the miraculous deeds of such gods as Vishnu, Shiva and Krishna. Other common subjects include stories of village guardians, local heroes and tribal deities, especially those connected with ancient fertility and animistic cults. A masked dance tradition derived from Tibetan Buddhism exists in the Buddhist monasteries of the Himalaya region. A separate tradition of non-functional metal temple masks (*mohrās*) has existed in the north-west of the subcontinent since the 11th century.

HANA KNÍŽKOVÁ

(i) Temple masks. Evidence for pre-18th-century temples in Himachal Pradesh and Ladakh is only indirect and takes the form of numerous silver and brass masks (*mohrās*) of divinities worshipped in villages. Some of these masks, which date from the 11th century on, are inscribed. According to the records from Kulu (formerly Sultanpur) state, more than 300 temples were represented by their masks at the annual Dashahra festival in the capital city; even in the late 20th century, nearly a hundred participated. Masks ranging in date from the 12th to the 17th century were held in a temple in Bail, near Nirmand, which was destroyed in the 20th century. A nondescript shrine in a village near Manali holds a silver mask of the god Vishnu, gilded and studded with hardstones. The mask bears a date corresponding to AD 1500 and the namd of Raja Siddha Pal Singh of Sultanpur (Kulu). Siddha Pal Singh was one of the most powerful rulers of Kulu, and the impressive mask and many others in the same shrine betoken the grandeur of his lost temple.

KIRIT MANKODI

(ii) Other. Modern masks are predominantly face masks used in dance or theatre; the use of helmet masks, helmets and other types of headdress is much less widespread. Although some mask traditions retain their original cultic or ritual character, others have succumbed to a gradual secularization, becoming more a form of general entertainment. Among the archaic forms of masked performance that survive are the exorcism and cultic dances connected with the worship of local guardian deities, nature spirits, ancestors and demons, as well as the ritual dance dramas organized at large temples, pilgrimage centres and village shrines. More common, however, is the use of masks in the classical and folk dance dramas performed during religious festivals. Most dances and dance dramas are performed once a year and are connected with the festivals of the annual cycle. The performances are organized in the dry season preceding the monsoon, before the beginning of work in the fields and after the harvest. They take place in the open spaces in front of temples and shrines, sometimes even within the temples themselves, and are also sometimes performed in the streets at village markets and fairs. Every performance is accompanied by music, the main, and sometimes the only instrument being the drum.

Because of the ritual nature of masks, both their makers and their wearers are bound by taboos, including abstinence from certain foods, alcohol and sex. In some places, the masks themselves are believed to be endowed with spirits that could prove harmful and are therefore offered propitiatory sacrifices. In addition, they are either kept at a sacred place near the temple or shrine or destroyed immediately after the performance. The making of masks is an exacting seasonal task demanding the participation of a considerable number of craftsmen, including carpenters, potters and painters. These hereditary craftsmen remain entirely anonymous, relying on local tradition and common principles of style. In consequence, masks, modelled on established schemes and painted according to predetermined iconographic rules, lack individualism even when they display technical excellence. The only examples of masks as products of free artistic creativity are found among the aboriginal peoples of the subcontinent. They include masks meant for general entertainment and ritual masks; since their execution depends on the talent and skill of the individual artist, the results vary widely in style, form and workmanship. Various materials—wood, paper, cloth, metal, wicker and gourd—are used in the manufacture of masks, depending on local availability. The fundamental material is wood (see fig. 361 below), preference being given to light, easily worked varieties. Another common procedure involves modelling masks from paper, which is laid in layers over a clay mould and then glued together. Masks are usually painted; natural pigments, both mineral and vegetable, were originally used, but these have since generally been replaced by powdered pigments or synthetic paints.

See also §XI, 2(ii) below.

BIBLIOGRAPHY

V. Elwin: 'The Mask', *The Tribal Art of Middle India* (London, 1951), pp. 136–50

G. S. Dutt: *Folk Dances of Bengal* (Calcutta, 1954)

V. Elwin: 'Pilgrimage and Pantomime', *The Art of the North-east Frontier of India* (Shillong, 1959), pp. 67–85

A. Bhattacharyya: *Chau Dance of Puruliva* (Calcutta, 1972)

H. Mode and S. Chandra: *Indische Volkskunst* (Leipzig, 1984)

S. R. Sarkar: *Masks of West Bengal* (Calcutta, 1990)

H. Knížková: 'India', *The World of Masks*, ed. E. Herold (London, 1992), pp. 116–50

S. Awasthi: 'Masks of India: Visions of Gods, Demons and Clowns', *A. Asia*, xxiii/5 (1993), pp. 144–54

HANA KNÍŽKOVÁ

15. METALWORK. From early times, metals have been worked at high levels of excellence on the Indian subcontinent. Surviving examples such as a figure of a dancing girl dated *c.* 2000 BC from Mohenjo-daro (see fig. 130 above), the probably contemporary Daimabad hoard, the 7th-century AD Sultanganj *Buddha* (Birmingham, Mus. & A.G.; *see* §V, 7(v) above) and the iron pillar at Delhi (*c.* AD 400; *see* DELHI, §III, 1) show mastery of technique. The development of decorative metalwork is largely the product of cultural factors. The almost endless variety of ritual implements needed for daily worship at the household shrine includes special spoons, bowls, plates, incense holders, mirrors, miniature baths and swings, stamps for marking the body and lamps. In addition, Hinduism has a marked tendency to see the activities of daily life as a ritual: washing, with its strong links to ideas of purity and pollution, requires water jars, coconut-oil pots, body scrapers, hair-dryers and combs, while marriage brings demands for dowry gifts, jewellery, sets of rice bowls, dowry boxes, jewellery boxes, cosmetic cases, betel-nut sets and special lamps. Although gold and silver were highly prized for jewellery, Indian metallurgists were always fascinated by alloys; indeed, their use was governed by the demands of religion. Bronze and brass are the most common, but special alloys such as *aṣṭadhātu* ('eight elements': zinc, tin, iron, gold, silver, lead, mercury and copper) and *pañcaloha* ('five irons': copper, gold, silver, zinc and tin or lead) are used for statues and ritual accessories. In such alloys the proportion of precious metals might be very small, as the reason for their inclusion is symbolic rather than practical. Bell metal (tin with a little copper) and various alloys of silver with up to 20% copper are also used. Brass is very popular, since it is the only acceptable alternative to precious metals for Hindu eating and cooking utensils; Muslims generally use tinned copper for food vessels.

See also BRASS, §III, 2, BRONZE, §II, 4, and METAL, §I.

DAVID JONES

(i) Gold. (ii) Silver. (iii) Base metals. (iv) Enamelled wares. (v) Inlaid and encrusted wares.

(i) Gold. Although such Classical writers as Herodotus described India as a land of fabulous wealth, gold deposits in the Indian subcontinent, mainly located in Karnataka, are relatively scant and have never been enough to supply the enormous home demand. The metal was, therefore, acquired through trading textiles and South-east Asian spices for African gold, which was absorbed to a degree that caused Pliny to complain about the drain of gold from the Roman world into South Asia. The importance of gold in the Indian subcontinent exceeded its material worth, as it held a central place in ritual and had a multi-layered symbolism. The frequent references to gold in Vedic literature were surveyed by Rajni Nanda, who observed that at all times obvious connections were made between gold and the sun and light. In the *Ṛg veda*, for example, the gods wear gold jewellery and have golden chariots and physical attributes of gold or of golden hue. The fire god Agni is specifically identified with gold, and aspects of other associations and other uses of the metal survive in Hinduism (see Sarpotdar and Subbarayappa). Gold jewellery was worn at all periods and is often classified systematically. The earliest literature indicates, as would be expected, that gold was obtained from alluvial deposits, but as early as the *Atharva veda* gold mining seems to be mentioned (Nanda, p. 119). Gold was also used in many auspicious rites and sometimes represented sacrificial fire, giving it a purificatory role: it was seen as an eternal cleanser. Gold and fire were considered necessary in a court of justice. In the later epic literature, gold maintained its central place, and its use was extended to include images, thrones and seats. Frequent reference is also made to gold in Buddhist and Jaina literature, with jewellery having the same crucial place. The ornaments here, too, are often classified in detail. The *Artha śāstra* of Kautilya, a 4th-century BC treatise on statecraft, contains important information on the technical aspects of purifying gold, on its properties and uses and on the goldsmith's work. Gold powder, used in medicine and in painting, also has an ancient history (see Dube).

The profuse literary evidence for gold is not matched by physical evidence, as artefacts would have been continually melted down and refashioned. Archaeological finds are usually small and consist overwhelmingly of ornaments, although coins are also important. There is also a small range of such Buddhist objects as miniature caskets and stupas, notably the 'Bimaran' casket (London, BM; *see* AFGHANISTAN, fig. 14) of the early to mid-1st century AD. Although there is literary evidence for the existence of gold images, none of any size has survived. A miniature headdress in Kushano-Sasanian style, set with rubies and sapphires, is probably from a small image (London, BM).

There are abundant references of the Mughal period (16th–19th century) for the use of gold in jewellery, in the decoration of arms and armour, in the manufacture and decoration of utensils (*see* GLASS, colour pl. V, fig. 1) and in architectural decoration, but physical evidence is again extremely limited, with the important exception of gold coins. Gold was also used extensively in book production and illustration. A spoon of *c.* 1600 (London, V&A), almost certainly produced for the court, is one of the earliest Mughal-period gold artefacts known. The same style, using flat-set stones and similar motifs, may be seen on other artefacts of the early 17th century, such as a dagger (Kuwait City, Mus. Islam. A.) and a thumb-ring (London, V&A; *see* JEWELLERY, colour pl. II, fig. 1). At this period gold was also important as a base for enamel decoration (*see* §(iv)(a) below), as it was the medium by which the characteristic combinations of brilliant translucent red, translucent green, translucent and opaque blues and white could be produced. According to contemporary texts, Shah Jahan (*reg* 1628–58) used gold copiously in the decoration of his buildings; none has survived, however. His most famous gold possession was the 'Peacock Throne', looted by Nadir Shah of Iran in 1739 and subsequently broken up. The same fate befell a gold throne owned by Tipu Sultan (*reg* 1782–99) and made between 1787 and 1793; pieces of it are now in the Royal Collection at Windsor Castle, Berks, and the National Trust Collection at Powis Castle, Powys (see Archer, Rowell and Skelton). However, the golden throne of the Sikh ruler Maharaja Ranjit Singh has survived intact (see fig. 344).

South Indian temples may represent the greatest repositories of gold on the subcontinent. A study of temple jewellery (see Filliozat and Pattabiramin) includes gem-encrusted artefacts, and a government-sponsored survey of temple holdings was undertaken by Indian scholars in 1993. The demand for traditional gold marriage jewellery and dowry goods also continues.

344. Golden throne of Maharaja Ranjit Singh, wood and resin core covered with sheets of embossed gold, 940×900 mm, early 19th century (London, Victoria and Albert Museum)

(ii) Silver. Although silver was not as important as gold in Indian society, it was used in vast amounts in the fabrication of jewellery, sumptuary artefacts and coinage. It was also used to embellish artefacts made of other materials and to decorate paintings. Silver is symbolically associated with the moon; like gold, it is regarded as incorruptible and is therefore used for ritual utensils and vessels. The profusion of jewellery worn by humans and animals at all times on the subcontinent, and other domestic and courtly demands for silver led to the use of enormous quantities of the metal, which, like gold, was acquired principally through trade.

Archaeological excavations have produced many silver finds, but these do not occur in sufficient quantity to enable the early history of Indian silver to be written. There is again a discrepancy between documentary evidence indicating the extensive use of silver in the Mughal period and the limited surviving material evidence. A mid-17th-century beaker with a Europeanizing form and floral decoration closely related to the architectural decoration of the Shah Jahan period is unique (see fig. 345). Apart from pieces made by European firms, few pre-19th-century silver artefacts are documented: Robert Clive's *pan* (betel leaf) set, listed in a 1766 inventory, is a rare exception (see Archer, Rowell and Skelton).

Silver was used to clad chairs, thrones and other furniture, to cover doors, to make or decorate images, perhaps most dramatically in the shaped coverings or 'cuirasses' used in the *kavacam* ritual in south Indian Hindu temples (Filliozat and Pattabiramin, pl. CXIII), and to decorate insignia such as fly whisks (*caurīs*) and ceremonial staffs (*chubs*). In all these cases gold could be substituted, or the silver could be gilded. Silver was used prolifically to inlay base metal (*see* §(v) below); it was also enamelled (*see* §(iv)(b) below), although the palette is markedly different from that of enamelled gold owing to the technical limitations of the material. The most successful results are obtained with translucent blue and green. The best enamelled silver is from Avadh and includes hookas, pan boxes and utensils, and decorations for furniture and weapons. Among the finer surviving pieces are an armchair and footstool (London, V&A) with silver cladding mounted with enamelled plaques. Although Indian silver was not hallmarked, European silversmithing firms established in India in the 18th and 19th centuries introduced their own 'pseudo-hallmarking'. This was not linked to a formal assaying system but was intended to reassure European customers and to advertise the firms involved (Wilkinson, 1973 and 1987).

Although there must have been many centres of silver production, each with its own definite style, little is known about them until the 19th century, when general surveying projects carried out by the British and the great international trade exhibitions led to data collection. Mukharji provides notes on centres of silver filigree production such as Cuttack and Dhaka, on metropolitan silversmithing centres such as Calcutta and Delhi and on many smaller centres, giving an outline of typical wares. Two more important silversmithing regions were Kashmir and Kutch (now Kachchh). Jaipur and Madras were other flourishing centres. In all these areas the same craftsmen would also have worked with gold. The foundation for the industry in specific localities was either active patronage from the local ruler—an aspect of the market that was beginning to

345. Silver beaker and cover, chased and engraved, the inside gilt, h. 142 mm, diam. 83 mm, mid-17th century (London, Victoria and Albert Museum)

disappear by the late 19th century—or demand in centres of trade and commercial wealth. European demand activated by the exhibitions provided a new and temporary stimulus to the market that had the effect of increasing production at the expense of quality and originality. Certain areas of the industry catering almost exclusively to European demand included production of the 'swami ware' of Madras, featuring images of Hindu deities (see fig. 342 above).

SUSAN STRONGE

(iii) Base metals. The most accomplished metalworking styles of the subcontinent are those associated with the cast-bronze statuary tradition of Kerala, Madurai and Thanjavur in south India (*see* §V, 7(vi) above). The product of a long period of development from the Chola period (9th–13th centuries AD) through Chalukya and Hoysala times (*c.* 10th–14th centuries), they seem to have taken their final form under the Vijayanagara empire (*c.* 14th–16th centuries) and its successor Nayaka states (*c.* 16th–17th centuries).

Apart from statuary, Keralan craftsmen produced enormous bronze cooking pots (*chavakku*; *varpu*) of a very distinctive shape consisting of a flattened coil body with minimally decorated lugs resting on a foot. Made for ceremonial feasts at temples, their simple but colossal proportions and the perfection of their form gives them considerable dignity. Made by the lost-wax process, they not only have an archaic grandeur but are also formidable technical achievements; most examples are believed to date from the 16th and 17th centuries. Even more noteworthy are Keralan lamps, of which there are three principal types: hanging, standard and hand-held. Most hanging lamps take the form of a circular oil dish, with a raised central island attached to a three-lobed arch that hangs from a central chain. The shape is beautifully proportioned, and the central island usually bears what is in effect a sculpture, sometimes of a god but more often of an elephant and groom, a rider on a rearing horse, a bird (see fig. 346) or a miniature temple. A very fine example found in the Yogeshvari Cave has been dated to the later Chalukya period (*c.* 12th century); it features an elephant figure. Standing lamps have a strong architectural feel and were often major elements in the design of sparsely furnished spaces. Their major interest is in the form and proportions of the pillar that supports a central oil dish, often with projecting oval lobes for individual wicks. There is commonly a reservoir in the centre of the oil dish containing extra oil, which is gravity-fed to the

346. Brass hanging lamp in the form of a bird, h. 395 mm including chain, from south India, 18th century or later (London, British Museum)

bowl. This reservoir may be finished with a bud or turned into a sculpture, usually of a bird of the *haṁsa* ('goose') type.

Some standing lamps have oil bowls placed at two different heights on either side of the column; these are designed for the use of a teacher seated on a platform and a pupil seated on the floor. In a special form of hand-held lamp, the whole of the lamp is in the form of a *haṁsa* bird, with the tail serving as the handle, the body as the oil container and the head as the hole for the wick. In general terms, the distinctive aspects of Keralan metalwork are an interest in smooth rounded shapes, in form and proportion and in single sculptural elements; these features seem to have been consolidated into a distinctive repertory in the 17th century.

Unlike this relatively restrained tradition, metalwork from Thanjavur and Madurai is marked by a love of the grotesque, of complex compositions and of floral surface decoration. Products include ritual implements, lamps, giant platters for wall decoration, water-containers, boxes, hair-dryers, betel-nut boxes, scissors and lime boxes. Repoussé work and the addition of copper and silver plates to brass vessels are typical Thanjavur techniques. Designs make frequent use of the gods of the south Indian pantheon ('swami ware'; *see* §12(iii) above). In Mysore, plates and bowls often combine a plain fluted border with alternating rings of plain and engraved bands based on a central floral pattern. Betel-nut cutters of the 19th century include such motifs as rearing horses and lions biting their own tails; handles ending in crocodilian (*makara*) mouths and betel-nut boxes in the form of monster-headed tortoises closely resemble the decoration of the remarkable weapons of the Thanjavur armoury. Gaja–Lakshmi lamps in which the leaf-shaped reservoir is backed by a scene of celestial elephants anointing the goddess Lakshmi seem to be another general south Indian type, while Dipa–Lakshmi lamps, in which the bowl is held by a standing woman, have a wide distribution in south India, Gujarat and Rajasthan. An early example of this type found at Warangal, Andhra Pradesh, has been ascribed to the Kakatiya dynasty (*c.* 11th–14th centuries). Long, twin-spiked hair-dryers, used for holding out wet hair to dry in the sun, occur throughout south India. Although extant examples of these dryers, which have handles in the form of graceful antelopes or female acrobats, are unlikely to be much older than the 19th century, their form probably goes back to medieval roots.

The first indications of a distinctively Indian Muslim style of metalwork are found in the medieval kingdoms of the Deccan. The aim of the master-craftsman was to provide accessories for the luxuries of court culture: ewers and bowls for washing, flasks and cups for wine, perfume and rosewater bottles and sprinklers, and the hooka (from *c.* 1604) for smoking. All these, together with the adoption by the Muslim nobility of the habit of chewing betel, provided opportunities for work showing the highest standards of technical skill and design. A number of interesting early examples clearly show a transitional stage in which Indian and Iranian or Turkish motifs appear on the same piece. In time, Mughal (16th–19th centuries) and post-Mughal styles influenced artefacts made for ordinary people in less expensive techniques. Hookas were particularly popular and were made in melon, coconut, flower-bud, mango or fish shapes. Cut and pierced mosque lamps and amuletic 'hands of Fatima' were made, perhaps at Ahmadabad. In Kashmir, distinctive teapots, coffeepots and samovars were made. Showing considerable Bukhara influence, they are decorated in all-over floral patterns using repoussé, cut brass and sometimes lacquer; dragon handles and spouts are quite common.

While Muslim courts built on the traditions of the Mughals, there was also a re-emergence of independent Hindu states, particularly of the Marathas and Rajputs, in the 18th century. New styles in metalwork appeared, along with human and animal forms. Human figures were shown in contemporary dress, and a strong love of humour or whimsy is apparent. Betel-nut cutters are made in the form of lovers, who embrace when the nut is cut, or a mother and child; cosmetic boxes take the form of a female face; a woman churning butter may decorate a brass foot-scraper (*vajrī*). Account books, pencases and inkwells were made in the shape of Ganesha, camel riders, elephants, carts, tortoises or birds. Hookas in the shape of birds and fish were made, as were sets of figures showing all the various contemporary types of warrior. Locks, stoves and braziers were also produced in animal shape or with applied animal figures. Special containers were made to hold sacred water from the River Ganga, and water spouts in the form of a cow's head were made for anointing the *liṅga* (phallic emblem of Shiva). Lamps were made in a dazzling array of types, all with a persistent underlying feeling of playfulness or romance. Parrots, associated with Kama (the god of love) and hence suitable for bedchambers, peacocks and the traditional *haṁsa* bird were very often used for hanging lamps. Ritual lamps often incorporate the animal associated with the worship of a particular divinity and sacred symbols such as the conch or tulsi leaf. They may be shaped like the female sexual organ (*yoni*) or even (in south India) incorporate the cross for Christians. Strange iron multiple lamp frames made for festivals and weddings in parts of Rajasthan were designed so that heated air rising from the lower lamps would make other lamps rotate like a ferris wheel. Elsewhere, lamps were mounted on gyroscopes, so that when they were rolled about, the flame remained upright. These were decorated with loving couples (*mithuna*) and may have been used at marriages. Multiple lamp trees with sockets for candles rather than bowls for oil seem to have been a feature of the later 19th century. Sometimes the sockets are set above the head rather than at waist-level, giving the impression of European influence.

Such features as size and skill of execution distinguish later court work from popular metalwork. Regional variations can also be detected. In Bengal, sets of wooden dowry rice measures were decorated with applied brass palmettes, iron vegetable cutters were made in the shape of birds, and in a late 19th-century innovation, brass imitation basketry was produced. The replacement of oil lamps by candle bearers also appears to be connected with Bengal. Flexible antimony containers in the form of fish were made in Bengal and Orissa. Decorated brass equipment for storing and taking opium was made in Malwa, Rajasthan. Meanwhile, the far south remained true to its heritage of medieval Hindu designs, and Muslim courts held on to their own styles. A very distinctive folk style existed in parts of western Bengal, Bihar, Orissa and Madhya Pradesh, where members of the Dhokra caste produced brass objects for rural Hindus and tribal people using a distinctive technique of lost-wax casting (see fig. 362 below). Decoration was made using a kind of pipette that squeezed out long strings of wax that could be applied as coils, spirals or long strips to the mould, rather like icing a cake. This technique was used for the production of figures of folk deities, votive horsemen, lamps (often in the form of a figure standing on an elephant holding an oil dish above its head), stacking sets of dowry rice bowls, animal figures and fish-shaped openwork brass purses. A very similar technique must have been used at Nadia, West Bengal, to produce the body stamps used by Vaishnava devotees.

DAVID JONES

BIBLIOGRAPHY

G. Birdwood: *The Industrial Arts of India* (London, 1880)

T. N. Mukharji: *Art-Manufactures of India* (Calcutta, 1888)

B. H. Baden-Powell: 'The Silver Workers of Cutch', *J. Ind. A. & Indust.*, v/45 (1894), pp. 59–62

G. Watt: *Indian Art at Delhi, 1903* (Calcutta, 1903)

R. Reeves: *Cire-perdue Casting in India* (New Delhi, 1962)

R. C. Sharma: *Brass and Copperware Industry in Uttar Pradesh with Special Reference to Varanasi* (Delhi, 1964)

J. Filliozat and P. Z. Pattabiramin: *Parures divines du sud de l'Inde* (Pondicherry, 1966)

R. Bussaberger and B. D. Robins: *The Everyday Art of India* (New York, 1968)

S. Kramrisch: *The Arts and Crafts of Kerala* (Cochin, 1970)

W. R. T. Wilkinson: *Indian Colonial Silver: European Silversmiths in India (1790–1860) and their Marks* (London, 1973)

J. Jain and J. Jain Neubauer: 'Treasures of Everyday Art: Raja Dinkar Kelkar Museum', *Marg*, xxx/3 (1978) [special issue]

Arts of Bengal: The Heritage of Bangladesh and Eastern India (exh. cat., London, Whitechapel A.G., 1979)

M. Sarpotdar and B. V. Subbarayappa: 'Gold in Vedic Society', *Indica*, xix/1 (1982), pp. 7–16

M. Zebrowski: 'The Indian Ewer', *Facets of Indian Art* (London, 1982), pp. 253–9

The Indian Heritage: Court Life and Arts under Mughal Rule (exh. cat., ed. R. Skelton; London, V&A, 1982)

C. Jain: 'Traditional Lamps of India', *A. Asia*, xiii/3 (1983), pp. 106–9

M. Jenkins: *Islamic Art in the Kuwait National Museum: The al-Sabah Collection* (London, 1983)

M. Archer, C. Rowell and R. Skelton: *Treasures from India: The Clive Collection at Powis Castle* (London, 1987)

W. R. T. Wilkinson: *A Register of European Goldsmiths, Silversmiths, Jewellers, Watchmakers and Clockmakers in India and their Marks, 1760–1860* (London, 1987)

Mughal Silver Magnificence (XVI–XIXth c.) (exh. cat., Brussels, Antalga, 1987)

A Golden Treasury: Jewellery from the Indian Subcontinent (exh. cat. by S. Stronge, N. Smith and J. Harle, Bradford, Cartwright Hall, 1988)

J. Guy and D. Swallow, eds: *Arts of India, 1550–1900* (London, 1990)

H. Brownrigg: *Betel Cutters from the Samuel Eilenberg Collection* (Stuttgart and London, 1991)

P. T. Craddock: 'Old Ways in the Kolar Gold Field', *Gold Bull.*, xxiv/4 (1991), pp. 127–31

R. K. Dube: 'Gold Powder: Its Preparation and Application as Described in Ancient Sanskrit Texts', *Gold Bull.*, xxiv/3 (1991), pp. 95–102

M. Spink: 'Silver Filigree from Cuttack', *Silver Soc. J.* (Winter 1991), p. 65

R. Nanda: *The Early History of Gold in India* (New Delhi, 1992)

The Crossroads of Asia: Transformation in Image and Symbol in the Art of Ancient Afghanistan and Pakistan (exh. cat., ed. E. Errington and J. Cribb; Cambridge, Fitzwilliam, 1992)

DAVID JONES, SUSAN STRONGE

(iv) Enamelled wares. The earliest known reference to enamelling in the Indian subcontinent is in the *Āyīn-i Akbarī* ('Annals of Akbar') of Abu'l-Fazl, completed *c.* 1596–1602 for the Mughal emperor Akbar (*reg* 1556–1605). The section on workmen in decorative art includes the enameller (*mīnākār*), who 'works on cups, flagons, rings and other articles with gold and silver. He polishes his delicate enamels separately on various colours, sets them in their suitable places, and puts them to the fire. This is done several times.' Although the art of enamelling was clearly well established by the end of the 16th century, nothing as yet is known of its earlier history. The lack of enamelling in the Hindu south suggests that it was a skill introduced after the advent of Muslim rule. Surviving enamelled artefacts do not pre-date *c.* 1600, and no additional information can therefore be gleaned from forms and motifs of foreign inspiration. Virtually all Indian enamelling, whether on gold, silver or copper, was done using the champlevé technique (*see* ENAMEL, §2(ii)).

(a) Gold. Enamelled gold was used for jewellery, weaponry and other luxury items such as *pan* boxes and rosewater sprinklers. One of the earliest surviving pieces is a Mughal thumb-ring (London, V&A; see 1988 exh. cat., no. 93). Datable to the early 17th century, it has a bejewelled and engraved outer surface, the enamelling being confined to the inner surface, a characteristic of Indian enamelled gold jewellery of all periods. The palette used for the thumb-ring is unusual by comparison with later enamels but may have been common at the time. Its scrolling motifs in opaque turquoise, leaf green and white on a black ground may derive from Renaissance ornament. However, the main motifs in turquoise, black, white and yellow on the narrow border of a hooka ring (Kuwait City, N. Mus.; Jenkins, p. 127) are more consistent with other surviving Mughal enamels inspired by architectural decoration. The translucent red and green poppies on a white ground echo the pietra dura of the main monuments of Shah Jahan's reign (1628–58), particularly the mausoleum of Jahangir at Lahore, where red cornelian and green jade poppy designs are inlaid into white marble. Another masterpiece with 'architectural' decoration is a *pan* box, cover and stand (St Petersburg, Hermitage; see Ivanov and others, no. 99), which have panels of flowering plants and Chinese clouds in translucent red and green on a white ground, framed by cypresses at the sides and by chevron borders at top and bottom. The cypresses cleverly conceal the structural joins in the box, which had to be fired in separate sections. In 1739 this box was looted from the Mughal treasury in Delhi by Nadir Shah (*reg* 1736–47) of Iran and was presented by him to Catherine the Great in 1741. Other sumptuous enamelled artefacts that reached the Hermitage by the same route include a 17th-century bejewelled armlet (*bāzūband*), which is notable for unusual enamelling on the inner surface: a scroll of white leaves and flowers with opaque yellow centres on a brilliant translucent green ground. Related objects are a jar and cover (Cleveland, OH, Mus. A.; see 1985 exh. cat., no. 181) and a box (priv. col., see 1982 exh. cat., *The Indian Heritage*, no. 329), both probably dating to *c.* 1700.

Considerably more material survives from the 18th and 19th centuries, and more information is also available on enamelling centres, particularly from the second half of the 19th century, when works were produced or collected for a series of international exhibitions. As central Mughal authority weakened following the death of Aurangzeb (*reg* 1658–1707), artists and craftsmen were attracted to the more powerful provincial courts, and the conventions of Mughal decorative style became widely diffused. As enamelling followed this general trend, it is impossible, without precise documentation, to deduce the provenance of particular pieces. Many courts must have produced enamelled work, but the specific characteristics of 18th-century enamelling from, for instance, Hyderabad in the Deccan, Murshidabad or Jaipur are not yet known. The difficulty in establishing the place of production is well illustrated by a set of turban jewels presented to Admiral Charles Watson on 26 July 1757, after the Battle of Plassey, by Mir Jaʿfar ʿAli Khan (London, V&A; see 1988 exh. cat., p. 51). These were almost certainly made at Murshidabad; a painting of *c.* 1750 (London, V&A; see 1979 exh. cat., no. 68) shows the previous nawab, ʿAlivardi Khan, wearing jewels of identical form. The enamelled backs of the jewels presented to Watson use the standard Mughal red and green flowers on a white ground, though the red is unusually dominant and there is strong Neo-classical influence. The enamel on the plume is closely similar to that on a contemporary turban aigrette (London, V&A) said to have come from the Jaipur treasury and to have been brought to Jaipur from the imperial Mughal workshops (see 1988 exh. cat., no. 39). Other pieces in the same group (all London, V&A) were held to be products of Jaipur and date from the mid-18th century to the early 19th.

In the late 19th century, the principal enamellers at Jaipur were Sikhs, and this remained true in the late 20th century (see Latif, p. 65). In a monograph published in the late 19th century, Thomas Hendley and Samuel Swinton Jacob stated that the Jaipur school was founded by Sikhs brought from Lahore by Maharaja Man Singh in the 16th century. However, it is more likely that the descendants of the original craftsmen were converted to Sikhism after their arrival in Jaipur (see Varney; Latif). Latif claims that the Jaipur archives record the establishment of a workshop (*kārkhāna*) in Amer in about 1560 by five enamellers brought from Lahore by Man Singh; four of the craftsmen are named, although the date of the reference is unclear. Hendley's description of the process of manufacturing enamelled artefacts in Jaipur applies to wares produced in most centres in the subcontinent. His survey of Jaipur wares included jewellery, cups, plates and weaponry, with about a third of the demand coming from Europeans.

Another major gold-enamelling centre was Varanasi. Rai Krishnadasa recorded that the craft was introduced to Avadh during the reign of Asaf al-Daula (*reg* 1775–97) by Kaisar Agha, an enameller from Kabul whose technique was Iranian. The enamellers of Varanasi copied his vibrant, painted polychrome style but gave prominence to a dusky rose-pink, often grinding the powder with attar of roses. The style was said to have disappeared from Varanasi in 1923 when the last hereditary master, Babbu Singh, died, but in recent years it has been revived (see Untracht). Enamelling in a similar style, probably done by Iranian craftsmen (e.g. London, V&A; see 1982 exh. cat., *The*

347. Enamelled hooka, silver, partly gilt, consisting of five pieces set with topazes and rubies, probably from Avadh, before 1766 (Powis Castle, Powys, NT)

Indian Heritage, no. 438), was found in Sind under the Talpur emirs (1783–1843), who also commissioned enamel in the standard Mughal palette of translucent red and green on a white ground.

(b) Silver. The court of Avadh—originally at Faizabad but moved to Lucknow in 1775—had established, by at least the mid-18th century, its own style of vibrant translucent blue and green enamelling on silver, which was sometimes gilt. A hooka of imperial quality, owned by Robert Clive, is listed in an inventory of 1766 and is almost certainly Avadh work (see fig. 347). On the underside is a rosette enamelled in translucent pale violet, gold and opaque leaf green; these colours are also found on Lucknow enamels in the collections of the Victoria and Albert Museum, London, all of which were bought from 19th-century exhibitions or collected in India in 1881–2. A second, related hooka (Powis Castle, Powys, NT) owned by Clive is not of the same high standard but is listed in an inventory of 1774; it may have been one of four undescribed hookas in the 1766 inventory. Other documented Avadh enamels with motifs similar to those on the Clive pieces include a sword that reputedly belonged to Shujaʿ al-Daula (London, Wallace; see 1982 exh. cat., *Islamiske vaben i dansk privateje*, fig. 3) and a box from the collection of Wajid ʿAli Shah (London, V&A; see 1982 exh. cat., *The Indian Heritage*, no. 332). Hendley also lists Multan, Bhawalpur, Kashmir, Kangra, Kulu, Lahore, Hyderabad (Sind), Karachi, Abbottabad, Nurpur, Lucknow, Kutch and Jaipur as centres of enamelling on silver in the late 19th century.

(c) Copper. The technique used to enamel copper in all periods was champlevé, although only a few examples predate the 19th century. The earliest, a ribbed box and cover dating from the early 17th century (London, V&A; see 1982 exh. cat., *The Indian Heritage*, no. 493), is so far unique; each rib of the box and cover has gently swaying copper flowers reserved against a pale lilac-blue ground and a flat, white roundel at the centre of the lid painted with flowers and leaves. The lid has black enamelled details with gilt leaves. On the underside of the box are blue and white flowers and leaves on a plain copper ground. Inside the lid, eight enamelled cypresses converge on a central floral medallion. In a fine piece from the 18th century (London, V&A), the enamel is again used as a ground for the relief decoration; the flowering plant motifs show traces of gilding. In the 19th century, Kashmir was the main centre for copper enamelling; a group of items including hookas of various forms dating from *c.* 1880 (London, V&A) uses colours including light and dark cobalt and turquoise blue, yellow, white, leaf green, black and brick red. The motifs relate to those on contemporary shawls and are cast in high relief; many of the pieces are gilded. Copper enamelling does not seem to have been practised to any great extent elsewhere, although Hendley notes Jaipur as a centre, the artisans producing 'copper eyes for idols', as they continued to do in the late 20th century.

BIBLIOGRAPHY

Abu'l-Fazl: *Āyīn-i Akbarī* [Annals of Akbar] (*c.* 1596–1602); Eng. trans. in 3 vols: iii, trans. H. S. Jarrett, ed. J. Sarkar (Calcutta, 1948–9/*R* Delhi, 1972–3)

S. S. Jacob and T. H. Hendley: *Jeypore Enamels* (London, 1886)

R. J. Varney: 'Enamelling in Rajasthan', *Roopa-Lekha*, xxix/1–2 (1958), pp. 31–9

R. Krishnadasa: 'The Pink Enamelling of Banaras', *Chhavi, Golden Jubilee Volume, Bharat Kala Bhavan, 1920–1970*, i (Varanasi, 1971), pp. 327–34

Arts of Bengal (exh. cat., ed. R. Skelton and M. Francis; London, Whitechapel A.G., 1979)

M. Latif: *Bijoux mogholes/Mogol juwelen/Mughal Jewels* (Brussels, 1982)

The Indian Heritage (exh. cat., ed. R. Skelton and others; London, V&A, 1982)

Islamiske vaben i dansk privateje [Islamic arms and armour from private Danish collections] (exh. cat., Copenhagen, Davids Saml., 1982)

M. Jenkins: *Islamic Art in the Kuwait National Museum: The al-Sabah Collection* (London, 1983)

A. A. Ivanov, V. G. Lukonin and L. S. Smesova: *Yuvelirniye izdeliya vostoka* [Oriental jewellery], St Petersburg, Hermitage cat. (Moscow, 1984)

India (exh. cat. by S. C. Welch, New York, Met., 1985)

M. Archer, C. Rowell and R. Skelton: *Treasures from India: The Clive Collection at Powis Castle* (London, 1987)

A Golden Treasury: Jewellery from the Indian Subcontinent (exh. cat. by S. Stronge, N. Smith and J. Harle, Bradford, Cartwright Hall, 1988); review by O. Untracht in *Jewel. Stud.*, iv (1990), p. 91

(v) Inlaid and encrusted wares. The catalogues of the large international exhibitions of the second half of the 19th century and the early 20th invariably include sections on the 'damascened', 'koftgari' and 'encrusted' metal wares of the Indian subcontinent. The term damascened usually referred to wares in which silver, brass or gold wire or shaped pieces of sheet silver or brass were inlaid into an engraved line or small area, a technique sometimes also called *teh-i nishān*. An overlay of fine wires hammered on to a crosshatched ground was known variously as 'koftgari' (Pers. *kūftkārī*), false damascene or counterfeit damascene (see Bauer). The term encrusted referred either to these techniques or to applied metal decoration fixed by soldering or pegging. By the 19th century particular areas were renowned for specific techniques, such as the *kūftkārī* ware of the Punjab.

The inlay or overlay of brass and silver on to base metal was used for centuries in sculpture, and the techniques are generally thought to be the result of foreign influence. However, it is not possible to trace their early development in the decorative arts because of the paucity of material before the Mughal period (16th–19th century) and the problems of dating uninscribed and unprovenanced pieces. The *Āyīn-i Akbarī* ('Annals of Akbar'), written by Abu'l-Fazl *c.* 1596–1602 for the Mughal emperor Akbar (*reg* 1556–1605), includes the gold-inlayer (*zarnishān*) and gold-beater (*kūftkār*) in a list of workmen in decorative art.

The gold-inlayer worked on silver and steel as well as hardstones, ivory, bone and tortoiseshell; the gold-beater, who commanded a lower price, was said to have worked principally on weapons. In fact, both techniques were used on weapons, which provide datable examples from the early 17th century onwards. Inlay and overlay techniques were used purely for decorative embellishment or to add emphasis to inscribed poems or prayers or to inscriptions giving the names of the weapon's owner or maker. The lack of a systematic history of arms and armour from the subcontinent precludes detailed analysis, but mention may be made of important royal Mughal weapons such as the jade-hilted dagger inscribed in gold to Shah Jahan (*reg* 1628–58; priv. col., see 1982 exh. cat., no. 406) and the sword of Dara Shikoh, dated *c.* 1640–41 (London, V&A; see fig. 325 above). The latter has an inlaid Persian verse on the back of the blade, a gold-inlaid umbrella (symbol of royalty) on the flat of the blade and gold-inlaid floral decoration on the blued steel hilt. Historic collections often include finely decorated arms and armour featuring both inlay and overlay techniques. Notable among these is the Clive collection (Powis Castle, Powys, NT), which includes a late 17th-century gold-overlaid steel armguard and a collection of swords made for Tipu Sultan (*reg* 1782–99) and the extensive armouries of the palace–forts of India (Jaipur, Alwar etc). The largely unpublished Royal Collection, Windsor Castle, also includes inlaid swords of Tipu Sultan.

In the 19th century, inlay and overlay techniques were divided into classes relating to specific cities or regions, the three main divisions being damascene work, encrusted wares and bidri ware.

(a) Damascene work. Thomas Hendley's monograph of 1892 gives the best survey of *kūftkārī* and metal-inlaying in India, noting the decline in the quality of work caused by the demand for damascened arms and ornaments for Europeans in the late 19th century. This forced craftsmen to turn out large quantities of inferior work rather than to concentrate their efforts on producing fewer but better items for connoisseurs. The Punjab, a prolific source of *kūftkārī*, was surveyed by Baden Henry Baden-Powell (1872). At the time that he compiled his survey, Punjabi craftsmen catered mainly to European taste, producing such items as weapons, hookas, trinkets, inkstands and bookstands. In Sialkot and Gujrat, the main centres, craftsmen had formerly worked almost exclusively on weapons, but with the decline of Sikh power after the annexation of the Punjab in 1849, they were forced to turn to decorating ornaments for domestic use. Lahore was another centre, and a small industry was said to have existed at Multan for over 200 years. According to Hendley, Rajasthan produced the most artistic work; the main centres were Jaipur and Alwar. George Watt, writing in 1903, noted a cheaper version of inlay known as 'dewali', which consisted of gold leaf rubbed into etched lines.

(b) Encrusted wares. The main towns producing this class of ware, according to Trailokyanatha Mukharji, were Tirupatti and Thanjavur in south India. Typically, objects made of brass or copper were decorated with applied copper or silver that was usually chased or had repoussé ornamentation. In Tirupatti, this contrasting decoration was inlaid so that it was smooth and level with the surface of the basic form, while in Thanjavur the decoration was in relief, the panels or small motifs having been worked by hand before being applied (several good examples in Birdwood). Where the repoussé was in particularly high relief, the panels had to be soldered or pegged on; this technique was reserved for the applied figures of Hindu deities used in 'swami' work. It has been suggested that originally only brass and copper were used at these two centres and that the use of silver was a European-inspired innovation (see Watt). By the 20th century, hand-chased pieces had largely been replaced by die-blocked sections, again reflecting the increase in demand and the consequent fall in standards of craftsmanship.

(c) Bidri ware. Although incorporating both inlaid and overlaid decoration (and even, in some Lucknow wares, decoration that could be called encrusted), the production of bidri ware—seemingly unique to the Indian subcontinent—should be seen as a separate technique because of its peculiarities of materials and production. The name of the technique is derived from the Deccani city of Bidar, and although it has been claimed that it was introduced by 'Ala' al-Din Bahmani (*reg* 1436–58) from Iran, there is no evidence for this, the earliest surviving pieces dating from the late 16th century.

To produce bidri ware, objects are first cast from an alloy in which zinc predominates but which may include small amounts of lead as well as copper and tin. The surface of the object is smoothed and a solution of copper sulphate applied to darken it temporarily for the next stage, engraving. The engraved design is lighter in colour than the darkened surface, enabling the pattern to be seen more clearly. The piece is passed on to the inlayer, who uses silver or brass, the brass often having a goldlike appearance owing to its high zinc content. The inlay may be of wire or sheet metal, and some of the finest pieces have a design cut out of sheet silver so that it appears silhouetted against the body of the object. In pieces of later date the decoration may be hammered on to a crosshatched surface. The final stage of the process is to blacken the dull grey of the zinc alloy so that the inlay is seen in dramatic contrast. This is done by applying a paste of ammonium chloride, potassium nitrate, sodium chloride, copper sulphate and mud, which darkens the body while having no effect on the inlay. The paste is removed, and the piece is rubbed with oil to deepen the matt black ground.

No documentary references have so far been discovered that would establish the existence of bidri ware much before 1600, although this may simply suggest that it was known by another name. The earliest written allusion to the industry is in the *Chahār gulshan* ('Four rose gardens'), a history of India written in Persian in 1759 and probably based on a text of *c.* 1720 (see Stronge). Here Bidar is listed as the place where 'the fine and rare bidri vessels are made', the items mentioned including *pan* boxes, bowls and ewers. Seventeenth-century pieces have survived (see fig. 348), although dating is on the basis of decoration and form rather than inscriptions. Such objects provide evidence for the use of metallic zinc on the Indian subcontinent nearly two centuries before it could be made in the West. Archaeological evidence pushes this back still further and proves that zinc was being smelted on an industrial scale in Rajasthan in the 14th century (see Craddock). It is not possible to determine where the surviving 17th-century pieces were made, though Deccani decorative features are seen, even when mixed with strongly Mughal design; craftsmen taken into Mughal service from Hyderabad in the Deccan may have taken the technique north. Not until the 18th century does more information on the centres of bidri production become available. On the evidence of the *Chahār Gulshān* Bidar was a flourishing

348. Bidri-ware ewer, inlaid with brass and silver, h. 285 mm, Deccan, mid-17th century (London, Victoria and Albert Museum)

centre, and in 1770 an atlas prepared for the French Colonel Gentil illustrated the items being made there (see Stronge). These included hookas with mouthpieces and tobacco holders, ewers and basins, boxes and covers, spittoons, backscratchers, various vessels, carpet weights and dishes. By this date, bidri ware was also being produced at Purnia in Bihar (see Buchanan).

The 19th century provides the clearest picture of bidri production, largely owing to detailed accounts given in exhibition catalogues from 1851 onwards. The Crystal Palace exhibition held in London in that year included bidri ware of high quality from Bidar; the Paris exhibition followed in 1855. Details of bidri ware shown at both exhibitions were singled out for illustration in Owen Jones's influential book, *The Grammar of Ornament* (London, 1856). As a result, bidri ware was exposed to new markets, which stimulated a demand that led to the opening up of new centres of production, including Surat, Bombay, Aurangabad and Benares (now Varanasi), although these appear to have been short-lived and only produced wares of poor quality. After 1875 Liberty and Co. of London also imported bidri ware, probably from the Deccan and Bengal. This international demand inevitably led to a decline in standards, with repetitious forms and patterns taking the place of individually commissioned and designed pieces. In decoration, the poppy pattern predominated, becoming coarser as the century wore on. In general, bidri decoration consists of floral, arabesque and non-figurative motifs, with the inclusion of small animals, birds and fish in Lucknow wares. Rare exceptions include a hooka base (New Delhi, N. Mus.) that depicts narrative scenes from the *Padmāvat*, a 16th-century Hindi poem by Muhammad Jayasi of Avadh. In the 20th century, bidri production became limited to the Deccan region. Modern production is largely confined to Hyderabad, with a small industry remaining at Bidar. As well as such items as buttons, jewellery, cigarette- and pill-boxes and decorative ornaments, 20th-century craftsmen are turning back to traditional forms, making, for example, hooka bases in 18th-century style.

BIBLIOGRAPHY

B. H. Baden-Powell: *Handbook on the Manufactures and Arts of the Punjab* (Lahore, 1872)
G. Birdwood: *The Industrial Arts of India* (London, 1880)
T. N. Mukharji: *Art-Manufactures of India* (Calcutta, 1888) [compiled for the Glasgow International Exhibition]
T. H. Hendley: *Damascening on Steel or Iron as Practised in India* (London, 1892)
G. Watt: *Indian Art at Delhi, 1903* (Calcutta, 1903)
F. Buchanan: *An Account of the District of Purnea in 1809–10* (Patna, 1928)
O. Untracht: *Metal Techniques for Craftsmen* (New York, 1968)
H. S. Jarrett: *The Ain-i Akbari by Abu'l Fazl 'Allami*, iii, rev. J. Sarkar (New Delhi, 1978)
W. Bauer: 'A Scientific Examination of the Applied Decoration on Two Indian Swords', *Islamic Arms and Armour*, ed. R. Elgood (London, 1979), pp. 1–4
The Indian Heritage: Court Life and Arts under Mughal Rule (exh. cat., ed. R. Skelton; London, V&A, 1982)
S. Stronge: *Bidri Ware: Inlaid Metalwork from India* (London, 1985)
M. Archer, C. Rowell and R. Skelton: *Treasures from India: The Clive Collection at Powis Castle* (London, 1987)
P. T. Craddock, ed.: *2000 Years of Zinc and Brass*, British Museum Occasional Paper; l (London, 1990)
K. Lal: *National Museum Collection: Bidri Ware* (New Delhi, 1990)
S. Markel: 'Bidri Ware: Lyric Patterns', *Golconda and Hyderabad*, ed. S. H. Safrani (Bombay, 1992)

SUSAN STRONGE

16. PUPPETS. Although puppetry in India does not have a written history, it is known that certain rulers, such as the Satavahana (late 1st century BC–early 3rd century AD) and Vijayanagara (14th–16th century) kings, patronized the puppet theatre. The general belief that puppets are one of the oldest forms of theatre in India is substantiated by Sanskrit texts that refer to the director of drama as *sūtradhāra* ('someone pulling strings'), a word that clearly derives from puppetry. In more recent times, puppet shows have become part of the rural folk culture of the subcontinent, and puppets are also used in religious rituals and festivals, commonly in supplicatory and magical roles; the puppet-theatre repertory is composed of Puranic texts, local legends and the *Mahābhārata* and *Rāmāyaṇa* epics. Puppetry suddenly declined at the beginning of the 20th century, but was revived after 1947 by government patronage and active programmes by cultural institutes such as the Sangeet Natak Academy, New Dehli. Several types of puppets—hand puppets, rod puppets, marionettes and shadow puppets—are used mainly in the southern states, although the puppets of Rajasthan and Orissa are also famous. Puppet shows, which have a sung narrative interspersed with dialogue, are accompanied by a small orchestra dominated by percussion instruments; the music played generally unites folk melodies with classical music.

Once found over a wider area, hand puppets remain only in Orissa and Kerala. The puppets from Orissa (*kandhai nāc* or *kandhai nata*), which re-create the popular love story of Krishna and Radha, are made of wood and paper and dressed in costumes inspired by temple sculptures. They are operated by a single puppeteer accompanied by a tambour player. The puppets of Kerala (*pava-kuthu*) developed around the 18th century under the influence of the *kathakali* dance form and assumed its style, music and repertory. The stylized puppets are made of clay, paper and wood and have painted *kathakali*-style make-up; they wear thorny crowns (*kiritams*) and elaborate, colourful costumes. The puppet team comprises four people, but the puppets are operated by a single puppeteer seated on the floor.

Rod puppets are found in western Bengal and Orissa. The puppets of western Bengal (*putul-nācs*) measure 0.3–1.2 m high and are fixed on a long bamboo pole that the animator tucks into his waistband. Each puppet comprises a bamboo frame pasted with hay and rice husks mixed with clay and covered with banana leaves. Make-up and costumes are brightly coloured, in keeping with the traditions of folk theatre. The puppets' shoulders are animated with the aid of rods, while the head is moved with a string. The *kaṭhakandhai nācs* (*kaṭha*: 'wooden') of Orissa are smaller (h. 0.30–0.45 m). The head is fixed to a rod, but the shoulders are moved using strings hidden inside the puppet.

Marionettes are most popular in the states of Rajasthan, Tamil Nadu and Karnataka. The *kathaputalī* puppets of Rajasthan (*kathaputalīs*) measure *c.* 0.6 m tall; their heads, necks and chests are carved from a single piece of wood, and their bodies and hands are of stuffed cloth. Normally made without legs, they are suspended by a single thread attached to the puppet's head and the back of its waist; there may also be two threads for the hands. The stylized faces, usually painted yellow, have large eyes, and the puppets wear medieval Rajasthani costumes. The *sakhi nāc* (*sakhi*: 'girl') puppets from Orissa are similar. The *bommalāṭa* puppets of Tamil Nadu flourished during the 18th and 19th centuries under the patronage of the rulers of Thanjavur. On average, they stand *c.* 0.75–0.9 m tall and weigh *c.* 10 kg. The articulated limbs are suspended by threads attached to a metal ring on the puppet's turban. Their hands are moved using rods from above, and their costumes and jewellery follow the *kathakali* dance tradition. The *gombe-atta* puppets from Karnataka imitate local folk opera in both costume and repertory.

Shadow puppets (*chhāyānāṭaka*) are of two types: opaque silhouettes and transparent coloured figures. The *rāvanachhāyā* puppets of Orissa are used to relate the legends of Rama. Made from opaque deerskin, they delineate only the silhouette of the figure. Their limbs, made from a single piece of wood, cannot be moved. Measuring up to 0.75 m tall, the puppets are supported by a bamboo pole. The shadow of the puppet is cast on to a screen composed of a piece of fabric, usually a *sāṛī*, hung over two bamboo rods. In front of it, the leader of the company recites and sings the narrative, beating out the rhythm on a small drum. The similar *chamdyacha bahulye* figures of Maharashtra include large-scale groupings combining several figures surrounded by ornamentation. Opaque *tholu pava-kuthu* shadow figures from Kerala, in a ritual dedicated to the goddess Bhadrakali, are made of goat- and deerskin and are painstakingly cut out and painted, although spectators do not see the colours. *Tolubommalāṭa* puppets from Andhra Pradesh (see fig. 349) existed as early as the 2nd century BC and flourished during the 16th century. They are among the largest Indian shadow figures, measuring between 0.9 and 1.8 m high depending on the status of the character. The articulated puppets are composed of many pieces of opaque goat-, buffalo- or deerskin and painted with plant pigments. Each figure is reinforced by a bamboo pole that supports it from both sides; the hands are moved by means of separate rods. Similar puppets with the same name are found in Tamil Nadu. The *togalu gombe atta* shadow puppets of Karnataka are smaller (h. up to 1.05 m), unarticulated and colourful, with faces characterized by eyes with enormous pupils.

Public collections of puppets are held by the Darpana Academy of Performing Arts, Ahmadabad; the Research Institute of Folk Culture, Calcutta; the Government Museum and National Art Gallery, Madras; and the Sangeet Natak Academy, New Dehli.

BIBLIOGRAPHY

R. Pischel: *Die Heimat des Puppenspiels* (Halle, 1900)
J. Tilakasiri: *The Puppet Theatre of Asia* (Colombo, 1968)
Marg, xxi/3 (1968) [Indian puppets issue]
K. X. Robbins: 'Indo-Asian Shadow Figures', *A. Asia*, xiii/5 (1983), pp. 64–75
J. Pani: *Living Dolls: The Story of Indian Puppets* (New Delhi, 1986)
F. Seltmann: *Schattenspiel in Kerala* (Stuttgart, 1986)
I. N. Solomonik: *Traditsionnyy teatr kukol vostoka* [Traditional puppet theatre of the East] (Moscow, 1992)

HENRYK JURKOWSKI

349. *Tolubommalāṭa* shadow puppet representing the *Rāmāyaṇa* character Sita, painted leather, h. 965 mm, Andhra Pradesh, early 20th century (New York, American Museum of Natural History)

17. Tents. Temple canopies may have been used from an early date in India. Free-standing tents, however, are not well documented until the Islamic period (*c.* 1200–1857; *see* Tent, §§II, 2, and III, 1 and 2(ii)): by the 11th century they belong within the urban and military tradition of the Middle East, including the Central Asian trellis tent. Much of the terminology used is Persian. The camp and its royal precinct were most elaborately developed in India, being essential in a vast territory for both military and administrative control. They also served in the transferral of the court to a cooler region each summer. Palace buildings, too, were shaded by large, often ostentatiously expensive awnings and other tentage.

From the Ghaznavid period the main types were the *khayma* and *dihlīz*, or vestibule used for public audience; both were of canvas stretched by guy ropes, like the great enclosure screen, *sarāy-parde*, around them. The trellis tent, *khargāh*, was also present. By the 13th century a marquee-like *bārgāh* was used as a tent of state. Royal tents distinguished by size, majesty, richness of materials and their red colour, a royal privilege, were thus established as a topos.

Ibn Battuta records that a suite of tents sent to Muhammad Tughluq (*reg* 1325–51) consisted of an enclosure, an awning to shade its interior, a guyed tent with an annexe and a retiring tent, all in appliqué work decorated with gold leaf. Tents other than royal ones at this time were white embroidered with blue. Firuz Shah (*reg* 1351–88) prohibited the depiction of people or animals on tents, an indication that at least some of this decoration was figurative. Babur (*reg* 1526–30) undoubtedly preferred a trellis tent of the domed Central Asian type as a retiring room. Mughal book paintings depict such tents with a bulbous dome in Timurid style and coverings of rich textiles in lieu of felt. A guyed audience tent was often set a little in front. Under Humayun (*reg* 1530–40, 1555–6) the *dihlīz* appeared for the last time. The military camp included tents of state, *bārgāh*, as well as a treasury, a bedding store, kitchens, buttery, stables, tents for ablutions and latrine tents. Another *bārgāh* served the royal harem. In 1534 Humayun developed for his own presence chamber a zodiac tent (*Khargāh-i davāzdah burj*), with 12 towers through which the stars could shine. A demountable three-storey pavilion, the Qasr-i Ravan (Moving Palace), open on six sides with multicoloured hangings, was used for palace festivities.

Under Akbar (*reg* 1556–1605) tents reached a new level of eclectic magnificence (see fig. 350), but the reorganization of the imperial camp was his most notable innovation. The entire camp precinct was laid out as a series of rectangular spaces of successively greater privacy from west to east (adumbrating the layout used later for the Red Fort at Delhi), 1275 m long. The women's quarters at the eastern end were protected by a wooden trellis adapted from the Central Asian tradition, enclosing a tent of state, trellis tents and wooden pavilions. Fronting the public audience courtyard at the west end was a larger tent of state for the élite, surrounded by 50 awnings. A courtyard at the centre was used for relaxation and for private audience in the evening. The imperial complex was made in duplicate so that an advance camp could be sent ahead to the next site. The tents of officers and men

350. *Camp of the Emperor Akbar on Campaign*, showing an enclosure screen, a marquee top used as an audience tent, an awning and a private trellis tent, 366×199 mm; miniature from *Akbarnāma*, *c.* 1590 (London, Victoria and Albert Museum, IS 2–1896, fol. 52)

extended in a 30-km circuit around the royal centre. Book paintings of the period show that most royal tents were a plain red externally, with eaves valances in yellow or diapered white; the principal tent of state might have elaborate appliquéwork medallions. Gold brocade seems to have been reserved for trellis tents and awnings. Double-nap velvet, already used in 1535, Portuguese broadcloth and various brocades were probably imported from Europe or Turkey. In 1605 the tent department was valued at ten million rupees.

Developments under Jahangir (*reg* 1605–27) and Shah Jahan (*reg* 1628–58) mainly affected palace tents. The tent of state, now devoid of its walls, was rigged as two distinct roofs, one above the other, on two tall main poles, with a throne canopy on four slender poles below making a third stage. Its awnings were arranged in a continuous series around the eaves, and a pair of trellis tents, their woodwork sheathed in silver, were set symmetrically behind (see Tent, fig. 1). The eaves assumed a bowed line, probably under Bengali influence. The most famous new tent of this type, known as *aspak*, of gold-brocaded velvet on silver and gold-sheathed poles, was first pitched at Agra in 1628. An even finer example was pitched at Agra in 1635 to house the new Peacock Throne. Comparable tents were used in front of the audience halls of the Red Fort at Delhi; at its inauguration in 1648 the tent for public audience matched the building in length (57 m) and, with a width of 37 m, could accommodate 10,000 courtiers. These tents were planned as part of the building from its inception, as must also have been true in earlier settings. More indigenous materials, notably chintz from Machilipatnam (Masulipatam), were used in the mid-17th century, especially under Aurangzeb (*reg* 1658–1707), as material excesses were reduced. In his reign the trellis tent finally went out of fashion, but the trellis enclosure was extended to fence off the entire royal precinct.

Among the few surviving tents from the 17th century are the roof of a small tent of state of silk brocade woven in arched panels (Ahmadabad, Calico Mus. Textiles), a tent of crimson silk velvet set off with gilt embroidery, which is surrounded by cusped arcades (Jodhpur Fort; see Welch), and a small ridged tent of crimson velvet ornamented with gold leaf and lined with a delicate pattern of pink silk flowers against a golden ground (Jaipur Palace). Examples from the 18th and 19th centuries show extensive use of coloured embroidery, such as floral designs in pink and turquoise on quilted white cotton (e.g. Jodhpur Fort). Animal and human figures were sometimes used in non-Muslim contexts, as in an example in cherry-coloured silk from Dhrangadhra (on loan to Ahmadabad, Calico Mus. Textiles). Tents remain in use in modern times to house public meetings, often with geometric appliquéwork in bright colours. Block-printing is also used, especially for temple canopies.

BIBLIOGRAPHY

Ibn Battuta: *The Travels of Ibn Baṭṭūṭa*; Eng. trans. H. A. R. Gibb (Cambridge, 1958–71), iii, pp. 672–6, 752–5

Abu'l-Fazl: *Āyīn-i Akbarī* [Annals of Akbar], (*c.* 1596–1602); Eng. trans. in 3 vols: i, trans. H. Blochmann, ed. S. L. Gloomer ([Calcutta], 1871/*R* Delhi, 1965), *āyīns* 16, 17 and 21; ii and iii, trans. H. S. Jarrett, ed. J. Sarkar (Calcutta, 1948–9/*R* Delhi, 1972–3)

F. Gladwin: *The Persian Moonshee* (Calcutta, 1801), pp. 69–74 [incl. extracts transl. into Eng. from Ray Chandar Bhan Brahman's *Qavā'id al Salṭanat* ('Rules of the sultanate') on tents at the time of Shah Jahan]

W. Irvine: *The Army of the Indian Moghuls, its Organization and Administration* (London, 1903)

Abdul Aziz: *Thrones, Tents and their Furniture Used by the Indian Mughuls* (Lahore, n.d.)

India: Art and Culture, 1300–1900 (exh. cat. by S. C. Welch, New York, Met., 1985)

P. A. Andrews: 'The Generous Heart or the Mass of Clouds: The Court Tents of Shah Jahan', *Muqarnas*, iv (1987), pp. 149–65

——: *Felt Tents and Pavilions* (Cologne, in preparation)

P. A. ANDREWS

18. TERRACOTTA. Indian artisans have fashioned objects from terracotta since at least the 3rd millennium BC. Their art has ranged from the ephemeral (made for seasonal observances or use in everyday life) to the permanent (meant to endure as long as the monumental architecture it adorns). Because clay is abundant, inexpensive and easily shaped, artisans working in terracotta have enjoyed greater liberty to improvise and experiment than have sculptors in stone or bronze. The result has been a wider variety of objects (including images meant for worship, pilgrimage souvenirs and toys) as well as a greater diversity in techniques and styles. These have co-existed over long periods, making it difficult in some cases to tell the art of one era from that of another.

(i) Materials and techniques. (ii) Historical survey.

(i) Materials and techniques. The clay used for terracottas is the same as that used for common pottery. The ideal clay comes mainly from riverbeds, but alternative sources may be selected for other, perhaps ritualistic, reasons. First the clay must be cleaned by removing pebbles and other extraneous matter, then mixed with rice husk or some other tempering material (such as ash, sand, cattle dung or a combination of these), which reduces the shrinkage, warping or splitting that may occur in firing. The clay is then kneaded by hand. Local methods for working the clay vary. The object may be pressed into shape, moulded or coil-built, or assembled by a combination of these techniques (see Saraswati). Various tools are used to shape and decorate terracotta objects, including wooden beaters, moulds, fabrics for wiping or smoothing the clay surface, shaping tools, blades for carving decoration (a technique comparable to incising wood or ivory) and various wood and clay stamps for impressing surface decoration.

When the clay is in the 'leather-hard' stage of drying before firing, the surface is ready for shaving or smoothing, stamping or impressing with decoration, or applying a slip made of finely grained clay mixed with water, as in Maurya-period figures (4th–3rd century BC) and Gupta-period panels and larger images (4th–5th century AD). The surface may be burnished after the application of slip to heighten its lustre. Mica powder is sometimes sprinkled on the surface at this stage, and large pieces may be painted.

To ensure durability, clay images are fired in open pits, ovens or kilns, depending on the locality. The colour of fired specimens ranges from red to biscuit to black; if the kiln is sealed, the result is grey; if exposed to air it is red, usually with a grey core. In general, men shape and decorate the objects, and women paint them (see Jayaswal and Krishna). The names of artists are usually not recorded, although several undeciphered Gupta-period inscriptions may contain the maker's name. Most inscriptions either identify the subject or indicate the placement of the piece in its architectural setting.

(ii) Historical survey. Although terracottas are difficult to date, some objects can be stylistically grouped according to iconographic and regional distinctions. Examples from stratified excavations provide fixed points of reference with which other terracottas can be compared. For example, a Maurya-period mother goddess discovered at Mathura compares with other terracottas that may be ascribed to Mathura on the basis of style (see 1986 exh. cat., nos 19–20). Although no two examples are identical, the Maurya-period Mathura group is technically and stylistically consistent. The same comparative method may be used with Shunga-period (*c.* 184–75 BC) plaques from Mathura, Kausambi and Tamluk and with Kushana and Gupta-period figures. A brief overview of the historical and regional development of the terracotta tradition based on such stylistic analysis follows.

(a) Pre- and protohistoric periods. Among the earliest Indian terracottas are those from the Indus River Valley in Pakistan (*see* §IV, 2(iii) above), where several excavated

sites such as Mohenjo-daro, Harappa and Chanu-daro provide evidence of urbanization as early as 2500 BC. Mostly simple, hand-modelled figures of females and animals, particularly bulls (e.g. New Delhi, N. Mus.; Karachi, N. Mus. Pakistan), these terracotta figures occur in large numbers and are often considered to reflect the sophistication of culture in this early period. They have been found as far east as Rajasthan, as far south as sites in Gujarat and as far west as Balakot, a Harappan site on the Makran coast of the Arabian Sea, where excavated pottery kilns contained bull figures (see Jarrige and Meadow). Although many scholars encourage restraint in ascribing religious significance to terracotta figures from the Harappan sites until more is known about the civilization, it is difficult not to see the numerous female figures as fertility figures, particularly in view of the significance of terracotta figurines in the Ancient Near East and the Classical world.

Evidence of terracotta production in the sparsely documented period between the decline of the Indus Valley civilization and *c.* 6th century BC is scarce. However, excavated sites such as Inamgaon and Nevasa in Maharashtra have yielded crude figures that appear to be associated with fertility (Pune, Deccan Coll., Maratha Hist. Mus.; see Dhavalikar). Examples found in the north-west, for instance a figurine from a tomb at Katelai, Swat (Rome, Pal. Brancaccio), continue the tradition of the hand-formed female type of the Harappan civilization. A torso of a male figure from Pandu Rajar Dhibi (Burdwan District) in West Bengal (Calcutta, Victoria Mus.), datable to the early 2nd millennium BC, documents the survival of the early terracotta tradition in eastern India.

(b) Early historic period–1st century BC. The establishment of the Maurya empire brought a period of increased trade and prosperity. The Maurya capital, Pataliputra (now Patna in Bihar), has yielded some of this period's finest terracottas, representing significant technological and stylistic changes in an increased number of types. A celebrated female dancing figure (Patna Mus.) from Bulandibagh, near the site of Pataliputra, represents a standard terracotta type found throughout eastern India at this time. Distinguished by their fine craftsmanship and profusion of naturalistic detail, these figures are generally represented standing with one arm raised and the other held akimbo at the waist. Their innovative character lies in their relatively large size (ranging from 220 to 280 mm), in their combination of moulded and hand-formed parts and in their lively and naturalistic poses. Similar figures have been found in fragmented form at Chandraketugarh, Tamluk and Patna.

These sensuous, naturalistic images contrast with a second group of Maurya-period female figures found mainly in Mathura (but also at sites in the Ganga Valley), in which the auspicious female is represented as an awesome static presence. Such images range from simple, flat standing figurines (see 1986 exh. cat., nos 18–20) to elaborate figures in seated postures. Finds have included few male images of this type, but many varieties of animals as well as fragments of animals with human riders. Their glossy black surfaces can be associated with the pottery known as Northern Black Polished Ware (*see* §5(i) above) discovered in the same context. The figures' faces, featuring high cheekbones, small mouths and elongated, almond-shaped eyes, are moulded; their narrow-waisted bodies and prominent breasts are hand-formed; and their elaborate hair and dress ornaments are composed of applied pellets and strips.

The emphasis on nudity and surface detail continued in the Shunga period in central and eastern India. The use of the mould became more popular, with complete figures and narrative subjects appearing in moulded plaques. An increased variety of types and decorative motifs is evident in objects excavated at such sites as Tamluk, Kausambi, Mathura and Chandraketugarh (see 1986 exh. cat., nos 23, 25–26, 30, 35 and 39). Perhaps the finest extant terracotta is a female figure represented on a Shunga-period plaque from Tamluk (see fig. 351). Although its lacelike fretwork

351. Moulded terracotta plaque, 210×99 mm, from Tamluk, West Bengal, Shunga period, *c.* 100 BC (Oxford, Ashmolean Museum)

scheme of surface embellishment is a common characteristic of moulded terracottas from the eastern region of the Ganga Valley, the richness of the jewelled decoration on this piece is unmatched by any other example. The figure's bicornate headdress wrapped with pearled fabric is set with the five emblematic hairpins (*pañcacuda*) thought to symbolize the five elements. Although Shunga-period terracottas are sometimes regarded as the stylistic precursors of stone sculpture, comparison reveals that the impact of terracottas comes from intricate surface play, while in contemporary stone and bronze images of the same subjects the emphasis is on voluptuous form and contour.

(c) 1st–3rd centuries AD. Numerous small human and animal figures moulded as hollow two-sided images are associated with the Satavahana period (late 1st century AD–early 3rd). However, while Satavahana power was centred in Andhra Pradesh, these images are also found in Maharashtra and further south (see 1986 exh. cat., nos 46–9). Their clay is often a refined white kaolin or reddish terracotta. These images are less obviously religious than some earlier examples; however, the commonest animals, horses, are often shown richly caparisoned with bridles, reins, saddles and ornaments, suggesting a possible reference to rites of the royal horse sacrifice (*aśvamedha*). Other animals represented include elephants, bulls and rams. The sculpting of small terracottas was never again as refined in central or south India as it was during this period. Examples datable to the 4th century from the Deccan are crude and moulded from inferior clay.

During the Kushana period (1st–3rd century AD) in north India the mould was not as widely used, and hand-modelled figures, with parts turned on a wheel, were more in evidence. As in contemporary stone sculpture, the number of subjects increased, and the iconography grew more complex, resulting in more definitive regional styles. Narrative reliefs were less common in terracotta than in stone, and emblematic and decorative approaches prevailed. Judging by dress and ornament, some images seem to have been secular. The numerous life-size terracotta heads found throughout Uttar Pradesh and the Gandhara region (e.g. Allahabad Mus.) show a variety of freely delineated ethnic features and individual expressions, indicating both an increased mastery of technical skills and a concern for portraiture.

The fashioning of female figures associated with fertility, including female nature-spirits (*yakṣi*s), persisted. Examples dating to the 1st century have been found at Sirkap and around Taxila in Pakistan. These north-western *yakṣī*s are often hollow, double-moulded figures that have shed their characteristic Indian voluptuousness for a narrow-waisted, flat-chested form similar to Greek and Iranian prototypes. The earliest known monumental figures in terracotta were produced in the late Kushana period. Three life-size cult figures found in a monastery at Kausambi (Allahabad U., Archaeol. Mus.) have been identified as Lakshmi, Hariti and Kubera. They are hollow, were fired on a grain core and are decorated with detailed hand-finished ornaments.

(d) 4th–12th centuries. A proliferation of terracotta work in north and central India marks the Gupta period (4th–5th century AD), an era of political stability that saw a flowering of cultural and artistic production. Many monumental brick temples were decorated with large terracotta relief panels. Human figures, in particular, demonstrate a new aesthetic: surface detail is reduced and decoration simplified. Compositions are often dramatic with a remarkable sense of vitality. The mood is theatrical and narrative rather than descriptive, reflecting the dramatic literature of the period. Among the finest Gupta terracottas are the late 5th-century examples from Ahichchhatra. One of the largest terracottas, a monumental relief depicting the river goddess Ganga (New Delhi, N. Mus.), was originally placed at the entrance to a Shiva temple at the site. Although the goddess is shown in a traditional pose, standing on her crocodilian mount (*makara*), she has a relaxed, natural posture and a voluptuousness seldom evident in more formal stone sculptures of the subject.

The identification of regional styles in Gupta relief panels from temple architecture is often difficult, but the influence of the two principal Gupta-period artistic schools in central India is evident in some terracotta examples. The style of Mathura-school stone sculpture is apparent in the terracottas of Uttar Pradesh and Haryana (see Zaheer), and the style of the Sarnath school spread to sites in eastern India. The widespread nature of terracotta art in this period is reflected by the remains of Buddhist monasteries at Mirpur Khas (in Sind, Pakistan) and Devni Mori (northern Gujarat) and the terracottas depicting Hindu themes from Rang Mahal in Rajasthan.

In the post-Gupta era, especially during the period of Pala rule in eastern India (8th–12th century), terracottas were produced for many purposes, including brick architecture. Monumental brick-built monasteries extensively decorated with terracotta reliefs dating to the 8th century and early 9th existed at such sites in eastern India as Antichak in Bihar and Paharpur and Mainamati in Bangladesh (see 1986 exh. cat., nos 114–15). The stylistic innovations of these friezes include a new, more dynamic figural treatment, more rigid compositions and larger constructions. Small Buddhist votive plaques (see 1986 exh. cat., nos 118–21) were also produced in great numbers.

(e) 13th–20th centuries. Terracottas continued to be produced following the Muslim conquest of north India (*c.* 1200), though they were rarely used in Muslim art. The main exception was in eastern India, where geometric and foliate patterns were incorporated into the design of brick mosques and tombs. Hindu temples were also covered with moulded bricks and carved terracotta tiles, often depicting epic and narrative themes (see 1986 exh. cat., nos 122–4). These were made well into the 19th century, after which they were replaced by cheaper stuccowork.

Although the tradition of decorating temples with sculpted bricks waned, terracotta continued as a folk art throughout India in the late 20th century. Toys and votive figures (see fig. 355 below) are the most prevalent objects, but simple, hand-modelled mother goddess and animal figurines of the archaic types found in archaeological contexts are also fashioned across India. In Tamil Nadu, potter-priests make monumental horses and equestrian figures as offerings to the local hunter-deity Ayyanar, and in West Bengal the artisans who fashion Bankura horses preserve a centuries-old village art. Often the only way to identify Indian terracotta images as modern is by their costume and ornament (see 1986 exh. cat., nos 126–7). While representing the continuity of a 4000-year tradition, 20th-century Indian terracottas also often reflect changes taking place in the Indian subcontinent. In Gorakhpur District, Uttar Pradesh, for instance, hand-modelled terracotta animal figures that were once made for local rituals continue to be mass-produced as household decorations and exported to various parts of the country.

See also §IX below and TERRACOTTA, §II, 5.

BIBLIOGRAPHY

A. K. Coomaraswamy: 'Early Indian Terracottas', *Bull. Mus. F.A., Boston*, xxv (1927), pp. 90–96

——: 'Archaic Indian Terracottas', *Jb. Prähist. Ethnog. Kst* (1928), pp. 64–76

E. J. H. Mackay: *Further Excavations at Mohenjo-daro, 2 vols* (Delhi, 1937–8)

S. Kramrisch: 'Indian Terracottas', *J. Ind. Soc. Orient. A.*, vii (1939), republished in *Exploring India's Sacred Art: Selected Writings of Stella Kramrisch*, ed. B. Stoler Miller (Philadelphia, 1983), pp. 69–84

V. S. Agrawala: 'The Terracottas of Ahichchatra', *Anc. India*, iv (1947–8), pp. 104–79

C. C. Dasgupta: *Origin and Evolution of Indian Clay Sculpture* (Calcutta, 1961)

S. A. Shere: *Terracotta Figurines in Patna Museum, Patna* (Patna, 1961)

B. Saraswati: *Pottery-making Cultures and Indian Civilization* (New Delhi, 1966)

D. McCutchion: 'Styles of Bengal Temple Terracottas: A Preliminary Analysis', *South Asian Archaeology*, ed. N. Hammond (London, 1971), pp. 265–78

H. Härtel: 'Some Results of the Excavations at Sonkh: A Preliminary Report', *German Scholars on India*, ii (New Delhi, 1976), pp. 69–99

M. C. Joshi and C. Margabandhu: 'Some Terracottas from Excavations at Mathura: A Study', *J. Ind. Soc. Orient. A.*, n. s., viii (1976–7), pp. 16–32

M. K. Dhavalikar: *Masterpieces of Indian Terracottas* (Bombay, 1977)

D. Desai: 'Social Background of Ancient Indian Terracottas', *History and Society: Essays in Honour of Professor Niharranjan Ray*, ed. D. Chattopadhyaya (Calcutta, 1978), pp. 143–68

G. Dales: 'Of Dice and Men', *Ancient Cities of the Indus*, ed. G. Possehl (New Delhi, 1979), p. 141

J.-F. Jarrige and R. H. Meadow: 'The Antecedents of Civilization in the Indus Valley', *Sci. American*, ccxliii/2 (1980), pp. 122–33

S. C. Kala: *Terracottas in the Allahabad Museum* (New Delhi, 1980)

S. S. Biswas: *Terracotta Art of Bengal* (Delhi, 1981)

M. Zaheer: *The Temple of Bhitargaon* (Delhi, 1981)

G. Mitchell, ed.: *Brick Temples of Bengal, from the Archives of David McCutchion* (Princeton, 1983)

S. L. Huntington: *The Art of Ancient India: Buddhist, Hindu, Jain* (New York, 1985)

V. Jayaswal and K. Krishna: *An Ethno-archaeological View of Indian Terracottas* (Delhi, 1986)

From Indian Earth: 4,000 Years of Terracotta Art (exh. cat. by A. G. Poster, New York, Brooklyn Mus., 1986)

P. Jayakar: *The Earthen Drum: An Introduction to the Ritual Arts of Rural India* (New Delhi, n.d.)

AMY G. POSTER

19. WOODWORK. Although no evidence survives, it can be inferred that the arts of wood-carving and timber construction were already highly evolved in the Indus Valley civilization of the 3rd millennium BC, as the *Ṛg veda* (*c.* 1500–*c.* 1200 BC) makes metaphorical reference to timber and carpentry work in its description of the building of heaven and earth. Hemachandra, court poet, adviser and historian at the court of the Solanki king Jayasimha Siddharaja (*reg c.* 1093–1145) mentions an image of the Jaina *tīrthaṅkara* Mahavira (6th–5th century BC) that had been carved out of sandalwood during his lifetime, and Megasthenes, the Greek ambassador to the court of Chandragupta Maurya (*reg c.* 321–*c.* 297 BC), refers to the wooden pillars in the spacious halls of the imperial residence at Pataliputra (modern Patna). Throughout the subsequent periods, cult images, furniture, tools and domestic articles continued to be made of wood. Wood was also the chief building material until the knowledge of stoneworking became widespread during the last centuries BC. During this period, the use of wooden beams in the rock-cut caves of western India, the woodlike appearance of many decorations and other architectural parts, the employment of unnecessarily large blocks in structures such as stupa railings and the absence of any knowledge of cement all point to the primacy of wood in early India (*see also* §III, 1(i)(a) above).

(i) Materials and techniques. In the different regions of the subcontinent various kinds of timber were and are used for woodwork, the selection being determined by the objects to be carved. The most durable and popular timbers, used throughout India, are teak (*Tectonia grandis*), shisham (*Dalbergia sissoo*) and rosewood (*Dalbergia latifolia*). Sandalwood (*Santalum album*) is valued for its fragrance and resistance to insects in the south and west, where it is used to make small household objects and carvings. Although ebony (*Diospyros ebenum*) is rare, it has traditionally been prized by Muslim craftsmen for carving ornamental combs, furniture, picture frames and walking sticks. Large blocks of the jackfruit tree (*Artocarpus integrifolia*) are used in Karnataka, especially the coastal regions, for carving monumental anthropomorphic and theriomorphic sculptures of heroes, spirits, deities and animals. In Kashmir, wooden buildings and carvings commonly employ Himalayan spruce (*Picea morinda*), walnut (*Juglans regia*) and deodar (*Cedrus deodara*). In this region, as in other Himalayan states, pine (*Pinus excelsa*) and Himalayan ash (*Fraxinus floribunda*) are often used. In Bihar and other parts of eastern India buildings are constructed of the abundant local palm wood, which is also used for small carved items. Other timbers traditionally used in the Indian subcontinent include acacia (*Acacia arabica*), nim (*Azadirachta indica*), tamarind (*Tamarindus indica linn.*) and mango (*Mangifera indica*); mango is especially popular because of its ready availability and softness. Rattan and bamboo canes are also used.

Seasoning is usually done by keeping cut timber in the open air or, in the case of bamboo, water for several months or even years. To aid preservation, sesame oil is applied. Wooden objects are normally ornamented by carving the surface in low or high relief, by inlaying ivory, tin, bronze or silver into grooves cut into the surface (sandalwood and ebony being most suitable for this purpose) or by veneering, painting or lac-turnery (*see* LACQUER, §I, 2).

(ii) Regional survey.

(a) North. Punjab and the Himalayan states have an extensive tradition of wood-carving and timber construction owing to the ready availability of local timber, notably ash, spruce, pine, walnut and cedar (deodar). Houses in Kulu, Himachal Pradesh, have a lower storey of stone and an upper storey of wood, with balconies, sloping roofs

supported on carved pillars and intricately carved ceilings and interiors. Hoshiarpur and other towns in the Punjab are known for furniture of deodar, rosewood and walnut, decorative pieces and small domestic items inlaid with bone or ivory. Kashmir is famous for its panelled domestic interiors, in which intricately carved panels, often of spruce, are attached by means of double-grooved battens to the walls and especially the ceilings. Outside, carved wooden façades feature windows of fine latticework skilfully joined by thin laths of wood carved with intricate geometric motifs. At the beginning of the 20th century, European influence encouraged the wood-carvers of Kashmir to produce decorative boxes, screens and panels of walnut, which has a heavy dark grain ideally suited to decoration by undercutting. Owing to the importance of boats for transportation and communication in the region, boatmaking in Jammu and Kashmir has developed into a matchless skill. Made from planks of cedar, the various types of boats created for specific requirements include houseboats, transportation barges and slim, fast-moving passenger boats. In addition, Rajouri District, Jammu, is famous for fine combs of boxwood (*Buxus sempervirens*). Ladakh has a long tradition of architectural woodwork—doorways, door panels, archways, posts and wooden interiors—all carved with scenes from the Buddhist pantheon, along with flower, bird and animal motifs. Besides architectural woodwork, Ladakh is also known for its carved and painted wooden furniture.

(b) West. Apart from an established tradition of architectural woodwork, the western states of Gujarat and Rajasthan were and are prolific producers of wooden objects for household and ritual purposes. Carpenters who carved columns, pillars, brackets, doors, windows, niches, wall and ceiling panels, balcony railings and entire house façades also made chests, cabinets, jewellery boxes, benches, mortars and pestles, spice containers, measuring bowls, laundry beaters, hand mirrors, cradles and small tables. Occasionally pieces of mica or mirror were inlaid into the carved designs on decorated pieces. Brass-bound wooden chests and dowry boxes measuring up to 1 m long are a typical feature of Gujarati woodwork. Such objects as chests, cash boxes, spice containers, bread moulds, opium grinders and cloth beaters were decorated with low-relief carvings of intricate geometric and floral patterns and motifs including interlocking circles, lotus medallions and diaper, dogtooth and chevron patterns. The arid climate of the region influenced the choice of timber for specific purposes: acacia (known as *babul* or *baval*) was used for building, khau (*Olea ferruginea*), lohero (*Tecoma andulata*) and nim for architectural woodwork and rosewood for small carved items. Acacia is also the chief wood used for lac-turned objects such as bedsteads, mortars and pestles, chair legs, cradle legs, cotton reels, spindles, rolling pins, ladles and handles. At the residences of prosperous merchants (*hāvelīs*) extensive use is made of wooden framing and bonding in combination with brick walls, as well as intricate, delicately carved wooden façades, balconies and doors.

The extremely soft wood of the Indian coral tree (*Erythrina indica*) is used by the Chitaris (hereditary painters) of Sawantwadi in Maharashtra to make brightly coloured imitation fruits and vegetables as well as small boxes painted with scenes from Hindu mythology. Elsewhere, the tribal groups inhabiting the hills around Chota Udaipur in eastern Gujarat and Alirajpur in the adjoining state of Madhya Pradesh carve votive images and ancestor figures, which are usually placed in shrines under trees.

(c) East. Throughout eastern India wooden images, mainly of nim, are made of the popular divine trinity of Jagannatha, Balabhadra and Subhadra; these are represented in a pillar-like form with facial and bodily features but no arms. Narrative scenes from the Krishna legend and other themes from Hindu mythology are commonly carved on wooden panels used in temples, temple chariots, shrine doors, household shrines and elsewhere. Orissa is famous for wooden chests and boxes painted with scenes from mythology. Tribal groups such as the Nagas, who inhabit the remote hilly tracts of north-eastern India (*see* §XI, 2(i) below), carve warrior figures, often holding guns; mother-and-child figures; animal figures, including lizards, boar, hornbills, pythons and deer; and skulls intended to be worn as trophies around the neck. Beautifully carved domestic articles, including bowls and other utensils, rice-pounding tables, musical instruments, ladles and spoons, are also produced. Wooden masks for ceremonial dances are carved by the Mongpas of Kameng in Arunachal Pradesh, the carpenters of Puruliya District in West Bengal and in Saraikela in Bihar; other traditions exist elsewhere in the subcontinent, notably in western India and in Kerala (*see* §14 above).

(d) South. Because of the abundance and variety of timber available in Kerala, wood, especially teak, is very prominent in houses, temples, mosques and palaces (*see also* §III, 7(ii)(g) above). Such architectural elements as ceilings, gables, lintels, door panels, brackets and pillars are usually intricately carved with reliefs of religious images and narrative episodes from well-known epic tales. In addition, monumental chariots, open ceremonial halls, domestic shrines and divine images were all carved in wood. An early example of exquisite wood-carving is the 13th-century pillared hall in front of the central shrine of the Mahadeva Temple in Katinamakulam. Later examples are at Chattankulangara, Kazhukkuta near Trivandrum, Padmanabhapuram and Ettumanur (*see* §III, 6(i)(h) above). Another is the *c.* 18th-century Shiva Temple at Kaviyur (see fig. 352). In the 20th century, gables, eaves and pillars of houses all along the Malabar coast had beautiful carvings representing mythological, religious and secular themes; many houses also have wooden screens carved in a variety of designs.

Houses belonging to the Chettinar community of Tamil Nadu are renowned for the exquisite carvings that completely cover the façades as well as pillars, balconies, brackets, frames and beams around the inner courtyard and niches in walls. The Gudipars ('dollmakers') of Karnataka are well known for their sandalwood carvings, including divine images, animals, picture frames, jewellery boxes, papercutters, tables and trays. The village of Kinnal (Raichur District, Karnataka) is known for its painted wooden figures; these are typically mythological images or women shown dancing or holding a child. Another

352. Carved wooden wall (detail), Shiva Temple, Kaviyur, Kerala, ?18th century

important industry of Karnataka is the inlay of ivory pieces into rosewood for a variety of furniture and utility items. In Kondapalle, Andhra Pradesh, a very light white wood is used to create delightful painted toys, including figures of the incarnations of Vishnu, women and animals. Wooden toys made in the villages around the famous temple of Tirupathi are sold to pilgrims as souvenirs.

BIBLIOGRAPHY

S. Kramrisch, J. H. Cousins and V. Poduval: *The Arts and Crafts of Travancore* (Oxford, 1952)
R. K. Trivedi: *Wood Carving of Gujarat*, Census of India 1961, v, pt VII-A(2) (New Delhi, 1965)
M. S. Mate: *Deccan Woodwork*, Deccan College Building Centenary and Silver Jubilee Series, xlix (Pune, 1967)
K. K. Dasgupta: *Tribal Woodcarvings of India*, Census of India, 1971, series I, paper no. 1 (New Delhi, 1973)
——: *Catalogue of Wood Carvings in the Indian Museum* (Calcutta, 1981)
J. Jain and A. Agarwal: *The National Handicrafts and Handlooms Museum: Catalogue* (Middletown and Ahmadabad, 1989)
V. S. Pramar: *Haveli: Wooden Houses and Mansions of Gujarat* (Middletown and Ahmadabad, 1989)
L. S. Thakur: 'An Iconographic Study of Six Wooden Sculptures from Gajan, Kulu District, and Some Connected Problems', *S. Asian Stud.*, vii (1991), pp. 83–90
G. Michell, ed.: *Living Wood: Sculptural Traditions of Southern India* (Bombay, 1992)
R. Vohra: 'Dating a Maitreya Relief of the Mid-8th Century: From Sum̱ da Chen', *S. Asian Stud.*, ix (1993), pp. 97–103

JYOTINDRA JAIN

IX. Colonial-period decorative arts.

The enormous wealth of the MUGHAL empire attracted craftsmen, architects and builders to the imperial workshops, not only from throughout the Indian subcontinent but also from other parts of Asia. These workshops were attached to the major centres of government (Agra, Delhi and Lahore), and in them goldsmiths, painters and weavers produced artefacts for the court. The provincial centres followed the Mughal model, each workshop answering the needs of a particular noble or ruler. Commercial centres also existed for products traded with the rest of India and exported to Iran, the Middle East and (with the increasing involvement of the European East India companies) to the West; Kashmir had an established shawl industry, Golconda was famed for its chintzes, Gujarat for its inlaid mother-of-pearl wares and carved wood, and Cambay (modern Khambhat) for its hardstone-carving. Crafts brought from Europe during the Mughal period also affected imperial workshops. European royal gifts influenced the Mughal style in painting and the decorative arts. A fusion of indigenous Indian and imported Iranian and European styles took place. The ceaseless flow of European artefacts to the court, the strong Iranian cultural and political ties and the arrival of European and Iranian artisans, who were taken into the workshops to join the Hindu and Muslim craftsmen already there, not only influenced the style and decoration of objects but also seem to have created entirely new industries.

With the stability and wealth that developed in his reign from the mid-16th century, Akbar (*reg* 1556–1605) encouraged the manufacture in the imperial workshops of copies of artefacts that came from abroad or appealed to him or for which there was a demand. The state wealth at this period was so great that court-patronized crafts were unparalleled: workshops were established to produce jewellery, stone-carving, metalwork, carpets and textiles, featuring combinations of indigenous Indian and traditional Islamic designs. Specialized designers conceived each work of art. Pile carpets, Kashmir shawls, textiles, wall hangings, floor coverings, tent panels, robes, sashes, chintzes, arms and armour, ivory and mother-of-pearl inlay on wood were some of the items introduced or improved under Akbar's patronage.

Textiles were one of the major reasons for the European interest in trade with the Indian subcontinent (*see* §§I, 6(i), and VII above). Portuguese merchants, who had established a trading post at Hooghly in Bengal in the 16th century, dealt in rich, backstitched quilts made in and around Satgaon, the old mercantile capital of Bengal. Worked in yellow silk on a cotton or jute ground, quilted in running stitch and embroidered in chain stitch, these 'Bengalla' or 'Sutgonge' quilts were highly prized as bed covers and bed hangings in England and Portugal. In 1632 the increasingly hostile relations between the Portuguese and their hosts culminated in the siege and fall of the Portuguese settlement at Hooghly. Thereafter Portuguese influence and power in Asia declined and other Europeans, anxious to avail themselves of India's merchandise, took advantage of the situation. The English and the French rapidly expanded their ports, and with the new ports came an increased demand for goods. Indian wares flooded European shops and warehouses, creating fashions and changing styles in every field. Textiles were among the most important exports (see fig. 353; *see also* EMBROIDERY, colour pl. I, fig. 2, and TEXTILE, colour pl. VI, fig. 2): chintz, calico, gingham, muslin, silk, satin, velvet and brocade as well as quilts, embroideries and carpets. A steady export of fabrics from India to Europe continued for 300 years, with Indian embroideries growing in popularity and demand. Initially, the embroidered articles were largely confined to the bedchamber: canopies for the beds and quilts as covers, embroidered carpets, tablecloths and curtains. In the late 17th century in Europe there was a fashion for complete sets of Indian furnishings in chintz, embroidery or a combination of both techniques. Some purchasers were content to acquire only a coverlet, or chintz yardage to line a small room, such as was bought by Samuel Pepys in 1663. In addition to the places from which exporting was easiest, Gujarat and Bengal were the main bulk producers and suppliers. Although many Gujarati items at this period were made by women for their personal use, there was also undoubtedly an organized industry producing for commercial purposes under the pressure of foreign demand.

By the mid-17th century Bengal's textiles had gained ascendancy over those from Surat and Madras, not only for their quality but also because the availability of fine cotton and cheap, skilled labour ensured a low cost of production. These textiles included fine assortments for royalty, medium-range muslins that were the latest fashion in Europe and coarse goods for the African market. During the 17th and 18th centuries foreign travellers commented on the wealth and prosperity of Dacca (now Dhaka), its flourishing commerce based on the production of cotton goods. The fineness of Dacca's *jāmdānī* muslins was explainable only by the genetic descent of manual dexterity from father to son and the local availability of the raw materials to produce these elegant, gauzelike fabrics. However, medium-grade cloth of all types provided the bulk of piece-goods exported to Europe. The finest silks and the most delicate muslins, plain, figured in the loom or embroidered, were reserved for the Mughal courts of Delhi and Murshidabad. The fine muslins exported to Europe were said to be coarse in comparison with those woven for Mughal court ladies. In the Company period, the best Bengal muslins came from Dacca and Santipore, and, as in earlier centuries, the finest went to the Indian courts. From *c.* 1770 it became fashionable for European women to wear over their shoulders fine shawls, the best of which were woven from goats' fleece by the twill-tapestry technique (see fig. 319 above). Shawls of this kind had been made in Kashmir for centuries. In India they were mainly male dress but were used as wraps for women in the cold season. When adapted for European use, they became regarded as essentially a female accessory and were a coveted possession. They were imitated in Europe from the end of the 18th century.

Other important trade goods exported to Europe were jewellery, gold, silver and brassware, precious woods, cabinetry, arms and armour. The detailed accounts kept by English, French, Portuguese and Italian travellers provide valuable descriptions of rural artisan communities and of their means of production. High-quality enamelwork was influenced by Europe, as were jewellery settings and cameos. The Mughal emperors are known to have employed European lapidaries, and several European travellers mention French and Italian jewellers and lapidaries at court. Jahangir (*reg* 1605–27) received a European-made enamelled jewel from the governor of Surat, and a European jeweller, Augustin of Bordeaux, was in the service of the Mughal emperors. A cameo relief portrait of Shah Jahan (*reg* 1628–58) from the 1630s is probably by a French–Flemish hand (London, V&A; see fig. 341 above). A Florentine panel of *Orpheus* in the Divan-i Am at Agra suggests an Italian source. Agate and crystal items were made in quantity, and a glassmaking centre was set up in Gujarat before 1669.

353. Colonial-period wall hanging, painted and dyed cotton, 2.59×1.52 m, from the Madras-Pulicat region, *c.* 1640–50, borders 18th century (London, Victoria and Albert Museum)

Silversmiths in India catered for the varying tastes and requirements of Europeans and Indians. Grand silversmiths such as Hamilton's in Calcutta and Orr and Sons of Madras made good-quality silverware for the princes of India, British royalty and government officials and their families. In Bombay in 1864 there were over 10,000 goldsmiths, but only 20 Europeans catered to the requirements of the British lifestyle in India by providing products—made in the Western style but by local craftsmen—that were virtually indistinguishable from their Regency counterparts in England. The metalworking technique known as bidri (*see* §VIII, 15(v)(c) above) was developed in Bidar in the Deccan. Other centres of production were Lucknow, Purnea and Murshidabad. Indian craftsmen adapted their wares for the European market in India—based in Calcutta and Dacca—and executed commissions for customers who wished to have, for example, their initials incorporated into the design. Hooka bases were a popular item, as were boxes.

Ivory-sheeted wood caskets were among early state and diplomatic gifts of the Portuguese period, some with Christian scenes. Two Indian polychrome ivory female European figures, possibly from Goa, shown dressed in the Portuguese manner of the 18th century, are rare survivors from the period when the foreigner in India was still an object of curiosity. Goa had a strong tradition of carving in both wood and ivory, particularly of religious images. As with other depictions of foreigners it is not unlikely that these figures were commissioned by a local patron. Large ivories of female figures are also known from Rajasthan, and well into the 19th century ivory was often used to make flat, circular, disclike, polychrome Indian playing cards (see von Leyden). Eastern India is known to have had an ivory-carving tradition from at least the 10th century. It became important in the 18th century when Murshidabad was a regional capital. Robert Clive had an ivory and partly coloured chess set, made in Murshidabad *c.* 1760 (Powys, Powis Castle, NT). Two Bengal ivory groups from the early 19th century represent an elephant procession and a bullock cart with bulls pulling a carriage with seated figures. The industry always seems to have been dependent on local patronage. At the end of the 18th century the focus changed from Murshidabad to nearby Berhampore, an army cantonment town where the increased demand for ivories was from Europeans, as Fanny Parks noted in 1836. Another material used decoratively was sandalwood inlaid with bone and ivory. A chess set (*c.* 1800) is known from Vizagapatam, which was an important furniture-making centre for elaborate and intricately inlaid furniture of a type popular with European purchasers in the 18th century (*see also* §VIII, 8 above).

Furniture, boxes and toys were often of painted wood. The Victoria and Albert Museum, London, possesses the famous Tipu's Tiger (*c.* 1795), a mechanical toy made for Tipu Sahib, Sultan of Mysore (*reg* 1782–99). This life-size carved and painted wooden tiger mauls a prostrate European (for illustration *see* COLONIALISM). A door in the animal's flank reveals a small organ keyboard. The locally made bodywork is similar to that of painted wooden toys still produced at centres in south India; the mechanism was probably by a French artisan in the Sultan's service. In Rajasthan in the 19th century, large polychrome wooden elephants were popular children's toys. Models of clay and wood, frequently of caste types, are found in different parts of India based, perhaps, on the model toys of Europe in the 18th century. By 1830, painted and clothed models of Indians of various castes, sects and occupations, made in Krishnagar near Calcutta, appeared in the collection of the Peabody Museum of Salem, Salem, MA. A pair of wood, clay and cloth models showing the methods of Thuggees murdering their victims, made for a Jaipur museum by a Madras artist *c.* 1847, were actually teaching aids used for rehabilitation of Thuggees (London, BM; see 1990–91 exh. cat., nos 294(i) and (ii)). Toy miniatures of Indian caste or regional types, usually from Lucknow or Krishnagar (see 1990–91 exh. cat., nos 364–5), were also an attempt by the colonists to understand and categorize the diversity of the Indian peoples. A splendid north Indian folk bronze known as the *Cavalcade of the King of Avadh (Oudh)* (*c.* 1820; see fig. 354) is a late and rare example of a kind of small bronze sculpture or decorative toy that was quite widely found throughout north and south India from the mid-18th century to *c.* 1830. They are believed to have been influenced both by French toy soldiers of the 18th century and by indigenous chess pieces.

During the course of the 19th century, craftsmen increasingly responded to the demands of Europeans and manufactured goods specifically for their use, ranging from furniture to such smaller items as cuff-links, card-cases, matchboxes, scarf rings and brooches. In some crafts this market became a significant part of the local production. By the 1880s Europeans purchased possibly a third of the enamelware produced in Jaipur. The British continued to be fascinated by the skills of the Delhi miniature painters, commissioning painted copies of photographic portraits on ivory. Such work, originally much larger in scale and on paper, became scaled down during the course of the century as painters began working on ivory tablets, often oval or circular. The inspiration was probably from European miniature portraits. The ivory miniatures of Delhi were very fashionable in the second quarter of the 19th century and were mounted as box lids or set into jewellery. Ivory was a more practical material than paper in the climate and more easily preserved. Company painters in Murshidabad and Patna (*see* §VI, 4(ix)(b) and (c) above) also developed a technique of painting on mica, a flexible transparent mineral used in talc. Sets of paintings were prepared in advance for sale to tourists, often showing different castes or activities (see 1990–91 exh. cat., nos 289–90), means of transportation or dress. These were approximately of postcard size and were available, as picture postcards would be to later generations, in places patronized by the British.

Where traditional patronage of the arts was established, for example at the great Rajput courts, it continued. In Jaipur the court remained the largest and most important purchaser of enamel-work in traditional forms: handles for swords, daggers, fans, yak-tail or peacock-feather whisks, horse, camel and elephant trappings and, of course, jewellery. Ceremonial weapons continued to be produced. India's rulers maintained high standards of aesthetic influence through the constant labour of gifted artisans, and armies of jewellers, weavers, embroiderers and tailors continued to ply their hereditary crafts. The Great Exhibition in London of 1851 and the exhibitions that followed showed historical artefacts from the collections of princes and magnates as well as contemporary products. Their impact was complex, creating new markets and therefore themselves affecting Indian design.

354. Colonial-period bronze: *Cavalcade of the King of Avadh (Oudh)*, h. 191 mm, north India, *c.* 1820 (Oxford, Ashmolean Museum)

A vicious circle was set in motion. Increased and uncritical demand led to a decline in the very standards and qualities that had created the initial demand. By the 1870s, people such as GEORGE BIRDWOOD feared deterioration in quality, loss of artistic integrity and destruction of the traditional modes of production in the decorative arts in India. Birdwood had a romantic image of the Indian craftsman living in a democratic village community and working with simple tools in his own home. His anxiety about the dangers of market exploitation and official encouragement of industrial development in India was identical to that of contemporary design critics and the leaders of the Arts and Crafts movement in England. During the 1870s and 1880s there was much debate on the state of Indian crafts. In Calcutta there were token attempts to support a few surviving traditional art industries, but there was also a new emphasis on training in the techniques of Western academic art. However, after the decline in arts and crafts in the late 19th century, a revival took place in the earlier part of the 20th century, helped in part by the artistic Bengal Renaissance led by such intellectuals as Rabindranath Tagore (*see* TAGORE, (1)) and the later political counterpart to this movement (*see also* §VI, 4(x) above).

BIBLIOGRAPHY

M. Archer and W. G. Archer: *Indian Painting for the British* (Oxford, 1955)
V. Ions: *Indian Mythology* (London, 1967)
R. F. Bussabarger and B. D. Robins: *The Everyday Art of India* (New York, 1968)
S. Chaudhuri: *Trade and Commercial Organization in Bengal, 1650–1720: With Special Reference to the English East India Company* (Calcutta, 1975)
Y. Vequaud: *The Art of Mithila* (London, 1977)
P. Woodford: *Rise of the Raj* (Speldhurst, 1978)
Arts of Bengal (exh. cat., ed. R. Skelton; London, Whitechapel A.G., 1979)
J. M. Gutman: *Through Indian Eyes* (New York, 1982)
R. von Leyden: *Ganjifa: The Playing Cards of India* (London, 1982)
The Indian Heritage: Court Life and Arts under Mughal Rule (exh. cat. by R. Skelton and others, London, V&A, 1982)
S. P. Huyler: *Village India* (New York, 1985)
N. Patnaik: *A Second Paradise: Indian Courtly Life, 1590–1947* (New York, 1985)
Woven Air: The Muslin and Kantha Traditions of Bangladesh (exh. cat., London, Whitechapel A.G., 1988)
J. Guy and D. Swallow, eds: *Arts of India, 1500–1900* (London, 1990)
J. P. Losty: *Calcutta, City of Palaces* (London, 1990)
The Raj: India and the British, 1600–1947 (exh. cat., ed. C. A. Bayly; London, N.P.G., 1990–91)

GERALDINE SMITH-PARR

X. Village art.

A rich variety of arts and crafts are produced in the subcontinent's villages, where over four-fifths of the population lives. Two aspects of society in particular shape the close relationship between rural and urban popular arts. The first is the close tie through kinship of rural and urban populations. Even city dwellers, who are a relatively small minority, generally consider their true home to be their family's village of origin, maintaining connections with it, especially at times of festivals and rites of passage (Skt *saṃskāra*). The second is the subcontinent's cultural continuity, which unites village and city, allowing them to share many of the same myths and rituals. 'It is because they perform and know the same stories that we can say that villager and urbanite belong to the same culture and civilization' (Marriott, p. 75). Thus artistic expressions of the simplest villager and the most sophisticated urbanite may have certain similarities. Links with the distant past reflect cultural continuity over the centuries. For example, the pinchwork sun-baked clay 'bird-mothers' made by Bengali women as ritual objects (see fig. 355 and below) are similar to terracotta figurines coming from the Indus region and dating from the 2nd millennium BC.

A division between the religious and secular poses difficulties, as everyday life in the Indian subcontinent is permeated with religious significance and symbolism. Some types of goods such as wearing apparel, jewellery and objects used in the home can be termed 'secular'. However, a constant awareness of the forces of nature and a desire for connection with such favourable aspects as wealth and fertility often mark even the most humble domestic artefact. The performing arts also bridge the sacred and profane, entertaining but often with the intent to inspire or instruct. The discussion below cannot be exhaustive, but brings together various examples of the subcontinent's rural arts grouped together by broad category or function. Because of modern trends, some of these works are no longer made. Others have been revived or are encouraged through government efforts. (For textiles *see also* §VII above; for dress and masks *see* §VIII, 7 and 14 above. *See also* INDIA, Republic of, §§VI–VIII; PAKISTAN, §§V and VI; and BANGLADESH, §§5 and 6.)

355. Votive figure or toy, terracotta, h. 90 mm, from Mymensingh, Bangladesh (Chester, CT, private collection)

1. Personal arts. 2. Domestic arts. 3. Sacred places and images. 4. Ritual objects. 5. Sacramental and festival arts. 6. Entertainment and theatre arts.

1. PERSONAL ARTS. Jewellery is an important part of personal adornment as well as an indication of social standing. Often worn in abundance, it may take on a variety of forms. In Bihar, women in Monghyar District wear multiple rows of geometrically designed silver 'flowers' in a girdle (*kardhanī*) fastened with large filigree clasps. In the Punjab, armlets may have links of brass and copper pinned together. Armbands may also include cotton threads for flexible fit, such as the *bājūband* ('arm ties') of Mina and Jat women of Rajasthan and the cast silver armlets from Andhra Pradesh. The large hollow silver or brass anklets seen often in early Indian sculpture (e.g. the Didarganj whisk bearer, *c.* 3rd century BC; see fig. 139 above) were worn by village women until the late 20th century in various parts of India. The custom prevails in some areas.

Both sexes and persons of any age, from infants to the elderly, may wear talismans. Small (50–100 mm) lockets, they have been blessed to protect the wearer against evil and often contain a prayer written on rolled-up paper. They may be of cast or beaten metal and generally indicate the divinity worshipped. Hanuman, the monkey god and carrier of healing herbs, would be worn, for instance, to ward off disease.

Combs, used for grooming hair or beard, were an art form until well into the 20th century. Most were of wood but some of ivory or bone, the handle often carved as an animal. Modern materials and ever-easier village–city travel have made this art form nearly obsolete.

2. DOMESTIC ARTS. The rural home is most often of impermanent materials such as earth or grasses. Decorative features generally consist of wall paintings and floor patterns. Women of Mithila in Bihar have long been known for their colourful folk renditions of divinities and myths, which they paint on domestic walls. The tradition is passed on from mother to daughter, as is that of abstract floor patterning called by various names: *ālpanā* in Bengal, *āripan* in Bihar, *māṇḍanā* in Rajasthan and *kolam* in south India, for instance. Traced in rice paste, these ephemeral designs may be part of daily ritual, bringing good luck to

the home. They are always part of important life sacraments (*saṃskāra*), even in urban settings.

By making *kānthā*s (embroidered quilts), Bengali women bring a new and artful wholeness to worn out and discarded clothing. The designs, sewn in coloured thread, include geometric patterns (often similar to those of auspicious floor patterns), mythological subjects and imagery from daily life (*see also* BANGLADESH, §5).

In moist regions such as Bihar, Bengal and Assam, the art of mat weaving is widely practised. In Assam floor-sized mats called *śītalpāṭi* ('cool matting') are often included among wedding gifts. Stylized bird and plant motifs are produced by contrasting natural rice straw with strips dyed red, blue or green. This tradition is particularly popular in Sylhet in Bangladesh. Arabic lettering is sometimes woven into examples made as Muslim prayer-rugs. Large mats, some measuring about 1.75×1.50 m, as well as small fans with turned wood handles are made in large enough numbers to be sold in nearby towns. Baskets are often made by women not only for their own use but also to help the economy of their family or community. Large bowl-shaped baskets easily carried on the head are produced all over the subcontinent. The coil technique is often used. In Bihar women produce trays and lidded containers from dried date-palm leaves (*khajūr*) and local *mūnj* grass. In north-eastern India, where pliable *sikki* grass grows wild, Bihari women have traditionally coiled and stitched together these fine golden-coloured grasses, sometimes dyed red, black, blue or green, to form small trays and baskets. *Sikki* products include 'sculptures' of human and animal forms, often given as gifts, particularly in connection with weddings. If made by the bride herself, they can stand as proof of her creative abilities.

Vessels for domestic use, made of clay or metal, have many local variations. Simple round shapes are familiar throughout the subcontinent in rural and urban homes, the vessels ranging in height from under 50 mm to over 500 mm. Terracotta vessels modelled in the 'slab' technique are made by village women in Manipur, north-eastern India. Women potters in Bangladesh use the clay coil method to make shallow bowls and narrow-necked water containers.

Metalwork is practised mainly by men. Pots may be made of beaten sheets of copper or brass or cast in the lost-wax technique. The simplest-shaped metal vessel is the *loṭā*, its rounded form resembling that of a gourd. It comes in many sizes and has various uses, including cooking, washing, drinking and storing. It has a broad flaring rim for ease in lifting and pouring. Spouted vessels are often of cast brass and range in size from about 200 to 300 mm. Especially common in Gujarat is the *vāḍhī*, a squat vessel, generally lidded, used to pour oil or *ghī* (clarified butter). *Vāḍhī* are sometimes made of clay. In Bengal a round-bellied water-pot with narrow neck and sweeping spout is used for washing the hands. Small hand-sized vessels (called *toyalī* in Gujarat) with S-shaped spouts are used to feed water to infants.

The popular leisure tradition of chewing betel gives rise to many specialized containers. Some of these have different compartments within one lidded box. The condiments for this activity are betel leaves, lime paste and

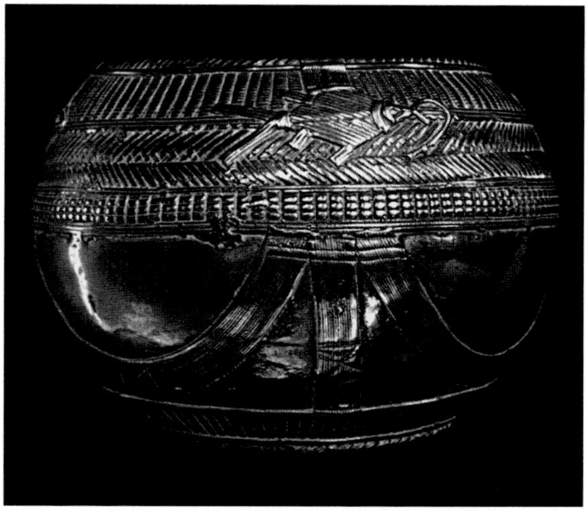

356. Measuring bowl, bell metal, h. 104 mm, from Bihar, early 20th century (Chester, CT, private collection)

areca-nut. The latter must be cut, often by fancifully decorated metal nutcrackers (*see also* §VIII, 15(iii) above).

Metal objects for the home are long-lasting items, often passed down in families as heirlooms. In north-eastern India and south-eastern Madhya Pradesh itinerant metalsmiths employ a special technique called *dhokra*. Containers, measuring bowls and ornaments (particularly heavy curved anklets), as well as deities and ritual objects, are fashioned in the *dhokra* technique (see fig. 356; see also Reeves, where both process and products are discussed and illustrated). Practice of the lost-wax technique in the subcontinent is thought to date to at least the Harappa civilization (*c.* 2550–*c.* 2000 BC). The unusual added feature of *dhokra* work is its raised designs created through the use of many small wax 'threads', extruded through a metal press. These grasslike filaments are placed tightly together over a wax-covered clay core and are cut or twisted to create the desired pattern. The process is similar to the *sikki* grass technique, which undoubtedly was its model. *Dhokra* bowls, most often used to measure rice, are generally made in nesting sets of three to five. Their *sikki*-type designs tend to include fish, crayfish or birds. In this context, the animal imagery may indicate the ingredients of a cooked rice dish, although many household items are decorated with such auspicious animals to bring good fortune to the family.

Containers of all sizes for dry foods as well as for jewellery, clothing and cosmetics are used by village and city dwellers alike. They may be made of woven straw and grasses; of wood that has been carved, painted or lacquered; of beaten or cast metal; or even of stone. As with most everyday artefacts, the difference between rural and urban examples lies mainly in degree of sophistication.

3. SACRED PLACES AND IMAGES. The humblest village hut will always have a shrine. The icon may be only a roughly painted terracotta plaque, the ritual objects simple clay receptacles to hold flowers, water and oil for a lamp. Rural shrines may have a painted uncut stone (*see* SHRINE,

As clay is an abundant and easily formed material, it is not surprising that terracotta 'mother goddesses' have been made in the subcontinent from at least the 2nd millennium BC to the present (*see also* §VIII, 18 above). The 'bird' or 'duck' mothers made by women in rural Bengal (see fig. 355 above) are part of the rituals involving vows (Bengali *brata*; Skt *vrata*). Such rites are performed only by women in order to fulfil various desires throughout the year and throughout their lives (see Ray). The animal-like forms of these mother-figures place them between animism and the mother-goddess cults. Their simple hand-formed bodies show quick cuts in wet clay, their features are pinched and their eyes formed from pricked pellets. Such images, baked only by the sun, may be ritually destroyed or immersed on completion of their votive use. Women may make large numbers at festival times, some of which are sold in the bazaar as toys for children.

The major divinities known throughout India, particularly Shiva and his consort Devi (also known by such names as Parvati, Durga and Kali) and Vishnu with his incarnations (*avatāras*), are worshipped as much in villages as in the great urban temples. The forms that these

357. *Nāgakal* (serpent stone), h. 380 mm, south India, 18th–19th century (Zurich, Universität Zürich, Völkerkundmuseum)

colour pl. III, fig. 2) or a clay image. More elaborate temples may be financed by all village members collectively or may be donated by a former member who has flourished in the city but maintained allegiance to his or her origins. Larger villages may also have wooden *rathas* (movable wheeled shrines), which carry images through the main road at festival times. In south India such *rathas* have long been known for their richly carved panels depicting deities and mythological subjects.

The belief that all living things possess a soul is indicated by the numerous tree-shrines scattered throughout most of the subcontinent. Linked closely with the tree is the serpent. Women address the wealth- and fertility-granting properties of both by commissioning carved 'serpent stones' (*nāgakals*) to be set beneath sacred trees (see fig. 357). This act is thought to bestow fertility, especially to the barren. Stone or terracotta *nāgakals* bearing Shaivite or Vaishnavite symbolism may be found side by side under the same tree-shrine. Because there is little call for stone-carving in the village setting, the local craftsmen of such votive offerings may be wood-carvers or jewellers.

358. *Shiva and Parvati*, bronze, h. 148 mm, Madhya Pradesh, 18th–19th century (Oxford, Ashmolean Museum)

359. Village potter with his terracotta image for a shrine of the god Ayyanar, Tamil Nadu

divinities take may differ widely according to medium and local style. Depending on materials at hand, wood or clay, both often brightly painted, may be the choice of a rural community, or cast bronze images may be made by travelling metalworkers for those villages or rural homes wishing more lasting icons. The solid cast image of *Shiva and Parvati* illustrated (fig. 358) has much the same iconography as the more sophisticated images of large temples. Shiva holds his trident, and the couple is further identifiable by Shiva's bull Nandi in the centre foreground. However, simplified in form, the god and goddess appear nearly identical in physiognomy and gender. Further, the work is an unrefined example of the lost-wax method, combining wax-thread, pellet and impression techniques.

Aside from the well-known deities of the larger Indian community, local divinities are important objects of villagers' devotions. Most rural populations have their own protecting goddess (*grām devī*), who in turn may resemble one of the main Hindu goddesses. However, many images of village goddesses may not conform with the *śilpa śāstra*s (iconographic texts; *see* §I, 10 above), but display attributes specific to the locale. An elaboration of the single goddess is the 'seven-sisters' motif, appearing as crudely formed terracotta images set up near ponds in south Indian open-air sanctuaries. They have power over both death and birth. Villagers offer them clay horses to gain the sisters' collective blessings and protection.

The horse has special significance in rural iconography, as both sacred mount and votive gift (see Kramrisch, 1968). The foreign origins of this animal, which was probably brought into India through the north-west *c.* 1500 BC, add to its mythic powers. Folk bronze horses with riders, coming from Madhya Pradesh and Rajasthan, may represent various local hero-protectors, such as Rao Dev and Hardaul, or ancestral spirits. These small metal equestrian images are often created in *dhokra* technique.

For centuries south Indian potter-priests have made clay figures, sometimes over life-sized, of the local protecting god Ayyanar and his retinue of warriors and horses (see fig. 359). Ayyanar, 'the Lord', blends two religious traditions. He is the son of the god Shiva and the god Vishnu who took the form of a woman, Mohini. Ayyanar's outdoor sanctuary is at a village border, often near a sacred tree.

4. Ritual objects. Various objects and accessories are required for daily rituals or special rites. In villages these objects are often made of clay. However, rural patrons, either individually or as a community, may (as with icons) commission an itinerant metalworker for more lasting works.

Some ritual objects come directly from nature, needing only a stand. For example, stones of various sizes employed as natural *liṅga*s are often placed in ring-shaped holders, part of which may extend up over the *liṅga* ending in a flared serpent hood. *Śālagrāma*s, fossilized ammonites symbolizing the god Vishnu, come mainly from the northern river of Gandaki and are more likely to be seen in shrines of the north and north-east. Their stands, some 300 mm high, generally consist of an elaborate cast metal base holding a circular tray. The base may be decorated with the sunbird, Garuda, vehicle of Vishnu, or with a fantastic lion. The conch (*śaṅkha*), an important attribute of Vishnu, may hold holy water or act as a trumpet, sounded particularly to announce birth, marriage and death. Sacred conches may be ornamented with brass or be carved with geometric patterns or mythological imagery. Metal conch-shaped vessels, small enough to fit in a mother's hand, are made for the ritually important 'first feeding' of an infant.

Metal utensils and ritual accessories often derive directly from natural products such as gourds, coconut shells and lotus flowers, or their designs may be based on terracotta models. Items for ritual use found in both metal and terracotta include pots for holy water, flower trays, incense burners, bells and lamps. The small ladle (*ācamanī*) used to pour oblations into the ceremonial fire is generally made of solid cast metal. Measuring about 160 mm from bowl to handle tip, the *ācamanī* often has a fluted cup reminiscent of a lotus. It may also have a braid-patterned handle ending in a popular divinity such as Ganesha, son of Shiva and Parvati, or Vishnu's *avatāra* Krishna.

All shrines and home altars have at least one lamp (*dīpa*), in order to bring the element of fire into the worship. The simplest cup of terracotta or even a coconut shell can suffice. Numerous metal examples exist, however, some of which are elaborate displays of complex and refined workmanship. Female figures, sometimes recognized as Lakshmi, Vishnu's wealth-bestowing consort, are often chosen as light-bearers. Cast metal images of varying sizes and quality called *dīpalakṣmī* show the goddess holding one wick-cup or a trayful. Throughout north-western India, *dīpa*s in the form of elephant and rider are prevalent. The Vedic god Indra, whose vehicle is the elephant Airavata and whose powerful weapon is the lightning-bolt, is their inspiration. *Dīpa*s of a size and weight able to be carried may have a handle at the back. Such lamps are held by the priest or worshipper and waved before the icon in the ritual of *āratī*, or invocation of the deity.

5. SACRAMENTAL AND FESTIVAL ARTS. Important times in life are marked by special rites and may also require specific artefacts. Their religious symbolism may be subtle, but their use indicates a bridging of spiritual and mundane life. Mother and child images can act as votive figures of thanksgiving for a birth as well as a request for fertility. In Tamil Nadu, large painted hollow clay male or female figures are commissioned by new parents. Rituals are performed before the pupils of the eyes of these votive figures are painted, and thereafter the images are placed in the sanctuary of the village god, Ayyanar.

Terracotta animal figures on wheels (resembling those found at Harappan sites) and other similar toys may first be offered at a village shrine by a family giving thanks for a blessing or requesting divine favour. After the *pūjā* (worship) is completed, the votive figure may have its function changed to that of play. Animal images of bronze, often made in the *dhokra* technique, may also have originated as votive figures. It has also been suggested that they were part of child weddings, being 'playthings for the use of the bridegroom' (see Kramrisch, 1968, p. 77, n. 42).

Certain local customs mark the honoured relationship between sister and brother, probably as training for young girls to respect their future husbands. In Madhubani, Bihar, unbaked clay images of the goddess Shyana, considered to be the daughter of Krishna, and other related figures are made by young girls for their brothers to ensure their well-being. This ritual occurs during the autumn festival of Chhathi. On the day of the full moon the gift images are turned back into earth (see Jain and Aggarawala, p. 187). In Rajasthan lidded peacock-shaped painted wood offering containers are presented to a brother by his sister at the celebration of Phuli (see Kramrisch, 1968, no. 37).

Handwork created for a dowry by the bride and her mother generally takes years of labour. Bengali embroidered *kānthā*s, made for bedcovers, *sikki*-grass objects from Bihar and *śītalpāṭi* floor-matting from Assam are just some of the household items brought into a marriage. Gifts may include all manner of containers, vessels and objects for the bride and her home. Auspicious symbols of wealth and fertility decorate most of these works. Necessary for the wedding itself is the *sindūr* (sacred vermilion powder) which a woman must wear to indicate her married state. This is kept in a small lidded container, often of wood and painted red. Elaborate wedding crowns worn by bride and groom indicate that for this special occasion they are princess and prince, even goddess and god. The *mukuṭ*s (crowns) of couples in Assam and West Bengal are made from *solā* pith, reeds carved to paper thinness and worked into fanciful constructions.

Death also has its artistic expressions. 'Bullposts' are erected in parts of West Bengal as memorials. Such a post may be carved with a stylized likeness of the deceased as well as with symbols of deities and objects of worship. Priest-painters of West Bengal, called *jādu-* or *duari-paṭuā*, are commissioned by bereaved relatives to paint a picture of the dead. The performance of the ceremony of *cakṣur-dāna* ('bestowal of eyesight') ensures that the spirit of the deceased will no longer wander blindly in the afterworld. A cult honouring spirits (*bhūta*) and known for its large sculptures is located in Udipi, southern Karnataka. Over life-size images of fierce deified heroes, mother goddesses and animals are among the forms carved from the wood of the jackfruit tree; these polychromed icons are set up in shrines near sacred trees. *Nāgakal*s are often within the precinct as well.

Many of the craft goods made for festivals are sold at *melā*s (fairs), which draw large numbers of village and city dwellers alike to share in a great mixing of cultural products and experiences. Special votive images and crafts such as *brata* images are always among the merchandise, some being sold only on these special occasions. Other simple painted wood carvings, papier mâché or terracotta images of animals, patrons in the form of married couples (*dampatī*) and deities may be bought at fairs throughout India to be taken back to village and domestic shrines. Inexpensive ritual objects such as bells, lamps and flower-offering containers, often of painted terracotta, are also available.

A continual 'fair' atmosphere may prevail at pilgrimage places. Folk images of the local divinities, sculpted or painted by unsophisticated urban or village artists, can be bought by pilgrims. Particularly famous are the painted sized cloth *paṭṭa*s (scrolls) from Puri in Orissa depicting Vaishnavite subjects, especially Jagannatha, a form of Vishnu-Krishna. At Nathdwara, Rajasthan, *pichvāī* (temple hangings painted on cloth) are produced depicting Krishna as Sri Nathji.

6. ENTERTAINMENT AND THEATRE ARTS. Entertainment can be held in private and public settings and always features at fairs and festivals. Dance and puppet performances (*see* §VIII, 16 above) often (but not always) express religious themes. 'Secular' forms of entertainment frequently have some religious aspect. Dice, for example, figure strongly in the great epic, the *Mahābhārata*. Board games played with dice include *caupaṛ* and *pachisi*. Both use a cruciform board and counters, with moves determined by a dice-throw. Another board game using dice is 'snakes and ladders', which stresses a lesson of morality. It is particularly popular in Jaina communities.

Cards (*ganjīfā*) were probably introduced into India at the time of the Mughal empire, around the 16th–17th century. Early examples were round in shape and made of ivory or ragboard. Heroic figures or Hindu deities are among the main subjects painted on playing cards. After the 16th century, European square-style cards appeared. These small cherished works of art were generally kept in wooden boxes painted with relevant themes.

The travelling story-teller, using the visual arts to relate the epics, religious myths or local folk-tales, has been an integral part of Indian education for many centuries. Long picture rolls may be held up for public view to illustrate narrated episodes (*see also* SCROLL, §2(ii)). Painted toys and dolls can also be used for instruction. In the Warangal District, Andhra Pradesh, brightly painted images of divinities and animals made of wood, cow dung, sawdust and clay are used in narrations of Hindu myths and local legends (see Jain and Aggarawala, p. 194). Small painted wooden shrines may be carried around in rural areas by itinerant priests or tribal poet-singers. Such folding box altars are sometimes small enough to be hung around the neck of the bard. If it is larger, the box is held on the head of an assistant. As the priest teaches, he can open out the shutters of the shrine to reveal the central deity within as well as the narrative scenes painted on the inner wings. A story-telling priest from Andhra Pradesh may add a theatrical dimension by wearing a brightly painted mask.

BIBLIOGRAPHY

M. Marriott, ed.: *Village India: Studies in the Little Community* (Chicago, 1955)
S. Kramrisch: 'Traditions of the Indian Craftsman', *Traditional India: Structure and Change*, ed. M. Singer (Philadelphia, 1959)
S. K. Ray: *The Ritual Art of the Bratas of Bengal* (New Delhi, 1961)
R. Reeves: *Cire Perdue Casting in India* (New Delhi, 1962)
Marg, xx/1 (1966) [full issue on Bihar]
R. F. Bussabarger and B. D. Robins: *The Everyday Art of India* (New York, 1968)
Unknown India: Ritual Art of Tribe and Village (exh. cat. by S. Kramrisch, Philadelphia, 1968)
M. Singer: *When a Great Tradition Modernizes: An Anthropological Approach to Indian Civilization* (New York, 1972)
K. C. Aryan: *Folk Bronzes of Northwestern India* (Delhi, 1973)
J. Jain and J. Jain Neubauer: 'Treasures of Everyday Art', *Marg*, xxxi/3 (1978) [full issue]
M. K. Pal: *Crafts and Craftsmen in Traditional India* (New Delhi, 1978)
J. Jain: *Folk Art and Culture of Gujarat* (Ahmadabad, 1981)
P. Jayakar: *The Earthen Drum: An Introduction to the Ritual Arts of Rural India* (New Delhi, 1981)
D. N. Saraf: *Indian Crafts and Development Potential* (New Delhi, 1982)
J. Jain: *Utensils: An Introduction to the Utensils Museum, Ahmedabad* (Ahmadabad, 1984)
S. Huyler: *Village India* (New York, 1985)
S. Kramrisch: 'The Ritual Arts of India', *Adidti: The Living Arts of India* (exh. cat., Washington, DC, Smithsonian Inst., 1985), pp. 247–69
H. Mode and S. Chandra: *Indian Folk Art* (Bombay, 1985)
H. Shah: *Form and Many Forms of Mother Clay: Contemporary Indian Pottery and Terracotta* (New Delhi, 1985)
S. Huyler: 'Terracotta Traditions in Nineteenth- and Twentieth-century India', *From Indian Earth: 4,000 Years of Terracotta Art* (exh. cat., ed. A. Poster; New York, Brooklyn Mus., 1986)
J. Jain and A. Aggarawala: *National Handicrafts and Handloom Museum* (New Delhi, 1989)
C. R. Bolon and A. V. Sarin: 'Bastar Brasses', *Asian A.*, v/3 (1992), pp. 35–52

ANN WOOD NORTON

XI. Tribal art.

About 7% of Indians, between 60 and 65 million people, are officially classified into 'Scheduled Tribes'. With few exceptions, their art has been unappreciated by critics, curators, collectors, dealers and other arbiters of taste, though other forms of Indian art enjoy international esteem. It is not some deficiency of tribal art, however, but outsiders' assumptions about it that best explains this relative neglect. A simplistic model of how Indian tribal and non-tribal societies interact underlies both insensitivity to and romanticization of tribal art. Inappropriate comparisons with the South Asian 'Great Tradition' or with admired tribal creativity elsewhere impede an appreciation of this art on its own terms. More subtly, non-tribal society has determined what outsiders perceive as tribal art by supplying the terms in which it is defined and interpreted.

In tribal society, aesthetic expressions are geared to the values and practices that make them meaningful for the people themselves. As these values and practices are modified under pressure from inside or outside the community, the expressions and their forms may also change. Only a fraction of artistic inspiration—not necessarily the most important to the people themselves—is given material form in art objects; much more creativity may be channelled into music, oral literature and dance. Moreover, their mundane functions tend to obscure the aesthetic element in the design of a vast range of utilitarian artefacts, while others, even if more obviously 'art objects', are too ephemeral, unelaborate or immobile to appeal to outside connoisseurs.

Below, a consideration of the non-tribal context of tribal art and of how this art might best be defined and appreciated is followed by a selective review of the art itself and a survey of its key characteristics. The latter relies on evidence for the uses and meanings given to tribal art objects by their producers or those inferred by outside observers.

1. Context and definition. 2. Peoples and art forms.

1. CONTEXT AND DEFINITION. From the rise of agriculture in the 2nd millennium BC, Indian tribal peoples have been increasingly dominated by the occupational specialism and hierarchy of the majority population. As tribal territory is invaded by an expanding peasantry or in the interests of industry or social planning, its inhabitants tend to lose not only their land but often their cultural identity as well. Land for the tribal peoples is a cultural as well as an economic resource. Some tribal groups have so far escaped cultural extinction, largely because they occupy remote regions or ecological zones with little to offer peasant farmers. Others have been able to respond flexibly by abandoning some aspects of their traditional way of life while retaining others. But the main, accelerating trend is for tribal peoples to become absorbed into dominant Hindu society at the lowest caste levels.

Even those who retain their land and most of their traditions cannot escape outside influence channelled through trade, bureaucracy and mass media. Some cultural features have doubtless been shared between tribes and castes from early times, but they are hard to distinguish from the effects of subsequent contact. Whatever the causes, even the most isolated and independent tribal peoples bear some cultural resemblance to their caste-organized neighbours. Everyone, for instance, has some concept of ritual purity, although few tribes elaborate this, in theory or in practice, to the extent that peasants do. Like tribes, castes acknowledge local deities and organize most aspects of daily life around kinship relations (*see* §I, 7(i) and (ii) above).

For most tribal peoples, the outside world is both threatening and attractive. New commodities, materials, colours, patterns and textures and new functions for existing tools and implements have edged their way into the local economy or have been eagerly sought out. Some beliefs and practices have been disrupted, while extraneous elements have been incorporated into others. Many objects considered characteristic of local tribes are not, in fact, produced by them; tribal groups may depend entirely on client artisan (caste) communities for certain types of ornament or ritual items. This is generally true of metal-work but also extends to other materials. The Bengali *jādu-paṭuā* and *citrakāra*, for example, traditionally paint for the tribal Santal (see 1968 exh. cat., pp. 70–71). The non-tribal artisans generally work for no-one else and tailor the product to their patrons' taste. Catering for tribal clients or subjects has also meant adjustments for non-tribal neighbours. Thus, Rajputs found themselves used as the generic model for equestrian figures made by and distinctive of the Bhil. By adding decoration to cloth made by local Hindus, Toda women transformed it into an expression of their own identity. Perhaps more strikingly, the Hindu cult of Jaganath in Puri (Orissa) seems to be an elaboration of an originally tribal deity and system of worship. In short, Hindu and tribal relations have almost always included a degree of mutuality.

The overall trend, however, has been generally one-sided: a long and complex process of dominance, compromise, resistance and retreat. Its result has been the transformation of cultures and the loss of much distinctive tribal art, even though many tribal people have been obliged or inspired to recreate their ethnic identities in both new and recycled forms. A symptom of awareness of this experience, and especially of a heightened appreciation of what still survives from one or two generations ago, is the emergence of *ādivāsī* (original inhabitants) as a respectful term to replace the often (though not necessarily) pejorative 'tribal'. To assume that the ancestors of the contemporary tribal peoples of India were necessarily its first settlers, however, is hazardous in view of the complex history of tribal/non-tribal relations and the paucity of relevant archaeological evidence. The term *ādivāsī* also connotes a harmonic ideal acting against problems of violence and fragmentation in modern India. Tribal peoples may once again find themselves stereotyped rather than acknowledged in the actual circumstances in which they live. Their art and artefacts are easily decontextualized and can then serve as props for this idealized image.

However their cultures may change, the tribal peoples or *ādivāsī* are likely to remain distinct from their neighbours if not indefinitely then for several more decades; and their art forms are likely to remain distinctive too. Most interpreters, however, limit their attention (or at least their appreciation) to products and activities falling within a restrictive and essentially nostalgic notion of 'authenticity'. They ignore what tribal groups do to make sense of their lives by creative means as well as the efforts of officials and entrepreneurs to direct or invent artistic performances by tribal peoples. However, older cultural forms perpetuated unaided by tribal peoples themselves have never exhausted the *ādivāsī* aesthetic repertory; adaptation to new circumstances, along with loss and innovation and even a degree of selfconsciousness and pastiche, are by no means new to tribal art traditions. Purists should therefore rethink their terms. However outside interpreters respond, both 'tourist art' and restored performance have a place in the 'living expressions' of real tribal peoples (see Schechner). Tribal traditions show vitality even in their opportunism, from the faking of bronzes by the Bastar of Madhya Pradesh, bought as antiques by tourists and collectors, to the adaptation of painting from walls and floors to paper by the Warli of Maharashtra and the Pardhan Gond of Madhya Pradesh.

2. Peoples and art forms.

(i) Naga. (ii) Tribes of eastern and central India. (iii) Bhil. (iv) Toda and Kota.

(i) Naga. Because of north-east India's isolation and topography, its tribal traditions have resisted outside influence for longer than those of most other parts of the subcontinent. Yet links with non-tribal peoples are well established and are manifested, for instance, in the elaborately decorated 'elephant cloths' of the Manipur Naga, which possibly derive from an alliance with a local ruler in the 17th century. More usual, however, is separation between tribal groups, which has led to many distinctive local variations of material culture.

The main visual art of the Naga was largely organized around collective activities: headhunting, the *morung* (bachelors' dormitory) and agricultural, political or social festivals or ritual occasions, such as family- or clan-centred funerals. Body decoration in tribal north-east India encompassed tattooing, painting, jewellery and forms of clothing including textiles and basketry headgear. Some groups developed artistic production in special fields: Manipur, for example, became known for its textiles, while the graphic designs of the Lushai people have been especially admired.

Some Naga groups were more hierarchical than most Indian tribes, and artistic expression was therefore subject to social or religious restriction. Thus, in some Wancho groups, weaving was monopolized by the wife and daughters of a chief, while elsewhere local aristocrats prevented commoners from making or using certain kinds of objects. Among some groups, it was necessary to sacrifice a dog or pig when a wood-carving was made, lest the artist become ill or die; this probably related to an earlier tradition dictating that only a man who had taken a head (i.e. proved his manhood) was allowed to carve a human figure in a *morung*.

Dances were major social festivals and always occasions for display of status symbols. Among the Wancho and Nocte they could also be used to celebrate victory in war, promote crop fertility or add lustre to feasts or weddings. For other groups, ritual dance was a means of enacting oral tradition. Decorative use was made of a wide variety of materials: hair, fur, shells, cane, ivory, carved and polished wood and monkeys' skulls. In some areas human hair was valued, probably because of its association with earlier headhunting; elsewhere bear fur or the hair of monkeys, dogs or goats was used instead. Hats, baskets, the hilts and sheaths of *dao* (all-purpose knife-swords), ceremonial sashes, gauntlets, textiles and wooden figures were all ornamented with red-dyed hair. Cowrie shells were applied to a variety of clothing accessories, such as belts and aprons, and in some groups were especially favoured by warriors. In earlier times, certain tattoos indicated that the wearer had taken an enemy's head.

Weaving was practised on narrow back-strap looms among most Naga tribes, but only by women. Woven designs were largely geometric, from simple lines and bands (e.g. among the Adi and Ara Juang) to more resourceful variations on the lozenge (e.g. among the Mishmi). Despite the limited colour range—black, yellow, dark blue and green, sometimes enlivened by the addition of scarlet and madder—dramatic effects were often possible, for instance by contrasting broad and narrow bands. Animal or human forms only rarely feature in woven or embroidered textiles, except on the bags or sashes of the Khampti or Wancho; anthropomorphs were usually associated with headhunting.

Some of the most specialized and sophisticated weaving was done in the central part of the region occupied by Naga peoples. Within this area textiles, basketry and bamboowork were produced but no masks or other forms of woodworking (Elwin, 1959, p. 102). The plateau-based Apa Tani favoured natural-dyed cloths of yellow, green and red and formerly wove shawls and coats from the unravelled and redyed wool of blankets of the Bhutia people. Apa Tani men wore their hair in knots on the forehead, pinned in place. Close-fitting cane hats adorned with projections, plumes and birds' feet were commonly worn by the Apa Tani and other peoples.

The costumes and ornaments of the different hill peoples were not worn simply for aesthetic effect but served as complex signifying systems. Few Naga ornaments were freely available for anyone to wear; most were considered 'powerful' and therefore subject to definite rules of acquisition and display because of their restriction to certain groups or situations. Some objects allowed discrimination within groups; thus the men of the various Ao Naga clans had different rights (hereditary or achieved) to wear different numbers of ivory armlets. Other ornaments or practices differentiated between groups; for instance, Angami men who had taken a head wore an ear ornament made of hair and a beetle's wing, while those of the adjacent Sema Naga wore a boar's-tusk necklace.

Its permanence makes tattooing a particularly emphatic way of signifying differences; thus among the Konyak, men of the Thendu sub-group had tattooed faces, while the Thenkoh Konyak men were tattooed on the arms and chest. Favoured especially by the eastern and northern peoples, tattooing encompassed a wide range of geometric and figurative designs, some of which were reproduced in painted form on the surfaces of carved wooden figures.

The same type of object could be used by the various Naga tribes on different occasions. For example, among the Ao, a hornbill feather worn in the headdress signified participation in a raid or the sacrifice of a buffalo, whereas among the Lhota it signified that the wearer had either taken a head or touched an enemy's dead body. This implies that the feathers were understood to signify, in general terms, male prowess but that how they did so in specific instances depended on a further set of conventions. The same applied to the other main kinds of male status insignia (Jacobs, pp. 103–10).

Whatever signifying function attached to personal dress, however, costume was also utilitarian. Thus war helmets were made of tightly woven cane for protection; coats might be ornamented but were also meant for warmth; and the back-flaps of Adi loincloths were for both modesty and sitting on.

Other specialist production was also associated with this area. One example was the distinctive *beyop*, a flat disc of cast bell-metal with an embossed design of dense concentric rings and a cross through the middle. Several of these were worn on a string as a waist ornament by young women and girls.

Wood-carving was especially geared to male group activities. After headhunting was abandoned in the late 19th or early 20th century, bravery and a man's status were signified by a diminutive carved wood head (see fig. 360) or by a brass version obtained from Hindu metalworkers and worn as a pendant or fixed to a basket. The ideological focus on the head meant that even when full figures were carved, the head was larger and rendered in more detail (especially the face) than the rest of the body. Carvings on drinking mugs, smoking-pipes and *morung* pillars, and of human figures attached to baskets or kept in the house as trophies, also drew inspiration from this source. Often decorated with cloth, hair or beads and mostly coloured black or red, these heads and figures were somewhat formalized and had restrained expressions, like faces of the dead.

In the *morung*, carvings were for prestige and magic, so that while the surroundings were generally admired, the young occupants might also acquire some of the characteristics of the men and animals represented. The main elements of the structure to be carved were the pillars and the horizontal beam extending across the front of the building. Favoured motifs included warriors, often with their guns; dancing couples; powerful or mischievous animals (elephants, tigers, dogs, monkeys); and fantasy animals, such as tigers with two heads or horns. Carved

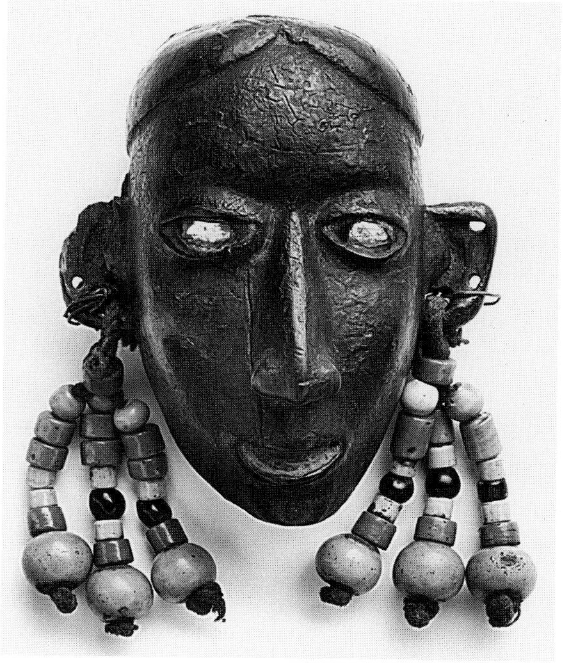

360. Head, carved wood, beads and glass inlaid eyes, Naga tribe (London, British Museum)

scenes were also meant for amusement or commemorated past incidents. The Konyak, especially, carved erotic motifs. Designs based on the *mithuna* (Skt: loving couple) or buffalo, usually consisting of conventionalized horns, were widely popular in *morung*s and other buildings; the *mithuna* symbolized wealth and sometimes fertility. Some designs were restricted, however. Among the more hierarchical groups, only the chief's *morung* might be carved with the hornbill motif.

Most of the Naga tribes formerly carved effigies of the dead to place in front of the tomb, although the forms used were cruder than those designed for the *morung*, usually with only the head carved in any detail. The tomb itself was often festooned with clothes and articles of daily use, said to be for the deceased to use in the after-life. Occasionally, instead of a solid wooden figure, the effigy was made of a framework of bamboo and placed in a hut. Mortuary figures seem to have been a sort of motel for the souls of the deceased, remaining dangerous and subject to various prohibitions until the completion of rituals designed to prepare the soul for the remainder of its journey to the afterworld. From this point, the figures themselves were neglected and fell into decay.

(ii) Tribes of eastern and central India. Much artistic elaboration in West Bengal, Bihar, Orissa and Madhya Pradesh is directed towards the body itself and those artefacts closely associated with it, such as clothes, jewellery, headgear and masks. Other categories include domestic and ritual equipment made of grasses, wood or metal; wall surfaces and paper are often decorated with two-dimensional designs.

361. Mask, terracotta, *c.* 254×203 mm, Gond tribe, from Kotrahi, Sarguja District, Madhya Pradesh (New Dehli, Crafts Museum)

An individual's body may be ornamented by tattooing or painting—the latter, being temporary, is especially used for ceremonies. Other examples include elaborate hairstyles among women, often including hairpins and combs and ear, nose, neck and chest decorations. Combs also emerge as independent motifs in other contexts, whether on carved doors (among the Saora), as love-tokens (for the Juang) or as special symbols of married status (among the Muduva and others). Among the Juang or Muria, the flat surfaces of the comb may be covered with figurative images or simple geometric shapes, and by exaggerating functional elements, striking sculptural forms are occasionally produced.

Finger, wrist and arm ornaments are also common, but legs and feet remain largely unadorned. The use of certain materials for ornament carries magical as well as aesthetic implications. Iron, for instance, has been reported as a cure for headache and as protection from lightning or, in some contexts, from witchcraft. Similar beliefs attach to the use of cowries in personal adornment. Iron objects and cowries may well attract such ideas because of their special association with two itinerant groups—ironworkers and Lambadi nomads, respectively—whose marginal status lends them special power.

Tribal peoples have worn garments of shell-girdles, leaves, bark cloth or narrow warp-striped textiles, but none is especially elaborate. Some Orissan tribes traditionally wore shawls or skirts derived from purchased yarn, which they spun before sending it to be woven by Hindus. Sometimes such weaving was carried out under the close supervision of tribal patrons such as the Saora.

Elaborate personal adornment is especially evident at communal festivals and dances, which are among the most distinctive aspects of tribal life and which allow the fullest expression of traditional social activity. Best known of these were the horned headdresses of the Maria or Dorla, formerly using real horns of buffalo or other animals and more recently using wooden or cast-brass ones. The Kondh used the beak and casque of a hornbill, while the Saora and Baiga preferred feathers. In all cases the effect was to produce a striking extension of the human body, creating a dramatic effect that would be increased by the movement of dance. These headdresses also emphasized the ritual significance of the animal or bird to the group as a whole.

Masks (*see also* §VIII, 14 above) also played an important role in tribal society. Large wooden ones were generally preferred by the Gond and Baiga, although terracotta examples are also found (see fig. 361), while Muria and Bhuiya versions are smaller and lighter and often made of gourds. Features are typically simple and expressions limited; emphasis is usually on the eyes and nose, with the mouth and ears not necessarily indicated. Teeth, perhaps represented by seeds or grains of rice, and hair are often attached to the mask; the latter may be taken from various animals, preferably from a bear. These characteristics give tribal Indian masks an elemental quality that may assist them in performing various functions.

Among the Muria, masks were used by young men to perform comical or moralizing sketches when visiting other members of the community; similar, if less controlled reversals of normal behaviour were sanctioned by mask-wearing among the Baiga and Bastar Muria. Such events simultaneously upheld the social order and entertained those taking part. Some uses of masks had further significance: for the Bhuiya, masquerades were held to ensure successful hunting, while Kondh masks seem to refer to the former practice of human sacrifice.

A priest of the Kuttia Kondh of Orissa is said to have claimed that Dharni Pinnu, the earth mother, told him in a dream that masks should be offered to her at the annual or triennial sacrifice (*meriah*) in her honour. This would have been in lieu of the skulls used by the Kondh as substitutes for human victims since the suppression of this practice in the mid-19th century. Also associated with the *meriah* were stones symbolizing Dharni Pinnu and tall, carved, often forked wooden pillars of the kind to which sacrificial victims had formerly been tied. The mask-offering then became a new tradition, accompanied by the slaughter of a fowl. The masks themselves were of gourds decorated with beads and hair; some were shaped roughly to resemble skulls.

A similar theme is evident in another case, where tribal innovators subverted myths from the ancient Puranas to their own ends. The Gond of the Mandla area used a version of the story of Krishna (one of the manifestations of the Hindu god Vishnu) and the cow-herd to justify their own masked dancing tradition as a way of commemorating Krishna's decapitation of certain demons (Elwin, 1951, pp. 138–40; *see also* §II, 1(iii) and 5 above).

If these examples illustrate the capacity of tribal peoples to protect the core concepts of their religion by controlling its expression in new conditions, other masking practices serve the similar objective of strengthening a sense of tribal identity by the alternative means of lampooning the Hindu 'other'. At the finale of the Laru Kaj ritual, observed by various tribes in the Mandla area, someone acts the role of a Hindu ascetic: his body is smeared with ashes, and his mask, if available, bears an appropriate mark on the forehead (see Elwin, 1951, fig. 160). He is offered pork and alcohol, and his ostentatious refusal causes great amusement.

(iii) Bhil. The Bhil of western India, one of the largest tribes, inhabit parts of Rajasthan, Gujarat and Maharashtra. The personal ornaments of the women, now mainly of pewter or silver, were formerly of brass and are an investment as well as for beautification. Many Bhil are Hinduized, but others, such as the Jhabua Bhil, recognize a personal supreme god, Bhagavan or Bholo Iswor, and retain a belief in minor deities, to whom they offer terracotta models of horses at modest shrines on hilltops or under trees (Fuchs, 1982).

Veneration of Bhagavan is focused on uncarved symbolic stones located in the settlement's central sanctuary, but it is to the human-orientated cult of the dead, the main ritual of which, Nukto, is performed before the house of the deceased, that the Bhil devote their metalworking skill. This ritual is meant to purify the dead person's spirit and unite it with Bhagavan.

From about the 6th century AD, their political fortunes having been tied to those of the dominant Rajputs, the image of the mounted horseman was added to the Bhil's sculptural repertory. Warriors killed in fights or cattle raids were traditionally memorialized as mounted figures carved in shallow relief on stone slabs. This practice reflected Bhil resistance to the Rajputs and other castes, which was protracted enough to engender strong self-reliance and respect for heroes.

362. Equestrian figure of Gothriz Purvez, cast brass, Bhil tribe (private collection)

Another form of memorial sculpture, that of Gothriz Purvez, the collective ancestor, is a small equestrian figure (see fig. 362). These are cast by the lost-wax technique out of brass that includes copper from the anklets of the dead man's widow. Together with a small figure of a cow, which is made in the same way and out of the same material, the 'spirit rider' plays a key role in Nukto ritual. Like the priest who is temporarily 'inhabited' by the spirit while in a trance, the figure of Gothriz Purvez accommodates the spirit on a stage of its journey to the afterworld. The anklets probably symbolize both the marriage and the clan it perpetuates. The occupation of the brass image by the spirit of the deceased may therefore reaffirm clan solidarity against the threat of disruption posed by his death.

(iv) Toda and Kota. One of the best-known tribal people of south India are the Toda of the Nilgiri Hills in Tamil Nadu. Besides ornaments and clothing, body decoration among the Toda amounted to tattooing for women, limited scarification for men and occasional forehead-painting by men or women using red or yellow vegetable pigments. Tattoo patterns, consisting of simple lines of dots and circles, were most conspicuous on the backs of the hands, the chin, the upper arms, the area above the breasts and on the feet, and extended to the legs and back. The tattooing of Toda women was a normal sign of adulthood until well after India became independent in 1947. Tattoo patterns may be imitated in soot on an untattooed female corpse before it is cremated. Similarly, the small scar or scars that were once raised on a boy's wrist or elbow or

under his shoulder were signs that he had attained the status required for milking buffaloes.

Forehead-decoration was probably done in imitation of Hindu practice, and like scarification and tattooing was meant to signify status or to serve a magical purpose. Although there was certainly an aesthetic component involved, this was not elaborated. Likewise, while women's hair was almost always worn in long ringlets, and men's hairstyles varied according to clan observances or personal taste, no ornaments were added for artistic effect. Some Toda men shaved their heads after a funeral, but most tied their hair into frontal knots until the obsequies for a dead clan member were completed. A man might also tie his hair behind to keep it out of his face, whereas another style signified that the wearer had made a vow.

Toda women wore more jewellery of more varied types than the men, who were usually restricted to a silver finger-ring and earrings, often of gold. For women, once common gold jewellery was replaced by silver and brass. A brass circlet round the waist might be accompanied by heavy brass armlets, a necklace of silver coins, earrings, other armlets, often with cowrie shells attached, and bracelets or bangles. Prior to the period of British rule, however, most jewellery worn by the Toda appears to have been made by metalsmiths of the Kota tribe, with whom the Toda had a dominant but largely symbiotic relationship. Among the most outstanding of Kota ornaments were probably small gold pendants and elaborate caparisons for sacrificial buffalo.

One such pendant, perhaps with magical functions, is said to have been worn suspended through a silver tube to which gold plates were attached; these take the form of a stylized buffalo mask, the back of which is ornamented with a plant motif. The buffalo trapping, by appropriate contrast, is a large composite ornament consisting of three great rosettes made up of hundreds of tightly packed cowrie shells sewn on to black cotton cloth over a wicker frame. These are connected by means of a thick cotton rope on which heavy, angular silver and gold beads are strung, while silver pendants extend from the perimeter of each cowrie-shell disc. It is reported that this elaborate structure was hung in the form of a triangle between the animal's forelegs with one large disc fixed to each horn; the triangle is said to symbolize the mother goddess, Thekkis (1985 exh. cat., pp. 85–7).

Perhaps best known of all artefacts associated with the Toda, however, are the large cloaks (*putkhuḷi*) worn by both men and women, although in slightly different ways. These cloaks consist of a double layer of cotton cloth sewn together to leave a large pocket inside. The cloak was normally worn wrapped completely around the body, but in ritual contexts it was worn with the right arm and shoulder exposed. At certain phases of funerary ritual, it covered the head. Among some Toda, higher status was signified by wearing a grey cloth garment of a sort in which corpses used to be wrapped, but this was of plain, unadorned material.

Neither these cloaks nor the simple loincloth that was normally worn beneath it (and is still, in certain circumstances) were made by the Toda themselves. Beginning at least in the 19th century, the cloaks were made by Hindus and acquired by the Toda indirectly, perhaps via their

363. Embroidered cloaks (*putkhuḷis*), Toda, south India

tribal 'partners', the Kota, from whom such garments were certainly obtained for the cremation of corpses (Walker, p. 31). Other cloths play an important role in funerary rituals but, unlike the cloaks, are not a focus of artistic skill.

In the 19th century, the Toda preferred cloths embellished with thin lines of red and blue, but later they developed a taste for wider bands of these colours. Traditionally, cloaks were embroidered by Toda women, using long stripes of serial lozenges, zigzags or similar motifs to supplement the limited existing ornamentation. The preferred colours for this embroidery were red and black, but yellow, blue and green have been added in recent decades. This additional work converted the textile (which they had not made) into a distinctively Toda garment (see fig. 363).

BIBLIOGRAPHY

C. W. Crooke: *The Tribes and Castes of the North-western Provinces and Oudh* (Calcutta, 1896)

W. H. R. Rivers: *The Todas* (London, 1906)

E. Thurston: *Ethnographic Notes in Southern India* (Madras, 1906)

——: *Castes and Tribes of Southern India*, 7 vols (Madras, 1909)

S. C. Roy: *The Mundas and their Country* (Calcutta, 1912)

R. V. Russell and H. Lal: *Tribes and Castes of the Central Provinces of India*, 4 vols (London, 1916)

R. E. Endhoven: *The Tribes and Castes of Bombay*, 3 vols (Bombay, 1920–22)

L. K. A. K. Iyer: *Mysore Tribes and Castes*, 4 vols (Mysore, 1928–35)

V. Elwin: *The Baiga* (London, 1939)
D. N. Bhagvat: *Tribal Culture of the Central Provinces* (Bombay, 1942)
V. Elwin: *The Tribal Art of Middle India: A Personal Record* (London, 1951)
T. B. Naik: *The Bhils: A Study* (Delhi, 1956)
V. Elwin: *The Art of the North-east Frontier of India* (Shillong, 1959)
S. Fuchs: *The Gond and Bhumia of Eastern Mandla* (New York, 1959)
Y. V. S. Nath: *Bhils of Ratanmal* (Vadodara, 1960)
R. Redfield: *Peasant Society and Culture* (Chicago, 1960)
C. von Furer-Haimendorf: *Naked Nagas* (Calcutta, 1962)
R. Reeves: *Cire Perdue Casting in India* (New Delhi, 1962)
Unknown India: Ritual Art in Tribe and Village (exh. cat. by S. Kramrisch, Philadelphia, PA, Mus. F.A.; San Francisco, CA, de Young Mem. Mus.; St Louis, MO, A. Mus.; 1968)
E. Fischer and H. Shah: *Mogra Dev—Tribal Crocodile Gods: Wooden Crocodile Images of Chodhri, Gamit and Vasava Tribes, South Gujarat (India)* (Ahmadabad, 1971)
K. S. Singh, ed.: *Tribal Situation in India* (Simla, 1972)
S. Fuchs: *The Aboriginal Tribes of India* (New Delhi, 1973)
L. P. Vidyarthi and B. K. Rai: *The Tribal Culture of India* (Delhi, 1977)
S. Fuchs: 'The Bhils: People of the Bow: An Aboriginal Tribe of Western North-India', *Gods of the Byways: Wayside Shrines of Rajasthan, Madhya Pradesh and Gujarat* (exh. cat., Oxford, MOMA, 1982), pp. 33–47
P. Jayakar: *The Earthen Drum: An Introduction to the Ritual Arts of Rural India* (New Delhi, 1982)
J. P. Barbier-Muller: *The Art of Nagaland* (exh. cat., Los Angeles, CA, Co. Mus. A., 1984)
A. L. Dallapiccola, ed.: *Kult und Alltag: Gelbguss in der Volkskunst Indiens*, Heidelberger Akten der von-Portheim-Stiftung, n. s., i (Heidelberg, 1984)
J. Jain: *Painted Myths of Creation: Art and Ritual of an Indian Tribe* (New Delhi, 1984)
C. von Furer-Haimendorf: *Tribal Populations and Cultures of the Indian Subcontinent* (Leiden and Cologne, 1985)
H. Mode and S. Chandra: *Indian Folk Art* (New York, 1985)
R. Schechner: *Between Theatre and Anthropology* (Philadelphia, 1985)
India: Art and Culture, 1300–1900 (exh. cat. by S. C. Welch, New York, Met., 1985)
A. R. Walker: *The Toda of South India: A New Look* (Delhi, 1986)
J. Swaminathan: *The Perceiving Fingers* (Bhopal, 1987)
The Art of the Adivasi (Indian Tribal Art) (exh. cat. by J. Swaminathan and J. Jain, Tokyo, 1988)
J. Jacobs: *The Nagas: Society, Culture and the Colonial Encounter* (London, 1990)
Adivasi, het andere India (exh. cat., ed. F. Cowan; Amsterdam, 1992)

BRIAN DURRANS

XII. Patronage.

Even before the mature phase of the Indus civilization (*c.* 2550–*c.* 2000 BC) there was a significant demand for terracotta figurines, votive objects, toys, simple ornaments and other minor objects. The patrons of this work, like the craftsmen themselves, remain anonymous, but the artefacts suggest that ordinary individuals were patrons of art from earliest times. With the appearance of stone sculpture and monumental architecture, documentation becomes more precise and focuses attention on the nobility and the leading institutions of ancient Indian society; the subsequent production of sumptuously illuminated manuscripts, jades and other luxury objects points directly to kings and historical personalities of power. Despite the élite's importance, a broad spectrum of crafts continued to be supported, a forum of patronage that accelerated with the growth of a middle class in the 18th and 19th centuries.

See also §I, 9 above.

1. Architecture and sculpture. 2. Painting.

1. Architecture and sculpture. Evidence for the patronage of architecture and sculpture stretches back to the 3rd century BC, when the Maurya dynasty established control over most of the subcontinent. The principal monuments of this period are a number of stone columns with animal capitals, which were often incised with royal edicts and were probably inspired by Achaemenid prototypes. The use of stone for the first time (in most cases from a single quarry) and a uniform sculptural style point to the existence of a central workshop under imperial control. The columns, placed at crossroads or Buddhist sites, served as emblems of state, Buddhism being used as an instrument to maintain the cohesion of the empire. Little Mauryan architecture survives, but the caves at Barabar in Bihar (*see* BARABAR AND NAGARJUNI) and the vestiges of a palace at Pataliputra (modern Patna) are the result of imperial patronage.

Although the art styles of the last two centuries BC have often been named after subsequent dynasties, inscriptional evidence indicates that the monuments of this period did not owe their origin to direct royal patronage. At SANCHI, for example, although a Mauryan column and the core of the main stupa point to imperial activity in the 3rd century BC, later additions were the product of popular piety. This is shown not only by the eclectic character of the iconography, which incorporates many folk deities and objects of worship, but by the inscriptions recording donations by private individuals or groups. Similar inscriptions at other early Buddhist sites also indicate that these monuments owed their origin to common followers of Buddhism; the proximity of many sites to major centres and routes of communication meant that such establishments could draw donations from a wide geographical area.

The popular support that helped these Buddhist sites flourish was also responsible for the development of centres of Jainism. At MATHURA, for example, a number of Jaina monuments and monasteries were constructed between the 1st century BC and 3rd century AD. A broad-based theism is also in evidence at this site, where Shiva, Vishnu and other gods of the Brahmanical pantheon were represented for the first time. A similar coexistence of Vaishnavism and several Buddhist sects is found at NAGARJUNAKONDA, where inscriptions indicate that the Buddhist monuments owed much to women of noble lineage. The pattern of patronage that emerged in the post-Mauryan era is therefore one in which the architectural monuments and sculptures were commissioned by a wide range of people from ordinary citizens to powerful guilds and nobles. The ruling monarchs, in contrast, were involved in the performance of such elaborate Vedic rituals as horse sacrifices (Skt *aśvamedha*). While there were supposed to be no tangible residues of these rituals, memorials were occasionally made, as shown by the sacrificial posts (*yūpa*s) found at Isapur, near Mathura. Although such Vedic rituals were the primary domain of royal patronage, other dynastic undertakings were apparently deemed necessary. Sanctuaries at Mat, near Mathura, and Surkh Kotal in Afghanistan contained royal portraits of Kushana rulers, but both sites were razed in ancient times, and consequently the exact nature of the cult is not entirely clear. In the case of Mat, however, inscriptions establish that the patrons of the shrine were Kushana functionaries rather than royalty. At Nanaghat a similar pattern is seen in a cave that once contained images of the SATAVAHANA family. Among the representations of kings, princes and their consorts was an officer, Tranakayira, whose inclusion suggests he was responsible for the cave. The advantage of delegating authority in such matters was that the king could retain appropriate ritual detachment while enjoying the prestige that a monumental public image of himself and his forebears provided.

During the 4th century AD, Kushana power gradually disintegrated in northern and western India. Successor states, principally the Gupta dynasty of the 4th–5th century, modified certain points of detail in matters of patronage but did not overthrow established patterns. The continuance of royal portraiture is documented by gold coins carrying images of the imperial Gupta rulers (*see* §VIII, 6(ii) above). The Guptas were also involved in the performance of Vedic rituals, notably the horse sacrifice. A number of stone horses appear to be memorials of these rituals; the best-preserved example is in the State Museum, Lucknow. In addition the Gupta monarchs erected columns of glory (*kīrtistambha*) lauding the king and his achievements; the most remarkable example is the iron pillar at Delhi (*see* DELHI, §III, 1). Imperial patrons did not, however, build temples or establish devotional images. Monarchs may have made grants to Brahmans at celebrated holy spots, but the actual business of construction appears to have been left to a wide variety of individuals, ranging from monks to powerful nobles. Thus, while there were many innovations in iconography, style and architectural practice during the Gupta period, the kings themselves do not appear to have been directly involved in them. However, arguments have been put forward that the celebrated Varaha at UDAYAGIRI (ii) can be read as an allegory of kingship, specifically that of Chandragupta II (*reg c.* 380–415). He is known from inscriptions to have visited the site while on campaign, and his successes in western India have been equated with Vishnu's rescue of the earth goddess as represented in the Udayagiri relief. While experimentation with this kind of imagery cannot be ruled out, the unequivocal use of allegory did not fully emerge until the 7th century. The only undisputed inscriptional evidence of imperial patronage is from the Vishnu temple at Bhitari in Uttar Pradesh, fragments of which are found in the Bharat Kala Bhavan at Banaras Hindu University, Varanasi. The wording of the inscription suggests that the idea of constructing the temple was a personal innovation of Skandagupta (*reg c.* 455–67).

The collapse of the Gupta dynasty brought significant changes to the nature of Indian polity and patronage. During the 6th century, Vedic rites ceased to figure among the royal duties, while religious imagery was incorporated into the ideals of kingship. These changes clearly emerged in the 7th century under three remarkable kings: Harsha (*reg* 606–47), whose power was centred in the Gangetic plain; Pulakesin II (*reg* 609/10–42), an early Chalukyan ruler who controlled the Deccan (*see* CHALUKYA, §1); and Mahendravarman I (*reg c.* 570–630), the PALLAVA king of Tamil Nadu. The Pallava material is the most complete and shows that a number of images were given a dual meaning, which applied equally to the gods and to the king (*see* §IV, 7(vi)(a) above). The monument most expressive of these ideas is the Adi Varaha cave at MAMALLAPURAM. Probably created for Narasimhavarman I (*reg c.* 630–68), it contains portraits of his father, Mahendravarman I, and his grandfather Simhavishnu flanking an image of Varaha that can be understood as an allegorical representation of Narasimhavarman himself; beside the Varaha figure are images of Lakshmi and Durga as consorts providing prosperity and victory. The overall iconographic scheme clearly shows that royal power was legitimized through the incarnation of the god as king.

While the allegorical use of religious images for royal purposes was entrenched by the 7th century, it was never a universal practice. There are, for example, no epigraphic references indicating that temples were built by the imperial monarchs of the 8th–11th-century Gurjara-Pratihara dynasty; although they occasionally provided grants of land to temples of note, the actual construction was undertaken exclusively by feudatories and their subjects. This seems to show that the Pratiharas, like their Gupta forerunners, maintained a certain aloofness as part of their ideal of kingship. The rest of the population, in contrast, was actively involved, and inscriptions provide a wealth of information about the individuals and groups who erected temples and provided gifts for their maintenance. The old standards of imperial detachment were finally eroded in the 10th century with the disintegration of Pratihara power and the emergence of strong regional dynasties. That the kings of these houses were extraordinary patrons is attested by the 10th- and 11th-century temples at such sites as THANJAVUR in Tamil Nadu and UDAIPUR and KHAJURAHO in Madhya Pradesh.

Although the intrusion of Islam in the 12th century destroyed this kind of patronage in north India, it continued under the indigenous dynasties of the south. The Tughluq conquest in the 14th century brought a momentary hiatus, but royal patronage was vigorously revived in the 14th–16th century by the VIJAYANAGARA kings of the Deccan. In the Islamic courts, however, ideals of patronage were derived from those developed in west Asia. Although Islamic strictures against figural representation largely limited sculpture to decorative reliefs, such houses as the Mughals (1526–1858) were enthusiastic patrons of architecture (*see* §III, 7(i) above). Away from the influence of these courts, however, India remained deeply traditional, fostering an indigenous art based on ancient popular beliefs. Between the 18th and 20th centuries, new patrons arose in the form of colonial powers, commercial interests and the rulers of princely states (*see* §§III, 7(iii), 8(i) and IV, 8 above).

BIBLIOGRAPHY

J. P. Vogel: 'The Sacrificial Posts of Īsāpur', *Archaeol. Surv. India, Annu. Rep.* (1910–11), pp. 40–48
——: *La Sculpture de Mathura*, Ars Asiatica xv (1930)
J. Marshall and A. Foucher: *The Monuments of Sanchi*, 3 vols (London, 1940)
J. C. Heesterman: *The Ancient Indian Royal Consecration* (The Hague, 1957)
J. Gonda: *Ancient Indian Kingship from the Religious Point of View* (Leiden, 1966)
J. Rosenfield: *The Dynastic Art of the Kushans* (Berkeley, 1967)
V. S. Agrawala: *The Deeds of Harṣa* (Varanasi, 1969)
P. L. Gupta: *The Imperial Guptas*, 2 vols (Varanasi, 1974–9)
S. P. Gupta: *The Roots of Indian Art* (New Delhi, 1980)
D. Schlumberger, M. Le Berre and G. Fussman: *Surkh Kotal en Bactriane* (Paris, 1983)

G. Verardi: 'The Kuṣāṇa Emperors as *Cakravartins*—Dynastic Art and Cults in India and Central Asia: History of a Theory, Clarifications and Refutations', *E. & W.*, xxxiii (1983), pp. 224–94
N. B. Dirks: *The Hollow Crown* (New York, 1988)
M. Rabe: 'Royal Portraits and Personified Attributes of Kingship at Mamallapuram', *J. Acad. A. & Archit., Mysore*, i (1991), pp. 1–4
C. Talbot: 'Temples, Donors and Gifts: Patterns of Patronage in Thirteenth-century South Asia', *J. Asian Stud.*, l (1991), pp. 308–40
B. S. Miller, ed.: *The Powers of Art: Patronage in Indian Culture* (New Delhi, 1992)
M. Willis: 'Religious and Royal Patronage in North India', *Gods, Guardians and Lovers*, ed. V. Desai (New York, 1993), pp. 48–65

MICHAEL D. WILLIS

2. PAINTING. Donative inscriptions at the Ajanta caves, the site of the earliest extant Indian paintings, establish both royal and monastic patronage. An inscription on the verandah of Cave 16, for example, names the donor as Varahadeva, minister of the Vakataka king Harisena (*reg c.* AD 460–78), and gives Varahadeva's motivation as the gaining of merit 'for the sake of his father and mother'. This association of a single donor with a comprehensive decorative scheme is unusual. Most of the sponsors of the large narrative paintings at the site remain anonymous. The inscription also describes the decoration of the cave, stating that it was adorned with beautiful picture galleries as well as sculpture and other ornamentation. Monastic donors include two monks, Bapuka and Dharmadatta, who recorded their offering of a series of iconic Buddha images in the same cave (though slightly later, possibly late 5th century or early 6th) with inscriptions painted prominently in a cartouche and discreetly on the lotus pedestal of each figure. The growing numbers of such hieratic images and the assertive presence of the patron's name and Buddhist votive formula on them seem to signal a change in the conception of the most efficacious type of Buddhist image and the means by which its merit was bestowed upon the believer. It has been suggested that such inscriptions may have been required for an image to be considered complete (see Begley).

The sacredness of scripture seems to have outweighed the potency of images in the commissioning of palm-leaf manuscripts of Buddhist and Jaina texts for monastic use. However, illustrated copies of these texts are outnumbered by unillustrated ones, and donors' names appear not beneath the small images in the centre of the folios but in the manuscript's colophon. An eastern Indian manuscript of the *Pañcarakṣā* (*c.* 1057; Cambridge, U. Lib., Add. MS. 1688), a text with hymns addressed to five Buddhist protective goddesses copied at the behest of Queen Uddaka, exemplifies the occasional royal patron. More often this role fell to monks or devout laymen who, as in the case of a manuscript of the *Aṣṭasāhasrikā prajñāpāramitā* ('Perfection of wisdom'; London, V&A, IS.4–10. 1958), dedicated the ensuing merit to their parents' souls. Although the lavishness of a manuscript's decoration was probably considered a measure of piety, colophons do not mention the aesthetic quality of these books nor even the presence of paintings.

Jaina manuscripts, originally copied to preserve learning and generate religious merit, developed an aesthetic dimension over the course of centuries of pictorial embellishment. Illustrations increased in both size and number, to the extent that nearly half of the 73 folios of the famous *Kalpa sūtra* manuscript (New Delhi, N. Mus., MS. 49.175) copied at Mandu in 1439–40 are illustrated. The colophon notes that the Jaina disciple Ksemahamsagani 'had this illustrated manuscript written for his own reading. May the text impart pleasure for a long time.'

A copy of the *Vasanta vilāsa* (1451–2; Washington, DC, Freer, MS. 32.24), a quasi-erotic poem describing love in the spring season, is the earliest known illustrated text not commissioned in a strictly religious context. The patron is named as Shah Sri Chandrapala of Ahmadabad, and a connoisseurly motivation for its commission is implied at the end of the lengthy scroll: 'the wise pass their time in the diversions of song and learning'. The absence of pious dedications and the occurrence of inscriptions naming both artist and patron in manuscripts illustrated in the style indigenous to north India in the late 15th century and early 16th suggest that pictorial delectation became a major impetus for patronage. Named patrons are not necessarily royal. A loosely structured and rendered *Āranyakaparvan* ('Forest book' of the *Mahābhārata*, 1516; Bombay, Asiat. Soc., MS. B.D.245) states that it was painted by Bhavanidas for the tax-collector Bhanadas Chaudhari. Some scholars, however, have posited a direct correlation between the wealth and interest of the patron and the quality of a painting. This has led to attempts to identify potential sources of royal patronage in the area between Delhi and Jaunpur for a superb contemporary *Caurapañcāśikā* (Ahmadabad, Cult. Cent., Mehta Col.) and dispersed *Bhāgavata purāṇa* series (*see* §VI, 4(i)(a) above).

After the establishment of Muslim rule in India *c.* 1200, Muslim patrons commissioned copies of Persian literary classics and treatises of worldly knowledge written in the Arabic script and often illustrated in Persian-influenced styles. Painting in the Sultanate period (*c.* 1200–1526) varied greatly in style and quality. The connection between high quality and royal patronage is supported by the firm association of two Muslim rulers of Mandu, Ghiyath al-Din Khalji (*reg* 1469–1500) and his son Nasir Shah (*reg* 1500–10), with three of the finest illustrated manuscripts of the period. Interestingly diverse in subject-matter, the three include the *Miftāḥ al-Fuẓulā* (London, BL, Or.MS. 3299), a glossary of rare words from ancient Persian poems; the *Būstān* of Saʿdi (New Delhi, N. Mus., MS. 48.6/4), a classic of Persian poetry; and the *Niʿmatnāma* (London, BL, Orient. & India Office Lib., Pers. MS. 149), a gourmet recipe book in Persian. Yet the difference in the quality of the work of two painters who contributed to the *Niʿmatnāma* shows that even when patron and provenance remained constant, local availability of accomplished artists and their understanding of an imported style profoundly affected the final result.

Abundant visual and literary evidence has encouraged some scholars to stress the role of the patron's personality in the development of style, particularly in the case of the Muslim states of the Deccan and the Mughal empire. In this view, the patron Ibrahim ʿAdil Shah II (*reg* 1579–1627) of Bijapur not only had the means and desire to summon talent to his court but also the force of personality to transmit his own poetical and musical interests to his painters, who translated them into melancholic colour schemes, fantastic landscape forms and sensitive rhythms of drapery and pattern. Likewise, the physically vital and intellectually inquisitive nature of Emperor Akbar (*reg* 1556–1605) is thought to be expressed in the lively naturalism of Mughal painting. Some proponents of this view link specific manuscripts and stylistic developments to changes in the Emperor's philosophy or emotional state. Court chronicles extol the Emperor's interest in painting, describing his personal selection of each scene to be illustrated in dozens of manuscripts and his weekly inspections of the workshop. Some recent studies, however, regard these accounts as panegyric and assign Akbar a primarily initiatory role, citing workshop instructions and schedules as evidence of many levels of authority between imperial patron and artist. Under Jahangir (*reg* 1605–27), large-scale projects of manuscript illustration were abandoned in favour of albums of single paintings by individual artists. Although Jahangir refers to only five artists in his voluminous memoirs, he boasts of his ability to distinguish the work of a given artist in even the tiniest detail, making him the first Indian patron to assert the systematic exercise of connoisseurship. (For further discussion of Mughal and Sub-imperial patronage, *see* §VI, 4(i) and (ii) above.)

The prestige of painting in Mughal culture led their vassals in Rajasthan, central India and the Punjab Hills to increase greatly the scope of painting in the 17th century, adding portraits and scenes of courtly activities to the illustration of traditional texts. As in the case of the Mughal court, painting is often perceived as the prerogative of these rulers, to whom the Jahangiri model of the discerning patron is applied indiscriminately. Thus, the sudden production of high-quality painting by small local workshops is construed as evidence of an inspirational and sensitive patron, and the intermittent influx of formal elements drawn from Mughal or other regional styles into a given centre is related to his diplomatic or military travels. It is more likely that a variety of factors contributed to stylistic developments, including the migration of artists, absorption of local idioms and organization of workshops. Rajasthani painting, particularly in traditional genres, changed slowly and presents clear regnal distinctions almost exclusively in portraits and ceremonial scenes with labelled personages. Nevertheless, rulers such as Jagat Singh I (*reg* 1628–52) of Mewar, Ram Singh II (*reg* 1827–66) of Kota and Savant Singh (*reg* 1748–64) of Kishangarh are commonly singled out as great patrons by virtue of the unusual amount of painting produced during their reigns.

Fluctuating financial and political conditions often influenced a royal patron's ability to attract and retain artists. Careful study of government records and inscribed paintings of the Punjab Hills suggests, however, that occasionally a patron's interest in painting could override such factors (see Goswamy). An exceptionally close personal relationship existed between the painter Nainsukh and Balwant Singh (1724–63), prince of Jasrota, despite the latter's limited means; similarly, Sansar Chand (*reg* 1775–1823) maintained a number of artists well after Kangra's fortunes had declined precipitously. Apart from the indulgence of personal taste and the display of courtly splendour, painting in this region also fulfilled a strong religious function. In some cases it appears that the personal devotion of the ruler and his family to Vishnu or the Goddess influenced the choice of texts to be copied and illustrated. The colophon of a dispersed *Rasamañjarī* dated 1695 expresses a more general religious motivation for commissioning paintings: 'In order to see the creation of God and to realize the hollowness of the world this illustrated *Rasamañjarī* containing many pictures, [which are] the wealth of the mind, was caused to be prepared by Raja Kirpal.' (For discussions of patronage with regard to particular schools of painting *see* §V above; for patronage in the 20th century *see* INDIA, REPUBLIC OF, §IX.)

BIBLIOGRAPHY

G. Yazdani: *Ajanta*, 4 vols (London, 1930–55)
W. Begley: *Chronology of Mahāyāna Buddhist Architecture and Painting at Ajaṇṭā* (diss., Philadelphia, U. PA, 1966)
B. N. Goswamy: 'Of Patronage and Pahari Painting', *Aspects of Indian Art*, ed. P. Pal (Leiden, 1972), pp. 130–38
W. G. Archer: *Indian Painting from the Punjab Hills*, 2 vols (London, 1973)
A. Topsfield: *Paintings from Rajasthan*, Melbourne, N.G. Victoria cat. (Melbourne, 1980)
The Art of the Book in India (exh. cat. by J. P. Losty, London, BL, 1982)
M. Zebrowski: *Deccani Painting* (London, 1983)
S. Doshi: *Masterpieces of Jain Painting* (Bombay, 1985)
India: Art and Culture, 1300–1900 (exh. cat. by S. C. Welch, New York, Met., 1985)
L. Leach: *Indian Miniature Paintings and Drawings*, Cleveland, OH, Mus. A. cat. (Cleveland, 1986)
J. Seyller: 'Scribal Notes on Mughal Manuscript Illustrations', *Artibus Asiae*, xlviii/3–4 (1987), pp. 247–77
B. N. Goswamy and E. Fischer: *Pahari Masters: Court Painters of Northern India* (Zurich, 1992)

JOHN SEYLLER

XIII. Collectors and collections.

Indian art has been collected for centuries. Hindu, Jaina and Buddhist temples and Muslim shrines were repositories of art. Rulers, merchants (Indian and other) and connoisseurs of all varieties also amassed significant collections. For example, the Mughal emperors Akbar (*reg* 1556–1605) and Jahangir (*reg* 1605–27) commissioned, purchased and preserved manuscripts, albums of miniatures, jades, jewels, metalwork, textiles and other precious items (*see also* §XII, 2 above). Rajput rulers also formed collections, many now displayed in former palaces converted to museums. The complex and varied reasons for collecting range from religious, political or social motives to aesthetic pleasure and a true love of art. The following survey looks mainly at collectors of the modern period and the fate of the treasures they gathered—some collections bequeathed to museums, others dispersed to a variety of institutions and to a new generation of collectors.

1. PRIVATE COLLECTIONS. Among the items collected at an early date by European missionaries, diplomats and merchants in India were illustrated manuscripts and illustrations of peoples and customs. These were occasionally painted to the specific requirements of European travellers. Paintings from India entered several collections in Europe as early as the 17th century. The missionary activities of the Jesuits led to Indian miniatures entering Italian collections such as those of Athanasius Kircher and Giovanni Antonio Baldini (1654–1725). Baldini's collection, later dispersed, was notable for containing mainly Indian and East Asian items and was, in this

respect, exceptional in Italy. The Venetian traveller Niccolo Manucci (1639–1717) acquired paintings in India, including depictions of Mughal emperors and Deccan notables. British and Dutch East India Company employees also took items back to Europe. Archbishop William Laud (1573–1645) in England requested that the ships of the British East India Company return with manuscripts, some of which were illustrated. Many of Laud's manuscripts and albums are now in the Bodleian Library, Oxford. The collection of Mughal paintings that belonged to Rembrandt probably arrived in Holland in Dutch Company vessels. The mission of Johan Ketelaar, the ambassador of the Dutch East India Company to the Mughal court in the years 1711–13, also returned to Holland with paintings. Among the items of trade brought to Europe were carpets and printed cottons from the Coromandel coast. Once in Europe, Indian paintings continued to change hands. Some of Rembrandt's Mughal paintings, for example, were acquired by Nicolaas Witsen, the burgomaster of Amsterdam. In 1728 Witsen's Indian paintings were auctioned, and some of them eventually found their way to the Rijksprentenkabinet, Amsterdam, and the Musée Napoléon, Paris. Others went into the possession of Empress Maria-Theresa to decorate her palace at Schönbrunn, Vienna.

After the Battle of Plassey in 1757 the British East India Company asserted itself more forcefully in India, especially in Bengal, which rose to become the senior of the Company's presidencies. As a result, a greater range of artefacts and manuscripts was collected by Company officials. Robert Clive, the victor at Plassey, who was in India from 1744 to 1767, acquired paintings, textiles and arms. Items from his collection are now displayed at Powis Castle, Powys, while two albums of his paintings are in the Victoria and Albert Museum, London (48–1956; 133–1964). Warren Hastings (1732–1818), who arrived in India in 1750 and was Governor-General of Bengal from 1774 to 1785, also acquired manuscripts and miniature paintings, as did his associate Elijah Impey (1732–1809), the Chief of Justice of Bengal from 1774 to 1783. Impey's Indian paintings included family scenes (still in the possession of his descendants) and Hindu subject-matter in local Bengal styles. From 1776 to 1782 he and his wife Mary employed three artists from Patna to draw natural history subjects. A number of these are in the collection of Sven Gahlin, Bristol. Some examples auctioned in London in 1984 went to a range of public and private collections. The Company official who collected the largest number of Indian manuscripts and paintings, however, was RICHARD JOHNSON, whose career in India spanned the years 1770–90. His collection, formed in Calcutta, Lucknow and Hyderabad and now in the Oriental and India Office Library, British Library, London, consisted of 716 manuscripts and 64 albums of paintings containing over 1000 items.

Among other Europeans forming collections in India at this time was the Frenchman Jean Baptiste Gentil (1726–99), who worked for the nawab Shujaʿ al-Daula (*reg* 1754–75) at Faizabad from 1763 to 1775; he collected manuscripts, miniatures, arms and medals and employed artists to illustrate the treatises he was writing. Much of Gentil's collection is in the Bibliothèque Nationale, Paris; works in other collections include an illustrated manuscript on the customs and people of India in the Victoria and Albert Museum, London. The Swiss engineer–architect Antoine Polier (1741–95), who worked for Shujaʿ al-Daula from 1773 to 1775 and then lived in Lucknow during the reign of Asaf al-Daula (*reg* 1775–97), also formed a collection of Indian miniatures. Many of Polier's paintings are now in the Islamisches Museum, Berlin, though a number of manuscripts, mainly unillustrated, are in the Bibliothèque Nationale and in the British Library, London. Claude Martin (1735–1800), a Frenchman who became adviser to Asaf al-Daula and superintendent of his arsenal, likewise collected antiquities and manuscripts, many of which are in the Bibliothèque Nationale.

As the East India Company secured its position in India, patronage among its officials became more widespread and diverse. Richard, Marquis Wellesley (1760–1842), for example, Governor-General of Bengal from 1798 to 1805, encouraged the creation in 1804 of an institution for natural history at Barrackpur, Calcutta, where, under the supervision of Francis Buchanan-Hamilton (1762–1829), Indian artists recorded natural history specimens, including animals and birds. In response to the collections being formed by its employees, the East India Company founded a library and museum in London in 1801. In India, the Asiatic Society of Bengal was at hand to receive items. A museum was founded by the Society in 1814; this is now the Indian Museum, Calcutta (*see* INDIA, Republic of, §XI, 1(v)). Manuscripts were also acquired by military conquest. Nearly 2000 volumes and other items including jewellery, for example, were acquired by the East India Company in the campaign against Tipu Sultan (*reg* 1782–99) at Seringapatam in 1799. Later, the British suppression of the uprising of 1857–8 led to the acquisition of the remnants of the Mughal library by the British government.

A taste for Indian sculpture was somewhat slower to develop than the arts of the book. A notable collector was Charles 'Hindoo' Stuart (1757/8–1828), who lived in India from 1777 until his death in Calcutta in 1828. His house was filled with sculptures collected in Bihar and Orissa. Most of them were sold at Christie's in London in 1830. They were bought by James Bridge, whose heirs gave the sculptures as a gift to the British Museum in 1872.

The international exhibitions in Europe, beginning with the Great Exhibition in London in 1851, raised the profile of Indian artefacts as 'industrial' arts. This outlook largely conditioned the purchases of the South Kensington Museum, London, which opened in 1857. Among the attempts by this museum to acquire Indian items was the visit to India of Caspar Purdon Clarke (1846–1911) in 1881–2; he was authorized to spend £2000 by the South Kensington Museum and a further £3000 by the India Office. He acquired about 3400 items, among which were *Hamzanāma* ('Tales of Hamza') paintings on cotton that he purchased in Srinagar.

Meanwhile, John Lockwood Kipling (1837–1911), principal of the Mayo School of Art in Lahore from 1875 to 1893 and curator of the Lahore Central Museum (now Lahore Museum), acquired traditional Indian artefacts for that museum. He also formed a small collection of his own that included bazaar art. Lockwood Kipling's friend

Thomas Hendley (1847–1917), the Residency surgeon at Jaipur, also had a personal collection, consisting largely of copies of Rajasthani portraits by artists he employed. Like Lockwood Kipling's personal collection, this is now in the Victoria and Albert Museum, London. Ernest Binfield Havell (*see* HAVELL, (3)), principal of the Calcutta School of Art and Keeper of the Art Gallery from 1896 to 1905, also purchased traditional Indian artefacts for the purpose of teaching and formed his own collection of Indian art. Havell's associate in Calcutta, the Indian painter Abanindranath Tagore, collected Indian art along with his elder brother Gaganendranath; some items from this collection are now in the Kasturbhai Lalbhai private collection in Ahmadabad. The artist William Rothenstein, who became acquainted with Havell and the Tagores, formed a fine collection of Mughal, Rajasthani and Pahari paintings, now also in the Victoria and Albert Museum.

Many connoisseurs of art living in France in the early 20th century collected Indian items, especially miniature paintings. Among them were Victor Goloubew (1879–1945), whose collection of Indian and Persian paintings went to the Boston Museum of Fine Arts in 1912. Maurice de Rothschild (1881–1957) and Jean Pozzi also collected Indian paintings. The dealer Charles Vignier (1863–1934) handled Indian art and donated items to the Musée Guimet, Paris. In Switzerland, the collection of Eduard von der Heydt included Indian sculptures that later entered the Museum Rietberg, Zurich. The Hungarian dealer Imre Schwaiger (1869–1940), who had lived in India in his early youth, specialized in Mughal and Rajput art and also sold textiles, jades and other items. In addition to supplying other dealers and collectors with Indian art, he was also responsible for enriching the Ferenc Hopp Museum of Oriental Art, Budapest, with donations. In Russia, the Indian items that were in the collections of Piotr Shchukin and Konstantin Nekrasov entered the Museum of Oriental Art, Moscow, after the Revolution of 1917.

In the 20th century some fine collections have been formed by Indian collectors, a number of whom used the international art market to acquire works. Even in the late 19th century, a collector such as Khuda Bakhsh (1842–1948), whose library is located in Patna, had agents in the Middle East. From his father (*d* 1876) Khuda Bakhsh inherited 1400 manuscripts, along with his father's wish that the collection should become public. This occurred in 1891, when it opened as the Khuda Baksh Oriental Public Library with nearly 4000 manuscripts. Patna was also the home of the lawyer P. C. Manuk, who formed an important collection of paintings, especially from the courts of the Punjab Hills. In Varanasi, RAI KRISHNADASA, a connoisseur of all aspects of Indian art, expanded his ancestral collection, and in 1950 it passed to Banaras Hindu University. B. N. Treasuryvala's miniatures and bronzes went to the National Museum, New Delhi, as did most of the fine miniature paintings in the collection of Motichand Khajanchi of Bikaner. A collection rich in miniature paintings was also formed by the businessman GOPI KRISHNA KANORIA of Patna. N. C. Mehta's collection of Indian miniature paintings is now in the Cultural Centre, Ahmadabad. Other important private collectors in Ahmadabad include Kasturbhai Lalbhai and Gautam Sarabhai. In Bombay, the large bequest of the house of Tata provided the basis for the Prince of Wales Museum of Western India. Significant collections were also formed by Madhuri Desai, C. D. Gujarati, A. C. Ardeshir, Cowasji Jehangir and the historian of Indian art Karl Khandalawala. Works acquired by Jagdish Goenka form the core collection of the Goenka Academy of Art and Music, New Delhi; and works collected by the Birla family are in the Birla Academy of Art and Culture, Calcutta. The extensive collection developed by Salar Jung in Hyderabad formed the basis for the Salar Jung Museum there. The Jagdish and Kamla Mittal Museum of Indian Art in Hyderabad was formed from the Mittal collection.

A number of 20th-century British collectors were inspired by meeting their Indian counterparts. William George Archer (*see* ARCHER, (1)) of the Indian Civil Service, who in 1949 became the keeper of the Indian section of the Victoria and Albert Museum, London, was a district magistrate in Patna in the early 1940s and there became acquainted with P. C. Manuk, Rai Krishnadasa and Gopi Krishna Kanoria. Archer was responsible for the acquisition by the Victoria and Albert Museum of the Rothenstein collection and parts of the collections of J. C. French and of T. G. Gayer-Anderson. The latter's collection of Indian paintings and drawings is now divided between the Victoria and Albert Museum, London, and the National Library of Australia in Canberra. W. B. Manley, a lawyer who had been in the Indian police force and later took up medicine, and F. B. P. Lory of the Indian Educational Service also formed collections in India. Dealers who went from India to the USA include Khan Monif and NASLI M. HEERAMANECK. Heeramaneck, a Parsi, acquired *en bloc* the stock of the dealer Georges Demotte containing important Mughal material. Heeramaneck's own collection was substantial; the most important part went to the Los Angeles County Museum of Art.

Denman Waldo Ross (1853–1935) was an important catalyst in the USA in the early 20th century; he not only gave his own items of Indian art to the Museum of Fine Arts, Boston, but as a lifelong trustee of the museum was instrumental in acquiring both the Victor Goloubew collection (see above) in 1912 and the ANANDA KENTISH COOMARASWAMY collection in 1917. As a result of this latter collection and the subsequent additions made to it by Coomaraswamy, who served as curator at the Boston Museum of Fine Arts until his death in 1947, Boston retained its primacy in Indian art in America until the 1960s. Miniatures acquired by Coomaraswamy were also sold to other museums in the eastern USA and abroad; Laurence Binyon of the sub-department of Oriental Prints and Drawings at the British Museum purchased Rajput paintings from Coomaraswamy before World War I.

The first Indian purchases of Charles Lang Freer (1856–1919) were made in 1907, when he bought a small ivory carving from Orissa and a collection of miniatures of various Indian schools that had been assembled in India in the late 19th century by Henry Bathhurst Hanna (*d* 1914). Many of these miniatures had at one time been in the royal libraries at Delhi and Agra and most are now in the Freer Gallery of Art, Washington, DC. Indian items were also purchased by collectors such as Henry Walters (1848–1931; now in the Walters Art Gallery, Baltimore, MD), John Frederick Lewis (1860–1932), the President of the Pennsylvania Academy of the Fine Arts, Philadelphia, John D. Rockefeller III (1906–78), who made gifts to the Asia Society Galleries, New York, Avery Brundage (1887–1975), whose collection forms the core works of the Asian Art Museum of San Francisco, and Christian Humann (1929–81). The mathematician Samuel Eilenberg (*b* 1913) acquired South Asian and South-east Asian art for his New York collection, as did Norton Simon (*b* 1907) of Los Angeles, most of whose collection is in the Norton Simon Museum in Pasadena. CHESTER BEATTY, the American mining engineer who moved to England in 1911, acquired an impressive collection of Mughal manuscripts in later years. His library of Oriental manuscripts is now in Dublin. George P. Bickford's wide-ranging Indian collection included paintings, sculptures, bronzes and ivories. Most of it was bequeathed to the Cleveland Museum of Art.

Wolf Ladejinsky (1899–1975), born in the Ukraine, arrived in the USA in 1922 and from 1964 until his death worked for the World Bank in India; he bequeathed his items, which included Rajasthani and Punjab Hills paintings, Tantric hangings and a variety of Indian sculptures, to the Israel Museum, Jerusalem. Edwin Binney III (1925–86) formed a comprehensive collection of Indian miniature paintings that eventually consisted of nearly 1400 items. Most were bequeathed to the San Diego Museum of Art, though several important works are in the Los Angeles County Museum of Art. Paul F. Walter (*b* 1935) of New York also initially collected Indian paintings then broadened his interests to include, for example, British Indian art, from 1970 becoming a generous patron of the Los Angeles County Museum of Art. Dr and Mrs William K. Ehrenfeld of San Francisco developed from the late 1970s a collection (now dispersed) of Indian paintings of the 16th–19th century from all major schools. By the late 20th century one of the most extensive and wide-ranging collections in the USA was the Kronos Collection, New York. As the century drew to a close the diverse collectors of Indian art included scholars such as Stuart Cary Welch, titled collectors such as Prince Sadruddin Aga Khan, political figures such as John Kenneth Galbraith and cinema 'moguls' such as James Ivory and Ismail Merchant.

See also INDIA, REPUBLIC OF, §XI, 2.

BIBLIOGRAPHY

F. Sarre: 'Rembrandts Zeichnungen nach indisch-islamischen Miniaturen', *Jb. Kön.-Preuss. Kstsamml.*, xxv (1904), pp. 143–58
——: 'Ein neues Blatt von Rembrandts indischen Zeichnungen', *Jb. Kön.-Preuss. Kstsamml.*, xxx (1909), pp. 283–90
V. A. Smith: 'Colonel H. B. Hanna's Collection of Indo-Persian Pictures and Manuscripts', *Ind. Antiqua.*, xxxix (1910), pp. 182–4
E. Blochet: *Les Peintures orientales de la collection Pozzi* (Paris, 1928)
A. K. Coomaraswamy: *Les Miniatures orientales de la collection Goloubew*, Ars Asiatica, xiii (1929)
T. W. Arnold: *The Library of A. Chester Beatty: A Catalogue of the Indian Miniatures*, 3 vols, rev. and ed. by J. V. S. Wilkinson (Oxford, 1936)
Miniature Paintings from the Sri Motichand Khajanchi Collection (exh. cat. by K. Khandalavala, M. Chandra and P. Chandra, New Delhi, Lalit Kala Akad., 1960)
Indian Miniatures from the Collection of Mildred and W. G. Archer, London (exh. cat., ed. N. Curtis; Washington, DC, Smithsonian Inst., 1963–4)
K. Khandalavala and M. Chandra: *Miniatures and Sculptures from the Collection of the Late Sir Cowasji Jehangir, Bart.* (Bombay, 1965)
The Arts of India and Nepal: The Nasli and Alice Heeramaneck Collection (exh. cat., Boston, MA, Mus. F.A., 1966)
J. M. Hartman: 'The Brundage Collection in San Francisco', *Orient. A.*, xiii (1967), pp. 113–24
E. Binney III and W. G. Archer: *Rajput Miniatures from the Collection of Edwin Binney III* (Portland, 1968)
R. W. Lightbown: 'Oriental Art and the Orient in Late Renaissance and Baroque Italy', *J. Warb. & Court. Inst.*, xxxii (1969), pp. 228–79
M. Archer: 'Company Painting in South India: The Early Collections of Niccolao Manucci', *Apollo*, xcii (1970), pp. 104–13
M. S. Young: 'Treasures of the Orient: A Rockefeller Collection', *Apollo*, xcii (1970), pp. 329–39
P. Pal: 'Indian Art from the Paul Walter Collection: Catalogue', *Allen Mem. A. Mus. Bull.*, xxviii/2 (1971), pp. 66–103
E. Binney III: *Indian Miniature Painting from the Collections of Edwin Binney, III: The Mughal and Deccani Schools with Some Related Sultanate Material* (Portland, 1973)
P. J. Marshall: 'Warren Hastings as Scholar and Patron', *Statesmen, Scholars and Merchants: Essays in Eighteenth Century History Presented to Dame Lucy Sutherland*, ed. A. Whiteman (Oxford, 1973)
Richard Johnson (1753–1807): Nabob, Collector and Scholar (exh. cat., London, India Office Lib., 1973)
Indian Art from the George P. Bickford Collection (exh. cat. by S. Czuma, Cleveland, OH, Mus. A.; Austin, U. TX, A. Mus.; Champaign, U. IL, Krannert A. Mus.; and elsewhere; 1975–7)
The Sensuous Line: Indian Drawings from the Paul F. Walter Collection (exh. cat. by P. Pal and C. Glynn, Los Angeles, CA, Co. Mus. A.; Vancouver, A.G.; Winnipeg, A.G.; and elsewhere; 1976–8)
The Classical Tradition in Rajput Painting from the Paul F. Walter Collection (exh. cat. by P. Pal, New York, Pierpont Morgan Lib.; and elsewhere; 1977–80)
A. N. Heeramaneck: *Masterpieces of Indian Sculpture from the Nasli M. Heeramaneck Collections* (Verona, 1979)
The Wolf Ladejinsky Collection of Asian Art (exh. cat. by P. D. Moynihan and others, Jerusalem, Israel Mus., 1980)
A. N. Heeramaneck: *Masterpieces of Indian Painting formerly in the Nasli M. Heeramaneck Collections* (Verona, 1984)
The Flame and the Lotus: Indian and Southeast Asian Art from the Kronos Collection (exh. cat. by M. Lerner, New York, Met., 1984)
J. Fisch: 'A Solitary Vindicator of the Hindus: The Life and Writings of General Charles Stuart (1757/58–1828)', *J. Royal Asiat. Soc. GB & Ireland* (1985), no. 1, pp. 35–57
Indian Miniatures: The Ehrenfeld Collection, (exh. cat. by D. J. Ehnbom, New York, Amer. Fed. A., 1985)
S. C. Welch: 'Private Collectors and Islamic Arts of the Book', *Treasures of Islam* (exh. cat., ed. T. Falk; Geneva, Mus. A. & Hist., 1985)
P. Pal, ed.: *American Collectors of Asian Art* (Bombay, 1986)
M. Archer, C. Rowell and R. Skelton: *Treasures from India: The Clive Collection at Powis Castle* (London, 1987)
K. Khandalavala and S. Doshi: *A Collector's Dream: Indian Art in the Collections of Basant Kumar and Saraladevi Birla and the Birla Academy of Art and Culture* (Bombay, 1987)

2. MUSEUMS. Items of Indian art, particularly paintings and illustrated manuscripts, began to enter European collections in increasing numbers from the 17th century. They were at first brought to Europe by Italian and Portuguese travellers, including Jesuit missionaries, but as trade developed British, Dutch and French travellers became more involved. As the British East India Company asserted itself in India from the 18th century, its employees were placed in a strong position to acquire works of art. This dominant position of Britain as far as collecting in India was concerned remained until Indian Independence in 1947. The development of substantial Indian collections in museums in other countries of the world, particularly the United States, has been largely a phenomenon of the 20th century.

In Asia itself, other than the museums of the subcontinent (*see* BANGLADESH, §8; INDIA, REPUBLIC OF, §XI, 1(v); and PAKISTAN, §VIII), the Kabul Museum had an important collection of ivories excavated at Begram, and the Gulistan Palace Library, Tehran, had major holdings of Mughal paintings. In the Middle East the National

Museum, Kuwait, has Indian Islamic art, and the Indian collection of the Israel Museum, Jerusalem, includes sculptures and paintings that belonged to Wolf Ladejinsky (1899–1975), who began to donate pieces from 1962, with the remainder of his collection arriving after his death. For holdings of Indian art in Japan *see* §(ii) below.

(i) Europe. (ii) North America and the Pacific.

(i) Europe. Before public museums were established in Europe in the 18th and 19th centuries, Indian manuscripts and paintings entered university or church libraries such as the Bodleian Library, Oxford, the Biblioteca Nazionale Marciana, Venice, and the Biblioteca Apostolica Vaticana, Rome. Items other than manuscripts and paintings were generally displayed in 'cabinets of curiosities'. However, acquisition intensified with the growth of European scholarly enquiry in India, especially after the founding of the Asiatic Society of Bengal in 1784, and a greater range of repositories for Indian art was established. The Orientalist societies founded in Europe in the early 19th century also promoted scholarship and accepted Indian pieces.

The museum of the East India Company in London, established in 1801, became the first important repository for Indian art in Britain. Some of the artefacts that arrived in its first decade were formerly in the possession of Tipu Sultan (*reg* 1782–99) and had been captured at Seringapatam in 1799. There was also a library, and the manuscript collection developed with the acquisition of a gift from William Kirkpatrick (1754–1812; British East India Company's Resident at Hyderabad, 1795–7) in 1804, Tipu Sultan's manuscripts in 1806, Richard Johnson's collection in 1807 and manuscripts belonging to Warren Hastings (Governor-General, 1774–85) in 1809. Johnson's collection was by far the largest of these collections (*see* §1 above). In 1857 the South Kensington Museum, now the Victoria and Albert Museum, opened in London. It was the first museum of 'industrial' art in Europe, and as it embraced for this purpose items from non-European lands, it quickly developed a collection of Indian 'manufactures' purchased from the Great Exhibition of 1851 and subsequent international exhibitions. The same emphasis on 'industrial' art characterized the museum of the East India Company. Following the Indian uprising against British rule in 1857, the East India Company was taken over by the British government and the museum became part of the newly formed India Office. Then, in 1880, it was divided; items of 'industrial' art went to the South Kensington Museum and antiquities—including the important Amaravati sculptures—to the British Museum. The manuscripts and paintings remained in the India Office Library, now a part of the British Library.

The antiquities sent to the British Museum in 1880 joined a number of others already in the collection, including sculptures collected in India by Charles 'Hindoo' Stuart (*see* §1 above). By the late 19th century the museum had an unrivalled collection of Indian sculptures, which has since been developed; it remains the most important centre outside India for the study of Amaravati sculpture. The British Museum also houses a fine collection of paintings, while illustrated manuscripts are in the collections of the British Library. The Victoria and Albert Museum has likewise broadened the scope of its collection to include numerous sculptures. A sandstone torso dated *c.* AD 900 was acquired as early as 1910, at a time when the aesthetic qualities of Indian art were beginning to be re-evaluated. This torso originated from a figure of the *bodhisattva* Avalokiteshvara that once stood in a small Buddhist temple at Sanchi in central India. In addition to other sculptures of stone and bronze, the Victoria and Albert Museum has collections of miniature paintings, notably from the Mughal, Rajasthani and Punjab Hill courts; textiles, including painted cottons from Golconda, shawls from Kashmir and carpets; and decorative arts such as glass, ivory, jewellery, furniture, enamelled metalwork, lacquer, crystal and jade.

Smaller collections of Indian art are to be found in other centres in Britain. In Oxford, the Indian collection at the Ashmolean Museum was developed after the transfer of items from the Indian Institute in 1962. Indian items can also be found at the Fitzwilliam Museum, Cambridge, the City of Birmingham Museum and Art Gallery, the City Art Gallery, Manchester, Durham University Oriental Museum and the Royal Museum of Scotland, Edinburgh. In Wales, the Clive Museum, Powis Castle, Powys, contains items that belonged to the 18th-century governor of Bengal, Robert Clive. In Ireland there are Indian exhibits at the National Museum of Ireland, Dublin, while the Chester Beatty Library and Gallery of Oriental Art, also in Dublin, is notable for its fine collection of Indian manuscripts.

In France, as in Britain, Indian art began to be acquired with a greater interest in its aesthetic qualities from the late 19th century. The Musée du Louvre in Paris was the original repository for artefacts, while illustrated manuscripts entered the Bibliothèque Nationale in the same city. The Musée Guimet, established in the late 19th century in Lyon and Paris as a museum of religions, acquired items that were primarily iconographic in nature, including bronzes and wooden chariot decorations from south India. By the 1920s and 1930s other items had arrived, notably the gifts of the dealer Charles Vignier, C. T. Loo and Gabriel Jouveau-Dubreuil; these included sculptures from Mathura, Buddhist reliefs from the Amaravati region and south Indian bronzes. The Musée Guimet also received the photographic archive of the collector Victor Goloubew, which reflected his interest in Indian art. After World War II, the Guimet was greatly enlarged when it received the Asian collections of the Louvre, including miniature paintings and Gandharan pieces brought from Peshawar in 1910 by Alfred Charles Auguste Foucher; it has since acquired items from Bengal, Orissa and Rajasthan.

Dutch collections of Indian art such as that of the Museum van Aziatische Kunst of the Rijksmuseum, Amsterdam, are more limited than those of Britain and France. However, the Kern Institute at Leiden, founded in 1925, has been responsible for the creation of a library and a photographic collection for research in Indian and Indonesian archaeology. Portugal, Spain and Italy also have limited collections of Indian art, again reflecting historical circumstances; inlaid furniture from Goa is displayed at the Museu Nacional de Arte Antiga, Lisbon. In Denmark, the Nationalmuseet, Copenhagen, founded in 1807, is notable for sculptures from Halebid in south

India and bronzes from Tranquebar, Tamil Nadu, where there had been a Danish colony since the 17th century. In Germany, Indian items have slowly accumulated over the last 200 years, although it was not until 1963 that the Museum für Indische Kunst, Berlin, was founded. In 1971, a new building was opened for the display of objects from South, Central and South-eastern Asia that had originally been in the museum's ethnological collection. Elsewhere in Berlin, illustrated manuscripts and albums are found in the Staatsbibliothek zu Berlin Preussischer Kulturbesitz. In Munich, the Staatliches Museum für Völkerkunde has an Indian collection that includes sculptures, ivories, lacquer, metalwork, textiles and paintings. Other notable Indian collections in Germany include those at the Folkwang Museum, Essen, the Museum für Kunst und Gewerbe and the Museum für Völkerkunde in Hamburg and the Museum des Kunsthandwerks, Leipzig. In addition, there are illustrated manuscripts in the Bayerische Staatsbibliothek, Munich.

In Switzerland, the Museum Rietberg Zürich, which opened in 1952, contains Indian sculptures from the collection of Eduard von der Heydt; all the main periods of Indian sculpture are represented, including outstanding pieces from Bhubaneshwar and Konarak, and good Pala-period sculptures (8th–12th century). There are also Indian exhibits in the Kunstgewerbemuseum, Zurich, the Museum für Völkerkunde und Schweizerisches Museum für Volkskunde, Basle, and the Historisches Museum, Berne. In Austria, the Österreichisches Museum für Angewandte Kunst, Vienna, has some rugs of Indian origin and important Indian paintings, including 60 from the *Hamzanāma* of the Mughal emperor Akbar (*reg* 1556–1605). At Schloss Schönbrunn, Vienna, built between 1696 and 1713 and altered in the 1740s, a small room on the upper floor is known for the Indian miniature paintings acquired by the 18th-century Habsburg empress Maria-Theresa that formed part of its decorative scheme.

In Hungary, the Indian collection in the Ferenc Hopp Museum of Oriental Art, Budapest, was enriched by the donations of Imre Schwaiger, a Hungarian who settled in India in his youth and became a dealer in Delhi. In the Czech Republic, a selection of the Asian collection of the Náprstek Museum of Asian, African and American Culture opened to the public in 1977 in the castle of Libechov near Mělník, north of Prague. This collection includes Buddhist art of the Mathura and Gandhara schools, metalwork, south Indian temple hangings and miniatures.

In Russia, the Indian items in the *Kunstkammer* created by Tsar Peter I (*reg* 1682–1725) were largely transferred to the Hermitage Museum, St Petersburg. In 1920, the Oriental Department was created by bringing together items formerly distributed throughout a number of sections of the museum; its relatively small collection of Indian art mainly comprises items of the 17th–20th century, including arms and armour, textiles, metalwork, ivory, woodwork and Mughal and Rajput miniatures. By the 1960s, this collection occupied four rooms and was supplemented with modern Indian paintings. In Moscow, at the Museum of Oriental Art (founded in 1918) the bulk of the Indian art collection was accumulated before the 1917 Revolution by the collectors Piotr Shchukin and Konstantin Nekrasov. This collection, important for miniatures, textiles, lacquer and woodwork, also includes 20th-century Indian paintings.

(ii) North America and the Pacific. In the USA, the foremost collection of Indian art up to the 1960s was the Museum of Fine Arts, Boston, where an important figure in the early 20th century was the historian and collector Denman Waldo Ross. Ross not only gave a large number of Asian items, including Indian art, to the museum, but as a trustee he was instrumental in acquiring Victor Goloubew's collection of Indian and Persian paintings from Paris in 1912 and Ananda Kentish Coomaraswamy's collection of Indian art in 1917; the latter collection was the first major collection of Indian art to enter an American museum. The strength of the Boston Museum's Indian collection has since increased, especially with the acquisition of more Rajasthani paintings through the generosity of John Goelet. The sculptures in the museum include Buddhist pieces from Gandhara and Mathura, reliefs from Amaravati and a range of works from the medieval period. Fine ivory sculptures from Kashmir and Orissa and jewellery are also represented.

Other museums in the USA followed the lead of Boston. For example, the Cleveland Museum of Art, founded in 1915, started to acquire Indian paintings in earnest from 1925, when Coomaraswamy sold it items from his own collection. The museum's collection continued to grow from the 1930s to the 1960s and included purchases from the dealer–collector Nasli M. Heeramaneck. From the 1950s the collector George P. Bickford, who was a trustee, became an important figure in the museum's acquisitions policy; in 1961 the director, Sherman E. Lee, recognized and purchased most of a *Ṭuṭīnāma* manuscript prepared for Akbar *c.* 1560–65, and in 1971 a large group of Mughal paintings was purchased from the collection of John MacDonald. At the Philadelphia Museum of Art, a stone section of a 16th-century temple hall from Madurai was received as a gift in 1919, and the first paintings were a gift from Lydia Thompson Morris in 1925. The president of the Pennsylvania Academy of the Fine Arts in Philadelphia, John Frederick Lewis, gave his important group of Indian paintings to the Free Library of Philadelphia in 1933.

There are many more museum collections of Indian art in the USA. In the north-east these include the Fogg Art Museum, Cambridge, MA, and the Worcester Art Museum, Worcester, MA. The latter contains a small collection of Indian miniatures and of Indian sculptures ranging in date from the Gandhara to the Vijayanagara periods. In New York there are notable Indian collections in the Metropolitan Museum of Art and the Brooklyn Museum, while the Newark Museum, NJ, has a large collection of Tibetan art as well as South Asian artefacts. The Walters Art Gallery in Baltimore possesses a fine collection of Mughal manuscripts and paintings, including an album with signed paintings by ABU'L-HASAN, DAULAT and MANOHAR, and a bound section of the *Baburnāma*; attempts have also been made to expand its collection of Indian sculptures. In Washington, DC there are major collections at the Freer Gallery of Art and the Arthur M. Sackler Gallery, and there are also notable holdings at the Detroit Institute of Arts, the Art Institute of Chicago and the Cincinnati Art Museum. Further south, the Virginia Museum of Fine Arts, Richmond, has some Indian sculptures that came from Nasli M. Heeramaneck. The Museum of Art and Archaeology at the University of Missouri, Columbia, MO, has a notable collection of Gandhara and east Indian sculpture that has developed since the 1960s through the generosity of its donors, particularly Samuel Eilenberg. In Kansas City, MO, the Nelson–Atkins Museum of Art contains a range of Indian sculptures and Mughal and Rajput paintings. The foremost collection on the west coast is that of the Los Angeles County Museum of Art, which acquired the bulk of the Heeramaneck collection in 1969; since then, through a vigorous acquisitions policy and the generosity of such donors as Paul F. Walter of New York, it has managed to double its South Asian holdings. The Asian Art Museum of San Francisco, which opened in 1966 as part of the M. H. de Young Memorial Museum, became a separate institution in 1969. Its collection includes temple sculptures, reliefs, stelae, bronzes, wood-carvings and paintings. Further north, the Portland Art Museum and Seattle Art Museum both have Indian collections. In Canada there are Indian pieces at the Montreal Museum of Fine Arts and the Royal Ontario Museum, Toronto.

In Japan, several museums contain collections of Indian art, often with a special emphasis on Buddhist material. The Matsuoka Art Museum, Tokyo, founded in 1975 to house the collection of Matsuoka Seijirō, contains Gandharan and medieval sculptures. By contrast, the Sankōkan Museum at Tenri has an ethnographic emphasis: its Indian collections include textiles, bronze figures of Hindu deities and musical instruments. In Osaka, the Masaki Art Museum contains Gandhara sculptures and early Indian coins. Other museums containing Indian works are the Fujii Yurinkan Museum, Kyoto, the Faculty of Letters Archaeological Collection at Kyoto University, the Hoppō Bunka (Northern Culture) Museum in the village of Yokogoshi near Niigata, the MOA Museum of Art at Atami, the Matsunaga Memorial Hall at Odawara, the Okura Shūkokan Museum, Tokyo, and the Shitennōji, Osaka.

Indian collections have also been formed in some Australian museums. Rajasthani paintings, for example, are found in the National Gallery of Victoria in Melbourne. There are also Indian paintings in the Art Gallery of New South Wales, Sydney, and the National Library of Australia, Canberra.

BIBLIOGRAPHY

EUROPE

H. H. Cole: *Catalogue of the Objects of Indian Art Exhibited in the South Kensington Museum* (London, 1874)
J. Strzygowski: *Die indische Miniatüren im Schlosse Schönbrunn* (Vienna, 1922)
L. Binyon, W. Rothenstein and H. Read: *Examples of Indian Sculpture at the British Museum* (London, [1923])
H. Goetz: 'Die indischen Miniatüren der Berliner Museen', *Der Cicerone*, xiii (May 1923), pp. 419–26
——: 'Indische Miniatüren im Münchener Völkerkunde Museum', *Münchn. Jb. Bild. Kst*, xiii/2 (1923), pp. 61–91
J. Hackin: *La Sculpture indienne et tibétaine au Musée Guimet* (Paris, 1931)
R. Chanda: *Medieval Indian Sculpture in the British Museum* (London, 1936)
E. Kühnel: *Indische Miniaturen aus dem Besitz der staatlichen Museen zu Berlin* (Berlin, 1937)
A. J. Arberry: *The Library of the India Office: A Historical Sketch* (London, 1938)
V. S. Agrawala: 'A Note on Asiatic Art in the Museums of Europe', *J. Ind. Mus.*, vi (1950), pp. 11–19
D. Barrett: *Sculptures from Amaravati in the British Museum* (London, 1954)
A. Banck: *The Oriental Collections at the Hermitage Museum* (Leningrad, 1960) [in English and Russian]
J. E. van Lohuizen-de Leeuw: *Indische Skulpturen der Sammlung Eduard von der Heydt* (Zurich, 1964)
H. Härtel, V. Moeller and G. Bhattacharya: *Museum für Indische Kunst Berlin: Katalog 1971—Ausgestellte Werke* (Berlin, 1971)
S. Settar: *Hoysala Sculpture in the National Museum* (Copenhagen, 1975)
Rarities of the Musée Guimet (exh. cat. by J. Auboyer and others, New York, Asia Soc. Gals; Kansas City, MO, Nelson–Atkins Mus. A.; San Francisco, CA, Asian A. Mus.; 1975)
R. Skelton: 'The Indian Collections: 1798 to 1978', *Burl. Mag.*, cxx (1978), pp. 296–304
Die Meisterwerke aus dem Museum für indische Kunst, Berlin, Staatliche Museen preussischer Kulturbesitz (Stuttgart and Zurich, 1980)
R. Desmond: *The India Museum, 1801–79* (London, 1982)
J. Ayers, A. Topsfield and J. Lowry: *Oriental Art in the Victoria and Albert Museum* (London, 1983)
J. C. Harle and A. Topsfield: *Indian Art in the Ashmolean Museum* (Oxford, 1987)
N. Sychova and others: *The Museum of Oriental Art, Moscow* (Leningrad, 1988)

NORTH AMERICA AND THE PACIFIC

A. K. Coomaraswamy: *Catalogue of the Indian Collections in the Museum of Fine Arts, Boston*, 4 vols (Boston, 1923–30)
Handbook of the Collections in the William Rockhill Nelson Gallery of Art and Mary Atkins Museum of Fine Arts (Kansas City, 1959)
S. Kramrisch: *Indian Sculpture in the Philadelphia Museum of Art* (Philadelphia, 1960)
R. Ettinghausen: *Paintings of the Sultans and Emperors of India in American Collections* (New Delhi, 1961)
H. Trubner: *Royal Ontario Museum: The Far Eastern Collection* (Toronto, 1968)
P. Pal and J. Fontein: *Museum of Fine Arts, Boston: Oriental Art* (Boston, 1969)
A. Lippe: *The Freer Indian Sculptures* (Washington, DC, 1970)
R. S. Teitz: 'Indian Sculpture at the Worcester Art Museum', *A. Asia*, ii/6 (1972), pp. 28–34
V. P. Dwivedi: 'Mathura Art in the Museums of United States of America', *J. Ind. Mus.*, xxix (1973), pp. 22–9
H. Trubner: *Asiatic Art in the Seattle Art Museum: A Selection and Catalogue* (Seattle, 1973)
M. C. Beach: 'New Asian Galleries, Walters Art Gallery Baltimore', *Orient. A.*, xxi/3 (1975), pp. 275–9
P. Pal: 'The Asian Collection in the Los Angeles County Museum of Art', *A. Asia*, v/3 (1975), pp. 47–58
M. Lerner: 'Treasures of South Asian Sculpture [in the Norton Simon Museum of Art]', *Connoisseur*, cxciii (Nov 1976), pp. 196–203
P. Pal: 'South Indian Sculptures in the Museum', *Bull. LA Co. Mus. A.*, xxii (1976), pp. 30–57
S. J. Czuma: 'Mathura Sculptures in the Cleveland Museum Collection', *Bull. Cleveland Mus. A.*, lxiv/3 (March 1977), pp. 83–112
R.-Y. Lefebvre d'Argencé, ed.: *Asian Art: Museum and University Collections in the San Francisco Bay Area* (New Jersey, 1978)
A. Topsfield: *Paintings from Rajasthan in the National Gallery of Victoria* (Melbourne, 1980)
E. B. Findly: *From the Courts of India: Indian Miniatures in the Collection of the Worcester Art Museum* (Worcester, MA, 1981)
C. K. Gairola: 'Manifestations of Śiva: Indian Śiva Images in the Virginia Museum of Fine Arts', *Orient. A.*, xxvii/3 (1981), pp. 316–22
S. D. Nagar: *Gandhāran Sculpture: A Catalogue of the Collection in the Museum of Art and Archaeology, University of Missouri-Columbia* (Columbia, 1981)
P. Pal: *Indian Paintings in the Los Angeles County Museum of Art* (New Delhi, 1982)
J. C. Y. Watt and others: *Asiatic Art in the Museum of Fine Arts, Boston* (Boston, 1982)
L. Y. Leach: *Indian Miniature Paintings and Drawings: The Cleveland Museum of Art* (Cleveland, 1986)
P. Pal: *Indian Sculpture: A Catalogue of the Los Angeles County Museum of Art Collection*, i (Berkeley and London, 1986)

M. B. Heston: 'The South Asian Collections at the Newark Museum', *A. Asia*, xix/5 (1989), pp. 119–29

□

XIV. Exhibitions.

Since the mid-19th century exhibitions have presented an ever-increasing range of Indian art to the public, reflecting India's changing political status and growing sense of heritage. European interest in Indian items as colonial 'manufactures' has been superseded by an awareness of the intellectual and aesthetic significance of the Indian artistic tradition. Exhibitions demonstrating the richness and breadth of Indian art have also stimulated scholarship in neglected areas of study.

The success of Indian exhibits at the Great Exhibition in London in 1851 marked the beginning in Europe of a greater public interest in Indian artefacts. Items from India were also displayed at the Exposition Universelle in Paris in 1855 and at the International Exhibition in London in 1862. At the Exposition Universelle in Paris in 1867 the Indian collection included some 500 photographs selected by JAMES FERGUSSON to illustrate styles of Indian architecture. (The Archaeological Survey of India was formed in 1862 with the aim of examining and preserving such monuments.)

The Exposition Universelle in Paris in 1878 included over 12,000 Indian items. The Indian Court was designed by Caspar Purdon Clarke, and the exhibits were organized by GEORGE BIRDWOOD. John Lockwood Kipling, the principal of the Mayo School of Art in Lahore and curator of the Lahore Central Museum, came to Paris for the occasion. One outcome was a letter drafted by WILLIAM MORRIS and signed by a number of sympathizers making a plea for measures to preserve Indian handicrafts. Birdwood became concerned about the introduction into India of imported designs and machinery, which were destroying the quality of Indian artefacts and encouraging the loss of traditional techniques. Yet, following the emphasis on 'manufactures' advocated by the South Kensington Museum and propagated at the schools of art in India, he did not accept that there were Indian equivalents of the European 'fine' arts of sculpture and painting. Smaller exhibitions were also arranged in India itself. The Punjab Exhibition, for example, was held in 1864, the Jaipur Exhibition in 1883 and the Calcutta International Exhibition in 1883–4.

By the early 20th century, Ernest Binfield Havell (*see* HAVELL, (3)), ANANDA KENTISH COOMARASWAMY and the artist WILLIAM ROTHENSTEIN, in particular, were responsible for launching a campaign to encourage an awareness of the aesthetic qualities of Indian art. This reassessment is reflected in the exhibitions of the early 20th century. At the Delhi Durbar Exhibition of 1902–3, for example, the conventional emphasis on 'manufactures' remained, and no miniature paintings were displayed. At the Coronation Durbar Exhibition at Delhi from 1911–12, however, there was a separate section of miniature paintings. Similarly, the Indian Court of the Festival of Empire and Imperial Exhibition at Crystal Palace in 1911 demonstrated a greater interest in the artistic legacy of India, especially Indian painting.

This re-evaluation also applied to contemporary art. In 1914 more than 200 works from artists of the New Calcutta School, including Abanindranath Tagore (*see* TAGORE, (3)), had their first international show. The exhibition, which included items on loan from the collections of Havell and Coomaraswamy, was staged first in Paris, at the 22nd exhibition of the Société des Peintres Orientalistes Français, then at the Victoria and Albert Museum in London, before continuing to Chicago and Tokyo in 1915.

After World War I, William Rothenstein in particular helped to organize exhibitions of Indian art, notably the Indian Pavilion at the British Empire Exhibition at Wembley in 1924, which included his own collection of Indian paintings, and the 'Exhibition of the Art of India' for the Burlington Fine Arts Club in 1931. The latter included carved seals and small sculptures that had recently been excavated under the auspices of John Marshall at Harappa in the Indus Valley; their high quality and early date challenged current conceptions of Indian art. The exhibition presented a comparatively small number of particularly fine examples, especially of sculpture and painting.

'The Art of India and Pakistan' at Burlington House in London from November 1947 to February 1948, organized to mark independence, rightly claimed to be the most important exhibition to that date of the arts of the subcontinent. A number of large and important pieces of sculpture were transported to Britain for it. Contributions came from museums and collectors in India (a consignment of 239 cases was brought by sea from Bombay), France, Holland and the United States, as well as Britain. Afterwards, when items were returned to India, some went to form the foundation collection of the new National Museum, which was established in 1949 in President House, New Delhi. Both the exhibition and the museum were important for promoting a sense of India's cultural heritage.

In 1959 '5000 Years of Art from India', a large exhibition initiated by the Krupp Concern and including works sent by the Indian government, was held at Villa Hügel in Essen, Germany. The exhibition travelled in 1959 to the Kunsthaus, Zurich, and in 1960 opened at the Petit Palais, Paris. In 1962–3 an exhibition with a similar title, '5000 Years of Art in Pakistan', sponsored by the German Arts Council, was held at Darmstadt, Augsburg and Bonn. These exhibitions stressed the long duration of a national heritage as well as the strong tradition of Indian scholarship in Germany.

In the United States, interest in Indian art developed rapidly in the 1960s. A number of exhibitions were organized by the Asia House Galleries of the Asia Society in New York (now the Asia Society Galleries), which had been founded in 1956 'to promote greater understanding between the United States and the peoples of Asia'. In 1960, for example, exhibitions of Gandhara sculpture and Rajput painting were held at Asia House. 'The Art of Mughal India', organized by Stuart Cary Welch and opened in 1964, was the first major loan exhibition of Mughal art in the United States, though significant examples of Mughal painting had been known and displayed since Coomaraswamy's time, for example at the Boston Museum of Fine Arts. The important role of the Asia House Galleries as a venue for Indian art has continued since the 1960s. Exhibitions have ranged from 'The Ideal Image:

The Gupta Sculptural Tradition and its Influence' in 1978 to an exhibition of the Islamic arts of the book in the collection of Prince Sadruddin Aga Khan in 1982–3, and 'Gods, Guardians, and Lovers: Temple Sculptures from North India, A.D. 700–1200' in 1993, part of a renewed interest in serious exhibitions of Indian art.

New themes in Indian art have come to the fore in a variety of exhibitions. For example, at the Museum of Art, Philadelphia, in 1968 the exhibition 'Unknown India: Ritual Art in Tribe and Village', organized by STELLA KRAMRISCH, presented a hitherto neglected aspect of Indian culture. This exhibition later moved on to the M. H. de Young Memorial Museum in San Francisco and the City Art Museum of St Louis. At the Hayward Gallery, London, in 1971, the influential 'Tantra' exhibition included paintings and sculpture from the collection of Ajit Mookerjee. In the early 1990s the art of the 'tribal' communities, or *ādivāsī*, was celebrated in exhibitions in the Netherlands and Japan; the exhibition 'Living Wood: Sculptural Traditions of Southern India' held at the Whitechapel Art Gallery, London, in 1992 (travelling to Bradford and Hamburg) featured for the first time outside India the stark and powerful *bhūta* figures of south Kanara. There have also been exhibitions on religious themes that featured Indian art: these included exhibitions on Buddhism and Hinduism at the British Museum in 1985 and 1993 respectively, and on Buddhism and Jainism at the Los Angeles County Museum in 1984 and 1994 respectively.

Shows of private collections in India included that of paintings belonging to Sri Motichand Khajanchi in 1960 at the Lalit Kala Akademi, New Delhi (travelling to Bombay and Calcutta), and in the United States those of Edwin Binney III (1925–86) in the 1960s and George P. Bickford in the mid-1970s. HOWARD HODGKIN's collection of Indian painting was exhibited at the Sackler Gallery, Washington, DC, and the Ashmolean Museum, Oxford, in the early 1990s.

In Asia, Tokyo has perhaps been the most important exhibition site outside India. Since the 1960s exhibitions have included 'The Ancient Art of India' in 1964 and 'The Ancient Sculpture of India' in 1984. In India, meanwhile, exhibitions have been motivated by a variety of considerations and sometimes have had a different character from those held in the Western world. It is in this light, for example, that the exhibition 'Islamic Heritage of India', which honoured the 1400th anniversary of the Hijra era, can be considered. This exhibition was organized by the National Museum, New Delhi, and items were collected for it throughout India.

It was with the Festival of India celebrated in London and various other centres in Britain in 1982 that the potential of holding a series of exhibitions and other cultural events in unison was realized. This festival attempted to give 'the fullest possible picture of Indian culture from the earliest times to the present day', not only through exhibitions of art of the past but also by incorporating the 'living traditions' of Indian craftsmen, artists, photographers, dancers and musicians. The centre-piece in London was the exhibition 'In the Image of Man' at the Hayward Gallery, subtitled 'The Indian Perception of the Universe through 2000 Years of Painting and Sculpture' and focusing on themes rather than a historical or stylistic presentation. At the Victoria and Albert Museum, 'The Indian Heritage' presented the court art of the Mughals, and, at the Tate Gallery, 'The Modern Indian Artists' featured the work of Magbool Fida Husain, Bhupen Khakhar, Jamini Roy, Amrita Sher-Gil, K. G. Subramanyan and Rabindranath Tagore.

The success of the Festival of India of 1982 in Britain became immediately apparent, and many similar festivals followed. In 1984–5, there was a festival in Australia, which included the exhibition 'The Spirit of India' at the Art Gallery of Western Australia, Perth. The Festival of India held in the United States in 1985–6 was the largest and most comprehensive of the Indian festivals of the 1980s. Its numerous exhibitions included 'The Sculpture of India', at the National Gallery of Art, Washington DC, organized by Pramod Chandra, presenting Indian sculpture from *c.* 3000 BC to AD 1300, and at the Metropolitan Museum of Art, New York, 'India: Art and Culture, 1300–1900', organized by Stuart Cary Welch, showing arts from the period after the arrival of Islam. In France, where there had been important exhibitions of Indian art at the Petit Palais, Paris, in 1960 and 1978–9, a 'L'Année de l'Inde' was held in 1986. This festival included the exhibition 'A la cour du Grand Moghol', organized by Monique Cohen, Amina Okada and Francis Richard, and 'Rasa, les neuf visages de l'art indien', organized by B. N. Goswamy and later shown in San Francisco. The following year, the festival 'India in Switzerland '87' included the exhibition 'Wonders of a Golden Age', at the Rietberg Museum, Zurich, organized by B. N. Goswamy and Eberhard Fischer, which displayed Mughal art of the 16th and 17th centuries from collections in Switzerland. An Indian festival held in the Soviet Union in 1987 was balanced by a festival of the Soviet Union in India, the two marking the 40th anniversary of the independence of India and the 70th anniversary of the Russian Revolution respectively. This use of exhibitions illustrates again their potential for affirming national identities and strengthening political relationships. Perhaps even more important, however, is the ongoing exposure of Indian art to the general public and the stimulation of scholarship (including that preserved in catalogues) that such exhibitions engender.

BIBLIOGRAPHY

EUROPE

G. C. M. Birdwood: *Paris Universal Exhibition of 1878: Handbook to the British Indian Section* (London, 1878)

'Festival of Empire and Imperial Exhibition', *J. Ind. A. & Indust.*, xv (1912–13)

Catalogue of Paintings of the New Calcutta School (exh. cat. by A. J. D. Campbell, London, V&A, 1914)

Catalogue of an Exhibition of the Art of India (exh. cat., London, Burlington F.A. Club, 1931)

L. Ashton, ed.: *The Art of India and Pakistan: A Commemorative Catalogue of the Exhibition Held at the Royal Academy of Arts, London, 1947–8* (London, 1949)

5000 Years of Art from India (exh. cat. by E. Boehringer, K. Fischer and H. Goetz, Essen, Villa Hügel, 1959; Eng. trans., London, 1964)

Kunst aus Indien: Von der Indus-Tal-Kultur im 3. Jahrtausend v. Chr. bis zum 19. Jahrhundert (exh. cat., Zurich, Ksthaus, 1959–60)

Trésors d'art de l'Inde (exh. cat., Paris, Petit Pal., 1960)

5000 Years of Art in Pakistan (exh. cat. by K. Schmidt and others, Darmstadt, Mathildenhöhe; Augsburg, Altes Rathaus; Bonn, Rhein. Landesmus.; 1962–3)

Tantra (exh. cat. by P. Rawson, London, Hayward Gal., 1971)

Inde: Cinq mille ans d'art (exh. cat., Paris, Petit Pal., 1978–9)

Contemporary Indian Art (exh. cat., London, RA, 1982)
The Indian Heritage: Court Life and Arts under Mughal Rule (exh. cat., ed. R. Skelton; London, V&A, 1982)
In the Image of Man: The Indian Perception of the Universe through 2000 Years of Painting and Sculpture (exh. cat. by G. Michell, L. Leach and T. S. Maxwell, London, Hayward Gal., 1982)
The Art of the Book in India (exh. cat. by J. P. Losty, London, BL, 1982)
Buddhism: Art and Faith (exh. cat., ed. W. Zwalf; London, BM, 1985)
A la Cour du Grand Moghol (exh. cat., Paris, Gal. Mansart, 1986)
Essence of Indian Art/Rasa, les neuf visages de l'art indien (exh. cat. by B. N. Goswamy, Paris, Grand Pal.; San Francisco, CA, Asian A. Mus.; 1986)
Wonders of a Golden Age: Painting at the Court of the Great Mughals (exh. cat. by B. N. Goswamy and E. Fischer, Zurich, Rietberg Mus., 1987)
Calcutta, City of Palaces: A Survey of the City in the Days of the East India Company, 1690–1858 (exh. cat. by J. P. Losty, London, BL, 1990)
Pahari-Meister (exh. cat. by B. N. Goswamy and E. Fischer, Zurich, Mus. Rietberg, 1990)
Adivasi, het andere India (exh. cat., ed. F. Cowan; Amsterdam, 1992)
The Crossroads of Asia: Transformation in Image and Symbol in the Art of Ancient Afghanistan and Pakistan (exh. cat., ed. E. Errington and J. Cribb; Cambridge, Fitzwilliam, 1992)
Living Wood: Sculpture Traditions of South India (exh. cat., ed. G. Michell; London, Whitechapel A.G., 1992)
Silk Road Coins in the Hirayama Collection (exh. cat. by K. Tanabe, London, BM, 1993)

NORTH AMERICA

Gandhara Sculpture from Pakistan Museums (exh. cat. by B. Rowland, Boston, MA, Mus. F.A.; Ann Arbor, U. MI, Mus. A.; New York, Asia Soc. Gals; and elsewhere; 1960)
Rajput Painting (exh. cat. by S. Lee, New York, Asia Soc. Gals, 1960)
The Art of Mughal India: Painting & Precious Objects (exh. cat. by S. C. Welch, New York, Asia Soc. Gals, 1963/*R* 1976)
Gods, Thrones, and Peacocks. Northern Indian Painting from Two Traditions: Fifteenth to Nineteenth Centuries (exh. cat. by S. C. Welch and M. C. Beach, New York, Asia Soc. Gals; Baltimore, MD, Mus. A. Utica, NY, Munson–Williams–Proctor Inst.; 1965–6)
Unknown India: Ritual Art in Tribe and Village (exh. cat. by S. Kramrisch, Philadelphia, PA, Mus. A.; San Francisco, CA, de Young Mem. Mus.; St Louis, MO, A. Mus.; 1968)
Indian Art from the George P. Bickford Collection (exh. cat. by S. Czuma, Cleveland, OH, Mus. A.; Austin, U. TX, A. Mus.; Urbana, U. IL, Krannert A. Mus., and elsewhere; 1975–7)
The Ideal Image: The Gupta Sculptural Tradition and its Influence (exh. cat. by P. Pal, New York, Asia Soc. Gals, 1978)
The Grand Mogul: Imperial Painting in India, 1600–60 (exh. cat. by M. C. Beach, Williamstown, MA, Clark A. Inst.; Baltimore, MD, Walters A.G.; Boston, MA, Mus. F.A.; New York, Asia Soc. Gals; 1978–9)
Room for Wonder: Indian Painting during the British Period 1760–1880 (exh. cat. by S. C. Welch, New York, Asia Soc. Gals, 1978–9)
The Imperial Image: Paintings for the Mughal Court (exh. cat. by M. C. Beach, Washington, DC, Freer, 1981–2)
Light of Asia: Buddha Sakyamuni in Asian Art (exh. cat. by P. Pal, Los Angeles, CA, Co. Mus. A., 1984)
Akbar's India: Art from the Mughal City of Victory (exh. cat. by M. Brand and G. D. Lowry, New York, Asia Soc. Gals, 1985)
Contemporary Indian Art from the Chester and Davida Herwitz Family Collection (exh. cat., New York, Grey A.G., 1985)
Festival of India in the United States, 1985–1986 (New York, 1985)
India: Art and Culture, 1300–1900 (exh. cat. by S. C. Welch, New York, Met., 1985)
Indian Miniatures: The Ehrenfeld Collection (exh. cat. by D. J. Ehnbom, New York, Amer. Fed. A., 1985)
Kushan Sculpture: Images from Early India (exh. cat. by S. Czuma, Cleveland, OH, Mus. A., 1985)
Life at Court: Art from India's Rulers, 16th–19th Centuries (exh. cat. by V. N. Desai, Boston, MA, Mus. F.A., 1985)
Pride of the Princes: Indian Art of the Mughal Era in the Cincinnati Art Museum (exh. cat. by E. S. Smart and D. S. Walker, Cincinnati, OH, A. Mus., 1985)
The Sculpture of India, 3000 B.C.–1300 A.D. (exh. cat. by P. Chandra, Washington, DC, N.G.A., 1985)
From Indian Earth: 4,000 Years of Terracotta Art (exh. cat. byA. Poster, New York, Brooklyn Mus., 1986)
Romance of the Taj Mahal (exh. cat. by P. Pal and others, Los Angeles, CA, Co. Mus. A., 1989)
A. Topsfield and M. Cleveland Beach: *Indian Paintings and Drawings from the Collection of Howard Hodgkin* (New York, 1991/*R* London, 1992)
Gods, Guardians and Lovers: Temple Sculptures from North India, A. D. *700–1200* (exh. cat., ed. V. N. Desai and D. Mason; New York, Asia Soc. Gals, 1993)

ASIA

T. H. Hendley: *Memorials of the Jeypore Exhibition*, 4 vols (London, 1883)
Indian Art at Delhi, 1903: Being the Official Catalogue of the Delhi Exhibition, 1902–1903 (exh. cat. by G. Watt and P. Brown, New Delhi, Qudsia Gdns, 1902–3)
Loan Exhibition of Antiquities, Coronation Durbar, 1911 (exh. cat. by J. P. Thompson, Delhi, Archaeol. Mus., 1911–12)
Miniature Paintings from the Sri Motichand Khajanchi Collection (exh. cat. by K. Khandalavala, M. Chandra and P. Chandra, New Delhi, Lalit Kala Akad., 1960)
Islamic Heritage of India (exh. cat. by K. Khandalavala, N. Nath and S. Puri, New Delhi, N. Mus., 1981)
S. Doshi, ed.: *Pageant of Indian Art: Festival of India in Great Britain* (Bombay, 1983)
The Crucible of Compassion and Wisdom, Special Exhibition Catalogue of the Buddhist Bronzes from the Nitta Group Collection (exh. cat., Taipei, N. Pal. Mus., 1987) [Gandhara sculpture]
The Art of the Adivasi (Indian Tribal Art) (exh. cat. by J. Swaminathan and J. Jain, Tokyo, 1988)

S. J. VERNOIT

XV. Copies and forgeries.

According to the orthodox Indian view, all knowledge is contained in the texts known as the Vedas and their attendant literature. These works are regarded as complete in themselves, and thus any change in human understanding of them can bring only corruption and degeneration; there is no concept of progress in the modern sense, and change is seen as necessary only to rephrase ancient truths in contemporary terminology. This has meant that repetition and copying have long been sanctioned as a proper way of perpetuating sacred tradition. Texts were faithfully memorized, manuscripts were copied (often with errors dutifully preserved), and the principal iconographic features of the main divinities, once fixed, were repeated again and again without significant modification. This conservatism accounts for the durability of such motifs as the amorous couple, the lotus flower and the woman-and-tree, which have continuous histories of more than 2000 years. The deliberate forgery of art objects for monetary gain was an innovation of the 20th century.

1. COPIES. Copying of an explicit nature is evident after the 9th century AD, by which time conventions in iconography and artistic practice were deeply entrenched. For example, the numerous Jaina sculptures made in western India between the 12th and 15th centuries and transported to other areas retained their distinctive style and iconographic features over the history of their production. Most of the figures give the impression of having been copied in a workshop, and fidelity to the original seems to have been the main concern. The same repetitious quality pervades manuscript paintings of the western Indian school (*see* §VI, 3(ii)(a) above). Artistic conventions were codified in manuals that perpetuated iconography and encouraged subsequent generations to copy their predecessors (*see* §I, 10 above). Furthermore, certain works deliberately referred to ancient prototypes, as in the case of the railing posts at Bodhgaya in Bihar (*see* BODHGAYA AND GAYA). The original railing was carved about the 1st century BC, but by the 5th century AD some of the uprights

evidently needed repair and were replaced with new pieces carefully patterned after the old in every respect. The modelling of the forms, however, displays the unmistakable delicacy and suppleness of 5th-century sculpture. The Mahabodhi Temple at the same site enjoyed a similar sanctity: models of the temple and seals carrying its image were made in considerable numbers and were apparently the basis for temples elsewhere.

The monolithic pillars and capitals of the Maurya period (3rd–4th century BC) were regarded with considerable awe through the ages, as indicated by the numerous inscriptions incised on them, by accounts of Chinese pilgrims and by their relocation and reuse in later buildings. While features of the capitals were employed as early as the 1st century BC (for instance on one of the Sanchi gateways), wholesale copies were apparently made only in the Gupta period (4th–5th century AD). The most notable example, a large 5th-century lion capital (Gwalior, Archaeol. Mus.) from UDAYAGIRI (ii), closely follows the Maurya prototype, but the overall proportions of the capital are more attenuated than the original, and the lions' manes are modelled in a more supple and repetitious manner. A smaller Gupta-period copy of a Maurya capital is also found at Sanchi (Sanchi, Archaeol. Mus.). Important works of the Gupta age inspired copies in their turn. The most remarkable instance is the 11th-century Varaha temple at DEOGARH; though ruined, the main images and architectural features were copied directly from the nearby 5th-century temple. In the colossal standing figure of Vishnu at ERAN, probably a 10th-century copy of 5th-century sculpture, all the features, particularly the decorative scrolls on the arm-bands and crown, have been imitated with great care. Such precise revival styles are rare, but later examples occur in the temples at Chittaurgarh, Rajasthan, where in the Kalika Mata Temple some 15th-century pillars are remarkably close studies of originals dating to the 7th century. The copying seen in these pillars was part of a general revival of western Indian temple architecture that drew its inspiration from the great age of temple building in the 11th century (see Dhaky).

Copies and revivals also occur in the later Islamic architecture of India. The tomb of the Mughal emperor Humayun (*reg* 1530–40, 1555–6) in Delhi (*see* DELHI, fig. 6) was much imitated, most notably in the small 16th-century building known as the Barber's Tomb in the complex, as well as the 18th-century mausoleum of Safdar Jang.

Paintings (some copies of lost originals) in a revived 16th-century manner also appeared in the 18th century. These works form a remarkable parallel to the 18th-century classicism of Europe and seem to be indicative of an attempt by the nawabs, the great oligarchs of 18th-century India, to revive the glories of the Mughal past.

2. FORGERIES. Copying of earlier Mughal paintings continued in the 19th century under the Delhi school (*see* §VI, 4(ix)(g) above). Although the tradition persisted into the 20th century, its aim shifted away from the perpetuation of tradition to pecuniary gain on the international art market, and copies became blatant forgeries made to deceive. The demand for Buddhist sculpture in the Gandhara style motivated craftsmen in Pakistan to produce images of remarkably good quality: a number of forged Buddha heads and *bodhisattva* images that have appeared on the London art market have proved difficult to detect. Terracotta seals with Buddhist themes and inscriptions, often made from antique moulds, also abound. In stone, copies of humble Kushana-period images have been produced in considerable numbers, the rugged style being relatively easy to imitate. More exceptional are two pillars (Los Angeles, CA, Co. Mus. A.; see Pal) that were probably made in Gujarat and closely ape the 5th-century style of Sarnath. The flaccid rendering of the scrollwork and wobbly shafts leave little doubt that these pillars are forgeries.

Paintings predominate in forgery because they can be produced and carried over international boundaries with relative ease. Many pictures are made for the tourist trade and are readily identified as forgeries by their modern paper, pigments, fake worm holes and absurd inscriptions. Quite often such forgeries appear soon after the original work has been reproduced in a scholarly publication. If the reproduction was in black and white, the fake often exhibits an imaginative palette verging on the ridiculous. One such example is a page in the Art Institute of Chicago that is based on a miniature in a late 16th-century copy of the *Bāburnāma* (London, BL). Other fakes often involve the repainting of heavily damaged pictures; an example in the *Caurapañcāśikā* style (*see* §VI, 3(ii)(e) above) appeared in the early 1990s. The technical abilities of forgers have improved dramatically since the late 1970s, and as long as present conditions prevail in the art market, there seems reason to suppose that forgeries of increasing sophistication will continue to be produced.

BIBLIOGRAPHY

A. K. Coomaraswamy: *La Sculpture de Bodhgaya* (Paris, 1935)
R. Krautheimer: 'Introduction to an "Iconography of Medieval Architecture"', *J. Warb. & Court. Inst.*, v (1942), pp. 1–33
M. A. Dhaky: 'Renaissance and the Late Māru-Gurjara Temple Architecture', *J. Ind. Soc. Orient. A.* (1965–6), pp. 4–22 [special issue]
P. O. Sompura: 'The Vāstuvidyā of Viśvakarmā', *Studies in Indian Temple Architecture*, ed. P. Chandra (Delhi, 1975), pp. 47–56
The Ideal Image (exh. cat. by P. Pal, New York, Asia House Gals, 1978)
C. Clunas: *Superfluous Things: Material Culture and Social Studies in Early Modern China* (Oxford, 1991)

MICHAEL D. WILLIS

Indochina. *See* SOUTH-EAST ASIA.

Indo-Greeks. *See* BACTRIAN AND INDO-GREEK MONARCHIES.

Indonesia, Republic of [formerly Dutch East Indies]. Country in South-east Asia comprising over 13,700 islands that extend in an arc straddling the equator, from Sumatra, west of Peninsular Malaysia, to the island of New Guinea, north of Australia (see fig. 1). Irian Jaya, the easternmost province of Indonesia, comprises the western half of the island of New Guinea; its population and cultures are Melanesian rather than Indonesian, and it is therefore treated elsewhere (*see* IRIAN JAYA). Kalimantan, in the centre of the archipelago, comprises most of the island of Borneo (the Malaysian states of Sabah and Sarawak, with Brunei, account for the remainder). The three next largest islands are Sumatra (see fig. 2), Sulawesi (Celebes) and Java (see fig. 3). Of the groups of smaller islands, the

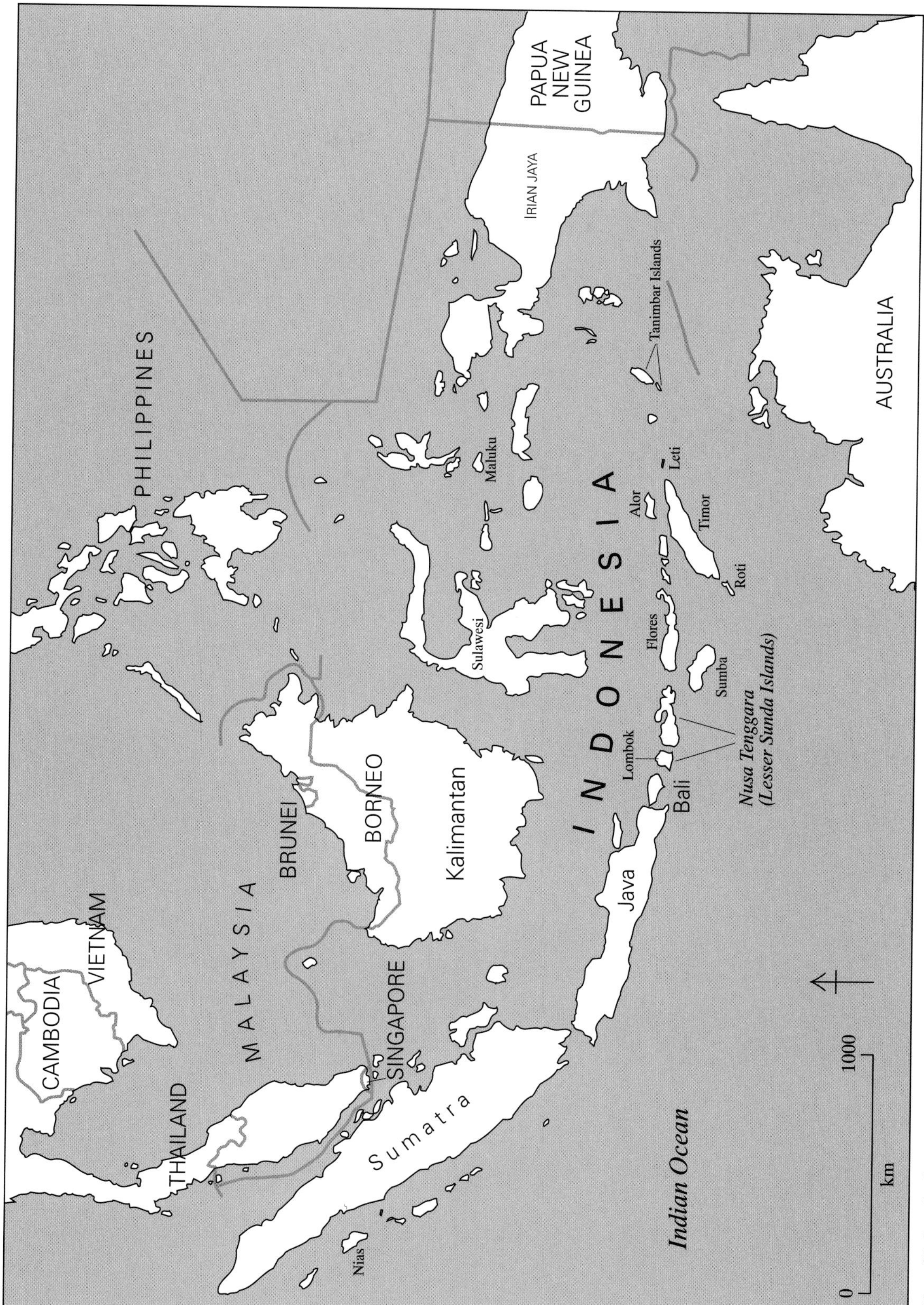

1. Map of Indonesia; the region IRIAN JAYA has a separate entry in this dictionary

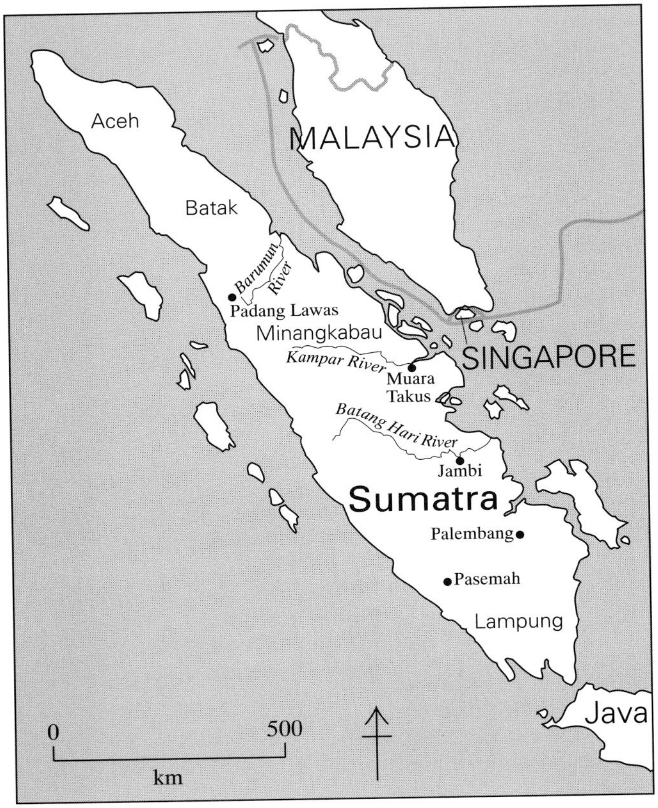

2. Map of Sumatra

largest are Maluku (Moluccas)—a term formerly used to denote only the five small clove-producing islands of Tidore, Ternate, Motir, Makian and Bacan but now embracing all the islands between Sulawesi, Timor and Irian Jaya—and Nusa Tenggara (Lesser Sundas), a chain of islands stretching from Bali (see fig. 4) in the west to Timor in the east. The capital is JAKARTA, on the north-west coast of Java. This article discusses aspects of Indonesian art specific to the archipelago. For a discussion of those shared features that make up the broader regional context and of such institutional aspects as patronage, collections and museums *see* SOUTH-EAST ASIA.

I. Introduction. II. Architecture. III. City planning. IV. Sculpture. V. Textiles. VI. Theatre. VII. Painting and drawing. VIII. Other arts. IX. Art education.

DETAILED TABLE OF CONTENTS

I. Introduction.

1. Geography, peoples and languages. 2. History. 3. Religion, iconography and subject-matter.

1. Geography, peoples and languages. Geologically, Indonesia constitutes one of the world's most diverse and complex regions, with some 300 active and inactive volcanoes crowning the mountain backbone of the island chain; the eruption of Krakatoa, west of Java, in 1883 was the most catastrophic of modern times. The volcanic soils of the lowlands of Central and East Java are among the richest in South-east Asia and helped to support a succession of early kingdoms, from that of the Shailendras in the 8th and 9th centuries to the Majapahit, with its capital in the area now known as Trawulan in the fertile Brantas Valley, from the late 13th century to the 16th. Contrasts between the mountain and the sea have greatly influenced the life and art of Indonesia, especially in the Hindu enclave of Bali. In 1990 the population of Indonesia was *c.* 200 million, of whom more than half live on the island of Java, which comprises less than 7% of Indonesia's total land area. Elsewhere, except on Bali, population densities are much lower, and the government has tried to encourage migration from Java to other, less densely populated islands. This has exacerbated the problem of deforestation, which has become a serious environmental issue throughout Indonesia, where a wide variety of tropical forest types once flourished. There is a large range of indigenous peoples, speaking some 25 principal languages, most of them of Malayo-Polynesian type, with more than 250 dialects. Among the most numerous peoples are the Malays, Bataks and Minangkabaus in Sumatra; the Javanese and Sundanese in Java; the Madurese, Balinese and Dayaks in Kalimantan; and the Buginese and Torajas in Sulawesi; there are also Indian, European, Arab, Chinese and Papuan communities. In order to forge a sense of national identity Bahasa Indonesia, a Malay dialect that has been used as a commercial lingua franca throughout South-east Asia for several centuries, has been adopted as the official language of Indonesia; it is spoken by almost the entire population as a second language and by an increasing number as a first language.

BIBLIOGRAPHY

C. A. Fisher: *South-east Asia: A Social, Economic and Political Geography* (London, 1964, 2/1966/*R* 1971)

D. W. Fryer and J. C. Jackson: *Indonesia* (London, 1977)

D. Wilhelm: *Emerging Indonesia* (London, 1980)

PHILIP STOTT

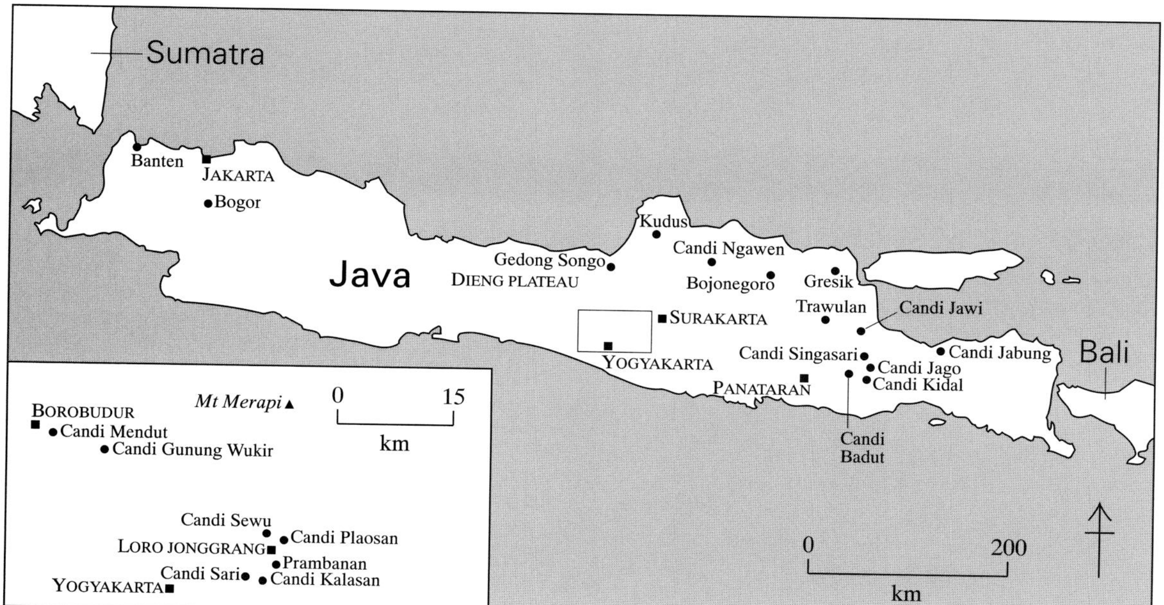

3. Map of Java; those regions with separate entries in this dictionary are distinguished by CROSS-REFERENCE TYPE

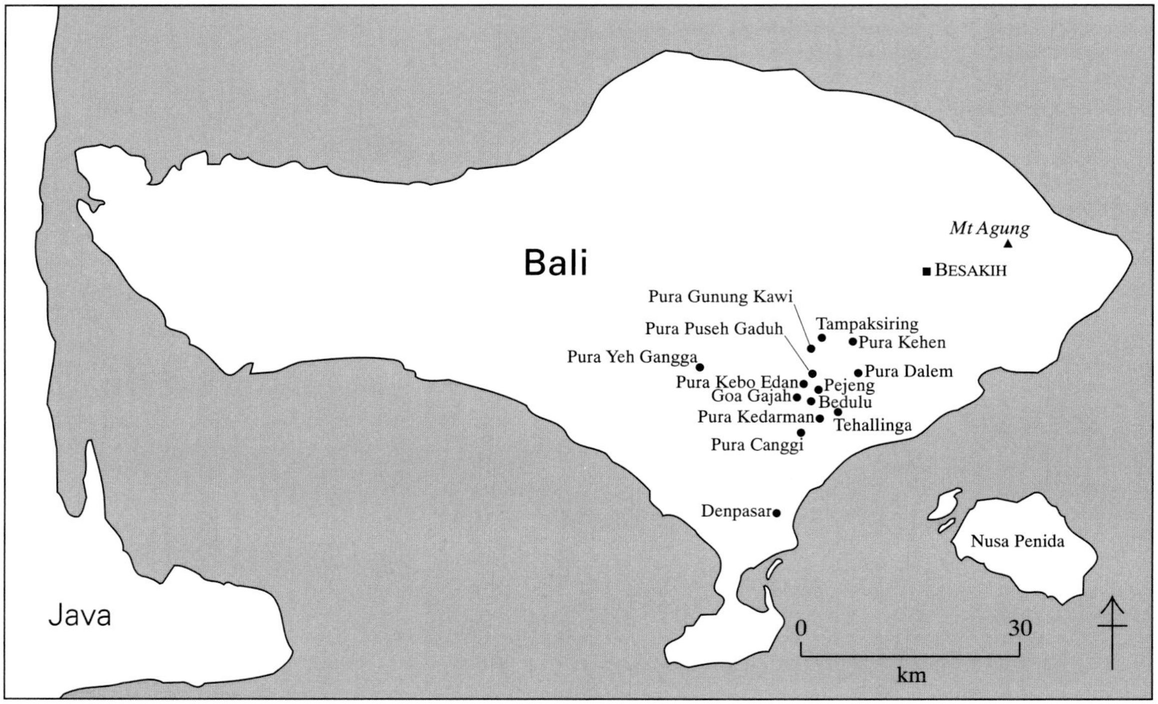

4. Map of Bali; the site BESAKIH has a separate entry in this dictionary

2. HISTORY. The western islands of the archipelago have seen the rise and fall of advanced civilizations of great richness and diversity, while the peoples of some of the eastern islands retained their Neolithic culture intact until the late 20th century. There was a gradual drift of peoples into Indonesia from the north-west between *c.* 5000 and *c.* 1000 BC. The most important of these migrations is thought to have been from the Yunnan region of China. Megaliths associated with the ancient religious beliefs of these peoples and dating from this period have been found in southern Sumatra, Nias, Sumba and Flores, and ceremonial rectangular axes of hardstone, terraced burial mounds and stone skull troughs were scattered throughout the region. The migrants also brought with them certain important technological advances, notably the construction of houses on piles, irrigated rice agriculture and pottery made by the coiling technique. Polished stone axes, adzes and other tools dating from *c.* 2500 BC have been unearthed, as have intricately incised ceremonial bronze drums clearly related to the drums of the DONG SON culture and thought to be 1000–2000 years old. By the 2nd century BC bronze and iron weapons, drums, bells, jewellery and ornaments were being manufactured, and bronze-casting by the lost-wax and closed-mould methods was practised in many parts of the archipelago.

The date of the first contacts between Indonesia and India is unknown, but already in the 3rd century AD Indianized principalities evidently existed in Sumatra, Java and Borneo. One of these was the mercantile Buddhist state of Srivijaya, which was probably centred in the region of present-day Palembang on the south-east coast of Sumatra, from where it dominated the maritime trade routes through the Straits of Malacca and the Sunda Straits. By the 7th century Srivijaya had developed strong links with the Buddhist monasteries of north-eastern India. The Chinese Buddhist pilgrim Yi Jing visited Srivijaya and another Sumatran state that has been identified as Malayu (Jambi) in 671 on his way to the monastery of Nalanda in Bengal and, after leaving Nalanda in 685, spent ten years in Srivijaya translating Sanskrit Buddhist texts into Chinese and writing an account of contemporary Buddhism. Regular embassies travelled from Srivijaya to the Chinese court between the 10th and 12th centuries. Fine bronze images of the Buddha and *bodhisattvas* from Srivijaya similar in style to the Indian Amaravati style (2nd–5th century) have been found throughout South-east Asia. Srivijaya seems to have been at the height of its power in the early 11th century, controlling the Straits of Malacca from both Sumatra and the isthmian region of southern Thailand, but a series of attacks by the south Indian Chola state reduced its international importance. Few archaeological remains from Srivijaya have been discovered; this has prompted much debate among scholars. In the 7th century the Shaivite kingdom of Mataram, ruled by the Sanjaya dynasty, was established in Central Java, where it co-existed with the neighbouring dynasty of the Shailendras ('Kings of the Mountain') (*c.* 775–864). The Shailendras were Mahayana Buddhists, and it was during this period that the great religious monuments of Central Java were constructed, including BOROBUDUR, one of the greatest Buddhist monuments in Asia, and the Hindu

Candi LORO JONGGRANG at Prambanan (*see* §II, 1(i) below). A struggle for supremacy in the region apparently culminated in the defeat of the Shailendras by Mataram, and the last Shailendra king withdrew to Sumatra, where he later became a ruler of Srivijaya.

In the early 10th century, for reasons unknown, but possibly as a result of some natural disaster, the centre of power of the Mataram kingdom moved from Central to East Java, where there was a resurgence of indigenous ancestor and spirit cults that flourished alongside Shaivism. The kingdoms of Kediri (929–1222), about which almost nothing is known, Singhasari (1222–92) and Majapahit (1292–*c.* 1500) became powerful. The 14th-century Javanese panegyric *Nagarakertagama* claims that at that time Hindu Majapahit exerted authority over much of the Indonesian archipelago and even parts of mainland South-east Asia. Although such claims are almost certainly exaggerated, it is certain that Bali was conquered by Majapahit between 1331 and 1351. As a result of this conquest, Bali developed its own highly idiosyncratic form of Hinduism and is the only Indonesian island to have remained uninfluenced by Islam. Marco Polo reported the existence of a Muslim town on the north coast of Sumatra in 1292. However, it was not until the 14th and 15th centuries, when Arab and Muslim Indian trade with the archipelago increased, that Islam gained followers in large numbers in Indonesia, with the Sunnis of the Shafi'ite legal school predominating. Islamic culture developed in a highly syncretic form that incorporated Buddhist, Hindu and indigenous elements and particularly influenced textile and weapon design, calligraphy and manuscript painting. The second Mataram kingdom, established in Central Java in the 16th century, was a Muslim power. In 1755 it was divided by the Dutch into two sultanates, ruled by the Yogyakarta and Surakarta (Solo) royal houses.

The Arabs, Indians and Chinese were drawn to Indonesia by the lucrative spice trade, and in the 16th century the Europeans followed. The Portuguese were the first Europeans to enter the region, setting up fortified outposts among the islands from which they attempted unsuccessfully to monopolize the spice trade. Uninterested in territorial expansion, the Portuguese nevertheless left a legacy of ship-building techniques, weaponry, costumes and loan-words that still survives in parts of the archipelago, especially the eastern islands. By the mid-17th century the Portuguese had been overtaken by the Dutch and the English, who continued in direct competition for 200 years; the British East India Company was formed in 1600 and the Dutch East India Company (Vereenigde Oostindische Compagnie or VOC) in 1602. In 1619 the VOC established their headquarters in Jakarta, a vassal of the sultan of Banten, and changed its name to Batavia. By the mid-18th century the Dutch had gained complete ascendancy in much of the region, and, assisted by autocratic Javanese rulers, they introduced forced labour in many areas and developed the cultivation both of spices and of such introduced crops as sugar, tea, coffee and rubber in large plantations to provide the Netherlands with revenue. In 1779 the VOC collapsed, and as a result of the wars that followed the French Revolution Java came under the direct rule of the Dutch government. Subsequent Dutch involvement in the Napoleonic wars led to the British occupation of Java under Stamford Raffles from 1811 to 1816, when Dutch rule was restored. During the 19th century the Dutch gradually extended their control throughout the archipelago, subjugating Bali only in 1906–8 and the Bugis states in Sulawesi and the Bataks in northern Sumatra in 1907. Dissatisfaction with Dutch rule led to local revolts, and by the outbreak of World War II the seeds of nationalism had been sown. After the Japanese occupation of 1942–5 the Dutch attempted to regain their former colony, but after the proclamation of an independent republic in 1945 and four more years of violent conflict with the nationalist forces they were obliged to admit defeat. Indonesia became independent under President Sukarno in 1949.

With independence came the problem of unifying the peoples of a vast archipelago into a single nation. Sukarno declared a Marxist–nationalist–Islamic state and was remarkably successful in forging a sense of nationhood among the many diverse peoples of the archipelago; however, his increasingly extreme nationalist policies abroad and unrealistic domestic projects led to economic collapse. This, together with migration to Java from the outer islands, led to poverty and overcrowding in the slums of Jakarta and Surabaya. An abortive coup in 1965 resulted eventually in Sukarno's downfall in 1968. President Suharto took control of the country, and progress became steadier; nevertheless, unrest still sometimes occurs in outlying islands, and complaints of Javanese 'imperialism' continue as territorial disputes abound. Irian Jaya was administered by Indonesia under United Nations authority from 1963 until 1969, when it was formally incorporated into the republic. In East Timor (Timor Timur, formerly Portuguese East Timor) an armed independence movement resisted the Indonesian occupying forces after the Portuguese left the territory in 1975. In the late 20th century tourism brought a boost to the economy and a resurgence of such traditional crafts as weaving, batik, carving and painting.

BIBLIOGRAPHY

A. H. Christie: 'The Megalithic Problem in South East Asia', *A History of South-east Asia*, ed. D. G. E. Hall (London, 1955, rev. 4/1981)

T. G. T. Pigeaud and H. J. de Graaf: *Islamic States in Java, 1500–1700* (The Hague, 1967)

R. Allen: *A Short Introduction to the History and Politics of Southeast Asia* (New York and London, 1970)

J. Pluvier: 'Indonesia: History', *South East Asia: An Introduction* (London, 1973), pp. 37–41

Boechari: 'Some Considerations on the Problem of the Shift of Mataram's Centre of Government from Central to East Java in the 10th Century', *Early South East Asia*, ed. R. B. Smith and W. Watson (Oxford, 1979), pp. 473–91

B. Bronson: 'The Archaeology of Sumatra and the Problem of Srivijaya', *Early South East Asia*, ed. R. B. Smith and W. Watson (Oxford, 1979), pp. 395–405

R. Soekmono: 'The Archaeology of Central Java before 800 AD', *Early South East Asia*, ed. R. B. Smith and W. Watson (Oxford, 1979), pp. 457–72

M. Ricklefs: *A History of Modern Indonesia, c. 1300 to the Present* (London, 1981)

K. R. Hall: *Maritime Trade and State Development in Early Southeast Asia* (Honolulu, 1985)

K. W. Taylor: 'The Early Kingdoms: Srivijaya', *The Cambridge History of South East Asia*, ed. N. Tarling (Cambridge, 1992), pp. 173–6

MIRANDA BRUCE-MITFORD

3. RELIGION, ICONOGRAPHY AND SUBJECT-MATTER. The iconography and subject-matter of Indonesian

religious art are extremely diverse and complex. The religion of the earliest inhabitants of Indonesia was based on magic and mythical tales and on sacred traditions from which the customs (*adat*) of the different communities evolved and which were guarded by the mythical deified ancestors. These beliefs led to the making of stone axes for sacral purposes, such as the ritual slaughter of sacrificial animals, and to the erection of megaliths to honour the dead and commemorate important events, such as the consecration of a chief. In many islands, notably Nias, Sumba and Flores, these megalithic monuments have continued to be erected right up to the end of the 20th century. The earliest of them include menhirs, dolmens and terraced burial mounds and are often associated with cemeteries. Stone sarcophagi and graves were later made, in which bronze and iron objects were placed. Hinduism and Buddhism were introduced from India and spread through the western islands of Indonesia in the 3rd–7th century AD, exercising their most profound influence in Sumatra, Java and Bali, and helping to legitimize the power of the rulers of the region. Initially, Hinduism seems to have met with more favour than Buddhism, perhaps because the *liṅga*, symbol of the creative power of Shiva, could be more easily identified with the megaliths erected by the adherents of earlier religions than could the image of the Buddha. Indonesia's principal Hindu and Buddhist monuments were constructed in the 7th–15th century (*see* §II, 1 below). During the 15th century Islam began to penetrate the archipelago from the west, and by 1530 it was widespread throughout the region. Roman Catholic and Protestant missionaries have been active in Indonesia since the arrival of the Portuguese in the early 16th century, and some islands (e.g. Flores) and ethnic groups (e.g. the central group of Bataks of north Sumatra and the Menadonese of north-east Sulawesi) are now predominantly Christian. In the late 20th century Indonesia was the largest Islamic nation in the world, over 80% of its population being Muslim. In some areas, however, Islam has become involved with pre-Islamic religious beliefs and practices and is consequently somewhat heterodox.

(i) Pre-Hindu–Buddhist. One of the most important megalithic sites in Indonesia is at Pasemah in southern Sumatra, where as well as menhirs and terraced sanctuaries, huge stones carved into the shape of human and animal figures have been found. The human figures are adorned with necklaces and bracelets and carry weapons. These megalithic monuments are the precursors of the statues of ancestors and deities of Hindu–Buddhist Java (*see* HINDUISM, §II), the seats of the gods (*padmāsana*) in Balinese temples, and the Islamic tombstones or *maesan* of East Java. Among the bronze objects belonging to the DONG SON culture, which seems to have spread throughout South-east Asia from its origins in the area of north Vietnam in the last 200 years BC, are drums on which are portrayed ceremonial axes with sacrificial animals and human figures. Some of these axes, which evidently served the same function as their stone predecessors, have survived: one of the most remarkable is an extremely thin and intricately decorated axe from Landu, on the small island of Roti in the Lesser Sunda Islands (Jakarta, N. Mus.). Also portrayed on the Dong Son drums are flat-bottomed boats; these are thought to be representations of the Ship of the Dead, in which it was believed that the souls of the dead went to the other world (*see* §VIII, 2 below). This belief still survives among some Indonesian peoples, for example the Kroes of southern Sumatra, who portray such ships on the floating weft textiles that they use in various rites of passage.

□

(ii) Hindu. The first iconographic manifestations of Hinduism occur in four rock inscriptions carved in the 5th century by order of King Purnavarman of the West Javanese kingdom of Taruma in the Jakarta region near Bogor. On the rock of Ci Aruton the inscription is accompanied by the carved print of the King's feet and indicates that they are similar to those of the god Vishnu. On the rock of Kebon Kopi two prints of elephant feet are carved similar to those of Airavata, the elephant mount of the god Indra. At the temples on the Dieng Plateau and at Gedong Songo (*see* §II, 1(i) below), dating from the 8th century, the emergence of a distinct style of iconographic sculpture can be discerned. These two temples are dedicated to Shiva. In the main cella stands a *liṅga* embedded in a plinth, the upper surface of which forms a basin to collect the water that has washed it. On the north side of the basin is a drain spout, linked in some temples (in Candi Arjuna on the Dieng Plateau, for example) to a conduit taking the water outside. In the outside of the temple walls are carved niches sheltering statues. On either side of the door facing east is a guardian figure: on the south, Agastya, the supreme master and teacher *par excellence*, sometimes considered to be a form of Shiva; on the west, Ganesha, the son of Shiva and his consort Parvati, with a human body, four arms, and the head of an elephant. Ganesha, the god of wisdom and prosperity, is very popular and is represented sitting and holding in one hand the shield smashed in the battle in which he opposed his father. On the north side is Durga, one of the consorts of Shiva and associated with death, who is usually portrayed standing on the body of a buffalo that she has just defeated and from which she is extracting the demon Mahisha, who inhabited it. When the temple complex was complete, the central temple was flanked by two secondary temples, one to the south sheltering an image of Brahma, the other to the north sheltering a Vishnu image. Finally, facing the *liṅga*, there is a statue of the bull Nandi, Shiva's mount.

In the 9th century this iconography remained substantially unchanged, with only a few exceptions: by this time the main cella no longer contained a *liṅga* but a statue of the deity; the cult had become more clearly defined and no longer conformed to Indian models. The king had become a direct emanation of the deity whom he represented during his life; and achieved his apotheosis after death by returning to him. This is expressed in the images made of the king in his deified form. In this way, the kingdom was conceived as a *maṇḍala*, a space with fluid frontiers but a fixed centre where the ruler's court was situated and where the gods might reside and which was represented diagrammatically by the temple. Delimiting this holy space became an essential function of the temple, realized in the nine *liṅga*s placed in the centre, at the corners and on the axes. The iconography was completed by reliefs representing stories from the Indian epics the *Rāmāyaṇa* and the *Kṛṣṇāyāṇa*.

During the 10th century, power moved from Central to East Java. Shaivism, in the form of a cult directly associated with the royal family, remained dominant at least until the end of the 13th century, despite the appearance of an important cult of Vishnu at Candi Kali. As a consequence of this change, King Kertanagara (*reg* 1268–92) secularized the monarchy and tried to syncretize Buddhism and Shaivism. This syncretism is well represented in the statue in the cella of the main sanctuary of Candi Jawi (*c.* 1290), which is half Shiva and half the *bodhisattva* Lokeshvara (*see* §II, 1(iii) below). The limits of the space are no longer marked by small *liṅgas* but by statues, sometimes very elaborate, of the guardians of the cardinal points: at Candi Singasari they appear mounted on fabulous animals. In the 14th century the narrative reliefs ceased to be sculpted in a way that allowed a consecutive reading of the text, but by the way they were located they contributed to the general significance of the temple, the symbolism of which became increasingly complicated.

(iii) Buddhist. In some parts of Indonesia, such as Sulawesi, Buddhism appeared without any transition from the previous religions, and it is likely that the large bronze images discovered there were imported from Sri Lanka. This first cult was probably Theravada Buddhism, but at the end of the 8th century a new, esoteric system of Tantric Buddhism appeared. This was the Vajrayana (the 'Diamond Path'), in which the meditations of the Supreme Buddha Vajradhana ('Holder of the Thunderbolt') are believed to have produced the five Jinas (Dhyani or Conqueror Buddhas)—Vairochana, Amoghasiddhi, Ratnasambhava, Akshobhya and Amitabha—who are Buddhas of all eternity, never having been anything else. The Jinas constitute the body of the universe; Vairochana is associated with the centre and the other four with the four cardinal directions. Each one is mirrored in a celestial *bodhisattva* and a terrestrial Buddha. This cult superseded all preceding forms of Buddhism and led to the adoption of a new iconography in all Buddhist temples built in Central Java in the late 8th century and early 9th (e.g. Candi Kalasan and Candi Sewu). In Candi Borobudur (*see* §II, 1(ii) below) images of the Jinas are distributed according to the points of the compass, with Vairochana, seated in the preaching gesture (*dharmachakra mudrā*), in the centre, under latticed stupas. The walls and balustrades of Candi Borobudur support reliefs: those of the first gallery describe the previous lives of the Buddha and the story of his last incarnation as Prince Siddhartha, the historical Buddha, ending with the crucial event of the First Sermon in the Deer Park at Sarnath. This last episode is also represented by three statues in Candi Mendut: the Buddha in the preaching gesture (to avoid misinterpretation, the sculptor carved a Wheel of the Law and two gazelles on the base) and two Jinas as *bodhisattvas*, Avalokiteshvara and Vajrapani, who were present, although invisible, at the First Sermon.

At the end of the 9th century, Buddhism evolved in a manner similar to Hinduism. The temples built in this period, such as Candi Plaosan Lor, are idealized representations of the kingdom, but the shift in political power towards the east resulted in an audience that was diminished considerably, probably to the court alone. Under the pressure of Islam, these Indian religions disappeared from Java during the 15th century, but they persisted in Bali, Sumatra and among the Balinese population in Lombok. Buddhism in particular survived in Sumatra, in the Palembang and Jambi areas; at Muara Jambi, near modern Jambi, a vast complex of *c.* 30 monuments was constructed, including Candi Astana, Candi Kedaton and Candi Kemberbatu.

BIBLIOGRAPHY

A. J. Bernet Kempers: *Ancient Indonesian Art* (Amsterdam and Cambridge, MA, 1959)
C. Geertz: *The Religion of Java* (Glencoe, 1960)
T. Pigeaud: *Java in the Fourteenth Century* (The Hague, 1963)
C. Hooykaas: *Religion of Bali* (Leiden, 1973)
Buddhism: Art and Faith (exh. cat., ed. W. Zwalf; London, BM, 1985)
J. Dumarçay: *The Temples of Java* (Singapore, 1986)
The Sculpture of Indonesia (exh. cat. by J. Fontein, R. Soekmono and E. Sedyawati, Washington, DC, N.G.A., 1990)

J. DUMARÇAY

(iv) Islamic. The design and siting of mosques show considerable regional variation. In Kudus and Gresik, in northern Java, there are examples of early mosques representing Mt Meru, the Hindu and Buddhist cosmic mountain. The Kudus mosque also has a substantial Hindu–Buddhist-inspired minaret in red brick, which may originally have supported a drum (Jav. *bedug*) used for summoning assemblies. The *bedug* is still used to announce prayer times in traditionalist mosques, for example in East Java. In Gresik the mosque–tomb complex of Sunan Giri, one of the early Muslim missionaries to the region, is built on a hilltop, with the saint's burial chamber positioned as if at the head of a congregation that consists of both the dead in the cemetery (all of whom are buried facing Mecca to the north-west) and the living (who make up the daily prayer congregations assembled at the back of the mosque itself). The saint's tomb is enclosed in a wooden chamber decorated with embossed lotuses, while the entrance to the sacred enclosure is guarded by sculptured wooden dragon–snake figures (*nāgas*). The gateway to the stairway leading to the hilltop cemetery is guarded by monumental stone *nāgas*. The minbar or pulpit in the mosque is in the form of a Hindu chariot, a style visible elsewhere in South-east Asia. In modern times the *meru* form of mosque has been largely replaced by Middle Eastern and South Asian domed forms.

Although literacy in Arabic has a long history among religious teachers, most Indonesians know at best only a few Arabic phrases, for use in devotions. Nevertheless, the Arabic script (known as Jawi) was adopted soon after the arrival of Islam for the writing of Malay and, in some cases, Javanese and Sundanese (all now written in the Roman alphabet). Islamic calligraphy, particularly in wood-carving, became a notable feature of the decorative arts in both Indonesia and Malaysia. Unfortunately, the use of wood and other perishable materials for grave markers, mosques and other structures has resulted in a relatively meagre archaeological legacy of Islamic antiquities. The design of the ancient ceremonial dagger, the *keris* (*see* §VIII, 10 below), was also influenced by Islamic ideas.

Although the hilt of the *keris* has traditionally been compared by the Javanese to the human body, the increasing simplicity of that part of the dagger may be attributable to the aniconic influence of Islam. It is likely that Islam also inspired the more abstract textile designs in areas where it was strongly embraced, such as Central Java (*see* §V, 1 below).

BIBLIOGRAPHY

Enc. Islam/2: 'Masdjid' [mosque]
J. F. Pijper: 'The Minaret in Java', *India Antiqua: A Volume of Oriental Studies Presented. . .to Jean Philippe Vogel* (Leiden, 1947), pp. 274–83
F. A. Wagner: *Indonesia: The Art of an Island Group* (Baden-Baden, 1959, rev. New York, 2/1967)
A. H. Johns: 'Islam in Southeast Asia: Reflections and New Directions', *Indonesia*, xix (1975), pp. 33–55
U. Hasyim: *Sunan Giri* (Kudus, 1979) [useful photographs]
A. Rochym: *Mesdjid dalam karya arsitektur nasional Indonesia* [The mosque in the national architectural legacy of Indonesia] (Bandung, 1983)

FREDERICK MATHEWSON DENNY

II. Architecture.

1. Hindu and Buddhist. 2. Islamic. 3. Formal Dutch Colonial. 4. Domestic.

1. HINDU AND BUDDHIST. Although some sacred bathing places and stepped sanctuaries built into the slopes of hills are of pre-Hindu origin, the oldest extant free-standing buildings in Indonesia are Hindu and Buddhist monuments built of stone and traditionally known as *candi*. This name is ultimately derived from one of the names of Durga, the Hindu goddess associated with death, and its literal meaning is therefore a sepulchral monument or a monument erected in commemoration of a dead person, but it is now commonly used to denote various kinds of ancient religious monument, especially in Java. The symbolism of the *candi* clearly reveals the strong influence of the two great Indian religions, Hinduism and Buddhism. This influence probably began to exert itself during the first centuries AD, although the oldest evidence, in the form of Sanskrit inscriptions written in south Indian Pallava script (e.g. the Taruma inscriptions; *see* §I, 3(ii) above) dates from the 5th century. The object of worship in the *candi* was the statue of a deity; such images depicted deceased kings and queens, who were believed to have become one with the gods on death and who at the same time represented the ancestors who had crossed over into the nether world. The *candi* was therefore a sanctuary of the gods, where ceremonies were performed at which the gods were thought to be present, and a place of worship, where homage was paid to them at the same time as to deified royalty and to the ancestral spirits. The *candi* is a symbolic replica of the cosmic mountain (*Mahāmeru*), which, according to Hindu mythology, rises from the centre of the universe and connects heaven and earth. The abode of the gods was believed to be located at its summit. The tectonic subdivision of the *candi* into the base, the main body of the temple and the superstructure corresponds to the three spheres of the universe. The base represents the sphere of the mortals (*bhurloka*); the body of the temple, containing the cella with its statuary, represents the sphere of the purified (*bhuvarloka*), the realm between heaven and earth in which the worshipper could meet with his ancestors, manifested in the statuary; the superstructure, which in many *candi* incorporates a stepped roof, symbolizes the heavenly sphere of the gods (*swarloka*).

From the early 8th century to the mid-10th, dozens of religious monuments were constructed in Java, ranging from small, solitary buildings to such vast complexes as Candi Borobudur and Candi Loro Jonggrang at Prambanan in Central Java, and consequently this period of Hindu and Buddhist architecture is commonly known as the Central Javanese period. However, temples were also built during the same period in the eastern part of Java, so the term is somewhat misleading. Modern Indonesian architectural historians, following the example set by other historians, have therefore renamed this period the Early Classical period. After the 10th century the centre of power shifted from Central Java to East Java, possibly as a result of the eruption of Mt Merapi or some other natural disaster. No *candi* from the 11th and 12th centuries have survived in Java, but a number of rock-cut *candi* were built in Bali during this period. It is difficult to establish with certainty whether building activity in Java did actually diminish around this time, or whether there was a continuous stylistic evolution that has been obscured by the extreme paucity of material evidence. In any case, there is unmistakable evidence of a renewed momentum in temple construction during the period from the mid-13th century to the end of the 15th. This period is usually called the East Javanese period because building activity was chiefly concentrated in East Java; no new temples were constructed in the central part of the island before the 15th century. However, construction was not limited to East Java, and some important monuments in central and northern Sumatra and in Bali also date from this period, which is therefore more appropriately called the Late Classical period.

(i) *c.* 700–*c.* 950: Early Classical period. (ii) *c.* 950–*c.* 1250. (iii) *c.* 1250–*c.* 1500: Late Classical period.

(i) c. *700*–c. *950: Early Classical period.* The group of *candi* on the Dieng Plateau, the Gedong Songo group and Candi Gunung Wukir are all in Central Java and are generally considered to be the earliest surviving architectural monuments in Indonesia. Candi Gunung Wukir was founded in AD 732, so the beginning of architectural history in Java can be placed around the beginning of the 8th century. Feverish building activity in the two following centuries resulted in the construction of a large number of *candi* in Central Java, which was the centre of the powerful agrarian monarchies of the Shaivite Sanjaya and Buddhist Shailendra dynasties. Generally speaking, the *candi* of Central Java, in spite of their somewhat squat appearance, give an impression of strength and grandeur. However, the emphasis on horizontal lines of the heavy mouldings and cornices, which is enhanced by the abruptly receding silhouette of the roof, is only to some extent balanced by the vertical elements of the façades, and the relatively small difference between the height and the width of the temple does little to create a monumental effect.

(a) Origins and early examples, *c.* 700–*c.* 775. (b) Shailendra dynasty, *c.* 775–864. (c) A late example: Candi Loro Jonggrang.

(a) Origins and early examples, c. *700*–c. *775.* Of the eight somewhat imperfectly preserved *candi* on the DIENG

PLATEAU, Candi Bima, with its roof shaped like a shikhara (see fig. 5) resembles north Indian prototypes. On the other hand, Candi Arjuna and the other *candi* on the plateau, with their squat shapes and pronounced horizontal mouldings, are at first sight reminiscent of temples in south India. However, closer scrutiny reveals that there are more differences than similarities. There is no temple in India that could have served as a prototype, especially for their decoration. For example, the Indonesian version of the *kāla-makara* motif (*see* §IV, 2(i)) is vastly different from the Indian *kīrttimukha* (lion mask) and the Indian way of rendering the *makara* (a mythical aquatic creature, part crocodile, part elephant). Moreover, the reliefs representing Shiva on the east wall of Candi Srikandi, flanked by Brahma on the south wall and Vishnu on the north, represent an arrangement that is manifestly Indonesian. Indian influence is apparent only in the temples' broad outlines, the execution of decoration and all small details having evidently been left in the hands of native Indonesian artists. Most remarkable is that, even where there are elements of unquestionably Indian origin, closer inspection often reveals that they are derived from two different parts of India and sometimes even belong to two different periods. It is clear that the design and decoration of the *candi* were not transplanted from India but constituted an indigenous Indonesian art form, rooted in Indian religious concepts but created and developed by the Indonesians in a variety of ways in different areas and at different periods, but always in accordance with their own tradition.

On the slopes of Mt Ungaran, *c.* 20 km south-east of Semarang on the north coast of Central Java, are the nine temples known as Gedong Songo. Several have been almost completely reconstructed. They are higher in relation to their width than the Dieng Plateau temples and have a three-tiered superstructure, but this only slightly diminishes the generally squat impression created by the horizontal mouldings. The building techniques and the way in which the different components have been put together are similar to those of the *candi* of Dieng. The presence of a temple of the same type as Candi Sĕmar at Dieng and the similarly random arrangement of both groups of temples suggests that they are of the same or very similar date. Epigraphic evidence suggests that there is one temple—Candi Gunung Wukir, 10 km south-east of Borobudur—that may be even older than the temples of Dieng and Gedong Songo. The oldest inscription from Dieng is dated 802, whereas the Canggal inscription, which mentions the founding of Candi Gunung Wukir, is dated 732. Only the base of the temple remains, and it is therefore impossible to establish its shape and compare it with that of other monuments. However, the carving, especially of the *kāla-makara* ornament, represents a development subsequent to that of the Dieng temples. The mouldings that usually occur on the lower part of these temples, and are often repeated higher up on the monument, are completely absent.

Candi Badut, north-west of Malang in East Java, also has a plain base. The foundation of this temple is probably connected with an inscription datable to 760. It has been reconstructed up to the lower section of the roof, so that the principal features of its architectural style are apparent. The base, the body of the temple and the roof are clearly differentiated, as are the stepped storeys of the roof. As in the *candi* of the Dieng and Gedong Songo groups, in an attempt to reduce the effect of horizontality the walls of the body of the temple are divided into three parts separated by vertical bands. The central section of the façade is reserved for the entrance porch, while on the other three walls it has been used for niches housing statuary. The principal image at Candi Badut, the *liṅga*, the phallic symbol of Shiva, is enshrined in the centre of the cella. The carved floral decoration on the walls of the body of the temple and the *kāla-makara* framing the niches and the doorway are stylistically more advanced than in the Dieng and Gedong Songo temples. Candi Badut is, therefore, probably of slightly later date.

5. Candi Bima, Dieng Plateau, Central Java, *c.* AD 730–80

(*b*) *Shailendra dynasty,* c. *775–864.* The most conspicuous difference between the oldest *candi* in Java, described above, and those of the Shailendra period is that the latter were much larger in scale, more complex in construction and more lavishly decorated. Determined efforts were also made to emphasize the slender elevation of these temples by increasing the number of vertical bands, both plain and decorated with spiral motifs, while at the same time continuing to use horizontal mouldings. The most characteristic monuments of the Shailendra period consist of a plain plinth, a bell-shaped ogee and semicircular moulding.

Borobudur. The most important structure built in Central Java during the Shailendra period is Candi Borobudur, *c.* 40 km north-west of Yogyakarta and not far west of

Candi Gunung Wukir. In its shape and structure, this Buddhist monument is not a true *candi*, and it lacks the basic component of a cella in which to enshrine a sacred image. Candi Borobudur is a virtually solid monument in the form of a stepped pyramid crowned by a stupa (*see* BOROBUDUR, fig. 1). Its main function was the worship of royal ancestors, namely the founders of the Buddhist Shailendra dynasty, who were believed to have merged with the Jīnas (*see* §I, 3(iii) above) after death. Built on top of a low hill above a wide plain, Candi Borobudur looks like a low dome. It consists of nine levels, the lowest of which, built on a redented square plan and with unadorned walls, functions as its base. On the sides of the original base of the monument, now concealed by the later addition of stones to form a processional path, were reliefs illustrating the law of *karma*, by which human behaviour produces its appropriate effect in future rebirths, when crime is punished and virtue receives its proper reward. (For a discussion of the Borobudur reliefs *see* §IV, 2(i) below.) The second, stepped, part that makes up the main body of the monument consists of five levels of diminishing size but on the same redented square plan. Each of the four lower levels is surrounded by a gallery with a balustrade. In the middle of each gallery is a staircase that gives access to all levels of the *candi*. The walls and balustrades of the galleries are covered with narrative reliefs. The upper levels, comprising the third part of the monument, are quite different from those of other *candi*, which usually have a roof. Here they consist of three circular, instead of square, terraces. All the stones are smooth and entirely devoid of decoration, except for the seventy-two latticed stupas arranged in circles on the three terraces that lead to the central stupa.

The differences in treatment between the lower, middle and upper parts of Candi Borobudur reflect the tripartite division of the Buddhist world, in which the Buddha manifests himself in different guises. The lowest level symbolizes the sphere of desire (*kāmadhātu*), in which the human spirit is still chained to greed and desire. Above this lies the sphere of forms (*rūpadhātu*), in which the human spirit has succeeded in liberating itself from greed but is still unable to transcend the phenomenal world. The upper part, consisting of the circular terraces, symbolizes the sphere of formlessness (*arūpadhātu*), in which the liberated human spirit has left all earthly considerations behind. The resemblance in symbolism and in the representation of the universe between Borobudur and other *candi* does not necessarily imply that all performed the same religious function. People visited *candi* primarily in order to pay homage to the gods and to their ancestors, but they would visit Candi Borobudur as pilgrims, to meditate and immerse themselves in the Buddha's teachings by studying the narrative reliefs and following the pilgrim's path round the terraces up to the central stupa at the summit.

Mendut. It is thought that before visiting Borobudur pilgrims paid homage at Candi Mendut, a few kilometres to the east. The three huge stone statues enshrined at Mendut fill almost the entire space of the cella of the temple. Candi Mendut is built on a square base 3.6 m high, each side measuring 22 m. On the front is a projection 3.6 m deep, accommodating a flight of steps that projects out even further. The square body of the temple measures only 15 m on each side and stands on a platform *c.* 1 m high. Surrounding the base is a balustrade, creating a terrace round the entire body of the temple. The walls of the *candi* are decorated with reliefs representing various *bodhisattva*s and gods. Only two levels of the roof have been preserved, giving the monument an incomplete, truncated appearance. Candi Mendut is not significantly different in shape or structure from the *candi* discussed above, although variations occur, such as the double base (also seen at Candi Puntadewa, Dieng Plateau) and an entrance in the shape of a cella (another example is at Candi Bima, also on the Dieng Plateau). The mouldings have the typical Shailendra profile. Below the semicircular moulding is a row of dentils comparable to that on the original, hidden base of Candi Borobudur. The similarity with Candi Borobudur extends to the magnificent sculpture and the reliefs.

Pawon. In the same group as Candi Borobudur and Candi Mendut and situated between them is the small temple of Candi Pawon, where pilgrims also paid homage. This *candi* has been completely restored, including even the top of the roof, which has been reconstructed in the shape of a stupa. The typical Shailendra combination of mouldings is found not only on the base, but also repeated at the foot of the body of the temple. The sensitive carving and the suppleness of the figures in high relief are typical of the Shailendra style.

Ngawèn. Not far to the south-east of Candi Borobudur, near Candi Gunung Wukir, lies another group of Buddhist *candi* consisting of five structures of different sizes, standing in a row aligned north–south. The largest, Candi Ngawèn II (i.e. the second temple from the north), is 11 m square in plan. The temple has been restored, but only up to the first level of the roof. Stylistically, Candi Ngawèn belongs to the Early Classical period, but there are several features that indicate it may be later than the examples discussed above. For example, there is a multiplication of structural elements and types of decoration that make the temple seem larger than it is. The separation of the entrance gateway from the main body of the temple is another new development. The placing of miniature buildings, each complete in the detail of its structure and outline, in the corners between the stairs and the temple base, foreshadows temples of the Later Classical style in East Java. The placement of statues of lions standing on their hindlegs at the four corners of the base of the temple is a feature also of Candi Kidal, to the east of Malang, East Java. These elements characteristic of the Late Classical style suggest that this group of Buddhist shrines, if it does belong to the Shailendra period, marks its conclusion.

Kalasan. A flat, undecorated foundation appears to be a typical architectural feature of 8th-century temples. It is a feature of the original temple of Candi Kalasan, *c.* 12 km east of Yogyakarta, which was subsequently completely enveloped by another structure, notable for the beauty of its stone carvings. Indeed, there are probably two *candi* encapsulated within the monument visible today. Of these, only parts of the base remain. However, an inscription dating from 778 that records the founding of a shrine dedicated to the Buddhist goddess Tārā in the village of Kalasa refers definitely only to the first of these structures. Little is known about this first temple of Tārā, except that it had a plain, undecorated base. Although it is in a poor state of preservation, Candi Kalasan unmistakably displays the style of the Early Classical period, with its squat shapes and pronounced horizontal mouldings. Nevertheless, the architects evidently attempted to give the monument greater verticality. Additional support is given to the base of the temple, some 3 m high, by a platform over 1 m high, while the difference between the square plan of the temple (16.5×16.5 m) and that of the entire structure (27×27 m) leaves a wide terrace round the body of the temple, enhancing its slender appearance. This impression is augmented by the plain double pilasters on the walls of the body of the temple, flanking pilasters with a carved decoration of floral scrolls. In the centre of each wall, between the double pilasters, is a niche flanked by columns supporting a flattened arch with a *kāla* head, behind which is a relief depicting a temple with a tiered roof that reaches almost to the cornice (see fig. 6). The entrance porch leading into the cella projects from the central part of the façade. On the porch the *kāla-makara* motif occurs twice, once over the entrance and again higher up, where its elaborate carvings interrupt the mouldings that define the cornice of the temple roof. Candi Kalasan is the earliest of the *candi* of the Early Classical style with five cellas, a principal cella in the centre and four subsidiary cellas in the four projections of the building. Each of the four side chapels has its own entrance, the one in the east façade acting as an antechamber to the central cella, where all that remains is an empty lion throne, deprived of its icon. All five cellas were once covered by a single stepped roof crowned by a stupa. Of this roof only part of the first level has been preserved, but this is enough to prove that its plan was octagonal, not square like that of the body of the building and its base. On each side is a niche, in front of which has been placed a miniature building decorated with a stupa as if to fill the open space.

6. Candi Kalasan, Central Java, south façade, *kāla-makara* ornament over a niche, late 8th century

Sari. Often associated with Candi Kalasan is Candi Sari. The two temples are situated close to each other, and the style of carving and sculpture is very similar. The same cannot be said of their architecture. With the exception of its base, Candi Sari has been reconstructed almost completely. The building is rectangular in form and has two storeys, each of which contains three rooms in a row and connected to each other by narrow doorways. The second storey originally had wooden floors, and the stairs leading to it were likewise made of wood. There are three separate roofs covering the three interior spaces. Each of these three roofs is decorated with a row of stupas, and they are linked by the row of niches immediately below. On both storeys the walls are divided into sections, the middle one of which has a rectangular window flanked by graceful figures of heavenly beings, creating an impression of slenderness.

Sewu. Coeval with Candi Kalasan is Candi Sewu, not far to the north in the plain of Prambanan. It is a complex of buildings consisting of a principal shrine and 250 subsidiary temples arranged in concentric squares around it. The shrine is probably the sanctuary referred to in the Kelurak inscription, which records the founding of a temple in 782. Another inscription, found inside the temple precinct, states that the temple was enlarged in the year 792; the same inscription gives the name of the *candi* as Mañjuśrīgrha, i.e. a shrine dedicated to the *bodhisattva* Mañjuśrī. The plan of the principal temple is the same as that of Candi Kalasan. However, here the chapels are separated by narrow passageways encircling the body of the temple. Each chapel has its own separate roof crowned by a stupa. A programme of reconstruction was initiated in the early 1990s and completed in February 1993. The main temple is in the Early Classical style, and an effort was made to enhance its verticality by the use of plain pilasters to divide the walls into vertical zones alternating with tall niches. Another hallmark of the Early Classical style evident at Candi Sewu is the luxuriant splendour of detail in the structure and decoration of all the buildings in the complex. The subsidiary temples are all identical in form. They have a single cella, and a stepped roof set on an octagonal base and terminating in a stupa. The base of the stupa is surrounded by smaller stupas, giving the entire superstructure a pointed, slender profile. This effect is balanced by the body of the temple, the walls of which are flanked by ornamental columns that appear to support the cornice of the roof.

Plaosan. About 2 km east of Candi Sewu is a pair of Buddhist temple complexes, Candi Plaosan Lor and Plaosan Kidul. Plaosan Lor consists of twin main shrines on a north–south axis and surrounded by three rows of subsidiary buildings, arranged in concentric rectangles. Two of these rows consist of stupas and one of small shrines. The two principal shrines closely resemble Candi Sari and similarly consist of three rooms on each of the two floors. They also have windows flanked by figures of heavenly beings in high relief. However, while Candi Sari has three roofs, the twin temples of Plaosan Lor each have a single tapering roof, culminating in a stupa, that covers the entire structure. Another significant difference is that, while all the cellas and niches of Candi Sari are empty, those of Candi Plaosan have beautiful statuary, enthroned on lotus pedestals placed close to the back wall. Neither Candi Sari nor Candi Plaosan is typical of a specific architectural style or period. Just as at Candi Borobudur, the shape and structure that distinguish these twin shrines are connected with their religious function, which is different from that of other *candi.* However, the sculptural style of their decoration definitely places these *candi* among the Shailendra monuments. The minor variations between monuments of the period result from small differences in age and from local traditions. One of the principal shrines was reconstructed during the 1960s. The reconstruction of the second began in 1993.

(c) A late example: Candi Loro Jonggrang. Candi Loro Jonggrang near the village of Prambanan, 17 km north-east of Yogyakarta, is a Hindu and not a Buddhist monument. Most authorities date this complex to the beginning of the 10th century, making it the last of the important temples of the Early Classical period. However, this view is inconsistent with the inscription of the principal shrine, dedicated to Shiva, which is dated 856 and seems to refer to Loro Jonggrang. If so, this would imply that the temple complex existed almost a century before the end of the Early Classical period. On the other hand, the architecture itself furnishes several arguments to strengthen the supposition that Loro Jonggrang really is the last creation of the Early Classical period. The efforts of the architects to give the *candi* a slender appearance are immediately evident (for illustration *see* LORO JONGGRANG). The foundation, which is *c.* 3 m high, serves as a base for the body of the building; upon it is set an additional base, decorated with mouldings. The body of the buildings has been divided into two parts, as if it were two-storeyed, by a belt of horizontal mouldings. The roof is constructed in such a way that the transitions between the false storeys have become indistinct. They are brought even closer together visually by filling the intervening space with rows of bell-shaped finials. All these are typical features of architecture of the Late Classical period in eastern Java (*see* §(iii)(a) below). The blurring of the distinction between Buddhist and Hindu elements, evident from the shape of the stupa- or bell-shaped decorative pieces as well as from the finial of the spire, also indicates a late date for these buildings. Another indication is the fact that the subsidiary temples occupying the corners of the squares have been given two entrances and therefore face two directions. This can only mean that the architects of the complex were preoccupied with external symmetry, forgetting the deeper symbolic meaning of the monument. Such symptoms occur when an art form has passed its prime and is approaching a phase of stagnation and rigidity. Candi Loro Jonggrang is also unusual in that it has separate shrines for each of the gods of the Hindu Trimūrti (Trinity): the principal shrine in the centre dedicated to Shiva, the one on Shiva's right (to the south) dedicated to Brahma and the one on his left dedicated to Vishnu.

Facing the temples of the three gods of the Trimūrti are three smaller temples. The middle one, facing the Shiva temple, enshrines a statue of the recumbent bull Nandi, Shiva's mount. This arrangement is found frequently in such other Hindu temples as Candi Gunung Wukir and Candi Badut. Yet another architectural feature characteristic of Candi Loro Jonggrang and not found elsewhere is the presence of the two so-called *candi apit* or court temples. These face each other across the space between the two rows of the six main temples on the square terrace and are raised above the rows of subsidiary shrines. The most noteworthy feature of these two temples is their slender elevation. They are also divided into two levels, and they have roofs in the shape of steep pyramids.

Although many architectural elements of the Candi Loro Jonggrang complex place it in the transition between the Early and Late Classical periods, there are also several features typical of the earlier period. The combination of plinth, S-shaped ogee and semicircular moulding that is a basic component of the profile of the buildings, the style of the statuary, and the treatment of the *kāla-makara* and other decorative motifs, give the complex an undeniably early character. The rows of reliefs representing the *Rāmāyaṇa* and *Kṛṣṇāyāṇa*, carved on the inside of the balustrades of the three main temples, represent the same style. The plan of the principal shrine, a central cella surrounded by four side chapels, is reminiscent of Candi Kalasan. The presence of stairways into the main cella as well as into the side chapels recalls the arrangement in the main temple of Candi Sewu, and the four rows of subsidiary temples surrounding the central enclosure is another feature that establishes a direct connection with Candi Sewu. The configuration of such complexes as Candi Sewu, Candi Loro Jonggrang and Candi Plaosan Lor, which are built round a central principal shrine, may reflect a world of thought based upon a system of centralized government of the kind thought to have been characteristic of Shailendra rule. In 1953 the reconstruction of the Shiva temple was completed and in 1993 the reconstruction of all eight temples in the central courtyard.

(ii) c. *950–*c. *1250.* No architectural remains have survived in Java from the period of the Kediri kingdom (mid-10th century–early 13th) and the early part of the Singhasari dynasty (1222–92). There is thus little evidence, even from East Java, of how architecture developed in the period between the mid-10th century and the mid-13th, which marks the beginning of the Late Classical period. Nevertheless, Javanese influence is evident during this period in

7. 'Queens' Tombs', Pura Gunung Kawi, Bali, *c.* 1080

the religion and culture of Bali, partly as a result of dynastic marriages between the royal families of Bali and East Java, and several temples survive in Bali from this time. These deviate from the usual Javanese type, however, in that they are not free-standing structures but are carved in high relief from the steep rocky banks of rivers. The best known of these 'rock *candi*' is the *pura* (temple complex) of Gunung Kawi at Tampaksiring, which is thought to date from the late 12th century. The art of carving buildings from the rock-face was, however, apparently known in Bali at least 100 years earlier. For example, not far west of Bedulu, south of the road to Peliatan, on the north bank of the Petanu River, lies the bathing place known as Goa Gajah (Elephant Cave), which is thought to date from the 11th century. It consists of three parts: the bathing places in the centre with their water spouts in the shape of female figures, excavated in 1954; a cave to the north, with a head of a huge demon emerging from a forest above the entrance; and, to the south, parts of a relief of a triple stupa which evidently broke away from the rock-face and fell into the ravine, where the fragments were discovered in 1931. The place where the relief once stood is still visible, indicating that it was carved on a square base. The stupas have pinnacles in the shape of multiple parasols, one having as many as 13. These stupas may be regarded as the Buddhist counterparts of the Hindu rock-cut *candi*; both the *candi* and the stupas were probably associated with the cults of deceased rulers and their relations.

The complex of Pura Gunung Kawi is situated at Tampaksiring in east-central Bali. Epigraphic evidence suggests that it dates from *c.* 1080, and, if so, it may be the funerary monument of King Anak Wungsu (*reg* 1050–*c.* 1078), his queens and concubines. It consists of ten *candi* set in vaulted niches hewn out of the solid rock at the bottom of a deep ravine formed by the Pakerisan River. They are grouped in two rows: five standing on a common base cut from the east bank of the river (the royal tombs); four, also on a common base reached by a staircase, cut into the west bank of the same river (the 'Queens' Tombs'; see fig. 7) and one further south, the so-called Tenth Tomb, carved from a rock that does not form part of the river bank. In addition there are caves excavated from the river bank that were probably inhabited by hermits. To the south-east of the group of five *candi* there is a monastery (Skt *vihāra*) consisting of courtyards, small chambers and niches hewn from the stone in such a way that parts were excavated to create space and others were left standing to form the buildings. The ten *candi* are all of the same form; their façades closely resemble *candi* of the Early Classical style, while their roofs are more like those of the Late Classical style (*see* §(iii) below). Heavy horizontal lines clearly define the different components of the buildings and the tiers of the roofs. The base of each *candi* is very low, as is the body of the temple. The squat shape of the body is made to appear slender by the use of broad vertical bands, each with a false door indicated on it in relief, in the centre of each wall, which cut through the mouldings of the base and the cornice. The roof is stepped, but the transitions between the tiers of the roofs are hidden behind rows of triple turrets shaped like *liṅgas* on *yoni* pedestals.

There are several other rock temples in Bali, all smaller and more slender than at Gunung Kawi; their roofs are constructed like those of the Late Classical style in Java. All have been carved from the rocks of riverbanks, recessed and sheltered by vaulted porticos. At Tegallinggah near Gianyar in central Bali are some unfinished rock *candi* with a *vihāra* also cut out of the rock-face, in a steep cliff on the banks of the Pakerisan River. They were probably abandoned before being completed, because of an earthquake or a volcanic eruption.

(iii) c. *1250–*c. *1500: Late Classical period.* By the mid-13th century in Java the characteristic features of the Early Classical style had disappeared completely and been replaced by new elements. For example, the solid, heavy horizontal mouldings such as the plinth-ogee-semicircular sequence of the earlier period were replaced by flat bands. Of the *kāla-makara* motif only the *kāla* (also called *banaspati*) remained, now, however, complete with lower jaw. The vertical bands on the body of the temple, introduced to balance the horizontality of the mouldings, were typically replaced by small shallow projections or porches containing niches that look as if they have been stuck to the walls. A larger structure of similar shape provides the entrance to the cella in the interior of the *candi.* Both niches and doorway have columns and a plain lintel supporting the head of a *banaspati* installed above. The porches also have a flight of steps flanked by string walls culminating in a heavy volute. The walls of the body of the temple are often decorated with carved round medallions. The greatest changes are in the shape of the roof. While in earlier Javanese *candi* the roof was constructed in such a way that each storey had ample open space on all sides, in temples of Late Classical date the transition from one level to the other is disguised by means of rows of stupas or bell-shaped ornaments. The more slender profile of *candi* of the Late Classical period is enhanced by the division of the base, which is of considerable height, into several layers. The body of the temple itself is a square block divided into two parts by a horizontal band of mouldings in the middle, which gives it a rather squat appearance. Notwithstanding the thickness of the flat mouldings above and below the cella block, which may be said to be exaggerated, they succeed in overcoming this impression of squatness. While the Late Classical style is closely associated with the late Singasari and Majapahit (1292–*c.* 1500) kingdoms in East Java, its influence is also evident in the architecture of Sumatra and Bali.

(a) Java. (b) Sumatra. (c) Bali.

(a) Java.

Singasari. Because of the hiatus in architectural remains in Java between the 10th and the 13th centuries, Candi Kidal, which may be considered the prototype of the Late Classical style, gives the false impression that changes occurred suddenly. This *candi* is located *c.* 24 km east of the city of Malang, East Java. According to the Javanese panegyric poem *Nāgarakṛtāgama* (1365) and the chronicle *Pararaton* ('Book of Kings'), it served as the commemorative shrine for King Anusapati (*reg* 1227–47). Candi Kidal has none of the characteristics of the Early Classical style, except, perhaps, in the general layout of the temple complex. The roof is an accumulation of layers that diminish in size with height, the already minor differentiation between layers being further disguised by the use of rows of miniature structures or turrets. While the courses and layers of stone in the structure of the roof stand out, emphasizing the horizontal lines, the general impression is of slender verticality. This is probably enhanced by the flat bands that support the roof and form a cornice crowning the walls of the *candi*, maintaining a balance with the mouldings that encircle the base of the body of the temple.

Candi Singasari, *c.* 19 km north of Malang, East Java, which was built shortly before 1292, does not have the tall, slender profile or the single cella of most Late Classical Javanese *candi.* It is built on a square platform and is supported by a base. The *candi* has projections on all four sides, each containing a side chapel, so that, including the main cella, the temple has five cellas. Unusually, these chapels are in the base of the monument and not in its body. The body of the temple is also unusual in that it has no entrance doorway. Its walls are decorated with tall narrow niches crowned by *banaspati* heads, which appear to support the roof. All five cellas were originally covered by separate tiered roofs, giving Candi Singasari five spires. Candi Singasari was partially restored in 1935–6, but it has been possible to reconstruct only the central roof, and that only partially. Several of the *banaspati* heads are unfinished, as are some of the other components of the building, which suggests that the carving of decorative details was done from the top downwards. Candi Jawi is located near the town of Pandakan, midway between Malang and Surabaya. The temple rises gracefully to a height of 24 m from a square base with sides of 9.5 m. The square precinct is surrounded by a moat. Another special feature of the temple is the form of its double finial: a square block surmounted by a stupa. This clearly indicates that Candi Jawi is dedicated to Shiva–Buddha in accordance with the account given in the *Nāgaṛakṛtāgama.* It is a commemorative shrine for Kĕrtanagara, the last king of the Singasari dynasty (*reg* 1268–92), who adhered closely to the syncretic Shiva–Buddha cult. It was completely restored in 1980 and entirely reconstructed in 1992.

Majapahit. A few kilometres north of Candi Kidal, and not far separated from it in date, is Candi Jago. According to the *Nāgaṛakṛtāgama* and the *Pararaton*, this is the commemorative shrine for King Vishnuvardhana (*d* 1268), who is portrayed here in a statue as the Buddhist deity Amoghapasha. Despite its proximity to Candi Kidal, Candi Jago in its present form is totally different, in both shape and structure, and this suggests that in its present form it dates not from the Singasari period, but from the Majapahit period, one century later. This view is supported by the evidence of the reliefs carved on the walls. They are executed in a style close to that of the Majapahit period, and in some of them all five of the *punakawan*, the clownish pages who accompany Arjuna and other heroes in the Old Javanese poem *Arjunavivāha*, appear for the first time. The body of the *candi* is in ruins. It may originally have been surmounted by a set of tiered roofs of progressively diminishing size made of palm fibres or grass thatch on a wooden frame, similar to the superimposed roofs of the Balinese sanctuary (*meru*). The base displays some unusual characteristics. It is built on three levels rising one behind the other as one enters the precinct of the temple from the west. The *candi* itself stands in the centre of the uppermost level. The front part of each level has consequently been transformed into a kind of porch, providing ample space for the two flights of steps. These are narrow and flanked by string walls with a heavy volute at the top. The walls of all three levels are covered with narrative reliefs. At the bottom level the story of *Kunjarakarna*, a *yakṣa* (guardian of treasure) who freed his friend from the tortures of hell, is illustrated. At the second level is the *Parthayajna*, the tale of the adventures of the Pandavas, the heroes of the Hindu epic, the *Mahābhārata*, before Arjuna's penance on Mt Indrakila, while on the uppermost level, which also functions as the base of the body of the *candi*, the story of Arjuna's wedding is depicted.

The stepped structure of Candi Jago signals the reappearance of original Indonesian elements found in the prehistoric stepped sanctuaries built on the slopes of hills. This tendency towards a return to pre-Hindu concepts exerted a strong influence on the subsequent development of Indonesian architecture. The temple complex of PANATARAN, on the south-western slope of Mt Kelut, 12 km north of Blitar, East Java, which was known under the name of Palah as early as 1197 and which remained an important sanctuary well into the Majapahit period, may be seen as a direct precursor of the modern Balinese temple. The buildings are no longer laid out round a principal shrine in the centre, as at Candi Sewu and Candi Loro Jonggrang, but are arranged towards the rear of the temple precinct, with the principal shrine, on a stepped foundation, occupying the place furthest to the back. Various kinds of structure are scattered over the three courtyards, running west-north-west to east-north-east, into which the temple precinct is divided, including open-sided halls or pavilions (*pendopo*), of which now only the square or rectangular platforms remain. On the left of the first courtyard is the Naga Temple, so called because of the coiling snakes (Skt *nāga*) that encircle its body. It was reconstructed in 1917–18 except for the roof, which was presumably made of perishable materials. In the centre of the courtyard is the Dated Temple, which has almost no base, a richly decorated body and a steep, multi-tiered stone roof (see fig. 8), and which derives its name from the date (corresponding to 1369) inscribed on the lintel above the entrance. It was also reconstructed in 1917–18. The principal shrine of Panataran, which stands at the far end of the complex nearest to Mt Kelut, resembles that of Candi Jago in that it has a triple base. Its second level has been shortened in front, creating space for a terrace. The smaller third level is in the centre of the second, while the *candi* itself stands in the centre of the third platform. Nothing remains of the roof, which, it may be assumed, was constructed, like the Naga Temple, in wood covered with palm fibre or grass thatch and had several superimposed roofs, like a Balinese *meru*. Sculptures of garuḍas (the winged mount of Vishnu) and of winged *nāga*s cover

8. The Dated Temple, Candi Panataran, East Java, 1369; reconstructed 1917–18

the walls of the third level of the base. The walls of the two lower levels are decorated with reliefs of scenes from the *Rāmāyaṇa* and *Kṛṣṇāyāṇa*.

The capital of the Majapahit kingdom, in the area now known as Trawulan in central East Java, is one of the few capitals of the Classical period of which the location is known. Few of the buildings, all of which were built in brick, have been preserved. Candi Brahu still displays traces of its former glory, although it is in a very ruinous condition. Candi Tikus, a bathing place with several pools, is also so ruined that it contributes little to knowledge of Majapahit architecture. Candi Wringin Lawang is a gate of a type known as *candi běntar* ('split gate'). Although imperfectly preserved, it gives an idea of the original appearance of such buildings. Candi Bajangratu is also a gate, but of a different type, resembling a *candi* structure perforated in the base and body of the temple by the aperture of the doorway. The structure, which is more than 15 m high, is still largely in its original condition, complete with roof and finial. A gateway similar in shape to Candi Bajangratu, but less slender and tall, is Candi Jedong, situated to the south of Trawulan on the northern slope of Mt Penanggungan. It bears an inscribed date corresponding to 1385.

Temples of yet another shape, consisting of a cylindrical body rising from a square base, were built in Java during the Majapahit period. One temple of this type is Candi Jabung, on the north coast of the eastern tip of Java, near

9. Candi Sukuh, Central Java, first half of the 15th century

Kraksaan, *c.* 60 km east of Pasuruan, which dates from 1354. On the axes of the building are projections that, because their construction differs from that of the building itself, appear to be later additions. The projection on the west side functions as a doorway to the square cella; the other three projections contain niches. Both doorway and niches are crowned by horned *banaspati* heads that seem to support the cornice. The roof is so completely ruined that neither its shape nor its structure can be ascertained. North-east of Wlingi, *c.* 22 km to the east of Blitar in the south of East Java, lies another gateway, Candi Plumbangan. A date is inscribed above the doorway corresponding to 1390. Although coeval with Candi Jedong and although both have winged gateways (*see* §(iv) below), Candi Plumbangan is totally different in form. It has the usual doorway with a plain frame and a roof in the form of a truncated pyramid surmounted by an upright rectangular element. At first sight the shape resembles that of the niches flanking the entrance to Candi Kidal. It was restored in 1921.

The re-emergence of pre-Hindu elements continued throughout the decline of the Majapahit dynasty during the 15th century. Many of the buildings on the slopes of Mt Penanggungan and its vicinity a few kilometres to the north-west of Candi Jawi have the shape of stepped sanctuaries, built to follow the slope of the mountain. The Late Classical style of these buildings can be seen from the decoration and the reliefs, and also from the shape of the altar, which resembles the body of a temple of that period. In Central Java, at a height of 910 m on the western slopes of Mt Lawu east of Surakarta (Solo), lies a temple of yet another architectural style, although its basic form is a stepped sanctuary. Candi Sukuh can be dated to the first half of the 15th century on the evidence of inscriptions. It is a truncated pyramid, with an extremely narrow gateway giving access by means of a flight of steps to a platform on top (see fig. 9).

(b) Sumatra. The influence of Singasari and Majapahit also found a response in Sumatra. In the vicinity of the village of Muara Jambi, not far from the provincial capital of Jambi, on the banks of the Batang Hari River in the south-east of the island, are a number of Buddhist *candi*, probably dating from the early 13th century. They are built of brick within spacious precincts and scattered in apparently random clusters. Although architecturally they do not display many signs of East Javanese influence, many of their decorative patterns, as well as statues and sculptural fragments associated with them are reminiscent of the art styles of Singasari. They all have stepped platforms and all lack a cella. A deviation from the Late Classical style is the presence of *makara*, often of large dimensions, in which the wings on either side of the stairs terminate. Architectural remains of uncertain date but probably older than the Muara Jambi group are found in the interior of Sumatra, close to the equator. At a bend in the Kampar River lies the Muara Takus group of temples, consisting of four brick and stone buildings inside a square walled precinct measuring 74×74 m. Three of them have been reduced to heaps of brick, but one, known as Candi Mahligai, still stands. It is in the form of a tower standing on a rectangular platform *c.* 1.8 m high. The height of the stepped base of the temple has been increased by inserting a lotus pedestal. The cylindrical body of the temple is crowned by a stupa, with a separate base, decorated with stone sculptures of lions. The entire structure is *c.* 12 m high.

Further to the north-east, in the Batak region of Padang Lawas ('Great Plain') on the upper course of the Barumun River, near the town of Padangsidempuan, lies a group of brick *candi* in the Late Classical style, all built on a high base. Called *biaro* (Skt *vihāra*) by the local population, they are scattered over the plain without any apparent plan. Two inscriptions found at Padang Lawas are dated 1245 and 1372, and this, together with the Tantric character of the monuments and the sculpture associated with them (*see* §IV, 4(ii) below), suggests that they were built in the 13th and 14th centuries. On the other hand, an inscription found near by at Jorang Belanga is dated 1179, and it is possible that some of the temples, particularly Biaro Bahal I, date from the 12th century. This earlier date is also suggested by the elements borrowed from Central Java, such as the *makara* ornaments that, as in the Muara Jambi *candi*, terminate the wings of the staircases. The whole group appears to constitute the only remains of a Batak Buddhist kingdom that is probably the same as the kingdom called Panai in the inscriptions. Biaro Bahal I, which served as the main shrine of a group of several temples built within a walled precinct (57×49 m), is the most complete. Erected on top of a square platform 1.8 m high, and missing its finial, it stands more than 9 m tall. The decoration of the platform consists of vertical bands dividing the wall into a row of square panels that are decorated with brick reliefs of lions. The projecting part of the platform, built to accommodate a flight of steps, is decorated with brick reliefs representing dancing *yakṣa*s or *rākṣasa*s (guardian wealth deities) in different poses. The base of the body of the temple consists of an accumulation of flat mouldings in a very simple style. The body of the temple is also undecorated, except for flat mouldings and two figures, now headless, in high brick relief flanking the entrance to the cella. Unlike the other temples of Padang Lawas, the roof of Biaro Bahal I is crowned by a cylindrical component that, because it is placed on top of a lotus cushion, most probably represented a stupa. Biaro Bahal II, 460 m to the east, is in ruinous condition. Nevertheless, it is still possible to see that its superstructure had an octagonal base and niches in the walls facing the four cardinal points that housed stone statues of guardian lions. Most remarkable is the 1 m-high stone statue discovered inside the cella. When the broken fragments were pieced together the statue could be identified as Heruka, the Drinker of Blood, a demonic figure from the Tantric pantheon, shown dancing on top of a (now missing) corpse. Biaro Bahal III, 365 m further east again, is of similar dimensions but even more ruined. The few parts of the walls of the body of the temple that are still standing are plain except for flat mouldings at the base and cornice.

The largest of all the Padang Lawas temples is Biaro Si Pamutung, the principal shrine of a group of temples in a large walled precinct (55×60 m). Although it is largely in a ruinous state, the remains of a double platform can still be discerned. A remarkable feature of this temple is that 2 rows of stupas, 16 in the lower row and 12 in the upper, appear in the ruins of the superstructure. South of Biaro Si Pamutung lies Biaro Si Joreng Belangah, which is similar to the other *biaro*s in shape, being square with flat, plain walls and rising high on its tall platform. In addition to the remains of buildings, several of the walled precincts of Padang Lawas have yielded carved stone pillars or miniature buildings (*stambha*s) 1–1.5 m tall. The shape of some of these recalls those of Candi Biaro Bahal I and Candi Mahligai at Muara Takus, although there are also considerable differences. It is unclear what the function of these miniature structures was. On the whole, the *biaro* of Padang Lawas show many points of resemblance to the temples of East Java. There are also elements borrowed from Central Java, such as the use of the *makara* on the wings of staircases. Elements derived from the art of South India likewise make an appearance, although less in architecture than in sculpture (*see* §IV, 4(ii) below). There is, however, no doubt that this temple architecture in central Sumatra belongs to the late style, as is also evident from its religious background and from the dated inscriptions found in the vicinity of many of the *biaro*.

(c) Bali. According to the 14th-century Javanese panegyric *Nāgarakṛtāgama*, the last king of Singasari sent an expedition against Bali in 1284 and conquered it, and the same source recounts a second conquest of Bali by Majapahit in the early 14th century, after which the Balinese followed 'all the customs of Java'. The political influence of Singasari and Majapahit led to the adoption in Bali of many stylistic and iconographic features of East Javanese architecture and sculpture. An interesting example of this gradual change is the temple of Pura Yeh Gangga at Perean, *c.* 12 km from Mengwi in central Bali, which is transitional between the *candi* of Java and the *meru* of Bali and gives an idea of how such East Javanese temples as Candi Jongo and the main temple of Panataran looked when they were still crowned by a multiple roof. The base and body of Pura Yeh Gangga are of stone, while the seven-tiered roof is of wood and palm fibre. A

10. Split gate (*candi bĕntar*), Pura Kehen, Bali, ?early 20th century

stone discovered in the precinct bears a date corresponding to 1334, which definitely places the temple in the Late Classical period. Indeed, the structure, the mouldings and the decoration all display characteristics familiar from architectural remains of the Majapahit period in Java.

The spread of Islam into Central and East Java during the 15th century brought ever more people from Java (*Wong Mojopahit*) into Bali, bringing their Hindu–Javanese culture and art forms with them. As a result this culture was preserved in Bali after its demise in Java, and a synthesis took place between East Javanese and ancient pre-Hindu Balinese traditions that led to the emergence of many distinctive new art forms and a highly idiosyncratic form of Hinduism (*see* HINDUISM, §II). An illustration of this process is provided by the great temple complex of Besakih, 1000 m above sea-level on the slopes of Gunung Agung, the sacred mountain of Bali. At Besakih there are shrines to many indigenous deities in addition to the principal *meru* of the Hindu gods of the Trimurti (Trinity), and their names and titles are in Old Balinese rather than Javanese or Sanskrit. As at Pura Yeh Gangga, the *meru* have stone bases and many-tiered wood and palm-fibre roofs (for illustration *see* BESAKIH). One important feature of Balinese temple architecture clearly derived from East Javanese models is the *candi bĕntar* (split gate), which almost always forms the entrance to the outer courtyard of the temple. It is in the shape of a tall East Javanese *candi* split into two halves, which are separated to create a passage (see fig. 10). Like the *candi* themselves, these split gates may be representations of the cosmic mountain, Mt Meru.

BIBLIOGRAPHY

W. F. Stutterheim: *Oudheiden van Bali* [Antiquities of Bali], 2 vols (Singaraja, 1929)

——: 'The Meaning of the Hindu-Javanese *Candi*', *J. Amer. Orient. Soc.*, ii (1931), pp. 1–15

F. M. Schnitger: *The Archaeology of Hindoo Sumatra* (Leiden, 1937)

——: *Forgotten Kingdoms in Sumatra* (Leiden, 1939)

A. J. Bernet Kempers: *Tjandi Kalasan dan Sari* (Jakarta, 1954)

J. Fontein: *The Pilgrimage of Sudhana* (The Hague, 1967)

S. S. Satari: 'Senirupa dan Arsitektur Zaman Klasik di Indonesia' [Art and architecture in Indonesia during the Classical period], *Kalpataru*, i (1975), pp. 5–38

R. Soekmono: *Chandi Borobudur* (Assen and Amsterdam, 1976)

A. J. Bernet Kempers: *Monumental Bali* (The Hague, 1978, rev. Berkeley and Singapore, 1991)

L. Chandra: 'Chandi Mendut and Pawon: A New Interpretation', *Bijdr. Taal-, Land- & Vlkenknd.*, cxxxvi (1980), pp. 313–20

R. Mulia: 'The Ancient Kingdom of Panai and the Ruins of Padang Lawas (North Sumatra)', *Bull. Res. Cent. Archaeol. Indonesia*, xiv (1980) [whole issue]

P. Worsley: 'Narrative Bas-reliefs at Candi Surawana', *Southeast Asia in the 9th to 14th Centuries* (Singapore, 1986), pp. 353–67

J. Dumarçay: *The Temples of Java* (Singapore, 1987)

P. Atmadi: *Some Architectural Design Principles of Temples in Java* (Yogyakarta, 1988)

J. Fontein: 'The Resurrection of a Thousand Temples', *Orientations* (Dec 1993), pp. 54–8

R. Soekmono: *The Javanese Candi: Function and Meaning* (Leiden, 1995)

JAN FONTEIN, R. SOEKMONO

11. Winged gateway, Sendangduwur, Bojonegoro, East Java, mid-16th century

2. ISLAMIC. With the advent of Islam in the late 15th century, Hindu–Buddhist architecture was superseded, except in Bali and western Lombok, where the Hindu religion continued to be practised. Here the classical tradition continued in temple architecture, most notably in the temple buildings with stone bases and many-tiered, timber-framed superstructures (*meru*) that became a familiar feature of the modern Balinese landscape. Elsewhere in Indonesia, Islamic architectural forms became dominant, although certain pre-Islamic elements survived, especially in Java, in the design and decoration of mosques.

The 16th-century cemetery at Sendangduwur, an early Islamic centre on the north coast of East Java, is a terraced monument built on a hill like many late Hindu-Javanese monuments. It also has gateways with wings on either side (see fig. 11) similar to, although more elaborately carved than, the winged gateways of such East Javanese Hindu temples as Belahan (13th century), Jedong (late 14th century) and Plumbangan (1390). The oldest surviving mosque in Indonesia is in Demak, a town on the north coast of Central Java. Demak was the island's first Muslim state, and the mosque dates from 1477–9, when Islam was beginning to supplant Hinduism in Java. This remarkable building, which has been restored several times, was a prototype for the Indonesian mosque. Like Indonesian Islam itself, Islamic architecture in Indonesia is heterodox, deriving for the most part not from Middle Eastern models but from the square, pillared open pavilion (*pendopo*; probably derived from Skt *maṇḍapa*), that pre-dates Indian influences and is depicted in the reliefs of the 9th-century Buddhist monument of Borobudur. It is to be found both in such Late Classical Hindu temples as Candi Panataran in East Java and in traditional palaces and houses in Java (*see* (§II, 2(iii) below), Bali (where it is known as *balé*), Lombok and the Lesser Sunda Islands. Until recently the Indonesian mosque was usually an enclosed adaptation of the *pendopo*. With its high and often multi-tiered roof, it is well suited to the hot climate and in harmony with Java's mountainous landscape. An exceptionally graceful 17th-century example of the form survives in Banten, west of Jakarta in West Java, while 18th- and 19th-century village examples abound. Another distinctive characteristic of the Indonesian mosque is the *surambi*, a broad, pillared, verandah-like structure extending out from the entrance façade. It is used for teaching and informal meetings, extending the function of the mosque into secular life. From the 19th century some mosques were built in traditional Middle Eastern style, with a bulbous dome, and that form was adopted for the national Istiqlal Mosque in Jakarta, completed in the 1980s. The intensification of Muslim orthodoxy in Indonesia in the late 20th century hastened the trend away from the indigenous *pendopo* form, and in many villages the uppermost roof of a two- or three-tiered mosque was replaced by a galvanized-iron onion dome, threatening the survival of a unique national heritage.

BIBLIOGRAPHY

R. Abikoesno: 'Masjid Agoeng te Cheribon' [The Grand Mosque in Cirebon], *Ind. Bouwknd. Tijdschr. Locale Tech.*, iv/3 (1935), pp. 14–20
L.-C. Damais: 'Etudes javanaises, I: Les Tombes musulmanes datées de Trâlâjâ', *Bull. Ecole Fr. Extrême-Orient*, xlviii (1957), pp. 353–415
A. H. Johns: 'Islam in Southeast Asia: Reflections and New Directions', *Indonesia*, xix (1975), pp. 33–55
M. C. Ricklefs: 'Six Centuries of Islamization in Java', *Conversion to Islam*, ed. N. Levtzion (New York, 1979), pp. 100–28
——: 'The Coming of Islam', *A History of Modern Indonesia: c. 1300 to the Present* (Basingstoke, 1981, 2/1987), pp. 3–13
Uka Tjandrasasmita: 'Le Rôle de l'architecture et des arts decoratifs dans l'islamisation de l'Indonésie', *Archipel.*, xxix (1985), pp. 203–11
Z. M. Wiryoprawiro: *Perkembangan arsitektur masjid di Jawa Timur* [Development of mosque architecture in East Java] (Surabaya, 1986)
R. S. Kipp and S. Rodgers, eds: *Indonesian Religions in Transition* (Tucson, 1987)

3. Formal Dutch Colonial. There was little significant building by the Dutch in Indonesia in the 17th century, and both the city planning and the architecture of the few surviving monuments from this period are Dutch East India Company (VOC) projects clearly derived from Dutch models. The oldest, the ruins of Fort Speelwijk in Banten in West Java (early 17th century), is a massive construction of unadorned stone. Plastered brick warehouses in the capital, Batavia (Jakarta), with gabled façades and steep roofs were modelled on contemporary structures in Amsterdam. The Batavia Town Hall (1707–10; now the Museum of the History of Jakarta) by W. J. van der Welde and Reinier de Klerk House (1760; now part of the National Archives), also in Jakarta, were influenced by contemporary Dutch architecture, the former by the recently completed town hall of Amsterdam and the latter by the typical detached country house (*landhuis*). Eighteenth-century engravings of now demolished Dutch buildings in Java show a preponderance of gabled façades in the urban style of the Netherlands. By the mid-19th century another trend had developed. To emphasize their growing imperial power, the Dutch adopted a grandiose Neo-classical style with colonnades and pediments for such buildings as the two official residences of the governor-general of the Dutch East Indies, both now presidential palaces, the Koningsplein Palace in Jakarta (Istana Merdeka, 1873–9) and Buitenzorg Palace in Bogor, *c.* 60 km south of Jakarta (see fig. 12). The latter houses most of the art collection formed by President Sukarno, first president of Indonesia. Other important public buildings in Jakarta built in this style are the Willemskerk (Gereja Emmanuel, 1834–9) by J. H. Hoost, the Justice Building (now the Fine Arts Museum, 1866–70) and the headquarters of the Batavian Society for Arts and Sciences (now the National Museum, 1862–88).

The Dutch population of Java grew rapidly with the expansion of trade in the 20th century. The increased proportion of women and children among them indicated a more permanent and stable society, a situation reflected in architecture, which again turned to models in the Netherlands. The influence of the Amsterdam architect H. P. Berlage was strong on many of the architects who early in the century designed office buildings such as those for the *Surabaya Handelsblad* in Surabaya, for N. V. de Bouwploeg in 1912 in Batavia (by P. A. J. Mooijen (1879–after 1930)) and for the plantation company, Cultuurmaatschappij der Voorstenlanden, in Semarang; all of these have domed towers and arched windows reminiscent of Berlage's work in the 1890s. The architectural firm of

12. Buitenzorg Palace, Bogor, West Java, 1856 (rebuilt several times)

EDUARD CUYPERS, M. J. Hulswit (1862–1921) and A. A. Fermont (*c.* 1890–1954) designed many buildings for the Java Bank in this style. Between 1920 and 1942 the International Style became increasingly influential in urban architecture. Functionalist buildings were created, most notably by R. L. A. Schoemaker (1886–1942) in the residence (1915–16) for the army commandant in Bandung and by J. F. L. Blankenberg (1888–1958) in an office (1938) in Semarang for the Borsumij Company. Fine examples of Art Deco abound; most notable are the Villa Isola (1933) in Lembang by C. P. Wolff Schoemaker (1882–1949) and the DENIS (De Eerste Nederlandsch-Indië Spaarkas) office (1935) and Hotel Savoy Homann (1939) in Bandung by A. F. Aalbers (1898–1961). The most interesting architects of the colonial period were Henri Maclaine Pont (1884–1971) and Herman Thomas Karsten (1885–1945). Both argued that indigenous architecture, particularly the pillared open-sided pavilion (*pendopo*) that is one of its most characteristic forms, could be adapted to the needs of an increasingly international and industrialized Indonesia. They believed that, aesthetically and climatically more suitable than Western types, it could protect cultural integrity in a changing society. Maclaine Pont's Institute of Technology (1919–24), Bandung, and a church (1936–7) in Pohsarang, East Java, incorporated *pendopo* structural techniques in the roofs. In his Sobokartti Folk Theatre (1922), Sisters Railway Company office (1928) and municipal abattoir (1929), all in Semarang, Karsten similarly applied indigenous construction principles to modern building. However, late 20th-century architecture in Indonesia embraced international modernism and showed few traces of the indigenous stylistic heritage.

BIBLIOGRAPHY

H. D. H. Bosboom: *Oude woningen in de stad Batavia* [Old dwellings in the town of Batavia] (The Hague, 1898)

Netherlands East Indian San Francisco Committee: Architecture in Netherlands East India, Department of Agriculture, Industry and Commerce Report, xi (Semarang, 1914)

H. T. Karsten: 'Van *pendopo* naar volksschouwburg' [From *pendopo* to people's theatre], *Djawa*, i (1921), pp. 20–30

J. Koning: 'Moderne bouwwerken in Indië' [Modern buildings in the Indies], *Ned.-Indië Oud & Nieuw*, vii/5 (1922), pp. 135–54

H. Maclaine Pont: 'Het inlandsch bouwambacht, zijn beteekenis . . . en toekomst?' [The domestic building trade, its importance. . . and future?], *Ind. Bouwknd. Tijdschr.*, x (1923), pp. 215–25

——: 'Javaansche architectuur', *Djawa*, iii/3 (1923), pp. 112–59; 4 (1923), pp. 159–70; iv/1 (1924), pp. 44–73

C. P. Wolff Schoemaker: 'Indische bouwkunst en de ontwikkelingsmogelijkheid van een Indo-Europeeschen architectuurstijl' [Indonesian architecture and the possibilities for the development of an Indo-European architectural style], *Ind. Bouwknd. Tijdschr.*, x/5 (1923), pp. 188–94

H. P. Berlage: 'De Europeesche bouwkunst op Java' [The European architecture of Java], *De Ingenieur*, xxxix (1924), pp. 399–408

E. H. de Roo: 'Raadhuis en gemeentekantoren van Bandoeng' [Town hall and municipal offices of Bandoeng], *Ind. Bouwknd. Tijdschr. Locale Tech.*, iii/4 (1934), pp. 82–9

H. T. Karsten: 'Opmerkingen over de laat-Javaanse bouwkunst naar aanleiding van de bouw van het Museum Sånå Boedåjå' [Comments on late Javanese architecture with reference to the construction of the Museum Sånå Boedåjå], *Djawa*, xv/6 (1935), pp. 221–8

Th. P. Galestin: *Houtbouw op Oost Javaansche tempelreliefs* [Wooden construction in East Javanese temple reliefs] (The Hague, 1936)

A. Heuken: *Historical Sites of Jakarta* (Jakarta, 1982)

H. I. Jessup: 'Four Dutch Buildings in Indonesia', *Orientations*, xiii (1982), no. 9, pp. 32–8; no. 10, pp. 24–32; no. 11, pp. 24–31; no. 12, pp. 22–34

T. E. Behrend: *Kraton and Cosmos in Traditional Java* (MA diss., Milwaukee, U. WI, 1983)

H. I. Jessup: 'Dutch Colonial Visions of the Indonesian Tradition', *Muqarnas: An Annual on Islamic Art and Architecture*, iii (Leiden, 1985), pp. 138–61

H. Akihary: *Architectuur & stedebouw in Indonesië, 1870–1970* [Architecture and town building in Indonesia, 1870–1970] (Zutphen, 1990)

H. I. Jessup: *Netherlands Architecture in Indonesia, 1900–1942* (in preparation)

HELEN IBBITSON JESSUP

4. DOMESTIC.

(i) Introduction. (ii) Sumatra. (iii) Java. (iv) Bali. (v) Kalimantan. (vi) Sulawesi. (vii) Other islands.

(i) Introduction. Many ethnic groups of Indonesia still inhabit 'great' houses built according to ancient traditional designs. Community halls, shrines, charnel-houses, ceremonial poles, rice granaries and field-houses or huts similarly employ traditional forms. The characteristic traditional house, depicted in engravings on bronze objects over 2000 years old, is a large dwelling, raised on posts, with a distinctive saddle roof, curved in the centre with projecting gable ends. Sometimes the roof is shown in one extended piece, or in tiered sections with a raised central element and one or two lower sections or half-roofs at each end slotted into the part(s) above. In those islands where the custom of living in 'great' houses does not obtain, dwelling houses are generally smaller and are built to accommodate less extended family units. In Java the structure of the traditional house derives from the pillared open pavilion (*pendopo*), which is also an important element of both mosque and palace architecture (*see* §(iii) below). In Bali the form of the different buildings within the family compound is also derived from the open pavilion, known in Bali as *balé*. Neither type of domestic building has a saddle roof. Materials employed in traditional domestic architecture include bamboo, used in frames, its tensile strength exploited in the curved roof, and woven to form walls; leaves, particularly coconut-palm, used in roofing; fibres from the sugar-palm; *cogon* grass; and wood. Carved wood is used as a decorative element in larger domestic buildings in many islands, especially Bali.

The construction of traditional houses usually entails a series of rites performed at successive stages, such as selecting the site, erecting the main support posts, raising the roof, completion and inauguration. Dwellings often have symbolically significant decorative motifs carved or painted on gable ends, outer wall panels, roof ridges and posts. The spatial orientation of the house, its layout and the sequence of construction usually relate to indigenous dualistic concepts of the cosmos. East–west, high–low, inner–outer, male–female, cool–hot, good–evil and right–left are common symbolic pairs in Indonesian classifications in which house structure and orientation are embedded and given meaning. However, the traditional architectural forms, both of the 'great' house and the smaller Malay-style dwellings for the nuclear family, have declined with the abandonment of old forms of socio-economic organization, the introduction of new ideas and techniques and the availability of modern building materials.

BIBLIOGRAPHY

P. H. van der Kemp: 'Over kunst in Indische woningbouw' [On art in house construction in the Indies], *Ned.-Indië Oud & Nieuw*, ii/2 (1915), pp. 1–7

H. Maclaine Pont: 'Volkswoningbouw', *Ind. Bouwknd. Tijdschr.*, ix (1922), pp. 351–5, 378–83
H. T. Karsten: 'Gesloten bebouwing voor woningbouw', *Locale Belangen*, iii (1934), pp. 12–16
R. Goris: *The Religious Character of the Village Community* (The Hague and Bandung, 1960)
G. T. Sergeant and R. Saleh: *Traditional Buildings of Indonesia*, 3 vols (Bandung, 1973)
P. Sørensen: 'A Brief Survey of East and Southeast Asian Prehistoric Houses', *The House in East and Southeast Asia: Anthropological and Architectural Aspects*, ed. K. G. Izikowitz and P. Sørensen (London and Malmö, 1982)
J. Dumarçay: *The House in South-East Asia* (Singapore, 1987)

(ii) Sumatra. A typical house of the Bataks, a group in the interior of northern Sumatra, is rectangular or square in plan, compact and raised on stout wooden posts *c.* 1.5 m high. The wooden entrance ladder or stone steps are at the front of the house or under the flooring between the posts. The low plank walls lean outwards, and the gently curved saddle roof has decorated triangular gables. The roof is about ten times the height of the walls. Traditionally the gables were held firm by a vertical strut fixed in the centre of the roof-ridge. Because of the tendency of horizontal beams to bend under the weight of vertical roof supports, the roof sags, and this is an early and widespread feature of South-east Asian architecture. Batak society is patrilineal, and alliances are maintained by 'wife-giving' and 'wife-taking' lineages. The Toba Batak village (*huta*) usually comprises a main street bordered on either side by 6–10 houses, each of which accommodates several related families. Sometimes the houses are arranged in a single row facing a line of rice granaries of the same general design but much smaller in scale. In contrast, Karo Batak villages have no focal village street, and their houses are arranged at random in relation to one another, although they are usually orientated east–west or have their front doors facing the source of the nearby river. There are various types of Karo house: these include the simple hip-and-saddle house (*rumah beru-beru*), which has a saddle roof with its lower part doubled, to produce a two-storey effect (*rumah tersek*); and a four-gabled variant, comprising two saddle roofs at right angles to each other (*rumah si empat ayo*). Karo houses are traditionally very large, measuring 18×12×12 m, and accommodate 20–60 people or 4–12 related families.

The Karo Batak house is divided longitudinally by a central walkway or 'gutter', which is at a lower level than the living-quarters and connects bamboo verandahs to front and rear, from which access ladders descend to the ground; the verandahs form a meeting and reception area. On either side of the central walkway are the apartments (*jabu*) of the individual families. These are not separated from each other by interior walls, and each pair of adjacent families shares a hearth sunk into the main floor. The apartment comprises a living space, where everyday activities and domestic rituals take place, and a sleeping area at the rear, divided from the living area by a curtain and from adjacent sleeping areas by mats hung over bamboo rods. The outer support posts, usually set in stone and enclosed in palisades, rise through the floor to carry enormous circular crossbeams supporting the roof and upper storage platform. These in turn act as cantilevers to bear the ring-beams on which the sloping roof rests. The rafters are covered and cross-braced for strength with bamboo, to

13. Minangkabau meeting house (*balai desa*), highlands of central Sumatra

which thatch is attached. The gable ends are filled with woven bamboo panels which are sometimes painted; other posts carry the floor. A cantilevered beam runs round the outer edge of the floor on which the low walls are fixed. The floor is supported by cantilevered crossbeams pegged and wedged into the tops of the support posts. The 'great' houses (*rumah gadang*) and meeting houses (*balai desa*) of the Minangkabau people in the highlands of central Sumatra are wood, bamboo and palm-fibre constructions (see fig. 13), generally larger than those of the Bataks. They are rectangular in plan and have a curved saddle roof, but with long, hornlike upturned ends. The tiered roof projects over a long front balcony and is usually divided into four or five sections. The house normally faces east and is raised a modest distance off the ground on solid ironwood posts, ideally 30 in number. The longer sides constitute the front and rear of the building. The entrance stairway (sometimes of stone, otherwise of wood) is located at the front of the house. The outer walls are decorated with carved or painted floral motifs, usually in panels at floor level. The house is divided into two main parts: the front half, containing a hearth, is a communal room or open space (*tangah rumah*), used for everyday activities, meetings and ceremonies, and as a dormitory for older children, elderly women and guests. The rear half, which is usually a little higher than the communal room, is divided into apartments, usually seven in number, although there may be as many as seventeen. The Minangkabaus are matrilineal, and each house is the seat of a matrilineage or sublineage. These apartments are each reserved for the married daughters of the lineage with their smaller children; it is also the place where the husband, who lives elsewhere with his matrilineage, comes to visit his wife at night. Expansion and segmentation of the matrilineage leads to the construction of extra apartments with curved roofs at the end of the house. Adding elements to a house can lead to the construction of up to six gable ends, and traditionally 70–80 people could be accommodated there. If pressure of numbers becomes too great, a new house is built. Beyond the apartments are the kitchens; they are partly separate but joined to the apartments by walkways. In front of the house are the separate rice granaries: saddle-roofed, on stilts, with floors and walls of planks or bamboo. Many support posts continue through the floor to the roof and divide up the living space into roughly 3-m squares. Apartments may be separated from each other by plank walls, bamboo or hung cloth fixed to the posts. Partitions can usually be easily taken down, so that the internal space can be rearranged when necessary.

BIBLIOGRAPHY

E. M. Loeb: *Sumatra: Its History and People* (Vienna, 1935)
M. Singarimbun: *Kinship, Descent and Alliance among the Karo Batak* (Berkeley, CA, 1975)
T. Kato: *Matriliny and Migration: Evolving Minangkabau Traditions in Indonesia* (Ithaca, NY, and London, 1982)

VICTOR T. KING

(iii) Java. The construction of traditional Javanese houses derives from the physical characteristics of locally available materials. The tensile strength of bamboo is often invoked for the ridge-pole and beams of the roof-frame, which is covered with coconut-palm thatch (*atap*), wood shingles (*sirap*) or terracotta tiles. The typical village house has a steep hipped roof with a less steep surrounding roof. A verandah supported by slender poles often projects from the front and rear façades, offering a cool place for such daytime activities as cooking. The essential element in Javanese architecture is not the wall, as in Western architecture, but the central column and beam system that supports a hanging roof. In this design, which has its origins in the open, pillared *pendopo*, instead of load-bearing walls, panels made of split and woven bamboo (*gedek*) enclose the interior space. There are no windows, but gaps between the *gedek* strips and the loose covering of the unlined roof permit the circulation of air. A few small rooms open off the main central space, and there is usually a small alcove, or sometimes merely a carved panel, designated as a shrine for Dewi Shri, the goddess of rice and fertility. Traditional aristocratic residences, notably the palaces of Muslim sultans and other rulers, clearly reveal their *pendopo* origin and often comprise several small pavilions around a large ceremonial *pendopo* with a marble-tiled stone or concrete plinth bearing central columns (*soko guru*) arranged on either a square (*joglo*) or a rectangular (*limasan*) ground-plan. The central columns support a beam framework, which bears the roof load by means of tensile strength. Many *pendopo* have multiple roofs, all depending from the central roof, and these are traditionally covered with shingles. The soaring interiors of such pavilions have great majesty, as in the Pendopo Agung of the Mangkunagaran Palace in SURAKARTA.

The colonial domestic architecture of the 17th and 18th centuries was directly derived from Dutch models. Houses were built of plastered brick and lacked eaves or verandahs to offer protection from tropical sun and rain; their enclosed nature restricted air circulation and contributed to unhealthy living conditions. In rural areas there was some borrowing from indigenous styles, as in the Jepang House built near Batavia (Jakarta) in the late 18th century for Andries Hartsinck. In the 19th century the Neo-classicism dominating public architecture also affected colonial houses, many of which had formal pediments and covered colonnades at front and rear, that created a cool, open space where much of the daily life of the household took place. This arrangement possibly owes as much to the indigenous *pendopo* as to Neo-classical forms. Modern urban housing is usually clustered in small groups (*kampung*) resembling rural village (*desa*) patterns within the city. Originally the dwellings were similar to their rural counterparts, but in the 1920s the colonial municipal authorities assumed responsibility for public housing, and indigenous structures were gradually replaced by semi-detached or terraced houses based on European models, with solid walls and without verandahs. Since these utilized neither traditional construction methods nor traditional materials, the inhabitants were unable to carry out maintenance and repair, and consequently slum conditions developed in many cities.

BIBLIOGRAPHY

P. H. van der Kemp: 'Over kunst in Indische woningbouw' [On art in house construction in the Indies], *Ned.-Indië Oud & Nieuw*, ii/2 (1915), pp. 1–7
H. F. Tillema: *Kromo Blanda: Over het vraagstuk van 'Het Wonen' in Kromo's groote land* [Kromo Blanda: On the question of 'the home' in Kromo's great land] (The Hague, 1915–23)
S. Kalff: 'Europeesche huizen te Batavia' [European houses in Batavia], *Ned.-Indië Oud & Nieuw*, ii/4 (1917–18), pp. 77–89
E. Cuypers: 'De moderne ambtenaarswoning in Nederlandsch-Indië' [The modern government official's residence in Dutch Indonesia], *Ned.-Indië Oud & Nieuw*, iv/4 (1919), pp. 117–24
Soerjo Winoto: 'De regentswoning' [The regent's residence], *Ned.-Indië Oud & Nieuw*, iv/5 (1919), pp. 131–41
F. F. van Hoytema: 'Comment les hollandais vivent actuellement aux Indes néerlandaises', *Ned.-Indië Oud & Nieuw*, xviii (1933), pp. 373–80
W. Lemei: *Moderne woning: Architectuur in Nederlands Indië: Villa Isola* [Modern home: Architecture in Dutch Indonesia: Villa Isola] (Bandung, 1934)
V. I. van de Wall: *Oude Hollandsche bouwkunst in Indonesië. Bijdrage tot de kennis van de Hollandsche koloniale bouwkunst in de VIIe en VIIIe eeuw: Antwerp, 1942* [Old Dutch architecture in Indonesia. Contributions to the knowledge of Dutch colonial architecture in the 7th and 8th centuries: Antwerp, 1942]
H. A. Breuning: *Het voormalige Batavia: Een Hollandse stedestichting in de tropen, anno 1619* [Former Batavia: A Dutch city settlement in the tropics, 1619] (Utrecht, 1954/*R* 1981)
Hamzuri: *Rumah tradisionil Jawa* (Jakarta, [1983])
H. I. Jessup: 'The Dutch Colonial Villa', *Mimar*, xiii (1984), pp. 35–42

HELEN IBBITSON JESSUP

(iv) Bali. A traditional Balinese village generally consists of a number of rectangular family compounds, each surrounded by walls. On two opposite sides the walls run along the roads that follow the axes between mountain and sea and between sunrise and sunset. Behind the loam or brick walls only the roofs of the buildings can be seen. The square formed by the crossroads at the centre of the village has a magic significance. Within it are one or two village temples, an assembly hall, a market, a signal tower containing a gong, a sacred banyan tree (*waringin*) and the residence of any nobility who live there. The basic form of all family compounds is the same: a simple, walled, rectangular enclosure containing a number of open-sided pavilions (*balé*). The most esteemed part of the compound is the high or pure (*utama*) area. This is orientated towards the mountain and the east and contains the family shrine or house temple, which has one or several altars and a

place for sacrificial offerings. The sacred zone is staked out before building work begins, and an altar is set up in it. The first dwelling to be erected, in the middle third of the *utama* area, is the *umah metèn*, the sleeping-quarters of the head of the family and the place where the family's treasures are kept.

The platform or 'foot' of the building is built from stones or bricks and filled with earth. Set on it is a brick enclosure with a door, reached by a flight of steps: the 'body'. Eight wooden posts, inserted into stone or cement bases and standing clear of the walls, support the roof ('head'); this floats above the enclosed space and over a projecting verandah. The roof is covered with several layers of cogon grass that are tied on to the long ribs of coconut-palm leaves and attached to the bamboo roof-frame and rafters. These are supported at the centre by a carved wooden figure, often a winged lion. The roof structure is stabilized by battening made from the dark brown wood of the sugar-palm, by rafters leading from the corner-posts into the roof and by beams that run round the roof. Bamboo pantiles or, on the coast where coconut-palms are plentiful, palm leaves are used for the roof. In the 20th century tiles have become more common. Fibres from the inner bark or bast of the sugar-palm are reserved for sacred buildings.

The roof construction of the typical *balé* can be seen most clearly in the asymmetrical group of pavilions that, with the *umah metèn*, surround the court in the centre of the village compound, since they are open on three or all four sides and the walls are kept separate from the posts and the rest of the building to minimize the risk of earthquake damage. The name and function of the *balé* are determined by the number of pillars supporting the roof. The smallest type of buildings, the *balé sakepat*, has four posts. These rest on a rectangular foundation measuring approximately 3.0×2.5 m and are sometimes linked by stabilizing central wooden platforms. The *balé sakenem* (pavilion with six posts) is very common; three posts stand on either side of the foundations, which are three times as long as they are wide (6×2 m); here too the posts are often linked by wooden platforms. The *balé sakepat* and *sakenem* are in the east of the middle zone, and the latter also occurs on the north side of the court opposite the *umah metèn*. They are used for weaving by the women, as sleeping areas and for the performance of family ceremonies. In the house temple they are used for laying out votive offerings and decorating cult objects. The *astasari*, which like the *umah metèn* has eight posts, measures approximately 4×5 m and is used for receiving guests and for customary ceremonies. Rectangular buildings with nine and twelve posts (*tiang sanga* and *sakaroras*) are found in compounds belonging to members of higher castes and are used to receive guests and perform ceremonies. The *astasari*, *tiang sanga* and *sakaroras* are ornamented with stone carvings; the wooden posts, which are always in three sections, and in particular the gable-shaped pieces that link them to the roof-frame, are carved. The kitchen, the pigsty, the rice granary and the entrance are in the lower area nearest the sea, the impure and most public part of the compound. The high, narrow entrance is covered with a roof. Often there are steps leading up to the living area, and, since motorcycles have come into use, ramps.

BIBLIOGRAPHY

M. Covarrubias: *Island of Bali* (London, 1937/*R* Kuala Lumpur, 1972)

R. Goris: *The Religious Character of the Village Community* (The Hague and Bandung, 1960)

J. L. Swellengrebel, ed.: *Bali: Studies in Life, Thought and Ritual* (The Hague and Bandung, 1960)

U. Ramseyer: *The Art and Culture of Bali* (Oxford, New York and Jakarta, 1977/*R* Singapore, Oxford and New York, 1986)

I. Nyoman Gelebet, ed.: *Arsitektur tradisional daerah Bali* (Denpasar, 1981–2)

Madé Wijaya: *Balinese Architecture: Towards an Encyclopaedia* (Sanur, 1984)

Eko Budihardjo: *Architectural Conservation in Bali* (Yogyakarta, 1986)

URS RAMSEYER

(v) Kalimantan. The characteristic dwelling of the Dayaks of Kalimantan and Sarawak is the longhouse (*rumah, uma, betang*; *see* MALAYSIA, §II, 2), though there are groups in southern Kalimantan, such as the Ma'anyan, that have apparently never known longhouses and instead build large houses on posts, square or rectangular in plan, accommodating extended families. A typical Dayak longhouse is a single, elongated structure raised off the ground on posts under a single unbroken pitched roof, which slopes at an angle of *c.* 30°-40°; it is not saddle-shaped. The roof comprises a longitudinal roof ridge supported by perpendicular struts placed on transverse roof-ties. Horizontal roof-plates are fitted on to the main posts, which run from ground to roof. Rafters and purlins are attached between the ridge and the roof-plates, as well as longitudinal wooden strips on to which wooden shingles are tied. Subsidiary posts support the main crossbeams of the floor. Joints are usually mortice-and-tenon and bound with rattan, or dowelled, pinned and spliced. They are flexible and allow for a certain amount of movement without causing serious damage to the frame.

Each longhouse accommodates a group of families related by descent and by marriage (up to 60 families). They are segregated from each other in apartments arranged in rows. Additional apartments can be attached to one end of the house. Among the traditionally more mobile, egalitarian Dayaks, such as the Ibans, longhouses are generally of lighter materials—softwoods, bamboo, bark and leaves—and are built low off the ground so that they can be easily dismantled. The more settled, aristocratic groups, such as the Kayans and Kenyahs, tend to use hardwoods, constructing massive houses from hewn planks on high, thick posts.

The longhouse usually comprises two main parts: a rear section made up of family living-quarters, divided from each other by walls of bark or timber, and a front-covered gallery, separated from the apartments by a continuous timber and bark wall. Sometimes there is a connecting door between contiguous apartments, especially if the families are closely related. The hearth may be located against one of the walls of the living-room, in a kitchen at the rear behind a bamboo or bark partition or in a separate roofed kitchen connected to the house by a covered walkway. Sometimes there are skylights in the roof section above the apartment. The apartment, in which family members eat and sleep, is connected to the gallery by a door, sprung so that it closes automatically. Part of the covered gallery constitutes a kind of village street, giving

14. Toraja house (*tongkonan*), Palawa, central Sulawesi, early 20th century

access at each end and sometimes at the front also, to entrance ladders. Much of the gallery, however, is used for receiving guests, holding ceremonies and village meetings, relaxation and performing everyday tasks. Among some groups, such as the Ibans, individual families may enclose the space adjacent to their apartment and beyond the 'street' with low wooden or bamboo walls, which serve as convenient backrests. Families often construct storage areas above the living-quarters and part of the adjacent gallery, either as an enclosed loft or as a simple, open platform. The Ibans store their rice there in round bark bins. Others, such as the Kenyahs, build separate roofed rice granaries or huts on stilts, with walls and a door. Some barns have decorated walls and carved and painted roof ridges.

Iban longhouses also have an open verandah at the front adjoining the covered gallery and running the whole length of the house. The verandah, floored with planks or bamboo and enclosed by a railing, is connected to the covered gallery by doors, which can be closed over at night. The Bidayuh Dayaks, however, sometimes construct apartments in two rows facing each other on to a single, open verandah. The houses of stratified Dayak groups sometimes have architectural variations. For example, a Kenyah chief's apartment may have a raised roof and an area of covered gallery larger than others for meetings and rituals. Other Dayak structures include the circular, elevated Bidayuh house, with a conical roof, formerly used for storing headhunting trophies and for the performance of male rites, and the square or rectangular charnel-house, built by such groups as the Kayans, Kenyahs and Ot Danums, on one or more substantial posts with a carved roof ridge and painted walls. Dayaks also put up massive carved funeral posts for their aristocratic chiefs. Most Dayaks construct simple square or rectangular raised houses or huts near their swidden fields, sometimes enclosed with walls and a door if occupied for a period, or roofed with open sides if only used for temporary shelter.

BIBLIOGRAPHY

V. T. King, ed.: *Essays on Borneo Societies* (Oxford, 1978)

J. Avé and V. T. King: *People of the Weeping Forest: Tradition and Change in Borneo* (Leiden, 1986)

V. T. King: *The Peoples of Borneo* (Oxford, 1993)

(vi) Sulawesi. Like the Minangkabaus and the Bataks of Sumatra, the Torajas of central Sulawesi erect large, solid, compact houses (*tongkonan*) with the roof in the shape of a great swooping arc (see fig. 14). The house is rectilinear and set on rectangular or octagonal posts. In contrast to Sumatran houses, the weight of the Torajan roof is supported not so much by the internal structure of posts, rafters and beams as by vertical posts erected around the house and outside the living area. Two posts (*tulak somba*), at the front and rear, underpin the projecting roof-ends. Others (*bantuli*) run along both sides of the house under the eaves. A staircase is located at either the front or the side. Some short inner posts, set in stone corbels, support the floor, tenoned in horizontal beams. One horizontal beam runs longitudinally down the centre of the house at floor level, supported by a central row of posts. Running parallel to it and above is another beam supporting the attic; the curved roof ridge is attached to this beam with rattan ropes. The roof covering comprises split bamboo, sewn together lengthwise with rattan fibre so that a convex bamboo alternates with a concave one. Shorter bamboos are placed towards the eaves, longer ones nearer the ridge. Sometimes wood shingles or palm fibres are used. Wall panels are fixed on the horizontal beams at floor level and between the vertical piles that run to the roof-beams. Details of Torajan houses often vary depending, in part, on the rank of the occupants. Aristocratic families are allowed to place a decorated post, sometimes made of stone, in the earth under the centre of the house, to build a porch supported by one of the *tulak somba* under the projecting roof, and to have elaborate wood-carving and sometimes painting (see fig. 33 below) on the walls and gable ends.

These ancestral houses are the dwelling-places of family groupings that trace their descent by means of their connections with particular family houses. There are usually three rooms within the house, partitioned from each other. Traditionally the central room, accommodating the hearth, was lower than the other two: here slaves and guests slept and heirlooms were stored. The rear room provides sleeping-quarters, the front room, a refectory and reception area. The separate rice granaries are simply smaller versions of the houses.

BIBLIOGRAPHY

H. Nooy-Palm: *The Sa'dan Toraja: A Study of their Social Life and Religion*, i (Leiden, 1979)

T. A. Volkman: *Feasts of Honor, Ritual and Change in the Toraja Highlands* (Urbana, IL, 1985)

(vii) Other islands. In some Indonesian islands, such as Enggano and Nias, off the west coast of Sumatra, Flores and Timor to the east, and in the Lesser Sunda Islands, round or oval houses are found. In Enggano, houses are small, round, on posts and *c.* 3 m in diameter, with no internal partitions. In northern Nias, circular houses are constructed on stone terraces with a central communal room and smaller rooms at the side. Traditionally, Nias houses were fortified, with village walls, gates and carved entrance stairs. Village streets were paved with stone, and stone megaliths were erected at symbolically significant points. In southern Nias, houses were usually rectangular, the roof being large and comprising two planes—a very steeply pointed central structure breaking sharply at a

lower level to a gently sloping section overhanging the walls. Pillars surround the living space of the raised house at the perimeter. The Atonis of Timor build rectangular houses as well as beehive houses, with high conical roofs of grass thatch reaching almost to the ground and thus serving as house walls. The Emas of Timor also construct circular or oval houses built on low posts on stone terraces. Again, the roof runs to the ground, and an entrance is cut into the roof. Inside there is a large multipurpose room connected to an entrance platform by an inner door. Elsewhere in eastern Indonesia different forms occur. In Savu (Sawu), roofs are usually oval or rectangular in plan with a characteristic extended ridge line which the Savunese call 'leaf neck' (*rukoko*). In the domain of Rindi, Sumba, rectangular houses are covered by a roof with four gently sloping sides rising to a very steep central point immediately above an inner central hearth.

BIBLIOGRAPHY

D. Freeman: *Report on the Iban* (London, 1970)

A. G. Schulte Nordholt: *The Political System of the Atoni of Timor* (Leiden, 1971)

J. A. Feldman: 'The House as World in Bawömatalua, South Nias', *Art, Ritual and Society in Indonesia*, ed. E. M. Bruner (Ohio, 1979)

B. Clamagirand: 'The Social Organization of the Ema of Timor', *The Flow of Life: Essays on Eastern Indonesia*, ed. J. J. Fox (Cambridge, MA, 1980)

N. L. Kana: 'The Order and Significance of the Savunese House', *The Flow of Life: Essays on Eastern Indonesia*, ed. J. J. Fox (Cambridge, MA, 1980)

G. L. Forth: *Rindi: An Ethnographic Study of a Traditional Domain in Eastern Sumba* (Leiden, 1981)

VICTOR T. KING

III. City planning.

In many respects, traditional urban settlements in Indonesia resembled their rural counterparts. Each quarter of the city had a council and headman, selected by the inhabitants, who were responsible for local security and the repair and maintenance of public facilities. Usually the only truly urban sections of these cities were the quarters occupied by foreign traders, notably the Chinese. Historically, Indonesian political and cultural life was focused on the agrarian-based *kraton* (palace) or holy town. The core comprised the *kraton* and the main temples surrounded by the houses of the nobility and religious leaders. Traditionally, the royal cities comprised a series of settlements clustered around the seat of government of the local sultan or raja. While the palace and its adjoining buildings and courtyards were often encircled by a perimeter wall, the outer limits of the city were usually not walled, and consequently there was no clear division between urban and rural areas. Among the most important surviving *kraton* are those of YOGYAKARTA and SURAKARTA (Solo), both in Central Java. In Yogyakarta the buildings of the *kraton*, thought to have been built over a period of 40 years during the 18th century, lie within the heart of the modern city. Covering an area of *c.* 1 sq. km, the palace complex is surrounded by whitewashed walls 4 m high by 3 m thick; much of the original moat has been filled in. It is essentially a rectangle orientated to the four cardinal points. The complex is really a city within a city, which, according to the British former lieutenant-governor of Java, Thomas Stamford Raffles, writing in the early 19th century, had 10,000–15,000 inhabitants; by the end of the 20th century the figure may be as high as 25,000. Many of the residents are artisans (especially batik-makers, silversmiths and puppet-makers) whose forebears were encouraged to settle around the court.

The Javanese traditionally associate centrality with purity, and for this reason the innermost group of buildings in the *kraton* comprises the private residence of the sultan and his family. This has interconnecting courtyards, flanked by open-sided pavilions, some of which house *gamelan* orchestras (*see* §VIII, 9 below). The central area is linked by a series of walled courtyards to a southern gate opening on to a large grassy square (*alun-alun*). This square, still used for shadow-puppet performances, lies within the perimeter walls of the *kraton*. In contrast, the northern square lies mainly outside the confines of the palace; it is connected to the sultan's quarters by the main gate. To the west of the inner sanctum, but still within the perimeter walls, lies the sultan's bathing place of Tamansari. It has tunnels leading to both the royal residence and a hidden entrance beyond the fortifications of the *kraton*.

The Grand Mosque is located to the west of the northern square, facing Mecca. Completed in 1773, it was designed by the court architect Wiryokusumo on the orders of Sultan Hamengkubuwono I (*reg* 1749–92). There is an 18th-century Dutch stronghold, Fort Vredenburg, to the north of the palace, near the southern end of Jalan Malioboro, the name of which is popularly believed to derive from Marlborough. The Pakualam Palace, belonging to the junior line of the Yogyakarta royal family, is located on Jalan Sultan Agung, to the north-east of the *kraton*. In common with other Indonesian capitals, the markets are located outside the palace walls. In Surakarta, the *kraton*, known as the Kashunanan Palace, similarly has open squares to the north and south of the inner sanctum with pavilions and courtyards, and a Grand Mosque west of the northern square. The Mangkunagaran Palace, belonging to the junior royal line, lies to the north-west. All the markets, including the bird market, lie outside the palace boundary.

Royal towns and cities elsewhere in Indonesia are generally not on the scale of those of central Java. Ujung Pandang (formerly Makassar), on the island of Sulawesi, was the capital of one of the archipelago's great mercantile powers, the twin sultanates of Gowa and Tallo'. Work began on the capital in the 16th century, but in 1669 the Dutch East India Company seized the port and dismantled most of its defences. The central citadel of Sultan Hassanudin (*reg* 1629–69), close to the harbour, was occupied by the Dutch and renamed Fort Rotterdam. The Grand Mosque is in the east of the capital, while the shrines belonging to Ujung Pandang's Chinese community are close to the old centre. Makassar also held sway over several neighbouring states to the south, including Bima, on the island of Sumbawa, which later emerged as a powerful independent sultanate. The town of Bima has two palaces, one belonging to the sultan, the other to the prime minister; near by lies a Grand Mosque. The quarters of the experts of Biman customary law were located in the west of the town, close to a rock reputed to be the place where the mythical founder of the royal dynasty first appeared. Another important centre of royal power was at Klungkung in Bali. The heir to the kingdom of Gelgel, it was recognized as the senior court by the other Balinese principalities and assumed pre-eminence in the early 18th century. Unfortunately, much of the palace was damaged by Dutch artillery in 1908, although the gateway and Royal Courts of Justice survived. The law court's pavilions, which are situated close to Klungkung's main road intersection, have ceilings decorated with murals depicting the punishment of miscreants in Hell. Amlapura (formerly Karangasem) was another important royal centre in Bali. The raja controlled neighbouring Lombok, following the Balinese conquest of that island, until the establishment of a separate administration in the town of Mataram. In addition to the raja's palace, Puri Kanginan, built in the early 20th century, there is a water-palace built by the raja in 1947 at Tirtagangga, *c.* 5 km from Amlapura (*see* GARDEN, fig. 33). The Balinese village is laid out according to principles that are different from, but every bit as sophisticated as, those that guided the planners of a great *kraton*.

BIBLIOGRAPHY

T. S. Raffles: *The History of Java* (London, 1817)

C. E. Cunningham: 'Order in the Atoni House', *Bijdr. Taal-, Land- & Vlkenknd.*, cxx/1 (1964), pp. 34–68

H. E. Evers: 'Cities as a "Field of Anthropological Studies" in South-East Asia', *Unity in Diversity: Indonesia as a Field of Anthropological Study*, ed. P. E. Josselin de Jong (Dordrecht, 1984)

A. van Beek: *Life in the Javanese Kraton* (Singapore, 1990)

MICHAEL HITCHCOCK

IV. Sculpture.

1. Introduction. 2. Java. 3. Bali. 4. Sumatra. 5. Other islands.

1. INTRODUCTION. Sculpture in Indonesia from the period before the arrival of Hinduism and Buddhism from India has been found at locations in many parts of the archipelago. The earliest sculptures, of bronze and stone, cannot be dated precisely, but on stylistic grounds they can be tentatively ascribed to the end of the 1st century BC. Throughout the archipelago, especially in Nusa Tenggara Timur (eastern Lesser Sunda Islands), objects have been found that either antedate the arrival of Hinduism and Buddhism or were produced in areas unaffected by Indian religious influences. In many Indonesian islands, especially the outer islands, there is still a tradition of megalithic sculpture associated with animist beliefs and ancestor worship dating from prehistoric times. Megaliths are still made, for example, in Nias and Sumba, but it is in wood-carving that the tradition has been most lively and productive in the late 20th century, and it has survived best in the areas least affected by Hinduism and Buddhism. In Java, Bali and Sumatra, on the other hand, a Classical sculptural style emerged from the 7th century that was closely related to the Classical Hindu and Buddhist architecture of the period (*see* §II, 1(i) and (iii) above). This reached its zenith in Java between the mid-8th century and the mid-10th and then flourished again during the 13th century under the Singhasari dynasty. It also spread to Sumatra and Bali.

Like the architects with whose buildings their work was associated, the stone sculptors of the Early Classical period presumably had neither first-hand experience nor original examples of Indian stone sculpture as models. For this reason, indigenous Indonesian styles were adopted from the beginning for Hindu and Buddhist stone sculpture. On the other hand, small bronze statuettes were easily transportable, and pilgrims returning from India must have brought large numbers back to Indonesia. Consequently, the influence of Indian sculptural styles and Indian iconographical traditions is most clearly visible in Indonesian bronze statuary. Even in the bronzes, however, different local Indian styles were blended to create a new style. Buddhist and Hindu bronzes have been discovered in Java, Sumatra, Lombok, north-east Kalimantan (Kutei), Sulawesi and many other islands, often in areas where no other remains of Indianized culture have been found. They are often stylistically related to others found in Thailand, Malaysia and Vietnam. Some are large, such as the images of the Buddha from Kota Bangun in eastern Kalimantan and Sikendeng on the west coast of Sulawesi (both Jakarta, N. Mus.). Some display stylistic characteristics of the school of Amaravati in Andhra Pradesh, India, notably in the linear treatment of the drapery folds, while others reflect the Gupta-influenced styles of Buddhapad or Nagappattinam.

As the Amaravati school flourished during the 2nd–5th centuries AD, it used to be thought that most of these Buddha statues were among the earliest examples of Buddhist art imported into the archipelago. The fact that they were often discovered in places far from the main cultural centres but always close to the coast led many scholars to suppose that they provided evidence of early Buddhist expansion overseas. However, not only have ideas about the spread of Indian civilization been revised, but it has also become clear that the Amaravati and Gupta styles continued in Indonesia long after the first introduction of Indian religions. Consequently, these much discussed statues are now attributed to the 7th and 8th centuries. Many come not directly from India but from such centres as Anuradhapura in Sri Lanka, where a local school influenced by the art of Amaravati flourished after the style had gone out of fashion in India itself. Although the Buddha images from Sikendeng and Kota Blater, near Jember, East Java (Amsterdam, Rijksmus.), are among the finest examples of Buddhist sculpture found in Indonesia, the Amaravati treatment of drapery found no favour with Indonesian bronze-casters, and the style did not enter the mainstream of Buddhist sculpture of the Early Classical period. In the course of the 9th century distinctly Indonesian styles, based on an amalgamation of Indian styles, began to emerge in bronze sculpture in both Java and Sumatra. Deviations from orthodox Buddhist and Hindu iconography, relatively rare in the sculpture of the Early Classical period in Central Java, became increasingly common as direct contacts with India diminished and Buddhism declined in its country of origin. This dilution of influences was carried still further in Bali. Although modern Indonesian sculptors working in traditional styles usually remain anonymous, some individual masters are known by name, especially in Bali.

BIBLIOGRAPHY

A. J. Bernet Kempers: *Ancient Indonesian Art* (Amsterdam and Cambridge, MA, 1959)

C. Holt: *Art in Indonesia: Continuities and Change* (Ithaca, NY, 1967)

A. Le Bonheur: *La Sculpture indonésienne au Musée Guimet* (Paris, 1971)

T. Bodrogi: *Art in Indonesia* (Greenwich, CT, 1972)

E. M. Bruner and J. Becker, eds: *Art, Ritual and Society in Indonesia*, Ohio U. Papers in International Studies, Southeast Asia Series, 53 (Athens, OH, 1979)
Art of the Archaic Indonesians (exh. cat., Dallas, TX, Mus. F.A., 1982)
Indonesian Primitive Art (exh. cat. by J. P. Barbier, Dallas, TX, Mus. A., 1984)
The Eloquent Dead: Ancestral Sculpture of Indonesia and Southeast Asia (exh. cat., ed. J. Feldman; Los Angeles, UCLA, Mus. Cult. Hist., 1985)
Divine Bronzes: Ancient Indonesian Bronzes from AD 600 to 1600 (exh. cat. by P. L. Scheurleur and M. J. Klokke, Amsterdam, Rijksmus., 1988)
Islands and Ancestors: Indigenous Styles of Southeast Asia (exh. cat., ed. J. P. Barbier and D. Newton; New York, Met., 1988)

2. JAVA. Although no stone sculpture from the period before the arrival of Hinduism and Buddhism in Java is known, a bronze sculpture that has associations with the DONG SON culture of Vietnam has been found at Satus, near Cibarusah, West Java (Jakarta, N. Mus.); it is a figure of a man clad in short trousers, his feet planted firmly on the ground and his arms akimbo. The pose is very similar to that of figures on bronze daggers excavated in Vietnam and at Changsha, Hunan Province, China. Although its archaeological context is unclear, this, the earliest known bronze statue of a Javanese man, could well date from the Bronze or Iron Age. Although the earliest epigraphic evidence of local Indianized cultures in West Java dates from the 5th century AD, with the exception of a few imported pieces, the earliest examples of stone sculpture on the island are from Central Java and date from the 8th century, when the first stone *candi* (ancient Hindu and Buddhist monuments; *see* §II, 1 above) to have survived were built on the Dieng Plateau.

(i) Hindu–Buddhist. (ii) Other traditions.

(i) Hindu–Buddhist.

(a) Early Classical period. (b) Late Classical period.

(a) Early Classical period. Even in the 8th century, at the beginning of the Early Classical period, sculpture in Java displayed elements that were not derived from Indian models. In the temples of the DIENG PLATEAU (*see also* §II, 1(i)(a) above) this tendency is evident from the reliefs of the walls of Candi Srikandi, where the arrangement of the figures of Brahma, Shiva and Vishnu, the gods of the Hindu Trimurti (Trinity), does not seem to have any parallel in India itself. The architectural style of Candi Bima combines elements traceable to both north and south India, but the shape of the heads placed in the arched frames of the false windows owes little to Indian sculpture and seems to prefigure the carved and painted wooden masks of later times for which the Indonesians have always shown a special talent. Typical of Indonesian sculpture of the Early Classical period is the use of the *kāla-makara* motif to frame an arched door or niche. This consists of a *kāla* (a demon's mask with no lower jaw) in the centre of the arch, symbolizing light and fire, and, on either side of its base, two *makara*s (fantastic aquatic animals, combining features of a crocodile and an elephant), symbolizing darkness and water. On both sides scrollwork connects the *kāla* with the *makara.* In the architecture of the Early Classical period the sculptural ornament applied to the façade of the *candi* never competed with the architectural elements but merely filled the space between them and provided visual support with subtle accents. In the course of the period this coordination of architectural and decorative elements was gradually perfected. Unfinished monuments such as Candi Asu, west of Mt Merapi in Central Java, demonstrate that the architects learnt to select the size of their stone building blocks, anticipating the decoration that was to be applied to them. This trend may foreshadow developments during the Late Classical period, when the sculptural ornament sometimes seems to cover the entire structure and has no direct visual relationship with the architectural elements.

Statuary. Early Classical stone statues generally follow the iconographical rules prescribed by Indian texts. There are, however, several as yet not fully explained deviations. At BOROBUDUR the 504 images of the Buddha reveal the bodily characteristics (Skt *lakṣaṇa*) prescribed by the Buddhist texts, such as the cranial protuberance (*uṣṇīṣa*), the curly hair twisting in a clockwise direction and the curl in the centre of the forehead (*ūrṇā*), as well as others, such as elongated ear lobes, which are not specified in the texts but are almost invariably portrayed. While clearly derived from Indian Gupta statues, the round faces of the Buddhas of Borobudur are of the Javanese ethnic type and have a softer, more humane quality than their Indian prototypes. The symbolic gestures (*mudrās*) of the Buddhas conform to Indian precedent, but the way they have been assigned to the Buddhas, which face different directions and are placed on different levels, reveals an iconographical programme that does not seem to be based on one of the transmitted Indian or Indonesian texts. The gesture of teaching or argumentation (*vitarkamudrā*), for example, seems to have been accorded greater importance than it was in the Indian systems.

Early Classical images of Hindu gods reveal a slightly different tendency. While their attributes almost always adhere to the iconographical rules, their poses frequently deviate from Indian models, and this has important effects on the overall composition of the statues. For example, the Indian texts require that representations of Vishnu as Narasimha show the demon-king Hiranyakashipu stretched out on his left thigh, whereas in the statue found at Candi Ijo, Yogyakarta (now Kalasan, Suaka Peninggalan Sejarah dan Purbakala), he is placed on the right thigh, creating a totally different type of composition (see fig. 15). Similarly, representations of Durga, the slayer of the buffalo demon Mahisha (Durga Mahishasuramardini), do not show the goddess in actual combat with the demon, as is common in India, but standing, the battle already won, in one instance even seated in a relaxed pose, on top of the reclining animal, from whose head the dwarfish figure of the slain Mahisha emerges.

At Borobudur and at Candi Sewu and Candi Plaosan almost all the statues were carved in stone: while many have been lost or damaged, the effect that they must once have created can still be imagined. However, at Candi Sewu and Candi Kalasan the principal image in the central cella of the temple was cast in bronze. These huge statues were some 4 m and 6 m tall respectively. They were removed, destroyed and melted down in later times. A few curls of the hair of a bronze statue of the Buddha, perhaps the main image from Candi Sewu, have been preserved (Jakarta, N. Mus. and Surakarta, Radya Pustaka Mus.). At Candi Mendut the three huge statues of Jinas in

15. Vishnu as Narasimha, andesite, 860×390 mm, from Candi Ijo, Central Java, *c.* 9th century (Kalasan, Suaka Peninggalan Sejarah dan Purbakala)

the cella (h. 3 m, 2.4 m and 2.6 m respectively) were carved in stone and have consequently been preserved *in situ*. The central figure of the Shakyamuni Buddha in Candi Mendut (see fig. 16) is closely related stylistically to smaller bronze images such as the altarpiece in the Rijksmuseum voor Volkenkunde, Leiden. The two other flanking statues represent the *bodhisattvas* Avalokiteshvara and Vajrapani. All three, the noblest Buddhist statues in Central Javanese art, are seated on lion thrones, facing each other.

Remains of Hindu *candi* dating from the Early Classical period have been found in many areas throughout Central Java, whereas Buddhist remains are concentrated in only a few areas, which suggests that Hinduism was more widespread than Buddhism at that time. On the other hand, the provenance of the more easily transportable bronze statuettes suggests the opposite: Buddhist statuettes are far more common than those of Hindu gods, and their geographical distribution is much wider. Many scholars have nevertheless assumed that large parts of Central Java, including the entire northern part, were preponderantly Brahmanic, while Buddhism was restricted to relatively small pockets. The scope, size and artistic quality of the Buddhist remains suggests that Buddhism may have been the religion of the ruling élite and Hinduism that of the mass of the people. The two religions seem to have co-existed peacefully, although this mutual tolerance did not preclude competition, as is shown by the presence of major Buddhist temples and Hindu shrines in close proximity to each other. Candi Sewu, one of the largest Buddhist monuments, is only a short distance from Candi Loro Jonggrang at Prambanan, the greatest Hindu shrine in Java. Close to Candi Borobudur once stood the Hindu Candi Banon, where the statues (Jakarta, N. Mus.) are among the largest and finest of the Early Classical period. At Selomerto, not far from the Dieng Plateau, the heartland of Javanese Hinduism, recent excavations have unearthed massive Buddhist stone statuary, although neither at Banon nor at Selomerto have extensive temple ruins been found. It is possible that no *candi* were ever built there and that

16. Shakyamuni Buddha in *dharmacakra mudrā*, stone, h. 2.4 m, Candi Mendut, Central Java, *c.* AD 800

the statues stood in the open or under an open-sided wooden pavilion (*pendopo*).

The Buddhist *candi* of Sari, Kalasan and Plaosan, all situated in the vicinity of Prambanan, have standing figures of deities flanking the doorways and windows. Those of Candi Sari, especially, are among the finest creations of the period. At Candi Kalasan parts of the decorated façade are still covered with a thin, hard layer of plaster. This *vajralepa* ('plaster as hard as diamond') has a double function. By filling the pores of the porous andesite, the volcanic stone used for temple façades, it prevented the growth of moss, fungi and other vegetation. It retained moisture and prevented it from penetrating the stone and may also have served as a ground for colours, although no trace of these has been preserved in Java's humid tropical climate.

In Central Java there was apparently no tradition of inscribing stone images. Even the relatively rare inscriptions on bronze statues consist merely of a standard formula, the so-called Buddhist credo. Only towards the end of the period are inscriptions found, on a few stone statues from East Java, which contain dates of the Shaka era. The Ganesha statue of Kĕtanen bears a date equivalent to 904 and the Ganesha of Kinwu one equivalent to 907.

Reliefs. Both Buddhist sacred books and the ancient Hindu epics the *Rāmāyaṇa* and the *Mahābhārata* exerted a deep and lasting influence on Indonesian culture. These texts not only provided the foundations on which the rich tradition of Old Javanese literature was built but also the subject-matter for narrative reliefs at Borobudur and Candi Loro Jonggrang on a scale unprecedented in the Buddhist and Hindu world. At Candi Borobudur in Central Java, the walls and balustrades of the galleries are covered with 1460 panels of reliefs, illustrating four or more Buddhist texts. Subjects were carefully selected to provide the perambulating pilgrim with a sequence, some 3 km in length, leading to a religious climax. The 160 panels illustrating the Buddhist text *Karmavibhangga*, expounding the law of *karma*, or cause and effect, were covered by a stone terrace before they were completed. The unfinished state of several panels makes it possible to reconstruct some of the procedures adopted for this vast project. First the architects and scholars in charge of construction and decoration assigned the space allotted to a text. Next it was decided which passage was to be illustrated on each individual relief. A brief inscription was carved in the border of the frame to remind the sculptors. These instructions (e.g. 'banner', 'adoration of a sanctuary', 'meeting with great men') were erased on completion of the reliefs; they were not intended to serve as explanatory labels for the spectator. Faithful adherence to the texts required extensive planning. There is some evidence to suggest that planning skills improved as the project progressed. However, the sculptural quality of the earliest panels on the hidden base and the first gallery of Borobudur is far superior to that of the third and fourth galleries, which may have been carved later.

On the first gallery the reliefs of both the main wall and the balustrade are arranged in two superimposed registers. The upper register of the main wall shows the life of the Buddha according to the *Lalitavistara*, ending not with his entrance into *nirvāṇa* but with his Enlightenment. These 120 panels constitute by far the most elaborate illustration of the Buddha's life in the world. The balustrade opposite and the balustrade of the second gallery are devoted to illustrations of edifying stories from the Buddha's previous incarnations (Skt *jātaka*s), in part based on Aryasura's *Garland of Birth Stories* (*Jātakamālā*). All the reliefs of the higher galleries illustrate the *Gandavyuha*, a text describing in detail the encounters with saints and *bodhisattva*s of a pilgrim in search of Supreme Enlightenment. The decision to devote almost one third of all panels to the *Gandavyuha* indicates that this text was held in high esteem. It obliged the sculptors to illustrate the last part of the text almost word by word.

The illustrations combine the monoscenic or isolated method, in which the entire story is represented by one characteristic scene (e.g. the *Story of the Young Quail* from the *Jātakamālā*), and the cyclic or continuous method, in which each panel depicts a different episode of the story in a series of panels separated by vertical bands of scrollwork. The *Karmavibhangga* reliefs, particularly, depict daily life in ancient Java in rich detail. The reliefs illustrating *jātaka*s seem to depict life in India as the sculptors imagined it to be and are therefore not entirely reliable as a source of information on the life and culture of ancient Java. The reliefs of the upper galleries represent a fantastic dream world in which miracles are commonplace, a faithful reflection of the repetitive description in the *Gandavyuha* of the rarefied atmosphere in the miraculous palace of the *bodhisattva*s Maitreya and Samantabhadra.

The location of the unfinished reliefs on the hidden base suggests that the sculptors generally worked clockwise round the monument, following the circumambulatory route (*pradakṣiṇapatha*) prescribed for pilgrims. However, it is also clear that different sculptors or teams of sculptors were active in different places at the same time. Recurrent figures, such as the pilgrim Sudhana in the *Gandavyuha* reliefs, are represented as types, as members of a class identified by their costume, headdress or attributes, not as individuals. The portrayal of the protagonists varies greatly, but although occasionally the work of an individual sculptor can be identified by the use of particular motifs or techniques of representation, the reliefs on the whole represent a remarkably consistent style. The stones used for the reliefs are of small size, and the sculptors generally avoided carving the faces of the figures so that the seams cut through them. Moreover, the protocol requiring that persons of high status be accompanied by a retinue commensurate with their rank led the sculptors to crowd the reliefs with servants and guards, all of whom had to be shown lower than their masters and more or less on the same level. These considerations contribute to a certain monotony of composition and a choice of scenes in keeping with the repetitive character of the texts. In the texts, to which the sculptors adhered so faithfully, there are numerous inconsistencies, scribal errors, interpolations and accretions, and, because the illustrations are so detailed, almost any discrepancy between the reliefs and the texts is an obstacle to correct interpretation and full understanding. Consequently, many panels, especially among those illustrating *jātaka*s, continue to defy adequate interpretation.

At Candi Loro Jonggrang, near the village of Prambanan, narrative reliefs decorate the inner surface of the balustrades of the three main temples dedicated to Shiva, Vishnu and Brahma. Those decorating the Shiva and Brahma temples illustrate the *Rāmāyaṇa*. The manner in which the material has been organized reveals a keen appreciation of the epic story and its dramatic potential. The reliefs of the Shiva temple deal with events taking place on the mainland, concluding with the building of the causeway to Langka by the monkey army. The first half of the reliefs at Candi Brahma illustrate the battles, the deaths of Kumbakarna and Ravana and the victorious home-coming of Rama and Sita. The second half illustrates the subsequent adventures of Sita, her rejection by Rama, her arrival at Valmiki's hermitage, the birth of her sons, their recital of the *Rāmāyaṇa* and their accession to the throne. The reliefs seem to follow a narrative close to Indian versions and quite different from the Old Javanese text thought to be coeval with the temple sculpture. On the other hand, a number of deviations from the Indian versions can be explained only by referring to much later Malay versions in which similar traditions have been preserved. On the balustrade of Candi Vishnu the life of Krishna is illustrated. As at Candi Brahma, the narrative is divided into two. The first half illustrates the well-known acts of heroism performed by the youthful Krishna, ending with the slaying of Kamsa. The reliefs of the second half have not yet been identified.

While the reliefs of Borobudur and Loro Jonggrang reveal many stylistic parallels, there is a marked contrast in spirit. To some extent these differences may be attributed to the contrast in style, content and spirit between the Buddhist *sūtra*s and the Indian epics. This contrast was emphasized by the sculptors of Borobudur, who deliberately played down what little drama there was in their texts in order not to distract the devout spectators from the lofty thoughts evoked by contemplation of the reliefs. At Loro Jonggrang, on the other hand, the sculptors obviously took delight in the tension and drama of the story and availed themselves of every opportunity to depict action, violent or otherwise. The liveliness of the Loro Jonggrang reliefs is further enhanced by the larger size of the stone slabs, which gave the sculptors a freedom of composition not available to their colleagues at Borobudur. Moreover, whereas most of the processions and rows of servants and guards in the Borobudur reliefs do not seem to be integrated with the actions of the protagonists, most of the figures in the Loro Jonggrang reliefs, who are far fewer in number than at Borobudur, play a more active role.

(b) Late Classical period.

Statuary. Towards the end of the 10th century the production of bronze images ceased. The reasons for this are unclear, especially since the art of carving large stone statuary continued without interruption and many bronze ceremonial objects, such as bells, censers, finials, lamps and dishes, often elaborately decorated and engraved, continued to be made. The statues of Bhatara Guru, Surya and Chandra excavated at Gurah near Kediri, East Java (all Jakarta, N. Mus.), have been tentatively dated to the 11th or 12th century. Yet they already reveal many of the characteristics of the sculpture of the 13th and 14th centuries. In the sculpture of the Late Classical period details of dress and jewellery are portrayed in great detail. The batik-like patterns incised in the costumes, the elaborate pectoral ornaments, the sashes tied into bows or floating upwards in defiance of gravity, and the conical crowns (*kiritamukuṭa*) and elaborate headdresses of intricately matted hair (*jaṭāmukuṭa*) lend an air of sumptuousness in striking contrast to the contemplative, inward-looking and noble features of the faces. This contrast and the harmonious blending of the human and the divine have given rise to the long-held view that these are 'portrait statues', images that combine all the iconographical marks of a god or goddess and the facial features of a mortal king or queen believed to have become one on death with the god with whom he or she had been associated when alive. Especially when it was still generally believed that Javanese *candi* were royal tombs, attempts were made to identify statues that were associated with particular sanctuaries as portrait statues of specific royal persons. Since it has become accepted that the function and meaning of the *candi* was commemorative rather than funerary, the concept of a 'portrait sculpture' has been questioned. There is no evidence in the statues believed to be portraits of any attempt to produce likenesses of members of the royal house. At the time it was first seen by Europeans, only one statue, the Prajnaparamita ('Perfection of Wisdom', sometimes thought of as the 'mother' or source of all Buddhas) from Candi Singasari (Jakarta, N. Mus.), was considered by the Javanese to be a portrait of a queen. The only indisputable 'portrait statue' is that of King Kertanagara of Singasari (*reg* 1268–92), portrayed as the Jina (Buddha) Akshobhya, now standing in a park in the centre of Surabaya, East Java. Popularly known as Joko Dolok ('Brother Fatso'), it is inscribed with a hymn to the King and a date, corresponding to 1289, proving the statue to have been carved during the King's lifetime. A slightly smaller, uninscribed, version of the same statue stands in front of the PAKRI building in Malang, south of Surabaya. Damage to the faces and crude efforts at restoration of both statues have made it impossible to establish any facial resemblance between the two.

Statues identified with specific royal persons are executed in a style inconsistent with the dates of those rulers they are thought to represent. It is generally accepted that statues dating from the Singasari kingdom (1222–92) show standing kings and queens, or gods and goddesses, flanked by lotuses growing from tubers on the lotus pedestals, whereas those of the subsequent Majapahit period show lotuses growing from pots or jars. Only in the image of a standing goddess or queen from Jebuk, Tulungagung (see fig. 17), does the lotus, symbol of rebirth, occupy the entire back of the statue. Some scholars have attempted to distinguish between 'portrait statues' and images of gods. It has been suggested that the empty conch is an attribute of the god Vishnu, while a conch with a live snail in it (as in the statue from Candi Sumberjati; Jakarta, N. Mus.) indicates a 'portrait statue'. Another suggestion is that 'portrait statues' wear conical headgear, whereas icons of gods have the tall *jaṭāmukuṭa*. These distinctions have not gained universal acceptance. A special type of 'portrait

17. Standing goddess or queen, andesite, h. 1.56 m, from Jebuk, Tulungagung, East Java, late 14th century or early to mid-15th (Jakarta, National Museum)

sculpture' is represented by two statues from Jebuk (both Jakarta, N. Mus.). The group of a divine or royal couple represents a humanized version of the Indian Alinganamurti (seated Shiva with his consort Parvati on his lap). The attributes of the gods have been dispensed with, and the sculptor has created an intimate human scene. The queen is thought to be Queen Suhita, who ruled the Majapahit kingdom from 1429 to 1447 and who may also be the subject of the statue of the standing queen. There is indeed a facial resemblance between the two figures. Such human, almost non-iconic, statuary appears to be represented only from this site.

The greatest masterpieces of East Javanese sculpture were originally enshrined in a group of *candi* at Candirenggo, Singasari, near Malang. From the one surviving *candi* (which was left unfinished), all but one of the statues were taken to the Netherlands early in the 19th century; two other statues were removed from ruins of other temples in the immediate vicinity. The finest of these statues, an image of Prajnaparamita, was returned to Indonesia in 1978. Three similar statues, all now headless, represent the same goddess. The entire Prajnaparamita is thought to portray Dedes, first queen of Singasari (and wife of Rajasa (*reg* 1222–7)), from whom all subsequent rulers of Singasari and Majapahit were descended. A statue of the demonic Chakrachakra, probably a form of the god Bhairava (Leiden, Rijksmus. Vlkenknd.), from one of the subsidiary Singasari temples, illustrates the importance of the cult of Bhairava at the East Javanese court. This cult spread to Sumatra and Bali (*see* §§3(ii) and 4(i) below). About 150 statues of Durga Mahishasuramardini, one of the most popular figures of the Hindu pantheon, have been preserved in Central and East Java. The two finest representations of Durga are from Candi Singasari (Leiden, Rijksmus. Vlkenknd.) and from Candi Jawi (Surabaya, Mus. Negeri Jawa Timur Mpu Tantular). The first gives a highly theatrical, dramatic interpretation of the ancient epic story, whereas the second achieves a more elegant, aesthetic effect. Both follow the same iconographical tradition and date from the early 14th century.

Towards the end of the Majapahit kingdom (late 13th century), the expressive movement of the statues began to stiffen, and the figures stand rigidly erect without flexion of the body. Statues such as the Shiva Mahadeva and the Parvati from Jugo, Mojoroto, Kediri (Jakarta, N. Mus., nos 6347 and 6348), are typical of this style. In the final years of the Late Classical period (late 15th century), a new, dynamic style of sculpture, parallel to similar developments in narrative reliefs, originated in the sanctuaries on Mt Lawu in Central Java at Candi Sukuh and Candi Ceto. At Candi Sukuh (see fig. 9 above) are two statues of winged figures, half-man, half-bird, one dated in accordance with the year 1441, the other with 1442. The standing figure of Bhima (Surakarta, Radya Pustaka Mus., K.R.T. Hardjonagoro Col.) bears a date corresponding to 1443. The bold, monumental style is quite different from any of the earlier sculpture. At Candi Ceto kneeling figures in the same manner have been found. It is possible that this last style of the Hindu–Buddhist period spread to West Java, where remains of Indo-Javanese culture before the 14th and 15th century are scarce. The stone sculpture from Gunung Cibodas in West Java reveals features similar to 15th-century statues in Central Java and Sumatra.

Reliefs. Sixteen reliefs incorporating waterspouts have been found at the bathing-place Jalatunda on the west slope of Mt Penanggungan in East Java (several now Jakarta, N. Mus.). They illustrate legends from the lives of the ancestors of the legendary Indian king Udayana and their spouses. An inscription *in situ* consists of a date corresponding to 977. The bathing-place was therefore constructed during the lifetime of a late 10th-century Javanese prince, Udayana, who reigned in Bali from *c.* 989 to *c.* 1022 and was the father of King Airlangga (*reg* 1019–49). The Javanese perceived a close analogy between the pedigree of the legendary Udayana, illustrated in the reliefs, and the ancestors of their own royal house. The reliefs mark a radical departure from the Early Classical style and represent a style transitional between the narrative reliefs of Central Java and those of the Late Classical period. The tendency to reduce carving from a three- to a two-dimensional representation, typical of the Late Classical period, is not yet apparent: the carving is deep and round, suggesting a style borrowed from techniques perfected in more malleable media such as clay or wood. The retinue that crowds the reliefs of Borobudur has been dispensed with, and even the kings and queens no longer appear in royal attire.

The first half of the Late Classical period, when the kingdom of Kediri flourished (929–1222), roughly coincides with the golden age of Javanese literature, when many great poems (*kakawin*) were created at the East Javanese courts. Hardly any sculpture or monuments have been preserved from this time, but the poets seem to have provided a new source of inspiration for subsequent sculptors, and many 14th- and 15th-century monuments in East Java are decorated with reliefs illustrating stories from Javanese literature. Just as the Javanese poets transformed the themes borrowed from the Indian epics by placing them in a Javanese setting, so the sculptors transformed the exploits of the legendary heroes and heroines into new art forms in which the characters, dressed as Javanese, are set against a lush background of tropical vegetation. Among the most popular themes are the adventures of Arjuna, based on the Javanese poem *Arjunawiwaha*, composed by Mpu Kanwa in the early 11th century, the descent into hell of Sri Tanjung and Kunjarakarna, and the Javanese versions of the Indian epics *Rāmāyaṇa* and *Kṛṣṇāyāṇa*.

The style of East Javanese reliefs is often called the *wayang* style, after the shadow-puppet plays that deal with closely related themes (*see* §VI below). Although the 'lobster claw' (Jav. *supit urang*) headdress of the heroes from epic literature and the shallow depth of the carving are reminiscent of the leather puppets of the *wayang*, there is no evidence that the sculptors imitated them directly. The two art forms seem to have existed independently, although it is likely that the versions of the stories that the *wayang* puppeteers invented found their way on to the reliefs. The relatively small scale of most East Javanese *candi* seems to have invited a less structured arrangement of the reliefs, and instead of the rigid, clockwise sequences characteristic of the great Central Javanese monuments, the narrative of the principal series of reliefs is interrupted

18. Ganesha in a smithy, volcanic stone, 1.62×2.18 m, Candi Sukuh, Central Java, 15th century

by subsidiary tales that provide reflection and commentary to the main themes. Such series of narrative reliefs occur at Candi Jawi (*c.* 1292), at the 14th-century *candi* of Jabung, Kedaton, Panataran, Tigawangi, Surawana and Jago and several 15th-century monuments on Mt Penanggungan.

During the 15th century, as Islam spread over Java from its early strongholds on the north coast, the adherents of the old religion retreated to mountain sanctuaries such as Candi Sukuh. In Central Java, where for most of the Late Classical period no narrative reliefs were produced, sculptors created a new, forceful style. In the precincts of the temple are several obelisks, with reliefs on the base representing the story of Garuda and other, as yet unidentified scenes.

There are also other unidentified reliefs, the most famous of which depicts Ganesha in a smithy (see fig. 18). The sandstone reliefs at Candi Sukuh all deal with the theme of deliverance, either in the form of redemption from slavery (Garuda's mother, Vinata), liberation from a terrible curse (Durga) or magic recovery from blindness (Tambrapetra). This general theme, treated in many different ways, is represented in deeply carved reliefs of a forceful, dynamic quality. Lacking the delicate elegance of East Javanese reliefs, they are sometimes considered to be more akin to folk art than to formal religious art, but their strength and vitality are remarkable in an art form on the brink of extinction.

(ii) Other traditions. The existence of sculptures portraying animals on early Islamic monuments and graves, such as the winged gateway of Sendangduwur (see fig. 11 above), on which deer similar to those at Candi Sukuh are depicted instead of *makara* heads in association with the *kāla* motif, indicates that the Islamic injunction against the representation of human and animal forms was not immediately accepted in Java. Nevertheless, Islam did eventually extinguish the Hindu–Javanese tradition of figurative sculpture in Java itself, and it survived only in Bali in a much modified form. The sculptor's art in Java is now confined almost exclusively to the purely decorative carving of wood, ivory and bone on such objects as *keris* and musical instruments, the making of wooden *wayang golek* and *wayang klitik* figures and images such as the traditional *loro blonyo* figures of the goddess Shri and her consort Sadono (sometimes said to represent Vishnu) that are placed in front of the ritual marriage bed (*kobongan*) in Java (see fig. 19). Sculpture was also applied to architecture, for example in the carving of geometric and foliated patterns on doors, shutters and screens, especially in Cirebon, Japara, Kudus and other cities on the north coast of Java.

19. *Loro blonyo* figures, wood, pigment, gold leaf, fish glue, copper gilt and silk thread, h. 540 mm and 580 mm, from Yogyakarta, Central Java, early 19th century (Leiden, Rijksmuseum voor Volkenkunde)

BIBLIOGRAPHY

A. J. Bernet Kempers: 'Hindu–Javanese Bronzes', *Ind. A. & Let.*, ix/2 (1935), pp. 92–100
J. Blom: *The Antiquities of Singasari* (Leiden, 1939)
J. Fontein, R. Soekmono and S. Suleiman: *Ancient Indonesian Art of the Central and East Javanese Periods* (New York, 1971)
B. Ashabranner and M. Ashabranner: '*Loro Blonyo*: Traditional Sculpture of Central Java', *A. Asia* (May–June 1986), pp. 112–19

JAN FONTEIN, R. SOEKMONO

3. BALI. Although Balinese sculpture has adopted ideas, forms and elements from other cultures, these have always been adapted to the Balinese people's own way of living and thinking and have always been powerfully imbued with their beliefs and rituals and the strength of their socio-religious institutions.

(i) Before 1343. (ii) After 1343.

(i) Before 1343. Before the advent of Hinduism and Buddhism, the Balinese, like most Indonesian peoples, were animist in religion, worshipping their ancestors and believing in the sacredness of high places. Their funerary customs were characterized by the burial of the dead in stone sarcophagi, sometimes decorated with knobs in the form of grotesque human heads reminiscent of later Balinese demonic masks. One such sarcophagus from Taman Bali, now in the Pejeng Museum, Bedulu, is in the form of two strange creatures, one on top of the other, with crudely carved human heads, long necks and the outline of four legs incised on the stone. Some of these sarcophagi were found with various objects in them, such as miniature bronze hoes, for the dead person to use in the next world. A number of bronze objects of Dong Son type have also been found in Bali, notably the famous kettle gong known as the 'Moon of Pejeng' (Pejeng, Archaeol. Mus.). This gong, which is of exceptional height for a Dong Son gong (1.86 m), is decorated with incised geometric patterns. There is no evidence, however, to determine whether it was made in Bali or imported, although fragments of a stone mould for impressing the

design of a drum on to a wax layer was discovered in 1932 at Manuaba, in Gianyar district.

From the 7th century AD Buddhist monks reached Bali. The Balinese rulers gained information from them concerning Indian methods of state organization and began to summon Indian advisers and priests to their courts, hoping thereby to legitimize and consolidate their authority. All the dynasty's claims received superterrestrial sanction by religious consecration and a genealogical tree that traced its descent from the Indian pantheon, while at the same time the rulers themselves became temporary incarnations of Hindu deities or manifestations of the Buddha. Some of the most impressive early Hindu sculpture in Bali has survived as a result of this deification of Balinese rulers. In particular, important monuments incorporating stone sculpture were constructed by the rulers in the area now occupied by the villages of Intaran, Pejeng and Bedulu. However, the earliest epigraphic evidence of Indianization in Bali dates only from the late 9th century. Hindu and Buddhist influences became particularly strong after the marriage in 989 of a Balinese prince Udayana to an East Javanese princess Mahendradatta, an event generally considered to mark the beginning of a process of 'Javanization' of Balinese culture. In the 12 years during which Udayana and Mahendradatta ruled together, Tantric rites and the practice of magic were introduced, a process with which Mahendradatta is particularly associated. Her funeral monument is at Pura Kedarman on a hill near Kutri. In accordance with her reputation as a witch, Mahendradatta is represented in the form of a 2 m-high image of the goddess Durga slaying the buffalo demon Mahisha (Durga Mahishasuramardini), encircled by fluttering ribbons and with leaping flames licking round her, further signs of her superhuman energies. In her six hands she holds a javelin, an arrow, a bow, a flaming disc (*cakra*), a shield and a winged flaming conch. A characteristic stylistic feature of this figure is the horizontal cylindrical ornament on the lower part of the crown above the forehead. The only other place where decorations of this kind have been found is the series of seven water-spouts at Goa Gajah (Elephant Cave), near Bedulu, which from the early 11th century was a retreat for meditating Shaivites. It is probable that these spouts date from the same period or shortly after. They stand against the rear wall of the bathing-place south of the cave of Goa Gajah, which was excavated and renovated in 1954–5. Six of them are statues of volcanic tufa in the form of female deities, with large round water-spouts in their bellies. The seventh is a figure of Ganesha. The style of the figures, particularly their facial expression, is decidedly Javanese.

Less evidently derived from any Javanese model is the exuberantly carved entrance, one of the best-known examples of early Hindu sculpture in Bali. Above the narrow 2 m-high door a demon with large, round eyes and powerful incisor teeth is forcing its head through the rock, which it has already split in two and pushed asunder with its hands. The rock wall is completely covered with carvings of rocks, plants and waves; there are figures of people and animals fleeing in terror symbolizing man's insignificance and powerlessness in the face of the demonic forces of nature. A pavilion in front of the cave entrance contains another important sculpture from the same period, a figure of the ogress Hariti, which is thought to date from about the year 1000. It may have belonged to a nearby Buddhist settlement and been erected in front of Goa Gajah at a later date. According to a *jātaka* story, Hariti was a feared child-eater who, after being converted by the Buddha himself, became the goddess of fecundity and the patron deity of children. She is portrayed surrounded by a swarm of children, although her small sharp teeth and large round eyes reveal her former demonic character. Hariti and her husband entered Balinese folklore as Men and Pan Brayut and have been portrayed by countless masons throughout Balinese history.

King Udayana probably died in 1011, some years after his wife. The double portrait of a standing king and queen in the highest mountain temple of Bali (Pura Tegeh Koripan on the edge of the crater of Mt Batur) dates from that year. The facial features of the royal couple can be clearly distinguished. They each stand on a lotus pedestal and carry a ritual object in their colossal hands, which are held clasped in front of the stomach. They are separated by a dividing wall. However, it has not been definitely established whether this work is a joint monument to Udayana and Mahendradatta. The nine huge royal tombs in the temple complex of Pura Gunung Kawi (*see* §II, 1(ii) above) provide the most impressive evidence of the strong Javanese influence at the Balinese courts and of the growing importance of royal funeral cults in the early 11th century. Royal cults and the worship of deified ancestors continued to play an important part in Balinese religion in the 12th–14th centuries, as is shown by the great number of images of deities and royal portrait statues dating from this period. It is evident that these statues, which are clearly distinguished from each other by various individual characteristics, were created as temporary vessels for the souls of deceased kings and queens, by means of which those who remained behind could make contact with their dynastic ancestors. The soft, friable volcanic tufa from which these were made deteriorates rapidly, and many of those that have survived in a relatively good state have done so only because they have been reinforced with a thin layer of cement.

At Pura Tegeh Koripan on Mt Penulisan in northern Bali, Pura Gaduh in Blahbatuh, Gianyar, central Bali, and Pura Canggi near Sakah, also in central Bali, are whole series of deliberately grouped portrait figures in stone, bronze and wood that appear to be images of royal wives, priests and ministers as well as of deities, including Ganesha, the Shiva *liṅga* and the *caturkāya*s (four-sided images). These images are not, however, associated with the worship of the Hindu deities they represent, but with court ancestor worship; they symbolize the character and deeds of the dead person, who is portrayed in the form of the god whom he was believed to incarnate during his lifetime. Wooden burial figures of the 13th and 14th centuries also have attributes of royalty, such as crowns with aureoles, earrings and lotus buds, which they hold with their two hands placed one above the other. Examples of these rare and often badly worn figures, which are the earliest known Balinese wooden sculptures, may be seen in Bali, Leiden and Switzerland. They are 290–410 mm tall. During the 13th and 14th centuries a gradual amalgamation of Hindu and indigenous Balinese elements took place, particularly in the portrait statues of rulers. These figures can be seen as Hinduized versions of ancient pre-Hindu ancestor figures, which they also resemble externally in their solid, hieratic and stylized appearance. The Indonesian artists endeavoured to imbue their statues with the power and energy that they attributed to the ancestors, and the same striving left its mark on the style of many of the royal portraits.

A number of demonic figures in the temple of Kebo Edan, near the village of Intaran in Pejeng, have their roots in a different spiritual climate and can be regarded as the departure point for a development that persisted to modern times, finding artistic expression in countless demonic sculptures and masks. The temple of Kebo Edan is probably a Balinese version of the Tantric magic temples at Bhairawa in southern Nepal. It is known that the Javanese king Kertanagara, who ruled over Bali for several years, sought salvation in magic cults of the Kalaohakra sects and gave court religion a Bhairawa-like slant, and that Shaivite and Buddhist cults, which increasingly overlapped and fused with one another, were influenced by Tantric concepts and practices. The demonic character of the religious ideas can be clearly seen in the few sculptures dating from this period. Towering above the inner courtyard of Pura Kebo Edan is a 3 m-tall figure (now badly damaged) of Bhairava, Shiva in his terrifying aspect. It is accompanied by *rākṣasas*, demonic guard figures in a threatening stance and adorned with skulls, a mark of Singhasari art. One of the demons is holding a large skull in front of him as a drinking vessel. Accompanying the Bhairava figure are a female and a male buffalo with their heads thrown back and Ganesha statues, also decorated with skulls.

One of the first works of Balinese sculpture to depart from Hindu-Javanese norms in favour of an original indigenous iconography can be found in a small pavilion of the temple of Pura Puseh Gaduh in Blahbatuh. This is a stone demon's head *c.* 1.2 m high, with pouting lips, a wide nose, large round eyes and wearing a cylindrical headdress that shows Buddhist influence. According to popular belief, this sculpture represents the powerful, legendary builder and minister Kebo Iwa, who is thought to have served the King of Bedahulu in the 14th century, immediately before he was overthrown by the East Javanese Majapahit empire. Kebo Iwa is also reputed to have used his fingernails to scratch out from the rock the stylistically unique life-size scenes depicted in relief on a 27 m-long tufa wall at Yeh Pulu, near Bedulu. These narrate the story of a wild boar hunt, and they depict horsemen, huntsmen armed with spears and machetes, and people carrying liquor in earthenware jugs. Other details include an old woman peeping out of a half-open door and another trying to grab a horse's tail. These brief scenes from everyday life are, however, depicted in a crude, almost rustic style that has no visible connection with modern Balinese art.

(ii) After 1343. After the subjection of Bali to the Majapahit empire in 1343, the colonizers found a society in which the values and contents of the Indian and Javanese epics had already reached a wider public beyond the court, and this was to have a lasting impact on the spread of the plastic arts. The new rulers' policy of rapprochement with the villages was far removed from the remote god-kingship of earlier times. It is therefore not surprising that the huge sculptures of deified royal ancestors characteristic of earlier times disappeared from art in Bali.

From the mid-14th century Balinese sculpture began to reflect the influence of the informal art characteristic of Majapahit Java. On the Majapahit model, groups of artists and artisans were employed in and around the fortified royal villages (*kraton*) of Samprangan and Gelgel and the courts of the regional governors and their associated temples. In the larger villages and towns the local district associations (*banjar*) had taken over, as part of their duties, the increasingly widespread cults of the dead and the many and varied artistic activities linked with them. Thus, through their cremation ceremonies, the population of the villages experienced the influence of the new art. At the same time, the refined, formal and sometimes mannered style of the court showed itself more in decoration and ornamentation than in subject-matter. This court art did not develop any truly popular forms or styles that were adopted in vernacular sculpture until after the Dutch had seized power in the 19th century (northern Bali) and early 20th (southern Bali). Following political restructuring, many of the palaces lost their traditional role of lavishly proclaiming their owners' status, and masons subsequently confined themselves to decorating public buildings in their own communities, in particular the doors, walls and shrines of temples. The influence of tourism, together with the artistic requirements of private and state institutions and the relative affluence of many Balinese from all social levels and castes, meant that artisan skills (especially stone-carving) underwent a revival in the 20th century. Batubulan, for example, became a well-known centre of stone-carving. The names of some modern masons are widely known. A village, a district council, a hotel, a bank or a state institution would bring such a specialist, sometimes from a considerable distance, to design pilasters and antefixes, coordinate the work and even execute it alongside a group of craftsmen and masons. The resulting figures and decorative elements are often derived from the repertory of Indian or Hindu-Javanese epics and legends, especially the *Rāmāyaṇa* and the *Mahābhārata.*

One of the specialities of modern Balinese masons is sculpture in the round, particularly in the form of guardian figures placed in front of entrance doors. These are mainly demon figures, often fashioned in an exaggeratedly expressive and grotesque way. Other common places for sculptures in the round are the bases of pillars acting as roof supports in larger temples or residential buildings. Heroes from the *Rāmāyaṇa* and the *Mahābhārata*, figures of priests or musicians flank temple terraces and stairways. The most favoured areas for stone reliefs are the walls of temples and palaces. These are mainly scenes in low relief drawn from the great epics, heroic legends and fairy tales or, in the case of temples to the dead, harsh portrayals of existence in hell (see fig. 20).

Wood-carvers observe a similar iconography. Doors and windows are richly adorned with relief carving, sometimes painted or gilded. The frames are decorated with flower or foliage motifs, and the wings with mythical birds, scenes from the *Rāmāyaṇa* epic, figures in the

20. Relief depicting the punishment of sinners in hell, volcanic tufa, *c.* 1.00×0.55 m, Pura Dalem (temple to the dead), Bangli, Bali, 1920–30

21. Crowned Bhoma head, wood, painted red, h. 425 mm, from Bali, probably 19th century (Basle, Museum für Volkerkunde und Schweizerisches Museum für Volkskunde)

wayang style, fabulous animals such as winged lions and, at the bottom, chthonic creatures such as crabs. Above, at the centre of the frame, a *bhoma* head, derived from the kāla head of Central Javanese temple architecture, keeps guard, its lower jaw often merging into vegetal ornamentation or forming the starting point for intricate volutes and leaf-and-flower arabesques (see fig. 21). Much of the plant ornamentation is based on the motif of the creeping tendrils of the lotus and its root at the centre. This symmetrical type has given rise to numerous subsidiary forms, some showing Chinese and others Dutch influence. Wooden rafters, especially the supporting socle of the ridge pillar, provide a favourite surface for wooden sculptures, which draw mainly on the religious idiom of Hinduism but also reveal Chinese influence, especially in their representation of winged lions. The socles often show a combination of different *karang* motifs. At the centre of a patterned section may be found demons' heads with one or two protruding eyes above a row of upper incisors, tusks and a hanging tongue. Corners may be embellished with a *karang curing*, the upper part of a bird's beak with sharp teeth and one eye; or a *karang asti*, an elephant's head, sometimes without a lower jaw. Many wooden sculptures show gods and heroes, demons and animals full-length and again reveal the strong influence of the *Rāmāyaṇa* and the *Mahābhārata*. One form of sculpture with a clearly defined function is the wooden stand for holding the *keris* or dagger (*see* §VIII, 9 below). This may either be in the form of a god, a hero or a demon, in whose hand or mouth the *keris* is placed, or may be in a more informal, imaginative style and represent an infant or a frog or toad with open mouth.

Also characteristic of Bali is the use of individual decorative elements carved from *paras*, a form of volcanic tufa. These are fluently interwoven and overlapped, with anthropomorphic or zoomorphic head motifs usually dissolving into plant decorations in the form of interlacing scrolls, leaves and flowers. As tufa can be worked almost like wood, it is not surprising that works created from both materials are notable for the same rich ornamentation.

BIBLIOGRAPHY

P. de K. Angelino: 'De bouwerken van Kebo-Joewa', *Ned.-Indië Oud & Nieuw*, vi/3 (1921), pp. 70–83

P. A. J. Moojen: *Kunst op Bali: Inleidende studie tot de bouwkunst* (The Hague, 1926)

W. O. J. Nieuwenkamp: 'De olifantsgrot bij Bedoeloe', *Ned.-Indië Oud & Nieuw*, x/11 (1926), pp. 333–41

——: *Beeldhouwkunst van Bali* (The Hague, 1928), ii of *Inlandsche kunst van Nederlandsch Oost-Indie*

W. F. Stutterhiem: *Oudheden van Bali: Het oude rijk van Pejeng*, 2 vols (Singaraja, 1929–30)

——: *Indian Influences in Old Balinese Art* (London, 1935)

M. Covarrubias: *Island of Bali* (London, 1937/*R* Oxford, 1972)

R. Goris: *Prasasti Bali*, 2 vols (Bandung, 1954)

U. Ramseyer: *The Art and Culture of Bali* (Oxford, New York and Jakarta, 1977/*R* Singapore, Oxford and New York, 1986)

G. Spitzing: *Bali: Tempeln, Myth und Volkskunst auf der tropischen Insel zwischen indischen und pazifischen Ozean* (Cologne, 1983)

URS RAMSEYER

4. SUMATRA.

(i) Pre-Classical. Among the most remarkable sculptures that pre-date the arrival of Hinduism and Buddhism are the megalithic stone statues from the Pasemah Plateau, near Pagaralam in southern Sumatra. Some of these are associated with slab graves, as at Tegurwangi. Some statues are carved in the round, as for example the figure from Pematang of a man riding a buffalo. Others are carved in low relief, using the natural shape of the boulder, as in the stones from Airpurah and Batugajah (Palembang, Mus. Badaruddin), the latter of which shows a warrior riding an elephant. The stone from Airpurah shows two warriors carrying a kettledrum. The sculptures, carved in a vigorous and dynamic manner, are the products of a local late prehistoric (approx. 2000-year-old) culture, and the kettledrum depicted on the stone is of a type associated with the Dong Son style of bronzeworking (*see* §VIII, 9 below). The technique used is very similar to that used in reliefs found near the tumulus of the Chinese general He Quping (*d* 117 BC) in Shaanxi Province, China. Examples of the bronze kettledrums themselves have been discovered at several places in Sumatra; it is not known whether they were made locally or imported. In the district of Kerinci, central Sumatra, a ceremonial bronze vessel of Dong Son type has also been found, and at Bangkinang, in South Sumatra, 14 bronze figurines were found 4 m below ground. They are furnished with suspension loops, and their style is unique and presumed to be local. In 1991 another Dong Son drum was discovered in Tampung, southernmost Sumatra. Another drum and well-preserved bronze flask were also found at another site in the same province.

(ii) Classical. Two concentrations of Classical sculpture have been found in Sumatra, at Palembang and at Padang Lawas, in addition to scattered discoveries elsewhere. Palembang was probably the capital of Srivijaya, a Mahayana Buddhist state that flourished in Sumatra, Peninsular Malaysia and western Borneo from the 7th century to the 11th (*see* THAILAND, §IV, 2). Buddhist and Hindu sculptures have both been found there. The statuary displays elements comparable to those of several Indian schools (Gupta, post-Gupta, Pallava and Pala). Some art historians detect a unique Srivijayan style, but too few images can certainly be associated with Srivijaya to make it possible to describe such a style convincingly. Srivijaya was a powerful maritime trading state and a centre of Buddhist learning, but its artistic influence as well as its precise extent are still debated.

The oldest statue from Palembang is a granite image of the Buddha in a style similar to that of Amaravati (2nd–5th centuries) but probably dating from the late 7th century or early 8th. A stone head of Vishnu from Bangka may be older; it resembles 6th-century Pallava art and similar images found in West Java, perhaps carved during the period of the Sundanese Taruma kingdom. Other important bronzes from Palembang are a group of the Buddha, Maitreya, and Avalokiteshvara, ascribed to the 9th or 10th century and thought to have been locally made. Another group of three bronzes portraying Vishnu, Brahma and Shiva is in 14th- or 15th-century Majapahit style, reflecting Majapahit domination of Sumatra during the reign of Hayam Wuruk (Rajasanagara; *reg* 1350–89). Padang Lawas, in the hinterland of North Sumatra, was a centre of Tantric Buddhism from at least the 11th century. A bronze statue of a four-armed Avalokiteshvara or Lokanatha (h. 455 mm; Jakarta, N. Mus.) found at Gunungtua bears an inscription in Old Malay, indicating local manufacture, and, most unusually, giving the name of the smith, Surya, and the date (corresponding to 1039). Stone statuary includes an image (h. 1.18 m) of Heruka, one of the most terrifying deities of Kalachakra Buddhism, associated with sorcery and human sacrifice, found in the central chamber of Biaro Bahal II, Padang Lawas. Other images include Bhairava (Shiva in his terrifying aspect) and his consort Bhairavi, dating from the 13th or 14th century. Some brick temples were adorned with sculpted reliefs of dancing *yakṣa*s, humans with animal heads, which may represent masks.

Several important images have been found in the adjacent provinces of Jambi and West Sumatra. At Jambi, besides a post-Gupta Buddha image, a *makara* bearing a date equivalent to 1064 has been found as well as a beautiful image of the female Buddhist deity Prajnaparamita. The style of this statue is very close to another found in East Java and made in the 13th-century kingdom of Singasari. A statue of the eight-armed Avalokiteshvara, Amoghapasha, has been found, which was sent in 1286 from the kingdom of Singasari as a token of political domination. An enormous Bhairava from Sungailangsat probably depicts Adityavarman, ruler of the kingdom of Malayu (Dharmasraya) in the mid-14th century. At Batusangkar, near Adityavarman's former palace, are pieces of two statues now mistakenly cemented together that may date from the 8th or 9th century. One of Sumatra's most beautiful images is an isolated discovery: a head of Lokeshvara with three figures of the Jina Buddha Amitabha in his crown, found in Aceh, the northernmost province of Sumatra.

BIBLIOGRAPHY

Nik Hasan Shuhaimi: 'The Bukit Seguntang Buddha: A Reconsideration of its Date', *J. Malay. Branch Royal Asiat. Soc.*, lii/2 (1979), pp. 33–40
O. W. Wolters: 'Studying Srivijaya', *J. Malay. Branch Royal Asiat. Soc.*, lii/2 (1979), pp. 1–32
M. C. Subhadradis Diskul, ed.: *The Art of Srivijaya* (Kuala Lumpur, 1980)

JOHN N. MIKSIC

(iii) Continuing traditions. As elsewhere in Indonesia, in Sumatra the Hindu–Buddhist sculpture of the Classical period did not completely displace the indigenous pre-Classical tradition or prevent other influences from being absorbed. At Pugungraharjo, Lampung Province, southern Sumatra, a 'Polynesian-style' stone statue with some characteristics resembling Late Classical sculpture has been found in association with a megalithic complex, large earthworks and ceramics and statuary dating from the late 15th century. The continuation of indigenous traditions into modern times is particularly evident in the wooden sculpture of the Bataks of central Sumatra, such as in ritual objects used by the *datu*, a person who can manipulate the protective or destructive powers of magic. The containers (*naga morsarang*) for magic substances and the *datu*'s staff often show rows of human figures and representations of the *singa*, a mythical being combining features of the buffalo, elephant and serpent that, according to Batak myth, carries the world on its back. The *singa* also appears on the façades of Toba Batak houses, where its head decorates one end of the major load-bearing beam. Characteristically, the *singa* representation has a highly ornamental, composite form, with large, circular eyes and a long tongue; it is also covered with ornate, intricate surface decorations. Its tongue and head may incorporate small human figures. Quite different from the ornamental nature of these objects are the wooden masks used in funeral rituals, in particular by the Toba, Karo, Simalungun and Pakpak Bataks. They are carved in well-defined contours, with a precise curve from eyebrows to the nose and large facial planes. Frequently hair is attached. The Toba and Pakpak Bataks have also developed a stone-carving tradition, expressed chiefly in sarcophagi and figures set up as funerary monuments. The *singa* image often decorates the sarcophagi. Stone figures of the deceased, often riding a horse or other animal, are also found.

BIBLIOGRAPHY

Art of the Archaic Indonesians (exh. cat., Dallas, TX, Mus. F.A., 1982)
J.-P. Berbier: 'The Batak of Sumatra', *Indonesian Primitive Art* (exh. cat. by J.-P. Berbier, Dallas, TX, Mus. A., 1984), pp. 46–75
——: 'A Stone Rider of the Batak of Sumatra', *Islands and Ancestors. Indigenous Styles of Southeast Asia* (exh. cat., ed. J.-P. Berbier and D. Newton; New York, Met., 1988), pp. 50–66
A. Sibeth: *Batak* (London, 1991)

5. OTHER ISLANDS. Sculpture in the pre-Classical tradition is still made in some more remote areas of western Indonesia and in the eastern islands. Here the social organization focuses especially strongly on the lineage linking a particular group of people together, and artistic representations are therefore produced for the village communities, for lineages or for individuals, but not generally for the entire region. The iconography of such sculpture is primarily concerned with ancestral lineage, fertility and continuity. Apart from male and female ancestor figures, the most widespread form is the protective image of the dragon–snake. In contrast to the production of textiles, the carving of wood and stone are male activities. It is always difficult and sometimes impossible to establish a chronology for the sculpture of the Outer islands. The documentation of the material only began at the end of the 19th century, and art historical research *in situ* is a recent development. While some stylistic and iconographic interpretations formerly concentrated on demonstrating external prehistoric and historic influences on Indonesia's indigenous artistic traditions, modern archaeological evidence and reinterpretations of ancient inter-island trade, together with the presence of certain distinctive designs in early pottery, indicate the continuity of prehistoric indigenous tradition.

In the south of Nias, an island off the west coast of Sumatra, there is a well developed stone-carving tradition. The right to set up stone seats and commemorative columns is reserved for the nobility (*si'ulu*) and is associated with the performance of 'feasts of merit'. Representations of a mythical serpent–dragon called *Iasara* are also found in Nias. Ancestor representations in stone, however, are confined to south-eastern and western parts of the island; in other regions they are carved in wood. The ancestor sculptures are named *adu zatua* ('ancient soul'). The older statues are usually in a squatting position, while more recent representations show the figures sitting or standing. The figures are always naked, with well-defined sexual organs, although they sometimes wear an elaborate headdress representing a golden crown worn by the nobility. Men wear one earring, women two. Wooden effigies made as magic protection usually have a forked headdress reflecting the forked ceremonial posts associated with feasts of merit.

In Kalimantan a rich wood-carving tradition was developed by the different peoples of the interior collectively known as Dayaks. Representations of human figures serve both protective and commemorative functions. Protective images include the *hampatong biji* of the Ngajus, a figure set up in the rice-fields to enhance fertility, while commemorative sculpture includes funerary posts with effigies of the deceased. The Ibans consider the hornbill (*burong kenyalang*) as their link to the ancestors, and large figures of the bird, carved with elaborate scroll designs and painted, are carried at the Feast of the Hornbill, a headhunting ceremony. Certain Dayak groups also have a masquerade tradition, involving the use of highly ornamental, elaborately carved facial masks, associated with harvest rituals. No systematic account yet exists of stylistic and iconographic distinctions between the wood-carvings of different Dayak societies. They are all characterized by highly ornate forms that seem to be based on figural representation but then separate and reintegrate different elements in a curvilinear, often asymmetric style. The dragon–snake, here called *aso* ('dog'), is the same as the serpentine, long-tongued creature of the Nias islanders and the Bataks. Fangs, spirals and large, staring eyes are carved on doors, house panels and coffins.

In the highlands of central Sulawesi stands a complex of pre-Classical sculptures of uncertain date. These are mainly simple images of males with faces, arms and genitals outlined on monoliths, some as tall as 4.5 m. The Sa'dan Torajas of Sulawesi are well known for their wooden images of ancestors (*tau-tau*) of high status, in which the deceased person's individual characteristics are represented in an attempt at portrayal. They are large, nearly life-size figures, either male or female, and are ceremonially dressed and set up in cliff caves above the villages. 20th-century carved figures have separate, movable limbs. Apart from these three-dimensional figures, the Torajas decorate their traditional large houses and rice granaries with relief carvings, both geometrically stylized and realistic, containing scenes from daily life. There are, however, certain proscribed positions for either style. In addition the front of the house has a realistic, three-dimensional carving of a buffalo's head. The buffalo is the most important sacrificial animal but is also the guardian of the structure and content of house and granary. Its representation on the granary door, for example, may be combined with the Tree of Life, symbolizing fertility and wealth.

Eastern Indonesia may be divided into four stylistic areas: Sumba, Flores, Alor and southern Maluku including the Leti and Tanimbar island groups. Sumba has a stone-carving tradition in which images of particular ancestors and founders of lineages or villages are made. The human form is carved in a simplified style, often combined with geometric designs in shallow relief on the supporting stele. This combination of styles also appears in the wood sculpture of central Flores, which includes ancestor figures of village founders, sometimes riding on a horse. Alor once had a thriving wood-carving tradition, but this was largely destroyed by Protestant missionaries. Commemorative sculptures play a less important part than representations of the mythical serpent (*nāga*), known locally as *haerd* or *ten*. The figure is highly ornate and abstracted from a 'realistic' image. The dragon–snake, once common as a protective image, was also carved on functional objects such as drums, rice mortars and bamboo containers. The southern Maluku islanders once produced ancestor sculptures in another variation of the ornate, curvilinear style. In Leti figural representations of seated figures with their arms on their knees and often wearing ornate headdresses were placed on graves. These figures also occurred on Tanimbar in reliefs in which the human form is the basis for an abstract shape filled with scrolls and spirals. Such carvings were formerly set up inside the house, as altars to the ancestors. The prows of boats were also carved, usually with the same ornate scroll designs used for the ancestor figures. Boats, as a means of travelling through time and space, are frequently associated throughout Indonesia with a link to the ancestors (*see* §VIII, 2 below).

BIBLIOGRAPHY

A. N. J. Th. à Th. van der Hoop: *Megalithic Remains in South Sumatra* (Zutphen, 1933)
E. Vatter: 'Der Schlangendrache auf Alor', *Jb. Prähist. Ethnog. Kst*, ix (1934), pp. 119–48
W. Kaudern: *Megalithic Finds in Central Celebes* (Göteborg, 1938)
A. J. Bernet Kempers: *Ancient Indonesian Art* (Amsterdam and Cambridge, MA, 1959)
J. Fontein, R. Soekmono and Satyawati Suleiman: *Ancient Indonesian Art of the Central and East Java Periods* (New York, 1971)
T. Bodrogi: *Art in Indonesia* (Greenwich, CT, 1972)
E. M. Bruner and J. Becker, eds: *Art, Ritual and Society in Indonesia*, Ohio U. Papers in International Studies, Southeast Asia Series, 53 (Athens, OH, 1979)
Art of the Archaic Indonesians (exh. cat., Dallas, TX, Mus. F.A., 1982)
Indonesian Primitive Art (exh. cat. by J. P. Barbier, Dallas, TX, Mus. F.A., 1984)
The Eloquent Death: Ancestral Sculpture of Indonesia and Southeast Asia (exh. cat., ed. J. Feldman; Los Angeles, UCLA Mus. Cult. Hist., 1985)
Islands and Ancestors: Indigenous Styles of Southeast Asia (exh. cat., ed. J. P. Barbier and D. Newton; New York, Met., 1988)

RUTH BARNES

V. Textiles.

Indonesian textiles are celebrated throughout the world for their fine craftsmanship, variety of techniques and range of colour and design. Two resist-patterning techniques—batik, chiefly associated with Java, and ikat (a term of Indonesian origin meaning 'tie', 'bind')—are particularly associated with Indonesia, and both are of great antiquity. Other techniques represented in the archipelago are supplementary weft, supplementary warp, tapestry weave, embroidery, appliqué, twining and beadwork (for the last, *see* §VIII, 8 below). Apart from their practical function as clothing, textiles are important indicators of status and ethnicity and are used as trade goods, heirlooms and ritual objects.

BIBLIOGRAPHY

J. E. Jasper and M. Pirngadie: *De weefkunst* (1912), ii of *De inlandsche kunstnijverheid in Nederlandsch Indië* (The Hague, 1912–30)
L. Langewis and F. A. Wagner: *Decorative Art in Indonesian Textiles* (Amsterdam, 1964)
Textiles of the Indonesian Archipelago (exh. cat. by B. Solyom and G. Solyom, Honolulu, HI, Acad. A., 1973)
Splendid Symbols: Textiles and Tradition in Indonesia (exh. cat. by M. Gittinger, Washington, DC, Textile Mus., 1979)

Textile Traditions of Indonesia (exh. cat., ed. M. H. Kahlenberg; Los Angeles, CA, Co. Mus. A., 1979)
Indonesian Textiles: Irene Emery Roundtable on Museum Textiles: Washington, DC, 1979
Indonesische Textilien: Wege zu Göttern und Ahnen (exh. cat. by B. K. Majlis, Cologne, Rautenstrauch-Joest-Mus., 1984)
S. Fraser-Lu: *Handwoven Textiles of South-east Asia* (Singapore, 1988)
M. Gittinger, ed.: *To Speak with Cloth: Studies in Indonesian Textiles* (Los Angeles, 1989)
R. Maxwell: *Textiles of Southeast Asia: Tradition, Trade, and Transformation* (Melbourne, 1990)
J. W. Christie: 'Ikat to Batik? Epigraphic Data on Textiles in Java from the Ninth to the Fifteenth Centuries', *Weaving Patterns of Life. Indonesian Textile Symposium: Basle, 1991*, pp. 11–29
M. Hitchcock: *Indonesian Textiles* (Berkeley and Singapore, 1991)

□

1. Java. 2. Bali. 3. Sumatra. 4. Other islands.

1. JAVA. Although the technique of batik has been used for centuries in many parts of the world, no country is so closely associated with it as Indonesia, and more specifically Java. Two other techniques employed in Java, *pelangi* and *teritik*, like batik, involve the resist-dyeing of woven cloth.

(i) Batik. (ii) Other techniques.

(i) Batik. In the batik process a resist substance, usually molten wax, is applied to the surface of a cloth in order to reserve specific areas for different colours. After dyeing, this wax is scraped away, the area beneath remaining the colour of the foundation (*see* DYE, colour pl. IV, fig. 1). The Javanese elaborated this basic procedure by applying multiple layers of wax to different areas of cloth, which were then scraped away in an ordered sequence between baths of different coloured dyes. In another variation of the technique, one layer of wax was scraped or boiled off after dyeing, and new designs were marked out with resist for subsequent dye baths. Accurate application of the liquid wax was facilitated by the use of the *canting*, a tool invented by the Javanese. This is a small, spouted metal reservoir held by a bamboo stem. The shape of the spout governs the type and fineness of the wax line. In traditional Javanese batik the design is waxed on both sides of the cloth, so that the pattern is clear on both sides, although it is always finer on the face patterned first. Cotton is the preferred fabric, but silk is occasionally used in some centres on the north coast of Java. Batik made by this process is called *kain tulis* or *batik tulis* (literally, 'written cloth' or 'written batik').

Rouffaer, the first serious Western scholar of the subject, states that the creators of *batik tulis* in the early 16th century were considered to be painters and were usually men. *Canting* batik work has been done by men in centres such as Cirebon on the north coast, but elsewhere *batik tulis* was traditionally allotted to women only. Not until the *cap*, a metal stamp, was invented in the mid-19th century, were men employed in batik production in significant numbers. The patterned stamps were used to apply molten wax to large areas of the surface of the cloth, dramatically increasing the rate and lowering the cost of production. However, use of the *cap* is akin to printing and lacks the creative potential of the *canting*. Both techniques continue to be practised, as well as more industrialized printing techniques. (For further discussion of the *canting* and *cap*, *see* TEXTILE, §III, 1(ii)(b).) Another form of batik patterning was known in parts of West Java until the early 20th century. In the place of wax, a rice paste resist was applied with a bamboo nib, and a single red dye was used to colour the handspun and woven cotton cloth. It is not known if this was the original form of batik or a peripheral manifestation of more complex processes.

The early history of batik in Java is not clear. It is known from 10th-century inscriptions that the Javanese used red, black, blue and yellow dyes, and by the 12th century the term *tulis* is used to distinguish certain cloth patterns, which may indicate batik was being practised in some form (Christie, 1991, p. 16). Rouffaer interpreted the term *tulis* on a palm-leaf manuscript of *c.* 1520 as the earliest mention of batik textiles. The first recorded use of the word batik appears relatively late, in a cargo manifest of a ship sailing between Java and Sumatra in 1641. The term, which has entered into many other languages, derives from the Indonesian–Malay word *tik*, meaning dot or spot and, possibly by association, small drops of wax. The word *tik* is also used in the context of tattooing.

Regional styles were formerly distinguished by the colours of their natural dyes. In the more conservative sultanates of Central Java indigo blue (from *Indigofera*) and a warm brown known as *soga* (from *Peltophorum ferrugineum*) were used singly and in combination to create a blue–black shade. In Yogyakarta these colours are used on a white ground, and in Surakarta on a cream ground. A red dye known as 'Turkey red', from the *mengkudu* tree (*Morinda citrifolia*), is also used in Java and in its most brilliant hue is associated with Lasem in East Java. In Madura it is combined with *soga* to make a rich reddish brown. The colours of traditional batiks made on the north coast are strikingly different. In addition to blues and browns, bright red, pink, yellow and green dyes are used; in the past these were often made from closely guarded family recipes that are now lost. Because of the reputation of certain local dyes, the same cloth might be dyed in two or three different places. These cloths were known as 'two-region' (*dua negeri*) or 'three-region' (*tiga negeri*). Once synthetic dyes became available, regional distinctions grew blurred, and the palette of such coastal centres as Pekalongan became unlimited.

The various regions also tend to favour their own particular designs. Geometric designs in grids or strong diagonals predominate in Central Java. In the 18th century, in the sultanates of Surakarta and Yogyakarta, some designs, known as *larangan* ('forbidden'), were reserved for the exclusive use of the royal family. They included '*garuda* wings' (*sawat*) and 'broken knife' (*parang rusak*) patterns and one, *semen* (from *semi*, 'bud', 'young shoot'), of forest scenes containing budding vegetation. These proscriptions were honoured near the courts but ignored elsewhere. The batik producers on the north coast knew the designs of the central areas but preferred a broader range of subject-matter that reflected the region's contacts with Indian, Chinese, European and Islamic traders. For centuries before the arrival of the Europeans, much of the trade of South-east Asia had been in Indian textiles (*see* SOUTH-EAST ASIA, §I, 3). From the early 17th century textiles began to be produced in India specially for export to Europe. The Javanese adopted techniques and motifs

22. *Kain panjang* ('long cloth'), cotton batik combining *semen* pattern of floral motifs and birds with *kawung* (circular) design (detail), 2.62×1.06 m, from Central Java, 20th century (Washington, DC, Textile Museum)

from both types. Floral designs and fantastic animal motifs were often inspired by Chinese embroidery and ceramics, while Chinese painting was instrumental in the development of the *megamendung* ('spiralling cloud') patterns of Cirebon, in which a basic colour, usually blue, was rendered in a series of progressively lighter shades, ending in white.

Europeans also played an important role in the development of batik designs in centres along the north coast of Java, where in the 19th century a sizeable population of Dutch and Eurasians developed. Some of the women supplemented their incomes by establishing batik workshops in their homes, where they controlled the quality of the dyes and the workmanship. In time they introduced new designs, often using illustrations in European magazines and postcards as their models. This gave rise to the large floral cluster motifs that came to dominate the design schemes of coastal centres such as Pekalongan. These women, many of whom had Dutch names such as Jans, Metzelaar and Van Zuylen, signed their work as a guarantee of quality rather than as artists, but their technique and designs had a profound influence on batik production in the metropolitan centres from *c.* 1875 to 1941. During the Japanese occupation (1942–5) a new style emerged, called Hokokai after a political organization. Hokokai batiks are much bolder in colour, and their minutely worked patterns are superimposed one upon another to create a riot of forms and colours. Some of them show the influence of Japanese taste. Another development after 1850 was the commercialization of batik. Whereas formerly batik had largely been a household craft for personal consumption, by the early 20th century it had become a commercial commodity marketed by Chinese, Arab and Indo-European traders. These businesses dictated pattern types and exerted some quality control but did not change working methods. They merely brought workers together under one roof or systematically farmed out the different stages of the batik-making process to village craftsmen.

Batik cloth is used for the sarong, the *kain panjang* ('long cloth') and the *selendang* ('scarf', 'shawl'). In the *kain panjang*, the entire rectangular cloth (*c.* 2.5×1.06 m) is treated as a single area to be patterned. The sarong (*c.* 2.15×1.06 m) is divided in the weft direction into two principal design areas; the wider is known as the 'body' (*badan*) and the narrower as the 'head' (*kepala*). The latter often has a motif of facing isosceles triangles known as *tumpal* (*see* TEXTILE, colour pl. XI). The *kain panjang* (see fig. 22) is wrapped about the body, often with an arrangement of pleats in front, while the sarong is sewn into a tube that is folded in front when worn. The *selendang* (*c.* 3.0×0.6 m) is used as shoulder-cloth in women's formal costume and as a sling for carrying a child or other burdens. Other items include headcloths, ceremonial court wraps and wall hangings. Batik is also increasingly used by artists in Java as a pictorial medium.

While batik is the signature textile of Java, the technique was also practised in a few villages of the Jambi region in Sumatra and in a very simple form in Central Sulawesi. It is thought the technique was introduced into the former area by batikers brought from the north coast of Java in the 19th century to serve the Jambi court. In the late 20th century there have been efforts to revive the traditional skills and patterns in this region.

(ii) Other techniques. Two other types of resist patterning known in Java are *pelangi* (sometimes written *plangi*) and *teritik* (sometimes written *tritik*). *Pelangi* involves tying off small areas of a cloth with a dye-resistant binding. After dyeing, the tied-off areas are opened and appear in the colour of the foundation fabric. Small circles, squares, lozenges etc can be arranged to create larger forms and relatively complex patterns. *Teritik* utilizes the same principles, but a thread is sewn through the cloth along a pattern margin and the cloth is subsequently pulled up tight along the thread. The creases and tight folds resist the penetration of the dye, leaving a wavy line. In Java both these resist techniques are often applied to a single cloth. *Pelangi*, alone or combined with *teritik*, is most often worked on silk to create shoulder-cloths, sashes and breast-cloths. Although it is still seen in formal costume, its chief use remains in dance costumes. *Teritik* may be found on cotton or silk and is used to outline the large central lozenge motif typical of the *kain kembangan* ('floral cloth') textiles worn as headcloths, large ceremonial wraps, breast-cloths or sashes at the courts of Central Java.

The origin of these techniques in Java is unknown. The earliest mention of *kain kembangan* dates from 1580, and the honoured status afforded to these textiles in the Central Javanese courts proves their antiquity. Some forms were reserved for royalty, some were required garments at weddings, and others were used as special offerings at marriage and circumcision ceremonies. Both these forms of resist patterning are now employed on imported woven cloth. Although the Javanese do weave their own cloth, this—with a few rare exceptions, such as the more elegant silks and some fine cottons, which are worked in ikat in various geometric and floral designs—tends to be patterned by other means than resist dyeing. For example, *kain lurik*, a sturdy cotton cloth, is patterned with simple stripes or plaids.

Ikat is a resist form of patterning in which portions of the warp or weft yarns are tied off to resist the penetration of the dye with which the yarns are treated before weaving (*see* DYE, colour pl. III, fig. 1). Cutting off certain ties and retying areas before dyeing in a different colour allow the use of a wide range of colours in the design. This labour-intensive process is now often abbreviated by means of the *cetak* process, in which chemical dyes are painted on to the yarns (usually the weft) to create the details of the pattern. The painted lengths are then tied to protect them, and the yarns are immersed in the dye that provides the background colour. Warp ikat was formerly done on Java to produce large ceremonial hangings. Ikat has been known in Java at least since the 10th century AD. It is traditionally associated with centres along the north coast, such as Gresik, Pekalongan and Banjumas. These places had an early association with Muslim traders from the Indian Ocean, so the ikat technique may have been introduced by Muslims from India's west coast. Cotton weft ikats continue to be made as a household industry in Gresik, while in Troso (near Japara) there are both weft ikats similar to those made in Gresik and warp ikats in imitation of patterns from Indonesia's outer islands. The ikat is woven on a frame loom with a hand-operated flying shuttle, which was formerly also used for *lurik*. Machine-powered looms are now in general use, but the traditional Javanese body-tension loom, which utilizes a reed, or comb, and a discontinuous warp, can still be found in some areas. With rare exceptions, embroidery and appliqué are seldom used to pattern textiles in Java. In the Central Javanese courts women of noble birth would often add appliqué to an imported silk textile over the plain central lozenge form of their breast-cloth (*kemben*) and ceremonial wraps.

Textiles play a crucial part in Javanese rituals and are used not merely for display or for cosmetic reasons but as symbols of a family's wealth, both material and spiritual. Some are heirlooms, and others are used only in the earlier stages of the life of the family, often serving as talismans for its continued well-being. Particular textiles gain their spiritual power through use in rites of passage, such as marriage, pregnancy and circumcision. In parts of Java the plain white cotton *kain* worn by the bride and groom at their pre-nuptial ritual baths are subsequently dyed with identical batik designs and are especially venerated by the couple. In rituals held in the seventh month of a woman's first pregnancy the expectant mother exchanges her *kain* seven times, the final breast-cloth being a *kain lurik*. The woman then wears *lurik* until the time of her confinement, when she changes to a batik. During circumcision rites, the boy dresses in batik garments suitable to his new status. The designs of the textiles used on these and other ceremonial or ritual occasions are dictated by their function. The bride's parents wear the *teruntum*, a repeated pattern of a small star or flower, while the bridal pair may wear a design conferring wishes for prosperity and a life free of worries, *sida mukti*. In court circles in Central Java, close relatives of a royal couple wear *nitik* patterns, which imitate woven ikat patterns in batik and are extremely difficult to make. The royal couple wear voluminous ceremonial garments worked with images of sacred forest animals. The use of specific textile types and patterns may originally have been dictated by complex conceptual categories extending even to the different stages in making the textiles. In this structuring the sombre *lurik* was placed in complementary opposition to batik, and the use of each type of textile was prescribed according to cosmological principles. These more profound aspects of textile usage have largely been forgotten, and custom alone dictates usage.

BIBLIOGRAPHY

G. P. Rouffaer and H. H. Juynboll: *De batikkunst in Nederlandsch Indië* (Utrecht, 1914)

J. E. Jasper and M. Pirngadie: *De batikkunst* (1916), iii of *De inlandsche kunstnijverheid in Nederlandsch Indië* (The Hague, 1912–30)
A. Bühler: 'Plangi: The Tie and Dye Work', *Ciba Z.* (1954), no. 54, pp. 3722–48
N. Tirtaamidjaja and B. R. O'G. Anderson: *Batik: Pola and Tjorak* (Jakarta, 1966)
J. L. Lenor and others: *The Dyer's Art: Ikat, Batik, Plangi* (New York, 1976)
D. Geirnaert-Martin: 'Ask Lurik Why Batik: A Structural Analysis of Textiles and Classifications (Central Java)', *The Future of Structuralism: Papers of the IUAES-Intercongress: Amsterdam, 1983*, pp. 155–201
H. Veldhuisen: 'Ontwikkelingen in de batik van Java: Javaanse batik?', *Handwk. Zonder Grenzen* (1983), no. 4, pp. 27–35; (1983), no. 5, pp. 27–33; (1984), no. 1, pp. 52–9; no. 2, pp. 26–33; no. 3, pp. 42–7; no. 4, pp. 50–55
I. M. Elliott: *Batik: Fabled Cloth of Java* (New York, 1984)
A. Veldhuisen-Djajasoebrata: *Bloemen van het heelal: De kleurrijke wereld van de textiel op Java* [Flowers of the universe: The colourful world of textiles in Java] (Amsterdam, 1984); abridged Eng. trans. as *Weavings of Power and Might: The Glory of Java* (Rotterdam, 1988)
S. Fraser-Lu: *Indonesian Batik: Processes, Patterns and Places* (Singapore, 1986)
R. Heringa: 'Dye Process and Life Sequence: The Coloring of Textiles in an East Javanese Village', *To Speak with Cloth: Studies in Indonesian Textiles*, ed. M. Gittinger (Los Angeles, 1989), pp. 107–30
J. W. Christie: 'Ikat to Batik? Epigraphic Data on Textiles in Java from the Ninth to the Fifteenth Centuries', *Weaving Patterns of Life. Indonesian Textile Symposium: Basle, 1991*, pp. 11–29
Een schitterende geschiedenis: Weefsels en batik van Palembang en Djambi [A glorious history: Woven cloth and batik from Palembang and Jambi] (exh. cat. by R. Heringa, The Hague, Gemeentemus., 1994)

2. BALI. In Bali the correct use of textiles as garments and as adornments for temples and images of the deities is one of the ways in which the Balinese strive for the blessings of gods and ancestors. Like some other aspects of Balinese art and culture, the textile arts may be indebted to Javanese influences introduced to the island during the Majapahit period (1292–*c.* 1500), when a strong Javanese presence was established on Bali. However, the great diversity of textiles and the richness of their usage bear witness to a 'continuous evolution within the context of the island. . .and its culture' (Hauser-Schäublin, Nabholz-Kartaschoff and Ramseyer, p. 5). Some of the most sumptuous Balinese textiles are the silks known as *kain songket*, in which the pattern is formed by the insertion of supplementary wefts of metallic yarns and which are worn as waist-cloths and shoulder-cloths. They tend to have geometric patterns, but designs with stylized birds and floral motifs also occur, as well as complex figural compositions in *wayang* (shadow-puppet) style. The weaving of these textiles was once carried out by women of noble birth, and the courts of Gelgel and Klungkung were notable centres for their production. Equally spectacular are the ceremonial *kain prada*, textiles with patterns in gold leaf glued to the surface or, more frequent in the modern period, patterns worked in gold dust or gold paint. They appear most often in dancers' costumes and at weddings and temple festivals. Silks with *pelangi* and *teritik* designs (*see* §1(ii) above) are also used as shoulder- and breast-cloths by dancers and others on ceremonial occasions.

Weft ikat, known as *endek*, is an important patterning technique used for both silk and cotton cloths. Designs range from large animal and *wayang* figures to small repeated geometric patterns. In creating the latter, the Balinese frequently combine the staccato outline of ikat with colour gradations that together give a pulsating visual effect. Silk weft ikat is often used in combination with metallic supplementary weft yarns. These textiles in the form of hip-wrappers and breast- and shoulder-cloths, once the prerogative of noble families, are now worn by all social classes on ceremonial occasions. For everyday wear Balinese purchase local, commercially made cotton weft ikat sarongs known as *enduk*, or batiks from Java. Although much more modest in texture and appearance, a type of cotton cloth patterned with weft ikat known as *kamben cepuk* has a ritual value seemingly much greater than that of the silk and gold cloths. These cloths, once thought to have been woven only on the small offshore island of Nusa Penida, are also made in Bali proper. Related in format and many design details to the Indian *patola* of Gujarat in north-western India (*see* §3 below), *kamben cepuk* are a sombre brick- or rust-red or brown, with muted designs in yellow, blue, purple, green and black. They are credited with strong powers of protection and exorcism and are called into use at rites of passage and purification rituals for the dead.

No less important to the Balinese are the *kain geringsing*, cotton cloths patterned by double ikat. This exacting work is done only in the village of Tenganan Pegeringsingan, a traditional religious community ruled by a complex ritual system in which textiles are an element in maintaining the sacred order. The same technique of double ikat is employed in the *patola*, although the relationship between Gujarat and Bali is not known. The colours of *geringsing* are a mellow ecru lent by the unbleached cotton, a deep brick-red (from *Morinda citrifolia*) and purplish-black (from *Indigofera*). Between the end borders the field is patterned with geometric and stylized floral elements in a grid or check pattern. In other *geringsing* large four-pointed stars divide the centre field into semicircular zones that frame temple forms and anthropomorphic figures in a pictorial style related to East Javanese temple reliefs and *wayang* figures.

In Tenganan Pegeringsingan the suitability of a *kain geringsing* for a particular use depends more on the quality of the dyes and whether the textile has been used than on the nature of the design. When the textile is taken from the loom it is tubular, because the back-tension loom on which it is woven utilizes a continuous warp. *Geringsing* retaining this form are considered to be suitable offerings to deities and ancestors. Men and boys also wear a narrow tube-shaped *geringsing* as a belt or neck-cloth for certain rituals. Women's ritual costume utilizes *geringsing* that have been cut open to be used as shoulder- or breast-cloths and, when two are joined, as large wraps. *Geringsing* and other cotton textiles with patterns of simple stripes and plaids are made into various costumes appropriate to particular groups at specific ritual occasions in Tenganan Pegeringsingan. Elsewhere in Bali *geringsing* are considered sacred and are used at tooth-filing ceremonies and weddings and to adorn temples and cremation towers.

BIBLIOGRAPHY

R. Bolland: 'A Comparison between the Looms Used in Bali and Lombok for Weaving Sacred Cloths', *Tropical Man*, iv (1971), pp. 173–82
A. Bühler, U. Ramseyer and N. Ramseyer-Gygi: *Patola und Geringsing* (Basle, 1975)
U. Ramseyer: 'Clothing, Ritual and Society in Tenganan Pegeringsingan (Bali)', *Verhand. Natforsch. Ges. Basel*, xcv (1984), pp. 191–241

M.-L. Nabholz-Kartaschoff: 'A Sacred Cloth of Rangda: *Kamben Cepuk* of Bali and Nusa Penida', *To Speak with Cloth: Studies in Indonesian Textiles*, ed. M. Gittinger (Los Angeles, 1989), pp. 181–98

B. Hauser-Schäublin, M.-L. Nabholz-Kartaschoff and U. Ramseyer: *Balinese Textiles* (London, 1991)

3. SUMATRA. The rich array of techniques and functions in Sumatran textiles makes the island a paradigm for understanding textiles elsewhere in the archipelago. This variability is partly the result of geographical features that have allowed groups of peoples living in the island's interior to perpetuate certain skills and customs in relative isolation, while coastal groups have been more subject to change fostered by international contact. There are profound differences between the various groups regarding preferred material, decorative techniques and design. Silk, most of which is imported, is woven in centres on or near the east coast such as Palembang and Jambi, in Muntok on the nearby island of Bangka, and Aceh in the north. In other places where silk-weaving is found, as on the Pasemah Plateau and among the Minangkabaus of West Sumatra, there has been long-standing contact with coastal centres. Silk is traditionally patterned by supplementary wefts and/or weft ikat; *pelangi*, *teritik* (*see* §1(ii) above) and embroidery are also known. Supplementary weft patterning is used in the making of the renowned silk and gold cloths called *kain songket*. On the east coast the finest of these cloths also have a weft-ikat-patterned centre field with gold margins. The dominant colour is red with ikat design details worked in blue, yellow and green. Among the Minangkabaus the textile may be patterned entirely with gold supplementary yarns, leaving little foundation weave visible. In Aceh patterns utilize less gold, and the predominant colour is dark purple. Cotton is used by all the peoples of Sumatra, but it has been the principal fibre employed by groups in the interior, such as the Bataks, who make mantles and shoulder-cloths of sombre blue or earth red patterned with warp ikat designs of simple arrowheads or interlocking lozenges. Supplementary weft patterning and borders worked by weft twining are also important decorative techniques. The Angkola Bataks weave a twill foundation and work patterns in supplementary wefts and tapestry weave.

In Sumatra, as elsewhere in the archipelago, weft ikat patterning is predominantly associated with silk, and warp ikat with cotton. The two materials are also woven on slightly different types of back-tension loom. Silk-weavers use a loom with a reed, or comb, and wind up the discontinuous warp on a warp beam. Cotton-weavers tend to use a loom without a reed, the warp forming a continuous circle between the warp beam and the weft beam. Because this type of loom is found among more remote peoples of the archipelago, such as the Bataks, it is thought to be older than the reed loom. When the reed loom first appeared in coastal areas is not known, but it may have been during the second half of the 1st millennium AD, at the time of strong Indian influence. With few exceptions the textiles woven on both types of loom are used as untailored garments wrapped about the body, draped over the shoulder or tied as a head-cloth. Simple jackets or blouses tend to be found in the same areas where silk-weaving is established. In format and design the silk textiles of the east coast of Sumatra incorporate elements of Indian textiles, primarily the *patola*, a silk, double-ikat cloth made in Gujarat (*see* INDIAN SUBCONTINENT, §VII, 3(iii)(a)). In the 17th century, and probably earlier, *patola* were highly prized items of exchange throughout the archipelago, reckoned as being worth half a ton of cloves each. They are large rectangular cloths with borders parallel to the selvages and deep end borders framing a large centre field, which is filled with fine geometric patterning. The *patola* format was adopted by silk-weavers on the east coast of Sumatra, who worked them in all patterning techniques. It is thought that most textiles in the archipelago had previously been ornamented with simple patterns in the warp.

In addition to their use as garments, textiles in Sumatra, as elsewhere in the archipelago, are major items of ritualized gift exchange. Among groups such as the Bataks, textiles are deemed to be female goods, and custom dictates that they be given as the pre-eminent gift of the bride and her family to the groom and his family in exchange for goods regarded as male. The pattern of exchange established at the marriage is repeated at all subsequent rites of passage, and 200 or more pieces of cloth may be given at a time. It is probable that textiles are categorized as female goods because all stages of their manufacture are regarded as women's labour. When textiles are given to the bride's family by the groom, it is usually because they are imported and have been purchased rather than crafted within the family. Textiles often play a critical role during rituals. Thus in the marriage ceremony of the Toba Bataks the bride and groom are enveloped in a large cloth wrapped about their shoulders by the bride's father. He also symbolically conveys the superior spiritual power of the bride's family to the groom's by draping one

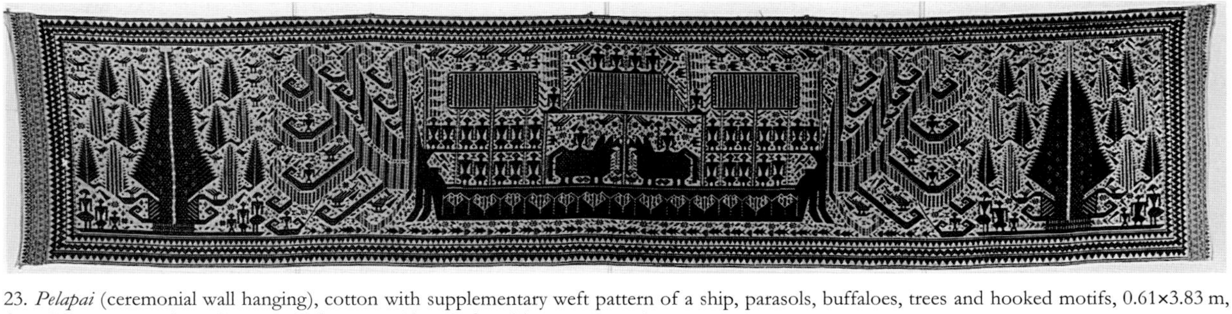

23. *Pelapai* (ceremonial wall hanging), cotton with supplementary weft pattern of a ship, parasols, buffaloes, trees and hooked motifs, 0.61×3.83 m, from Lampung, southern Sumatra, 20th century (Amsterdam, Tropenmuseum)

or more members of that family in cloth. The textile used on these occasions is chosen according to the age and standing of the recipient from a repertory of over 120 different types of Batak cloth.

In the extreme south of Sumatra certain textiles were woven for use within a specific ritual context: small cotton squares with supplementary weft patterns (*tampan*) and a long narrow cotton hanging (*pelapai*; see fig. 23). Use of the latter—as a backdrop to the principal actor in such rites as weddings, circumcisions or ceremonies celebrating advancement in social rank—was the prerogative of heads of lineage. Their patterns of large ships and animals may be seen as transition symbols. The smaller *tampan* had many functions, including use as obligatory gifts at all rites of passage, when they passed between bride's and groom's families in a prescribed manner. Their designs range from simple geometric patterning to complex narrative scenes. Although these textiles were still in use in the early 1970s, they have not been woven in Sumatra since the beginning of the century. A few examples of textiles similar to the *tampan* are known from Lombok and from parts of mainland South-east Asia, but their relationship is unclear. In the mountainous interior of southern Sumatra, warp ikat and embroidery were used to pattern women's sarongs (*tapis*). Lozenge and related forms—very rarely a ship—appear in red-brown and blue ikat, while the principal motif worked in satin stitch embroidery is a ship filled with figures. South of the mountains the *tapis* lack ikat but have designs made with metallic yarns and/or sequins couched on to a cotton foundation. Here and on the west coast small pieces of mirror glass are important patterning elements. Embroidery was also used on ceremonial pillows found in coastal centres and on some Palembang shoulder-cloths, and still occurs on simple blouses among the Gayo. Appliqué has played a relatively small role in the textile arts of Sumatra, although it was used in women's costume on the offshore island of Nias.

BIBLIOGRAPHY

J. E. Jasper and M. Pirngadie: *De weefkunst* (1912), ii of *De inlandsche kunstnijverheid in Nederlandsch Indië* (The Hague, 1912–30)

M. Gittinger: 'The Ship Textiles of South Sumatra: Functions and Design System', *Bijdr. Taal-, Land- & Vlkenknd.*, cxxxii (1976), pp. 207–27

S. A. Niessen: *Motifs of Life in Toba Batak Texts and Textiles* (Dordrecht, 1985)

4. OTHER ISLANDS. The textile traditions of other islands in the archipelago mirror those of Sumatra in varying degrees. In the eastern part of the dry island of Sumba, men's large mantles (*hinggi*) patterned in warp ikat (see fig. 24 and DYE, colour pl. III, fig. 1) and women's sarongs in warp ikat and supplementary warp patterning were used in ritual exchanges at all formal gatherings. These boldly patterned textiles with motifs of human figures, horses, deer, snakes, birds, rampant lions etc became sought after by collectors as early as the 19th century. The mantles were blue and white for commoners, a more complex red, blue and yellow for nobles. Knowledge of the red-dye recipes was kept secret among noblewomen and forbidden to commoners. The stages of textile manufacture metaphorically paralleled those of childbirth, an illustration of the important conceptual role of textiles on Sumba. Warp ikat was the predominant means of patterning cotton textiles in eastern Flores,

24. Man's warp ikat cotton mantle (*hinggi*), 2.90×1.42 m, from Sumba, ?early 20th century (Washington, DC, Textile Museum)

Lembata, Savu and Roti. The designs (see fig. 25) were strongly influenced by the Indian *patola*, not only in format but also in specific design elements. Some designs have become indicators of sub-clan membership. The women on these islands knew the complex technique of dyeing with 'Turkey red' (*see* §1(i) above).

The people of Timor knew warp ikat but also commanded an impressive range of other patterning techniques, including warp-faced alternating float weave, two types of supplementary weft patterning, twining and tapestry weave. Warp ikat patterns of interlocking scrolls, reptiles, birds and anthropomorphic forms were used on men's mantles and some women's tubular sarongs in warp bands flanked by multicoloured stripes. Patterning, dye range and technique varied widely and indicated particular group affiliation. Twining and tapestry weave were used on mantles and were a primary technique in the creation of warriors' costumes and men's small bags. The exchange of mantles and sarongs was particularly important at funerals. Warp ikat is also important to the Toraja people in the interior of Sulawesi, for blanket-sized textiles used as hangings, shrouds or skirts. The Torajas have rich traditions built around sacred cloths, some of which were formerly made locally and others the origins of which are cloaked in myth. These textiles are a crucial element in rituals associated with cults of the dead. One type of

25. Rotinese women in warp ikat sarongs and *selendangs*; from a photograph of 1926

sacred cloth, the *sarita* or ceremonial banner, was patterned with a resist in the manner of batik. The interior of Sulawesi, together with Jambi in Sumatra, are thought to be the only locations in the archipelago other than Java where batik was made, although the *sarita* batik was extremely primitive in execution. Until well into the 20th century, the Torajas also made headbands, head wrappers, full skirts and blouses from bark-cloth. The blouses were patterned with painted figures, embroidery and pieces of bark-cloth and mica. The resemblance of the tailoring to Western women's dress is startling, but the origin of this costume in the mountainous interior remains a mystery. (*See* §1(iii) above for the patterns and colours of *sarita* and bark-cloth.)

The textile traditions of coastal Sulawesi were different from those of the interior. Many have disappeared, but one that remains, indeed seems to flourish, is the weaving of silk sarongs by the Buginese in the vicinity of Ujung Pandang, south-west Sulawesi. Utilizing local as well as imported silk, they make colourful sarongs of plaid and weft ikat. It is thought that ikat has only recently been introduced into Sulawesi, and that silk-weaving in this area may be a considerably older tradition. Southern Sulawesi and nearby islands may have been the points of dispersal for certain textile techniques in the eastern part of the archipelago. In Kalimantan, where there are numerous ethnic groups, there were once many different textile patterning techniques. These included forms of supplementary weft and supplementary warp, twining, appliqué and extensive beadwork. The large cotton warp ikat blankets (*pua*) and skirts (*bidang*) of the Ibans, however, have received the most acclaim. These have intricate interlocking patterns of geometric forms, lizards and anthropomorphic figures. The tying of certain ikat designs was considered to be a dangerous undertaking and was pursued only by older women. Weaving *pua* was seen as a creative act parallel to men's activities in headhunting. These patterned textiles were used by the Ibans only for certain important celebrations or when a person sought spiritual aid from the beyond.

BIBLIOGRAPHY

J. E. Jasper and M. Pirngadie: *De weefkunst* (1912), ii of *De inlandsche kunstnijverheid in Nederlandsch Indië* (The Hague, 1912–30)

S. Kooijman: *Ornamented Bark-cloth in Indonesia* (Leiden, 1963)

M. J. Adams: *System and Meaning in East Sumba Textile Design: A Study in Traditional Indonesian Art* (New Haven, 1969)

——: 'Work Patterns and Symbolic Structures in a Village Culture, East Sumba, Indonesia', *SE Asia*, i (1971), pp. 321–34

J. J. Fox: 'Roti, Ndao and Savu', *Textile Traditions of Indonesia*, ed. M. Hunt Kahlenberg (Los Angeles, 1977), pp. 97–104

H. Nooy-Palm: 'The Role of the Sacred Cloths in the Mythology and Ritual of the Sa'dan-Toraja', *Indonesian Textiles: Irene Emery Roundtable on Museum Textiles: Washington, DC, 1979*, pp. 81–95

C. Vogelsanger: 'A Sight for the Gods: Notes on the Social and Religious Meaning of Iban Ritual Fabrics', *Indonesian Textiles: Irene Emery Roundtable on Museum Textiles: Washington, DC, 1979*, pp. 115–26

Early Indonesian Textiles from Three Island Cultures: Sumba, Toraja, Lampung (exh. cat. by R. J. Holmsren and A. E. Spertus, New York, Met., 1980)
D. C. Geirnaert: 'Textiles of West Sumba: Lively Renaissance of an Old Tradition', *To Speak with Cloth: Studies in Indonesian Textiles*, ed. M. Gittinger (Los Angeles, 1989), pp. 57–80
L. E. Visser: 'Foreign Textiles in Sahu Culture', *To Speak with Cloth: Studies in Indonesian Textiles*, ed. M. Gittinger (Los Angeles, 1989)

MATTIEBELLE GITTINGER

VI. Theatre.

Indonesia has a dramatic tradition, chiefly derived from Java and Bali, dating back some 1000 years, with puppet (especially shadow-puppet) theatre playing a central part. The word *wayang* (literally 'shadow') denotes a dramatic performance (whether enacted by people or by puppets) or the puppets themselves. The principal forms of puppet theatre are *wayang kulit*, in which flat leather puppets are manipulated behind a white screen, and *wayang golek*, which makes use of three-dimensional wooden puppets and is performed without a shadow screen; in *wayang beber* ('unfolding') the *dalang* (puppeteer) unrolls a series of long painted scrolls supported by two poles as he narrates the story. Mask plays and dance dramas have been much influenced by puppet theatre.

BIBLIOGRAPHY
C. Holt: *Art in Indonesia: Continuities and Change* (Ithaca, NY, 1967)
V. M. Clara van Groenendael: *Wayang Theatre in Indonesia: An Annotated Bibliography* (Dordrecht, 1987) [succinct descriptions of literature in Indonesian, Javanese and major Western languages on all forms of *wayang* theatre]
J. O. Miettinen: *Classical Dance and Theatre in South-east Asia* (Singapore, 1992)

□

1. *Wayang kulit*. 2. *Wayang golek* and *wayang kerucil*. 3. *Wayang beber*. 4. Dance drama and masks.

1. Wayang kulit. In *wayang kulit*, each puppet, intricately carved and elaborately painted, is supported by a central rod of buffalo horn. The *dalang*, sitting cross-legged beneath a lamp fired traditionally by coconut oil but today more often by electricity, narrates the story while animating the figures' arms, which pivot at shoulder and elbow, by means of two further rods attached to the hands. The audience sees only the puppets' shadows, not their bright colours, though these are visible to casual spectators gathered behind the *dalang* and the *gamelan* (orchestra). Most of the stories are taken from the Hindu epics, the *Mahābhārata* and the *Rāmāyaṇa*, which supports the widely held view that the shadow theatre of Java and Bali originated in India. Some scholars, however, argue that it came from China or that it is an indigenous invention.

(i) Java. (ii) Bali.

(i) Java. Shadow plays are the most prestigious of Java's many performing arts. While the Central Javanese courts have long supported the *wayang kulit* tradition, commissioning large and beautiful sets of puppets, appointing *dalang* to give court performances and fostering the development of the repertory of stories, the *wayang* also has a large popular following in rural areas, and it would be tendentious to ascribe a prior origin to either village or court. Nevertheless, court and urban influence in the 20th century has increased the size and importance of the *gamelan* in all performances, including those held in villages. There are many regional *wayang kulit* traditions, but the predominant styles are those of the court cities of Surakarta (Solo) and Yogyakarta. Most performances start with *gamelan* music at *c.* 7.30 in the evening, the play itself beginning at 9.00 and lasting until at least 5.00 the next morning. Village performances are often preceded by a six- or seven-hour daytime performance as well, though these are thought less important than those held at night.

A complete set of *wayang kulit* consists of at least 200 puppets, often many more (see fig. 26); court sets can include 400 or 500. It is possible that the stylization of the *wayang* puppets is due to the Islamic prohibition of representing the human form. The iconography of the

26. *Wayang kulit* performance at Kraton Ngayogyakarta Hadiningrat, Yogyakarta, 1989

27. *Wayang kulit* puppet figure of Bima, buffalo hide, pigment, gold leaf, fish-glue medium, buffalo horn, bone studs, 950×550×22 mm, from Cirebon, West Java, 19th century (Cirebon, Kraton Kasepuhan)

figures is determined by the status of the characters they represent (god, king, priest, knight, princess, acolyte, demon, male or female servant, or animal), and there are three categories of style (refined, bold or crude). Each physical feature and each article of dress or adornment will take one of several possible forms. For example, eyes are either long, narrow and almond-shaped (refined), fully rounded (bold) or outsized and glaring (crude). Feet may be slippered or bare, and close together or spread apart. Gods' heads are turbaned, kings' are crowned, while knights wear their hair in an elaborate coiffure. The tilt of a character's head is particularly telling. Downcast eyes indicate the character's sensitivity to the demands of Javanese etiquette, in particular that one should show a self-effacing acceptance of one's proper place in the social hierarchy. However, neither such willingness to show deference nor the delicate proportions of a refined knight's form should be taken as signs of weakness. On the contrary, they indicate the character's great spiritual strength, all the more impressive for its self-control. Although the iconography is highly conventionalized, each of the 60 or more characters appearing regularly in performances is readily recognizable.

In the case of individual figures, the puppets of Yogyakarta and Surakarta differ in subtle ways. Overall, Yogyakarta puppets tend to be slightly larger than those from Surakarta and favour darker colours and much gold leaf, whereas Surakarta prefers lighter pastels. The puppets of Cirebon, West Java (see fig. 27), are of particular interest stylistically. Many *dalang* are accomplished puppet-makers but frequently leave puppet-making to others, often to relations. Puppets are almost invariably made by tracing the outline and details of an old puppet on to a new piece of hide, so that the new one is as nearly as possible a replica of it.

The stories related in performance are based on Javanese versions of the Indian epics, the *Rāmāyaṇa* and the *Mahābhārata*, which is particularly popular in Java. The *dalang* usually relies on one of a limited number of formulaic stories that relate the romantic adventures of one character, for example, or one of the many tales in which the Kaurawas try to cheat the Pandawas out of their patrimony. Particularly popular in the modern *wayang* are the stories of the competition between the Pandawas and Kaurawas to obtain some mystical gift, a competition inevitably ending in the triumph of the righteous Pandawas. The story to be performed may be chosen either by the sponsors of a performance or by the *dalang*. Usually, little effort is made to tie the story closely to the event marked by the performance, although certain categories of stories would be inappropriate or inauspicious for some occasions. A story concerning a mystical gift, for example, can be used on virtually any occasion, but one including the death of an important character is only considered suitable for a funerary ritual. Stories from the *Bratayudha* cycle, which deals with a cataclysmic war, are considered powerful and dangerous and are performed only on occasions when their influence will be exerted over so many people as to be rendered benign, as in a collective village ritual or on radio broadcasts.

No matter what the story, virtually every performance has a given structure, beginning with a long opening scene at court, followed by a series of set-pieces. Yogyakarta and Surakarta performances have slightly different structures, but at least one other formal court scene is included in both traditions. There is a set number of battle sequences, and at about 1.00 a.m. the servants of the Pandawas, much loved by the Javanese, appear for the first time, occasioning the singing of light, popular songs and much joking. Most of the important episodes are performed between about 3.00 and 5.00 a.m., the earlier part of the performance having advanced the story relatively little.

Most performances are now sponsored by families, usually to mark important rites of passage such as a daughter's wedding, a son's circumcision or the fulfilment of a vow. In the past, many villages sponsored performances collectively to celebrate the harvest or the annual village purification ritual, but the frequency of such village-sponsored performances appears to be decreasing. Nevertheless, daytime ritual performances to ward off spiritual attack on certain categories of people are still occasionally sponsored. Important events in both government and commercial circles, such as Indonesian Independence Day or the opening of a new building, are likely to be marked by a *wayang kulit* performance. When a performance is held to mark a family ritual occasion, the male guests, who together with their wives have contributed money or labour towards the event, are seated on the shadow side of the screen, their age and status determining their proximity to it. Traditionally these guests sat on mats; in modern times they are more likely, especially in Surakarta performances, to be seated on metal chairs. Young people of the neighbourhood serve them snacks and a meal cooked by relatives and neighbours on behalf of the sponsors. Once they have finished eating, the invited guests take their leave. At this time, about midnight, many of the young men and boys who have been watching outside, from behind the *gamelan*, stream into the area their elders have vacated.

The audience tends to watch a performance only intermittently. Since the plot is usually of a conventional nature, and few spectators stay until the end, the stories seem to matter less to most spectators than the music, jokes and battles that run through the performance. The great respect that the Javanese accord to the *wayang* seems, in fact, to depend less on the content of any single performance than on the figure of the *dalang* himself, whose control over all aspects of the performance is total, yet whose presence is disguised by the screen and the diversity of voices he adopts. Still immensely popular in Central Java, shadow plays continue to be performed frequently. However, the proliferation of cassette tapes made by Java's four or five most popular *dalang* has raised standards, making it difficult for less renowned *dalang* to find sponsors. At the same time, competing forms of conspicuous consumption tend to discourage all but the very wealthiest of Javanese from marking important events with *wayang kulit* performances.

BIBLIOGRAPHY

G. A. J. Hazeu: *Bijdrage tot de kennis van het Javaansche tooneel* [Contribution to the knowledge of Javanese theatre] (Leiden, 1897)

J. Kats: *Wajang poerwa* (1923), i of *Het Javaansche tooneel* [The Javanese theatre] (Weltevreden, 1923); rev. as *De wajang poerwa, een vorm van Javaans tooneel* (Dordrecht, 1984)

W. H. Rassers: 'Over de oorsprong van het Javaansche tooneel' [On the origins of the Javanese theatre], *Bijdr. Taal-, Land- & Vlkenknd.*, lxxxviii (1931), pp. 317–450; Eng. trans. in *Pañji: The Culture Hero* (The Hague, 1959), pp. 95–215

R. L. Mellema: *Wayang Puppets: Carving, Colouring and Symbolism* (Amsterdam, 1954)

J. Brandon: *On Thrones of Gold: Three Javanese Shadow Plays* (Cambridge, MA, 1967)

B. R. O'G. Anderson: *Mythology and the Tolerance of the Javanese* (Ithaca, NY, 1969)

J. Scott-Kemball: *Javanese Shadow Puppets: The Raffles Collection in the British Museum* (London, 1970)

J. J. Ras: 'The Historical Development of the Javanese Shadow Theatre', *Rev. Indon. & Malay. Affairs*, x/2 (1976), pp. 50–76

A. L. Becker: 'Text-building, Epistemology, and Aesthetics in Javanese Shadow Theatre', *The Imagination of Reality: Essays in Southeast Asian Coherence Systems*, ed. A. L. Becker and A. A. Yengoyan (Norwood, NJ, 1979), pp. 211–43

V. M. Clara van Groenendael: *The Dalang behind the Wayang: The Role of the Surakarta and Yogyakarta Dalang in Indonesian–Javanese Society* (Dordrecht, 1985)

——: *Wayang Theatre in Indonesia: An Annotated Bibliography* (Dordrecht, 1987)

W. W. Keeler: *Javanese Shadow Plays, Javanese Selves* (Princeton, 1987)

——: *Javanese Shadow Puppets* (Singapore, 1993)

WARD KEELER

(ii) Bali. The shadow play, the most venerated theatre genre in Bali, seems to have come to the island from Java some time between the 11th and 14th centuries, and, though related, it is clear that Balinese and Javanese shadow theatres developed separately. While the Javanese puppets evolved into extremely stylized, ornate forms, those from Bali are naturalistic and sturdy, having a lingering affinity with figures in the so-called '*wayang* style' found on reliefs of East Javanese temples from the 13th and 14th centuries. The rustic style of the puppets reflects the fact that the shadow theatre in Bali belongs predominantly to Balinese folk tradition, whereas its counterpart in Java is more closely associated with the court. The main occasion for a performance is during the celebration of the anniversary of a temple, which may occur on any of the 210 days of the Hindu–Balinese year, when it is paid for by the temple congregation. Throughout the island it is customary to have a form of entertainment on each of the three final days of the anniversary. The shadow theatre is often chosen for one of the nights because its moral and religious content make it appropriate for the festival, during which the gods are invited to descend to the temple for a few days to witness the celebrations. A performance may also take place during the celebration of rites of passage such as a birth or marriage. The sponsor hires a *dalang* to give a performance, partly for its own sake, but partly also to enhance his own prestige in the eyes of the community, since it indicates his awareness of the traditional culture. A performance may also be given when a sponsor, in fulfilment of a vow (*mesesangi*), wishes to show his gratitude to the gods for granting him a request (e.g. for the restoration to health of a child or for a good harvest after a drought).

The *dalang* has a priestly function and must therefore be consecrated before he is allowed to perform. This is done in a special rite, exorcist in intent, called *sudamala*, which seems mainly to deal with death, illness or danger. The rite also indicates that magical power is attributed to the puppets, for the *dalang* prepares purificatory water by dipping into it the handles of high-ranking puppets, while reciting ritual incantations. The puppets principally used for this seem always to be the gods Tunggal and Shiva, the Tree of Life (*kekayon*) and the wisest of the servants, Tualen. The Balinese consider the puppets to be sacred, so the puppet chest, when not in use, is kept in the household shrine, and small offerings are given to the puppets throughout the year.

A standard collection contains between 80 and 130 puppets. In the *Mahābhārata* stories there are four main groups of characters. The first two are the celestial beings, who ideally embody the noblest spiritual values, but like the Greek gods can succumb to human passions, and the nobles (Kshatriyas), who are the warriors and administrators and constitute the largest group. The heroes of the *Mahābhārata* are the five Pandawa brothers, and their opponents are their first cousins, the hundred Kaurawa brothers. The Pandawas tend to be refined in looks, while the Kaurawas are cruder and larger. The mentor of the Pandawas is the elegant prince Krishna, an incarnation of the god Vishnu. The male servants (*panasar*) form the third group, the principal characters being Tualen, Merdah, Delem and Sangut. In contrast to most of the other characters, who belong to the epic, they belong to the folk tradition and act as clowns and jokers to embellish and give comic relief to the otherwise serious tone of the main plots evolving around the Kshatriyas. They also function as commentators, translating into colloquial Balinese what the mythic characters say in Old Javanese, the language of the texts, which has little affinity to the Balinese spoken by the villagers. The servants are uncouth and highly idiosyncratic in appearance. Finally, there are the ogres, who are sturdy figures with wild hair and coarse features.

Most of the puppets are recognizably human in form, yet their features also symbolize important social and cultural values. The most striking index of status and role is the often sumptuously decorated headdress. Two of these, the *ketu* and *candi utama*, are worn only by senior figures, such as sages and kings, including Krishna. The word *candi* is associated with the temple and *utama* means 'eminent', so this name implies both spiritual and secular power. The puppets have two basic eye shapes: slit (*sumpé*) eyes, such as many of the Pandawa princes have, indicate refined and controlled characters; large, round (*dedelingan*) eyes denote coarse, hot-headed and haughty characters, such as the Kaurawa princes and ogres. Hand positions are among the most eloquent parts of the puppets, and tense gestures punctuate all the speeches. Scholarly Balinese say that the stylized finger positions represent ritual hand gestures (*mudra*s). The gesture called *redaya-mudra* represents the creation of the world by the supreme god Sang Hyang Widi, who is seen as a manifestation of a higher or transcendental truth. With the *sika-mudra*, ogres supplicate Saraswati, the goddess of literature, so that in their next incarnation they may learn to read and write and thereby become civilized. *Dalang* point out that it is important for ogres to make ritual hand gestures in order to beg pardon from the gods for their destructive and base behaviour. The gestures of most of the Pandawa princes, whose orientation is essentially virtuous, are in *saro-mudra*, which indicates a desire to protect the land by calling on the goddess Ganga, the deified River Ganga.

Puppets' body colours are, however, their most significant feature, as they are said to reflect the gods. Five basic colours—white, red, yellow, blue and black—are linked with the Hindu–Balinese pantheon of gods (Ishvara, Brahma, Mahadeva, Vishnu and Sambu respectively). All the bodies of the puppets, with a few exceptions, are painted with different mixtures of these colours and so subtly express the mystic aspects of the gods associated with them. The majority of the audience do not, of course, see the colours, but only the shadows, which are often called by the Sanskrit term *maya* ('illusion', 'deceit', 'magic', 'play'), and have profound metaphysical meaning for the Balinese. The shadow theatre gains religious significance as the elusive shadows on the screen point to the illusory nature of appearance. It is only on the stage that the puppets come alive or, as the villagers say, wake up from their sleep in the puppet chest. The narration adds a further dimension to the plays. The speech of the different characters tends to accord in tonal quality and content with their appearance, whether refined and noble or coarse, uncontrolled and proud.

BIBLIOGRAPHY

C. Holt: *Art in Indonesia: Continuities and Change* (Ithaca, NY, 1967)
C. Hooykaas: *Kama and Kala: Materials for the Study of the Shadow Theatre in Bali*, Verhand. Kon. Ned. Akad. Wet., lxxix (1973)
H. I. R. Hinzler: 'Bima Swarga in Balinese Wayang', *Verhand. Kon. Inst. Taal-, Land- & Vlkenknd.*, xc (1981)
W. D. O'Flaherty: *Dreams, Illusion, and Other Realities* (Chicago, 1984)
A. Hobart: *Dancing Shadows of Bali: Theatre and Myth* (London, 1987)
M. S. Zurbuchen: *The Language of Balinese Shadow Theatre* (Princeton, 1987)
A. Hobart: 'The Enlightened Prince Sutasoma: Transformations of a Buddhist Story', *Power, Nature and Culture in Indonesia*, ed. R. McVey [in preparation]

ANGELA HOBART

2. WAYANG GOLEK AND WAYANG KERUCIL. *Wayang golek* is a puppet theatre performed in full view of the audience, without a screen. Each wooden puppet, carved in the round, is dressed with a long cloth concealing the hand of the *dalang* (puppeteer) as he manipulates its head by means of a wooden rod that runs through the body and into the neck. With his other hand the *dalang* manipulates the movable wooden arms by means of two rods attached to the puppet's hands (see fig. 28). Except for those from Japara on the north coast of Java, *wayang golek* puppets do not have legs or feet. The stage consists of two banana trunks, placed horizontally in front of the *dalang c.* 0.6 m above the floor, into which the puppets are stuck and to which a wooden frame is sometimes fastened to mark off the stage more clearly. The *dalang* sits cross-legged facing the audience and is clearly visible behind his puppets. At his back the *gamelan* (orchestra) and one or more female singers are seated. As in the *wayang kulit*, the

28. *Wayang golek* puppet of a dancer (*tayub* or *gambyong*), wood, cotton, cloth, diamonds, pigment, gold leaf, fish-glue medium, fibre fastenings, 490×180×160 mm, from Surakarta, Central Java, 19th century (Surakarta, Radya Pustaka Museum)

dalang directs the performance, which is held for both secular and ritual purposes, as well as speaking all the roles.

According to Surakarta court tradition, *wayang golek* was created by a Muslim saint from Kudus, in northern Java, in 1584. The example of Chinese puppetry is believed by some to have influenced its development. From the north coast it spread throughout most of Java and Madura. In Sunda (West Java), where it replaced the *wayang kulit*, certain regents of Bandung played an important role in its dissemination. Chiefly owing to their patronage, in the mid-19th century the Sundanese *wayang golek purwa* was developed with puppets and a repertory (from the Hindu epics, the *Rāmāyaṇa* and the *Mahābhārata*) that imitate the *wayang kulit*. In northern Java, from Indramayu east to Kudus, and in Kebumen in the south, *wayang golek cepak*, in which stories of Muslim heroes and Javanese legends are enacted, seems to be best preserved. *Wayang golek* was popular for a time in the Yogyakarta area, but since the death of its only *dalang* in the 1980s it seems to have gone out of fashion there. *Wayang golek cepak* is performed in West Java (notably around Bogor), but *wayang golek purwa* is by far the most popular puppet theatre there, and the Bandung style has become pre-eminent. In Madura, as far as is known, *wayang golek* has disappeared.

Wayang kelitik or *kerucil* ('small') is a similar type of theatre in Java (in the past the names *golek* and *kerucil* were sometimes used interchangeably) that uses flat, painted wooden puppets, carved in low relief (although a few have more or less three-dimensional heads), and usually with leather arms jointed at the shoulders and the elbows and moved by means of a pair of rods attached to the hands. There is no screen, and the stage resembles that of *wayang golek*. This form of *wayang* was a late development. Although some sources mention the last king of Majapahit (*d c.* 1478) as the inventor of this *wayang*, others attribute its creation to Pakubuwono (Pakubawana) II of Kartasura (*reg* 1726–49). He is said to have copied in wood a set of leather puppets, specially made for the performance of stories of the legendary hero Damar Wulan, and to have called his new set *wayang kerucil*.

In the last quarter of the 19th century *wayang kerucil* was found in some parts in the south of Central Java and in much of East Java. The stories enacted were mainly legendary histories of Java (Panji and Damar Wulan) and Arab stories (Menak). By the late 20th century it was almost extinct. In 1985–6 there were in East Java only a few *dalang* who still performed it, and they did so rarely. In Kediri and Nganjuk in East Java performances were given at the yearly harvest festival, in which were enacted, respectively, a Menak story and the exorcistic ritual Murwakala. A farmer of Pagu, near Kediri, possessed, as a sacred heirloom, a *wayang kerucil* set called *wayang gandrung*, to which great healing power is ascribed owing to its reputedly miraculous origin.

BIBLIOGRAPHY

H. H. Juynboll: 'Wajang kelitik oder kerutjil; Mit Tafel V–XIV', *Int. Archvs Ethnog.*, xiii (1900), pp. 4–17, 97–119

M. K. Foley: *The Sundanese 'Wayang Golèk': The Rod Puppet Theatre of West Java* (diss., Honolulu, U. HI, 1979)

P. Buurman: *Wayang golek: De fascinerende wereld van het klassieke West-Javaanse poppenspel* (Alphen aan den Rijn, 1980; Eng. trans., Singapore, Oxford and New York, 1988)

F. Seltmann and W. Gamper: *Stabpuppenspiel auf Java: Wayang Golèk (Mit besonderer Berücksichtigung der Amir-Hamza-Zyklus von Mitteljava)* (Zurich, 1980) [on the *wayang golek cepak* from Yogyakarta area]

U. Wickert and T. Purbaya: *Wayang Stories Photographed, Retold and Edited by Utta Wickert, Adapted from Wayang Plays Performed by Tizar Purbaya, Translated into English by Lilo Oldenburg* (Jakarta, 1980) [based on the *wayang golek purwa* of Sunda]

3. WAYANG BEBER. The *wayang beber* uses a painted scroll rather than puppets or human actors, but like other forms of *wayang* theatre in Java it requires a storyteller, as well as employing parts of the same repertory. Like *wayang kerucil*, it seems to survive only in the region near Pacitan on the south coast of East Java. The storyteller recites, sometimes to the accompaniment of a few musical instruments, the story painted on a series of scrolls, interspersing his account with sung fragments from Old Javanese poems. The scrolls (see fig. 29), made of very strong but transparent bark paper, are clamped at both ends between rods slotted upright into the wooden chest in which the scrolls are stored. During the performance the storyteller sits cross-legged behind the chest and unrolls the scroll scene by scene from one rod to the other. The audience sits facing the pictures.

29. *Wayang beber* scroll showing an episode from the Prince Panji cycle, watercolour and ink on paper, wood batons, 0.71×2.89 m, from Java, before 1852 (Leiden, Rijksmuseum voor Volkenkunde)

According to Surakarta court tradition, *wayang beber* dates from 1361. The earliest known account of a performance in Java comes from a Chinese source dated 1433. From the 17th century the popularity of *wayang beber* diminished, and by the 1970s only one example survived in Java. It consists of six or seven scrolls depicting a Panji story. For many generations it has been the sacred heirloom of one family in Pacitan, reputedly given to an ancestor in the 15th century by a king of Majapahit in gratitude for the healing of his daughter. A 19th-century copy is in the library of the Mangkunagaran Palace in Surakarta. Curative powers are attributed to the scrolls, and offerings are regularly made to them. A peculiarity of this set is that in every generation only one member of the family is entitled to conduct the performance, which is usually given at circumcision feasts, often in fulfilment of a vow. The chest containing the scrolls also circulates yearly among the members of the extended family, so that each in turn enjoys its supposedly benevolent influence.

BIBLIOGRAPHY

B. Anderson: 'The Last Picture Show: Wayang Bèbèr', *Conference on Modern Indonesian Literature: Madison, 1974*, pp. 33–81 [description of the *wayang beber* of Pacitan]

M. Kant-Achilles, F. Seltmann and R. Schumacher: *Wayang beber: Das wiederentdeckte Bildrollen-Drama Zentral-Javas* (Stuttgart, 1990)

VICTORIA M. CLARA VAN GROENENDAEL

4. DANCE DRAMA AND MASKS. Dance, with or without masks, is important throughout Indonesia. The classical dance drama of the Javanese and Balinese courts shows powerful overlapping influences from India (Hinduism, Buddhism and the great epics) and the shadow-puppet theatre (*wayang kulit*). The costumes and particularly the masks of *wayang topeng* are especially fine. Other traditions—some related to ancestor cults, some, more recent, from China—have entered into the popular theatre in rural areas in Bali, Sumatra and other islands.

(i) Java. (ii) Bali. (iii) Other islands.

(i) Java. The Javanese dance theatre with masks, *wayang topeng* ('masked shadow'), was probably introduced to the royal courts in the 16th century by Sunan Kalijaga, a coastal prince revered as one of the seven *wali*, sages of Islam. The invention of the dance theatre without masks, *wayang wong* ('human shadows'), on the other hand, is ascribed to an 18th-century ruler. Both of these genres of dance theatre were formalized, and their costumes enriched, at the Central Javanese courts of Surakarta and Yogyakarta during the 18th–20th centuries. The costumes generally follow the conventions established for the shadow-puppet theatre. Clothing, hairstyle, headdress and ornaments indicate the character portrayed. Princes wear a long waist-cloth but no trousers. Gods, priests and bureaucrats are usually dressed in trousers, a shorter waist-cloth and a coat or blouse. Warriors of the upper class wear a very short waist-cloth and trousers, sometimes with shorts. A long dress is typical for women of royal status. Ladies tie their hair in a knot on top; princes dress theirs upwards in an arc. A crown, either high (*mahkota*) or low (*topong*), is worn by kings, the latter also by gods. State officials wear a cap (*ketu*), whereas priests, and occasionally gods, wear a turban (*songkok*). All but the more refined figures wear bracelets and rings around the upper arm. A large wing-shaped ornament (*praba*) worn at the back indicates a ruling prince, while young princes wear crescent-shaped pendants. Actors of *wayang topeng* and *wayang wong* (a form of dance drama created by Sultan Hamengkubuwono I (*reg* 1755–92) in which men and women dance without masks) make much use of the *sampur*, a long shawl attached to the waist. With its two free ends hanging from the centre of the female's waist and from the hips of the male, actors can convey grace or force and imply emotions.

In *wayang wong* make-up is of major importance, since it indicates, together with miming, a character's status and condition. White denotes goodness, purity, patience, intelligence, holiness and youth; black indicates wisdom, concentration and asceticism; greedy and uncontrolled figures show red faces; gold denotes dignity, love and rank, and is also the colour used by gods. In *wayang topeng* miming is impossible; instead the mask shows clear, often exaggerated traits. Status and character are thus fixed and can be influenced only slightly by movements of the body and head. If a character undergoes an essential change in status or condition, another mask has to be used, and so important characters will have several, in up to five different colours.

The stories enacted in *wayang topeng* are taken mainly from the Javanese cycle of Prince Panji tales, those of *wayang wong* from the Hindu epics and from indigenous tales and myths. Both genres are chiefly arts of the courts, where they are still performed. Many of their features, including masks and costumes, have been adopted in the modern Indonesian theatre, merging there with Western elements. In the countryside masked plays continue to be performed that have no connection with court theatre, although some were once part of that tradition. A notable example features the *barongan*, a beast of prey represented by a huge mask with a movable lower jaw that is worn by two men in animal costume. Often connected with trance dances, it usually makes its appearance at a moment of crisis in the story and has to be overcome to make room for a positive outcome, the essential theme in Javanese theatre.

BIBLIOGRAPHY

Tjan Tjoe Siem: 'Masques javanais', *A. Asiat.*, xx (1969), pp. 185–208

H. Lucas: *Java-Masken: Der Tanz auf einem Bein* (Kassel, 1972)

WOLFGANG MARSCHALL

(ii) Bali. Balinese masks are ritual objects instilled with soul and life, and they derive vitality and energy (*taksu*), which are transmitted to their wearers, from the wood of which they are made, especially that of the *pulé* tree (*Alsonia scholaris*). This tree traditionally grows close to the cemetery and the temple to the dead (*pura dalem*), places ruled by the most magic of the Balinese mask characters, Barong and Rangda. The power of a Rangda mask consecrated by a priest and charged with magic energy is of vital importance for its wearer, as the mask, the embodiment of the feared primordial witch, is subject to repeated murderous attacks by enraged men armed with *kric* daggers. The terror mask (see fig. 30) has prominent, wide-open eyes with pupils outlined in red, black and white. The principal colour of the face is white. Below inflated nostrils, a gaping mouth is framed by deep red lips from which jut a row of bared upper teeth and long

30. Mask of the supreme wicked witch, Rangda, Bali (Basle, Museum für Volkerkunde und Schweizerisches Museum für Volkskunde)

curved fangs. The usual anatomical order is inverted, setting Rangda in the sphere of the non-human, the demonic. A fire-red tongue of leather, covered with stylized flame motifs and circular mirrors, hangs from the open mouth to below the stomach, possessing protective magic to ward off spirits and opponents of all kinds, and, at the same time, enhancing the figure's own magic power. Flames, symbols of magic energy, also emerge from the corners of the mouth and from the parting of the wig, which is made of white marbled goat's hair and falls over the back almost to the ground. Rangda's costume is a white, long-sleeved shirt and long trousers, striped (as are the shirt-sleeves) in black, white and red, the colours of the Trimurti, the Hindu trinity of Brahma, Vishnu and Shiva (Ishvara). A magic hip-cloth (*cepuk*) is worn over the trousers. Hair is attached to the torso, which has loose hanging breasts, and to the white gloves with their long fingernails. All these iconographic features place the masked figure, with its malice and unfettered passions, in the realm of demonic beings and black magic.

The Balinese are protected by Rangda's eternal opponent, Barong, the ruler of white magic, who enjoys the respect of one superior protecting deity, Bhatara Gedé, and is associated with another, Banaspati Raja, king of the forest, which is thought of as the intermediate realm between civilization and nature. The *pulé* tree, whose wood is used to carve the Barong masks, is imbued with the spirit of Barong. Banaspati Raja is also identified in Bali with the placenta, the most powerful of the four brothers and sisters (*Kanda mpat*) who accompany and protect man's life from the womb to the afterlife. The Barong mask is generally kept in the chthonic temple (*pura paseh*). 'Barong' is a generic term usually accompanied by a specific animal name. Common Barong figures are Barong Bangkal (wild boar), Barong Macan (tiger) and Barong Lembu (cow). The best-known and ritually the most significant is the Barong Ket or Keket, a mask that is strongly reminiscent of the head of Bhoma in Balinese temple architecture (see fig. 21 above), but which also seems to incorporate elements of Chinese lion masks. The body of the mythical animal is operated, as in China, by two men. It is 3–4 m long, covered with fibres of the pineapple plant and chicken or heron feathers, and decorated with hanging pieces of leather covered with gold leaf, coloured glass and mirrors. The relatively small head, like all Barong masks, has a mobile lower jaw with handles held with both hands by the front wearer. The face, of an intense, glowing red, is dominated by protruding eyes, inflated nostrils and a large mouth with two rows of giant incisors and fangs arranged in an unnatural order. Above the curved eyebrows is the trident (*karawista*), symbol of the god Shiva and of the Hindu Trimurti. The face is flanked by two spoon-shaped cow's ears and is surmounted by a towering, ornate headdress. The black beard, made from human hair, hangs from the lower jaw of the mask; it contains the essence of the figure's magical power, and water which comes into contact with the beard can be used as medicine or as consecrated water.

Barong and Rangda are two large theatrical figures, with accentuated superhuman or non-human, sinister and grotesque qualities who appear whenever conflict breaks out in the magic world. Thus Durga, goddess of the dead, sometimes appears in the figure of Rangda, and the widow Calon Arang, in the drama of the same name, fights in the figure of Rangda against the exorcist priest Mpu Paradah, who for his part assumes the figure of Barong. Other masks appearing in the Calon Arang drama are those of pupils of Rangda (*sisya*); *jauk*, a group usually composed of four dancers with wild (*galak*) expressions and round eyes, and wearing dark costumes and white trousers; and four *sandaran*, boyish figures with delicate white masks, finely cut, 'sweet' (*manis*) eyes and dressed in light-coloured costumes. Special forms of Barong include the Barong Landung, two colossal masked figures of an old married couple, Jero Gedé and Jero Luh, danced and played by two men. Barong Landung figures, which are mostly kept in temples, are sometimes regarded as especially sacred. Performances of the Barong Landung take place in particular during the New Year (*Galungan*) festival period, when the masked figures travel from village to village singing folk songs (often very coarse in content) as they dance.

In contrast to the demonic masks and abundant energy of the Barong and Rangda drama is the restrained solemnity of the masks of the *topeng* chronicle play, representing ancient kings, ministers, generals, priests and folk heroes of the Majapahit Empire and the court of Gelgel (Bali). At the same time *topeng* is an ancestor cult, often performed in temples and residences of the nobility; it belongs to the category of *bebali*, sacred performances given as part of ritual offerings. Also in this category are the *wayang lemah*, a leather-puppet theatre performed by day without a screen, the old courtly *gambuh* dance theatre and *wayang wong* (*see* §(i) above), in which demonic powers, apes, Jatayu and, above all, Rawana appear in masks, together with unmasked heroes and gods. In its oldest and purest form, the ritual *topeng* is a mute performance by a single priest who dances one role after another. Since the early 20th century, the *topeng pañca*, where the roles are distributed among five dancers, has also become established. Each masked figure in the *topeng* appears accompanied by appropriate music, which was formerly performed on the sacred *gamelan gong gedé* ('great gong') but is now more often played by the modern *gamelan gong kebyar*, with its *reyong* (row of pot gongs) of two and a half octaves (*see* §VIII, 9 below). All the characters wear the same colourful ceremonial clothing—a sequin-covered jacket, long narrow trousers and a shawl worn high above the chest—but their masks, headdresses and wigs differ. A complete set of masks (*tapel*) always includes a few heroic figures of different ages, an old man, a king, a queen, a priest, a few leading characters from the ordinary people and a number of comic or bizarre figures. The sacred *topeng pajegan* always ends with the masked figure of Sidhakary, an old man with a grinning white face, at once friendly and repulsive, with protruding teeth (including two sharp upper canines) and bushy hair. This half-demonic, half-human holy figure dances a final, unpredictable dance that in particular frightens children, to whom he afterwards gives coins.

In the *topeng* chronicle play, the audience is first shown a few mute figures (*pengelembar*) with full masks representing among others energetic ministers or generals with dark (often red or red-brown) faces, moustaches and spherical eyes, which give them a powerful and aggressive appearance, and the old man *Tua*, a forebear of the tribe, whose veteran's dance is interspersed with bouts of youthful vitality. In several interludes, village idiots with nervous tics, buffoons with hare-lips or effeminate dandies with special walks and a repertoire of stereotyped movements appear in front of the curtain. The plot (*lakon*) is unfolded by speaking figures in brown half-masks with prominent noses and fantastic moustaches. They are leading representatives of the people or attendants (*penasar*) of the king, and, as well as narrating the story, they glorify, speak for or interpret the mute figure. It culminates in their encounter with the mute figure of the king (*tapel* Dalem), whose mask is white or orange-yellow, with a distinguished and gentle smile. It is in this mask above all that the mask-carver (*sangging tapel*) demonstrates his skill. The quality of the mask is determined by the choice of the appropriate wood and by the skill, energy and inspiration of the mask-carver, who never sees the mask as a static form but as part of a dynamic process in which the dancer's ability plays its part.

BIBLIOGRAPHY

M. Covarrubias: *Island of Bali* (London, 1937)

H. Neuhaus: 'Barong', *Djawa*, xvii (1937), pp. 230–39

B. Zoete and W. Spies: *Dance and Drama in Bali* (London and Kuala Lumpur, 1938/*R* London, 1952, 1973)

J. Belo: *Bali: Rangda and Barong* (New York, 1949)

Bali: Studies in Life, Thought and Ritual: Selected Studies on Indonesia by Dutch Scholars (The Hague, 1960)

C. McPhee: *Music in Bali* (New Haven, 1966)

——: 'Dance in Bali', *Traditional Balinese Culture*, ed. J. Belo (New York, 1970)

C. Hooykaas: *Cosmogony and Creation in Balinese Tradition* (The Hague, 1974)

U. Ramseyer: *The Art and Culture of Bali* (Oxford, 1977)

A. Forge: 'Tooth and Fang in Bali', *Canberra Anthropol.*, iii/1 (1980), pp. 1–16

I. Madé Bandem and F. E. de Boer: *Kaja and Kelod: Balinese Dance in Transition* (Kuala Lumpur, 1981)

E. Schlager: 'Ein Beispiel: Der Barong', *Bali: Insel der Götter* (exh. cat., ed. U. Ramseyer; Basle, Mus. Vlkerknd., 1983), pp. 101–6

URS RAMSEYER

(iii) Other islands. Javanese court dance traditions spread to other islands after independence in 1949. Some islands, predominantly those in the western part of Indonesia, have their own forms of masked drama, although they are not common everywhere. Ritual dancing, however, is found throughout Indonesia. Relatively well documented are the carved wooden masks of the Bataks in Sumatra and those of the Kayans and Kenyahs of Kalimantan. The masked performances of the Bataks take place at the funerals of important men. The masks (*hudoq*) represent either a horse with a hornbill face or a human, and the ceremony enacts the accompanying of the deceased to the next world. The carving of the Batak masks is generally plain, with strong but simple accentuation of facial features. By contrast, the Kalimantan masks have the composite features found in much Kayan and Kenyah iconography. They may combine the anthropomorphic characteristics of three-dimensional ancestor representations with elaborate open scrollwork framing the face (*kitaq* masks). Protective demonic features are found in the masks, which combine animal and mythical aspects, including the hornbill and *aso* (dragon–snake) motif. These are used in agricultural ceremonies as well as for curing illnesses. Less well known are the hood masks used by Kenyah women, which incorporate beadwork, textiles and feathers, and the Kenyah 'wild boar' mask carried by a group of young men or boys. The performances seem intended to ward off evil and to harness benevolent spiritual powers. During the 1970s some very simple masks from Timor came on to the art market, but their use was unclear.

BIBLIOGRAPHY

H. H. Bartlett: *The Labors of the Datoe*, Michigan Papers on South and Southeast Asia, v (Ann Arbor, 1973)

N. Revel-Macdonald: 'La Danse des "hudoq" (Kalimantan Timur)', *Obj. & Mondes*, xviii/1–2 (1978), pp. 31–44

The Eloquent Dead: Ancestral Sculpture of Indonesia and Southeast Asia (exh. cat., ed. J. Feldman; Los Angeles, UCLA, Mus. Cult. Hist., 1985)

Islands and Ancestors: Indigenous Styles of Southeast Asia (exh. cat., ed. J.-P. Barbier and D. Newton; New York, Met., 1988)

RUTH BARNES

VII. Painting and drawing.

In Java and Bali, traditional court styles of painting and drawing owe much to the influence of the shadow-puppet theatre (*wayang kulit*). Indeed, all forms of *wayang* theatre employ the painter's skills. The traditional arts of Indonesia and of South-east Asia generally were largely untouched by Islamic culture until the 15th century, when Islam first gained a foothold in the archipelago. Thereafter, traditional painting largely comprised manuscript illumination, and this was chiefly confined to Java and Bali. The painted decoration of houses and other pictorial arts in Sumatra and other islands belong to a separate tradition. In many Muslim courts illuminated manuscripts of the Koran were made, and examples of these are to be found in the palace collections of Tidore and Sumbawa Besar as well as Surakarta and Yogyakarta. Dutch and other Western artists also played a role in the development of painting, particularly in Java and Bali, and in the later part of the colonial period and after independence painting became one of Indonesia's most vigorous art forms.

1. Traditional. 2. Colonial and modern.

1. Traditional.

(i) Java. Manuscript illumination and illustration in Java are subject to conventions that relate to place, date and type of text. Illustration and illumination in manuscripts with writing in Perso-Arabic characters are relatively rare. In accordance with their Islamic subject-matter, only decorative frames around the text are common, particularly on initial facing pages. Sometimes these frames are illuminated with colours and gilt. One notable example is the gilded letter (London, PRO, C.O. 77/14, p. 111) sent from Sultan Abdul Fatah of Banten, West Java, to King Charles II of England in 1683. On the other hand, in manuscripts in Javanese characters, illumination is often more elaborate and illustrations more common. The art of manuscript illumination reached its peak in the Yogyakarta courts between the second half of the 18th century and the early 20th. In the Yogyakarta tradition, ornamental frames, called *wadana* ('head'), are found not only on initial facing pages—as in other regional traditions—but also as chapter headings in the body of the text. Double-page *wadana* are most common on the first and last pages. They usually have a rectangular outline on to which one or more rhomboids are mapped. The outlines, drawn in ink, are filled in with geometrical, foliate and floral patterns, coloured and gilt. Single-page *wadana* may also be shaped as buildings or ships. Stanza and canto markers are embellished with foliate patterns and occasionally animal heads, and are sometimes coloured and gilt. Illustration of narrative poems is found most often in manuscripts from

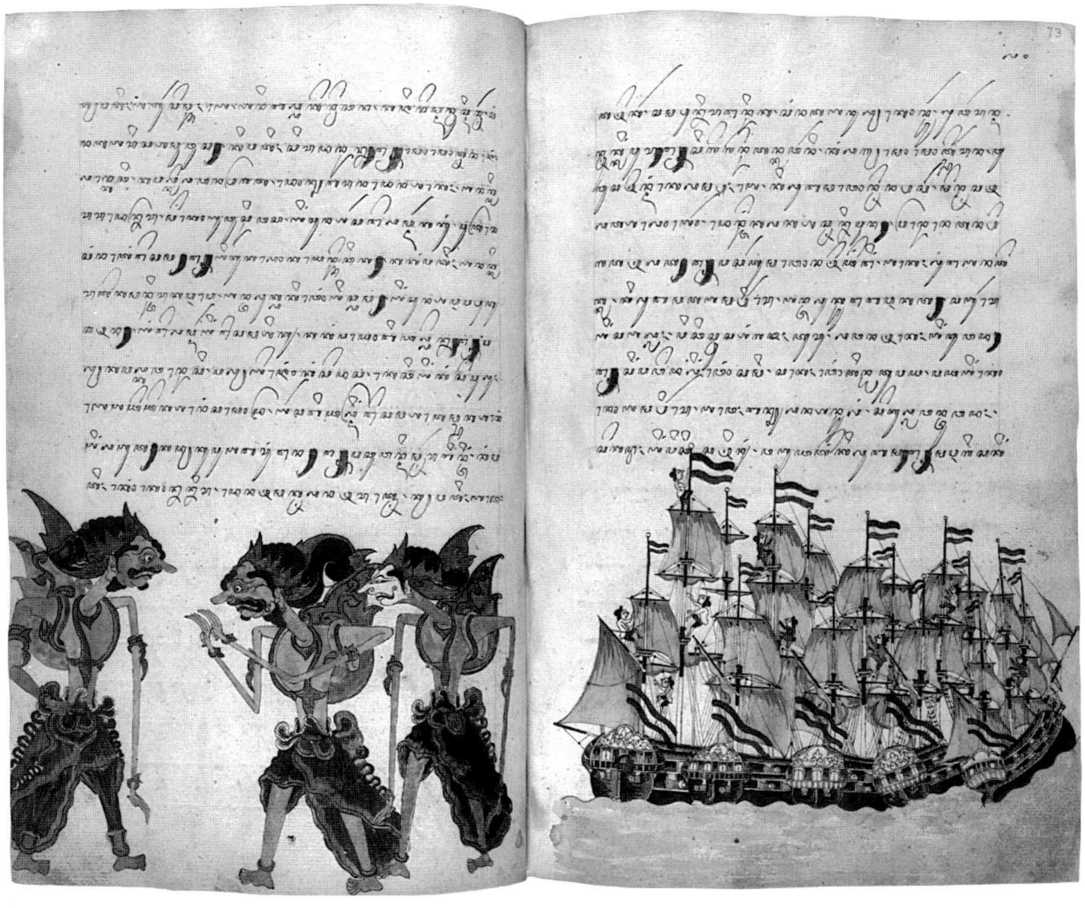

31. Manuscript of *Sela Rasa*, ink, polychrome watercolour and gold leaf on European paper, each folio 403×200 mm, from Java, 1804 (London, British Library)

the north coast and from the Yogyakarta courts. Figures of high-ranking humans and deities usually have a stylized form resembling shadow-puppets (*wayang kulit*), which means that they are shown in profile. More lowly figures, buildings, ships, flora and fauna are depicted more realistically and in great detail (see fig. 31). *Pawukon* (divination almanacs) are the most common illustrated genre in all regional traditions. Each of 30 *wuku* weeks has a set of attributes, such as a deity, a bird or a mystical tree, that symbolically represents its nature and is depicted in *wayang* style. The traditonal style remained dominant in painting (on paper and wood) and drawing by Indonesian artists until the 1930s.

BIBLIOGRAPHY

L. M. Coster-Wijsman: 'Illustrations in a Javanese Manuscript', *Bijdr. Taal-, Land- & Vlkenknd.*, cix (1953), pp. 153–63, 276

Th. G. Th. Pigeaud: *Illustrations and Facsimiles of Manuscripts, Maps, Addenda and a General Index of Names and Subjects* (1970), iii of *Literature of Java* (The Hague, 1967–80)

Golden Letters: Writing Traditions of Indonesia (exh. cat. by A. Teh Gallop with B. Arps, London, BL, 1991)

BERNARD ARPS

(ii) Bali. Traditional Balinese paintings and drawings have fixed stylistic elements, ornaments, motifs and rules of composition, largely derived from the highly idiosyncratic religious and literary tradition of Balinese Hinduism. As in Java, human figures are represented in *wayang* style (*see* §VI, 1(ii) above), and their physical features, clothes, jewellery, coiffures and headdresses indicate their class, age and character. Sky, rocks and ground are indicated by specific ornamental motifs. There is no perspective. The scenes in a narrative picture are separated by rock ornaments or indicated by the back-to-back arrangement of the figures. Important scenes are placed in the centre; those in which gods appear should be at the top and those with demons or animals at the bottom, to express the idea of hierarchy. The subject-matter is derived from religious texts, in particular the Old Javanese and Balinese versions of the Indian epics the *Mahābhārata* and *Rāmāyaṇa*, the *Pañcatantra*, the Javanese stories of Prince Panji (see fig. 32) and Balinese folk-tales such as *Brayut.* Cloth paintings are displayed only during religious ceremonies. The subject-matter is intended to harmonize with the symbolic character of the ceremony.

32. Ida Madé Tlaga: *Princess Nawang Rum and her Servant Madukara*, polychrome drawing on paper, 418×340 mm, late 19th century (Leiden, Bibliotheek der Rijksuniversiteit Leiden)

Painting materials are cloth, wood, paper (Javanese, Chinese and, since the 19th century, European), bark and glass. Wood and glass paintings are mounted in shrines and pavilions in temples and domestic sanctuaries, and on walls of bedchambers, particularly in palaces. Paintings on paper, initially made on demand for Westerners, are kept in albums or displayed on the walls of houses. The paint was originally handmade from natural dyes, but chemical dyes are now also used. Traditional drawings are made on palm leaves (*lontar*), Chinese paper, potsherds, thin leaves of gold and silver, and on cloth. Black ink (made from soot), Chinese ink and, in modern times, felt-tip pens are used for drawing on paper and cloth. The palm leaves, potsherds and metal pieces are inscribed with a stylus; the engravings on palm leaves are blackened with soot. The majority of the drawings are for ritual and magic purposes, though palm-leaf drawings may also illustrate literary texts in Old Javanese and Balinese. Painting and drawing skills and conventions were generally passed on from father to son and in workshops. Most traditional painters work anonymously, as they are considered craftsmen rather than artists. In the past their patrons were primarily noblemen and temple authorities, but now they are mainly tourists. In contrast, the makers of magical drawings (available to any Balinese) are witch-doctors and priests. An important centre of traditional Balinese painting is Kamasan, near Gelgel. The craftsmen here were in the service of the former rulers of Bali, who had settled in Gelgel (from the 15th century to 1710) and in nearby Klungkung (1710–1908). Other centres of traditional painting and drawing were the courts of the rulers at Gianyar, Bangli, Karangasem, Tabanan, Sanur and Singaraja.

BIBLIOGRAPHY

A. Forge: *Balinese Traditional Painting* (Sydney, 1978)

A. A. Madé Djelantik: *Balinese Painting* (Singapore, 1986)

H. I. R. HINZLER

(iii) Sumatra and other islands. The traditional painting of the Indonesian islands other than Java and Bali is chiefly significant as architectural decoration. The panel to be painted is usually first carved in relief, and the ornaments are then highlighted with colour. The painting is executed in a linear, strictly two-dimensional style, even in realistic scenes such as those sometimes found on the houses and ceremonial banners (*sarita*) of the Torajas of central Sulawesi. The dominant colours are red, black and white, which have a different symbolic significance in different

Indonesian societies, or even within one society, depending on circumstances. Black often appears to be associated with the physical, including the human, world, while white is the colour of spirits and ancestors. Red is ambiguous; it may represent the blood of warfare and violent death but also that of descent, and so be a symbol of fertility and life-giving principles. Spectacularly painted houses are made by the Minangkabaus in central Sumatra and the Toba Bataks in northern Sumatra, and by the Sa'dan Torajas (see fig. 33). The exterior walls of Dayak longhouses in Kalimantan may also be painted with the curvilinear, asymmetric designs characteristic of much of their art (*see* §II, 4(v) above). Although apparently abstract, the patterns are in fact representational. For example, the stylized figure of a mythical dragon-snake frequently occurs on Toba Batak and Dayak houses. Called *sanga* by the Toba Bataks and *aso* ('dog') in Kalimantan, it is thought to have protective powers and is therefore also painted on the shields of Dayak warriors.

Certain Toraja groups used to wear garments of bark cloth brightly painted—not in the usual colour triad, but in yellow, purple, pink and black with geometric and vegetal patterns. The Torajas also paint the patterns on their ceremonial banners with a resist paste before dyeing, in a technique similar to batik. The patterns combine geometric designs and realistic scenes similar to those on Toraja ceremonial houses. In addition to true painting, decoration by incision is practised. Bamboo containers are elaborately decorated in this manner, with the designs picked out by the addition of pigments. In Kalimantan the designs are executed in the same ornate curvilinear style as that used in the region's wood-carving and house-panel decoration. The result is two-dimensional and restricted by the tubular shape of the bamboo, of which the artist takes advantage by drawing the elaborate scroll designs round the container. A similar effect is achieved with coconut containers, which are incised and then have white chalk rubbed in, a technique used in Timor and Pantar in the eastern Nusa Tenggara (Lesser Sundas).

BIBLIOGRAPHY

A. R. Hein: *Die bildenden Künste bei den Dayaks auf Borneo: Ein Beitrag zur allgemeinen Kunstgeschichte* (Vienna, 1890) [for drawings of Borneo designs]

T. Bodrogi: *Art in Indonesia* (Greenwich, CT, 1972)

Islands and Ancestors: Indigenous Styles of Southeast Asia (exh. cat., ed. J.-P. Barbier and D. Newton; New York, Met., 1988)

RUTH BARNES

2. COLONIAL AND MODERN. Developments in painting and drawing during the colonial period and after independence were concentrated in Java and Bali. An important influence was the work of resident European artists, reinforced by the experiences of Indonesian artists who studied in Europe. Already some late 19th-century drawings from Sanur and Singaraja have perspective, there is naturalism in the treatment of figures and landscape, and the composition is less stereotyped. More important innovations date from the late 1920s. A naive, naturalistic style mixed with elements from the *wayang* was developed in the Gianyar area. As well as the traditional subject-matter, scenes from daily life were also depicted. Paper and crayon or gouache were the main media used. Two European artists, the German painter-musician Walter Spies (1895–1942), who settled in Campuan, near Ubud in Gianyar, in 1927, and the Dutchman Rudolf Bonnet (1895–1978), who settled in Ubud in 1931, strongly influenced Balinese painters: Spies by his landscapes, characterized by trees with bright leaf-tips, stylized animal and human figures and double or triple horizons, and Bonnet by his naturalistic, romantic portraits. Bonnet also taught anatomy, composition, sketching, drawing and the use of oil paint. The Mexican painter Miguel Covarrubias (in Bali 1930–33) was also influential.

33. Painting on a Sa'dan Toraja house, Sulawesi, 20th century

(i) Java. From the 18th century, draughtsmen and painters, mainly Dutch and many of them amateurs, were engaged in technical drawing and in portrait and landscape drawing and painting. Some painters influenced talented Javanese. The Belgian A. A. J. Payen (1792–1853) lived in Java from 1817 to 1826 and inspired the Javanese RADEN SALEH, who went to The Hague to study portrait painting with Cornelis Kruseman, landscape painting with Andreas Schelfhout and drawing in the service of the Dutch government (1829–37). Raden Saleh became the first Indonesian painter whose work was known abroad, an exponent of a form of romanticism in his portraits and landscapes and of a form of orientalism in his rendering of wild animals and scenery. He travelled through Europe between 1838 and 1851 and frequented court circles in Germany and France before returning to Java. Despite being widely known and acclaimed, however, he had no pupils.

In the early 20th century some Dutch-trained Indonesian draughtsmen and artists, including Mas Pirngadie (1875–1936), Abdullah Surio Subroto (1878–1941) and Wakidi (*b* 1889), trained small groups of Javanese and Sumatrans. These adopted the naturalistic style of their teachers and the subject-matter favoured at that period. This 'Beautiful Indies' style, characterized by pleasant landscapes and still-lifes with exotic flowers, was rejected in the early 1930s by certain young painters living mainly in the big cities of Java (Batavia, Yogyakarta, Bandung), among them Affandi (*b c.* 1910), Sudjojono (1913–86), Agus Djaja (*b* 1913), Otto Djaja (*b* 1916) and Basuki Resobowo (*b* 1916). Many of these artists were self-taught, but some of them were influenced by the ideas of Ki

Hadjar Dewantoro (1889–1959), who founded the Taman Siswa schools (*see* §IX below). They sought to bring art to the people, and to express their rejection of tradition they chose modern oil painting in Western naturalistic and realistic styles (see fig. 34), which they had seen at exhibitions of French, Italian and Russian painters organized by the Union of Dutch Indies Art Societies in Batavia in the 1930s. Their subjects, however, were Indonesian. After their work had been criticized for inferior technique, the artists organized the Union of Indonesian Painters (Persatuan Ahli Gambar or PERSAGI) in 1937 under Sudjojono and Agus Djaja, and in 1941 the Union organized a special exhibition of Indonesian painters. Other associations of painters were founded, such as the Group of Five in Bandung, which included Affandi, Hendra (1918–86) and Barli (*b* 1921) and whose work was impressionist in style. During the 1930s a few painters studied at academies in the Netherlands or elsewhere abroad: Salim (*b* 1908) studied in Paris, Abdullah (*b* 1915) in The Hague and Rusli (*b* 1916) in Shantiniketan (India), at an establishment founded by Tagore.

During the Japanese occupation (1942–5) many painters, including Affandi and Sudjojono, but also younger artists such as Zaini (1924–77) and Trubus (1926–66), were forced to depict propaganda scenes. Although these artists were initially encouraged by the facilities and recognition afforded them by the Japanese, a sense of nationalism grew, especially during the late 1940s, when many of these same artists produced anti-Dutch posters and guerilla scenes in naturalistic, realistic styles. During the late 1940s and early 1950s a broad and highly influential debate began in Indonesia between the 'traditionalists', such as Ki Hadjar Dewantoro and President Sukarno (1901–70), who argued that traditional themes and forms should be used in order to retain continuity and the consciousness of national identity, and the modernists, such as the writer Takdir Alisjahbana, who argued that the value of art in modern Indonesian society lay in its relevance for the future development of society. This debate continued into the late 1980s. Central Java in particular became a stronghold of Indonesian nationalism, in contrast to other regions, which retained closer affinities with the West: in Bandung, for example, the Cubism of Ries Mulder was influential on such artists as Mochtar Apin (*b* 1923), Achmad Sadali (1924–87), But Muchtar (*b* 1930), Srihadi S(udarsono) (*b* 1932) and Popo Iskandar (*b* 1927). In the late 20th century Java remained the centre of Indonesian modern art, with the formation of many new associations such as the Gerakan Seni Rupa Baru, founded in 1974 by Jim Sunpangkat. Other artists experimented with such styles as New Realism and naive painting, and with new media such as batik, feathers and glass.

34. Sudjojono: *Before the Open Kelambu*, oil on canvas, 1939 (private collection)

BIBLIOGRAPHY

C. Holt: *Art in Indonesia: Continuities and Change* (Ithaca, NY, and London, 1967)

Articles on Art in the Indonesian Press, i–iv (Leiden, 1986–8)

A. Wright: *Soul, Spirit, and Mountain: Preoccupations of Contemporary Indonesian Painters* (Singapore, 1993)

(ii) Bali. During the late 19th century, as Dutch control in Bali increased and the authority of the local rulers declined, and more particularly after the final subjugation of Bali by the Dutch in 1906–8, the traditional arts were affected by the need to find new patrons, and modern influences began increasingly to make themselves felt.

Three important modern art centres with characteristic styles and subject-matter developed in the 1930s. The first of these, in the Ubud area, produced work in which refined, polychrome figures in *wayang* style are surrounded by scenery derived from Spies's landscapes, or in which men and women similar to those painted by Bonnet are depicted barebacked and surrounded by plants and trees. The figures are seen harvesting, planting, making offerings and dancing. Witches and scenes from Old Javanese and Balinese literature and folk-tales are also depicted. Prominent artists working in Ubud include Ida Bagus Kembeng (1897–1952), his son Ida Bagus Madé (Poleng) (*b* 1915), Anak Agung Gedé Soberat (*b* 1917), who learnt much from Spies, his cousin Anak Agung Gedé Meregeg (*b* 1902) and Wayan Tohjiwa (*b* 1916). The second centre was Sanur, on the coast close to Denpasar. The artists here produced softly coloured or black-and-white drawings of figures in ink in half-*wayang*, half-naturalistic style, animals in human dance poses, huge insects and birds (notable exponents being I Sukaria, Gusti Madé Rundu and I Regig) or naive, coloured and black-and-white drawings of village and rural scenes, in which the trees have large, indented leaves (as in the work of Ida Bagus Madé Pugug, Ida Bagus Rai). The work of the artists of the third centre, Batuan, is characterized by stylized figures, also in half-*wayang*, half-naturalistic style, featuring pronounced, blackish, heavily shadowed vertebrae, leafy trees similar to those of Spies, and an idiosyncratic use of perspective that makes buildings and walls appear spread across the paper. Originally only black ink and crayon were used, on paper; the idea of colouring with crayon came from the brothers Hans Neuhaus and Rolf Neuhaus from Munich, who sold Batuan drawings from 1935. Watercolours, gouache and cloth were later used as well. Typical representatives of this centre are Ida Bagus Madé Djata(sura) (1910–46) and Ida Bagus Madé Togog (*b* 1916).

The majority of these modern painters had initially been taught painting in the traditional way and later came to work together with small groups, often imitating each other's designs, styles and subject-matter. Some painters, however, refused to imitate Spies or Bonnet. I Gusti Nyoman Lempad (1875 or 1862–198?) produced naturalistic but flat and highly stylized human figures almost without scenery, and I Gusti Madé Deblog (1906–87) used black and white paint to depict naturalistic figures dressed in *wayang* costume in romantic, perspectival scenery.

From 1934 to 1937 paintings and drawings were sold to tourists by the sales department of the Bali Museum in Denpasar (founded in 1932). It was temporarily closed as the result of a controversy with the Neuhaus brothers, who had started an art gallery (Toko Neuhaus) in Sanur in 1935. Spies, Bonnet and the archaeologist Willem Frederik Stutterheim, who feared the negative effects of tourism on the quality of painting and drawing in the new styles, founded the Pita Maha artists' association in Ubud in 1936 with the help of two noblemen, Cokorda Raka and Cokorda Gedé Soekawati. About 150 painters and sculptors became members, Lempad playing an important role among them. The main aim was to make artists more aware of the quality of their work and to organize sales exhibitions in Java and abroad. In this way modern Balinese art became widely known and began to be bought by collectors and museums in Europe and the USA. In 1942, following the Japanese occupation, the Pita Maha ceased to exist and, as there was no tourism, the market for art disappeared. Bonnet, who returned to Bali from a Japanese prison camp in 1947, tried to reorganize the artists. He settled in Ubud and founded the Ubud Painters' Club with the help of Cokorda Gedé Soekawati; in 1956 it was renamed Ratna Warta. Some painters from Batuan and Sanur also started to work again.

A new style of painting was introduced by the Dutch painter Arie Smit (*b* 1916), who became an Indonesian citizen and moved to Bali in 1956. In Panestanan near Ubud he taught small numbers of talented young boys, who formed themselves into a group called Young Artists. Their naive style, characterized by strong colours and naturalistic but stylized human figures, became well known. Their subject-matter included scenes from daily life, festivals, animals and birds. After 1965, Bali became increasingly open to tourism, and young Balinese painters and sculptors, as well as Javanese, Sumatran and Western artists, settled in the area between Mas and Ubud, which is much frequented by tourists. New styles, such as Pop art, Macro art and Magic Realism, emerged, and new materials (e.g. batik and screenprint) became fashionable. For instance, Dewa Nyoman Batuan from Pengosekan and his followers took their subject-matter from nature and produced large, colourful paintings with monumental depictions of leaves, grasses, insects and birds.

Only a few modern Balinese painters received formal art training, notable examples being Madé Wianta (*b* 1945) and Nyoman Gunarsa (*b* 1943). The styles and subject-matter of such artists are in complete contrast to those of other Balinese painters, but the main difference between the majority of the non-academic painters who began working in the 1920s and the academic painters lies in their subject-matter. The work of the former is heavily influenced by stories from the epics and folk-tales, so that it cannot be understood without a knowledge of Balinese literature. However, painters of both schools often depict religious ceremonies, dance and drama performances and other scenes of Balinese daily life, and some familiarity with Balinese culture is also necessary for an understanding of these. The majority of non-academic painters in Bali regard tourists as their main customers and therefore produce works that are neither large nor expensive. Many less skilful Balinese, often children, are engaged in the mass production for the tourist market of uninspired imitations of works by more talented colleagues.

BIBLIOGRAPHY

Hedendaagse kunst van Bali [Modern art of Bali] (exh. cat. by Th. P. Galestin, Utrecht, Cent. Mus., 1962)

H. Rhodius and J. Darling: *Walter Spies and Balinese Art* (Amsterdam and Zutphen, 1980)

A. A. Madé Djelantik: *Balinese Painting* (Singapore, 1986)

G. Kam: *Perceptions of Paradise: Images of Bali in the Arts* (Ubud, 1993)

H. I. R. HINZLER

VIII. Other arts.

In other arts, often expressed in artefacts that are relatively portable, parts of Indonesia beyond the world of the royal courts of Java and Bali excel. The great variety of materials and techniques employed and of functions served is a reflection of distinct artistic traditions that continue to be active in different parts of Indonesia. One art form particularly strong among many ethnic groups in Kalimantan (Indonesian Borneo), for example, is tattooing. However, this is part of a tradition shared also with Sarawak in Malaysian Borneo; to avoid duplication, therefore, it is discussed in MALAYSIA, §X, 1.

BIBLIOGRAPHY

H. I. Jessup: *Court Arts of Indonesia* (New York, 1991)

P. M. Taylor and L. V. Aragon: *Beyond the Java Sea: Art of Indonesia's Outer Islands* (New York, 1991)

□

1. Basketwork. 2. Boats. 3. Ceramics. 4. Coins. 5. Cremation towers and temple offerings. 6. Dress. 7. Dutch colonial furniture and silver. 8. Jewellery and beadwork. 9. Musical instruments. 10. Weapons.

1. BASKETWORK. Basket-weaving is a highly developed art in Indonesia. All known techniques are represented, some—such as three-way plaiting—unique to South-east Asia. Mats and containers are usually plaited, using screw-pine (*Pandanus*), split bamboo, palm leaves, rattan and grass. In Java, Madura, Bali and Lombok

bamboo is the most plentiful material available for basket-weaving; in Kalimantan, Sulawesi and Sumatra rattan, and in Nusa Tenggara (Lesser Sunda Islands) *lontar* palm leaves are more widely used. Bamboo lends itself particularly well to the making of such kitchen utensils as rice baskets and rice steamers, coconut-milk strainers and flour sieves. In Palembang, south-east Sumatra, baskets are often coated with several layers of red and black lacquer, sometimes with a layer of gold leaf beneath, to make food containers for ceremonial use. In Bali young coconut leaves are used for the decoration of temple offerings such as the *sampian*, a plaited ornament with long streamers, which is placed on the top of food offerings or suspended from tall bamboo poles known as *penjor*, and the *lamak*, a long panel bearing a stylized representation of Shri, goddess of the earth and fertility, which is placed under the offering and hangs down in front of it (*see also* §5 below). Young coconut leaves are also used to make the plaited ornaments symbolizing beauty and fertility that are employed in Javanese wedding ceremonies.

In the outer islands betel and tobacco containers, in particular, are often elaborately decorated with both geometric abstract patterns and representations of human or animal figures. Eastern Indonesia (Timor, Sumba and Flores) has a tradition of finely ornamented baskets made for everyday and ceremonial use. The patterns, picked out in fibres dyed red and black on a natural ground, can be linked to certain textile designs. Sleeping mats from Halmahera in northern Maluku (Moluccas) are part of the gift exchange at marriages, serving a function apparently similar to that of textiles in many other parts of rural Indonesia. They have patterns that closely imitate the designs of imported Indian cloths, originally introduced as items of exchange in the spice trade with eastern Indonesia (*see* §V, 3 above). Also directly linked to textiles is the ornamentation of carrying baskets made in Kalimantan. These are usually worked in black fibres on white ground; occasionally red is used instead. The patterns are abstract, although usually with a name suggesting a representational image. Hats and headdresses are important plaited items. Large, round hats, often decorated with beads, paintwork, pieces of fabric or mica, occur in Sulawesi and Kalimantan. In Ambon (northern Maluku) baskets and decorative objects are sometimes made entirely of cloves.

BIBLIOGRAPHY

J. E. Jasper and M. Pirngadie: *Het vlechtwerk* [Basketwork] (1912), i of *De inlandsche kunstnijverheid in Nederlandsch Indië* (The Hague, 1912–30)

A. M. Klausen: *Basket-work Ornamentation among the Dayaks*, Studies Honouring the Centennial of Universitetets Etnografiske Museum, Oslo, iii (Oslo, 1957)

I. Emery: *The Primary Structure of Fabrics* (Washington, DC, 1966) [for techniques]

Art of the Archaic Indonesians (exh. cat., Dallas, TX, Mus. F.A., 1982)

B. Solyom and G. Solyom: *Fabric Traditions of Indonesia* (Washington, DC, 1984) [for illustrations]

J. Ave and others, eds: *The Crafts of Indonesia* (Singapore, 1988), pp. 54–79

RUTH BARNES

2. BOATS. The boat has been an important symbol in the Indonesian archipelago since early times, and it may be that some of the forms used in their traditional houses derive from the designs of boats. Boat-building and house-building are closely related activities, the same vocabulary often being used for similar house and boat parts. Cloths hung from the rafters of new houses are said to represent sails, and many of the motifs found on textiles and baskets, especially the hook motif, symbolize boats. Many textiles, such as those of Lampung in southern Sumatra, depict the boats that take the souls of the dead to the afterlife. Depictions of Indonesian boats with curved prow and stern appear on some DONG SON drums (*c*. 3rd century BC–1st century AD), and the village of Sikka in Flores in the Lesser Sunda Islands owns a bronze model of such a boat, believed to date from the same period. The 9th-century AD reliefs at Borobudur show several different kinds of Indonesian boat, ranging from simple canoes to large ships with sails, lateral rudders and outriggers. There are no modern Indonesian boats like this; the closest is the *kora kora*, an outrigger canoe found in Maluku and originally used in naval warfare.

The boats of the Hindu–Javanese rulers often had carved dragon-snake (*nāga*) figureheads symbolizing royal power. Drawings made in the 19th century (e.g. London, BL) and showing such boats with carvings of a *nāga* head at the prow and a *nāga* tail at the stern indicate that they were still used in that period. An example of such a figurehead, probably dating from the 19th century, exists in the Hadiningrat court (*kraton*) in Surakarta. Carved from teak, it is gilded and painted in red and black and bears a *nāga* head with a crown similar to the headdresses worn by Balinese and Javanese dancers. In the back of the head, as a talisman of protection, there is a rear-facing head of a *garuḍa* swallowing a fish. Similar dragon-headed prow ornaments were used by the rulers of Banjarmasin in southern Kalimantan and Makassar in south-west Sulawesi. They displayed Chinese and Malay as well as Javanese stylistic influences (e.g. Jakarta, N. Mus.). On boats still used by many Dayak groups in Kalimantan (Jakarta, Mus. Bahari) the *nāga* carvings are more stylized. The ceremonial warships of the ruling families of northern Sumatra also had dragon figureheads. Models of these boats, called yellow boats (*perahu lancang kuning*), were used to present food offerings during rituals. An example in the National Museum, Jakarta, has a dragon head with painted scales and carved and painted floral motifs, and bears the royal insignia of Asahan, northern Sumatra, on the posts and masts.

The use of carved ornamentation on the prow is widespread. For example, the Tanimbar islanders make several types of boat, from simple outrigger canoes to large plank-built boats, and these were formerly equipped with carved prow and stern boards that extended the line of the boat into a graceful upturned arc. These boards were carved in open fretwork, mainly with spiral motifs, but with birds (symbolizing ancestral spirits), fish and various monsters towards the base. The cockerel (said to be the sign of a nobleman) is a very common motif on such boards (e.g. Geneva, Mus. Barbier–Mueller). Some were further embellished with shells (e.g. Jakarta, N. Mus.). Sketches of Balinese outriggers from 1906 show their bows carved and painted to represent monster faces, and with 19th-century European designs. The figures are said to represent the god Gajahmina, half-elephant, half-fish. Madurese and Javanese *perahu* of many types are generally very brightly painted, the bows and stern pieces often being highly decorated with carved and painted floral motifs, and sometimes with designs from Dutch coats of arms, Art Nouveau and other European-influenced patterns. The sail-rests (*sanggen*) of these *perahu* consist of a post with an X-shaped piece at the top, and each village or building yard may have its own design. Bangkalan in Madura, for example, has a cockerel.

BIBLIOGRAPHY

A. Horridge: *Sailing Craft of Indonesia* (Oxford, 1986)

——: *Outrigger Canoes of Bali and Madura, Indonesia* (Honolulu, 1987)

S. McKinnon: 'Tanimbar Boats', *Islands and Ancestors: Indigenous Styles of Southeast Asia*, ed. J. P. Barbier and D. Newton (New York, 1988)

SIAN E. JAY

3. CERAMICS. The oldest ceramics found in Indonesia are prehistoric, utilitarian earthenware pots and funerary objects. Production of simple earthenware for domestic use has continued into modern times, although the limited extent of modern production suggests that other materials, such as wood, bamboo and other fibres and gourds, were preferred for use as containers. The terracotta figures in the shapes of humans, mythological creatures and animals found at Trawulan, centre of the Majapahit kingdom (1292–*c.* 1500), developed out of the unglazed tradition. Strategically situated on the trade route from China to India, Java and Sumatra are rich sources of foreign ceramics. Chinese celadon and white-glazed stoneware excavated at various, mostly coastal, sites verify that direct trade between China and Sumatra was established by the 10th century AD. Kota Cina, on the east coast of North Sumatra, was an important commercial centre for Chinese trade ceramics from the 12th century to the 14th (*see* CHINA, §VII, 4(iv)). Most of the early Chinese ceramics found in Java are monochrome wares. Blue-and-white porcelain dominates finds from after the 14th century. Quantities of Vietnamese blue-and-white architectural tiles and Thai celadons were shipped to Java in the 15th and 16th centuries. Japanese blue-and-white porcelain and enamelled ware were traded in Java during the 17th century through the Dutch East India Company (VOC) in Batavia. A broad range of foreign ceramics that includes Chinese monochromes, blue-and-white porcelain and brown-glazed storage jars, and Thai and Vietnamese wares has been found at sites in Aceh (North Sumatra), Banten (West Java), Sanur (Bali) and in Sulawesi. In Kalimantan large, brown-glazed stoneware storage jars, originally imported from southern China and from other parts of South-east Asia, have been treasured heirlooms for centuries. Later, at the instigation of Chinese immigrants, kilns were set up in Kalimantan to manufacture the jars.

Ceramic centres situated throughout modern Java produce unglazed earthenware. Typical forms are fanciful animal-shaped flowerpots and sculptures depicting daily life. Glazed ware fired at high temperatures for commercial purposes was not produced until the 20th century. Potters specialize in copies of antique Chinese ware (Yixing teapots, blue-and-white Ming-style vases, polychrome dishes), Vietnamese ceramics and Thai glazed stoneware. Ceramic centres in modern Bali produce utilitarian earthenware and abstract figures, both human and mythical.

BIBLIOGRAPHY

S. Adhyatman: *Antique Ceramics Found in Indonesia: Various Uses and Origins* (Jakarta, 1981)

B. Harrisson: *Pusaka: Heirloom Jars of Borneo* (Singapore, 1986)

D. Rooney: *Folk Pottery in South-east Asia* (Singapore, 1987)

DAWN F. ROONEY

4. COINS. The earliest coinage of insular South-east Asia, a silver sandalwood-flower series, originated in south Central Java during the late 8th century AD, replacing irregular stamped silver ingots. These somewhat thick and dumpy coins were struck in a single denomination, the 2.4 g *māṣa*. By the late 9th century, the coins were struck from a broader scyphate flan in multiple denominations, including the 0.6 g *kupang*, with a distribution ranging from central and eastern Java to Bali. A cubical gold coinage, the *piloncito*, was struck in central and eastern Java during the same period and was current in Bali (it is not known if Bali possessed mints of its own). In Java both series were supplanted in the late 13th century by imported *caxa*s, Chinese cash coins of low value made of copper alloy and with a square hole in the centre. Gold and electrum sandalwood-flower coins, datable to the late 1st millennium, have been recovered along Sumatra's west coast and from Muara Jambi in the east, a possible site of Srivijaya's capital from the late 12th century. Sumatran examples are smaller than their Javanese counterparts and share characteristics with specimens from southern Thailand (*see* THAILAND, §X, 4).

Beginning in the 14th century a remarkable series of cast bronze temple tokens appeared in Java. Similar in shape to Chinese cash, the tokens are large (average 38–42 mm diam.) and usually display two *wayang* figures in profile below a stylized tree, around a central square hole. Cast tin and bronze pieces with a central hole that is either hexagonal, pentagonal or round and a wide, flat outer rim imitative of Chinese cash appeared at Banten in West Java during the 16th and 17th centuries. The first coins in the series are inscribed (on one side only, the reverse is blank) in Javanese, replaced by Arabic in the early 17th century. During the 17th and 18th centuries, a number of other localities, such as Cirebon on Java's northern shore, also cast reduced versions of Chinese *caxa*s, chiefly in tin or tin alloy, some with romanized inscriptions. During the politically tumultuous 18th and 19th centuries, English, Dutch and local mints issued hammer-struck silver, gold, tin and copper coins. Most were imitations of European trading coinage, with the addition of Javanese and Arabic inscriptions. An emergency series of copper *bonken* was also struck in Java in the late 18th century and early 19th.

South-east Asia's first Islamic coinage was struck in northern Sumatra, at Samudra-Pase, by the end of the 14th century. The gold coins are inscribed with three lines of a simplified Arabic script, the name of the ruler on the obverse and his honorific titles on the reverse. Called *mas* (Indon.: 'gold'), the coins were struck to the 0.6 g *kupang* standard borrowed from Java. They were issued by rulers of Aceh in the north until the late 17th century. In the early 15th century, this gold series was supplemented by a cast coinage of tin, frequently dated and indicating its place of origin. Other centres, such as Palembang, Siak and Jambi, also issued cast base-metal coins, most often with Arabic inscriptions, until the mid-19th century. The coins are exceedingly thin and brittle, often hexagonal or octagonal with a circular hole. In addition to the Islamic issues of Sumatra proper, Chinese mining associations involved in tin production on the island of Bangka in the 18th and 19th centuries cast a large number of very large Chinese-style coins in tin. Silver and copper pieces were issued between 1786 and 1804 during the British occupation of Sumatra, some with the name of Fort Marlbro (Marlborough) on the obverse. On the south-western coast of Sulawesi, the Islamic sultans of Makassar issued a short-lived series of gold and copper struck coins (*mas* and *kupang*) during the 17th century. The coins are broader and possess longer inscriptions than the Sumatran gold series. A related issue was struck *c.* 1680 by the Sultan of Bima.

BIBLIOGRAPHY

H. C. Millies: *Recherches sur les monnaies des indigènes de l'archipel indien et de la péninsule malaie* (The Hague, 1871)

A. Ligtvoet: 'Zijn de munten nos. 287 en 288 van het werk van prof. Millies: Recherches etc., van Makassaarschen oorsprung?', *Tijdsch. Ind. Taal-, Land- & Vlknknd.*, xxiii (1876), pp. 159–60

J. Hulsoff Pol: 'De gouden munten (mas) van noord-Sumatra', *Jb. Munt- & Penningknd.*, xxvi (1929), pp. 1–32

C. Scholten: 'De gouden munten (mas) van noord-Sumatra (addenda)', *Jb. Munt- & Penningknd.*, xxxvi/2 (1949), pp. 176–9

L. Blussée: 'Trojan Horse of Lead: The Picis in Early 17th Century Java', *Between People and Statistics: Essays on Modern Indonesian History, Presented to P. Crentzburg*, ed. F. van Anroij and others (The Hague, 1979), pp. 33–47

R. S. Wicks: *A Survey of Native Southeast Asian Coinage circa 450–1850: Documentation and Typology* (PhD thesis, Ithaca, NY, Cornell U., 1983)

——: 'Monetary Developments in Java between the Ninth and Sixteenth Centuries: A Numismatic Perspective', *Indonesia*, xlii (1986), pp. 42–77

——: *Money, Markets, and Trade in Early Southeast Asia* (Ithaca, 1992), pp. 219–99

ROBERT S. WICKS

5. Cremation towers and temple offerings. The ephemeral arts associated with the religious ceremonial and ritual of the Hindu Balinese, especially the funerary towers and coffins, are among the most colourful and spectacular in Indonesia. Burial, cremation and subsequent purification involve the most complex rituals. When the corpse is ready to be cremated, it is brought to a cremation tower, an elaborate bier of wood and bamboo, crowned by pagoda-like roofs that symbolize the world of the gods. The number of roofs indicates the deceased person's caste and wealth. Towers are sumptuously decorated with gold tinsel, small mirrors, paintings and carvings, which include the celestial bird Garuda, Vishnu's mount, which will bear away the purged soul. The tower is then carried by a noisy crowd of men to the cremation grounds, where the corpse is placed in a coffin (*patulungan*). Caste prescriptions that traditionally determined the shape of the coffin have become laxer in modern times; winged lions (see fig. 35), black bulls, white cows and elephant fish may be used by all castes, although Brahman priests are still usually cremated in bamboo lotus thrones (*padmāsana*). The coffin, made with skill and at great cost over weeks, ignites instantaneously.

Palm-leaf hangings (*lamak*) adorn altars and shrines during festive days. Intricately woven by women, these often have as their central motif an elongated and stylized female figure (*cili*) with a fan-shaped headdress, or a mountain or tree symbol. This delicate figure represents the Great Mother Goddess, identified in Bali with the rice goddess, Shri. *Lamak* may also be hung from decorated tall bamboo poles (*penjor*) at the entrances to temples.

35. Winged-lion coffin, painted and decorated wood, from Bali; from a photograph of 1992

Together the *lamak* and *penjor* represent the divine couple Shiva and Shri, Mountain and Lake, and the unity of the male and female principles. Offerings presented to gods and spirits, often strikingly beautiful, are made mostly from natural materials such as banana or coconut-palm leaves (sometimes woven into containers), flowers, rice and rice cakes, fruit and betel nuts. They may be as much as 2 m high. Other offerings are fashioned from rice-dough in the form of mythical creatures, faces or dancing figurines.

BIBLIOGRAPHY

U. Ramseyer: *The Art and Culture of Bali* (Oxford, 1977)

F. Brinkgrove: 'The Cili and Other Female Images in Bali', *Indonesian Women in Focus*, ed. E. Locher-Scholten and A. Niehof (Dordrecht, 1987), pp. 135–51

ANGELA HOBART

6. Dress. Traditionally, Javanese costume comprises untailored rectangular cloths, usually decorated with batik designs. In modern times these garments, based on traditional court dress, are reserved for formal occasions. The *kain panjang* ('long cloth') is wrapped around the waist; when worn by women the end of the fabric may be arranged in a series of pleats that fan out as the wearer moves. Aristocrats and court dancers formerly wore a very long garment known as the *dodot.* Men wore it knee-length

over silk trousers, while women used it as a long dress. Noblewomen wore the breast-cloth (*kemben*), a narrow piece wound tightly round the chest, leaving the shoulders bare. Women also draped a shawl or scarf (*selendang*) around the head or upper half of the body, and men wore a starched cloth (*iket*) folded as a turban. There is regional variation in both the design of the textiles and the way in which these garments are worn.

The Balinese wear rectangular pieces of cloth tied, wrapped or draped around the body. These fabrics are decorated with a variety of techniques, including ikat, batik, supplementary weft and gilding. Although men often wear the *kain panjang* knee-length, with elaborate folds hanging in front, women usually wear it as a long wrap-around skirt. Traditionally, women were not obliged to cover the upper half of their body in public, but this changed from the mid-19th century as a result of increasing contact with European Christians and Indonesian Muslims. Many women have adopted the Malay blouse (*kebaya*). During festivals a Balinese woman's hair is often adorned with flowers; men use headcloths, tied in a variety of regional styles. Balinese dress, because of the strength of rural traditions, has been less heavily influenced by court fashions than that of Java. The most elaborate costumes are worn at religious festivals or important social events, such as marriage.

In Sumatra the sarong, a sewn fabric tube, is worn. The wearer steps into the sarong before pulling it up around the waist, where it is secured with folds and tucks. Sarongs are often made of brightly coloured chequered cloth, although fabrics embellished with silk and precious-metal supplementary wefts are esteemed. Ikat, couching and embroidery are among other techniques used, and there are many regional costume styles. Men often wear the sarong pulled above the knee, on top of a jacket and breeches, while women frequently combine it with the Malay blouse. Headcloths are worn chiefly by men, although some women, such as those of the Minangkabaus, make elaborate fabric headdresses. Modern wedding and festival dress often imitates old court styles. Similar patterns of dress can be seen in southern Sumatra, Bima (Sumbawa) and southern Kalimantan. Further inland in Kalimantan, a short sarong is worn by women, sometimes with a beaded or ikat-decorated waistcoat. Among the indigenous peoples of Kalimantan, men often wear loincloths (*cawat*) instead of sarongs. Ikat sarongs are also worn on the islands of Flores, Sumba, Sawu, Roti (see fig. 25 above) and Timor in Nusa Tenggara (Lesser Sunda Islands), where they are often combined with highly decorated shoulder-blankets (*selimut*). The latter, which are reserved for formal occasions, are symbols of prestige. Headgear may also be elaborate, especially in Roti, where Portuguese influence can be detected.

See also §V above.

BIBLIOGRAPHY

B. de Zoete and W. Spies: *Dance and Drama in Bali* (Oxford, 1973)
Textiles of the Indonesian Archipelago (exh. cat. by B. Solyom and G. Solyom, Honolulu, HI, Acad. A., 1973)
M. Gittinger: *Splendid Symbols: Textiles and Tradition in Indonesia* (Washington, DC, 1979)
Art of the Archaic Indonesians (exh. cat., Dallas, TX, Mus. F.A., 1982)
B. K. Majlis: *Indonesische Textilien: Wege zu Göttern und Ahnen* (Cologne, 1984)
S. Fraser-Lu: *Indonesian Batik: Processes, Patterns and Places* (Singapore, 1986)
L. S. Dubin: *The History of Beads from 30,000 BC to the Present* (New York, 1987)
M. Hitchcock: *Indonesian Textiles* (Berkeley and Singapore, 1991)

MICHAEL HITCHCOCK

7. Dutch colonial furniture and silver. The most distinctive period of colonial decorative arts in Indonesia was from the mid-17th century until the second quarter of the 18th. During this time a unique style emerged that is now often associated with the Dutch East India Company (VOC). The style, consisting of European forms and ornaments fused with Eastern decoration, was most clearly expressed in furniture and silver. Later in the 18th century, and especially during the 19th, strict imitation of European styles became dominant. Most Dutch colonial pieces were made in Batavia (now Jakarta), the location of the headquarters of the Dutch East India Company since 1619. They were intended for use by Company officials or for export. Craftsmen from Java, Madura, Bali, India and Sri Lanka worked together with Europeans in the Company workshops in the Ambachtskwartier district. Independent Chinese craftsmen were also established in the city.

In furniture, the predominant material used from the second half of the 17th century until early in the 18th was ebony. Typical of this period are the low, broad chairs and settees with spirally turned legs and stretchers, baluster backs and caned seats. The floral motifs in low relief, decorating the back rails and seat rails, became larger in size and were carved in half-relief after 1680. Similarities with work from the Coromandel Coast of south-east India and from Sri Lanka are evident. Teak, amboyna-wood, Indian black-wood and, under Chinese influence, lacquered wood were common during the 18th and 19th centuries. Fashionable pieces include the 'burgomaster' chair, with its circular plan, its six cabriole legs and its back set with three carved medallions, and the Raffles chair, based on designs in the style of Thomas Sheraton and named after the English lieutenant-governor of Java.

Little remains of the silver from this period, and few silversmiths are known by name. Even though the craftsmen were obliged to have their products assayed, only part of the silver carries the Batavian town mark (sword in wreath) and a maker's mark. Unlike the custom in Europe, where date letters were used, an additional mark was used between 1667 and 1730 to indicate the assayer's term of office. Among extant pieces is a baptismal font in Régence style in the Gereja Emmanuel, Jakarta, executed in 1749 by Elias Albertus Meiszner (*fl* 1745–61). There are also surviving examples of commemorative plates and trays, called *schenkpiring*, dating from the late 17th century until the mid-18th, that were presented at or after funerals. Silver mounts are found on cabinets, small chests and betel boxes. These boxes, made of ivory, amboyna-wood, tortoiseshell or silver, contained the implements and ingredients necessary for the local habit of betel-chewing and were used in combination with spittoons.

BIBLIOGRAPHY

Wonen in de wijde wereld [Living in the wide world] (exh. cat., Amsterdam, Tropenmus., 1964)
J. Veenendaal: 'Het derde merkteken op V.O.C.-zilver' [The third mark on V.O.C. silver], *Verslagen en aanwinsten van de stichting CNO* [Reports

and acquisitions of the CNO Foundation] (Amsterdam, 1982–3), pp. 39–45
S. M. Voskuil-Groenewegen: *Zilver uit de periode van de Verenigde Oostindische Compagnie, 17de en 18de eeuw* (The Hague, 1983)
J. Terwen-de Loos: *Het Nederlands koloniale meubel* (Franeker, 1985)
J. Veenendaal: *Furniture from Indonesia, Sri Lanka and India during the Dutch Period* (Delft, 1985)
J. K. Kwisthout: 'De schenkpirings ter nagedachtenis aan Cornelis Chastelein' [The *schenkpirings* in commemoration of Cornelis Chastelein], *Antiek*, xxiii (1989), pp. 342–52

DANIËLLE GROSHEIDE

8. JEWELLERY AND BEADWORK. In Java and Bali jewellery has long been made for all parts of the body from the head to the ankles and includes chest ornaments (*hiasan dada*) and so-called modesty plates (*badong* or *cupeng*), as can be seen from carvings on the reliefs of such 9th-century Central Javanese temples as Candi Pawon and Candi Mendut. Much Indonesian jewellery, both traditionally and in modern times, is made of gold, which serves throughout the archipelago as an expression of success or merit. On Nias, for example, the aristocratic regalia of gold crown, necklaces and bracelets belong to the man or woman of high status, and on Timor a successful headhunter traditionally gained the right to wear a gold headdress and neck ornament. Cold-working techniques such as chasing and repoussé are used, as well as granulation and soldering. Gold earrings and finger-rings are popular throughout the archipelago, as are gilded bracelets and belt buckles.

Other materials include garnets, crystals, pearls and amethysts (in Java) and rubies, baroque pearls and red coral (in Bali). Imported ivory is frequently turned into bracelets: on Flores and among the Lamahalot these are part of the bridewealth gift. Shell bracelets are sometimes used for the same purpose. Bone and tortoiseshell are also carved, but this practice seems to be somewhat localized. Mother-of-pearl is used for neck pendants and is frequently decorated with incised patterns. The jewellery of village societies traditionally incorporates non-indigenous objects and gives them a specific, highly indigenous interpretation. The widespread use of Dutch and Chinese coins in jewellery is one example. A few prehistoric bronze items, found in ceremonial use in some parts of eastern Indonesia, are spectacular cases of this incorporation. The stringing or restringing of imported beads is another longstanding tradition. Trade in glass and coral beads seems to be of ancient origin: Roman beads have been found on Flores. Particularly fine and complex beadwork occurs in Kalimantan, where jackets, baby-carriers and hats are often encrusted with bead designs. Woven cloth adorned with beadwork is found in several societies, notably in Sumba and among the Ngada of Flores. Elaborately worked bead necklaces and headbands are also traditionally worn by wealthy women on the island of Alor in Nusa Tenggara.

Some of the most elaborate jewellery is that worn by brides and court dancers. A Balinese bride may wear gilded armlets, earrings and necklaces and adorn her hair with real and precious-metal flowers. A groom's hair is also usually decorated with metal flowers, and, as well as carrying an elaborate heirloom dagger (*keris*), he may wear numerous finger-rings. Signet-rings are also worn. Balinese dancers wear elaborate jewellery, which may include filigree collars and headdresses embellished with chasing and repoussé. In West Java, brides wear gilded headdresses and silver belts, whereas in Central and East Java, extensive use is made of real flowers, gilded hairpins and combs. Grooms usually wear finger-rings and necklaces, as well as heirloom *keris*. Signet-rings are also valued. Javanese court dancers wear skilfully crafted bracelets, anklets, metal headdresses and beaten silver armbands. In the northern Sumatran province of Aceh, women use numerous gilded medallions and hairpins, while in the neighbouring province of North Sumatra brides wear gilded headdresses from which hang pendants. The headdresses of Minangkabau women are particularly elaborate: a tiny model of a traditional house is often hung among the numerous hairpins. Large gilded headdresses can be seen in Lampung in southern Sumatra, while in the nearby Riau Archipelago both men and women wear jackets festooned with medallions.

Like the inhabitants of Sumatra, the peoples of southern Kalimantan wear jewellery based on court styles. Gilded bangles and medallions are esteemed, as well as elaborate necklaces. Further inland a wider range of materials is used. Beadwork necklaces and armbands are popular, sometimes decorated with locks of hair, boars' tusks or claws. Coin pendants and twisted precious-metal anklets are worn. Intricately worked bead necklaces and headbands are also traditionally worn by wealthy women on the island of Alor in Nusa Tenggara (Lesser Sundas). In southern Sulawesi, Makassarese and Bugis brides dress as princesses and wear numerous pearl-headed hairpins and gold chains; the forearms are virtually concealed by bracelets and bangles, and embellished metal plates sewn on to cloth are usually tied to the upper arms. The groom wears medallions, sometimes including a representation of a double-headed eagle. In Bima (west Sumbawa) similar jewellery is worn, although young children wear necklaces bearing square black patches, to which are ascribed talismanic properties. In islands further east, jewellery is equally important, especially the crescent headdresses worn by Timorese brides.

Classical Javanese and Balinese court jewellery had a complex iconography, often derived from such creatures of Hindu mythology as the *nāga* and the *kāla* head. In modern times the imagery represented in jewellery is closely related to the iconography specific to a region or island. Thus, among the Toba Bataks of Sumatra metal ornaments frequently include the winged-lion (*sanga*) motif, a common feature of architectural and sculptural designs. The Dayaks of Kalimantan cast brass ornaments (usually earrings) that have the same asymmetric scroll patterns as their wood-carvings; they sometimes include the *aso* motif, the regional version of the mythical dragon–snake. However, certain basic features recur throughout the islands. Most pervasive is a type of gold or silver earring that has the shape of an open oval with reflexed ends. It appears among the Bataks, and in particular in Central Sulawesi, in Sumba (where it is called *mamuli* and refers to female fertility), Flores and the Lamaholot islands. Cast by the lost-wax method, it is often embellished in the local style (see fig. 36). Among the Torajas of Sulawesi, it takes the form of a buffalo head, with prominent horns that may sprout leaves, while among the Toba Bataks the open oval may have the head of the *sanga* at one end.

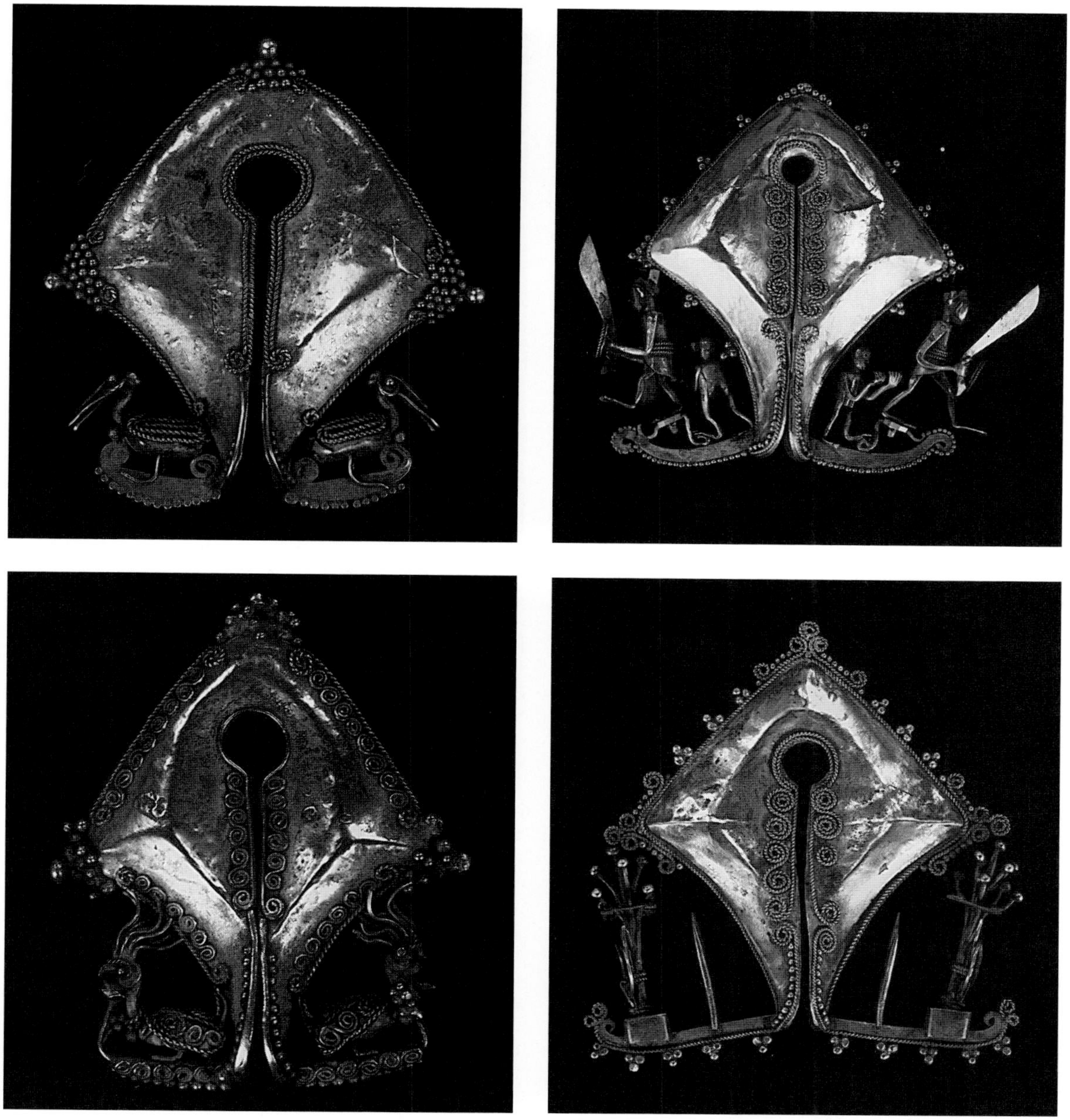

36. Gold *mamuli* (ear ornaments) from Sumba, Indonesia: (top left) 100×93×20 mm (New York, private collection); (top right) 80×65×16 mm (New York, Metropolitan Museum of Art); (bottom left) 100×102×22 mm (New York, private collection); (bottom right) 70×60×14 mm (New York, Metropolitan Museum of Art)

Metal neck or head ornaments that employ a motif based on a boat or on the curve of buffalo horns are found in Sumatra, Flores, Sumba and Timor. They are always associated with high rank and are passed on as lineage heirlooms. In eastern Indonesia, braided silver or gold thread is sometimes worked into a chain, often with small snake heads at the end. Originally these subjects were meant to be worn as necklaces, but in modern times they are rarely displayed. Instead they are stored as clan treasures. The snake represents the spirit of the lineage and is thought to be alive.

BIBLIOGRAPHY

J. E. Jasper and M. Pirngadie: *De goud- en zilversmeedkunst* (1927), iv of *De inlandsche kunstnijverheid in Nederlandsch Indië* (The Hague, 1912–30)

E. Vatter: *Ata Kiwan: Unbekannte Bergvölker im tropischen Holland* (Leipzig, 1932)

M. Raats: 'Römisch-ägyptische Glasperlen im Ngada-Gebiet auf Flores', *Anthropos*, liii (1958), pp. 1023–4

F. A. Wagner: *Indonesia: The Art of an Island Group* (London, 1959)
W. Marschall: 'Die metallenen Öllampen von Süd-Nias', *Ethnol. Z. Zürich*, ii (1976), pp. 5–26
T. Newman: *Contemporary South-east Asian Arts and Crafts* (New York, 1977) [jewellery in Java]
J. Fox: 'Island of Gold- and Silversmiths', *Hemisphere*, xx/12 (1978), pp. 24–7
S. Rodgers: *Power and Gold: Jewellery from Indonesia, Malaysia and the Philippines* (Geneva, 1985)
L. S. Dubin: *The History of Beads from 30,000 BC to the Present* (New York, 1987)
J. Mack, ed.: *Ethnic Jewellery* (London, 1988)
N. Hoch: 'Southeast Asia', *Beauty, Wealth and Power: Jewels and Ornaments of Asia* (San Francisco, 1992), pp. 29–37

RUTH BARNES, MICHAEL HITCHCOCK

9. MUSICAL INSTRUMENTS. The oldest musical instruments in Indonesia are the large, bronze ritual kettledrums found throughout the archipelago. Most are products of the Bronze Age DONG SON culture, named after its type site in northern Vietnam, which spread throughout South-east Asia from the 4th century BC to the 1st century AD. The drums in Indonesia are of two principal types; both are cast by the lost-wax process and both are waisted. The 'Heger I' type (named after the Austrian ethnologist Rolf Heger, who proposed a classification in 1902) is cast in one, and has a bulbous upper part and a conical foot. The 'Pejeng' type (named after the 'Moon of Pejeng' drum at Pura Penataran Sasih at Pejeng, Bali) is cast in two parts and is more slender. Motifs decorating the drums include human and other animal figures, Ships of the Dead, abstract feather-like shapes, stars, circles, loops and spirals. Four cast frogs usually appear on the rim of Heger I-type drums, reflecting the drums' function in rain-making rituals. On the island of Alor in Nusa Tenggara, Pejeng-type drums known as *moko*, most of which are modern and made in East Java, some probably as late as the end of the 19th century, are still used in ceremonies and rituals and as dowries.

The main elements of traditional Indonesian music are those found combined in the *gamelan* (orchestra). This is an ensemble of as many as 35 or more instruments, including idiophones (bronze gongs, gong-chimes and forms of metallophone), aerophones (flutes) and cordophones or stringed instruments. The principal instruments probably originated in the 2nd–1st century BC. Gong-chime instruments have probably been used in Java at least since the 9th century AD. *Gamelan* instruments are depicted in reliefs at Borobudur, dating from the 8th–9th century, and in 14th-century reliefs at Candi Panataran, East Java, although not until the 16th century is there definite evidence of *gamelan* ensembles playing in Java. The *gamelan* was probably introduced into Bali by immigrants from Majapahit (East Java) in the 16th century, although archaic types dating from the 11th century also exist. Other types were also introduced in the 16th century from Central Java into South Kalimantan, West Java (Sunda) and Madura. Elaborate *gamelan* are still used in the courts; some very old examples are considered sacred and used only at special ceremonies. Village *gamelan* are more simply decorated.

Bronze gongs are hand-forged, and their wooden racks and stands are often highly decorated. Court examples are carved, painted (usually red) and gilded. The stand of the *gong ageng* (great gong) in the Raffles Collection (*c*. 1800; London, BM), for example, is in the form of a double fish (a royal motif of the Majapahit kingdom) with crowned serpents (*nāgas*) and *garuḍas*. Other examples have coiled *nāgas* on the crossbeam, foliage and flowers. Other bronze idiophones are the gong-kettles (*bonang* and *kenong*) and metallophones with thick (*saron*) and thin (*gender*) plates or keys, and the multi-octave *gambang gangsa*. They rest on wooden bases, often with carved, painted and gilded foliage or depictions of scenes from the *wayang* (shadow) theatre. Very fine examples (e.g. Raffles Collection) incorporate carvings of mythical creatures such as the *garuḍa*, *kāla-makara*, *nāga* and *singha*. Examples from the Cirebon court in West Java have Chinese-influenced motifs such as rocks and clouds. A more unusual bronze instrument is the *reyong*, which consists of a wooden bar with a gong attached to each end; it is common in Bali, but it is also represented on 13th- and 14th-century East Javanese temple reliefs and on a relief at Padang Lawas. Modern 12-gong *reyong* are laid out horizontally.

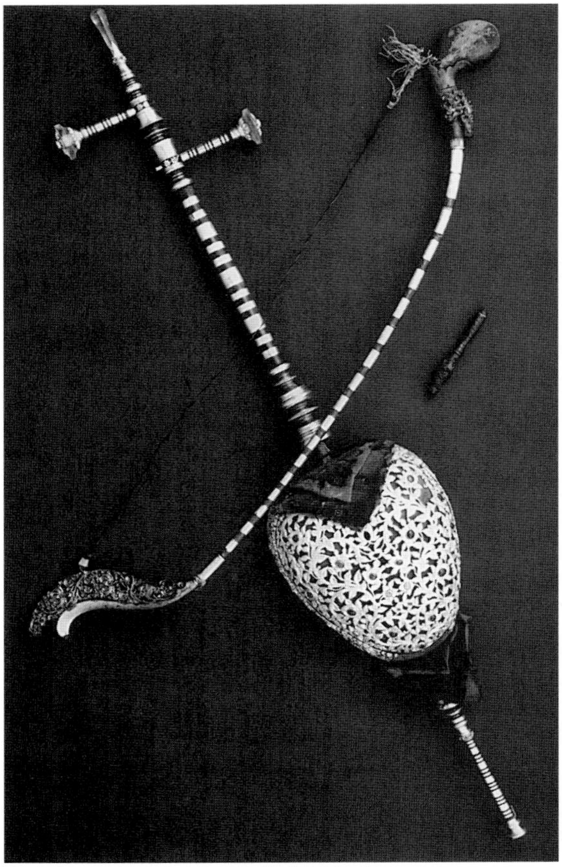

37. *Rebab* and bow, wood, coconut shell, gold, silver, rubies, sapphires, hardstones, crystal, horsehair, gut, parchment, velvet, 920×184×85 mm, from Klungkung, Bali, 19th century (Jakarta, National Museum)

Among the cordophones in the *gamelan*, the *rebab*, a two-stringed spike fiddle of Middle Eastern origin, has a heart-shaped sound-box of wood or coconut shell and a parchment membrane. Often the spike and neck are of turned wood, although court examples may be decorated with gold leaf, be set with precious stones and hardstones, and have gilded wooden bows (e.g. from Klungkung, Bali, 19th century; see fig. 37). Their stands may also be carved and gilded. Javanese zithers (*celempung*), which are sometimes used in large *gamelan*, also have carved and gilded frames. Some other instruments are similarly decorated. The wooden bodies of court drums (*kendang*), for example, are carved with foliage and flower motifs and gilded. *Gamelan* drums in Java are tapering or barrel-shaped; in Bali they taper more gently. Among the aerophones, the flute (*suling*) is usually made of wood or bamboo, although rare examples (e.g. from Klungkung, 19th century) are covered with gold, precious stones, hardstones and tortoiseshell.

There is also a wide array of instruments that do not belong to the *gamelan*. An unusual rattle instrument, the *angklung*, is particularly associated with West Java but is also found in South Sumatra and in South and West Kalimantan. It consists of a series of bamboo tubes, tuned to a basic note or its octaves, loosely held in a bamboo frame; these produce a harmonious sound when shaken. Bamboo tubes or wooden slats may also be grouped together on a wooden frame to form a type of xylophone (*calung*), the frame of which is sometimes decorated with figures from the *wayang* theatre. Balinese examples, called *grantang*, are often highly decorated. Plucked instruments are found throughout the archipelago. In Sumatra the body of the *gambus*, a 7- to 12-stringed lute with a pear-shaped body, may be carved with foliage and flowers. The Toba Bataks often use another form of lute (*hasapi*) for trance ceremonies and entertainment, and this may have a winged lion and anthropomorphic figures, representing spirits, carved on the back and front (e.g. Jakarta, N. Mus.). In Kalimantan the Dayaks also play a form of lute, which is sometimes brightly painted with traditional designs. The Dayak *kledi* or mouth organ is still used in a form depicted on the reliefs at Borobudur. The bamboo body may be incised, and a hornbill casque often forms the top. Jew's harps are played throughout Indonesia, and the cases in which they are kept are often elaborately decorated. Drums are also widely used and may take many forms, ranging from the simple slit drums of Nias to the shamanic drums of the Dayaks, carved and painted with motifs depicting the Tree of Life.

BIBLIOGRAPHY

Grove 6: 'Indonesia'

W. Fagg: *The Raffles Gamelan: A Historical Note* (London, 1970)

M. J. Kartomi: *Musical Instruments of Indonesia: An Introductory Handbook* (Melbourne, 1985)

J. Lindsay: *Javanese Gamelan* (Singapore, 1985)

E. Taylor: *Musical Instruments of South-east Asia* (London, 1989)

N. Sorrell: *A Guide to the Gamelan* (London, 1990)

M. Tenzer: *Balinese Music* (Berkeley and Singapore, 1991)

SIAN E. JAY

10. WEAPONS. The most characteristic traditional weapon in Indonesia, as in Malaysia, is the *keris*, a long dagger with a straight or wavy steel blade. The blade of the *keris* is made of nickel-bearing iron, most of which is now mined in Sulawesi and is known as *pamur luwu*. The term *pamur* (Mal. *pamor*) denotes the damascened patterns applied to *keris* blades of most types. Some iron is also extracted from a meteorite that fell near Prambanan in Central Java in 1749 (*pamur prambanan*), and *keris* made from this iron are considered to contain specially powerful magic. *Keris* blades differ widely in length and width and may be either completely straight or have as many as 13 waves (*luk*). The blade of the Balinese *keris* is usually appreciably longer and heavier than that of the *keris majapahit*, which is possibly the oldest form, dating from before the 16th century, and is an all-metal, one-piece weapon with a blade 150–250 mm long and a figural hilt. The Sumatran *keris*, with its long thin, usually straight blade (*see* MALAYSIA, §VI, 2), was widely used for executions in precolonial times and later became popular with collectors, leading to the production of many simplified replicas for the tourist market. The third type (see fig. 38) is particularly associated with the Bugis people of Sulawesi.

A great variety of *pamur* techniques and markings are used on the blade. Javanese *pamur* is particularly complex. The metal is laminated into 32, 64 or even more than 100 layers, using two or three different types of iron, each of

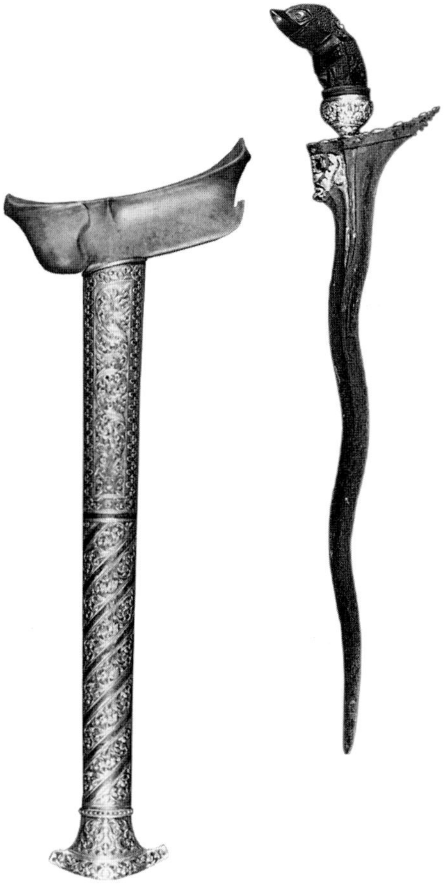

38. *Keris* and sheath, iron, wood and gold, 482×145×70 mm, Bugis, from South Sulawesi (Amsterdam, Tropenmuseum)

which has to be forged, separated, reforged and etched with lemon juice and arsenic. Every *pamur* marking has its own symbolic significance, but most scholars agree that they all derive from five main motifs: *beras wos wutah* (Jav.: 'scattered grains of rice'), *sekar pala* (nutmeg flowers), *sekar ngadeg* (straight-standing flowers), *blarak ngirid* (parallel coconut leaves) and *sekar temu* (ginger flowers). The hilt of the *keris* is generally made of wood and shaped like a boat. The sheath is also made of wood, or sometimes of ivory, and both the crosspiece (*wrangka*) and the shank (*gandar*) are usually encased in metal, which is often decorated with incised or repoussé motifs and adorned with jewels. The Bugis *keris* has a medium, damascened blade and an upright, half-cranked *jawa demam* ('fever-stricken') hilt, depicting a bent human figure with a birdlike head. The sheath has a boat-shaped crosspiece and is made either of wood with the lower part bound with rattan, or of wood cased in metal, the base of which is either straight or flared into a crescent moon. The metal casing, which is often elaborately decorated with leaf, tendril and floral motifs, may cover the crosspiece as well as the lower sheath. On the reverse there is often a braided cord for attaching the sheath to the waist.

In some parts of Indonesia all weapons are believed to be endowed with magical properties, and they have therefore traditionally either been made specifically for ceremonial and ritual use or have subsequently acquired those functions. Weapons form part of the collections of regalia and heirlooms (Indon. *pusaka*) of many Indonesian rulers. Some of the most splendid of these *pusaka* are the lances or spears (*tombak*). Made of gold, silver and iron with gold inlay work or *pamur* designs in nickel or zinc, and wooden shafts, they are found in the Riau Islands, in Sumatra, Java, Sulawesi, Sumbawa and other islands. Their decoration is often similar to that found on the *keris* and includes such Hindu motifs as *nāgas* (mythical serpents), cocks (a symbol of courage), the Tree of Life (a symbol of fertility and power), inscribed texts and depictions of characters from the *wayang* (shadow play). They often have two (*dwisula*) or three (*trisula*) prongs, and these are sometimes wavy like the blade of a *keris*. One notable 17th-century Central Javanese example in the Tropenmuseum, Amsterdam, has a three-pronged head and thirteen *luk* on the central prong.

Swords (*parang*) are also found among the regalia of Indonesian rulers, such as the 17th-century *parang*, called La Teya Riduni, which formerly belonged to the sultans of Bone in southern Sulawesi and is now in the possession of the Kabupaten of Watampone, South Sulawesi, or the sumptuous *parang* made by the famous goldsmith Palina Sape for Sultan Amrullah of Semawa in Sumbawa (*reg* 1836–82) and still in the possession of his descendants. The supernatural powers attributed to a fighting knife (*golok*) in Bima, Sumbawa, called La Ngyunti Rante, have led to its adoption since the 16th century as a kind of palladium of the kingdom of Bima.

BIBLIOGRAPHY

J. Groneman: *Der Keris der Javaner* (Yogyakarta, 1910)
G. B. Gardner: *Keris and Other Malay Weapons* (Singapore, 1936)
Shahrum bin Yub: *Keris dan senjata pendek* [*Keris* and other short weapons] (Kuala Lumpur, 1967)
G. B. Solyum: *The World of the Javanese Keris* (Honolulu, 1978)
E. Frey: *The Kris: Mystic Weapon of the Malay World* (Singapore, 1986, 2/1988)
Court Arts of Indonesia (exh. cat. by H. I. Jessup, New York, Asia Soc. Gals, 1990)
M. D. Coe and others: *Swords and Hilt Weapons* (London, 1993), pp. 198–204

LEWIS G. HILL

IX. Art education.

Formal art education did not exist in Indonesia until 1947 and was initially mainly concentrated in Java. Before this date talented young artists were trained either by locally based European (mainly Dutch) painters or by Indonesians who had been trained by the Dutch and had become draughtsmen in their service. For example, the draughtsman Mas Pirngadie (1875–1936) took lessons from Du Chattel; the painter Sudjojono (1913–86) from Pirngadie; and Affandi (*b c.* 1910) from Sudjojono. Occasionally such artists had the opportunity to study at a fine arts academy in the Netherlands. These included Abdullah Surio Subroto (1878–1941) in Amsterdam, his son Basuki Abdullah (*b* 1915) in The Hague in 1933 and Agus Djaja (*b* 1913) in Amsterdam in the late 1920s. The Dutch governmental and semigovernmental bodies were interested in Indonesian draughtsmen only for technical drawings and book illustrations and considered formal art education to be unnecessary in Indonesia. An influential figure in the 1920s and 1930s was Ki Hadjar Dewantoro (1889–1959). Born in Yogyakarta, he was exiled to the Netherlands from 1913 to 1919 because of his nationalist sympathies. While in exile he studied the works of such educationalists as Maria Montessori (1870–1952) and Rudolf Steiner, and in 1922 he used their ideas to found the Taman Siswa schools for teacher training. Here creativity was stressed, and in the 1920s and 1930s many young Indonesians were encouraged by this approach to become self-taught painters, rejecting tradition but concentrating on Indonesian subject-matter (*see* §VII, 2(i) above).

During their internment in a Japanese prison camp (1942–5), the Dutch painter Siem Admiraal and the architect Jack Zeijlemaker planned the eventual establishment of an art academy in Indonesia. In 1947 the first courses, sanctioned by the Ministry of Higher Education, started at the Institute for the Training of Art Teachers in Secondary Schools in Bandung; this institution was connected with the Technical College. The curriculum, based on the Dutch art-educational system, included drawing, painting, ceramics, sculpture and art history. The accent was on oil painting. The teacher Ries Mulder, influenced by the French Cubist painter Jacques Villon, dominated the style of the Indonesian students in Bandung in the 1950s. After independence in 1949 the academy was renamed, and it later became the Faculty of Fine Arts and Design in the Bandung Institute of Technology (ITB). Most of the Dutch teachers left in 1953–4 following political unrest over the sovereignty of New Guinea (Irian Jaya), but the curriculum remained Western-orientated, because these teachers were succeeded by their former pupils. In Yogyakarta a second art academy, the Indonesian Academy for the Plastic Arts (Akademi Seni Rupa Indonesia or ASRI; from 1986 the Institut Seni Indonesia or ISI), was founded in 1950. The main subjects taught here were painting, sculpture, handicrafts and graphic arts.

Traditional craftsmanship was stressed: silver- and metal-working, sculpture and batik were taken as starting-points to emphasize continuity with the cultures of Indonesia's past. Only later, in 1965, was an Academy of Fine Arts attached to the Faculty of Technics of the Udayana University in Denpasar (Bali); drawing and painting in a naturalistic style are taught there. These three academies only are classified as higher education institutes; they are controlled directly by the Ministry of Education and Culture.

In 1968 the Jakarta Institute for Art Education (Lembaga Kesenian Jakarta or LKJ) was founded as part of the non-departmental governmental services of Indonesia. In addition to organizing exhibitions, the LKJ set up an art school in Jakarta (Institut Kesenian Jakarta or IKJ), and other art schools are now established in cities and capitals of provinces in Java (Surakarta, Surabaya) and outside (Ujung Pandang in Sulawesi and Jayapura in Irian Jaya).

H. I. R. HINZLER

Indo-Parthian [Pahlava]. Dynasty that replaced Shaka or Indo-Scythian rule in south-east Afghanistan and the north-western region of the Indian subcontinent in the 1st century AD. The origins of the dynasty are uncertain, and the suggestion that the Indo-Parthians came from the eastern borders of the Parthian empire remains unsubstantiated. Iranian influence is already evident in Afghanistan during the Shaka period. Vonones (*c.* 75–50 BC), for example, was apparently a Shaka king ruling with his associates in Arachosia (south-east Afghanistan), but he bears the same name as later Parthian kings and has the Iranian title 'king of kings' on his coinage.

The founder of the Indo-Parthian dynasty appears to have been Gondophares (*reg c.* AD 20–50), who took control of the TAXILA and adjacent territories, although some Shaka satraps of the region apparently retained a degree of autonomy. The so-called TAKHT-I-BAHI inscription, dated in the year 103 (probably of the Vikrama Era of 57 BC) during the '26th year of the reign of Guduvhara', is thought to establish the first year of Gondophares as AD 20. A date in the first half of the 1st century is corroborated in Christian tradition by the account that St Thomas was employed as a slave in the court of Gondophares, building a palace for the king (*Acts of St Thomas*). The account of the travels in India by Apollonius of Tyana, the Pythagorean philosopher and holy man from Cappadocia, also records that a Parthian king was ruling in Taxila *c.* AD 45 (Philostratus: *Life of Apollonius*, II, xxvi).

Numismatics provides the names of a further eight Indo-Parthian rulers: Abdagases, Orthagnes, Gudana, Ubouzanes, Sarpedanes, Sasan, Pakores and Sanabares. The Panjtar inscription of the year 122 (AD 65) from the Peshawar Valley and the Taxila silver scroll of the year 136 (AD 79) show that both these regions had fallen to the KUSHANA dynasty by the second half of the 1st century. The Indo-Parthians, however, retained control of Sistan and Arachosia until the 3rd century, when the territories became part of the Sasanian empire.

See also INDIAN SUBCONTINENT, §IV, 5(ii)(b).

BIBLIOGRAPHY

S. Konow: *Kharoshṭhī Inscriptions with the Exception of those of Aśoka*, Corp. Inscr. Indic., ii/1 (Calcutta, 1929/*R* Delhi, 1991), nos XX, XXVI–XXVII, pp. 57–62, 67–77, pls XII.1, XIII.4, XIV

M. Mitchiner: *Establishment of the Scythians in Afghanistan and Pakistan*, v of *Indo-Greek and Indo-Scythic Coinage* (London, 1976), pp. 391–402, 439–63

——: *The Indo-Parthians, their Kushan Neighbours*, viii of *Indo-Greek and Indo-Scythic Coinage* (London, 1976), pp. 697–700

J. Cribb: 'New Evidence of Indo-Parthian Political History', *Coin Hoards*, vii (1982), pp. 282–300

The Crossroads of Asia: Transformation in Image and Symbol in the Art of Ancient Afghanistan and Pakistan (exh. cat., ed. E. Errington and J. Cribb; Cambridge, Fitzwilliam, 1992), pp. 6, 14–17, 64–6

E. ERRINGTON

Indo-Saracenic style. *See* MOORISH STYLE.

Induno. Italian family of painters.

(1) Domenico Induno (*b* Milan, 14 May 1815; *d* Milan, 4 Nov 1878). He began his artistic career as a goldsmith working under Luigi Cossa, who subsequently sponsored his studies at the Accademia di Belli Arti di Brera, Milan, under Francesco Hayez and Luigi Sabatelli. Under their influence Domenico produced works based on religious or historical themes, such as *Alexander Drains the Cup of Medicine* (1836; Milan, Brera). From the 1840s Domenico developed an interest in genre painting, initially inspired by such 18th-century specialists as Giacomo Ceruti and Giovanni Battista Piazzetta, which developed into an overwhelmingly sentimental, anecdotal realism. He produced such paintings as *Falling Leaves* (1858; Milan, Civ. Mus. A. Contemp.) in vast quantities, and these were extremely popular with his extensive Milanese clientele. In 1848 Domenico participated in the Milan uprising against Austrian rule. His involvement with the Risorgimento led him to produce a number of semi-anecdotal paintings based on modern Italian history, which were also very successful. The best of these, *News of the Peace of Villafranca*, exists in many versions (e.g. 1862; Milan, Mus. Risorgimento).

(2) Gerolamo Induno (*b* Milan, 13 Dec 1825; *d* Milan, 18 Dec 1890). Brother of (1) Domenico Induno. Like his brother, Gerolamo enrolled at the Accademia di Belli Arti di Brera to study under Luigi Sabatelli but left to participate in the uprising against Austrian rule in 1848. He joined in the 1849 defence of Rome, enlisted for the Crimea in 1855 and followed Garibaldi on his 1859 campaign. Much of his work derived from these military experiences (e.g. *Garibaldi at Capua*, 1861; Milan, Mus. Risorgimento), and, upon his return to Milan, he received many official commissions for paintings of Italian patriotic themes, for example *Departure of the Conscripts* (1881; Milan, Civ. Mus. A. Contemp.), and for portraits of important figures of the Risorgimento, such as *Victor Emmanuel II* (1867; Milan, Brera). Gerolamo's anecdotal genre pieces were also popular. These included scenes of contemporary everyday life and costume pieces in 18th-century settings, for example *Kissing Hands at the Carriage* (1881; Milan, Gal. A. Mod.).

BIBLIOGRAPHY

Luciani

A. M. Comanducci: *Dizionario illustrato dei pittori, desegnatori e incisori italiani moderni e contemporanei*, 5 vols (Milan, 1934, rev. 4/ 1970–74)

G. Nicodemi: *Domenico e Gerolamo Induno* (Milan, 1945)

L. Caramel and C. Pirovano: *Opere dell'ottocento*, Milan, Gal. A. Mod. cat., i (Milan, 1975), p. 338
1886–1986. La Permanente: Un secolo d'arte a Milano (exh. cat., Milan, Pal. Permanente, 1986)

CLARE HILLS-NOVA

Industrial design. Design process applied to goods produced, usually by machine, by a system of MASS PRODUCTION based on the division of labour. The terms 'industrial design' and 'industrial designer' were first coined in the 1920s in the USA to describe those specialist designers who worked on what became known as product design. The history of industrial design is usually taken to start with the industrialization of Western Europe, in particular with the Industrial Revolution that began in Britain in the second half of the 18th century. The main focus of attention then moved to the USA and Germany when they industrialized and, in the second half of the 19th century, began to challenge Britain's supremacy as 'the workshop of the world'. After World War II, Italy, the former Federal Republic of Germany and Japan each challenged the USA for world supremacy in industrial design.

1. Before *c.* 1850. 2. *c.* 1850–1915. 3. 1915–45. 4. After 1945.

1. BEFORE *c.* 1850.

(i) The emergence of the designer. In the period before 1850 Britain became established as 'the workshop of the world', exporting manufactured goods to a host of other nations. There was a gradual separation in most areas of manufacture between design, entrepreneurial activities and the craft process, all of which had generally been carried out by one person in earlier periods. This led to the emergence of the professional designer on the one hand and the entrepreneur or business manager on the other—a basic division that still prevails.

Such entrepreneurs as Josiah Wedgwood (*see* WEDGWOOD, §1), Matthew Boulton and Thomas Chippendale (i) realized the vital role design played not only in differentiating their products in an increasingly competitive world but also in dictating or tuning in to the changing fashions of a market that was constantly increasing due to the general growth of population, overseas trade and the cheaper ranges of such goods as quality Staffordshire pottery that were available to a wider range of social groups. Robert Campbell's trade guide of 1747 stated that a young cabinetmaker who could not design and invent new fashions was unlikely to become either rich or eminent in his profession. Entrepreneurs who did not design their own goods hired specialists to 'beautify' their products or copied designs from the many pattern books that were published at the time, such as Chippendale's *The Gentleman and Cabinetmaker's Director* (1754). Wedgwood was one of the new breed of businessmen who no longer had time to work at his craft but concentrated on increasing the division of labour within his workshop in order to use less skilled labour and to make the products more uniform. In his highly successful 'Queen's Ware' range, a limited number of standard shapes could be decorated in many different patterns set out in specially prepared catalogues or pattern books, which customers could consult (see fig. 1). Much of the design work at Wedgwood's Etruria

1. 'Queen's Ware' teapots, jugs and tureens; from a catalogue issued by Josiah Wedgwood, Staffordshire, 1774

factory in Staffordshire was carried out by the firm's own designers—or modellers as they were called in the pottery trade—who were regarded so highly that such men as William Greatbach (1735–1813) became the highest-paid workers in the firm. Wedgwood's success lay in his recognition of the importance of design and in developing new glazes and simpler forms that suited the new Neo-classical taste for purity and simplicity. As he turned increasingly to Neo-classical design in the 1760s, he had difficulty finding modellers who were familiar with the style and capable of adapting it. He was forced to go outside the industry to such artists as John Flaxman, whose familiarity with Neo-classical forms enabled him to make acceptable new products that had no classical precedents. Such was Flaxman's talent that from 1817 to 1826 he was also hired to design Neo-classical silver and silver-plate for Rundell, Bridges & Rundell, one of London's largest silver firms. Although Flaxman and other freelance designers employed on a commission basis produced successful designs, Wedgwood preferred to use his own 'in-house' modellers who fitted in better with his rigid work schedules.

(ii) The Society of Arts. The society was founded in 1754 by William Shipley to encourage 'Arts, Manufacture and Commerce', but by the late 18th century design and other matters related to commercial production were largely ignored until profits were threatened. The fears of British manufacturers—particularly textile manufacturers—about competition from well-designed foreign, mainly French, goods were voiced in the House of Commons after the

1832 Reform Act, and a Select Committee on Arts and Manufactures met in 1835 to hear evidence from designers, manufacturers and artisans on the state of the British manufacturing industry. The ensuing Ewart Report (1836) recommended the establishment of Government schools of design along the lines of those in France and Germany. The first school opened at Somerset House, London, in 1837 (among its pupils was CHRISTOPHER DRESSER), and by 1843 six branch schools had been set up in the provinces. Despite some valiant efforts to relate to the needs of the commercial world, the schools mainly relied on fine-art training, and in 1846 another report declared the schools had completely failed to meet the needs of manufacturers.

Under the influence of Prince Albert, Queen Victoria's consort and Prince of Saxe-Coburg, who became its President in 1843, and HENRY COLE, the Society of Arts again mounted exhibitions of manufactured goods in an effort to improve the standards of British product design. Cole collaborated with Herbert Minton (1793–1858) on a design for a tea-service for the exhibition of 1846, and in 1847 Cole established the Summerly's Art Manufactures, a venture that brought together such manufacturers as the Coalbrookdale Iron Co., Holland & Sons, the Wedgwood and Minton potteries and Rodgers, Joseph & Sons cutlery company, and such artists as Richard Redgrave, Richard Westmacott, John Bell and Daniel Maclise. Once again the designers were criticized for not fully understanding the materials and processes involved, and the hoped-for fusion of art and commerce in the newly named art manufactures was not successful. These art-manufactures exhibitions were the forerunners of the Great Exhibition of 1851, more properly known as the Great Exhibition of the Industry of All Nations. Organized largely by Cole and Prince Albert, helped by a group of design reformers that included Owen Jones, the exhibition had the aim partly to display British pre-eminence (half the exhibits were British), partly to show the benefits of applying arts, science and technology to commerce and partly to assess the state of British design, which was generally found wanting, as was most European design. One result of the exhibition was the establishment in 1857 of a museum in South Kensington (now the Victoria and Albert Museum), where contemporary designers and manufacturers could see the very best in world design, past and present, and so improve their own design practice.

2. *c.* 1850–1915.

(i) The American System of Manufacture. The American section of the Great Exhibition revealed a new approach to design and manufacture that came to be known as the American System of Manufacture, in which goods using standardized and interchangeable parts were mass-produced by machine. Developments in precision tool-making helped perfect identical components in a society that

2. 'New Family' sewing-machine, manufactured by I. M. Singer & Co., New York, 1865–85 (London, Science Museum)

experienced a shortage of craft skills and high labour costs. Although there had been European precedents for this type of production, they had not been developed, and the British Government recognized that its systematic development in the USA from about 1800 had led to American supremacy in the production of fire-arms (where interchangeable parts meant repairs could take place on the battlefield), locks and machinery. Samuel Colt (1814–62) and Alfred C. Hobbs (1812–91) recognized gaps in the British market and established their own firms in Britain. In 1853 the Enfield Fire-arms Factory was established using American machine tools, and in the same year a commission was sent to America to investigate the new economic threat. The subsequent Report of the Commission on the Machinery of the United States noted the drive towards innovation in the USA—particularly labour-saving machinery—whereas Britain still enjoyed cheap, abundant labour.

In the USA the use of standardized interchangeable parts spread. In 1850 Aaron L. Dennison, founder of the American Horologe Co., Roxbury, MA, expressly visited fire-arms factories to apply their techniques to clock and watch production, and by the end of the century watches were a major American product.

A key feature of American product design in the second half of the 19th century was the proliferation of new products, many of which—for example sewing-machines and typewriters—were mechanical devices for what had previously been hand skills (see fig. 2). Others—the camera, the telephone, the motor- car—were new developments. Many of the companies that became familiar brand-names—Singer, Kodak (the Eastman Co. was founded by George Eastman in 1881, known as Eastman Kodak from 1892), Ford—developed into major industries with large national and international sales. Such entrepreneurs as Isaac Singer (1811–75), Samuel Colt and Philo Remington (1816–89) all combined an understanding of technical developments with business and marketing acumen. Singer used hire-purchase to sell his goods; during the slump in the fire-arms industry following the Civil War, Remington diversified into typewriters, which the firm's mechanics redesigned for mass production in 1874, by which time the American system formed the basis of more than 20 industries, including precision instruments and tools, machine tools, cutlery and musical instruments.

The success of the motor-car business started in 1903 by Henry Ford (1863–1947), and in particular his Ford 'Model T' (1908), was based on an unvarying standard

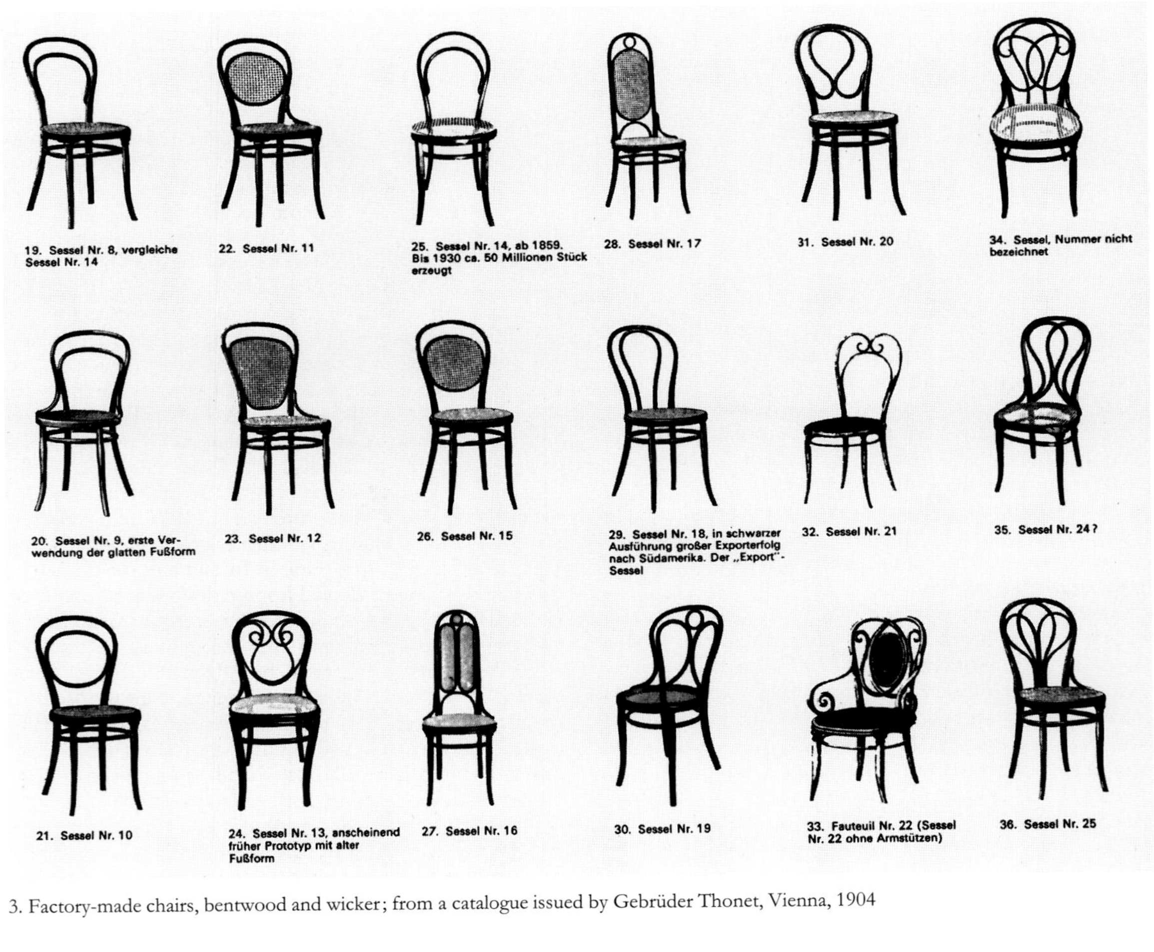

3. Factory-made chairs, bentwood and wicker; from a catalogue issued by Gebrüder Thonet, Vienna, 1904

4. Electric kettles, designed by Peter Behrens for AEG, 1909

design, which kept down the cost of what had previously been expensive items. From 1914 it was mass-produced using a moving assembly line and a standardized design with interchangeable parts; as a result costs fell dramatically (*see* MASS PRODUCTION, fig. 1). In 1921 Ford still produced half of all the cars made in the USA but declining sales forced him to abandon a single design and bring out new models at regular intervals. Manufacturers were confronted with a dilemma: cheapness demanded standardization for long enough to recoup capital-investment costs; demands for novelty meant rapid changes. The solution was to maximize superficial changes related only to appearance, a new mode of operating that came to be known as 'styling' and distinguished American, and later international, design for many years.

(ii) The Arts and Crafts Movement. The development of industrial design was also influenced by the ARTS AND CRAFTS MOVEMENT, which, by the late 19th century, had sown the seeds of design reform. The movement was a reaction against what were seen as the evils of industrialization in Britain in the second half of the 19th century: the division of labour, the irresponsible use of machinery and the mass production of shoddy goods. Despite its attacks on the effects of industrialization, the movement's emphasis on quality, honesty of production, the necessity for well-designed everyday objects and the importance of designers who understood the materials and techniques involved in the process for which they were designing was to inspire many of those who strove to improve commercial product design in Britain, Germany, Italy and the USA in the early 20th century.

By the late 19th century Arts and Crafts practitioners were frustrated that their ideals had led them into producing, by hand, one-off expensive items for rich clients, and that the ideals of democratizing design had not been achieved. The second generation of Arts and Crafts designers, in particular W. R. Lethaby, developed William Morris's concern for the everyday object into a theory and definition of art focused on the design of well-made objects that could be commercially produced at affordable prices. The emphasis was on quality in both hand and machine production, both of which were encompassed in the design education reforms that advocated direct links between colleges of art and design and local manufacturers. These reforms took place in Britain, Austria and Germany from about 1898 to 1903, with Lethaby at the new Central School of Arts and Crafts, London (1898–1903), August Spencer and Benjamin Fletcher at the Leicester School of Art (from 1898 and 1900 respectively), PETER BEHRENS at the Kunstgewerbeschule, Düsseldorf (from 1903), and Josef Hoffman at the Kunstgewerbeschule, Vienna (from 1899).

The widespread dissemination of the Arts and Crafts ideals led to an emphasis on the importance of the designer as opposed to the fine artist, and many young people deliberately turned from fine art to design work, which they felt was more appropriate to the needs of the new century. Architects also became increasingly concerned with wider issues of design. From *c.* 1900 to 1914 in Vienna the painters and architects who formed the Vienna Secession (*see* SECESSION, §3), a group established in opposition to the official academy, turned to product design. Josef Hoffman, Hans Vollmer, Kolo Moser and others were involved in designing bentwood furniture for the firms of the Gebrüder Thonet (see fig. 3) and J. & J. Kohn and also cane furniture, in particular for the Prag-Rudniker company that, from its bases in Prague and Rudnik, Poland, employed hundreds of craftworkers and sold thousands of relatively cheap items. These and similar well-made objects were designed in Germany by Peter Behrens, Henry Van de Velde and RICHARD RIEMERSCHMID for commercial production as early as 1905 and were produced in such large numbers that they threatened the domestic wicker-furniture trade in Britain and the USA.

The employment of well-known designers by commercial firms in Germany before the establishment of the Deutscher Werkbund and the engagement in 1907 of Peter Behrens as designer at the Allgemeine Elektrizitäts-Gesellschaft (AEG) by Emil Rathenau were not isolated incidents but part of a wider movement to democratize design. The Deutscher Werkbund was founded in 1907 to improve the quality of both hand- and machine-made German goods through cooperation between designers and manufacturers, thereby helping to forge a national culture and to make the economy of the new nation state more competitive. Cooperation between certain manufacturers and designers was evident both in such projects as

Riemerschmid's cutlery designs for Peter Bruckmann and in Peter Behrens's brief from Emil Rathenau at AEG to design what is usually seen as the first example of a corporate image. He designed a logo, buildings, brochures, prospectuses, exhibition displays, advertising, kettles, fans and arc lamps. The kettles had standardized parts that could be combined in a variety of ways to produce over 80 variations, although only 30 were put into production. The three kettle forms came in three sizes, in three different materials, each with three different surface finishes and a choice of two lids, two handles and two plinths (see fig. 4): plugs and heating elements were uniform. Behrens's use of standardized parts to provide variety was an innovation in the history of industrial design.

3. 1915–45.

(i) Britain. The Design and Industries Association (DIA) was established in London in 1915 as a British version of the Werkbund. Its founding statement set the cooperation between manufacturers, designers and distribution in the context of national development and Britain's need to gain greater shares in world markets. At the outbreak of World War I the DIA emphasized to the government the threat to the post-war British economy of German quality goods as well as the well-known competition from cheap goods. Some business firms (Wedgwood, Heal & Son, Stevens & Williams, Gordon Russell) took up the aims and ideals of the DIA, but it was Frank Pick's implementation of them at the London Passenger Transport Board that is best known. Pick (1878–1941) believed that good design improved the public environment and sought to develop a corporate image that not only included a new logo and clear typography but also the remodelling or construction of 50 London Underground stations between 1924 and 1939. Many private firms were more sympathetic towards DIA views in the lean economic years of the 1930s, and in the period just before World War II the association's stress on good design leading to economic viability, and even increased profits, heightened its appeal.

(ii) Germany. Industrial design in the inter-war years was marked by an increasing tendency for such progressive firms as Karl Bosch to Americanize their systems of production. Opel moved to 'Fordism' and was taken over by General Motors in the 1920s. In direct contrast Benz remained in the quality-car market and was typical of those German firms that resented the American influence and continued to use traditional methods of organization and production.

The Bauhaus school of art and design (1919–33) aimed to weld together art and technology in forms appropriate to the new machine age. Although it played an important part in the Modern Movement, many items designed there were never put into industrial production. Walter Gropius (director from 1923) described its workshops as laboratories, in which prototypes of products suitable for mass production and typical of the time were carefully developed and constantly improved. Despite the emphasis on form following function, visual considerations frequently outweighed those of function. The dominant aesthetic of abstract geometric form was to influence future generations of architects and designers, particularly after Bauhaus staff and former students became established in the USA after fleeing Nazi Germany, yet this 'purist' Modernism often only appeared in products made and bought by a discerning élite.

5. Volkswagen 'Beetle' automobile, after a prototype designed by Ferdinand Porsche, 1933

(iii) USA. The inter-war years saw the rise of the new profession of industrial designer. During the massive consumer boom in the five years after World War I, many new companies mass-produced technological goods, and by the 1920s competition necessitated differentiation within each type. From 1927, when the first effects of economic recession were felt, designers began to play a crucial role in American industry. After the Wall Street crash (1929) and during the Depression of the 1930s, goods were made to look more attractive to increase sales. The new industrial designers were mainly commercial artists who worked in advertising—Walter Dorwin Teague, Raymond Loewy, Donald Deskey (*b* 1894)—and stage designers—Norman Bel Geddes and Henry Dreyfuss (1904–72). The Ford Motor Co. was one of the first firms to call in the new breed of designers when it was forced to abandon its single design. Such firms as Eastman Kodak and Gestetner employed industrial designers as consultants, while others (for example the electrical company Westinghouse) took on staff designers. In the 1930s such leading industrial designers as Gilbert Rohde set up their own agencies. The new designers worked with engineers and market researchers as part of a wider team. They tuned in with 'streamlining', which both connected with popular taste and symbolized the Modern Movement through references to speed and dynamism. Popularized by Norman Bel Geddes, streamlining—sometimes known as the teardrop shape—became synonymous with styling, although it was severely criticized as being applied indiscriminately, regardless of how an object functioned. The streamlining forms are best represented by the Boeing 247 (1933), the Hotchkiss stapler (1936) and the Dymaxion cars (1933–4) of R. Buckminster Fuller. His cars were too futuristic for popular consumption, and the motor-car industry was careful to make its streamlined forms acceptable to the general public. In 1927 General Motors of Detroit appointed Harley T. Earl (1893–1969) to design their Cadillacs as part of their attempt to cut into the Ford market. Earl subsequently became Head of the Styling

Division, which employed 1400 people by the time he retired in 1959. However, the best-known streamlined car design of the pre-war period is the German prototype of the Volkswagen 'Beetle' (1933; see fig. 5), designed by Ferdinand Porsche, which was to become one of the major success stories of the automobile industry and of mass production.

One of the new industrial designers was Walter Dorwin Teague, who moved from graphic design to product design in the mid-1920s and in 1927 was commissioned by Eastman Kodak to redesign not only cameras but also packaging. In 1928 he developed the 'Vanity' Kodak, which was produced in a range of colours and finished with chromium-plated trim. The 'Bantam Special' small, hand-held camera (1936) is a good example of his ability to grapple with technological problems as well as aesthetic form.

In 1929 Raymond Loewy was given five days to redesign a duplicating machine for Gestetner. His solution—what he described as a face-lift—remained the basic design well into the 1950s. His equally famous Coldspot refrigerator (1935) for the Sears Roebuck Co. dramatically changed the appearance of the product and increased sales from 15,000 to 275,000 in five years. The success of the design lay in encasing composite parts in a unified whole, in this case a plain, flush-doored, white enamelled steel cabinet trimmed with chrome. The interior had many 'extras' to tempt the suburban consumer—an array of containers, a semi-automatic defrosting device, instant-release ice-cube trays and a glass rolling-pin that could be filled with ice-cubes.

The design of office furniture and equipment and mechanical 'mod cons' led designers to think about how human beings used machines. Such American designers as Henry Dreyfuss took the study of ergonomics seriously, as did some of the anonymous staff designers working in kitchen-unit furniture and equipment, a great growth area in the inter-war years and after World War II.

4. After 1945.

(i) USA. After 1945 American industrial expansion continued, and increasing wealth led to greater demands for 'modern' goods. Although trained as an architect and painter respectively, the husband-and-wife team of Charles Eames and Ray Eames (*see* Eames) sought to fuse aesthetics with technological developments in their efforts to design reasonably priced mass-produced furniture (see fig. 6). They emphasized the constraints imposed by the design brief, and their workshop epitomized the Bauhaus idea of the studio as an industrial laboratory where they constantly experimented with, and tested, their designs. Their collaboration with the furniture firm of Herman Miller Inc., Zeeland, MI, was a model client/designer relationship where respect for the designers allowed them complete control over their work. The good, modern designs that the Eames brought into American homes and offices were widely copied abroad.

6. Glass-reinforced plastic chair with metal legs, designed by Charles Eames and Ray Eames for Herman Miller Inc., 1949

7. Modular glass containers, designed by Wilhelm Wagenfeld, 1938

(ii) Federal Republic of Germany. The economy was slow to recover after World War II, but the economic aid provided by the Marshall Plan (£1.5 billion by 1952) meant that by 1950 production had reached pre-war levels, and the *Wirtschaftswunder*—the German economic miracle—took off. Under the Marshall Plan industrialists who were not already convinced of the superiority of the American system of organizing capitalist production visited the USA; converts set about modernizing their companies. From 1950 the USA influenced not only West German production processes but also product design and advertising. The Opel 'Kadets' of the 1950s were little more than replicas of American cars. The German government saw

8. 'Valentine' typewriter, designed by Ettore Sottsass for Olivetti, 1969

9. 'B8' 125 cc motor-cycle, manufactured by the Kawasaki Corp., 1962

industrial design as a key factor in economic regeneration, and in 1951 the Rat für Formgebung was set up under the control of the Ministry of Economics and established professorships of industrial design at technical universities. It was after hearing a lecture at the Technische Hochschule Darmstadt on the links between art and industry, given in 1954 by Wilhelm Wagenfeld, a former member of the Bauhaus, many of whose designs had been put into industrial production (see fig. 7), that Artur Braun (*b* 1925) and Erwin Braun reassessed their firm's design policy. Braun AG already had a reputation for technical excellence, and the name was soon to become synonymous with good design. They made contact with the Hochschule für Gestaltung, Ulm, the first graduate school of design in Germany, established in 1955. From Ulm they employed Fritz Eichler (*b* 1911) as Head of Design, and Hans Gugelot (1920–65) and Otl Aicher (*b* 1922) as design consultants. Together they produced a new corporate image and designed new products. Although not formally associated with the Ulm school, the work of Dieter Rams (*b* 1932), perhaps the best-known Braun designer, fitted into the restrained, balanced, functionalist, monochromatic units—white, grey or black and increasingly black or grey in the 1960s and 1970s—that encased a variety of mechanical products, including a succession of electric shavers, the Braun calculator (1977) and the innovative voice-controlled alarm-clock (1986).

(iii) Italy. American cultural influences were also important in Italy, although it received less American aid after World War II. 'Functionalism' and 'rationalism' dominated Italian industrial design as industry modernized (1945–50), and such firms as Olivetti competed with IBM on the international markets. Existing Olivetti products—the 'Lexikon 80' standard typewriter (1948), the portable 'Lettera 22' (1950)—were redesigned by Marcello Nizzoli (1887–1969). In 1959 ETTORE SOTTSASS designed Olivetti's first computer, 'Elea 9003', on rationalist, modernist lines. New types of product were introduced: the Vespa (designed by Corradino d'Ascanio, 1947) and the Lambretta scooters (designed by Cesare Pallavicino and Pierluigi Torre, 1947), both originally designed to use aircraft motors left over from the war and to travel short distances in narrow city streets, met an international demand for cheap, individual, motorized transport. Their sculptural forms reflected designers' interest in organic forms and expressed a feeling of youthful modernism. Small cars were another successful Italian design. The emphasis on compactness went hand in hand with increased efforts to industrialize and automate the production process. The result was the Fiat 'Ritmo' (1978), produced on a fully automatic production line and advertised as 'hand-built by robots'.

The Italian consumer boom of the 1950s was boosted by discoveries of gas and oil and the growth of the chemical and plastics industries. Numerous design philosophies were hotly debated by artists and intellectuals, and Milan became the centre of world debate on design; its famous Triennale exhibitions, with large sections devoted to consumer products, were key events in the design world.

Ettore Sottsass was the best-known theoretical and practical post-war Italian designer. His work is difficult to categorize because it changed as his critique of design and society developed. He insisted that colour and symbolism should re-enter the world of product design as he tried to make new products, for example the red plastic 'Valentine' typewriter (1969, e.g. in London, Des. Mus.; see fig. 8) for Olivetti. His later designs in the Post-modern style for the Memphis group challenge existing ideas about what constitutes design suitable for the home (e.g. 'Tatar' table, 1985; New York, Met.).

(iv) Japan. In the immediate post-war years, Japanese goods were considered cheap and inferior. Massive industrial expansion took place after World War II, and early products simply copied American technology and styling, including chromium trimmings. Although still using imported technology, by the mid-1960s Japanese companies were producing cars, motor-cycles (see fig. 9), cameras, televisions and other technically efficient and also cheap products. The 'high tech' style adopted had, at its worst, excessive cheap-looking detail. However, such firms as

10. TR610 transistor radio, manufactured by the Sony Corp., 1958

the Sony Corp. soon became aware of the need to make their products look more sophisticated, partly in order to counteract their low cost.

Japanese designers worked as part of a close-knit team with marketing and sales staff. They were acutely aware of consumers' needs, and they emphasized attractive design and packaging as well as vigorous advertising and selling. There was a synthesis between Western design influences and traditional aesthetic values, with particular emphasis on miniaturization, multi-functionality and attention to detail as well as overall form (see fig. 10). Japanese post-war product design was increasingly successful, from the Sony TR610 (a pocket transistor radio, 1958) to its Micro television set with a 125 mm screen (1962). In 1955 Toyota advertised Western-looking cars occupied by Japanese women wearing Western clothes; just 17 years later in 1972 Honda made its first impact on the Western market. Many European manufacturers adopted Japanese policies and production methods, and there was direct Japanese investment in British industry, for example Nissan Motors Manufactory (UK).

BIBLIOGRAPHY

S. Giedion: *Mechanization Takes Command* (New York, 1948)
R. Loewy: *Never Leave Well Enough Alone* (New York, 1951)
C. Singer, E. J. Holmyard and A. R. Hall, eds: *A History of Technology*, 5 vols (Oxford, 1954–8)
C. Harvie, G. Martin and A. Scharf, eds: *Industrialization and Culture, 1830–1914* (London, 1970)
G. Naylor: *The Arts and Crafts Movement: A Study of its Sources, Ideals and Influence on Design Theory* (London, 1971, 2/1990)
R. Banham: *Theory and Design in the First Machine Age* (London, 1972)
Italy: The New Domestic Landscape (exh. cat., ed. E. Ambasz; New York, MOMA, 1972)
R. Caplan: *The Design of Herman Miller* (New York, 1973)
A. Forty and G. Newman: *British Design* (Milton Keynes, 1975)
N. Carrington: *Industrial Design in Britain* (London, 1976)
S. Katz: *Plastics: Designs and Materials* (London, 1978)
S. Bayley: *In Good Shape: Style in Industrial Products, 1900–1960* (London, 1979)
J. Meikle: *Twentieth Century Limited: Industrial Design in America, 1925–1939* (Philadelphia, 1979)
P. Garner: *Twentieth-century Furniture* (Oxford, 1980)
J. Heskett: *Industrial Design* (London, 1980, 2/1984)
A. Windsor: *Peter Behrens: Architect and Designer* (London, 1981)
S. Sanders: *Honda: The Man and his Machines* (Tokyo, 1982)
P. Sparke: *Ettore Sottsass Jnr* (London, 1982)
S. Bayley: *Harley Earl and the Dream Machine* (London, 1983, 2/1990)
E. Lucie-Smith: *A History of Industrial Design* (Oxford, 1983)
P. Sparke: *Consultant Design: The History and Practice of the Designer in Industry* (London, 1983)
J. M. Woodham: *The Industrial Designer and the Public* (London, 1983)
T. Buddensieg and H. Rogge: *Industriekultur: Peter Behrens and the AEG, 1907–1914* (Cambridge, MA, 1984)
A. Forty: *Objects of Desire: Design and Society, 1750–1980* (London, 1986)
J. Heskett: *Design in Germany, 1870–1918* (London, 1986)
P. Sparke: *An Introduction to Design and Culture in the Twentieth Century* (London, 1986)
H. Conway, ed.: *Design History: A Student Handbook* (London and Boston, 1987)
P. Kirkham, R. Mace and J. Porter: *Furnishing the World: The East London Furniture Trade, 1830–1980* (London, 1987)
D. Miller: *Material Culture and Mass Consumption* (Oxford and New York, 1987)
P. Sparke: *Japanese Design* (London, 1987)
N. Oliver and B. Wilkinson: *The Japanization of British Industry* (London, 1988)
J. Neuhart, M. Neuhart and R. Eames: *Eames Design: The Office of Charles and Ray Eames, 1941–1978* (London and New York, 1989)
Design of the Times: One Hundred Years of the Royal College of Art (exh. cat., ed. C. Frayling and C. Catterall; London, Royal Coll. A., 1996)

PAT KIRKHAM

Industrial scenes. Type of subject-matter that formed a major theme in Western art from the beginnings of the Industrial Revolution in the mid-18th century until the decline of heavy industry in the mid-20th century.

1. Introduction. 2. Depictions of industrial landscape. 3. Depictions of the industrial worker. 4. Prints and photographs.

1. INTRODUCTION. Before the 18th century the theme of industry was only periodically and peripherally important. Scenes of labour appeared in Egyptian reliefs and paintings, but in Greek and Roman art the subject was largely absorbed into such mythological tales as those of the Forge of Vulcan and the Labours of Hercules. The prevalence of slavery in the ancient world may have rendered labour a theme unworthy of extensive artistic attention. During the Middle Ages the belief that labour was a punishment for original sin probably had a similar effect. Themes relating to industry, such as the Labours of the Months, appeared with greater frequency in later medieval art, both in manuscript illustrations and on the sculpted portals of churches. Portrayals of urban craftsmen, such as those presented in the windows of Chartres Cathedral, reflect the growing prominence of guilds in the later Middle Ages.

By the 16th century an increase in mining and forging attracted artistic attention, both in the illustrations of printed books and in paintings. Georgius Agricola's publication *De re metallica* of 1556, with its woodcut illustrations of mining activities, marked the beginning of an alliance between industry and the graphic arts that would survive well into the industrial age. Landscape paintings of the Liège industrial region by Lucas van Valckenborch I and Marten van Valckenborch (1534/5–1612) introduced the theme of industry's transformation of nature. The common labourer was depicted as early as 1570–75 in the series of frescoes showing various industries painted by Giorgio Vasari and others for the *studiolo* of Francesco I de' Medici in the Palazzo Vecchio, Florence (*in situ*). Though such scenes usually retained mythological references through the 17th century, a growing acknowledgement of the reality of heavy labour began to emerge. Paintings of the Forge of Vulcan by such important and diverse artists as Jan Breughel I, Velázquez and Louis Le Nain all reflect this ambivalence between the myth of industry and its reality.

In response to the massive industrialization of Western society in the 18th and 19th centuries, each of these pre-industrial themes achieved considerable artistic importance. The industrial landscape and the modern labourer became major subjects of paintings, and a special alliance between industry and the graphic arts developed, ultimately transformed by the invention of photography.

2. Depictions of industrial landscape. The increasing importance of landscape as a theme in 18th- and 19th-century painting was accompanied by a marginal but persistent recognition of industry's growing intrusion into nature. During the Romantic era artists tended to incorporate industry into the aesthetic landscape categories of the time, especially those of the Picturesque and the Sublime. Such sites as Coalbrookdale, Salop, where scenic countryside was subjected to massive industrialization, were often the focus of this imagery. During the later 18th century such landscape painters as Paul Sandby began to incorporate evidence of early industry in nature in a Picturesque manner. The first major painter of Sublime views of the industrial landscape was Philippe Jacques de Loutherbourg (*see* Landscape painting, colour pl. III, fig. 2). In general, the Picturesque approach suggested a degree of acceptance of industry into nature, while the more Sublime imagery of blast furnaces and blackened skies tended to express a sense of danger.

During the 19th century the Sublime approach reached its climax in John Martin's spectacular scenes inspired by industry (for example, Martin's *Great Day of his Wrath*, 1852; London, Tate). The Picturesque inclusion of industry in nature gradually evolved into a more straightforward, realistic approach. Factories and railroads appeared only occasionally and Picturesquely in landscapes of the Hudson River school, but by the 1850s such subjects began to be presented more insistently by such American painters as George Inness. In Germany Karl Blechen's painting of the *Ironworks at Neustadt-Eberswalde* (*c.* 1834; Berlin, Tiergarten, N.G.) and Adolph Menzel's overview of the *Berlin–Potsdam Railway* (1847; Berlin, Alte N.G.) introduced a new degree of topographical frankness to the industrial landscape. A similar objectivity characterized the numerous paintings of factories by the French artist François Bonhommé. This more objective approach to industrial topography was often encouraged by industry itself as a tool of self-promotion. Inness's most famous industrial landscape, the *Lackawanna Valley* (*c.* 1855; Washington, DC, N.G.A.), was commissioned by the local railway company. Bonhommé produced most of his works in the employ of such powerful industries as the Fourchambault Iron Works.

During the late 19th century progressive landscape painters began to develop a harsher, more critical portrayal of the effects of industrialization. Among the landscape painters who exhibited with the Impressionists in the 1870s, Armand Guillaumin was the most attentive to industry. He concentrated on depicting the heavily industrialized banks of the Seine east of Paris, where nature was often dominated by industry and the expanding city. This interest in the industrial suburbs was generally not shared by Guillaumin's Impressionist colleagues, but was pursued avidly by the younger, more politically radical group of Neo-Impressionists. During the 1880s such Neo-Impressionists as Georges Seurat, Paul Signac and Maximilian Luce frequently depicted the factories and gas tanks of the grim, working-class districts surrounding Paris, as in Signac's *Gasometers at Clichy* (1886; Melbourne, N.G. Victoria; see fig. 1).

By the end of the 19th century the concentration of industry in major urban centres resulted in the emergence of the cityscape as a primary source of industrial imagery. At the beginning of the 20th century Berlin was one of the most industrialized cities in Europe, and, as such, it inspired considerable artistic attention. The factories and railways of Berlin were portrayed by such realist painters as Hans Baluschek (1870–1935), as well as by the younger and more radical Expressionists. In the intense, distorted depictions by such Expressionists as Ernst Ludwig Kirchner and Ludwig Meidner the industrial city was seen as a menacing and dehumanizing force. In Paris Cubism provided artists with a means of responding to various aspects of the urban-industrial experience. Among French Cubist painters who focused on this theme, Robert Delaunay expressed the kaleidoscopic complexity of the modern city, while Fernand Léger emphasized the mechanization imposed by industry. Such Italian Futurists as Umberto Boccioni adopted Cubism as a method of expressing their celebration of the dissolution of traditional values in the face of a rapidly accelerating, mechanized world.

In the USA, New York emerged as the centre of progressive art and the focus of industrial imagery. Early in the 20th century such artists associated with the Ashcan school as John Sloan and George Bellows frequently portrayed industrial New York in a blunt, realistic style. Joseph Stella adopted a more European, Cubo-Futurist style in his dynamic visualizations of New York's industrial structures. During the 1920s and 1930s various styles were applied to the American industrial landscape, and distinctly different attitudes were sometimes expressed. Such realists as Thomas Hart Benton portrayed industry as a heroic symbol of power and progress, while others, such as Edward Hopper and Charles Burchfield, presented a mostly bleak and alienating industrial landscape. The Precisionists utilized a sleek, machine-like style perfectly suited to the theme of industry. In the work of Charles Demuth the result could be ironic and pessimistic, while Charles Sheeler's industrial scenes tend to celebrate enthusiastically the order and precision of modern industry. As

1. Paul Signac: *Gasometers at Clichy*, oil on canvas, 648×788 mm, 1886 (Melbourne, National Gallery of Victoria)

was the case in the 19th century, the most positive scenes of industry were often painted on commission and reflect the outlook of powerful patrons. Many of Sheeler's most exemplary depictions of industry were related to projects commissioned by *Fortune* magazine and the Ford Motor Corp.

The rise of abstract art in the 1940s and 1950s, combined with the subsequent decline of heavy industry, reduced substantially the importance of the industrial landscape as a subject in modern art. Among abstract artists, however, significant echoes of the theme persisted in the paintings of Franz Kline and the sculptures of David Smith. Kline's bold black-and-white patterns evolved from earlier industrial landscape scenes and evoke massive industrial structures. Smith's use of welded steel related directly to industry, and in such sculptures as *Hudson River Landscape* (1951; New York, Whitney) he participated directly, though abstractly, in the long tradition of industrial landscape.

3. Depictions of the industrial worker. The representation of the industrial worker evolved parallel to, but generally distinct from, the theme of the industrial landscape. While the latter was largely concerned with industry's relation to nature, paintings of the industrial labourer focus on the individual's relation to industry. The two principal, contrasting themes entailed in this subject are the portrayal of the worker as a heroic individual controlling the vast powers of industry and the acknowledgement of industry's dehumanizing impact on the individual.

The mythological context that dominated most pre-industrial portrayals of workers was decisively cast off by Joseph Wright in the 1770s, in a group of paintings of forges and blacksmith shops (e.g. of 1771; New Haven, CT, Yale Cent. Brit. A.). The lingering association of such scenes with ancient myths survived well into the industrial age, however, and was occasionally used to lend a heroic aura to the modern labourer. Menzel changed the title of his vividly realistic painting of German factory workers from the *Iron-rolling Mill* to a *Modern Cyclops* (1872–5; Berlin, Alte N.G.) before sending it to the Salon in Paris in 1880. In the second half of the 19th century British and American painters struggled to balance the realistic and the heroic in portrayals of workers. Ford Madox Brown's *Work* (1852, 1851–63; Manchester, C.A.G.) and *Iron and Coal* (1861; Wallington House, Northumb., NT; see fig. 2) by William Bell Scott (i) are two prominent examples of the British tendency to glorify labour. A somewhat greater

2. William Bell Scott (i): *Iron and Coal*, oil on canvas, 1.8×1.4 m, 1861 (Wallington House, Northumbria, NT)

emphasis on realism characterizes the paintings of industrial workers by the American artists John Ferguson Weir and Thomas Anshutz. During the late 19th century the glorification of the worker was also a theme of sculpted monuments, most notably in the work of the Belgian sculptor Constantin Meunier.

During the 20th century the image of the industrial worker became increasingly politicized within the general artistic category of social realism. In countries with Marxist governments this image developed into a virtual icon of officially sanctioned art, as exemplified in paintings of the 1920s and 1930s by the Soviet artists Yury Pimenov and Alexander Deineka (*b* 1899). In non-Communist countries the theme of the industrial worker was emphasized most often by artists with strong Socialist beliefs. Among the most influential examples are the monumental murals painted in Mexico and the USA during the 1920s and 1930s by the Mexican artists Diego Rivera, José Clemente Orozco and David Alfara Siqueiros. Rivera's mural *Detroit Industry* (*see* RIVERA, DIEGO, fig. 1), painted at the Detroit Institute of Arts in 1932–3, effectively glorifies the industrial worker, while at the same time criticizing the mechanistic dehumanization of the modern factory. Such American artists as Ben Shahn and William Gropper (1897–1977) were inspired by these Mexican painters to produce similar murals in the 1930s. Shahn's employment poster *Welders* (Trenton, NJ State Mus.), designed in 1944 for the Congress of Industrial Organizations, combined the heroic scale of the Mexican muralists and the realism of photography, which was used as a source for the figures.

4. PRINTS AND PHOTOGRAPHS. Throughout the early years of industrialization printmaking was the artistic method most closely allied with industry. The development of new print techniques during this era paralleled the early evolution of industry itself. Printmakers were generally quicker than painters to depict newly emerging industries, and popular illustrated travel books include many of the earliest views of industrialized landscapes and towns. Industries soon began to employ printmakers, not only for purposes of technical illustration, but also for promotion. The lithographer John Cooke Bourne produced impressive promotional albums of prints for both the London and Birmingham Railway (London, 1839) and the Great Western Railway (London, 1846).

The proliferation of illustrated journals during the 19th century contributed substantially to widening the range of industrial scenes produced by printmakers. Such weekly news journals as the *Illustrated London News*, *L'Illustration* and *Harper's Weekly* frequently included wood-engravings of various aspects of the industrial scene. Most of the pictures and articles in these popular weeklies were supportive of industrial progress, but a growing body of critical, reform-minded images also began to appear in left-wing journals during the later 19th century. Scenes that emphasized poor working conditions, labour strikes and the poverty that accompanied industry appeared frequently in such journals as *The Graphic*.

By the early 20th century photographs had begun to replace prints in illustrated journals and other publications. A growing number of commissions to illustrate industrial scenes went to photographers, but some painters and printmakers continued to work in this area. Joseph Stella was commissioned by the journal *The Survey* in 1908 to produce an extensive series of charcoal illustrations of the industrial scene in Pittsburgh. The continuing role of printmaking was highlighted when the etcher Joseph Pennell published his compendium of industrial illustrations, *Pictures of the Wonder of Work* (Philadelphia and London, 1916). For the most part, however, photography had taken over as the principal medium for the depiction of industry.

The earliest photographers were drawn to industrial subjects, and by the 1850s photographers were being hired to document such major projects as the construction and launching of the Great Eastern steamship in England (1852–8). During the 1860s the building of transcontinental railway lines in the USA was illustrated in albums of photographs by Alexander Gardner and A. J. Russell (1830–1902). The construction of the great Forth Bridge in Scotland during the 1880s was documented in nine albums of photographs by Evelyn Carey. These industrial commissions all served the dual purpose of documentation and promotion. Throughout the late 19th century and early 20th a proliferation of popular, commercial types of photographs (including stereoscopic views, lantern slides and postcards) focused on industry's more sensational scenes, such as mining disasters.

During the early 20th century photographs of industry were characterized by two contrasting approaches. The photographs of Lewis W. Hine, aimed at social reform, defined one approach. His images of working conditions in factories and mines were produced in the employ of such organizations as the National Child Labor Committee and the American Red Cross as well as the journal *The Survey*. The other approach is best exemplified in the work of Margaret Bourke-White. While Hine focused on workers, Bourke-White emphasized the mechanisms and architectural structures of industry. In contrast to Hine's spirit of critical reform, Bourke-White's pictures celebrated industry as a source of order, progress and power. Like Charles Sheeler, Bourke-White worked for *Fortune*, a magazine established in the 1930s to promote business and industry. After a flurry of photographs of the war industries established during World War II, industrial photography gradually became redundant because of the rise of electronic technology during the second half of the 20th century.

BIBLIOGRAPHY

R. W. Schmidt: *Art and Industry: 96 Masterpieces of Art Illustrating the Technical Achievements of the Ages* (New York, 1923)

P. Brandt: *Schaffende Arbeit und bildende Kunst im Altertum und Mittelalter* (Leipzig, 1927)

F. D. Klingender: *Art and the Industrial Revolution* (London, 1947, rev. 1968)

R. Evrard: *Les Artistes et les usines à fer: Oeuvres d'art inspirées par les usines à fer* (Liège, 1955)

F. Schnack: *Die Welt der Arbeit in der Kunst* (Stuttgart, 1965)

Industrie und Technik in der deutschen Malerei von der Romantik bis zur Gegenwart (exh. cat. by S. Salzmann, Duisburg, Lehmbruck-Mus., 1969)

La Représentation du travail: Mines, forges, usines (exh. cat. by M. Evrard and P. Le Nouëne, Le Creusot, Ecomus., 1977)

A. Briggs: *Iron Bridge to Crystal Palace: Impact and Images of the Industrial Revolution* (London, 1979)

F. J. Hurley, ed.: *Industry and the Photographic Image: 153 Great Prints from 1850 to the Present* (New York, 1980)

American Realism and the Industrial Age (exh. cat. by M. Doezema, Cleveland, OH, Mus. A.; Lakewood, OH, Kenneth C. Beck Cent. Cult. A.; Columbus, OH, Mus. A.; 1980–81)

R. L. Herbert: 'Industry in the Changing Landscape from Daubigny to Monet', *French Cities in the Nineteenth Century*, ed. J. Merriman (New York, 1981), pp. 141–64

M. A. Bessonowa: 'Technik und Kunst: Das Bild der industriellen Umwelt in der sowjetischen und französischen Malerei der zwanziger Jahre', *Bild. Kst*, iii (1984), pp. 135–7

Industrial Image: British Industrial Photography, 1843 to 1986 (exh. cat. by F. Pugh and S. Stebbing, London, Photographers' Gal., 1986)

The Machine Age in America (exh. cat. by R. G. Wilson and others, New York, Brooklyn Mus., 1986)

Industrial Images/Images industrielles (exh. cat. by R. Donegau, Hamilton, Ont., A.G., 1987)

S. Danly and L. Marx, eds: *The Railroad in American Art: Representations of Technological Change* (Cambridge, MA, 1988)

DENNIS COSTANZO

Ineb hedj. *See* GIZA.

Inerti. *See* GEBELEIN.

Infantado, Duques del. *See under* MENDOZA.

Infante, Francisco [Francisko; Fransisko] (*b* Vasil'yevka, Saratov region, 4 June 1943). Russian installation artist and theorist. The son of a Spanish Republican émigré, Infante studied at the Surikov Art Institute in Moscow from 1956 to 1962. From 1962 to 1968 he was a member of the group Dvizheniye (Movement), which elaborated the principles of kinetic art. In 1970, together with his wife, the artist Nonna Goryunova (*b* 1944), and the designer Valery Osipov (*b* 1941), he organized his own group, ARGO, which became prominent in the Moscow avant-garde of the period. Characteristic of his work in the 1960s are abstract geometric paintings, blueprints for his subsequent three-dimensional compositions. Underlying these compositions is the notion of the artefact, the handmade object, symbolizing the harmony of art, the technosphere and nature. Although to some extent he continued the traditions of Russian Constructivism, he succeeded in infusing his work with a sense of ideal ecological balance, free from technocratic utopianism. His work comprises series of numerous temporary landscape installations, for example *Life of a Triangle* (a triangle placed in the landscape, 1977; outskirts of Moscow; see Ludwigshafen exh. cat., pp. 36–7), in which a major role is usually played by synthetic mirror film on a light framework reflecting the surrounding environment. The next stage in the life of these installations is represented by corresponding cycles of photographs and slides that Infante uses in lectures and articles, giving his art a distinctly didactic character.

WRITINGS

'Iz opyta osvoeniya geometricheskoy formy' [From the experience of mastering geometric form], *Trudy VNIITTE*, xxviii (1981), pp. 67–74

'Nature and Art: The Natural and Artificial', *The Structurist*, xxiii–xxiv (1983–4), pp. 95–8

'Artificially Created Spaces: The Projects and Realizations of the ARGO Group', *J. Dec. & Propaganda A.*, v (1987), pp. 112–25

BIBLIOGRAPHY

'Fransisko Infante', *A-Ya*, i (1979), pp. 9–10, 38–41

Francisco Infante: Artefakty a kresby [Francisco Infante: artefacts and drawings] (exh. cat., Louny, Benedikt Rejt Gal.; Brno, House A.; 1987)

Francisco Infante (exh. cat., Sewickly, PA, Int. Images Ltd, 1989)

Francisko Infante: Artefakten (exh. cat., ed. B. Attman and R. W. Gassen; Ludwigshafen, Hack-Mus. & Städt. Kstsamml., 1989)

Francisco Infante: Artefakty (Moscow, 1990) [cat. of unrealized exh.]

M. N. SOKOLOV

Informalism. *See* ART INFORMEL.

Information art. *See* CONCEPTUAL ART.

Ingannati, Pietro degli (*fl* Venice, 1529–48). Italian painter. Probably from the Veneto, he was formerly confused with Francesco Bissolo, whose work sometimes resembles Ingannati's. He possibly trained in the workshop of Alvise Vivarini. The *Virgin and Child with Four Saints* (ex-Kaiser-Friedrich Mus., Berlin; destr. 1945) and the *Virgin and Child with Two Saints* (Vercelli, Mus. Civ. Borgogna), both datable for stylistic reasons to the first decade of the 16th century, are his earliest signed works. The paintings show the influence of Giovanni Bellini with regard to composition, but stylistically Ingannati's work is closer to the figurative language, first of Lazzaro Bastiani and later of Marco Basaiti and Benedetto Diana. He was strongly influenced by the later works of Giovanni Bellini and Vincenzo Catena and superficially acknowledged the innovations of Giorgione. Ingannati also looked to the work of Palma Vecchio in, for example, the *Portrait of a Man* (Venice, Coin priv. col.). Like Rocco Marconi, Ingannati adapted the compositional type known as the SACRA CONVERSAZIONE to show half- or full-length figures seated in a landscape, the composition dependent upon Titian, but the figurative types repeating those of Giovanni Bellini. In his later years he continued to exploit techniques from 50 years earlier, as is shown by the fact that, beyond the rounded shapes and rich, fresh colours, the Virgins of his last *sacre conversazioni* are based on

Giovanni Bellini's *Madonna and Child* (*Madonna of the Meadow*; London, N.G.). Other works by Ingannati include the signed *Female Martyr* (Portland, OR, A. Mus.), *Christ Giving a Blessing with Four Saints* (Milan, Marinotti priv. col.), the *Adoration of the Magi* (Perugia, G.N. Umbria), the *Portrait of a Woman* (Berlin, Staatl. Museen Preuss. Kultbes.) and the *Virgin and Child with Mary Magdalene* (ex-Gentner priv. col., Worcester, MA). Other works include various *sacre conversazioni* as well as several paintings derived from Giovanni Bellini's *Virgin and Child with a Bird* (Zurich, Schrafl priv. col.). His last signed work, the *Holy Family with St John the Baptist and St Ursula* (untraced, see Caccialupi, fig. 25), is dated 1548.

BIBLIOGRAPHY

Thieme–Becker
A. Venturi: *Storia* (1901–40), vii/4, p. 584
B. Berenson: *Venetian School* (1957), i, pp. 91–2
F. Heinemann: *Giovanni Bellini e i Belliniani*, 2 vols (Venice, 1962), i, pp. 107–11
P. Caccialupi: 'Pietro degli Ingannati', *Saggi & Mem. Stor. A.*, 11 (1978), pp. 21–43, 147–62 [incl. bibliog.]

ANCHISE TEMPESTINI

Ingapirca. Village and site of Pre-Columbian Andean ruins 16 km from Cañar in the Sierra Sur, Ecuador. The site is in a rugged area between the River Silante and the village of Ingapirca, *c.* 3200 m above sea-level. An early Cañari settlement, dating from the 10th century AD, was conquered by the Incas at the end of the 15th century. Its Inca name is believed to have been Hatun Cañar. The site had been known and visited since the 18th century but was not excavated until 1968, by G. J. Hadden. Further work was conducted by Juan Cueva in 1970, José Alcina in 1974–5 and Antonio Fresco in 1978–82.

The identification of architectural structures has proved difficult, as some are Inca and others earlier. The outstanding feature of the site is the Castillo complex, comprising a large oval building and a series of rectangular dwellings. The Castillo itself is a pyramidal structure in which the main platform is formed by a finely carved wall *c.* 4 m high of rectangular masonry blocks of the type found at CUZCO (ii). Access to this platform is from the south, where an entrance with a double jamb is reached by four steps. Behind the entrance twin stairways, each with seven steps, rise towards the east and the west. Such staircases are relatively common in Andean architecture, the earliest example being found at CHAVÍN DE HUANTÁR. On the upper platform is the *'Cuerpo de Guardia'* (guardroom), an almost square structure having two rooms separated by a wall with high niches, each room having two more niches on the north and south sides. The entrances, in the east and west walls, are flanked by niches of similar proportions to the door. The general arrangement of the building suggests that it was an *ushnu* (or *usnu*; Quechua: ceremonial platform and place of justice) with a temple dedicated to the Sun on it; this hypothesis is supported by the orientation of the doors to the east and west. It is likely that a *pacarina*, or Cañari *huaca* (holy site containing cult objects), existed on the site of the Castillo.

Near the Castillo is the Condamine group, comprising a rectangular building with a long central corridor lined by large storehouses (*galpones*) or rectangular rooms. The complex was built over a Cañari cemetery in which 39 graves were found. Not far from this group, on Pilaloma hill, a *kancha* (walled compound) was discovered. It was built on a trapezoidal plan, rounded on one side, with its longitudinal axis running approximately east–west. The interior comprises eight rooms; six of these are built around a patio with a central monolith (*huanca*), indicating the existence of a great shaft tomb. The burial chamber contained a multiple interment, with 11 skeletons arranged in a circular fashion and accompanied by a large quantity of grave furniture and offerings. The importance and sacred character of the enclosure are inferred from the number of carved stone tenoned heads found in the area, many of which represent birds, possibly macaws. Since female skeletons are predominant in the burial, a possible hypothesis is that the Pilaloma *kancha* was the residence of a priestess dedicated to the cult of an important *huaca*. This would have led to the *kancha* itself assuming the status of a secondary cult centre.

In the Vaguada sector, between the Condamine group and Pilaloma, two complexes, Las Bodegas and Gran Kancha, have been identified, with four and ten enclosures respectively. These may have served as stores, residences and workplaces. A long paved road connects the Condamine group and Pilaloma, and a stairway and some Inca baths are situated on the west side of Pilaloma. In sectors further away from the central zone are ancient remains such as the Ingachungana, a carved rock associated with the water cult.

BIBLIOGRAPHY

J. Alcina Franch: 'Ingapirca: Arquitectura y áreas de asentamiento', *Rev. Esp. Antropol. Amer.*, viii (1978), pp. 127–46
A. Fresco: *La arqueología de Ingapirca (Ecuador): Costumbres funerarias, cerámica y otros materiales* (Cuenca, 1978)
J. Alcina Franch: 'Las cabezas-clava de Ingapirca (Ecuador)', *Indiana*, viii (1983), pp. 229–42
A. Fresco: 'Excavaciones en Ingapirca (Ecuador): 1978–1982', *Rev. Esp. Antropol. Amer.*, xiv (1984), pp. 85–101
M. S. Ziolkowski and R. M. Sadowski: 'Informe acerca de las investigaciones arqueoastronómicas en el área central de Ingapirca', *Rev. Esp. Antropol. Amer.*, xiv (1984), pp. 103–25
J. H. Hyslop: *Inka Settlement Planning* (Austin, 1990)

JOSÉ ALCINA FRANCH

Ingen Ryūki [Yinyuan Longqi] (*b* Fuqing County, Fujian Province, 1592; *d* Uji, 1673). Chinese monk, poet and calligrapher, active in Japan. Along with his disciples MOKUAN SHŌTŌ and SOKUHI NYOITSU, he was extolled as one of the Ōbaku no Sanpitsu ('Three Brushes of Ōbaku'), the three principal calligraphers of the Ōbaku Zen school. He was a leading southern Chinese Buddhist master who, not long after the end of the Ming period (1368–1644), emigrated to Nagasaki where, in the early 17th century, a community of Chinese merchants had established three Chinese Buddhist temples. In Japan Ingen quickly became a religious figure of national reputation, and was later celebrated as the founding patriarch of the Japanese Ōbaku Zen lineage (*see* BUDDHISM, §III, 10). A search for his father, who had disappeared when he was five, brought him at the age of 20 to a temple on Mt Putuo (Zhoushan Archipelago, off the coast of Zhejiang Prov.), where, it is recorded, he served tea to the monks. It was not until he was about 28, however, after the death of his mother, that he was able to be ordained as a Buddhist monk at his family temple, Wanfusi, on Mt

Huangbo. He trained under the eminent monks Miyun Yuanwu (1566–1642) and Feiyin Tongrong (1593–1661), receiving '*dharma* transmission' (i.e. recognition as an heir in the spiritual lineage) from the latter in 1633. Ingen first served as abbot of Wanfusi in 1637, but it was during his long second tenure, beginning in 1646, that Mt Huangbo was transformed into a thriving monastic complex. When the Chinese community in Nagasaki heard of Ingen's renown, ITSUNEN SHŌYŪ, abbot of the Chinese temple Kōfukuji in that city, invited him to Japan. Ingen departed for Nagasaki in 1654 with some 30 monks and artisans, promising, however, to return to Mt Huangbo in three years.

At that time the shogunate's policy of national seclusion meant that the only foreigners allowed in Japan proper in any numbers were the Chinese and Dutch, who were restricted to Nagasaki. Among certain Japanese prelates Ingen found disfavour, in part because their own prestige, authority and financial resources were threatened, and in part because of cultural differences. In addition to such political and social factors, the Japanese had misgivings about the doctrinal and meditative teachings espoused by the Chinese monks. It was only through the efforts of the monk Ryōkei Shōsen (1602–70) of Myōshinji, religious teacher to the retired emperor GoMizunoo (*reg* 1611–29) and adviser to the shogun Tokugawa Ietsuna (1641–80), that Ingen gradually gained official sanction. Granted land at Uji, near Kyoto, and permission to build a major monastery, in 1661 Ingen established MANPUKUJI (the Japanese pronunciation of Wanfusi), named the site Mt Ōbaku (the Japanese pronunciation of Huangbo), and was inaugurated founding abbot. His teachings quickly became a model of religious practice and institutional reform for older Japanese Zen institutions. In 1664, at the age of 72, Ingen retired to a hermitage within the Manpukuji compound. He was never to return to China. Nine years later he received from GoMizunoo the honorary title Daikō Fushō Kokushi (*kokushi* ('national teacher') was an honorary title bestowed by the court on eminent ecclesiastics). The day after receiving this honour Ingen wrote out the customary death poem and died.

Ingen brought with him to Japan many books of ink rubbings showing the work of early Chinese master calligraphers, as well as actual examples of fine Ming period calligraphy. His own calligraphy, which combined fluency and power, was much admired and emulated. Like that of other Chinese masters in Edo period (1600–1868) Japan, it was derived from Late Ming period literati styles and was strikingly different from the accepted Japanese style known as Oie ryū ('official school'). It was particularly suited to the monumental inscriptions profusely displayed in Ōbaku monasteries and is known in Japan as Ōbaku-style calligraphy. For the wooden nameboards over temple halls the master's calligraphy would be transcribed into carving; maxims and statements of faith might likewise be carved in wood or brushed on banner-sized pieces of paper. A representative work in large characters is the triptych of three hanging scrolls (see fig.), the central scroll of which reads *Katsu kai shō bō gen* (Chin. *Huo kai zheng fa yan*; 'Opening the true *dharma* eye'). The flanking scrolls form a couplet: *Ki tō un sui gō* (Chin. *Ji tou yun shui he*; 'The pivotal moment/The wandering monks commune'),

Ingen Ryūki: three hanging scrolls, ink on paper, each 1319×364 mm, *c.* 1661–73 (Uji, Manpukuji)

Dō kei sei ken rin (Chin. *Dao qi sheng xian lin*; 'Falling in with the Way/The sages and worthies are manifest'). Also notable is the cursive-script (Jap. *sōsho*) composition in the style of the Ming period artist and connoisseur Wang Duo (1592–1652), *Nenkōge* (Chin. *Nian xiang jie*; 'Buddhist verses on lighting incense'; hanging scroll, ink on paper; 1669; Uji, Manpukuji).

Ingen was a charismatic and multi-talented man, who, together with his disciples, influenced many aspects of Japanese culture in the Edo period; these include not only monastic art and architecture, but also the literary arts of calligraphy, poetry, painting, seal-carving, and the infused tea (Jap. *sencha*) ceremony. His influence in cultural matters was magnified by the fact that Chinese Neo-Confucianism was the official philosophy of the government, which in turn stimulated a renewed passion for Chinese learning and arts among Japanese literati. Ingen summoned to Japan Chinese monks and craftsmen of all trades to construct temple buildings and fill them with sculpture, painting, calligraphy and ritual paraphernalia, duplicating in Japan the environment of monastery life in south China during the late Ming period. Manpukuji, with its holdings of Chinese texts, paintings and calligraphies and of Ming-style Buddhist art, served as a reservoir in Japan of hitherto unknown or unavailable Chinese cultural artefacts.

BIBLIOGRAPHY

G. Toyama: 'Minmatsu no kikasō to Nihon bunka' [Late Ming period naturalized monks and Japanese culture], *Shodō zenshū* [Complete collection of calligraphy], xxii (Tokyo, 1959), pp. 26–31, pls 64–5

Masters of Japanese Calligraphy, 8th–19th Century (exh. cat. by Y. Shimizu and J. M. Rosenfield, New York, Japan House Gal. and Asia House Gals, 1984), pp. 160–61

M. Ōtsuki, S. Katō and Y. Hayashi, eds: *Ōbaku bunka jinmei jiten* [Biographical dictionary of Ōbaku cultural figures] (Kyoto, 1988)

S. Addiss: *The Art of Zen: Paintings and Calligraphy by Japanese Monks, 1600–1925* (New York, 1989), pp. 74–81

J. Stanley-Baker: *The Transmission of Chinese Idealist Painting to Japan: Notes on the Early Phase (1661–1799)* (Ann Arbor, 1992)
H. Baroni: *Buddhism in Early Tokugawa Japan: The Case of Obaku Zen and the Monk Tetsugen Dōkō* (PhD thesis, New York, Columbia U., 1993)
E. Horton Sharf: *Obaku Zen Portrait Painting: A Revisionist Analysis* (PhD diss., Ann Arbor, U. MI, 1994)

ELIZABETH HORTON SHARF

Ingham, Charles Cromwell (*b* Dublin, 1796; *d* New York, 10 Dec 1863). American painter of Irish birth. He was trained in Dublin, and his early work was in the style of Sir Martin Archer Shee. He arrived in New York in 1816 and became a leading figure in its artistic and social circles. Ingham was particularly successful with his flattering portraits of fashionable women and completed over 200 such works between 1826 and 1845. A meticulous draughtsman, Ingham developed a technically advanced style, building up layers of glazes and varnishes to create a glossy surface. Such portraits as *Fidelia Marshall* (Washington, DC, N. Mus. Amer. A.) demonstrate Ingham's careful attention to the rendering of textures and details of dress. Several of his better-known works, including *Flower Girl* (1846; New York, Met.), carry allegorical overtones. Although his reputation rested on his portraits of women and children, Ingham painted a considerable number of men as well.

Ingham was a founder-member of and frequent exhibitor at the National Academy of Design, New York, and belonged to the American Academy of Fine Arts. When the National Academy acquired Browere's Stables on Broadway in 1848, Ingham was chairman of the building committee and designed the grand staircase known then as 'Ingham's Stairs'. He is credited with originating the idea for the Sketch Club, established in 1827, and was its first President; when it reorganized and expanded to become the Century Club in 1847, Ingham was among its earliest members.

BIBLIOGRAPHY

DAB
W. Dunlap: *History of the Rise and Progress of the Arts of Design in the United States*, ii (New York, 1834/*R* 1969), pp. 271–4
T. S. Cummings: *Historic Annals of the National Academy of Design* (Philadelphia, 1865)
A. T. E. Gardner: 'Ingham in Manhattan', *Bull. Met.*, n.s., x (1952), pp. 245–53

ELEANOR HARVEY JONES

Inglada, José Aparicio. *See* APARICIO INGLADA, JOSÉ.

Inglés, Jorge (*fl c.* 1544–85). Painter and illuminator, active in Spain. His name suggests that he was of English origin, and he may have been trained in the Netherlands. His work shows the influence of Rogier van der Weyden and of Netherlandish tapestries and manuscript illumination (see Post). He employed a vigorous drawing technique, and his figures are sculptural and expressive, particularly the faces and hands. The sumptuous clothes show that he understood the characteristics of Spanish brocades. The settings are enlarged by an ambitious use of perspective and are filled with carpets, flagstones and canopies; details such as books give a sense of atmosphere, and openings are used to reveal landscape. He was the first painter in Castile known by name to employ the Netherlandish technique of oil on panel.

Jorge Inglés: *St Jerome in his Study*, central panel from an altarpiece, oil on panel, 1.73×0.82 m, *c.* 1469–85 (Valladolid, Museo Nacional de Escultura)

In a codicil to his will of 5 June 1455 Iñigo López de Mendoza, Marqués de Santillana, ordered that a retable already completed by Jorge Inglés should be placed on the high altar in the church of the Hospital de S Salvador in Buitrago, his ancestral village. It illustrated a poem that the Marqués had written in honour of the Virgin, and the choice of Inglés to execute the work suggests that he must already have been a famous painter. The sculpted parts and the panel depicting *St George* are untraced, but the other paintings survive (Madrid, Col. Marqués de Santillana). Four *Fathers of the Church* are depicted half-length on the predella. The portraits of the *Marqués and Marquesa de Santillana* praying before a sculpted Virgin (untraced) appear on the main panel; they are lavishly dressed, set off by a canopy and accompanied by a page and a maid. On two of the panels are 12 angels bearing verses; another panel shows the Marqués holding the last stanza of his poem, a clear indication that the altarpiece was in celebration of his writing. Jorge Inglés also executed several miniatures in manuscripts in the Marqués's collection (e.g. the opening pages of Spanish translations of Plato's *Phaedo* and St Augustine's *De vita beata*, Madrid, Bib.N.).

The retable of *St Jerome* from the Hieronymite monastery of La Mejorada at Olmedo (Valladolid, Mus. N. Escul.) seems to have been made for Alonso de Fonseca, Bishop of Avila (1469–85). The seven predella panels include a *St Sebastian* who wears a curious hat, similar to that worn by the Marqués of Santillana in the retable in Buitrago. The main panel shows *St Jerome in his Study*, with three monks who are depicted on a much smaller scale (see fig.). A liking for anecdotal detail (bookcases, a large chest, the lion devouring a piece of meat) bears out Inglés's Netherlandish background. The setting, which is extended into a landscape, is enlarged by the oblique perspective construction. The four lateral panels, representing episodes from the *Life of St Jerome*, also show an appreciation of landscape. Vigorous colours are employed for the flagstones and ochres for the monks' habits.

According to Gudiol, the retable in the parish church of Villasandino (Burgos), fragments of which survive, is Inglés's last work (after 1485). The forms are soft and the faces more lifelike. Post attributes a *Virgin and Child* (Paris, priv. col.) to Jorge Inglés, as well as the paintings on a hexagonal paschal candlestick (New York, Cloisters), an unusual object that has three tiers of paintings on each face. The *Bestowal of the Chasuble on St Ildefonso* (ex-Bilbao, priv. col.) is a doubtful attribution, although Post linked the figure of St Ildefonso with the Fathers of the Church on the predella of the Buitrago retable and related the three diminutive acolytes serving the Saint to the three monks of the St Jerome altarpiece. Post also noted some relationship between the kneeling figure of the Marqués in the Buitrago retable with a figure in the same position on the retable of the Ermita de la Fuensanta in Sopetrán near Hita (Guadalajara), although this must be the work of a different painter.

BIBLIOGRAPHY

F. J. Sánchez Cantón: 'Maestro Jorge Inglés, pintor y miniaturista del Marqués de Santillana', *Bol. Soc. Esp. Excurs.*, xxv (1917), pp. 99–105; xxvi (1918), pp. 27–31

C. R. Post: *A History of Spanish Painting* (Cambridge, MA, 1930–60), iv, pp. 65–83; vii, p. 840; ix, p. 793

J. Gudiol: 'Una obra inédita de Jorge Inglés', *Bol. Semin. Estud. A. & Arqueol. [U. Valladolid]*, x (1943), pp. 159–63

J. J. Martín González: 'En torno a la nacionalidad de Jorge Inglés', *Bol. Semin. Estud. A. & Arqueol. [U. Valladolid]*, xix (1953), p. 140

J. J. MARTÍN GONZALEZ

Inglott, Anton (*b* 1915; *d* 15 Aug 1945). Maltese painter. He studied in Malta at the Government School of Art and in Rome at the Regia Accademia di Belle Arti and at the Accademia Serale del Nudo in Via Margutta. The impending outbreak of hostilities with Italy forced his return to Malta in 1940. Despite his youth he quickly established himself as the leading painter on the island, where his works impressed by their deep spirituality and intense religious fervour. He was, however, already terminally ill with the diabetes from which he died, shortly after completing the huge apse painting of the *Death of St Joseph* (Msida, parish church), which represents an important contribution to 20th-century Maltese art.

MARIO BUHAGIAR

Ingolstadt. Bavarian fortified town halfway between Munich and Nuremberg, on the left bank of the Danube at its confluence with the Schutter. It was originally fortified in the 16th century, and there is a fine contemporary model of those defences by Jakob Sandtner in the Bayerisches Nationalmuseum in Munich, depicting a walled town stiffened in places by large semicircular-headed drum towers similar to those drawn by Albrecht Dürer in the first printed book on fortification (1527).

Ingolstadt was completely refortified in four phases during the 19th century. Between 1828 and 1832 a scheme, somewhat reminiscent of Dürer's work, was begun to provide a curving front and detached oval towers. On the east bank of the river, the splendid Tilly Redoubt (1828) was built in the form of a large semicircle backing on to the river, and this was supported by detached oval towers. The redoubt was elaborately detailed by Leo von Klenze, court architect to Ludwig I. In 1833 the curved front was replaced by powerful free-standing multi-gun caponiers flanking straight sections of wall, backed by defensible barracks originally designed as artillery cavaliers. This was the polygonal German system (*see* GERMERSHEIM), but to some extent it was a return to earlier German practice. There are significant remains of the south-west front displaying beautiful craftsmanship with precise detailing in brick and stone. In the 1860s detached forts were built surrounding the town, and in the 1870s an outer ring of large polygonal forts was constructed some 7 km out, of which one, Fort Prinz Karl, survives. The fortifications of Ingolstadt were largely demolished in the 1920s in accordance with the provisions of the Treaty of Versailles.

BIBLIOGRAPHY

A. Dürer: *Etliche Underricht zu Befestigung der Stett, Schloss und Flecken* (Nuremberg, 1527)

A. F. von Reitzenstein: *Ingolstadt* (Munich, 1967)

QUENTIN HUGHES

Ingres, Jean-Auguste-Dominique (*b* Montauban, 29 Aug 1780; *d* Paris, 14 Jan 1867). French painter. He was the last grand champion of the French classical tradition of history painting. He was traditionally presented as the opposing force to Delacroix in the early 19th-century confrontation of Neo-classicism and Romanticism, but subsequent assessment has shown the degree to which Ingres, like Neo-classicism, is a manifestation of the Romantic spirit permeating the age. The chronology of Ingres's work is complicated by his obsessive perfectionism, which resulted in multiple versions of a subject and revisions of the original. For this reason, all works cited in this article are identified by catalogue raisonné number: Wildenstein (W) for paintings; Naef (N) for portrait drawings; and Delaborde (D) for history drawings.

I. Life and work. II. Working methods and technique. III. Character and personality. IV. Critical reception and posthumous reputation.

I. Life and work.

1. Montauban, Toulouse and Paris, 1780–1806. 2. Rome, 1806–10. 3. Italy, 1811–15. 4. Rome, 1815–20. 5. Florence, 1820–24. 6. Paris, 1824–34. 7. Rome, 1835–41. 8. , 1841–55. 9. Paris, 1856–67.

1. MONTAUBAN, TOULOUSE AND PARIS, 1780–1806. His father, Jean-Marie-Joseph Ingres (1755–1814), a decorative painter and sculptor as well as an amateur

musician, taught him the basics of drawing and also the violin. In accord with contemporary academic practice, Ingres devoted much of his attention to copying from his father's collection of prints after such masters as Raphael, Titian, Correggio, Rubens, Watteau and Boucher; none of these copies survives. The earliest known drawings, some signed *Ingres fils*, are portrait sketches and miniatures of family members and Montauban acquaintances (N 1–8). He studied at the academy in Toulouse with the history painter Guillaume-Joseph Roques and the sculptor Jean-Pierre Vigan (*d* 1829): only a selection of school drawings remains and some records of prizes for excellence in 'composition', 'figures and antique', 'rounded figure' and 'life studies'. He studied landscape painting with Jean Briant (1760–99) and continued his musical training. His entry into the Paris studio of David in 1797 brought him into contact with the most talented artists of his generation—among David's former students still frequenting the studio were Jean-Germain Drouais, François-Xavier Fabre, Anne-Louis Girodet and Antoine-Jean Gros; studying at the same time as Ingres were Lorenzo Bartolini, Etienne-Jean Delécluze, Auguste Forbin, François-Marius Granet, Jean-Pierre Granger (1779–1840), Charles Langlois, Fleury Richard and Pierre Revoil. Signed and/or dated works from this period are scarce. It was in David's studio that the principles of the German theorist Johann Joachim Winckelmann and his apotheosis of Greek art became part of Ingres's artistic credo and that he first became aware of the beauty inherent in the work of such Italian painters as Giotto, Masaccio, Fra Angelico and Perugino. During the next five years Ingres found his own eclectic balance of these stylistic contradictions, to which he added a personal elevation of Raphael as the ultimate classical ideal. He trained his eye to be as acute as David's and sought an even greater degree of historical authenticity.

In 1801 Ingres won the Prix de Rome with the *Envoys of Agamemnon* (W 7, 1801; Paris, Ecole N. Sup. B.-A.; *see* PARIS, fig. 44), which John Flaxman described as the best painting he had seen from the modern French school. Subsequently Flaxman's illustrations to Homer and Dante became a staple in Ingres's artistic diet, reinforcing his natural proclivity for abstract linearity. *Venus Wounded by Diomedes* (W 28, *c.* 1804–6; Basle, Kstmus.) was painted in direct emulation of Flaxman. Ingres could not immediately claim his prize as the Académie de France in Rome had yet to be funded by the government. He was given a small bursary and studio space and a share of available government portrait and copy commissions. In July 1803 he received the commission for a portrait of *Bonaparte as First Consul* (W 14, 1804; Liège, Mus. B.-A.) for the city of Liège, the first acknowledgement that he was becoming one of the leading portraitists of his time.

At the end of 1805 funds were made available for the Prix de Rome stipends. However, Ingres delayed his departure until the last possible moment, submitting five portraits to the Salon of 1806 just before it opened: a *Self-portrait Aged 24* (W 17, 1804; Chantilly, Mus. Condé); portraits of *Philibert Rivière*, *Mme Philibert Rivière* and *Mlle Caroline Rivière* (W 22–4, 1806; all Paris, Louvre) and a portrait of *Napoleon I on the Imperial Throne* (W 27, 1806; Paris, Mus. Armée). An additional incentive for him to remain in Paris was his engagement in June 1806 to Julie Forestier (*b* 1789), a painter and musician.

2. ROME, 1806–10. *En route* to Rome, Ingres stayed briefly with Lorenzo Bartolini's family in Florence, where he received letters with news of the adverse criticism his paintings had received at the Salon. After his arrival in Rome in October 1806, he discovered that even David had found his *Napoleon* 'unintelligible'. Stunned, Ingres realized that he could not leave Rome until he had proved himself to the Parisian art establishment. On 26 December 1806 he moved into the small pavilion of S Gaetano in the grounds of the Villa Medici (home of the Académie de France from 1803). It had a magnificent view of Rome and gave him the privacy he needed to work. A series of landscape drawings and small oil paintings records his response to the city (see 1960 exh. cat.).

In 1807 Ingres began two history paintings. Pen-and-ink sketches (Montauban, Mus. Ingres, 867.2302, 2303) show the evolution of the *Venus Anadyomene* (W 257, completed 1848; Chantilly, Mus. Condé), which was inspired by Botticelli's *Birth of Venus* (Florence, Uffizi). In a letter (Feb 1806) he stated his intention of painting a half life-size *Antiochus and Stratonice*, later (29 May) mentioning that he was going to invite Lucien Bonaparte to his studio to see it as soon as it was finished, although it was not until 1808 that the meeting actually took place (portrait drawing of *Lucien Bonaparte*, N 45; New York, priv. col.). The relationship between the wealthy patron and the ambitious young artist soured, however, when Bonaparte requested Ingres's services not as a history painter but as a copyist. Ingres executed few portraits during these early years in Rome. He continued to work on the *Antiochus and Stratonice* (W 232; Chantilly, Mus. Condé) for the next 30 years, until he finished it for Ferdinand-Philippe, Duc d'Orléans, in 1840; the *Venus* remained unfinished until 1848. These works set a characteristic pattern of procrastination in a search for perfection.

In 1808 Ingres prepared three compositions, all focusing on his expertise with the nude figure, for the annual *envoi* to the Ecole in Paris. The first, now known as the Valpinçon *Bather* (W 53, 1808; Paris, Louvre), is a female bather seen from behind and is derived from the study of a *Half-length Bather* (W 45, 1807; Bayonne, Mus. Bonnat); both of these seem inspired by the nudes of Flaxman and Bronzino and reveal for the first time the cool sensuality that became characteristic of Ingres's vision. The second *envoi* was *Oedipus and the Sphinx* (W 60, 1808; Paris, Louvre). A third painting, *Reclining Woman* (later called the '*Sleeper of Naples*', W 54, 1808; lost in 1815), was listed in the Villa Medici catalogue of 1808 but was not sent to Paris, being bought by Joachim Murat, King of Naples. The criticism of the paintings for their unorthodox stylizations and departure from academic propriety left Ingres puzzled and angry at the lack of appreciation for his talents.

During his last two years at the Villa Medici, Ingres continued to establish potentially useful connections. Among fellow winners of the Prix de Rome, for instance, was Jacques-Edouard Gatteaux with whom he formed a lifelong friendship and through whom he was introduced to Charles Marcotte d'Argenteuil (1787–1864). The resultant portrait (W 69, 1809; Washington, DC, N.G.A.) clearly reveals what a congenial spirit Ingres found his sitter to be. Commissions from several other French government officials followed, and Ingres's income in Rome was assured.

3. ITALY, 1811–15. Encouraged by the steadiness of commissions in Rome, in November 1810 Ingres took an apartment at 40 Via Gregoriana at the end of his tenure at the Villa Medici. Living near by was Granet, of whom there are several portrait drawings (e.g. N 86, 1812; Aix-en-Provence, Mus. Granet), and the two painters had free government studios in the church of S Trinità dei Monti. Ingres was still completing his last *envoi*, the large-scale *Jupiter and Thetis* (W 72, 1811; Aix-en-Provence, Mus. Granet), a subject he had first considered in 1806. He envisioned a 'divine painting' that would convey the full beauty of the god-like forms and expressions. His Jupiter is a masterly image of male power; the sensuous curves and pliant posture of Thetis express eloquently the sensual intimacy between the two immortals. To Ingres's distress, the painting was severely criticized: in his attempt to reconcile prevailing taste and the classical spirit, he failed to see how unorthodox his painting was in combining an intimate love theme with a massive scale and in introducing wildly manneristic exaggerations of contour and proportion.

For the next two years Ingres devoted himself to three monumental decorative paintings: *Romulus Victorious over Acron* (W 82, 1812; Paris, Ecole N. Sup. B.-A.) and the *Dream of Ossian* (W 87, 1813; Montauban, Mus. Ingres), both for the Palazzo di Monte Cavallo, and *Virgil Reading from the 'Aeneid' before Augustus and Livia* (W 83, 1812; Toulouse, Mus. Augustins) for the residence of General François de Miollis (1759–1828), the French lieutenant-governor who oversaw the renovation of Monte Cavallo (the pontifical palace on the Quirinal was being made into the residence of the King of Rome). The programme was an ambitious mixture of painting and sculpture in the Neo-classical style: its theme was the parallel between Roman and Napoleonic history. Antonio Canova oversaw the selection of artists, which included the Danish sculptor Bertel Thorvaldsen. This commission marked the acceptance of Ingres as a history painter. *Romulus Victorious over Acron* was one of three antique battle scenes for the salon of the Empress. Ingres followed Plutarch's *Life of Romulus* closely, striving for archaeological correctness. The archaisms of the work's stylized composition and the flat colouring were intended to imitate an antique low relief. The *Dream of Ossian*, begun in 1812 in collaboration with Jose Alvarez y Priego, was intended as an oval ceiling decoration for the Emperor's bedroom. (When Ingres bought it back in the 1830s he began to rework it into a rectangular format; it was in his studio with its perimeters unfinished at his death.) *Virgil Reading from the 'Aeneid' before Augustus and Livia*, a night scene painted for General Miollis's bedroom in the Villa Aldobrandini, is perfectly attuned to the traditional Neo-classical approach to subject-matter: action is frozen, emotion is held in check, gestures tell all. (It too was repurchased, reworked and left unfinished: see below.)

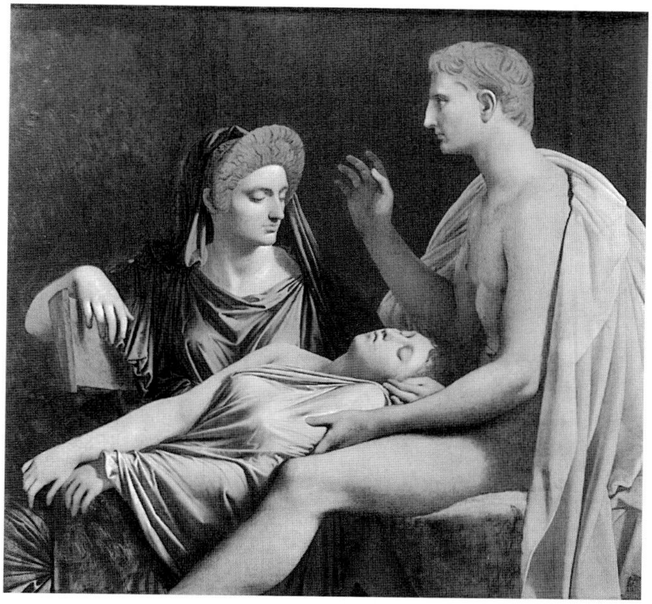

1. Jean-Auguste-Dominique Ingres: *Tu Marcellus eris*, fragment (1.38×1.42 m) cut from a version of *Virgil Reading from the 'Aeneid' before Augustus and Livia*, oil on canvas, 1813–14 (Brussels, Musées Royaux d'Art et d'Histoire)

The large commissions were completed by May 1813. Having firmly established his reputation in Rome, Ingres looked to secure a place in Paris. He set to work on an ambitious plan for the Salon of 1814, at which he hoped to outshine the popular historical genre painters. In a letter of July 1813 he mentioned plans to send two *grands tableaux*, two portraits, a painting of the *Interior of the Sistine Chapel* (W 91, 1814; Washington, DC, N.G.A.), which had been commissioned in 1812 by Marcotte, and a small painting of *Raphael and La Fornarina* (W 86, 1813; untraced). Neither of the *grands tableaux* was completed: *Tu Marcellus eris* (W 128; Brussels, Musées Royaux A. & Hist.; see fig. 1) is a fragment of the three central figures from a revised *Virgil Reading* cut down (at a later date) from the composition Ingres intended to send to this Salon; it is uncertain what the second *tableau* was to have been. The *Interior of the Sistine Chapel* was finished in summer 1814 and was sent to the Salon accompanied only by another historical genre piece, *Don Pedro of Toledo Kissing the Sword of Henry IV* (W 101, exh. Salon 1814; untraced). It was hardly the *tour de force* that Ingres intended. *Raphael and La Fornarina* reached Paris just days before the Salon closed.

While preparing for the Salon, on 4 December 1813 Ingres married Madeleine Chapelle (1782–1849), beginning 36 years of personal security and happiness. A series of portraits shows his contentment within this new family circle (N 98–111). Another diversion from preparations for the Salon was a summons to Naples, where he spent February to May 1814, painting the *Grande Odalisque* (W 93, 1814; Paris, Louvre) as a pendant to the *'Sleeper of Naples'*. A full-length oil portrait of *Caroline Murat, Queen of Naples* (W 90, 1814) and the *Sleeper* were lost from the palace in May 1815 with the fall of the Murat régime, but a series of portrait drawings of the family remains (N 116–21). He also painted two smaller Troubadour style love scenes for Caroline Murat—the *Betrothal of Raphael* (W 85, 1813; Baltimore, MD, Walters A.G.), which Ingres boasted he completed in just 20 days, and the first version of *Paolo and Francesca* (W 100, *c*. 1814; Chantilly, Mus. Condé).

4. ROME, 1815–20. As the withdrawal of the Napoleonic forces from Italy cut off avenues of financial support, Ingres was forced to turn to drawing portraits of tourists and later a host of new officials of the French Restoration government. Eventually these connections led to new historical commissions, but in the meanwhile he was distressed by having to waste time on such portraits. In contrast to these, many of the portrait drawings Ingres did of friends are exquisite in the loving detail he lavished on them. One of the most intimate, and a perfect example of the type, is his portrait of the *Guillon-Lethière Family* (N 140, 1815; see fig. 2). In the winter of 1816–17 Ingres received a commission from the Alba family for three small paintings with subjects taken from Spanish history. For *Philip V and the Marshal of Berwick* (W 120, 1818; Madrid, Pal. Liria, Col. Casa de Alba), a scene from 18th-century Alba family history, Ingres raided the Gobelins tapestry series the *Story of the King* for stylistic prototypes. The figures, diminutive in comparison with his other work, are subordinated to the props of the scene, dressed in period costumes, each playing their assigned role. The subject—the Spanish king rewarding a loyal subject—is purely anecdotal, and Ingres had little personal commitment to it. The subject of the second painting moved Ingres from disinterest to disgust. The *Duque de Alba at Ste Gudule, Brussels* (W 102, 1816–17; Montauban, Mus. Ingres) had as its 'hero' the man who led the Catholic campaign in the Low Countries against the Protestant Reformation and who was responsible for the slaughter of hundreds of innocent people. At first Ingres had in mind a horizontal composition with the protagonist receiving honours from the archbishop. Infra-red photographs reveal that the original format of the canvas was identical with that of a drawing (D 216; ex-Paul Rosenberg & Co., New York) done as a model. Then he switched to a vertical format in order to put as much distance as possible between the viewer and the Duque, the latter becoming almost a speck on the horizon in a long view down the nave of Ste Gudule. Even that did not ease his scruples, and in 1819 Ingres abandoned the canvas. The third painting never reached the drawing phase.

2. Jean-Auguste-Dominique Ingres: *Guillon-Lethière Family*, pencil drawing, 278×219 mm, 1815 (Boston, MA, Museum of Fine Arts)

Ingres made concerted efforts to build up connections with the new French Restoration circles in Rome. Commissions were not only smaller but less frequent than in the glorious days of the Empire. It may be fortuitous, or it may reflect a political astuteness for which Ingres does not often receive credit, that the paintings he sent to the first Restoration Salon (1814) were particularly appropriate to a post-Napoleon environment: the *Sistine Chapel* (W 91) and *Don Pedro of Toledo* (W 101). He lost no time in ingratiating himself with the new leadership. He enjoyed the friendship of three diplomatic secretaries, Gabriel de Fontenay (1784–1855), Artaud de Montor and Augustin Jordan (1773–1849), and profited from their acquaintance in many ways. He drew their portraits, made gifts of drawings of his latest genre subjects, and even made a rare venture into printmaking, transforming the portrait of the ambassador *Mgr de Pressigny* (N 170; priv. col.) into an etching, which he hand-tinted. Mgr de Pressigny (1745–1823) was soon replaced by Pierre-Louis-Casimir, Comte (later Duc) de Blacas, a man of independent fortune, powerfully connected to the inner circle of government. Ingres's relationship with this patron yielded two exquisite Bourbon cabinet pictures for Blacas's personal collection, *Henry IV Playing with his Children* (W 113, 1817; Paris, Petit Pal.), a classic of the Restoration Troubadour style that shows Henry IV down on his knees in a cosy domestic scene, and its pendant, the *Death of Leonardo da Vinci* (W 118, 1818; Paris, Petit Pal.), which depicts the artist dying in the arms of Francis I.

In July 1816 Charles Thévenin (1764–1838), the new director of the Académie de France, began successfully to lobby the Direction des Beaux-Arts in Paris on Ingres's behalf. In January 1817 Blacas chose Ingres as one of the artists for the renovation and the decoration of Trinità dei Monti, the focus of the French colony in Rome. *Christ Giving the Keys to St Peter* (W 132; Montauban, Mus. Ingres) was completed in March 1818 for a fee of 3000 francs. Ingres certainly knew the versions of the subject by Raphael (tapestry cartoon, 1515; London, V&A) and Poussin (*Ordination*, 1639–40; Belvoir Castle, Leics), but while they included all twelve Apostles, Ingres reduced the number to six, while retaining the symbolic position of Judas, who stands apart from the others. (Characteristically, he retouched the painting in the 1840s when the Dames du Sacré-Coeur exchanged it with the French government for a copy.) The Comte de Blacas acted as an intermediary in the acquisition by Louis XVIII of *Roger Freeing Angelica* (W 124, 1819; Paris, Louvre), Ingres's first sale to the State and also the first work by him to enter a public collection (by 1824 it had been moved to the Musée du Luxembourg, Paris). With his confidence as a history painter re-established by these commissions, Ingres sent *Roger Freeing Angelica* to the Salon of 1819 with the *Grande Odalisque*. James-Alexandre, Comte de Pourtalès-Gorgier, acquired the latter from the Salon, as he had *Raphael and La Fornarina* in 1814, but critics and public alike found the arbitrariness of the odalisque's anatomical structure shocking and found so little to interest them in the *Angelica* as to misidentify the scene as representing Perseus and Andromeda. Ingres felt that the three public exhibitions of his work in 1806, 1814 and 1819 had ridiculed him in Paris, and he determined to stay in Italy.

5. FLORENCE, 1820–24. In August 1820 Ingres moved to Florence, where he hoped to renew contact with Bartolini and to explore the artistic and architectural wealth of the city. Bartolini had become a famous sculptor, and the friendship did not survive. Immediately after his installation at Bartolini's home, Ingres finished a variant of the *Sistine Chapel* (W 131, 1820; Paris, Louvre). He made a copy of Titian's *Venus of Urbino* (W 149, 1822; Baltimore, MD, Walters A.G.) for Bartolini to use as a model for his *Recumbent Venus* (1822; Montpellier, Mus. Fabre) and did a portrait of *Bartolini* (W 142, 1820; Paris, Louvre). He also copied a painting in the Uffizi that he believed to be a self-portrait by Raphael (W 163; Montauban, Mus. Ingres), drew the churches of Florence and the gardens and visited Lucca, Siena and Pisa. In 1821 Ingres did two portrait commissions, *Count Nicolas Dmtrievitch de Gouriev* (W 148; St Petersburg, Hermitage) and *Mlle Jeanne Gonin* (W 147; Cincinnati, OH, Taft Mus.). The Gonin family became lifelong friends, their household being a model of Ingres's ideal world: a patriarchal merchant husband, a devoted wife, clever children and a wide circle of worthy friends and relatives.

One of the commissions Ingres had 'in progress' when he arrived from Rome was from the Comte de Pastoret (1791–1859) for a small history painting of the *Entry into Paris of the Dauphin, the Future Charles V* (W 146, 1821; Hartford, CT, Wadsworth Atheneum) derived from that of 1358 by Jean Froissart. The figure welcoming the Dauphin was one of Pastoret's relatives. The medieval prototypes Ingres sought in developing the painting are to be found in the vignettes from the *Grandes Chroniques de France* (Paris, Bib. N., MS.fr.6465), which Ingres traced from Bernard de Montfaucon's *Les Monumens de la monarchie française* (Paris, 1729–33, iii, pl. XXII and XXXIX). He also borrowed from Jean Fouquet's *Reception of the Emperor Charles IV* (*Grandes Chroniques*, fol. 419) and Franz Pforr's *Entry of Rudolf I of Habsburg into Basle in 1273* (1808–9/10; Frankfurt am Main, Städel. Kstinst; for illustration *see* PFORR, FRANZ). Though finished in 1821 and listed in the Salon catalogue for 1822, the *Entry into Paris* was not shown until two years later, when it received critical acclaim.

Shortly after his arrival in Florence, Ingres received word from Thévenin of a government commission for a religious painting on a grand scale. The official request was for a painting for the choir of Montauban Cathedral; Ingres's response was a plan for a confrontation at the Salon of 1822. The mayor had asked for a work that would show the King placing the royal family of France under the protection of the Virgin at the time of her Assumption. At first Ingres protested that these were two distinct subjects; later he realized the concept was perfect for the Raphaelesque solution he found in the *Vow of Louis XIII* (W 155, 1824; see fig. 3). His representation of the Virgin and Child is a reversal of the *Madonna of Foligno* (1511–12; Rome, Pin. Vaticana) by Raphael. His image of Louis XIII is from a painting of the same name by Philippe de Champaigne (1637–8; Caen, Mus. B.-A.). Ingres had these borrowings firmly in place with an oil sketch by 1822 (W 156; Montauban, Mus. Ingres), but he failed to deliver the painting for two more years because once again his grandiose intentions inhibited his ability to realize the dream. In late 1821 Ingres mentioned that he expected to cover the cost of personally bringing his *Vow* to Paris by finishing a painting begun in 1807, the *Venus Anadyomene*. By January 1822 he had found a buyer for the work, Jacques-Louis Leblanc (1774–1846), a man of patience who advanced funds against the intended purchase and yet never questioned that the *Vow* would take precedence over his commission. By December 1823 the *Vow* had progressed to the point where Ingres expected to bring it to Paris by the spring. However, it was not until November 1824 that he arrived.

6. PARIS, 1824–34. The *Vow of Louis XIII* appeared at the Salon on 12 November 1824. Its favourable reception was essentially a tribute to the long-absent artist. Also, the work was sufficiently orthodox in its presentation of traditional values to stand against such Romantic incursions as Delacroix's *Massacre at Chios* (1824; Paris, Louvre). In early 1825 Ingres received the Cross of the Légion d'honneur, was invited to attend the coronation of Charles X and was elected to the Académie des Beaux-Arts. By July Ingres was installed in a two-room studio with his prints, books, earlier canvases and drawings to inspire, and distract, him. In November 1825 he opened a studio for students, foremost among whom were Eugène-Ammanuel Amaury-Duval, Paul Chenavard, Armand Cambon (1819–85), Raymond Balze (1818–1909) and Paul Balze (1815–84), Auguste Flandrin and Hippolyte Flandrin, Henri Lehmann, Franz Adolph von Stürler (1802–81) and Sébastien Cornu. One of the first fruits of his new place as champion of the classical tradition was a commission from the Bishop of Autun for a monumental religious subject, the *Martyrdom of St Symphorian* (W 212, 1827–34; Autun Cathedral). Shortly afterwards he received the commission for the *Apotheosis of Homer* (W 168, 1827–33; Paris, Louvre; *see* CLASSICISM, fig. 2) for the ceiling of one of the nine rooms dedicated to Egyptian and Etruscan antiquities in the Musée Charles X (now Musée du Louvre) to be inaugurated in 1827. The transport of the *Vow of Louis XIII* to Montauban was delayed by Ingres's efforts to keep the work in Paris at one of the more prestigious churches. Abandoning that plan, he kept it for several months so that the engraver Luigi Calamatta could make a drawing of it. The painting was unveiled in the city hall

3. Jean-Auguste-Dominique Ingres: *Vow of Louis XIII*, oil on canvas, 4.21×2.62 m, 1824 (Montauban Cathedral)

in Montauban on 12 November 1826, the only time Ingres ever returned to his birthplace. On his way back to Paris, he stopped in Autun, where he made studies of the old Roman wall for the *St Symphorian*: an oil sketch (W 202, 1827; New York, priv. col.) was completed by February, by which time a watercolour study of *Homer* (D 178, Lille, Mus. B.-A.) was also well advanced.

During this ten-year period in Paris Ingres carefully manipulated his connections with French society: portrait drawings from this time onwards were exclusively for friendship and/or favour (the two were often linked) and never directly for money. His oil portraits of *Mme Marcotte de Sainte Marie* (W 166, 1826; Paris, Louvre) and *Comte Amédée-David de Pastoret* (W 167, 1826; Chicago, IL, A. Inst.) were sent to the Salon of 1827. A portrait of *Charles X* (W 206, 1829; Bayonne, Mus. Bonnat) was followed by paintings that mark the passage from the Restoration to the bourgeois government of the July Monarchy (1830): both the founder and director of the *Journal des Débats* (*Louis-François Bertin*, W 208, 1832; Paris, Louvre) and Louis-Philippe's prime minister (*Comte Louis-Mathieu Molé*, W 225, 1834; priv. col.) symbolized the new age. Painfully aware that the work he had produced during the previous two decades was virtually unknown in France, Ingres was determined to launch prints of his work soon after his arrival in Paris. James Pradier bought engraving rights to *Virgil Reading the 'Aeneid'* and *Raphael and La Fornarina* in February 1825; Pierre Sudre (1783–1866) bought lithographic rights for the *Grande Odalisque* in 1826; Théodore Richomme (1785–1849) had engraving rights to *Henry IV Playing with his Children* and Charles-François Sellier to the *Death of Leonardo*. These contracts ended financial need, yet Ingres's fussing over the details of how these prints were done, coupled with obsessive reworking of earlier compositions in replicas and revisions from 1828 to 1833, resulted in a marked decline in his artistic output.

The deadline for the Louvre commission, the *Apotheosis of Homer*, was linked to the opening of the 1827 Salon. While Ingres was still laying in preliminary contours on the canvas, the other artists agreed they could be ready in time. Though in place when the Salon opened, the painting was finished only in grisaille; Ingres eventually completed it for the opening of the Salon of 1833. He was now ready to take up again the *Martyrdom of St Symphorian*, depicting the moment at which the young Christian is led out of the city gate to be beheaded. Although the format had been resolved by February 1827, and Ingres listed it in the Salon catalogue of that year, it was not shown until the Salon of 1834; its discordances of space, perspective, emotion and colour were deemed contrary to academic practice, and the painting was damned as an unsuccessful marriage of Raphael and Michelangelo. Profoundly discouraged, Ingres decided to abandon the Paris art scene. He requested, and received on 5 July 1834, the directorship of the Académie de France in Rome. His Paris studio was abruptly closed. He swore that he would neither submit his works to public exhibition nor undertake government commissions ever again; henceforth he would do only small paintings for friends.

7. ROME, 1835–41. Ingres replaced Horace Vernet as director at the Villa Medici. He and his wife soon gathered round them an intimate circle of young artists, including the composer Ambroise Thomas (1811–96), the architect Victor Baltard, the painter Hippolyte Flandrin and the sculptor Pierre-Charles Simart. At first Ingres buried himself in administrative details. In January 1836 his direct superior Adolphe Thiers asked him to return to Paris to work on paintings for the church of La Madeleine. Ingres politely declined; but he did have a new project in mind, the *Odalisque with Slave* (W 228, Cambridge, MA, Fogg), which he completed in 1839, part token of his friendship with Marcotte, and part repayment for Marcotte's advance in 1825 to Calamatta for engraving the *Vow*. Ingres also had another commitment. In 1834 Ferdinand-Philippe, Duc d'Orléans, eldest son of Louis-Philippe and a prominent Parisian art collector, had commissioned an *Antiochus and Stratonice* as an unlikely pendant to Paul Delaroche's *Death of the Duc de Guise* (1834; Chantilly, Mus. Condé). Ingres had begun work on this subject in 1807 and had reconsidered it several times in the 1820s.

Despite a period of debilitating illness, Ingres continued to work as much as possible. He resumed painting in September 1837, and he was still involved with the *Antiochus* in January 1839; pressure for completion was being applied by Pradier, who had been promised reproduction rights. It was August 1840 before the painting was sent back to Paris. By then the simple cast of three in a narrow rectangular format had developed into a theatrical cast of characters in a room, the architecture of which was based on designs by Victor Baltard and mostly executed by the Balze brothers. The impressive array of auxiliary characters and the splendour of the room reflect Ingres's attempt to match the *juste-milieu* style of Delaroche. The Musée Ingres, Montauban, has more than 100 sheets containing over 300 drawings showing his search for the right balance of detail; there are over 40, for instance, for the position of the arm of Antiochus. Gatteaux delivered the painting to the Duc d'Orléans, who wrote personally to thank Ingres and included payment of 18,000 francs, nearly double the agreed price. The Duc authorized a showing of the completed *Antiochus and Stratonice* each day in the most beautiful Salon of the Tuileries. Never had a work by Ingres excited such admiration.

8. PARIS, 1841–55. In May 1841 Ingres returned to Paris, where he was received with acclaim following the favourable reception of the *Antiochus and Stratonice*. In November that year he began a portrait of *Ferdinand-Philippe, Duc d'Orléans* (W 239; Louveciennes, priv. col.), which was delivered to the Palais-Royal by May 1842. At the request of Queen Marie-Amélie (1782–1866), Louis-Philippe commissioned a religious painting for the chapel of the château at Bezy (*Christ among the Doctors*, W 302, completed 1862; Montauban, Mus. Ingres), and in June 1842 he purchased *Cherubini with the Muse of Lyric Poetry* (W 236, 1842; Paris, Louvre) for the State collection.

Ingres declined to reopen his studio on his return to Paris as he was assured of a secure income not only from such commissions as the *Golden Age* (see below) but also from society portraits. At the end of June 1842 he was doing an oil sketch (W 238, Paris, priv. col.) for the portrait of the *Comtesse d'Haussonville* (W 248, completed 1845; New York, Frick) and was about to have his first sitting with the Baronne James de Rothschild (1805–86). Despite his many complaints about the inconvenience such portraits caused, he still gave them the same attention as his history paintings. With the accidental death of the Duc d'Orléans in July 1842, Ingres lost a patron who had shown him much respect and understanding. Shortly afterwards Louis-Philippe asked for a copy of his son's portrait (W 242, 1843; Versailles, Château), and within a year five more copies of the portrait, in varied formats, were requested. The Queen erected a memorial chapel dedicated to St Ferdinand at Dreux and commissioned designs for its stained-glass windows from Ingres. He completed his cartoons (in colour) for the 25 windows with incredible speed in August and September 1842 (Camesasca, 1971, no. 135a–q; Paris, Louvre). In November 1843 he received a request for stained-glass window designs for the royal chapel of St Louis at Dreux, which held the tombs of the Orléans family (Camesasca, 1971, no. 136a–h; Paris, Louvre), and the designs were completed by June 1844.

Meanwhile in 1843 Ingres had begun work on the largest commission of his career. The Duc de Luynes wanted pendant murals of the *Golden Age* and the *Iron Age* (unfinished; each mural 4.8×6.6 m) as the principal decorations of the Salon de Minerva, a large room on the second floor of the family château at Dampierre. The theme of the *Golden Age* was intended to compare 19th-century Paris with the ideal world at the beginning of time. The literary and artistic sources ranged from Ovid and Hesiod to Mantegna, Raphael, Agostino Carracci, Poussin, Watteau and Anton Raphael Mengs, and Ingres found further inspiration in Milton's *Paradise Lost.* The project was to occupy him for several years. When Gatteaux asked to see the work in progress in the summer of 1844 Ingres refused, as not even the Duc de Luynes had been admitted to the gallery.

In June 1845 Ingres brought the portrait of the *Comtesse d'Haussonville* to a remarkable conclusion. It attracted virtually all Parisian high society to his studio, including the sitter's brother, the Prince de Broglie (1785–1870), who immediately commissioned a portrait of his wife the *Princesse de Broglie* (W 272, 1853; New York, Met.). About this time Ingres did cameo portrait pendants in grisaille of the Queen and her daughter-in-law, the *Duchesse d'Orléans* (Camesasca, nos 141–2; Paris, Mus. A. Déc.). By the summer of 1845 the *Golden Age* was progressing steadily, and both Gatteaux and Marcotte were invited to see it in late October. By June 1847 *Christ among the Doctors* was well advanced, and Ingres had again taken up the *Venus Anadyomene* (begun 1807), now for Etienne Delessert (1735–1816). In October 1847 Henri-Eugène-Philippe-Louis, Duc d'Aumale (Louis-Philippe's fifth son), offered Ingres a commission for cartoons for the stained-glass windows of a chapel he wanted to restore in his château at Chantilly. The project was cut short by the Revolution of February 1848; Ingres also lost his client for *Christ among the Doctors*, when Louis-Philippe was deposed and his art collection dispersed.

In the opening months of 1848 social life in Paris halted, and Ingres found the solitude he needed to finish the *Venus Anadyomene* and the portrait of *Baronne James de Rothschild* (W 260, priv. col.). Delessert dared to complain of irregularities in the Venus's proportions, and the work was sold in an instant to Frédéric Reiset (1815–91). Ingres excused himself from work on the murals at Dampierre that summer, claiming that the political climate made work impossible. In October he accepted an invitation to be on the Commission des Beaux-Arts, where, remembering his own painful entry into the artistic establishment, he abandoned his conservatism and argued for an open Salon. He was named vice-president of the Ecole des Beaux-Arts for 1849.

When his wife Madeleine died on 27 July 1849, Ingres seems to have felt that his own life had come to an end also. The families of his friends and students placed him under attentive care, and portrait drawings of this supportive circle show the artist being nurtured back into life (N 414–21). One of his disciples, Albert Magimel (1799–1877), suggested that Ingres should prepare his collected works for publication in outline format (Magimel, 1851). Ostensibly a simple exercise in line reproduction based on tracings of his compositions from his portfolios, the project gave Ingres new life. By June 1851 he had returned to portrait painting, blocking in the portrait of the *Princesse de Broglie* and working on the first of two portraits of *Mme Moitessier* (W 266, 1851; Washington, DC, N.G.A.). As soon as Ingres finished the view of Mme Moitessier standing, he resumed work on a portrait of her seated (W 280, completed 1856; London, N.G.; *see* PORTRAITURE, fig. 9), which he had begun in 1844 as a double portrait of her and her daughter. At this time Ingres believed that his career was nearly at an end. He had abandoned the Dampierre commission in 1850, much to the disappointment of the Duc de Luynes. In July 1851 he donated his art collection to the museum at Montauban, and in October he resigned from the Ecole des Beaux-Arts. However, the beginning of the Second Empire and his marriage on 15 April 1852 to Delphine Ramel (1808–87; portrait drawing, N 427; Bayonne, Mus. Bonnat) rejuvenated him. Close friends realized how painful the loss of his first wife had been and how necessary a second wife was. The only disadvantage of the new marriage was the 'swarm of portraits' required for his extended family (N 428–32, 435–8, 441–2, 448).

In 1851 Guisard, the Directeur des Beaux-Arts, had asked Ingres to paint a subject of his choice for the State. The only stipulation was that Ingres submit a drawing for the approval of the government. Ingres rejected the offer, proposing instead to finish two works already under way in his studio. Guisard agreed, and paintings of the *Virgin with the Host* (W 276) and *Joan of Arc* (W 273; both Paris, Louvre) were delivered in 1854. Both works were repetitions of subjects that he had executed in the 1840s: a painting of the former had been commissioned by the future Tsar Alexander II (W 234, 1841; Moscow, Pushkin Mus. F.A.); the latter is based on his drawing (1844; Paris, Louvre) engraved in the second edition of Mannechet's *Le Plutarque français: Vies des hommes et femmes illustrés de la France* (Paris, 1844–7). An infra-red examination of the *Virgin with the Host* reveals that it began as a rectangular composition and was changed into a circular one, with the paired columns becoming two angels and curtains. In Ingres's painting of *Joan of Arc* the heroine is shown surrounded by her pages and followers, among them Ingres, witnessing the coronation of King Charles VII in Reims Cathedral.

The *Apotheosis of Napoleon* (W 270, 1853; destr.) was one of only two exceptions to the pledge Ingres had made in 1834 never again to work on a monumental scale. In March 1853 he accepted a commission from the government of Napoleon III for a ceiling painting for the Salon Napoléon in the Hôtel de Ville in Paris. The work had to be completed by the end of the same year. It was delivered on time, but was destroyed in the fires of the Commune of 1871: an oil study (W 271; Paris, Carnavalet) remains of the composition together with several drawn versions (e.g. Paris, Louvre, RF 3608). It is also known through photographs taken at the Exposition Universelle (Paris, 1855), where all Ingres's important works were hung in a separate gallery. Paranoid as ever, he believed that he had been humiliated by the jury's decision to award gold medals to other artists in addition to himself, including one to Delacroix, 'the apostle of the ugly'. His anger was modified only slightly by being named Grand Officer of the Légion d'honneur, but he vowed again to abandon the public arena.

9. PARIS, 1856–67. From 1856 Ingres's work was directed primarily towards a private audience. At his summer residence at Meung-sur-Loire he worked on two drawings: a watercolour of the *Birth of the Muses* (D 28, 1856; Paris, Louvre), painted in imitation of a fresco to ornament the cella of a little Greek temple for Prince Napoléon-Jérôme Bonaparte; and a drawing of *Homer Deified* (D 180; Paris, Louvre, RF 5273), 'reseen and redrawn' and meant to be the model for an engraving after his 1827 ceiling painting by Calamatta. Although he expected to finish it by the end of the summer, it was in progress for nine more years, when Ingres had it photographed by Charles Marville and sent signed copies of it in a limited edition to his friends. He also painted a number of late versions in oil of his early subjects for private clients. For example, the *Turkish Bath* (W 312, completed 1863; Paris, Louvre) is an elaboration of his many earlier bather compositions. The canvas had been in the studio from the early 1850s, when Prince Anatole Demidov was listed as the client; by the time he considered it to be finished in 1859, however, it was claimed by Prince Napoléon-Jérôme. Much to Ingres's dismay, the painting was returned as Princesse Clotilde found it unsuitable for a family residence. Frédéric Reiset, Director of the Louvre and a friend of both Ingres and the Prince, averted disaster by negotiating an exchange for Ingres's *Self-portrait* of 1806. A photograph (see 1983–4 exh. cat., p. 125) records the *Turkish Bath* as it was then, nearly square in format. Once back in the studio it met the fate common to returned works. In his reworking Ingres increased the number of figures to 23 and gave the composition its circular format (see fig. 4). The final painting was sold in 1863 to Khalil-Bey, the Turkish ambassador to France.

Ingres created a private gallery of his work for his wife. The collection (complete list in 1983–4 exh. cat., p. 252) included the *Antiochus and Stratonice* (W 322; Montpellier, Mus. Fabre), which he painted in watercolour and oil over a drawing on tracing paper (affixed to canvas in 1866), a technique that was also used in the *Martyrdom of St Symphorian* (W 319, 1865; Philadelphia, PA, Mus. A.). He gave away some of his works, again all reductions or variants of earlier subjects, as tokens of his friendship: Mme Marcotte (1798–1862) received a *Virgin with the Host with SS Helen and Louis* (W 268; London, priv. col.); Théophile Gautier received a reworked study for the *Apotheosis of Homer, Three Greek Tragedians, Aeschylus, Sophocles and Euripedes* (W 324; Angers, Mus. B.-A.). In 1861 several of Ingres's friends organized an exhibition of about 100 of his historical and portrait drawings in the Salon des Arts Unis, Paris. It was the first time Ingres had consented to let his drawings be shown, as he had previously felt that their popular appeal would distract from his paintings.

Christ among the Doctors was finished in 1862, after Ingres was released from his original contract of the 1840s and given the right to dispose of it as he pleased. A large exhibition of his work, organized by Armand Cambon, opened in Montauban on 4 May 1862; on 25 May Ingres became the first artist since Joseph-Marie Vien to be named Senator. His last will and testament was signed on 28 August 1866. In it he bequeathed to the city of Montauban his art collection (paintings, prints, drawings, plaster casts, antique fragments, terracottas) and illustrated art books, in addition to the contents of his studio (including the large paintings of *Christ among the Doctors* and the *Dream of Ossian*) and over 4000 of his study drawings. He left the huge canvas of *Virgil Reading the 'Aeneid'*, which had been in his Paris studio for reworking since the 1840s, to the Musée des Augustins, Toulouse. He made provision for his wife's financial security after his death by working closely with his dealer, Etienne-François Haro, to assemble a body of work from his studio for sale. Haro bought 31 oil studies for the history paintings and assorted drawn copies and studies for 50,000 francs. On 6–7 May 1867 the remaining contents of Ingres's studio were sold.

II. Working methods and technique.

Marjorie B. Cohn (intro. to 1983–4 exh. cat.) divided Ingres's working method into the generative phase (in which the original idea was conceived) and the extended and obsessive executive phase. The latter included not only the process of realizing the painting, but was extended by Ingres to include a lifetime of reworking favourite compositions in preparation for reproductive prints, in finished drawings and paintings for friends and clients, and in reductions to partial compositions, which were sent into the world, often decades after the original product, as works in their own right. These habits reflected Ingres's profound esteem for repetition as a means of understanding. He was very much governed by traditional Ecole des Beaux-Arts practices. He began with quick pen-and-ink sketches of a general idea and then explored all possible artistic prototypes for the composition. He worked next in a combination of life studies from the model for individual figures and detailed studies of archaeological furnishings from his library of engraved models after antiquity and the Renaissance. He suited his style to the

4. Jean-Auguste-Dominique Ingres: *Turkish Bath*, oil on canvas affixed to panel, diam. 1.08 m, 1863 (Paris, Musée du Louvre)

subject, imitating 15th-century primitive oil painting for Troubadour subjects, emulating fresco technique in oil for antique battle scenes, and used every conceivable drawing material on a wide variety of papers—charcoal for light and shadow studies, pen with ink or a sharp graphite for contour drawings. He was especially partial to working on a translucent tracing paper that aided his endless manipulations of the composition. Some of his drawings are built up of layers of paper types over one another as revision followed revision; other drawings were spontaneously completed in a few perfect contours.

Major history paintings were preceded by relatively finished drawings of the whole composition, by oil sketches of the whole and by detailed studies in oil of the individual figures. When faced with a new commission, Ingres assembled all possible relevant historical documentation, then slowly laboured to dominate the model with his own vision by rebuilding it from the ground up with studies from life. A good example of this approach is the *Golden Age* mural for the Duc de Luynes. In 1843 Ingres started on the commission, alternately working at the château at Dampierre (usually from June to October) and at the studio in Paris (November to June). He worked on the subject for several years (1843–8), especially in the quiet evening hours, making over 500 drawings. During the first year at Dampierre he had a model made of the major figures so that he could study the effects of light and shadow. As he was unable to work from the live model in the gallery, detailed drawings for the major figures were made in Paris. In such later paintings as *Antiochus and Stratonice* and *Odalisque with Slave*, which required elaborate interiors, Ingres began his studies from nature. He prepared the rough sketch on the canvas, and his students then worked on less important parts such as the architecture, mosaics, rugs and furniture, some of which might need repositioning if he decided to change the figures. Since the figures were completed by Ingres, he alone undertook to harmonize the ensemble with innumerable carefully applied layers of colour. His concern for the final touches extended to the last coats of varnish and the exact choice of frame.

A normal day consisted of work in the studio from nine to six, followed, preferably, by dinner and a quiet evening in preparation for the next day, but more often in Paris by the exigencies of social life. The time devoted to portraits was carefully scheduled and followed a set pattern. Ingres and the sitter met for an hour and a half in the morning, then broke for lunch. While the sitter relaxed, Ingres looked for mannerisms, gestures or opinions that could throw light on the sitter's character. They returned to the studio for a two-and-a-half hour session. At four the sitting was over, the drawing finished. Patience was essential as, regardless of the status of the sitter, the finished portrait might be delivered up to seven years later, or not at all.

Ingres wrote of his working habits, 'I force myself to press ahead by every sort of study, and each step further that I make in the understanding of nature makes me see that I know nothing. The more I reach toward perfection, the more I find myself ... measuring ... what I lack. I destroy more than I create' (letter, 24 Dec 1822). Justifying his obsessive reworking, he also noted 'if my works have a value and are deserving, it is because ... I have taken them up twenty times over again, I have purified them with an extreme of research and sincerity' (Delaborde, 1870, p. 100).

III. Character and personality.

Ingres was the staunchest, most conservative defender of the classical tradition, preaching an inflexible, if sometimes contradictory, doctrine of ideal beauty and the absolute supremacy of line and pure form over colour and emotion. He described himself as generally affable but with a 'white hot' temper if he felt himself wronged. His personality, like his art, was marked by a preference for the order of a familiar universe. He adjusted slowly to changes in daily habits and remained the worst sort of provincial traveller, comparing everything that was new to him unfavourably with the home equivalent.

According to Charles Blanc, Ingres's friend and biographer, 'In him genius is will.... Here was a man for whom invention was painful, but who bent his faults by a prodigious love of the beautiful' (1870, pp. 92–3). In times of stress, Ingres was likely to react with a whole variety of physical symptoms, for example boils and atrocious headaches during the last few months of 1833, while he was working on the *Apotheosis of Homer*. There were times, however, when the pleasures of work were sweeter than ever before: 'Every day I am shut away in my studio from morning to night. I am love struck by painting, I don't possess it, it possesses me' (letter, May 1827). He was not at all the 19th-century bohemian artist; he loved every bourgeois comfort and expected his wife to look after his domestic needs.

In a letter of 7 July 1862 to Hippolyte Fockedey (Naef, 1977–81, iii, p. 371) Victor Mettez described 'le Père Ingres' as 'choleric, impatient, obstinate, good, naive, righteous, lazy ... by moments eloquent and sublime ... an incredible mélange'. This 'mélange' was echoed in an intimate sketch of Ingres by the composer Charles Gounod: 'He had an enthusiasm which sometimes approached eloquence. He had the tenderness of a child and the indignations of an apostle. He was naive and sensitive. He was sincerely humble before the great masters, but fiercely proud of his own accomplishments' (*Mémoires d'un artiste*, Paris, 1896).

Ingres's passions for music (Gluck, Haydn, Mozart and Beethoven), for literature (Plutarch, Virgil, Homer, Shakespeare, Dante and Vasari) and the visual arts (Raphael and Michelangelo) were deep and lifelong. His friends were friends for life, unless they crossed him, and nothing pleased him more than his favourite music in the company of a select circle of friends. As a student, he was seen as too serious, intolerant of the usual studio antics; as a teacher, although he often acted as a father figure to his favourite students, he brooked no opposition: 'Discussion was, unfortunately, not possible with M. Ingres' (Amaury-Duval, 1878, 2/1924, p. 61). And M. Ingres he remained, even to his family and closest friends.

IV. Critical reception and posthumous reputation.

Ingres alternated between pride and self-doubt, confidence and crisis. This insecurity was fuelled, and his development thwarted, both in early and mid-career, by constant harsh criticism. At first, he was considered too radical; later he was seen as representative of the moribund old guard. In one year only—1825—did he receive critical acclaim, when he was given the Cross of the Légion d'honneur, following the success of the *Vow of Louis XIII* that welcomed him back to France as champion of the classical style.

There is a marked difference between Ingres's posthumous reputation as a leading figure of his school and the difficulty he had establishing and holding that place during his lifetime. Equally ironic, given Ingres's absolute devotion to his calling as a history painter, is the fact that his portraits are now more widely appreciated than his history paintings. A retrospective exhibition of his work, including 587 paintings, drawings and oil sketches, was held in May 1867 at the Ecole des Beaux-Arts during the Exposition Universelle. It attracted 40,000 visitors.

WRITINGS

R. Cogniet, ed.: *Ingres, écrits sur l'art: Textes recueillis dans les carnets et dans la correspondance d'Ingres* (Paris, 1947)

T. B. Brumbaugh: 'A Group of Ingres Letters', *J. Walters A.G.*, xlii–xliii (1984–5), pp. 90–96 [five letters, 1845–54]

See also Delaborde (1870), Courtheon, i (1947) and Ewals (1984).

BIBLIOGRAPHY

GENERAL

E. Delécluze: *David, son école & son temps: Souvenirs de soixante années* (Paris, 1862)

E. A. Amaury-Duval: *L'Atelier d'Ingres* (Paris, 1878, 2/1924)

H. Lapauze: *Histoire de l'Académie de France à Rome*, 2 vols (Paris, 1924)

W. Friedlaender: *Von David bis Delacroix* (Bielefeld, 1930); Eng. trans. by R. Goldwater (Cambridge, MA, 1952)

David, Ingres, Géricault et leur temps (exh. cat., Paris, Ecole N. Sup. B.-A., 1934)

F. Lugt: *Ventes* (The Hague, 1938–64), iii, pp. 83–4, 563

J. Alazard: *Ingres et l'Ingrisme* (Paris, 1950)

P. Angrand: *Monsieur Ingres et son époque* (Lausanne, 1967)

The Age of Neo-classicism (exh. cat., foreword J. Pope-Hennessy; ACGB, 1972)
French Painting, 1774–1830: The Age of Revolution (exh. cat., preface P. Rosenberg; Paris, Grand Pal.; Detroit, MI, Inst. A.; New York, Met., 1974–5)
The Second Empire: Art in France under Napoleon III (exh. cat., ed. G. H. Marcus and J. M. Iandola; Philadelphia, PA, Mus. A.; Detroit, MI, Inst. A.; Paris, Grand Pal.; 1978–9)

CATALOGUES RAISONNÉS

H. Delaborde: *Ingres: Sa vie, ses travaux, sa doctrine, d'après les notes manuscrites et les lettres du maître* (Paris, 1870) [D]
D. Wildenstein: *The Paintings of J.-A.-D. Ingres* (London, 1954, rev. 2/1956) [W] [the most useful source for tracing provenance]
E. Camesasca: *L'opera completa di Ingres*, intro. by E. Radius (Milan, 1968); Fr. trans. with add. mat. as *Tout l'oeuvre peint d'Ingres*, intro. by D. Ternois (Paris, 1971)
H. Naef: *Die Bildniszeichnungen von J.-A.-D. Ingres*, 5 vols (Berne, 1977–81) [N]

MONOGRAPHS

A. Magimel, ed.: *Oeuvres de J.-A. Ingres, gravées au trait sur acier par A. Réveil, 1800–1851* (Paris, 1851)
C. Blanc: *Ingres: Sa vie et ses oeuvres* (Paris, 1870)
E. Gatteaux: *Collection des 120 dessins, croquis et peintures de M. Ingres classés et mis en ordre par son ami Edouard Gatteaux*, 2 vols (Paris, 1875)
L. Frölich-Bum: *Ingres: Sein Leben und sein Stil* (Vienna, 1911)
H. Lapauze: *Ingres: Sa vie, et son oeuvre* (Paris, 1911)
W. Pach: *Ingres* (New York, 1939)
P. Courtheon: *Ingres raconté par lui-même et par ses amis*, i: *Pensées et écrits du peintre*; ii: *Ses contemporains, sa postérité* (Geneva, 1947)
H. Naef: *Ingres. Rom* (Zurich, 1962)
R. Rosenblum: *Jean-Auguste-Dominique Ingres* (New York, 1967)
J. Whiteley: *Ingres* (London, 1977)
D. Ternois: *Ingres* (Paris, 1980)

MUSEUM AND EXHIBITION CATALOGUES

Ingres (exh. cat., Paris, Gal. Martinet, 1861)
A. Cambon: *Catalogue du Musée de Montauban* (Montauban, 1885)
H. Lapauze: *Les Dessins de J.-A.-D. Ingres du Musée de Montauban* (Paris, 1901)
Portraits par Ingres et ses élèves (exh. cat. by C. Sterling, Paris, Gal. Jacques Seligmann, 1934)
A Loan Exhibition of Paintings and Drawings from the Ingres Museum at Montauban (exh. cat., intro. A. Mongan and D. Ternois; New York, Knoedler's, 1952)
Ingres et ses maîtres, de Roques à David (exh. cat. by P. Mesplé and D. Ternois, Toulouse, Mus. Augustins; Montauban, Mus. Ingres; 1955)
Rome vue par Ingres (exh. cat., ed. H. Naef; Lausanne, 1960; Zurich, 1962; Montauban, Mus. Ingres, 1973)
D. Ternois: *Montauban, Musée Ingres: Peintures, Ingres et son temps* (1965), xi of *Inventaire des collections publiques françaises* (Paris, 1957–)
Ingres Centennial Exhibition, 1867–1967: Drawings, Watercolors and Oil Sketches from American Collections (exh. cat., ed. A. Mongan and H. Naef; Cambridge, MA, Fogg, 1967)
Ingres et son temps: Exposition organisée pour le centenaire de la mort d'Ingres (exh. cat. by D. Ternois and J. Lacambe, Montauban, Mus. Ingres, 1967)
Ingres (exh. cat., ed. L. Duclaux, J. Foucart, H. Naef and D. Ternois; Paris, Petit Pal., 1967–8) [with excellent bibliog.]
Ingres in Italia: 1806–1824, 1835–1841 (exh. cat. by J. Foucart, Rome, Villa Medici, 1968)
M. Cohn and S. Siegfried: *Works by J.-A.-D. Ingres in the Collection of the Fogg Art Museum* (Cambridge, MA, Fogg, 1980)
Ingres (exh. cat. by M. Ikuta and others, Tokyo, N. Mus. W. A.; Osaka, N. Mus. A.; 1981)
In Pursuit of Perfection: The Art of J.-A.-D. Ingres (exh. cat., ed. P. Condon; Louisville, KY, Speed A. Mus.; Fort Worth, TX, Kimbell A. Mus.; 1983–4)

SUBJECT-MATTER AND ICONOGRAPHY

J. Alazard: 'Ce que J.-D. Ingres doit aux primitifs italiens', *Gaz. B.-A.*, ii (1936), pp. 167–75
E. King: 'Ingres as a Classicist', *J. Walters A.G.*, v (1942), pp. 69–113
A. Mongan: 'Ingres and the Antique', *J. Warb. & Court. Inst.*, x (1947), pp. 1–13
D. Ternois: 'Les Sources iconographiques de *l'Apothéose d'Homère*', *Bull. Soc. Archéol. Tarn-et-Garonne* (1954–5), 97–108
H. Naef: 'Paolo und Francesca: Zum Problem der schöpferischen Nachahmung bei Ingres', *Z. Kstwiss.*, x (1956), pp. 97–108
N. Schlenoff: *Ingres, ses sources littéraires* (Paris, 1956)
Ingres and the Comtesse d'Haussonville (exh. cat. by E. Munhall, New York, Frick, 1985)

SPECIALIST STUDIES

H. Delaborde: 'Les Dessins de M. Ingres au Salon des Arts-Unis', *Gaz. B.-A.*, ix (1861), pp. 257–69
C. Blanc: 'Du Style et de M. Ingres', *Gaz. B.-A.*, xiv (1863), pp. 5–23
H. Schwarz: 'Die Lithographien J. A. D. Ingres', *Mitt. Ges. Vervielfält. Kst* (1926), pp. 74–9
Bull. Mus. Ingres (1956–)
E. Bryant: 'Notes on J. A. D. Ingres' *Entry into Paris of the Dauphin, Future Charles V*', *Wadsworth Atheneum Bull.*, 5th ser., iii (1959), pp. 16–21
M. J. Ternois: 'Les Oeuvres d'Ingres dans la collection Gilibert', *Rev. A.* [Paris], iii (1959), pp. 120–30
H. Naef: 'Un Tableau d'Ingres inachevé: *Le Duc d'Albe à Sainte-Gudule*', *Bull. Mus. Ingres*, 7 (1960), pp. 3–6
——: 'Ingres as Lithographer', *Burl. Mag.* (1966), pp. 476–9
Actes du colloque Ingres et son temps: Montauban, 1967
D. Ternois: 'Ingres et sa méthode', *Rev. Louvre*, iv (1967), pp. 195–208
——: 'Napoléon et la décoration du palais impérial de Monte Cavallo en 1811–13', *Rev. A.* [Paris], vii (1970), pp. 68–89
J. Connolly: *Ingres Studies: Antiochus and Stratonice, the Bather and Odalisque Themes* (diss., Philadelphia, U. PA, 1974)
Actes du colloque Ingres et le néo-classicisme: Montauban, 1975
C. Duncan: 'Ingres's *Vow of Louis XIII* and the Politics of the Restoration', *Art and Architecture in the Service of Politics*, ed. H. Millon and L. Nochlin (Cambridge, MA, 1978), pp. 80–91
M. Lader: 'Gorky, De Kooning and the "Ingres Revival" in America', *A. Mag.* (March 1978), pp. 94–9
S. Symmons: 'J. A. D. Ingres: The Apotheosis of Flaxman', *Burl. Mag.*, cxxi (1979), pp. 721–5
Actes du colloque Ingres et son influence: Montauban, 1980
M. Méras: 'Théophile Gautier critique officiel d'Ingres au Moniteur', *Bull. Mus. Ingres*, 47–8 (1980), pp. 205–19
S. Siegfried: *Ingres and his Critics, 1806–1824* (diss., Cambridge, MA, Harvard U., 1980)
P. Angrand: 'Le Premier Atelier de Monsieur Ingres', *Bull. Mus. Ingres*, 49 (1982), pp. 19–58 [with bibliog.]
F. Haskell: 'A Turk and his Pictures in Nineteenth-century Paris', *Oxford A. J.*, v/1 (1982), pp. 40–47
C. Ockman: *The Restoration of the Château of Dampierre: Ingres, the Duc de Luynes and an Unrealized Vision of History* (diss., New Haven, CT, Yale U., 1982)
A. D. Rifkin: 'Ingres and the Academic Dictionary: An Essay on Ideology and Stupefaction in the Social Formation of the Artist', *A. Hist.*, vi (1983), pp. 153–70
L. Ewals: 'Ingres et la réception de l'art français en Hollande avec des lettres inédites de David, Gérard, Ingres, Vernet, Delaroche, Decamps et Rousseau', *Bull. Mus. Ingres*, 53–4 (1984), pp. 21–42
A. Boime: 'Declassicizing the Academic: A Realist View of Ingres', *A. Hist.*, viii (1985), pp. 50–65
C. de Cououssin: 'Portraits d'Ingres: Examen du laboratoire', *Rev. Louvre*, xxxiv (1985), pp. 197–206
P. Condon: *J.-A.-D. Ingres: The Finished History Drawings* (diss., Providence, RI, Brown U., 1986)
D. Ternois: 'La Correspondance d'Ingres: Etat des travaux et problèmes de méthode', *Archvs A. Fr.*, n. s., xxviii (1986), pp. 161–200
B. Ivry: 'Right under his Nose', *Connoisseur*, ccxx (1990), pp. 126–9, 156

PATRICIA CONDON

Ingushetia. *See under* RUSSIA, §XVII, 1.

Initial, manuscript. Enlarged or otherwise accentuated letter that introduces sentences, paragraphs or major divisions of a text. The use of initials, accentuated by size, placement or decoration, evolved in the Late Antique or Early Christian period in conjunction with the growing prevalence of texts written in the codex format. Perhaps as a result of an increased dependence on the authority of the written word occasioned by the growing needs of the Christian Church, combined with a developing sense of the aesthetic and practical requirements of the codex, various devices were invented to mark significant divisions

1. Chi-rho monogram, initial page from the Book of Kells, 330×250 mm, from ?Iona, late 8th century (Dublin, Trinity College Library, MS. 58, fol. 34*r*)

of the text. In the late 4th-century Codex Sinaiticus (London, BL, Add. MS. 43725) the divisions between books are marked by *explicit* (ending) inscriptions; in the 5th-century Codex Alexandrinus (London, BL, Royal MS. 1. D. V–VIII) sentences are introduced by larger letters moved into the margins, and the *explicit* is accompanied by penned decoration. At about the same time a Vergil manuscript, the so-called Augusteus (Rome, Vatican, Bib. Apostolica, Cod. Vat. lat. 3256), was provided with initials, four lines in height, containing wash-coloured panels within the structure of the letter. Here, by its scale and decoration, the initial is emancipated from the text and serves as a major visual accent for the beginning of a block of text. In the Valerianus Gospels (Munich, Bayer. Staatsbib., Clm. 6224), produced in north-east Italy *c.* 675, a decorative *explicit* is combined with a larger, more ornamented initial, accompanied by the appropriate Evangelist symbol.

From this point decorated initials developed in various ways. In products of Irish and English monasteries from *c.* 600 to 800, beginning with the Cathach of St Columba (Dublin, Royal Irish Acad., s.n.), large penned initials, accompanied by interior and exterior penwork, introduce several successively smaller letters of the first words leading into the normal-sized letters of the text of the psalms. In the Book of Durrow (Dublin, Trinity Coll. Lib., MS. 57; *see* INSULAR ART, fig. 3), the LINDISFARNE GOSPELS (London, BL, Cotton MS. Nero D. IV) and ultimately in the Book of Kells (Dublin, Trinity Coll. Lib., MS. 58), this led to the treatment of the first letter, word and even phrase as a large elaborate monogram to open the text. The letters themselves, composed of framed panels, the area that they enclose and the field against which they are set, are decorated with myriad geometric interlace, knot, spiral and even zoomorphic forms derived from contemporary metalwork and stone-carving. The most fully developed and complex manifestation of this tradition occurs in the late 8th-century Book of Kells, in the chi-rho page (see fig. 1), which comprises the first three letters of Christ's name (XPI). Letters, interior ground and exterior field have become one, a resplendent mystic talisman to introduce the narrative of the birth of Christ (Matthew 1:18). A parallel continental development resulted in the decorative elaboration of the structure of the letter itself. In the Merovingian manuscripts of 8th-century France, fishes, birds and quadrupeds are depicted bent and attached to each other in incongruous juxtapositions. The shape of the letter might frame the animals, beasts or plant forms that are contained within its structure, or forms might be combined to approximate the shape of the letter itself.

This kind of initial was revived with special exuberance during the Romanesque period, when zoomorphic and figured letters were combined with plant forms, vine scrolls and tendrils, which not only extended the letter into the margin, but also took over the interior ground (*see* ROMANESQUE, §IV, 2 and fig. 61). Inhabited initials are those in which the figures and animals spill over into the foliage and become enmeshed in the vine scrolls, struggling against them and with each other. Some initials of this type have no particular thematic content, and perhaps simply reflect the persistence of intertwined, fighting animals and figures found in earlier non-Christian art (*see* MIGRATION PERIOD); but others seem to be

2. Inhabited initial V, opening to the Book of Job from a Bible, 525×360 mm, from Winchester, *c.* 1160–80 (Oxford, Bodleian Library, MS. Auct. E. inf. 1, fol. 304*r*)

3. Historiated initial P, opening to St Paul's Epistle to the Romans from a *Commentary on St Paul's Epistles*, 475×340 mm, from Corbie, 1163–4 (Paris, Bibliothèque Nationale, MS. lat. 11575)

generally related to the text, as in the male figure caught up in a vine scroll and attacked by a dog that opens the Book of Job in an English Romanesque Bible (Oxford, Bodleian Lib., MS. Auct. E. inf. 1, fol. 304*r*; see fig. 2), which perhaps symbolizes the tribulations of Job. A 12th-century copy of St Gregory's *Moralia in Job*, which was produced at Cîteaux, includes some figured initials, such as a Q made up of a monk and a laybrother chopping a log (Dijon, Bib. Mun., MS. 170, fol. 59*r*) or another Q with a falconer riding in a landscape with water-fowl splashing in a pond on the tail of the letter (Dijon, Bib. Mun., MS. 173, fol. 174*r*); these narrative vignettes of the daily life of the monks have little to do with the text.

The introduction of narrative scenes into the ground surrounded by the initial may have originated in such Insular manuscripts as the 8th-century Vespasian Psalter (London, BL, Cotton MS. Vesp. A. I), where *David Fighting the Lion* is enclosed within a letter D (fol. 53*r*). On the Continent the illustrative content of some figured initials in the Corbie Psalter (*c.* 800; Amiens, Bib. Mun., MS. 18), which includes letters composed of *David and Goliath* or *Jonah and the Whale*, may represent an early step in this direction. These historiated initials seem to have been perfected in Carolingian manuscripts. For example, in the Harley Gospels (London, BL, Harley MS. 2788) an interlace Q frames a representation of the *Annunciation to Zacharias* (fol. 109*r*; for illustration *see* GOSPEL BOOK). Such historiated initials, in contrast to the ambiguous content of inhabited initials or the less precise content of many figured initials, not only maintain a distinction between the letter and the scene represented within it, but also present an identifiable incident, usually narrated within or germane to the text that they introduce (see fig. 3 and MANUSCRIPT, colour pl. V, fig. 1). The variety of historiated initials from the 9th to the 15th centuries is immense. They often take the place of miniatures to introduce the beginning of textual divisions, and they are found in a wide range of liturgical (e.g. *see* CHOIR-BOOK, fig. 1), devotional and secular (e.g. *see* ICELAND, fig. 2) manuscripts.

Once the initial had become more than just a slightly larger letter with some embellishment, executed in the same ink as the text, it usually became the responsibility of someone other then the scribe. This might be a different person in a monastic scriptorium, or, in the Gothic period, when books were increasingly written in lay scriptoria, a member of an artisan's workshop nearby. The scribe would leave blank spaces at the beginning of the text, indicating the letter to be executed with a minute penned letter and occasionally suggesting appropriate subject-matter with additional sketches or instructions.

By the end of the Middle Ages various lesser decorative initials were used to adorn the text and indicate its subdivisions. Wash initials, simple one-line initials in ink touched with wash, began sentences. Flourished initials, usually one or two lines high in blue with red pen flourishes or gold embellished with black pen flourishes, are often found in alternating sequences at the beginning of sentences or verses. Dentelle or filigree initials, found in all sizes, consist of gold letters set against blue or red fields with red or blue interior grounds decorated with white filigree. The field and ground would often alternate between red and blue as the letters appeared in the text. A variant of this form, with red, magenta or blue initials decorated with filigree and set against a gold field, might also appear in alternating sequences. A more elaborate version, appearing in all sizes, consisted of painted letters with white filigree set against a gold field with an interior ground filled with red and blue vines, ivy leaves and flowers. At the end of the 15th century this repertory of initials was replaced by brushed gold letters on alternating red and blue grounds, or grey-white letters, often made up of scroll-like forms, against painted fields. These initials are used in a strict hierarchical order, with larger, more elaborate letters opening major sections of the text, often following miniatures, while smaller ones indicate subordinate parts or sentences. The major initials were often accompanied by border decoration, frequently a reduced variant of the borders accompanying the major initials that open significant divisions of the text (for further discussion and illustration *see* BORDER, MANUSCRIPT). Thus the size of the initials, the sequence of types of decoration and the presence of accompanying border decoration all worked together to signal the location and hierarchy of the parts of the text.

BIBLIOGRAPHY

A. Schardt: *Das Initial* (Berlin, 1938)

C. Nordenfalk: *Die spätantiken Zierbuchstaben* (Stockholm, 1970)

J. D. Farquhar: 'The Manuscript as a Book', *Pen to Press: Illustrated Manuscripts and Printed Books in the First Century of Printing* (exh. cat. by S. Hindman and J. D. Farquhar, College Park, U. MD A.G., 1977), pp. 68–72

J. J. G. Alexander: *The Decorated Letter* (London and New York, 1978)

O. Pächt: *Buchmalerei des Mittelalters* (Munich, 1984; Eng. trans., New York, 1986), pp. 45–128

ROBERT G. CALKINS

Injae. *See* KANG (ii), (1).

Injalbert, (Jean-)Antoine [Antonin] (*b* Béziers, 23 Feb 1845; *d* Béziers, Jan 1933). French sculptor. After serving an apprenticeship with an ornamental sculptor, Injalbert entered the Ecole des Beaux-Arts in Paris in 1866 with a municipal scholarship. His teacher was Augustin-Alexandre Dumont. In 1874 he won the Prix de Rome with a figure of *Orpheus* (1874; Paris, Ecole N. Sup. B.-A.). He exhibited with the Société des Artistes Français only at the beginning and end of his career, otherwise remaining faithful to the Société Nationale des Beaux-Arts. Although he produced many portrait busts and playful allegorical statuettes, Injalbert concentrated on public sculpture. His decorative work, heavy and majestic, adorns many of the most prestigious buildings in Paris, including the Hôtel de Ville (1880) and the Palais de Justice (1913). His statue of the *City of Nantes* for the Gare d'Orsay (1900) is an example of his collaboration with the architect Victor Laloux. The monument to *Octave Mirbeau* in the Panthéon is important, if atypical, since Injalbert produced far more decorative works than commemorative monuments. Most of his sculptures are in the département of Hérault; notable examples include the two stone groups known as *Love Taming Strength* at the main entrance of the Promenade du Peyrou in Montpellier and a fountain with the bronze figure of *Atlas Carrying the World* in Béziers, both in a decorative style reminiscent of 18th-century sculpture.

BIBLIOGRAPHY

C. Ponsonnailhe: *Injalbert* (Paris, 1892)

O. Uzanne: *Figures contemporaines tirées de l'album Mariani*, 11 vols (Paris, 1896–1908), ii

D. Cady Eaton: *A Handbook of Modern French Sculpture* (New York, 1913), pp. 259, 291

A. B. [?Alfred Bachelet]: 'Jean-Antonin Injalbert', *Acad. B.-A., Bull. Annu.* [Paris], 17 (Jan–June 1933), pp. 43–8

H. Bouchard: *Notice sur la vie et les oeuvres de Jean-Antonin Injalbert* (Paris, 1935)

PENELOPE CURTIS

Ink. Imprecise term applied to a number of more or less fluid materials that are used for either writing or printing the written word or have evolved for a variety of illustrative and artistic purposes. Most inks for the written and printed word have always been black, or nearly so, but coloured inks also evolved for some writing, for embellishment and for pictorial work.

See also PIGMENT, especially §§II and IV.

I. Types and properties. II. Uses. III. Conservation.

I. Types and properties.

A primary distinction can be made between inks used for writing and drawing and those used for printing. The former are usually water-based and are sometimes barely distinguishable from watercolour paints, especially in the case of coloured inks. Printing inks may be water-, oil- or solvent-based. Ink for writing and drawing must flow freely from the pen or brush and must be of adequate tinting strength. These properties can be provided by black pigments held in suspension or by solutions that are or become black, but in each case only a few preparations have been found adequate, at least before modern times. Carbon, in various forms, has provided the usual black pigment. Historically, however, the most important aqueous solutions used as inks have been those of metal tannates, which evolved into iron-gall (iron gallotannate or gall-nut) ink. Ink is also judged by its stability, either in the sense of its adhesion to the support or the permanence of its colour over time.

1. Writing and drawing. 2. Printing.

1. Writing and drawing.

(i) Asia. (ii) Middle East and the Western world.

(i) Asia.

(a) Black. Chinese ink (Chin. *mo*; Jap. *sumi*; Kor. *mŏk*) is not the earliest carbon-based ink, but it became the most highly perfected, and its development is well documented. Essentially, it is an intimate mixture of soot or lampblack with animal glue (other constituents have been added, but they are more variable). Such a mixture, differing only in details from later recipes, was described in the *Qimin yaoshu* ('The essential ways for living of the common people'), an agricultural encyclopedia of the 6th century AD by Jia Sixie. Some historical accounts refer to the earlier use of lacquer for writing and also to a material called 'stone ink' (Chin. *shimo*), but their existence or importance remains uncertain. In any event, extant inscriptions on wood, bamboo and silk, as well as wall paintings from the Han period (221 BC–AD 220), suggest the use of a fluid black ink, which was applied with a brush and did not differ in its general properties from later versions.

The earliest recorded type of carbon is pinesoot black, which was made with considerable care from pine-wood soot. Various accounts describe and illustrate structures designed to burn the wood in a restricted air supply, then to cause the soot so formed to drift through a series of chambers or down an extended tunnel-like arrangement. This process eliminated impurities such as fly ash and tarry materials, leaving the very fine carbon particles produced by a sooting flame. The soot that drifted the furthest was considered to be of the best quality, while soot that drifted shorter distances through the structure was deemed of progressively lower quality. The use of lampblack, made by burning oil at a wick, began from about the Song period (960–1279). Typically, a simple lamp made from a bowl of oil with a wick at the edge had an inverted funnel or heavy saucer propped over the flame to catch the lampblack. Vegetable oils, such as tung, rapeseed, hemp or sesame oil, were used, as were other fuels: for instance, spoiled lacquer is supposed to have afforded a good product, and later accounts suggest that pigs' fat and petroleum products were also effective. In modern ink-making practice, commercially produced carbon blacks are often preferred.

For the best ink, much care was also taken over the selection of the second main constituent, the animal glue. When the protein collagen (the main constituent of animal connective tissue such as skin and tendon) is heated in water, the protein chains are disarranged and dispersed to give a solution that gels on cooling and acts as an effective adhesive and sizing agent (*see* ADHESIVES, §1(i)). The skins of bovine animals were apparently the main raw material, but in China, specifically, fish skins and other fish products may have featured, besides less common materials such as horn and antler. Up to 1100 other additives are known (Franke). Some are vegetable extracts, such as that of the bark of the tree *Fraxinus pubinervus*, which may have helped disperse the carbon. Others are natural dyes, which may have modified or 'toned' the colour. Perfumes such as camphor or musk recur and may have helped retard or disguise the effects of bacterial decomposition. Such secondary constituents were usually added when the carbon was mixed with an aqueous solution of the animal glue. All accounts stress that the mixing process is important and must be performed thoroughly and at length to obtain a good product. The pasty mixture, about the consistency of potters' clay, was repeatedly steamed, sprinkled, pounded and rolled. Carbon itself is a hydrophobic (water-repellent) substance, and the thoroughness of the compounding with glue is clearly one of the secrets of modifying it so that it disperses readily in water to form a stable suspension.

Portions of the carbon and glue paste were moulded under pressure into sticks or cakes, usually in wooden moulds carved with characters or designs that were impressed on the surface of the sticks. The inksticks were then dried carefully and slowly to avoid the ever-present danger of cracking. They were also commonly painted or gilded, resulting in decorative pieces that have often been collected for their own sake (*see* CHINA, §XIII, 12). Many connoisseurs claim that inksticks improve with aging, and that lighter sticks are better than denser ones. A purple glint off a fractured surface has also been considered by some to indicate the best-quality ink.

The same process of making ink spread to Korea and Japan at an early date: it was introduced into Japan in the 7th century AD, according to the *Nihon shoki* ('Chronicle of Japan'; completed AD 720), and it was certainly known in Korea before then. The Koreans apparently had available both a very suitable pine-wood for the soot and a high-quality animal glue for the binding medium, which resulted in a particularly fine version of ink. In the 20th century Chinese ink in stick form was made in Japan, Korea and Taiwan, as well as on the Chinese mainland.

Being based on carbon as the pigment, Chinese ink has always been free of fading or similar chemical changes. Mechanical stability, or resistance to flaking and powdering, is related both to the adhesive strength of the binder and to the degree of penetration of the ink into the support. The second factor is helped by the widespread use in East Asia of silk or paper supports that, except when heavily sized, are more or less readily penetrated by ink. In addition, selection of a finely divided carbon and high-quality glue, combined with great thoroughness in the blending, gives an ink that disperses very finely to afford the best attainable penetration and adhesion. When viewed through an electron microscope, ink that has penetrated the support well is seen as small carbon particles spread over the surface in a matted layer or small groups (see fig. 1).

The black inks that gradually came into use in India were based on carbon in the form of lampblack and of charcoal from various plant materials, but they otherwise owe little to Chinese inksticks. One type of ink for writing on birch bark was made by boiling charred almond shells with cows' urine, but, more usually, plant gums such as acacia gum were the dispersal and binding medium. Carbohydrate-based, these are more readily soluble and have less adhesive strength than the animal glues of East Asia. Inks seem usually to have been made in liquid form, and writing was with pens (made, for example, from reeds) rather than with the brush.

Inks from other areas of Asia show affinities either with those from China, those from India, or both. In South-east Asia, especially Indo-China, Chinese ink was imported, while accounts of Thai painting materials suggest that a black ink similar to that of India may have been made there. There is evidence in Central Asia for the use of plant gums in addition to animal glues for watercolour paintings and perhaps therefore for inks, reflecting the intrusion of Indian practice. The Mongols appear to have borrowed their ink from China, and in Tibet domestic as well as imported Chinese ink has long been used. From

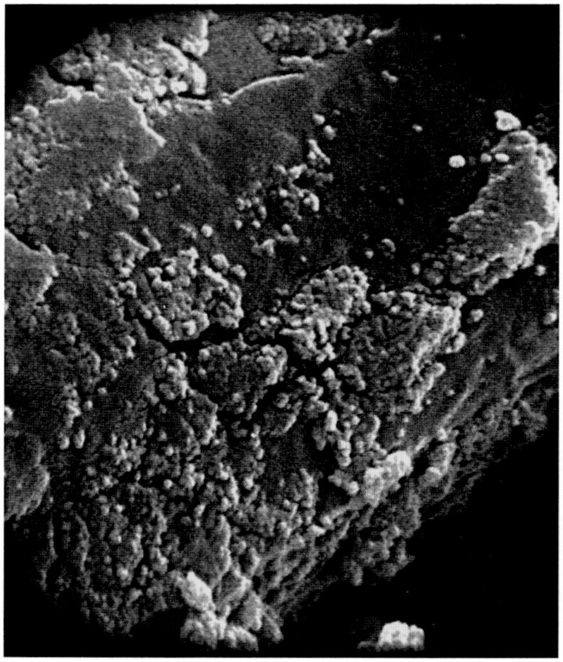

1. Scanning electron micrograph of the surface of a single paper fibre with Chinese ink, 8000×; removed from a painting by Wang Jian: *Landscape*, ink and colours on paper (Washington, DC, Freer Gallery of Art)

the evidence of their brass inkpots, the Tibetans may often have kept ink in liquid form.

An oil-based black ink, with lampblack or charcoal the usual pigment, was used in South and South-east Asia for palm-leaf manuscripts. Writing on palm leaves was frequently incised, then made more legible by applying the ink and wiping off the excess to leave the incisions filled with black.

(b) Coloured. Coloured inks in East, South and Central Asia are essentially the same as watercolour paints, being a dispersion of finely divided pigment in a solution of the same binders as noted above. Gold and silver inks have often been used for religious writings and are most often found in areas and periods where religions, especially Buddhism, have been strongly established. Gold is chemically very stable and also adheres to most supports well, but silver tarnishes readily and has often turned quite black. It survives best where it is well protected, such as in handscrolls that have been infrequently unrolled. In addition, silver often causes brown discolorations on paper supports. In South-east Asia, white and yellow inks have frequently been used to write on black paper. There have been differing, and generally unsubstantiated, claims for the pigments used. Red inks have long been used in many parts of Asia, the most common pigment being vermilion (red mercuric sulphide). When they are employed for writing, the same water-based media are employed as for black ink, and in East Asia red, as well as other, pigments have sometimes been made up into stick form.

A rather different red ink in East Asia is that used for impressing seals on paintings, documents etc. Chinese seals were usually impressed into clay until silk and paper came into widespread use for writing, when vermilion seal ink was introduced. The earliest version was probably dispersed in water, and some accounts indicate that honey was used as the dispersing medium and binder. The use of oil-based ink later become dominant, especially after the development of the seal pad in the 12th century. A punk of dried moxa leaves (*Artemisia moxa*) was mixed with oil and vermilion to give a pasty mass that served to ink the seal after the fashion of a modern inkpad. Castor, rapeseed and some other oils have been used, but in modern times linseed oil is favoured because of its better drying properties.

(ii) Middle East and the Western world.

(a) Black and brown. The history of the development of black writing ink in the world of Islam and Judaism parallels that of western Europe. In both cases, carbon-based inks came first. They later co-existed for some time with metal tannate preparations, which eventually largely displaced them for ordinary writing, although not entirely for artistic purposes. The earliest known type of ink is the carbon-based ink of ancient Egypt, a type that continued to be used in the Mediterranean area throughout Classical times. The Romans made soot by burning resin in special furnaces, as well as using charcoal, yeast black (made by roasting wine sediment) and probably lampblack and ivory black (carbonized ivory or, more usually, bone). Plant gums were probably the dispersing and binding medium for most of these early inks. The mixture was dried to give cakes that were either mulled with water or wetted before a pen was rubbed on the surface. Preparations such as these are readily water-soluble and are known to have been easily erasable with water. This property was due in part to the impenetrable nature of the papyrus or parchment used as supports. The ink remained largely on the surface and rather weakly attached to it, unlike the Chinese ink used in East Asia (*see* §(i) above).

In the Middle East, inks based on carbons mixed with plant gums also form the earliest known types, which date, at least in the Jewish case, to biblical times. Acacia and tragacanth gums have been cited as media and lampblack from olive oil or soot from burning resin, pine-wood or other fuels as the pigments. These preparations clearly had the same erasable property.

The introduction of metal tannates as inks did not happen quickly or simply. Tannins are a group of vegetable products that occur widely. Many (though not all) of them form a deep blue-black colour with iron in the ferric (trivalent) state; the colour forms after oxidation by atmospheric oxygen of the soluble product with ferrous (divalent iron) sulphate solution. Eventually, extracts of gall-nuts or oak-apples (an abnormal growth found on certain trees and a rich source of suitable tannins) mixed with a solution of an iron salt came to be used for the writing ink known as iron-gall ink. Such mixtures may be connected to the use of metal salts as mordants for vegetable dyes, some of which are based on tannins. However, the earliest recipes involving these materials usually include them in mixtures with a carbon-based preparation and often seem to specify salts of metals other than iron—for example alum or copper sulphate (blue vitriol). In this period of experimentation, the objective may have been to improve the notoriously poor adhesion of a carbon and gum ink to the underlying surface. Mixtures of metal salts and tannins produce small amounts of acid, depending on the exact materials and proportions, and this, by corroding or biting into the support surface, may have been found to make the writing more permanent.

From the 9th century, authors in the Islamic world knew and distinguished between carbon-based and metal tannate inks, even though many recipes were mixtures (*see* ISLAMIC ART, §III, 2(i)). A wide variety of recipes has been preserved, perhaps because inks were made up by scribes themselves rather than by specialists as in China. Authors such as the Zirid prince al-Mu'izz ibn Badis (*reg* 1016–62) describe inks in both solid and liquid form and of various qualities, as well as the *liq*, an ink-soaked felt or wool pad for use with the pen. A generally similar evolution took place in Europe, where the practice of using metal tannates may have been introduced from the Arabs. *De diversis artibus* by Theophilos (11th or 12th century) describes an iron tannate preparation; before that time all recipes were carbon-based. From the 13th century, iron-gall inks were described and in common use, and by the 16th century the texts are all based essentially on the same model: an extract of galls with gum arabic and vitriol (though it is still not always clear whether copper sulphate or ferrous sulphate was intended). In due course ferrous sulphate and gall extracts, with the recommended addition of gum arabic or other materials, formed the standard basis for writing inks.

Because a solution of ferrous sulphate with tannin is only slightly coloured and may take several days to develop its typical blue-black colour, ink manufacturers since about the 18th century have added a provisional colour such as indigo (later synthetic dyes) to make the writing easily visible at once. Before this was done, it was usual to oxidize the ink deliberately to give enough ferric tannate complex to make the ink usable. This complex is, however, insoluble, forming in effect a dispersed pigment, and the function of the gum present in virtually all recipes was probably to stabilize this dispersion and attach it to the support. It thus had the same drawback as a carbon pigment, even though the soluble ferrous tannate could penetrate the support slightly before being oxidized and thus become more firmly attached to it. Indeed, it seems to have been recognized that an ink that was quite pale at the writing stage would ultimately prove the most stable.

Iron tannates, blue-black to fully black after the initial oxidation, fade somewhat in time to a brown or greyish-brown colour (the exact shade may depend on impurities). They tend therefore to be more mechanically stable but less lightfast than carbon-based inks. Moreover, it has long been known that they can sometimes chemically attack and destroy supports, some preparations being quite markedly acid (*see* §III below).

Other important black or brown inks are sepia and bistre. Bistre is more of a watercolour paint than an ink and is made from wood soot, often using beech-wood. The soot, collected from close to the fire, contains much tarry material as well as carbon particles. The coarser material is removed by extracting with water, decanting and allowing the solution to evaporate. The colour varies from yellowish-brown to dark brown, depending on the wood and the exact method of preparation. Although bistre contains carbon, it is not lightfast, since the tarry materials fade with exposure, usually making the overall colour cooler and paler. The first known literary mention of bistre was by Jehan Le Begue in 1431.

True sepia is made from the dried ink sacs of various cephalopods, the best known being the Mediterranean cuttlefish (*Sepia officinalis*). It was described by Roman authors, but it is not clear how far it may have been used as an ink at that time. It was introduced by Seydelmann in Dresden sometime after 1778 and appears to have displaced bistre and carbon-based inks for wash drawings. Sepia is prepared by pulverizing the dried ink sacs, then dissolving the pigment in alkali, filtering, reprecipitating with acid, washing and drying. The product consists chiefly of the nitrogenous compound melanin and is not lightfast. Many modern products marketed as 'sepia' are, in fact, watercolour paints based on earth pigments.

Carbon-based ink in the form of Chinese inksticks was imported into Europe, possibly as early as the 16th century. Frequently referred to as 'Indian' or 'India' ink, it began to be mentioned in art manuals in the 17th century. These Chinese carbon-based inks were soon imitated, for example in the Netherlands, and the term 'Indian' ink began to be used also for the European product. This process resulted in an improvement in the technical standard of the ink: it has become the draughtsman's ink of more recent times and is also used by artists requiring a heavy, dense black.

(b) Coloured. A red ink, based on red iron oxide, was used in ancient Egypt for the rubrication of headings, notes etc. The Arabs used a wider variety of coloured inks for rubrics, capitals and various embellishments, using either pen or brush. According to al-Muʿizz ibn Badis, red, yellow and green were the most important colours, though others were also used. Vermilion and red lead were used as red pigments, orpiment for yellow and verdigris for green; the media were the same plant gums as before. Yellow inks may sometimes have been intended to mimic gold, though gold inks, as well as those of silver, tin and even copper, were also employed.

Colours were used to illuminate and embellish European manuscripts, but these are essentially paints. From the 19th century, a variety of synthetic colouring materials began to be used for Western inks to give reds, violets or other colours, though these were usually light-fugitive. Better-quality synthetic dyes developed in the later 20th century have led to the production of felt-tipped or fibre-tipped pens in a wide variety of colours, including black.

2. Printing.

(i) Asia. Printing with ink, usually on to paper, began in East Asia, probably in China. The black ink used was the same mixture of lampblack or soot with glue as used for writing and painting, though the quality of the materials may not have been as high as that used for the finest calligraphy. This water-based ink worked well on the carved woodblocks with which the majority of East Asian printing was done. Metal type was also introduced, especially in Korea, where it is known to have been in use by 1234: this implies the use of an oil-based printing ink (water-based inks do not spread properly on metal surfaces), but little seems to be known of its composition. The concurrent use of oil-based vermilion seal inks suggests that such a preparation would have been technically feasible.

Colour-printing from woodblocks was also practised in East Asia. The earliest known example is a Diamond Sutra printed in 1341 in red and black by the Zifu Temple in modern Hebei province. Polychrome book printing was under way in China at the beginning of the 17th century, a notable example being the prints in the *Treatise on Calligraphy and Painting of the Ten Bamboo Studio*, produced between 1619 and 1633. The best-known East Asian colour prints are those of the Japanese *ukiyoe* school centred on Edo (now Tokyo; *see* Japan, §IX, 3(ii)). Printing in two colours (in addition to black) began there around 1742, that in multiple colours in the mid-1760s. Colour printing (like any other printing) requires finely divided colorants of high tinting strength, which has precluded the use of some of the pigments used for painting. Many of the traditional print colours have been organic dyestuffs. In Japan they have included *beni* (safflower pink from *Carthamus tinctorius*), *ukon* (turmeric yellow from *Curcuma longa*), *ai* (indigo from *Polygonum tinctorium*), *aigami* (dayflower blue from *Commelina communis*), *suō* (sappan-wood red from *Caesalpina sappan*), *kihada* (yellow from *Phellodendron amurense*), *enji* (red from various scaled insects, including cochineal) and various others. Common inorganic pigments have been red lead (orange), iron oxides (reds and browns) and, from about the beginning of the 19th century, Prussian blue. However, less is known about the sources and history of colorants in *ukiyoe* and other East Asian prints than is the case with painting materials.

(ii) Western world. Inks are used for all four basic types of printing: relief, intaglio, planographic and porous printing. Although relief prints, such as woodcuts and wood-engravings, can be printed with a water-based ink, nearly all printing processes in Europe and the West required the development of oil-based inks. Aqueous vehicles will not spread uniformly and reliably on the metal surfaces of types and plates, and the process of movable type printing attributed to Johann Gutenberg *c.* 1450 depended on, among other things, the development of a suitable ink. The ink used in Gutenberg's productions is considered to be of very high quality, being densely black and free of an oily halo formation around the letters. Inks for typographic and other relief-printing generally used a lampblack as the pigment, often made by burning resins and pitches. For the best product, the black first obtained from the burning was reheated at a high temperature in a closed vessel in order to rid the pigment of incompletely carbonized materials. It was then washed and ground to a fine powder, removing gritty impurities. Other fuels used to make lampblack were animal fats and, later, coal tar; these blacks have been superseded by industrial carbon blacks, first manufactured in 1872 from natural gas. The addition of blue pigments, such as indigo or, later, Prussian blue, has sometimes been described as a way of giving a blacker appearance to the ink in typographic and line printing. Inks for certain printing methods, such as intaglio work, have often used other carbons, such as yeast black, vine black (carbonized vine twigs) or ivory black.

The vehicle used is oleo-resinous. A variety of resins have been tried at times, including mastic, dammar and Copaiba balsam. Other additives include varieties of soap, which help the ink 'lift' from the printing surface on to the paper. The major component, however, is the oil, the usual types being linseed and walnut oil. To give the oil satisfactory drying properties, it had to be 'boiled' or heated in a large vessel to a high temperature. The boiling process was both unpleasant, since acrid fumes were produced, and dangerous, since the oil could easily froth over and ignite; indeed, recipes often required it to be deliberately ignited or 'burnt'. Boiling the oil was nevertheless important for making good ink. In many cases it was done with the addition of siccatives such as litharge (lead monoxide), and a recurring theme is the insertion into the hot oil of breadcrusts and sometimes onions. These may have absorbed and helped remove mucilagenous impurities. Until the second half of the 19th century, many printers made their own ink, often moving temporarily to an open place to boil the oil. Modern methods are based on the use of super-heated steam. Inks for intaglio and planographic printing are similar in principle to those for relief printing, but with some adjustment of the detailed properties.

Printing ink is a thick, pasty material. Its physical behaviour during printing is expressed by the empirical concepts of 'length' and 'tack'. A 'long' ink is stretchy and elastic when pulled out; a 'short' one is rather buttery. 'Tack' indicates the tendency to stick to a surface on contact. Both properties must be optimized for best results. Intaglio inks, for example, are quite 'short' to avoid the ink being pulled from the incisions when the plate is wiped of surplus ink. In fine art printing, the artist usually adjusts his own ink in the light of the properties of the plate and the effect for which he is striving.

Two distinct materials have been referred to as lithographic inks: that used by the artist to draw his design on the stone (usually a crayon but sometimes a liquid, and almost always black) and that used to print from the stone. They are, however, of rather similar composition, both being oleo-resinous with a high proportion of oil. Lithographic printing inks are formulated to 'take' readily on the oleophilic areas of the stone or plate and to be repelled by the wetted areas without having any tendency to emulsify with water. They need a high enough 'tack' to keep printing consistently through a run and are usually rather slow drying. Many coloured pigments, if of fairly high tinting strength and sufficiently finely ground, work well in lithographic printing.

'Porous printing' embraces stencil and silkscreen methods, for which water-based, oil-based and solvent-based inks have all been used. Screenprinting is based on pushing an ink across the screen, which has non-printing areas blocked out. The ink type chosen may depend on the blocking out method, and it is formulated 'short' so as not to drag on the squeegee and to release cleanly from the screen after the printing pass.

II. Uses.

The basic uses of ink are for writing and printing. However, the materials and their uses have both undergone an evolution as artists began employing inks for artistic purposes. Those purposes have themselves evolved, resulting in the blurring of the distinction between ink and paint. This evolution is more marked in the Western world than in Asia, where black ink has changed little. In the West, writing is normally done with the PEN, which distinguishes it from painting; but as fine writing began to demand embellishment and associated pictorial work evolved, artists who began with pen and ink soon found the need for effects produced with the BRUSH. Thus drawing evolved towards watercolour painting, and the distinction between the two sometimes tends to be arbitrary. Inks for Western printing have changed less as basic types, though printing methods have also evolved, and modern methods such as screenprinting do not distinguish sharply between ink and paint. Such developments have resulted in considerable artistic diversity, as well as imprecise terminology.

1. EAST ASIA.

(i) Painting and calligraphy. Both these art forms have a long history in China. They use the same instrument—the brush—and, to a large extent, the same black ink. Ink and brush together offer great flexibility and precision and in China have served as a constant means of expression for writing, drawing and painting (*see* CHINA, §§IV–V), while in the West several tools and materials have been produced

2. *Clearing out a Mountain Forest* by an anonymous Chinese artist, handscroll, ink on paper, Ming dynasty, 15th–16th centuries (Washington, DC, Freer Gallery of Art); detail showing the versatility of the ink and brush system, from the precise, careful strokes with which the animals and pine needles are rendered to the deliberately broken, uneven outlines of the demons and the very bold outlines and *cun* strokes of the tree-trunks and rocks

to meet the same ends. Although Chinese ink is arguably the most important single material in both painting and calligraphy, its use cannot be divorced from the characteristics of either the brush or the support (*see also* PAPER and SILK).

Good-quality Chinese ink results from grinding the inkstick with water on the inkstone to yield a dense black, free-flowing and stable dispersion. It is usual to grind at least as much ink as will be needed for the proposed work, as the necessity to regrind may result in differences of ink density. The dispersion may be diluted, either in the well of the inkstone or after pouring off the ink into a separate dish. Calligraphy is usually done with a fairly dense ink, though the brush may be charged fully to allow a 'wet' ink effect, or only partially to produce a 'dry' effect. A wide variety of types and styles of ink painting has been produced in East Asia. In the highly conservative tradition of Buddhist temple paintings, ink is used to form outlines that are filled in with colour. However, it is with paintings in ink only, or with slight additions of colour, that the full versatility of the material is revealed. Such painting is often held to be essentially linear in concept. Many types of ink lines and dots have been distinguished and named, and their uses in building up different painting features have been discussed in Chinese manuals, as in the *Jiezi yuan huazhuan* ('Mustard seed garden manual'), compiled by Wang Gai (1679–1701). Outlines are differentiated from shorter strokes used for modelling and shaping (*cun*) and from dots (*dian*). Lines may be regular and even or irregular, sometimes with spaces in the line (Chin. *pomo*: 'broken ink' styles). The latter techniques include such effects as 'splashed ink', in which the ink is applied with particularly broad and forceful movements of the brush, and 'flying white', in which a rapidly moving brush opens up to leave white streaks in the line. Many other ink techniques have been distinguished and classified. All linear methods may, of course, be performed with different ink densities, and true washes added to complete the modelling. The use of wash without outlines is one form of *mogu* (Chin.: 'boneless painting') and may sometimes be seen in renditions of flowers. Several techniques can be used in a single work (see fig. 2).

(ii) Printing. Traditional East Asian printing in black uses the same conventional Chinese ink as for calligraphy and painting, though not necessarily of the same quality. The

usual printing elements were wooden blocks carved in relief with the characters or design to be printed. The relief surface had the liquid ink applied with a brush and the piece of paper laid on it and burnished down firmly using either a brush or a burnisher. The earliest surviving examples of woodblock-printing appear to be Buddhist images or charms dating to the latter part of the 6th century AD. The earliest known example of the printed word is a Buddhist text fragment that was enclosed in 751 AD in a stone stupa in the temple of Pulguksa, in Kyŏngju, Korea.

Woodblock colour-printing uses a separate block for each colour, with black most often serving for the outline. In the traditional *ukiyoe* technique, a dispersion of the colorant in animal glue is placed on the block along with a little starch paste, and the two are mixed and spread over the printing surface with a soft brush. Shading effects are achieved either by wiping away part of the ink or by a preliminary graded damping of certain areas to decrease the amount of ink taken over those areas. Other printing methods have been incorporated. Gold can be applied by first printing a wet adhesive mixture, then sprinkling and brushing out gold powder over it. Mica could be applied in the same way, but a better method was to brush in the mica and glue mixture through a stencil.

2. WESTERN WORLD.

(i) Writing and drawing. Writing in the West usually involves ink applied with a pen rather than a brush. During the Middle Ages, up to about the 15th century, SCRIPT was an important art form. Illumination and embellishment of both religious and secular manuscripts were either executed with the same pen-and-ink system as used for the script or by the addition of colours and gilding. From the early Renaissance period, however, DRAWING became independent of textual illustration and evolved into an art form in its own right. Drawing, as opposed to script or calligraphy, thus became dominant in terms of the artistic use of ink, the emphasis on script diminishing in any case after the introduction of typographical printing in the 15th century. Iron-gall ink, already firmly established as the standard writing material, was naturally used for drawings, for which bistre and true sepia were also eventually available. These inks are all intermiscible and were almost certainly sometimes used as mixtures. Depending on the tool chosen, the same ink, in various dilutions, produced different effects. Pen and ink produces an incisive line, eliminating all but linear essentials and retains this character even when it is used to describe shading and texture. The brush-and-ink system is more flexible, allowing expressive variations, and is, of course, necessary for applying washes.

(ii) Printing. The WOODCUT, the main relief process, can use either water- or oil-based inks. Those that predate the development of typographic PRINTING in the mid-15th century may well have used a water-based carbon ink. Line-blocks, incorporated into text as illustrations, were inked at the same time as the text. The later development of half-tone blocks for printing continuous tones is almost entirely commercial in nature but in any event uses a similar ink, usually with a rather softer body.

Many ways of making intaglio plates have been devised, the most direct being ENGRAVING, which dates back to at least 1446, and ETCHING, from the early 16th century. The earliest engravings may well have been printed with a water-based carbon ink. However, intaglio printing was developed at roughly the same time as text printing from movable type and soon began using a similar oil-based ink. After an engraved or etched plate is inked, the surplus ink is wiped from the relief surface. To be successful, this requires an ink that is 'short', heavily pigmented and unlikely to streak during the wiping. A very fine pigment such as lampblack tends not to meet the last criterion. Earth pigments, such as umber, may be added to give a warmer tone. The properties and versatility of carbon pigments have made it easy to formulate black inks for a variety of intaglio applications, leading to a concentration on monochrome black. However, colours can perfectly well be printed, and in more recent times several methods of printing different colours from the same plate have been used. These have included the application of inks that do not mix readily to different areas of the same plate, which can then be printed in one pull through the press. A suitable ink will also enable an intaglio plate to be printed from the relief areas, so that the same plate can fill empty space with a desired colour.

In LITHOGRAPHY an image is created on a suitable surface (originally, and for the fine arts often still, a slab of limestone) using water-repellent crayons and inks, treating the surface to make the non-image parts receptive to water, damping and then inking the surface so that the oil-based ink 'takes' only on those parts where the image was drawn and is repelled from the water-receptive parts. The alternative procedure of drawing the image in water-soluble ink, desensitizing the stone or plate to water, and inking using a water-soluble ink was apparently also achieved by the inventor of lithography, Alois Senefelder, in the late 18th century but has not been used as a practical method.

The STENCIL method uses almost any kind of 'ink', while various kinds can be employed for SCREENPRINTING, providing they are compatible with the blocking-out method used on the silkscreen. A common blocking-out method is based on the use of a water-soluble glue, applied to the screen after the design has been drawn in a waxy resist. Water-soluble inks are incompatible with this technique as they would damage or dissolve the glue block. Oil paints or solvent-based poster paints have often been favoured as the inks. Solvent-based types have the advantage of being fairly quick-drying, so that successive colours can be printed without undue delay.

III. Conservation.

For the conservator the problems posed by inks fall into the following categories: lack of adhesion between ink and support; attack of the support material by the ink; changes in colour; and biological attack. Cleaning or repair procedures also have to take account of the properties of any ink present.

Lack of adhesion leads to flaking or powdering of the ink and can be a problem with some carbon-based types. Much depends on the quality of the binder and the extent

3. Guercino: *Shepherds Peering into a Chasm*, brush and brown (iron-gall) ink wash on paper, *c.* 1630 (Washington, DC, National Gallery of Art); detail, seen in raking light before treatment, showing the severe attack of the iron-gall ink on the underlying paper, which has resulted in losses and cracking of the support

to which the carbon has penetrated the support. East Asian paintings on heavily sized paper may have the ink lying entirely on the surface, when it sometimes tends to flake off. Treatments are based on reattachment and consolidation with various natural and synthetic adhesives. Some scroll paintings and calligraphy, especially from China, show 'smearing' of the ink as a result of over-vigorous cleaning or demounting operations in the past.

Iron-gall inks, being more or less acidic, are liable to attack paper supports, which are particularly vulnerable to acids. (Proteins such as vellum survive such conditions much better.) The amount of acid in ink varies according to the materials and method of preparation, and some papers have enough alkaline reserve to neutralize the acid present. Many drawings and passages of writing in iron-gall ink thus survive quite well, but some undergo serious attack (see fig. 3). White pigments used for highlighting, which are usually carbonates such as lead white, can also be destroyed by the underlying ink. Treatment usually calls for repair of the support and perhaps inpainting of losses. A number of deacidification procedures are available, but their feasibility depends on the individual case and is a matter for the experienced conservator.

Changes in colour, such as fading, affect iron-gall ink, bistre, true sepia and many coloured inks. It should be remembered that bistre and sepia have been imitated by other pigments, generally earth colours, that are much more lightfast. Many, perhaps most, Old Master drawings in ink have faded and no longer show the same colours as when they were produced. Such changes are irreversible and largely a function of light exposure, which should be limited for both drawings and prints. Faded writing in iron-gall ink can be chemically intensified; these methods, however, also change the ink's colour, making their use unacceptable for works of art. Some coloured inks fade quite badly, among the most sensitive being those in Japanese pre-Modern prints. Apart from inpainting faded areas, no longer considered an ethical conservation practice, there is no cure for these changes, only prevention.

Microbiological attack is not usually a serious problem but may occasionally happen. Such attack is inhibited by iron gallotannates. It is preventable by the avoidance of high atmospheric humidities, or by the use of fungistats such as thymol; it is treated by sterilizing the affected areas and removing any existing mould growth.

See also DRAWING, §VI, and PRINTS, §VI.

BIBLIOGRAPHY

E. S. Lumsden: *The Art of Etching* (London, 1925/*R* New York, 1962), pp. 85–98

B. March: *Some Technical Terms of Chinese Painting* (Baltimore, 1935)

C. A. Mitchell: *Inks: Their Composition and Manufacture* (London, 1937)

H. J. Plenderleith: *The Conservation of Prints, Drawings and Manuscripts* (London, 1937)

Mai-mai Sze, ed.: *The Mustard Seed Garden Manual of Painting: 'Chieh tzŭ yüan hua chuan', 1679–1701* (New York, 1956, rev. 1963)

J. Watrous: *The Craft of Old-master Drawings* (Madison, WI, 1957)

F. van Briessen: *The Way of the Brush* (Rutland, VT, 1962)

H. Franke: 'Kulturgeschichtliches über die chinesische Tusche', *Abh. Philos.-Hist. Kl. Bayer. Akad. Wiss.*, n. s., liv (1962) [whole issue]

M. Levey: 'Mediaeval Arabic Bookmaking and its Relation to Early Chemistry and Pharmacology', *Trans. Amer. Philos. Soc.*, n. s., lii/4 (1962), pp. 1–79 [commentary on and trans. of early 11th-century text by Ibn Badis]

——: 'Some Black Inks in Early Medieval Jewish Literature', *Chymia*, ix (1964), pp. 27–31

C. H. Bloy: *A History of Printing Ink, Balls and Rollers, 1440–1850* (London, 1967)

D. M. Mendelowitz: *Drawing* (New York, 1967)

F. Eichenberg: *The Art of the Print: Masterpieces, History, Techniques* (New York, 1976)

Pochoir: Flowering of the Hand-color Process in Prints and Illustrated Books (exh. cat., Santa Barbara, U. CA, A. Mus., 1977)

M. Zerdoun Bat-Yehouda: *Les Encres noires au moyen âge (jusqu'à 1600)* (Paris, 1983)

R. L. Feller, M. Curran and C. W. Baillie: 'Identification of Traditional Organic Colorants Employed in Prints and Determination of their Rates of Fading', *Japanese Woodblock Prints: A Catalogue of the Mary A. Ainsworth Collection* (exh. cat., Oberlin Coll., OH, Allen Mem. A. Mus., 1984), pp. 253–66

T. H. Tsien and J. Needham: *Chemistry and Chemical Technology, Pt 1: Paper and Printing* (1985), v of *Science and Civilisation in China* (Cambridge, 1954–)

R. van Gulik and N. E. Kersten-Pampiglione: 'A Closer Look at Iron Gall Ink Burn', *Restaurator*, xv (1994), pp. 173–87

JOHN WINTER

Inkhuk [Institut Khudozhestvennoy Kultury; Rus.: 'Institute of Artistic Culture']. Soviet institute for research in the arts that flourished from 1920 to 1926. Inkhuk was a dominant force in the development of Soviet art, architecture and design in the 1920s. Founded in Moscow in May 1920, with affiliations in Petrograd (now St Petersburg) and Vitebsk, it attracted many members of the avant-garde, especially LYUBOV' POPOVA and ALEKSANDR RODCHENKO; its key administrative positions were occupied by Vasily Kandinsky (Moscow), Vladimir Tatlin (Petrograd) and Kazimir Malevich (Vitebsk). At one time Inkhuk maintained contact with Berlin (through El Lissitzky and the journal *Veshch'/Gegenstand/Objet*), the Netherlands, Hungary and Japan, although it never really had the chance to develop these international connections. One of the principal aims of Inkhuk was to reduce the modern movements such as Suprematism and Tatlin's concept of the 'culture of materials' (*see* TATLIN, VLADIMIR) to a scientifically based programme that could be used for educational and research purposes—a development analogous to the initial endeavours of the Russian Formalist school of literary criticism, which attempted to analyse literature in terms of formal structures. In its aspiration to elaborate a rational basis for artistic practice, Inkhuk encouraged discussions on specific issues of artistic content and form, such as the debate on 'composition versus construction' in 1921.

The practical contribution of Inkhuk was twofold, for it investigated both the intrinsic, formal components of the artistic process ('laboratory art') and also its utilitarian application ('production art'). The former, advocated by Kandinsky, Inkhuk's first chairman, was soon rejected by the majority of the Inkhuk members as being too aesthetic and irrelevant to the needs of a technological society, especially when Kandinsky emphasized the need to take account of intuitive and occult responses as well as physical and material elements. Kandinsky soon left Inkhuk and in the summer of 1921 entered the commission for the establishment of the State Academy of Artistic Sciences (GaKhn), where he presented a version of the Inkhuk proposals.

Towards the end of 1920 Inkhuk was reorganized by Rodchenko, Varvara Stepanova, the sculptor Aleksey Babichev (1887–1963) and the musician Nadezhda Bryusova (1881–1951). Babichev and his Working Group of Objective Analysis compiled a new programme that gave primary consideration to scientific analysis and the material organization of the work of art. But even Babichev's call for an 'exact aesthetics' underwent serious criticism, since some artists felt that the very notion of the independent, 'beautiful' work of art was outmoded, and that the real justification of art lay in its functional applicability. This opinion, identifiable with the Productionists (or Productivists), was voiced by the most influential faction within Inkhuk and contributed directly to the rise and consolidation of Constructivism in 1921 (*see* CONSTRUCTIVISM, §2). The concern with concrete materials and the object (Rus. *veshch'*), shared by such artists as Georgy and Vladimir Stenberg and Rodchenko, and the ideological publications by its apologists Boris Arvatov, Osip Brik (who became head of Inkhuk in 1922), Aleksey Gan (1889–*c.* 1940), Boris Kushner and Nikolay Tarabukhin, left a deep imprint on the evolution of early Soviet culture.

The exhibition *5×5 = 25*, organized at Inkhuk by Rodchenko in September 1921, expressed the belief that studio art had to be replaced by a utilitarian creative process. Typical of the five works shown by each of the five participants (Alexandra Exter, Popova, Rodchenko, Stepanova and Aleksandr Vesnin) was Rodchenko's painted series of three monochrome panels in red, yellow and blue (all untraced). The artists' statements in the catalogue, such as Stepanova's that 'technology and industry have confronted art with the problem of construction not as contemplative representation, but as an active function', also epitomized the new ideas. At a plenary session of Inkhuk in November 1921, the majority of the participants, together with their associates, condemned studio painting as outmoded and useless and promoted new artistic values in the 'absoluteness of industrial art and Constructivism as its only form of expression'. As a result, many artists entered the world of industrial design and production: for example, Popova and Stepanova turned to textile design, Rodchenko to graphic design and photography and Vesnin to architecture.

Inkhuk was attached to GaKhn at the beginning of 1922 and quickly lost its autonomy, but its Petrograd affiliation, Ginkhuk (Rus. Gosudarstvenny Institut Khudozhestvennoy Kultury: 'State Institute of Artistic Culture'), assumed its formal status only in October 1924. An extension of the Museum of Artistic Culture in Petrograd, Ginkhuk was divided into five sections: Formal and Theoretical Systems under Malevich, Material Culture under Tatlin, Organic Culture under Mikhail Matyushin, General Ideology under Nikolay Punin and the Experimental Department under Pavel Mansurov. Although Ginkhuk was smaller than its Moscow counterpart, it attracted a number of Malevich's and Matyushin's most promising students and, through its exhibitions and tabulations, made an especially valuable contribution to the elaboration of colour theory (*see* MATYUSHIN, MIKHAIL). Ginkhuk was closed by official decree at the end of 1926.

BIBLIOGRAPHY

A. Z. Rudenstine, ed.: *Russian Avant-garde Art: The George Costakis Collection* (London, 1981)

C. Lodder: *Russian Constructivism* (New Haven, 1983)

S. O. Khan-Magomedov: *Rodchenko: The Complete Work* (London, 1986)

JOHN E. BOWLT

Inkyo. *See* NAGASAWA ROSETSU.

Inman, Henry (*b* Whitestown, nr Utica, NY, 28 Oct 1801; *d* New York, 17 Jan 1846). American painter. The son of an English land agent who had emigrated to America in 1792, he studied under an itinerant drawing-master before moving to New York with his family in 1812. Two years later he obtained an apprenticeship with the city's leading portrait painter, John Wesley Jarvis, drawn to the artist not only for his skill but also for his collection of pictures, which at that time included Adolf Ulric Wertmüller's *Danaë and the Shower of Gold* (1787; Stockholm, Nmus.). Inman worked closely with Jarvis, eventually accompanying him on his travels and serving more as a collaborator than an apprentice. Within this partnership Inman established a speciality in miniature painting. In 1823 he set up his own practice in New York and ceded miniature painting to his student and eventual partner Thomas Seir Cummings (1804–94).

Instrumental in founding the National Academy of Design in New York in 1825, Inman became vice-president of the new organization and found himself at the centre of the so-called 'Knickerbocker society', New York's rapidly developing cultural circle. He began to receive portrait commissions from prominent families and city government but also painted literary, historical and genre subjects, such as *Young Fisherman* (1829–30; New York, Met.). Many of these were engraved for illustration in journals and popular gift books, furthering his renown. He moved to Philadelphia in 1831 and joined the engraver Cephas G. Childs (1793–1871) as a partner in the lithographic firm Childs & Inman, providing meticulously drafted designs in pencil and watercolour that were reproduced by the firm's talented lithographer, Albert Newsam (1809–64), for example *Mount Vernon* (1832; see 1987 exh. cat., p. 175). He continued to paint portraits despite the presence of Thomas Sully, Philadelphia's reigning artist and an acknowledged master of women's portraits. Inman had greater success with male sitters, such as *John Marshall* (1831; Philadelphia, PA, Bar Assoc.), whom he portrayed with quiet yet forceful dignity, without the suave elegance of Sully's style.

After three years in Philadelphia, Inman returned to New York and from 1834 to 1839 was at the height of his career. For a while he was New York's leading portrait painter, yet he decried the public's 'rage for portraits', which prevented artists from exercising their full powers. Like Sully in Philadelphia, Inman in New York was called 'the American Lawrence', in reference to the English portrait painter Thomas Lawrence. His romantic style is marked by softened contours and a restrained brush, and he often gave his sitters a genial expression or glint of humour. His propensity towards sweetness in depictions of women and children, such as *Georgianna Buckham and her Mother* (1839; Boston, MA, Mus. F.A.), rarely slipped into sentimentality, a quality that never coloured his portraits of men, which are painted with vigour if not bravura (e.g. *Richard Channing Moore*, *c.* 1844; priv. col., see 1987 exh. cat., p. 24). His later subjects exhibit a clarified style that anticipated the insistent materiality of mid-19th-century American portraiture and the rise of a photographic standard of naturalism.

Financial reverses and deteriorating health contributed to a decline in Inman's productivity in his later years. Although no longer prosperous he continued to paint, creating some of his most accomplished and beautiful works, including *Angelica Singleton Van Buren* (1842; Washington, DC, White House Col.), and returning to literary compositions and such genre subjects as *Mumble the Peg* (1842; Philadelphia, PA Acad. F.A.). In 1844 he travelled to England, briefly reviving his spirits and health. After painting several portraits and visiting William Wordsworth at Rydal Mount, Cumbria, Inman considered remaining in London to pursue his career. He returned to New York in 1845, however, and died the following year.

BIBLIOGRAPHY

T. Bolton: 'Henry Inman: An Account of his Life and Work', *A. Q.*, iii (1940), pp. 353–75

The Art of Henry Inman (exh. cat. by W. Gerdts and C. Rebora, Washington, DC, N.P.G., 1987) [additional bibliog.]

SALLY MILLS

Inner Asia. *See* CENTRAL ASIA.

Innes, James Dickson (*b* Llanelli, 27 Feb 1887; *d* Swanley, Kent, 22 Aug 1914). Welsh painter. He studied first at Carmarthen Art School, and then at the Slade School of Fine Art, London, from 1906 to 1908, where he met Derwent Lees (1885–1931). Innes made several trips abroad in order to paint, most importantly to Collioure, France, in 1908 where he produced works such as *Town of Collioure* (1908; Bradford, Cartwright Hall), and again in 1911. He is, however, best known for his paintings of Wales. In 1907 he had begun a friendship with Augustus John, whose fascination with gypsies had drawn him to Wales and to a nomadic life. With John and Lees, Innes wandered over a remote and unfashionable part of North Wales in pursuit of a romantic freedom; Innes slept out of doors despite the fact that he had been diagnosed as a consumptive.

In works in an essentially Post-Impressionist style such as *Portrait of a Gypsy* (*c.* 1912; Aberdeen, A.G.) Innes developed a poetic intensity comparable to that found in Samuel Palmer's work. Using a notational method and painting for the most part on a small scale, as in *Bala Lake* (*c.* 1911; Manchester, C.A.G.), he developed a style notable for its lucidity and immediacy of touch. He is most often associated with the mountain he painted repeatedly, *Arenig* (*c.* 1911–13; Cambridge, Fitzwilliam), on the top of which he buried a casket of love letters from Euphemia Lamb. He painted at speed, using chopped brushstrokes to render foliage, clouds or light reflections on water. His career was cut short by his tuberculosis.

BIBLIOGRAPHY

James Dickson Innes (exh. cat., intro. J. Hoole; Southampton, C.A.G.; Cardiff, N. Mus.; London, F.A. Soc.; Manchester, C.A.G.; 1978)

Some Miraculous Promised Land: J. D. Innes, Augustus John and Derwent Lees in North Wales, 1910–12 (exh. cat., Llandudno, Mostyn A.G., 1982)

J. D. Innes, 1887–1914 (exh. cat., essay by C. Hampton; Llanelli, Pub. Lib., Nevill Mem. Gal., 1987)

FRANCES SPALDING

Inness, George (*b* Newburgh, NY, 1 May 1825; *d* Bridge of Allan, Central Scotland, 3 Aug 1894). American painter. He grew up in Newark, NJ, and New York City, and received his first artistic training with John Jesse Barker (*fl* 1815–56), an itinerant artist claiming to be a student of Thomas Sully. Between 1841 and 1843 Inness was apprenticed to the engravers Sherman & Smith in New York. More significant was his study in 1843 with Régis-François Gignoux, a student of Paul Delaroche and a recent immigrant from France, whose landscapes were delicate and sweet. Though Gignoux seems to have had little influence on the development of Inness's style, the Frenchman did provide him with a knowledge of European masters. Inness's early attraction to the Old Masters, especially to Claude Lorrain, is evident in his landscapes of the 1840s, and it prompted him to visit Italy in 1851–2. His *Bit of the Roman Aqueduct* (*c.* 1852; Atlanta, GA, High Mus. A.) is especially derivative of Claude in its classical composition and descriptive details.

In 1853 Inness returned to Europe for two years. In France he was impressed by the Barbizon school of landscape painting which had a decisive influence on his art. The Barbizon style became pronounced in his work after 1860 when he moved from New York, home to the dominant Hudson River school of landscape painting, to Medfield, MA, a village where he could work in isolation. Pictures such as *Clearing up* (1860; Springfield, MA, Smith A. Mus.; see fig.) have the sketch-like brushwork, loosely structured composition and rustic themes associated with the Barbizon work of Théodore Rousseau.

Inness travelled to Europe a third time in 1870, settling in Rome, where he painted *The Monk* (1873; Andover, MA, Phillips Acad., Addison Gal.). With its ambiguous spaces, enigmatic theme and brooding colours enlivened with chromatic flourishes, it is the most avant-garde American painting of the 1870s. Upon his return to America in 1875, Inness worked for a while in New Hampshire, where he painted such pictures as *Saco Ford: Conway Meadows* (1876; South Hadley, MA, Mount Holyoke Coll. A. Mus.), which shows a heightened confidence

George Inness: *Clearing up*, oil on canvas, 375×625 mm, 1860 (Springfield, MA, George Walter Vincent Smith Art Museum)

in the use of swirling, textured brushwork and a temporary concern for the majesty of open spaces.

Beginning in the late 1870s Inness turned to the thoughtful, personal, non-topographic landscapes that are the trademark of his late style. In many respects these landscapes were the result of his religious beliefs. As early as the mid-1860s, when he was living at Eagleswood, NJ, the site of the Raritan Bay Union utopian community, Inness began to study spiritualism. Spurred by Marcus Spring, leader of the Eagleswood community, and by the painter William Page, he became a disciple of the teachings of Emanuel Swedenborg. Believing that all material objects were spiritually charged and that the earthly realm was continuous with the heavenly, Inness arrived in the late 1870s and 1880s, after years of effort, at a uniquely spiritual imagery. Though still derived from Barbizon painting, Inness's late work is an effort to convert Swedenborgianism into art. Travelling between Montclair, NJ, his permanent home after 1878, and seasonal retreats in California, Florida and Nantucket, MA, where he went to improve his chronically poor health, he painted highly moving, personal pictures. In *Niagara Falls* (1893; Washington, DC, Hirshhorn) he depicted the Falls dissolved in mists of iridescent colour, in contrast to the highly representational Hudson River style in which it had traditionally been painted, for instance by Frederic Church (1857; Washington, DC, Corcoran Gal. A.). Instead of conveying Church's image of power, Inness's *Niagara Falls* expresses a brooding inner passion through heavy paint surfaces and dematerialized forms. In *Home of the Heron* (1893; Chicago, IL, A. Inst.) Inness constructed a twilight world of hazy forms cast halfway between substance and nothingness. Space and detail were virtually eliminated in favour of a flat and indistinct landscape of softly vibrating colours and gauzy paint surfaces. Though there is nothing in Swedenborg's writings to account for Inness's late imagery in a specifically iconographic way, pictures like this are redolent of the 'correspondence' Swedenborg claimed existed between the material and the spiritual worlds.

Inness's early works received mixed critical reviews. In the 1840s and 1850s he was often criticized for not adhering to the prevailing taste for the Hudson River school. Instead of imitating nature, the critics claimed, Inness was imitating art. Though Hudson River painters such as Asher B. Durand were equally influenced by Claude, in the critics' eyes Inness made the act of imagination unacceptably overt by stressing broad handling of paint, eccentric colours and palpable atmosphere. Nonetheless, Inness's early pictures were promoted by George Ward Nichols (1831–85), a devotee of French art and the owner of the Crayon Gallery in New York. Inness's early patrons included Ogden Haggerty, who financed his first trip to Europe, and the Rev. Henry Ward Beecher (1813–87). The critical response to Inness's art improved greatly during the 1880s and 1890s, though the American Pre-Raphaelites, led by the critic Clarence Cook, condemned his lack of interest in replicating nature. In his later years Inness attracted the attention of Thomas B. Clarke, the leading collector of American art, who purchased works by Inness.

BIBLIOGRAPHY

E. Daingerfield: *George Inness: The Man and his Art* (New York, 1911)
G. Inness jr: *The Life, Art and Letters of George Inness* (New York, 1917)
E. McCausland: *George Inness: An American Landscape Painter, 1825–1894* (New York, 1946)

L. Ireland: *The Works of George Inness: An Illustrated Catalogue Raisonné* (Austin, TX, 1965)
N. Cikovsky jr: *George Inness* (New York, 1971)
A. Werner: *Inness Landscapes* (New York, 1973)
N. Cikovsky jr: *The Life and Work of George Inness* (New York, 1977)
George Inness (exh. cat. by N. Cikovsky jr and M. Quick, Los Angeles, CA, Co. Mus. A., 1985)

PAUL J. STAITI

Innocent III, Pope [Lotario dei Conti di Segni] (*b* Gavignano, nr Anagni, ?1160–61; elected 8 Jan 1198; *d* Perugia, 16 July 1216). Italian pope and patron. He was educated in Rome, Paris and Bologna and wrote several major theological and philosophical works, but as Pope his influence was most widely spread through his many sermons and letters. He reasserted control over the Papal States and notably over Rome itself by 1208. Outstanding among his religious concerns were crusades against pagans, heretics and infidels and the development of Christian unity through Church reform, for which in 1213 he convened the Fourth Lateran Council, which was then held in 1215. He also encouraged some of the new religious groups and can justifiably be regarded as the founder of the Franciscans and Dominicans.

Evidence of Innocent's artistic patronage comes from the *Gesta Innocentii Tertii*, a biography written by an anonymous cleric in the Papal Chancery before 1209. Innocent's taste was clearly influenced by a journey he made in 1187 to Grandmont, near Limoges, where seven great champlevé basilica shrines stood on the high altar. In 1190 he became Cardinal-Deacon; within two years he had restored the fabric of his titular church SS Sergio e Bacco (destr. *c.* 1562), near the Arch of Septimius Severus in Rome, and, when Pope, he donated a champlevé basilica shrine of Limoges work (*see* LIMOGES, §1(i)), a silver-gilt chalice and rich altar vestments.

Innocent's considerable personal fortune derived from his time as Cardinal and especially from his maternal relations, the Scotti. He showed his political awareness when, with his wealthy brother Riccardo, and in the well-established tradition of Italian tower building, he erected early in his pontificate the strategically placed Tor de' Conti, a fortified compound and great brickwork tower by the Forum of Nerva. Its base has striped bands of small black and white stones, a facing common in the Campagna, and is valued for its striking decorative qualities. The political situation within Rome and the Tower Wars of 1199–1205 between patrician factions led Innocent to enclose the papal palace at the Vatican within walls, erecting towers at the gates. He strengthened the earlier construction of Eugenius III and enlarged the papal suite, building on three floors in small tufa blocks, faced on one side with brickwork (*opus saracinescum*). A five-storey corner tower was constructed overlooking the south side of the Cortile del Pappagallo.

A former Canon of St Peter's, Innocent centred much of his interest on the basilica. He granted the canons the right to strike pilgrim badges in tin or lead and to keep the proceeds. His decoration of St Peter's should perhaps be seen in the perspective of the Fourth Lateran Council (Gautier). He protected the confessio of St Peter with a bronze screen enriched with Limoges enamel. On the new protective covering for the Niche of the Pallia, he placed an inscription rich in theological significance, identifying himself as the patron. He reworked the apse mosaic, with the figures of himself as Bishop of Rome and the Roman Church (*Ecclesia Romana*) flanking a gemmed throne on which stood the Lamb of God bleeding into a chalice. The metrical inscription along the outer rim of the mosaic was designed to celebrate the basilica and its clergy, attributing to St Peter's the title 'Mother of all churches' previously given to S Giovanni in Laterano alone. To further his ideal of creating co-equal seats at the Lateran and the Vatican, he raised St Peter's to cathedral status.

At the Lateran the Sancta Sanctorum was described by Innocent's biographer as being richer in precious objects than had ever before been seen. Innocent especially venerated the image of the Saviour there, known as the *Acheiropoita* ('icon made without human hands'), and added a silver cover, which concealed all but the head and neck. He protected the relics beneath the altar with a grille and provided a new reliquary for the heads of SS Peter and Paul (now Rome, Vatican, Cappella di S Pio V). He repaired the roof of the Lateran Baptistery and added extra summer chambers (*camerae estivae*) to the Lateran Palace.

Innocent's charitable artistic interest extended in 1204 to the building of the Ospedale di S Spirito (destr. 1471) on the site of the former Saxon school by the Tiber, endowing its church of S Maria in Sassia with rich books and ornaments. In 1208 he instituted the liturgical procession of the Veronica on the second Sunday after Epiphany from St Peter's to S Spirito. His most extensive project was the creation of the convent of S Sisto Vecchio for which he donated 50 ounces of royal gold and 1100 pounds. Begun in 1207, the campaign was still incomplete in 1216. The 5th-century basilica was partially demolished, and the ground-level of the nave was raised by 3.45 m. The new church and convent became part of Innocent's plan for a new, large convent in which to house all the nuns of Rome; merged with the nearby convent of S Maria in Tempulo, S Sisto became the first convent of Dominican nuns in Rome.

Innocent's biographer lists more than 45 separate entries for his donations to churches in Rome and Lazio, ranging from gifts of 100 pounds to the Cistercian monasteries of Fossanova (nr Priverno) and of 200 ounces of gold to Casamari (nr Veroli) for the construction of the church there, to many small acts that he considered to be of religious importance. Among these, he presented to all the churches of Rome that lacked them silver chalices (133 in all), valuable vestments, orphreys and precious liturgical ornaments. Innocent saw all his acts of patronage, both great and small, as unifying the Church and glorifying God.

BIBLIOGRAPHY

Gesta Innocentii P.P.III (before 1209); ed. in *PL*, ccxiv (1855), pp. xvii–ccxxviii
D. Redig de Campos: 'Les Constructions d'Innocent III et de Nicolas III sur la colline vaticane', *Mél. Archéol. & Hist.: Ecole Fr. Rome*, lxxi (1959), pp. 359–76
V. J. Koudelka: 'Le *Monasterium tempuli* et la fondation dominicaine de San Sisto', *Archv Fratrum Praedicatorum*, xxxi (1961), pp. 5–81
J. Ruysschaert: 'Le Tableau Mariotti de la mosaïque absidale de l'ancien S Pierre', *Rendi. Pont. Accad. Romana Archeol.*, lx (1967–8), pp. 295–317

M. M. Gautier: 'La Clôture émaillée de la Confession de Saint Pierre au Vatican, lors du Concile de Latran IV, 1215', *Synthronon*, ii of Bibliothèque des Cahiers Archéologiques: Art et archéologie de la fin de l'antiquité et du moyen âge, ed. A. Grabar (Paris, 1968), pp. 237–46
M. Bonfioli: 'La diacona dei SS Sergio e Bacco nel Foro Romano', *Riv. Archaeol. Crist.*, l (1974), pp. 55–85
R. Krautheimer: *Rome: Profile of a City, 312–1308* (Princeton, 1980)
C. Rebecchini: 'Il ritrovamento del palazzo d'Innocenzo III in Vaticano', *Boll. Mus. & Gal. Pont.*, ii (1981), pp. 39–52
J. E. Barclay Lloyd: 'Masonry Techniques in Medieval Rome *c.* 1080–*c.* 1300', *Pap. Brit. Sch. Rome*, iii/1 (1985), pp. 225–77
M. Maccarrone: 'La *Cathedra Sanct Petri* nel medioevo: Da simbolo a reliquia', *Rivista di storia della Chiesa in Italia*, xxxix (1985), pp. 349–447

BRENDA M. BOLTON

Innocent VIII, Pope [Cibo, Giovanni Battista] (*b* Genoa, 1432; elected 29 Aug 1484; *d* Rome, 25 July 1492). Italian pope and patron. Though he was a poor administrator and left the church in a state of disarray, he did not neglect the renovation of Rome and the Vatican begun by his predecessors. He commissioned the ciborium of the Holy Lance for St Peter's (fragments, Rome, Grotte Vaticane), rebuilt S Maria in Via Lata and continued the restoration and embellishment of S Giovanni in Laterano. At St Peter's he continued the Benediction loggia begun by Pius II, built a palace adjoining the atrium for the Curia, erected the fountain to the right of the obelisk in St Peter's Square and in 1486 commissioned from Gian Cristoforo Romano a statue of *St Peter* for the steps in front of the façade (untraced; possibly unexecuted).

Innocent's major architectural project at the Vatican was the Villa Belvedere that he built between 1485 and 1487 at the northern end of the Vatican hill. In the 16th century the villa was connected with the Vatican palace by Bramante's Cortile del Belvedere. The villa was altered by Pius VI, and its loggia is now the Galleria delle Statue of the Musei Vaticani. The original exterior was crowned by a crenellated parapet. Its long central segment containing the loggia and framed by shallow projecting blocks at either side had its prototype in Late Antique imperial villas. The loggia is decorated with a rich stucco vault in the manner of Roman vaults in the then recently discovered Golden House of Nero and with illusionistic frescoes by Pinturicchio, of which only fragments remain, imitating the mural decorations in ancient Roman villas. These transformed the loggia into an airy hall with views of Monte Mario to the north and of imaginary landscapes 'in the Flemish manner' (Vasari) of Rome, Milan, Genoa, Florence, Venice and Naples to the south. In the lunettes Pinturicchio painted pairs of putti with musical instruments and the Cibo arms. The interior of the villa's chapel contained frescoes and an altarpiece with the *Baptism* by Andrea Mantegna (destr.). From his accession Innocent had sought to secure the services of Mantegna, who was in the employ of Francesco Gonzaga, 4th Duke of Mantua; Mantegna finally came to Rome in 1486. He was there again in 1487 and is recorded as leaving the city in 1490.

Innocent VIII was the first pope to enter into diplomatic relations with the Ottoman empire, when in 1489 he agreed to detain Sultan Bayezid II's brother and potential rival, Jem, in Rome, in return for an annual payment of 40,000 ducats and the gift of the relic of the Holy Lance that was supposed to have pierced Christ's side at his Crucifixion. The reception of the relic by Innocent VIII in Rome on 31 May 1492 marked the high point of his pontificate. To house it he commissioned a tabernacle with a fresco by Pinturicchio (completed 1495; destr.), and in the seated image that Antonio Pollaiuolo sculpted for his tomb (1492–8) at St Peter's he is shown holding the relic of the Holy Lance aloft in his right hand.

BIBLIOGRAPHY

G. Vasari: *Vite* (1550, rev. 2/1568); ed. G. Milanesi (1878–85)
L. Pastor: *Geschichte der Paepste seit dem Ausgang des Mittelalters*, iii (Freiburg, 1895, 11/1955), pp. 207–335
E. Muentz: *Les Arts à la cour des papes Innocent VIII, Alexandre VI, Pie III* (Paris, 1898), pp. 13–138
D. Redig de Campos: *Il Belvedere di Innocenzo VIII in Vaticano* (Vatican City, 1958)
S. Sandstroem: 'The Programme for the Decoration of the Belvedere of Innocent VIII', *Ksthist. Tidskr.*, xxix (1960), pp. 35–75
J. Schulz: 'Pinturicchio and the Revival of Antiquity', *J. Warb. & Court. Inst.*, xxv (1962), pp. 35–55
D. R. Coffin: 'Pope Innocent VIII and the Villa Belvedere', *Studies in Late Medieval and Renaissance Painting in Honor of Millard Meiss*, ed. I. Lavin and J. Plummer (New York, 1978), pp. 88–97
J. Alexander: 'Fragments of an Illuminated Missal of Pope Innocent VIII', *Pantheon*, xxxviii (1980), pp. 377–82

HELLMUT WOHL

Innocent X, Pope. *See* PAMPHILI, (1).

Innocent XI, Pope. *See* ODESCALCHI, (1).

Innocent XII, Pope [Pignatelli, Antonio] (*b* nr Spinazzola, Puglia, 13 March 1615; elected 12 July 1691; *d* Rome, 27 Sept 1700). Italian pope and patron. Born into an aristocratic family in southern Italy, he became a cardinal (1681) under Innocent XI, obtained the archiepiscopal see of Naples in 1686 and was elected Pope in 1691. He took a lively interest in the arts, most notably in architecture. In Rome he inaugurated significant architectural programmes whose execution ran concurrently during his pontificate. Carlo Fontana was employed as his official architect. The first commission was for a new baptismal font in the Cappella Battesimale, St Peter's, a project that he put out to competitive tender, inviting Rome's leading artists (including Fontana, Carlo Maratti, Domenico Guidi and Mattia de Rossi) to submit designs and models (Bonnani; Dowley; Braham and Hager). However, in the event this caused delay while the Pope decided that almost none of the proposals were satisfactory. Despite his efforts to supervise expenditure wisely, the commission became a complex decorative scheme, requiring a team of artists and involving expensive renovations throughout the chapel. It was not until 1696 that Fontana was finally appointed to design and oversee works on the new font, the chapel architecture and its decoration, including the bronze Pignatelli coat of arms (*c.* 1698; *in situ*). Fontana's reports on the project (*Descrizzione della nobilissima cappella*, 1697; *Verdico racconto*, MS., 1704) describe his often difficult relationship with his patron.

During 1692 Fontana was engaged to restore the harbour and aqueduct at Civitavecchia (completed 1702), and the Pope's subsequent inspection of the site (1696) was commemorated in engravings by both Pietro Sante Bartoli (Donati, figs 276–7) and Fontana (*Veduta de' nuovi aquedotti di Civitavecchia*, 1699). In 1692 Fontana also erected Innocent XII's unpretentious tomb monument in

St Peter's (destr.), but following the Pope's death considered embellishing the memorial with a full-length standing figure of the pontiff (drawings, *c.* 1700; Windsor Castle, Berks, Royal Col.). In 1693 Innocent XII assumed control of the Ospizio di S Michele (Ripa Grande, Rome), a hospice for orphaned boys founded in 1686 by the Odescalchi. He considerably enlarged the premises, at first under the direction of Mattia de Rossi, and after 1695 under Fontana. The Pope's inspection of the site on 64 occasions bears witness to his commitment to the project and to his close scrutiny of his architectural projects. In the same year (1693) he rejected Fontana's proposals for the new Sacristy at St Peter's.

With the purchase of the Palazzo di Montecitorio (formerly Ludovisi) in 1694, Innocent XII began the most important architectural and administrative reform of his pontificate: a new complex to house the Curia Innocenziana, alongside the palazzo, which accommodated the customs office and the newly centralized offices of the papal tribunals. The drawn-out building campaign was begun in 1694 under Mattia de Rossi, but Fontana assumed overall control by the end of that year. The Curia was to prove his most arduous and elaborate undertaking for the Pope (see Fontana, 1694 and 1708).

In 1696 Innocent XII commissioned the marble and bronze tomb monument of *Christina of Sweden* (1697–1702; Rome, St Peter's) from Fontana in collaboration with Jean Théodon, Lorenzo Ottone and Giovanni Giardini. Despite his much-criticized demolition (1697) of the famous Tor di Nona Theatre, that had been designed (early 1670s) by Fontana under the patronage of Queen Christina, Innocent XII was interested in the preservation of monuments. According to Bellori, he appointed Maratti guardian of the Vatican frescoes by Raphael and Michelangelo. Numerous portraits of the Pope were executed, but among the most important visual records of his pontificate are the bronze medallions (London, BM; Oxford, Ashmolean) commemorating his reign and his achievements.

BIBLIOGRAPHY

C. Fontana: *Alla santità di nostro signore Innocenzo XII: Discorso del cavalier Carlo Fontana sopra il Monte Citatorio* (Rome, 1694)

F. Bonnani: *Numismata summorum pontificum templi vaticani fabricam* (Rome, 1696, 2/1700)

C. Fontana: *Descrizione della nobilissima cappella del fonte battismale nella Basilica Vaticana* (Rome, 1697)

——: *Discorso sopra l'antico Monte Citatorio* (Rome, 1708)

G. P. Bellori: *Le vite de' pittori, scultori et architetti moderni*, iii (Pisa, 1821), pp. 210–11

U. Donati: *Artisti ticinesi a Roma* (Bellinzona, 1942)

L. von Pastor: *History of the Popes*, xxxii (London, 1957), pp. 584–91

F. H. Dowley: 'Carlo Maratti, Carlo Fontana, and the Baptismal Chapel in Saint Peter's', *A. Bull.*, xlvii (1965), pp. 57–81

F. Borsi, A. Gambuti and G. Limiti: *Immagini di Montecitorio* (Rome, 1970)

Il Palazzo di Montecitorio (exh. cat., ed. M. del Piazzo; Rome, Pal. Montecitorio, 1970)

A. Braham and H. Hager: *Carlo Fontana: The Drawings at Windsor Castle* (London, 1977) [incl. Fontana's *Verdico racconto* (MS., 1704), pp. 46–51]

□

Innocent XIII, Pope [Conti, Michelangelo] (*b* Poli, 13 May 1655; elected 1721; *d* Rome, 7 March 1724). Italian pope and patron. He studied at the Collegio Romano and then became chamberlain to Alexander VIII (*reg* 1689–91). He became a priest under Innocent XII and was successively appointed governor of Ascoli, Frosinone and Viterbo and nuncio in Switzerland and then in Lisbon. He became a cardinal in 1706 and on his election as Pope took the name of his ancestor INNOCENT III (*reg* 1198–1216). Despite the brevity of his pontificate Innocent XIII was able to enrich the Vatican library with East Asian manuscripts and a valuable collection of medals bought from Cardinal Alessandro Albani. In Rome he had the Ponte Sant'Angelo, the Vatican obelisk and the church of S Eustachio restored. He also commissioned decorations (e.g. four garden scenes; 3.5×4 m, 1722) for the Palazzo Quirinale from Giovanni Paolo Panini and gave his support to the construction of Francesco de' Sanctis's Spanish Steps (1723–6) below Trinità dei Monti on the western slopes of the Pincian Hill.

BIBLIOGRAPHY

L. von Pastor: *Geschichte der Päpste*, xv (Freiburg, 1931), pp. 389–460

A. Blunt: *Guide to Baroque Rome* (London, 1982)

T. A. Marder: 'The Decision to Build the Spanish Steps: From Project to Monument', *Projects and Monuments in the Period of the Roman Baroque*, ed. H. Hager and S. S. Munshower (Philadelphia, 1984), pp. 82–99

OLIVIER MICHEL

Innocenzo da Imola [Francucci, Innocenzo] (*b* Imola, *c.* 1490; *d* Bologna, *c.* 1545). Italian painter. He probably trained with Francesco Francia in Bologna *c.* 1508 and then with Mariotto Albertinelli in Florence for a period between 1510 and 1515. His earliest known work, the *Virgin and Child with SS Sebastian, Roch, Cosmas and Damian*, signed and dated 1515, is in the Chiesa Archipretale at Bagnara, Ravenna. It is a classical composition of Florentine derivation, with the Virgin and Child appearing on a cloud above the four saints. His Florentine training is even more evident in the *Virgin and Child with SS John, Apollinaris and Catherine and a Bishop*, signed and dated 1516, for S Apollinare at Cásola Valsenio, near Bologna.

In 1517 Innocenzo moved to Bologna, where he painted frescoes for the chapel of the Sacristy of S Michele in Bosco, representing the *Assumption of the Virgin*, the *Annunciation*, the *Resurrection* and *St Michael* (damaged). The use of Florentine models is enriched here by a monumental, classicist accent suggested by Raphael's *Ecstasy of St Cecilia* (1515; Bologna, Pin. N.), which was in Bologna from that time. A Raphaelesque prototype, *St Michael* (Paris, Louvre), directly inspired the *Virgin in Glory with St Michael the Archangel between SS Peter and Benedict* (1521–2; Bologna, Pin. N.), also painted for S Michele in Bosco. In 1526 Innocenzo began working on commissions for Faenza. He painted an altarpiece, the *Virgin and Child with Saints and the Archangel Raphael with Tobias* (1527; Forlì, Pin. Civ.), for S Francesco. The formula of Florentine grace plus the more modern Raphaelesque classicism appears again in the *Virgin with Child and Saints* (1532; St Petersburg, Hermitage). One of the best works by Innocenzo in Bologna, the altarpiece of the *Virgin and Child with the Eternal Father and Saints* (dismantled), painted for S Mattia, introduces a new attention to colour, which approaches the work of Girolamo da Carpi. Its original form has been reconstructed by Zeri.

Among the works of Innocenzo's maturity was the important commission of 1533 for S Giacomo Maggiore in Bologna: the altarpiece of the *Virgin and Child with Saints* (*in situ*) and the frescoes representing the *Assumption of the Virgin, Christ and St Paul* (*in situ*). A greater freedom in his use of models and increased attention to colour modulation can be seen in the *Crucifixion* (1539; Bologna, S Salvatore), although the faces, especially that of St John, still reflect the influence of Raphael. Innocenzo's artistic career ended with an ambitious project, the decoration of the Palazzino della Viola in Bologna, begun after 1541, where for the first time he dealt with mythological subjects including *Diana and Actaeon* and *Apollo and Marsyas* (damaged; some *in situ*), and here again he looked to the model of Raphael. His pupils included Prospero Fontana.

BIBLIOGRAPHY

Thieme–Becker: 'Francucci, Innocenzo'

G. Vasari: *Vite* (1550, rev. 2/1568); ed. G. Milanesi (1878–85), v, p. 185; vii, p. 406

C. C. Malvasia: *Felsina pittrice* (1678); ed. G. Zanotti (1941), p. 118

R. Galli: 'Innocenzo da Imola: I tempi, la vita, le opere', *La Mercanzia*, vi/2–4 (1951)

Mostra delle opere di Innocenzo da Imola (exh. cat. by R. Buscaroli, Imola, Pin. Civ., 1951)

R. Longhi: *Opere complete*, v (Florence, 1956), pp. 161, 191

F. Zeri: 'Two Fragments by Innocenzo da Imola', *J. Walters A.G.*, xxxiii–xxxiv (1970–71), pp. 59–63

D. Ferriani: 'Innocenzo Francucci detto da Imola', *Pittura bolognese del '500*, ed. V. Fortunati Pietrantonio, i (Bologna, 1986), pp. 59–66 [good bibliog.]

FRANCESCA CAPPELLETTI

Innsbruck. Austrian city, capital of the Bundesland of the Tyrol, with a population of *c.* 128,800 (1994). It is situated at the confluence of the Sill and Inn rivers, in a basin-shaped widening of the Inn valley. The valley, which connects the north and south Tyrol, extends from Bressanone in Italy to Innsbruck by the Brenner Pass and has thus been since Roman times an important trade and traffic link between Italy and the countries north of the Alps. Unlike those of other Austrian provincial capitals, the old centre of Innsbruck has remained essentially Late Gothic in style.

1. History and urban development. 2. Art life and organization. 3. Buildings.

1. History and urban development.

(i) To 1420. The first settlements in the Innsbruck basin, from the Bronze Age to the high Middle Ages, were on the slopes and rim of the Inn valley. The flat central plains were avoided by settlers until the 12th century. Thus the Roman military station was situated on the southern edge of the valley at Wilten (Lat. Veldidena), where the Chorherrenstift was founded *c.* 1138. The Bavarian counts of Andechs established a trading settlement on the narrow left bank of the Inn (*c.* 1165–70) and built the first bridge across the river, hence the name Innsbruk (bridge over the Inn), recorded in documents of 1167–83. The Markgraf Berchtold V of Andechs-Istrien (*d* 1188) acquired land on the right bank of the Inn in 1180, moved his market there and enlarged it. This area is now known as the Altstadt; St Jakobskirche was built there (1180–1266) as a daughter church of Wilten, no doubt in Romanesque style. Berchtold and his son of the same name built a castle (destr.) to the west, close to the bridge, and surrounded the new market with a circular wall radiating from the castle. Gradually the old market on the left bank became a municipal suburb. In 1281 the city was enlarged by the Neustadt, reaching from Maria-Theresien-Strasse to the Altes Landhaus; later (by 1440) it incorporated the southernmost part of the Neustadt and the Saggen to the east of the Altstadt, towards the River Sill.

Shaped in an irregular semicircle, the Altstadt has a diameter formed by the right or southern bank of the Inn: the area formerly served as a fortified bridgehead as well as a market. There was formerly a gate-tower at the bridge, and another at the southern end of the main street, the Herzog-Friedrich-Strasse (as it has been called since 1873), leading to the suburbs. Other gate-towers were at the eastern end of the Hofgasse (the Saggentor) and the western end of the Seilergasse (the Pickentor, erected *c.* 1340), leading to the landing stage for rafts and timber on the banks of the Inn and also to the fields of Wilten. The Rathaus (from 1358) is the oldest in the Tyrol. Around the city wall was a narrow outer ward and a wide moat. In 1363 the Tyrol passed into the hands of the Habsburg Dukes of Austria. The Altstadt was destroyed by fire in 1390.

(ii) 1420–1665. The favourable location of Innsbruck led to its adoption as a provincial capital in 1420, when Duke Frederick IV (*reg* 1406–39) purchased two houses on the Stadtplatz and had them converted into his residence, the Neuer Hof. The presence of a court between 1420 and 1665 had not only political, economic and cultural advantages but also led to the construction of several important buildings and monuments. Frederick's son Sigismund (*reg* 1446–90), who found the Neuer Hof too modest, erected (*c.* 1450–60) the spacious Hofburg on the eastern edge of the fortified Altstadt. In the Altstadt itself most of the present-day buildings are from the 15th and 16th centuries (see fig. 1). During the 15th century the Romanesque St Jakobskirche was replaced by a fine Gothic church. The arcades (from *c.* 1420) along the Herzog-Friedrich-Strasse, the broad main street of the Altstadt, originated as the houses gradually had their upper floors projected forward, while the recesses provided by the vaulted arcades at ground-level preserved the original circulation area to its full extent, at least for pedestrians. Looking over the arcades is the Stadtturm, erected by the citizens in 1442–50 as an annex to the Rathaus. The numerous rectangular or polygonal oriels, with their projecting shape and rich relief decoration, give life and variety to the otherwise smooth façades.

Maximilian I, who ruled the Tyrol from 1490 to 1519, had the Hofburg further enlarged and adorned by the Wappenturm (now incorporated into the south tower of the main building during the 18th-century works). This work was presumably executed by his master builder and mason, Nikolaus Türing the elder (*d* 1517/18); the picturesque inner court is depicted in two informative watercolours (*c.* 1494–5; Vienna, Albertina) by Dürer. In 1494–6, on the occasion of his second marriage, he converted the older rectangular oriel at the Neuer Hof into the princely

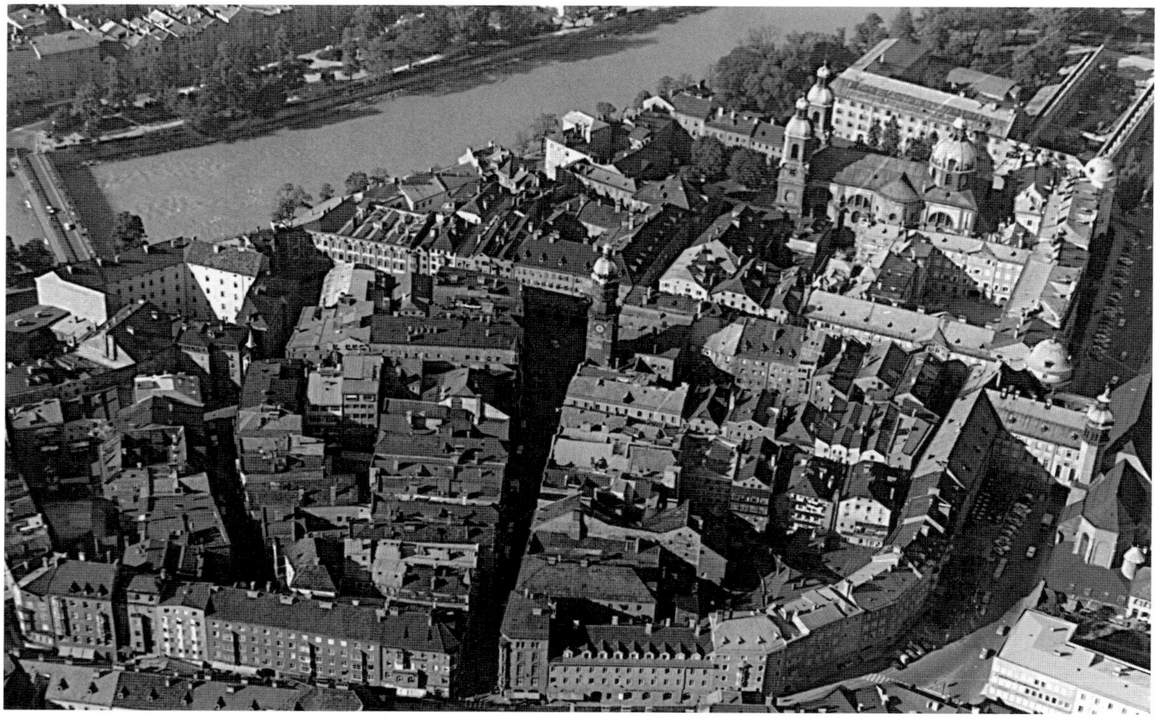

1. Innsbruck, aerial view of the Altstadt from the south-east, showing the bridge over the River Inn on the left, St Jakobskirche (1717–24), the Hofburg (from 1453) and the Hofkirche (1553–63) on the right, and the Rathaus (from 1358) in the centre

splendour of the Goldenes Dachl, a lavishly decorated Gothic loggia set over an oriel window and surmounted by a roof composed of burnished copper tiles. In one of the two central reliefs of the loggia, on the second floor, Maximilian is represented in profile with his two wives: the bust of Maria Bianca Sforza of Milan (1472–1510) appears next to him, while that of his first wife, Mary, Duchess of Burgundy, is in the right-hand corner. The escutcheons below—the arrangement of which was largely altered after Maximilian became Holy Roman Emperor in 1508—indicate the territories to which he laid claim. The primary function of the Goldenes Dachl was to mark the presence of the ruler in the city, even during periods of absence. It also established the vogue for decorating oriels with reliefs. The reliefs of tourneys and minstrels on the corner oriel of the Katzunghaus (*c*. 1500–50) are a vivid reminder that the square in front of the Goldenes Dachl and the Rathaus was once used as a tiltyard.

As Innsbruck was untouched by war, from 1500 the owners of houses adjoining the city wall on the inside were allowed to let doors and windows into it, so that the fabric, albeit pierced in places, remained basically intact. Between 1500 and 1506 Maximilian built an arsenal on the River Sill. The 16th-century buildings within the Altstadt include the Kolbenturm, the Deutschordenshaus (house of the Teutonic Knights, 1532), the Trautsonhaus (1541), the Innsbruck Gymnasium (1562) and the Altes Regierungsgebäude (old government house) of 1569, which was rebuilt in Baroque style after the earthquake of 1689. Among other important buildings and monuments are the Hofkirche (1553–63; *see* §3(i) below); the religious houses, endowed by the princes and their consorts, of the Jesuits (1561), Franciscans (1564), Capuchins (1593) and Servites (1614–16); Schloss Ambras (remodelled by Archduke Ferdinand from 1565; *see* §3(ii) below); the legislative building, the Ständehaus (1615); the bronze tomb (1620) of *Archduke Maximilian III* (*reg* 1602–18) in St Jakobskirche, executed by Heinrich Reinhart (1575–1629) to the design of Caspar Gras; the Leopold Fountain (1623–30) with the bronze equestrian statue of *Archduke Leopold V* (*reg* 1619–32), in the Rennweg, which was also designed by Caspar Gras and built by Heinrich Reinhart and Friedrich Reinhart; and the Claudia Hall (1645) in the wing behind the Altes Regierungsgebäude. It was thanks to the court that the first opera house in German-speaking lands was founded at Innsbruck in 1629–30, with a permanent company for operatic as well as theatrical performances (see Senn). The Baroque Mariahilfkirche, a domed building of 1647–9, is by Christoph Gumpp.

(iii) From 1665. In 1665 the younger Tyrolean line died out with Sigismund Francis, and the Tyrol was then governed from Vienna. Innsbruck University (now Leopold-Franzens Universität) was founded in 1669 by Emperor Leopold I to give the populace a sound Catholic education. The famous Annasäule by Cristoforo Benedetti (*b* 1660) was erected in 1704–6 in the Maria-Theresien-Strasse near the Landhaus (see fig. 2). After earthquake damage St Jakobskirche was rebuilt (1717–24) in Baroque style after plans by Johann Jakob Herkomer (1648–1717). The Landhaus, the finest Baroque palace in the city, was

built in 1725–8, to the designs of Georg Anton Gumpp, the chief Innsbruck architect of the time (for illustration *see* GUMPP, (4)). Though Gothic in origin, the Helblinghaus in Herzog-Friedrich-Strasse was adorned with a richly decorated Rococo façade *c.* 1730. Maria-Theresa, consort of the Emperor Francis I (*reg* 1745–65) and herself ruler of the Austrian hereditary domains, rebuilt the Hofburg in two phases (1754–6; 1763–73) in the contemporary Rococo taste. Innsbruck thus assumed for the last time the brilliance of an Austrian court that in reality had ceased to exist. In 1756 the moat around the city walls was filled in (and now serves as a street area with single-storey shops).

In 1844–6 the court theatre, the Tiroler Landestheater, was built by Giuseppe Segusini as a successor to the 17th-century opera house. In 1849 Innsbruck was constitutionally proclaimed the provincial capital, a status previously given to Meran (now Merano, Italy). Ecclesiastically, Innsbruck had traditionally belonged to the diocese of Brixen in south Tyrol. However, the partition of 1919 following World War I put Brixen (now Bressanone) into Italy, and ultimately Innsbruck was raised to a see with St Jakobskirche as its cathedral (1964). From 1904 various villages were incorporated into Innsbruck: Wilten (1904), Pradl (1904), Amras (1938), Hötting (1938), Mühlau (1938), Arzl (1940), Vill (1942) and Igls (1942). In 1944–5 more than half of the buildings in Innsbruck were damaged by bombing. Rebuilding continued for many years, and in addition some new suburbs were created (from 1952). After World War II the city became an international sporting, cultural and conference centre, with a congress hall built in 1973.

BIBLIOGRAPHY

J. Probst: *Geschichte der Universität in Innsbruck seit ihrer Entstehung bis zum Jahre 1860* (Innsbruck, 1869)
O. Trapp: *Die Kunstdenkmäler Tirols in Not und Gefahr, 1938–1945* (Innsbruck, 1947)
H. Hammer: *Kunstgeschichte der Stadt Innsbruck* (Innsbruck, 1952)
F. Huter: *Die Matrikel der Universität Innsbruck* (Innsbruck, 1952)
W. Senn: *Musik und Theater am Hof zu Innsbruck: Geschichte der Hofkapelle vom 15. Jahrhundert bis zu deren Auflösung im Jahre 1748* (Innsbruck, 1954)
F.-H. Hye: 'Zur Geschichte des Goldenen-Dachl-Gebäudes, des "Neuen Hofes" zu Innsbruck', *Tirol. Heimatbl.*, xxix–xxx (1966), pp. 149–59
V. Oberhammer: *Das Goldene Dachl zu Innsbruck* (Innsbruck, 1970)
E. Egg: *Das Landhaus der Tiroler Stände in Innsbruck* (Innsbruck, 1971)
F.-H. Hye: *Stadtpfarrkirche und Dom zu St Jakob in Innsbruck* (Innsbruck, 1974)
——: 'Die Städte Tirols am Ausgang des Mittelalters', *Beitr. Gesch. Städte Mitteleuropas*, iii (1974), pp. 155–72
——: 'Meran und Innsbruck: Das Problem der Landeshauptstadt in Tirol', *Alpenregion und Österreich*, ed. E. Widmoser and H. Reinalter (Innsbruck, 1976), pp. 47–55
——: 'Die alten Städte Tirols: Grundzüge ihrer Entstehungsweise und ihres Erscheinungsbildes', *Innsbrucker Geographische Studien*, vi (Innsbruck, 1979), pp. 57–73
——: 'Bundesland Tirol', *Österreichisches Städtebuch*, ed. A. Hoffmann, v (Vienna, 1980), pp. 71–132
——: 'Innsbruck: Geschichte und Stadtbild bis zum Anbruch der Neuen Zeit', *Tirol. Heimatbl.* (1980) [issue dedicated to 800th anniversary of Innsbruck]
——: 'Die "Gauhauptstadt" Innsbruck in der Zeit von 1938–1945', *Tirol, 1938: Voraussetzungen und Folgen* (Innsbruck, 1988), pp. 56–73

FRANZ-HEINZ HYE

2. ART LIFE AND ORGANIZATION. The most important patrons in the Middle Ages were the rulers of the Tyrol, who lived in Innsbruck from 1420 to 1665; Maximilian I (*see* HABSBURG, §I(3)) and Ferdinand II (*see* §3(ii) below) were particularly important. Metal founding flourished in the 15th and 16th centuries (*see* AUSTRIA, §IX, 2); Hans Seelos (1452–1514), Stefan Godl, Peter Löffler (1488–1530) and Gregor Löffler (1490–1565) cast bells, cannons and statues, while Ludwig Seelos (*d* 1486) was a master armourer. Painters active in the 16th century included Sebastian Schel (Scheel) (*fl c.* 1479–1554), Paul Dax the elder (1503–61) and Wolfgang Polhamer (*fl c.* 1540–*c.* 1580).

2. Innsbruck, Maria-Theresien-Strasse, view looking north, with the Annasäule (1704–6) in the centre

The presence of ALEXANDER COLIN from 1562 contributed to the rise of Innsbruck as an important sculptural centre. Painting was influenced by Egid Schor, who brought the style of Cortona to the town and taught Kaspar Waldmann. The rebuilding of St Jakobskirche (1717–24; now the cathedral) provided commissions for a variety of artists, including Cosmas Damian Asam, Egid Quirin Asam, Caspar Gras, Johann Georg Grasmeir (1691–1751) and Nikolaus Moll (1676–1754), whose son, Balthasar Ferdinand Moll, also executed sculptures for Innsbruck. Matthäus Günther (1705–88), Johann Michael Strickner (1720–59) and Martin Knoller (1725–1804) painted altarpieces and frescoes for the town's churches.

In 1772 the painter Johann Peter Denifle (1739–1808) founded a drawing school. In the 19th century the Tiroler Glasmalereianstalt (1861) and the state Gewerbliche Zeichen- und Modellierschule (1877; now Höhere Technische Bundes-Lehr- und Versuchsanstalt) were founded. Innsbruck was adorned with such works as the monument to *Andreas Hofer* (erected 1893) on the Bergisel by Heinrich Natter (1844–92) and the fountains by Franz Santifaller (1894–1953) in front of the Landschaftliche parish church (1926), while Raphael Thaler (1870–1947), Ernst Nepo (1895–1971) and Oswald Haller (1908–89) frescoed the façades of numerous houses.

In the first half of the 20th century a variety of artistic organizations was established, including the Künstlerbund Tyrol (1903) and the private school of painting (1919–63)

run by Anton Kirchmayr (1887–1965). Frescoes by Rudolf Stolz (1874–1960) in the railway station were destroyed (1943–4) and replaced by those of Max Weiler (*b* 1910). Hans Andre (1902–91) provided sculptures (1941–60) for the façade of the cathedral. The city has a variety of public museums (e.g. Schloss Ambras, Tiroler Landesmuseum Ferdinandeum, Tiroler Volkskunstmuseum) and commercial galleries (e.g. Stadtturm-Galerie, Theresiengalerie). Increasingly, banks and insurance companies sponsor galleries and exhibitions, and in 1989 the first of a series of arts festivals known as *Innsbruck Sommer* was held. Since 1991 the Galerie im Andechshof has provided a free venue for young artists to exhibit their work.

BIBLIOGRAPHY

H. Hammer: *Kunstgeschichte der Stadt Innsbruck* (Innsbruck, 1952)

E. Egg: *Kunst in Tirol*, 2 vols (Innsbruck, Vienna and Munich, 1970–71)

Malerei und Graphik in Tirol, 1900–1940 (exh. cat., Innsbruck, Kongresshaus; Vienna, Sezession, 1973)

M. Krapf: *Die Baumeisterfamilie Gumpp* (Vienna, 1979)

Barock in Innsbruck (exh. cat. by E. Egg and G. Amman, Innsbruck, Tirol. Landesmus., 1980)

W. Auer and K. Gamper: *Tirol: Schöpferisches Land* (Innsbruck, 1984)

JOSEFINE JUSTIĆ

3. Buildings.

(i) Hofkirche. The Hofkirche (1553–63), immediately to the east of the Hofburg, is a hall church with a nave and two aisles all of the same height, articulated by red marble columns. There is a polygonal choir and a single side tower. Late Gothic elements (the nave, aisles and choir) are skilfully combined with Renaissance ones (the porch and the nave columns) in a design attributed to the Italian architects Andrea Crivelli (*fl* from 1528) and Alessio Longhi (*fl* from 1522) and executed by the master builder Nikolaus Türing the younger (*fl* from 1549). The Heiligen Kreuz-Kirche at Augsburg served as a model.

The Hofkirche owes its fame to the fact that it houses the monument to *Maximilian I*, although it was in fact the wish of the Emperor that the tomb be erected in the Schlosskirche at Wiener Neustadt, where he is actually buried (*see* HABSBURG, §I(3)). The first-floor location of that church, however, above the entrance passage of the castle, made this technically impossible, and Emperor Ferdinand I decided to locate the monument to his grandfather in the Hofkirche, where it stands in the nave. A massive marble sarcophagus rests in the centre, flanked by 28 bronze statues, ranged between the nave columns, representing the Emperor's ancestors and contemporaries, to a scheme devised by Maximilian himself in 1502. The figures (1509–50) were cast in various workshops, mostly in Innsbruck, and are represented as mourners carrying funeral torches (for attributions *see* AUSTRIA, §IV, 2 and fig. 20).

Archduke Ferdinand of Austria, Count of Tyrol, commissioned Giovanni Luchese to add the Silberne Kapelle (1577/8, 1586/7); in it are the tombs of *Archduke Ferdinand* and his first wife, *Philippine Welser* (*d* 1580), both by Alexander Colin. The present Baroque stucco ceiling of the church dates from the repair of the vault following earthquake damage in 1689.

BIBLIOGRAPHY

E. Egg: *Die Hofkirche in Innsbruck: Das Grabdenkmal Kaiser Maximilians I und die Silberne Kapelle* (Innsbruck, 1974)

F.-H. Hye: 'Der Inhalt der Turmkugel der Innsbrucker Hofkirche und das Erdbeben am 22 Dezember 1689' *Tirol. Heimatbl.*, lvi (1981), pp. 44–53

——: 'Neues zur Geschichte des Innsbrucker Erdbebens am 22.–24. Dezember 1689 und des Innsbrucker Franziskanerklosters', *Innsbruck. Hist. Stud.*, ix (1986), pp. 91–9

FRANZ-HEINZ HYE

(ii) Schloss Ambras. The castle, which consists of several buildings, is situated in a park south of Innsbruck (*see* fig. 3). The name Ambras is primarily associated with the collection of armour, *objets d'art* and curiosities assembled there by Archduke Ferdinand, ruler of the Tyrol from 1564 (*see* HABSBURG, §I(9)). He had laid the foundations for this collection during his period as Governor of Bohemia (1547–64). In 1563 he acquired the 10th-century Schloss Ambras and converted it into a Renaissance pleasure palace. The Hochschloss (the original castle) was remodelled from 1565 onwards to form the Archduke's family residence. It is a massive, four-winged building with an inner courtyard painted in grisaille. In 1572 the Spanischer Saal was built. The first monumental (43 m long, 10 m wide and 5 m high) and free-standing banqueting hall north of the Alps, it has rich interior decoration: a carved wooden ceiling and inlaid doors (1572) by Conrad Gottlieb (*fl* from 1560), grotesques attributed to Dionys Hallaert (*fl* 1570), portraits of the Landesfürsten by Giovanni Battista Fontana (ii), and plasterwork by Antonis van Brackh (*see* AUSTRIA, fig. 24). On completion of the Spanischer Saal work began on the building of the Unterschloss with its so-called Kornschütt, which housed the library, antiquarium and small armoury at first-floor level. Thereafter the museum buildings were built. Originally, these consisted of three blocks of differing heights. A fourth building, by an unknown architect, was added in 1586 and removed again in the 19th century.

The complete museum consisted of five rooms, one behind the other, for the armoury collection, and an adjoining wing housing the *Kunst- und Wunderkammer.* A partial inventory of 1583 records the contents and display of the armouries, while the inventory made in 1596 after Archduke Ferdinand's death lists the entire collection. These records show that a tour of the museum began at the first armoury, where the Archduke kept contemporary jousting armour as well as racing equipment and weaponry inherited from his great-grandfather Emperor Maximilian I. Since much of the armour was still in use, the room had the double function of storeroom and museum. Next, beyond a transverse wooden wall, came the Historische Rüstkammer, where, besides suits of armour belonging to Maximilian I, the boyhood armour of King Philip I (1478–1506) and his son Emperor Charles V was exhibited. Among curiosities displayed here were suits of armour—complete with figurine and costume—formerly belonging to the court giant Giovanni Bona and the court dwarf Thomerle (untraced). In the corner to the right a few steps led up to the third and largest room, which was Archduke Ferdinand's personal armoury. Here an imposing row of nine suits of war armour and seven suits of parade armour were displayed in chronological sequence, facing each other on horseback, while along the sides of the room stood suits of jousting armour on wooden crosses together with festival masks and costumes. From the ceiling hung

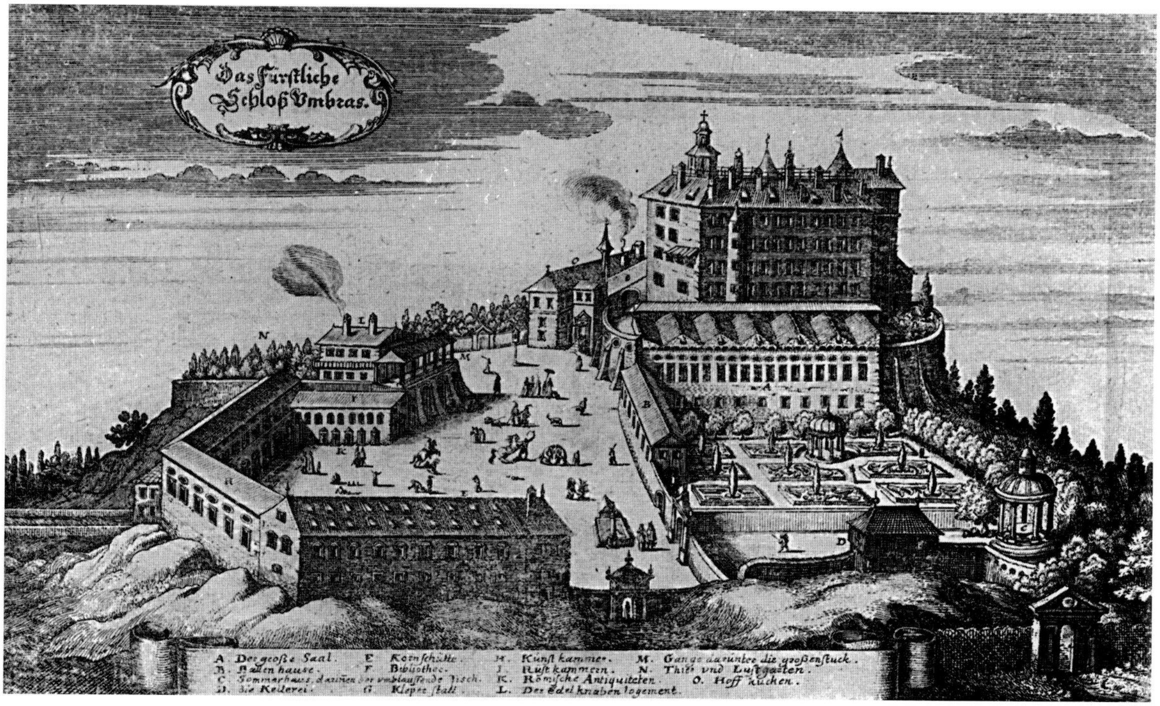

3. Innsbruck, Schloss Ambras, remodelled from 1565; engraving attributed to Matthäus Merian (i), from *Topographia provinciarum Austriacarum* (Frankfurt am Main, 1649)

12 banners with depictions of Hercules, the emblem of Archduke Ferdinand.

The real heart of the collection lay in the fourth room, the Heldenrüstkammer. Here the armour and weapons of emperors and kings were arranged according to the rank and merit of their owners in individual showcases, while suits belonging to minor aristocrats were kept in large cases. Above them hung the armour and weapons of commanders, with small portraits beside them as documentation. For this fourth room, which is also known as the Ehrliche Gesellschaft, Ferdinand devised an illustrated catalogue, the *Armamentarium heroicum* (1601; Ger. trans., 1603), with engravings by Giovanni Battista Fontana (ii) and text by Jakob Schrenck von Notzing. The last of the five rooms was the Türkenkammerl, formed by dividing off a small compartment in the third room. This contained objects of Turkish provenance, booty from Archduke Ferdinand's Turkish campaign of 1556 and gifts from the imperial commander Lazarus Schwendi (1522–84).

In the *Kunst- und Wunderkammer* the exhibits were grouped according to their material in 18 cases, placed back to back along the main axis of the room and painted to harmonize with their contents. The walls were covered with portraits, and natural-history specimens were also on display. The exhibits received the best possible lighting from adjacent windows. The Ambras *Kunstkammer* was the first museum north of the Alps to be organized from an aesthetic point of view for public viewing. Among the most impressive sections were the exotica (including Pre-Columbian feather pieces from America and Chinese Ming porcelain), natural and carved corals, turned work in wood and ivory, figure scenes in glass, gold- and silverwork (e.g. Cellini's salt cellar, 1540–43; Vienna, Ksthist. Mus.) and the collection of objects inherited from Emperor Maximilian I and his father Frederick III. Some of these treasures were taken to Vienna in 1806 as a result of the Napoleonic wars and are now in the Kunsthistorisches Museum. In 1918 Schloss Ambras became the property of the Republic of Austria; the museum is a branch of the Kunsthistorisches Museum, Vienna.

BIBLIOGRAPHY

A. Primisser: *Die kaiserlich-königliche Ambraser Sammlung* (Vienna, 1819/*R* Graz, 1972)
L. Luchner: *Denkmal eines Renaissancefürsten* (Vienna, 1958)
Die Kunstkammer, Führer durch das Kunsthistorische Museum, Kunsthistorisches Museum Sammlungen Schloss Ambras (Innsbruck, 1977)
E. Scheicher: *Die Kunst- und Wunderkammer der Habsburger* (Vienna, Munich, and Zurich, 1979)
Die Rüstkammern, Führer durch das Kunsthistorische Museum, Kunsthistorisches Museum Sammlungen Schloss Ambras (Vienna, 1981)
A. Auer: 'Das Inventarium der Ambraser Sammlungen aus dem Jahr 1621', *Jb. Ksthist. Samml. Wien*, lxxx (1984), pp. 191–312
E. Scheicher: 'The Collection of Archduke Ferdinand II at Schloss Ambras: Its Purpose, Composition and Evolution', *The Origins of Museums*, ed. O. Impey and S. MacGregor (Oxford, 1985), pp. 29–38
Österreichisches Künstler-Lexikon, xlvii (Vienna, 1986), pp. 509–614

ELISABETH SCHEICHER

Innuit. *See* INUIT.

Inpainting. Term used in the conservation of paintings or objects for the toning or imitative matching of an area of paint loss, without obscuring any original paint.

RUPERT FEATHERSTONE

Installation [Environment]. Term that gained currency in the 1960s to describe a construction or assemblage conceived for a specific interior, often for a temporary period, and distinguished from more conventional sculpture as a discrete object by its physical domination of the entire space. By inviting the viewer literally to enter into the work of art, and by appealing not only to the sense of sight but also, on occasion, to those of hearing and smell, such works demand the spectator's active engagement. As an art form, installations are particularly associated with movements of the 1960s and 1970s such as Pop art, Nouveau Réalisme, Minimalism, conceptual art and process art, but in theory they can be conceived within the terms of virtually any style.

The notion of the installation can be traced back to the second half of the 19th century and in particular to Richard Wagner's concept of the *Gesamtkunstwerk* as a synthesis of sensory impressions overwhelming the spectator. Whistler's decorative scheme of the same period, *Harmony in Blue and Gold: The Peacock Room* (1876–7; Washington, DC, Freer), originally designed for the dining-room of his patron F. R. Leyland, sought a similar immersion of the spectator in an experience of beauty encompassing the whole of his or her field of vision; as such it went beyond the impulse to decorate, narrate or instruct, characteristic of church or palace architecture during the medieval period or in the Renaissance.

The most direct predecessors of the installation in its narrower sense, however, are to be found in the international Surrealist exhibitions held during and after the 1930s, notably in London (1936) and at the Galerie Beaux-Arts in Paris (1938); on the latter occasion, music and smells pervaded an entirely enclosed space that included coal sacks on the ceiling, assemblages, plants and paintings.

One of the earliest installations, in the historically precise sense of the term, was Yves Klein's *The Void* (Paris, Gal. Iris Clert, 1958), a presentation of the empty white interior of a commercial gallery; a year later another sculptor associated with Nouveau Réalisme, Arman, created *Fullness* in the same gallery interior by filling the space with rubbish so that it could be viewed only through the outside window. In New York some of the first installations, such as Claes Oldenburg's *The Street* and Jim Dine's *The House* (both exh. New York, Judson, 1960), each assembled from discarded items found in the streets of the city, were

Installation by Claes Oldenburg: *Bedroom Ensemble*, wood, vinyl, metal, artificial fur, cloth and paper, 3.00×6.50×5.25 m, 1963 (Ottawa, National Gallery of Canada)

closely linked to performance-art events known as Happenings, which also sought to expand the realm of art by drawing the audience into the physical environment as a total entity. One of the most influential of the artists involved with both Happenings and installations was Allan Kaprow; for his installation *Words* (New York, Smolin Gal., 1961) he combined numerous sheets and rolls of paper containing random arrangements of words with music played by several record-players, allowing spectators to walk right through this chaotic jumble. Joseph Beuys's arcane installations, such as *Room Sculpture*, a collection of his earlier works gathered together for the specific gallery space at *Documenta IV* (Kassel, 1968), emerged from a similar background of actions and Happenings.

In contrast to these temporary or changeable displays, installations that were more fixed in form were made by other artists as early as the 1960s. In works such as *The Beanery* (1965; Amsterdam, Stedel. Mus.), for example, Edward Kienholz created detailed environments of real places through which the spectator could walk. Modelled on an actual bar in Los Angeles and built to half-scale, it reproduced its architectural source together with assembled figures, most of them heads in the form of clocks and tape-recorded sounds. As permanent, self-contained structures, such installations do not relate closely to the surrounding gallery space but could in principle be housed anywhere. *She*, a temporary work created by Niki de Saint-Phalle, Jean Tinguely and Per Olof Ultvedt for an exhibition held in 1966 at the Moderna Museet in Stockholm, was similarly enclosed. It consisted of a huge reclining female figure, which could be entered between the legs, with a variety of rooms with machines and further installations inside.

Oldenburg followed his installation *The Street* with *The Store*, housing it in a rented shop in New York for two months from December 1961. In this space, which functioned as both a studio and a commercial gallery, that is to say as source of production and as retail outlet, he sold sculptural replicas of ordinary manufactured objects and items of food displayed as if they formed part of a typical shop. This equation of commerce and mass production with the work of art, central to Pop art, was pursued also by Andy Warhol in an installation of sculptures replicating stacked supermarket cartons (New York, Stable Gal., 1964). At the Leo Castelli Gallery, New York, in April 1966, Warhol created two separate installations: one consisting of a room containing only silver-coloured helium-filled pillow shapes known as *Silver Clouds*, the other of walls covered in Warhol's *Cow Wallpaper*, each in its way marking the artist's removal from his work and renunciation of traditional painting. Oldenburg, for his part, created *Bedroom Ensemble* (1963; Ottawa, N.G.; see fig.), an arrangement of furniture and other items in synthetic materials and false perspective: the ultimate Pop-art interior.

In the late 1960s and 1970s installations became a favoured form for artists working against the notion of the permanent, and therefore collectable, art object. It was essential, for instance, for Minimalists such as Dan Flavin, who modified the viewer's perception of interior spaces through the precise placement of fluorescent light tubes of different colours, or Carl André, whose exhibitions of floor sculptures were designed in part to articulate the architectural setting in which they were housed. Installations of a temporary or changeable nature, such as Richard Serra's *Splashing* (1968; for illustration *see* PROCESS ART) or Eva Hesse's *Rope Piece* (1970; New York, Whitney; for illustration *see* SOFT ART), were produced by artists involved with process art. Even land artists, when working indoors, found installations to be a natural form for their work; Walter de Maria's *New York Earth Room* (1977; New York, Dia A. Found.), a pristine-white gallery space filled with a deep layer of dirt, is perhaps the best-known example. In CONCEPTUAL ART, installations assumed paramount importance, given the fact that in replacing the art object with an idea it was only through its specific context that it could take form. In such works the installation as a complete entity, rather than as a collection of objects, becomes the work of art.

BIBLIOGRAPHY

A. Kaprow: *Assemblages, Environments and Happenings* (New York, 1966)
Räume und Environments (exh. cat., Leverkusen, Schloss Morsbroich, 1969)
A. Henri: *Environments and Happenings* (London, 1974)

□

Institute of Artistic Culture. *See* INKHUK.

Instruments, musical. *See* MUSICAL INSTRUMENTS.

Insula [Lat.: 'island']. Multi-storey Roman apartment building. *Insulae* appeared in Rome as early as the 3rd century BC. These were insubstantial wood and mud structures, up to ten storeys high, that were largely replaced after the fire of AD 64. Building codes under Nero prescribed safer brick-faced concrete structures of only four to five storeys. Similar buildings later supplanted single-family houses as the principal form of accommodation in large, densely populated cities throughout the Empire.

The origin of the *insula* is unclear. It appears to have been a pragmatic response to increased population density. The best-preserved *insulae* (mainly 2nd century AD) occur at Ostia, the port of Rome (see fig.). These buildings, generally three to five storeys high, often included ground-floor shops or workshops. They do not follow any specific plan but vary considerably in form and scale. Some are small and free-standing, while others are vast amalgams occupying an entire city block. The Insula delle Volte Dipinte (AD 120) had only one flat on each of its three floors, while the Caseggiato degli Aurighi (AD 140) was a much larger building with a central porticoed courtyard, a ground floor mostly given over to commercial uses and apartments of varying sizes on several floors above. Larger still were such complexes as the Casa a Giardino quarter (AD 128), where several *insulae* surrounded a large rectangular courtyard containing two free-standing *insulae* and most of the apartments had standardized plans. Since *insulae* housed all but the wealthiest classes, the standard of accommodation varied considerably, from crowded rooming houses to large luxury apartments. Most were rented out by absentee landlords, though the proprietor might occupy a lavish ground-floor apartment.

The *insulae* at Ostia, like those built after AD 64 in Rome, were of brick-faced concrete, with floors resting

Insula, Ostia, 2nd century AD; reconstruction

on either concrete vaults or wooden beams. Stone, concrete or wooden staircases provided access from the street or courtyard to upper levels, while large windows provided light and air. Some apartments also had balconies, supported on cantilevered wooden beams or stone corbels and vaults. Roofs were of terracotta tiles, and external walls were often of exposed brick decorated with mass-produced terracotta mouldings, though some may have been stuccoed. Doorways were given particularly elaborate treatment, often being framed by brick pilasters or engaged columns. *Insulae* were, however, essentially utilitarian structures with simple, uniform exteriors that gave Roman cities their characteristic appearance and provided a backdrop for more monumental public and religious buildings.

Although the forms of individual *insulae* and the nature of the accommodation they provided were diverse, apartments within them generally shared the same basic layout. Most of the best-preserved examples at Ostia (on the lower floors) are organized around a narrow hall (*medianum*) with one long wall facing a street or courtyard, letting in light through several large windows. Rooms opened on to the other three sides of the *medianum*, the largest and most important being at either end. The latter were particularly elaborately decorated, with floor mosaics and wall and ceiling frescoes. The remaining rooms were small and windowless and were probably used for sleeping. Some more luxurious apartments had two levels, with large, double-height end rooms and a private stairway to the upper floor above the *medianum* and bedrooms.

BIBLIOGRAPHY

B. M. Felletti Maj: 'Ostia, la casa delle Volte Dipinte: Contributo all'edilizia privata imperiale', *Boll. A.*, 2nd ser., xlv (1960), pp. 45–65

J. E. Packer: 'The Insulae of Imperial Ostia', *Mem. Amer. Acad. Rome*, xxxi (1971) [whole volume]

B. N. Frier: *Landlords and Tenants in Imperial Rome* (Princeton, 1980)

G. Hermansen: *Ostia: Aspects of Roman City Life* (Edmonton, 1981)

C. M. Watts and D. Watts: 'Geometrical Ordering of Garden Houses at Ostia', *J. Soc. Archit. Hist.*, xlvi (1987), pp. 265–76

CAROL MARTIN WATTS

Insular [Hiberno-Saxon] **art.** Term commonly applied to the art of Britain and Ireland from *c.* AD 500 to the 9th century; the style lingered in Ireland until *c.* 1000. Accounts of the period have been dominated by controversies, fuelled by national loyalties, about whether particular works were manufactured in Ireland, Northumbria or Scotland. As a neutral term, Insular avoids the danger of exaggerating geographical distinctions and underlines the fact that north Britain and Ireland belonged within the same cultural and ecclesiastical sphere.

1. Introduction. 2. Metalwork. 3. Manuscript illumination. 4. Sculpture.

1. INTRODUCTION. The period was one of great cultural ferment, which began with the establishment of the Anglo-Saxons in England and the migration of the Irish into western Scotland (the kingdom of Dal Riada). The period also coincided with the spread of Christianity throughout the British Isles. Much (but by no means all) of the surviving art was made in the service of the Church: it includes a series of sumptuously decorated Gospel books, much fine liturgical metalwork and numerous elaborate stone crosses and cross slabs. The most outstanding secular art of the day survives in the form of personal jewellery.

An important development in Insular art occurred in 563 with the foundation by St Columba (*c.* 521–97) of IONA, a monastery that served as a mission station for northern Britain. During the course of the 7th century, the Saxon kingdoms of England were converted to Christianity, in part by Irish missionaries and in part by missions associated with Rome. The Christian faith was successfully implanted in Northumbria after the foundation of a bishopric at Lindisfarne (635), established by Aidan (*d* 651), an Irishman from Iona. Irish missionary activity remained strong in England for much of the 7th century. The Irish connection worked both ways, for the historian Bede (673–735) commented on the number of Anglo-Saxons who travelled to Ireland to study the Christian faith. Yet the Anglo-Saxon Church increasingly looked for guidance to the Mediterranean world, particularly after Theodore of Tarsus (*c.* 602–90) became Archbishop of Canterbury in 669. Benedict Biscop (*c.* 623 –*c.* 690), founder of the twin monasteries of Monkwearmouth (674) and Jarrow (681–2), made no fewer than five visits to Rome, returning to Northumbria with books, panel paintings and relics. The Pictish peoples of Scotland were also drawn into this expanding Christian culture. As early as 565, St Columba had travelled from Iona on a missionary expedition to the Moray Firth, and Christianity appears to have been well established in Pictland by 710, when King Nechton (*reg* 706–24) sought the help of masons from Northumbria.

The travels of ecclesiastics and their craftsmen, together with the artefacts they made, led to a remarkable cultural fusion, combining the pre-Christian traditions of northern Europe with the post-Classical traditions of the Mediterranean. Following the collapse of Roman rule in Britain, there had been a revival of Celtic curvilinear styles (circles, spirals, triskeles etc), and this phase, more accurately known as Ultimate La Tène (*see* CELTIC ART), formed one of the basic ingredients of Insular art. With the consolidation of the Saxon kingdoms in the early 7th century, Germanic animal ornament began to exert an influence. At the same time, a taste for complex patterns of interlace was introduced, the exact background of which remains controversial. During the 8th century, Insular artists exploited the older traditions in a highly imaginative way, adding a variety of animal and human forms to the existing repertory. Insular ornament is usually highly disciplined, with many patterns being dependent on an underlying geometrical structure that was exploited to give the impression of relentless movement and energy. Many of the forms employed were the product of extraordinary technical proficiency, a point well illustrated in metalwork. The ornament reflects a taste for minute and highly intricate designs, almost as if this was an aesthetic aim in its own right. It is clear that metalwork, and the status associated with it, had a powerful impact on the other arts. Indeed the incorporation of non-Christian ornament into Gospel books appears to have been a means of enhancing the status of the Gospels, by equating them with the secular treasures of the time.

Throughout the period, abstract values tended to predominate, even in the depiction of religious subjects, and there was a heavy emphasis on colour, line and pattern. Yet where Mediterranean influence was strong, figural compositions could be surprisingly Classical in appearance. Most of the inspiration for the Christian figural subjects was derived from the Mediterranean world, particularly from Italy, although some scholars believe that the Carolingian *renovatio* also had a significant influence after 800. Indeed, much research has been devoted to establishing the type of models, particularly books, that found their way north to the monasteries of Britain and Ireland. When confronted with Classical models, the general instinct of the Insular artist was to ignore the representational elements and to reduce the human form to two-dimensional patterns.

Many aspects of Insular art are poorly understood. Much remains to be discovered about the working methods of the scribes and artists, their training and the length of time it took to complete the illuminated manuscripts. The exact function of such sumptuous Gospel books as the Lindisfarne Gospels (London, BL, Cotton MS. Nero D. IV) and the Book of Kells (Dublin, Trinity Coll. Lib., MS. 58) remains unclear, as do the circumstances in which they were commissioned and the type of audience they addressed. Many of the Christian subjects in the manuscripts and sculpture raise difficult issues of interpretation, particularly in relation to contemporary biblical exegesis. With regard to metalwork, questions of sequence and date continue to raise intractable problems, which have tended to deflect attention away from broader issues, such as the social context of the lavishly decorated brooches. Among other issues is the extent to which pre-Christian decorative forms retained their pagan associations and the extent to which abstract and zoomorphic themes were interpreted in Christian terms. Indeed, the relationship between the various arts and the mixture of pagan and Christian themes are among the most fascinating aspects of this dynamic era in European art.

See also ANGLO-SAXON ART.

BIBLIOGRAPHY

T. D. Kendrick: *Anglo-Saxon Art to AD 900* (London, 1938)

M. de Paor and L. de Paor: *Early Christian Ireland* (London, 1958)

F. Henry: *Irish Art during the Early Christian Period to 800 AD* (London, 1965)

——: *Irish Art during the Viking Invasions, 800–1020 AD* (London, 1967)

B. Colgrave and R. A. B. Mynors, eds: *Bede's Ecclesiastical History of the English People* (Oxford, 1969)

L. Laing: *The Archaeology of Late Celtic Britain and Ireland, c. 400 AD–1200 AD* (London, 1975)

Treasures of Ireland: Irish Art, 3000 BC–1500 AD (exh. cat., ed. M. Ryan; Dublin, Royal Irish Acad., 1983)

C. L. Neuman de Vegvar: *The Northumbrian Renaissance: A Study in the Transmission of Style* (Cranbury, 1987)

'The Work of Angels': Masterpieces of Celtic Metalwork, 6th–9th Centuries AD (exh. cat., ed. S. Youngs; London, BM, 1989)

ROGER STALLEY

2. METALWORK. Although in Insular art there was much cross-fertilization of media, particularly between metalwork and manuscript illumination, many of the most characteristic motifs were those of metalwork, which exerted the strongest influences. In the early years the curvilinear motifs characteristic of the abstract art of northern Britain and Ireland were mingled with some provincial Roman influence: the new style that emerged is sometimes referred to as Ultimate La Tène. A number of variants appeared, and these are best exemplified on the decorative escutcheons of hanging bowls known mainly from Saxon graves (e.g. U. Bergen, Hist. Mus.). An early style (6th century) characterized by fine reserved metal spiral scrolls (often with bird-head endings), set in a field of champlevé red enamel, was succeeded in the 7th century by more fleshy combinations of trumpet scrolls and more lavish enamels. These stylistic changes are found in Ireland on objects known as 'latchets' (dress fasteners), handpins and penannular (gapped ring) brooches with animal-head or zoomorphic terminals. During the 6th century *millefiori* work was adopted by Irish craftsmen. It was often used at first in the form of small decorative tesserae floated in

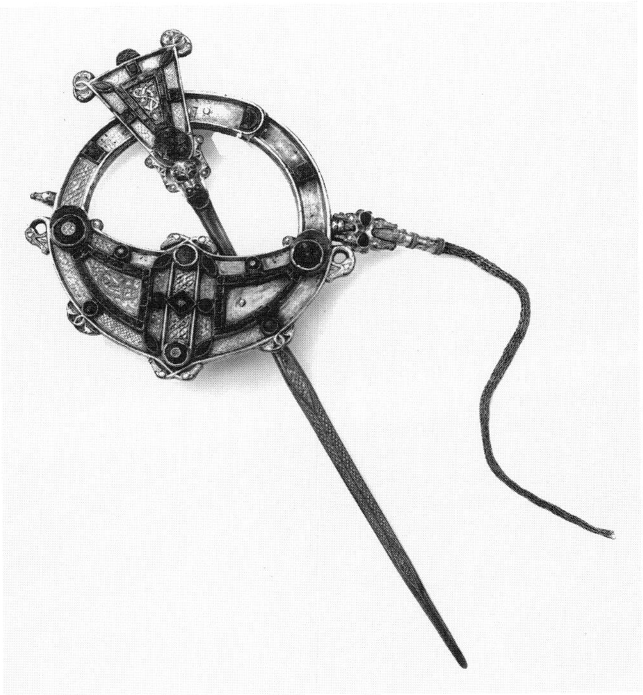

1. Tara Brooch, silver gilt bronze with gold filigree, enamels and amber, ring diam. 87 mm, pin l. 222 mm, from Bettystown, Co. Meath, 8th century AD (Dublin, National Museum of Ireland)

fields of red enamel. A good example is the penannular brooch from Ballinderry Crannog, Co. Offaly (Dublin, Trinity Coll. Lib.), which in its use of *millefiori* and decoratively ribbed moulding has a close counterpart in the mounts of a hanging bowl (London, BM) from the great Anglo-Saxon 7th-century ship burial of Sutton Hoo. A 6th-century workshop-area, in which *millefiori* was used and enamel- and bronze-casting performed, was excavated at Garranes, Co. Cork. Workshop debris of later date has been found at both secular and monastic sites, for example at Armagh (Belfast, Ulster Mus.). The practice of the Ultimate La Tène style in Ireland is further shown by a substantial monolith carved with characteristic motifs (now Dublin, N. Mus.), which formerly stood at Mullaghmast, Co. Kildare.

In the later 6th century and the 7th, elements of Germanic animal ornament were slowly being added to the bird head and trumpet scroll widespread in earlier Celtic art. This resulted from contact with the Anglo-Saxon and Frankish worlds, probably through trade, as is suggested by the fittings, perhaps serving as saddle mounts, recovered from the River Shannon near Athlone. Little, apart from casual references in 7th-century hagiography, is known of early ecclesiastical metalwork. The cross-fertilization of the 7th century, evident in manuscript illumination, led to a remarkable flowering of the metalworker's craft in Ireland in the 8th century, which is marked by the appearance of a dazzling array of new techniques and materials. The first known mature product is the pseudo-penannular Tara Brooch (Dublin, N. Mus.; see fig. 1), which retains the penannular form in the layout of its ornaments, but the gap in the ring is now closed and the broad 'terminals' are used for sumptuous ornament. Pseudo-penannular brooches are an Irish type, and the silver Tara Brooch, with its magnificent filigree, cast, gilded and overlaid ornaments, gem-set enamels and amber, stands at the head of the series. The front is dominated by filigree entwined and interlaced animals and plain interlace ornament, while cast animals and birds and Ultimate La Tène designs cover the reverse. The entwined animal motifs and use of Ultimate La Tène designs relate the Tara Brooch to the style of the Lindisfarne Gospels and suggest that it, too, dates to the early 8th century. More than 20 other silver pseudo-penannulars of varying quality are known, of which the closest to the Tara Brooch is the Hunterston Brooch from Ayrshire (Edinburgh, N. Mus. Ant.). The Tara–Lindisfarne style of contorted animal is closely matched on the tinned-bronze disc of an animal head, possibly a door-handle (Dublin, N. Mus.), found in a hoard at Donore, Moynalty, Co. Meath, which is a sophisticated adaptation to Insular taste and technique of a Classical lion-head ring-handle. The sources of inspiration drawn on by craftsmen and the variety of raw materials and techniques available enabled them to produce work that rivalled the delicacy of manuscript painting; this is shown most clearly in a second Ultimate La Tène disc from the same hoard.

During the 8th century goldsmiths produced ambitious pieces in the service of the Church. Outstanding among these are the Ardagh Chalice and Derrynaflan Paten (both Dublin, N. Mus.), in which local tastes are combined to produce distinctively Irish forms. Metalworkers generally avoided the human figure, and decoration followed the norms of secular pieces, but a characteristic Irish Crucifixion iconography was reproduced in an openwork, cast-bronze plaque (Dublin, N. Mus.; see fig. 2) from St John's Rinnagan (near Athlone, Co. Westmeath), which was designed for fastening to a large wooden altar or cross. The later 8th-century, cast-bronze, silvered and gilt shrine crest from Killua Castle, Co. Westmeath (Dublin, N. Mus.), shows an *orans* (Christ or Daniel) between two beasts. This motif also occurs on the shaft of a composite wood and bronze cross (*c.* 800). Reliquaries, frequently small, gabled caskets shaped like a tomb or house, were common. They may be made of wood inlaid with metal, such as the Emly Shrine (8th century; Boston, MA, Mus. F.A.; for illustration *see* SHRINE (i), fig. 1), covered with metal plates, for example the Lough Erne Shrine (8th century; Dublin, N. Mus.), or entirely of metal (e.g. early 9th century; Bologna, Mus. Civ. Med.). House-shaped shrines sometimes contained corporeal relics. A remarkable 8th-century reliquary from Moylough, Co. Sligo (Dublin, N. Mus.), preserves in its hinged bronze segments the leather girdle of an unknown saint. Its dummy buckle and counterplate mimic the form of Frankish buckles of the later 6th century, and its appliqué cruciform and rectangular ornaments recall the metal stiffeners of continental belts in the Late Roman tradition. Its polychrome gem-set, cast enamels, *millefiori* and superb die-stamped silver panels make it one of the most important pieces of the 8th-century 'Golden Age'.

2. Crucifixion plaque, gilt bronze, 211×139 mm, from St John's Rinnagan, Co. Roscommon, 8th century AD (Dublin, National Museum of Ireland)

The best 8th-century work achieved its effects by a stunning deployment of colour and remarkable artistry, in which animal ornament, Ultimate La Tène scrollwork, interlace, key and fret patterns all played their part. During the 9th century this brilliance was in decline, but this should not be attributed to the disruption of the Viking raids that began at the close of the 8th century and were most intensive in the 9th. A significant amount of Irish material has been found in graves of the Viking period in Norway. The closest parallels to a set of harness mounts (Dublin, N. Mus.) from Navan, Co. Meath, for example, have been found at Gausel, Norway. The availability of silver in fairly generous quantities—often from Viking trade—led to experimentation with decorations of solid metal. Enamel and filigree fell from favour, although such ambitious polychrome pieces as the Derrynaflan Chalice (Dublin, N. Mus.) were still commissioned. The development is clearly shown in pseudo-penannular brooches as single, semi-naturalistic animal patterns were introduced; amber and, later, solid bosses replaced the earlier enamels. In the later 9th century the penannular brooch enjoyed a revival in the form of 'bossed' brooches with engraved animal ornament, which betray strong Anglo-Saxon influence. Another form, the 'thistle' brooch, has large ball-shaped terminals and was popular in Ireland, northern Britain and even Scandinavia. Some brooches made in the 10th century, often with pins of extravagant length, are known as 'kite' brooches from the shape of their hinged pendants. By the end of the century large silver brooches seem to have gone out of fashion and been replaced by a variety of simpler pins. A change of dress in the 9th century, probably introduced by the Scandinavians of Dublin and York, led to the adoption in Ireland of cross-gartering of leggings; a large number of decorative bronze strap-ends for these have been found, many from the early levels of the excavations at Dublin (Dublin, N. Mus.).

Ecclesiastical metalwork of the later 9th century and the 10th is known principally from some characteristic Irish walking-stick crosiers. The early work on the composite British Museum Crosier (London, BM) betrays a naturalistic element that may derive from the same tradition as the earlier Derrynaflan Chalice. Scandinavian influence is absent from the metalwork of the 9th and 10th centuries, but it became significant in the 11th, when traditional secular centres of production finally gave way to the more organized workshops of the great monasteries and the new secular town of Dublin. Much of the style of the earlier period was to be revived and reinterpreted during the renaissance of the 11th and 12th centuries.

BIBLIOGRAPHY

M. Stokes: *Early Christian Art in Ireland* (London, 1887/*R* Dublin, 1932)
G. Coffey: *Guide to the Celtic Antiquities of the Christian Period in the National Museum, Dublin* (Dublin, 1909)
A. Mahr and J. Raftery: *Christian Art in Ancient Ireland*, 2 vols (Dublin, 1932–41)
Treasures of Early Irish Art: Irish Art, 1500 BC to 1500 AD (exh. cat. by G. F. Mitchell and others, New York, Met., 1977)
M. Ryan, ed.: *Ireland and Insular Art, AD 500–1200* (Dublin, 1987)

For further bibliography *see* §1 above.

MICHAEL RYAN

3. MANUSCRIPT ILLUMINATION. The full literacy brought by the conversion to Christianity offered a new vehicle for artistic production: the book. Nowhere is the fusion of Celtic, Germanic, antique, Mediterranean and Eastern elements that characterizes Insular art more apparent than in manuscript production. The earliest extant decorated Insular manuscript is the Codex Usserianus Primus (Dublin, Trinity Coll. Lib., MS. 55), widely thought to date to the early 7th century, which is embellished simply by a cross within a panel of 'colophon' decoration (fol. 149*v*), an antique practice of highlighting information on title, authorship or production with graphic surrounds, generally in red. The next early landmark, a copy of the Psalms, the so-called Cathach of St Columba (Dublin, Royal Irish Acad., s.n.), is controversially dated *c.* 625. It features enlarged initials with following letters gradated down to the script of the main text ('diminuendo'), incorporating vestigial Ultimate La Tène motifs, and crosses and fishes inspired by contemporary Roman manuscripts. The Insular concern with integrating script and ornament with text was already apparent. Both manuscripts were made in Ireland, where the foundations of Insular manuscript production were laid, but the origin of the first of the luxury Insular Gospel books, the Book of Durrow (second half of the 7th century; Dublin, Trinity Coll. Lib., MS. 57), is disputed. It has a medieval Irish provenance and employs Celtic ornament, but shares close affinities with Germanic metalwork, such as that from

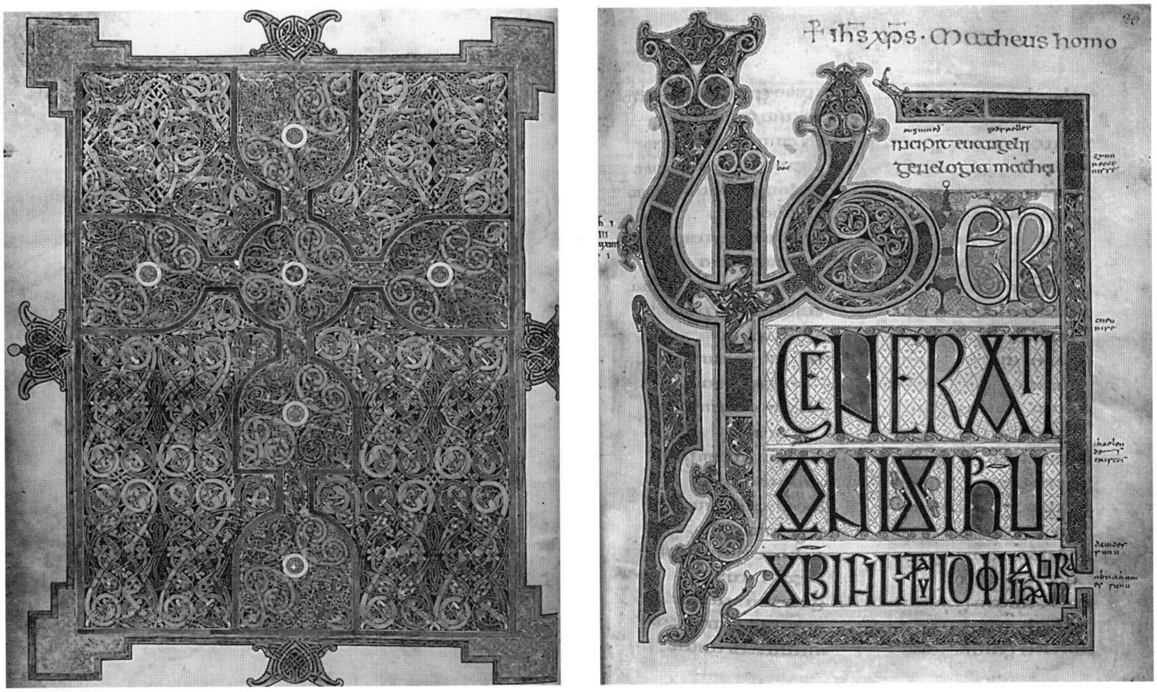

3. Carpet and incipit pages from the Lindisfarne Gospels, 340×240 mm, *c.* AD 700 (London, British Library, Cotton MS. Nero D. IV, fols 26*v*–27

Sutton Hoo (London, BM). Textually it is related to another of the greatest, and most anomalous, Insular manuscripts, the BOOK OF KELLS, which is thought possibly to have been made at Iona, and the Book of Durrow may also originate from there (although origins in Ireland, Pictland and Northumbria are also advanced as possibilities). The Book of Durrow is the first to show the characteristic Insular programme of Gospel decoration: carpet pages (pages of abstract ornament preceding major textual openings, probably of Coptic inspiration); Evangelist miniatures (here distinctive full-length zoomorphic or 'terrestrial' symbols, some displaying Pictish affinities); enlarged major initials and display script at the Gospel openings (incipit pages, often combining Celtic curvilinear ornament and Germanic zoomorphic interlace; *see* INITIAL, MANUSCRIPT, fig. 1). It is also prefaced by a page carrying all four Evangelist symbols, of Coptic or Eastern inspiration.

The next three great Gospel books, the Durham (Durham, Cathedral Lib., MS. A.II.17), Echternach (Paris, Bib. N., MS. lat. 9389) and Lindisfarne Gospels (London, BL, Cotton MS. Nero D. IV), all dating from around 700, are closely related in decoration and script, but whether they were produced in the same scriptorium remains disputed. The damaged Durham Gospels contains the earliest extant Insular narrative miniature, a *Crucifixion* (fol. 38*v*) of Eastern inspiration. The Echternach Gospels lacks carpet pages, but features dynamic stylized Evangelist symbols within rectilinear tracery frames. The LINDISFARNE GOSPELS, a pinnacle of Insular art, carries a full programme of Evangelist miniatures, carpet pages, opening pages (incipits), many decorated minor initials with zoomorphic terminals, and canon tables in the form of architectural arcades (see fig. 3). The Evangelists are depicted as scribes, identified by their accompanying symbols, in a style that may represent a response to a Late Antique trend towards linearization. New types of beast also infiltrate the interlace, with recognizable birds, dogs and cats replacing their amorphous Germanic ancestors. Mediterranean influence is further apparent in the extensive palette, which replaced the characteristic red, yellow and green, and in the Neapolitan textual exemplar (Backhouse).

The portrait of *St Matthew* (fol. 25*v*; *see* BOOK, fig. 3) in the Lindisfarne Gospels is adapted from a miniature of *Ezra*, or its Mediterranean Cassiodoran model, in the Codex Amiatinus (Florence, Bib. Medicea-Laurenziana, MS. Amiatinus 1, fol. V*r*), one of three Bibles commissioned by Ceolfrith, Abbot of the Northumbrian monasteries of Monkwearmouth and Jarrow, before departure for Rome in 716. So proficient were the members of the Wearmouth/Jarrow team in their uncial script and painterly, illusionistic style that the Codex Amiatinus was long considered a Mediterranean product. Other products from Wearmouth and Jarrow include the Durham Cassiodorus (Durham, Cathedral Lib., MS. B.II.30), with its delicate tinted drawings, exemplifying what was to become a popular Anglo-Saxon technique (*see* ANGLO-SAXON ART, §IV, 2).

Eighth-century Insular work is represented by such books as the Lichfield, or Chad, Gospels (Lichfield, Cathedral Lib., s.n.), with its iconic, stylized Evangelist portraits. This was exchanged by one Gelhi for his best horse and given to the altar of St Teilo (Llandeilo-fawr) in the early 9th century, probably having reached Wales via an Irish presence, rather than by raids into Mercia. Its stylistic links are with Northumbrian and Irish works. Later examples made in Ireland include the St Gall Gospels (St Gall, Stift.-Bib., Cod. 51), the Macregol Gospels (Oxford, Bodleian Lib., MS. Auct. D.2.19) and a series of 8th-century pocket Gospel books, for example the Book of Dimma (Dublin, Trinity Coll. Lib., MS. 59). A rare Welsh response to the style may be seen in the Hereford Gospels (Hereford, Cathedral Lib., MS. P.I.2) and a Scottish response in the Book of Deer (Cambridge, U. Lib., MS. Ii.6.32). Brittany also evolved a provincial version of the Insular style (Paris, Bibl. N., MS. nouv. acq. lat. 1587 may be an example of this).

The Book of Kells, made probably *c.* 800, represents the culmination of the style, forming an encyclopedia of Insular art. It has stylistic affinities with the Book of Armagh (Dublin, Trinity Coll. Lib., MS. 52), dated 807. Some Carolingian influence has been discerned (notably the beast canon tables), but a Carolingian intermediary is not necessary to explain such features. The wealth of incidental detail in initials and line-fillers finds echoes in Frankish and Byzantine art, and in contemporary 'Southumbrian' art. The Insular programme of decoration is supplemented by narrative and iconic images, such as the *Virgin and Child*, the *Temptation of Christ* (*see* IRELAND, fig. 7) and the *Betrayal of Christ*. Many contain various levels of meaning drawn from exegesis, the *Temptation of Christ* (fol. 202*v*), for example, simultaneously representing the Communion of Saints with Christ as the head (literally) of the Church.

Insular styles were also carried to the Continent, often as part of the Anglo-Saxon and Irish missions, where they fused with indigenous trends. Important examples of such works include the products of Bobbio and St Gall Abbey, the Trier Gospels (Trier, Domschatz, Cod. 61) and other books made at Echternach during the 8th century and the Cutbercht Gospels (Vienna, Österreich. Nbib., Cod. 1224) probably from Salzburg. Such works as the Valenciennes Apocalypse (Valenciennes, Bib. Mun., MS. 99) bear witness to lost Insular narrative cycles in their exemplars. Insular art played a formative role in the early Carolingian *renovatio* (*see* CAROLINGIAN ART, §IV, 3), and characteristic features such as interlace were absorbed into a 'Franco-Saxon' style, which was later reimported to Anglo-Saxon England.

In southern England another major centre of romanization was formed at Canterbury, base of the Augustinian mission (*see* CANTERBURY, §II). The ST AUGUSTINE GOSPELS (Cambridge, Corpus Christi Coll., Lib. MS. 286), produced in Rome in the late 6th century, was traditionally thought to have accompanied Augustine to England in 596–7. It contains a portrait of a bearded Evangelist (*St Luke*; fol. 129*v*; *see* EARLY CHRISTIAN AND BYZANTINE ART, fig. 57), enthroned beneath an architectural arch carrying a bust of his symbol, the bull, in its tympanum. The portrait is flanked by scenes from the *Life of Christ*, in registers. Such works influenced the earliest surviving illuminated manuscripts from Kent: the Vespasian Psalter (London, BL, Cotton MS. Vesp. A.I), made in Canterbury *c.* 730, and the Stockholm Codex Aureus (mid-8th century; Stockholm, Kun. Bib., MS. A. 135). Both employ arches as frames, for a scene of *David and his Musicians* (fol. 30*v*) in the former, and for evangelist portraits in the latter (e.g. *St John*; fol. 150*r*), and in both the figures are naturalistic and well modelled. The Codex Aureus is penned in gold and silver uncials on purple pages, in Byzantine fashion, and in both registers of golden display capitals are preferred to Insular lacertine display scripts, although Celtic motifs and interlace make a limited appearance. These two books are the earliest members of the important Southumbrian 'Tiberius' group of 8th- and 9th-century manuscripts, named from the Tiberius Bede (first half of the 9th century; London, BL, Cotton MS. Tib. C.II). The alternative term, the 'Canterbury' group, obscures the more general Southumbrian context of production, some members having probably originated in the Mercian heartland (with Kent forming part of Mercia politically for much of the period in question).

The next important member of the group, chronologically, is the Barberini Gospels (late 8th century; Rome, Vatican, Bib. Apostolica, MS. Barb. lat. 570), which displays a taste for exotic eastern Mediterranean styles in its painterly bearded Evangelists in their landscaped settings (e.g. *St John*; fol. 124*v*). Such taste enjoyed broader currency in Southumbria during the late 8th century and the 9th, influencing other works, such as the sculptures of St Mary's church, Breedon on the Hill, Leics. This splendid manuscript may be the finest surviving book from the once-powerful kingdom of Mercia, although a Northumbrian origin (perhaps York) cannot be excluded. It also introduces panels of lacertine display script linked by biting beast heads and grotesques (fol. 125*r*). This is a characteristic feature of later 'Tiberius' group members, notably the Tiberius Bede and the Royal Bible (second quarter of the 9th century; London, BL, Royal MS. 1.E.VI), both from Canterbury, and three prayerbooks intended for private devotional use: the Royal Prayerbook (London, BL, Royal MS. 2.A.XX), the Book of Nunnaminster (London, BL, Harley MS. 2965) and the Book of Cerne (Cambridge, U. Lib., MS. Ll.1.10), all from Mercia (?Lichfield and ?Worcester). The mischievous use of zoomorphic features is particularly evident in Cerne with its worm-like run-over symbols. Similar beasts are found in contemporary Southumbrian metalwork (*see* TREWHIDDLE HOARD), the silver-niello technique of which is reflected in the white-on-black panels of ornament in the 'Tiberius' manuscripts. As with earlier Insular art, many stylistic features were used in several different media.

The Book of Cerne features unusual Evangelist miniatures, in which full-length zoormorphic symbols (of Insular type) are accompanied by an anthropomorphic bust above (features which may be explained by certain exegetical sources and liturgical practices). The bull of *St Luke* (fol. 21*v*) was partly modelled on the same Mediterranean or Carolingian Court school exemplar as a more painterly, classicizing half-length bull in the Royal Bible (fol. 43). Cerne was probably made for Aethelwald, Bishop of Lichfield (818–30), whose colleague, Wulfred, Archbishop of Canterbury (805–32), was introducing reforms along Carolingian lines. The sharing of a continental exemplar between these two centres is not, therefore, unlikely. Although reduced to Gospel fragments, the Royal Bible is particularly classicizing in style, with its purple pages and gold and silver display capitals identifying lost narrative New Testament miniatures.

At the end of the Insular period, on the eve of the Viking occupation, Insular art was flourishing and responding actively to the Carolingian developments it had helped to foster. At the end of the 9th century Alfred the Great's cultural revival was to be as heavily influenced by earlier Southumbria as by the Continent, assuring a continuing Insular input into later Anglo-Saxon art, and thereby into Romanesque and Gothic art.

BIBLIOGRAPHY

E. H. Zimmermann: *Vorkarolingische Miniaturen* (Berlin, 1916)
E. A. Lowe: *Codices Latini Antiquiores: A Palaeographical Guide to Latin Manuscripts prior to the Ninth Century*, 12 vols (Oxford, 1934–71)
G. L. Micheli: *L'Enluminure du haut moyen âge* (Brussels, 1939)
M. Rickert: *Painting in Britain: The Middle Ages* (Har 2/1965)
F. Henry: *Irish Art in the Early Christian Period* (London, 1965)
C. Nordenfalk: *Celtic and Anglo-Saxon Painting* (New York, 1976)
J. J. G. Alexander: *Insular Manuscripts, 6th to the 9th Century*, Survey of Manuscripts Illuminated in the British Isles (London, 1978)
C. D. Verey, T. J. Brown and E. Coatsworth, eds: *The Durham Gospels (Durham, Cathedral Library, MS. A.II.17)*, Early English Manuscripts in Facsimile, xx (Copenhagen, 1980); review by D. ó Cróinín in *Peritia*, i (1982), pp. 352–62
J. M. Backhouse: *The Lindisfarne Gospels* (Oxford, 1981)
M. P. Brown: *Anglo-Saxon Manuscripts* (London, 1991)
G. Henderson: *From Durrow to Kells: The Insular Gospel Books* (London, 1991)
The Making of England: Anglo-Saxon Art and Culture, AD 600–900 (exh. cat., ed. L. Webster and J. Backhouse; London, BM, 1991)

MICHELLE P. BROWN

4. SCULPTURE. The quality of stone-carving fostered by the early Irish monasteries was among the finest in pre-Romanesque Europe. By the 10th century, if not long before, such major monasteries as Clonmacnois, Kells, Monasterboice and Armagh were equipped with well-modelled 'scripture crosses', placed at various points around their precincts. This development was remarkable given that Irish craftsmen, unlike those in other countries, had no experience of Roman sculpture on which to base their work. Patronage was concentrated on pillar stones and monumental crosses, but stone sculptors also manufactured hundreds of recumbent grave-slabs (*see* CLONMACNOIS MONASTERY, §2) as well as a curious group of stelae in north-west Ulster.

Precedents for stone-carving in Ireland go back to prehistory, and Irish Neolithic tombs (e.g. NEWGRANGE) are renowned for their abstract decoration, spirals, zigzags etc. The first Christian carvings appear on standing stones and take the form of simple incised crosses, sometimes with the addition of a chi-rho or alpha and omega monogram or even an ecclesiastical figure, as at Ballyvourney, Co. Cork. The spiral decoration on the outstanding example at Reask, Co. Kerry, can be related to initials in the so-called Cathach of St Columba (*see* §3 above), a decorated Psalter of the early 7th century. The distribution of the engraved pillar stones is concentrated in the west, and, while many are attributed to the 6th and 7th centuries, it is likely that such simple incised designs continued for a long time, especially in remote areas.

By the 8th or 9th centuries the free-standing cross had appeared, constructed of carefully shaped blocks, with designs cut vigorously in relief (*see* CROSS, §I, 1(ii)).

4. Base of cross showing the *Three Hebrews in the Fiery Furnace*, the *Flight into Egypt* and the *Miracle of the Loaves and Fishes*, granite, Moone, Co. Kildare, *c.* AD 800

Whether the sculptors' new confidence was the consequence of accumulated experience or some unknown intervention from abroad is much debated. On many crosses major elements in the design project forward of the main plane, indicating that substantial quantities of stone had to be cut away before detailed carving could begin, a point that emphasizes the amount of planning and forethought that was required. The technique is well illustrated on the Unfinished Cross at Kells, Co. Meath. The cutting of a pierced ring also called for delicate and skilful handling.

It is generally presumed that those crosses decorated principally with abstract designs, such as at Ahenny (*see* CROSS, fig. 1) and a group at Clonmacnois (*c.* 800), preceded those with figure sculpture, but this is far from certain. Differences in style and approach may reflect local traditions as well as chronological distinctions. Almost all crosses include some ornamental panels, and popular designs include spirals, whorls, bosses, interlace, a variety of animals, entangled humans, frets and foliage scrolls. At Monasterboice and Ahenny these patterns were executed with breathtaking precision. Many designs were derived from manuscripts and metalwork, and the methods of the goldsmiths (e.g. rivets, bosses and chip-carving) were reproduced unaltered in stone.

Figure-carving falls into a number of stylistic categories. At one extreme are the granite sculptures of Moone, Co. Kildare (see fig. 4), where human bodies are reduced to blunt geometrical forms, naive, albeit charming, pictograms. At the other extreme are the smooth, well-proportioned figures of the Monasterboice–Clonmacnois–Durrow workshop, active at the beginning of the 10th century. In such panels as the *Ecce homo* on Muiredach's Cross at MONASTERBOICE, figures move with ease and freedom and there is a sensitive delineation of human form (see fig. 5, lowest panel). The long ornamental cloak, pulled deftly around the shoulders, appears regularly, as do the round cherubic faces with curly hair and the somewhat sterner individuals with long moustaches, the latter evidently a reflection of Irish male fashion. In less weathered panels, much local detail survives, such as the penannular and kite brooches (*see* §2 above) in the *Ecce homo* scene. The BOOK OF KELLS contains hints of this figure style, but manuscript illumination cannot account for the bold modelling, which reaches a depth of 60 mm (on figures 300 mm high) on Muiredach's Cross. Confidence acquired in wood-carving might go some way to explain it. On other crosses the so-called 'Kells profile' is more prominent, in which angular faces with pointed noses and chins are covered with hair flowing down to a curl at the nape of the neck. The roots of this style have been sought in such divergent locations as Pictish Scotland and Visigothic Spain.

Much effort has been devoted to deciphering and explaining the iconography of the crosses. About 90 different biblical subjects, divided between the Old and New Testaments, have been identified. Old and New Testament scenes often appear on opposite faces. The *Crucifixion* is the most common subject, normally carved on the cross arms, with the *Last Judgement* or *Christ in Majesty* on the reverse side. Stress is placed on the idea of the Redemption and the suffering and sacrifice of Christ. Thus there are panels devoted to the *Passion* as well as miracles relating to the eucharistic theme. This also explains the popularity of *St Paul* and *St Antony Receiving Bread in the Desert.* The most frequent Old Testament subject is the *Fall of Man*, included as an essential prologue to the Incarnation. A number of typological scenes occur with regularity: the *Death of Abel*, the *Sacrifice of Isaac*, *David and Goliath*, *Daniel in the Lions' Den* etc. Some of these have been explained by reference to the Roman prayer 'commendatio animae', in which Old Testament 'deliverance' episodes are invoked as encouragement for the faithful. The inclusion of several scenes associated with the life of David reflects not only his typological role but also the importance of the psalms in Irish monastic life. Some panels have never been interpreted satisfactorily, but older views that they might represent events from Irish history or hagiography have been discredited. Only on the bases of some crosses are there enigmatic carvings of such secular subjects as warriors, chariots and processions. The sources of this rich iconography have provoked much discussion. Irish illuminated manuscripts rarely provide models and scholars have therefore searched

5. Muiredach's Cross, west face, with *New Testament* scenes, Monasterboice, *c.* AD 920

abroad for prototypes. A widely held view is that Irish sculpture is an offshoot of the Carolingian *renovatio*, and comparisons have been made with 9th-century ivories and wall paintings (Harbison, 1984, 1992). No Carolingian ivories or manuscripts have been found in Ireland, however, and a number of important Carolingian subjects are conspicuously absent. An alternative view places more stress on Early Christian sources. The Irish Church had plenty of opportunities from the 5th century onwards to acquire manuscripts and panel paintings of Mediterranean origin. Moreover, the scholarly fame of Irish monasteries presupposes the existence of excellent libraries. The crosses may reflect an older tradition of wood-carving and panel painting, which would also explain some of the iconographic idiosyncracies.

Whatever the correct answer (and it may be a combination of both points of view), it is difficult to envisage exactly what models or pattern-books the sculptors were using. Although subjects are repeated from cross to cross, the selection varies and the sequence of scenes is never the same. Many of these issues anticipate those that arise in the study of Romanesque art, with which the Irish crosses have much in common. The architectonic emphasis of the crosses, the orderly arrangement of panels, the firm dividing frames, the relief techniques of the carvers and the balance attained in figure sculpture between naturalism and abstract form all foreshadow Romanesque sculpture in a remarkable way. The isolated geography of Ireland, however, ensured that the range and quality of these carvings remained unknown elsewhere in Europe.

See also ANGLO-SAXON, §III.

BIBLIOGRAPHY

H. S. Crawford: *Irish Carved Ornament* (Dublin, 1926)
A. K. Porter: *The Crosses and Culture of Ireland* (New Haven, 1931)
F. Henry: *La Sculpture irlandaise pendant les douze premiers siècles de l'ère chrétienne* (Paris, 1933)
E. H. L. Sexton: *Irish Figure Sculpture of the Early Christian Period* (Portland, 1946)
H. M. Roe: 'The "David Cycle" in Early Irish Art', *J. Royal Soc. Antiqua. Ireland*, lxxix (1949), pp. 39–59
R. Flower: 'Irish High Crosses', *J. Warb. & Court. Inst.*, xvii (1954), pp. 87–97
R. B. K. Stevenson: 'The Chronology and Relationship of some Irish and Scottish Crosses', *J. Royal Soc. Antiqua. Ireland*, lxxxvi (1956), pp. 84–96
F. Henry: *Irish High Crosses* (Dublin, 1964)
K. Hughes and A. Hamlin: *The Modern Traveller to the Early Irish Church* (London, 1977), pp. 80–101
A. Hamlin: 'Early Irish Stone Carving: Content and Context', *The Early Church in Western Britain and Ireland: Studies Presented to C. A. Ralegh Radford*, Brit. Archaeol. Rep., 102 (Oxford, 1982), pp. 283–96
P. Harbison: 'Earlier Carolingian Narrative Iconography: Ivories, Manuscripts, Frescoes and Irish High Crosses', *Jb. Röm.-Ger. Zentmus.*, xxxi (1984), pp. 455–71
——: 'A Group of Early Christian Carved Stone Monuments in County Donegal', *Early Medieval Sculpture in Britain and Ireland*, ed. J. Higgitt, Brit. Archaeol. Rep., 152 (Oxford, 1986), pp. 49–85
A. Hamlin: 'Crosses in Early Ireland: The Evidence from Written Sources', *Ireland and Insular Art, AD 500–1200*, ed. M. Ryan (Dublin, 1987), pp. 138–40
P. Harbison: 'The Carolingian Contribution to Irish Sculpture', *Ireland and Insular Art, AD 500–1200*, ed. M. Ryan (Dublin, 1987), pp. 105–10
——: *The High Crosses of Ireland: An Iconographical and Photographic Survey* (Bonn, 1992)

ROGER STALLEY

Intaglio. Process in which the design is hollowed out, the opposite of relief. The term is applied to gemstones (*see* GEM-ENGRAVING) and to a class of printmaking techniques, most notably ENGRAVING and ETCHING (*see* PRINTS, §III, 2).

Intarsia [tarsia]. Decorative wood technique in which the design or pattern is made by assembling small, shaped pieces of veneer. The term, which derives from 15th-century Italy, is commonly used on the Continent to describe both marquetry, in which the entire surface is veneered (*see* MARQUETRY, §1), and inlay, in which the pattern pieces are laid into a solid ground (*see* AUSTRIA, fig. 29).

Intensity. The quantity of light from a light source, measured by scientists in units of milliamberts. Intensity is also used to refer to the psychological perception of colour brightness due to high saturation. *See* LIGHT.

□

Intention. What is meant, or intended, by a work of art: what this comprises, and how to interpret it, is an issue entailing some of the central and most vexed questions of modern criticism. Intention has emerged as a major problem in modern theories of interpretation for several reasons. Most simply, when artefacts are used by members of a group or culture, their meaning is largely unproblematical: a Renaissance Florentine understood the meaning of a *Virgin and Child* and a Yoruba understands the meaning of a Gelede society mask, even if some specific details might have to be explained. In the modern world, however, both may be encountered in museums, as 'art', and although the viewer may feel that he knows how to deal with them as such, he confronts them in situations far in space and time from the situations in which their use and understanding were 'second nature'. In such circumstances questions of 'meaning' and origin come to the fore, and with them the problem of how such meaning is to be reclaimed. This article is concerned not with the question of what an intention might be, rather with the problem of intention as it bears on the interpretation of art.

1. The commonsense notion and its earlier history. 2. Formalist and Post-modernist critiques. 3. Reclaiming the concept.

1. THE COMMONSENSE NOTION AND ITS EARLIER HISTORY. At the simplest level, the search for intention is usually understood to mean the search for 'what the artist had in mind' before a work was made. This commonsense notion of intention conceals three assumptions: that the artist is in some sense the origin and agent of the work; that there is a kind of symmetry between intention and result; and that intention is mental. Common sense thus agrees with Aristotle, who argued that things made by art are different from things made by nature in that whereas works of nature have their origin in themselves, works of art have theirs in the artist. This origin is a form in the imagination of the artist, which, having been imagined, is subsequently realized in matter. The preceding mental form not only determines the configuration of the work,

it is the final cause of the work, towards which it tends as a limit in its realization. If the origin of the work is to be understood, it is necessary to understand that prior mental image, as it came to be called in the Renaissance, that 'idea' or 'concept'.

The Classical formulation of what is now called 'intention' (though this is not a Classical issue) makes the artist's concept only one of a number of causes. The artist in antiquity typically made art *for* someone and may have been little concerned with the reasons for its being made. A sculptor carving a marble statue of Augustus may be supposed to have cared or understood little about the political occasion for doing so. Materials and tools were also listed as causes of the work, but these were generally discussed as secondary to the concept. That is, skill was measured by the degree to which the artist manipulated tools in such a way as to give materials the form of the mental concept.

Ideas about art such as Aristotle's were repeated in one way or another for some 2000 years, but during the Renaissance, with the emergence of modern ideas of 'genius' and 'creativity', the artist's concept began to assume characteristically different dimensions. In the Renaissance the interconnected emergence of naturalism and personal style yielded the idea of art as the expression of personal 'vision'. At the same time, art was cut away from the direct civic or religious patronage of earlier periods; this had the effect of broadening the responsibility of the artist for the origin of the work, whence the metaphor of 'creation'. The artist, speculating in personal *ingenium* (genius or mental power), represented the world imaginatively and at will. The concept was now a spontaneous re-creation of the world, expressed in the work of art.

These ideas assumed sublime proportions with the emergence of Romantic historicist idealism and its attendant reifications of culture, nation and race (*see* HISTORICISM, §3). The 'genius' now 'created' the 'world-view' of a people or period. According to the general idealist position, the representation of the world takes place at a level immediate to sensation (that is, at an 'aesthetic' level) and it is at this preconscious level of contact between the forces of nature and the radically constructive or formative imagination that the constituting principles of mind itself are first to be encountered. The artist became one who makes the processes of formation and representation evident in themselves, and the 'formal' or 'abstract' elements of artistic representation (line, shape, colour, value and their combinations) emerged as the true elements of artistic 'vision'. The traditional goal of the imitation of nature became secondary. Formal elements were regarded as not only constructive but expressive, the means by which the 'vision' of the artist is made apparent to others. Such 'visions' were not only held to be personal but carried all the baggage of modern historicism, synthesizing racial or national predispositions as well as the historical 'influences' of other cultural expressions and taking their place in the developmental series to which forms themselves were thought to be subject. It is important to stress that all these new dimensions of artistic imagination were understood as preconscious (if not explicitly unconscious). The conscious, on the other hand, tended to be identified both with intention and with subject-matter, which, like imitation, became secondary, the occasion and vehicle for deeper expression.

2. FORMALIST AND POST-MODERNIST CRITIQUES. The foregoing sets the stage for the modern dispute regarding intention. The historicist–idealist ('formalist') position implied that, since the successful work of art is realized precisely as aesthetic form, form alone should be addressed in the interpretation of the work (*see* FORMALISM). Such a view makes the reconstruction of intention in principle extremely difficult or impossible and in any case misdirects criticism from its real purpose and object. Even if there is a 'unity of form and content' in the successful work of art, primary concern with intention leaves the most important aspects of the work, the properly aesthetic aspects, unexamined and unexaminable. There is an obvious problem of circularity in identifying the finished work of art with the artist's preceding concept, and even if that concept might be reclaimed, the factors bearing on its formation and determining its character cannot be presumed to have been intentional in the old sense. This was the tack taken by M. C. Beardsley (1914–42) and W. K. Wimsatt (1907–75) in their influential article 'The Intentional Fallacy' (1946), which became a cornerstone of the 'New Criticism' in literature. Such arguments could easily be extended and deepened as a critique of the traditional notion of intention (or of artistic agency taken altogether). The artist–genius did not *intend* to express the spirit of race, nation or age, or to display the 'influence' of other art or ideas, or to fashion a transitional phase between Classic and Baroque at the time that the artist might be said to have intended to paint an *Annunciation*; rather this expression simply came about in the synthesis of the work, and it is the character of that synthesis that is there to be seen in the forms of the work itself. This prerational significance of form has obvious potential connections with what Ricoeur (1970) termed the 'hermeneutics of suspicion', that is, with such highly developed modern interpretative schemes as those descending in various ways from Freud and Marx. Reinforced by such schemes, the essential prerational aspect of art might be at least partially explained as more explicitly unconscious or historically situated. On this view artistic agency, or the significance of artistic agency, cannot be explained by the recovery of intention since intention itself merely betrays deeper motivations, that is, deeper principles of explanation determined by unconscious desires or class interests.

Formalist criticism presumed a sensitive viewer (or 'reader'), a specialist in 'aesthetic distance' able to interpret the forms of art to non-specialists. Historicism and idealism had always offered the possibility that the experience of the work of art is in its turn largely determined by historical circumstances or by the subjectivity of the viewer, and the notion that the meaning of the worlds constituted by forms in art are in one way or another unconscious clearly points to the possibility that the act of criticism itself is 'situated' in some 'context' of pre-intentional motivation, that it is not 'distant' or 'removed' or 'objective' at all. Since subjectivity and interests (or gender, to add a third major, later category) are not themselves held to be unstructured, this position need not entail the dissolution of criticism into the 'merely subjective'; rather it raises the possibility that criticism is a simultaneous explication of work of art and critic. This 'hermeneutic' possibility opens the way to a number of interpretative options, which have been pursued into Post-modernist criticism. In all such criticism, even more than in earlier formalist criticism, the traditional notion of intention not only plays no role but is explicitly rejected for illegitimately presupposing the existence of a limiting presence (the artist's concept) that prevents the exploration of the dialectic in the present of work of art and situated viewer or critic. The distance of this position from the idea that the task of criticism is the recovery of intention may be gauged by considering the Post-modern and counter-Romantic notion of the 'death of the author', according to which the importance of authorial agency is minimized, the author becoming the locus for the permutational play of language, *topoi* and genres, an activity arising from psychological and sociological forces, fulfilled in acts of viewing and criticism.

3. Reclaiming the concept. Both the formalist and Post-modernist positions presuppose that the encounter of a work of art and an interpreter is one point of view (the artist's in the work) coming into contact with another point of view (the interpreter's). Formalist criticism is optimistic about what might be called the expressive adequacy of the work, the possibility of explicating the artist's point of view on the basis of the forms of the work itself; Post-modernist criticism, on the other hand, is guarded to pessimistic, finding the substance of criticism inevitably in some form of reception. In both cases, intention is secondary to irrelevant. It is, however, possible to save an important aspect of intention, namely the possibility of the historical reconstruction of first meaning, by questioning two principles: the traditional idea that an intention is a simple mental counterpart to the finished work, and the formalist idea that the work of art is in itself adequately expressive.

As noted earlier, identification of the finished work with its putative mental cause is inherently circular, and the expressive adequacy of the work is open to simple and obvious objections. In art historical literature both Erwin Panofsky and Ernst Gombrich have argued that historical reconstruction is necessary to understand, for example, that a woman shown holding a peach is an allegory of veracity. Although response to the image may have all kinds of significance in its own right, none of these is equivalent to what might be understood by placing it in relation to a series of similar images (including one in an iconological handbook), by finding out that abstract nouns in Latin are feminine in gender or by investigating the long Western traditions of allegory and personification. Nor will the viewer look at or respond to the image in the same way once he has done these things. The historical particular, the immediate object of interest and interpretation, is thus effectively changed by reconstruction. The validity of such inference, which basically places images in traditions of meaning and use, is assumed by interpreters of all kinds. Even those who might question the historical enterprise itself as ideologically charged make use of chronologies or iconographic identifications in their own interpretations, proceeding as if such knowledge were given with the work itself.

This bears fundamentally on issues usually clustered around the idea of intention. If the reconstruction of intention is separated from the assumption that what is being reclaimed is the artist's mental concept, and is replaced with the more limited aim of finding out what elements of a work of art meant in the circumstances in which it was made, many of the problems surrounding intention can be avoided; at the same time, the scepticism regarding historical reconstruction that is attendant to the rejection of intention can also be avoided. This solution involves the assumption that making art is meaningful in culturally specific ways in all circumstances in which art is made (as opposed to being simply expressive of those circumstances), but that these meanings of art are not radically determined by the artist since, if they were, the artist would have to be supposed in each case to have invented all the significant elements of the work, which is obviously never the case. The artist is rather a specialist in the construction of understood kinds of meaning. Even if artistic activity be viewed as subversive of dominant conventions (as modernism is often held to be), it is essential that these conventions be understood in order to plot deviation from them.

To take a familiar example, Panofsky defined iconography as the recovery of conventional subject-matter, by which he meant what was understood both by artists and by members of the group or groups for which they made works. Such a principle might be extended far beyond iconography. Historical analysis may seriate the elements of works of art (formats, constructive devices such as proportion or perspective, ornamental, stylistic or technical traditions), and inferences drawn from these procedures point to a broader notion of meaning, encompassing both iconography and the contexts of use, also understood by artist and audience alike, for which works of art are made. By this means procedures and rules of discourse may be established by which to gain some understanding of what works of art 'meant' and why they were made just as they were, without supposing that in so doing the act of interpretation has been completed or that what was 'in the artist's mind' has been reclaimed.

See also Communication theory.

BIBLIOGRAPHY

W. K. Wimsatt and M. C. Beardsley: 'The Intentional Fallacy', *Sewanee Rev.*, liv (1946), pp. 468–88
E. D. Hirsch jr: *Validity in Interpretation* (New Haven, 1967)
P. Ricoeur: *Freud and Philosophy: An Essay on Interpretation* (New Haven and London, 1970)
E. H. Gombrich: 'Aims and Limits of Iconology', *Symbolic Images: Studies in the Art of the Renaissance*, ii (Chicago, 1972), pp. 1–25
M. Baxandall: *Patterns of Intention: On the Historical Explanation of Pictures* (New Haven and London, 1985)
M. Roskill: *The Interpretation of Cubism* (Philadelphia, 1985), pp. 185–222, 284–92
D. Summers: 'Intentions in the History of Art', *New Lit. Hist.*, xvii (1986), pp. 305–21

DAVID SUMMERS

Interguglielmi, Elia (*b* Naples, 1746; *d* Palermo, 16 May 1835). Italian painter. He is documented in Naples until 1762, where he formed his style by working as a draughtsman at the Reale Opificio delle Pietre Dure and trained in the studios of Giuseppe Bonito and of Antonio Dominici (*b* 1730), a Sicilian painter active in Naples. He then moved to Palermo, where his first paintings, of scenes from the *Life of St Anne* (1767; Palermo, S Anna della Misericordia), were influenced by Vito d'Anna (*c.* ?1729–69), who had taught Dominici and who was a leading figure in the art world of 18th-century Palermo. The scenes from the *Life of the Virgin* (Palermo, Chiesa degli Agonizzanti, 1782) are directly influenced by Neapolitan painting, especially that of Luca Giordano and Francesco Solimena. Between *c.* 1780 and 1810, Interguglielmi executed decorative frescoes in palazzi and villas in Palermo and in Piana dei Colli (Bagheria), becoming one of the leading figures in the transition from the late Baroque to Neo-classicism. Among such works are frescoes in the Palazzi Santa Croce–S Elia (*c.* 1790), Gangi (1792), Mirto (1793) and Coglitore (1796), all in Palermo. In the frescoes in the Villa Bordonaro Adriana at Colli, also attributed to Interguglielmi, he created an illusion of deep space through the classical device of a perspective of colonnades. Towards the end of the 18th century Interguglielmi moved his workshop to Bagheria, where the aristocracy from Palermo built their country houses. In his later years he responded to a central European decorative style, which had already spread to Naples, in which Rococo and Neo-classical elements were harmoniously united. The fresco *Glory of the Virtuous Prince* (*c.* 1785–90; Bagheria, Villa Valguarnera) initiated this successful period. There followed frescoes (1796–7) in the Villa Trabia, Bagheria, where the unity of the architecture is emphasized by the painted decoration, which was inspired by recent discoveries in Herculaneum and by the Pompeian style of the Adam brothers and the porcelain of Wedgwood.

BIBLIOGRAPHY

C. Siracusano: *La pittura del '700 in Sicilia* (Rome, 1986), pp. 363–6

——: 'La pittura del '700 in Sicilia', *La pittura in Italia: Il settecento*, ed. G. Briganti, 2 vols (Milan, 1989, rev. 1990), pp. 751–2 [with bibliog.]

DONATELLA GERMANÒ SIRACUSA

Interián de Ayala, Juan (*b* Madrid, 1656; *d* Madrid, 1730). Spanish theorist. He studied first at Alcalá de Henares, where he entered the Order of the Mercedarians. Later he took his doctorate in arts and theology at the University of Salamanca, where later he held the chairs of philosophy, Greek and Hebrew. He was Vicario Provincial of Castile, Predicador de su Majestad and Theologian on the Real Junta de la Concepción. He was admitted into the Real Academia Española, participating in the completion of the *Diccionario de la lengua castellana.* Author of a vast and varied literary output written in Latin and Castilian, Padre Interián de Ayala became famous on the publication in Madrid in 1730 of an essay on religious iconography, *Pictor Christianus eruditus, sive de erroribus qui passim admittuntur circa pingendas, atque effigendas Sacras Imagenes.* The Castilian translation was not published until 1782, and the extent of its influence has been much debated, although it must have circulated widely in the religious circles of Catholic Europe, since an edition was published in Paris in 1764 and an abridged version in Italian appeared in Ferrara in 1854, with a reprint in 1883 in Barcelona.

El Pintor Christiano, y erudito, the title of the 1782 Castilian edition by Padre Luis de Durán y de Bastero, is a wide-ranging and rather confused essay on sacred iconography with extensive disquisitions on Catholic liturgical subjects. It is written in the spirit of the moralizing essays of the Counter-Reformation, which specialized in, among other things, the orthodoxy of sacred images, and followed the example of the writings of Cardinal Gabriele Paleotti. Interián de Ayala had little interest in specifically artistic subjects and gave few details about the formal characteristics of a work or about the artist's personality, concentrating almost exclusively on the religious and moral aspects of the appropriate representation of sacred themes. The subject of religious iconography was taken up at varying length and with varying authority in several treatises on Spanish Baroque art, the most important being Francisco Pacheco's *Arte de la pintura* (Seville, 1649) and Antonio Acisclo Palomino y Velasco's *Museo pictórico y escala optica* (Madrid, 1715–24). In this context Interián de Ayala's work remains an essential source and provides evidence of the survival of Counter-Reformation ideology in the art of southern Catholic Europe.

BIBLIOGRAPHY

C. Dejob: *De l'influence du Concile de Trente sur la littérature et les Beaux Arts chez les peuples catholiques* (Paris, 1884)

M. Menéndez Pelayo: *Historia de las ideas estéticas en España* (Madrid, 1889)

F. J. Sánchez Cantón: *Fuentes literarias para la historia del arte español*, v (Madrid, 1941)

E. Male: *L'Art religieux de la fin du XVIe siècle, du XVIIe siècle et du XVIIIe siècle: Etude sur l'iconographie après le Concile de Trente: Italie-France-Espagne-Flandres* (Paris, 1972)

J. A. Gaya Nuño: *Historia de la crítica de arte en España* (Madrid, 1975)

S. Sebastián: *Contrarreforma y barroco: Lecturas iconográficas e iconológicas* (Madrid, 1981)

FRANCISCO CALVO SERVALLER

Interlace. Design that creates an illusion of strands, ribbons or the limbs and bodies of animals passing over and under each other. With the exception of the reef knot (a universal motif by virtue of the symbolism of joining and uniting), most interlacing designs do not portray real cords, plaiting or knotting and have no symbolic meaning.

Twist and plait motifs, also known as cable, guilloche or entrelac, appear as important motifs on cylinder seals in northern Syria in the second millennium BC (Collon, 1987, pp. 52–7). The motifs occur, mainly as borders and frames, on ivory objects (e.g. in Baghdad, Iraq Mus.; London, BM; New York, Met.) found in the North-west Palace at Nimrud as part of tribute and loot collected by Neo-Assyrian rulers in the 9th century BC. The designs were constructed on compass-drawn grids (see fig. 1a). This motif group was further developed in Greek art to provide a variety of architectural decoration. The decorated terracotta revetments on the treasury of Gela (first half 5th century BC) at Olympia, for example, include elaborate interlacing borders (Lawrence, fig. 117).

Roman mosaic designs used geometrical constructions as the framework into which decorative borders, often of twists and plaits, and emblematic motifs were fitted. The framework could also become an interlacing design when the construction lines passed over and under each other. This was particularly the case in the northern provinces of the Roman Empire.

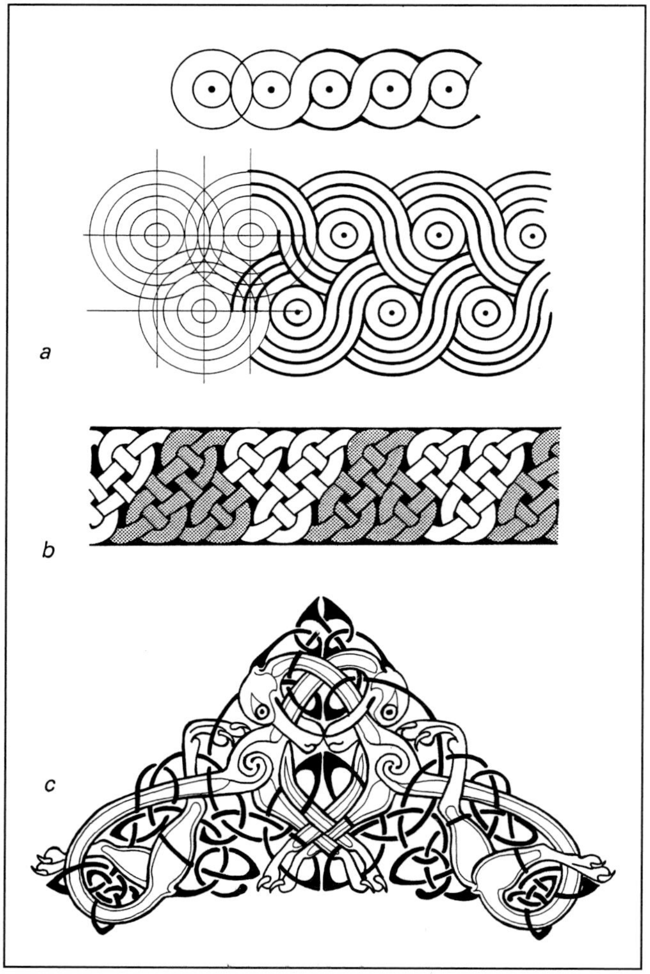

1. Interlace designs: (a) details from ivory panels found in the North-west Palace, Nimrud, Assyria, showing the methods of construction on compass-drawn grids, 9th century BC (London, British Museum); (b) border (detail) from the Book of Durrow, second half of the 7th century AD (Dublin, Trinity College Library, MS. 57, fol. 84*v*); (c) detail of a carpet page from the Lindisfarne Gospels, late 7th century AD (London, British Library, Cotton MS. Nero D.IV, fol. 94*v*)

More intricate ribbon interlacing became a major motif in Early Christian art. The choir-screen panels and capitals of S Vitale (consecrated AD 547) in Ravenna are examples of this style of interlace. In the Early Christian art of the Germanic kingdoms of post-Roman Europe, ribbon interlace and other motifs of Mediterranean derivation were combined with interlacing animal motifs from the late 5th century. Insular art was characterized by the use of these motifs, together with spiral scrolls, as in the Book of Durrow (second half of the 7th century; Dublin, Trinity Coll. Lib.; see fig. 1b; *see also* INSULAR ART, fig. 3), the LINDISFARNE GOSPELS (late 7th century; London, BL; see fig. 1c) or the Book of Kells (*c.* 721–806; Dublin, Trinity Coll. Lib., MS. 58; *see* INITIAL, MANUSCRIPT, fig. 1). This style influenced contemporary art in continental Europe and continued until the 11th century. Complicated ribbon interlace and knot patterns as representative of a Celtic heritage were revived in the CELTIC REVIVAL movement in 19th-century Ireland.

In Islamic art decoration was part of a larger and, in the main, geometrically based system, which involved all expressions of art and architecture. The grid lines of the geometrical figures, or the designs superimposed on them, generally feature a regular over–under interlace, which contributes to a high degree of elaboration and sophistication (e.g. *c.* 950 in London, BL, Add. MS. 11735; *see* ISLAMIC ART, fig. 102). Many motifs from Islamic decoration were adopted in European countries and feature in pattern books that were produced from the 15th century for the use and inspiration of craftsmen; for example the 'Academy of Leonardo da Vinci', a collection of engravings published *c.* 1495 to serve as models for craft workers, with designs apparently adapted from Islamic metalwork then produced in Venice (see fig. 2).

Interlacing ornament has also occasionally been used in the art of other cultures: for example a sophisticated use of interlacing ornament developed in the Kuba (i) kingdom of Zaïre, while interlacing dragons are popular motifs in Borneo (Wilson, 1994).

BIBLIOGRAPHY

R. D. Barnett: *A Catalogue of the Nimrud Ivories* (London, 1957)
I. El-Said and A. Parman: *Geometric Concepts in Islamic Art* (London, 1976)
J. J. G. Alexander: *Insular Manuscripts: 6th to the 9th Century*, A Survey of Manuscripts Illuminated in the British Isles (London, 1978)

2. Interlace design from the 'Academy of Leonardo da Vinci', *c.* 1495 (London, British Museum, PD 1877. 1–13.364)

J. Sheehy: *The Rediscovery of Ireland's Past: The Celtic Revival, 1830–1930* (London, 1980)
D. S. Neal: *Roman Mosaics in Britain*, Britannia Monograph Series, i (London, 1981)
A. W. Lawrence: *Greek Architecture*, Pelican Hist. A. (Harmondsworth, 1983)
D. M. Wilson: *Anglo-Saxon Art from the Seventh Century to the Norman Conquest* (London, 1984)
D. Collon: *First Impressions: Cylinder Seals in the Ancient Near East* (London, 1987)
R. Ettinghausen and O. Grabar: *The Art and Architecture of Islam, 650–1250*, Pelican Hist. A. (Harmondsworth, 1987)
E. Wilson: *8000 Years of Ornament: An Illustrated Handbook of Motifs* (London, 1994), pp. 173–96

EVA WILSON

International exhibition. Large-scale industrial and cultural exhibition in which several nations participate. The first was the Great Exhibition of Products of Industry of All Nations held at the Crystal Palace in London in 1851 (see fig. 1), succeeded by an international exhibition held every few years in a major city. The principal ones include:

London 1851	Paris 1900
New York 1853	St Louis 1904
Dublin 1853	Liège 1905
Paris 1855	Milan 1906
London 1862	Brussels 1910
Paris 1867	Turin 1911
Vienna 1873	Ghent 1913
Philadelphia 1876	San Francisco 1915
Paris 1878	Paris 1925
Sydney 1879–80	Barcelona 1929
Melbourne 1880–81	Chicago 1933–4
Antwerp 1885	Paris 1937
Melbourne 1888–9	New York 1939–40
Paris 1889	Brussels 1958
Chicago 1893	Seattle 1962
Antwerp 1894	Montreal 1967
Brussels 1897	Osaka 1970

Prior to the Great Exhibition national industrial shows had been held in most European countries. The Society of Arts in London had mounted such exhibitions since 1761 but had included only models and drawings of industrial machinery rather than the products themselves. The first true industrial exhibition, the Exposition Publique des Produits de l'Industrie Française, was held in Paris in 1798 as part of the series of festivals celebrating the Revolution of 1789; between 1798 and 1849 France sponsored 11 such events. With the expansion of markets in the mid-19th century, customs barriers and strict controls on foreign trade were relaxed, and from the necessity of selling products internationally came the idea of holding major international industrial exhibitions. Conceived as encyclopedic in nature, encompassing products from all nations, they were a natural extension of the 18th-century passion for the organization of knowledge and the 19th-century optimism about the benefits of industrial development. In addition to the didactic motivation, which particularly marked the earlier ones, international exhibitions were used to assert the economic and cultural dominance of the host nation. They have also been used to divert national attention away from failings in these areas.

In its organization the Great Exhibition adopted the classification of the French national shows, a structure that, though subsequently somewhat modified, nonetheless remained standard with four broad divisions: raw materials, machinery, manufactures and fine arts and, within these, at least 30 subdivisions. The Great Exhibition differed from its national predecessors in that it was the first to include the fine arts as a category *per se* (*see* PRINTS, colour pl. VII, fig. 1); previous industrial exhibitions had included them only to demonstrate materials and techniques used in art production (e.g. paints, tools, casting, printing). Painting was nonetheless excluded in 1851 because the commissioners felt that 'being but little affected by material conditions, it seemed to rank as an independent art'. Only in 1855 at the Exposition Universelle in Paris, the first French international exhibition, was a full-scale fine arts exhibition included among the categories. After this the fine arts were always represented but the displays, chosen by each country's national committees, tended to favour official art and have been of little interest to art historians. There were, however, exceptions to this general conservatism, the most noteworthy of which was Picasso's *Guernica* (1937; Madrid, Prado), commissioned from the artist by the Republican government of Spain.

Beginning with Joseph Paxton's Crystal Palace for the Great Exhibition, international exhibitions have been important showcases for the latest architecture, design ideas and engineering techniques (see fig. 2). The Eiffel Tower, at a height of 300 m (for illustration *see* EIFFEL, GUSTAVE), and the Galerie des Machines, at that time the building with the longest span in the world, were built for the Exposition Universelle in Paris in 1889. For the World's Columbian Exposition in 1893 in Chicago, Louis Sullivan designed the Transportation Building, and George Washington Ferris created the Ferris Wheel. At the Exposició Internacional de Barcelona in 1929 Ludwig Mies van der Rohe designed the German pavilion, which introduced his concept of flowing space. International exhibitions also popularized traditional architectural styles: Japan regularly sent tea houses, Switzerland chalets. The Rue des Nations at the Exposition Universelle in Paris in 1878 served as an architectural museum with the building styles of all participating countries represented in one long façade, a concept repeated in later exhibitions.

International exhibitions have also helped propagate wide-ranging design styles. The influence of Art Nouveau was greatly enhanced by the Exposition Universelle in Paris in 1900 (e.g. armchair by Louis Majorelle; *see* FRANCE, fig. 61), especially through the displays from Austria. Josef Hoffmann designed the room for the exhibition of products of the Kunstgewerbeschule in Vienna, while Joseph Maria Olbrich showed a room designed for a luxury steamer. Decorative works by such designers as Emile Gallé and René Lalique were also displayed. The Exposition Internationale des Arts Décoratifs et Industriels Modernes held in Paris in 1925 popularized the Art Deco style named after it.

The contemporaneous state of industry and design can be studied through the numerous official and unofficial publications that accompanied the exhibitions. Virtually every invention or design principle was introduced at an international exhibition, from the washing machine at the

1. Interior of the Crystal Palace by Henry Courtney Selous: *The Inauguration of the Great Exhibition, 1st May 1851*, oil on canvas, 1.70×2.37 m, 1851–2 (London, Victoria and Albert Museum)

2. Pavillon de l'Air at the Exposition Internationale des Arts et Techniques dans la Vie Moderne, Paris, 1937, showing the mural painted by Robert Delaunay and others

Great Exhibition of 1851 to the television at the New York World's Fair of 1939–40. In addition to the art, architecture and manufactured goods of the participating countries, other aspects of their cultures were also represented; food, dress, music and customs were demonstrated, displayed and sampled. As a result, in addition to the commercial sector, international exhibitions commanded a broad general audience from all social strata.

Although the great age of international exhibitions really ended with the New York World's Fair of 1939–40, such exhibitions continue to be held regularly. They are increasingly dominated by multinational corporations and the desire to promote tourism, though these features have their roots in earlier exhibitions. One notable characteristic of the international exhibitions since the Exposition Universelle et Internationale de Bruxelles in 1958 has been the widespread use of audio-visual environmental displays, which bombard the audience with a wealth of sounds and images.

See also EXHIBITION ARCHITECTURE.

BIBLIOGRAPHY

R. Isay: *Panorama des expositions universelles* (Paris, 1937)

K. Luckhurst: *The Story of Exhibitions* (London, 1951)

R. Poirier: *Des Foires, des peuples, des expositions* (Paris, 1958)

E. Kroker, ed.: *Die Weltausstellungen im 19. Jahrhundert*, Studien zur Naturwissenschaft, Technik und Wirtschaft im neunzehnten Jahrhundert, iv (Göttingen, 1975)

W. Plum: *Weltausstellungen im 19. Jahrhundert: Schauspiele des sozio-kulturellen Wandels* (Bonn and Bad Godesberg, 1975; Eng. trans., Bonn and Bad Godesberg, 1977)

H. Neuberg: *Conceptions of International Exhibitions* (Zurich, 1976)

J. Allwood: *The Great Exhibitions* (London, 1977)

P. Ory: *Les Expositions universelles de Paris: Panorama raisonné, avec des aperçus nouveaux et des illustrations par les meilleurs auteurs* (Paris, 1982)

W. Friebe: *Architektur der Weltausstellungen, 1851 bis 1970* (Stuttgart, 1983; Eng. trans., Leipzig, 1985)

——: *Vom Kristallpalast zum Sonnenturm: Eine Kulturgeschichte der Weltausstellungen* (Leipzig, 1983; Eng. trans., Leipzig, 1985)

Le Livre des expositions universelles, 1851–1989 (exh. cat. by R. Bordaz and others, Paris, Mus. A. Déc., 1983)

P. Greenhalgh: *Ephemeral Vistas: The Expositions Universelles, Great Exhibitions and World's Fairs, 1851–1939* (Manchester, 1988)

E. G. Holt, ed.: *Universal Expositions and State-sponsored Fine Arts*, i of *The Expanding World of Art, 1874–1902* (New Haven and London, 1988)

J. E. Findling, ed.: *Historical Dictionary of World's Fairs and Expositions, 1851–1988* (New York, Westport and London, 1990)

PATRICIA MAINARDI

International Exhibition of Modern Art. *See* ARMORY SHOW.

International Gothic. *See under* GOTHIC, §IV, 5(xi).

International Style. Term applied to architecture of the MODERN MOVEMENT after 1932. That year the first architectural exhibition at the Museum of Modern Art (MOMA), New York, was held following a visit to Europe by historian Henry-Russell Hitchcock and Philip Johnson, Director of Architecture at MOMA; the term was enshrined in the title of the accompanying book and catalogue *The International Style: Architecture since 1922*. Buildings selected for inclusion in the exhibition, with some notable exceptions (see below), had certain formal characteristics in common, being mostly rectilinear, undecorated, asymmetrical and white.

The idea of an international architecture, partly inspired by the symbolic socialist use of the word 'international', had been suggested by Walter Gropius in his title *Internationale Architektur* for the first *Bauhausbuch* (Munich, 1925). It was also used by Ludwig Hilberseimer in the title of his book *Internationale neue Baukunst* (Stuttgart, 1927), published a year or two before he was appointed to teach at the Bauhaus, and its validity was confirmed by successful international participation in the Siedlungaustellung (1927) at Weissenhof, Stuttgart (for further discussion and illustration *see* DEUTSCHER WERKBUND; *see also* MODERN MOVEMENT, §4). After the foundation of CIAM (Congrès Internationaux d'Architecture Moderne) in 1928, Hitchcock accepted this position when he used the phrase 'international style' in referring to the work of European avant-garde architects in his book *Modern Architecture: Romanticism and Reintegration* (New York, 1929) and again in the MOMA exhibition catalogue.

While the work of 48 architects, firms and official groups from 15 countries was shown at MOMA, the exhibition was dominated by that of European avant-garde architects of the Modern Movement. More than half of them were from Germany, including Marcel Breuer, Walter Gropius, Ernst May, Erich Mendelsohn, Mies van der Rohe and Hans Scharoun. The Netherlands was represented by the work of J. J. P. Oud, Mart Stam, Johannes Brinkman and L. C. van der Vlugt; Italy by Luigi Figini and Gino Pollini; France by Le Corbusier and André Lurçat; Spain by José Manuel de Aizpúrua and Joaquín Labayen; Finland by Alvar Aalto and Erik Bryggman; Sweden by Gunnar Asplund and Sven Markelius; Switzerland by Werner Moser; Britain by Joseph Emberton; and Japan by Mamoru Yamada. The most notable of the six American architects whose work was shown were Raymond Hood and J. André Fouilhoux (1879–1945), George Howe with the Swiss emigré architect William Edmond Lescaze, and another recent immigrant, Richard Neutra.

In analysing the exhibited work in stylistic terms, Hitchcock and Johnson purged it of the ideological connotations implicit in the socio-cultural origins of the Modern Movement. They saw the International Style as a 'frame of potential growth rather than as a fixed and crushing mould', with only three controlling 'principles': the first, 'the conception of architecture as volume rather than mass', premised a gridded structure divided into volumes by non-load-bearing (lightweight) planes and wrapped in a smooth skin, producing an aesthetic of surface. The second, 'regularity rather than symmetry as the chief means of ordering design', was related to the underlying discipline of arranging façades according to a regularly disposed structure, and it seemed to oppose the emerging Functionalist ethic in its assertion that the prime architectural problem is 'to adjust the irregular and unequal demands of function to regular construction and the use of standard parts'. The third principle, 'proscribing arbitrary applied decoration', completed the description of a new architecture that claimed already to exist in a 'set of actual monuments, not a vague corpus of theory'. While by far the majority of buildings exhibited at MOMA—such as Le Corbusier's Villa Savoye (1929–31), Poissy (*see* VILLA, fig. 10), and Mies van der Rohe's Tugendhat House (1928–30), Brno—conformed to the then mainstream

1. Alvar Aalto: tuberculosis sanatorium at Paimio, Finland, 1929–32

prismatic 'white architecture', however, the way to a major extension of the boundaries of the International Style was opened by the inclusion of such buildings as Mendelsohn's curved, glazed Schocken Store (1928) at Chemnitz (*see* MENDELSOHN, ERICH, fig. 2) and the skyscrapers by Hood and Fouilhoux for McGraw-Hill (1931), New York, and by Howe and Lescaze for the Philadelphia Savings Fund Society (PSFS; completed 1933), Philadelphia.

Reversion to a formalized concept of style nevertheless ran counter to the anti-aestheticism of such radical European avant-garde architects as Hannes Meyer, and in the very year of the MOMA exhibition even Le Corbusier had successfully pleaded with Alberto Sartoris to change the name of a forthcoming book to *Gli elementi dell'architettura funzionale* (Milan, 1932; preface by Le Corbusier) instead of *razionale*. This was important in helping to make the term FUNCTIONALISM a convenient one for architects wishing to justify the new and unfamiliar forms without reference to style. Buildings in the International Style may also be characterized as having structures independent of the articulation of enclosed space, although in many of the buildings shown at MOMA this characteristic was formalized rather than real. The effect of independent structure results in adaptability to function rather than its overt expression, and, taken together with the economy and technological convenience of rectilinear geometry, this was one of the main causes of the anonymity and banal appearance often ascribed to buildings of the International Style.

It was, however, the simple, white cubic forms that first caught the international imagination in the 1930s and early 1940s, when several notable examples were built in Europe, including a tuberculosis sanatorium (1929–32; see fig. 1), Paimio, Finland, by Aalto, medium-rise flats in Doldertal (1935–6), Zurich, by Alfred Roth and Emil Roth (with Marcel Breuer), and the two Highpoint blocks (1933–8) in north London by Tecton; and private houses in the Netherlands by Brinkman and van der Vlugt and in Hungary by Farkas Molnár and József Fischer. In the same period buildings of this general character, often adapted to climate or tinged with regional features, can be found as far apart as Mexico City (e.g. Luis Barragán's duplex houses and Juan O'Gorman's standardized schools, both 1933–4); Rio de Janeiro (e.g. Oscar Niemeyer's Obra do Berço day nursery and maternity clinic, 1937); Tokyo (e.g. Yamada's Communications Ministry Hospital, 1937); Moscow (e.g. the Vesnin brothers' Zil Club, 1937); and Tel Aviv (e.g. Arieh Sharon's cooperative housing, 1939).

The buildings of the Italian *Razionalismo* movement (*see* RATIONALISM (ii)), notably Giuseppe Terragni's Casa del Fascio (now Casa del Popolo; completed 1936), Como (*see* ITALY, fig. 24), and Ignazio Gardella's Dispensario Antitubercolare (1936), Alessandria, strongly influenced developments elsewhere: an example is Jorge Hardoy's Virrey del Pino flats (1943), Buenos Aires, one of numerous rectilinear, multi-storey, reinforced-concrete buildings erected around the world in which the appearance was determined by *brise-soleil* systems. On the other hand a more baroque approach to the 'white' style was taken by Oscar Niemeyer and Lúcio Costa in their Brazilian Pavilion (with Paul Lester Weiner) for the New York World's Fair of 1939 (*see* BRAZIL, fig. 6) and in Niemeyer's lakeside buildings at Pampulha (1942–6), Belo Horizonte, Brazil (*see* NIEMEYER, OSCAR, fig. 1).

After World War II the International Style moved into the more practically orientated mode foreshadowed in the MOMA exhibition. Absence of historical reference was *de rigueur* as a matter of economy in dealing concurrently with post-war reconstruction in Europe and Asia and with increasingly rapid urbanization and a growing demand worldwide for schools, housing and other social buildings of all kinds. The Athens Charter, which originated at CIAM IV (1933), was revised and published by Le Corbusier in 1943 and, although subsequently widely criticized for its emphasis on zoning and the use of widely spaced multi-storey blocks as vital ingredients of urbanization, it had significant implications for Latin American, South-east Asian and African countries with exploding urban populations or in their first years of post-colonial independence between 1945 and *c.* 1960. Multi-storey mass housing is found all over the world, from Hong Kong to Caracas, where Carlos Raúl Villanueva's elegant Banco Obrero housing climbs the hills behind the city. The principal monument to Corbusian urbanism, however, is BRASÍLIA, the capital city of Brazil, inaugurated in 1960 (urban plan 1957; for illustration see COSTA, LÚCIO). Despite its functional failings, its open phalanx of identical ministry buildings and the formalism of the executive offices and Congresso Nacional (1960; *see* NIEMEYER, OSCAR, fig. 2) constitute one of the most memorable images of 20th-century architecture.

In Europe and the USA developments in structural techniques using steel and concrete frames with prefabricated infill panels, which were designed to expedite the construction of housing and schools, added to the increasingly standardized appearance of many buildings; this can be seen in the more than 100 schools built in 1947–55 by

C. H. Aslin (1893–1959) to a system developed for Herts County Council in England (*see* RATIONALIZED CONSTRUCTION, §2). The mainstream of the International Style, however, reached its apogee in the work of Mies van der Rohe in the USA, for example his Lake Shore Drive Apartments (1948–51), Chicago (*see* UNITED STATES OF AMERICA, fig. 10). The development of the curtain wall (*see* CURTAIN WALL (ii)) as a practical method of construction changed the character of the International Style in the late 1940s and early 1950s to one of undecorated rectilinear formalism, with surface structure and materials (usually mainly glass) consistently articulated. Many of the gridded patterns of curtain walling systems nevertheless reflect the sophisticated detailing and refined proportions of Mies's exposed steel or bronze frames, which were mostly not curtain walls. Particularly characteristic of this corporate 'glass box' International Style is the work of SKIDMORE, OWINGS & MERRILL in the 1950s (see fig. 2), during which period office buildings of this genre changed the appearance of every major city in the world, from New York (e.g. United Nations Headquarters, 1947–53, by an international committee under the chairmanship of Wallace K. Harrison; *see* GOVERNMENT BUILDING, fig. 2) to Melbourne (e.g. ICI Building, 1958, by Bates, Smart & McCutcheon) or Mexico City (e.g. Torre Latino Americano, 1957, by Augusto H. Alvarez and Adolfo Zeevaert).

2. Gordon Bunshaft and Skidmore, Owings & Merrill: Lever House, New York, 1950–52

Meanwhile Le Corbusier had begun to develop new, more sculptural forms of expression, particularly in reinforced concrete, in his buildings of the 1950s in France and India (*see* LE CORBUSIER, §I, 1(v)). Together with the contemporary reinforced-concrete work of Kenzo Tange in Japan, these buildings soon became associated with BRUTALISM and such related developments as New Brutalism and New Empiricism, which represented a new honesty of expression stemming from the work and precepts of members of TEAM TEN, who had thrown CIAM into disarray and led to its demise in 1959. The NEO-LIBERTY movement in Italy kindled the wrath of the orthodox Modernists in 1957, with the firm BBPR daring to revive historical reference overtly in a gesture of contextualism in their Torre Velasca (completed 1958), Milan (for illustration *see* BBPR ARCHITECTURAL STUDIO). Although orthodox International Style buildings continued to be constructed in the 1960s, this was the beginning of a growing pluralism in Modernism—subsequently ranging from the more rhetorical buildings of late Modernism to the mechanistic expressions of HIGH TECH—that defied collective characterization. By 1963, when early evidence of Post-modernism had already appeared in architecture (*see* POST-MODERNISM, §1), for example in the Guild House Retirement Home (1960–62), Philadelphia, by Venturi, Rauch & Scott Brown, Hitchcock had concluded that 'the International Style is over' (see Hitchcock, 1963, epilogue).

BIBLIOGRAPHY

H.-R. Hitchcock and P. Johnson: *The International Style: Architecture since 1922* (New York, 1932, rev. 2/1966)
A. Roth: *La Nouvelle Architecture* (Zurich, 1940)
S. Giedion: *A Decade of New Architecture* (Zurich, 1951)
H.-R. Hitchcock: *Architecture, Nineteenth and Twentieth Centuries*, Pelican Hist. A. (Harmondsworth, 1958, rev. 2/1963)
P. R. Banham: *The New Brutalism: Ethic or Aesthetic?* (London, 1966)
J. Jacobus: *Twentieth-century Architecture, 1940–65* (London, 1966)
J. Joedicke: *Architecture since 1945* (London, 1969)
W. H. Jordy: *American Buildings and their Architects*, iii–iv (New York, 1970–73)
C. Jenks: *Modern Movements in Architecture* (London, 1973, rev. 2/1985)
A. Smithson and P. Smithson: *Without Rhetoric: An Architectural Aesthetic, 1955–1972* (London, 1973)
P. R. Banham: *The Age of the Masters* (London, 1975)
A. M. Vogt: *Arkitektur 1940–1980* (Frankfurt am Main, 1980)
W. J. R. Curtis: *Modern Architecture since 1900* (Oxford, 1982, rev. 2/1987) [esp. pt 2, chaps 13–18, and pt 3, chaps 19–22]
H. Searing, ed.: *In Search of Modern Architecture* (New York, 1982)
M. Tafuri: *Storia dell' architettura italiana, 1944–1985* (Turin, 1982; Eng. trans., 1989) [esp. pt 1, chaps 1–4]
B. Bognar: *Contemporary Japanese Architecture: Its Development and Challenge* (New York, 1985)
D. P. Handlin: *American Architecture* (London, 1985) [esp. chaps 6–9]
G. Monnier: *L'Architecture en France: Une Histoire critique, 1918–1950* (Paris, 1990) [esp. pts 2 and 3]
D. Sharp: *Twentieth Century Architecture: A Visual History* (London, 1991)

For further bibliography *see* MODERN MOVEMENT.

ANDREW BALLANTYNE

Intimisme. Term applied to paintings depicting everyday life in domestic interiors, usually referring to the work of PIERRE BONNARD and EDOUARD VUILLARD. It was first used in the 1890s, although the type of paintings to which it refers had been produced earlier by such artists as Johannes Vermeer and Jean-Siméon Chardin. The *intimiste* style is aptly characterized by André Gide's comment on Vuillard's four decorative panels, *Figures and Interiors* (1896; Paris, Petit Pal.), that the artist was 'speaking in a low tone, suitable to confidences' ('Promenade au Salon d'Automne', *Gaz. B.-A.*, xxxiv, 1905, p. 582). Bonnard and Vuillard were both members of the mystical brotherhood of the NABIS, but their commitment to the esoteric, symbolist side of the Nabi aesthetic was not as strong as their interest in the group's technical ideas on painting, and often their subject-matter was tranquil, bourgeois interiors. An example is Bonnard's *Le Déjeuner* (1899; Zurich, Stift. Samml. Bührle), in which the technique owes much to Impressionism, though, influenced by the theory of Paul Sérusier, the leader of the Nabis, more muted colours are employed. Their interest in decoration and pattern is evident, and the figures in their paintings often merge with the décor of their interiors, which in turn reflect the contemporary taste for rich patterned effects, as in Vuillard's *Mother and Sister of the Artist* (1893; New York, MOMA). Even when dealing with exterior scenes, Bonnard and Vuillard often create a sense of domestic intimacy (e.g. Vuillard's *The Park*, 1894; New York, priv. col.; see Preston, p. 60). Vuillard's style remained predominantly *intimiste* throughout his career, whereas Bonnard's later paintings exhibit a more expansive approach with a use of brighter colours; nevertheless, some of the latter's late paintings (e.g. *Nu dans le bain*, 1936; Paris, Petit Pal.) still retain the *intimiste* quality of his earlier works.

BIBLIOGRAPHY

A. Carnduff Ritchie: *Edouard Vuillard* (New York, 1954)

Bonnard and his Environment (exh. cat. by J. T. Soby and others, New York, MOMA, 1964)

J. Russell and others: *Bonnard* (London, 1984)

S. Preston: *Edouard Vuillard* (London, 1985)

J. Warnod: *Edouard Vuillard* (Näfels, 1989)

□

Intonaco. Term used in the true fresco technique for the final, smooth coat of plaster to which the pigments are applied, while the plaster is still wet (*see* FRESCO, §1).

RUPERT FEATHERSTONE

Intrados [soffit]. Term for the inner curve or underside of an arch or voussoir (*see* ARCH, fig. 1f).

Inuit [Innuit; 'the real people']. Indigenous people mainly of GREENLAND and the Arctic coasts of Canada (*see under* NATIVE NORTH AMERICAN ART). They form the largest group of the so-called Eskimo peoples but prefer not to use the term 'Eskimo' of themselves. The Inuit language is also spoken by the Inupiat of northern Alaska.

□

Investment. The purchase of a work of art in the expectation of an increase in its value. Any investment is based on two fundamental expectations: the return, in the form of interest, on any capital invested, and capital gain when the investment is realized. Obviously there is no return in interest on a work of art, therefore the profit on sale must be greater than the total of the capital gain on conventional stock plus the total annual dividends that would have accrued. Art is a useful investment commodity when political or economic circumstances make conventional investment in stocks or shares less desirable. At such times jewellery, especially those pieces whose value lies in precious materials rather than craftsmanship, is popular as it is highly portable. Other investment involves speculative venture into areas of the art market that have been thought to be undervalued. Generally speaking, the return on works of art is modest. For example, the investment portfolio of works of art acquired by the British Railways Pension Fund on the advice of Sotheby's in the 1970s and early 1980s produced a marginally poorer yield than would have been achieved by a similar sum invested on the stock market. Two factors militate against the success of such investment: first, the question of whether an auction house, whose legal obligation is to the vendor, can represent both vendor and buyer without inflating the market price and thereby benefit from a larger commission and buyer's premium; and second, the fact that when such items are resold buyers will often discount their bids in the knowledge of the role of the auction house.

An item that is not from a private source and that may have appeared comparatively recently on the market will almost always lead to a lower hammer price than one that has been in a particular collection for a number of years. Conversely, the price of an object that is to be bought by a museum, and will therefore disappear from the market, is often inflated. However, during recession, prices in the ART MARKET both decline less fast than those on the international stock markets and recover more quickly, as demonstrated by the *Times*–Sotheby index. In general, two areas of the art market hold their value: historical and contemporary masterpieces in the long term and fashionable items in the short term. The entry of the J. Paul Getty Museum, Malibu, CA, and such Japanese companies as Yasuda Fire and Marine Insurance have kept up the price of the former. The market for the latter is more volatile and can fluctuate wildly according to the presence or absence of one customer. In London in the late 1980s investment in the newly fashionable graduates from the Glasgow School of Art, whose work was more highly priced than that of established artists, produced only short-term gains as the international market for lesser-known contemporary work collapsed during the economic recession that followed. By contrast Titian's *Venus and Adonis* (*c.* 1555) was sold by auction in December 1991 at Christie's London saleroom for £7,480,000, more than three times the pre-sale estimate. The vagaries of taste may also affect value. Profitable investment in works of art may be helped by tax concessions on loans to museums, as in the USA, or by a sympathetic policy regarding taxable status as in Monaco or Switzerland.

BIBLIOGRAPHY

G. Reitlinger: *The Economics of Taste*, 3 vols (London, 1961–70)

R. H. Rush: *Art as an Investment* (Englewood Cliffs, NJ, 1962)

G. Keen: *The Sale of Works of Art: A Study based on the Times–Sotheby Index* (London, 1971)
F. Herrmann: 'The Art Market: Now and Then', *Art at Auction, 1974–75*, ed. A. Jackson (London, 1975), pp. 9–22
Conference Proceedings of the Law and Business Forum: Collecting and Investing in Fine Art: London, 1990

BRUCE TATTERSALL

Inwood. English family of artists. William Inwood (*b* ?London, *c.* 1771; *d* London, 16 March 1843) became the steward of Edward Abbot, later 1st Baron Colchester. He practised as a surveyor, publishing *Tables for the Purchasing of Estates. . .and for the Renewal of Leases* (London, 1811), which ran into many editions. According to Papworth he was also widely employed as an architect, but few specific commissions are recorded. His three sons all attended the Royal Academy Schools, London. By far the most successful was the eldest, Henry William Inwood (*b* London, 22 May 1794; *d* at sea, March 1843), who trained with his father; in 1818 the two were awarded the commission to build St Pancras New Church in the Euston Road, London. That year Henry went on an expedition to Italy and Greece; in Athens he measured some of the most important buildings on the Acropolis. On his return in 1819 he and his father collaborated on the design of St Pancras New Church, which drew heavily on the Erectheion and other Greek prototypes and became the best-known church of the Greek Revival. In 1827 Henry published *The Erectheion at Athens*, which became the standard reference work on the building and forms his most important contribution to English architecture. His later London works, most of which were credited to 'W. & H. W. Inwood', include All Saints' Church (1822–4), Camden Town, St Peter's Chapel (1822–5; destr. 1967), Regent Square, both classical, and St Mary's Chapel (1824–7), Somers Town, a thin Gothic building that was held up to derision in A. W. N. Pugin's *Contrasts*. William Inwood's two other sons were Charles Frederick Inwood (*b* 28 Nov 1798; *d* 1 June 1840), who became an architect and assisted his father on Westminster Hospital (1832–4; destr. 1951), and Edward Inwood (*c.* 1800–40), a monumental sculptor whose only known work is a memorial to the *Rev. J. S. Breedon* (*d* 1826) and his wife, at Pangbourne, Berks.

WRITINGS

H. W. Inwood: *The Erectheion at Athens* (London, 1827; Ger. trans., Potsdam, 1843)

BIBLIOGRAPHY

Colvin; Papworth

NEIL BURTON

Inza, Joaquín (*b* Agreda, Soria, 1736; *d* Madrid, 1811). Spanish painter. He trained at the Real Academia de Bellas Artes de S Fernando in Madrid from 1752 and must have concentrated on portraiture soon after, as signed and dated portraits exist from 1758. He painted members of the Madrid aristocracy and enjoyed the patronage of both the Duquesa de Arcos, for whom he worked in 1781–2, and the Conde de Fernán Núñez, whose portrait he painted in 1784 (priv. col.). He also painted portraits of many noblemen at the court in Madrid and was especially close to the Iriarte family; one of his finest and most expressive portraits is of the celebrated poet, *Tomás Iriarte* (*c.* 1790; Madrid, Prado), which was engraved by Luis Salvador Carmona in 1792. Inza executed several commissions for successive Spanish monarchs, including portraits of *Charles III* (Madrid, Real Acad. S Fernando, Mus.) and other members of the royal family. He also painted canvases for several institutions and a portrait of the prime minister, *Manuel Godoy* (Aránjuez, Pal. Real), in which his style is formal and unobtrusive.

Inza's work is precise and restrained, although his draughtsmanship is a little harsh. His ability to handle colour is evident, despite a certain coldness in the tonalities. His portraits are often hieratic and lacking in emotion and show the influence of courtly images from Jean Ranc to Anton Raphael Mengs, of French engravings and of some contact with Francisco de Goya, to whom some portraits probably by Inza have been dubiously attributed. Despite his technical limitations, Inza appears to have enjoyed as much commercial success as some of his more eminent contemporaries.

BIBLIOGRAPHY

E. Lafuente Ferrari: *Antecedentes, coincidencias e influencias del arte de Goya* (Madrid, 1947)
J. Valverde Madrid: 'El pintor Joaquín Inza', *Goya*, 152 (1979), pp. 90–93

JUAN J. LUNA

Ioannina [Yannina]. Greek city in Epiros, capital of the Ioannina district. The site, on a rocky promontory on the west bank of Lake Pamvotis, is probably, according to Prokopios (*Buildings* VI.i.39–42), where Justinian I (*reg* AD 527–565) resettled the citizens of ancient Euria, who were suffering from barbarian raids.

Ioannina is first documented in 1020. In 1082 it was taken by the Normans, who repaired the walls around the promontory to withstand attack from the Byzantine forces. Few sections of these walls survive, although a circular tower (11th century), known as Bohemond's tower, stands in what later became the inner keep of the Turkish fortress. When Michael I Angelos Doukas Komnenos (*reg* 1204–15) founded the Despotate of Epiros, Ioannina became its second most important city after Arta, and it became the home of some of the Byzantine nobility following the Latin conquest of Constantinople in 1204. Such families as the Philanthropinoi and Stratigopouloi formed a powerful aristocracy that made Ioannina into a self-governing state and gave it a rich cultural and artistic tradition. Among the few extant foundations from this period are two monastery churches on the island in Lake Pamvotis: Hagios Nikolaos Philanthropinoi (1292), a single-aisle, barrel-vaulted basilica with porches on three sides, and the tiny, wooden-roofed Hagios Nikolaos Stratigopoulos or Dilios (13th century). Other remains include a 13th-century bathhouse built on the ruins of a Hellenistic building within the fortified area of the promontory.

In 1318 Ioannina acknowledged the suzerainty of Andronikos II (*reg* 1282–1328), who conceded numerous commercial privileges, as a result of which the city flourished. In 1345, however, the city was taken by Stephen Uroš IV Dušan (*reg* 1331–55; emperor 1346). Much is known about Ioannina during the 14th and 15th centuries from the Ioannina and Tocco Chronicles. In addition to the names of successive city governors, the chronicles describe the city's cultural and artistic life, including references to the workshops of painters and metalworkers.

They also record 18 churches (all destr.) within the fortified area.

In 1430 the city was captured by the Turks, under whom it thrived as a commercial and cultural centre. Between the 15th and 17th centuries there were major developments in the working of silver and gold, for which the city remains famous; gold embroidery from Ioannina was exported throughout the region during the 19th and 20th centuries (*see* GREECE, §V). Numerous high-quality wall paintings also survive from this period, including those in Hagios Nikolaos Stratigopoulos (1543) and in Hagios Nikolaos Philanthropinoi (1531–2, 1542 and 1560; *see* POST-BYZANTINE, §II, 2). In the latter church the south annexe includes portraits of seven Greek philosophers, while the paintings in the narthex (1542 or later) and annexes (1560) have been attributed to George and Frangos Kontari. The same artists may also have been responsible for the earliest wall paintings (late 16th century) in the Eleousa monastery church (early 16th century) on the island in Lake Pamvotis; the latest paintings in this church date to 1759. In 1507 the brothers Nektarios and Theophanis Apsarades, both monks, built the monastery of the Prodromos (St John the Baptist), also on the island; its church combines the transverse vaulted plan with the cross-in-square type. The walls were first painted in 1798 and repainted in 1824 and 1891. Another 16th-century foundation is the monastery of Hagios Panteleimon.

Among the Turkish buildings that survive within the fortified area are the Aslan Pasha Mosque (1618), the Fetiye Mosque (rest. 1795), the Soufari Saray and the Turkish baths. Between 1789 and 1822, Ali Pasha made Ioannina his headquarters, restored its fortress and used it as a base in his unsuccessful bid for independence from the Sultan. The city remained in Turkish hands until 1913, when it became part of the Greek state.

BIBLIOGRAPHY

L. Vranoussi: *Istorika kai topographika tou mesaionikou kastrou ton Ioanninon* [History and topography of the medieval fortress at Ioannina] (Athens, 1968)

M. Acheimastou-Potamianou: *I moni ton Philanthropinon kai i proti phasi tis metavyzantinis zographikis* [The monastery of the Filanthropinoi and the first phase of Post-Byzantine painting] (Athens, 1980)

T. Liva-Xanthaki: *I tihografies tis Monis Diliou* [The wall paintings of the Dilios Monastery] (Ioannina, 1980)

P. Soustal and J. Koder: 'Ioannina', *Nikopolis und Kefallenia* (1981), iii of *Tabula Imperii Byzantini*, ed. H. Hunger (Vienna, 1976–), pp. 165–7

D. Nicol: *The Despotate of Epiros, 1267–1479* (Cambridge, 1984)

S. Dakari: *To nisi ton Ioanninon* [The island of Ioannina] (Ioannina, 1986)

BARBARA PAPADOPOULOU

Iofan, Boris (Mikhaylovich) (*b* Odessa, 28 April 1891; *d* Barvikha, nr Moscow, 1976). Ukrainian architect, active in Russia. He studied at the School of Art, Odessa, and subsequently graduated as an architect from the Regio Istituto Superiore di Belle Arti, Rome, in 1916. From 1917 he practised in Rome, where he designed the Soviet Embassy (1923), before returning to the Soviet Union in 1924.

Iofan's early works manifest a synthesis of Neo-classical and Modern Movement architectural concepts. The residential complex (1928–30) on the Bersenevskaya Embankment, Moscow, designed with his elder brother Dmitry Iofan, draws on Constructivist ideas concerning the incorporation of shared facilities into the design of housing schemes. This massive and densely populated housing scheme, comprising 500 flats, consists of 11-storey blocks surrounding a series of courtyards, among which are interspersed various collective facilities, such as a laundry and supermarket. The southern side of the site is completed by the Udarnik Cinema, with an innovative reinforced-concrete barrel vault; whereas the northern façade, facing the River Moskva, prefigures Iofan's emergence as a Neo-classicist in the 1930s, with its repetitive use of heavy vertical piers. His most overtly modernist building is a sanatorium (1929–34), at Barvikha, near Moscow. This richly engineered building, planned as a set of three-storey interlocking horizontal blocks, is a complex of bedrooms, dining-rooms and social facilities, such as an internal winter garden. The combination of steel-gridded balconies, semicircular bedroom plans orientated towards the sun, steel windows and white concrete frame, give the building a light, elegant and machine-like quality.

In stark contrast is Iofan's most famous design: the Palace of the Soviets (1933–8; with Vladimir Shchuko and Vladimir Gel'freykh; unexecuted), destined for Moscow. Conceived as a synthesis of architecture, sculpture and the decorative arts, the design consists of a tower composed of diminishing cylindrical drums, articulated with columns, mounted on two square plinths and crowned with a statue of Lenin; the gigantic overall height was to be *c.* 470 m. Although the design refers obliquely to Vladimir Tatlin's *Monument to the Third International* (1919–20; unexecuted, *see* TATLIN, VLADIMIR, fig. 2) it contains little of Tatlin's progressive vision and desire for new forms of expression. Rather, in its inhuman scale, it symbolizes the ascendancy of Stalin's omnipotent state. The victory of Iofan's design over proposals by Moisey Ginzburg, Walter Gropius and Le Corbusier also signalled the institutionalization of a hybrid form of classicism as the official style of STALINIST ARCHITECTURE, and simultaneously marked the final defeat of the alternative visions of the Constructivists and Rationalists. Of similar conception to the Palace of the Soviets is Iofan's Soviet Pavilion (1937) at the Exposition des Arts et Techniques dans la Vie Moderne, Paris, a Neo-classical extravaganza surmounted by Vera Mukhina's thrusting statue of the *Worker and Collective Farm Woman* (1937). He spent the last phase of his career working on housing schemes, including a more modest prefabricated 16-storey housing complex (1962–9) on Sherbakov Street, Moscow.

WRITINGS

'Kak ya rabotayu nad proyektom Dvortsa sovetov' [How I work on the project of the Palace of Soviets], *Arkhit. SSSR*, 5 (1933), pp. 30–31

BIBLIOGRAPHY

E. Melnikov: 'Boris Mikhaylovich Iofan', *Arkhit. SSSR*, 5 (1971), pp. 39–42

S. O. Chan-Magomedov: *Pioniere der sowjetischen Architektur* (Dresden, 1983); Eng. trans. as S. O. Khan-Magomedov: *Pioneers of Soviet Architecture* (London, 1987)

A. V. Ikonnikov: *Arkhitektura Moskvy—dvadtsatyy vek* [The architecture of Moscow of the 20th century] (Moscow, 1984), pp. 94–106

A. V. Ryabushin and I. V. Shishkina: *Sovetskaya arkhitektura* [Soviet architecture] (Moscow, 1984), pp. 12, 45, 54, 59–60, 64, 73

A. M. Shuravlev, A. V. Ikonnikov and A. G. Rochegov: *Arkhitektura Sovetskoy Rossii* [The architecture of Soviet Russia] (Moscow, 1987)

A. V. Ikonnikov: *Russian Architecture of the Soviet Period* (Moscow, 1988)

Zodchiye Moskvy [The architects of Moscow] (Moscow, 1988)

JONATHAN CHARNLEY

Ioganson, Boris (Vladimirovich) (*b* Moscow, 25 July 1893; *d* Moscow, 25 Feb 1973). Russian painter. He was trained in the 19th-century Realist tradition of the WANDERERS and became one of the most important artists in establishing SOCIALIST REALISM as the official art of the USSR. He studied with Pyotr Kelin in 1912 and at the Moscow School of Painting, Sculpture and Architecture (1913–18) under Nikolay Kasatkin (1859–1930), Abram Arkhipov and Konstantin Korovin. He then served in the Red Army and worked as a stage designer in the province of Kherson from 1919 to 1922. In 1922 he participated in the 47th Wanderers' exhibition in Moscow and became one of the members of AKhRR (the Association of Artists of Revolutionary Russia), promoting Realism and attacking the abstract experiments of the avant-garde. Ioganson argued that 'the Russian painter is an innovator. . .not an innovator of form divorced from content, but a true innovator, reflecting the new tendencies of reality'.

Ioganson produced highly detailed canvases depicting the new industrial enterprises associated with the building of Socialism, for example the *Building of the Zemo-Achalay Hydroelectric Power Station* (1925; Moscow, Cent. Mus. Revolution), and also a series of narrative paintings, at once anecdotal and idealized, depicting the new way of life, including *Trial in a Soviet Court* (1928; Moscow, Tret'yakov Gal.). He also painted numerous historical works, glorifying the class struggle of Tsarist times and the heroes of the Revolution. The most famous of these was the *Interrogation of the Communists* (1933; Moscow, Tret'yakov Gal.), commissioned by the Revolutionary Military Council to mark the 15th anniversary of the Red Army. It shows Bolsheviks captured by Tsarist forces in the civil war facing death fearlessly as heroes and ultimate victors.

Ioganson taught at the Moscow Graphics Institute (1932–5) and at the Moscow Institute of Fine Arts (1935–9). He occupied numerous official positions and received several marks of recognition from the government, serving as Vice-President (1953–8) and President (1958–62) of the USSR Academy of Arts. He acted as a member of the presidium and organizational committee of the Union of Artists of the USSR (1939–57), as first secretary to the Board of the Union (1965–8), and also as the Director of the Tret'yakov Gallery in Moscow (1952–4).

WRITINGS

O zhivopisi [Concerning painting] (Moscow, 1960)

BIBLIOGRAPHY

M. Sokol'nikov: *Boris Vladimirovich Ioganson: Zhizn' i tvorchestvo* [Boris Vladimirovich Ioganson: Life and work] (Moscow, 1957)

N. Sokolova and N. Ioganson: *Boris Ioganson* (Leningrad, 1982)

CHRISTINA LODDER

Iol. *See* CHERCHEL.

Iolkos [now Volos]. Site in Thessaly on the north-eastern coast of Greece. Iolkos is located on a mound within the boundaries of modern Volos near Mt Pelion on the Gulf of Volos. Systematic excavations carried out in 1921–2 by A. Arvanitopoulos and in 1956–61 by D. Theochares revealed intriguing archaeological correspondence for Iolkos' legendary fame as the point of departure for the voyage of the Argonauts. The site comprises an artificial mound evincing continuous occupation from Early Helladic (*c.* 3600/3000–*c.* 2050 BC) to Late Helladic (LH, or Mycenaean; *c.* 1600–*c.* 1050 BC) and Protogeometric (*c.* 1000–*c.* 900 BC) times. Among the abundant pottery remains was a Middle Helladic (*c.* 2050–*c.* 1600 BC) Matt-painted sherd decorated with ships that prefigured both the later maritime importance of Iolkos as Thessaly's best port and the launching of the *Argo*. The mound also revealed a Mycenaean palatial structure with fine white-stuccoed floors and frescoed walls preserved over 1 m high, recalling the palace of King Pelias, who sent Jason on the quest for the Golden Fleece. The building was constructed in LH IIIB (*c.* 1335–1180 BC) on top of an earlier (LH IIIA) palace and was destroyed by fire not long after, around 1200 BC. Large rooms yielded hundreds of small kylikes and fragments of a vase painted with warriors (Volos, Athanassakeion Archaeol. Mus.). At nearby Kapakli, a rich tholos tomb containing many small gold ornaments attests the prosperous past of the Mycenaean settlement. Iolkos was also the home of Eumelos, whose wife Alcestis was immortalized in Euripides' play.

BIBLIOGRAPHY

K. Kourouniotis: 'Anaskaphe tholotou taphou en Volo' [Excavations of tholos tomb in Volos], *Archaiol. Ephimeris* (1906), pp. 211–40, pls 12–15

D. Theochares: annual reports in *Praktika Athen. Archaiol. Etaireias* (1956–61) and *Ergon* (1956–61)

——: 'Iolkos, Whence Sailed the Argonauts', *Archaeology*, xi (1958), pp. 13–18

S. Immerwahr: 'Some Pictorial Fragments from Iolkos in the Volos Museum', *Archaiol. Ephimeris* (1987), pp. 85-94

SUSAN LANGDON

Iommi, Ennio (*b* Rosario, 20 March 1926). Argentine sculptor. His father was a sculptor, and Iommi studied in his father's workshop and attended metalwork courses. He was a founder-member of the ASOCIACIÓN ARTE CONCRETO INVENCIÓN and is one of the most representative Constructivist sculptors in Argentina. In 1954 he created *Continual Forms* (white concrete, 2.0×0.8×1.2 m), a sculpture for a house in La Plata designed by Le Corbusier. His highly formal work was characterized at first by an economy of means, rigorous logic and dynamic rhythms and tensions, with an intelligible and rational structure of form that was optimistic in tone. It was with such works that he won a gold medal in Brussels at the Exposition Universelle et Internationale in 1958, took part in the exhibition *Concret Art* at the Kunsthaus, Zurich, in 1958, and participated hors concours in the São Paulo Biennale in 1961 and Venice Biennale in 1964.

Iommi completely changed direction in 1977, using coarse elements and distressed materials without aestheticizing them in any way. While he had always been interested in the relationship between the artist and society, he now categorically rejected consumerism and saw technology as a negative force that contributed to contemporary anxieties. He continued to exhibit internationally and in 1981 erected *Spatial Construction* (stainless steel, 4.0×1.2×0.7 m) in the Plaza Argentina in Brasília.

BIBLIOGRAPHY

C. Córdova Iturburu: *80 años de pintura argentina* (Buenos Aires, 1978), pp. 145–7

N. Perazzo: *El arte concreto en la Argentina* (Buenos Aires, 1983), pp. 159–64

NELLY PERAZZO

Iona. Island adjacent to the larger island of Mull off the west coast of Scotland. The Irish monk Columba or Colum Cille (*c.* AD 521–97) founded a monastery here in 563 (*see* INSULAR ART, §1). It became the main religious centre of the kingdom of Dal Riada and head of a confederation of monasteries founded by Columba and his successors in Ireland, in the Pictish territory in eastern Scotland and, from *c.* 635 to 664, in Northumbria. The internal buildings were of timber, but impressive remains survive of the enclosing bank and ditch. The *Life of Columba* by Abbot Adomnan (*d* 704) portrays writing as an important activity in the monastery, and the so-called Cathach of St Columba (Dublin, Royal Irish Acad., s.n.), a Psalter with simple penwork decoration, is probably typical of the calligraphy of Iona and its related houses in the late 6th century or early 7th (*see* INSULAR ART, §3). Excavations have shown evidence of leather-, wood- and metalworking on the monastic site.

The principal remains of the early monastery are about 100 carved stones, ranging from simple cross-incised gravemarkers to the great high crosses erected in the mid- or late 8th century. Originally St John's Cross (see fig.) resembled in form the Northumbrian crosses of Ruthwell and Bewcastle (*see* RUTHWELL CROSS) but surpassed them in scale and used a repertory of Celtic ornament emulating the decoration of ecclesiastical metalwork. The composite ring was probably added to strengthen the cross after an early collapse, and in this revised form it may stand at the beginning of the Irish series of ringed high crosses (*see* CROSS, §II, 1(ii)). Its spiralwork and snake-and-boss ornament are closely related to the BOOK OF KELLS (Dublin, Trinity Coll. Lib., MS. 58), and both cross and Gospel book were probably created to honour the cult of St Columba, perhaps marking the enshrinement of his relics. A series of Viking raids from 795 led the abbots to move to a new foundation at Kells (Co. Meath) during the 9th century, while relics of St Columba were divided in 849 between Kells and Dunkeld (Tayside). The surviving monastery on Iona remained a focus for pilgrimage, however, and sculpture continued to be produced, some of it in Norse style.

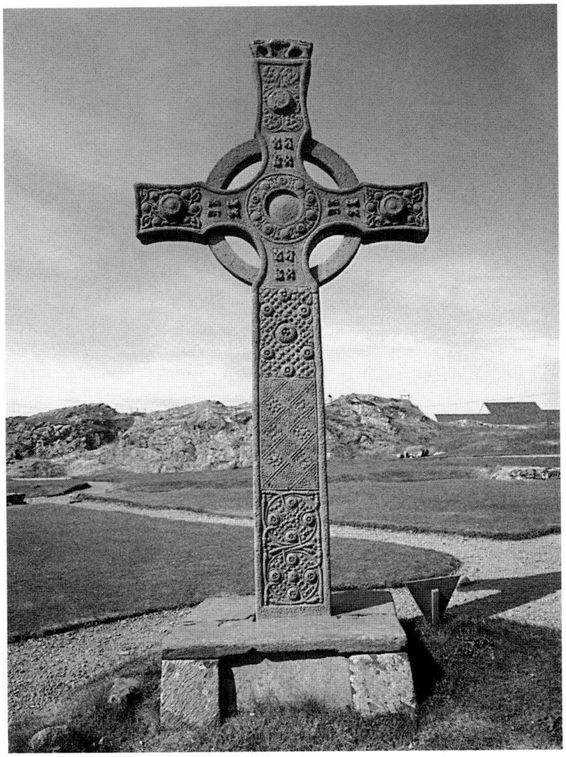

Iona, St John's Cross, green chlorite-schist, 5.30×2.17 m, second half of the 8th century; partially reconstructed

The Celtic community was replaced *c.* 1200 by a Benedictine abbey under the patronage of the family who later became the MacDonald Lords of the Isles. The abbey church, although retaining Romanesque and Early Gothic portions, was largely rebuilt *c.* 1450–90 under the master mason Donald Ó Brolchán. The nearby nunnery, a priory of Augustinian canonesses, retains the well-preserved ruin of a Romanesque church with many architectural features of Irish character. A new school of monumental carving, apparently based on Iona, was active from *c.* 1350 to *c.* 1500, producing numerous effigies, graveslabs and crosses in a distinctive local style, many of which remain on the island.

The religious houses fell into decay after the Scottish Reformation of 1560, despite an attempt to repair the abbey church as the cathedral of the Isles in the 1630s. It was restored for worship by the Iona Cathedral Trust between 1902 and 1910, the architect of the largely rebuilt nave being P. MacGregor Chalmers (1859–1922). The adjacent monastic buildings were sympathetically restored by Ian Gordon Lindsay (1906–66) for the Iona Community between 1938 and 1965.

From the second half of the 18th century Iona and the nearby island of Staffa became popular with travellers, including the topographical artists Moses Griffith (1747–1819), John Frederick Miller (*fl* 1768–80), William Daniell and David Roberts. During the late 19th century and the early 20th it was also a favoured resort of such artists as D. Y. Cameron and F. C. B. Cadell (1883–1937), who produced a series of 'scintillating views' (Halsby) inspired by the brilliant colours of the sea and beaches.

BIBLIOGRAPHY

Adomnan: *Life of Columba* (MS; *c.* 688–92); ed. A. O. Anderson and M. O. Anderson (London, 1961, rev. Oxford, 1991)

M. Martin: *A Description of the Western Islands of Scotland* (London, 1703/*R* 1934, rev. 2/1716/*R* 1981)

J. Drummond: *Sculptured Monuments in Iona and the West Highlands* (Edinburgh, 1881)

R. R. Anderson and others, eds: *Examples of Scottish Architecture from the 12th to the 17th Century*, iv, National Art Survey of Scotland (Edinburgh and London, 1933) [measured drgs]

K. A. Steer and J. W. M. Bannerman: *Late Medieval Monumental Sculpture in the West Highlands* (Edinburgh, 1977)

J. W. Barber: 'Excavations on Iona, 1979', *Proc. Soc. Antiqua. Scotland*, cxi (1981), pp. 282–380

Iona (1982), iv of *Argyll: An Inventory of the Monuments*, Royal Comm. Anc. & Hist. Mnmts Scotland (Edinburgh, 1971–92) [full bibliog.]

J. Halsby: *Scottish Watercolours, 1740–1940* (London, 1986), pp. 204–6

I. Henderson: 'The Book of Kells and the Snake-boss Motif on Pictish Cross-slabs and the Iona Crosses', *Ireland and Insular Art, AD 500–1200*, ed. M. Ryan (Dublin, 1987), pp. 56–65
H. Richardson and J. Scarry: *An Introduction to Irish High Crosses* (Cork, 1990)

IAN FISHER

Ionescu, Grigore (*b* Floreşti, Prahova, 11 Jan 1904; *d* 26 June 1992). Romanian architect, architectural historian and teacher. He studied (1924–30) at the Ion Mincu Academy of Architecture, Bucharest, where he later became a professor, teaching mainly the history of Romanian architecture, first as a lecturer (1935–42) and then as a professor (1942–). In the beginning he also held courses on restoration and assisted in the drawing/planning course.

Ionescu's main architectural work was in the medical field. The Turia Sanatorium (1935–8), Covasna, designed with a curve at one extremity, was innovative. Other projects include the school (1937–8) for Red Cross nurses built within the grounds of the military hospital, Bucharest. Another important commission was for the Emilia Irza Clinical Institute for Paediatrics, Bucharest, which started in 1949 as a design for a day nursery and was enlarged and adapted the following year. It is distinguished by its U-shaped layout, with simple buildings around a wide inner court and with a horizontal main façade marked with a row of windows and devoid of any decorative element. The sobriety of expression corresponds with the International Style of the 1930s and characterizes Ionescu's other works. Ionescu also attained eminence through his study of Romanian architectural history. His series of reference books on the subject served to promote the traditional and authentic values of Romanian architecture.

WRITINGS

Istoria arhitecturii româneşti [The history of Romanian architecture] (Bucharest, 1937)
Arhitectura in România în perioada anilor 1944–1969 [Architecture in Romania, 1944–1969] (Bucharest, 1969)
Arhitectura pe teritoriul României de-a lungul veacurilor [Architecture in Romania through the centuries] (Bucharest, 1982)
Arhitectura românească: Tipologii, creaţii, creatori [Romanian architecture: typologies, creations, creators] (Bucharest, 1986)

BIBLIOGRAPHY

P. Constantin: *Dicţionar universal al arhitecţilor* [Universal dictionary of architects] (Bucharest, 1986)

CODRUŢA CRUCEANU

Ionescu-Valbudea, Sţefan. *See* VALBUDEA, ŞTEFAN.

Ionia. Ancient region covering the central part of the west coast of Asia Minor (modern Turkey) from the Bay of Izmir south to Bargyla. It included the cities of Miletos, Myous, Priene, Ephesos, Kolophon, Teos, Lebedos, Erythrai, Klazomenai, Phokaia and Smyrna, and the adjacent islands of Samos and Chios. Herodotos (*Histories* I.cxlv–cxlviii) and Thucydides (*History of the Peloponnesian War* I.xii) claimed that Greeks fleeing the Dorian invasion colonized the region in the 11th century BC, but excavators have discovered Late Bronze Age (13th century BC) Mycenaean objects in the area, and Miletos may have been a Mycenaean trading port.

There is evidence for small urban settlements at about 1000 BC at Miletos as well as at Old Smyrna (*see* SMYRNA, §1), where one-room oval mud-brick cottages with straw roofs were replaced, probably in the 8th century BC, by small rectangular mud-brick houses on stone foundations. By then other urban enclaves existed in the region, and in the late 9th century BC the Ionian cities united to form the Pan-Ionian League.

The Ionian cities prospered from the 8th to the 6th century BC, striking coins after the Lydian practice. Most cities were probably walled, though only the circuit at Old Smyrna has been studied in detail. The most significant sacred areas often lay outside the walls; during the 8th century BC the first monumental building was undertaken at such an area: the 'hundred-footer' (*hekatompedos*), at Samos (*see* SAMOS, §1), was dedicated to Hera. In the mid-7th century BC the earlier temple to Artemis at Ephesos (*see* EPHESOS, §II) was replaced by a *hekatompedos*; the first temple to Apollo at DIDYMA was erected at the same time.

These early temples were long and narrow, often with a single row of columns down the middle that supported the roof beams. The external colonnade, the peristyle, probably developed soon afterwards. In the 6th century BC the dipteral plan with two peristyles was employed at Samos for Rhoikos' and Theodoros' new temple to Hera and, at Ephesos, for the temple to Artemis dedicated by the Lydian king Croesus. This arrangement was typical of the great temples in the Ionic order (*see* GREECE, ANCIENT, §II, 1(i)(a)). During the 6th century BC, Aiolic capitals using a leaf motif with volutes, and Ionic capitals with two volutes linked by an egg-and-dart motif decorating the echinus, were employed. These complemented the sculpted quality of the Ionic base of two convex tori which was developed simultaneously (*see also* ORDERS, ARCHITECTURAL, §I, 1 (ii)).

Monumental figural sculpture from Ionia in the 6th century BC was also associated with sanctuaries: examples are Cheramyes' *kore* (*c*. 570 BC; Paris, Louvre) and the Geneleos group (*c*. 560 BC; Samos, Archaeol. Mus., and Berlin, Pergamonmus.), both from Samos, and the *Branchidai* (*c*. 570–*c*. 550 BC; London, BM) on the Sacred Way leading to Didyma. While rare, the kouros type has been found: a fragment from Samos (*c*. 560–*c*. 550 BC; Samos, Archaeol. Mus.) and a small bronze of a similar type (*c*. 570 BC; Stockholm, Nmus., Sk 314). Ionian sculpture was softer and fleshier than contemporary Attic work and often exhibited elaborate drapery patterns, as on a series of korai holding birds (*c*. 540–*c*. 530 BC; Samos, Archaeol. Mus., I.217). Similar stylistic qualities are found on the small votive figurines of ivory and gold.

Ionian cities also produced distinctive painted pottery (*see* GREECE, ANCIENT, §V, 4(iv) and 5(v)). Wild Goat ware, bearing Black-figure friezes of real and imaginary animals interspersed with floral motifs, was manufactured in several local varieties. Phokaian artists painted human figural scenes, some perhaps narratives, and artists at Klazomenai produced terracotta sarcophagi painted on the top with registers of decoration.

The Persian conquest (547 BC) and the suppression of the Ionian revolt of 494 BC ended Ionian artistic exploration. Nevertheless, Ionian artists probably worked on the Achaemenid projects at Pasargadae and Persepolis, and

Ionia, Temple of Hadrian, Ephesos, 2nd century AD

wealthy Ionian cities in the 5th century BC lured Attic and other Greek artists to the region, as evidenced by the *Amazon* competition at Ephesos in which Pheidias and Polykleitos allegedly took part (Pliny: *Natural History* XXXIV.xix.53). Greek control of the Near East after the conquests of Alexander the Great (334–323 BC) brought new patrons and wealth to the Ionian cities. In the 4th century BC several cities adopted the orthogonal plan attributed to Hippodamos of Miletos. Priene (*see* PRIENE, §1) and the harbour district of MILETOS acquired grander and more regular public spaces set off by stoas. PYTHEOS (4th century BC) and HERMOGENES (*c.* 200 BC) revitalized Ionian architecture by grafting Doric elements on to the Ionic order. Thus Pytheos' Temple of Athena at Priene included a Doric opisthodomos, and Hermogenes' pseudo-dipteral Ionic Temple of Artemis at MAGNESIA ON THE MAEANDER had Doric mouldings along the base of the cella walls and around the bases of the columns. Great temples were also begun at Sardis (*see* SARDIS, §1), Didyma and Ephesos. The region's increased wealth is apparent also in domestic architecture such as the fine peristyle houses at Priene.

The Ionian cities suffered under the Roman administration after being bequeathed to Rome by the will of Attalos III of Pergamon (133 BC), though Augustus (*reg* 30 BC–AD 14) ended the exploitation. Earthquakes in AD 17 and 178 caused much damage, but imperial funds helped pay for the rebuilding, and the cities reached their greatest size under Roman rule. New building forms were developed or introduced, including the bath-gymnasium, the forum and the apartment house. Traditional Greek structures such as the theatre, bouleuterion, agora and temple were built on an even larger scale. In the 2nd century AD architects began to build in the aedicular style with cheap local and imported marbles, creating façades of columns, entablatures and pediments with niches for sculptural displays (see fig.). Public structures were decorated with both free-standing and relief sculpture that often recalled the pre-Roman origins of the city, such as a statue of the founder-hero *Androklos Hunting the Wild Boar* in the Gymnasium of Vedius at Ephesos (*c.* AD 300; Selçuk, Ephesos Archaeol. Mus).

The foundation of Constantinople in AD 324 restored the region's prosperity after the turmoil of the 3rd century. Large churches graced several cities, such as the basilica of St John at Ephesos (*c.* AD 400, enlarged 527–65). At Sardis the Jewish population lavishly redecorated their major synagogue (*c.* AD 400), and a new shopping area was built. The Persian invasions of the mid-6th century AD ended the prosperity of many of the Ionian cities.

BIBLIOGRAPHY

E. Akurgal: *Die Kunst Anatoliens von Homer bis Alexander* (Berlin, 1961)
——: 'The Early Period and the Golden Age of Ionia', *Amer. J. Archaeol.*, lxvi (1962), pp. 369–79
J. M. Cook: *The Greeks in Ionia and the East* (London and New York, 1962)
E. Akurgal: *Ancient Civilizations and Ruins of Turkey* (Istanbul, 1969, rev. 8/1985)
G. M. A. Hanfmann: *From Croesus to Constantine: The Cities of Western Asia Minor and their Arts in Greek and Roman Times* (Ann Arbor, 1975)
E. Akurgal: *Wohnschichten und Athenatempel* (1983), i of Alt-Smyrna (Ankara, 1983–)
The Anatolian Civilizations, II: Greek, Roman, Byzantine (exh. cat. by N. Asgari, B. Madra and M. Soysal, Council of Europe 18th European Art Exhibition, Istanbul, 1983)

WILLIAM E. MIERSE

Ionic order. *See under* ORDERS, ARCHITECTURAL.

Ionides. British family of patrons of Greek origin. Constantine Ioannou Ipliktzis (*b* Constantinople [now Istanbul], 1775; *d* Athens, 1852) was the founder of the family fortune. In the 1820s he settled in Manchester, where he established himself as a textile merchant. His eldest son, Alexander Constantine Ionides (*b* Constantinople, 1 Sept 1810; *d* Hastings, E. Sussex, 10 Nov 1890), changed the family name to Ionides. He settled in Manchester, where he founded the firm Ionides & Co. in 1833. The following year he moved to London, where he served as Consul-General for Greece (1854–66) and as a director of the Crystal Palace. Alexander patronized several artists, in particular G. F. Watts, who became the chief portrait painter of the family. From the 1860s, influenced by his son Aleco, Alexander extended his patronage to Whistler, George Du Maurier, Edward John Poynter, Alphonse Legros and Henri Fantin-Latour, who were frequent guests in his house. On his death his collection was distributed to his children, with the exception of Watts's *Psyche* (early 1870s; Athens, N. Pict. Gal.), which he bequeathed to the National Library of Athens.

Alexander's son Constantine Alexander Ionides (*b* Cheetham Hill, nr Manchester, 14 May 1833; *d* Hove, E. Sussex, 29 June 1900) entered his father's firm in Manchester in 1850 and later represented the firm in Greece, Turkey and the Balkans. In 1864 he settled in London at 8 Holland Villas Road (later added to by Philip Webb) and entered the Stock Exchange. (He was a registered member from 1865 to 1900.) He began collecting on a large scale in 1878 and made most of his major purchases before 1884. He bequeathed his entire collection of over 1000 items (oils, watercolours, drawings and prints) to the

South Kensington Museum (now the Victoria and Albert Museum), London, on the condition that it be kept as a separate collection. The wide-ranging collection contains works from the early Italian Renaissance (e.g. Botticelli's *Smeralda Brandini*, *c.* 1470; previously owned by Dante Gabriel Rossetti), from the 17th century (e.g. Louis Le Nain's *Landscape with Figures*, *c.* 1640–48) and from the 19th century.

Through his close friendship with Legros, professor at the Slade School of Art, London, Constantine developed an interest in 19th-century French paintings and collected works by Delacroix, Ingres, Théodore Rousseau, Jean-François Millet, Courbet, Degas and Henri Fantin-Latour, as well as sculpture by Jules Dalou. In 1879 he commissioned D. G. Rossetti, a friend of his sister Aglaia (1834–1906), to paint a *Day Dream* (1880; London, V&A). He also collected ancient Greek coins, gems, cameos, porcelain, ivories and other objects of vertu, which he bequeathed to his eight children.

Constantine's brother Aleco [Alexander Alexander] Ionides (*b* Tulse Hill, London, 1 Jan 1840; *d* London, *bur* 4 Aug 1898) was a merchant and Consul-General for Greece. During an extended stay in Paris he became friendly with several art students, including Whistler. He assumed possession of his father's house at 1 Holland Park, London—the family house since 1864—and from 1870 had it decorated by Philip Webb, Thomas Jeckyll, William Morris and Walter Crane. An early showpiece of the Aesthetic Movement, the house contained Aleco's collection of pottery and contemporary pictures by such artists as Whistler, Dante Gabriel Rossetti, Edward Burne-Jones, Simeon Solomon and Albert Joseph Moore. His collection of early Hellenistic Tanagra figurines strongly influenced Whistler, who had a photographic album of them (Glasgow, Hunterian). After his death, Aleco's collection was auctioned at Christie's on 13 and 15 March 1902 and, with the exception of a few items, is dispersed.

BIBLIOGRAPHY

C. Monkhouse: 'The Constantine Ionides Collection: From David to Millet', *Mag. A.*, vii (1884), pp. 36–44 [contemp. account of the col.]

G. White: 'An Epoch-making House', *The Studio*, xii (1898), pp. 102–12 [Aleco's house]

L. Ionides: *Memories* (Paris, 1925) [privately printed]

B. S. Long: *Victoria and Albert Museum: Catalogue of the Constantine Alexander Ionides Collection* (London, 1925)

A. C. Ionides jr: *Ion: A Grandfather's Tale* (Dublin, 1927) [privately printed]

C. M. Kauffmann: *Victoria and Albert Museum: Catalogue of Foreign Paintings*, 2 vols (London, 1973)

A. Leoussi: *The Ionides Circle and Art* (diss., U. London, 1982)

Additional information supplied by K. Metaxas, editor of the *Greek Gazette* and administrator of the Greek archives, London.

ATHENA S. E. LEOUSSI

Iosifo-Volokolamsky Monastery. Monastery at Teryayevo in Russia, some 110 km north-west of Moscow. It was founded in 1479 by Iosif Volotsky (1439–1515), who successfully resisted the 15th-century movement to secularize monastic properties, and was partially paid for by the Grand Princes of Moscow, who helped to establish it as a centre for icon painting and manuscript illumination and who established its collection of ancient reliquaries. Between 1484 and 1500 DIONISY painted an extensive series of icons for the monastery.

The monastery's first stone church was built between 1484 and 1486 and was surrounded by brick walls *c.* 1543–66. The whole complex, which is enclosed on two sides by a lake, was completely rebuilt between the 1670s and 1690s and is a fine example of 17th-century Russian architecture, with its numerous white walls and towers and well-proportioned stone-stepped roofs. A two-storey building pierced by two asymmetrically placed gates, the Holy Gates, serves as the main entrance to the monastery. The five-domed church of the Dormition (1688–92), with its three eastern apses and a gallery, stands in the centre on a high wooden base. Four internal piers support the central cupola, which is decorated on the exterior with *kokoshniki* arches. The triple division of the façades and the use of polychrome tile decoration framing the entrances are typical of late 17th-century Russian Baroque architecture. Nearby is the monastery refectory with the church of the Epiphany (1504–30; rebuilt 1682) and the remains of a multi-storey bell-tower (15th–17th century: destr. World War II).

BIBLIOGRAPHY

Nektary: *Istoricheskoye opisaniye Iosifo-Volokolamskogo monastyrya* [Historical description of the Iosifo-Volokolamsky Monastery] (Moscow, 1887)

S. Toropov: *Iosifo-Volokolamsky monastyr'* (Moscow, 1946)

N. Voronov: 'Novyye materialy ob arkhitekturnom ansamble Iosifo-Volokolamskogo monastyrya' [New material on the architectural ensemble of the Iosifo-Volokolamsky Monastery], *Arkhit. Nasledstvo*, vi (1956), pp. 107–32

V. Pavlichenkov: '"Ansamble" Iosifo-Volokolamskogo monastyrya', *Arkhit. Nasledstvo*, x (1958), pp. 127–52

B. Al'tshuller: *Pamyatniki arkhitektury Moskovskoy oblasti* [Architectural monuments in the Moscow region] (Moscow, 1975), pp. 33–7

D. O. SHVIDKOVSKY

I Ping-shou. *See* YI BINGSHOU.

Ipoustéguy, Jean (Robert) (*b* Dun-sur-Meuse, nr Verdun, 6 Jan 1920). French sculptor, painter, architect and printmaker. Virtually self-taught, he took evening classes in drawing with Robert Lesbounit in 1938 in Paris before turning to architecture. The post-war debates about Picasso and modernism aroused his interest in sculpture, to which he devoted himself from 1949, when he moved to Choisy-le-Roi, a suburb of Paris. One of his early bronzes, the *Split Helmet* (1958; artist's col.), was a kind of manifesto that he later described as the breaking of 'Brancusi's egg'. All his subsequent work was to be marked by a dichotomy between a full, pure, quasi-abstract form and its burst shell, bloody and visceral, simultaneously recalling both foetal and seismic images. In 1960 he began to combine forms derived from architecture with those of the human figure, for instance in the bronze *Beach and Cliffs* (1960; Paris, Gal. Claude Bernard).

A trip to Greece led to Ipoustéguy's appreciation of the fullness of the forms of ancient statuary, particularly with regard to the human figure. His over life-size bronze *Man with Three Legs* (1964; artist's col., see 1979 exh. cat., pl. 37) is a modern avatar of the archaic kouros, a pendant to the female deity suggested by *The Earth* (1963; artist's col., see 1979 exh. cat., pl. 34). During this period he also made small bronzes such as *The Mafia* (1961; Paris, Gal. Claude Bernard), cast from potter's clay, which he called

Tactiles because they appealed to the sense of touch and were intended to be handled.

In 1965 Ipoustéguy began to integrate the human figure more explicitly into its architectural setting, using tables and vertical partitions. One such bronze, *Ecbatana* (1965; artist's col., see 1979 exh. cat., pl. 47), was later realized on a monumental scale as *Alexander before Ecbatana* (1979) for the Internationales Kongresszentrum in Berlin. In 1967 he returned to painting and engraving, for example in *Adriatic* (oil on canvas, 1967; artist's col., see 1979 exh. cat., pl. 107). His interest in the qualities of different surfaces, combined with the influence of the *Tactiles*, encouraged him to work in marble. This resulted in some large-scale compositions, freely derived from history and mythology, such as *Mother's Agony* (1970–71; Paris, Fonds N. A. Contemp.). The *Death of Bishop Neumann* (1976–7; artist's col., see 1979 exh. cat., pl. 97) combines marble and bronze. After 1975, the artist divided his time between printmaking and bronze sculptures, including public commissions such as *Val de Grâce* (bronze, 1977), for the military hospital of that name in Paris, and the monument to Rimbaud, *L'Homme aux semelles devant* (1984; Paris, Place de l'Arsenal).

BIBLIOGRAPHY

Ipoustéguy (exh. cat. by M. Tronche, Paris, Fond. N. A. Graph. & Plast., 1978)

Ipoustéguy: Werke, 1956–1978 (exh. cat., ed. D. Ruckhaberle; W. Berlin, Staatl. Ksthalle, 1979)

JEAN CLAIR

Ippitsusai Bunchō [Mori] (*fl* Edo [now Tokyo], 1760–94; *d c.* 1794). Japanese print designer and book illustrator. He may have been a pupil of the *ukiyoe* ('pictures of the floating world') artist Ishikawa Yukimoto. He is principally known for prints of the following types: *hosōban* ('narrow format', *c.* 320×150 mm); *yakushae* ('pictures of actors') and *bijinga* ('pictures of beautiful women'). In its eclecticism, his style resembles that of his contemporaries, Katsukawa Shunshō (*see* KATSUKAWA, (1)) and SUZUKI HARUNOBU, who incorporated a lyricism with a naturalistic depiction of the subject. In 1770 Bunchō collaborated with Harunobu and Shunshō to produce *Ehon butai ōgi* ('Picture book of stage fans'; untraced), which featured a new type of *yakushae*, *yakusha nigaoe* ('pictures of likenesses of actors') and challenged the traditional dominance of theatre illustration by the TORII school. In *Ehon butai ōgi*, Bunchō depicted *onnagata* (*kabuki* actors playing female roles), while Shunshō illustrated *kata keyaki* (*kabuki* villains). Bunchō abandoned *yakushae* in 1772. From 1769 to 1774 he designed *bijinga*, including *Chayamusume Kasamori Osen* ('Osen of the Kasamori teahouse'; untraced) and *Miko no Ohatsu* ('The *miko* Ohatsu'; untraced). His women have high noses, pointed eyes, flat foreheads, thick eyebrows and pursed lips, giving them a cynical, sterile charm. His movements after 1774 are unknown, but a memorial *surimono* ('printed object'; de luxe print) printed after his death suggests that he remained active in the art world until his death. His students included Kitsu Bunchō, Bunkō and Tamagawa Shūchō.

BIBLIOGRAPHY

Genshoku ukiyoe daihyakkajiten [Encyclopedia of *ukiyoe*, illustrated], Genshoku ukiyoe dihyakka jiten iinkai, 11 vols (Tokyo, 1980–82)

TADASHI KOBAYASHI

Ippō. *See* IKENAGA DŌUN.

Ippolito del Donzello. *See* DONZELLO, (2).

Ippu. *See* SIN YUN-BOK.

Iran, Islamic Republic of [Pers. Jumhūrī-yi Islāmī-yi Īrān]. Country in the Middle East with its capital at TEHRAN. Iran has an area of *c.* 1,648,000 sq. km, bordered in the north by Armenia, Azerbaijan, Turkmenistan and the Caspian Sea, in the east by Afghanistan and Pakistan, in the south by the Persian Gulf and the Gulf of Oman and in the west by Turkey and Iraq (see fig. 1). Large areas of the country consist of mountainous regions or desert; only about 10% of the land is arable and habitable. Iran has a population of *c.* 49,875,000 (1986 estimate), the majority being Shi'a Muslim (the religion of the State) and the remainder comprising Sunni Muslims, Armenian Christians and other religious minorities. The official language is Farsi (Persian), and about 25% of Iranians speak Turkic languages. The principal Turkic groups are the Turkmen in the north-east and the Qashga'i in the Shiraz region. In the north-west the Kurds, who constitute about 5% of the population, have a distinct culture and language, and distinct traditions are also maintained by the Lur and Bakhtyari tribes in the west and the Baluchs in the east. Oil, discovered in the early 20th century, is an important source of revenue, and there are reserves of natural gas, coal, copper and iron ore. As well as oil refining, the manufacture of carpets is a major industry.

Under the Qajar dynasty (*reg* 1779–1924) Iran experienced a period of relative peace and renewed contact with the Western world: Nasir al-Din (*reg* 1848–96) was the first Iranian monarch to visit Europe, travelling there three times. His son, Muzaffar al-Din (*reg* 1896–1907), however, was forced by popular unrest to convene the Majlis (National Assembly), which met for the first time in 1906 and provided Iran with a constitution. Muhammad 'Ali (*reg* 1907–9) resorted to absolute rule, but he was deposed and replaced by Ahmad (*reg* 1909–24), aged 11. During World War I, Turkish, Russian and British forces intervened in Iran. In 1921 a coup d'état was staged by the army officer Riza Khan and two years later he was appointed Prime Minister. In 1924 the Majlis declared that the rule of the Qajar dynasty was terminated, and the monarchy was entrusted to Riza Khan, who ascended the throne as Riza Shah Pahlavi. During the 1920s and 1930s he introduced a series of measures to modernize Iran and develop its economy, including the expansion of educational facilities. In 1941 he was succeeded by his son Muhammad Riza (*reg* 1941–79) after British and Russian forces invaded the country. The occupying armies withdrew at the end of World War II, and a planned economic development was initiated in 1949. This political and economic phase lasted until the Revolution of 1979, when an exiled religious leader, Ayatollah Ruhollah Khomeini, returned to Iran and established an Islamic republic. There followed a period of rapid cultural change and upheaval, exacerbated by a war with Iraq (1980–88) that devastated the economy. This article covers the art produced in the country in the 20th century. For its earlier history *see* IRAN, ANCIENT and ISLAMIC ART.

1. Map of Iran; those areas with separate entries in this dictionary are distinguished by CROSS-REFERENCE TYPE

1. Architecture. 2. Painting, sculpture and calligraphy. 3. Decorative arts. 4. Archaeological sites, museums and collections.

1. ARCHITECTURE. Compared with the range of religious and secular buildings erected in the 19th century, Qajar patronage in the early 20th century was slight, although the palace of Dowshantepe constructed for Muzaffar al-Din to the east of Tehran was a notable amalgam of Iranian and European conventions. With the commencement of Pahlavi rule, new priorities came to the fore and buildings dating from the Qajar era or earlier began to be replaced by modern structures. Programmes of urbanization and town planning were introduced in which broad avenues and apartment blocks altered the character of traditional urban life. This trend continued into the 1970s when large-scale investment in housing resulted in the construction of ill-suited prefabricated buildings.

Aware of this dislocation of traditional values, such architects as NADER ARDALAN and KAMRAN DIBA began to confront the issue in their work. Ardalan linked an appreciation of traditional architecture with such modern requirements as the prevention of energy waste. His Iran Centre for Management Studies (1972) in Tehran, for example, was designed in the form of a madrasa and used local construction methods and labour. Diba was concerned with the preservation of traditional Iranian culture through urban renewal projects. His work included the new town of Shushtar (1974–80) and the campus of Jondi Shapour University (1968–78) at Ahwaz. He also designed the Museum of Contemporary Art (1976; with Ardalan) in Tehran and became the museum's first director (1976–8). Successful restoration projects in Iran included work on the Safavid monuments of ʿAli Qapu, Chihil Situn and Hasht Bihisht (completed in 1977) in Isfahan, by the Istituto Italiano per il Medio ed Estremo Oriente (IsMEO)

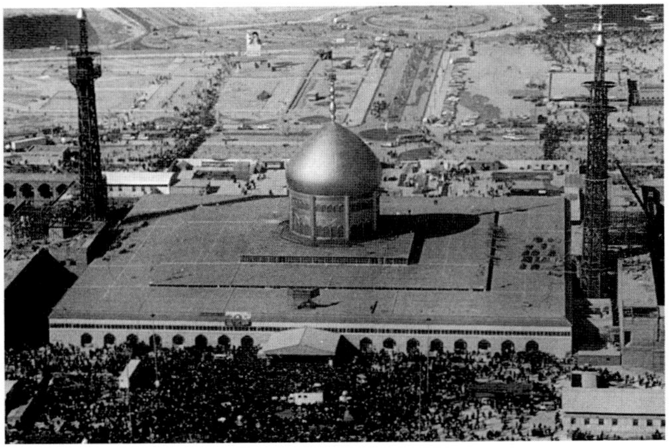

2. Mausoleum of Ayatollah Khomeini, Tehran, Iran, begun 1989

on behalf of the National Organization for Conservation of Historic Monuments of Iran (NOCHMI). Less successful was the artificial isolation of conserved buildings in such cities as Hamadan, Mashhad and Shiraz, which disfigured the urban setting. The upheaval of the 1979 Revolution and the war with Iraq put a halt to many architectural projects, although the construction of the large mausoleum (begun in 1989; see fig. 2) of Ayatollah Khomeini to the south of Tehran was an important enterprise.

Vernacular architecture in Iran displays regional characteristics (*see* VERNACULAR ARCHITECTURE, §II, 7(viii)). In those parts of the country with high rainfall and an abundance of timber, especially on the shores of the Caspian Sea and the northern slopes of the Elburz Mountains, buildings are designed to shed rain and sloping roofs are common. Such buildings contrast with those of the plateau where mud is used. If timber is available flat roofs are constructed but in other regions roofs are made of mud-brick or more durable baked brick to create an astonishing variety of domes and vaults. Not only mosques and shrines but houses, cisterns, mills and animal shelters receive this treatment. Also noteworthy is the wide range of vernacular structures, which include the WIND CATCHER, the ICE HOUSE and the pigeon tower.

2. PAINTING, SCULPTURE AND CALLIGRAPHY. In the late 19th century and the early 20th Iranian painting was influenced by European art, especially in the works of the poet laureate Mahmoud Khan (1813–93) and Muhammad Ghaffari (*see* GHAFFARI, (3)), who studied in Europe and adopted a naturalistic style. In 1911 Muhammad Ghaffari established an art school in Tehran that promoted Western-style painting, and he directed the school until 1928. He was instrumental in introducting easel painting to Iran and fostered basic changes in Iranian painting and art appreciation. When the College of Fine Arts opened at Tehran University in 1938 a number of Muhammad Ghaffari's disciples occupied key positions on the staff.

Revivalism in Iranian painting was also prominent in the early 20th century. One of the main representatives of revivalism or the 'traditional' school of painting was Husayn Bihzad (1894–1968). He served an apprenticeship with painters in the Tehran bazaar and specialized in works in the style of Timurid and Safavid paintings (15th–17th century), for both Western and Iranian patrons. In 1935 he visited Paris for 13 months where he studied Islamic manuscripts in French collections. He also developed a more personal style, which was a simplified version of the Safavid style incorporating elements of Western pictorial conventions, and sometimes worked on the scale of easel paintings. In 1946 he became an employee of the Office of Archaeological Works; he also taught painting and participated in exhibitions at home and abroad.

Popular art, meanwhile, continued in Iran in the 'coffee-house' genre of murals and oil paintings inspired by folk traditions, with their themes taken from the *Shahnama* ('Book of kings'), romances or from accounts of the lives of Shi'ite imams. Many of the artists who worked in this style were anonymous, but some signed their works and gained recognition, including Muhammad Mudabber and Husayn Qullar-Aghasi.

After World War II a greater number of Iranian painters studied in Europe and the United States, and by the 1950s the modernist movement in Iran had received official backing from the Department (later Ministry) of Fine Arts. An important advocate of modernism was Jalil Ziapur (*b* 1928), a graduate of the College of Fine Arts who studied in France under André Lhôte. He founded an art society and the monthly publication *Khurus-i Jangi* ('The Fighting Cock'), which championed modernism and was a rallying-point for avant-garde painters and writers. In 1954 the painter Marcos Gregorian (*b* 1925) returned to Iran after training in Italy and opened the first art gallery (1954–9) in Tehran. In 1958 he also organized the first of the five Tehran Biennale exhibitions undertaken by the Department of Fine Arts. The last Biennale, held in 1966, included works by 37 Pakistani and Turkish artists, which was a step towards creating an Asian Biennale.

In 1960 the College of Decorative Arts was established in Tehran, which fostered a less formal approach to art than the College of Fine Arts and was an influential training ground for artists. At this time an art movement known as the SAQQAKHANA school developed. Its artists, among whom were the painters HUSSEIN ZENDEROUDI and Faramarz Pilaram (1937–83) and the sculptor PARVIZ TANAVOLI, combined motifs derived from Shi'ite iconography and folklore with Western techniques. Other artists in the 1960s and 1970s who combined Iranian subject-matter with modern Western styles and techniques included Mas'ud Arabshahi (*b* 1935), Nasser Ovissi (*b* 1934), Mansur Qandriz (1935–65), Jazeh Tabatabai and Sadeq Tabrizi (*b* 1938). Compositions inspired by calligraphy increasingly preoccupied such artists as Zenderoudi (see fig. 3). Traditional forms of calligraphy were promoted by the Iranian Calligraphers Association, which became active in 1966 and organized calligraphy classes in major Iranian cities.

After 1979 paintings affirming the spirit and ideals of the Revolution became important, as did poster art (which had developed in Iran since the 1940s), backed by official sponsorship. Works that illustrated the theme of martyrdom were notable for incorporating Surrealist elements. Naturalism and traditionalism in art continued in the works of such painters as Mansur Negargar Husayni

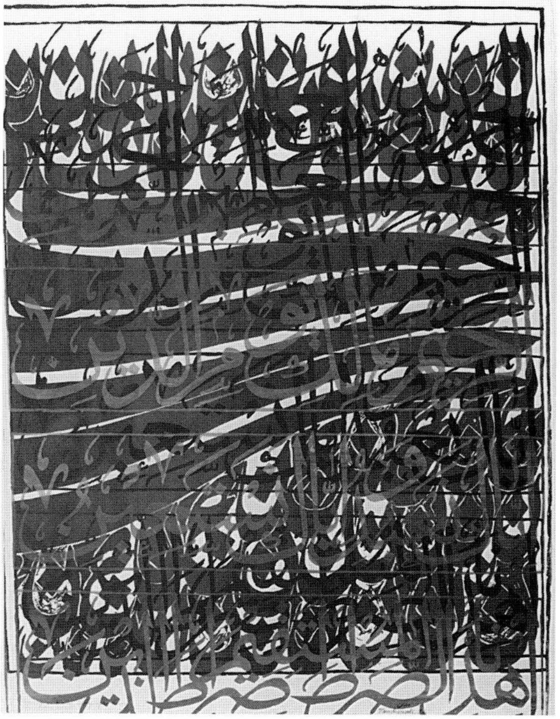

3. Hussein Zenderoudi: untitled etching, 760×560 mm, 1986 (Amman, National Gallery of Fine Art)

(*b* 1951), a graduate of the College of Fine Arts. Calligraphy also flourished in Iran and abroad. Shams Anwari Alhuseyni (*b* 1937), for example, who studied calligraphy under the brothers Husayn Mirkhani and Hasan Mirkhani at the College of Fine Arts (1953–6) and settled in West Germany in 1957, staged his first one-man exhibition at the Rautenstrauch-Joest-Museum, Cologne, in 1990.

3. DECORATIVE ARTS. Foremost among the decorative arts is the manufacture of carpets. Made in a great variety of sizes and shapes, with a wide range of motifs and patterns, they are woven on fixed vertical looms in towns and villages and on light horizontal looms among tribes on migration. The revival of the Iranian carpet industry began in the 1870s, when Tabriz merchants produced carpets for export and foreign firms such as Ziegler and Company of Manchester became involved in carpet-weaving. In the 20th century the carpet industry expanded further and underwent such changes as the increasing use of synthetic dyes instead of vegetable dyes. In 1935 the Iranian Carpet Company was founded to produce quality carpets. Important carpet manufacturing centres in the late 20th century included Arak, Isfahan, Kashan, Kirman, Mashhad, Na'in, Qum, Tabriz and Yazd. Each centre or area has its own characteristic designs and methods of production. In 1975 a monumental Isfahan carpet measuring *c.* 10 m sq., woven by 28 women simultaneously, was ordered by the Shah for the Parliament Building in Tehran. Kurdish textiles are made in Bijar, Senna (Sanandaj) and the Zanjan, Hamadan, Songur and Varamin regions. They have strong deep hues and geometric renditions of floral patterns, insects, animals and abstract forms, with the exception of the Sennas, which have fine textures and elegant curved floral designs.

A wide range of metalwork is made in Iran, including caskets, plates, bowls and trays, often worked in relief and with embossing and chasing. There are various regional variations; distinct belts, buckles, jewellery and weapons, for example, were traditionally produced by the Kurds. High-quality metalwork, including jewellery and regalia in precious metals, was also encouraged by royal patronage. Pottery is manufactured in small, localized workshops in a number of centres. Wares with underglaze designs painted in blue were produced at Na'in (until 1935) and Maibud. In the early 20th century ceramic tiles were an important feature in architectural decoration. When the Takiyya Mu'avin al-Mulk in Kirmanshah was restored and refurbished *c.* 1917–25, for example, it was decorated with painted tiles under the supervision of Hasan Tihrani, a tilemaker who came from Tehran with four assistants and constructed kilns near the site. The tiles depict the tragedy of Karbala, portraits of leaders, dervishes, landscapes and ancient Iranian monuments. The art of inlaying wood with ivory, bone, mother-of-pearl, brass, silver or different shades of wood is still practised by craftsmen in such centres as Isfahan and Shiraz, especially for tables, boxes, picture frames and similar items. Painted lacquer, which flourished under the Qajars, has declined since the early 20th century. The lacquer painters who used the name Simiruni at the turn of the century painted single figures and scenes of almost photographic realism under the influence of imported Russian pieces, and other work was executed in the revived Safavid style; some finely painted lacquer, for example, was produced by ʿAbd al-Latif and ʿAbd al-Husayn, both of whom enjoyed the title *sanīʿ humāyūn* ('royal painter').

4. ARCHAEOLOGICAL SITES, MUSEUMS AND COLLECTIONS. European travellers began to study monuments and remains in Iran from the 17th century onwards, and the first archaeological excavations were conducted in the 19th century; the most important was undertaken by French archaeologists at SUSA, the Elamite capital. In 1928 ANDRÉ GODARD was invited by the Iranian government to establish an archaeological service, make an inventory of historic monuments and commence restoration work. In the 1930s such scholars as ERNST HERZFELD and ARTHUR UPHAM POPE were also active in Iran, and excavations took place at BISHAPUR, NISHAPUR, PERSEPOLIS, RAYY and other sites. Since World War II excavations have also been carried out at HASANLU, PASARGADAE, TAKHT-I SULAYMAN and elsewhere.

In Tehran, the Ethnographical Museum and Crown Jewels Museum (displayed in the Bank Melli) both date from 1938. The Iran Bastan Museum, founded in 1946, is the principal archaeological collection. In 1957 the State acquired a collection of art formed by Abdullah Rahimi, which formed the nucleus of the Decorative Arts Museum, inaugurated in 1961; the majority of items in this museum date from the 19th and 20th centuries. Other collections in the capital include the Riza ʿAbbasi Museum, Gulistan Palace Museum and the Nigaristan Museum, the latter founded in 1975 when Queen Farah Pahlavi acquired a collection of Qajar paintings (ex-Julian Amery priv. col.). In the 1970s the Farah Pahlavi Foundation funded several museums and cultural centres, including the Museum of Contemporary Art (1976). Specific arts are displayed in the Carpet Museum (opened 1978) and the Museum of Glass and Ceramics (inaugurated 1978). The latter, in a 19th-century building renovated in 1976 by HANS HOLLEIN, houses glassware and ceramics from prehistoric times to the 20th century. Outside the capital museums are located in such centres as Isfahan, Mashhad (Iman Riza Shrine Mus.), Qazvin, Qum and Shiraz (Pars Mus.).

Collections of 20th-century Iranian art were formed by Queen Farah, which she donated to various museums; by the prime minister ʿAbbas Hovaida, who amassed in the 1960s and 1970s a collection for his office; and by such individuals as Kamran Diba, Ibrahim Gulistan and the Lajevardi family. By the 1970s corporate collectors had also emerged, led by the Behshahr Industrial Group, which collected *c.* 400 Iranian paintings. Under Pahlavi rule, government ministries commissioned artists to produce work for public institutions, and exhibition halls were opened. Various commercial galleries also opened in the 1960s and 1970s. After the Revolution the Museum of Contemporary Art in Tehran displayed pro-Revolutionary art and propaganda but later re-installed some of its permanent collection and exhibited the work of prominent Iranian artists. Other museums halted their activities after 1979 to revise their policies.

BIBLIOGRAPHY

Enc. Iran: 'Hosayn Behzad'
B. W. Robinson: 'Some Modern Persian Miniatures', *The Studio*, cxxxv (1948), pp. 78–85
A. C. Edwards: *The Persian Carpet: A Survey of the Carpet-weaving Industry of Persia* (London, 1953)
R. W. Ehrich, ed.: *Relative Chronologies in Old World Archaeology* (Chicago, 1954); rev. as *Chronologies in Old World Archaeology*, 2 vols (Chicago, 1965/*R* 1992)
N. Naderpour: *Nasser Ovissi* (Tehran, 1966)
H. E. Wulff: *The Traditional Crafts of Persia: Their Development, Technology, and Influence on Western Civilizations* (Cambridge, MA and London, 1966)
A. Tadjvidi: *L'Art moderne en Iran* (Tehran, 1967)
V. B. Meen and A. D. Tushingham: *Crown Jewels of Iran* (Toronto, 1968)
Modern Persian Painting (exh. cat. by K. Emani, New York, Columbia U., Cent. Iran Stud., 1968)
M. Centlivres-Demont: *Une Communauté de potiers en Iran: Le Centre de Meybod (Yazd)* (Wiesbaden, 1971)
E. Yarshater, ed.: *Iran Faces the Seventies* (New York, 1971)
D. Behnam: *Cultural Policy in Iran* (Paris, 1973)
Iranian Calligraphy: A Selection of Works from 15th to 20th Century: The Aydin Aghdashloo Collection in Negaristan Museum of Eighteenth and Nineteenth Century Iranian Art (exh. cat. by A. Aghdashloo, Tehran, Nigaristan Mus., 1975)
L. S. Diba, J. Bahnam and A. Aghdashlu: *Iranian Wedding Contracts of the Nineteenth and Twentieth Centuries* (Tehran, Nigaristan Mus., 1976)
Calligraphy from Iran (exh. cat., London, Commonwealth Inst., 1976)
The Qashqāʾi of Iran: World of Islam Festival 1976 (exh. cat., U. Manchester, Whitworth A.G., 1976)
J. Gluck and S. H. Gluck, eds: *A Survey of Persian Handicraft: A Pictorial Introduction to the Contemporary Folk Arts and Art Crafts of Modern Iran* (New York, 1977)
R. Rainer: *Traditional Building in Iran* (Graz, 1977)
Saqqakhaneh (exh. cat. by K. Emami and P. L. Wilson, Tehran, Mus. Contemp. A., 1977)
W. Eilers: 'Educational and Cultural Development in Iran during the Pahlavi Era', *Iran under the Pahlavis*, ed. G. Lenczowski (Stanford, CA, 1978)
Y. Zoka and M. H. Semsar: *Iranian Art Treasures in the Prime Ministry of Iran's Collections* (Tehran, 1978)
Les Peintres populaires de la légende persane (exh. cat., Paris, Maison Iran, n.d.)
Poster Art in Iran (exh. cat. by N. Rohani and M. Momayez, Tehran, Mus. Contemp. A., 1978)
J. Dhamija: *Living Tradition of Iran's Crafts* (New Delhi, 1979)
E. Yarshater: 'Contemporary Persian Painting', *Highlights of Persian Art*, ed. R. Ettinghausen and E. Yarshater (Boulder, CO, 1979)
K. Diba: *Kamran Diba: Buildings and Projects* (Stuttgart, 1981)
E. Beazeley and M. Harverson: *Living with the Desert: Working Buildings of the Iranian Plateau* (Warminster, 1982)
W. L. Hanaway jr: 'The Symbolism of Persian Revolutionary Posters', *Iran since the Revolution*, ed. B. M. Rosen (Boulder, CO, 1985)
P. Tanavoli: *Shahsavan: Iranian Rugs and Textiles* (New York, 1985)
W. Eagleton: *An Introduction to Kurdish Rugs and Other Weavings* (Buckhurst Hill, 1988)
A. Sreberny-Mohammadi and A. Mohammadi: 'The Islamic Republic and the World: Images, Propaganda, Intentions, and Results', *Post-Revolutionary Iran*, ed. H. Amirahmadi and M. Parvin (Boulder, CO and London, 1988), pp. 75–104
W. Ali, ed.: *Contemporary Art from the Islamic World* (London, 1989), pp. 150–58
A. Schimmel: 'Shams Anwari Alhuseyni', *A. & Islam. World*, 19 (1990), pp. 25–8

Iran, ancient [Persia]. Region in which several cultures and civilizations flourished from the Palaeolithic period until the Arab conquest in AD 651. There is evidence that ancient Iran was inhabited from *c.* 100,000 BC, but the earliest named inhabitants were ELAMITE (*c.* 3000–mid-6th century BC), whose language, insofar as it has been deciphered, bears no relation to any known group. The ancestors of the present Indo-European or Indo-Aryan inhabitants of Iran, including the Medes and Persians, entered the country only in the second half of the 2nd millennium BC. Besides the Elamites, the three major Iranian dynasties of the pre-Islamic period are the ACHAEMENID or Persian (550–331 BC), the PARTHIAN (250 BC–AD 224) and the SASANIAN (*c.* AD 224–651).

This article covers the major art forms in pre-Islamic Iran. Each major bold subsection has cross-references to individual sites that have made a particular contribution at a certain period or in a given field. The development of some types of object, such as seals or jewellery, and the use of some materials (e.g. faience, glass and ivory) are best seen in the wider context of the ANCIENT NEAR EAST. For the later history of ancient Iran *see* ISLAMIC ART and IRAN.

I. Introduction. II. Architecture. III. Sculpture. IV. Rock reliefs. V. Metalwork. VI. Ceramics. VII. Painting. VIII. Museums and collections. IX. Exhibitions.

I. Introduction.

1. Geography and trade. 2. Chronology. 3. Religion and iconography.

1. GEOGRAPHY AND TRADE. The country is bounded on the north by the Caspian Sea and on the south by the Gulf (see fig. 1). Its western frontier with ancient Mesopotamia and present-day Iraq is marked by the natural barrier of the Zagros mountains. Less well defined, however, are the borders with eastern Turkey and the Caucasus in the mountainous north-west. In the south-west the Mesopotamian plain extends into Khuzistan, and the lack of a natural boundary has made this a disputed frontier throughout history. In Khorasan in the north-east the

1. Map of ancient Iran; those areas with separate entries in this dictionary are distinguished by CROSS-REFERENCE TYPE

country lies open to invaders from the deserts of Turkestan, and there are also no clearly defined natural features to mark the eastern limits of Iran (towards present-day Afghanistan and Pakistan).

Within these borders Iran resembles a saucer, with a high plateau, mostly above 1000 m, surrounding a central depression that forms one of the most arid deserts on earth. This desert was once an inland sea, and the northern part is called the Dasht-i Kavir while the southern is the Dasht-i Lut. The rim of the saucer is formed by high mountain ranges: to the west the Zagros running north-west to south-east, to the north, along the Caspian, the Elburz mountains, and to the south the Makran chain. Fertile valleys fan out from these mountains, and in periods of prosperity and political stability irrigation meant that large areas could be settled. For instance, the province of Sistan in the east was densely populated in Sasanian and early Islamic times, as large numbers of ruin mounds and underground water channels called *qanat* testify, but *c.* AD 1400 the Mongols destroyed the irrigation system and turned the area into the desert it is now.

The mountainous nature of the terrain has had a twofold impact on the history and art of Iran. Isolated mountain valleys tended to develop their own individual cultures with little contact with, or influence from, the outside world; and the major trade routes through Iran avoided the more difficult mountainous areas by running north or south of the desert. One east–west route still passes such sites as YARIM TEPE (i) and Tureng Tepe, along the coastal plain south of the Caspian, past MARLIK, through the AMLASH REGION and across into Azerbaijan and the rich sites around Lake Urmia (e.g. YANIK TEPE and HASANLU). A second route runs south of the Elburz mountains and north of the desert through TEPE HISSAR and either joins the first route or goes further south through Hamadan (anc. Ecbatana), BISITUN and on into Mesopotamia. A third route runs south of the desert and, according to texts of the 3rd millennium BC and early 2nd, carried trade from Meluhha (probably the Indus Valley), and Magan (a name that has survived in the present toponym Makran), past BAMPUR and TEPE YAHYA, along the foothills of the Makran range and into Khuzistan, where the city of SUSA grew up to handle the trade and pass it on to Mesopotamia. A maritime route was also in operation through the Indian Ocean and Gulf, hugging the Makran coast. These east–west routes were intersected by a north–south route which still runs along the edge of the central desert, through TEPE SIALK and down into Fars, where the ancient capitals of the Elamites (Anshan, now TALL'I MALYAN) and Persians (PASARGADAE and PERSEPOLIS) were situated. A pass through the Makran range leads to the port of Bandar Abbas on the coast.

The most spectacular item of trade to have been carried along these routes (and to have survived in the archaeological record) was lapis lazuli. This rich blue stone was mined in the Badakhshan district of Afghanistan and reached Mesopotamia by the middle of the 4th millennium BC. A millennium later it was traded in large quantities, judging from the evidence of jewellery and other artefacts in the Royal Cemetery of Ur in Mesopotamia (e.g. London, BM), and epics tell of expeditions to obtain the mineral. Workshops where the raw lapis lazuli was worked have been found at SHAHR-I SOKHTA in Sistan. Tin may have travelled along the same route, but it is still uncertain where the Ancient Near East obtained the tin it needed for making bronze. Copper, ivory, cornelian and agate probably came from the Indus and beyond. In the second half of the 3rd millennium BC chlorite bowls were being manufactured at Tepe Yahya for markets in Mesopotamia and Syria (*see also* ANCIENT NEAR EAST, §I,1).

Ancient Iran had its own natural resources, however. The chlorite bowls were made of stone from local quarries. Copper was mined on the plateau and used for producing metal artefacts, the best-known of which are the bronzes of the LURISTAN region. Wood was plentiful in the mountain valleys and led to a predilection for columned architecture, which was later translated into the soaring stone columns of the Achaemenid palaces at Susa and Persepolis. Good-quality, fine-grained stone also enabled the carving of fine reliefs (e.g. at Persepolis), and there was a thriving tradition of rock-carving.

BIBLIOGRAPHY

Enc. Iran.
E. Herzfeld: *Iran in the Ancient East* (London, 1941)
H. Frankfort: *The Art and Architecture of the Ancient Orient*, Pelican Hist. A. (Harmondsworth, 1954, rev. 4/1970)
R. Ghirshman: *Iran from the Earliest Times to the Islamic Conquest* (Harmondsworth, 1954)
——: *Iran: Parthes et Sassanides* (Paris, 1962; Eng. trans., London, 1962); and as *Persian Art: The Parthian and Sassanian Dynasties, 249 BC–AD 651* (New York, 1962)
A. Godard: *L'Art de l'Iran* (Paris, 1962; Eng. trans., New York and Washington, DC, 1965)
E. Porada: *Alt-Iran: Die Kunst in vorislamischer Zeit* (Baden-Baden, 1962); Eng. trans. as *Ancient Iran: The Art of Pre-Islamic Times*, A. World (London, 1965); *The Art of Ancient Iran: Pre-Islamic Cultures* (New York, 1965)
R. Ghirshman: *Perse: Proto-Iraniens, Mèdes, Achéménides*, A. Mankind (Paris, 1963); Eng. trans. as *The Art of Ancient Iran from its Origins to the Time of Alexander the Great* (London, 1964)
A. U. Pope and P. Ackerman, eds: *Survey of Persian Art* (2/1964–7), i and ii
P. Amiet: *Elam* (Auvers-sur-Oise, 1966)
J.-L. Huot: *From the Origins to the Achaemenids* (1970), i of *Persia*, Archaeologia Mundi (Geneva, 1967–)
V. G. Lukonin: *From the Seleucids to the Sassanids* (1970), ii of *Persia*, Archaeologia Mundi (Geneva, 1967–)
S. A. Matheson: *Persia: An Archaeological Guide* (London, 1972, rev. 1976)
W. Orthmann: *Der alte Orient*, Propyläen-Kstgesch., xiv (Berlin, 1975)
P. Amiet: *L'Art antique du Proche Orient* (Paris, 1977; Eng. trans. 1980)
G. Herrmann: *The Iranian Revival*, The Making of the Past (Oxford, 1977)
P. Amiet: *L'Age des échanges inter-iraniens, 3500–1700 avant J.-C.*, Notes et documents des Musées de France, xi (Paris, 1986)

DOMINIQUE COLLON

2. CHRONOLOGY.

(i) Prehistoric period. (ii) Historic period.

(i) Prehistoric period.

(a) Palaeolithic. Unlike prehistoric Europe, Palaeolithic Iran has no known graphic art. Only utilitarian artefacts have survived, consisting mainly of stone and bone tools and a few ornaments. The presence of ochre and exotic shells suggests this lack is due to an accident of survival rather than to a dearth of artistic imagination. There are not many known Palaeolithic sites, and of these few have been excavated and fewer still published.

The earliest Palaeolithic chopping tools and scrapers in ancient Iran come from the Kashaf Rud Basin in Khorasan. Problematic collections are known from Baluchistan. Isolated hand-axes have been located on hilltops near Kirmanshah and in Azerbaijan. Chopping tools and small hand-axes, from *c.* 100,000 BC, were found at Pal Barik in Hulaylan. Approximately sixteen Middle Palaeolithic sites are known from Zagros areas, and six more, unevenly distributed, from the rest of the country. Points, borers, scrapers and a few burins were found, and these belong to the flint industry known as the Mousterian. There is considerable uniformity in the flint industry of the Middle Palaeolithic throughout the country.

In the Zagros the Upper Palaeolithic era is subdivided into two imperfectly understood periods. The Baradostian (*c.* 38,000–*c.* 25,000 BC) has a much greater variety of tool types than the Mousterian of the Middle Palaeolithic and is one of the earliest known blade industries in which flakes or blades are struck from specially prepared flint cores. This was a major technological advance in the manufacture of more sophisticated tools. Bone tools, particularly awls, are also common in the period. The presence of ochre on stones and human bones attests to the use of colour. Pebbles, sometimes polished, coated with ochre and drilled, were used as ornaments. The Zarzian period, which terminated around 10,000 BC, is characterized by an elegant flint industry with a rich variety of blade tools, frequently of diminutive size. Imported seashells were used as ornamentation, and bone tools, particularly awls, have been found. The delicate craftsmanship of everyday tools presages the flowering of artistic expression seen in the Neolithic period.

A number of sites that fall between the Upper Palaeolithic period and the Neolithic in terms of style and development, belonging to neither but sharing attributes with both, are assigned to the Epipalaeolithic (formerly Mesolithic) period. These sites are scattered along the shores of the Caspian Sea and in the south and west of the country.

BIBLIOGRAPHY

P. E. L. Smith: *Palaeolithic Archaeology in Iran*, The American Institute of Iranian Studies, i (Philadelphia, 1986)

(b) Neolithic. Late in the Upper Palaeolithic period many hunter-gatherers began to experiment with new ways of exploiting their environment. They selected and sowed grains, managed livestock and conserved a surplus. The Neolithic villagers were thus less mobile than their forefathers. The structure of society became more complex, and the beginning of specialization is evident in functionally determined architecture, expressive graphic design on pottery, simple sculpture and more elaborate rituals.

Permanent buildings were built of clay and mud and housed storage facilities, religious centres and burials, as well as people (*see* §II, 1(i) below). The houses were decorated, and their owners manufactured and accumulated possessions, examples of which have been found in villages of the Zagros, the Caspian and the Iranian plateau. A few crude 8th-millennium BC potsherds were discovered at Ganj Dareh. These are exceptionally early, and pottery does not become common until the 7th millennium BC. Other containers were made of carved and polished stone or reeds lined with asphalt. Some of the earliest painted pottery is from Tepe Guran. By the 6th millennium BC the ceramic tradition was firmly established in the Zagros and Khuzistan.

The 5th-millennium BC sites of TEPE GIYAN and Dalma have become type sites for two widespread pottery traditions with geometric designs. From Tepe Sialk and related sites on the Iranian plateau come a greater variety of pottery shapes and decoration (*see* §VI, 1(i) below). Clay and occasionally stone animal and human figurines, such as the large steatite bisexual figurine from Tepe Yahya (Tehran, Archaeol. Mus.; see fig. 2), have also been found at a number of sites (*see* §III, 1(i) below). Finely made flint tools, reminiscent of those of the Upper Palaeolithic period, are present at the early Neolithic sites of Asiab, GANJ DAREH, Ali Kosh and Abdul Hosein (see Pullar). Bone tools, plain or decorated, are widespread throughout the period.

Many artefacts have been found in burials. Neolithic funerary practices in ancient Iran varied, but there seems to have been a belief in the afterlife. Skeletons coloured with red ochre are known both from the Zagros and further east from Tepe Zagheh and Tepe Sialk. Grave goods such as polished stone vessels and personal ornaments are common, and at Ali Kosh such ornaments included native copper and turquoise beads, stone bracelets, bell-shaped clay pendants that formed part of a loincloth, cowrie shell beads and pendants of boar tusk, mussel

2. Neolithic figurine from Tepe Yahya, steatite, h. 277 mm, *c.* 4900 BC (Tehran, Archaeological Museum)

shell and pebbles. The grave goods also suggest a degree of religious ceremony.

BIBLIOGRAPHY

F. Hole, K. V. Flannery and J. A. Neely: *Prehistory and Human Ecology of the Deh Luran Plain* (Ann Arbor, 1969)

J. Mellaart: *The Neolithic of the Near East* (London, 1975)

P. Mortensen and others: 'Excavations at Tepe Guran, Luristan', *Acta Archaeol.* [Copenhagen], xxxiv (1975), pp. 97–133

F. Hole: *Studies on the Archaeological History of the Deh Luran Plain* (Ann Arbor, 1977)

P. E. L. Smith: 'An Interim Report on Ganj Dareh Tepe, Iran', *Amer. J. Archaeol.* [Copenhagen], lxxxii/4 (1978), pp. 538–40

M. Voigt: *Hajji Firuz Tepe, Iran: The Neolithic Settlement* (Philadelphia, 1983)

C. C. Lamberg-Karlovsky, ed.: 'Excavations at Tepe Yahya, Iran, 1967–75: The Early Periods', *Amer. Sch. Prehist. Res. Bull.*, xxxviii (1986) [whole issue]

J. Pullar: *Tepe Abdul Hosein: A Neolithic Site in Western Iran*, Brit. Archaeol. Rep., Int. Ser., dlxiii (Oxford, 1990)

D. Schmandt-Besserat: *Before Writing*, 2 vols (Austin, 1992)

JUDITH PULLAR

(c) Chalcolithic. The end of the Neolithic period in south-west Iran was marked, as in nearby Mesopotamia, by an event of vital importance to all human history: the emergence of an urban, state-based, potentially literate civilization. The large town of CHOGHA MISH had developed in the 6th and 5th millennia BC, and Susa was founded about 4000 BC. Susa had connections with the highland communities of the plateau to the east, and to the north, in Luristan. Certain villages in the centre of the plateau—Tall-i Iblis in Kirman and Tepe Qabristan near Qazvin—developed metalworking skills sufficiently to allow production for export. Long-distance trade movements were thus initiated, to the advantage of Susa, which lay at the crossroads of the trade routes from the plateau.

The ties between the civilization at Susa and that of the highland communities are seen in the beautiful ceramics, painted with heavily stylized animal decoration (see fig. 13a below), which is more elaborate than that of contemporary Ubaid ceramics in south Mesopotamia (*see* §VI, 1(i) below). Another link can be seen in the engraved seals from both Susa and Luristan, which have common iconographical motifs such as genies depicted as 'Masters of the animals' (*see* §III below).

Shortly after Susa was founded, an enormous stepped terrace was built at a site for the temple, the economic and administrative heart of the community. The extreme stylization seen in the art of this period, however, reflects a material culture still within the prehistoric Neolithic tradition. During the 4th millennium BC Susa broke with the plateau and united with Proto-Sumerian Mesopotamia, and particularly with the city of Uruk. The buildings of this period at Susa have disappeared, but sealed clay balls are marked with signs that illustrate the preliminary stages in the development of accounting and writing (*see also* ANCIENT NEAR EAST, §I, 3).

The leading figure in this society is depicted on seals and sculpture from Susa, Chogha Mish and Uruk. He is recognizable by his browband, his beard and his bell-shaped skirt. He is normally referred to as 'priest-king' since he seems to have fulfilled the roles of war leader, or king, and of priest. His duties are comparable with those of the Sumerian kings as described in texts of the 3rd millennium BC. Seal impressions from Susa show him as a conqueror showering arrows upon his enemies who are at the foot of a high wall surrounding a temple. A number of other seals give an animated picture of the population's everyday activities—hunting, stock-raising, farming (especially gathering the harvest into granaries) and weaving. Worship and war are more rarely shown. The realism of these representations implies a profound change in mentality and a break with prehistoric archaism. The change was also expressed in the emergence of refined statuary in the form of small animals and figures (*see* §III, 2 below) and of metalwork using the lost-wax process for modelling small animals and pins decorated with human figures.

This civilization was exported by merchant-colonists, to the north (GODIN TEPE) and to the east (Tepe Sialk). It died out towards the end of the 4th millennium BC, probably overwhelmed by highland nomads who came down from the Fars plateau and founded the Proto-Elamite civilization.

BIBLIOGRAPHY

P. Amiet: *L'Age des échanges inter-iraniens, 3500–1700 avant J.-C.*, Notes et documents des Musées de France, xi (Paris, 1986), pp. 24–90

(ii) Historic period.

(a) 3000–1000 BC. (b) 1000 BC–AD 651.

(a) 3000–1000 BC. By *c.* 3000 BC the Elamites had settled on the plateau of Fars and laid the foundations of the Proto-Elamite civilization by founding the historical capital of Elam at Anshan (Tall-i Malyan). They annexed Susa and inherited its trade network. Clay tablets, inscribed in the as yet undeciphered Proto-Elamite script, have been found at Tepe Sialk to the north, Tepe Yahya to the east and Shahr-i Sokhta on the borders of Afghanistan. This trade network extended into Turkmenia and to the borders of India. At the same time a new tradition, characterized by grey pottery, arose to the south-east of the Caspian at Tepe Hissar and on the Gorgan plain, at Yarim Tepe (i).

About 2800 BC the Proto-Elamite civilization collapsed and the people of Fars returned to a nomadic way of life. Susa became part of the Mesopotamian Early Dynastic sphere of influence and trade network. In response to this new situation, Luristan to the north-west began exploiting local copper resources and developed a new metalworking industry in copper and even bronze. Stone-lined tombs in Luristan contained collective burials and were arranged in cemeteries far from any settlement, suggesting a partly nomadic population. Painted pottery from Luristan (see fig. 13b below) is related to that of Susa, indicating that the city had a mixed population.

In south-central Iran the village of Tepe Yahya housed workshops where stone vessels, decorated with dense patterns, were carved from soft, green chlorite, which was quarried near by. Some of the patterns are geometric, possibly inspired by architecture, and some are mythological with figures associated with leopards, lions, scorpions and lion-headed snakes. These vessels were highly prized in Susa, Mesopotamia and even Mari (now in Syria) and were probably exported via the Gulf. To the north of Tepe Yahya, on the edge of the Dasht-i Lut desert at Shahdad, potters, bronzesmiths and workers in chlorite and alabaster are attested, and clay funerary statues resembling sculpture from Mesopotamia have been found.

Around 2300 BC the Mesopotamian kings of Akkad annexed Susa and introduced their Akkadian cuneiform script. About 2100 BC, after this empire had collapsed, a ruler named Puzur-Inshushinak created an Elamite state that included the plain of Susa and the southern plateau. He was defeated by the kings of the 3rd Dynasty of Ur, who had established the last Sumerian empire *c.* 2112 BC. Again trade flourished, with craftsmen in the Iranian hinterland enjoying exceptional prosperity. A trans-Elamite civilization developed which absorbed the previously independent cultures of the Gorgan plain, of Turkmenia and even of Bactria. About 2004 BC the Elamites brought about the downfall of the 3rd Dynasty of Ur and annexed Susa.

With the annexation of Susa, the Elamites were able to reconstruct their empire; once again it was centred on Anshan (Tall-i Malyan), which became a large capital city covering 150 ha. It was a major staging-post on the trade routes with eastern Iran. At the end of the 20th century BC the Elamite sovereigns adopted the title 'Grand Vizier' or 'King of Anshan and of Susa'. However, from the 18th century BC the population of Fars returned to a nomadic way of life, although they remained masters of the plain of Susa. Their princes built two open-air places of worship in Fars at Kurangun and Naqsh-i Rustam, where the supreme god of the Elamites was depicted on rock reliefs enthroned on a serpent. This god was also introduced at Susa. At the same time, a wide-ranging development was affecting the whole Iranian world and reaching as far as India; all the prosperous sites in Kirman, Sistan and Gorgan were abandoned, although a much impoverished civilization survived in other areas. In Luristan the nomads became settled and their tradition of metalwork fell into disuse for some five centuries.

After an obscure period in the middle of the 2nd millennium BC, Elam experienced a new period of prosperity, which began at Kabnak (now HAFT TEPE) near Susa in the 15th century BC and was at its height from the second half of the 14th century to the 12th BC at CHOGHA ZANBIL under the new kings of Anshan and of Susa, the 'Extenders of the Kingdom', who conquered Kassite Babylon towards 1160 BC. After this classical age of Elamite art a number of peoples, whose language belonged to the Indo-European group and who were to give the country its name of Iran, started to move on to the north of the plateau. They must have come from the plain of Gorgan, bringing with them beautiful grey ceramics often similar to those typical of Gorgan before its civilization died out towards the 18th century BC. These new ceramics, which could also sometimes be red or orange, spread first to Marlik, south of the Caspian Sea, to Khurvin, west of Tehran, and to the necropolises of Tepe Sialk in central Iran. A princely necropolis at Marlik contained grave goods representative of the new civilization. The potters there made animal-shaped rhyta of great originality, while the goldsmiths started a tradition of ceremonial vessels that was to continue until Achaemenid and Sasanian times. They apparently lacked any very strong artistic tradition and were greatly influenced by the art of Babylon, Assur and Mitanni and sometimes that of Elam. This is illustrated by gold and silver vessels showing animals and winged monsters, but rarely humans. The animals are shown passant or rampant, sometimes with the head full face in high relief. The same population movement may once more have brought nomadism to Luristan towards the 12th century BC. The tradition of ornate bronzes revived and developed extensively during the 1st millennium BC. Initially the most remarkable pieces were ceremonial axes with multiple points on the heel; some of these have inscriptions naming Babylonian kings.

BIBLIOGRAPHY

L. Vanden Berghe: 'La Nécropole de Bani Surmah', *Archeologia*, xxiv (1968), pp. 53–63
——: 'La Nécropole de Kalleh Nisar', *Archeologia*, xxxii (1970), pp. 64–73
——: 'Prospections dans la région de Badr', *Archeologia*, xxxvi (1970), pp. 1–21
A. Hakemi: *Catalogue de l'exposition LUT Xabis (Shahdad)* (Tehran, 1972)
C. C. Lamberg-Karlovsky: 'Urban Interaction on the Iranian Plateau', *Proc. Brit. Acad.*, lix (1973), pp. 283–319
L. Vanden Berghe: 'Le Luristan à l'âge du bronze', *Archeologia*, lxiii (1973), pp. 24–36
P. Amiet: *L'Age des échanges inter-iraniens, 3500–1700 avant J.-C.*, Notes et documents des Musées de France, xi (Paris, 1986), pp. 120–214

PIERRE AMIET

(b) 1000 BC–AD *651.* In the early centuries of the 1st millennium BC western Iran was divided among numerous peoples: those along the western border, mentioned in Assyrian texts, included the Elamites in the lowlands of south-west Iran, and in the mountains (from north to south) the URARTIANS, Manaeans, Medes and Persians. During what is known as the Neo-Elamite period (8th–mid-7th centuries BC) the Elamites were allies of the Babylonians against the Assyrians until about 640 BC, when they were defeated by the Assyrian king Ashurbanipal (*reg* 668–627 BC). There is evidence for local rule continuing, but with the rise of Achaemenid power in the 6th century BC Elam became a province of the Persian empire. The Urartians expanded into north-west Iran in the late 9th century BC and built fortresses, including those at BASTAM and HAFTAVAN TEPE. The precise extent of the territory of the Manaeans has not been determined, though the site of Hasanlu has been suggested as one of its centres. Whether the ZIWIYEH 'treasure' with its mixture of artistic traditions belonged to Manaea or Media is disputed.

By the 7th century BC the Medes, who were descended from Indo-European invaders of the previous millennium, had become the most important power in western Iran and, in alliance with the Babylonians, defeated the Assyrians and captured Nineveh in 612 BC. Thereafter Median power expanded in the west into central Turkey and probably covered most of the Iranian plateau. Surprisingly few works of art of the Median period have been identified, but the architecture is well represented at the sites of TEPE NUSH-I JAN and Godin Tepe (see fig. 5c below). An unidentified group living in what is now Luristan in the first half of the 1st millennium BC used the lost-wax technique to produce what are known as the Luristan bronzes. The site of BABA JAN, which shows evidence of Median occupation in level II, may have been used by these people.

The Persians, like the Manaeans and the Medes, are first mentioned in Assyrian texts of the 9th century BC. There is evidence that more than one region was called Parsua but the most important was the ancient territory of Anshan, which still bears their name (Old Pers. Parsa; Gr. Persis; now Fars). In the early 6th century the Persians were vassals of the Medes, but in 550 BC the Median king Astyages (*reg* 585–550 BC) was overthrown by his grandson Cyrus II (*reg* 550–530 BC), the ruler of the Persians. The vast Median empire was extended by Cyrus, who defeated Croesus of Lydia in 547 BC and occupied Babylon in 539 BC, by his son Cambyses II (*reg* 529–522 BC), who captured Egypt in 525 BC, and by the usurper Darius I (*reg* 521–486 BC), who added the Indus Valley and Thrace to the Persian empire but was defeated by the Greeks at Marathon (490 BC). Cyrus built a monumental city at Pasargadae, where he was buried. Darius was the greatest of the Achaemenid builders. At Bisitun his inscription and relief record his version of his accession to the throne. He completed a canal from the River Nile to the Red Sea. At Susa he revived the ancient Elamite capital, building a palace dominated by an apadana, an enormous porticoed columned hall (see fig. 5e below), and he started the building of Persepolis, near which he was buried. The palaces of Persepolis (see fig. 5f below) were completed by Darius' son Xerxes I (*reg* 485–465 BC) and his grandson Artaxerxes I (*reg* 464–424 BC). The later Achaemenid kings managed to keep the empire almost intact except for Egypt, which rebelled at the end of the 5th century BC.

The Achaemenid Persian empire was defeated by Alexander the Great, who captured Persepolis in 330 BC. After Alexander's death in 323 BC, his conquests were split up among his generals. Seleucus I Nicator (*reg* 305–281 BC) seized Babylon in 312 BC and acquired the eastern part of Alexander's conquests (*see* SELEUCIDS). The main interests of Seleucus and his successors lay in the west towards the Mediterranean; evidence for their presence in Iran is sparse, although there is a fine rock relief of Herakles at Bisitun. In 246 BC the Seleucid governor of Bactria founded an independent Greco-Bactrian kingdom (*see* BACTRIAN AND INDO-GREEK MONARCHIES), which survived for more than a century, retaining close cultural ties with the Greek world, as is shown by the finds from Ai Khanum beside the River Oxus.

Also in the mid-3rd century BC the neighbouring province of Parthia was overrun by the Iranian tribe of the Parni under the leadership of one Arsaces. This tribe adopted the name of the province and as the Parthians repulsed the Seleucids. They moved their capital from NISA (near Ashkhabad, Turkmenistan) to Hecatompylos (probably SHAHR-I QUMIS in northern Iran) at the end of the 3rd century BC, and in the 1st century BC to KTESIPHON, the later Sasanian capital in central Iraq. As Seleucid control diminished, independent kingdoms arose in Persis, ELYMAIS and Characene, which became vassals of the Parthians under Mithradates I (*reg* 171–138 BC), whose victories included the invasion of Babylonia in 141 BC. In the 2nd century BC a series of tribal movements in China precipitated the invasion of the Shaka (Scythians) into eastern Iran, where they overthrew the Greco-Bactrian kingdom *c.* 130 BC; they then continued into south-east Iran, where they gave their name to the province of Sistan (Sacastene), which includes the extraordinary site of KUH-I KHWAJA, and into India, where they founded the Indo-Scythian kingdom. In the long reign of Mithradates II (123–87 BC) Parthian control was established as far as the Euphrates River, and sites such as DURA EUROPOS, HATRA and ASSUR were subject to the Parthians. Mithradates even exchanged ambassadors and gifts with Wudi, the emperor of the Chinese Han dynasty (206 BC–AD 220). In 64 BC Pompey (106–48 BC) established Roman rule in Syria, and for the next 700 years there was almost constant conflict between the Parthian rulers of Iran and the Romans. The defeat of the invading Romans at the Battle of Carrhae in 53 BC halted Roman expansion to the east. Later Roman rulers struck deep into the heart of Parthia: Mark Anthony (*c.* 83–30 BC) invaded north-west Iran in 36 BC but was forced to retreat, Trajan (*reg* AD 98–117) reached the Gulf in AD 116, Lucius Verus (*reg* AD 161–9) destroyed the Parthian king's palace in Ktesiphon in AD 164 and Septimius Severus (*reg* AD 193–211) also sacked Ktesiphon in AD 198. Information about the east of Iran is minimal, but in the early 1st century AD the Kushanas, a dynasty of Central Asian origin, took control of the eastern Parthian provinces and extended their rule southwards into Afghanistan and the Indian subcontinent. Parthian rule was surprisingly long-lived and yet it was not heavy. Even more than that of the earlier Achaemenids or the later Sasanians, it was based on tribal allegiances with considerable autonomy given to local dynasties who were effectively independent rulers, like that of QAL'EH-I YAZDEGERD.

The rebellion of one of the Parthian vassals brought an end to their rule. Ardashir (the later version of the name Artaxerxes) was probably ruler of Persis; with his defeat of the last Parthian king *c.* AD 224 he founded the Sasanian dynasty (named after Ardashir's grandfather Sasan), which ruled Iran until the Islamic conquest. Both Ardashir I (*reg* AD 224–41) and his son Shapur I (*reg* AD 241–72) were great military leaders and builders. Ardashir re-established Iranian power both in the east, ending the rule of the Kushans, and in the west, capturing Hatra and other towns allied to the Romans. He built a new circular city at FIRUZABAD. Shapur consolidated and extended his father's conquests, killing the emperor Gordian III (*reg* AD 238–44), capturing Valerian (*reg* AD 253–60) in AD 259 and sacking Antioch. At Firuzabad, at BISHAPUR, which was built by Shapur I using captured Roman workmen, and at Naqsh-i Rustam, the burial place of the Achaemenid kings near Persepolis, the early Sasanian kings carved spectacular bas-reliefs illustrating their victories (see fig. 10 below). An account of Shapur's conquests was inscribed in three languages on the Achaemenid tower at Naqsh-i Rustam.

During the long reign of Shapur II (*reg* AD 309–79), who was crowned while still in the womb, Iran was attacked both from the east by yet another invader from the direction of China, the Chionites or Red Huns, and from the west by the Roman emperor Julian the Apostate (*reg* AD 360–63), who reached the gates of Ktesiphon, before his death in battle and the capitulation by his successor Jovian (*reg* AD 363–4). A second wave of Huns, the Hephthalites or White Huns, invaded eastern Iran at the end of the 4th century. For the following century the Sasanians were preoccupied with events in the east and were largely unsuccessful until the reign of Chosroes I (*reg* AD 539–71), who first reformed the administration and taxation systems and then extended Iranian rule, defeating the Huns in the east, reducing Byzantine power in the west and even annexing the Yemen. His grandson, Chosroes II (*reg* AD 591–628), in later tradition exemplified the typical Sasanian monarch surrounded by luxury, and many stories were told about his court, such as the frequently illustrated story of Khusraw and Shirin. He may also have been responsible for the reliefs at TAQ-I BUSTAN. Chosroes had been helped to the throne by the Byzantine emperor Maurice (*reg* AD 582–602), who was overthrown by Phocas (*reg* AD 602–10). Chosroes invaded the Levant and in a series of campaigns captured Jerusalem in AD 614, Egypt in 619 and reached the Asiatic shore opposite Constantinople in 626. Heraclius (*reg* AD 610–41) counter-attacked from the Black Sea and sacked the religious sanctuary of Shiz (TAKHT-I SULAYMAN); in a later campaign he destroyed Chosroes' palace near Ktesiphon, whereupon the Persian nobles murdered Chosroes and made peace with Heraclius. The final years of the Sasanians were marked by dynastic squabbles and a succession of weak rulers. The beneficiaries were not the Byzantines, however, but the Arabs, who under the banner of Islam carried all before them, defeating the Sasanians at the battles of Qadisiyeh in AD 637 and Nihavand in 642. The last Sasanian king, Yazdegerd III (*reg* AD 633–51), took refuge in Merv and was murdered there in 651.

BIBLIOGRAPHY

E. Yarshater, ed.: *The Seleucid, Parthian and Sasanian Periods* (1983), iii/1–2 of *The Cambridge History of Iran* (Cambridge and London, 1968–)

E. Carter and M. Stolper: *Elam: Surveys of Political History and Archaeology*, Near Eastern Studies, xxv (Berkeley, 1984)

I. Gershevitch, ed.: *The Median and Achaemenian Periods* (1985), ii of *The Cambridge History of Iran* (Cambridge and London, 1968–)

J. Boardman and others, eds: *Persia, Greece and the Western Mediterranean c. 525 to 479 BC*, Cambridge Anc. Hist., iv (Cambridge, 2/1988)

MICHAEL ROAF

3. RELIGION AND ICONOGRAPHY. Written sources concerning the religion of ancient Iran are either totally lacking or extremely scant. Iconographic evidence is therefore of prime importance despite difficulties in interpretation.

(i) Before 3000 BC. Terracotta nude females, with their sexual characteristics emphasized, for instance the 'Venus of Tepe Sarab' (6th millennium BC; Tehran, Archaeol. Mus.), bear witness to a cult of the mother goddess in the early Neolithic communities of Iran. Animal figurines associated with hunting rituals were endowed with magical properties. From the 5th millennium BC animals painted on pottery and engraved on seals symbolized supernatural powers. The major protagonist on archaic stamp seals from Luristan and Susa was the 'Master of the animals', who had horns or a caprid's head and was probably a genie or masked sorcerer rather than a deity. The development of an urban society towards the end of the 4th millennium BC led to the building of temples; a seal impression from Susa depicts one decorated with horns (Paris, Louvre).

(ii) 3000–1000 BC. Urbanization was reflected in an iconography that emphasized stability, with representations of bulls and lions in human posture (e.g. New York, Brooklyn Mus.; see fig. 6 below). The primacy of female deities in Elam and on the plateau (e.g. on seals from Tepe Yahya and Shahdad; Tehran, Archaeol. Mus.) in the 3rd millennium BC was inherited from the prehistoric cult of the mother goddess.

During the 2nd millennium BC goddesses tended to make way for male deities associated with royalty. The names of many Elamite deities are known; the most important are Inshushinak (the great god of Susa), Napirisha and Kiririsha (the divine couple of Anshan) and Pinikir (the great goddess of Awan); however, the deities depicted on the monuments are rarely identifiable. Throughout most of the 2nd millennium BC divine imagery was dominated by a fertility god seated on a coiled snake; this god appears on cylinder seals, on the stele of King Untash-Napirisha (for illustration *see* ELAMITE) and on rock reliefs at Kurangun and Naqsh-i Rustam. The importance of the snake in the iconographies of Elam, Luristan and the eastern plateau suggests a common source of religious beliefs. A bronze model of the 12th century BC, known as the *Sit Shamshi* (Akkad.: 'rising sun'; Paris, Louvre; for illustration *see* SUSA), reproduces the sacred enclosure of Susa with a ziggurat, a temple, a stele, a basin, a large water container and a sacred grove. An actual sacred enclosure and ziggurat (see fig. 4 below) have been excavated at CHOGHA ZANBIL.

The Hasanlu Gold Bowl (Tehran, Archaeol. Mus.; *see* HASANLU, fig. 2) probably dates from the late 2nd millennium BC; it may indicate that the pantheon of north-west Iran was dominated by three great gods in chariots, but the tombs at Marlik contained goldwork illustrating a world of good and evil demons. Figurines of naked male and female worshippers were also found at Marlik (Tehran, Archaeol. Mus.).

(iii) 1000 BC–AD *651*. The iconographic repertory of the LURISTAN bronzes (*c*. 1200–600 BC) reflects an essentially independent tradition that survived remarkably unchanged from the period of the prehistoric stamp seals onwards. The religious thought of the Luristan nomads was mainly expressed through a few themes that were closely connected with nature. 'Standards' with ibex on either side of a tree illustrate the theme of fertility. Pastoral order is symbolized by standards with confronted lions, by idols, openwork discs decorating the heads of votive pins and by the cheek-pieces of horses' bits depicting the 'Master of the animals' grasping two menacing lions round the neck. Figurines of naked men and women also emphasize fertility. The same themes are repeated on other bronzes decorated in repoussé, such as the disc-shaped heads of pins, the plaques on quivers, and vessels, but with the addition of ritual scenes and mythical animals. Ritual scenes of a very different kind are depicted on contemporary Neo-Elamite rock reliefs at the open-air sanctuary at Kul-i Farah (10th–6th century BC) in western Iran (see figs 3 and 9 below), which illustrate religious ceremonies, accompanied by music and song. Median art (7th century–550 BC) inherited the fantastic bestiary depicted on the Marlik metal vessels of the 2nd millennium BC.

Achaemenid art (550–331 BC) is the symbolic expression of royal power. The traditional 'Master of the animals' is depicted on the reliefs at Persepolis and on cylinder seals as a royal hero wearing Persian dress (*see* ANCIENT NEAR EAST, fig. 34(l)). Apotropaic figures, genii and mythical

3. Religious procession on a rock relief at Kul-i Farah, h. 2.5–3 m, Neo-Elamite, 8th–7th centuries BC

animals protected the palaces at Pasargadae, Susa and Persepolis. The only Achaemenid ritual scene is the adoration of fire, the visible symbol of divinity, which is depicted on seals and on the royal tombs at Naqsh-i Rustam and Persepolis (*see* ZOROASTRIANISM, fig. 1). The upper part of a male figure emerging from a winged disc appears frequently. It is uncertain whether this symbol represents Ahura Mazda (the supreme deity of Zoroastrianism) or the *khvarnah* (divine grace, the equivalent of the Greek Tyche and Roman Fortuna). Votive plaques in the OXUS TREASURE show figures holding the ritual *barsom* (a bundle of rods) or a flower.

Alexander the Great and the Seleucids (312–150 BC) were fervent worshippers of Herakles, who was depicted on a rock-carving at Bisitun and whose cult survived in Elymais into the first centuries AD (e.g. at Masjid-i Suleiman). Parthians (250 BC–*c.* AD 224) made use of Greek imagery (e.g. Tyche and Nike on the reverse of coins), but it is difficult to evaluate the influence of Hellenism on Iranian religion. The absence of a Zoroastrian figurative tradition led to the borrowing of themes and motifs, which it would be rash to take as proof of syncretism in religious beliefs.

Under the Sasanians, Zoroastrianism became the state religion. The anthropomorphic representations of Ahura Mazda, Anahita, Mithra and Ahriman appear on rock reliefs solely in royal investiture scenes (e.g. at Bishapur). The decoration of mosaic panels from Bishapur and some silver vessels (see fig. 12 below) depict Dionysiac motifs; such scenes may be connected with the cult of Anahita, goddess of water and fertility. Seals and bullae show the fire cult and frequently represent astral symbols, and real or fantastic animals, which probably had astrological or religious significance. The Zoroastrian fire altar is depicted on the reverse of coins.

BIBLIOGRAPHY

J. Duchesne-Guillemin: *La Religion de l'Iran ancien* (Paris, 1962)
W. Hinz: *Das Reich Elam* (Stuttgart, 1964)
D. Schlumberger: *L'Orient hellénisé* (Paris, 1970)
P. Amiet: *Les Antiquités de Luristan* (Paris, 1976)
M. A. R. Colledge: *Parthian Art* (New York and London, 1977)
P. Amiet: 'L'Iconographie archaïque de l'Iran: Quelques documents nouveaux', *Syria: Revue d'art oriental et d'archéologie*, lvi (1979), pp. 333–52
P. O. Harper: *Royal Imagery*, i of *Silver Vessels of the Sasanian Period* (New York, 1981–)
P. de Miroschedji: 'Le Dieu élamite au serpent et aux eaux jaillissantes', *Iran. Antiq.*, xvi (1981), pp. 1–25
E. De Waele: *Bronzes du Luristan et d'Amlash: Ancienne collection Godard* (Louvain-la-Neuve, 1982)
Reliefs rupestres de l'Iran ancien (exh. cat. by L. Vanden Berghe, Brussels, Musées Royaux A. & Hist., 1983)
M. Boyce: *Zoroastrians: Their Religious Beliefs and Practices* (London, 1986)
F. Vallat: 'Religion et civilisation élamites en Susiane', *Doss. Hist. & Archéol.*, 138 (May 1989), pp. 46–9

ERIC DE WAELE

II. Architecture.

Fragmentary archaeological records make it difficult to establish trends in ancient Iranian architecture: information is often derived from single sites, or even single buildings, and some periods and areas are not represented at all. From the outset, however, the indigenous builders of Iran absorbed and transformed, to striking effect, a long succession of external influences. Clay and mud were the principal building materials throughout most of ancient Iran's history. Buildings are first attested in the Neolithic period, in the second half of the 8th millennium BC, and monumental mud-brick architecture appeared for the first time in the 4th millennium BC (the Chalcolithic period).

1. Before 3000 BC. 2. 3000–1000 BC. 3. 1000 BC–AD 651.

1. Before 3000 BC.

(i) Neolithic. The architecture of this early period varies in complexity. Walls made of mud bricks bonded with a mortice-and-tenon technique and cubicles made of prefabricated mud slabs were features of the early building levels at GANJ DAREH in the Zagros mountains of western Iran. Domed ovens are common and there are some mud benches. Often rooms were small and entry difficult, as at TEPE YAHYA, in south-east Iran, where access to some of the earliest structures may have been through the roof. At Ganj Dareh part of the complex network of small rooms, possibly storage rooms, may have been capped by a second storey. Sometimes floors or walls were covered with coloured plaster; at YANIK TEPE, west of the Caspian, floors were coated with lime plaster, while at Tepe Guran, not far from Ganj Dareh, floors and a courtyard were covered with a mosaic of white felspar and red clay. Reed mats were often used as floor coverings. At Ganj Dareh a niche, possibly of religious significance, was decorated with two sheep or goat skulls, one above the other. This ritualistic use of animal decoration is reminiscent of the much more dramatic shrines of ÇATAL HÜYÜK in Anatolia.

JUDITH PULLAR

(ii) Chalcolithic. The most important surviving architectural undertaking of this period—and the largest edifice in the ancient world—is the enormous stepped terrace built *c.* 4000 BC at SUSA, in south-west Iran, as a site for the city's temple and annexes. The monumental mud-brick terrace was at least 80 m long, probably as wide, and 10 m high. Other buildings at Susa completely escaped the notice of early archaeologists due to poor excavating techniques.

Architecture in Susiana, the area surrounding Susa, in the second half of the 4th millennium BC (the Uruk period) is known from designs on seal impressions. At Susa one of these shows a temple decorated with horns and surrounded by a wall, and another shows a two-storey house, while at CHOGHA MISH a third represents a fortress surrounded by two walls. During the same period merchant–colonists settled further north at GODIN TEPE and built a little circular citadel that housed a small residence heated by a fireplace on one wall and lit by two narrow windows.

2. 3000–1000 BC.

In the Proto-Elamite period (*c.* 3000–2800 BC) administrative buildings with storerooms on the ground floor appear at several sites. In the capital, Anshan (now TALL'I MALYAN), a building of this type was probably a palace and was decorated with paintings. Little is known of the architecture of the remainder of the 3rd millennium BC, but the base of a large granary, ventilated by vaulted galleries, adjoined the largest temple at Susa in the Akkadian period (*c.* 2300 BC). It bears an interesting resemblance to those of the same period at Mohenjo daro and Harappa in the Indus Valley. In roughly the same period at TEPE HISSAR in north-east Iran a local ruler built himself a residence with a relatively simple design; it was about 27 m long and had an entrance stairway flanked by towers. A little to the north, at Tureng Tepe, an enormous stepped terrace was built, which is still 25 m high; its resemblance to a ziggurat is misleading, and its true function remains obscure.

Elamite power reasserted itself with the annexation of Susa *c.* 2004 BC. At this time a new quarter was added to the city, with simple, well-built houses. One of these, in the middle of the quarter, contained a small sanctuary. The central paved courtyard gave access to two living-rooms and to the sanctuary, all heated by fireplaces. At the far end of the sanctuary was a podium on which an idol could be placed. Later the aristocracy moved into the neighbourhood, replacing the poorer inhabitants, and their homes resembled small palaces, with a paved main courtyard beyond which lay a very wide hall heated by a fireplace and often with pilasters supporting the roof. This hall, which resembled the throne-room of a palace, gave access to various apartments, which were arranged round small courtyards and which suggest a large staff of servants. During Susa's decline in the 15th century BC, the Elamite king Tepti-Ahar built a temple at Kabnak (now HAFT TEPE). The temple consisted of an entrance, a courtyard for open-air worship and a portico giving access to what appear to be two parallel twin sanctuaries. This complex was connected to two vaulted cellars where a large number of bodies were deposited. The temple was doubtless used for a funerary cult.

The largest known Elamite architectural complex was built by King Untash-Napirisha in the second half of the 14th century BC at CHOGHA ZANBIL, south-east of Susa. The first building was a temple dedicated to Inshushinak, the patron god of Susa. It was square with a central courtyard and storerooms arranged round three sides. On the fourth side there were two sanctuaries, one opening to the outside and the other opening on to the inner courtyard. The building looks less like a temple than an economic complex in which religious facilities not provided for by the architect were subsequently installed. It was later transformed into a stepped tower, the stages of which were not superposed but slotted into one another in the former central courtyard (see fig. 4). A vaulted staircase, perpendicular to the south-east side, cut through the structure to allow access to the little temple built on the summit, dedicated to Napirisha, patron of Anshan, and to Inshushinak. This cult was doubtless designed to ensure cohesion between the two different halves of the Elamite empire. The building must have been over 54 m high, with sides twice as long. An irregular surrounding

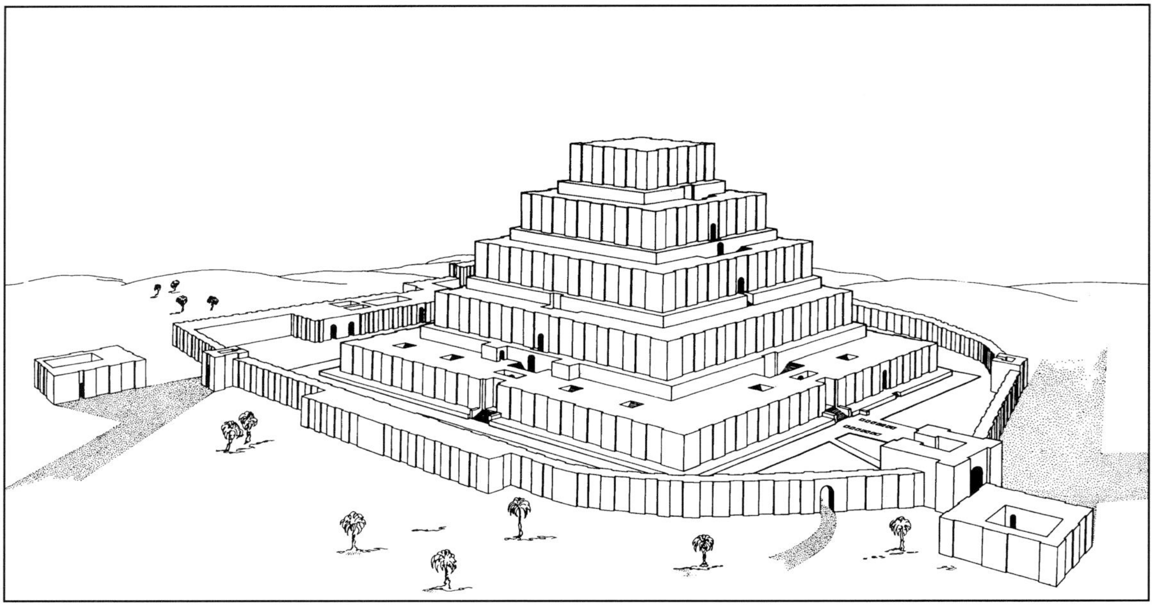

4. Stepped tower at Chogha Zanbil, south-west Iran, Elamite, second half of the 14th century BC; reconstruction as seen from the south

wall enclosed the courts at the foot of the tower and united the temples of the goddess-consorts of the two major gods and a minor god. These temples had the overall design of houses with a small central courtyard, as if the Elamites had no separate specifically religious architecture. A second surrounding wall (470×380 m) marked the boundary of the sacred area. Several temples to provincial deities were built within this second area. A third surrounding wall would have protected the city itself, of which only a series of palaces—no more functional than the first great temple, which they resemble—was ever built. They must have been temporary residences used during ceremonies and could not have housed a full administration. A more complex palace was designed for the funerary cult of the royal family, who were cremated and then buried in underground vaults. To the south stood a temple on its own, comprising an antechamber and a large cella open to the sky; the cella had an altar in the centre used in a fire cult, fire being personified by the god Nusku. This Elamite cult is remarkably similar to that of the Iranians a few centuries later (*see* ZOROASTRIANISM).

In the 12th century BC the conqueror Shutruk-Nahhunte I and his two sons built temples at Susa, which are now almost completely destroyed. The façade of one was in brick, moulded to represent the alternating figures of goddesses giving blessings and of bull-men who guarded the sacred grove. The interior of the temple was decorated with reliefs in moulded brick glazed green and yellow, representing royal couples (*see* ANCIENT NEAR EAST, §II, 5). At the same time on the plateau, in the almost deserted city of Anshan, there was a building that served as a warehouse for long-distance trade. Its layout is similar to that of the first great temple at Chogha Zanbil.

BIBLIOGRAPHY

R. Ghirshman: 'L'Architecture élamite et ses traditions', *Iran. Antiq.*, v (1965), pp. 93–100
——: *La Ziggurat*, Mémoires de la Délégation Archéologique en Iran: Mission de Susiane, xxxix (1966), i of *Tchoga Zanbil (Dur-Untash)* (Paris, 1966–70)
R. Ghirshman and M. J. Stève: 'Suse: Campagne de l'hiver, 1964–65', *A. Asiatiques*, xiii (1966), pp. 3–32
R. Ghirshman: 'Suse: Campagne de l'hiver, 1965–66: Rapport préliminaire', *A. Asiatiques*, xv (1967), pp. 3–27
——: *Temenos, temples, palais, tombes*, Mémoires de la Délégation Archéologique en Iran: Mission de Susiane, xl (1968), ii of *Tchoga Zanbil (Dur-Untash)* (Paris, 1966–70)

PIERRE AMIET

3. 1000 BC–AD 651. The architecture of Iran during this period is marked by both invention and continuity. Among the more significant structures of the early Iron Age are the columned buildings (*c.* 900 BC and after) of HASANLU, most of which formed a coherent complex round a central court. These constructions have no evident antecedents in Bronze Age Iran and may owe their columnar style to a highland architectural tradition that stretched from north-west Iran to central Anatolia and beyond. The larger buildings at Hasanlu are characterized by a plan that includes a short entrance portico, an antechamber and a lofty columned hall with two rows of four free-standing wooden columns (see fig. 5a). This is the form in which the long-lived columned halls of Iran first appeared.

As early as *c.* 800 BC a stone-footed 'manor' house from BABA JAN in central Luristan documents the introduction of a columned central room in a building partly flanked by projecting corner towers (see fig. 5b). Not long after, oblong hypostyle 'audience halls' of considerable size emerge, for example at Godin Tepe (see fig. 5c). They are characteristic of a late Iron Age style of architecture that cannot be regarded as Median alone, but is visibly at home in the core area of Median authority near Hamadan. The main strength of this traditional architecture comes from its scale, as is amply confirmed by such buildings as the

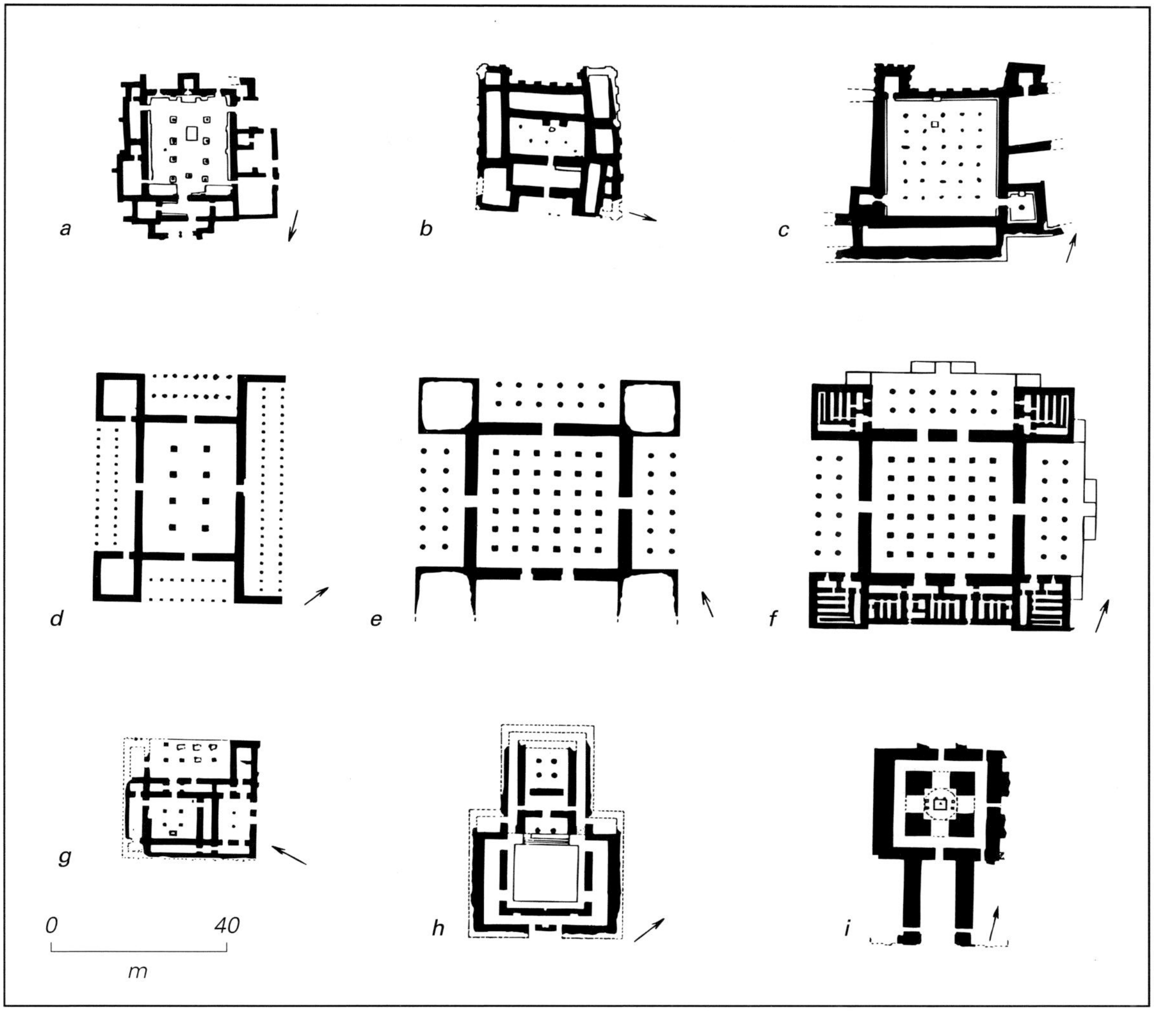

5. Plans of ancient Iranian buildings: (a) columned building, Hasanlu, early Iron Age, *c.* 900 BC; (b) stone-footed 'manor' house, Baba Jan, late Iron Age, *c.* 800 BC; (c) oblong hypostyle 'audience hall', Godin Tepe, possibly Median, 7th century BC; (d) Palace S, Pasargadae, Achaemenid, *c.* 640 BC; (e) apadana, Susa, Achaemenid, late 6th century BC; (f) apadana, Persepolis, Achaemenid, 6th–5th centuries BC; (g) detail of temple, near Persepolis, late Achaemenid or post-Achaemenid; (h) 'Ayadana', near Susa, Parthian, late 2nd century BC; (i) detail of *chahār ṭāq* ('four arched') sanctuary, Takht-i Sulayman, Sasanian, *c.* 6th century AD. Scale approximate only, (e) and (f) are shown at half the scale of the other buildings

'Central Temple' and the 'Fort' at TEPE NUSH-I JAN, with their soaring, buttressed façades and massive mud-brick walls. Long, curved mud-brick struts were used for vaulting, and this distinctively Iranian technique continued to be used in Achaemenid and Parthian times.

When Cyrus II (*reg* 559–530 BC) defeated in close succession the Medes, the Lydians and the Babylonians, the Achaemenid Persians (550–331 BC) became masters of the Ancient Near East. They lacked any strong tradition of monumental architecture, but were rapidly successful in creating an architectural synthesis that at once signalled their own identity and the extent to which, through conquest, they had absorbed other lands. The inclusion of Lydia and the eastern Greek cities of Ionia within the limits of Cyrus' empire greatly influenced the technical basis of this new synthesis. Large-scale masonry, as in the high platform of the Tall-i Takht, a dominant feature of Cyrus' new capital, PASARGADAE, is notably close in character, for example, to that from a palace platform at Lydian Sardis. Pasargadae also documents a number of experiments in form and design. Among these are the simple, dignified tomb of Cyrus and a four-sided palace (Palace S), the clear plan of which shows a distinctive marriage of the architectural traditions of Ionia and Iran. This palace combines low, flanking, almost stoa-like colonnades with a tall, oblong columned hall (see fig. 5d). The spacious, yet symmetrical distribution of much of this elegant construction within the geometric framework of an early Persian park, replete with stone water channels, underlines the unique appeal of this almost 'landscaped' royal residence.

Darius I (*reg* 521–486 BC) largely created the subsequent, mature phase of Achaemenid architecture. At the beginning of his reign Darius embarked on the construction at Susa of a new square form of audience hall, for which the term 'apadana' was used. This now much denuded building (see fig. 5e) measures an impressive 109 m on each side. Its main chamber, which stood over 19 m high, was originally flanked by four corner towers and at least three columned porticos, each of which rose to the full height of the central hall. The columns in these side porticos display a novel form of bell-shaped base and other striking and typically Achaemenid elements such as double protome capitals.

The most spectacular of all Achaemenid building projects was at PERSEPOLIS, in the heart of the Persian homeland. Here, on a partly fortified stone terrace-platform, 14 m high, Darius and a number of his successors, including Artaxerxes III Ochus (*reg* 358–338 BC), planned, completed or reshaped a host of monumental buildings, the more significant of which were adorned with painted stone reliefs. These buildings include the exquisite palace of Darius, the free-standing Gate of Xerxes and the dominant apadana (see fig. 5f and PERSEPOLIS, fig. 2), a pre-eminent symbol of Achaemenid rule. This last structure was founded on a projecting core of bedrock and is justly renowned for its 80 m long mirror-image reliefs, which originally depicted 23 gift-bearing delegations being led into the presence of the enthroned king and his standing crown prince. At the nearby cliff face of Naqsh-i Rustam, Darius chose to locate his relief-decorated, rock-cut tomb. With its new cruciform façade, the horizontal panel of which depicts a columned portico, it provided a funerary model not only for his successors until the fall of Persepolis in 331 BC, but also for local dynasts of the post-Achaemenid period whose smaller, cruder tombs were at first taken to be ancestral to, rather than descended from, Darius' monument.

Cult installations of Achaemenid date are rare, but a late- or post-Achaemenid building near Persepolis, with a distinctive podium set in a four-columned hall (see fig. 5g), is conceivably representative of a type of closed temple that Artaxerxes II Memnon (*reg* 404–358 BC) introduced in honour of the goddess Anahita. It is evident that much of the ancient Iranian world adopted a 'four-columned cella' as a prominent element in religious buildings for several centuries after the fall of the Achaemenid empire. For example, this four-column design characterizes the 'Ayadana' near Susa (see fig. 5h) from the Parthian period (for this date see Stronach, Leiden, 1985) and arguably this same design is echoed in the standard Sasanian *chahār ṭāq* (Pers.: 'four arched') sanctuary (see fig. 5i).

The influence of Hellenism on Iranian architecture was considerable, but uneven. Within Iran no site from the period of the Seleucid dynasty (*c.* 330–mid-2nd century BC) has yielded structures of the order of those from Ai Khanum in Afghanistan or even of those on the island of Faylaka (Dilmun) in the Gulf. Until more is known of the urban foundations of Seleucus I Nicator (*reg* 305–281 BC) and his son, Antiochus I Soter (*reg* 281–261 BC), which lay along the strategic high road that traversed northern Iran, it will remain difficult to distinguish construction of Seleucid date from that which is Parthian (250 BC–*c.* AD 224) or even Sasanian (*c.* AD 224–651). For instance, the stone terrace and colonnade at Kangavar once thought to be 'Seleucid' is now firmly dated on palaeographic grounds to the late Sasanian period (Lukonin).

In the 1st century AD a quick-drying gypsum mortar that allowed the construction, without wooden centering, of pitched brick vaults of imposing size was introduced in Parthian Mesopotamia. At sites such as Assur and Seleucia-on-the-Tigris this new technology led to the appearance of the iwan, a three-sided, barrel-vaulted hall in which the open end usually faced on to a wide court. This bold and simple design retained its popularity through both the Sasanian and Islamic periods. Relatively few major sites of assured middle and late Parthian date are known in Iran, but their architecture, although often regional, is innovative. At SHAHR-I QUMIS (probably anc. Hecatompylos) part of the mud-brick exterior of a building of possible early 1st-century BC date (Site V) already exhibits engaged arches, and, in the western-central Zagros, a late Parthian palatial structure within the mountain stronghold of QAL'EH-I YAZDEGERD documents a dramatic taste for elaborate, all-over stucco decoration.

Following the establishment of the Sasanians, ancient Iran once again came under the rule of a strong centralized administration. Ardashir I (*reg* 224–41 AD), the founder of the dynasty, set about creating a vigorous, new style of art and architecture. He was inspired by the Achaemenids, and the Egyptian-style cavetto cornices that are prominent in his early building programme (imitating similar mouldings at Persepolis) underscored his claim to be directly descended from them. As one of several preferred methods of construction, the Sasanians turned, where suitable stone was available, to mortar masonry. In this economical and durable medium, which was often given a richly worked stucco facing, rough stone cobbles were set in gypsum mortar and raised in successive lifts between forms of planks. Certain features of the palaces of Ardashir at FIRUZABAD can also be seen to have inspired various elements in Islamic architecture. These include the introduction of specifically Iranian cone-shaped squinches, which allowed a dome to be placed over a square room, and the equally successful experiment of placing a dominant dome directly behind an iwan. The unusual concentric plan of Ardashir's circular capital at Firuzabad may have inspired the layout of various later circular cities such as al-Mansur's Baghdad, but most Sasanian cities, including Shapur I's mid-3rd-century foundation at BISHAPUR, were built on some form of rectangular grid system. Typically such Sasanian towns were defended by strong walls with rounded bastions.

Much less is known of mid-Sasanian architecture than was hitherto supposed, because long-held dates for individual 'Sasanian' structures cannot always be trusted (Huff). It now appears, for instance, that a possibly religious building at Sarvistan in eastern Fars may be of 9th- rather than 5th-century date (Bier). However, the excavation of a sizeable stucco-decorated 'manor' house at Hajjiabad, east of Sarvistan, promises to document provincial, non-royal architecture from the middle years of Sasanian rule (Azarnoush). A lively discussion still surrounds the precise function of almost all religious monuments of Sasanian date (*see also* ZOROASTRIANISM).

In one view, the Zoroastrian sanctuaries of this period included both a free-standing *chahār ṭāq*, beneath the dome and between the arches of which the sacred fire could be witnessed at times of worship, and a small closed chamber (Pers. *ātishgāh*: 'fire temple'), located some distance away, within which a second, permanent fire was maintained. According to a more favoured second view, however, there was but one type of sanctuary, namely a closed chamber in which the fire was permanently maintained by priests, with adjacent ambulatories or rooms being used for worship. Unfortunately the preservation of the key 6th-century and later architectural remains at TAKHT-I SULAYMAN, a remote yet principal sanctuary of the empire, is such that any ascription of function must be strictly provisional. In the late Sasanian period baked brick construction began to appear more often; it was used for the parabolic, pitched brick vault of the great palace at KTESIPHON, which for a long time was the largest single-span vault of unreinforced brick in the world.

BIBLIOGRAPHY

Enc. Iran.
H. Frankfort: *The Art and Architecture of the Ancient Orient*, Pelican Hist. A. (Harmondsworth, 1954, rev. 4/1970), pp. 348–78
R. Ghirshman: *Bîchâpour*, 2 vols (Paris, 1956–71)
L. Vanden Berghe: 'Récentes Découvertes de monuments sassanides dans le Fars', *Iran. Antiq.*, i (1961), pp. 163–98
O. Reuther: 'Parthian Architecture: A History', *Survey of Persian Art*, ed. A. U. Pope and P. Ackerman (2/1964–7), i
T. C. Young jr: 'Thoughts on the Architecture of Hasanlu IV', *Iran. Antiq.*, vi (1966), pp. 48–71
C. Goff: 'Excavations at Baba Jan, 1967: Second Preliminary Report', *Iran*, vii (1969), pp. 115–30
C. Nylander: *Ionians in Pasargadae: Studies in Old Persian Architecture* (Uppsala, 1970)
F. Krefter: *Persepolis Rekonstruktionen* (Berlin, 1971)
K. Schippmann: *Die iranischen Feuerheiligtümer* (Berlin, 1971)
D. Huff: '"Sasanian" Čahar Taqs in Fars', *Proceedings of the 3rd Annual Symposium on Archaeological Research in Iran: Tehran, 1974*, pp. 243–54
E. J. Keall: 'Some Thoughts on the Early Eyvan', *Near Eastern Numismatics, Iconography, Epigraphy and History: Studies in Honour of George C. Miles* (Beirut, 1975), pp. 123–30
P. Bernard: 'Les Traditions orientales dans l'architecture gréco-bactrienne', *J. Asiat.*, cclxiv (1976), pp. 245–76
B. Finster and J. Schmidt: 'Sasanidische und frühislamische Ruinen im Iraq', *Baghdad. Mitt.*, viii (1976), pp. 1–167
R. Boucherlat: 'La Forteresse sassanide de Tureng-Tepe', *Le Plateau iranien et l'Asie centrale des origines à la conquête islamique*, ed. J. Deshayes (Paris, 1977), pp. 329–42
R. H. Dyson jr: 'The Architecture of Hasanlu: Periods I to IV', *Amer. J. Archaeol.*, lxxxi (1977), pp. 548–52
V. Lukonin: 'Khram Attakhaty v Kangavare' [The temple of Anahita in Kangavar], *Vestnik Drevney Istor.*, ii (1977), pp. 105–11
D. Stronach and M. Roaf: 'Excavations at Tepe Nush-i Jan. Part 1: A Third Interim Report', *Iran*, xvi (1978), pp. 1–11
J. Kroger: *Sasanidischer Stückdekor* (Mainz, 1982)
M. Azarnoush: 'Excavations at Hajiabad, 1977: First Preliminary Report', *Iran. Antiq.*, xviii (1983), pp. 159–79
E. Porada: 'Classic Achaemenian Architecture and Sculpture', *The Median and Achaemenian Periods*, ed. I. Gershevitch (1985), ii of *The Cambridge History of Iran* (Cambridge and London, 1968–), pp. 793–827
D. Stronach: 'The Apadana: A Signature of the Line of Darius I', *De l'Indus aux Balkans: Recueil Jean Deshayes* (Paris, 1985), pp. 433–45
——: 'On the Evolution of the Early Iranian Fire Temple', *Papers in Honour of Professor Mary Boyce* (Leiden, 1985), pp. 605–27
P. Amandry: 'Le Système palatial dans la Perse achéménide', *Le Système palatial en Orient, en Grèce et à Rome*, ed. E. Lévy (Strasbourg, 1986), pp. 159–72
L. Bier: *Sarvistan: A Study in Early Iranian Architecture* (University Park, PA, 1986)
D. Stronach: 'Parterres and Stone Watercourses at Pasargadae: The Achaemenid Contribution to the Evolution of Garden Design', *J. Gdn Hist.*, 14 (1994), pp. 3–12

DAVID STRONACH

III. Sculpture.

Ancient Iran was a source of a variety of stones and clays that were suitable for carving and moulding. The resulting sculptures and architectural reliefs will be treated in this section. In addition, many rock outcrops and mountainsides in the western part of the country were carved into reliefs to a far greater extent than was the case in any other part of the Ancient Near East. These rock reliefs will be dealt with separately below in §IV. Much of the sculpture discussed here is in the Archaeological Museum in Tehran and some from Susa is in the Louvre in Paris.

1. Before 3000 BC. 2. 3000–1000 BC. 3. 1000 BC–AD 651.

1. BEFORE 3000 BC.

(i) Neolithic. From the 8th millennium BC clay geometric objects, used as calculi in a primitive form of accounting, or as gaming pieces, are common. Crude clay animal figurines are also widely distributed, and rudimentary human figurines, generally female, have been found at Asiab, Sarab, GANJ DAREH, Ali Kosh, Chogha Sefid and Hajji Firuz. Occasionally stone was used in preference to clay for figurines, as at YANIK TEPE. Four stone phalli are known. One of the most striking sculptures is the large steatite bisexual figurine found at TEPE YAHYA (see fig. 2 above).

For bibliography *see* §I, 2(i)(b) above.

JUDITH PULLAR

(ii) Chalcolithic. True sculpture appeared in ancient Iran in the Proto-urban period, during the second half of the 4th millennium BC. Like the first examples of monumental architecture, it has been found mainly at SUSA and is part of the same pattern of development as that which produced monumental sculpture in contemporary Mesopotamia during the Uruk period (*see* MESOPOTAMIA, §III, 1). Small vases, shaped like animals, such as birds, piglets and frogs, were beautifully and often humorously carved in gypseous alabaster. Statuettes, which were placed in temples, depict male and female worshippers, often shown kneeling in their skirts.

2. 3000–1000 BC.

In the Proto-Elamite period (*c.* 3000–*c.* 2800 BC) humans were no longer depicted, but animals were often shown adopting human postures, both on seals (*see* ANCIENT NEAR EAST, §II, 1(ii)) and in sculpture. Musculature is strongly marked, and the figures are often twisted. There are three examples of sculpture from Susa and also a particularly fine lioness (New York, Brooklyn Mus.; see fig. 6) of unknown provenance. The statuary of the succeeding Early Dynastic period (*c.* 2800–*c.* 2300 BC) in Susa seems to have been a provincial interpretation of that of Mesopotamia. At first it was stylized and angular, but later it gained a greater realism, as exemplified by a statue of a man carrying a kid and wearing his hair in the royal style with browband and chignon (Paris, Louvre). During the same period green chlorite was used in south-central Iran to carve a small

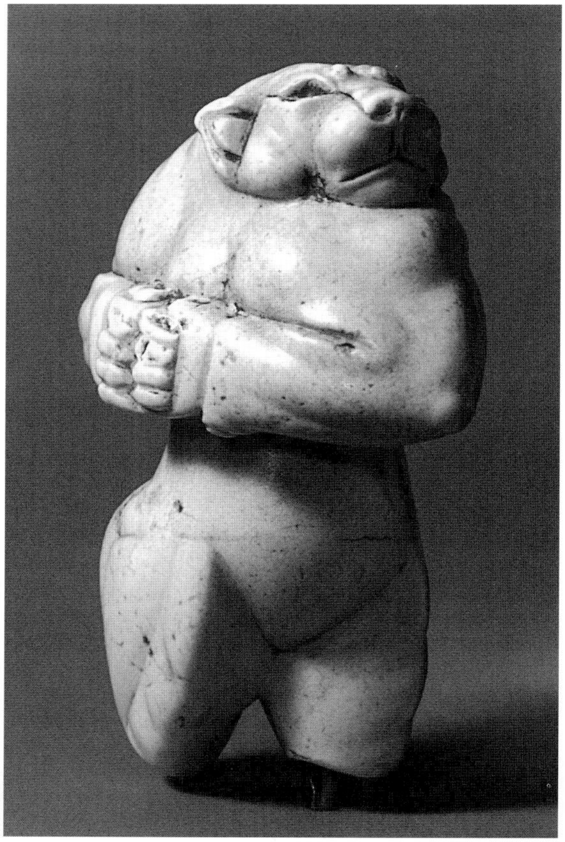

6. Sculpture of a lioness, magnesite, h. 84 mm, Proto-Elamite, *c.* 2900 BC (Washington, DC, Guennol Collection, on loan to New York, The Brooklyn Museum)

number of statues and numerous heavily decorated vessels. Some of this decoration is geometric and resembles architectural designs, and some of it depicts humans associated with snakes and lions, illustrating what is probably an eastern, Trans-Elamite mythology. Towards 2100 BC a ruler named Puzur-Inshushinak established an Elamite empire, and the sculptures and bas-reliefs (Paris, Louvre) of his reign are closely related to those of the contemporary Neo-Sumerian empire in Mesopotamia (e.g. the monuments of Gudea of Lagash).

The Elamite civilization of the 2nd millennium BC remained culturally dependent on that of Mesopotamia. Few stone, clay or terracotta sculptures have survived in Susa, but there are some Elamite rock reliefs (*see* §IV below) and some statues in gold, silver and bronze (*see* §V below). At the same time, further east in Bactria, which was then effectively a distant dependency of Elam, chlorite and white limestone stylized statuettes, carved in an archaizing style, were shown wearing the crinoline dress of Elamite princesses. On the edges of the Dasht-i Lut desert, clay funerary portraits drew their inspiration from earlier Mesopotamian models, and in the 15th century BC clay funerary portraits were placed in tombs at Susa. They were painted, and realistically depict austere Elamite faces above which the hair bulges in typical Elamite fashion. The rich graves found at MARLIK in north Iran date to the late 2nd and early 1st millennia BC and contained clay stylized animals (for illustration *see* AMLASH REGION), and female figurines whose simplified naked figures with developed buttocks belong to a prehistoric tradition and are quite unlike the products of Elam's urbanized art.

BIBLIOGRAPHY

P. Amiet: *Elam* (Auvers-sur-Oise, 1966)

PIERRE AMIET

3. 1000 BC–AD 651. Little sculpture in the round survives from the early centuries of the 1st millennium BC, although there are some interesting rock reliefs (*see* §IV below). However, three-dimensional sculpture is found in the second half of the millennium and up to the advent of Islam. The phases of development associated with the three major dynasties, the Achaemenids (550–331 BC), the Parthians (250 BC–*c.* AD 224) and the Sasanians (*c.* AD 224–651), were linked by underlying philosophical and religious tenets, most fully documented in Persian Zoroastrian sources of the Sasanian and post-Sasanian periods (*see* ZOROASTRIANISM).

Early Achaemenid sculpture was profoundly influenced by the art of antecedent cultures of the Ancient Near East. By contrast, contemporary influences, for example from ancient Greece and Egypt, are perceptible in the later years

7. Relief showing an enthroned king (detail), black limestone, h. 2.6 m, Achaemenid, from Persepolis, early 5th century BC (Tehran, Archaeological Museum)

8. Ivory rhyton, carved with human figures, tallest plaque 124×33 mm, Parthian, from Ol'viya, Black Sea coast, 1st century AD (St Petersburg, Hermitage)

of the dynasty. It is even possible to speak of an 'international style' sponsored by the Achaemenids to reflect their growing empire, which from 525 BC included Egypt. The high point of Achaemenid sculpture was reached in the later years of the reign of Darius I (*reg* 521–486 BC) and in the reign of Xerxes I (*reg* 485–465 BC). The stone statue of Darius I (originally 3 m high, now 1.95 m, on a rectangular base 0.51 m; Tehran, Archaeol. Mus.), which was produced in Egypt, shares the oversize dimensions, proportional ratios, formal details and solemn dignity of the royal image in the relief sculptures of audience scenes at Persepolis (see fig. 7).

These famous reliefs, originally designed for the apadana but later relegated to the treasury (*in situ* and in Tehran, Archaeol. Mus.), were connected to a series of reliefs (mostly still *in situ*) depicting a procession of peoples of the empire bringing gifts to the king. These reliefs support the idea of a secure and orderly regime by showing the cordial relations between Persian ushers and the foreign delegations. This theme is reiterated in the gesture of voluntary support expressed by the figures of subject nations on the socle of the statue of Darius I and in the rock relief (*see* §IV below) on the tomb of Darius I at Naqsh-i Rustam near Persepolis. The latter provided a lasting model for Achaemenid tomb sculpture in its depiction of subject nations actually supporting the king's couch or throne (for an example *see* ZOROASTRIANISM, fig. 1).

Parthian sculpture survives in a variety of media, found largely in the provinces of Kurdistan and Khuzistan in west and south-west Iran. Terracotta sculptures often depict horsemen, with distinctive pellets of clay added to indicate eyes, jewellery and other features. The Greco-Iranian style of early Parthian art is exemplified by finds (now St Petersburg, Hermitage) from Nisa (nr Ashkhabad, Turkmenistan; for illustration *see* NISA) and Ol'viya (see fig. 8) of carved ivory rhyta, decorated with friezes depicting sacrificial processions, and of three-dimensional protomes of humans and monsters. Parthian art underwent a dramatic transformation in the 1st and 2nd centuries AD. The adoption of flat, stylized, disconnected elements grouped together into compositions and the introduction of frontality has been attributed to the rejection of Hellenistic values (Avi-Yonah) by the Parthians and their contemporaries in the Near East.

Although little Sasanian three-dimensional sculpture has been found, its existence is suggested by the very high relief found in the carving of some of the dynasty's well-known rock reliefs. For instance, in a relief at Taq-i Bustan the equestrian figure of King Khusro II (*reg* AD 591–628) is partly carved in the round (for illustration *see* TAQ-I BUSTAN). One of the few surviving three-dimensional Sasanian works is the colossal (8 m high) statue of Shapur I (*reg* AD 241–72) carved from a stalactite in a cave near BISHAPUR.

BIBLIOGRAPHY

M. Avi-Yonah: *Oriental Art in Roman Palestine*, Studi Semitici, v (1961)

M. C. Root: *The King and Kingship in Achaemenid Art: Essays on the Creation of an Iconography of Empire*, Acta Iran. 19, 3rd ser., ix (Leiden, 1979)

M. Roaf: 'Sculpture and Sculptors at Persepolis', *Iran*, xxi (1983) [whole issue]

E. Porada: 'Classical Achaemenian Architecture and Sculpture', *The Median and Achaemenian Periods*, ed. I. Gershevitch (1985), ii of *The Cambridge History of Iran* (Cambridge, 1985), pp. 793–827 (815–21)

H. E. Mathieson: *Sculpture in the Parthian Empire: A Study in Chronology*, 2 vols (Aarhus, 1992)

GUITTY AZARPAY

IV. Rock reliefs.

Figurative rock-carving is an integral part of the art of ancient Iran. Just over 100 reliefs are known, spread over two and a half millennia from the late 3rd millennium BC (there was also a revival under the QAJAR shahs in the 19th century AD). All the reliefs are concentrated in about 30 sites in western Iran from Kurdistan in the north to the province of Fars in the south. Many are situated in open-air sanctuaries, often close to springs, near cities or in places of particular historical or political importance; most are cut on the sides of mountains. The state of preservation of a relief naturally varies depending on its age, position, orientation, the quality of the rock, the way the rock face was dressed and the depth of carving; some have been damaged or destroyed in modern times.

The rock reliefs illuminate the art of eight of the successive cultures and civilizations in ancient Iran and are a prime source of information on history, politics, social history, religion, customs, dress, arms and furnishings. Their importance is increased by the fact that in some periods they provide the only evidence for a particular historical event or for the geographical location of a kingdom.

1. Introduction. 2. Lullubi (*c.* 2100–1600 BC). 3. Elamite (*c.* 2000–mid-6th century BC). 4. 'Median' (7th century–550 BC) and Achaemenid (550–331 BC). 5. Seleucid (312–*c.* 250 BC) and Parthian (250 BC–*c.* AD 224). 6. Elymaean (2nd century BC–3rd century AD). 7. Sasanian (*c.* AD 224–651).

1. INTRODUCTION. The iconography of the rock reliefs is royal and the king is only absent on a few post-Achaemenid reliefs. Women, whether goddesses, queens or priestesses, appear rarely, on the reliefs of the Lullubi, Elamites and Sasanians. Children occur on a very few Elamite, Elymaean and Sasanian reliefs.

The composition is generally linear with figures arranged on one plane or, if they are numerous, in several superimposed registers. It was further used to convey the idea of royal power: antithetical or convergent grouping might emphasize the importance of one figure; the figures may vary in size according to their importance (social perspective); or the most important figures in a scene might be ordered so that they are at the head of a procession, or at the centre or top of a group. Although there were chronological and geographical preferences, the type of composition used depended entirely on the theme, iconography and number of figures depicted. The hierarchical nature of the figures is reflected in a static style that was governed by well-defined laws, and the symbolic essence of the chosen theme was conveyed, rather than the precise moment in time. Figures were not individualized and the same model was often repeated with stereotyped gestures, so that identification rests on hierarchical traits such as dress, headdress, weapons, attributes and emblems.

The reliefs are often accompanied by inscriptions, which may be dated with some accuracy if they bear known royal names. Iconographical features can also provide chronological indicators: for instance the influence of Classical iconography can be seen in the winged victories, putti and genii with cornucopias adopted, from the 2nd century BC, by the Parthians, Elymaeans and Sasanians. The rock reliefs are the products of distinct, although chronologically overlapping, cultures and this is reflected in the following subdivisions.

2. LULLUBI (*c.* 2100–1600 BC). The five earliest rock reliefs are attributed to the Lullubi, a mountain people who lived in the Zagros mountains on one of the main trade routes between Mesopotamia and Iran. Four reliefs at Sar-i Pul-i Zuhab show, often in antithetical compositions, the triumphs in war of little-known kings, identified in cuneiform inscriptions, frequently aided by the goddess Inanna/Ishtar. They are difficult to date but are probably contemporary with Ur III and the Old Babylonian dynasties of Mesopotamia (2112–1595 BC) and seem to be based on Mesopotamian royal iconography as represented by the stele depicting the conquest of the Lullubi by Naram-Sin of Akkad (*reg* 2254–2218 BC; Paris, Louvre; *see* AKKADIAN, fig. 1). The most famous rock-carving shows King Anubanini, armed with a bow and sickle-sword, facing the goddess Ishtar in her warrior aspect; both are trampling a fallen enemy. A lower register depicts six small prisoners and Ishtar leads a further two by a leash attached to rings through their noses.

3. ELAMITE (*c.* 2000–mid-6th century BC). There are 15 Elamite rock reliefs, all of which are votive in character, treat religious themes and are found in open-air sanctuaries. Early Elamite (first half of the 2nd millennium BC) and Middle Elamite reliefs (second half of the 2nd millennium BC) represent deities enthroned in association with water and serpents, and also the royal family in adoration. Most Neo-Elamite rock reliefs (first half of the 1st millennium BC) depict a complex liturgy, including processions and ritual banquets with musicians, animal sacrifice, and offerings on an altar (see figs 3 and 9). They introduce a very large number of small figures arranged in rows in several registers over vast surfaces, with important figures up to six times larger. In some of these reliefs the figures are in complete profile.

4. 'MEDIAN' (7TH CENTURY–550 BC) AND ACHAEMENID (550–331 BC). The five so-called 'Median' rock reliefs (probably 4th–3rd centuries BC), all of which are found in Kurdistan, are funerary in character, generally with a worshipper before a fire altar, sometimes associated with a carved façade. There are nine Achaemenid rock reliefs. It is remarkable that, even when the Achaemenid empire encompassed the whole of Iran, Achaemenid reliefs were only cut in areas with an earlier tradition of rock-carving. The triumph of Darius I (*reg* 521–486 BC) is recorded on a mountainside at BISITUN (*see* ACHAEMENID, fig. 1), accompanied by a trilingual cuneiform inscription (dated 520–519 BC). This rock-carving echoes the theme of the Lullubi reliefs, but all the other Achaemenid rock-carvings are, like the 'Median' examples, funerary in character. Most decorate the rock-cut tombs of the Achaemenid kings in Fars: four at Naqsh-i Rustam (5th century BC) and three at nearby PERSEPOLIS (4th century BC). The reliefs are cut on a recessed cruciform area of rock (h. *c.* 23 m) and the lower part is left blank. In the upper part of the cross is a divine figure in a winged disc; beneath it, the king faces an altar; both king and altar are raised on stepped podia, which stand on a richly decorated bed supported by smaller figures representing the different parts of the empire (satrapies). In the broad part of the cross is carved the façade of a columned building with a doorway leading into the rock-cut tomb-chamber (*see* ZOROASTRIANISM, fig. 1). As with some Neo-Elamite reliefs, figures are in complete profile. A 4th-century BC tomb façade at Akhor-i Rustam in Fars is carved with two columns, their capitals decorated with addorsed bull protomes.

5. SELEUCID (312–*c.* 250 BC) AND PARTHIAN (250 BC–*c.* AD 224). Two rock reliefs belong to the period of Seleucid domination. One, in Fars, depicts an archer. The other, at Bisitun, shows a life-size reclining figure of Herakles in high relief, accompanied by a Greek inscription of 148 BC. Four Parthian rock reliefs are found in Kurdistan: three at Bisitun, one at Sar-i Pul-i Zuhab. Several themes originated at this period and were later adopted by the Sasanians. A battle scene is symbolically represented by an equestrian duel between the king and

9. Rock relief at Kul-i Farah, showing a ritual banquet attended by the king, h. 2.8 m, Neo-Elamite, 10th–9th centuries BC

an enemy chief. Various Parthian kings, identified by Greek or Parthian inscriptions, are depicted receiving homage; later examples show the king on horseback. One of the Bisitun reliefs shows a king making an offering on an altar. The PARTHIANS introduced a strict rule of frontality, thereby establishing a link with the spectator but precluding interdependent relationship between the figures. As a result the compositions are remarkably static.

6. ELYMAEAN (2ND CENTURY BC–3RD CENTURY AD). About twenty rock reliefs are located in ELYMAIS (north-east Khuzistan). Although difficult to date, they belong to the Parthian period but are more closely related by subject-matter to a separate, Elymaean group, and several are accompanied by inscriptions in Elymaean written in the Aramaic script. Elymaean reliefs are grouped in open-air sanctuaries dedicated to ancestor worship in association with a royal cult, thus endorsing the king's legitimacy. The image of the king reclining on a couch alternates with that of the royal diadem, the symbol of power. The royal hunt and equestrian scenes are occasionally depicted. Elymaean reliefs show reverence for deities, but the only deity who can be identified with any certainty is Herakles. Some of the reliefs are found on large boulders, a practice already attested for Elamite reliefs.

7. SASANIAN (*c.* AD 224–651). There are more rock reliefs from this period than any other: *c.* 40 have been recorded, most in Fars (*see* SASANIAN). Occasionally reliefs were left unfinished, and as some bear traces of a plaster coating, which must have been painted, they are now lacking an important stylistic element. Antithetical and convergent compositions were popular. On some reliefs figures are systematically smaller than life-size but most depict over life-size figures. Profile heads are often found on frontal bodies but the king 'in majesty' is strictly frontal. The changes in royal headdress from reign to reign make it possible to date reliefs to a specific ruler. In the second half of the 3rd century AD, western influence led to the Sasanians using higher and more rounded relief and, for a brief period, the folds in the garments were indicated, thus giving the figures more vitality. From the beginning of the 4th century AD the figures are frequently almost in the round with overlaid, incised details, and are often set in rock-cut architecture (for illustration *see* TAQ-I BUSTAN).

Several themes initiated by the Parthians and the Elymaeans continued. The king is often depicted in equestrian duels with the enemy chief. He may also be shown seated frontally, on horseback or standing, surrounded by an entourage on foot, comprising his court, subjects, officials or members of his family. In one case, at Taq-i Bustan, Shapur III (*reg* AD 383–8) is depicted with his father as a proclamation of legitimacy.

Scenes of triumph in war generally show the king on horseback (see fig. 10). With the exception of some Lullubi rock reliefs, the theme of the king's investiture by a god is restricted to Sasanian times and is sometimes combined with the theme of triumph. The deity endorses the divine origins of the king's power and affirms the divine order of Sasanian kingship.

In common with some Elymaean reliefs, the Sasanians depicted fights with lions or royal hunts. These representations are symbolic and glorify the king's courage and his

10. Rock relief at Bishapur, showing Shapur I triumphing over the Roman emperors Gordian III, Philip the Arab and Valerian, h. 2.5 m, Sasanian, *c.* AD 260–72

fight against the unruly elements of the world. However, in the latest rock reliefs, at Taq-i Bustan, the purpose of the hunting scene is to illustrate one of the king's favourite pastimes; the scenes show greater realism and even some attempts at perspective. Aerial views of the *paradeisoi* (hunting parks) enclosures are combined with the continuous narrative style of the hunting scenes. They reflect the influence of palace wall paintings and were placed in the enclosed space of a grotto, thus partly losing the close association between natural, open-air settings and rock-carving that had survived for millennia.

BIBLIOGRAPHY

E. F. Schmidt: *The Royal Tombs and other Monuments* (1970), iii of *Persepolis* (Chicago, 1953–70), pp. 79–141

H. von Gall: 'Beobachtungen zu den sogenannten medischen Felsgräbern', *Proceedings of the 2nd Annual Symposium on Archaeological Research in Iran: Tehran, 1973*, pp. 139–54

P. Calmeyer: 'Zur Genese altiranischer Motive, III: Felsgräber', *Archäol. Mitt. Iran*, viii (1975), pp. 99–113

G. Herrmann: *The Iranian Revival*, The Making of the Past (Oxford, 1977), pp. 87–94

R. Börger: *Die Chronologie des Darius-Denkmals am Behistun-Felsen* (Göttingen, 1982)

J. Börker-Klähn: *Altvorderasiatische Bildstelen und vergleichbare Felsreliefs*, 2 vols (Mainz, 1982)

Reliefs rupestres de l'Iran ancien (exh. cat. by L. Vanden Berghe, Brussels, Mus. Royaux A. & Hist., 1983), pp. 155–64 [good bibliog.]

D. Huff: 'Das Felsrelief von Qir, Fars', *Archäol. Mitt. Iran*, xvii (1985), pp. 221–47

L. Vanden Berghe and K. Schippmann: *Les Reliefs rupestres d'Elymaïde (Iran) de l'époque parthe* (Ghent, 1985)

E. De Waele: 'Les Trois Reliefs rupestres de Pol-e Abguineh près de Kazerun', *Iran. Antiq.*, xxi (1986), pp. 167–88

U. Siedl: *Die elamischen Felsreliefs von Kürängün und Naqš-e Rustam* (Berlin, 1986)

E. De Waele: 'L'Investiture et le triomphe dans la thématique de la sculpture rupestre sassanide', *Archaeologia Iranica et Orientalis: Miscellanea in Honorem L. Vanden Berghe*, ed. L. De Meyer and E. Haerinck (Ghent, 1989), pp. 811–30

——: 'Musicians and Musical Instruments on the Rock Reliefs in the Elamite Sanctuary of Kul-e Farah (Izeh)', *Iran*, xxvii (1989), pp. 29–38

H. von Gall: *Das Reiterkampfbild in der iranischen und iranisch beeinflussten Kunst partischer und sasanidischer Zeit*, vi of Teheraner Forschungen (Berlin, 1990)

H. E. Mathiesen: *Sculpture in the Parthian Empire*, 2 vols (Århus, 1992)

ERIC DE WAELE

V. Metalwork.

The origins of metalwork in ancient Iran date to the 7th millennium BC (the Neolithic period). The earliest metal objects are made of copper, most likely native copper rather than copper extracted from ore. Iranian smiths had mastered the lost-wax technique by the late 5th millennium BC or early 4th, as is proved by a unique, shaft-hole mace head from a grave at Parchinah (Luristan, Pusht-i Kuh mountains). Lead, silver and gold were in use from the second half of the 4th millennium BC. In order to make copper easier to work at a lower temperature, smiths soon learnt to add to it a high percentage of lead (up to 20%), and possibly also arsenic. By the beginning of the Proto-Elamite period (3000 BC) basic skills in most metalworking processes and techniques had been acquired, and smiths were producing a wide range of metal objects. Tin–copper alloys were introduced in the 3rd millennium BC, but since tin was a rare ore that had to be imported (possibly from Afghanistan), the alloy most commonly produced in Iran continued to be arsenical copper. The production of bronzes reached its peak in the second half of the 2nd millennium BC, the same time that iron first appeared.

1. BEFORE 3000 BC. The earliest metal object so far excavated is a copper bead from an aceramic level at Ali Kosh in south-west Iran. Evidence of metalwork during the 6th millennium BC comes from early pottery settlement sites, such as Chogha Sefid in south-west Iran, TEPE SIALK near Kashan, Tepe Zagheh in the Qazvin plain and Tall-i Mushki in the province of Fars. These sites produced simple objects such as pins, awls and beads.

From the end of the 5th millennium BC and especially from the 4th millennium (Chalcolithic period) onwards, copper objects are found in some quantity. The best surviving material, consisting of a variety of tools and objects, including flat axes, chisels, mirrors and tanged daggers, comes from graves at SUSA (60 flat axes and 7 mirrors), from Tepe Qabristan in the Qazvin plain, from level III of Tepe Sialk and level I B–C of TEPE HISSAR near Damghan. All were cast in open moulds, as were finds made in a workshop at Tepe Qabristan, where 20 kg of ore intended for smelting was also discovered. Susa is the only site from the second half of the 4th millennium BC to yield important material; there are pins topped with the figure of a naked woman, a mountain goat or a seated feline.

2. 3000–1000 BC. Owing to the wide variety of metal wares produced from this date onwards, it is possible to differentiate between the objects manufactured in different

regions. South-west and west Iran (Luristan) often produced objects related to those of Mesopotamia. South-east and east Iran (TEPE YAHYA, Shahdad and SHAHR-I SOKHTA) and north-east Iran (Tepe Hissar and Shah Tepe) were closer to eastern cultures, for example the Bactrian.

There is little archaeological information for the first half of the 2nd millennium BC. It is clear that the eastern parts of ancient Iran became less densely settled and that urban centres were abandoned. However, during the second half of the 2nd millennium BC, the classical age of the Elamite empire, the production of bronze objects reached its peak. The skill of the Elamite smiths is illustrated by several objects from Susa (all Paris, Louvre): the statue of a smiling god wearing a flounced robe, the 12th-century BC Sit Shamshi (Akkad.: 'rising sun') votive offering (for illustration *see* SUSA) and the cast bronze statue of Queen Napir-Asu, with her hands clasped on her bell-like skirt (see fig. 11), which is life-size and weighs nearly two tonnes. Statuettes in gold, silver and bronze, some of them solemn and others smiling, reveal two opposed tendencies in Elamite art. The bronzes typical of the Luristan region, such as finials of rampant goats, whetstone sockets, flanged daggers and spike-butted axes, also belong to this period (*see* LURISTAN REGION, figs 1

11. Cast bronze statue of Queen Napir-Asu, h. 1.29 m, Middle Elamite, from Susa, *c.* 1250BC (Paris, Musée du Louvre)

and 2); such objects, with their distinctive fantastic decoration, continued to be produced in the region in the early 1st millennium BC.

In the north, particularly at Gilan, there is also ample evidence of extensive metal production in the second half of the 2nd millennium BC. Numerous decorated vessels of bronze, silver and gold bear witness to the highly inventive and developed skills of smiths at such northern sites as Kaluraz and Marlik (for illustration *see* MARLIK). Probably also contemporary are two objects from Hasanlu, a gold bowl decorated with mythological events and a silver vessel with a battle scene (both Tehran, Archaeol. Mus.; for illustration of the gold bowl *see* HASANLU, fig. 2).

3. 1000 BC–AD 651. By the beginning of the 1st millennium BC the use of iron had become common. Whereas initially only small objects had been made of the material, from the 9th or 8th century BC onwards it was used for almost all weapons and tools (bronze, however, continued to be used for vessels and decorative elements). In the early phase of the Iron Age there were some bi-metallic objects, made of both bronze and iron. Early iron production in Iran is best illustrated by the more than 2000 iron objects from the 9th century BC found in level IV at Hasanlu.

The metalwork produced in Iran in the first half of the 1st millennium BC was affected not only by new metal technologies, but also by the invaders, such as Urartians, Scythians and Assyrians, who occupied or influenced the western regions of Iran at this time. Urartian objects have been found in north-west Iran, Scythian ones in the central Zagros, and Assyrian or related objects most frequently in Luristan. The eclectic style that resulted from so many external influences is best exemplified by objects from the famous site of ZIWIYEH. Little material is available for the 7th to 5th centuries BC. Metalwork produced during the Median dynasty may yet be discovered in the central Zagros, but there is currently no material available (the objects found at Ziwiyeh cannot, unfortunately, be used as evidence for a 'Median' style).

Like the other arts in ancient Iran, metalwork from the second half of the 1st millennium BC until the Arab conquest can be categorized according to the major pre-Islamic dynasties of the period. From this time onwards coins also represent an important form of metal production (*see* ANCIENT NEAR EAST, §II, 8). Metal vessels from the later years of the Achaemenid dynasty (550–331 BC) are outstanding, both technically and artistically (*see* METAL, colour pl. II, fig. 1). Gold and silver gadrooned bowls and rhyta were widespread throughout the empire, and though few have been found in Iran itself, they are depicted on the Persepolis reliefs. Few objects survive from the Seleucid (*c.* 330–mid-2nd century BC) and Parthian (250 BC–*c.* AD 224) periods. However, a chance find at Shami in the Bakhtiari mountains in south-west Iran brought to light a large bronze statue (h. 1.92 m) of a Parthian noble or prince, with a separately cast head (Tehran, Archaeol. Mus.; *see* PARTHIAN, fig. 2). With its emphasis on native ideals of beauty and dress and its assertive frontality, it epitomizes the late Parthian period, when the natives of Mesopotamia and Iran apparently

12. Sasanian silver gilt plate showing King Shapur hunting deer, diam. 179 mm, h. 45 mm, 4th century AD (London, British Museum)

rejected the stylistic and aesthetic values of Hellenistic art. Metal armour and jewellery were also highly developed during the reign of the Parthians, as can be seen in several rock reliefs of the period. Most characteristic of the Sasanian period (*c.* AD 224–651) are numerous silver or gold dishes, plates and flasks. These are usually decorated with scenes of an equestrian king or nobles hunting (see fig. 12), or with dancing girls. There are also a few bronze heads of Sasanian rulers. Depictions on rock reliefs, for instance at TAQ-I BUSTAN and BISHAPUR, provide further evidence of the production of metalwork in the Sasanian period.

BIBLIOGRAPHY

P. Amandry: 'Orfèvrerie achéménide', *Ant. Kst*, i (1958), pp. 9–23
——: 'Toreutique achéménide', *Ant. Kst*, ii (1959), pp. 38–56
A. U. Pope and P. Ackerman, eds: *Survey of Persian Art* (2/1964–7), i–ii [see especially chapters by P. Ackerman, S. Casson and J. Orbeli]
L. Vanden Berghe and E. Haerinck: *Bibliographie analytique de l'archéologie de l'Iran ancien* (Leiden, 1979); *Supplément*, i (Leiden, 1981); and *Supplément*, ii (Leuven, 1987)
O. W. Muscarella: 'Excavated and Unexcavated Achaemenian Art', *Ancient Persia: The Art of an Empire*, ed. D. Schmandt-Besserat (Malibu, 1980), pp. 23–4
V. Pigott: 'The Iron Age in Western Iran', *The Coming of the Age of Iron*, ed. T. A. Wertime and J. D. Muhly (New Haven, 1980), pp. 417–61
P. R. S. Moorey: 'Archaeology and Pre-Achaemenid Metalworking in Iran: A Fifteen Year Retrospective', *Iran*, xx (1982), pp. 81–101

VI. Ceramics.

Pottery was a major art form in ancient Iran, and its complex pattern of different decorative techniques and styles is unmatched elsewhere in the Ancient Near East. The size of the country and its environmental variety have led to major differences in the material culture of the various regions. The range and complexity of the surviving material, which covers such an exceptionally long time-span, also accounts for the lack of a detailed study of the different pottery styles. A chronology is well established for some regions, but other sequences are incomplete and there are also major gaps.

E. HAERINCK

1. Before 3000 BC. 2. 3000–1000 BC. 3. 1000 BC–AD 651.

1. BEFORE 3000 BC.

(i) Neolithic. Iran's pottery tradition dates from the 8th millennium BC at GANJ DAREH, where a few crude potsherds were discovered. It was not until the 7th millennium BC, however, that pottery became common. Decoration resembling basketwork on some of the earliest painted pottery, from Tepe Guran, reflects the older tradition of basketry containers. Early decoration is crude, with red slips, which were sometimes burnished, blobbed linear patterns and basic geometric designs. By the 6th millennium BC bowls, often carinated, with geometric designs of zigzags, lozenges, triangles and chevrons, were present at many sites in Hulaylan, Khuzistan and Azerbaijan. In the Zagros in the 5th millennium BC, at TEPE GIYAN, animal motifs on pottery were introduced. Dalma ware, called after the type site south of Lake Urmia, is characterized by hole-mouth bowls decorated with bold geometric designs over the entire exterior, and sometimes with a red slip on the interior; this pottery is widely distributed. Sites on the Iranian plateau have produced a greater variety of shapes and decoration. At TEPE SIALK and related sites pedestalled bowls and goblets, as well as conical beakers decorated with birds, goats, onager, gazelle, and human figures, complemented more mundane bowls covered with chequerboards and lozenges.

JUDITH PULLAR

(ii) Chalcolithic. The use of different styles of painted pottery, common before 4000 BC, continued and reached its peak during the late Chalcolithic period (4th millennium BC), when exceptionally fine pottery was produced. Each style was characterized by its own shapes and motifs. Forms are usually quite simple, but decoration is of a high standard, covering the whole vessel or the upper two-thirds. The paste is usually buff and covered by a brown or black design. Particularly characteristic of the SUSA I style of south-west Iran are elegant tall beakers, with very thin walls, on a flat base, decorated with highly stylized animals, particularly goats with enormous horns (see fig. 13a), birds with long necks, dogs and snakes, or elaborate geometrical motifs. The fine pottery from Tall-i Bakun in southern Iran is typified by pointed bowls or beakers, decorated with elaborate motifs, such as schematized human and animal forms, including goats with exaggeratedly curly horns. Whereas the Susa I pottery is notable for its simplicity, clarity and sobriety, with a dominant sense of line, the Bakun pottery is characterized by its broken line and complicated motifs, which produce a sense of 'horror vacui'. Although slightly different in manufacture and shapes, the Tepe Sialk III and TEPE HISSAR I styles of central and north-east Iran can be considered as a single pottery province. Besides simple shapes, there are bowls or jars on a high pedestal foot, often with a slightly carinated body. There is a rich variety of decorative forms, particularly of animals, which are represented in a simpler and more realistic way than the

southern styles. Tepe Hissar ware is usually cruder in execution than that from Tepe Sialk III.

2. 3000–1000 BC. During the early 3rd millennium BC the painted Sialk/Hissar style was replaced by a plain grey ware (Hissar II A). This fine, highly burnished ware, which often imitates metal prototypes, characterized north-east Iranian production for a long time.

By contrast, in south-west Iran a polychrome pottery type was produced early in the 3rd millennium BC, which was painted after firing, so that the paint can easily be rubbed off. It was related to Mesopotamian Early Dynastic Scarlet Ware. In the second quarter of the 3rd millennium BC a monochrome painted pottery (Susa II) was produced, often of crude execution, but this had disappeared by *c.* 2400 BC. From then on no more painted pottery was made in south-west Iran. Other products of the 3rd millennium BC include the BAMPUR/Khurab style of south-east Iran as well as painted pottery at SHAHR-I SOKHTA in the east, characterized by small pear-shaped jars.

The long sequence of Giyan painted pottery of the 3rd and 2nd millennia BC (*see* GIYAN, TEPE) in west-central Iran is well known. Excavations at GODIN TEPE have revealed an almost uninterrupted sequence of painted pottery. Typical examples of the Giyan IV style (2200–1900 BC) are rounded and bag-shaped vessels with carinated shoulders, painted with 'bird-comb' motifs (see fig. 13b) and eagles with outstretched wings. The polychrome Giyan III style (2000–1600 BC) is characterized by tripods, Giyan II (1600–1400 BC) by footed goblets with bird and sun motifs. Tall beakers with simple geometric or floral motifs are typical of Giyan I A (1400–1200 BC). Pottery types from the south during the 2nd millennium BC include those from Kaftari, Qaleh and Taimuran. Polychrome painted pottery from north-west Iran, which is related to Transcaucasian pottery, is known as 'Urmia' ware. A unique, polychrome style was found at Sakkizabad (*c.* 1600–1200 BC), south of Qazvin. This is usually handmade and often shows broken lines, meanders, zigzags or swastikas in brown-black paint on a red slipped and burnished body.

From the second half of the 2nd millennium BC, painted pottery became rare and was replaced, particularly in north-west and central Iran, by polished grey-black or red ware, the decoration of which was less important than the shape or design. Major sites illustrating this elegant pottery are HASANLU, Khurvin, Tepe Sialk, MARLIK and Kaluraz. Long beak-spouted pitchers were typical. A particularly fine series of thin-walled vessels from the Amlash region are in the form of humans or stylized animals, mainly humped bulls (for illustration *see* AMLASH REGION).

3. 1000 BC–AD 651. A new style of painted pottery, Sialk VI (10th–7th centuries BC), was made in central Iran using shapes similar to the earlier burnished types. Long-spouted pitchers decorated with painted bulls or running horses are of particular interest (see fig. 13c). During the Achaemenid period (550–331 BC) the most typical shape was the carinated bowl; some rhyta with animals' heads also belong to this period. Painted pottery continued to be made in some western areas until well into the Parthian period (250 BC–*c.* AD 224), for example the Ardabil style, but from the 3rd century BC glazed pottery became more common, and Hellenistic shapes, such as fishplates or double-handled jars, were introduced. Glaze colours included white, yellow, green and blue. Other areas, such as Germi in north-west Iran, continued to produce animal-shaped vessels. There has been little research into pottery of the Sasanian period (*c.* AD 224–651), which often featured incised decoration and was covered with a dark green glaze.

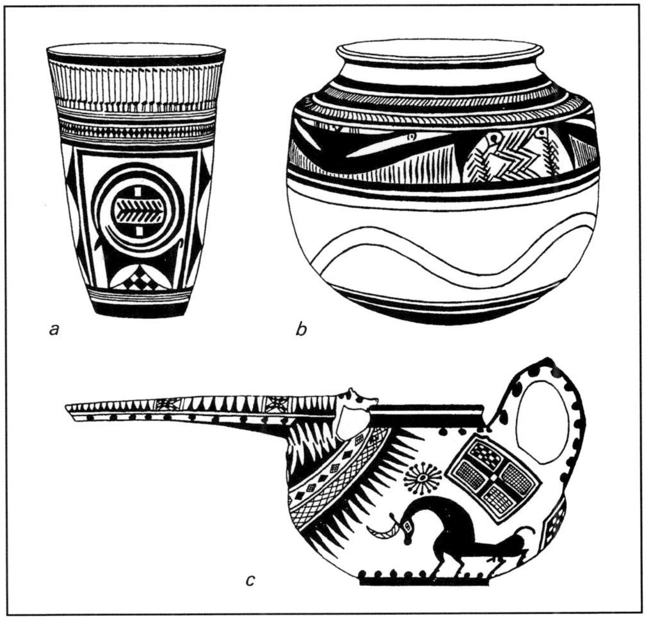

13. Ancient Iranian ceramics: (a) Susa I style beaker with brownish-red paint on yellow ground, h. 232 mm, Chalcolithic, *c.* 3800 BC (Paris, Musée du Louvre); (b) Giyan IV style vessel with painted motifs, h. *c.* 280 mm, 2200–1900 BC; (c) Sialk VI style pitcher with wine-red paint on pink ground, h. 130 mm, 1000–700 BC

BIBLIOGRAPHY

E. Herzfeld: *Iran in the Ancient East* (London, 1941)

D. E. McCown: *The Comparative Stratigraphy of Early Iran*, Studies in Ancient Oriental Civilization, xxiii (Chicago, 1942)

L. Vanden Berghe: 'De beschilderde ceramiek in Iran van de oudste tijden tot ca. 2000 voor onze jaartelling', *Gentse Bijdr. Kstgesch.*, xv (1954), pp. 5–84; xvi (1955), pp. 5–54 [Fr. summary]

——: *L'Archéologie de l'Iran ancien* (Leiden, 1959)

E. Porada: *Alt-Iran: Die Kunst in vorislamischer Zeit* (Baden-Baden, 1962); Eng. trans. as *Ancient Iran: The Art of Pre-Islamic Times*, A. World (London, 1965); *The Art of Ancient Iran: Pre-Islamic Cultures* (New York, 1965)

A. U. Pope and P. Ackerman, eds: *Survey of Persian Art* (London, 2/1964–7), i, pp. 225–48; ii, pp. 664–80 [chapters by G. Contenau and R. Ettinghausen]

T. C. Young jr: 'A Comparative Ceramic Chronology for Western Iran, 1500–500 BC', *Iran*, iii (1965), pp. 53–85

R. H. Dyson: 'The Archaeological Evidence of the Second Millennium BC on the Persian Plateau', *The Middle East and the Aegean Region, c. 1800–1380 BC*, Cambridge Anc. Hist., ii/1, ed. I. E. S. Edwards, N. G. L. Hammond and E. Sollberger (Cambridge, 1973), pp. 686–715

A. Cattenat and J. C. Gardin: 'Diffusion comparée de quelques genres de poterie caractéristique de l'époque achéménide sur le plateau iranien et en Asie centrale', *Colloques internationaux du Centre National de la Recherche Scientifique, no. 567. Le Plateau iranien et l'Asie centrale des origines à la conquête islamique: Leurs relations à la lumière des documents archéologiques: Paris, 1976*, pp. 225–48

E. Haerinck: *La Céramique en Iran pendant la période parthe (ca. 250 av. J.C. à ca. 225 après J.C.): Typologie, chronologie et distribution* (Ghent, 1983)

E. Carter and M. W. Stolper: *Elam: Surveys of Political History and Archaeology*, Near Eastern Studies, xxv (Berkeley, 1984)

E. HAERINCK

VII. Painting.

Apart from painted decoration on ceramics (*see* §VI, 2 above), the only surviving paintings before 1000 BC are murals from a building at TALL'I MALYAN (anc. Anshan) in the province of Fars, from the Proto-Elamite period *c.* 3000–2800 BC. The decoration in black, white, grey, yellow and red consists of friezes of opposed S-shaped volutes and stepped cross-shaped motifs combined with floral motifs.

In the 1st millennium BC the earliest substantial remains of painting from the Iranian plateau are on baked-brick ceiling tiles (each *c.* 515×470×60 mm) decorated with geometric designs in red on a buff ground. These are from the 'Fort' at BABA JAN in the central Zagros and date from the period of Median expansion in the 8th century BC. Mention in textual sources of the use of pictorial narration in wall paintings of the Achaemenid period (550–331 BC) finds little support in the fragmentary murals uncovered at Persepolis, Susa and Babylon. These exhibit the brilliant colours and subjects of glazed tile panels and painted stone sculpture of that period (*see* ANCIENT NEAR EAST, §II, 5).

Pictorial narration in painting is first found in murals from the Parthian period (250 BC–*c.* AD 224), uncovered at sites both outside Iran, for example at Dura Europos in Syria (*see* DURA EUROPOS, fig. 2), and at the palace complex of Kuh-i Khwaja in Iranian Sistan (for illustration *see* KUH-I KHWAJA). Hellenistic naturalism, notable in early Parthian painting such as the reclining figures painted at the latter site (1.54×1.90 m; New Delhi, N. Mus.), is replaced in later Parthian murals by flat, frontal and fragmented compositions. Fragmentary murals from the Sasanian period (*c.* AD 224–651) are known from various sites throughout the Iranian plateau (e.g. Damghan, Ayvan-i Karkha, Susa and Hajjiabad). The pictorial epic seen in Sogdian painting, which was developed as a corollary to the popular literature of entertainment in the east Iranian world (*see* CENTRAL ASIA, §I, 4(ii)(a) and (iii)(a)), was largely ignored by Sasanian painters. They turned instead to the stylistic principles and conventional subjects of official Sasanian court art.

BIBLIOGRAPHY

E. F. Schmidt: *Excavations at Tepe Hissar, Damghan* (Philadelphia, 1937), pp. 336–7

R. Ghirshman: *Iran: Parthes et Sassanides* (Paris, 1962; Eng. trans., London, 1962); and as *Persian Art: The Parthian and Sassanian Dynasties, 249 BC–AD 651* (New York, 1962)

J. Lerner: 'A Painted Relief from Persepolis', *Archaeology*, xxvi (1973), pp. 118–22

M. A. R. Colledge: *Parthian Art* (New York and London, 1977)

C. Goff: 'Excavations at Baba Jan', *Iran*, xv (1977), pp. 103–40 (133–40)

R. Boucharlat and A. Labrousse: 'Le Palais d'Artaxerxès II sur la rive droite du Chaour à Suse', *Cah. Dél. Archéol. Fr. Iran*, x (1979), pp. 67–8

G. Azarpay: *Sogdian Painting: The Pictorial Epic in Oriental Art* (Los Angeles, 1981), pp. 81–94

M. Azarnoush: 'Excavations at Hajiabad, 1977: First Preliminary Report', *Iran. Antiq.*, xviii (1983), pp. 159–79 (172–9)

GUITTY AZARPAY

VIII. Museums and collections.

The antiquities of ancient Iran are spread throughout the museums of the world, but the largest single holding is in the Tehran Archaeological Museum (Muzeh Iran Bastan), which houses objects from excavations as well as some acquired on the antiquities market. The museum was built following the appointment in 1931 of the Frenchman André Godard as Director of the Iranian Archaeological Service (a post he held until 1960). Until then, most objects excavated at the principal archaeological site of SUSA had been either stored on the site in a huge castle, known as the Château, which was built by 19th-century French archaeologists (but badly damaged and looted in the 1980s during the Iraq–Iran war), or sent to Paris, to the Musée du Louvre, which has the second largest collection of ancient Iranian antiquities. Once the Tehran Archaeological Museum opened, the objects excavated by foreign expeditions were systematically divided between the excavators and the museum. The French had a long-standing interest in Iran, and under Roman Ghirshman (1895–1979) they remained foremost in the field. Other museums and institutions that have benefited from antiquities officially excavated by foreign expeditions in Iran include the British Museum, London, the University Museum, Philadelphia, the Metropolitan Museum of Art, New York, and the Oriental Institute Museum, University of Chicago.

All major public collections contain some Iranian antiquities of unknown provenance, some of them acquired in the 19th century, but many obtained more recently. The major private collections of Ancient Near Eastern antiquities, such as the Leo Pomerance and Norbert Schimmel collections in New York, the former Mohsen Foroughi (1907–84) collection in Tehran and the Borowski collection in Jerusalem, contain a large number of objects from ancient Iran, and there are now many private collections in Japan. Much of Godard's own collection, mainly bronzes from the LURISTAN region, is in the Ullens de Schooten collection and in the Musées Royaux d'Art et d'Histoire, both in Brussels.

Many objects in public and private collections are still the focus of fierce debate concerning their authenticity. Major 'discoveries' have led, from time to time, to the creation of markets in, for instance, Luristan bronzes, ZIWIYEH 'treasures' and pottery and metalwork from the AMLASH REGION. Such labels became so popular among dealers and collectors that they were attached indiscriminately to antiquities illicitly acquired in completely different areas of Iran. The Ziwiyeh objects, for example, were said to have been burial goods found in a large bronze coffin, but it has been estimated that the objects in museums and collections bearing this provenance would fill several such coffins. The situation is aggravated both by the physical geography of Iran, which has facilitated the looting of isolated cultures, and by the appearance on the market of forgeries, some of which are of spectacular quality.

BIBLIOGRAPHY

D. W. Muscarella: '"Ziwiye" and Ziwiye: The Forgery of a Provenience', *J. Field Archaeol.*, iv/2 (1977), pp. 197–219

For further bibliography *see* §IX below; ANCIENT NEAR EAST, §III, 3; and under individual sites.

IX. Exhibitions.

In 1931 the *International Exhibition of Persian Art* opened at the Royal Academy in London and was a revelation to those who saw it. C. J. Gadd, in his chapter on 'Early Persian Art' in the small introductory book that accompanied the exhibition, devoted just two pages to the pre-Achaemenid periods. He mentioned the Elamites, discussed the prehistoric pottery of Susa in a paragraph and then summed up Iranian history as follows: 'Elam became an artistic appanage of the plains, and simply copied the contemporary Babylonian types during the whole of two millennia.' Only two of the fourteen exhibition rooms were devoted to pre-Islamic exhibits. Four years later, in 1935, an exhibition was organized in Leningrad (now St Petersburg) in conjunction with the Third International Congress of Iranian Art. The treasures of the Hermitage Museum that were exhibited on the occasion consisted largely of Scythian, Sarmatian and Siberian discoveries from outside Iran (although many were culturally linked to 1st-millennium BC Iranian artefacts), and a spectacular collection of Sasanian silver bowls of the 3rd to early 7th centuries AD. In 1938 Sasanian and Islamic objects from French museums and collections were exhibited in Paris. In 1948 objects drawn from the imperial collections and museums of Tehran were shown at the Musée Cernuschi in Paris, but only a small number of exhibits belonged to the early periods of Iranian art. This also applied to a similar exhibition that was sent to New York, Boston and various American cities in 1949–50. The exhibition in Rome, in 1956, of a further selection of objects from the Tehran Archaeological Museum included, for the first time, a sufficient number of LURISTAN bronzes to give some idea of this lively style.

The art of ancient Iran was revealed to the world in the 1960s in a major touring exhibition, consisting of more than 1100 exhibits drawn from the collections of the Archaeological Museum in Tehran and from major public and private collections worldwide. In striking contrast to the earlier exhibitions, almost three-quarters of the exhibits were pre-Islamic and were illustrated on 98 of the 120 plates in the catalogue. Unfortunately, many of the most spectacular pieces were subsequently declared to be forgeries, thus highlighting the problem of authenticity (the exhibition had been organized by no less an authority than Roman Ghirshman, the Director of the French excavations in Iran). Since then smaller exhibitions have concentrated on different aspects of ancient Iranian art.

BIBLIOGRAPHY

E. Denison Ross, ed.: *Persian Art* (London, 1930)

Catalogue of the International Exhibition of Persian Art (exh. cat., London, RA, 1931)

Les Arts de l'Iran (exh. cat., Paris, Bib. N., 1938)

Exposition d'art iranien (exh. cat., Paris, Mus. Cernuschi, 1948)

Iranian Art: Treasures from the Imperial Collections and Museums of Iran (exh. cat. by M. Bahrami, New York, Met., 1949)

Mostra d'arte iranica (exh. cat. by M. Tucci, Rome, Pal. Brancaccio, 1956)

Sept Mille Ans d'art en Iran (exh. cat., Paris, Petit Pal., 1961) [the exh. was also circulated in Germany as *7000 Jahre Kunst Iran* (Essen, Villa Hügel, 1962); throughout the USA as *7000 Years of Iranian Art* (exh. cat., Washington, DC, Smithsonian Inst., 1964–5); and in Switzerland as *Trésors de l'ancien Iran* (Geneva, Mus. Rath, 1966)]

Art iranien ancien: Préhistoire, protohistoire (exh. cat. by L. Vanden Berghe, Brussels, Musées Royaux A. & Hist.; Utrecht, Cent. Mus.; 1966)

The Pomerance Collection of Ancient Art (exh. cat., New York, Brooklyn Mus., 1966), nos 27–61

The Art Called Amlash, an Art of Ancient Iran: A Loan Collection in the New York–New Jersey Metropolitan Area (exh. cat., Newark, NJ, Mus., 1969)

Catalogo de la exposición de antigüedades des Persas (exh. cat., Madrid, Mus. Arqueol. N., 1971)

O. W. Muscarella, ed.: *Ancient Art: The Norbert Schimmel Collection* (Mainz, 1974), nos 136–68

——: *Ladders to Heaven: Art Treasures from the Lands of the Bible* (Toronto, 1981), nos 153–78 [cat. of the Elie Borowski col. pubd on occasion of the exh. *Ladders to Heaven: Our Judeo-Christian Heritage, 5000 BC–AD 500*, Toronto, Royal Ont. Mus., 1979]

Luristan, een verdwenen bronskunst uit West-Iran (exh. cat. by L. Vanden Berghe, Ghent, Cent. Kst & Cult., 1982)

Les Reliefs rupestres de l'Iran ancien (exh. cat. by L. Vanden Berghe, Brussels, Musées Royaux A. & Hist., 1984)

Treasures of the Bible Lands: The Elie Borowski Collection (exh. cat. by R. Merhav, Tel Aviv Mus. A., 1987), nos 50–57

DOMINIQUE COLLON

Illustration Acknowledgements

We are grateful to those listed below for permission to reproduce copyright illustrative material and to those contributors who supplied photographs or helped us to obtain them. The word 'Photo:' precedes the names of large commercial or archival sources who have provided us with photographs, as well as the names of individual photographers (where known). It has generally not been used before the names of owners of works of art, such as museums and civic bodies. Every effort has been made to contact copyright holders and to credit them appropriately; we apologize to anyone who may have been omitted from the acknowledgements or cited incorrectly. Any error brought to our attention will be corrected in subsequent editions. Where illustrations have been taken from books, publication details are provided in the acknowledgements below.

Line drawings, maps, plans, chronological tables and family trees commissioned by the *Dictionary of Art* are not included in the list below. All of the maps in the dictionary were produced by Oxford Illustrators Ltd, who were also responsible for some of the line drawings. Most of the line drawings and plans, however, were drawn by the following artists: Diane Fortenberry, Lorraine Hodghton, Chris Miners, Amanda Patton, Mike Pringle, Jo Richards, Miranda Schofield, John Tiernan, John Wilson and Philip Winton. The chronological tables and family trees were prepared initially by Kate Boatfield and finalized by John Johnson.

Hungary *19* Iparmüvészeti Múzeum, Budapest (inv. no. 76.197); *20* Iparmüvészeti Múzeum, Budapest (inv. no. 17.640); *21* Iparmüvészeti Múzeum, Budapest, (inv. no. 3283); *22* Iparmüvészeti Múzeum, Budapest (inv. no. 23.312); *23* Iparmüvészeti Múzeum, Budapest (inv. no. E.60.14); *24* Photo: Országos Müemléki Hivatal, Budapest; *25* Magyar Nemzéti Múzeum, Budapest; *26* Iparmüvészeti Múzeum, Budapest

Hunt: (1) William Morris Hunt Museum of Fine Arts, Boston, MA (Bequest of Elizabeth Howes)

Hunt: (2) Richard Morris Hunt *1* Preservation Society of Newport County, Newport, RI/Photo: John W. Corbett; *2* North Carolina Division of Archives and History, Raleigh, NC

Hunt, William Holman *1* Manchester City Art Galleries; *2* Board of Trustees of the National Museums and Galleries on Merseyside, Liverpool

Hurrian Photo: © RMN, Paris

Huygens: (2) Constantijn Huygens (ii) Fondation Custodia/Institut Néerlandais, Paris (Collection Frits Lugt)

Huysum, van: (1) Jan van Huysum Rijksmuseum, Amsterdam

Hyderabad British Library, London

Iberian art *1* Museo Arqueológico Nacional, Madrid

Ibibio *1–4* Photo: Jill Salmons

Iceland *2* Stofnun Arna Magnússonar á Íslandi, Reykjavík (AM 350, fol. 51*r*)/Photo: Jóhanna Ólafsdóttir; *3* Photo: National Gallery of Iceland, Reykjavík/Photo: K.P. Gudnason; *4–5* National Museum of Iceland, Reykjavík

Icon *1–2* Photo: Temple Gallery, London

Icon cover © Hellenic Institute of Byzantine and Post-Byzantine Studies in Venice, 1975

Iconoclasm *1* Photo: T. Richard Blurton; *2* National Portrait Gallery, London

Iconographic programmes *1* Photo: © RMN, Paris; *2* Photo: Arch. Phot. Paris/© DACS, 1996

Iconography and iconology *1, 10* Rijksmuseum, Amsterdam; *2* Biblioteca Apostolica Vaticana, Rome; *3* Museo Civico d'Arte Antica, Turin; *4* Bibliothèque Nationale de France, Paris; *5* Metropolitan Museum of Art, New York (Elisha Whittelsey Collection; Elisha Whittelsey Fund; no. 51.501.3467); *6* Trustees of the British Museum, London; *7* Museo dell'Opera del Duomo, Siena; *8* Metropolitan Museum of Art, New York (Bequest of Michael Friedsam, 1931; Friedsam Collection; no. 32.100.35); *9* Mauritshuis, The Hague

Idoma Photo: Sidney Littlefield Kasfir

Idromeno, Kol Galeria Arteve, Tiranë

Ife *1–4* Detroit Institute of Arts, Detroit, MI (Founders Society Purchase; Miscellaneous Memorials Fund)/Photo: © Dirk Bakker, 1990

Igalu Photo: J.S. Boston

Igbo *1* Photo: Dr G.I. Jones; *2, 4* Photo: Herbert M. Cole; *3* Fowler Museum of Cultural History, UCLA, Los Angeles, CA; *5* Seattle Art Museum, Seattle, WA (Gift of Katherine White and the Boeing Company)

Igbo-Ukwu *1–3* National Commission for Museums and Monuments, Lagos; *4* Department of Archaeology and Anthropology, University of Ibadan/Photo: Frank Speed

Ijo *1–2* Pitt Rivers Museum, Oxford

Ike: (1) Ike Taiga Kawabata Yasunari Memorial Museum, Kamakura

Ikkyū Sōjun *1* Hatakeyama Collection, Tokyo; *2* Shinjuan Daitokuji, Kyoto

Illusionism *1* Photo: Archivi Alinari, Florence; *2* Metropolitan Museum of Art, New York (Catharine Lorillard Wolfe Collection; Catharine Lorillard Wolfe Fund, 1963; no. 63.85)

Imperiali National Trust, Stourhead/Photo: Courtauld Institute of Art, London

Impresa Society of Antiquaries, London

Impressionism *1* Musée Marmottan, Paris; *2* Wadsworth Atheneum, Hartford, CT (Bequest of Anne Parrish Titzell; no. 1957614)/Photo: Joseph Szaszfai

Inca *2* Photo: W. Iain MacKay, Edinburgh

India *1* Photo: Martin Charles, Isleworth; *2, 6* Board of Trustees of the Victoria and Albert Museum, London; *3* © Satish Gujral, New Delhi; *4* © S. Nandagopal; *5, 7* Trustees of the British Museum, London

Indian subcontinent *2, 5, 13, 17, 23–7, 30, 37–45, 48, 50–52, 54–0–52, 54–177, 60, 62–3, 70–72, 75–6, 80, 85, 122–3, 131–2, 135, 139–41, 143–5, 149, 151, 153–4, 159, 166, 168, 170–75, 177, 179, 189–90, 192–3, 195, 225–31, 239* Photo: © American Institute of Indian Studies, Varanasi; *3* Philadelphia Museum of Art, Philadelphia, PA (Given by Mrs N.R. Norton, Mrs Richard Wain Mairs, Mrs Edwin N. Benson Jr and Mrs William A.M. Fuller in memory of Mrs Jones Wister); *4, 313, 351, 354, 358* Ashmolean Museum, Oxford; *6–7, 161–2, 306–7, 329, 331, 338, 346, 360* Trustees of the British Museum, London; *8* Museum of Fine Arts, Boston, MA (Helen and Alice Colburn Fund); *9* Los Angeles County Museum of Art, Los Angeles, CA (Gift of Dr and Mrs Pratapaditya Pal); *10* Museum Rietberg, Zurich (Sammlung von der Heydt)/Photo: Wettstein and Kauf; *12* British Library, London (Add. MS. 15296(i)); *14* Cleveland Museum of Art, Cleveland, OH (John L. Severance Fund; no. 69.34); *15, 147, 157, 235, 247–8, 251, 256, 262, 286, 290, 297, 301, 314, 316–23, 325, 333–4, 337, 339, 341–2, 344–5, 348, 350, 353* Board of Trustees of the Victoria and Albert Museum, London; *16* Photo: Dr Padma Kaimal; *18, 21* Photo: © Michael W. Meister; *22* Photo: © German Research Project Mohenjo-Daro, Aachen University; *28, 84* Photo: © Archaeological Survey of India, New Delhi; *29, 34–5, 78, 142, 180–83, 191, 196, 330* Photo: Michael D. Willis; *31, 127* Photo: Gary Michael Tartakov; *32, 61, 73–4* Photo: Adam Hardy; *47* British Library, London (no. ASIO 867); *64–5, 83, 207–9, 212–14, 222* Photo: Michael D. Rabe; *67, 87–90, 92–6* Photo: © Mehrdad Shokoohy; *68–9, 121* Photo: Kirit Mankodi; *77* Photo: John Irwin; *79* Photo: Gerard Foekema, Amsterdam; *81, 120* Photo: George Michell; *82, 111, 327* Photo: Douglas Dickens, London; *86* British Library, London (no. W.P. 5616); *91* British Library, London (no. 1710.b.1/19); *98–104,*

109 Photo: Catherine B. Asher; *105–6* Photo: Subhash Parihar, Kot Kapura; *107* Photo: Rosie Llewellyn-Jones; *108* British Library, London (India Office photo no. 45.29); *110* British Library, London (no. ASIM 1812); *112–17* Photo: G.H.R. Tillotson; *119* Photo: Miki Desai; *124, 215, 217, 233* Photo: M.E. Heston; *125* Photo: Geraldine Smith-Parr Banerji; *126* Photo: British Architectural Library, RIBA, London; *128* British Library, London (India Office photo no. P1601); *130* National Museum, New Delhi/Philadelphia Museum of Art; *133* Department of Archaeology, Indian Museum, Calcutta; *134* Philadelphia Museum of Art, Philadephia, PA; *136* British Library, London (no. 685/346A); *137* British Library, London (India Office no. W2271); *138, 253* Photo: © RMN, Paris; *146* British Library, London (no. AS10 596); *148* British Library, London (no. ASE 471); *150, 352* Photo: Yale University Press Photo Library, London/© Archaeological Survey of India, New Delhi; *152, 155, 163, 258* Harvard University Art Museums, Cambridge, MA; *156* Photo: © J. Biltgen, Paris; *158* Peshawar Museum/Photo: Warburg Institute, London; *160, 178* Photo: Frederick M. Asher; *164* Government Museum, Mathura; *165* Los Angeles County Museum of Art, Los Angeles, CA (Given in memory of Christian Humann by Tobert Hatfield Ellsworth); *167* Los Angeles County Museum of Art, Los Angeles, CA (Nasli and Alice Heeramaneck Collection; Museum Associates Purchase); *169, 249* National Museum, New Delhi; *176* Allahabad Museum; *184* Dogra Art Gallery, Jammu; *185, 292* Government Museum and Art Gallery, Chandigarh; *186* © American Institute of Indian Studies, Varanasi/Photo: Cynthia P. Atherton; *187–8* Photo: Cynthia P. Atherton; *194* Photo: Dr Harvey Stahl; *197, 202–3, 206* Photo: John C. Huntingdon; *198–9* Patna Museum, Government of Bihar, Patna/Photo: John C. Huntingdon; *200–01* Indian Museum, Calcutta/Photo: John and Susan Huntingdon; *204–5* Photo: ©: Prof. Thomas Donaldson; *210* Royal Ontario Museum, Toronto; *211* Department of Archaeology, Government of Tamil Nadu, Madras; *216, 218, 223* Los Angeles County Museum of Art, Los Angeles, CA; *219, 246, 257, 299* Prince of Wales Museum of Western India, Bombay; *220–21, 224* Photo: Andrew L. Cohen; *232, 298* Photo: Sotheby's, London; *234* British Library, London (Or. MS. 6902); *236* British Library, London (Add. MS. 15296); *237* Commissioner, Archaeology and Museums, Madhya Pradesh; *238, 240* Photo: Prof. Walter Spink; *241* British Library, London (no. ASIO 5852); *242, 308* Arte Photo/ Photo: Maurice Babey; *243, 309* Asian Art Archives of the University of Michigan, Ann Arbor, MI; *244* French Institute/Ecole Française d'Extrême-Orient, Pondicherry; *245* Photo: Mr John Siudmak; *250* Bayly Art Museum, University of Virginia, Charlottesville, VA/Photo: Robert Browning; *252* Arthur M. Sackler Gallery, Smithsonian Institution, Washington, DC; *254* British Library, London (MS. ETHE 2775, fol. 100*v*; *255* Photo: A.C. Cooper Ltd, London; *259* Cincinnati Art Museum, Cincinnati, OH (Gift of John Warrington); *260* Museum of Fine Arts, Boston, MA (Frances Bartlett Donation of 1912 and Special Contribution); *261, 263, 265, 267, 270* Freer Gallery of Art, Smithsonian Institution, Washington, DC; *266* Museum of Fine Arts, Boston, MA; *268* Royal Collection, Windsor Castle/© Her Majesty Queen Elizabeth II; *269* Bodleian Library, Oxford; *271* British Library, London; *272* Photo: John Seyller; *274* British Library, London (Add. MS. 15287); *275* National Gallery of Victoria, Melbourne; *276* Private collection; *277–8* Gopi Krishna Vinod Krishna Kanoria Collection, Patna; *279–81* Photo: Dr Joachim Bautze; *282, 293* Bharat Kala Bhavan, Varanasi Hindu University; *264, 283–4* Maharaja Sawai Man Singh II Museum, Jaipur; *285* from E. Dickinson and K. Khandavala: *Kishangarh Painting* (New Delhi, 1959), pl. ix; *287* Elvehjem Museum of Art, University of Wisconsin, Madison, WI (Gift of Mrs Earnest C. Watson); *288* Photo: A.L. Dallapiccola; *291* Himachal State Museum, Simla; *294* San Diego Museum of Art, San Diego, CA; *295* Museum Rietberg, Zurich/Photo: Wettstein and Kauf; *296* Museum of Fine Arts, Boston, MA (Ross–Coomaraswamy Collection); *300* Photo: Yale University Press Photo Library, London/© Kronos Collections; *302* British Library, London; *303* British Library, London (Or. MS. 11612, 19*v*–20*r*; *305, 343* Bibliothèque Nationale de France, Paris; *310* Museum für Völkerkunde, Hamburg; *311* British Library, London (Add. MS. 7763); *312* British Library, London (Add. Or. MS. 3229); *315* National Gallery of Modern Art, New Delhi; *324* Photo: T. Richard Blurton; *326* Photo: South Asia Microform Project, Joseph Regenstein Library, University of Chicago, Chicago, IL/Nineteenth Century Hindi Project; *328* Metropolitan Museum of Art, New York (Purchase, Bequest of Florance Waterbury and Rogers Fund, 1970; no. 1970.321); *332* British Library, London (no. 2775 (1.0.149)); *335* Rijksmuseum, Amsterdam; *336* Virginia Museum of Fine Arts, Richmond, VA; *340* Metropolitan Museum of Art, New York (Gift of the Kronos Collection, 1981; no. 1981.398.4); *347* Photo: National Trust, North Wales Regional Office/© Mrs V. Shreiber, Southampton; *349* Department of Library Services, American Museum of Natural History; *355, 357* Völkerkundemuseum der Universität, Zurich; *356* Photo: Dr Ann Norton; *359* Photo: © Stephen P. Huyler; *361* Crafts Museum, New Delhi; *362* Photo: Hans-Joerg Soldan; *363* Photo: Anthony R. Walker, 1974 (from: *The Toda of South India: A New Look*, 1986)

Indonesia *5, 8* Photo: Robert Harding Picture Library, London; *6, 12* Photo: © Tettoni, Cassio and Associates Pte Ltd, Singapore; *7* Photo: Amir Sidharta; *9, 11, 15–18* Photo: © Dirk Bakker, 1990; *10, 20* Photo: Urs Ramseyer; *12* Photo: Photobank, Bangkok; *13* Photo: Hyko Laeyendecker; *14, 33, 35* Photo: Angela Hobart; *19* Rijksmuseum voor Volkenkunde, Leiden; *21–2* Textile Museum, Washington, DC (no. 1977.18.1); *23, 38* Royal Tropical Institute (K.I.T.), Tropenmuseum, Amsterdam/Photo: L. Lange; *24* Textile Museum, Washington, DC (no. 68.1); *25* Photo: Kitlv-Leiden; *26* Asia Society Galleries, New York/Photo: John Gollings; *27* Asia Society Galleries, New York/ Yayasan Nusantara Jaya for P.R.A. Maulana Pakuningrat, SH Kraton Kasepuhan, Cirebon/© 1990/Photo: John Gollings; *28* Asia Society Galleries, New York; *29* Asia Society Galleries, New York/Rijksmuseum voor Volkenkunde, Leiden/© 1990/Photo: Dirk Bakker; *30* Museum für Völkerkunde und Schweizerisches Museum für Volkskunde, Basle; *31* British Library, London (no. JAV 28; Mackenzie Collection); *32* Legatum Warnerianum, Library, University of Leiden; *34* Photo: Dr H.I.R. Hinzler; *36* Asian Cultural History Program, Smithsonian Institution, Washington, DC/Photo: Diane L. Nordeck; *37* Asia Society Galleries, New York/National Museum, Jakarta/© 1990/Photo: John Gollings

Industrial design *1* Courtesy of the Trustees of the Wedgwood Museum, Barlaston, Staffs; *2* Trustees of the Science Museum, London/Photo: Science and Society Picture Library; *3* Photo: Archiv Gebrüder Thonet GmbH, Frankenberg/Eder; *4* Photo: Photoarchiv AEG, Frankfurt am Main; *5* Photo: Motoring Picture Library, National Motor Museum, Brockenhurst; *6* Photo: © Herman Miller, London; *7* Trustees of the British Museum, London; *8* Design Museum, London; *9* Photo: Kawasaki Heavy Industry Ltd, Tokyo; *10* Photo: Sony Corp., Tokyo

Industrial scenes *1* National Gallery of Victoria, Melbourne (Felton Bequest, 1948); *2* Wallington Hall, Northumberland/Photo: Bridgeman Art Library, London

Ingen Ryūki Obakusan Manpukuji Bunkaden, Kyoto

Inglés, Jorge Museo Nacional de Escultura, Valladolid

Ingres, Jean-Auguste-Dominique *1* Photo: © ACL Brussels; *2* Museum of Fine Arts, Boston, MA (Purchased from the Maria Antoinette Evans Fund); *3* Photo: Giraudon, Paris; *4* Photo: © RMN, Paris

Initial, manuscript *1* Board of Trinity College, Dublin; *2* Bodleian Library, Oxford (MS. Auct. E.inf.1, fol. 304*r*); *3* Bibliothèque Nationale de France, Paris

Ink *1* Freer Gallery of Art, Smithsonian Institution, Washington, DC; *2* Freer Gallery of Art, Smithsonian Institution, Washington, DC (no. 17.184-5); *3* National Gallery of Art, Washington, DC (Gift of Nicholas Brown, J. Carter Brown and Angela B. Fisher: Tenants in Common)

Inness, George George Walter Vincent Smith Art Museum, Springfield, MA

Innsbruck *1* Photo: Frischauf Bild, Innsbruck; *2* Photo: Anthony Kersting, London; *3* Bildarchiv, Österreichische Nationalbibliothek, Vienna

Installation © Oldenburg, 1995/Photo: Van Bruggen

Insula Photo: Archivi Alinari, Florence

Insular art *1–2* National Museum of Ireland, Dublin; *3* British Library, London (Cotton MS. Nero IV); *4–5* Commissioners of Public Works in Ireland, Dublin

Interlace *2* Trustees of the British Museum, London

International exhibition *1* Board of Trustees of the Victoria and Albert Museum, London; *2* Photo: Arch. Phot. Paris/© ADAGP, Paris, and DACS, London, 1996

International Style *1* Museum of Finnish Architecture, Helsinki; *2* Photo: Ezra Stoller/© Esto

Iona Royal Commission on Ancient Monuments, Scotland/© Crown Copyright

Ionia Photo: Turkish Tourist Office, London

Iran *2* Photo: Range/Reuter/Bettmann; *3* Jordan National Gallery of Fine Arts, Amman

Iran, ancient *2* C.C. Lamberg-Karlovsky/Iran Bastan Museum, Tehran/ Photo: Dev Kernan; *3, 9–10* Photo: Prof. Eric De Waele; *6* Brooklyn Museum, Brooklyn, NY (Collection of Robin B. Martin; no. L48.7.9); *7* Photo: Guitty Azarpay; *8* Hermitage Museum, St Petersburg; *11* Photo: © RMN, Paris; *12* Trustees of the British Museum, London